D1188671

NON-LEAGUE DIRECTORY 1995

PUBLISHER: TONY WILLIAMS

EDITOR: JAMES WRIGHT

Published by:
Tony Williams

Copyright in this edition:
Tony Williams

All rights reserved.
No part of this publication may be reproduced, stored in a retrieval system or transmitted, in any form or by any means, electronic, mechanical, photocopying, recording or otherwise without the permission of the copyright holder.

ISBN 1-869833-22-8

Typeset by:
Stop-the-Clock
(Bury St Edmunds)

Printed by:
Hillman Printers (Frome) Ltd.
Frome, Somerset

Distributed by:
Little Red Witch Book Distribution, 24a Queen Square, North Curry, Taunton TA3 6LE. Tel: 0823 491 069. Fax: 0823 490 281.

Cover photograph:
Clevedon Town's Dave Bright gets airborne during a goalless against Leicester United in the Beazer Homes League at the Hand Stadium.

Photo - Colin Rozee/PictureSport.

EDITORIAL PREFACE

This is the seventeenth edition of the *Non-League Club Directory*. The book covers all levels of football below the Endsleigh, from the top reserve team competitions through the senior semi-professional non-League game to local parks football. 313 leagues, national and local cup competitions, and over 2,700 clubs are featured.

James Wright

PUBLISHER:
Tony Williams

EDITOR:
James Wright

PRODUCTION CO-ORDINATOR:
Michael Williams

ADVERTISING/PUBLIC RELATIONS:
Greg Tesser (0823 490080)

EDITORIAL TEAM:
James Wright, Steve Whitney, Greg Tesser, Kerry Miller, Tony Williams

EDITORIAL ADDRESS:
Football Directories, 24a Queen Square, North Curry, TAUNTON, Somerset TA3 6LE
(Tel: 0823 490469. Fax: 0823 490281)

PHOTOGRAPHIC TEAM:

Eric Marsh, Colin Stevens, Dennis Nicholson, Dave West, Gavin Ellis-Neville, Mick Cheney, Francis Short, Paul Dennis, Roger Turner, Ged Rule, Keith Gillard, Ian Morseman, Alan Coomes, David Collins, Victor Robertson, Neil Whittington, Nick Robinson, Steve Daniels, Martin Wray, Keith Clayton, Richard Brock, Paul Barber, Derrick Kinsey, Alan Watson, Barry Lockwood, Rob Ruddock, John Diamond, Rachel Wilson, John Vass, Tim Lancaster.

CONTRIBUTORS:

Mike Ford - 'Bureau of Non-League Football' (League Tables & County Cup Results), Mandy Sabat & Steve Clark (Football Association), Nick Robinson (Diadora League), Dennis Strudwick (Beazer Homes League), Duncan Bayley (Northern Premier League), Wally Goss (Amateur Football Alliance), Mike Simmonds (Schools Football), Jeremy Biggs, Trevor Bailey (Sunday Football), Bob Morrison - 'First XI Sports Agency', Dudley Jackson, Stewart Davidson (Scottish Football), Bill Berry - 'Non-League Traveller' (League & Club Addresses), Robert Errington, Gareth Davies (North Wales Football), Rob Kelly, Peter Bentley, Paul Bates, Basil Stallard, Mike Wilson, Leslie G Moore (Ten Year Records), Richard Ralph, Andy Molden (Programme cover, league tables), Peter Dridge, Pat Brunning, Steve Layzell, G E Andrews, P R Shelton, Steve Durham, Graham Showell, F P Wye, David Robinson, Brian Byles, David Walton, Nigel Davis, Cliff Sparkes, Malcolm McDonald, Jon Weaver, John Bullen, Rex Bennett (Channel Islands), Mike Odgers & Dave Deacon (Cornish Football), Dave Edmunds, Kevin Folds, Steve Carr, Steve Davies, Colin Timbrell, Paul Gardner, Mike Amos, Arthur Clark, Alan Turvey, Keith Masters, David Halford, Rod Harrington, Walter Morris, N Bainbridge, Malcolm Pagan (Scottish Football), Cathy Gibb (Womens' Football).

All League Secretaries & Officials - names accompany relevant pieces

All Club Secretaries & Officials who completed questionnaires

Acknowledgements

There can few annual publications into which more people have an input than the *Directory.* This year's mail-shot to clubs and leagues amounted to 1,500 letters, so, with the subtraction of non-respondents being offset by the addition of many individual contributors, I think it can be safely assumed that over a thousand people contribute in some way to the book. Therefore they cannot all be listed here, but I would like to take this opportunity of thanking some of the many people who have made my mission possible this summer.

League Secretaries:

The response from the top 24 Pyramid leagues was fabulous with all providing the information requested. I know that the summer months are a very busy time for non-League administrators, so thank you for finding the time to help.

Club Secretaries:

In May, questionnaires were sent to the secretaries of over 800 clubs, and so a warm thank you goes to those that replied.

Contributors:

In addition to the League and Club Secretaries, many other individuals contribute in some way to the *Directory*, and all should have been listed on page 3. If anyone has been left out, I apologise profusely. Special thanks, however, go to John Bullen, Nigel Davis, Bill Berry and Andy Molden who have gone out of their way to help with this edition.

Character Graphics (Taunton):

The clarity of the photographs in last season's *Directory* was without doubt the best yet, so we were delighted that Character Graphics again agreed to do the 'repro' this time. They have to work around the clock in the week between the book leaving us and hitting the printers, so our thanks go to Graham and his hard-working team.

Photographers:

The dedication of our 'Photographic Team' continues to astound all. Scores of photographers have their efforts - duly credited - published in this book, but we have a small 'hard core' of enthusiasts who travel the length and breadth of the country each week chasing the action for the *Directory* and *Team Talk.* I would imagine that Paul Dennis' annual input into British Rail's coffers alone would be sufficient to settle the Signal Workers' pay demands! In passing my personal thanks to the photographers, I would hope that future policy will see their efforts appropriately rewarded.

The Football Association:

As you will read in Tony's enlightening passage on pages 8 and 9, this publication no longer has any direct link with the Football Association. I can, however, always rely on the full support of Steve Clark in the Competitions Department and Mandy Sabat for details on the England Semi-Pro and FA Rep. sides, so I would like to record my gratitude to them for their help.

'The Team':

I was somewhat aghast at the start of the season when a reshuffle of responsibilities in the office left me 'going solo' on the *Directory*. However, support, if largely moral rather than direct, was always at hand in the office. Particular thanks must go to Jenny Gullick who typed much of the 'straight text', Steve Whitney whose unrivalled knowledge of non-League players has enabled the re-introduction of squad details for senior clubs, and Kerry Miller whose indefatigible telephoning hauled in much missing information. But the biggest help I received from my colleagues was the fact they deflected all other responsibilities away from me allowing me to concentrate 100% on the *Directory.*

CONTENTS

Konica Wales 995

EDITORIAL

The essence of the 1993-94 season was perhaps encapsulated in the two showcase Wembley finals. Despite a deluge of rain on each occasion, the four finalists - Diss Town, Taunton Town, Woking and Runcorn - served up a feast of compelling and skilful football. That is how I will remember this particular season - wet, wet, wet - but immensely enjoyable none-the-less.

The first postponement I personally had to endure was as early as the Preliminary Round of the FA Vase, on a Friday night at Sheppey United's borrowed home in Faversham. From then on in there was hardly an occasion when one could travel to a game without first having made a series of phone calls to verify that the pitch was playable. Postponements persisted until the end of the season (the Parasol Combined Counties League report one on 26th May - surely a record) as the rain fell unabated, and the fact that virtually all the senior leagues were completed is a great tribute to their fixture secretaries and the co-operation of the clubs.

From a non-League angle, the FA Cup was particularly memorable. You know it is going to be a good year when struggling sides such as Nuneaton and Yeovil still manage to raise their game sufficiently to beat League teams. Four of our clubs made it to the Third Round, where all performed heroically, but pride of place went to Kidderminster Harriers who continued to the last sixteen (further than Arsenal, Leeds, Liverpool, Everton etc) where West Ham were forced to play extremely well to win on a never-to-be-forgotten afternoon at Aggborough.

Kidderminster's Cup run coupled with their Conference championship success made them the outstanding team of 1993-94. Here is perhaps not the place to delve into the politics of their rejection by the Football League. Suffice to say that, after the 'Bad Old Days' of the end-of-season ballot constantly leaving non-League applicants out in the cold, we have lived through a 'Golden Age' in which for seven consecutive seasons the GMV Conference champions have been promoted. This has invigorated football from the lower half of the Fourth Division right through to the feeder leagues. (Would the incredible on and off-field happenings at clubs such as Rushden, Stevenage and Sittingbourne have occurred had the old doors remained closed?). It is infuriating that the clock should now be turned back, and issues be settled in committee rooms as opposed to on the field of play.

Throughout this book, you will find other, lower profile, cases of clubs being denied promotion (Marine, Stocksbridge Park Steels, Durham City). Again, it would be wrong to comment on individual cases, especially not being in full possession of the facts, and I hope that we do not become too obsessed by the Pyramid and promotion, and that these clubs find it in them to swallow any disappointment and to celebrate fully deserved championships. Only a handful of non-League clubs have the resources, fan-base and potential to harbour realistic Conference/Football League ambitions. For the remainder, supremacy at local level must be the ultimate aim.

Three wishes for 1994-95, then; that the high standard of entertainment on offer throughout the Pyramid is maintained; that the important promotion and relegation issues are settled, as far as possible, on the field of play; and, of course, a little less rain.

James Wright

PUBLISHER'S FOREWORD

The 1993-94 season cannot be described as memorable as far as football in the Pyramid of leagues are concerned.

Sadly the most discussed topic was Kiddeminster Harriers' failure to gain a place in the Endsleigh League despite proving their undoubted quality on the pitch within the Conference and of course in the FA Cup.

Ignoring sentiment, it could be said that Harriers knew the rules of entry and hadn't matched them. However, the whole principle of promotion and relegation throughout the Pyramid, whether it is at the much publicised peak - from Vauxhall Conference to Division Three - or from junior feeder leagues into Diadora, Beazer or NPL, must surely be made much more cut and dried.

It doesn't help the image of Non-League football if no-one knows at the end of the season whether certain clubs have qualified for promotion or not, or maybe they are appealing against decisions!

If we look back to the time when automatic promotion and relegation was achieved for the 'Alliance' champions, we can remember the thrill of satisfaction that justice had at last been done. This situation should now exist at all levels where leagues and their clubs should know exactly what must be achieved for promotion to be automatic.

Just because the Football League have in some ways 'pulled up the ladder', the 'Pyramid' world must not be seen to do likewise. Lets make sure our world conducts itself in a fair, open and understandable way in which we all know for what clubs are aiming and there are no double standards.

The fact that Kidderminster Harriers won the Conference last season was a just reward for the long term building of chairman Dave Reynolds and his long-serving manager Graham Allner. The stability and spirit at Aggborough could well act as an example to football in general.

However this season may see a much stronger challenge coming from Altrincham, Bath City, Dover Athletic, Kettering, Woking and possibly Stevenage Borough. It should be a very competitive championship.

Rumour has it that the recession is really on its way out but whether this proves to be fact or not, may we all take this opportunity to thank the thousands of regular purchasers of this Directory for your support through the difficult years.

James Wright has certainly developed the publication in superb fashion, but continued excellent sales which make the Directory a best seller every Autumn give us the solidity on which to base our publishing business.

We obviously enjoy our work and hope that the Non-League Club Directory will carry on giving many more years of pleasure to readers. Our monthly non-League Football Magazine 'Team Talk' is now into it's fourth year - a record for this type of magazine - and hopefully the publicity we give the game at this level has helped widen the general appeal.

As usual we will welcome any new ideas for our books or magazine, so please write to us if you have any interesting views.

The season ahead promises to be particularly lively and will be affected by the World Cup attitudes both from players and referees. We are looking forward to it, and we wish you all a happy and successful year.

Tony Williams

ANNUAL....YEARBOOK....DIRECTORY SEVENTEEN HAPPY YEARS!

The idea to produce an annual for non-League football wasn't perhaps a suprise as I had managed to persuade an agent and publisher to launch the Rothman's Football Yearbook in 1970, and had enjoyed working with Greg Tesser on his 'Amateur Footballer' magazine in the late sixties.

Having played with a number of senior non-League clubs in the Isthmian, Athenian and Southern Leagues, and also having enjoyed managing and coaching at this level, the game was in my blood.

So, with the encouragement of Ted Croker at the Football Association and a little financial help, the first FA Non-League Football Annual was published as a Playfair Annual by Queen Anne Press for the 1978-79 season. It was a 252 page pocket book that cost 70p!

Blyth Spartans had thrilled the football world with their great FA Cup run when they featured in the Sixth Round draw, and our Editorial Committee was Ted Powell from Herefordshire, the chairman of the FA Publications Committee, and Adrian Titcombe of the FA who I am pleased to say has helped us ever since. On our first advisory committee were others who still give valuable support; Steve Clark and Glen Kirton (FA), Peter Grave, Bill Mitchell, Brian Lee, Barry Lenton (Marine FC) and Greg Tesser who has moved to Somerset to work with us.

'The Annual' increased to 304 and then 336 pages in the next two years being published by Macdonald & James (a part of Queen Anne) and then by myself, as confidence had eroded at the big publishing house. The FA now supported without a financial input, but a sponsor helped the 1980-81 edition in the form of Duripanel, an uncombustible building material suitable for the construction of stands. This issue also recorded the successful start of 'The Alliance' with the ex-amateurs of the Isthmian League resisting changes.

A significant boost to the publication's development came in 1981 when Rothmans sponsored the new 'Yearbook'. Geoff Peters co-ordinated this sponsorship and the book was published by Rothmans Publications. During my time with the company when we were the first sponsors of football leagues in the Seventies, I had helped run the Rothmans Football Yearbook and introduced the Rothmans Rugby Union and Rugby League Yearbooks, so this was a fitting and very welcome liaison.

The front cover showed action from Liverpool v Altrincham in the FA Cup and the Rothmans FA Non-League Football Yearbook really took off. I was 'in the depths' after a divorce which left me penniless, so the help of Geoff Peters and Rothmans will always be remembered with gratitude.

Rothman's sponsored for three years and during this time we published some hard backed editions which were a joy to see on the shelf. The size went from 336 (A5) pages to 512 pages, but Queen Anne Press, under the 'leadership' of Robert Maxwell, had persuaded Rothmans to hand over their sports publishing department to a 'proper publishers'. Geoff Peters, having been asked to go with his books, was promptly squeezed out by 'the chairman'. Prices of the books soared and there was no understanding of or desire for a non-League publication, so once again the title reverted to me.

It was at this stage that another friend, Barry Hugman, influenced the book's future. Barry introduced me to a director of Newnes Books, Tony Bagley, who commissioned two directories from me; 'The FA (they still encouraged their name to be associated with the book) Non-League Directory 1985' and 'The Football League Club Directory 1985' (which was later to be sponsored by Barclays and then Endsleigh).

Regular monthly payments for these books also enabled me to have my own rented flat for the first time in three years, so Tony Bagley's faith and Newnes Books will always have a special place in my memory.

The 1985 edition was 602 pages large but a real tragedy struck as Tony, who was diabetic, had a blackout and died in an accident on holiday. His colleagues, with no understanding or faith in Non-League football, relinquished the publishing rights so, after reducing the size of the 1986 edition (576 pages) despite having another sponsor in 'Safestand', the publishing rights again reverted to me.

The 1987 edition edged up to 640 pages with Composite Grandstands (the same parent company) sponsoring. Once again the book was shown as the 'Official Football Association Publication', although I remember we were instructed to ensure that 'views expressed in the book were not necessarily those of 'The Football Association'. They never change!

The 1988 book was the first with the now well known bright red cover, and much appreciated sponsorship was offered by Vauxhall-Opel whose parent company continued its involvement for five years during which time the size increased from 736 pages to over the magic 1,000 mark, and the price from £8.98 to £11.95.

Kidderminster Harriers featured on the covers of the first and last editions sponsored by Vauxhall and the attitude, the football played, and the development of that club probably mirrors the spirit in which I feel the Annual/YearBook/Directory has also developed.

The 1993 edition was edited by James Wright, a lover of all that is good in our national winter sport throughout the Pyramid. I knew 'my baby' would be in good hands while I had to cope with the problems of keeping a small publishing house 'on the rails' during a recession.

During these recent difficult financial years 'The Non-League Club Directory' has continued to be a best seller with WH Smiths, Sportspages, the book trade in general and of course our Mail Order customers. It is the flagship of our business and I know, from our letters, that it gives hours of enjoyment to our readers.

James has poured hours of love into its continued development and we are all very proud that this edition covers a wider span throughout the Pyramid and beyond than ever before.

We are a little sad that the FA Publications Committee feel that the FA should no longer be seen to be involved and while, appreciating Lucozade's support last season, we were disappointed that although they appreciated all we did for them, they didn't have the sales force resources to capitalise, so have withdrawn their sponsorship!

So the saga goes on! When all is said and done, we are still probably the only organisation that has a complete faith in this level of football and an understanding of the people, the spirit, and the unique family attitudes and comradeship that exist within the game. We try to publicise all major competitions and how the Pyramid works. The fabulous work that the FA does undertake for football outside the full-time game is probably promoted better within our publications than by the FA themselves, who give the impression of worrying more about finances than the game itself or the development or caring for football at its less glamorous levels.

Thank goodness we <u>do</u> appreciate these facets as we have enjoyed seventeen wonderfully happy and fulfilling years, and we aim to enjoy many more.

Tony Williams

INTRODUCTION

Sorting 2,500 club entries, tables from 500 different leagues, and the results of scores of other competitions stretching from the Western Isles to the Weald of Kent into the structured framework of a book is the biggest challenge I have ever faced.

This year we have reorganised the Directory to a large extent. The book can now be split into three main parts; The Football Association section, the Pyramid section and the County Associations and a Miscellaneous section.

FOOTBALL ASSOCIATION SECTION

This remains largely unchanged, kicking-off with an extensive statistical and photographic review of non-League involvement in the FA Cup, and the Trophy and Vase. The FA Sunday Cup is also included for reasons that will become apparent. This section concludes with an annual report of the England Semi-Professional side who experienced their most active season for a number of years.

THE PYRAMID SECTION

This starts with the usual exhaustive analysis of the GMV Conference, including a six page feature on each club, but is followed immediately this year by the three main feeder leagues (Beazer, Diadora and NPL). Next follow the twenty regional feeder leagues (fifteen of which feed directly into either the Beazer, Diadora or NPL). These are listed in no particular order, though the parent league is marked in all cases.

COUNTY ASSOCIATIONS AND MISCELLANEOUS SECTION

County Associations are the administrative divisions of our sport, so I saw no reason why they should not be used to 'sort' the Directory. Each county has a 'chapter' which starts with results from county FA competitions. Senior (or intermediate) leagues are then covered in the same depth as in previous years (co-operation from the leagues permitting), and the chapter concludes with tables from junior and Sunday leagues (hence the abolition of the county cups and Sunday sections). One of the advantages in this new system is that it allows local association competitions such as the Reading Senior Cup, the Isle of Wight cups or the Daventry Charity Cup, to be logically incorporated.

Inserted alphabetically among the county associations are the usual array of miscellaneous chapters such as the Amateur Football Alliance, English Schools FA etc. Please refer to the contents page at the front of the book, and the league and club indices at the rear, for more detailed guidance.

IMPORTANT NOTES

LEAGUE ENTRIES

All Senior Leagues were invited to submit material such as a season's review, result grids and League Cup results. The response, as you will see, was fabulous and I cannot thank the various Secretaries/Press Officers/Chairmen enough for their co-operation. Conversely, the response to requests for tables from Junior Saturday Leagues and Sunday Leagues was disappointing (see further notes below).

One important thing to bear in mind after this one of the wettest seasons in living memory was that a number of minor Leagues were uncompleted. All the tables published in this book are final even if some games remain unplayed. 'Awarded' results are marked on result grids with 'W' as the score for the winning team and 'L' for the losers.

As in the past two editions of the Directory, tables from all divisions of Saturday leagues are published in full, but only the top divisions of Sunday leagues are printed. However, for Sunday leagues we have listed, where notified, lower division champions. Numbers in brackets in these sections denote the number of teams in the particular division.

The new 'county orientated' lay-out did pose a problem with leagues which come under the jurisdiction of more than one association. In the case of senior leagues, we have endeavoured to place the league in the county to which the majority of its club are affiliated, for example to Jewson South Western League section is located in the Cornwall chapter and the Lovewell Blake Anglian Combination in Norfolk. 'Multi-County' junior leagues were inserted wherever space permitted, so all I can do is point you in the direction of the League Index which starts on page 1201.

CLUB ENTRIES

Nearly all clubs in the Pyramid Section, together with a number in the County Associations Section, received questionnaires. The response was 'fair' (again, see further notes below). Sadly, time constraints allowed us to chase up by telephone only the major clubs, i.e. those in the top four leagues.

The main innovation in this field was the granting of a second page to clubs in the Premier Divisions of the Northern Premier, Beazer and Diadora Leagues. The new page includes a chronological list of all games played in the 1993-94 season, and playing squad details - brought back by popular demand. Again there is a very important observation to make here - the squads are only up-to-date as at the end of the 1993-94 season because it was impossible to log in the hundreds of summer transfers. I sincerely hope that in future editions we will be able to; (A) include summers transfer, and (B) extend squad details to include clubs in the lower divisions of the Beazer, Diadora and Northern Premier Leagues.

Letters received from readers during the season indicate that some of the categories in club entries require clarification. The years given in the "Previous Leagues" category are the year joined and the year departed. So, an entry "Isthmian 91-93" would indicate that the club played in the Isthmian League for two seasons; 1991-92 and 1992-93. The same annotation applies in the "Previous Names", "Previous Grounds" and "Honours" categories.

In club honours, the words "champions" and "winners" are assumed. Thus the entry "Northumberland Senior Cup(3) 73-76 (R-up 77-78)", would indicate that the club in question won the Northumberland Senior Cup in seasons 1973-74, 1974-75 and 1975-76, and were beaten finalists in 1977-78.

The syntax for the "Club Colours" category is as follows: Shirt colour/shorts colour/socks colours. (If just two colours are listed, e.g. Tangerine/black, then colours are tangerine shirts, black shorts).

The "Record Win" category gives the club's biggest winning margin, not necessarily their highest goals tally. Hence a 7-0 victory would override an 8-3 win. In the case of identical margins, the goals total comes in to play, a 9-2 win superseding an 8-1 win, etc. The same applies in reverse for the "Record Defeat" entry - a 0-5 score-line would take precedence over a 1-6 defeat.

The "Club Record Scorer" category has caused some confusion. When I put it on the questionnaire, I intended it to be read as the club's all-time record goalscorer in a career, but it became apparent from the returns that many respondants had taken it as the player who had scored the most goals in a season. Whatever information was provided has been entered, and the numbers should give the game away in most cases - totals of sixty or below will generally indicate a seasonal, as opposed to a career, tally.

If, having read the above, you feel that the information on your club may be inaccurate, please drop me a line as soon as possible. I tinker with the club entries throughout the season, not just during the summer months. In fact, where some research is required it is preferrable that it be undertaken during comparatively tranquil periods.

RESPONSES/APATHY

The most soul-destroying aspect of compiling the Directory is noting how many League/Club Secretaries fail to respond to requests for information. Now, it is pointless getting on a high horse and preaching here because the 'Apathetic Ones' will not be Directory readers - if they were they would realise the importance of having up-to-date information from their club/league published therein.

The only thing I can do is appeal to readers. We now have a computer database of club contacts to whom we mail questionnaires. If (and only if) your club has failed to respond this year (the giveaway clue is whether the "Captain/Top Scorer/Player of the Year 93-94" slots have been filled in) please get in touch with me between now and April 1995 and I will ensure the relevant forms are sent to you instead.

Likewise, if you are involved as a player or spectator in a Sunday or Junior Saturday league, please send tables (either clipped from a newspaper, photocopied from a League Newsletter, or even hand-written) next Spring. It was in this field (Sunday and Junior Leagues) that we experienced the poorest response-rate (less than 50%), so we will have to seriously consider whether it is worthwhile doing a mail-out at all.

Incidently, if any club secretary who failed to return a questionnaire doeshappen to read this, please write and let me know why as I am quite fascinated by the psychology of someone accepting a position to promote his/her club and then declining a gilt-edged, and free, opportunity to do just that!

AND FINALLY..

Whilst every practical measure to ensure accuracy has been taken, I do have to work 12-15 hours a day every day during the three summer months, and it would be outrageous to assume that fatigue has induced no errors. If it was your club that I cocked-up, I apologise most sincerely and pledge to get it right, with your help, next time.

If you have any comments about the book, in particular the new format, please drop me a line or have a chat if our paths cross at a match. Enjoy the season.

James Wright

THE NON-LEAGUE CLUB DIRECTORY AWARDS 1993-94

PLAYER OF THE YEAR

Chris Brindley

* * * * *

INDIVIDUAL MERIT AWARDS

Simon Smith
Bill Punton
T W Fox

* * * * *

REGIONAL CLUB AWARDS

NORTH EAST	Spennymoor United
NORTH WEST	Marine
MIDLANDS	VS Rugby
EAST of ENGLAND	Sudbury Town
HOME COUNTIES NORTH	Marlow
HOME COUNTIES SOUTH	Chertsey Town
WEST of ENGLAND	Tiverton Town
WALES	Barry Town
F.A. CUP	Kidderminster Harriers

PLAYER OF THE YEAR

Chris Brindley
(Kidderminster Harriers)

Whilst their attacking flair was there for all to see, like all great teams Kidderminster based their success on a rock solid defence. From Kevin Rose in goal through full-backs Paul Bancroft and Simeon Hodson to the central defensive pairing of Martin Weir and Chris Brindley, they exuded confidence gained from years of experience in the Conference and Football League.

Chris Brindley became Kidderminster's record signing when Graham Allner paid Telford £20,000 for his services in 1992 and, though success on the the field, particularly in the non-League game, cannot be equated in monetary terms, few at Aggborough would argue that Chris has not amply repaid this outlay. He has been ever-present for two seasons as the Harriers have progressed from being relegation candidates in 1992 to champions in 1994, and his central defensive partnership with Martin Weir is widely regarded as the soundest in the Conference.

Chris learned his trade at Wolverhampton Wanderers in late the 1980s and, like several other members of Kidderminster's championship squad, has used his early career experience gained in the full-time game to become a polished performer in the Conference. He is a thoroughly deserving recipient of this year's award.

Photo - Dave West

INDIVIDUAL MERIT AWARDS 1993-94

Simon Smith (Gateshead)

One very familiar pair of gloves will be missing from Conference grounds this season - those of Simon Smith who, at the age of 31 and after 450 appearances, has announced his retirement nine years after making his Gateshead debut.

As the Tyneside club have yo-yoed between the Conference and Northern Premier League, a string of managers and players have passed through the International Stadium, but Simon remained a sign of stability throughout, showing loyalty that is no longer commonplace at this level of football. He can take a large slice of the credit for the fact that Gateshead have at last established themselves as a top-half Conference outfit, but will be sorely missed by the club's small but equally loyal band of supporters.

Bill Punton (Manager, Diss Town)

When Diss Town lifted the FA Vase after an enthralling Wembley final against Taunton, the whole of East Anglian football rejoiced for their amicable manager Bill Punton. Bill is one of the most shrewd and experienced non-League managers on the circuit having enjoyed a long and successful League career as a player, and then given Great Yarmouth magnificent service steering them to many successes during a twenty-year spell as manager. In four seasons at Brewers Green Lane, he has established Diss Town as a major force in the Jewson League and nationally in the FA Vase. When I spoke to Bill moments after the dramatic Vase semi-final win over Atherton LR at VS Rugby, he was more eager to talk in generous terms about the qualities of Diss Town's two recently vanquished Vase opponents - Tiverton and Atherton - than wallow in his own club's success. Such magnanimity make him one of 1994's most popular winners.

T W Fox (Secretary, Carr & Carr Sunday League)

Of the hundreds of letters we send out requesting final league tables for the Directory each year, we can be sure that one of the first to elicit a reply will be that sent to Mr Fox of the Carr & Carr Sunday League. He has been involved with local leagues in the Grimsby area since 1920, and still combines his duties with the Carr & Carr Sunday with working on the boardroom door in uniform for Grimsby Town FC on matchdays. Mr Fox is typical of so many other league and club officials who work tirelessly, and sadly often thanklessly, to ensure the smooth running of the game for us all to enjoy. We hope this award serves as a small tribute to his many years of dedication to local football.

REGIONAL CLUB AWARDS 1994-95

NORTH EAST - SPENNYMOOR UNITED

Spennymoor United showed their hand in 1990 when, frustrated by the Northern League's continued absence from the Pyramid, they switched to the Northern Counties (East) set-up - geographically less appropriate but at least offering a route to the Northern Premier League and higher. Here was an ambitious club willing to take risks. In their first two seasons in the NCEL, Spennymoor had to play second fiddle to exceptionally good Guiseley and North Shields sides, but the championship was won at the third attempt. To say that the Moors took the NPL by storm in their first season would be the under-statement of the year. They beat four Premier Division sides (including champions-elect Marine and old rivals Bishop Auckland) to win the League Cup, lifted the Durham Challenge Cup, and, most significantly, just edged out Ashton United to book the second Division One promotion berth behind champions Guiseley. A sparkling new stand has been built at the Brewery Field ground confirming that the club has certainly come a long way since the difficult decision to quit their beloved Northern League four years ago.

NORTH WEST - MARINE

Marine have been perhaps the most consistent performers in the Northern Premier League Premier Division over recent seasons. It is a decade since the Mariners last finished outside the top ten, and during that period they have enjoyed some exhilarating runs in both the FA Cup and FA Trophy. The championship however, has always somehow eluded Roly Howard and his team. That is until 1993-94 when Marine were to the fore throughout the season and eventually managed to hold off a strong challenge in the New Year from Leek Town to lift the crown. The Crosby club knew that the title would not earn them promotion to the GMV Conference as their three-sided ground could never meet that competition's strict requirements, but that did not blunt their determination to achieve supremacy in local football. The finest of Roly Howard's twenty seasons at Rossett Park was capped by a win over deadly rivals Southport in the final of the Liverpool Senior Cup.

MIDLANDS - V.S. RUGBY

When the 1994 Non-League Club Directory went to the printers on the eve of the season we had to put a note on the VS Rugby page saying the club might not be in a position to commence the campaign. The keys to the ground were in the hands of the liquidator, and it looked very much as if the Warwickshire town was going to lose a second Southern League club, Rugby Town having slipped into the abyss in the early 1970s. Thankfully, a new board launched a successful rescue bid, and, significantly, manager Ron Bradbury remained loyal to the club. Against all the odds, VS Rugby enjoyed a marvellous season. They reached the First Round Proper of the FA Cup, and just edged out Weston-super-Mare on the final day of the season to reclaim their Beazer Homes League Premier Division place at the first attempt.

EAST OF ENGLAND - SUDBURY TOWN

Sudbury Town's rise to prominence over the past decade has been steady but sustained. Their protracted FA Vase runs helped increase already staunch local support, and a major milestone was passed in 1990 when, twelve months after the club's appearance at Wembley, they earned promotion to the Southern League. After three years of consolidation in the Southern Division, 1993-94 was the season when it all clicked for Sudbury Town. The club thrashed Premier Division Gresley Rovers 5-1 on aggregate to lift the Barclays Commercial Services (League) Cup, reached the final of the Suffolk Premier Cup and, most significantly, clinched promotion to the top flight behind champions Gravesend & Northfleet. Sudbury Town have achieved a lot under manager Richie Powling, and are still upwardly mobile.

HOME COUNTIES NORTH - MARLOW

Marlow are another small town club whose progress in recent season's has been sustained rather than prolific. When they achieved promotion to the Premier Division of the Isthmian League in 1988, few thought they would stick around for long, and relegation was only just avoided in their first two seasons. However their progress has been such in the early 1990s that for much of last season they were the bookmakers' favourites for the title, before being edged out by fast-finishing big guns Stevenage Borough and Enfield in the run-in. A third consecutive appearance in the First Round Proper of the FA Cup brought Plymouth Argyle to the Alfred Davis Memorial Ground (one of the most beautifully maintained grounds in the Pyramid), and Match of the Day viewers saw Marlow battle magnificently before going down by a 0-2 scoreline that flattered the Devonians. A successful season for Marlow was concluded by the capture of the Berks & Bucks Senior Cup from Chesham United.

HOME COUNTIES SOUTH - CHERTSEY TOWN

Chertsey Town completed a Diadora 'double' that may never be repeated by winning both the domestic cups they entered. They were always among the favourites to take the lower divisions' Carlsberg Trophy, and duly obliged, but for a Second Division team to win the League Cup was a remarkable achievement. The wonder was that they didn't just beat Premier Division clubs - they thrashed them! I was privileged to witness their 5-0 quarter-final demolition of St Albans. Carshalton were then despatched 5-1 on aggregate, and title-chasing Enfield 3-0 in the final. Needless to say, Jim Kelman's team also achieved their main objective - promotion to Division One.

WEST OF ENGLAND - TIVERTON TOWN

When Clevedon Town went through the entire 1992-93 Great Mills League season undefeated, drawing just four games, one thought it an achievement that would not be unequalled, let alone bettered, for many years. However, just twelve months later Tiverton Town were looking at a undefeated league record that had seen them held to a draw on only three occasions. Averaging very nearly four goals a game, Martyn Rogers has assembled one of the most powerful teams the Western League has seen for years. To cap a remarkable campaign, Tivvy retained the two cups won in 1992-93; the Les Phillips (League) Cup and the Devon St Lukes Cup.

WALES - BARRY TOWN

When Barry Town were forced into exile by their unwillingness to join the League of Wales in 1992, things looked very bleak for the Linnets. It became obvious they could not survive on miniscule gates at distant Worcester, so pride was swallowed and the club joined the Abacus League for 1993-94. A squad of immense talent and experience was assembled, and it was little suprise that the title was won at a canter. The League Cup and FAW Trophy completed a treble trophy haul, but the club still had to prove they were more than a big fish in a small pool. This they did in the Allbright Bitter Welsh Cup defeating a string of Konica League clubs, including champions-elect Bangor City, and then Endsleigh League Cardiff City in a memorable Arms Park final.

PAST NON-LEAGUE DIRECTORY AWARDS

CLUB AWARDS 1977-1983.

	Team of the Year	Special Merit Awards	FA Cup	FA Vase
1978	Blyth	Enfield	Blyth	Barton Rvrs
1979	Barking	Worcester City	Altrincham	Billericay
1980	Dagenham	Altrincham, Stamford	Harlow	Guisborough
1981	Altrincham	Bishop's Stortford, Runcorn, Slough	Enfield	Willenhall
1982	Leytonstone-Ilford	Shepshed, Enfield, Runcorn, Wealdstone	Altrincham	Rainworth
1983	England Semi-Pro	Enfield, Sutton Utd, Gateshead, Harrow	B. Stortford	Harry Rudge (Halesowen sec.)

REGIONAL CLUB AWARDS

	Nth East	Nth West	Midlands	East	Home Cos (Nth/Sth)		West/Wales	FA Cup
1984	Whitby	S Liverpool	Shepshed	Stansted	Maidstone United		Exmouth	
1985	Bishop Auck.	Fleetwood	Telford	Boston Utd	Wealdstone		Exmouth	
1986	Gateshead	Altrincham	Kidderminster	Wisbech	Enfield		Barry T.	
1987	Scarboro.	Macclesfield	Burton A.		Barnet	Fareham	Merthyr Tyd.	Caernarfon
1988	Blyth	Colne	Kettering	Lincoln C.	Barnet	Bashley	Yeovil	Sutton Utd
1989	Bishop Auck.	Hyde	Tamworth	Kettering	Leyt.-Ilford	Maidstone	Merthyr Tyd.	Sutton Utd
1990	Darlington	Colne	Leek	Wivenhoe	Barnet	Welling	Newport AFC	Whitley B.
1991	Guiseley	Witton	Stourbridge	Colchester	Barnet	Littlehampton	Gloucester	Woking
1992	Blyth	Stalybridge	Bromsgrove	Colchester	Stevenage	Hastings	Wimborne	Farnborough
1993	Whitby	Southport	Nuneaton	Canvey Is.	Chesham	Peacehaven	Clevedon/Cwmbran	Yeovil

INDIVIDUAL MERIT AWARDS

1978 Dave Clark (Blyth Spartans), Gary Stewart (Boston United), Paul Gover (Bath City), John King (Altrincham), Keith Searle (Enfield).

1979 Jim Arnold (Stafford Rangers), Tony Jennings (Enfield), Billy Kellock (Kettering Town), Chris Tudor (Almondsbury Greenway), Howard Wilkinson (England semi-pro Manager).

1980 Ted Hardy (Manager of Enfield), Leo Skeete (Stamford), Mike Roberts (Winsford United), Graham Smith (Northwich Victoria), Adrian Titcombe (The Football Association).

1981 Tony Sanders (Manager of Altrincham), Larry Pritchard (Sutton United), Terry Moore (Bishop's Stortford), Colin Williams (Northwich Victoria Victoria), Keith Wright (England semi-pro Manager).

1982 Mickey Burns (Forest Green Rovers), Barry Howard (Altrincham), John Williams (Manager of Runcorn), Keith Barrett (Enfield), Graham Bennett (Bangor City).

1983 John Watson (Maidstone United), John Davison (Altrincham), John Barley (Maidstone United), Ken Jones (Northwich Victoria), Tommy Dixon (Blyth Spartans), Bill Dellow (Secretary of the Southern League).

1984 Paul Culpin (Nuneaton Borough), Tommy Robson (Stamford), Mark Newsom (Maidstone United), Dave Ryan (Northwich Victoria).

1985 Paul Culpin (Nuneaton Borough), David Howells (Enfield), Paul & Lee Joinson (Halesowen Town).

1986 Kim Casey (Kidderminster Harriers), Paul Shirtliff (Frickley Athletic), Cyril Whiteside (Chairman of Clitheroe), Barrie Williams (Manager of Sutton United).

1987 Paul Davies (Kidderminster Harriers), Barry Fry (Manager of Barnet), Peter Hunter (Secretary of GMV Conference), Jim Thompson (Chairman of Maidstone United) + Special 'Pyramid' creation award.

1988 Kevin Verity (England semi-pro Manager), Steve Burr (Macclesfield Town), Bill McCullough (Chairman of Barrow).

1989 Barrie Williams (Manager of Sutton United), Stan Storton (Manager of Telford United), Mickey Roberts (Macclesfield Town), Nigel Ransom (Welling United).

1990 Gary Wager (Merthyr Tydfil), Ray Wilkie (Manager of Barrow), Gordon Bartlett (Manager of Yeading), Gary Simpson (Altrincham).

1991 Dereck Brown (Woking), Frank Northwood (Manager of Gresley Rovers), Ted Pearce (Manager of Farnborough Town), Noel White (Liverpool and the Football Association).

1992 Gordon Rayner (Manager of Guiseley), James Bowdidge (Chairman of Colchester United), Tony Ricketts (Manager of Bath City), Paul Cavell (Dagenham & Redbridge), Roly Howard (Manager of Marine).

1993 David Leworthy (Farnborough Town), Martin O'Neill (Manager of Wycombe Wanderers), Brian Ross (Marine), Hedley Steele (Tiverton Town).

PLAYER OF THE YEAR

1984 Brian Thompson (Maidstone)
1985 Alan Cordice (Wealdstone)
1986 Jeff Johnson (Altrincham)
1987 Mark Carter (Runcorn)
1988 David Howell (Enfield)
1989 Steve Butler (Maidstone)
1990 Phil Gridelet (Barnet)
1991 Mark West (Wycombe Wdrs)
1992 Tommy Killick (Wimborne)
1993 Steve Guppy (Wycombe Wdrs)

Right: Steve Guppy of Wycombe Wanderers receives the Player-of-the-Year award for 1992-93 from editor James Wright.
Photo - Paul Dennis.

WIRRAL PROGRAMME CLUB AWARDS 1993-94

Secretary: I W R Runham, 3 Tansley Close,
Newton, West Kirby, Wirral, Merseyside L48 9XH (051 625 9554)

19th NON-LEAGUE PROGRAMME SURVEY

Entries were received from 1,188 clubs - 29 more than last season and a new record. The standards are again high with many clubs showing improvements on last season's efforts, and it is also pleasing to see many clubs issuing for the first time. All clubs who issue a programme are to be congratulated, a single sheet being much better than nothing.

The winning club receives a framed certificate, and the winners for each league also receive a certificate. Please note, the programmes have been surveyed, not voted on. Marks were awarded to each programme as follows:-

Cover 15 (design 10, match details 5); Page size 10; Team layout and position within programme 10; Results 10; League tables 10; Price 15; Pictures 15; Printing quality and paper used 20; Frequency of issue 20; Value for money 20 (this takes into account ratio of adverts to articles, the club's league etc), Contents 105 (other than those listed) taking into account relevance to club, its league, environs etc, the size of print used, spacing between lines, size of margins and if the contents are originals or reproduced (from league bulletins etc).

Further notes: To gain full marks in the frequency of issue section, programmes from ten different matches were required (allowances were made if a club did not play ten homes games before the closing date, if we were informed of this fact and if programmes were received from all home games played). As many programmes varied from issue to issue, all programmes were surveyed and the marks in each section were totalled and divided by the number of programmes received to get a final mark for each section. The marks for each section were then totalled together to get the final score. A new standard of marks is set each seaon, so this survey should not be compared with those of previous years.

We have listed the winners for each league below. For more detailed results including divisional break-downs for each league and a complete list of the 1,188 entrants, please send an SAE to the address above.

NATIONAL WINNER: NORTHWOOD (Diadora League)
RUNNERS-UP: RAUNDS TOWN and HODDESDON TOWN

LEAGUE (No. of entries)	**1st**	**Pts**	**2nd**	**Pts**	**3rd**	**Pts**
GMV Conference (22)	Woking	139	Bath City	133	Halifax Town	131
Beazer Homes Lge (66)	Crawley Town	139	Weymouth	133	Baldock Town	131
Diadora Lge (82)	Northwood	176	Aldershot Town	172	Sutton United	150
Northern Prem. (41)	Boston United	153	Lancaster City	141	Ashton United	129
Hereward SUCL (24)	Raunds Town	174	Potton United	155	Stotfold	139
Minerva SML (45)	Hoddesdon Town	174	Sandy Albion	171	Arlesey Town	123
Spartan Lge (15)	St Andrews	120	Cockfosters	119	St Margaretsbury	109
Parasol Comb. Co's (14)	Peppard	161	Ash United	122	Ashford Town (Middx)	107
Essex Senior Lge (13)	Concord Rgrs	104	Romford	99	Maldon Town	98
Unijet Sussex Lge (39)	Lancing	153	Stamco	145	Langney Sports	132
Winstonlead Kent (20)	Whitstable Town	140	Thamesmead T.	121	Folkestone Invicta	108
Jewson Eastern (35)	Somersham Town	147	Gorleston	115	Wroxham	113
Skol Mids Comb. (38)	Boldmere St M.	143	Meir KA	131	Barwell	126
Great Mills Lge (31)	Exmouth Town	116	Clyst Rovers	111	Mangotsfield United	108
Hellenic Lge (31)	Swindon S'marine	148	Cinderford T.	111	Purton	103
West Mids Lge (27)	Blakenall	145	Pelsall Villa	136	Hinckley Athletic	126
Jewson Wessex (20)	AFC Lymington	125	Portsmouth RN	92	Bournemouth	91
Carling NWCL (36)	Newcastle Town	162	Atherton Colls	132	Kidsgrove Athletic	120
Middlesex Lge (4)	CAV Northolt	101	Cockfosters Res.	87	St Clarets/ Hounslow	=60
Northern CE Lge (31)	Denaby United	128	=Liversedge	122	=Pickering Town	122
Fed. Northern Lge (21)	Chester-le-Str.	110	Billingham T.	104	Consett	101
Herts Senior Lge (22)	Bovingdon	115	Sandridge R.	112	Colney Hth/Knebworth	=79
SC Johnson Surrey (3)	Walton Casuals	112	Netherne	91	Ottershaw	86
Char'gton Chiltonian (13)	Finchampstead	113	Finchamp. Res.	99	Penn & Tylers Green	93
Essex Intermediate (5)	Broomfield	98	Runwell Hosp.	87	Springfield Res.	84
British Sugar S&IL (12)	Needham Market	104	Stonham Aspal	94	Achilles/Parkside Utd	=86
Refuge Midland Lge (9)	Audley	122	=Brocton	116	=Eccleshall	116
Glos County (7)	Smiths Athletic	119	Wotton Rovers	105	Ellwood	90
Everards Leics (21)	Lutterworth T.	130	Birstall Utd	114	Oadby Town	109
Westward Devon (4)	Plymouth Parkway	76	Plymstock Utd	73	Newton Abbot	65
Jewson Sth Western (11)	Holsworthy	104	D & C Police	102	Wadebridge Town	81
Dorset Combination (9)	Bournemouth Spts	108	Weymouth Spts	91	Flight Refuelling	82
Kershaw Cambs (3)	Stple Bumpstead	127	Gamlingay	119	Cottenham United	57

CBH Hants (22)	Colden Common 128	Bishopstoke S. 109	Saint Mary's 104
Anglian Comb. (10)	Dereham Town 92	Loddon United 77	Aylsham W./Blofield U. =75
Mid-Cheshire Lge (7)	Rylands 118	Garswood Utd 113	Knutsford/Wilmslow =109
West Lancs (6)	Hesketh Bank 102	Padiham 79	Thornton I'national 70
Perkins Shropshire (4)	Meole Brace 102	Wellington Amtr 53	Oakengates Town 48
TSW Printers Lincs (5)	Lincoln Moorlands 105	Grimsby Amtrs 64	Spilsby Town 55
West Riding (8)	Brighouse T. 126	Wibsey 109	Wibsey 'A' 94
West Yorkshire (8)	Horsforth St M. 122	Knaresborough 120	Beeston St Anthony 95
Notts Alliance (10)	Rainworth MW 167	Rainworth Res. 126	Dunkirk 124
John Smiths CML (36)	Sth Normanton A. 170	Derby C&W R. 126	Derby C&W Reck. Res. 121
Vaux Wearside (11)	North Shields 126	Fulwell Myers 95	Marske United 72
Northern Alliance (9)	Benfield Park 131	W Allotment C. 84	Amble Town 74
CSS Reading Lge (3)	Cantley Manor 75	Reading Exiles 56	Marlow United 45
Cheltenham Lge (3)	Smiths Ath. Res. 98	Smiths Ath. 'A' 97	Smiths Ath. 'B' 96
Other English Lges (45)	Longwell Gn Spts 141	Colden C. Res. 127	Longwell Gn Spts Res. 121
Reserves (44)	Colden Common 127	Rainworth MW =126	Stamco =126
Youth Clubs (6)	Silsden 110	Marford/Gresford 109	Teversal Grange Colts 97
Youth XIs (3)	Worcester City 94	Blackfld/Langley 67	Dulwich Hamlet 53
FA Youth Cup (8)	Warrington T. 80	Wokingham T. 72	Worcester City 66
FA Sunday Cup (52)	Carnforth 108	AD Bulwell 106	BRSC Aidan/Leic CB =88
Sunday Leagues (30)	Yarnfield College 159	ICLU 156	Sutherland Arms Muxt. 150
Kidderminster SL (5)	Kingswinford 76	William Stevens 71	Round Oak 67
WOMEN's Overall (39)	Doncaster Belles 136	Wigan Ladies 121	Epsom & Ewell LFC 113
Womens Nat. Lge (19)	Doncaster Belles 136	Epsom & Ewell 113	Millwall Lionesses 106
North West WL (6)	Wigan Ladies 121	Stockport Co. 98	Winsford Utd Ladies 83
Gtr London WL (6)	Chelsea Ladies =106	Southend Mnr =106	Walton & Her. Ladies =106
Eastern WL (22)	Colch. Eagles 89	Col Utd Hawks 81	Harlow Town 62
Other Ladies' Lges (5)	Crowborough 105	Bristol Rvrs 101	City Roses 84
Womens' FA Cup (35)	Doncaster Belles 127	Horsham LFC =102	Wigan Ladies =102
SCOTLAND Overall (22)	Largs Thistle 118	Caledonian 116	Tayport 114
P & J Highland Lge (8)	Caledonian 116	Buckie This. 112	Inverness Thistle 105
East of Scot. Lge (6)	Gala Fairydean 73	Manor Thistle 67	Whitehill Welfare 65
Ayrshire JL (9)	Largs Thistle 118	Auchinleck T. 85	Ardeer Thistle 83
Central Reg. JL (14)	Pollok 100	Arthurlie =81	Cumbernauld Utd =81
Eastern JL (10)	Blackburn Utd 99	Broxburn A. 78	Bathgate Thistle 69
Tayside Reg. JL (5)	Tayport 114	Scone Thistle 84	Dundee St Josephs 82
Other Scottish Lges (3)	Lochore Welfare 92	West Lothian =65	Kelty Hearts =65
WALES Overall (81)	Porthmadog 146	Connah's QN 133	Gresford Athletic 120
Konica League (19)	Porthmadog 146	Connah's QN 106	Flint Town Utd 131
Abacus League (18)	Pontllanfraith 99	Risca United 89	Newport YMCA 83
Cymru Alliance (10)	Gresford Ath. 120	Cefn Druids =107	Rhyl =107
Sealink Alliance (7)	Llanfairfechan 109	Llandrynog Utd 62	Prestatyn Town 60
RC Wrexham Lge (22)	Lex XI Res. 94	Oswestry Town 86	Penycae 76
Sth Wales Amateur (5)	FC Cwmaman 84	Pencoed A. 72	Llantwit Major 69
Richards Mid-Wales (3)	Morda United 75	Waterloo Rvrs 71	Berriew 41
Copywrite Gwynedd (7)	Hotpoint 88	Pwllheli & D. 86	Penrhosgarnedd Utd 71
Other Welsh Lges (3)	Chepstow Town 112	Rhyl Delta 92	Denbigh Town 69

The closing date for next season's (1994-95) survey is 31st January 1995, and for special issues (for one-offs, big cup ties, friendlies, testimonials etc) it is 31st May 1995. The minimum entry for the survey is one programme, but to gain full marks in the 'frequency of issue' section please send programmes from at least ten different matches for each team entered to the address at the top of the previous page. These can be league, cup etc. If ten games have not been played by the closing dates, please let us know with your entry so that allowances can be made.

To avoid disappointment, please package your entries carefully and, if you wish, send them by Recorded Delivery.

Details of next season's survey will be sent to League Secretaries in September/October for hopeful onward delivery to their clubs. If you would like information sent directly to you, please let us have a large SAE by the end of September 1995.

Ian Runham, Secretary

THE FOOTBALL ASSOCIATION CHALLENGE CUP

REVIEW 1993-94

Featuring Non-League Clubs.

Preliminary Round

(SAT. 28th AUG. 1993)

(Attendances in brackets)

Consett	5-2	Willington (44)
Billingham Town	1-1	Alnwick Town (78)
Alnwick Town	1-2	Billingham T. (85)
Yorkshire Amateur	2-1	Brandon Utd (82)
Billingham Syn.	3-0	Darlington CS (75)
Harrogate Town	5-2	Peterlee Newtown (249)
Evenwood Town	3-1	Ferryhill Ath. (71)
Esh Winning	0-1	Gretna (30)
Horden CW	4-4	Hebburn (100)
Hebburn	2-1	Horden CW
Ryhope CA	0-3	Prudhoe EE (25)
Shildon *(w/o)*		South Shields *(scr)*
Pickering Town	5-2	Penrith (92)
Workington	0-2	Crook Town (234)
Tow Law Town	1-0	West Auckland (118)
Lancaster City	3-1	Whickham (90)
Murton	3-2	Durham City (120)
Atherton LR	1-1	Blackpool Rvrs (100)
Blackpool Rovers	1-6	Atherton LR
Alfreton Town	3-2	Armthorpe Welf. (100)
Blidworth MW	1-4	Arnold Town (120)
Belper Town	1-2	Bamber Bridge (159)
Caernarfon Town	0-0	Burscough (59)
Burscough	2-0	Caernarfon (150)
Clitheroe	1-0	Congleton Town (111)
Warrington T.	5-0	Bradford PA (248)
Flixton	2-0	Farsley Celtic (115)
Glasshoughton W.	0-2	Glossop NE (110)
Eccleshill Utd	2-2	Denaby Utd (90)
Denaby Utd	2-1	Eccleshill U. (90)
Hucknall Town	4-0	Chadderton (260)
Gt Harwood T.	1-5	Guiseley (210)
Ossett Town	5-3	Harworth CI (120)
Immingham Town	1-3	Ilkeston Town (112)
Newcastle Town	1-1	Ossett Albion (55)
Ossett Albion	1-2	Newcastle T. (111)
Maine Road	0-1	Maltby MW (64)
Lincoln United	4-2	Mossley (144)
Oldham Town	1-3	Nth Ferriby (72)
Skelmersdale Utd	0-1	Thackley (100)
Rossendale U.	3-0	Rossington Main (184)
Radcliffe Borough	1-3	Salford City (145)
Stocksbridge PS	1-2	St Helens T. (192)

(played 29-8-93)

Below: Stocksbridge's Andy Tibbenham races past Derek McCartney of St Helens. Photo - Colin Stevens.

Wednesfield	1-0	Eastwood Town (50)
West Brom Town	1-3	Willenhall T. (92)

(played at Sutton Coldfield Town)

Winterton Rgrs	2-0	Prescot (70)
Bilston Town	0-2	Bridgnorth T. (88)
Armitage '90	1-0	Banbury Utd (48)
Chasetown	2-1	Barwell (89)
Boldmere St Mich.	2-0	Blakenall (101)
Halesowen Harriers	2-4	Leicester Utd (70)
Dudley Town	2-1	Eastwood Han. (127)
Desborough T.	1-0	Evesham Utd (69)
Hinckley Town	2-1	Hinckley Ath. (303)
Long Buckby	2-2	Redditch U. (130)
Redditch United	3-1	Long Buckby (122)
Lye Town	1-2	Northampton S. (142)

(played 27-8-93)

Daventry Town	0-3	Oldbury United (47)
RC Warwick	1-2	Pershore Town (136)
Stewarts & Lloyds	1-3	Stratford Town (142)
Rothwell Town	2-0	Rushall Olym. (120)
Rocester	0-1	Rushden & D. (169)
Stourport Swifts	0-0	Stourbridge (128)
Stourbridge	2-1	Stourport S. (173)
Brightlingsea Utd	1-3	Canvey Island (143)
Bishop's Stortford	4-0	Boston (354)

Below: The Boston goalkeeper shows great bravery in thwarting Leo Fortune-West of Bishop's Stortford.
Photo - Robbie Pragnell.

Billericay Town	5-2	Bourne Town (233)
Bury Town	1-2	Burnham Rblrs (189)
Haverhill Rovers	1-2	Eynesbury R. (109)
Felixstowe Town	1-1	Gorleston (63)
Gorleston	0-2	Felixstowe T. (112)

(played at Diss Town)

Fakenham Town	2-2	Gt Yarmouth (90)
Gt Yarmouth T.	3-1	Fakenham T. (126)
Histon	0-9	Heybridge S. (73)
Stamford	4-1	Tiptree United (94)
Mirrlees Blackstone	0-1	King's Lynn (175)
March Town Utd	3-2	Saffron Walden (140)
Sudbury Town	4-1	Stowmarket Town (285)
Watton United	3-1	Barking (120)

(played at Diss Town)

Wisbech Town	3-1	Brimsdown Rvrs (302)
Lowestoft Town	3-2	Tamworth (266)
Brook House	2-1	Boreham Wood (55)
Chatteris Town	2-3	Cornard United (66)
Biggleswade Town	0-3	Barton Rovers (87)

(played at Letchworth Garden City)

Dunstable	2-2	Collier Row (87)
Collier Row	0-1	Dunstable (121)
Edgware Town	3-0	Feltham & HB (100)
Clapton	1-1	Cheshunt (61)
Cheshunt	2-1	Clapton (85)
Hertford Town	0-1	Kempston Rovers
Hanwell Town	1-2	Harefield Utd
Ford United	1-1	Haringey Boro. (120)
Haringey Borough	2-0	Ford United (85)
Hornchurch	1-1	Hoddesdon Town
Hoddesdon Town	0-3	Hornchurch *(at Ware)*

Opposite (right): Hornchurch's Mark Sexton (white shirt) gets past Stuart Parker during the 1-1 draw with Hoddesdon Town in Essex. Pablo Ardiles (son of Ossie) runs back to cover.

Photo - Rob Monger.

A goalmouth scramble as Portfield (black shorts) defeat Steyning 1-0. *Photo - Peter Lirettoc.*

Langford	2-1	Leighton Town (168)
Northwood	3-0	Royston Town (128)
Ruislip Manor	4-3	Letchworth GC (125)
Rainham Town	1-5	Purfleet (92)
Walthamstow Pennant	2-3	Wingate & Finchley (65)
Tilbury	1-1	Tring Town (31)
Tring Town	0-4	Tilbury
Staines Town	1-0	Uxbridge (203)
Southall	1-0	Ware
Bracknell Town	3-3	Bognor Regis T. (106)
Bognor Regis Town	5-0	Bracknell Town (289)
Burgess Hill Town	3-0	Arundel (157)
Bedfont *(w/o)*		Beckenham Town *(scr)*
Horsham YMCA	2-2	Croydon Athletic (75)
Croydon Athletic	5-2	Horsham YMCA (42)
Eastbourne United	5-1	Egham United (100)
Croydon	5-0	Corinthian-Casuals (52)
Hailsham Town	1-4	Epsom & Ewell (142)
Faversham Town	3-0	Fisher '93
(Faversham expelled - ineligible player)		
Erith & Belvedere	2-1	Godalming & Gfd (86)
Horsham	1-2	Herne Bay (152)
Merstham	1-4	Pagham (100)
Lewes	3-1	Littlehampton T. (127)
Langney Sports	2-1	Malden Vale (150)
Oakwood	1-1	Met. Police (43)
Met. Police	3-1	Oakwood (350)
Portfield	1-0	Steyning Town (50)
Redhill	1-2	Ringmer (122)
Ramsgate	1-1	Selsey (61)
Selsey	3-3	Ramsgate
Selsey	0-1	Ramsgate (140)
(Ramsgate expelled - ineligible player)		
Southwick	2-1	Slade Green (160)
Whyteleafe	5-1	Three Bridges
Tooting & Mitcham	7-0	Tunbridge Wells (203)

Above: Whitehawk's Simon Edwards (left) outjumps Steve Hearn, but his side still lose 1-4 at Tonbridge. *Photo - Alan Coomes.*

Tonbridge	4-1	Whitehawk (344)
Windsor & Eton	1-4	Wick (134)
Cove	2-1	Walton & Hers. (109)
Bournemouth	0-1	Brockenhurst (110)
Shoreham	0-2	Buckingham Town (60)
Fareham Town	1-1	Eastleigh (113)
Eastleigh	4-1	Fareham Town (142)
Newbury Town	6-1	Lancing (164)
Gosport Borough	0-3	Hungerford T. (146)
Peacehaven & Tel.	2-1	Fleet Town (151)
Oxford City	0-7	Newport IOW (240)
AFC Totton	1-1	Ryde Sports (63)
Ryde Sports	1-3	AFC Totton (65)
Poole Town	5-0	Swanage T&H (192)
Petersfield Utd *(scr)*		Thame United *(w/o)*
Wimborne Town	5-0	Westbury United
Barnstaple Town	4-0	Exmouth Town (123)
Bridport	4-0	Bristol Mnr F. (209)
Bideford	2-2	Chippenham T. (130)
Chippenham Town	3-0	Bideford (145)
Elmore	2-1	Devizes Town (61)
Melksham Town	1-0	Falmouth Town (110)
Frome Town	3-3	Glastonbury (113)
Glastonbury	0-1	Frome Town (133)
Odd Down	1-1	Ilfracombe Town (85)
Ilfracombe Town	2-2	Odd Down (110)
Odd Down	1-0	Ilfracombe Town
Moreton Town	2-0	Minehead
Torrington	1-4	Yate Town (140)
Shortwood United	3-2	St Blazey (85)
Dawlish Town	0-12	Taunton Town (152)
Weston-super-Mare	6-1	Welton Rovers (300)

First Qualifying Round

(SAT. 11th SEPT. 1993)

(Attendances in brackets)

Billingham Town	0-3	Billingham Syn. (310)
Yorkshire Amateur	1-3	Dunston Feds
Gateshead	4-0	Blyth Spartans (728)
Chester-Le-Street. T.	2-3	Consett (102)
Evenwood Town	0-0	Hebburn (76)
Hebburn	0-3	Evenwood Town
Gretna	3-1	Seaham Red Star (101)
Barrow	3-1	Guisborough (826)
Harrogate Railway	1-2	Harrogate Town (634)

Below: Brian Duffy of Harrogate Railway effects a sliding tackle on John Deacey during the Harrogate Cup derby. *Photo - Ackrills Newspapers, Harrogate*

Shildon	0-1	Easington Coll. (90)
Pickering T.	0-2	Northallerton (147)
Bishop Auckland	1-4	Netherfield (208)
Newcastle Blue Star	3-2	Prudhoe E E (85)
Tow Law Town	3-3	Murton
Murton	1-2	Tow Law Town (77)
Lancaster City	2-1	Stockton (73)
Whitley Bay	1-6	Spennymoor U. (320)
Whitby Town	5-1	Crook Town
Alfreton Town	2-3	Bamber Bridge (133)
Arnold Town	1-3	Leek Town (347)
Northwich Victoria	2-2	Emley (709)
Emley	2-0	Northwich V. (358)
Ashton Utd	4-0	Atherton LR (201)
Clitheroe	2-2	Curzon Ashton (122)
Curzon Ashton	0-1	Clitheroe (133)
Warrington T.	3-0	Matlock Town (302)
Stalybridge C.	6-0	Fleetwood T. (517)
Bootle	5-1	Burscough
Glossop North End	2-2	Goole Town (200)
Goole Town	1-0	Glossop NE (184)
Denaby United	0-4	Morecambe (124)
Bridlington Town	2-0	Frickley Athletic
Darwen	1-1	Flixton (97)
Flixton	3-0	Darwen (158)
Guiseley	3-1	Ilkeston Town (563)
Ossett Town	1-1	Winsford Utd (210)
Winsford Utd	3-1	Ossett Town (184)
Buxton	2-1	Gainsborough (282)
Heanor Town	1-2	Hucknall Town (218)
Maltby MW	1-1	Nth Ferriby Utd (100)
North Ferriby Utd	4-2	Maltby MW (100)
Lincoln Utd	2-0	Nantwich Town (173)
Chorley	3-1	Horwich RMI (407)
Liversedge	3-2	Newcastle Town
Rossendale Utd	1-1	St Helens T. (212)
St Helens Town	1-0	Rossendale U. (120)
Salford City	1-1	Knowsley Utd (120)
Knowsley United	6-0	Salford City (127)

Colwyn Bay	4-1	Hyde United (209)
Sheffield	1-4	Thackley
Willenhall Town	1-2	W Mids Police (100)
Winterton Rangers	1-7	Nuneaton Boro. (305)
Droylsden	1-1	Brigg Town (136)
Brigg Town	0-1	Droylsden (89)
Worksop Town	1-1	Wednesfield (233)
Wednesfield	0-2	Worksop Town (210)
Armitage '90	3-0	Boldmere St M. (60)
Chasetown	0-1	Solihull Boro. (181)
Bromsgrove Rovers	1-1	Gresley Rovers (902)
Gresley Rovers	0-1	Bromsgrove R. (1,222)
Bedworth United	2-1	Bridgnorth T. (161)
Dudley Town	1-1	Hinckley Town (175)
Hinckley Town	2-3	Dudley Town (101)
Desborough Town	1-3	Raunds Town (112)
Telford Utd	4-0	Halesowen Town (903)
Grantham Town	3-1	Leicester Utd (320)
Northampton Spencer	0-1	Pershore Town
Oldbury United	1-1	Pelsall Villa (107)
Pelsall Villa	3-0	Oldbury Utd (254)
Atherstone United	2-1	Hednesford Town (524)
Paget Rangers	1-1	Redditch Utd (106)
Redditch Utd	2-1	Paget Rangers (144)
Rothwell Town	7-1	Stourbridge (143)
Rushden & Diamonds	2-0	Sutton Coldfield (536)
Burton Albion	2-1	Moor Green (508)
Sandwell Borough	5-0	Stratford Town (42)
Bishop's Stortford	2-0	Burnham Rblrs (479)
Billericay	1-1	Aveley (301)
Aveley	1-3	Billericay Town
Boston United	1-1	Braintree Town (802)
Braintree Town	1-2	Boston United (420)
Basildon Utd	1-1	Canvey Island (240)
Canvey Island	1-0	Basildon Utd (405)
Felixstowe Town	1-1	Heybridge Sw. (110)
Heybridge Swifts	5-1	Felixstowe T.
Great Yarmouth Town	2-2	Hendon (215)
Hendon	4-2	Gt Yarmouth (232)
Cambridge City	4-1	Berkhamsted T. (223)
Harwich & Parkeston	4-1	Eynesbury R. (203)
King's Lynn	2-1	Sudbury Town (909)
March Town Uited	3-6	Wivenhoe Town (140)
Chelmsford City	0-0	Newmarket T. (438)
Newmarket Town	1-1	Chelmsford C. (302)
Chelmsford City	3-0	Newmarket T. (489)

Below: Newmarket's Martin Pammenter chases Matt Jones as the Jockeys earn an excellent 0-0 draw at Chelmsford City. *Photo - Martin Wray.*

Spalding Utd	1-2	Stamford (210)
Wisbech Town	1-1	East Thurrock (348)
East Thurrock	1-0	Wisbech Town (161)
Lowestoft Town	1-0	Witham Town (184)
Stevenage Borough	2-2	Wembley
Wembley	1-1	Stevenage B. (260)
Wembley	0-1	Stevenage B. (282)
Corby Town	4-0	Watton United (202)
Cornard Utd	0-1	Halstead Town (190)
Barton Rovers	1-0	Arlesey Town
Dagenham & Red.	1-0	Hitchin Town (580)
Baldock Town	6-0	Brook House (157)
Edgware Town	2-0	Flackwell Hth (116)
Cheshunt	0-2	Burnham (70)
Chesham United	5-0	St Albans City (1,004)
Chalfont St Peter	1-0	Dunstable (93)

Kevin Hales (left) scores Welling United's only goal in their surprise defeat at Enfield. Photo - Keith Gillard.

Harefield United	1-2	Hornchurch
Haringey Borough	0-0	Hampton (50)
Hampton	1-2	Haringey Boro. (155)
Enfield	4-1	Welling Utd (938)
Hemel Hempstead	2-1	Kempston Rovers
Langford	1-4	Purfleet (114)
Ruislip Manor	3-1	Leyton (163)
Grays Athletic	0-2	Yeading (183)
Kingsbury Town	2-1	Northwood (93)
Tilbury	3-2	Southall (42)
Staines Town	1-2	Chertsey Town (393)
Harrow Borough	3-1	Wealdstone (555)
Viking Sports	3-0	Wingate & Finch. (47)
Burgess Hill	0-1	Chatham Town (151)
Bedfont	0-1	Canterbury C. (88)
Kingstonian	2-1	Ashford Town (396)
Banstead Athletic	0-3	Bognor Regis (114)
Eastbourne Utd	0-2	Greenwich Borough
Croydon	4-1	Chipstead (70)
Hastings Town	1-5	Molesey (336)
Corinthian	3-0	Croydon Athletic
Fisher '93	3-3	Herne Bay (124)
Herne Bay	3-2	Fisher '93 (409)
Erith & Belvedere	4-3	Deal Town (97)
Sittingbourne	1-1	Dover Athletic (3,583)
Dover Athletic	1-2	Sittingbourne (3,016)
Gravesend & Nthflt	3-0	Epsom & Ewell (350)
Lewes	1-1	Met. Police (98)
Metropolitan Police	3-2	Lewes (94)
Langney Sports	3-8	Leatherhead (168)
Bromley	3-1	Dulwich Hamlet (541)
Margate	6-0	Pagham (343)
Ringmer	1-0	Southwick (106)
Selsey	2-3	Basingstoke T. (82)
Carshalton Athletic	2-0	Havant Town (371)
Sheppey United	1-1	Portfield (41)
Portfield	0-3	Sheppey United (49)
Tooting & Mitcham U.	3-1	Wick (219)
Tonbridge	3-0	Bemerton Heath (412)
Dorking	4-1	Worthing (298)
Whitstable Town	2-1	Whyteleafe (160)
Brockenhurst	1-4	Eastleigh (133)
Buckingham Town	0-1	Andover (118)
Bashley	2-1	Abingdon Town (240)
Calne Town	5-1	Cove (71)
Hungerford Town	0-2	Newport IOW (111)
Peacehaven & Tel.	1-1	AFC Lymington (152)
AFC Lymington	2-0	Peacehaven (76)
Dorchester Town	1-0	Wokingham T. (489)
Maidenhead United	1-2	Newbury Town
Poole Town	0-0	Wimborne Town (456)
Wimborne Town	2-0	Poole Town (710)
Thame United (152)	1-1	Witney Town
Witney Town	1-2	Thame United (172)
Waterlooville	1-0	Salisbury City (295)
Thatcham Town	4-2	AFC Totton (128)
Bridport	2-3	Elmore (252)

Chippenham Town	0-5	Weymouth (332)
Gloucester City	1-2	Clevedon Town (346)
Cinderford Town	1-1	Barnstaple T. (105)
Barnstaple Town	3-1	Cinderford T. (218)
Frome Town	0-0	Moreton Town (128)
Moreton Town	1-0	Frome Town (123)
Odd Down Athletic	2-2	Forest Green (87)
Forest Green Rovers	1-3	Odd Down Ath. (106)
Trowbridge Town	1-1	Newport AFC (477)
Newport AFC	0-5	Trowbridge T. (244)
Mangotsfield United	3-0	Melksham Town (138)
Shortwood United	1-3	Weston-s-Mare (105)
Taunton Town	3-0	Saltash United (253)
Worcester City	1-1	Tiverton Town (823)
Tiverton Town	4-2	Worcester C. (518)
Paulton Rovers	2-1	Yate Town (140)

The two matches between Kent rivals Sittingbourne and Dover caused a big stir in the 'Garden of England'. Below Sittingbourne striker Steve Lovell rises above Tony Dixon to get in a header during the goalless first game. Photo - Paul Dennis.

Second Qualifying Round

(SAT. 25th SEPT. 1993)

(Attendances in brackets)

Dunston Feds	1-1	Billingham Syn. (125)
Billingham Synthonia	1-0	Dunston Feds (128)
Gateshead	3-1	Consett
Gretna	8-1	Evenwood Town (65)
Barrow	6-1	Harrogate Town (998)
Northallerton	4-1	Easington Coll. (124)
Netherfield	3-2	Newcastle BS (184)
Lancaster City	3-2	Tow Law Town (155)
Spennymoor United	2-3	Whitby Town (417)
Leek Town	5-3	Bamber Bridge (394)
Emley	2-0	Ashton United (407)

Below: Carl Bradshaw (left) of Emley holds off Ian Redman as the Yorkshire side ease to a 2-0 victory over Ashton United at the Welfare Ground.

Photo - Colin Stevens.

Warrington Town	2-2	Clitheroe (259)
Clitheroe	0-2	Warrington T. (224)
Stalybridge Celtic	2-2	Bootle (426)
Bootle	1-3	Stalybridge C. (313)
Morecambe	3-2	Goole Town (354)
Bridlington Town	2-1	Flixton (121)
Winsford Utd	2-1	Guiseley (271)
Buxton	2-0	Hucknall Town (320)
Lincoln Utd	1-5	North Ferriby (115)
Chorley	2-1	Liversedge (273)
Knowsley United	2-1	St Helens Town (191)
Colwyn Bay	4-1	Thackley (188)
Nuneaton Borough	3-3	W Mids Police (1,073)
West Mids Police	0-3	Nuneaton Boro' (300)
Droylsden	1-1	Worksop Town (254)
Worksop Town	3-0	Droylsden (276)
Solihull Borough	2-2	Armitage '90 (146)
Armitage '90	2-3	Solihull Boro. (125)
Bromsgrove Rovers	2-0	Bedworth Utd (701)
Raunds Town	3-1	Dudley Town (78)
Telford Utd	2-2	Grantham Town (665)
Grantham Town	1-3	Telford Utd (557)
Pelsall Villa	1-2	Pershore Town
Atherstone United	0-0	Redditch Utd (290)
Redditch United	1-1	Atherstone Utd (302)
Redditch United	1-3	Atherstone Utd (445)
Rushden & Diamonds	1-1	Rothwell Town (990)
Rothwell Town	0-2	Rushden & D. (929)
Burton Albion	3-2	Sandwell Boro' (425)
Billericay Town	1-3	Bishop's Stfd (567)
Boston United	2-3	Canvey Island (855)
Hendon	5-2	Heybridge Sw. (171)
Cambridge City	3-0	Harwich & P. (327)
Wivenhoe Town	2-2	King's Lynn (324)
King's Lynn	1-4	Wivenhoe Town (1,019)

Chelmsford City	5-2	Stamford (486)
Lowestoft Town	1-2	East Thurrock (285)
Stevenage Borough	4-3	Corby Town (707)
Barton Rovers	1-2	Halstead Town

Below: Halshead Town (white shirts) attack the Barton Rovers defence as they win 2-1 at Sharpenhoe Road to reach the Third Qualifying Round for the first time.

Photo - Martin Wray.

Dagenham & Red.	2-1	Baldock Town (677)
Burnham	1-3	Edgware Town (118)
Chesham United	5-0	Chalfont St P. (538)
Haringey Borough	1-3	Hornchurch (68)
Enfield	1-0	Hemel Hemp. (623)
Ruislip Manor	1-1	Purfleet (172)
Purfleet	1-0	Ruislip Manor (97)
Yeading	5-2	Kingsbury T. (130)
Chertsey Town	2-0	Tilbury (268)
Harrow Borough	6-0	Viking Sports (185)
Canterbury City	1-4	Chatham Town (104)
Kingstonian	1-1	Bognor Regis T.
Bognor Regis	1-6	Kingstonian (450)
Croydon	0-1	Greenwich B. (80)
Molesey	2-0	Corinthian (138)
Erith & Belvedere	2-1	Herne Bay (187)
Sittingbourne	0-2	Gravesend & N. (2,044)
Leatherhead	3-5	Met. Police
Bromley	0-3	Margate (343)
Basingstoke Town	3-0	Ringmer (185)
Carshalton Athletic	5-1	Sheppey United (474)
Tonbridge	0-2	Tooting & Mit. (552)
Dorking	4-0	Whitstable Town
Andover	3-0	Eastleigh (221)
Bashley	3-1	Calne Town (263)
AFC Lymington	0-1	Newport IOW (215)
Dorchester Town	0-3	Newbury Town (449)
Thame United	2-3	Wimborne Town (189)
Waterlooville	3-0	Thatcham Town (140)
Weymouth	3-0	Elmore (622)
Clevedon Town	2-2	Barnstaple T. (474)
Barnstaple Town	2-1	Clevedon Town (410)
Odd Down Athletic	0-2	Moreton Town (213)
Trowbridge Town	0-0	Mangotsfield (432)
Mangotsfield Utd	2-2	Trowbridge T. (420)
Trowbridge Town	2-3	Mangotsfield (497)
Taunton Town	2-4	Weston-s-Mare (493)
Tiverton Town	2-1	Paulton Rovers (454)

PHOTOS OPPOSITE

Top: *Tim Hope attempts a spectacular overhead kick for Tooting & Mitcham in the 2-0 win at Tonbridge.*

Photo - Dennis Nicholson.

Centre: *Greenwich Borough substitute Steve Scott heads just wide at Croydon, but his side still win 1-0 to reach the penultimate qualifying round for the first time.*

Photo - Alan Coomes.

Foot: *Another spectacular overhead kick, and this time a specular goal - the first for Erith & Belvedere against Herne Bay - scored by Simon Piere.*

Photo - Keith Gillard.

LONDON CREDITPOINT CENTRE
FINANCE CONSULTANTS

Third Qualifying Round

(SAT. 9th OCT. 1993)

Andover 0 v 2 Bashley
Att:517 — Whale 47, Morrell 69

Basingstoke Town 1 v 3 Carshalton A.
Woods, Att:417 — Bolton, Richards, Annon

Billingham Syn. 1 v 1 Gateshead
Allen 41 Att:409 — Dobson 33

Gateshead 0 v 1 Billingham S.
(Played 12-10-93)
Att:409 — O'Brien 21

Bishop's Stortford 0 v 1 Canvey Island
Att:921 — Newbury 38

Chatham Town 1 v 2 Kingstonian
Hume 39(p) Att:498 — Harlow 5 75

Chertsey Town 1 v 3 Harrow Boro'
Turner Att:556 — Westley, Fraser, Shaw

East Thurrock U. 1 v 5 Stevenage B.
Lewis Att:622 — Gittings (4), Venables

Edgware Town 1 v 2 Chesham Utd
Thompson 25 Att:631 — Webley 48, Dawber 75

Erith & Belvedere 0 v 1 Gravesend
Att:742 — Gubbins 48

Greenwich Boro. 0 v 4 Molesey
Att:280 — Pearson(4)
(played at Bromley FC, 10-10-93)

Gretna 2 v 1 Barrow
Gorman 3 89(p) Att:732 — Doherty 87(p)

Halstead Town 1 v 3 Dagenham
Streatley 7 Att:850 — Watts 2, Crown 22, Desouza 44

Hendon 0 v 1 Cambridge C.
Att:382 — Grogan 45

Hornchurch 1 v 4 Enfield
Nelson Att:554 — Ryan, Hobson(p), Collins, Greene

Below: Micky Linnell (white shirt) of Hornchurch is crowded out by Paul Hobson and Graham Roberts of Enfield. *Photo - Rob Monger.*

Knowsley United 3 v 0 Colwyn Bay
Waring 25, Green 30, Stanton 70 Att:254

Lancaster City 1 v 2 Whitby Town
Diggle 39 Att:213 — Linacre 46 65

Leek Town 1 v 0 Emley
Twigg 19 Att:572

Met. Police 5 v 2 Margate
Russo 4 30, Pendry 5, Carruth 70 85 Att:217 — Cuggy 19, Cordice 89

Morecambe 2 v 0 Bridlington T.
Grimshaw 58, Holden 74 Att:405

Moreton Town 1 v 1 Mangotsfield
Rose 66 Att:225 — Saunders 83(OG)

Mangotsfield Utd 1 v 2 Moreton Town
(Played 12-10-93)
Birkby 76 Att:324 — Spittle 45, Tucker 63

Newport I.O.W. 4 v 2 Newbury Town
(Played 18-10-93)
Soares 9 46 65, Ritchie 22(p) Att:548 — McDonnell 3, Parr 83

Northallerton T. 4 v 3 Netherfield
Gill 53 71, Warrior 57, Dowson 84 Att:226 — Whittaker 18 20 73

North Ferriby Utd 1 v 1 Chorley
McKenzie 16 Att:284 — Hamilton 70

Chorley 2 v 1 North Ferriby
(Played 12-10-93)
M Payne 4, Grant 40 Att:347 — Tennison 63

Nuneaton Boro' 4 v 1 Worksop Town
Bullock 64 90, Culpin 83, Wharton 89(OG) Att:1382 — Rowlands 60

Pershore Town 1 v 0 Atherstone T.
Knight 37(OG) Att:709

Purfleet 1 v 2 Yeading
Cobb Att:153 — Charles (2)

Raunds Town 0 v 4 Telford United
Att:354 — Niblett 37, Parrish 42, Taylor 74, Whitehouse 90

Rushden & Dia. 4 v 0 Burton Albion
Nuttell 26, Mann 65, Richardson 78, Watkins 83 Att:1201

Solihull Borough 1 v 2 Bromsgrove R.
Canning 18 Att:816 — Carter 74, Crisp 80

Tooting & Mit. 2 v 0 Dorking
Hope 29, Cowan 50 Att:524

Warrington Town 0 v 1 Stalybridge C.
Att:654 — Kirkham 39

Weston-s.-Mare 0 v 0 Tiverton Town
Att:845

Tiverton Town 0 v 2 Weston-s.-M.
(Played 12-10-93)
Att:891 — Tapp 8 80

Weymouth 2 v 1 Barnstaple T.
(Played 14-10-93)
Gibson 11, Senior 46 Att:707 — Nichols 43

Wimborne Town 0 v 1 Waterlooville
Att:796 — Burnside 88

Winsford Utd 6 v 1 Buxton
Byrne 2 47, Bishop 9 38 48, Blain 86 Att:322 — Lowe 64

Wivenhoe Town 2 v 0 Chelmsford C.
Ashurst 20, Guyon 34 Att:676

Gretna's Paul Gorman dramatically scores an injury-time penalty winner against Barrow.Photo - Alan Watson.

Jubilant Canvey Island celebrations in the dressing-room at Bishop's Stortford. Photo - Gavin Ellis-Neville.

Gary Fletcher (left) of Wimborne chases a ball with Waterlooville's Kevin Murphy. Photo - Paul Dennis.

Fourth Qualifying Round

(SAT. 23rd OCT. 1993)

Witton Albion	**2 v 1**	**Northallerton**
Maynard 14, Burke 90	Att: 706	Gill 54
Winsford United	**0 v 0**	**Gretna**
	Att: 347	
Gretna	**5 v 0**	**Winsford Utd**
	(Played 26-10-93)	
Walker 19, Dobie 37 82, Gorman 57, Halpin 77	Att: 754	
Macclesfield T.	**5 v 3**	**Southport**
Wood 7, Alford 23(p) 31 76, Sharratt 89	Att: 1190	Goulding 10, Gamble 32 90(ps)
Altrincham	**0 v 2**	**Accrington S.**
	Att: 956	Beck 77 89
Stalybridge C.	**0 v 0**	**Whitby Town**
	Att: 1521	
Whitby Town	**0 v 1**	**Stalybridge**
	(Played 27-10-93)	
	Att: 887	Allen 34
Stafford Rangers	**1 v 1**	**Knowsley Utd**
Burr 69	Att: 973	Jones 88
Knowsley United	**2 v 2**	**Stafford Rgrs**
	(Played 26-10-93)	
Green 23 88(p)	Att: 612	Hemming 3,
Knowsley United	**1 v 0**	**Stafford Rgrs**
	(Played 01-11-93)	
Jones 85	Att: 951	
Billingham Syn.	**1 v 1**	**Leek Town**
Maloney 83(p)	Att: 469	Smith 31
Leek Town	**2 v 1**	**Billingham S.**
	(Played 26-10-93)	
Wheaton 31, Twigg 55	Att: 876	O'Brien 51,
Chorley	**0 v 2**	**Marine**
	Att: 740	Camden 16, Proctor 65
Telford Utd	**2 v 0**	**Morecambe**
Parrish 62, Myers 82	Att: 901	
Wivenhoe Town	**1 v 2**	**Enfield**
Prior 73	Att: 532	Green 7, Collins 38
Hayes	**0 v 2**	**Slough Town**
	Att: 877	M Scott 29, Fiore 49
Cambridge City	**2 v 2**	**Dagenham & Red.**
Wilkin 6, Ryan 90	Att: 1026	Richardson 12 36
Dagenham & R.	**0 v 2**	**Cambridge C.**
	(Played 25-10-93)	
	Att: 1410	Grogan 18, Conner 43(OG)
Stevenage B.	**1 v 2**	**Nuneaton B.**
Debham 33	Att: 2187	Bullock 74, Rosegreen 89
Kettering Town	**3 v 1**	**Canvey I.**
Thorpe 6, Wright 26 55	Att: 2191	Jones 58
VS Rugby	**2 v 2**	**Harrow Boro'**
Warner 16, King 52(p)	Att: 826	Fraser 9, Westley 27(p)
Harrow Borough	**1 v 2**	**VS Rugby**
	(Played 27-10-93)	
Westley 41(p),	Att: 640	King 49 68
Aylesbury Utd	**1 v 2**	**Marlow**
Blencowe 88	Att: 926	Watkins 4, Lay 56
Pershore Town	**1 v 3**	**Yeading**
Rawle 84	Att: 1356	Welsh 12(p) 90, Charles 29
Rushden & Dia.	**1 v 3**	**Bromsgrove**
Kirkup 76	Att: 1521	Wardle 45, Carter 73, Radburn 90
Chesham United	**1 v 4**	**Kidderminster**
Dawber 89	Att: 1500	Humphreys 5 90, Brindley 60, Grainger 67
Kingstonian	**0 v 1**	**Met. Police**
	Att: 689	Pendry 43
Waterlooville	**1 v 3**	**Gravesend**
James 34	Att: 683	Cotter 30, Portway 40 89
Crawley Town	**2 v 1**	**Merthyr Tyd.**
Whitington 58, Vansittart 80	Att: 1623	James 24
Cheltenham T.	**1 v 1**	**Bath City**
Eaton 11	Att: 1020	Adcock 88
Bath City	**4 v 2**	**Cheltenham**
	(Played 26-10-93)	
Noble 28, Cousins 61, Crowley 79, Adcock 83	Att: 1166	Eaton 49, J Smith 55(p)
Bashley	**1 v 1**	**Carshalton A.**
Stickler 35	Att: 615	Riley 78
Carshalton Ath.	**4 v 2**	**Bashley**
	(Played 25-10-93)	
Warden 8, Beste 30 49, Bolton 66	Att: 971	Morrell 37(p), Harbut 52
Sutton United	**0 v 0**	**Moreton Town**
	Att: 804	
Moreton Town	**0 v 2**	**Sutton Utd**
	(Played 26-10-93)	
	Att: 706	Newman 13 63
Molesey	**0 v 0**	**Tooting & M.**
	Att: 461	
Tooting & Mit.	**1 v 2**	**Molesey**
Stephens,	Att: 702	Worrall, Rattue
Weymouth	**1 v 4**	**Farnborough**
Aston 34	Att: 1283	Read 9 32, Horton 47, Boothe 74
Weston-s.-Mare	**2 v 0**	**Newport IOW**
Bowering 60, Bonaparte 88	Att: 700	

PHOTOS OPPOSITE

Top: *Christer Green of Cheltenham Town prepares to take on Bath City defender Richard Crowley. The Robins were unlucky to be denied victory by a late equaliser for the Conference side in this Whaddon Road clash.*
Photo - Gavin Ellis-Neville.

Centre: *Paul Tomlinson and Ollie Parillon combine to clear a Telford United attack at Bucks Head, but the Lancashire side still go down 0-2.*
Photo - Colin Stevens.

Foot: *Dave Johnson of Rushden & Diamonds holds off Bromsgrove's semi-pro international full-back Stewart Brighton during the keenly contested tie at Nene Park.*
Photo - Paul Dennis.

AMILY
ENCLOSURE
Gulf

a pint of the Midlands

shden & Diamonds

First Round Proper

(SAT. 13th NOV. 1993)

Accrington Stan. 2 v 3 Scunthorpe Utd
Connor 66, Beck 93 — Toman 31, Goodacre 82 94
(Played at Burnley FC, 14-11-93)
Ref: T Heilbron (Newton Aycliffe) Att: 5,858
Accrington: Armfield, Wood, Cooper, Connor, Moss, Williams, Grimshaw, Hughes (Senior 74), Lutkevitch (Lampkin 88), Beck, Hoskin. Unused sub: Henry.
Scunthorpe: Samways, Alexander, Mudd, Hope, Knill, Carmichael, Thompstone, Martin, White (Goodacre 64), Toman, Smith. Unused subs: Thornber, Wilmot.

Barnet 2 v 1 Carshalton Ath.
Haag 56, Close 72 — Annon 15
Ref: D Orr (Iver) Att: 2,690
Barnet: Phillips, Wilson, Haylock (Cooper 62), Hoddle (Alexander 84), Walker, Barnett, Marwood, Rowe, Haag, Close, Scott. Unused sub: Pape.
Carshalton: Cleevely, Stevens, Richards, Priddle, Riley, Cooper, Warden, Bowyer, Bolton, Annon (Cox 62), Beste. Unused subs: Carney, Norman.

Cambridge City 0 v 1 Hereford United
Pike 85
(Played 14-11-93)
Ref: P Alcock (South Merstham) Att: 2,325
Cambridge: Murray, Tovey, Scott, Fallon, Beattie, Gawthorpe, Wilkins, Pincher, Ryan, Grogan, Coe. Unused subs: Hope, Goddard, Piggott.
Hereford: Judge, Clark, Anderson, Downs, Smith, Reece, Hall, Fry, Pike, Pickard, Nicholson. Unused subs: Morris, Abraham, Thomas.

Colchester Utd 3 v 4 Sutton United
McGavin 40, Brown 52, English 87 — Quail 18, Smart 31, Newman 84, Morah 88
Ref: N Barry (Scunthorpe) Att: 3,051
Colchester: Keeley, Betts, Roberts, Kinsella, English, Cawley, Dickens, Brown, McDonough, McGavin, Smith. Unused subs: Ball, Richardson, Schults.
Sutton: McCaulsky, Gates, Smart, Golley, Costello, Jones, Anderson, Newman, Morah, Quail, Byrne. Unused subs: McKinnon, Edwards, Harris.

Enfield 0 v 0 Cardiff City
Ref: A Smith (Birmingham) Att: 2,374
Enfield: McCann, Francis, Engwell, Roberts, Heald, St Hilaire, Hobson, Pye (Bailey 80), Turner, Collins, Ryan. Unused subs: Ridout, White.
Cardiff: Williams, Brazil, Searle, Millar, Perry, Aizelwood, Thompson (Bird 75), Richardson, Stant, Blake, Griffith. Unused subs: Wigg, Grew.

Farnborough T. 1 v 3 Exeter City
Jones 42 — Worthington 76, Jepson 81, Ross 83
Ref: G Pooley (Bishop's Stortford) Att: 2,069
Farnborough: Taylor, Stemp, Pratt, Broome, Coney, Jones, Boothe, Read, Baker, Turkington, Horton. Unused subs: Walters, Savage, Grainger.
Exeter: Fox, Minett, Robinson (Daniels 46), Bailey, Brown, Whiston, Wigley, Coughlin, Jepson, Ross, Phillips (Worthington 66).

Gretna 2 v 3 Bolton Wdrs
Townsley 11, Dobie 25 — McGinlay 14, Coyle 79 84
(Played at Bolton)
Ref: E Lomas (Manchester) Att: 6,447
Gretna: Priestley, Armstrong, McCartney, Gorman, Gardiner, Townsley, Halpin, Walsh, Walker (Eagling 89), Dobie, Potts (Monaghan 89). Unused sub: Sweeting.
Bolton: Davison, Brown, Phillips, McAteer, Stubbs, Winstanley, Lee, Green (Kelly 71), Coyle, McGinlay, Thompston. Unused subs: Seagraves, Hoult.

Halifax Town 2 v 1 West Bromwich
Peake 6, Saunders 37 — Hunt 82
(Played 14-11-93)
Ref: A Flood (Stockport) Att: 4,250
Halifax: Hayes, German, Craven, Edwards, Boardman, Barr, Peake, Ridings, Lambert, Patterson (Constable 85), Saunders. Unused subs: Filson, Brown.
West Brom: Lange, Coldicott, Ampadu (Reid 74), McNally, O'Regan, Burgess, Hunt, Hamilton, Taylor, Ashcroft, Donovan (Mellon 62). Unused sub: Naylor.

Kidderminster 3 v 0 Kettering Town
Brindley 66, Forsyth 68(p), Davies 89
Ref: T Holbrook (Walsall) Att: 3,775
Kidderminster: Rose, Hodson, Bancroft, Weir, Brindley, Forsyth, Cartwright, Grainger, Humphreys, Davies, Palmer. Unused subs: Gillett, Deakin, Carrington.
Kettering: Benstead, Muckleborough, Ashby, Price, Oxbrow, Taylor, Wright (Thorpe 75), Brown, Martin, Donald, Clark. Unused subs: Roderick.

Knowsley Utd 1 v 4 Carlisle United
Reeves 29(og) — Arnold 8 66, Reeves 33, Davey 28
(Played at Everton FC)
Ref: M Peck (Kendal) Att: 4,800
Knowsley: Johnston, Wareing, Diggle, O'Brien, Jackson, Barton (King 66), McMahon, R Kilshaw (Siddell 46), B Kilshaw, Green, Gelling. Unused sub: Duffy.
Carlisle: Day, Burgess, Gallimore, Walling, Joyce, Edmondson (Fairweather 77), Thomas, Arnold, Reeves, Davey, Reddish. Unused subs: McCreery, Elliott.

Leek Town 2 v 2 Wigan Athletic
Sutton 70 93 — Skipper 35, Morton 67
(Played 12-11-93)
Ref: J A Kirkby (Sheffield) Att: 2,785
Leek: Mayfield, S R Jones, Sankey, Holmes (Finney 73), Norris, Diskin, Wheaton (Mitchell 66), Somerville, D Sutton, S M Jones, Smith. Unused sub: S Sutton.
Wigan: Farnworth, Carragher, Rennie, Kennedy, Skipper, Johnson, Duffy, Rimmer (Langley 66), Gavin, Morton (Robertson 80), McKearney. Unused sub: Pennock.

Leyton Orient 2 v 1 Gravesend & N.
Lakin 42, Hackett 77 — Portway 40
Ref: M Bailey (Cambridge) Att: 5,461
Orient: Newell, Hendon, Austin, Hackett, Harriott, Okai, Tomlinson, Ryan, Cooper, West, Lakin. Unused subs: Taylor, Bellamy, Turner.
Gravesend: Turner, Harrop, Land, Gubbins, Gibbs, Cant, Schweiso, Hunt, Graves (Coffil 81), Portway, Ullathorne. Unused subs: Leahy, Carlton.

Macclesfield T. 2 v 0 Hartlepool Utd
Sorvel 39, McDonald 45
Ref: E Wolstenholme (Blackburn) Att: 2,747
Macclesfield: Farrelly, Shepherd, Bimson, Kendall, Lillis, Sorvel, Askey, Wood (McDonald 23), Alford, Adams, Sharratt. Unused sub: Heron, Williams.
Hartlepool: Carter, Cross, Skedd, McGuckin, McPhail, Olsson, Gilchrist, Wratten (Honour 55), Houchen, Johnrose, West (Southall 61). Unused sub: Jones.

Marlow 0 v 2 Plymouth Argyle
Dalton 64 89
Ref: M J Brandwood (Lichfield) Att: 2,700
Marlow: K Mitchell, S Mitchell, Holmes, Baron, Ferguson, Regan (Malins 76), Lay, Catlin (Dell 46), Blackman, Buzaglo, Watkins. Unused sub: Lester.
Plymouth: Nicholls, Patterson, Naylor, Burrows, Comyn, McCall, Burnett, Castle, Nugent, Skinner (Marshall 46), Dalton. Unused subs: Edworthy, Newland.

PHOTOS OPPOSITE

Top: *Cambridge City's Andy Beattie gets the better of Chris Fry of Hereford United during the Sunday afternoon tie at Milton Road.*
Photo - Dave West.

Centre: *Neil Sorvel is mobbed by ecstatic team-mates after scoring the first goal to put Macclesfield Town on the road to a shock result against Hartlepool United.*
Photo - Colin Stevens.

Foot: *Steve Portway heads Gravesend & Northfleet into a surprise lead away to Leyton Orient.*
Photo - Keith Gillard.

six days a
week
FRED R
LAW COSTS DRAFT
TEL. CAMBRIDGE
MUSIC

BUKTA

Met. Police 0 v 2 Crawley Town
Whitington 52, Vansittart 61

Ref: B Hill (Kettering) Att: 1,561
Police: Land, Towler, Mullings (Wright 65), Naylor, Carrugh, Reed, Adams, Pendry, Russo, Holding, Richardson (Clarke 65). Unused sub: Young.
Crawley: Taylor, Pearson, N Turner, Shepherd, Vessey, Jeffrey, Payne, Ford, Vansittart (L Turner 85), Whitington, Dack. Unused subs: Adam, Caulfield.

Molesey 0 v 4 Bath City
Mings 13, Boyle 14, Adcock 34 45

Ref: G Singh (Wolverhampton) Att: 913
Molesey: Brace, Langley, Woods, Dodman, Boorman (Callaghan 62), Patullo, Wilgoss (White 78), McCoy, Rose, Pearson, Rattue. Unused subs: Swift, Agboola, Read.
Bath: Mogg, Banks, Brooks, Boyle, Crowley, Cousins (Batty 78), Williams, Gill, Adcock (Vernon 78), Mings, Chenoweth. Unused sub: Torrez.

Northampton T. 1 v 2 Bromsgrove Rvrs
Aldridge 89 — Shilvock 35, Carter 85

Ref: B Coddington (Sheffield) Att: 3,382
Northampton: Sherwood, Parsons, Gillard, Phillips, Terry, Chard, Harmon (Fleming 72), Aldridge, Gilzean, Bell. Unused subs: Stackman, Richardson.
Bromsgrove: Cooksey, Webb, Brighton, Richardson, Wardle, Skelding, Shilvock, Stott, Radburn (Pearce 71), Crisp, Carter. Unused subs: Carty, Powell.

Runcorn 0 v 1 Hull City
Atkinson 29
(Abandoned after 29 minutes)

Ref: K Lynch (Lincoln) Att: 2,194
Runcorn: Williams, Bates, Robertson, Brady, Lee, Anderson, Thomas, Connor, McInerny, McKenna, Brabin. Unused subs: Parker, Wall, Curtis.
Hull: Fettis, Mail, Miller, Warren, Dewhurst, Abbott, Norton, Hargreaves, Brown, Windass, Atkinson. Unused subs: Allison, Wilson.

Runcorn 0 v 2 Hull City
Brown 7, Hargreaves 12
(Played at Witton Albion FC, 23-11-93)

Ref: K Lynch (Lincoln) Att: 1,131
Runcorn: Williams, Bates, Robertson, Brady, Lee, Anderson, Thomas, Connor, McInerny, McKenna, Carroll. Unused subs: Parker, Wall, Curtis.
Hull: Fettis, Allison, Miller, Warren, Dewhurst, Abbott, Norton, Hargreaves, Brown, Windass, Atkinson. Unused subs: Moran, Wilson, Lee.

Slough Town 1 v 2 Torquay United
M Scott 65 — Sale 10, Moore 40

Ref: P Don (Hanworth) Att: 2,371
Slough: Bunting, Quamina, Hancock, Manning, Lee, Edwards, Stanley (Walker 81), S Scott, M Scott, Sayer, Fiore. Unused subs: Dilly, Briley.
Torquay: Bayes, Barrow, Colcombe, O'Riordan, Moore (Burton 73), Curran, Trollope, Kelly, Foster (Darby 90), Sale, Hathaway. Unused sub: Lowe.

Stalybridge C. 1 v 1 Marine
Aspinall 27 — Rowlands 20

Ref: T West (Hull) Att: 1,525
Stalybridge: Hughes, Bennett, Coathup, Dixon, Aspinall, Booth, Brown, Leicester (White 74), Shaughnessy, Bunn, Locke (Jackson 21). Unused sub: Kirkham.
Marine: Holcroft, Ward, Hansen, Roche, Draper, Gautrey, Murray, Rowlands, Ross, Camden, Dawson. Unused subs: Doherty, McBride, Hollywood.

Swansea City 1 v 1 Nuneaton Boro'
Torpey 90 — Shearer 79

Ref: J Holbrook (Ludlow) Att: 3,532
Swansea: Freestone, Clode, Cook, Walker, Harris (Ford 19), Pascoe, Bowen (McFarlane 74), Chapple, Torpey, Perrett, Hayes. Unused sub: Miles.
Nuneaton: Attwood, Byrne, McGorry, Bullock, Tarry, Keogh, Simpson, Bradder, Green, Rosegreen (Shearer 68), Wade. Unused subs: London, Manuel.

Telford United 1 v 1 Huddersfield T.
Bignot 17 — Rowe 5

Ref: G Cain (Bootle) Att: 2,257
Telford: Acton, Pritchard, Parrish, Niblett, Gaunt, Fergusson, Bignot, Taylor, Whitehouse, Myers, Ford. Unused subs: Holmes, Gernon, Hughes.
Huddersfield: Francis, Trevitt, Billy, Hicks, Mitchell, Jackson, Rowe, Robinson, Roberts, Onuora, Wells. Unused subs: Dyson, Collins, Blackwell.

V.S. Rugby 0 v 3 Brentford
Allon 38(p) 79, Gayle 54

Ref: I Hemley (Ampthill) Att: 3,006
Rugby: Batchelor, Yang, McGinty, Smithers, Statham (Magill 15), Smith, Mason, King, Martin, Warner, Harriman (Alsop 69). Unused sub: Gawman.
Brentford: Dearden, Hutchings, Grainger, Westley, Bates, Stephenson, Ratcliffe, Smith, Mundee, Gayle, Allon. Unused subs: Ravenscoft, Millen, Williams.

Witton Albion 0 v 2 Lincoln City
West 72, Lormor 90

Ref: R Poulain (Huddersfield) Att: 1,450
Witton: Mason, Senior, Thomas, Edey, Walker (Blackwood 77), Garton, Gallagher, Rose, Maynard, Burke, Hall. Unused subs: Holt, Williams.
Lincoln: Pollitt, Smith, Barraclough, Hill, Brown, Schofield, West, Loughlin (Mardenborough 68), Lormor, Matthews, Johnson. Unused subs: Clarke.

Woking 2 v 2 Weston-s-Mare
Wye 8, Dennis 53 — Elson 20, Bowering 30

Ref: K Cooper (Swindon) Att: 2,766
Woking: Batty, Clement, Steele, Berry, K Brown, S Wye, D Brown, Biggins, Dennis, Fielder, Walker. Unused sub: Swift, Agboola, Read.
Weston: Stevens, Holt, Chattoe, Stearnes, Bowering, Rogers, Hooker, Patterton, Withey, Elson, Tapp. Unused subs: Sweeney, Purnell.

Yeading 0 v 0 Gillingham
(Played at Hayes FC)

Ref: K Morton (Bury St Edmunds) Att: 2,285
Yeading: McKenzie, Ardren, Dicker, Cordery, Croad, Denton, Oatway, James, Welsh (Williams 90), Hippolyte, Charles (Baker 86).
Gillingham: Banks, Martin, Palmer, Butler, Green, Dunne, Carpenter, Forster, Baker (Arnott 88), Smith, Reinelt. Unused subs: Watson, Barrett.

Yeovil Town 1 v 0 Fulham
Wallace 90
(Played 15-11-93)

Ref: C Wilkes (Gloucester) Att: 6,180
Yeovil: Coles, Coates, Ferns, Sherwood, Bye, Leonard, Sanderson, Wallace, Wilson, Spencer, Harrower (Cooper 67). Unused subs: McPherson, Bush.
Fulham: Stannard, Jupp, Ferney, Eckhardt, Angus, Thomas, Hails, Bedroussian, Farrell, Brazil, Baah. Unused subs: Tierling, Kelly, Harrison.

FIRST ROUND REPLAYS

Cardiff City 1 v 0 Enfield
Blake 89
(Played 30-11-93)

Ref: A Smith (Birmingham) Att: 3,232
Cardiff: Grew, Brazil, Searle, Aizelwood, Baddeley, Perry (Wigg 67), Bird (Thompson 73), Millar, Stant, Blake, Griffith. Unused sub: Kite.
Enfield: McCann, Francis, Engwell, Ridout (Britwell 88), Heald, Pye (Boyce 88), Hobson, St Hilaire, Turner, Ryan, Collins. Unused sub: White.

Gillingham 3 v 1 Yeading
Smith 11, Micklewhite 28, Baker 38 — James 85
(Played 30-11-93)

Ref: K Morton (Bury St Edmunds) Att: 3,231
Gillingham: Banks, Carpenter, Butler, Dunne, Clark, Palmer, Smith, Micklewhite, Smillie, Forster (Reinelt 77), Baker. Unused subs: Breen, Barrett.
Yeading: McKenzie, Denton, Dicker, Croad, Ardren, James, Oatway (Williams 73), Cordery, Welsh, Hippolyte, Charles (Baker 66).

Huddersfield T. 1 v 0 Telford United
Jackson 50
(Played 23-11-93)

Ref: G Cain (Bootle) Att: 3,517
Huddersfield: Francis, Trevitt, Billy, Mitchell, Hicks, Jackson, Rowe, Robinson, Roberts, Dunn, Wells. Unused subs: Starbuck, Collins, Blackwell.
Telford: Hughes, Pritchard, Parrish, Niblett, Mitchell (Whitehouse 81), Fergusson, Bignot, Taylor, Ford, Myers, Statham. Unused subs: Acton, Gernon.

Marine 4 v 4 Stalybridge C.
Camden 29 32, Murray 83, Doherty 107(p) — Hill 6, Shaughnessy 30, Aspinall 62, Kirkham 113
(Stalybridge won 4-2 on pens)
(Played 29-11-93)

Ref: T West (Hull) Att: 853
Marine: Holcroft, Baines, Ward, Roche, McBride (sub: Doherty), Gautrey, Murray, Rowlands, Ross, Camden, Dawson. Unused subs: Hanson, Hollywood.
Stalybridge: Hughes, Edmonds, Coathup, Dixon, Aspinall, Booth, Brown, Bunn, Shaughnessy (Leicester 109), Kirkham, Hill (Bennett 20). Unused sub: White.

Nuneaton Boro' 2 v 1 Swansea City
Simpson 83 99 — Torpey 9
(Played 23-11-93)

Ref: J Holbrook (Ludlow) Att: 4,443
Nuneaton: Attwood, Byrne, McGorry, Keogh, Tarry, Wade (Symonds 69), Simpson, Bradder, Green, Rosegreen, Shearer. Unused subs: London, Manuel.
Swansea: Freestone, Clode (Ford 79), Cook, Walker, Harris, Pascoe, Bowen, Chapple, Torpey, Cornforth, Hayes (McFarlane 90). Unused sub: Miles.

Weston-s-Mare 0 v 1 Woking
Clement 57
(Played 23-11-93)

Ref: D Frampton (Poole) Att: 2,350
Weston: Stevens, Holt, Jones (Chattoe 73), Stearnes, Bowering, Rogers, Hooker, Patterton, Withey, Elson, Tapp (Banks 80). Unused sub: House.
Woking: Batty, Clement, Steele, Berry, K Brown, S Wye, D Brown, Biggins, Fielder, Dennis, Walker. Unused sub: Swift, Tucker, Read.

Wigan Athletic 3 v 0 Leek Town
McKearney 17(p), Diskin 50(og), Duffy 82
(Played 30-11-93)

Ref: J A Kirkby (Sheffield) Att: 1,807
Wigan: Farnworth, Rennie, Wright (Ogden 75), Langley, Skipper, Johnson, Carragher, McKearney, Daley (Furlong 84), Gavin, Duffy. Unused sub: Pennock.
Leek: S Sutton, S R Jones, Banks, Norris (S M Jones 65), Clowes, Diskin, Beeby, Somerville, Twigg, D Sutton, Smith (Finney 65). Unused sub: Mayfield.

Brentford's Paul Stephenson (left) wades his way through the mire at VS Rugby. Photo - Richard Brock.

Fulham goalkeeper Jim Stannard punches clear in his side's defeat at Yeovil Town. Photo - Paul Dennis.

Second Round Proper

(SAT. 4th DEC. 1993)

Bath City 2 v 1 Hereford United
Brooks 45, Batty 78 — Hall 55
(Played 5-12-93)
Ref: V G Callow (Solihull) Att: 3,086
Bath: Mogg, Gill, Dicks, Boyle, Crowley, Cousins, Williams, Chenoweth, Adcock (Smart 86), Mings, Brooks (Batty 75). Unused sub: Torrez.
Hereford: Judge, Clark, Downs, Davies, Smith (Anderson 38), Reece, Hall, Harrison (May 80), Pike, Pickard, Nicholson. Unused sub: Thomas.

Bournemouth 1 v 1 Nuneaton Boro'
Watson 51 — Green 79
Ref: K Cooper (Pontypridd) Att: 7,000
Bournemouth: Bartram, Chivers, Masters, Morris, Watson, Parkinson, O'Connor, McGorry, Beardsmore, Wood, Leadbitter. Unused subs: Cotterill, Murray, Moss.
Nuneaton: Attwood, Byrne, McGorry, Keogh, Tarry, Wade, Simpson, Bradder, Green, Rosegreen, Shearer. Unused subs: Symonds, London, Manuel.

Carlisle United 3 v 1 Stalybridge C.
Edmondson 23, Gallimore 38, Arnold 50 — Kirkham 68
Ref: R Shepherd (Leeds) Att: 5,546
Carlisle: Elliott, Burgess, Gallimore, Walling, Joyce, Edmondson, Thomas, Arnold, Joyce, Reeves, McCreery, Reddish. Unused subs: Oghani, Caig, Curran.
Stalybridge: Hughes, Edmonds, Coathup, Dixon, Aspinall, Booth, Brown, Bunn, Shaughnessy, Kirkham, Bennett. Unused subs: Leicester, White, Locke.

Crawley Town 1 v 2 Barnet
Ford 86 — Rowe 53, Hoddle 71
Ref: M Pierce (Drayton) Att: 4,104
Crawley: Taylor, Pearson, N Turner, Shepherd, Vessey, Jeffrey, Payne, Ford, Vansittart, Adam, Dack. Unused subs: L Turner, O'Shaughnessy, Caulfield.
Barnet: Phillips, Wilson, Newson, Hoddle, Walker, Barnett, Marwood, Rowe, Haag, Close, Scott. Unused subs: Cooper, Alexander, Pape.

Below: Crawley Town's Micky Turner chases a Barnet forward in front of a record crowd at Town Mead.
Photo - Peter Lirettoc.

Crewe Alex. 2 v 1 Macclesfield T.
Lennon 25, Whalley 30 — Askey 49
Ref: K A Leach (Wolverhampton) Att: 6,007
Crewe: Smith, Booty, Gardiner, Evans, Hughes, Wilson, Whalley, Naylor, Collins, Lennon, Rowbotham. Unused sub: Tierney, Abel, Wilkinson.
Macclesfield: Farrelly, Shepherd, Bimson, Kendall, Lillis, Sorvel, Askey, McDonald, Alford, Adams, Sharratt. Unused sub: Green, Heron, Williams.

Kidderminster 1 v 0 Woking
Forsyth 81(p)
Ref: S Dunn (Bristol) Att: 4,411
Kidderminster: Rose, Hodson, Bancroft, Weir, Brindley, Forsyth, Cartwright, Grainger, Humphreys, Davies, Purdie. Unused subs: Deakin, Palmer, Steadman.
Woking: Batty, Clement, Steele, Berry, K Brown, S Wye, D Brown, Biggins, Gray, Fielder, Walker. Unused sub: Dennis, L Wye, Read.

Stockport Co. 5 v 1 Halifax Town
Frain 39, Francis 51 73, Beaumont 80, Wallace 87 — Barr 85(p)
Ref: M Peck (Kendall) Att: 5,502
Stockport: Edwards, Todd, Wallace, Frain, Flynn, Gannon, Miller, Emerson, Francis, Beaumont, Preece. Unused subs: Barras, Ryan, Ironside.
Halifax: Hayes, German, Craven, Edwards, Boardman, Megson, Peake, Barr, Ridings, Patterson, Saunders. Unused subs: Constable, Cameron, Brown.

Torquay United 0 v 1 Sutton United
Jones 77
Ref: C Wilkes (Gloucester) Att: 3,414
Torquay: Bayes, Barrow, Colcombe, O'Riordan, Moore, Curran, Trollope, Kelly, Foster, Sale, Hathaway. Unused sub: Darby, Lowe, Gayle.
Sutton: McCaulsky, Gates, McKinnon, Golley, Costello, Jones, Anderson, Newman, Morah, Quail, Byrne. Unused subs: Thomas, Feltham, Harris.

Yeovil Town 0 v 2 Bromsgrove R.
Webb 4, Radburn 7
Ref: J Griffiths (Chippenham) Att: 5,462
Yeovil: Coles, Coates, Ferns, Sherwood, Bye, Leonard (McPherson 70), Sanderson (Connor 59), Wallace, Wilson, Spencer, Harrower. Unused sub: Bush.
Bromsgrove: Cooksey, Webb, Brighton, Richardson, Wardle, Skelding, Shilvock, Stott, Radburn (Pearce 77), Crisp, Carter. Unused subs: Hanks, Powell.

SECOND ROUND REPLAY (15-12-93)

Nuneaton Boro' 0 v 1 Bournemouth
Cotterill 11
Ref: D Gallagher (Banbury) Att: 4,127
Nuneaton: Attwood, Byrne, McGrory, Keogh, Tarry, Symonds (Wade 70), Simpson, Bradder, Green, Rosegreen, Shearer. Unused subs: Ridding, Manuel.
Bournemouth: Bartram, Pennock, Masters, Morris, Watson, Parkinson, O'Connor, McGorry, Fletcher (Murray 83), Cotterill, Wood. Unused subs: Chivers, Moss.

PHOTOS OPPOSITE

Top: *Halifax Town's Steve Saunders shields the ball from an opponent during the defeat away to Second Division promotion challengers Stockport County.*
Photo - Richard Brock.

Centre: *The Sutton United celebrations at Plainmoor centre on David Jones, scorer of the only goal against Torquay.*
Photo - Paul Dennis.

Foot: *Hereford United defender Kevan Smith clears the ball under pressure from Adie Mings, but his side were still beaten in front of the 'Sky Sports' TV cameras.*
Photo - Dave West.

securicor

BATH
ADVERTISER
605717

Third Round Proper

(SAT. 8th JAN. 1994)

Birmingham C. 1 v 2 Kidderminster H.
Harding 9 — Cartwright 28, Purdie 64

Ref: T West (Hull) Att: 19,666
Birmingham: Bennett, Hiley, Cooper, Parris, Dryden, Whyte, Lowe, Harding (Smith 67), Saville, Donowa (Willis 61), McMinn. Unused sub: Miller.
Kidderminster: Rose, Hodson, Bancroft, Weir, Brindley, Forsyth, Cartwright, Grainger, Humphreys, Deakin, Purdie. Unused subs: Woodall, Palmer, Steadman.

Bromsgrove R. 1 v 2 Barnsley
Crisp 31 — Rammell 88, Archdeacon 90

Ref: J Lloyd (Wrexham) Att: 4,893
Bromsgrove: Green, Webb, Brighton (Hanks 46), Richardson, Wardle, Skelding, Shilvock, Stott, Radburn, Crisp, Carter. Unused subs: O'Meara, Powell.
Barnsley: Butler, Eaden, Fleming, Wilson, Taggart, Bishop, O'Connell (Liddell 78), Redfearn, Rammell, Payton, Archdeacon. Unused subs: Snodin, Watson.

Notts County 3 v 2 Sutton United
Draper 1, Agana 10, Devlin 78 — Barrowcliffe 61, Smart 69

Ref: K Barratt (Coventry) Att: 6,805
Notts County: Cherry, Wilson, Dijstra, Cox, Johnston, P Turner, Devlin, Draper, Lund, McSwegan (Legg 65), Agana (Matthews 87). Unused sub: Catlin.
Sutton: McCaulsky, Gates, Smart, Golley, Costello, Jones, Anderson (Newman 84), Barrowcliffe, Morah, Quail, Byrne (Thomas 81). Unused sub: Harris.

Stoke City 0 v 0 Bath City

Ref: P Wright (Northwich) Att: 14,159
Stoke: Marshall, Clarkson, Sandford, Cranson, Overson, Orlygsson (Sturridge 78), Foley, Bannister, Regis, Butler, Gleghorn. Unused sub: Glynn, Prudhoe.
Bath: Mogg, Gill, Dicks, Batty, Hedges, Cousins, Banks, Chenoweth (Smart 76), Adcock, Mings (Vernon 80), Brooks. Unused sub: Torres.

THIRD ROUND REPLAY (18-1-94)

Bath City 1 v 4 Stoke City
Chenoweth 89 — Regis 4 57, Cranson 36, Orlygsson 81

Ref: P Wright (Northwich) Att: 6,213
Bath: Mogg, Gill, Dicks, Batty, Hedges, Cousins (Smart 77), Banks, Chenoweth, Adcock (Vernon 60), Mings, Brooks. Unused sub: Torres.
Stoke: Marshall, Clarkson, Sandford, Cranson, Overson, Orlygsson (Sturridge 78), Foley, Bannister, Regis, Butler, Gleghorn. Unused sub: Glynn, Prudhoe.

Kidderminster Harriers goalscorers Jon Purdie (left) and Neil Cartwright celebrate after the Conference club's magnificent victory away to First Division Birmingham City.

Photo - Paul Dennis.

Nick Eaden takes on the Bromsgrove defence during Barnsley's fortunate victory. *Photo - Richard Brock.*

Stoke keeper Gordon Marshall plucks the ball off the head of Bath's Adie Mings. *Photo - Paul Dennis.*

Sutton United's Mark Costello helps clear a first-half Notts County attack. *Photo - Dave West.*

Fourth Round Proper  (SAT. 29th JAN. 1994)	**Fifth Round Proper**  (SAT. 19th FEB. 1994)

Kidderminster 1 v 0 Preston Nth End
Humphreys 47
Ref: P E Alcock (Redhill) Att: 7,000
Kidderminster: Rose, Hodson, Bancroft, Weir, Brindley, Forsyth (Deakin 46), Cartwright, Grainger, Humphreys, Davies, Purdie. Unused subs: Woodall, Steadman.
Preston: Woods, Fensome, Kidd, Lucas, Nebbeling, Moyes, Ainsworth, Cartwright, Conroy, Ellis (Norbury 63), Raynor. Unused subs: Whalley, O'Hanlon.

Kidderminster 0 v 1 West Ham United
Chapman 69
Ref: G Pawley (Bishop's Stortford) Att: 7,850
Kidderminster: Rose, Hodson, Bancroft, Weir, Brindley, Forsyth, Cartwright (Deakin 75), Grainger, Humphreys, Davies, Purdie. Unused subs: Woodall, Steadman.
West Ham: Miklosko, Breacker, Rowlands, Potts, Martin, M Allen, Marsh, Bishop, Chapman, C Allen (Morley 68), Holmes. Unused subs: Kelly, Brown.

Kidderminster's FA Cup run gripped the whole nation. **Above:** *Delwyn Humphreys slots home the winning goal against Preston. Photo - Dennis Nicholson.* **Below:** *Chris Brindley tackles West Ham's Matt Holmes during the unforgettable Fifth Round afternoon at Aggborough.* *Photo - Paul Dennis.*

THE FOOTBALL ASSOCIATION CHALLENGE TROPHY

REVIEW 1993-94

First Qualifying Round

(SAT. 18th SEP. 1993)

Bridlington Town	**4 v 0**	**Ferryhill A.**
Radford, Harvey Woodcock, Bell	Att: 63	
Peterlee Newtown	**0 v 2**	**Workington**
	Att: 46	Campbell, Atkinson
Ashton United	**1 v 2**	**Chester-le-St.**
Hulme	Att: 223	Carroll, Latimer
Dunston F.B.	**3 v 0**	**Easington Coll.**
Nicholson, Redhead, Mulholland	Att: 105	
Fleetwood Town	**0 v 6**	**Gt Harwood T.**
	Att: 145	Horsfield, Smith 2, Baker 2, Dunn
Durham City	**0 v 1**	**Tow Law Town**
	Att: 150	Laidler
Whitley Bay	**1 v 1**	**Chorley**
Kiddie	Att: 184	Outterside (og)
Chorley	**3 v 1**	**Whitley Bay**
	(Played 21-9-93)	
Pilkington, Kent, Morgan	Att: 266	Bone
Shildon	**1 v 1**	**Harrogate T.**
Anderson	Att: 126	Daly

Below: Shildon's Micky Taylor (left) contests a high ball with Gary Edmunds of Harrogate Town as the Northern League side hold their NPL visitors to a 1-1 draw.
Photo - Colin Stevens.

Harrogate Town	**4 v 2**	**Shildon**
	(Played 21-9-93)	
Price, Greenhough 2, Philpott	Att: 202	Anderson, Huban
Consett	**2 v 2**	**Hebburn**
Clark, Candlish	Att: 49	Muir, Powers
Hebburn	**1 v 2**	**Consett**
	(Played 22-9-93)	
Tynemouth		McLeod, Quinn(p)
Brandon United	**0 v 2**	**Seaham Red S.**
	Att: 46	Milner, Kirby
Matlock Town	**0 v 0**	**Knowsley Utd**
	Att: 351	
Knowsley Utd	**1 v 1**	**Matlock Town**
	(Played 21-9-93)	
Jackson	Att: 128	Reed
Matlock Town	**3 v 0**	**Knowsley Utd**
	(Played 27-9-93)	
Evans 2, Reed	Att: 376	
Tamworth	**3 v 2**	**Worksop Town**
Bodkin(p), Straw, Anderson	Att: 480	Waller, Pickering
Buxton	**0 v 0**	**Curzon Ashton**
	Att: 268	
Curzon Ashton	**2 v 4**	**Buxton**
	(Played 21-9-93)	
Lowrie, Holt	Att: 136	Heywood 2, Lowe, Hurlstone
Dudley Town	**3 v 2**	**Mossley**
Grainger, Cartwright, Ingham(p)	Att: 192	Diamond, Sivori,
Grantham Town	**5 v 2**	**Bedworth Utd**
Ward 2, Grocock, Harris, Barker	Att: 335	Landon, Cairns
Burton Albion	**3 v 0**	**Caernarfon T.**
Doughty, Brain, Barks	Att: 398	
Horwich R.M.I.	**0 v 2**	**Congleton T.**
	Att: 67	Oliver 2
Gainsborough T.	**5 v 3**	**Eastwood T.**
Brook 4, Shaw	Att: 337	Wiggins 2, Clarke
Gresley Rovers	**1 v 2**	**Goole Town**
Weston(p)	Att: 701	Walmsley 2
Sutton Coldfield	**1 v 1**	**Colwyn Bay**
Long	Att: 138	Brett(p)
Colwyn Bay	**4 v 0**	**Sutton C'field**
	(Played 21-9-93)	
Jones, Brett, Nicholas 2	Att: 177	
Atherstone U.	**1 v 1**	**Redditch U.**
Randle	Att: 305	Moss
Redditch Utd	**2 v 0**	**Atherstone U.**
	(Played 21-9-93)	
Williams, Moss	Att: 194	
Leicester Utd	**0 v 2**	**Moor Green**
	Att: 127	Jones, Brown
Droylsden	**2 v 0**	**Solihull Boro'**
Grimes, Bunter	Att: 195	
Barking	**0 v 1**	**Billericay T.**
	Att: 206	Allen

Bromley's John Raffington and keeper Curtis Hayes deny Trevor McCoy of Molesey. Photo - Alan Coomes.

Bishop's Stort.	**1 v 0**	**Braintree Town**
Fortune-West	Att: 490	
Hitchin Town	**0 v 2**	**Boreham Wood**
	Att: 366	Hann, Liburd
Hendon	**1 v 2**	**Marlow**
Cherry	Att: 247	Caesar, Buzaglo
Ruislip Manor	**1 v 4**	**Chelmsford C.**
Bastien	Att: 203	Jones, Restarick, Garvey, Howard
Sudbury Town	**3 v 3**	**Purfleet**
Barker, Farthing, Cutmore	Att: 352	Donovan, Cobb 2
Purfleet	**3 v 0**	**Sudbury Town**
(Played 20-9-93)		
Brett, Georgiou 2	Att: 191	
Leyton	**6 v 4**	**Chalfont St P.**
Samuels 3, Chick, Frain, Braithwaite	Att: 89	Abercrombie 2, Hooper, Wallace

Below: Leyton's Steve Carney slides in to dispossess Terry Hall during the thriller against Chalfont.
Photo - Dave West.

Berkhamsted T.	**1 v 1**	**Yeading**
Dicker (og)	Att: 105	Cordery
Yeading	**2 v 0**	**Berkhamsted**
(Played 21-9-93)		
Welsh, Charles	Att: 168	
Uxbridge	**1 v 2**	**Harrow Boro'**
Downes	Att: 225	Metcalfe, Pearce
Ashford Town	**3 v 1**	**Windsor & E.**
Stanton 2, Pearson	Att: 354	Dodds
Bromley	**0 v 2**	**Molesey**
	Att: 365	Wilgoss, Pearson
Gravesend & N.	**3 v 0**	**Bognor Regis**
Cotter, Portway 2(1p)	Att: 448	
Tooting & Mit.	**3 v 1**	**Whyteleafe**
Stephens, Cowan, Hope	Att: 200	Jones
Dorking	**1 v 5**	**Sittingbourne**
George	Att: 526	Jones 2, Beard, Arter, Ross
Margate	**0 v 2**	**Worthing**
	Att: 360	Stevens, Brown
Fisher '93	**1 v 0**	**Walton & Her.**
Huntley	Att: 73	
Croydon	**3 v 0**	**Canterbury C.**
Brenton 2, Nohilly	Att: 30	
Dulwich Hamlet	**2 v 1**	**Hastings Town**
Murphy, Best	Att: 232	O'Shaughnessey
Wokingham Town	**1 v 0**	**Maidenhead U.**
Biggs	Att: 275	
Fareham Town	**1 v 2**	**Weston-s-Mare**
Sampson	Att: 119	Tapp, Bowering
Salisbury City	**1 v 3**	**Poole Town**
Odey	Att: 256	Jones 2(1p), Wilson
Newport A.F.C.	**1 v 0**	**Havant Town**
Foley	Att: 253	
Basingstoke T.	**0 v 2**	**Abingdon Town**
	Att: 138	Appleton(p), Connolly
Weymouth	**0 v 2**	**Witney Town**
	Att: 799	Clarke 2

Second Qualifying Round

(SAT. 16th OCT. 1993)

Abingdon Town 1 v 1 Wokingham T.
Martin 41 Att:238 Hampstead 85

Wokingham Town 2 v 1 Abingdon T.
(Played 19-10-93)
Devereux 38, Martin 41(OG) Att:206 Kemp 78

Alfreton Town 2 v 0 Congleton T.
Ridsdale 28, Maybury 44(p) Att:111

Ashford Town 1 v 1 Gravesend
Stanton 62 Att:633 Cotter 23

Gravesend & N. 2 v 0 Ashford Town
(Played 19-10-93)
Portway 22, Cotter 65 Att:721

Baldock Town 2 v 3 Purfleet
Bulzis 45, Bruce 88 Att:175 Brett 36 64, Reece 71

Bishop's S'ford 1 v 2 Billericay T.
Das Att:449 S Warner, Potts

Buxton 1 v 6 Colwyn Bay
Wood 3 Att:215 Nicholas 5 20 30, Woods 34, Jones 42 78

Cambridge City 1 v 1 Chelmsford C.
Covey 54 Att:344 Davidson

Chelmsford City 3 v 2 Cambridge C.
(Played 18-10-93)
Rogers 19, Davidson 44 75 Att:452 Gawthrop 35, Tovey 90

Consett 3 v 0 Chester-le-Str.
Rowell 35, Bayles 57, Cowley 87 Att:59

Croydon 1 v 7 Worthing
Kempster Quirk (3), Carroll (2), Tiltman, Quinn

Dunston Feds 2 v 1 Newcastle B.S.
Ditchburn 31, Mullholland 80 Att:98 Pidgeon 25

Fisher '93 0 v 2 Dulwich Ham.
Att:210 Best 85, Hinds 90(OG)

Gainsboro' Trin. 1 v 2 Matlock Town
Moore 46 Att:362 Burton 39, Tilly 44

Goole Town 3 v 1 Dudley Town
Rookyard 23 36, Wood 89 Att:156 Grainger 55

Grantham Town 3 v 2 Droylsden
Tomlinson 1, Williams 30(p) 50 Att:343 Bunter 8, Norris 20

Guiseley 4 v 3 Tow Law Town
Colville 17 90, Allen 62, Stevenson 76 Att:486 Laidler 23 31, Pickford 48

Harrogate Town 3 v 1 Chorley
Gallagher 24, Philpott 51 90 Att:244 Grant 6

Harrow Borough 0 v 0 Boreham Wood
Att:233

Boreham Wood 1 v 2 Harrow Boro'
(Played 19-10-93)
Fox Att:122 Fraser, Prutton

Marlow 1 v 1 Hayes
Cattlin 31 Att:260 Walton 45

Hayes 2 v 3 Marlow
(Played 19-10-93)
Goodliffe 51, Kelly 69 Att:177 Lay 65(p), Cattlin 67 69

Molesey 0 v 4 Sittingbourne
Att:342 Arter 48 72, Lovell 57, Ross 82

Poole Town 1 v 1 Waterlooville
Jones 33 Att:153 Morley 34(OG)

Waterlooville 2 v 0 Poole Town
(Played 19-10-93)
Boyce 55 65(p) Att:168

Redditch Utd 2 v 0 Moor Green
Taylor 40, Donnelly 77 Att:218

Rushden & D. 0 v 1 Burton Albion
Att:812 Redfern 36(p)

Seaham Red Star 3 v 1 West Auckland
Ould 14, Coxall 27, Walker (p) Att:95 Skirving 60(p)

Stockton 2 v 1 Gt Harwood
May 81, Wynn 83 Att:79 Dunn 79

Stourbridge 0 v 1 Halesowen T.
Att:835 Abell 63

Tamworth 2 v 2 Emley
Deacey 28, Eccleston 57 Att:562 Bradshaw 29 38

Emley 4 v 0 Tamworth
(Played 18-10-93)
Bradshaw 24 64, Reynolds 38 61 Att:409

Tooting & Mit. 1 v 2 Erith & Bel.
Collins 90(p) Att:187 Cowan 25(OG), Smales 83

Wembley 1 v 1 Staines Town
Bates Att:73 Williams

Staines Town 1 v 0 Wembley
(Played 19-10-93)
Reilly Att:202

Weston-s-Mare 2 v 0 Newport A.F.C.
Sweeney 1, Chattoe 42 Att:405

Witney Town 0 v 1 Dorchester T.
Att:121 Manson 34

Workington 0 v 2 Bridlington T.
Att:282 Roberts 13, Bell 37

Yeading 1 v 1 Leyton
Charles 65 Att:107 Frain 62

Leyton 1 v 3 Yeading
(Played 19-10-93)
Braithwaite Sheldrick, Denton, Welsh

PHOTOS OPPOSITE

Top: *Tamworth's equalising goal, scored by Tony Eccleston, floats into the net in the 2-2 draw against Tamworth.* *Photo - Paul Barber.*

Centre: *Michael Montague of Worthing (left) races past Mark Bushby as the Sussex side romp to a 7-1 win at Croydon.* *Photo - Dave West.*

Foot: *Workington's Nigel Dustin closes down Alan Radford, but the Cumbrians slide to a 0-2 home defeat against Bridlington Town.* *Photo - Colin Stevens.*

602351
65544

Third Qualifying Round

(SAT. 27th NOV. 1993)

Alfreton Town 4 v 1 Bridlington T.
Stafford 53 90, Ridsdale 72, Johnson 87 — Att:148 — Crawford 38

Barrow 2 v 2 Emley
Oldroyd 72, Higginbotham 90 — Att:1020 — Tunnacliffe 31 62

Emley 2 v 1 Barrow
(Played 29-11-93)
Bradshaw 10, Clarke 47 — Att:408 — Addenbrook 45

Billericay Town 2 v 0 Yeading
Allen 13, Payne 85 — Att:283

Bishop Auckland 2 v 2 Murton
(Played 1-12-93)
Coverdale 28, Motler 55 — Att:279 — Robson 12, Thompson 78

Murton 1 v 4 Bishop Auck.
(Played 6-12-93)
Evans 75 — Att:190 — Todd 30, Borthwick 40, Mockler 48, Hyde 77

Burton Albion 1 v 2 Halesowen T.
Bradley 38(og) — Att:709 — Brown 45, Wright 80

Colwyn Bay 2 v 2 Guisborough
Nicholas 65, Jones 75 — Att:114 — Moore 29, Peel 35

Guisborough T. 2 v 3 Colwyn Bay
(Played 1-12-93)
Davies 38, Peel 60 — Att:281 — Nicholas 11 21, Morgan 89

Consett 1 v 3 Billingham S.
(Played 1-12-93)
Staff 90 — Att:37 — Butler 2, Roberts 55, Fletcher 87

Dorchester Town 0 v 0 Bashley
Att:372

Bashley 3 v 0 Dorchester T.
(Played 6-12-93)
Walters 20, Adams 21, Woolley 60 — Att:214

Dulwich Hamlet 2 v 1 Gloucester C.
Egan 7, Vines 8 — Att:312 — Bayliss 4

Dunston Feds 1 v 5 Frickley Ath.
Ditchburn 68 — Att:281 — Lacey 6, Hayward 60 64, Templeton 78, Garnham 85

Enfield 2 v 1 Corby Town
St Hilaire 44 45 — Att:440 — McInerney 57

Erith & Belvedere 1 v 4 Weston-s.-M.
Young 55 — Att:364 — Chattoe 24, Tilley 44, Tapp 74, Elson 76

Goole Town 1 v 1 Northallerton
Hotte 50 — Att:147 — Lee 1

Northallerton 1 v 0 Goole Town
(Played 1-12-93)
Woods 13 — Att:227

Gravesend & N. 1 v 4 Marlow
Portway 6 — Att:604 — Watkins 4, Regan 41, Buzaglo 62, Caesar 87

Harrogate Town 3 v 4 Guiseley
Deane 48 53, Ottley 79, — Att:505 — Allen 55, Hogarth 56, W Roberts 67, Bottomley 74

Hyde United 2 v 0 Accrington S.
Thornton 71 89 — Att:355

Leek Town 0 v 2 Stevenage B.
Att:485 — Gittings 11, Venables 50

Matlock Town 1 v 3 Blyth Spartans
Evans 44 — Att:530 — Peatie 31 40, Palmer 64

Nuneaton Boro' 2 v 2 Aylesbury Utd
Simpson 21, Rosegreen 65 — Att:1375 — Bashir 33, Stacey 77

Aylesbury Utd 1 v 2 Nuneaton B.
(Played 30-11-93)
Hercules 8 — Att:537 — Rosegreen 63, Green 74

Purfleet 3 v 2 Heybridge Sw.
Donovan 16, Grainger 46, Cobb 85 — Att:138 — May 4, Matthews 77

Redditch Utd 1 v 1 Hednesford T.
Hawkins 65 — Att:163 — Berks 76

Hednesford T. 1 v 0 Redditch Utd
(Played 29-11-93)
O'Connor 67 — Att:224

Seaham Red S. 0 v 3 Gretna
Att:119 — Armstrong 27 40, Dobie 80

Sittingbourne 1 v 2 Kingstonian
Lovell 63 — Att:1248 — Ndah 17, Harlow 42(p)

Staines Town 0 v 3 St Albans City
Att:321 — Gurney 20 32, Clark 77

Stockton 0 v 3 Spennymoor U.
(Played 1-12-93)
Att:121 — Saunders 63, Gorman 64 85

Trowbridge T. 1 v 1 Cheltenham T.
Freegard 75 — Att:467 — Mortimer 89

Cheltenham T. 1 v 0 Trowbridge T.
(Played 30-11-93)
J Smith 76 — Att:489

V.S. Rugby 0 v 3 Chelmsford C.
Att:426 — Rogers 38, Davidson 53, Restarick 90

Waterlooville 3 v 0 Wokingham T.
Elley 3, Sowerby 30, Hore 86 — Att:233

Wealdstone 2 v 2 Harrow Boro'
Hedge 38, Mellor 72 — Att:364 — Westley 51, Knight 78

Harrow Boro' 3 v 0 Wealdstone
(Played 1-12-93)
Westley 2, Ripley 26 40 — Att: 557

Wivenhoe Town 1 v 2 Grantham T.
Bullimore 4(og) — Att:152 — Williams 17, Harris 18

Worcester C. 1 v 1 Crawley Town
Donovan 45 — Att:612 — Crawley 28

Crawley Town 1 v 2 Worcester C.
(Played 30-11-93)
Turner 86 — Att:445 — Davidson 45, Donovan 77

Worthing 3 v 0 Carshalton A.
Quinn 39, Riley 47, Barrett 90 — Att: 432

Ansil Bushay scores St Albans's first goal in the First Round thriller against Merthyr. Photo - Eric Marsh.

Mark Underdown tackles Wayne Kerrins of Dulwich in Kingstonian's First Round win. Photo - Paul Dennis.

Robin Beste (left) races Worthing's Spencer Mintram in Carshalton's shock defeat. Photo - Graham Cotterill.

First Round Proper

(SAT. 22nd JAN. 1994)

Alfreton Town 0 v 5 Runcorn
Att:502 — McKenna 8 22 44 65, Atkinson 54(og)

Gretna 1 v 1 Warrington T.
Townsley 40 — Att:102 — Knop 31

Warrington T. 2 v 3 Gretna
(Played 25-1-94)
Finley 28(p), Nicely 83 — Att:244 — Armstrong 7, Eagling 55, Dobie 79

Halifax Town 2 v 1 Emley
Paterson 14, Lambert 47 — Att:1579 — Clark 44(p)

Halesowen Town 0 v 2 Gateshead
Att:936 — Lamb 57, Sharpe 58

Stalybridge C. 1 v 1 Colwyn Bay
Anderson 56 — Att:422 — Roberts 89

Colwyn Bay 2 v 2 Stalybridge C.
(Played 1-2-94)
S Jones 55, G Roberts 85 — Att:220 — Anderson 24, Blain 80(p)

Colwyn Bay 2 v 1 Stalybridge
(Played 3-2-94)
S Roberts 60, Jones 110 — Att:138 — Kirkham 1

Winsford United 0 v 1 Guiseley
Att:332 — R Roberts 76

Grantham Town 3 v 2 Witton Albion
Speed 49, Watson 79, Grocock 88 — Att:527 — Blackwood 22 73

Billingham Syn. 2 v 1 Frickley Ath.
Butler 31, Allen 71 — Att:238 — Gabbiadini 18

Spennymoor Utd 2 v 1 Hyde United
Ainsley 52, Gorman 59 — Att:529 — Kimmins 66

Blyth Spartans 1 v 3 Bishop Auck.
English 60 — Att:622 — Cramman 15(p), Borthwick 58, Bond 77

Hednesford T. 1 v 0 Whitby Town
Fitzpatrick 88 — Att:517

Boston United 1 v 1 Macclesfield T.
Morrow 24 — Att:1559 — Alford 50

Macclesfield T. 1 v 0 Boston United
(Played 25-1-94)
Alford 86(p) — Att:590

Morecambe 2 v 1 Northwich Vic.
McCluskie 43, Lavelle 80 — Att:693 — Parker 87

Telford Utd 2 v 1 Northallerton
Roberts 40(p), Whitehouse 84 — Att:926 — Gill 90

Marine 0 v 0 Southport
Att:1179

Southport 3 v 1 Marine
(Played 25-1-94)
Walmesley 5, Brennan 16, Gamble 38 — Att:818 — Ross 85

Altrincham 0 v 2 Stafford Rgrs
Att:790 — Bradshaw 36, Williams 44

Cheltenham T. 1 v 0 Nuneaton B.
Jones 33 — Att:1118

Dulwich Hamlet 1 v 2 Kingstonian
Fisher 61 — Att:705 — Underdown 45 86

Welling Utd 6 v 1 Chelmsford C.
Robbins 45, White 53, Copley 60, Abbott 63 77, Robinson 86 — Att:1108 — Keen 51

Kettering Town 2 v 1 Stevenage B.
Wright 12, Reed 90 — Att:2414 — Gittings 61

St Albans C. 4 v 5 Merthyr Tydfil
Bushay 9, Clark 55, Pluckrose 57, Brett 76, — Att:1017 — Davies 4, Coates 32, Drewitt 45, Tucker 65, Benbow 86,

Billericay T. 0 v 2 Slough Town
Att: 709 — M Scott 28, Sayer 59

Kidderminster H. 0 v 2 Dagenham & R.
Att: 1587 — Greene 51, Cavell 53

Waterlooville 1 v 1 Bromsgrove R.
Ogburn 32 — Att:300 — Webb 75(p)

Bromsgrove R. 2 v 1 Waterlooville
(Played 25-1-94)
Carter 25, Burgher 84 — Att:1026 — Milkins 4

Farnborough T. 1 v 1 Grays Athletic
Pratt 47 — Att:521 — Durrant 55

Grays Athletic 2 v 0 Farnborough
(Played 25-1-94)
Mitchell(2) — Att:277

Bashley 2 v 4 Woking
Stickler 10, Adams 40 — Att:1102 — Walker 34(p), Dennis 37 58, S Wye 86

Weston-s.-Mare 0 v 2 Dover Athletic
Att:575 — Browne 49, Leworthy 90

Yeovil Town 3 v 3 Bath City
Wilson 2, Spencer 14, Leonard 70 — Att:2611 — Boyle 45, Mings 59 61

Bath City 4 v 0 Yeovil Town
(Played 25-1-94)
Cousins 7, Gill 45, Boyle 54, Adcock 84 — Att:1148

Sutton United 2 v 0 Chesham Utd
Morah 40, Feltham 83 — Att: 1029

Enfield 2 v 0 Purfleet
Collins 60, St Hilaire 74 — Att:486

Harrow Boro' 3 v 3 Worcester C.
Fraser 16, Westley 65 75 — Att:486 — Smith 43 85, Rutter 80

Worcester C. 5 v 3 Harrow Boro'
(Played 24-1-94)
Green 64, 87, Rutter 69 81, Benton 76 — Att:1021 — Benstead 38, Westley 44, Booker 83

Worthing 3 v 0 Marlow
(Played 7-2-94)
Montague, Benson, Tiltman — Att:564

A shot from Gretna's Derek Townsley sqirms past Warrington keeper Steve Parsonage. Photo - Alan Watson.

Billericay keeper Dave Cass saves bravely from Morrys Scott of Slough Town. Photo - Martin Wray.

A Waterlooville defender makes a goal-line clearance to deny Bromsgrove a goal. Photo - Graham Cotterill.

Second Round Proper

(SAT. 12th FEB. 1994)

Runcorn 2 v 1 Telford United
McInerny 58, Thomas 89 — Att:844 — Whitehouse 49

Grantham Town 1 v 2 Bishop Auckland
Harris 55 — Att:815 — Borthwick 61 70

Colwyn Bay 0 v 3 Southport
Att:660 — Gamble 51, Withers 54, Haw 85

Kettering Town 2 v 2 Billingham Syn.
Donald 8, Graham 52 — Att:2076 — Butler 41 85

Billingham Syn. 3 v 1 Kettering Town
(played 28-2-94)
Butler 18, O'Brien 44(p), Banks 78 — Att:842 — Stringfellow 12

Dagenham & Red. 1 v 2 Woking
Richardson 68 — Att:1769 — Walker 14, Rattray 20

Below: Paul Bottomley surges past Stafford defender Chris Hemmings as Guiseley spring a major surprise by defeating the Conference side 3-2.
Photo - Colin Stevens.

Worcester City 0 v 0 Macclesfield T.
Att:1578

Macclesfield T. 3 v 2 Worcester City
(Played 21-2-94)
Askey 33, McGrath 40(OG), Power 45 — Att:704 — Benton 80, Donovan 90

Worthing 1 v 1 Enfield
Duchossoy — Att:837 — Hobson

Enfield 2 v 0 Worthing
Whale 34, St Hilaire 65 — Att:583

Below: Mark Costello closes in on Bath City's ball-juggling Paul Adcock as Sutton United run up a staggering six goal tally against the GMVC side.
Photo - Peter Lirettoc.

Sutton United 6 v 1 Bath City
Golley 13, Feltham 50 85, Morah 58 68, Barrowcliffe 89 — Att:1188 — Brooks 3

Cheltenham Town 1 v 0 Hednesford T.
N Smith 72 — Att:965

Morecambe 1 v 0 Slough Town
Holden 72 — Att:831

Welling United 1 v 3 Dover Athletic
Robbins 75 — Att:1726 — Bartlett 44, Lewis 57 61

Guiseley 3 v 2 Stafford Rgrs
Essex 39(OG), Roberts 64 73 — Att:1209 — Williams 20, Foy 44

Gateshead 0 v 0 Gretna
Att:402

Gretna 0 v 1 Gateshead
(Played 15-2-94)
Att:205 — Dobson 110(p)

Spennymoor Utd 1 v 2 Halifax Town
Gorman 86 — Att:1426 — Peterson 61, Peake 68

Kingstonian 0 v 2 Merthyr Tydfil
Att:844 — Robbie James 14, Coates 73

Grays Athletic 1 v 2 Bromsgrove R.
Goldstone 10 — Att:494 — Crisp 50, Carter 75

PHOTOS OPPOSITE

Top: *Phil Mason of Worcester City dribbles the ball past the home team 'dug-out' during the goalless against Macclesfield Town at St Georges Lane.*
Photo - Paul Dennis.

Centre: *Jason Walker (right) of Grays Athletic takes on Steve Scott as the Diadora League side give Bromsgrove Rovers a scare before eventually going down 1-2.*
Photo - Alan Coomes.

Foot: *Mark Tucker, with Woking team-mate Lenny Dennis looking on, tries to squeeze a shot through a packed Dagenham & Redbridge defence as the Cards win 2-1 at Victoria Road.*
Photo - Roger Turner.

WHEN WE SET SAIL, WE SET STANDARDS.
WHAT WOULD YOU DO FOR A PINT?

CARLING

Third Round Proper

(SAT. 5th MAR. 1994)

Macclesfield T. 0 v 1 Billingham Syn.
Att:909 Banks 26

Cheltenham Town 0 v 0 Guiseley
Att:1117

Guiseley 1 v 0 Cheltenham T.
(Played 8-3-94)
Bottomley 2 Att:1138

Gateshead 3 v 2 Merthyr Tydfil
Dobson 71 73 86 Att:502 Coates 13, Jones 15

Sutton United 0 v 0 Dover Athletic
Att:1578

Dover Athletic 2 v 3 Sutton United
(Played 8-3-94)
Browne 67 81 Att:2207 Jones 16 94, Morah 77

Runcorn 1 v 1 Halifax Town
Thomas Att:1302 Brabin 89(OG)

Halifax Town 0 v 2 Runcorn
(Played 8-3-94)
Att:1406 Anderson 5, Thomas 81

Bishop Auckland 2 v 2 Enfield
Adams 35, Hyde 44 Att:830 Hobson 7, St Hilaire 43

Enfield 2 v 1 Bishop Auck.
(Played 8-3-94)
Collins 1, Turner 85 Att:890 Todd 40

Woking 3 v 2 Bromsgrove R.
Brown 40, Dennis 66, Lakin 84 Att:2342 Webb 32(p) 60

Morecambe 2 v 1 Southport
McCluskie 38, Grimshaw 74 Att:2246 Withers 76

Arthur Williams makes a fine save for Runcorn against Halifax at Canal Street. *Photo - Paul Dennis.*

Sutton's Ollie Morah unleashes a fierce shot past Tony Dixon of Dover. *Photo - Peter Lirettoc.*

Fourth Round Proper

(SAT. 26th MAR. 1994)

Gateshead 0 v 3 Runcorn
Thomas 14(p) 83, Corner 21(og)

Ref: Mr Parker Att: 1,807
Gateshead: Smith, Farrey, Higgins (Cole 59), Hine, Corner, Nobbs, Proudlock, Dobson, Lamb, Watson (Sharpe 59), Wrightson.
Runcorn: Williams, Bates, Hill, Brady, Lee, Anderson, Thomas, Connor, McInerney, McKenna, Brabin. Unused subs: Parker, Robertson.

Sutton United 1 v 1 Enfield
Moran 64 — Anderson 70(og)

Ref: Gary Willard (Worting) Att: 1,813
Sutton: McCaulskey, Gates, Smart, N Golley, Costello, Jones, Anderson, Barrowcliff (Feltham 68), Morah, Quail, Byrne. Unused sub: McKinnon.
Enfield: Pape, Chester, Ridout, Ryan, Heald, Bailey, Hobson, Pye, Britnell, St Hilaire, Collins. Unused subs: Brotherton, Telfer.

Enfield 1 v 0 Sutton United
Roberts 54

Att: 1,255
Enfield: Pape, Britnell, Ryan, Roberts, Heald, Bailey, Hobson, Pye, Turner, St Hilaire, Collins. Unused subs: Chester, Engwell.
Sutton: McCaulskey, Gates, Smart, N Golley (Feltham 70), Costello, Jones, Anderson, Barrowcliff, Morah, Quail (McKinnon 82), Byrne.

Woking 1 v 1 Billingham S.
Walker 40 — Butler 16

Ref: G R Pooley (Bishop's Stortford) Att: 2,767
Woking: Batty, Tucker (Lakin 52), L Wye, Berry, K Brown, Fielder, D Brown, Rattray, Steele, Bennett (Hislop 75), Walker.
Billingham Synthonia: Popple, O'Gorman, O'Brien, Roberts, Harbron, Lynch (Connor 63), Corkain, Malone, Butler, Allen, Banks. Unused sub: Davis.

Billingham Syn. 1 v 2 Woking
Allen 44 — K Brown 62 67

Att: 1,776
Billingham Synthonia: Popple, O'Gorman, O'Brien, Roberts, Harbron, Lynch, Corkain (Davies 84), Malone, Butler, Allen, Banks. Unused sub: Connor.
Woking: Batty, Clement, L Wye, Berry, K Brown, Fielder, D Brown, Rattray, Steele, Puckett, Walker. Unused subs: Swift, Lakin.

Guiseley 3 v 2 Morecambe
Colville 10, W Roberts 27 80 — Cain 70, McCluskie 84

Att: 1,805
Guiseley: Dickinson, Atkinson, Hogarth, Brockie, Bottomley, Stevenson, James, Allen, Colville, Noteman, W Roberts. Unused subs: Richards, Armitage.
Morecambe: Thornley, Tomlinson, Middlemass, Harvey, Lavelle, Dullaghan (Burns 69), Richardson, Grimshaw, McCluskie, Holden, Cain. Unused sub: Coleman.

Morecambe's Ian Cain in spectacular action at Guiseley. *Photo - Colin Stevens.*

Clive Walker of Woking is tackled by Billingham Synthonia's Andy Harbron. *Photo - Graham Cotterill.*

Semi-Finals (Two Legs)

(16th MAR. 1994)
(23rd MAR. 1994)

WOKING 1 *(Roberts 1(og))*
ENFIELD 1 *(Tucker 75(og)* **Att:** Att: 3,841

This game was always going to be a closely fought battle with two in-form teams meeting on a heavily sanded Kingfield pitch. With the game only two minutes old, Enfield player-manager Graham Roberts scored, to his horror, an own-goal when a low cross from the exciting Darran Hay canoned into the the net off his right leg giving former England semi-pro 'keeper Andy Pape little chance.

The remainder of the half settled down with very few chances created. Woking's evergreen Clive Walker failed to hit the target after half-an-hour with a shot from eight yards which flew high and wide, and Scott Steele managed the same 'feat' for the home side five minutes before the break.

The second-half was a very different game with Enfield attacking with the wind at their backs. Chances fell to Darren Collins, and Laurence Batty made one outstanding save at his feet.

John Bailey was hurt in a collision with Batty after 53 minutes and his replacement, Martin Chester, was himself later taken off injured. This was significant as the second sub, Gary Britnell, played a major role in securing Enfield's 75th minute equaliser. His header after a goalmouth scramble was deflected in by Mark Tucker for the afternoon's second own-goal.

Enfield pressed hard to secure a priceless away win, and were aggrieved by the decision of referee Ron Groves not to award a penalty when Tucker appeared to bring down Roberts in the box - Paul Hobson was booked for expressing his displeasure too frankly. Despite failing to capitalise on their late pressure, however, the Diadora side were best pleased with the outcome of this enthralling first-leg. *(Dave West).*

Woking: Batty, Fielder, L Wye, Berry, K Brown, Tucker, D Brown, Lakin, Steele (Rattray 75), Hay, Walker. Unused sub: Puckett.
Enfield: Pape, Engwell, Ryan, Roberts, Heald, Bailey (Chester 53 (Britnell 75)), Hobson, Pye, Turner, St Hilaire, Collins.

ENFIELD 0
WOKING 0 **Att:** 3,319

Woking and Enfield are fine attacking sides, but in this second-leg they got it all wrong. Enfield were hindered by the absence of Martin St Hilaire, injured from the previous leg, leaving Graham Roberts and Darren Collins to forage alone up front. They did OK, but the midfield was too slow pushing up in support. Woking, for their part, still seemed shell-shocked by the eight goals that Dagenham had stuffed past them in the week. They were happy to sit back and absorb what little the home side had to throw at them, and prod back with over-eleborate breaks.

To their credit, Enfield risked St Hilaire after the break, and the powerful striker would have spared us extra-time had not he missed from a couple of yards out having been set up after an electrifying run by Collins in the very last minute. In another bold move, Enfield brought on Leroy Whale, out injured since the Third Round tie against Bishop Auckland, in extra-time. But it was to no avail - it was an afternoon of stultifying boredom in which the two physios saw far more action than the goalkeeper, and a replay became necessary. *(James Wright)*

Enfield: Pape, Ryan, Francis (St Hilaire 45), Roberts, Heald, Bailey, Hobson, Pye (Whale 106), Turner, Britnell, Collins.
Woking: Batty, Tucker, L Wye, Berry, K Brown, Clement, D Brown, Fielder, Steele (Puckett 111), Hay, Walker. Unused sub: Rattray.

WOKING 3 *(Hay 41 89, Steele 66)*
ENFIELD 0 **Att:** 2,674
(at Wycombe Wanderers FC, 26-4-94)

Enfield committed footballing suicide at Adams Park - Lee Francis and Graham Roberts were both sent off as Woking made their numerical advantage tell to cruise into a Wembley final.

Within three minutes, Francis was cautioned for giving Fielder a back-hander, and less than ten minutes later was sent off for a trip on Darren Hay. Enfield, with Martin St Hilaire ploughing a lone furrow up front, eventually succumbed to Clive Walker's trickery, failing to cut out his pin-point cross, and allowing Darran Hay to bullet a header home from six yards.

The second-half was one-way traffic with Walker, Hay and Scott Steele tormenting an overworked defence, and it was no surprise when those three combined to make it 2-0, Steele finishing the move. Immediately, Roberts substituted himself, but only lasted ten minutes on the bench as he joined Francis in the dressing-room for continually abusing the linesman. With Enfield in disarray, Woking sealed the game a minute from time with a sweet lob from Hay, to set off scenes of wild celebration. *(Kerry Miller).*

Woking: Batty, Tucker, L Wye, Berry, K Brown, Clement, D Brown, Fielder, Steele (Rattray 90), Hay, Walker (Puckett 90).
Enfield: Pape, Ryan, Francis, Roberts (Britnell 66), Heald, Bailey (Whale 68), Hobson, Pye, Turner, St Hilaire, Collins.

Below: Woking's Kevan Brown (right) tackles Martin St Hilaire during the second-half of the goalless second-leg at Southbury Road. St Hilaire, in fact, had the best chance of the afternoon when he hit a post in the last minute of normal time. *Photo - Alan Coomes.*

RUNCORN 1 *(McKenna 3)*
GUISELEY 1 *(Allen 72)* **Att:** 1,595
(played at Chester City FC)

When Runcorn raced into a fourth minute lead, Ken McKenna latching onto a titanic kick from 'keeper Arthur Williams to run on and bury the ball past Steve Dickinson, one could not help thinking that Runcorn would submerge their NPL opponents under an avalanche of goals.

Despite having had to concede home advantage because of the Canal Street fire - this match was played at Chester City's Deva Stadium - they looked the far more assured of the two sides in the early stages. Even after Gary Brabin had been dismissed, in the 24th minute, for his second booking, Runcorn's ten men posed the greater threat in attack and it took two breath-taking saves on the half-hour to keep Guiseley in contention. First Dickinson raced across his goal to turn behind a McKenna header from Joe Connor's free-kick, and then he was equally agile in tipping over an Andy Lee headed effort from the resultant corner.

But as the game progressed, and Runcorn tired, Guiseley became more dangerous. Initially they could not develop enough possession, giving the ball away too cheaply but, as the realisation dawned that the Linnets were there to be shot down, they started to carve open the Conference side in the final quarter. The equaliser arrived after 72 minutes. Lutel James picked out Bob Colville with a long cross from the right, and the Welsh semi-pro international's far post header wrong-footed Williams and Calvin Allen was just able to squeeze the ball over the line from close-range. *(James Wright).*

Runcorn: Williams, Bates, Hill, Shaw, Lee, Anderson, Thomas, Connor, McInerny (Robertson 70), McKenna, Brabin. Unused sub: Smith.
Guiseley: Dickinson, Atkinson, Hogarth, Brockie, Bottomley, Stevenson, James, Allen, Colville, Noteman, W Roberts. Unused subs: Richards, Wilson.

GUISELEY 0
RUNCORN 1 *(McKenna 120)* **Att:** 2,176

Runcorn started this second-leg strongly, with Guiseley having a major scare after only two minutes when Steve Dickinson handled a back-pass. The free-kick was scrambled out, but the visitors still dominated the remainder of the half. However, Bob Colville did have one excellent chance to give Guiseley the lead, firing wide from ten yards having been found by a pin-point cross from Billy Roberts.

The Conference side were still to the fore after the interval, but Karl Thomas and Ken McKenna were closely marked, and Guiseley came strong midway through the half with the skilful Lutel James causing a lot of problems for Runcorn.

A goal-line clearance by Peter Atkinson took Guiseley into extra-time, but they were to suffer a heart-break in the very last minute when McKenna met a free-kick with a glancing header to send Runcorn back to Wembley. *(Colin Stevens).*

Guiseley: Dickinson, Atkinson, Hogarth, Brockie, Bottomley (Richards 105), Stevenson, James, Allen, Colville, Noteman, W Roberts. Unused sub: Armitage.
Runcorn: Williams, Bates, Robertson, Hill, Lee, Anderson, Thomas, Connor, McInerny, McKenna, Brabin. Subs: Shaw, Parker.

Above: *Guiseley's Lutel James in action during the second-leg.*
Below: *Runcorn celebrate another semi-final win.*
Photos - Paul Dennis.

F.A. TROPHY FINAL

Saturday 21st May, At Wembley Stadium

Woking 2 v 1 Runcorn

D Brown (19), Hay (29) — Shaw (75 penalty)

Attendance: 15,818

Woking: Laurence Batty, Mark Tucker, Lloyd Wye, Gwynne Berry, Kevan Brown, Andy Clement, Dereck Brown (Kevin Rattray 32), Colin Fielder, Scott Steele, Darran Hay (David Puckett 46), Clive Wilson. Manager: Geoff Chapple.
Runcorn: Arthur Williams, Jamie Bates, Paul Robertson, Nigel Shaw, Andy Lee, Garry Anderson, Karl Thomas, Joe Connor, Ian McInerney (Graham Hill 71), Ken McKenna, Gary Brabin. Unused sub: Neil Parker. Manager: John Carroll.

Referee: Mr Paul Durkin (Portland)

Linesmen: Mr John Elwin (Norwich), Mr Robert Jeavons (Coseley).

On a lush pitch, heavy to overflowing after constant rain had fallen for days, the faintly ludicrous scene of referee Mr Paul Durkin being interviewed in the centre circle seconds before the kick-off greeted the two sets of supporters, who generated a surprisingly good atmosphere considering their sparseness. Woking lined up, in a formation indicating that they were to play with a sweeper, with Darren Hay and Clive Walker up front. Runcorn had Ken McKenna in a forward role, with league leading scorer Karl Thomas and Joey Connor joining from deeper positions. The first 10 minutes could easily have been choreagraphed to Swan Lake, with the players sliding around, unable to obtain even the most basic of grips underfoot. Ken McKenna made inroads into the Cards' penalty area only to lose his balance as the ball slid away. Runcorn settled much earlier, and it seemed they had learned from last season's early debacle. Their play seemed more positive, although the break-through did not come. Off the field however, the view was decidedly negative as many had doubts whether the match could go to completion if the rain continued to fall.

Woking soaked up the early pressure and, with their first meaningful sortie, took the lead courtesy of a catalogue of errors. Gary Brabin attempted to play the ball out of trouble but only succeeded in knocking it against the falling Andy Lee. The ball broke to Scott Steele who crossed for Dereck Brown to side-foot into the near side of the goal with keeper Arthur Williams slow to cover. It was a cruel blow to the Linnets who had been so dominant. Woking sensed the kill and Darran Hay tried a cross shot which Williams was glad to field comfortably. As the rain eased, Runcorn were dealt a mortal blow when Clive Walker played a delightful reverse ball to Scott Steele who gathered himself on the goalline before rolling the ball to Dereck Brown. His mishit shot was similarly mishit by Darran Hay, the ball rolling almost apologetically in off the inside of the post.

Dereck Brown lasted but three minutes more, retiring with a groin strain having made one and scored one. Darran Hay could and should have sealed the match, misdirecting a clear header from another glorious cross from the ageless Clive Walker two minutes later, and Runcorn were glad to hear the half-time whistle.

Woking's tactics of soaking up pressure, then countering swiftly were borne out by the half-time stats, which gave Runcorn the balance of the possession and a higher shot count. Darran Hay failed to appear for the second-half to be replaced by Dave Puckett, which bought the combined age of Woking's forward line to 69. The first ten minutes of the second period were a replica of the first, Woking on the defensive, with Kevan Brown going close with a back-pass wide of Laurence Batty and Joe Connor shooting across the goal. Runcorn soon wilted as the much needed goal failed to materialise and, although pressing forward, their attacks lacked any kind of invention, reminiscent of a cricket team facing a score of 400-3 bowling for a run-out.

They almost got their run-out on the hour when their Man of the Match, Paul Robertson, rocked the bar from 25 yards. With less than 20 minutes to go, Graham Hill replaced Ian McInerney and, within minutes, a long throw from the boundary caught out Gwynne Berry who handled in the box. Nigel Shaw tucked away the spot kick. Runcorn reverted to route one in a desperate attempt to salvage the game, and Woking wobbled slightly, Lloyd Wye flirting with Mr Durkin's notebook with back-to-back late tackles but, with Andy Lee having a header saved seconds from time, the Cards held on to claim the trophy.

Kerry Miller

Ken McKenna splashes his way past Woking's Andy Clement. *Photo - Paul Dennis.*

Nigel Shaw nets Runcorn's consolation goal from the penalty spot. *Photo - Dennis Nicholson.*

Julilant post-match scenes in the Woking dressing-room. *Photo - Gavin Ellis-Neville.*

Andy Clement dribbles the ball towards the corner flag as Woking are nearly home. Photo - Paul Dennis.

PAST F.A. CHALLENGE TROPHY FINALS

1970 MACCLESFIELD TOWN 2 (Lyond, B Fidler) **TELFORD UNITED 0** Ref: K Walker
Macc: Cooke, Sievwright, Bennett, Beaumont, Collins, Roberts, Lyons, B Fidler, Young, Corfield, D Fidler. *Telford:* Irvine, Harris, Croft, Flowers, Coton, Ray, Fudge, Hart, Bentley, Murray, Jagger. *Att: 28,000.*

1971 TELFORD UTD 3 (Owen, Bentley, Fudge) **HILLINGDON BORO. 2** (Reeve, Bishop) Ref: D Smith
Telford: Irvine, Harris, Croft, Ray, Coton, Carr, Fudge, Owen, Bentley, Jagger, Murray. *H'don:* Lowe, Batt, Langley, Higginson, Newcombe, Moore, Fairchild, Bishop, Reeve, Carter, Knox. *Att: 29,500.*

1972 STAFFORD RANGERS 3 (Williams 2, Cullerton) **BARNET 0** Ref: P Partridge
Staff: Aleksic, Chadwick, Clayton, Sargeant, Aston, Machin, Cullerton, Chapman, Williams, Bayley, Jones. *Barnet:* McClelland, Lye, Jenkins, Ward, Embrey, King, Powell, Rerry, Flatt, Easton, Plume. *Att: 24,000.*

1973 SCARBOROUGH 2 (Leask, Thompson) **WIGAN ATHLETIC 1** (Rogers) *aet* Ref: H Hackney
Scarboro: Garrow, Appleton, Shoulder, Dunn, Siddle, Fagan, Donoghue, Franks, Leask (Barmby), Thompson, Hewitt. *Wigan:* Reeves, Morris, Sutherland, Taylor, Jackson, Gillibrand, Clements, Oats (McCunnell), Rogers, King, Worswick. *Att: 23,000.*

1974 MORECAMBE 2 (Richmond, Sutton) **DARTFORD 1** (Cunningham) Ref: B Homewood
M'cambe: Coates, Pearson, Bennett, Sutton, Street, Baldwin, Done, Webber, Roberts (Galley), Kershaw, Richmond. *D'ford:* Morton, Read, Payne, Carr, Burns, Binks, Light, Glozier, Robinson (Hearne), Cunningham, Halleday. *Att: 19,000.*

1975 MATLOCK TOWN 4 (Oxley, Dawson, T Fenoughty, N Fenoughy) **SCARBOROUGH 0** Ref: K Styles *Matlock:* Fell, McKay, Smith, Stuart, Dawson, Swan, Oxley, N Fenoughy, Scott, T Fenoughty, M Fenoughty. *Scarborough:* Williams, Hewitt, Rettitt, Dunn, Marshall, Todd, Houghton, Woodall, Davidson, Barnby, Aveyard. *Att: 21,000.*

1976 SCARBOROUGH 3 (Woodall, Abbey, Marshall(p)) **STAFFORD R. 2** (Jones 2) *aet* Ref: R Challis *S'boro:* Barnard, Jackson, Marshall, H Dunn, Ayre (Donoghue), HA Dunn, Dale, Barmby, Woodall, Abbey, Hilley. *S'ford:* Arnold, Ritchie, Richards, Sargeant, Seddon, Morris, Chapman, Lowe, Jones, Hutchinson, Chadwick. *Att: 21,000.*

1977 SCARBOROUGH 2 (Dunn(p), Abbey) **DAGENHAM 1** (Harris) Ref: G Courtney *S'boro:* Chapman, Smith, Marshall (Barmby), Dunn, Ayre, Deere, Aveyard, Donoghue, Woodall, Abbey, Dunn. *D'ham:* Hutley, Wellman, P Currie, Dunwell, Moore, W Currie, Harkins, Saul, Fox, Harris, Holder. *Att: 21,500.*

1978 ALTRINCHAM 3 (King, Johnson, Rogers) **LEATHERHEAD 1** (Cook) Ref: A Grey *A'cham:* Eales, Allan, Crossley, Bailey, Owens, King, Morris, Heathcote, Johnson, Rogers, Davidson (Flaherty). *L'head:* Swannell, Cooper, Eaton, Davies, Reid, Malley, Cook, Salkeld, Baker, Boyle (Bailey). *Att: 20,000.*

1979 STAFFORD RANGERS 2 (A Wood 2) **KETTERING TOWN 0** Ref: D Richardson *S'ford:* Arnold, F Wood, Willis, Sargeant, Seddon, Ritchie, Secker, Chapman, A Wood, Cullerton, Chadwick (Jones). *K'ring:* Lane, Ashby, Lee, Eastell, Dixey, Suddards, Flannagan, Kellock, Phipps, Clayton, Evans (Hughes). *Att: 32,000.*

1980 DAGENHAM 2 (Duck, Maycock) **MOSSLEY 1** (Smith) Ref: K Baker *D'ham:* Huttley, Wellman, Scales, Dunwell, Mooore, Durrell, Maycock, Horan, Duck, Kidd, Jones (Holder). *M'ley:* Fitton, Brown, Vaughan, Gorman, Salter, Polliot, Smith, Moore, Skeete, O'Connor, Keelan (Wilson). *Att: 26,000.*

1981 BISHOP'S STORTFORD 1 (Sullivan) **SUTTON UNITED 0** Ref: J Worrall *S'ford:* Moore, Blackman, Brame, Smith (Worrell), Bradford, Abery, Sullivan, Knapman, Radford, Simmonds, Mitchell. *Sutton:* Collyer, Rogers, Green, J Rains, T Rains, Stephens (Sunnucks), Waldon, Pritchard, Cornwell, Parsons. *Att: 22,578.*

1982 ENFIELD 1 (Taylor) **ALTRINCHAM 0** Ref: B Stevens *Enfield:* Jacobs, Barrett, Tone, Jennings, Waite, Ironton, Ashford, Taylor, Holmes, Oliver (Flint), King. *A'cham:* Connaughton, Crossley, Davison, Bailey, Cuddy, King (Whitbread), Allan, Heathcote, Johnson, Rogers, Howard. *Att: 18,678.*.

1983 TELFORD UTD 2 (Mather 2) **NORTHWICH VICTORIA 1** (Bennett) Ref: B Hill *Telford:* Charlton, Lewis, Turner, Mayman (Joseph), Walker, Easton, Barnett, Williams, Mather, Hogan, Alcock. *N'wich:* Ryan, Fretwell, Murphy, Jones, Forshaw, Ward, Anderson, Abel (Bennett), Reid, Chesters, Wilson. *Att: 22,071.*

1984 NORTHWICH VICTORIA 1 (Chesters) **BANGOR CITY 1** (Whelan) *Att: 14,200.* Ref: J Martin
replay at Stoke: NORTHWICH 2 (Chesters(p), Anderson) **BANGOR 1** (Lunn) *Att: 5,805*
N'wich: Ryan, Fretwell, Dean, Jones, Forshaw (Power 65), Bennett, Anderson, Abel, Reid, Chesters, Wilson. *Bangor:* Letheren, Cavanagh, Gray, Whelan, Banks, Lunn, Urqhart, Morris, Carter, Howat, Sutcliffe (Westwood 105). *Same teams in replay.*

1985 WEALDSTONE 2 (Graham, Holmes) **BOSTON UNITED 1** (Cook) Ref: J Bray *W'stone:* Iles, Perkins, Bowgett, Byatt, Davies, Greenaway, Holmes, Wainwright, Donnellan, Graham (N Cordice 89), A Cordice. *Boston:* Blackwell, Casey, Ladd, Creane, O'Brien, Thommson, Laverick (Mallender 78), Simpsom, Gilbert, Lee, Cook. *Att: 20,775.*

1986 ALTRINCHAM 1 (Farrelly) **RUNCORN 0** Ref: A Ward *A'cham:* Wealands, Gardner, Densmore, Johnson, Farrelly, Conning, Cuddy, Davison, Reid, Ellis, Anderson. Sub: Newton. *Runcorn:* McBride, Lee, Roberts, Jones, Fraser, Smith, S Crompton (A Crompton), Imrie, Carter, Mather, Carrodus. *Att: 15,700.*

1987 KIDDERMINSTER HARRIERS 0 BURTON ALBION 0 *Att: 23,617.* Ref: D Shaw
replay at West Brom: KIDDERMINSTER 2 (Davies 2) **BURTON 1** (Groves) *Att: 15,685*
K'minster: Arnold, Barton, Boxall, Brazier (sub Hazlewood in rep), Collins (sub Pearson 90 at Wembley), Woodall, McKenzie, O'Dowd, Tuohy, Casey, Davies. sub: Jones. *Burton:* New, Essex, Kamara, Vaughan, Simms, Groves, Bancroft, Land, Dorsett, Redfern, (sub Wood in replay), Gauden. Sub: Patterson.

1988 ENFIELD 0 TELFORD UNITED 0 *Att: 20,161.* Ref: L Dilkes
replay at West Brom: ENFIELD 3 (Furlong 2, Howell) **TELFORD 2** (Biggins, Norris(p)) *Att: 6,912*
Enfield: Pape, Cottington, Howell, Keen (sub Edmonds in rep), Sparrow (sub Hayzleden at Wembley), Lewis (sub Edmonds at Wembley), Harding, Cooper, King, Furlong, Francis. *Enfield:* Charlton, McGinty, Storton, Nelson, Wiggins, Mayman (sub Cunningham in rep (sub Hancock)), Sankey, Joseph, Stringer (sub Griffiths at Wembley, Griffiths in rep), Biggins, Norris.

1989 TELFORD UNITED 1 (Crawley) **MACCLESFIELD TOWN 0** Ref: T Holbrook *Telford:* Charlton, Lee, Brindley, Hancock, Wiggins, Mayman, Grainger, Joseph, Nelson, Lloyd, Stringer. Subs: Crawley, Griffiths. *Macclesfield:* Zelem, Roberts, Tobin, Edwards, Hardman, Askey, Lake, Hanton, Imrie, Burr, Timmons. Subs: Devomshire, Kendall. *Att: 18,102.*

1990 BARROW 3 (Gordon 2, Cowperthwaitee) **LEEK TOWN 0** Ref: T Simpson. *Barrow:* McDonnell, Higgins, Chilton, Skivington, Gordon, Proctor, Doherty (Burgess), Farrell (Gilmore), Cowperthwaite, Lowe, Ferris. *Leek:* Simpson, Elsby (Smith), Pearce, McMullen, Clowes, Coleman (Russell), Mellor, Somerville, Sutton, Millington. *Att: 19,011.*

1991 WYCOMBE WANDERERS 2 (Scott, West) **KIDDERMINSTER HARRIERS 1** (Hadley) Ref: J Watson *Wycombe:* Granville, Crossley, Cash, Kerr, Creaser, Carroll, Ryan, Stapleton, West, Scott, Guppy (Hutchinson). *Kidderminster:* Jones, Kurila, McGrath, Weir, Barnett, Forsyth, Joseph (Wilcox), Howell (Whitehouse), Hadley, Lilwall, Humphries. *Att: 34,842.*

1992 COLCHESTER UTD 3 (Masters, Smith, McGavin) **WITTON ALBION 1** (Lutkevitch) Ref: K P Barratt *Colchester:* Barrett, Donald, Roberts, Knsella, English, Martin, Cook, Masters, McDonough (Bennett 65), McGavin, Smith. *Witton:* Mason, Halliday, Coathup, McNeilis, Jim Connor, Anderson, Thomas, Rose, Alford, Grimshaw (Joe Connor), Lutkevitch (McCluskie). *Att: 27,806.*

1993 WYCOMBE W. 4 Cousins, Kerr, Thompson, Carroll) **RUNCORN 1** Shaughnessy) Ref: I J Borritt *Wycombe:* Hyde, Cousins, Cooper, Kerr, Crossley, Thompson (Hayrettin 65), Carroll, Ryan, Hutchinson, Scott, Guppy. Unused sub: Casey. *Runcorn:* Williams, Bates, Robertson, Hill, Harold (Connor 62), Anderson, Brady (Parker 72), Brown, Shaughnessy, McKenna, Brabin. *Att: 32,968.*

F.A. TROPHY
1993-94 At a Glance

1st Rnd Proper

Kidderminster	0
Dagenham & R.	2
Bashley	2
Woking	4
Farnborough	1;0
Grays Ath.	1;2
Waterlooville	1;1
Bromsgrove	1;2
Harrow B.	3;3
Worcester C.	3;5
Boston Utd	1;0
Macclesfield	1;1
Kettering T.	2
Stevenage B.	1
Billingham S.	2
Frickley Ath.	1
Sutton United	2
Chesham United	0
Yeovil T.	3;0
Bath City	3;4
Welling United	6
Chelmsford C.	1
Weston-s-Mare	0
Dover Ath.	2
Grantham T.	3
Witton Albion	2
Blyth Spartans	1
Bishop Auckland	3
Worthing	3
Marlow	0
Enfield	2
Purfleet	0
Cheltenham T.	1
Nuneaton Boro.	0
Hednesford T.	1
Whitby Town	0
Winsford Utd	0
Guiseley	1
Altrincham	0
Stafford Rgrs	2
Morecambe	2
Northwich V.	1
Billericay T.	0
Slough T.	2
Stalybdge	1;2;1
Colwyn B.	1;2;2
Marine	0;1
Southport	0;3
Halesowen T.	0
Gateshead	2
Gretna	1;3
Warrington	1;2
Dulwich Hamlet	1
Kingstonian	2
St Albans City	4
Merthyr Tydfil	5
Alfreton Town	0
Runcorn	5
Telford United	2
Northallerton	1
Spennymoor Utd	2
Hyde United	1
Halifax Town	2
Emley	1

2nd Rnd Proper

Dagenham & R.	1
Woking	2
Grays Athletic	1
Bromsgrove R.	2
Worcester	0;2
Macclesfield	0;3
Kettering	2;1
Billingham S.	2;3
Sutton United	6
Bath City	1
Welling United	1
Dover Athletic	3
Grantham Town	1
Bishop Auckland	2
Worthing	1;0
Enfield	1;2
Cheltenham T.	1
Hednesford T.	0
Guiseley	3
Stafford Rgrs	2
Morecambe	1
Slough Town	0
Colwyn Bay	0
Southport	3
Gateshead	0;1
Gretna	0;0
Kingstonian	0
Merthyr Tydfil	2
Runcorn	2
Telford United	1
Spennymoor Utd	1
Halifax Town	2

3rd Rnd Proper

Woking	3
Bromsgrove Rvrs	2
Macclesfield	0
Billingham S.	1
Sutton Utd	0;3
Dover Ath.	0;2
Bishop Auck.	2;1
Enfield	2;2
Cheltenham	0;0
Guiseley	0;1
Morecambe	2
Southport	1
Gateshead	3
Merthyr Tydfil	2
Runcorn	1;2
Halifax Town	1;0

4th Rnd Proper

Woking	1;2
Billingham Syn.	1;1
Sutton United	1;0
Enfield	1;1
Guiseley	3
Morecambe	2
Gateshead	0
Runcorn	3

Semi-final

Woking	1;0;3
1st leg at Woking	
Enfield	1;0;0
Guiseley	1;0
1st leg at Runcorn	
Runcorn	1;1

Final

Woking	2
Runcorn	1

THE FOOTBALL ASSOCIATION CHALLENGE VASE

REVIEW 1993-94

Extra Preliminary Round

(SAT. 4th SEP. 1993)

(Attendances in brackets)

Shotton Comrades	0-5	Ponteland Utd (25)
Heaton Stannington	1-6	Cleator Moor C. (14)
W Allotment Celtic	4-1	Bedlington T. (101)
Kennek Roker	2-4	Walker (26)
Marske United	0-2	Holker Old Boys
Wolviston	2-6	Seaton Delaval Amtrs
Seaton Terrace	1-3	Newton Aycliffe (17)
Mickleover RBL	0-5	North Trafford (62)
(played at North Trafford)		
Hall Road Rgrs	2-1	Heswall (42)
Clipstone Welfare	5-0	Westhoughton (75)
Priory (Eastwood)	5-2	Ayone
Christleton	1-3	Waterloo Dock (35)
(played at Waterloo Dock)		
Poulton Victoria	3-3	Rainworth MW (46)
Rainworth MW	1-2	Poulton Vics (94)
Maghull	1-1	General Chemicals
General Chemicals	1-3	Maghull
Nettleham	2-3	Merseyside Police (52)
Borrowash Vics	1-0	Wythenshaw Ams (42)
Grove United	0-1	Ashfield Utd (40)
Kimberley Town	3-2	Worsbrough Bdge (42)
Shirebrook Town	1-5	Hallam (140)
RES Parkgate	3-1	Cheadle Town
St Dominics	1-4	Vauxhall
Lucas Sports	5-1	Ashville (56)
(played at Ashville)		
Louth United	1-0	Castleton Gabriels
Atherton Collieries	1-2	Liversedge (50)
Blackpool Mechanics	1-4	Ellesmere Port (40)
Walsall Wood	1-0	Lutterworth T. (48)
Holswell Sports	3-1	Barwell (100)
Alvechurch Sports	3-0	Meir KA (79)
St Andrews	0-0	Bolehall Swifts (110)
Bolehall Swifts	0-4	St Andrews (45)
Pegasus Juniors	2-2	Westfields (148)
(at Hereford United)		
Westfields	5-2	Pegasus Juniors (126)
Dunkirk	6-1	Cradley Town (42)
Stapenhill	2-1	Brierley Hill Town
Knowle	4-1	Kings Heath (38)
Oadby Town	1-1	Anstey Nomads
Anstey Nomads	1-3	Oadby Town (187)
Gedling Town	2-1	Birstall United
Sawbridgeworth T.	5-3	Hadleigh United
Clacton Town	1-0	Brightlingsea (104)
Warboys Town	1-2	Brantham Ath. (92)
Somersham Town	1-0	Stanway Rovers (46)
Ely City	7-0	Downham Town (70)
Woodbridge Town	0-3	Ipswich Wdrs (164)
Long Sutton Ath.	1-5	Gt Wakering R. (92)
Beaconsfield Utd	1-3	Brook House
St Margaretsbury	1-2	London Colney (34)
(played at Hertford Town)		
Wootton Blue Cross	1-5	Tower Hamlets
Concord Rangers	3-0	Bowers Utd
Totternhoe	2-0	Luton Old Boys (29)
Hillingdon Boro.	3-1	Welwyn GC (32)
Stansted	0-2	East Ham Utd
Romford	1-2	Potton United (145)
(played at East Ham United)		
Leverstock Green	3-1	Potters Bar T. (57)
Barkingside	3-1	Cockfosters
Rayners Lane	2-1	Harpenden Town (62)
Slade Green	2-1	Eastbourne Utd
Cray Wanderers	2-3	Ashford T. (Middx) (72)
Furness	1-0	Cranleigh (40)
Broadbridge Heath	3-1	Hartley Wintney (55)
Newhaven	4-2	St Andrews (100)

Right: Newhaven's Tony Towner uses some of his vast Football League experience to beat Andrew Silk (left) of St Andrews.

Photo - Colin Stevens.

Crowborough Ath.	3-1	Worthing Utd (98)
West Wickham	1-4	Alma Swanley (60)
Farleigh Rovers	2-0	Eastbourne Town (39)

Below: Farleigh Rovers forward Rob Wadey rides a crunching tackle in the first minute of the game against Eastbourne Town. Photo - Dave West.

Folkestone Invicta	3-2	Ash United (156)
Shoreham	0-3	Cobham
Arundel	2-1	Ditton (57)
Thamesmead Town	4-0	Beckenham Town
Petersfield Utd *(scr)*		Christchurch *(w/o)*
Swindon Supermarine	5-1	Clanfield (35)
Sandhurst Town	1-1	Flight Refuelling (57)
Flight Refuelling	0-1	Sandhurst Town (28)
BAT Sports	1-2	Sherborne Town (53)
Sholing Sports *(scr)*		North Leigh *(w/o)*
Whitchurch Utd	1-3	Peppard
Tuffley Rovers	1-4	Keynsham Town (84)
DRG	0-1	Bishop Sutton
Almondsbury Town	1-3	Larkhall Ath. (42)
Patchway Town	0-5	Brislington
Old Georgians	1-0	Wotton Rovers (50)
Clyst Rovers	0-1	Cirencester Town (48)
Porthleven	0-2	Newquay
Hallen	2-1	Ellwood (79)
Moreton Town	1-0	Backwell United
Crediton United	2-0	Bridgwater Town (134)

PHOTOS OPPOSITE

Top: *A despairing dive by Ashville keeper Steve Aspinall cannot keep out a free-kick from John Conway of Lucas Sports. Photo - Rob Ruddock.*

Centre: *Peter Smith of Alma Swanley surges forward as his side end AFA interest in the Vase by winning 4-1 at West Wickham. Photo - Dennis Nicholson.*

Foot: *Johnstone, the Ditton goalkeeper, is beaten by the Mark Norrell effort that gives Arundel a 2-1 win. Photo - Graham Cotterill.*

Preliminary Round

(SAT. 2nd OCT. 1993)

(Attendances in brackets)

Walker 1-3 Eppleton CW (65)
Horden CW 0-3 Penrith
Darlington CS 1-2 Evenwood Town (14)
Pickering Town 7-3 Holker OB (81)
Billingham Town 4-0 Cleator Moor C. (46)
Newton Aylcliffe 1-4 Crook Town (25)
Whickham 1-0 Netherfield (60)
Prudhoe East End 4-3 Norton & Stockton A.

Below: Norton's Gary Cawley opens the scoring after rounding Prudhoe goalkeeper Damien Boyd but, despite trailing 0-3 midway through the second-half, the home side fought back to win in extra-time.
Photo - Alan Watson.

Ponteland Utd 2-0 Alnwick Town (26)
Harrogate RA 3-0 West Allotment C.
Annfield Plain 0-2 Seaton Delaval A.
Langley Pk S&S 0-1 Willington (33)
Esh Winning 2-1 Ryhope CA
Nantwich Town 2-0 Ossett Town
Clitheroe 1-0 Maine Road
Tadcaster Albion 1-3 Louth Utd (33)
Chadderton 0-4 Ossett Albion
Blidworth MW 2-4 Kimberley T. (27)
Lincoln United 3-2 Skelmersdale (114)
Belper Town 1-0 Bradford PA (185)
Armthorpe Welfare 4-1 Harworth CI (58)
Hallam 2-0 St Helens T. (117)
Lancaster City 0-1 Ilkeston T. (151)
Garforth Town 1-1 Maghull
Maghull 2-1 Garforth Town
Selby Town 2-4 Bacup Borough (38)

Below: Craig Dewhurst (left) of Bacup is chased by Selby's Pollington. *Photo - Colin Stevens.*

Prescot 3-1 Hucknall Town (82)
Thackley 3-0 Clipstone Welf. (147)
Salford City 2-0 Poulton Vics (80)
Heanor Town 1-3 Stocksbridge PS
Priory (Eastwood) 2-5 Rossendale U. (102)
Merseyside Police 2-1 Farsley Celtic (150)
Glossop North End 2-1 Hatfield Main (195)
Borrowash Victoria 1-2 Eccleshill Utd (54)
Immingham Town 2-6 Maltby MW (55)
Liversedge 3-0 Winterton R. (88)
North Trafford 2-1 Lucas Sports (81)
Sheffield 2-0 Hall Road Rgrs (13)
Bootle 3-1 Ellesmere Port T.
Waterloo Dock 0-2 RES Parkgate
Rossington Main 0-1 Pontefract Col. (56)
Oldham Town 1-3 Darwen
Formby 1-2 Radcliffe B. (55)
Ashfield United 0-4 Vauxhall (91)
Yorks Amateur 2-0 Blackpool Rovers
Glasshoughton W. 2-3 Denaby United
St Andrews 0-1 Boldmere SM (49)
Northampton S. 3-2 Banbury United
Gedling Town 3-3 Walsall Wood
Walsall Wood 3-0 Gedling Town
Stapenhill 3-1 Pershore Town '88
Long Buckby 3-1 Knowle (57)
Rushall Olympic 1-0 Sandwell Boro. (43)
Alvechurch Sports 4-2 Halesowen H. (84)
Chasetown 4-1 Stourport Sw. (102)
Highgate United 1-2 Holwell Sports (42)
Daventry Town 0-3 Dunkirk
RC Warwick 3-0 Wellingborough T.
Raunds Town 4-2 Wednesfield (86)
Lye Town 1-0 Stratford Town
Willenhall Town 0-3 West Bromwich T.
Westfields 4-2 Mile Oak Rvrs (62)
Cogenhoe Town 6-1 Northfield T. (35)
Paget Rangers 3-2 Desborough T. (76)
Blakenall 1-1 Oadby Town (45)
Oadby Town 6-0 Blakenhall (144)
Hinckley Town 5-1 Stewart & Lloyds (50)
Rocester 4-0 Newport Pagnell (137)
Watton United 1-3 Witham Town (95)
Sawbridgeworth 2-1 Bury Town (80)
Fakenham Town 5-5 Boston (199)
Boston 2-1 Fakenham T. (85)
Halstead Town 4-0 Norwich Utd (220)
Spalding Utd 1-1 Holbeach United
Holbeach Utd 3-4 Spalding Utd
Gt Wakering Rvrs 4-1 Gorleston (109)
Cornard United 1-1 Felixstowe Town (47)
Felixstowe T. 0-2 Cornard Utd (85)
Brantham Athletic 5-4 Ely City (46)
Histon 3-0 Tiptree United (30)
Soham Town R. 5-3 Basildon Utd (125)
Mirrlees B'stone 0-1 Sudbury Wanderers
(abandoned at half-time)
Mirrlees B'stone 3-1 Sudbury Wanderers
March Town Utd 1-0 Bourne Town (121)
King's Lynn 1-0 Clacton Town (458)
Stowmarket Town 5-2 Ipswich Wdrs (131)
Chatteris Town 2-2 Stamford
Stamford 1-2 Chatteris T. (128)
Eynesbury Rovers 2-3 Haverhill Rovers
Newmarket T. 4-0 Somersham T. (78)
Arlesey Town 2-0 Flackwell Hth (45)
Hornchurch 2-0 East Ham Utd (94)

Below: East Ham's Cornel Dobbs (left) takes on Lee O'Connor of Hornchurch. *Photo - Rob Monger.*

Roy Boon forces home one of Stotfold's six goals against Barkingside. *Photo - Neil Whittington.*

Hemel Hempstead	4-2	Haringey Boro. (67)
Kingsbury Town	1-2	Cheshunt (53)
East Thurrock	2-4	Concord Rgrs (178)
Ware	3-2	Tower Hamlets (60)
Kempston Rovers	0-2	Ford United
Wingate & Fin.	2-10	Hatfield Town
Brook House	2-4	Royston Town (65)
Viking Sports	3-4	Leverstock Green (40)
Letchworth GC	4-0	Hertford Town
Hillingdon Boro'	1-1	Potton United (62)
Potton United	1-0	Hillingdon Boro. (140)
London Colney	1-2	Feltham & Hounslow
Stotfold	6-2	Barkingside (90)
Biggleswade Town	1-3	Rayners Lane (51)
Leighton Town	2-0	Totternhoe (177)
Southall	1-5	Burnham
(played at Burnham)		
Rainham Town	2-5	Hanwell Town
Shillington	2-1	Langford
Hampton	0-1	Collier Row
Clapton	2-1	Dunstable (58)
Three Bridges	2-2	Horsham YMCA (116)
(Three Bridges expelled)		
Burgess Hill T.	3-1	Pagham (168)
Bracknell Town	6-0	Steyning Town
Bedfont	2-1	Egham Town
Merstham	1-1	Arundel
Arundel	3-1	Merstham
Leatherhead	0-1	Whitehawk (160)
(played at Whitehawk)		
Epsom & Ewell	1-1	Ashford T. (Middx)
Ashford T.(Middx)	3-1	Epsom & Ewell (94)
(played at Walton & Hersham)		
Newhaven	2-1	Furness (105)
Farleigh Rovers	0-3	Corinthian (55)
Cobham	0-2	Crowborough A. (35)
Chipstead	1-0	Chichester C. (21)
Lancing	2-1	Horsham (171)
Faversham Town	1-3	Croydon Athletic
Chatham Town	2-1	Southwick (102)
Greenwich Borough	1-4	Alma Swanley (86)
Corinthian-Casuals	4-0	Broadbridge Heath
Redhill	1-3	Godalming & G. (66)
Portfield	3-1	Ramsgate (85)
Whitstable Town	2-3	Wick

Right: Peter Venn chips Micky Phillips to give Whitstable the lead at home to Wick. *Photo - Paul Dennis.*

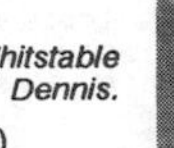

Selsey	0-1	Herne Bay (85)
Slade Green	3-2	Ringmer (47)
Thamesmead Town	2-4	Folkestone Invicta
Sheppey United	8-0	Langney Spts (56)
Oakwood	3-0	Deal Town (28)
Swindon S'marine	1-2	Eastleigh (40)
Sandhurst Town	1-0	AFC Totton (34)
Swanage T.&H.	1-3	North Leigh (101)
Bournemouth	0-1	First Tower United
Newbury Town	4-1	Westbury United (315)

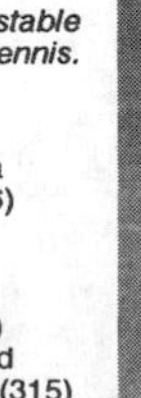

Thatcham Town	1-1	Brockenhurst (48)
Brockenhurst	1-1	Thatcham Town (98)
Brockenhurst	0-3	Thatcham Town (172)
Aldershot Town	7-0	Gosport Boro. (1,701)
Thame United	9-0	Kintbury Rangers (85)
Sherborne Town	2-2	Horndean
Horndean	1-3	Sherborne Town (62)
Calne Town	1-0	Bicester Town (38)
Bemerton Hth H.	1-2	Christchurch
Abingdon United	2-5	Cove
Hamworthy United	1-5	Ryde Sports (101)
Milton United	1-0	Wantage Town (72)
Peppard	5-2	Fleet Town
Frome Town	3-1	Ilfracombe T. (70)
Chard Town	2-1	Cinderford T. (75)
Crediton United	1-2	Torpoint Ath. (131)
Mangotsfield Utd	3-0	Brislington (153)
Moreton Town	0-2	Taunton Town (130)
Liskeard Athletic	1-2	Melksham Town (130)
Fairford Town	1-2	Bridport (40)
Glastonbury	1-3	Falmouth Town (95)
Cirencester T.	3-1	Wellington (35)
Bristol Mnr Farm	0-2	Keynsham Town
Dawlish Town	1-5	Torrington (32)
Odd Down	2-2	Chippenham T. (71)
Chippenham Town	2-1	Odd Down (185)
Minehead	5-2	Hallen (70)
(played at Hallen)		
Shortwood United	1-2	St Blazey
Exmouth Town	0-2	Bishop Sutton (89)
Elmore	4-3	Newquay
Larkhall Ath.	2-0	Devizes Town
Old Georgians	0-2	Barnstaple Town

First Round

(SAT. 31st OCT. 1993)

(Attendances in brackets)

Whickham	3-2	Billingham T. (58)
Harrogate Railway	1-4	Pickering Town (92)
Penrith	2-1	Eppleton CW (114)
Esh Winning	2-7	South Shields
Willington	0-1	Prudhoe E End (23)
Ponteland United	2-1	Seaton Delaval Am.
Crook Town	1-0	Evenwood Town
Eccleshill United	1-2	Belper Town (37)
Prescot	2-0	Hallam (90)
Rossendale United	2-4	Bootle (168)
Vauxhall	2-1	Denaby United (38)
Salford City	0-0	RES Parkgate (15)
RES Parkgate	4-1	Salford City (51)
Liversedge	4-1	North Ferriby (74)
Thackley	0-0	Stocksbridge (85)
Stocksbridge PS	0-2	Thackley (71)
Pontefract Coll.	2-4	Maltby MW (48)
Merseyside Police	4-5	Louth United
Ossett Albion	1-1	Sheffield (112)
Sheffield	4-0	Ossett Albion
Bacup Borough	1-1	Clitheroe (110)
Clitheroe	1-2	Bacup Borough (251)
Lincoln United	2-0	Darwen (121)
Kimberley Town	1-2	Nantwich Town
Yorks Amateur	1-0	Armthorpe Welf. (48)
Newcastle Town	3-4	Glossop Nth E. (55)
(played at Eastwood Hanley)		
Radcliffe Borough	2-0	North Trafford (118)
Maghull	0-1	Ilkeston Town (164)
Friar Lane OB	1-1	Cogenhoe United (141)
Cogenhoe Utd	2-0	Friar LOB (129)
Northampton Spen.	3-0	Walsall Wood (87)
Arnold	3-0	Boldmere St M. (170)
Bridgnorth Town	1-0	Lye Town (133)
Westfields	1-0	RC Warwick (81)
Armitage	1-2	Chatteris Town (41)
Raunds Town	5-2	Stapenhill (110)
Chasetown	3-1	Long Buckby (98)
Dunkirk	4-4	Rushall Olym. (40)
Rushall Olympic	2-3	Dunkirk
Rocester	4-2	West Brom Town (122)
Hinckley Town	0-3	Oadby Town (85)
Holwell Sports	1-1	Paget Rangers (120)
Paget Rgrs	2-4	Holwell Sports (48)
Oldbury United	3-3	Alvechurch (102)
Alvechurch	1-0	Oldbury Utd (62)
March Town Utd	4-0	Witham Town (100)
Spalding United	1-4	Sawbridgeworth (162)
Lowestoft Town	10-1	Brantham Ath. (147)
Harwich & Park.	2-3	Newmarket Town (178)
(Harwich protest overturned)		
Boston	2-1	Mirrlees Black. (96)
Haverhill Rovers	2-1	Tilbury (122)
King's Lynn	2-1	Gt Yarmouth T. (492)
Stowmarket Town	2-5	Soham Town Rgrs
Halstead Town	5-0	Histon (220)
Gt Wakering Rvrs	4-1	Cornard United (159)
Edgware Town	1-0	Feltham & H. (128)
Tring Town	5-2	Hatfield Town (56)
Leverstock Green	1-2	Brimsdown Rovers (57)
Burnham	0-1	Hemel Hempstead
Concord Rangers	0-2	Letchworth GC (90)
Ware	0-1	Arlesey Town
Cheshunt	1-1	Royston Town (85)
Royston Town	0-2	Cheshunt (72)
Hornchurch	4-0	Leighton Town (76)
Harefield United	0-3	Aveley
Shillington	2-0	Burnham Rblrs (60)
Clapton	0-1	Barton Rovers (73)
Northwood	1-0	Stotfold (157)
Collier Row	4-1	Rayners Lane
Potton United	0-0	Ford United (156)
Ford United	1-1	Potton United
Ford United	1-0	Potton United (52)
Ashford T. (Middx)	0-2	Bedfont (85)
Burgess Hill T.	2-0	Chatham Town (113)

Dave Boyton of Tonbridge is tackled by Matt Wiltshire during the BHL club's win at Newhaven.
Photo - Roger Turner.

Newhaven	2-3	Tonbridge AFC (320)
Croydon Athletic	3-1	Littlehampton T. (85)
Arundel	0-3	Lewes (67)
Sheppey United	0-2	Corinthian-Cas. (101)
Portfield	2-0	Oakwood (56)
Alma Swanley	0-1	Tunbridge Wells
Crowborough Ath.	2-0	Slade Green
Hanwell Town	2-3	Lancing (31)
Corinthian	0-3	Whitehawk (31)
Wick	3-1	Hailsham Town
Godalming & G.	2-2	Chipstead (44)
Chipstead	2-3	Godalming & G. (40)
Bracknell Town	3-0	Folkestone Invicta
Herne Bay	3-0	Horsham YMCA (225)
Cove	1-3	Eastleigh (102)
Newbury Town	2-0	Sandhurst Town (210)
AFC Lymington	0-2	Thame United (94)
Hungerford Town	2-3	Melksham Town (89)
North Leigh	3-1	Christchurch (101)
Peppard	1-0	Oxford City (113)
(Peppard expelled)		
Ryde Sports	0-3	Andover (32)
Milton United	4-2	Calne Town (49)
First Tower Utd	1-0	Sherborne Town
Thatcham Town	0-1	Aldershot T. (1,138)
St Blazey	3-1	Chard Town
Chippenham Town	2-2	Torpoint Ath. (129)
Torpoint Ath.	3-0	Chippenham T. (121)
Yate Town	2-1	Cirencester T. (109)
Saltash United	1-1	Barnstaple T. (132)
Barnstaple T.	2-1	Saltash Utd (207)
Mangotsfield Utd	3-1	Minehead (115)
Larkhall Athletic	0-1	Frome Town (62)
Bishop Sutton	1-2	Bideford (74)
Elmore	2-1	Torrington
Taunton Town	2-0	Keynsham Town (302)
Bridport	1-2	Falmouth Town (303)

PHOTOS OPPOSITE

Top: *Paul Brett scores for Merseyside Police, but his side lose narrowly at home to Louth United in a quite remarkable match.*
Photo - Colin Stevens.

Centre: *Stotfold keeper Steve Young watches hopelessly as Northwood's winner crosses the line.*
Photo - Paul Dennis.

Foot: *Trace Norton heads Saltash United's equalizer at home to Barnstaple Town.*
Photo - Richard Brock.

Second Round

(SAT. 20th NOV. 1993)

(Attendances in brackets)

Atherton L.R.	3-0	Prudhoe East End
Ponteland United	3-1	Liversedge
Yorkshire Amateur	3-2	Sheffield (77)
Burscough	2-3	Penrith (120)
Cammell Laird	6-2	Bootle (150)
Brigg Town	3-1	Flixton (126)
Bamber Bridge	4-2	Vauxhall (346)
South Shields	2-3	Maltby MW
Thackley	2-1	Prescot
Pickering Town	0-1	Bacup Borough (89)
RES Parkgate	0-3	Whickham (49)
Radcliffe Borough	3-1	Crook Town (133)
Chasetown	3-4	Oadby Town (109)
Arnold Town	1-2	Lincoln United (267)
Cogenhoe United	0-0	Evesham United (105)
Evesham United	1-2	Cogenhoe United (164)
Belper Town	1-0	Ilkeston Town (404)
Dunkirk	4-2	Louth United (94)
Pelsall Villa	1-1	Alvechurch
Alvechurch	2-3	Pelsall Villa
Bridgnorth Town	5-1	Chatteris Town (104)
Westfields	1-1	Northampton Spencer
Northampton Spen.	3-0	Westfields
Holwell Sports	1-6	Nantwich Town (143)
Rothwell Town	1-1	Eastwood Hanley
Eastwood Hanley	2-1	Rothwell Town (121)
Hinckley Athletic	2-1	W Mids Police (159)
Rocester	1-2	Glossop NE (147)
Bilston Town	2-2	Raunds Town (102)
Raunds Town	4-0	Bilston Town (102)
Walthamstow Pennant	1-4	Saffron Walden (77)
Arlesey Town	2-1	Haverhill Rovers (100)
Brimsdown Rovers	2-1	Shillington
Edgware Town	1-2	Wisbech Town (208)
Tring Town	0-0	Diss Town (95)
Diss Town	2-0	Tring Town (267)
Collier Row	3-2	Newmarket Town

Below: Newmarket Town's Dave Brown (right) tussles for possession with two Collier Row opponents.
Photo - Martin Wray.

Lowestoft Town	0-2	Buckingham T. (126)
Letchworth Gdn City	2-3	Soham Town Rangers
Hoddesdon Town	1-4	Cheshunt (175)
Hemel Hempstead	0-1	Ford United (90)
King's Lynn	7-1	Hornchurch (398)
Halstead Town	3-1	Sawbridgeworth (260)
Boston	3-1	Barton Rovers (64)
March Town United	0-2	Gt Wakering R. (175)
Aveley	2-4	Canvey Island
Goldalming & G.	2-4	Bracknell Town (142)
Wick	0-1	Malden Vale (140)
Burgess Hill Town	0-3	Met Police
Thame United	2-1	North Leigh (99)
Aldershot Town	2-1	Herne Bay (1,965)
Whitehawk	4-1	Portfield (100)
Eastleigh	1-2	Peacehaven (93)
Crowborough Ath.	1-4	Corinthian-Cas. (135)
Chertsey Town	0-3	Newbury Town (311)
Tunbridge Wells	2-0	Lewes (198)
Bedfont	1-1	Northwood (75)
Northwood	1-2	Bedfont
Newport IOW	2-2	Banstead Ath. (297)
Banstead Athletic	0-0	Newport IOW (55)
Banstead Athletic	1-1	Newport IOW (60)
Newport IOW	1-6	Banstead Ath. (213)
Lancing	3-4	Tonbridge (246)
Croydon Athletic	2-0	Oxford City
Forest Green R.	0-0	Barnstaple T. (112)
(Forest Green expelled)		
Torpoint Ath.	2-0	First Tower (205)
Melksham Town	0-6	Taunton Town
Welton Rovers	0-1	Wimborne Town (134)
Mangotsfield United	0-5	Tiverton Town (240)
Yate Town	1-2	Elmore (125)
Andover	6-2	Bideford (204)
Milton United	1-4	Falmouth Town (119)
Paulton Rovers	2-1	Frome Town (127)
Clevedon Town	4-0	St Blazey (372)

Below: Clevedon's Shaun Penny (left) in action as his side cruise to victory against St Blazey.
Photo - Colin Rozee/PictureSport.

PHOTOS OPPOSITE

Top: *Thackley's Stuart Taylor fires in a shot during his side's 2-1 home win over visiting Prescot.*
Photo - Colin Stevens.

Centre: *Chertsey Town goalkeeper John Granville safely clutches a cross, but his side go down 0-3 at home to their DFL Division Two title rivals Newbury Town in the 'tie of the round'.*
Photo - Paul Dennis.

Foot: *Portfield's Chad Franklin challenges Whitehawk keeper Malcolm Judge for a high cross as his side slip to defeat at East Brighton Park.*
Photo - Dave West.

BNFS

Third Round

(SAT. 11th DEC. 1993)

(Attendances in brackets)

Thackley	2-1	Lincoln United (213)
Cammell Laird	2-3	Glossop Nth End (155)
Oadby Town	2-0	Ponteland Utd (170)
Nantwich Town	2-0	Bacup Borough (220)
Belper Town	2-1	Brigg Town (202)
Radcliffe Borough	2-0	Yorkshire Amtr (149)
(played 18-12-93)		
Penrith	0-1	Atherton LR (89)
Whickham	1-0	Bamber Bridge (135)
Dunkirk	2-1	Maltby MW (103)
Wisbech Town	1-2	Collier Row (410)
Gt Wakering Rvrs	3-3	Hinckley Ath. (159)
Hinckley Athletic	2-1	Gt Wakering R. (323)
(played 18-12-93)		
Northampton Spen.	1-2	Cogenhoe United (185)

Below: Roy Wilmott of Northampton Spencer clears the ball upfield as Cogenhoe United's Neil Westland tries to intervene during this keenly contested local derby.
Photo - Paul Dennis.

Boston	6-1	Bedfont (55)
Ford United	1-2	Diss Town
Saffron Walden T.	1-4	Raunds Town (137)
Bridgnorth Town	3-1	Cheshunt (145)
Soham Town Rgrs	3-0	Brimsdown Rvrs (155)
Buckingham Town	1-2	King's Lynn (260)
Pelsall Villa	0-0	Halstead Town
(abandoned after 57 mins)		
Pelsall Villa	2-4	Halstead Town
(played 14-12-93)		
Eastwood Hanley	1-2	Arlesey Town (120)

Canvey Island	2-1	Corinthian-Cas. (381)
Taunton Town	2-0	Barnstaple T. (284)
Elmore	1-2	Thame United (120)
Croydon Athletic	0-2	Paulton Rovers

Below: Paul Slocombe of Paulton Rovers wins an aerial duel with Dave Bygraves as the Western League side record a surprise win against Croydon Athletic at Mayfield Road.
Photo - Dennis Nicholson.

Tonbridge AFC	0-1	Tiverton Town (536)
Aldershot Town	1-0	Malden Vale (1,697)
Tunbridge Wells	2-6	Torpoint Ath. (278)
Clevedon Town	3-4	Wimborne Town (392)
Bracknell Town	1-2	Newbury Town (165)
Banstead Athletic	1-0	Peacehaven (45)
Falmouth Town	3-1	Andover (418)
Whitehawk	3-2	Met Police (175)

PHOTOS OPPOSITE

Top: *King's Lynn goalkeeper Gary Groom gets above a Buckingham Town forward as the Norfolk team score an excellent win in the all-Beazer Homes League clash at Ford Meadow.*
Photo - Richard Brock.

Centre: *Ian Pendry of Metropolitan Police is crowded out by Whitehawk defenders as the Diadora League side slip to a surprise defeat in Sussex.*
Photo - Dave West.

Foot: *Mike Davidson salutes the crowd after heading the first of Torpoint Athletic's astounding six goals at Tunbridge Wells.*
Photo - Francis Short.

Fourth Round

(SAT. 15th JAN. 1994)

Boston defender Pat Clarke outjumps Radcliffe's Gary Stewart as the UCL side earn an exciting 3-3 draw.
Photo - Colin Stevens.

Radcliffe Boro. 3 v 3 Boston
Wardle 3, Horwood 68(og), Glendon 103 — Att: 216 — Clarke 38, McDonald 49, Horwood 97(p)

Boston 2 v 1 Radcliffe Boro.
(Played 18-1-94)
Horwood 28, Smaller 85 — Att: 160 — Wardle 84

Atherton LR 0 v 0 Thackley

Thackley 2 v 3 Atherton LR
(Played 18-1-94)
A Taylor 44, Hall 78 — Att: 250 — Parker 20 43 95

Raunds Town 1 v 2 Belper Town
Westley 41 — Att: 330 — Allen 68 111

Whickham 0 v 0 Dunkirk
Att: 356

Dunkirk 1 v 0 Whickham
(Played 22-2-94)
Cassidy — Att: 380

King's Lynn 1 v 0 Nantwich Town
Jones 21 — Att: 886

Bridgnorth Town 3 v 2 Glossop N.E.
Beddow 21, Taylor 30, Pound 71 — Att: 310 — Smallwood 57, Morgan 88

Oadby Town 5 v 1 Cogenhoe Utd
(Played at Leics FA Ground, Holmes Park)
Cook 26 66, Culpin 46 70, Tonge 89 — Att: 400 — Cunningham 81

Halstead Town 1 v 5 Wimborne T.
Hollocks 56 — Att: 463 — Allen 32, Sturgess 47 82, Turner 68, Lovell 86

Canvey Island 1 v 2 Newbury Town
(Played 22-1-94)
Jones 5 — Att: 782 — Gardner 50, Kemp 75

Taunton Town 1 v 1 Banstead Ath.
Graddon 79 — Att: 479 — Yetzes 86

Banstead Ath. 0 v 2 Taunton Town
(Played 22-1-94)
Att: 135 — Palfrey 73, West 89

Whitehawk 3 v 2 Thame United
Carr 9, Somers 50, Brown 58 — Att: 285 — Sweales 76, Shepherd 84

Torpoint Ath. 0 v 3 Diss Town
(Played 22-1-94)
Att: 329 — Bugg 15, Miles 47, Fletcher 84

Aldershot Town 5 v 0 Soham Town R.
Holmes 8, Calvert 67, Stairs 71 80, Frampton 82 — Att: 2284

Tiverton Town 5 v 0 Paulton Rvrs
Smith 13 14 90, Everett 52, M Saunders 85 — Att: 810

Hinckley Ath. 4 v 2 Collier Row
Hodgkins 41 43, Sinden 80 85 — Att: 440 — Simon 57, Christodoulou 85

Arlesey Town 5 v 3 Falmouth T.
Howell 12 44, Long 44(og), Cochrane 75, Donnelly 84 — Att: 350 — Babb 7, Mattews 19, Gosling 55

PHOTOS OPPOSITE

Top: *Simon Cook rises to head an excellent opening goal for Oadby Town in their impressive 5-1 win over Cogenhoe United.*
Photo - Chris Monument.

Centre: *Thame United's Richard Gregory (left) tries to guess which way Ashley Carr of Whitehawk is going go.*
Photo - Roger Turner.

Foot: *High-flying action in the high-scoring game between Arlesey Town and Falmouth Town (stripes).*
Photo - Dennis Nicholson.

ETHERIDGE
ELECTRICS

Fifth Round

(SAT. 5th FEB. 1994)

Simon Pierce tries to shield the ball from Derrick Nuttell of Boston.

Photo - Dave West.

Hinckley Ath.	**0 v 3**	**Newbury Town**
	Att: 636	Gardner 76, Masters 35 43
Atherton LR	**1 v 0**	**Bridgnorth T.**
Parker 42	Att: 567	
Oadby Town	**1 v 2**	**Arlesey Town**
Culpin 77	Att: 600	Gyalog 85, Cardines 100
Dunkirk	**0 v 2**	**Tiverton Town**
	Att: 814	Everett 14 80
Diss Town	**2 v 0**	**King's Lynn**
Warne 65, Gibbs 80	Att: 1492	
Whitehawk	**2 v 3**	**Boston**
Somers 60, Pierce 63	Att: 485	Clarke 42, Smaller 84 89
Aldershot Town	**1 v 0**	**Wimborne T.**
Lampkin 89	Att: 3420	
Belper Town	**1 v 3**	**Taunton Town**
Woolley 44	Att: 1050	Perrett 86, Durham 40, Jarvis 52

Below: Darren Prior of King's Lynn eludes a tackle from Paul Warne of Diss Town.

Photo - Paul Dennis.

PHOTOS OPPOSITE

Top: *Hinckley Athletic top-scorer Mark Hodgkins beats Newbury keeper Danny Honey to the ball, but his header goes wide.*

Photo - Keith Clayton.

Centre: *Dean Culpin gets in a shot for Oadby Town despite the close attention of Nigel Cardines, Arlesey's eventual match-winner.*

Photo - Chris Monument.

Foot: *Kevin Leonard can only watch in disbelief as an effort from Mark Frampton (on floor, extreme right) gives Aldershot Town a last-gasp winner.*

Photo - Eric Marsh.

Dunkirk's Alan Douglas tests the Tiverton Town defence. *Photo - Gavin Ellis-Neville.*

JEWSON
JEWSON

Sixth Round

(SAT. 26th FEB. 1994)

Arlesey Town 2 v 3 Boston
Howell 53, Gyalog 58 — Smaller 39, McDonnell 75, Shaw 90

Ref: Graham Barber (Guildford) Att:
Arlesey: Hawkins, Hall, Mullins (Tansley 45), Cardines, Kelly, Burgess, Gyalog, Cochrane, Marshall, Ford (Glasgow 58), Howell.
Boston: Foxcroft, Vince, Horwood (Walker 60), Cooper, Clarke, Nuttell, Shaw, Stevenson (Burns 67), McDonnell, C Smaller, P Smaller.

Diss Town 1 v 0 Tiverton Town
Bugg 69

Ref: G Pawley (Bishop's Stortford) Att: 1,256
Diss: Woodcock, Carter, Musgrave, Casey, Hartle, Smith, Barth (Bugg 45), Mendham, Miles, Warne (Fletcher 84), Gibbs.
Tiverton: Nott, Tregedeon, N Saunders, M Saunders, Scott (Carpenter 55), Steele, Annunziata, Smith, Everett, Daly, Hynds. Unused sub: Cole.

Taunton Town 2 v 0 Newbury Town
(Played 5-3-94)
Fowler 8(p)
Perrett 18

Att: 1,472
Taunton: Maloy, Morris, Walsh, Ewens, Graddon, Palfrey, West, Fowler, Durham, Perrett, Jarvis. Unused subs: Ward, Hendy.
Newbury: Honey, Kemp, Richardson, Gribben, Hicks, Gardner (Denton 33), Rhoades-Brown, Seymour, Masters, McDonnell, Parr. Unused sub: Deaner.

Aldershot Town 0 v 0 Atherton L.R.
Ref: D Orr (Iver, Bucks) Att: 4,246
Aldershot: Burns, O'Neill (May 105), Shrubb, Harris, Udal, Baker, Calvert, Osgood, Frampton (Stairs 67), Holmes, Butler.
Atherton: Hills, Southern, Evans, Holgate, Feeley, Stewart, Burrows, Pemberton, Liptrot (Ingham 108), Parker, Humphries (Pizelis 118).

Atherton L.R. 0 v 0 Aldershot Town
(Played 5-3-94)
Att: 1,856
Atherton: Hills, Southern, Evans, Holgate, Feeley, Stewart, Burrows, Pemberton (Ingham 80), Liptrot, Parker (Pizelis 31), Humphries.
Aldershot: Burns, O'Neill, Sutton, Harris, Udal, Baker, Calvert, Osgood, Stairs, Holmes, Butler. Unused subs: May, Frampton.

Aldershot Town 0 v 2 Atherton L.R.
(Played 8-3-94)
Unsworth 31,
Stewart 77

Ref: Stephen Dunn (Bristol) Att: 4,439
Aldershot: Burns, O'Neill, Sutton (May 41), Harris, Udal, Baker, Calvert, Osgood (Frampton 60), Stairs, Holmes, Butler. Unused subs: May, Frampton.
Atherton: Hills, Southern, Evans, Holgate, Feeley, Stewart, Burrows, Unsworth (Pemberton 78), Liptrot, Ingham (Pizelis 93), Humphries.

PHOTOS OPPOSITE

Top: *Andy Perrett (far left) cracks home Taunton's second goal against competition favourites Newbury.* *Photo - Tony Smith.*

Centre: *Paul Burrows of Atherton LR takes on Aldershot's Dave Sutton during the first replay of this marathon tie.* *Photo - Colin Stevens.*

Foot: *Boston substitute Stuart Burns gets in a cross despite the close proximity of Nigel Cardines of Arlesey Town.* *Photo - Dave West.*

Carl Smaller strokes the ball into an unguarded net for Boston's first goal. *Photo - Dennis Nicholson.*

Alford HOMES
Building
For Better Living

D.SCOTT & SON
BUILDING CONTRACTORS

Semi-Finals
(Two legs)
(SAT. 19th MAR. 1994)
(SAT. 26th MAR. 1994)

Diss Town 3 v 1 Atherton L.R.
Casey 14, Gibbs 40, Bugg 72 — Liptrot 55

Ref: G S Willard (Worthing) Att: 1,700
Diss: Woodcock, Carter, Musgrave, Casey (Mortimer 55), Hartle, Smith, Barth, Mendham, Miles (Bugg 79), Warne, Gibbs.
Atherton: Hills, Southern, Evans, Holgate (Unsworth 85), Feeley (Ree 75), Stewart, Burrows, Pemberton, Liptrot, Ingham, Humphries.

Atherton L.R. 2 v 0 Diss Town
Liptrot 14, Burrows 57

Att: 1,341
Atherton: Hills, Southern, Evans, Holgate, Feeley, Stewart, Burrows, Pemberton, Liptrot (Ingham 108), Parker, Humphries (Pizelis 118).
Diss: Woodcock, Carter (Clements 82), Musgrave, Woolsey, Hartle, Smith, Barth (Bugg 72), Mendham, Miles, Warne, Gibbs.

SEMI FINAL REPLAY

Diss Town 2 v 1 Atherton LR
(played at VS Rugby FC, 30-3-94)
Smith 83, Manning 84 — Stewart 52

Ref: P S Danson (Blaby) Att: 736
Diss: Woodcock, Carter, Musgrave, Clements (Manning 64), Hartle, Smith, Mortimer, Mendham, Miles, Warne, Gibbs. Unused: Bugg.
Atherton: Hills, Southern, Evans, Holgate, Feeley, Stewart, Burrows, Pizelis, Liptrot, Ingham (Quigg 80), Humphries. Unused sub: Ree.

Taunton Town 1 v 0 Boston
Durham 4

Ref: P E Alcock (Redhill) Att: 1,369
Taunton: Maloy, Morris, Walsh, Ewens, Graddon, Palfrey, West, Fowler, Durham, Perrett (Ward 72), Jarvis. Unused sub: Hendy.
Boston: Foxcroft, Vince, Horwood, Cooper, Clarke, Nuttell, Walker, Shaw, Roddis, C Smaller, P Smaller. Unused subs: Stephenson, Burns.

Boston 0 v 1 Taunton Town
(Played 27-3-94)
Perrett 56

Ref: T E West (Hull) Att: 1,700
Boston: Foxcroft, Vince (Stephenson 56), P Smaller, Cooper, Clarke, Nuttell, Walker, Shaw (Burns 77), Horwood, C Smaller, Roddis.
Taunton: Maloy, Morris, Walsh, Ewens, Graddon, Palfrey (Thaws 92), West, Fowler, Durham (Ward 88), Perrett, Jarvis.

PHOTOS OPPOSITE

Top: *Atherton's Keith Ingham carries the ball upfield closely pursued by Stephen Miles of Diss.*
Photo - Paul Dennis.

Centre: *Tom Casey (partly hidden) scores the opening goal of the first leg.*
Photo - Paul Dennis.

Foot: *Happy scenes in the Taunton Town dressing-room after their win at Boston.*
Photo - Paul Dennis.

Andy Perrett rounds Dale Foxcroft to score and send Taunton to Wembley. *Photo - Dave West.*

F.A. VASE FINAL

Saturday 7th May, At Wembley Stadium

Diss Town 2 v 1 Taunton Town

Gibbs (90 penalty), Mendham (108) — Fowler (12)

Attendance: 13,450

Diss: Robert Woodcock, Jason Carter, Martin Wolsey (Rob Musgrave 59), Tom Casey (Phil Bugg 75), Paul Hartle, Garry Smith, Kelly Barth, Peter Mendham, Stephen Miles, Paul Warne, Paul Gibbs. Manager: Bill Punton.
Taunton: Kevin Maloy, Wayne Morris, Alan Walsh, Dave Ewens, Keith Graddon, Damon Palfrey, Paul West (Nicky Hendy 115), Derek Fowler, John Durham, Andy Perrett (Jamie Ward 53), Nigel Jarvis. Manager: Terry Rowles.

Referee: Mr Kelvin Morton (Bury St Edmunds)
Linesmen: Mr Phil Joblin (Newark), Mr Phil Richards (Preston).

From the first thirty seconds when Paul West sprinted down the right flank setting up John Durham to force an athletic save out of Robert Woodcock with an equally acrobatic shot, you had the impression that this was going to be a classic. It did not disappoint, and in years to come those who were privileged to be present will talk about this match in the same breath as many of Wembley's most famous finals.

Much of the talk, particularly in Somerset, will centre on one piece of equipment - the referee's stop-watch. Kelvin Morton was playing the eighth minute of added time when he awarded Diss the penalty that took them to extra-time and ultimate victory.

"There were an unusual amount of stoppages," the arbiter recognised afterwards. "I don't know how long I did play. I just stopped my watch every time the trainer was on - I have a duty to play 45 minutes football in each half." He went on to state that there were only eighteen seconds remaining when he whistled the penalty.

The second-half hold-ups included an almost five-minute delay as Keith Graddon was brought around after deflecting a fierce shot behind for a corner with his face, and had the injury-time not been played the better side would have been deprived of victory. Over 90, 99 or 120 minutes, Diss where the more penetrative and inventive of two very good teams.

Both clubs had been plagued by injury in the month preceding the match, which made its high quality all the more commendable. Taunton had been without four highly influential campaigners - Dave Ewens, Nigel Jarvis, Andy Perrett and Wayne Morris - for the majority of the fifteen games they had contested since the semi-final, whilst Diss had been without Kelly Barth for a number of matches and had to wait on late fitness tests on Peter Mendham and Tom Casey.

Taunton settled quickest and took the lead in the thirteenth minute when West's long throw was flicked on by Derek Fowler at the near post. Andy Perrett won his header turning the ball back towards Fowler whose second attempt found the far corner of the net despite Woodcock getting a hand on the ball. With all the long-time absentees back together at last, the Westerners were playing their most controlled football for many weeks, and should have extended their lead when the Diss defence opened for West, but the stocky midfielder blazed over with only Woodcock to beat.

Diss, meanwhile, looked lethal on the break with Paul Warne impressing yet again with his pace and vision. He was equally effective on both flanks, jinking in from the right in the twentieth minute to force Kevin Maloy into a low save, then cropping up on the left a few moments later to tee up a header for Stephen Miles that was tipped just over.

In the second-half, Diss's dominance became more pronounced with their opponents unable to muster a single effort on target. Time and again Maloy was the saviour for Taunton, diving courageously at the feet of Peter Mendham in the fiftieth minute, then tipping over a bullet-header from Paul Hartle following a Kelly Barth corner a quarter of an hour later.

However, as the game moved closer to, then beyond, the ninety-minute mark, Diss's hopes seemed to be evaporating. Twice in injury-time the Taunton fans thought their side had wrapped it up; firstly when John Durham headed home deftly at the near-post only for the ball to be adjudged already over the goal-line before West had hooked it back; then when the side-netting bulged as Damon Palfrey ended a 'four-on-two' break by blasting the wrong side of the post.

How costly that last miss proved! The Taunton defence was caught cold by a desperate last-ditch punt upfield and suddenly Miles was in on Maloy with Barth alongside him in support. The custodian clattered the on-rushing forward and, though he made a valiant attempt to reach Paul Gibbs's rifled spot-kick, Taunton's Vase dream had turned into a nightmare.

The Western League side enjoyed territorial advantage in the first period of extra-time, but they were clearly distraught and one sensed that Diss, like a coiled cobra, were preparing for one last killer strike. It came in the 108th minute when Mendham got on the end of an in-swinging corner from the right. His initial effort was pushed out but, at the second attempt, the former Norwich City star, and perhaps the most consistent performer in Diss Town's historic run, rammed home what must surely be the most significant goal of his long career.

James Wright

Rob Musgrave fires a fierce shot at goal with Dave Ewens attempting to block. Photo - Gavin Ellis-Neville.

Paul Gibbs slides his way past Taunton full-back Wayne Morris. *Photo - Gavin Ellis-Neville.*

Diss Town - FA Challenge Vase winners 1993-94. *Photo - Paul Dennis.*

Taunton Town's 1994 Wembley goalscorer Derek Fowler rises to the occasion. *Photo - Paul Dennis.*

PAST F.A. CHALLENGE VASE FINALS

1975 HODDESDON T. 2 (Sedgwick 2) **EPSOM & EWELL 1** (Wales) *Att: 9,500.* Ref: R Toseland
Hoddesdon: Galvin, Green, Hickey, Maybury, Stevenson, Wilson, Bishop, Picking, Sedgwick, Nathan, Schofield. *Epsom:* Page, Bennett, Webb, Wales, Worby, Jones, O'Connell, Walker, Tuite, Eales, Lee.

1976 BILLERICAY TOWN 1 (Aslett) **STAMFORD 0** *(aet)* *Att: 11,848.* Ref: A Robinson
Billericay: Griffiths, Payne, Foreman, Pullin, Bone, Coughlan, Geddes, Aslett, Clayden, Scott, Smith. *Stamford:* Johnson, Kwiatkowski, Marchant, Crawford, Downs, Hird, Barnes, Walpole, Smith, Russell, Broadbent.

1977 BILLERICAY TOWN 1 (Clayden) **SHEFFIELD 1** (Coughlan OG) *(aet)* *Att: 14,000.* Ref: J Worrall
B'cay: Griffiths, Payne, Bone, Coughlan, Pullin, Scott, Wakefield, Aslett, Clayden, Woodhouse, McQueen. Sub: Whettell *Shef.:* Wing, Gilbody, Lodge, Hardisty, Watts, Skelton, Kay, Travis, Pugh, Thornhill, Haynes. Sub: Strutt.

Replay at Nottm Forest. BILLERICAY 2 (Aslett, Woodhouse) **SHEFFIELD 1** (Thornhill) Ref: J Worrall
Billericay: Griffiths, Payne, Pullin, Whettell, Bone, McQueen, Woodhouse, Aslett, Clayden, Scott, Wakefield. *Sheffield:* Wing, Gilbody, Lodge, Strutt, Watts, Skelton, Kay, Travis, Pugh, Thornhill, Haynes. *Att: 3,482.*

1978 NEWCASTLE BLUE STAR 2 (Dunn, Crumplin) **BARTON ROVERS 1** (Smith) Ref: T Morris
Blue Star: Halbert, Feenan, Thompson, Davidson, S Dixon, Beynon, Storey, P Dixon, Crumplin, Callaghan, Dunn. Sub: Diamond. *Barton:* Blackwell, Stephens, Crossley, Evans, Harris, Dollimore, Dunn, Harnaman, Fossey, Turner, Smith. Sub: Cox. *Att: 16,858.*

1979 BILLERICAY TOWN 4 (Young 3, Clayden) **ALMONDSBURY GREENWAY 1** (Price) Ref: C Seel
Billericay: Norris, Blackaller, Bingham, Whettell, Bone, Reeves, Pullin, Scott, Clayden, Young, Groom. Sub: Carrigan. *Almondsbury:* Hamilton, Bowers, Scarrett, Sullivan, Tudor, Wookey, Bowers, Shehean, Kerr, Butt, Price. Sub: Kilbaine. *Att: 17,500.*

1980 STAMFORD 2 (Alexander, McGowan) **GUISBOROUGH TOWN 0** Ref: Neil Midgley
Stamford: Johnson, Kwiatkowski, Ladd, McGowan, Bliszczak I, Mackin, Broadhurst, Hall, Czarnecki, Potter, Alexander. Sub: Bliszczak S. *Guisborough:* Cutter, Scott, Thornton, Angus, Maltby, Percy, Skelton, Coleman, McElvaney, Sills, Dilworth. Sub: Harrison. *Att: 11,500.*

1981 WHICKHAM 3 (Scott, Williamson, Peck OG) **WILLENHALL 2** (Smith, Stringer) *(aet)* Ref: R Lewis
Whickham: Thompson, Scott, Knox, Williamson, Cook, Ward, Carroll, Diamond, Cawthra, Robertson, Turnbull. Sub: Allon. *Willenhall:* Newton, White, Dams, Woodall, Heath, Fox, Peck, Price, Matthews, Smith, Stringer. Sub: Trevor. *Att: 12,000.*

1982 FOREST GREEN ROVERS 3 (Leitch 2, Norman) **RAINWORTH M.W. 0** Ref: K Walmsey
Forest Green: Moss, Norman, Day, Turner, Higgins, Jenkins, Guest, Burns, Millard, Leitch, Doughty. Sub: Dangerfield. *Rainworth:* Watson, Hallam, Hodgson, Slater, Sterland, Oliver, Knowles, Raine, Radzi, Reah, Comerfield. Sub: Robinson. *Att: 12,500.*

1983 V.S. RUGBY 1 (Crawley) **HALESOWEN TOWN 0** Ref: B Daniels
Rugby: Burton, McGinty, Harrison, Preston, Knox, Evans, Ingram, Setchell, Owen, Beecham, Crawley. Sub: Haskins. *Halesowen:* Coldicott, Penn, Edmonds, Lacey, Randall, Shilvock, Hazelwood, Moss, Woodhouse, P Joinson, L Joinson. Sub: Smith. *Att: 13,700.*

1984 STANSTED 3 (Holt, Gillard, Reading) **STAMFORD 2** (Waddicore, Allen) Ref: T Bune
Stansted: Coe, Williams, Hilton, Simpson, Cooper, Reading, Callanan, Holt, Reeves, Doyle, Gillard. Sub: Williams. *Stamford:* Parslow, Smitheringale, Blades, McIlwain, Lyon, Mackin, Genovese, Waddicore, Allen, Robson, Beech. Sub: Chapman. *Att: 8,125.*

1985 HALESOWEN TOWN 3 (Moss, L Joinson 2) **FLEETWOOD TOWN 1** (Moran) Ref: C Downey
Halesowen: Caldicott, Penn, Sherwood, Warner, Randle, Heath, Hazelwood, Moss (Smith), Woodhouse, P Joinson, L Joinson. *Fleetwood:* Dobson, Moran, Hadgraft, Strachan, Robinson, Milligan, Hall, Trainor, Taylor (Whitehouse), Cain, Kenneley. *Att: 16,715.*

1986 HALESOWEN TOWN 3 (Moss 2, L Joinson) **SOUTHALL 0** Ref: D Scott
Halesowen: Pemberton, Moore, Lacey, Randle (Rhodes), Sherwood, Heath, Penn, Woodhouse, P Joinson, L Joinson, Moss. *Southall:* MacKenzie, James, McGovern, Croad, Holland, Powell (Richmond), Pierre, Richardson, Sweales, Ferdinand, Rowe. *Att: 18,340.*

1987 ST HELENS 3 (Layhe 2, Rigby) **WARRINGTON TOWN 2** (Reid, Cook) Ref: T Mills
St Helens: Johnson, Benson, Lowe, Bendon, Wilson, McComb, Collins, (Gledhill), O'Neill, Cummins, Lay, Rigby. Sub: Deakin. *Warrington:* O'Brien, Copeland, Hunter, Gratton, Whalley, Reid, Brownville (Woodyer), Cook, Kinsey, Looker (Hill), Hughes. *Att: 4,254.*

1988 COLNE DYNAMOES 1 (Anderson) **EMLEY 0** Ref: A Seville
Colne: Mason, McFafyen, Westwell, Bentley, Dunn, Roscoe, Rodaway, Whitehead (Burke), Diamond, Anderson, Wood (Coates). *Emley:* Dennis, Fielding, Mellor, Codd, Hirst (Burrows), Gartland (Cook), Carmody, Green, Bramald, Devine, Francis. *Att: 15,000.*

1989 TAMWORTH 1 (Devaney) **SUDBURY TOWN 1** (Hubbick) *aet* Ref. C Downey
Tamworth: Belford, Lockett, Atkins, Cartwright, McCormack, Myers, Finn, Devaney, Moores, Gordon, Stanton. Subs: Rathbone, Heaton. *Sudbury:* Garnham, Henry, G Barker, Boyland, Thorpe, Klug, D Barker, Barton, Oldfield, Smith, Hubbick. Subs: Money, Hunt. *Att: 26,487.*

Replay at Peterborough. TAMWORTH 3 (Stanton 2, Moores) **SUDBURY TOWN 0**
Tamworth: Belford, Lockett, Atkins, Cartwright, Finn, Myers, George, Devaney, Moores, Gordon, Stanton. Sub: Heaton. *Sudbury:* Garnham, Henry, G Barker, Boyland, Thorpe, Klug, D Barker, Barton, Oldfield, Smith, Hubbick. Subs: Money, Hunt. *Att: 11,201.*

1990 YEADING 0 BRIDLINGTON TOWN 0 *Att: 7,932.* Ref: R Groves
Replay at Leeds. YEADING 1 (Sweales) **BRIDLINGTON TOWN 0** *Att: 5,000.* Ref: R Groves
Yeading: MacKenzie, Wickens, Turner, Whiskey (sub McCarthy at Wembley), Croad (sub McCarthy in rep), Denton (Schwartz in rep), Matthews, James (sub Charles at Wembley), Sweales, Impey (sub Welsh in rep), Cordery. *Bridlington:* Taylor, Pugh, Freeman, McNeil, Warburton, Brentano, Wilkes (sub Hall at Wembley, Brown in rep), Noteman, Gauden (sub Downing in rep), Whiteman, Brattan (sub Brown at Wembley).

1991 GRESLEY ROVERS 4 (Rathbone, Smith 2, Stokes)
GUISELEY 4 (Tennison 2, Walling, A Roberts) Ref: C Trussell
Replay at Bramall Lane. GUISELEY 3 (Tennison, Walling, Atkinson) **GRESLEY 1** (Astley) Ref: C Trussell
Guiseley: Maxted, Bottomley (Annan in rep), Hogarth, Tetley, Morgan, McKenzie (sub Bottomley in rep), Atkinson (sub Annan at Wembley), Tennison (sub Noteman in rep), Walling, A Roberts, B Roberts (sub Annan at Wembley). *Gresley:* Aston, Barry, Elliott (sub Adcock at Wembley), Denby, Land, Astley, Stokes (sub Weston in rep), K Smith, Acklam, Rathbone, Lovell (sub Weston at Wembley, Adcock in rep). *Att: 11,314 at Wembley, 7,585 at Sheffield.*

1992 WIMBORNE TOWN 5 (Richardson, Sturgess 2, Killick 2)
GUISELEY 3 (Noteman 2, Colville) Ref: M J Bodenham
Wimborne: Leonard, Langdown, Wilkins, Beacham, Allan, Taplin, Ames, Richardson, Bridle, Killick, Sturgess (Lovell), Lynn. *Guiseley:* Maxted, Atkinson, Hogarth, Tetley (Wilson 68), Morgan, Brockie, A Roberts, Tennison, Noteman (Colville 80), Annan, W Roberts. *Att: 10,772*

1993 BRIDLINGTON TOWN 1 (Radford) **TIVERTON TOWN 0** Ref: Mr R A Hart
Bridlington: Taylor, Brentano, McKenzie, Harvey, Bottomley, Woodcock, Grocock, A Roberts, Jones, Radford (Tyrell 85), Parkinson. Unused sub: Swailes. *Tiverton:* Nott, J Smith, N Saunders, M Saunders, Short (Scott 83), Steele, Annunziata, K Smith, Everett, Daly, Hynds (Rogers 75). *Att: 9,061*

F.A. VASE
1993-94 At a Glance

Third Round

Tunbridge W.	2
Torpoint Ath.	6
Ford United	1
Diss Town	2
Buckingham T.	1
King's Lynn	2
Nantwich Town	2
Bacup Borough	0
Whickham	1
Bamber Bridge	0
Dunkirk	2
Maltby MW	1
Tonbridge	0
Tiverton T.	1
Croydon Ath.	0
Paulton Rvrs	2
Aldershot T.	1
Malden Vale	0
Soham Town R.	3
Brimsdown R.	0
Pelsall Villa	2
Halstead Town	4
Clevedon Town	3
Wimborne Town	4
Penrith	0
Atherton LR	1
Thackley	2
Lincoln Utd	1
Bridgnorth T.	3
Cheshunt	1
Cammell Laird	2
Glossop NE	3
Saffron Walden	1
Raunds Town	4
Belper Town	2
Brigg Town	1
Taunton Town	2
Barnstaple T.	0
Banstead Ath.	1
Peacehaven	0
Gt Wakering	3;1
Hinckley A.	3;2
Wisbech Town	1
Collier Row	2
Canvey Island	2
Corinthian-Cas.	1
Bracknell Town	1
Newbury Town	2
Oadby Town	2
Ponteland Utd	0
Northampton S.	1
Cogenhoe Utd	2
Eastwood Hanley	1
Arlesey Town	2
Falmouth Town	3
Andover	1
Whitehawk	3
Met Police	2
Elmore	1
Thame United	2
Radcliffe Boro.	2
Yorkshire Am.	0
Boston	6
Bedfont	1

Fourth Round

Torpoint Ath.	0
Diss Town	3
King's Lynn	1
Nantwich Town	0
Whickham	0;0
Dunkirk	0;1
Tiverton Town	5
Paulton Rovers	0
Aldershot Town	5
Soham Town R.	0
Halstead Town	1
Wimborne Town	5
Atherton LR	0;3
Thackley	0;2
Bridgnorth Town	3
Glossop NE	2
Raunds Town	1
Belper Town	2
Taunton Town	1;2
Banstead Ath.	1;0
Hinckley Ath.	4
Collier Row	2
Canvey Island	1
Newbury Town	2
Oadby Town	5
Cogenhoe Utd	1
Arlesey Town	5
Falmouth Town	3
Whitehawk	3
Thame United	2
Radcliffe B.	3;1
Boston	3;2

Fifth Round

Diss Town	2
King's Lynn	0
Dunkirk	0
Tiverton Town	2
Aldershot Town	1
Wimborne Town	0
Atherton LR	1
Bridgnorth T.	0
Belper Town	1
Taunton Town	3
Hinckley Ath.	0
Newbury Town	3
Oadby Town	1
Arlesey Town	2
Whitehawk	2
Boston	3

Sixth Round

Diss Town	1
Tiverton Town	0
Aldershot	0;0;0
Atherton	0;0;2
Taunton Town	2
Newbury Town	0
Arlesey Town	2
Boston	3

Semi-final

Diss Town	3;0;2
1st leg at Diss	
Atherton	1;2;1
Taunton Town	1;1
1st leg at Taunton	
Boston	0;0

Final

Diss Town	2
Taunton Town	1

F.A. SUNDAY CUP 1993-94

First Round (31-10-93)

Croxteth/Gilmoss RBL	3-0	Bedini Altone
Baildon Athletic	2-3	Newfield
Carnforth	1-0	Almithak
Humbledon Pl. Farm	1-1	Clubmoor Nalgo
Clubmoor Nalgo	1-2	Humbledon PF
Dudley & Weetslade	4-5	Framwellgate Moor PM
East Levenshulme	4-0	East Bowling Unity
Littlewoods Athletic	3-2	Mitre
Green Man '88	0-2	Lion Hotel
Moorland Hotel	1-2	Allerton
Hartlepool Lion Hotel	5-0	Iron Bridge
Woodlands '84	0-3	BRNESC
Royal Oak	0-1	Bolton Woods
Waterloo SC Blyth	1-4	Northwood
Sandon	2-4	Western Approaches
Cork & Bottle	2-1	Berner United
Bournville Warriors	1-2	Broad Plain House
Dulwich	2-3	Sawston Keys
Brookville Ath.	2-0	Clifton Athletic
Poringland Wanderers	2-4	Ford Basildon
Kenwick Dynamo	0-1	Courage
Olton Royale	1-1	Inter Volante
Inter Volante	0-2	Olton Royale
Leic. City Bus	2-3	St Clements Hosp.
Hobbies	1-0	Continental
Elliott Bull/Tiger	1-1	AD Bulwell
AD Bulwell	2-4	Elliott Bull/Tiger
Corby Phoenix	4-1	Ansells Stockland Star
BRSC Aidan	1-1	Ford Utd Supporters
Ford Utd Supporters	2-1	BRSC Aidan
Caversham Park	2-0	Chapel United
Lebeq Tavern	5-0	Olympic Star
Hammer	3-0	Sandwell
Inter Royalle	2-2	Fryerns Community
Fryerns Community	3-2	Inter Royalle
Hanham Sunday	2-4	Kerria Sports
S & N Fairway	0-3	Leavesden S & S
Oakwood Sports	4-0	Sheerness Steel Utd
Oxford Road Social	1-2	Northfield Rgrs
Ouzavich	8-1	Poole Town Social
Tottenham Wine	1-3	Vosper
Somerset Ambury VE	3-0	Thorn Walk Tavern
Slade Celtic	4-0	London Boys
St Josephs (S Oxhey)	2-0	St Josephs (Bristol)

Second Round (21-11-93)

Newfield	4-3	Croxteth/Gilmoss
Allerton	4-0	Western Approaches
Golden Eagle	1-3	Carnforth
Oakenshaw	3-0	Northwood
East Levenshulme	3-0	A3
Albion Sports	1-5	Hartlepool Lion Hotel
B & A Scaffolding	4-0	Bolton Woods
Dock	2-2	BRNESC
BRNESC	1-2	Dock
Lobster	1-2	Nicosia
Nenthead	2-5	Lion Hotel
Marston Sports	1-1	Gibraltar
Gibraltar	6-3	Marston Sports
Seymour	2-1	Manfast Kirby
Framwellgate M & PM	3-1	Littlewood Athletic
Etnaward	0-1	Humbledon Plains Fm
St Josephs (Luton)	2-1	Olton Royale
Elliott Bull/Tiger	1-0	Corby Phoenix
St Clements Hosp.	9-1	Sawston Keys
Hobbies	5-3	Courage
Forest Athletic	2-1	Ford Basildon
Heathfield	3-1	Brookvale Athletic
Lodge Cottrell	3-3	Broad Plain House
(Broad Plain House expelled)		
Cork & Bottle	5-1	Hundred Acre
Bedfont Sunday	0-4	Lobeq Tavern
Hammer	3-2	Bly Spartans
Oakwood Sports	2-0	Northfield Rangers
St Josephs (S Oxhey)	0-2	Fryerns Community
Marine (Sussex)	0-1	Ouzavich
Vosper	1-0	Kerria Sports
Slade Celtic	2-1	Leavesden Spts & Soc.
Reading Borough	0-1	Theale
Somerset Ambury VE	1-4	Ranelagh Sports
Caversham Park	1-2	Ford United Supporters

Third Round (12-12-93)

Seymour	5-1	Carnforth
Oakenshaw	1-0	Nicosia
East Levenshulme	1-0	Newfield
B & A Scaffolding	5-3	Gibraltar
Hartlepool Lion Hotel	1-0	Humbledon P. Farm
Allerton	2-1	F'gate Moor & Pity Me
Dock	1-2	Lion Hotel
Hammer	3-5	St Clements Hospital
Slade Celtic	1-2	Ranelagh Sports
St Josephs (Luton)	2-0	Vosper
Ouzavich	2-1	Forest Athletic
Ford Utd Supporters	2-1	Hobbies
Oakwood Sports	1-3	Lodge Cottrell
Elliott Bull/Tiger	1-4	Theale
Cork & Bottle	1-3	Lebeq Tavern
Fryerns Community	1-2	Heathfield

Fourth Round (16-1-94)

Seymour	0-0	Allerton
Allerton	3-2	Seymour
Hartlepool Lion Hotel	2-0	Oakenshaw
Lion Hotel	5-1	East Levenshulme
Lodge Cottrell	1-3	B & A Scaffolding
St Josephs (Luton)	2-0	Heathfield
St Clements Hospital	3-2	Lebeq Tavern
Ranelagh Sports	4-3	Theale
Ford Utd Supporters	2-3	Ouzavich

Fifth Round (13-2-94)

Lion Hotel	0-1	Hartlepool Lion Hotel
B & A Scaffolding	2-3	Ranelagh Sports
Allerton	0-1	Ouzavich
St Clements Hospital	2-3	St Josephs (Luton)

Semi-Finals (20-3-94)

Ranelagh Sports	3-1	Ouzavich
(at Carshalton Athletic, attendance 350)		
St Josephs (Luton)	1-1	Hartlepool Lion Hotel
(at Hitchin Town, attendance 450)		
Hartlepool Lion Hotel	4-1	St Josephs (Luton)
(at Peterlee Newtown, 27-3-94, att: 433)		

Final (8-5-94)

Ranelagh Sports	2-0	Hartlepool Lion Hotel
(at Woking FC)		

Left: *Lion Hotel keeper Keith Halse makes a timely clearance during the final.*

Photo - Gavin Ellis-Neville.

Ranelagh Sports - FA Sunday Cup winners 1993-94. *Photo - Gavin Ellis-Neville.*

Hartlepool Lion Hotel - FA Sunday Cup runners-up 1993-94. *Photo - Gavin Ellis-Neville.*

The England semi-professional squad selected to play Wales at Bangor. Back Row (L/R): Jimmy Conway (Physio), Steve Holden, Stewart Brighton, Kevin Richardson, Mark Hone, Graham Benstead, Kevin Rose, Brian Ross, Darren Collins, Ron Reid (Asst Manager). Front Row: Gary Brabin, David Leworthy, Paul Webb, Wayne Simpson, Dave Venables, Terry Robbins, Delwyn Humphreys, Simeon Hodson, Tony Jennings (Manager).
Photo - Dennis Nicholson.

INTERNATIONAL & F.A. REPRESENTATIVE FOOTBALL

The England Semi-Professional International side that lost 1-2 to the Norway under-21 International side in Slemmestad. Back Row (L/R): Mark Hone (Welling Utd), Corey Browne (Dover Athletic), Darren Collins (Enfield), Graham Benstead (Kettering Town), Colin Jones (FA Representative Match Committee), Mandy Sabat (FA Administration), Alan Turvey (FA Rep. Match Committee), Kevin Rose (Kidderminster Harriers), Nick Ashby (Kettering Town), Gary Brabin (Runcorn), Dereck Brown (Woking), Jim Conway (Kidderminster Harriers, Physio). Front: Tony Jennings (Manager), Kevin Richardson (Bromsgrove Rovers), Wayne Simpson (Stafford Rangers), Paul Webb (Bromsgrove Rovers), Terry Robbins (Welling Utd), Major T C Knight (FA Rep. Match Committee Chairman), Simeon Hodson (Kidderminster Harriers), Delwyn Humphreys (Kidderminster Harriers), Russell Milton (Dover Athletic), Stephen Holden (Kettering Town).

Photo - James Wright

England played three full semi-pro internationals during the season. The annual match against Wales was won at Bangor, and an exciting end-of-season tour to Scandinavian was embarked upon. In addition, the England side played as an 'FA XI' in a match to celebrate the centenary of the Guernsey FA, winning 3-1.

WALES 1, ENGLAND 2

(at Bangor City FC, Tuesday 22nd March 1994)

It was the bleakest of nights at Farrar Road, Bangor, on Tuesday 22nd February. Snow started to fall about an hour before kick-off. It turned to rain halfway through the match, but soon reverted, and by the time the England party had set off on their return trip to the National Sports Centre at Lilleshall, blizzards were howling in from the Irish Sea.

Attendances for semi-pro internationals have proved disappointing in recent seasons in the best of conditions. This year just 536 huddled into the ground, scores of locals doubtless having been deterred by the wintry weather. Peering through the ludicrous meshed fences that make watching football at Farrar Road more like a visit to the zoo, the hardy few prayed for entertainment that would drive out the cold.

Wales can always be relied on to make a spirited start in these matches, and Paul Giles warmed the home fans by a couple of degrees with early thrusts down the left flank. In the third minute he picked out Dave Taylor with a well-weighted cross, but the Porthmadog striker, who has nearly thirty Konica League goals to his name this season, headed too close to 'keeper Graham Benstead. England's feathers were further ruffled three minutes later when their debutant goalkeeper was again called into action, this time to push behind a fierce 25-yard shot from Andrew Ellis.

Whilst the reds' captain and number nine Giles was first to threaten for Wales, his counterpart, Terry Robbins, filled a similar role for England. He sliced wide the whites' first shooting chance in the fourth minute then, after seventeen minutes, wriggled clear of the Welsh defence. Neil O'Brien pulled him down on the edge of the area and, from the free-kick, England took the lead with a special goal; Darren Collins rolled the ball short to Stephen Holden, the Kettering player stopped it dead, and Mark Deegan was left clawing thin air as **Paul Webb** curled a delicious shot into the top right-hand corner of his net.

Delwyn Humphreys celebrates his winning goal in Bangor.
Photo - Dennis Nicholson.

The goal boosted England, and they controlled the remainder of the half, though the only chances of note both fell to David Leworthy in the final minute. Firstly, he was thwarted bravely by Deegan when receiving an excellent centre from Delwyn Humphreys, then he fired inches over after a losing his marker with skilful turn.

England made their first substitution at the interval, replacing debutant Simeon Hodson with Mark Hone, and the reorganisation at the back may have explained their only lapse of the evening. In the 47th minute Giles had a choice of two unmarked forwards in the centre at whom to aim. Wisely he chose **Taylor**, and the lethal Porthmadog striker gave Benstead little chance with a bullet header.

With their tails up, the Welsh enjoyed their best period of the game and, in the 63rd minute, they came within an inch of taking the lead. A twice-taken free-kick on the edge of the England area ricocheted out to Dewi Parry, and the Flint player, who had been on the field for less than ten minutes, rattled the cross-bar with a vicious shot from a tight angle.

The home players appeared to fatigue first on the claggy surface, and England were allowed to boss the final twenty minutes of the game. After 71 minutes, Tony Jennings delighted the small but vociferous band of Marine supporters present by sending on Brian Ross in place of Leworthy, and within two minutes Rossy had helped instigate the winning goal. He raced down the right flank and rolled a low centre towards Robbins, winning a corner. Stewart Brighton flighted the kick long to the far side of the box, his Bromsgrove cohort Kevin Richardson knocked it down, and **Humphreys** turned it home from close-range.

Ten minutes from time, another substitution nearly reaped dividends for England. Dave Venables, a late replacement in the squad for Dagenham's injured Jason Broom, was sent on in place of fellow Diadora Leaguer Darren Collins. Collins had looked lively early in the match but, generally, had been starved of possession. Venables, on the other hand, made an immediate impact with some scintillating bursts and, two minutes from time, Robbins was inches away from cashing in when he could not quite connect with a low centre from the Stevenage debutant.

"3-1 would have been a fairer reflection," mused coach Ron Reid afterwards, but both he and Jennings felt that their charges had displayed great character in difficult conditions, and were delighted by the fact that the goals had stemmed from well-rehearsed set-plays; "For a coach, that is most satifying," beamed Reid. The debutants also pleased the England management, with the tigerish display by Gary Brabin in midfield, and the competent performances turned in by Kettering duo Graham Benstead and Stephen Holden, meriting special praise.

Wales: Mark Deegan (Holywell (sub Pat O'Hagan (Cwmbran) 86)), Jim Blackie (Cwmbran), Michael Foster (Porthmadog), Brian Gullett (Ton Pentre (sub Dewi Parry (Flint) 55)), Neil O'Brien (Aberystwyth (sub Andrew Harper (Conwy) 86)), Andrew Ellis (Inter Cardiff), Marc Lloyd-Williams (Porthmadog), John Morgan (Inter Cardiff), Paul Giles (Inter Cardiff), Paul Evans (Inter Cardiff), David Taylor (Porthmadog). Unused sub: David Evans (Bangor).

England: Graham Benstead (Kettering), Simeon Hodson (Kidderminster (sub: Mark Hone (Welling) 46)), Stewart Brighton (Bromsgrove), Kevin Richardson (Bromsgrove), Stephen Holden (Kettering), Gary Brabin (Runcorn), Delwyn Humphreys (Kidderminster), Paul Webb (Bromsgrove), Terry Robbins (Welling), David Leworthy (Dover (sub: Brian Ross (Marine) 72)), Darren Collins (Enfield (sub: David Venables (Stevenage) 81)). Unused subs: Kevin Rose (Kidderminster), Wayne Simpson (Stafford).

FINLAND under-21s 2, ENGLAND 0

(at Aanekoski, Monday 5th May 1994)

England really could not have got off to a worse start. Inside the first four minutes they had missed an excellent opportunity to take the lead, Delwyn Humphreys screwing a right-foot shot over from an unmarked position, and fallen a goal behind when a misread high bounce in their area presented the lethal **Mika Kottila** with the chance to head a very soft goal over the advancing goalkeeper Graham Benstead.

The early strike by the Finns fuelled the carnival atmosphere that had reigned at the Liikuntapuistossa ground for the two hours preceding kick-off. This game really did mean a lot to the folk of the small lakeside town of Aanekoski. 1,335 paying spectators were present, but the actual attendance was twice that, tickets having been distributed to many local organisations, in particular the local schools.

The locals were not slow to give loud vocal support to their team, and after half-an-hour had more to celebrate when England conceded another sloppy goal. Petri Kokko flighted in a corner from the right and **Kottila** flicked on the ball at the near post and was on hand to slam it into the net after the England defence had declined a couple of chances to clear during the ensuing scramble.

When Danish referee Knud Fasker awarded a penalty against Darren Collins five minutes into the second-half one feared that the tour may be starting with a heavy defeat. However Kevin Rose, who had come in place of Benstead at the interval, had other ideas and flung himself to his right to smother Jussi Nuorela's kick. The save seemed to rejuvenate the tourists who went on to dominate the remainder of the match.

Before the game, Tony Jennings had stated that one of his main fears centred on his players' fitness - or rather lack of it. All but Trophy finalists Dereck Brown and Gary Brabin had been out of action for nearly three weeks, and that after a long and particularly gruelling season. Happily his fears looked unfounded as the England players began to cross the rutted surface with more zest than their more youthful opponents and monopolised possession as the match wore on.

In the final twenty minutes England at last started to convert their possession into clear chances and could feel aggrieved that at least one goal did not go their way. In a particularly agonising four minute spell, Collins saw three gilt-edged opportunities go begging. In the 73rd minute he waltzed around substitute goalkeeper Jani Viander but his shot was scrambled behind for a corner. Three minutes later the forceful Enfield striker was picked out by a delightful chip by Humphreys but, on the stretch, put his volley over an open goal, and he fired wide of the mark again thirty seconds later after Brabin had opened the Finnish defence with a thrilling run.

"We think that in making an attacking game of it we deserved a goal," said a slightly disappointed Tony Jennings, but he declared himself very happy with the overall team performance and in particular that of debutant Nick Ashby. "Considering it was his first cap, he appeared to understand exactly what was required and was very effective."

Finland coach Jyrki Heliskoski saw the game as useful warm-up to the forthcoming UEFA Under-21 Championship qualifiers: "I am very pleased with not only the final result, but because it was an excellent occasion to get used to the British style of playing as our next game is against Scotland on 6th September."

Finland: Jussi Jaaskelainen (Jani Viander 46), Anni Heinola, Sami Hyypia, Jussi Nuorela, Lasse Karjalainen (Sasu Iivonen 46), Mika Kottila, Petri Kokko, Joonas Kolkka (Toni Huttenen 55), Sami Vaisanen (Juuso Kangaskorpi 55), Sami Ristila (Jesse Jalonen 64), Jari Javaja (Teemu Ingi 60).

England: Benstead (Rose 46), Simpson (Hodson 46), Nick Ashby (Kettering), Holden (Hone 61), Richardson, Webb (Corey Browne (Dover) 61), Russell Milton (Dover), Humphreys, Robbins (Dereck Brown (Woking) 75), Collins, Brabin.

NORWAY under-21s 2, ENGLAND 1

(at Slemmestad, Wednesday 1st June 1994)

It couldn't happen again - could it? It did! England began the second game of their tour in exactly the same way as they had the first - by letting in a sloppy goal before the contest had really started. And, like the second goal in Finland, it stemmed from a near-post corner. Gunnar Norebo swung in the kick, **Ousman Nyan** got the decisive flick, Simeon Hodson on the far-post was just unable to block, and England were behind with less than three minutes played.

The whole atmosphere at the Norway game contrasted starkly to that in Finland. Played at 4.30 on a Wednesday afternoon, and only a few hours before the Norwegian World Cup side played their final home send-off game for the USA, the crowd was very thin compared to that in Aanekoski. The ground, that of Third Division side Slemmestad, was also less grandiose than Aanekoski's former First Division set-up having no seats or cover. The opposition, too, was less exalted being only the second string of Norway's under-21 squad, the 'first team' having beaten their Danish counterparts the the previous evening.

There was, however, one significant improvement - the playing surface which seemed almost marble-smooth compared to the Aanekoski's pitch which bore all the signs of a ravaging winter in central Finland.

On Slemmestad's lush pitch, England were quicker to get into their stride than against Finland, and soon began to make inroads into the Norwegian defence, particularly down the right flank where Hodson, pushing up from right-back, Delwyn Humphreys and Dereck Brown, this time on from the start, were very effective. However, parallels with the first game could again be drawn as, despite a marked territorial advantage, England failed to create many clear chances. Those that did come their way went begging. Humphreys fired high following Kevin Richardson's knock-down from a corner, Gary Brabin headed over after another flag-kick and, just before the interval, Darren Collins shot wide to add to his catalogue of unfortunate misses.

The Norwegians enjoyed a very bright start to the second-half. With Kevin Rose stranded, Stephen Holden, who had come on for Mark Hone midway through the first period, bravely flung himself in front of Thomas Hafstad in the 56th minute to deflect a fierce shot for a corner. Three minutes later, Rose surpassed even his penalty stop in Finland to pull off the 'save of the tour', tipping behind a shot from Rune Buer Johansen after a well worked free-kick by Norway. A second goal appeared inevitable, but it was most unfortunate that it should come from the boot of **Kevin Richardson**, skewing the ball over the Kidderminster goalkeeper under severe pressure from a Norway forward.

For the third consecutive half, England grew in stature after starting shakily. At the interval, Corey Browne had replaced Terry Robbins, who had working tirelessly in a foraging role up front for a game and a half, and soon the tricky Dover forward began to get the measure of the Norwegian defence, and it was he who netted England's long overdue first goal of the tour. Following a half-cleared 73rd minute corner from Nick Ashby, Holden and Brown combined to free Humphreys on the right. The Kidderminster forward delivered a perfect centre to the near-post and **Browne** was able to poke the ball beyond the advancing 'keeper.

England made a valiant attempt to save the game. In injury-time, Brabin met a corner from Ashby but directed his typically fierce header too close to the goalkeeper, then Humphreys had a shot pushed behind for a corner after being set up by an excellent break by Paul Webb.

But it was not to be. The statistics will show two games and two defeats despite two very solid performances. "We played well but wasted chances. You cannot afford to do that in any level of football," reflected Tony Jennings.

Norway: Andre Ulla, Frank Tonnesen, Steinar Pedersen (Trygve Nygard 61), Thomas Wehler, Berdon Sunderland, Ousman Nyan, Gunnar Norebo (Karl Oskar Fjortoft 67), Thomas Hafstad, Ole Solskjaer, Aksel Kolle (Bernt Birkeland 67), Eivind Karlsbakk.
England: Rose (Benstead 72), Hodson, Ashby, Hone (Holden 26), Richardson, Brown, Milton (Simpson 60), Humphreys, Robbins (Browne 46), Collins (Webb 72), Brabin.

Reports by James Wright

Dover Athletic supporters Simon Harris (left), Andy Bushby (right) and Gary Constable (photographer) travelled to Scandinavia to support England in the games against Norway and Finland.

FOUR NATIONS TOURNAMENTS 1979-87 and other Internationals

1979 (England)
Knock - out basis, England won final.

S/Final	England	5 v 1	Scotland
S/Final	Holland	3 v 0	Italy
3rd Place	Scotland	1 v 2	Italy
Final	England	1 v 0	Holland

1980 (Holland)	P	W	D	L	F	A	PTS
Scotland	3	2	1	0	7	2	5
England	3	2	0	1	6	5	4
Italy	3	0	2	1	2	4	2
Holland	3	0	1	2	3	7	1

1981 (Italy)	P	W	D	L	F	A	PTS
England	3	1	2	0	3	1	4
Italy	3	1	2	0	2	1	4
Scotland	3	0	3	0	2	2	3
Holland	3	0	1	2	2	5	1

1982 (Scotland)	P	W	D	L	F	A	PTS
Scotland	3	1	2	0	5	4	4
England	3	1	2	0	2	1	4
Italy	3	0	2	1	4	6	2
Holland	3	1	0	2	5	5	2

1983 (England)	P	W	D	L	F	A	PTS
England	3	3	0	0	10	1	6
Scotland	3	1	1	1	7	6	3
Holland	3	1	1	1	6	11	3
Italy	3	0	0	3	3	8	0

1984 (Italy)	P	W	D	L	F	A	PTS
Italy	3	2	1	0	4	1	5
England	3	1	1	1	5	4	3
Holland	3	1	1	1	8	8	3
Scotland	3	0	1	2	2	6	1

1985 (Holland)	P	W	D	L	F	A	PTS
Scotland	3	2	0	1	4	4	4
England	3	1	1	1	6	5	3
Italy	3	1	1	1	4	4	3
Holland	3	1	0	2	4	5	2

1986 (Scotland)
Competition cancelled - Italy withdrew.

1987 (Scotland)	P	W	D	L	F	A	PTS
Italy	3	2	1	0	6	3	5
England	3	2	0	1	7	3	4
Scotland	3	1	0	2	4	6	2
Holland	3	0	1	2	0	5	1

OVERALL FOUR NATIONS TROPHY RECORD

	P	W	D	L	F	A	PTS
England	23	13	6	4	45	21	32
Italy	23	7	9	7	27	31	23
Scotland	23	7	8	8	33	37	22
Holland	23	5	5	13	31	47	15

OTHER RESULTS

v. WALES

		Eng.	Wales
1984	Newtown	1	2
1985	Telford	1	0
1986	Merthyr	1	3
1987	Gloucester	2	2
1988	Rhyl	2	0
1989	Kidderminster	2	0
1990	Merthyr	0	0
1991	Stafford	1	2
1992	Aberystwyth	1	0
1994	Bangor	2	1

v. REPUBLIC OF IRELAND

		Eng.	Ire.
1986	Kidderminster	2	1
1986	Nuneaton	2	1
1990	Dublin	2	1
1990	Cork	3	0

v. GIBRALTAR

		Eng.	Gib.
1982	Gibraltar	3	2

v. FINLAND (under-21)

		Eng.	Fin.
1993	Woking	1	3
1994	Aanekoski	0	2

v. ITALY

		Eng.	Italy
1989	La Spezia	1	1
1990	Solerno	0	2
1991	Kettering	0	0

v. NORWAY (under-21)

		Eng.	Nor.
1994	Slemmestad	1	2

ENGLAND'S Overall International Record

P	W	D	L	F	A
45	24	10	11	75	47

England Semi-Pro Caps 79-94 (Max 45)

(I - Italy, S - Scotland, W - Wales, H - Holland, E - Eire, F - Finland, G - Gibralter, N - Norway)

Gary Abbott (Welling) 87 I(s), S(s), 92 W(s) (3)
David Adamson (Boston Utd) 79 SH, 80 ISH (5)
Tony Agana (Weymouth) 86 E (1)
Jim Arnold (Stafford Rangers) 79 SH (2)
Nick Ashby (Kettering) 94 FN (2)
Noel Ashford (Enfield & Redbridge For.) 82 GHS, 83 IHS, 84 WHSI, 85 WI(s), 86 EE, 87 W(s), IHS, 90 WE, 91 I(s) (21)
John Askey (Macclesfield) 90 W, (1)
Paul Bancroft (Kidderminster) 89 IW, 90 IWE, 91 W (6)
Keith Barrett (Enfield) 81 HSI, 82 GIHS, 83 IHS, 84 W(s)HS, 85 IHS (16)
Laurence Batty (Woking) 93 F(s) (1)
Mark Beeney (Maidstone) 89 I(s) (1)
Graham Benstead (Kettering) 94 WFN(s) (3)
Gary Brabin (Runcorn) 94 WFN (3)
Colin Brazier (Kidderminster) 87 W (1)
Stewart Brighton (Bromsgrove) 94 W (1)
Steve Brooks (Cheltenham) 88 W(s), 90 WE (3)
Derek Brown (Woking) 94 F(s)N (2)
Corey Browne (Dover) 94 F(s)N(s) (2)
David Buchanan (Blyth) 86 E(s)E (2)
Brian Butler (Northwich) 93 F (1)
Steve Butler (Maidstone) 88 W, 89 IW (3)
Mark Carter (Runcorn & Barnet) 87 WIHS, 88 W, 89 IW, 90 IE, 91 IW(s) (11)
Kim Casey (Kidderminster) 86 WEE(s), 87 WI (5)
Paul Cavell (Redbridge) 92 W, 93 F (2)
Kevin Charlton (Telford) 85 WI (2)
Andrew Clarke (Barnet) 90 EE (2)
David Clarke (Blyth Spartans) 80 IS(s)H, 81 HSI, 82 IHS, 83 HS, 84 HSI (14)
Gary Clayton (Burton) 86 E (1)
Robert Codner (Barnet) 88 W (1)
John Coleman (Morecambe) 93 F(s) (1)
Darren Collins (Enfield) 93 F(s), 94 WFN (4)
Steve Conner (Dartford, Redbridge & Dagenham & R) 90 I, 91 IW, 92 W, 93 F (5)
David Constantine (Altrincham) 85 IHS, 86 W (4)
Robbie Cooke (Kettering) 89 W(s), 90 I (2)
Alan Cordice (Wealdstone) 83 IHS, 84 WS(s), I(s), 85 IHS (9)
Paul Cuddy (Altrincham) 87 IHS (3)
Paul Culpin (Nuneaton B) 84 W, 85 W(s) IHS (5)
Paul Davies (Kidderminster) 86 W, 87 WIS, 88 W, 89 W (6)
John Davison (Altrincham) 79 SH, 80 IS, 81 HSI, 82 GIHS, 83 IHS, 84 WHIS, 85 IHS, 86 WEE (24)
John Denham (Northwich Victoria) 80 H (1)
Peter Densmore (Runcorn) 88 W, 89 I (2)
Phil Derbyshire (Mossley) 83 H(s)S(s) (2)
Mick Doherty (Weymouth) 86 W(s) (1)
Mick Farrelly (Altrincham) 87 IHS (3)
Trevor Finnegan (Weymouth) 81 HS (2)
Paul Furlong (Enfield) 90 IEE, 91 IW (5)
John Glover (Maidstone Utd) 85 WIHS (4)
Mark Golley (Sutton) 87 H(s)S, 88 W, 89 IW, 92 W (6)
Phil Gridelet (Hendon + Barnet) 89 IW, 90 WEE (5)
Steve Guppy (Wycombe) 93 W (1)
Steve Hancock (Macclesfield) 90 W (1)
Tony Hemmings (Northwich) 93 F (1)
Andy Hessenthaler (Dartford) 90 I (1)
Kenny Hill (Maidstone Utd) 80 ISH (3)
Simeon Hodson (Kidderminster) 94 WFN (3)
Stephen Holden (Kettering) 94 WFN(s) (3)
Mark Hone (Welling) 90 I, 93 F, 94 W(s)F(s)N (5)
Gary Hooley (Frickley) 85 W (1)
Keith Houghton (Blyth Spartans) 79 S (1)
Barry Howard (Altrincham) 81 HSI, 82 GIHS (7)
David Howell (Enfield) 85 H(s)S(s), 86 WE, 87 WIHS, 88 W, 89 IW, 90 IEE (14)
Delwyn Humphreys (Kidderminster) 91 W(s), 92 W, 94 WFN (5)
Steve Humphries (Barnet) 87 H(s) (1)
Nicky Ironton (Enfield) 83 H(s), 84 W(2)
Tony Jennings (Enfield) 79 SH, 80 ISH, 81 HSI, 82 GIHS (12)
Jeff Johnson (Altrincham) 81 SI, 82 GIHS, 83 IHS, 84 HSI, 84 IHS, 86 W(s)EE (18)
Tom Jones (Weymouth) 87 W (1)
Anton Joseph (Telford Utd + Kidderminster) 84 S(s), 85 WIHS, 86 W(s), 87 WI(s)H, 88 W, 89 IW, 90 IEE (14)
Andy Kerr (Wycombe) 93 W (1)
Mike Lake (Macclesfield) 89 I (1)
Andy Lee (Telford/Witton) 89 I(s), 91 IW (3)
David Leworthy (Farnborough) 93 W, 94 W (2)
Kenny Lowe (Barnet) 91 IW (2)
John McKenna (Boston Utd) 88 W(s), 90 IEE, 91 IW, 92 W (7)
Bobby Mayes (Redbridge) 92 W (1)
Paul Mayman (Northwich Vic) 80 IS (2)
Stewart Mell (Burton) 85 W (1)
Neil Merrick (Weymouth) 80 I(s)S (2)
Russell Milton (Dover) 94 FN (2)
Trevor Morley (Nuneaton) 84 WHSI, 85 WS(s) (6)
Les Mutrie (Blyth Spartans) 79 SH, 80 ISH (5)
Mark Newson (Maidstone U) 84 WHSI, 85 W (5)
Doug Newton (Burton) 85 WHS (3)
Paul Nicol (Kettering T) 91 IW, 92 W (3)
Steve Norris (Telford) 88 W(s) (1)
Eamon O'Keefe (Mossley) 79 SH (2)
Frank Ovard (Maidstone) 81 H(s)S(s)I(s) (3)
Andy Pape (Harrow + Enfield) 85 W(s)HS, 86 W(s)E 87 WIHS, 88 W, 89 IW, 90 IWE (15)
Brian Parker (Yeovil Town) 80 S (1)
Trevor Peake (Nuneaton Bor) 79 SH (2)
David Pearce (Harrow Bor) 84 I(s) (1)
Brendan Phillips (Nuneaton B, Kettering) 79 SH, 80 S(s)H (4)
Gary Philips (Barnet) 82 G (1)
Ryan Price (Stafford) 92 W(s) 93 WF (3)
Simon Read (Farnborough) 92 W(s) (1)
Carl Richards (Enfield) 86 E (1)
Derek Richardson (Maidstone U) 83 I, 84 W, 86 E (4)
Kevin Richardson (Bromsgrove) 94 WFN (3)
Paul Richardson (Redbridge) 92 W, 93 WF (3)
Terry Robbins (Welling) 92 W, 93 WF, 94 WFN (6)
Peter Robinson (Blyth S) 83 IHS, 84 WI, 85 W (6)
John Rogers (Altrincham) 81 HSI, 82 I(s)S (5)
Paul Rogers (Sutton) 89 W, 90 IE(2), 91 IW (6)
Kevin Rose (Kidderminster) 94 F(s)N (2)
Brian Ross (Marine) 93 W(s)F(s), 94 W(s) (3)
Neil Sellars (Scarboro) 81 HSI, 82 GH(s)S, 83 IHS (9)
Mark Shail (Yeovil) 93 W (1)
Peter Shearer (Cheltenham) 89 I(s) (1)
Paul Shirtliff (Frickley & Boston) 86 EE, 87 WIH, 88 W, 89 IW, 90 IWEE, 92 W, 93 WF (15)
Paul Showler (Altrincham) 91 I(s)W (2)
Gordon Simmonite (Boston Utd) 79 S(s)H(s), 80 ISH (5)
Gary Simpson (Stafford) 86 EE, 87 IHS, 90 IWEE (9)
Wayne Simpson (Stafford) 94 FN(s) (2)
Glenn Skivington (Barrow) 90 IWE, 91 IW (5)
Alan Smith (Alvechurch) 82 GIS (3)
Ian Smith (Mossley) 80 ISH(s) (3)
Ossie Smith (Runcorn) 84 W(1)
Tim Smithers (Nuneaton), 85 W(s)I, 86 W (3)
Simon Stapleton (Wycombe) 93 W (1)
Mickey Stephens (Sutton), 82 GS(s), 86 WEE(s) (5)
Bob Stockley (Nuneaton Bor) 80 H (1)
Peter Taylor (Maidstone) 84 HSI (3)
Shaun Teale (Weymouth) 88 W (1)
Brian Thompson (Yeovil & Maidstone) 79 SH, 81 HSI, 82 IHS, 83 IHS, 84 WHSI (15)
Steve Thompson (Wycombe) 93 W (1)
Kevin Todd (Berwick Rangers) 91 W (1)
Tony Turner (Telford) 85 W (1)
David Venables (Stevenage) 94 W(s) (1)
David Waite (Enfield) 82 G (1)
Paul Walker (Blyth) 86 WEE(s), 87 S(s) (4)
Mark Ward (Northwich Victoria) 83 S(s) (1)
John Watson (Wealdstone, Scarborough & Maidstone) 79 S(s)H, 80 ISH, 81 HSI, 82 IHS, 83 IHS, 84 W(s)HSI (18)
Paul Watts (Redbridge Forest) 89 W, 90 IEE, 91 I, 92 W, 93 WF (8)
Paul Webb (Bromsgrove) 93 F, 94 WFN(s) (4)
Mark West (Wycombe W) 91 W (1)
Barry Whitbread (Runcorn & Altrincham) 79 SH, 80 ISH, 81 I (6)
Russ Wilcox (Frickley) 86 WE (2)
Colin Williams (Scarboro & Telford) 81 HS, 82 IHS (5)
Roger Willis (Barnet) 91 I(s) (1)
Paul Wilson (Frickley) 86 W (1)

Gary Brabin in the thick of the action as England lose in Finland. *Photo - Matti Kautto.*

England captain Terry Robbins is sandwiched by two Finnish defenders. *Photo - Matti Kautto.*

Delwyn Humphreys (left) of England challenges Finland's Antti Heinola. *Photo - Matti Kautto.*

F.A. REPRESENTATIVE MATCHES 1993-94

F.A. XI 6 *(Cook 2, Purdie 2, Webb, Preedy)*
HEREFORDSHIRE F.A. XI 2

(Herefordshire FA Centenary Match, at Hereford United, Wednesday 29th September 1993)

FA XI: Scott Cooksey *(Bromsgrove (*sub: Andrew Watkins *(Solihull Borough)),* Paul Bloomfield *(Gloucester City),* Ashley Vickers *(Worcester City),* Kevin Richardson *(Bromsgrove Rovers),* Richard Clark *(Cheltenham Town),* Paul Webb *(Bromsgrove Rovers),* Jon Purdie *(Kidderminster Harrier (*sub: James Watkins *(Hereford Utd)),* Dave Hodges *(Worcester City (*sub: Phil Preedy *(Hereford Utd)),* Paul Davies *(Kidderminster Harriers),* Tony Cook *(Gloucester City),* Gary Smith *(Worcester City).* Manager: John Layton *(Hereford Utd),* Trainer/Physio: Peter Isaacs *(Hereford Utd)*

F.A. XI 1 *(Batty)*
GREAT MILLS WESTERN LEAGUE XI 4

(Western League Centenary Match, at Tiverton Town, Tuesday 19th October 1993)

FA XI: Mark Teasdale *(Trowbridge Town (*sub: Nathan Bush *(Yeovil Town)),* Russell Bowles *(Cinderford Town),* Jeff Meacham *(Shortwood Utd),* Paul Thorpe *(Trowbridge Town),* Mike Kilgour *(Trowbridge Town),* Nigel Gillard *(Clevedon Town),* Keith Knight *(Trowbridge Town),* Paul Batty *(Bath City),* Malcolm McPherson *(Yeovil Town),* Steve Dann *(Weymouth (*sub: Steve Rutter *(Yeovil Town)),* Steve Harrower *(Yeovil Town).* Manager: Tony Passey, Trainer/Physio: Jimmy Green *(Glastonbury)*

F.A. XI 1 *(Burr)*
BEAZER HOMES SOUTHERN LEAGUE XI 4

(Southern League Centenary Match, at Nuneaton Borough, Wednesday 3rd November 1993)

FA XI: Scott Cooksey *(Bromsgrove (*sub: Mark Carrington *(Kidderminster Harriers)),* Simeon Hodson *(Kidderminster Harriers* (sub: *David Pritchard (Telford Utd)),* Sean Parrish *(Telford Utd),* Martin Weir *(Kidderminster Harriers),* Chris Brindley *(Kidderminster Harriers),* Gary Butterworth *(Dagenham & Redbridge),* Danny Williams *(Stafford Rgrs),* Marcus Bignot *(Telford Utd (*sub: Martin Bodkin *(Stafford Rgrs)),* Steve Burr *(Stafford Rgrs),* Paul Davies *(Kidderminster Harriers),* Jon Purdie *(Kidderminster Harriers).* Manager: Graham Allner, Trainer/Physio: Jimmy Conway *(both Kidderminster Harriers)*

F.A. XI 0
NORTHERN PREMIER LEAGUE XI 2

(at Chorley, Tuesday 13th November 1993)

FA XI: Keith Mason *(Witton Albion (*sub: Russell Hughes *(Stalybridge Celtic)),* George Sheppard *(Macclesfield Town),* Stuart Bimson *(Macclesfield Town),* Brian Butler *(Northwich Victoria),* Jeff Parker *(Northwich Victoria),* Kevin Mooney *(Souuthport (*sub: Leroy Dove *(Southport)),* Shaun Constable *(Halifax Town),* Carl Alford *(Macclesfield Town),* John Askey *(Macclesfield Town),* Brendan Burke *(Witton Albion),* David Gamble *(Southport* (sub: Gary Brabin *(Runcorn)).* Manager: Peter Wragg *(Halifax Town)*

F.A. XI 1 *(Broom)*
DIADORA ISTHMIAN LEAGUE XI 2

(at Enfield, Tuesday 7th December 1993)

FA XI: Darren Williams *(Welling Utd (*sub: Laurence Batty *(Woking)),* Gary Stebbing *(Dagenham & Redbridge* (sub: Mark Keen *(Chelmsford City)),* Paul Watts *(Dagenham & Redbridge),* Mark Hone *(Welling Utd),* Steve Conner *(Dagenham & Redbridge),* Mark Biggins *(Woking (*sub: Russell Milton *(Dover Athletic)),* Joe Jackson *(Dover Athletic),* Jason Broom *(Dagenham & Redbridge),* Gary Abbott *(Welling Utd (*sub: Colin Fielder *(Woking)),* David Leworthy *(Dover Athletic),* Mark Fiore *(Slough Town).* Manager: John Still, Trainer/Physio: Jim Payne *(both Dagenham & Redbridge)*

F.A. XI 2 *(Lamb, Ord)*
COMBINED SERVICES 2

(at Spennymoor United, Tuesday 11th January 1994)

FA XI: Gary Popple *(Billingham Synthonia (*sub: David Race *(Durham City)),* Peter Atkinson *(Guiseley),* Sean O'Brien *(Billingham Synthonia* (sub: Don Peattie *(Blyth Spartans)),* Jason Ainsley *(Spennymoor Utd* (sub: Ged Parkinson *(Gateshead)),* Jeff Wrighton *(Gateshead),* Colin Alcide *(Emley),* Michael Farrey *(Gateshead),* Derek Ord *(Durham City),* Alan Lamb *(Gateshead),* Jarrod Suddick *(Whitley Bay),* Wes Saunders *(Spennymoor Utd).* Managers: Colin Richardson *(Gateshead)* & Ron Reid, Trainer/Physio: William Thomson *(Gateshead)*

F.A. XI 3 *(Browne 2, Venables)*
GUERNSEY 1

(Guernsey FA Centenary Match, at St Martins FC, Monday 14th March 1994)

FA XI: Kevin Rose *(Kidderminster Harriers* (sub: Darren Williams *(Welling Utd*)), Wayne Simpson *(Stafford Rgrs),* Stewart Brighton *Bromsgrove Rovers* (sub: Jason Bartlett *(Dover Athletic)),* Mark Hone *(Welling Utd),* Kevin Richardson *(Bromsgrove Rovers* (sub: Simeon Hodson *(Kidderminster Harriers)),* Gary Brabin *(Runcorn (*sub: Paul Webb *(Bromsgrove Rovers)),* Dave Venables *(Stevenage Borough),* Dereck Brown *(Woking),* Terry Robbins *(Welling Utd),* Corey Browne *(Dover Athletic),* Russell Milton *(Dover Athletic).* Manager: Tony Jennings. Assistant Manager: Ron Reid. Trainer/Physio: Jimmy Conway *(Kidderminster Harriers)*

G.M. VAUXHALL CONFERENCE

Founded: 1979

President: J C Thompson

Chairman: W J King

Vice-Chairman: G E Smith

Secretary: P D Hunter,
24 Barnehurst Road, Bexleyheath, Kent DA7 6EZ

KIDDERMINSTER CLAIM THEIR FIRST TITLE

In the end, a tense last Saturday saw Kidderminster Harriers confirmed as champions of the GM Vauxhall Conference while Slough Town joined already doomed Witton Albion in being relegated.

In Harriers' case, a fixture backlog almost caused them to slip up at the end and let in Kettering Town, their only really serious challengers, but, ironically, both lost their final matches at home. Harriers were indeed worthy champions, and it is very sad and disappointing that they will not be replacing Northampton Town in the Third Division next term.

Merthyr Tydfil escaped the drop because neither champions Marine nor runners-up Leek Town of the Northern Premier League could meet the criteria for promotion to the GM Vauxhall Conference.

Many people, myself included, felt that this season's competition was not as good as in previous campaigns. Whether or not that was because, with all due respect to Kidderminster and Kettering, there wasn't a side which totally dominated the league as the likes of Barnet, Colchester and Wycombe have done recently, I don't know. But it did seem to me that when the league possessed a really outstanding team or teams the others raised their game increasing the overall standard of the competition.

This season saw a really open league, with everyone capable of beating everyone else. The closeness of the final league table shows this with only eight points separating fourth-from-bottom Yeovil Town and sixth-placed Dagenham & Redbridge.

Another example of this can be seen with Dover Athletic who, after looking like championship contenders for three quarters of the season, still required points towards the end to ensure staying up!

Next season will see no relegated club appear from the Endsleigh Football League, and everything points towards Harriers, Kettering and possibly Southport making the running again. It looks like being another close and very even campaign, and let's hope that this time we see a GM Vauxhall Conference club make the step up - the just reward for winning the 'Fourth Division'.

Steve Whitney

G.M. Vauxhall Conference

Final League Table 1993-94

	HOME				AWAY					
	P	W	D	L	W	D	L	F	A	Pts
KIDDERMINSTER HARRIERS	42	13	5	3	9	4	8	63	35	75
KETTERING TOWN	42	9	7	5	10	8	3	46	24	72
WOKING	42	12	5	4	6	8	7	58	58	67
SOUTHPORT	42	10	7	4	8	5	8	57	51	66
RUNCORN	42	12	6	3	2	13	6	63	57	61
DAGENHAM & REDBRIDGE	42	12	5	4	3	9	9	62	54	59
MACCLESFIELD TOWN	42	7	8	6	9	3	9	48	49	59
DOVER ATHLETIC	42	9	3	9	8	4	9	48	49	58
STAFFORD RANGERS	42	10	7	4	4	8	9	56	52	57
ALTRINCHAM	42	8	5	8	8	4	9	41	42	57
GATESHEAD	42	10	6	5	5	6	10	45	53	57
BATH CITY	42	6	8	7	7	9	5	47	38	56
HALIFAX TOWN	42	7	9	5	6	7	8	55	49	55
STALYBRIDGE CELTIC	42	6	6	9	8	6	7	54	55	54
NORTHWICH VICTORIA	42	7	9	5	4	10	7	44	45	52
WELLING UNITED	42	7	7	7	6	5	10	47	49	51
TELFORD UNITED	42	8	7	6	5	5	11	41	49	51
BROMSGROVE ROVERS	42	5	8	8	7	7	7	54	66	51
YEOVIL TOWN	42	7	4	10	7	5	9	49	62	51
MERTHYR TYDFIL	42	8	7	6	4	8	9	60	61	49
SLOUGH TOWN	42	8	8	5	3	6	12	44	58	47
WITTON ALBION	42	4	8	9	3	5	13	37	63	34

Merthyr Tydfil -2 points

RESULTS CHART 1993-94

HOME TEAM	1	2	3	4	5	6	7	8	9	10	11	12	13	14	15	16	17	18	19	20	21	22
1. Altrincham	*	0-2	2-3	1-2	2-0	0-3	0-0	1-1	1-0	0-1	3-0	2-2	2-1	2-0	1-2	0-0	0-0	2-0	2-0	1-3	0-2	1-0
2. Bath	0-1	*	0-1	0-0	0-0	2-3	2-2	0-3	4-0	5-1	0-3	0-0	0-0	3-0	2-1	2-3	1-1	3-0	0-0	1-1	0-1	3-0
3. Bromsgrove	1-2	0-1	*	2-0	1-2	3-0	1-0	0-4	0-3	3-0	3-3	0-0	0-0	0-1	2-2	3-3	2-0	0-5	1-1	3-3	0-0	1-2
4. Dagenham	3-0	3-0	4-2	*	2-1	1-1	3-0	2-3	1-1	1-1	0-1	1-1	2-1	1-0	3-3	1-0	0-1	4-1	2-0	2-1	3-4	2-1
5. Dover	1-0	0-3	4-3	1-1	*	3-1	1-2	0-1	3-1	1-2	1-0	2-0	2-3	0-0	0-2	2-0	1-1	0-1	0-1	1-0	5-0	0-2
6. Gateshead	2-1	1-0	0-1	3-1	1-2	*	2-1	0-0	0-2	1-0	0-0	1-0	2-2	0-0	1-3	0-0	2-1	0-2	1-0	3-0	1-1	2-1
7. Halifax	0-0	0-0	3-0	0-1	0-1	3-1	*	0-0	1-0	1-2	2-1	1-2	1-1	1-0	2-2	1-1	2-1	6-0	1-1	0-0	2-3	1-1
8. Kettering	1-0	0-1	0-1	1-1	1-0	0-0	0-1	*	1-1	0-1	0-0	0-0	2-2	2-0	2-0	2-0	3-2	1-2	2-2	1-0	3-0	1-0
9. Kidderminster	0-1	0-0	1-1	2-1	3-0	1-1	2-1	0-2	*	2-1	2-0	2-0	3-0	0-0	2-0	2-0	1-0	2-0	1-0	0-0	3-1	2-3
10. Macclesfield	1-0	0-0	4-3	3-0	0-2	6-1	0-1	0-0	0-0	*	1-2	0-0	0-0	2-2	0-1	0-0	1-3	1-0	1-0	2-0	1-1	1-2
11. Merthyr	0-0	1-1	2-1	0-0	0-0	3-0	2-1	0-1	1-4	2-1	*	5-0	1-1	5-1	2-2	2-0	1-2	0-3	0-1	4-3	2-3	1-1
12. Northwich	2-0	3-1	1-1	2-2	0-1	1-2	0-2	1-1	3-0	1-1	1-2	*	1-1	1-1	2-1	0-0	2-0	1-0	3-1	0-1	0-0	1-1
13. Runcorn	2-1	0-0	4-1	2-1	2-1	1-1	5-0	0-0	0-5	2-1	1-1	1-2	*	3-2	3-0	2-2	1-1	3-2	2-4	1-0	2-1	4-0
14. Slough	0-2	0-0	1-1	3-1	1-0	2-1	2-0	0-2	1-5	1-1	3-2	2-2	3-0	*	0-0	3-0	2-3	0-0	1-1	0-1	0-0	5-2
15. Southport	3-1	1-1	1-2	0-0	3-2	1-1	2-2	0-1	1-1	1-0	3-2	0-0	1-0	1-0	*	0-2	0-2	1-0	2-1	2-1	2-1	1-1
16. Stafford	0-1	2-0	0-0	2-0	2-2	3-1	1-1	1-0	2-3	2-3	5-1	3-1	2-2	0-0	0-2	*	2-2	1-1	3-0	1-0	3-0	4-2
17. Stalybridge	1-3	1-3	0-2	5-0	0-0	2-1	1-1	1-1	0-2	0-2	2-2	1-1	1-2	0-1	3-1	1-2	*	1-0	2-1	2-1	2-2	1-2
18. Telford Utd	0-2	0-0	0-0	0-0	0-1	0-0	3-2	1-2	1-0	1-3	1-0	2-1	1-1	4-1	1-3	2-1	0-2	*	2-0	2-2	2-0	1-1
19. Welling	2-1	0-0	1-1	0-0	2-0	1-2	0-2	2-0	0-3	0-1	1-1	0-1	1-1	6-2	0-2	2-1	1-2	0-0	*	2-1	2-2	2-0
20. Witton A.	0-1	0-3	4-1	1-1	1-2	1-0	2-2	0-1	2-0	0-2	2-2	1-1	1-1	1-0	0-2	1-1	0-3	0-0	0-5	*	0-0	1-2
21. Woking	1-1	4-1	0-0	1-8	3-0	1-0	2-6	0-0	1-0	3-0	2-1	2-1	1-1	2-1	1-0	4-0	3-0	0-0	0-2	3-1	*	1-2
22. Yeovil	0-0	1-2	2-3	2-1	1-3	0-2	0-0	1-0	0-1	4-0	2-2	0-3	4-2	0-2	3-2	0-1	0-0	1-0	0-1	2-0	0-1	*

G.M. Vauxhall Conference

LEADING GOALSCORERS 1993-94

	CONFERENCE	FAC	FAT	DC	Total
PAUL DOBSON (*Gateshead*)	**25**	(3	4	2	34)
KARL THOMAS (*Runcorn*)	**23**	(-	5	2	30)
PAUL ADCOCK (*Bath City*)	**17**	(4	1	-	23)
TERRY ROBBINS (*Welling United*)	**17**	(-	2	2	21)
CLIVE WALKER (*Woking*)	**16**	(-	3	-	19)
MICKEY SPENCER (*Yeovil Town*)	**16**	(-	1	1	18)
DAVID LEWORTHY (*Dover Athletic*)	**15**	(1	1	3	20)
DAVID GAMBLE (*Southport*)	**15**	(2	2	-	19)
CARL ALFORD (*Macclesfield Town*)	**14**	(3	2	6	25)
PAUL DAVIES (*Kidderminster Harriers*)	**14**	(1	-	3	19)
MORRYS SCOTT (*Slough Town*)	**14**	(2	1	-	17)

Paul Dobson, pictured here trying to find a path between three Halifax Town defenders during a league fixture at the International Stadium, did exceptionally well to lead the Conference goalscoring charts as Gateshead were never among the front-runners in the table.

Photo - Gavin Ellis-Neville.

DRINKWISE (LEAGUE) CUP

First Round (2 Legs)

ALTRINCHAM	1	v	3	GATESHEAD	Att: 378
GATESHEAD	3	v	1	ALTRINCHAM	Att: 251
KETTERING TOWN	0	v	0	WELLING UNITED	Att: 961
WELLING UNITED	2	v	1	KETTERING TOWN	Att: 457
MERTHYR TYDFIL	0	v	2	DOVER ATHLETIC	Att: 303
DOVER ATHLETIC	2	v	0	MERTHYR TYDFIL	Att: 967
SOUTHPORT	1	v	4	RUNCORN	Att: 912
RUNCORN	2	v	1	SOUTHPORT	Att: 509
STALYBRIDGE CELTIC	2	v	0	TELFORD UNITED	Att: 352
TELFORD UNITED	2	v	1	STALYBRIDGE CELTIC	Att: 408
WITTON ALBION	1	v	2	MACCLESFIELD TOWN	Att: 826
MACCLESFIELD TOWN	4	v	1	WITTON ALBION	Att: 466

BYES TO SECOND ROUND:

Bath City, Bromsgrove Rovers, Dagenham & Redbridge, Halifax Town, Kidderminster Harriers, Northwich Victoria, Slough Town, Stafford Rangers, Woking, Yeovil Town.

Second Round

BATH CITY	0	v	1	YEOVIL TOWN	Att: 584
BROMSGROVE ROVERS	2	v	1	SLOUGH TOWN	Att: 692
DOVER ATHLETIC	1	v	2	DAGENHAM & REDBRIDGE	Att: 749
HALIFAX TOWN	3	v	0	GATESHEAD	Att: 749
NORTHWICH VICTORIA	1	v	0	STALYBRIDGE CELTIC	Att: 521
RUNCORN	0	v	4	MACCLESFIELD TOWN	Att: 471
WELLING UNITED	1	v	0	WOKING	Att: 616
KIDDERMINSTER HAR.	3	v	0	STAFFORD RANGERS	Att: 774

Third Round

NORTHWICH VICTORIA	3	v	2	KIDDERMINSTER HAR.	Att: 474
DAGENHAM & REDBRIDGE	1	v	2	YEOVIL TOWN	Att: 466
WELLING UNITED	1	v	2	BROMSGROVE ROVERS	Att: 320
HALIFAX TOWN	1	v	2	MACCLESFIELD TOWN	Att: 621

Semi Finals (First & Second Legs)

BROMSGROVE ROVERS	1	v	2	YEOVIL TOWN	Att: 1,175
YEOVIL TOWN	0	v	1	BROMSGROVE ROVERS	Att: 1,922

(after extra-time, Yeovil won on away goals rule)

MACCLESFIELD TOWN	2	v	1	NORTHWICH VICTORIA	Att: 578
NORTHWICH VICTORIA	0	v	1	MACCLESFIELD TOWN	Att: 1,008

Final (First & Second Legs)

MACCLESFIELD TOWN	4	v	1	YEOVIL TOWN	Att: 651
YEOVIL TOWN	0	v	0	MACCLESFIELD TOWN	Att: 1,241

G.M. Vauxhall Conference

TEN YEAR CLUB RECORD

	84/85	85/86	86/87	87/88	88/89	89/90	90/91	91/92	92/93	93/94
ALTRINCHAM	5	4	5	14	14	16	3	18	10	10
AYLESBURY UNITED	-	-	-	-	20	-	-	-	-	-
BARNET	15	14	2	2	8	2	1	-	-	-
BARROW	18	22	-	-	-	14	10	22	-	-
BATH CITY	4	12	10	20	-	-	20	9	7	12
BOSTON UNITED	17	13	6	16	3	18	18	8	22	-
BROMSGROVE ROVERS	-	-	-	-	-	-	-	-	2	18
CHELTENHAM TOWN	-	11	11	13	15	11	16	21	-	-
CHORLEY	-	-	-	-	17	20	-	-	-	-
COLCHESTER UNITED	-	-	-	-	-	-	2	1	-	-
DAGENHAM	19	19	15	22	-	-	-	-	-	-
DAGENHAM & REDBRIDGE	-	-	-	-	-	-	-	-	3	6
DARLINGTON	-	-	-	-	-	1	-	-	-	-
DARTFORD	3	21	-	-	-	-	-	-	-	-
DOVER ATHLETIC	-	-	-	-	-	-	-	-	-	8
ENFIELD	7	1	4	12	13	22	-	-	-	-
FARNBOROUGH TOWN	-	-	-	-	-	21	-	5	21	-
FISHER ATHLETIC	-	-	-	15	18	19	22	-	-	-
FRICKLEY ATHLETIC	11	2	21	-	-	-	-	-	-	-
GATESHEAD	21	-	22	-	-	-	17	14	14	11
HALIFAX TOWN	-	-	-	-	-	-	-	-	-	13
KETTERING TOWN	12	9	16	3	2	5	4	3	13	2
KIDDERMINSTER HARRIERS	8	3	12	7	5	13	13	19	9	1
LINCOLN CITY	-	-	-	1	-	-	-	-	-	-
MACCLESFIELD TOWN	-	-	-	11	7	4	7	13	18	7
MAIDSTONE UNITED	13	17	3	9	1	-	-	-	-	-
MERTHYR TYDFIL	-	-	-	-	-	9	9	4	16	20
NORTHWICH VICTORIA	9	10	17	17	10	15	12	11	11	15
NUNEATON BOROUGH	2	18	18	-	-	-	-	-	-	-
REDBRIDGE FOREST	-	-	-	-	-	-	-	7	-	-
RUNCORN	14	6	8	4	6	3	8	16	19	5
SCARBOROUGH	6	15	1	-	-	-	-	-	-	-
SLOUGH TOWN	-	-	-	-	-	-	19	20	5	21
SOUTHPORT	-	-	-	-	-	-	-	-	-	4
STAFFORD RANGERS	-	7	13	6	19	17	15	17	6	9
STALYBRIDGE CELTIC	-	-	-	-	-	-	-	-	12	14
SUTTON UNITED	-	-	7	8	12	8	21	-	-	-
TELFORD UNITED	10	8	9	5	16	12	6	6	15	17
WEALDSTONE	1	10	19	21	-	-	-	-	-	-
WELLING UNITED	-	-	20	19	11	6	11	12	20	16
WEYMOUTH	16	5	14	10	21	-	-	-	-	-
WITTON ALBION	-	-	-	-	-	-	-	10	17	22
WOKING	-	-	-	-	-	-	-	-	8	3
WORCESTER CITY	20	-	-	-	-	-	-	-	-	-
WYCOMBE WANDERERS	-	20	-	18	4	10	5	2	1	-
YEOVIL TOWN	22	-	-	-	9	7	14	15	4	19

G.M. Vauxhall Conference

PREVIOUS SEASONS' TOP FOUR

Season	Max Pts	Champions Pts	Champions	Runners-up Pts	Runners-up	3rd Place Pts	3rd Place	4th Place Pts	4th Place
1979/80	76	56	Altrincham	54	Weymouth	49	Worcester C.	45	Boston Utd.
1980/81	76	54	Altrincham	51	Kettering T.	47	Scarborough	45	Northwich V.
1981/82	126	93	Runcorn	86	Enfield	77	Telford Utd.	71	Worcester C.
1982/83	126	84	Enfield	83	Maidstone U.	79	Wealdstone	72*	Runcorn
1983/84	105	70	Maidstone U.	69	Nuneaton Bor.	65	Altrincham	62*	Wealdstone
1984/85	105	62	Wealdstone	58	Nuneaton Bor.	57*	Dartford	57*	Bath City
1985/86	105	76	Enfield	69	Frickley Ath.	67	Kidderminster	63	Altrincham
1986/87	126	91	Scarborough	85	Barnet	73	Maidstone Utd.	70	Enfield
1987/88	126	82	Lincoln City	80	Barnet	75	Kettering Town	74	Runcorn
1988/89	126	84	Maidstone Utd.	76	Kettering Town	74	Boston Utd.	71	Wycombe W.
1989/90	126	87	Darlington	85	Barnet	70	Runcorn	66	Macclesfield T.
1990/91	126	87	Barnet	85	Colchester U.	82	Altrincham	80	Kettering T.
1991/92	126	94	Colchester Utd	94	Wycombe Wdrs	73	Kettering Town	68	Merthyr Tydfil
1992/93	126	83	Wycombe Wdrs	68	Bromsgrove R.	67	Dagenham & R.	66	Yeovil Town

* Indicates position achieved through goal difference.

FOOTBALL LEAGUE MOVEMENTS

1987	Promoted to 4th Div.:	**Scarborough**	Relegated to Conference:	**Lincoln City**
1988	Promoted to 4th Div.:	**Lincoln City**	Relegated to Conference:	**Newport County**
1989	Promoted to 4th Div.:	**Maidstone United**	Relegated to Conference:	**Darlington**
1990	Promoted to 4th Div.:	**Darlington**	Relegated to Conference:	**Colchester United**
1991	Promoted to 4th Div.:	**Barnet**	No relegation from 4th Div.	
1992	Promoted to 4th Div.:	**Colchester United**	No relegation from 4th Div.	
1993	Promoted to 3rd Div.:	**Wycombe Wanderers**	Relegated to Conference:	**Halifax Town**
1994	No promoted to 3rd Div.		No relegation from 3rd Div.	

BOB LORD TROPHY

(NOW DRINKWISE CUP)

	Winner	Runner-up
1979/80	Northwich Victoria	Altrincham
1980/81	Altrincham	Kettering Town
1981/82	Weymouth	Enfield
1982/83	Runcorn	Scarborough
1983/84	Scarborough	Barnet
1984/85	Runcorn	Maidstone United
1985/86	Stafford Rangers	Barnet
1986/87	Kettering Town	Hendon (Isthmian)
1987/88	Horwich RMI (NPL)	Weymouth
1988/89	Barnet	Hyde United (HFS)
1989/90	Yeovil Town	Kidderminster H.
1990/91	Sutton United	Barrow
1991/92	Wycombe Wdrs	Runcorn
1992/93	Northwich V.	Wycombe Wdrs
1992/93	Macclesfield T.	Yeovil Town

CHAMPIONSHIP SHIELD

Conference Champions v Trophy Winners

	Winner	Runner-up
1980	Northwich V	Altrincham
1981	Altrincham	Kettering T.
1982	runcorn	Weymouth
1983	Enfield	Runcorn
1984	Maidstone U.	Scarborough
1985	Runcorn	Wealdstone
1986	Stafford R.	Enfield
1987	Kidderminster H.	Scarborough
1988	Lincoln City	Enfield
1989	Maidstone Utd.	Telford Utd.
1990	Darlington	Barrow
1991	Wycombe W.	Barnet
1992	Wycombe W.	Colchester Utd
1993	Wycombe W.	Northwich Vics

PREMIER INTER-LEAGUE CUP

(also CLUBCALL CUP/ G.M.A.C. CUP - no longer contested)

	Winner	Runner-up
1987	Kettering Town	Hendon (Isthmian)
1988	Horwich RMI (NPL)	Weymouth
1989	Barnet	Hyde Utd. (HFS)

COMPLETE CONFERENCE TABLE 1979-1994 # - Founder Member.

	No. of Seasons	P	W	D	L	F	A	Pts
ALTRINCHAM #	15	620	264	160	196	939	766	865
KETTERING TOWN #	15	620	249	61	202	920	829	852
TELFORD UNITED #	15	620	249	149	220	862	838	840
RUNCORN	13	544	233	156	155	862	709	827
NORTHWICH VICTORIA #	16	620	218	170	232	827	825	766
BOSTON UNITED #	14	578	222	136	220	881	911	740
BARNET #	12	494	209	114	174	759	658	688
BATH CITY #	13	538	189	150	199	687	698	661
KIDDERMINSTER HARRIERS	11	460	188	107	165	761	810	644
STAFFORD RANGERS #	12	536	164	172	210	682	752	627
MAIDSTONE UNITED #	10	410	179	113	118	684	492	589
YEOVIL TOWN #	12	494	158	122	214	656	783	556
ENFIELD	9	376	169	80	127	672	541	553
WEYMOUTH #	10	410	164	102	144	603	553	524
WYCOMBE WANDERERS	7	292	133	73	86	480	386	465
SCARBOROUGH #	8	328	136	101	91	471	393	450
MACCLESFIELD TOWN	7	292	110	83	99	384	361	413
WELLING UNITED	8	334	107	91	138	446	509	406
WEALDSTONE #	8	328	113	99	116	444	443	387
BARROW #	9	370	108	103	159	452	575	387
CHELTENHAM TOWN	7	292	93	92	107	420	458	358
FRICKLEY ATHLETIC	7	290	108	69	113	432	458	337
NUNEATON BOROUGH #	7	286	104	79	103	425	408	333
GATESHEAD	7	294	82	78	144	357	508	311
DAGENHAM	7	294	87	70	137	374	494	307
MERTHYR TYDFIL	5	210	76	62	72	299	320	288
WORCESTER CITY #	6	244	93	58	93	347	376	288
SUTTON UNITED	5	208	76	59	73	352	305	287
SLOUGH TOWN	4	168	55	37	76	211	275	202
COLCHESTER UNITED	2	84	53	20	11	166	75	179
FISHER ATHLETIC	4	166	41	46	79	206	283	169
FARNBOROUGH TOWN	3	126	40	35	51	196	213	155
BANGOR CITY #	4	160	44	45	71	201	273	150
WITTON ALBION	3	126	34	40	52	162	188	142
DAGENHAM & REDRIDGE	2	84	34	25	25	137	101	126
WOKING	2	84	35	21	28	116	120	126
DARTFORD	3	126	35	31	60	155	199	122
BROMSGROVE ROVERS	2	84	30	29	35	121	115	119
GRAVESEND & NORTHFLEET #	3	118	40	28	50	148	168	118
STALYBRIDGE CELTIC	2	84	27	29	28	102	110	110
TROWBRIDGE TOWN	3	126	29	25	72	127	229	109
CHORLEY	2	82	26	12	44	99	138	90
DARLINGTON	1	42	26	9	7	76	25	87
LINCOLN CITY	1	42	24	10	8	86	48	82
A P LEAMINGTON #	3	118	21	32	65	119	234	78
SOUTHPORT	1	42	18	12	12	57	51	66
REDBRIDGE FOREST	1	42	18	9	15	69	56	63
DOVER ATHLETIC	1	42	17	7	18	48	49	58
HALIFAX TOWN	1	42	13	16	13	55	49	55
AYLESBURY UNITED	1	40	9	9	22	43	71	36
REDDITCH UNITED #	1	38	5	8	25	26	69	18
(NEWPORT COUNTY - deleted record		29	4	7	18	31	62	19)

G.M.V. CONFERENCE DIARY 1993-94

COMPILED BY STEVE WHITNEY

1 - 23 AUGUST

Dagenham & Redbridge are installed as 7/2 favourites to win the Vauxhall Conference title by Ladbrokes with relegated **Halifax** as 4/1 second favourites. Former Sunderland boss Malcolm Crosby is appointed as coach at **Gateshead** while ex-England left-back Derek Statham joins **Telford** from Walsall as a player. Another former international, Scotland's Kenny Burns, also joins United as Gerry Daly's number two. Farnborough Town striker David Leworthy joins new boys **Dover** for a new Pyramid record fee of £50,000. **Halifax** 'keeper Lee Bracey makes a swift return to the League by joining Bury for £20,000 after making just one appearance in the Conference. **Gateshead**'s goalkeeper Simon Smith ends his run of 406 consecutive appearances by losing his place to ex-Spurs custodian Peter Guthrie. The opening day fixtures see **Bath**'s new striker Paul Adcock hit a hat-trick in the 5-1 demolition of **Macclesfield**. Leworthy starts life with his new club in style by netting two of **Dover**'s three goals in their win over **Kidderminster**. Fellow newcomers **Southport** begin with a 3-3 draw at favourites **Dagenham** while **Halifax** are held to a goalless draw at The Shay by **Kettering**.

Jason Peake shields the ball from Kettering Town's Gareth Price as Halifax Town make a goalless start to Conference life.

Photo - Paul Dennis.

Bath's early-season scoring sensation Paul Adcock dribbles the ball past Mark Hayde as the Romans win 2-0 at Altrincham on 28th August.

Photo - Paul Dennis.

24 AUG - 6 SEP

Stalybridge offer manager Phil Wilson a new two-year contract. **Southport** attract their highest attendance (2,423) since leaving the Football League in 1978 for the home game against **Halifax**. **Slough** relinquish the last remaining 100% record with a 1-0 reversal at **Dagenham**. Welshmen **Merthyr Tydfil** start with five straight draws. **Kettering**'s on loan 'keeper Russell Hoult concedes his first goal in 449 minutes when **Telford** convert a penalty in injury-time in the 2-1 away win for the Poppies. BHL champions **Dover** are the early season league leaders.

7 - 20 SEPTEMBER

Malcolm Crosby leaves **Gateshead** to join Dennis Smith at Oxford United. **Northwich**'s Tony Hemmings joins Wycombe Wanderers for £25,000. **Yeovil** set a new Pyramid record with season ticket sales passing the 1,200-mark. **Welling** give a Drinkwise Cup debut to 17-year-old YT graduate Steve Finnan against **Kettering**. The FA Cup first qualifying round sees early exits for **Welling**, beaten 4-1 at Diadora League Enfield, **Dover**, who are beaten in a replay at home by Beazer Homes League neighbours Sittingbourne and **Northwich**, who bow out at Northern Premier League Emley also after a replay. Wycombe Wanderers' striker Mark West breaks his leg on his loan debut for **Kidderminster**, whose 1-0 success at Aggborough against **Stalybridge** ends a 438-minute wait for a league goal. **Merthyr** extend their draw sequence and record to an unusual played 7 drawn 7, goals for 7 goals against 7! **Kettering** are the other unbeaten side and have conceded just once goal in 7 games.

21 SEP - 4 OCT

Welling suffer a break-in at their Park View Road ground and lose the control box and bulbs from one of their floodlight pylons. **Halifax** record their first victory of the season - a 6-2 success at **Woking**. Russell Hoult, who kept seven clean sheets in eight games for **Kettering**, returns to Leicester City after breaking a bone in his hand. Poppies boss Graham Carr obtains Brentford's experienced custodian Graham Benstead in his place. **Bromsgrove** sign prolific scorer Recky Carter from BHL club Solihull Borough for a four-figure fee, only the second time manager Bobby Hope has paid such a fee in his 13-year spell at the Victoria Ground. There are no real shocks in the FA Cup second qualifying round, although **Telford** and **Stalybridge** are held at home by Grantham and Bootle respectively. Both come through their replays successfully, but it isn't enough to save Gerry Daly from getting the sack at the Buck's Head after almost four years with the club. **Halifax** sell defender Chris Lucketti to Bury for £50,000 then end their seven month wait for a home win by beating Telford 6-0. Wilf Rostron replaces Malcolm Crosby as coach at **Gateshead**. **Kettering** are the last remaining side in Britain's senior league competitions to remain unbeaten. **Dover** remain top with **Slough** second.

5 - 18 OCTOBER

Merthyr appoint former Welsh international Robbie James as player-manager in succession to Wynford Hopkins who retired. **Witton** sign the ex-Spurs and Manchester City midfielder Neil McNab from Derry City. **Kettering**'s unbeaten run ends with a 1-0 defeat at **Stafford**, ironically managed by a former Poppies player, Brendan Phillips. **Macclesfield** end their 376-minute spell without a goal when new signing from **Stalybridge**, Phil Power, notches the first in a 2-0 success at **Witton**. All Conference sides come through the third qualifying round of the FA Cup, although **Gateshead** are held at Northern League neighbours Billingham Synthonia. John Docherty resigns as manager of **Slough** for "personal and professional reasons". Les Briley takes over as player-manager. **Kidderminster** extend their run of victories to six with a 2-0 win at **Stalybridge**. **Gateshead** bow out of the FA Cup when Billingham Synthonia win 1-0 at the International Stadium in a replay.

19 OCT - 1 NOV

Telford appoint George Foster as their new manager. He had previously been in charge at Mansfield for five years until early October. **Yeovil** announce a profit of £40,147 for the year ending May 1993. The fourth qualifying round of the FA Cup sees a few shocks. **Altrincham** are beaten at home by Accrington, **Merthyr** lose at Crawley and **Dagenham**, **Bath**, **Stafford** and **Stalybridge** all draw. **Merthyr** are told that they must pay Cardiff City £10,000 for new manager Robbie James by a transfer tribunal. Wycombe beat **Northwich** 1-0 to win the Championship Shield. **Kidderminster** boss Graham Allner celebrates 10 years in charge by keeping his team at the top of the table with a 5-1 victory at **Slough**. Cambridge City dump **Dagenham** out of the FA Cup after a replay. **Stalybridge Celtic** and **Bath** come through their replays but **Stafford** must try again after being held by Knowsley for the second time.

8 - 15 NOVEMBER

Altrincham sack Gerry Quinn after 18 months in charge at Moss Lane. **Gateshead**'s Tommy Cassidy resigns and is replaced by former Bridlington Town and North Shields boss Colin Richardson. **Witton** sign ex-Manchester United defender Billy Garton, who retired from the full-time game through ME. He had been player-manager at North West Counties League side Salford City. **Southport** set a new seasonal record when a 2-0 win at **Stafford** extends their unbeaten run to 11 games. Rangers' misfortunes continue when Knowsley win the FA Cup second replay 1-0. Former player Paul Rowlands, latterly player manager at Konica League of Wales club Bangor, is the new boss at **Altrincham**. **Halifax** record their first FA Cup win since 1990 by beating First Division West Bromwich Albion 2-1 in the first round proper. There are other notable successes for **Macclesfield**, 2-0 winners over Hartlepool, and **Bromsgrove** who beat Northampton 2-1 at the County Ground, while **Telford** hold Huddersfield 1-1 at Buck's Head. The big all-Conference tie between **Kidderminster** and **Kettering** goes the way of the former, 3-0 winners at Aggborough.

Maurice Munden makes a spectacular save for Dover in their Conference debut at home to Kidderminster.

Photo - Dave West.

16 NOV - 6 DEC

Southport's run of eleven games without defeat ends when they lose 2-0 to **Kettering. Yeovil** cause yet another FA Cup shock by beating Second Division Fulham 1-0, courtesy of a last minute Andy Wallace goal at Huish Park. Soon afterwards, manager Steve Rutter stands down. He had been in charge at Huish Park since April 1991. Experienced defender Phil Ferns takes over as caretaker-manager. **Kettering** go top of the table after a 2-0 win at **Slough Town. Woking** progress to the Second Round of the FA Cup after beating Weston-super-Mare 1-0. **Macclesfield**'s Sammy McIlroy wins the 'Mail on Sunday' manager of the month award for November. Welsh semi-pro international Ceri Williams leaves **Merthyr Tydfil** after seven years to join Barry. **Yeovil** appoint Brian Chambers as Ferns' number two. **Welling** make YT graduate midfielder Steve Finnan their first full-time player. There are Second Round FA Cup wins for **Bath**, who beat Third Division Hereford 2-1, **Bromsgrove**, who put out fellow Conference side **Yeovil**, and **Kidderminster**, who also defeat a fellow Conference outfit, **Woking. Stalybridge, Macclesfield** and **Halifax** all bow out to League opposition. **Merthyr Tydfil** are beaten 2-1 by Swansea City in a third round replay of the Welsh Cup. Midfielder Andy Reid returns to **Altrincham** from Bury.

Steve Finnan, with Chairman Barrie Hobbins (left) and Player-Manager Terry Robbins, becomes the first player to sign professional forms for Welling United.
Photo - Keith Gillard.

7 - 20 DECEMBER

Bath relinquish Britain's last remaining unbeaten away record by losing 4-1 at **Woking**. The leadership changes hands for the 14th time when **Kidderminster** return to the top by defeating **Dover** 3-0. **Telford** set a seasonal record of 12 matches without success when losing to **Southport**. **Northwich** reach the semi-final of the Drinkwise Cup by beating **Kidderminster** 3-2. They are joined by **Yeovil** and **Bromsgrove**, who beat **Dagenham** and **Welling** respectively. **Merthyr** are ordered to pay Cardiff City £10,000 for player-manager Robbie James following a tribunal hearing. Former Macclesfield striker Steve Burr joins **Halifax** from **Stafford** for a £4,000 fee. **Telford** end their run without a victory with a 2-1 win against **Stafford**. **Macclesfield** goalkeeper Steve Farrelly scores with a drop kick against **Halifax**. **Runcorn** midfielder Gary Brabin becomes the latest Conference player to attract interest from the League with Port Vale wanting to take the 22-year-old on trial.

21 DEC - 10 JAN

Bromsgrove sell their highly rated goalkeeper Scott Cooksey to Peterborough for £25,000. **Yeovil** striker Malcolm McPherson could be the next Conference player to move into the full-time ranks with West Ham showing an interest. **Woking** announce that they are looking into the possibilities of moving to a new ground. **Halifax** sign Scunthorpe 'keeper Richard Wilmott for a five-figure fee. **Kidderminster** produce the shock of the FA Cup Third Round by beating Birmingham City 2-1 at St Andrews. **Bath** also do well to hold Stoke City to a goalless draw at the Ground. **Bromsgrove** go out, however, losing 2-1 at home to Barnsley. **Yeovil**'s 19-year-old striker Malcolm McPherson moves to West Ham in a deal which could eventually be worth £200,000 to the Somerset club. **Woking** set a seasonal record when they extend their run of unbeaten matches to 12 with a 2-0 success at **Altrincham**. **Stalybridge** try to halt a run of three successive defeats by signing three new players, Mike Lutkevitch from Accrington Stanley, Ian Harold from **Runcorn** and Alan Richards from **Altrincham**.

11 - 24 JANUARY

Dagenham sell striker Miguel Desouza to Birmingham City for a potential £75,000 fee. 46-year-old veteran Tommy Hutchison finally hangs up his boots to concentrate on his other duties at **Merthyr Tydfil**. Another former Scottish international, midfielder Neil McNab, joins **Witton** from Irish club Derry City. **Dagenham** snap up defender Martin Filson from **Halifax**. Both **Halifax** and **Yeovil** are better off financially following further appearance-related payments received for former players Lee Bracey, who moved to Bury from The Shay, and Mark Shail, who joined Bristol City from Huish Park. Meanwhile, returning to **Yeovil** as manager is Brian Hall, who has been scouting for Martin O'Neill at Wycombe recently. There are some new faces in the England semi-professional squad. **Kettering**'s Graham Benstead and Stephen Holden, **Kidderminster**'s Simeon Hodson and Kevin Rose, **Runcorn**'s Gary Brabin and **Stafford**'s Wayne Simpson are the new faces named by manager Tony Jennings. **Bath** make their exit from the FA Cup, losing 4-1 at Twerton Park to Stoke in front of a crowd of 6,213 - City's biggest gate for a quarter of a century. **Welling** defender Nigel Ransom records his 1,000th game for the Kent club in the 6-1 FA Trophy win over Chelmsford City. There are Trophy exits for **Witton**, at Grantham, and **Northwich**, away to Morecambe, while all-Conference ties see **Stafford** beat **Altrincham** and **Dagenham** defeat **Kidderminster** at Aggborough. **Kettering**, who beat Stevenage in the Trophy after the Diadora side have been reduced to nine men, announce a new five-figure sponsorship deal with Danish pharmaceutical company Ferrosan.

25 JAN - 7 FEB

Kidderminster's marvellous FA Cup run continues with a 1-0 win over Third Division Preston in the Fourth Round. **Yeovil** sign experienced defender Glyn Creaser from Wycombe on loan. **Woking** suffer their first defeat for four months, losing 2-0 at **Telford**, ending a 14-match unbeaten run. **Halifax** become the latest Conference club to view a move to a new all-purpose stadium. **Kidderminster** set a seasonal attendance record when a crowd of 4,358 watch the 2-1 win over **Dagenham**. **Witton** sign Gainsborough's highly-rated striker Simon Grayson. **Southport**, however, are unsuccessful in their bid to sign **Runcorn**'s Karl Thomas. **Stalybridge** lose 2-1 to Colwyn Bay in a Trophy first round second replay.

8 - 21 FEBRUARY

Halifax dispense with the services of manager Peter Wragg, despite a run of one defeat in 12 matches. **Slough** appoint ex-Crystal Palace player Martin Hinshelwood as number two to Les Briley. The pair were together at Brighton. The second round of the FA Trophy sees exits for **Dagenham**, at home to **Woking**, **Slough** at Morecambe, **Telford**, who lose at **Runcorn**, and **Welling** who lose the Kent derby to **Dover** at Park View Road, while **Bath** are hammered 6-1 at Sutton and **Stafford** lose at Guiseley. Championship chasers **Kettering** are held at home by Northern Leaguers Billingham Synthonia. Paul Rowlands' five month term as manager at **Altrincham** ends and old favourite John King returns to Moss Lane from Bury to take charge for the third time. **Kidderminster**'s FA Cup run finally ends when a Lee Chapman goal sees FA Premiership West Ham scrape through 1-0 at Aggborough in front of 7,850. **Halifax** appoint the former York manager John Bird as their new boss. Striker Danny Dichio makes an outstanding debut for **Welling**. The on loan QPR player scores four in the Wings' 6-2 victory over **Slough**. West Bromwich Albion offer the Hawthorns to **Kidderminster** as a possible groundshare in the event of the Harriers winning promotion

22 FEB - 7 MAR

Telford sell full-back Dave Pritchard to Bristol Rovers for a five-figure fee and **Halifax**'s midfielder Dave Ridings joins Lincoln City for £10,000. Meanwhile, **Yeovil**'s Dave Leonard and Ian Wilmott and **Welling**'s Paul Copley are the latest Conference players to attract League interest. **Yeovil** reach the final of the Drinkwise Cup by beating **Bromsgrove** on the away goals rule. **Slough** record their first away win since the opening day of the season by beating **Yeovil** 2-0 at Huish Park. Billingham Synthonia cause an FA Trophy upset by beating **Kettering** 3-1 in a second round replay. In the third round there are wins for **Gateshead** at home to **Merthyr** and **Woking**, who beat fellow Conference side **Bromsgrove** 3-2 at Kingfield. **Macclesfield** follow Kettering by becoming victims of Northern League Billingham.

Slough goalkeeper Trevor Bunting clears under pressure as the Rebels win 2-0 at Yeovil to record their first away victory since the opening day of the season.

Photo - Tim Lancaster.

8 - 21 MARCH

Witton become the latest club to lose their manager as Mike McKenzie resigns. Former Watford, AC Milan and England striker Luther Blissett joins **Southport** on loan from Bury. **Kidderminster** open a five point advantage at the top of the table, the widest margin of the campaign to date, with a 2-0 win against **Southport**. Sutton follow their second round Trophy win over Bath by beating **Dover** in a third round replay at the

Crabble. **Runcorn** come out on top of the other replay by winnng 2-0 at **Halifax**. Yet another manager departs, this time **Stalybridge**'s Phil Wilson, while **Witton** replace Mike McKenzie with ex-Morecambe boss Bryan Griffiths. Fire destroys **Runcorn**'s main stand. **Halifax** announce a £127,907 profit. **Runcorn**'s 540-minute spell without conceding a goal finally ends when **Gateshead**'s Paul Dobson nets in a 1-1 draw at Canal Street. **Yeovil** chairman Bryan Moore is elected to the FA Council.

22 MAR - 5 APRIL

Stalybridge appoint recently sacked **Halifax** manager Peter Wragg as their new boss. Prolific Conference scorer Mark West joins **Yeovil** on loan from Wycombe. **Runcorn** remain on course for a Wembley return with a 3-0 away win at **Gateshead** in the quarter-finals of the FA Trophy. **Woking** are held at home by giant-killers Billingham Synthonia. Jason Peake becomes the fifth **Halifax** player to move back into the Football League this season by joining Rochdale in a straight swap for centre-half Alex Jones. Former Northern Ireland international defender John McClelland, 38, joins **Yeovil** from Wycombe. **Runcorn** turn down a substantial bid for midfielder Gary Brabin from a Third Division club and **Welling** refuse a £25,000 offer from Southend for England defender Mark Hone. **Woking** finally put an end to Billingham's Trophy run by winning 2-1 in a replay. The transfer deadline passes with only 34 deals registered - the lowest total this decade. Busiest clubs on the day are **Altrincham** and **Dagenham**. Most notable transfers involve Billericay winger Chris Payne's £6,000 move to Victoria Road and **Macclesfield**'s Chris Sharratt moving to Moss Lane in exchange for striker Gary Powell. **Telford** striker Mark Whitehouse joins **Kettering**, who had lost the impressive Peter Costello through injury in a county cup tie against Rushden & Diamonds. The loanee returned to Lincoln City having scored five goals in seven games for the Northamptonshire club.

6 - 18 APRIL

Southport announce a £500,000 programme of ground improvements which will transform Haig Avenue into a fully covered arena. **Runcorn**'s run of 15 games without defeat ends when **Dagenham** win 2-1 at Victoria Road. The Canal Street club also announce that secretary George Worrall, who has been connected with the Linnets since the 1930s, is to relinquish his post and will be replaced by Warrington's Graham Ost. **Macclesfield** take a firm grip on the Drinkwise Cup by beating **Yeovil** 4-1 in the first-leg at Moss Rose.

19 APRIL - 7 MAY

Witton become the first club to be relegated following a 3-0 home defeat by improving **Stalybridge**. **Runcorn** reach Wembley for the second season running by beating Guiseley 2-1 on aggregate. The other finalist will be **Woking**, who come through a replay against Enfield after a goalless draw left the two sides level on aggregate. **Macclesfield** duly win the Drinkwise Cup after a goalless draw at **Yeovil**. It represented Sammy McIlroy's first major honour in management. The final Saturday of the season sees five clubs involved in the relegation dogfight to join already doomed Witton. At the top of the table, **Kettering** need to win by a large margin to stop **Kidderminster** claiming the title. Harriers are duly crowned as champions despite losing at home to **Altrincham** as the Poppies lose at home to **Bromsgrove**, who needed to win to be sure of staying up.

Yeovil save themselves with a home win over **Telford**, who are rescued by the fact that **Slough** and **Merthyr Tydfil** both finish in the relegation zone. However, due to the fact that no Northern Premier League club is to be promoted, Merthyr are saved from the drop.

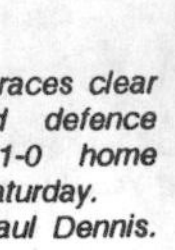

Right: *Scott Steele races clear of the Gateshead defence during Woking's 1-0 home victory on Easter Saturday.*
Photo - Paul Dennis.

ALTRINCHAM

Formed: 1891

President:
Noel White

Chairman:
John Maunders

Vice-Chairman
Gary Corbett

Football Secretary:
Jean Baldwin

Manager:
John King

Assistant Manager:
Graham Heathcote

Physiotherapist:
Mandy Johnson

Trainer:
Les Attwood

Commercial Manager:
Barbara Maunders

Press Officer:
Mark Harris

What looked like being Altrincham's worst season for over thirty years was saved, if not at the eleventh hour then mighty close, by the return to Moss Lane of the near-legendary figure of John King to become the third occupant of the manager's chair in six months.

Robins had been knocked out in the first rounds of four cup competitions, were anchored in second-bottom place and had just eighteen games left to play when King's assistant Graham Heathcote and coach Les Atwood took up a challenge which would have made a good 'Mission Impossible' script. The up-turn in fortunes was amazing; a 1-0 win at Bath gave the manager a dream start, and when Dover were dumped 2-0 the following Saturday, there was little doubt that the Robins would not give up unbroken Conference status without a fight.

Things had begun badly as the team failed to pick up where it had left off at the end of the 92/93 season, with a chronic lack of goals proving the undoing of manager Gerry Quinn. The axe finally fell on the likeable Yorkshireman following a 0-2 home FA Cup defeat at the hands of Accrington Stanley, and within 48 hours, Bangor City's Paul Rowlands, skipper of the Altrincham side which so narrowly missed out on promotion to the Football League in 1991, was installed at Moss Lane's first player-manager for thirty years.

Despite a brief revival under the new boss, the bad weather prevented Rowlands' new signings from knitting together, and after 13 games in charge had brought just two wins, the Moss Lane board decided that the situation was one which only one man could remedy. The players reacted magnificently to the motivational and tactical skills of the new management; goalkeeper Paul Collins kept eleven clean sheets in eighteen starts whilst savvy signings bolstered a depleted squad. The arrivals of Barrow full back Darren Heesom and ex-Macclesfield man Mark Dempsey proved particularly telling.

By the time that safety was finally clinched against Welling, four matchs from the end, Robins had fielded an incredible 43 players. Paul France, Ricky Harris and Mick Carmody were the only Quinn signings still at the club, with Carmody demolishing all opposition to take both players' and supporters 'Player of the Year Awards' after taking over as skipper from Mark Ogley, transferred to Stalybridge, at Christmas.

The lack of a reliable goalscorer nearly proved the side's undoing for a second consecutive season. Eight different players wore the number 9 shirt during the season, with top scorer Harris notching seven from midfield, and despite the arrival of Andy Green from Morecambe in February, the manager's main priorities lie in recruiting a striker.

Mark Harris, Press Officer

Altrincham FC. *Photo - Eric Marsh.*

ALTRINCHAM *MATCHFACTS 93-94* ***ALTRINCHAM*** *MATCHFACTS 93-94* ***ALTRINCHAM*** *MATCHFACTS 93-94*

Key: Home fixtures are denoted by bold capitals. Numbers in brackets after players names indicate goals scored (asterisks by the results denote own goals). Only used substitutes are listed - substituted players are *italicised*.

Key to Competitions: GMVC: GM Vauxhall Conference. **CSC**: Cheshire Senior Cup. **DC**: Drinkwise (GM Vauxhall Conference) Cup. **FAC**: FA Cup. **FAT**: FA Trophy.

Date	Opponents	Comp.	Res	Gate	1.	2.	3.	4.	5.	6.	7.	8.	9.	10.	11.	Sub.	Sub.
21/08	Merthyr Tydfil	GMVC	0-0	670	Clarke	Woodhead	Smith	France	Hayde	Ogley	Bell	Harris	Tunnacliffe	Carmody	*Saunders*		Jones
24/08	**STALYBRIDGE**	GMVC	0-0	758	Clarke	Woodhead	Smith	France	Hayde	Ogley	*Bell*	Harris	Tunnacliffe	Carmody	Saunders		Jones
28/08	**BATH CITY**	GMVC	0-2	706	Clarke	*Woodhead*	Smith	France	Hayde	Ogley	Hughes	Harris	Tunnacliffe	Carmody	Saunders		Richards
21/08	Bromsgrove R.	GMVC	2-1	963	Clarke	Woodhead	Smith	France	Hayde	Ogley	Bell(2)	Saunders	Tunnacliffe	Carmody	Harris		
04/09	Welling United	GMVC	1-2	930	Clarke	Woodhead	*Smith*	France	Hayde	Ogley(1)	Bell	*Saunders*	Tunnacliffe	Carmody	Harris	Hughes	Richards
07/09	**GATESHEAD**	DC1(1)	1-3	378	Clarke	Woodhead	Smith	France	Hayde	Ogley	Bell	*Raymond*	*Tunnacliffe*	Richards(1)	Harris	Hughes	Green
11/09	**KIDDERMINSTER**	GMVC	1-0	688	Clarke	Woodhead	Hayde	France	Ogley(1)	Green	*Bell*	Richards	Harris	Carmody	Hughes	Raymond	
18/09	Dover Athletic	GMVC	0-1	1,670	Clarke	Woodhead	Hayde	France	Green	Ogley	*Bell*	Richards	Tunnacliffe	Carmody	Hughes	*S Strange*	Raymond
22/09	Gateshead	DC1(2)	*1-3	251	Clarke	Woodhead	Hayde	France	Green	Ogley	Smith	Richards	Tunnacliffe	Carmody	Hughes		
25/09	**STAFFORD R.**	GMVC	0-0	758	Clarke	Woodhead	*Wright*	France	Green	Ogley	Hayde	Richards	Tunnacliffe	Carmody	*McFadzean*	Hughes	Smith
02/10	**DAGENHAM & R.**	GMVC	1-2	641	Clarke	Woodhead	Hayde	Wright	Green	Ogley	*Raymond*	*Richards(1)*	Tunnacliffe	Carmody	Smith	S Strange	Harris
09/10	Yeovil Town	GMVC	0-0	2,917	Clarke	Ogley	Hayde	France	Green	Smith	Woodhead	A Strange	Harris	Carmody	Wright		
12/10	Southport	GMVC	1-3	1,230	Clarke	Ogley	Hayde	France	Green	Smith	Woodhead	A Strange(1)	*Harris*	Carmody	Tunnacliffe		Donachie
16/10	**SLOUGH TOWN**	GMVC	2-0	678	Clarke	Ogley	Hayde	France(1)	Green	Smith	Woodhead	*Richards(1)*	Harris	Carmody	*A Strange*	S Strange	Jones
23/10	**ACCRINGTON**	FAC4q	0-2	956	Spencer	Ogley	Hayde	France	Green	Smith	Woodhead	Richards	Harris	Carmody	*Jones*	A Strange	
30/10	Kettering Town	GMVC	0-1	1,681	Gorton	A Smith	Hayde	France	Ogley	J Smith	Woodhead	Richards	Green	S Strange	*A Strange*		Jones
13/11	**NORTHWICH V.**	GMVC	2-2	1,019	Baker	Cross(2)	Hayde	France	Ogley	J Smith	*Woodhead*	Harris	Green	Carmody	Terry		A Smith
20/11	Runcorn	GMVC	1-2	627	Gorton	Cross	A Strange(1)	*France*	Ogley	J Smith	Woodhead	Harris	Green	Carmody	Terry	Rowlands	
27/11	**GATESHEAD**	GMVC	0-3	565	Baker	Cross	A Strange	France	Ogley	*J Smith*	Woodhead	Harris	Green	Carmody	Terry	Rowlands	
30/11	**MACCLESFIELD**	CSC2	0-1	333	Baker	Cross	A Strange	*France*	Ogley	Rowlands	Woodhead	Harris	Green	Carmody	Terry	Richards	
18/12	Witton Albion	GMVC	1-0	856	Collings	Cross	Hayde	France	Ogley	Reid	Esdaille	Harris	Powell	Carmody	Terry(1)		

05/01	Macclesfield T.	GMVC	0-1	742	Collings	Cross	*Hayde*	France	Green	Reid	Esdaille	Harris	Pennington	Carmody	Terry	Woodhead			
08/01	**WOKING**	GMVC	0-2	788	Collings	Cross	Hayde	*France*	Green	Reid	Esdaille	Harris	Pennington	Carmody	Terry	Woodhead			
15/01	**MERTHYR TYD.**	GMVC	*3-0	696	Collings	Cross	Hayde	France	Green	*Esdaille*	Powell	Harris	*Pennington(1)*	Carmody	Terry	Rowlands	Woodhead		
22/01	**STAFFORD R.**	FAT1	0-2	790	Collings	Reid	Hayde	France	*Green*	*Esdaille*	Powell	Harris	Pennington	Carmody	Terry	Rowlands	Woodhead		
29/01	Dagenham & Red.	GMVC	0-3	1,047	Collings	Cross	Hayde	France	Rowlands	Reid	Woodhead	Harris	Powell	Doherty	Terry				
02/02	Gateshead	GMVC	1-2	146	Collings	Cross	Hayde	France	Rowlands	Reid	Pennington	Harris	Powell	Doherty(1)	Terry				
05/02	**BROMSGROVE**	GMVC	2-3	673	Collings	Cross	Hayde	France(1)	Rowlands	Reid	*Mellish*	Harris	Powell	Doherty	Terry(1)	A Strange			
12/02	**WITTON ALBION**	GMVC	1-3	647	Collings	Cross	*Hayde*	France	Woodhead	Reid	Doherty	Harris(1)	Powell	Carmody	Terry	Pennington			
19/02	Bath City	GMVC	1-0	639	Collings	Cross	Heesom	France	Reid	*A Green*	*Doherty*	Harris(1)	Powell	Carmody	Terry	Esdaille	R Green		
26/02	**DOVER ATH.**	GMVC	2-0	723	Collings	Cross	Heesom	France	Reid	*Cockram*	A Green	Harris(1)	Powell(1)	Carmody	Terry	Doherty	R Green		
01/03	**MACCLESFIELD**	GMVC	0-1	1,030	Collings	Cross	Heesom	France	Reid	*Doherty*	A Green	*Harris*	Powell	Carmody	Terry	May	R Green		
05/03	Stafford Rgrs	GMVC	1-0	808	Collings	Cross	Heesom	France	*Reid*	Cockram	A Green	Harris	May	Carmody	Terry	R Green(1)	Powell		
12/03	Woking	GMVC	1-1	1,816	Collings	Cross	Heesom	France	Reid	*Cockram*	A Green(1)	Harris	May	Carmody	Terry	R Green	Dempsey		
15/03	Stalybridge C.	GMVC	3-1	510	Collings	Cross	Heesom	France	Reid	Dempsey	A Green(2)	Harris(1)	Doherty	Carmody	Terry				
19/03	**YEOVIL TOWN**	GMVC	1-0	747	Collings	Cross	Heesom	France(1)	Reid	Dempsey	A Green	Harris	*Doherty*	Carmody	*Burton*	R Green	Terry		
29/03	Northwich Vics	GMVC	0-2	1,037	Collings	Cross	Heesom	France	Reid	Dempsey	*Burton*	Harris	*Doherty*	Carmody	Terry	R Green	Powell		
02/04	**SOUTHPORT**	GMVC	1-2	982	Collings	Cross	Heesom	France	Reid	Dempsey	*Terry*	Harris	R Green	Carmody	Sharratt(1)		Cockram		
04/04	Telford United	GMVC	2-0	904	Collings	Cross	Heesom	France	Reid	Dempsey	Terry	*Harris*	R Green(1)	Carmody	Sharratt(1)		Cockram		
07/04	Halifax Town	GMVC	0-0	1,018	Collings	Cross	Heesom	France	Reid	Dempsey	A Green	*Terry*	R Green	Carmody	Sharratt		Cockram		
12/04	**RUNCORN**	GMVC	2-1	659	Collings	Cross	Heesom	France	Reid	*Dempsey*	A Green(1)	Harris(1)	Butler	Carmody	Sharratt		Terry		
16/04	**TELFORD UTD**	GMVC	2-0	684	Collings	Cross	Heesom	France	Reid	Terry(1)	A Green(1)	Harris	*R Green*	Carmody	Sharratt		Cockram		
23/04	Slough Town	GMVC	2-0	674	Collings	Cross	Heesom	France	Reid	Dempsey	*A Green*	Harris(1)	Terry	Carmody	Sharratt	Cockram(1)			
26/04	**WELLING UTD**	GMVC	*2-0	642	Collings	Cross	Heesom	France	Reid	Dempsey	A Green	Harris	Terry(1)	*Carmody*	Sharratt	R Green			
30/04	**HALIFAX TOWN**	GMVC	0-0	799	Collings	Cross	Heesom	France	Reid	*Dempsey*	A Green	Harris	Terry	Carmody	Sharratt	R Green			
02/05	**KETTERING T.**	GMVC	1-1	979	Collings	Cross	Heesom	France	Reid	Dempsey	A Green	Harris	Terry	Carmody	Sharratt(1)				
07/05	Kidderminster H.	GMVC	1-0	4,114	Collings	Cross	Heesom	France	Reid	Dempsey	A Green	Harris	Terry(1)	Carmody	Sharratt				

Altrincham

JOHN KING

John King returned to Moss Lane to begin his third spell as manager towards the end the 1993-94 season. His arrival saw a dramatic change in fortunes as the Robins, facing relegation for the first time, displayed championship form to end the campaign on a high note and finish well away from the bottom places.

King started his playing career as a junior with both Everton and Shrewsbury Town before joining the non-League ranks with Kirkby Town, Wigan Athletic and Northwich Victoria. He then joined Altrincham in 1977 to begin a highly successful spell at Moss Lane. The tough-tackling midfielder helped the Robins win the Alliance Premier League championship twice and the Bob Lord Trophy, and also featured in their many FA Cup exploits. His playing career was ended by an injury sustained during his third FA Trophy final, in 1982.

He cut his managerial teeth with South Liverpool before almost inevitably taking over at Altrincham in January 1984. FA Trophy success came again as a manager in 1986 when the Robins beat neighbours Runcorn but, surprisingly, the very next day King joined the Linnets. He returned to Moss Lane early in the 1988-89 season.

During the summer of 1990, King accepted an offer to join Bury as assistant-manager. He stayed there until February 1994 when he rejoining the Robins and master-minded their miraculous escape from relegation.

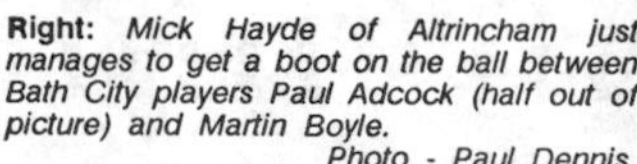

Right: *Mick Hayde of Altrincham just manages to get a boot on the ball between Bath City players Paul Adcock (half out of picture) and Martin Boyle.*
Photo - Paul Dennis.

Programme details:
32 pages for £1
Editor - Mark Harris/ Terry Surridge

Any other club publications:

Local Newspapers:
Sale & Altrincham Messenger
Sale & Altrincham Express
Manchester Evening News
Manchester Metro News

Local Radio Stations:
GMR (BBC)

ALTRINCHAM - PLAYING SQUAD

Player	Honours	Birthplace and date	Transfer Fees	Previous Clubs
GOALKEEPERS				
Paul Collings		Liverpool 30/9/68		Ellesmere Pt, Tranmere, Altrincham, Bury
DEFENDERS				
Ray Sidderley		Manchester 29/8/60		Stockport, Droylsden, Cheadle, Adswood Am, Droylsden, Acc.Stanley
Simon Woodhead		Dewsbury 26/12/63		Mansfield, Crewe, Emley, Burnley, Shepshed Chart., Frickley
Paul France		Holmfirth 10/9/68		Huddersfield, Bristol C, Burnley
Russell Green		Barnsley 6/10/70		Barnsley, Emley
Mick Hayde		St Helens 20/6/71		Liverpool, Chester C, St Helens T.
Darren Heesom		Warrington 8/5/68		Burnley, Altrincham, Macclesfield T, Witton Alb, Hyde Utd, Barrow.
Steve Cross				Bangor City
MIDFIELDERS				
Andy Reid	CSC	Davyhulme 4/7/62		Everton, Witton Alb, Southport, Runcorn, Altrincham, Bury
Mick Carmody		Huddersfield 9/2/66		Huddersfield, Emley, Tranmere R, Emley
Steve Terry				Bangor City
Mark Dempsey		Manchester 14/1/64		Manchester Utd, Sheffield Utd, Rotherham, Macclesfield T, Buxton
David Esdaille		Manchester 22/7/63		Wrexham, Bury
FORWARDS				
Mick Doherty	ESP, SLP, ILP, CSC, DSC, HSC	Liverpool 8/3/61		B'stoke, Reading, Weymouth, Maidstone, Yeovil, Runcorn, Farnboro, Maccsfld, Marine
Chris Sharratt		West Kirby 13/8/70		Bangor C, Caernarfon, Stalybridge C, Wigan, Macclesfield T
Ricky Harris		Manchester 12/7/67		Ashton Utd, Altrincham, Hyde Utd, Runcorn, Hyde Utd
Andy Green		Liverpool 23/8/69		Bootle, Sth Liverpool, Binche (Belg), Macclesfield, Morecambe, Knowsley Utd
Dave Cockram	CSC	Liverpool 6/8/67		Poulton V, Caernarfon, Mold Alex.

Departures during season:
John Smith (Fleetwood), Alan Richards (Stalybridge), David Jones (Released), Paul Rowlands (Worcester C), Steve Pennington (St Helens), Leroy May (Stafford R), Mark Ogley (Stalybridge), Gary Powell (Macclesfield), Andy Gorton (Released), Ian Tunnacliffe (Emley), Tim Clarke (Shrewsbury), Mark Wright (Released).

Players on loan during season:
Simon Burton (Preston), Alan Fahy & Steve Birks (Bury).

Moss Lane, Altrincham

Address and telephone number: Moss Lane, Altrincham, Cheshire WA15 8AP. Tel: 061 928 1045. Fax: 061 926 9934.

Simple directions: M6 junction 19; A556/M56 (Manchester Airport) to junction 7; signs Hale and Altrincham; through 1st traffic lights and 3rd right into Westminster Road and continue into Moss Lane. Ground on right.

Capacity: 3,500 **Seated:** 1,000 **Covered terracing:** Yes

Record Attendance: 10,275 - Altrincham Boys v Sunderland Boys - English Schools Shield 3rd Round 28.02.25.

Club Shop: Open on matchdays only; programmes, badges, shirts, books & souvenirs.

Social Facilities: Four snack bars on ground for pies, crisps, soft drinks and chocolate etc; bar open on match days only.

Previous Grounds: Pollitts Field - 1903-1910

Altrincham Fact File

Nickname: The Robins

Club Sponsors: Maunders Homes

Previous Leagues: Manchester League 1903-1911, Lancashire Combination 1911-1919, Cheshire County League 1919-1968, Northern Premier League 1968-1979.

Club colours: Red & white striped shirts, black shorts and white socks.

Change colours: Sky blue shirts, dark blue shorts and sky blue socks.

Reserve team league: North West Combination.

Youth team league: Altrincham Independent Insurance League.

Midweek home matchday: Tuesday.

Record win: Unknown.

Record defeat: Unknown.

Record transfer fee: To Telford United for Ken McKenna - 1990.

Record transfer fee received: From Crewe Alexandra for Paul Edwards - 1988.

1993-94 Captain: Mark Ogley (pre-Christmas)/ Mick Carmody

1993-94 Top scorer: Ricky Harris

1993-94 Player of the Year: Mick Carmody

Club record goalscorer: Jack Swindells 252 - 1965-71

Record appearances: John Davison 677 - 1971-86.

Past players who progressed to the Football League: Graham Barrow (Wigan Athletic, 1981), Eddie Bishop (Tranmere Rovers, 1988), Frank Carrodus (Manchester City, 1969), Peter Conning (Rochdale, 1986), Robert Dale (Bury, 1951), Nicky Daws (Bury, 1992), Paul Edwards (Crewe, 1988), Brian Green (Exeter City, 1962), John Hughes (Stockport County, 1976), Steve Johnson (Bury, 1977), Joe Kennedy (West Brom, 1948), Andy Kilner (Stockport County, 1990), Stan March (Port Vale, 1959), Charlie Mitten (Halifax Town, 1965), Brian Phillips (Middlesbrough, 1954), Andy Reid (Bury, 1992), Eric Robinson (West Brom, 1957), John Rogers (Wigan Athletic, 1982), Paul Showler (Barnet, 1991), Nelson Stiffle (Chesterfield, 1954), Jeff Street (Barrow, 1969), Clive Freeman (Doncaster, 1993).

Club Honours: Alliance Premier League Champions 1980,1981; FA Trophy Winners 1978,1986; Bob Lord Trophy Winners 1981; N.P.L. Cup Winners 1970; N.P.L. Shield Winners 1980; Cheshire County League Winners 1966,1967; Cheshire County League Cup Winners 1951,1953,1964; Cheshire Senior Cup Winners 1905,1934,1967,1982; Manchester League Champions 1905;

BATH CITY

Formed: 1889

President:
Mr F Entwistle

Chairman:
Mr R C Stock

Vice-Chairman:
Mr C Jefferis

Chief Executive:
Mr P Britton

Manager:
Mr A Ricketts

Physiotherapist:
Rachel Jackson

Commercial Manager:
Paul Cater

Press Officer:
Paul Britton

A SEASON OF PROMISE

City began the season in fine style with a 5-1 home win over Macclesfield Town and followed this up with a convincing home win over eventual champions Kidderminster Harriers on Bank Holiday Monday. New signings Paul Batty, Paul Chenoweth and Paul Adcock made an immediate impact, with Paul Adcock hitting a hat-trick in the aforementioned win over Macclesfield and finishing the campaign with 23 goals.

Defeat by Gateshead at Twerton Park in September signalled the beginning of a worrying run of home games without a win, although the club remained unbeaten on their travels until mid-December when they lost at Woking.

Once again, though, Bath enjoyed a successful FA Cup run. After coming within two minutes of defeat in a fourth round qualifying round tie at Cheltenham, a 4-2 win in the replay secured a first round tie at Moseley and a 4-0 victory. Herefore United were beaten 2-1 in round two and City played magnificently to hold Stoke to a goalless draw in the third round, though they failed to make home advantage pay in the replay and went down 4-1.

After a heavy defeat at the hands of Sutton United in the FA Trophy, league form dipped and at one stage City failed to score in six consecutive league fixtures. A succession of injuries badly affected form and confidence. Most significant of these was the wrist injury sustained by goalkeeper Dave Mogg, at a crucial stage of the season forcing him to miss seven games in total. His consistency between the sticks was recognised by fans and players alike as he picked up both awards for 'Player of the Season'.

A season which began in style ended somewhat disappointingly, though a win over tenants Bristol Rovers in the Somerset Premier Cup went some way towards making up for this. With the nucleus of an excellent side retained, the addition of two or three quality players during the summer could see City making a strong title challenge in 1994-95.

Paul Britton.

Bath celebrate their memorable FA Cup Second Round victory against Hereford. *Photo - Paul Dennis.*

BATH CITY MATCHFACTS 93-94 *BATH CITY MATCHFACTS 93-94* *BATH CITY MATCHFACTS 93-94*

Key: Home fixtures are denoted by bold capitals. Numbers in brackets after players names indicate goals scored (asterisks by the results denote own goals).

Key to Competitions: GMVC: G.M. Vauxhall Conference. **SPC**: Somerset Premier Cup. **DC**: Drinkwise (G.M. Vauxhall Conference) Cup. **FAC**: F.A. Cup. **FAT**: F.A. Trophy.

Date	Opponents	Comp.	Res	Gate	1.	2.	3.	4.	5.	6.	7.	8.	9.	10.	11.	Sub.	Sub.
21/08	**MACCLESFIELD**	GMVC	5-1	667	Mogg	Hedges	Dicks	Cousins	Crowley	Batty	Banks	Chenoweth	Boyle(1)	*Adcock(3)*	*Smart(1)*	Mings	Noble
24/08	Merthyr Tydfil	GMVC	1-1	567	Mogg	Hedges	Dicks	*Batty*	Crowley	Cousins	Banks	Chenoweth	*Adcock*	Boyle	Smart(1)	Mings	Noble
28/08	Altrincham	GMVC	2-0	706	Mogg	Hedges	Dicks	Batty	Crowley	Cousins(1)	Banks	Chenoweth	Adcock(1)	*Boyle*	*Smart*	Mings	Noble
30/08	**KIDDERMINSTER**	GMVC	4-0	941	Mogg	Hedges	Noble	Gill(2)	Crowley(1)	*Cousins*	Banks	Chenoweth	*Adcock(1)*	Mings	Smart	Batty	Boyle
04/09	**STALYBRIDGE**	GMVC	1-1	861	Mogg	Hedges	Noble	Gill	Crowley	Cousins	Banks	Chenoweth	Boyle	Mings(1)	Smart		
11/09	Southport	GMVC	1-1	1,129	Mogg	Gill	Noble	Batty	Crowley	Cousins	Banks	Ch'weth(1)	Adcock	Boyle	Smart		
18/09	**GATESHEAD**	GMVC	2-3	703	Mogg	Gill	Noble	*Batty*	Crowley	Cousins(1)	Banks	Chenoweth	Adcock(1)	Boyle	Smart	Mings	
25/09	Witton Albion	GMVC	3-0	688	Mogg	Hedges	Noble	Batty(1)	Crowley(1)	Cousins	Williams	Chenoweth	Adcock(1)	*Boyle*	*Smart*	Mings	Gill
28/09	**WELLING UTD**	GMVC	0-0	722	Mogg	Hedges	Noble	Batty	Crowley	Cousins	Williams	Chenoweth	Adcock	Mings	*Smart*		Boyle
02/10	**KETTERING T.**	GMVC	0-3	864	Mogg	Hedges	Noble	Batty	Crowley	Cousins	Williams	Chenoweth	Adcock	*Mings*	*Smart*	Boyle	Vernon
09/10	Slough Town	GMVC	0-0	1,334	Mogg	Hedges	Dicks	Batty	Crowley	Cousins	Williams	*Chenoweth*	Adcock	Gill	Boyle		Vernon
16/10	**STAFFORD R.**	GMVC	2-3	656	Mogg	Hedges	Dicks	*Batty*	Crowley	Cousins(1)	Williams	*Gill*	Adcock(1)	Vernon	Smart	Mings	Brooks
23/10	Cheltenham Town	FAC4q	1-1	1,020	Mogg	Hedges	Dicks	Batty	Crowley	Cousins	Williams	Gill	Adcock(1)	Mings	*Smart*		Vernon
26/10	**CHELTENHAM**	FAC4qr	4-2	1,166	Mogg	Hedges	Dicks	*Batty*	Crowley(1)	Cousins(1)	Williams	Gill	Adcock(1)	Mings	*Noble(1)*	Smart	Vernon
30/10	**HALIFAX T.**	GMVC	2-2	712	Mogg	Hedges	Dicks	*Weston*	Crowley	Cousins	Banks	Gill	Adcock	*Boyle(1)*	Noble(1)	Smart	Vernon
02/11	**YEOVIL TOWN**	DC2	0-1	584	Mogg	Hedges	Dicks	*Weston*	Brooks	Cousins	Banks	Gill	Adcock	Boyle	Noble		Thaws
06/11	Telford United	GMVC	0-0	721	Mogg	Hedges	*Noble*	*Weston*	Crowley	Cousins	Banks	Dicks	Adcock	Boyle	Gill	Chenoweth	Mings
10/11	Clevedon Town	SPC2	2-0	502	Mogg	Gill	Williams	Brooks	Crowley	*Cousins*	Banks	Chenoweth	Mings(2)	*Boyle*	Vernon	Batty	Noble
13/11	Molesey	FAC1	4-0	913	Mogg	Banks	Brooks	Boyle(1)	Crowley	*Cousins*	Williams	Gill	*Adcock(2)*	Mings(1)	Chenoweth	Batty	Vernon
20/11	**BROMSGROVE**	GMVC	0-1	642	Mogg	Gill	*Williams*	Boyle	Crowley	Chenoweth	Banks	Brooks	*Adcock*	Mings	Cousins	Batty	Vernon
27/11	Dover Athletic	GMVC	3-0	1,820	Mogg	Gill	Williams	*Boyle*	Crowley(1)	Cousins	Banks	Ch'weth(1)	*Adcock*	Mings(1)	Brooks	Batty	Smart
30/11	**SLOUGH TOWN**	GMVC	3-0	541	Mogg	Gill	Dicks	*Boyle(1)*	Crowley	Cousins	Banks	Ch'weth(1)	Adcock	Mings	*Brooks*	Smart(1)	Batty
05/12	**HEREFORD UTD**	FAC2	2-1	3,086	Mogg	Gill	Dicks	Boyle	Crowley	Cousins	Williams	Chenoweth	*Adcock*	Mings	*Brooks(1)*	Smart	Batty(1)
11/12	Woking	GMVC	1-4	1,437	Mogg	Gill	Dicks	Boyle	Crowley	Cousins	Williams	*Chenoweth*	Adcock	*Mings*	Brooks(1)	Smart	Batty
18/12	**NORTHWICH V.**	GMVC	0-0	514	Mogg	Hedges	Dicks	*Boyle*	Crowley	*Cousins*	Banks	Chenoweth	Adcock	Batty	Brooks	Gill	Vernon

27/12	Yeovil Town	GMVC	2-1	3,371	Mogg	Hedges	Dicks	*Boyle*	Gill	Cousins	Banks	*Chenoweth*	Batty(1)	Mings	Brooks	Adcock(1)	Vernon
01/01	Kidderminster H.	GMVC	0-0	2,157	Mogg	Gill	Dicks	Batty	Hedges	Cousins	Banks	*Chenoweth*	*Adcock*	Mings	Brooks	Smart	Vernon
03/01	**YEOVIL TOWN**	GMVC	3-0	1,518	Mogg	Hedges	Dicks	Batty	Smart	Cousins	Banks	*Ch'weth(1)*	Adcock(2)	*Mings*	Gill	Williams	Vernon
08/01	Stoke City	FAC3	0-0	14,159	Mogg	Gill	Dicks	Batty	Hedges	Cousins	Banks	*Chenoweth*	Adcock	*Mings*	Brooks	Smart	Vernon
18/01	**STOKE CITY**	FAC3r	1-4	6,213	Mogg	Gill	Dicks	Batty	Hedges	*Cousins*	Banks	Ch'weth(1)	*Adcock*	Mings	Brooks	Boyle	Vernon
22/01	Yeovil Town	FAT1	3-3	2,611	Mogg	Gill	Dicks	Batty	Hedges	Cousins	Banks	Chenoweth	Mings(2)	Boyle(1)	Brooks		
25/01	**YEOVIL TOWN**	FAT1r	4-0	1,148	Mogg	Gill(1)	Dicks	Batty	Hedges	Cousins(1)	Banks	*Chenoweth*	Adcock(1)	*Boyle(1)*	Brooks	Smart	Vernon
29/01	Stalybridge C.	GMVC	3-1	508	Mogg	Gill	Dicks	*Batty(1)*	Hedges	Cousins(2)	Banks	Chenoweth	Adcock	*Boyle*	Brooks	Smart	Vernon
05/02	**RUNCORN**	GMVC	0-0	698	Mogg	Gill	Dicks	Batty	Hedges	Cousins	Banks	Chenoweth	Adcock	Boyle	Brooks		
08/02	Kettering Town	GMVC	1-0	2,044	Torrez	Gill	Williams	Batty	Hedges	Cousins	Crowley	Smart	Adcock(1)	*Mings*	Brooks	Chenoweth	
12/02	Sutton United	FAT2	1-6	1,188	Torrez	Gill	Williams	*Batty*	Hedges	Cousins	*Crowley*	Smart	Adcock	Boyle	Brooks(1)	Chenoweth	Mings
19/02	**ALTRINCHAM**	GMVC	0-1	637	Rudgley	Gill	Williams	Chenoweth	Hedges	Cousins	Harrison	*Smart*	Adcock	Mings	Brooks	*Boyle*	Thaws
23/02	Bristol City	SPCqf	3-1	258	Torrez	Gill	Dicks	Crowley	Hedges	Cousins	Vernon	Chenoweth	*Adcock(1)*	Mings(1)	*Brooks(1)*	Ricketts	Williams
26/02	Northwich Vict.	GMVC	1-3	648	Rudgley	Gill	Dicks	Crowley(1)	*Hedges*	Cousins	Harrison	Chenoweth	Thaws	Mings	*Smart*	Williams	Vernon
05/03	**WITTON ALBION**	GMVC	1-1	482	Torrez	Gill	Dicks	Crowley	Vernon	Cousins	Banks	Chenoweth	Adcock	Thaws	Smart		
12/03	Macclesfield T.	GMVC	0-0	757	Torrez	Gill	Dicks	Short	Crowley	Cousins	Banks	Chenoweth	Adcock	Thaws	Vernon		
15/03	**YEOVIL TOWN**	SPCsf	1-0	322	Mogg	Gill	Dicks	Smart	Crowley	Cousins	Banks	Ch'weth(1)	Brooks	Mings	*Harrison*	Adcock	
19/03	**SOUTHPORT**	GMVC	2-1	615	Mogg	Gill	*Dicks*	Smart(1)	Crowley	Cousins	Banks	Chenoweth	Brooks	Mings	Harrison	Adcock(1)	
26/03	Halifax Town	GMVC	0-0	1,008	Mogg	Gill	Dicks	Crowley	*Smart*	Cousins	Banks	Chenoweth	Adcock	*Thaws*	Vernon	Ricketts	Lucas
30/03	Dagenham & Red.	GMVC	0-3	823	Mogg	Gill	Dicks	Crowley	Smart	Cousins	Banks	Chenoweth	Adcock	*Thaws*	*Brooks*	Ricketts	Batty
02/04	**TELFORD UTD**	GMVC	3-0	473	Mogg	Gill	Dicks	Crowley	*Smart*	*Cousins*	Banks	Chenoweth	Adcock(3)	Mings	Brooks	Vernon	Batty
04/04	Welling United	GMVC	0-0	800	Mogg	Gill	Dicks	Brooks	Crowley	Cousins	Banks	Chenoweth	Adcocks	*Mings*	*Smart*	Vernon	Batty
12/04	**WOKING**	GMVC	0-1	691	Mogg	Gill	Dicks	Crowley	Smart	Cousins	Banks	*Chenoweth*	Adcock	*Mings*	Brooks	Vernon	Batty
16/04	Gateshead	GMVC	0-1	401	Mogg	Gill	Dicks	Batty	Crowley	Cousins	Banks	*Chenoweth*	Adcock	Vernon	Smart	Ricketts	
19/04	**MERTHYR TYD.**	GMVC	0-3	512	Mogg	Gill	Dicks	Crowley	Smart	Cousins	Banks	*Chenoweth*	Adcock	Vernon	*Batty*	Thaws	Lucas
21/04	**BRISTOL RVRS**	SPCf(1)	3-2	307	Mogg	Gill	Dicks	*Crowley*	Smart(2)	Lucas	Banks	Chenoweth	*Adcock*	Vernon	Batty	Boyle(1)	Forbes
26/04	**DOVER ATH.**	GMVC	0-0	448	Mogg	Gill	Dicks	Cousins	Smart	Brooks	Banks	Chenoweth	Adcock	*Vernon*	*Batty*	Boyle	Thaws
28/04	Runcorn	GMVC	0-0	284	Mogg	Gill	Dicks	Brooks	*Vernon*	Cousins	Banks	Chenoweth	Adcock	Boyle	Smart	Lucas	
30/04	Bromsgrove R.	GMVC	*1-0	843	Mogg	Gill	Dicks	Brooks	*Lucas*	Cousins	Banks	Chenoweth	Adcock	*Bayliss*	Smart	Ricketts	Vernon
03/05	**BRISTOL RVRS**	SPCf(2)	2-2	509	Mogg	Gill	Dicks	Brooks(1)	Lucas	Cousins	Banks	Chenoweth	*Adcock*	Boyle(1)	*Smart*	Vernon	Forbes
07/05	**DAGENHAM & R.**	GMVC	0-0	454	Mogg	Gill	Dicks	Brooks	*Lucas*	Cousins	Banks	Chenoweth	Adcock	Boyle	*Vernon*	Ricketts	Batty

Bath City

TONY RICKETTS

Tony's playing career began with local side Clandown before he joined City as a player for the first time. He later enjoyed a successful spell with local rivals Yeovil Town before returning to Twerton Park.

He was appointed player-manager midway through the 1990/91 season at a time when relegation to the Beazer Homes League looked a distinct possibility. He helped City avoid the drop by just three points, and in his first full season he led the side to ninth position in the Conference. With virtually an unchanged squad, he improved on that in 1992/93 by achieving 7th place.

Tony brought a number of new players to the club during the summer of 1993 and, although a final placing of twelfth was a slight disappointment after a bright first half of the season and a fine FA Cup run, he encouraged his team to play a passing game and was unfortunate in that injuries to a number of key players occurred at crucial times during the season.

His ambition to bring success to the club will undoubtedly see more new faces arrive at the club before the start of the new campaign which, City supporters hope, see a sustained effort for the title.

Richard Crowley climbs highest to clear the danger during Bath's early season win at Altrincham.
Photo - Paul Dennis.

Programme details:
40 pages for £1
Editor - Keith Brookman.

Local Newspapers:
Bath Chronicle
Evening Post
Western Daily Press

Local Radio Stations:
Radio Bristol
GWR
Brunel

BATH CITY - PLAYING SQUAD

Player	Honours	Birthplace and date	Transfer Fees	Previous Clubs
GOALKEEPERS				
David Mogg	ES, FAXI	Bristol 11/2/62		Bristol C, Atvidaberg (Swe), Abbotonians, Bath C, Cheltenham T, Gloucester C
Raphael Torres				
DEFENDERS				
Grantley Dicks		Bristol 17/10/66		Clandown, Paulton Rovers
Ian Hedges		Bristol 5/2/69	£7,500	Bristol Manor Farm, Gloucester C, AFC Bournemouth
Jerry Gill	SSC	Clevedon 8/9/70		Backwell Utd, Trowbridge T, Leyton Orient, Weston-Super-Mare
Chris Banks		Stone, Staffs 12/11/65		Port Vale, Exeter C
Tony Ricketts	ILP, AC Delco Cup	Bath 21/6/59	£10,000	Clandown, Bath C, Yeovil T
MIDFIELDERS				
Gary Smart		Kingston, Jam. 1/4/62		Glenside Hospital, Bristol R, Cheltenham T
Rob Cousins		Bristol 9/1/71		Bristol C
~~Paul Batty~~	Div.4	Doncaster 9/1/64		Swindon T, Chesterfield, Exeter C, Yeovil T
Paul Chenoweth		Bristol 5/2/73		Bristol R
Nicky Brooks		Bristol		Bristol C, Barnstaple T, Mangotsfield Utd, Clevedon T
FORWARDS				
Paul Adcock		Ilminster 2/5/72		Plymouth Argyle
Adie Mings		Chippenham 17/10/68	£2,000	Melksham T, Chippenham T
Deion Vernon		Bristol		Bristol C
Martin Boyle	WL	Bristol		Bristol R, Trowbridge T, Mangotsfield Utd

Departures during season:
Colston Gwyther (Released), Steve Book (Brighton), Kevin Thaws (Taunton), Wayne Noble (Taunton), Gary Williams, Ian Weston (Released)

Players on loan during season:
Gerry Harrison (Bristol City), Donald Forbes (Avon St Phillips), Simon Rudgeley (non contract).

Twerton Park, Bath

Address and telephone number: Twerton Park, Twerton, Bath Avon BA2 1DB. Tel: 0225 423087. Fax: 0225 481391.

Simple directions: Twerton Park is situated on the A4/A36 Lower Bristol Road - on the Bristol side of Bath City Centre (Approx 2.5 miles). The area is serviced by J18 on the M4. From the centre of Bath the bus route is No.5 - Twerton High Street.

Capacity: 9,899 **Seated:** 1,017 **Covered terracing:** 4,800

Record Attendance: 18,020 v Brighton & Hove Albion, FA Cup.

Club Shop: Contact Mr P Cater or Mr K Sellick.

Social Facilities: Several bars open all week and full service with menu on match-days catering for up to 250 people.

Previous Grounds: The Belvoir Ground/ Lambridge - 1889-1932

Bath Fact File

Nickname: Romans

Club Sponsors: Bath Advertiser.

Previous Leagues: Beazer Homes (Southern League)

Club colours: Black/white striped shirts, black shorts & black/white socks.

Change colours: All sky blue

Midweek home matchday: Tuesday

Record win:

Record defeat:

Record transfer fee: £15,000 for Micky Tanner from Bristol City.

Record transfer fee received:

1993-94 Captain: Richard Crowley

1993-94 Top scorer: Paul Adcock

1993-94 Player of the Year: David Mogg

Club record goalscorer: Paul Randall

Record appearances:

Past players who progressed to the Football League: Alan Skirton (Arsenal), Tony Book (Plymouth Argyle, Manchester City), Kenny Allen (Bournemouth, Swindon Town), Peter Rogers (Exeter City), R Bourne (Torquay), Dave Wiffil (Manchester City), Stan Mortensen (Blackpool), Brian Wade (Swindon Town), Jeff Meacham (Bristol Rovers), Martin Hirst (Bristol City), Paul Bodin (Swindon), Graham Withey (Coventry), Jason Dodd (Southampton).

Club Honours: Southern League (2); League Cup, Somerset Premier Cup (13); Anglo-Italian Cup finalists.

BROMSGROVE ROVERS

Formed:
1885

President:
Charles W Poole

Chairman:
Keith MacMaster

Football Secretary:
Brian Hewings

Manager:
Bobby Hope

Assistant Manager:
Doug Griffiths

Physiotherapist:
Paul Sunners

Commercial Manager:
Rebecca O'Neill

Press Officer:

This was a truly amazing season with Rovers continuing to break or set records. Firstly, ones that they didn't want, like going fifteen matches without a win between 22nd March and 5th May. There were home defeats of 0-4 and 0-5, and no wins at all in September or April.

August saw a slow start including a dramatic 3-4 defeat, but in September we had wins in two FA Cup ties, and October was kind with no defeats and wins in the FA Cup putting us into the first round proper for the ninth time.

Club records came thick and fast in November; progress into round two of the FA Cup and a first-ever Cup win over a league club. We beat Slough in the Drinkwise Cup, but managed only four points out of twelve in the league. Decemberr brought FAC glory at Yeovil, further progress in the Drinkwise Cup and, in the league, six points out of nine. The most stunning event, however, was the sale of goalkeeper Scott Cooksey to Peterborough, mainly due to its awful timing.

January arrived, and FA Cup glory was snatched away when Barnsley hit 88th and 90th minute goals to win 2-1 having been outplayed for the first 88 minutes. We did, however, win through to the semi-finals of the Drinkwise and Worcestershire Senior Cups and made progress in the FA Trophy.

February brought four points out of six, and we progressed into the third round of the FA Trophy only to lose to Woking, but March was a real disaster, losing to Yeovil on the away goals rule in the semi-final of the Drinkwise Cup and registering two record home defeats. A win on March the 22nd was to be our last win until May!

April saw five draws and five defeats - what a nightmare! Mid-table with matches in hand, then bang! Suspensions, injuries and a total loss of form brought a dive down the league in the style of a sinking submarine! May arrived, a cruicial match at Merthyr was lost. We lost Stuart Brighton, one of our three semi-pro Internationals, with a broken leg and it looked near impossible to pull out of the dive. Only two wins would do from our last two matches. Our horrific run ended on the 5th with only our 5th home win of the season, and victory at Kettering on the last day saved us.

The season ended on a high note with a 5-1 aggregate win against Kidderminster to take the Worcestershire Senior Cup. Steve Stott won four different Player-of-the-Year trophies - a great season for this popular player.

Brian Perry

Bromsgrove Rovers pictured after beating Kidderminster Harriers 4-0 (5-1 on aggregate) to win the Worcestershire Senior Cup. Back Row (L/R): R Carter, P Masefield, S Taylor, B Gray, R Green, N Clarke. Front: C Radburn, C Gaunt, C Pearce, L Young, K Richardson, S Stott.

Photo - Brian Perry.

BROMSGROVE MATCHFACTS 93-94 *BROMSGROVE* MATCHFACTS 93-94 *BROMSGROVE* MATCHFACTS 93-94

Key: Home fixtures are denoted by bold capitals. Numbers in brackets after players names indicate goals scored (asterisks by the results denote own goals). Only used substitutes are listed - substituted players are *italicised*.

Key to Competitions: GMVC: G.M. Vauxhall Conference. **WSC**: Worcestershire Senior Cup. **DC**: Drinkwise (G.M. Vauxhall Conference) Cup. **FAC**: F.A. Cup. **FAT**: F.A. Trophy.

Date	Opponents	Comp.	Res	Gate	1.	2.	3.	4.	5.	6.	7.	8.	9.	10.	11.	Sub.	Sub.
21/08	**YEOVIL TOWN**	GMVC	1-2	1,157	Cooksey	Skelding	Brighton	Webb	Wardle	Shilvock	Carty	Stott	*Hanks*	Crisp(1)	B Gray	O'Meara	
24/08	Macclesfield T.	GMVC	3-4	697	Cooksey	Skelding	Brighton	Webb(1)	Wardle	Burgher	Carty	Stott	Carter(2)	Crisp	*B Gray*		Hanks
28/08	Southport	GMVC	2-1	1,238	Cooksey	Skelding	Brighton	Webb	O'Meara	Shilvock	Carty	Stott	*B Gray*	Crisp(1)	Carter(1)		Hanks
30/08	**ALTRINCHAM**	GMVC	1-2	953	Cooksey	*Skelding*	Brighton	Richardson	O'Meara	Shilvock	*Carty*	Stott(1)	Webb	Crisp	B Gray	Wardle	Hanks
04/09	Witton Albion	GMVC	1-4	739	Cooksey	Skelding	Brighton	Richardson	Wardle	Shilvock(1)	Carty	Stott	Webb	Crisp	*Radburn*	O'Meara	
07/09	**STAFFORD RGRS**	GMVC	3-3	929	Cooksey	Skelding	Brighton	Richardson	O'Meara(1)	*Webb(1)*	Stott	Shilvock	Hanks(1)	Crisp	*Pearce*	Wardle	Radburn
11/09	**GRESLEY RVRS**	FAC1q	*1-1	902	Cooksey	Skelding	Brighton	Richardson	O'Meara	Shilvock	Carty	Webb	Hanks	Crisp	Pearce		
14/09	Gresley Rovers	FAC1qr	1-0	1,222	Cooksey	Skelding	Brighton	Richardson	Wardle	Shilvock	O'Meara	Webb	Hanks	Crisp(1)	Pearce		
18/09	**WOKING**	GMVC	0-0	1,097	Cooksey	Skelding	Brighton	Richardson	Wardle	Shilvock	O'Meara	Webb	*Hanks*	Crisp	Pearce	Devery	
25/09	**BEDWORTH UTD**	FAC2q	2-0	701	Cooksey	Skelding	Brighton	Richardson	Wardle	O'Meara	Carty	Webb	Crisp(1)	Carter	*Pearce*	Radburn(1)	
02/10	**WELLING UTD**	GMVC	1-1	751	Cooksey	O'Meara	Brighton	Richardson	*Wardle*	Skelding	Carter(1)	Webb	Radburn	Crisp	*B Gray*	Pearce	Shilvock
09/10	Solihull Boro.	FAC3q	2-1	816	Cooksey	O'Meara	Brighton	Richardson	Scandrett	Skelding	Carty	Webb	*Radburn*	Crisp(1)	Carter(1)	Pearce	
12/10	Northwich Victoria	GMVC	1-1	667	Cooksey	O'Meara	Brighton	Richardson	Scandrett	Skelding	Burgher	Webb	Crisp	Carter(1)	*Radburn*	Pearce	
16/10	**GATESHEAD**	GMVC	3-0	824	Cooksey	O'Meara	Brighton	Richardson	Scandrett	Skelding	Webb	Stott	*Radburn(1)*	Crisp	Carter(2)	Pearce	
23/10	Rushden & Diam.	FAC4q	3-1	1,521	Cooksey	O'Meara	Brighton	Richardson	Wardle(1)	Skelding	Webb	Stott	*Pearce*	Crisp	Carter(1)	Radburn(1)	
30/10	Stalybridge Celtic	GMVC	2-0	596	Cooksey	Webb	Brighton	Richardson	Wardle	Skelding	Carty	Shilvock(1)	*Pearce*	Crisp(1)	Carter	Radburn	
02/11	**SLOUGH TOWN**	DC2	2-1	692	Cooksey	*Webb(1)*	Brighton	Richardson	Wardle	Skelding	Carty	Shilvock	Radburn	Crisp	Carter	Hanks(1)	
06/11	Halifax Town	GMVC	0-3	1,003	Cooksey	*Stott*	Brighton	Richardson	Wardle	Skelding	Carty	Shilvock	Hanks	Crisp	Radburn		Pearce
13/11	Northampton Town	FAC1	2-1	3,382	Cooksey	Webb	Brighton	Richardson	Wardle	Skelding	Shilvock(1)	Stott	*Radburn*	Crisp	Carter(1)	Pearce	
20/11	Bath City	GMVC	1-0	623	Cooksey	Webb(1)	Brighton	Richardson	Wardle	Skelding	Shilvock	Stott	*Radburn*	Crisp	Carter	Pearce	
27/11	**MERTHYR TYDFIL**	GMVC	3-3	914	Cooksey	Webb	Brighton	Richardson	Shilvock	Skelding	Pearce	Stott(2)	Radburn	Crisp	Carter(1)		
04/12	Yeovil Town	FAC2	2-0	5,462	Cooksey	Webb(1)	Brighton	Richardson	Wardle	Skelding	Shilvock	Stott	*Radburn(1)*	Crisp	Carter		Pearce
11/12	Yeovil Town	GMVC	3-2	1,721	Cooksey	Webb	Brighton	Richardson	Wardle	Skelding	Radburn	Stott	*Hanks*	Crisp	Carter(3)		Carty
14/12	Welling United	DC3	2-1	320	Cooksey	Webb	Brighton	Richardson	Wardle	Skelding	Radburn(1)	Stott(1)	*Taylor*	Crisp	Carter		Hanks
18/12	**STALYBRIDGE C.**	GMVC	2-0	1,695	Cooksey	Webb	Brighton	Richardson	Wardle(1)	Skelding	Radburn	Stott	Hanks(1)	Crisp	*Carter*		Carty
27/12	**KIDDERMINSTER**	GMVC	0-3	3,938	Cooksey	Radburn	Webb	Richardson	Wardle	Skelding	Burgher	Stott	*Hanks*	Crisp	Carter		Carty
01/01	Dover Athletic	GMVC	3-4	1,586	Green	Webb	Shilvock	Richardson	Wardle	Skelding	*Radburn(1)*	Stott	Hanks(1)	Crisp(1)	*Carter*	Taylor	Carty

03/01	Stafford Rangers	GMVC	0-0	989	Green	Webb	Brighton	Richardson	Wardle	Skelding	Radburn	Stott	Taylor	Crisp	Carter			
08/01	**BARNSLEY**	FAC3	1-2	4,893	Green	Webb	*Brighton*	Richardson	Wardle	Skelding	Shilvock	Stott	Radburn	Crisp(1)	Carter		Hanks
15/01	Gateshead	GMVC	1-0	561	Green	Webb	Shilvock	Richardson	Wardle	Skelding	*Radburn*	Stott(1)	Taylor	Crisp	B Gray		Hanks
18/01	**MOOR GREEN**	WSC2	3-0	725	Green	Webb	Shilvock	Richardson	Wardle	*Skelding*	Radburn	Stott	Taylor	Crisp(1)	Hanks(2)		O'Meara
22/01	Waterlooville	FAT1	1-1	300	Green	Webb(1)	Brighton	Richardson	Wardle	Skelding	Shilvock	Stott	Taylor	*Crisp*	*Hanks*	Pearce	Carter
25/01	**WATERLOOVILLE**	FAT1r	2-1	1,026	Green	Webb	Brighton	Richardson	Wardle	Skelding	Burgher(1)	Stott	*Taylor*	Crisp	Carter(1)		Pearce
29/01	**MACCLESFIELD**	GMVC	3-0	1,701	Green	Webb(1)	Brighton	Richardson(1)	Wardle	Skelding	*Pearce*	Stott	Taylor	Crisp	Carter	Devery(1)	
01/01	**YEOVIL TOWN**	DCsf(1)	1-2	1,175	Green	Webb(1)	Brighton	Richardson	Wardle	Skelding	Shilvock	Stott	Taylor	*Burgher*	Carter	Devery	
05/02	Altrincham	GMVC	3-2	673	Green	Webb(1)	Brighton	Richardson	Wardle	Skelding	Shilvock	Stott(1)	*Radburn*	Crisp	Carter(1)		Pearce
12/02	Grays Athletic	FAT2	2-1	494	Green	Webb	Brighton	Richardson	Wardle	Skelding	Shilvock	Stott	*Radburn*	Crisp(1)	Carter(1)		Pearce
19/02	**NORTHWICH V.**	GMVC	0-0	1,017	Green	Webb	Brighton	Richardson	Wardle	Skelding	Shilvock	Stott	Pearce	*Crisp*	Carter		B Gray
01/03	Yeovil Town	DCsf(2)	1-0	1,922	Green	Skelding	Brighton	Richardson	*Wardle*	Clarke	Radburn	Stott	*Taylor*	Webb	Carter	B Gray(1)	Burgher
05/03	Woking	FAT3	2-3	2,342	Green	Skelding	Brighton	Richardson	Wardle	Clarke	B Gray	Stott	*Taylor*	Webb(2)	Carter		Devery
08/03	**SOLIHULL BOR.**	WSCsf	3-0	798	Green	Skelding	Brighton	Richardson	Webb	Clarke	Burgher	Wardle	*Taylor(1)*	*B Gray(1)*	Carter(1)	Shilvock	Pearce
12/03	**RUNCORN**	GMVC	0-0	998	Green	Skelding	Brighton	Richardson	Wardle	Clarke	Webb	Stott	Taylor	*B Gray*	*Carter*	Shilvock	Pearce
15/03	Woking	GMVC	0-0	1,192	Green	Skelding	Brighton	Richardson	Wardle	Burgher	O'Meara	*Hodges*	Devery	Stott	Webb		B Gray
19/03	**KETTERING T.**	GMVC	0-4	1,253	Green	Skelding	Brighton	Webb	Wardle	Masefield	O'Meara	Stott	Devery	*Crisp*	*Shilvock*	Pearce	B Gray
22/03	**DAGENHAM & R.**	GMVC	2-0	739	Green	Skelding	Brighton	Richardson	Wardle	Burgher	*Masefield*	Stott(1)	Webb	Crisp(1)	*Radburn*	Pearce	Devery
26/03	Dagenham & Red.	GMVC	2-4	763	Green	Skelding	Brighton	Richardson	Wardle	Masefield	Webb	Stott(1)	*Devery*	Crisp	*Radburn(1)*	M Gray	B Gray
29/03	**TELFORD UTD**	GMVC	0-5	808	Green	Webb	McKeever	Burgher	Wardle	Skelding	*Masefield*	Stott	*B Gray*	Crisp	Radburn	Pitcher	Devery
02/01	**SLOUGH TOWN**	GMVC	0-1	752	Green	Skelding	O'Meara	Webb	Holmes	Gaunt	Carter	Stott	*Masefield*	Crisp	*Radburn*	Pearce	Devery
05/04	Kidderminster H.	GMVC	1-1	4,438	Green	Skelding(1)	O'Meara	Webb	Holmes	Gaunt	Burgher	Stott	Crisp	B Gray	Carter		
09/04	**WITTON ALBION**	GMVC	3-3	725	Green	Skelding	Brighton	Richardson	Holmes	Gaunt	*Crisp*	Stott(1)	Webb	*B Gray(1)*	Carter(1)	Taylor	Radburn
12/04	Telford United	GMVC	0-0	676	Green	Skelding	Brighton	Richardson	Holmes	Gaunt	Burgher	*Stott*	Taylor	Webb	Carter		Crisp
14/04	Slough Town	GMVC	1-1	538	Green	Skelding	Brighton(1)	Richardson	Holmes	Gaunt	Burgher	*Webb*	Taylor	Crisp	Carter	Masefield	
16/04	**SOUTHPORT**	GMVC	2-2	890	Green	Skelding	Brighton	Richardson	Holmes	Gaunt	Webb	Stott	Taylor(1)	*Crisp*	Radburn(1)	Masefield	
19/04	**DOVER ATH.**	GMVC	1-2	867	Green	*Masefield*	Brighton	Richardson	Holmes	*Skelding(1)*	Burgher	Stott	Taylor	Webb	*Radburn*	Pearce	O'Meara
23/04	Welling United	GMVC	1-1	655	Green	Skelding	O'Meara	Richardson	Holmes	Gaunt	Brighton	Stott	Taylor(1)	Webb	*Devery*		Young
26/04	Runcorn *(at Witton)*	GMVC	1-4	348	Green	Skelding	O'Meara	Richardson	Holmes	Gaunt	Burgher(1)	Stott	Taylor	Webb	Brighton		
30/04	**BATH CITY**	GMVC	0-1	843	Green	Skelding	Brighton	Richardson	Clarke	Gaunt	*Radburn*	Stott	Taylor	Webb	*Carter*	Shilvock	B Gray
02/05	Merthyr Tydfil	GMVC	1-2	514	Green	Skelding	*Brighton*	Richardson	Clarke	*Gaunt*	Young	Stott(1)	Taylor	Burgher	Carter	Masefield	B Gray
04/05	**HALIFAX TOWN**	GMVC	1-0	1,050	Green	Skelding	Young	Richardson	Clarke	Gaunt	B Gray	Stott(1)	Taylor	Burgher	Carter		
07/05	Kettering Town	GMVC	1-0	2,620	Green	Skelding	Carter	Richardson	Clarke(1)	Gaunt	Young	Stott	Taylor	Shilvock	B Gray		
11/05	Kidderminster H.	WSCf(1)	1-1	1,235	Green	Masefield	Carter(1)	Richardson	Clarke	Gaunt	Young	Stott	Taylor	Shilvock	Burgher		
13/05	**KIDDERMINSTER**	WSCf(2)	4-0	1,796	Green	Masefield	Carter(2)	Richardson	Clarke	Gaunt	*Burgher*	Stott	Taylor(1)	Young	Pearce(1)		Radburn

Bromsgrove Rovers

BOBBY HOPE

Bobby Hope was born in Bridge of Allan, Scotland. He began his playing career with West Bromwich Albion whom he joined in 1959 as a junior. He went on to make over 330 appearances at The Hawthorns before moving on to Birmingham City and Sheffield Wednesday. Bobby represented Scotland at Schoolboy, Under-23 and twice at Full International level.

He is now in his second spell in charge of Bromsgrove Rovers after leaving for a brief period with Burton Albion. His excellent leadership qualities carried the club to the Beazer Homes League championship in 1992 and thus into the GM Vauxhall Conference for the first time.

Rovers have continued to excel under Bobby Hope in the top flight of non-League football. In their first season they finished runners-up behind Martin O'Neill's Wycombe Wanderers, then in 1993-94, despite indifferent league form, they won the Worcestershire Senior Cup beating Conference champions Kidderminster in the final and enjoyed a sensational run to the Third Round Proper of the FA Cup.

Steve Stott hits the ball upfield as Bromsgrove win 3-1 at Rushden & Diamonds in the FA Cup.
Photo - Paul Dennis.

Programme details:
40 pages for £1

Any other club publications:

Local Newspapers:
Bromsgrove Advertiser
Bromsgrove Messenger

Local Radio Stations:
BBC Hereford & Worcester.

BROMSGROVE ROVERS - PLAYING SQUAD

Player	Honours	Birthplace and date	Transfer Fees	Previous Clubs
GOALKEEPERS				
Ron Green		Birmingham 3/10/56		Alvechurch, Walsall, Shrewsbury, Bristol R, Scunthorpe, Walsall, Kidderminster, Colchester
DEFENDERS				
Kevin Richardson	ESP, BHL FAXI	Walsall 22/11/62		Pelsall V, Sutton C, Stafford R, Worcester, Sutton C, Alvechurch, Hednesford T
Stewart Brighton	ESP, BHL, FAXI	Bromsgrove 3/10/66		Crewe Alexandra
Paul Wardle	BHL	Burton 1/2/70		Belper T, Denaby Utd
Jimmy Skelding	BHL	Bilston 30/5/64		Bilston T, Wolves, Bromsgrove R, Burton Alb, Worcester C
Scott McKeevor				Youth team
MIDFIELDERS				
Paul Webb	ESP, BHL, FAXI	Wolverhampton 30/11/67		Bilston T, Shrewsbury
Symon Burgher	BHL	Birmingham 29/10/66		Exeter C, Redditch Utd
Rob Shilvock	SLM, SLC, WML, BSC	Birmingham 26/10/61		Halesowen T, Bromsgrove R, Kidderminster H, Halesowen T
Shaun O'Meara	BHL, WSC	Bromsgrove		Bromsgrove R, Stourbridge, Alvechurch, Bromsgrove R, Worcester C
Mark Crisp	BHL	Birmingham		Smethwick, Redditch Utd, Bromsgrove R, Alvechurch
Steve Stott	BHL	Leeds 3/2/65		Bromsgrove R, Alvechurch
Lee Young		Stourbridge 9/3/71		Dudley T, Lye T, Halesowen T, Dudley T, Stourbridge
FORWARDS				
Brian Gray		Birmingham		Birmingham City
Steve Taylor		Birmingham	Small Fee	Rushall Olympic
Recky Carter	SLM	Birmingham 19/10/71	4-fig	Northfield T, Fairfield V, Kidderminster H, Worcester C, Malvern T, Solihull B
Chris Pearce		Birmingham		Aston Villa
Colin Radburn		Birmingham		Sutton Coldfield T
Brendan Devery		Birmingham		Birmingham C, Moor Green
Scott Crane		Birmingham		Evesham Utd

Departures during season:
Scott Cooksey (Peterborough Utd), Chris Hanks (Gresley Rovers), Paul Carty (Stafford Rangers).

Players on loan during season:
Nicky Clarke (Mansfield T.), Paul Masefield & Steve Holmes (Preston), Craig Gaunt (Scarborough).

Victoria Ground, Bromsgrove

Address and telephone number: Victoria Ground, Birmingham Road, Bromsgrove, Worcs, B61 0DR Tel: 0527 876949 (Office + fax), 0527 878260 (Social Club). Club Newsline: 0891 884496.

Simple directions: The Victoria Ground is situated on the north side of Bromsgrove on the Birmingham Road, which is off the A38 Bromsgrove by pass. The M5 and M42 join the A38 to the north of the town making it easy to get to the ground without having to go into town. The 144 Midland Red bus runs from New Street Station Birmingham and passes the ground.

Capacity: 4,893 **Seated:** 400 **Covered terracing:** 2,152

Record Attendance: 7,389 v Worcester City - 1957.

Club Shop: Sells all kinds of replica clothing & souvenirs. Contact Doug Bratt (0527 874997).

Social Facilities: Victoria Club (0527 878260) - Serves hot & cold food. Big screen satellite TV, pool table & darts. Open matchdays, Sunday 12.00-2.00 and week-day evenings.

Previous Grounds: Old Station Road 1885-1887, Recreation Ground 1887-1889, Churchfields 1889-1891, Well Lane 1891-1910.

Bromsgrove Fact File

Nickname: Rovers or Greens

Club Sponsors: All Saints of Bromsgrove.

Previous Leagues: Birmingham Combination 1910-1953, Birmingham/West Midlands League 1953-1973, Southern League (Northern Division) 1973-1979, Southern League (Midland Division) 1979-1986, Southern League (Premier Division) 1986-1992.

Club colours: Green & white stripes/black/green.

Change colours: All red.

Reserve team's league: Midland Combination Reserve Division.

Midweek home matchday: Tuesday (7.30pm)

Record win: 11-0; v Hinckley Ath. 1970; v Halesowen Town 'A' 1939.

Record defeat: 0-12 v Aston Villa 'A' 1939.

Record transfer fee paid: £3,000 for Recky Carter (Solihull Borough) 93-94.

Record transfer fee received: Undisclosed for Scott Cooksey (Peterborough) December 1993.

1992/93 Captain: Kevin Richardson

1992/93 Top scorer: Recky Carter

1992/93 Player of the Year (Sponsors', Players' & Supporters'): Steve Stott

Club record goalscorer: Chris Hanks 238, 1983-84

Record appearances: Shaun O'Meara 763, 1975-94

Past players who progressed to the Football League: Mike McKenna (Northampton 1946), Ray Hartle (Bolton 1952), Angus McLean (Bury 1953), Alan Smith (A.Villa 1954), Mike Deakin (C Palace 1954), Brain Puster (Leicester 1958), Tom Smith (Sheff Utd 1978), Malcolm Goodman (Halifax 1979), Steve Smith (Walsall 1980), Gary Hackett (Shrewsbury 1983), Bill McGarry, Martyn O'Connor (C Palace 1992), Scott Cooksey (Peterborough 1993)

Club Honours: Vauxhall Conference R-up 1992-93; Southern League Premier Champions 1991-92; Southern League Prem. R-up 1986-87; Southern League Mid. Champions 1985-86; Bill Dellow Cup Winners 1985-86; Southern League Champions v Cup Winners Cup Winners 1992-93; Worcester Senior Cup Winners 1946-47, 1947-48, 1959-60, 1986-87, 1993-94; Birmingham Senior Cup Winners 1946-47; West Midlands League Champions 1960-61; Birmingham Combination Champions 1946-47.

DAGENHAM & REDBRIDGE

Formed:
1992

President:
Barry East BSC

Joint Chairmen:
Dave Andrews
Norman Sparrow

Football Secretary:
Derek Almond

Manager:
Dave Cusack

Physiotherapist:
Jim Stannard

Press Officer:
Steve Warren

A season of promise and high expectation turned sour early on for the championship favourites as injuries to a number of key players contributed to the Essex club's inauspicious start to their campaign.

The loss of the experienced and influential skipper Tony Pamphlett, who ultimately missed the entire season, and Paul Cavell, top-scorer for the last two seasons, who didn't kick a ball for the Reds until the turn of the year, badly disrupted manager John Still's plans. Add to this the absense of newly appointed skipper Jason Broom for half the season, and it is easy to appreciate why the club failed to live up to its pre-season billing.

The cup competitions provided mixed fortunes with good progress in the FA Cup undone with a very disappointing 4th qualifying round replay defeat at home to Cambridge City. Likewise, the FA Trophy yielded an excellent victory at Kidderminster in the 1st Round but despair followed with a home defeat at the hands of the competition's eventual winners, Woking, at the next stage.

Grays Athletic eliminated the club at the 2nd round stage of the Essex Senior Cup, whilst the semi-final was reached in the newly entered London Challenge Cup, but Uxbridge were the surprise victors on that occasion by 3 goals to 1.

Early in 1994, following a run of defeats, the club were struggling just one place off the bottom of the league table albeit with several matches in hand over the clubs above them. Happily, improved form which saw just two defeats in their remaining fourteen fixtures, lifted the club to a respectable final placing of sixth. Highlights were few and far between, but the 8-1 trouncing of Woking, which was born out of one of the best attacking performances ever seen in the Conference, made up for many indifferent displays throughout the season.

The club also benefitted financially from the sale of striker Juan Miguel Desouza to Football League side Birmingham City, and the consistent performances of other players attracted scouts from top clubs from all over the country.

All in all though the season was largely unsuccessful, but the club remains ambitious in its immediate aim of achieving a football league place and the new season is eagerly awaited by all at Victoria Road when a strong challenge for the Conference title is expected.

Steve Warren, Press Officer

Dagenham & Redbridge. Back Row (L-R): Physio, T Pamphlett, P Richardson, J McKenna, M Nuttell (now Rushden), S Conner, M Walsh, B Mayes, G Owers, J Broom, P Cavell, J Still (Manager, now Peterborough). Front Row: G Butterworth, G Blackford, P Watts, P Shirtliff (now Gateshead), G Stebbing. Photo - V J Robertson.

DAGENHAM *MATCHFACTS 93-94* ***DAGENHAM*** *MATCHFACTS 93-94* ***DAGENHAM*** *MATCHFACTS 93-94*

Key: Home fixtures are denoted by bold capitals. Numbers in brackets after players names indicate goals scored (asterisks by the results denote own goals). Only used substitutes are listed - substituted players are *italicised*.

Key to Competitions: GMVC: GM Vauxhall Conference. **DC**: Drinkwise (GM Vauxhall Conference) Cup. **ESC**: Essex Senior Cup. **LCC:** London Challenge Cup. **FAC**: FA Cup. **FAT**: FA Trophy. **Fr.**: Friendly.

Date	Opponents	Comp.	Res	Gate	1.	2.	3.	4.	5.	6.	7.	8.	9.	10.	11.	Sub.	Sub.
21/08	**SOUTHPORT**	GMVC	3-3	1,234	McKenna	Stebbing	Watts(1)	Butterworth	Conner	Richardson	Owers	*Bacon*	Jones(1)	Crown	Blackford	De Souza(1)	
24/08	Yeovil Town	GMVC	1-2	3,349	McKenna	Stebbing	Watts	Butterworth	Conner	Rich'son	De Souza(1)	Bacon	Crown	Jones	*Blackford*		Martin
28/08	Stafford Rangers	GMVC	0-2	884	McKenna	Stebbing	Watts	Butterworth	Conner	Richardson	*Bacon*	*Ramage*	Crown	Jones	De Souza	Crowley	Martin
30/08	**SLOUGH TOWN**	GMVC	1-0	1,371	McKenna	Stebbing	Watts	Butterworth	Conner	Richardson	Reed	Martin	Jones	Crown	De Souza(1)		
04/09	Macclesfield T.	GMVC	0-3	633	McKenna	Stebbing	Watts	Butterworth	Conner	Richardson	*Reed*	De Souza	Jones	*Crown*	Broom	Stimson	Owers
11/09	**HITCHIN TOWN**	FAC1q	1-0	580	McKenna	Stebbing	Watts	Butterworth	Conner	Richardson	Broom	Owers	De Souza(1)	*Crown*	*Blackford*	Cavell	Martin
18/09	**TELFORD UTD**	GMVC	4-1	752	McKenna	Stebbing	Watts	Butterworth	Conner	Reed	Broom(1)	Owers	Cavell(1)	De Souza	Richardson(2)		
20/09	**COLLIER ROW**	ESC1	6-4	346	Foster	Stebbing	Devereux	Fowler	Reed	Parratt	Martin	*Potts(2)*	*Crown(2)*	Kimble(1)	Tekell(1)	Sinclair	Ramage
25/08	**BALDOCK T.**	FAC2q	2-1	677	McKenna	Stebbing	Watts	Butterworth	Conner	Reed	Broom(1)	Owers	De Souza(1)	Cavell	Richardson		
27/09	**DOVER ATH.**	GMVC	2-1	1,423	McKenna	Stebbing	Watts	Butterworth	Conner	Reed	Broom	Diverts	Cavell(2)	De Souza	Blackford		
02/10	Altrincham	GMVC	2-1	641	McKenna	Stebbing	Watts	Butterworth	Conner	Reed	Broom	Owers	*Cavell*	De Souza(2)	Blackford		Crown
09/10	Halstead Town	FAC3q	3-1	850	McKenna	Stebbing	Watts(1)	Butterworth	Conner	Reed	Broom	Owers	Crown(1)	De Souza(1)	Parratt		
12/10	Welling United	GMVC	0-0	895	McKenna	Stebbing	Watts	Butterworth	Conner	Reed	Broom	Owers	Crown	De Souza	Richardson		
16/10	**HALIFAX TOWN**	GMVC	3-0	1,303	McKenna	Stebbing	Watts	Butterworth	Conner	Reed	Broom(2)	Owers	Crown	De Souza(1)	Rich'son		
18/10	**GRAYS ATH.**	ESC2	1-3	280	Foster	Tekell	Devereux	Reed	Fowler	Martin	Parratt	Richardson	Kimble(1)	Ramage	Blackford	Double	
23/10	Cambridge City	FAC4q	2-2	1,026	McKenna	Stebbing	Watts	Butterworth	Conner	Reed	Broom	Owers	Crown	De Souza	Richardson(2)		Kimble
25/10	**CAMBRIDGE C.**	FAC4qr	0-2	1,410	McKenna	Stebbing	Watts	Butterworth	Conner	*Reed*	Broom	Owers	*Crown*	De Souza	Blackford	Martin	Kimble
30/10	Witton Albion	GMVC	1-1	692	McKenna	Stebbing	Watts	Butterworth	Conner	Reed	Broom	*Owers*	Walsh	De Souza	Blackford(1)		Parratt
02/11	Dover Athletic	DC2	2-1	749	McKenna	Stebbing	Ramage	Butterworth	Conner	Reed	Broom(2)	Parratt	Walsh	De Souza	Blackford		
06/11	**KIDDERMINSTER**	GMVC	1-1	1,164	McKenna	Stebbing	Watts	Butterworth	Conner	Reed	Broom	*Parratt*	Walsh	De Souza	*Martin*	Owers(1)	Crown
13/11	**WEST HAM UTD**	Fr.	1-1	2,200	Foster	Stebbing	Watts	Butterworth	Conner	Reed	Broom	Owers	Walsh	De Souza	Richardson(1)		
20/11	Gateshead	GMVC	1-3	441	McKenna	Stebbing	Watts	Butterworth	Conner	Reed	Broom	*Owers*	Walsh	De Souza(1)	Rich'son	Blackford	
27/11	**NORTHWICH V.**	GMVC	1-1	686	McKenna	Stebbing	Watts	Butterworth	Conner	Richardson(1)	Broom	Owers	*Walsh*	De Souza	Blackford		Crown
04/12	**CHARLTON RES.**	Fr.	1-3	150	Foster	Stebbing	Watts	Butterworth	Conner	*Reed*	Broom	Richardson	De Souza(1)	Cox	Blackford		Owers
11/12	Merthyr Tydfil	GMVC	0-0	486	McKenna	Stebbing	Watts	Butterworth	Conner	Richardson	Broom	Owers	Mettioui	De Souza	Blackford		
13/12	**YEOVIL TOWN**	DC3	1-2	455	McKenna	Stebbing	Watts	Butterworth	Conner	*Blackford*	Broom	*Owers*	Mettioui	De Souza	Richardson	Crown(1)	Parratt

18/12	Telford United	GMVC	0-0	647	McKenna	Stebbing	Watts	Butterworth	Conner	Richardson	Broom	Parratt	Crown	De Souza	Blackford		
27/12	**KETTERING T.**	GMVC	2-3	1,376	McKenna	Stebbing	Watts	Butterworth	Conner	Richardson	Broom(1)	*Parratt*	Crown(1)	De Souza	*Blackford*	Mettioui	Owers
01/01	Slough Town	GMVC	1-3	975	McKenna	Stebbing	Watts	Butterworth	Conner	Richardson	Broom	*Parratt*	Green	De Souza	Blackford		Crown(1)
15/01	Southport	GMVC	0-0	1,472	McKenna	Stebbing	Watts	Butterworth	Conner	Filson	Broom	Greaves	*Cavell*	Green	Blackford		Crown
22/01	Kidderminster	FAT1	2-0	1,587	McKenna	Stebbing	Watts	Butterworth	Conner	Filson	*Broom*	Greaves	Cavell(1)	Greene(1)	Blackford	Richardson	
26/01	Barnet	LCC1	1-0	217	Foster	Fowler	Watts	Butterworth	Logan	*Turnbull*	Parratt	Richardson	Cavell	Crown(1)	*Blackford*	Lingley	Double
29/01	**ALTRINCHAM**	GMVC	3-0	1,047	McKenna	Stebbing	Watts	Butterworth	Conner	Filson	Richardson	*Greaves*	Cavell	Greene(2)	Blackford		Crown(1)
05/02	Kidderminster	GMVC	1-2	4,358	McKenna	Stebbing	Watts	Butterworth	Conner	Filson	Richardson	*Greaves*	Cavell(1)	Greene	Blackford		Crown
12/02	**WOKING**	FAT2	1-2	1,769	McKenna	Stebbing	Watts	Butterworth	Conner	Filson	Broom	Richardson(1)	Cavell	Greene	*Blackford*	Crown	Greaves
19/02	**STALYBRIDGE**	GMVC	0-1	820	McKenna	Stebbing	Watts	Butterworth	Richardson	Filson	Broom	*Greaves*	Cavell	*Green*	Crown	Wordsworth	Blackford
26/02	Kettering Town	GMVC	1-1	2,161	McKenna	Stebbing	Watts	Butterworth	Conner(1)	Fowler	Richardson	Greaves	Cavell	*Greene*	Blackford		Crown
01/03	Dover Athletic	GMVC	1-1	1,163	McKenna	Stebbing	Watts	Butterworth	Conner	Fowler	Greaves	Richardson	Cavell	Wordsworth(1)	Blackford		
03/03	Erith & Belve.	LCCqf	7-1	175	Foster	Fowler	Turnbull	*Parratt*	Watts	Greaves	Richardson(2)	Crown(2)	Greene(2)	Sorrell	*Cooper*	Wordsworth(1)	Double
05/03	**ARSENAL RES.**	**Fr.**	1-2	300	Foster	Blackford	Greaves	Watts	Fowler	Conner	Sorrell	Stebbing	Cavell	Richardson	*Wordsworth*	Greene	Crown(1)
08/03	**WOKING**	GMVC	3-4	894	McKenna	Stebbing	Watts	Butterworth	Conner	*Filson*	Richardson	Sorrell	Cavell	*Wordsworth(1)*	Blackford	Greene(1)	Crown(1)
12/03	**MERTHYR TYD.**	GMVC	0-1	764	McKenna	Stebbing	Blackford	Butterworth	Conner	Fowler	Richardson	Sorrell	Cavell	*Greene*	Crown	Wordsworth	
19/03	**WITTON ALBION**	GMVC	2-1	708	McKenna	Stebbing	Watts	Butterworth	Conner	Fowler	Richardson	Sorrell	Cavell	Crown(2)	Blackford		
22/03	Bromsgrove Rvrs	GMVC	0-2	709	McKenna	*Parratt*	Watts	Butterworth	Conner	Sorrell	Richardson	Stebbing	Cavell	Crown	Blackford		Greene
26/03	**BROMSGROVE**	GMVC	4-2	763	McKenna	Stebbing	Watts	Butterworth(2)	Conner(1)	Fowler	Richardson	Sorrell	Cavell	Greene(1)	Blackford		
30/04	**BATH CITY**	GMVC	3-0	823	Foster	Stebbing	Watts	Butterworth	Conner	Fowler	Richardson(1)	Sorrell(1)	*Cavell*	*Greene(1)*	Blackford	Wordsworth	Crown
02/04	Runcorn	GMVC	1-2	496	McKenna	Stebbing	Watts	Butterworth	Conner	Livett	Richardson	Sorrell	Cavell	Greene(1)	*Blackford*		Crown
04/04	**YEOVIL TOWN**	GMVC	2-1	923	McKenna	Stebbing	Watts	Butterworth	Conner	Livett	Richardson	Crown(2)	*Cavell*	Greene	Blackford	Wordsworth	
06/04	**RUNCORN**	GMVC	2-1	815	McKenna	Stebbing	Watts	Butterworth	Pearson	Livett	Richardson	Crown	Cavell(2)	Greene	Blackford		
13/04	**WELLING UTD**	GMVC	2-1	854	McKenna	Stebbing	Watts	Butterworth	Conner(1)	Fowler	Richardson	Livett(1)	*Cavell*	*Greene*	Blackford	Payne	Crown
17/03	Northwich Vics	GMVC	2-2	718	McKenna	Fowler	Watts	Butterworth	Conner	Livett(1)	Richardson	Stebbing	Cavell	Greene	Blackford(1)		
19/04	Woking	GMVC	8-1	1,127	McKenna	Stebbing	Watts	Butterworth	Conner(1)	Livett(1)	Richardson(3)	Sorrell	*Cavell(1)*	Greene(2)	*Blackford*	Wordsworth	Payne
21/04	**UXBRIDGE**	LCCsf	1-3	292	Foster	Blackford	*Davis*	Watts	*Fowler*	Richardson	Stebbing	Devereux	Flint	Wordsworth	Payne	Cooper	Mudd
24/04	**MACCLESFIELD**	GMVC	1-1	889	McKenna	Stebbing	Watts	Butterworth	Conner	Livett(1)	Richardson	Sorrell	Cavell	*Greene*	*Blackford*	Payne	Crown
26/04	Stafford Rgrs	GMVC	1-0	547	McKenna	Stebbing	Watts	Butterworth	Conner	Livett	Richardson	Sorrell	Cavell	*Greene*	Blackford		Crown(1)
29/04	Halifax Town	GMVC	1-0	643	McKenna	Stebbing	Watts	Butterworth	Blackford	Livett	Richardson	Sorrell	Cavell	Crown	Payne(1)		
01/05	Stalybridge C.	GMVC	0-5	596	McKenna	Stebbing	Watts	Butterworth	Blackford	Livett	Richardson	Sorrell	Cavell	Crown	Payne		
03/05	**GATESHEAD**	GMVC	1-1	803	McKenna	Stebbing	Watts	Butterworth	Blackford	Livett	Richardson(1)	Sorrell	Cavell	Crown	*Payne*	Wordsworth	
07/05	Bath City	GMVC	0-0	454	McKenna	Stebbing	Watts	Butterworth	Blackford	Livett	Richardson	Sorrell	Cavell	Crown	Wordsworth		

Dagenham & Redbridge

DAVE CUSACK

Dave was appointed as manager at Victoria Road during the summer of 1994 after John Still's move to Peterborough United. His playing career began with Sheffield Wednesday and he went on to make almost 500 Football League appearances for the Owls, Southend, Millwall, Doncaster and Rotherham.

He obtained his first experience of management as player-manager at both Doncaster and Rotherham before joining Boston United midway through the 1989-90 season. Dave then took over as caretaker boss at York Street following the departure of George Kerr and guided the Pilgrims to Vauxhall Conference safety. His reward for that was to be given the post on a permanent basis and he led United to 8th position in the league in his first full season in charge, the club's best finishing position for three years.

However, at the end of that 1991-92 campaign, Dave resigned and joined rivals Kettering. Sadly, it was a trouble-torn time at Rockingham Road and, just two months into the season, he was dismissed by the administrators and replaced by Graham Carr. Dave then resumed his playing career and had spells with both Harworth Cl and Grays Athletic *(where he captained them to success in the Essex Senior Cup - photo opposite)* last term before accepting the post at Dagenham & Redbridge.

David Crown Crown hits a left-foot shot at goal as Dagenham & Redbridge beat Yeovil Town 2-1.
Photo - Paul Dennis.

Programme details:
40 pages for £1
Editor - John Hillier

Any other club publications:
Raise Your Game - Fanzine

Local Newspapers:
Dagenham Post
Waltham Forest Guardian
Ilford Recorder

Local Radio Stations:
Breeze AM
BBC Radio Essex
Capital Radio

DAGENHAM & REDBRIDGE - PLAYING SQUAD 1993-94

Player	Honours	Birthplace and date	Transfer Fees	Previous Clubs
GOALKEEPERS				
John McKenna	ESP, FAXI LSC	Liverpool 21/3/62	5-fig	Everton, Formby, Morecambe, Durban (SA), Mamelodi (SA), Nuneaton B, Boston Utd
DEFENDERS				
Paul Watts	ESP, FAXI, ILP, IL1	London 20/9/62		Barking
Steve Conner	ESP, ILP	Essex 14/7/64	£3,500	Grays Ath, East Thurrock Utd, Tilbury, Dartford
Tony Pamphlett	GMVC, SLP, ILP	London 13/4/60		Cray W, Dartford, Maidstone Utd
Gary Stebbing	EY	Croydon 11/8/65		Crystal Palace, KV Ostend (Belg), Maidstone Utd, Kettering T
Gary Butterworth		Peterborough 8/9/69		Peterborough Utd
Martin Filson	NPL	Manchester 25/6/68		Wrexham, Rhyl, Stalybridge C, Halifax T
MIDFIELDERS				
Jason Broom	ESP, ILP	Essex 15/10/69	£3,000	Eton Manor, Billericay T
Ian Richardson		London		Reserves
Tony Sorrell	GMVC	Bromchurch 17/10/66		Bishop's Stortford, Barking, Maidstone Utd, Peterborough, Colchester, Barnet, Brentford
Gary Blackford		Redhill 25/9/68		Whyteleafe, Croydon, Fisher Ath, Barnet
Lee Fowler		London		Leyton Orient
FORWARDS				
Paul Cavell	ESP, Middx W	Worksop 13/5/63	5-fig	Worksop T, Goole T, Stafford R, Boston Utd
Chris Payne		Brentwood 16/7/69	£6,000	Brentwood, Harlow T, Billericay T
Dennis Greene	GMVC, BLT	Stoke Newington 14/4/65		B Stortford, Harlow, Basildon, Ware, B Stortfd, Saffron W, Chelmsfd, Wycombe
David Crown		Enfield 16/2/58		Walthamstow Ave, Brentford, Portsmouth, Reading, Camb Utd, Southend, Gillingham
Dean Wordsworth		London		Greenwich Borough

Departures during season:
Adrian Owers (Chelmsford), Miguel DeSouza (Birmingham), Steve Greaves (Released), Paul Bacon (Brentford), Danny Tripp (Grays), Eddie Martin (Chelmsford), Kevin Foster (B Stortford), Gary Kimble (Purfleet), Mario Walsh (Heybridge S), Andy Ramage (Released).

Players on loan during season:
Gary Jones (Southend), Ahmed Mettioui (Stafford R), Dennis Greene (Wycombe W), Simin Livett (Camb Utd).

Victoria Road, Dagenham

Address and telephone number: Victoria Road, Dagenham RM10 7XL.
Tel: 081 592 7194. Fax: 081 593 7227. Daggersline: 0891 101965. Fanzline: 0891 101955.
Simple directions: On A112 between A12 & A13. Buses 103 & 174 or, exit Dagenham East tube station, turn left and after approximately 500 yards take 5th turning left into Victoria Road.
Capacity: 5,500 **Seated:** 700 **Covered terracing:** 3,000
Record Attendance: 5,300 v Leyton Orient - FA Cup 1st Rnd - 14.11.92.
Club Shop: Sells programmes, badges, replica shirts, scarves, hats etc. Contact John Hillier for more details.
Social Facilities: Clubhouse open 11.00am -11.00pm on match days. Hot & cold food available.

Dagenham & Red. Fact File

Nickname: Reds or Daggers

Club Sponsors: Barking & Dagenham Post

Previous Grounds: None

Previous Leagues: None

Club colours: Red shirts, red shorts (blue trim), and blue socks.

Change colours: All yellow (navy blue trim).

Reserve team league: Essex & Herts Border Combination.

Midweek home matchday: Monday

Record win: 8-1 v Woking (A), GMV Conference 19/4/94.

Record defeat: 0-5 v Stalybridge Celtic (A), GMV Conference 31/4/94.

Record transfer fee: £30,000 to Boston United for Paul Cavell & Paul Richardson - 1991.

Record transfer fee received: £65,000 from Watford for Andy Hessenthaler - 1991.

1993-94 Captain: Jason Broom

1993-94 Top scorer: David Crown - 13 goals.

1993-94 Player of the Year: Gary Stebbing

Club record goalscorer: Paul Cavell - 31

Record appearances: John McKenna - 106

Past players who progressed to the Football League: Juan Mequel DeSouza (Birmingham City) 1994.

Club Honours: None since amalgamation.

DOVER ATHLETIC

Formed:
1983

Chairman:
Mr J T Husk

Football Secretary:
Mr J F Durrant

Manager:
Chris Kinnear

Physiotherapist:
Frank Brooks

Commercial Manager:
Mr B Greenfield

Press Officer:
Mr J F Durrant

Dover Athletic completed their first season in the GM Vauxhall Conference by finishing a creditable 8th in the table.

Just a few days before the season began, the club paid £50,000 for David Leworthy from Farnborough Town, breaking the transfer record fee paid between non-League teams.

Dover started the new campaign by beating the eventual champions Kidderminster Harriers 3-1 with new signing Leworthy endearing himself to the home fans by scoring twice. By the beginning of September, Dover led the league and, although the home form was good, results away were rather indifferent, but by Christmas the club were maintaining a top six spot.

After the turn of the year, Dover's form at home started to desert them, picking up just one point from the last seven games. By contrast, away performances improved with the team extending a run of seven wins and two draws from the last eight games on the road.

In the FA Cup, a 1st Qualifying round defeat by Kent rivals Sittingbourne after a home replay proved very disappointing. Both games drew crowds in excess of 3,500 and possibly created a record combined crowd 7,000 to watch an FA Cup tie at this early stage of the competition.

In the FA Trophy another disappointing performance, this time in a 3rd round replay at home to Sutton United, ended any hopes of reaching Wembley. After a 0-0 draw at Sutton, Dover held high hopes of progressing further than they had ever been in the competition, but then crashed 3-2 in front of another big home gate.

The cup disappointments continued until the end of the season, losing 2-1 to Margate in the Kent Senor Cup Final.

With the club working very hard during the summer months in complying with the Football League ground grading criteria, confidence of challenging for the title this season is high, and progress into the Football League no longer such a distant dream.

A G Husk, Director

Back Row (L-R): Tom Terry (Asst Physio), Bob Jennings (Physio), David Scott, Tony Dixon, Jason Bartlett, Joe Jackson, Maurice Munden, Nicky Dent, Dave Walker, Steve Cuggy, Corey Browne, Kevin Raine (Scout), Chris Kinnear (Manager). Front Row: Richmond Donkor, Colin Blewden, Tim Dixon, Steve Warner, Barry Little, Nigel Donn, Iain O'Connell, Tony MacDonald, Russell Milton, Paul O'Brien.

***DOVER** MATCHFACTS 93-94*   ***DOVER** MATCHFACTS 93-94*   ***DOVER** MATCHFACTS 93-94*

Key: Home fixtures are denoted by bold capitals. Numbers in brackets after players names indicate goals scored (asterisks by the results denote own goals). Only used substitutes are listed - substituted players are *italicised*.

Key to Competitions: GMVC: G.M. Vauxhall Conference. **DC**: Drinkwise (G.M. Vauxhall Conference) Cup. **KSC**: Kent Senior Cup. **BHCM:** Beazer Homes League Championship Match. **FAC**: F.A. Cup. **FAT**: F.A. Trophy.

Date	Opponents	Comp.	Res	Gate	1.	2.	3.	4.	5.	6.	7.	8.	9.	10.	11.	Sub.	Sub.
14/08	**STOURBRIDGE**	BHCM	2-1	770	Munden	Scott	Bartlett	A Dixon	O'Connell(1)	Walker	Jackson	Browne	Blewden	T Dixon	Milton(1)		
21/08	**KIDDERMINSTER**	GMVC	3-1	1,729	Munden	Scott	Bartlett(1)	A Dixon	O'Connell	Walker	Jackson	Lewis	Blewden	Leworthy(2)	Milton		
24/08	Slough Town	GMVC	0-1	1,074	Munden	*Scott*	Bartlett	A Dixon	O'Connell	Walker	Jackson	*Lewis*	Blewden	Leworthy	Milton	T Dixon	Donn
28/08	Macclesfield T.	GMVC	2-0	836	Munden	Scott	Bartlett	A Dixon	O'Connell	Walker	Jackson	Browne(2)	Lewis	*Leworthy*	Milton		Dent
30/08	**WOKING**	GMVC	5-0	2,220	Munden	Scott(1)	Bartlett	A Dixon	O'Connell	Walker	*T Dixon*	Lewis(1)	Browne(1)	Leworthy(1)	Milton(1)		Donn
04/09	**GATESHEAD**	GMVC	3-1	1,911	Munden	Scott	Bartlett	A Dixon	O'Connell	Walker	Jackson	Browne(2)	Lewis	Leworthy(1)	Milton		
07/09	Merthyr Tydfil	DC1(1)	2-0	330	Munden	Scott	Bartlett	A Dixon	O'Connell(1)	Walker	T Dixon	Lewis	Browne(1)	Leworthy	Milton		
11/09	Sittingbourne	FAC1q	1-1	3,583	Munden	Scott	Bartlett	A Dixon	O'Connell	Walker	T Dixon	Jackson	Browne	Leworthy(1)	Milton		
14/09	**SITTINGBOURNE**	FAC1qr	1-2	3,016	Munden	Scott	Bartlett	A Dixon	O'Connell(1)	Walker	Lewis	Jackson	Browne	Leworthy	Milton		
18/09	**ALTRINCHAM**	GMVC	1-0	1,670	Munden	Scott	Bartlett	A Dixon	O'Connell	Walker	Jackson	Lewis	Blewden	Leworthy(1)	Milton		
21/09	**MERTHYR TYD.**	DC1(2)	2-0	867	Munden	Scott	Bartlett	A Dixon	O'Connell	Walker	T Dixon	Jackson	Browne	Leworthy(2)	Milton		
27/09	Dagenham & Red.	GMVC	0-1	1,423	Munden	Scott	Bartlett	A Dixon	O'Connell	Walker	Jackson	Lewis	*Blewden*	Leworthy	Milton	*Darlington*	T Dixon
02/10	**WITTON ALBION**	GMVC	1-0	1,563	Munden	Scott	Bartlett	A Dixon	O'Connell	Walker	Jackson	Browne(1)	Blewden	Leworthy	Milton		
09/10	**NORTHWICH V.**	GMVC	2-0	1,630	Munden	Scott	Bartlett	A Dixon	O'Connell	Walker	Jackson	Browne(1)	Blewden	Leworthy(1)	Milton		
12/10	Woking	GMVC	0-3	1,822	Munden	Scott	Bartlett	A Dixon	O'Connell	Walker	Jackson	Browne	Leworthy	Milton	*T Dixon*	Darlington	
16/10	Runcorn	GMVC	1-2	637	Munden	Scott	Bartlett(1)	A Dixon	O'Connell	Walker	Jackson	Browne	Blewden	Leworthy	*Milton*		T Dixon
26/10	Bromley	KSC1	3-1	363	Munden	Donn	Bartlett	A Dixon	Scott	Walker	Jackson	Browne	Blewden	Leworthy(2)	Milton(1)		
30/10	Southport	GMVC	2-3	1,569	Munden	Scott	Bartlett	A Dixon	O'Connell	Walker	Jackson	Browne(1)	Blewden	Leworthy	Milton(1)		
02/11	**DAGENHAM & R.**	DC2	1-2	749	Munden	Scott	Bartlett	A Dixon	O'Connell	Walker	Jackson	Browne	Blewden	Leworthy(1)	Milton		
06/11	**MERTHYR TYD.**	GMVC	1-0	1,301	Munden	Donn	Bartlett	A Dixon	O'Connell	Walker	Jackson	Browne(1)	Lewis	Leworthy	Milton		
13/11	Merthyr Tydfil	GMVC	0-0	556	Munden	Donn	Bartlett	A Dixon	O'Connell	Walker	Jackson	*Browne*	Lewis	Leworthy	Milton	Blewden	
20/11	Yeovil Town	GMVC	3-1	2,730	Munden	Donn	Bartlett	A Dixon	O'Connell(1)	Walker	Jackson	T Dixon(1)	Lewis	Leworthy(1)	*Darlington*		O'Brien
27/11	**BATH CITY**	GMVC	0-3	1,820	Munden	*Donn*	Bartlett	*A Dixon*	O'Connell	Walker	Blewden	T Dixon	Lewis	Leworthy	Darlington	Milton	Scott
04/12	**SLOUGH TOWN**	GMVC	0-0	1,119	Munden	Donn	Bartlett	A Dixon	O'Connell	Walker	Jackson	*Blewden*	Lewis	Leworthy	Milton		Scott

11/12	Kidderminster	GMVC	0-3	1,379	*Munden*	Donn	Bartlett	A Dixon	O'Connell	Walker	Jackson	Walsh	Lewis	Leworthy	Milton	T Dixon	
18/12	**HALIFAX TOWN**	GMVC	1-2	1,340	Chivers	*Donn*	Bartlett	*A Dixon*	O'Connell	Walker	Jackson	Walsh	Lewis	Leworthy(1)	Milton	Blewden	Scott
27/12	Welling United	GMVC	0-2	2,022	Chivers	Scott	Bartlett	A Dixon	O'Connell	Walker	Jackson	Walsh	Lewis	Leworthy	*Browne*		Milton
01/01	**BROMSGROVE**	GMVC	4-3	1,586	Chivers	Scott	Bartlett	A Dixon	O'Connell	Walker(1)	Jackson(1)	*Walsh(1)*	Lewis	Leworthy(1)	*Darlington*	O'Brien	Milton
15/12	**TELFORD UTD**	GMVC	0-1	1,525	Chivers	Scott	Bartlett	A Dixon	O'Connell	Walker	Jackson	Walsh	Lewis	Leworthy	Darlington		
22/01	Weston-s.-Mare	FAT1	2-0	575	Chivers	Scott	Bartlett	A Dixon	O'Connell	Walker	Jackson	Browne(1)	Lewis	Leworthy(1)	Milton		
29/01	**STAFFORD R.**	GMVC	2-0	1,270	Munden	Scott	Bartlett	A Dixon	O'Connell(1)	Walker	Jackson	*Browne*	Lewis	Leworthy	Milton(1)		
01/02	Ashford Town	KSCqf	3-0	584	Munden	Scott(1)	Bartlett	A Dixon	O'Connell	Walker	T Dixon	Browne(1)	Lewis	Leworthy(1)	Milton		
05/02	Witton Albion	GMVC	2-1	650	Munden	Scott	Bartlett	A Dixon	O'Connell	Walker	Jackson	Browne	Lewis(1)	Leworthy(1)	Milton		
12/02	Welling United	FAT2	3-1	1,726	Munden	Scott	Bartlett(1)	A Dixon	O'Connell	Walker	Jackson	Browne	Lewis(2)	Leworthy	Milton		
19/02	Stafford Rgrs	GMVC	2-2	760	Munden	*Scott*	Bartlett	A Dixon	O'Connell	Walker	Jackson	Blewden(1)	Lewis	Leworthy	Milton(1)		O'Brien
26/02	Altrincham	GMVC	0-2	743	Munden	Scott	Bartlett	A Dixon	O'Connell	Walker	Jackson	Blewden	*T Dixon*	*Leworthy*	Milton	O'Brien	Donn
01/03	**DAGENHAM & R.**	GMVC	1-1	1,163	Munden	Scott	Bartlett	A Dixon	O'Connell	Walker	Jackson	Browne	Blewden	Donn	Milton		
05/03	Sutton United	FAT3	0-0	1,989	Munden	Scott	Bartlett	A Dixon	O'Connell	Walker	Jackson	Browne	Donn	Blewden	Milton		
08/03	**SUTTON UTD**	FAT3r	2-3	2,207	Munden	Scott	Bartlett	A Dixon	O'Connell	Walker	Jackson	Browne(2)	Blewden	Leworthy	Milton		
12/03	Halifax Town	GMVC	1-0	760	Munden	Scott	Bartlett	*Donn(1)*	O'Connell	Walker	Jackson	*Browne*	Blewden	Leworthy	Milton	Darlington	Hambly
16/03	Welling United	KSCsf	1-0	1,726	Munden	Scott	Bartlett	Donn	O'Connell	Walker	Jackson(1)	Browne	Blewden	Leworthy	Milton		
19/03	**STALYBRIDGE**	GMVC	1-1	1,003	Munden	Scott	Bartlett	Donn	O'Brien	Walker	Jackson	Browne	Blewden(1)	Leworthy	Milton		
22/03	**KETTERING**	GMVC	0-1	947	Munden	Scott	Bartlett	Donn	O'Brien	Walker	Jackson	Browne	Blewden	Leworthy	Milton		
26/03	Telford United	GMVC	1-0	905	Munden	Scott	Bartlett	Donn	O'Connell	Walker	Jackson	O'Brien	Blewden	Leworthy(1)	Milton		
29/03	**WELLING UTD**	GMVC	0-1	953	Munden	Scott	Bartlett	Donn	*O'Connell*	Walker	Browne	O'Brien	Blewden	Leworthy	Milton		Hambly
02/04	**MACCLESFIELD**	GMVC	1-2	942	Munden	Scott	Bartlett	Donn	O'Connell	Walker	Jackson	Browne	Blewden	Leworthy	Milton(1)		
04/04	Kettering Town	GMVC	0-1	2,134	Munden	Scott	Bartlett	Donn	O'Connell	Walker	*Jackson*	*Browne*	Blewden	Leworthy	Milton	Donn	Hambly
09/04	**SOUTHPORT**	GMVC	0-2	942	Munden	Scott	Bartlett	A Dixon	O'Connell	Walker	Donn	Browne	Blewden	Leworthy	Milton		
16/04	Stalybridge C.	GMVC	0-0	594	Munden	Scott	Donn	A Dixon	O'Connell	Walker	Jackson	Browne	Blewden	Leworthy	*Milton*		O'Brien
19/04	Bromsgrove R.	GMVC	2-1	867	Munden	Scott	*Donn*	A Dixon	O'Connell	Walker	Jackson	Browne(1)	Blewden(1)	Leworthy	*Milton*	Bartlett	O'Brien
23/04	**YEOVIL TOWN**	GMVC	0-2	849	Munden	Scott	Bartlett	A Dixon	O'Connell	Walker	Jackson	Browne	Blewden	Leworthy	Lewis		
26/04	Bath City	GMVC	0-0	448	Munden	Scott	Bartlett	A Dixon	O'Connell	Walker	Jackson	Browne	Blewden	Leworthy	Lewis		
30/04	Gateshead	GMVC	2-1	456	Munden	*Scott*	Bartlett	A Dixon	O'Connell	Walker	O'Brien	Browne(1)	Blewden	Leworthy(1)	Lewis		Milton
02/05	MARGATE *	KSCf	1-2	2,300	Munden	Scott	Bartlett	A Dixon	O'Connell	Walker	Jackson	Browne	Blewden(1)	Leworthy	Milton		
04/05	Northwich Vics	GMVC	1-0	416	Munden	O'Brien	Bartlett	A Dixon	O'Connell	Walker	Jackson	Browne	Blewden(1)	Leworthy	Lewis		
07/05	**RUNCORN**	GMVC	2-3	739	Munden	O'Brien	Bartlett	A Dixon	O'Connell	Walker	Jackson	Browne	Blewden	Leworthy(2)	Milton		

* - Played at Gillingham FC

Dover Athletic

CHRIS KINNEAR

Chris Kinnear joined Dover Athletic eight years ago as a player but unfortunately broke his leg. He was appointed manager in November 1985 and won trophies in every season up to 1993-94, Dover's first in the GM Vauxhall Conference. Chris is now recognised as one of the best non-League managers around.

Chris began his playing career with West Ham United as an apprentice professional. He moved on to Leyton Orient before he joined the non-League game with Wealdstone. Successful spells with Maidstone United, Barnet and Dagenham followed before joining Dover Athletic. Whilst with Maidstone and playing in the Alliance Premier League (GMVC), Chris twice won the club's player of the year trophy.

Chris twice guided Dover to the Beazer Homes League championship, the second success, in 1993, earning the the club their long-awaited promotion to the Conference. The first season in the top flight started spectacularly with the club even topping the table. Although they tailed off somewhat in the latter part of the campaign, Chris could still be satisfied with the GMVC debut.

Dover Athletic defender David Scott centre challenges Yeovil Town forwards Paul Wilson and Mark West during the end-of-season Conference fixture at the Crabble.

Photo - Tim Lancaster.

Programme details:
32 pages.
Editor - Chris Collings - 0304 822074

Any other club publications:
'Tales from the River End'
'Dover Sole' (both fanzines)

Local Newspapers:
Dover Express.
East Kent Mercury.

Local Radio Stations:
Radio Kent
Invicta FM

DOVER ATHLETIC - PLAYING SQUAD 1993-94

Player	Honours	Birthplace and date	Transfer Fees	Previous Clubs
GOALKEEPERS				
Maurice Munden	SLP	East London 8/11/63		Charlton Ath, Folkestone, Welling Utd
DEFENDERS				
Jason Bartlett	ESP, SLP	Kent		Folkestone
David Scott	SLP, SLS, E Univ.	Carlisle 15/4/67		Penrith, Hastings T, Canterbury C, Hastings T
Tony Dixon	SLP	London		Erith & Bevedere, Gravesend
Nigel Donn	SLP	Maidstone 2/3/62		Gillingham, Leyton Orient, Maidstone Utd
David Walker	SLP	London		West Ham United
MIDFIELDERS				
Iain O'Connell	SLP	Southend 9/10/70		Southend Utd
Tim Dixon	SLP	Dover 31/12/65		Southampton, Waterford Utd
Corey Browne	ESP, SLP	Enfield 2/7/70		Spurs(Sch), Watford(Sch), Wealdstone, Exeter C, Fulham
Tim Hambley		London		Woodford T, Tower Hamlets
Joe Jackson	SLP	Wolverhampton 22/4/66	£13,000	Wolves, Bilston T, Hednesford T, Willenhall T, Gresley R, Worcester C, Yeovil T
FORWARDS				
David Leworthy	ESP, FAY	Portsmouth 22/10/62	£50,000	Portsmouth, Fareham T, Spurs, Oxford U, Reading, Farnborough T
Russell Milton	ESP KG	London		Arsenal, Double Flower (HK), Instant Dict (HK)
Colin Blewden	SLP, SLC	Pembury 12/8/65	£6,000	Gillingham, Tonbridge, Gravesend
Jermaine Darlington		London 11/4/74		Charlton Athletic
Junior Lewis		Middlesex 9/10/73		Fulham

Departures during season:
Steve Warner (Billericay), Mark Harrop (Gravesend), Steve Cuggy (Margate).

Players on loan during season:
Mario Walsh (Dagenham & Redbridge).

Crabble Athletic Ground, Dover Athletic

Address and telephone number: Crabble Athletic Ground, Lewisham Road, River, Dover. Tel: 0304 822373
Simple directions: Main A2 from Canterbury to Hammonds roundabout, follow directions to Town Centre, left at mini-roundabout right at traffic lights where ground is sign-posted.
Nearest station - Dover Priory. Regular bus service from Town Centre to the ground.
Capacity: 6,240 **Seated:** 1,000 **Covered terracing:** 4,900
Record Attendance: 4,035 v Bromsgrove Rovers, Beazer Homes League April 1992.
Club Shop: Open match days only. Sells home/away programmes, replica shirts home/away, general souvenirs - mugs, bagdes etc. Contact Jean Haves 0304 240041.
Social Facilities: Social Club open 7 days a week. Meals available.
Steward - Gavin Hughes 0304 822306.
Previous Grounds: None

Dover Fact File

Nickname: Lilywhites

Club Sponsors: Countrywide Derv Ltd.

Previous Leagues: Kent League, Southern League.

Club colours: White shirts, black shorts and socks.

Change colours: Yellow shirts, green shirts and yellow socks.

Reserve team league: Winstonlead Kent League Div.2.

Midweek home matchday: Tuesday

Record win: 7-0 v Weymouth 3rd April 1990.

Record defeat: 1-7 v Poole Town.

Record transfer fee: £50,000 for David Leworthy from Farnborough Town - 1993.

Record transfer fee received: £11,500 for Tony Rogers from Chelmsford City 1992.

1993-94 Captain: David Leworthy

1993-94 Top scorer: David Leworthy - 17 goals.

1993-94 Player of the Year: Russell Milton.

Club record goalscorer: Lennie Lee - 160.

Record appearances: Jason Bartlett - 530.

Past players who progressed to the Football League:

Club Honours: Beazer Homes League Premier Division Champions 1989/90, 1992/93; Beazer Homes League Southern Division Champions 1987/88; Beazer Homes League Championship Cup Winners 1990/91; Premier Inter League Cup Winners 1990/91; Southern League Cup Winners 1990/91; Kent Senior Cup Winners 1990/91, Runners-up 1993/4; Knight Floodlit Cup Winners 1987/88, 1988/89.

FARNBOROUGH TOWN

Formed:
1967

Chairman:
Richard Molden
President:
Maurice O'Brien
Football Secretary:
Terry Parr

Directors:
Brian Blewett
Gerry Darcey
John Davies
Alan Gillespie
Peter Gough
Terry Parr
Alan Spaven

Manager:
Alan Taylor
Assistant Manager:
Ken Ballard
Coaches: Mike Savage/Mike Critchell
Physiotherapist:
Alan Morris

Commercial Manager:
Graham Willis

Press Officer:
V Curtis

FARNBOROUGH TOWN BOUNCE STRAIGHT BACK AGAIN

After two seasons in the Vauxhall Conference, we fell backwards to the Beazer Homes League once again. A team had to be brought together with the news that we were to have a new manager - Ted Pearce had retired at the end of the season and Alan Taylor, previously the senior coach took the helm. He produced a squad of players, both young and old, with strategic signings from smaller teams, and brought all these players to the top level.

There were probably three really penetrative signings, those of Chris Boothe from Hanwell Town, Wayne Stemp returning from Bognor and the experienced Trevor Senior joining in November from Weymouth. The defence was tightened up with Dean Coney reverting back to central defence, and the team conceded only 44 goals in their 42 league matches, including five at Bashley and four goals at Gresley and not forgetting the amazing game at home to Chelmsford City with us leading 5-2 at half-time and just scrapping through 7-6. It was one of the memorable games ever at Farnborough.

As the season's end arrived, our last away trip was to Corby. An astonishing 6-0 win, coupled with Cheltenham and Crawley - our closest rivals over most of the season - both losing at home, put Boro's destiny in the hands of the players. A revenge victory of 5-0 at home to Gresley, and the champagne started to flow once again in North East Hampshire. There is no doubt that 'there just ain't no stopping Farnborough Town'.

Farnborough Town - Beazer Homes League champions 1993-94. *Photo - Eric Marsh.*

Key: Home fixtures are denoted by bold capitals. Numbers in brackets after players names indicate goals scored (asterisks by the results denote own goals).

Key to Competitions: BHL: Beazer Homes (Southern) League Premier Division. **DC**: Doctor Martens (Southern League) Cup. **FAC**: FA Cup. **FAT**: FA Trophy. **EFL:** Eastern Floodlit League. **HSC:** Hampshire Senior Cup.

Date	Opponents	Comp.	Res	Gate	1.	2.	3.	4.	5.	6.	7.	8.	9.	10.	11.	Sub.	Sub.
21/08	Atherstone Utd	BHL	0-2	364	Taylor	Stemp	Walters	Broome	Coney	Woods	*Boothe*	Terry	Baker	Read	Horton		Traylen
24/08	**CRAWLEY TOWN**	BHL	1-2	453	Taylor	Stemp	Walters	Broome	Coney	Woods	Traylen	Hanlan	Baker	*Read(1)*	Horton		Terry
28/08	**WORCESTER C.**	BHL	3-1	404	Taylor	Pratt(1)	*Walters*	Broome	Coney	Terry	Traylen(1)	Hanlan	Baker	Turkington	Horton(1)		Jones
30/08	Dorchester T.	BHL	1-0	752	Taylor	Stemp	Pratt	Broome	Coney	Terry	Traylen(1)	Hanlan	Baker	Turkington	Horton		
04/09	**MOOR GREEN**	BHL	1-0	381	Taylor	Stemp	Pratt	Broome	Coney	Terry	Traylen	Read(1)	Baker	*Turkington*	Horton		Jones
07/09	**SOLIHULL B.**	BHL	1-1	343	Taylor	Stemp	Pratt	Broome	Coney	Terry	Traylen(1)	*Read*	Baker	*Turkington*	Horton	Boothe	Jones
18/09	Hednesford T.	BHL	2-0	469	Taylor	Stemp	Pratt	Broome(1)	Coney	Terry	*Jones*	*Read(1)*	Baker	Turkington	Horton	Traylen	Walters
25/09	**CHELTENHAM T.**	BHL	1-1	535	Taylor	Stemp	Pratt	Broome	Coney	Terry(1)	Jones	*Traylen*	Baker	Turkington	Horton	Newbery	
02/10	Burton Albion	BHL	1-2	577	Taylor	Stemp	Pratt	Broome	Coney	Terry	Jones	*Read*	Baker	*Turkington*	Horton(1)	Boothe	Traylen
09/10	**HASTINGS T.**	BHL	3-1	464	Taylor	Stemp	Pratt	*Broome*	Coney	Terry	*Boothe(1)*	Read	Baker	Turkington(1)	Horton(1)	Walters	Traylen
16/10	Worcester City	BHL	2-0	829	Taylor	Stemp	Walters	Jones	Coney	Terry(1)	Boothe(1)	*Read*	Baker	Turkington	Horton		Newbery
23/10	Weymouth	FAC4q	4-1	1,283	Taylor	Stemp	Walters	Jones	Coney	*Terry*	Boothe(1)	Read(2)	Baker	Turkington	Horton(1)		Traylen
26/10	Waterlooville	DC1(1)	2-2	148	Granger	Stemp	Walters	*Broome*	Coney	Traylen	Boothe(1)	Newbery(1)	Baker	Turkington	Horton		Savage
30/10	**CORBY TOWN**	BHL	1-0	461	Taylor	Stemp	Walters	Jones	Coney	Broome	Boothe(1)	Read	Baker	Turkington	Horton		
02/11	**BOURNEMOUTH**	HSC2	7-0	209	Granger	Stemp	Walters	*Broome(2)*	Pratt(1)	*Savage*	Smith(1)	Newbery(2)	Baker	Traylen(1)	Horton	McCaskill	Nash
06/11	Nuneaton Boro.	BHL	1-2	1,140	Taylor	Stemp	Pratt	*Jones*	Coney	Broome	Boothe	Read	Baker	Turkington(1)	Horton		Walters
09/11	**WATERLOOVILLE**	DC1(2)	2-4	279	Taylor	Stemp	Pratt(1)	Terry	Walters	Broome	Boothe(1)	*Traylen*	Baker	*Turkington*	Horton	Newbery	Savage
13/11	**EXETER CITY**	FAC1	1-3	2,069	Taylor	Stemp	Pratt	Broome	Coney	Jones(1)	Boothe	Read	Baker	Turkington	Horton		
20/11	**GLOUCESTER C.**	BHL	1-0	426	Taylor	Stemp	Pratt	Broome	Coney	*Jones*	Boothe(1)	Senior	Baker	Turkington	Horton		Terry
27/11	Hastings Town	BHL	0-1	415	Taylor	Stemp	Pratt	Broome	Coney	Jones	Boothe	Senior	Baker	Turkington	Horton		
30/11	**HORNDEANn**	HSC3	4-0	115	Granger	Smith	Walters	Stemp	Savage(1)	Pratt	Terry	*Jones*	*Newbery*	Senior(2)	Baker	Boothe(1)	McCaskill
04/12	Cambridge City	BHL	5-1	330	Taylor	Stemp	Pratt	Broome	Coney	Jones	Boothe(1)	Senior(1)	Baker	*Turkington*	Horton(2)	Terry(1)	Savage
11/12	**ATHERSTONE**	BHL	1-0	356	Taylor	Stemp	Pratt	Broome	Coney	*Jones*	Boothe	Senior	Baker	Turkington	Horton	*Terry(1)*	Walters
18/12	**HEDNESFORD**	BHL	1-0	440	Taylor	Stemp	Pratt	Broome	Coney	Jones	Boothe	Senior(1)	Baker	Turkington	Horton		

Date	Opponent	Comp	Score	Att	1	2	3	4	5	6	7	8	9	10	11	Sub	Sub
21/12	Crawley Town	BHL	0-1	633	Taylor	Stemp	Pratt	Broome	Coney	Jones	Boothe	Senior	Baker	Turkington	Horton		
27/12	Bashley	BHL	0-5	448	Taylor	Stemp	Pratt	Broome	Coney	Jones	Boothe	Senior	Baker	*Turkington*	Horton	Terry	
01/01	**WATERLOOVILLE**	BHL	3-0	602	Taylor	Stemp	Pratt	*Broome*	Terry	Jones	Boothe	Senior(3)	Baker	Turkington	Horton		Savage
03/01	Sittingbourne	BHL	3-1	1,321	Taylor	Stemp	Pratt	Broome	Terry	Jones	Boothe(1)	Senior(1)	Baker	Turkington	Horton(1)		
11/01	**ALDERSHOT T.**	HSCqf	1-1	2,493	Taylor	Stemp	Pratt	*Broome*	Terry	*Jones*	Boothe	Senior	Baker	Turkington	Horton(1)	Savage	Walters
15/01	Halesowen Town	BHL	3-2	920	Taylor	Stemp	Pratt	Broome	Coney	Jones	Boothe(2)	Senior	Baker(1)	Turkington	*Horton*		Savage
18/01	Aldershot Town	HSCqfr	1-0	4,502	Taylor	Stemp	Pratt	*Broome*	*Coney*	Jones	Boothe(1)	Senior	Baker	Turkington	Savage	Walters	Traylen
22/01	**GRAYS ATH.**	FAT1	1-1	521	Taylor	Stemp	Pratt(1)	*Broome*	Savage	Jones	Boothe	Traylen	Baker	Turkington	Walters		Terry
25/01	Grays Athletic	FAT1r	0-2	277	Granger	Stemp	Walters	Broome	Jones	Terry	Boothe	*Traylen*	Baker	Turkington	Horton	Denny	
29/01	**NUNEATON B.**	BHL	1-2	578	Taylor	Stemp	Walters	Broome	Jones	Terry	*Boothe*	Senior(1)	Baker	Turkington	Horton		Read
05/02	Moor Green	BHL	2-1	252	Taylor	Stemp	Walters	Broome	Jones	Terry	Boothe	Senior(2)	Baker	Turkington	Horton		
08/02	**CHELMSFORD C.**	BHL	7-6	527	Granger	Stemp	Walters	Broome	Jones(1)	*Read(1)*	Boothe(3)	Senior	Baker	Turkington	Horton(1)	Terry(1)	
19/02	**CAMBRIDGE C.**	BHL	2-2	523	Taylor	Stemp	Walters	*Broome*	Pratt	Jones	Boothe(2)	Senior	Baker	Turkington	Horton		Terry
22/02	**DORCHESTER**	BHL	0-0	362	Granger	Stemp	Walters	Broome	Pratt	Jones	Boothe	Senior	Baker	Terry	Horton		
01/03	Trowbridge T.	BHL	0-0	422	Granger	Stemp	Walters	Broome	Pratt	Jones	Boothe	Senior	Baker	Terry	Savage		
05/03	**HALESOWEN T.**	BHL	3-0	529	Taylor	Stemp	Walters	Turkington(1)	Pratt	Coney	Boothe(1)	Senior(1)	*Baker*	Terry	*Jones*	Savage	Read
12/03	Gloucester C.	BHL	1-0	486	Taylor	Stemp	Walters	Turkington	Pratt	Coney	Boothe	Senior(1)	Baker	Jones	*Horton*		Terry
16/03	WATERLOOVILLE	*HSCsf	4-2	168	Taylor	Stemp	Walters	Turkington	Pratt	*Coney*	Boothe(3)	Senior(1)	Baker	Terry	Horton	Broome	
26/03	**BURTON ALB.**	BHL	2-0	538	Taylor	Stemp	Walters	Turkington	Pratt	Coney	Boothe(2)	Senior	Baker	Jones	Horton		
29/03	Cheltenham T.	BHL	1-1	1,559	Taylor	Stemp	Walters	Turkington	Pratt	*Coney*	Boothe(1)	Senior	Baker	Jones	Horton		Terry
02/04	**BASHLEY**	BHL	3-1	529	Taylor	Stemp	Walters	Turkington	Pratt	Terry	Boothe	Senior(1)	Baker(1)	Jones	Horton(1)		
09/04	**SITTINGBOURNE**	BHL	2-1	776	Taylor	Stemp	Walters	Turkington	Pratt	Coney	Boothe(1)	*Senior*	Baker	Jones	Horton(1)		Terry
11/04	Chelmsford City	BHL	0-1	907	Taylor	Stemp	Walters	Turkington	Pratt	Coney	Boothe	Senior	Baker	Jones	Horton		
14/04	Waterlooville	BHL	3-2	336	Taylor	Stemp	Walters	Turkington	Pratt(1)	*Coney*	Boothe(1)	Senior(1)	Baker	Jones	Horton		Terry
16/04	Gresley Rovers	BHL	0-4	656	Taylor	Stemp	Walters	Turkington	Pratt	*Terry*	Boothe	Senior	*Baker*	Jones	Horton	Broome	Read
20/04	Solihull Boro.	BHL	0-0	178	Taylor	Stemp	Walters	Turkington	Pratt	Coney	Boothe	Senior	Baker	Jones	Horton		
25/04	HAVANT TOWN #	HSCf	0-1	932	Taylor	Stemp	Walters	Turkington	Pratt	Coney	Boothe	*Senior*	Baker	*Jones*	Horton	Terry	Read
30/04	Corby Town	BHL	6-0	301	Taylor	Stemp	Walters	Turkington	Pratt	*Coney*	Boothe(3)	Senior(2)	Baker	Jones	*Horton(1)*	Broome	Read
02/05	**GRESLEY R.**	BHL	5-0	818	Taylor	Stemp	Walters	Turkington(1)	Pratt(1)	Coney	Boothe	Senior(2)	Baker	Jones	Horton(1)		
07/05	**TROWBRIDGE T.**	BHL	1-0	784	Taylor	Stemp	Walters	Turkington	Pratt(1)	Coney	Boothe	Senior	Baker	Jones	Horton	Savage	

* - Played at Andover FC # - Played at Southampton FC

Farnborough Town

ALAN TAYLOR

In his playing days, Alan had a promising career with West Ham United and AFC Bournemouth before being forced out of the full-time game by injury.

After a short time at Hillingdon Borough he went to Craven Cottage where he served as Fulham's youth team coach for nine years. It was from Fulham that Alan joined Farnborough Town in 1986 and, apart from a brief spell as manager at Chesham United, he has been at Cherrywood Road ever since serving as Assistant Manager to the long-serving Ted Pearce.

When Pearce stood down in 1993, Taylor took over the top spot. Alan's first season at the helm was more than successful. The club reached the First Round Proper of the FA Cup (leading Exeter City for a long time) and the Hampshire Senior Cup final, and won a second Beazer Homes League championship to earn promotion back to the GM Vauxhall Conference.

Chris Boothe takes the ball around Gresley 'keeper Bob Aston during Farnborough's championship-deciding win.
Photo - Paul Dennis.

Programme details:
40 pages for £1
Editor - Graham Willis (0252 549328)

Any other club publications:
Simon Read's Haircut - Fanzine

Local Newspapers:

Local Radio Stations:

FARNBOROUGH TOWN - PLAYING SQUAD

Player	Honours	Birthplace and date	Transfer Fees	Previous Clubs
GOALKEEPERS				
Maik Taylor	Army Rep BHLP	8/11/63		Basingstoke Town
DEFENDERS				
Bradley Pratt	ILP, BHLP ACDC	Surrey 25/7/63		Camberley, Wokingham, Bracknell, Egham, Farnborough, Nth.Shore(NZ), Woking, Chertsey Town
Wayne Stemp	BHLP	Epsom 9/9/70		Brighton, Woking, Staines T, Bognor Regis Town
Dean Coney	BHLP	Dagenham 18/9/63		Fulham, QPR, Norwich City, Ernest Borel (HK)
Derek Walters	BHLP	Surrey		Staines Town, Egham Town, Windsor & Eton
Mark Jones	Div 2, Div 3, BHLP	Oxford 26/9/61		Oxford Utd, Swindon T, Cardiff C
MIDFIELDERS				
Peter Terry	BHLP	Edmonton 11/9/72		Basingstoke Town, Aldershot, Basingstoke Town
Steve Baker	BHLP	Newcastle 2/12/61		Southampton, Leyton Orient, Aldershot
Brian Broome	BHLP, HiSC, FAXI	Reading 14/4/60		A'shot, Camberley, Farnboro, Wokingham, Farnboro, Bracknell, Aldershot T
Ian Savage	BHLP	Berkshire 30/4/74		Southampton
Jamie Horton	BHLP, HiSC, FAXI	Aldershot 20/4/63		Godalming Town, Ash United
Mark Turkington	BHLP, HiSC,	Aldershot 31/1/64		Chelsea, Farnboro, Woking, Leatherhead, Farnboro, Slough, Farnboro, Aldershot T
FORWARDS				
Chris Boothe	BHLP	London		Hanwell Town
Simon Read	ESP, BHLP, HiSC, HSC	Windlesham 4/4/61		Staines Town, Wycombe Wanderers
Richard Denny		London		Hanwell Town

Departures during season:
Mark Woods (Basingstoke Town), Derek Traylen (Staines Town), Trevor Senior (Weymouth).

Players on loan during season: None.

Guide to honours:
ESP = England Semi-Pro Int., BHLP = Beazer Homes League premier div, ILP = Isthmian League premier division, HiSC = Hitachi Cup, HSC = Hants Senior Cup, ACDC = AC Delco Cup.

Cherrywood Road, Farnborough

Address and telephone number: John Roberts Ground, Cherrywood Road, Farnborough, Hampshire GU14 8UD.
Tel: 0252 541469. Club Newsline: 0898 88 44 07.
Simple directions: M3 exit 4, A325 towards Farnborough, right into Prospect Avenue (club signposted), 2nd right into Cherrywood Rd, ground on right. 20-30 min walk from Farnborough Main, Farnborough North and Frimley BR stations. Whippet mini-bus route 19 passes ground.
Capacity: 4,900 **Seated:** 561 **Covered terracing:** 1,350
Record Attendance: 3,069 v Colchester Utd 9/11/91 (GMV Conference).
Club Shop: Boro' Leisurewear shop sells all types of club leisurewear and matchballs (contact Commercial Manager (0252 549328)). Supporters Club shop sells old progs, scarves, badges etc (contact Sandy Turnball).
Social Facilities: Clubhouse open pub hours and matchdays. Hot pies, bar meals, crisps etc. Darts, pool, fruit machines & jukebox.

Club Fact File

Nickname: The "Boro"

Colours: Yellow (blue pinstripe)/blue/yellow

Change colours: Red/black/red.

Previous Leagues: Surrey Senior 68-72/ Spartan 72-76/ Athenian 76-77/ Isthmian 77-89/ Alliance Premier (GMV Conference) 89-90 91-93/ Southern 90-91 93-94.

Midweek matchday: Tuesday

Reserve Team's League: Suburban League (Western Division)

Best FA Cup season: 3rd Rd Proper replay 91-92 (lost 0-1 at West Ham United after 1-1 draw).

League Clubs defeated in FA Cup: Torquay United 91-92.

Record win: 11-0 v Chertsey Town (H), Spartan League 72-73.

Record defeat: 2-10 v Worplesdon (H), Surrey Senior League Division One 68-69.

Record Fee Paid: £6,000 to Runcorn for Mick Doherty, October 1990.

Record Fee Received: £50,000 from Dover Athletic for David Leworthy, August 1993.

Players progressing to Football League: Dennis Bailey (Crystal Palace & Birmingham City), Paul Mortimer (Charlton Athletic), Tommy Jones (Aberdeen & Swindon Town), Allan Cockram (Brentford).

Club Record Goalscorer (career): Simon Read 200, 1986-1994.

Club Record Goalscorer (season): Simon Read 53, 1988-89.

Club Record Appearances: Brian Broome 500, 1980-1994.

1993-94 Captain: Dean Coney

1993-94 Player of the Year: Steve Baker/ Wayne Stemp.

1993-94 Top scorer: Chris Boothe.

Honours: Southern Lg 90-91 93-94, Isthmian Lg R-up 88-89 (Div 1 84-85, Div 2 78-79), Athenian Lg Div 2 78-79, Spartan Lg 72-73 73-74 74-75 (Lg Cup 74-75), London Spartan Lg 75-76 (Lg Cup 75-76), Hants Snr Cup 74-75 81-82 83-84 85-86 90-91 (R-up 93-94), FA Trophy QF 92-93, FA Vase SF 75-76 76-77.

GATESHEAD

Formed:
1977

President:
J C Thomas

Chairman:
J Gibson

Vice Chairman
P Robinson

Football Secretary:
Clare Tierney

Manager:
Colin Richardson

Coach:
George Cook

Physiotherapist:
Billy Thomson

Press Officer:
Jeff Bowron

Commercial Manager:
Peter Mole

Gateshead recorded their best season since losing their Football League status in 1960. A second consecutive appearance in the Quarter-Finals of the FA Trophy and a final placing of 11th confirmed a continued improvement. However, when a disappointing start realised only one point from the first five games, and the club was still languishing in a relegation position two months later, former Northern Ireland International Tommy Cassidy was replaced by the most successful non-League manager in the North-East, Colin Richardson.

Twice an FA Vase winner at Wembley, the 50-year old wasted no time in improving fortunes. An eight game unbeaten run saw Gateshead enter the New Year just below mid-table. An FA Trophy win over Halesown Town, followed by a hard earned extra-time replay triumph at Gretna, also helped to keep the momentun going. Much travelled striker Paul Dobson was frequently the Tynesiders' scoring hero and, in the third round, it was his superb late hat-trick that saw Gateshead overcome a two goal deficit to reach the last eight of the Trophy at the expense of a shell-shocked Merthyr. A first appearance at Wembley beckoned, only for a needless penalty and a bizarre own-goal to gift Runcorn victory in front of a near 2,000 Tyneside crowd.

Unlike the previous season's unlucky Quarter-Final exit at Wycombe, the response to this latest setback was positive. Indeed, only defeat in the final game against Southport prevented Gateshead from clinching a coverted top six placing. Leading scorer Dobson went on to record an impressive 34 goals, a feat that earned him the *Mail on Sunday* Vauxhall Conference Goalscorer of the Year Award. While the ink was still to dry on that record, another was brought to a close when long-serving goalkeeper Simon Smith announced his retirement from the game at the age of 31 - 450 appearances and 9 years after making his Gateshead debut.

The club received a boost in the close season when main sponsors Cameron Hall Developments extended their backing for another two years. With key players Paul Shirtliff and Michael Farrey due to return after long-term injuries, a sprinkling of new signings, and Colin Richardson about to embark on his first full season at the helm, the Tynesiders are well placed to continue their move towards the top echelons of the Conference.

Jeff Bowron

Back Row (L/R): Simon Smith, Phil Sharpe, Steve Higgins, Keith Notts, Michael Farrey, John Tindler, George Cook (Coach). Centre: Billy Thomson (Physio), Paul Shirtliff, Paul Sweeney, Paul Proudlock, Paul Dobson, Mark Hine, Brian Rowe, Gary Nicholson, Ian Bruce (Kitman). Front: David Corner, Ged Parkinson, Clive Thirkell (Vice-Chairman), John Gibson (Chairman), Colin Richardson (Manager), Peter Robinson (Director), Jeff Bowron (Press Officer), Alan Lamb, Jeff Wrightson.

Key: Home fixtures are denoted by bold capitals. Numbers in brackets after players names indicate goals scored (asterisks by the results denote own goals). Only used substitutes are listed - substituted players are *italicised*.

Key to Competitions: GMVC: GM Vauxhall Conference. **DC**: Drinkwise (GM Vauxhall Conference) Cup. **FAC**: FA Cup. **FAT**: FA Trophy.

Date	Opponents	Comp.	Res	Gate	1.	2.	3.	4.	5.	6.	7.	8.	9.	10.	11.	Sub.	Sub.
21/08	**RUNCORN**	GMVC	2-2	510	Guthrie	Shirtliff	Sweeney	Nicholls	Nobbs	Wrightson	Farrey(1)	Dobson(1)	Borthwick	Proudlock	Adams		
24/08	Witton Albion	GMVC	0-1	706	Guthrie	Shirtliff	*Sweeney*	*Nicholls*	Nobbs	Wrightson	Farrey	Dobson	Borthwick	Proudlock	Higgins	Dalziel	Adams
28/08	**TELFORD UTD**	GMVC	0-2	478	Guthrie	Shirtliff	Dalziel	Higgins	Nobbs	Wrightson	Farrey	Dobson	*Borthwick*	Proudlock	Askew		Rowe
30/08	Stalybridge C.	GMVC	1-2	605	Guthrie	Shirtliff	Dalziel	Nobbs	Corner	Wrightson	*Farrey*	Dobson(1)	Higgins	Proudlock	Askew	Borthwick	
04/09	Dover Athletic	GMVC	1-3	1,911	Guthrie	Shirtliff	Sweeney	*Nobbs*	Corner	Wrightson	Rowe	Dobson(1)	*Payne*	Proudlock	Hine	Borthwick	Higgins
07/09	Altrincham	DC1(1)	3-1	346	Smith	Shirtliff	*Sweeney*	Nobbs	Corner	Wrightson	Farrey(1)	Dobson(1)	*Rowe*	Proudlock(1)	Lamb	Borthwick	Higgins
11/09	**BLYTH SPAR.**	FAC1q	4-0	728	Smith	Higgins	Sweeney	Nobbs(1)	Corner	Wrightson	Farrey	Dobson(1)	*Rowe*	Proudlock	Lamb(2)	Nicholls	
18/09	Bath City	GMVC	3-2	703	Smith	Rowe	*Sweeney*	Nobbs	Corner	Wrightson	Farrey	Dobson(1)	Hine(1)	Proudlock(1)	Lamb		Dalziel
22/09	**ALTRINCHAM**	DC1(2)	3-1	251	Smith	*Rowe*	Sweeney	Nobbs	*Corner*	Wrightson	Farrey	Dobson(1)	Hine	Proudlock(1)	Lamb(1)	Higgins	Cullen
25/09	**CONSETT**	FAC2q	3-1	305	Smith	Shirtliff	*Sweeney*	Nobbs	Higgins	Wrightson(1)	Farrey	Dobson(1)	*Rowe*	Proudlock	Lamb(1)	Borthwick	Nicholls
28/09	Southport	GMVC	1-1	1,237	Smith	Shirtliff	Dalziel	Hine	*Higgins*	Wrightson	Farrey	Dobson(1)	*Nobbs*	Proudlock	Lamb	Borthwick	Cullen
02/10	**SLOUGH TOWN**	GMVC	0-0	618	Smith	Shirtliff	Dalziel	Hine	Corner	Wrightson	Farrey	Dobson	Cullen	Proudlock	Lamb		
09/10	Billingham Syn.	FAC3q	1-1	481	Smith	Shirtliff	Dalziel	Hine	Corner	Wrightson	Farrey	Dobson(1)	*Cullen*	Proudlock	*Lamb*	Borthwick	Nobbs
12/10	**BILLINGHAM S.**	FAC3qr	0-1	383	Smith	Shirtliff	Dalziel	Hine	Corner	Wrightson	Farrey	Dobson	*Nobbs*	Proudlock	Lamb	Borthwick	
16/10	Bromsgrove R.	GMVC	0-3	824	Smith	Higgins	Dalziel	Hine	Corner	Wrightson	Farrey	Dobson	Tinkler	*Proudlock*	Lamb	McDonald	
27/10	**WITTON ALBION**	GMVC	3-0	307	Guthrie	Higgins	Dalziel	Hine	Corner	Wrightson	Farrey	Dobson(3)	Nobbs	Tinkler	*Lamb*	McDonald	
30/10	Yeovil Town	GMVC	2-0	2,747	Guthrie	Shirtliff	Dalziel	Hine	Corner	Higgins	Farrey(2)	Dobson	Nobbs	Tinkler	*Lamb*	McDonald	
02/11	Halifax Town	GMVC	0-3	749	Guthrie	Shirtliff	Dalziel	Hine	*Corner*	Higgins	Farrey	Dobson	Nobbs	*Tinkler*	Lamb	McDonald	Nicholls
06/11	Macclesfield T.	GMVC	1-6	1,033	Guthrie	Shirtliff	Sweeney	*Nicholls*	Corner	Higgins	Farrey	Dobson(1)	Nobbs	Proudlock	Lamb	Dalziel	
20/11	**DAGENHAM & R.**	GMVC	3-1	441	Smith	Shirtliff	Higgins	Hine	Wrightson	Nobbs	Farrey	Dobson(1)	Lamb(1)	*Proudlock*	Parkinson		Rowe(1)
27/11	Altrincham	GMVC	3-0	565	Smith	Shirtliff	*Higgins*	Hine	Wrightson	Nobbs	Farrey	*Dobson(1)*	Lamb(1)	Rowe	Parkinson(1)	Corner	Proudlock
04/12	**STAFFORD R.**	GMVC	0-0	470	Smith	Shirtliff	Higgins	Hine	Wrightson	Nobbs	*Farrey*	*Dobson*	Lamb	Rowe	Parkinson	Corner	Proudlock
11/12	Kettering Town	GMVC	0-0	1,763	Smith	Shirtliff	*Higgins*	Hine	Wrightson	Nobbs	Farrey	*Proudlock*	Lamb	Rowe	Parkinson	Corner	Sharpe

18/12	**WOKING**	GMVC	1-1	579	Smith	Shirtliff	Higgins	Hine(1)	Wrightson	Nobbs	*Nicholson*	*Proudlock*	Lamb	Rowe	Parkinson	Corner	Dobson
01/01	**NORTHWICH V.**	GMVC	1-0	410	Smith	*Shirtliff*	Higgins	Hine	Wrightson	Nobbs	Nicholson	Dobson	Lamb(1)	*Tinkler*	Parkinson	Corner	Proudlock
03/01	**STALYBRIDGE**	GMVC	2-1	572	Smith	Corner	*Higgins*	Hine	Wrightson	Nobbs(1)	Proudlock	Dobson(1)	Lamb	*Tinkler*	Parkinson	Sweeney	Farrey
08/01	Telford United	GMVC	0-0	1,014	Smith	Corner	Higgins	Hine	Wrightson	Nobbs	Farrey	*Dobson*	Lamb	*Rowe*	Parkinson	Tinkler	Proudlock
15/01	**BROMSGROVE**	GMVC	0-1	561	Smith	Corner	Higgins	Hine	Wrightson	Nobbs	*Watson*	Dobson	Lamb	*Nicholson*	Parkinson	Tinkler	Proudlock
22/01	Halesowen Town	FAT1	2-0	936	Smith	Watson	Higgins	Hine	Corner	Nobbs	Sharpe(1)	*Dobson*	Lamb(1)	*Rowe*	Wrightson	Tinkler	Proudlock
29/01	Merthyr Tydfil	GMVC	0-3	421	Smith	Watson	*Higgins*	Hine	Corner	Nobbs	Sharpe	Dobson	Lamb	Gibson	Wrightson		Proudlock
02/02	**ALTRINCHAM**	GMVC	2-1	416	Smith	Watson	*Higgins*	Hine	*Wrightson*	Nobbs	Sharpe(1)	Corner	Lamb	Rowe	Parkinson	Dobson	Proudlock
05/02	**YEOVIL TOWN**	GMVC	2-1	552	Smith	Watson	Higgins	Hine	*Corner*	Nobbs	Sharpe	Dobson	Lamb	Gibson	Parkinson	Proudlock(2)	
12/02	**GRETNA**	FAT2	0-0	402	Smith	Watson	Gibson	Hine	Corner	Nobbs	Sharpe	Dobson	Lamb	Proudlock	Higgins		
15/02	Gretna	FAT2r	1-0	305	Smith	Watson	Gibson	Hine	Corner	Nobbs	Sharpe	Dobson(1)	*Lamb*	Rowe	Higgins		Proudlock
05/03	**MERTHYR TYD.**	FAT3	3-2	503	Smith	Higgins	Cole	Watson	*Corner*	Nobbs	*Sharpe*	Dobson(3)	Lamb	Rowe	Wrightson	Nicholls	Gibson
12/03	**KETTERING T.**	GMVC	0-0	553	Smith	Watson	*Cole*	Nicholls	Wrightson	Nobbs	Proudlock	Dobson	*Lamb*	Rowe	Parkinson	Gibson	Sharpe
15/03	Runcorn	GMVC	1-1	443	Smith	Watson	Cole	Hine	Higgins	Nobbs	Proudlock	*Dobson(1)*	Lamb	Rowe	Parkinson		Sharpe
19/03	**MERTHYR TYD.**	GMVC	0-0	442	Smith	Watson	*Cole*	Hine	Higgins	Nobbs	Proudlock	Dobson	Lamb	Rowe	Parkinson		Nicholls
23/03	**KIDDERMINSTER**	GMVC	0-2	473	Smith	*Wrightson*	Cole	Hine	Higgins	Nobbs	Proudlock	Dobson	*Sharpe*	Rowe	Parkinson	Farrey	Nicholls
26/03	**RUNCORN**	FATqf	0-3	1,807	Smith	Farrey	*Higgins*	Hine	Corner	Nobbs	Proudlock	Dobson	Lamb	*Watson*	Wrightson	Cole	Sharpe
30/03	**MACCLESFIELD**	GMVC	1-0	306	Smith	Wrightson	*Gibson*	Hine	Corners	Nobbs	Proudlock	*Dobson(1)*	Lamb	Watson	Parkinson	Sharpe	Nicholls
02/04	Woking	GMVC	0-1	1,669	Smith	Wrightson	Cole	*Hine*	*Corner*	Nobbs	Watson	Proudlock	Lamb	Rowe	Parkinson	Whitmarsh	Nicholls
04/04	**HALIFAX TOWN**	GMVC	2-1	659	Smith	Watson	Wrighton	Hine	Corner	*Harvey*	*Farrey*	Dobson(2)	Proudlock	Rowe	Parkinson	Whitmarsh	Nobbs
09/04	Stafford Rgrs	GMVC	1-3	685	Smith	*Watson*	Cole	Hine	Corner	Nobbs	Proudlock	Dobson(1)	*Lamb*	Rowe	Parkinson	Whitmarsh	Harvey
12/04	Northwich Vics	GMVC	2-1	536	Smith	Higgins	*Sweeney*	Wrightson	Corner	Nobbs	Proudlock	*Dobson(1)*	Sharpe(1)	Rowe	Parkinson	Lamb	Nicholls
16/04	**BATH CITY**	GMVC	1-0	401	Smith	Watson	*Sweeney*	Wrighton	Corner	Nobbs	Proudlock	*Dobson*	Sharpe	Rowe(1)	Parkinson	Lamb	Nicholls
19/04	Welling United	GMVC	2-1	526	Smith	Watson	*Sweeney*	Hine	Corner	Nobbs	Proudlock	*Dobson(2)*	Sharpe	Rowe	Wrightson	Whitmarsh	Lamb
23/04	Halifax Town	GMVC	1-3	760	Smith	Higgins	*Sweeney*	*Hine*	Wrightson	Nobbs	Proudlock	Dobson(1)	Sharpe	Rowe	Parkinson	Harvey	Lamb
25/04	Kidderminster H.	GMVC	1-1	2,468	Smith	Watson	Wrightson	Hine	Corner	Nobbs	Whitmarsh	Dobson(1)	Lamb	Rowe	Parkinson		
28/04	**WELLING UTD**	GMVC	1-0	303	Smith	Watson	Sweeney	Hine	Corner	Nobbs	*Proudlock*	Dobson	Lamb(1)	Rowe	Wrightson	Whitmarsh	
30/04	**DOVER ATH.**	GMVC	1-2	456	Smith	Watson	Sweeney	*Hine*	Corner	Nobbs	Proudlock	Dobson	*Lamb*	Rowe	Parkinson	Whitmarsh(1)	Cole
02/05	Slough Town	GMVC	1-2	705	Armstrong	Watson	*Sweeney*	Hine	Wrightson	Nobbs	*Whitmarsh*	Dobson	Lamb	Rowe(1)	Parkinson	Proudlock	Corner
03/05	Dagenham & Red.	GMVC	1-1	803	Smith	Parkinson	Cole	Harvey	Corner	Nobbs	Proudlock	*Dobson(1)*	Sharpe	Rowe	Wrightson		Lamb
07/05	**SOUTHPORT**	GMVC	1-3	508	Smith	Parkinson	Cole	*Watson*	Corner	Harvey	Proudlock	Dobson(1)	Sharpe	Rowe	Wrightson	Whitmarsh	

Gateshead

COLIN RICHARDSON

Colin Richardson became Gateshead's fourth manager in four years when he replaced former Northern Ireland international Tommy Cassid in November 1993. He went on to guide the Tynesiders to their highest Vauxhall Conference final placing - eleventh - and the quarter-finals of the FA Trophy.

The most successful manager in North East non-League football, he has won 25 trophies at the five clubs under his guidance; Ferryhill Athletic, Whickham, Blue Star, North Shields and Bridlington Town.

With both Whickham and Bridlington Town he won the FA Vase at Wembley. The Wearside League and Northern League Second Division titles were carried off during a nine year spell at Blue Star. During the 1990s, Colin won the Northern Counties (East) League at North Shields and the Northern Premier League Division One at Bridlington Town. Now 50, his is facing his first full season of Conference management at Gateshead.

Gateshead's Ged Parkinson has to work hard to dispossess Dave Hanson during the Tynesiders' 2-1 home win over Halifax Town on Easter Monday.

Photo - Gavin Ellis-Neville.

Programme details:
28 pages for 80p
Editor - Jeff Bowron (091 482 3242)

Any other club publications:
Supporters Club Broadsheet
'A Different Corner' - Fanzine

Local Newspapers:
Gateshead Post
Newcastle Chronicle & Journal

Local Radio Stations:
BBC Radio Newcastle
Metro Radio

GATESHEAD - PLAYING SQUAD

Player	Honours	Birthplace and date	Transfer Fees	Previous Clubs
GOALKEEPERS				
Simon Smith	NPL, NL, FAXI	Newton Aycliffe 16/9/62		Newcastle Utd, Whitley Bay, Gateshead, Blyth Spartans
DEFENDERS				
David Corner	EY, GMVC, Div 4	Sunderland 15/5/66		Sunderland, Leyton Orient, Darlington
Steve Higgins	NPL, FAT, FAXI	Gateshead 6/10/60		Gateshead, Barrow, Newcastle Blue Star
Paul Shirtliff	ESP, LSC	Hoyland 3/11/62	£5,000	Sheff Wed, Northampton, Frickley Ath, Boston Utd, Dagenham & Redbridge
Anthony Cole		Gateshead 18/9/72		Midlesbrough, St.Johnstone
Ged Parkinson	FAV, NCEL, NPL1	Sunderland 14/11/63		Dawdon CW, Seaham Red Star, North Shields, Bridlington T, Durham C
MIDFIELDERS				
Keith Nobbs		Bishop Auckland 19/9/61		Middlesbrough, Halifax T, Bishop Auckland, Hartlepool Utd
Jeff Wrightson	FAYC	Newcastle 18/5/68		Newcastle Utd, Preston NE
Michael Farrey	Wearside Lge	Gateshead 17/8/65		Chester-le-Street, Whickham
Brian Rowe		Bromsgrove 24/10/71		Doncaster Rovers
Lee Harvey	FAV, NPLC, ERSC	Barnsley 8/6/64		Barnsley, Huddsfld, Scunthorpe, Gainsboro' T, Goole T, Bridlington T, Bradford PA
FORWARDS				
Alan Lamb		Gateshead 30/10/70		Nottm F, Hartlepool U, Halifax (loan), Brandon Utd
Paul Dobson		Hartlepool 17/12/62		Newcastle, Hartlepool, Horden CW, Torquay, Doncaster, Scarborough, Lincoln, Darlington
Phil Sharpe		Leeds 26/1/68		Doncaster, Halifax, Eendracht Wervik(Belg), Union De Centre(Belg), Farsley Celtic
Paul Proudlock		Washington 8/11/63		Sunderland, Birmingham C, Walsall, Carlisle Utd, Darlington

Departures during season:
Steve Adams (Macclesfield), Billy Askew (Spennymoor Utd), Lee Payne (Holland), John Borthwick (Bishop Auckland), Gary McDonald (North Shields), Peter Guthrie (Whitley Bay), Tony Cullen (Jarrow Roofing), Ian Dalziel (Dunston Feds), John Tinkler (Fleetwood), Gary Nicholson (Newcastle Blue Star)

Players on loan during season:
Mark Hine (Doncaster), John Watson (Scunthorpe), Paul Whitmarsh (Doncaster).

International Stadium, Gateshead

Address and telephone number: International Stadium, Neilson Road, Gateshead, NE10 0EF Tel: 091 478 3883 Fax: 091 410 0070.

Simple directions: from the South follow A1(M) to Granada services (Birtley), take right hand fork off motorway marked A194 (Tyne Tunnel, South Shields) follow A194 to first roundabout. Turn right at traffic lights into Neilson Road. By Rail to Newcastle Central Station transfer to Metro System to Gateshead Stadium.

Capacity: 11,750 **Seated:** 11,750 **Covered terracing:** 3,300

Record Attendance: 5,012 v Newcastle United 20/08/84 (Testimonial).

Club Shop: Yes, selling replica shirts, baseball caps, sweatshirts, badges, scarves, programmes, coffee mugs, pennants, fanzines, ski hats. Contact: Tommy Doleman (091 469 688).

Social Facilities: Bar inside Tyne & Wear stand open before, during and after matches. The Stadium Public House adjacent to ground.

Gateshead Fact File

Nickname: The Tynesiders

Club Sponsors: Cameron Hall Developments Ltd

Previous Leagues: Football League Division 3 North 1930-1958, Football Lge Div.4 1958-1960, Northern Counties League 1960-1962, North Regional League 1962-1968, Northern Premier League 1968-1970, Wearside League 1970-1971, Midland League 1971-1972, Northern Premier League 1973-1983, Alliance Premier League 1983-1985, Northern Premier League 1985-1986, Vauxhall Conference 1986-1987, Northern Premier League 1987-1990.

Club colours: Black & white halved shirts, black shorts and socks.

Change colours: All yellow.

Midweek home matchday: Wednesday

Record win: 8-0 v Netherfield, Northern Premier League.

Record defeat: 0-9 v Sutton United - 22/09/90 - GMVC.

Record transfer fee paid: £5,000 for Paul Shirtliff (Dagenham & Redbridge) 1993.

Record transfer fee received: £3,000 from Sunderland for John McGinley - 1981.

1993-94 Captain: Jeff Wrightson

1993-94 Top scorer: Paul Dobson - 34

1993-94 Player of the Year: Paul Dobson

Club record goalscorer: Bob Topping

Record appearances: Simon Smith - 450 - 1985-1994

Past players who progressed to the Football League: Osher Williams (Southampton, Stockport, Port Vale, Preston), John McGinley (Sunderland, Lincoln), Billy Askew (Hull City, Newcastle United), Lawrie Pearson (Hull City, Port Vale), Ian Johnson (Northampton Town), Ken Davies (Stockport).

Club Honours: Football League Division 3 North R-up 1931-32, 1949-50; FA Cup Quarter-Finalists 1952-53; Northern Premier League Champions 1982-83, 1985-86; Northern Premier League R-up 1989-90; Northern Premier League Cup Finalists 1989-90.

Formed:
1911

President:
J S Crowther

Chairman:
S J Brown

Vice Chairman
D C Greenwood

Football Secretary:
Mr B Fielding

Manager:
John Bird

Coach:
Mick Rathbone

Physiotherapist:
Mick Rathbone

Commercial Manager:
Nick Beaumont

HALIFAX TOWN

Season 1993-94 was Halifax Town's first venture into the GM Vauxhall Conference, and everyone's hopes were raised when they won the pre-season Yorkshire Electricity Cup beating Bradford City 4-2.

The season started with the experienced non-League boss Peter Wragg as Manager, but sadly it didn't work out and he left the club at the end of January. John Bird, ex-York City and Hartlepool United was duly appointed.

The highlight of the season was beating West Bromwich Albion in the First Round of the FA Cup in a game screened "live" on SKY television.

In the FA Trophy, after beating Northern Premier League clubs Emley and Spennymoor United, Town went out to eventual finalists Runcorn in a replay at the Shay. Runcorn appear to have been Halifax's "bogey" side as they also inflictd their worst defeat of the season; 5-0.

The transition from the Football League brought many changes on the playing side with Lee Bracey, Jason Peake, Chris Lucketti and David Ridings all being transferred to League Clubs. The balance was re-dressed with Craig Boardman and Alex Jones joining the Shaymen from Peterborough United and Rochdale respectively.

To their credit, the Directors have decided to retain a full-time playing staff for the new season and, with John Bird's desire to bring to the club proven Football League players, the future looks bright as Halifax Town attempt to regain League Status.

The pleasing factor from last season was the tremendous away support this, being highlighted by over 200 going all the way to Dover in the middle of winter.

Halifax Town.

HALIFAX TOWN *MATCHFACTS 93-94* ***HALIFAX TOWN*** *MATCHFACTS 93-94* ***HALIFAX TOWN*** *MATCHFACTS 93-94*

Key: Home fixtures are denoted by bold capitals. Numbers in brackets after players names indicate goals scored (asterisks by the results denote own goals). Only used substitutes are listed - substituted players are *italicised*.

Key to Competitions: GMVC: GM Vauxhall Conference. **DC**: Drinkwise (GM Vauxhall Conference) Cup. **FAC**: FA Cup. **FAT**: FA Trophy.

Date	Opponents	Comp.	Res	Gate	1.	2.	3.	4.	5.	6.	7.	8.	9.	10.	11.	Sub.	Sub.
21/08	**KETTERING**	GMVC	0-0	1,810	Bracey	Barr	Craven	Edwards	Filson	Lucketti	Peake	Ridings	Cameron	Paterson	Gregory		
24/08	Southport	GMVC	*2-2	2,423	Brown	Barr	Craven	Edwards	Filson	Lucketti(1)	Peake	*Ridings*	*Cameron*	Paterson	Gregory	Constable	German
28/08	Slough Town	GMVC	0-2	1,170	Heyes	Barr	Craven	Edwards	Filson	Lucketti	Peake	Greenwood	*Ridings*	Paterson	Gregory	Constable	
30/08	**STAFFORD R.**	GMVC	1-1	1,228	Brown	German	Hardy	Barr	Lucketti	Gregory	Peake	Greenwood	*Constable*	Paterson(1)	Craven	Cameron	
04/09	**YEOVIL TOWN**	GMVC	1-1	1,152	Heyes	German	Hardy	Barr	Lucketti	Constable	Peake	*Greenwood*	*Gregory*	Paterson	Craven	Filson(1)	Megson
11/09	Runcorn	GMVC	0-5	732	Heyes	Craven	*Hardy*	Edwards	Lucketti	*Ridings*	Peake	Saunders	Hanson	Paterson	Constable	Edwards	Gregory
17/09	**WITTON ALBION**	GMVC	0-0	1,099	Heyes	*German*	Barr	Lucketti	Edwards	Megson	Peake	Saunders	Constable	Paterson	Craven		Filson
25/09	Woking	GMVC	6-2	1,848	Heyes	Filson	Lucketti	Edwards	*Barr*	Megson	Peake(1)	Constable	Craven	*Paterson(2)*	Saunders(2)	Hanson(1)	German
02/10	**TELFORD UTD**	GMVC	6-0	1,118	Heyes	Filson	Barr	Edwards	*Lambert*	Megson	Peake(1)	Saunders(2)	Constable	Paterson(3)	*Craven*	German	Hardy
05/10	Stalybridge	GMVC	1-1	1,233	Heyes	Filson	German	Edwards	Lambert	Megson(1)	Peake	Saunders	Constable	Paterson	Craven		
09/10	Merthyr Tydfil	GMVC	1-2	911	Heyes	*Filson*	German	Edwards	Megson	Lambert(1)	Peake	Saunders	Paterson	*Constable*	Craven	France	Crosby
16/10	Dagenham & Red.	GMVC	0-3	1,303	Heyes	*Rathbone*	Craven	Edwards	Lambert	Megson	Barr	*Saunders*	Constable	Paterson	Filson	Ridings	France
23/10	**WOKING**	GMVC	2-3	1,201	Brown	German	Craven	Barr	*Filson*	Lambert(1)	Peake	Costello	*Constable*	Paterson(1)	Megson	Edwards	Hardy
30/10	Bath City	GMVC	2-2	712	Heyes	Barr	Craven	Edwards	Filson	Megson	Peake(1)	Costello	*Lambert*	Paterson(1)	*Saunders*	Constable	German
02/11	**GATESHEAD**	DC2	3-0	749	Heyes	German	Craven	Barr	Filson	*Cunningham*	Peake	Costello(1)	Ridings	Paterson(2)	Saunders		Megson
06/11	**BROMSGROVE**	GMVC	3-0	1,003	Heyes	German	*Craven*	Edwards	Boardman	Barr	Peake	Saunders(2)	Ridings	*Paterson*	Megson(1)	Constable	Hardy
14/11	**WEST BROM.**	FAC1	2-1	4,250	Heyes	German	Craven	Edwards	Boardman	Barr	Peake(1)	Ridings	Lambert	*Paterson*	Saunders(1)	Constable	
20/11	**WELLING UTD**	GMVC	1-1	1,035	Heyes	*German*	Craven	Edwards	Boardman	Barr	Peake	Ridings	Lambert(1)	Paterson	*Saunders*	Constable	Filson
26/11	Witton Albion	GMVC	2-2	846	Heyes	Barr	Craven	Edwards	Boardman	Constable	Peake	Ridings	Lambert(2)	Paterson	Saunders		
04/12	Stockport Co.	FAC2	1-5	5,496	Heyes	*German*	Craven	Edwards	*Boardman*	Megson	Peake	Barr(1)	Ridings	Paterson	Saunders	Constable	Cameron
18/12	Dover Ath.	GMVC	2-1	1,348	Heyes	Barr	Craven	Edwards	Boardman	Megson	Peake(1)	Burr	Ridings	*Paterson(1)*	Saunders		German
21/12	**MACCLESFIELD**	DCqf	1-2	621	Heyes	German	Craven	Barr	Filson	Megson	Peake	Ridings	Constable	Saunders(1)	*Cunningham*		Cameron

04/01 Kidderminster	GMVC	1-2	2,016	Wilmot	Barr	Craven	Edwards	Boardman	*Ridings*	Peake(1)	*Burr*	Lambert	Paterson	Saunders	Constable	Megson
08/01 Kettering T.	GMVC	1-0	2,409	Wilmot	Barr	Craven	Edwards	Boardman	Ridings(1)	Peake	Burr	Lambert	Paterson	*Saunders*		Megson
11/01 **STALYBRIDGE**	GMVC	2-1	1,012	Wilmot	Barr	Craven	Edwards	Boardman	Ridings(2)	Peake	Burr	Lambert	Paterson	Megson		
15/01 **RUNCORN**	GMVC	1-1	1,196	Wilmot	Barr	Craven	Edwards	Boardman	Ridings	Peake	Collins	Lambert(1)	Paterson	Burr	Constable	
22/01 **EMLEY**	FAT1	2-1	1,579	Wilmot	Barr	Craven	Edwards	Boardman	Ridings	Peake	Collins	Lambert	Paterson(1)	*Burr*		Megson
29/01 Welling United	GMVC	2-0	1,263	Wilmot	Barr	Craven	Edwards	Boardman	Megson(1)	Peake	Ridings(1)	Lambert	*Paterson*	Burr	Collins	
02/02 **SOUTHPORT**	GMVC	2-2	1,310	Wilmot	Barr(1)	Craven	Edwards	Boardman	Megson	Peake	Ridings	Lambert(1)	Paterson	Burr		
05/02 Stafford Rgrs	GMVC	1-1	1,082	Wilmot	Barr	Craven	Edwards	Boardman	Megson	Peake	Ridings	Lambert	*Paterson*	Burr	Collins	
12/02 Spennymoor Utd	FAT2	2-1	1,426	Wilmot	Megson	Craven	Barr	Boardman	Ridings	Peake(1)	*Burr*	Lambert	Paterson(1)	Collins		Hanson
19/02 Telford United	GMVC	2-3	1,072	Wilmot	Barr	Prindiville	Edwards(1)	Boardman	Megson	Peake	Lormor(1)	Lambert	Paterson	Craven		
05/03 Runcorn	FAT3	*1-1	1,302	Wilmot	Barr	Prindiville	Edwards	Boardman	*Craven*	Peake	*Lormor*	Lambert	Paterson	Hanson	Higgins	German
08/03 **RUNCORN**	FAT3r	0-2	1,406	Wilmot	Barr	Prindiville	Edwards	Boardman	*Craven*	Peake	Lormor	Lambert	Paterson	*Hanson*	German	Higgins
12/03 **DOVER ATH.**	GMVC	0-1	760	Wilmot	Barr	Prindiville	Edwards	Boardman	*Constable*	Peake	Lormor	Lambert	Paterson	Hanson	Higgins	
19/03 Macclesfield T.	GMVC	1-0	1,115	Wilmot	Barr	Prindiville	Edwards	Boardman	German	Peake(1)	Lormor	Lambert	Paterson	Hanson		
26/03 **BATH CITY**	GMVC	0-0	1,008	Wilmot	Barr	Prindiville	Jones	Boardman	Megson	German	Lormor	Lambert	Paterson	Hanson		
29/03 **MERTHYR TYD.**	GMVC	2-1	771	Wilmot	Barr	Prindiville	Jones	Boardman	Megson	Smith	Hanson(2)	*Lambert*	Paterson	Constable		German
02/04 Northwich Vics	GMVC	2-0	927	Wilmot	German	Prindiville	Jones	Boardman	Megson	Smith	Hanson(1)	Barr(1)	Paterson	Constable		
04/04 Gateshead	GMVC	1-2	659	Wilmot	German	Prindiville	Jones	Boardman	Megson	*Lormor*	*Hanson*	Barr	Paterson(1)	Constable	Horsfield	Gray
07/04 **ALTRINCHAM**	GMVC	0-0	1,019	Wilmot	German	Prindiville	Jones	Boardman	Megson	Horsfield	*O'Toole*	Barr	Paterson	Constable	Higgins	
16/04 Yeovil Town	GMVC	0-0	1,823	Wilmot	German	Prindiville	Jones	Boardman	Megson	Lormor	*Hanson*	Barr	Paterson	Horsfield	Constable	
19/04 **NORTHWICH V.**	GMVC	1-2	809	Wilmot	Barr	Prindiville	Jones	Boardman	Megson	Lormor	*Higgins*	Barr	Paterson	*Smith(1)*	Horsfield	O'Toole
23/04 **GATESHEAD**	GMVC	3-1	760	Wilmot	Barr(1)	Prindiville	*Jones*	Boardman	Megson	Constable	Hanson	O'Toole	Paterson(2)	Smith		German
26/04 **MACCLESFIELD**	GMVC	1-2	732	Wilmot	Barr	Prindiville	Jones	Boardman	Megson	Constable	Hanson	O'Toole	Paterson	Smith(1)		
29/04 **DAGENHAM & R.**	GMVC	0-1	643	Heyes	German	Prindiville	Barr	Boardman	Megson	Constable	Hanson	O'Toole	Paterson	Smith		
30/04 Altrincham	GMVC	0-0	799	Heyes	German	Prindiville	Barr	Boardman	Megson	Rathbone	Horsfield	O'Toole	Paterson	Constable		
02/05 **KIDDERMINSTER**	GMVC	1-0	1,141	Heyes	German	Prindiville	Jones	Boardman	Megson	Horsfield	Barr(1)	Hanson	Paterson	Hardy		
05/05 Bromsgrove R.	GMVC	0-1	1,050	Heyes	German	Prindiville	Jones	Boardman	Megson	*Smith*	Barr	Horsfield	Paterson	*Hardy*	Higgins	O'Toole
07/05 **SLOUGH TOWN**	GMVC	1-0	935	Wilmot	German	Prindiville	Jones	Boardman	Megson	Horsfield	Barr	Hook	Paterson(1)	*Higgins*	Constable	

Halifax Town

JOHN BIRD

John was appointed as manager early in 1994 following the dismissal of Peter Wragg. His playing career began at Doncaster Rovers and he went on to make over 400 League appearances with Rovers, Preston North End, Newcastle United and Hartlepool United. A hard, uncompromising centre-half, John's managerial career started at his last club, Hartlepool, where he took on the role of assistant-manager to Billy Horner before eventually succeeding him as boss in November 1986. Two years later, John was sacked and replaced by Bobby Moncur and, since that time, he has held coaching posts at a number of clubs, most latterly Doncaster Rovers, before taking over at The Shay.

Dave Hanson (centre) of Halifax Town is squeezed out by Jeff Wrighton (left) and Ged Parkinson (right) during the Shaymen's 1-2 defeat at Gateshead on Easter Bank Holiday Monday.

Photo - Gavin Ellis-Neville.

Programme details:
32 pages for £1.
Editor - Nick Beaumont (0422 363336)

Any other club publications:

Local Newspapers:
Halifax Courier
Yorkshire Post
Telegraph Argus

Local Radio Stations:
Pennine Radio
Radio Leeds

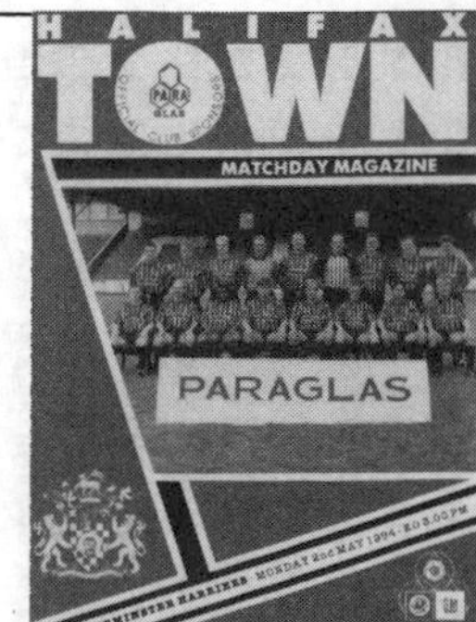

HALIFAX TOWN - PLAYING SQUAD

Player	Honours	Birthplace and date	Transfer Fees	Previous Clubs
GOALKEEPERS				
Richard Wilmot		London 29/8/69	£20,000	Pirton, Hitchin T, Stevenage Borough, Scunthorpe Utd
Nick Brown		Northampton 25/1/73		Norwich City
DEFENDERS				
Steve Prindiville		Harlow 26/12/68		Leicester C, Chesterfield, Mansfield, Doncaster R, Wycombe W
Alex Jones		Blackburn 27/11/64	Player/ Exchange	Oldham Ath, Preston NE, Carlisle U Rochdale, Motherwell, Rochdale
Craig Boardman		Barnsley 30/11/70		Nottingham Forest, Peterborough Utd
Mick Rathbone	FY	Birmingham 6/11/58		Birmingham C, Blackburn R, Preston NE
Billy Barr		Halifax 21/1/69		From Trainee
Scott Longley		Halifax 16/7/73		YTS
MIDFIELDERS				
Kevin Megson		Halifax 1/7/71		Bradford City
Colin Lambert		Manchester 21/9/63	£5,000	Flixton, Winsford Utd, Macclesfield T
Peter Craven		Hanover 30/6/68		Eccleshill Utd, Farsley Celtic, Eccleshill Utd, Guiseley
David German		Sheffield 16/10/73		Sheffield Wednesday
Jason Hardy		Burnley 14/12/69		Burnley
Pat O'Toole		Dublin 2/1/65		Shelbourne, Leicester C, Exeter C, Shrewsbury T, Shamrock Rovers
Shaun Constable	British Students			None
FORWARDS				
Steve Saunders		Warrington 29/9/64	£5,000	Bolton, Crewe, Preston, Northwich V, Grimsby, Scarboro, Runcorn, Altrincham
Steve Hook		Yorkshire		YTS
Jamie Paterson		Dumfries 26/4/73		YTS
Geoff Horsefield		Barnsley 1/11/73		Scarborough
David Hanson		Yorkshire		YTS

Departures during season:
Lee Bracey (Bury), Nigel Greenwood (Bamber Bridge), Tony Gregory (Buxton), Steve Circuit (Boston Utd), Chris Lucketti (Bury), Steve Burr (Hednesford T), Martin Filson (Dagenham & Redbridge), Jim Cameron (Winsford Utd), Dave Ridings (Lincoln C), Jason Peake (Rochdale), Elfyn Edwards (Southport), Harvey Cunningham (Released).

Players on loan during season:
Tony Lormor (Lincoln C), Peter Costello (Lincoln C).

The Shay, Halifax Town

Address and telephone number: The Shay, Halifax, West Yorkshire HX1 2YS. Tel: 0422 353423. Fax: 0422 349487

Simple directions: From North: Take A629 to Halifax Town Centre. Take 2nd exit at roundabout into Broad Street and follow signs for Huddersfield (A629) into Skircoat Road. From South, East & West: Exit M62 junction 24 and follow Halifax (A629) signs to Town centre into Skircoat Road for ground.

Capacity: 8,041 **Seated:** 1,878 **Covered terracing:** 6,000 (Approx)

Record Attendance: 36,885 v Tottenham - 5th Round FA Cup - 14.02.53

Club Shop: Contact Nick Beaumont on 0422 363336 for details.

Social Facilities: No facilities on the ground.

Halifax Fact File

Nickname: The Shaymen

Club Sponsors: Westgrove

Previous Grounds: Sandhall Lane 1911-15, Exley 1919-21.

Previous Leagues: Yorkshire Combination 1911-12, Midland League 1912-21, Division 3 North 1921-58, Division 3 1958-63, 1969-76, 1992, Division 4 1963-69.

Club colours: Blue & white

Change colours: White/green & purple

Reserve team league: Midland Senior League

Midweek home matchday: Tuesday

Record win: 12-0 v West Vale Ramblers - 1st Qualifying Round FA Cup - 1913-14

Record defeat: 0-13 v Stockport County - Division 3 North - 1933-34

Record transfer fee: £50,000 for Ian Juryeff (Hereford United).

Record transfer fee received: £250,000 for Wayne Allison (Watford).

1993-94 Captain: Alex Jones.

1993-94 Top scorer: Jamie Paterson.

1993-94 Player of the Year: Craig Boardman.

Club record goalscorer: Albert Valentine

Record appearances: John Pickering

Past players who progressed to the Football League: N/A

Club Honours: Promoted to Division 3 1968-69

KETTERING TOWN

Formed:
1872

President:
S Chapman

Vice-President:
T F Bradley

Chairman:
P Mallinger

Vice-Chairman
P Oliver

Secretary/Press Officer:
G P Knowles

Manager:
Graham Carr

Coach
Clive Walker

Physiotherapist:
Richie Norman

Commercial Manager:
Mrs P J Knowles

After the horrors of the 1992-93 season which saw the Poppies avoid extinction only with the help of High Court Administrators it was desperately hoped that 1993-94 season would see some kind of recovery in our fortunes. The scale of the subsequent turn-arround is still difficult to believe.

Manager Graham Carr started July 1993 with only two registered players and, with no chairman, things still looked grim at Rockingham Road. However, with the arrival of Peter Mallinger as the Poppies' new Chairman immediate, improvements were seen. Players were quickly signed and to most people's surprise a Championship challenge was mounted. The long-awaited dream of League football was missed by only one victory and several GMVC Conference records were smashed, not least away from home where only 10 goals were conceded in 21 matches. The first round proper of the FA Cup being reached for a 38th time.

Many ground improvements have been carried out and a Football League 'A' grading has been achieved. A new Sponsors Lounge has been built offering a high standard of hospitality to sponsors and guests, and a new Executive Members scheme has been successfully launched.

A staged plan for future building work has been prepared. A new covered terrace at the Cowper Street end of the ground together with development work under the Main Stand will shortly be commenced.

Having now been GMVC bridesmaid on three occasions, hope is high at Rockingham Road that with a slightly strengthened squad the Poppies will go one better and take their place in the Football League at the end of the 1994/95 season.

Gerry Knowles

Back Row (L/R): John Ashdjian, Jon Graham, Martin Roderick, Graham Benstead, Owen Wright, Adrian Thorpe. Centre: Richie Norman (Physio), Dean Martin, Darren Oxbrow, Nicky Ashby, Simon Clarke, Graham Reed, Robin Taylor, Colin Walker (Coach). Front: Richard Davis (Financial Director), Gareth Price, Graham Carr (Manager), Warren Donald (Captain), Peter Mallinger (Chairman), Phil Brown, Peter Oliver (Vice-Chairman).

KETTERING *MATCHFACTS 93-94* ***KETTERING*** *MATCHFACTS 93-94* ***KETTERING*** *MATCHFACTS 93-94*

Key: Home fixtures are denoted by bold capitals. Numbers in brackets after players names indicate goals scored (asterisks by the results denote own goals). Only used substitutes are listed - substituted players are *italicised*.

Key to Competitions: GMVC: GM Vauxhall Conference. **NSC**: Northamptonshire Hillier Senior Cup. **DC**: Drinkwise (GM Vauxhall Conference) Cup. **FAC**: FA Cup. **FAT**: FA Trophy. **MC:** Maunsell Cup.

Date	Opponents	Comp.	Res	Gate	1.	2.	3.	4.	5.	6.	7.	8.	9.	10.	11.	Sub.	Sub.
07/08	**NORTHAMPTON**	MC	2-0	1,818	Hoult	Mason	Platneaur	Price	Oxbrow(1)	Taylor	Wright	Brown	*Donovan*	Donald	*Thorpe*	Loughlan(1)	Clarke
21/08	Halifax Town	GMVC	0-0	1,810	Hoult	Reed	Ashby	Price	Oxbrow	Taylor	Wright	Brown	*Loughlan*	Donald	Roderick		Clarke
23/08	Kidderminster H.	GMVC	2-0	1,264	Hoult	Reed	Ashby	Price	Oxbrow	Taylor(1)	Wright	Brown	Loughlan(1)	Donald	Roderick		
28/08	**NORTHWICH VIC.**	GMVC	0-0	1,767	Hoult	Reed	Ashby	Price	Oxbrow	Taylor	Wright	Brown	*Loughlan*	Donald	*Roderick*	Donovan	Clarke
30/08	**WITTON ALBION**	GMVC	1-0	1,680	Hoult	Reed	Ashby	Price	Oxbrow	Taylor	Wright	Brown	Loughlan	Donald	Thorpe(1)		
04/09	Telford United	GMVC	2-1	970	Hoult	Reed	Ashby	Price	Oxbrow(1)	Taylor	Wright	Brown	*Loughlan*	Donald	*Thorpe*	Roderick	Clarke(1)
07/09	**WELLING UTD**	DC1(1)	0-0	961	Hoult	Muckleberg	Ashby	Price	Oxbrow	Taylor	Wright	Brown	*Clarke*	Donald	*Thorpe*	Roderick	Donovan
11/09	**MERTHYR TYD.**	GMVC	0-0	1,702	Hoult	Reed	Ashby	Price	Oxbrow	Taylor	Wright	*Brown*	Martin	Donald	*Roderick*	Thorpe	Clarke
19/09	Macclesfield T.	GMVC	0-0	938	Hoult	Reed	Ashby	Price	Oxbrow	Taylor	Wright	Brown	Martin	Donald	*Roderick*		Thorpe
21/09	Welling United	DC1(2)	1-2	457	Trinder	Muckleberg	Ashby	Price	Oxbrow	*Reed*	Taylor	Clarke	*Donovan*	Donald	Thorpe(1)	Brown	Wright
25/09	**RUNCORN**	GMVC	2-2	1,476	Benstead	Reed	Ashby	Price	Oxbrow	Taylor	Wright	Brown(1)	Martin(1)	Donald	*Thorpe*		Donovan
02/10	Bath City	GMVC	3-0	864	Benstead	Reed	Ashby	Price	Oxbrow	Taylor	Wright	Brown(1)	*Martin(1)*	Donald	*Roderick(1)*	Donovan	Clarke
09/10	Stafford Rangers	GMVC	0-1	1,456	Benstead	Reed	Ashby	Price	Oxbrow	Taylor	Wright	Brown	Martin	Donald	*Roderick*		Thorpe
16/10	**YEOVIL TOWN**	GMVC	1-0	1,949	Benstead	Reed(1)	Ashby	Price	Oxbrow	Taylor	*Wright*	Brown	Martin	Donald	*Roderick*	Clarke	Thorpe
23/10	**CANVEY ISLAND**	FAC4q	3-1	2,191	Benstead	Reed	Ashby	Price	Clarke	Taylor	Wright(2)	Brown	Martin	Donald	Thorpe(1)		
30/10	**ALTRINCHAM**	GMVC	1-0	1,681	Benstead	Reed	Ashby	Price	Oxbrow	Clarke	Wright	Brown	Graham	Donald	Roderick(1)		
06/11	Stalybridge C.	GMVC	1-1	630	Benstead	Reed	Ashby	Price(1)	Taylor	Clarke	Wright	Brown	Graham	Donald	*Roderick*	Muckleberg	*Donovan*
13/11	Kidderminster H.	FAC1	0-3	3,775	Benstead	Muckleberg	Ashby	Price	Oxbrow	Taylor	*Wright*	*Brown*	Martin	Donald	Clarke	Roderick	Thorpe
20/11	**SOUTHPORT**	GMVC	2-0	1,980	Benstead	Price	Ashby	Holden	Oxbrow	Taylor(1)	Wright	*Graham*	Clarke	Donald	Thorpe(1)	Brown	
27/11	Slough Town	GMVC	2-0	1,122	Benstead	Price	Ashby	Holden	Oxbrow	Taylor(1)	Wright	Brown(1)	Clarke	Donald	Thorpe		
04/12	Welling United	GMVC	0-2	924	Benstead	Price	Ashby	Holden	Oxbrow	Taylor	Wright	*Brown*	Clarke	Donald	*Thorpe*	Martin	Ashdjian
11/12	**GATESHEAD**	GMVC	0-0	1,783	Benstead	Price	Ashby	Holden	Oxbrow	Taylor	*Wright*	*Brown*	Martin	Donald	Thorpe	Clarke	Ashdjian
18/12	**WELLING UTD**	GMVC	2-2	1,811	Martin	Price	Ashby	Holden	Oxbrow	Taylor	Clarke	Brown	*Martin*	Donald(1)	*Ashdjian*	Graham(1)	Wright

27/12	Dagenham & Red.	GMVC	3-2	1,376	Benstead	Price	Ashby	Holden	Oxbrow	Taylor	Wright	Brown(2)	Clarke	Donald	*Thorpe*	Graham(1)	
01/01	**TELFORD UTD**	GMVC	1-2	3,120	Benstead	Price(1)	Ashby	*Holden*	Oxbrow	Taylor	Wright	Brown	Clarke	*Donald*	Graham	Ashdjian	Martin
03/01	Woking	GMVC	0-0	3,130	Benstead	Price	Ashby	Holden	Oxbrow	Taylor	Wright	Brown	Martin	Donald	Graham		
08/01	**HALIFAX TOWN**	GMVC	0-1	2,409	Benstead	Price	Ashby	Holden	Oxbrow	*Taylor*	Wright	Brown	Martin	Donald	*Graham*	Asdhdjian	Reed
15/01	Witton Albion	GMVC	1-0	798	Benstead	Price	Ashby	Holden	Oxbrow	Clarke	*Graham(1)*	Brown	Martin	Donald	*Roderick*	Ashdjian	Thorpe
22/01	**STEVENAGE B.**	FAT1	2-1	2,414	Benstead	Price	Ashby	Holden	Oxbrow	Clarke	Wright(1)	*Brown*	Martin	Donald	*Roderick*	Ashdjian	Reed(1)
29/01	Yeovil Town	GMVC	0-1	2,382	Benstead	Price	Ashby	Holden	Oxbrow	Clarke	*Graham*	Murphy	Martin	Donald	Roderick	*Brown*	Wright
05/02	**STALYBRIDGE**	GMVC	3-2	1,949	Benstead	Price	Ashby	Holden	Oxbrow(1)	Clarke(1)	Martin(1)	Stringfellow	Murphy	Donald	Taylor		
08/02	**BATH CITY**	GMVC	0-1	2,044	Benstead	Price	Ashby	Holden	Oxbrow	Clarke	Martin	Stringfellow	*Murphy*	*Donald*	Taylor	Graham	Brown
12/02	**BILLINGHAM S.**	FAT2	2-2	2,076	Benstead	Reed	Ashby	Holden	Oxbrow	*Wright*	Martin	Stringfellow	Murphy	Donald(1)	*Roderick*	Graham(1)	Clarke
19/02	**WOKING**	GMVC	3-0	2,054	Benstead	*Reed*	Ashby	Holden	Oxbrow	*Clarke*	Martin(1)	Stringfellow	Brown(1)	Donald	Price	Graham(1)	Murphy
26/02	**DAGENHAM & R.**	GMVC	1-1	2,161	Benstead	Reed	Ashby	Holden	Oxbrow	Price	Martin	*Brown(1)*	*Stringfellow*	Donald	Graham	Taylor	Murphy
28/02	Billingham Syn.	FAT2r	1-3	842	Benstead	Reed	Ashby	Holden	Oxbrow	Price	*Martin*	Brown	Stringfellow(1)	Donald	*Taylor*	Ashdjian	Kilber
05/03	**KIDDERMINSTER**	GMVC	1-1	2,922	Benstead	Reed	Ashby	*Holden*	Oxbrow	Taylor	*Wright*	Brown	Stringfellow	Costello(1)	Dempsey	Martin	Donald
12/03	Gateshead	GMVC	0-0	553	Benstead	Reed	Ashby	Holden	Oxbrow	Taylor	Donald	Costello	Stringfellow	*Brown*	Dempsey	Graham	
15/03	**SLOUGH TOWN**	GMVC	2-0	1,434	Benstead	Reed	Ashby	Holden	Oxbrow	Taylor	Donald	Graham	Stringfellow	Costello(2)	Dempsey		
19/03	Bromsgrove R.	GMVC	4-0	1,235	Benstead	Reed	Ashby	Holden	Oxbrow	Taylor(1)	Donald	Graham(1)	Stringfellow	Costello(1)	Dempsey(1)		
22/03	Dover Athletic	GMVC	0-0	974	Benstead	Reed	Ashby	Holden	Oxbrow	Taylor	Donald	Graham(1)	Stringfellow	Costello	Dempsey		
26/03	**MACCLESFIELD**	GMVC	0-1	2,158	Benstead	Reed	Ashby	Holden	Price	Taylor	*Donald*	Graham	Stringfellow	Costello	Dempsey		Martin
29/03	Rushden & D.	NSCsf	2-3	2,450	Benstead	Reed	Ashby	Holden	Oxbrow	Taylor	Donald	Brown	Stringfellow	Costello	Dempsey(2)		
02/04	Merthyr Tydfil	GMVC	1-0	527	Benstead	Reed	Ashby	Holden	Oxbrow	Taylor	Donald	*Graham*	*Stringfellow*	Whitehouse	Dempsey(1)	Martin	Brown
04/04	**DOVER ATH.**	GMVC	1-0	2,134	Benstead	Reed	Ashby(1)	Holden	Oxbrow	Taylor	Donald	Graham	Stringfellow	Whitehouse	*Dempsey*		Martin
09/04	Northwich Vics	GMVC	1-1	783	Benstead	Reed	Ashby	Holden	Oxbrow	*Taylor*	Donald	Graham	Price	*Whitehouse(1)*	Martin	Brown	Wright
16/04	**STAFFORD R.**	GMVC	2-0	1,701	Benstead	Reed	Ashby	Holden	Oxbrow	Taylor(1)	Donald	Brown(1)	Price	Whitehouse	Dempsey		
19/04	Southport	GMVC	1-0	1,015	Benstead	Reed	Ashby	Holden	Oxbrow	Taylor	Donald	Brown	Price	Whitehouse(1)	Dempsey	Stringfellow	
30/04	Runcorn	GMVC	0-0	464	Benstead	Reed	Ashby	Holden	Oxbrow	Taylor	*Donald*	Brown	Price	*Whitehouse*	Dempsey	Stringfellow	Graham
02/05	Altrincham	GMVC	1-1	979	Benstead	Reed(1)	Ashby	Holden	Oxbrow	Taylor	*Wright*	Martin	Price	Graham	Dempsey	Brown	
07/05	**BROMSGROVE R.**	GMVC	0-1	2,620	Benstead	Reed	Ashby	Holden	Oxbrow	Taylor	Donald	*Graham*	Price	Brown	Wright		Martin

Kettering Town

GRAHAM CARR

One of the most respected managers in the league, Graham was appointed as manager by the administrators in September 1992 and, with an extremely low budget to work within, managed to attract enough quality players to Rockingham Road to keep them safely in the Vauxhall Conference. After the club came out of administration, Graham was rewarded with a well-deserved three-year contract.

A hard, uncompromising defender, Graham made 160 Football League appearances with Northampton Town, York City and Bradford Park Avenue, winning England Youth caps as well, before going non-League with the likes of Dartford, Telford United, Altrincham, Tonbridge and Weymouth. His managerial career began as player-boss at Weymouth and Dartford before taking over at Nuneaton where he led the club to runners-up spot in the Alliance Premier League (Conference). Whilst at Nuneaton, Graham brought on the likes of Trevor Morley, Eddie McGoldrick, Paul Culpin and Richard Hill who all went on to enjoy League careers. Since then he has managed in the Football League at Northampton Town (winning the Fourth Division title in 1987), Blackpool and Maidstone United.

Darren Oxbrow beats Steve Sherwood from the spot as Kettering triumph 2-0 at home to Northampton Town to win the pre-season Maunsell Cup.

Photo - Mick Cheney.

Programme details:
32 pages for £1.00
Editor: Paul Harrison

Any other club publications:
Poppies at the Gates of Dawn (Fanzine)

Local Newspapers:
Evening Telegraph
Chronicle & Echo
Herald & Post
Citizen

Local Radio Stations:
Radio Northampton
Northants 96
KCBC

KETTERING TOWN - PLAYING SQUAD

Player	Honours	Birthplace and date	Transfer Fees	Previous Clubs
GOALKEEPERS				
Graham Benstead	ESP, EY	Aldershot 20/8/63		QPR, Norwich C, Sheffield Utd, Brentford
DEFENDERS				
Nick Ashby		Northampton 29/12/70	£3,000	Nottingham Forest, Rushden T, Aylesbury Utd
Graham Reed	Div 4	Doncaster 24/6/63		Barnsley, Frickley Ath, Northampton T, Aylesbury Utd, VS Rugby
Stephen Holden	ESP	Luton 4/9/72		Leicester C, Carlisle Utd
Darren Oxbrow		Ipswich 1/9/69		Ipswich T, Maidstone Utd, Colchester Utd, Barnet
Gareth Price		Swindon 21/2/70		Mansfield T, Bury
MIDFIELDERS				
Warren Donald	GMVC, FAT Div 4	Hillingdon 7/10/64		West Ham Utd, Northampton T, Colchester Utd
Robin Taylor	British Students	Leicester		Cambridge C, Hinckley T, Shepshed Alb, Kettering T, Peterborough Utd
Simon Clarke		Chelmsford 23/9/71		West Ham United
Ian Stringfellow		Nottingham 8/5/69	£5,000	Mansfield Town
FORWARDS				
Phil Brown	GMVC, Div 4, FAXI	Sheffield 16/1/66		Chesterfield, Stockport County, Lincoln City
John Ashdjian		Hackney 13/9/72		Northampton Town, Scarborough
Owen Wright		Birmingham 8/3/67		Bedworth U, Aylesbury U, Worcester C, Leicester U, Shepshed Alb
Dean Martin		London 31/8/72		Fisher Athletic, West Ham United
Jon Graham		Leicester 24/11/66	£3,000	Kettering Town, Boston Utd

Departures during season:
Sean Wood (Released), Tony Loughlan (Wycombe W), Neil Donovan, Terry Muckleburg & Phil Mason (Worcester C), Mark Whitehouse, Simon Guthrie & Martin Roderick (Released).

Players on loan during season:
Matt Murphy (Oxford Utd), Stephen Holden (Carlisle Utd), Graham Benstead (Brentford), Peter Costello (Lincoln C), Mark Dempsey (Gillingham).

Rockingham Road, Kettering

Address and telephone number: Rockingham Road, Kettering, Northants, NN16 9AW. Tel: 0536 83028/410815 (Office). 0536 410962 (Social Club). Fax: 0536 412273.
Simple directions: M1 junction 15, A43 to Kettering use A14 and Kettering Northern by pass, turn right A6003, ground half a mile. From North M1 or M6 use junction 19 then A14 to Kettering. A1 use A14 at Huntingdon then as above. British Rail - Inter-City Midland - 50mins from London (St.Pancras), 20mins from Leicester.
Capacity: 6,100 **Seated:** 1,800 **Covered terracing:** 3,000
Record Attendance: 11,536 Kettering v Peterborough (pre-Taylor report).
Club Shop: Open before and after matches, and office staff will open on request on non-match days. Situated in front of main stand.
Social Facilities: Social Club (Poppies), Vice-Presidents Bar.
Previous Grounds: North Park/ Green Lane.

Kettering Fact File

Nickname: Poppies

Club Sponsors: Healthcrafts

Previous Leagues: Southern League, Northants League, Midland League, Birmingham League, Central Alliance, United Counties League.

Club colours: All red.

Change colours: All blue.

Midweek home matchday: Tuesday

Record win:

Record defeat:

Record transfer fee paid: £25,000 to Macclesfield for Carl Alford, 1994.

Record transfer fee received: £150,000 from Newcastle United for Andy Hunt.

1993-94 Captain: Graham Reed

1993-94 Top scorer: Phil Brown.

1993-94 Player of the Year: Stephen Holden.

Club record goalscorer: A Woolhead.

Record appearances: Roger Ashby.

Past players who progressed to the Football League: B.Kellock (Peterborough), G.Wood (Notts Co.), D.Longhurst (Nott'm Forest), S.Endersby (ipswich), S.Fallon (Cambridge Utd), J.Sellers (Manchester Utd), A.Rogers (Plymouth), M.Foster (Northampton), J.Brown (Chesterfield), Cohen Griffith (Cardiff City), Andy Hunt (Newcastle).

Club Honours: Premier Inter League Cup winners; FA Trophy finalists; Alliance Premier League r-up (x3); Southern League Winners, County Cup Winners, Daventry Charity Cup Winners (x2); Northants Senior Cup (x2); Maunsell Cup Winners.

KIDDERMINSTER HARRIERS

Formed:
1886

Chairman:
David L Reynolds

Vice-Chairman
J. Richard Painter

Secretary/Press Officer:
Ray Mercer

Manager:
Graham Allner

Asst Manager/Physio:
Jimmy Conway

Commercial Manager:
Mark Searl

That was the season that was! The most memorable in the history of Kidderminster Harriers.

Formed in 1886, the Harriers will always look back to the 1993/94 season as the highlight since they were formed 108 years ago. In their eleventh season in the Conference, the Harriers became champions - and who will ever forget the FA Cup exploits?

The Harriers were deserving champions, although not many would have given them much chance after a disastrous start to the season. The end of the season was disappointing in the hectic programme in the closing weeks, but the middle of the season took them from the bottom to the top - and that is where they stayed.

For manager Graham Allner, it was the highlight of his managerial career. The side played the way he has always said that football should be played. It was attacking football, it was stylish football and it was entertaining football. And it was played in the way that Graham Allner has always indicated - and that was proved with the winning of the Trophy for Sportsmanship.

Most of the squad will look back upon a never-to-be-forgotten season. Delwyn Humphreys started the season on the transfer list and also on the injured list, but fought back to claim his place in the side - and regained his place in the England Non-League International side. Captain Simeon Hodson and goalkeeper Kevin Rose both playing their first season in non-League after coming from League sides, and both gained their first-ever 'caps' in the England Non-League team. Long-serving Paul Davies, in his eleventh season with Kidderminster, the town where he was born, has now made 530 appearances and scored 250 goals, and earned a deserving benefit game at the end of the season against Aston Villa.

The Harriers had reached the Third Round of the FA Cup for the first time an earned an away win against Birmingham City and a Fourth Round home win over Preston North End before going down by one goal before a crowd of nearly 8,000 against West Ham in the Fifth Round.

To win the Conference, promotion to the Football League is the 'prize'. But for the Harriers - disappointment, deprived of the honour they richly deserved. Disappointment in not being the first club in Football League club from Worcestershire. Disappointment for the loyal supporters. Disappointment for the players, and disappointment for chairman David Reynolds.

David Reynolds fought hard off the field to obtain the Football League rightful position, but he, like Graham Allner, says "We'll do it again this season".

Ray Mercer, Secretary.

KIDDERMINSTER HARRIERS MATCHFACTS 93-94 *KIDDERMINSTER HARRIERS* MATCHFACTS 93-94

Key: Home fixtures are denoted by bold capitals. Numbers in brackets after players names indicate goals scored (asterisks by the results denote own goals). Only used substitutes are listed - substituted players are *italicised*.

Key to Competitions: GMVC: G.M. Vauxhall Conference. **WSC**: Worcestershire Senior Cup. **DC**: Drinkwise (G.M. Vauxhall Conference) Cup. **FAC**: F.A. Cup. **FAT**: F.A. Trophy.

Date	Opponents	Comp.	Res	Gate	1.	2.	3.	4.	5.	6.	7.	8.	9.	10.	11.	Sub.	Sub.
21/08	Dover Athletic	GMVC	1-3	1,729	Rose	Hodson	Bancroft	Weir	Brindley	Forsyth	Deakin	*Cartwright*	Gordon(1)	Davies	*Purdie*	Williams	Grainger
23/08	**KETTERING T.**	GMVC	0-2	1,274	Rose	Hodson	*Bancroft*	Weir	Brindley	Forsyth	*Deakin*	Cartwright	Hadley	Davies	Purdie	Williams	Grainger
28/08	**WELLING UTD**	GMVC	1-0	918	Rose	Hodson	Williams	Weir	Brindley	Wolsey	*Cartwright*	Grainger(1)	Hadley	Davies	Purdie		Gillett
30/08	Bath City	GMVC	0-4	941	Rose	Hodson	Williams	*Weir*	Brindley	*Wolsey*	Cartwright	Grainger	Hadley	Gordon	Purdie	Sirk	Gillett
04/09	**SLOUGH TOWN**	GMVC	0-0	1,009	Rose	Hodson	Williams	Weir	Brindley	Forsyth	Cartwright	Grainger	Gordon	Davies	Purdie		
11/09	Altrincham	GMVC	0-1	688	Rose	Hodson	Williams	Weir	Brindley	Forsyth	Cartwright	Grainger	*Gordon*	Davies	Purdie		Hadley
14/09	Witton Albion	GMVC	0-2	615	Rose	Hodson	Williams	Weir	Brindley	Forsyth	Cartwright	Grainger	*Gillett*	Gordon	Purdie		Hadley
18/09	**STALYBRIDGE C.**	GMVC	*1-0	921	Rose	Hodson	Bancroft	Weir	Brindley	Forsyth	Cartwright	Grainger	*West*	Davies	Purdie		Gillett
25/09	**MERTHYR TYD.**	GMVC	2-0	1,026	Rose	Hodson	Williams	Weir	Brindley(1)	Forsyth	Cartwright	Grainger	*Hadley*	Davies	Purdie(1)	Humphreys	
02/10	Stafford Rangers	GMVC	3-2	1,187	Rose	Hodson	Bancroft	Weir	Brindley	Forsyth	Cartwright(1)	Grainger	*Humphreys*	Davies(1)	Purdie(1)		Palmer
09/10	**RUNCORN**	GMVC	3-0	1,208	Rose	Hodson	Bancroft	Weir	Brindley	Forsyth	Cartwright	Grainger	*Palmer(2)*	Davies	Purdie	Humphreys(1)	
11/10	**MACCLESFIELD**	GMVC	2-1	1,228	Rose	Hodson	Bancroft	Weir	Brindley(1)	Forsyth	Cartwright	Grainger	*Humphreys*	Davies	Purdie(1)		Palmer
16/10	Stalybridge Celtic	GMVC	*2-0	654	Rose	Hodson	Bancroft	Weir	Brindley	Forsyth(1)	Cartwright	Grainger	*Palmer*	Davies	Purdie	Humphreys	
18/10	**NORTHWICH V.**	GMVC	2-0	1,514	Rose	Hodson	Bancroft	Weir	Brindley	Forsyth	Cartwright(1)	Grainger	Humphreys	Davies(1)	Purdie		
23/10	Chesham United	FAC4q	4-1	1,144	Rose	Hodson	Bancroft	Weir	Brindley(1)	Forsyth	Cartwright	Grainger(1)	Humphr.(2)	*Davies*	Purdie		Palmer
30/10	Slough Town	GMVC	5-1	1,191	Rose	Hodson	Bancroft	Weir	Brindley	Forsyth(1)	Cartwright	Grainger	Humphr.(3)	Palmer	*Purdie(1)*		Deakin
06/11	Dagenham & Red.	GMVC	1-1	1,729	Rose	Hodson	Bancroft	Weir	Brindley	Forsyth	*Cartwright*	Grainger	Humphr.(1)	Davies	Palmer		Deakin
08/11	**WORCESTER C.**	WSC2	4-2	918	Carrington	*Hodson*	Bancroft	Weir	Brindley(1)	Forsyth	Stirk(1)	Deakin	*Humphr.(1)*	Davies	Palmer	Gillett	Wolsey
13/11	**KETTERING T.**	FAC1	3-0	3,775	Rose	Hodson	Bancroft	Weir	Brindley(1)	Forsyth(1)	Cartwright	Grainger	Humphreys	Davies(1)	Palmer		
15/11	**STAFFORD RGRS**	DC2	3-0	774	Rose	*Hodson*	Bancroft	Weir	Brindley	Forsyth	Cartwright	Deakin	Humphr.(1)	Davies(2)	*Palmer*	Stirk	Purdie
20/11	**WITTON ALBION**	GMVC	0-0	1,536	Rose	Hodson	Bancroft	Weir	Brindley	Forsyth	Cartwright	Grainger	Humphreys	Davies	Palmer		Purdie
27/11	Woking	GMVC	0-1	1,726	Rose	Hodson	Bancroft	Weir	Brindley	Forsyth	*Cartwright*	Grainger	Humphreys	*Davies*	Purdie	Deakin	Palmer
04/12	**WOKING**	GMVC	1-0	4,411	Rose	Hodson	Bancroft	Weir	Brindley	Forsyth(1)	*Cartwright*	Grainger	Humphreys	Davies	Purdie		Palmer
07/12	Northwich Vict.	DC3	2-3	474	Rose	Hodson	*Williams*	Weir	Brindley	Deakin(1)	Cartwright	Grainger	Humphreys	Davies(1)	Purdie		Stirk
11/12	**DOVER ATH.**	GMVC	3-0	1,379	Rose	Hodson	Bancroft	Weir	Brindley	Forsyth	Deakin(1)	Grainger	Humphreys	Davies(2)	Purdie		

18/12	Southport	GMVC	1-1	1,739	Rose	Hodson	Bancroft	Weir	Brindley	Forsyth	Deakin	Grainger	Humphreys	*Davies(1)*	Purdie		Palmer
27/12	Bromsgrove Rvrs	GMVC	3-0	3,938	Rose	Hodson	Bancroft	Weir	Brindley	Forsyth	Deakin	Grainger	Humphr.(1)	Davies(1)	Purdie(1)		
01/01	**BATH CITY**	GMVC	0-0	2,517	Rose	Hodson	Bancroft	Weir	Brindley	Forsyth	*Deakin*	Grainger	Humphreys	Davies	Purdie	Cartwright	
04/01	**HALIFAX TOWN**	GMVC	2-1	2,016	Rose	Hodson	Bancroft	Weir	Brindley	Forsyth	Deakin	Grainger	Humphr.(1)	*Davies*	Purdie	Cartwright(1)	Grainger
08/01	Birmingham City	GMVC	2-1	19,666	Rose	Hodson	Bancroft	Weir	Brindley	Forsyth	Cartwright(1)	Grainger	Humphreys	Deakin	Purdie(1)		
15/01	**YEOVIL TOWN**	GMVC	2-3	3,812	Rose	Hodson	Bancroft	Weir	Brindley	Forsyth	Cartwright	Grainger	Humphreys	*Deakin*	Purdie(2)		Davies
22/01	**DAGENHAM & R.**	FAT1	0-2	1,587	Rose	Hodson	Bancroft	Weir	Brindley	Forsyth	Cartwright	Grainger	Humphreys	Deakin	Purdie		
29/01	**PRESTON N.E.**	FAC4	1-0	7,000	Rose	Hodson	Bancroft	Weir	Brindley	*Forsyth*	Cartwright	Grainger	Humphr.(1)	Davies	Purdie		Deakin
05/02	**DAGENHAM & R.**	GMVC	2-1	4,358	Rose	Hodson	Bancroft	Weir	Brindley	Forsyth	Cartwright	Grainger	Humphr.(1)	Davies(1)	Purdie		
19/02	**WEST HAM U.**	FAC5	0-1	7,850	Rose	Hodson	Bancroft	Weir	Brindley	Forsyth	*Cartwright*	Grainger	Humphreys	Davies	Purdie		Deakin
26/02	**STAFFORD R.**	GMVC	2-0	2,186	Rose	Hodson	Bancroft	Weir(1)	Brindley	Forsyth	Deakin	Grainger	*Palmer*	Davies(1)	*Purdie*	Cartwright	Woodall
01/03	Merthyr Tydfil	GMVC	4-1	710	Rose	Hodson	Bancroft(1)	Weir	Brindley	Forsyth	Deakin	Grainger	Humphreys	Davies(3)	Purdie		
05/03	Kettering T.	GMVC	1-1	2,922	Rose	Hodson	Bancroft	Weir	Brindley	Forsyth	Deakin	Grainger	Humphreys	Davies(1)	*Purdie*	Cartwright	
12/03	**SOUTHPORT**	GMVC	2-0	3,877	Rose	Hodson	Bancroft	Weir(2)	Brindley	Forsyth	*Deakin*	Grainger	Palmer	Davies	*Purdie*	Cartwright	Woodall
19/03	**WOKING**	GMVC	3-1	2,705	Rose	Hodson	Bancroft	Weir	Brindley	Forsyth	Cartwright	Grainger	Palmer(2)	Davies(1)	Woodall		
23/03	Gateshead	GMVC	2-0	473	Rose	Hodson	Bancroft	Weir	Brindley	Forsyth	Cartwright(2)	Grainger	Palmer	Davies	Woodall		
29/03	Redditch Utd	WSCsf	3-2	1,128	Rose	*Hodson(1)*	Bancroft	Weir	Brindley	Forsyth	Cartwright(1)	Grainger	Palmer(1)	*Humphreys*	Woodall	Gillett	Hadley
02/04	Yeovil Town	GMVC	1-0	2,835	Rose	Hodson	Bancroft	Weir	Brindley	Forsyth	*Cartwright*	Grainger	*Palmer*	Humphreys(1)	Woodall	Purdie	Deakin
05/04	**BROMSGROVE**	GMVC	1-1	4,438	Rose	Hodson	Bancroft	Weir	Brindley	Forsyth	Woodall	*Grainger(1)*	Humphreys	Davies	*Palmer*	Purdie	Deakin
16/04	Macclesfield T.	GMVC	0-0	1,125	Rose	Hodson	Bancroft	Weir	Brindley	Forsyth	*Woodall*	Grainger	Humphreys	Davies	Purdie		Deakin
20/04	Runcorn *	GMVC	5-0	594	Rose	Hodson	Bancroft	*Weir*	Brindley	Forsyth(1)	Woodall	Grainger	*Humphr.(1)*	Cartwright(2)	Purdie(1)	Palmer	Deakin
23/04	**TELFORD UTD**	GMVC	2-0	2,746	Rose	Hodson	Bancroft	Woodall	Brindley	Forsyth(1)	*Deakin*	Grainger	Humphr.(1)	Cartwright	Purdie		Palmer
25/04	**GATESHEAD**	GMVC	1-1	2,438	Rose	Hodson	Bancroft	Weir	Brindley	Forsyth	*Woodall*	Grainger	Humphr.(1)	Cartwright	Purdie		Palmer
30/04	Welling United	GMVC	3-0	941	Rose	Hodson	Bancroft	Weir	Brindley	Forsyth	*Cartwright(1)*	Grainger	Humphr.(1)	Davies(1)	*Purdie*	Woodall	Palmer
02/05	Halifax Town	GMVC	0-1	1,141	Rose	Hodson	Bancroft	*Weir*	Brindley	Forsyth	*Cartwright*	Grainger	Humphreys	Davies	Palmer	Deakin	Woodall
04/05	Telford United	GMVC	0-1	2,083	Rose	Hodson	Bancroft	Woodall	Brindley	Forsyth	Cartwright	Grainger	Humphreys	*Davies*	Purdie		Palmer
07/05	**ALTRINCHAM**	GMVC	0-1	4,114	Rose	Hodson	Bancroft	*Weir*	Brindley	Forsyth	*Woodall*	Grainger	Humphreys	Davies	Purdie	Cartwright	Palmer
11/05	**BROMSGROVE**	WSCf(1)	1-1	1,235	Rose	Hodson	Bancroft	Woodall	Brindley	Forsyth	Cartwright	Grainger	Humphreys	Davies(1)	*Purdie*		Palmer
13/05	Bromsgrove R.	WSCf(2)	0-4	1,994	Rose	Hodson	Bancroft	Woodall	Brindley	Forsyth	*Cartwright*	Grainger	*Humphreys*	Davies	Palmer	Wolsey	Deakin

* - Played at Witton Albion FC

Kidderminster Harriers

GRAHAM ALLNER

Graham Allner joined Kidderminster Harriers as manager in October 1983. Formerly assistant manager at Cheltenham Town, he had won the Southern League championship when manager of the now defunct AP Leamington.

Graham's playing days began at Walsall where he gained England Youth honours. He then moved into non-League football where he played at Worcester City, Stafford Rangers and Alvechurch.

1993-94 was, without doubt, Graham's most successful as a manager, steering Kidderminster to the GM Vauxhall Conference championship and through to the last sixteen of the FA Cup.

During his time at Aggborough, Graham has encouraged youth through their YT programme and many of his young players have come through to the first team.

Kidderminster captain Simeon Hodson (left) and Neil Cartwright combine to shut out Matt Holmes of West Ham United during the emotion-charged FA Cup Fifth Round tie at Aggborough.

Photo - Paul Dennis.

Programme details:
36 pages for £1.20. Editor - Roger Barlow

Any other club publications:
None

Local Newspapers:
Kidderminster Shuttle/Times
Kidderminster Chronicle
Evening Mail
Express & Star
Worcester Evening News

Local Radio Stations:
BBC Hereford & Worcester
Radio Wyvern
Beacon Radio, BRMB

KIDDERMINSTER HARRIERS - PLAYING SQUAD 1993-94

Player	Honours	Birthplace and date	Transfer Fees	Previous Clubs
GOALKEEPERS				
Kevin Rose	GMVC	Evesham 23/11/60		Ledbury T, Lincoln C, Ledbury T, Hereford, Bolton W, Rochdale
Darren Steadman	ES	Kidderminster 26/1/70		From YTS
DEFENDERS				
Paul Bancroft	ESP, GMVC	Derby 10/9/64		Derby Co, Northampton T, Nuneaton B, Burton Alb, Kidderminster H, Kettering T
Chris Brindley	GMVC, FAT, FAXI	Stoke 5/7/69	£20,000	Hednesford T, Wolves, Telford United
Simeon Hodson	ESP, GMVC	Lincoln 5/3/66		Notts Co, Charlton, Lincoln, Newport Co, WBA, Doncaster, Kidderminster, Mansfield
Martin Weir	GMVC, FAXI, Middx Wand.	Birmingham 4/7/68		Birmingham City
Wayne Williams		Delford 17/11/63		Shrewsbury T, Northampton T, Walsall
Craig Gillett		Dudley 17/10/72		From Youth Team
MIDFIELDERS				
Neil Cartwright	GMVC	Stourbridge 20/2/71		West Bromwich Albion
Richard Forsyth	GMVC, FAXI	Dudley 3/10/70		Stourbridge
John Deakin	GMVC	Sheffield 29/9/66		Barnsley, Doncaster, Grimsby, Frickley A, Shepshed, Birmingham, Carlisle, Wycombe
Paul Grainger	GMVC, FAT, FAXI	Walsall 28/1/68	£10,000	Aston Villa, Mile Oak Rovers, Wolves, Telford United
Mark Wolsey		Birmingham 27/12/73		From YTS
FORWARDS				
Paul Davies	ESP, GMVC, FAT, FAXI	Kidderminster 9/10/60		Cardiff C, Trowbridge T, SC Hercules (Holl)
Jon Purdie	Es, GMVC	Corby 22/2/67		Arsenal, Wolves, Oxford U, Brentford, Shrewsbury, Worcester C, Cheltenham T
Les Palmer	GMVC	Birmingham 5/9/71		West Bromwich Albion
Delwyn Humphreys	ESP, GMVC, SSC	Shrewsbury 13/2/65	£10,000	Newtown, Bridgnorth Town
David Hadley	GMVC	Birmingham 7/12/64	£10,000	Tamworth, Mile Oak Rovers, Moor Green

Departures during season:
David Benton (Worcester City), Colin Gordon (Released).

Players on loan during season:
Mark West (Wycombe W).

Aggborough, Kidderminster Harriers

Address and telephone number: Aggborough Staduim, Hoo Road, Kidderminster, DY10 1NB. Tel: 0562 823931 (Ground). 0562 740198 (Social Club). Fax: 0562 823931.

Simple directions: From North - exit M5 at junction 3, follow A456 to Kidderminster and on reaching the town at first traffic lights turn left into Chester Road. At next traffic lights turn right into Comberton Road, continue past station and Hoo Road is on the left halfway down the hill. From the South & West - exit M5 at junction 6. Follow A449 to Kidderminster. At first roundabout (Adjacent to railway viaduct) turn right into Chester Road and first left into Hoo Road. From London direction via M42 then follow M5 north to junction 4 (Lydiate Ash). Exit motorway turn left and follow A491 towards Stourbridge. At Hagley roundabout turn left and follow A456 to Kidderminster as above.

Capacity: 6,290 **Seated:** 1,100 **Covered terracing:** 4,690

Record Attendance: 9,155 - Hereford United - FA Cup 1st Round Proper 27.11.48.

Club Shop: Open Monday to Friday 9am-5pm, plus 1st XI match days.

Social Facilities: Vice Presidents lounge bar for members, officials & players. Social & supporters club (3 bars) open to visiting supporters before & after the match, temporary admission fee 50p. Hot & cold food available.

Kidderminster Fact File

Nickname: Harriers

Previous Grounds: None

Previous Leagues: Birmingham League 1889-1890, 1891-1939, 1947-1948, 1960-1962, Midland League 1890-1891, Southern League 1939-1945 (Abandoned - World War II), 1948-1960, 1972-1983, Birmingham Combination 1945-1947, West Midlands League 1962-1972.

Club colours: Red & white

Change colours: Yellow & blue

Reserve team league: Midland Combination Reserve Division

Midweek home matchday: Mondays 7.45pm.

Record win: 25-0 v Hereford (H) - 12.10.1889 - Birmingham Senior Cup 1st Rnd.

Record defeat: 0-13 v Darwen (A) - 24.01.1891 - FA Cup 1st Rnd Proper.

Record transfer fee: £20,000 for Chris Brindley from Telford - 1992

Record transfer fee received: £60,000 each for Paul Jones from Wolves - 1991 & Steve Lilwall from W.B.A - 1992.

1993-94 Captain: Simeon Hodson

1993-94 Top scorer: Paul Davies, Delwyn Humphreys

1993-94 Player of the Year: Chris Brindley

Club record goalscorer: Peter Wassall 432 - 1963-1974

Record appearances: Brendan Wassall 686 - 1962-1974

Past players who progressed to the Football League: To numerous to list.

Club Honours: GMV Conference Champions 1994; FA Trophy Winners 1987, Runners-up 1991; Welsh FA Cup finalists 1986, 1989; Southern League Cup 1980; Worcester Senior Cup (19); Birmingham Senior Cup (7); Staffordshire Senior Cup (4); West Midland League Champions (6), Runners-up (3); Southern Premier Runners-up (1); West Midland League Cup winners (7); Keys Cup winners (7); Border Counties Floodlit League Champions (3), Camkin Floodlit Cup Winners (3); Bass County Vase Winners (1).

MACCLESFIELD TOWN

Formed:
1874

Chairman:
A Jones
Vice Chairman
N Bardsley
Football Secretary:
C Garlick

Directors:
R Isherwood
R Higginbotham
J Brooks
N Bardsley
A Masheder
B Lingard
R Curran
A Cash

Manager:
Sammy McIlroy
Assistant Manager:
Gil Prescot

Physiotherapist:
Eric Campbell

Commercial Manager:
Ray Smith

Press Officer:
A Garlick

Macclesfield Town had an indifferent start to the season as new manager Sammy McIlroy looked to settle his squad. A number of heavy defeats away from the Moss Rose caused some early concern but, as the squad settled, an attractive style of football evolved. This brand of football started with six straight victories and a period where the Silkmen scored at least a goal a game in a 21 match unbroken sequence. During this time, Carl Alford and John Askey won the *Mail on Sunday* Goalscorer of the Month Award, and Sammy McIlroy won Manager of the Month recognition.

Macclesfield were entered for five cup competitions. They had differing fortunes in the two County Senior Cups. In the Cheshire, a narrow victory against Altrincham was followed by a 7-1 thrashing of Colwyn Bay. Unfortunately, due to a technical problem, Macclesfield took no further part in the competition. The Staffordshire Senior Cup caused fixture problems and will be concluded prior to the 94/95 season as Macclesfield have progressed all the way to the final.

In the FA Trophy, Macclesfield travelled to Boston United and Worcester City in rounds one and two. Both teams were brought back to the Moss Rose before Macclesfield progressed to round three. Billingham Synthonia were Macclesfield's conquerors at this stage, and were only beaten by the eventual winners, Woking.

In the 4th qualifying round of the FA Cup Macclesfield entertained Southport and emerged 5-3 victors in a very entertaining tie. Their reward was a home tie against Hartlepool United in the first round proper. Macclesfield added another league scalp to their collection as they were comfortable 2-0 winners which set up a visit to Gresty Road to face high-flying Crewe Alexandra. Although 2-0 down at half-time, the Silkmen pulled a goal back early in the second-half and were unlucky not to earn at least a replay when a second goal was controversially ruled out for offside.

The cup success of the season came in the Drinkwise Cup with impressive victories over Witten Albion, Runcorn and Halifax Town. In the semi-final they gained revenge for the previous season's defeat against Northwich Victoria to take their place in the final. At the Moss Rose in the first-leg of the final, Macclesfield took charge of the tie and took a 4-1 advantage to Yeovil Town. A goalless draw in the second leg was a formality as Macclesfield lifted the Bob Lord Trophy for the first time.

In the final quarter of the season, the Silkmen made steady progress up the table collecting their best Conference away record of nine victories and eventually finishing a very creditable 7th. Overall, a very successful first season for Sammy McIlroy; a major trophy in the cabinet with the possibility of another to follow and hopefully a very firm foundation upon which to build.

Macclesfield - Drinkwise Cup winners 1993-94. *Photo - Keith Clayton.*

MACCLESFIELD TOWN *MATCHFACTS 93-94* ***MACCLESFIELD TOWN*** *MATCHFACTS 93-94*

Key: Home fixtures are denoted by bold capitals. Numbers in brackets after players names indicate goals scored (asterisks by the results denote own goals). Only used substitutes are listed - substituted players are *italicised*.

Key to Competitions: GMVC: GM Vauxhall Conference. **CSC**: Cheshire Senior Cup. **DC**: Drinkwise (GM Vauxhall Conference) Cup. **FAC**: FA Cup. **FAT**: FA Trophy. **SSC:** Staffordshire Senior Cup.

Date	Opponents	Comp.	Res	Gate	1.	2.	3.	4.	5.	6.	7.	8.	9.	10.	11.	Sub.	Sub.
21/08	Bath City	GMVC	1-5	667	Sutton	Shepherd	Bimson	Lillis	*Allardyce*	Dempsey	*Leicester*	Wood	Alford	Roberts	Sharrat(1)	Sorvel	Green
25/08	**BROMSGROVE R.**	GMVC	4-3	695	Lennon	Shepherd	Bimson	Lillis	Alford(2)	*Dempsey*	Leicester	Wood	Green(2)	Roberts	Sharrat	Sorvel	
28/08	**DOVER ATH.**	GMVC	0-2	864	Lennon	Shepherd	Bimson	Lillis	Alford	Dempsey	Leicester	*Wood*	Green	Roberts	Sharrat	Sorvel	
30/08	Runcorn	GMVC	1-2	737	Lennon	Shepherd	Bimson	Lillis	Allardyce	Dempsey	*Roberts*	Sorvel	Alford(1)	Mitchell	Sharrat	Leicester	
04/09	**DAGENHAM & R.**	GMVC	3-0	633	Farrelly	Shepherd	Bimson	Lillis	Howarth	Dempsey	Roberts	Sorvel(1)	Alford(1)	Adams	Sharrat(1)		
07/09	Witton Albion	DC1(1)	2-1	837	Farrelly	Shepherd	Bimson	Lillis	Howarth	Dempsey	Roberts(1)	Sorvel	Alford(1)	Adams	Sharrat		
11/09	Woking	GMVC	0-3	1,566	Farrelly	Shepherd	Bimson	Lillis	Howarth	Dempsey	*Roberts*	Sorvel	Alford	Adams	*Sharrat*	Leicester	Mitchell
18/09	**KETTERING T.**	GMVC	0-0	933	Walker	Shepherd	Bimson	Lillis	Howarth	Dempsey	*Leicester*	Sorvel	Alford	Adams	Sharrat		Askey
21/09	**WITTON ALBION**	DC1(2)	4-1	466	Walker	Shepherd	Bimson	Lillis	Howarth	Dempsey	Wood	Askey(2)	Alford(1)	Adams	Sharrat(1)		
25/09	Yeovil Town	GMVC	0-4	2,516	Walker	Brown	Bimson	Kendall	Howarth	Dempsey	*Wood*	Askey	*Alford*	Adams	Sharrat	Sorvel	Mitchell
28/09	Sutton Coldfield	SSC1	5-2	150	Walker	Vigon	Bimson	Kendall(1)	Lillis	*Wood(2)*	Leicester	*Askey*	Mitchell(2)	Sorvel	Adams	Dempsey	Alford
02/10	**SOUTHPORT**	GMVC	0-1	1,002	Walker	Shepherd	Bimson	Kendall	Alford	Dempsey	Sorvel	Askey	*Roberts*	Adams	Sharrat	Mitchell	
09/10	Witton Albion	GMVC	2-0	1,068	Farrelly	Shepherd	Bimson	Kendall	Lillis	Roberts(1)	Askey	Sorvel	Alford	Power(1)	Adams		
11/10	Kidderminster H.	GMVC	1-2	1,228	Farrelly	Shepherd	Bimson	Kendall	Lillis	Roberts	Askey	*Sorvel*	Alford	*Power(1)*	Heron	Mitchell	Dempsey
16/10	**MERTHYR TYD.**	GMVC	1-2	835	Farrelly	Shepherd	Bimson	*Kendall*	Lillis	Roberts	Askey	Sorvel	Alford	Power(1)	*Adams*	Wood	Green
23/10	**SOUTHPORT**	FAC4q	5-3	1,190	Farrelly	Shepherd	Bimson	Kendall	Lillis	Roberts	Askey	Sorvel	Alford(3)	Wood(1)	Sharrat(1)		
26/10	**TELFORD UTD**	GMVC	1-0	731	Farrelly	Shepherd	Bimson	Kendall	Lillis	Sorvel	Askey	Wood	Alford(1)	*Roberts*	Sharrat		Power
30/10	Stafford Rgrs	GMVC	3-2	1,249	Farrelly	Shepherd	Bimson	Kendall	Lillis	Sorvel	Askey	Wood	Alford(3)	Power	Sharrat		
02/11	Runcorn	DC2	4-0	471	Farrelly	Shepherd(1)	Bimson	Kendall	Lillis	Sorvel	Askey(2)	Wood(1)	Alford	Adams	Sharrat		
06/11	**GATESHEAD**	GMVC	6-1	1,033	Farrelly	*Shepherd*	Bimson	Kendall	Lillis	Sorvel	Askey(3)	Wood(1)	Alford	Power(1)	Sharrat(1)	Heron	
13/11	**HARTLEPOOL U.**	FAC1	2-0	2,747	Farrelly	Shepherd	Bimson	Kendall	Lillis	Sorvel(1)	Askey	*Wood*	Alford	Adams	Sharrat	McDonald(1)	
15/11	Pelsall Villa	SSC2	1-1	441	Williams	Vigon	Cunningham	Kendall	Heron	Sorvel	Adams	McDonald	Green	Atkinson	Izakoboh(1)		
20/11	**SLOUGH TOWN**	GMVC	2-2	1,033	Farrelly	Shepherd	Bimson	Kendall	Lillis	Sorvel	Askey	McDonald	Alford(1)	*Adams*	Sharrat(1)		Green
27/11	Welling United	GMVC	1-0	773	Farrelly	Shepherd	Bimson	Kendall	Lillis	Sorvel(1)	Askey	McDonald	Alford	Power	Sharrat		
30/11	Altrincham	CSC2	1-0	369	Farrelly	Shepherd	Bimson	Kendall	Lillis	Sorvel	Askey	McDonald	Alford	Power(1)	Sharrat		Adams
04/12	Crewe Alexandra	FAC2	1-2	6,007	Farrelly	Shepherd	Bimson	Kendall	Lillis	Sorvel	Askey(1)	McDonald	Alford	Adams	Sharrat		
07/12	**PELSALL VILLA**	SSC2r	3-1	149	Farrelly	Heron	Bimson	Kendall	*Lillis*	Sorvel	*Askey(1)*	McDonald	Alford	Power(2)	Sharrat	Vigon	Adams
11/12	**STALYBRIDGE**	GMVC	1-3	776	*Farrelly*	Shepherd	Bimson	Kendall	Heron	Sorvel	Askey	McDonald	Alford(1)	*Power*	Sharrat	Mitchell	Adams
18/12	Merthyr Tydfil	GMVC	1-2	425	Farrelly(1)	Shepherd	Bimson	Kendall	Lillis	Sorvel	Askey	McDonald	Alford	Adams	Sharrat		
21/12	Halifax Town	DCqf	2-1	778	Farrelly	Shepherd	Bimson	Kendall	Lillis(1)	Sorvel	Askey	McDonald	Alford(1)	*Kinsey*	Sharrat		Adams

01/01	Stalybridge C.	GMVC	2-0	1,059	Farrelly	Shepherd	Bimson	Kendall	Lillis	Sorvel(1)	Askey	McDonald	Alford	Power(1)	Adams		
05/01	**ALTRINCHAM**	GMVC	1-0	742	Farrelly	Shepherd	Bimson	Kendall	Lillis	Sorvel	Askey	McDonald	Alford	*Power*	Adams(1)		Thorpe
15/01	**WOKING**	GMVC	1-1	1,053	Farrelly	Shepherd	Bimson	*Kendall*	Lillis	Sorvel	Askey	McDonald	Alford	Power(1)	Adams		Thorpe
22/01	Boston United	FAT1	1-1	1,559	Farrelly	*Shepherd*	Bimson	Kendall	Lillis	Sorvel	Askey	McDonald	Alford(1)	Power	Adams		Wood
25/01	**BOSTON UTD**	FAT1r	1-0	590	Farrelly	Thorpe	Bimson	Kendall	Lillis	Sorvel	Askey	McDonald	Alford(1)	Power	Adams		
29/01	Bromsgrove R.	GMVC	0-3	1,701	Farrelly	Thorpe	Bimson	Kendall	Lillis	Sorvel	Askey	McDonald	Alford	Power	Lyons		
05/02	**NORTHWICH V.**	GMVC	0-0	1,141	Farrelly	Shepherd	Bimson	Kendall	Howarth	Sorvel	Askey	McDonald	*Alford*	Power	Lyons		Wood
08/02	**COLWYN BAY**	CSCqf	#7-1	384	Farrelly	*Shepherd*	Bimson	Thorpe	Lillis	Sorvel	Wood	*McDonald*	Lyons(4)	Askey(1)	Sharrat(1)	Atkinson(1)	Vigon
12/02	Worcester City	FAT2	0-0	1,537	Farrelly	Shepherd	Bimson	Kendall	Howarth	Sorvel	Wood	McDonald	Lyons	Askey	Sharrat		
19/02	**RUNCORN**	GMVC	0-0	1,004	Farrelly	Shepherd	Bimson	Kendall	Howarth	Sorvel	Askey	McDonald	*Lyons*	Power	Sharrat		Adams
21/02	**WORCESTER C.**	FAT2r	*3-2	704	Farrelly	*Shepherd*	Bimson	Kendall	Howarth	Sorvel	Askey(1)	McDonald	Alford	*Power(1)*	Sharrat	Lyons	Lillis
26/02	Telford United	GMVC	3-1	1,108	Farrelly	Thorpe	Bimson	Kendall	Howarth	Sorvel(1)	Askey	Lillis	Alford(2)	*Power*	Sharrat		Lyons
01/03	Altrincham	GMVC	1-0	1,030	Farrelly	Thorpe	Bimson	Kendall	Howarth	Sorvel	Askey	Lillis	Alford	Power(1)	Sharrat		
05/03	**BILLINGHAM S.**	FAT3	0-1	909	Farrelly	Shepherd	Bimson	Kendall	Howarth	Sorvel	Askey	McDonald	Alford	*Power*	*Sharrat*	Adams	Thorpe
08/03	**NORTHWICH V.**	DCsf(1)	2-1	578	Farrelly	Shepherd	Bimson	Kendall	Howarth	Sorvel	Askey	McDonald	Alford(1)	Lyons(1)	Adams		
12/03	**BATH CITY**	GMVC	0-0	757	Farrelly	Shepherd	Bimson	Kendall	Howarth	Sorvel	Askey	McDonald	Adams	*Lyons*	Sharrat		Lillis
15/03	Northwich Vics	DCsf(2)	1-0	1,008	Farrelly	Shepherd	Bimson	Kendall	Howarth	Sorvel	Askey	McDonald	*Alford(1)*	Lillis	*Sharrat*	Lyons	Adams
19/03	**HALIFAX TOWN**	GMVC	0-1	1,115	Farrelly	Shepherd	Bimson	Kendall	Howarth	Sorvel	*Askey*	McDonald	Lillis	*Power*	Sharrat	Adams	Lyons
22/03	Southport	GMVC	0-1	1,012	Farrelly	Locke	*Bimson*	Kendall	Howarth	Sorvel	Askey	McDonald	Lillis	Power	Sharrat		Lyons
26/03	Kettering Town	GMVC	1-0	2,158	Farrelly	Locke	Lillis	*Kendall*	Howarth(1)	Sorvel	Askey	McDonald	Alford	*Power*	Sharrat	Adams	Wood
30/03	Gateshead	GMVC	0-1	306	Farrelly	Locke	Lillis	Adams	Howarth	Sorvel	*Askey*	McDonald	Alford	Power	Sharrat		Lyons
02/04	Dover Athletic	GMVC	2-1	942	Farrelly	Shepherd	Lillis	Locke	Howarth	Sorvel	Askey	McDonald	Alford(2)	*Power*	Adams		Powell
06/04	**HALESOWEN T.**	SSCqf	4-1	251	Farrelly	*Vigon*	Lillis	Locke	Howarth	Sorvel	Lyons	Wood(1)	Alford(1)	*Power(1)*	Adams	McDonald(1)	Askey
09/04	Slough Town	GMVC	1-1	584	Farrelly	Shepherd	Lillis	Locke	Howarth(1)	Sorvel	Askey	McDonald	Alford	Lyons	Adams		
12/04	**YEOVIL TOWN**	DCf(1)	4-1	651	Farrelly	Shepherd	Bimson	Lillis	Howarth	Sorvel	Askey	*McDonald(1)*	Alford(1)	Lyons(2)	Adams		Wood
16/04	**KIDDERMINSTER**	GMVC	0-0	1,114	Farrelly	Shepherd	Lillis	Locke	Howarth	Sorvel	Askey	McDonald	Alford	Lyons	*Adams*		Wood
19/04	Yeovil Town	DCf(2)	0-0	1,241	Farrelly	Shepherd	Lillis	Wood	Howarth	Sorvel	Askey	McDonald	*Alford*	Lyons	Adams		Powell
23/04	**WITTON ALBION**	GMVC	2-0	720	Farrelly	Shepherd	Lillis	Locke	Howarth	Sorvel(1)	*Askey*	Wood	Alford	Lyons(1)	Adams		Power
24/04	Dagenham & Red.	GMVC	1-1	829	Farrelly	Shepherd	Bimson	Kendall	Howarth	Sorvel	*Lyons*	McDonald(1)	Alford	Powell	Adams		Wood
26/04	Halifax Town	GMVC	2-1	723	Farrelly	Shepherd	Bimson	Lillis	Howarth	Sorvel	Lyons	McDonald	*Alford*	Power(2)	Adams		Powell
30/04	**YEOVIL TOWN**	GMVC	1-2	732	Farrelly	Shepherd	Bimson	Lillis	Howarth(1)	Sorvel	*Lyons*	McDonald	Powell	Power	Adams		Wood
02/05	**WELLING UTD**	GMVC	1-0	577	Farrelly	Shepherd	Bimson	Lillis	Howarth	Sorvel	Lyons	McDonald	Powell(1)	Power	Adams		
04/05	**STAFFORD R.**	GMVC	0-0	542	Farrelly	Shepherd	Bimson	Lillis	Howarth	Sorvel	*Lyons*	McDonald	Powell	Power	Adams		Wood
07/05	Northwich Vics	GMVC	1-1	1,002	Farrelly	Shepherd	Bimson	Lillis	Howarth	Sorvel	Askey	McDonald	Powell(1)	Power	Adams		
10/05	**DUDLEY TOWN**	SSCsf	2-0		Farrelly	Wood	Bimson	Lillis	Locke	Sorvel	Askey	McDonald	*Powell*	Power(1)	Adams		Lyons(1)
10/08	Wednesfield	SSCf(1)															
13/08	**WEDNESFIELD**	SSCf(2)															

- Tie awarded to Colwyn Bay because Macclesfield Town fielded an ineligible player - Darren Lyons.

Macclesfield Town

SAMMY McILROY

The last of the 'Busby Babes', Sammy followed in the footsteps of the legendary George Best when he moved from his native Belfast to join Manchester United as a raw teenager in the late sixties. He became an established member of the highly successful and exciting United side built by Tommy Docherty. In all he made 418 appearances for United, the highlight being the 1977 FA Cup Final success over Liverpool.

In 1982 he moved to Stoke City where he played 144 times before heading back to Manchester to join United's deadly rivals, City. His time at Maine Road was curtailed when he accepted an offer to join Bury, then managed by Martin Dobson, whom he was to succeed at Northwich Victoria. He then took up a post as player-coach with Preston, but a severe knee injury virtually ended his playing days.

In July 1991, he was appointed as manager at Northwich Victoria. Coming into the job cold with virtually no experience of the non-league scene, everyone at the club was delighted with his and his team's performance. Happily his own injuries recovered sufficiently for him to make a welcome, and most effective, comeback as a player with the Vics towards the end of the season. The experience of playing in a green shirt again no doubt brought back memories of his 78 appearances in an emerald shirt for his country, Northern Ireland.

Sammy left Northwich Victoria in 1992 and became manager of Ashton United for short spell before joining Macclesfield Town for the start of the 1993-94 season, a season that was to bring him his first managerial - the Drinkwise Cup.

John Askey and Carl Alford join scorer Neil Sorvel to celebrate Macclesfield's first goal in their excellent 2-0 win at home to Hartlepool United in the FA Cup.

Photo - Colin Stevens.

Programme details:
36 pages for £1
Editor - Dennis Johnson. (Asst Editor: Joanne Foy)

Any other club publications:
Silk Yarns (Fanzine)

Local Newspapers:
Macclesfield Express
Manchester Evening News
Manchester Evening News Pink

Local Radio Stations:
GMR (BBC)
BBC Radio Stoke
Piccadilly Radio
Signal Radio

MACCLESFIELD TOWN - PLAYING SQUAD

Player	Honours	Birthplace and date	Transfer Fees	Previous Clubs
GOALKEEPERS				
Steve Farrelly	DC, CCS, Middx Wand.	Manchester		Chester City, Knowsley Utd
DEFENDERS				
George Shepherd	DC, CSC	Manchester 25/2/67	£6,000	Manchester City, Bolton W, Hyde United
Stuart Bimson	DC, NPLC, LSC, CSC	Liverpool 29/9/69	£5,000	Prescot, Ellesmere Port, Southport
Paul Kendall	DC, GMVC	Halifax 19/10/64		Halifax T, Scarborough, Halifax T
Mick Farrelly	ES, ESP, FAT	Manchester 1/11/62		Preston NE, Altrincham
Stuart Locke	MCSC	Manchester		Man.City, Crewe, Northwich V, Stalybridge C
Mark Lillis	DC	Manchester 17/1/60		Huddersfield, Man.City, Derby, A.Villa, Scunthorpe, Stockport, Witton Alb
MIDFIELDERS				
Neil Sorvel	DC	Widnes 2/3/73		Crewe Alexandra
Steve Adams	GMVC, DC	Sheffield 7/9/59		Rotherham, Worksop, Scarboro, Doncaster, Boston U, Kettering, Gateshead, Witton Alb
John Askey	ESP, NPL, DC, CSC	Stoke 4/11/64		Port Vale, Milton Utd
Steve Wood	DC	Manchester 23/6/63		Chadderton, Mossley, Droylsden, Stalybridge C
Graham Roberts	WSP	Wales		Mold Alexandra, Flint Town, Colwyn Bay
Aidan Brodigan		Manchester		From Reserves
Martin McDonald	DC	Glasgow		Glasgow Celtic, Stockport Co
FORWARDS				
Darren Lyons		Manchester 9/11/66	Player/ Exchange	Oldham, Rhyl, Droylsden, Macclesfield, Leek, Mossley, Ashton Utd, Bury, Southport
Phil Power	DC, GMAC	Salford 25/7/66	Player/ Exchange	Northwich V, Witton A, Crewe, Horwich, Chorley, Barrow, Stalybridge C
Carl Alford	DC	Manchester 11/2/72	£1,700	Rochdale, Stockport Co, Burnley, Witton Alb
Gary Powell		Hoylake 2/4/69	Player/ Exchange	Everton, Wigan Ath, Bury, Altrincham

Departures during season:
John Timmons (Witton Alb), Pat Lennon (Canada), Roy Green (Worcester C), Steve Kinsey (Released), Richard Mitchell (Southport), Chris Sharratt (Altrincham), Mike France (Northwich V).

Players on loan during season:
Andy Thorpe (Witton Alb), Craig Allardyce (Preston), Neil Howarth (Burnley), Gary Walker & Gary Brown (Buxton).

Moss Rose, Macclesfield

Address and telephone number: Moss Rose, London Road, Macclesfield, Cheshire SK11 7SP. Tel: 0625 511545 (Commercial Office). 0625 424324 (Social Club). 0891 12 15 46 (Club Call).
Simple directions: Approximately 1 mile south of the Town Centre on the A523 (Leek Road). British Rail Macclesfield approximately 1.5 miles, regular bus service on Match day. Ample unrestricted parking around the ground.
Capacity: 6,000 **Seated:** 600 **Covered terracing:** 2,500
Record Attendance: 9,003 v Winsford United - Cheshire Senior Cup 2nd Round 04.02.48.
Club Shop: Open Monday - Friday 10.00 to 4.00 and on match days. Contact Andy Ridgway on 0625 423099 for more details.
Social Facilities: The Blues Club - open match days and functions.
Previous Grounds: None

Macclesfield Fact File

Nickname: Silkmen

Club Sponsors: Zeneca Pharmaceutical

Previous Leagues: Manchester League, Cheshire League, Northern Premier League.

Club colours: Blue & white

Change colours: Yellow/blue/yellow

Reserve team league: North West Alliance League

Midweek home matchday: Tuesday (7.45pm)

Record win: 15-0 v Chester St.Marys - Cheshire Senior Cup 2nd Round 16.02.1886.

Record defeat: 13-1 v Tranmere Rovers Reserves 03.05.1929.

Record transfer fee: £7,000 to Binche for Andy Green - 1991.

Record transfer fee received: £40,000 for Mike Lake from Sheffield United - 1988.

1993-94 Captain: Stuart Bimson.

1993-94 Top scorer: Carl Alford.

1993-94 Supporters' Player of the Year: Martin McDonald

1993-94 Players' Player of the Year: Steve Farrelly

Club record goalscorer: Albert Valentine 84 - 1933-34.

Record appearances: Keith Goalen - 1957-1970.

Past players who progressed to the Football League: Numerous.

Club Honours: FA Trophy Winners 1970, Runners-up 1989, 1986; Bord Lord Trophy winners 1994; NPL Challenge Cup 1986; Presidents Cup 1986; Cheshire Senior Cup 1890, 1891, 1894, 1896, 1911, 1930, 1935, 1951, 1952, 1954, 1960, 1964, 1969, 1971, 1973, 1983; Cheshire County League 1932, 1933, 1953, 1961, 1964, 1968.

MERTHYR TYDFIL

Formed:
1945

Joint President:
The Archbishop of Cardiff
His Grace John Aloysious Ward
The Lord Bishop of Llandaff
The Right Rev. Roy Davies

Chairman:
John Reddy

Football Secretary:
Howard King

Manager:
Gerald Aplin

Physiotherapist:
Ken Davey

Commercial Manager:
Howard King

Press Officer:
Anthony Hughes

Saved from drop by Leek Town

After the signing of Robbie James from Cardiff City in October 1993 (James was soon appointed Player-Manager), Merthyr Tydfil's hopes of success were very high. Robbie James was injured himself, however, in the match against Kidderminster Harriers, and was not to play again all season.

After the the club had been knocked out of the FA Challenge Trophy at Gateshead, things went from bad to worse. They finished the season third from bottom after losing five games on the trot, and were only spared relegation because Leek Town, second in the Northern Premier League, were rejected by the GM Vauxhall Conference.

The club will play in the Conference again in 1994-95, but under a new manager. Gerald Aplin, the man who guided Chesham United to the Diadora Isthmian League Premier Division title in 1993 has taken over the managerial reigns and brough several new players to the club.

Howard King

(Howard King, the former FIFA and Premier League referee, has taken over as Secretary of Merthyr Tydfil combining the role with that of Commercial Manager)

Merthyr Tydfil pictured before their remarkable 5-4 success away to St Albans City in the First Round of the FA Challenge Trophy.

Photo - Eric Marsh.

MERTHYR *MATCHFACTS 93-94* **MERTHYR** *MATCHFACTS 93-94* **MERTHYR** *MATCHFACTS 93-94*

Key: Home fixtures are denoted by bold capitals. Numbers in brackets after players names indicate goals scored (asterisks by the results denote own goals). Only used substitutes are listed - substituted players are *italicised*.

Key to Competitions: GMVC: GM Vauxhall Conference. **WC**: Allbright Bitter Welsh Cup. **DC**: Drinkwise (GM Vauxhall Conference) Cup. **FAC**: FA Cup. **FAT**: FA Trophy. **SWS:** South Wales Senior Cup.

Date	Opponents	Comp.	Res	Gate	1.	2.	3.	4.	5.	6.	7.	8.	9.	10.	11.	Sub.	Sub.
21/08	**ALTRINCHAM**	GMVC	0-0	643	Wager	M Williams	M Davies	Rogers	Trick	D Lewis	Tucker	*M Jones*	Drewitt	*C Williams*	Benbow	Holtham	Owen
24/08	**BATH CITY**	GMVC	1-1	543	Wager	M Jones	M Davies	Holtham	Trick	D Lewis	Tucker	Benbow	Drewitt	C Williams	Rogers(1)		
28/08	Witton Albion	GMVC	2-2	751	Wager	M Jones	M Davies	Holtham	Trick	D Lewis	Tucker(1)	Rogers	*Drewitt*	C Williams(1)	Benbow	Ry James	
03/09	Welling Utd	GMVC	1-1	1,081	Wager	M Williams	M Davies	*Holtham*	M Jones	D Lewis	Tucker	Rogers	Drewitt	C Williams(1)	Benbow	Ry James	
04/09	**SOUTHPORT**	GMVC	2-2	607	Wager	M Williams	M Davies	D Lewis	*Trick*	M Jones	Tucker(1)	Rogers	Drewitt(1)	C Williams	*Benbow*	Holtham	Coates
07/09	**DOVER ATH.**	DC1(1)	0-2	303	Wager	M Williams	M Davies	Holtham	Trick	Ry James	Tucker	Coates	Drewitt	C Williams	Benbow		
11/09	Kettering Town	GMVC	0-0	1,702	Wager	M Williams	M Davies	Holtham	Trick	R James	Tucker	Coates	Drewitt	C Williams	Benbow		
18/09	**RUNCORN**	GMVC	1-1	516	Wager	M Williams	Rogers(1)	Holtham	Trick	M Jones	Tucker	Coates	Drewitt	C Williams	Lewis		
21/09	Dover Athletic	DC1(2)	0-2	867	Wager	M Williams	M Jones	Lewis	*Owen*	Rogers	Holtham	Benbow	Coates	Drewitt	Ry James	Hutchison	
25/09	Kidderminster	GMVC	0-2	1,026	Wager	M Williams	*James*	M Jones	Trick	Rogers	Tucker	Holtham	Benbow	Drewitt	Lewis		Coates
02/10	Taffs Well	WC2	7-1		Wager	M Williams	*M Jones*	Holtham(2)	Trick	Lewis	Tucker(1)	Coates(1)	Benbow(1)	C Williams(2)	Rogers	M Davies	
21/08	Woking	GMVC	1-2	1,266	Wager	M Williams	*M Davies*	Holtham	Trick	Lewis	Tucker	Coates	Benbow	C Williams(1)	Rogers	Hutchison	
09/10	**HALIFAX TOWN**	GMVC	2-1	911	Wager	M Williams	M Davies	Lewis	Trick	Rogers(1)	Holtham	*Ro James*	Coates	Tucker	C Williams(1)	Ry James	
12/10	Slough Town	GMVC	2-3	763	Wager	M Williams	M Davies	Lewis	Trick	*Rogers*	Holtham	Ro James	Coates(2)	Ry James	*Drewitt*	Hutchison	Benbow
16/10	Macclesfield T.	GMVC	2-1	835	Wager	M Williams	Ry James	Lewis	Trick	Tucker	Holtham	Ro James	Coates	*C Williams(1)*	Rogers	Drewitt(1)	
23/10	Crawley Town	FAC4q	1-2	1,623	Wager	M Williams	M Davies	*Lewis*	*Trick*	Ry James(1)	Holtham	Ro James	Coates	C Williams	Rogers	Hutchison	Drewitt
30/10	**NORTHWICH V.**	GMVC	5-0	602	Wager	*M Williams*	N Jones	Lewis	M Davies	Ry James	Holtham(1)	Ro James	Coates(1)	*C Williams*	Rogers(2)	Drewitt(1)	Owen
06/11	Dover Athletic	GMVC	0-1	1,301	Wager	M Williams	N Jones	Lewis	M Davies	Ry James	Holtham	Tucker	Coates	*Benbow*	*Rogers*	Hutchison	Drewitt
09/11	Swansea City	WC3	0-0	2,450	Wager	M Williams	Ry James	Lewis	M Davies	Hutchison	Holtham	Tucker	Coates	Rogers	Drewitt		
13/11	**DOVER ATH.**	GMVC	0-0	556	Wager	M Williams	N Jones	Lewis	M Davies	Ry James	Holtham	Tucker	Coates	*C Williams*	*Rogers*	Hutchison	Drewitt
20/11	**STAFFORD R.**	GMVC	2-0	561	Wager	M Williams	N Jones	Lewis	M Davies	Ry James(1)	Holtham	Tucker	Coates	Drewitt(1)	*Hutchison*		Rogers
27/11	Bromsgrove R.	GMVC	3-3	914	Wager	M Williams	N Jones	Lewis	M Davies(2)	Ry James	Holtham	Tucker(1)	Coates	Rogers	Drewitt		
02/12	**SWANSEA CITY**	WC3r	1-2	2,106	Wager	M Williams	James	Lewis	M Davies	*Hutchison*	Holtham	Tucker	Coates	Rogers	Drewitt(1)	Benbow	Owen
04/12	Northwich Vics	GMVC	2-1	670	Wager	M Williams	N Jones	Lewis	M Davies	Ry James	*Holtham*	Tucker	Coates(1)	Rogers	Drewitt	Benbow(1)	
11/12	**DAGENHAM & R.**	GMVC	0-0	478	Wager	M Williams	N Jones	Lewis	M Davies	*Ry James*	Tucker	Ro James	Coates	Benbow	Drewitt		Holtham

18/12	**MACCLESFIELD**	GMVC	2-1	425	Wager	M Williams(1)	N Jones	Lewis	M Davies	Tucker	Holtham(1)	Ro James	Benbow	Rogers	Drewitt			
21/12	**ABERAMAN**	SWSC	6-1		Wager	M Williams	N Jones	Lewis	M Davies	Tucker	Holtham(1)	Ro James	Benbow(2)	Rogers	*Drewitt(2)*	Coates(1)		
01/01	**YEOVIL TOWN**	GMVC	1-1	1,068	Wager	M Williams(1)	N Jones	David	M Davies	Ry James	Tucker	Ro James	Benbow	*Coates*	Drewitt			Rogers
03/01	**TELFORD UTD**	GMVC	0-3	726	Wager	M Williams	N Jones	David	M Davies	Ry James	Tucker	Ro James	Benbow	*Rogers*	Drewitt			Coates
08/01	Stalybridge C.	GMVC	2-2	445	Wager	M Williams	N Jones	Lewis	M Davies	Ry James(1)	Tucker	Ro James	Benbow(1)	Rogers	Drewitt			
15/01	Altrincham	GMVC	0-3	696	Wager	M Williams	N Jones	Lewis	M Davies	Ry James	Tucker	Ro James	Benbow	*Rogers*	Drewitt			Coates
18/01	**PONTLOTTYN**	SWSC	8-0		Wager	M Williams	Ry James	Lewis	M Davies(2)	Rogers	Tucker(1)	Ro James	Coates(2)	*Benbow(1)*	Drewitt(2)			M Jones
22/01	St Albans C.	FAT1	5-4	1,017	Wager	M Williams	N Jones	Lewis	M Davies(1)	*Ry James*	Tucker(1)	Ro James	Benbow(1)	Coates(1)	Drewitt(1)			Rogers
29/01	**GATESHEAD**	GMVC	3-0	421	Wager	M Williams(1)	N Jones	Lewis	M Davies	Ry James	Tucker	Ro James	Benbow	Dyer(2)	Drewitt			
01/02	Telford United	GMVC	0-1	909	Wager	M Williams	N Jones	Lewis	M Davies	*Ry James*	Tucker	Ro James	Benbow	Dyer	*Drewitt*	Coates		Rogers
05/02	**SLOUGH TOWN**	GMVC	5-1	430	Wager	M Williams	N Jones	David	M Davies	Ry James	Tucker	*Ro James*	Benbow(1)	Dyer(2)	Coates(2)	Drewitt		
08/02	**TAFFS WELL**	SWSCqf	3-0		Wager	M Williams	N Jones	Ry James	M Davies	Rogers	Tucker	*M Jones*	Benbow(2)	Coates	Drewitt(1)	Hutchison		Ro James
12/02	Kingstonian	FAT2	2-0	853	Wager	M Williams	N Jones	Lewis	M Davies	Ry James	Tucker	Ro James(1)	Benbow	Dyer	Coates(1)			
19/02	Southport	GMVC	2-3	1,150	Wager	M Williams	N Jones	Lewis	M Davies	*Ry James*	Tucker	Ro James	Benbow	Dyer(1)	Coates(1)	Drewitt		
01/03	**KIDDERMINSTER**	GMVC	1-4	710	Wager	*M Williams*	N Jones	Lewis	M Davies	Ry James	Tucker	*Ro James(1)*	Benbow	Dyer	Coates	Drewitt		Rogers
05/03	Gateshead	FAT3	2-3	520	Wager	Ry James	N Jones(1)	Lewis	M Davies	Rogers	Tucker	M Jones	Benbow	Dyer	Coates(1)			
12/03	Dagenham & Red.	GMVC	1-0	764	Wager	Ry James	N Jones	A Lewis	M Davies	Rogers	Tucker	M Jones	Benbow	Dyer(1)	Coates			
19/03	Gateshead	GMVC	0-0	422	Wager	M Williams	N Jones	A Lewis	M Davies	Ry James	Tucker	Holtham	Benbow	Dyer	*Coates*	Rogers		
22/03	**WOKING**	GMVC	2-3	490	Mo Williams	M Williams	N Jones	A Lewis	M Davies	Ry James(1)	Tucker	*Holtham*	Benbow	Dyer(1)	*Drewitt*	Rogers		M Jones
29/03	Halifax Town	GMVC	1-2	771	Mo Williams	M Williams	N Jones	*D Lewis*	M Davies	A Lewis	Tucker	*Holtham*	Benbow	Dyer(1)	Ry James	Drewitt		M Jones
02/04	**KETTERING T.**	GMVC	0-1	527	Mo Williams	M Williams	N Jones	A Lewis	M Davies	Ry James	Tucker	Holtham	Benbow	Dyer	*Drewitt*	Rogers		
04/04	Runcorn	GMVC	1-1	407	Mo Williams	Gorman	N Jones	A Lewis	M Davies	Ry James	Tucker	*Holtham*	Benbow	*Dyer(1)*	Rogers	Drewitt		D Lewis
12/04	Grange Quins	SWSCsf	3-0	217	Wager	M Williams	N Jones(1)	M Davies	A Lewis	Ry James	Tucker	Holtham	Benbow	Dyer(1)	Drewitt(1)			
16/04	**WELLING UTD**	GMVC	0-1	416	Wager	Gorman	N Jones	A Lewis	M Davies	Ry James	Tucker	*Holtham*	Benbow	Dyer	Rogers	Drewitt		
19/04	Bath City	GMVC	3-0	512	Wager	Gorman	N Jones	A Lewis	M Davies	Ry James	Tucker	Holtham(1)	Benbow(1)	Dyer	Rogers(1)			
23/04	**STALYBRIDGE**	GMVC	1-2	531	Wager	Gorman	N Jones	A Lewis	*M Davies*	Ry James	*Tucker*	Holtham	Benbow	Dyer(1)	Rogers	Drewitt		D Lewis
26/04	Yeovil Town	GMVC	2-2	2,030	Wager	M Williams	*Gorman*	A Lewis	M Davies	Ry James	Tucker	Holtham	Benbow	N Jones	Drewitt(1)	Rogers(1)		
30/04	Stafford Rgrs	GMVC	1-5	921	Wager	M Williams	N Jones	A Lewis	M Davies	Ry James	Tucker	*Holtham*	Benbow	*Rogers*	Drewit1(1)	D Lewis		Dyer
02/05	**BROMSGROVE**	GMVC	2-1	514	Wager	M Williams	*N Jones*	D Lewis	M Davies	Ry James	Tucker	*Holtham*	Benbow(1)	Dyer	Drewitt	Rogers(1)		Gorman
07/05	**WITTON ALBION**	GMVC	4-3	526	Wager	M Williams	*Gorman*	A Lewis	M Davies	Ry James	Tucker(1)	Dyer(1)	Benbow	Rogers	Drewitt(2)	Holtham		N Jones
	BARRY TOWN	SWSCf	*held over until 1994-95 season*															

Merthyr Tydfil

GERALD APLIN

Gerald was appointed as manager during the close season for his first spell in the Conference. Born locally, Gerald's football pedigree started in the local leagues in Wales where he enjoyed great success. However, his managerial career really took off when he agreed to join Chesham United, where his brother Tony was Chairman, in March 1992. During those last few months of the 1991-92 season, Gerald led Chesham to fourth spot in the Diadora League premier division and also to victory in the Berks & Bucks Cup, the club's first success in that competition since 1976. The following season saw Chesham enjoy the best campaign in their 114-year history. They won the premier division by a five-point margin and retained the Berks & Bucks Cup, although promotion to the Conference was denied through ground inadequacies at Meadow Park. 1993-94 saw Chesham again amongst the leading pack with a team including a number of commuting Welshmen. At the season's end though, Gerald decided that travelling to and from his Welsh home was becoming too much and he reluctantly resigned his post, only to be asked to help Merthyr to improve upon their poor showing of 1993-94.

Merthyr Tydfil's vastly experienced goalkeeper Gary Wager claims the ball under pressure from Welling United's Kevin Hales as five of his team-mates look on.

Photo - V J Robertson.

Programme details:
32 pages for £1.00
Editor - Anthony Hughes (0685 359921 H)
(0685 874221 B)
Any other club publications:
Dial 'M' for Merthyr (Fanzine)
The Junior Martyr - For Junior Members
Local Newspapers:
Merthyr Express
Merthyr Herald and Post
South Wales Echo
Western Mail
Wales on Sunday
Local Radio Stations:
Radio Wales
Red Dragon Radio

Official Programme
1993-1994
MERTHYR TYDFIL
A.F.C.
"The Martyrs"
Penydarren Park, Merthyr Tydfil
V
WITTON ALBION
Issue No. 20

MERTHYR TYDFIL - PLAYING SQUAD

Player	Honours	Birthplace and date	Transfer Fees	Previous Clubs
GOALKEEPERS				
Gary Wager	WSP, BHL WC	Bridgend 21/5/62		Bridgend Town
DEFENDERS				
Andy Gorman		Cardiff 13/9/74	Player/ Exchange	Cardiff City, Yeovil Town
Dudley Lewis	WI, W-u21, WS	Swansea 17/11/62		Swansea C, Huddersfield T, Wrexham, Halifax T, Torquay Utd
Allan Lewis		Pontypridd 31/5/71		Cardiff City, Ebbw Vale
Ryan James		Blackwood 3/12/71		Blackpool
Nathan Jones		Cardiff		Cardiff City, Ton Pentre
Richard David		Cardiff		Aberaman
Mark Williams	WSP, WY, WS	Merthyr 11/8/70		Aston Villa
MIDFIELDERS				
Robbie James	WI, W-u21	Swansea 23/3/57	£10,000	Swansea C, Stoke, QPR, Leicester, Swansea C, Bradford C, Cardiff C
Mark Tucker	WSP, WY, WS	Pontypool 10/2/63		Abergavenny Thursdays
Kevin Rogers	WSP, BHL	Merthyr 23/9/63		Aston Villa, Birmingham C, Wrexham, Rhyl
Mark Jones		Warley 22/10/61		Aston Villa, Brighton, Birmingham C, Shrewsbury, Hereford, Worcester C
Matthew Holtham	WY	Cardiff		Luton Town
FORWARDS				
Ian Benbow	WC	Hereford 9/1/69	£5,000	Hereford Utd, Telford Utd
Ian Drewitt		Cardiff		Ferndale Ath, Ton Pentre, Weymouth
Simon Dyer		Swansea		Briton Ferry

Departures during season:
Ceri Williams (Barry T), Marc Coates (Yeovil T), Tommy Hutchison (Retired).

Players on loan during season:
None.

Penydarren Park, Merthyr Tydfil

Address and telephone number: Pennydarren Park, Merthyr Tydfil, Mid Glamorgan. Tel: 0685 384102. Fax: 0685 382882.

Simple directions: South A470 Express Way to Merthyr Tydfil, through Town Centre to Pontmorlais (traffic lights) turn left then first right, first right at Catholic Church and right again into Park Terrace to ground. North Heads of the Valley road to Town Centre, to Pontmorlais (traffic lights) turn right, then first right again first right at Catholic Church and right again into Park Terrace to ground.

Capacity: 10,000 **Seated:** 1,500 **Covered terracing:** 5,000

Record Attendance: 21,000 v Reading - FA Cup 2nd Rnd - 1949/50

Club Shop: Sells replica kits, clubs souvenirs & programmes. Contact Mr Mel Jenkins 0443 692336.

Social Facilities: Open Monday to Sunday 6-30 to 11-00pm. Two club cafes open on match days for hot food.

Previous Grounds: None

Merthyr Fact File

Nickname: Martyrs

Club Sponsors: Hoover PLC

Previous Leagues: Southern League, Beazer Homes (Midland Division), Beazer Homes (Premier Division).

Club colours: Grey Black & white

Change colours: All red

Midweek home matchday: Tuesday (7.45pm)

Record win: 11-0

Record defeat: 9-2

Record transfer fee paid: £10,000 to Cardiff City for Robbie James - 1992

Record transfer fee received: £12,000 for Ray Pratt from Exeter City - 1981

1993/94 Captain: Dudley Lewis

1993/94 Top scorer: Ian Drewitt

1993/94 Player of the Year: Mark Davies

Club record goalscorer: Not known

Record appearances: Not known

Past players who progressed to the Football League: Syd Howarth (Aston Villa), Cyril Beech, Gilbert Beech, Bill Hullet, Ken Tucker (Cardiff City), Nick Deacy (Hereford United), Gordon Davies (Fulham), Ray Pratt (Exeter City), Peter Jones, Paul Giles (Newport County).

Club Honours: Welsh FA Cup Winners 1948/49, 1950/51, 1986/87; Southern League 1947/48, 1949/50, 1950/51, 1951/52, 1953/54; Southern League (Midland) Winners 1987/88; Southern League (Premier) Winners 1988/89; Southern League Cup Winners 1947/48, 1950/51.

NORTHWICH VICTORIA

Formed:
1874

Chairman:
Dave Stone

Vice Chairman:
Rod Stich

Directors:
John Stich
Jim Rafferty
Rod Stich
Colin Adshead
Peter Morgan
Roger Stubbs
Graham Cookson
Dave Edgeley

Company Secretary:
Graham Fenton

Football Secretary:
Derek Nuttall

Manager:
John Williams

Coach:
Ossie Smith

Reserve Team Manager:
Nigel Deeley

Physiotherapist:
Phil Lea

General Manager:
Dave Thomas

A DRAWING PICTURE

With the future at their historic Drill Field home finally secured, Northwich were at last able to settle down and fix their attention on matters of a purely footballing nature. Fifteenth place may not seem to represent great progress, but it is largely disguised by the pressures of end-of-season fixture congestion.

With only a handful of new faces added to the Drinkwise Cup winning squad, Vics started against Woking full of optimism. August was memorable, if only for Vics quite literally paying the penalty for a lack of defensive discipline. Remarkably, no fewer than five spot-kicks were conceded during the month's four games! September saw Vics lose a treasured outlet when popular winger Tony Hemmings was transferred to Wycome for a £25,000 fee, only three days after signing off with a winner at Runcorn. October saw Jeff Parker return from a summer spent in Brunei and his presence firmed up the backline. Vics completed their 3500th league fixture in their history during November, when they drew 1-1 at the appropriately named Victoria Ground of Dagenham. As Christmas came, Vics were perilously close to the danger zone, but the New Year was to bring a change to their fortunes.

January saw winger Trevor Snowden sign on loan from Rochdale and, with Darren Tinson finally recovered from a nasty pre-season injury, Vics began to look a stronger unit. This strength was enhanced further the following month when big striker Dele Adebola was signed from Crewe, again on a temporary basis. Vics had lacked firepowesr all season but the efforts of Adebola (11 goals in 23 games) and Snowden (6 in 13) helped them to safety. The season went flat towards the end, yet this was largely due to the fixture pile-up that was epitomised by the final two days of the season. Having travelled to Woking on a Friday night, Vics were back at the Drill Field some 17.5 hours later to play out the final game with Macclesfield.

In the Cup competitions, the ignominy of First Round exits in the FA Cup and FA Trophy were somewhat offset by achievements elsewhere. A good defence of the Drinkwise Cup was finally curtailed at the Semi-Final stage, and silverware came with May, in the shape of the Cheshire and Mid-Cheshire Senior Cups.

Vics simply drew far too many games. A look at the final table reveals they drew a remarkable 19 matches and, in fact, only lost one more game than the champions.

Vics' supporters will have been happy with a season of consolidation on the field after seasons of drama off it. With the addition of a couple of new faces to the squad, the club may well be making the running in the future era of non-league football.

William Hughes

Back Row (L/R): Phil Lea (Physio), Jim Sewell (released), Mark Jones, Malcolm O'Connor, Neil Hardy, Alastair Monk (released), Tony Bullock, Peter Donnelly, Tommy Lloyd (released), Darren Tinson, Ossie Smith (Coach). Front: Kane Westray, Charlie Boyd, Mark Hancock, John Williams (Manager), Brian Butler, Tony Hemmings (now Wycombe), Tony McGee (realeased).

NORTHWICH *MATCHFACTS 93-94* ***NORTHWICH*** *MATCHFACTS 93-94* ***NORTHWICH*** *MATCHFACTS 93-94*

Key: Home fixtures are denoted by bold capitals. Numbers in brackets after players names indicate goals scored (asterisks by the results denote own goals). Only used substitutes are listed - substituted players are *italicised*.

Key to Competitions: GMVC: GM Vauxhall Conference. **CSC**: Cheshire Senior Cup. **MCSC**: Mid-Cheshire Senior Cup. **DC**: Drinkwise (GM Vauxhall Conference) Cup. **CS:** GM Vauxhall Conference Championship Shield. **FAC**: FA Cup. **FAT**: FA Trophy.

Date	Opponents	Comp.	Res	Gate	1.	2.	3.	4.	5.	6.	7.	8.	9.	10.	11.	Sub.	Sub.
21/08	**WOKING**	GMVC	0-0	1,041	Bullock	Butler	Simms	Hancock	Boyd	Jones	Hardy	Donnelly	*Lloyd*	*O'Connor*	Hemmings	Westray	Sewell
24/08	Stafford Rgrs	GMVC	1-3	1,064	Bullock	Butler	Simms	Hancock	Boyd	Jones	Westray	Donnelly	Lloyd	Hardy(1)	Hemmings		
28/08	Kettering Town	GMVC	0-0	1,767	Bullock	Butler	Simms	Hancock	Boyd	Jones	Westray	Donnelly	Paxton	Hardy	Hemmings		
30/08	**SOUTHPORT**	GMVC	2-1	1,266	Bullock	*Butler*	Simms	Hancock	Boyd	Jones	Westray(1)	Donnelly	Hardy(1)	Mulligan	*Hemmings*	O'Connor	Sewell
04/09	Runcorn	GMVC	2-1	1,044	Bullock	Smith	Simms	Hancock	Boyd	Jones	Westray	Donnelly	Hardy(1)	*O'Connor*	Hemmings(1)		Lloyd
11/09	**EMLEY**	FAC1q	2-2	709	Bullock	Smith	Simms	Hancock	Boyd	Jones	Hardy	Donnelly(1)	Mulligan(1)	O'Connor	*Paxton*		Lloyd
13/09	Emley	FAC1qr	0-2	420	Monk	Smith	McGee	Hancock	Boyd	Jones	*Sewell*	Donnelly	Mulligan	O'Connor	Hardy		Lloyd
18/09	**SLOUGH TOWN**	GMVC	1-1	825	Bullock	Smith	McGee	Hancock	Butler	Jones	Hardy	Boyd	Mulligan	O'Connor(1)	*Berks*		Sewell
02/10	**YEOVIL TOWN**	GMVC	1-1	939	Bullock	Smith	Simms	Hancock	Butler	Jones	Westray	Boyd	Lewin	O'Connor(1)	*Hardy*	Donnelly	
09/10	Dover Athletic	GMVC	0-2	1,630	Bullock	*Smith*	Simms	Hancock	Butler	Jones	*Westray*	Boyd	Lewin	O'Connor	Hardy	Donnelly	Sewell
12/10	**BROMSGROVE**	GMVC	1-1	667	Bullock	Smith	Simms	Hancock	Butler(1)	Jones	Westray	Boyd	Hardy	*O'Connor*	Christie	Donnelly	
18/10	Kidderminster	GMVC	0-2	1,514	Bullock	Norman	Simms	Hancock	Butler	Jones	*Westray*	*Boyd*	Hardy	O'Connor	Christie		
23/10	Welling Utd	GMVC	1-0	811	Bullock	Norman	Simms	Hancock	Parker	Jones	Butler	Boyd	Donnelly	*O'Connor*	*Christie*	Hardy(1)	Westray
26/10	**WYCOMBE W.**	CS	0-1	805	Bullock	Norman	Simms	Donnelly	Parker	Jones	Butler	Boyd	Hardy	O'Connor	Christie		
30/10	Merthyr Tydfil	GMVC	0-5	602	Bullock	Norman	McGee	Donnelly	Parker	Jones	Butler	Boyd	Hardy	*O'Connor*	*Christie*	Westray	Lewin
02/11	**STALYBRIDGE**	DC2	1-0	521	Greygoose	Norman	Simms	Hancock	Parker	Jones	Butler	Boyd(1)	Lewin	Donnelly	Hardy		
06/11	**RUNCORN**	GMVC	1-1	1,122	Greygoose	Norman	Simms	Hancock	Parker	Jones	Butler	Boyd	*Lewin*	Donnelly(1)	Hardy	Westray	
13/11	Altrincham	GMVC	2-2	1,019	Greygoose	Norman	Simms	Hancock	*Parker*	Jones	Westray	*Boyd*	Anders(1)	Donnelly	Butler	Lewin(1)	Hardy
20/11	**TELFORD UTD**	GMVC	1-0	748	Greygoose	Norman	Simms	Hancock	Boyd	Jones	Westray	Butler	O'Connor(1)	*Anders*	*Christie*	Parker	Hardy
27/11	Dagenham & R.	GMVC	1-1	686	Greygoose	Norman	Parker	Hancock	Boyd	Jones	Westray	Butler	O'Connor(1)	Anders	*Christie*	Hardy	
30/11	Vauxhall	CSC2	4-3	142	Greygoose	Norman	Parker	Hancock	Boyd	Jones	Westray	Butler	O'Connor(3)	*Anders*	*Hardy*	Lewin(1)	Simms
04/12	**MERTHYR TYD.**	GMVC	1-2	670	Greygoose	Norman	Parker	Hancock	Donnelly(1)	Jones	*Westray*	Butler	O'Connor	Bunter	Abercrombie	Hardy	
07/12	**KIDDERMINSTER**	DCqf	3-2	474	Greygoose	Norman	Parker	Hancock	Donnelly	Jones	Hardy(1)	Butler	*O'Connor(1)*	Bunter(1)	Abercrombie	Lewin	
18/12	Bath City	GMVC	0-0	514	Greygoose	Norman	Parker	Hancock	*Donnelly*	Jones	Hardy	Butler	O'Connor	Bunter	*Abercrombie*	Lewin	Simms
27/12	**WITTON ALBION**	GMVC	0-1	2,897	Greygoose	Norman	Parker	Hancock	*Donnelly*	Jones	Hardy	Butler	O'Connor	Bunter	*Abercrombie*	Lewin	Simms

01/01	Gateshead	GMVC	0-1	410	Greygoose	Norman	Parker	Hancock	Boyd	*Jones*	Hardy	Butler	O'Connor	Bunter	*Simms*	Lewin	Tinson
03/01	Southport	GMVC	0-0	1,606	Greygoose	Norman	Parker	Hancock	Tinson	Jones	Westray	*Boyd*	Bunter	O'Connor	*Simms*	Donnelly	Lewin
15/01	**WELLING UTD**	GMVC	3-1	717	Greygoose	Norman	Parker	Tinson	Boyd	Jones	Hardy	*Butler*	Bunter(1)	O'Connor(1)	Snowden(1)	Donnelly	
22/01	Morecambe	FAT1	1-2	693	Greygoose	*Norman*	Parker(1)	Tinson	Boyd	Jones	Hardy	Butler	*Lewin*	O'Connor	Snowden	Donnelly	Westray
02/02	Winsford Utd	CSCqf	6-0	317	Greygoose	Norman(1)	Parker	Hancock	*Tinson*	Jones	*Boyd*	Butler	Bunter(2)	O'Connor(2)	Snowden(1)	Westray	Simms
05/02	Macclesfield T.	GMVC	0-0	1,141	*Greygoose*	Norman	Parker	Hancock	Tinson	Jones	Boyd	Butler	Bunter	O'Connor	*Snowden*	Adebola	Hardy
08/02	**WITTON ALBION**	MCSCsf	4-0	834	Bullock	Norman	*Parker*	Hancock	Tinson	Jones	Boyd	Bunter	Adebola(1)	O'Connor	Snowden(2)	Hardy(1)	
12/02	Stalybridge C.	GMVC	1-1	668	Bullock	*Norman*	Parker	Hancock	Tinson	Jones	Boyd	Adebola(1)	Bunter	Butler	*Snowden*	Hardy	O'Connor
19/02	Bromsgrove R.	GMVC	0-0	1,017	Bullock	Norman	Parker	Hancock	*Donnelly*	Jones	O'Connor	Boyd	Bunter	Adebola	Snowden	Hardy	
26/02	**BATH CITY**	GMVC	3-1	625	Bullock	Tinson	Simms	Hancock	*Boyd*	Parker(1)	Adebola(2)	*Butler*	Bunter	O'Connor	Snowden	Hardy	Norman
01/03	Colwyn Bay	CSCsf(1)	0-0	254	Bullock	Norman	Simms	Hancock	Tinson	Parker	Boyd	Butler	Bunter	Adebola	*Snowden*	Hardy	
05/03	**STALYBRIDGE**	GMVC	2-0	929	Bullock	Norman	Parker	Hancock	Tinson	Jones	Boyd	Butler	O'Connor(1)	Adebola	Snowden(1)		
08/03	Macclesfield T.	DCsf(1)	0-1	1,008	Bullock	Tinson	Parker	Hancock	Boyd	Jones	Bunter	Butler	Hardy	Adebola	Snowden		
12/03	Yeovil Town	GMVC	3-0	2,029	Bullock	Tinson	Parker	Hancock	Boyd	Jones	Bunter	Butler	*O'Connor*	Adebola(2)	Snowden(1)	Hardy	
15/03	**MACCLESFIELD**	DCsf(2)	0-1	1,008	Bullock	Tinson	Parker	Hancock	Boyd	Jones	Bunter	Butler	Hardy	Adebola	Snowden		
19/03	**STAFFORD R.**	GMVC	0-0	752	Bullock	Tinson	Parker	Hancock	Boyd	Jones	*Norman*	Butler	Bunter	Adebola	Hardy	Westray	
22/03	**COLWYN BAY**	CSCsf(2)	3-2	517	Bullock	Tinson	Parker	Hancock	Boyd	Jones	*Norman*	Butler	Bunter	Adebola(2)	*Simms*	Westray(1)	Donnelly
26/03	Slough Town	GMVC	2-2	605	Bullock	Tinson	Parker	Hancock	Boyd	Jones	*Westray*	Butler	Bunter(2)	*Adebola*	Jones	Hardy	Norman
29/03	**ALTRINCHAM**	GMVC	2-0	1,037	Bullock	Tinson	Simms	Hancock(1)	Boyd	Jones	Westray	Butler	Bunter	Hardy(1)	T Jones		
02/04	**HALIFAX TOWN**	GMVC	0-2	927	Bullock	Tinson	Parker	Hancock	Boyd	Jones	*Hardy*	Butler	Bunter	Adebola	*Westray*	Norman	T Jones
04/04	Witton Albion	GMVC	1-1	1,564	Bullock	Tinson	Parker	Hancock	Boyd	Jones	Norman	Butler(1)	Bunter	Adebola	*T Jones*	Westray	
09/04	**KETTERING**	GMVC	1-1	783	Bullock	Norman	Parker	Tinson	Boyd	Jones	Westray	*Butler*	Bunter	Hardy(1)	*T Jones*	Birchall	Simms
12/04	**GATESHEAD**	GMVC	1-2	532	Bullock	Norman	Simms	Tinson	Boyd	Jones	*Birchall*	Hardy	Bunter(1)	Adebola	Westray		O'Connor
17/04	**DAGENHAM & R.**	GMVC	2-2	718	Bullock	Norman	Parker	Tinson	Boyd	Jones	*Westray*	Butler(1)	Bunter(1)	*Adebola*	Simms	Hardy	O'Connor
19/04	Halifax Town	GMVC	2-1	809	Bullock	Tinson	Simms	Hancock	Boyd	Parker	Westray	Norman	Bunter	Adebola(1)	Hardy(1)		
27/04	**KIDDERMINSTER**	GMVC	3-0	980	Bullock	Tinson	Parker	Hancock	Boyd	Jones	Westray	*Norman*	Bunter(1)	Adebola(1)	Hardy(1)		O'Connor
30/04	Telford United	GMVC	1-2	831	Bullock	Tinson	Simms	Hancock	Boyd	Parker(1)	Westray	*O'Connor*	Bunter	Adebola	Hardy		Butler
02/05	RUNCORN *	CSCf	1-0	1,238	Bullock	Tinson	Parker	Hancock	Boyd	Jones	*Westray*	Butler	Bunter	Adebola(1)	Hardy		O'Connor
04/05	**DOVER ATH.**	GMVC	0-1	416	Bullock	Tinson	Parker	Hancock	Boyd	Jones	Westray	Butler	O'Connor	Adebola	Hardy		
06/05	Woking	GMVC	1-2	692	Bullock	Butler	Parker	Hancock	Boyd	Jones	Birchall	Hardy	Bunter	O'Connor	Westray		
07/05	**MACCLESFIELD**	GMVC	1-1	1,002	Bullock	Tinson	Parker	Hancock	Boyd	Jones	Westray	*Butler*	Bunter(1)	*O'Connor*	Hardy	Birchall	Norman
09/05	**WINSFORD UTD**	MCSCf	2-0	469	Bullock	Tinson	Norman	Hancock	Boyd	Jones	Westray(1)	Butler	Bunter	O'Connor(1)	Hardy		

* - played at Witton Albion FC

Northwich Victoria

JOHN WILLIAMS

Undoubtedly the most experienced manager in the Conference, John Williams' pedigree in the non-League game is virtually second to none. After finishing his playing career - which encompassed spells with Everton, Crewe and Ellesmere Port - John took charge of Welsh side Portmadoc with no little success. His next move was to Vics' near neighbours Winsford United where he produced an outstanding team which included the likes of Neville Southall. Trophy after trophy duly arrived at the Barton Stadium, but in 1980 Runcorn made him an offer he could not refuse. In just over six seasons at Canal Street he guided the Linnets to the Conference & NPL titles, two Bob Lord Trophy wins, the FA Trophy final and last, but not least, two Cheshire Senior Cup successes, not to mention unearthing such players as Ossie Smith and Mark Carter.

In the summer of 1986 he moved to Altrincham but this proved to be an unhappy time and, after just over a year at Moss Lane. John was sacked. Subsequent moves took him to Stafford, Chorley and Fleetwood, but he found success at these clubs elusive.

He arrived at the Drill Field in late October 1992 as care-taker manager when the club was in turmoil both on and off the field, but his quiet and firm style quickly changed the club's fortunes and, after being appointed to the job on a permanent basis in early December, he promptly won the 'Manager of the Month' award.

This early success proved to be no fluke, and John's side went on to produce some of the best football that many Vics' fans could remember. To cap it all he guided the Vics to their first major Trophy since 1984 when they beat double winners Wycombe in the final at the 1993 Drinkwise Cup, and further silverware followed twelve months later in the form of the Cheshire and Mid-Cheshire Senior Cups.

Northwich striker Malcolm O'Connor takes on Jim Harvey during Vics' 2-1 victory over Southport.
Photo - Paul Dennis.

Programme details:
28 pages for £1. Editor - Terry Mortram (0744 57726)

Any other club publications:
A Team for All Seasons - Club History
Hardback £14.95 plus p&p. Available from club shop.
Not in the Same League - Fanzine, £1.
1994 Handbook (edited by William Hyder) £2.50

Local Newspapers:
Northwich Guardian (Wednesday) 0606 43333
Northwich Chronicle (Wednesday) 0606 42272
Daily Post
Manchester Evening News Pink (Saturday evenings)

Local Radio Stations:
GMR (BBC Manchester)
Piccadilly Radio, Signal Radio

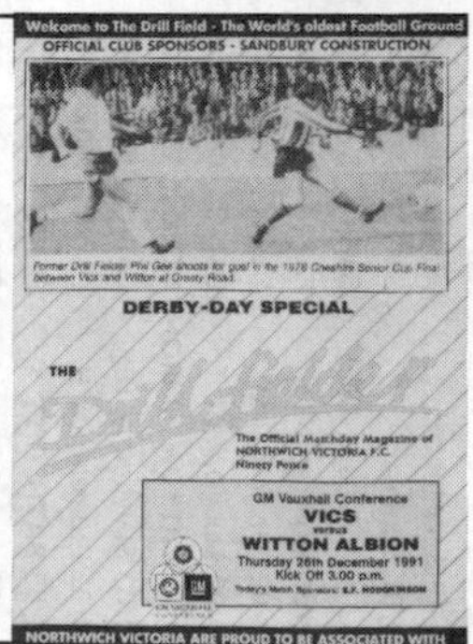

NORTHWICH VICTORIA - PLAYING SQUAD

Player	Honours	Birthplace and date	Transfer Fees	Previous Clubs
GOALKEEPERS				
Dean Greygoose	EY	Thetford 18/12/64		Camb.Utd, Leyton Orient, Crystal Palace, Crewe Alexandra, Holywell T
Tony Bullock	DC SSC	Manchester		Barnton
DEFENDERS				
Mark Jones	DC, SSC, MCSC, FAXI	Liverpool 16/9/60		Runcorn, Preston NE, Southport
Jeff Parker	DC	Liverpool 23/1/69		Everton, Crewe Alexandra, Northwich V, Brunei Darussalam
Darren Tinson		Wales		Connah's Quay Nomads, Colwyn Bay
Mark Hancock	FAT, DC, MCSC, FAXI	Ellesmere Pt 30/9/60	£3,000	Van Leer, Telford Utd
Dave Norman		Wales		Llansanffraid
Mark Simms	BLT	Southport 17/10/70		Blackburn Rovers, Preston NE, Bury, Fleetwood Town
MIDFIELDERS				
Neil Hardy	DC	Manchester		Crewe Alexandra
Kane Westray	BLT	Manchester		Middlewich Athletic
Charlie Boyd	BLT	Liverpool 20/9/69		Liverpool, Chesterfield, Bristol R, Chorley, Runcorn, Droylsden
Brian Butler	ESP, BLT, MSC, FAXI	Salford 4/7/66		Blackpool, Stockport Co, Halifax Town
FORWARDS				
Malcolm O'Connor	NPLC, SSC, MCSC, FAXI	Ashton 25/4/65	£10,000	Curzon Ashton, N. Forest, Rochdale, Curzon Ashton, Hyde Utd
George Oghani		Manchester 2/9/60		Hyde, Bolton, Wrexham, Burnley, Stockport, Hereford, Scarborough, Evagoras, Carlisle United.
John Berks		Stoke		Stoke City, Carlisle United

Departures during season:
Tony Hemmings (Wycombe W), Alistair Monk (Released), Tommy Lloyd (Bangor C), Jim Sewell (Released), Dave Christie (Ashton Utd), Tony McGee (Caernarfon T), Peter Donnelly (Colwyn Bay), Mike Bennett (Witton Alb), Craig Nixon (Altrincham), Steve Simms (Southport), Steve Bunter (Droylsden).

Players on loan during season:
Jimmy Mulligan (Stoke City), Jason Anders (Rochdale), Trevor Snowden (Rochdale), Dele Adebola (Crewe Alexandra).

Drill Field, Northwich Victoria

Address and telephone number: The Drill Field, Drill Field Road, Northwich, Cheshire. Tel: 0606 41450. Fax: 0606 330577.

Simple directions: Leave M6 at Junc.19 and follow A556 towards Chester. At second roundabout (approx. 6 miles), turn right onto A533. Ground on right 1.5 miles behind Volunteer Public House.

Capacity: 10,000 (currently limited to 3,500) **Seated:** 660 **Covered terracing:** 2,000

Record Attendance: 11,290 v Witton Albion, Cheshire League, Good Friday 1949.

Club Shop: Located inside ground. Open match days. Manager: Andy Dakin.

Social Facilities: Large social club with members lounge and seperate function room - both available for hire Tel: 0606 43120. Food available on matchdays with prior notice. Bass beers, Pool, Darts, TV.

Previous Grounds: None

Northwich Fact File

Nickname: The Vics

Club Sponsors: Morgan Contractors.

Previous Leagues: The Combination 1890-1892, Football League Div.2 1892-94, The Combination 1894-1898, The Cheshire League 1898-1900, Manchester League 1900-12, Lancashire 1912-19, Cheshire County League 1919-68, Northern Premier League 1968-79.

Club colours: Green & white shirts, green shorts and white socks.

Change colours: Claret shirts, sky blue shorts and claret socks.

Midweek home matchday: Tuesday

Record transfer fee: £10,000 to Hyde United for Malcolm O'Connor - August 1988.

Record transfer fee received: £50,000 from Chester City for Neil Morton - October 1990.

Club record goalscorer: Peter Burns 160 - 1955-65.

Record appearances: 970 by Ken Jones 1969-85.

Past players who progressed to the Football League: To numerous to list.

Club Honours: Welsh Cup Runners-up 1881/82,1888-89; FA Trophy Winners 1983/84, Runners-up 1982/83; Bob Lord Trophy Winners 1979/80, 1992/93; Northern Premier League Runners-up 1976/77; Northern Premier League Cup Winners 1972/73, Runners-up 1978/79; Cheshire County League Champions 1956/57, Runners-up 1924/25,1947/48; Cheshire County League Cup Winners 1925/35; Manchester League Champions 1902/03, Runners-up 1900/01,1903/04,1907/08,1908/09,1911/12; The Combination Runners-up 1890/91;
Cheshire Senior Cup Winners 1880-81,1881/82,1882/83,1883/84,1884/85,1885/86,1928/29,193-.6/37,1949/50,1954/55,1971/72,1976/77,1978/79,1983/84,1983/84.
Runners-up 1891/92,1896/97,1905/06,1908/09,1947/48,1950/51,1963/64, 1965/66,1969,1970/71,1977/78,1985/86;
Staffordshire Senior Cup Winners 1978/79, 1979/80, 1989/90, Runners-up 1986/87, 1990/91;
Cheshire Amateur Cup Winners 1901/02, Runners-up 1898/99,1902/93,
Northwich Senior Cup Winners 1948/49,1958/59,1959/60,1963/64,1964/65,1965/66,1967/68,-1968/69,1969/70,1971/72,1974/75,
Runners-up 1953/54,1954/55,1955/56,1957/58,1960/61,1961/62.1972/73; Mid Cheshire Senior Cup Winners 1984/85,1985/86,1987/88,1989/90, Runners-up 1982/83,1983/84,1990/91,-1992/93,1993/4; North-West Floodlit League Winners 1966/67,1975/76; Cheshire League Lancashire Combination Inter-League Cup Winners 1961/62; Guardian Charity Shield Winners 1985/86,1986/87,1987/88.

RUNCORN

Formed:
1918

President:
Mr G Worrall

Chairman:
Mr D Robinson

Vice-Chairman
Mr P Saunders Lee

Football Secretary:
Mr G Ost

Manager:
Mr J F Carroll

Assistant Manager:
Mr B Rodaway

Physiotherapist:
Mr J Graham

Commercial Manager:
Mr J Graham

Press Officer:
Mr P Saunders Lee

Season 1993/94 can be divided into two sections, one of satisfaction for a greatly improved performance on the field culiminating with the club's third appearance at Wembley, having reached the final of the Cheshire Building Society Senior Cup and achieved a highly respectable position in the final league placings. However, in the cold light of day the records will show that nothing was won, not withstanding the scintillating performances on the road to Wembley and the impressive away performances at Halifax, Gateshead and Guiseley.

Off the field - disaster. Against Hull City in the FA Cup, a section of the pitch perimeter fence collapsed, an incident which unleashed the concentrated attentions of various authorities on the club's facilities. Much has been written about the incident and nothing will be achieved by further observations. Nature then took a hand and promptly blew off a section of the roof covering the remaining terrace available to us following the authorities ongoing investigations and, as if this was not enough, the main stand was gutted by a fire of such speed and intensity that one can only reflect on what would have happened had the incident taken place on the previous evening when Gateshead were the visitors. The cause of the fire is unknown. All these incidents were aggravated by sundry, but costly, acts of burglary and vandalism.

Let us hope that the fable about the phoenix rising from the ashes proves prophetic in our situation.

Finally Runcorn AFC are indebted to our good neighbours Chester City, Northwich Victoria and Witton Albion for their unstinting help in staging our outstanding games.

George Worrall, President

Back Row (L-R): Terry Bratt (Kit Manager), Andy Lee, Mike Smith, Ian Brady, Neil Parker, Arthur Williams, M Gallagher, Joe Connor, Garry Anderson, Paul Robertson, Jimmy Graham (Physio). Centre: A Armstrong (Asst Physio), Ken McKenna, Ian McInerny, Justin Wall, Gary Brabin (now Doncaster Rovers), Karl Thomas, Jamie Bates, Billy Rodaway (Asst Manager). Front: A Loftus (Director), A Reilly (Asst Secretary), Dr D Robertson (Director), P Saunders-Lee (Vice-Chairman), John Carroll (Manager), D Robertson (Chairman), George Worrall (President), A Bamber (Director), K Moss (Director).

RUNCORN *MATCHFACTS 93-94* ***RUNCORN*** *MATCHFACTS 93-94* ***RUNCORN*** *MATCHFACTS 93-94*

Key: Home fixtures are denoted by bold capitals. Numbers in brackets after players names indicate goals scored (asterisks by the results denote own goals). Only used substitutes are listed - substituted players are *italicised*.

Key to Competitions: GMVC: GM Vauxhall Conference. **CSC**: Cheshire Senior Cup. **DC**: Drinkwise (GM Vauxhall Conference) Cup. **FAC**: FA Cup. **FAT**: FA Trophy.

Date	Opponents	Comp.	Res	Gate	1.	2.	3.	4.	5.	6.	7.	8.	9.	10.	11.	Sub.	Sub.
21/08	Gateshead	GMVC	2-2	510	Williams	Bates	Wall	Lee	Hill	*Robertson*	Thomas	Connor	*McInerny(1)*	Brady	Brabin(1)	Smith	Parker
24/08	**TELFORD UTD**	GMVC	3-2	628	Williams	Bates	Wall	*Lee*	Hill	Smith	Thomas(2)	Connor(1)	McInerny	Brady	Brabin	McKenna	
28/08	Woking	GMVC	1-1	1,520	Williams	Bates	Wall	Parker	Hill	Smith	Thomas(1)	Connor	*McInerny*	Brady	Brabin(1)	McKenna	
30/08	**MACCLESFIELD**	GMVC	2-1	737	Williams	Bates	Wall	*Parker*	Hill	*Smith*	Thomas	Connor	McInerny(1)	Brady	Brabin	McKenna(1)	Brown
04/09	**NORTHWICH V.**	GMVC	1-2	1,044	Williams	Bates	Robertson	*Parker*	Hill	*Smith*	Thomas(1)	Connor	McInerny	Brady	Brabin	McKenna	Brown
07/09	Southport	DC1(1)	4-1	912	Williams	Bates	Robertson	Brady(2)	Hill	Brown	*Thomas(1)*	Connor	McInerny	McKenna(1)	Brabin		Parker
11/09	**HALIFAX TOWN**	GMVC	*5-0	732	Williams	Bates	Robertson	Brady(1)	Hill	Brown	Thomas	Connor(1)	McInerny(1)	*McKenna*	Brabin	Parker(1)	
18/09	Merthyr Tydfil	GMVC	1-1	531	Williams	Bates	Robertson	Brady	Hill	Brown	Thomas(1)	Connor	McInerny	*McKenna*	Brabin		Lee
21/09	**SOUTHPORT**	DC1(2)	2-1	509	Williams	Bates	Robertson	*Brady*	Hill	Brown	Thomas(1)	Connor	McInerny	McKenna	Brabin		Lee(1)
25/09	Kettering Town	GMVC	2-2	1,475	Williams	Bates	Robertson	Brady	Hill	Brown	Thomas	Connor(1)	McInerny	McKenna	Brabin(1)		
02/10	**STALYBRIDGE C.**	GMVC	1-1	712	Williams	Bates	Robertson	Brady	Hill	Brown	Thomas(1)	Connor	McInerny	McKenna	Lee		
09/10	Kidderminster H.	GMVC	0-3	1,208	Williams	Bates	Robertson	Brady	Hill	Brown	Thomas	Connor	McInerny	McKenna	Lee		
16/10	**DOVER ATH.**	GMVC	2-1	637	Williams	Bates	Robertson	Lee	Hill	Brady	Thomas(1)	Connor	McInerny(1)	*McKenna*	Anderson		Parker
23/10	Yeovil Town	GMVC	2-4	2,475	Williams	Bates	Robertson	Brady	*Hill*	Anderson	Thomas(1)	Connor	McInerny(1)	McKenna	Brabin		Wall
30/10	**WELLING UTD**	GMVC	2-4	572	Williams	Bates	Robertson	Brady	*Hill*	Anderson	Thomas(1)	Connor	McInerny	McKenna	Brabin(1)	Smith	
02/11	**MACCLESFIELD**	DC2	0-4	471	Williams	Bates	Robertson	Brady	Gallagher	Anderson	Thomas	Connor	Parker	Wall	Brown		
06/11	Northwich Victoria	GMVC	1-1	1,122	Williams	Bates	Robertson	Brady	Lee	Anderson	Thomas	Connor	McInerny	McKenna(1)	Brabin		
13/11	**HULL CITY**	FAC1	*0-1*	*2,194*	*Williams*	*Bates*	*Robertson*	*Brady*	*Lee*	*Anderson*	*Thomas*	*Connor*	*McInerny*	*McKenna*	*Brabin*	*(aband. 29 mins.)*	
20/11	**ALTRINCHAM**	GMVC	2-1	510	Williams	Bates	Robertson(1)	Brady	Lee	Anderson	Thomas(1)	Connor	McInerny	McKenna	Carroll		
23/11	**HULL CITY** *	FAC1	0-2	1,131	Williams	Bates	Robertson	Brady	Lee	Anderson	Thomas	Connor	McInerny	McKenna	Carroll		
27/11	Telford United	GMVC	1-1	726	Williams	Bates	Robertson	Brady	Lee	Anderson	Thomas	Connor	McInerny(1)	McKenna	Carroll		
30/11	**HYDE UNITED**	CSC2	2-1	272	Williams	Bates	*Robertson*	Brady	Lee	Anderson	Thomas(1)	Connor	McInerny(1)	McKenna	Gallagher	Smith	
04/12	**SOUTHPORT**	GMVC	3-0	603	Williams	Bates	Robertson	Brady	Lee	Anderson	Thomas(1)	Connor	McInerny	McKenna(2)	Brabin		
11/12	Slough Town	GMVC	0-3	675	Williams	Bates	Robertson	Brady	Lee	Anderson	Thomas	Connor	McInerny	McKenna	Brabin		
27/12	**STAFFORD R.**	GMVC	2-2	715	Williams	Bates	Robertson	Brady	Lee	Anderson	Thomas	Connor	McInerny(1)	McKenna(1)	Brabin		
01/01	Stafford Rgrs	GMVC	1-1	1,111	Williams	Bates	Robertson	*Brady*	Lee	Anderson	Thomas(1)	Connor	McInerny	McKenna	Brabin		Hill
08/01	**SLOUGH TOWN**	GMVC	3-2	563	Williams	Bates	Robertson	*Brady*	Lee	Anderson	Thomas(3)	Connor	McInerny	McKenna	Brabin		Hill

Date	Opponent	Comp	Score	Att												Sub	Sub
11/01	Witton Albion	GMVC	1-1	883	Williams	Bates	Hill	Brady(1)	Lee	Anderson	Thomas	Connor	McInerny	McKenna	Brabin		
15/01	Halifax Town	GMVC	1-1	1,196	Williams	Bates	Hill	Brady(1)	Lee	Anderson	Thomas	Connor	McInerny	McKenna	Brabin		
19/01	Nantwich Town	CSCqf	3-1	360	Williams	Bates	Hill	Brady(1)	Lee	Anderson	Thomas(1)	Connor	McInerny	McKenna(1)	Brabin		
22/01	Alfreton Town	FAT1	5-0	502	Williams	Bates	Hill	Brady	Lee	*Anderson*	*Thomas*	Connor	Smith	McKenna(4)	Brabin	Robertson	Baldwin
29/01	**WITTON ALBION**	GMVC	1-0	869	Williams	Bates	Hill	Brady	Lee	Anderson	Thomas	Connor	Smith(1)	McKenna	Brabin		
05/02	Bath City	GMVC	0-0	698	Williams	Bates	Hill	Brady	Lee	Anderson	Thomas	Connor	McInerny	McKenna	Brabin		
12/02	**TELFORD UTD**	FAT2	2-1	844	Williams	Bates	Hill	Brady	Lee	Anderson	Thomas(1)	Connor	McInerny(1)	McKenna	Brabin		
19/02	Macclesfield T.	GMVC	0-0	1,004	Williams	Bates	Hill	Brady	Lee	Anderson	Thomas	Connor	McInerny	McKenna	Brabin		
26/02	**YEOVIL TOWN**	GMVC	4-0	427	Williams	Bates	Hill	Brady	Lee	*Anderson(1)*	Thomas(1)	Connor	*McInerny*	McKenna(2)	Brabin	Robertson	Parker
01/03	Warrington Town	CSCsf(1)	0-0	327	Williams	Bates	Hill	Brady	Lee	Anderson	Thomas	Connor	McInerny	Shaw	Brabin		
05/03	**HALIFAX TOWN**	FAT3	1-1	1,302	Williams	Bates	Hill	Brady	Lee	Anderson	Thomas(1)	Connor	McInerny	McKenna	Brabin		
08/03	Halifax Town	FAT3r	2-0	1,406	Williams	Bates	Hill	Brady	Lee	Anderson	Thomas(1)	Connor(1)	McInerny	*McKenna*	Brabin		Shaw
12/03	Bromsgrove R.	GMVC	0-0	998	Williams	Bates	Hill	Brady	*Lee*	Anderson	Thomas	Connor	McInerny	McKenna	Brabin	Robertson	
15/03	**GATESHEAD**	GMVC	1-1	432	Williams	Bates	Robertson	Brady	Hill	Anderson	Thomas(1)	*Connor*	*McInerny*	McKenna	Brabin	Smith	Shaw
19/03	Welling United	GMVC	1-1	808	Williams	Bates	Lee	*Brady*	Gallagher	Anderson	Thomas(1)	Connor	McInerny	McKenna	Brabin	Robertson	
22/03	**WARRINGTON**	CSCsf(2)	2-0	402	Williams	Bates	Hill	*Brady*	Lee	Robertson	*Thomas(1)*	Connor	Shaw	McKenna	Brabin(1)	Smith	Parker
26/03	Gateshead	FATqf	*3-0	1,807	Williams	Bates	Hill	Brady	Lee	Anderson	Thomas(2)	Connor	McInerny	McKenna	Brabin		
02/04	**DAGENHAM & R.**	GMVC	2-1	496	Williams	Bates	Robertson	Brady(1)	Hill	Anderson	Thomas	Connor(1)	*McInerny*	McKenna	Brabin	Smith	
04/04	**MERTHYR TYD.**	GMVC	1-1	467	Williams	Bates	Hill(1)	Brady	Lee	Anderson	Thomas	Connor	Parker	Smith	Brabin		
06/04	Dagenham & Red.	GMVC	1-2	832	Williams	Bates	Robertson	Shaw(1)	Lee	Hill	Thomas	Smith	*McInerny*	McKenna	*Brabin*	Anderson	Connor
09/04	**WOKING**	GMVC	2-1	532	Williams	Bates	Robertson	Brady	*Lee*	Anderson	Thomas(2)	Connor	Shaw	McKenna	Hill	McInerny	
12/04	Altrincham	GMVC	1-2	659	Williams	Bates	Robertson	*Brady*	Rowlands	Shaw	Thomas(1)	Connor	McInerny	McKenna	Brabin	Anderson	
16/04	**GUISELEY #**	FATsf(1)	1-1	1,595	Williams	Bates	Hill	Shaw	Lee	Anderson	Thomas	Connor	*McInerny*	McKenna(1)	Brabin	Robertson	
20/04	**KID'MINSTER ***	GMVC	0-5	595	Williams	Bates	Robertson	Rowlands	*Carroll*	*Anderson*	Smith	Connor	Parker	McKenna	Brabin	O'Brien	Shaw
23/04	Guiseley	FATsf(2)	1-0	2,176	Williams	Bates	Robertson	Hill	Lee	Anderson	Thomas	Connor	McInerny	McKenna(1)	Brabin		
26/04	**BROMSGROVE ***	GMVC	4-1	348	Williams	Bates	Robertson	Shaw(1)	*Lee*	Anderson	Thomas	Connor(2)	*McInerny(1)*	McKenna	Brabin	Parker	Smith
28/04	**BATH CITY ***	GMVC	0-0	284	Williams	Bates	Carroll	Shaw	Rowlands	Anderson	*Thomas*	Connor	Parker	*Smith*	Brabin	Robertson	McKenna
30/04	**KETTERING**	GMVC	0-0	464	Williams	Bates	Robertson	Shaw	Carroll	Anderson	Parker	O'Brien	McInerny	McKenna	Brabin		
02/05	NORTHWICH V. *	GMVC	0-1	1,238	Williams	Bates	Robertson	Shaw	Carroll	Anderson	Thomas	Connor	*McInerny*	McKenna	*O'Brien*	Parker	Lee
04/05	Southport	GMVC	0-1	723	Williams	*Bates*	Robertson	Shaw	Carroll	Anderson	Thomas	Parker	McInerny	McKenna	O'Brien	Smith	
07/05	Dover Athletic	GMVC	3-2	739	Williams	O'Brien	Robertson	Shaw	Carroll	Anderson	Thomas(1)	Parker	Smith	McKenna(2)	Brabin		
21/05	WOKING +	FATf	1-2	15,818	Williams	Bates	Robertson	Shaw(1)	Lee	Anderson	Thomas	Connor	*McInerny*	McKenna	Brabin		Hill

* - Played at Witton Albion FC

- Played at Chester City FC

+ - Played at Wembley Stadium

JOHN CARROLL

During the 1991-92 season, John Carroll became Runcorn's third manager in a year when he was appointed to take over permanently at Canal Street after a short period as caretaker-manager. Peter O'Brien had filled the vacancy left by Barry Whitbread but, left to take over at Witton Albion after only a short spell at Canal Street.

Carroll, aged 34, played for South Liverpool and Weymouth and has now made well over 200 appearances for the Linnets. Although his playing appearances are now limited, he is still regarded as one of the best centre-backs in the Vauxhall Conference.

Carroll's record in his two and a half years as manager cannot be questionned - he has guided Runcorn to two consecutive FA Trophy Finals and steadied them into one of the most solid and consistent Conference outfits.

The goal that sent Runcorn back to Wembley - Ken McKenna rises above Calvin Allen to head home the dramatic 120th minute winner in the FA Trophy semi-final second-leg at Guiseley.

Photo - Colin Stevens.

Programme details:
32 pages for £1
Editor: Peter Saunders-Lee,
c/o Halton Print 0928 560269

Any other club publications:
The Jolly Green Giant (Fanzine)

Local Newspapers:
Runcorn Weekly News
Liverpool Echo
Runcorn World

Local Radio Stations:
Radio Merseyside
Radio City

RUNCORN - PLAYING SQUAD

Player	Honours	Birthplace and date	Transfer Fees	Previous Clubs
GOALKEEPERS				
Arthur Williams		Widnes 14/7/64		General Chemicals
DEFENDERS				
Jamie Bates		Manchester		Maine Road
Paul Robertson		Manchester 5/2/72		York C, Stockport Co, Bury
Graham Hill		Manchester		Curzon Ashton
Ian Brady		Liverpool		Bootle, Heswall
John Carroll	CSC	Liverpool 6/8/59		South Liverpool, Weymouth
Andy Lee Runcorn, Altrincham,	ESP, FAT, Telford, NPL	Liverpool 4/7/62		L'pool, Wrexham, Bangor, Stafford,Camb.U, Colne D, Witton A, Altrincham, Telford
Justin Wall		Manchester		Crewe Alexandra
MIDFIELDERS				
Gary Anderson	FAT, CSC	Liverpool 5/1/60		Altrincham, Sth Liverpool, Altrincham, Runcorn, Altrincham
Joe Connor	NPL	Stockport	Player/ Exchange	Stockport Co, Hyde Utd, Mossley, Hyde Utd, Witton Alb
Mike Smith		Liverpool		Tranmere Rovers
Nigel Shaw	NPL, NPLC	Stoke 13/2/63		Stoke C, Nantwich T, Congleton T, Macclesfield T, Altrincham
FORWARDS				
Ken McKenna	FAT, CSC, SSC	Birkenhead 2/7/60		Poulton V, Tranmere R, Telford U, Tranmere Runcorn, Telford U, Altrincham, Barrow
Karl Thomas	NPL	Liverpool 11/9/63	5-fig	South Liverpool, Colne Dynamoes, Witton Albion
Ian McInerny		Liverpool 26/1/64		Newcastle Blue Star, Huddersfield T, Stockport Co
Neil Parker		Liverpool		Caernarfon T, Waterloo Dock

Departures during season:
Ian Vickers (Stafford Rangers), Jimmy Brown (Stalybridge Celtic), Gary Brabin (Doncaster Rovers).

Players on loan during season:
None.

Canal Street, Runcorn

Address and telephone number: Canal Street, Runcorn, Cheshire. Tel: 0928 560076. Fax: 0928 560076.

Simple directions: South: M6. Take M56 to junction 11. Follow signs for Warrington. Left at min-roundabout (signed Liverpool/Runcorn) for 3 miles. Sign at slip road Runcorn Old Town, right at junction, follow road to Egerton Arms, turn right and right again to ground. North: leave M62 at Widnes, through Widnes to Runcorn/Widnes bridge, turn left, through town to Egerton Arms.

Capacity: TBA **Seated:** TBA **Covered terracing:** TBA

Club Shop: Sells scarves, hats, shirts, flags etc. Contact Mrs Redican 0928 560076.

Social Facilities: Clubhouse open before and after matches. Pies & sandwiches available.

Runcorn Fact File

Nickname: The Linnets

Previous Grounds: None

Previous Leagues: Lancashire Combination 1918-19, Cheshire County League, Northern Premier League, Alliance Premier League.

Club colours: Yellow/green

Change colours: Red/white

Midweek home matchday: Tuesday

Record win: 11-0 v Congleton

Record defeat: 8-0 v South Shields

Record Attendance: 10,111 v Preston North End - FA Cup - 1938/39

Record transfer fee paid: £17,000 to Hyde for Simon Rudge

Record transfer fee received: £80,000 from Nottingham Forest for Ian Woan

1993-94 Captain: Gary Brabin

1993-94 Top scorer: Karl Thomas

1993-94 Player of the Year: Paul Robertson

Club record goalscorer: Alan Ryan

Players progressing to Football League: Mark McCarrik, Eddie Bishop, Jimmy Cumbes, Graham Abel, Barry Knowles, Mark Jones, Don Page, David Pugh, Ian Woan, Gary Brabin.

Club Honours: Lancs Junior Cup 1918/19; Cheshire League Champions 1919/20, 1936/37, 1938/39, 1939/40, 1962/63; Cheshire Senior Cup Winners 1924/25, 1935/36, 1961/62, 1964/65, 1967/68, 1973/74, 1974/75, 1984/85, 1985/86, 1986/87, 1987/88, 1988/89, Runners-up 1993/94; Cheshire County Bowl Winners 1937/38; Northern Prem. League Champions 1975/76, 1980/81; NPL Challenge Cup Winners 1974/75, 1979/80, 19080/81; NPL Challenge Shield Winners 1980/81, 1981/82; Alliance Premier League Champions 1981/82; Gola League Championship Shield champions 1982/83, 1985/85; Bob Lord Trophy winners 1982/83, 1984/85, Runners-up 1991/92; FA Trophy Runners-up 1985/86, 1992/93, 1993/94.

SOUTHPORT

Formed:
1881

President:
Jack Carr

Chairman:
Charles Clapham

Football Secretary:
Roy Morris

Manager:
Brain Kettle

Assistant Manager
Steve Joel

Physiotherapist:
Dave Knight

Press Officer:
Roy Morris

AN IMPRESSIVE FIRST SEASON

A superb first season at the top of the non-League Pyramid saw Southport finish in fourth spot after being in contention for the title for most of the campaign.

Manager Brian Kettle kept faith with his Northern Premier League championship winning squad, and in fact nine of that side regularly featured in the 'Port line up throughout the season. Strikers Steve Haw and Peter Withers, so prolific in the NPL, found goals a little harder to come by in the top flight, but still did well and midfielder Dave Gamble regularly attracted the League scouts. The signing of ex-England star Luther Blissett caused great interest in the town, but failed to lift the side when fortunes on the field were wavering a little.

It was in defence that Southport struggled. Conceding 51 goals compared to Kidderminster's total of 34 and Kettering's miserly 24 was the major reason why the club failed to stay in the title fight to the end. The season ended with double disappointment when Southport were surprisingly defeated in the finals of both their county cup competitions by Northern Premier League opposition. Morecambe defeated them 4-3 in a gripping Lancashire ATS Challenge Trophy final at Burnden Park, whilst Marine avenged defeat in two earlier competitions by winning the final of the Liverpool Senior Cup 2-1 at Goodison Park.

A great deal of building work was completed at the club's Haig Avenue ground during the season, and the stadium is now ready to host League football once again. If Kettle can strengthen his defence there is no reason why they shouldn't mount a challenge again next term, although again, the second season is always the hardest.

Steve Whitney, *Team Talk* magazine.

Southport's 1993-94 squad with the impressive array of trophies won the previous year including the Northern Premier League championship, the Liverpool Senior Cup and the Lancashire ATS Challenge Trophy. Back Row (L/R): M Morgan (Director), C Walmsley, S Joel (Assistant Manager), D Gamble, A McDonald, P Lodge, P Cornstive, P Moore, D Goulding, L Williams, D Knight (Physio), A Pope (Director), T Medcroft (Director), B Kettle (Manager). Front: D Fuller, P Withers, R Morris (Secretary), C Clapham (Chairman), S Haw, L Dove, P Quinlan, R Mitchell. Photo - Paul Maher.

SOUTHPORT *MATCHFACTS 93-94* ***SOUTHPORT*** *MATCHFACTS 93-94* ***SOUTHPORT*** *MATCHFACTS 93-94*

Key: Home fixtures are denoted by bold capitals. Numbers in brackets after players names indicate goals scored (asterisks by the results denote own goals). Only used substitutes are listed - substituted players are *italicised*.

Key to Competitions: GMVC: GM Vauxhall Conference. **DC**: Drinkwise (GM Vauxhall Conference) Cup. **FAC**: FA Cup. **FAT**: FA Trophy. **NPL:** Northern Premier League Championship Shield. **LSC:** Liverpool Senior Cup. **ATS:** Lancashire ATS Challenge Trophy.

Date	Opponents	Comp.	Res	Gate	1.	2.	3.	4.	5.	6.	7.	8.	9.	10.	11.	Sub.	Sub.
14/08	**WINSFORD UTD**	NPL	5-0	593	Moore	Harvey	Fuller	Mooney	Goulding	Dove	Lyons(1)	Comstive	*Haw(1)*	*Walmsley(1)*	Withers(2)	McDonald	Mullen
21/08	Dagenham & Red.	GMVC	3-3	1,234	Moore	Dove	Fuller	Mooney	Goulding	Harvey	Lyons	*Walmsley(1)*	*Haw*	Comstive(1)	Withers(1)	McDonald	Mullen
24/08	**HALIFAX TOWN**	GMVC	2-2	2,423	Moore	Dove	Fuller	Mooney	Goulding	Harvey	Lyons	Walmsley	*Haw(1)*	*Comstive(1)*	Withers	McDonald	Mullen
28/08	**BROMSGROVE**	GMVC	1-2	1,238	Moore	Dove	Fuller	Mooney	Goulding	Harvey	*Lyons*	*Walmsley*	Haw	Comstive	Withers(1)	McDonald	Gamble
30/08	Northwich Vict.	GMVC	1-2	1,266	Moore	Dove	Fuller	Mooney	Goulding	Harvey	Mullen	*Walmsley*	Haw	Comstive	Withers	Gamble(1)	
04/09	Merthyr Tydfil	GMVC	2-2	607	Moore	Dove	Fuller	Mooney	Goulding	*Harvey*	*Gamble*	McDonald	Haw	Comstive	Withers(2)	Todhunter	Walmsley
07/09	**RUNCORN**	DC1(1)	1-4	912	Moore	*Todhunter*	Fuller	Mooney	Goulding	Dove(1)	McDonald	*Walmsley*	Withers	Comstive	Gamble	Quinlan	Mullen
11/09	**BATH CITY**	GMVC	*1-1	1,102	Moore	*Appleton*	Fuller	Dove	Goulding	Harvey	Walmsley	Comstive	*Haw*	Gamble	Withers	Quinlan	Mullen
18/09	Welling United	GMVC	2-0	1,130	Moore	McDonald	Fuller	Dove	Goulding	Harvey	Walmsley	Comstive	Haw	Gamble	Quinlan(2)		
21/09	Runcorn	DC1(2)	1-2	509	Moore	McDonald	Fuller	Dove	*Goulding*	Pilling	Quinlan(1)	Comstive	Chadwick	Gamble	*Walsh*	Withers	Mullen
25/09	**SLOUGH TOWN**	GMVC	1-0	1,224	Moore	McDonald	Fuller	Mooney	Dove	Pilling	Walmsley	Comstive	Haw	Gamble	Quinlan(1)		
28/09	**GATESHEAD**	GMVC	1-1	1,237	Moore	McDonald	Mullen	Mooney	*Walmsley*	Pilling	*Quinlan*	Comstive	Haw	Gamble	Withers(1)	Chadwick	Lyons
02/10	Macclesfield T.	GMVC	1-0	1,002	Moore	McDonald	Fuller	Mooney	Pilling	Mullen	Walmsley(1)	*Comstive*	*Quinlan*	Gamble	Withers	Haw	Lyons
09/10	**WOKING**	GMVC	2-1	1,526	Moore	McDonald	Fuller	Mooney	Goulding	Walmsley	Lyons	Comstive	Haw	Gamble(1)	Withers(1)		
12/10	**ALTRINCHAM**	GMVC	3-1	1,230	Moore	McDonald	Fuller	Mooney	Goulding	Walmsley	*Lyons*	Comstive	*Haw*	Gamble(1)	Withers(2)	Quinlan	Dove
16/10	Telford United	GMVC	3-1	855	Moore	Dove	Fuller	Mooney	Goulding	Walmsley	*McDonald*	Comstive	Haw(2)	Gamble	Withers(1)	Quinlan	Pilling
23/10	Macclesfield T.	FAC4q	3-5	1,190	Moore	Dove	Fuller	Mooney	Goulding(1)	Walmsley	*McDonald*	Comstive	*Haw*	Gamble(2)	Withers	Lyons	Pilling
30/10	**DOVER ATH.**	GMVC	3-2	1,569	Moore	Dove	Fuller	Mooney	Goulding	*McDonald*	Lyons	Comstive	Haw(2)	Gamble(1)	Withers		Pilling
06/11	Stafford Rangers	GMVC	2-0	1,159	Moore	Halliday	Fuller	Mooney	Dove	Walmsley	*Lyons*	Comstive	Haw(1)	Gamble(1)	Withers	McDonald	
20/11	Kettering Town	GMVC	0-2	1,980	Moore	Halliday	Fuller	Mooney	Dove	Walmsley	*Lyons*	Comstive	Haw	Gamble	Withers	McDonald	Lodge
27/11	**YEOVIL TOWN**	GMVC	1-1	1,303	Moore	Halliday	Fuller	*Mooney*	Dove	Walmsley	Lodge	Comstive	Haw(1)	Gamble	*Withers*	McDonald	Quinlan
04/12	Runcorn	GMVC	0-3	603	Moore	Halliday	Fuller	Mooney	Dove	Walmsley	Lodge	*Comstive*	Haw	Gamble	Withers		Quinlan
11/12	**TELFORD UTD**	GMVC	1-0	902	Moore	McDonald	Fuller	Goulding	Dove	Lodge	Lyons	*Quinlan*	Haw	*Gamble*	Withers(1)	Walmsley	Brennan
18/12	**KIDDERMINSTER**	GMVC	1-1	1,739	Moore	McDonald	Fuller	Goulding	Dove	Lodge	*Lyons*	Comstive	Haw	Gamble(1)	Withers	Walmsley	Quinlan
01/01	Witton Albion	GMVC	2-0	1,144	Moore	McDonald	Fuller	Dove	Goulding(2)	Lodge	Lyons	Brennan	Haw	*Quinlan*	Withers	Walmsley	

03/01	**NORTHWICH V.**	GMVC	0-0	1,606	Moore	*McDonald*	Fuller	Dove	Goulding	Lodge	Lyons	Brennan	Haw	*Quinlan*	Withers	Walmsley	Gamble
08/01	**EVERTON RES.**	LSC2	2-1	713	Moore	Halliday	Fuller	Mooney	Goulding	*Lodge*	Lyons	Comstive	Haw	Quinlan	Withers(2)		Gamble
11/01	**MARINE**	ATS2	2-1	809	Moore	Halliday	Fuller	Dove	Goulding	Lodge	*Lyons*	*Brennan*	Haw	Gamble(2)	Withers	Comstive	Quinlan
15/01	**DAGENHAM & R.**	GMVC	0-0	1,472	Moore	Halliday	Fuller	Dove	Goulding	Lodge	*Lyons*	*Comstive*	Haw	Gamble	Withers	Walmsley	Quinlan
22/01	Marine	FAT1	0-0	1,179	Moore	McDonald	Fuller	Dove	Goulding	Lodge	Walmsley	Brennan	Haw	*Gamble*	*Withers*	Comstive	Quinlan
25/01	**MARINE**	FAT1r	3-1	878	Moore	Mcdonald	Fuller	Dove	Goulding	*Lodge*	*Walmsley*	Brennan(1)	Haw	Gamble(2)	Withers	Comstive	Quinlan
29/01	Woking	GMVC	0-1	2,571	Moore	McDonald	Fuller	Dove	Goulding	Lodge	*Walmsley*	*Brennan*	Haw	Gamble	Withers	Comstive	Quinlan
02/02	Halifax Town	GMVC	2-2	1,310	Moore	McDonald	Fuller	Dove	Goulding	Lodge	*Mitchell*	Comstive	Haw	Gamble	*Withers*	Quinlan(2)	Williams
05/02	**WELLING UTD**	GMVC	2-1	1,115	Moore	McDonald	Fuller	Dove	Goulding	Lodge	*Mitchell*	Comstive	Quinlan(1)	Gamble(1)	Withers	Williams	
09/02	Accrington S.	ATSqf	1-0	449	Moore	McDonald	Fuller	Dove(1)	Goulding	Walmsley	Mitchell	Comstive	Haw	Gamble	*Quinlan*	Withers	
12/02	Colwyn Bay	FAT2	3-0	640	Moore	McDonald	Fuller	Dove	Goulding	Lodge	Walmsley	Comstive	*Haw(1)*	Gamble(1)	*Withers(1)*	Mitchell	Quinlan
19/02	**MERTHYR TYD.**	GMVC	3-2	1,150	Moore	McDonald	Fuller	Dove	Goulding	Lodge	*Mitchell(1)*	Comstive	*Haw*	Gamble(2)	Withers	Walmsley	Quinlan
26/02	**WITTON ALBION**	GMVC	2-1	1,417	Moore	McDonald	Fuller	Dove	Goulding	Lodge	*Walmsley*	Comstive	Haw(1)	Gamble(1)	Withers		Mitchell
01/03	**HORWICH R.M.I.**	AFSsf	2-0	521	Moore	McDonald(1)	Fuller	Dove	Mooney	*Lodge*	Walmsley(1)	Comstive	Haw	Gamble	*Quinlan*	Withers	Mitchell
05/03	Morecambe	FAT3	1-2	2,246	Moore	McDonald	Fuller	Dove	Goulding	Lodge	*Walmsley*	Comstive	Haw	*Gamble*	Withers(1)	Mitchell	Quinlan
12/03	Kidderminster	GMVC	0-2	3,877	Moore	McDonald	Fuller	Dove	Goulding	Lodge	*Williams*	*Comstive*	Haw	Gamble	Withers	Mitchell	Quinlan
14/03	**TRANMERE R.**	LSCsf	4-1	519	Moore	McDonald	Fuller	Dove	Mooney	Lodge	*Williams*	Brennan	Haw(3)	Gamble	Mitchell	Quinlan(1)	Walmsley
19/03	Bath City	GMVC	1-2	615	Moore	McDonald	Fuller	Dove	Mooney	Lodge	Walmsley	Brennan	*Haw(1)*	Gamble	Withers		Quinlan
22/03	**MACCLESFIELD**	GMVC	1-0	1,012	Moore	McDonald	Fuller	Dove	Mooney	Lodge(1)	*Walmsley*	*Quinlan*	Haw	Gamble	Withers	Mitchell	Comstive
26/03	Yeovil Town	GMVC	2-3	1,472	Moore	McDonald(1)	Comstive	Mooney	Dove	Lodge	Blissett(1)	Walmsley	*Mitchell*	*Gamble*	Withers	Goulding	Fuller
02/04	Altrincham	GMVC	2-1	982	Moore	McDonald	Fuller	Mooney	Goulding	Edwards	Lodge	Blissett(1)	Haw(1)	Gamble	*Withers*	Williams	
04/04	**STALYBRIDGE**	GMVC	0-2	1,422	Moore	McDonald	*Fuller*	Mooney	Goulding	Edwards	Lodge	Blissett	Haw	Gamble	*Williams*	Walmsley	Quinlan
09/04	Dover Athletic	GMVC	2-0	942	Moore	Farley	Mooney	Dove	Edwards	Lodge	McDonald(1)	Walmsley(1)	Haw	*Gamble*	*Blissett*	Withers	Comstive
12/04	Stalybridge C.	GMVC	1-3	593	Moore	Farley	Mooney	*Dove*	Edwards	Lodge	McDonald	Walmsley	Haw	Gamble(1)	*Blissett*	Withers	Comstive
16/04	Bromsgrove R.	GMVC	2-2	890	Moore	Farley	Mooney	Dove	Edwards	Lodge	Walmsley(1)	*McDonald*	Haw	Gamble(1)	*Quinlan*	Mitchell	Fuller
19/04	**KETTERING**	GMVC	0-1	1,026	Moore	Farley	Fuller	Dove	Edwards	Lodge	*Williams*	Walmsley	Haw	Gamble	*McDonald*	Blackhurst	Mitchell
23/04	**STAFFORD R.**	GMVC	0-2	707	Moore	McDonald	Fuller	Mooney	Goulding	*Edwards*	Walmsley	*Mitchell*	Haw	Gamble	Withers	Blackhurst	Williams
26/04	# MORECAMBE	ATSf	3-4	1,000	Moore	McDonald	*Fuller*	Dove	Edwards	*Lodge*	*Walmsley*	Comstive(1)	Haw(1)	*Gamble(1)*	Withers	Mitchell	Mooney
30/04	Slough Town	GMVC	0-0	663	Moore	Farley	Dove	*Edwards*	Goulding	Lodge	Fuller	Comstive	Haw	Gamble	*Withers*	Walmsley	McDonald
04/05	**RUNCORN**	GMVC	1-0	723	Moore	McDonald	Fuller	Edwards	Goulding	Dove	Lodge	Walmsley	Haw	Gamble(1)	*Comstive*	Withers	
07/05	Gateshead	GMVC	3-1	508	Moore	McDonald	Fuller	Edwards	Goulding	Lodge	Walmsley	*Mitchell*	Haw	Gamble(2)	*Withers(1)*	Williams	Farley
09/05	* MARINE	LSCf	1-2	1,535	Moore	McDonald	Fuller	Edwards	Goulding	Lodge	Blackhurst(1)	Comstive	Haw	Gamble	Withers		

- Played at Bolton Wanderers FC * - Played at Everton FC

Southport

BRAIN KETTLE

Brian, a former England Youth International, began his career as an apprentice with Liverpool. However, due to the tremendous strength in depth in the Anfield squad during the early 1970s, Brian's first team appearances were restricted to just three matches.

In August 1980, Brian transferred to Wigan Athletic where he made fourteen League appearances before joining the North American Soccer League circus with Houston Hurricane.

Upon his return to England, Brian played semi-professionally for Runcorn and South Liverpool before taking over as player-manager at the latter. He then joined Southport four years ago with the Northern Premier League championship in 1993 being the culmination of three years of steady progress.

Brian likes to play attacking football, and his principles have not changed now that the club are only one step away from reclaiming the Football League place they lost in 1979.

A David Gamble curled free-kick gives Southport their winner at home to Witton Albion.

Photo - Paul Maher.

Programme details:
36 pages for £1
Editor - Derek Hitchcock (0704 579458)
Assistant Editor - Martin Hagan

Any other club publications:
I've Seen the Sea (Fanzine)

Local Newspapers:
Southport Visitor
Southport Star

Local Radio Stations:
Radio Merseyside
Red Rose
Radio City

SOUTHPORT - PLAYING SQUAD

Player	Honours	Birthplace and date	Transfer Fees	Previous Clubs
GOALKEEPERS				
Paul Moore	NPL, NPLC, LSC, WSC	Liverpool 1/4/61		Rhyl, Worcester C, Alvechurch, Morecambe
DEFENDERS				
Alan McDonald	NPL, NPLC, LSC	Liverpool 17/12/63		St Helens T, General Chemicals, Southport, Witton Alb, Accrington Stanley, Altrincham
Derek Goulding	GMVC, NPL, NPLC, SSC	Liverpool 6/5/63		Altrincham, Bangor C, Stafford R, Oswestry T, Bangor C, Chorley
Dave Fuller	NPL	Burton Strather 20/11/64		Bangor C, Gainsborough Trinity, Bangor C, Witton Alb
Kevin Mooney	NPL, BLT, NPLC, LSC	Liverpool 23/8/59		Bangor C, Bury, Karlskrona(Swe), Telford U, Tranmere, Stafford R, Bangor C
Elfyn Edwards	WSP, WY, GMVC, NPL	Aberystwyth 4/5/60		Wrexham, Tranmere R, Runcorn, Altrincham, Macclesfield T, Halifax T
MIDFIELDERS				
Leroy Dove	NPL	Manchester 27/4/63		Prestwich Heys, Droylsden, Buxton
Paul Lodge	ES, NPL	Liverpool 13/2/61	£3,000	Everton, Preston, Bolton, Stockport, Barrow, Southport, Macclesfield, Witton, Morecambe
David Gamble	NPL	Liverpool 23/3/71		Grimsby T, Altrincham
Chris Walmsley	NPL	Wigan 21/7/66		Daisy Hill, Horwich RMI, Atherton LR, Horwich RMI, Fleetwood T
Paul Comstive		Southport 25/11/61		Blackburn, Wigan, Wrexham, Burnley, Bolton W, Chester C
FORWARDS				
Richard Mitchell		Stoke 14/9/73	Player/ Exchange	Port Vale, Macclesfield Town
Steve Haw	NPL	Liverpool 9/11/62		Wigan, Runcorn, Kirkby T, Marine, Altrincham, Marine
Peter Withers	NPL, LSC	Huyton 2/5/66		South Liverpool, Runcorn
Phil Quinlan	NPL	Southport 14/4/71		Everton, Doncaster Rovers

Departures during season:
Steve Appleton (Hyde Utd), Stuart Todhunter (Workington), Mark Henshaw (Hyde Utd), Darren Lyons (Macclesfield T), Mike Halliday (Ashton Utd), Stuart Mellish (Winsford Utd), Paul Mullen (Knowsley Utd), Jimmy Harvey (Released), Dave Chadwick (Chadderton), Mark Brennan (Chorley).

Players on loan during season:
Luther Blissett (Bury).

Haig Avenue, Southport

Address and telephone number: Haig Avenue, Southport, Merseyside (0704 533422).
Simple directions: Signposted from all entrances to town.
Capacity: 5,500 **Seated:** 1,880 **Covered terracing:** 1,100
Record Attendance: 20,000 v Newcastle United - FA Cup - 1932
Club Shop: Scarves, replica kits, programmes and various other souvenirs for sale. Contact Southport FC.
Social Facilities: Open 7.30-11.00 every night and match days. (Tel: 0704 530182).

Southport Fact File

Nickname: The Sandgrounders

Club Sponsors: Apollo Leisure

Previous Grounds: Ash Lane

Previous Leagues: Northern Premier League, Football League, Lancashire Combination

Club colours: Old Gold & black

Change colours: White & black

Midweek home matchday: Tuesday

Record win: 8-1 v Nelson - 01.01.31.

Record defeat: 0-11 v Oldham - 26.12.62

Record transfer fee: £6,000 for Malcolm Russell

Record transfer fee received: £25,000 from Rochdale for Steve Whitehall - 1991

1993-94 Captain: Leroy Dove.

1993-94 Top scorer: David Gamble.

1993-94 Player of the Year: Paul Moore.

Club record goalscorer: Alan Spence 98

Record appearances: Arthur Peat 401 - 1962-72

Club Honours: Football League Division Four Champions 1972/73 (Runners-up 1966/67); Northern Premier League Champions 1992/93 (League Cup Winners 1990/91, League Shield 1993/94); Third Division North Section Cup Winners 1937/38; Liverpool Senior Cup Winners 1930/31, 1931/32, 1943/44, 1957/58 (shared), 1963/64 (shared), 1974/75, 1990/91, 1992/93 (Runners-up 1993/94); Lancashire Senior Cup Winners 1904/05; Lancashire Junior Cup (now ATS Challenge Trophy) Winners 1919/20, 1992/93 (Runners-up 1993/94).

Formed:
1876

President:
R N Heath

Chairman:
R J Horton

Vice-Chairman
C Went

Football Secretary:
Mr M T Hughes

Manager:
Brendan Phillips

Physiotherapist:
Barrie Whittaker

Commercial Manager:
George Berry

Press Officer:
Chris Godwin

STAFFORD RANGERS

The 1993/94 GM Vauxhall Conference campaign saw the good work started by previous manager Dennis Booth continued in Brendan Phillips' first full season in charge.

For the first time for a number of years there was no nail-biting fight against relegation as Stafford hardly dropped out of the top ten throughout the whole season. The team eventually finished ninth. Home form was excellent (only four league defeats), but only two victories were gained away from Marston Road.

Rangers were out of luck in the three national cup competitions, suffering early exits in the FA Cup, FA Trophy and Bob Lord Trophy to Knowsley United, Guiseley and Kidderminster Harriers respectively. Progress, however, was made in the Staffordshire Senior Cup as victories at Oldbury United and Stourbridge set up a home semi-final tie with Dudley Town. After the game at Marston Road finished 1-1, Rangers never recovered from three Dudley goals during the opening thirteen minutes of the replay and bowed out of the competition.

During the season, Ryan Price's club record run of consecutive appearances that stretched from his debut in August 1988 to November 1994 came to an end at 294. In total the 24-year old keeper made 325 first team appearances for the club. His performances attracted attention from numerous Football League clubs over the years and in August he joined Barry Fry's Birmingham City.

Chris Bedford, Programme Editor.

Stafford Rangers - 1993-94.

STAFFORD RANGERS *MATCHFACTS 93-94* ***STAFFORD RANGERS*** *MATCHFACTS 93-94*

Key: Home fixtures are denoted by bold capitals. Numbers in brackets after players names indicate goals scored (asterisks by the results denote own goals). Only used substitutes are listed - substituted players are *italicised*.

Key to Competitions: GMVC: GM Vauxhall Conference. **DC**: Drinkwise (GM Vauxhall Conference) Cup. **FAC**: FA Cup. **FAT**: FA Trophy. **SSC**: Staffordshire Senior Cup.

Date	Opponents	Comp.	Res	Gate	1.	2.	3.	4.	5.	6.	7.	8.	9.	10.	11.	Sub.	Sub.
21/08	Welling Utd	GMVC	1-2	885	Price	Hemming	Bradshaw	Simpson	Essex(1)	Berry	Williams	Hanlon	Burr	Massey	*Mettioui*	Boughey	
24/08	**NORTHWICH V.**	GMVC	3-1	1,064	Price	Hemming	Bradshaw	Simpson	Essex	Berry	Williams	Hanlon	*Burr(1)*	Massey	*Mettioui(1)*	Boughey	Clayton
28/08	**DAGENHAM & R.**	GMVC	2-0	885	Price	*Hemming*	Bradshaw	Simpson	Essex	Berry	*Williams*	Hanlon	Burr	Massey	Mettioui(2)	Boughey	Clayton
30/08	Halifax Town	GMVC	1-1	1,228	Price	Wood	Bradshaw	Simpson	Hope	Hemming	Williams	Hanlon	Burr(1)	*Massey*	*Mettioui*	Boughey	
04/09	**WOKING**	GMVC	3-0	1,071	Price	Boughey	Bradshaw	Simpson(1)	Essex	Berry	Williams	Hanlon(1)	Burr	*Massey*	*Mettioui(1)*	Palgrave	Clayton
07/09	Bromsgrove R.	GMVC	3-3	929	Price	Boughey	Bradshaw	Simpson	Essex	Williams	Mettioui(1)	Hanlon	Burr(1)	Berry	*Palgrave(1)*		Hope
11/09	Slough Town	GMVC	0-3	907	Price	Hemming	Bradshaw	Simpson	Essex	*Berry*	Boughey	Hanlon	Burr	Palgrave	*Mettioui*	Massey	Clayton
18/09	**YEOVIL TOWN**	GMVC	4-2	1,064	Price	Boughey	Bradshaw	Simpson(3)	Essex	*Hemming*	Williams(1)	Hanlon	Burr	Palgrave	Clayton		Hope
21/09	Oldbury Utd	SSC1	2-0	146	Price	Boughey	Bradshaw(1)	Wood	*Essex*	Hope(1)	*Williams*	Hanlon	Dawson	Palgrave	Clayton	Simpson	Burr
25/09	Altrincham	GMVC	0-0	758	Price	Boughey	Bradshaw	Simpson	Essex	Hope	Williams	Hanlon	*Burr*	Massey	Mettioui	Clayton	
02/10	**KIDDERMINSTER**	GMVC	2-3	1,187	Price	Boughey	Bradshaw	Simpson	Essex	*Hemming*	Williams	Hanlon	Clayton	Burr(1)	*Mettioui*	Wood(1)	Hope
09/10	**KETTERING**	GMVC	1-0	1,456	Price	Hemming	Bradshaw	Simpson	Essex	Hope	Williams	*Hanlon*	Clayton(1)	Burr	Mettioui	Griffiths	
16/10	Bath City	GMVC	3-2	656	Price	Boughey	Bradshaw	Simpson	Essex	Hope	*Williams*	*Hanlon*	Clayton(2)	Burr(1)	Mettioui	Griffiths	Bodkin
23/10	**KNOWSLEY UTD**	FAC4q	1-1	977	Price	Boughey	Bradshaw	Simpson	Essex	Hope	Williams	Foy	Clayton	Burr(1)	*Mettioui*	Griffiths	
26/10	Knowsley United	FAC4qr	2-2	612	Price	Boughey	Bradshaw(1)	Simpson	Hemming(1)	Hope	Wood	Foy	*Clayton*	Burr	*Griffiths*	Williams	Hanlon
30/10	**MACCLESFIELD**	GMVC	2-3	1,249	Price	Simpson(1)	Bradshaw	*Wood*	*Hemming*	Hope	Williams	Bodkin	Boughey	Burr(1)	Hanlon	Berry	Foy
01/11	Knowsley Utd	FAC4qr	0-1	951	Price	Hemming	Bradshaw	Simpson	Hope	Berry	Williams	Hanlon	Boughey	Burr	*Griffiths*	Mettioui	
06/11	**SOUTHPORT**	GMVC	0-2	1,159	Price	Berry	Bradshaw	Simpson	Essex	Hemming	*Williams*	Bodkin	Boughey	Burr	Hope		Foy
15/11	Kidderminster	DC2	0-3	774	Price	Berry	Hope	Simpson	Essex	Hemming	Williams	Bodkin	*Boughey*	Burr	Griffiths		Mee
20/11	Merthyr Tydfil	GMVC	0-2	561	Davies	Berry	Bradshaw	Simpson	Essex	Hemming	Boughey	Bodkin	Kabia	Burr	Mettioui		
27/11	**STALYBRIDGE**	GMVC	2-2	685	Davies	Boughey	Bradshaw	Simpson(1)	Essex	Hemming	Bodkin(1)	Shepstone	Kabia	Burr	*Mettioui*		Foy
04/12	Gateshead	GMVC	0-0	470	Price	*Boughey*	Bradshaw	Simpson	Essex	Hemming	Foy	Bodkin	Kabia	Burr	*Mettioui*	Griffiths	Williams
07/12	Stourbridge	SSC2	2-1	152	Price	Boughey	Bradshaw	Simpson(1)	Hope	Hemming	Williams	Bodkin	Foy	Burr(1)	*Griffiths*		Mee

11/12	**WITTON ALBION**	GMVC	1-0	580	Price	Boughey	Bradshaw	Simpson	Essex	Hemming	Williams	Bodkin	Foy	Burr(1)	Finney		
14/12	Telford Utd	GMVC	1-2	733	Price	Boughey	Bradshaw	*Griffiths*	Essex	Hemming	*Williams*	Bodkin	Clayton(1)	Finney	Foy	Hope	Mee
19/12	**SLOUGH TOWN**	GMVC	0-0	671	Price	Boughey	Bradshaw	Simpson	Essex	Hemming	Mee	Bodkin	Clayton	Foy	Finney		
27/12	Runcorn	GMVC	2-2	715	Price	Boughey	Bradshaw	Foy	Essex	Berry	Mee(1)	Bodkin	Clayton	*Harrison*	*Finney(1)*	Williams	Mee
01/01	**RUNCORN**	GMVC	2-2	1,111	Price	Boughey(2)	Bradshaw	Hemming	Essex	Hope	*Williams*	Bodkin	*Vickers*	Mee	Finney	Griffiths	Berry
03/01	**BROMSGROVE**	GMVC	0-0	989	Price	Berry	Bradshaw	Foy	Essex	Hemming	Williams	Griffiths	Boughey	*Mee*	*Finney*	Clayton	Hope
15/01	**BATH CITY**	GMVC	2-0	810	Price	Simpson	Bradshaw	Hemming	Essex	Hope	Williams	Griffiths	Clayton	Boughey	*Finney*	Mettioui(2)	
22/01	Altrincham	FAT1	2-0	790	Price	Boughey	Bradshaw(1)	Simpson	Essex	*Hope*	Williams(1)	Hemming	Clayton	*Mettioui*	Finney	Griffiths	Mee
29/01	Dover Athletic	GMVC	0-2	1,270	Price	Boughey	Bradshaw	Simpson	Essex	*Hemming*	Williams	Griffiths	*Clayton*	Mee	Finney	Ward	Hope
05/02	**HALIFAX TOWN**	GMVC	1-1	1,082	Price	Berry	Bradshaw	Simpson	Essex	Hemming	*Williams*	Bodkin	Boughey	Mettioui(1)	Foy		Mee
12/02	Guiseley	FAT2	2-3	1,209	Price	Berry	Bradshaw	*Griffiths*	Essex	*Hemming*	Williams(1)	Finney	Boughey	Mettioui	Foy(1)	Clayton	Wood
19/02	**DOVER ATH.**	GMVC	2-2	760	Price	Boughey	Bradshaw	Simpson	Essex	Hope	*Williams*	Foy(1)	Burton	Mettioui(1)	*Finney*	Bodkin	Mee
26/02	Kidderminster	GMVC	0-2	2,196	Price	Boughey	Bradshaw	Simpson	*Essex*	Foy	Williams	Bodkin	Burton	Mettioui	Shepstone	Griffiths	
01/03	**TELFORD UTD**	GMVC	1-1	905	Price	Boughey	Bradshaw	Simpson	Hope	Foy	Williams	Bodkin	Burton(1)	Mettioui	Shepstone		
05/03	**ALTRINCHAM**	GMVC	0-1	808	Price	Boughey	Bradshaw	Simpson	Hope	Foy	Mee	*Bodkin*	*Burton*	Mettioui	Shepstone	Griffiths	Williams
08/03	Witton Albion	GMVC	1-1	613	Price	Boughey	Bradshaw(1)	Simpson	Essex	Foy	Williams	*Bodkin*	Burton	Mettioui	Shepstone		Mee
12/03	Stalybridge C.	GMVC	2-1	458	Price	*Boughey*	Bradshaw	Simpson	Essex	Shepstone	Williams	Bodkin(1)	Foy	Mettioui(1)	*Burton*	Griffiths	Berry
19/03	Northwich Vics	GMVC	0-0	752	Price	Berry	Bradshaw	Simpson	Essex	Foy	Williams	Bodkin	Boughey	Mettioui	Shepstone		
22/03	Yeovil Town	GMVC	1-0	1,405	Price	Boughey	Bradshaw	Simpson	Essex	Foy	Williams	*Griffiths*	May(1)	*Mettioui*	Shepstone	Griffiths	Berry
02/04	**WELLING UTD**	GMVC	3-0	781	Price	Boughey	Bradshaw	Simpson	Essex	Foy	Williams	*Bodkin*	May(2)	Mettioui(1)	Shepstone	Griffiths	
09/04	**GATESHEAD**	GMVC	3-1	686	Price	Boughey	Bradshaw	Simpson	Essex	Foy	Williams(1)	*Bodkin*	May(1)	*Mettioui*	Shepstone	Griffiths	Berry
16/04	Kettering Town	GMVC	0-2	1,701	Price	Boughey	Bradshaw	Simpson	Essex	Foy	Williams	Griffiths	May	Mee	Shepstone		
19/04	**DUDLEY TOWN**	SSCqf	1-1	348	Price	Boughey	Bradshaw	Luby	Essex	Berry	*Williams*	Griffiths	May	Mee	Shepstone(1)	Wilkinson	
23/04	Southport	GMVC	2-1	707	Price	Boughey	Bradshaw	Simpson	Essex	*Berry*	*Williams*	Griffiths	May(1)	Mee	Shepstone(1)	Foy	Luby
26/04	Dagenham & Red.	GMVC	0-1	547	Price	Boughey	Bradshaw	Simpson	Berry	Luby	Williams	Griffiths	May	*Mee*	Shepstone	Mettioui	
30/04	**MERTHYR TYD.**	GMVC	5-1	921	Price	Boughey	Bradshaw	Simpson(1)	Berry	Foy(1)	Williams	Griffiths	May(2)	*Mettioui*	Shepstone(1)		Mee
02/05	Dudley Town	SSCqfr	1-3	238	Price	Luby	Bradshaw	Simpson	Berry(1)	Foy	Williams	Griffiths	May	Boughey	Shepstone		
04/05	Macclesfield T.	GMVC	0-0	542	Price	Luby	Bradshaw	Simpson	Berry	Foy	Williams	Griffiths	May	Mee	Shepstone		
07/05	Woking	GMVC	0-4	1,428	Price	Boughey	Bradshaw	Simpson	Berry	Williams	Griffiths	Foy	Mettioui	*Luby*	*Bodkin*	Essex	Mee

Stafford Rangers

BRENDAN PHILLIPS

Brendan was appointed as manager at Marston Road towards the end of the 1992-93 season after Dennis Booth departed for Bristol Rovers. Prior to his appointment at Stafford, Brendan had been in charge of Beazer Homes League club Bedworth United for two years, guiding them to a top six finish in the Midland Divisionin both seasons.

During his playing career, Brendan served 12 clubs, played in the Football League for Mansfield Town and representing the England semi-professional side on four occasions. A skilfull midfield player, Brendan took in spells with Peterborough United, Burton Albion, Nuneaton Borough (twice), Kettering Town, Boston United (twice), Mansfield, Scarborough (twice), Shepshed, Corby Town, Aylesbury United and Atherstone United before joining Bedworth.

He will look back on his first season of Conference management with a degree of satisafaction as Stafford's league form showed a marked improvement on recent campaigns.

Stafford Rangers have to defend in depth during their FA Trophy tie away to Guiseley.

Photo - Colin Stevens.

Programme details:
40 pages for £1.00
Editor - C & W Bedford

Any other club publications:

Local Newspapers:
Staffordshire Newsletter
Express & Star
Evening Sentinel

Local Radio Stations:
Radio Stoke
Beacon Radio
Signal Radio

STAFFORD RANGERS - PLAYING SQUAD 1993-94

Player	Honours	Birthplace and date	Transfer Fees	Previous Clubs
GOALKEEPERS				
Ryan Price	ESP, SSC, FAXI	Wolverhampton 13/3/70		Bolton Wanderers
DEFENDERS				
George Berry	WI, FLC	Rostrup, Ger 19/11/57		Wolves, Stoke, Peterborough, Preston, Aldershot
Mark Bradshaw	SSC	Ashton 7/9/69		Blackpool
Chris Hemming		Newcastle 13/4/66		Stoke, Hereford, Merthyr Tydfil
Steve Essex	BLT, BSC, FAXI	Walsall 2/10/60	£8,000	Gresley Rovers, Burton Albion, Aylesbury United
Paul Carty	BSC	Birmingham 22/10/66		Everton, Stourbridge, Nuneaton Boro, VS Rugby, Bromsgrove Rovers
MIDFIELDERS				
Darren Boughey	E-u19	Stoke 30/11/70		Stoke City
David Foy		Birmingham		Birmingham City, Scunthorpe Utd
Martin Bodkin		Birmingham		Coventry, Bedworth, Stratford, C.Sporting, RC Warwick, Atherstone, Tamworth
Wayne Simpson	ESP, FAXI	Newcastle, 19/9/68		Port Vale
Tony Griffiths	FAT	Stoke 1/4/63		Stafford R, Leek T, Telford U
Kevin Finney		Newcastle 19/10/69		Port Vale, Lincoln City, Leek Town
Paul Shepstone	FA School	Coventry 8/11/70		Coventry C, Birmingham C, Atherstone Utd, Motherwell, Crewe Alex, WBA
Sean Luby		Birmingham		Coleshill, Chelmsley, Hinckley T, Chelmsley, Redditch U, Cradley, Armitage
FORWARDS				
Danny Williams		Birmingham 29/10/68		Wolverhapton Utd, Bloxwich, Harrisons, North Park, Blakenall, Bilston T
Mark Hope				Plymouth Argyle, Bradford City, Kilmarnock, Falmouth Town
Leroy May		Wolverhapton 12/8/69		Tividale, Walsall, Tividale, Hereford, Tividale, Altrincham
Ahmed Mettioui	Morrocco u-21	Tangier 3/11/65		Faith Union SC, Crewe Alexandra
Jason Dawson		Stoke 9/2/71		Port Vale, Rochdale, Macclesfield Town
Andy Mee		Coventry 15/3/75		Coventry City (Sch), Bedworth United

Departures during season:
Simon Mason (VS Rugby), Paul Clayton (Stalybridge C), Steve Hanlon (Released), Ian Vickers (Released), Jason Kabia (Malta).

Players on loan during season:
Mark Davies (Coventry C), Mike Harrison (Port Vale), Chris Burton (Solihull Borough).

Marston Road, Stafford Rangers

Address and telephone number: Marston Road, Stafford St16 3BX. Tel: 0785 42750. Fax: 0785 54050.

Simple directions: From M6 junction 14, A34 (Stone) to roundabout, straight over into Beaconside, take third right into Common Road, ground one mile ahead. From Town Centre, follow signs for B5066 (Sandon) turn left by Lotus shoe factory. Two miles from railway station.

Capacity: 6,000 **Seated:** 426 **Covered terracing:** 3,000

Record Attendance: 8,536 v Rotherham United FA Cup Third Round - 4.1.1975

Club Shop: Two shops, one containing a large stock of old programmes and one specialising in souvenirs run by Jim & Irene Dalglish.

Previous Grounds: Lammascotes, Stone Road, Newtown, Doxey (until 1896)

Stafford Fact File

Nickname: Boro

Club Sponsors: Sentinal Newspapers

Previous Leagues: Shropshire 1891/93, Birmingham 1893/96, 1921/40, North Staffordshire 1896/1900, Cheshire 1900/01, Birmingham Combination 1900/12, 1946/52, Cheshire County 1952/69, Northern Premier 1969/79, 1983/85, Alliance Premier 1979/83.

Club colours: Black & white striped shirts, black shorts & socks

Change colours: All yellow

Midweek home matchday: Tuesday

Record win: 11-0 v Dudley Town, FA Cup - 6.9.58

Record defeat: 0-12 v Burton Town, Birmingham Lge - 13.12.30

Record transfer fee: £13,000 for Stephen Butterworth from VS Rugby - 1990

Record transfer fee received: £100,000 from Crystal Palace for Stan Collymore - 1990

1993-94 Captain: Steve Essex

1993-94 Top scorer: Ahmed Mettioui

1993-94 Player of the Year: Chris Hemming

Club record goalscorer: M Cullerton 176

Record appearances: Jim Sargent

Past players who progressed to the Football League: M Alckisie (Plymouth, Luton, Spurs), J Arnold (Blackburn, Everton, Port Vale), R Williams, M Cullerton, T Bailey (all Port Vale), K Barnes (Man. City), A Lee (Tranmere Rovers), E Cameron, (Exeter), W Blunt (Wolves), G Bullock (Barnsley), K Mottershead (Doncaster), McIlvenny (WBA), S Collymore (Crystal Palace), P Devlin (Notts County), R Price (Birmingham City).

Club Honours: Birmingham Combination Champions 1912-13; Birmingham League Champions 1925-26; Northern Premier League Champions 1971-72, 1984-85; FA Trophy Winners 1971-72, 1978-79, Runners-up 1975-76; Bob Lord Trophy 1985-86; Wednesday Charity Cup Winners 1920-21; Midland Floodlight Cup Winners 1970-71; NPL Championship Shield Winners 1984-85; Jim Thompson Shield Winners 1986-87; Staffs Senior Cup Winners 1954-55, 1956-57, 1962-63, 1971-72, 1977-78, 1986-87, 1991-92.

STALYBRIDGE CELTIC

Formed:
1909

President:
J Knott
Chairman:
Peter Barnes
Vice Chairman
Derek Wolsterholme
Football Secretary:
Martyn Torr
Manager:
Peter Wragg
Assistant Manager:
Dave Denby
Physiotherapist:
Dave Stevens
Commercial Manager:
Martyn Torr
Press Officer:
Martyn Torr

Saved by Cup run and Peter Wragg

Stalybridge Celtic's season was been fraught with worry about the relegation issue ... but there was one magnificent high spot - the FA Cup run.

For the first time in almost 60 years, Celtic reached the second round proper of this the most prestigious knockout competition in the history of the game. It was a tortuous road to Carlisle, and ultimately defeat, but consider this: Celtic have been knocked out, indirectly by cup winners Manchester United!

We lost at Carlisle, who went out against Sunderland, whose conqueors were Wimbledon, beaten by Manchester United who progressed past Charlton and Oldham. Just think ... it could have been us facing Chelsea in front of the old Twin Towers.

Seriously, the campaign started in September with a 6-0 demolition of Fleetwood, Phil Power scoring a hat-trick. That earned a home draw with Bootle, who scored two late goals at Bower Fold to force a replay at Netherton, which we won 3-1, the highlight being a stunning volley by Paul Kirkham. Kirkham then hit another stunning goal to earn a 1-0 win at Warrington. This set up a final qualifier with Whitby Town at Bower Fold, which after a goalless draw was won by a Paul Allen goal in the replay.

The draw for the first round wasn't particularly kind, pairing us with another non-league side, Marine. In front of 1,500 fans in pouring rain at Bower Fold, a John Aspinall equaliser cancelled out a Marine goal and took the replay to Crosby. This was probably the single most memorable game I can remember in 29 years of watching Celtic. We led 2-0, and were seconds away from history when they levelled at 3-3 in the last minute of normal time. Marine went ahead for the first time in extra time, but Kirkham's header sent the game to a penalty shootout which was won 8-6 by Celtic thanks to Paul Bennett's cool nerve.

And so to Carlisle and honourable defeat, by 3-1, Kirkham scoring his fourth goal of the campaign, a classic diving header from a Stuart Leicester cross. The 5,546 stood and applauded off the teams at the end of a day full of memories.

In the league at the end of March, hopes of surviving the dreaded drop were dwindling. Peter Wragg took over the managerial reins with twelve games to go, and his record was:- P12 W9 D1 L2 F24 A9 Pts 28. That proves that miracles can and do happen!

Martyn Torr

STALYBRIDGE MATCHFACTS 93-94 *STALYBRIDGE* MATCHFACTS 93-94 *STALYBRIDGE* MATCHFACTS 93-94

Key: Home fixtures are denoted by bold capitals. Numbers in brackets after players names indicate goals scored (asterisks by the results denote own goals). Only used substitutes are listed - substituted players are *italicised*.

Key to Competitions: GMVC: GM Vauxhall Conference. **CSC**: Cheshire Senior Cup. **DC**: Drinkwise (GM Vauxhall Conference) Cup. **FAC**: FA Cup. **FAT**: FA Trophy.

Date	Opponents	Comp.	Res	Gate	1.	2.	3.	4.	5.	6.	7.	8.	9.	10.	11.	Sub.	Sub.
21/08	**SLOUGH TOWN**	GMVC	0-1	679	Hughes	Bennett	Coathup	Dixon	*Aspinall*	Booth	Anderson	*Kirkham*	Bunn	Power	Locke	Jackson	Brown
24/08	Altrincham	GMVC	0-0	758	Hughes	Bennett	Coathup	Dixon	Aspinall	Booth	Anderson	*Kirkham*	Bunn	*Power*	Locke	Jackson	Brown
28/08	Yeovil Town	GMVC	0-0	3,102	Hughes	Bennett	Coathup	Dixon	Aspinall	Booth	Anderson	Kirkham	Bunn	Power	Locke		
30/08	**GATESHEAD**	GMVC	2-1	605	Hughes	Bennett(1)	Coathup	Dixon	Aspinall	*Booth*	Anderson	Kirkham	*Jackson*	Power(1)	Locke	Boyle	Brown
04/09	Bath City	GMVC	1-1	861	Hughes	Bennett	Coathup	Dixon	Aspinall	Edmonds	Anderson	Kirkham	Bunn(1)	*Power*	Locke	Jackson	
07/09	**TELFORD UTD**	DC1(1)	2-0	352	Hughes	Bennett	Brown	Dixon	Boyle	Booth	Anderson	Kirkham	Jackson(1)	Power	Locke(1)		
11/09	**FLEETWOOD T.**	FAC1q	6-0	517	Hughes	Bennett	Coathup	*Dixon*	Boyle	Booth	Anderson	Jackson(1)	Bunn(1)	Power(3)	Locke		Brown(1)
18/09	Kidderminster H.	GMVC	0-1	921	Hughes	Bennett	Coathup	Dixon	Boyle	*Booth*	Anderson	Jackson	Brown	Power	Locke	Kirkham	
21/09	Telford United	DC1(2)	1-2	408	Hughes	*Bennett*	Coathup	Boyle	Aspinall	Allen	Anderson	Jackson	Kirkham	Brown	Locke(1)		Booth
25/09	**BOOTLE**	FAC2q	2-2	426	Hughes	Brown(1)	Coathup	Boyle	Aspinall	Booth	Anderson	*Jackson*	Kirkham	Power	Locke(1)		Allen
28/09	Bootle	FAC2qr	3-1	330	Hughes	Bennett	Coathup	Dixon(1)	Aspinall	*Booth*	Anderson(1)	Jackson	Kirkham(1)	Allen	Locke		Brown
02/10	Runcorn	GMVC	1-1	713	Hughes	Bennett	Allen	Dixon	Aspinall	Boyle	Anderson	Jackson	Bunn	Kirkham(1)	Locke		
05/10	**HALIFAX TOWN**	GMVC	1-1	1,233	Hughes	Bennett	Coathup	Dixon	Aspinall	Boyle	*Anderson*	Kirkham	Bunn	Jackson(1)	Locke		Brown
09/10	Warrington Town	FAC3q	1-0	654	Hughes	Bennett	Coathup	*Dixon*	Aspinall	Boyle	Anderson	Jackson	Bunn	*Kirkham(1)*	Locke	Allen	Brown
16/10	**KIDDERMINSTER**	GMVC	0-2	654	Hughes	Bennett	Coathup	Dixon	Aspinall	Boyle	Anderson	*Jackson*	Bunn	Leicester	*Locke*	Kirkham	Booth
23/10	**WHITBY TOWN**	FAC4q	0-0	740	Hughes	Bennett	Coathup	Dixon	Aspinall	Boyle	Anderson	*Leicester*	Bunn	Kirkham	Allen	Shaughnessy	*Booth*
27/10	Whitby Town	FAC4qr	1-0	887	Hughes	Brown	Coathup	Dixon	Aspinall	Allen(1)	Anderson	Leicester	Shaughnessy	Kirkham	Locke		
30/10	**BROMSGROVE R.**	GMVC	0-2	596	Hughes	Brown	Coathup	Dixon	Aspinall	*Allen*	Anderson	Leicester	Shaughnessy	Kirkham	Locke		Bunn
02/11	Northwich Vics	DC2	0-1	521	Hughes	Brown	Coathup	*Dixon*	Aspinall	Booth	Anderson	*Leicester*	Shaughnessy	Bunn	Locke	Bennett	Kirkham
06/11	**KETTERING T.**	GMVC	1-1	630	Hughes	Bennett	Coathup	Dixon(1)	Brown	Booth	*Anderson*	*Leicester*	Shaughnessy	Bunn	Locke	Jackson	Kirkham
13/11	**MARINE**	FAC1	1-1	1,525	Hughes	Bennett	Coathup	Dixon	Aspinall(1)	Booth	Brown	*Leicester*	Shaughnessy	Bunn	*Locke*	Jackson	Kirkham
20/11	**WOKING**	GMVC	2-2	524	Hughes	Edmonds	Coathup	Dixon	Aspinall	Booth	*Brown(1)*	*Jackson*	Shaughnessy	Kirkham	Hill	Leicester	Bunn(1)
27/11	Stafford Rgrs	GMVC	2-2	778	Hughes	Edmonds	Coathup	Dixon(1)	Aspinall	Booth	Brown	*Leicester*	Sh'nessy	Kirkham(1)	Hill		Bunn
29/11	Marine	FAC1r	x4-4	895	Hughes	Edmonds	Coathup	Dixon	Aspinall(1)	Booth	Brown	Bunn	*Sh'nessy(1)*	Kirkham(1)	*Hill(1)*	Leicester	Bennett
04/12	Carlisle United	FAC2	1-3	5,546	Hughes	Edmonds	Coathup	*Dixon*	Aspinall	Booth	Brown	*Bunn*	Sh'nessy	Kirkham(1)	Bennett	Leicester	Locke

07/12	Colwyn Bay	CSC2	1-4	110	Hughes	Edmonds	Coathup	Locke	Aspinall	Booth	Brown	*Leicester*	Sh'nessy	Kirkham(1)	*Bennett*	Jackson	Blain
11/12	Macclesfield T.	GMVC	3-1	788	Hughes	Edmonds	Coathup	Locke	Aspinall	Booth	Brown	Woods	Sh'nessy(2)	Kirkham(1)	*Anderson*	Leicester	
18/12	Bromsgrove R.	GMVC	0-2	1,695	Hughes	Edmonds	Coathup	Dixon	Aspinall	Locke	Brown	Woods	Shaughnessy	*Kirkham*	*Anderson*	Leicester	Bunn
01/01	**MACCLESFIELD**	GMVC	0-2	1,059	Hughes	Edmonds	Locke	Dixon	Aspinall	Ogley	Brown	*Woods*	Shaughnessy	Kirkham	*Bunn*	Jackson	Leicester
03/01	Gateshead	GMVC	1-2	572	Hughes	Bennett	*Blain*	Dixon	Aspinall	Ogley	Brown	Leicester	*Shaughnessy*	Jackson(1)	Anderson	Locke	Kirkham
08/01	**MERTHYR TYD.**	GMVC	2-2	445	Hughes	Harold	Richards	Dixon	Aspinall	Ogley	Anderson	Leicester	Lutkevitch	Jackson(2)	Blain		
11/01	Halifax Town	GMVC	1-2	1,012	Hughes	Harold	Richards	Dixon	Aspinall(1)	Ogley	Anderson	Leicester	Lutkevitch	Jackson	Blain		
15/01	Slough Town	GMVC	3-2	743	Hughes	Harold	Coathup	Booth	Aspinall	Ogley	Anderson(1)	Leicester(1)	*Lutkevitch*	*Jackson*	Blain(1)	Bennett	Bunn
22/01	**COLWYN BAY**	FAT1	2-2	422	Hughes	Harold	Coathup	Booth	Aspinall	Ogley	Anderson(1)	Leicester	*Bunn*	Jackson	Blain(1)	*Shaughnessy*	Bennett
29/01	**BATH CITY**	GMVC	1-3	508	Hughes	Harold	Coathup	Booth	Aspinall	*Ogley*	Anderson(1)	Leicester	Lutkevitch	Jackson	*Blain*	Dixon	Hill
01/02	Colwyn Bay	FAT1r	2-2	202	Hughes	Harold	Coathup	Dixon	Aspinall	Ogley	*Anderson(1)*	Booth	*Leicester*	Jackson	Blain(1)	Kirkham	Hill
03/01	Colwyn Bay	FAT1r(2)	1-2	138	White	Harold	Coathup	Dixon	Aspinall	Ogley	*Hill*	Booth	Kirkham(1)	Jackson	*Blain*	Leicester	Richards
05/02	Kettering Town	GMVC	2-3	1,967	Hughes	Harold	Coathup	Booth	Aspinall	Ogley	Anderson(1)	Leicester	*Lutkevitch*	Arnold(1)	Edwards	Kirkham	
12/02	**NORTHWICH V.**	GMVC	1-1	668	Hughes	Harold	Coathup	Booth	Aspinall	Ogley	Anderson	*Leicester*	Lutkevitch	Arnold	Edwards(1)	Jackson	
19/02	Dagenham & Red.	GMVC	1-0	820	Hughes	Harold	Coathup	Dixon	Booth	Ogley	Anderson	Clayton	*Lutkevitch*	Arnold(1)	*Edwards*	Shaughnessy	Blain
26/02	Woking	GMVC	0-3	1,727	Hughes	Harold	Coathup	Dixon	Booth	Ogley	Anderson	Clayton	Lutkevitch	*Shaughnessy*	*Blain*	Leicester	Bennett
05/03	Northwich Vics	GMVC	0-2	929	Hughes	Harold	Coathup	Dixon	Booth	*Ogley*	Anderson	Clayton	*Lutkevitch*	Arnold	Bennett	Shaughnessy	Leicester
08/03	Telford United	GMVC	2-0	823	Hughes	Harold	Coathup	Leicester(1)	Booth	Ogley	Anderson	Clayton(1)	Shaughnessy	Arnold	Bennett		
12/03	**STAFFORD R.**	GMVC	1-2	458	Hughes	Harold	Coathup	Leicester	Aspinall	Booth	Anderson	Clayton	*Shaughnessy*	Arnold(1)	Bennett	Lutkevitch	
15/03	**ALTRINCHAM**	GMVC	1-3	510	Hughes	Harold	Coathup	Leicester	Aspinall	Booth	Anderson	*Clayton*	Sh'nessy(1)	Arnold	Bennett	Dulson	
19/03	Dover Athletic	GMVC	1-1	1,003	Hughes	Harold(1)	Coathup	Ogley	Aspinall	Booth	Anderson	Leicester	*Shaughnessy*	Arnold	Bennett	Jackson	
22/03	**TELFORD UTD**	GMVC	*1-0	344	Hughes	Harold	Coathup	Ogley	Aspinall	Booth	Anderson	Leicester	*Shaughnessy*	*Arnold*	Bennett	Jackson	Blain
26/03	Welling Utd	GMVC	2-1	703	Hughes	*Harold*	Coathup	Ogley	Booth	Brown	Anderson	Kirkham(1)	Clayton(1)	Arnold	Bennett		Prokas
29/03	**RUNCORN**	GMVC	1-2	573	Hughes	Edmonds	Coathup	Ogley	Booth	*Aspinall*	*Brown*	Bennett	Clayton	Arnold	Kirkham(1)	Sh'nessy	Leicester
02/04	**WITTON ALBION**	GMVC	2-1	537	Hughes	Edmonds	Coathup	Ogley	Booth	Anderson	*Ward*	Bennett	Clayton	Arnold(1)	*Kirkham(1)*	Sh'nessy	Leicester
04/04	Southport	GMVC	2-0	1,422	Hughes	Edmonds	Coathup	Ogley	Aspinall	Anderson	*Brown(1)*	Bennett	Clayton(1)	Arnold	*Kirkham*	Blain	Leicester
12/04	**SOUTHPORT**	GMVC	3-1	593	Hughes	Edmonds	*Brown*	Ogley	Aspinall	Anderson	Dixon	Bennett	Clayton(1)	Arnold(2)	*Kirkham*	Shaughnessy	Leicester
16/04	**DOVER ATH.**	GMVC	0-0	597	Hughes	Edmonds	Brown	Ogley	Aspinall	Anderson	Dixon	Bennett	Clayton	Arnold	*Leicester*	Shaughnessy	
19/04	Witton Albion	GMVC	3-0	641	Hughes	Edmonds(1)	Coathup	Ogley	Aspinall	Anderson	Dixon	Bennett	Clayton	*Arnold(1)*	*Kirkham*	Brown(1)	Leicester
23/04	Merthyr Tydfil	GMVC	2-1	531	Hughes	Edmonds(1)	Coathup	Ogley	Aspinall	Dixon	Bennett	Anderson	Clayton(1)	*Shaughnessy*	*Leicester*	Jackson	Brown
28/04	**YEOVIL TOWN**	GMVC	1-2	515	Hughes	Edmonds	Coathup	Ogley	Aspinall	Dixon	Bennett	Anderson(1)	Clayton	*Shaughnessy*	Leicester		Jackson
01/05	**DAGENHAM & R.**	GMVC	5-0	596	Hughes	Edmonds(1)	Coathup	Ogley	*Aspinall*	Dixon	Bennett	Anderson	Clayton(1)	Kirkham(3)	*Leicester*	Jackson	Brown
07/05	**WELLING UTD**	GMVC	2-1	653	Hughes	Edmonds	Coathup	*Ogley*	Aspinall	Dixon	Bennett	Anderson(1)	Clayton	*Kirkham(1)*	Leicester	Jackson	Brown

PETER WRAGG

Peter played for Leek Town, winning the Cheshire League. He became manager when injury ended his career and the club came 4th and 2nd during his two years in charge. He then had spells with Stalybridge Celtic, Chorley and Hyde United, taking the latter to the First Round of the FA Cup for the first time in 20 years.

In early 1986 he joined Macclesfield Town and took them to an unprecedented treble of Northern Premier League, League Cup and Presidents Cup and promotion to the Conference. After consolidating in the Conference, the Silkmen went from strength to strength, reaching Wembley for the 1989 FA Trophy Final - his proudest moment to date.

When Halifax were relegated from the Football League in 1993, they turned to Peter Wragg's Conference experience. In his brief stop at the Shay, Wragg led Halifax to an astounding FA Cup win against West Brom, but he was surprisely sacked soon after Christmas.

However, Wragg was soon back in the Conference scene taking over from Phil Wilson at Stalybridge and master-minding a miraculous escape from relegation.

Left: *The travelling Stalybridge Celtic supporters who trekked all the way to South Somerset to watch the goalless draw against Yeovil Town on 28th August. Photo - Dave West.*

Programme details:
40 pages for £1
Editor - Nick Shaw (061 633 1117)

Any other club publications:

Local Newspapers:
Manchester Evening News
Manchester Evening News Pink (Saturday evenings)

Local Radio Stations:
GMR (BBC Manchester)
Piccadilly Radio, Signal Radio

STALYBRIDGE CELTIC - PLAYING SQUAD

Player	Honours	Birthplace and date	Transfer Fees	Previous Clubs
GOALKEEPERS				
Russ Hughes	NPL	Manchester		Tranmere R, South Liverpool, Caernarfon Town
DEFENDERS				
John Aspinall	NPL	Birkenhead 15/3/59		Cmll Ld, Tranmere, Altrincham, Bangor C, Tranmere, Bangor C, Northwich V, Chorley
Lee Coathup		Singapore 2/5/67		Everton, Newtown, Vauxhall GM, Stalybridge C, Witton Alb
Neil Edmonds	NPL	Accrington 18/10/68		Oldham Ath, Rochdale, Chorley, Stalybridge C, East Bengal (Ind)
Mark Ogley		Barnsley 10/3/67	4-fig	Barnsley, Carlisle U, Aldershot, York C, Altrincham
Kevin Booth	NPL	Ashton-U-Lyne		Stalybridge C, Bacup Borough, Stalybridge C, Curzon Ashton
Ian Harold		Liverpool 16/1/69		Newton, Runcorn
Paul Dixon	NPL, Brit.Fire Serv.	Oldham		Chadderton
MIDFIELDERS				
Stuart Anderson	FAT, FAV, NPL, NWCL	Manchester 20/11/59	£2,500	Chadderton, Colne Dynamoes, Witton Alb, Morecambe
Jimmy Brown		Liverpool		Bootle, Vauxhall GM, Morecambe, Runcorn
Paul Bennett	NPL	Liverpool 30/1/61	£900	Everton, Port Vale, Northwich V, Telford U, Northwich V, Buxton
Jonathan Hill		Wigan 26/8/70		Crewe A, Rochdale, Preston, Witton Albion
Colin Blain	MSC, SSC	Davyhulme 7/3/70		Curzon Ashton, Halifax T, Northwich V, Hyde Utd, Macclesfield T
FORWARDS				
Frank Bunn		Birmingham 6/11/62		Luton T, Hull C, Oldham Ath
Stuart Leicester	NPL	Altrincham 11/8/66	Player/ Exchange	Irlam T, Stalybridge C, Macclesfield T
Steve Shaughnessy		Manchester	Player/ Exchange	Tranmere R, Maine Road, Runcorn
Paul Kirkham	NPLC, CSC	Manchester 5/7/69	4-fig	East Manchester, Manchester Utd, Huddersfield T, Hyde Utd
Paul Clayton	FAYC	Dunstable 4/1/65		Norwich, Darlington, Crewe Alex, Stafford Rangers
Robert Jackson		Altrincham 9/2/73		Manchester C, Walsall, Altrincham, Radcliffe Borough
Alan Richards		Preston 1/10/71		Luton T, Altrincham
Colin Heywood		Sheffield 18/9/72		Sheffield U, Hyde U, Mossley, Accrington S, Leek T, Buxton, Mossley

Departures during season:
Paul Higginbotham (Barrow), Martin White (Curzon Ashton), Andy Gayle (Accrington Stanley), Paul Allen (Released), Gary Boyle (Released), Stuart Locke (Macclesfield T), John Brown (Leek T), Mike Lutkevitch (Accrington Stanley).

Players on loan during season:
Kenny Woods (Bury), Ian Arnold (Carlisle Utd), Mike Edwards (Tranmere R), Richard Prokas (Carlisle Utd), Richard Ward (Huddersfield T).

Bower Fold, Stalybridge Celtic

Address and telephone number: Bower Fold, Mottram Road, Stalybridge, Cheshire SK15 2RT. Tel: 061 338 2828

Simple directions: M6 to A556 to M63 to M67; end of Motorway through roundabout to traffic lights, left; left at end into Molttram Road, up hill, down hill into Stalybridge, ground on left next to Hare & Hounds pub.

Capacity: 6,000 **Seated:** 407 **Covered terracing:** 1,300

Record Attendance: 9,753 v WBA - FA Cup replay - 1922-23

Club Shop: Contact Martyn Torr for details (061 338 2828)

Social Facilities: Clubhouse open matchdays and evenings during the week. Food available on matchdays.

Previous Grounds: None

Stalybridge Fact File

Nickname: Celtic

Club Sponsors: Hickson Manro Ltd

Previous Leagues: Lancashire Combination 1911-12, Central Lge 1912-21, Football Lge 1921-23, Cheshire Co. Lge 1923-1982, North West Co's 1982-87, Northern Prem. Lge 1987-92.

Club colours: Blue & white quarters/blue

Change colours: Black & white stripes/black or all green.

Midweek home matchday: Tuesday

Record win: 16-2 twice; v Manchester NE 1/5/26; v Nantwich 22/10/32

Record defeat: 0-6 v Northwich Victoria

Record transfer fee paid: To Runcorn for Steve Shaughnessy, 1993

Record transfer fee received: £3,000 for Martin Filson from Halifax Town

1993-94 Captain: Paul Bennett

1993-94 Top scorer: Paul Kirkham, 16

1993-94 Player of the Year: Stewart Anderson

Club record goalscorer (in a season): Chris Camden 45, 1991-92

Record appearances: Kevin Booth 354

Past players who progressed to the Football League: Too numerous to list.

Honours: Northern Premier League Premier Division Champions 91-92, NPL Runners-up 90-91 (Div.1 runners-up 87-88); Cheshire County League 79-80 (Runners-up 77-78), League Cup 21-22 (Runners-up 46-47,81-82); Challenge Shield 77-78 (runners-up 79-80), Reserves Division runners-up 81-82), NW Counties League 83-84, 86-87 (Lge Cup Runners-up 83-84), Champions v Cup Winners Trophy 83-84, (reserves Division Runners-up 82-83; Lancashire Combination Division 2 11-12; Cheshire Senior Cup 52-53 (runners-up 54-55, 80-81; Manchester Senior Cup 22-23 (Intermediate Cup 57-58, 68-69 (runners-up 56-57, 67-68, 69-70)); Challenge Shield 54-55, (Junior Cup 62-63), Lancashire Floodlit Cup 88-89 (runners-up 89-90); Reporter Cup Runners-up 74-75; Edward Case Cup 77-78.

STEVENAGE BOROUGH

Formed:
1976

President:
Rod Resker

Chairman:
Victor Green

Vice-Chairman
Ken Vale

Secretary:
John Jackson
(0438 362045)

Manager:
Paul Fairclough

Coach:
Paul Peterson

Physiotherapist:
Ray Lainchbury

Press Officer:
Martin Rosenberg
(0438 743482)

Ten years in the making, Borough's affair with the Isthmian League culminated with the greatest prize of them all, the Premier Division title, their third championship in four seasons under the guidance of Paul Fairclough. Having moved Stevenage from the obscurity of Division Two North football they are now just one step from the club's long-term ambition of a place in the Football League.

1993-94 will go down in the annals of the club as the greatest in its history to date, Borough, in only their second term in the top flight, sweeping all before them and accumulating 31 wins and 97 points to claim a place in the excellence of non-League football - the GM Vauxhall Conference.

The league season began with a tough trip to Sutton United, a goal-less draw at the start of an impressive run of 15 games in all competitions without defeat, including nine successive victories in the league to firmly establish themselves, if a little unexpectedly, as the Division's top side, opening up a large points lead at the head of the table.

The commanding series of victories left their rivals clambering to keep up; indeed only a mid-season blip ever really tested Borough's ability to win the league. Having been caught for the first time since the early part of the season, just after Christmas, Borough then put together a run of just two defeats in their last 19 league games to comfortably win the Division.

And what a wonderful way to end the season! Despite being aware of their fate, with nearest rivals Enfield having failed to win the previous evening, nothing was going to spoil Borough's Championship party. Even the rain couldn't dampen the spirits of the large 3,005 crowd - the largest gate ever recorded at Stevenage Stadium - who enjoyed themselves in a memorable 3-0 win over Harrow Borough.

In addition to a memorable league season, Borough enjoyed a variable amount of success in the Cup competitions, achieving their best ever run in the FA Cup and reaching both County Cup Finals; the Senior Cup Final against Watford to be played early next season. Perhaps the measure of the Borough success has been the terrific work of the Management and backroom staff - from the committee, ground staff, programme team to the tea bar staff and helpers alike, who have all played their part in the continuing Borough success story. No more help, however, than the extraordinary support of the club's fans at both home and away games, whether vocally or in presence. This has been worth at least a point to the team every game.

Stevenage Borough - Diadora League Premier Division champions 1993-94. *Photo - Eric Marsh.*

***STEVENAGE** MATCHFACTS 93-94* ***STEVENAGE** MATCHFACTS 93-94* ***STEVENAGE** MATCHFACTS 93-94*

Key: Home fixtures are denoted by bold capitals. Numbers in brackets after players names indicate goals scored (asterisks by the results denote own goals).

Key to Competitions: DFL: Diadora (Isthmian) League Premier Division. **DLC**: Diadora League Cup. **CC:** Carlsberg (Diadora League Full Members) Cup. **FAC**: FA Cup. **FAT**: FA Trophy. **EFL:** Eastern Floodlit League. **HCC:** Hertfordshire Charity Cup. **HSC:** Hertfordshire Senior Cup.

Date	Opponents	Comp.	Res	Gate	1.	2.	3.	4.	5.	6.	7.	8.	9.	10.	11.	Sub.	Sub.
14/08	Hertford Town	HCC2	6-2		Gallagher	Wilkinson	Joyce	Debnam	Blackwell	Smith	Alzapiedi	Shanley	Gittings(3)	Venables(1)	Pearson(2)	Brown	Parker
21/08	Sutton United	DFL	0-0	622	Gallagher	Wilkinson	Joyce	Debnam	Blackwell	Smith	Alzapiedi	Shanley	Gittings	Venables	Pearson	Brown	Edwards
23/08	**DULWICH HAM.**	DFL	2-0	602	Gallagher	Wilkinson	Joyce	Debnam	Blackwell	Smith	Graham	Shanley	Gittings	Venables(1)	Pearson(1)	Brown	Cardines
28/08	**YEADING**	DFL	4-1	506	Gallagher	Wilkinson	Joyce	Debnam	Nugent	Smith	Graham(1)	Shanley	Gittings(1)	Venables(2)	Pearson	Blackwell	Cardines
31/08	Dorking	DFL	5-1	283	Gallagher	Wilkinson	Joyce	Debnam	Nugent	Smith	Graham	Shanley(2)	Gittings(1)	Venables(2)	Pearson	Brown	Blackwell
04/09	**BASINGSTOKE**	DFL	2-1	379	Gallagher	Wilkinson	Joyce	Debnam	Nugent	Smith	Graham(1)	Cardines	Gittings(1)	Venables	Pearson	Blackwell	Edwards
06/09	**SUTTON UTD**	DFL	3-2	936	Gallagher	Wilkinson	Joyce	Debnam	Nugent	Smith	Graham	Cardines	Gittings(2)	Venables(1)	Pearson	Nunn	Edwards
11/09	**WEMBLEY**	FAC1q	2-2	557	Gallagher	Wilkinson	Joyce	Debnam	Nugent(1)	Smith	Graham	Cardines(1)	Gittings	Venables	Pearson	Brown	Nunn
14/09	Wembley	FAC1qr	1-1	260	Gallagher	Wilkinson	Joyce	Debnam(1)	Nugent	Smith	Graham	Cardines	Gittings	Venables	Nunn	Brown	Edwards
18/09	St Albans C.	DFL	2-1	852	Gallagher	Hedman	Joyce	Debnam	Nugent	Smith	Graham	Wilkinson	Gittings	Venables(2)	Alzapiedi	Brown	Blackwell
20/09	Wembley	FAC1qr(2)	1-0	282	Gallagher	Wilkinson	Joyce	Debnam	Nugent	Smith	Alzapiedi	Shanley	Gittings(1)	Venables	Pearson	Brown	Blackwell
25/09	**CORBY TOWN**	FAC2q	4-3	707	Gallagher	Wilkinson	Joyce	Debnam	Nugent	Smith	Alzapiedi	Shanley	Gittings(1)	Venables(2)	Pearson	Brown(1)	Nunn
27/09	**GRAYS ATH.**	DFL	1-0	567	Gallagher	Hedman	Joyce	Debnam	Nugent	Smith	Brown	Shanley	Gittings(1)	Venables	Pearson	Alzapiedi	Nunn
02/10	Hendon	DFL	2-1	551	Gallagher	Hedman	Joyce	Debnam	Nugent	Smith	Alzapiedi	Shanley	Gittings(2)	Venables	Graham	Wilkinson	Brown
04/09	**MARLOW**	DFL	4-2	941	Gallagher	Hedman	Joyce	Debnam	Nugent(1)	Smith	Alzapiedi	Shanley	Gittings(3)	Venables	Graham	Wilkinson	Brown
09/10	E Thurrock U.	FAC3q	5-1	622	Gallagher	Wilkinson	Joyce	Debnam	Nugent	Smith	Alzapiedi	Shanley	Gittings(4)	Venables(1)	Graham	McCauley	Brown
11/10	**CARSHALTON**	DFL	2-4	1,066	Wallduck	Hedman	Joyce	Debnam	Nugent	Smith	Alzapiedi	Shanley	Gittings(2)	Venables	Graham	Brown	Nunn
19/10	Saffron Walden	DLC1	0-2	176	Fairbairn	Wilkinson	Joyce	Debnam	Wakefield	Graham	Alzapiedi	Shanley	Mays	McComb	Nunn	Beavor	Dowden
23/10	**NUNEATON B.**	FAC4q	1-2	2,187	Gallagher	Wilkinson	Joyce	Debnam(1)	Blackwell	Smith	Alzapiedi	Shanley	Gittings	Venables	Graham	Brown	McComb
26/10	Aylesbury Utd	DFL	1-0	673	Fairbairn	Hedman	Joyce	Debnam	Blackwell	Smith	Alzapiedi	Brown	Gittings	Venables(1)	Graham	Pearson	McComb
30/10	**CHESHAM UTD**	DFL	0-0	947	Fairbairn	Hedman	Joyce	Debnam	Nugent	Smith	Alzapiedi	Brown	Gittings	Venables	Graham	Wilkinson	Shanley
02/11	Berkhamsted T.	HSC1	0-0	157	Gallagher	Hedman	Joyce	Debnam	Nugent	Smith	Alzapiedi	Brown	Gittings	Venables	Pearson	Graham	Shanley
06/11	Bromley	DFL	2-1	472	Gallagher	Hedman	Joyce	Debnam	Nugent	Smith	Pearson	Brown	Gittings(2)	Venables	Graham	Alzapiedi	Blackwell
08/11	**BERKHAMSTED**	HSC1r	2-1	325	Gallagher	Hedman	Joyce	Debnam(1)	Nugent	Smith	Pearson	Brown(1)	Gittings	Blackwell	Graham	Bertie	Shanley
13/11	**WIVENHOE T.**	DFL	*6-0	729	Gallagher	McGill	Joyce	Debnam(1)	Nugent	Smith	Cuffie	Brown	Gittings(3)	Venables	Graham(1)	Alzapiedi	Pearson
20/11	Hayes	DFL	3-1	356	Gallagher	Hedman	Joyce	Debnam	Nugent(1)	Smith	Cuffie	Brown	Gittings(2)	Venables	Graham	Alzapiedi	Blackwell
27/11	Leek Town	DFL	2-0	485	Gallagher	McGill	Joyce	Debnam	Nugent	Smith	Cuffie	Brown	Gittings(1)	Venables(1)	Alzapiedi	Howell	Blackwell
30/11	Kingstonian	DFL	5-3	738	Gallagher	McGill	Joyce	Debnam	Nugent(1)	Smith	Shanley	Parker	Gittings	Venables(3)	Howell(1)	Dowden	Blackwell
04/12	Harrow Boro.	DFL	0-1	450	Gallagher	Hedman	Joyce	Debnam	Nugent	Smith	Brooks	Brown	Gittings	Venables	Graham	Howell	Blackwell

06/12	**SAFFRON WAL.**	EFL	3-0	328	Gallagher	Hedman(1)	Joyce	Blackwell	Nugent(1)	Smith	Brooks	Shanley	Howell	Parker(1)	Graham	Brown	McGill
11/12	**DORKING**	DFL	4-3	634	Gallagher	Hedman	McGill	Debnam	Nugent	Smith	Shanley	Howell	Gittings(1)	Venables(1)	Graham(2)	Parker	Blackwell
04/12	**B. STORTFORD**	EFL	1-0	246	McCauley	McGill	Cretton	Vega	Blackwell	Brown	Cuffie	Parker(1)	Bertie	Bates	Graham	Venables	Gittings
18/12	Enfield	DFL	0-3	943	Gallagher	McGill	Cuffie	Debnam	Nugent	Smith	Brown	Howell	Gittings	Venables	Graham	Parker	Blackwell
27/12	**HITCHIN T.**	DFL	1-2	2,483	Gallagher	Hedman	Joyce	Debnam	Nugent	Smith	Shanley	Hobbs	Gittings(1)	Venables	Graham	Brown	Cuffie
01/01	Carshalton A.	DFL	0-2	1,244	Gallagher	Hedman	Joyce	Cuffie	Blackwell	Smith	Debnam	Graham	Gittings	Venables	Hobbs	Alzapiedi	Parker
15/01	Dulwich Hamlet	DFL	2-0	338	Gallagher	Hedman	Joyce	Debnam	Clark	Smith	Alzapiedi	Crawshaw	Gittings(2)	Venables	Graham	Hobbs	Parker
17/01	**BOREHAM WD**	HSCqf	0-0	331	Gallagher	Blackwell	Joyce	Debnam	Nugent	Smith	Cuffie	Parker	Gittings	Venables	Graham	Brown	Shanley
22/01	Kettering T.	FAT1	1-2	2,414	Gallagher	Hedman	Joyce	Debnam	Nugent	Smith	Brown	Alzapiedi	Gittings(1)	Venables	Graham	Parker	Blackwell
25/01	Boreham Wood	HSCqfr	2-1	123	Gallagher	Hedman	Joyce	Blackwell	Nugent	Smith	Parker(1)	Alzapiedi	Gittings	Venables	Graham	Brown(1)	Shanley
29/01	Yeading	DFL	2-0	403	Gallagher	Hedman	Joyce	Clark	Nugent	Smith	Alzapiedi	Crawshaw(1)	Gittings	Venables	Hobbs(1)	Brown	Parker
31/01	**HEYBRIDGE S.**	CC2	1-2	403	Wild	Blackwell	Joyce	Debnam	Nugent	Clark	Smith	Crawshaw	Gittings	Brown(1)	Shanley	Howell	Parker
06/02	**BASINGSTOKE**	DFL	0-0	638	Wilkerson	Hedman	Joyce	Alzapiedi	Nugent	Clark	Smith	Crawshaw	Brown	Parker	Hobbs	Howell	Graham
19/02	**St ALBANS C.**	DFL	3-0	876	Gallagher	Hedman	Joyce	Debnam	Nugent	Clark	Smith(1)	Crawshaw	Hobbs	Venables(1)	Stein(1)	Simpson	Hayles
26/02	Molesey	DFL	2-1	431	Gallagher	Hedman	Joyce	Alzapiedi	Nugent	Clark	Smith(1)	Crawshaw(1)	Hobbs	Venables	Stein	Simpson	Hayles
28/02	**B. STORTFORD**	HCCsf	2-0	529	Wilkerson	Hedman	Joyce	Debnam	Nugent	Clark	Smith	Crawshaw(1)	Gittings	Graham	Hayles(1)	Parker	Brown
06/03	**KINGSTONIAN**	DFL	4-1	909	Gallagher	Hedman	Joyce	Simpson	Nugent	Clark	Smith	Crawshaw(1)	Hobbs	Stein(3)	Venables	Gittings	Hayles
10/03	Saffron Walden	EFL	0-3		C Morgan	Dowden	Nolan	McGill	Wakefield	Cretton	Reed	Plummer	Brown	Sellar	Bertie	R Phillips	Hutchins
12/03	Marlow	DFL	0-0	1,020	Gallagher	Hedman	Joyce	Simpson	Nugent	Clark	Smith	Crawshaw	Hobbs	Stein	Venables	Gittings	Hayles
15/03	Bish. Stortford	HSCsf	4-0	194	Gallagher	Hedman	Joyce	Simpson	Hayles	Clark	Smith	Crawshaw(2)	Gittings(1)	Stein(1)	Graham	Parker	Brown
19/03	**HENDON**	DFL	3-0	815	Gallagher	Hedman	Joyce	Simpson	Nugent	Clark	Smith	Crawshaw	Hayles	Stein(3)	Graham	Gittings	Brown
21/03	**BROMLEY**	DFL	0-1	823	Gallagher	Hedman	Joyce	Simpson	Nugent	Clark	Hayles	Crawshaw	Gittings	Stein	Graham	Debnam	Brown
26/03	Chesham Utd	DFL	2-1	939	Gallagher	Hedman	Joyce	Simpson(1)	Nugent	Clark	Smith	Crawshaw(1)	Hayles	Stein	Venables	Gittings	Debnam
29/03	Grays Athletic	DFL	2-1	251	Gallagher	Hedman	Joyce	Simpson	Nugent	Clark(1)	Smith	Crawshaw	Hayles	Stein(1)	Venables	Gittings	Debnam
31/03	Bish. Stortford	EFL	2-1		C Morgan	Cretton	Reed(1)	McGill	Burgess	Dowden	Walker(1)	Debnam	Gittings	Parker	Graham	Brown	Vega
02/04	**AYLESBURY**	DFL	*4-0	869	Gallagher	Hedman	Joyce	Simpson	Nugent	Clark(1)	Smith	Crawshaw(1)	Hayles	Stein(1)	Venables	Gittings	Debnam
04/04	Hitchin Town	DFL	3-1	2,503	Gallagher	Hedman	Joyce	Simpson	Nugent	Clark	Smith(1)	Crawshaw	Hayles(1)	Stein	Venables	Gittings(1)	Debnam
06/04	Baldock Town	EFL	2-1	245	C Morgan	Burgess	McGill	Southon	Blackwell	Walker	Debnam	Brown	Gittings	Parker(2)	Graham	Venables	Dowden
09/04	**ENFIELD**	DFL	0-1	1,905	Thompson	Hedman	Joyce	Simpson	Nugent	Clark	Smith	Crawshaw	Hayles	Stein	Lynch	Gittings	Venables
11/04	**WOKINGHAM**	DFL	1-0	836	Thompson	Hedman	Joyce	Simpson	Nugent	Clark	Smith	Gittings(1)	Hayles	Stein	Lynch	Debnam	Venables
16/04	Wivenhoe Town	DFL	1-0	368	Thompson	Venables	Joyce	Simpson	Nugent	Clark	Smith	Gittings	Hayles	Stein(1)	Lynch	Crawshaw	Debnam
18/04	**MOLESEY**	DFL	4-2	1,004	Thompson	Hedman	Joyce	Simpson(1)	Nugent	Clark	Smith	Crawshaw	Gittings(1)	Venables(1)	Lynch	Stein(1)	Debnam
21/04	Heybridge Sw.	EFL	1-5		C Morgan	McGill	Reed	Cretton	Blackwell	Graham	Southon(1)	Walker	Bates	Parker	Beeke	Dowden	Bertie
23/04	**HAYES**	DFL	2-1	1,214	Thompson	Hedman(1)	Joyce	Simpson	Nugent	Clark	Smith(1)	Crawshaw	Gittings	Venables	Lynch	Debnam	Stein
26/04	Baldock Town	HCCf	1-2		McCauley	McGill	Cretton	Blackwell	Reed	Southon	Debnam	Hayles	Bates	Parker(1)	Graham	Dowden	Beeke
30/04	Wokingham T.	DFL	1-0	619	Gallagher	Hedman	Joyce	Simpson	Nugent	Clark	Smith	Stein(1)	Gittings	Venables	Lynch	Crawshaw	Thompson
07/05	**HARROW BORO.**	DFL	3-0	3,005	Gallagher	Hedman	Graham	Simpson	Nugent	Clark	Smith(1)	Stein(1)	Gittings	Venables	Hayles	Crawshaw(1)	Blackwell
09/08	WATFORD	HSCf	*to be played at St Albans City FC*														

Stevenage Borough

PAUL FAIRCLOUGH

1993-94, the most successful in Stevenage Borough's short history, was Paul Fairclough's fourth season at Broadhall Way. After making the short journey from Hertford Town in the summer of 1990, he has been at the helm as the club have risen from the Isthmian League Second Division to a new beginning in the GMV Conference. Three championship successes has earned Paul a new five year contract as the first full-time manager of Stevenage Borough. Fairclough, who hails from Liverpool and is an Everton fanatic, is very ambitious to see Borough through to even greater achievements.

As a player, Fairclough was a member of Harlow Town's famous 1979-80 FA Cup squad which reached the Fourth Round Proper - he scored the winning goal in the First Round clash with Leytonstone-Ilford. Among other clubs, he also played for St Albans and Hertford.

His first taste of management came at Hertford Town when he succeeded Tony Woodrow at the start of the 1986-87 season. After four seasons in charge he had led them to their first County Cup success for 23 years and to third in Division Two North of the Isthmian League. At the start of 1990-91 he replaced Brian Williams at Stevenage, and the rest is history.

Stevenage's England semi-pro international Dave Venables in the thick of the action during the Boxing Day derby clash with Hitchin Town at Broadhall Way. *Photo - Paul Dennis.*

Programme details:
48 pages for £1
Editor - Simon Mortimer (0438 725263)

Any other club publications:

Local Newspapers:
Stevenage Gazette
Comet
Herald & Post

Local Radio Stations:
Chiltern Radio
Three Counties Radio

STEVENAGE BOROUGH - PLAYING SQUAD

Player	Honours	Birthplace and date	Transfer Fees	Previous Clubs
GOALKEEPERS				
Des Gallagher	ILP	London		Watford, Eaton Bray Utd, Stevenage Borough, Dunstable
DEFENDERS				
Noel Blackwell	ILP, IL1, FAXI	Luton		Barnet, Barton R, Dunstable, Chesham U, Tring T, Vauxhall Mtrs
Tony Joyce	ILP	Wembley 24/9/71		QPR, Aldershot, Woking, Staines T, Leighton T
Simon Clark	ILP	Boston		Lincoln C, Boston FC, Holbeach U, King's Lynn, Hendon
Rudi Hedman	ILP	Lambeth 16/11/64		Charlton Ath, Crystal Palace, Dulwich Hamlet
Mark Smith	ILP	Luton		Hitchin, Letchworth, Hitchin, Woking, Hitchin
Richard Nugent	GMVC, ILP	Birmingham 20/3/64		Royston, Stevenage B, Hitchin, Barnet, St Albans C, Barnet, Woking
MIDFIELDERS				
Shaun Debnam	ILP	London		Hertford Town
David Brown	ILP	Herts		Royston, Hitchin, Vauxhall M, Stevenage B, Hertford, Baldock, Royston
Steve Graham	ILP	London		Enfield, Basildon Utd, Wembley
Glen Alzapeidi	ILP	London		Birmingham C, Southend U, Woodford, Cheshunt, Ware, Harlow, Ware
Adam Parker		Herts		From Youth Team
FORWARDS				
Brian Stein	EI, E-u21, ILP	South Africa 19/10/57		Edgware T, Luton T, Caen (Fr), Luton T, Barnet
David Venables	ESP, ILP	Horsham 6/11/67		Eastbourne United, Crawley Town, Wealdstone
Gary Crawshaw	ILP	Reading 4/2/71		Luton Town, Wycombe Wanderers, Staines Town, Hendon
Martin Gittings	ILP	London		Stevenage, Hitchin, Barnet, Hertford, Harlow, Wivenhoe, Baldock, Wivenhoe
Greg Howell		Middlesex		Tottenham Hotspur, Southend United

Departures during season:
Mickey Nunn (Stotfold), Mark Shanley (Ware), Adam Wilkinson (Boreham Wood), Tony Craig (Hertford T), Sean Pearson (Hitchin T), Roy Edwards (Dulwich Hamlet), Steve Wallduck (Harlow T), Mick Cuffie (Yeading), Paul Hobbs (Berkhamsted T).

Players on loan during season:
None.

Guide to honours:
GMVC = GM Vauxhall Conference, ILP = Isthmian League premier div., IL1 = Isthmian League div 1, ESP = England Semi-Pro Int., EI = England Full Int., E-u21 = England under-21 Int.

Broadhall Way, Stevenage

Address and telephone number: Stevenage Stadium, Broadhall Way, Stevenage, Herts SG2 8TH (0438 367059).
Simple directions: Stevenage South exit off A1(M) - ground on right at second roundabout. One mile from Stevenage BR station. Buses SB4 and SB5.
Capacity: 3,700 **Seated:** 488 **Covered terracing:** 2,000
Record Attendance: 3,005 v Harrow Borough, Isthmian League Premier Division 7/5/94.
Club Shop: Yes, selling programmes, scarves and other club merchandise. Contact Mrs Lynn Gamby.
Social Facilities: Clubhouse at ground open Mon-Fri 6-11pm, Sat noon-2.30 & 4-11pm, Sub noon-3 & 7-10.30pm.

Stevenage Fact File

Nickname: Boro'

Reserve Team's League: Essex & Herts Border Combination.

Previous Leagues: Clithern Youth 76-79/ Wallspan South Combination 79-80/ United Counties 80-84/ Isthmian 84-94.

Club colours: Red & white stripes/red/red.

Change colours: All blue.

Midweek home matchday: Monday

Record win: 11-1 v British Timken Athletic (H), United Counties League 80-81.

Record defeat: 0-7 v Southwick (H), Isthmian League 87-88.

Record transfer fee paid: Undisclosed.

Record transfer fee received: Undisclosed.

1993-94 Captain: Richard Nugent.

1993-94 Top scorer: Martin Gittings.

1993-94 Player of the Year: Martin Gittings.

Club record goalscorer: Martin Gittings.

Record appearances: Martin Gittings.

Past players who progressed to the Football League: Richard Wilmot & Neil Trebble (Scunthorpe Utd) 1993, Simon Clark (Peterborough United) 1994.

Honours: Isthmian Lg 93-94 (Div 1 91-92 (Div 2 (North) 85-86 90-91)), Utd Counties Lg Div 1 80-81 (Div 1 Cup 80-81), Herts Snr Cup R-up 85-86, Herts Charity Cup R-up 93-94, Herts Charity Shield R-up 83-84, Televised Sports Snr Floodlit Cup 89-90, Eastern Professional F'lit Cup Group winners 81-82 85-86 86-87 88-89 90-91 91-92, South Co's Comb. Cup 91-92.

TELFORD UNITED

Formed:
1876

President:
G E Smith

Chairman:
A H Esp

Football Secretary:
M J Ferriday

Manager:
George Foster

Assistant Manager:
Alan Ashman

Physiotherapist:
C McBride

Commercial Manager:
Richard Jones

Press Officer:
Robert Cave

The enigma club of the Vauxhall Conference. Telford have always captured the imagination of the footballing public with their cup expolits, both FA Cup and FA Trophy, but have always fallen short of expectations in the bread-and-butter of the league. This season almost saw the club exit the Conference for the first time in a real topsy-turvy campaign for the Buck's Head faithful.

By the end of September, former Manchester United star Gerry Daly had been sacked with the club at rock bottom of the pile. Ex-Mansfield player-manager George Foster came in and after a while took the club through a tremendous run which saw them head the form table and, amazingly in February, saw them quoted by Ladbrokes as tenth favourites for the title!

The changes to the squad were minimal, but acquiring the services of striker Darren Roberts from Wolves on loan proved a shrewd move. However, a poor end-of-season run saw United tumble down the table again and they only just managed to avoid the drop, finishing a couple of points ahead of third-from-bottom Merthyr Tydfil. However, considering the position earlier in the season, that could represent success.

Trying to predict Telford United's league future is almost impossible. Suffice to say that they will still be in the Vauxhall Conference this time next year!

Steve Whitney, *Team Talk* magazine.

Telford United's 1994-95 squad.

TELFORD MATCHFACTS 93-94 *TELFORD MATCHFACTS 93-94* *TELFORD MATCHFACTS 93-94*

Key: Home fixtures are denoted by bold capitals. Numbers in brackets after players names indicate goals scored (asterisks by the results denote own goals). Only used substitutes are listed - substituted players are *italicised.*

Key to Competitions: GMVC: G.M. Vauxhall Conference. **DC**: Drinkwise (G.M. Vauxhall Conference) Cup. **FAC**: F.A. Cup. **FAT**: F.A. Trophy.

Date	Opponents	Comp.	Res	Gate	1.	2.	3.	4.	5.	6.	7.	8.	9.	10.	11.	Sub.	Sub.
21/08	**WITTON ALBION**	GMVC	2-2	933	Acton	Pritchard	Statham	Fergusson	Gernon	Parrish(1)	Bignot	Holmes	Whitehouse(1)	Taylor	*Miller*		Niblett
24/08	Runcorn	GMVC	2-3	628	Acton	Pritchard	Statham	Fergusson	Gernon	Niblett	Bignot	Mitchell(1)	Wh'house	Taylor(1)	Parrish		
28/08	Gateshead	GMVC	2-0	478	Acton	Pritchard	Statham	Fergusson	Gernon	Niblett	Bignot	Mitchell(1)	Wh'house(1)	*Taylor*	*Parrish*	Hunter	Miller
30/08	**YEOVIL TOWN**	GMVC	1-1	931	Acton	Pritchard	Statham	*Fergusson*	Gaunt	Niblett	Bignot	Mitchell	Whitehouse(1)	Taylor	*Parrish*	Myers	Hunter
04/09	Kettering Town	GMVC	1-2	970	Acton	Pritchard	Statham	*Fergusson*	Gaunt	Niblett	Bignot	Mitchell	Whitehouse(1)	Taylor	*Parrish*	Myers	Hunter
07/09	Stalybridge Celtic	DC1(1)	0-2	352	Hughes	Pritchard	Statham	Myers	Parrish	Niblett	Bignot	Holmes	*Miller*	Taylor	Mitchell		Hunter
11/09	**HALESOWEN T.**	FAC1q	4-0	903	Acton	Pritchard	*Statham*	Myers	Gaunt	Niblett	Bignot(1)	Fergusson	Whitehouse	Taylor(3)	Parrish		Hughes
18/09	Dagenham & Red.	GMVC	1-4	792	Acton	Pritchard	Gernon	Niblett	Gaunt	Parrish	Bignot	Ferg'son(1)	Whitehouse	*Taylor*	Muir		Myers
21/09	**STALYBRIDGE C.**	DC1(2)	2-1	408	Acton	Pritchard	Gernon	Niblett	Gaunt	Parrish	Bignot	Holmes	Whitehouse(2)	Myers	Muir		
25/09	**GRANTHAM T.**	FAC2q	2-2	665	Acton	Pritchard	Statham	Fergusson	Gaunt	Parrish(1)	Bignot	Holmes	*Whitehouse*	Myers(1)	Muir		Taylor
28/09	Grantham Town	FAC2qr	3-1	571	Acton	Pritchard	Statham	Fergusson	Gaunt	*Parrish(1)*	Bignot	Mitchell	Whitehouse(2)	Myers	Muir		Gernon
02/10	Halifax Town	GMVC	0-6	1,118	Acton	Pritchard	*Statham*	Fergusson	Gaunt	Parrish	Bignot	*Mitchell*	Whitehouse	Myers	Muir	Taylor	Gernon
09/10	Raunds Town	FAC3q	4-0	354	Acton	Pritchard	Parrish(1)	*Niblett(1)*	Gaunt	Fergusson	Bignot	Taylor(1)	Whitehouse(1)	Myers	Holmes		Gernon
12/10	Witton Albion	GMVC	0-0	534	Acton	Pritchard	Parrish	Statham	Gernon	Fergusson	Bignot	Taylor	Whitehouse	Myers	Holmes		
16/10	**SOUTHPORT**	GMVC	1-3	855	Acton	*Pritchard*	Parrish	Fergusson	Gernon	Hindmarch	Bignot	Taylor(1)	Whitehouse	Myers	*Holmes*	Mitchell	Hunter
23/10	**MORECAMBE**	FAC4q	2-0	901	Acton	Pritchard	*Parrish(1)*	Niblett	Hindmarch	Fergusson	Bignot	Taylor	Whitehouse	Myers(1)	Gernon		
26/10	Macclesfield T.	GMVC	0-1	731	Acton	Pritchard	Foster	Niblett	Fergusson	Parrish	Bignot	Myers	Whitehouse	*Taylor*	Gaunt		Holmes
30/10	Woking	GMVC	0-0	1,753	Acton	*Pritchard*	Parrish	Fergusson	Foster	Gaunt	Bignot	Taylor	Whitehouse	Myers	Gernon		Holmes
06/11	**BATH CITY**	GMVC	0-0	721	Acton	Pritchard	Parrish	Gaunt	Niblett	Fergusson	Bignot	*Mitchell*	*Whitehouse*	Myers	Gernon	Taylor	Holmes
13/11	**HUDDERSFIELD**	FAC1	1-1	2,257	Acton	Pritchard	Parrish	Niblett	Gaunt	Fergusson	Bignot(1)	Taylor	Whitehouse	Myers	Ford		
20/11	Northwich Vict.	GMVC	0-1	748	Acton	Pritchard	Parrish	Niblett	*Gaunt*	Fergusson	Bignot	Taylor	Whitehouse	*Myers*	Ford	Gernon	Holmes
23/11	Huddersfield T.	FAC1r	0-1	3,517	Hughes	Pritchard	Parrish	Niblett	*Mitchell*	Fergusson	Bignot	Taylor	Ford	Myers	Statham	Whitehouse	
27/11	**RUNCORN**	GMVC	1-1	726	Hughes	Pritchard	Parrish	Niblett	*Mitchell*	Fergusson	*Bignot*	Taylor	Ford(1)	Myers	Statham	Whitehouse	Gernon

11/12	Southport	GMVC	0-1	902	Hughes	Pritchard	Parrish	Niblett	Gernon	Holmes	Ford	*Roberts*	Whitehouse	*Myers*	Statham	Taylor	Bignot
14/12	**STAFFORD R.**	GMVC	2-1	733	Hughes	Pritchard	Parrish	Niblett	Gaunt	Holmes	Bignot	Roberts(1)	Ford	Taylor(1)	Statham		
18/12	**DAGENHAM & R.**	GMVC	0-0	647	Acton	Pritchard	Parrish	Niblett	Gaunt	*Holmes*	Bignot	Roberts	Ford	Taylor	Myers	Statham	Lemon
01/01	Kettering Town	GMVC	2-1	3,120	Hughes	Pritchard	Parrish	Niblett(1)	Ford	Fergusson	Bignot	Myers	Whitehouse	*Roberts(1)*	*Statham*	Taylor	Lemon
03/01	**MERTHYR TYD.**	GMVC	3-0	726	Hughes	Pritchard	Parrish	Niblett	Ford	Fergusson	Bignot	Roberts(1)	*Whitehouse(1)*	Myers	*Statham*	Taylor(1)	Lemon
08/01	**GATESHEAD**	GMVC	0-0	1,014	Hughes	Pritchard	Parrish	Niblett	Ford	Fergusson	Bignot	Roberts	*Whitehouse*	Myers	*Statham*	Taylor	Holmes
15/01	Dover Athletic	GMVC	1-0	1,525	Hughes	Pritchard	Parrish	Niblett	Ford	Fergusson	Bignot	Roberts	*Taylor(1)*	Myers	Statham	Whitehouse	
22/01	**NORTHALLERTON**	FAT1	2-1	926	Hughes	*Pritchard*	Parrish	Niblett	Ford	Fergusson	Bignot	Roberts(1)	*Taylor*	Myers	Statham	Whitehouse(1)	Foster
29/01	**SLOUGH TOWN**	GMVC	4-1	833	Hughes	Pritchard	Parrish	Niblett	Ford	Fergusson(1)	Bignot(1)	Roberts(1)	*Taylor(1)*	Myers	*Statham*	Whitehouse	Foster
01/02	**MERTHYR TYD.**	GMVC	1-0	909	Hughes	Pritchard	Parrish	Niblett	Ford	Fergusson	Bignot	*Roberts*	Taylor(1)	Myers	*Statham*	Whitehouse	Foster
05/02	**WOKING**	GMVC	2-0	1,222	Hughes	Pritchard	Parrish	Niblett	Ford	Fergusson	Bignot(1)	*Roberts(1)*	Taylor	Myers	Statham	Whitehouse	
12/02	Runcorn	FAT2	1-2	844	Hughes	Pritchard	Parrish	Niblett	Ford	Fergusson	Bignot	Whitehouse(1)	Taylor	Myers	Foster		
19/02	**HALIFAX TOWN**	GMVC	3-2	1,072	Hughes	Pritchard	Parrish	Niblett	Ford	Fergusson	Bignot(1)	*Whitehouse*	Taylor	Myers	*Statham*	Steeuwenhoek(2)	Foster
26/02	**MACCLESFIELD**	GMVC	1-3	1,108	Hughes	Foster	Parrish	Niblett	Ford(1)	Fergusson	Bignot	Sleeuwenhoek	*Whitehouse*	Myers	*Statham*	Mitchell	Gernon
01/03	Stafford Rangers	GMVC	1-1	905	Hughes	Foster	Parrish	Niblett	*Ford*	Fergusson	Bignot	Sleeuwenhoek	Whitehouse(1)	Myers	Statham		Gernon
05/03	Welling United	GMVC	0-0	832	Acton	Foster	Parrish	Niblett	Ford	*Gernon*	Bignot	*Bradbury*	Whitehouse	Myers	Statham	Sleeuwenhoek	Taylor
08/03	**STALYBRIDGE**	GMVC	0-2	823	Acton	Foster	Parrish	Niblett	Ford	*Bradbury*	Bignot	*Sleeuwenhoek*	Taylor	Myers	Statham	Whitehouse	Frisby
19/03	Slough Town	GMVC	0-0	575	Hughes	Foster	Parrish	Niblett	Ford	Fergusson	Bignot	Taylor	*Bradbury*	Myers	Statham	Whitehouse	
22/03	Stalybridge C.	GMVC	0-1	344	Hughes	Foster	Parrish	Niblett	*Davidson*	Fergusson	Bignot	Taylor	Wilson	Myers	*Statham*	Bradbury	Frisby
26/03	**DOVER ATH.**	GMVC	0-1	905	Hughes	Foster	Parrish	Niblett	Ford	Fergusson	Bignot	Taylor	*Wilson*	Myers	Statham	Bradbury	
29/03	Bromsgrove R.	GMVC	5-0	808	Hughes	Foster	Parrish	Niblett	Ford	Fergusson(1)	Bignot(1)	Taylor(1)	Wilson(2)	Myers	Statham		
02/04	Bath City	GMVC	0-3	473	Hughes	Foster	Davidson	Niblett	Ford	Fergusson	Bignot	*Taylor*	Wilson	Myers	Statham	Sleeuwenhoek	
04/04	**ALTRINCHAM**	GMVC	0-2	904	Hughes	Foster	Parrish	Niblett	Ford	Fergusson	Bignot	*Taylor*	Wilson	Myers	*Statham*	Sleeuwenhoek	Gernon
09/04	**WELLING UTD**	GMVC	2-0	611	Hughes	Foster	Parrish	Niblett	Ford	Fergusson	Bignot	Taylor(1)	Wilson(1)	*Myers*	Davidson		Joseph
12/04	**BROMSGROVE**	GMVC	0-0	676	Hughes	Foster	Parrish	Niblett	Ford	Fergusson	Bignot	Taylor	Wilson	Myers	Davidson		
12/04	Altrincham	GMVC	0-2	694	Hughes	Foster	Parrish	Niblett	Davidson	Fergusson	Bignot	*Taylor*	Wilson	Myers	*Statham*	Sleeuwenhoek	Joseph
23/04	Kidderminster	GMVC	0-2	2,746	Hughes	Foster	Parrish	Niblett	Davidson	Bowen	Bignot	Taylor	Wilson	Sleeuwenhoek	Statham		
30/04	**NORTHWICH V.**	GMVC	2-1	831	Hughes	Foster	Parrish	Niblett	Davidson	Bowen	Bignot	*Taylor(2)*	Wilson	Myers	Statham	Sleeuwenhoek	
04/05	**KIDDERMINSTER**	GMVC	1-0	2,088	Hughes	Foster	Parrish	Niblett	Davidson	Fergusson	Bignot	Taylor	Wilson(1)	Myers	Statham		
07/05	Yeovil Town	GMVC	0-1	2,783	Hughes	Foster	Parrish	*Niblett*	Davidson	Fergusson	Bignot	Taylor	Wilson	Myers	Statham	Sleeuwenhoek	

Telford United

GEORGE FOSTER

After the departure of Gerry Daly, Telford United turned to the managerial experience of George Foster to guide them away from what had become a perilous position at the foot of the table. Foster took over after the club had found themselves at rock-bottom by November, and led them to safety with an excellent run of results, even though, in the end, relegation was only just avoided.

His playing career began with his home town club, Plymouth Argyle, with whom he made over 200 League appearances. He moved to Derby County in June 1982 before joining Mansfield Town a year later. He stayed at Field Mill for ten years, making in excess of 350 appearances, and spent from February 1989 until the early part of last season as player-manager with the Stags. After his dismissal from the post, he spent a brief spell with Beazer Homes League club Burton Albion before accepting the post at the Buck's Head.

Mark Whitehouse (on floor) just fails to connect with a cross during Telford's FA Cup win against Morecambe. Photo - Colin Stevens.

Programme details:
32 pages for £1
Editor - T Andem

Any other club publications:

Local Newspapers:
Shropshire Star
Telford Journal

Local Radio Stations:
BBC Radio Shropshire
Beacon Radio

TELFORD UNITED - PLAYING SQUAD 1993-94

Player	Honours	Birthplace and date	Transfer Fees	Previous Clubs
GOALKEEPERS				
Ken Hughes		Barmouth 9/1/66		Crystal Palace, Shrewsbury Town, Wrexham
Darren Acton		Birmingham		From YTS
DEFENDERS				
Nigel Niblett	SLC, BSC, MFC, FAXI	Stratford 12/8/67	4-fig	Snitterfield Sports, Stratford T, VS Rugby
George Foster	FRT	Portsmouth 24/9/57		Plymouth Argyle, Derby County, Mansfield T, Burton Albion
Derek Statham	EI, E-u21, EY	Wolverhampton 24/3/59		WBA, Southampton, Stoke City, Walsall
Irvin Gernon	E-u21, EY	Birmingham 30/12/62		Ipswich T, Gillingham, Reading, Northampton T, Kettering T
Gary Ford		York 8/2/61		York C, Leicester C, Port Vale, Mansfield T
MIDFIELDERS				
Sean Parrish		Wrexham 14/3/72		Shrewsbury Town
Steve Fergusson	WSC	Birmingham 21/4/61	£6,000	Bromsgrove R, Redditch U, Alvechurch, Redditch U, Worcester C, Gloucester C
Marcus Bignot		Birmingham 22/8/74		Birmingham City
Martin Myers		Birmingham 10/1/66		Shrewsbury Town, Tamworth
Mickey Holmes		Blackpool 9/9/65		Bradford C, Burnley, Wolves, Huddersfield, Camb Utd, Rochdale, Torquay, Carlisle, Northampton Town.
FORWARDS				
Colin Taylor	EY	Liverpool 25/12/71		Wolverhampton Wanderers
Kris Sleeuwenhoek		Oldham 2/10/71		Wolverhampton Wanderers, Derby County, Brierley Hill

Departures during season:
Dave Pritchard (Bristol Rovers), Paul Hunter (Released), Rob Hindmarsh (Released), Mark Whitehouse (Kettering Town), Paul Lemon (Released).

Players on loan during season:
Darren Roberts (Wolves), Sean Bradbury (Wolves), Lee Wilson (Mansfield Town), Jon Davidson (Preston NE).

Bucks Head, Telford United

Address and telephone number: Bucks Head Ground, Watling Street, Wellington, Telford, Shropshire TF1 2NJ.
Tel: 0952 223838. Fax: 0952 246431.
Simple directions: M54 Junction 6, A518 to B5061 (Watling Street). Ground is on several bus routes.
Capacity: 6,400 **Seated:** 1,200 **Covered terracing:** 2,500
Record Attendance: 13,000 v Shrewsbury Town - Birmingham League - 1936.
Club Shop: Contact Shirley Finnigan on 0952 223838 for details.
Social Facilities: Social club adjacent to ground - open matchdays and selected other hours.

Telford Fact File

Nickname: Lilywhites

Club Sponsors: National Power

Previous Leagues: Southern League, Cheshire League, Birmingham League.

Previous Grounds: None

Previous Name: Wellington Town (prior to 1969).

Club colours: White shirts, blue shorts and white socks.

Change colours: Yellow shirts, red shorts and yellow socks.

Midweek home matchday: Tuesday

Record win:

Record defeat:

Record transfer fee: £10,000 to Northwich Victoria for Paul Mayman.

Record transfer fee received: £50,000 from Scarborough for Stephen Norris.

1993-94 Captain: Steve Ferguson

1993-94 Top scorer: Colin Taylor

1993-94 Player of the Year: Nigel Niblett

Club record goalscorer:

Past Players who progressed to the Football League: A.Walker (Lincoln City), G.French (Luton Town), K.McKenna (Tranmere Rovers), S.Norris (Scarborough).

Club Honours: Birmingham League 1920-21, 1934-35, 1935-36; Cheshire League 1945-46, 1946-47, 1951-52; Edward Case Cup 1952-53, 1954-55; Welsh Cup 1901-02, 1905-06, 1939-40; Birmingham Senior Cup 1946-47; Walsall Senior Cup 1946-47; Birmingham League Challenge Cup 1946-47; Shropshire Senior Cup (30); Southern League Cup 1970-71; Midland Floodlit Cup 1970-71; Midland Floodlit Cup 1970-71, 1982-83, 1988-89, Runnser-up 1969-70, 1987-88.

WELLING UNITED

Formed:
1963

President:
E.Brackstone
Chairman:
P.Websdale
Vice Chairman
S.Pain
Football Secretary:
Barrie Hobbins
Manager:
Terry Robbins
Assistant Manager
Ray Burgess
Coach:
Paul Haverson
Physiotherapist:
Peter Green
Commercial Manager:
G.Hobbins
Press Officer:
Paul Carter

The season began brightly for the Wings, with the early season league results indicating a successful 93/94 campaign, but an early FA cup exit, in what was an awkward opening tie at Enfield, set the scene for what was an up and down year.

Whilst holding a position in the top half of the table until well after the start of the New Year, results took a turn for the worst at around the time of the FA Trophy competition proper. Defeat in the second round of that cup came against Kent rivals Dover Athletic, with the final third of the season turning out to be extremely disappointing.

Player/Manager Terry Robbins' own form followed a similar pattern to that of his team - when he was amongst the goals all was well, but without his frequent goalscoring achievements, successes were hard to come by.

Having guided the Wings through to league safety in his first full season, following the survival battle of the previous year, Terry has seen the need to introduce new faces in time for the start of the 94/95 campaign. Although he may need to look outside of the club for experienced recruits, the one major plus for Welling followers during the past two seasons has been the success of the YT scheme, with four of the all-conquering youth team making the progression from trainee status to that of full-time professional. Two of them, Steve Finnan and Steve Barnes, figured in the Conference line-up frequently during the second half of last season, at the age of 17, and much is expected of them in the future.

Welling have also realised the need to re-introduce a second team in a competitive grade of football, and have therefore re-entered the Capital League for season 1994/95, offering spectators at Park View Road three grades of soccer this season.

Barrie Hobbins, Secretary

WELLING UTD *MATCHFACTS 93-94* ***WELLING UTD*** *MATCHFACTS 93-94* ***WELLING UTD*** *MATCHFACTS 93-94*

Key: Home fixtures are denoted by bold capitals. Numbers in brackets after players names indicate goals scored (asterisks by the results denote own goals). Only used substitutes are listed - substituted players are *italicised*.

Key to Competitions: GMVC: G.M. Vauxhall Conference. **DC**: Drinkwise (G.M. Vauxhall Conference) Cup. **KSC**: Kent Senior Cup. **LCC:** London Challenge Cup. **FAC**: F.A. Cup. **FAT**: F.A. Trophy.

Date	Opponents	Comp.	Res	Gate	1.	2.	3.	4.	5.	6.	7.	8.	9.	10.	11.	Sub.	Sub.
21/08	**STAFFORD R.**	GMVC	2-1	885	Williams	Hone	Robinson	Collins	*Brown*	Copley	White	Hales	Abbott(1)	Robbins(1)	*Reynolds*	Clemmence	Dennis
24/08	Woking	GMVC	2-0	1,833	Williams	Hone	Robinson	Collins	Brown	Copley	White	Hales	*Abbott*	Robbins(2)	Reynolds		Dennis
28/08	Kidderminster	GMVC	0-1	918	Williams	Hone	Robinson	Collins	Brown	Copley	White	Hales	Abbott	Robbins	Reynolds		
30/08	**MERTHYR TYD.**	GMVC	1-1	1,081	Williams	Hone	*Robinson*	Ransom	Brown	Copley	White	Hales	Abbott	Robbins(1)	Reynolds		Slater
04/09	**ALTRINCHAM**	GMVC	2-1	930	Williams	Hone(1)	*Robinson*	Collins	Brown	Copley	White	Hales	Abbott	Robbins(1)	Reynolds	Clemmence	
07/09	Kettering Town	DC1(1)	0-0	961	Williams	Hone	Clemmence	Ransom	*Brown*	Copley	White	*Burgess*	Abbott	Slater	Reynolds	Robbins	Finnan
11/09	Enfield	FAC1q	1-4	938	Williams	Hone	Robinson	*Ransom*	Clemmence	Copley	White	Hales(1)	Abbott	Robbins	Reynolds		Slater
14/09	Yeovil Town	GMVC	1-0	3,083	Williams	Hone	Robinson	Ransom	*Clemmence*	Copley	White	Hales	Abbott	Robbins(1)	Reynolds		Burgess
18/09	**SOUTHPORT**	GMVC	0-2	1,130	Williams	Hone	*Robinson*	Ransom	Brown	Copley	White	Hales	Abbott	Robbins	Reynolds		Slater
21/09	**KETTERING**	DC1(2)	2-1	457	Williams	Hone	Robinson	Collins	*Brown*	Clemmence	White	*Hales*	Abbott	Robbins(2)	Reynolds	Copley	Slater
28/09	Bath City	GMVC	0-0	722	Williams	Hone	Robinson	Collins	Brown	Copley	*Clemmence*	Hales	Abbott	Robbins	Reynolds		White
02/10	Bromsgrove R.	GMVC	1-1	751	Williams	Hone	Robinson	*Collins*	Brown	Clemmence	White(1)	*Hales*	Abbott	Robbins	Reynolds	Ransom	Slater
12/10	**DAGENHAM & R.**	GMVC	0-0	895	Williams	Hone	Robinson	Ransom	Brown	Clemmence	White	*Hales*	Abbott	Robbins	Reynolds		Slater
23/10	**NORTHWICH V.**	GMVC	0-1	811	Williams	Hone	Robinson	Ransom	Brown	Clemmence	White	Hales	*Abbott*	Robbins	*Steffe*	Finnan	Slater
30/10	Runcorn	GMVC	4-2	572	Williams	Hone	Robinson	Ransom	Brown(1)	Clemmence	White	Hales	Abbott	Robbins(2)	Reynolds(1)		
02/11	**WOKING**	DC(2)	1-0	616	Williams	Hone	Robinson	Ransom	Brown	*Clemmence*	White	Hales	*Abbott(1)*	Robbins	Reynolds	Finnan	Steffe
06/11	**YEOVIL TOWN**	GMVC	2-0	930	Williams	Hone	Robinson	Ransom	Brown	Clemmence	White	Hales	Abbott	Robbins(2)	Reynolds		
16/11	**CRAY WDRS**	KSC1	3-1	407	Williams	Hone	Steffe	Ransom	Brown	*Clemmence*	Finnan	Hales	Abbott(1)	*Robbins(1)*	Reynolds(1)	Smith	Slater
20/11	Halifax Town	GMVC	1-1	1,035	Williams	Steffe	Robinson	Ransom	Burgess	Clemmence	White	Hales	*Abbott(1)*	Robbins	Reynolds		Slater
27/11	**MACCLESFIELD**	GMVC	0-1	773	Williams	Hone	Robinson	Ransom	*Steffe*	Clemmence	White	Hales	*Abbott*	Robbins	Reynolds	Finnan	Slater
04/12	**KETTERING**	GMVC	2-0	924	Williams	Hone	*Robinson*	Ransom	Finnan	Clemmence	White	Hales	*Abbott*	*Robbins(2)*	Reynolds	Steffe	Slater
14/12	**BROMSGROVE**	DCqf	1-2	320	Williams	Hone	Robinson	Ransom	Finnan	Clemmence	White	*Hales*	Abbott(1)	*Robbins*	Reynolds	Copley	Steffe
18/12	Kettering Town	GMVC	**2-2	1,811	Williams	Hone	Robinson	Ransom	Finnan	Clemmence	White	Copley	Abbott	Robbins	Reynolds		
27/12	**DOVER ATH.**	GMVC	2-0	2,022	Williams	Hone(1)	Robinson	Ransom	Copley	Clemmence	White	*Finnan*	Abbott	Robbins	Reynolds(1)		Hales
01/01	**WOKING**	GMVC	*2-2	1,762	Williams	Hone	Robinson	Ransom	Copley	Clemmence	White	Hales	*Abbott(1)*	Robbins	Reynolds		Finnan
08/01	**WITTON ALBION**	GMVC	2-1	1,001	Williams	Hone	Robinson	Ransom	Copley(1)	Clemmence	White(1)	Hales	Abbott	Robbins	*Reynolds*		Finnan

11/01	**BOREHAM Wd**	LCC1	2-1	226	Williams	Hone	Robinson	Forst	Copley	Clemmence	White(1)	Steffe(1)	Abbott	*Finnan*	Barnes		Smith
15/01	Northwich Vics	GMVC	1-3	717	Williams	Hone	Robinson	Ransom	Copley	Clemmence	White	*Finnan*	Abbott(1)	*Steffe*	Reynolds	Burgess	Smith
18/01	**GRAVESEND**	KSCqf	1-1	715	Williams	Hone	Rutherford	Ransom	Copley	Clemmence	White	Barnes	*Abbott*	*Robbins(1)*	Reynolds	Steffe	Smith
22/01	**CHELMSFORD C.**	FAT1	6-1	1,108	Williams	Hone	Robinson(1)	Ransom	Copley(1)	Clemmence	White(1)	Rutherford	*Abbott(2)*	*Robbins(1)*	Reynolds	Finnan	Steffe
29/01	**HALIFAX TOWN**	GMVC	0-2	1,121	Williams	Hone	Robinson	Ransom	*Copley*	Clemmence	White	Rutherford	*Abbott*	Robbins	Reynolds	Smith	Finnan
01/02	Slough Town	GMVC	1-1	650	Williams	Hone	Robinson	Finnan	Copley	Clemmence	White	Rutherford	*Abbott*	Robbins(1)	Reynolds		Smith
05/02	Southport	GMVC	1-2	1,115	Williams	Hone	Robinson	Finnan	Copley	Clemmence	White	Rutherford	*Abbott*	Robbins(1)	Barnes		Smith
08/02	Gravesend & N.	KSCqfr	1-1	861	Williams	Hone	Robinson	Finnan	Holman	*Clemmence*	White	Rutherford	Barnes(1)	Robbins	*Reynolds*	Burgess	Powell
12/03	**DOVER ATH.**	FAT2	1-3	1,726	Williams	Hone	Robinson	Ransom	Copley	Clemmence	White	Rutherford	*Abbott*	Robbins(1)	Reynolds	Finnan	Barnes
19/03	**SLOUGH TOWN**	GMVC	6-2	770	Williams	Hone	Robinson	Ransom	Copley	Finnan	White	Rutherford(1)	Dichio(4)	Robbins(1)	*Reynolds*		Barnes
01/03	**BROMLEY**	LCCqf	4-1	406	Williams	Hone	Holman	Hales	Copley	*Clemmence*	White	*Rutherford(1)*	Smith	Robbins(3)	Barnes	Reynolds	Brown
05/03	**TELFORD UTD**	GMVC	0-0	832	Williams	Hone	*Robinson*	Ransom	Copley	*Finnan*	White	Rutherford	Dichio	Robbins	Barnes	Reynolds	Brown
09/03	Gravesend & N	KSCqfr	+0-0	659	Williams	Hone	Holman	Brown	Copley	Hales	White	Rutherford	Dichio	*Robbins*	*Barnes*	Reynolds	Abbott
12/03	Witton Albion	GMVC	5-0	593	Williams	Hone	Robinson	Ransom	Copley	Brown	White(1)	Rutherford	Dichio(2)	Robbins	Reynolds(2)		Abbott
16/03	**DOVER ATH.**	KSCsf	#0-1	523	Williams	Hone	Robinson	Ransom	Copley	Brown	White	*Rutherford*	*Dichio*	Robbins	Reynolds	Hales	Abbott
19/03	**RUNCORN**	GMVC	1-1	808	Williams	Hone	*Robinson*	Ransom	*Brown*	Copley	White	Rutherford	Abbott	Robbins	Reynolds(1)	Hales	Finnan
22/03	Tooting & Mit.	LCCsf	3-0	217	Williams	Brown	Reynolds	Hales	Copley	Clemmence	*White*	Rutherford(2)	Abbott	Smith	Barnes	Finnan(1)	
26/03	**STALYBRIDGE**	GMVC	1-2	703	Williams	Hone	*Robinson*	Ransom	Copley	Brown	White	Rutherford	Abbott	Robbins(1)	*Reynolds*	Hales	Barnes
29/03	Dover Athletic	GMVC	1-0	940	Williams	Hone	Robinson	Ransom	Brown	*Copley*	White	Hales	*Abbott(1)*	Robbins	Reynolds	Finnan	Barnes
02/04	Stafford Rgrs	GMVC	0-3	781	Williams	Hone	Robinson	Ransom	Brown	*Hales*	White	Rutherford	*Abbott*	Robbins	Reynolds	Smith	Finnan
04/02	**BATH CITY**	GMVC	0-0	800	Williams	Hone	Robinson	Ransom	Brown	Copley	White	Hales	Abbott	Robbins	Reynolds		
09/04	Telford Utd	GMVC	0-2	611	Williams	Hone	Robinson	Ransom	Brown	Copley	White	Hales	Abbott	*Smith*	Reynolds	Finnan	
13/04	Dagenham & Red.	GMVC	0-2	854	Williams	Hone	Barnes	Ransom	Brown	Copley	White	Hales	Abbott	Robbins	*Finnan*	Robinson	
16/04	Merthyr Tydfil	GMVC	1-0	416	Williams	Hone	Robinson	Ransom	Brown	Copley(1)	White	Hales	Abbott	Robbins	Barnes		Reynolds
19/04	**GATESHEAD**	GMVC	1-2	526	Williams	Hone(1)	Robinson	Ransom	Brown	Copley	White	*Hales*	*Smith*	Robbins	Reynolds	Finnan	Barnes
23/04	**BROMSGROVE**	GMVC	1-1	665	Williams	Hone	Robinson	Ransom	Brown	Copley	White	Reynolds	*Smith*	Robbins(1)	Barnes		Finnan
26/04	Altrincham	GMVC	0-2	568	Williams	Hone	Robinson	Ransom	Brown	Copley	*White*	Hales	Clemmence	Robbins	Reynolds	O'Keefe	
28/04	Gateshead	GMVC	0-1	303	Williams	Hone	Robinson	Ransom	Brown	Copley	White	Finnan	Smith	*Robbins*	Barnes		Abbott
30/04	**KIDDERMINSTER**	GMVC	0-3	941	Williams	Hone	Robinson	Ransom	Brown	Copley	White	*Rutherford*	*Abbott*	Robbins	Finnan	Smith	Barnes
02/05	Macclesfield T.	GMVC	0-1	577	Williams	Hone	Robinson	Ransom	*Brown*	Barnes	White	Rutherford	Abbott	Robbins	Reynolds		Copley
07/05	Staltbridge C.	GMVC	1-2	589	Williams	Hone	Robinson	Ransom	Brown	*Copley*	White(1)	Rutherford	*Abbott*	Robbins	Reynolds	Smith	Barnes

- After extra-time

+ - Won 7-6 on penalties, after extra-time

Welling United

TERRY ROBBINS

Has been with the club for eight years as a player, and more recently as player-manager.

Terry joined 'The Wings' from Crawley Town for £8,000 and has been top goal-scorer for the club in every season since then. It was this goalscoring record that gained him International recognition, and he has spear-headed the attack of the England semi-professional team for the past two seasons, captaining his country on the 1994 tour of Scandinavia.

When poor Conference form, and a shock FA Cup defeat, culminated in Nicky Brigden parting company with Welling during the 1992-93 season, Terry Robbins took over as player-manager. At 27-years-old Terry became the youngest manager in senior football.

Terry's first term as manager was successful in that relegation was avoided, and in 1993-94 Welling were tucked in behind the pace-setters for most of the season before a very disappointing run-in saw them finish in a position that did not do justice to their overall campaign.

Player-manager Terry Robbins (left) looks on as Steve Finnan eludes the tackle of Kettering Town's Steve Holden. Photo - Keith Gillard.

Programme details:
32 pages for £1
Editor - Paul Carter

Any other club publications:
Wings Review
'Winning isn't Everything' (Fanzine)

Local Newspapers:
Kentish Times
Bexleyheath & Welling Mercury

Local Radio Stations:
Radio Kent
Radio Invicta

WELLING UNITED - PLAYING SQUAD 1993-94

Player	Honours	Birthplace and date	Transfer Fees	Previous Clubs
GOALKEEPERS				
Darren Williams	ESC	Plaistow 11/5/66		Dagenham, Barnet, Wealdstone, Sorrento (Australia), Chelmsford City
DEFENDERS				
Mark Hone	ESP	Sidcup 31/3/68	£5,000	Crystal Palace
Paul Collins	SLP, SLC, LSC, KSC	Bermondsey 27/12/63		Millwall, Fisher Athletic
Nigel Ransom	SLP, LSC, KSC, Middx W.	Hammersmith 12/3/59		None
Paul Copley		Kent		Slade Green, Crockenhill
Richard Powell		Kent		From YTS
Mark Holman		London		Crystal Palace
Wayne Brown		London 12/5/70		From Youth Team
Steve Robinson	SLP	London 7/9/63	£3,500	Arsenal, Dartford, Leytonstone & Ilford
MIDFIELDERS				
Stuart White	SLP, KSC, LSC	Ashford 30/11/63		Charlton Athletic
Neil Clemmence	SLP, LSC, KSC	Gravesend 29/7/64		Dartford
Kevin Hales		Dartford 13/1/61		Chelsea, Leyton Orient
Ray Burgess	SLP, LSC, KSC	London 14/10/56		None
Danny Smith		Kent		From YTS
Steve Finnan		Kent		From YTS
FORWARDS				
Terry Robbins	ESP, LSC, Middx Wand.	Southwark 14/1/65	£8,000	Tottenham Hotspur, Gillingham, Maidstone United, Crawley Town
Gary Abbott	ESP, KSC LSC	Catford 7/11/64	£30,000	Welling United, Barnet, Enfield
Tony Reynolds	LSC	Ashford 25/4/63		Folkestone, Ashford Town, Maidstone United
Mike Rutherford		Sidcup 6/6/72		Queen's Park Rangers
Steve Barnes		London		From YTS

Departures during season:
John Glover (Erith & Belvedere), Paul Steffe (New Zealand).

Players on loan during season:
Danny Dichio (QPR).

Park View Road, Welling

Address and telephone number: Park View Road Ground, Welling, Kent DA16 1SY. Tel: 081 3011196. Fax: 081 3015676. Welling Wingsline: 0891 800 654.
Simple directions: M25, then A2 towards London. Take Welling turn-off, ground 1 mile. By rail to Welling station (BR) - ground 3/4 mile.
Capacity: 5,500 **Seated:** 500 **Covered terracing:** 1,500
Record Attendance: 4,100 v Gillingham, FA Cup
Club Shop: On sale programmes (League & non-League), scarves, mugs, caps, hats, badges, replica kits - matchday manager Peter Mason.
Social Facilities: Clubhouse open on match days
Previous Grounds: Butterfly Lane, Eltham - 1963/78

Welling Fact File

Nickname: The Wings

Club Sponsors: Welling Building Services Ltd

Previous Leagues: Eltham & District League 1963/71, London Spartan League 1971/77, Athenian League 1977/79, Southern League 1979/86.

Club colours: Red shirts & shorts

Change colours: All white

Midweek home matchday: Tuesday

Record win: 7-1

Record defeat: 0-7

Record transfer fee paid: £30,000 for Gary Abbott from Enfield

Record transfer fee received: £22,000 from Barnet for Duncan Horton

1993-94 Captain: Nigel Ransom

1993-94 Top scorer: Terry Robbins

1993-94 Player of the Year:

Club record goalscorer: John Bartley - 533

Record appearances: Ray Burgess - 1,000+

Past players who progressed to the Football League: Paul Barron (Plymouth, Arsenal, Stoke, WBA, C. Palace, QPR), Andy Townsend (Southampton, Norwich, Chelsea), Ian Thompson (AFC Bournemouth), John Bartley (Millwall), Dave Smith (Gillingham, Bristol City), Murray Jones (C. Palace, Bristol City, Exeter City), Kevin Shoemaker (Peterborough), Tony Agana (Watford, Sheffield Utd), Duncan Horton (Barnet)

Club Honours: London Spartan League 1978; Southern League Premier Division 1985/86; Kent Senior Cup 1985/86; London Senior Cup 1989/90; London Challange Cup 1991/92, Runners-up 1993/94.

Formed:
1889

President:
L A Gosden MBE

Chairman:
A E Hills

Vice Chairman
P J Ledger

Football Secretary:
P J Ledger JP

Manager:
Geoff Chapple

Coach:
C Lippiatt

Physiotherapist:
Barry Kimber

Press Officer:
P J Ledger

WOKING

A Season Transformed

At the beginning of October, no-one could have predicted that Woking were embarking upon the most successful season in their 105-year history. After eight Conference games, a team showing several changes from last term had just one victory, and had suffered humiliating defeats to newcomers Dover and Halifax. With talk of a rapid return to the Diadora League circulating, manager Geoff Chapple kept faith with his squad and, with the addition of two important loan signings (Jodie Craddock from Cambridge United and Andy Gray from Reading), the side gradually turned the corner. A 3-0 home win against Dover heralded a Conference run of 14 games without defeat lifting the club 15 places in under three months.

New signing, the evergreen Clive Walker, rapidly came to terms with Conference football with a string of classy performances and some vital goals, while the defence improved beyond recognition with last season's 'Player of the Year' Kevan Brown and Mark Tucker both outstanding. The return of the club's longest-serving players, brothers Shane and Lloyd Wye, helped maintain momentum, and despite a congested programme in the final week of the season (three home games in the last three days) Woking amassed a highly creditable 67 points to finish third in only their second season in the GM Vauxhall Conference.

The turn around in form may have come too late to claim league honours but it made a dramatic impact in the cup competitions, with the Cards achieving a 'double' - lifting the Surrey Senior Cup and the FA Trophy.

The Club had seen little success in the Trophy in recent years - just one victory in three seasons - but there was a feeling around Kingfield that this could be the year. The road to Wembley was far from straightforward, with just one victory at home, and Conference teams being the opposition on three occasions. A very tight two-legged semi-final against Diadora high-fliers Enfield was only resolved after a replay at Adams Park, giving the Cards their first Wembley appearance for 38 years.

The final was a fine advertisement for non-League football with goals from Darran Hay and Dereck Brown putting Woking 2-0 up in the first half hour. With both goal scorers substituted by half-time, a rearguard action was needed but they hung on to lift the Trophy for the first time.

A 3-1 victory over Sutton in the Surrey Senior Cup Final ensured a Cup double. Progress in this competition was relatively smooth with The Cards scoring three goals in each of the four rounds, conceding just two in the entire competition.

There can be little doubt that the season was the most successful in the club's history and one which should give Woking the opportunity to progress in their quest for Football League status.

Mike Deavin

Woking pictured before their FA Trophy semi-final against Enfield. Back Row (L/R): Darran Hay, Laurence Batty, Clive Walker, Gwynne Berry, Scott Steele, Kevan Brown, Dereck Brown. Front: Colin Fielder, Kevin Rattray, Scott Steele, Barry Lakin, David Puckett, Mark Tucker. *Photo - Eric Marsh.*

WOKING *MATCHFACTS 93-94* ***WOKING*** *MATCHFACTS 93-94* ***WOKING*** *MATCHFACTS 93-94*

Key: Home fixtures are denoted by bold capitals. Numbers in brackets after players names indicate goals scored (asterisks by the results denote own goals). Only used substitutes are listed - substituted players are *italicised*.

Key to Competitions: GMVC: GM Vauxhall Conference. **SSC**: Surrey Senior Cup. **DC**: Drinkwise (GM Vauxhall Conference) Cup. **FAC**: FA Cup. **FAT**: FA Trophy.

Date	Opponents	Comp.	Res	Gate	1.	2.	3.	4.	5.	6.	7.	8.	9.	10.	11.	Sub.	Sub.
21/08	Northwich Victoria	GMVC	0-0	1,041	Batty	Clement	Agboola	K Brown	Tucker	Berry	D Brown	*Biggins*	Morah	Puckett	Walker	Del Brown	
24/08	**WELLING UTD**	GMVC	0-2	1,833	Batty	Clement	Agboola	K Brown	Tucker	Berry	D Brown	*Biggins*	Del Brown	Puckett	Walker		Steele
28/08	**RUNCORN**	GMVC	1-1	1,520	Batty	Clement	Fielder	K Brown	Tucker	Berry	D Brown(1)	*Puckett*	Dennis	Greene	*Walker*	Biggins	Steele
30/08	Dover Athletic	GMVC	0-5	2,220	Batty	Clement	Fielder	K Brown	*Tucker*	Berry	D Brown	*Puckett*	Dennis	Greene	Walker	Biggins	Steele
04/09	Stafford Rangers	GMVC	0-3	1,071	Batty	Fielder	Agboola	K Brown	Tucker	Clement	D Brown	Biggins	Walker	Dennis	*Steele*	Del Brown	
11/09	**MACCLESFIELD**	GMVC	3-0	1,566	Batty	Clement	Fielder	K Brown	Berry	Rattray	D Brown	*Steele*	*Dennis(1)*	Swift	Walker(2)	Biggins	Haylock
18/09	Bromsgrove Rovers	GMVC	0-0	1,097	Batty	Clement	Fielder	K Brown	Berry	*Rattray*	D Brown	Steele	Heritage	*Puckett*	Walker	Biggins	Greene
25/09	**HALIFAX TOWN**	GMVC	2-6	1,848	Batty	Clement	Fielder	K Brown	Berry	Biggins	D Brown	*Steele*	Heritage	*Swift*	Walker(1)	Puckett(1)	Rattray
05/10	**MERTHYR TYD.**	GMVC	2-1	1,266	Batty	Clement	Agboola	Craddock	Berry	K Brown	D Brown	Biggins	*Heritage*	Rattray(1)	Walker(1)	Puckett	
09/10	Southport	GMVC	1-2	1,526	Batty	Clement	Fielder	K Brown	Craddock	*Berry*	D Brown	Biggins	Gray(1)	Agboola	Walker	Puckett	
12/10	**DOVER ATH.**	GMVC	3-0	1,836	Batty	Clement(1)	*Steele*	K Brown	Craddock	Berry	D Brown	Biggins(1)	Gray	Rattray	Walker(1)		Fielder
16/10	**WITTON ALBION**	GMVC	3-1	1,615	Batty	Clement	*Steele*	Craddock(1)	K Brown	Berry	*D Brown*	Biggins	Gray(1)	Rattray	Walker(1)	Puckett	Fielder
23/10	Halifax Town	GMVC	3-2	1,201	Batty	Clement(1)	Agboola	Tucker(1)	Berry	K Brown	D Brown	Puckett(1)	Gray	Rattray	Walker		
30/10	**TELFORD UTD**	GMVC	0-0	1,876	Batty	Clement	Steele	Craddock	K Brown	Berry	D Brown	*Puckett*	Gray	Rattray	Walker	Biggins	
02/11	Welling United	DC2	0-1	616	Batty	Clement	Steele	Craddock	K Brown	Berry	D Brown	Puckett	*Gray*	Rattray	Walker	Biggins	
13/11	**WESTON-s.-M.**	FAC1	2-2	2,766	Batty	Clement	Steele	Berry	K Brown	S Wye(1)	D Brown	Biggins	Fielder	Dennis(1)	Walker		
20/11	Stalybridge Celtic	GMVC	2-2	524	Batty	Clement	Steele	Craddock(1)	K Brown	S Wye	D Brown	Fielder	Gray	Dennis	Walker(1)		
23/11	Weston-super-Mare	FAC1r	1-0	2,623	Batty	Clement(1)	Steele	Berry	K Brown	S Wye	D Brown	Biggins	Fielder	Dennis	Walker		
27/11	**KIDDERMINSTER**	GMVC	1-0	1,726	Batty	*Clement*	Steele	Craddock	K Brown	S Wye	D Brown	*Biggins*	Gray	Fielder	Walker(1)	Dennis	Berry
04/12	Kidderminster H.	FAC2	0-1	4,411	Batty	Clement	Steele	Berry	K Brown	S Wye	D Brown	*Biggins*	Gray	Fielder	Walker	Dennis	
11/12	**BATH CITY**	GMVC	*4-1	1,463	Batty	Tucker	L Wye	Berry	K Brown	S Wye(1)	D Brown	Rattray(2)	Steele	Dennis	Walker		
14/12	**DORKING**	SSC1	3-1	622	Batty	Tucker	L Wye	Berry	K Brown	S Wye	*D Brown*	Rattray	Steele(1)	*Dennis*	Walker(2)	Biggins	Gray
18/12	Gateshead	GMVC	1-1	579	Batty	Tucker	L Wye	Berry	K Brown	S Wye	D Brown	Rattray	Steele(1)	Puckett	Walker		
27/12	**SLOUGH TOWN**	GMVC	2-1	2,913	Batty	Tucker	L Wye	Berry	K Brown	S Wye	D Brown	Rattray(1)	Steele	Dennis(1)	Walker		
01/01	Welling United	GMVC	2-2	1,762	Batty	Tucker	L Wye	Berry	K Brown	S Wye	D Brown(1)	Rattray	Steele(1)	Dennis	*Walker*		Puckett
03/01	**KETTERING T.**	GMVC	0-0	3,130	Batty	Tucker	L Wye	Berry	K Brown	S Wye	D Brown	Rattray	Steele	Dennis	Walker		
08/01	Altrincham	GMVC	2-0	632	Batty	Tucker	L Wye	Berry	K Brown	S Wye	D Brown	Rattray	Steele	Dennis	*Walker(1)*	Puckett(1)	

15/01	Macclesfield T.	GMVC	1-1	1,053	Batty	Tucker	Clement	Berry	K Brown	S Wye	D Brown	*Rattray*	Steele	Dennis(1)	Walker		Fleming
19/01	**WALTON & H.**	SSCqf	3-0	1,022	Batty	Tucker	Clement	Berry	*K Brown*	S Wye	D Brown	Biggins	Steele(1)	*Dennis(2)*	Puckett	Fielder	Swift
22/01	Bashley	FAT1	4-2	1,102	Batty	Tucker	Clement	Berry	K Brown	S Wye(1)	D Brown	Agboola	Steele	*Dennis(2)*	Walker(1)		Fleming
29/01	**SOUTHPORT**	GMVC	1-0	2,571	Batty	Tucker	L Wye	Berry	K Brown	Fielder	D Brown	Rattray	Steele	Dennis	Walker(1)		
05/02	Telford United	GMVC	0-2	1,222	Batty	Tucker	L Wye	Berry	K Brown	Fielder	D Brown	Rattray	*Steele*	Dennis	Walker		Fleming
12/02	Dagenham & Red.	FAT2	2-1	1,769	Batty	Tucker	L Wye	Berry	K Brown	Clement	*Lakin*	Rattray(1)	Steele	Dennis	Walker(1)	Fielder	
19/02	Kettering Town	GMVC	0-3	2,054	Batty	Tucker	L Wye	Berry	K Brown	Clement	Lakin	*Rattray*	*Steele*	Dennis	Walker	Biggins	Hislop
26/02	**STALYBRIDGE**	GMVC	3-0	1,727	Batty	Tucker	L Wye	Berry	K Brown	Clement	D Brown	*Rattray*	Steele	Dennis(2)	Walker(1)	Lakin	Hislop
01/03	Molesey	SSCsf	3-0	925	Batty	Tucker	L Wye	Berry	K Brown	Clement	D Brown	Fielder	*Steele*	Dennis(1)	*Walker(2)*	Biggins	Swift
05/03	**BROMSGROVE R.**	FAT3	3-2	2,342	Batty	Tucker	L Wye	Berry	K Brown(1)	Clement	Lakin(1)	D Brown	*Steele*	Dennis(1)	Walker		Hislop
08/03	Dagenham & Red.	GMVC	4-3	894	Batty	Tucker	L Wye	Berry	Fielder	Clement	D Brown(1)	Lakin	Puckett	Dennis(1)	Walker(2)		
12/03	**ALTRINCHAM**	GMVC	1-1	1,816	Batty	Tucker	L Wye	Berry	K Brown	Clement	D Brown	Lakin(1)	*Steele*	*Dennis*	Walker	Fielder	Puckett
15/03	**BROMSGROVE R.**	GMVC	0-0	1,192	Batty	Tucker	L Wye	Berry	K Brown	Clement	D Brown	Fielder	Steele	Bennett	Walker		
19/03	Kidderminster	GMVC	1-3	2,705	Batty	Tucker	L Wye	Berry	K Brown	Clement	D Brown	Lakin	Puckett	Bennett(1)	Walker		
22/03	Merthyr Tydfil	GMVC	3-2	490	Batty	Tucker	L Wye(1)	Berry	K Brown	Fielder	D Brown	Lakin	Steele	Bennett	Walker(2)		
26/03	**BILLINGHAM S.**	FATqf	1-1	2,767	Batty	*Tucker*	L Wye	Berry	K Brown	Fielder	D Brown	Rattray	Steele	*Bennett*	Walker(1)	Hislop	Lakin
30/03	Billingham Syn.	FATqfr	2-1	1,176	Batty	Clement	L Wye	Berry	K Brown(2)	Fielder	D Brown	Rattray	Steele	Puckett	Walker		
02/04	**GATESHEAD**	GMVC	1-0	1,669	Read	Clement(1)	L Wye	Berry	K Brown	Fielder	D Brown	Rattray	Steele	*Puckett*	Walker		Swift
04/04	Slough Town	GMVC	0-0	1,433	Batty	Clement	L Wye	Berry	K Brown	Fielder	D Brown	Rattray	*Steele*	*Puckett*	Hay	Lakin	Swift
09/04	Runcorn	GMVC	1-2	555	Batty	Clement	L Wye	Berry	K Brown	Fielder	*D Brown*	Rattray	Lakin	Hay(1)	Walker		Steele
12/04	Bath City	GMVC	1-0	691	Batty	Tucker	L Wye	Berry	K Brown	Fielder	D Brown	Lakin	Steele	Hay(1)	Walker		
16/04	**ENFIELD**	FATsf(1)	*1-1	3,841	Batty	Tucker	L Wye	Berry	K Brown	Fielder	D Brown	Lakin	*Steele*	Hay	Walker	Rattray	
19/04	**DAGENHAM & R.**	GMVC	1-8	1,127	Batty	Tucker	L Wye	*Berry*	K Brown	Clement	D Brown	Rattray	Puckett	*Hay(1)*	Steele	Fielder	Lakin
23/04	Enfield	FATsf(2)	0-0	3,319	Batty	Tucker	L Wye	Berry	K Brown	Clement	D Brown	Fielder	*Steele*	Hay	Walker	Puckett	
26/04	ENFIELD +	FATsfr	3-0	2,674	Batty	Tucker	L Wye	Berry	K Brown	Clement	D Brown	Fielder	*Steele(1)*	Hay(2)	Walker	Puckett	Rattray
30/04	Witton Albion	GMVC	0-0	454	Batty	Tucker	*L Wye*	Berry	K Brown	Clement	*D Brown*	Fielder	Hay	Steele	Puckett	Lakin	Rattray
02/05	Yeovil Town	GMVC	*1-0	2,208	Batty	*Tucker*	L Wye	Berry	K Brown	Clement	D Brown	Fielder	Steele	Hay	Puckett	Del Brown	Rattray
05/05	**YEOVIL TOWN**	GMVC	1-2	1,265	Read	Fielder	L Wye(1)	Berry	K Brown	Clement	D Brown	Rattray	*Steele*	Hay	Puckett		Walker
06/05	**NORTHWICH V.**	GMVC	2-1	692	Read	Tucker	L Wye	Berry	K Brown	Clement	D Brown	Fielder	Rattray	Hay(1)	*Walker(1)*		Lakin
07/05	**STAFFORD R.**	GMVC	4-0	1,428	Read	Tucker	*L Wye*	Berry	K Brown(1)	Clement	*D Brown*	Fielder	Steele	Del Brown	Puckett(2)	Hutchinson	Lakin(1)
10/05	SUTTON UTD #	SSCf	3-1	1,959	Batty	Tucker(1)	*L Wye*	Berry	K Brown	Clement	D Brown	Fielder	Steele(1)	*Hay(1)*	Puckett	Del Brown	Rattray
21/05	RUNCORN x	FATf	2-1	15,818	Batty	Tucker	L Wye	Berry	K Brown	Clement	*D Brown(1)*	Fielder	Steele	*Hay(1)*	Walker	Puckett	Rattray

- played at Kingstonian FC

x - played at Wembley Stadium

+ - played at Wycombe Wanderers FC

Woking

GEOFF CHAPPLE

The 87 supporters who witnessed Woking's 1-0 victory over Clapton on 29th September 1984 probably had little idea that the game would become a landmark in the history of the club. Not because it was the first game of the season that didn't end in defeat, but because it was the first match for the new manager Geoff Chapple.

Chapple joined Aldershot from school but did not play first team football. He played for Woking in the 1970's and also had a spell with Guildford City. He broke a leg whilst playing for Windsor & Eton in 1980 and then became manager of that club before moving to Kingfield in 1984. The game referred to above was in Division One of the Isthmian League and ended a run of seven consecutive defeats. Even Chapple was unable to prevent relegation that season and for the first time in their history Woking played Division Two football.

Chapple, however, used the time to build a firm foundation which was to produce arguably one of the best-ever Isthmian sides. Promotion to Division One came in the 86/87 season when the club won the title scoring 110 goals in the process. The Cards reclaimed their place in the Premier Division in 1990 and two seasons later won promotion to the Conference.

Chapple's finest hour came at Wembley on 21st May 1994 when his master-minded Woking to their first FA Trophy triumph.

Dereck Brown rides a determined challenge from Gateshead's Brian Rowe. *Photo - Paul Dennis.*

Programme details:
32 pages for £1
Editor - Mike Deavin

Any other club publications:
'Wubble Yoo' (Fanzine)

Local Newspapers:
Woking News/Mail
Surrey Advertiser
Woking Herald

Local Radio Stations:
County Sound

WOKING - PLAYING SQUAD

Player	Honours	Birthplace and date	Transfer Fees	Previous Clubs
GOALKEEPERS				
Laurence Batty	ESP, FAT, ILP	Westminster 15/2/64		Maidenhead Utd, Fulham, Brentford, Farense (Port)
DEFENDERS				
Reuben Agboola	Nigeria I	London 30/5/62		Southampton, Sunderland, Swansea City
Kevan Brown	Div 3, FAT	Andover 2/1/66		Southampton, Brighton, Aldershot
Mark Tucker	FAT	Woking 27/4/72		Fulham
Andy Clement	WY, FAT	Cardiff 12/11/67		Wimbledon, Woking, Plymouth Argyle
Gwynne Berry	FAT	Ystrad Mynach 18/12/63		Sutton Utd, Whyteleafe, Sutton Utd, Dorking
Lloyd Wye	FAT, ILP, NZL, FAXI	Wokingham 14/5/67		Southampton, Woking, Wanganui Athletic (NZ)
MIDFIELDERS				
Colin Fielder	FAT, SLP, HSC	Winchester 5/1/64	Player/ Exchange	Aldershot, Farnborough Town, Slough Town
Kevin Rattray	FAT	London		From Youth Team
Dereck Brown	ESP, FAT, ILP	London		Wembley, Crystal Palace, Hendon, Wembley, Hendon
Jason Cook	GMVC	Edmonton 29/12/69		Tottenham Hotspur, Southend Utd, Colchester Utd, Braintree T
Mark Biggins	ILP, FAXI	Middlesbrough 18/4/63	£2,500	Hampton, Hanwell, Feltham, Maidenhead U, St Albans C, Windsor & Eton
FORWARDS				
Clive Walker	ES, FAT	Oxford 26/5/57		Chelsea, Sunderland, QPR, Fulham, Brighton
Lennie Dennis	ILP, SSC	Lewisham 13/11/64		Bromley, Dulwich Hamlet, Sutton Utd, Umea (Sweden), Welling Utd
Gary Bennett	GMVC	Enfield 2/9/69		Colchester Utd, Braintree T, Doncaster R, Braintree T
David Puckett	Div 3, FAT	Southampton 29/10/60		Southampton, Bournemouth, Aldershot, Bournemouth
Scott Steele	SS, FAT	Motherwell 19/9/71		Airdrie
Delroy Brown		London		Local Football

Departures during season:
Ollie Morah (Sutton Utd), Shane Wye (New Zealand), Peter Heritage (Hastings T), Paul Haylock (Released).

Players on loan during season:
Jodie Craddock (Camb Utd), Andy Gray (Reading), Dave Fleming (Enfield), Dennis Greene (Wycombe W), Barry Lakin (Leyton Orient), Darren Hay (Camb Utd).

Kingfield Sports Ground, Woking

Address and telephone number: Kingfield Sports Ground, Kingfield, Woking, Surrey. Tel: 0483 772470
Simple directions: M25 J10 or 11, signposted from outskirts of Town. Ground 1 mile. Woking B.R.Station & buses from Woking.
Capacity: 6,000 **Seated:** 500 **Covered terracing:** 2,000
Record Attendance: 6,000 v Swansea, FA Cup - 1978/79
Club Shop: Phone 0483 772470 for details.
Social Facilities: Clubhouse open on matchdays. Food available.
Previous Grounds: Wheatsheaf, Ivy Lane (pre 1923)

Woking Fact File

Nickname: The Cards

Club Sponsors: O.L.C.
Previous Leagues: Isthmian 1991/92
Club colours: Red/white halves & black shorts
Change colours: All yellow
Reserve team's league: Capital/Suburban League
Midweek home matchday: Tuesday
Record win: 17-4 v Farnham, 1912-13.
Record defeat: 0-16 v New Crusaders, 1905-06.
Record transfer fee: £15,000 for Steve Milton (Fulham) - 1991/92
Record transfer fee received: £4,000 from Marlow for Tim Buzaglo - 1993
1993/94 Captain: Kevan Brown
1993/94 Top scorer: Clive Walker 23
1993/94 Player of the Year: Clive Walker
Club record goalscorer: C Mortimore 331, 1953-65
Record appearances: B Finn 564, 1962-74
Past players who progressed to the Football League: Ray Elliott (M'wall 1946), Charlie Mortimore (A'shot 1949), Robert Edwards (Chelsea 1951), Ron Newman (Portsmouth 1955), Mervyn Gill (Southampton 1956), John Mortimore (Chelsea 1951), Reg Stratton (Fulham 1959), George Harris (Newport 1961), Norman Cashmore (A'shot 1963), Alan Morton (C.Palce 1967), William Holmes (Millwall 1970), Richard Forbes (Exeter 1979).

Honours: FA Trophy 93-94; FA Amateur Cup 57-58; Isthmian League R-up 56-57, Lge AC Delco Cup 90-91, Div.1 R-up 89-90, Div.2 South 86-87, Reserve Section (2); West Surrey Lge (4), London Senior Cup R-up 82-83; Surrey Senior Cup 12-13, 26-27, 55-56, 56-57, 71-72, 90-91, 93-94; Surrey Senior Shield (9); Surrey Premier Cup (2); Surrey Invitation Cup 66-67; Surrey Intermediate Cup (2); Channel Islands Victory Cup (2); Suburban Lge (2), Lge Cup (2); Diadora Premier Division 91-92; Isthmian League Charity Shield 91-92, 92-93.

YEOVIL TOWN

Formed:
1895

President:
Norman Burfield

Chairman:
Bryan Moore

Vice-Chairman
Allan Houghton

Football Secretary:
Roger Brinsford

Manager:
Brian Hall

Physiotherapist:
Tony Farmer

Commercial Manager:
Alan Skirton

Press Officer:
Secretary

TOO EXCITING FOR COMFORT

The beautiful ground and palatial facilities make Huish Park a very special non-League venue, so unfortunately it is assumed that any club with such a lovely home should be able to field a team to match.

Yeovil Town's move from the old sloping ground left them £750,000 in debt. Finances have improved to leave them a mere £400,000 in arrears, but this means the club cannot really lure any senior expensive players to play their football in the South West.

With this in mind, the club's start to the season was excellent seeing them in second position (their highest ever Conference place) in September. But gradually form deteriorated and, although a brilliant goal from Andy Wallace gave Yeovil Town another FA Cup scalp as Fulham were defeated live on Sky, manager Steve Rutter decided enough was enough and it was time to give someone else the chance to motivate a squad that he had been with as player and manager for four seasons.

A period of indecision and negotiations didn't help anyone, and Bromsgrove Rovers deservedly won at Yeovil in the FA Cup and form was patchy. Phil Ferns bravely tried to hold things together, but it was decided to call on Brian Hall's expeience to keep the club in the Conference and, after a disastrous six games without a goal, the end of season form was a revelation.

Jeff Sherwood and Paul Wilson enjoyed superb seasons. Newcomers Marc Coates, Peter Mason, Chris White and the experienced John McClelland showed excellent form, and Micky Spencer was again top goalscorer.

There is no doubt the coming season will again be difficult, but two or three new faces, added to a great deal of experience under the guidence of one of non-League football's wisest managers, could still make Yeovil Town difficult to beat.

Tony Williams, Director.

Yeovil Town 1994/95 - Back Row (L-R): Steve Perkins, Matthew Leonard, David Morris, David Coles, Peter Mason, Marc Coates, Richard Evans, Mark Thompson. Centre: Rhys Hamer, Wayne Dobbins, Matthew Francis, Neil Cordice, Ian Benbow, Nick Flory, Steve Sivell, Mickey Spencer, Adi Searl. Seated: Lee Groves, Tony Farmer (Physio), Peter Conning, Jeff Sherwood, Brian Hall (Manager), Phil Ferns, Paul Wilson, Anne Read (Physio), Wayne Farnell-Jack. Front: Danny Burwood, Christian Gallo-Cornish, Nick Williams, Wayne Lewis, Matthew Longden, Stuart Munroe, Chris Visick, Andy Flory.

Photo - Tilzey Studios, Yeovil.

YEOVIL MATCHFACTS 93-94 *YEOVIL* MATCHFACTS 93-94 *YEOVIL* MATCHFACTS 93-94

Key: Home fixtures are denoted by bold capitals. Numbers in brackets after players names indicate goals scored (asterisks by the results denote own goals). Only used substitutes are listed - substituted players are *italicised.*

Key to Competitions: GMVC: GM Vauxhall Conference. **SPC**: Somerset Premier Cup. **DC**: Drinkwise (GM Vauxhall Conference) Cup. **FAC**: FA Cup. **FAT**: FA Trophy.

Date	Opponents	Comp.	Res	Gate	1.	2.	3.	4.	5.	6.	7.	8.	9.	10.	11.	Sub.	Sub.
21/08	Bromsgrove Rvrs	GMVC	2-1	1,157	Coles	*Dobbins*	Ferns	Sherwood	Bye	*Leonard*	Sanderson(1)	Wallace	Wilson	Spencer(1)	Harrower	Connor	Coates
24/08	**DAGENHAM & R.**	GMVC	2-1	3,349	Coles	Dobbins	Ferns	Sherwood	Bye	Leonard	Sanderson	Wallace(1)	Wilson(1)	Spencer	Harrower		
28/08	**STALYBRIDGE**	GMVC	0-0	3,012	Coles	Dobbins	Ferns	Sherwood	Bye	Leonard	Sanderson	Wallace	Wilson	Spencer	*Harrower*	Connor	
30/08	Telford United	GMVC	1-1	931	Coles	Dobbins	Ferns	Sherwood	Bye	Leonard	Sanderson	Wallace	*Wilson(1)*	Spencer	Harrower	Connor	
04/09	Halifax Town	GMVC	1-1	1,152	Coles	*Dobbins*	Ferns	Sherwood	Bye	Leonard	Sanderson(1)	Wallace	Connor	Spencer	Harrower		Coates
11/09	**WITTON ALBION**	GMVC	2-0	2,849	Coles	Coates	Ferns	Sherwood	Bye	Leonard	Sanderson	Wallace(1)	*McPherson*	Spencer(1)	Harrower		Nevin
14/09	**WELLING UTD**	GMVC	0-1	3,083	Coles	Coates	Connor	Sherwood	Bye	Leonard	*Sanderson*	*Wallace*	McPherson	Spencer	Harrower	Gorman	Nevin
18/09	Stafford Rangers	GMVC	2-4	1,064	Coles	Coates	Flory	Sherwood	Bye	Leonard	Sanderson	*Wallace*	McPherson	Spencer(2)	*Harrower*	Connor	Nevin
21/09	Slough Town	GMVC	2-5	1,313	Coles	*Coates*	Rutter	Sherwood	Bye	Leonard(1)	Wilson	Wallace(1)	*McPherson*	Spencer	Harrower	Sanderson	Connor
25/09	**MACCLESFIELD**	GMVC	4-0	2,516	Coles	Coates	Ferns	Sherwood	Bye	Leonard	Sanderson(2)	Wallace	*Wilson(1)*	*Spencer(1)*	Harrower	McPherson	Connor
02/10	Northwich Vict.	GMVC	1-1	939	Coles	Coates	Ferns(1)	Sherwood	Bye	*Leonard*	Sanderson	Wallace	Wilson	Spencer	Harrower	McPherson	*Cooper*
09/10	**ALTRINCHAM**	GMVC	0-0	2,917	Coles	Coates	Ferns	Sherwood	Bye	Leonard	Sanderson	Wallace	Wilson	*Spencer*	*Harrower*	McPherson	Connor
16/10	Kettering Town	GMVC	0-1	1,949	Coles	*Coates*	Ferns	Sherwood	Bye	Connor	Sanderson	Wallace	Wilson	Spencer	*Rutter*	Harrower	Nevin
23/10	**RUNCORN**	GMVC	4-2	2,475	Coles	Coates	Ferns	Sherwood	Bye	*Rutter(1)*	Sanderson	Wallace	*Wilson*	Spencer(1)	Connor	McPherson(2)	Gorman
25/10	Frome Town	SPC2	6-0	310	Coles	Coates	*Ferns*	Sherwood	Bye(1)	Taylor(1)	Sanderson(1)	Gorman	*McPher.(1)*	Spencer(1)	Harrower(1)	Rowe	Flory
30/10	**GATESHEAD**	GMVC	0-2	2,787	Coles	Coates	Ferns	Sherwood	Bye	*Connor*	Sanderson	Wallace	McPherson	Spencer(1)	Rutter		Harrower
02/11	Bath City	DC2	1-0	584	Coles	Coates	Ferns	Sherwood	Bye	Taylor	Sanderson	Wallace	*McPherson*	Spencer(1)	Harrower	Cooper	Gorman
06/11	Welling United	GMVC	0-2	930	Coles	Coates	Gorman	Sherwood	Bye	Taylor	Sanderson	*Connor*	McPherson	Spencer	Cooper		Flory
15/11	**FULHAM**	FAC1	1-0	6,180	Coles	Coates	Ferns	Sherwood	Bye	Leonard	Sanderson	Wallace(1)	Wilson	Spencer	*Harrower*	Cooper	
20/11	**DOVER ATH.**	GMVC	1-3	2,730	Coles	Coates	Ferns	Sherwood	Bye	Leonard	*Sanderson*	Wallace	Wilson	Spencer(1)	Harrower	McPherson	
27/11	Southport	GMVC	1-1	1,303	Coles	Coates	Ferns	Sherwood	Bye	Leonard	*Thwaites*	Wallace	Wilson	Spencer(1)	Harrower	McPherson	
04/12	**BROMSGROVE**	FAC2	0-2	5,462	Coles	Coates	Ferns	Sherwood	Bye	*Leonard*	*Sanderson*	Wallace	Wilson	Spencer	Harrower	McPherson	Connor
11/12	**BROMSGROVE**	GMVC	2-3	1,721	Coles	Coates	Ferns	*Sherwood(1)*	Bye	Leonard(1)	Thwaites	Wallace	Wilson	McPherson	*Harrower*	Connor	Spencer
13/12	Dagenham & Red.	DC3	2-1	466	Coles	Coates	Flory	Nevin	Bye	Leonard	Thwaites	Cooper	Wilson(1)	*McPherson(1)*	*Harrower*	Taylor	Spencer

27/12 **BATH CITY**	GMVC	1-2	3,371	Coles	*Coates*	Flory	Sherwood	Bye	Leonard	*Thwaites*	Cooper	Wilson(1)	McPherson	Harrower	Taylor	Nevin
01/01 Merthyr Tydfil	GMVC	1-1	1,068	Coles	Coates	Ferns	Sherwood	Bye	Leonard	Nevin	Cooper	*Taylor*	Spencer	Sanderson(1)		Thwaites
03/01 Bath City	GMVC	0-3	1,518	Coles	Coates	Flory	Sherwood	*Bye*	Leonard	Nevin	Cooper	*Taylor*	Spencer	Sanderson	Wallace	Thwaites
15/01 Kidderminster H.	GMVC	3-2	3,812	Coles	*Coates*	Ferns	Sherwood	Bye	Leonard	Nevin	Cooper	Wilson(1)	Spencer(1)	Wallace(1)	Sanderson	
22/01 **BATH CITY**	FAT1	3-3	2,611	Coles	*Coates*	Ferns	Sherwood	Nevin	Leonard(1)	Sanderson	Wallace	Wilson(1)	Spencer(1)	Cooper		Harrower
25/01 Bath City	FAT1r	0-4	1,148	Coles	*Harrower*	Ferns	Sherwood	*Nevin*	Leonard	Sanderson	Wallace	Wilson	Spencer	Cooper	Bye	Coates
29/01 **KETTERING T.**	GMVC	1-0	2,382	Coles	Sherwood	*Harrower*	Creaser	Willmott	Leonard	Sanderson	Wallace	Wilson	Spencer(1)	Cooper		Coates
01/02 Bromsgrove Rvrs	DCsf(1)	2-1	1,175	Coles	Coates	*Willmott*	Sherwood	Creaser	*Leonard*	Sanderson(1)	Wallace	Wilson(1)	Spencer	Cooper	Nevin	Gorman
05/02 Gateshead	GMVC	1-2	552	Coles	Coates	Willmott	Sherwood	Creaser	Leonard	Sanderson	Wallace	Wilson	Spencer(1)	Cooper		
17/02 Weston-s.-Mare	SPC3	3-1	240	Coles	Coates	Ferns	Sherwood	Nevin	*Leonard*	*Sanderson*	Wallace(1)	Wilson	Dobbins	Cooper(2)	Gorman	Harrower
19/02 Witton Albion	GMVC	2-1	643	Coles	Coates	Ferns	Sherwood	Creaser	*Willmott*	Dobbins	Wallace	*Wilson(1)*	Cordice(1)	Cooper	Sanderson	Harrower
26/02 Runcorn	GMVC	0-4	427	Coles	Coates	Ferns	Sherwood	Creaser	Leonard	*Sanderson*	Wallace	Wilson	Cordice	Cooper		Willmott
01/03 **BROMSGROVE**	DCsf(2)	0-1	1,922	Coles	Coates	Ferns	Sherwood	*Rutter*	Leonard	*Knight*	Wallace	Wilson	Spencer	Cooper	Cordice	Harrower
05/03 **SLOUGH TOWN**	GMVC	0-2	2,021	Coles	Coates	Willmott	Sherwood	Rutter	*Cordice*	*Harrower*	Wallace	Wilson	Spencer	Cooper	Dobbins	Knight
12/03 **NORTHWICH V.**	GMVC	0-3	2,029	Coles	*N Coates*	Ferns	Sherwood	Willmott	*Dobbins*	Knight	Wallace	Wilson	Spencer	Cordice	Harrower	Leonard
15/03 Bath City	SPC4	0-1	322	Coles	Coates	Harrower	Sherwood	Cordice	Leonard	*Knight*	Dobbins	*Wilson*	Spencer	Cooper	Taylor	Flory
19/03 Altrincham	GMVC	0-1	870	Coles	Harrower	Willmott	Sherwood	Cordice	Leonard	Knight	Dobbins	M Coates	Spencer	Cooper		
22/03 **STAFFORD R.**	GMVC	0-1	1,405	Coles	White	Willmott	Sherwood	Cordice	Leonard	Knight	Dobbins	M Coates	*Spencer*	Cooper		Burke
26/03 **SOUTHPORT**	GMVC	3-2	1,978	Mason	*White*	Ferns	Sherwood	Cordice	Cooper	West(1)	Wallace	M Coates(1)	Spencer(1)	Dobbins	Harrower	
02/04 **KIDDERMINSTER**	GMVC	0-1	2,835	Mason	Harrower	Ferns	Sherwood	Cordice	Cooper	*West*	Wallace	M Coates	Spencer	Dobbins	N Coates	
04/04 Dagenham & Red.	GMVC	1-2	923	Mason	*Harrower*	Ferns	Sherwood	Cordice	Cooper	West	Wallace	M Coates	Spencer(1)	*Dobbins*	Leonard	Wilson
12/04 Macclesfield T.	DCf(1)	1-4	651	Mason	White	Ferns	Sherwood	McClelland(1)	Cordice	West	Cooper	Wilson	*Spencer*	*Dobbins*	Leonard	Wallace
16/04 **HALIFAX TOWN**	GMVC	0-0	1,823	Mason	White	Ferns	Sherwood	McClelland	Cordice	*N Coates*	Wallace	M Coates	Wilson	Dobbins		West
19/04 **MACCLESFIELD**	DCf(2)	0-0	1,241	Mason	White	Ferns	Sherwood	McClelland	Cordice	West	Cooper	Wilson	Spencer	Leonard		
23/04 Dover Athletic	GMVC	2-0	849	Mason	White	Ferns	Sherwood	McClelland	Cordice	West(1)	Wallace(1)	*M Coates*	Wilson	Leonard		Spencer
26/04 **MERTHYR TYD.**	GMVC	2-2	2,030	Mason	White	Ferns	Sherwood	McClelland	Cordice	West	*Wallace*	*M Coates(1)*	Wilson(1)	Leonard	Spencer	Cooper
28/04 Stalybridge C.	GMVC	2-1	515	Mason	White	Ferns(1)	Sherwood	McClelland	Cooper	*West*	Cordice	M Coates	Wilson	*Leonard*	Spencer(1)	Dobbins
30/04 Macclesfield T.	GMVC	2-1	617	Mason	White	Ferns	Sherwood	McClelland	Cooper	*West*	Cordice	*M Coates*	Wilson(1)	Leonard	Spencer(1)	Dobbins
02/05 **WOKING**	GMVC	0-1	2,208	Mason	*White*	Ferns	Sherwood	McClelland	Cordice	West	Cooper	Spencer	Wilson	Leonard	N Coates	
05/05 Woking	GMVC	2-1	1,265	Mason	White	Ferns	Sherwood	McClelland	Cooper	*West*	Cordice	M Coates	Wilson(1)	*Leonard*	Spencer(1)	Dobbins
07/05 **TELFORD UTD**	GMVC	1-0	2,783	Mason	White	Ferns	Sherwood	McClelland	Cooper(1)	*West*	Cordice	M Coates	Wilson	Spencer		Dobbins

Yeovil Town

BRIAN HALL

Brian was re-appointed as manager at Huish Park after the resignation of Steve Rutter in early 1994. His career in coaching began with Walton & Hersham in 1973 before moving to Wimbledon where he, along with manager Allen Batsford, laid the foundations for their entry into the Football League. Spells with Slough Town, Wycombe Wanderers and Metropolitan Police followed before he joined Wealdstone, initially as coach again under Batsford, then as manager in 1983. He proceeded to lead the Stones through the most successful period in their history, winning the Gola League and FA Trophy double. In 1987 he joined Yeovil Town, who had been relegated from the Conference, and led them to the Isthmian League and Cup double 18 months later. However, in October 1990, after a disappointing start to the campaign, the club decided to part company with Brian and replace him with Clive Whitehead. Almost immediately, Brian was back in charge at Wealdstone, who by now were playing in the Beazer Homes League. When he left the Stones for the second time, he continued in the game as scout for Wycombe Wanderers before receiving the call to return to Huish Park last season.

Yeovil 'keeper David Coles is forced to stretch to tip the ball over during the 0-4 defeat at Runcorn.
Photo - Tim Lancaster.

Programme details:
52 pages for £1. Editor - Roger Brinsford

Any other club publications:
Fanzine

Local Newspapers:
Western Gazette, Western Daily Press
Somerset Express & Star
Sunday Independent

Local Radio Stations:
Radio Bristol
Somerset Sound
Orchard FM
Radio Camelot (Hospital)

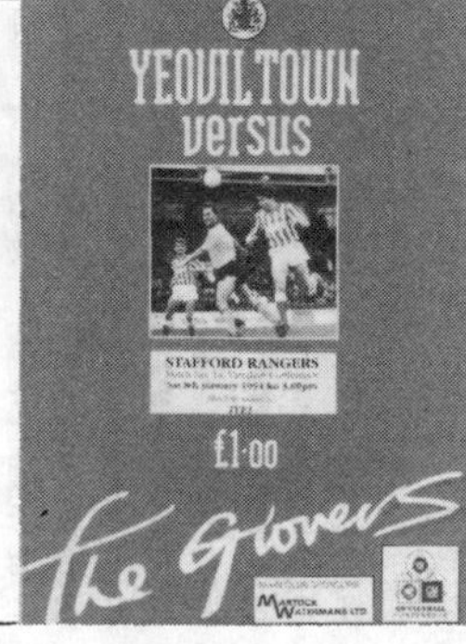

YEOVIL TOWN - PLAYING SQUAD

Player	Honours	Birthplace and date	Transfer Fees	Previous Clubs
GOALKEEPERS				
David Coles	FPL	Wandsworth 15/6/64		Birmingham, Aldershot, HJK Helsinki (Fin), C.Palace, Brighton, Aldershot, Fulham
Peter Mason		Wales		Cwmbran Town, Newport AFC, Albion Robers, Forest Green Rovers
DEFENDERS				
Phil Ferns	ILP, ACDC	Liverpool 12/9/61		Bournemouth, Charlton, Blackpool, Aldershot, Yeovil T, Poole T
Jeff Sherwood	ILP, BLT, FAXI	Bristol 5/10/59		Minehead, Taunton T, Bath C, Bristol R, Bath C, Yeovil T, Gloucester C
Steve Harrower	Div 4	Exeter 9/10/61		Dawlish Town, Exeter City
John McClelland	NI, SLC, Skol C	Belfast 7/12/55		Cardiff C, Bangor (NI), Mansfield T, Rangers, Watford, Leeds, St Johnstone, Wycombe W
Wayne Dobbins		Bromsgrove 30/8/68		West Bromwich Albion, Torquay United
Mike McEvoy		Wigan 5/7/73		Yeovil Town, Wakaito (NZ)
Neil Coates	BLT	Templecombe 15/1/68		Watford, Bournemouth, Yeovil T, Dorchester T
MIDFIELDERS				
Richard Cooper		London 7/5/65		Sheff Utd, Lincoln C, Exeter C, Weymouth
Andy Wallace	ILP, BLT, ACDC, Middx	London 30/6/64		Metropolitan Police, Kingstonian, Wealdstone
Neil Cordice	GMVC, FAT, ILP, ACDC	Amersham 7/4/60		Flackwell H, Northampton T, Wycombe W, Yeovil T, Wealdstone
Dave Leonard		Devon		Saltash Utd
FORWARDS				
Mickey Spencer	Comb Serv, BLT	Manchester 27/11/62		Bury, Wokingham Town
Paul Wilson	ESP, BLT	Doncaster 16/11/60	£13,000	Frickley Ath, Heidelburg (Australia), Boston United
Marc Coates		Swansea	Player/	Swansea City, Merthyr Tydfil

Departures during season:
Nigel Thwaites (Falmouth T), Malcolm McPherson (West Ham Utd), Terry Connor (Calne T), Andy Bye (Bashley), Andy Gorman (Merthyr Tydfil), Keith Knight (Trowbridge T), Steve Rutter (Trowbridge T).

Players on loan during season:
Glyn Creaser (Wycombe W), Mark West (Wycombe W), Chris White (Exeter C).

Guide to honours:
FPL = Finnish Premier League, ILP = Isthmian League Premier Div., ACDC = AC Delco Cup, BLT = Bob Lord Trophy, NI = Northern Ireland International, SLC = Scottish League Cup, Skol C = Skol Cup, GMVC = GM Vauxhall Conference, FAT = FA Trophy, Middx = Middlesex Wanderers, Comb Serv = Combined Services Representative.

Huish Park, Yeovil Town

Address and telephone number: Huish Park, Lufton Way, Yeovil, Somerset BA22 8YF Tel: 0935 23662. Fax: 0935 73956

Simple directions: Leave A303 at Cartgate roundabout and take A3088 signposted Yeovil. Take first exit at next roundabout and first exit again at next roundabout into Lufton Way. Railway Station - Yeovil Pen Mill (Bristol/Westbury to Weymouth) 2.5 miles from ground. Yeovil Junction (Waterloo - Exeter - 4 miles). Bus service - from both stations on Saturday - matchdays.

Capacity: 8,720 **Seated:** 5,212 **Terracing:** 3,508

Record Attendance: 8,612 v Arsenal - 3rd Round FA Cup - 02/01/93

Club Shop: Sells replica kits, badges, stickers, pennants, books, *Team Talk* magazines, subbuteo teams, hats etc.

Social Facilities: Matchdays - hot and cold food available. Meals can be ordered provided advance notice is given. All-weather astro-turf pitch available for bookings 9am-10pm.

Yeovil Fact File

Nickname: Glovers

Club Sponsors: Tesco Social Club

Previous Name: Yeovil & Petters United 1895-1946.

Previous Grounds: Pen Mill 1895-1920/ The Huish 1920-1990.

Previous Leagues: Western League, London Combination, Southern League, Alliance Premier, Isthmian League.

Club colours: Green & white striped shirts, white shorts and white socks.

Change colours: Old gold and black.

Reserve team league: Football Combination.

Midweek home matchday: Tuesday

Record transfer fee: £15,000 to Worcester City for Joe Jackson - 1990.

Record transfer fee received: £75,000 from Bristol City for Mark Shail - 1993.

1993-94 Captain: Jeff Sherwood

1993-94 Top scorer: Mickey Spencer.

1993-94 Player of the Year: Mickey Spencer.

Club record goalscorer: Dave Taylor 285 - 1960-69

Record appearances: L Harris

Past players who progressed to the Football League: Over 40 players + 18 mangers including, since 1985: Nigel Jarvis (Torquay); Ian Davies (Bristol Rovers); Alan Pardew (Crystal Palace); Paul Miller (Wimbledon); John McGinlay (Shrewsbury); Guy Whittingham (Portsmouth); Mark Shail (Bristol City); Malcolm McPherson (West Ham).

Honours: Southern League 1954/55, 1963/64, 1970/71, Runners-up 1923/24, 1931/32, 1934/35, 1969/70, 1972/73; Southern League Cup: 1948/49, 1954/55, 1960/61, 1965/66. Vauxhall-Opel League 1987/88, Runners-up 1985/86, 1986/87; AC Delco Cup 1987/88; FA Cup 5th Round 1948/49; Bob Lord Trophy 1989/90, Runners-up 1993/4.

NORTHERN PREMIER LEAGUE

President: N White, Esq.
Chairman: K Marsden, Esq.
Vice-Chairman: K F Brown Esq.
Secretary/Treasure: R D Bayley, Esq.
22 Woburn Drive, Hale, Altrincham, Cheshire WA15 8LZ
(061 980 7007 - Fax: 061 980 7007)

Following the runaway successes of the past few seasons by such clubs as Southport, Stalybridge, Witton and Colne, the 1993-94 NPL Premier Division was a much closer fought affair. Boston United, Bishop Auckland and Frickley all flirted with aspiration but, in the end, it became a two horse race between the perennial consistency of Marine and Neil Baker's Leek Town who, at last, put the promise of the past few campaigns into practice

The "Mariners" were unhindered by long cup runs in any of the major competitions and took full advantage to get their fixtures played and points on the board. By contrast, Leek fought their way to a First Round Proper FA Cup replay with Wigan, reached the semi-final of the NPL Challenge Cup and the Final of the President's Cup in a period that was beset by postponements due to the monsoon winter. Success left them with a backlog of fixtures that was to prove their undoing. The Staffordshire club's failure to land a major trophy was scant reward for their endeavours and, at the time of writing, even their elevation to the GMV Conference as runners-up was in considerable doubt.

At the other end of the table, Fleetwood got off to a horrendous start and were never able to recover despite some improved results under new boss Phil Staley. Promotion, rather than relegation, must have been on the minds of Bridlington as they made a healthy debut in their first season of Premier Division football, but financial disaster lay just around the corner for the 1993 FA Vase winners and they plummeted down the table as fast as a stone in water. Strange to relate then, that it was Bridlington who finally presented the title to Marine when they held Leek to a 1-1 draw in the penultimate game of the season after their own relegation had been confirmed. Their fate, however, was worse than relegation for, as soon as they had completed their fixtures, Bridlington Town resigned from the League twelve months after lifting the Vase at Wembley.

Of the other clubs, Morecambe, as so often, flattered only to deceive, Accrington had a desperately disappointing campaign just twelve months after being the darlings of the media with their nostalgic FA Cup run, Boston were never quite able to sustain good runs long enough to make the impact expected of them, and Chorley's end of season form when they were beating all of the top teams must have had manager Glen Buckley wishing the campaign had started in March!

In the First Division, there was little doubt about the team of the season although Spennymoor may wish to dispute that accolade being given to Guiseley. The new boys beat no fewer than five Premier Division Clubs, including Hyde in the Final, to lift the NPL Challenge Cup at the first attempt as well as becoming the first club from outside the top flight to lift the trophy. The North-East side also won promotion and landed the Durham Senior Cup to complete a great first season, but Guiesely had an even better time of it. Ray McHale's team won the title in a canter, beat Leek in both legs of the President's Cup Final and almost put the icing on the cake by matching GMVC outfit Runcorn stride for stride in three and a half hours of FA Trophy semi-final action only to loose to a goal deep into time added on as the Twin Towers beckoned.

But, in this Division, spare a thought for Ashton United who were pipped for promotion on the very last day of the 1992-93 season. This time, after winning the First Division Cup, they got even closer to their burning ambition of Premier Division football as, with six minutes of the 1993-94 term left, the Hurst Cross club were up, only to concede two goals in those vital few minutes to finish third again. All their despair, however, paled into insignificance compared to the tragedy that hit the club with the death of their ever-present, ever-popular player, Ian Redman from a suspected heart attack. The shadow cast over the NPL fraternity served starkly to remind everybody in the most painful way possible that football is only a game.

At the bottom, Eastwood Town's defensive record was better than half of the other teams in the league but they could only muster 47 goals themselves. Every picture tells a story, or does it? Strangely, Eastwood twice took four goal leads only to finish up level and leave their fans in a state of apoplexy. Harrogate Town's goal-scoring problems were even worse. They went 13 hours 6 minutes without finding the net at one stage during March and April! Harrogate, however, were saved from relegation by Bridlington's plight.

In the FA Cup, Accrington, Gretna, Knowsley and Leek all took on Football League opposition and, whilst Knowsley were given a lesson in finishing by Carlisle, the other three all gave their loftier opponents a fright. Accrington lost in the sixth minute of injury time to Scunthorpe United, Leek took Wigan to a replay and First Division minnows, Gretna, gave Bolton Wanderers the shock of their lives when leading 2-1 until their legs gave up in the last ten minutes enabling the Wanderers to grab a 3-2 victory that set them on the path to success over Everton, Aston Villa and Arsenal. How thin is the line between success and failure!

R D Bayley, League Secretary

NORTHERN PREMIER LEAGUE CHALLENGE CUP 1993-94

Preliminary Round

Great Harwood Town v Worksop Town	4-1	Radcliffe Borough v Curzon Ashton	1-2

First Round

Alfreton Town v Harrogate Town	4-2	Goole Town v Ashton United	2-2,3-5
Bamber Bridge v Spennymoor United	1-3	Curzon Ashton v Guiseley	0-1
Congleton Town v Farsley Celtic	1-1,0-3	Great Harwood Town v Netherfield	1-0
Mossley v Gretna	1-1,3-4	Lancaster City v Warrington Town	1-1,4-2
Workington v Eastwood Town	1-2		

Second Round

Accrington Stanley v Guiseley	6-4	Alfreton Town v Droylsden	0-1
Ashton United v Farsley Celtic	5-2	Barrow v Buxton	2-3
Boston United v Fleetwood Town	6-0	Bridlington Town v Bishop Auckland	4-7
Emley v Lancaster City	3-0	Frickley Athletic v Gretna	0-1
Gainsborough Trinity v Colwyn Bay	0-2	Horwich RMI v Great Harwood Town	1-1,1-2
Hyde United v Matlock Town	4-0	Eastwood Town v Knowsley United	1-1,0-2
Leek Town v Caernarfon Town	3-1	Morecambe v Chorley	5-2
Spennymoor United v Marine	3-0	Whitley Bay v Winsford United	2-0

Third Round

Boston United v Buxton	1-0	Accrington S. v Ashton Utd	2-2,0-0*(Acc on pens)*
Emley v Droylsden	1-0	Gretna v Bishop Auckland	1-1,2-2*(B Auck on pens)*
Hyde United v Colwyn Bay	2-1	Leek Town v Knowsley United	2-1
Morecambe v Great Harwood Town	0-2	Spennymoor United v Whitley Bay	2-1

Quarter Finals

Bishop Auckland v Spennymoor United	1-2	Emley v Accrington Stanley	0-0,1-3*(aet)*
Boston United v Leek Town	0-1	Hyde United v Great Harwood Town	5-2

Semi-Finals (Two Legs)

Hyde United v Leek Town	3-1,2-3	Spennymoor United v Accrington Stanley	3-1,4-1

Final *(at Harrogate Town FC)*: Spennymoor United 3, Hyde United 1

NORTHERN PREMIER LEAGUE PRESIDENT'S CUP 1993-94

First Round

Barrow v Warrington Town	3-1	Bridlington Town v Frickley Athletic	0-3
Curzon Ashton v Morecambe	0-3	Accrington Stanley v Gt Harwood Town	2-2,3-2
Marine v Guiseley	0-0,0-1	Hyde United v Knowsley United	3-1
Gretna v Leek Town	0-0,0-4	Winsford United v Ashton United	0-3

Quarter Finals

Barrow v Accrington Stanley	0-1	Guiseley v Frickley Athletic	3-0
Hyde United v Leek Town	0-0,0-5	Morecambe v Ashton United	1-1,3-4

Semi-Finals (Two Legs)

Guiseley v Winsford United	0-0,1-0	Leek Town v Accrington Stanley	3-1,1-1

Final: Guiseley 3, Leek Town 1; Leek Town 1, Guiseley 2 *(Guiseley won 5-2 on aggregate)*

NORTHERN PREMIER LEAGUE FIRST DIVISION CUP 1993-94

First Round

Caernarfon Town v Spennymoor United	1-4	Congleton Town v Radcliffe Borough	2-0
Netherfield v Curzon Ashton	0-0,2-3	Farsley Celtic v Mossley	4-0
Workington v Eastwood Town	2-1		

Second Round

Curzon Ashton v Alfreton Town	2-2,0-1	Ashton United v Workington	2-1
Bamber Bridge v Congleton Town	1-0	Great Harwood Town v Worksop Town	2-3
Goole Town v Harrogate Town	0-0,5-2	Lancaster City v Guiseley	1-1,1-1*(Guiseley on pens)*
Warrington Town v Spennymoor United	1-2	Farsley Celtic v Gretna	4-2

Quarter Finals

Ashton United v Spennymoor United	3-2	Bamber Bridge v Farsley Celtic	3-0
Worksop Town v Goole Town	0-0,0-1	Guiseley v Alfreton Town	1-2

Semi-Finals (Two Legs)

Bamber Bridge v Alfreton Town	4-3,0-0	Ashton United v Goole Town	0-1,2-0

Final: Ashton United 3, Goole Town 1

NORTHERN PREMIER LEAGUE PREMIER DIVISION ATTENDANCES 1993-94

HOME TEAM	1	2	3	4	5	6	7	8	9	10	11	12	13	14	15	16	17	18	19	20	21	22
1. Accrington	*	452	434	569	454	492	527	420	359	643	560	411	388	337	467	421	425	537	536	633	317	471
2. Barrow	972	*	491	810	513	434	1255	426	720	1063	665	954	1161	1268	792	862	826	935	1310	1185	1606	1275
3. B Auckland	366	235	*	325	150	290	319	211	257	251	247	235	270	402	320	291	303	269	235	230	338	270
4. Boston Utd	651	885	1149	*	935	648	1100	1028	1174	881	880	850	1602	884	920	902	741	1418	784	434	908	772
5. Bridlington	84	72	29	170	*	70	59	37	47	91	20	178	297	32	84	24	118	64	90	64	39	31
6. Buxton	454	373	202	456	279	*	319	290	309	340	186	267	208	252	400	266	634	374	349	251	161	352
7. Chorley	360	377	161	302	233	180	*	250	225	101	361	230	451	294	194	190	325	240	266	367	160	235
8. Colwyn Bay	207	220	144	115	101	152	145	*	131	206	161	106	210	104	159	110	158	280	102	256	119	179
9. Droylsden	386	336	169	157	115	87	266	237	*	475	133	108	255	227	313	300	256	336	272	138	237	303
10. Emley	684	164	346	433	310	173	305	153	312	*	257	701	330	168	317	204	289	334	184	329	336	337
11. Fleetwood	151	216	148	255	289	157	157	135	196	190	*	150	374	181	120	75	237	366	156	268	187	153
12. Frickley	272	256	208	257	475	238	256	202	226	256	276	*	297	199	206	193	213	226	254	280	183	244
13. Gainsboro.	563	474	431	1421	626	418	514	380	409	586	336	828	*	383	378	320	486	375	466	542	370	415
14. Horwich	185	232	158	243	258	159	363	148	160	151	153	352	158	*	168	96	163	264	207	213	151	185
15. Hyde	401	447	242	379	222	352	413	325	467	255	245	289	249	291	*	294	434	326	269	325	297	319
16. Knowsley	260	249	124	73	151	178	132	111	103	81	112	75	73	168	145	*	169	396	47	102	116	145
17. Leek	419	701	544	409	396	573	549	364	476	515	480	622	443	447	324	349	*	1030	448	547	452	448
18. Marine	636	503	383	382	489	317	417	674	525	435	337	340	381	377	474	551	361	*	345	537	381	339
19. Matlock	428	400	298	658	490	406	459	445	392	426	354	436	435	385	422	357	531	434	*	237	320	264
20. Morecambe	311	1423	402	306	301	319	340	413	461	319	362	410	235	234	274	231	456	412	359	*	348	407
21. Whitley Bay	250	264	343	346	207	201	204	134	202	240	223	196	226	202	271	200	246	276	170	303	*	199
22. Winsford	224	560	217	247	123	154	270	372	313	244	173	243	173	249	279	222	282	194	222	206	251	*

FIRST DIVISION ATTENDANCE CHART 1993-94

HOME TEAM	1	2	3	4	5	6	7	8	9	10	11	12	13	14	15	16	17	18	19	20	21
1. Alfreton	*	139	148	111	128	100	218	113	107	123	114	256	100	105	145	123	172	171	141	137	178
2. Ashton Utd	304	*	312	188	302	487	318	285	271	320	310	560	315	275	545	307	310	489	261	293	269
3. Bamber B.	370	480	*	435	403	348	214	343	264	629	304	502	281	461	387	350	403	576	456	311	333
4. Caernarfon	65	201	80	*	118	109	65	71	69	100	59	158	78	74	196	72	78	97	101	91	87
5. Congleton	71	105	149	102	*	89	103	109	113	126	123	230	127	172	134	131	85	122	175	185	121
6. Curzon Ash.	144	450	123	100	132	*	118	80	124	140	153	115	105	122	257	83	143	141	136	197	103
7. Eastwood T.	247	114	103	91	115	77	*	94		111	90	118	84	125	111	78	124	142	126	103	189
8. Farsley	100	269	129	115	91	119	67	*	112	174	129	459	156	89	131	79	72	112	159	87	186
9. Goole T.	110	185	102	145	148	135	146	219	*	178	160	238	182	172	195	146	130	251	145	101	230
10. Gt Harwood	148	176	176	152	125	83	168	152	128	*	80	296	146	148	147	148	114	138	126	315	100
11. Gretna	106	94	115	90	103	126	120	127	87	84	*	100	75	94	101	160	85	187	64	201	74
12. Guiseley	283	705	405	491	488	393	695	674	524	291	525	*	637	408	420	487	489	624	452	505	471
13. Harrogate	185	250	243	194	217	197	231	344	212	205	169	635	*	259	204	255	195	210	197	258	243
14. Lancaster	182	163	214	157	139	111	115	119	114	159	215	123	102	*	182	186	125	171	170	158	137
15. Mossley	191	335	225	206	154	252	203	190	161	186	185	363	238	191	*	176	189	245	212	201	215
16. Netherfield	126	121	156	177	104	114	147	117	107	110	147	308	95	172	135	*	111	145	168	363	181
17. Radcliffe	108	132	143	94	72	85	92	138	72	121	72	151	126	70	146	129	*	130	102	89	125
18. Spennymoor	341	914	304	316	247	308	326	126	207	363	223	309	206	367	308	252	268	*	231	449	367
19. Warrington	162	285	203	216	274	256	186	169	135	287	201	248	208	168	141	236	236	248	*	201	220
20. Workington	140	235	289	245	266	149	202	228	201	193	422	181	198	234	244	278	254	216	249	*	166
21. Worksop	383	320	226	233	190	250	308	225	285	241	232	310	275	213	378	230	192	226	175	230	*

'MAIL ON SUNDAY' MANAGER OF THE MONTH AWARDS

Month	Premier Player	Premier Manager	Div. 1 Player	Div. 1 Manager
Sept.	Steve Bunter (Droylsden)	Bryn Jones (Colwyn B.)	Tim Hotte (Goole)	Tony Hesketh (Netherfield)
Oct.	Stacy Reed (Matlock)	Ronnie Glavin (Frick.)	Steve Learoyd (H'gate)	Ray McHale (Guiseley)
Nov.	Simon Grayson (Gainsb.)	Ronnie Glavin (Frick.)	Danny Campbell (Worksop)	Kevin Keelan (Ashton)
Dec.	Neil Grayson (Boston)	Tony Lee (Bishop A.)	Mark Dobie (Gretna)	Matty Pearson (S'moor)
Jan.	John Brady (Barrow)	Neil Baker (Leek)	Stuart Diggle (Lanc.)	Matty Pearson (S'moor)
Feb.	Phil Hutchinson (Acc'ton)	Leighton James (M'cambe)	Ian Monk (Ashton)	Ray McHale (Guiseley)
Mar.	Tony McDonald (Chorley)	Pete O'Brien (Hyde)	Paul Bottomley (Guiseley)	Ray McHale (Guiseley)
Apr.	Jeremy Smith (Bridlington)	Tony Lee (Bishop A.)	Derek Townley (Gretna)	Matty Pearson (S'moor)

FIVE GOALS IN A GAME:

Andy Green for Knowsley v Salford City (FA Cup, 15/9/93)
David Woodcock for Bishop Auckland at Bridlington Town (League Cup, 11/12/93)
Kenny Clark for Worksop Town against Farsley Celtic (7/5/94)
Andy Whittaker for Netherfield at Farsley Celtic (4/12/93)
Tony Carroll for Radcliffe Borough at Harrogate Town (5/3/94).

FOUR GOALS IN A GAME:

Gary Brook for Gainsborough Trinity against Eastwood Town (FA Trophy, 18/9/93)
Neil Doherty for Barrow against Harrogate Town (FA Cup, 25/9/93)
Stacy Reed for Matlock Town against Fleetwood Town (30/10/93)
Brian Ross for Marine at Chorley (4/12/93)
Andy Whittaker for Netherfield at Bishop Auckland (FA Cup, 11/9/93).
Gary Dalgleish for Bamber Bridge against Mossley (5/10/93)
Andy Shaw for Spennymoor against Goole Town (20/10/93)

SEQUENCES:

Consecutive wins: 12 - Leek Town (Division One: 15 - Guiseley)
Consecutive games without defeat: 16 - Leek Town (Division One: 16 - Guiseley & Spennymoor)
Consecutive defeats: 10 - Bridlington Town (Division One: 7 - Gretna)
Consecutive games without a win: 18 - Bridlington Town (Division One: 10 - Caernarfon & Eastwood)

N.P.L. ATTENDANCE ANALYSIS 1993-94

PREMIER DIVISION Club	Ave 92-93	Ave 93-94	% Change	Highest Crowd	Low
Accrington Stanley	581	471	-18.9	643 v Emley	317
Barrow	1,241	930	-25.1	1,606 v Whitley Bay	426
Bishop Auckland	279	277	-0.7	402 v Horwich RMI	150
Boston United	1,041	928	-10.9	1,602 v Gainsborough Trinity	434
Bridlington Town	238	81	-66.0	297 v Gainsborough Trinity	20
Buxton	351	320	-8.8	634 v Leek Town	161
Chorley	244	259	+6.1	451 v Gainsborough Trinity	101
Colwyn Bay	186	160	-14.0	280 v Marine	101
Droylsden	260	241	-7.3	475 v Emley	87
Emley	350	320	-8.6	701 v Frickley Athletic	153
Fleetwood Town	194	195	+0.5	374 v Gainsborough Trinity	75
Frickley Athletic	227	248	+9.3	475 v Bridlington Town	183
Gainsborough Trinity	400	512	+28.0	1,421 v Boston United	320
Horwich RMI	219	198	-9.6	363 v Chorley	96
Hyde United	358	326	-8.9	467 v Droylsden	222
Knowsley United	106	143	+34.9	396 v Marine	47
Leek Town	436	502	+15.1	1,030 v Marine	324
Marine	460	437	-5.0	674 v Colwyn Bay	317
Matlock Town	364	408	+12.1	658 v Boston United	237
Morecambe	452	393	-13.1	1,423 v Barrow	231
Whitley Bay	227	233	+2.6	346 v Boston United	134
Winsford United	442	256	-42.1	560 v Barrow	123

DIVISION ONE Club	Ave 92-93	Ave 93-94	% Change	Highest Crowd	Low
Alfreton Town	119	139	+16.8	256 v Guiseley	100
Ashton United	268	336	+25.4	560 v Guiseley	188
Bamber Bridge	n/k	393	n/k	629 v Great Harwood Town	214
Caernarfon Town	98	98		201 v Ashton United	59
Congleton Town	143	129	-9.8	230 v Guiseley	71
Curzon Ashton	140	144	+2.9	450 v Ashton United	80
Eastwood Town	135	118	-12.6	247 v Alfreton Town	77
Farsley Celtic	158	142	-10.1	459 v Guiseley	67
Goole Town	227	166	-26.9	251 v Spennymoor United	101
Great Harwood Town	177	153	-13.6	315 v Workington	80
Gretna	138	110	-25.5	201 v Workington	64
Guiseley	493	498	+1.0	705 v Ashton United	283
Harrogate Town	229	245	+7.0	635 v Guiseley	169
Lancaster City	101	154	+52.5	215 v Gretna	102
Mossley	331	211	-26.3	363 v Guiseley	154
Netherfield	161	155	-3.7	363 v Workington	95
Radcliffe Borough	105	112	+6.7	151 v Guiseley	70
Spennymoor United	n/k	322	n/k	914 v Ashton United	126
Warrington Town	210	214	+1.9	287 v Great Harwood Town	135
Workington	183	230	+25.7	422 v Gretna	140
Worksop Town	311	256	-17.7	383 v Alfreton Town	175

Left: *Mark Dobie of Gretna receives the December 'Mail on Sunday' Division One Player-of-the-Month award from Warrington Town secretary Graham Ost before the FA Trophy tie between the two clubs. See page 241 for a complete list of all the 'Mail on Sunday' awards for 1993-94.*

Photo - Alan Watson.

PREMIER DIVISION 1993-94

	P	W	D	L	F	A	PTS
Marine	42	27	9	6	106	62	90
Leek Town	42	27	8	7	79	50	89
Boston United	42	23	9	10	90	43	78
Bishop Auckland	42	25	9	10	73	58	78
Frickley Athletic	42	21	12	9	90	51	75
Colwyn Bay	42	18	14	10	74	51	68
Morecambe	42	20	7	15	90	56	67
Barrow	42	18	10	14	59	51	64
Hyde United	42	17	10	15	80	71	61
Chorley	42	17	10	15	70	67	61
Whitley Bay	42	17	9	16	61	72	60
Gainsborough Trin.	42	15	11	16	64	66	56
Emley	42	12	16	14	63	71	52
Matlock Town	42	13	12	17	71	76	51
Buxton	42	13	10	19	67	73	49
Accrington Stanley	42	14	7	21	63	85	49
Droylsden	42	11	14	17	57	82	47
Knowsley United	42	11	11	20	52	66	44
Winsford United	42	9	11	22	50	74	38
Horwich RMI	42	8	12	22	50	75	*35
Bridlington Town	42	7	10	25	41	91	***28
Fleetwood Town	42	7	7	28	55	114	28

* - 1 point deducted

TOP SCORERS

	Lge	Cup	Tot
Darren Twigg (Leek Town)	24	16	40
Andy Hayward (Frickley Ath.)	26	8	34
Steve Jones (Colwyn Bay)	21	13	34
Tony McDonald (Chorley)	31	2	33
Chris Camden (Marine)	26	6	32
Jim McCluskie (Morecambe)	21	11	32
Brian Ross (Marine)	26	3	29
Neil Grayson (Boston Utd)	25	4	29

Below: *Marine pictured with the championship trophy before they completed a 'double' by beating GMVC side Southport 2-1 in the Liverpool Senior Cup final at Goodison Park. Back Row (L/R): Roly Howard (Manager), Keith Proctor, Brian Ross, Chris Camden, Andy Draper, Kevin O'Brien, Graham Rowlands, Paul Dawson, Neil Hansen, Roger Patience (Coach). Front: Paul McNally, Tony Ward, Sean Lundon, John Roche, Mascot, John Gautrey, Eddie Murray, Ian Baines, John Bradshaw (Physio).*

Photo - Liverpool Post & Echo.

RESULT CHART 1993-94

HOME TEAM	1	2	3	4	5	6	7	8	9	10	11	12	13	14	15	16	17	18	19	20	21	22
1. Accrington	*	0-5	1-2	1-3	2-1	3-1	1-1	5-5	2-0	1-2	3-1	2-4	2-4	1-0	4-1	2-1	0-3	0-2	0-2	3-2	0-1	4-2
2. Barrow	1-0	*	0-2	0-2	4-0	4-0	3-1	0-2	2-2	1-2	1-1	1-3	1-1	0-2	1-4	2-1	3-0	2-1	2-1	1-2	1-0	1-1
3. Bishop Auck.	0-0	2-1	*	1-1	1-1	2-1	3-1	3-2	3-1	2-1	3-2	3-1	1-0	1-0	1-2	1-2	2-2	1-4	2-0	2-1	2-0	4-2
4. Boston Utd	0-1	0-0	1-2	*	5-0	2-2	4-0	6-1	2-0	4-0	4-1	2-2	6-1	2-1	3-1	4-1	3-3	4-2	2-0	2-0	0-1	1-1
5. Bridlington	1-1	1-2	0-4	0-1	*	2-3	0-1	2-0	1-1	1-2	4-1	0-3	0-0	0-2	4-0	0-1	1-1	1-2	2-2	0-4	1-1	3-2
6. Buxton	3-0	3-0	0-2	0-1	3-1	*	2-3	1-0	0-3	2-2	4-1	1-1	2-5	4-4	3-0	3-1	1-2	2-2	4-1	0-2	5-4	1-0
7. Chorley	4-1	3-0	2-5	2-0	1-2	0-0	*	2-2	6-1	1-1	5-2	2-1	1-1	1-1	4-2	4-1	3-1	0-4	1-2	2-2	0-2	1-0
8. Colwyn Bay	2-2	2-3	6-0	1-1	5-0	3-1	2-0	*	4-0	1-0	2-2	1-1	1-2	1-0	2-1	0-0	0-1	0-0	3-0	2-3	1-0	0-0
9. Droylsden	2-1	0-0	4-2	0-2	1-0	2-1	3-1	0-0	*	3-3	1-1	2-2	1-4	1-2	3-3	2-1	1-3	2-0	2-4	0-3	3-2	0-0
10. Emley	4-2	0-0	2-2	1-1	1-1	1-4	0-3	3-3	1-1	*	3-2	0-0	0-2	1-1	2-2	2-1	1-1	6-2	4-4	2-0	3-1	2-0
11. Fleetwood	1-2	2-3	1-2	1-3	1-0	1-2	1-2	0-3	1-1	2-2	*	1-1	1-2	2-3	1-0	0-3	2-1	2-3	3-1	0-6	0-1	1-3
12. Frickley	2-0	0-0	5-0	0-1	5-0	3-1	5-0	0-1	3-0	1-0	2-2	*	1-0	5-2	4-1	1-0	1-3	5-2	1-0	3-3	6-1	2-2
13. Gainsboro.	0-1	2-1	0-0	2-2	3-1	1-1	1-1	0-1	1-2	2-0	5-1	2-3	*	4-0	1-1	2-1	3-5	1-2	2-2	0-1	1-3	3-1
14. Horwich	2-4	0-2	2-1	0-5	0-1	1-0	2-2	2-3	2-2	1-1	2-3	1-1	1-2	*	0-1	3-0	0-1	3-5	1-1	1-3	1-1	0-2
15. Hyde Utd	1-4	2-1	1-1	2-1	6-1	1-1	2-1	1-2	4-2	2-1	5-2	4-0	4-0	1-1	*	0-0	5-0	1-3	1-0	2-3	6-0	1-1
16. Knowsley	0-0	2-0	1-1	1-2	0-0	1-1	0-1	1-5	2-0	2-0	0-1	0-2	1-1	1-0	2-1	*	0-0	1-1	5-1	2-3	1-1	3-1
17. Leek Town	2-1	0-0	2-1	2-1	0-2	2-1	1-0	2-0	4-2	2-0	3-0	1-0	2-0	2-0	3-0	3-2	*	1-4	2-1	2-0	2-1	3-1
18. Marine	2-1	2-2	3-1	3-2	3-0	1-0	4-1	1-1	2-1	4-1	4-0	4-1	3-0	1-1	1-1	3-2	3-2	*	0-0	4-2	6-3	2-2
19. Matlock	3-3	0-2	0-2	2-1	3-0	1-1	2-1	3-1	1-1	2-3	6-1	1-5	5-2	1-0	1-2	2-2	3-3	1-2	*	3-1	1-1	3-0
20. Morecambe	5-0	1-2	0-2	1-2	7-1	4-1	0-1	1-1	1-2	1-0	8-0	1-2	3-0	1-1	2-3	5-0	0-0	3-2	2-2	*	0-0	1-0
21. Whitley Bay	4-1	0-2	2-1	2-1	4-3	1-0	0-0	1-1	1-1	2-0	4-3	2-2	0-1	3-1	2-0	1-3	0-4	0-4	3-0	3-1	*	2-1
22. Winsford	3-1	1-2	0-0	1-0	2-2	2-1	0-4	0-1	4-1	1-3	1-4	1-0	0-0	1-3	2-2	4-3	1-2	2-3	0-3	0-1	2-0	*

1968 **ACCRINGTON STANLEY** Reds

ACCRINGTON STANLEY

The Accrington Stanley side that took on Fleetwood Town on February 26th.

Chairman: John S Alty **President:** J C Prescott/ J Hudson.
Secretary: Philip Terry, 8 Princess Street, Colne, Lancs BB8 9AN (0286 866768).
Manager: Eric Whalley **Asst Manager:** Neil Hanson **Physio:** Alan Crane
Coach: Tony Keyes. **Press Officer:** John S Alty (061 339 2487)
Commercial Advisor: John de Maine
Ground: Crown Ground, off Livingstone Road, Accrington (0254 383235).
Directions: Arriving on A680 from Clayton-le-Moors Livingstone Road is on left 50 yds past Crown Hotel. From M62/M66, through town centre on A680 - Livingstone Road 500 yds on right after Victoria Hospital. One and a half miles from Accrington (BR).
Capacity: 2,420 **Cover:** 1,650 **Seats:** 200 **Floodlights:** Yes **Metal Badges:** Yes
Club Shop: Yes, selling replica kits, sweaters, t-shirts, videos, photos and general souvenirs. Contact Keith Morton (0282 831144).
Colours: Red/white/red **Change colours:** All sky
Previous Leagues: Lancs Combination 70-78/ Cheshire County 78-82/ North West Counties 82-87.
Midweek home matchday: Wednesday **Reserve Team's League:** North West Alliance.
Sponsors: Hollands Pies, Baxenden.
Record Attendance: 2,096 v Fleetwood Town, FA Cup 4th Qualifying Rd 27/10/90 *(10,081 v Crewe Alexandra, F.A. Cup Second Round Proper 5/12/92 - played at Ewood Park, Blackburn).*
Best FA Cup season: Second Rd Proper 92-93 (lost 1-6 at home to Crewe Alexandra).
League clubs defeated in FA Cup: None.
Record win: 9-0 v Ashton Town, Lancashire Combination 75-76.
Record defeat: 1-9 v Runcorn (A), F.A. Cup 2nd Qualifying Rd replay 85-86.
Record Fees - Paid: £2,250 for Bernie Hughes (Droylsen 90-91).
Received: £10,000 for Martin Clark (Crewe A. 92-93).
Players progressing to Football League: David Hargreaves (Blackburn Rovers 1977), Ian Blackstone (York City), Gus Wilson (Crewe), Glen Johnstone (Preston), Darren Lyons (Bury), Martin Clark (Crewe 92-93), Mark Wright (Wigan 93-94).
Clubhouse: Open two nights and matchdays. Private functions. Well stocked tea bar in ground.
Club Record Scorer: David Hargreaves 318
Club Record Appearances: David Hargreaves 310.
93-94 Captain: Charlie Cooper.
93-94 P.o.Y.: Ashley Hoskin.
93-94 Top scorer: Paul Beck.
Local Press: Accrington Observer (0254 871444), Lancashire Evening Telegraph (0254 63588).
Local Radio Stations: Radio Lancashire, Red Rose Radio.
Newsline: 0898 122 921.
Honours: North West Counties Lg R-up 86-87, Cheshire County Lg Div 2 80-81 (R-up 79-80), Lancs Combination 73-74 77-78 (R-up 71-72 75-76, Lg Cup 71-72 72-73 73-74 76-77), George Watson Trophy 71-72 73-74 74-75, John Duckworth Trophy 85-86, Lancs Junior Cup (now ATS Trophy) R-up 85-86, FA Trophy 1st Rd 72-73 78-79 92-93, Lancs under-18 Yth Cup 89-90.

PROGRAMME DETAILS
Pages: 32 **Price:** £1
Editor: Secretary/David Ellis.
(0282 866768 - David Ellis)

ACCRINGTON's 1993-94 CAMPAIGN

Date	Opponents	Comp.	Res	Gate	Goalscorers
21/08	Hyde United	NPL	4-1	401	Beck(2), Johnston, Moss
25/08	**MORECAMBE**	NPL	3-2	644	Burns(2), B Hughes
28/08	**MATLOCK TOWN**	NPL	0-2	536	
30/08	Knowsley United	NPL	0-0	209	
04/09	Leek Town	NPL	1-2	419	Williams
08/09	**HORWICH R.M.I.**	NPL	1-0	337	Lutkevitch
11/09	**MARINE**	NPL	0-2	537	
18/09	**BOSTON UNITED**	NPL	1-3	569	Hoskin
21/09	Droylsden	NPL	1-2	396	Beck
25/09	Fleetwood Town	NPL	2-1	213	Hoskin(2)
29/09	**Gt HARWOOD T.**	PC1	2-2	539	Moss, Beck
02/10	**BISHOP AUCKLAND**	NPL	1-2	434	Lutkevitch
05/10	Barrow	NPL	0-1	972	
09/10	Marine	NPL	1-2	636	Lutkevitch
12/10	**WHITLEY BAY**	NPL	0-1	317	
16/10	**FRICKLEY ATH.**	NPL	2-4	411	Cooper, Lutkevitch
19/10	Chorley	NPL	1-4	360	Lutkevitch
23/10	Altrincham	FAC4q	2-1	956	Beck(2)
30/10	Gt Harwood Town	PC1r	3-2	483	B Hughes(3)
03/11	**BARROW**	NPL	0-5	452	
06/11	Buxton	NPL	0-3	454	
14/11	**SCUNTHORPE UTD**	FAC1	2-3	5,879	Wood, Connor *(played at Burnley FC)*
20/11	**BRIDLINGTON T.**	NPL	2-1	454	Lutkevitch, Beck
27/11	Hyde United	FAT3q	0-2	355	
01/12	Winsford United	NPL	1-3	224	Grimshaw
04/12	Colwyn Bay	NPL	2-2	207	Gayle(2)
07/12	Barrow	PC2	1-0	522	Williams
11/12	**GUISELEY**	NPLC2	6-4	452	Byron, Rogerson, Moss, Gayle(3)
27/12	Emley	NPL	2-4	684	Byron, Gayle
01/01	**EMLEY**	NPL	1-2	643	Moss
08/01	**GAINSBOROUGH Tr.**	NPL	2-4	388	Cooper, Hoskin
19/01	**NELSON**	ATS2	4-1	340	Beck, Senior, Gayle, Hoskin
22/01	**LEEK TOWN**	NPL	0-3	425	
29/01	**KNOWSLEY UTD**	NPL	2-1	421	Quick, Beck
02/02	**ASHTON UNITED**	NPLC3	2-2	317	Hutchinson, Gayle
05/02	Bishop Auckland	NPL	0-0	366	
09/02	**SOUTHPORT**	ATS3	0-1	449	
12/02	**BUXTON**	NPL	3-1	492	Hutchinson(3)
19/02	Matlock Town	NPL	3-3	428	Beck, Hutchinson(2)
21/02	Ashton United	NPLC3r	0-0	205	*(abandoned after 45 minutes)*
26/02	**FLEETWOOD TOWN**	NPL	3-1	560	Williams, Kirkham, Hutchinson
01/03	Leek Town	PCsf(1)	1-3	381	Kirkham
05/03	Whitley Bay	NPL	1-4	250	Kirkham
07/03	Ashton United	NPLC3r	0-0	332	*(Accrington won 5-4 on penalties)*
12/03	**DROYLSDEN**	NPL	2-0	359	Kirkham, Hoskin
14/03	Emley	NPLCqf	0-0	273	
19/03	**WINSFORD UNITED**	NPL	4-2	471	Hutchinson(2), Quick, Williams
23/03	**EMLEY**	NPLCsfr	3-1	309	Hoskin, Hutchinson(2)
26/03	Frickley Athletic	NPL	0-2	272	
28/03	Bridlington Town	NPL	1-1	84	Beck
31/03	**LEEK TOWN**	PCsf(2)	1-1	313	Hoskin
02/04	**COLWYN BAY**	NPL	5-5	420	Hoskin(3), Senior, Lampkin
04/04	Gainsborough Trin.	NPL	1-0	563	Lutkevitch
06/04	Spennymoor Utd	NPLCsf(1)	1-3	403	Hoskin
13/04	**SPENNYMOOR UTD**	NPLCsf(2)	1-2	363	Hutchinson
16/04	**HYDE UNITED**	NPL	4-1	467	Beck(3), Hutchinson
23/04	Horwich RMI	NPL	4-2	185	Beck(2), Hoskin, Procter
30/04	Boston United	NPL	1-0	651	Beck
05/05	Morecambe	NPL	0-5	311	
07/05	**CHORLEY**	NPL	1-1	527	Procter

Key: NPL: Northern Premier League Premier Division, NPLC: Northern Premier League Cup, PC: (Northern Premier League) Presidents Cup, FAC: F.A. Cup, FAT: F.A. Trophy, ATS: Lancashire ATS Challenge Trophy. Numbers after cup competitions denote rounds (r: replay, qf: Quarter-Final, sf: Semi-Final, f: Final. Numbers in brackets indicate legs, i.e. (1): 1st leg).
Home fixtures are denoted by bold capitals, away matches by lower case. (p): penalty, og: Own goal.

SQUAD MEMBERS *(previous clubs listed in chronological order)*

GOALKEEPERS: John Armfield *(Man Utd, Blackpool, Fleetwood, Wren Rovers, Runcorn, Lancaster, Blackpool Rovers, Barrow)*

DEFENDERS: Steve Lampkin *(Bradford C., Oswestry, Colne D., Chorley, Rossendale)*, **Neil Peters** *(Irlam, Horwich, Witton, Chorley, Hyde, Horwich, Winsford)*, **Shaun Weatherhead** *(Huddersfield, York)*, **Eddie Johnston** *(South Liverpool, Bangor)*, **Chris Wood** *(Grove Utd)*, **Terry Williams** *(Oldham Ath., Bramhall, Grove Utd)*, **R Procter** *(Chorley, Clitheroe)*, **Darren Quick** *(Blackpool, Salford)*, **R Wilson** *(Bradford City)*, **Paul Moss** *(Darwen, Stalybridge, Winsford, Horwich, Chorley, Horwich)*, **Paul Byron** *(Barrow, Blackburn, Hartlepool, Southport, Fleetwood, Bamber Bridge, Morecambe)*

MIDFIELD: Rob Mulloy *(Colne Dynamoes, Nelson)*, **Chris Grimshaw** *(Burnleyy, Crewe, Bury, Accrington, Colne Dynamoes, Accrington, Rossendale, Fleetwood, Haslingden)*, **Charlie Cooper** *(Huddersfield, Horwich, Chorley, Horwich, Chorley, Emley)*, **Jon Senior** *(Bolton, Horwich, Northwich, Horwich, Southport)*, **Lee Rogerson** *(Clitheroe, Wigan Ath., Morecambe, Great Harwood, Chorley, Clitheroe)*

FORWARDS: Paul Beck *(Darwen, Accrington, Rossendale, Clitheroe, Rossendale)*, **Paul Hutchinson** *(Tempest Utd)*, **Andy Gayle** *(Oldham A., Crewe, Bury, Horwich, Naxaar Lions(Malta), Horwich, Stalybridge)*, **Mike Lutkevitch** *(Curzon Ashton, Hyde, Witton, Accrington, Stalybridge)*, **Ashley Hoskin** *(Burnley, Wrexham, Burnley Bank Hall)*, **John Harris** *(Bacup)*

Founded: 1901

BARROW

Nickname: Bluebirds

The old stand at Holker Street, which was sadly demolished in the summer of 1994.

Chairman: J Barker **President:** W A McCullough.
Secretary: Pat Brewer, c/o The Club (below)(0229 820316).
Manager: Tony Hesketh **Coach:** Peter Farrell/ Mick Cloudsdale.
Physio: N/A **Press Officer:** Phil Yelland (031 445 1010)
Ground: Holker Street Ground, Wilkie Rd, Barrow-in-Furness, Cumbria LA14 5UH (0229 820346/823839). Commercial Office: 102 Scott Str., Barrow-in-Furness (0229 823061 - Manager Mrs Linda Barker).
Directions: M6 to junction 36, A590 to Barrow, enter Barrow on Park Road and after about 2 miles turn left into Wilkie Rd - ground on right.
Capacity: 5,500 **Cover:** 1,200 **Seats:** **Floodlights:** Yes **Metal Badges:** Yes
Club Shop: Yes - on popular side of ground.
Colours: White/royal/royal **Change colours:** Purple/white/white.
Previous Leagues: Lancs Combination 01-21/ Football League 21-72 / Northern Premier 72-79 83-84 86-89/ GMV Conference 79-83 84-86 89-92.
Previous Grounds: The Strawberry & Little Park, Roose.
Midweek home matchday: Tuesday **Reserve Team's League:** Furness Premier Lge.
Record Attendance: 16,840 v Swansea Town, FA Cup Third Round 1954. For non-League game: 6,002 v Enfield, FA Trophy Semi-Final, April 1988.
Best FA Cup season: Third Round Proper on nine occasions including once as a non-League club (90-91, lost 0-1 at Bolton Wanderers).
Record win: 12-0 v Cleator, FA Cup 1920.
Record defeat: 1-10 v Hartlepools United, Football League Division Four 1959.
Record Fees - Paid: £9,000 for Andy Whittaker (Ashton United, July 1994).
Received: £40,000 for Kenny Lowe (Barnet, January 1991).
Players progressing to Football League: Ian McDonald, Neil McDonald, John Laisby, Barry Diamond, Frank Gamble, Barry Knowles, Glen Skivington, Paul Byron, Levi Edwards, Kenny Lowe, Mark Dobie, Tony Rigby, Neil Doherty.
Clubhouse: Barrow Sports & Leisure centre next to ground (0229 823839). Snack bars around ground.
Club Record Goalscorer: Colin Cowperthwaite 282 (Dec '77-Dec '92)
Club Record Appearances: Colin Cowperthwaite 704
93-94 Captain: Barry Butler.
93-94 P.o.Y.: Ian Senior/ Barry Butler/ Tony Edwards (various awards).
93-94 Top scorer: John Brady 21.
Sponsors: Prudential.
Local Press: North West Evening Mail (0229 821835), Barrow & West Cumberland Advertiser (0229 832032).
Local Radio Stations: BBC Radio Furness, BBC Radio Cumbria, Red Rose, Bay Radio.
Newsline: 0898 888 620.
Honours: FA Trophy 89-90 (SF 87-88), Northern Premier League 83-84 88-89 (League Cup Runners-up 87-88, League Shield 84-85), Bord Lord Trophy Runners-up 90-91, Cumbrian Cup 82-83 83-84 (Runners-up 84-85), Lancs Floodlit Cup Runners-up 86-87, Lancs Senior Cup 54-55 (Runners-up 51-52 65-66 66-67 69-70), Lancs Challenge Trophy 48-49(reserves) 80-81 (Runners-up 81-82 84-85), Lancs Combination 20-21 (Runners-up 13-14, Div 2 Runners-up 04-05 10-11).

PROGRAMME DETAILS:
Pages: 32 **Price:** £1
Editor: D Gardner

BARROW's 1993-94 CAMPAIGN

Date	Opponents	Comp.	Res	Gate	Goalscorers
21/08	Winsford United	NPL	2-1	560	Oldroyd, Brady
24/08	**HORWICH R.M.I.**	NPL	0-2	1,268	
28/08	**EMLEY**	NPL	1-2	1,063	Watt
30/08	Marine	NPL	2-2	503	Brady(2)
04/09	Hyde United	NPL	1-2	447	Doherty
07/09	**KNOWSLEY UTD**	NPL	2-1	862	Doherty, Brady
11/09	**GUISBOROUGH T.**	FAC1q	3-1	826	Oldroyd, Brady(2)
15/09	Fleetwood Town	NPL	3-2	213	Brady(2), Higginbotham
18/09	Frickley Athletic	NPL	0-0	256	
21/09	**MORECAMBE**	NPL	1-2	1,185	Brady
25/09	**HARROGATE TOWN**	FAC2q	6-1	998	Doherty(4), Butler, Watt
29/09	Bishop Auckland	NPL	1-2	235	Butler
02/10	**WARRINGTON TOWN**	PC1	3-1	642	Brady(2), Nugent
05/10	**ACCRINGTON STAN.**	NPL	1-0	972	Addenbrook
09/10	Gretna	FAC3q	1-2	732	Doherty
16/10	**LEEK TOWN**	NPL	3-0	826	Oldroyd, Watt(2)
19/10	Whitley Bay	NPL	2-0	264	Watt(2)
23/10	Horwich RMI	NPL	2-0	232	Oldroyd, Higginbotham
26/10	**CHORLEY**	NPL	3-1	1,255	Doherty, Watt, Higginbotham
30/10	Knowsley United	NPL	0-2	249	
03/11	Accrington Stanley	NPL	5-0	452	Brady(3), Higginbotham, Addenbrook
06/11	**MATLOCK TOWN**	NPL	2-1	1,310	Butler, Higginbotham
13/11	**GAINSBOROUGH Tr.**	NPL	1-1	1,161	Rooney
20/11	Boston United	NPL	0-0	885	
27/11	**EMLEY**	FAT3q	2-2	1,020	Higginbotham, Oldroyd
29/11	Emley	FAT3q	1-2	408	Addenbrook
01/12	Blackpool Rovers	ATS1	2-1	72	Addenbrook, Doherty
04/12	Droylsden	NPL	0-0	336	
07/12	**ACCRINGTON STAN.**	PC2	0-1	522	
11/12	**BUXTON**	NPLC2	2-3	647	Brady, own-goal
18/12	Colwyn Bay	NPL	3-2	220	Doherty, Brady(2)
27/12	Morecambe	NPL	2-1	1,423	Parkin
01/01	**WHITLEY BAY**	NPL	1-0	1,606	Brady
03/01	**WINSFORD UTD**	NPL	1-1	1,275	Doherty
15/01	Buxton	NPL	0-3	373	
18/01	**HORWICH R.M.I.**	ATS2	1-2	387	Brady
29/01	**FRICKLEY ATH.**	NPL	1-3	954	Doherty
05/02	Gainsborough Trin.	NPL	1-2	474	Higginbotham
12/02	**BOSTON UNITED**	NPL	0-2	810	
19/02	**MARINE**	NPL	2-1	935	Chilton, Brady
05/03	**DROYSLDEN**	NPL	2-2	720	McMahon, Booth(og)
12/03	Bridlington Town	NPL	2-1	72	Watt(2)
19/03	**FLEETWOOD TOWN**	NPL	1-1	665	McMahon
26/03	Matlock Town	NPL	2-0	400	Higginbotham(2)
02/04	**HYDE UNITED**	NPL	1-4	792	McGarvey
04/04	Chorley	NPL	0-3	377	
09/04	**BISHOP AUCKLAND**	NPL	0-2	491	
16/04	**BUXTON**	NPL	4-0	434	Butler, Watt, Higginbotham, Hopper
23/04	Leek Town	NPL	0-0	701	
25/04	Emley	NPL	0-0	164	
30/04	**COLWYN BAY**	NPL	0-3	426	
07/05	**BRIDLINGTON TOWN**	NPL	4-0	513	Livingstone, Watt, Proctor, Brady

Key: NPL: Northern Premier League Premier Division, NPLC: Northern Premier League Cup, PC: Northern Premier League Presidents Cup, FAC: F.A. Cup, FAT: F.A. Trophy, ATS: Lancashire ATS Challenge Trophy. Numbers after cup competitions denote rounds (r: replay, qf: Quarter-Final, sf: Semi-Final, f: Final. Numbers in brackets indicate legs, i.e. (1): 1st leg).
Home fixtures are denoted by bold capitals, away matches by lower case. (p): penalty, og: Own goal.

SQUAD MEMBERS *(previous clubs listed in chronological order)*

GOALKEEPERS: Ian Senior *(Prestwich Heys, Stalybridge Celtic, Oldham Ath., Mossley, Bolton W., Radcliffe Boro., Rochdale, Horwich RMI, Mossley, Rossendale, Bury, Horwich RMI, Ashton Utd., Man. City, Altrincham, Witton Alb., Leek, Southport, Chorley, Buxton, Curzon Ashton, Accrington Stanley, Chorley, Droylsden, Chorley)*, **Darrek Hoyland** *(Youth Team).*

DEFENDERS: Tony Edwards *(Liverpool, Skelmersdale Utd., Witton Alb., Marine, Runcova, Altrincham)*, **Andy Rooney** *(Everton, Crewe, Runcorn, Altrincham, Marine)*, **Glen Skivington** *(Barrow, Derby, Southend)*, **Steve McMahon** *(QPR, Swansea, Carlisle Utd.)*, **Mike Brown** *(Barrow, Millom)*, **Tim Parkin** *(Blackburn R., Malmo(Swe), Almondsbury, Bristol R., Swindon, Port Vale, Darlington)*, **Tony Chilton** *(Sunderland, Burnley, Whitley Bay, Hartlepool, Workington, Gretna, Barrow, Newcastle Blue Star, Barrow, Altrincham, Gateshead, Gretna).*

MIDFIELD: David Hamilton *(Sunderland, Blackburn R., Wigan, Chester, Burnley, Chorley)*, **Darren Oldroyd** *(Everton, Wolves, Southport, Fleetwood)*, **Kevin Proctor** *(Barrow, Holker OB, Dalton Utd.)*, **Colin McArthur** *(Glaxo, Netherfield, Glaxo)*, **Steve Livingstone** *(Vickers SC)*, **Barry Butler** *(Atherton LR, Chester)*

FORWARDS: John Brady *(Preston, Burscough, Southport, Altrincham, Southport, Buxton, Chorley, Altrincham)*, **Stuart Mason** *(Barrow, Ulverston R.)*, **Paul Higginbotham** *(Altrincham, Witton Alb., Flixton, Witton Alb., Glossop, Stalybridge C.)*, **Dave Addenbrook** *(Barrow Wanderers, Crooklands Casuals)*, **Steve Watt** *(Vickers SC, Barrow, Netherfield)*, **Scott McGarvey** *(Man. Utd., Portsmouth, Carlisle Utd., Grimsby, Bristol C., Oldham Ath., Paris FC., Derry City, Witton Alb.).*

Formed: 1886

BISHOP AUCKLAND

Bishops

George Adams (left) dances with Grantham's Tim Preece during the Second Round FA Trophy tie.
Photo - Dave West.

Chairman: S Newcomb **Vice-Chairman:** C Backhouse **President:** W B Botcherby
Secretary: N Postma, 18 Wynyard Grove, Bishop Auckland DL14 8RF (0388 608330).
Manager: Tony Lee **Asst Mgr:** Tony Boylan **Coach:**
Press Officer: Secretary **Physio:** J Moore. **Commercial Manager:** Tony Lee.
Ground: Kingsway, Bishop Auckland, County Durham (0388 603686).
Directions: A1 to Scotch Corner (or M6 to Barnard Castle) then follow signs to Bishop Auckland. Ground in town centre (rear of Newgate Str). Half mile from station.
Capacity: 3,500 **Cover:** 2,000 **Seats:** 600 **Shop:** Yes **Metal Badges:** £3.00
Colours: Sky & Navy blue **Change colours:** Red & white. **Sponsors:** E Bac Ltd
Previous Leagues: N East Counties 1889-90/ Northern Alliance 1890-91/ Northern 1893-1988.
Midweek home matchday: Wednesday **Reserve Team:** None.
Record Attendance: 17,000 v Coventry, FA Cup 2nd Rd 6/12/52.
Record win: 13-0 **Record defeat:** 1-7.
Best FA Cup season: 4th Rd 54-55 (lost 1-3 at home to York City).
League clubs beaten in FA Cup: Crystal Palace, Ipswich 54-55, Tranmere 56-57.
Record Fees - Paid: £2,000 **Received:** £6,000 for Andy Toman.
Players progressing to Football League: Bob Paisley (Liverpool), Fred Richardson & Seamus O'Connell (Chelsea 1946 & 54), Robert Hardisty & Ken Williamson (Darlimgton 1946 & 52), William Shergold (Newport 1947), Norman Smith (Fulham 1948), Ron Steel & Ken Murray (Darlington 1950), Arthur Adey (Doncaster 1950), Frank Palmer & Alan Stalker (Gateshead 1951 & 58), Arthur Sewell (Bradford City 1954), Gordon Barker (Southend 1954), Jack Major (Hull 1955), Harry Sharratt (Oldham 1956), Frank McKenna (Leeds 1956), John Barnwell (Arsenal 1956), Derek Lewis (Accrington Stanley 1957), Corbett Cresswell (Carlisle 1958), Warren Bradley (Man Utd), Laurie Brown (Northampton), Paul Baker (Southampton), Micky Gooding (Rotherham), Keith Nobbs & Andy Toman (Hartlepool), Peter Hinds (Dundee Utd).
Clubhouse: Open every lunchtime and evening noon-4 & 7-11pm, and Saturday matchdays noon-4 & 5-6 & 7-11pm. Large bar, pool, juke box. Also snack bar within grounds sells hot & cold pies & drinks.
Club Record Appearances: Bob Hardisty
93-94 Captain: Kevin Todd.
93-94 P.o.Y.: Kevin Todd.
93-94 Top scorer: Gary Hyde.
Local Newspapers: Northern Echo, Evening Gazette, N'castle Journal.
Local Radio Stations: Radio Cleveland, Radio Tees.
Honours: FA Amateur Cup(10) 1895-96, 1899-1900 13-14 20-22 34-35 38-39 54-56 57-58 (R-up(8) 01-02 05-06 10-11 14-15 45-46 49-51 53-54), FA Trophy QF 78-79 88-89, Northern Lg(19) 1898-99 1900-02 08-10 11-12 20-21 30-31 38-39 46-47 49-52 53-56 66-67 84-86 (R-up(16) 03-04 05-06 14-15 19-20 21-23 36-38 39-40 47-49 52-53 60-61 72-73 78-79 86-87, Lg Cup(7) 49-51 53-55 59-60 66-67 75-76), D'ham Chall Cup 1891-92 98-99 1930-31 38-39 51-52 55-56 61-62 66-67 84-85 85-86 87-88, HFS Loans Lg Div 1 R-up 88-89. Plus tournaments in Isle of Man, Spain, Portugal etc.

PROGRAMME DETAILS:
Pages: 28 **Price:** 70p
Editor: N Postma
(0388 608330)

BISHOP AUCKLAND's 1993-94 CAMPAIGN

Date	Opponents	Comp.	Res	Gate	Goalscorers	
21/08	Gainsborough Trinity	NPL	0-0	431		
25/08	**WHITLEY DAY**	NPL	2-0	338	Gamble, McDonald	
28/08	Colwyn Bay	NPL	0-6	144		
30/08	Morecambe	NPL	2-0	402	McDonald(2)	
04/09	**CHORLEY**	NPL	3-1	319	McDonald, Cramman(2)	
07/09	Whitley Bay	NPL	1-2	343	Hyde	
11/09	**NETHERFIELD**	FAC1q	1-4	208	McDonald	
15/09	**BRIDLINGTON TOWN**	NPL	1-1	150	Bond	
18/09	**MARINE**	NPL	1-4	269	Tupling	
21/09	Frickley Athletic	NPL	0-5	208		
25/09	Horwich	NPL	1-2	158	Bond	
29/09	**BARROW**	NPL	2-1	235	Hyde, Cramman	
02/10	Accrington Stanley	NPL	2-1	434	Hockley, Adams	
06/10	**EMLEY**	NPL	2-1	251	Cramman, Todd	
09/10	Fleetwood Town	NPL	2-1	148	Hyde, Mockler	
12/10	Droylsden	NPL	2-4	169	Coverdale, Cramman	
16/10	**WINSFORD UTD**	NPL	4-2	270	Hyde(3), Borthwick	
20/10	**MATLOCK TOWN**	NPL	2-0	235	Cass, Bond	
23/10	**BOSTON UNITED**	NPL	1-1	325	Borthwick	
30/10	**BUXTON**	NPL	2-1	290	Cramman, Borthwick	
06/11	Boston United	NPL	2-1	1,149	Woodcock, Coverdale	
13/11	**HORWICH R.M.I.**	NPL	1-0	402	Cramman	
20/11	**LEEK TOWN**	NPL	2-2	299	Woodcock, Hyde	
01/12	**MURTON**	FAT3q	2-2	279	Mickler, Coverdale	
04/12	Knowsley United	NPL	1-1	166	Hyde	
06/12	Murton	FAT3qr	4-1	190	Mockler, Todd, Borthwick, Hyde	
11/12	Bridlington Town	NPLC2	7-4	37	Coverdale, Bell, Woodcock(5)	
15/12	**FERRYHILL ATH.**	DCC1	3-0	163	Woodcock, Borthwick, Bond	
18/12	Chorley	NPL	5-2	161	Woodcock(2), Mockler(2), Bond	
12/01	Silksworth	DCC2	5-1	330	Mockler(2), Borthwick, Hyde, Waller	
15/01	**HYDE UNITED**	NPL	1-2	326	Adams	
22/01	Blyth Spartans	FAT1	3-1	622	Borthwick, Bond, Cramman	
29/01	Emley	NPL	2-2	366	Waller, Borthwick	
02/02	**GRETNA**	NPLC3	1-1	275	Todd	
05/02	**ACCRINGTON STAN.**	NPL	0-0	361		
07/02	Gretna	NPLC3r	2-2	158	Todd, Lobb	*(won 5-3 on penalties)*
12/02	Grantham Town	FAT2	2-1	815	Borthwick(2)	
19/02	**KNOWSLEY UTD**	NPL	1-2	290	Borthwick	
26/02	Marine	NPL	1-3	383	West	
28/02	**HARTLEPOOL TOWN**	DCCqf	2-1	129	Todd, Bond	
05/03	**ENFIELD**	FAT3	2-2	830	Adams, Hyde	
08/03	Enfield	FAT3r	1-2	890	Todd	
12/03	Winsford United	NPL	0-0	217		
16/03	**SPENNYMOOR UTD**	NPLCqf	1-2	401	Bell	
19/03	**COLWYN BAY**	NPL	3-2	211	Laws(2), Todd	
21/03	Bridlington Town	NPL	4-0	29	Hyde, Parkinson, Bond, West	
23/03	**HEBBURN**	DCCsf	6-1	153	Hyde(3), Bond(2), Johnson	
26/03	**FLEETWOOD**	NPL	3-2	247	Chapman(og), Hyde, Laws	
30/03	**FRICKLEY ATH.**	NPL	3-1	240	Cramman, Parkinson, Laws	
04/04	**DROYLSDEN**	NPL	3-1	257	Parkinson, Bond, Laws	
09/04	Barrow	NPL	2-0	491	Laws, Lobb	
13/04	**MORECAMBE**	NPL	2-1	230	Parkinson, Hyde	
16/04	**GAINSBOROUGH**	NPL	1-0	270	Parkinson	
23/04	Hyde United	NPL	1-1	242	Laws	
26/04	Matlock Town	NPL	2-0	298	Bond(2)	
30/04	Buxton	NPL	2-0	202	Cramman, Bell	
02/05	SPENNYMOOR UTD	DCCf	2-3		Woods, Bond	*(played at Darlington FC)*
07/05	Leek Town	NPL	1-2	544	Lobb	

Key: NPL: Northern Premier League Premier Division, NPLC: Northern Premier League Cup, PC: Northern Premier League Presidennts Cup, FAC: F.A. Cup, FAT: F.A. Trophy, DCC: Durham Challenge Cup. Number after cup competitions denote rounds (r: replay, qf: Quarter-Final, sf: Semi-Final, f: Final. Numbers in brackets indicate legs, i.e. (1): 1st leg).
Home fixtures are denoted by bold capitals, away matches by lower case. (p): penalty, og: Own goal.

SQUAD MEMBERS *(previous clubs listed in chronological order)*

GOALKEEPERS: Simon Bishop *(Newcastle Utd, Guisborough, Whitby, Northallerton)*, **Peter Gardner** *(Langley Park, Blyth Spartans)*

DEFENDERS: Shaun Elliott *(Sunderland, Norwich, Blackpool, Colchester Utd, Gateshead)*, **Steve West** *(Youth Team)*, **Mark Cass** *(Berwick R.)*, **Michael Waller** *(Middlesbrough, South Bank, Northallerton)*, **Garry Parle** *(Bootle, Shildon, Bishop Auckland, Shildon)*,

MIDFIELD: Derek Bell *(Newcastle Utd, Gateshead, North Shields, Gateshead, Bridlington)*, **Dale Anderson** *(Darlington, Middlesbrough, Bishop Auckland, King's Lynn)*, **George Adams** *(Shildon)*, **Robert Lake** *(Middlesbrough, Whitley Bay)*, **Dave Woodcock** *(Sunderland, Darlington, Newcastle Blue Star, North Shields, Bridlington)*, **Andy Mockler** *(Arsenal, Scarborough)*, **David Lobb** *(Peterlee Newtown, Hartlepool T.)*, **Phil Oliver** *(Shildon)*

FORWARDS: John Borthwick *(Hartlepool Utd, Darlington, York, Gateshead)*, **Gary Hyde** *(Darlington, Leicester, Scunthorpe, Whitby)*, **Kevin Todd** *(Ryhope, Newcastle Utd, Darlington, Newcastle Blue Star, Whitley Bay, Berwick R.)*, **Kenny Cramman** *Hartlepool Utd, Dunston Fed.)*, **Richie Bond** *(Blyth Spartans, Blackpool, Carlisle Utd)*

Founded: 1934

BOSTON UNITED

The Pilgrims

Boston United FC. Back Row (L/R): Ernie Moss (Asst Manager 93-94), Gary Lee, Robbie Curtis, Tim Preece (now Grantham), Paul Nicol, Paul Bastock, Darren Bloodworth (now King's Lynn), Dean Trott, Noel Luke, Steve Chambers. Front: Dean West (now Lincoln City), Jon Graham (now Kettering), Jamie Hardwick, David Riley, Peter Morris (Manager 93-94), Neil Grayson, Mick Matthews (now in Hong Kong), Darren Munton, Paul Casey.
Photo - courtesy of A & K Markham.

President: Mr A E Bell **Chairman:** Mr Pat Malkinson **Vice-Chairman:** Mr S Burgess.
Secretary: John Blackwell, 14-16 Spain Place, Boston, Lincs PE26 6HN (0205 364406(club office)).
Manager: Mel Sterland **Asst Manager:** Ron Reid.
Commercial Manager: Secretary. **Press Officer:** The Club Offices
Ground: York Street, Boston, Lincs (0205 364406-office, 365524/5-matchday no., 354063-fax).
Directions: A1 to A17 Sleaford-Boston, over rail crossing, bear right at Eagle pub to lights over haven Bridge, thru lights opposite B & Q, right into York Street. Ground just off town centre.
Capacity: 8,771 **Cover:** 8,771 **Seats:** 1,826 **Floodlights:** Yes **Metal Badges:** Yes
Club Shop: Yes, but at club office (as secretary's address, above) not ground.
Colours: Amber/black/amber **Change colours:** All blue or white & green.
Previous Leagues: Midland 21-58 62-64/ Southern 58-61/ Central Alliance 61-62/ United Counties 65-66/ West Midlands (Regional) 66-68/ Northern Premier 68-79/ Alliance Premier (Conference) 79-93.
Previous Grounds: None. **Previous Names:** Boston Town/ Boston Swifts.
Midweek home matchday: Wednesday **Reserve Team's League:** Lincolnshire League.
Sponsors: Batemans Brewery.
Record Attendance: 10,086 v Corby Town, floodlight inauguration 1955.
Best FA Cup season: Third Rd Proper replay 73-74 (lost 1-6 at home to Derby County after 0-0 draw).
League clubs defeated in FA Cup: Derby 55-56, Southport 70-71, Hartlepool 71-72, Crewe 82-83.
Record win: 14-0 v Spilsby Town, Grace Swan Cup, 1992-93.
Record Fees - Paid: £14,000 for Micky Nuttell (Wycombe Wanderers).
Received: £25,000 for Gary Jones (Southend United, 1993).
Players progressing to Football League: Jim Smith (Colchester), Steve Thompson (Lincoln), Brendon Phillips (Mansfield), Gordon Simmonite (Blackpool), Simon Garner (Blackburm), John Froggatt & Bobby Svarc (Colchester), David Gilbert, Neil Grayson, Jamie Pascoe, Robbie Curtis, Dean Trott (Northampton), Tim Dalton (Bradford City), Gary Jones (Southend).
Clubhouse: (0205 362967) Open every day except Tuesday. Live entertainment Saturday, pool, darts, dominoes, Sunday football teams.
Club Record Scorer: Jimmy Rayner 55, 66-67.
Club Record Appearances: Billy Howells, 500+.
93-94 Captain: Paul Casey/ Noel Luke.
P.o.Y. 93-94: Neil Grayson.
93-94 Top scorer: Neil Grayson.
Newsline: 0898 121 539.
Honours: FA Trophy R-up 84-85, Northern Premier Lg 72-73 73-74 76-77 77-78 (R-up 71-72, Lg Cup 73-74 75-76 (R-up 77-78), Challenge Shield 73-74 74-75 76-77 77-78), Lincs Snr Cup 34-35 36-36 37-38 45-46 49-50 54-55 55-56 76-77 78-79 85-86 87-88 88-89, East Anglian Cup 60-61, Central Alliance 61-62 (Lg Cup 61-62), Utd Counties Lg 65-66 (Lg Cup 65-66), West Midlands (Regional) Lg 66-67 67-68, Eastern Professional Floodlit Cup 71-72 (R-up 76-77), Non-League Champion of Champions Cup 72-73 73-74 76-77 77-78, Midland Lg R-up 55-56, Lincs Lg(reserves) R-up 81-82 82-83.

PROGRAMME DETAILS:
Pages: 44 **Price:** £1
Editor: Secretary

BOSTON UNITED's 1993-94 CAMPAIGN

Date	Opponents	Comp.	Res	Gate	Goalscorers
21/08	Marine	NPL	2-3	392	Grayson, Graham
24/08	**FRICKLEY ATH.**	NPL	2-0	850	Trott, Riley
28/08	**KNOWSLEY UTD**	NPL	4-1	902	West(2), Luke, Graham
31/08	Matlock Town	NPL	1-2	683	Grayson
04/09	Horwich RMI	NPL	5-0	243	Trott(2), West, Hardwick, Fee
08/09	**LEEK TOWN**	NPL	3-3	741	Munton, Riley(2)
11/09	**BRAINTREE TOWN**	FAC1q	1-1	802	Munton
14/09	Braintree Town	FAC1qr	2-1	420	Luke, Trott
18/09	Accrington Stanley	NPL	3-1	569	Grayson(2), West
22/09	**EMLEY**	NPL	2-2	881	Grayson, West
25/09	**CANVEY ISLAND**	FAC2q	2-3	885	Fee, Riley
28/09	Buxton	NPL	1-0	456	Trott
02/10	**FLEETWOOD TOWN**	NPL	4-1	880	Munton(3), Riley
06/10	Bridlington Town	NPL	1-0	170	Trott
09/10	Hyde United	NPL	1-2	379	Riley
14/10	**HYDE UNITED**	NPL	3-1	920	Grayson(2), Munton
16/10	**MARINE**	NPL	4-2	1,418	Fee(2), Riley(2)
19/10	Leek Town	NPL	1-2	409	Grayson
23/10	Bishop Auckland	NPL	1-1	325	Riley
30/10	**CHORLEY**	NPL	4-0	1,100	Luke(2), Fee, Munton
06/11	**BISHOP AUCKLAND**	NPL	1-2	1,149	Grayson
13/11	Whitley Bay	NPL	1-2	346	Fee
20/11	**BARROW**	NPL	0-0	885	
23/11	Grimsby Town	LSCf	0-1	183	
27/11	Morecambe	NPL	2-1	306	Orton, Munton
04/12	**HORWICH R.M.I.**	NPL	2-1	884	Grayson, Fee
11/12	**FLEETWOOD TOWN**	NPLC2	6-0	576	Grayson(3), Luke, Fee, Pascoe
18/12	Winsford United	NPL	0-1	246	
27/11	Gainsborough Tr.	NPL	2-2	1,421	Grayson(2)
01/01	**GAINSBOROUGH**	NPL	6-1	1,602	Munton(2), Morrow(2), Grayson, Bairstow(og)
08/01	**DROYLSDEN**	NPL	2-0	1,174	Grayson, Luke
15/01	Emley	NPL	1-1	433	Fee
22/01	**MACCLESFIELD**	FAT1	1-1	1,559	Morrow
25/01	Macclesfield Town	FAT1r	0-1	590	
29/01	**COLWYN BAY**	NPL	6-1	1,028	Fee, Grayson, Luke, Morrow, Munton, Orton
05/02	Fleetwood Town	NPL	3-1	255	Grayson, Morrow, Chambers
12/02	Barrow	NPL	2-0	810	Grayson, Munton
16/02	**BUXTON**	NPLC3	1-0	626	Grayson
19/02	Colwyn Bay	NPL	1-1	115	Grayson
05/03	**BRIDLINGTON**	NPL	5-0	935	Grayson(2), Munton(2), Fee
12/03	Chorley	NPL	0-2	302	
16/03	**LEEK TOWN**	NPLCqf	0-1	715	
19/03	**WHITLEY BAY**	NPL	0-1	908	
26/03	**WINSFORD UNITED**	NPL	1-1	722	Munton
02/04	Frickley Athletic	NPL	1-0	250	Grayson
06/04	**MATLOCK TOWN**	NPL	2-0	784	Luke, Munton
16/04	Knowsley United	NPL	2-1	73	Grayson, Riley
23/04	**BUXTON**	NPL	2-2	648	Trott(2)
30/04	**ACCRINGTON S.**	NPL	0-1	651	
02/05	**MORECAMBE**	NPL	2-0	434	Riley, Grayson
07/05	Droylsden	NPL	2-0	137	Grayson(2)

Key: NPL: Northern Premier League Premier Division, NPLC: Northern Premier League Cup, PC: (Northern Premier League) Presidents Cup, FAC: F.A. Cup, FAT: F.A. Trophy, LSC: Lincolnshire Senior Cup. Numbers after cup competitions denote rounds (r: replay, qf: Quarter-Final, sf: Semi-Final, f: Final. Numbers in brackets indicate legs, i.e. (1): 1st leg).
Home fixtures are denoted by bold capitals, away matches by lower case. (p): penalty, og: Own goal.

SQUAD MEMBERS *(previous clubs listed in chronological order)*

GOALKEEPERS: Paul Bastock *(Coventry, Cambridge Utd, Kettering)*

DEFENDERS: Paul Casey *(Sheffield Utd, Boston Utd, Lincoln City)*, **Paul Nicol** *(Scunthorpe, Kettering)*, **Gary Lee** *(Doncaster, Gainsborough, Armthorpe, Goole)*, **Tim Preece** *(Hucknall)*, **Robbie Curtis** *(Shirebrook)*, **Greg Fee** *(Bradford City, Kettering, Boston Utd, Sheffield Wednesday, Mansfield Town)*.

MIDFIELD: Noel Luke *(WBA, Mansfield, Peterborough)*, **Steve Chambers** *(Sheffield Wednesday, Mansfield)*, **Robbie Orton** *(Ashfield Utd)*, **Neil Grayson** *(Doncaster, Rowntree Mackintosh, York, Chesterfield)*, **Steve Marshall** *(Eynesbury)*, **Jamie Hardwick** *(local)*

FORWARDS: Darren Munton *(Oakham, Melton, Bourne)*, **Steve Circuit** *(Sheffield Utd, Stafford Rgrs, Halifax)*, **Jamie Pascoe** *(Oakham, Sutton Town, Worksop, Ashfield)*, **Grant Morrow** *(Rowntree Mackintosh, Doncaster, Colchester)*, **Dean Trott** *(Pontefract, Emley, North Shields, Ossett Town)*, **David Riley** *(Keyworth Utd, Nottm Forest, Port Vale, Peterborough, Kettering, FC Ponsonby(NZ))*.

Formed: 1877

BUXTON

The Bucks

The main stand at Buxton's imposing Silverlands ground.

Photo - Colin Stevens.

Chairman: G S Worth **Vice Chairman:** S Dakin.
Secretary/Press Officer: D Belfield, 20 Hereford Road, Buxton SK17 9PG (0298 26033).
Manager: Gary Walker **Asst Manager:** **Physio:** K Perrins
General Manager:
Ground: The Silverlands, Buxton, Derbyshire (0298 24733).
Directions: Within 200 yards of Buxton Market Place, opposite County Police HQ. Half mile from Buxton (BR).
Capacity: 4,000 **Cover:** 2,500 **Seats:** 490 **Floodlights:** Yes **Club Shop:** No
Colours: All white (blue trim) **Change colours:** All yellow (blue trim).
Sponsors: Josiah Tetley.
Previous Leagues: The Combination 1891-99/ North Derbyshire/ E Cheshire/ Manchester 1907-32/ Cheshire County 32-73.
Midweek home matchday: Tuesday
Record Attendance: 6,000 v Barrow, FA Cup 1st rd 51-52.
Best FA Cup season: 3rd Rd 51-52. Also 2nd Rd 58-59, 1st Rd 62-63.
League clubs defeated in FA Cup: Aldershot 51-52.
Best FA Trophy season: Quarter Finals 70-71 71-72.
Record Fees - Paid: £5,000 for Gary Walker (Hyde United, 1989)
Received: £16,500 for Ally Pickering (Rotherham, 1989).
Players progressing to Football League: Peter Robinson (Notts Co 1950), John Higgins (Bolton 1950), Maurice Brooks (Stockport 1951), Ray Parker (Bradford City 1951), Fred Marlow (Grimsby 1951), Ian Greaves (Man Utd 1953), John Brindley (Chesterfield 1953), Les Ferriday (Walsall 1954), John Good (Tranmere 1955), Jimmy Anders (Bradford PA 1956), William Haydock (Man City 1959), Anthony Parkes (Blackburn 1970), Andy Proudlove (Sheffield Wednesday 1975), Graham Collier (York City 1978), Harry Charlton (Darlington 1979), Ally Pickering (Rotherham 1990).
Clubhouse: (0298 23197). Open nightly + Sunday lunchtimes. Tetleys beers, no hot food.
Club Record Goalscorer: Dave Herbert
Club Record Appearances: Mick Davis.
93-94 Captain:
Supporters' P.o.Y. 93-94: David Bainbridge.
Players' P.o.Y. 93-94: Wayne Goodison.
93-94 Top scorer:
Local Newspapers: Buxton Advertiser (0298 22118/22119), Matlock Mercury (Matlock 2432/3).
Local Radio Stations: Radio Derby.
Honours: Northern Premier Lg Cup 90-91 (Presidents Cup R-up 81-82), Cheshire County 72-73 (R-up 46-47 62-63, Lg Cup 56-57 57-58 68-69), Manchester Lg 31-32 5-60(reserves)(R-up 04-05 28-29 29-30 30-31, Lg Cup 25-26 26-27), Derbyshire Senior Cup 38-39 44-45 45-46 56-57 59-60 71-72.

PROGRAMME DETAILS:
Pages: 36 **Price:** 60p
Editor: Tony Tomlinson
(0484 718907)

BUXTON's 1993-94 CAMPAIGN

Date	Opponents	Comp.	Res	Gate	Goalscorers
21/08	Knowsley United	NPL	1-1	178	Downes
24/08	**WINSFORD UNITED**	NPL	1-0	352	Goodison
28/08	**HORWICH**	NPL	4-4	252	Lowe (2), Heywood(2)
30/08	Leek Town	NPL	1-2	573	Lowe
04/09	Fleetwood Town	NPL	2-1	157	Coe
07/09	**HYDE UNITED**	NPL	3-0	400	Hurlstone, Barnsley
11/09	**GAINSBOROUGH Tr.**	FAC1q	2-1	282	Geelan, Lowe
14/09	Gainsborough Trinity	NPL	1-1	418	Heywood
18/09	**CURZON ASHTON**	FAT1q	0-0	268	
20/09	Curzon Ashton	FAT1qr	4-2	136	Heywood(2), Low, Hurlstone
25/09	**HUCKNALL TOWN**	FAC2q	2-0	320	Goodison, Barnsley
28/09	**BOSTON UNITED**	NPL	0-1	456	
02/10	Whitley Bay	NPL	0-1	201	
05/10	**DROYLSDEN**	NPL	0-3	309	
09/10	Winsford United	FAC3q	1-6	322	Lowe
12/10	Frickley Athletic	NPL	1-3	283	Dwyer
14/10	**COLWYN BAY**	FAT2q	1-6	215	Wood
19/10	**GAINSBOROUGH Tr.**	NPL	2-5	208	Hughes(2)
23/10	Bridlington Town	NPL	3-2	70	Hughes(2) Dawson
30/10	Bishop Auckland	NPL	1-2	290	Barnsley
06/11	**ACCRINGTON STAN.**	NPL	3-0	454	Hughes, Lowe, Nisbett
09/11	Chorley	NPL	0-0	180	
13/11	Colwyn Bay	NPL	1-3	152	Barnsley
20/11	**MORECAMBE**	NPL	0-2	251	
23/11	**WHITLEY BAY**	NPL	5-4	161	Hughes(3), Goodison, Lowe
04/12	**EMLEY**	NPL	2-2	340	Blackwood(2)
11/12	Barrow	NPLC2	3-2	647	Hopkinson, Blackwood, Bainbridge
18/12	Marine	NPL	0-1	317	
03/01	**COLWYN BAY**	NPL	1-0	290	Lowe
08/01	Hyde United	NPL	1-1	352	Eley
15/01	Barrow	NPL	3-2	352	Hopkinson, Blackwood, Bainbridge
22/01	**KNOWSLEY UNITED**	NPL	3-1	266	Wood(20), Dempsey
05/02	**BRIDLINGTON TOWN**	NPL	3-1	279	Brown, Dempsey, Wood
08/02	Belper Town	DSC3	1-1	221	Bainbridge
12/02	Accrington Stanley	NPL	1-3	492	Lowe
16/02	Boston United	NPLC3	0-1	625	
22/02	**BELPER TOWN**	DSC3r	2-1	153	Hopkinson, Blackwood
05/03	**FRICKLEY ATHLETIC**	NPL	1-1	267	Bainbridge
12/03	Morecambe	NPL	1-4	319	Hughes
15/03	Gresley Rovers	DSCqf	0-1	402	
19/03	Horwich RMI	NPL	0-1	159	
22/03	**CHORLEY**	NPL	2-3	319	Blackwood, Lowe
26/03	**MARINE**	NPL	2-2	374	Blackwood, Lowe
02/04	Emley	NPL	4-1	173	Goodison (2), Eley, Blackwood
16/04	Barrow	NPL	0-4	434	
19/04	**LEEK TOWN**	NPL	1-2	634	Blackwood
21/04	Matlock Town	NPL	1-1	406	Blackwood
23/04	Boston United	NPL	2-2	648	Hopkinson, Goodison
25/04	**FLEETWOOD TOWN**	NPL	4-1	186	Blackwood(3), Wood
27/04	Winsford United	NPL	1-2	154	Wood
30/04	**BISHOP AUCKLAND**	NPL	0-2	202	
02/05	**MATLOCK TOWN**	NPL	4-1	349	Williams, Blackwood(3)
05/05	Droylsden	NPL	1-2	87	Eley

Key: NPL: Northern Premier League Premier Division, NPLC: Northern Premier League Cup, PC: Northern Premier League Presidennts Cup, FAC: F.A. Cup, FAT: F.A. Trophy, DSC: Derbyshire Senior Cup. Number after cup competitions denote rounds (r: replay, qf: Quarter-Final, sf: Semi-Final, f: Final. Numbers in brackets indicate legs, i.e. (1): 1st leg).

SQUAD MEMBERS *(previous clubs listed in chronological order)*

GOALKEEPERS: Gary Walker *(Ashton Utd., Stockport, Man. City, Hyde Utd., Buxton, Radcliffe Boro.).*

DEFENDERS: Jim Connor *(Stockport, Northwich V., Napier City(NZ), Mossley, Macclesfield, Witton Alb.),* **Ken Geelan** *(Sheff. Utd., Shepshed Alb., Burton Alb.),* **Andy Taylor** *(Rotherham, Scarborough),* **Wayne Goodison** *(Barnsley, Crewe, Rochdale, Hyde Utd., Accrington Stanley),* **Robert Brown** *(Irlam, Buxton, Winsford),* **Gary Barnsley** *(Frickley Ath., Sheffield FC).*

MIDFIELD: Gary Mallender *(Barnsley, Boston Utd., Frickley Ath., Gainsborough T.),* **Kevin Eley** *(Rotherham, Chesterfield, Gainsborough T.),* **Ian Scott** *(Bury, Mossley),* **Kevin Birchall** *(Local Football),* **Dave Bainbridge** *(Biggin R., Buxton, Stalybridge C., Leek).*

FORWARDS: Mark Hughes *(Irlam, Altrincham, Witton Alb., Congleton),* **Mark Hopkinson** *(Sheffield Aurora, Bridlington),* **Stuart Lowe** *(Huddersfield, Goole, Sheffield FC, Buxton, Gainsborough T., Leek),* **Bevon Blackwood** *(Salford, Hyde Utd., Lancaster, Winsford, Witton Alb.).*

Formed: 1883

CHORLEY

The Magpies

Chorley's Keith Johnson challenges for a high ball with Paul Clowes of Leek Town. The Magpies' 3-1 in this fixture on Saturday 26th February brought to an end their opponents' run of fifteen straight wins.
Photo - Colin Stevens.

Chairman: TBA **Vice Chairman:** TBA **President:** Dr P J Wren.
Secretary/Press Officer: Alan Robinson, 55 Janice Drive, Fulwood, Preston, Lancs PR2 4TY (0772 719266).
Manager: Glen Buckley **Assistant Manager:** Les Rigby **Physio:** Dr Philip Earl
Commercial Manager: G Haydock.
Ground: Victory Park, Duke Street, Chorley, Lancs (0257 263406).
Directions: M61 jct 6, A6 to Chorley, going past Yarrow Bridge Hotel on Bolton Rd turn left at 1st lights into Pilling Lane, 1st right into Ashley Str., ground 2nd left. From M6; jct 27, follow signs to Chorley, left at lights, continue for two and a half miles on A49, right onto B5251, on entering Chorley turn right into Duke Street 200yds after Plough Hotel. Quarter mile from Chorley (BR).
Capacity: 9,000 **Cover:** 4,000 **Seats:** 900 **Floodlights:** Yes **Club Shop:** No
Colours: White & black stripes/black/black & white **Change colours:** Red/white/red.
Previous Leagues: Lancs Alliance 1890-94/ Lancs 94-1903/ Lancs Comb. 03-68 69-70/ Northern Premier 68-69 70-72 82-88/ Cheshire County 72-82/ GMV Conference 88-90.
Previous Grounds: Dole Lane 1883-1901/ Rangletts Park 01-05/ St George's Park 05-20.
Midweek home matchday: Tuesday **Reserve Team's League:** Alliance League.
Sponsors: Trust Inns **Record Gate:** 9,679 v Darwen, 1931-32.
Best FA Cup year: 2nd Rd 86-87 (lost in replay at Preston), 90-91 (lost at Shrewsbury).
League clubs defeated in FA Cup: Accrington 46-47/ Wolves 86-87/ Bury 90-91.
Record Fees - Paid: £5,000 for Tony McDonald (Horwich RMI, 1993)
Received: £22,500 for Paul Mariner (Plymouth, 1973).
Players progressing to Football League: Charles Ashcroft (Liverpool 1946), William Healey (Arsenal 1949), Stan Howard (Huddersfield 1952), Derek Hogg (Leicester 1952), William Norcross (Southport 1959), Micky Walsh (Blackpool 1971), Paul Mariner (Plymouth 1973), Graham Barrow (Wigan 1976), Steve Galliers (Wimbledon 1977), Kevin Tully (Bury 1980), Geoff Twentyman (Preston 1983), Gary Buckley (Bury 1984), Chris Hunter (Preston 1984).
Clubhouse: (0257 275662). Open every evening. Entertainment at weekends. Snacks available.
Club Record Goalscorer: Peter Watson.
93-94 Captain: Keith Johnson.
93-94 P.o.Y.: Tony McDonald.
93-94 Top scorer: Tony McDonald.
Local Newspapers: Lancs Evening Post, Chorley Guardian (0257 264911).
Local Radio Stations: Radio Lancs, Red Rose.
Honours: Northern Premier Lg 87-88, Cheshire Co. Lg 75-76 76-77 81-82, Lancs Comb. 19-20 22-23 27-28 28-29 32-33 33-34 45-46 59-60 60-61 63-64 (R-up 21-22 26-27 48-49 62-63 64-65 65-66, Lg Cup 24-25 58-59 62-63), Lancs Lg 1896-97 98-99, Lancs Alliance 1892-93 (R-up 93-94), Lancs Jnr Cup 1893-94 1908-09 23-24 39-40 45-46 57-58 58-59 60-61 63-64 64-65 75-76 79-80 81-82 82-83, FA Tphy QF (replay) 76-77.

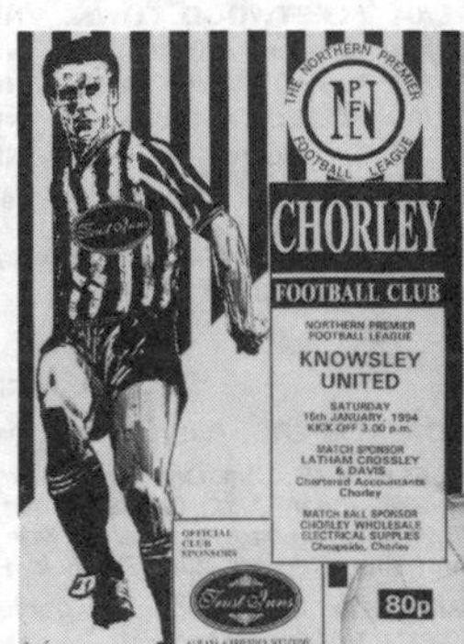

PROGRAMME DETAILS:
Pages: 18 **Price:** 80p
Editor: TBA

CHORLEY's 1993-94 CAMPAIGN

Date	Opponents	Comp.	Res	Gate	Goalscorers
21/08	Whitley Bay	NPL	0-0	204	
24/08	**FLEETWOOD TOWN**	NPL	5-2	301	Schofield, McCrae, Grant(2), Hamilton
28/08	**GAINSBOROUGH Tr.**	NPL	1-1	451	Schofield
30/08	Hyde United	NPL	1-2	413	M Payne
04/09	Bishop Auckland	NPL	1-3	319	Schofield
07/09	**WINSFORD UTD**	NPL	1-0	235	McCrae
11/09	**HORWICH R.M.I.**	FAC1q	3-1	407	R Payne, M Payne, Grant
14/09	Marine	NPL	1-4	417	Critchley
18/09	Whitley Bay	FAT1q	1-1	184	Outerside(og)
21/09	**WHITLEY BAY**	FAT1qr	3-1	266	Kent, Pilkington, Morgan
25/09	**LIVERSEDGE**	FAC2q	2-1	273	M Payne, Pilkington
29/09	Fleetwood Town	NPL	2-1	190	M Payne, Rogerson
02/10	**BRIDLINGTON T.**	NPL	1-2	233	Grant
05/10	**MORECAMBE**	NPL	2-2	367	M Payne, McCrae
09/10	North Ferriby Utd	FAC3q	1-1	284	Hamilton
12/10	**NORTH FERRIBY U.**	FAC3qr	2-1	347	Grant, M Payne
16/10	Harrogate Town	FAT2q	1-3	244	Grant
19/10	**ACCRINGTON STAN.**	NPL	4-1	300	Schofield, McCrae(2), Hamilton
23/10	**MARINE**	FAC4q	0-2	740	
26/10	Barrow	NPL	1-3	1,255	Grant
30/10	Boston United	NPL	0-4	1,100	
06/11	**COLWYN BAY**	NPL	2-2	250	Schofield, Critchley
09/11	**BUXTON**	NPL	0-0	139	
13/11	Winsford United	NPL	4-0	270	R Payne, Schofield, McDonald, Conlon
20/11	Frickley Athletic	NPL	0-5	256	
04/12	**MARINE**	NPL	0-4	240	
11/12	Morecambe	NPLC1	2-5	221	Tyrrell, Conlon
18/12	**BISHOP AUCKLAND**	NPL	2-5	161	McCrae, Conlon
01/01	**FRICKLEY ATH.**	NPL	2-1	230	McDonald, Schofield
03/01	Gainsborough Trin.	NPL	1-1	514	Conlon
08/01	Matlock Town	NPL	1-2	459	McDonald
15/01	**KNOWSLEY UNITED**	NPL	4-1	190	McDonald(2), Conlon(2)
17/01	Clitheroe	ATS2	2-1	384	McDonald, Conlon
22/01	Droylsden	NPL	1-3	266	Schofield
29/01	**MATLOCK TOWN**	NPL	1-2	266	Conlon
05/02	**HYDE UNITED**	NPL	4-2	194	Critchley, McDonald(3)
12/02	Bridlington Town	NPL	1-0	59	McDonald
26/02	**LEEK TOWN**	NPL	3-1	325	McDonald(2), Conlon
05/03	**HORWICH R.M.I.**	NPL	1-1	294	Schofield
08/03	Lancaster City	ATSqf	0-3	202	
12/03	**BOSTON UNITED**	NPL	2-0	302	McDonald(2)
19/03	Emley	NPL	3-0	305	Tyrrell(2), Eyre
22/03	Buxton	NPL	3-2	319	McDonald(2), Hopkinson(og)
26/03	Horwich R.M.I.	NPL	2-2	363	McDonald(2)
02/04	Knowsley United	NPL	1-0	132	Conlon
04/04	**BARROW**	NPL	3-0	377	Tyrrell, Conlon, McDonald
16/04	**DROYLSDEN**	NPL	6-1	225	Eyre, McDonald(3), Conlon(2)
19/04	Morecambe	NPL	1-0	340	McDonald
23/04	Colwyn Bay	NPL	0-2	145	
28/04	Leek Town	NPL	0-1	549	
30/04	**WHITLEY BAY**	NPL	0-2	160	
07/05	Accrington Stanley	NPL	1-1	527	McDonald

Key: NPL: Northern Premier League Premier Division, NPLC: Northern Premier League Cup, FAC: F.A. Cup, FAT: F.A. Trophy, ATS: Lancashire ATS Challenge Trophy. Numbers after cup competitions denote rounds (r: replay, qf: Quarter-Final, sf: Semi-Final, f: Final. Numbers in brackets indicate legs, i.e. (1): 1st leg). Home fixtures are denoted by bold capitals, away matches by lower case. (p): penalty, og: Own goal.

SQUAD MEMBERS *(previous clubs listed in chronological order)*

GOALKEEPERS: Andy Gill *(local football)*

DEFENDERS: Keith Johnson *(Prescot, Marine)*, **Danny Kent** *(Bury)*, **Paul Booth** *(Bolton Wanderers, Crewe Alexandra, Horwich RMI)*, **Adam Critchley** *(Preston North End)*,

MIDFIELD: Steve Eyre *(Burnley, Wigan Athletic, Stockport County)*, **Andy Westwell** *(Leyland Motors, Horwich RMI)*, **Mark Schofield** *(Wigan Athletic, Horwich RMI, Southport)*, **Mark Brennan** *(South Liverpool, Bootle, South Liverpool, Morecambe, Southport)*, **Kevin Mooney**

FORWARDS: Russell Payne *(Liverpool, Skelmersdale United)*, **Peter McCrae** *(Blackburn Rovers, Oldham Athletic, Runcorn, Lancaster City, Northwich Victoria, Ghent(Belgium), Lancaster City)*, **Tony McDonald** *(Radcliffe Borough, Horwich RMI)*, **Carl Conlon** *(Stalybridge Celtic, Ashton United, Flixton, Irlam Town, Runcorn, Witton Albion, Altrincham)*, **Neil Williams** *(Chorley, Durham University)*, **Peter Withers** *(South Liverpool, Runcorn, Southport)*

Formed: 1885

COLWYN BAY

'Bay' or 'Seagulls'

Colwyn Bay pictured before their match at Hyde United on February 14th. Back Row (L/R): Steph Rush (Assistant Manager), Timmy Williams, Mark Woods, Colin Caton, Steve Morgan, Alan Nicholas, Mark Price, Richie Roberts, Gareth Drury, Neil Clarke. Front: Craig Dulson, Steve Mann, Lee Harley, Dave Brett, Neil Rigby.
Photo - John Newton.

Chairman: Mr G Owens **Vice Chairman:** Mr J A Humphreys
Secretary/Press Officer: Mr A J Banks, 15 Smith Avenue, Old Colwyn, Clwyd LL29 8BE (0492 516941).
Manager: Bryn Jones **Assistant Manager:** Steph Rush
Physio: John Carmichael.
Ground: Llanelian Road, Old Colwyn, Clywd, North Wales (0492 516554).
Directions: M55 North Wales Coast - approaching Colwyn Bay take 1st exit signposted Old Colwyn, left at bottom slip road, straight over r'bout into Llanelian Rd - ground half mile on right. 2 miles from Colwyn Bar BR station.
Capacity: 5,000 **Seats:** 200 **Cover:** 700 **Floodlights:** Yes **Metal Badges:** Yes
Club Shop: Yes - contact secretary.
Colours: Sky/maroon/sky **Change colours:** Red/white/red. **Sponsors:** TBA
Previous Grounds: Eiras Park 1930-82/ Llanelian Road 82-92/ Northwich Victoria FC 92-93/ Ellesmere Port Stadium 93-94 *(two years in exile due to dispute with FAW over the League of Wales).*
Previous Leagues: Nth Wales Coast 01-21 33-35/ Welsh National 21-30/ Nth Wales Comb. 30-31/ Welsh Lg (Nth) 45-84/ North West Counties 84-91.
Midweek home matchday: Tuesday **Reserve Team:** None.
Record Attendance: 5,000 (at Eiras Park) v Borough United, 1964.
Best FA Cup season: First Round Proper 87-88.
League clubs defeated in FA Cup: None.
Clubhouse: Open before and after matches. Usual club food (pies etc).
93-94 Captain: Dave Brett.
93-94 P.o.Y.: Richie Roberts.
93-94 Top scorer: Steve Jones, 34.
Local Newspapers: North Wales Weekly News, North Wales Pioneer.
Honours: Northern Premier Lg Div 1 91-92 (Div 1 Cup 91-92), North West Counties Lg R-up 90-91 (Div 3 R-up 83-84, Lg Cup 88-89, Floodlit Cup 90-91), Welsh Cup SF 91-92, Welsh National Lg R-up 27-28 29-30, Nth Wales Comb. 30-31, Welsh Lg Nth 64-65 82-83 83-84 (R-up 35-36 45-46 63-64, Lg Cup 27-28), Alves Cup 63-64, Cookson Cup 73-74 79-80 80-81 81-82 83-84, Barritt Cup 79-80 81-82 83-84, Nth Wales Coast Chal. Cup 30-31 31-32 81-82 82-83 83-84, Nth Wales Coast Jnr Cup 1898-99.

PROGRAMME DETAILS:
Pages: 28 **Price:** 70p
Editor: M Richardson
(0492 878953)

COLWYN BAY's 1993-94 CAMPAIGN

Date	Opponents	Comp.	Res	Gate	Goalscorers
21/08	Frickley Athletic	NPL	1-0	202	Nicholas
24/08	**MARINE**	NPL	0-0	280	
28/08	**BISHOP AUCKLAND**	NPL	6-0	144	Jones(3), Nicholas, Brett, Caton
30/08	Winsford United	NPL	1-0	375	Morgan
04/09	Matlock Town	NPL	1-3	435	Jones
07/09	**FLEETWOOD TOWN**	NPL	2-2	161	Brett, Nicholas
11/09	**HYDE UNITED**	FAC1q	4-1	209	Nicholas(2), Jones, Morgan
18/09	Sutton Coldfield T.	FAT1q	1-1	138	Brett
21/09	**SUTTON COLDFIELD**	FAT1q	4-0	177	Nicholas(2), Jones, Brett
25/09	**THACKLEY**	FAC2q	4-1	188	Jones(2), Nicholas, Caton
29/09	Horwich RMI	NPL	3-2	148	Dulson, Jones, Morgan
02/10	**GAINSBOROUGH**	NPL	1-2	210	Caton
05/10	Leek Town	NPL	0-2	364	
09/10	Knowsley United	NPL	0-3	254	
16/10	Buxton	FAT2q	6-1	215	Nicholas(3), Jones(2), Woods
19/10	**HYDE UNITED**	NPL	2-1	159	Nicholas, Jones
23/10	Fleetwood Towb	NPL	3-0	135	Dulson, Jones, Rigby
30/10	**EMLEY**	NPL	1-0	206	Jones
06/11	Chorley	NPL	2-2	250	Morgan, Rigby
13/11	**BUXTON**	NPL	3-1	154	Nicholas, Roberts, Morgan
16/11	**WINSFORD UTD**	NPL	0-0	179	
20/11	Droylsden	NPL	0-0	237	
27/11	**GUISBOROUGH T.**	FAT3q	2-2	114	Nicholas, Jones
01/12	Guisborough Town	FAT3qr	3-2	281	Nicholas(2), Morgan
04/12	**ACCRINGTON STAN.**	NPL	2-2	207	Jones(2)
07/12	**STALYBRIDGE C.**	CSC2	4-1	110	Rigby, Morgan, Jones, Roberts
11/12	Gainsborough Trin.	NPLC2	2-0	313	Nicholas, Jones
18/12	**BARROW**	NPL	2-3	220	Nicholas(2)
27/11	Marine	NPL	1-1	674	Jones
01/01	**MORECAMBE**	NPL	2-3	256	Nicholas, Roberts
03/01	Buxton	NPL	0-1	290	
15/01	Morecambe	NPL	1-1	413	Morgan
22/01	Stalybridge Celtic	FAT1	1-1	422	Roberts
29/01	Boston United	NPL	1-6	1,028	Nicholas
01/02	**STALYBRIDGE C.**	FAT1r	2-2	220	Jones, Roberts
03/02	**STALYBRIDGE C.**	FAT1r2	2-1	138	Jones, Roberts
05/02	**LEEK TOWN**	NPL	0-1	158	
08/02	Macclesfield Town	CSCqf	1-7	384	Jones *(Macclesfield Town later expelled)*
12/02	**SOUTHPORT**	FAT2	0-3	660	
14/02	Hyde United	NPLC3	1-2	138	Nicholas
19/02	**BOSTON UNITED**	NPL	1-1	115	Roberts
01/03	**NORTHWICH VICS**	CSCsf(1)	0-0	254	
05/03	Gainsborough Trin.	NPL	1-0	000	Dulson
08/03	Knowsley United	NPL	5-1	111	Jones(2), M Jones(og), Dulson, Donnelly
12/03	**WHITLEY BAY**	NPL	1-0	119	Donnelly
19/03	Bishop Auckland	NPL	2-3	211	Jones, Nicholas
22/03	Northwich Victoria	CSCsf(2)	2-3	517	Morgan, Jones
26/03	**DROYLSDEN**	NPL	4-0	131	Donnelly, Brett, Nicholas, Jones
29/03	**MATLOCK TOWN**	NPL	3-0	102	Caton, Morgan, Jones
02/04	Accrington Stanley	NPL	5-5	420	Donnelly(2), Morgan, Brett, Jones
09/04	Hyde United	NPL	2-1	325	Morgan, Jones
12/04	**BRIDLINGTON TOWN**	NPL	5-0	101	Morgan(2), Donnelly, Jones, Armor
16/04	Bridlington Town	NPL	0-2	37	
19/04	**HORWICH R.M.I.**	NPL	1-0	104	Brett
21/04	Emley	NPL	3-3	153	Caton, Brett, Jones
23/04	**CHORLEY**	NPL	2-0	145	Roberts, Caton
26/04	**KNOWSLEY UNITED**	NPL	0-0	110	
28/04	**FRICKLEY ATH.**	NPL	1-1	106	Caton
30/04	Barrow	NPL	2-0	585	Donnelly, Jones
04/05	Whitley Bay	NPL	1-1	134	Caton

Key: NPL: Northern Premier League Premier Division, NPLC: Northern Premier League Cup, PC: (Northern Premier League) Presidents Cup, FAC: F.A. Cup, FAT: F.A. Trophy, CSC: Cheshire Senior Cup. Numbers after cup competitions denote rounds (r: replay, qf: Quarter-Final, sf: Semi-Final, f: Final. Numbers in brackets indicate legs, i.e. (1): 1st leg).
Home fixtures are denoted by bold capitals, away matches by lower case. (p): penalty, og: Own goal.

SQUAD MEMBERS *(previous clubs listed in chronological order)*

GOALKEEPERS: Richie Roberts *(Christleton)*

DEFENDERS: Steve Mann *(Connahs Quay, Upton, Newtown, Mold, Caernarfon)*, **Mark Woods** *(United Services, Flint, Colwyn Bay, Pieksamaki(Fin))*, **Mark Price** *(Connahs Quay)*, **Neil Clarke** *(Christleton)*, **Alan Schumaker** *(Everton, Ellesmere Port, Witton, Vauxhall GM, Caernarfon)*, **Neil Rigby** *(Everton, Tranmere, Chester, Marine, Vauxhall GM, Southport, Holywell)*.

MIDFIELD: Colin Caton *(Rhyl)*, **Les Armor** *(Colwyn Bay, Rhyl, Bangor, Stalybridge, Caernarfon)*, **Tim Williams** *(Flint, Rhyl)*, **Lee Harley** *(Flint)*, **Phil Owens** *(Rhyl, local football)*, **Dave Brett** *(Colwyn Bay, Chester)*

FORWARDS: Steve Jones *(Pilkingtons, Bethesda Utd, Colwyn Bay, Rhyl)*, **Peter Donnelly** *(Chester, Oswestry, Rhyl, Colwyn Bay, Northwich)*, **Alan Nicholas** *(Everton, Malpas, Llay RBL, Rhyl, Bangor, Hyde)*, **Steve Morgan** *(Oldham, Rochdale, Stalybridge)*, **Neil Young** *(Tranmere, Altrincham, Warrington, Southport, Vauxhall GM, Barrow, Winsford Utd, Bangor)*

Formed: 1892

DROYLSDEN

The Bloods

Droylsden's Butchers Arms Ground.

Photo - James Wright.

Chairman: David Pace
Secretary: B King, 22 Hart Street, Droylsden, Manchester M43 7AW (061 371 9880).
Manager: Peter O'Brien **Asst Manager:** Billy Dodds/ Jim Walker.
General Manager: Ray Lee.
Ground: The Butchers Arms Ground, Market Street, Droylsden, Manchester (061 370 1426).
Directions: 4 miles east of Manchester via A662 Ashton New Road, behind Butchers Arms Hotel.
Capacity: 3,500 **Cover:** 2,000 **Seats:** 500 **Shop:** Yes **Metal Badges:** Yes.
Colours: Red/white/red **Change colours:** Green/white/green.
Previous Leagues: Manchester/ Lancs Com 36-39 50-68/ Cheshire County 39-50 68-82/ NW Counties 82-87.
Midweek home matchday: Tuesday **Reserve Team:** None.
Sponsors: Alpha Court Windows/ Hastings Taxis.
Record Attendance: 4,250 v Grimsby, FA Cup 1st rd 1976.
Best FA Cup season: 2nd Rd 78-79.
League clubs defeated in FA Cup: Rochdale 78-79.
Record transfer fees received: £11,000 for Tony Naylor (Crewe).
Record win: 13-2 v Lucas Sports Club.
Players progressing to Football League: Albert Butterworth & F Letchford (Blackpool 1931), William Davies & Maurice Randall (Crewe 1947), William Mellor (Accrington 1950), Geoff Tonge (Bury 1960), David Campbell (WBA 1962), Kevin Randall (Bury 1965), Peter Litchfield (Preston 1979), Tony Naylor (Crewe 1990).
Clubhouse: Pub hours except atchdays. Pool and darts.
Club Record Scorer: E Gillibrand 78 (1931-32)
93-94 Captain: Phil Wardle.
93-94 P.o.Y.: Aeon Lattie.
93-94 Top scorer: Steve Bunter.
Local Newspapers: Droylsden Reporter (061 303 1910), Advertiser.
Local Radio Stations: BBC Manchester.
Honours: Northern Prem League Division 1 Runners-up 89-90 (Division 1 Cup 87-88), NW Counties League Division 2 86-87, Cheshire County League Runners-up 39-40 45-46 (League Cup 77-78 (Runners-up 76-77)), Lancs Comb Division 2 Runners-up 55-56 58-59 62-63, Manchester League 30-31 32-33 (League Cup 23-24 33-34), Manchester Premier Cup 80-81 (Runners-up 83-84 90-91 93-94), Manchester Senior Cup 72-73 75-76 78-79 (Runners-up 72-73 75-76 78-79), Manchester Intermediate Cup 59-60 64-65 69-70, Manchester Challenge Shield 46-47.

PROGRAMME DETAILS:
Pages: 20 **Price:** 50p
Editor: TBA

DROYLSDEN's 1993-94 CAMPAIGN

Date	Opponents	Comp.	Res	Gate	Goalscorers
21/08	Morecambe	NPL	2-1	461	Mellor, Short
24/08	**KNOWSLEY UNITED**	NPL	2-1	300	Woodcock, Bunter
28/08	**MARINE**	NPL	2-0	296	Short, Bunter
30/08	Fleetwood Town	NPL	1-1	196	Short
04/09	Gainsborugh Trinity	NPL	2-1	409	Bunter(2)
07/09	**EMLEY**	NPL	3-3	475	Bunter, Wardle, Washington
11/09	**BRIGG TOWN**	FAC1q	1-1	136	Wardle
15/09	Brigg Town	FAC1qr	1-0	89	Grimes
18/09	**SOLIHULL BOROUGH**	FAT1q	2-0	195	Grimes
21/09	**ACCRINGTON STAN.**	NPL	2-1	396	Bunter(2)
25/09	**WORKSOP TOWN**	FAC2q	1-1	254	Washington
27/09	Worksop Town	FAC2qr	0-3	276	
02/10	**MATLOCK TOWN**	NPL	2-4	272	Lattie, Bunter
05/10	Buxton	NPL	3-0	309	Bunter, Washington(2)
09/10	Frickley Athletic	NPL	0-3	226	
12/10	**BISHOP AUCKLAND**	NPL	4-2	169	Schofield, Washington, Bunter
14/10	Grantham Town	FAT2q	2-3	343	Bunter, Norris
19/10	**WINSFORD UNITED**	NPL	0-0	303	
23/10	Matlock Town	NPL	1-1	392	Bunter
25/10	Hyde United	NPL	2-4	467	Schofield, Grimes
30/10	**GAINSBOROUGH Tr.**	NPL	1-4	255	Burns
06/11	**WHITLEY BAY**	NPL	3-2	237	Washington, Bunter, Norris
19/11	**OLDHAM TOWN**	MPC1	1-1	97	Washington
13/11	Bridlington Town	NPL	1-1	47	Washington
15/11	Emley	NPL	1-1	312	Washington
20/11	**COLWYN BAY**	NPL	0-0	237	
27/11	Oldham Town	MPC1r	4-1	70	Lattie(2) Washington(2)
04/12	**BARROW**	NPL	0-0	336	
01/01	Winsford United	NPL	1-4	313	Woodcock
08/01	Boston United	NPL	0-2	1,174	
15/01	**LEEK TOWN**	NPL	1-3	256	Wilkin
19/01	Alfreton Town	NPLC2	1-0	101	Washington
22/01	**CHORLEY**	NPL	3-1	266	Morris, Cavill, Lattie
29/01	Whitley Bay	NPL	1-1	202	McKenzie(og)
31/01	Emley	NPLC2	1-2	254	Gavin
05/02	**HORWICH R.M.I.**	NPL	1-2	227	Wardle
12/02	Knowsley United	NPL	0-2	103	
19/02	Horwich RMI	NPL	2-2	160	Manning, Gavin
05/03	Barrow	NPL	2-2	720	Gavin, Chadwick
08/03	Leek Town	NPL	2-4	476	Gavin, Schofield
12/03	Accrington Stanley	NPL	0-2	359	
15/03	**RADCLIFFE BOROUGH**	MPCqf	1-0	86	Hughes
19/03	**FRICKLEY ATHLETIC**	NPL	2-2	108	Washington, Morris
22/03	**FLEETWOOD TOWN**	NPL	1-1	133	Woodock
26/03	Colwyn Bay	NPL	0-4	131	
28/03	**HYDE UNITED**	NPL	3-3	313	Grimes, Short, Norris
02/04	**BRIDLINGTON TOWN**	NPL	1-0	115	Schofield
04/04	Bishop Auckland	NPL	1-3	257	Schofield
06/04	**CURZON ASHTON**	MPCsf	3-3	160	Woodcock, Gavin(2)
13/04	Curzon Ashton	MPCsfr	2-1	89	Norris, Shaw
16/04	Chorley	NPL	1-6	225	Schofield
23/04	**MORECAMBE**	NPL	0-3	138	
30/04	Marine	NPL	1-2	525	Gavin
04/05	HYDE UNITED	MPCf	1-4	350	Washington *(played at Ashton Utd FC)*
05/05	**BUXTON**	NPL	2-1	87	Washington

Key: NPL: Northern Premier League Premier Division, NPLC: Northern Premier League Cup, PC: Northern Premier League Presidennts Cup, FAC: F.A. Cup, FAT: F.A. Trophy, MPC: Manchester Premier Cup. Number after cup competitions denote rounds (r: replay, qf: Quarter-Final, sf: Semi-Final, f: Final. Numbers in brackets indicate legs, i.e. (1): 1st leg).
Home fixtures are denoted by bold capitals, away matches by lower case. (p): penalty, og: Own goal.

SQUAD MEMBERS *(previous clubs listed in chronological order)*

GOALKEEPERS: Ted Hinnigan *(Chester, Burscough)*

DEFENDERS: Carl Hodgert *(Salford, Atheton C., Altrincham, Hyde Utd., Runcorn, Hyde Utd, Mossley, Altrincham* **Graham Hughes** *(Maghull)* **Phil Wardle** *(Chorlton, Cheadle)*, **Steve Baines** *(Newtown, Southport, Knowsley Utd.)*, **Liam Crosby** *(Chester)*, **Colin Booth** *(Bacup Boro., Stalybridge C., Curzon Ashton, Stalybridge C., Cheadle, Stalybridge C.)*

MIDFIELD: Ged Manning *(North Trafford, Winsford Utd.)*, **Andy Woodcock** *(Oldham Ath., Northwich V., Buxton)*, **Jon Mayo** *(Oldham Ath., Bolton W., Stalybridge C.)*, **Darren Schofield** *(Horwich RMI, Curzon Ashton, Droylsden, Accrington Stanley, Mossley, Warrington)*, **John Burns** *(Buxton, Droylsden, Accrington Stanley)*, **Chris Short** *(Vauxhall GM)*, **Peter Mellor** *(Hyde Utd, Radcliffe Boro. Barrow)*, **Barry Norris** *(Everton, Chester)*,.

FORWARDS: Aeon Lattie *(Droylsden, Irlam)*, **Gary Washington** *(Vauxhall GM)*, **Tyrone Grimes** *(Everton, Bromborough Pool)*, **Scott James** *(Tranmere R.)*

Formed: 1903

EMLEY

Emley pictured before their home fixture against Colwyn Bay on April 21st. Back Row (L/R): Daryl Brook (Physio), Ian Tunnacliffe, Richard Hopley, Colin Alcide, David Redfern, Robert Mellor, Hanson Jerome, Stephen Codd (Manager), Stephen Dyson (Coach). Front: Simon Jones, Andrew Palmer, Gary Lockwood, John Dysart, Matthew Johnson, Michael Reynolds, Bob Clarke, Andy Bondswell.

Chairman: Peter Matthews **Vice Chairman:** Roy Shirley **President:** Peter Maude
Secretary: Gordon Adamson, 219 Rowley Lane, Lepton, Huddersfield HD8 0EH (0484 602720).
Manager: Steve Codd **Asst Manager:** Stephen Dyson **Coach:** Daryl Brook.
Physio: Daryl Brook. **Press Officer:** Alan Blackman (0924 403959).
Ground: Emley Welfare Sports Ground, Emley, Huddersfield (0924 848398. Office: 840087).
Directions: Follow Huddersfield signs from M1 junction 38, left onto A636 at r'bout, then right after about three quarters of a mile for Emley. From M62 jct 23 to Huddersfield ring-road, follow Wakefield signs for 5 miles, thru Lepton, past White Horse pub on left and turn right at top of next hill - just under 3 miles to Emley. Floodlights unmissable in small village. Seven miles from Huddersfield (BR) station - buses to Emley Cross.
Capacity: 3,000 **Cover:** 1,000 **Seats:** 250 **Floodlights:** Yes **Metal Badges:** Yes.
Club Shop: Yes. On ground, stocks all Emley souvenirs and sportswear, programmes and magazines. Contact Mrs Linda Sykes through club number.
Colours: Sky & maroon/sky/sky **Change colours:** All white. **Sponsors:** TBA.
Previous Leagues: Huddersfield/ Yorkshire 69-82/ Northern Counties East 82-89.
Midweek home matchday: Monday **Reserve Team's League:** Northern Co's (East) Reserve Div.
Record Attendance: 5,134 v Barking, FA Amateur Cup Third Round Proper 1/2/69. *9,035 v Bolton Wanderers, FA Cup First Round Proper 17/11/92; matched staged at Huddersfield Town FC.*
Best FA Cup season: First Round Proper 91-92 (lost 0-3 at home to Bolton Wanderers in a match played at Huddersfield).
Record Fee Received: £10,000 for John Francis (Sheffield United, 1988).
Players progressing to Football League: Alan Sweeney (Hartlepool United 1979), Graham Cooper (Huddersfield Town 1984), John Francis (Sheffield United 1988), Shaun Smith (Crewe Alexandra 1992).
Clubhouse: (0924 848398). Members' social club open five nights a week and Saturday & Sunday. Bingo, discos, occasional caberet.
Club Record Goalscorer: Mick Pamment 305
Club Record Appearances: Ray Dennis 711.
93-94 Captain: Charlie Bradshaw.
93-94 P.o.Y.: Gary Lockwood.
93-94 Top scorer: Charlie Bradshaw 20.
Local Newspapers: Huddersfield Examiner (0484 430000), Huddersfield & District Chronicle.
Local Radio Stations: Radio Leeds, Radio Sheffield.
Honours: FA Vase R-up 87-88 (SF 86-87), FA Trophy 4th Rd 90-91, FA Amateur Cup 3rd Rd replay 69-70, Northern Premier Lg Div 1 R-up 90-91, Northern Counties East Lg(2) 87-89 (R-up 85-86, Reserve Div 82-83 83-84 84-85 87-88, Reserve Div Cup 82-83 85-86), Yorkshire Lg 75-76 77-78 79-80 81-82 (R-up(5) 72-74 76-77 78-79 80-81, Lg Cup 69-70 78-79 81-82, Div 2 R-up 69-70, Reserve Div 79-80 81-82, Reserve Div Cup 81-82), Sheffield & Hallamshire Senior Cup 75-76 79-80 80-81 83-84 88-89 90-91 91-92, Huddersfield Challenge Cup 82-83 83-84 85-86, Huddersfield Lg(4) 65-69.

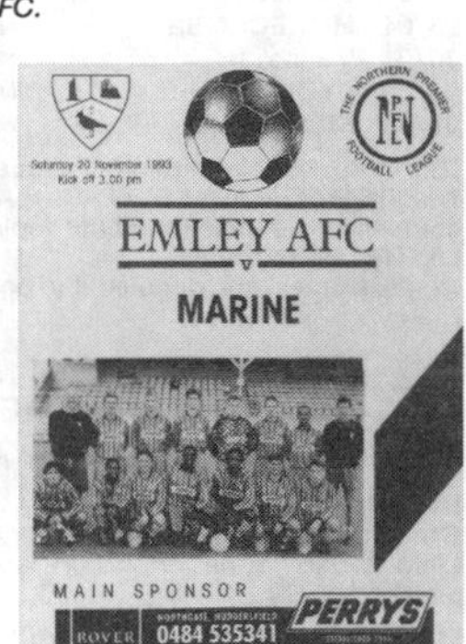

PROGRAMME DETAILS:
Pages: 34 **Price:** 80p
Editor: Alan Blackman
(0924 403959)

EMLEY's 1993-94 CAMPAIGN

Date	Opponents	Comp.	Res	Gate	Goalscorers
21/08	Fleetwood Town	NPL	2-2	193	Bradshaw, Clarke
23/08	**HYDE UNITED**	NPL	2-2	317	Clarke, Drewery
28/08	Barrow	NPL	2-1	1,063	Reynolds, Alcide
30/08	Gainsborough Trin.	NPL	0-2	584	
04/09	**MORECAMBE**	NPL	2-0	329	Clarke, Burrows
07/09	Droylsden	NPL	3-3	475	Bradshaw, Pritchard(2)
11/09	Northwich Victoria	FAC1q	2-2	709	Burrows, Reynolds
13/09	**NORTHWICH VICT.**	FAC1qr	2-0	358	Clarke, McGee(og)
22/09	Boston United	NPL	0-4	881	
25/09	**ASHTON UNITED**	FAC2q	2-0	407	Reynolds, Bradshaw
02/10	**WINSFORD UNITED**	NPL	2-0	337	Pritchard, Reynolds
06/10	Bishop Auckland	NPL	1-2	251	Baker
09/10	Leek Town	FAC3q	0-1	572	
11/10	**GAINSBOROUGH Tr.**	NPL	0-2	330	
16/10	Tamworth	FAT2q	2-2	562	Bradshaw(2)
18/10	**TAMWORTH**	FAT2qr	4-0	409	Bradshaw(2), Reynolds(2)
23/10	**WHITLEY BAY**	NPL	3-1	336	Clarke, Bradshaw, Tunnacliffe
25/10	**FRICKLEY ATHLETIC**	NPL	0-0	701	
30/10	Colwyn Bay	NPL	0-1	206	
06/11	**LEEK TOWN**	NPL	1-1	289	Burrows
09/11	Frickley Athletic	S&H1	1-2	322	Bradshaw
13/11	Matlock Town	NPL	3-2	426	Bradshaw, Clarke, Alcide
15/11	**DROYLSDEN**	NPL	1-1	312	Clarke
20/11	**MARINE**	NPL	6-2	334	Alcide, Bradshaw(2), Clarke, Tunnacliffe, Bondswell
27/11	Barrow	FAT3q	2-2	1,020	Tunnacliffe(2)
29/11	**BARROW**	FAT3qr	2-1	408	Bradshaw, Clarke
04/12	Buxton	NPL	2-2	387	Clarke, Tunnacliffe
11/12	**LANCASTER CITY**	NPLC2	3-0	355	Johnson, Tunnacliffe(2)
21/12	Chorley	NPL	1-1	101	Clarke
27/11	**ACCRINGTON STAN.**	NPL	4-2	684	Tunnacliffe, Bradshaw(2), Johnson
01/01	Accrington Stanley	NPL	2-1	643	Alcide, Bradshaw
03/01	**BRIDLINGTON T.**	NPL	1-1	310	Bradshaw
15/01	**BOSTON UNITED**	NPL	1-1	433	Tunnacliffe
18/01	Knowsley United	NPL	0-2	88	
22/01	Halifax Town	FAT1	1-2	1,575	Clarke(p)
29/01	**BISHOP AUCKLAND**	NPL	2-2	346	Tunnacliffe(2)
31/01	**DROYLSDEN**	NPLC3	2-1	254	Bradshaw, Clarke
05/02	Morecambe	NPL	0-1	319	
12/02	Marine	NPL	1-4	435	Bondswell
19/02	Winsford United	NPL	3-1	244	Burrows, Bondswell(2)
21/02	**KNOWSLEY UTD**	NPL	2-1	204	Tunnacliffe, Bondswell
05/03	**FLEETWOOD TOWN**	NPL	3-2	251	Bondswell, Bradshaw(2)
12/03	Hyde United	NPL	1-2	253	Reynolds
14/03	**ACCRINGTON S.**	NPLC4	0-0	273	
19/03	**CHORLEY**	NPL	0-3	305	
24/03	Accrington Stanley	NPLC4r	1-3	307	Johnson
26/03	Whitley Bay	NPL	0-2	242	
02/04	**BUXTON**	NPL	1-4	173	Reynolds
04/04	Leek Town	NPL	0-2	515	
09/04	**MATLOCK TOWN**	NPL	4-4	184	Tunnacliffe, Alcide, Jones, Jerome
16/04	**HORWICH R.M.I.**	NPL	1-1	168	Jerome
18/04	Bridlington Town	NPL	2-1	91	Clarke(2)
21/04	**COLWYN BAY**	NPL	3-3	158	Bondswell(2), Reynolds
23/04	Frickley Athletic	NPL	0-1	256	
25/04	**BARROW**	NPL	0-0	164	
30/04	Horwich RMI	NPL	1-1	151	Mellor

Key: NPL: Northern Premier League Premier Division, NPLC: Northern Premier League Cup, FAC: F.A. Cup, FAT: F.A. Trophy, S&H: Sheffield & Hallamshire Senior Cup. Numbers after cup competitions denote rounds (r: replay, qf: Quarter-Final, sf: Semi-Final, f: Final. Numbers in brackets indicate legs, i.e. (1): 1st leg). Home fixtures are denoted by bold capitals, away matches by lower case. (p): penalty, og: Own goal.

SQUAD MEMBERS *(previous clubs listed in chronological order)*

GOALKEEPERS: Dave Redfern *(Sheffield Wednesday, Rochdale, Gainsborough, Stockport County, Buxton),* **Robert Wraight** *(Huddersfield Town),* **Ray Dennis** *(Emley, Altrincham, Emley, Barrow, Ossett Albion),* **Scott Winstanley** *(Farsley Celtic).*

DEFENDERS: Steve Codd *(Long Eaton Utd, Boston FC, Guiseley, Denaby Utd),* **Matthew Johnson** *(Huddersfield T., Bradley Rgrs),* **Neil Griffiths** *(Halifax Town),* **Richard Hopley** *(local),* **Martin Baker** *(Berkhamsted Town, Watford, Rhyl, Altrincham),* **Hanson Jerome** *(local),* **Robert Mellor** *(local),* **Gary Lockwood** *(Hatfield Main, Bridlington Town, Goole Town, Bishop Auckland).*

MIDFIELD: Andy Bondswell *(Leeds Utd, Halifax Town, Thackley, Guiseley, Harrogate Town, Accrington Stanley, Witton Albion),* **Colin Alcide** *(Emley, Altrincham),* **Lee Burrows** *(Southampton, Bradley Rgrs, Guiseley),* **Simon Jones** *(local),* **Tony Gregory** *(Halifax, Buxton),* **Jason Drewery** *(local)*

FORWARDS: Bob Clarke *(Bradley Rgrs, Brackenhall Utd, Bradley Rgrs),* **Charlie Bradshaw** *(Ossett Town, Accrington Stanley, Emley, Altrincham),* **Michael Reynolds** *(local),* **John Dysart** *(Huddersfield T.),* **Ian Tunnacliffe** *(Storthes Hall, Emley, Altrincham).*

1866 FRICKLEY ATHLETIC The Blues

The refurbished main stand at Frickley Athletic's ground.

Chairman: Mike Twiby **President:** M High.
Secretary: Bob Bates, 2 Lincoln Crescent, South Elmsall, Pontefract WF9 2TJ (0977 644575).
Manager: Ronnie Glavin **Physio:** T McCroakam **Coach:** TBA
Financial Secretary: D Fisher.
Ground: Westfield Lane, South Elmsall, Pontefract (0977 642460/644453).
Directions: Follow signs for South Elmsall from A1 and A638. Left at Superdrug warehouse, right at T junction and immediately left up Westfield Lane (signposted Frickley Colliery). Left into Oxford Road (opposite Westfield Hotel) - ground at bottom on right. Two miles from South Elmsall (BR).
Capacity: 6,000 **Cover:** 2,500 **Seats:** 800 **Floodlights:** Yes **Club Shop:** Yes.
Colours: All blue **Change colours:** Yellow & black.
Previous Leagues: Sheffield/ Yorkshire 22-24/ Midland Counties 24-33 34-60 70-76/ Cheshire County 60-70/ Northern Premier 76-80/ GMV Conference (Alliance Premier) 80-87.
Midweek home matchday: Tuesday **Sponsors:** Ramset Construction.
Record Attendance: 6,500 v Rotherham United, FA Cup First Round 1971.
Previous Name: Frickley Colliery Athletic.
Best FA Trophy season: Quarter-Finals 84-85.
Best FA Cup season: 3rd Rd 1985-86 (lost 1-3 at home to Rotherham). 2nd Rd 84-85 (0-1 at Darlington). 1st Rd 36-37 57-58 63-64 71-72 73-74 83-84 86-87 88-89.
League clubs defeated in FA Cup: Hartlepool United 85-86.
Record Fees - Paid: £1,800
Received: £12,500 for Paul Shirtliff (Boston Utd).
Players progressing to Football League: Dennis Smith & Jack Brownsword (Hull 1946), Stan Scrimshaw (Halifax 1947), William Callaghan (Aldershot 1949), Leo Dickens 1950), John Ashley & Graham Caulfield (York 1950 & 67), Ron Barritt (Leeds 1951), John Pickup (Bradford PA 1955), Tom Hymers & Arthur Ashmore & Stewart Gray (Doncaster 1958 & 66 & 78), Colin Roberts (Bradford City 1959), Derek Downing (Middlesbrough 1965), Graham Reed & Russell Wilcox (Northampton 1985 & 86), Will Foley (Swansea 1986), Gary Brook (Newport 1987), Wayne Scargill (Bradford City 93-94).
Clubhouse: Harlequin Club outside ground. TV, pool, other facilties.
Club Record Scorer: K Whiteley
Captain 93-94: Neil Lacey.
Top Scorer 93-94: Andy Hayward
Player of the Year 93-94: Ian Thompson.
Local Newspapers: S Yorks Times (0977 642214), Hemsworth & S Elmsall Express (0977 640107).
Local Radio Stations: Radio Sheffield, Radio Hallam, Radio Leeds.
Honours: Alliance Premier Lg R-up 85-86, Midland Counties Lg R-up 72-73, (Lg Cup 75-76), Yorkshire Lg R-up 23-24, Sheffield & Hallamshire Senior Cup 27-28 56-57 60-61 62-63 66-67 78-79 85-86 87-88 89-90, Sheffield Association Lg 20-21 (R-up 11-12).

PROGRAMME DETAILS:
Pages: 40 **Price:** 50p
Editor: D Fisher

FRICKLEY ATHLETIC's 1993-94 CAMPAIGN

Date	Opponents	Comp.	Res	Gate	Goalscorers
21/08	**COLWYN BAY**	NPL	0-1	202	
25/08	Boston United	NPL	2-2	850	Thompson, Lacey
28/08	**LEEK TOWN**	NPL	1-3	213	Whitehurst
30/08	**WHITLEY BAY**	NPL	6-1	183	Garnham, Hayward(3), Fuller, Hatto
04/09	Marine	NPL	1-4	340	Hatto
07/09	**GAINSBOROUGH Tr.**	NPL	1-0	297	Templeton
12/09	Bridlington Town	FAC1q	0-2	335	
14/09	Matlock Town	NPL	5-1	436	Fuller, Hatto(2), Whitehurst, Templeton
18/09	**BARROW**	NPL	0-0	256	
21/09	**BISHOP AUCKLAND**	NPL	5-0	208	Hayward(3), Hancock, Fuller
25/09	Hyde United	NPL	0-4	289	
29/09	Bridlington Town	PC1	3-0	115	Whitehurst(2), Hayward
02/10	**FRICKLEY ATHLETIC**	NPL	5-2	199	Hayward, Fuller(2), Lloyd, Kelly
05/10	Whitley Bay	NPL	2-2	196	Templeton (2)
09/10	**DROYLSDEN**	NPL	3-0	226	Hayward, Templeton, Kelly
12/10	**BUXTON**	NPL	3-1	238	Templeton, Whitehurst, Hatto
13/10	Accrington Stanley	NPL	4-2	411	Templeton(2), Hayward(2)
20/10	Bridlington Town	NPL	3-0	178	Thompson, Kelly, Hayward
25/10	Emley	NPL	0-0	701	
02/11	Gainsborough Trinity	NPL	3-2	828	Thompson(2), Hayward
06/11	**MORECAMBE**	NPL	3-3	280	Whitehurst, Lacey, Hayward
09/11	**EMLEY**	SHSC(1)	2-1	322	Hayward(2)
13/11	Morecambe	NPL	2-1	410	Whitehurst, Hayward
16/11	**BRIDLINGTON**	NPL	5-0	475	Hancock, Templeton, Hayward(2), Hatto
20/11	**CHORLEY**	NPL	5-0	256	Templeton, Thompson, Hayward(2), Lacey
22/11	Guiseley	PC2	0-3	475	
27/11	Dunston Fed. Brewery	FAT3q	5-1	281	Lacey, Hayward(2), Templeton, Garnham
04/12	Winsford United	NPL	0-1	243	
11/12	**GRETNA**	NPLC2	0-1	180	
29/12	Hallam	SHSC2	6-2	150	Hayward(3), Thompson, Kelly, Templeton
01/01	Chorley	NPL	1-2	230	Hayward
03/01	**MATLOCK TOWN**	NPL	1-0	254	Lloyd
08/01	Frechville CA	SHSCqf	3-1	95	Lacey, Fuller, Garnham
15/01	**FLEETWOOD TOWN**	NPL	2-2	276	Gabbiadini(2)
22/01	Billingham Synthonia	FAT1	1-2	238	Gabbiadini
29/01	Barrow	NPL	3-1	954	Garnham, Hancock, Thompson
05/02	**WINSFORD UNITED**	NPL	2-2	244	Hayward(2)
07/02	Sheffield	SHSCsf(1)	1-2	110	Thompson
12/02	Horwich RMI	NPL	1-1	352	Thompson
19/02	Leek Town	NPL	0-1	622	
01/03	**SHEFFIELD**	SHSCsf(2)	0-0	211	
05/03	Buxton	NPL	1-1	267	Thompson
12/03	**KNOWSLEY UNITED**	NPL	1-0	193	Hatto
19/03	Droylsden	NPL	2-2	108	Fuller, Hayward
26/03	**ACCRINGTON STAN.**	NPL	2-0	272	Hatto, Hayward
30/03	Bishop Auckland	NPL	1-3	235	
02/04	**BOSTON UNITED**	NPL	0-1	257	
13/04	**MARINE**	NPL	5-2	226	Hayward, Templeton, Rayson(2), Thompson
16/04	Fleetwood Town	NPL	1-1	150	Rayson
19/04	**HYDE UNITED**	NPL	4-1	206	Hayward(2), Rayson(2)
23/04	**EMLEY**	NPL	1-0	256	Hatto
28/04	Colwyn Bay	NPL	1-1	106	Hatto
30/04	Knowsley United	NPL	2-0	75	Thompson(2)

Key: NPL: Northern Premier League Premier Division, NPLC: Northern Premier League Cup, PC: Northern Premier League Presidennts Cup, FAC: F.A. Cup, FAT: F.A. Trophy, SHSC: Sheffield & Hallamshire Senior Cup. Number after cup competitions denote rounds (r: replay, qf: Quarter-Final, sf: Semi-Final, f: Final. Numbers in brackets indicate legs, i.e. (1): 1st leg).
Home fixtures are denoted by bold capitals, away matches by lower case. (p): penalty, og: Own goal.

SQUAD MEMBERS *(previous clubs listed in chronological order)*

GOALKEEPERS: Ian Wardle *(Barnsley, Maltby MW).*

DEFENDERS: Peter Heaney *(Goole, Ossett T., Frickley, Buxton, Denaby Utd.),* **Neil Lacey** *(Denaby Utd., Goole),* **Gary Hatto** *(Huddersfield, Doncaster, Frickley, Ossett T.),* **Andy Barnsley** *(Denaby Utd., Rotherham, Sheff. Utd., Rotherham, Carlisle Utd., Buxton),* **Tim Wragg** *(Worksop, Matlock, Gainsborough T., Goole, Ossett T., Bridlington),* **Paul Brown** *(Local Football),* **Ian Thompson** *(Gainsborough T., Worksop, Goole, Worksop, Goole, Frickley, Altrincham)*

MIDFIELD: Kevin Kelly *(Huddersfield, Goole),* **Ian Garnham** *(RES Parkgate),* **Chris Audsley** *(Ossett Alb., Frickley, Ossett Alb.),* **Mike Thompson** *(Scunthorpe, Goole),* **Mark Hancock** *(Grimethorpe, Wharncliffe Arms),* **Stuart Bentley** *(Local Football),* **Henry Templeton** *(St Mirren, Ayr Utd., Falkirk, Queen of the South),*

FORWARDS: Simon Fuller *(Bradford C., Ossett T.),* **Andy Hayward** *(Pontefract Coll.),* **Viv Rayson** *(Local Football),* **Billy Whitehurst** *(Middlesbrough, Hull, Newcastle Utd., Oxford Utd., Reading, Sunderland, Hull, Sheff. Utd., Doncaster, Hartfield Main, Kettering, Goole, Stafford R., Mossley, South China(HK))*

1873 **GAINSBOROUGH TRINITY** Blues

The 'Northolme' ground.

Chairman: John Davis **Vice Chairman:** P F C Lobley **President:** Ken Marsden
Secretary: Frank Nicholson, 9 North Street, Morton, Gainsborough, Lincs DN21 3AS (0427 615239).
Joint Managers: Gary Brook/ Alastair Miller **Coach:** C Gaffney.
Physio: E Beaumont **Commercial Manager:** Barry Martin.
Ground: The Northolme, North Street, Gainsborough, Lincs DN21 2QW (0427 613295).
Directions: Ground situated in town centre, 250 yds from the Post Office and magistrates court. Two miles from Lea Road (BR).
Capacity: 7,500 **Cover:** 5,000 **Seats:** 238 **Floodlights:** Yes **Club Shop:** Yes.
Colours: Royal blue (white trim)/white/blue & white **Change colours:** White/black/black.
Previous Leagues: Mids Counties 1889-96 1912-60 61-68/ Football League 1896-1912/ Central Alliance 60-61.
Club Sponsors: National Power West Burton.
Midweek home matchday: Tuesday **Record Gate:** 9,760 v Scunthorpe Utd, Midland Lge 1948.
Best FA Trophy season: 2nd Rd 2nd rep. 86-87.
Best FA Cup season: 3rd Rd 1886-87. 1st Rd on 33 occasions; 1885-86 97-98 1905-14 27-34 35-36 37-39 45-47 48-49 50-54 59-60 66-67 83-84.
League clubs defeated in FA Cup: Rotherham United 1894-95/ Stockport County 1913-14/ Crewe 28-29 31-32/ Port Vale 37-38/ Gateshead 38-39/ Mansfield Town 45-46.
Record Fees - Paid: £3,000 for Stuart Lowe (Buxton 89-90)
Received: £20,000 for Tony James.
Record win: 7-1 v Whitley Bay
Record defeat: 2-7 v Hyde United.
Players progressing to Football League: A Morton & S Foxall & J Cockcroft (West Ham), Arthur Hall (Chesterfield 1947), Jack Haigh (Liverpool 1949), Norman Curtis (Sheffield Wednesday 1950), Des Thompson & Steve Richards (York 1951 & 86), Terry Farmer & Barry Webster & John Woodall (Rotherham 1952 & 56 & 74), Maurice Robinson & Roy Brown (Doncaster 1952 & 53), John Burnett & Robert Ham (Grimsby 1958 & 64), Robert Pashley & Mike Woldworth (Scunthorpe 1959 & 76), Simon Jones (Rochdale 1963), William Purton (Bradford City 1975), Keith Ripley (Huddersfield 1978), Stewart Evans (Sheffield United 1980), Tony James & Ian Bowling & John Scofield (Lincoln 1988), David Redfearn (Stockport), Richard Logan (Huddersfield 1993).
Clubhouse: Executive 'Club on the Park' (0427 615625) open nightly and Saturday matchday lunctimes. Full license and restaurant facilties.
Club Record Scorer: Monty Brown
Club Record Appearances: Monty Brown.
Local Newspapers: Gainsborough News, Lincolnshire Echo.
Local Radio Stations: BBC Radio Lincs.
93-94 Captain: C Bishop.
93-94 Top Scorer: Gary Brook.
93-94 Supporters' P.o.Y.: Gary Brook.
93-94 Players' P.o.Y.: Andy Moore.
Hons: Northern Premier Lg Cup 81-82 (R-up 71-72), Midland Co's Lg 1890-91 1927-28 48-49 66-67 (R-up 1891-92 95-96 1913-14 28-29), Lincs Snr Cup(15) 1889-90 92-93 94-95 97-98 1903-05 06-07 10-11 46-49 50-51 57-59 63-64.

PROGRAMME DETAILS:
Pages: 28 **Price:** 70p
Editor: K Croft
(0427 615625)

GAINSBOROUGH's 1993-94 CAMPAIGN

Date	Opponents	Comp.	Res	Gate	Goalscorers
21/08	**BISHOP AUCKLAND**	NPL	0-0	431	
25/08	Bridlington Town	NPL	0-0	297	
28/08	Chorley	NPL	1-1	451	Brook
30/08	**EMLEY**	NPL	2-0	586	Grayson, Bishop
04/09	**DROYLSDEN**	NPL	1-2	409	Toone
07/09	Frickley Athletic	NPL	0-1	297	
11/09	Buxton	FAC1q	1-2	282	Grayson
14/09	**BUXTON**	NPL	1-1	418	Moore
18/09	**EASTWOOD TOWN**	FAT1q	5-3	337	Brook(4), Shaw
20/09	Hyde United	NPL	0-4	249	
25/09	**MARINE**	NPL	1-2	375	Bishop
02/10	Colwyn Bay	NPL	2-1	210	Brook(2)
05/10	**MATLOCK TOWN**	NPL	2-2	466	Grayson(2)
09/10	**WHITLEY BAY**	NPL	1-3	370	Grayson
11/10	Emley	NPL	2-0	330	Grayson(2)
16/10	**MATLOCK TOWN**	FAT2q	1-2	453	Moore
19/10	Buxton	NPL	5-2	208	Fox, Bishop, Brook, Grayson(2)
23/10	**HYDE UNITED**	NPL	1-1	378	Grayson
26/10	**BRIDLINGTON T.**	NPL	3-1	628	Grayson(2), Brook
30/10	Droylsden	NPL	4-1	255	Brook(2), Grayson, Logan
02/11	**FRICKLEY ATH.**	NPL	2-3	828	Grayson, Brook
06/11	Marine	NPL	0-3	381	
13/11	Barrow	NPL	1-1	1,161	Bishop
20/11	**FLEETWOOD TOWN**	NPL	5-1	386	Grayson(2), Margerison, Bishop, Hart
27/11	**KNOWSLEY UNITED**	NPL	2-1	320	Toone, Brook
04/12	Matlock Town	NPL	2-5	435	Grayson, Brook
11/12	**COLWYN BAY**	NPLC2	0-2	313	
27/12	**BOSTON UNITED**	NPL	2-2	1,421	Pascoe(og), Brook
01/01	Boston United	NPL	1-6	1,602	Toone
03/01	**CHORLEY**	NPL	1-1	514	Hart
08/01	Accrington Stanley	NPL	4-2	388	Brook(3), Margerison
15/01	**WINSFORD UNITED**	NPL	3-1	415	Hardy, Toone, Brook
22/01	Horwich RMI	NPL	2-1	158	Brook, Toone
29/01	Fleetwood Town	NPL	2-1	374	Brook, Grayson
01/02	**LEEK TOWN**	NPL	3-5	486	Brook, Shaw, Grayson
05/02	**BARROW**	NPL	2-1	474	Brook(2)
12/02	Whitley Bay	NPL	1-0	226	Margerison
19/02	**MORECAMBE**	NPL	0-1	542	
05/03	**COLWYN BAY**	NPL	0-1	380	
12/03	**HORWICH R.M.I.**	NPL	4-0	383	Bairstow, Brook(2), Toone
19/03	Leek Town	NPL	0-2	443	
02/04	Winsford United	NPL	0-0	173	
04/04	**ACCRINGTON STAN.**	NPL	0-1	563	
09/04	Morecambe	NPL	0-3	235	
16/04	Bishop Auckland	NPL	0-1	270	
23/04	Knowsley United	NPL	1-1	73	Grayson

Key: NPL: Northern Premier League Premier Division, NPLC: Northern Premier League Cup, FAC: F.A. Cup, FAT: F.A. Trophy. Numbers after cup competitions denote rounds (r: replay, qf: Quarter-Final, sf: Semi-Final, f: Final. Numbers in brackets indicate legs, i.e. (1): 1st leg).
Home fixtures are denoted by bold capitals, away matches by lower case. (p): penalty, og: Own goal.

SQUAD MEMBERS *(previous clubs listed in chronological order)*

GOALKEEPERS: Giles Newcombe *(Rotherham)*, **Gary Ingham** *(Rotherham, Gainsborough T., Shepshed Chart., Goole, Bridlington, Maltby MW, Boston Utd).*

DEFENDERS: Andy Moore *(Grimsby, Lincoln, Western Suburbs (Aust), Boston Utd, Grantham)*, **Darrell Fox** *(Hallam, Harworth CI, Hallam)*, **Paul Watson** *(Ossett T.)*, **Mark Pennant** *(Oakham Utd., Sutton T., Eastwood T., Sutton T.)*, **Gary Middleton** *(Rotherham), Barnsley, Belper).*

MIDFIELD: Colin Bishop *(Frickley Ath., Bridlington)*, **Lee Margerison** *(Bradford C., Slough)*, **Aidan Hart** *(Boston FC, Lincoln Moorlands)*, **Kyle Talbot** *(Grimsby, Grantham)*, **Andy Shaw** *(Worksop, Wellington (NZ))*, **Scott Bairstow** *(Bradford C., Guiseley)*, **Richard Toone** *(Leicester C., Lincoln Utd, Boston Utd).*

FORWARDS: Gary Brook *(Ossett Alb., Frickley Ath., Newport Co., Scarborough, Blackpool, Frickley Ath.)*, **Simon Grayson** *(Sheff. Utd, Chesterfield, Hartlepool, Sheffield FC)*, **Jeff Hardy** *(Local Football)*, **Mark Culley** *(Stapenhill, Long Eaton, Sutton T.)*, **Brian Peach** *(Local Football).*

Formed: 1909

GUISELEY

Guiseley had a remarkable season winning the Division One title and coming within a hair's breadth of becoming the first former FA Vase winners to reach an FA Trophy final. Here Paul Bottomley (left), himself bidding to return to Wembley for the second consecutive season, battles with Chris Hemming during the Second Round victory over Stafford Rangers.

Photo - Colin Stevens.

Chairman: Gary Douglas **President:** David Brotherton.
Sec.: Philip Rogerson, 8 Viewlands Cres., Chevin End, Menston, Ilkley, W Yorks LS29 6BH (0943 879236).
Manager: Ray McHale **Asst Manager:** Garry Watson.
Physio: John Rhodes **Commercial Manager:** John Holmes. **Press Officer:** Secretary
Ground: Nethermoor, Otley Road, Guiseley, Leeds LS20 8BT (0943 873223).
Directions: Via M1 to M62 junction 28, follow Leeds road to Leeds ring-road to junction of A65 at Horsforth. At r-about turn left onto A65 through Rawdon to Guiseley centre. Ground quarter of a mile past traffic lights, on the right, entrance on A65 opposite Silver Cross factory. Additional car parking available off Ings Crescent. Five mins walk from Guiseley (BR/Metro) station.
Capacity: 3,000 **Cover:** 1,040 **Seats:** 427 **Floodlights:** Yes **Metal Badges:** Yes
Club Shop: Yes, selling programmes, various items of clothing, key rings, badges, mugs etc. Phone either club office no. (above) or clubhouse (below).
Colours: White/blue/white **Change colours:** All yellow. **Sponsors:** Laser Care Clinics Ltd.
Previous Leagues: West Riding Co. Amtr/ West Yorks/ Yorkshire 68-82/ Northern Co's (East) 82-91.
Midweek home matchday: Monday **Reserves' League:** Northern Co's (East) Reserve Div.
Record Attendance: 2,486 v Bridlington Town, FA Vase Semi Final 1st Leg 89-90.
Best FA Cup season: First Round Proper 1991-92 (lost 0-1 at Chester City).
Players progressing to Football League: Keith Walwyn (York City), Frank Harrison (Halifax Town), Dean Walling (Carlisle United), Richard Annan (Crewe Alexandra).
Clubhouse: (0943 872872) Open before and after all games (closes 11pm). Snack bar within ground open before and during matches.
93-94 Captain: Paul Bottomley. **93-94 P.o.Y.:** Paul Stevenson
Supporters' P.o.Y. 93-94: Peter Atkinson.
Players' P.o.Y. 93-94: Steve Dickinson. **93-94 Top scorer:** Billy Roberts.
Local Newspapers: Yorkshire Evening Post, Bradford Telegraph & Argus, Airedale & Wharfdale Observer, Wharfe Valley Times.
Honours: FA Vase 90-91 (R-up 91-92, SF 89-90), FA Trophy SF 93-94, Northern Premier Lg Div 1 93-94 (Presidents Cup 93-94, Div 1 Cup 92-93), Northern Counties (East) Lg 90-91 (Lg Cup 90-91), West Riding County Cup(5 inc 93-94), Yorkshire Lg R-up 79-80 81-82 (Lg Cup 79-80).

PROGRAMME DETAILS:
Pages: 40 **Price:** £1
Editor: Les Wood
(0532 509181)

SQUAD MEMBERS

GOALKEEPERS: Steve Dickinson *(Bradford C.)*, **Phil Hughes** *(Man Utd, Leeds, Bury, Wigan, Scarborough, Rochdale)*

DEFENDERS: Colin Hogarth *(Thackley, Otley, Guiseley, Harrogate T., Guiseley, Lancaster)*, **Andy Armitage** *(Leeds, Rochdale, Guiseley, Farsley C., Mt Gravatt(NZ))*, **Calvin Allen** *(Farsley, Harrogate RA, Farsley)*, **Peter Atkinson** *(Otley)*, **Paul Bottomley** *(Garforth, Guiseley, Bridlington)*, **Brendan Hudson** *(Baildon, Guiseley, Hyde, Thackley)*, **Steve Richards** *(Hull, York, Gainsborough, Lincoln, Cambridge U., Scarborough, Halifax, Doncaster)*, **Phil Wilson** *(Bolton, Huddersfield, York, Macclesfield, Scarborough, Stafford, Witton, Guiseley, Winnipeg(Can))*. *(cont. opposite)*

GUISELEY's 1993-94 CAMPAIGN

Date	Opponents	Comp.	Res	Gate	Goalscorers
21/08	**WORKINGTON**	NPL	6-2	505	Colville(2), Allen(2), Richards, James
28/08	Great Harwood Town	FACpr	5-1	210	Stevenson(2), Allen, B Roberts, James
30/08	**RADCLIFFE BORO.**	NPL	2-0	489	Colville(2)
04/09	Mossley	NPL	6-1	363	Outhart, Colville, Allen, Roberts, Richards, Whellans
06/09	**EASTWOOD TOWN**	NPL	1-0	695	B Roberts
11/09	**ILKESTON TOWN**	FAC1q	3-1	563	B Roberts, Allen, Armitage
18/09	Netherfield	NPL	0-3	308	
20/09	**SPENNYMOOR UTD**	NPL	2-0	624	Noteman, Allen
25/09	Winsford United	FAC2q	1-2	271	Colville
02/10	Marine	PC1	1-1	253	Hogarth
06/10	Spennymoor United	NPL	2-1	309	James(2)
09/10	**ASHTON UNITED**	NPL	1-0	705	Allen
12/10	Eastwood Town	NPL	2-0	118	Noteman, Colville
16/10	**TOW LAW TOWN**	FAC2q	4-3	486	Colville(2), Allen, Stevenson
18/10	**CAERNARFON TOWN**	NPL	4-0	491	Allen(3), Richards
23/10	Curzon Ashton	NPLC1	1-0	160	Atkinson
27/10	Alfreton Town	NPL	1-3	256	Colville
30/10	**MARINE**	PC1r	1-0	561	Stevenson
02/11	Farsley Celtic	NPL	2-0	459	B Roberts, Outhart
06/11	**CONGLETON TOWN**	NPL	2-2	438	Allen, Brockie
08/11	**GARFORTH TOWN**	WRC1	0-0	501	
13/11	Bamber Bridge	NPL	2-3	502	Outhart(2)
15/11	**WORKSOP TOWN**	NPL	1-1	471	Colville
18/11	**GARFORTH TOWN**	WRC1r	7-1	332	B Roberts(3), Allen(2), Whellans(2)
20/11	**WARRINGTON T.**	NPL	2-0	452	Stevenson, B Roberts
22/08	**FRICKLEY ATH.**	PCqf	3-0	475	Allen(3)
27/11	Harrogate Town	FAT3q	4-3	505	Allen, Hogarth, B Roberts, Bottomley
04/12	Lancaster City	D1C2	1-1	120	Colville
09/12	Farsley Celtic	WRC2	1-0	319	Aitkin
11/12	Accrington Stanley	NPLC2	4-6	452	B Roberts(2), Allen, Richards
20/12	Curzon Ashton	NPL	2-0	150	Colville, Atkinson
01/01	Congleton Town	NPL	2-0	230	Allen, Colville
10/01	**CURZON ASHTON**	NPL	2-0	393	Allen(2)
19/01	**TADCASTER ALBION**	WRCqf	3-1	286	Noteman, B Roberts, Stevenson
22/01	Winsford United	FAT1	1-0	332	B Roberts
25/01	Goole Town	NPL	2-1	238	B Roberts, Olney(og)
05/02	**MOSSLEY**	NPL	3-2	420	B Roberts(2), A Roberts
12/02	**STAFFORD RGRS**	FAT2	3-2	1,209	Essex(og), B Roberts(2)
14/02	**ASHTON UNITED**	PCsf(1)	0-0	273	
19/02	Great Harwood Town	NPL	2-1	296	B Roberts, Brockie
21/02	**LANCASTER CITY**	D1C2r	1-1	302	Allen *(won on penalties)*
05/03	Cheltenham Town	FAT3	0-0	1,117	
08/03	**CHELTENHAM TOWN**	FAT3r	1-0	1,139	Bottomley
10/03	Ashton United	PCsf(2)	1-0	347	Bottomley
12/03	**NETHERFIELD**	NPL	4-0	487	B Roberts(2), Hogarth, Colville
14/03	Caernarfon Town	NPL	5-0	158	A Roberts, Allen, B Roberts, Colville, Marshall
19/03	Ashton United	NPL	2-0	560	B Roberts(2)
21/03	**ALFRETON TOWN**	D1Cqf	1-2	487	Armitage
23/03	Ossett Albion	WRCsf	4-3	138	Marshall, Outhart, Flanagan, Armitage
26/03	**MORECAMBE**	FATqf	3-2	1,805	Colville, B Roberts(2)
28/03	**HARROGATE TOWN**	NPL	2-0	607	B Roberts, Colville
31/03	**BAMBER BRIDGE**	NPL	3-2	405	Baldwin(og), Allen, Bottomley
02/04	**FARSLEY CELTIC**	NPL	4-0	674	Colville, B Roberts, Outhart, James
04/04	Harrogate Town	NPL	1-0	600	Colville
06/04	**GRETNA**	NPL	1-0	525	A Roberts
07/04	Worksop Town	NPL	2-3	310	James, Outhart
12/04	Gretna	NPL	2-1	90	Allen, Wilson
16/04	Runcorn	FATsf(1)	1-1	1,595	Allen *(played at Chester City FC)*
19/04	Warrington Town	NPL	1-1	248	B Roberts
23/04	**RUNCORN**	FATsf(2)	0-1	2,176	
25/04	**LEEK TOWN**	PCf(1)	3-1	411	Richards, Stevenson(2)
26/04	Radcliffe Borough	NPL	2-2	150	Allen, B Roberts
28/04	**GOOLE TOWN**	NPL	2-0	524	Allen, James
30/04	Workington	NPL	0-3	181	
02/05	Leek Town	PCf(2)	2-1	524	Colville, Brockie
03/05	**Gt HARWOOD TOWN**	NPL	1-1	291	James
04/05	Lancaster City	NPL	2-1	123	James, Colville
05/05	**ALFRETON TOWN**	NPL	3-1	390	Colville(2), Brockie
07/05	**LANCASTER CITY**	NPL	1-1	408	Bottomley
09/05	GOOLE TOWN	WRCf	1-0	771	B Roberts *(played at Halifax Town FC)*

Key: NPL: Northern Premier League Division One, NPLC: Northern Premier League Cup, D1C: (Northern Premier League) Division One Cup, PC: (Northern Premier League) Presidents Cup, WRC: West Riding County Cup.

SQUAD *(continued from opposite page)*
MIDFIELD: Vince Brockie *(Leeds, Doncaster, Goole)*, **Paul Stevenson** *(Farsley, Harrogate T., Farsley, Blackpool, Farsley, Bridlington)*, **Andy Clarkson** *(Bradford C.)*, **Tony Outhart** *(Bridlington Trinity, Scarborough, Harrogate RA, Harrogate T., Brigg)*

FORWARDS: Billy Roberts *(Frasley, Rochdale, Farsley, Guiseley, Bridlington, Farsley)*, **Andy Lamb** *(Farsley, Thackley, Farsley)*, **Bob Colville** *(Rossendale, Oldham, Bury, Stockport, York, Darlington, Northwich, Bangor, Barrow, Guiseley, Bangor)*, **Allan Roberts** *(Thackley, Ossett A., Thackley, Farsley, Pontefract, Harrogate, Bradford PA, Guiseley, Bridlington, Bradford PA)*, **Wayne Noteman** *(Yorkshire Main, Harrogate RA, Goole, Farsley, Harrogate, Frickley, Bridlington, Bishop Auckland)*, **Lutel James** *(Yorkshire Am.)*

HORWICH R.M.I.

Formed: 1896 — Railwaymen

A Horwich RMI defender is left trailing in the wake of an Emley forward, but the Railwaymen still pick up a useful point with a 1-1 April draw in Yorkshire.

Photo - Barry Lockwood.

Chairman: Garry Culshaw **President:** G H Fisher, Esq.
Secretary: Brian Hart, 'Meadow View', 7 Rectory Gdns, Daisy Hill, Westhoughton, Bolton BL5 2RG (0942 818669).
Manager: Mick Holgate **Asst Manager:** TBA **Coach:** TBA
Press Officer: P O'Berg
Ground: Grundy Hill, Ramsbottom Road, Horwich, Bolton BL6 5NH (0204 696908). *****Important note - Horwich RMI's ground has been sold for development and the club intend to move to Leigh Rugby League club during the course of the 1994-95 season*****
Directions *(to Grundy Hill)*: M61 junction 6, follow Horwich signs at r-about, bear left then right, just before zebra crossing, into Victoria Road, ground alongside road on left. 3 miles from Blackrod (BR). Buses - 126 from Preston, 517 from Wigan, 575 from Bolton.
Capacity: 5,000 **Cover:** 3 sides **Seats:** 500 **Floodlights:** Yes **Club Shop:** Yes
Colours: Blue & white stripes/blue/blue
Change colours: Maroon & white/maroon/maroon.
Sponsors: Dunhall Financial Services, Horwich.
Previous Leagues: Lancs Alliance 1891-97/ Lancs 1897-1900/ Lancs Combination 17-18 19-39 46-68/ Cheshire County 68-82/ North West Counties 82-83.
Midweek home matchday: Wednesday
Reserve Team's League: Northern Football Combination.
Record Attendance: 4,500.
Best FA Cup season: 1st Rd 28-29 82-83.
League clubs defeated in FA Cup: None.
Record Fee Received: £2,000 for Tony Caldwell (Bolton).
Players progressing to Football League: Harold Lea & David Holland & Jim Cunliffe (Stockport 1958 & 59 & 60), Frank Wignall (Everton 1958), Gary Cooper (Rochdale 1973), Tony Caldwell (Bolton 1983), Raymond Redshaw (Wigan 1984), Tony Ellis (Oldham 1986).
Clubhouse: Open every evening.
Local Newspapers: Bolton Evening News (Bolton 22345).
Local Radio Stations: Radio Lancs, Red Rose Radio.
Honours: FA Trophy QF 90-91, Premier Inter League (GMAC) Cup 87-88, Cheshire County Lg 78-79 (Challenge Shield 78-79), Lancs Combination 57-58 (R-up 29-30 55-56 66-67, Lg Cup 28-29 53-54 56-57 65-66, Div 2 R-up 48-49 50-51), West Lancs Lg 10-11 11-12, Lancs Junior Cup 24-25 29-30 (R-up 53-54 57-58 62-63 82-83), Lancs Floodlit Trophy 84-85 (R-up 83-84), Lancs FA Cup 84-85.

PROGRAMME DETAILS:
Pages: 28 **Price:** 50p
Editor: Garry Culshaw

HORWICH R.M.I's 1993-94 CAMPAIGN

Date	Opponents	Comp.	Res	Gate	Goalscorers
21/08	**MATLOCK TOWN**	NPL	1-1	207	McDonald
24/08	Barrow	NPL	2-0	1,268	Dobson, McDonald
28/08	Buxton	NPL	4-4	252	Barnsley(og), McLachlan, McDonald, Goodison(og)
30/08	**BRIDLINGTON TOWN**	NPL	0-1	258	
04/09	**BOSTON UNITED**	NPL	0-5	243	
08/09	Accrington Stanley	NPL	0-1	337	
11/09	Chorley	FAC1q	1-3	407	McDonald
15/09	**MORECAMBE**	NPL	1-3	213	Wright
18/09	**CONGLETON TOWN**	FAT1q	0-2	67	
25/09	**BISHOP AUCKLAND**	NPL	2-1	158	Hill, Hallows
29/09	**COLWYN BAY**	NPL	2-3	148	Griffin, Clarke
02/10	Frickley Athletic	NPL	2-5	199	Curwen, McDonald
06/10	**FLEETWOOD TOWN**	NPL	2-3	153	Thomas, McDonald
09/10	Matlock Town	NPL	0-1	385	
11/10	Winsford United	NPL	3-1	249	Leach, McDonald(2)
23/10	**BARROW**	NPL	0-2	232	
26/10	Marine	NPL	1-1	372	Leach
30/10	Whitley Bay	NPL	1-3	202	Thomas
06/11	**WINSFORD UNITED**	NPL	0-2	185	
09/11	Knowsley United	NPL	0-1	168	
13/11	Bishop Auckland	NPL	0-1	402	
20/11	**HYDE UNITED**	NPL	0-1	168	
27/11	Fleetwood Town	NPL	3-2	181	Holman, Nugent
30/12	**FLEETWOOD TOWN**	ATS1	3-0	30	Hallows, Curwen(2)
04/12	Boston United	NPL	1-2	884	Diamond
11/12	**Gt HARWOOD TOWN**	NPLC2	1-1	48	Irvine
01/01	Leek Town	NPL	0-2	447	
05/01	**LEEK TOWN**	NPL	0-1	163	
15/01	**WHITLEY BAY**	NPL	1-1	151	Diamond
18/01	Barrow	ATS2	2-1	387	Diamond, Thomas
22/01	**GAINSBOROUGH Tr.**	NPL	1-2	158	Diamond
29/01	Hyde United	NPL	1-1	291	Redshaw
05/02	Droylsden	NPL	2-1	227	Hodgert(og), Diamond
08/02	Bamber Bridge	ATSqf	2-1	299	Diamond(2), Nugent
12/02	**FRICKLEY ATHLETIC**	NPL	1-1	352	Diamond
19/02	**DROYLSDEN**	NPL	2-2	160	Diamond
28/02	Southport	ATSsf	0-2	521	
03/03	Gt Harwood Town	NPLC2r	1-2	62	Diamond
05/03	Chorley	NPL	1-1	294	Diamond
12/03	Gainsborough Trinity	NPL	0-4	383	
19/03	**BUXTON**	NPL	1-0	159	Diamond
26/03	**CHORLEY**	NPL	2-2	363	Johnson(og), Leach
02/04	**MARINE**	NPL	3-5	264	Phoenix(2), Leach
13/04	**KNOWSLEY UNITED**	NPL	3-0	96	Diamond(2), Leach
16/04	Emley	NPL	1-1	168	Diamond
19/04	Colwyn Bay	NPL	0-1	104	
23/04	**ACCRINGTON STAN.**	NPL	2-4	185	Diamond, McLoughlin
26/04	Bridlington Town	NPL	2-0	32	Marsden, Diamond
30/04	**EMLEY**	NPL	1-1	151	Diamond

Key: NPL: Northern Premier League Premier Division, NPLC: Northern Premier League Cup, PC: Northern Premier League Presidennts Cup, FAC: F.A. Cup, FAT: F.A. Trophy. ATS: Lancashire ATS Challenge Trophy. Number after cup competitions denote rounds (r: replay, qf: Quarter-Final, sf: Semi-Final, f: Final. Numbers in brackets indicate legs, i.e. (1): 1st leg).
Home fixtures are denoted by bold capitals, away matches by lower case. (p): penalty, og: Own goal.

SQUAD MEMBERS *(previous clubs listed in chronological order)*

GOALKEEPERS: Richard Bibby *(Accrington Stanley, Congleton).*

DEFENDERS: Chris Molloy *(York, Witton Alb., St Helens, Altrincham, Mossley, Hyde Utd.),* **Stuart Phoenix** *(Wigan, St Helens),* **Paul Cuddy** *(Man. City, Bolton W., Rochdale, Huddersfield, Blackpool, Chorley, Altrincham, Witton Alb., Barrow),* **Nigel Cudworth** *(Chorley, Morecambe, Leyland Daf., Darwen, Ashton Utd., Chorley),* **Ian Curwen** *(Preston).*

MIDFIELD: Andy Leach *(Youth Team),* **Jamie Fahey** *(St. Helens),* **Graham Haddon** *(Horwich RMI, Leyland Motors, Radcliffe Boro., Horwich RMI., Bamber Bridge),* **Neil McLachlan** *(Wrexham, Morecambe, Horwich RMI, Chorley, Horwich RMI, Atherton LR),* **Denis Haslam** *(Horwich RMI, Chorley),* **Glenn Walker** *(Burnley, Crewe, Horwich RMI, Marine, Horwich RMI, Warrington, Horwich RMI, Fleetwood, St. Helens),*. .gap 5
FORWARDS: Ray Redshaw *(Salford, Prestwich Heys, Glossop, Hyde Utd., Southport, Glossop, Horwich RMI, Wigan, Northwich V., Auckland(NZ), Northwich V., Chorley, Salford, Rossendale, Horwich RMI, Redcliffe Boro.),* **Peter Cottam** *(Westhoughton),* **Steve Nugant** *(Wigan, Halifax, Barrow),* **Paul Griffin** *(Bolton W., Chorley, Mossley, Chorley, Hyde Utd., Mossley),* **Barry Diamond** *(Gillingham, Dumbarton, Barrow, Workington, Barrow, Ollum Palliosuera(Fin.), Rochdale, Halifax, Gainsborough T., Morecambe, Colne D., Mossley, Hyde Utd., Altrincham, Chorley, Stalybridge C., Curzon Ashton, Rossendale, Mossley).*

Formed: 1919

HYDE UNITED

The Tigers

Back Row (L/R): P O'Brien (Manager), R Blackman, B Hudson, A Waugh, A Graham, S Marsh, D Christie, L Potts, C Hall, P Chadwick. Front: J Walker (Trainer), D Nolan, G Wilson, G Kimmins, N Slater (Mascot), G Henshaw, I Callaghan, D Thornton, B Dodd (Trainer). Photo - John Newton.

Chairman: S C Hartley **Vice Chairman:** A Slater
Secretary: Alan Slater, 83 King Edward Road, Hyde, Cheshire SK14 5JJ (061 368 3687).
Manager: Mike McKenzie **Asst Manager:** TBA
Physio: C I Wych. **Coach:** TBA
Press Officer: Secretary **Commercial Manager:** Brian Slater.
Ground: Tameside Stadium, Ewen Fields, Walker Lane, Hyde SK14 5PL (061 368 1031).
Directions: On entering Hyde follow signs for Tameside Leisure Park - in Walker Lane take second car park entrance near Leisure Pool and follow road around to the stadium. Quarter of a mile from Newton (BR).
Capacity: 4,000 **Cover:** 2,000 **Seats:** 400 **Floodlights:** Yes **Metal Badges:** Yes
Colours: Red/white/black **Change colours:** Azure/black.
Club Shop: Yes. Replica shirts, scarves, sports shirts, baseball caps, bronx hats, badges. Contact either Alan Slater (061 368 3687) or Brian Slater (061 303 8891).
Previous Leagues: Lancashire & Cheshire 19-21/ Manchester 21-30/ Cheshire County 30-68 70-82/ Northern Premier 68-70. *Predecessors, Hyde FC: Lancs Lg 1889-90/ Lancs Combination 1906-17.*
Midweek home matchday: Monday **Record Attendance:** 9,500 v Nelson, FA Cup 1952.
Best F.A. Cup season: 1st Rd 54-55 (v Workington), 83-84 (v Burnley). *Hyde FC: 1st Rd 1887-88.*
Record Fee Paid: £8,000 for Jim McCluskie (Mossley, 1989).
Record Fee Received: £17,500 for Simon Rudge (Runcorn, 1989).
Record Defeat: (as Hyde F.C.) 0-26 v Preston North End, F.A. Cup.
Players progressing to Football League: Charles McClelland & John Webber & Patrick Barry (B'burn 1946 & 47 & 48), L Battrick (Manc. City 1968), Jack Hilton (Wrexham 1950), David Teece (Hull 1952), Ray Calderbank & William Bell & Neil Colbourne (R'dale 1953 & 74 & 80), Jeff Johnson (Stockport 1976), David Constantine & Donald Graham (Bury 1979), George Oghani (Bolton 1983), Kevin Glendon (Burnley 1983), Peter Coyne (Swindon 1984).
Club Sponsors: TMI Metals.
Clubhouse: (061 368 1621). Open most nights, full facilities, 150 seats. Stewards: Lil & Doug.
Club Record Scorer: P O'Brien 247
Club Record Appearances: S Johnson 623.
93-94 Captain: G Henshaw
93-94 Top scorer: Phil Chadwick 27.
93-94 Players' P.o.Y.: Ian Callaghan
93-94 Supporters' P.o.Y.: Dave Nolan.
Local Newspapers (+Tel.Nos.): North Cheshire Herald & Hyde Reporter (061 368 3595).
Local Radio Stations: GMR, Picadilly.
Honours: FA Trophy SF 88-89, Premier Inter-Lge Cup R-up(2) 88-90, NPL R-up(2) 87-89 (Lg Cup 85-86 88-89 (R-up 83-84 93-94), Chal. Shield R-up 86-87 90-91), Cheshire Co. Lg(3) 54-56 81-82 (Lg Cup 33-34 52-53 54-55 72-73 81-82, Lg Chal. Shield(2) 80-82 Manchester Lg(5) 20-23 28-29 29-30 (Lg (Gilgryst) Cup(4) 27-29 49-50 70-71), Cheshire Snr Cup 45-46 62-63 69-70 80-81 89-90, Manchester Prem. Cup 93-94 (Snr Cup 74-75, Int Cup 55-56 56-57(jt), Junior Cup 21-22 68-69), Lancs & Cheshire F'lit Cup(2) 54-56, Ashton Chal. Cup(6) 30-34 39-40 47-48, Hyde Chal. Cup(2) 27-29, Reporter Cup(3) 72-74 75-76, Gavin Nicholson Mem Trophy 79-80, Lancs F'lit Trophy(2) 86-88, Edward Case Cup(4) 56-8 59-60 80-81.

PROGRAMME DETAILS
Pages: 32 **Price:** 60p
Editor: M Dring

HYDE UNITED's 1993-94 CAMPAIGN

Date	Opponents	Comp.	Res	Gate	Goalscorers
21/08	**ACCRINGTON S.**	NPL	1-4	401	Graham
23/08	Emley	NPL	2-2	317	Daughtry(2)
28/08	Bridlington Town	NPL	0-4	84	
30/08	**CHORLEY**	NPL	2-1	413	Thornton, Nolan
04/09	**BARROW**	NPL	2-1	447	Henry, Graham
07/09	Buxton	NPL	0-3	400	
11/09	Colwyn Bay	FAC1q	1-4	209	Chadwick
18/09	Winsford United	NPL	2-2	279	Graham, Chadwick
20/09	**GAINSBOROUGH**	NPL	4-0	249	Kimmins(2), Graham, Wilson
25/09	**FRICKLEY ATH.**	NPL	4-0	289	Appleton, Chadwick, Nolan, Kimmins
02/10	**KNOWSLEY UTD**	PC1	3-1	256	Chadwick(2), Kimmins
04/10	**MARINE**	NPL	1-3	326	Callaghan
09/10	**BOSTON UNITED**	NPL	2-1	379	Chadwick(2)
14/10	Boston United	NPL	1-3	902	Nolan
16/10	**MORECAMBE**	NPL	2-3	325	Graham, Chadwick
19/10	Colwyn Bay	NPL	1-2	159	Chadwick
23/10	Gainsborough Trin.	NPL	1-1	378	Chadwick
25/10	**DROYLSDEN**	NPL	4-2	467	Henshaw, Kimmins, Rowson, Graham
30/10	**WINSFORD UTD**	NPL	1-1	319	Graham
02/11	Morecambe	NPL	3-2	267	Waugh, Graham, Nolan
06/11	Knowsley United	NPL	1-2	145	Graham
13/11	Fleetwood Town	NPL	0-1	120	
15/11	**LEEK TOWN**	PC2	0-0	222	
20/11	Horwich RMI	NPL	1-0	168	Nolan
27/11	**ACCRINGTON S.**	FAT3q	2-0	355	Thornton(2)
30/12	Runcorn	CSC2	1-2	272	Callaghan
07/12	Leek Town	NPL	0-3	324	
11/12	**MATLOCK TOWN**	NPL	4-0	231	Chadwick(2), Kimmins(2)
01/01	**KNOWSLEY UTD**	NPL	0-0	294	
03/01	Whitley Bay	NPL	0-2	271	
08/01	**BUXTON**	NPL	1-1	352	Chadwick
15/01	Bishop Auckland	NPL	2-1	320	Chadwick(2)
22/01	Spennymoor Utd	FAT1	1-2	529	Kimmins
29/01	**HORWICH R.M.I.**	NPL	1-1	291	Graham
31/01	* Caernarfon Town	MPC1	5-0	163	Kimmins(2), Graham, Thornton(2) *(see note)*
05/02	Chorley	NPL	2-4	194	Chadwick, Graham
12/02	Matlock Town	NPL	2-1	422	Graham, Chadwick
14/02	**COLWYN BAY**	NPLC3	2-1	154	Wilson, Nolan
19/02	**BRIDLINGTON T.**	NPL	6-1	222	Kimmins, Hall(2), Thornton(3)
22/02	Leek Town	PC2r	0-5	262	
07/03	**MATLOCK TOWN**	NPL	1-0	359	Chadwick
12/03	**EMLEY**	NPL	2-0	255	Thornton(2)
14/03	**Gt HARWOOD TOWN**	NPLCqf	5-2	222	Thornton, Graham, Chadwick(3)
17/03	Mossley	MPCqf	4-0	215	Callaghan, Graham, Thornton, Kimmins
19/03	Marine	NPL	1-1	474	Thornton
26/03	**LEEK TOWN**	NPL	5-0	434	Thornton, Graham, Chadwick, Nolan, Key(og)
28/03	Droylsden	NPL	3-3	313	Kimmins, Graham, Chadwick
31/03	**ASHTON UNITED**	MPCsf	3-0	324	Nolan(2), Thornton
02/04	Barrow	NPL	4-1	792	Graham, Chadwick, Nolan, Kimmins
04/04	**WHITLEY BAY**	NPL	6-0	297	Bancroft, Chadwick, Graham, Kimmins, Nolan(2)
07/04	**LEEK TOWN**	NPLCsf(1)	3-1	324	Thornton(3)
09/04	**COLWYN BAY**	NPL	1-2	325	Thornton
13/04	Leek Town	NPLCsf(2)	2-3	296	Graham, Thornton
16/04	Accrington Stanley	NPL	1-4	467	Nolan
19/04	Frickley Athletic	NPL	1-4	206	Kimmins
23/04	**BISHOP AUCKLAND**	NPL	1-1	242	Nolan
28/04	SPENNYMOOR UTD	NPLCf	1-3	585	Nolan *(played at Harrogate Town)*
30/04	**FLEETWOOD TOWN**	NPL	5-2	245	Kimmins(2), Chadwick(2), Graham
04/05	DROYLSDEN	MPCf	4-1	350	Graham(2), Kimmins, Nolan *(at Ashton Utd)*

** - Match played at home. Result was declared void because Hyde fielded an ineligible player, but they progressed because Caernarfon could not raise a team for the replay.*

Key: NPL: Northern Premier League Premier Division, NPLC: Northern Premier League Cup, PC: (Northern Premier League) Presidents Cup, FAC: F.A. Cup, FAT: F.A. Trophy, CSC: Cheshire Senior Cup, MPC: Manchester Premier Cup. Numbers after cup competitions denote rounds (r: replay, qf: Quarter-Final, sf: Semi-Final, f: Final. Numbers in brackets indicate legs, i.e. (1): 1st leg).

SQUAD MEMBERS *(previous clubs listed in chronological order)*

GOALKEEPERS: Simon Marsh *(Blackpool)*

DEFENDERS: Alan Waugh *(Ford Motors)* **Steve Appleton** *(Wigan, Southport)* **Stuart Owen** *(Grove Utd, Rossendale Utd, Accrington Stanley, Ashton Utd,)* **Ricky Blackman** *(Chadderton, Stalybridge C., Ashton Utd)* **Brendan Hudson** *(Baildon Ath., Guiseley)* **Terry Megram** *(Northwich V., Curzon Ashton, Witton Alb., Hyde Utd, Winsford Utd)* **Jez Rowson** *(Droylsden, Ashton Utd, Droylsden, Ashton Utd Droylsden, Ashton Utd, Warrington)* **Graham Lang** *(Mitchell Shackleton)* **Russ Hooton** *(Stockport, South Liverpool, Mossley, Droylsden, Witton Alb., Northwich V., Runcorn, Oswestry, Hyde Utd, Witton Alb., Mossley)*

MIDFIELD: Ian Callaghan *(Bolton W., Northwich V.)* **Greg Henshaw** *(Grimsby, Bolton W., Swansea, Chorley, Runcova)* **Darren Thornton** *(Salt GSOB, Baildon Ath.)* **Dave Nolan** *(Prescot, Bromborough Pool, Chester, Barrow)* **Paul Whitty** *(Gorton, Mossley)* **Greg Wilson** *(Oldham Ath.)* **Gary Butterworth** *(Man. Utd (A), Rochdale, Curzon Ashton, Stalybridge C., Accrington Stanley, Ashton Utd)*

FORWARDS: Ged Kimmins *(Salford C.)* **Phil Chadwick** *(Droylsden)* **Dave Christie** *(Preston, Bury, Ashton Utd, Northwich V.)* **Dave Bancroft** *(Stockport, Witton Alb., Leek)* **Rick MacNamara** *(Dukinfield)*, **Andy Graham** *(Bramhall, Oldham Ath., Lancaster, Hyde Utd, Wealdstone, Wycombe W., Staines, Northwich V.)*

Formed: 1984 **KNOWSLEY UNITED** The Reds

Knowsley United FC. Back Row (L/R): P Orr (Manager), S O'Brien, W Loughlin, R Birch, A Johnston, K McDonald, P Elliss, A Diggle, B Haughton (Kit Man). Front: B Orr (Mascot), P Edwards, D O'Brien, J McMahon (Captain), B Kilshaw, C Stanton, M Jones.

Photo - John L Newton.

Chairman: Mr P G Orr **President:** The Mayor of Knowsley.
Secretary K O'Brien, 153 Church Road, Litherland L21 7LJ (Phone/Fax: 051 474 3808).
Manager: P J Orr **Coach:** R Willingham **Physio:** L Blasberry
Press Officer: Ken O'Brien **Commercial Manager:** D Johnstone.
Ground: Alt Park, Endmoor Road, Huyton, Merseyside L36 3LV (051 480 2529).
Directions: Come off M62 at junction 6 onto M57. Leave at junction 2 (Prescot), onto Liverpool Rd at r'bout, 3rd right at 3rd set of lights into Seth Powell Way. From Jct 3 (Huyton), go straight across r-about onto Huyton link road (Seth Powell Way) and turn right at lights. From Liverpool; East Prescot Rd-Liverpool Rd (6 miles) - turn left into Seth Powell Way. Buses 10, 10a, 8, 210 to Page Moss. Nearest station is Huyton 2 miles away - bus from station to Page Moss.
Capacity: 9,000 **Cover:** 3,500 **Seats:** 350 **Floodlights:** Yes **Club Shop:** Due
Colours: Red & black hoops **Change colours:** Yellow & black hoops.
Sponsors: Rogersons (Builders).
Previous Name: Kirkby Town (pre-1988) **Previous Leagues:** North West Counties 84-91.
Previous Grounds: Simonswood Lane, Kirkby 84-86/ Kirkby Sports Centre 86-88.
Midweek matchday: Tuesday **Reserve Team's League:** Liverpool Co. Comb.
Women's Team League: F.A. National League, Premier Division.
Record Attendance: 5,015 v Carlisle United at Everton FC, FA Cup First Round 13/11/93. At Alt Park: 900 v Everton, Liverpool Senior Cup, 1984.
Best FA Cup season: First Round Proper 93-94 (lost 1-4 v Carlisle United).
Best FA Trophy season: First Qual. Round second replay 93-94 (lost 0-3 at Matlock Town).
Record win: 10-1 v Flixton
Record defeat: 1-7 v Colwyn Bay.
Record Fee Paid Received: Undisclosed for Mike Marsh (Liverpool).
Players progressing to Football League: Phil Daily (Wigan), Mike Marsh (Liverpool), Rodney McDonald (Walsall), Steve Farrelly (Chester City).
Clubhouse: Lounge, 2 Function Suites, Sponsors Box, Directors Room. Clubhouse open normal licensing hours - filled rolls available. Refreshment bar in ground sells pies, rolls, chips, tea, coffee oxo etc.
Club Record Goalscorer: Jimmy Bell, 50.
93-94 Captain: John McMahon.
93-94 P.o.Y.:
93-94 Top scorer:
Local Press: Liverpool Daily Post/Liverpool Echo (051 227 2000), Knowsley Challenger (051 548 0710).
Local Radio Stations: Radio Merseyside (051 708 5500), Radio City.
Hons: FA Vase 5th Rd 90-91 91-92, Northern Premier Lg Div 1 R-up 92-93, North West Counties Lg 90-91 (R-up 88-89 89-90, Div 2 85-86, Div 3 84-85, Raab Karcher Cup 89-90, Champions v Cup Winners Trophy 89-90).

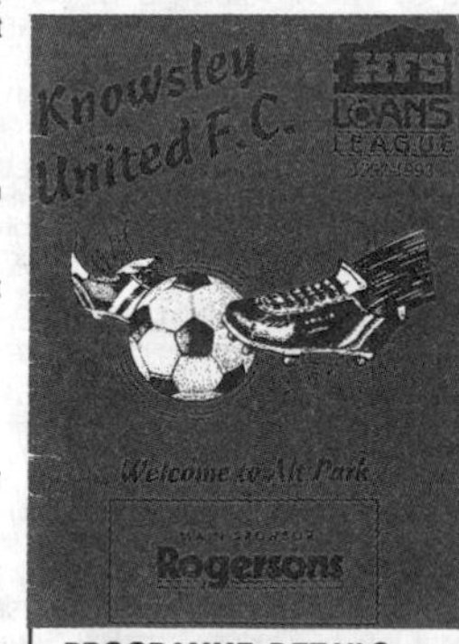

PROGRAMME DETAILS:
Pages: 32 **Price:** 70p
Editor: Dave Cookson
(0772 749 768)

KNOWSLEY UNITED's 1993-94 CAMPAIGN

Date	Opponents	Comp.	Res	Gate	Goalscorers	
21/08	**BUXTON**	NPL	1-1	178	Barton	
24/08	Droylsden	NPL	1-2	300	Kilshaw	
28/08	Boston United	NPL	1-4	902	Siddell	
30/08	**ACCRINGTON STAN.**	NPL	0-0	260		
04/09	**BRIDLINGTON TOWN**	NPL	0-0	151		
07/09	Barrow	NPL	1-2	862	Siddell	
11/09	Salford City	FAC1q	1-1	120	Barton	
15/09	**SALFORD CITY**	FAC1qr	6-0	127	Green(5), Barton	
18/09	Matlock Town	FAT1q	0-0	351		
20/09	**MATLOCK TOWN**	FAT1qr	1-1	128	Jackson	
25/09	**St HELENS TOWN**	FAC2q	2-1	191	Green, Quigley	
27/09	Matlock Town	FAT1qr	0-3	376		
02/10	Hyde United	PC1	1-3	256	Edwards	
05/10	**WINSFORD UNITED**	NPL	3-1	145	Green(2), Kilshaw	
09/10	**COLWYN BAY**	FAC3q	3-0	254	Waring, Green, Stanton	
13/10	Fleetwood Town	NPL	3-0	75	Kershaw, McMahon, Green	
16/10	Whitley Bay	NPL	3-1	200	Kilshaw(2), Mullen	
19/10	**MARINE**	NPL	1-1	396	Barton	
23/10	Stafford Rangers	FAC4q	1-1	973	Jones	
26/10	**STAFFORD RANGERS**	FAC4qr	2-2	612	Green(2)	
01/11	**STAFFORD RANGERS**	FAC4qr	1-0	951	Jones	
06/11	**HYDE UNITED**	NPL	2-1	145	Green, Waring	
13/11	**CARLISLE UNITED**	FAC1	1-4	5,015	Jackson	*(played at Everton FC)*
15/11	**St HELENS TOWN**	LSC1	1-3	168	Jackson	
20/11	**WHITLEY BAY**	NPL	1-1	116	King	
27/11	Gainsborough Trinity	NPL	1-2	320	McMahon	
04/12	**BISHOP AUCKLAND**	NPL	1-1	124	Kilshaw	
07/12	Morecambe	NPL	0-5	231		
11/12	Eastwood Town	NPLC2	1-1	90	Green	
18/12	Leek Town	NPL	2-3	349	Green, McMahon	
01/01	Hyde United	NPL	0-0	294		
03/01	Marine	NPL	2-3	551	Kilshaw, McDonald	
12/01	Winsford United	NPL	3-4	222	McMahon(2), Kilshaw	
15/01	Chorley	NPL	1-4	190	Kilshaw	
18/01	**EMLEY**	NPL	2-0	81	Edwards, Orr	
22/01	Buxton	NPL	1-3	266	Siddell	
29/01	Accrington Stanley	NPL	1-2	421	Siddell	
01/02	**EASTWOOD TOWN**	NPLC2r	2-0	59	Edwards, Birch	
05/02	Matlock Town	NPL	2-2	357	Siddell, Kilshaw	
01/02	Leek Town	NPLC3	1-2	273	McMahon	
12/02	**DRYLSDEN**	NPL	2-0	103	Siddell, McDonald	
19/02	Bishop Auckland	NPL	2-1	291	Parker, Siddell	
21/02	Emley	NPL	1-2	204	Birch	
05/03	**LEEK TOWN**	NPL	0-0	169		
08/03	**COLWYN BAY**	NPL	1-5	111	Donnelly(og)	
12/03	Frickley Athletic	NPL	0-1	193		
26/03	Bridlington Town	NPL	1-0	n/k	McMahon	
02/04	**CHORLEY**	NPL	0-1	132		
13/04	Horwich RMI	NPL	0-3	96		
16/04	**BOSTON UNITED**	NPL	1-2	73	Birch	
23/04	**GAINSBOROUGH TR.**	NPL	1-1	73	Birch	
26/04	Colwyn Bay	NPL	0-0	110		
28/04	**MATLOCK TOWN**	NPL	5-1	47	Kilshaw, Birch, Jones(2), Siddell	
30/04	**FRICKLEY UNITED**	NPL	0-2	75		
02/05	**FLEETWOOD TOWN**	NPL	0-1	112		
07/05	**MORECAMBE**	NPL	2-3	102	Jones, Kilshaw	

Key: NPL: Northern Premier League Premier Division, NPLC: Northern Premier League Cup, PC: Northern Premier League Presidennts Cup, FAC: F.A. Cup, FAT: F.A. Trophy, LSC: Liverpool Senior Cup. Number after cup competitions denote rounds (r: replay, qf: Quarter-Final, sf: Semi-Final, f: Final. Numbers in brackets indicate legs, i.e. (1): 1st leg).
Home fixtures are denoted by bold capitals, away matches by lower case. (p): penalty, og: Own goal.

SQUAD MEMBERS *(previous clubs listed in chronological order)*

GOALKEEPERS: Andy Johnson *(Wigan, St. Helens).*

DEFENDERS: Andy Diggle *(Skelmersdale),* **Peter Orr** *(Prescot, Northwich V., Southport),* **Will Loughlin** *(Bootle, Morecambe),* **Andy Taylor** *(Liverpool, Winsford, Runcorn, Winsford),* **Chris Waring** *(Local Football),* **Paul Mullen** *(Heswall, South Liverpool, Caernarfon, South Liverpool, Runcorn, Southport),* **Tommy King** *(Runcorn),* **Dave O'Brien** *(Everton, Marine, Southport).*

MIDFIELD: John McMahon *(Everton, Southport, S. Liverpool, Altrincham, Witton Alb., Runcorn, Altrincham, Morecambe, Macclesfield),* **Joe Barton** *(Northwich V., Warrington),* **Stuart Gelling** *(Liverpool),* **Peter Edwards** *(Knowsley, Bootle),* **Ronnie Kilshaw** *(Liverpool, Tranmere, Runcorn, Prescot, Southport, South Liverpool, Kirkby, Witton Alb., Knowsley, Ellesmere Port, Skelmersdale, Rossendale Utd., Colwyn Bay),* **Ray Birch** *(Halifax, Bradford C., Tranmere, Stamford, Rushden, Corby, Kettering, Fleetwood, Colne D., Morecambe, Rhyl, Fleetwood, Rhyl, Caernarfon, Bangor C., Newtown, Accrington Stanley, Droylsden, Bootle).*

FORWARDS: Dave Siddell *(Local Football),* **Brian Kilshaw** *(Skelmersdale, Altrincham, St. Helens),* **Neil Parker** *(Waterloo Dock, Caernarfon, Runcorn),* **Chris Stanton** *(Lucas Sports).*

Formed: 1894

MARINE

The Mariners

Eddie Murray heads goalwards for Marine in their 1-1 draw against in-form Hyde United in March.
Photo - Rachel Watson.

Chairman: Tom Culshaw **President:** D Hargreaves.
Secretary: John Wildman, 4 Ashbourne Avenue, Blundellsands, Liverpool L23 8TX (051 924 5248).
Manager: Roly Howard **Asst Mgr/Coach:** Roger Patience **Physio:** John Bradshaw
Commercial Manager: Tony Wake. **Press Officer:** David Wotherspoon
Ground: Rossett Park, College Road, Crosby, Liverpool (051 924 1743).
Directions: College Road is off main Liverpool-Southport road (A565) in Crosby. Ground ten minutes walk from Crosby & Blundellsands (Mersey Rail). Bus No. 92.
Capacity: 2,500 **Cover:** 1,900 **Seats:** 400 **Floodlights:** 210 lux **Metal Badges:** Yes.
Club Shop: Yes, selling replica kit, baseball caps, polo shirts, scarves, mugs, pens/pencils, bookmarks, car stickers, combs, tax disc holders.
Colours: White/black/black **Change:** Yellow/green/green
Sponsors: Murphys Irish Stout. **Reserve Team's League:** Lancashire League Division One.
Previous Lges: I Zingari/ Liverpool Co. Comb./ Lancs Combination 35-39 46-69/ Cheshire County 69-79.
Prev. Name: Waterloo Melville 1894-1903 **Previous Ground:** Waterloo Park 1894-1903.
Midweek home matchday: Tuesday **Record Gate:** 4,000 v Nigeria, Friendly 1949.
Record win: 14-2 v Rossendale United (A), Cheshire County League 25/2/78.
Record defeat: 1-7 v Dulwich Hamlet, FA Amateur Cup final at West Ham United, 1932.
Best FA Cup year: 3rd Rd 92-93 (lost 1-3 at Crewe Alexandra). Also 2nd Rd rep. (v Hartlepool) 75-76. Also 1st Rd 32-33 45-46 46-47 47-48 74-75 89-90.
League clubs defeated in FA Cup: Barnsley 75-76, Halifax Town 92-93.
Record Fee Paid: £3,000 for Brian Ross (Chorley, November 1991).
Record Fee Received: £12,250 for Ian Nolan (Tranmere Rovers, 1991).
Players progressing to Football League: James Veacock & Anthony Sharrock & Steve Brooks (Southport 1947 & 73 & 77), Sam Parker (Accrington 1948), Harry Conner (Stoke 1953), Alf Jones (Leeds 1960), Gary Williams (Preston 1972), John Lacy (Fulham & Spurs), Paul Beesly (Sheffield Utd), Mark Kearney (Everton 1981), Alan Finlay (Shrewsbury 1981), Paul Cook (Norwich), Paul Edwards (Crewe & Coventry), Ian Nolan (Tranmere).
Clubhouse: Open daily. Concert Hall (250 seats), Members Lounge (100 seats). **Club Record Goalscorer:** Paul Meachin 200
Club Record Appearances: Peter Smith 952
93-94 Captain: John Gautrey **93-94 Top Scorer:** Chris Camden 33.
Player of the Year 93-94: Brian Ross (r-up: Paul Dawson)
Local Press: Crosby Herald, Liverpool Echo, Daily Post (051 227 2000).
Local Radio Stations: BBC, Radio Merseyside, Radio City.
Hons: FA Amtr Cup R-up 31-32 (SF 46-47), FA Trophy SF 83-84 91-92, Northern Prem Lg 93-94 (R-up 85-86 91-92, Lg Cup 84-85 91-92 (R-up 80-81 85-86), Presidents Cup R-up 83-84 86-87), Cheshire Co. Lg 73-74 75-76 77-78 (R-up 72-73), Lancs Comb. R-up 46-47 (Lg Cup 46-47 63-64 68-69), Liverpool Comb. 27-28 30-31 33-34 34-35 (Lg Cup 30-31), Lancs Tphy 87-88 90-91, Lancs Jnr Cup 78-79, Lancs Amtr Cup 21-22 25-26 30-31 31-32 32-33, Liverpool Snr Cup 78-79 84-85 87-88 89-90 93-94, Liverpool Non-Lge Cup 68-69 75-76 76-77, Liverpool Chal. Cup 42-43 44-45 71-72.

PROGRAMME DETAILS:
Pages: 24 **Price:** 70p
Editor: David Wotherspoon

MARINE's 1993-94 CAMPAIGN

Date	Opponents	Comp.	Res	Gate	Goalscorers
21/08	**BOSTON UNITED**	NPL	3-2	392	Doherty(3)
24/08	Colwyn Bay	NPL	0-0	280	
28/08	Droylsden	NPL	0-2	296	
30/08	**BARROW**	NPL	2-2	503	Gautrey(p), Camden
04/09	**FRICKLEY ATH.**	NPL	4-1	340	Ross(3), Gautrey
07/09	Morecambe	NPL	2-3	412	Baines, Camden
11/09	Accrington Stanley	NPL	2-0	537	Murray, Baines
14/09	**CHORLEY**	NPL	4-1	417	Camden(2), Ross(2)
18/09	Bishop Auckland	NPL	4-1	269	Camden(3), Doherty
21/09	**FLEETWOOD TOWN**	NPL	4-0	337	Ross(2), Camden, Proctor
25/09	Gainsborough Trin.	NPL	2-1	375	Gautrey(p), Rowlands
02/10	**GUISELEY**	PC1	1-1	253	Ross
04/10	Hyde United	NPL	3-1	326	Baines, Ross, Camden
09/10	**ACCRINGTON STAN.**	NPL	2-1	636	Doherty, Hanson
12/10	**LEEK TOWN**	NPL	3-2	361	Doherty, Rowlands, Gautrey
16/10	Boston United	NPL	2-4	1,418	Rowlands, Ward
19/10	Knowsley United	NPL	1-1	376	Camden
23/10	Chorley	FAC4q	2-0	740	Camden, Proctor
26/10	**HORWICH R.M.I.**	NPL	1-1	372	Camden
30/10	Guisley	PC1r	0-1	561	
03/11	Winsford United	NPL	3-2	194	Murray, Rowlands(2)
06/11	**GAINSBOROUGH Tr.**	NPL	3-0	381	Rowlands(2), Baines
09/11	**BURSCOUGH**	LSC1	4-0	236	Camden(2), Rowlands, McDonough
13/11	Stalybridge Celtic	FAC1	1-1	1,525	Rowlands
20/11	Emley	NPL	2-6	334	Camden, McBride
27/11	**WINSFORD UNITED**	NPL	2-2	339	Ross, Camden
29/11	**STALYBRIDGE C.**	FAC1r	4-4	853	Camden(2), Murray, Doherty(p) *(2-4 on pens)*
04/12	Chorley	NPL	4-0	240	Ross(4)
11/12	Spennymoor Utd	NPLC2	0-3	303	
18/12	**BUXTON**	NPL	1-0	317	Ross
27/11	**COLWYN BAY**	NPL	1-1	674	Doherty
01/01	Fleetwood United	NPL	3-2	366	Gautrey(p), Rowlands, Camden
03/01	**KNOWSLEY UTD**	NPL	3-2	551	Gautrey(p), Camden, Ross
11/01	Southport	ATS2	1-2	809	Camden
15/01	**MATLOCK TOWN**	NPL	0-0	345	
18/01	**BOOTLE**	LSC2	3-0	244	Baines, Doherty, Murray
22/01	**SOUTHPORT**	FAT1	0-0	1,169	
25/01	Southport	FAT1r	1-3	818	Ross
29/01	Bridlington Town	NPL	2-1	64	Ross(2)
05/02	**WHITLEY BAY**	NPL	6-3	381	Ross(3), Camden, McNally, Murray
12/02	**EMLEY**	NPL	4-1	405	Murray, Gautrey(2(1p)), Ward
19/02	Barrow	NPL	1-2	935	Camden
26/02	**BISHOP AUCKLAND**	NPL	3-1	383	Ross(2), Camden
05/03	**MATLOCK TOWN**	NPL	2-1	434	Camden, Ross
12/03	Leek Town	NPL	4-1	1,030	Roche, Murray(2), Gautrey
19/03	**HYDE UNITED**	NPL	1-1	474	Camden
21/03	**LIVERPOOL RES.**	LSCsf	2-0	308	Ross, McNally
26/03	Buxton	NPL	2-2	374	Rowlands, Ross
02/04	Horwich RMI	NPL	5-3	264	Camden, Roche, Ross, Murray(2)
09/04	Whitley Bay	NPL	4-0	276	McKenzie(og), Ross, Gautrey, Camden.
13/04	Frickley Athletic	NPL	2-5	226	Rowlands, Camden
16/04	**MORECAMBE**	NPL	4-2	537	Camden(2), Murray, Rowlands
23/04	**BRIDLINGTON TOWN**	NPL	3-0	489	McNally, Gautrey, Murray
30/04	**DROYLSDEN**	NPL	2-1	525	Gautrey, Camden
09/05	SOUTHPORT	LSCf	2-1	1,535	Baines(2) *(played at Everton FC)*

Key: NPL: Northern Premier League Premier Division, NPLC: Northern Premier League Cup, PC: (Northern Premier League) Presidents Cup, FAC: F.A. Cup, FAT: F.A. Trophy, LSC: Liverpool Senior Cup, ATS: Lancashire ATS Challenge Trophy. Numbers after cup competitions denote rounds (r: replay, qf: Quarter-Final, sf: Semi-Final, f: Final. Numbers in brackets indicate legs, i.e. (1): 1st leg).
Home fixtures are denoted by bold capitals, away matches by lower case. (p): penalty, og: Own goal.

SQUAD MEMBERS *(previous clubs listed in chronological order)*

GOALKEEPERS: Kevin O'Brien *(Everton, Maghull, Rhyl, Burscough, Runcorn, Chorley, South Liverpool)*, **Rob Holcroft** *(Liverpool)*.

DEFENDERS: Tony Ward *(Everton, Wigan Athletic, Chorley)*, **Andy Draper** *(local football)*, **Sean Lundon** *(Everton, Chester, Bath City, Runcorn, Worcester City)*, **Keith Proctor** *(youth team)*, **Ian Barnes** *(Kirkby Town, Southport, Knowsley Utd, Rhyl, Knowsley Utd, Southport)*.

MIDFIELD: Graham Rowlands *(Preston North End, Southport, Formby, Southport, Coastal(USA))*, **Jon Gautrey** *(Bolton Wanderers, Southport)*, **John Roche** *(Skelmersdale Utd, Kirkby Town, Warrington Town, Caernarfon Town)*, **Joey Murray** *(Liverpool, Wrexham)*, **Terry McDonough** *(Heswall, Stork, Burscough)*, **Paul McNally** *(Oswestry Town, Runcorn, Stalybridge Celtic, Southport, Warrington Town)*, **Neil Hanson** *(Preston North End, Halifax Town, Chorley, Accrington Stanley, Morecambe, Great Harwood Town, Accrington Stanley, Rossendale Utd, Burscough)*.

FORWARDS: Chris Camden *(Tranmere Rovers, Oswestry Town, Chorley, Tranmere Rovers, Ellesmere Port, South Liverpool, Stafford Rangers, Macclesfield Town, Cheltenham Town, Stalybridge Celtic)*, **Brian Ross** *(Manchester Utd, Rochdale, Northwich Victoria, Winsford Utd, Chorley)*, **Eddie Murray** *(Maghull, Stork, Tranmere Rovers, Altrincham)*.

MATLOCK TOWN

Formed: 1885 — The Gladiators

Matlock Town come under some pressure in their FA Trophy First Qualifying Round tie at home to Knowsley United in September. Here Brian Kilshaw gets in a shot for the visitors who were making their first-ever appearance in the competition. Matlock eventually won through in a second replay.

Chairman: Donald T Carr
Secretary: K F Brown, 'Barncroft', 1 Malvern Gardens, Matlock DE4 3JH (0629 584231).
Manager: David Vaughan **Physio:**
Press Officer: G M Tomlinson.
Commercial Manager: Mrs S Tomlinson.
Ground: Causeway Lane, Matlock, Derbyshire (0629 583866).
Directions: On A615, 500 yds from town centre and Matlock (BR).
Capacity: 7,500 **Cover:** 2,000 **Seats:** 240 **Floodlights:** Yes **Club Shop:** Yes
Colours: Royal blue/white/royal blue **Change colours:** All yellow.
Sponsors: Westons of Wirksworth/ Panasonic.
Previous Ground: Hall Leys (last century).
Previous Leagues: Midland Counties 1894-96 1961-69/ Matlock & District/ Derbys Senior/ Central Alliance 24-25 47-61/ Central Combination 34-35/ Chesterfield & District 46-47.
Midweek home matchday: Tuesday
Record Attendance: 5,123 v Burton Albion, FA Trophy 1975.
Best FA Cup season: 3rd Rd 76-77. Also 1st Rd 1885-86 86-87 86-87 87-88 1959-60 74-75 75-76 89-90.
League clubs defeated in FA Cup: Mansfield Town 76-77.
Record Fees - Paid: £300 for Mick Chambers (Grantham)
Received: £10,000 for Ian Helliwell (York).
Players progressing to Football League: Keith Haines (Leeds 1959), Wayne Biggins (Burnley 1984), Darren Bradshaw (Chesterfield 1987), Les McJannet (Scarborough 1987), Ian Helliwell (York 1987).
Clubhouse: Gladiators Social Club, on ground, open six nights per week.
Local Newspapers: Matlock Mercury, Derbyshire Times.
Local Radio Stations: Radio Derby.
Captain 93-94: John Shepherd/ Dave McNicholas.
Player of the Year 93-94: Martin Hardy.
Players' Player of the Year 93-94: David McNicholas.
Top Scorer: Stacy Reed.
Honours: FA Trophy 74-75, Northern Premier League Runners-up 83-84 (League Cup 77-78, Shield 78-79), Midland Counties League 61-62 68-69, Central Alliance (North) 59-60 60-61 (Runners-up 61-62 62-63, Division 1 Cup Runners-up 61-62, Division 2 59-60, Division 2 Cup 59-60 60-61), Derbyshire Senior Cup 74-75 76-77 77-78 80-81 83-84 84-85 91-92 (Runners-up 60-61 72-73 73-74 75-76 80-81 81-82 82-83 89-90 93-94), Derbshire Divisional Cup (North) 61-62 (Runners-up 62-63), Evans Halshaw Floodlit Cup 88-89, Anglo-Italian Non-League Cup 1979.

PROGRAMME DETAILS:
Pages: 32 **Price:** 50p
Editor: D Phillips

MATLOCK TOWN's 1993-94 CAMPAIGN

Date	Opponents	Comp.	Res	Gate	Goalscorers
21/08	Horwich RMI	NPL	1-1	207	Reed
24/08	**LEEK TOWN**	NPL	3-3	531	Sheppard, Evans(2)
28/08	Accrington Stanley	NPL	2-0	536	Burton, Evans
01/09	**BOSTON UNITED**	NPL	2-1	658	R Taylor, D Tomlinson
04/09	**COLWYN BAY**	NPL	3-1	445	McNicholas, Sheppard, Evans
08/09	Bridlington Town	NPL	2-2	90	Burton, Reed
11/09	Warrington Town	FAC1q	0-3	302	
14/09	**FRICKLEY ATH.**	NPL	1-5	436	Reed
18/09	**KNOWSLEY UNITED**	FAT1q	0-0	351	
21/09	Knowsley United	FAT1qr	1-1	128	Reed
25/09	**WHITLEY BAY**	NPL	1-1	320	Reed
27/09	**KNOWSLEY UNITED**	FAT1qr2	3-0	376	Evans(2), Reed
02/10	Droylsden	NPL	4-2	272	R Taylor, Tilly, Reed, Burton
05/10	Gainsborough Trin.	NPL	2-2	466	Reed(2)
09/10	**HORWICH R.M.I.**	NPL	1-0	385	Reed
12/10	**BRIDLINGTON TOWN**	NPL	3-0	490	Evans(2), Reed
16/10	Gainsborough Trin.	FAT2q	2-1	362	Burton, Tilly
20/10	Bishop Auckland	NPL	0-2	235	
23/10	**DROYLSDEN**	NPL	1-1	392	Reed
30/10	**FLEETWOOD TOWN**	NPL	6-1	354	Reed(4), Burton, McJannet
02/11	**ASHFIELD UTD**	EHFC	1-2	214	Evans
06/11	Barrow	NPL	1-2	1,310	Reed
08/11	**LEEK TOWN**	NPL	1-2	448	R Taylor
13/11	**EMLEY**	NPL	2-3	426	Reed(2)
20/11	Winsford United	NPL	3-0	247	Cheetham, Evans(2)
27/11	**BLYTH SPARTANS**	FAT3q	1-3	530	Evans
01/12	Ashfield United	EHFC	4-2		R Taylor, Cheetham, Tilly, own-goal
04/12	**GAINSBOROUGH Tr.**	NPL	5-2	435	McJannet, Reed, R Taylor, Cheetham, Sheppard
11/12	Hyde United	NPLC2	0-4	231	
03/01	Frickley Athletic	NPL	0-1	254	
08/01	**CHORLEY**	NPL	2-1	459	Evans, Reed
15/01	Marine	NPL	0-0	345	
18/01	**HUCKNALL TOWN**	EHFC	4-0	99	Evans, R Taylor, Reed, Tilly
29/01	Chorley	NPL	2-1	266	Reed, Evans
05/02	**KNOWSLEY UNITED**	NPL	2-2	357	R Taylor, Tilly
12/02	**HYDE UNITED**	NPL	1-2	422	Reed
19/02	**ACCRINGTON STAN.**	NPL	3-3	428	Sheppard, Reed, Cheetham
22/02	Eastwood Town	EHFC	0-1		
26/02	Morecambe	NPL	2-2	359	Evans, Cheetham
05/03	**MARINE**	NPL	1-2	434	Tilly
07/03	Hyde United	NPL	0-1	269	
09/03	**EASTWOOD TOWN**	EHFC	4-2	92	Tilly(2), R Taylor(2)
12/03	Fleetwood Town	NPL	1-3	156	Sheppard
15/03	**MEIR K.A.**	DSC4	4-0	153	McJannet, Tilly, Sheppard, Mullins
26/03	**BARROW**	NPL	0-2	400	Higginbotham(2)
29/03	Colwyn Bay	NPL	0-3	102	
06/04	Boston United	NPL	0-2	784	
09/04	Emley	NPL	4-4	184	Tilly, Cheetham, Evans, Thompson
12/04	Glapwell	DSCsf	0-0	300	
16/04	**WINSFORD UNITED**	NPL	3-0	264	Cheetham, Taylor(2)
19/04	**GLAPWELL**	DSCsfr	1-0	353	Taylor
21/04	**BUXTON**	NPL	1-1	406	Tomlinson
23/04	Whitley Bay	NPL	0-3	170	
26/04	**BISHOP AUCKLAND**	NPL	0-2	298	
28/04	Knowsley United	NPL	0-5	47	
30/04	**MORECAMBE**	NPL	3-1	237	Cheetham, Evans, Thompson
02/05	Buxton	NPL	1-4	349	Mullins
04/05	**GRESLEY ROVERS**	DSCf(1)	0-1	437	
10/05	Gresley Rovers	DSCf(2)	1-3	847	

Key: NPL: Northern Premier League Premier Division, NPLC: Northern Premier League Cup, FAC: F.A. Cup, FAT: F.A. Trophy, DSC: Derbyshire Senior Cup, EHFC: Evans Halshaw Floodlit Cup. Numbers after cup competitions denote rounds (r: replay, qf: Quarter-Final, sf: Semi-Final, f: Final. Numbers in brackets indicate legs, i.e. (1): 1st leg).
Home fixtures are denoted by bold capitals, away matches by lower case. (p): penalty, og: Own goal.

SQUAD MEMBERS *(previous clubs listed in chronological order)*

GOALKEEPERS: Richard Harrison *(Sheff. Utd., Frickley Ath., Farsley C.)*

DEFENDERS: Les McJannet *(Mansfield, King's Lynn, Matlock, Burton Alb., Scarborough, Darlington, Boston Utd.),* **Spencer Taylor** *(Ecclesfield, Stannington Coll.),* **Martin Hardy** *(Notts. Co., Worksop, Boston Utd.),* **Dave McNicholas** *(Barnsley, Goole, Matlock, Goole),* **Ian Batten** *(Scarborough),* **David Vaughan** *(Boston FC, Mossley, Burton Alb., Boston Utd.).*

MIDFIELD: John Sheppard *(Sheffield FC),* **Richard Taylor** *(Scarborough),* **Mick Cheetham** *(Hatfield Main),* **Paul Burton** *(Scarborough),* **Paul Bennett** *(Rotherham, Caernarfon),* **Nick Tilly** *(Crookes, Matlock, Sheffield FC, Matlock, Belper),* **Craig Thompson** *(Boston Utd., Gainsborough T., King's Lynn, Worksop, Gainsborough T.).*

FORWARDS: Stacy Reed *(Sheffield Aurora),* **Scott Cordner** *(Chesterfield, Burton Alb., Rocester),* **Mark Mullins** *(Chesterfield, Alfreton, Staveley),* **Gary Evans** *(Goole, Frickley Ath., Thorne Coll., Chesterfield, Goole),* **Roger McKenzie** *(Scarborough, Northampton, Boston Utd., Mossley).*

Formed: 1920

MORECAMBE

The Shrimps

Morecambe fans out in force for the FA Trophy Quarter-Final at Guiseley. The Shrimps lost 2-3, ending hopes of returning to Wembley exactly twenty years after their 1974 victory over Dartford.

Photo - Colin Stevens.

Chairman: Eddie Weldrake **Vice Chairman:** Fred O'Brien.
Secretary: Neil Marsdin, 6 Palmer Grove, Bare, Morecambe, Lancs LA4 2BQ (0524 833358-h, 582520-b).
Manager: Jimmy Harvey **Coach:** Dickie Danson **Physio:** David Edge
Press Officer: Neil Marsden (0524 833358).
Chief Executive: Nigel Webster.
Ground: Christie Park, Lancaster Road, Morecambe LA4 4TJ (0524 411797/832230).
Directions: Ground on main town centre road, on left arriving from Lancaster. BR to Morecambe Promenade station.
Capacity: 3,500 **Seats:** 1,000 **Floodlights:** Yes **Metal Badges:** Yes
Colours: Red (black pin stripes) **Change colours:** Jade/black/black.
Newsline: 0891 446 826. **Sponsors:** Promotional Printing Machinery.
Previous Ground: Woodhill Lane 1920. **Previous Leagues:** Lancs Combination 20-68.
Club Shop: Yes, with over 10,000 programmes and a full range of leisure wear and souvenirs.
Midweek home matchday: Tuesday **Record Gate:** 9,383 v Weymouth, FA Cup 3rd Rd 13/1/62.
Best FA Cup year: 3rd Rd 61-62. 1st Rd(13) 36-37 56-57 58-59 61-63 66-67 68-69 74-77 78-80 85-86 91-92.
League clubs defeated in FA Cup: Chester 61-62.
Record win: 16-0 v Rossendale Utd, Lancs Combination Sept 1967 (Arnold Timmins scored eight).
Record Fees - Paid: £7,500 to Fleetwood for Ian Cain, 1988
Received: £6,000 from Colne Dynamoes for Barrie Stimpson.
Players progressing to Football League: Fred Blondel & Malcolm Darling (Bury 1946 & 78), Herbert Harrison (Accrington 1947), Gordon Milne (Preston 1956), Ray Charnley (Blackpool 1957), Geoff Slack (Stockport 1958), Ron Mitchell (Leeds 1958), Derek Armstrong (Carlisle 1961), Alan Taylor (Rochdale 1973), John Coates (Southport via Burscough & Skelmersdale 1975), Keith Galley (Southport 1975), Brian Thompson (West Ham 1977), David Eyres (Blackpool), Kenny Lowe (Barnet via Barrow), Steve Gardner (Bradford City), Dave Lancaster (Chesterfield).
Clubhouse: The Shrimps Club. Open every evening 7-11pm, Sat 1-2.45 & 4.45-11pm, Sun 7-10.30pm. All types of food available.
Club Record Scorer: Keith Borrowdale 289
Club Record Appearances: Steve Done 579.
93-94 Captain: Andy Grimshaw.
93-94 P.o.Y.: Jim McCluskie.
93-94 Top scorer: Jim McCluskie.
Local Newspapers: Lancashire Evening Post, Morecambe Visitor (0524 414531).
Local Radio: Radio Lancs, Red Rose Radio, Bay Radio.
Hons: FA Trophy 73-74 (QF 93-94), Northern Premier Lg Presidents Cup 91-92, Lancs Combination(5) 24-25 61-63 66-68 (R-up 25-26, Lg Cup 26-27 45-46 64-65 66-68), Lancs Jnr Cup (now ATS Tphy)(8) 25-27 61-63 68-69 85-87 92-93, Lancs Snr Cup 67-68, Lancs Lg Div 2 83-84.

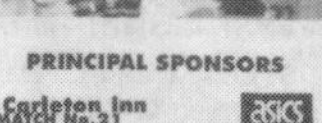

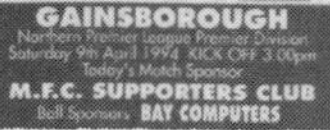

PROGRAMME DETAILS:
Pages: 40 **Price:** £1
Editor: Secretary

MORECAMBE's 1993-94 CAMPAIGN

Date	Opponents	Comp.	Res	Gate	Goalscorers
21/08	**DROYLSDEN**	NPL	1-2	471	Grimshaw
25/08	Accrington Stanley	NPL	2-3	663	Holden, Cain
28/08	**WINSFORD UTD**	NPL	1-0	407	Holden
30/08	**BISHOP AUCKLAND**	NPL	0-2	402	
04/09	Emley	NPL	0-2	329	
07/09	**MARINE**	NPL	3-2	412	Holden(2), Lodge
11/09	Denaby United	FAC1q	4-0	124	Holden(3), Dullaghan
15/09	Horwich RMI	NPL	3-1	213	McCluskie, Holden, Grimshaw
18/09	**LEEK TOWN**	NPL	0-0	456	
21/09	Barrow	NPL	2-1	1,185	McCluskie, Parillon
25/09	**GOOLE TOWN**	FAC2q	3-2	354	Lodge, King, Grimshaw
28/09	**WHITLEY BAY**	NPL	0-0	358	
02/10	Curzon Ashton	PC1	3-0	162	McNally, King, Tomlinson
05/10	Chorley	NPL	2-2	367	Holden(2)
09/10	**BRIDLINGTON T.**	FAC3q	2-0	405	Grimshaw, Holden
16/10	Hyde United	NPL	3-2	325	Holden(2), McCluskie
19/10	**FLEETWOOD TOWN**	NPL	8-0	362	Grimshaw(2), Holden(2), McCluskie, Tomlinson
23/10	Telford United	FAC4q	0-2	902	
27/10	Fleetwood Town	NPL	6-0	267	Cain(2), McCluskie, Parillon, Eaves(2)
30/10	**ASHTON UNITED**	PCqf	1-1	302	Holden
02/11	**HYDE UNITED**	NPL	2-3	267	Grimshaw(2)
06/11	Frickley Athletic	NPL	3-3	290	Lodge, Cain, McNally
13/11	**FRICKLEY ATH.**	NPL	1-2	416	Eaves
20/11	Buxton	NPL	2-0	251	Eaves, Cain
27/11	**BOSTON UNITED**	NPL	1-2	306	Lee(og)
04/12	Bridlington Town	NPL	4-0	63	Holden, Cain, McCluskie, Parillon
07/12	**KNOWSLEY UTD**	NPL	5-0	232	McCluskie(3), Holden, King
11/12	**CHORLEY**	NPLC2	5-2	234	McCluskie(2), Holden(2), Cain
13/12	Ashton United	NPL	3-4	PCqfr	McCluskie(2), Parillon
27/12	**BARROW**	NPL	1-2	1,423	Holden
01/01	Colwyn Bay	NPL	3-2	256	McCluskie(2), Cain
15/01	**COLWYN BAY**	NPL	1-1	413	McCluskie
18/01	**BACUP BOROUGH**	ATS2	4-0	178	Tomlinson, Richardson, McNally, McCluskie
22/01	**NORTHWICH VICS**	FAT1	2-1	793	McCluskie, Lavelle
29/01	Leek Town	NPL	0-2	547	
05/02	**EMLEY**	NPL	1-0	319	McCluskie
12/02	**SLOUGH TOWN**	FAT2	1-0	831	McCluskie
19/02	Gainsborough Trin.	NPL	1-0	546	McCluskie
22/02	**RADCLIFFE BORO.**	ATSqf	2-0	177	Holden(2)
26/02	**MATLOCK TOWN**	NPL	2-2	359	McCluskie, Burns
05/03	**SOUTHPORT**	FAT3	2-1	2,246	Grimshaw, McCluskie
08/03	**Gt HARWOOD TOWN**	NPLC3	0-2	187	
12/03	**BUXTON**	NPL	4-1	319	Holden(2), McCluskie, Harvey
15/03	Lancaster City	ATSsf	0-0	539	
19/03	**BRIDLINGTON T.**	NPL	7-1	301	Cain(2), Coleman(2), McCluskie, Dullaghan(2)
22/03	**LANCASTER CITY**	ATSsfr	3-0	661	McCluskie(2), Holden
26/03	Guiseley	FATqf	2-3	1,805	Cain, McCluskie
02/04	Whitley Bay	NPL	1-3	303	Smith(og)
04/04	**HORWICH R.M.I.**	NPL	1-1	234	McCluskie
06/04	Winsford United	NPL	1-0	206	McCluskie
09/04	**GAINSBOROUGH**	NPL	3-0	235	Coleman(3)
13/04	Bishop Auckland	NPL	1-2	230	Coleman
16/04	Marine	NPL	2-4	537	McCluskie, Coleman
19/04	**CHORLEY**	NPL	0-1	340	
23/04	Droylsden	NPL	3-0	138	Coleman(2), Cain
26/04	SOUTHPORT	ATSf	4-3		McCluskie, Dullaghan, Cain, Coleman *(at Bolton)*
30/04	Matlock Town	NPL	1-3	237	Coleman
02/05	Boston United	NPL	0-2	434	
05/05	**ACCRINGTON STAN.**	NPL	5-0	311	McCluskie, Colen(3), Tomlinson
07/05	Knowsley United	NPL	3-2	102	McCluskie, Coleman(2)

Key: NPL: Northern Premier League Premier Division, NPLC: Northern Premier League Cup, PC: (Northern Premier League) Presidents Cup, FAC: F.A. Cup, FAT: F.A. Trophy, ATS: Lancashire ATS Challenge Trophy. Numbers after cup competitions denote rounds (r: replay, qf: Quarter-Final, sf: Semi-Final, f: Final. Numbers in brackets indicate legs, i.e. (1): 1st leg).
Home fixtures are denoted by bold capitals, away matches by lower case. (p): penalty, og: Own goal.

SQUAD MEMBERS *(previous clubs listed in chronological order)*

GOALKEEPERS: Mike Allison *(Horwich, Chesterfield)*, **Mark Thornley** *(Alfreton, Belper, Sutton T., Alfreton, Stafford, Matlock, Fleetwood)*

DEFENDERS: Paul Tomlinson *(Burscough, Mossley)*, **Gary Dullaghan** *(South Liverpool, Ford Motors, Witton, Oswestry, Rhyl)*, **Matthew Lambert** *(Preston, Bury)*, **Scott Middlemass** *(Burnley, Ashton Utd, Bamber Bridge)*, **Robbie Armstrong** *(Kirkby, Southport, Rhyl)*, **Ollie Parillon** *(Leyland Motors, Horwich RMI)*

MIDFIELD: Andy Grimshaw *(Colne D., Rossendale, Colne Dynamoes, Witton)*, **Ben Lavelle** *(Southport, Blackpool Rovers, Morecambe, Fleetwood)*, **John McNally** *(Vauxhall GM)*, **Carl Parker** *(Burnley, Colne D., Rossendale, Rochdale)*, **Jimmy Harvey** *(Glenavon, Arsenal, Hereford, Bristol C., Tranmere, Crewe, Southport)*, **Peter King** *(Liverpool, Crewe, Southport, Marine, Stafford, Chorley, Barrow, Marine, Stalybridge)*

FORWARDS: Jim McCluskie *(Rochdale, Mossley, Hyde, Witton, Accrington)*, **Paul Burns** *(Grimsby, Burscough, Prescot, Altrincham, Caernarfon, Accrington)*, **Ian Cain** *(Fleetwood, Blackpool Mechs, Fleetwood)*, **Steve Holden** *(Fleetwood, Blackpool Mechs, Runcorn, Northwich, Fleetwood, Taranaki(NZ), Fleetwood, Morecambe, Southport)*, **John Coleman** *(Kirkby, Burscough, Marine, Southport, Runcorn, Macclesfield, Rhyl, Witton)*

1904 **SPENNYMOOR UNITED** The Moors

Spennymoor United - Northern Premier League Challenge Cup winners 1993-94.

Chairman: Mr J B Hindmarsh **Vice Chairman:** Mr J Norman **President:** Mr T Beaumont, MA
Secretary: Mr J Nutt, 41 Warwick Close, Grange Estate, Spennymoor, County Durham DL16 6UU (0388 812179).
Manager: Matty Pearson **Asst Manager:** Dave Barton **Physio:** Alan Jackson
Coach: Managerial team.
Commercial Mgr: Des Beamson **Press Officer:** Mr J B Hindmarsh (0388 815168).
Ground: Brewery Field, Durham Road, Spennymoor, County Durham DL16 6JN (0388 811934).
Directions: From South; A1(M), A167, A688, straight on at mini-r'bout, 3rd exit at next large r'bout (St Andrews church opposite), pass Asda on left, straight on at junction, pass Salvin Arms (Durham Rd), ground 200 yds on left. From A167 North - leave at Croxdale (N.E.S.S. factory), right at cemetary on left - this is Durham Rd - ground half mile on right. Nearest rail station is Durham - buses from there.
Seats: 300 **Cover:** 2,000 **Capacity:** 7,500 **Floodlights:** Yes
Club Shop: Yes, selling replica kit, memorabilia, programmes etc. Contact Bill Forster (0388 814100).
Club colours: Black & white stripes/black/black **Change colours:** All red
Midweek home matches: Tuesday
Sponsors: Home: Rothmans (Spennymoor). Away: Welland Medical (Leicester)
Reserve Team: None **Previous Ground:** Wood Vue 1901-1904.
Previous Leagues: Northern 05-08 60-90/ North Eastern 08-37 38-58/ Wearside 37-38/ Midland Counties 58-60/ Northern Counties (East) 90-93.
Record Gate: 7,202 v Bishop Auckland, Durham County Challenge Cup 30/3/57.
Local Press: Northern Echo/ The Journal.
Best FA Cup season: 3rd Rd 36-37 (lost 1-7 at West Bromwich Albion).
League clubs defeated in FA Cup: Hartlepool 27-28, Southport 75-76.
Best FA Trophy season: Semi Final 77-78.
Record win: 19-0 v Eden Colliery, North Eastern Lge 6/2/37.
Record defeat: 0-16 v Sunderland 'A', Durham Snr Cup 4/1/02 (Half-time: 0-10).
Players progressing to Football League: Over fifty, including: Harold Hubbick (Burnley, March 1925), Tommy Dawson (Charlton, March 1939), Tommy Flockett (Charlton, April 1949), Jimmy Smallwood (Chesterfield, Dec. 1949), Jack Oakes (Aldershot, May 1954), Jimmy Adams (Luton Town, 1953), Alan Moore (Chesterfield), Michael Heathcote (Sunderland, May 1987).
Record transfer fee paid: £2,500 for Dean Gibb (Seaham Red Star, 1991).
Record Transfer Fee Received: £20,000 for Michael Heathcote (Sunderland, 1988).
Clubhouse: (0388 814100) Open nightly 7-11pm, Sat noon-11pm, Sun noon-2 & 7-10.30pm. Bar snacks available. Private functions. Well stocked tea bar in ground.
Club Record Scorer: Dougie Humble 200+
Club Record Appearances: Ken Banks 600+
93-94 Captain: Brian Healy.
Player of the Year 93-94: Wes Saunders.
93-94 Top scorer: Andrew Shaw, 31.
Hons: Northern Premier Lg Cup 93-94 (Div 1 R-up 93-94), Northern Lg(6) 67-68 71-72 73-74 76-79 (R-up(3) 74-75 79-81, Lg Cup(5) 65-66 67-68 79-81 86-87, Turney Wylde Cup 80-81, J R Cleator Cup 80-81 86-87), Northern Counties (East) Lg 92-93 (Lg Cup 92-93), Durham Challenge Cup 29-30 44-45 45-46 53-54 62-63 67-68 72-73 73-74 74-75 75-76 78-79 82-83 93-94; Durham Benevolent Bowl 26-27 29-30 31-32 47-48 58-59 60-61, North Eastern Lg(4) 09-10 44-46 56-57 (Lg Cup 28-29); FA Trophy SF 77-78.

PROGRAMME DETAILS:
Pages: 32 **Price:** 80p
Editor: Peter Mains
(091 378 0135)

SPENNYMOOR UNITED's 1993-94 CAMPAIGN

Date	Opponents	Comp.	Res	Gate	Goalscorers
21/08	**WARRINGTON TOWN**	NPL	1-2	231	Cooke
24/08	Goole Town	NPL	1-2	251	Shaw
28/08	**NETHERFIELD**	NPL	1-3	252	Veart
04/09	Bamber Bridge	NPL	2-0	576	Healey, Veart
11/09	Whitley Bay	FAC1q	6-1	320	Shaw(3), Tucker, Goodrick, Healey
14/09	Harrogate Town	NPL	5-2	210	Powell, Cowell, Daly(og), Hewitt, Healey
18/09	**RADCLIFFE BOROUGH**	NPL	4-1	268	Hewitt(2), Cowell, Healy
20/09	Guiseley	NPL	1-2	624	Hewitt
25/09	**WHITBY TOWN**	FAC2q	2-3	417	Shaw(2)
29/09	**GRETNA**	NPL	4-0	223	Hewitt, Cooke, Shaw, Tucker
02/10	Alfreton Town	NPL	2-2	171	Shaw, Ainsley
06/10	**GUISELEY**	NPL	1-2	309	Healey
09/10	Curzon Ashton	NPL	2-1	141	Cooke, Shaw
12/10	Farsley Celtic	NPL	3-1	112	Shaw, Ainsley, Gorman
16/10	**BAMBER BRIDGE**	NPL	2-1	304	Healy, Shaw
20/10	**GOOLE TOWN**	NPL	5-3	207	Shaw(4), Veart
23/10	Bamber Bridge	NPLC1	3-1	336	Cowell(2), Cooke
30/10	**ALFRETON TOWN**	NPL	2-2	341	Shaw, Healy
03/11	**HARROGATE TOWN**	NPL	5-0	206	Saunder, Cooke(2), Askew, Gorman
06/11	Mossley	NPL	2-0	245	Shaw, Ainsley
13/11	Caernarfon Town	N1C1	4-1	69	Shaw, Corman, Healy, Cooke
20/11	**CONGLETON TOWN**	NPL	0-0	247	
30/11	Stockton	FAT3q	3-0	121	Saunders, Gorman(2)
04/12	Warrington Town	N1C2	2-1	149	Gorman(2)
11/12	**MARINE**	NPLC2	3-0	303	Healy, Ainsley, Shaw
14/12	**HERRINGTON C.W.**	DSC1	4-0	132	Shaw, Cooke, Gorman(2)
01/01	**WORKINGTON**	NPL	5-3	449	Gorman(3), Ainsley(2)
03/01	Gretna	NPL	2-1	187	Ainsley, Healey
08/01	**Gt HARWOOD TOWN**	NPL	4-0	363	Healy(2), Veart, Pettitjohn
12/01	Billingham Synthonia	NPL	3-2	305	Ainsley, Healy, Veart
15/01	Warrington	NPL	2-2	248	Saunders, Gorman
22/01	**HYDE UNITED**	FAT1	2-1	529	Ainsley, Gorman
29/01	**LANCASTER CITY**	NPL	1-0	367	Fletcher
02/02	**WHITLEY BAY**	NPLC3	2-1	358	Veart, Gorman
05/02	Ashton United	NPL	2-1	489	Fletcher, Gorman
07/02	Ashton United	N1C3	2-3	296	Cooke, Shaw
12/02	**HALIFAX TOWN**	FAT2	1-2	1,426	Gorman
19/02	**WORKSOP TOWN**	NPL	0-0	007	Pettitjean, Gorman, Fletcher
02/03	**BILLINGHAM TOWN**	DSCqf	8-3	152	Shaw(3), Cooke(3), Gorman, Cowell
05/03	Great Harwood Town	NPL	6-0	138	Cooke, Veart, Shaw, Gorman(2), Fletcher
12/03	**CAERNARFON TOWN**	NPL	1-3	316	Fletcher
16/03	Bishop Auckland	NPLCqf	2-1	401	Fletcher, Saunders
19/03	Shildon	DSCsf	4-0	356	Askew, Taylor(og), Saunders, Goodrick
22/03	Radcliffe Borough	NPL	2-4	n/k	Ainsley, Veart
26/03	**MOSSLEY**	NPL	3-0	308	Fletcher(2), Ainsley
28/03	Caernarfon Town	NPL	5-3	97	Healey(2), Ainsley, Nelson(og), Gorman
02/04	Worksop Town	NPL	1-0	226	Healy
04/04	**EASTWOOD TOWN**	NPL	2-1	326	Veart, Shaw
06/04	**ACCRINGTON STAN.**	NPLCsf(1)	3-1	403	Fletcher(2), Ainsley
13/04	Accrington Stanley	NPLCsf(2)	4-1	363	Healey, Shaw, Fletcher, Holmes
16/04	Eastwood Town	NPL	2-0	142	Shaw, Saunders
19/04	Netherfield	NPL	0-1	145	
21/04	Congleton Town	NPL	1-0	122	Cooke
23/04	**CURZON ASHTON**	NPL	2-1	308	Saunders, Gorman
26/04	Workington	NPL	4-0	216	Saunders(2),Gorman(2)
26/04	Workington	NPL	4-0	216	Saunders(2), Gorman(2)
28/04	HYDE UNITED	NPLCf	3-1	585	Gorman, Healy, Shaw *(at Harrogate Town FC)*
30/04	Lancaster City	NPL	0-1	171	
02/05	Bishop Auckland	DSCf	3-2	n/k	Cowell, Veart, Healey *(played at Darlington FC)*
07/05	**ASHTON UNITED**	NPL	3-1	914	Gorman(2), Shaw

Key: NPL: Northern Premier League Division One, NPLC: Northern Premier League Cup, PC: Northern Premier League Presidents Cup, N1C: (Northern Premier League) Division One Cup, DSC: Durham Senior Challenge Cup. FAC: F.A. Cup, FAT: F.A. Trophy. Number after cup competitions denote rounds (r: replay, qf: Quarter-Final, sf: Semi-Final, f: Final. Numbers in brackets indicate legs, i.e. (1): 1st leg).
Home fixtures are denoted by bold capitals, away matches by lower case. (p): penalty, og: Own goal.

Formed: 1897

WHITLEY BAY

The Bay

Whitley Bay's Jarrod Suddick (stripes) beats Gary Dullaghan of Morecambe to the ball as the North Easterners record a 3-1 home win on Easter Saturday.

Photo - Gavin Ellis-Neville.

Chairman: John Gray **Vice Chairman:** P Harrison **President:** J Hedworth.
Secretary: Rob Harding, 22 Cambridge Avenue, Whitley Bay NE26 1BB (091 251 5179).
Manager: Bobby Graham **Asst Manager:** Keith Twennce **Coach:**
Physio: Joe Jars **Press Officer:** Dave Folkes
Commercial Manager: Secretary.
Ground: Hillheads Park, Hillheads Road, Whitley Bay, Tyne & Wear (091 251 3680).
Directions: 1 mile walk from bus station - leave St Pauls Church southward, turn right at r-about, ground 3rd left at rear of ice rink. Whitley Bay (25 mins from Newcastle) or Monkseaton metro stations, both 1 mile.
Capacity: 4,500 **Cover:** 650 **Seats:** 450 **Floodlights:** Yes **Metal Badges:** Yes
Club Shop: Yes, selling programmes, club scarves, hats etc. Contact Tom Moony (091 252 0087).
Colours: Blue & white stripes/blue/blue **Change colours:** All yellow
Record Fee Paid: £500
Previous Leagues: Tyneside 09-10/ Northern Alliance 50-55/ North Eastern 55-58/ Northern 58-88.
Previous Name: Whitley Bay Athletic 1950-58.
Midweek home matchday: Wednesday **Record Gate:** 7,301 v Hendon, FA Amateur Cup 1965.
Record win: 12-0 v Shildon 1961 **Record defeat:** 1-8 v Bishop Auckland 1979.
Best FA Cup season: 3rd Rd 89-90 (lost 0-1 at Rochdale). 2nd Rd 90-91 (lost 0-1 at home to Barrow).
League clubs defeated in F.A. Cup: Scarborough, Preston North End 89-90.
Players progressing to Football League: William Dodd (Burnley 1956), William Younger (Nottm Forest 1957), Ron Brown (Blackpool 1965), John Ritchie (Port Vale 1965), John Brodie & Aiden McCaffery (Carlisle 1967 & 88), Mike Spelman (Wolves 1969), Tony Harrison (Southport 1977), Mark Miller (Gillingham 1981), Garry Haire (Bradford City 1983), Stewart Ferebee (Darlington 1987).
Clubhouse: Open every night except Wednesday & Sunday 7-11pm. Bar and concert room. Darts, pool, 5-a-side courts.
Club Record Goalscorer: Billy Wright 307
Club Record Appearances: Bill Chater 640.
93-94 Captain: Andy Gowans.
93-94 Player of the Year: Ian Chandler.
93-94 Top scorer: Jarrod Suddick.
Local Newspapers: The News, Guardian, Herald & Post.
Local Radio: Radio Newcastle, Metro.
Honours: FA Amateur Cup SF 65-66 68-69, FA Trophy 3rd Rd 86-87, Northern Premier Lg Div 1 90-91 (Div 1 Cup 88-89 90-91), Northern Lg 64-65 65-66 (R-up 59-60 66-67 68-69 69-70, Lg Cup 64-65 70-71 (R-up 67-68)), Northern Alliance 52-53 53-54 (Lg Cup 52-53 53-54), Northumberland Senior Cup 52-53 60-61 63-64 64-65 67-68 68-69 69-70 70-71 72-73 86-87 (R-up 53-54 54-55 55-56 65-66 76-77 85-86 90-91).

PROGRAMME DETAILS:
Pages: 24 **Price:** 60p
Editor: Len Bone
(091 262 6234)

WHITLEY BAY's 1993-94 CAMPAIGN

Date	Opponents	Comp.	Res	Gate	Goalscorers
21/08	**CHORLEY**	NPL	0-0	204	
25/08	Bishop Auckland	NPL	0-2	338	
28/08	**FLEETWOOD TOWN**	NPL	4-3	223	Williams, Chandler(2), Suddick
30/08	Frickley Athletic	NPL	1-6	183	Suddick
04/09	Winsford United	NPL	0-2	251	
11/09	**SPENNYMOOR UTD**	FAC1q	1-6	320	Suddick
18/09	**CHORLEY**	FAT1q	1-1	184	Kiddie
21/09	Chorley	NPL	1-3	266	Bone
25/09	Matlock Town	NPL	1-1	320	Suddick
28/09	Morecambe	NPL	0-0	348	
02/10	**BUXTON**	NPL	1-0	201	Chandler
05/10	**FRICKLEY ATHLETIC**	NPL	2-2	196	Chandler(2)
09/10	Gainsborough Trinity	NPL	3-1	370	Hutchinson, Lobban, Alderson
12/10	Accrington Stanley	NPL	1-0	317	Suddick
16/10	**KNOWSLEY UNITED**	NPL	1-3	200	Warham
19/10	**BARROW**	NPL	0-2	264	
23/10	Emley	NPL	1-3	336	Suddick
30/10	**HORWICH**	NPL	3-1	202	McDowell(2), Chandler
06/11	Droylsden	NPL	2-3	237	Bone, Suddick
13/11	**BOSTON UNITED**	NPL	2-1	346	Suddick, Hutchinson
20/11	Knowsley United	NPL	1-1	116	Stephenson
27/11	Buxton	NPL	4-5	161	Bone, Warham(2), Suddick
04/12	**LEEK TOWN**	NPL	0-4	246	
11/12	**WINSFORD UNITED**	NPLC2	2-0	120	Suddick(2)
27/12	**BRIDLINGTON TOWN**	NPL	2-0	209	Gowans, Henderson(2), Hutchinson
01/01	Barrow	NPL	0-1	1607	
03/01	**HYDE UNITED**	NPL	2-0	271	Henderson, Suddick
10/01	Newcastle Blue Star	NSC2	2-6	259	Suddick(2)
15/01	Horwich RMI	NPL	1-1	151	Nicholas
29/01	**DROYLSDEN**	NPL	1-1	202	Suddick
02/02	Spennymoor United	NPLC3	1-2	358	Henderson
05/02	Marine	NPL	3-6	381	Hall, Suddick, Gowans
12/02	**GAINSBOROUGH Tr.**	NPL	0-1	226	
10/02	Fleetwood Town	NPL	1-0	187	Henderson
05/03	**ACCRINGTON STAN.**	NPL	4-1	250	Henderson, Chandler, Gowans, Cooper
12/03	Colwyn Bay	NPL	0-1	119	
19/03	Boston United	NPL	1-0	908	Suddick
26/03	**EMLEY**	NPL	2-0	240	Bone, Stephenson
02/04	**MORECAMBE**	NPL	3-1	303	Henderson(?), Robson
04/04	Hyde United	NPL	0-0	297	
09/04	**MARINE**	NPL	0-4	276	
16/04	Leek Town	NPL	1-2	452	Stephenson
23/04	**MATLOCK TOWN**	NPL	3-0	170	Suddick, Stephenson, Henderson
30/04	Chorley	NPL	2-0	160	Stevenson, Gowens
02/05	Bridlington Town	NPL	1-1	39	Henderson
04/05	**COLWYN BAY**	NPL	1-1	134	Suddick
07/05	**WINSFORD UNITED**	NPL	2-1	199	Chandler, Henderson

Key: NPL: Northern Premier League Premier Division, NPLC: Northern Premier League Cup, PC: Northern Premier League Presidennts Cup, NSC: Northumberland Senior Cup. FAC: F.A. Cup, FAT: F.A. Trophy. Number after cup competitions denote rounds (r: replay, qf: Quarter-Final, sf: Semi-Final, f: Final. Numbers in brackets indicate legs, i.e. (1): 1st leg).
Home fixtures are denoted by bold capitals, away matches by lower case. (p): penalty, og: Own goal.

Founded: 1883

WINSFORD UNITED

Blues

The Winsford United side that lifted the 1992-93 Cheshire Senior Cup.

Photo - Keith Clayton.

Chairman: Chris Clarke **Vice Chairman:** George Sankey **President:** J Deans.
Secretary: Peter Warburton, 3 Maisey Avenue, Winsford, Cheshire CW7 3DU (0606 554295).
Manager: Larry Gaffney **Asst Manager:** John Imrie.
Ground: Barton Stadium, Wharton, Winsford, Cheshire CW7 3EU (0606 593021).
Directions: From north; M6 junction 19, A556 towards Northwich to Davenham, then A5018 to Winsford. From south; M6 junction 18, A54 through Middlewich to Winsford. Ground quarter mile off main road in Wharton area of town. 1 mile from Winsford (BR).
Capacity: 6,000 **Cover:** 5,000 **Seats:** 250 **Floodlights:** Yes **Club Shop:** No.
Colours: Royal/white/royal **Change colours:** Maroon/white/white.
Sponsors: Dickson Motors Ltd, Winsford (Ford).
Previous Name: Over Wanderers (prior to 1914).
Previous Leagues: The Combination 02-04/ Cheshire County 19-40 47-82/ North West Counties 82-87.
Midweek home matchday: Wednesday **Record Attendance:** 7,000 v Witton Albion 1947.
Best F.A. Cup season: 2nd Rd 1887-88. Also 1st Rd 1975-76 1991-92.
League clubs defeated in F.A. Cup: None.
Record Fees - Paid: Nil
Received: £6,000 for Neville Southall from Bury.
Players progressing to Football League: William Foulkes (Chester 1948), Cliff Marsh (Leeds 1948), Bennett Nicol (Rochdale 1949), Eric Johnson (Coventry 1952), Walter Hughes (Liverpool 1954), Reg Lewis (Luton 1954), William Heggie (Accrington 1955), Joe Richardson (Birmingham City 1959), John Abbott (Crewe Alexandra 961), Robert Walters (Shrewsbury 1962), Phil Mullington (Rochdale 1978), Neville Southall (Bury 1980), Mark Came (Bolton Wanderers 1984), Dave Bamber (Blackpool), Bob Sutton (West Ham United), J Richardson (Sheffield United), Stanley Wood (West Bromwich Albion), R Pearce (Luton Town).
Clubhouse: Mon-Sat 8-11pm, Sun 8-10.30pm
Club Record Goalscorer: Graham Smith 66
Club Record Apps: Edward Harrop 400.
93-94 Captain: Cec Edey
93-94 P.o.Y.:
93-94 Top scorer: Bevon Blackwood.
Local Newspapers: Winsford Chronicle, Winsford Guardian.
Local Radio Stations: Signal, Piccadilly.
Honours: Northern Premier Lg R-up 92-93 (Div 1 R-up 91-92, Lg Cup 92-93, Presidents Cup 92-93, Div 1 Cup SF 89-90), Cheshire County Lg 20-21 76-77 (R-up 74-75 79-80, Lg Cup 49-50 55-56 59-60 76-77 78-79 79-80 80-81 (R-up 36-37 68-69 77-78)), Cheshire Senior Cup 58-59 79-80 92-93, Mid-Cheshire Snr Cup 90-91 92-93 (R-up 88-89), Cheshire Amateur Cup 00-01 02-03, Lancs Comb/Cheshire County Inter-Lg Cup 62-63, FA Trophy QF 77-78.

PROGRAMME DETAILS:
Pages: 24 **Price:** 50p
Editor: Ernie Maylor

WINSFORD UNITED's 1993-94 CAMPAIGN

Date	Opponents	Comp.	Res	Gate	Goalscorers
14/08	Southport	NPLCS	0-5	587	
21/08	**BARROW**	NPL	1-2	560	Williams
24/08	Buxton	NPL	0-1	352	
28/08	Morecambe	NPL	0-1	407	
30/08	**COLWYN BAY**	NPL	0-1	372	
04/09	**WHITLEY BAY**	NPL	2-0	281	Stewart, Newton
08/09	Chorley	NPL	0-1	235	
11/09	Ossett Town	FAC1q	1-1	200	Bishop
15/09	**OSSETT TOWN**	FAC1qr	3-1	185	Blain, Bishop, Mellish
18/09	**HYDE UNITED**	NPL	2-2	279	Talbot, Stewart
25/09	**GUISELEY**	FAC2q	2-1	287	Williams, Brown
29/09	**ASHTON UNITED**	PC1	0-2	162	
02/10	Emley	NPL	0-2	337	
05/10	Knowsley United	NPL	1-3	145	Bishop
09/10	**BUXTON**	FAC3q	6-1	275	Blain, Byrne(2), Bishop(3)
11/10	**HORWICH R.M.I.**	NPL	1-3	249	Russell
16/10	Bishop Auckland	NPL	2-4	270	McCarrick, Bishop
19/10	Droylsden	NPL	0-0	336	
23/10	**GRETNA**	FAC4q	0-0	446	
26/10	Gretna	FAC4qr	0-5	754	
30/10	Hyde United	NPL	1-1	319	Panton
03/11	**MARINE**	NPL	2-3	194	Russell, Daughtry
06/11	Horwich RMI	NPL	2-0	185	Russell, Daughtry
13/11	**CHORLEY**	NPL	0-4	346	
20/11	**MATLOCK TOWN**	NPL	0-3	247	
27/11	Marine	NPL	2-2	339	O'Loughlin, Russell
01/12	**ACCRINGTON STAN.**	NPL	3-1	224	McCarrick, Talbot, Russell
04/12	**FRICKLEY ATH.**	NPL	1-0	244	O'Loughlin
11/12	Whitley Bay	NPLC2	0-2	120	
18/12	**BOSTON UNITED**	NPL	1-0	247	Russell
01/01	**DROYLSDEN**	NPL	4-1	312	O'Loughlin, Russell(2), Bell
03/01	Barrow	NPL	1-1	1,265	Newton
12/01	**KNOWSLEY UNITED**	NPL	4-3	222	Bryne, Russell(2), Bell
15/01	Gainsborough Trin.	NPL	1-3	415	Cameron
22/01	**GUISELEY**	FAT1	0-1	332	
02/02	**NORTHWICH VICS**	CSC3	0-6	317	
05/02	Frickley Athletic	NPL	2-2	244	Shaw(2)
19/02	**EMLEY**	NPL	1-3	244	Byrne
12/03	**BISHOP AUCKLAND**	NPL	0-0	217	
19/03	Accrington Stanley	NPL	2-4	471	Byrne, Shaw
23/03	**LEEK TOWN**	NPL	1-2	282	Byrne
26/03	Boston United	NPL	1-1	722	O'Loughlin
29/03	Leek Town	NPL	1-3	448	O'Loughlin
02/04	**GAINSBOROUGH Tr.**	NPL	0-0	173	
04/04	Bridlington Town	NPL	2-3	31	Maynard, Shaw
06/04	**MORECAMBE**	NPL	0-1	206	
13/04	Fleetwood Town	NPL	3-1	163	Maynard, O'Loughlin, Newton
16/04	Matlock Town	NPL	0-3	264	
23/04	**FLEETWOOD TOWN**	NPL	1-4	173	O'Loughlin
27/04	**BUXTON**	NPL	2-1	154	Maynard, O'Loughlin
04/05	**BRIDLINGTON T.**	NPL	2-2	123	O'Loughlin, Byrne
07/05	Whitley Bay	NPL	1-2	199	Danskin

Key: NPL: Northern Premier League Premier Division, NPLC: Northern Premier League Cup, NPLCS: Northern Premier League Championship Shield, PC: (Northern Premier League) Presidents Cup, FAC: F.A. Cup, FAT: F.A. Trophy, CSC: Cheshire Senior Cup. Numbers after cup competitions denote rounds (r: replay, qf: Quarter-Final, sf: Semi-Final, f: Final. Numbers in brackets indicate legs, i.e. (1): 1st leg).
Home fixtures are denoted by bold capitals, away matches by lower case. (p): penalty, og: Own goal.

SQUAD MEMBERS *(previous clubs listed in chronological order)*

GOALKEEPERS: Steve Crompton *(Crewe, Stockport, Mossley, Hyde, Cheadle),* **Ray Curtis** *(Merseyside Police, Runcorn)*

DEFENDERS: Gary Talbot *(local football),* **Chris Blundell** *(Oldham Ath., Rochdale, Northwich),* **Vinny Panton** *(Buxton, Cheadle),* **Russell Sang** *(Stalybridge, Runcorn, Caernarfon, Warrington, Chorley, Caernarfon),* **Mark McCarrick** *(Witton, Birmingham, Lincoln, Crewe, Runcorn, Tranmere, Northwich, Bangor, Marine).*

MIDFIELD: John Smith *(Tranmere, Northwich, Altrincham, Fleetwood),* **Dave Maynard** *(Army, Winsford, Witton),* **Ged Byrne** *(Salford, Maine Rd, Winsford, Maine Rd, Winsford, Witton),* **Paul Newton** *(Man City, Flixton, Stockport, Cheadle, Radcliffe B.),* **John Imrie** *(Bury, Nantwich, Northwich, Runcorn, Altrincham, Macclesfield, Runcorn, Mossley, Droylsden).*

FORWARDS: John Russell *(Broadheath Central, North Trafford, Barrow, North Trafford),* **Willie Bell** *(Maine Rd, Altrincham),* **Colin O'Loughlin** *(Maine Rd, Flixton, Cheadle, Winsford, Witton),* **Jason Danskin** *(Everton, Mansfield, Winsford, Northwich),* **Paul Dougherty** *(Portsmouth, Buxton, Hyde)*

Formed: 1887

WITTON ALBION

The Albion

Witton's Brendan Burke (right) tussles for possession with Gareth Price during Albion's away fixture at Kettering Town in the GMV Conference last season.

Photo - Keith Clayton.

President: T Stelfox **Chairman:** G D Shirley **Vice-Chairman:** D T Lloyd.
Secretary: David Leather, 34 Grosvenor Ave., Hartford, Northwich, Cheshire (0606 76488).
Manager: Bryan Griffiths **Coach:** John Davison. **Physio:** Keith Higgins.
Commercial Mgr: Jackie Birks **Press Officer/General Manager:** Rod Price (0606 43008).
Ground: Wincham Park, Chapel Street, Wincham, Northwich (Tel/Fax: 0606 43008. Newsline: 0891 12 27 67).
Directions: M6 junction 19. Follow A556 towards Northwich, after 3 miles turn onto A559 at beginning of dual carriageway, after three-quarters of a mile turn left opposite Black Greyhoud Inn and ground is half a mile on left immediately after crossing Canal Bridge.
Capacity: 4,500 **Seated:** 650 **Cover:** 2,300 **Floodlights:** Yes.
Colours: Red & white stripes **Change colours:** All mauve
Midweek home matchday: Tuesday **Reserve Team's League:** None.
Record Attendance: 3,940 v Kidderminster Harriers - FA Trophy Semi-Final.
Club Shop: Yes. Contact Rod Price at club.
Record win: 6-0 v Stafford Rangers - 1992/93
Record defeat: 0-5 v Welling United (H), GMV Conference 12/3/94.
Record transfer fee: £10,000 (twice) for Karl Thomas from Colne Dynamoes and for Jim McCluskie from Hyde United both 1990.
Record fee received: £11,500 for Peter Henderson from Chester City.
Previous Grounds: Central Ground, Witton Street, Northwich.
Club Sponsors: Tetley Bitter.
Previous Leagues: Lancs Comb./ Cheshire County/ Northern Premier/ GMV Conference 91-94.
Past players who progressed to the Football League: P Henderson (Chester City), Chris Nicholl (ex-Southampton manager), Phil Powell (Crewe), Neil Parsley & Mike Whitlow (Leeds).
Social Facilities: Concert room and Vice-Presidents room open matchdays, Tuesday, Thursday, Friday and Sunday evenings. Food available for private functions.
1993-94 Captain: Steve McNeilis
1993-94 Top scorer: Brendan Burke
1993-94 Player of the Year: Cec Edey
Club record goalscorer: Frank Fidler - 122
Record appearances: John Gorle - 652
Honours: Northern Premier League 90-91; Cheshire County League 48-49 49-50 53-54 (R-up 50-51, League Cup 53-54 75-76); Cheshire County Senior Cup winners five times; FA Trophy R-up 91-92 (SF 90-91 92-93).

PROGRAMME DETAILS:
Pages: 32 **Price:** £1
Editor: Rod Price
(0606 43008)

WITTON ALBION's 1993-94 CAMPAIGN

Date	Opponents	Comp.	Res	Gate	Goalscorers
21/08	Telford United	GMV	2-2	933	Cunningham, Burke
24/08	**GATESHEAD**	GMV	1-0	706	Timmons
28/08	**MERTHYR TYDFIL**	GMV	2-2	751	Matnard, Cunningham
30/08	Kettering Town	GMV	0-1	1,680	
04/09	**BROMSGROVE R.**	GMV	4-1	739	Burke(2), Blackwood, Gallagher
07/09	**MACCLESFIELD T.**	DC1(1)	1-2	826	Senior
11/09	Yeovil Town	GMV	0-2	2,849	
14/09	**KIDDERMINSTER**	GMV	2-0	613	Blackwood, Burke
18/09	Halifax Town	GMV	0-0	1,099	
21/09	Macclesfield Town	DC1(2)	1-4	466	Burke
25/09	**BATH CITY**	GMV	0-3	688	
02/10	Dover Athletic	GMV	0-1	1,563	
09/10	**MACCLESFIELD T.**	GMV	0-2	1,068	
12/10	**TELFORD UNITED**	GMV	0-0	534	
16/10	Woking	GMV	1-3	1,615	
23/10	**NORTHALLERTON**	FAC4q	2-1	706	Maynard, Burke
27/10	Gateshead	GMV	0-3	320	
30/10	**DAGENHAM & R.**	GMV	1-1	692	Burke
06/11	Slough Town	GMV	1-0	781	Maynard
13/11	**LINCOLN CITY**	FAC1	0-2	1,450	
20/11	Kidderminster H.	GMV	0-0	1,536	
26/11	**HALIFAX TOWN**	GMV	2-2	846	Burke(2)
11/12	Stafford Rangers	GMV	0-1	580	
18/12	**ALTRINCHAM**	GMV	0-1	856	
27/12	Northwich Victoria	GMV	1-0	2,897	Rose
01/01	**SOUTHPORT**	GMV	0-2	1,144	
08/01	Welling United	GMV	1-2	1,001	Walker
11/01	**RUNCORN**	GMV	1-1	883	Tobin
15/01	**KETTERING TOWN**	GMV	0-1	798	
18/01	Warrington Town	CSC3	1-2	303	Burke
22/01	Grantham Town	FAT1	2-3	505	Blackwood(2)
29/01	Runcorn	GMV	0-1	869	
05/02	**DOVER ATHLETIC**	GMV	1-2	650	Burke
08/02	Northwich Victoria	MCSC	0-4	844	
12/02	Altrincham	GMV	3-1	640	Harris(og), Edey, Burke
19/02	**YEOVIL TOWN**	GMV	1-2	643	Pritchard
26/02	Southport	GMV	1-2	1,417	Goulding(og)
05/03	Bath City	GMV	1-1	482	Grayson
08/03	**STAFFORD RGRS**	GMV	1-1	613	Shaw
12/03	**WELLING UNITED**	GMV	0-5	593	
19/03	Dagenham & Redbdge	GMV	1-2	708	Burke
02/04	Stalybridge Celtic	GMV	1-2	537	Burke
04/04	**NORTHWICH VIC.**	GMV	1-1	1,564	McNeilis
09/04	Bromsgrove Rovers	GMV	3-3	725	Shaw(2), Hall
16/04	**SLOUGH TOWN**	GMV	1-0	489	Edey
19/04	**STALYBRIDGE C.**	GMV	0-3	641	
23/04	Macclesfield Town	GMV	0-2	720	
30/04	**WOKING**	GMV	0-0	454	
07/05	Merthyr Tydfil	GMV	3-4	526	Hall, Rose, Tobin

Key: GMV: GM Vauxhall Conference, DC: Drinkwise (GM Vauxhall Conference) Cup, FAC: F.A. Cup, FAT: F.A. Trophy, CSC: Cheshire Senior Cup, MCSC: Mid-Cheshire Senior Cup. Numbers after cup competitions denote rounds (r: replay, qf: Quarter-Final, sf: Semi-Final, f: Final. Numbers in brackets indicate legs, i.e. (1): 1st leg). Home fixtures are denoted by bold capitals, away matches by lower case. (p): penalty, og: Own goal.

SQUAD MEMBERS *(previous clubs listed in chronological order)*

GOALKEEPERS: Keith Mason *(Lutterworth, Wigston, Leicester City, Huddersfield, Colne D.)*

DEFENDERS: Billy Garton *(Man Utd, Salford)*, **Steve Senior** *(York, Northampton, Wigan, Preston)*, **Andy Thorpe** *(Stockport, Tranmere, Stockport, Melbourne(Aust))*, **Jason Gallagher** *(Marine, Ternia(Bel), Newton)*, **Cec Edey** *(Lancaster, Chorley, Lancaster, Morecambe, Winsford)*, **Steve McNeilis** *(Formby, Burscough, Northwich, Colne D.)*

MIDFIELD: Neil Hall *(Winsford)*, **Dean Pritchard** *(Ovenden, Emley, Accrington, Emley)*, **Colin Rose** *(Crewe)*, **Warren Godfrey** *(Liverpool, Barnsley)*, **Gary Thomas** *(Bury, Luton, Maine Road, Buxton, Winsford)*, **Dave Richardson** *(Marine, Morecambe)*, **Neil McNab** *(Morton, Spurs, Bolton, Brighton, Man City, Tranmere, Derry City)*, **Peter Mellor** *(Hyde, Radcliffe, Barrow, Droylsden)*

FORWARDS: Brendan Burke *(Man Utd, Oldham Town, Mossley)*, **Chris Shaw** *(Radcliffe, Oldham Town, Ashton Utd)*, **Matthew Holt** *(Blackburn, Mossley)*, **Mark Savage** *(Maghull)*, **Darrell McCarty** *(Chorley, Horwich, Bolton, Marine, Morecambe, Horwich, Runcorn)*

Northern Premier League Premier Division Ten Year Records

	84/5	85/6	86/7	87/8	88/9	89/0	90/1	91/2	92/3	93/4
Accrington Stanley	–	–	–	–	–	–	–	8	6	16
Bangor City	10	13	2	7	4	10	18	20	–	–
Barrow	–	–	15	5	1	–	–	–	8	8
Bishop Auckland	–	–	–	–	–	11	7	11	10	4
Boston United	–	–	–	–	–	–	–	–	–	3
Bridlington Town	–	–	–	–	–	–	–	–	–	21
Burton Albion	6	5	12	–	–	–	–	–	–	–
Buxton	22	19	13	16	15	16	8	5	14	15
Caernarfon Town	–	17	3	3	12	21	–	–	–	–
Chorley	19	20	9	1	–	–	14	21	18	10
Colne Dynamoes	–	–	–	–	–	1	–	–	–	–
Colwyn Bay	–	–	–	–	–	–	–	–	12	6
Droylsden	–	–	–	–	–	–	13	15	20	17
Emley	–	–	–	–	–	–	–	6	16	13
Fleetwood Town	–	–	–	–	7	8	4	10	19	22
Frickley Athletic	–	–	–	10	9	13	10	14	7	5
Gainsborough Trinity	11	4	20	20	17	12	20	18	11	12
Gateshead	–	1	–	18	21	2	–	–	–	–
Goole Town	16	22	16	12	6	19	12	12	22	–
Grantham Town	21	–	–	–	–	–	–	–	–	–
Horwich RMI	9	16	22	13	20	14	16	13	13	20
Hyde United	4	10	11	2	2	4	11	9	9	9
Knowsley United	–	–	–	–	–	–	–	–	–	18
Leek Town	–	–	–	–	–	–	9	4	5	2
Macclesfield Town	2	9	1	–	–	–	–	–	–	–
Marine	5	2	4	9	5	9	6	2	4	1
Matlock Town	13	21	7	19	13	6	17	19	15	14
Morecambe	18	3	6	4	16	15	3	3	3	7
Mossley	15	12	10	17	10	18	15	16	21	–
Oswestry Town	14	18	17	21	–	–	–	–	–	–
Rhyl	17	14	18	8	8	22	–	–	–	–
Shepshed Albion	–	–	–	–	18	20	21	22	–	–
South Liverpool	20	15	5	15	11	5	19	–	–	–
Southport	12	6	8	14	14	7	5	7	1	–
Stafford Rangers	1	–	–	–	–	–	–	–	–	–
Stalybridge Celtic	–	–	–	–	19	17	2	1	–	–
Whitley Bay	–	–	–	–	–	–	–	17	17	11
Winsford United	–	–	–	–	–	–	–	–	2	19
Witton Albion	3	11	14	11	3	3	1	–	–	–
Workington	8	8	21	22	–	–	–	–	–	–
Worksop Town	7	7	19	6	22	–	–	–	–	–
No. of Clubs	**22**	**22**	**22**	**22**	**22**	**22**	**21**	**22**	**22**	**22**

Hyde United (striped shirts) win the ball on this occasion, but ultimately lose 1-2 to a last minute goal against Colwyn Bay in this Premier Division game at Ewen Fields.

Photo - Tim Lancaster.

DIVISION ONE 1993-94

	P	W	D	L	F	A	PTS
Guiseley	40	29	6	5	87	37	93
Spennymoor Utd	40	25	6	9	95	50	81
Ashton United	40	24	7	9	85	41	79
Lancaster City	40	20	10	10	74	46	70
Netherfield	40	20	6	14	68	60	66
Alfreton Town	40	18	10	12	83	70	64
Warrington Town	40	17	11	12	52	48	62
Goole Town	40	16	11	13	72	58	59
Gt Harwood Town	40	15	14	11	56	60	59
Gretna	40	16	7	17	64	65	55
Workington	40	14	10	16	70	74	52
Worksop Town	40	14	9	17	79	87	51
Bamber Bridge	40	13	11	16	62	59	50
Curzon Ashton	40	13	8	19	62	71	47
Congleton Town	40	12	9	19	53	68	45
Radcliffe Borough	40	10	14	16	62	75	44
Mossley	40	10	12	18	44	68	*39
Caernarfon Town	40	9	11	20	54	88	38
Farsley Celtic	40	6	16	18	42	77	34
Harrogate Town	40	8	9	23	40	86	33
Eastwood Town	40	7	11	22	47	63	32

* - 3 points deducted

TOP SCORERS

	Lge	Cup	Tot
Kenny Clark (Worksop Town)	32	11	43
Andy Whittaker (Ashton/Netherfield)	29	9	38
Mark Dobie (Gretna)	21	16	37
Mark Edwards (Ashton United)	19	16	35
Billy Roberts (Guiseley)	17	14	31
Phil Stafford (Alfreton Town)	22	8	30
Mark Rookyard (Worksop Town)	18	12	30
Andy Shaw (Spennymoor Utd)	16	14	30
Calvin Allen (Guiseley)	17	12	29

Below: *Champions Guiseley, whose remarkable season also comprised a run to the semi-finals of the FA Trophy. Back Row (L/R): John Rhodes (Physio), Tony Marshall, Calvin Allen, Paul Stevenson, Steve Dickinson, Paul Bottomley (Captain), Allan Roberts, Steve Richards, Colin Hogarth, Andy Armitage. Front: Vince Brockie, Bob Colville, Peter Atkinson, Billy Roberts, Ray McHale (Manager).*

Photo - Wharfedale & Airedale Observer.

RESULT CHART 1993-94

HOME TEAM	1	2	3	4	5	6	7	8	9	10	11	12	13	14	15	16	17	18	19	20	21
1. Alfreton Town	*	0-3	2-0	3-3	4-0	4-3	4-1	4-0	1-4	4-1	5-3	3-1	2-2	3-0	2-3	2-5	2-0	2-2	1-4	1-2	3-1
2. Ashton United	3-2	*	2-0	4-2	2-0	4-1	3-0	5-2	4-2	2-2	2-1	0-2	4-1	1-1	1-1	4-0	2-2	1-2	1-0	1-1	5-0
3. Bamber Bridge	2-2	1-2	*	2-0	1-1	3-1	0-0	1-1	2-2	3-2	1-1	3-2	1-0	0-3	7-1	3-2	2-2	0-2	1-1	3-2	6-0
4. Caernarfon Town	0-0	2-1	1-1	*	2-0	2-2	4-4	2-1	2-2	1-4	2-2	0-5	2-0	2-2	0-0	1-2	4-1	3-5	1-0	2-1	0-4
5. Congleton Town	2-1	0-5	3-0	4-2	*	1-1	2-1	2-0	1-3	1-2	1-2	0-2	0-2	0-2	1-0	2-1	3-1	0-1	0-0	2-0	0-1
6. Curzon Ashton	0-2	1-3	5-1	2-1	5-2	*	1-0	1-0	1-1	1-1	1-0	0-2	3-2	4-2	4-2	1-2	0-0	1-2	0-1	1-1	1-3
7. Eastwood Town	1-3	1-2	0-2	1-1	0-3	3-0	*	1-1	0-1	1-1	2-0	0-2	3-0	0-2	0-0	1-2	2-2	0-2	1-1	2-0	4-4
8. Farsley Celtic	2-3	0-2	1-1	1-0	1-1	0-3	0-5	*	0-3	2-2	2-0	0-2	1-2	1-2	2-1	4-5	2-2	1-3	0-0	1-0	3-3
9. Goole Town	1-1	0-1	1-0	6-1	2-2	2-0	0-0	0-1	*	0-1	2-1	1-2	2-2	2-0	1-3	2-0	4-0	2-1	2-2	1-4	0-0
10. Gt Harwood T.	2-2	1-1	1-1	2-0	2-1	3-2	2-1	0-0	0-2	*	4-2	1-2	0-1	1-1	2-1	4-1	0-0	0-6	0-0	3-1	1-2
11. Gretna	1-2	1-4	1-0	4-1	2-1	3-1	1-0	2-0	2-1	2-1	*	1-2	1-1	2-2	3-1	1-1	4-0	1-2	4-1	1-2	1-3
12. Guiseley	3-1	1-0	3-2	4-0	2-2	2-0	1-0	4-0	2-0	1-1	1-0	*	2-0	1-1	3-2	4-0	2-0	2-1	2-0	6-2	1-1
13. Harrogate Town	1-3	1-0	0-4	1-1	1-1	0-3	4-2	1-1	1-4	0-1	2-0	0-1	*	0-4	0-0	1-5	2-6	2-5	0-1	1-4	1-0
14. Lancaster City	5-0	0-1	1-0	2-1	3-0	5-2	2-1	0-0	1-2	3-0	1-2	1-2	4-1	*	2-0	1-1	2-2	1-0	1-0	1-1	5-2
15. Mossley	1-1	2-2	0-2	2-0	1-0	1-2	3-2	2-2	1-1	0-1	1-3	1-6	1-1	0-2	*	1-3	1-0	0-2	0-2	1-1	2-0
16. Netherfield	3-0	1-0	4-3	2-1	3-5	1-1	0-1	1-2	2-1	1-2	2-0	3-0	0-0	4-1	0-1	*	0-3	1-0	3-2	0-0	2-0
17. Radcliffe B.	0-0	2-1	1-0	2-1	2-2	1-1	0-2	1-1	2-1	1-1	2-3	2-2	3-0	0-2	2-4	2-0	*	4-2	1-2	0-3	5-2
18. Spennymoor Utd	2-2	3-1	2-1	1-3	0-0	2-1	2-1	1-1	5-3	4-0	4-0	1-2	5-0	1-0	3-0	1-3	4-1	*	1-2	5-3	3-3
19. Warrington Town	0-2	1-0	2-0	2-0	2-1	1-3	1-0	1-1	1-2	2-2	1-3	1-1	3-2	1-1	0-1	1-0	2-1	2-2	*	2-1	4-2
20. Workington	1-3	1-2	1-0	2-3	5-2	2-1	2-1	2-2	4-2	0-2	1-1	3-0	3-1	4-3	1-1	1-1	2-2	0-4	3-1	*	2-6
21. Worksop Town	2-1	0-3	1-2	4-0	1-4	3-1	2-2	6-2	4-4	4-0	2-2	3-2	0-3	1-2	1-1	0-1	5-4	0-1	1-2	2-1	*

ALFRETON TOWN

Formed: 1959

The Reds

Alfreton Town FC. Back Row (L/R): Sean Egan (Chairman), Steve Howson (Physio), Craig Weston, John Peach, Phil Stafford, Paul Norton, Scott Ridsdale, Bob Dawes, Andy Glenister, Glen Bowin of Mayfield Furniture (Sponsor). Front: Paul Eshelby, Tim Atkinson, Steve Johnson (Mascot), John McFadzean, Matt Walsh, John Rocca.

Chairman: Sean Egan **Vice Chairman:** David Bearder.
Secretary: Roger Taylor, 9 Priory Rd, Alfreton, Derbyshire DE55 7JT (0773 835121).
Joint Managers: Danny Hague/ Paul Mitchelle.
Physio: Steve Howson. **Press Officer:** Chris Tacey (0773 511012).
Commercial Manager: Linden Davison.
Ground: Town Ground, North Street, Alfreton, Derbyshire(0773 830277).
Directions: M1 junction 28 and follow A38 towards Derby for 1 mile, left onto B600, right at main road to town centre and after half a mile turn left down North Street - ground on right. Half mile from Alfreton & Mansfield Parkway (BR) station. Buses 242 & 243 from both Derby and Mansfield.
Capacity: 5,000 **Cover:** 1,000 **Seats:** 172 **Floodlights:** Yes **Metal Badges:** Yes
Club Shop: Yes, selling programmes (English & Scottish Lge + non-Lge), club badges, pens, key rings, ties, sewn-on badges. Contact Mr Brian Thorpe, 13 Oakland Str., Alfreton, Derbyshire (0773 836251).
Colours: Red & white/white/red **Change colours:** Yellow (green trim)/green/yellow.
Previous Leagues: Central Alliance *(before reformation 21-25)* 59-61/ Midland (Counties) *25-27* 61-82/ Northern Counties (East) 82-87.
Midweek home matchday: Wednesday **Reserve Team's League:** East Mids Regional Alliance.
Sponsors: Mayfield Furniture.
Record Attendance: 5,023 v Matlock Town, Central Alliance 1960.
Best FA Cup season: 1st Rd 3rd replay 69-70. Also 1st Rd 73-74.
League clubs defeated in FA Cup: Lincoln 24-25, but none since club's reformation in 1959.
Record win: 15-0 v Loughborough
Record defeat: 2-9 v Worksop 1961, 0-8 v Bridlington 1992.
Record Fees - Paid: £1,000 for R Mountain (Matlock)
Received: £1,500 for T Henson (Chesterfield), for Matt Walsh (Leek Town).
Players progressing to Football League: Martin Wright (Chesterfield 1968), Alan Woodward (Grimsby Town 1970), Alan Taylor (Chelsea 1972), Andy Kowalski (Chesterfield 1973), Tony Henson (Chesterfield 1981), Ricky Greenhough (Chester City 1985), Philip Greaves (Chesterfield 1986), Keith Smith (Exeter City 1989).
Clubhouse: Clubhouse on ground for members. Hot & cold food & drinks available on ground. Supporters Clubs just outside ground open 11am-4pm matchdays and 7-11pm at night.
Record Goalscorer: J Harrison 303.
Record Appearances: J Harrison 560.
93-94 Captain: Steve Johnson
93-94 Top Scorer & P.o.Y.: Phil Stafford.
Local Newspapers: Derbyshire Times, Derby Evening Telegraph, Nottingham Evening, Ripley/Heanor News, Mansfield Chad.
Local Radio Stations: Radio Derby.
Honours: FA Trophy 1st Rd Proper 93-94, Northern Counties (East) Lg 84-85 (Lg Cup 84-85), Midland (Counties) Lg 69-70 73-74 76-77 (R-up 71-72 80-81 81-82, Lg Cup 71-72 72-73 73-74), Derbyshire Senior Cup 60-61 69-70 72-73 73-74 81-82 (R-up 92-93), Derbyshire Divisional Cup (North) 64-65, Evans Halshaw Floodlit Cup 87-88. *Before reformation in 1959: Central Alliance 23-24 (Lg Cup 22-23).*

PROGRAMME DETAILS:
Pages: 32 **Price:** 60p
Editor: Chris Tacey
(0773 511012)

Formed: 1878

ASHTON UNITED

Robins

The Ashton defence have trouble containing the skilful Lutel James (right) of championship rivals Guiseley.
Photo - P Suthers.

Chairman: John Milne **Vice Chairman:** Mrs A Cummings **President:** Sid Sykes.
Secretary: Ernest Jones, 2 Anderton Grove, Hurst Cross, Ashton-under-Lyme OL6 9EF (061 339 9987).
Manager: Kevin Keelan **Asst Manager:** Steve Waywell **Physio:** Ronnie Fox
Press Officer: T Liverside **Commercial Manager:** TBA
Ground: Surrey Street, Hurst Cross, Ashton-u-Lyne OL6 8DY (061 339 4158. Fax-061 652 6413).
Directions: M62 jct 20, A627(M) to Oldham, keep in righthand 2 lanes, leave at Ashton sign after 2 miles passing Belgrade Hotel, take A627 at next island, keep in left lane and take slip road signed Ashton-under-Lyme, at island follow Stalybridge/Park Road sign, go straight ahead for 3 miles to ground at Hurst Cross. BR to Charles Street (Ashton), or Stalybridge. Buses 331, 332, 337, 408 (Ashton-Stalybridge) all pass ground.
Seats: 250 **Cover:** 750 **Capacity:** 4,500 **Floodlights:** Yes
Club Shop: Yes - contact Mr K Lee (061 330 9800).
Cols: Red & white halves/black/red **Change colours:** Blue/white/blue.
Record Attendance: 11,000 v Halifax Town, FA Cup First Round 1952.
Midweek matches: Monday.
Club Sponsors: Coral Travel.
Previous Name: Hurst 1878-1947 **Previous Ground:** Rose Hill 1878-1912.
Previous Leagues: Manchester/ Lancs Combination 12-23 48-64 66-68/ Midland 64-66, Cheshire Co. 23-48 68-82/ North West Counties 82-92.
Record Transfer Fees - Paid: £9,000 for Andy Whittaker (Netherfield, 1994).
Received: £15,000 for Karl Marginson (Rotherham, March 1993).
Best FA Cup season: 1st Rd replay 52-53 (lost 1-2 at Halifax after 1-1 draw). Also 1st Rd 55-56 (lost 1-6 at Southport).
Players progressing to Football League: Alan Ball (Blackpool, Everton, Arsenal & England), John Mahoney (Stoke City & Wales), Barney Daniels (Manchester City), Rodney Jones (Rotherham United), Alf Arrowsmith (Liverpool), Nelson Stiffle (Crystal Palace & Bournemouth).
Clubhouse: Open 11am-11pm. Refreshment bar open matchdays.
93-94 Captain: Mike Halliday/ Steve Byrne
93-94 Top Scorer: Andy Whittaker.
93-94 P.o.Y.: Ian Monk.
Clun Record Scorer: Mark Edwards, 37.
Club Record Appearances: Micky Boyle, 462.
Hons: Northern Premier League Division 1 Cup 93-94, Manchester Senior Cup 1884-85 13-14 75-76 77-78, Manchester League 11-12, Lancs Comb. Div 2 60-61 (League Cup 62-63), Manchester Prem. Cup 79-80 82-83 92-93, North West Counties League 91-92 (Challenge Cup 91-92, Div 2 87-88, Floodlit League 90-91, Challenge Shield 92-93), Manchester Challenge Shield 35-36 38-39 49-50 53-54 (R-up 34-35 39-40), Manchester Intermediate Cup 58-59 62-63 65-66 (R-up 60-61 64-65), Manchester Jnr Cup(4) 1893-94 10-12 32-33.

PROGRAMME DETAILS:
Pages: 46 **Price:** 70p
Editor: Steve Lee

1954 **ATHERTON LABURNUM ROVERS** Rovers

Tony Pemberton of Atherton is pursued by Danny Holmes during Rovers' goalless draw at Aldershot Town in the first leg of their three-game FA Vase Quarter-Final saga.

Photo - Eric Marsh.

President: Pat Mulcahy **Chairman:** Derek Halliwell.
Vice Chairman/Treasuer: A Grundy
Secretary: Steve Hartle, 32 Greensmith Way, Westhoughton, Bolton BL5 3DR (0942 840906).
Manager: Dave Morris **Assistant Manager:** Peter Lee **Coach:** Gerry Luczka.
Ground: Crilly Park, Spa Road, Atherton, Greater Manchester (0942 883950).
Directions: M61 to Jct 5, follow signs for Westhoughton, left onto A6, right onto A579 (Newbrook Rd/Bolton Rd) over the railway bridge, right into Upton Rd passing Atherton Central Station, left into Springfield Rd and left again into Hillside Rd into Spa Rd and ground.
Seats: 250 **Cover:** 3 sections **Capacity:** 3,000 **Floodlights:** Yes
Club Shop: Yes, selling programmes etc.
Record Gate: 1,856 v Aldershot Town, FA Vase Quarter-Final replay 5/3/94.
Colours: Yellow/royal/royal **Change colours:** Royal/yellow/yellow.
Previous leagues: Bolton Combination/ Cheshire County 80-82/ North West Counties 82-94.
Reserve Team's League: North West Alliance.
Club Sponsors: Norweb (Retail).
Previous Name: Laburnum Rovers 54-79
Previous Grounds: Laburnum Road 54-56/ Hagfold 56-66.
Best FA Cup season: Second Qualifying Round replay 90-91 (lost 0-4 at Bangor City after 0-0 draw).
Best FA Vase season: Semi-Final replay 93-94 (lost 1-2 to Diss Town).
Best FA Trophy season: Not entered to date.
Clubhouse: Open normal licensing hours.
Midweek Matches: Tuesday
Players progressing to Football League: Barry Butler (Chester).
Local Newspapers: Bolton Evening News, Manchester Evening News, Leigh Reporter.
Club Record Scorer: Sean Parker
Club record appearances: Jim Evans.
Captain 93-94: Jim Evans.
Top Scorer 93-94: Dave Liptrot.
Player of the Year 93-94: Rob Holgate.
Honours: North West Counties Lg 92-93 93-94 (Champions Cup 92-93), FA Vase Semi-Finalists 93-94.

PROGRAMME DETAILS:
Pages: 48 **Price:** TBA
Editor: Peter Jones
(0942 883950)

Founded: 1952

BAMBER BRIDGE

Brig

Bamber Bridge FC. Back Row (L/R): Scott Middlemass, Jez Baldwin, Ian Pilkington, Mark Milligan, Tony Greenwood (Manager), Phil Enthistle (Asst Manager), John Whittaker, Steve Berryman, Graham Waddon, Kenny Mayers. Front: Dave Leaver, Darren Brown, Neil Kennedy, Neil Doherty, Andy Hayes, Stuart Proctor, Tony Black.
Photo - Richard Brock.

President: Harold Hargreaves **Chairman:** D Allan **Vice Chairman:** H Milburn.
Secretary/Press Officer: D G Spencer, 11 Tennyson Place, Walton-le-Dale, Preston, Lancs PR5 4TT (0772 34355).
Manager: Tony Greenwood **Asst Manager:** Phil Entwhistle **Coach:**
Physio: A Jones **Commercial Manager:** D Dundersdale.
Ground: Irongate, Brownedge Road, Bamber Bridge, Preston, Lancs (0772 627387).
Directions: M6 Junct 29, A6 (Bamber Bridge Bypass) towards Walton-le-Dale, to r'bout, A6 London Road to next r'bout, 3rd exit signed Bamber Bridge (Brownedge Road) and first right. Ground 100 yds at end of road on left. Just over a mile from Bamber Bridge (BR).
Seats: 150 **Cover:** 650 **Capacity:** 2,500 **Floodlights:** Yes **Metal badges:** Yes.
Club Shop: Yes - a Supporters Club caravan on ground. Sells hats, cups, scarves, key rings, badges etc plus large selection of programmes. Contact Kevin Walker (0772 30685).
Colours: White/black/white. **Change colours:** All yellow. **Sponsors:** Baxi Ltd
Midweek Matches: Tuesday
Reserve Team's League: North West Alliance.
Previous Leagues: Preston & District 52-90/ North West Counties 90-93.
Previous Ground: King George V Ground, Higher Walton 1952-86.
Best FA Vase season: Semi Finalists 91-92 (lost 0-2 on aggregate to Wimborne Town).
Best FA Cup season: Second Qualifying Round 92-93 (lost 0-4 at home to Spennymoor United).
Record Attendance: 2,241 v Preston North End 1988. Competitive: 2,020 v Wimborne Town, FA Vase Semi Final 1st leg 21/3/92.
Clubhouse: On ground, open all day Saturday matchdays, every evening except Monday and Sunday lunchtimes. Refreshment cabin on ground serves hot & cold drinks, pies, sandwiches crisps etc during matches.
93-94 Captain: Jez Baldwin.
93-94 P.o.Y.: Dave Leaver/ Steve Berryman (shared).
93-94 Top scorer: John Whittaker.
Hons: FA Vase SF 91-92, North West Co's League Runners-up 92-93 (Div 2 91-92, F'lit Cup Runners-up 91-92), Preston & Dist League(4) 80-81 85-87 89-90 (Runners-up 78-79 82-83 84-85), Guildhall Cup 78-79 80-81 84-85 89-90 (Runners-up 77-78 79-80 87-88), Lancs Amtr Shield 81-82 (Runners-up 80-81 89-90), Lancastrian Brigade Cup 76-77 89-90 90-91.

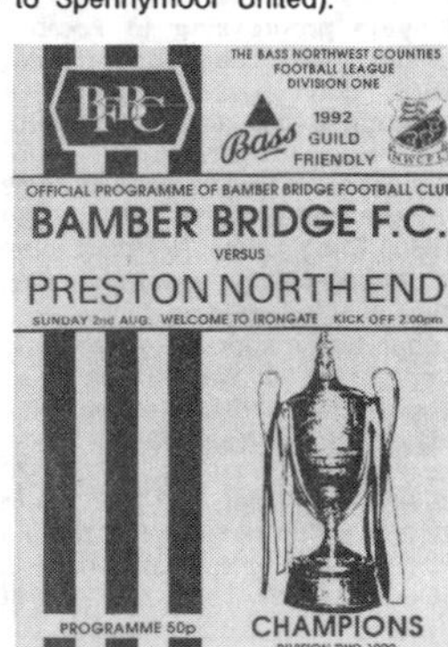

PROGRAMME DETAILS:
Pages: TBA **Price:** 50p
Editor: Rob Gillies
(0772 769348)

Formed: 1899

BLYTH SPARTANS

Spartans

Croft Park

Photo - Alan Watson.

Chairman: Jim Telford
Secretary: Bob Cotterill, 34 Solingen Estate, Blyth, Northumberland NE24 3ER (0670 361057).
Manager: Harry Dunn **Assistant Manager:** Dave Robertson
Press Officer: Bill Lowery.
Ground: Croft Park, Blyth, Northumberland. (0670) 354818
Directions: Through Tyne tunnel heading north on A19, take Cramlington turn, follow signs for Newsham/Blyth. Right fork at railway gates in Newsham, down Plessey Rd, ground can be seen on left behind chip shop and before Masons Arms. Buses X24, X25, X26, X1 from Newcastle.
Seats: 300 **Cover:** 2,500 **Capacity:** 6,000 **Floodlights:** Yes
Colours: Green & white stripes **Change colours:** All white (green trim).
Previous leagues: Northumberland 01-07/ Northern Alliance 07-13/ 46-47/ North Eastern 13-14 19-39 47-58 62-64/ Northern Combination 45-46/ Midland 58-60/ Northern Counties 60-62/ Northern 62-94.
Sponsors: Federation Brewery.
Souvenir Shop: Yes, selling hats, pennants, programmes etc. Contact Ronnie Clark (0670 353416).
Record transfer fee received: £30,000 for Les Mutrie (Hull City) 1979.
Midweek Matches: Tuesday
Best FA Trophy season: Quarter-Final replay 79-80 82-83.
Best FA Amateur Cup season: Semi-Final 71-72.
Best FA Cup season: 5th Rd replay 77-78 (lost to Wrexham). Competition Proper on 25 occasions.
League Clubs defeated in FA Cup: Ashington, Gillingham 22-23/ Crewe Alexandra, Stockport County 71-72/ Chesterfield, Stoke City 77-78.
Players progressing to Football League: William McGlen (Manchester United 1946), Joe Roddom (Chesterfield 1948), Henry Mills (Huddersfield 1948), John Allison (Reading 1949), James Kelly (Watford 1949), Robert Millard (Reading 1949), Jim Kerr (Lincoln 1952), James Milner (Burnley 1952), John Hogg (Portsmouth 1954), John Allison (Chesterfield 1955), John Inglis (Gateshead 1957), John Longland (Hartlepool 1958), Alan Shoulder (Newcastle) 1979, Les Mutrie (Hull City) 1979, Steve Carney (Newcastle) 1980, Craig Liddle (Middlesbrough) 1994.
Clubhouse: Open every night plus Saturday & Sunday lunch & matchdays. Available for wedding functions. Pies & sandwiches available.
Local Newspapers: Newcastle Journal & Evening Chronicle.
Captain 93-94: Warren Teasdale.
Top Scorer 93-94: Stephen Pile.
Player of the Year 93-94: Craig Liddle.
Hons: Northern Lg(10) 72-73 74-76 79-84 86-88 (R-up 71-72 73-74 77-78 84-85 93-94, Lg Cup(5) 72-73 77-79 81-82 91-92), North Eastern Lg 35-36 (R-up 22-23, Lg Cup 49-50 54-55), Northumberland Lg 03-04, Northern All. 08-09 12-13 (R-up 46-47), Northumberland Snr Cup(19) 13-15 31-32 33-37 51-52 54-55 58-59 62-63 71-72 73-75 77-78 80-82 84-85 93-94.

PROGRAMME DETAILS:
Pages: 50 **Price:** 50p
Editor: Ronnie Clark
(0670 353416)

1876 **CAERNARFON TOWN** Canaries

Caernarfon Town FC. Back Row (L/R): Ron Hughes (Kit Manager), John Bishop, Danny Gee, Steve Jackson, Ian Haigh, Archie Lloyd, Ian Johnson, John Stringer, Ian Humphrey (Physio). Front: Martin Faulkner, Sean Hegarty, Paul Nelson, Simon Connolly, Jimmy Brown. Mascot: Michael. Missing from photo: Terry Murphy (Manager), Jimmy Williams, Steve Bullock.

President: Jack F Thomas.
Chairman: Dr Emrys Price-Jones **Vice-Chairman:** Eilian Angel/ Geriant Lloyd-Owen.
Football Secretary: J E Watkins, 20 South Penrallt, Caernarfon, Gwynedd LL55 1NS (0286 674045).
Manager: Terry Murphy **Coach:** Jimmy Williams
Physio: Ian Humphreys
Commercial Manager: James Edwards **Press Officer:** Dr Emrys Price-Jones (0286 830631).
Ground: The Oval, Marcus Street, Caernarfon, Gwynedd (0286 5002).
Directions: A55 coast road to A487 bypass to Caernarfon. At inner relief road r'bout follow Beddlegert sign, then 2nd right - ground opposite. Nearest BR station is 9 miles distant at Bangor. Local buses to Hendre estate.
Capacity: 3,678 **Seats:** 178 **Cover:** 1,500 **Floodlights:** Yes **Metal Badges:** Yes.
Club Shop: Yes, selling scarves, programmes & badges.
Colours: Yellow/green/green **Change colours:** Red/white/red **Sponsors:** TBA
Previous Leagues: North Wales Coast 06-21/ Welsh National 26-30/ North Wales Combination 32-33/ Welsh Lg (North) 37-76 77-80/ Lancs Combination 80-82/ North West Counties 82-85.
Previous Ground: Curzon Ashton FC 92-94 (two seasons in exile due to conflict with FA of Wales over the League of Wales).
Previous Name: Caernarfon Athletic. **Reserve Team:** None.
Midweek home matchday: Tuesday **Record Gate:** 6,002 v Bournemouth, FA Cup 2nd Rd 1929.
Best FA Trophy season: 1st Round replay 87-88.
Best FA Cup season: 3rd Rd replay 86-87 (lost 0-1 at Barnsley). Also 2nd Rd 29-30.
League clubs defeated in FA Cup: Darlington 29-30/ Stockport County, York City 86-87.
Record win: 16-2 v Holyhead, Cookson Cup 11/3/39.
Record defeat: 0-18 v Colwyn Bay (A), North Wales Coast League 14/3/08.
Record Transfer Fee Received: £2,500.
Players progressing to Football League: Ernie Walley (Spurs), Gwyn Jones (Wolves 1955), Wyn Davies & Haydn Jones (Wrexham 1960 & 64), Tom Walley (Arsenal 1964), Paul Crooks (Stoke 1986), David Martindale & Steve Craven & David Higgins (Tranmere 1987).
Clubhouse: Yes. 2 snooker tables, darts, pool, fruit machines and live entertainment.
Club Record Goalscorer: Walter Jones 255 (1906-26)
Club Record Appearances: Walter Jones 306.
93-94 Captain: Steve Bullock.
93-94 P.o.Y.: Steve Bullock.
93-94 Top scorer: Jimmy Bell 11.
Local Newspapers: Caernarfon Herald, Liverpool Daily Post.
Local Radio Stations: Radio Cymru/Wales.
Honours: North West Co's Lg R-up 84-85 (Div 2 R-up 82-83), Lancs Comb 81-82 (Lg Cup 80-81), Welsh Lg (North)(4) 46-47 65-66 77-79 (R-up(4) 56-58 72-73 79-80, Alves Cup(4) 38-39 74-75 77-79, Cookson 56-57 77-78, North Wales Combination 32-33, Welsh National Lg 26-27 29-30 (R-up 28-29), North Wales Coast Lg 11-12.

PROGRAMME DETAILS:
Pages: 44 **Price:** 50p
Editor: Dr Emrys Price-Jones (0286 830631)

Formed: 1901

CONGLETON TOWN

Humbugs/Bears

Congleton Town's Steve Hibbert (left) just beats Derek Townsley to the ball, but his side go down 1-2 to Gretna in this Division One fixture at Booth Street on Saturday 15th January.

Photo - Alan Watson.

Chairman: Peter Farrow
Secretary: Carolyne Slater, 1 Crossways Road, Sneyd Green, Stoke-on-Trent ST6 2ND (0782 280377).
Manager: Steve Crowther **Physio:** N/A.
Press Officer: N/A.
Ground: Booth Street Ground, Crescent Road, Congleton, Cheshire (0260 274460).
Directions: On approach to Congleton via Clayton bypass take second right after fire station, into Booth Street. Two miles from Congleton (BR).
Capacity: 5,000 **Cover:** 1,200 **Seats:** 250 **Floodlights:** Yes **Club Shop:** Yes
Colours: White & black stripes/black/black & white **Change colours:** All blue.
Previous Leagues: Crewe & Dist/ North Staffs/ Macclesfield/ Cheshire 20-39 46-65 78-82/ Mid Cheshire 68-78/ North West Counties 82-87.
Previous Name: Congleton Hornets *(prior to current club's formation in 1901).*
Reserve Team: Congleton Town Hornets - Refuge Assurance Midland League.
Midweek home matchday: Wednesday
Record Attendance: 7,000 v Macclesfield, League 53-54.
Best FA Trophy season: 3rd Qualifying Rd 89-90 90-91
Best FA Vase season: 4th Rd 76-77 80-81.
Best FA Cup season: 1st Rd 89-90 (lost 0-2 at Crewe).
League clubs defeated in FA Cup: None.
Record Fees - Paid: None
Received: £5,000 for D Frost (Leeds).
Players progressing to Football League: Ron Broad (Crewe 1955), Jack Mycock (Shrewsbury 1958), Steve Davies (Port Vale 1987), L Hamlet (Leeds), Jimmy Quinn (West Ham, N Ireland), Ian Brightwell (Man City).
Clubhouse: Open every day.
Club Record Goalscorer: Mick Biddle (150+)
Club Record Appearances: Ray Clack (600+)
Captain 93-94: Graham Harrison.
Player of the Year: Richard Bland.
Top Scorer 93-94: Rick Griffiths.
Local Newspapers: Congleton Chronicle (0260 273737), Staffs Evening Sentinel (0782 289800).
Local Radio Stations: Radio Stoke, Signal.
Honours: North West Counties League Runners-up 85-86, Cheshire County League Runners-up 20-21 21-22 (Div 2 81-82), Mid Cheshire League 73-74 75-76 77-78 (Runners-up 69-70 71-72 76-77, League Cup 71-72), Cheshire Senior Cup 20-21 37-38.

NO PROGRAMME

COVER AVAILABLE

PROGRAMME DETAILS:
Pages: 32 **Price:** 50p
Editor: P Warren

Formed: 1963

CURZON ASHTON

Curzon

Curzon Ashton FC. Back Row (L/R): David 'Taffy' Jones (Manager), Paul Wroe, Peter Smythe, Iain McLellan, Anthony Briffa, Kenny Clements (Captain), Colin McCrory, Peter Sharp, Scot Moore, Peter Tilley (Assistant Manager), Jackie McDonald (Physio), Martin White. Front: Pat Sales, Keith Evans, Danny Jones, Jamie Holt, Steve Platts, Andy Lowrie, Malcolm Wagstaffe, Martin White.

Photo - John L Newton.

Chairman: Harry Twamley **Vice Chairman:** Peter Booth **President:** Peter Mayo.
Secretary: Alun Jones, 36 Forrest Road, Denton, Manchester M34 1RL (061 336 8004).
Manager: David 'Taffy' Jones **Assistant Manager:** Peter Tilley.
Physio: Jackie McDonald **Press Officer:** David Murray (061 7757509)
Ground: National Park, Katherine Street, Ashton-under-Lyne OL7 6DA (061 330 6033).
Directions: Behind Ashton police station off Manchester Rd (A635), Ashton-under-Lyne, one and a half miles from Ashton-under-Lyne (BR).
Capacity: 5,000 **Cover:** 450 **Seats:** 350 **Floodlights:** Yes **Nickname:** Curzon.
Club Shop: Due to be opened during 1994-95 season - contact club number.
Colours: All royal blue **Change colours:** Yellow/black/black.
Sponsors: Byford Computer Services/ P M Communications/ M L Electro Optics Ltd/ Stoneswood Engineering Group Ltd.
Previous Lges: Manchester Amtr/ Manchester (until 1978)/ Cheshire Co. 78-82/ North West Co's 82-87.
Midweek home matchday: Monday **Record Gate:** 1,826 v Stamford, FA Vase SF 1980.
Best FA Cup season: Third Qualifying Round replay 89-90 (lost 1-3 at Mossley after 1-1 draw)
Record win: 6-1 v Radcliffe Borough **Record defeat:** 1-5 v Knowsley United.
Record Transfer Fees - Paid: £1,000 for Garry Stewart (Witton Albion, 1993)
Received: £1,500 for Steve Wigley (Nottm Forest, 1981).
Players progressing to Football League: Gordon Taylor (Bolton 1962), Steve Wigley (Nottm Forest 1981), Malcolm O'Connor (Rochdale 1983), Eric Nixon (Man. City 1983).
Clubhouse: Open every night. Food on matchdays. Function room for private hire. Also, five-aside astro pitch available for hire every day.
Club Record Goalscorer: Alan Sykes
Club Record Appearances: Alan Sykes 620.
93-94 Captain: Kenny Clements.
93-94 P.o.Y.: Jamie Holt.
93-94 Top scorer: Keith Evans.
Local Newspapers: Ashton Reporter, Ashton Advertiser.
Local Radio Stations: Manchester Radio, Piccadilly.
Honours: FA Vase SF 79-80, Cheshire County League Div 2 R-up 78-79 (Reserve Div 81-82), Manchester League 77-78 (R-up 74-75 75-76, League Cup 77-78 (R-up 74-75 75-76), Murray Shield R-up 75-76, Reserve Div 74-75 75-76 76-77 77-78), Manchester Amateur League 63-64 65-66 (R-up 64-65 79-80(Res) 80-81(Res)), Manchester Premier Cup 81-82 83-84 85-86 86-87 89-90, Manchester Intermediate Cup 71-72 72-73 73-74 (R-up 70-71), Manchester Amateur Cup R-up 63-64, Ashton Challenge Cup 64-65 67-68, Philips F'lit Cup R-ups 77-78, FA Trophy 2nd Qualifying Rd 82-83 84-85, North West Counties Reserve Div 82-83 84-85 (R-up 83-84, League Cup 84-85 (R-up 83-84 85-86)), Northern Combination Supplemently Cup 87-88 88-89, South East Lancs League Shield R-up 84-85.

PROGRAMME DETAILS:
Pages: 16 **Price:** 50p
Editor: Ian Seymour

Formed: 1953

EASTWOOD TOWN

The Badgers

Back Row (L/R): Martin Connelly, Mark Clarke, Mark Jones, John Knapper, Graham Bush, Richard Wilson, Mark Richardson, Shaun Browne, Supporters' Club Representative, Mark Place. Front: David Clarke, Graham Merryweather, Tony Holgate, Kevin Leatherday, Dean Smith. Mascots: Philip & Graeme Langley.

Chairman: George Belshaw **Vice Chairman:** Richard James **President:** Vacant.
Sec./Press Off.: Paddy Farrell, 7 Primrose Rise, Newthorpe, Notts NG16 2BB (Tel/Fax: 0773 715500).
Manager: Bryan Chambers **Reserves' Mgr:** Paul McFarland **Physio:** Derek Myatt.
Ground: Coronation Park, Eastwood, Notts (0773 715823).
Directions: From North - M1 junction 27 then follow Heanor signs via Brinsley to lights in Eastwood. Turn left then first right after Fire Station - ground entrance on Chenton Street. From South - M1 jct 26, A610 to Ripley, leave at 1st exit (B6010), follow to Eastwoos, left at lights, first left at 'Man in Space' - ground entrance on Chenton Street. Nearest rail station is Langley Mill. Buses every 10 mins (R11, R12 or R13) from Victoria Centre, Nottingham. Journey time 40 mins.
Capacity: 5,500 **Cover:** 1,150 **Seats:** 200 **Floodlights:** Yes **Metal Badges:** Yes
Club Shop: Yes, selling programmes, mugs, scarves, badges etc. Contact Sean Burns (0773 769860).
Colours: Black & white stripes/black/black **Change colours:** All yellow or all white.
Previous Leagues: Notts Alliance 53-61/ Central Alliance 61-67/ East Midlands 67-71/ Midland Counties 71-82/ Northern Counties (East) 82-87.
Previous Names: None - predecessors Eastwood Collieries disbanded in 1953.
Previous Ground: Also Coronation Park 1953-65 - previous pitch now town bowling green.
Midweek home matchday: Tuesday**Record Attendance:** 2,723 v Enfield, FA Amateur Cup, February 1965.
Best F.A. Cup season: Final Qualifying Rd replay 75-76 (lost 0-1 at Wycombe Wanderers).
Record win: 26-0 **Record defeat:** 1-7.
Record Fees - Paid: £500 for Jamie Kay, Gainsborough Trinity 90-91.
Received: £35,000 for Richard Liburd (Middlesbrough 92-93).
Players progressing to Football League: John Butlet (Notts County 1957), Tony Woodcock (Nottm Forest), Paul Richardson (Derby), Alan Buckley, Steve Buckley (Luton), Richard Liburd (Middlesbrough 92-93), Martin Bullock (Barnsley 93-94).
Clubhouse: Large social club open daily - normal licensing hours (Sat 11am-11pm, midweek matches 6.30-11pm). Hot & cold food available.
Steward: Mr Peter Leadwood.
Club Record Goalscorer: Martin Wright
Club Record Appearances: Arthur Rowley, over 800 1st team games, but not a single booking, 1955-76.
93-94 Captain: Everton Marsh.
93-94 P.o.Y.:
93-94 Top scorer: Mark Richardson.
Sponsors: Melfin (UK) Ltd.
Local Newspapers: Eastwood Advertiser (0773 713563), Nottingham Evening Post (0602 482000), Derby Telegraph (0332 291111).
Local Radio Stations: Radio Nottingham, Radio Trent.
Honours: Northern Counties (East) Lg R-up 82-83 84-85, Midland Counties Lg 75-76 (R-up 74-75 77-78, Lg Cup 77-78 79-80), Central Alliance 63-64 (R-up 64-65), Notts Alliance 56-57 (R-up 53-54 54-55 55-56 57-58 58-59 59-60, Lg Cup 55-56), East Midlands Lg R-up 68-69, Notts Senior Cup 75-76 77-78 78-79 79-80 82-83 83-84 88-89 89-90 91-92 (R-up 57-58 63-64 65-66), Evans Halshaw Floodlit Cup R-up 89-90 93-94, Notts Intermediate Cup 86-87, Ripley Hospital Charity Cup(6) 76-81, FA Trophy 1st Rd 78-79, FA Amateur Cup 3rd Rd replay 67-68.

PROGRAMME DETAILS:
Pages: 24 **Price:** TBA
Editor: TBA

Formed: 1908

FARSLEY CELTIC

Villagers

The main stand at the Throstle Nest.

Photo - James Wright.

Chairman: John E Palmer **Vice Chairman:** Paul Glover.
Secretary: Mrs Margaret Lobley, 29 Spring Bank Road, Farsley, Leeds, West Yorks LS28 5LS (0532 575675).
Manager: Eugene Lacy **Coach:** Alun Jones.
Physio: Ian McGready **Press Officer:** Eugene Lacy.
Ground: Throstle Nest, Newlands, Farsley, Pudsey, Leeds LS28 5BE (0532 561517).
Directions: From North East: A1 south to Wetherby, A58 to Leeds, at 1st island (approx 8 miles) take 3rd exit (A6120 ring-rd), follow Bradford signs to 12th r'bout (approx 12 miles) - 1st exit (B6157 Stanningley). From M62 jct 26, M606 (Bradford) to r'bout, 4th exit (A6177) passing Rooley pub on left, continue on Rooley Lane - Sticker Lane passing Morrisons store on left to lights (approx 3 miles) - right onto A647 (Leeds) to 2nd r'bout, 2nd exit (B6157 Stanningley). Continue 800yds passing Police & Fire Stations on left. Turn left down New Street at Tradex warehouse before turning right into Newlands. Ground at bottom of road. 1 mile from New Pudsey (BR).
Capacity: 4,000 **Cover:** 1,000 **Seats:** 430 **Floodlights:** Yes **Metal Badges:** Yes.
Club Shop: Yes. League and non-League programmes and magazines. Club badges, scarves, ties, sweaters, training suits, polo and T-shirts. Various souvenirs and photographs. Contact Brian Falkingham (0532 550749) at 27 Rycroft Court, Leeds LS13 4PE.
Colours: Sky & navy stripes/navy/navy **Change colours:** All yellow.
Previous Grounds: Red Lane, Farsley/ Calverley Lane, Farsley (prior to 1948).
Prev. Lges: West Riding County Amateur/ Leeds Red Triangle/ Yorkshire 49-82/ Northern Counties (East) 82-87.
Midweek home matchday: Wednesday **Reserve Team's League:** Northern Counties (E) Reserve Div.
Record Attendance: 11,000 (at Elland Road) v Tranmere Rovers, FA Cup 1st Rd 1974.
Best FA Cup season: 1st Rd 74-75 (see above). Lost 0-2.
League clubs defeated in FA Cup: None.
Best FA Amateur Cup season: Third Round, 34-35.
Players progressing to Football League: Barry Smith (Leeds 1951), Paul Madeley (Leeds 1962), William Roberts (Rochdale 1988), Stuart McCall (Bradford City, Everton, Scotland).
Clubhouse: Lounge, games room and committee room open every evening and Friday and weekend lunchtimes. New multi-purpose Leisure Centre available evenings and afternoons.
Steward: Stuart Shaw.
93-94 Captain: Mick Adams.
93-94 P.o.Y.: Mick Adams.
93-94 Top scorer: Jamie White.
Local Newspapers: Yorkshire Evening Post, Telegraph & Argus, Pudsey Times.
Local Radio Stations: Radio Leeds, Radio Aire, Radio Pennine.
Honours: FA Vase QF 87-88, West Riding County Cup 57-58 59-60 66-67 70-71 83-84 87-88, Yorkshire League 59-60 68-69 (R-up 57-58 58-59 70-71 71-72, Div 2 51-52, League Cup 62-63 63-64 66-67).

PROGRAMME DETAILS:
Pages: 26 **Price:** 60p
Editors: Mark Threlfal/ Ron Kitchen.

1977 FLEETWOOD Fishermen

David Gough salutes the Flaatwood supporters after scoring the second goal in the home win over Leek Town. Alan Hughes runs to congratulate him.

Chairman: Stuart Kay **Vice Chairman:** Trevor Fisher **President:** Reg Apperley.
Secretary/Press Officer: Peter Jose, 18 South Strand, Rossall, Fleetwood, Lancashire FY7 8RL (0253 872018).
Manager: Stan Allen **Asst Manger:** TBA
Commercial Manager: Tony Mason.
Ground: Highbury Stadium, Park Avenue, Fleetwood, Lancs (0253 876443/ 771402).
Directions: M55 jct 3, A585 to Fleetwood, at r'bout at Nautical College carry straight on the new road towards Fleetwood, at next r'bout (after Fisherman's Friends Factory), turn left and follow road round, just before town centre there is a fire station on left where road crosses tram tracks - turn back past fire station and then turn right - ground straight ahead on Park Avenue. Nearest rail station is seven miles distant at Poulton-le-Fyle. Tram stop - Nansen Rd, 400yds.
Capacity: 6,000 **Cover:** 1,000 **Seats:** 220 **Floodlights:** Yes **Club Shop:** No.
Colours: Red & white/white/red **Change colours:** TBA.
Previous Leagues: Cheshire County 78-82/ North West Counties 82-87.
Previous Grounds: None *(predecessors Fleetwood FC played at Euston Ground 1937-38).*
Midweek home matchday: Tuesday **Previous Name:** Fleetwood Town, 1977-94.
Reserve Team: None. **Sponsors:** Pricebusters.
Record Attendance: 3,000 v Exmouth Town, FA Vase Semi Final 2nd Leg 84-85. *Ground Record: 6,000 - Fleetwood v Rochdale, FA Cup First Round Proper 65-66.*
Best FA Trophy season: 1st Rd 88-89 90-91.
Best FA Cup season: First Rd Proper 80-81 (0-4 at Blackpool), 90-91 (1-4 at Atherstone United).
League clubs defeated in FA Cup: None.
Record win: 10-0 v Sutton Town (H), NPL Division One 19/9/87.
Record defeat: 0-8 v Morecambe (A), NPL Premier Division 19/10/93.
Record Fees - Paid: £5,000 for Rob Wakenshaw (Southport).
Received: £25,000 for Steve Macauley (Crewe Alexandra).
Players progressing to Football League: Paul Sanderson (Manchester City), Phil Clarkson & Steve Macauley (Crewe Alexandra 1991), Andy Lyons (Crewe Alexandra 1992). *Frank Swift (Manchester City) from predecessors Fleetwood FC.*
Clubhouse: Open normal licensing hours.
Club Record Scorer: David Barnes 101.
Club Record Appearances: Stuart Robinson 388.
93-94 Captain: John Gamble.
93-94 Top scorer: David Gough.
Player of the Year 93-94: David Gough.
Local Press: West Lancashire Evening Gazette, Fleetwood Weekly News.
Local Radio Stations: Radio Lancashire, Red Rose Radio.
Honours: FA Vase R-up 84-85, Northern Premier League Div 1 87-88 (Presidents Cup 89-90 (R-up 90-91), League Cup R-up 88-89), North West Counties League Div 2 83-84.

PROGRAMME DETAILS:
Pages: 20 **Price:** 60p
Editor: Steve Presnail
(0253 886883)

Formed: 1900

GOOLE TOWN

Town or Vikings

Goole Town's Shaun Almey finds tackling Les Armstrong of Gretna a hair-raising experience.
Photo - Alan Watson.

Chairman: Christopher J Raywood **President:**
Vice President: E Shaw **Vice Chairman:** D O'Hearne.
Secretary/Press Officer: Graeme Wilson, 12 Thorntree Close, Goole, North Humbs DN14 6LN (0405 763316).
Manager: David Jones **Asst Manager:** Rod Hindmarsh **Physio:** Colin Naylor
Coach: TBA **Commercial Manager:** Mr Paul Smith.
Ground: The Victoria Pleasure Ground, Carter Street, Goole (0405 762794 - matchdays).
Directions: M62 junction 36, then A614. On entering Goole turn left at second set of lights - Carter Street is the sixth right. 400 yds from Goole Town (BR).
Capacity: 4,500 **Cover:** 4,000 **Seats:** 200 **Floodlights:** Yes **Shop:** Yes
Colours: Blue & red stripes/blue/red **Change colours:** All green.
Previous Leagues: Yorkshire 24-48/ Midland Counties 48-60 61-68/ Central Alliance 60-61.
Midweek home matchday: Tuesday **Record Fee Received:** £10,000 for Tony Galvin (Spurs).
Record Attendance: 8,700 v Scunthorpe United, Midland Counties League 1950.
Best FA Trophy season: Third Round 74-75.
Best FA Cup season: 3rd Rd 1956-57 (lost at Nottm Forest). Also 1st Rd on eight other occasions; 14-15 49-50 51-52 55-56 57-58 67-69 76-78 84-85.
League Clubs defeated in FA Cup: Workington 56-57.
Players progressing to Football League: Eric Binns (Burnley 1949), Arthur Hall & Les Bloadley & John Kaye & Steve Shutt (Scunthorpe 1951 & 52 & 60 & 85), William Linacre & Malcolm Thompson & David Stewart (Hartlepool 1953 & 68 & 83), Bernard Shaw (Lincoln 1953), Eric Cousans (Walsall 1954), Brian Handley (Aston Villa 1957), Gordon Robbins (Crewe Alexandra 1958), Alan Darby (Doncaster 1959), Mitchell Dournie (Bradford City 1959), Arthur Taylor (Hull 1962), Stan Marshall (Middlesbrough 1963), John Woodall (York 1967), Ian Pearson (Plymouth 1974), Tony Galvin (Spurs 1978), Brian Ferguson (Southend 1983), Chris Maples (Chesterfield 1986), I Sampson (Sunderland), J Smith (Wigan).
Club Record Scorer: Brian Howard
Club Record Appearances: Jimmy Kelly 475.
Local Newspapers: Goole Times (763391), Hull Mail (762647), Goole Courier (763073).
Local Radio Stations: BBC Radio Radio Humberside, Viking FM.
Honours: Northern Premier League Cup 87-88, Yorkshire League 27-28 36-37 47-48 (League Cup 33-34 48-49), West Riding County Cup 38-39 50-51 51-52 56-57 68-69 69-70 75-76 76-77 77-78 86-87 88-89 91-92, West Riding Snr Cup(1)(Runners-up 93-94).

PROGRAMME DETAILS:
Pages: 16 **Price:** 50p
Editor: G Wilson, A Lawson

1978 **GREAT HARWOOD TOWN** Robins

Great Harwood Town's 'Showground' which has always been the venue of senior football in the town having been previously the home of the now defunct Great Harwood FC who also played in the Northern Premier League. Photo - John Dunn.

Chairman: C R Hickey
Secretary: Peter Birtwistle, 23 Dryden Grove, Great Harwood, Lancs (0254 886754).
Manager: Ian Rishton **Asst Manager:** Mick Higgins **Coach:** Mick Higgins
Press Officer: K Lambert **Commercial Manager:** J Dobson.
Ground: The Showground, Wood Street, Great Harwood, Lancs (0254 883913).
Directions: M66 from Manchester to Haslingden exit, A680 through Baxenden, Accrington to Clayton-le-Moors, left at the Hyndburn Bridge Hotel into Hyndburn Road and right into Wood Street to ground. Or M6 jct 31, Clitheroe/Skipton road to Trafalgar Hotel, A677 to Blackburn, left at Moat House Hotel and follow ring-road to M65 junction, A678 to Rishton, left at lights (B6536) to Gt Harwood, right at Town Gate into Queen Str., follow signs for Lomax Square, left into Park Rd, right into Balfour Street to ground. 3 miles from Rishton (BR), 6 miles from Blackburn (BR). Various buses from Heyes Lane & Park Road to Blackburn & Accrington.
Seats: 200 **Cover:** 700 **Capacity:** 2,500 **Floodlights:** Yes
Colours: All red **Change colours:** All blue.
Club Shop: Yes, selling programmes, badges, key rings, shirts. Contact Roy Smith (0254 877908).
Reserve Team: West Lancs Lge **Record Gate:** 5,397 v Manchester Utd, 1980
Midweek Matches: Wednesday **Club Sponsors:** None at present.
Previous Name: Great Harwood Wellington.
Previous Leagues: West Lancashire/ Lancs Combination 79-82/ North West Counties 82-92.
Previous Ground: Park adjacent to the Showground until demise of Great Harwood FC in 1978.
Record win: 7-0 v Farsley Celtic (H), NPL Division One 1992-93.
Record defeat: 0-6 v Spennymoor United (H), NPL Division One, 1993-94.
Best FA Cup season: 1st Qualifying Round replay 92-93 (lost 1-2 at home to Atherton LR after 1-1 draw).
Best FA Vase season: Quarter Finals 90-91 (lost 1-2 at Littlehampton Town).
Clubhouse: Yes - The Sportsman just outside ground. Normal licensing hours. Full bar facilities. Squash courts and gym. Hot & cold snacks and drinks on matchdays from tea bar within ground.
93-94 Captain: S Westwell
93-94 Top Scorer: P Baker.
93-94 Player of the Year: P Smith.
Hons: North West Counties League R-up 91-92 (Div 2 90-91, Lamot Pils Tphy 89-90 (R-up 90-91), Tennents Floodlit Trophy 91-92), Lancs ATS Challenge Trophy 91-92 (R-up 90-91).

PROGRAMME DETAILS:
Pages: 20 **Price:** 50p
Editor: Barry Marsden

1946 **GRETNA** Black & whites

GRETNA

Gretna FC - Cumberland Senior Cup winners 1993-94. Back Row (L/R): Graham Emerson, Duncan Armstrong, Paul Cooke, Derek Townsley, David Adamson, Jim Mulholland, Mike McCartney, Leslie Armstrong. Front: Craig Potts, Derek Walsh, Andrew Walker, Anthony Monaghan, Mark Dobie, William Bentley.

Photo - John L Newton.

Chairman: Ian B Dalgleish **Vice Chairman:** Jack Gass **President:** Thomas Kerr.
Secretary: Keith Rhodes, 8 Graitney, Gretna, Dumfriesshire DG16 5AR (0461 337447).
Physio: William Bentley **Manager:** Michael McCartney **Asst Manager:** N/A
Press Officer/ Commercial Manager: Fred Sheckley (0461 337602).
Ground: Raydale Park, Dominion Rd., Gretna, Dumfriesshire (0461 337602).
Directions: 8 miles north of Carlisle on A74. Take slip road to Gretna over border bridge, left at Crossways Inn for Township along Annan Rd for quarter of a mile, left into Dominion Rd, ground on right. Buses leave Carlisle on the half hour. Also trains from Carlisle.
Seats: 385 **Cover:** 800 **Capacity:** 2,200 **Floodlights:** Yes
Club Shop: Yes, selling pennants, programmes, sweaters, scarves, hats, magazines, balls, T-shirts, badges. Contact Mr Fred Sheckley (0461 337602).
Club colours: Black & white hoops/black/black & white
Change colours: All blue. **Midweek Matches:** Tuesday
Record Gate: 2,307 v Rochdale, F.A. Cup First Round Proper, 16/11/92.
Previous Leagues: Dumfriesshire Amateur 47-47/ Carlisle & District 47-51/ Cumberland 51-52/ Northern 83-92.
Midweek matchday: Tuesday
Previous Ground: Station Park 1946-47.
Club Sponsors: Gables Hotel.
Record win: 13-0 **Record defeat:** 1-5.
Best season in FA Trophy: Third Round 90-91.
Best season in FA Cup: 1st Round Proper 1991-92 (lost 1-3 in replay at Rochdale).
Players progressing to Football League: John Hamilton (Hartlepool United) 1982, Russell Black & Don Peattie (Sheffield United) 1984, Mark Dobie (Cambridge United).
Clubhouse: Bar, lounge, TV room, concert room. Cooked meals available. Open every day. Late bar at weekends.
Club record scorer: Denis Smith
Club record appearances: William Cross.
Captain 93-94: Paul Gorman.
Top Scorer 93-94: Mark Dobie.
P.o.Y. 93-94:
Local Newspapers: Cumberland News
Honours: Northern Lg 90-91 91-92 (Lg Cup 90-91), Cumberland Senior Cup (9), JR Cleator Cup 89-90 90-91 91-92, Craven Cup 91-92, Carlisle & Dist. Lg (28)(Charity Shield(25), Lg Cup(20), Benevolent Cup(15)).

PROGRAMME DETAILS:
Pages: 8 **Price:** 50p
Editor: Fred Sheckley (0461 337602)

Formed: 1919

HARROGATE TOWN

The 350-seat main stand, constructed in 1990, at Harrogate Town's ground.

Photo - Alan Watson.

Chairman: George Dunnington **President:** C Margolis.
Secretary: Roy Dalby, 123a Dene Park, Harrogate, North Yorkshire HG1 4JX (0423 567973).
General Manager: Alan Smith **Manager:** John Deacey.
Ground: Whetherby Road, Harrogate. (0423 883671 (880675-press)).
Directions: From Leeds turn right at traffic lights (Appleyard's) into Hookstone Road, continue to Woodlands Hotel (traffic lights) turn left into Wetherby Road, ground on the right. From Harrogate (BR), turn left and left again, cross road (Odeon Cinema), proceed for about 400yds to main road, cross over to The Stray (open land) using footpath which leads to Wetherby Rd, ground 200yds on left.
Capacity: 3,800 **Cover:** 600 **Seats:** 450 **Floodlights:** Yes **Metal Badges:** Yes
Club Shop: Yes, selling scarves, ties, pens shirts and other common souvenirs.
Colours: Yellow/black/yellow **Change colours:** All blue.
Previous Names: Harrogate FC 26-34/ Harrogate Hotspurs 36-50.
Previous Ground: Starbeck Lane 1919-20.
Previous Leagues: Yorkshire 20-21 22-31 51-82/ Midland 21-22/ Northern 31-32/ Harrogate & District 36-46/ West Yorkshire 46-51/ Northern Counties (East) 82-87.
Midweek home matchday: Tuesday **Reserve Team's Lge:** Northern Co's (East) Reserve Div.
Club Sponsors: Crystal Motors.
Record Attendance: 3,208 v Starbeck LNER (now Harrogate R.A.), Whitworth Cup final 1948.
Best FA Vase season: 4th Round 89-90.
Best FA Cup season: 3rd Qualifying Rd 87-88 (lost 0-2 at Bishop Auckland after a 1-1 draw).
League clubs defeated in FA Cup: None.
Record win: 9-1 v Winsford
Record defeat: 0-7; v Hyde Utd & v Lancaster City.
Players progressing to Football League: Tony Ingham (Leeds) 1947, Stewart Ferebee (York City 1979), Tim Hotte (Halifax Town 1985), Andy Watson (Halifax Town 1988).
Clubhouse: On ground, open Tuesday, Thursday and every other Wednesday in addition to every matchday. Sandwiches available.
93-94 Captain: Steve Learoyd.
93-94 P.o.Y.: Steve Learoyd.
93-94 Top scorer:
Local Newspapers: Yorkshire Post, Harrogate Herald Advertiser.
Local Radio Stations: Radio Leeds, Radio York, local hospital radio.
Honours: Northern Premier League Division 1 Cup 89-90, Northern Counties (East) Division 1 (Nth) R-up 84-85 (Reserve Division 85-86, Reserve Division Cup 86-87), Yorkshire League Division 1 26-27 (Division 2 81-82, Division 3 R-up 71-72 80-81), West Riding County Cup 62-63 72-73 85-86, West Riding Challenge Cup 24-25 26-27.

PROGRAMME DETAILS:
Pages: 48 **Price:** 60p
Editor: R Chambers/ T Moseley

1902 # LANCASTER CITY

Dolly Blues

Lancaster City have an effort cleared off the line by Alfreton Town defender Steve Johnson with goalkeeper Paul Norton stranded. However, they still ran in five goals without reply in this January home fixture.
Photo - Alan Watson.

Chairman: John Bagguley **Vice-Chairman:** K Lancaster. **President:** M Woodhouse.
Secretary: Barry Newsham, 104 Willow Lane, Forest Park, Lancaster LA1 5QF (0524 35774).
Manager: Alan Tinsley **Coach:** Mike Hoyle **Physio:** D McKevitt/F Charlton
Commercial Mgr: Mike Hoyle. **Press Officer:** Dave Henig (c/o the club).
Ground: Giant Axe, West Road, Lancaster LA1 5PE (0524 382238).
Directions: From south: M6 junction 33, follow into city, left at lights immediately after Waterstones bookshop, second right, pass railway station on right, follow road down hill, ground 1st right. From north: M6 jct 34, left on to A683, follow into city on one-way system, pass police station, at next lights by Alexandre pub follow road back down in centre, then follow as from south. 5 mins walk from both bus & rail stations.
Capacity: 5,000 **Cover:** 800 **Seats:** 500 **Floodlights:** Yes **Metal Badges:** Yes
Club Shop: Yes - selling metal badges, programmes etc. Contact Dave Henig at club.
Colours: Blue/white/blue **Change colours:** All yellow **Sponsors:** Reebok UK
Previous Leagues: Lancs Combination 05-70/ Northern Premier 70-82/ North West Counties 82-87.
Reserve Team's League: North Western Alliance.
Previous Names: Lancaster Town **Previous Ground:** Quay Meadow 05-06 (club's 1st 2 games only!)
Midweek home matchday: Wednesday **Record Attendance:** 7,500 v Carlisle, FA Cup 1936.
Best FA Cup season: 2nd Rd 46-47 (0-4 v Gateshead) 72-73 (1-2 v Notts County). Also 1st Rd on 8 other occasions; 28-29 29-30 30-31 31-32 33-34 37-38 38-39 47-48.
League Clubs defeated in FA Cup: Barrow, Stockport County 21-22.
Record win: 8-0 v Leyland Motors (A), 83-84.
Record defeat: 0-7 v Newtown (H), NPL Division One, 89-90.
Players progressing to Football League: John McNamee (Workington 1975), Brendan O'Callaghan (Stoke City), Ian Stevens (Stockport County 1986), Glenn Johnstone (Preston North End 1993), Martin Clark & Wayne Collins (Crewe Alexandra), Gus Wilson (Crewe Alexandra).
Club Fanzines: The Mad Axeman, Bambula Azzurri.
Clubhouse: New clubhouse opened July 1994.
Club Record Appearances: Edgar J Parkinson.
93-94 Captain: Barrie Stimpson.
93-94 Top Scorer/Supporters' P.o.Y.: Stuart Diggle.
93-94 Players' P.o.Y.: Steve Hartley
Local Newspapers: Lancaster Guardian, Morcambe Visitor, Lancaster Evening Post.
Local Radio Stations: Lancaster Radio, Red Rose.
Honours: Northern Premier Lg Cup R-up 79-80 (Div 1 Cup R-up 90-91), Lancs Combination 21-22 29-30 34-35 35-36 (R-up 19-20 22-23 27-28 51-52, Lg Cup 21-22, Div 2 R-up 14-15), Lancs Junior Cup (ATS Challenge Trophy) 27-28 28-29 30-31 33-34 51-52 74-75 (R-up 06-07 08-09 19-20 26-27), FA Vase 2nd Rd 86-87 90-91, FA Trophy 3rd Rd 74-75 75-76, Lancs Yth (under 18) Cup 87-88 88-89 (R-up 86-87 89-90).

PROGRAMME DETAILS:
Pages: 32 **Price:** 50p
Editor: D Henig
(c/o the club)

MOSSLEY

Formed: 1903 Lillywhites

Mossley's Wayne Roberts (white shirt) heads clear from Andy Walker of Gretna. The Scots came away from their first league visit to Seel Park with a 3-1 win on 12th March.

Photo - Alan Watson.

Chairman: Roger Finn **President:** J Anderson.
Secretary: Les Fitton, 25 Rushmere, 18th Fairway, Ashton-under-Lyme OL6 9EB (061 330 2182).
Manager: Richard Dawson **Coach:** N/A **Physio:** Ron Fox
Commercial Manager: Tom Harrop (061 624 5151).
Ground: Seel Park, Market Street, Mossley, Ashton-under-Lyme (0457 832369).
Directions: Off M62; from west via Oldham, Lees and Grotton; from east via Saddleworth. From M1 or Sheffield via Stalybridge then Mossley. Half mile from Mossley (BR), buses 153 from Manchester, 343 from Oldham or 350 from Ashton.
Capacity: 4,500 **Cover:** 1,500 **Seats:** 200 **Floodlights:** Yes **Club Shop:** Yes
Colours: White/black/black **Change colours:** Yellow/blue/yellow.
Previous Leagues: Ashton/ South East Lancs/ Lancs Combination 18-19/ Cheshire County 19-72.
Previous Names: Park Villa 03-04/ Mossley Juniors 04-09.
Previous Ground: Luzley.
Midweek home matchday: Tuesday **Record Attendance:** 7,000 v Stalybridge, 1950.
Best FA Cup season: 2nd Rd replay 49-50. Also 2nd Rd 80-81, 1st Rd 69-70 77-78 78-79 79-80 81-82 83-84.
League clubs defeated in FA Cup: Crewe Alexandra, 80-81.
Record Fees - Paid: £2,300 **Received:** £25,000 for Eamon O'Keefe (Everton, 1979).
Players progressing to Football League: John Wright (Blackpool 1946), Tom Bell & Albert Wadsworth (Oldham 1946 & 49), Albert Lomas (Rochdale 1950), Arthur Tyrer (Leeds 1946), Eric Williams (Halifax 1951), John Willis (A Villa 1958), Mike Eckershall (Torquay 1959), Alan Roberts (Bradford PA 1969), Gary Pierce (Huddersfield 1971), Eamon O'Keefe (Everton 1979), David Young (Wigan 1983).
Clubhouse: Open nights and matchdays.
Captain & Player of the Year 93-94: Micky Boyle.
Top Scorer 93-94: Phil Hulme.
Local Newspapers: Oldham Evening Chronicle, Saddleworth & Mossley Reporter.
Local Radio Stations: Radio Manchester, Piccadilly.
Honours: FA Trophy Runners-up 79-80, Northern Premier League 78-79 79-80 (Runners-up 80-81 81-82 82-83, League Cup 78-79 88-89 (Runners-up 75-76 81-82), Challenge Shield 88-89 (Runners-up 78-79 79-80 80-81 81-82)), Cheshire County League Runners-up 19-20 69-70 (League Cup 20-21 60-61), Manchester Premier Cup 88-89 90-91, Manchester Intermediate Cup 60-61 66-67 67-68 (Runners-up 58-59 63-64 70-71 78-79), Manchester Challenge Shield 14-15 33-34 37-38 48-49 (Runners-up 36-37 38-39 50-51), Reporter Floodlit Cup 74-75 88-89, North West Floodlit Cup Runners-up 76-77.

PROGRAMME DETAILS:
Pages: 28 **Price:** 50p
Editor: Julian Thomas

Formed: 1920

NETHERFIELD

The Field

The Netherfield side that recorded an excellent early-season 3-0 home win over Guiseley.
Photo - Gavin Ellis-Neville.

Chairman: David Willan **President:** Ty Power.
Secretary: John Wharton, 3 Vicars Hill, Kendal, Cumbria LA9 5DA (0539 734209).
Manager: Leighton James **Asst Manager:** TBA
Physio: TBA **Commercial Manager:** Malcolm Spowart
Press Officer: Peter Savage (0539 726488).
Ground: Parkside Road, Kendal, Cumbria (0539 722469).
Directions: M6 junction 36, follow signs for Kendal (South), right at lights, left at r-bout to shoe factory - Parkside Rd on right opposite factory main offices - ground 400 yds. One and a half miles from Oxenholme (BR) station - bus service to shoe factory.
Capacity: 4,800 **Cover:** 1,000 **Seats:** 250 **Floodlights:** Yes **Club Shop:** No.
Colours: White/black/red **Change colours:** Yellow/green/yellow. **Sponsors:** 'K' shoes
Previous Leagues: Westmorland/ North Lancs/ Lancs Combination 45-68/ Northern Premier 68-83/ North West Counties 83-87.
Midweek home matchday: Tuesday **Reserve Team's League:** North West Alliance.
Record Attendance: 5,184 v Grimsby Town, FA Cup 1st Rd 1955.
Record win: 11-0 v Great Harwood 22/3/47.
Record defeat: 0-10 v Stalybridge Celtic 1/9/84.
Record transfer fee paid: Undisclosed for Tom Brownlee (Bradford City, 1966).
Record transfer fee received: £9,000 for Andy Whittaker (Ashton United, 1994).
Best FA Vase season: 3rd Rd 89-90
Best FA Trophy season: 2nd Rd 80-81.
Best FA Cup season: 2nd Rd replay 63-64 (lost 1-4 at Chesterfield after 1-1 draw). Also 2nd Rd 49-50, 1st Rd 45-46 48-49 52-53 54-55 55-56 64-65.
Players progressing to Football League: John Laidlaw (Carlisle 1946), Louis Cardwell (Crewe 1947), Herbert Keen (Barrow 1953), Alec Aston (Preston 1955), Horace Langstreth (Torquay 1956), John Simpson (Lincoln 1957), Dennis Rogers (Accrington 1959), Tom Brownlee (Bradford City 1965), Peter McDonnell (Bury 1973), Keith Silken (Workington 1973), Roger Wicks (Darlington 1981), Andy Milner (Man City).
Clubhouse: The Park, open all matchdays. Pies & pasties available.
Club Record Goalscorer: Tom Brownlee
93-94 Captain: Wayne Maddock.
93-94 P.o.Y.: Gavin Boyd.
93-94 Top scorers: Andy Whittaker.
Local Press: Westmorland Gazette (0539 720555), Lancaster Evening Post.
Local Radio Stations: Radio Cumbria, Red Rose.
Hons: Lancs Comb. 48-49 64-65 (R-up 45-46 53-54 61-62 63-64, Lg Cup 55-56 60-61), Westmorland Snr Cup(12) 24-25 31-33 35-36 46-48 63-64 65-66 71-72 86-87 89-89 90-91.

PROGRAMME DETAILS:
Pages: 36 **Price:** 60p
Editor: P Savage
(0539 726488)

1949 **RADCLIFFE BOROUGH** Boro'

Radcliffe Borough FC 1993-94.

Photo - John Newton.

President: A A Swarbrick. **Chairman:** Bernard Manning Jnr
Secretary: Graham E Fielding, 93 Callender Street, Ramsbottom, Bury, Lancs BL0 9DU (0706 825299).
Manager: Kevin Glendon **Asst Manager/Coach:** Jimmy Golder **Physio:** Roy Davies
Press Officer: M Collins **Commercial Manager:** N/A.
Ground: Stainton Park, Pilkington Road, Radcliffe, Lancs M26 0PE (061 725 9197).
Directions: M62 junction 17 - follow signs for Whitefield and Bury then A665 to Radcliffe. Through town centre, turn right into Unsworth Street (opposite Turf Hotel), ground half mile on left, Colshaw Close Easy. Half a mile from Radcliffe (BR).
Capacity: 3,000 **Cover:** 1,000 **Seats:** 350 **Floodlights:** Yes
Club Shop: Yes - contact A Mitchell at ground.
Colours: All blue **Change colours:** All red.
Sponsors: Comet Copiers.
Previous Ground: Bright Street 1949-70.
Previous Leagues: South East Lancs/ Manchester 53-63/ Lancs Combination 63-71/ Cheshire County 71-82/ North West Counties 82-87.
Midweek home matchday: Tuesday **Reserve Team:** None.
Record Attendance: 1,468 v Caernarvon Town, North West Counties League 1983.
Best FA Trophy season: First Round 72-73.
Best FA Cup season: Second Qualifying Rounds replay 75-76 (lost 1-4 at Rossendale United after 2-2 draw).
Record Fees - Paid: £5,000 for Gary Walker (Buxton, 1991)
Received: £5,000 for Kevin Hulme (Bury, 1989).
Players progressing to Football League: Jim Hayman (Bury 1950), Ian Wood (Oldham Athletic 1965), Robert Hutchinson (Rochdale 1974), Gary Hawarth (Rochdale 1984), Kevin Hulme (Bury 1989).
Clubhouse: (061 723 4181). 'The Footballers' - public house on ground. No food available.
Club Record Goalscorer: Gary Haworth
Club Record Appearances: Chris Lilley.
93-94 Captain: Craig Wardle.
93-94 P.o.Y.: Phil Melville.
93-94 Top scorer: Tony Carroll.
Local Newspapers: Radcliffe Times, Bolton Evening News, Manchester Evening News.
Local Radio Stations: Greater Manchester Radio (GMR), Piccadilly.
Honours: North West Counties Lg 84-85 (Div 2 82-83), Lancs Combination Lg Cup 69-70), Manchester Lg R-up 55-56 (Lg Cup 58-59(joint)).

PROGRAMME DETAILS:
Pages: 28 **Price:** 50p
Editor: Mervyn Collins

1949 **WARRINGTON TOWN** The Town

Warrington Town FC. Back Row (L/R): Graham Ost (Secretary, now Runcorn), Gavin McDonald, Mike Tandy, Don Nicely, Steve Parsonage, John O'Neil, Phil Lambert, Kenny Saunders, Chris Henshall. Front: Neil Cook, Joey Dunn, Gary Finley, Neil Williams, Alan Blair, Andy O'Connor.

Chairman: R Smith **Vice Chairman:** M P McShane **President:** R Smith.
Secretary: Peter Rowe, 5 Beech Avenue, Thelwall, Warrington, Cheshire WA4 2HU (0925 860223).
Manager: Derek Brownbill **Asst Manager:** Alan Blair
Coach: Malcolm Liptrot **Press Officer:** Colin Serjent
Physio: Lynda Roberts.
Ground: Cantilever Park, Loushers Lane, Latchford, Warrington WA4 2RS (0925 631932).
Directions: M6 junction 20, then A50 towards Warrington. After 2 miles turn left immediately after swing bridge into Station Road, ground 600yds on left. From town centre travel 1 mile south on A49, left at lights into Loushers Lane, ground quarter mile on right. 2 miles from Warrington Bank Quay (BR).
Capacity: 2,500 **Cover:** 500 **Seats:** 300 **Floodlights:** Yes
Club Shop: Yes, selling badges, scarves, pennants, past & present League and non-League programmes, *Team Talk* magazines, fanzines. Contact Matthew Dale, 11 Mullion Grove, Padgate, Warrington, Cheshire WA2 0QW (0925 811307).
Colours: Yellow/blue/yellow **Change colours:** All purple. **Sponsors:** TBA.
Previous Name: Stockton Heath 1949-62. **Previous Ground:** London Road, Stockton Heath, Warrington.
Best FA Cup season: 3rd Qualifying Rd 88-89 (lost 1-2 at home to Leek Town).
Best FA Vase season: Finalists 86-87 (lost 2-3 to St Helens Town).
Best FA Trophy season: Quarter-Finalists 92-93 (lost 1-2 at Sutton United).
Previous Leagues: Warrington & Dist. 49-52/ Mid-Cheshire 52-78/ Cheshire Co. 78-82/ North West Co's 82-90.
Midweek home matchday: Tuesday **Reserve Team's League:** Mid-Cheshire.
Record Attendance: 3,000 v Halesowen Town, FA Vase Semi Final 1st leg 85-86.
Record win: 14-0 v Crosfields (H), Depot Cup 1951-52.
Record defeat: 0-10 v Eastwood (A), Mid-Cheshire Challenge Cup 1967-68.
Record transfer fee paid: £2,000; for Paul McNally (Southport) 1992; for Darren Schofield (Mossley) 1993.
Record transfer fee received: £60,000 for Liam Watson (Preston North End) 1992-93.
Players progressing to Football League: Sam Morris (Chester 1951), John Green (Tranmere 1958), Roger Hunt (Liverpool 1959), John Richards (Wolves), John Bramhall (Tranmere 1976), Mark Leonard (Everton, Stockport, Bradford City), Neil Whalley & Liam Watson (Preston North End) 92-93.
Clubhouse: Weekdays 1pm-11pm, Sat. noon-11pm, Sun. 12-3pm, 7pm-10.30pm. Whitbread & guest beers. Lounge, concert room & Sports room. Rooms for hire for all occasions. Pools, darts, dominoes & indoor bowls. Traditional bar food on matchdays.
Club Record Goalscorer: L Arnold 60
Captain 93-94: Gary Finley
Supporters' P.o.Y. 93-94: Mike Tandy
Management P.o.Y. 93-94: Neil Williams
Top Scorer 93-94: Gavin McDonald
Local Newspapers: Warrington Guardian (0925 33033), Warrington Mercury, Manchester Evening News, Liverpool Post & Echo.
Local Radio Stations: Radio Merseyside, Radio Manchester (GMR).
Honours: FA Vase R-up 86-87 (SF 85-86), FA Trophy QF 92-93, North West Counties Lg 89-90 (Lg Cup 85-86 87-88 88-89 (R-up 89-90), Div 2 R-up 86-87, Div 3 R-up 82-83, Reserve Div West 89-90), Mid-Cheshire Lg 60-61 (R-up 57-58, Lg Cup 54-55 55-56) 11-12 72-73, Altrincham Amateur Cup 54-55, Warrington Yth Chall. Cup 93-94.

PROGRAMME DETAILS:
Pages: 36 **Price:** 50p
Editor: Garry Clarke

WORKINGTON

1884 (reformed 1921) **WORKINGTON** Reds

Workington AFC. Back Row (L/R): Alan Cook (Manager), Gary Messenger, Paul Campbell, Lee Copeland, Martin Henderson, Jason Prins, Danny Wheatley, Billy Gilmour. Front: Lee Chambers, Stuart Todhunter, Graham Flynn, Paddy Atkinson, Mascot, Nigel Dustin, Paul Doolan, David Gray, Graham Caton, Reg Carther (Physio). Photo - Steve Durham.

Chairman: Jackie Donald **President:** Eric Fisher.
Secretary: Tom Robson, 12 Derwent Bank, Seaton, Workington CA14 1EE (0900 605208).
Manager: Alan Cook **Asst Manager:** TBA
Press Officer: Steve Durham (0946 61380) **Physio:** Reg Carther.
Commercial Manager: Jackie Donald.
Ground: Borough Park, Workington, Cumbria CA14 2DT (0900 602871).
Directions: A66 into town, right at 'T' junction, follow A596 for three quarters of a mile - ground is then visible and signposted. Ground is to north of town centre quarter of a mile from Workington (BR) station and half mile from bus station in town centre.
Capacity: 2,500 **Cover:** 800 **Seats:** 200 **Floodlights:** Yes **Metal Badges:** Yes
Club Shop: Yes, selling programmes, badges, magazines, pennants, photographs, replica kit, T-shirts. Contact Martin Wingfield (0900 818346).
Colours: Red/white/red **Change colours:** All sky. **Sponsors:** TBA
Reserve Team's League: West Cumberland.
Previous Leagues: Cumberland Association 1890-94/ Cumberland Snr 94-1901 03-04/ Lancs Lge 1901-03/ Lancs Combination 04-10/ North Eastern 10-11 21-51/ Football League 51-77.
Midweek home matchday: Tuesday **Previous Grounds:** Various 1884-1921/ Lonsdale Park 21-37.
Record Attendance: 21,000 v Manchester United, FA Cup 3rd Rd 4/1/58.
Best FA Cup season: 4th Rd, 1933-34. Competition Proper on 53 other occasions.
Best FA Trophy season: 1st Round replay 77-78.
Record win: 17-1 v Cockermouth Crusaders, Cumberland Senior League 19/1/01.
Record loss: 0-9 v Chorley (A), NPL Prem. Division, 10/11/87.
Record Fees - Paid: £6,000 for Ken Chisholm (Sunderland, 1956).
Received: £33,000 for Ian McDonald (Liverpool, 1974).
Players progressing to Football League: Numerous, the best known being John Burridge.
Clubhouse: Open matchdays and for private functions. Food on matchdays restricted menu.
Club Record Goalscorer: Billy Charlton 193
Club Record Apps: Bobby Brown 419.
93-94 Captain: Graham Flynn
93-94 P.o.Y.: Keith Glover
93-94 Top scorer: Martin Henderson 23.
Local Press: Evening News & Star, Times & Star (John Walsh 0900 601234).
Local Radio Stations: BBC Radio Cumbria (0228 31661).
Honours: Football League Cup QF 63-64 64-65, Football League: 5th in Div 3 65-66, 3rd Div 4 63-64, Northern Premier League Presidents Cup 83-84, North Eastern League Runners-up 38-39 (League Cup 34-35 36-37 (Runners-up 37-38)), Cumberland County Cup 1886-87 87-88 88-89 89-90 90-91 95-96 96-97 97-98 98-99 1906-07 07-08 09-10 24-25 34-35 36-37 37-38 49-50 53-54 67-68 85-86 (Runners-up 1885-86 91-92 1899-1900 00-01 02-03 08-09 11-12 23-24 26-27 29-30 46-47 68-69 78-79).

PROGRAMME DETAILS:
Pages: 28 **Price:** 60p
Editor: Steve Durham (0946 61380)

Formed: 1861

WORKSOP TOWN

The Tigers

Worksop Town goalkeeper Lee Fuller makes a brave save to deny Rob Alleyne during the Tigers' FA Trophy defeat at Tamworth on 18th September.

Photo - Paul Barber.

Chairman: Mel Bradley **Vice Chairman:** Vacant
Secretary: W E Peace, 72 Woodburn Drive, Chapeltown, Sheffield S30 4YT (0742 468160).
Manager: Tommy Spencer **Asst Manager:** John Stokes **Physio:** Tommy Watson.
Press Officer: Mel Bradley **Commercial Manager:** Don Ayscough.
Ground: Babbage Way, off Sandy Lane, Worksop, Notts S80 1UJ (0909 501911).
Directions: M1 jct 31 (from north) jct 30 (from south), follow Worksop signs, join A57 and follow signs for Sandy Lane Industrial Estate - ground on left. 5 mins walk from station.
Capacity: 2,500 **Cover:** 1,000 **Seats:** 360 **Floodlights:** Yes. **Metal Badges:** Yes.
Club Shop: The Tigershop selling badges, scarves, magazines, programmes. 30 page catalogue from Steve Jarvis, 10 Wood End Drive, Ravenshead, Notts NG15 9EJ.
Colours: Amber/black **Change colours:** Blue/white.
Previous Grounds: Netherton Road/ Bridge Meadow/ Central Avenue (prior to 1989)/ The Northolme (Gainsborough Trinity F.C.) (shared) 89-92.
Previous Leagues: Midland (Counties) 1896-98 1900-30 49-60 61-68 69-74/ Sheffield Association 1898-99 1931-33/ Central Combination 33-35/ Yorkshire 35-39/ Central Alliance 47-49 60-61/ Northern Premier 68-69.
Midweek home matchday: Monday
Sponsors: Hooleys of Worksop/ Eyres of Worksop.
Reserve Team's League: Sheffield County Senior (Youth Team: Notts Youth League).
Record Attendance: 1,503 v Sheffield United, friendly. *At Central Avenue: 8,171 v Chesterfield, FA Cup 1925.*
Record win: 20-0 v Staveley, 1/9/1894
Record defeat: 1-11 v Hull City Reserves, 55-56.
Best FA Trophy season: 2nd Rd replay 73-74.
Best FA Cup year: Last 64; 1907-08 v Chelsea (A) 1-9, 21-22 v Southend (H) 1-2, 22-23 v Spurs (A) 0-0 & 0-9, 55-56 v Swindon (A) 0-1. 2nd Rd, 25-26 v Chesterfield (H) 1-2. 1st Rd; 20-21 v Bristol Rovers (A) 0-9, 26-27 v York (A) 1-1, 1-4, 61-62 v Workington (A) 0-2, 78-79 v Barnsley (A) 1-5.
League Clubs defeated in FA Cup: Rotherham Town 1893-94/ Grimsby Town 94-95/ Nelson 1921-22/ Chesterfield 22-23/ Coventry City 25-26/ Bradford City 55-56.
Record Fees - Paid: None.
Received: £10,000 for Martin Hardy (Boston U. 1987).
Players progressing to Football League: Jack Brown (Sheff Wed & England), Gordon Dale (Chesterfield 1948), Alan Daley (Doncaster 1950), Kevin Wood (Grimsby 1951), Harry Jarvis (Notts County 1951), Brian Taylor (Leeds 1951), Stan Rhodes & Dennis Gratton & Alan Hodgkinson & John Harrison (Sheffield United 1951 & 52 & 53 67), Stanley Lloyd & Peter Marshall (Scunthorpe 1954), Albert Rhodes (QPR 1954), Robert Moore (Rotherham 1955), Harold Mosby (Crewe 1956), Les Moore (Derby 1957), Herbert Bowery (Nottm Forest 1975), Tony Moore (Rochdale 1984), Steve Adams (Scarborough 1987), David Moss (Doncaster 1993).
Clubhouse: Tigers Club. Normal licensing hours. Pool, quiz nights, disco etc.
Club Record Goalscorer: Kenny Clark, 193.
Club Record appearances: Dave Cunnington, 315.
93-94 Captain: Neil Pickering.
93-94 P.o.Y.: Lee Howard (Players'), Kenny Clark (Supporters').
93-94 Top scorer: Kenny Clark 42.
Local Press: Worksop Guardian (500500), Worksop Star (486335), Nottingham Football Post (0602 475221).
Local Radio Stations: Radio Sheffield, Radio Hallam, Radio Lincoln.
Hons: Northern Prem. Lg Presidents Cup 85-86, Midland Co's Lg 21-22 65-66 72-73 (R-up 62-63 66-67 73-74), Sheffield Association Lg 1898-99, Sheffield & Hallamshire Snr Cup 23-24 52-53 54-55 65-66 69-70 72-73 81-82 84-85, Mansfield Charity Cup 22-23.

PROGRAMME DETAILS:
Pages: 28-32 **Price:** 50p
Editor: Mel Bradley
(0909 500491/500500)

Northern Premier League Division One Seven Year Records

	87/8	88/9	89/0	90/1	91/2	92/3	93/4
Accrington Stanley	4	6	3	4	–	–	–
Alfreton Town	11	20	18	22	20	9	6
Ashton United	–	–	–	–	–	3	3
Bamber Bridge	–	–	–	–	–	–	13
Bishop Auckland	–	2	–	–	–	–	–
Bridlington Town	–	–	–	9	6	1	–
Caernarfon Town	–	–	–	14	5	16	18
Colne Dynamoes	–	1	–	–	–	–	–
Colwyn Bay	–	–	–	–	1	–	–
Congleton Town	9	10	6	11	17	20	15
Curzon Ashton	18	13	8	10	11	7	14
Droylsden	6	4	2	–	–	–	–
Eastwood Hanley	7	8	21	–	–	–	–
Eastwood Town	17	12	11	6	15	14	21
Emley	–	–	5	2	–	–	–
Farsley Celtic	5	14	12	21	12	17	19
Fleetwood Town	1	–	–	–	–	–	–
Goole Town	–	–	–	–	–	–	8
Gretna	–	–	–	–	–	6	10
Great Harwood Town	–	–	–	–	–	8	9
Guiseley	–	–	–	–	4	4	1
Harrogate Town	10	8	9	19	10	10	20
Irlam Town	13	15	15	17	21	–	–
Knowsley United	–	–	–	–	8	2	–
(City of) Lancaster	16	7	10	8	16	18	4
Leek Town	3	3	1	–	–	–	–
Mossley	–	–	–	–	–	–	17
Netherfield	19	21	20	12	9	15	5
Newtown	–	9	14	13	14	–	–
Penrith	14	16	22	–	–	–	–
Radcliffe Borough	12	17	17	16	13	12	16
Rhyl	–	–	–	5	18	–	–
Rossendale United	–	–	13	15	19	21	–
Shepshed Albion	–	–	–	–	–	19	–
Spennymoor United	–	–	–	–	–	–	2
Stalybridge Celtic	2	–	–	–	–	–	–
Sutton Town	15	22	–	–	–	–	–
Warrington Town	–	–	–	7	7	5	7
Whitley Bay	–	5	4	1	–	–	–
Winsford United	8	19	7	18	2	–	–
Workington	–	11	16	20	22	13	11
Worksop Town	–	–	19	3	3	11	12
No. of Clubs	19	22	22	22	22	21	21

Netherfield goalkeeper Graham Bryan makes a competent catch under pressure from a Guiseley forward. The Kendal side beat previously undefeated Guiseley 3-0 in this fixture on 18th September.

Photo - Gavin Ellis-Neville.

BEAZER HOMES SOUTHERN LEAGUE

President: G E Templeman

Chairman: D S R Gillard

Hon. Secretary: D J Strudwick,
11 Welland Close, Durrington, Worthing, West Sussex
BN13 3NR (0903 267788).

SECRETARY'S REPORT

Once again the Competition proved to be so fierce in the Beazer Homes League that not a single award winning issue was settled until the last week of the season. After a 38-week campaign, only five days remained when Farnborough Town put five past Gresley Rovers, without reply, to earn their second Championship success in four years.

In my Report last year I welcomed back Farnborough Town following the club's relegation from the Football Conference, saying almost prophetically, that I hoped their stay with us would be as enjoyable as their last sojourn in the Beazer Homes League. Farnborough Town have now spent two seasons with us and have won the championship on each occasion. But having said that, on both occasions, no club has won the Premier Division in its present format with fewer points. Town won the 1990-91 Championship with 85 points following a late winner at Atherstone United. After opening this year's campaign with a 2-0 defeat, ironically at Atherstone, 82 points proved enough for Farnborough's second triumph.

Unfortunately for Cheltenham, Farnborough's win over Gresley condemned the Robins to runners-up sport for the second consecutive year despite losing one match fewer than their rivals. How they must be regretting the 24 points dropped in drawn matches.

Halesowen Town could also be feeling some form of penitence. The Yeltz finished third - their highest ever position in football - in spite of losing to Bashley, Moor Green and Solihull Borough; all teams who spent much of the season either close to, or in, the relegation zone. Just one point behind Halesowen came Atherstone United. The Adders completed the season with an amazing 15 wins and two draws from their final matches. Crawley Town were 5th, behind Atherstone on goal difference.

By a double coincidence, Rushden & Diamonds won the Midland Division also on May's first Bank Holiday Monday with a win over Forest Green Rovers, and also by a 5-0 margin. Following a floodlight failure at the magnificently developing Nene Park Stadium, the game finished in the fading light of early evening. Fortunately, the game had started at 7.00pm rather than the customary 7.30 or 7.45. A decision with vision on the part of the two club Secretaries.

The remaining three honours in the regional divisions were still available on the final day for a number of clubs to take advantage. Chasing runners-up place in the Midland Division, Weston-super-Mare could only draw with Redditch United during the final midweek of the season. This handed the initiative to VS Rugby. Both clubs entered their final fixtures knowing that only a victory was good enough to keep alive their promotional hopes. Weston, though, needed Rugby to drop points at Racing Club Warwick. It wasn't to be; VS Rugby won 2-0 whilst Weston-super-Mare convincingly beat Bridgnorth Town to finish in third place with 91 points!

The Southern Division was even closer. Despite leading the table for much of the season, Gravesend & Northfleet still needed a point from their last game to clinch the title. Bury Town, bottom of the table with just 14 points and 3 wins from the year's work, were Northfleet's opponents. The favourites won a predictable victory, 3-0, to collect the Trophy.

Having lost 2-1 on the penultimate Saturday, to late promotion challengers Havant Town, Sudbury Town then dropped two midweek points at Fisher. In the same midweek Witney collected six points from outings against Buckingham Town and Fareham Town to take them three points clear of Sudbury in the race for second spot. A single point from their last game would secure the silver medals. Nothing but a win would keep Sudbury's promotion hopes alive. Their respective problem was that they were playing each other! Sudbury won the titanic battle 2-1, and Witney finished third for the second year running.

Although only finishing in fifth place, it is worthy of notice that Havant Town plundered 101 goals. Only a twelve goal glut in their final two matches by Rushden & Diamonds denied Havant from receiving the Merit Cup for the most League goals scored and, therefore, taking some consolation from the long season.

After Stourbridge's success against a Premier Division side in last year's League Cup Final, another regional division side repeated the feat this year. The Southern Division's Sudbury Town defeated Gresley Rovers 2-0 (at home) and 3-1 (away) in the inaugural Dr Marten's Cup Final. In front of a vociferous and partisan home crowd, Rovers reduced the deficit from the first-Leg with a 39th minute goal, but their familiar patient football was not, perhaps, conducive to sustaining the more intense pressure required to make Sudbury's resolute defence succumb a second time. At the end of a fiercely contested final it was generally felt that the stronger of the two teams over two legs had won the tie. Sudbury Town's celebrations were spontaneous and commenced at fever pitch immediately referee Paul Roberts concluded the clash.

Progress and success in national competitions this season was comparatively isolated and sparse. The advancement of Crawley Town and Nuneaton Borough to second Round of the FA Cup was undoubtedly the highlight. Six clubs reached the First Round proper. Farnborough Town lost at home to Alan Ball's Exeter City, Gravesend & Northfleet were narrowly defeated by the odd goal in three at Leyton Orient, VS Rugby lost 3-0 at home to Brentford and Weston-super-Mare lost 1-0 in a replay against Woking after holding the Conference club on their own ground 2-2. Crawley Town, meanwhile, were beating Metropolitan Police 2-0 with the aid of one of Craig Whitington's last goals for the club (Whitington joined Scarborough shortly afterwards for a £50,000 fee). Nuneaton Borough led Swansea City at the Vetch Field with a goal from Shearer, but they were pulled back in the last few minutes of the game. Swansea's reprieve was short-lived; a brace from Simpson in the replay earned Boro' a trip to Bournemouth in Round Two.

A repeat performance looked on the cards when an 80th minute strike from Green earned Boro' a home replay. But under the gaze of 'live' television coverage by Sky, an 11th minute goal by Cotterill (formerly a Beazer League player with Burton Albion) earned the Cherries a Third Round trip to Preston North End.

Unfortunately, Crawley Town also slipped up in the Second Round. Despite having what looked to be a less daunting task than their Beazer colleagues, the Newtowners went down 2-1 at home to Barnet. Ford grabbed Crawley's goal in a dramatic finish but it was Barnet who were invited to entertain Chelsea, one of the eventual finalists, in Round Three

Successes in the FA Trophy and the FA Vase were harder to come by. Only Cheltenham Town reached the Third Round of the Trophy and left the Competition when losing a replay to Guiseley, 1-0. The Robins had defeated Hednesford Town and Nuneaton Borough by the same margin in the previous two rounds.

Worcester City lost in the Second Round after a replay at Macclesfield, 3-2, following a goalless draw at St George's Lane. This match followed a tremendous win by George Rooney's men against Harrow Borough in the previous round. Despite trailing by two goals at Harrow, Worcester fought back for a 3-3 draw. In the replay, Harrow again led by two clear goals but City recovered to win a thrilling match, 5-3.

Grantham Town were the only other Beazer club to reach the Second Round. Following an excellent 3-2 victory over Football Conference club Witton Albion, Grantham lost 2-1 to Bishop Auckland. It must be said, however, that the apparent lack of impact in this year's tournament by Beazer clubs was largely due to the 'luck of the draw'. In the Third Qualifying Round, 22 of our clubs were drawn against one another.

In the FA Vase, King's Lynn and Bridgnorth Town both reached the Fourth Round and defeated Nantwich 1-0, and Glossop 3-0, respectively. Both, however, came to grief in the last sixteen. Bridgnorth Town fell to Atherton LR by the only goal of the game (Atherton went on to reach the Semi-Final) and King's Lynn were eclipsed 2-0 by their local rivals and eventual winners of the competition, Diss Town.

Perhaps the most bizarre result in the FA Vase this year was reserved for Newport IOW and Banstead. The teams had been drawn together in last year's tournament and Newport suffered a couple of dismissals. A close encounter was, therefore, expected this year. And that is certainly what the teams produced. After three matches they were still even. But for the third replay Banstead travelled to the Island and won 6-1!

Looking back at the League, last year's newcomers endured varying degrees of success. Tonbridge achieved a comfortable mid-table postion in the Southern Division, and Clevedon Town finished a creditable 5th in the Midland Division whilst their colleagues Armitage enjoyed several early triumphs before plummeting down the table. Good fortune, has however, shone on the clubs finishing at the foot of the regional divisions. With long-standing members Canterbury City (1960) and Dunstable (1965) both withdrawing from the League and only two clubs, Ilkeston Town and Rothwell Town, proving eligible for promotion, relegation blushes have been saved. At this point, therefore, I extend a warm welcome to next season's freshmen from Derbyshire and Northamptonshire, together with Leek Town who have transferred from the Northern Premier League.

Along with the departing clubs already mentioned, I bid a fond farewell to Farnborough Town, for the second time. Farnborough, please do not 'read between the lines', I wish you no ill-luck, when I say that you are welcome back in the Beazer any time. Good luck in the Football Conference next season!

This review of the playing year would not be complete without thanks to everyone involved in organising the five Representative Matches staged during this, the Southern Football League's Centenary Year. I will avoid naming names because of the risk of offending anyone that I may accidentally miss. I must, however, single out Management Committee member Keith Allen for the extraneous duties he has undertaken on this aspect of the League's affairs. Otherwise, I offer a blanket 'thank you' to everyone who took part.

In the games specifically organised to celebrate our Centenary, the League Representative side enjoyed a satisfying 4-1 win over an FA XI at Nuneaton, a creditable 0-0 draw against Wimbledon at Dorchester and an honourable 2-1 defeat at the hands of Millwall at Ashford. In reciprocal celebration events, a Midland Area team shared Dudley Town's Centenary and shared the score, too, 1-1. And in a mutual celebration with the Middlesex Wanderers, Cambridge City represented the League and won 2-0.

Dennis Strudwick

DOC MARTENS
SOUTHERN LEAGUE CHALLENGE CUP

1st Round

Sudbury	1;1
Baldock	0;0
Buckingham	0;1
Braintree	2;1
Gravesend	5;0
Crawley T.	1;1
Burnham	5;1
Bury Town	0;2
Hastings	0;6
Erith & Bel.	0;0
Tonbridge	3;2
Sittingbourne	2;0
Ashford T.	4;7
Canterbury	2;0
Margate	0;1
Fisher '93	0;1
Poole Town	1;1
Salisbury C.	5;0
Weymouth	1;0
Newport IW	0;0
Weston-s-M.	3;1
Cheltenham	1;4
Trowbridge	2;0
Worcester C.	1;0
Wealdstone	1;3
Dunstable	0;3
Waterlooville	2;4
Farnborough	2;2
Fareham T.	2;2
Dorchester	3;2
Havant T.	3;1
Bashley	0;1
Clevedon T.	5;0
Halesowen T.	2;4
Redditch	0;0
Dudley Town	0;3
Forest GR	2;2
Bridgnorth	4;1
Hinckley T.	0;0
Gresley R.	4;6
Bilston T.	1;5
Leicester U.	2;0
Atherstone	1;0
Corby Town	1;1
Rushden & D.	2;0
Bedworth	0;0
Cambridge C.	4;3
King's Lynn	1;0
VS Rugby	2;0
Hednesford	1;4
Nuneaton	4;2
Solihull	1;1
Evesham Utd	1;0
Yate Town	0;0
Gloucester	2;1
Witney T.	1;1
Sutton C'field	1;1
Gravesend	1;0
Margate	3;2
Tamworth	2;2
Burton A.	3;6
Armitage	0;3
Newport AFC	1;2
Stourbridge	3;1

2nd Round

Sudbury T.	3
Braintree T.	1
Gravesend & N.	3
Burnham	0
Hastings T.	0
Tonbridge AFC	2
Ashford Town	0
Margate	2
Salisbury	2;3
Weymouth	2;1
Cheltenham T.	2
Trowbridge T.	3
Wealdstone	0
Waterlooville	2
Dorchester T.	2
Havant Town	1
Halesowen T.	2
Dudley Town	1
Bridgnorth T.	0
Gresley Rovers	4
Bilston Town	1
Corby Town	3
Rushden & D.	2;1
Cambridge C.	2;3
Hednesford	1;3
Nuneaton B.	1;1
Evesham United	1
Gloucester C.	3
Sutton C'field	1
Moor Green	3
Burton Albion	2
Stourbridge	1

3rd Round

Sudbury *(reinst.)*	0
Gravesend *(exp.)*	1
Tonbridge AFC	4
Margate	1
Salisbury City	1
Trowbridge T.	0
Waterlooville	1
Dorchester T.	2
Halesowen T.	2
Gresley Rovers	3
Corby Town	2
Cambridge City	1
Hednesford T.	0
Gloucester City	1
Moor Green	0
Burton Albion	3

Quarter-final

Sudbury Town	2
Tonbridge AFC	1
Salisbury City	4
Dorcester Town	0
Gresley Rvrs	0;3
Corby Town	0;1
Gloucester City	0
Burton Albion	1

Semi-final

Sudbury Town	2;4
1st leg at Sudbury	
Salisbury City	2;1
Gresley Rovers	1;1
1st leg at Gresley	
Burton Albion	0;0

Final

Sudbury Town	**2;3**
Gresley Rovers	**0;1**

Prel. Rd: Chelmsford 2;1 Buckingham 1;2 *(2-4 pens)* Grantham 1;2 Rushden 3;3 *(away goals rule applies throughout)*

PREMIER DIVISION 1993-94

	P	W	D	L	F	A	PTS
Farnborough Town	42	25	7	10	74	44	82
Cheltenham Town	42	21	12	9	67	38	75
Halesowen Town	42	21	11	10	69	46	74
Atherstone United	42	22	7	13	57	43	73
Crawley Town	42	21	10	11	56	42	73
Chelmsford City	42	21	7	14	74	59	70
Trowbridge Town	42	16	17	9	52	41	65
Sittingbourne	42	17	13	12	65	48	64
Corby Town	42	17	8	17	52	56	59
Gloucester City	42	17	6	19	55	60	57
Burton Albion	42	15	11	16	57	49	56
Hastings Town	42	16	7	19	51	60	55
Hednesford Town	42	15	9	18	67	66	54
Gresley Rovers	42	14	11	17	61	72	53
Worcester City	42	14	9	19	61	70	51
Solihull Borough	42	13	11	18	52	57	50
Cambridge City	42	13	11	18	50	60	50
Dorchester Town	42	12	11	19	38	51	47
Moor Green	42	11	10	21	49	66	43
Waterlooville	42	11	10	21	47	69	43
Bashley	42	11	10	21	47	80	43
Nuneaton Borough	42	11	8	23	42	66	41

TOP SCORERS

L Ryan (Cambridge City)	28
T Senior (Farnborough Town)	26
C Boothe (Farnborough Town)	24
P Joinson (Halesowen Town)	22
L McRobert (Sittingbourne)	21
S Restarick (Chelmsford City)	21

Below: *Jubilant scenes in the Farnborough Town dressing-room after their title-clinching 5-0 victory over Gresley Rovers. Farnborough's second Southern League championship success means they join Gateshead as being one of only two teams in the history of the Pyramid to have won promotion to the Conference on three separate occasions.*

Photo - Eric Marsh.

RESULT CHART 1993-94

HOME TEAM	1	2	3	4	5	6	7	8	9	10	11	12	13	14	15	16	17	18	19	20	21	22
1. Atherstone	*	4-0	3-1	0-1	3-0	3-2	2-0	2-0	1-0	2-0	2-1	3-0	1-2	1-1	0-2	0-1	1-0	0-1	4-1	0-1	1-0	2-1
2. Bashley	1-2	*	1-0	0-2	1-5	2-1	2-1	1-1	0-1	5-0	4-5	2-0	2-1	1-5	1-1	2-0	1-0	0-3	2-3	1-1	2-1	2-2
3. Burton A.	1-2	2-1	*	1-1	0-0	1-1	1-0	0-1	0-0	2-1	4-1	1-0	0-2	2-0	3-0	1-0	6-1	1-2	2-1	1-1	1-0	2-1
4. Cambridge	0-0	1-1	0-0	*	1-3	1-1	1-1	0-1	1-2	1-5	2-0	1-0	3-2	1-0	4-1	1-3	3-0	2-2	0-2	2-0	3-0	4-3
5. Chelmsford	0-0	4-0	3-1	2-0	*	0-1	2-3	1-2	3-0	1-0	2-1	2-1	0-1	0-2	4-1	1-1	1-1	3-0	3-1	2-2	3-2	2-1
6. Cheltenham	5-1	2-0	1-0	2-1	5-0	*	4-1	1-3	0-1	1-1	0-1	1-1	3-1	1-0	3-0	3-1	1-0	0-0	1-2	0-1	1-0	1-0
7. Corby T.	1-0	1-2	2-1	0-0	0-0	1-1	*	5-1	0-0	0-6	2-1	2-1	2-1	0-1	4-2	2-1	1-0	3-2	1-0	1-0	0-1	3-2
8. Crawley T.	0-1	6-2	1-1	2-1	0-2	0-1	0-0	*	1-1	1-0	0-0	0-1	0-1	3-0	3-1	2-0	1-0	1-1	3-0	1-1	2-1	2-0
9. Dorchester	2-2	1-3	2-1	3-1	1-0	0-2	0-0	1-2	*	0-1	1-2	1-2	1-1	0-0	1-4	1-1	1-0	1-3	1-1	0-1	0-1	0-3
10. Farnborough	1-0	3-1	2-0	2-2	7-6	1-1	1-0	1-2	0-0	*	1-0	5-0	3-0	3-1	1-0	1-0	1-2	2-1	1-1	1-0	3-0	3-1
11. Gloucester	3-0	1-0	4-2	2-1	2-5	1-3	2-4	3-0	1-0	0-1	*	1-1	0-0	2-1	2-0	2-1	2-1	0-1	3-1	0-1	2-1	1-2
12. Gresley	1-1	1-1	0-4	2-1	2-1	1-1	1-0	1-1	0-2	4-0	2-0	*	1-1	3-0	0-2	3-3	5-3	1-1	2-1	1-3	2-1	3-4
13. Halesowen	0-0	2-0	2-2	3-0	3-1	1-1	2-0	2-2	2-0	2-3	1-0	2-1	*	2-1	2-1	0-1	3-1	2-1	1-3	1-1	4-0	2-1
14. Hastings	1-2	1-0	3-2	1-0	3-1	1-1	2-0	0-1	1-0	1-0	1-0	2-1	1-1	*	0-3	1-3	2-3	0-3	1-2	2-2	2-0	3-2
15. Hednesford	1-2	6-0	2-2	4-0	1-2	2-0	3-1	2-1	2-4	0-2	1-1	3-1	1-1	1-2	*	0-0	4-1	1-1	2-1	0-1	3-2	4-2
16. Moor Green	2-2	0-0	2-0	0-1	3-1	1-2	0-4	0-2	1-3	1-2	3-0	2-4	0-3	1-0	2-4	*	1-0	0-4	1-1	3-1	2-0	0-2
17. Nuneaton	0-1	1-1	1-2	0-1	1-1	2-1	2-1	2-1	0-2	2-1	1-3	2-3	1-1	0-2	0-0	1-0	*	2-1	0-3	2-0	3-0	1-1
18. Sit'bourne	2-0	1-1	0-0	3-2	1-2	1-3	2-0	2-3	1-2	1-3	0-0	1-2	3-2	2-1	3-0	5-2	2-2	*	1-0	1-0	0-0	4-0
19. Solihull	0-2	2-0	0-0	2-0	0-1	1-2	1-2	0-1	1-1	0-0	2-4	4-2	0-2	2-2	0-0	2-1	1-0	1-0	*	0-2	1-1	1-0
20. Trowbridge	4-1	3-0	3-2	0-0	2-1	2-2	1-1	0-0	1-0	0-0	2-0	2-0	3-1	1-1	3-2	2-2	0-0	0-0	2-2	*	0-0	2-2
21. Wat'ville	0-3	1-1	1-0	2-2	0-1	0-3	2-1	1-2	2-0	2-3	1-1	2-2	1-4	4-1	2-0	0-0	3-2	2-2	2-2	2-0	*	3-2
22. Worcester	3-0	2-0	0-4	2-0	1-1	1-1	2-1	2-0	1-0	0-2	2-0	2-2	0-2	3-1	0-0	3-3	0-1	1-1	0-4	2-1	1-2	*

Beazer Homes (Southern) League Premier Division Ten Year Records

	84/5	85/6	86/7	87/8	88/9	89/0	90/1	91/2	92/3	93/4
Alvechurch	15	4	8	7	14	21	–	–	–	–
Ashford Town	–	–	–	12	18	19	–	–	–	–
Atherstone United	–	–	–	–	–	6	15	13	15	4
Aylesbury United	–	8	3	1	–	–	–	–	–	–
Bashley	–	–	–	–	–	–	10	4	9	21
Basingstoke Town	–	15	16	–	–	–	–	–	–	–
Bath City	–	–	–	–	9	2	–	–	–	–
Bedworth United	12	10	12	14	22	–	–	–	–	–
Bromsgrove Rovers	–	–	2	4	10	10	5	1	–	–
Burton Albion	–	–	–	16	8	4	7	10	8	11
Cambridge City	–	–	6	3	5	8	3	5	14	17
Chelmsford City	9	2	5	19	–	18	18	18	12	6
Cheltenham Town	1	–	–	–	–	–	–	–	2	2
Corby Town	11	13	9	10	16	20	–	14	3	9
Crawley Town	3	6	13	6	12	15	19	17	=6	5
Dartford	–	–	4	2	2	3	13	6	w/d	–
Dorchester Town	–	–	–	11	13	14	11	11	18	18
Dover Athletic	–	–	–	–	6	1	4	2	1	–
Dudley Town	–	12	21	–	–	–	–	–	–	–
Fareham Town	14	19	14	9	19	–	–	–	–	–
Farnborough Town	–	–	–	–	–	–	1	–	–	1
Fisher Athletic	8	3	1	–	–	–	–	21	–	–
Folkestone	7	9	22	–	–	–	–	–	–	–
Gloucester City	10	–	–	–	–	9	2	12	13	10
Gosport Borough	–	18	18	15	7	22	–	–	–	–
Gravesnd & Northfleet	13	20	–	–	–	7	21	22	–	–
Gresley Rovers	–	–	–	–	–	–	–	–	–	14
Halesowen Town	–	–	–	–	–	–	8	8	10	3
Hastings Town	16	–	–	–	–	–	–	–	16	12
Hednesford Town	–	–	–	–	–	–	–	–	4	13
King's Lynn	2	14	20	–	–	–	–	–	–	–
Leamington	20	–	–	–	–	–	–	–	–	–
Leicester United	–	–	–	8	20	–	–	–	–	–
Merthyr Tydfil	–	–	–	–	1	–	–	–	–	–
Moor Green	–	–	–	–	15	11	16	9	19	19
Nuneaton Borough	–	–	–	21	–	–	–	–	–	22
Poole Town	–	–	–	–	–	–	17	20	–	–
Redditch United	–	–	7	18	21	–	–	–	–	–
Road Sea Southampton	5	16	–	–	–	–	–	–	–	–
Rushden Town	–	–	–	–	–	–	14	–	–	–
Salisbury	–	–	19	–	–	–	–	–	–	–
Shepshed Charterhouse	10	7	11	13	–	–	–	–	–	–
Sittingbourne	–	–	–	–	–	–	–	–	–	8
Solihull Borough	–	–	–	–	–	–	–	–	=6	6
Trowbridge Town	19	–	–	–	–	–	–	7	5	7
V.S. Rugby	–	–	–	17	3	5	9	3	20	–
Waterlooville	–	–	–	–	17	16	20	15	11	20
Wealdstone	–	–	–	–	11	12	12	19	–	–
Welling United	6	1	–	–	–	–	–	–	–	–
Weymouth	–	–	–	–	–	17	22	–	21	–
Willenhall Town	4	11	15	20	–	–	–	–	–	–
Witney Town	17	17	17	22	–	–	–	–	–	–
Worcester City	–	5	10	5	4	13	6	16	17	15
No. of Clubs	**20**	**20**	**22**	**22**	**22**	**22**	**22**	**22**	**22**	**22**

Crawley keeper Neil Taylor tips over a header from Steve Lovell of Hastings. *Photo - Roger Turner.*

1979 **ATHERSTONE UNITED** The Adders

Nigel Fry scores Atherstone United's second goal in their 4-1 home win over Solihull Borough on 22nd January. Photo - Paul Barber.

Chairman: Mr K Haskins **Vice Chairman:** Mr P Barber **President:** Mr C Culwick
Secretary: Keith Allen, 19 Hathaway Drive, Nuneaton CV11 6NU (0203 349989).
Manager: M Brookes **Asst Manager:** L Spencer **Physio:** D Looms
Press Officer: John Harman **Commercial Manager:** Phil Bellinger.
Ground: Sheepy Road, Atherstone, Warks CV9 1HG (0827 717829)
Directions: Half mile north of town centre on B4116 Twycross/Ashby road.
Capacity: 3,500 **Cover:** 1,000 **Seats:** 373 **Floodlights:** Yes **Metal Badges:** Yes
Club Shop: Yes. Programmes, magazines, souvenirs etc. Contact John Harman (021 358 1681).
Colours: Red & white **Change colours:** Yellow & blue
Club Sponsors: Lloyds Chemist. **Previous Leagues:** West Midlands 1979-87
Midweek home matchday: Tuesday **Reserve's Lge:** Midland Comb. Reserve Div.
Record Attendance: 2,873 v V.S. Rugby, F.A. Cup 1st Round Proper 1987-88
Record win: 12-2 v Tipton Town (H), West Midlands (Regional) League Premier Division 86-87.
Record defeat: 0-5 v Solihull Borough (A), Southern League Premier Division 92-93.
Best F.A. Cup season: 2nd Rd Proper 1990-91 (lost 0-1 at Crewe Alexandra)
Record Fee Paid: £4,500 to Gloucester City for Gary Bradder, 1989.
Record Fee Received: £40,000 for Andy Rammell from Manchester United, September 1989.
Past Players who have progressed into The Football League: Andy Rammell (Manchester United).
Clubhouse: Normal hours, all usual facilities.
Record Goalscorer: Alan Bourton
Record Appearances: Lee Spencer
93-94 Captain: Steven Jackson.
93-94 P.o.Y.: Steve Campbell.
93-94 Top scorer: Robbie Ellison.
Local Newspapers: Tamworth Herald (0827 60741), Evening News (0203 353534), Atherstone Herald, Coventry Telegraph (0203 382251).
Local Radio Stations: Mercia Sound, CWR.
Honours: Southern Lg Midland Div 88-89, West Mids Lg 81-82 86-87 (Lg Cup 81-82, Premier Div Cup 86-87, Div 2 Cup (Reserves) 86-87), Walsall Snr Cup 83-84, Midland Comb. Reserve Division 87-88, Birmingham Snr Cup R-up 89-90, FA Tphy 1st Rd 88-89 91-92.

PROGRAMME DETAILS:
Pages: 28 **Price:** 70p
Editor: Phil Bellinger

ATHERSTONE UNITED's 1993-94 CAMPAIGN

Date	Opponents	Comp.	Res	Gate	Goalscorers
21/08	**FARNBOROUGH T.**	BHL	2-0	364	Baddams, Stemp(og)
23/08	Chelmsford City	BHL	0-0	552	
28/08	Waterlooville	BHL	3-0	349	Ellison, Wallace(2)
30/08	**GRESLEY ROVERS**	BHL	3-0	805	Campbell, Wallace, Fry
04/09	Hastings Town	BHL	2-1	450	Donovan(2(1p))
07/09	**CAMBRIDGE CITY**	BHL	0-1	421	
11/09	**HEDNESFORD TOWN**	FAC1q	2-1	524	Thurman, Campbell
18/09	**REDDITCH UTD**	FAT1q	1-1	305	Randall
21/09	Redditch United	FAT1qr	0-2	194	
25/09	**REDDITCH UTD**	FAC2q	0-0	290	
28/09	Redditch United	FAC2qr	1-1	302	Jackson
02/10	Trowbridge Town	BHL	1-4	312	Howell(og)
04/10	Redditch United	FAT1qr2	3-1	445	Randall, Judd(2)
09/10	Pershore Town	FAC3q	0-1	709	
16/10	**CHELTENHAM TOWN**	BHL	3-2	362	Ellison(2), Baddams
19/10	**CORBY TOWN**	DMC1(1)	1-1	235	Ellison
23/10	Moor Green	BHL	2-2	323	Campbell, Thurman
25/10	Boldmere St Mich.	BSC1	2-2	101	Baddams, Wileman
27/10	Corby Town	DMC1(2)	0-1	110	
30/10	**SITTINGBOURNE**	BHL	0-1	402	
01/11	**BOLDMERE ST M.**	BSC1r	0-0	182	*(lost 1-4 on penalties)*
06/11	Dorchester Town	BHL	2-2	461	Wallace, Thurman
16/11	Gresley Rovers	BHL	1-1	804	Campbell
20/11	Cheltenham Town	BHL	1-5	468	Campbell
27/11	**MOOR GREEN**	BHL	0-1	263	
01/12	**HALESOWEN TOWN**	BHL	1-2	316	Horne
04/12	**HEDNESFORD TOWN**	BHL	0-2	289	
07/12	Hinckley Town	MFC1	0-1	74	
11/12	Farnborough Town	BHL	0-1	356	
18/12	**WATERLOOVILLE**	BHL	1-0	201	Campbell
01/01	Corby Town	BHL	0-1	335	
08/01	Gloucester City	BHL	0-3	577	
15/01	Sittingbourne	BHL	0-2	1,009	
18/01	**ASTON VILLA xi**	Fr.	2-2	130	Gordon(2)
22/01	**SOLIHULL BORO'**	BHL	4-1	261	Campbell(2), Ellison, Fry
29/01	Worcester City	BHL	0-3	938	
02/02	**WILLENHALL TOWN**	MFC1	2-2	154	Thurman, Ellison
05/02	**HASTINGS TOWN**	BHL	1-1	212	Tuppenny(og)
09/02	Solihull Borough	BHL	2-0	153	Thurman, Ellison
12/02	**CHELMSFORD CITY**	BHL	3-0	306	Thurman, Russell, Whitehurst
19/02	**BASHLEY**	BHL	4-0	246	Russell(p), Ellison(2), Thurman
02/03	**NUNEATON BORO'**	BHL	1-0	1,145	Russell
05/03	Bashley	BHL	2-1	298	Thurman, Ellison
12/03	**TROWBRIDGE TOWN**	BHL	0-1	312	
16/03	**BURTON ALBION**	BHL	3-1	362	Ellison, Campbell, Russell
19/03	Cambridge City	BHL	0-0	176	
26/03	**WORCESTER CITY**	BHL	2-1	361	Merchant, Russell
02/04	Nuneaton Borough	BHL	1-0	1,365	Russell
09/04	Burton Albion	BHL	2-1	553	Ellison, M Owen
11/04	Hednesford Town	BHL	2-1	436	Russell, Wileman
16/04	**GLOUCESTER CITY**	BHL	2-1	277	Ellison, Russell
18/04	Tamworth	HGT	3-3	679	Wilman, Knight, Broadhurst
20/04	**CRAWLEY TOWN**	BHL	2-0	323	Ellison, Whitehurst
23/04	Halesowen Town	BHL	0-0	849	
25/04	**CORBY TOWN**	BHL	2-0	301	Ellison, Russell
28/04	**TAMWORTH**	HGT	1-2	619	Russell
30/04	Crawley Town	BHL	1-0	722	Merchant
07/05	**DORCHESTER TOWN**	BHL	1-0	375	Russell

Key: BHL: Beazer Homes League Premier Division, DMC: Doctor Martens (Beazer Homes League) Cup, FAC: F.A. Cup, FAT: F.A. Trophy, BSC: Birmingham Senior Cup, MFC: Midland Floodlit Cup (1st Rd on 'group' basis), HGT: Harry Godfrey Trophy, Fr.: Friendly. Numbers after cup competitions denote rounds (r: replay, qf: Quarter-Final, sf: Semi-Final, f: Final. Numbers in brackets indicate legs, i.e. (1): 1st leg).
Home fixtures are denoted by bold capitals, away matches by lower case. (p): penalty, og: Own goal.

SQUAD MEMBERS *(previous clubs listed in chronological order)*

GOALKEEPERS: Richard Williams *(Birmingham City)*

DEFENDERS: Craig Knight *(Rushall Olympic)*, **Steve Jackson** *(Bedworth Utd)*, **Leigh Everitt** *(Nuneaton Borough)*, **Matthew Wideman** *(Stoke City)*, **Paul Upton** *(Coventry Sporting, Bedworth Utd, Stafford Rgrs)*, **Malcolm Randle** *(Hurley Daw Mill, Bedworth Utd)*.

MIDFIELD: Nick Whitehurst *(Arnold)*, **Darren Horne** *(local football)*, **David Travis** *(Aston Villa, Tamworth, Hednesford Town)*, **Micky Thurman** *(Nuneaton Borough, Atherstone Utd, Bolehall Swifts, Nuneaton Borough, Bolehall Swifts)*, **Keith Russell** *(Walsall, Tamworth)*.

FORWARDS: Nigel Fry *(yth team)*, **Robbie Ellison** *(Mile Oak Rovers, Tamworth)*, **Steve Campbell** *(Knowle, Redditch Utd)*, **Shaun Merchant** *(Stafford Rgrs, Halesowen Harriers)*, **Carl Rathbone** *(Mile Oak Rovers, Armitage, Tamworth, Bromsgrove Rovers, Gresley Rovers, Alvechurch, Sutton Coldfield Town)*, **Micky Perry** *(West Bromwich Albion, Torquay Utd, Stafford Rgrs, Wealdstone, Worcester City, Redditch Utd, Tamworth, Hednesford Town, Moor Green)*

Formed: 1950

BURTON ALBION

Brewers

The main stand at Burton Albion's Eton Park ground.

Chairman: Jock Gordon **Vice Chairman:** W Royall
Secretary: Tony A Kirkland, 40 Hurst Drive, Stretton, Burton-on-Trent DE13 0ED (0283 36510).
Manager: John Barton **Coach:** TBA **Physio:** M Brown
Press Officer: David Twigg (0283 62013) **Commercial Mgr:** Committee.
Ground: Eton Park, Princess Way, Burton-on-Trent DE14 2RU (0283 65938)
Directions: 1) From south - M1 jct 22, A50 (Ashby) follow to Burton over Trent bridge, thru 3 sets of lights, right at mini-r'bout (Derby Turn Pub), left at next island - ground on left. 2) From M42 - A38 (Lichfield), follow signs for Burton, take 2nd turn for Burton (A5121), right at island - ground on left. 3) From north M1 jct 28 (A38 Derby), A38 to Burton, take 1st turning to Burton A5121 then as (2). 4) From M6 north - jct 15 and follow A50 for Stoke and Uttoxeter, follow A50 signs to Burton, ob reaching Burton continue under bypass, left into Shakespeare Rd after canal bridge (opposite Navigation Inn), ground at end.
Capacity: 4,500 **Cover:** 2,500 **Seats:** 300 **Club Shop:** Yes **Metal Badges:** Yes
Cols: Yellow & black stripes/black **Change colours:** Red & white.
Sponsors: Inde Coope Burton Brewery Ltd.
Previous Leagues: West Midlands 1950-58/ Southern 58-79/ Northern Premier 79-87
Midweek matchday: Tuesday **Previous Ground:** Wellington Street 50-57.
Record Attendance: 5,860 v Weymouth, Southern Lg Cup Final 2nd leg, 1964 *(22,500 v Leicester City, F.A. Cup 3rd Rd 1984 - played at Derby County F.C.).*
Best F.A. Cup season: 3rd Rd Proper, 1955-56 and 1984-85. 1st Rd on nine occasions.
League clubs defeated in F.A. Cup: Halifax (55-56), Aldershot (84-85)
Record Fees - Paid: £21,000 to for R Jones and J Pearson (Kidderminster).
Received: £60,000 for Darren Carr (Crystal Palace, 19889).
Past players progressing to Football League: Ray Russell (Shrewsbury 1954), David Neville (Rochdale 1955), Derek Middleton (York 1958), Tom McGlennon (Barrow 1959), Les Green & Tony Parry (Hartlepool 1965), George Hunter (Lincoln 1965), Stan Aston (Hartlepool 1966), David Jones (Newport 1968), Richie Barker & Jeff Bourne & Tony Bailey (Derby 1967 & 69 & 70), Maitland Pollock & Steve Buckley (Luton 1974), Peter Ward (Brighton 1975), Tony Moore (Sheffield Utd 1979), Carl Swan & Gary Clayton (Doncaster 1980 & 86), Richard Jobson (Watford 1982), Paul Haycock (Rotherham 1986), Alan Kamara (Scarborough 1987), Paul Groves (Leicester City 1988), Steve Cotterill & John Gayle (Wimbledon 1989), Darren Carr (Crystal Palace 1989), Darren Smith & Darren Roberts (Wolves 1990 & 92).
Clubhouse: 'The Football Tavern' - open normal pub hours. Full hot & cold menu.
Steward: Brian Finch
Club Record Goalscorer: Ritchie Barker, 157
Club Record Appearances: Phil Annable, 567
93-94 Captain: Simon Redfern.
93-94 P.o.Y.: Nick Goodwin.
93-94 Top scorer: Jason Rhodes.
Local Newspaper: Burton Daily Mail (0283 43311).
Local Radio: Radio Derby.
Honours: Southern Lg Cup 63-64 (R-up 88-89, Div 1 (Nth) R-up 71-72 73-74), Northern Premier Lg Challenge Cup 82-83 (R-up 86-87, Presidents Cup R-up 85-86 (SF 86-87), Birmingham Snr Cup 53-54 70-71 (R-up 86-87), FA Trophy R-up 86-87 (SF 74-75), GMAC Cup SF 86-87, Bass Charity Vase 81-82 85-86, Bass Challenge Cup 84-85, West Midlands Lg R-up 53-54, Staffordshire Senior Cup 55-56.

PROGRAMME DETAILS:
Pages: 48 **Price:** 80p
Editor: David Twigg
(0283 62013)

BURTON ALBION's 1993-94 CAMPAIGN

Date	Opponents	Comp.	Res	Gate	Goalscorers
21/08	**TROWBRIDGE TOWN**	BHL	1-1	588	Rhodes
24/08	Gloucester City	BHL	2-4	569	Briscoe, Rhodes
28/08	Hastings Town	BHL	2-3	475	Redgate, Rhodes
30/08	**NUNEATON BORO.**	BHL	6-1	1,078	Payne(2), Gretton, Briscoe(3(1p))
04/09	**CHELMSFORD CITY**	BHL	0-0	614	
07/09	Moor Green	BHL	0-2	312	
11/09	**MOOR GREEN**	FAC1q	2-1	508	Gretton(2)
14/09	**HALESOWEN TOWN**	BHL	0-2	472	
18/09	**CAERNARFON TOWN**	FAT1q	3-0	398	Doughty, Brain, Barks
25/09	**SANDWELL BOROUGH**	FAC2q	3-2	425	Gretton(2), Payne
02/10	**FARNBOROUGH T.**	BHL	2-1	577	Redfern, Briscoe
05/10	**ARMITAGE '90**	DMC1(1)	3-0	284	Rhodes, Redfern(2)
09/10	Rushden & Diamonds	FAC3q	0-4	1,201	
12/10	**SOLIHULL BOROUGH**	BSC1	4-0	193	Davis, Payne, Briscoe, Howell
16/10	Rushden & Diamonds	FAT2q	1-0	812	Redfern(p)
19/10	Armitage '90	DMC1(2)	6-0	163	Rhodes(2), Gretton(4)
23/10	**CORBY TOWN**	BHL	1-0	523	Gretton
26/10	**GLOUCESTER CITY**	BHL	4-1	526	Rhodes, Redfern, Callinan(og), Redding
30/10	Worcester City	BHL	4-0	778	Gretton(3), Briscoe
06/11	Waterlooville	BHL	0-1	353	
09/11	**STOURBRIDGE**	DMC2	2-1	297	Redfern, Payne
13/11	**SITTINGBOURNE**	BHL	1-2	761	Payne
16/11	**COVENTRY CITY**	BSC2	1-0	315	Rhodes
27/11	**HALESOWEN TOWN**	FAT3q	1-2	709	Bradley(og)
01/12	Solihull Borough	BHL	0-0	209	
04/12	Cheltenham Town	BHL	0-1	701	
06/12	Moor Green	DMC3	3-0	187	Gretton, Howell, Rhodes
11/12	Trowbridge Town	BHL	2-3	434	Gretton, Briscoe
14/12	**BEDWORTH UTD**	BSC3	1-0	187	Davis
18/12	**MOOR GREEN**	BHL	1-0	503	Briscoe
27/12	Gresley Rovers	BHL	4-0	2,409	Briscoe, Gretton, Rhodes, Mottram
01/01	**HEDNESFORD TOWN**	BHL	3-0	1,044	Rhodes, Redfern, Howell
08/01	**BASHLEY**	BHL	2-1	750	Gretton, Briscoe
15/01	**CAMBRIDGE CITY**	BHL	1-1	735	Rhodes
18/01	**BIRMINGHAM CITY**	BSC4	1-3	501	Howell
22/01	Dorchester Town	BHL	1-2	627	Redfern
25/01	Gloucester City	DMCqf	1-0	314	Gretton
29/01	**CRAWLEY TOWN**	BHL	0-1	713	
01/02	Nuneaton Borough	BHL	2-1	1,081	Attwood(og), Rhodes
05/02	Corby Town	BHL	1-2	324	Rhodes
08/02	**WORCESTER CITY**	BHL	2-1	538	Gretton, Howell
15/02	Gresley Rovers	DMCsf(1)	0-1	1,019	
19/02	Halesowen Town	BHL	2-2	822	Payne, Rhodes
22/02	**WATERLOOVILLE**	BHL	1-0	358	Rhodes(p)
26/02	**DORCHESTER TOWN**	BHL	0-0	576	
05/02	Cambridge City	BHL	0-0	264	
08/03	**GRESLEY ROVERS**	DMCsf(2)	0-1	1,738	
12/03	**HASTINGS TOWN**	BHL	2-0	422	Redfern, Rhodes
16/03	Atherstone Utd	BHL	1-3	362	Redfern
19/03	Chelmsford City	BHL	1-3	550	Redfern
26/03	Farnborough Town	BHL	0-2	538	
02/04	**GRESLEY ROVERS**	BHL	1-0	1,109	Howell
09/04	**ATHERSTONE UTD**	BHL	1-2	553	Rhodes
16/04	Bashley	BHL	0-1	144	
23/04	**CHELTENHAM TOWN**	BHL	1-1	706	Shearer
30/04	Sittingbourne	BHL	0-0	728	
02/05	Crawley Town	BHL	1-1	579	Howell
07/05	**SOLIHULL BORO.**	BHL	2-1	481	Howell, Shearer

Key: BHL: Beazer Homes League Premier Division, DMC: Doctor Martens (Beazer Homes League) Cup, FAC: F.A. Cup, FAT: F.A. Trophy, BSC: Birmingham Senior Cup. Numbers after cup competitions denote rounds (r: replay, qf: Quarter-Final, sf: Semi-Final, f: Final. Numbers in brackets indicate legs, i.e. (1): 1st leg).
Home fixtures are denoted by bold capitals, away matches by lower case. (p): penalty, og: Own goal.

SQUAD MEMBERS *(previous clubs listed in chronological order)*

GOALKEEPERS: Nicky Goodwin *(Graham Street Prims, Kettering Town, Shepshed Charterhouse, Kettering Town, Corby Town).*

DEFENDERS: Steve Nelson *(Northwich Victoria, Leek Town, Macclesfield Town, Telford Utd)*, **John Williams** *(Bromsgrove Rovers, Bilston Town)*, **Robbie Briscoe** *(Derby County, Gresley Rovers)*, **Gary Redgate** *(Atherstone Utd, VS Rugby)*, **Brian Donnelly** *(VS Rugby, Armitage)*, **Darren Robinson** *(Hull City, Loughborough University).*

MIDFIELD: Simon Redfern *(local)*, **Allan Davies** *(Manchester City)*, **Darren Grocutt** *(Northfield Town, Moor Green, Evesham Utd)*, **Karl Payne** *(youth)*, **Paul Simpson** *(Bilston, Tamworth, Hednesford, Armitage).*

FORWARDS: Peter Howell *(Aston Villa, Kidderminster Harriers)*, **Paul Gretton** *(local)*, **Nigel Mottram** *(Rocester)*, **Ian Doughty** *(youth)*, **Jason Rhodes** *(Birmingham City, Worcester City, Willenhall Town, Sandwell Borough, Armitage)*, **Danny Levers** *(local football).*

Formed: 1908

CAMBRIDGE CITY

Lilywhites

The Cambridge City side tnat took on Hereford United in the FA Cup First Round.

Photo - Eric Marsh.

Chairman: Dennis Rolph **President:** Sir Neil Westbrook, CBE MA FRICS
Secretary: Stuart Hamilton, 55 Crowhill, Godmanchester, Huntingdon, Cambs (0480 412266).
Manager: Steve Fallon **Asst Manager:** Tom Finney **Physio:** Colin Pettit
Press Officer: Secretary **Commercial Manager:** Jim Mills
Ground: City Ground, Milton Road, Cambridge CB4 1UY (0223 357973)
Directions: 50 yards on left from beginning of A1309, Cambridge to Ely Road. Half hour walk from Cambridge BR station.
Capacity: 5,000 **Cover:** 1,400 **Seats:** 400 **Floodlights:** Yes **Metal Badges:** Yes
Club Shop: Yes, selling programmes, club history, badges, scarves, pennants, replica shirts etc. Contact Neil Harvey (0223 235991).
Colours: White/black/white **Change colours:** All sky
Club Sponsors: Lancer UK **Previous Name:** Cambridge Town 1908-51.
Previous Leagues: Bury & Dist. 08-13 19-20/ East Anglian 08-10/ Southern Olympian 11-14/ Southern Amateur 1913-35/ Spartan 35-50/ Athenian 50-58.
Midweek matchday: Wednesday **Reserve Team's League:** Jewson Eastern Counties.
Record Attendance: 12,058 v Leytonstone, FA Amateur Cup 1st Rd, 1949-50.
Best FA Cup season: 1st Rd; v Ashford 1966, v Swindon 1946, v Walthamstow Ave. 1948, v Hereford 1993.
Record Fee Paid: £7,000 for Andy Beattie (Barnet, 1991).
Record Fee Received: £15,500 for Kevin Wilkin (Northampton Town, 1991).
Players who have progressing to Football League: Ken Wright (West Ham 1946), Antonio Gallego (Norwich 1947), Alf Stokes (Watford 1961), Derek Weddle (Middlesbrough 1961), Dave Hicksen (Bury 1962), Bryan Harvey (Blackpool 1962), Robert Whitehead (Darlington 1962), George Cummins (Hull 1962), Reg Pearce & Dom Genovese (Peterborough 1963 & 88), Alan Banks (Exeter 1963), Tom Carroll (Ipswich 1966), Roy Jones (Swindon), Winston Dubose (Oldham).
Clubhouse: 11am-11pm Mon-Sat, 12-3pm & 7pm-10.30pm Sun. Bingo, Dances, Pool, Stag nights, Darts.
Club Record Scorer: Gary Grogan
Club Record Appearances: Mal Keenan
93-94 Captain: Steve Gawthrop.
93-94 Top Scorer: Laurie Ryan.
93-94 Players' P.o.Y.: Laurie Ryan.
93-94 Supporters' P.o.Y.: Laurie Ryan.
Local Press: Cambridge Evening News 35877
Local Radio: BBC Radio Cambridge
Honours: Southern Lg 62-63 (R-up 70-71, Southern Div 85-86, Div 1 R-up 69-70, Championship Cup 62-63), East Anglian Cup 30-31 35-36 42-43 43-44 45-46 47-48 59-60 64-65 75-76, Eastern Professional Floodlit Lg 65-66 72-73, Cambs Professional Cup 60-61 61-62 62-63 70-71 72-73 74-75, Cambs Invitation Cup 50-51 76-77 78-79 85-86 88-89 89-90, Spartan Lg 47-48 48-49 (R-up 49-50, Eastern Div Champs 45-46), Southern Amateur Lg 20-21 27-28 28-29 30-31 31-32, Bury & Dist. Lg 09-10 10-11 12-13 19-20, East Anglian Lg 09-10 39-40 40-41 41-42 42-43 44-45, AFA Snr Cup 30-31 46-47 47-48(shared) 48-49 49-50, AFA Invitation Cup 50-51, Hunts Premier Cup 62-63 64-65, Suffolk Senior Cup 09-10, FA Trophy 2nd Rd 86-87 87-88, FA Amateur Cup SF 27-28, Addenbrookes Hospital Cup 87-88, The Munns Youth Cup 82-83 83-84 84-85, Chiltern Youth League Cup R-up 75-76, South Mids Lg Youth Trophy 82-83, Robinson Cup 87-88 89-90, Jim Digney 89-90, Essex & Herts Youth Lg 89-90.

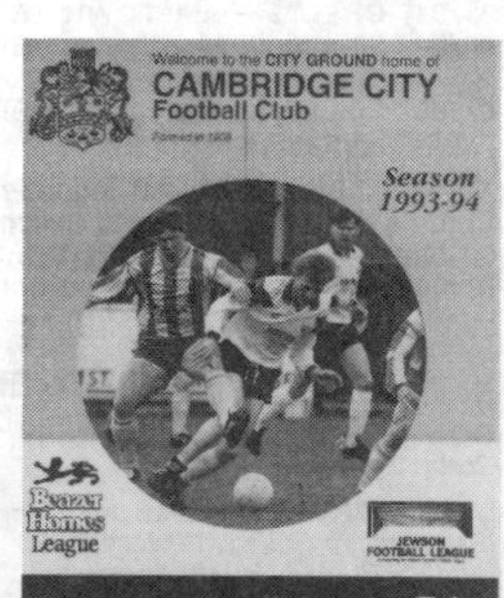

PROGRAMME DETAILS:
Pages: 28 **Price:** 50p
Editor: Dave Crane
(0223 233057)

CAMBRIDGE CITY's 1993-94 CAMPAIGN

Date	Opponents	Comp.	Res	Gate	Goalscorers
21/08	**MOOR GREEN**	BHL	1-3	281	Grogan
24/08	Gresley Rovers	BHL	1-2	835	Goddard
28/08	Trowbridge Town	BHL	0-0	387	
30/08	**HASTINGS TOWN**	BHL	1-0	321	Gawthrop
04/09	**CHELTENHAM TOWN**	BHL	1-1	333	Coe
07/09	Atherstone United	BHL	1-0	421	Coe
11/09	**BERKHAMSTED T.**	FAC1q	4-1	223	Grogan, Coe, Wilkin(2)
18/09	**HALESOWEN TOWN**	BHL	3-2	330	Ryan, Wilkin, Coe
25/09	**HARWICH & PARK.**	FAC2q	3-0	327	Ryan, Coe, Tovey
02/10	Worcester City	BHL	0-2	783	
06/10	**KING'S LYNN**	DMC1(1)	4-1	176	Ryan(4)
09/10	Hendon	FAC3q	1-0	382	Grogan
16/10	**CHELMSFORD CITY**	FAC2q	1-1	344	Covey
18/10	Chelmsford City	FAT2qr	2-3	452	Gawthrop, Tovey
23/10	**DAGENHAM & R.**	FAC4q	2-2	1,026	Wilkin, Ryan
25/10	Dagenham & Redbridge	FAC4qr	2-0	1,410	Grogan, Conner(og)
30/10	Bashley	BHL	2-0	241	Grogan, Ryan
02/11	King's Lynn	DMC1(2)	3-0	242	Pincher(2), Wilkin
06/11	**GLOUCESTER CITY**	BHL	2-0	447	Ryan(2)
09/11	Rushden & Diamonds	DMC2	2-2	419	Ryan(2)
14/11	**HEREFORD UNITED**	FAC1	0-1	2,325	
20/11	**HEDNESFORD TOWN**	BHL	4-1	297	Ryan(2), Pincher, Coe
27/11	**GRESLEY ROVERS**	BHL	1-0	308	Ryan
30/11	Hertford Town	EAC1	4-2	39	Tovey, Pincher, Goddard, Wilkin
04/12	**FARNBOROUGH T.**	BHL	1-5	330	Ryan
07/12	**RUSHDEN & DIAM.**	DMC2	3-1	167	Ryan(2), Wilkin
09/12	Histon	CIC1	2-5	47	Ryan, Baker
11/12	Moor Green	BHL	1-0	217	Ryan
15/12	Corby Town	DMC3	1-2	97	Ryan
18/12	**CRAWLEY TOWN**	BHL	0-1	315	
27/12	**CORBY TOWN**	BHL	1-1	344	Wilkin
01/01	Nuneaton Boro.	BHL	1-0	1,408	Gawthrop
03/01	**CHELMSFORD CITY**	BHL	1-3	445	Beattie
08/01	Solihull Boro	BHL	0-2	184	
15/01	Burton Albion	BHL	1-1	735	Ryan
18/01	Sittingbourne	BHL	2-3	1,107	Beattie, Lockhart
22/01	**TROWBRIDGE TOWN**	BHL	2-0	227	Edey, Ryan
25/01	Biggleswade	EAC2	3-0	134	Wilkins, Fallon, Pincher
29/01	Cheltenham Town	BHL	1-2	839	Ryan
05/02	Halesowen Town	BHL	0-3	638	Howells, S Jones
09/02	**SITTINGBOURNE**	BHL	2-2	323	Edey, Tovey
12/02	**DORCHESTER TOWN**	BHL	1-2	249	Ryan
19/02	Farnborough Town	BHL	2-2	523	Scott, Ryan
26/02	**WORCESTER CITY**	BHL	4-3	218	Gawthrop, Ryan(2), Wilkin
05/03	**BURTON ALBION**	BHL	0-0	264	
12/03	Hednesford Town	BHL	1-4	287	Lockhart
16/03	Harlow Town	EAC3	3-0	32	Pope(2), Lockhart
19/03	**ATHERSTONE UTD**	BHL	0-0	176	
20/03	Crawley Town	BHL	1-2	903	Ryan
02/04	Corby Town	BHL	0-0	282	
09/04	Chelmsford City	BHL	0-2	547	
16/04	**SOLIHULL BORO.**	BHL	0-2	224	
19/04	**WATERLOOVILLE**	BHL	3-0	201	Pope(2), Ryan
21/04	**NUNEATON BORO.**	BHL	3-0	222	Scott(2), Ryan
23/04	Gloucester City	BHL	1-2	455	Fallon
26/04	Dorchester Town	BHL	1-3	415	Scott
30/04	**BASHLEY**	BHL	1-1	210	Lockhart
02/05	Hastings Town	BHL	0-1	375	
04/05	Wroxham	EACqf	2-0	93	Grogan, McLean
07/05	Waterlooville	BHL	2-2	176	Lockhart, Pammenter
08/05	**MIDDLESEX WDRS**	CENT	2-0		

East Anglian Cup Semi-Final - held over to 1994-95

Key: BHL: Beazer Homes League Premier Division, DMC: Doctor Martens (Beazer Homes League) Cup, FAC: F.A. Cup, FAT: F.A. Trophy, EAC: East Anglian Cup, CIC: Cambridgeshire Invitation Cup, CENT: Centenary Match.

SQUAD MEMBERS *(previous clubs listed in chronological order)*

GOALKEEPERS: Kevin Murray *(Camb. C., Saffron Walden)*, **Vince Garner** *(Histon)*, **Barry Piggott** *(Royston).*

DEFENDERS: Steve Fallon *(Kettering, Camb. Utd., Histon)*, **Chris Tovey** *(Letchworth GC, Royston, Camb. C., Royston)*, **Mark Scott** *(Potton Utd.)*, **Andy Beattie** *(Camb. Utd., Barnet, Maidstone Utd., Barnet, Camb. C., Hendon)*, **Wayne Goddard** *(Histon).*

MIDFIELD: Steve Gawthrop *(Youth Team)*,, **Keith Lockhart** *(Camb. Utd., Wolves, Hartlepool, Camb. C., Sudbury)*, **Andy Pincher** *(Camb. Utd.)*, **Gary Haylock** *(Histon)*,, **Neil O'Donohue** *(Camb. C., Eynesbury R., St Ives)*, **John McLean** *(Northallerton, Whitby, Histon, Camb. C., Newmarkest, Eynesbury R).*

FORWARDS: Laurie Ryan *(Chesham Utd., Dunstable, Camb. Utd.)*, **Gary Grogan** *(Camb. C., Soham, Camb. C., Barnstaple, Ely)*, **Martin Pammenter** *(Histon)*, **Paul Wilkin** *(Histon)*, **Neil Pope** *(Camb. Utd., Peterborough, Camb. C., St Ives, Eynesbury R.).*

Formed: 1938

CHELMSFORD CITY

Clarets

Chelmsford defender Mark Keen tackles Welling's Stuart White in an FA Trophy tie. *Photo - Keith Gillard.*

CHELMSFORD CITY HAVE LIVED THROUGH A TRAUMATIC SUMMER DURING WHICH THE CLUB ALMOST FOLDED. AT THE TIME OF GOING TO PRESS, NO PERSONNEL INFORMATION WAS AVAILABLE.

Ground: The Stadium, New Writtle Street, Chelmsford CM2 0RP (0245 353052).
Directions: A1016 (Chelmsford) exit off A12, follow Colchester signs to 3rd r'bout, left (B1007, New London Rd), left at 2nd lights (signed County Cricket Ground), ground 100 yds on right. Residents only parking in New Writtle Street, but there is public car park next to ground (£1.30). 5 mins walk from Chelmsford (BR) station.
Capacity: 2,850 (Police limit) **Seats:** 1,296 **Cover:** 1,700 **Metal Badges:** Yes
Club Shop: Yes, selling League & non-League programmes, badges, scarves, mugs etc. Contact Helen Williams or Rob Wigley via club.
Colours: White/claret/white. **Change colours:** Claret/white/claret. **Sponsors:** TBA.
Midweek home games: Monday **Reserve Team's League:** Essex & Herts Border Comb.
Previous Name: None (Brentwood Town were incorporated in 1968).
Previous Leagues: None **Record Gate:** 16,807 v Colchester, Southern League 10/9/49.
Best FA Cup season: 4th Rd Proper, 1938-39 (v Birmingham City). 1st Rd Proper on 25 occasions.
League clubs defeated in FA Cup: Darlington 38-39, Southampton 38-39, Oxford Utd 67-68.
Record win: 10-3 v Billericay Town (H), Essex Senior Cup, 4/1/93.
Record defeat: 2-10 v Barking (A), FA Trophy, 11/11/78.
Record Fee Paid: £10,000 for Tony Rogers (Dover Athletic, 1992).
Received: £20,000 from Ian Brown (Bristol City, 1993).
Players progressing to Football League: Geoff Merton (Watford 1948), George Adams (Orient 1949), William O'Neill (Burnley 1949), Brian Farley & Sid McClellan (Spurs 1949), Oscar Hold (Everton 1950), Reuben Marden (Arsenal 1950), Cecil McCormack (Barnsley 1950), Les Dicker (Spurs 1951), Dave Sexton (Luton 1951), Wally Bellet & Robert Mason & Anthony Nicholas (Orient 1961 & 63 & 65), Robin Gladwin (Norwich 1966), Brian King (Millwall 1967), Peter Collins (Spurs 1968), John O'Mara (Bradford City 1974), Nigel Spink (Aston Villa 1977), Mark Dziadulewicz (Wimbledon 1979), Mervyn Cawston (Southend 1984), Phil Coleman (Exeter 1984), John Keeley & Adrian Owers (Brighton 1986 & 87), Ian Brown (Bristol City 1993).
Clubhouse: Open matchdays & every evening except Sunday (open Sunday lunchtimes). Pool, darts, satellite TV. Available for private hire. Playing facilities also available for private hire. Snacks served.
Club Record Goalscorer: Tony Butcher, 287 (1957-71).
Club Record Appearances: Derek Tiffin, 550 (1950-63).
Captain 93-94: Steve Mosely.
Top Scorer 93-94: Steve Restarick.
Player of the Year 93-94: Tony Rogers.
Local Newspapers: Essex Chronicle (0245 262421), Chelmsford Weekly News (0245 493444), East Anglian Daily Times (0473 230023).
Local Radio Stations: Essex Radio/Breeze AM, BBC Essex.
Hons: Southern Lg 45-46 67-68 71-72 (R-up 48-49 60-61 63-64 65-66, Southern Div 88-89, Lg Cup 45-46 59-60 (R-up 60-61), Merit Cup 71-72, Southern Lg War-Time (East) 39-40), Essex Professional Cup(5) 57-58 69-71 73-75, Essex Snr Cup 85-86 88-89 92-93, Non-League Champs Challenge Cup 71-72, E Anglian Cup 48-49, Eastern Co's Lg(3) 46-49 (Lg Cup 59-60), Eastern Floodlit Competition 66-67 74-75 77-78 81-82 82-83 86-87 (Cup 72-73 74-75), Metropolitan Lg 67-68 (Lg Professional Cup 67-68, Autumn Shield 70-71), Essex Snr Lg Cup 84-85 (Harry Fisher Memorial Tphy 88-89).

PROGRAMME DETAILS:
Pages: 32 **Price:** £1
Editor: Steve Dorrington
(0245 251667)

CHELMSFORD CITY's 1993-94 CAMPAIGN

Date	Opponents	Comp.	Res	Gate	Goalscorers
21/08	Cheltenham Town	BHL	0-5	731	
23/08	**ATHERSTONE UTD**	BHL	0-0	552	
28/08	**DORCHESTER TOWN**	BHL	3-0	487	Davidson(2), Restarick
30/08	Corby Town	BHL	0-0	253	
04/09	Burton Albion	BHL	0-0	614	
06/09	**BUCKINGHAM TOWN**	DMC1(1)	2-1	287	Morrison, Rogers
11/09	**NEWMARKET TOWN**	FAC1q	0-0	438	
14/09	Newmarket Town	FAC1qr	1-1	302	Moseley
18/09	Ruislip Manor	FAT1q	4-1	203	Jones, Restarick, Garvey, Howard
20/09	**NEWMARKET TOWN**	FAT2qr	3-0	489	Jenkins, Restarick, Rogers
25/09	**STAMFORD**	FAC2q	5-2	486	Garvey, Rogers(2), Jenkins, Restarick
28/09	Buckingham Town	DMC1(2)	1-2	85	Restarick *(lost 2-4 on penalties)*
02/10	**GLOUCESTER CITY**	BHL	2-1	525	Restarick, Davidson
09/10	Wivenhoe Town	FAC3q	0-2	676	
16/10	Cambridge City	FAT2q	1-1	344	Davidson
18/10	**CAMBRIDGE CITY**	FAT2qr	3-2	452	Rogers, Davidson(2)
23/10	**WORCESTER CITY**	BHL	2-1	503	Hoddy, Davidson
30/10	**WATERLOOVILLE**	BHL	3-2	570	Restarick, Morrison, Davidson
02/11	Braintree Town	ESC1	1-1	326	Jenkins
06/11	Halesowen Town	BHL	1-3	712	Davidson
08/11	**IPSWICH TOWN**	TEST	0-4	1,584	
13/11	**GRESLEY ROVERS**	BHL	2-1	465	Garvey(2)
15/11	**CORBY TOWN**	BHL	2-3	469	Restarick, Davidson
20/11	Nuneaton Borough	BHL	1-1	1,195	Symonds(og)
27/11	VS Rugby	FAT3q	3-0	426	Rogers, Davidson, Restarick
29/11	**BRAINTREE TOWN**	ESC1r	2-0	241	Brush, Restarick
01/12	**HALSTEAD TOWN**	EFC	0-5	104	
04/12	**TROWBRIDGE TOWN**	BHL	3-1	501	Davidson, Rogers, Baverstock(og)
11/12	**CHELTENHAM TOWN**	BHL	0-1	519	
18/12	Dorchester City	BHL	0-1	492	
21/12	Aveley	ESCqf	5-3	70	Rogers(2), Keen, Morrison(2)
27/12	Sittingbourne	BHL	2-1	1,795	Restarick(2)
01/01	**CRAWLEY TOWN**	BHL	1-2	851	Hannigan
03/01	Cambridge City	BHL	3-1	445	Restarick, Morrison, Rogers
08/01	**MOOR GREEN**	BHL	1-1	682	Rogers
15/01	Gloucester City	BHL	5-2	538	Rogers, Restarick, Jenkins, Garvey(2)
18/01	Sudbury Town	ETC	1-2	181	Fox
22/01	Welling United	FAT1	1-6	1,108	Keen
25/01	Halstead Town	EFC	3-3	170	Brooks, Fox, Hoddy
29/01	Bashley	BHL	5-1	212	Morrison, Restarick(3), Owers
31/01	**SUDBURY TOWN**	EFC	2-1	108	Fox, Rogers
05/02	**SOLIHULL BORO.**	BHL	3-1	670	Hannigan, Rogers, Restarick
08/02	Farnborough Town	BHL	6-7	527	Rogers(3), Hannigan, Restarick, Morrison
12/02	Atherstone United	BHL	0-3	306	
14/02	**HASTINGS TOWN**	BHL	0-2	319	
19/02	**NUNEATON BORO.**	BHL	1-1	635	Rogers
22/02	Billericay Town	ESCsf	1-2	304	Rogers
26/02	**HALESOWEN TOWN**	BHL	0-1	218	
02/03	Solihull Borough	BHL	1-0	77	Rogers
05/03	Waterlooville	BHL	1-0	274	Keen
07/02	**STANSTED**	EFC	6-0	108	Keen, Hannigan(2), Howard, Davidson, Morrison
12/03	Gresley Rovers	BHL	1-2	556	Rogers
19/03	**BURTON ALBION**	BHL	3-1	559	Restarick(2), Garvey
21/03	Hednesford Town	BHL	2-1	397	Restarick, Hoddy
26/03	Hastings Town	BHL	1-3	439	Howard
02/04	**SITTINGBOURNE**	BHL	2-3	703	Morrison, Hannigan
09/04	**CAMBRIDGE CITY**	BHL	2-0	547	Rogers, Martin
11/04	**FARNBOROUGH T.**	BHL	1-0	907	Rogers
16/04	Moor Green	BHL	1-3	226	Rogers
23/04	Worcester City	BHL	1-1	668	Restarick
26/04	Crawley Town	BHL	2-0	1,052	Rogers(2)
30/04	Trowbridge Town	BHL	1-2	332	Garvey
07/05	**HEDNESFORD TOWN**	BHL	4-1	583	Restarick(3), Rogers

Key: BHL: Beazer Homes League Premier Division, DMC: Doctor Martens (Beazer Homes League) Cup, FAC: F.A. Cup, FAT: F.A. Trophy, ESC: Dorset Senior Cup, EFC: Eastern Floodlit Competition, TEST: Don Walker Testimonial.

SQUAD MEMBERS *(previous clubs listed in chronological order)*

GOALKEEPERS: Micky Desborough *(Clapton, Hornchurch, Aveley, Purfleet).*

DEFENDERS: Steve Moseley *(Stambridge, Billericay, Barking, Dartford, Enfield),* **Robbie Garvey** *(Purfleet, Billericay, Grays, Dartford, Redbridge F., Hendon),* **Dean Crumpton** *(West Ham, Dagenham, Basildon, Grays, Billericay, Grays),* **Steve Tapley** *(Fulham, Wealdstone, Enfield, Yeovil, Wealdstone, Harrow, Wealdstone),* **Liam Cutbush** *(Tiptree, Braintree, Dartford, Grays, Braintree, Aveley, Heybridge),* **Eddie Martin** *(Spurs, Dulwich, Carshalton, Dagenham, Bishop's Stortford, Dagenham, Carshalton, Aveley, Dagenham & R.),* **David Jacques** *(Leytonstone-Ilford, Dartford, Enfield, Maidstone, Dagenham & R.)*

MIDFIELD: Kevin Hoddy *(Fulham, Charlton Athletic, FC Roselare(Belg.), Welling Utd.),* **Wayne Hannigan** *(Home Farm, Colchester Utd., Chelmsford C., Shamrock R.),* **Mark Keen** *(Witham T., Dartford, Enfield),* **Paul Goyette** *(West Ham Utd., Tilbury, Dagenham, Maidstone Utd., Wealdstone).* **Gary Howard** *(Gt Wakering R., Stambridge, Enfield, Grays Athletic, Brighton),* **Adrian Owers** *(Southend Utd., Chelmsford C., Brighton, Maidstone Utd., Dagenham & Redbridge),* **Mark Jenkins** *(Southend Utd., Southend Manor, Basildon Utd., Southend Manor, Billericay T.).*

FORWARDS: Steve Restarick *(West Ham, Colchester Utd.)* **Dave Morrison** *(Southend Utd),* **Kurt Davidson** *(Ford Utd., Barking, Hornchurch, Leytonstone-Ilford, Billericay, Dartford, Redbridge Forest, Hendon),* **Tony Rogers** *(Basildon Utd., Leytonstone-Ilford, Tilbury, Dartford, Barking Maidstone Utd., Dover Athletic).*

1892 **CHELTENHAM TOWN** Robins

Cheltenham Town's Steve Jones heads just over the Bath City cross-bar as he overcomes a challenge from Ian Hedges. The Robins were pegged back to a 1-1 draw by a last gasp City equaliser in this FA Cup Fourth Qualifying Round tie at Whaddon Road.

Photo - Gavin Ellis-Neville.

Chairman: Arthur Hayward **President:** Vacant
Secretary: Reg Woodward, 3 Harveys Lane, Winchcombe, Glos GL54 5QS (0242 602261).
Manager: Lindsay Parsons **Asst Manager:** TBA **Coach:**
Press Officer: Arthur Hayward **Physio:** John Atkinson
Commercial Manager: P G Cook.
Ground: Whaddon Road, Cheltenham, Gloucestershire GL52 5NA (0242 513397).
Directions: M5 jct 10, A4019 through Cheltenham centre and join B4632 Prestbury Road. Whaddon Rd turning on right. M5 jct 11, A40 into Cheltenham, join A46 Bath Road, follow through town and join Prestbury Road, Whaddon Rd on right. From London; A40 into Cheltenham and join A46 at Hewlett Rd then as above. Ground 1 mile from town centre and 2 miles from Cheltenham (BR).
Capacity: 5,000 **Cover:** 4,000 **Seats:** 1,000 **Floodlights:** Yes **Metal Badges:** Yes
Club Shop: Yes, selling souvenirs of all descriptions.
Colours: Red & white stripes **Change colours:** White (navy trim) **Sponsors:** TBA
Midweek home games: Tuesday **Reserve's Lge:** Neville Ovenden Football Combination.
Previous Leagues: Birmingham Combination/ Birmingham Lge/ Southern 35-85/ GMV Conference 85-92.
Record Attendance: 8,326 v Reading, FA Cup 1st Rd 56-57.
Best F.A. Cup season: 3rd Rd Proper 33-34 (lost 1-2 at Blackpool).
League clubs defeated in F.A. Cup: Carlisle United 33-34.
Record Fee Paid: £20,000 to Kidderminster Harriers (Kim Casey)
Received: £45,000 from Derby County (Brett Angell).
Players progressing to Football League: Paul Tester (Shrewsbury), Brett Angell (Derby), Keith Knight (Reading), Peter Shearer (Bournemouth), Simon Brain (Hereford), Chris Burns (Portsmouth).
Clubhouse: Open every evening. 3 bars; clubroom, lounge, Robin's Nest. Open before and after Saturday matches. Nest & clubroom Available for private hire.
Club Record Scorer: Dave Lewis 290 (1970-83)
Club Record Apps: Roger Thorndale 701 (58-76)
93-94 Captain: Neil Smith
93-94 P.o.Y.: Martin Thomas.
93-94 Top scorer: Jason Eaton, 19.
Local Newspapers: Echo/ Western Daily Press.
Local Radio Stations: Radio Glos/ Severn Sound.
Hons: Southern Lg 84-85 (R-up 92-93 93-94, Midland Div 82-83, Lg Cup 57-58 (R-up 68-69 84-85), Championship Shield 58-59, Merit Cup 84-85), Nth Glos. Snr Professional Cup(29), Midland Floodlit Cup 85-86 86-87 87-88.

PROGRAMME DETAILS:
Pages: 24 **Price:** £1
Editor: Paul Godfrey
(0242 517554)

CHELTENHAM TOWN's 1993-94 CAMPAIGN

Date	Opponents	Comp.	Res	Gate	Goalscorers
21/08	**CHELMSFORD CITY**	BHL	5-0	731	Iddles(2), Howells, N Smith, Hirons
24/08	Halesowen Town	BHL	1-1	923	Howells
28/08	Nuneaton Borough	BHL	1-2	1,212	Howells
30/08	**MOOR GREEN**	BHL	3-1	702	Lovell, Howells, Mortimore
04/09	Cambridge City	BHL	1-1	334	Mortimore
07/09	**HEDNESFORD TOWN**	BHL	3-0	665	N Smith, J Smith, Mortimore
11/09	**CRAWLEY TOWN**	BHL	1-3	827	J Smith
18/09	Corby Town	BHL	1-1	326	Mortimore
25/09	Farnborough Town	BHL	1-1	535	Weston
28/09	Weston-super-Mare	DMC1(1)	1-3	327	Howells
02/10	**GRESLEY ROVERS**	BHL	1-1	689	J Smith
16/10	Atherstone United	BHL	2-3	362	J Smith, Eaton
19/10	**WESTON-s.-MARE**	DMC1(2)	4-1	286	Eaton(2), N Smith, Howells
23/10	**BATH CITY**	FAC4q	1-1	1,020	Eaton
26/10	Bath City	FAC4qr	2-4	1,166	J Smith, Eaton
30/10	Solihull Borough	BHL	2-1	309	N Smith, Eaton
02/11	**GLOUCESTER CITY**	GSC	0-1	449	
06/11	**WORCESTER CITY**	BHL	1-0	738	J Smith
09/11	**TROWBRIDGE TOWN**	DMC2	2-3	353	Eaton, Bloomer
20/11	**ATHERSTONE UTD**	BHL	5-1	468	Bloomer, Howells, J Smith(2), Eaton
27/11	Trowbridge Town	FAT3q	1-1	467	Mortimore
30/11	**TROWBRIDGE TOWN**	FAT3qr	1-0	489	J Smith
04/12	**BURTON ALBION**	BHL	1-0	701	Warren
11/12	Chelmsford City	BHL	1-0	519	Howells
18/12	**NUNEATON BORO.**	BHL	1-0	863	S Jones
21/12	Moor Green	BHL	2-1	319	N Smith, Howells
27/12	**TROWBRIDGE TOWN**	BHL	0-1	1,444	
01/01	Gloucester City	BHL	3-1	1,239	Cooper, J Smith(2)
03/01	**DORCHESTER TOWN**	BHL	0-1	840	
08/01	Hastings Town	BHL	1-1	432	J Smith
15/01	Waterlooville	BHL	3-0	243	Eaton(2), Brown
18/01	**HALESOWEN TOWN**	BHL	3-1	759	Howells, J Smith, Eaton
22/01	**NUNEATON BORO.**	FAT1	1-0	1,118	S Jones
29/01	**CAMBRIDGE CITY**	BHL	2-1	839	Brown, J Smith
01/02	Crawley Town	BHL	1-0	1,356	Cooper
05/02	Gresley Rovers	BHL	1-1	811	Howells
12/02	**HEDNESFORD TOWN**	FAT2	1-0	965	N Smith
19/02	Sittingbourne	BHL	3-1	2,159	Bloomer, Lovell, Eaton
05/03	**GUISELEY**	FAT3	0-0	1,117	
08/03	Guiseley	FAT3r	0-1	1,139	
12/03	**BASHLEY**	BHL	2-0	775	Howells, S Jones
19/03	Worcester City	BHL	1-1	1,107	Howells
22/03	**SITTINGBOURNE**	BHL	0-0	1,071	
26/03	**CORBY TOWN**	BHL	4-1	866	Wring, Warren, Eaton(2)
29/03	**FARNBOROUGH T.**	BHL	1-1	1,559	Eaton
02/04	Trowbridge Town	BHL	2-2	598	J Smith, Eaton
04/04	**GLOUCESTER CITY**	BHL	0-1	1,806	
09/04	Dorchester Town	BHL	2-0	580	Warren, Eaton
16/04	**HASTINGS TOWN**	BHL	1-0	846	Eaton
18/04	Hednesford Town	BHL	0-2	515	
23/04	Burton Albion	BHL	1-1	706	Diaz
24/04	**WATERLOOVILLE**	BHL	1-0	1,065	Mortimore
30/04	**SOLIHULL BORO.**	BHL	1-2	1,062	Howells
07/05	Bashley	BHL	1-2	403	Wring

Key: BHL: Beazer Homes League Premier Division, DMC: Doctor Martens (Beazer Homes League) Cup, FAC: F.A. Cup, FAT: F.A. Trophy, GSC: North Gloucestershire Senior Professional Cup. Number after cup competitions denote rounds (r: replay, qf: Quarter-Final, sf: Semi-Final, f: Final. Numbers in brackets indicate legs, i.e. (1): 1st leg).
Home fixtures are denoted by bold capitals, away matches by lower case. (p): penalty, og: Own goal.

SQUAD MEMBERS *(previous clubs listed in chronological order)*

GOALKEEPERS: Martin Thomas *(Bristol Rovers, Newcastle Utd, Birmingham City).*

DEFENDERS: Steve Brown *(Birmingham),* **Bob Bloomer** *(Chesterfield, Bristol Rovers),* **Richsrd Clark** *(Cheltenham Town, Port Vale, Cheltenham Town, Moreton Town, Forest Green Rovers),* **Craig Dore** *(Cardiff City, Worcester City, Witney Town),* **Lee Howells** *(Bristol Rovers, Queensland(Aust)),* **Vaughan Jones** *(Bristol Rovers, Newport County, Cardiff City, Bristol Rovers).*

MIDFIELD: Neil Smith *(Shrewsbury Town, Redditch Utd, Lincoln City),* **Simon Cooper** *(YTS),* **Jimmy Wring** *(Bristol Rovers, Bath City, Mangotsfield),* **Matthew Lovell** *(Bournemouth),* **Steve Jones** *(Forest Green Rovers),* **Andy Tucker** *(YTS).*

FORWARDS: Jimmy Smith *(Torquay, Salisbury),* **Christer Warren** *(YTS),* **Jason Eaton** *(Trowbridge, Bristol Rovers, Bristol City, Gloucester),* **Paul Mortimore** *(YTS).*

Formed: 1948

CORBY TOWN

The Steelmen

Corby Town's Rockingham Triangle Stadium.

Photo - Jonathan Green.

Chairman: A Wetherell **President:** H Hqtterley.
Secretary: Roger Abraham, 68 Cornwall Rd, Kettering, Northants NN16 8PE (0536 522159).
Mgr: Gerry McElhinney/Bryn Gunn **Coach:** TBA
Commercial Mgr: Lorraine Sims **Physio:** Gerry Lucas.
Ground: Rockingham Triangle Stadium, Rockingham Road, Corby NN17 2AE (0536 401007).
Directions: On northern outskirts of town at junction of A6003 and A6116, opposite entrance to Rockingham Castle grounds. One and a half miles from Corby (BR).
Capacity: 3,000 **Cover:** 1,150 **Seats:** 960 **Floodlights:** Yes **Metal Badges:** Yes
Club Shop: Yes, selling metal badges & programmes etc. Contact C Woolmer (0536 260900).
Colours: White & black stripes **Change colours:** All yellow.
Midweek home matchday: Wednesday **Previous Leagues:** United Counties 35-52/ Midland 52-58.
Prev. Name: Stewart & Lloyds 1935-48. **Previous Ground:** Occupation Road 1935-85.
Club Sponsor: Mr Bips.
Reserve Team's League: Hereward Sports United Counties League Reserve Division.
Record Attendance: 2,240 v Watford, pre-season friendly 86-87. At Old Ground; 10,239 v Peterborough United, FA Cup Third Qualifying Round 52-53.
Record win: 14-0 v Gainsborough Trinity, 56-57. **Record defeat:** 0-9 v Merthyr Tydfil, 78-79.
Best FA Trophy season: 3rd Rd, 1986-87.
Best FA Cup season: 3rd Rd 65-66 (lost to Plymouth). 1st Rd on five occasions; 54-55 63-66 67-68.
League clubs defeated in F.A. Cup: Luton Town 65-66.
Record Fees - Paid: £2,700 for Elwyn Roberts (Barnet, 1981)
Received: £20,000 for Matt Murphy (Oxford United, 1993).
Players progressing to Football League: Andy McCabe (Chesterfield 1955), Les Clalmers (Leicester City 1956), Ken Brown (Nottm Forest 1956), Peter Kearns (Aldershot 1962), Norman Dean (Southampton 1963), Hugh Curran (Millwall 1964), Dixie McNeil & Andy McGowan & George Reilly (Northampton 1969 & 75 & 76), Phil Chard (Peterborough 1979), Trevor Morley (West Ham), J Flower (Sheffield Utd, Aldershot), Matt Murphy (Oxford United 1993), Chris McKenzie (Hereford 1994).
Clubhouse: No - only VP Lounge open matchdays only for one hour before game and two hours after.
Club Record Scorer: David Hofbauer 137 (1984-93)
Club Record Appearances: Derek Walker 600 (78-92).
93-94 Captain: Dougie Keast (now Rushden)/S Devine.
93-94 Player of the Year: C McKenzie.
93-94 Top scorer: Calvin Plummer.
Local Newspapers: Northampton Evening Telegraph (0536 81111).
Local Radio Stations: BBC Radio Northampton, Hereward and KCBC.
Hons: UCL 50-51 51-52 (R-up 37-38), Midland Lg R-up 52-53, Southern Lg Midland Div R-up 90-91 (Merit Cup 63-64 90-91), Northants Snr Cup 37-38 39-40 50-51 62-63 75-76 82-83, Maunsell Cup 83-84, Daventry Charity Cup 93-94, Midland Floodlit Cup 74-75, Evans Halshaw F'lit Cup 91-92, Anglia Floodlit Trophy 68-69 72-73, Chelmsford Invitation Cup 63-64 64-65 65-66(joint), Kettering & Dist Samaritan Cup 60-61(joint) 68-69, Wellingborough Charity Cup 50-51, Desborough Nursing Cup 48-49 50-51(joint), Bob Cumning Cup 85-86 86-87 87-88 88-89 92-93 93-94.

PROGRAMME DETAILS:
Pages: 32 **Price:** £1
Editor: C Smith
(0536 522159)

CORBY TOWN's 1993-94 CAMPAIGN

Date	Opponents	Comp.	Res	Gate	Goalscorers
21/08	**GLOUCESTER CITY**	BHL	2-1	350	Plummer(2)
24/08	Hednesford Town	BHL	1-3	490	Rayment
28/08	Halesowen Town	BHL	0-2	655	
30/08	**CHELMSFORD CITY**	BHL	0-0	253	
04/09	**BASHLEY**	BHL	1-2	243	Plummer
07/09	Gresley Rovers	BHL	0-1	765	
11/09	**WATTON UNITED**	FAC1q	4-0	202	Plummer(2), Archer, Rayment
18/09	**CHELTENHAM TOWN**	BHL	1-1	326	Thomas
25/09	Stevenage Borough	FAC2q	3-4	707	Plummer(2), Devine
02/10	Dorchester Town	BHL	0-0	463	
09/10	**WORCESTER CITY**	BHL	3-2	292	McInerney(2), Thomas
12/10	Daventry Town	NSC1	3-0	50	McInerney(2), Garner(og)
16/10	Trowbridge Town	BHL	1-1	347	Plummer
19/10	Atherstone Utd	DMC1(1)	1-1	235	Gunn
23/10	Burton Albion	BHL	0-1	523	
27/10	**ATHERSTONE UTD**	DMC1(2)	1-0	110	Keast
30/10	Farnborough Town	BHL	0-1	461	
06/11	**HASTINGS TOWN**	BHL	0-1	296	
13/11	Solihull Borough	BHL	2-1	196	Gunn, Plummer
15/11	Chelmsford City	BHL	3-2	469	Thomas(2), Keast
23/11	Bilston Town	DMC2	3-1	28	McInerney(3)
27/11	Enfield	FAT3q	1-2	440	McInerney
11/12	Gloucester City	BHL	4-2	289	Thomas(2), Plummer(2)
15/12	**CAMBRIDGE CITY**	BHL	2-1	98	Plummer, Thomas
18/12	**TROWBRIDGE TOWN**	BHL	1-0	201	Thomas
27/12	Cambridge City	BHL	1-1	344	Thomas
01/01	**ATHERSTONE UTD**	BHL	1-0	335	Thomas
03/01	Moor Green	BHL	4-0	238	Thomas(2), McInerney, Plummer
08/01	**CRAWLEY TOWN**	BHL	5-1	371	Thomas(3), Archer, Keast
12/01	**LONG BUCKBY**	NSCqf	2-0	84	McInerney, Thomas
15/01	**SOLIHULL BORO.**	BHL	1-0	390	Plummer
19/01	**CRANFIELD UTD**	DCC2	7-0	98	McInerney(2), Thomas, Harding, Archer, Cook
22/01	**GRESLEY ROVERS**	BHL	2-1	574	Thomas, Plummer
25/01	Gresley Rovers	DMCqf	0-0	504	
29/01	Sittingbourne	BHL	0-2	1,207	
02/02	**NORTHAMPTON SPEN.**	NSCsf	1-1	140	Plummer
05/02	**BURTON ALBION**	BHL	2-1	324	Cook(2)
09/02	**GRESLEY ROVERS**	DMCqfr	1-3	321	McInerney
19/02	Waterlooville	BHL	1-2	314	Devine
26/02	**SITTINGBOURNE**	BHL	3-2	420	Plummer(2), Cook
01/03	Rothwell Town	DCCqf	2-1	296	Keast, McInerney
05/03	**DORCHESTER TOWN**	BHL	0-0	240	
07/03	Hinckley Athletic	MFC	1-1	121	Cook
09/03	**BEDWORTH UTD**	MFC	2-2	70	Thomas(2)
12/03	Worcester City	BHL	1-2	659	Thomas
16/03	**NUNEATON BORO.**	BHL	1-0	311	Plummer
19/03	**HALESOWEN TOWN**	BHL	2-1	361	Devine, Thomas
22/03	Northampton Spencer	NSCsfr	1-3	121	Cook
26/03	Cheltenham Town	BHL	1-4	866	Cook
30/03	**HEDNESFORD TOWN**	BHL	4-2	246	Plummer(2), McInerney, Gunn
02/04	**CAMBRIDGE CITY**	BHL	0-0	282	
09/04	**MOOR GREEN**	BHL	2-1	221	Plummer, Archer
12/04	Willenhall Town	MFCqf	2-1	40	Riley, Cook
16/04	Crawley Town	BHL	0-0	955	
19/04	Bashley	BHL	1-2	157	Plummer
23/04	Nuneaton Borough	BHL	1-2	902	Plummer
25/04	Atherstone United	BHL	0-2	301	
30/04	**FARNBOROUGH T.**	BHL	0-6	301	
04/05	**WATERLOOVILLE**	BHL	0-1	110	
07/05	Hastings Town	BHL	0-2	307	
	Leicester United	MFCsf	2-2		*(lost 4-5 on penalties)*
	Long Buckby	DCCsf	3-1		
11/05	NEWPORT PAGNELL	DCCf	2-0		*(played at Daventry Town FC)*

Key: BHL: Beazer Homes League Premier Division, DMC: Doctor Martens (Beazer Homes League) Cup, FAC: F.A Cup, FAT: F.A. Trophy, DCC: Daventry Charity Cup, NSC: Hillier Northants Senior Cup, MFC: Midland Floodlit Cup.

SQUAD MEMBERS *(previous clubs listed in chronological order)*

GOALKEEPERS: Chris Mackenzie *(Desborough)*, **David Bolton** *(Gresley R., Stapenhill)*, **Des Elliott** *(Rothwell)*.

DEFENDERS: Gerry McElhinney *(Distillery, Bolton W., Plymouth, Peterborough Utd)*, **Bryn Gunn** *(Nottm Forest, Peterborough U., Chesterfield)*, **Graham Retallick** *(Peterborough Utd.)*, **Pat Rayment** *(Peterborough Utd., Cambridge Utd.)*, **Steve Collins** *(Peterborough Utd., Southend, Lincoln, Peterborough Utd., Kettering, Boston Utd.)*

MIDFIELD: Steve Devine *(Wolves, Derby, Stockport, Hereford Utd.)*, **Mike Cook** *(Coventry, Cambridge Utd., Wycombe W.)*, **Graeme Archer** *(Youth Team)*, **David Harding** *(Youth Team)*, **Ian Walker** *(Youth Team)*,

FORWARDS: Anton Thomas *(Northampton T., Kettering, Bedworth Utd., Leicester Utd)*, **Ian McInerney** *(Peterborough Utd)*, **Calvin Plummer** *(Nottm Forest Chesterfield, Derby, Nottm Forest, Barnsley, Reipns Lahden(Fin), Plymouth, Chesterfield, Gainsborough T., Shepshed Alb.)*,.

Formed: 1896

CRAWLEY TOWN

Red Devils

Crawley's Tony Vessey (right) is pressurised by Barnet striker Kelly Haag during the FA Cup Second Round at Town Mead in December.

Photo - Graham Cotterill.

Chairman: John Maggs **President:** K Symons
Secretary: Stan Markham, 105 Winchester Road, Tilgate, Crawley RH10 5HH (0293 522371).
Manager: Ted Shepherd **Asst Manager:** David Haining **Commercial Mgr:** Andy Bell.
Coach: Ted Shepherd **Physio:** John Poulshum.
Ground: Town Mead, Ifield Avenue, West Green, Crawley (0293 21800).
Directions: M23 exit 10, A264 for Horsham, left at 2nd island, over mini r-about, right at next island into Ifield Avenue and ground 150 yards on right behind fire station. 10 mins walk from Crawley (BR).
Capacity: 4,750 **Cover:** 1,800 **Seats:** 400 **Floodlights:** Yes **Metal Badges:** Yes.
Club Shop: Yes, selling programmes, metal badges, hats, scarves, mugs, replica kits. Contact Ian Hands.
Colours: Red/red/white **Change cols:** Blue/blue/white or red **Sponsors:** TBA
Previous Grounds: Malthouse Farm 1896-1914 38-39/ Victoria Hall + Rectory Fields 18-38/ Yetmans Field 45-52.
Previous Leagues: Sussex County 1951-56/ Metropolitan 56-63
Reserves' Lge: Suburban (Capital Lge also entered for 94-95, but the first team will play these fixtures).
Midweek matchday: Tuesday **Record Gate:** 4,104 v Barnet, FA Cup 2nd Round 4/12/93.
Best FA Trophy season: 2nd Rd 85-86 87-88.
Best FA Cup season: 3rd Rd Proper 91-92 (lost 0-5 at Brighton).
League Clubs defeated in FA Cup: Northampton Town 91-92.
Record win: 10-0 v Chichester United, Sussex County League Division Two 17/12/55.
Record defeat: 0-10 v Dartford (H), Mid-Surrey Prof. Floodlit Lge 8/4/75.
Record Fee Paid: £5,000 for David Thompson (Wokingham, May 1992)
Record Received: £50,000 for Craig Whitington (Scarborough 1993).
Players progressing to Football League: Ray Keeley (Mansfield 1968), Graham Brown (Mansfield 1969), Andy Ansah (Brentford 1987 (now Southend)), Craig Whitington (Scarborough 1993), Brian Sparrow as coach to Wimbledon 1992.
Clubhouse: Weekdays noon-3 & 6-11pm, Sat noon-11pm, Sun noon-3 & 7-10.30pm. Snacks available.
Club Record Goalscorer: Phil Basey 108.
Club Record Apps: John Maggs 652.
93-94 Captain: Tony Vessey.
93-94 P.o.Y.: Viv Jeffrey.
93-94 Top scorer: Paul Fishenden 29.
Local Newspapers: Crawley Observer (0293 526929), Crawley News (0293 526474).
Local Radio Stations: Radio Mercury, BBC Radio Sussex
Hons: Sussex Snr Cup(2) 89-91 (R-up 58-59), Sussex Intermediate Cup 26-27, Sussex Prof. Cup 69-70 (beat Brighton 1-0 in final), Southern Lg Southern Div R-up 83-84 (Merit Cup 70-71), Sussex Floodlit Cup(3) 90-93, Sussex Lg Div 2 R-up 55-56, Gilbert Rice Floodlit Cup 79-80 83-84, Southern Co's Comb. Floodlit Cup 85-86, Metropolitan Lg Chal. Cup 58-59, Mid-Sussex Snr 02-03, Montgomery Cup 25-26.

PROGRAMME DETAILS:
Pages: 40 **Price:** £1
Editor: Ian Hands

CRAWLEY TOWN's 1993-94 CAMPAIGN

Date	Opponents	Comp.	Res	Gate	Goalscorers
21/08	**NUNEATON BORO'**	BHL	1-0	763	Vessey
24/08	Farnborough Town	BHL	2-1	453	Pearson, Whitington
28/08	Gresley Rovers	BHL	1-1	774	Whitington
30/08	**GLOUCESTER CITY**	BHL	0-0	785	
04/09	**WORCESTER CITY**	BHL	2-0	586	Whitington(2)
11/09	Cheltenham Town	BHL	3-1	827	Fishenden(2), Whitington
15/09	Langney Sports	SFC1(1)	2-0	127	Fishenden(2)
18/09	**DORCHESTER TOWN**	BHL	1-0	667	Whitington
25/09	**MOOR GREEN**	BHL	2-0	532	M Turner, Fishenden
28/09	**LANGNEY SPORTS**	SFC1(2)	7-3	144	Pearson, Wilson, L Turner, Vansittart(3), Wales
02/10	Sittingbourne	BHL	3-2	1,603	Jeffery, Payne, Fishenden
05/10	Gravesend & N'fleet	DMC1(1)	1-5	411	Fishenden
20/10	**EAST GRINSTEAD**	SFC2(1)	2-0	148	Pearson, Whitington
23/10	**MERTHYR TYDFIL**	FAC4q	2-1	1,623	Whitington, Vansittart
26/10	**GRAVESEND & NFLT**	DMC1(2)	1-0	450	Dack
30/10	Hednesford Town	BHL	1-2	522	Whitington
03/11	East Grinstead	SFC2(2)	0-0	149	
06/11	**SOLIHULL BOROUGH**	BHL	3-0	706	M Turner, Payne, Whitington
13/11	Metropolitan Police	FAC1	2-0	1,561	Vansittart, Whitington
16/11	Gloucester City	BHL	0-3	430	
20/11	Chichester City	SSC2	3-0	250	L Turner(2), Dack
27/11	Worcester City	FAT3q	1-1	641	M Turner
30/11	**WORCESTER CITY**	FAT3qr	1-2	445	L Turner
04/12	**BARNET**	FAC2	1-2	4,104	Ford
11/12	Nuneaton Borough	BHL	1-2	1,083	M Turner
18/12	Cambridge City	BHL	1-0	315	Carroll
21/12	**FARNBOROUGH T.**	BHL	1-0	633	Fishenden
27/12	**HASTINGS TOWN**	BHL	3-0	1,165	Dack, Fishenden(2)
01/01	Chelmsford City	BHL	2-1	851	Dack(2)
08/01	Corby Town	BHL	1-5	371	Dack
15/01	**BASHLEY**	BHL	6-2	601	Payne(2), Carroll, Fishenden(3)
18/01	**BURGESS HILL T.**	SSC3	3-0	227	Carroll, Seagroatt, own-goal
22/01	**SITTINGBOURNE**	BHL	1-1	1,927	Carroll
25/01	**NEWHAVEN**	SFC3(1)	0-2	154	
29/01	Burton Albion	BHL	1-0	713	Dack
01/02	**CHELTENHAM TOWN**	BHL	0-1	1,376	
05/02	**WATERLOOVILLE**	BHL	2-1	925	Fishenden, Dack
08/02	Bashley	BHL	1-1	215	Fishenden
09/02	Newhaven	SFC3(2)	4-5	140	Vansittart(2), Willie, May
12/02	**PEACEHAVEN & TEL.**	SSC4	1-2	421	Fishenden
19/02	Dorchester Town	BHL	2-1	680	Fishenden, Payne
22/02	**GRESLEY ROVERS**	BHL	0-1	684	
05/03	**HEDNESFORD TOWN**	BHL	3-1	795	Payne(2), Dack
07/03	Worcester City	BHL	0-2	625	
12/03	Halesowen Town	BHL	2-2	892	Dack, Fishenden
19/03	Waterlooville	BHL	2-1	302	Payne, Fishenden
22/03	**TROWBRIDGE TOWN**	BHL	1-1	677	Thorpe(og)
26/03	**CAMBRIDGE CITY**	BHL	2-1	903	Ford, M Turner
20/03	**HALESOWEN TOWN**	BHL	0-1	714	
02/04	Hastings Town	BHL	1-0	595	Dack
16/04	**CORBY TOWN**	BHL	0-0	955	
20/04	Atherstone United	BHL	0-2	323	
23/04	Solihull Borough	BHL	1-0	206	Pearson
26/04	**CHELMSFORD CITY**	BHL	0-2	1,052	
30/04	**ATHERSTONE UTD**	BHL	0-1	722	
02/05	**BURTON ALBION**	BHL	1-1	579	Yetzes
04/04	Trowbridge Town	BHL	0-0	231	
07/05	Moor Green	BHL	2-0	261	Dack(2)

Key: BHL: Beazer Homes League Premier Division, DMC: Doctor Martens (Beazer Homes League) Cup, FAC: F.A. Cup, FAT: F.A. Trophy, SSC: Sussex Senior Cup, SFC: Sussex Floodlit Cup. Numbers after cup competitions denote rounds (r: replay, qf: Quarter-Final, sf: Semi-Final, f: Final. No.s in brackets indicate legs, i.e. (1): 1st leg). Home fixtures are denoted by bold capitals, away matches by lower case. (p): penalty, og: Own goal.

SQUAD MEMBERS *(previous clubs listed in chronological order)*

GOALKEEPERS: Colin Caulfield *(Addlestone, Wimbledon, Addlestone, Wokingham Town, Woking, Leatherhead),* **Neil Taylor** *(Raynes Park).*

DEFENDERS: Tony Vessey *(Brighton & Hove Albion, Vassalund(Sweden), Steyning Town, Worthing),* **Mark Jenkins** *(Sutton Utd),* **Stuart Hemsley** *(Croydon, Sutton Utd, Slough Town),* **Rob Shaughnessy** *(Bognor Regis Town, Sutton Utd, Staines Town),* **Damian Webber** *(Brighton & Hove Albion, Worthing),* **Matthew Pearson** *(Crystal Palace, Wimbledon, Kingstonian, Carshalton Athletic),* **Ashley Cook** *(local football).*

MIDFIELD: Mickey Turner *(Portsmouth, Peterborough Utd),* **Mark Ford** *(Sutton Utd),* **Viv Jeffrey** *(Banstead Athletic),* **David Shepherd** *(Tottenham Hotspur, Wimbledon, Sheffield Utd, Whyteleafe),* **Jimmy Dack** *(Epsom & Ewell, Sutton Utd),* **Paul Adam** *(Sutton Utd, Molesey),* **Robbie Carroll** *(Southampton, Gosport Borough, Brentford, Fareham Town, Yeovil Town, Woking, Worthing).*

FORWARDS: Paul Fishenden *(Hillingdon, Wimbledon, Crewe Alexandra, Wokingham Town),* **Steve Payne** *(Ware, Loughborough University, Ringmer),* **Joff Vansittart** *(youth team),* **Neil Willie** *(Brighton & Hove Albion),* **Robin Seagroatt** *(Redhill, Sutton Utd),* **Lee Turner** *(Horsham).*

Formed: 1880 **DORCHESTER TOWN** The Magpies

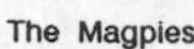

Tony Diaz holds off Jason Miller during Dorchester Town's FA Trophy win at Witney Town.
Photo - Richard Brock.

Chairman: P J Aiken **Vice Chairman:** C E Clark **President:** J Pitfield
Secretary: Albert Miller, 29 Shaston Crescent, Dorchester DT1 2EB (0305 264843)
Manager: Stuart Morgan **Physio:** Geoff Dine
Commercial Manager: Keith Kellaway (0305 262451).
Ground: Avenue Stadium, Weymouth Avenue, Dorchester DT1 2RY (0305 262451).
Directions: At junction of southern bypass (A35) and Weymouth road (A354).
Capacity: 7,210 **Cover:** 4,000 **Seats:** 710 **Floodlights:** Yes **Metal Badges:** Yes
Club Shop: Yes, selling replica shirts (£19.99/£24.99), club badges (£2.50/£2), bone china thimbles (£1.75), miniature bone china mugs (£1.75), porcelain lace plates (£19.95), bone china plate (£17.95), ashtrays (£3.25), hats (£2.50), mugs (£2.50), scarves (£3/£2.50).
Colours: Black & white stripes/black/black **Change colours:** All sky blue
Previous Leagues: Dorset/ Western 1947-72.
Previous Grounds: Council Recreation Ground, Weymouth Avenue 1880-1929/ The Avenue Ground, Weymouth Avenue 29-90.
Midweek home games: Tuesday **Reserve Team League:** Dorset Combination
Sponsors: Olds Motor Group **Best FA Trophy season:** 3rd Rd replay 71-72.
Record Attendance: 4,000 v Chelsea, official ground opening 1990. Competitive: 3,027 v Weymouth, Southern League Premier Division 26/12/92. *At old ground: 5,500 v York City, FA Cup Second Rd 1954).*
Best FA Cup season: 2nd Rd Replay 81-82 (lost 1-2 to A.F.C. Bournemouth after 1-1 draw). 2nd Rd 54-55 57-58, 1st Rd on seven occasions; 55-56 56-57 59-60.
League Clubs defeated in FA Cup: None.
Record win: 7-0 v Canterbury (A), Southern Lge Southern Div 86-87.
Record defeat: 0-6 on four occasions: v Kettering 7/4/79, Cambridge City 2/9/89, Bath City 6/2/90.
Record Fees: Paid: £12,000 for Chris Townsend (Gloucester City, 1990)
Received: £35,000 for Trevor Senior (Portsmouth, 1981)
Players progressing to The Football League: Len Drake (Bristol Rovers 1957), David Noake (Luton 1959), Mike Turner (Swindon 1961), Trevor Senior (Portsmouth 1981), David West (Liverpool 1983), Mike Squire (Torquay 1984), Jeremy Judd (Torquay 1984), Anthony White (Bournemouth 1985) + Graham Roberts (Spurs, Chelsea, Rangers, England) who progressed via Weymouth.
Clubhouse: Dorchester Lounge Club - access via main entrance to stadium. Cold food and snacks
Club Record Goalscorer: Dennis Cheney 61 (in one season)
Club Record Appearances: Trevor Townsend 377.
93-94 Captain:
93-94 P.o.Y.:
93-94 Top scorer:
Local Press: Dorset Evening Echo, Western Gazette, Western Daily Press.
Local Radio Stations: Two Counties Radio (2CR Bournemouth).
Newsline (Magpies Hotline): 0839 664412.
Hons: Southern Lg R-up 79-80 (Div 1 (Sth) R-up 77-78, Lg Cup 86-87 (R-up 91-92), Western Lg 54-55 (R-up 60-61, Div 2 R-up 49-50), Dorset Snr Cup 50-51 60-61 67-68 68-69 71-72 93-94, Dorset Lg 37-38.

PROGRAMME DETAILS:
Pages: 32 **Price:** 80p
Editor: David Martin
(0305 264740)

DORCHESTER TOWN's 1993-94 CAMPAIGN

Date	Opponents	Comp.	Res	Gate	Goalscorers
21/08	**GRESLEY ROVERS**	BHL	1-2	622	Taylor
24/08	Trowbridge Town	BHL	0-1	472	
28/08	Chelmsford City	BHL	0-3	487	
30/08	**FARNBOROUGH T.**	BHL	0-1	752	
04/09	Hednesford Town	BHL	4-2	398	Taylor, Manson(2), Foster(og)
07/09	**HASTINGS TOWN**	BHL	0-0	519	
11/09	**WOKINGHAM TOWN**	FAC1q	1-0	489	Taylor
18/09	Crawley Town	BHL	1-1	667	Manson
25/09	**NEWBURY TOWN**	FAC2q	0-3	449	
02/10	**CORBY TOWN**	BHL	0-0	463	
16/10	Witney Town	FAT2q	1-0	121	Manson
20/10	Fareham Town	DMC1(1)	3-2	79	Senior, Taylor, Manson
23/10	**SOLIHULL BORO.**	BHL	1-1	434	T Diaz
26/10	**FAREHAM TOWN**	DMC1(2)	2-2	479	Senior(2)
30/10	Gloucester City	BHL	0-1	405	
06/11	**ATHERSTONE UTD**	BHL	2-2	461	Manson, Senior
13/11	**QUEENS PARK RGRS**	Fr.	2-3	578	Waters(2)
16/11	**HAVANT TOWN**	DMC2	2-1	213	Conning, T Diaz
20/11	Halesowen Town	BHL	0-2	656	
25/11	Weymouth	DSC2	1-0	813	Manson
27/11	**BASHLEY**	FAT3q	0-0	372	
04/12	Northerners	DSC3	5-1		Coleman, Conning, Waters, Manson, Whalley
06/12	Bashley	FAT3qr	0-3	214	
11/12	Gresley Rovers	BHL	2-0	564	Manson, T Diaz
14/12	Waterlooville	DMC3	2-1	66	Conning, Waters
18/12	**CHELMSFORD CITY**	BHL	1-0	492	Conning
27/12	Waterlooville	BHL	0-2	303	
01/01	**BASHLEY**	BHL	1-3	1,002	Waters
03/01	Cheltenham Town	BHL	1-0	840	T Diaz
08/01	**WORCESTER CITY**	BHL	0-3	615	
11/01	**TROWBRIDGE TOWN**	BHL	0-1	541	
15/01	Moor Green	BHL	3-1	261	Manson, Waters, T Diaz
22/01	**BURTON ALBION**	BHL	2-1	627	Waters, Killick
26/01	Salisbury City	DMCqf	0-4	322	
29/01	Solihull Borough	BHL	1-1	212	Docherty(p)
02/02	**WEST HAM UTD**	Fr.	1-6	2,866	Diaz
05/02	**SITTINGBOURNE**	BHL	1-3	597	Birmingham
08/02	Hastings Town	BHL	0-1	297	
12/02	Cambridge City	BHL	2-1	249	Conning, Killick
19/02	**CRAWLEY TOWN**	BHL	1-2	680	Killick
22/02	Farnborough Town	BHL	0-0	362	
26/02	Burton Albion	BHL	0-0	576	
01/03	**GLOUCESTER CITY**	BHL	1-2	450	McPherson
05/03	Corby Town	BHL	0-0	240	
08/02	Bridport	DSCsf	1-0	484	Waters
12/03	**NUNEATON BORO.**	BHL	1-0	607	White
19/03	**HEDNESFORD TOWN**	BHL	1-4	451	Killick
26/03	Sittingbourne	BHL	2-1	954	McPherson(2)
02/04	**WATERLOOVILLE**	BHL	1-2	636	Coleman
04/04	Bashley	BHL	1-0	309	Killick
09/04	**CHELTENHAM TOWN**	BHL	0-2	580	
12/04	Nuneaton Borough	BHL	2-0	691	White, Waters
16/04	Worcester City	BHL	0-1	613	
19/04	**POOLE TOWN**	DSCf	1-0	252	Coleman *(played at Swanage Town & Herston)*
23/04	**MOOR GREEN**	BHL	1-1	500	Docherty
26/04	**CAMBRIDGE CITY**	BHL	3-1	415	Brooks, Docherty, Killick
30/04	**HALESOWEN TOWN**	BHL	1-1	650	Killick
07/05	Atherstone United	BHL	0-1	375	

Key: BHL: Beazer Homes League Premier Division, DMC: Doctor Martens (Beazer Homes League) Cup, FAC: F.A. Cup, FAT: F.A. Trophy, DSC: Dorset Senior Cup, Fr.: Friendly. Numbers after cup competitions denote rounds (r: replay, qf: Quarter-Final, sf: Semi-Final, f: Final. Numbers in brackets indicate legs, i.e. (1): 1st leg). Home fixtures are denoted by bold capitals, away matches by lower case. (p): penalty, og: Own goal.

SQUAD MEMBERS *(previous clubs listed in chronological order)*

GOALKEEPERS: Mark Coombe *(AFC Bournemouth, Bristol City, Colchester Utd, Torquay Utd, Salisbury)*, **Tony Oliver** *(Portsmouth, Brentford, Weymouth, Bournemouth Poppies)*

DEFENDERS: Phil Lloyd *(Middlesbrough, Barnsley, Darlington, Torquay)*, **Steve Harris** *(Sherborne)*, **Tony White** *(Dorchester Town, AFC Bournemouth)*, **Lee Bradford** *(AFC Bournemouth, Poole Town*, **Aaron Davis** *(Torquay Utd)*, **David Coleman** *(AFC Bournemouth, Farnborough Town, Woking)*, **Graham Kemp** *(Weymouth, Dorchester Town, Trowbridge Town, Portland Utd, AFC Lymington, Bashley)*.

MIDFIELD: Graham Waters *(Oxford Utd, Exeter City)*, **Peter Conning** *(Rochdale, Altrincha, Weymouth, Yeovil Town, Bashley)*, **Gary Borthwick** *(Portsmouth, Southend Utd, Aylesbury Utd, Barnet, AFC Bournemouth, Yeovil Town, Weymouth, Yeovil Town, Weymouth*, **Shaun Brooks** *(Crystal Palace, Leyton Orient, AFC Bournemouth, Wimborne Town, Salisbury)*, **Dave Whalley** *(West Bromwich Albion, Weymouth)*, **Mark Rednapp** *(AFC Bournemouth, Bashley)*.

FORWARDS: Gary Manson *(Wimborne Town, Parley Spts, Poole Town)*, **Tony Diaz** *(Weymouth)*, **Sean Docherty** *(Heart of Midlothian, Weymouth, AFC Bournemouth, Bashley, Newport IOW)*, **Tommy Killick** *(Poole Town, Swanage Town & Herston, Wimborne Town)*, **Rob Taylor** *(Portsmouth, Newport County, Weymouth, Torquay Utd, Dorchester Town, Fareham Town)*.

Formed: 1889

GLOUCESTER CITY

The Tigers

The main stand at Gloucester City's Meadow Park.

Photo - James Wright.

Chairman: Keith Gardner **Vice-Chairman:** George Irvine
President: R F Etheridge **Chief Executive:** Keith Gardner.
Secretary/Press Officer: Ken Turner, 24 Ladysmith Road, Cheltenham, GL52 5LQ (0242 522514).
Manager: John Murphy **Asst Manager:** Bob Baird **Coach:** Brian Hughes.
Assistant Secretary: Jason Mills **Physios:** Bernard & Adrian Tandy **Commercial Manager:** Chris Owen.
Ground: Meadow Park, Sudmeadow Road, Hempsted, Gloucester GL2 6HS (0452 523883. Commercial Office: 0452 421400).
Directions: From North: A40 then then A4301 towards City Centre & Historic Docks, right into Severn Road over swingbridge, right into Llanthony Road/Hempsted Lane, 2nd right into Sudmeadow Road, ground 50yds on left. Front South: A38 then A430 towards city centre, left at lights into Llanthony Rd third mile from centre, follow road and take 3rd right into Sudmeadow Rd then as above.
Capacity: 5,000 **Cover:** 2,000 **Seats:** 560 **Club Shop:** Yes **Metal Badges:** Yes
Colours: All Yellow **Change colours:** White/white/red
Midweek home games: Tuesday **Reserve Team's League:** None. **Sponsors:** TBA
Previous Leagus: Bristol & Dist. (now Western) 1893-96/ Gloucester & Dist. 97-1907/ Nth Glos. 07-10/ Glos. Nth Snr 20-34/ Birmingham Comb. 1935-39.
Previous Grounds: Longlevens 1935-1965/ Horton Road 65-86.
Previous Name: Gloucester Y.M.C.A.
Record Attendance: 10,500 v Spurs 1952 (at Meadow Park; 3,952 v Arsenal, July 1987)
Best FA Cup season: 2nd Rd 89-90 **Best FA Trophy season:** 3rd Rd 90-91.
Record Transfer Fee: Paid: £25,000 S Fergusson (Worcester City)
Received: £25,000 Ian Hedges (AFC Bournemouth, 1990)
Players progressing to The Football League: George Beattie & David Pugsley (Newport County 1950 & 53), John Boyd & Robert Etheridge & Charlie Cook (Bristol City 1950 & 56 & 57), David Jones (Leeds United1954), Mike Johnson (Fulham 1958), William Teague & Rod Thomas (Swindon 1961 & 64), John Layton (Hereford 1974), Ian Main (Exeter 1978), Mike Bruton (Newport 1979), Mel Gwinnett (Bradford City 1984), Steve Talboys (Wimbledon, 1991).
Clubhouse: Meadow Park Sports & Social Club at entrance to ground. Normal licensing hours. Hot & cold food available.
Club Record Goalscorer: Reg Weaver, 250
Club Record Apps: Stan Myers & Frank Tredgett in 1950s
93-94 Captain: Mark Buckland.
93-94 P.o.Y.: Paul Bywater.
93-94 Top scorer: Karl Bayliss 21.
Local Press: Gloucester Citizen, Gloucester Express, Western Daily Press
Local Radio Stations: Severn Sound, BBC Radio Gloucestershire
Hons: Southern Lg R-up 90-91 (Lg Cup 55-56 (R-up 81-82), Midland Div 88-89), Glos Nth Snr Lg 33-34, Glos Snr Prof. Cup 37-38 49-58 65-66 68-69 70-71 74-75 78-79 79-80 81-82 82-83 83-84 90-91 92-93 (R-up 93-94, Snr Amtr Cup (Nth) 31-32).

PROGRAMME DETAILS:
Pages: 44 **Price:** £1
Editor: Helen Lodge/ Debbie Dembny

GLOUCESTER CITY's 1993-94 CAMPAIGN

Date	Opponents	Comp.	Res	Gate	Goalscorers
21/08	Corby Town	BHL	1-2	358	Buckland
24/08	**BURTON ALBION**	BHL	4-2	569	Bayliss(2), Cook(2)
28/08	**SOLIHULL BORO.**	BHL	3-1	570	Bayliss(2), Cook
30/08	Crawley Town	BHL	0-0	785	
04/09	**GRESLEY ROVERS**	BHL	1-1	586	Cook
07/09	Halesowen Town	BHL	0-1	728	
11/09	**CLEVEDON TOWN**	FAC1q	1-2	438	Callinan
19/09	**WATERLOOVILLE**	BHL	2-1	475	Bayliss, Olner
25/09	Hednesford Town	BHL	1-1	402	Bayliss
28/09	**WITNEY TOWN**	DMC1(1)	2-1	286	Boyland, Fishlock
02/10	Chelmsford City	BHL	1-2	525	Callinan
09/10	**MOOR GREEN**	BHL	2-1	438	Buckland, Bayliss
16/10	**HASTINGS TOWN**	BHL	2-1	457	Cook, Bloomfield
19/10	Witney Town	DMC1(2)	1-1	132	Callinan
23/10	Sittingbourne	BHL	0-0	963	
26/10	Burton Albion	BHL	1-4	526	Cook
30/10	**DORCHESTER TOWN**	BHL	1-0	405	Bloomfield
02/11	Cheltenham Town	GSC1	1-0	449	Buckland
06/11	Cambridge City	BHL	0-2	447	
13/11	Trowbridge Town	BHL	0-2	390	
16/11	**CRAWLEY TOWN**	BHL	3-0	430	Buckland, Bayliss, Cook
20/11	Farnborough Town	BHL	0-1	426	
27/11	Dulwich Hamlet	FAT3q	1-2	313	Bayliss
11/12	**CORBY TOWN**	BHL	2-4	389	Bywater, Boyland
14/12	**SITTINGBOURNE**	BHL	0-1	352	
27/12	Worcester City	BHL	0-2	1,196	
01/01	**CHELTENHAM TOWN**	BHL	1-3	1,239	Cook
03/01	Bashley	BHL	5-4	465	Bayliss(2), Tilley, Callinan, N Hughes
08/01	**ATHERSTONE UTD**	BHL	3-0	577	Tilley, Bayliss, Cook
10/01	Evesham United	DMC2	3-1	140	Bayliss(2), Cook
15/01	**CHELMSFORD CITY**	BHL	2-5	538	Cook, Lee
19/01	Hednesford Town	DMC3	1-0	287	Boyland
28/01	**BURTON ALBION**	DMCqf	0-1	314	
29/01	Waterlooville	BHL	1-1	210	Buckland
05/02	**HEDNESFORD TOWN**	BHL	2-0	398	Bayliss, Buckland
08/02	**HALESOWEN TOWN**	BHL	0-0	458	
12/02	Hastings Town	BHL	0-1	333	
19/02	**TROWBRIDGE TOWN**	BHL	0-1	510	
01/03	Dorchester Town	BHL	2-1	450	Webb, Bayliss
05/03	Moor Green	BHL	0-3	253	
12/03	**FARNBOROUGH T.**	BHL	0-1	486	
15/03	Forest Green Rvrs	GSCsf	3-2	281	Bywater, Callinan, Porter
22/03	Nuneaton Borough	BHL	3-1	813	Webb, Bayliss, Bywater
26/03	Solihull Borough	BHL	4-2	246	Bayliss(2), Porter, Fishlock
02/04	**WORCESTER CITY**	BHL	1-2	624	Bayliss
04/04	Cheltenham Town	BHL	1-0	1,806	Bayliss
09/04	**BASHLEY**	BHL	1-0	472	Cook
12/04	**NEWPORT A.F.C.**	GSCf	0-1	401	
16/04	Atherstone United	BHL	1-2	277	Fishlock
23/04	**CAMBRIDGE CITY**	BHL	2-1	455	Buckland, Cook
30/04	Gresley Rovers	BHL	0-2	574	
07/05	**NUNEATON BORO.**	BHL	2-1	728	Callinan, Cook

Key: BHL: Beazer Homes League Premier Division, DMC: Doctor Martens (Beazer Homes League) Cup, FAC: F.A. Cup, FAT: F.A. Trophy, GSC: North Gloucestershire Senior Professional Cup. Number after cup competitions denote rounds (r: replay, qf: Quarter-Final, sf: Semi-Final, f: Final. Numbers in brackets indicate legs, i.e. (1): 1st leg).
Home fixtures are denoted by bold capitals, away matches by lower case. (p): penalty, og: Own goal.

SQUAD MEMBERS *(previous clubs listed in chronological order)*

GOALKEEPERS: Robbie Kemp *(Moreton, Worcester)*, **Steve Crompton** *(Man. City, Carlisle, Stockport, Wycombe, Harrow Boro., Hounslow, Harrow Boro.)*

DEFENDERS: Mark Saunders *(Moreton)*, **Kevin Willetts** *(Sharpness, Cheltenham, Forest Green R.)*, **Gary Kemp** *(Almondsbury P.)*, **Paul Bywater** *(Shrewsbury, Worcester)*, **Murray Fishlock** *(Swindon T., Gloucester, Trowbridge)*, **Phil Jones** *(Youth Team)*, **Mark Buckland** *(Cheltenham, AP Leamington, Wolves, Kidderminster, Cheltenham)*.

MIDFIELD: David Webb *(Supermarine, Wantage, Devizes, Stroud, Gloucester, Trowbridge)*, **Tommy Callinan** *(Cheltenham, Cheltenham Saracens, Cinderford)*, **Paul Bloomfield** *(St Marks, Cheltenham)*, **Danny Iddles** *(Sharpness, Yate, Forest Green R., Yate, Trowbridge, Cheltenham, Yate)*, **Brian Hughes** *(Swindon, Torquay, Cheltenham)*.

FORWARDS: Tony Cook *(Bristol C., Weymouth)*, **Karl Bayliss** *(Cheltenham, Forest Green R., Sharpness, Stroud)*, **Steve Crouch** *(Frampton Utd, Cheltenham, Stroud, Shepshed Alb.)*, **Nick Hughes** *(Moreton)*, **Darren Tilley** *(Bath, Trowbridge, Mangotsfield, Bath, Yate, York, Yate, Weston-super-Mare, Chippenham)*.

1946 **GRAVESEND & NORTHFLEET** The Fleet

Gravesend top-scorer Steve Portway is denied by an athletic catch by Ashford Town's Adrian Clewlow. Neither side was able to find the net in this Kentish derby at Stonebridge Road. *Photo - Alan Coomes.*

Chairman: L G F Ball **Vice Chairman:** D F Hockley **Manager:** Gary Aldous
Secretary: Bill Hornby c/o the club (H - 0474 363424).
Asst Manager: Peter Coffill **Coach:** Peter Coffill/ Chris Weller **Physio:** Micky Ward
Press Officer: Lionel R H Ball (0474 569985).
Ground: Stonebridge Road, Northfleet, Kent DA11 9BA (0474 533796)
Directions: From A2 take Northfleet/Southfleet exit (B262), follow to Northfleet then B2175 (Springhead Rd) to junction with A226, turn left (The Hill, Northfleet), road becomes Stonebridge Rd, ground is on right at bottom of steep hill after 1 mile - car parking behind for 400-500 cars. 2 mins walk from Northfleet BR station.
Capacity: 6,000 **Cover:** 5,000 **Seats:** 400 **Floodlights:** Yes **Metal Badges:** Yes
Club Shop: Yes, selling various supporters' items (hats, scarves etc), other football memorabilia, extensive selection of programmes. Contact Mick Hills or Simon Merton via the club.
Colours: Red/white/red **Change colours:** White/black/white
Sponsors: Sprint Eng. Services Ltd **Previous Names:** Gravesend Utd/ Northfleet Utd (merged 1946).
Previous Leagues: Kent (as Gravesend Utd)/ Southern 1946-79/ Alliance Prem. 79-80.
Previous Ground: Central Avenue (as Gravesend United) *(Northfleet Utd alway played at Stonebridge Rd).*
Midweek home matchday: Tuesday **Reserves' Lge:** Hurst Electrical Kent Midweek.
Record Attendance: 12,036 v Sunderland, FA Cup 4th Rd 62-63.
Best FA Trophy season: 3rd Rd 88-89.
Best FA Cup season: 4th Rd Replay 1963 (lost 2-5 at Sunderland after 1-1 draw at home).
League clubs defeated in FA Cup: Exeter City, Carlisle United (both 62-63).
Record Fees - Paid: £6,000 for Dave Boyce (Waterlooville, 1993).
Received: £15,000 for Lee Smelt (Nottm Forest, 1980).
Record win: 8-1 v Clacton Town, Southern League 62-63.
Record defeat: 0-9 v Trowbridge Town (A), Southern League Premier Division 1991-92.
Players progressing to Football League: James Wilson (Chelsea 1947), Fred Pincott (Newport 1947), Stan Aldows & Herbert Hawkins (Orient 1950 & 51), Harry Gunning (West Ham 1952), John Hills (Spurs 1953), Norman Lewis (Newport 1954), Kevin Baron (Aldershot 1960), Roy Dwight (Coventry 1962), Robert Cameron (Southend 1963), Robert McNichol (Carlisle 1965), Alan Humphreys (Mansfield 1964), Barry Thornley (Brentford 1965), Pat Jeavons (Lincoln 1966), Barry Fry (Orient 1966), Barry Gordine (Sheffield Utd 1968), Tommy Baldwin (Brentford 1977), Lee Smelt (Nottm Forest 1980), Tom Warrilow (Torquay 1987)
Clubhouse: Fleet Social Centre open before and after all matches, Sat 7-11pm, Sun noon-2.30, Tues & Thurs 7-11pm. Hot and cold food available at tea bars on matchdays.
Club Record Goalscorer (career): Bert Hawkins.
Club Record Goalscorer (season): Steve Portway, 61 (92-93).
Club Record Appearances: Ken Burrett 537.
93-94 Captain: Tommy Warrilow. **93-94 P.o.Y.:** Matt Gubbins.
93-94 Top scorer: Steve Portway 52.
Local Newspapers: Gravesend & Dartford Reporter, Kent Evening Post, Gravesend Extra, Leader
Local Radio Stations: Invicta Radio, Radio Kent, RTM.
Hons: Southern Lg 57-58 (Southern Div 93-94, Div 1 Sth 74-75 (R-up 70-71 88-89), Lg Cup 77-78 (R-up 57-58), Championship Cup 77-78), Kent Senior Cup 48-49 52-53 80-81 (R-up 47-48 76-77 90-91), Kent Floodlit Cup 69-70 (R-up 72-73), Kent Senior Shield R-up 47-48 51-52, Kent Intermediate Cup R-up 87-88, Kent Midweek Lg R-up 92-93, Kent Youth Lg Cup 82-83 86-87, John Ullman Cup 82-83.

PROGRAMME DETAILS:
Pages: 28 **Price:** £1
Editor: Lionel R H Ball
(0474 569985)

GRAVESEND's 1993-94 CAMPAIGN

Date	Opponents	Comp.	Res	Gate	Goalscorers
21/08	Buckingham Town	BHL	2-0	187	Cotter, Smale
24/08	**BALDOCK TOWN**	BHL	1-2	501	Warrilow
28/08	**WITNEY TOWN**	BHL	1-0	506	Warrilow
30/08	Canterbury City	BHL	5-0	220	Graves, Portway(2), Ullathorne(2)
04/09	**SALISBURY CITY**	BHL	0-0	611	
07/09	Fareham Town	BHL	0-0	151	
11/09	**EPSOM & EWELL**	FAC1q	3-0	350	Portway, Cotter, Cant
18/09	**BOGNOR REGIS**	FAT1q	3-0	448	Portway(2), Cotter
25/09	Sittingbourne	FAC2q	2-0	2,044	Portway, Cotter
02/10	**POOLE TOWN**	BHL	4-0	711	Portway(3), Warrilow
05/10	**CRAWLEY TOWN**	DMC1(1)	5-1	411	Ullathorne, Portway(2), Cotter(2)
09/10	Erith & Belvedere	FAC3q	1-0	742	Gubbins
16/10	Ashford Town	FAT2q	1-1	633	Cotter
19/10	**ASHFORD TOWN**	FAT2qr	2-0	721	Portway, Cotter
23/10	Waterlooville	FAC4q	3-1	683	Cotter, Portway(2)
26/10	Crawley Town	DMC1(2)	0-1	450	
30/10	**WEYMOUTH**	BHL	4-1	810	Schweiso, Portway(2), Cotter
02/11	**ERITH & BEL.**	BHL	0-0	777	
06/11	Tonbridge AFC	BHL	3-1	643	Portway, Graves, Ullathorne
09/11	**BURNHAM**	DMC2	3-0	428	Portway(2), Cant
13/11	Leyton Orient	BHL	1-2	5,461	Portway
16/11	**CANTERBURY CITY**	BHL	1-0	706	Boyce
20/11	Erith & Belvedere	BHL	1-0	528	Boyce
27/11	**MARLOW**	BHL	1-4	604	Portway
04/12	**FISHER '93**	BHL	1-0	554	Portway
07/12	Bury Town	BHL	5-2	179	Portway(3), Boyce, Graves
11/12	**DUNSTABLE**	BHL	1-0	614	Cant
27/12	Ashford Town	BHL	2-2	731	Portway, Warrilow
01/01	**BURNHAM**	BHL	6-0	777	Portway(3), Ullathorne(2), Boyce
15/01	**SUDBURY TOWN**	BHL	2-2	764	Portway, Warrilow
18/01	Welling United	KSCqf	1-1	715	Portway
22/01	**TONBRIDGE**	BHL	0-0	812	
25/01	Sudbury Town	DMC3	1-0	320	*(result declared void - Sudbury re-instated)*
29/01	Poole Town	BHL	1-1	210	Lamb
05/02	Salisbury City	BHL	4-1	492	Portway(3), Ullathorne
08/02	**WELLING UTD**	KSCqfr	1-1	861	Portway
12/02	**BUCKINGHAM T.**	BHL	0-0	684	
15/02	**WEALDSTONE**	BHL	4-1	507	Portway(2), Warrilow, Ullathorne
19/02	Dunstable	BHL	4-1	277	Portway(3), Graves
22/02	**FAREHAM TOWN**	BHL	2-0	553	Portway(2)
26/02	**NEWPORT I.W.**	BHL	0-1	725	
01/03	Baldock Town	BHL	2-1	452	Portway, Mawson
05/03	Weymouth	BHL	1-1	680	Watts
09/03	**WELLING UTD**	KSCqfr(2)	0-0	600	*(Welling United won 7-6 on penalties)*
12/03	Wealdstone	BHL	3-0	294	Portway(2), Mawson
19/03	**BRAINTREE TOWN**	BHL	4-0	666	Portway(2), Lamb, Mawson
22/03	Margate	BHL	2-0	488	Portway, Mawson
26/03	Witney Town	BHL	1-0	522	Warrilow
02/04	**ASHFORD TOWN**	BHL	0-0	876	
04/04	Burnham	BHL	1-1	292	Warrilow
09/04	**MARGATE**	BHL	4-1	736	Mawson, Ullathorne, Cotter, Watts
12/04	Braintree Town	BHL	4-1	255	Gubbins, Portway(3)
16/04	Havant Town	BHL	1-2	353	Cotter
23/04	**GRAVESEND & N..**	BHL	0-1	854	
26/04	Newport IOW	BHL	2-0	264	Boyce, Cotter
30/04	Fisher '93	BHL	2-0	423	Cotter, Mawson
02/05	**HAVANT TOWN**	BHL	3-1	1,154	Mawson(2), Cotter
07/05	**BURY TOWN**	BHL	3-0	1,775	Cotter(2), Portway

Key: BHL: Beazer Homes League Southern Division, DMC: Doctor Martens (Beazer Homes League) Cup, FAC: F.A. Cup, FAT: F.A. Trophy, KSC: Facit Kent Senior Cup.
Home fixtures are denoted by bold capitals, away matches by lower case. (p): penalty, og: Own goal.

SQUAD MEMBERS *(previous clubs listed in chronological order)*

GOALKEEPERS: Lee Turner *(Leyton Orient, Corinthian, Sittingbourne, Corinthian, Bury T.).*

DEFENDERS: Paul Lamb *(Ramsgate, Dartford, Margate, Ramsgate)*, **Ian Gibbs** *(yth team)*, **Lee Graves** *(Watford, Brentford)*, **Tommy Warrilow** *(Millwall, Tonbridge, Gravesend, Canterbury, Adelaide(Aust), Kuopio Elo(Fin), Torquay, Crawley, Hythe, Sittingbourne)*, **Mark Leahy** *(Ashford, Gillingham)*, **Mark Harrop** *(Ramsgate, Thanet Utd, Dover, Canterbury, Dover)*, **Dennis Abboh** *(Greenwich B., Alma Swanley, Welling, Alma Swanley, Erith, Welling)*

MIDFIELD: Wayne Schweiso *(Gravesend, Corinthian, Gravesend, Corinthian, Bury T.)*, **Ian Mawson** *(Sittingbourne, Canterbury, Faversham, Tonbridge)*, **Kevin Hunt** *(Gillingham)*, **Cliff Cant** *(Arsenal, Fulham, Carshalton, Crawley, Welling, Crawley, Horsham)*, **Lewis Watts** *(yth team)*, **Dean Wells** *(West Ham, Southend, Basildon, Dartford, Chelmsford, Purfleet, Gravesend, Enfield)*, **Gary Groom** *(Alma Swanley, Greenwich B., Erith, Gravesend, Fisher Ath., Darenth H., Croydon, Slade Green)*

FORWARDS: Simon Ullathorne *(Windscale Utd, Workington, Cleator Moor C., Croydon)*, **Dave Boyce** *(Crystal Palace, Fisher Ath., Dover, Crawley, Waterlooville)*, **Neil Pheasant** *(yth team)*, **Micky Cotter** *(Welling Utd, Erith, Dover)*, **Steve Portway** *(Dagenham, Walthamstow Ave., Bishop's Stortford, Brentwood, Witham, Boreham Wood, Barking)*, **Graham Brenton** *(Gillingham, Bromley, Sheppey, IFK Mariehamn(Fin), Margate, Erith, Croydon, Braintree)*

Formed: 1882

GRESLEY ROVERS

The Moatmen

Back Row (L/R): Malcolm Campion (Assistant Manager), Craig Weston, Martin Dick, Gil Land, Stuart Evans, Bob Aston, Nick Stanborough, Paul Acklam, Mark Hurst, Gordon Ford (Physio). Front: Simon Osborne, Dave Swainston, Mike Taplin, Steve Dolby (Manager), Richard Wardle, Christian Moore, Tony Marsden.

Photo - Derrick Kinsey.

Chairman: Peter Hall **Vice Chairman:** Dennis Everitt **President:** Gordon Duggins.
Secretary: Neil Betteridge, 88 Midway Road, Midway, Swadlincote, Derbys DE11 7PG (0283 221881).
Manager/Coach: Steve Dolby **Asst Manager:** Malcolm Campion **Physio:** Gordon Ford.
Press Officer: Secretary **Commercial Manager:** Frank McArdle.
Ground: Moat Ground, Moat Street, Church Gresley, Swadlincote, Derbys DE11 9RE (0283 216315).
Directions: Travel to A444 via either the A5, A38, A5121 or M42 North to Appleby Magna. On reaching A444 head for Castle Gresley. Turn onto A514 to Derby; at island take second exit (Church Street), then second left (School Street) then first left into Moat Street. Five miles from Burton-on-Trent (BR). Buses from Swadlincote and Burton.
Capacity: 2,000 **Cover:** 1,200 **Seats:** 400 **Floodlights:** Yes **Metal Badges:** Yes
Club Shop: Yes - wide range of programmes and other merchandise. Contact Shelley Holmshaw (0283 224493).
Cols: Red (white sleeves)/red/red **Change colours:** All royal blue
Sponsors: Building Builders.
Previous Lges: Burton leagues 1892-95 97-98 1910-12 43-44/ Derbyshire Senior 1895-97 1902-03/ Leicestershire Senior 1898-1901 08-10 35-39 40-42 46-49/ Notts 01-02/ Midland 03-06/ Central Alliance 12-25 49-53 59-67/ Birmingham Combination 25-33 53-54/ Birmingham (now West Mids) 54-59/ Central Combination 33-35/ East Mids 67-75/ 75-92.
Previous Names: None
Prev. Grounds: Mushroom Lane, Albert Village 1882-95/ Church Str., Church Gresley 95-1909.
Midweek home matchday: Tuesday **Reserve's Lge:** Midland Combination (Res. Div.)
Record Attendance: 3,950 v Burton Albion, Birmingham (now West Mids) Lg Division One, 57-58.
Best F.A. Cup season: 1st Rd Proper 30-31 (lost 1-3 at York City).
League clubs defeated in F.A. Cup: None.
Record win: 23-0 v Holy Cross Priory, Leicestershire Junior Cup 1889-90.
Record defeat: 1-15 v Burton Crusaders, 1886-87.
Record fees received: £12,500 for Mark Blount (Sheffield United, 1994).
Players progressing to Football League: Phil Gee (Derby County 1985), Mark Blount (Sheffield Utd 1994), Colin Loss (Bristol City 1994).
Clubhouse: Inside ground, open Mon, Tues & Thurs evenings and matchdays. Variety of food available from tea bar on ground.
Club Record Goalscorer: Gordon Juggins 306.
Club Record Appearances: Dennis King 579.
93-94 Captain: Richard Denby.
93-94 P.o.Y.: Stuart Evans.
93-94 Top scorer: Martin Devaney.
Local Newspapers: Burton Mail.
Hons: FA Vase R-up 90-91 (SF 92-93), West Mids Lg 90-91 91-92 (R-up 85-86 88-89, Lg Cup 88-89), Southern Lg Midland Div R-up 92-93, Derbys Snr Cup 87-88 88-89 89-90 90-91 93-94, Leics Snr Lg 46-47 47-48 (Lg Cup 46-47), Coalville Charity Cup 46-47, Derbys Divisional Cup 48-49, Bass Vase 10-11 28-28 30-31 48-49 49-50 66-67, Central Alliance 64-65 66-67 (Lg Cup 52-53), East Mids Regional Lg 67-68 69-70.

PROGRAMME DETAILS:
Pages: 36 **Price:** 70p
Editor: Brian Spare
(0332 862812)

GRESLEY's 1993-94 CAMPAIGN

Date	Opponents	Comp.	Res	Gate	Goalscorers
21/08	Dorchester Town	BHL	2-1	622	Devaney(2)
24/08	**CAMBRIDGE CITY**	BHL	2-1	835	Marsden, Hurst
28/08	**CRAWLEY TOWN**	BHL	1-1	774	Taplin
30/08	Atherstone United	BHL	0-3	805	
04/09	Gloucester City	BHL	1-1	572	Marsden
07/09	**CORBY TOWN**	BHL	1-0	765	Marsden
11/09	Bromsgrove Rovers	FAC1q	1-1	902	Osborne
18/09	**BROMSGROVE R.**	FAC1qr	0-1	1,222	
18/09	**GOOLE TOWN**	FAT1q	1-2	701	Weston
25/09	**HALESOWEN TOWN**	BHL	1-1	737	Devaney
02/10	Cheltenham Town	BHL	1-1	689	Osborne
09/10	**SITTINGBOURNE**	BHL	1-1	787	Acklam
16/10	Hinckley Town	DMC1(1)	4-0	412	Acklam(2), Devaney, Marsden
19/10	**HINCKLEY TOWN**	DMC1(2)	6-0	408	Rigg, Hurst, Devaney, Marsden, Moore(2)
23/10	Halesowen Town	BHL	1-2	894	Devaney
30/10	**MOOR GREEN**	BHL	3-3	723	Marsden, Acklam, Devaney
06/11	**TROWBRIDGE TOWN**	BHL	1-3	729	Weston
10/11	Bridgnorth Town	DMC2	4-0	125	Osborne, Acklam, Taplin(2)
13/11	Chelmsford City	BHL	1-2	465	Weston
16/11	**ATHERSTONE UTD**	BHL	1-1	804	Marsden
20/11	**HASTINGS TOWN**	BHL	3-0	601	Devaney(2), Hurst
27/11	Cambridge City	BHL	0-1	308	
04/12	**WATERLOOVILLE**	BHL	2-1	632	Devaney, Acklam
07/12	Halesowen Town	DMC3	3-2	488	Blount, Hurst, Devaney
11/12	**DORCHESTER TOWN**	BHL	0-2	564	
27/12	**BURTON ALBION**	BHL	0-4	2,409	
01/01	Solihull Borough	BHL	2-4	301	Rigg, Moore
11/01	Sittingbourne	BHL	2-1	763	Hurst, Loss
15/01	Worcester City	BHL	2-2	869	Devaney, Loss
22/01	Corby Town	BHL	1-2	574	Marsden
25/01	**CORBY TOWN**	DMCqf	0-0	504	
28/01	Hednesford Town	BHL	1-3	553	Marsden
05/02	**CHELTENHAM TOWN**	BHL	1-1	811	Blount
09/02	Corby Town	DMCqfr	3-1	321	Evans, Devaney, Marsden
15/02	**BURTON ALBION**	DMCsf(1)	1-0	1,019	Hanks
19/02	**HEDNESFORD TOWN**	BHL	0-2	676	
22/02	Crawley Town	BHL	1-0	684	Devaney
26/02	Hastings Town	BHL	1-2	402	Hurst
05/03	Trowbridge Town	BHL	0-2	339	
08/03	Burton Albion	DMCsf(2)	1-0	1,738	Denby
12/03	**CHELMSFORD CITY**	BHL	2-1	556	Hurst, Holmes
15/03	**BUXTON**	DSCqf	1-0	402	Hurst
19/03	Moor Green	BHL	4-2	376	Marsden(2), Straw, Hurst
26/03	**BASHLEY**	BHL	1-1	704	Holmes
29/03	Sudbury Town	DMCf(1)	0-2	540	
02/04	Burton Albion	BHL	0-1	1,109	
04/04	**SOLIHULL BORO.**	BHL	2-1	584	Devaney, Wardle
09/04	Nuneaton Borough	BHL	3-2	919	Stanborough, Hurst, Straw
13/04	**ALFRETON TOWN**	DSCsf	2-1	409	Holmes, Straw
16/04	**FARNBOROUGH T.**	BHL	4-0	656	Hurst(2), Holmes, Swainston
19/04	**SUDBURY TOWN**	DMCf(2)	1-3	1,089	Devaney
23/04	Waterlooville	BHL	2-2	226	Holmes
24/04	Bashley	BHL	0-2	309	
27/04	**NUNEATON BORO.**	BHL	5-3	946	Hurst(2), Holmes(2), Devaney
30/04	**GLOUCESTER CITY**	BHL	2-0	574	Hurst, Straw
02/05	Farnborough Town	BHL	0-5	818	
04/05	Matlock Town	DSCf(1)	1-0	437	Holmes
07/05	**WORCESTER CITY**	BHL	3-4	670	Dick, Evans, Holmes
10/05	**MATLOCK TOWN**	DSCf(2)	3-1	847	Holmes, Devaney, Dick

Key: BHL: Beazer Homes League Premier Division, DMC: Doctor Martens (Beazer Homes League) Cup, FAC: F.A. Cup, FAT: F.A. Trophy, DSC: Derbyshire Senior Cup. Number after cup competitions denote rounds (r: replay, qf: Quarter-Final, sf: Semi-Final, f: Final. Numbers in brackets indicate legs, i.e. (1): 1st leg).
Home fixtures are denoted by bold capitals, away matches by lower case. (p): penalty, og: Own goal.

SQUAD MEMBERS *(previous clubs listed in chronological order)*

GOALKEEPERS: Bob Aston *(Stoke City, Port Vale, Hanley, Oswestry, Welshpool, Congleton, Eastwood Hanley, Gresley, Leek).*

DEFENDERS: Nigel Simms *(Burton A., Rocester)*, **Nathan Foster** *(Burton A.)*, **Nick Stanborough** *(Hinckley Ath.)*, **Dave Swainston** *(Ilkeston, Heanor, Eastwood T., Alfreton, Grantham)*, **Martin Dick** *(Long Eaton, Hucknall, Borrowash)*, **Stuart Evans** *(Wolves, Derby)*, **Ian Straw** *(Southampton, Grimsby, Burton Albion, Buxton)*, **Gil Land** *(Nottm Forest, Mickleover RBL, Burton A., Worksop, Heanor, Gresley, Rocester)*, **John Barry** *(Slack & Parr, Kimberley, Scarborough, Burton A., Shepshed)*

MIDFIELD: Tony Marsden *(Burton A., Belper, Grantham)*, **Dave Reddin** *(Bourne, Shepshed, Kettering, Boston Utd, Shepshed, Burton A.)*, **Scott Elliott** *(Long Eaton)*, **Richard Wardle** *(Tamworth)*, **Graeme Rigg** *(Burton A., Mickleover RBL)*, **Richard Denby** *(Nottm Forest, Chesterfield, Boston Utd, Sutton T., Huthwaite, Alfreton)*

DEFENDERS: Chris Hanks *(Studley Sporting, Bromsgrove)*, **David Holmes** *(Scarborough)*, **Mark Hurst** *(Nottm Forest, Huddersfield, Grantham, Leicester Utd)*, **Keiron Smith** *(Huthwaite, Sutton Town)*, **Martin Devaney** *(Ilkeston, Hanford, Gresley, Tamworth, Leek)*, **Mike Taplin** *(Burton A., Mickleover RBL)*, **Simon Osborne** *(Army, Shepshed, Eastwood T., Ilkeston)*, **Paul Acklam** *(Sheff Utd, Long Eaton, Hucknall, Borrowash, Gresley, Shepshed).*

Formed: 1873

HALESOWEN TOWN

Yeltz

Halesowen Town. Back Row (L/R): John Snape, Henry Wright, Kevin Hickman, Lee Joinson, Ian Brown, Malcolm Hazlewood, Kevin Harrison, Eric Smith, Tony Rowe, Darren Marsh, Richard Massey, David Heywood, Ian Bettles, Gavin Blackwell (Physio). Front: Ian Hipkiss, Adam Patrick, Andrew Bradley, Shane Abell, Paul Joinson, Christopher Jones, Philip Wood, Stewart Bowen, Stuart Hall (Coach).

Chairman: Ron Moseley **Vice Chairman:** Roger Wood **President:** Laurence Wood.
Secretary: Stewart Tildesley, 83 Bloomfield Street, Halesowen B63 3RF (021 550 8443).
Manager: John Morris **Asst Manager:** Mick Tuohy **Coach:** Kevin Sweeney
Press Officer: Paul Floud (021 550 8999) **Physio:** Gavin Blackwell.
Commercial Manager: Nigel Pitt **Newsline:** 0898 122 910.
Ground: The Grove, Old Hawne Lane, Halesowen, West Midlands B63 3TB (021 550 2179).
Directions: M5 jct 3, A456 (signed Kidderminster) to 1st island turn right (signed A459 Dudley), left at 2nd island (signed A458 Stourbridge), at next island take 3rd left into Grammar School Lane, then Old Hawne Lane - ground 400 yds on left.
Capacity: 5,000 **Cover:** 1,420 **Seats:** 420 **Floodlights:** Yes **Metal Badges:** Yes.
Club Shop: Yes, selling replica strips, T-shirts, waterproof tops, coats, scarves, programmes etc.
Colours: Blue/white/blue **Change colours:** White/orange/orange.
Sponsors: D Berry & Co (Pipe Fitting Supplies) Ltd.
Previous Leagues: West Mids 1892-1905 06-11 46-86/ Birmingham Comb. 11-39.
Midweek home matchday: Tuesday **Reserve's League:** Skol Midland Comb. (Res. Div).
Record Gate: 5,000 v Hendon F.A. Cup 1st Rd Proper 1954. *(18,234 v Southall, 1986 FA Vase Final at Wembley).*
Best FA Cup year: 1st Rd 54-55 84-85 85-86(replay) 86-87 87-88(replay) 88-89 89-90 90-91 91-92(replay).
Best FA Trophy year: 1st Round Proper 93-94.
Record Fees - Paid: £5,000 for Richard Massey (Stourbridge, 1992)
Received: £30,000 for Dean Spink (Aston Villa, 1989).
Players progressing to Football League: Arthur Proudler (Aston Villa), Cyril Spiers (Aston Villa), Billy Morris (Wolves), Dean Spink (Aston Villa), Stuart Cash (Nottm Forest), Andrew Pearce & Tim Clarke & Sean Flynn (Coventry), Dean Stokes (Port Vale), Frank Bennett (Southampton).
Record win: 13-1 v Coventry Amateurs, Birmingham Senior Cup, 1956.
Record defeat: 0-8 v Bilston, West Midlands League, 7/4/62.
Clubhouse: (021 602 5305) 12-2.30 & 7-11pm daily (closes 10.30pm on Sundays). Cold snacks served.
Record Goalscorer: Paul Joinson 347
Record Appearances: Lee Joinson 544.
93-94 Captain: Chris Jones.
93-94 P.o.Y.: Andrew Bradley.
93-94 Top scorer: Paul Joinson.
Local Newspapers: Sports Argus, Express & Star, Birmingham Mail, Halesowen News, Stourbridge & Halesowen Chronicle.
Local Radio: B.R.M.B./BBC West Mids/Beacon.
Hons: Southern Lg Midland Div 89-90, W Mids Lg(5) 46-47 82-85 85-86 (R-up 64-65, Lg Cup 82-83 84-85), Birmingham Snr Cup 83-84 (R-up 51-52 67-68), Staffs Snr Cup 88-89 (R-up 83-84), FA Vase(2) 84-86 (R-up 82-83), Worcs Snr Cup 51-52 61-62 (R-up 87-88), Midland Comb. Res Div 89-90.

PROGRAMME DETAILS:
Pages: 44 **Price:** £1
Editor: R Pepper

HALESOWEN TOWN's 1993-94 CAMPAIGN

Date	Opponents	Comp.	Res	Gate	Goalscorers
21/08	Bashley	BHL	1-2	438	P Joinson
24/08	**CHELTENHAM T.**	BHL	1-1	923	Bradley
28/08	**CORBY TOWN**	BHL	2-0	655	Hazlewood, P Joinson
30/08	Solihull Borough	BHL	2-0	449	Massey, P Joinson
04/09	Sittingbourne	BHL	2-3	1,146	P Joinson, Harrison
07/09	**GLOUCESTER CITY**	BHL	1-0	728	P Joinson
11/09	Telford United	FAC1q	0-4	903	
14/09	Burton Albion	BHL	2-0	472	Hazlewood, Massey
18/09	Cambridge City	BHL	2-3	330	Bradley, P Joinson
25/09	Gresley Rovers	BHL	1-1	532	P Joinson
28/09	**HALESOWEN HARR.**	SSC1	3-1	723	Harrison, P Joinson(2)
02/10	**NUNEATON BORO.**	BHL	3-1	1,041	P Joinson(3)
06/10	Clevedon Town	DMC1(1)	2-5	354	Harrison, Hazlewood
12/10	Redditch United	BSC1	1-1	194	Bradley
16/10	Stourbridge	FAT2q	1-0	835	Abell
19/10	**CLEVEDON TOWN**	DMC1(2)	4-0	463	Hazlewood, Patrick, Wright(2)
23/10	**GRESLEY ROVERS**	BHL	2-1	894	Hazlewood, P Joinson
26/10	**REDDITCH UNITED**	BSC1r	4-2	442	P Joinson, Bowen, Abell, Hazlewood
30/10	Trowbridge Town	BHL	1-3	348	Harrison
06/11	**CHELMSFORD CITY**	BHL	3-1	712	P Joinson(2), Massey
09/11	**DUDLEY TOWN**	DMC2	2-1	423	P Joinson, Wright
13/11	Hastings Town	BHL	1-1	368	Brown
16/11	**WEST MIDS POLICE**	BSC2	2-1	420	Massey, Wright
20/11	**DORCHESTER TOWN**	BHL	2-0	656	Massey, P Joinson
23/11	**ROCESTER**	SSC2	4-0	242	Hazlewood(2), P Joinson, Wright
27/11	Burton Albion	FAT3q	2-1	709	Wright, Brown
01/12	Atherstone United	BHL	2-1	316	Hazlewood, Massey
07/12	**GRESLEY ROVERS**	DMC3	2-3	488	Snape, P Joinson
11/12	**BASHLEY**	BHL	2-0	694	Hazlewood(2)
18/12	**HASTINGS TOWN**	BHL	2-1	735	Bradley, P Joinson
01/01	**MOOR GREEN**	BHL	0-1	928	
08/01	Aston Villa	BSC3	0-2	167	
15/01	**FARNBOROUGH**	BHL	2-3	920	Bradley, Snape
18/01	Cheltenham Town	BHL	1-3	759	Massey
22/01	**GATESHEAD**	FAT1	0-2	936	
29/01	**TROWBRIDGE T.**	BHL	1-1	752	Wright
31/01	Worcester City	BHL	2-0	1,448	Hazlewood, Harrison
05/02	**CAMBRIDGE CITY**	BHL	3-0	638	P Joinson(3)
08/02	Gloucester City	BHL	0-0	459	
19/02	**BURTON ALBION**	BHL	2-2	822	P Joinson(2)
21/02	Hednesford Town	BHL	1-1	355	P Joinson
26/02	Chelmsford City	BHL	1-0	589	Harrison
05/03	Farnborough Town	BHL	0-3	529	
12/03	**CRAWLEY TOWN**	BHL	2-2	892	Wright(2)
19/03	Corby Town	BHL	1-2	392	Wood
22/03	**SOLIHULL BORO.**	BHL	1-3	582	Hazlewood
26/03	Nuneaton Borough	BHL	1-1	951	Mulders
29/03	Crawley Town	BHL	1-0	714	Harrison
02/04	**HEDNESFORD T.**	BHL	2-1	670	Hazlewood, Wright
04/04	Moor Green	BHL	3-0	491	Hazlewood, Wright, Brown
06/04	Macclesfield Town	SSCqf	1-4	231	Wright
09/04	**WORCESTER CITY**	BHL	2-1	772	Wright, Brown
16/04	Waterlooville	BHL	4-1	236	Wright(2), Robinson, Richards
23/04	**ATHERSTONE UTD**	BHL	0-0	849	
26/04	**WATERLOOVILLE**	BHL	4-0	531	Wright(2), Hazlewood, Robinson
30/04	Dorchester Town	BHL	1-1	660	Waters(og)
07/05	**SITTINGBOURNE**	BHL	2-1	790	Hazlewood, Brown

Key: BHL: Beazer Homes League Premier Division, DMC: Doctor Martens (Beazer Homes League) Cup, FAC: F.A. Cup, FAT: F.A. Trophy, SSC: Staffs Senior Cup, BSC: Birmingham Senior Cup. Number after cup competitions denote rounds (r: replay, qf: Quarter-Final, sf: Semi-Final, f: Final. Numbers in brackets indicate legs, i.e. (1): 1st leg).
Home fixtures are denoted by bold capitals, away matches by lower case. (p): penalty, og: Own goal.

SQUAD MEMBERS *(previous clubs listed in chronological order)*

GOALKEEPERS: Antonio Rowe *(Northfield, Solihull Borough, Redditch Utd, Worcester City)*, **Mick Martin** *(Hinckley Ath., Bedworth, Shepshed, Nuneaton, VS Rugby, Worcester, RC Warwick)*.

DEFENDERS: David Heywood *(Wolves, Kettering, Stafford Rgrs, Burton Albion, Halesowen Town, Worcester)*, **Phil Wood** *(Bilston Town, Rushall, Bilston Town, Dudley, Bilston Town, Pelsall)*, **Ian Bettles** *(VS Rugby, Southam Utd, RC Warwick)*, **John Delahaye** *(yth team)*, **Shane Abell** *(Kings Heath, Knowle, Northfield, Moor Green, RC Warwick, Alvechurch, Atherstone)*, **Chris Jones** *(Telford, Redditch, Halesowen Town, Bilston Town, Stourbridge, Kidderminster, Bromsgrove, Stourbridge)*.

MIDFIELD: Malcolm Hazlewood *(Walsall, Halesowen Town, Dudley, Kidderminster)*, **John Snape** *(WBA, Bromsgrove, Northfield, Stourbridge)*, **Richard Massey** *(Exeter, Kettering, Stourbridge)*, **Adam Patrick** *(Oldswinford, Lye)*, **Andy Bradley** *(Tividale)*, **Mark Clarke** *(Brierley Hill)*, **Darren Marsh** *(Cradley, Oldswinford, Tamworth)*, **Ian Brown** *(Stafford Rgrs, Telford, Stafford Rgrs, Burton Albion)*.

FORWARDS: Paul Joinson *(GEC Witton, Halesowen Town, Worcester, Redditch, Dudley, Malvern, Stourbridge)*, **Henry Wright** *(Wolves, Bilston Town, Springvale-Tranco, Stourbridge, Hednesford)*, **Kevin Harrison** *(Tividale, Stourbridge)*, **Simon Robinson** *(Aston Villa, Mansfield, Alvechurch, Blackpool, Alvechurch, Halesowen Town, Stourport Swifts)*.

Formed: 1894

HASTINGS TOWN

The Town

Steve Willard of Hastings Town moves in to tackle Crawley Town's Paul Adams in the Premier Division fixture at the Pilot Field.

Photo - Roger Turner.

Chairman: Dave Nessling **Vice Chairman:** Charles Pilbeam **President:** David Harding
Secretary/Press Officer: R A Cosens, 22 Baldslow Road, Hastings TN34 2EZ (0424 427867).
Manager: Dean White **Asst Manager:** Garry Wilson **Physio:** Ray Tuppen
Newsline: 0891 664 356.
Ground: The Pilot Field, Elphinstone Road, Hastings TN34 2AX (0424 444635).
Directions: From A21 turn left at 1st mini-r'bout into St Helens Rd, left after 1 mile into St Helens Park Rd, this leads into Downs Rd, at end of Downs Rd (T-junction) turn left, ground 200yds on right. From town centre take Queens Road (A2101). Right at roundabout into Elphinstone Road - ground 1 mile on right. One and a half miles from Hastings BR station - infrequent bus service from town centre to ground.
Capacity: 10,000 **Cover:** 1,750 **Seats:** 800 **Floodlights:** Yes **Metal Badges:** Yes
Club Shop: Yes, selling replica kits, scarves, programmes, pens, key-rings etc.
Colours: All white **Change colours:** All yellow
Sponsors: Video Star.
Previous Leagues: South Eastern 04-05/ Southern 05-10/ Sussex County 21-27 52-85/ Southern Amateur 27-46/ Corinthian 46-48.
Previous Name: Hastings & St Leonards Amateurs
Previous Ground: Bulverhythe Recreation Ground (until about 1976).
Midweek home matchday: Tuesday **Reserve Team's League:** Winstonlead Kent Div 2.
Record Attendance: 2,248 v Arsenal, friendly 25/7/92. *Competitive: 1,774 v Dover Athletic, Southern League Premier Division 12/4/93.*
Best FA Cup season: 4th Qualifying Rd 85-86, lost 2-3 at Farnborough Town.
League clubs defeated in FA Cup: None.
Record Fees - Paid: £2,000 for Darren Hare (Dover)
Received: £5,500 for Andy Blondrage (Sittingbourne).
Players progressing to Football League: Peter Heritage (Gillingham and Hereford United).
Clubhouse: Open matchdays and Tues, Thurs and Fri evenings from 7pm.
Club Record Goalscorer: Dean White 28
Club Record Appearances:
93-94 Captain: Tony Burt.
93-94 P.o.Y.: Steve Powell.
93-94 Top scorer: Keiran O'Shaughnessy 23.
Local Newspapers: Hastings Observer & News (0424 854242), Evening Argus (0273 606799).
Local Radio Stations: Radio Sussex, Southern Sound.
Hons: FA Vase 5th Rd rep. 90-91, FA Amateur Cup 3rd Rd 38-39, Southern Lg Southern Div 91-92 (Div 2 R-up 08-09 (Div 2(B) 09-10)), Sussex County Lg R-up 21-22 25-26 (Lg Cup 80-81, Div 2 79-80 (R-up 59-60), Div 2 Cup 79-80), Sussex Senior Cup 35-36 37-38, AFA Snr Cup 37-38, Gilbert Rice Floodlit Cup 89-90.

PROGRAMME DETAILS:
Pages: 44 **Price:** 80p
Editor: Tony Cosens
(0424 427867)

HASTINGS TOWN's 1993-94 CAMPAIGN

Date	Opponents	Comp.	Res	Gate	Goalscorers
21/08	Worcester City	BHL	1-3	915	Giles
24/08	**BASHLEY**	BHL	1-0	480	Hughes(og)
28/08	**BURTON ALBION**	BHL	3-2	475	Whyman(2), Callaway
30/08	Cambridge City	BHL	0-1	321	
04/09	**ATHERSTONE UTD**	BHL	1-2	440	Callaway
07/09	Dorchester Town	BHL	0-0	519	
11/09	**MOLESEY**	FAC1q	1-5	375	O'Shaughnessy
18/09	Dulwich Hamlet	FAT1q	1-2	232	O'Shaughnessy
25/09	**TOTTENHAM HOT.**	Fr.	2-2	435	Blondrage, T White
02/10	**SOLIHULL BORO.**	BHL	1-2	364	Blondrage
05/10	**ERITH & BELVEDERE**	DMC1(1)	0-0	138	
09/10	Farnborough Town	BHL	1-3	464	O'Shaughnessy
16/10	Gloucester City	BHL	1-2	457	O'Shaughnessy
19/10	Erith & Belvedere	DMC1(2)	6-0	114	D White, Heritage, O'Shaughnessy(4)
23/10	**HEDNESFORD TOWN**	BHL	0-3	368	
30/10	**NUNEATON BORO.**	BHL	2-3	420	T White, O'Shaughnessy
06/11	Corby Town	BHL	1-0	289	Tuppenney
13/11	**HALESOWEN TOWN**	BHL	1-1	368	Whyman
16/11	**TONBRIDGE**	DMC2	0-2	305	
20/11	Gresley Rovers	BHL	0-3	601	
27/11	**FARNBOROUGH T.**	BHL	1-0	415	Trott
30/11	**HORSHAM YMCA**	SSC2	1-1	96	Heritage
04/12	Solihull Borough	BHL	2-2	196	Heritage, O'Shaughnessy
07/12	Horsham YMCA	SSC2r	3-1	75	Henderson, Willard, Heritage
11/12	**WORCESTER CITY**	BHL	3-2	359	O'Shaughnessy, Miles, T White
18/12	Halesowen Town	BHL	1-2	735	T White
27/12	Crawley Town	BHL	0-3	1,165	
01/01	**SITTINGBOURNE**	BHL	0-3	956	
08/01	**CHELTENHAM TOWN**	BHL	1-1	432	O'Shaughnessy
22/01	**WHITEHAWK**	SSC3	0-1	241	
29/01	**MOOR GREEN**	BHL	1-3	297	T White
05/02	Atherstone United	BHL	1-1	212	Lovell
08/02	**DORCHESTER TOWN**	BHL	1-0	297	Powell
12/02	**GLOUCESTER CITY**	BHL	1-0	333	T White
14/09	Chelmsford City	BHL	2-0	319	Lovell(2)
19/02	Moor Green	BHL	0-1	205	
26/02	**GRESLEY ROVERS**	BHL	2-1	402	Powell(2)
05/03	Nuneaton Borough	BHL	2-0	909	Lovell, O'Shaughnessy
12/03	Burton Albion	BHL	0-2	422	
19/03	**TOTTENHAM HOT.**	Fr.	0-3	504	
22/03	Bashley	BHL	5-1	172	O'Shaughnessy(3), Willard, Lovell
26/03	**CHELMSFORD CITY**	BHL	3-1	439	T White, Lovell, O'Shaughnessy
29/03	Waterlooville	BHL	1-4	188	Willard
02/04	**CRAWLEY TOWN**	BHL	0-1	595	
04/04	Sittingbourne	BHL	1-2	925	O'Shaughnessy
16/04	Cheltenham Town	BHL	0-1	846	
21/04	**WATERLOOVILLE**	BHL	2-0	295	T White(2)
23/04	**TROWBRIDGE TOWN**	BHL	2-2	385	T White, O'Shaughnessy
30/04	Hednesford Town	BHL	2-1	294	Lovell, O'Shaughnessy
02/05	**CAMBRIDGE CITY**	BHL	1-0	375	O'Shaughnessy
07/05	**CORBY TOWN**	BHL	2-0	307	O'Shaughnessy, Powell

Key: BHL: Beazer Homes League Premier Division, DMC: Doctor Martens (Beazer Homes League) Cup, FAC: F.A Cup, FAT: F.A. Trophy, SSC: Sussex Senior Cup, Fr.: Friendly. Numbers after cup competitions denote rounds (r: replay, qf: Quarter-Final, sf: Semi-Final, f: Final. Numbers in brackets indicate legs, i.e. (1): 1st leg). Home fixtures are denoted by bold capitals, away matches by lower case. (p): penalty, og: Own goal.

SQUAD MEMBERS *(previous clubs listed in chronological order)*

GOALKEEPERS: James Creed *(Faversham Town).*

DEFENDERS: Tony Burt *(Hastings Utd)*, **Phil Henderson** *(Northampton Town, Wivenhoe Town, Eastbourne Utd)*, **Steve Powell** *(Eastbourne Utd, Crawley Town)*, **Robin Trott** *(Gillingham)*, **Dean White** *(Sidley Utd, Hastings Utd, Chelsea, Gillingham, Millwall, Hastings Utd, Maidstone Utd)*, **Steve Smith** *(Brighton & Hove Albion, Hastings Town, Southwick)*, **Steve Streeter** *(local football).*

MIDFIELD: Paul Giles *(Ashford Town, Dartford, Ashford Town, Hastings Town, Ashford Town, Hastings Town, Sittingbourne)*, **Paul Tuppenney** *(Hastings Town, Stamco)*, **Terry White** *(Hastings Town, Hythe Town)*, **Steve Willard** *(Sidley Utd)*, **Richard Calloway** *(Bristol City, Chester, Wokingham Town, Yate Town, Tunbridge Wells)*, **Keiran O'Shaughnessy** *(local football)*, **Liam Barham** *(Brighton & Hove Albion, Hastings Town, Dunstable, Windsor & Eton, Dunstable, Dover, VV Veendam (Holland), Kingstonian, Grays Ath., Hastings Town, Wealdstone)*, **Karl Elsey** *(Pembroke Borough, QPR, Newport County, Cardiff City, Gillingham, Maidstone Utd, Gillingham, Sittingbourne, Braintree Town, Ashford Town).*

FORWARDS: Steve Lovell *(Crystal Palace, Millwall, Gillingham, Sittingbourne, Braintree Town, St Albans City)*, **Peter Heritage** *(Hastings Utd, Hythe Town, Gillingham, Hereford Utd, Doncaster Rovers)*, **Danny Whyman** *(Sidley Utd, Hailsham Town, Hastings Town, Hythe Town)*, **Keith Miles** *(Hastings Utd, Eastbourne Utd, Hastings Town, Eastbourne Utd, Hailsham Town)*, **David Powell** *(Bromley, Margate)*, **Dale Seymour** *(Ringmer, Bexhill, Sidley Utd).*

1880 HEDNESFORD TOWN The Pitmen

Hednesford Town FC, pictured before the Birmingham Senior Cup final against Walsall. Back Row (L/R): John Baldwin (Manager), Paul Jones, Brendan Hackett, Nick Dunphy, Paul Hayward, Mark Freeman, Kevin Foster, Gary Fitzpatrick, Stuart Jones, John Allen (Asst Manager), Don Drakeley (Physio). Front: Paul Parker, Kevin Collins, Tyron Street, Steve Burr, Joe O'Connor.

Chairman: Mike Smith **Vice Chairman:** John Baldwin **President:** Nigel Tinsley
Secretary: Richard Murning, 26 Linden View, Chase Heights, Hednesford, Staffs WS12 5UA (0543 876887).
Manager: John Baldwin **Asst Manager/Coach:** John Allen.
Physio: Don Drakeley
Press Officer: Phil Lloyd. **Commercial Manager:** Steve Burr (0543 422870).
Ground: Cross Keys Ground, Hill Street, Hednesford (05438 422870). *A move to a new, adjacent, ground is planned to take place in January/February 1995.*
Directions: M6 junction 11 to Cannock, A460 to Hednesford. After 2 miles turn right opposite Shell garage, ground on right at bottom of hill.
Capacity: 4,000 **Cover:** 1,000 **Seats:** 500 **Floodlights:** Yes **Metal Badges:** Yes
Club Shop: Yes, selling clothing, ties, badges, replica shirts, t-shirts, mugs, pens, programmes. Contact Commercial Manager.
Cols: White & black halves/black/white **Change colours:** Yellow/navy/yellow.
Sponsors: Bridgetown Doors.
Previous Leagees: Walsall & District/ Birmingham Combination 08-15 45-53/ West Mids 19-39 53-72 74-84/ Midland Counties 72-74.
Previous Names: None - club the result of an 1880 amalgamation between West Hill and Hill Top.
Previous Ground: The Tins (behind Anglesey Hotel) until 1904.
Reserve Team's League: Midland Combination Reserve Division.
Midweek home matchday: Monday **Record Gate:** 10,000 v Walsall, FA Cup 1919-20.
Record Fees: Paid: £12,000 - Steve Burr (Macclesfield Town, 1991)
Received: £6,000 - Steve Biggins (Shrewsbury Town).
Record win: 12-1; v Birmingham City - Birmingham Wartime League Cup 40-41; v Redditch United, Birmingham Combination 52-53.
Record defeat: 0-15 v Burton, Birmingham League 24-25.
Best FA Cup season: 1st Rd 19-20.
Players progressing to Football League: Norman Allsop (West Bromwich Albion 1948), Ron Russon & George Heseltine & John Giles & Gordon Dyas (Walsall 1948 & 49 & 50 & 55), Dennis Jackson & Gordon Lee (Aston Villa 1954 & 55), Brian Horton (Port Vale 70), Steve Biggins (Shrewsbury 1977), Vernon Allatt (Halifax Town 1979), Chris Brindley (Wolves 1986).
Clubhouse: Open every day with a matchday extension.
Club Record Scorer: Tosh Griffiths
Club record appearances: Kevin Foster.
93-94 Captain: Mark Freeman.
93-94 P.o.Y.: Kevin Collins.
93-94 Top scorer: Tyron Street 24.
Local Newspapers: Express & Star (Wolverhampton 22351), Chronicle, Chase News, Hednesford Mercury.
Local Radio Stations: Radio West Mids, Beacon (Wolverhampton), Radio BRMB.
Club Hotline: 0891 12 29 35.
Hons: Welsh Cup R-up 91-92, FA Tphy 2nd Rd 2nd rep. 77-78, Southern Lg Midland Division R-up 91-92 (Lg Cup R-up 86-87), West Mids Lg 77-78 (R-up 83-84, Lg Cup 83-84), Birmingham Combination 09-10 50-51 (R-up 12-13 52-53), Staffs Senior Cup 69-70 73-74 (R-up 92-93), Birmingham Senior Cup 35-36 (R-up 93-94).

PROGRAMME DETAILS:
Pages: 26 **Price:** £1
Editor: Chris Southall

HEDNESFORD TOWN's 1993-94 CAMPAIGN

Date	Opponents	Comp.	Res	Gate	Goalscorers
21/08	Sittingbourne	BHL	0-3	1,108	
23/08	**CORBY TOWN**	BHL	3-1	490	Wright(2), Street
28/08	**BASHLEY**	BHL	6-0	304	Street(3), P Jones, Wright, O'Connor
30/08	Worcester City	BHL	0-0	1,361	
04/09	**DORCHESTER TOWN**	BHL	2-4	398	Berks, King
07/09	Cheltenham Town	BHL	0-3	665	
11/09	Atherstone United	FAC1q	1-2	524	Street
18/09	**FARNBOROUGH T.**	BHL	0-2	469	
21/09	Newcastle Town	SSC1	3-1	132	Hallam(2), Street
25/09	**GLOUCESTER CITY**	BHL	1-1	401	King
02/10	Waterlooville	BHL	0-2	256	
09/10	Trowbridge Town	BHL	2-3	287	Hallam, Street
12/10	VS Rugby	DMC1(1)	1-2	320	Simcox
16/10	**NUNEATON BORO.**	BHL	4-1	729	Street(2), Green, Hallam
18/10	**V.S. RUGBY**	DMC1(2)	4-0	352	O'Connor(2), Hallam, Green
23/10	Hastings Town	BHL	3-1	368	Street, P Jones, Freeman
30/10	**CRAWLEY TOWN**	BHL	2-1	522	Foster, Green
01/11	**LEEK TOWN**	SSC2	3-4	436	Green, O'Connor, P Jones
06/11	Moor Green	BHL	4-2	319	P Jones, Street, Hallam, O'Connor
08/11	**NUNEATON BORO.**	DMC2	1-1	547	Hallam
10/11	**DARLASTON**	BSC2	1-0	238	O'Connor
15/11	**WORCESTER CITY**	BHL	4-2	401	O'Connor(3), Street
20/11	Cambridge City	BHL	1-4	294	Rudge
27/11	Redditch United	FAT3q	1-1	163	Berks
29/11	**REDDITCH UTD**	FAT3qr	1-0	224	O'Connor
04/12	Atherstone United	BHL	2-0	289	Fitzpatrick, Fry(og)
07/12	Nuneaton Borough	DM2r	3-1	643	Street(2), Hallam
11/12	**SITTINGBOURNE**	BHL	1-1	417	P Jones
14/12	Dudley Town	BSC3	3-1	141	Street, Green, O'Connor
18/12	Farnborough Town	BHL	0-1	440	
01/01	Burton Albion	BHL	0-3	1,044	
15/01	Nuneaton Borough	BHL	0-0	1,281	
19/01	**GLOUCESTER CITY**	DMC4	0-1	267	
22/01	**WHITBY TOWN**	FAT1	1-0	517	Fitzpatrick
28/01	**GRESLEY ROVERS**	BHL	3-1	553	Street(2), Wallace
31/01	**ASTON VILLA**y	BSCqf	2-1	1,089	P Jones, Hallam
05/02	Gloucester City	BHL	0-2	396	
12/02	Cheltenham Town	FAT2	0-1	965	
19/02	Gresley Rovers	BHL	2-0	676	Hallam, Street
21/02	**HALESOWEN TOWN**	BHL	1-1	355	O'Connor
05/03	Crawley Town	BHL	1-3	795	Hallam
07/03	**MOOR GREEN**	BSCsf	3-1	500	P Jones, Burr, Street
12/03	**CAMBRIDGE CITY**	BHL	4-1	287	Yates, Hallam(2), Dunphy
14/03	**SOLIHULL BORO.**	BHL	2-1	297	Street, Hackett
19/03	Dorchester Town	BHL	4-1	451	Street(2), Burr, O'Connor
21/03	**CHELMSFORD CITY**	BHL	1-2	397	Street
26/03	**WATERLOOVILLE**	BHL	3-2	348	Yates, Burr, O'Connor
30/03	Corby Town	BHL	2-4	246	O'Connor, Hackett
02/04	Halesowen Town	BHL	1-2	670	Burr
04/04	**BURTON ALBION**	BHL	2-2	501	Hackett, Hallam
09/04	Solihull Borough	BHL	0-0	170	
11/04	**ATHERSTONE UTD**	BHL	1-2	436	Harrison
13/04	**MOOR GREEN**	BHL	0-0	172	
16/04	**TROWBRIDGE TOWN**	BHL	0-1	365	
18/04	**CHELTENHAM TOWN**	BHL	2-0	515	Street, O'Connor
23/04	Bashley	BHL	0-0	205	
26/04	Walsall	BSCf	0-3	2,555	
30/04	**HASTINGS TOWN**	BHL	1-2	294	O'Connor
07/05	Chelmsford City	BHL	1-4	583	Rudge

Key: BHL: Beazer Homes League Premier Division, DMC: Doctor Martens (Beazer Homes League) Cup, FAC: F.A. Cup, FAT: F.A. Trophy, SSC: Staffs Senior Cup, BSC: Birmingham Senior Cup. Number after cup competitions denote rounds (r: replay, qf: Quarter-Final, sf: Semi-Final, f: Final. Numbers in brackets indicate legs, i.e. (1): 1st leg).
Home fixtures are denoted by bold capitals, away matches by lower case. (p): penalty, og: Own goal.

SQUAD MEMBERS *(previous clubs listed in chronological order)*

GOALKEEPERS: Paul Hayward *(Paget, Worcester, Kidderminster, Redditch, Blakenall, Bilston).*

DEFENDERS: Mark Freeman *(Bilston, Wolves, Bilston, Willenhall),* **Kevin Foster** *(Stourbridge, Hednesford, Willenhall),* **Nick Dunphy** *(Rushall, Sutton Coldfield),* **Kirk Thomas** *(Boldmere St Michaels),* **Luke Yates** *(Nottm Forest, Halesowen T., Sandwell Borough, Brierley Hill, Bilston),* **Kevin Collins** *(Causeway Green, Boldmere, Shrewsbury, Alvechurch, Kidderminster, Burton A., Rushall, Stourbridge).*

MIDFIELD: Paul Jones *(Walsall, Wolves, Kettering, Stafford Rgrs),* **Martin Byrne** *(West Brom Town),* **Stuart Jones** *(local football),* **Dale Rudge** *(Wolves, Preston, Djerv(Norway), Hednesford, Brierley Hill),* **Gary Fitzpatrick** *(Leicester City, VS Rugby, Moor Green),* **Tyrone Street** *(Blakenhall, Willenhall, Bilston, Cradley, Bilston),* **Brendan Hackett** *(Bilston, Redditch, Stourbridge, Dudley, Archdales, Worcester, Gloucester, Telford)*

FORWARDS: Steve Burr *(Lichfield, Atherstone, Stafford Rgrs, Macclesfield, Hednesford, Stafford Rgrs, Macclesfield),* **Mark Hallam** *(Leicester Utd, Boston Utd),* **Joe O'Connor** *(Lye, Stafford Rgrs),* **Mike Harrison** *(Port Vale),* **Matthew Wallace** *(Shepshed, Atherstone),* **Neil Bannister** *(Darlaston),* **Andy Quinn** *(Boldmere, Tamworth, Solihull, Mile Oak, Paget).*

Formed: 1952

LEEK TOWN

The Blues

Leek Town's Dave Sutton takes on Paul Dawson during the Blues' disappointing 1-4 home defeat in their top-of-the-table home fixture against Marine.

Photo - Nick Kennedy.

President: Mr G Heath **Chairman:** Mr M Howson.
Secretary: Michael Rowley, 62 London Rd, Chesterton, Newcastle, Staffs ST5 7DY (0782 562890).
Manager: TBA **Asst Manager:** TBA **Physio:** Martin Parr
Coach: Steve Norris **Commercial Manager:** Mr A Carr
Press Officer: Mike Cope
Ground: Harrison Park, Macclesfield Road, Leek ST13 8LD (0538 399278. Fax 0538 399826).
Directions: Opposite Courtaults chemical works on A523 Macclesfield to Buxton road half a mile out of Leek heading towards Macclesfield.
Capacity: 3,800 **Cover:** 3,300 **Seats:** 625 **Floodlights:** Yes **Metal Badges:** Yes
Club Shop: Yes - contact club on 0538 399278.
Colours: Blue/white **Change colours:** Yellow/purple **Sponsors:** TBA.
Previous Leagues: Staffs County/ Manchester 51-54 57-73/ West Mids (B'ham) 54-56/ Cheshire County 73-82/ North West Counties 82-87/ Northern Premier 87-94.
Previous Names: Abbey Green Rovers/ Leek Lowe Hamil.
Midweek home matchday: Tuesday
Record Attendance: 3,512 v Macclesfield Town, F.A. Cup Second Qualifying Round 73-74.
Best FA Cup season: 2nd Rd replay 90-91 (lost 0-4 at Chester after 1-1 draw).
League clubs defeated in FA Cup: Scarborough 90-91.
Record Fees - Paid: £2,000 for Simon Snow (Sutton Town)
Received: £2,500 Tony Griffiths (Telford).
Players progressing to Football League: Geoff Crosby (Stockport 1952), Bill Summerscales & Mark Bright & Martyn Smith (Port Vale 1970 & 81 & 84), Paul Edwards (Crewe 1989).
Clubhouse: (0538 383734). Open nightly + weekend lunchtimes.
Club Record Goalscorer: Alan Vickers
Club Record Appearances: Gary Pearce 447.
Local Newspapers: Leek Post & Times (0538 399599), Evening Sentinel (0782 289800).
Local Radio Stations: Radio Stoke, Signal Radio.
Newsline: 0891 664 353.
Captain 93-94: Allan Somerville.
Top Scorer 93-94: Darren Twigg.
Player of the Year 93-94: Darren Twigg.
Honours: FA Trophy R-up 89-90 (QF 85-86), Northern Premier Lg R-up 93-94 (Div 1 89-90, Div 1 Cup R-up 88-89, Presidents Cup R-up 93-94, Lg Shield 90-91), North West Co's Lg Cup 84-85 (Charity Shield 84-85), Cheshire County Lg 74-75 (Challenge Shield 74-75), Manchester Lg 51-52 71-72 72-73 (Lg Cup 72-73), Staffs Snr Cup R-up 54-55 81-82 (Jnr Cup 51-52 70-71 (R-up 47-48 48-49 49-50)), Staffs Co. Lg 50-51 69-70 70-71 73-74 (R-up 47-48 49-50, Lg Cup 70-71 73-74), Leek Post Charity Shield 46-47, Leek Cup 47-48 52-53 70-71 71-72 (R-up 46-47), May Bank Cup 47-48 50-51 71-72, Hanley Cup 48-49 70-71 (R-up 49-5), Mid Cheshire Lg Div 2 87-88 (Div 2 Cup 87-88).

PROGRAMME DETAILS:
Pages: 36 **Price:** £1
Editor: Mike Cope

LEEK TOWN's 1993-94 CAMPAIGN

Date	Opponents	Comp.	Res	Gate	Goalscorers
21/08	**BRIDLINGTON**	NPL	0-2	396	
25/08	Matlock Town	NPL	3-3	531	Clowes, Wheaton, Twigg
28/08	Frickley Athletic	NPL	3-1	213	Taylor, Sutton, S M Jones
30/08	**BUXTON**	NPL	2-1	573	Finney, Sutton
04/09	**ACCRINGTON S.**	NPL	2-1	419	Somerville, Wheaton
08/09	Boston United	NPL	3-3	741	Wheaton, Somerville, Twigg
11/09	Arnold Town	FAC1q	3-1	347	Wheaton, Twigg(2)
18/09	Morecambe	NPL	0-0	456	
25/09	**BAMBER BRIDGE**	FAC2q	5-3	393	Twigg(3), Smith, Wheaton
28/09	Eastwood Hanley	SSC1	2-1	292	Twigg, Sutton
02/10	Gretna	PC1	0-0	101	
05/10	**COLWYN BAY**	NPL	2-0	384	Twigg(2)
09/10	**EMLEY**	FAC3q	1-0	572	Twigg
12/10	Marine	NPL	2-3	362	Twigg, Clowes
16/10	Barrow	NPL	0-3	826	
19/10	**BOSTON UNITED**	NPL	2-1	409	Twigg, Diskin
23/10	Billingham Syn.	FAC4q	1-1	469	Smith
26/10	**BILLINGHAM S.**	FAC4qr	2-1	893	Wheaton, Twigg
30/10	**GRETNA**	PC1r	4-0	362	Wheaton, Twigg, Sutton, Clowes
01/11	Hednesford Town	SSC2	4-3	436	Wheaton, Finney, Sutton, Foster(og)
06/11	Emley	NPL	1-1	259	Sutton
08/11	**MATLOCK TOWN**	NPL	2-1	440	Mitchell, S R Jones
12/11	**WIGAN ATHLETIC**	FAC1	2-2	2,785	Sutton(2)
15/11	Hyde United	PCqf	0-0	222	
20/11	Bishop Auckland	NPL	2-2	303	Wheaton, Twigg
27/11	**STEVENAGE BORO.**	FAT3q	0-2	485	
30/11	Wigan Athletic	FAC1r	0-3	1,807	
04/12	Whitley Bay	NPL	4-0	246	Sutton(3), Twigg
07/12	**HYDE UNITED**	NPL	3-0	320	Twigg(2), Sutton
18/12	**KNOWSLEY UTD**	NPL	3-2	349	Sutton, Twigg, Banks
01/01	**HORWICH R.M.I.**	NPL	2-0	447	Twigg, Sutton
05/01	Horwich RMI	NPL	1-0	163	S M Jones
11/01	**CAERNARFON TOWN**	NPLC2	3-1	260	Twigg(2), Sutton
15/01	Droylsden	NPL	3-1	256	Twigg(2), Clowes
22/01	Accrington Stanley	NPL	3-0	425	Sutton(2), S M Jones
29/01	**MORECAMBE**	NPL	2-0	547	Wheaton(2)
01/02	Gainsborough Trin.	NPL	5-3	486	Wheaton, S M Jones, Diskin, S R Jones, Key
05/02	Colwyn Bay	NPL	1-0	158	Sutton
08/02	**KNOWSLEY UTD**	NPLC3	2-1	273	Sutton, Brown
12/02	**FLEETWOOD TOWN**	NPL	3-0	480	Twigg, Brown, S M Jones
19/02	**FRICKLEY ATH.**	NPL	1-0	622	S M Jones
22/02	**HYDE UNITED**	PCqfr	5-0	262	Twigg(3), Brown, Diskin
26/02	Chorley	NPL	1-3	325	Sutton
01/03	**ACCRINGTON S.**	PCsf(1)	3-1	381	Twigg, S M Jones, Holmes
05/03	Knowsley United	NPL	0-0	169	
08/03	**DROYLSDEN**	NPL	4-2	485	Sutton(2), Holmes, S R Jones
12/03	**MARINE**	NPL	1-4	1,030	Brown
16/03	Boston United	NPLCqf	1-0	715	Wheaton
19/03	**GAINSBOROUGH**	NPL	2-0	443	Twigg, Wheaton
23/03	Winsford United	NPL	2-1	282	Twigg, Brown
26/03	Hyde United	NPL	0-5	434	
29/03	**WINSFORD UTD**	NPL	3-1	448	Diskin, Wheaton, Twigg
31/03	Accrington Stanley	PCsf(2)	1-1	313	S R Jones
02/04	Fleetwood Town	NPL	1-2	237	Twigg
04/04	**EMLEY**	NPL	2-0	515	Twigg(2)
07/04	Hyde United	NPLCsf(1)	1-3	324	Key
11/04	Paget Rangers	SSCqf	0-3	75	
13/04	**HYDE UNITED**	NPLCsf(2)	3-2	296	Brown, Twigg, Sutton
16/04	**WHITLEY BAY**	NPL	2-1	452	Sutton, Twigg
19/04	Buxton	NPL	2-1	634	Beeby, Sutton
23/04	**BARROW**	NPL	0-0	701	
25/04	Guiseley	PCf(1)	1-3	411	S M Jones
28/04	**CHORLEY**	NPL	1-0	549	Twigg
30/04	Bridlington Town	NPL	1-1	118	Beeby
02/05	**GUISELEY**	PCf(2)	1-2	524	Diskin
07/05	**BISHOP AUCKLAND**	NPL	2-1	544	Sutton, Washington

Key: NPL: Northern Premier League Premier Division, NPLC: Northern Premier League Cup, PC: (Northern Premier League) Presidents Cup, FAC: F.A. Cup, FAT: F.A. Trophy, SSC: Staffordshire Senior Cup.

SQUAD MEMBERS *(previous clubs listed in chronological order)*

GOALKEEPERS: Alex Mayfield *(Crewe, Winsford, Nantwich, Curzon Ashton)*, **Scott Healey** *(York, Salford, Colne D., Mossley, Bangor C.)*.

DEFENDERS: John Diskin *(Nantwich)*, **Andy Holmes** *(Stoke, Doncaster)*, **Steve R Jones** *(Stoke, Stafford R., Eastwood Hanley)*, **Martin Meylan** *(Rocester, Chesterfield)*, **Steve Norris** *(Port Vale, Winsford, Leek, Eastwood Hanley)*, **Paul Clowes** *(Port Vale)*, **Paul Allen** *(Bolton, Preston, Southport, Preston, Southport, Fleetwood, Buxton, Fleetwood, Stalybridge C.)*.

MIDFIELD: Allan Somerville *(Stafford R., Hednesford, Rocester)*, **Matthew Beeby** *(Port Vale, Leek CSOB)*, **Martyn Smith** *(Leek, Port Vale, Macclesfield, Eastwood Hanley)*, **Ian Banks** *(Port Vale)*, **John Brown** *(Liverpool, Winsford, Witton Alb., Stalybridge C.)*, **Dave Rushton** *(Port Vale)*, **Ali Kamara** *(Newcastle T., Meir KA., K. Chell)*,.

FORWARDS: Darren Twigg *(Audley, Eastwood Hanley)*, **Dave Sutton** *(Stoke (A), Crewe)*, **Darren Washington** *(Knypersley V., Eastwood Hanley, Congleton)*, **Ian Wheaton** *(Man. City, Crewe, Nantwich, Eastwood Hanley)*, **Gary Taylor** *(Meir KA)*, **Steve Jones** *(Kidsgrove Ath.)*,.

1992 **RUSHDEN & DIAMONDS** Diamonds

Rushden & Diamonds FC, Beazer Homes League Midland Division champions and Hillier Northants Senior Cup winners 1993-94. Back Row (L/R): Glenn Beech, Dougie Keast, Tim Wooding, Kevin Fox, John Flower, Lee Crane, Paul York, David Johnson, Billy Jeffery, Peter Brown (Physio). Front: Alan Kurila, Dale Watkins, Richard Bailey, Paul Coe, Roger Ashby (Manager), Adie Mann, Micky Nuttell, Andy Peaks, Darren Hillier. Missing player: Daryl Page. Photo - Peter Barnes.

Chairman: W M Griggs **Vice Chairman:** A C Jones.
Joint Presidents: D Attley & C Jones.
Secretary: David Joyce, 54 Ferrestone Rd, Wellingborough, Northants NN8 4EJ (0933 279466(h) /653574(b)).
Manager: Roger Ashby **Coach:** Billy Jeffrey **Physio:** Peter Brown
Press Officer: Bernard Lake (0933 57968).
Commercial Manager: Bernard Lake (0933 57968)/ Jenny Limmage.
Ground: Nene Park, Station Rd, Irthlingborough, Northants (0933 650345).
Directions: On A6 approx. 350yds north of A45 junction over bridge.
Capacity: 3,500 **Cover:** 2,000 **Seats:** 2,000 **Floodlights:** Yes **Metal Badges:** Yes
Club Shop: Yes, stocking football memorabilia etc. Contact Bernard Lake (number above).
Colours: Red/white/blue **Change colours:** All white **Sponsors:** Pittards Garner.
Previous Names: Irthlingborough Diamonds (formed 1946), Rushden Town (formed 1889) merged in 1992.
Previous Leagues: Rushden Town: Midland 1894-1901/ Utd Co's 01-04 19-56 61-83/ Central Alliance 61-83. *Irthlingborough Diamonds: Rushden Yth/ Rushden & District/ Kettering Amtr.*
Previous Ground: Rushden Town: Hayden Rd, Rushden (pre-1992).
Midweek home matchday: Tuesday **Reserve Team's League:** Skol Midland Comb. Reserve Division.
Record Gate: 2,352 v Kettering, Northamptonshire Senior Cup semi-final 29/3/94. *Ground record: 2,470 Irthingborough Diamonds v Dagenham, FA Cup 4th Qualifying Rd replay 1978.*
Best FA Cup season: 4th Qualifying Round 93-94 (lost 1-3 v Bromsgrove Rovers). As Rushden Town: 4th Qualifying Round 59-60 (lost 0-3 at Enfield). As Irthlingborough: 4th Qualifying Round replay 78-79 (lost 1-2 after 0-0 draw at Dagenham).
Record win: 7-0 home v Redditch United, Southern League Midland Division 7/5/94.
Record defeat: 0-4 away v Leicester United, Beazer Homes Midland Division 92-93.
Record transfer fee paid: £20,000 for Darren Collins (Enfield, 1994).
Players progressing to Football League: From Rushden Town: Gordon Inwood (WBA 1949), Robert Peacock (Northampton 1957). *From Irthlingborough Diamonds: Scott Endersby (Ipswich, Tranmere, Swindon, Carlisle), Steve Brown & Dave Johnson (N'hampton).*
Clubhouse: Lounge facilities. Open all day, every day. Full restaurant facilities.
Club Record Scorer: Dale Watkins 47l **Record Apps:** Darryl Page
93-94 Captain: Jon Flower
Player of the Year 93-94: David Johnson.
93-94 Top Scorer: Micky Nuttell 39.
Local Newspapers: Northants Evening Telegraph (0536 81111), Chronicle & Echo (0604 231122), Herald & Post, Northants Citizen
Local Radio Stations: Radio Northampton, Radio Northampton 96.6, KCBC
Hons: Southern Lg Midland Division 93-94, Northants Senior Cup 93-94, Daventry Charity Cup 92-93, Campri Leisurewear Cup 92-93. As Rushden Town: Southern Lg Midland Div R-up 88-89, Utd Co's Lg(10) 02-03 26-27 29-30 31-32 34-38 63-64 72-73 (R-up(12) 01-02 24-25 28-29 30-31 33-34 38-39 49-50 62-63 71-72 77-79 82-83, Lg Cup(5) 33-35 36-38 46-47, Northants Snr Cup(9) 25-28 29-31 34-35 36-37 57-58 77-78, FA Amtr Cup 2nd Rd 1893-94, FA Tphy 3rd Qual Rd 69-70, FA Vase QF 89-90. *As Irthlingborough Diamonds: Utd Co's Lg 70-71 76-77 78-79 82-83 (KO Cup 78-79 80-81 (R-up 90-91)), Northants Snr Cup 80-81.*

PROGRAMME DETAILS:
Pages: 32 **Price:** £1
Editor: Mark Rushton

RUSHDEN's 1993-94 CAMPAIGN

Date	Opponents	Comp.	Res	Gate	Goalscorers
21/08	**CLEVEDON TOWN**	BHL	2-0	641	Nuttell, Watkins
24/08	Tamworth	BHL	1-1	632	Nuttell
28/08	Rocester	FACpr	1-0	132	Nuttell
30/08	**BEDWORTH UNITED**	BHL	3-1	884	Nuttell(2), Flower
04/09	Stourbridge	BHL	1-0	284	Richardson
07/09	Grantham Town	DMCpr(1)	3-1	188	Kirkup, Flower, Watkins
11/09	**SUTTON COLDFIELD**	FAC1q	2-0	584	Watkins, Mann
14/09	**KING'S LYNN**	BHL	6-0	901	Nuttell, Mann(3), Kirkup, Diver
18/09	Bridgnorth Town	BHL	2-0	167	Mann, Diver
21/09	**GRANTHAM TOWN**	DMCpr(2)	3-2	621	Nuttell, Watkins, Kurila
25/09	**ROTHWELL TOWN**	FAC2q	1-1	990	Nuttell
28/09	Rothwell Town	FAC2qr	2-0	929	Watkins(2)
02/10	Dudley Town	BHL	2-2	235	Nuttell(2)
09/10	**BURTON ALBION**	FAC3q	4-0	1,201	Nuttell, Mann, Richardson, Watkins
12/10	**COGENHOE UNITED**	NSC1	4-2	437	Nuttell(3), Watkins
16/10	**BURTON ALBION**	FAT2q	0-1	812	
19/10	**BEDWORTH UNITED**	DMC1(1)	2-0	402	Nuttell, Watkins
23/10	**BROMSGROVE RVRS**	FAC4q	1-3	1,522	Kirkup
26/10	Bedworth United	DMC1(2)	0-0	216	
30/10	Redditch United	BHL	2-1	146	Mann, Watkins
06/11	**HINCKLEY TOWN**	BHL	2-3	647	Mann, Kirkup
09/11	**CAMBRIDGE CITY**	DMC2	2 2	419	Nuttell, Mann
13/11	**BILSTON TOWN**	BHL	5-1	637	Nuttell(2), Watkins, Mann, Diver
20/11	**TAMWORTH**	BHL	5-1	701	Nuttell, York, Watkins, Kirkup, Baines(og)
27/11	**STOURBRIDGE**	BHL	3-3	603	Watkins(3)
30/11	Rothwell Town	NSC2	1-0	203	Davis(og)
04/12	**DUDLEY TOWN**	BHL	2-1	738	Richardson, Kirkup
07/12	Cambridge City	DMC2r	1-3	167	Kirkup
18/12	Leicester United	BHL	2-0	191	Kirkup(2)
27/12	**V.S. RUGBY**	BHL	1-1	2,054	Nuttell
01/01	Grantham Town	BHL	1-0	502	Kirkup
03/01	**R.C. WARWICK**	BHL	1-1	1,019	Richardson
08/01	Armitage	BHL	3-0	117	Nuttell(2), Watkins
15/01	**SUTTON COLDFIELD**	BHL	2-0	906	Watkins, Bailey
22/01	Forest Green Rovers	BHL	5-3	287	Flower(2), Watkins, P Coe, Beech
26/01	Newport AFC	BHL	2-0	422	Beech, Watkins
29/01	Weston-super-Mare	BHL	1-2	495	Nuttell
05/02	**YATE TOWN**	BHL	3-0	810	Nuttell, Flower, Bailey
08/02	King's Lynn	BHL	1-1	383	Watkins
12/02	Evesham United	BHL	4-1	224	Nuttell(2), Flower, York
19/02	**NEWPORT A.F.C.**	BHL	1-1	991	Watkins
26/02	**LEICESTER UTD**	BHL	4-0	855	Nuttell, Mann(2), Bailey
01/03	Bedworth United	BHL	2-1	292	Nuttell, Watkins
05/03	Bilston Town	BHL	1-0	189	Watkins
08/03	**BRIDGNORTH TOWN**	BHL	2-0	844	Beech, P Coe
12/03	Yate Town	BHL	4-2	238	Beech, Bailey(2), Watkins
19/03	**WESTON-s.-MARE**	BHL	3-2	1,310	Nuttell, York, Watkins
23/03	Clevedon Town	BHL	0-0	469	
26/03	Hinckley Town	BHL	4-0	262	Nuttell, Watkins(2), Keast
29/03	**KETTERING TOWN**	NSCsf	3-2	2,352	Nuttell, Kirkup(2)
02/04	VS Rugby	BHL	2-2	1,233	Nuttell, Keast
09/04	RC Warwick	BHL	2-2	249	Watkins, P Coe
12/04	**GRANTHAM TOWN**	BHL	3-3	723	Nuttell(2), Watkins
13/04	Lutterworth Town	DCCqf	3-2	30	Bailey, Kirkup, Kurila
16/04	**ARMITAGE**	BHL	4-0	945	Nuttell(2), Johnson, Mann
23/04	Sutton Coldfield T.	BHL	2-1	345	Johnson, Flower
26/04	**N'PTON SPENCER**	NSCf	5-0	1,254	Watkins(3), Flower, Wooding
30/04	**EVESHAM UNITED**	BHL	1-0	1,186	Mann
02/05	**FOREST GREEN**	BHL	5-0	1,504	Nuttell(2), Mann, Watkins, P Coe
04/05	**NEWPORT PAGNELL**	DCCsf	0-1		
07/05	**REDDITCH UTD**	BHL	7-0	1,397	Mann(2), Nuttell, Watkins, Flower, Wooding, Keast

Key: BHL: Beazer Homes League Midland Division, DMC: Doctor Martens (Beazer Homes League) Cup, FAC: F.A. Cup, FAT: F.A. Trophy, DCC: Daventry Charity Cup, NSC: Hillier Northants Senior Cup.

SQUAD MEMBERS *(previous clubs listed in chronological order)*

GOALKEEPERS: Kevin Fox *(Lincoln, Kettering, Rushden, Wellingborough)*, **Dennis Burke** *(Stockport, Bromsgrove, Paget, Alvechurch, Redditch, Telford, Halesowen T., Burnham, Hinckley T.)*

DEFENDERS: Darryl Page *(Kettering, Rothwell, Burton PW, New Plymouth(NZ))*, **John Flower** *(Timken Duston, Brixworth, Corby, Sheff Utd, Aldershot, Aylesbury)*, **Tim Wooding** *(Norwich City)*, **David Johnson** *(Kettering, Irthlingborough, Northampton)*, **John Coe** *(Rothwell, VS Rugby)*, **Andy Peaks** *(Northampton, Bedworth)*, **Darren Hillier** *(Kettering, Long Buckby, Cogenhoe, Corby)*

MIDFIELD: Dougie Keast *(Hibernian, Shepshed, Kettering, Corby)*, **Paul York** *(Cogenhoe, Irthlingborough, Kettering, Aylesbury, Baldock)*, **Paul Richardson** *(Eastwood, Nuneaton, Derby, Kettering, Barnet, Boston Utd, Dagebham & Red.)*, **Adie Mann** *(Northampton, Torquay, Northampton, Barnet, Northampton Spencer)*, **Glenn Beech** *(Aston Villa, Stamford, Baker Perkins, Rushden, Grantham, Boston Utd, Kettering, Boston Utd, Stamford)*, **Alan Kurila** *(Birmingham, Bedford, Bromsgrove, Burton A., Stafford Rgrs, Kidderminster, Burton A.)*

FORWARDS: Dale Watkins *(Sheff Utd, Peterborough, Peterborough City, Grantham)*, **Richard Bailey** *(Yth team)*, **Andy Kirkup** *(Rushden, Corby, Rushden, Wellingborough)*, **Shaun Diver** *(Kettering, Desborough, Rothwell, Corby)*, **Paul Coe** *(Newmarket, Sudbury, Cambridge C., Scarborough, Cambridge C.)*, **Micky Nuttell** *(Peterborough, Cheltenham, Wycombe, Boston Utd, Kettering, Dagenham & Red.)*

SITTINGBOURNE

Formed: 1881 — Brickies

Sittingbourne pictured before their FA Trophy tie at Molesey.

Photo - Eric Marsh.

Chairman: Mick Fletcher **President:** E H Bennett.
Secretary: Ian Kingsnorth, c/o Sittingbourne FC
Manager: John Ryan **Coach:** Nicky Sparks **Physio:** Kevin Manser
Youth Development & Community Liaison Officer: Carl Laraman. **Newsline:** 0891 88 44 34.
Commercial Manager & Press Officer: Kevin Illand (c/o the club).
Ground: Central Park, Eurolink, Sittingbourne, Kent ME10 3SB (0795 475547. Fax: 0795 430776).
Directions: Through Sittingbourne on main A2, club signposted clearly and regularly from both east and west. 1 mile from Sittingbourne BR station.
Capacity: 8,000 **Cover:** 3,300 **Seats:** 2,000 **Floodlights:** 420 lux **Metal Badges:** Yes
Club Shop: Yes, selling match videos, action photos, college scarves, bar scarves, t-shirts, flat hats, bobble hats, badges, mugs, rosettes, tankards, pennants, car pennants & stickers, key rings, pens, coasters, replica home & away kits, club ties, programmes etc. Open matchdays, otherwise contact Ann Morrison (0795 664436) or Clive Phillips (0795 477108).
Colours: Red/black/red. **Change colours:** All yellow.
Club Sponsors: Harrisons (shirt sponsors: Medway Galvanising).
Previous Leagues: Kent 1894-1905 09-27 30-39 46-59 68-91/ South Eastern 05-09/ Southern 27-30 59-67.
Previous Names: Sittingbourne United 1881-86.
Previous Grounds: Sittingbourne Recreation Ground 1881-90/ Gore Court Cricket Ground 90-92/ The Bull Ground 1892-1990.
Midweek home matchday: Wednesday **Reserve's League:** None - friendly matches played.
Record Attendance: 5,951 v Tottenham Hotspur, friendly 26/1/93. *Competitive: 5,583 v Gravesend, F.A. Cup 1961 (at the Bull Ground).*
Record transfer paid: £20,000 to Ashford Town for Lee McRobert, 1993.
Record transfer received: £210,000 from Millwall for Neil Emblen and Michael Harle, 1993.
Best FA Cup season: Second Round Proper 25-26 (lost 0-7 at Swindon Town), 28-29 (lost 1-2 at Walsall). Also First Round Proper 26-27 30-31 62-63.
Players progressing to Football Lge: Jason Lillis (Walsall) 1993, Neil Emblen & Michael Harle (Millwall 1993), Jimmy Case (Brighton 1993), Lee Harper (Arsenal) 1994, Steve Forbes (Millwall) 1994.
Clubhouse: New updated clubhouse.
93-94 Captain: Dave Bourne
93-94 P.o.Y.: Simon Beard
93-94 Top scorer: Lee McRoberts 21 (including 14 for Ashford).
Local Newspapers: East Kent Gazette, Kent Today, Kent Messenger Extra, Sittingbourne & Maidstone Post, The Word Is Out.
Local Radio Stations: Invicta Supergold, BBC Radio Kent, Invicta FM.
Hons: Southern Lg Southern Div 92-93, Kent Lg 1897-98 1902-03 57-58 58-59 75-76 83-84 90-91 (Lg Cup 25-26 58-59 73-74 80-81, Div 2 Cup 54-55 57-58 83-84 86-87 87-88), Kent Senior Cup 01-02 28-29 29-30 57-58, Kent Senior Shield 25-26 27-28 53-54, Kent Senior Trophy 89-90, Thames & Medway Cup 55-56 58-59, Thames & Medway Comination 02-03 07-08 11-12 24-25 25-26, Chatham Charity Cup 03-04 19-20. Kent Midweek Lg(res) 91-92 (Lg Cup 90-91). *Unbeaten in Kent Lg 90-91.*

PROGRAMME DETAILS:
Pages: 48 **Price:** £1
Editor: William Rickson (c/o the club)

SITTINGBOURNE's 1993-94 CAMPAIGN

Date	Opponents	Comp.	Res	Gate	Goalscorers
21/08	**HEDNESFORD TOWN**	BHL	3-0	1,108	Barham, Lovell, Lillis
24/08	Waterlooville	BHL	2-2	410	Beard, Arter
28/08	Moor Green	BHL	1-0	312	Beard
30/08	**TROWBRIDGE TOWN**	BHL	1-0	1,369	Lovell
04/09	**HALESOWEN TOWN**	BHL	3-2	1,146	Lillis, Lovell(2)
07/09	Bashley	BHL	3-0	331	Arter, Wynter(2)
11/09	**DOVER ATHLETIC**	FAC1q	1-1	3,583	Jones
14/09	Dover Athletic	FAC1qr	2-1	3,016	Beard, Mudd
18/09	Dorking	FAT1q	5-1	526	Beard, Arter, Jones(2), Ross
25/09	**GRAVESEND & NFLT**	FAC2q	0-2	2,044	
02/10	**CRAWLEY TOWN**	BHL	2-3	1,603	Lovell(2)
06/10	Tonbridge A.F.C.	DMC1(1)	2-3	592	Arter(2)
09/10	Gresley Rovers	BHL	1-1	787	Arter
12/10	**ERITH & BELVEDERE**	KSC1	2-0	433	Arter, Beard
16/10	Molesey	FAT2q	4-0	342	Arter(2), Lovell, Ross
19/10	**TONBRIDGE A.F.C.**	DMC1(2)	0-2	853	
23/10	**GLOUCESTER CITY**	BHL	0-0	963	
30/10	Atherstone United	BHL	1-0	402	Arter
06/11	**BASHLEY**	BHL	1-1	1,060	Clarke
13/11	Burton Albion	BHL	2-1	761	Arter(2)
16/11	Trowbridge Town	BHL	0-0	495	
20/11	**SOLIHULL BOROUGH**	BHL	1-0	1,068	Lovell
27/11	**KINGSTONIAN**	FAT3q	1-2	1,248	Lovell
04/12	Worcester City	BHL	1-1	787	Clarke
11/12	Hednesford Town	BHL	1-1	417	Beard
14/12	Gloucester City	BHL	1-0	352	Beard
27/12	**CHELMSFORD CITY**	BHL	1-2	1,795	McRobert
01/01	Hastings Town	BHL	3-0	956	Arter(2), McRobert
03/01	**FARNBOROUGH T.**	BHL	1-3	1,321	Wynter
08/01	Nuneaton Borough	BHL	1-2	1,338	Beard
11/01	**GRESLEY ROVERS**	BHL	1-2	763	Buglione
15/01	**ATHERSTONE UTD**	BHL	2-0	1,009	Beard, McRobert
18/01	**CAMBRIDGE CITY**	BHL	3-2	1,107	Buglione, Bourne, McRobert
22/01	Crawley Town	BHL	1-1	1,927	Wynter
24/01	Charlton Athletic	KSC2	1-3	1,110	Barham
29/01	**CORBY TOWN**	BHL	2-0	1,207	McRobert(2)
05/02	Dorchester Town	BHL	3-1	597	Bourne, Arter, White(og)
09/02	Cambridge City	BHL	2-2	323	Buglione, Scott(og)
12/02	**MOOR GREEN**	BHL	5-2	1,198	Jones(2), Clarke, Buglione(2)
19/02	**CHELTENHAM TOWN**	BHL	1-3	2,159	Arter
26/02	Corby Town	BHL	2-3	420	Buglione, Barham
05/03	**WORCESTER CITY**	BHL	4-0	989	Arter, Ross, Buglione, Barham
12/03	Solihull Borough	BHL	0-1	281	
19/03	**ARSENAL XI**	Fr.	3-2	933	Jones, Buglione, McRobert
22/03	Cheltenham Town	BHL	0-0	1,071	
26/03	**DORCHESTER TOWN**	BHL	1-2	954	McRobert
02/04	Chelmsford City	BHL	2-3	703	Beard, Jones
04/04	**HASTINGS TOWN**	BHL	2-1	836	Smith, Daley
09/04	Farnborough Town	BHL	1-2	776	Beard
12/04	**WATERLOOVILLE**	BHL	0-0	541	
16/04	**NUNEATON BORO'**	BHL	2-2	755	Beard, Buglione
23/04	**MILLWALL XI**	Fr.	1-3	294	Bourne
30/04	**BURTON ALBION**	BHL	0-0	728	
07/05	Halesowen Town	BHL	1-2	790	Wynter

Key: BHL: Beazer Homes League Premier Division, DMC: Doctor Martens (Beazer Homes League) Cup, FAC: F.A. Cup, FAT: F.A. Trophy, KSC: Kent Senior Cup. Fr.: Friendly. Numbers after cup competitions denote rounds (r: replay, qf: Quarter-Final, sf: Semi-Final, f: Final. Numbers in brackets indicate legs, i.e. (1): 1st leg). Home fixtures are denoted by bold capitals, away matches by lower case. (p): penalty, og: Own goal.

SQUAD MEMBERS *(previous clubs listed in chronological order)*

GOALKEEPERS: Lee Harper *(Eltham)*, **Andy Hough** *(Sheppey)*, **Steve Williams** *(Gillingham)*

DEFENDERS: Brian Clarke *(Gillingham)*, **Kevin Mudd** *(Mount Grace, St Albans, Enfield, Finchley, Harrow, St Albans)*, **Keith Day** *(Aveley, Colchester, Leyton Orient)*, **Paul Kelly** *(West Ham)*, **Lloyd Hume** *(Chatham, Tonbridge, Whitstable)*, **Neil McLoughlin** *(yth team)*, **Simon Beard** *(West Ham)*, **Kevin Bond** *(AFC Bournemouth, Norwich, Seattle Sounders(US), Man City, Southampton, AFC Bournemouth, Exeter)*

MIDFIELD: David Bourne *(local football)*, **Andy Blondrage** *(Gravesend, Ashford, Gravesend, Hastings)*, **Scott Saunders** *(Charlton, Greenwich B.)*, **Carlton Wynter** *(Bromley Green, Ashford, Hastings, Ashford)*, **Mark Barham** *(Norwich, Huddersfield, Middlesbrough, WBA, Millwall, Brighton, Kitchee(HK))*, **Jason Eede** *(Gillingham, Gravesend)*, **Matt Stock** *(Charlton, Durban(SA), Maidstone, Hastings, Chelmsford, Hastings, Durban(SA), Gravesend, Maidstone, Sheppey, Ashford, Crawley, Sheppey, Hastings, Durban(SA), Sittingbourne, Faversham)*, **Tim Hulme** *(Hythe, Folkestone, Dover, Hythe, Ashford, Hythe, Crawley)*

FORWARDS: Lee McRobert *(Bromley Green, Ashford)*, **Martin Buglione** *(Enfield, Boreham Wood, Walthamstow Ave., Dagenham, Tonbridge, Welling, Margate, St Johnstone)*, **Leroy Ambrose** *(Croydon, Charlton, Hvidovre(Den), Kolding(Den), Esbjerg(Den), Fisher Ath., Dover, Erith)*, **Murray Jones** *(Southend, Welling, Epsom, Greenwich, Croydon, Carshalton, Crystal Pal., Bristol C., Exeter, Grimsby, Brentford)*.

1951 SOLIHULL BOROUGH Boro

A Solihull Borough player (right) fells David Bourne of Sittingbourne.

Photo - Phil Crowder.

Chairman: John Hewitson **Vice Chairman:** T Stevens **President:** Joe McGorian.
Secretary: John A France, 105 Coppice Walk, Cheswick Green, Shirley, Solihull B90 4HZ (05646 3011).
Manager: Ron Mason **Asst Manager:** **Coach:** D Clements.
Physio: John Price **Press Officer:** Richard Crawshaw (0564 702746).
Ground: Moor Green FC (see page 377). Solihull are groundsharing at Moor Green whilst awaiting planning permission for a stadium of their own
Directions & Capacity: See Moor Green **Club Shop:** Yes **Metal Badges:** Yes.
Colours: Red/white/red **Change colours:** Yellow/black/black.
Sponsors: Mitchells & Butlers. **Previous Leagues:** Mercian/ Midland Combination 69-91.
Previous Name: Lincoln FC **Previous Grounds:** Widney Stadium, Solihull 65-88.
Midweek matchday: Wednesday **Reserve's League:** Midland Combination Reserve Division.
Record Attendance: 1,360 v VS Rugby, FA Cup First Round 14/11/92. *At previous ground: 400 v Moor Green, Midland Combination Division Two, 1971.*
Bes FA Vase season: 5th Rd 74-75
Best FA Trophy season: 3rd Qualifying Rd 92-93.
Best FA Cup season: 1st Rd 92-93 (lost 1-3 at VS Rugby after 2-2 draw).
Record win: 6-1 v Hednesford (H), Southern Lge Midland Div 91-92.
Record defeat: 1-7 v V.S. Rugby (A), Birmingham Senior Cup.
Record Fees - Paid: £5,000 for Robin Judd (Atherstone United).
Received: £30,000 for Andy Williams (from Coventry City).
Players progressing to Football League: Kevin Ashley (Birmingham City, Wolverhampton Wanderers), Andy Williams (Coventry City, Rotherham United, Leeds United, Notts County), Geoff Scott (Leicester City, Birmingham City, Stoke City), Danny Conway (Leicester City), Alan Smith (Leicester City, Arsenal), Dean Spink (Aston Villa, Shrewsbury Town).
Clubhouse: The Borough Club, Tanworth Lane, Shirley; opened June 16th 1990. Two bars, dance floor, meeting room available for hire. Open every night, Sunday and bank holiday lunchtimes. **Steward:** Mark Dumelow.
Club Record Goalscorer: Chris Burton.
Club Record Appearances: Darrell Houghton.
93-94 Captain & P.o.Y.: Paul Dyson.
93-94 Top scorer: Kim Casey.
Local Press: Solihull Times, Solihull News, Sunday Mercury, Sports Argus.
Local Radio Stations: Radio WM, BRMB.
Hons: Southern Lg Midland Div 91-92, Midland Comb. R-up 90-91 (Chall. Cup R-up 74-75 90-91, Presidents Cup R-up 69-70), Lord Mayor of Birmingham Charity Cup 91-92 92-93 93-94, Worcs Senior Cup R-up 92-93.

PROGRAMME DETAILS:
Pages: 20 **Price:** 60p
Editor: Richard Crawshaw (0564 702746)

SOLIHULL BOROUGH's 1993-94 CAMPAIGN

Date	Opponents	Comp.	Res	Gate	Goalscorers
21/08	**WATERLOOVILLE**	BHL	1-1	254	Burton
24/08	Nuneaton Borough	BHL	3-0	1,254	Burton, Canning(2)
28/08	Gloucester City	BHL	1-3	570	Burton
30/08	**HALESOWEN TOWN**	BHL	0-2	449	
04/09	Trowbridge Town	BHL	2-2	327	Burton, Casey
07/09	Farnborough Town	BHL	1-1	343	Casey
11/09	Chasetown	FAC1q	1-0	185	Casey
14/09	Boldmere St Michaels	LMCqf	4-1		Casey(3), Canning
18/09	Droylsden	FAT1q	0-2	350	
25/09	**ARMITAGE**	FAC2q	2-2	156	Hopkins, Boxall
28/09	Armitage	FAC2qr	3-2	125	Casey(2), Hawker
02/10	Hastings Town	BHL	2-1	364	Burton, Casey
05/10	Nuneaton Borough	DMC1(1)	1-4	629	Canning
09/10	**BROMSGROVE R.**	FAC3q	1-2	816	Canning
12/10	Burton Albion	BSC1	0-4	193	
16/10	**BASHLEY**	BHL	2-0	91	Mulders, Burton
20/10	**NUNEATON BORO.**	DMC1(2)	1-2	155	Burton
23/10	Dorchester Town	BHL	1-1	434	Palgrave
27/10	**NUNEATON BORO.**	BHL	1-0	403	Crawley
30/10	**CHELTENHAM TOWN**	BHL	1-2	309	Burton
03/11	**SUTTON COLDFIELD**	WSC1	4-0	99	Burton, Powell, Hopkins, Clark
06/11	Crawley Town	BHL	0-3	706	
13/11	**CORBY TOWN**	BHL	1-2	198	Burton
20/11	Sittingbourne	BHL	0-1	1,068	
01/12	**BURTON ALBION**	BHL	0-0	209	
04/12	**HASTINGS TOWN**	BHL	2-2	196	Burton(2)
11/12	Waterlooville	BHL	2-2	327	Hopkins, Coogan
18/12	**WORCESTER CITY**	BHL	0-1	237	
27/12	Moor Green	BHL	1-1	595	Casey
01/01	**GRESLEY ROVERS**	BHL	4-2	301	Casey, Mulders, Dyson, Burton
08/01	**CAMBRIDGE CITY**	BHL	2-0	194	Burton, Wolsey
15/01	Corby Town	BHL	0-1	360	
19/01	Dudley Town	WSCqf	1-0	117	Burton
22/01	Atherstone United	BHL	1-4	261	Burton
29/01	**DORCHESTER TOWN**	BHL	1-1	212	Burton
05/02	Chelmsford City	BHL	1-3	670	Keen(og)
09/02	**ATHERSTONE UTD**	BHL	0-2	153	
12/02	**TROWBRIDGE TOWN**	BHL	0-2	232	
19/02	Worcester City	BHL	4-0	661	Green(2), Casey, Canning
02/03	**CHELMSFORD CITY**	BHL	0-1	77	
08/03	Bromsgrove Rovers	WSCsf	0-3	222	
12/03	**SITTINGBOURNE**	BHL	1-0	281	Canning
15/03	Hednesford Town	BHL	1-2	297	Marshall
19/03	Bashley	BHL	3-2	209	Casey(2), Canning
22/03	Halesowen Town	BHL	3-1	546	Casey, Dyson, Green
26/03	**GLOUCESTER CITY**	BHL	2-4	246	Casey, Canning
30/03	West Midlands Police	LMCsf	3-0	120	Ollis, Casey(2)
02/04	**MOOR GREEN**	BHL	2-1	361	Green, Clark
04/04	Gresley Rovers	BHL	1-2	584	Casey
09/04	**HEDNESFORD TOWN**	BHL	0-0	170	
16/04	Cambridge City	BHL	2-0	224	Casey, Judd
19/04	**FARNBOROUGH T.**	BHL	0-0	178	
23/04	**CRAWLEY TOWN**	BHL	0-1	500	
30/04	Cheltenham Town	BHL	2-1	1,062	Casey, Burton
07/05	Burton Albion	BHL	1-2	481	Hopkins
09/05	**SUTTON COLDFIELD**	LMCf	1-0	250	Casey

Key: BHL: Beazer Homes League Premier Division, DMC: Doctor Martens (Beazer Homes League) Cup, FAC: F.A. Cup, FAT: F.A. Trophy, LMC: Lord Mayor of Birmingham Charity Cup, BSC: Birmingham Senior Cup, WSC: Worcestershire Senior Cup, MFC: Midland Floodlit Cup. Number after cup competitions denote rounds (r: replay, qf: Quarter-Final, sf: Semi-Final, f: Final. Numbers in brackets indicate legs, i.e. (1): 1st leg).
Home fixtures are denoted by bold capitals, away matches by lower case. (p): penalty, og: Own goal.

SQUAD MEMBERS *(previous clubs listed in chronological order)*

GOALKEEPERS: Darrel Houghton *(Kidderminster, Coleshill).*

DEFENDERS: Alan Cook *(Birmingham, Worcester, Chelmsley),* **Paul Dyson** *(Coventry, Stoke, WBA, Darlington, Crewe, Telford Utd.),* **Jon Pearson** *(Leicester C., Kidderminster, Burton Alb., Stafford R.),* **Trevor Whittington** *(Northfield, Redditch Utd., Telford Utd., Evesham Utd.),* **Mickey Clarke** *(Barnsley, Scarborough, Burton Alb., Sutton Coldfield),* **Jan Mulders** *(Malvern, Kidderminster, Bromsgrove),* **Keith Brown** *(Birmingham, Wolves, Alvechurch, Evesham Utd., Stourbridge, Evesham Utd., Barri),* **Ian Pinner** *(Stoke C., Notts Co., Moor Green, Alvechurch, Nuneaton Boro., Burton Alb., Solihull Boro., Alvechurch).*

MIDFIELD: Robin Judd *(Birmingham, Kidderminster, Mile Oak, Redditch Utd., Atherstone),* **Marc Coogan** *(Birmingham, Kidderminster, Barri, Sherwood Celtic),* **Richard Naylor** *(Birmingham, Solihull Boro., Evesham Utd.),* **Robert Hopkins** *(WBA, Birmingham, Man. City, WBA, Birmingham, Shrewsbury, Instant Dict(HK)),* **Brian Palgrave** *(Walsall, Port Vale, Nuneaton Boro., Bromsgrove, Stafford C.),* **Alan Ollis** *(Aston Villa, Cheltenham, AP Leamington, Kidderminster, Moor Green, Kelmscott(Aust)).*

FORWARDS: Kim Casey *(Sutton Coldfield, AP Leamington, Gloucester, Kidderminster, Cheltenham, Wycombe W.),* **Chris Burton** *(Kidderminster),* **Kim Green** *(Coventry Sporting, VS Rugby, Nuneaton Boro., Atherstone, VS Rugby, Hednesford),* **Ricky Marshall** *(Chelmsley, Bilston),* **Andy Canning** *(Walsall, Port Vale, Boldmere, Redditch Utd., Sutton Coldfield, Redditch Utd., Kidderminster, Willenhall, Burton Alb.),* **Ian Mitchell** *(Solihull, Moor Green, Highgate Utd., Nuneaton, Willenhall, King's Heath, Banbury, Solihull, Barri, Telford).*

Formed: 1885

SUDBURY TOWN

The Borough

Sudbury Town's Mark Farthing heads the opening goal in the 2-0 home win over Weymouth on 26th March. Team-mate Don Cutmore (10) gains points for artistic impression. *Photo - Roger Leeks.*

Chairman: Phil Turner **President:** H D J Yallop.
Secretary: David Webb, 6 Melford Road, Sudbury, Suffolk CO10 6LS (0787 372352).
Manager: Richie Powling **Asst Mgr/Coach:** Graham Daniels. **Physio:** Tony Brightwell
Commercial Manager/Press Officer: Richie Powling, c/o the club (0787 370957).
Ground: Priory Stadium, Priory Walk, Sudbury, Suffolk (0787 379095).
Directions: Take Friars Street from town centre, pass cricket ground and continue to the 'Ship & Star'. Left into Priory Walk and continue to ground. Half mile and three quarters of a mile from bus and rail stations respectively.
Capacity: 5,000 **Cover:** 1,000 **Seats:** 300 **Floodlights:** Yes **Metal Badges:** Yes
Colours: All yellow **Change colours:** All red.
Sponsors: Fairview Homes/ DFDS Transport/ Wheelers (Timber & Building).
Club Shop: Open before and after first team games and at half-time. Items on sale include League and non-League programmes, scarves, hats, rosettes, badges, bags, fanzines, *Team Talk* magazines etc. Shop managed by Darren Witt, 4 Highfield Rd, Sudbury, Suffolk CO10 6QJ.
Previous Leagues: Suffolk & Ipswich/ Essex & Suffolk Border/ Eastern Counties 55-90.
Previous Ground: Friars Street (until 1951).
Midweek home matchday: Tuesday **Reserve Team's League:** Jewson Eastern Cos. Div 1.
Record Attendance: 4,700 v Ipswich Town, testimonial 1978.
Record win: 14-1 v Leiston (H), FA Cup First Qualifying Rd 24/9/55.
Record defeat: 0-9 v Tottenham Hotspur 'A', Eastern Counties League 25/2/61.
Record Transfer Fee Received: Undisclosed for Steve McGavin (Colchester United, 1991).
Best FA Cup season: Fourth Qualifying Rd on five occasions.
Players progressing to Football League: Gilbert Dowsett (Tottenham Hotpur 1952), John Taylor (Cambridge United 1988), Steve McGavin (promoted with Colchester United in 1992).
Clubhouse: Open on matchdays and for other functions. Pool, darts and dancehall.
93-94 Captain: Andy Crane.
93-94 P.o.Y.: Paul Catley (goalkeeper).
93-94 Top scorer: Steve Parnell.
Local Newspapers: Suffolk Free Press, East Anglian Daily Times.
Hons: FA Vase R-up 88-89 (SF 87-88 91-92), Southern Lg Cup 93-94 (Southern Div R-up 93-94), Eastern Counties Lg 73-74 74-75 75-76 85-86 86-87 88-89 89-90 (R-up 65-66 72-73 76-77 80-81 81-82 84-85, Lg Cup 69-70 76-77 82-83 86-87 88-89 89-90), Suffolk & Ipswich Lg 34-35 52-53, Suffolk Premier Cup 72-73 73-74 75-76 80-81 81-82 82-83 84-85 86-87 87-88 88-89 89-90 91-92 92-93 (R-up(7)), Suffolk Senior Cup 56-57 86-87, East Anglian Cup 85-86 86-87(retained - final not played) 91-92, Essex & Suffolk Border Lg 48-49 49-50 51-52 52-53 53-54.

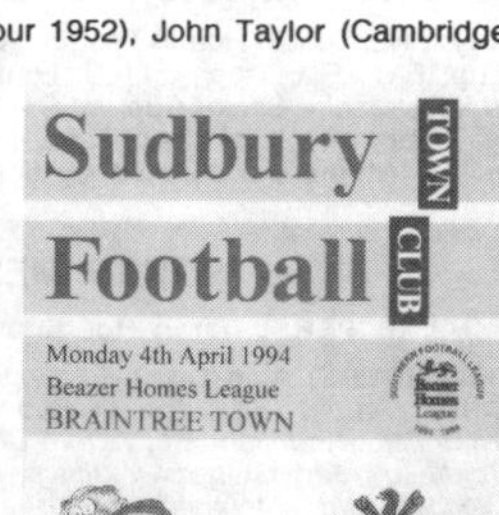

PROGRAMME DETAILS:
Pages: 32 **Price:** 75p
Editor: Darren Witt

SQUAD MEMBERS *(previous clubs listed in chronological order)*

GOALKEEPERS: Paul Catley *(Braintree, Bury T.)*

DEFENDERS: Trevor Gunn *(Bishop's Stortford, Harlow, Brantham, Braintree, Sudbury, Cambridge City),* **Brett Girling** *(Woodbridge),* **Clive Stafford** *(Ipswich, Diss, Colchester, Bury T.),* **Ian Williams** *(Brymbo, Rhyl, Bangor),* **Murray Osman** *(Ransomes, Harwich),* **Chris Tracey** *(Stanway, Harwich)*

(continued opposite)

SUDBURY TOWN's 1993-94 CAMPAIGN

Date	Opponents	Comp.	Res	Gate	Goalscorers
21/08	Canterbury City	BHL	0-3	59	
24/08	**MARGATE**	BHL	3-0	266	Parnell(2), Daniels
28/08	**STOWMARKET T.**	FACpr	4-1	285	Barker(2), Wallis, Osman
30/08	Baldock Town	BHL	3-1	385	Cutmore(2), Bailey
04/09	**WEALDSTONE**	BHL	3-2	379	Cutmore, Low, Barker
08/09	Burnham	BHL	4-1	85	Cutmore, Low, Osman, Smith
11/09	King's Lynn	FAC1q	1-2	909	Tracey
18/09	**PURFLEET**	FAT1q	3-3	352	Farthing, Barker, Cutmore
20/09	Purfleet	FAT1qr	0-3	190	
25/09	Poole Town	BHL	4-0	141	Parnell(2), Tracey(2)
28/09	**STANSTED**	EFCq	4-2	155	Parnell(2), Beacher, McIntosh
02/10	**ASHFORD TOWN**	BHL	4-5	401	Low, Smith, Tracey, Clewlow(og)
05/10	**BALDOCK TOWN**	DMC1(1)	1-0	259	Low
16/10	**DUNSTABLE**	BHL	5-2	294	Osman(3), Crane, Parnell
19/10	Baldock Town	DMC1(2)	1-0	210	McIntosh
23/10	**SALISBURY CITY**	BHL	1-3	404	Tracey
26/10	Margate	BHL	1-2	395	Smith
30/10	Fareham Town	BHL	2-0	103	Daniels, Wallis
02/11	**STOWMARKET T.**	SPC1	2-0	223	Smith(2)
06/11	**NEWPORT I.O.W.**	BHL	2-1	317	Wallis(2)
09/11	**BRAINTREE TOWN**	DMC2	3-1	384	Low, Girling, Wallis
16/11	**BALDOCK TOWN**	BHL	2-1	319	Osman, Barker
20/11	**HAVANT TOWN**	BHL	0-0	301	
23/11	**HADLEIGH UTD**	EAC1	2-3	240	Girling, Wallis
27/11	Buckingham Town	BHL	0-0	71	
07/12	**HALSTEAD TOWN**	EFCq	4-4	179	Parnell(2), Orvis, Wallis
11/12	**CANTERBURY C.**	BHL	3-1	249	Crane, Farthing, Smith
16/12	Stansted	EFCq	10-0	27	Parnell(3), Farthing(2), Bailey, Low, Wallis, Tracey, Daniels
18/12	Dunstable	BHL	1-0	80	Parnell
21/12	Halstead Town	BHL	4-2	180	Farthing, Parnell, Bailey, Orvis
27/12	**BURY TOWN**	BHL	4-1	502	Parnell(3), Wallis
01/01	Braintree Town	BHL	3-1	635	Wallis, Cutmore, Farthing
03/01	**TONBRIDGE A.F.C.**	BHL	2-1	443	Clarke(og), Farthing
08/01	Witney Town	BHL	1-1	233	Williams
15/01	Gravesend & Nflt	BHL	2-2	764	Stafford, Barker
18/01	**CHELMSFORD CITY**	EFCq	2-1	181	Farthing(2)
22/01	Wealdstone	BHL	1-0	191	Smith
25/01	**GRAVESEND & N.**	DMC3	0-1	320	*(result declared void - Sudbury re-instated)*
29/01	**BUCKINGHAM TOWN**	BHL	2-0	288	Wallis, Smith
31/01	Chelmsford City	EFCq	1-2	108	Orvis
05/02	Weymouth	BHL	2-2	845	Smith, Barker
08/02	**BURNHAM**	BHL	5-1	266	Parnell(2), Daniels, Smith, Barker
12/02	**FISHER '93**	BHL	2-0	356	Wallis, Smith
19/02	Ashford Town	BHL	2-2	346	Farthing, Wallis
22/02	**POOLE TOWN**	BHL	1-2	189	Osman
01/03	**FELIXSTOWE T.**	SPCsf	2-1	204	Farthing, Barker
05/03	Newport IOW	BHL	3-1	233	Watkins(2), Parnell
09/03	**TONBRIDGE A.F.C.**	DMCqf	2-0	275	Parnell(2)
12/03	Salisbury City	BHL	0-1	345	
15/03	**SALISBURY CITY**	DMCsf(1)	2-2	276	Parnell, Smith
19/03	**FAREHAM TOWN**	BHL	2-1	301	Reilly, Farthing
23/03	Salisbury City	DMCsf(2)	4-1	482	Farthing(2), Cutmore, Wallis
26/03	**WEYMOUTH**	BHL	2-0	321	Farthing, Osman
29/03	**GRESLEY ROVERS**	DMCf(1)	2-0	540	Farthing, Wallis
02/04	Bury Town	BHL	5-1	360	Parnell(2), Farthing(2), Cutmore
04/04	**BRAINTREE TOWN**	BHL	9-0	427	Farthing(3), Parnell(2), Osman, Wallis, Smith, Wilson(og)
07/04	**ERITH & BELVEDERE**	BHL	2-0	346	Wallis, Farthing
13/04	Tonbridge AFC	BHL	3-3	247	Parnell(2), Osman
19/04	Gresley Rovers	DMCf(2)	3-1	1,089	Barker, Smith, Farthing
23/04	**GRAVESEND & N..**	BHL	1-0	854	Smith
25/04	Erith & Belvedere	BHL	1-0	165	Smith
28/04	**WITHAM TOWN**	EFCqf	0-1	157	
30/04	Havant Town	BHL	1-2	333	Parnell
02/05	**NEWMARKET TOWN**	SPCf	1-2	445	Brown
04/05	Fisher '93	BHL	2-2	124	Parnell, Smith
07/05	**WITNEY TOWN**	BHL	2-1	805	Osman, Parnell

Key: BHL: Beazer Homes League Southern Division, DMC: Doctor Martens (Beazer Homes League) Cup, FAC: F.A. Cup, FAT: F.A. Trophy, SPC: Suffolk Premier, EFC: Eastern Floodlit Competition, EAC: East Anglian Cup.

(continuation of squad)

MIDFIELD: Andy Crane *(Ipswich, Shrewsbury, Hereford)*, **Jamie Reilly** *(Maidstone, Margate, Ashford)*, **Scott McIntosh** *(Gt Yarmouth, Sudbury, Wroxham, Diss)*, **Shane Bailey** *(Braintree, Bury T., Halstead)*, **Steve Low** *(Soham, Newmarket, Skel(Nor), Cambridge C.)*, **Dean Barker** *(Felixstowe, Bury T., Brantham, Sudbury, Kettering)*, **Justin Beacher** *(Leyton Orient, Chelmsford, Braintree, Chesham)*, **Nigel Wallis** *(Felixstowe)*

FORWARDS: Steve Parnell *(Tiptree, Halstead, Braintree, Halstead)*, **Andy Orvis** *(Hadleigh)*, **Tony French** *(Coggeshall, Brightlingsea, Sudbury, Wivenhoe, Brightlingsea)*, **Paul Smith** *(Woodbridge, Felixstowe, Sudbury, Bury T.)*, **Graham Daniels** *(Bridgend, Cardiff Corinthians, Cambridge Utd, Cambridge C.)*. **Don Cutmore** *(Halstead, Sudbury, Halstead)*, **Mark Farthing** *(Colchester, Heybridge, Braintree, Wivenhoe, Heybridge, Brantham, Heybridge, Brantham, Kemi(Fin), FC Volo(Fin), Tornavon 55 (Fin))*

Formed: 1880

TROWBRIDGE TOWN

The Bees

The covered end nearest to the entrance at Trowbridge Town's ground.

Photo - James Wright.

Chairman: A I Moore **Vice Chairman:** C Belcher **President:** A M Townley.
Secretary: Jeff Hooper, 8 Elm Close, North Bradley, Trowbridge BA14 0SF (0225 767187).
Manager: Steve Rutter **Asst Manager:** TBA **Coach:** TBA
Physio: TBA **Press Officer:** A Meaden (0225 755752).
Commercial Manager: G Phillips.
Ground: County Way, Trowbridge, Wilts BA14 0DB (0225 752076).
Directions: On entering town, follow inner relief road (County Way) signs towards Frome, ground on left 100 yds past Ship Inn near Bradley Rd r'bout. Ground on right if entering from Frome.
Capacity: 5,000 **Cover:** 2,000 **Seats:** 250 **Floodlights:** Yes **Metal Badges:** £1.55
Club Shop: Yes, selling hats, scarves, badges, mugs, sweaters, jumpers, replica kits, programmes.
Colours: Old gold/black/black **Change colours:** All white.
Sponsors: Bowyers (Wiltshire) Ltd.
Previous Leagues: Somerset Senior/ Trowbridge & Dist/ Western 1892-98 1901-07 13-58/ Wiltshire/ Southern 58-81/ Alliance Premier (GMV Conference) 81-84.
Previous Name: Trowbridge F.C.
Previous Grounds: Timbrell Street 1880-87/ Flower Show Field 87-1923/ Bythesea Rd 23-34.
Midweek home matchday: Tuesday. **Reserve Team's League:** None.
Record Attendance: 9,009 v Weymouth, F.A. 4th Qualifying Rd 49-50.
Best F.A. Cup season: 1st Rd replay (v Brighton) 47-48. 1st Rd 45-46 57-58 63-64.
Record win: 17-1 v Yeovil & Petters **Record defeat:** 0-10 v Barnet.
Record Fees - Paid: £7,000 for John Freegard (Gloucester City, 1991).
Received: £10,000 for Paul Compton (B'mouth), for Andy Feeley (Leicester City).
Players progressing to Football League: Alec Eisentrager (Bristol City 1950), Don Townsend (Charlton 1950), Cecil Dixon (Cardiff 1954), David Pyle & Jeff Meacham (Bristol Rovers 1955 & 87), Eric Weaver & Ken Skeen & Bryan Wade (Swindon 1961 & 64 & 85)), Paul Compton (Bournemouth 1980), John Layton (Newport 1984), Andy Feeley (Leicester 1984), Ray Cashley (Chester 1985).
Clubhouse: Open before and after games. Skittles, TV, pool, darts. Hot & cold pies and rolls.
93-94 Captain: Mike Kilgour.
93-94 P.o.Y.: Alan Bird.
93-94 Top scorer: Keith Knight.
Local Newspapers: Wiltshire Times (0225 777292), Bath Evening Chronicle, Western Daily Press.
Local Radio Stations: Radio Bristol, Wilts Radio, Wilts Sound.
Hons: F.A. Vase SF 90-91, F.A. Tphy 1st Rd rep 83-84, F.A. Amateurr Cup 2nd Rd 30-31, Southern Lg Southern Div R-up 90-91 (Lg Cup R-up 85-86), Western Lg(7) 27-28 29-30 38-40 46-48 55-56 (R-up 1892-93 1921-22 48-49 56-57, Lg Cup 56-57), Wilts Lg Div 2 11-12 30-31(jt)(R-up 03-04 06-07 08-09 19-20 88-89), Trowbridge & Dist Lg(3) 09-11 13-14, Wilts Snr Cup 1884-85 95-96(jt with Swindon T) 97-98 1921-22 25-26 33-34 37-38 (R-up 1886-87 89-90 92-93 96-97 1906-07 07-08 12-13), Wilts Prof. Shield(8) 45-47 49-50 68-70 72-73 92-94, Wilts F'lit Lg Cup(3) 91-94, Bristol Charity Cup 25-26, Wilts Jnr Cup 10-11 12-13, Trowbridge & Dist Jnr Cup 19-20, Allen Palmer Cup 23-24 24-25(joint), Swanborough Cup 33-34 34-35 35-36(jt), Somerset Snr Lg 30-31 (R-up 11-12 33-34 35-36), Western Co's F'lit Lg Cup 80-81 85-86, Coronation Cup 92-93, Mid Wilts Yth u-17 Lg 91-92 (Lg Cup 91-92, u-16 91-92 (R-up 88-89), u-15 R-up 88-89, u-14 88-89), National Assn of Supporters Clubs u-16 champions 88-89.

PROGRAMME DETAILS:
Pages: 48 **Price:** 60p
Editor: A Meaden
(0225 752076)

TROWBRIDGE TOWN's 1993-94 CAMPAIGN

Date	Opponents	Comp.	Res	Gate	Goalscorers
21/08	Burton Albion	BHL	1-1	588	Harris
24/08	**DORCHESTER TOWN**	BHL	1-0	475	Mitchell
28/08	**CAMBRIDGE CITY**	BHL	0-0	387	
30/08	Sittingbourne	BHL	0-1	1,369	
04/09	**SOLIHULL BORO.**	BHL	2-2	327	Knight(2)
07/09	Waterlooville	BHL	0-2	280	
11/09	**NEWPORT A.F.C.**	FAC1q	1-1	477	Mitchell
15/09	Newport AFC	FAC1qr	5-0	244	Bird, Baverstock, Harris(2), Knight
18/09	Nuneaton Borough	BHL	0-2	1,064	
25/09	**MANGOTSFIELD UTD**	FAC2q	0-0	432	
28/09	Mangotsfield Utd	FAC2qr	2-2	410	Webb, Lester
02/10	**ATHERSTONE UTD**	BHL	4-1	312	Webb, Taylor(2), Harris
04/10	**MANGOTSFIELD UTD**	FAC2qr2	2-3	497	Webb, Mitchell
09/10	**HEDNESFORD TOWN**	BHL	3-2	297	Knight(2), Mitchell
12/10	**WORCESTER CITY**	DMC1(1)	2-1	270	Knight, Taylor
16/10	**CORBY TOWN**	BHL	1-1	347	Knight
18/10	Worcester City	DMC1(2)	0-0	437	
26/10	Melksham Town	WFC	6-0		Lunt, Kilgour, Boden, Mitchell, Harris(2)
30/10	**HALESOWEN TOWN**	BHL	3-1	348	Mitchell, Webb, Taylor
06/11	Gresley Rovers	BHL	3-1	729	Bird(2), Harris
09/11	Cheltenham Town	DMC2	3-2	353	Thorpe, Mitchell, Knight
13/09	**GLOUCESTER CITY**	BHL	2-0	390	Thorpe, Mitchell
16/09	**SITTINGBOURNE**	BHL	0-0	495	
20/11	Moor Green	BHL	1-3	226	Adams
27/11	**CHELTENHAM TOWN**	FAT3q	1-1	467	Freegard
30/11	Trowbridge Town	FAT3qr	0-1	489	
04/12	**CHELMSFORD CITY**	BHL	1-3	501	Webb
07/12	**MELKSHAM TOWN**	WFC	3-0		Knight, Mitchell, Adams
11/12	**BURTON ALBION**	BHL	3-2	434	Adams(2), Mitchell
15/12	Salisbury City	DMC3	0-1	271	
18/12	Corby Town	BHL	0-1	201	
27/12	Cheltenham Town	BHL	1-0	1,444	Knight
01/01	**WORCESTER CITY**	BHL	2-2	551	Knight, Boden
11/01	Dorchester Town	BHL	1-0	541	Kilgour
15/01	**HASTINGS TOWN**	BHL	1-1	335	Kilgour
22/01	Cambridge City	BHL	0-2	227	
25/01	**CALNE TOWN**	WFC	2-0		Knight, Freegard
29/01	Halesowen Town	BHL	1-1	752	Mitchell
05/02	**BASHLEY**	BHL	3-0	348	Knight, Freegard(2)
08/02	**WATERLOOVILLE**	BHL	0-0	358	
12/02	Solihull Borough	BHL	2-0	232	Adams, Pinner(og)
19/02	Gloucester City	BHL	1-0	510	Jackson
01/03	**FARNBOROUGH**	BHL	0-0	434	
05/03	**GRESLEY ROVERS**	BHL	2-0	339	Mitchell, Adams
07/03	Swindon Town	WPSqf	2-1		Boden, Mitchell
12/03	Atherstone United	BHL	1-0	312	Mitchell
19/03	**NUNEATON BORO.**	BHL	0-0	362	
22/03	Crawley Town	BHL	0-0	677	
26/03	**MOOR GREEN**	BHL	2-2	345	Brogan (og), Mitchell
29/03	**SALISBURY CITY**	WPSsf	2-0	285	Knight, Harris
02/04	**CHELTENHAM TOWN**	BHL	2-2	598	Knight, Adams
04/04	Worcester City	BHL	1-2	837	Taylor
12/04	Bashley	BHL	1-1	88	Adams
14/04	**CHIPPENHAM TOWN**	WPSf	3-0	326	Knight(2), Adams
16/04	Hednesford Town	BHL	1-0	365	Kilgour
23/04	Hastings Town	BHL	2-2	358	Mitchell, Freegard
25/04	Calne Town	WFC	5-0		Boden, Knight(2), Mitchell, Freegard
30/04	**CHELMSFORD CITY**	BHL	2-1	332	Mitchell, Freegard
04/05	**CRAWLEY TOWN**	BHL	0-0	231	Mortimore
07/05	Farnborough Town	BHL	0-1	784	

Key: BHL: Beazer Homes League Premier Division, DMC: Doctor Martens (Beazer Homes League) Cup, FAC: F.A. Cup, FAT: F.A. Trophy, WFC: Wiltshire Floodlit Cup, WPS: Wiltshire Premier Shield. Number after cup competitions denote rounds (r: replay, qf: Quarter-Final, sf: Semi-Final, f: Final. Numbers in brackets indicate legs, i.e. (1): 1st leg).
Home fixtures are denoted by bold capitals, away matches by lower case. (p): penalty, og: Own goal.

SQUAD MEMBERS *(previous clubs listed in chronological order)*

GOALKEEPERS: Mark Teasdale *(St Josephs, Devizes, Oxford City, Gloucester, Hungerford).*

DEFENDERS: Paul Thorpe *(Newport County, Bristol City, Torquay, Yeovil, Dorchester),* **Toby Jackson** *(Larkhall, Bath),* **Jason Lunt** *(Westbury),* **Mark Adams** *(Bath, Larkhall),* **Mike Kilgour** *(Bath, Larkhall, Melksham, Trowbridge, Salisbury, Stroud),* **Ray Baverstock** *(Swaindon, Cheltenham, Gloucester, Worcester, Bath, Moreton, Gloucester)*

MIDFIELD: Ian Howell *(Swindon Town, Swindon Ath., Trowbridge, Hungerford),* **Alan Bird** *(Chippenham),* **Steve Lester** *(Frome, Backwell, Trowbridge, Mangotsfield),* **Marcus Bray** *(Trowbridge, Gloucester, Trowbridge, Newport AFC),* **Dave Mitchell** *(Trowbridge, Westbury, Chippenham, Trowbridge, Yate, Clevedon, Magotsfield)*

FORWARDS: John Freegard *(Bath, Chippenham, Trowbridge, Bath, Gloucester),* **Richard Boden** *(Wollen Sports),* **Keith Knight** *(Cheltenham, Reading, Gloucester, Trowbridge, Yeovil),* **Adie Harris** *(Dale Utd, Llandrindod Wells, Aberystwyth, Gloucester)*

Formed: 1956

V.S. RUGBY

The Valley

Considering their future was in doubt right up to the eve of the season, VS Rugby had a magnificent campaign, winning promotion back to the Premier Division at the first attempt. Their Boxing Day clash at title rivals Rushden & Diamonds attracted a 2,054 gate. Here Mickey Nuttell puts the home side ahead.

Photo - Neil Whittington.

Chairman: Peter Kilvert.
Secretary: Keith J Coughlan, 3 Evans Road, Rugby, Warwickshire CV22 7HT (0788 814746).
Manager: Ron Bradbury **Asst Manager:** Bob Stokley
Physio: Paul Miller. **Press Officer:** Derek Jenkins (0788 576804).
Ground: Butlin Road, Rugby, Warks CV21 3ST (0788 543692).
Directions: 1 mile walk from station. Ground off Clifton (B5414) on north side of Rugby.
Capacity: 6,000 **Cover:** 1,000 **Seats:** 240 **Floodlights:** Yes **Metal Badges:** Yes
Club Shop: Yes.
Colours: Sky & navy blue stripes/navy/navy
Change colours: White (red trim)/white/white(red trim)
Sponsors: T.B.A. **Previous Name:** Valley Sports/ Valley Sports Rugby.
Previous Leagues: Rugby & District 1956-63/ Coventry & Partnership/ North Warks 63-69/ United Counties 69-75/ West Midlands 75-83
Midweek matchday: Wednesday
Record Attendance: 3,961 v Northampton FA Cup 1984
Best FA Cup season: 1st Rd 84-85 85-86 86-87 93-94, 2nd Rd 87-88
League clubs defeated in FA Cup: None
Record Fees - Paid: £3,500 R Smith, I Crawley, G Bradder
Received: £15,000 T Angus (Northampton)
Players progressing to Football League: S Storer (Birmingham 1985), S Bicknell (Leicester), S Norris (Scarborough), T Angus (Northampton Town), Ashley Walker (Peterborough), Ian King (Stoke City).
Clubhouse: Every night and weekend lunchtimes. Entertainment Saturday nights. Excellent facilities include Long Alley Skittles, darts and pool.
Club Record Goalscorer: Danny Conway, 124
Club Record Appearances: Danny Conway, 374
93-94 Captain: Gary Statham.
93-94 P.o.Y.: Simon Mason.
93-94 Top scorer: Ashley Walker.
Local Newspapers: Rugby Advertiser (0788 535363), Coventry Evening Telegraph (0203 633633), Rugby Observer (0788 535147).
Local Radio Stations: Mercia Sound, CWR
Club Newsline: 0891 884 497.
Hons: Southern Lg Midland Div 86-87 (R-up 93-94, Lg Cup 89-90), FA Vase 82-83, Midland F'lit Cup 84-85 89-90 (R-up 86-87), Birmingham Snr Cup 88-89 91-92, Utd Co's Lg Div 3 Cup 69-70. (all-time record FA Trophy win; 10-0 away to Ilkeston Town, Preliminary Rd 85-86).

PROGRAMME DETAILS:
Pages: 20 **Price:** 60p
Editor: Bob Pinks

V.S. RUGBY's 1993-94 CAMPAIGN

Date	Opponents	Comp.	Res	Gate	Goalscorers
21/08	Redditch United	BHL	0-2	169	
25/08	**YATE TOWN**	BHL	1-1	437	Martin
30/08	**GRANTHAM TOWN**	BHL	3-0	386	Warner(2), Green
04/09	Bilston Town	BHL	3-0	180	Statham, Martin, Warner
07/09	Forest Green Rovers	BHL	5-0	161	Smith, Green(2), Harriman, Warner
11/09	**EVESHAM UNITED**	BHL	1-0	420	Warner
15/09	**BRIDGNORTH TOWN**	BHL	2-1	272	Green(2)
18/09	Clevedon Town	BHL	0-4	399	
25/09	Hinckley Town	BHL	1-0	126	Warner
02/10	**WESTON-SUPER-MARE**	BHL	4-1	355	McGinty, Smith, Warner(2)
09/10	**TAMWORTH**	BHL	1-0	493	Statham
12/10	**HEDNESFORD TOWN**	DMC1(1)	2-1	320	King, Warner
16/10	Armitage	BHL	1-0	151	Warner
18/10	Hednesford Town	DMC1(2)	0-4	352	
23/10	**HARROW BOROUGH**	FAC4q	2-2	826	Warner, King
27/10	Harrow Borough	FAC4qr	2-1	640	King(2)
30/10	**STOURBRIDGE**	BHL	2-0	524	Alsop, Warner
06/11	Sutton Coldfield Town	BHL	3-0	265	King(2), Smith
13/11	**BRENTFORD**	FAC1	0-3	3,006	
16/11	Boldmere St Michaels	BSC2	2-1	105	Magill, Warner
20/11	**LEICESTER UNITED**	BHL	0-0	372	
27/11	**CHELMSFORD CITY**	FAT3q	0-3	426	
03/12	Bedworth United	BHL	5-2	414	Smith, Warner(3), King
07/12	**NORTHFIELD TOWN**	BSC3	0-0	166	
11/12	**REDDITCH UNITED**	BHL	4-1	318	Smith, King(2)
18/12	Northfield Town	BSC3r	0-1	185	
21/12	Bridgnorth Town	BHL	4-0	215	Warner(2), Olner, Smith
27/12	Rushden & Diamonds	BHL	1-1	2,055	Warner
01/01	**NEWPORT A.F.C.**	BHL	1-1	747	King
03/01	King's Lynn	BHL	4-2	635	King(2), Young, Warner
08/01	**WEST BROMWICH A.**	Fr.	2-5	474	Warner, Alsop
15/01	**ARMITAGE**	BHL	6-1	348	Smith, Olner, King(2), Warner, Crawley
22/01	Leicester United	BHL	3-0	373	Warner, King (2)
26/01	**R.C. WARWICK**	BHL	2-1	490	Martin, King
29/01	Stourbridge	BHL	1-3	735	Warner
05/02	**CLEVEDON TOWN**	BHL	2-2	361	Warner, Statham
09/02	**FOREST GREEN R.**	BHL	1-1	340	King
12/02	Dudley Town	BHL	0-2	289	
19/02	**BILSTON TOWN**	BHL	2-0	336	Warner, Harriman
22/02	Grantham Town	BHL	3-2	201	Smith, Crawley, Warner
05/03	Weston-Super-Mare	BHL	1-1	453	King
12/03	**HINCKLEY TOWN**	BHL	3-0	383	Warner, Crawley(2)
23/03	Yate Town	BHL	5-1	144	Crawley, Mason, King, Warner(2)
26/03	**DUDLEY TOWN**	BHL	2-1	377	Mason, Martin
02/04	**RUSHDEN & DIAM.**	BHL	2-2	1,233	Warner, King
04/04	Newport AFC	BHL	0-2	614	
09/04	**KING'S LYNN**	BHL	3-1	375	King, Crawley, Russell(og)
16/04	Evesham United	BHL	5-1	273	Crawley, King(2), Statham, Warner
23/04	**BEDWORTH UNITED**	BHL	5-2	539	Olner, Martin, Warner(3)
30/04	Tamworth	BHL	4-1	740	Warner, Crawley(2), King
07/05	Racing Club Warwick	BHL	2-0	620	Mason, Warner

Key: BHL: Beazer Homes League Midland Division, DMC: Doctor Martens (Beazer Homes League) Cup, FAC: F.A. Cup, FAT: F.A. Trophy, BSC: Birmingham Senior Cup, Fr.: Friendly. Number after cup competitions denote rounds (r: replay, qf: Quarter-Final, sf: Semi-Final, f: Final. Numbers in brackets indicate legs, i.e. (1): 1st leg). Home fixtures are denoted by bold capitals, away matches by lower case. (p): penalty, og: Own goal.

SQUAD MEMBERS *(previous clubs listed in chronological order)*

GOALKEEPERS: Paul Batchelor *(VS Rugby, Long Buckby, Clifton)*

DEFENDERS: Tim Smithers *(Nuneaton Boro., Oxford Utd., Nuneaton Boro., Atherstone Utd., Bedworth Utd.),* **Keith Aston** *(Leicester C.),* **Tom McGinty** *(Coventry Sporting, Moor Green),* **Boyd Young** *(Coventry C., St Mirren, Tamworth, Hinckley Ath.),* **Gary Statham** *(Barwell, Barlestone St Giles, Hinckley FC, Shepshed Alb., Hinckley T).*

MIDFIELD: Paul Olner *(Atherstone Utd., VS Rugby, Gloucester),* **Robert Smith** *(Hillcroft, Aylesbury Utd.),* **John Halford** *(Birmingham C., Hinckley Ath., VS Rugby, Weymouth),* **Simon Mason** *(Leicester C., Enderby, Shepshed Chart., Leicester Utd., Aylesbury Utd., Stafford R.),* **Ian King** *(Aston Villa, WBA),* **Paul Sweeney** *(WBA, Worcester),* **Peter Wilkinson** *(Hinckley FC, Bedworth Utd.)*

FORWARDS: Danny Martin *(Stoke, Nuneaton Boro.),* **Ashley Warner** *(Coventry C., Anstey T., Hillcroft, Friar Lane OB, VS Rugby, Hinckley T.),* **Lee Harriman** *(Lutterworth, Highfield R., Hinckley Ath., Houghton R., Hinckley T.),* **Ian Crawley** *(Bedworth Utd., Nuneaton Boro., VS Rugby, Kettering, Telford Utd., VS Rugby, Tamworth, Solihull Boro.)*

Formed: 1902

WORCESTER CITY

The City

Worcester striker Gary Smith surges past George Shepherd as City hold GMV Conference side Macclesfield Town to a goalless draw in the FA Trophy in February. *Photo - Paul Dennis.*

Chairman: Dr Michael Sorenson **Vice Chairman:** N Collins **President:** R H Mann
Secretary: Stephen Bond, 4 Ferry Close, Worcester, Worcs WR2 5PQ (0905 423120/617887).
Manager: George Rooney **Asst Mgr:** Graham Selby/Alan Webb.
Coach: Steve Bond. **Physio:** Peter O'Connell **Newsline:** 0898 884476.
Commercial Manager: Nigel Collins, c/o Worcester City FC
Ground: St Georges Lane, Barbourne, Worcester WR1 1QT (0905 23003 (fax: 26668)).
Directions: M5 jct 6 (Worcester North), follow signs to Worcester, right at first lights, St Georges Lane is 3rd left. From South: M5 jct 6 (Worcester) A44 to Worcester, pass racecourse and follow A38 (towards Bromsgrove), ground on right. 1 mile from Foregate Street (BR) station.
Capacity: 4,749 **Cover:** 2,000 **Seats:** 1,223 **Floodlights:** Yes **Metal Badges:** Yes
Club Shop: Yes, selling programmes and souvenirs. Contact John Hawkins (0905 20660).
Colours: Blue & white/blue/blue **Change colours:** All red
Sponsors: MSF Gas. **Previous Grounds:** Severn Terrace/ Flagge Meadow.
Previous Leagues: West Mids (Birmingham) 1902-38/ Southern 38-79/ Alliance Premier 79-85.
Previous Names: Worcester Rovers, Berwick Rangers (merged in 1902).
Midweek home matchday: Monday **Reserve Team's League:** Skol Midland Combination Res. Div.
Record Attendance: 17,042 v Sheff Utd (lost 0-2), FA Cup 4th Rd 24/1/59.
Best FA Cup year: 4th Rd 58-59. 1st Rd (10) 05-06 25-26 28-29 50-51 57-58 60-61 78-79 82-84 87-88.
League clubs defeated in FA Cup: Millwall, Liverpool 58-59, Plymouth 78-79, Wrexham 82-83, Aldershot 83-84.
Record win: 18-1 v Bilston, Birmingham League 21/11/31.
Record defeat: 0-10 v Wellington, Birmingham League 29/8/20.
Record Fees - Paid: £8,500 for Jim Williams (Telford United, 1981)
Received: £27,000 for John Barton (Everton, 1979).
Players progressing to Football League: John Goodwin (Birmingham 1946), Tom Brown (Portsmouth 1946), Gordon Medd (Birmingham 1946), Henry Horton (Blackburn 1947), Ron Baynham (Luton 1951), Arthur Lawless (Plymouth 1955), Harry Knowles & Peter King (1959 & 60), Keith Ball (Walsall 1965), John Fairbrother (Peterborough 1965), David Tennant (Lincoln 1966), Roger Davies (Derby 1971), Neil Merrick (Bournemouth 1974), John Barton (Everton 1978), James Williams (Walsall 1979), Andy Awford (Portsmouth 1988), Andy Preece (Wrexham 1990), Mark Gayle (Walsall 1991), Des Lyttle (Swansea 1992).
Clubhouse: Open every evening and Saturday and Sunday daytime. Cold snacks available.
Club Record Goalscorer: John Inglis 189 (1970-77).
Club Record Appearances: Bobby McEwan 596 (1959-75).
93-94 Captain: John McGrath.
93-94 P.o.Y: Mick Davidson.
93-94 Top Scorer: Steve Rutter.
Local Press: Berrows Journal, Worcester Evening News, Worcester Source.
Local Radio Stations: Radio Wyvern & BBC Hereford & Worcester
Hons: Southern Lg 78-79 (Div 1 67-68, Div 1 Nth 76-77, Lg Cup R-up 45-46 59-60, Chal. Cup 39-40, Champs Cup 78-79), West Mids (B'ham) Lg(4) 13-14 24-25 28-30 (R-up(3) 31-34), Worcs Snr Cup(25) 07-14 28-30 32-33 45-46(jt) 48-49 55-59 60-61 62-63 64-65 69-70 77-78 79-80 81-82 83-84 87-88, B'ham Snr Cup 75-76, Staffs Snr Cup 76-77, Inter Lg Champs Cup 78-79, Welsh Cup SF 78-79, FA Tphy QF 69-70 73-74 80-81 81-82.

PROGRAMME DETAILS:
Pages: 32 **Price:** 70p
Editor: Julian Pugh
(0905 25844)

WORCESTER CITY's 1993-94 CAMPAIGN

Date	Opponents	Comp.	Res	Gate	Goalscorers
21/08	**HASTINGS TOWN**	BHL	3-1	917	Smith(2), McGrath
24/08	Moor Green	BHL	2-0	431	Walker, Hodges
28/08	Farnborough Town	BHL	1-3	432	Hodges
30/08	**HEDNESFORD TOWN**	BHL	0-0	1,361	
04/09	Crawley Town	BHL	0-2	586	
06/09	**NUNEATON BORO.**	BHL	0-1	1,261	
11/09	**TIVERTON TOWN**	FAC1q	1-1	823	Benton
15/09	Tiverton Town	FAC1qr	2-4	580	Walker, Richards
18/09	Bashley	BHL	2-2	276	Moverley, Smith
02/10	**CAMBRIDGE CITY**	BHL	2-0	783	Rutter, Richards
09/10	Corby Town	BHL	2-3	345	Rutter(2)
12/10	Trowbridge Town	DMC1(1)	1-2	270	Churchill
16/10	**FARNBOROUGH T.**	BHL	0-2	829	Davies
18/10	**TROWBRIDGE TOWN**	DMC1(2)	0-0	432	
21/10	Cradley Town	BSC1	2-2	175	Smith, Stephenson
23/10	Chelmsford City	BHL	1-2	503	Wilson
25/10	**MOOR GREEN**	BHL	3-3	717	Rutter(2), Daly
30/10	**BURTON ALBION**	BHL	0-4	776	
01/11	**CRADLEY TOWN**	BSC1r	0-2	321	
06/11	Cheltenham Town	BHL	0-1	739	
08/11	Kidderminster H.	WSC2qf	2-4	918	Benton, Wilson
15/11	Hednesford Town	BHL	2-4	624	Donovan
20/11	**BASHLEY**	BHL	2-0	508	Rutter, Donovan
27/11	**CRAWLEY TOWN**	FAT3q	1-1	614	Donovan
30/11	Crawley Town	FAT3qr	2-1	404	Davidson, Donovan
04/12	**SITTINGBOURNE**	BHL	1-1	767	Moverley
11/12	Hastings Town	BHL	2-3	359	Muckleberg, Rutter
18/12	Solihull Borough	BHL	1-0	206	Rutter
27/12	**GLOUCESTER CITY**	BHL	2-0	1,198	Smith, Donovan
01/01	Trowbridge Town	BHL	2-2	675	Smith, Rutter
08/01	Dorchester Town	BHL	3-0	615	Smith(2), Green
15/01	**GRESLEY ROVERS**	BHL	2-2	869	Mason, Rutter
22/01	Harrow Borough	FAT1	3-3	486	Smith(2), Rutter
24/01	**HARROW BOROUGH**	FAT1r	5-3	1,021	Rutter(2), Benton, Green(2)
29/01	**ATHERSTONE UTD**	BHL	3-0	938	Smith(3)
31/01	**HALESOWEN TOWN**	BHL	0-2	1,238	
05/02	Nuneaton Borough	BHL	1-1	1,153	Donovan
08/02	Burton Albion	BHL	0-2	538	
12/02	**MACCLESFIELD T.**	BHL	0-0	1,587	
19/02	**SOLIHULL BORO.**	BHL	0-4	661	
21/02	Macclesfield Town	FAT2r	2-3	704	Benton, Donovan
26/02	Cambridge City	BHL	3-4	218	Mason, Roderick, Rutter
05/03	Sittingbourne	BHL	0-4	987	
07/03	**CRAWLEY TOWN**	BHL	2-0	625	McGrath, Rutter
12/03	**CORBY TOWN**	BHL	2-1	659	Mason(2)
19/03	**CHELTENHAM TOWN**	BHL	1-1	1,107	Daly
26/03	Atherstone United	BHL	1-2	361	Mason
02/04	Gloucester City	BHL	2-1	624	Mason(2)
04/04	**TROWBRIDGE TOWN**	BHL	2-1	836	Daly, Smith
09/04	Halesowen Town	BHL	1-2	772	Daly
16/04	**DORCHESTER TOWN**	BHL	1-0	613	Daly
23/04	**CHELMSFORD CITY**	BHL	1-1	668	Smith
30/04	**WATERLOOVILLE**	BHL	1-2	657	Mason
02/05	Waterlooville	BHL	2-3	183	Rutter, Burns(og)
07/05	Gresley Rovers	BHL	4-3	670	Hayde, Daly(2), Donovan

Key: BHL: Beazer Homes League Premier Division, DMC: Doctor Martens (Beazer Homes League) Cup, FAC: F.A. Cup, FAT: F.A. Trophy, BSC: Birmingham Senior Cup, WSC: Worcestershire Senior Cup, MFC: Midland Floodlit Cup. Number after cup competitions denote rounds (r: replay, qf: Quarter-Final, sf: Semi-Final, f: Final. Numbers in brackets indicate legs, i.e. (1): 1st leg).
Home fixtures are denoted by bold capitals, away matches by lower case. (p): penalty, og: Own goal.

SQUAD MEMBERS *(previous clubs listed in chronological order)*

GOALKEEPERS: Kevin Shoemake *(Leyton Orient, Harlow, Chelmsford, Welling, Peterborough, Kettering, Rushden & D.)*

DEFENDERS: Terry Muckelberg *(Oxford Utd, Banbury, Oxford C., Brackley, Buckingham, Kettering),* **John McGrath** *(Shrewsbury, Worcester, Kidderminster),* **Nigel Richards** *(Leicester City, Paget, Sutton Coldfield, Tamworth),* **David Benton** *(Birmingham, Kidderminster),* **Nigel Larkins** *(Birmingham, Bromsgrove),* **Andy Wallbridge** *(Oxford Utd),* **John Ridding** *(Chelmsley, Worcester, Sutton Coldfield, Banbury, Sutton Coldfield, Redditch, Alvechurch, Worcester, Nuneaton),* **Paul Rowlands** *(Tranmere, Heswall, West Kirby, Runcorn, Bangor, Mt Maunganui(NZ), Altrincham, Bangor, Altrincham)*

MIDFIELD: Phil Mason *(Newcastle Utd, Kettering, Blyth Spartans),* **Mick Davidson** *(Telford, Bridgnorth),* **Ashley Vickers** *(Sheff Wed, Sheff Utd),* **Jason Wolverson** *(yth team)*

FORWARDS: Steve Rutter *(Maidstone, Kettering),* **Tommy Daly** *(Coleshill, Bromsgrove),* **Neil Donovan** *(Cogenhoe, Buckingham T., Daventry, Coventry),* **Gary Smith** *(Paget, Sutton Coldfield),* **Roy Green** *(Aston Villa, Lye, Oldbury, Dudley, Tamworth, Atherstone, Telford, Macclesfield)*

BEAZER HOMES PREMIER LEAGUE PREMIER DIVISION ATTENDANCES 1993-94

HOME TEAM	1	2	3	4	5	6	7	8	9	10	11	12	13	14	15	16	17	18	19	20	21	22
1. Atherstone	*	246	362	421	306	362	301	323	375	364	277	805	316	212	289	263	1245	402	261	312	201	361
2. Bashley	298	*	144	241	212	403	157	215	309	448	465	309	438	172	205	223	234	331	209	88	356	276
3. Burton A.	553	750	*	735	614	706	523	713	576	577	526	1109	472	422	1044	503	1078	761	481	588	358	538
4. Cambridge	176	210	264	*	445	333	344	315	249	330	447	308	330	321	297	281	222	323	224	227	201	218
5. Chelmsford	552	502	559	547	*	519	469	851	487	907	525	465	589	319	583	682	635	703	670	501	570	503
6. Cheltenham	468	775	701	839	731	*	866	827	840	1559	1806	689	759	846	665	702	863	1071	1062	1444	1065	738
7. Corby T.	335	243	324	282	253	326	*	371	240	301	358	574	361	289	246	221	311	420	390	201	110	292
8. Crawley T.	722	601	579	903	1052	1356	955	*	667	633	785	684	714	1165	795	532	763	1927	706	677	925	586
9. Dorchester	461	1002	627	415	492	580	463	680	*	752	450	622	650	519	451	500	607	597	434	541	636	615
10. Farnborough	356	476	538	527	535	461	453	153	362	*	426	375	529	464	440	381	578	776	343	784	602	404
11. Gloucester	577	476	569	455	538	1239	389	430	405	486	*	566	459	457	396	435	728	352	570	510	475	624
12. Gresley R.	804	704	2409	835	556	811	765	774	564	656	574	*	737	601	676	723	946	787	584	729	632	670
13. Halesowen T.	849	694	822	638	712	923	655	892	656	920	728	894	*	735	670	928	1041	790	582	752	531	772
14. Hastings	450	480	475	375	439	432	307	595	297	415	333	402	368	*	368	297	420	956	364	358	295	359
15. Hednesford	436	304	501	287	397	515	490	522	398	469	401	553	355	294	*	171	729	417	297	365	248	401
16. Moor Green	323	236	312	217	226	319	258	261	261	252	253	376	490	205	319	*	483	312	595	226	206	431
17. Nuneaton B.	1365	416	1081	1408	1195	1212	902	1083	691	1140	813	919	951	909	1281	769	*	1338	1240	1064	1112	1153
18. Sittingbourne	1009	1060	728	1107	1795	2159	1207	1603	954	1321	963	763	1146	925	1108	1198	755	*	1068	1369	541	989
19. Solihull B.	153	91	209	184	77	309	196	500	212	178	246	301	449	196	170	361	403	281	*	232	254	237
20. Trowbridge	312	348	434	387	332	598	347	231	471	422	390	339	348	335	287	345	362	495	327	*	366	551
21. Waterlooville	349	276	353	176	274	243	314	302	303	336	210	226	236	188	256	252	305	410	327	280	*	183
22. Worcester	938	508	778	783	668	1107	659	625	613	829	1198	866	1238	911	1361	717	1261	787	661	836	657	*

MIDLAND DIVISION ATTENDANCES 1993-94

HOME TEAM	1	2	3	4	5	6	7	8	9	10	11	12	13	14	15	16	17	18	19	20	21	22
1. Armitage	*	44	65	40	48	61	55	53	45	44	60	35	119	50	45	117	125	60	313	151	52	52
2. Bedworth	162	*	189	143	169	186	167	216	165	220	213	155	249	190	167	292	213	179	301	414	203	173
3. Bilston T.	122	109	*	91	161	132	124	102	104	103	112	82	212	124	131	189	155	133	190	180	126	105
4. Bridgnorth	112	128	165	*	131	172	137	138	112	102	118	102	275	127	147	165	172	102	310	215	158	138
5. Clevedon	203	263	245	325	*	170	348	187	322	318	207	360	447	232	415	469	326	364	348	399	680	461
6. Dudley T.	127	263	162	172	153	*	141	160	148	166	109	147	284	161	138	237	204	165	247	289	227	217
7. Evesham Utd	73	184	195	94	85	115	*	202	136	134	185	184	282	187	256	224	160	152	323	273	112	187
8. Forest GR	115	136	129	114	229	126	101	*	143	105	103	108	333	127	127	287	129	121	251	161	246	138
9. Grantham	103	204	219	204	260	270	223	186	*	300	210	228	443	188	291	502	215	331	238	201	345	195
10. Hinckley T.	78	93	72	64	78	79	70	90	51	*	51	63	172	70	63	262	98	75	174	126	100	54
11. King's Lynn	541	482	410	357	278	662	454	426	511	808	*	327	242	355	426	383	752	337	250	635	403	476
12. Leic. Utd	179	115	101	117	84	149	128	129	124	170	167	*	179	104	82	191	132	104	189	373	148	104
13. Newport AFC	264	275	275	366	317	325	306	352	203	327	200	280	*	421	212	422	239	315	486	614	267	318
14. RC Warwick	78	123	69	100	123	81	83	110	144	150	172	90	183	*	120	249	91	90	267	620	117	73
15. Redditch	132	146	142	118	103	78	164	108	122	113	104	138	245	65	*	146	117	140	318	169	209	112
16. Rushden	945	884	637	844	641	738	1186	1504	723	647	901	855	991	1019	1397	*	603	906	701	2055	1310	810
17. Stourbridge	112	124	204	153	162	279	182	191	159	135	141	167	271	154	180	284	*	126	285	404	160	156
18. Sutton CT	116	197	166	159	178	184	133	139	109	133	125	163	315	176	176	345	168	*	463	265	180	152
19. Tamworth	576	610	355	485	495	383	635	401	616	470	604	438	805	428	513	622	472	546	*	740	543	468
20. VS Rugby	348	539	336	272	361	377	420	340	386	383	375	372	747	490	318	1233	524	467	493	*	355	437
21. Weston SM	323	262	258	430	1260	383	284	410	272	365	325	275	565	310	335	495	276	240	265	453	*	415
22. Yate Town	170	84	198	110	287	111	112	287	148	128	115	110	317	118	114	238	159	114	158	144	335	*

SOUTHERN DIVISION ATTENDANCES 1993-94

HOME TEAM	1	2	3	4	5	6	7	8	9	10	11	12	13	14	15	16	17	18	19	20	21	22
1. Ashford	*	313	254	402	383	272	341	318	251	321	301	731	302	251	304	336	219	346	410	309	320	248
2. Baldock	150	*	362	265	201	232	339	287	268	232	193	452	253	235	247	201	301	358	272	285	439	206
3. Braintree	225	202	*	125	192	270	182	103	242	163	170	255	115	187	101	181	156	635	252	152	307	204
4. Buckingham	80	67	68	*	85	52	64	35	92	50	60	187	83	54	36	119	112	71	152	90	86	168
5. Burnham	145	136	124	103	*	104	94	81	82	97	89	292	91	79	85	99	164	85	180	174	192	135
6. Bury Town	111	244	153	70	110	*	101	111	36	128	184	162	118	95	91	97	160	360	74	130	120	119
7. Canterbury	250	42	65	34	35	40	*	44	34	38	51	220	48	134	47	52	63	59	129	42	38	58
8. Dunstable	96	139	150	105	125	85	40	*	128	56	76	277	56	85	72	107	88	80	126	158	90	77
9. Erith & B.	183	80	100	81	89	57	46	71	*	65	108	370	90	149	80	97	95	165	277	196	195	97
10. Fareham	111	110	108	96	78	78	87	119	85	*	106	151	223	95	77	184	217	103	118	102	121	84
11. Fisher '93	125	102	163	100	93	129	120	89	159	127	*	423	103	183	104	103	103	124	163	101	172	122
12. Gravesend	876	501	666	684	777	1775	706	614	777	553	554	*	1154	736	725	711	611	764	812	507	810	506
13. Havant T.	277	159	168	137	166	154	149	199	179	320	142	353	*	175	388	135	411	333	150	151	248	206
14. Margate	525	600	168	325	325	250	405	336	350	280	102	488	320	*	208	287	312	395	306	340	420	347
15. Newport IW	282	247	262	217	259	279	278	190	283	355	216	264	216	190	*	266	301	233	212	326	212	175
16. Poole T.	221	102	135	103	153	102	104	107	168	103	203	210	109	148	157	*	235	141	101	201	227	112
17. Salisbury	250	385	324	271	189	192	252	265	243	193	255	492	334	332	282	222	*	345	182	329	471	361
18. Sudbury T.	401	319	427	288	266	502	249	294	346	301	356	854	301	266	317	189	321	*	443	379	331	806
19. Tonbridge	376	435	388	348	445	415	347	354	409	269	444	643	440	546	306	404	551	247	*	416	344	453
20. Wealdstone	183	124	242	231	189	166	185	144	185	192	205	296	165	225	196	175	261	191	166	*	174	178
21. Weymouth	582	1244	649	343	444	458	467	823	415	514	776	680	713	619	742	913	680	845	514	767	*	1087
22. Witney	166	125	231	203	148	160	182	293	163	276	115	552	306	186	206	138	221	233	303	219	164	*

SPORTIQUE 'MANAGER OF THE MONTH' AWARDS 1993-94

MONTH	PREMIER DIVISION	MIDLAND DIVISION	SOUTHERN DIVISION
AUG.	Mick Brookes (Atherstone)	Graham Rogers (Newport)	Brian Chambers (Poole)
SEP.	John Barton (Nuneaton)	Ron Bradbury (VS Rugby)	Richie Powling (Sudbury)
OCT.	Brian Kenning (Burton)	Ron Bradbury (VS Rugby)	Neil Cugley (Ashford)
NOV.	Steve Fallon (Cambridge)	Steve Fey (Clevedon)	Andy Lynes (Witney)
DEC.	Lindsay Parsons (Cheltenham)	Ron Bradbury (VS Rugby)	Geoff Butler (Salisbury)
JAN.	Elwyn Roberts (Corby)	Paul Hendrie (Redditch)	Geoff Butler (Salisbury)
FEB.	Dean White (Hastings)	Roger Ashby (Rushden)	Gary Aldous (Gravesend)
MAR.	Joe Sullivan (Chelmsford)	Roger Ashby (Rushden)	Richie Powling (Sudbury)
APR.	Mick Brookes (Atherstone)	Graham Rogers (Newport)	Tony Mount (Havant)

PREMIER DIVISION MANAGER OF THE SEASON - ALAN TAYLOR (FARNBOROUGH)
MIDLAND DIVISION MANAGER OF THE SEASON - ROGER ASHBY (RUSHDEN & D.)
SOUTHERN DIVISION MANAGER OF THE SEASON - GARY ALDOUS (GRAVESEND)

MIDLAND DIVISION 1993-94

	P	W	D	L	F	A	PTS
Rushden & Diam.	42	29	11	2	109	37	98
VS Rugby	42	28	8	6	98	41	92
Weston-s.-Mare	42	27	10	5	94	39	91
Newport AFC	42	26	9	7	84	37	87
Clevedon Town	42	24	10	8	75	46	82
Redditch Utd	42	19	11	12	79	62	68
Tamworth	42	19	7	16	82	68	64
Bilston Town	42	16	10	16	65	73	58
Stourbridge	42	17	6	19	71	75	57
Evesham United	42	16	8	18	50	60	56
Grantham Town	42	16	6	20	77	73	54
Bridgnorth Town	42	15	6	21	56	68	51
RC Warwick	42	13	12	17	53	66	51
Dudley Town	42	13	10	19	64	61	49
Forest Green R.	42	12	12	18	61	84	48
Sutton Coldfield	42	12	8	22	53	75	44
Bedworth United	42	12	7	23	62	81	43
Hinckley Town	42	11	10	21	44	71	43
Leicester United	42	11	9	22	34	73	42
King's Lynn	42	9	11	22	47	72	38
Yate Town	42	10	6	26	48	86	36
Armitage '90	42	8	11	23	45	103	35

TOP SCORERS

A Warner (VS Rugby)	33
M Nuttell (Rushden & Diamonds)	32
D Watkins (Rushden & Diamonds)	26
P McBean (Tamworth)	24
C Moss (Redditch United)	23
I King (VS Rugby)	22

Below: *The Rushden & Diamonds squad celebrate after receiving the Beazer Homes League Midland Division Championship Shield at Nene Park.*

Photo - P C W Barnes.

RESULT CHART 1993-94

HOME TEAM	1	2	3	4	5	6	7	8	9	10	11	12	13	14	15	16	17	18	19	20	21	22
1. Armitage '90	*	0-1	1-0	2-7	0-2	0-0	1-3	0-2	4-3	0-1	3-3	2-1	2-1	4-1	0-2	0-3	2-2	1-2	2-11	0-1	0-2	0-3
2. Bedworth U.	5-3	*	4-2	1-3	1-3	0-3	0-1	4-1	0-2	1-2	1-1	1-1	0-2	1-2	2-1	1-2	3-1	1-2	1-2	2-5	0-1	2-1
3. Bilston Town	1-2	1-0	*	2-0	2-1	1-2	3-2	3-2	2-4	6-1	0-1	1-1	1-5	0-0	2-2	0-1	1-3	2-0	2-0	0-3	0-6	2-0
4. Bridgnorth	5-0	0-2	0-2	*	0-0	1-0	0-1	0-1	3-2	4-0	2-0	0-3	1-0	3-1	2-2	0-2	1-4	1-2	1-0	0-4	2-2	0-1
5. Clevedon T.	1-1	3-2	2-2	3-0	*	1-0	2-1	1-0	4-2	2-2	3-0	0-0	0-2	2-0	3-3	0-0	3-1	0-1	1-1	4-0	2-1	2-1
6. Dudley T.	4-0	1-1	1-2	3-4	0-1	*	2-0	0-1	3-6	0-0	1-4	5-0	2-2	0-2	0-3	2-2	0-3	2-4	3-3	2-0	1-1	1-1
7. Evesham U.	3-2	2-1	0-3	1-1	0-2	0-3	*	4-2	3-0	0-1	2-0	1-0	2-4	3-3	0-3	1-4	2-0	1-0	1-2	1-5	0-2	0-0
8. Forest G.R.	5-2	1-1	2-2	0-0	2-1	2-1	0-4	*	0-2	1-1	1-0	0-1	3-8	1-0	0-0	3-5	4-2	2-5	2-4	0-5	0-2	5-0
9. Grantham	2-2	2-4	0-3	4-1	2-3	0-1	1-1	1-1	*	1-1	2-1	0-2	0-2	1-2	2-1	0-1	4-0	1-0	2-0	2-3	0-1	3-2
10. Hinckley T.	3-0	3-3	0-1	1-1	4-1	0-0	0-0	1-0	2-4	*	1-2	1-0	2-3	0-1	0-2	0-4	2-0	2-2	1-2	0-1	2-2	0-3
11. King's Lynn	0-0	0-1	0-1	2-3	0-1	1-1	0-1	1-1	1-0	3-2	*	3-0	1-1	1-2	2-3	1-1	3-2	0-0	0-0	2-4	1-4	3-2
12. Leicester U.	2-2	3-0	0-0	0-2	0-4	0-5	1-1	1-1	1-3	0-2	1-0	*	1-2	1-2	2-1	0-2	3-2	0-0	3-1	0-3	0-6	0-1
13. Newport AFC	0-0	3-1	1-0	2-1	2-0	2-1	3-1	0-1	1-0	2-0	3-0	5-0	*	2-1	3-1	0-2	4-0	3-0	3-1	2-0	0-1	2-3
14. RC Warwick	1-1	2-2	2-2	2-3	0-1	1-2	0-2	1-1	1-4	2-0	2-1	0-2	0-0	*	1-0	2-2	0-2	3-2	1-2	0-2	2-1	4-2
15. Redditch U.	1-1	3-1	0-0	4-0	2-3	1-2	2-0	4-1	2-1	2-0	1-1	1-0	2-1	1-1	*	1-2	1-3	3-2	5-0	2-0	0-0	3-2
16. Rushden	4-0	3-1	5-1	2-0	2-0	2-1	1-0	5-0	3-3	2-3	6-0	4-0	1-1	1-1	7-0	*	3-3	2-0	5-1	1-1	3-2	3-0
17. Stourbridge	5-0	1-3	2-6	1-0	2-3	3-1	1-1	1-5	3-1	1-1	1-5	4-1	0-0	1-1	2-2	0-1	*	1-2	2-0	3-1	0-3	0-2
18. Sutton C.T.	1-3	2-2	3-1	2-1	0-1	0-3	1-1	3-3	2-4	0-1	2-3	0-1	1-1	4-1	1-5	1-2	0-2	*	0-1	0-3	0-3	2-2
19. Tamworth	0-0	2-0	9-2	1-0	3-3	2-1	1-2	4-1	3-1	4-0	2-2	2-1	0-1	0-2	3-4	1-1	1-0	2-0	*	1-4	1-2	6-0
20. VS Rugby	6-1	5-2	2-0	2-1	2-2	2-1	1-0	1-1	3-0	3-0	3-1	0-0	1-1	2-1	4-1	2-2	2-0	0-1	1-0	*	4-1	1-1
21. Weston-s-M.	3-0	2-1	1-1	4-1	0-1	2-1	4-0	1-1	0-0	1-0	3-2	3-0	3-3	2-0	3-3	2-1	1-2	2-0	5-1	1-1	*	4-2
22. Yate Town	0-1	1-2	2-2	0-1	0-2	1-0	1-0	2-1	0-5	2-1	1-0	0-1	0-1	2-2	1-2	2-4	1-2	2-3	0-2	1-5	1-2	*

Reformed: 1990

ARMITAGE '90

Nickname: The Tage

Armitage forward Patrick Jordan challenges Tamworth goalkeeper Dale Belford during the opening minutes of the Midland Division fixture at the Lamb Ground on Easter Monday. Armitage did exceptionally well to hold Tamworth to a goalless draw in this match as earlier in the season they had conceded eleven goals to the same opposition on their own pitch!

Photo - Martin Wray.

Chairman: Sid Osborn **President:** S G Osborn
Secretary: F J Rought, 25 Lebanon Rd, Chase Terrace, Burntwood, Staffs (Tel: Ground - below).
Manager: John Newell **Coach:** N/A
Physio: N/A.
General Manager: N/A
Commercial Manager: N/A.
Press Officer: N/A.
Ground: Kings Bromley Lane, Handsacre, Rugeley, Staffs WS15 4EB (0543 491077).
Capacity: 2,500 **Seats:** 300 **Cover:** 500 **Floodlights:** Yes
Colours: Green & white **Change Colours:** Blue & white.
Sponsors: Armitage Shanks/ Bass Mitchell & Butlers.
Previous Names: None *(predecessors Armitage FC, founded in 1915, ceased to operate in 1987).*
Previous League: Staffs Senior 90-91/ Midland Combination 91-93 *(predecessors: Staffs County/ West Midlands (Regional) 71-87).*
Record Gate: 800 v Notts County, friendly, August 1991.
Record defeat: 2-11 v Tamworth (H), Southern League Midland Division 4/1/94.
Best FA Cup season: Second Qualifying Rd replay 93-94 (lost 2-3 aet at home to Solihull Borough after 2-2 draw) *(predecessors: 3rd Qualifying Rd 82-83 (lost 1-3 at Grantham)).*
Best FA Vase season: Preliminary Rd 92-93 *(predecessors: 2nd Rd on two occasions).*
Best FA Trophy season: Never entered *(predecessors: 1st Qual Rd).*
Players progressing to Football League: P J Devlin (Notts County), D A Roberts (Wolverhampton Wanderers).
Clubhouse: Fully licensed Bar. Pool. Tea bar.
93-94 Captain: John Capaldi.
93-94 P.o.Y.:
93-94 Top scorer: Eric Sandiford.
Local Newspapers: Burton Daily Mail, Lichfield Mercury.
Hons: Midlands Combination 92-93 (R-up 91-92), Walsall Snr Cup 91-92, Tony Allden Cup R-up 92-93 *(predecessors: West Midlands Lg Div 1 73-74, Walsall Snr Cup).*

PROGRAMME DETAILS:
Pages: 24 **Price:** 50p
Editor: C Bailey

1947 # BEDWORTH UNITED Greenbacks

The recently constructed main stand at The Oval.

Chairman: Alan Robinson **Vice Chairman:** Roy Whitehead **President:** Harold Jones.
Secretary: Graham Bloxham, 43 Mount Pleasant Road, Bedworth, Nuneaton, Warks CV12 8EX (0203 317940).
Manager: Billy Hollywood **Asst Mgr:** Martin Smith **Physio:** John Roberts.
Press Officer: Alan Robinson
Ground: The Oval, Miners Welfare Park, Coventry Road, Bedworth CV12 8NN (0203 314302).
Directions: M6 jct 3, into Bedworth on B4113 Coventry to Bedworth road, ground 200yds past past Bedworth Leisure Centre on this road. Coaches should park at this Leisure Centre. Buses from Coventry and Nuneaton pass ground.
Capacity: 7,000 **Cover:** 300 **Seats:** 300 **Floodlights:** Yes **Metal Badges:** Yes
Club Shop: Yes, selling badges, scarves, programmes, shirts, hats, caps, club coats. Contact Tom Ison-Jacques (0203 314884).
Colours: Green & white **Change colours:** Yellow & green.
Sponsors: Double Vision.
Previous Leagues: Birmingham Comb. 47-54/ West Mids (at first Birmingham) Lg 54-72.
Previous Name: Bedworth Town 47-68 **Previous Ground:** British Queen Ground 11-39.
Midweek home matchday: Tuesday **Reserve's Lge:** Midland Floodlit Youth League.
Record Attendance: 5,127 v Nuneaton Borough, Southern Lg Midland Division 23/2/82.
Record win: 11-0 **Record defeat:** 1-10.
Record Fees - Paid: £1,750 for Colin Taylor (Hinckley Town, 1991-92)
Received: £30,000 for Richard Landon (Plymouth Argyle, January 1994).
Best FA Trophy season: Second Round 80-81.
Best FA Cup season: 4th Qualifying Rd 1983/89/90
League clubs defeated in F.A. Cup: None.
Players progressing to Football League: Phil Huffer (Derby County 1953), Geoff Coleman (Northampton Town 1955), Ian Hathaway (Mansfield Town 1989), Richard Landon (Plymouth Argyle 1994).
Clubhouse: Social club open every day 7.30-11pm and weekend lunchtimes noon-3pm. Hot and cold bar food, pool, darts.
Club Record Goalscorer: Peter Spacey (1949-69)
Club Record Appearances: Peter Spacey.
93-94 Captain: David Crowley.
93-94 P.o.Y.: Richard Landon.
93-94 Top scorer: Richard Landon.
Local Newspapers: Bedworth Echo (312785/319548), Coventry Evening Telegraph (0203 633633)
Local Radio Stations: Mercia Sound, BBC CWR.
Hons: Birmingham Comb.(2) 48-50, Birmingham Snr Cup(3) 78-79 80-82, Midland Floodlit Cup 81-82 92-93.

PROGRAMME DETAILS:
Pages: 30 **Price:** 50p
Editor: Peter Thompson
(0203 311538)

BILSTON TOWN

Formed: 1895

Steelmen or Boro

Bilston Town FC. Back Row (L/R): A Potts (Coach), K Bird, S Booth, M Turner, J Cooke, M Simms, R Attwood, P Berks, M Bowater, C Arnot. Front: W Campbell, G Jones, A Edwards, E Black, E Smith, S Phillips, D Wright. Photo - Peter Barnes.

Chairman: Mr I K Wymer **Vice-Chairman:** Mr A K Hickman **President:** Dennis Turner MP.
Secretary: Mr Jeff Calloway, 4 Mervyn Rd, Bradley, Bilston, West Midlands WV14 8DF (0902 491799).
Manager: John Wilson **Asst Manager:** Alan Potts **Coach:** I Painter/B Pope
Physio: Reg Pickering **Press Officer:** Mr A Owen.
Ground: Queen Street, Bilston WV14 7EX (0902 491498).
Directions: M6 junction 10, A454 towards Wolverhampton then pick up A563 towards Bilston and turn left into Beckett Street after a little over a mile, ground at bottom. 3 miles from Wolverhampton (BR), bus 45 from bus station passes ground. Buses 78 and 79 from Birmingham stop within quarter of a mile of ground.
Capacity: 4,000 **Cover:** 350 **Seats:** 350 **Floodlights:** Yes **Metal Badges:** Yes
Club Shop: Yes, selling badges, pennants, key rings, pens, old and new non-League progs. Contact Paul Galloway, 4 Mervyn Rd, Bradley, Bilston, West Mids WV14 8DF.
Colours: Tangerine & white **Change colours:** White/black/white.
Club Sponsors: Stowlawn Ltd and Second City.
Previous Names: Bilston Utd 1895-1932/ Bilston
Previous Ground: Pounds Lane 1895-1921.
Previous Leagues: Birmingham Comb. 07-21 48-54/ (Birmingham) West Mids 21-32 54-85.
Midweek home matchday: Tuesday **Reserve Team's League:** N/A.
Record Attendance: 7,500 v Wolverhampton Wanderers, floodlight opening 1953. *Competitive: 7,000 v Halifax Town, F.A. Cup First Round 1968.*
Record win: 12-2 v Tipton Town **Record defeat:** 0-8 v Merthyr Tydfil.
Best F.A. Cup season: 2nd Rd replay 72-73 (lost 0-1 at Barnet after 1-1 draw). Also 1st Rd 68-69.
League clubs defeated in F.A. Cup: None.
Record Fees - Paid: for Steve Gloucester.
Received: From Southend United for Ron Poutney, 1975.
Players progressing to Football League: R Ellows (Birmingham), James Fletcher (Birmingham 1950), Stan Crowther (A Villa 1955), Ron Pountney (Southend 1975), K Price (Gillingham), Campbell Chapman (Wolves 1984).
Clubhouse: Open every night and weekend lunchtimes (normal pub hours). Usual club activities.
Club Record Scorer: Ron McDermott 78.
93-94 Captain: Eric Smith.
93-94 P.o.Y.: Mark Bowater.
93-94 Top scorer: Jason Cooke.
Local Newspapers: Expess & Star, Evening Mail.
Local Radio Stations: Radio West Mids, WABC (Wolverhampton), Beacon (Wolverhampton), BRMB.
Honours: F.A. Tphy 2nd Rd 70-71 74-75, F.A. Vase QF 92-93, West Mids Lg 60-61 72-73 (R-up 22-23 70-71 73-74 74-75 75-76 84-85, Lg Cup 72-73 (R-up 65-66), Div 2 56-57), Birmingham Comb R-up 07-08 53-54, Staffs Senior Cup 57-58 59-60 60-61 61-62 (R-up 56-57 64-65 85-86), Birmingham Junior Cup 1895-96, Wednesbury Charity Cup 1981-81 81-82 82-83 84-85 (R-up 83-84).

PROGRAMME DETAILS:
Pages: 24 **Price:** 70p
Editor: Secretary

Formed: 1946

BRIDGNORTH TOWN

The Town

Bridgnorth Town FC. Back Row (L/R): M Pound, H Lander, C Hammond, P Bennett, D Blocksidge, D Nock, T Beddow, J Yates, A Garratt, C Marshall (Coach), J Stretton (Physio), J Chambers (Trainer). Front: C Robinson, J Hill, P Evans, K Bowen (Manager), P Tester, S Blakemore (Assistant Manager), I Sankey, K Seabury, M Minnikin.

Chairman: Paul Haden **Vice Chairman:** Bernard Durnin **President:** Mike Williams
Secretary/Press Off.: Gordon Thomas, 7 Meadow Close, Oldbury Wells, Bridgnorth WV16 5HY (0746 765178).
Manager: Kevan Bowen **Asst Mgr:** Steve Blakemore. **Coach:** Chris Marshall
Physio: Jenny Stretton **Commercial Manager:** Glynn Dobbs (0746 766884).
Ground: Crown Meadow, Innage Lane, Bridgnorth, Salop WV16 6PZ (0746 762747/766064).
Directions: Follow signs for Shrewsbury (A458) over river bridge on by-pass, turn right for town centre at island, right at T-junction, 1st left into Victoria Rd, right at cross-road, follow road into Innage Lane, ground on left.
Capacity: 1,600 **Cover:** 700 **Seats:** 250 **Floodlights:** Yes **Metal Badges:** Yes
Club Shop: Yes, selling programmes, badges, pennants, pens, scarves and hats.
Colours: Blue/white/blue **Change colours:** All red.
Club Sponsors: Premier Coaches.
Previous Name: St Leonards Old Boys (prior to the current club's formation in 1946).
Previous Leagues: Kidderminster & District (until 68)/ Midland Combination 68-83.
Midweek home matchday: Tuesday **Reserve's Lge:** Midland Combination (Reserve Div).
Record Attendance: 1,600 v South Shields, FA Vase 5th Rd 1976.
Best F.A. Cup season: 3rd Qualifying Rd 64-65.
League clubs defeated in F.A. Cup: None.
Record Fees - Paid: N/A **Received:** £10,000 for Delwyn Humphreys (to Kidderminster Harriers).
Players progressing to Football League: Roger Davies (Derby County).
Clubhouse: Open every evening and weekend lunchtimes. Darts, pool, fruit machines, dancehall. Hot meals on matchdays.
Club Record Scorer: Roger Davies 157
Club Record Appearances: Kevin Harris 426.
93-94 Captain: Paul Tester.
93-94 P.o.Y.: Martin Lander.
93-94 Top scorer: Jason Yates.
Local Newspapers: Shropshire Star, Bridgnorth Journal, Express & Star.
Local Radio Stations: Beacon, BBC Radio Shropshire.
Honours: FA Vase 5th Rd 75-76 93-94, Midland Combination 79-80 82-83 (R-up 76-77 80-81, Lg Cup 78-79, Tony Allden Memorial Cup R-up), Kidderminster & District Lg, Shropshire Snr Cup 85-86, Shropshire County Cup 70-71 75-76 76-77 78-79 79-80, Welsh Amateur Cup 70-71, Shropshire Junior Cup - Bridgnorth are the only Shropshire side to have won all three county cups.

PROGRAMME DETAILS:
Pages: 24 **Price:** 75p
Editor: Terry Brumpton
(0278 781683)

1883 BUCKINGHAM TOWN The Robins

Buckingham Town FC 1993-94.

Chairman: Chris Lawrence **Vice Chairman:** Ernie Seaton **President:** Robin Taylor
Secretary: E J Seaton, 20 Glebe Road, Deanshanger, Milton Keynes MK19 6LT (0908 562875).
Manager/Coach: Mick Foster **Assistant Manager:** Keith Searle
Physio: Willie Holman.
Press Officer: Philip Cornwall **Commercial Manager:** Mick Foster.
Ground: Ford Meadow, Ford Street, Buckingham (0280 816257).
Directions: From town centre take Aylesbury (A413) road and turn right at Phillips Garage after 400yds. By public transport: train to Milton Keynes, then bus to Buckingham.
Capacity: 4,000 **Cover:** 420 **Seats:** 420 **Floodlights:** Yes **Metal Badges:** Yes.
Club Shop: Yes, selling scarves, hats, badges and programmes. Contact Dave Newton at ground.
Colours: All red **Change colours:** All white. **Sponsors:** Busiprint.
Previous Lges: Aylesbury & Dist/ Nth Bucks/ Hellenic 53-57/ Sth Mids 57-74/ Utd Co's 74-86.
Midweek matchday: Tuesday **Reserve Team's League:** None.
Record Attendance: 2,451 v Orient, FA Cup 1st Rd 84-85.
Best FA Cup season: 1st Rd 84-85. **League clubs defeated in FA Cup:** None.
Record Fees - Paid: £7,000 for Steve Jenkins (Wealdstone, 1992)
Received: £1,000 for Terry Shrieves (Kettering).
Players progressing to Football League: None.
Clubhouse: Open every evening 7-11pm (4-11pm on Sat) and weekend lunchtimes 12-3pm. Concert room with stage for hire, capacity 150. Bingo, dominoes, ladies and mens darts, pool. Rolls ect available matchdays only.
93-94 Captain: Jess Mansfield.
93-94 P.o.Y.: Lee Attfield.
93-94 Top scorer: Danny Nicholls.
Local Newspapers: Buckingham Advertiser, MK Citizen, Herald & Post.
Local Radio Stations: Chiltern Radio, Fox FM (102.6 fm).
Newsline: 0891 884 431.
Hons: FA Vase QF 90-91 92-93, Southern Lg Southern Div 90-91, Utd Co's Lg 83-84 85-86 (Div 1 R-up 75-76, Div 2 R-up 74-75, Lg Cup 83-84, Div 2 Cup R-up 74-75), Nth Bucks Lg(8) 24-25 28-29 33-34 35-37 38-39 48-49 49-50, Aylesbury & Dist. Lg 02-03, Berks & Bucks Snr Cup 83-84, Berks & Bucks Jnr Cup 02-03 48-49 (R-up 38-39 72-73), Berks & Bucks Minor Cup 32-33, Buckingham Snr Charity Cup(18) 32-33 35-36 37-38 47-50 52-55 72-73 75-77 78-79 80-81 83-87 (R-up 31-32 36-37 39-40 73-74 81-82).

PROGRAMME DETAILS:
Pages: 32 **Price:** TBA
Editor: Phillip Cornwall

Formed: 1893 # DUDLEY TOWN The Robins

Dudley Town's Round Oak Stadium.

Chairman: Trevor Lester **Vice Chairman:** Philip Edwards **President:** N D Jeynes.
Secretary: Tony Turpin, 24 Andrew Drive, Short Heath, Willenhall WV12 5PP (0922 475541).
Manager: Malcolm Woodbine **Assistant Manager/Coach:** Graham Thompson
Press Officer: Secretary
Ground: The Round Oak Stadium, John Street, Brierley Hill, West Mids (0384 263478/78560).
Directions: From Dudley take the A461 towards Stourbridge for about 2 miles and on entering Brierley Hill turn right at traffic island onto on B4180 (John Street), ground 200 yds on right. Two and a half miles from Stourbridge BR station.
Capacity: 3,000 **Cover:** 300 **Seats:** 234 **Floodlights:** Yes **Metal Badges:** Yes
Club Shop: Yes, selling programmes and badges. Contact Frank Whitehouse.
Colours: Red/white/black **Change colours:** All yellow.
Sponsors: Dudley Building Society/ Thornleigh Freight.
Previous Leagues: West Mids (previously Birmingham) 1898-1915 35-38 53-82/ Midland (Worcs) Combination 29-32/ Birmingham Combination 32-35 45-53.
Previous Grounds: The Sports Centre, Birmingham Rd 1936-85.
Midweek home matchday: Wednesday **Reserves' League:** None.
Record Fee Received: £25,000 for Gary Piggott (West Bromwich Albion, March 1991).
Record Gate: 3,000 v West Bromwich Albion, pre-season friendly 1991. *(At old ground; 16,500 for the official opening (a representative game) in 1936).*
Best F.A. Cup season: 1st Rd replay 76-77 (v York).
League clubs defeated in F.A. Cup: None.
Record win: 8-0 v Banbury, 1965.
Players progressing to Football League: Albert Broadbent (Notts Co 1952), Joe Mayo (Walsall 1972), Ken Price (Southend 1976), Andy Reece (Bristol Rovers 1987), Russell Bradley (Nottm Forest 1988), John Muir (Doncaster 1989), Gary Piggott (West Bromwich Albion 1991).
Clubhouse: Dudley Town Sports & Social Club, John Street, Brierley Hill. Open nightly, all day Saturday and Sunday lunchtimes. Bar, lounge bar, ballroom, bowling green etc. Bar snacks available.
Club Record Scorer: Frank Treagust, 56 (47-48).
Club Record Appearances: Brendon Hackett & John Muir, 55.
93-94 Captain: Andy Crannage.
P.o.Y. 93-94: Philip Cartwright.
93-94 Top scorer: Alan Grainger.
Local Newspapers: Express & Star, Dudley Evening Mail, Birmingham Post, Sunday Mercury.
Local Radio Stations: Beacon Radio, BRMB, BBC Radio West Midlands.
Honours: FA Trophy 2nd Rd 84-85, Southern Lg Midland Div 84-85, Birmingham Comb 33-34 (R-up 34-35 47-48), Midland (Worcs) Comb 31-32 (R-up 29-30 30-31), West Mids Lg Cp R-up 75-76 (Div 2 Cp R-up 80-81), Birmingham Senior Cp 85-86 (R-up 64-65 83-84), Worcs Senior Cp 45-46(joint)(R-up 84-85), Camkin Cp 64-65, Worcs Junior Cp 83-84.

PROGRAMME DETAILS:
Pages: 36 **Price:** 50p
Editor: Bill Anthony
c/o the club

Formed: 1945

EVESHAM UNITED

The Robins

Evesham United. Back Row (L/R): John Busst (Manager), Graham Brown (Trainer), Carl Bannister, Paul Busst, Sean Cotterill, Billy Turley, John Baker, Mark Robinson, Micky Williams, Steve George, Chas Webb. Front: Chris Webber, Neil Emms, Tony Grealish, Chas Jones, Andy Ryan

Photo - Peter Barnes.

Chairman: Stuart Reeves **Vice Chairman:** Dave Bearcroft.
President: M E H Davies **Treasurer:** Dave Wright.
Secretary/Commercial Mgr: Mike J Peplow, 68 Woodstock Rd, St Johns, Worcester WR2 5NF (0905 425993).
Manager: John Busst **Asst Manager:** Nick Jordan **Coach:** Gerry Clarke.
Physio: Graham Brown **Press Officer:** Graham Hill (0905 351653)
Commercial Manager: Mike J Peplow (0905 425993).
Ground: Common Road, Evesham, Worcestershire WR11 4PU (0386 442303).
Ground Directions: From Evesham High Street turn into Swan Lane, continue down hill between Willmotts factory called Conduit Hill into Common Rd, ground 200yds down on right just before railway bridge. 5 minutes walk from Evesham BR station.
Seats: 350 **Capacity:** 2,000 **Cover:** 600 **Floodlights:** Yes **Metal Badges:** Yes
Club Shop: Yes, selling programmes, pennants, scarves and ties. Contact Darren Attwood c/o the club.
Cols: Red (white sleeves)/black/black **Change Colours:** All blue
Club Sponsors: Safeway.
Midweek home matches: Tuesday **Reserves' League:** No reserve team.
Previous Name: Evesham Town **Previous Ground:** The Crown Meadow (pre-1968).
Previous Lges: Worcester/ Birmingham Combination/ Midland Combination 51-55 65-92/ West Midlands Regional 55-62.
Record Gate: 2,338 v West Bromwich Albion, friendly 18/7/92.
Record win: 11-3 v West Heath United.
Record Fee Paid: £1,500; to Hayes for Colin Day, 1992.
Record Fee Received: £5,000 for Simon Brain (to Cheltenham Town).
Players who have progressed to Football League: Billy Tucker, Gary Stevens (Cardiff 1977), Kevin Rose (Lincoln 1978), Andy Preece (Northampton 1986), Simon Brain (Hereford, via Cheltenham Town).
Clubhouse: Open matchdays and training nights, and available for hire. Cold food available in club, and hot food from tea hut on matchdays.
Club Record Scorer: Sid Brain.
Club Record Appearances: Rob Candy.
93-94 Captain: Sean Cotterill
93-94 P.o.Y: Sean Cotterill
93-94 Top Scorer: John Baker.
Local Press: Evesham Journal (0386 765678), Worcester Evening News (0905 748200), Gloucester Echo.
Local Radio Stations: Radio Wyvern, BBC Hereford & Worcester.
Hons: FA Amateur Cup R-up 23-24, FA Vase QF 91-92, Worcestershire Snr Urn(2) 76-78 (R-up 90-91), Midland Combination(6) 52-53 54-55 65-66 67-69 91-92 (Chal. Cup 53-54 87-88 91-92 (R-up(5) 54-55 71-72 83-84 88-90)), Worcestershire Combination 52-53 54-55; B'gham Combination R-up 30-31, Evesham Hosp. Cup 89-90, Tony Allden Mem. Cup 1973 1988 1992.

PROGRAMME DETAILS:
Pages: 24 **Price:** 50p
Editor: Graham Hill (0905 351653)

1890 **FOREST GREEN ROVERS** Rovers

The new management team at Forest Green Rovers for 1994-95; Manager Frank Gregan (right) and his Assistant, Paul Collicutt.

Chairman: Trevor Horsley **President:** G C Mills, MBE.
Sec./Press Officer: Colin Peake, 25 Skylark Way, Painswick Rd, Gloucester GL4 9QY (0452 412668).
Manager: Frank Gregan **Asst Manager:** Paul Collicutt **Physio:** Adrian Tandy.
Ground: 'The Lawn', Nympsfield Road, Forest Green, Nailsworth, Glos. GL6 0ET (0453 834860).
Directions: About 4 miles south of Stroud on A46 to Bath. In Nailsworth turn into Spring Hill off mini r'bout - ground approximately half mile up hill on left. The nearest BR station is Stroud.
Capacity: 1,995 **Cover:** 800 **Seats:** 200 **Floodlights:** 138.4 lux
Club Shop: Yes - open matchdays.
Colours: Black & white stripes/black/red **Change colours:** Red & white stripes/white/white.
Sponsors: Sheffield Insulations.
Previous Lges: Stroud & Dist. 1890-1921/ Glos Northern Snr 22-67/ Glos Co. 67-73 /Hellenic 73-82.
Previous Name: Stroud FC, 1989-92.
Previous Ground: None.
Midweek matchday: Wed. (7.45pm)
Youth Team's League: Midland Floodlit Yth/ Glos Co. Yth.
Record Attendance: 2,200 v Wolverhampton Wanderers, floolight inauguration 1981.
Best FA Cup season: 3rd Qualifying Rd 87-88.
Best FA Trophy season: 3rd Round Proper 90-91.
Best FA Vase season: Winners 81-82.
Players progressing to Football League: Graham Rogers (Newport County 1985), Mike England (Bristol Rovers 1985), Kevin Gill (Newport County 1985).
Clubhouse: (0453 833295). Bar and lounge, open every night. Chairman: Bill Trueman: 0453 833141.
93-94 Club Captain: Russell Wilton.
93-94 Team Captain: Paul Collicutt.
93-94 P.o.Y.: Paul Collicutt
93-94 Top scorer: Andy Hoskins 14 in 20 matches.
Local Newspapers: Stroud News & Journal, Gloucester Citizen.
Local Radio Stations: Severn Sound, BBC Radio Gloucestershire.
Honours: FA Vase 81-82, Hellenic Lg 81-82, Stroud & Dursley Lg 02-03, Gloucestershire Northern Senior Lg 37-38 49-50 50-51, Gloucestershire Senior Cup 84-85 85-86 86-87, Gloucestershire Senior Amateur Cup (North) 26-27 45-46 71-72 75-76 77-78, Gloucestershire Senior Professional Cup 84-85 85-86.

PROGRAMME DETAILS:
Pages: 24 **Price:** 60p
Editor: Keith Sheppard

GRANTHAM TOWN

Formed: 1874

Gingerbreads

Grantham 'keeper Jon Goodwin and team-mate Warren Ward keep out the rampaging John Borthwick of Bishop Auckland. The Gingerbreads lost 1-2 in this FA Trophy Second Round tie.

Photo - Dave West.

Chairman: Allan Prince **President:** Baroness Thatcher of Kesteven.
Secretary: Mr Pat Nixon, 72 Huntingtower Road, Grantham, Lincs NG31 7AU (0476 64408).
Manager: Warren Ward **Asst Mgr:** Paul Buckthorpe **Physio:** Nigel Marshall.
Ground: The South Kesteven Sports Stadium, Trent Road, Grantham, Lincs (0476 62011).
Directions: Midway between A1 and A52 on edge of Earlesfield Industrial Estate; from A1 take A607 to Earlsfield Ind. Est and continue into Trent Rd. From Nottingham on A52 turn right into Barrowby Gate then into Trent Rd. From Boston on A52 follow A607 across two sets of lights to Trent Rd.
Capacity: 7,500 **Cover:** 1,950 **Seats:** 750 **Floodlights:** Yes **Metal Badges:** Yes
Club Shop: Yes, selling programmes and a wide range of souvenirs. Contact Andy Barton (0476 62011).
Colours: Black & white stripes **Change colours:** Yellow & blue or Red & white.
Sponsors: Academy Preservations.
Previous Leagues: Midland Amateur Alliance/ Central Alliance 11-25 59-61/ Midland Co's 25-59 61-72/ Southern 72-79/ Northern Prem. 79-85.
Prev. Name: Grantham FC, pre-1980's **Previous Ground:** London Road until October 1990.
Midweek home matchday: Tuesday **Reserve Team's League:** Lincolnshire.
Record Attendance: 1,402 v Ilkeston Town, FA Cup Preliminary Rd 91-92 *(At London Road: 6,578 v Middlesborough, FA Cup 3rd Rd 1974).*
Record win: 13-0 v Rufford Colliery (H), FA Cup Preliminary Rd 15/9/34.
Record defeat: 0-16 v Notts County Rovers (A), Midland Amateur Alliance 22/10/1892.
Record Fees - Paid: £1,000 for Gary Jones (Doncaster Rovers, 1989)
Received: £20,000 for Gary Crosby (Nottingham Forest, 1987)
Best FA Cup season: 3rd Rd 1883-84 86-87 1973-74. Competition Proper on 23 occasions; 1877-79 80-81 83-88 1928-29 35-36 45-46 47-48 49-50 61-62 65-71 72-74 75-76.
League clubs defeated in FA Cup: Stockport 70-71, Rochdale 73-74.
Players progressing to Football League: Archie Burgeon (Spurs 1930's), Syd Bycroft (Doncaster 1934), Ernest Morris (Halifax 1950), Peter Thompson & Robbie Cooke (Peterborough 1964 & 80), James Rayner (Notts County 1964), David Dall (Scunthorpe 1979), Nick Jarvis & Hugh Wood (Scunthorpe 1980), Devon White (Bristol Rvrs 1986), Terry Curran (Grimsby 1987), Gary Crosby (Nottm Forest 1987), Alan Kennedy (Wrexham 1987), Richard Wilson (Lincoln 1987).
Clubhouse: (0476 593506) Open evenings and weekends. Bar, darts, pool etc. Frequent live entertainment. Available for functions.
Club Record Goalscorer: Jack McCartney 416
Club Record Appearances: Chris Gardiner 664.
93-94 Captain: Adrian Speed
93-94 Top scorer/P.O.Y.: Ian Williams.
Local Newspapers: Grantham Journal (0476 62291), Nottingham Evening Post (0602 482000), Melton & Grantham Trader (0476 74433), Grantham Citizen, Lincolnshire Echo (0522 525252).
Local Radio Stations: Radio Lincolnshire, Lincs FM.
Hons: FA Tphy QF 71-72, Southern Lg R-up 73-74 (Div 1 Nth 72-73 78-79, Merit Cup 72-73), Midland Co's Lg(3) 63-64 70-72 (R-up 37-38 64-65 69-70, Lg Cup 68-69 70-71), Midland Amtr Lg 10-11 (Lg Cup R-up 10-11), Central All. 24-25 (Southern Div R-up 59-60), Lincs Snr Cup 1884-85 1936-37 (R-up(5) 34-36 39-40 45-47), Lincs Co. 'A' Cup(3) 53-54 60-62 (R-up 49-50 52-53 57-58), Lincs Co. Snr Cup 71-72 82-83 (R-up 80-81).

PROGRAMME DETAILS:
Pages: 36 **Price:** 70p
Editor: M Koranski

Formed: 1958

HINCKLEY TOWN

The Town

A Hinckley Town defender tackles Wayne Noble of Clevedon Town during the Leicestershire club's first visit to the Hand Stadium.

Photo - Colin Rozee/PictureSport.

Chairman: Kevin Downes **Vice Chairman:** Geoffrey Sutton. **President:** Frank Downes.
Secretary: Stuart Milliovie, c/o the club (below).
Manager: David Grundy **Assistant Manager:** Martin Sockett.
Coach: Jeavon Payne.
Physio: TBA **Commercial Manager:** TBA
Ground: Leicester Road Sports Ground, Leicester Road, Hinckley, Leics (0455 615062).
Directions: From M69 junction 1 take A447 then A47 towards Leicester. Ground on A47 about 2 miles from town centre (half way between Earl Shilton and Hinckley).
Capacity: 2,000 **Cover:** 200 **Seats:** 200 **Floodlights:** Yes
Club Shop: Yes, selling programmes, books, vidoes, badges, mugs. Contact Mr Brian Blockley (0455 635148).
Colours: Claret & blue **Change colours:** Yellow.
Sponsors: F E Downes Ltd.
Previous Name: Westfield Rovers 1958-66.
Previous Grounds: Westfield Playing Field 58-60/ Coventry Road Recreation Ground 60-68.
Previous Lges: Sth Leicester & Nuneaton Amtr/ Leics Snr 72-86/ Central Mids 86-88/ West Mids 88-90.
Midweek home matchday: Tuesday **Reserve Team's League:** None.
Record Attendance: 2,000 v Real Sociedad, floodlight opening, 1986. *Competitive: 1,022 v Nuneaton Borough, Southern League Midland Division 1/1/91.*
Best FA Vase season: Third Round 85-86.
Best FA Cup season: 4th Qualifying Rd replay 1988-89 (lost 0-3 after 1-1 draw at Welling United).
League clubs defeated in FA Cup: None.
Record win: 10-0 v Kettering Town Reserves, Central Midlands League B.E. Webbe Cup.
Record defeat: 0-10 v Barry Town, Southern League Midlands Division.
Record Fees - Paid: £1,600 for John Lane (V.S. Rugby)
Received: £1,750 for Colin Taylor (Bedworth United).
Clubhouse: Bar with facilities for functions. Open matchdays and training nights (Tuesday & Thursday). Sandwiches available.
Club Record Scorer: Paul Purser.
93-94 Captain: Tim Griffin.
93-94 P.o.Y.: Paul Purser.
93-94 Top scorer: Scott Machin.
Local Newspapers: Hinckley Times (0455 238383), Leicester Mercury (512512).
Local Radio Stations: Radio Leicester.
Honours: West Midlands (Regional) Lg 89-90, Central Midlands Lg 86-87 (R-up 87-88, B E Webbe Cup R-up 86-87 87-88, Gerry Mills Cup R-up 87-88), Leics Senior Lg R-up 83-84 (Div 2 72-73, Div 2 Cup 72-73), Leicestershire Challenge Cup 89-90 (R-up 90-91 93-94), Leics Senior Cup (Jelson Holmes) R-up 87-88, Leics Senior Cup 88-89, Midland Floodlit Cup 88-89 (R-up 91-92 93-94).

PROGRAMME DETAILS:
Pages: 16 **Price:** 60p
Editor: Alan Mason

ReFormed: 1945

ILKESTON TOWN

The Robins

Ilkeston Town's New Manor Ground, which witnessed a championship success in only its second year. Photo - Colin Stevens.

Chairman: Paul Millership **President:** Robert Lindsay
Secretary: Mr Anthony Cuthbert, 8 Darwin Road, Long Eaton, Nottingham NG10 3NW (0602 731531).
Manager: Bill Brindley **Asst Manager:** N/A **Coach:** Graham Collier.
Press Officer: John Richards
Commercial Manager: Danny Boyes.
Ground: New Manor Ground, Awsworth Rd, Ilkeston (0602 324094).
Directions: M42 to M1 junction 23A, continue on M1 to junction 26, exit left onto A610 towards Ripley, take 1st exit signed Awsworth and Ilkeston (A6096), continue thru Awsworth, right at top of hill into Newtons Lane (signed Cotmanhay & Heanor) - ground half mile on left before canal bridge. Or, A38 to Derby centre, A52 for Nottm to M5 junction 25, then follow as above from M1 junction 26. Rail to Nottingham or Derby then bus to Ilkeston. Ground about 1 mile from town centre.
Capacity: 3,000 **Seats:** 323 **Cover:** 750 **Floodlights:** Yes
Colours: Red/white/red **Change colours:** White/black/black
Club Shop: Yes, selling shirts, T-shirts, jumpers, caps, badges, programmes, scarves, 'Team Talk' magazine. Contact Roger Rosser or Janice Straw (0602 292537). Programme swaps welcome.
Record Gate: 1,641 v Alfreton Town, Derbys Snr Cup final 2nd leg 11/5/93. *At old ground: 9,800 v Rochdale, F.A. Cup 1st Rd 1951.*
Previous Leagues: Midland 1894-1902 25-58 61-71 73-82/ Central Alliance 47-61/ Central Midlands 82-90/ West Midlands (Regional) 90-94.
Best FA Cup season: 1st Rd 51-52 (lost 0-2 at home to Rochdale), 56-57 (1-5 at home to Blyth).
Sponsors: Manor House Furnishing **Previous Ground:** Manor Ground, Manor Rd (pre-1992).
Midweek home matchday: Tuesday
Reserve team's League: Mids Regional Alliance.
Record win: 14-2 **Record defeat:** 1-11
Record transfer fee paid: Nil **Received:** £11,750 for Chris Brookes (Luton Town, 1992).
Clubhouse: Open Wed-Fri 7-11pm, Sat-Sun noon-3 & 7-11pm, and Mon or Tue if there is a match. Snacks behind bar. Large tea bar open matchdays 2-5pm (6.30-9pm for night games).
Captain 93-94: Paul Fletcher.
Top Scorer 93-94: Mark Harbottle 30.
Player of the Year 93-94: Nigel Bailey.
Players' P.o.Y. 93-94: Mark Harbottle.
Supporters' P.o.Y. 93-94: Jason Campbell.
Hons: West Mids (Regional) Lg 93-94 (Div 1 91-92, Lg Cup 91-92 93-94), Central Mids Lg Cup 87-88, Midland Lg 67-68 (R-up 1898-99), Central All. 52-53 53-54 54-55 (R-up 47-48 55-56), Derbys Snr Cup 1894-95 95-96 96-97 97-98 1948-49 52-53 55-56 57-58 62-63 82-83 92-93.

PROGRAMME DETAILS:
Pages: 32 **Price:** 50p
Editor: Mick Capill
(0602 324257)

Formed: 1879

KING'S LYNN

The Linnets

The King's Lynn side that faced Diss Town in the Fifth Round of the FA Vase. Back Row (L/R): Simon Scarff, David Jones, Paul Willis, Steve Lewis, Darren Bloodworth, Gary West, Tim Webster, Jackie Gallagher. Front: Darren Rolph, Gus Russell, Mark Howard, Darren Prior, Clive Worthingtion.

Photo - Richard Brock.

Chairman: J Dollimore **President:** Jim Chandler.
Secretary: The Secretary, c/o the club.
Manager: Tony Godden **Asst Manager/Coach:** N/A
Physio: Simon Parsell.
Ground: The Walks Stadium, Tennyson Road, King's Lynn PE30 5PB (0553 760060).
Directions: At mini r-about arriving from A10/A47 take Vancouse Avenue. Ground on left after a half mile. Quarter mile from King's Lynn (BR), half mile from bus station.
Capacity: 8,200 **Cover:** 5,000 **Seats:** 1,200 **Club Shop:** Yes **Metal Badges:** Yes
Colours: Yellow & blue stripes **Change colours:** All red
Previous Leagues: Norfolk & Suffolk/ Eastern C'ties 35-39 48-54/ UCL 46-48/ Midland C'ties 54-58/ NPL 80-83.
Previous Name: Lynn Town **Previous Ground:** None.
Sponsors: TBA.
Midweek home matchday: Tuesday **Reserve Team's League:** Eastern Counties (Division One).
Record Attendance: 12,937 v Exeter, FA Cup 1st Rd 50-51. *(44,916 saw the Cup tie at Everton (below)).*
Best FA Trophy season: 2nd Rd 78-79.
Best FA Vase season: 5th Rd 93-94 (lost 0-2 at Diss Town).
Best FA Cup season: 3rd Rd 61-62 (lost 0-4 at Everton). Competition Proper on 14 occasions; 05-06 37-38 49-50 51-52 58-63 64-65 68-69 71-72 73-74 84-85.
League clubs defeated in FA Cup: Aldershot 59-60, Coventry 61-62, Halifax 68-69.
Players progressing to Football League: Norman Rowe (Derby 1949), Brian Taylor & Polly Ward (Bradford Park Avenue 54 & 55), Tom Reynolds (Darlington 54), Graham Reed (Sunderland 55), Peter McCall (Bristol City 55), John Neal (Swindon 57), Tom Dryburgh (Oldham 57), John Hunter (Barrow 59), John Stevens (Swindon), George Catleugh (Watford), George Walters (Chesterfield 64), Peter McNamee (Notts County 1966), Wayne Biggins (Burnley & Manchester City), Jackie Gallagher (Peterborough 80), Andy Higgins (Rochdale 83), Neil Horwood (Grimsby 86), Darren Rolph (Barnsley 87), Mark Howard (Stockport 88).
Clubhouse: Normal hours, extension for matchdays.
Club Record Appearances: Mick Wright 1,152 (British Record)
Club Record Goalscorer: Malcolm Lindsay 321.
93-94 Captain: Mark Howard
Club Captain 93-94: Clive Worthington.
93-94 P.o.Y.: Tim Webster.
93-94 Top scorer:
Local Newspapers: Lynn News & Advertiser (0553 761188), Eastern Daily Press (0603 628311).
Honours: FA Amateur Cup R-up 1900-01, Southern Lg R-up 84-85 (Div 1 R-up 63-64), NPL Presidents Cup 82-83, Eastern Co's Lg 53-54 (R-up 49-50 52-53 (Lg Cup 53-54), Norfolk & Suffolk Lg(8)(R-up(6)), East Anglian Lg R-up(2), Norfolk Snr Cup(19) 1882-84 86-87 89-90 98-99 1907-08 23-25 31-32 33-34 36-37 38-39 51-52 53-58 (R-up(20)), Norfolk Invitation Cup 93-94, Norfolk Premier Cup 68-69(jt) 73-74, East Anglian Cup(4) 65-68 84-85 (R-up(3)), Eastern Professional Floodlit Lg 68-69.

PROGRAMME DETAILS:
Pages: TBA **Price:** TBA
Editor: TBA

Formed: 1900

LEICESTER UNITED

United

Leicester United players in joyous mood after a 2-1 win over Hinckley Town at United Park had given them victory in the final of the Midland Floodlit Cup.

Photo - Chris Monument.

Chairman: John Potter **Vice Chairman:** Gary Glover.
Secretary: Gary Glover, 19 Bachelor Rd, Fleckney, Leicester LE8 OBE (0533 403271).
Manager: Glen McNulty **Asst Manager:** Ian Marsden **Coach:** Glen McNulty.
Physio: Brett Pruce **Commercial Manager/Press Officer:** Paul Martin.
Ground: United Park, Winchester Road, Blaby, Leicester LE8 3HN (0533 778998).
Directions: 2 miles from junct 21 M1 & M69. 1st exit on approach road onto B582. Left at 1st r-about, right at next r-about (Everards Brewery) towards Narborough. Left at r-bout (Huntsman PH), through Whetstone village to next r-about, across A426 into Blaby, through lights and go 100 yds to next junction, right and ground on left immediately after residential area.
Capacity: 4,000 **Cover:** 1,300 **Seats:** 252 **Club Shop:** Yes **Metal Badges:** Yes
Cols: Red & white/black/red **Change colours:** All blue. **Sponsors:** TBA
Previous Name: Enderby Town (1900-81).
Previous Ground: George Street (until 1985).
Previous Leagues: Leics Senior 49-50 51-69/ East Mids 69-72.
Midweek home matchday: Tuesday **Reserve Team's League:** Ansells Midland Combination.
Record Attendance: 1,058 v Hinckley Town, 26/12/90.
Best FA Cup season: 1st Rd 77-78 (lost 1-6 at AP Leamington).
Best FA Trophy season: 3rd Rd replay 78-79 (lost 2-4 at Bishop Auckland).
Record Fees - Paid: £1,000
Received: £22,500 for Keith Scott (Lincoln).
Players progressing to Football League: Richard Dixey (Burnley 1974), Cohen Griffith (Cardiff), Neil Lyne & Tony Loughlan (Nottm Forest), Dave Puttnam & Keith Scott (Lincoln), Graham Cross (Lincoln 1979), Robert Atkins (Sheffield Utd 1982).
Clubhouse: Open every day and evening. Meals available.
93-94 Captain: Steve Ross.
93-94 P.o.Y.: Chris Tonge.
93-94 Top scorer:
Local Newspapers: Leicester Mercury. Oadby & Wigston Mail.
Local Radio Stations: Radio Leicester.
Honours: Southern Lg Midland Div R-up 86-87, Leics Senior Lg 62-63 64-65 66-67 (R-up 59-60 63-64 65-66 67-68 68-69, Div 2 58-59 (R-up 51-52)), East Mids Regional Lg 70-71 71-72 (Lg Cup 70-71), Leics Snr Cup 61-62 64-65 66-67 70-71 72-73 78-79, Leics Challenge Cup 78-79 79-80 86-87 87-88, Midland Floodlit Cup 93-94, Rolleston Charity Cup 92-93.

PROGRAMME DETAILS:
Pages: 20 **Price:** 50p
Editor: Paul Martin

Formed: 1901

MOOR GREEN

The Moors

Guy Russell of Moor Green tries to stop a fine attacking run from Crawley Town's Mark Ford. The Moors lost 0-2 in this Beazer Homes League Premier Division fixture in Sussex on 25th September.

Photo - Paul Dennis.

Chairman: Geoff Hood **Vice-Chairman:** Martyn Alcott.
Secretary: Martyn Davis, 22 Collingdon Ave., Sheldon, Birmingham B26 3YL (021 743 0991).
Manager: Bob Faulkner **Asst Manager:** TBA **Coach:** Graham Clegg
Press Officer: Peter Clynes (021 745 3262) **Physio:** TBA
Commercial Manager: Rory Lynas (021 777 8961).
Ground: 'The Moorlands', Sherwood Road, Hall Green B28 0EX (021 777 2727).
Directions: Off Highfield Road, which is off A34 (B'ham to Stratford). Hall Green & Yardley (BR) half mile away.
Capacity: 3,250 **Cover:** 1,200 **Seats:** 250 **Floodlights:** Yes **Metal Badges:** Yes
Club Shop: Yes, selling scarves, mugs, stickers, programmes. Contact Craig Hochkins (021 745 3191).
Colours: Sky/navy/sky **Change colours:** All yellow **Sponsors:** Ansells.
Previous Leagues: (friendlies only 1901-21) Birmingham & Dist. A.F.A. 1908-36/ Central Amateur 36-39/ Birmingham Comb 45-54/ West Mids 54-65/ Midland Comb 65-83.
Previous Grounds: Moor Green Lane 1901-02/ numerous 02-22/ Windermere Road 1910-30.
Midweek home matchday: Tuesday **Reserve Team's League:** None.
Best F.A. Cup season: 1st Rd Proper 1979-80 (lost 2-3 at Stafford Rangers).
Record Gate: 5,000 v Romford, FA Amtr Cup 1951 *(15,000 v Ajax in Olympic Stadium, Amsterdam).*
Record Fees - Paid: £1,000 for Adrian O'Dowd (Alvechurch)
Received: £15,000 for Ian Taylor (Port Vale).
Players progressing to Football League: Herbert Smith & Ron Jefferies (Aston Villa 1947 & 50), Fred Pidcock (Walsall 1953), Peter Woodward (West Bromwich Abion 1954), Steve Cooper (Birmingham City 1983), Ken Barnes (Manchester City), Brian Mack (West Bromwich Albion), Paul Brogan (Mansfield Town), Ian Taylor (Pt Vale 1992), Stewart Talbot (Doncaster 1994).
Clubhouse: Two bars and dance floor. Open nightly and weekend lunchtimes.
93-94 Captain: Guy Russell.
93-94 P.o.Y.: C Gillard
93-94 Top scorer: P Davies 17.
Local Newspapers: Solihull News (021 626 6635), Solihull Times (021 704 3338), Birmingham Post & Mail (021 236 3366), Express & Star (0902 319461).
Local Radio Stations: Radio WM, BRMB.
Hons: Southern Lg Midland Div R-up 87-88, Mids Comb 80-81 (R-up(4) 74-76 79-80 82-83, Div 1 85-86, Presidents Cup(2) 66-68 78-79), Mids Comb Challenge Cup 80-81 (R-up 69-70 82-83), Lord Mayor of B'ham Charity Cup 90-91, Mids F'lit Cup(2) 90-92, Tony Allden Tphy 81-82, B'ham Snr Cup 57-58, Worcs Snr Cup R-up 86-87, B'ham Jnr Cup 66-67, Worcs Jnr Cup 85-86, Solihull Charity Cup 85-86, Smedley Crook Memorial Cup 87-88, Central Amateur Lg 36-37 37-38 38-39, Verviers (Belg) Tphy 32-33 36-37, AFA Challenge Cup 38-39, AFA Snr Cup 26-27 35-36, Mids F'lit Yth Lg Cup R-up 87-88, B'ham County Yth Lg Cup R-up 83-84.

PROGRAMME DETAILS:
Pages: 52 **Price:** 60p
Editor: Peter Denham
(021 777 3356)

NEWPORT A.F.C.

Formed: 1989 | The Exiles

Newport AFC pictured with the Gloucestershire Senior Cup after defeating landlords Gloucester City 1-0 in the final at Meadow Park. Back Row (L/R): Phil Coyne, Mark Price, Darren Porretta, David Cole, Brendan Dowd, Will Foley, Jon Roberts, Jason Hoskins, Graham Rogers (Manager), Jason Donovan, Tony Gilbert (Physio), Mark Evans. Front: Chris Townsend, John Lewis (Player-Coach), Mike Pengelly, Linden Jones, Dave Webley, Mark Spencer.

Chairman: David Hando **Vice-Chairman:** Wallace Brown **President:** Brian Toms, MBE.
Secretary: Mike Everett, 66 Gibbs Rd, Newport, Gwent NP9 8AU (0633 280932).
Manager: Graham Rogers **Asst Manager:** John Lewis **Physio:** Tony Gilbert
Trainer: David Williams **Press Officer:** Wallace Brown (0633 265500).
Community Director: Ray Taylor (0443 237545).
Club Headquarters: The King, 76 Somerton Road, Newport, Gwent NP9 0JX (0633 271771).
Ground: Spytty Park, Newport, Gwent.
Capacity: 3,800 **Cover:** 1,250 **Seats:** 1,250 **Floodlights:** Yes.
Club Shop: Yes. Open matchdays, selling metal badges, scarves, pennants, replica shirts, back issues of programme, sportswear, videos, mugs, bookmarks etc. These items are also available from the Club HQ (see above) during pub opening hours.
Colours: Amber black (sleeves)/amber/amber
Colours: Green & white/green/green
Sponsors: Courage
Previous Leagues: Hellenic 89-90.
Previous Grounds: London Road, Moreton-in-the-Marsh 89-90/ Somerton Park, Newport 90-92/ Gloucester City FC 92-94 *(period in exile due to dispute with FAW over the League of Wales).*
Previous Names: None. Newport AFC were formed after the demise of Newport County in 1988-89.
Midweek matchday: Wednesday **Reserve Team's League:** None.
Record Attendance: At Somerton Park: 2,354 v Moreton Town, friendly 13/8/90 (competitive game: 2,271 v Redditch Utd, Southern Lge 22/8/90). At Moreton: 594 v Pegasus Juniors, Hellenic Lge 19/8/89. At Gloucester: 810 v Sutton Utd, FA Cup 4th Qualifying Rd, 3/11/92. *Newport County had a crowd of 24,268 against Cardiff at Somerton Park in 1937.*
Best FA Cup season: 4th Qualifying Rd 92-93.
Best FA Trophy season: 1st Rd Proper 91-92.
Record win: 9-0 v Pontlottyn Blast Furnace (A), Welsh Cup First Round 1/9/90.
Record defeat: 0-5 v Trowbridge Town (H), FA Cup 1st Qualifying Round replay 15/9/93.
Clubhouse: Open 2 hours before kick-off and three hours after (approx). Pasties available in club. Burgers, hot dogs, hot drinks etc available within ground.
Club Record Goalscorer: Chris Lilygreen 93.
Club Record Appearances: C Lilygreen 196.
93-94 Captain: Linden Jones.
93-94 P.o.Y.: Brendan Dowd.
93-94 Top scorer: Will Foley 20.
Local Newspapers: South Wales Argus, South Wales Echo.
Local Radio Stations: Red Dragon.
Honours: Hellenic League 89-90 (League Cup 89-90), Gloucestershire Senior Cup 93-94.

PROGRAMME DETAILS:
Pages: 20 **Price:** TBA
Editor: Wallace Brown (0633 265500)

1937 NUNEATON BOROUGH The Boro

Nuneaton Borough fans at their Second Round FA Cup tie at Bournemouth.

Chairman: Howard Kerry **Vice Chairman:** Brendan Dodd.
Life President: Alf Scattergood.
Secretary: Peter Humphreys, 29 Amington Rd, Shirley, Solihull, West Mids B90 2RF (021 745 2031).
Manager: Elwyn Roberts **Asst Manager:** Andy McGowan **Physio:** Andy Cunningham
Press Officer: Gordon Chislett (0203 222106 office hrs)
Commercial Manager: Ray Dickinson (0203 325281(office hrs)).
Ground: Manor Park, Beaumont Road, Nuneaton, Warks CV10 0SY (0203 342690/385738. Fax: 342690).
Directions: A444 to Nuneaton from M6 junction 3, 2nd exit at 1st r-about, left at 2nd r-about then 2nd right into Greenmoor Road, turn right at the end and ground is on the left. From town centre ring-road ground is at the end of Queens Road. Parking for 100 cars at Manor Park School, Beaumont Rd, 50p each. Ground 1 mile from Nuneaton Trent Valley (BR) station.
Capacity: 5,000 **Cover:** 2,000 **Seats:** 600 **Floodlights:** Yes **Metal Badges:** Yes.
Club Shop: Yes. Numerous Boro' souvenirs, non-League & League programmes & fanzines. Current season programme exchanges welcome. Contact Andy Pace (0203 374043).
Colours: Royal & white stripes **Change colours:** Red & white **Sponsors:** Brew XI
Previous Leagues: Central Amateur 37-38/ B'ham Comb 38-52/ West Mids (B'ham) 52-58/ Southern 58-79 81-82/ GM Conference (Alliance Premier & Gola) 79-81 82-87.
Midweek home matchday: Tuesday **Reserves' League:** Ansells Midland Comb. (Res. Div.).
Record Gate: 22,114 v Rotherham, FA Cup 3rd Rd 1967 *(Best in Conference: 3,597 v Maidstone, 83-84).*
Best FA Cup season: 3rd Rd rep. 66-67. 1st Rd 19 times; 49-50 53-55 66-68 71-72 74-80 81-82 84-86 92-94.
League clubs defeated in FA Cup: Watford 53-54, Swansea T. 66-67, Oxford U. 77-78, Swansea C. 93-94.
Record Fees - Paid: £9,500 for Richard Dixey (Scarborough, 1981)
Received: £60,000 for Darren Bullock (Huddersfield Town, 1993).
Record win: 11-1 (45-46 & 55-56) **Record defeat:** 1-8 (55-56 & 88-89).
Players progressing to Football League: Richard Mason & Paul Culpin (Coventry 1946 & 85), Eric Betts (Walsall 1949), Frank Cruickshank (Notts Co. 1950), Ken Plant (Bury 1950), John Schofield (Birmingham 1950), Ron Howells (Wolves 1952), Frank Upton & Richard Hill (Northampton 1953 & 85), Ron Dickinson & Mike Gibson (Shrewsbury 1953 & 60), George Cattleugh (Watford 1954), Terry Wright (Barrow 1962), Mick Hartland (Oxford 1963), Ken Satchell & Barry Holbutt (Walsall 1965), Terry Bell (Hartlepool 1966), Alan Morton (Fulham 1970), Reg Edwards (Port Vale 1972), Kirk Stephens (Luton 1978), Trevor Peake (Lincoln 1979), Paul Sugrue (Manchester City 1980), Malcolm Shotton & Tim Smithers (Oxford 1980), Dean Thomas (Wimbledon 1981), Paul Richardson (Derby 1984), Trevor Morley (Northampton 1985), Eddie McGoldrick & Alan Harris (Northampton 1986), Darren Bullock (Huddersfield 1993).
Clubhouse: Stewardess - Jackie Salisbury (0203 383152). Open every evening, weekebd lunchtimes and matchdays (inc Reserve & Youth). Vice Presidents Lounge under main stand. Members only.
Club Record Scorer: Paul Culpin 201.
Record Record Scorer in one season: Paul Culpin 55 (92-93).
Club Record Appearances: Alan Jones 545 (1962-74).
93-94 Captain: Gary Bradder.
93-94 P.o.Y.: Matt Tarry.
93-94 Top scorer: Mark Rosegreen 15.
Local Newspapers: Hartland Evening News, Nuneaton Evening Telegraph, Neaton Weekly Tribune.
Local Radio: Mercia Sound, BBC CWR. **Boro' Newsline:** 0891 122 909.
Hons: FA Tphy QF 76-77(replay) 79-80 86-87, Alliance Premier Lge R-up(2) 83-85, Southern Lg R-up 66-67 74-75 (Midland Div 81-82 92-93, Lg Cup R-up 62-63, Merit Cup 92-93(joint)), Birmingham Lg 55-56 (Nth Div 54-55), Birmingham Comb. R-up 45-46 48-49 50-51, Birmingham Snr Cup 48-49 55-56 59-60 77-78 79-80 92-93 (R-up 52-53 66-67 90-91.

PROGRAMME DETAILS:
Pages: 36 **Price:** 80p
Editor: Editorial team
(contact 0203 374043)

1919 **RACING CLUB WARWICK** Racing

Racing Club Warwick's Townsend Meadow ground.

Chairman: Mr J Wright **Vice Chairman:** Mr E Jenkins.
Secretary: Patrick Murphy, 20 Dadglow Rd, Bishops Itchington, Leamington Spa CV33 0TG (0926 612675).
Manager: Wilson Barrett **Asst Manager:** Russell Ashendon.
Press Officer: Secretary **Commercial Manager:** Robin Lamb.
Ground: Townsend Meadow, Hampton Road, Warwick CV34 6JP (0926 495786).
Directions: On the B4095 Warwick to Redditch road (via Henley in Arden) next to owners' & trainers' car park of Warwick Racecourse. From M40 jct 15 (one and a half miles) take A429 into Warwick, left into Shakespeare Ave., straight over island, right at T-junction into Hampton Rd, ground 300yds on left. 2 miles from Warwick BR station.
Capacity: 1,000 **Cover:** 200 **Seats:** 200 **Floodlights:** Yes **Metal Badges:** Yes
Club Shop: Scarves, mugs, badges, programmes - contact Robin Lamb.
Colours: Gold/black/black **Change colours:** Red/white/white **Sponsors:** N/A.
Previous Leagues: Birmingham & West Midlands Alliance/ Warwickshire Combination/ West Midlands (Regional) 67-72/ Midland Combination 72-89.
Previous Name: Saltisford Rovers 1919-68/ Warwick Saltisford 68-70.
Midweek home matchday: Tuesday
Reserve Team's League: No Reserve team.
Record Attendance: 1,000 v Halesowen Town, FA Cup 1987.
League clubs defeated in FA Cup: None.
Record Fees - Paid: £1,000 for Dave Whetton (Bedworth United)
Received: £2,000 for Ian Gorrie (Atherstone Utd).
Record win: 9-1 **Record defeat:** 2-6.
Clubhouse: (0926 495786). Open every evening and and Fri/Sat/Sun & Mon lunchtimes.
Club Record Goalscorer: Steve Edgington.
Club Record Appearances: Steve Cooper 600.
93-94 Captain: Various.
93-94 P.o.Y.: Simon Williams.
93-94 Top scorer: Mark Jamieson.
Local Newspapers: Warwick Advertiser, Leamington Courier, Coventry Evening Telegraph.
Local Radio Stations: BBC Radio Coventry.
Hons: FA Vase 4th Rd 77-78, Midland Combination 87-88 (R-up 88-89), Warwick Lg 33-34 34-35 35-36, Birmingham & West Mids Alliance 48-49, Birmingham & Dist Alliance Senior Cup 49-50, Leamington & Dist Lg 37-38 45-46 46-47 47-48, Leamington Hospital Cup 37-38 46-47, Warwick Cinderella Cup 35-36 36-37 37-38 38-39 46-47, T G John Cup 36-37, Leamington Junior Cup 38-39 46-47.

PROGRAMME DETAILS:
Pages: 20 **Price:** TBA
Editor: Robin Lamb

Formed: 1900

REDDITCH UNITED

The Reds

Redditch United. Back Row (L/R - players' names only): Kevin Seivwright, Justin Taylor, Paul Molloy, Ron Walker, Tony Donnelly, Micky Andrews, Paul Levy. Front: Barry Williams, Paul Snowball, Jimmy Williams, Michael Warner, Dennis Mulholland, Robert Smith.

Photo - Keith Clayton.

Chairman: TBA **President:** Bob Thompson.
Secretary: M A Langfield, 174 Harport Road, Redditch, Worcs B98 7PE (0527 526603).
Manager: Paul Hendrie **Asst Manager:** Andy Dwyer **Physio:** Ginger Jordan.
Commercial Mgr: Dave Roberts **Press Officer:** R Newbold (0527 27516).
Ground: Valley Stadium, Bromsgrove Road, Redditch B97 4RN (0527 67450).
Directions: Access 7 on town centre ring-road takes you into Bromsgrove Road (via Unicorn Hill) - ground entrance 400yds past traffic lights on right. Arriving from Bromsgrove take first exit off dual carriageway. Ground 400 yds from Redditch BR station and town centre.
Capacity: 9,500 **Cover:** 2,000 **Seats:** 400 **Floodlights:** Yes **Club Shop:** No.
Colours: Red & white stripes/red/red
Change colours: White/black/black.
Sponsors: TBA.
Previous Leagues: Birmingham Combination 05-21 29-39 46-53/ West Midlands 21-29 53-72/ Southern 72-79/ GMV Conference (then Alliance Premier League) 79-80.
Previous Name: Redditch Town **Prev. Ground:** HDA Spts Ground, Millsborough Rd.
Midweek home matchday: Tuesday **Reserves' League:** Ansells Midland Comb. Res Div.
Record Attendance: 5,500 v Bromsgrove, league match 54-55.
Best FA Cup season: 1st Rd replay 71-72 (lost 0-4 at P'boro after 1-1 draw). Also 1st Rd 71-72.
League clubs defeated in FA Cup: None.
Record Fees - Paid: £3,000 for Paul Joinson
Received: £42,000 for David Farrell (Aston Villa, 1991).
Players progressing to Football League: N Davis (Aston Villa), Hugh Evans (Birmingham 1947), Trevor Lewes (Coventry 1957), David Gilbert (Chesterfield 1960), Mike Tuohy (Southend Utd 1979), Neil Smith (Liverpool), David Farrell (Aston Villa 1992).
Clubhouse: Large clubroom and lounge boardroom. Open matchdays and for private hire. Food availsable on matchdays; hot dogs, burgers, chips etc.
93-94 Captain: Paul Molloy.
93-94 P.o.Y.: Micky Andrews.
93-94 Top scorer: Chris Moss, 31.
Local Newspapers: Redditch Indicator (0527 63611), Redditch Advertiser, Birmingham Evening Mail, Redditch Weekly Mail.
Local Radio Stations: BBC Hereford & Worcester.
Hons: FA Trophy 1st Rd 78-79, Southern Lg Div 1 Nth 75-76 (Midland Div R-up 85-86), West Mids (B'ham) Lg Southern Sect. 54-55, Birmingham Comb. 13-14 32-33 52-53 (R-up 06-07 14-15 51-52), Staffs Snr Cup 90-91, Birmingham Snr Cup 24-25 31-32 38-39 76-77, Worcs Snr Cup 1893-94 1930-31 74-75 76-77 (R-up 1888-89 1929-30 52-53 73-74), Worcs Jnr Cup 90-91.

PROGRAMME DETAILS:
Pages: 48 **Price:** TBA
Editor: Roger Newbold
(0527 27516)

1896 **The Bones**

ROTHWELL TOWN

Rothwell Town - Hereward Sports United Counties League champions 1993-94. Back Row (L/R): Dave Kenney, Dave McHutchison, Chris Munns, Shaun McPolin, Bernie Geoghegan, John Coe, Simon Munns, Kevin McDonald, Chris Lund, Barry Price, Adie Spencer. Centre: Dick Dighton (Goalkeeping Coach), Mark Southon (Programme Editor), Peter Cassell (Treasurer), Nigel Bates, Ryan Smythe, Glyn Davies, Neil Edwards, Chris Miller, Danny Liquorish, Andy Wright, Stewart Marshall, Grant Mawby, Graham Simmonds (First Team Assistant Manager), Bob Mullan (Youth Team Manager), Roger Barratt (Secretary), Jeremy Freestone (Vice-Chairman). Front: Mick Callaghan, Andy Pawluk (Joint Reserve Team Managers), Adrian Sheerin, Kevin Shoemake, Mike Bearcroft (both NPS, main club sponsors), Stuart Andrews (Chairman), Jack Murray (First Team Manager), Les Hornby, Kim Davies (Coach), Peter Bradley (Press Officer). Seated: Shaun Wills, Mark Humphrey, John Mason, Gary Chambers (Mascot), Paul Murphy, Tommy Manson.

Chairman: Stuart Andrews **Vice-Chairman:** Jeremy Freestone **President:** Jack Covington.
Secretary: Roger Barratt, 18 Norton Street, Rothwell, Northants NN14 2DE (0536 711244).
Manager: Jack Murray **Asst Manager/Physio:** Graham Simmonds
Coach: Kim Davies.
Press Officer/Commercial Manager: Peter Bradley (0536 710925).
Club Newsline: 0891 88 44 14.
Ground: Cecil Street, Rothwell, Northants NN14 2EZ (0536 710694).
Directions: A14/A6 to Rothwell. At town centre roundabout turn into Bridge Street at Midland Bank (right if northbound, left if southbound), take 3rd left into Tresham Street, ground is at top on left. Three miles from Kettering (BR); Rothwell is served by Kettering to Market Harborough buses.
Capacity: 3,000 **Seats:** 264 **Cover:** 1,000 **Floodlights:** Yes **Club Shop:** No.
Colours: Blue (white sleeves)/blue/blue **Change Colours:** Red (white sleeves)/red/red
Metal Badges: Due 94-95
Midweek matchday: Tuesday **Club Sponsors:** National Physiotherapy Service.
Previous Grounds: None. **Previous Name:** Rothwell Town Swifts.
Previous Leagues: Northants 1896-1911 21-33/ Kettering Amateur 11-21 33-48/ Leicestershire Senior 48-50/ United Counties 50-56 61-94/ Central Alliance 56-61.
Record Attendance: 2,508 v Irthlingborough Diamonds, United Counties League 1971.
Reserve Team's League: Hereward Sports United Counties League Reserve Division.
Players progressing to Football League: Lee Glover (Nottingham Forest, Barnsley & Scotland under-21) 1987, Matty Watts (Charlton Athletic) 1990.
Best FA Cup season: Never past Second Qualifying Round.
Best FA Trophy season: Preliminary Round 74-75.
Best FA Vase season: Fifth Round 92-93 (lost 1-2 v Bridlington Town).
Record transfer fee paid: Undisclosed for Andy Wright (Aylesbury 1992).
Record transfer fee received: Undisclosed for Matty Watts (Charlton 1990).
Record win: 17-0 v Stamford, FA Cup Preliminary Round replay 1927.
Record defeat: 1-10 v Coalville Town, Leicestershire Senior League 1949.
Clubhouse: Rowellian Social Club, open every evening and weekend lunchtimes. Crisps and rolls available on matchdays (hot food and drinks available in ground). 'Top of the Town Ballroom', lounge seats 200.
Local Newspapers: Northants Evening Telegraph (0536 81111), Chronicle & Echo (0604 231122), Herald & Post.
Local Radio Stations: Radio Northants, KCBC.
Captain 93-94: Adrian Sheerin
Top Scorer 93-94: Shaun McPolin, 35.
Player-of-the-Year 93-94: Glyn Davies.
Hons: United Counties Lg 92-93 93-94 (R-up 69-70 70-71 87-88 89-90 90-91, KO Cup 55-56 70-71 71-72 91-92 92-93 (R-up 77-78 79-80 82-83), Div 2 52-53 53-54, Div 2 Cup 52-53 53-54, Benevolent Cup 92-93 93-94 (R-up 89-90 90-91)), Northants Lg 1899-1900 (R-up 1895-96 96-97 97-98), Northants Snr Cup 1899-1900 23-24 59-60 88-89 (R-up 24-25 71-72 87-88).

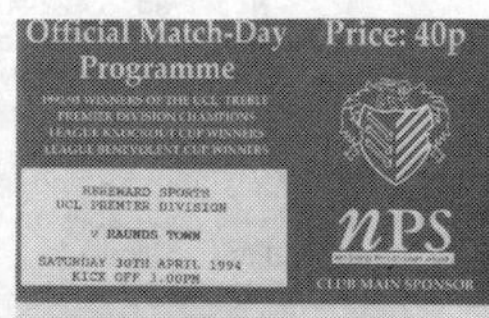

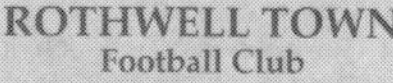

PROGRAMME DETAILS:
Pages: 52 **Price:** 40p
Editor: Mark Southon
(0533 774877)

Formed: 1876

STOURBRIDGE

The Glassboys

Stourbridge FC. Back Row (L/R): Alf Bowerman (then Manger), Russell Turley, Lee Young, Nigel Barrows, Mark Phillips, Toby Hall, Matt Davis, Lewis Claxton. Front: John Horne (Captain), Trevor Burroughs, Adrian Cooper, Jason Lowe, Alan Potter, Kevin Duckworth.

Chairman: Tony Spicer **Vice Chairman:** G Taylor **President:** J L Guest.
Secretary/Press Off.: Hugh Clark, 10 Burnt Oak Drive, Stourbridge, West Mids DY8 1HL (0384 392975).
Manager: Colin Gordon **Coach:** Gary Kirkwood **Physio:** Steve Kings
Commercial Manager: Peter Cooper.
Ground: War Memorial Athletic Ground, High Street, Amblecote, Stourbridge DY8 4EB (0384 394040).
Directions: Take A491, signposted Wolverhampton, from Stourbridge ring-road - ground 300yds on left immediately beyond traffic lights and opposite 'Royal Oak' pub. Buses 311, 313 from Dudley, and 256 from Wolverhampton, pass ground. One mile from Stourbridge Town (BR).
Capacity: 2,000 **Cover:** 1,250 **Seats:** 250 **Floodlights:** Yes **Metal Badges:** Yes
Colours: Red & white stripes **Change colours:** Yellow & blue (new for 93-94).
Club Shop: Yes. Thousands of programmes and souvenirs. Contact Nigel Gregg (0384 838334).
Previous Leagues: West Midlandss (previously Birmingham) 1892-1939/ Birmingham Combination 45-53.
Previous Grounds: None **Previous Name:** Stourbridge Standard
Sponsors: Bevan Contracts Ltd **Midweek home matchday:** Tuesday
Record Attendance: 5,726 v Cardiff City, Welsh Cup final 1st leg 1974.
Best F.A. Cup season: 4th Qual. Rd 3 times this century: v Arnold 67-68, v V.S. Rugby 84-85 & 85-86.
League clubs defeated in F.A. Cup: Crewe 1892-93, Burslem Port Vale 94-95, Burton Swifts 97-98.
Record Fee Received: £20,000 for Tony Cunningham (Lincoln City, 1979).
Players progressing to Football League: Doug Pinbley & Brian Farmer (Birmingham City 1946 & 54), Howard Edwards (Derby County 1947), James Pemberton (Luton Town 1947), Jack Boxley (Bristol City 1950), Antonio Rowley (Liverpool 1953), Colin Taylor & Keith Ball (Walsall 1958 & 72), Peter Clark (Stockport County 1965), Percy Freeman (West Bromwich Albion 1968), Chic Bates & Ray Harwood (Shrewsbury Town 1974), Les Lawrence (Shrewsbury Town 1975), Steve Cooper (Torquay 1978), Tony Cunningham (Lincoln 1979), Mel Gwinnet (Peterborough 1981).
Clubhouse: Open every evening from 8pm and Sunday lunchtimes.
Club Record Scorer: Ron Page, 269
Club Record Appearances: Ron Page 427.
93-94 Captain & P.o.Y: John Horne
93-94 Top scorer: John Hanson 18
Local Newspapers: Stourbridge News & County Express, Express & Star, Dudley Evening Mail.
Local Radio Stations: Radio West Wids, B.R.M.B., Beacon.
Honours: Welsh Cup R-up 73-74, FA Trophy QF 70-71, Southern Lg Midland Div 90-91 (Lg Cup 92-93, Div 1 North 73-74, Merit Cup 73-74), West Mids (prev. Birmingham) Lg 23-24 (R-up 01-02 37-38 55-56 62-63, Div 2 R-up(res) 80-81), Birmingham Comb. R-up 51-52, Birmingham Snr Cup 49-50 45-46 75-76 (R-up 10-11 45-46 75-76), Worcs Snr Cup 04-05 05-06 19-20 21-22 23-24 27-28 49-50 67-68 80-81 (R-up 03-04 09-10 10-11 13-14 20-21 24-25 25-26 36-37 48-49 55-56 78-79), Herefordshire Snr Cup 54-55, Camkin Cup R-up 69-70, Camkin Presidents Cup 70-71, Albion Shield 43-44, Kidderminster Cup 1887-88, Keys Cup 37-38 62-63, Dudley Guest Hosp. Cup 1891-92, Worcester Charity Cup 1887-88, Worcs Comb. R-up 27-28, Worcester Jnr Cup R-up 27-28, Tillotson Cup R-up 39-40, Brierley Hill Lg R-up 44-45 (Lg Cup R-up 44-45), Brierley Hill Yth Lg Coronation Cup 56-57.

PROGRAMME DETAILS:
Pages: 36 **Price:** 70p
Editor: Secretary

1897 # SUTTON COLDFIELD TOWN Royals

Sutton Coldfield Town FC. Back Row (L/R): Brendan Glynn (Physio), Stuart Randall, John Hunt, Tony Hadland, John Parsons, Carl Heeley, Tony Haddon, Adam Whitehouse, Andy Comerford (Trainer). Centre: Wayne Rowley, Paul Morton, Royston Richardson, Andy Ling, Andy Biddle, Micky Richards, Larry Chambers, Matthew Carroll, Steve Mead. Front: Pete Young, Bill Worship, Pat Garratt, Mike Harrison (Vice-Chairman), Gerry Shanahan (Chairman), Carlo Rossi (Manager), Tony Binns, Bernard Bent, Derek Garratt.

Chairman: Gerry Shanahan **Vice Chairman:** Mike Harrison.
Secretary: Gerry Shanahan, 34 Shipton Road, Sutton Coldfield B72 1NR (021 354 5152).
Manager: Carlo Rossi **Asst Mgr:** Tony Hadland **Physio:** Brendon Glynn.
Press Officer: Bryan Turner **Commercial Manager:** Pete Young.
Ground: Central Ground, Coles Lane, Sutton Coldfield B72 1NL (021 354 2997/021 355 5475).
Directions: A5127 into Sutton, right at Odeon cinema (Holland Road), then first right into Coles Lane - ground 150 yds on left. 10 mins walk from Sutton Coldfield (BR), bus 104 from Birmingham.
Capacity: 4,500 **Cover:** 500 **Seats:** 200 **Floodlights:** Yes **Metal Badges:** Yes
Club Shop: Yes, selling metal badges, scarves, hats, pens, rosettes, progs. Contact Paul Vanes (021 770 9835).
Colours: Royal/white/royal **Change colours:** White/royal/white.
Previous Leagues: Central Birmingham/ Walsall Senior/ Staffs County/ Birmingham Combination 50-54/ West Mids (Regional) 54-65 79-82/ Midlands Combination 65-79.
Previous Grounds: Meadow Plat 1879-89/ Coles Lane (site of current ambulance station) 90-1919.
Reserve Team's League: None. **Previous Name:** Sutton Coldfield FC 1879-1921.
Midweek home matchday: Wednesday
Record Fees - Paid: £1,500 twice in 1991, for Lance Morrison (Gloucester) & Micky Clarke (Burton A.)
Received: £25,000 for Barry Cowdrill (WBAl 1979).
Record Attendance: 2,029 v Doncaster Rovers, F.A. Cup 80-81 (Receipts £2,727).
Best FA Cup season: 1st Rd 80-81 (lost 0-1 to Doncaster), 92-93 (1-2 at Wanderers).
Players progressing to Football League: Arthur Corbett (Walsall 1949), Paul Cooper (Manchester City), Noel Blake (Leeds), Steve Cooper (Barnsley), Peter Latchford (WBA & Celtic), Mark Smith (Wolves), John Barton (Everton), Barry Cowdrill (WBA 1979), Colin Dryhurst (Halifax 1979), Dale Belford (Notts County 1987), Ellis Laight (Torquay 1992).
Clubhouse: Brick built lounge and concert room, fully carpeted and extensively decorated. Open daily, food available.
Club Record Goalscorer: Eddie Hewitt 288
Club Record Apps: Eddie Hewitt 465
93-94 Captain: Tony Hadland.
93-94 P.o.Y.: Carl Heeley.
93-94 Top scorer: John Hunt 19.
Local Newspapers: Sutton Coldfield News, Sutton Observer.
Local Radio Stations: BRMB, Radio WM.
Honours: Southern Lg Midland Div R-up 82-83, West Mids Lg 79-80 (Lg Cup 80-81 81-82), Midland Comb.(2) 77-79 (R-up(2) 69-71, Lg Cup 69-70), Walsall Snr Lg 46-47, Walsall Snr Cup(3) 77-80 (R-up 80-81), Staffs Senior Cup R-up 89-90 (SF 84-85 86-87), Lord Mayor of Birmingham Charity Cup R-up 93-94, Worcs Snr Cup SF 88-89, Walsall Challenge Cup R-up 46-47 47-48, Sutton Charity Cup 46-47 65-66 71-72 86-87 89-90 90-91, F.A. Trophy 1st Rd Replay 89-90, FA Amateur Cup 2nd Rd 70-71, Express & Star Cup 44-45.

PROGRAMME DETAILS:
Pages: 20 **Price:** 80p
Editor: TBA

Formed: 1933

TAMWORTH

Lambs or Town

Tamworth FC 1993-94.

Photo - Paul Barber.

Chairman: Bob Andrews **Vice Chairman:** Tony Reeves **President:** Len Gendle.
Secretary: Rod A Hadley, 38 Godolphin, Riverside, Tamworth B79 7UF (0827 66786).
Manager: Les Green **Asst Manager:** Derek Bond **Physio:** Peter Smith
Groundsman: Cliff Earp **Press Officer:** Sam Holiday.
Commercial Manager: Buster Belford.
Ground: The Lamb Ground, Kettlebrook, Tamworth, Staffs B79 1HA (0827 65798).
Directions: From town centre follow one-way road marked South into Kettlebrook Road - ground on right opposite railway arches. From M42 jct 10, A5 Watling Street to 'Bulls Head' at Two Gates traffic lights, left into Tamworth Road (A51), one mile to ground on left - entrance from car park at side of the Lamb Inn. 1 mile from Tamworth BR station.
Capacity: 2,500 **Cover:** 1,191 **Seats:** 391 **Floodlights:** Yes **Metal Badges:** Yes
Club Shop: Yes, selling replica shirts, sweat shirts, rugby-style shirt, lapel badges etc.
Colours: Red/black/black **Change colours:** All yellow **Sponsors:** Specsavers.
Previous Leagues: Birmingham Combination 33-54/ West Midlands (initially Birmingham Lg) 54-72 84-88/ Southern 72-79 83-84/ Northern Premier 79-83.
Midweek home matchday: Tuesday **Previous Grounds:** Jolly Sailor Ground 33-34.
Record Attendance: 4,920 v Atherstone Town, Birmingham Combination 3/4/48.
Best FA Cup season: 2nd Rd 69-70 (lost 0-6 at Gillingham). Also 1st Rd 66-67 70-71 87-88 90-91.
League clubs defeated in FA Cup: Torquay 69-70.
Record Fees - Paid: £5,000 for Steve Cartwright (Colchester United, November 1988).
Received: £7,500 for Martin Myers (Telford United, 1990).
Record Win: 14-4 v Holbrook Institute (H), Bass Vase 17/11/34.
Record Defeat: 0-11 v Solihull (A), Birmingham Comb. 13/4/40.
Players progressing to Football League: Peter Hilton (WBA 1949), Alan Godridge (Swansea 1950), W Ealing (Doncaster), Higgins (Fulham), P Weir (Cardiff), S Fox (Wrexham), Steve Cartwright (Colchester 1988).
Clubhouse: Club on ground open matchdays only, training nights and tote night (Monday) only, but club own the adjacent Lamb Inn which is open every day, normal licensing hours.
Club Record Goalscorer: Graham Jessop 195
Club Record Scorer in single season: Percy Vials 63 (33-37), Ray Holmes 60 (69-70).
Club Record Appearances: Dave Seedhouse 869.
93-94 Captain: Adrian Piggon.
93-94 P.o.Y.: Peter McBean.
93-94 Top scorer: Peter McBean.
Local Newspapers: Tamworth Herald (0827 60741).
Local Radio Stations: Radio WM, BRMB Radio.
Hons: FA Vase 88-89, West Mids Lg 63-64 65-66 71-72 87-88 (R-up(2) 67-69, Div 2 55-56, Lg Cup(5) 64-66 71-72 85-86 87-88 (R-up 70-71)), Birmingham Snr Cup 60-61 65-66 68-69 (R-up 36-37 63-64), Staffs Snr Cup 58-59 63-64 65-66 (R-up 55-56 66-67 70-71), Midland F'lit Cup R-up 71-72 72-73, Camkin Cup 71-72 (R-up 70-71), Birmingham County Youth Cup 88-89.

PROGRAMME DETAILS:
Pages: 24 **Price:** 70p
Editor: Secretary

SOUTHERN DIVISION 1993-94

	P	W	D	L	F	A	PTS
Gravesend & N.	42	27	11	4	87	24	92
Sudbury Town	42	27	8	7	98	47	89
Witney Town	42	27	8	7	69	36	89
Salisbury City	42	26	10	6	90	39	88
Havant Town	42	27	4	11	101	41	85
Ashford Town	42	24	13	5	93	46	85
Baldock Town	42	26	7	9	76	40	85
Newport IOW	42	22	8	12	74	51	74
Margate	42	20	8	14	76	58	68
Weymouth	42	18	9	15	71	65	63
Tonbridge AFC	42	19	5	18	59	62	62
Buckingham Town	42	14	14	14	43	42	56
Braintree Town	42	16	7	19	72	84	55
Fareham Town	42	12	12	18	54	75	48
Poole Town	42	13	6	23	54	86	45
Burnham	42	10	9	23	53	92	39
Fisher '93	42	9	10	23	52	81	37
Dunstable	42	9	7	26	50	91	34
Erith & Belvedere	42	9	5	28	40	72	32
Canterbury City	42	8	7	27	35	80	31
Wealdstone	42	6	7	29	45	95	25
Bury Town	42	3	5	34	36	121	14

TOP SCORERS

S Portway (Gravesend & Northfleet)	41
P Odey (Salisbury City)	34
A Jones (Havant Town)	31
K Phillips (Baldock Town)	29
D Fosbury (Havant Town)	25
S Saunders (Salisbury City)	23
M Stanton (Ashford Town)	23
S Parnell (Sudbury Town)	23
G Bennett (Braintree Town)	22
M Dent (Ashford Town)	22

Below: *A familiar sight - Steve Portway celebrates another goal (this one against Burnham was in fact his 90th for the club) as Gravesend & Northfeet head back to the Premier Division.*

Photo - Paul Dennis.

RESULT CHART 1993-94

HOME TEAM	1	2	3	4	5	6	7	8	9	10	11	12	13	14	15	16	17	18	19	20	21	22
1. Ashford	*	2-0	3-2	3-0	4-0	6-1	1-1	6-3	3-1	2-3	2-0	2-2	4-2	1-0	3-2	3-0	1-1	2-2	1-0	2-0	3-1	1-2
2. Baldock	1-1	*	1-0	2-1	4-0	2-1	2-0	0-0	2-2	2-0	3-2	1-2	4-2	1-1	3-2	3-1	2-0	1-3	0-2	1-0	1-1	2-0
3. Braintree T.	1-3	2-1	*	1-3	5-0	1-1	4-1	1-1	4-1	3-0	3-1	1-4	0-1	1-1	0-2	5-1	0-1	1-3	2-1	2-2	1-1	1-2
4. Buckingham	0-0	1-0	0-2	*	2-2	1-0	2-0	0-1	2-2	0-0	0-0	0-2	0-0	0-2	1-1	1-0	0-1	0-0	2-1	0-0	1-1	0-1
5. Burnham	1-1	1-4	6-1	1-1	*	4-2	1-1	3-2	0-3	1-2	0-0	1-1	1-0	0-2	0-2	3-1	1-2	1-4	1-0	3-0	1-3	1-2
6. Bury Town	0-4	0-4	0-2	0-3	1-4	*	2-1	3-3	1-2	0-3	2-3	2-5	1-3	0-2	0-3	0-0	1-5	1-5	0-2	4-0	1-1	0-1
7. Canterbury	0-4	0-3	1-4	0-1	3-2	3-2	*	1-3	3-0	0-2	2-3	0-5	0-3	0-2	0-4	1-1	0-2	3-0	1-2	1-2	3-1	0-1
8. Dunstable	3-2	1-2	2-1	0-2	2-2	0-3	0-2	*	0-3	3-2	2-1	1-4	0-1	1-1	0-4	1-2	1-1	0-1	1-4	1-0	2-4	1-2
9. Erith & B.	1-1	0-1	0-3	0-2	1-0	5-1	2-0	0-1	*	2-1	1-2	0-1	0-2	2-3	0-2	1-3	0-2	0-1	1-3	2-0	0-3	1-4
10. Fareham T.	2-3	0-3	1-0	4-2	0-1	3-1	1-1	2-2	1-0	*	3-3	0-0	0-5	4-2	1-4	1-4	1-1	0-2	1-0	1-0	3-2	1-2
11. Fisher '93	0-2	0-4	2-2	0-3	1-1	6-0	3-1	1-3	3-1	1-1	*	0-2	0-4	0-1	0-1	2-0	0-2	2-2	2-1	1-1	1-1	1-2
12. Gravesend	0-0	1-2	4-0	0-0	6-0	3-0	1-0	1-0	0-0	2-0	1-0	*	3-1	4-1	0-1	4-0	0-0	2-2	0-0	4-1	4-1	1-0
13. Havant Town	3-3	3-1	1-2	0-1	3-0	3-0	3-0	2-1	5-2	4-1	3-2	2-1	*	1-1	3-0	10-0	1-0	2-1	2-1	2-0	2-0	1-2
14. Margate	3-2	0-2	6-0	2-1	4-0	2-2	2-0	2-1	1-0	0-0	1-3	0-2	1-0	*	0-1	5-0	1-4	2-1	5-1	4-1	3-1	0-3
15. Newport IW	2-1	0-2	1-0	1-1	0-0	3-0	0-0	4-1	1-0	0-0	3-0	0-2	3-2	3-2	*	1-0	3-3	1-3	1-3	1-1	1-3	1-3
16. Poole T.	0-0	1-2	2-3	1-2	2-0	3-0	0-1	3-1	2-1	1-1	5-4	1-1	1-2	3-2	1-2	*	1-0	0-4	0-1	5-1	0-2	1-1
17. Salisbury	1-2	2-0	5-1	2-1	5-2	6-1	1-1	2-0	1-0	3-2	6-0	1-4	1-0	2-2	1-1	3-2	*	1-0	2-0	4-0	3-1	1-1
18. Sudbury T.	4-5	2-1	9-0	2-0	5-1	4-1	3-1	5-2	2-0	2-1	2-0	1-0	0-0	3-0	2-1	1-2	1-3	*	2-1	3-2	2-0	2-1
19. Tonbridge	1-2	0-0	0-3	0-0	5-3	2-0	2-0	1-0	0-2	3-3	2-1	1-3	0-8	2-1	4-1	2-0	0-5	3-3	*	3-0	2-0	0-1
20. Wealdstone	0-0	1-2	3-4	2-5	0-3	5-1	1-2	4-0	1-1	2-2	3-0	0-3	0-4	1-3	0-6	1-2	2-3	0-1	1-2	*	3-0	1-4
21. Weymouth	0-2	2-2	4-1	3-1	2-1	2-0	2-0	3-2	3-0	4-0	1-0	1-1	0-3	3-2	1-4	2-1	1-1	2-2	1-0	1-3	*	6-1
22. Witney T.	0-0	0-2	2-2	2-0	3-0	1-0	0-0	3-1	1-0	2-0	1-1	0-1	3-2	1-1	4-0	5-1	1-0	1-1	0-1	2-0	1-0	*

Formed: 1930

ASHFORD TOWN

Nuts & Bolts

Ashford Town's Andy Morris (left) challenges Paul Lamb of Gravesend & Northfleet during the FA Trophy Second Qualifying Round clash at The Homelands.

Photo - Roger Turner.

Chairman: Ernie A Warren **Vice Chairman:** Roger C West **President:** Ashley M Batt.
Secretary/Press Officer: Alan G Lancaster, 128 Kingsnorth Road, Ashford, Kent TN23 2HY (0233 621325).
Manager: Neil Cugley **Asst Manager/Coach:** Dave Williams
Commercial Manager: E A Warren (0233 634125). **Physio:** George Sergeant
Ground: The Homelands, Ashford Road, Kingsnorth, Ashford, Kent TN26 1NJ (0233 611838).
Directions: M20 jct 10, follow A2070 signs towards Brenzett & Lydd airport, dual carriageway to junction of old A2070, ground one mile on left through village of Kingsworth. 4 miles south of Ashford - special bus service leaves railway station at 13.35 (Saturday) and 18.35 (midweek matches).
Capacity: 3,200 **Cover:** 1,250 **Seats:** 500 **Floodlights:** Yes **Metal Badges:** Yes
Club Shop: Yes, selling old programmes, pennants, scarves, gloves, hats. Contact Martin Simmons on club number matchdays only.
Colours: White & green stripes/white/green (white tops) **Change colours:** TBA.
Previous Leagues: Kent 30-59. **Previous Ground:** Essella Park, Essella Rd 30-87.
Midweek home matchday: Tuesday **Reserve Team's League:** No Reserve team for 1994-95.
Record Attendance: 6,525 (at Essella Park, previous ground), v Crystal Palace, FA Cup 1st Rd 1959.
Best FA Cup season: 2nd Rd 61-62 (lost 0-3 at home to QPR), 66-67 (0-5 at Swindon). Also 1st Rd 34-35 58-59 59-60 60-61 74-75.
League clubs defeated in FA Cup: None.
Previous Names: Ashford United/ Ashford Railway/ Ashford F.C.
Record Fees - Paid: £2,000 for Tim Hulme (Hythe Town, August 1988)
Received: £25,000 for Jeff Ross & Dave Arter (Hythe Town, December 1990). *Individually: £20,000 for Lee McRobert (Sittingbourne, 1993).*
Record win: 10-1 v Barry Town, February 1964.
Record defeat: 0-8 v Crawley Town, November 1964.
Players progressing to Football League: Ollie Norris (R'dale 1961), Howard Moore (Coventry 1966), Tony Godden (WBA 1975).
Clubhouse: Open matchdays and for special functions. Licensed bar, pool, function room. Limited food available; sandwiches, sausage & chips, pie & chips etc.
Club Record Goalscorer: John Young 172
Club Record Appearances: Peter McRobert.
93-94 Captain: Jason Wheeler.
93-94 P.o.Y.: Andy Morris.
93-94 Top scorer: Mark Stanton.
93-94 Clubman o.Y: Steve Brignall.
Local Newspapers (+Tel.Nos.): Kentish Express (0233 623232), Ashford Citizen & Scene.
Local Radio Stations: Radio Kent, Radio Invicta.
Honours: FA Trophy SF 72-73, Southern Lg Southern Div R-up 86-87, Kent Lg 48-49 (R-up 31-32, Lg Cup 38-39), Kent Senior Cup 58-59 62-63 92-93.

NO PROGRAMME

COVER AVAILABLE

PROGRAMME DETAILS:
Pages: 24 **Price:** 80p
Editor: Ernie Warren

Formed: 1889

BALDOCK TOWN

Reds

The winning Baldock Town side that beat Diadora Premier champions Stevenage Borough 2-0 in the final of the Herts Charity Cup with goals from Nick Sweetman and Danny Howell. Back Row (L/R): Nick Sweetman, David Rolfe, Brad Gillham, Paul Olney, Paul England, Darren Fenton. Front: Steve Cook, Marcelle Bruce, Paddy Stanton, Paul Bowgett, Danny Howell, Kevin Phillips.

Photo - Grant Melton.

Chairman: Ray Childerstone **Vice Chairman:** Tony J Bottomley
Secretary: C T Hammond, 2 Elmwood Court, High Str., Baldock, Herts SG7 6AY (0462 894253).
Manager: Rob Eagles **Coach:** Dave Moseley **Physio:** Fred Day.
Press Officer: David Hammond (0462 892797) **Commercial Mgr:** Eddie Haeztman.
Ground: Norton Road, Baldock, Herts SG7 5AU (0462 895449).
Directions: Off A1(M) at Letchworth/Baldock sign, left to 3rd island, A505 to Baldock, Norton Road is left off A505, left past Orange Tree pub, ground on right after railway bridge. From North or East turn left into town, Hitchin Street, right into Norton then proceed as above. From Baldock station (Kings Cross to Royston line) - left down Ickneild Way and right into Norton Road.
Capacity: 3,000 **Cover:** 1,250 **Seats:** 250 **Club Shop:** No **Metal Badges:** Yes
Colours: Red/white/red **Change colours:** Yellow/blue/blue.
Sponsors: Happy Eater.
Previous Leagues: S Midlands 25-39 47-54 63-83/ Parthenon 54-59/ London 59-63/ United Counties 83-87.
Previous Ground: Bakers Close (until 1982).
Midweek home matchday: Tuesday **Reserve Team's League:** No reserve team.
Record Attendance: 1,200 v Arsenal, floodlight opening 1984.
Best F.A. Cup season: 4th Qualifying Round replay (lost 0-1 at Halesowen Town after 1-1 draw). 1991-92.
Record Fees - Paid: £2,000; for Colin Hull (Bishop's Stortford); for Glen Russell (Braintree 1993)
Received: £2,000 for Glen Russell (Windsor & Eton 1994).
Players progressing to Football League: Ian Dowie (Luton & West Ham), Alan Stewart (Portsmouth).
Clubhouse: Members' bar and seperate function room. Food available.
Club Record Goalscorer: Unknown.
Club Record Apps: Paddy Stanton 440
93-94 Captain:
93-94 P.o.Y.: Paddy Stanton.
93-94 Top scorer:
Local Newspapers: Comet, Gazette, Herald.
Local Radio: Radio Bedfordshire, Chiltern.
Hons: FA Tphy 2nd Qual. Rd 90-91, FA Vase 5th Rd 83-84, United Counties Lg R-up 83-84 86-87, South Mids Lg 27-28 65-66 67-68 69-70 (R-up 53-54 82-83, Lg Cup 65-66 69-70, Div 1 49-50, Reserve Div 1 66-67), Herts Charity Cup 91-92 93-94, Herts Charity Shield 57-58 69-70, Wallspan Floodlit Cup 85-86, Hinchingbrooke Cup 86-87, TSI Floodlit Cup 88-89, Woolwich Equitable Buliding Society Cup 83-84, Herts Intermediate Cup 86-87.

PROGRAMME DETAILS:
Pages: 48 **Price:** £1
Editor: TBA

Formed: 1947

BASHLEY

The Bash

The covered stands at Bashley's rural ground.

Chairman: Trevor Adams **Vice Chairman:** Richard Eastwood **President:** Len Farebrother
Secretary: Ray Murphy, Flat 10, Richmond Court, 122 Richmond Park Rd, Bournemouth BH8 8TH (0202 517607).
Manager: Frank Whitman **Asst Manager/Coach:** Paul Arnold.
Commercial Mgr: David Groom **Physio:** Kim Sturgess **Newsline:** 0898 446 881.
Press Officer: Tony Adams (0425 613859)
Ground: Recreation Ground, Bashley, Hants BH25 5RY (0425 620280)
Directions: A35 Lyndhurst towards Christchurch, turn left down B3058 towards New Milton, ground on left in Bashley village. Half hour walk from New Milton (BR) station
Capacity: 4,250 **Cover:** 1,200 **Seats:** 200 **Floodlights:** Yes **Metal Badges:** Yes
Colours: Yellow & black **Change colours:** Blue & white.
Club Shop: Open matchdays - contact Mrs L Murphy (address as secretary).
Club Sponsors: A.E. Insurance.
Previous Leagues: Bournemouth 50-83/ Hants 83-86/ Wessex 86-89.
Midweek home matchday: Tuesday **Reserve's League:** Jewson Wessex Combination.
Record Attendance: 3,500 v Emley, F.A. Vase S.F. 1st Leg 1987-88
Best FA Cup season: 4th Qualifying Rd 1990-91 (lost 0-1 at Welling United)
Record win: 21-1 v Co-operative (A), Bournemouth League, 1964.
Record defeat: 2-20 v Air Speed (A), Bournemouth League, 1957.
Record Fee Paid: £7,500.
Record Fee Received: £5,000 from Havant Town for John Wilson, 1990.
Past Players who have progressed into The Football League: Wayne Brown (Bristol City, 1994).
Clubhouse: Usual licensing hours. Snacks available.
Record Goalscorer: Colin Cummings
Record Appearances: John Bone
93-94 Captain: Jimmy Sheppard.
93-94 P.o.Y.: Jeremy Stagg.
93-94 Top scorer: Jeremy Stagg.
Local Newspapers: Bournemouth Echo, Southern Pink, New Milton Advertiser.
Local Radio Stations: 2CR Solent, Ocean Sound.
Honours: Southern Lg Southern Division 89-90 (Lg Cup SF 89-90), Wessex Lg 86-87 87-88 88-89, Hants Lg Div 3 84-85, Hants Lg Combination 88-89, Russell Cotes Cup 88-89 90-91 92-93, FA Vase SF 87-88 (QF 88-89), FA Tphy 2nd Rd 91-92.

PROGRAMME DETAILS:
Pages: 36 **Price:** 70p
Editor: Mark Barlow
(c/o Bashley FC)

BRAINTREE TOWN

Formed: 1898 The Iron

Back Row (L/R): Peter Collins (Joint-Manager), John Bishop, Justin Pearce, John Cheesewright (now Colchester), Dean Braybrook, Simon Roberts, Glen Adams, Tony Last (Physio), Frank Bishop (Joint-Manager). Front: Gary Culling, Mark Brewer, James Devlin, Jason Cook, Russell Tanner, Dave Fynn. Photo - Jon Weaver.

Chairman: George Rosling **Vice Chairman:** Ivan Kibble **President:** R F Webb.
Secretary: T A Woodley, 19a Bailey Bridge Road, Braintree, Essex CM7 5TT (0376 326234).
Mgr: Frank Bishop/Peter Collins **Coach:** Peter Collins **Physio:** Tony Last.
Press Officer: R F Webb (0376 325338) **Comm. Manager:** Mike Craig.
Ground: Cressing Road Stadium, Clockhouse Way, Braintree, Essex (0376 345617).
Directions: From all routes use Braintree by-pass and turn into Braintree at the McDonalds r'bout following signs for East Braintree Industrial Estates - floodlights visible on left half mile into town behind 'The Sportsman' snooker, entrance is next left in Clockhouse Way, then left again. 1 mile from Braintree & Bocking (BR). Bus 353 from Witham or town centre stops at 'The Sportsman'. Town centre is twenty minutes walk.
Capacity: 4,000 **Cover:** 1,500 **Seats:** 292 **Floodlights:** Yes **Metal Badges:** £2.00
Club Shop: Yes, selling thousands of programmes, fanzines, handbooks, magazines, photos, memorabilia, newspapers, shirts, caps, mugs, jumpers, kit bags, club ties, teddy bears, scarves, pennants, club badges, bobble hats, key fobs, car stickers, rosettes, matchbooks, medals, old books & directories, picture cards. Contact Jon Weaver (0376 340780).
Cols: Yel. & white stripes/blue/yellow **Change colours:** Red & black stripes/black/red.
Reserves' Lg: Essex/Herts Border Comb. **Sponsors:** Essex Electrical Wholesalers (Braintree) Ltd.
Previous Leagues: North Essex 1898-1925/ Essex & Suffolk Border 25-28 55-64/ Spartan 28-35/ Eastern Co's 35-37 38-39 52-55 70-91/ Essex Co. 37-38/ London 45-52/ Gtr London 64-66/ Metropolitan 66-70.
Previous Names: Manor Works 1898-1921/ Crittall Ath. 21-68/ Braintree & Crittall Ath. 68-81/ Braintree FC 81-82.
Previous Grounds: Kings Head Meadow 1898-1903/ Spaldings Meadow, Panfield Lane 03-23.
Midweek home matchday: Tuesday **Best FA Cup season:** 4th Qual. Rd 69-70 85-86.
Record Attendance: 6,000 - Saffron Walden v Rainham, Essex Jnr Cup final 1926. For Braintree game: 4,000 v Spurs, charity challenge match, May 1952.
Record Fees - Paid: £1,000 twice; for Gary Hollocks (Bury Town) and for Glenn Russell (Heybridge)
Received: £10,000 Matt Metcalf (Brentford) 1993.
Players progressing to Football League: John Dick (West Ham & Scotland) 1953, Steve Wright (Wrexham) 1983, John Cheesewright (Birmingham City) 1991 + Colchester 1994, Gary Bennett + Matt Metcalf (Brentford) 1993, Robbie Reinhelt (Gillingham) 1993, Steve Allen (Wimbledon - physio).
Record win: 15-3 v Hopes (Birmingham), friendly 28/1/39. Competitive: 12-0 v Thetford Town (H), Eastern Counties League 35-36.
Record defeat: 0-14 v Chelmsford City 'A' (A), Nth Essex Lge Div 1 10/2/23 *(weakened due to another simultaneous fixture.*
Clubhouse: Open every evening 7-11pm, Sunday lunchtimes noon-2pm and Saturday matchday lunchtimes. Full bar facilites, childrens games, darts, pool, video arcade, large satellite T.V. screen. Separate section for functions. Steward: Mrs Christine Thorogood.
Record Goalscorer: Chris Guy 211 (1983-90)
Seasonal Record Scorer: C Purkiss 55, 1927-28
Club Record Appearances: Paul Young 524 (1966-77).
93-94 Captain & P.o.Y.: Mark Cranfield
93-94 Top scorer: Gary Bennett 26.
Local Newspapers: Braintree & Witham Times (0376 551551).
Local Radio Stations: BBC Essex (103.5 fm), Essex Radio (102.6 fm).
Honours: Eastern Counties Lg 36-37 83-84 84-85 (R-up 86-87 87-88 88-89 90-91, Lg Cup 87-88 (R-up 35-36 74-75)), Essex County Lg R-up 37-38, London Lg (East) R-up 45-46 (Lg Cup 47-48(joint) 48-49 51-52 (R-up 49-50)), Metropolitan Lg Cup 69-70, Essex Elizabethan Tphy R-up 68-69, East Anglian Cup 46-47 68-69, Essex Senior Trophy 86-87 (R-up 90-91), Essex & Suffolk Border Lg 59-60 84-85 (Lg Cup 59-60), Nth Essex Lg 05-06 10-11 11-12, Essex Jnr Cup R-up 04-05 05-06 22-23, RAFA Cup 56-57, Gtr London Benevolent Cup 65-66, Worthington Evans Cup 62-63(joint) 71-72 75-76 (R-up 56-57 60-61 69-70 74-75), Eastern F'lit Cup 85-86 (R-up 93-94), Anglian F'lit Lg 69-70, Jan Havanaar International Tournament 93-94 (R-up 92-93).

PROGRAMME DETAILS
Pages: 36 **Price:** 70p
Editor: Len Llewellyn
(0277 363103llis)

Formed: 1878

BURNHAM

The Blues

Burnham FC 1993-94. Dave Brown, Justin Chandler, Darren Tough, Jamie Jarvis, Tim Cook, Neal Deamer, Noel Devereux, Phil Surridge, Mark O'Donnell, Colin Cooper, Del Clayton. Front: Steve Bunce, Gary Hall, Kenny Hughes, Dominic Gavin, Colin Barnes, Neil Foster, Tony Anglin, Carl Raynes, Paul Goodison.

Photo - Mike Swift.

Chairman: Malcolm Higton **Vice Chairman:** D C Eavis **President:** R J Laverick.
Secretary/Press Officer: M J Boxall, 39 Tockley Road, Burnham, Slough SL1 7DQ (0628 660265).
Manager: Barrie Gould **Asst Manager:** Kevin Hill **Coach:** Dave Brown
Physio: Colin Cooper **Commercial Manager:** Michael Broadley.
Ground: Wymers Wood Road, Burnham, Slough SL1 8JG (0628 602467/602697).
Directions: North west of village centre, 2 miles from Burnham BR station, 2 miles from M4 junction 7, 5 miles from M40 junction 2, 100yds north of Gore crossroads - fork right into Wymers Wood Rd and ground is immediately on right. Bee Line bus 66.
Capacity: 2,500 **Cover:** 250 **Seats:** 250 **Floodlights:** Yes
Club Shop: Yes, selling programmes and other club items.
Colours: Blue & white **Change colours:** All yellow.
Sponsors: TBA
Previous Leagues: Sth Bucks & East Berks/ Maidenhead Intermediate/ Windsor, Slough & Dist./ Gt Western Comb. 48-64/ Wycombe Comb. 64-70/ Reading Comb. 70-71/ Hellenic 71-77/ Athenian 77-84/ London Spartan 84-85.
Previous Name. Burnham & Hillingdon 1985-87
Previous Ground: Baldwin Meadow (until 20's).
Midweek home matchday: Tuesday
Reserve Team's League: Suburban.
Record Attendance: 2,400 v Halesowen Town, FA Vase 2/4/83.
Best FA Cup season: 3rd Qualifying Rd.
League clubs defeated in FA Cup: None.
Best FA Trophy season: Third Qualifying Rd replay 89-90.
Record win: 18-0 v High Duty Alloys, 70-71
Record defeat: 1-10 v Ernest Turners Sports, 63-64.
Players progressing to Football League: D Hancock (Reading), R Rafferty (Grimsby Town, Portsmouth), D Payne (Barnet, Southend United).
Clubhouse: Open every evening and weekend lunchtimes. Darts and pool, two bars, usual matchday food.
Club Record Scorer: Fraser Hughes 65, 69-70
93-94 Captain: Shane Chandler.
93-94 P.o.Y.: Darren Tough.
93-94 Top scorer: Steve Bunce, 15.
Local Newspapers: Slough Observer (0753 523355), South Bucks Express (0753 825111), Maidenhead Advertiser (0628 798048).
Local Radio Station: Star FM.
Hons: FA Vase SF 82-83 (QF 77-78), Athenian Lg R-up(2) 78-80, Hellenic Lg 75-76 (Div 1 R-up 72-73, Lg Cup 75-76, Div 1 Cup 71-72), London Spartan Lg 84-85 (Lg Cup 84-85), Reading Comb. Lg Cup 70-71 (All Champions Cup 70-71), Wycombe Comb. R-up(4) 65-67 68-70, various local cup competitions.

PROGRAMME DETAILS:
Pages: 24 **Price:** TBA
Editor: Cliff Sparkes
(0753 642490)

Formed: 1872

BURY TOWN

The Blues

Bury Town's Dale Brooks (left) steers the ball back to his 'keeper with Danny Walken of Braintree Town in hot pursuit. The Suffolk side achieved a 1-1 in this fixture at Cressing Road.

Photo - Jon Weaver.

Chairman: V J Clark **Vice Chairman:** TBA **President:** C Elsey.
Secretary: Brian Lafflin, 20 Ulster Ave., Ipswich, Suffolk IP1 5JT (0473 745640).
Manager/Coach: Phil Boyland **Asst Manager:** Tony Hall
Press Officer: C Hurley **Physio:** John Chandler **General Mgr:** Brian Lafflin.
Ground: Ram Meadow, Cotton Lane, Bury St Edmunds, Suffolk (0284 754721/754820).
Directions: Leave A45 at sign to central Bury St Edmunds, follow signs to town centre at exit r'bout, 1st exit into Northgate Street at next r'bout, left at 'T' junct. (2nd lights) into Mustow Street and left immediately into Cotton Lane - ground 350 yds on right, through 'Pay & Display' car park (n.b. fine for not displaying a 40p ticket is £15). 10 mins walk from station.
Capacity: 3,500 **Cover:** 1,500 **Seats:** 300 **Floodlights:** Yes **Metal Badges:** Yes
Club Shop: Yes - contact Ian Pinches (0284 769440).
Colours: Blue/white/blue **Change colours:** Red/black/red.
Sponsors: Greene King Plc.
Previous Lges: Norfolk & Suffolk/ Essex & Suffolk Border/ Eastern Co's 35-64 76-87/ Metropolitan 64-71.
Previous Names: Bury St Edmunds 1895-1902/ Bury Utd 02-06.
Previous Ground: Kings Road 1872-1978.
Midweek home matchday: Tuesday **Reserves' Lge:** Jewson (Eastern Co's) Div 1.
Record Attendance: 2,500 v Enfield, FA Cup 3rd Qualifying Rd 1986. (At Kings Road, previous ground, 4,710 v King's Lynn, 1950).
Best FA Cup season: 1st Rd replay 68-69 (lost 0-3 at AFC Bournemouth after 0-0 draw).
League clubs defeated in FA Cup: None.
Record Fees - Paid: £1,500 for Mel Springett (Chelmsford 1990).
Received: £5,500 for Simon Milton (Ipswich).
Players progressing to Football League: D Lewis (Gillingham, Preston), Larry Carberry (Ipswich & England), Terry Bly (Norwich 1956, Peterborough), Terry Pearce (Ipswich), Gary Stevens (Brighton, Spurs & England), Simon Milton (Ipswich 1990).
Clubhouse: Members'/Public Bars open at matchdays and evenings. Darts, pool, satellite TV, bar snacks, meeting facilities.
Club Record Goalscorer: Doug Tooley 58.
Club Record Appearances: Doug Tooley.
93-94 Captain:
93-94 P.o.Y.:
93-94 Top scorer:
Local Newspapers: East Anglian Daily Times (0473 230023), Bury Free Press (0284 768911).
Local Radio: BBC Radio Suffolk (0473 250000), S.G.R. Radio (0284 701511).
Honours: FA Vase QF 88-89, FA Trophy 2nd Rd 70-71, Eastern Counties Lg 63-64 (R-up 37-38, Lg Cup 61-62 63-64), Metropolitan Lg 65-66 (R-up 67-68 70-71, Lg Cup 67-68, Professional Cup 65-66), Suffolk Premier Cup 58-59 59-60 60-61 61-62 63-64 64-65 70-71 77-78, Suffolk Senior Cup 36-37 37-38 38-39 44-45 84-85.

PROGRAMME DETAILS:
Pages: 40 **Price:** 50p
Editor: TBA

Formed: 1880

CLEVEDON TOWN

The Seasiders

Ex-Torquay star Paul Hirons (second left) gets in a header as Clevedon Town defeat St Blazey 4-0 in the Second Round of the FA Vase on Saturday 20th November. The other Clevedon player looking on is Nigel Gillard. Photo - Colin Rozee/PictureSport.

President: Doug Hand **Chairman:** B K Baker **Vice-Chairman:** J Croft.
Secretary: Mike Williams, 34 Robinia Walk, Whitchurch, Bristol BS14 0SH (0272 833835).
Manager: Steve Fey **Physio:** Steve Tregale **Coach:** Steve Millard.
Press Officer: Steve Millard **Commercial Manager:** Terry Brumpton (0275 343446).
Ground: Hand Stadium, Davis Lane, Clevedon (0275 871636-club, 871636-office, 343446-Comm. Dept).
Directions: M5 Jct 20 - follow signs for Clevedon Town Sports Complex; first left into Central Way (at island just after motorway), 1st left at mini-r'bout into Kenn Rd, 2nd left Davis Lane; ground half mile on right. Or from Bristol (B3130) left into Court Lane (opposite Clevedon Court), turn right after 1 mile, ground on left. Nearest BR station: Nailsea & Backwell. Buses from Bristol.
Seats: 300 **Cover:** 1,600 **Capacity:** 3,650 **Floodlights:** Yes **Founded:** 1880
Club colours: Blue & white **Change colours:** Yellow. **Metal Badges:** Yes.
Midweek Matches: Wednesday **Reserve Team's League:** Somerset Senior.
Club Sponsors: Jarrett Construction.
Club Shop: Yes, selling all types of souvenirs, programmes and replica kit. Contact Mr J Anderson.
Previous Leagues: Weston & District/ Somerset Senior/ Bristol Charity/ Bristol & District/ Bristol Suburban/ Western 74-93.
Previous Grounds: Dial Hill (til early 1890's)/ Teignmouth Road (til 1991).
Previous Names: Clevedon FC, Ashtonians (clubs merged in 1974).
Record Gate: 1,295 v Tiverton Town, Western League Premier Division 17/4/93 *(At Teignmouth Road: 2,300 v Billingham Synthonia, FA Amateur Cup, 52-53).*
Record win: 18-0 v Dawlish Town (H), Western League Premier Division 24/4/93.
Best FA Cup season: 3rd Qual. Rd second replay 92-93 (lost 2-4 after two 1-1 draws with Newport AFC).
Football league Clubs defeated in FA Cup: None.
Best FA Amateur Cup season: 3rd Round Proper, 52-53.
Best FA Vase season: 5th Round 92-93 (lost 0-1 at Canvey Island).
Clubhouse: Open every day and evening. Separate function suite & lounge bar. Hot food available. Matchday refreshment bar within ground sells confectionary, teas & hot food.
93-94 Captain: Dave Singleton.
93-94 P.o.Y.: Darren Cann.
93-94 Top scorer: Shaun Penny.
Local Radio Stations: Radio Bristol
Local Newspapers: South Avon Mercury
Hons: Western League 92-93 (R-up 91-92, League Cup R-up 92-93), Bristol Charity League, Somerset Snr Cup 01-02 04-05 28-29 76-77, Somerset Snr League Div 1(reserves) 92-93.

PROGRAMME DETAILS:
Pages: 36 **Price:** 50p
Editor: Terry Brumpton
(0275 343446)

1922 **ERITH & BELVEDERE** Deres

Erith & Belvedere FC pictured before their league fixture at Poole Town.

Photo - Gavin Ellis-Neville.

Chairman: J McFadden **Vice Chairman:** R E Cowley **President:** L O'Connell.
Secretary: D Joy, 104 Overton Road, Abbey Wood, London SE2 9SE (081 311 0650).
Manager: Harry Richardson **Asst Manager:** **Physio:** Ron Bates
Ground: Park View, Lower Road, Belvedere, Kent DA17 6DF (081 311 4444).
Directions: From Dartford bridge follow signs for Crayford to Erith and follow A206. Ground half mile from Erith Blackwall tunnel: head for Abbey Wood and on to Belvedere. Entrance in Station Road, adjoining Belvedere (BR) station. Bus No. 469.
Capacity: 1,500 **Cover:** 1,000 **Seats:** 500 **Floodlights:** Yes **Metal Badges:** Yes
Club Shop: Yes, selling programmes, badges and pens.
Colours: Blue & white **Change colours:** All red.
Previous Leagues: Kent 22-29 31-39 78-82/ London 29-31/ Corinthian 45-63/ Athenian 63-78.
Previous Names: Erith FC/ Belvedere & District FC (clubs amalgamated in 1922).
Midweek home matchday: Tuesday **Reserves' League:** None.
Record Attendance: 8,000 v Coventry City, FA Cup First Round Proper 1932.
Best FA Trophy season: Third Qualifying Round second replay 89-89.
Best FA Vase season: Third Round 76-77.
Best FA Cup season: First Round Proper 24-25 32-33.
League clubs defeated in FA Cup: None.
Players progressing to Football League: Geoff Bray (Oxford Utd 1971), Tommy Ord (Chelsea 1972).
Clubhouse: Licensed social club open matchdays and weekends. Cold snacks available available, separate canteen provides hot food on matchdays.
93-94 Captain: Martin Johnson.
93-94 P.o.Y. Engin Salih.
Top scorer 93-94: John Leslie.
Local Newspapers: Kentish Times, Kentish Independant.
Local Radio Stations: Radio Kent, Radio Thamesmead.
Honours: FA Amateur Cup R-up 23-24 37-38, Athenian League Div 1 R-up 70-71 (League Cup 73-74, Memorial Shield 67-68), Corinthian League R-up 62-63 (League Cup 47-48 48-49 49-50), Kent League 81-82 (League Cup R-up 81-82), London Senior Cup 44-45 (R-up 38-39), Kent Amateur Cup 23-24 47-48 65-66 66-67 68-69 69-70 (R-up 33-34 35-35 51-52 73-74), Bromley Hospital Cup 38-39, Kent Floodlit League R-up 67-68, Kent Intermediate Cup R-up 90-91, Kent Junior Cup 67-68, Essex & Herts Border Comb Cup 73-74, Kent County Youth League 90-91, Kent Youth Cup 87-88.

PROGRAMME DETAILS:
Pages: 30 **Price:** 50p
Editor: Peter Bird

Formed: 1947

FAREHAM TOWN

The Town

Two Fareham Town defenders combine to close down Neil Grice (stripes) of Braintree Town, but they cannot prevent the Essex side winning 3-0 in this January fixture.

Photo - John Weaver.

Chairman: Michael K Jackson **President:** Vacant.
Secretary: K F Atkins, 4 Cedar Close, Elson, Gosport PO12 4AT (0705 583049).
Manager: Roger Kent **Asst Manager/Coach:** None
Press Officer: M Willis **Physio:** James McKay
Commercial Manager: None.
Ground: Cams Alders, Highfield Avenue, Fareham, Hants PO14 1JA (0329 231151).
Directions: From Fareham station follow A27 towards Southampton and take second left into Redlands Avenue. Turn right at Redlands Inn then left into Highfields Avenue.
Capacity: 5,500 **Cover:** 500 **Seats:** 450 **Metal Badges:** Yes
Colours: Red & black/black/red **Change colours:** All white.
Sponsors: Hellyers Coaches.
Club Shop: Yes, selling programmes, scarves & fanzines.
Previous Name: Fareham FC **Previous Leagues:** Portsmouth 47-49/ Hants 49-79.
Previous Ground: Bath Lane.
Midweek home matchday: Wednesday **Reserve Team:** None.
Record Gate: 2,650 v Wimbeldon, FA Cup 1965. *(at Southampton F.C.; 6,035 v Kidderminster Harriers, FA Trophy Semi Final Second leg 86-87).*
Best FA Cup season: 1st Rd replay 88-89 (lost 2-3 at home to Torquay after 2-2 draw).
League clubs defeated in FA Cup: None.
Record Fees - Paid: £1,000 for Peter Baxter (Poole)
Received: £43,000 for David Leworthy (Spurs).
Players progressing to Football League: Ray Hiron (Portsmouth 1964), John Hold (AFC Bournemouth), David Leworthy (Spurs 1984), Steve Claridge (AFC Bournemouth 1984), Darren Foreman (Barnsley), Kevin Bartlett (Cardiff City 1986), Domenyk Newman (Reading 1990).
Clubhouse: Open every evening except Sundays.
93-94 Captain: Sean New.
93-94 P.o.Y.: Kevin Murphy.
93-94 Top scorer: Paul Pinder.
Local Newspapers: Portsmouth Evening News, Southampton Evening Echo.
Hons: FA Trophy SF 86-87, FA Amateur Cup 2nd Rd 63-64 66-67 73-74, Hants Lg(8) 59-60 62-67 72-73 74-75 (R-up 55-56 60-61 67-68 71-72 76-77 78-79, Div 2 R-up 52-53, Eastern Div 24-25, Div 3 East 49-50), Hants Snr Cup 56-57 62-63 67-68 92-93, Russell Cotes Cup(6) 64-65 72-77, Gosport War Memorial Cup, SW Co's Cup(2), Pickford Cup(2), Hants I'mediate Cup (reserves), FA Sunday Cup (as Fareham Centipedes) 74-75.

PROGRAMME DETAILS:
Pages: 36 **Price:** 50p
Editor: Roy Grant

Formed: 1908

FISHER '93

The Fish

Fisher's Phil Collins (stripes) is tackled by Jason Peters during the derby match at Salter Road against Erith & Belvedere.

Photo - Alan Coomes.

President: Lord Mellish **Chairman:** Chris Georgiou **Vice-Chairman:** D Wilding
Secretary/General Manager: M J Wakefield, 146 Layard Square, Drummond Rd, Bermondsey SE16 0JG (071 237 2819).
Manager: Nicky Milo **Asst Manager:** Ossie Bayram **Coach:** Michael Marks
Press Officer: **Physio:** Joe Miller.
Commercial Manager: Bert Kite. **Press Officer:** Brian Parish.
Ground: The Surrey Docks Stadium, Salter Road, London SE16 1LQ (071 231 5144. Fax: 231 5536).
Directions: 8 minutes walk from Rotherhithe (tube), 2 miles from London Bridge (main line). Buses 188, P11, P14.
Capacity: 5,300 **Cover:** 4,283 **Seats:** 400 **Floodlights:** Yes **Club Shop:** Yes.
Colours: Black & white **Change colours:** All red. **Metal Badges:** Yes
Previous Leagues: Parthenon/ West Kent/ Kent Amateur/ London Spartan 76-82/ Southern 82-87/ GMV Conference 87-91.
Midweek home games: Tuesday **Reserve Team's League:** Kent Midweek.
Club Sponsors: Senator Travel. **Record Gate:** 4,283 v Barnet, GMV Conference 4/5/91.
Previous Name: Fisher Athletic 08-93.
Previous Ground: London Road, Mitcham.
Record win: 6-0 v Bury Town, 26/10/93.
Record defeat: 0-6 v Salisbury, 21/8/93.
Best FA Cup season: 1st Rd 84-85 (0-1 at home to Bristol City), 88-89 (0-4 at Bristol Rovers).
League Clubs Defeated in FA Cup: None.
Record Fees: Paid: £500 for Davis Regis.
Received: Undisclosed.
Players progressing to The Football League: John Bumstead (Chelsea), Trevor Aylott (Bournemouth), Paul Shinners (Orient 1984), Dave Regis (Notts County - via Barnet).
Clubhouse: (071 252 0590). Luxury clubhouse, Vice-President's club. Bar open 11am-3 & 5-11pm. Sandwiches, pies, sausage rolls, chips etc available. cold food.
Club Record Scorer: Paul Shinners 205
Club Record Appearances: Dennis Sharp 720.
93-94 Captain: Danny Davenport.
93-94 P.o.Y.: Brian Hinds.
93-94 Top scorer: Alan Montague/ Mark Beckett.
Honours: Southern Lg 86-87 (R-up 83-84, Southern Div 82-83, Lg Cp 84-85, Championship Cup 87-88, Merit Cup), London Spartan Lg 80-81 81-82 (R-up 78-79, Senior Div 77-78, Div 2 R-up 76-77), Parthenon Lg 61-62 (Lg Cup 63-64 65-66), Kent Amateur Lg 73-74 74-75 (R-up 72-73), London Senior Cup 84-85 87-88 88-89, London Intermediate Cup 59-60 (R-up 75-76), Kent Senior Cp 83-84, Kent Senior Trophy 81-82 82-83, Surrey Intermediate Cup 61-62, FA Trophy 3rd Rd 3rd replay 87-88, FA Vase 2nd Rd replay 82-83.

PROGRAMME DETAILS:
Pages: 16 **Price:** 50p
Editor: Ken Wenham

Formed: 1958

HAVANT TOWN

A Havant Town defender heads the ball back to his goalkeeper under pressure from Matt Metcalf of Braintree Town. Havant lost 1-2 in this August fixture at West Leigh Park.

Photo - Jon Weaver.

Chairman: Ray Jones **President:** George Jones.
Directors: Derek Pope, Paul Cummins, Ian Craig, Trevor Brock.
Secretary/Press Officer: Trevor Brock, 2 Betula Close, Waterlooville, Hants PO7 8EJ (0705 267276).
Manager: Tony Mount **Physio:** Gary Buckner
Ground: West Leigh Park, Martin Road, West Leigh, Havant PO9 5TH (0705 470918).
Directions: Take B2149 to Havant off the A27 (B2149 Petersfield Rd if coming out of Havant). 2nd turning off dual carriageway into Bartons Road then 1st right into Martins Road. 1 mile from Havant BR station.
Capacity: 6,000 **Cover:** 1,500 **Seats:** 240 **Floodlights:** Yes **Metal Badges:** Yes
Club Shop: Yes, selling various souvenirs and programmes.
Colours: Yellow **Change colours:** Blue **Sponsors:** Nynex Cablecomms.
Previous Leagues: Portsmouth 58-71/ Hants 71-86/ Wessex 86-91.
Previous Names: Leigh Park/ Havant & Leigh Park.
Previous Grounds: Front Lawn 1958-83.
Midweek home matchday: Monday **Reserves' Lge:** Jewson Wessex Combination.
Record Attendance: 3,500 v Wisbech Town, FA Vase QF 85-86.
Best FA Cup season: Third Qualifying Round 92-93 (lost 2-3 at Sillingbourne).
Record win: 10-0 three times; v Sholing Sports (H), FA Vase 4th Rd 85-86, v Portsmouth Royal Navy (H), Wessex League 90-91; v Poole Town, Southern League Southern Division 93-94.
Record defeat: 1-7 v Camberley Town (H), FA Vase 3rd Rd 88-89.
Record Fees - Paid: £5,750 for John Wilson (Bashley, 1990)
Received: £7,000 for Steve Tate (Waterlooville, 1993).
Players progressing to Football League: Bobby Tambling (Chelsea).
Clubhouse: Open every day, lunchtime and evening. 2 bars, function suites, hot & cold food available.
Club Record Goalscorer: Unknown.
Club Record Appearances: Tony Plumbley.
93-94 Captain: Clint Webbe.
93-94 P.o.Y.: Clint Webbe.
93-94 Top scorer: Andy Jones 32.
Local Newspapers: News (Portsmouth)(0705 664488).
Local Radio Stations: Ocean Sound, Radio Solent.
Honours: FA Sunday Cup 68-69, FA Vase QF 85-86, Wessex Lg 90-91 (R-up 88-89), Hampshire Lg Div 3 72-73 (Div 4 71-72), Hampshire Senior Cup R-up 91-92 93-94, Hampshire Intermediate Cup, Hampshire Junior Cup, Russell Cotes Cup 91-92, Portsmouth Senior Cup 83-84 84-85 91-92, Gosport War Memorial Cup 74-75 91-92 92-93 93-94, Southern Counties Floodlit Cup R-up 91-92, Hampshire Floodlit Cup 85-86, Portsmouth Lg.

PROGRAMME DETAILS:
Pages: 24 **Price:** 50p
Editor: Steve Cox
(0705 269072)

Formed: 1896

MARGATE

The Gate

Margate FC - Kent Senior Cup winners 1993-94. Back Row (L/R): Steve Cuggy, Terry Cordice, Kevin Hudson, Mark Weatherly, Ivan Haines, Joe Brayne, Billy Plews, Andy Allon. Front: Jason Eede, Matt Lemoine, Malcolm Smith, Phil Handford, Paul Malcolm.

Photo - Paul Bates.

Chairman: Gordon Wallis **Vice Chairman:** Keith Piper **President:** Mr R W Griffiths
Secretary: K E Tomlinson, 65 Nash Road, Margate CT9 4BT (0843 291040).
Managers: Bill Roffey **Coach:** Mark Weatherly/ Andy Woolford.
Press Officer: Chairman **Commercial Manager:** Cliff Egan
Ground: Hartsdown Park, Hartsdown Road, Margate CT9 5QZ (0843 221769).
Directions: A28 into Margate, turn right opposite hospital into Hartsdown Road, proceed over crossroads and ground is on left. Ten mins walk from Margate (BR).
Capacity: 6,000 **Cover:** 3 sides **Seats:** 400 **Floodlights:** Yes **Metal Badges:** Yes
Club Shop: Yes. Progs, books, magazines, fanzines, badges, scarves, car stickers, T-shirts, mugs, pens, key-rings, address books, tax disc holders, etc... Contact Paul Bates, 46 High Str., Minster, Ramsgate, Kent CT12 4BT (0843 821032).
Colours: Royal/white/royal **Change colours:** White/blue or yellow.
Previous Grounds: Margate College/ Dreamland, Northdown Rd/ Garlinge.
Previous Leagues: Kent 11-23 24-28 29-33 37-38 46-59/ Southern 33-37.
Sponsors: Westons Dairies.
Midweek home matchday: Tuesday **Reserve Team's League:** Kent Midweek Lg.
Previous Name: Thanet Utd 1981-89 **Record Gate:** 14,500 v Spurs, FA Cup 3rd Rd 1973.
Best FA Cup season: 3rd Rd 72-73 (lost 0-6 to Spurs), 36-37 (lost 1-3 at Blackpool).
League clubs defeated in F.A. Cup: Gillingham 29-30, Queens Park Rangers, Crystal Palace 35-36, Bournemouth & Boscombe Athletic 61-62, Swansea 72-73.
Record transfer fees paid: £5,000 for Steve Cuggy (Dover Athletic, 1993)
Record transfer fee received: Undisclosed for Martin Buglione (St Johnstone 92-93).
Players progressing to Football League: Pre-War; too numerous to mention, partly because Margate were Arsenal's nursery club between 1934 & 1938. Post-War: John Yeomanson (West Ham 1947), Doug Bing & George Wright (West Ham 1951), Tommy Bing (Spurs 1956), John Roche (Millwall 1957), Derek Hodgkinson (Manchester City 1961), Stan Foster (Crystal Palace 1961), John Fraser (Watford 1962), Robert Walker (Bournemouth 1965), Ken Bracewell (Bury 1966), Tom Jenkins & Ray Flannigan (Reading 1969-70), Mel Blyth (Millwall 1978), Martin Buglione (St Johnstone 1992).
Clubhouse: Flexible hours, private functions, matchday facilities.
Steward: Pam & Mark Weatherly.
Club Record Goalscorer: Dennis Randall 66 (season 1966-67).
Club Record Appearances: Bob Harrop.
93-94 Captain: Phil Handford.
93-94 P.o.Y.: Phil Handford (players'), Joe Brayne (supporters').
93-94 Top scorer: Joe Brayne 24.
Local Newspapers: Isle of Thanet Gazette, Thanet Times (0843 221313), Thanet Extra, Adscene.
Local Radio: Radio Kent, Invicta Radio.
Newsline: 0898 800 665.
Hons: Southern Lg 35-36 (Lg Cp 67-68 (R-up 61-62 74-75), Div 1 62-63 (R-up 66-67), Div 1 Sth 77-78, East Div R-up 33-34, Merit Cp 66-67 77-78, Midweek Sect. 36-37), Kent Lg(4) 32-33 37-38 46-48 (R-up 27-28 29-30 53-54 55-56 57-58, Div 2 37-38 53-54 56-57 89-90, Lg Cp 35-36 47-48 53-54 68-69), Kent Snr Cup(4) 35-37 74-75 93-94, Kent Snr Shield(8) 20-21 30-31 35-37 47-48 52-53 61-63, Kent F'lit Cp 62-63 66-67 75-76, Kent Jnr Cup 01-02, FA Tphy 3rd Rd rep 78-79.

PROGRAMME DETAILS:
Pages: 28 **Price:** 60p
Editor: TBA

Formed: 1888

NEWPORT I.O.W.

The Port

Newport's Clifton Soares (right) battles with Braintree Town defender Russell Tanner as the islanders chalk up a 1-0 home win in this Easter fixture.

Photo - Keith Gillard.

Chairman: K Lacey **Vice Chairman:** M Edwards **President:** W H J Bunday.
Secretary/Press Off.: Chris Cheverton, 127 Westhill Road, Ryde, Isle of Wight PO33 1LW (0983 567355).
Manager: Steve Mellor **Asst Manager:** Dave Wakefield **Coach:** Roger McCormack
Commercial Manager: Dave Hiscock. **Physio:** TBA
Ground: St George's Park, St George's Way, Newport, Isle of Wight PO30 2QH (0983 525027).
Directions: Roads from all ferry ports lead to Coppins Bridge R-about at eastern extremity of town. Take Sandown/Ventnor exit, proceed to small r-about, St George's way is first exit (straight on), ground immediately visible on left. Five minute walk from Newport bus station; along Church Litten (past old ground), turn left then right at r-about.
Capacity: 5,000 **Cover:** 1,000 **Seats:** 300 **Floodlights:** Yes **Metal Badges:** Yes.
Club Shop: Yes, selling clothes, programmes and novelties. Contact M Reader at ground.
Colours: Royal & gold halves **Change colours:** White & red/black.
Previous Ground: Church Litten (previously Well's Field) 1888-1988.
Previous Leagues: Isle of Wight 1896-1928/ Hants 28-86/ Wessex 86-90.
Midweek home matchday: Tuesday **Reserve Team's Lge:** Moreys Isle of Wight League.
Record Attendance: 1,700 v Fulham (official ground opening). *(6,000 v Watford, FA Cup 1st Round 56-57, at Church Litten (old ground)).*
Record win: 14-1, home to Thornycroft Athletic, Hampshire League Division One, 22/12/45.
Record defeat: 2-10, home to Basingstoke Town, Hampshire League Division One, 12/10/68.
Players progressing to Football League: Gary Rowatt (Cambridge City, Everton).
Best FA Cup season: 2nd Rd 35-36 45-46. 1st Rd another seven times; 45-46 52-55 56-59.
League clubs defeated in FA Cup: Clapton Orient 45-46.
Record Fees - Paid: £3,000 for Stuart Ritchie (Bashley, May 1991)
Received: £2,250 for Mick Jenkins (Havant, March 1992).
Clubhouse: Open normal licensing hours. 2 bars, full range of hot and cold bar snacks. Buffet inside ground.
Club Record Goalscorer: Eddie Walder.
Club Record Apps: Jeff Austin 540 (69-87).
93-94 Captain: Andy Leader.
93-94 Player of Year: Stuart Ritchie.
93-94 Top scorer: Eurshall Fearon.
Local Newspapers (+Tel.Nos.): Portsmouth Evening News, I.O.W. County Press, Southampton Evening Echo.
Local Radio Stations: Solent, Isle of Wight Radio, Ocean Sound.
Honours: FA Vase 5th Rd 91-92 93-93, Wessex Lg R-up 89-90 (Comb. 91-92(reserves)), Hants Lg(11) 29-30 32-33 38-39 47-48 49-50 52-54 56-57 78-81 (R-up(7) 30-32 35-36 51-52 54-55 58-59 77-78, Div 2 R-up 70-71), Hants Snr Cup(7) 31-33 54-55 60-61 65-66 79-81, Russell Cotes Cup(3) 77-80, Pickford Cup(4) 47-50 52-53, Isle of Wight Snr (Gold) Cup(29) 29-30 35-36 37-38 39-40 44-47 48-49 52-54 55-56 57-58 65-66 67-68 70-76 77-79 80-81 86-88 89-90 91-94, Hants F'lit Cup 76-77 77-78, Isle of Wight Lg(4) 07-10 23-24, Hants I'mediate Cup 31-32, Hants Comb. Cup 38-39.

PROGRAMME DETAILS:
Pages: 32 **Price:** 60p
Editor: Peter Ranger
(0983 526144)

Founded: 1880

POOLE TOWN

The Dolphins

Poole Town pictured before their last-ever match at Poole Stadium.

Photo - Gavin Ellis-Neville.

Chairman: Clive Robbins **Vice Chairman:** Chris Reeves **President:** Fred Yates
Secretary: Barry Hughes, 226 Malvern Road, Bournemouth, Dorset BH9 3BX (0202 536906).
Manager: Keith Miller **Asst Manager:** **Physio:** Dick Thomas.
Press Officer: Secretary.
Commercial Manager: Geoff Van de Velde (0202 301976).
Ground: Dean Court, Bournemouth BH7 7AF (202 395381). ****This is a temporary groundsharing arrangement. In the latter part of the 1994-95 season, spectators should check venue before travelling***.*
Directions: From North or East; A338 to r'bout junction with A3080, take 2nd exit then 1st from next r'bout into Littledown Ave., right into Thistlebarrow Rd for Dean Court. From West; A3049 to Bournemouth, in 2 miles after lights at Wallisdown turn left into Talbot Rd, 1st exit from r'bout into Queens Park Drive South, 2nd exit from next r'bout into Littledown Avenue then as above.
Capacity: 11,880 **Cover:** 6,750 **Seats:** 3,130 **Floodlights:** Yes **Metal Badges:** Yes
Colours: Red & white stripes/red/white **Change colours:** All blue.
Sponsors: Abba Roofing.
Previous Leagues: Hants 1903-04 05-10 11-14 20-23 29-30 34-35/ Western 23-26 30-34 35-39 46-57.
Previous Ground: Poole Stadium, Wimborne Road (prior to 1994).
Midweek home matchday: Tuesday
Reserve Team's League: Dorset Combination.
Record Attendance: 11,155 v Watford, FA Cup First Round replay 1962-63.
Best FA Cup season: 3rd Rd Proper 1926-27 (lost 1-3 at Everton). 1st Rd 7 times; 26-29 46-47 62-63 66-67 83-84).
League clubs defeated in FA Cup: Newport County, 26-27
Record Fees - Paid: £5,000 for Nicky Dent (Yeovil Town, 1990).
Received: £8,000 for Nicky Dent (Dover Athletic, 1992).
Players progressing to Football League: Derek Stround (Bournemouth & Boscombe Athletic 1950), Dave Lawrence (Bristol Rovers 1951), John Thomas (Bournemouth & Boscombe Athletic 1958), James Rollo (Oldham 1960), John Smeulders (AFC Bournemouth 1987), Bob Iles (Chelsea), Phil Ferns Jr (AFC Bournemouth), D Lyon (Southport).
Clubhouse: Open every evening & lunchtime.
Club Record Goalscorer: Tony Funnell
Club Record Appearances: Martyn Jones
93-94 Captain: Trevor Townsend.
93-94 P.o.Y.: Trevor Townsend.
93-94 Top scorer: Mattie Brown.
Local Newspapers: Evening Echo, Gazette.
Local Radio Stations: Radio Solent, 2CR
Honours: Southern Lg Div 1 R-up 61-62 (Southern Div R-up 88-89), Western Lg 56-57 (R-up 46-47 49-50 53-54 55-56, Lg Cup 54-55), Dorset Senior Cup 1894-95 96-97 1901-02 03-04 06-07 25-26 26-27 37-38 46-47 88-89, FA Trophy 1st Rd replay 69-70, FA Amateur Cup 2nd Rd 47-48 48-49.

PROGRAMME DETAILS:
Pages: 32 **Price:** 70p
Editor: Mr M J Willis
(0202 605089)

Formed: 1947

SALISBURY CITY

The Whites

Baldock Town are denied a goal against Salisbury City by an invisible defender's goal-line clearance. However, a Keith Phillips brace did give the Reds a 2-0 win in this vital promotion battle.

Photo - Neil Whittington.

Chairman: Mr P R McEnhill **Vice-Chairmam:** Mr K R Miller.
Secretary: Sean Gallagher, 49 Sunnyhill Road, Salisbury, Wilts SP1 3JQ (0722 324932).
Manager: Geoff Butler **Coach:** **Physio:** Conrad Parrott
Press Officer: David Macey (0264 773765)
Youth Development Officer: Kevin Jackson.
Commercial Manager: Geoff Butler, 38 Endless House, Salisbury (0722 326454).
Ground: Victoria Park, Castle Road, Salisbury SP1 3ER (0722 336689).
Directions: A345 (Amesbury) road north from city centre/ring-road, Victoria Park is on the left 800 yds after the ring road. One mile from Salisbury (BR). Buses 208 & 209 run every 15 mins from city centre.
Capacity: 3,400 **Cover:** 1,100 **Seats:** 320 **Floodlights:** Yes **Metal Badges:** Yes
Colours: White/black/black **Change colours:** Gold/white/black. **Sponsors:** TBA
Previous Leagues: Western 47-68. **Previous Name:** Salisbury FC (pre-1992).
Midweek home matchday: Wednesday **Reserve Team's League:** None.
Club Shop: Yes, selling programmes, scarves, metal badges, souvenirs. Contact Mr David Beavon (0747 828624).
Previous Ground: Hudson Field, Castle Rd, Salisbury - 1947-51.
Record Attendance: 8,902 v Weymouth, Western League 1948.
Best FA Amt. Cup year: 2nd Rd 49-50 **Best FA Trophy season:** 1st Rd 85-86 90-91 91-92.
Best FA Cup season: 2nd Rd 59-60, lost 0-1 at home to Newport County.
Record win: 9-0 v Westbury United (H), FA Cup 1st Qualifying Round 1972.
Record defeat: 0-7 v Minehead, Southern League 1975.
Record Fees - Paid: £5,750 for Peter Loveridge (Dorchester Town, 1990)
Received: £16,000 for Ian Thompson (AFC Bournemouth, 1983).
Players progressing to Football League: Eric Fountain (Southampton 1948), Cyril Smith (Arsenal & Southampton 1948), Graham Moxham (Exeter 1975), Tony Alexander (Fulham 1975), Eric Welch (Chesterfield) 1976), Ian Thompson (Bournemouth 1983), Trevor Wood (Port Vale 1988), Denny Mundee (B'mouth 1988), Matthew Carmichael (Lincoln 1990).
Clubhouse: Small bar on ground open matchdays. Main Supporters Club situated in Chatham Close, some 500yds from ground - normal pub hours. Two bars and a seperate function room, snooker, satellite TV, Discos etc.
Club Record Goalscorer: Allan Green 113 (Southern Lg)
Club Record Appearances: Barry Fitch 713.
93-94 Captain: Sean Sanders.
93-94 P.o.Y.: Sandy Baird.
93-94 Top scorer: Paul Odey 34.
Local Newspapers: Salisbury Journal, Sòuthern Evening & Sports Echo, Western Gazette, Western Daily Press.
Local Radio Stations: Wiltshire Sound, Radio Solent, Spire F.M.
Club Information Line: Cityline, 0891 122 905 (Sponsored by Spire F.M.).
Honours: Southern Lg Southern Div R-up 85-86 92-93, Western Lg 57-58 60-61 (R-up 58-59 59-60 60-61 61-62 67-68, Div 2 47-48, Lg Cup 55-56), Hants Senior Cup 61-62 63-64, Alan Young Cup 59-60 60-61 62-63, Wilts Premier Shield 56-57 59-60 60-61 61-62 66-67 67-68 70-71 77-78 78-79.

PROGRAMME DETAILS:
Pages: 48 **Price:** 70p
Editor: David Macey
(0831 395756)

Founded: 1948

TONBRIDGE A.F.C.

The Angels

Tonbridge with the Kent League Charity Shield, won against Ramsgate in the traditional seasonal curtain raiser between the champions and League Cup winners.

Photo - Eric Marsh.

Chairman: Nigel Rimmer **Vice Chairman:**
Secretary: Steve Wardhaugh, 39 Badger Rd, Lordswood, Chatham, Kent ME5 8TY (0634 669154).
Manager: Phil Emblen **Physio:** John Knapton **Coach:** Dave Boyton
Press Officer: Rob Kelly **Commercial Manager:** Rob Kelly (c/o the club).
Ground: Longmead Stadium, Darenth Avenue, Tonbridge, Kent TN10 3JW (0732 352417/ 358868).
Directions: From Tonbridge BR station, through High Street, north up Shipbourne Rd (A227 Gravesend road) to 2nd mini-r'bout ('The Pinnacles' pub), left into Darenth Avenue, ground at bottom approx. 1 mile at far side of sports ground car park.
Seats: 202 **Cover:** 640 **Capacity:** 5,000 **Metal Badges:** Yes. **Club Shop:** Yes.
Colours: Blue (white sleeves)/blue/blue **Change Colours:** All red.
Midweek matchday: Wednesday **Sponsors:** New Entreprises Coaches
Reserve Team's League: Winstonlead Kent Division Two.
Previous Leagues: Southern 48-89/ Kent 89-93.
Previous Ground: The Angel 48-80.
Previous Names: Tonbridge Angels, Tonbridge F.C.
Record Gate: 1,463 v Yeovil Town, FA Cup 4th Qualifying Round 26/10/91. *At the Angel Ground: 8,236 v Aldershot, FA Cup 1st Round 1951.*
Players progressing to Football League: R Saunders, M McMcDonald, T Burns, I Seymour, G Moseley, T Morgan.
Clubhouse: Open Mon-Sat evenings and Sunday lunchtimes. Hot food on matchdays from burger bar.
Club Record Goalscorer: Unknown
Club Record Appearances: Mark Gillham, 520 to date.
93-94 Captain: Dave Boyton.
93-94 P.o.Y.: Steve Campfield.
93-94 Top scorer: Ian Mawson.
Local Newspapers: Kent Messenger.
Local Radio Stations: Invicta, Radio Kent.
Honours: Kent League 93-94 (League Cup(2)), Southern League Cup Runners-up(2)(SF(1)), Kent Senior Cup 64-65 74-75 (Runners-up(2)), Kent Senior Shield 51-52 55-56 57-58 58-59 63-64, FA Cup 1st Rd Proper 50-51 51-52 52-53 67-68 72-73.

PROGRAMME DETAILS:
Pages: 28 **Price:** 50p
Editor: Ian White

Formed: 1905

WATERLOOVILLE

The Ville

Waterlooville pictured before their New Year's Day Hampshire derby at Farnborough Town.
Photo - Eric Marsh.

Chairman: F P Faulkner **Vice Chairman:** K L Ashman **President:** M Hibberd
Secretary: P Elley, 139 Chichester Rd, North End, Portsmouth, Hampshire PO2 0AQ (0705 665885).
Manager: Billy Gilbert **Asst Manager/Coach:** John Waugh **Physio:** Bill Pizey
Press Officer: 0705 263867 **Commercial Manager:** Terry Diddymus (0705 230114).
Ground: Jubilee Park, Aston Road, Waterlooville PO7 7SZ (0705 263867).
Directions: Turn right off town by-pass (B2150) at Asda r-about. Dual carriage to next island, and return back towards town (ground signposted). Aston Road is first left. Nearest stations; Havant (4 miles), Cosham (5).
Capacity: 7,000 **Cover:** 1,500 **Seats:** 480 **Floodlights:** Yes **Metal Badges:** Yes
Club Shop: Yes, selling usuals items. Contact Mrs B Tomkins.
Colours: White & navy **Change colours:** Yellow & green.
Previous Leagues: Waterlooville & District/ Portsmouth 38-53/ Hants 1953-71
Club Sponsors: None.
Previous Grounds: Convent Ground 10-30/ Rowlands Avenue Recreation Ground 30-63.
Midweek home matchday: Tuesday **Reserve Team's League:** Wessex Combination.
Record Attendance: 4,500 v Wycombe Wanderers, FA Cup 1st Rd 1976-77.
Best FA Cup season: 1st Rd 2nd replay 83-84 (lost 0-2 at Northampton Town after two 1-1 draws. Also 1st Rd 68-69 76-77 88-89.
League clubs defeated in FA Cup: None
Record Fees: Paid: £6,000 for Steve Tate (Havant Town, 1993)
Received: £6,000 for Dave Boyce (Gravesend & Northfleet, 1993).
Players progressing to Football League: Phil Figgins (Portsmouth 1973), Paul Hardyman (Portsmouth 1983), Guy Whittingham (Portsmouth via Yeovil Town 1988), Paul Moody (Southampton 1991).
Clubhouse: Jubilee Club, open to all for all games (first team and reserves). Food available.
93-94 Captain: Duncan Burns.
93-94 P.o.Y.: Paul Thomas.
93-94 Top scorer: N Selby.
Local Newspapers: The News & Sports Mail.
Local Radio Stations: BBC Solent, Ocean Sound.
Hons: Southern Lg Div 1 Sth 71-72 (Lg Cup 86-87, R-up 82-83), Hants Lg R-up 69-70 (Div 2 59-60 64-65, Div 3 (East) R-up 53-54), Hants Snr Cup 69-70 72-73 84-85 (R-up 75-76 90-91), Russell Cotes Cup 88-89, Portsmouth Lg 49-50 50-51 51-52 (Div 2 46-47, Div 3 38-39), Portsmouth Snr Cup 68-69, Portsmouth Victory Cup 59-60 69-70, FA Tphy 2nd Rd 76-77, FA Amtr Cup 1st Rd 59-60.

PROGRAMME DETAILS:
Pages: 32 **Price:** 50p
Ed.: Universal Leisure Ltd

Formed: 1889

WEALDSTONE

The Stones

Wealdstone FC 1993-94.

Photo - Eric Marsh.

Chairman: Paul Rumens **Vice Chairman:** Nick Dugard.
Secretary: Steve Hibberd, 17 Brancaster Rd, Newbury Park, Ilford, Essex IG3 7ER (081 597 7534).
Manager: Fred Callaghan **Asst Mgr:** Steve Frangou **Newsline:** 0891 88 44 73
Press Officer: Graham Sharpe **Fixture Secretary:** Alan Couch (0081 907 4421).
Sports Therapist: Alan Wharton **Commercial Manager:** Wayne Patterson.
Ground: As Yeading FC (see Diadora Lge section)(Wealdstone club office: 081 813 7800. fax: 813 7720).
Metal Badges: No. **Club Shop:** No
Colours: Blue & white quarters **Change colours:** Yellow & green.
Sponsors: Vandanel Sport & Leisure Co.
Previous Leagues: Willesden & Dist. 1899-1906 08-13/ London 1911-22/ Middx 13-22/ Spartan 22-28/ Athenian 28-64/ Isthmian 64-71/ Southern 71-79 81-82/ GMV Conference 79-81 82-88.
Previous Grounds: College Farm 03-10/ Belmont Rd 10-22/ Lower Mead Stadium 22-91/ Vicarage Rd (Watford FC) 91-93.
Midweek home matchday: Wednesday **Reserve Team's League:** None.
Record Attendance: 13,504 v Leytonstone FA Amateur Cup Fourth Round replay 5/3/49.
Best FA Cup season: 3rd Rd 77-78 (0-4 at Q.P.R.). 1st Rd on 13 occasions 49-50 65-67 68-69 75-80 82-84 85-87.
League clubs defeated in FA Cup: Hereford Utd and Reading, 77-78.
Record win: 22-0 v The 12th London Regiment (The Rangers)(H), FA Amateur Cup 13/10/23.
Record defeat: 0-14 v Edgware Town (A), London Senior Cup 9/12/44.
Record Fees: Paid: £15,000 for David Gipp (Barnet, 1990).
Received: £25,000; for Stuart Pearce (Coventry City 1983); for Sean Norman (Chesham, 1989).
Players progressing to Football League: Edward Smith (Chelsea 1950), Phil White (Orient 1953), Tom McGhee & John Ashworth (Portsmouth 1954 & 62), Charlie Sells (Exeter City 1962), Eddie Dilsworth (Lincoln City 1967), Colin Franks (Watford 1969), Stuart Pearce (Coventry City 1983), Vinnie Jones (Wimbledon 1986), Danny Bailey (Exeter 1989), Francis Joseph (Wimbledon & Brentford), Bobby Ryan.
Clubhouse: Yes, normal licensing hours.
Club Record Goalscorer: George Duck, 251
Club Record Appearances: Charlie Townsend, 514
93-94 Captain: Various.
93-94 P.O.Y.: Dermot Drummy.
93-94 Top scorer: Colin Tate 10.
Local Newspapers: Harrow Observer.
Local Radio: LBC, Capital, Greater London Radio.
Honours: FA Tphy 84-85, FA Amateur Cup 65-66 (R-up 67-68), GMV Conference 84-85, Southern Lg Southern Div 81-82 (Div 1 South 73-74, Lg Cup 81-82), Athenian Lg 51-52 (R-up 52-53 58-59 60-61), Spartan Lg R-up 22-23, London Lg Div 2 12-13 (R-up 11-12), London Snr Cup 61-62(joint)(R-up 39-40, 51-52 60-61), Middx Snr Cup(11) 29-30 37-38 40-43 45-46 58-59 62-64 67-68 84-85, Middx Senior Charity Cup(11) 29-31 37-42 49-50 63-64 67-68 80-81, Capital League 84-85 86-87.

PROGRAMME DETAILS:
Pages: 30 **Price:** £1
Editor: Roy Couch
(081 907 4421)

1948 **WESTON-SUPER-MARE** Seagulls

Weston-super-Mare FC. Back Row (L/R): Dean Holtham, Andy Hogg, Julian Stearnes, Paul Tatterton, Shaun Rouse (now Carlisle United), Mark Stevens, Jon Bowering, Lee Rogers, Paul Elson. Front: Steve Tapp, Steve Purnell, Alan Hooker, Steve Holt, Graham Withey.

Photo - Peter Barnes.

President: D A Usher **Chairman:** P T Bliss
Secretary/Press Officer: Keith Refault, 7 Somerdale Close, Weston-s-Mare BS22 8EB (0934 628068).
Manager: Peter Amos **Asst Manager:** **Coach:** Keith Christie.
Physio: Dave Lukins **Commercial Manager:** Dave Percy.
Ground: Woodspring Park, Winterstoke Road, Weston-super-Mare BS23 2YG (0934 6355665/621618).
Directions: From North: M5 Jct 21, A370 into Weston until junction A371 on left (at Heron pub), take A371 over railway bridge to r'bout, take right-hand exit and follow to 3rd r'bout, bear left for 100yds - club on right. From South: M5 Jct 22, follow Weston signs for approx 7 miles, right at first r'bout (by Hospital), left at next r'bout, ground 1 mile on left. Twenty minutes walk from Weston-super-Mare (BR).
Seats: 350 **Cover:** 1,000 **Capacity:** 4,000 **Metal Badges:** Yes
Club Shop: Yes, selling programmes, club ties, pullovers, badges, scarves, pens, pennants, Sweat Shirts and T-shirts. Contact Mrs Aileen Milsom, 12 Greenland Road, Milton, Weston-s-Mare BS22 8JP (0934 413059).
Club colours: White/blue/blue **Change colours:** All yellow
Midweek matches: Tuesday **Reserve Team's Lge:** Somerset Snr Lge Division One.
Previous Name: Borough of Weston-super-Mare.
Previous Grounds: The Great Ground, Locking Road 48-55, Langford Road 55-83.
Record Attendance: 2,623 v Woking, FA Cup First Round Proper replay 23/11/93. *At Langford Road: 2,500 v Bridgwater Town, FA Cup First Round Proper replay 1961-62.*
Best FA Cup season: First Round Proper replay 1961-62 (lost 0-1 after 0-0 draw at Bridgwater Town) 1993-94 (lost 0-1 after 2-2 draw at Woking).
Players progressing to Football League: Shaun Rowse (Carlisle United, March 1994), Ian Maine, John Palmer.
Previous League: Western 1948-92.
Club Sponsors: Uphill Motor Company.
Record win: 11-0 v Paulton Rovers
Record defeat: 1-12 v Yeovil Town Reserves.
Clubhouse: Mon-Fri 7-11pm, Sat 12-11pm, Sun 12-3 & 7-11pm. 2 skittle alleys, 3 bars. Bar meals available and cooked meals on matchdays.
Club Record Goalscorer: Matthew Lazenby, 180
Club Record Appearances: Harry Thomas, 740.
93-94 Captain: Jon Bowering
93-94 P.o.Y.: Jon Bowering.
93-94 Top scorer: Steve Tapp 26.
Local Newspapers: Bristol Evening Post, Western Daily Press.
Local Radio Stations: Somerset Sound.
Hons: Somerset Snr Cup 23-24 26-27, Western Lg 91-92 (R-up 76-77, Lg Cup 76-77 (R-up 89-90), Merit Cup 76-77 77-78), Somerset Snr Lg (Reserves) Div 1 87-88 (R-up 90-91), Div 2 R-up 85-86, Div 3 84-85).

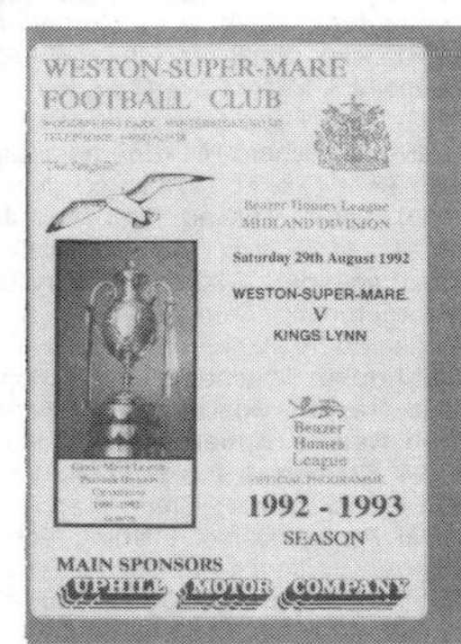

PROGRAMME DETAILS:
Pages: 32 **Price:** 60p
Editor: Secretary

Formed: 1890

WEYMOUTH

The Terras

Dave Aston milks the applause of the travelling fans in Weymouth's excellent 3-0 win at Erith & Belvedere. Photo - Alan Coomes.

Chairman: Matthew McGowan **Vice Chairman:** Peter Sapsworth.
Secretary: Terry Northover, 2 Stoke Rd, Weymouth, Dorset DT4 9JF (0305 771480).
Manager: William Coldwell **Coach:** Phil Simkin. **Physio:** Bob Lucas.
Commercial Manager: Fred Dunford.
Ground: Wessex Stadium, Radipole Lane, Weymouth, Dorset DT4 0TJ (0305 785558).
Directions: Arriving from Dorchester on A354, turn right following signs to Granby Industrial Estate at Safeway r'bout - ground on right as you enter estate.
Capacity: 10,000 **Cover:** All sides **Seats:** 900 **Floodlights:** Yes **Metal Badges:** Yes.
Club Shop: Yes, open matchdays. During week contact Andrew Millar at 4 Franklin Rd, Weymouth DT4 0JR (0305 772743). Progs & souvenirs.
Colours: Claret & blue **Change colours:** All yellow. **Sponsors:** Marlboro.
Previous Ground: Recreation Ground (until 1987).
Previous Lges: Dorset Lge/ Western 1907-23 28-49/ Southern 23-28 49-79/ Alliance Premier 79-89.
Midweek home matchday: Wednesday **Reserve Team's League:** Dorset Combination
Record Attendance: 4,995 v Manchester Utd, ground opening, 21/10/87.
Best FA Cup season: 4th Rd 61-62, 0-2 at Preston. 1st rd on 29 occasions 25-27 48-50 51-54 55-57 58-59 60-62 63-66 67-70 71-72 73-79 80-83 84-86.
League clubs defeated in FA Cup: Merthyr 24-25, Aldershot 49-50, Shrewsbury Town 56-57, Newport County 61-62, Cardiff City 82-83.
Record Fees: Paid: £15,000 for Shaun Teale (Northwich)
Received: £100,000 for Peter Guthrie (Spurs, 1988)
Players progressing to Football League: Reg Pickett & Brian Carter (Portsmouth 1949 & 56), Stan Northover (Luton 1950), Edward Grant (Sheffield United 1950), David Clelland (Scunthorpe 1950), Alex Corbett (Hartlepool 1953), William Holt (Barrow 1954), Alex Smith (Accrington 1961), Graham Bond, Terry Spratt, Andy Donnelly & Micky Cave (Torquay 1961, 65, 67 & 68), Peter Leggett (Swindon 1962), Ron Fogg (Aldershot 1963), Barry Hutchinson (Lincoln 1965), Terry Gulliver & Richard Hill (Bournemouth 1966 & 67), Alan Wool (Reading 1971), Alan Beer (Exeter 1974), Bob Iles (Chelsea 1978), Graham Roberts (Spurs 1980), Neil Townsend, Paul Morrell & John Smeulders (Bournemouth 1979, 83 & 84), Tony Agana (Watford), Andy Townsend & D Hughes (Southampton), S Claridge (Crystal Palace), B McGorry & Shaun Teale (Bournemouth), Tony Pounder & R Evans (Bristol Rvrs), Robbie Pethick (Portsmouth) 1993.
Clubhouse: Matchdays & functions. Hot & cold food available.
Club Record Goalscorer: W Farmer, Haynes. 275
Club Record Appearances: Tony Hobson 1,076
93-94 Captain & P.o.Y 93-94: Willie Gibson.
93-94 Top scorer: Chris Evans 17.
Local Press: Dorset Evening Echo. **Local Radio:** Wessex FM.
Honours: Alliance Premier Lg R-up 79-80 (Lg Cup 81-82), Premier Inter Lg Cup R-up 87-88 (QF 90-91), Southern Lg 64-65 65-66 (R-up 54-55 77-78, Lg Cup 72-73 (R-up 52-53 63-64 64-65 70-71 77-78), Southern Div R-up 91-92), Western Lg 22-23 (Div 2 33-34 36-37 (R-up 35-36 47-48)), Dorset Sen. Cup(25) 1893-94 98-1900 02-03 19-20 22-24 27-28 31-32 33-34 36-37 47-48 49-50 51-52 53-58 64-65 84-87 90-91 92-93, Mark Frowde Cup (12), FA Tphy 4th Rd rep. 76-77, FA Amateur Cup 1st Rd 1900.

PROGRAMME DETAILS:
Pages: 44 **Price:** 70p
Editor: Fred Danford
(784133)

Formed: 1885

WITNEY TOWN

The Town

Witney Town pictured before their fixture against Wealdstone at Yeading.
Photo - Eric Marsh.

Chairman: Brian Constable **Vice-Chairman:** Adrian Dunsby **President:** Sir Peter Parker
Secretary: Bob Watts, 16 Daubigny Mead, Brize Norton, Oxon OX18 3QE (0993 841210).
Manager: Andy Lyne **Asst Manager/Coach:** Richard Hill/
Press Officer: Adrian Bircher (0993 703257) **Physio:** Roger Alder
Commercial Manager: Paul Skidmore.
Ground: Oakey Park, Down Rd, Curbridge, Witney, Oxon (0993 702549).
Directions: From West on A40; take B4047 at island past Burford, follow signs for Witney West & N.W. Industrial Estates, thru Minster Lovell to West Witney, right into Downs Rd, ground on right. From the East on A40, 2nd turn off to Witney and follow signs for South & S.W. Industrial Estates, right at r'bout to traffic lights, left and proceed to r'bout, straight over, signs to West Witney Industrial Estate, left at lights onto B4047, left into Downs Rd, ground on right. Nearest BR station is Oxford 12 miles away.
Capacity: 3,500 **Cover:** 1,224 **Seats:** 224 **Floodlights:** Yes **Metal Badges:** Yes
Club Shop: Yes, selling programmes, t-shirts, sweatshirts, hats, scarves etc. Contact secretary.
Colours: Yellow/blue/yellow **Change colours:** Blue/white/white. **Sponsors:** TBA
Previous Leagues: Reading & Dist./ Oxfordshire Senior/ Hellenic 53-73.
Previous Name: Witney F.C.
Previous Ground: Marriotts Close, Welch Way - in Witney centre (pre-1992).
Midweek home matchday: Tuesday **Reserve Team's League:** Midland Combination.
Record Attendance: 2,000 (approx) v Aston Villa, ground opening 1992. Competitive: 544 v Salisbury, F.A. 4th Qual. Rd 24/10/92. *At Marriotts Close: 3,500 for Nottm Forest v West Bromwich Albion, Trevor Stokes benefit match 1965.*
Best F.A. Cup season: 1st Rd 71-72 (lost 0-3 at home to Romford).
League clubs defeated in F.A. Cup: None.
Record Fees - Paid: £3,000 for Steve Jenkins (Cheltenham Town)
Received: £5,000 for John Bailey (Worcester City).
Players progressing to Football League: Herbert Smith, Frank Clack (Birmingham City), Arthur Hall (Bristol Rovers 1959), David Moss (Swindon 1969), Jack Newman.
Clubhouse: Members bar open seven days a week except Christmas Day 6.30-11pm. Open all day Saturday. Hot food on matchdays.
Club record scorer: Kenny Clarke 133.
Club record appearances: Kenny Clarke 305 (+25 sub).
93-94 Captain: Andy Leach.
93-94 Top scorer: Kenny Clarke.
Players' Player of the Year 93-94: Keith Knight.
Supporters' Player of the Year 93-94: Keith Knight.
Local Newspapers: Witney Gazette (0993 704265), West Oxon Standard (0993 702175), Oxford Mail & Oxford Times (0865 244988).
Local Radio Stations: BBC Radio Oxford, Fox (FM) Oxford.
Hons: FA Tphy 2nd Rd 78-79, FA Amtr Cup 2nd Rd rep.(3) 66-67 71-73, Southern Lg Div 1 Nth 77-78, Hellenic Lg(8) 54-55 57-58 64-67 70-73 (R-up 53-54 67-68 69-70, Lg Cup(6) 56-57 63-65 69-70 71-73, Prem Div Benevolent Cup 59-60 63-64), Oxon Snr Lg(5) 28-30 31-32 51-53, Oxon Snr Cup(10) 1894-95 97-99 1952-53 54-56 58-59 70-71(jt) 72-73 93-94.

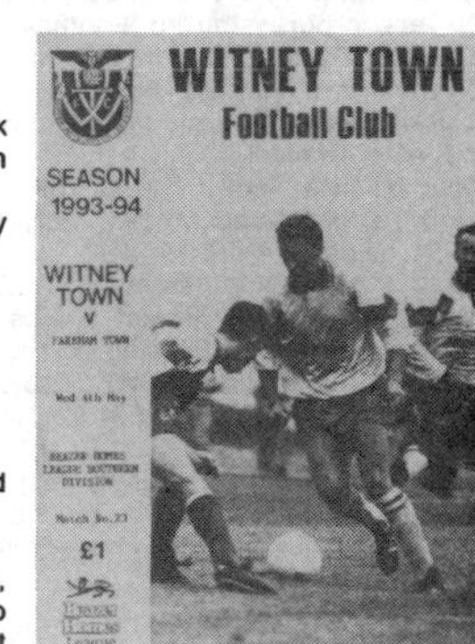

PROGRAMME DETAILS:
Pages: 40 **Price:** 50p
Editor: Adrian Bircher
(0993 703257)

YATE TOWN

Formed:, 1946

The Bluebells

Yate Town FC. Back Row (L/R): Alan Ball (goalkeeper & Coach), Paul Harrison (now Mangotsfield United), Richard Thompson, Wayne Hewitt, Glenn Thomas, Ian Beevor, Colin Towler, Richard Dunn, Terry Leslie (Physio), Pete Jackson (Manager). Front: Paul Dempsey, Russell Dunn, Richard Smith, Gary Hewlett, Darin Hunt, Gary Davis.

Chairman: R G Hawkins **Vice Chairman:** D A Phillips **President:** R Hewetson.
Secretary: T M Tansley, 1 Tyning Close, Yate, Bristol BS17 4PN (0454 324305).
Manager: Peter Jackson **Asst Manager:** Bobby Jones **Coach:** Jeff Meacham
Press Officer: TBA **Physio:** Steve Britton
Commercial Manager: Peter Last.
Ground: Lodge Road, Yate, Bristol BS17 5LE (0454 228103).
Directions: M4 jct 18, A46 towards Stroud, then A432 to Yate. Turn right at top of railway bridge into North Road, first left past traffic lights. Five miles from Bristol Parkway BR main line station, half mile from Yate BR station. Buses 329, X68 and 328.
Capacity: 2,000 **Cover:** 236 **Seats:** 236 **Floodlights:** Yes **Metal Badges:** Yes
Club Shop: Yes, selling programmes, metal badges, pens, rosettes, shirts, key rings etc. Contact Secretary.
Colours: White/navy/white **Change colours:** All tangerine.
Sponsors: Carlsberg/ Tetley.
Previous Leagues: Gloucestershire County 68-83/ Hellenic 83-89.
Previous Name: Yate YMCA 1946-70.
Previous Grounds: Yate Aerodrome 50-54/ Newmans Field 54-60/ Sunnyside Lane 60-84.
Midweek home matchday: Wednesday **Reserve Team's League:** Bristol Suburban.
Record Attendance: 2,000 for Bristol Rovers v Bristol Rovers Past, Vaughan Jones testimonial 1990.
Record Fees - Paid: None.
Received: £7,500; for Darren Tilley (York, 1991); for Mike Davis (Bristol Rovers, 1993).
Record win: 13-3 v Clevedon, Bristol Premier Combination 1967-68.
Players progressing to Football League: Richard Thompson (Newport County & Exeter City), Phil Purnell (Bristol Rovers), Darren Tilley (York City), Steve Winter (Walsall), Mike Davis (Bristol Rovers) 1993.
Clubhouse: Open every night and weekend lunchtimes. Skittles, darts, pool, live entertainment.
Club Record Scorer: Kevin Thaws.
Club Record Appearances: Gary Hewlett.
93-94 Captain: Gary Hewlett.
93-94 P.o.Y.: Gary Hewlett.
93-94 Top scorer: Stewart Phillips.
Local Press: Bristol Evening Post, Western Daily Press, North Avon Gazette.
Local Radio Stations: GWR, Radio Bristol.
Honours: FA Vase 5th Rd 91-92, Hellenic Lg(2) 87-89 (Div 1 R-up 84-85, Lg Skol Cup R-up 87-88), Glos Chal. Tphy 88-89 (R-up 78-79), Glos Snr Amtr Cup Sth 77-78 91-92(res) 92-93(res), Glos Snr Chal. Cup (Nth) R-up 89-90 92-93, Stroud Charity Cup R-up 74-75 81-82 84-85 (Sect. A Winners(6) 76-78 79-80 82-83 87-89), Berkeley Hosp. Prem. Cup(3) 73-75 80-81, S.W. Co's Sutton Vase 85-86.

PROGRAMME DETAILS:
Pages: 24 **Price:** 50p
Editor: Secretary

DIADORA ISTHMIAN LEAGUE

FOUNDED: 1905

President: B D East.

Chairman: Alan C F Turvey.

Hon. Secretary: Nicholas Robinson,
226 Rye Lane, Peckham, London SE15 4NL.

STEVENAGE - CHAMPIONS OF A WATERY SEASON

After four seasons without serious fixture problems due to bad weather our thoughts that global warming had put an end to bad weather winters were dispersed as numerous matches were lost due to waterlogged pitches. The only bright spot was that we did not have an extended freeze!

Enfield were probably the team most affected because they were also successful in the various cup competitions and found themselves having to play virtually every day of the week in the last ten days of the season. Notwithstanding this they did themselves great credit in finishing in the runners-up position once again. They were also finalists in the League Cup where Chertsey Town became only the second Associate Member to win the League Cup when they defeated Enfield 3-0 at Hayes FC on May Bank Holiday Monday in front of a crowd of just over 1,000 spectators who all saw a most entertaining game.

The champions were Stevenage Borough FC who had established their claim to the crown in the early part of the season and then, with the "transfer" of Victor Green as Chairman from Hendon, they then set about meeting the grading criteria of the Conference so as to ensure that they could be promoted if they achieved their ambitions and finished as champions. Several hundreds of thousands of pounds were spent on the ground which was virtually rebuilt in a period of a few weeks

Chertsey Town, who had a quite astonishing season, celebrate after their 3-0 victory over Enfield in the League Cup final at Church Road, Hayes.

Photo - V Hardwick.

and their promotion to the conference was confirmed at the beginning of June. This was a suitable end to what was a marvellous season for the club and particularly for Manager Paul Fairclough who rightly became the 'Manager of the Season'.

At the other end of the table, Wivenhoe Town had a fairly miserable season and were relegated to Division One along with Dorking, who found it difficult to compete with the Premier Division in their first season, and Basingstoke Town who faced various problems both on and off the pitch during the season.

Returning to the Premier Division are Bishop's Stortford after a short absence and they are promoted as champions of Division One together with two clubs who will be in the Premier Division for the first time, namely Walton & Hersham and Purfleet, the latter of whom have done so well in non-league football in the short period of time since they were founded.

At the wrong end of the table we see Chalfont St Peter, Windsor & Eton and Croydon dropping down to Division Two. Croydon had a particularly unenviable record with an enormous number of 192 goals scored against them with several clubs setting personal records against them and one club equalling the League record victory during the season. But all credit to the club who at one stage did not look as though they would complete the season, but did so well to field a team every week.

The three "Towns" of Newbury, Chertsey and Aldershot are the clubs making the jump from Associate to Full membership, and these clubs have really established themselves as the contenders in a three-horse race from very early on in the season, the only question really being as to which would be the champion club. This was not decided until the very last day of the season when Newbury Town were confirmed champions, Chertsey Town as runners-up and Aldershot occupied the third spot. A marvellous season in this Division with, once again, record attendances at virtually every ground Aldershot visited.

Rainham Town decided during the campaign that they would not be able to compete in the League next season and gave notice that they would be resigning at the end of the season. Their results were such that they did, in fact, finish in 22nd place. Lewes and Collier Row occupied the other two relegation places. Their places will be taken in the Second Division by Bracknell Town, who finished as champions of the Third Division, Cheshunt and Oxford City. Bracknell did exceptionally well to become champions after the season in 1992/93 when they did less then they would have wished.

The other two promoted clubs were spending their first season back in the League after both having left previously, and did extremely well in their first season back. The fourth-placed club were Harlow Town, who were another club who had spent the season away from competitive football having accepted the season's suspension to sort out their "off the pitch" problems.

In the cup competitions, mention has already been made of the feat by Chertsey Town in winning the League Cup and finishing as runners-up in Division Two, but they also had another success in winning the Carlsberg (Associate Members) Trophy in a close competitive final held at Hendon. One goal from Chertsey was sufficient to see them home against Hornchurch to win the magnificent trophy presented by Carlsberg in their first season of sponsorship of this competition.

Carlsberg took over sponsorship of both the Associate Members Trophy and the Full Members Cup, and in the now named Carlsberg Cup the final was played at Marlow FC between Hendon and Wokingham Town. It resulted in a win for Hendon by 2 goals to 1, so Chairlady Elaine Green had something to produce in response to husband Victor's Championship Trophy at Stevenage.

The award for 'Team of the Year' went to Chertsey Town, not only for the feats chronicled above but also for the fact that they were the first team to 100 goals, won the Mitre Team award for the season, and have qualified for the Charity Shield match against Stevenage at the beginning of next season.

This year we say goodbye to Rainham Town who have resigned and to Royston Town who return to the South Midlands League. We welcome in their places Canvey Island from the Essex Senior League and Bedford Town from the South Midlands League. We congratulate those who performed well during 1993/94, commiserate with those who did not, and wish everyone well for 1994/95.

Nick Robinson, Secretary.

DIADORA LEAGUE CUP 1993-94

Preliminary Round

Epsom & Ewell v Hungerford Town	1-0
Horsham v East Thurrock United	2-1
Newbury Town v Kingsbury Town	2-0
Aldershot Town v Clapton	5-1
Aveley v Ruislip Manor	0-0,1-3
Harefield United v Collier Row	0-1
Metropolitan Police v Rainham Town	3-0
Bracknell Town v Cheshunt	1-2
Oxford City v Egham Town	3-0
Cove v Flackwell Heath	5-3*(aet)*
Northwood v Witham Town	1-1,2-1*(aet)*
Ware v Camberley Town	0-2
Chertsey Town v Royston Town	1-0
Worthing v Hemel Hempstead	3-2*(aet)*
Leatherhead v Hornchurch	1-0
Feltham & Hounslow Borough v Thame United	2-3
Hertford Town v Lewes	1-3
Banstead Athletic v Edgware Town	1-0
Hampton v Berkhamsted Town	0-1
Malden Vale v Tilbury	2-1
Barton Rovers v Harlow Town	1-2
Saffron Walden Town v Southall	4-2
Leighton Town v Tring Town	0-1

First Round

Hendon v Boreham Wood	2-3*(aet)*
Walton & Hersham v Abingdon Town	2-1
Molesey v Newbury Town	1-1,3-2
Chalfont St Peter v Leyton	1-5
Aldershot Town v Kingstonian	0-4
Croydon v Thame United	1-2
Tooting & Mitcham United v Lewes	2-1
Collier Row v Whyteleafe	1-2
Metropolitan Police v Wokingham Town	3-4
Abingdon Town v Cheshunt	2-1*(aet)*
Malden Vale v Oxford City	2-3
Barking v Wembley	1-3
Sutton United v Purfleet	2-0
Harlow Town v Dorking	1-2*(aet)*
Saffron Walden Town v Stevenage Borough	2-0
Billericay Town v Tring Town	3-0
Epsom & Ewell v Chertsey Town	1-2*(aet)*
Horsham v Worthing	2-3
Leatherhead v Staines Town	1-3
St Albans City v Bromley	2-1
Hitchin Town v Uxbridge	4-3
Ruislip Manor v Harrow Borough	1-3
Carshalton Athletic v Wivenhoe Town	5-1
Banstead Athletic v Bishop's Stortford	0-6
Berkhamsted Town v Chesham United	1-4
Grays Athletic v Dulwich Hamlet	4-2
Heybridge Swifts v Basingstoke Town	1-2
Marlow v Yeading	2-0
Bognor Regis Town v Hayes	2-0
Cove v Enfield	1-5
Northwood v Windsor & Eton	1-3
Camberley Town v Maidenhead United	1-3

Second Round

Boreham Wood v Chertsey Town	2-3
Molesey v Staines Town	0-1
Kingstonian v Hitchin Town	4-3*(aet)*
Tooting & Mitcham United v Carshalton Ath.	0-3
Wokingham v Chesham	2-1*(W'gham expelled)*
Oxford City v Basingstoke Town	1-3
Sutton United v Bognor Regis Town	1-3
Saffron Walden Town v Windsor & Eton	2-1
Walton & Hersham v Worthing	0-1
Leyton v St Albans City	3-4
Thame Utd v Harrow Borough	4-4,3-3*(4-5 on pens)*
Whyteleafe v Bishop's Stortford	2-7
Aylesbury United v Grays Athletic	1-4
Wembley v Marlow	2-2,1-2
Dorking v Enfield	1-4
Billericay Town v Maidenhead United	1-1,1-0

Third Round

Chertsey Town v Worthing	3-0
Kingstonian v Harrow Borough	6-1
Chesham United v Grays Athletic	3-2
Bognor Regis Town v Enfield	2-3
Staines Town v St Albans City	0-1
Carshalton Athletic v Bishop's Stortford	1-0
Basingstoke Town v Marlow	1-1,2-3*(aet)*
Saffron Walden Town v Maidenhead United	3-1

Quarter-Finals

Chertsey Town v St Albans City	5-0
Chesham United v Marlow	0-3
Kingstonian v Carshalton Athletic	0-1
Enfield v Saffron Walden Town	3-1*(aet)*

Semi-Finals (two legs)

Carshalton Athletic v Chertsey Town	0-3,1-2
Marlow v Enfield	1-1,1-2

Final *(at Hayes FC, Monday 4th May)*: Chertsey Town 3, Enfield 0

Below: *Lee Charles of Chertsey holds off a challenge during the Third Round match against Worthing.* *Photo - Eric Marsh.*

CARLSBERG (FULL MEMBERS) CUP 1993-94

First Round

Berkhamsted Town v Yeading	1-2	Bishop's Stortford v Hayes	3-0
Borehamwood v Hitchin Town	1-3	Dulwich Hamlet v Tooting & Mitcham United	2-1
Chesham United v St Albans City	0-2	Barking v Enfield	0-2
Chalfont St Peter v Maidenhead United	1-1	Whyteleafe v Croydon	3-4*(aet)*
Marlow v Ruislip Manor	2-1	Bognor Regis v Carshalton	2-2*(aet, 1-4 on pens)*
Sutton United v Worthing	5-1	Staines Town v Basingstoke Town	1-3

Second Round

Wivenhoe Town v Yeading	1-3	Billericay Town v Bishop's Stortford	1-2
Enfield v Hendon	0-1	Wembley v Uxbridge	1-2
Harrow Borough v Aylesbury United	2-1*(aet)*	Grays Athletic v Hitchin Town	2-1
Dulwich Hamlet v Walton & Hersham	2-0	Kingstonian v Abingdon Town	4-0
St Albans City v Leyton	5-3	Stevenage Borough v Heybridge Swifts	1-3
Molesey v Maidenhead United	3-2*(aet)*	Bromley v Croydon	3-1
Marlow v Purfleet	0-1	Carshalton Athletic v Sutton United	3-1
Basingstoke v Wokingham	1-1*(aet, 3-4 on pens)*	Windsor & Eton v Dorking	0-2

Third Round

Yeading v Bishop's Stortford	0-1	Hendon v Uxbridge	1-0
Harrow Borough v Grays Athletic	1-4	Dulwich Hamlet v Kingstonian	1-0
St Albans v Heybridge S.	3-3*(aet, 4-3 pens)*	Molesey v Bromley	2-1
Purfleet v Carshalton	2-2*(aet, 8-7 pens)*	Wokingham Town v Dorking	2-1

Quarter-Finals

Grays Athletic v Dulwich Hamlet	1-2	Bishop's Stortford v Hendon	1-1*(aet, 3-1 on pens)*
St Albans City v Molesey	2-1	Purfleet v Wokingham Town	1-1*(aet, 4-5 on pens)*

Semi-Finals

Hendon v Dulwich Hamlet	2-1	St Albans City v Wokingham Town	0-2

Final *(at Marlow FC, Tuesday 3rd May)*: Hendon 2, Wokingham Town 1

CARLSBERG (ASSOCIATE MEMBERS) TROPHY 1993-94

First Round

Horsham v Feltham & Hounslow Borough	1-5	Saffron Walden Town v Northwood	2-1
Flackwell Heath v Southall	5-2	Harefield Hamlet v Camberley Town	1-0
Hungerford Town v Newbury United	0-1	Bracknell v Leatherhead	1-1*(aet, 4-5 pens)*
Tring Town v Hemel Hempstead	1-4	Cheshunt v East Thurrock United	2-1
Barton Rovers v Leighton Town	0-1	Kingsbury Town v Hornchurch	1-2*(aet)*
Collier Row v Rainham	1-1*(aet, 2-4 pens)*		

Second Round

Alershot Town v Malden Vale	2-0	Feltham & Hounslow Borough v Epsom & Ewell	1-3
Chertsey Town v Metropolitan Police	4-0	Thame United v Oxford City	2-0
Saffron Walden Town v Tilbury	2-1	Witham Town v Flackwell Heath	5-1
Harefield United v Cove	0-2*(aet)*	Banstead Athletic v Lewes	2-0
Egham Town v Newbury Town	0-1	Hampton v Leatherhead	1-0
Hemel Hempstead v Rainham Town	2-0*(aet)*	Cheshunt v Ware	5-2
Aveley v Clapton	3-2	Leighton Town v Hornchurch	1-3
Edgware Town v Rainham Town	2-1	Hertford Town v Harlow Town	0-2

Third Round

Aldershot Town v Epsom & Ewell	0-2	Chertsey Town v Thame United	7-3
Saffron Walden Town v Witham Town	1-2	Cove v Banstead Athletic	1-5
Newbury Town v Hampton	3-1	Hemel Hempstead v Cheshunt	2-1
Aveley v Hornchurch	0-2*(aet)*	Edgware Town v Harlow Town	3-0

Quarter-Finals

Epsom & Ewell v Chertsey Town	0-7	Witham Town v Banstead Athletic	0-1
Newbury Town v Hemel Hempstead	2-1	Hornchurch v Edgware Town	5-0

Semi-Finals

Chertsey Town v Banstead Athletic	1-0	Newbury Town v Hornchurch	0-2*(aet)*

Final *(at Hendon FC)*: Chertsey Town 1, Hornchurch 0

Left: *Epsom & Ewell celebrate with a crate of the sponsors wares after their excellent Third Round win at Aldershot Town.*
Photo - Eric Marsh.

PHOTOS OPPOSITE:

Top: *Hampton's Paul Reed tussles with a Barton Rovers defender during a Division Two fixture.* *Photo - Les Rance.*

Centre: *Purfleet - Division One runners-up.* *Photo - Eric Marsh.*

Foot: *Gary Sperry of Bognor Regis Town looks amazed as Colin Matthews makes a brilliant save to deny Windsor & Eton.* *Photo - Graham Cotterell.*

SPONSOR

MAIN SPONSOR
REYNOLDS FURNISHERS

PREMIER DIVISION 1993-94

	P	W	D	L	F	A	PTS
Stevenage Borough	42	31	4	7	88	39	97
Enfield	42	28	8	6	80	28	92
Marlow	42	25	7	10	90	67	82
Chesham United	42	24	8	10	73	45	80
Sutton United	42	23	10	9	77	31	79
Carshalton Athletic	42	22	7	13	81	53	73
St Albans City	42	21	10	11	81	54	73
Hitchin Town	42	21	7	14	81	56	70
Harrow Borough	42	18	11	13	54	56	65
Kingstonian	42	18	9	15	101	64	63
Hendon	42	18	9	15	61	51	63
Aylesbury Utd	42	17	7	18	64	67	58
Hayes	42	15	8	19	63	72	53
Grays Athletic	42	15	5	22	56	69	50
Bromley	42	14	7	21	56	69	49
Dulwich Hamlet	42	13	8	21	52	74	47
Yeading	42	11	13	18	58	66	46
Molesey	42	11	11	20	44	62	44
Wokingham Town	42	11	6	25	38	67	39
Dorking	42	9	4	29	58	104	31
Basingstoke Town	42	5	12	25	38	86	27
Wivenhoe Town	42	5	3	34	38	152	18

TOP SCORERS

	Lge	Cup	Tot
Jimmy Bolton (Carshalton Ath.)	29	6	35
Martin Gittings (Stevenage Boro.)	27		27
David Lay (Marlow)	21	6	27

Below: *Stevenage Borough in joyous mood after receiving the Premier Division title at their home game against Harrow Borough on Saturday 7th May. A record crowd of 3,005 - the biggest Diadora attendance of the season - turned up for the 'party'.*

RESULT CHART 1993-94

HOME TEAM	1	2	3	4	5	6	7	8	9	10	11	12	13	14	15	16	17	18	19	20	21	22
1. Aylesbury	*	4-4	2-1	3-0	0-2	2-0	1-3	1-0	0-1	0-1	1-0	2-3	1-1	3-6	1-5	2-1	1-2	0-1	1-2	3-0	3-0	1-1
2. Basingstoke	2-3	*	1-3	0-2	3-3	0-0	0-1	1-2	0-0	1-1	4-1	0-1	1-3	1-1	1-3	1-2	0-1	1-2	0-0	6-2	1-2	1-1
3. Bromley	0-0	3-0	*	0-2	1-2	2-1	3-2	1-2	0-2	0-3	0-0	3-3	0-0	2-2	2-3	0-1	2-0	1-2	1-4	6-0	1-0	2-1
4. Carshalton	1-3	2-0	2-1	*	1-1	1-2	0-1	0-3	3-0	2-1	2-0	3-0	1-4	1-4	2-1	0-1	3-3	2-0	1-0	4-3	1-0	2-0
5. Chesham U.	1-4	2-1	5-0	2-1	*	3-0	2-1	2-3	2-1	3-0	0-1	2-1	0-3	1-0	1-3	0-1	0-0	1-2	1-0	5-1	3-0	3-2
6. Dorking	1-4	1-2	0-3	1-4	3-4	*	0-1	1-3	3-3	4-3	0-1	1-2	3-1	2-0	2-3	3-1	1-2	1-5	1-3	4-1	1-3	4-3
7. Dulwich H.	2-0	1-1	1-2	2-1	0-2	1-1	*	2-2	2-3	1-2	3-2	0-1	0-0	1-7	2-3	1-0	1-2	0-2	0-3	0-1	2-2	1-1
8. Enfield	4-0	0-1	2-0	1-1	0-1	6-0	3-0	*	1-0	2-0	2-0	1-0	0-3	3-0	0-0	3-0	1-1	3-0	1-0	8-0	1-0	0-0
9. Grays Ath.	2-0	2-0	3-2	1-1	0-2	4-0	4-0	1-4	*	0-1	0-1	0-3	0-2	0-3	4-7	1-2	0-1	1-2	1-0	1-0	0-3	2-1
10. Harrow B.	0-1	4-0	0-0	3-0	0-4	3-2	2-1	1-1	1-1	*	3-3	2-1	1-1	2-4	2-0	1-1	0-0	1-0	0-1	3-0	1-1	1-0
11. Hayes	0-0	4-0	3-1	3-3	1-1	3-2	1-2	0-1	1-3	1-1	*	1-1	2-2	2-1	2-0	3-0	2-1	1-3	1-8	0-2	1-2	0-1
12. Hendon	2-2	6-0	2-1	1-1	0-1	3-1	2-1	0-2	2-1	0-2	0-2	*	2-4	0-0	0-1	2-0	1-0	1-2	0-1	0-2	1-1	5-2
13. Hitchin T.	5-1	1-0	1-0	1-0	2-1	2-3	2-3	2-3	2-3	0-1	3-2	0-0	*	1-3	2-1	2-0	1-3	1-3	0-0	6-2	1-0	4-2
14. Kingstonian	2-1	5-0	3-0	0-2	1-2	2-2	3-0	1-2	3-0	7-0	4-1	1-3	3-5	*	1-1	0-0	0-1	3-5	0-2	8-1	5-0	1-2
15. Marlow	1-0	2-0	3-4	0-6	0-2	2-1	4-2	2-1	3-1	0-1	4-3	2-1	1-0	3-3	*	2-1	4-2	0-0	3-2	3-1	3-1	1-1
16. Molesey	1-2	0-0	2-3	0-1	1-1	3-0	0-0	0-1	0-2	0-0	3-2	2-3	1-2	1-1	1-1	*	2-1	1-2	0-0	4-0	2-0	0-0
17. St Albans	1-1	6-1	2-0	1-3	1-1	3-0	4-3	2-1	5-3	3-1	4-0	0-0	2-1	1-4	1-2	4-1	*	1-2	0-0	9-1	2-0	1-1
18. Stevenage	4-0	0-0	0-1	2-4	0-0	4-3	2-0	0-1	1-0	3-0	2-1	3-0	1-2	4-1	4-2	4-2	3-0	*	3-2	6-0	1-0	4-1
19. Sutton U.	3-1	5-0	3-0	2-2	3-1	3-0	0-3	1-1	1-0	3-1	0-1	0-1	2-0	2-1	2-2	4-1	4-1	0-0	*	5-0	1-0	1-1
20. Wivenhoe	0-4	1-2	0-0	0-8	1-1	1-0	3-4	1-2	0-5	2-3	0-6	0-4	0-7	1-1	2-3	3-4	0-3	0-1	0-3	*	3-2	2-4
21. Wokingham	0-3	0-0	2-1	0-4	2-0	3-1	0-1	1-1	3-0	0-1	0-1	0-2	2-0	1-3	0-6	1-1	1-3	0-1	0-1	1-0	*	1-2
22. Yeading	1-2	3-1	2-3	2-1	0-2	1-2	0-0	1-2	1-1	2-0	2-3	1-1	2-1	2-3	2-0	3-0	1-1	0-2	0-0	4-1	1-3	*

Diadora (Isthmian) League Premier Division Ten Year Record

	84/5	85/6	86/7	87/8	88/9	89/0	90/1	91/2	92/3	93/4
Aylesbury United	-	-	-	-	-	3	3	7	10	12
Barking	19	18	8	19	10	20	21	-	-	-
Basingstoke Town	-	-	-	22	-	8	18	14	11	21
Billericay Town	18	21	-	-	-	-	-	-	-	-
Bishop's Stortford	16	7	10	13	7	9	13	22	-	-
Bognor Regis Town	6	15	5	16	9	19	17	21	22	-
Bromley	-	-	11	2	14	21	-	12	17	15
Carshalton Athletic	15	20	15	9	4	10	9	8	4	6
Chesham United	-	-	-	-	-	-	-	4	1	4
Croydon	12	4	7	18	22	-	-	-	-	-
Dagenham	-	-	-	-	18	6	14	9	-	-
Dorking	-	-	-	-	-	-	-	-	-	20
Dulwich Hamlet	7	9	18	20	16	22	-	-	14	16
Enfield	-	-	-	-	-	-	2	2	3	2
Epsom & Ewell	13	22	-	-	-	-	-	-	-	-
Farnborough Town	-	3	9	8	2	-	-	-	-	-
Grays Athletic	-	-	-	-	5	5	6	15	6	14
Harlow Town	22	-	-	-	-	-	-	-	-	-
Harrow Borough	8	5	6	12	19	18	20	18	8	9
Hayes	9	16	16	6	8	14	8	19	9	13
Hendon	17	19	4	10	12	12	15	17	11	11
Hitchin Town	20	17	20	21	-	-	-	-	-	8
Kingstonian	-	8	12	14	6	4	5	10	13	10
Leytonstone-Ilford	21	-	-	4	1			(see Redbridge)		
Leyton-Wingate	-	-	-	17	15	7	22	-	-	-
Marlow	-	-	-	-	20	17	7	6	15	3
Molesey	-	-	-	-	-	-	-	-	-	18
Redbridge Forest	-	-	-	-	-	11	1	-	-	-
St Albans City	-	-	14	15	17	15	16	13	2	7
Slough Town	14	6	3	3	3	1	-	-	-	-
Staines Town	-	-	-	-	-	16	19	20	20	-
Stevenage Borough	-	-	-	-	-	-	-	-	7	1
Sutton United	1	1	-	-	-	-	-	3	5	5
Tooting & Mitcham United	10	12	19	11	21	-	-	-	-	-
Walthamstow Avenue	11	13	22	-	-	-		(see Redbridge)		
Windsor & Eton	5	11	13	7	13	13	12	11	21	-
Wivenhoe Town	-	-	-	-	-	-	10	16	18	22
Woking	-	-	-	-	-	-	4	1	-	-
Wokingham Town	4	10	17	5	11	2	11	5	16	19
Worthing	2	14	21	-	-	-	-	-	-	-
Wycombe Wanderers	3	-	1	-	-	-	-	-	-	-
Yeading	-	-	-	-	-	-	-	-	19	17
Yeovil Town	-	2	2	1	-	-	-	-	-	-
No. of clubs competing	22	22	22	22	22	22	22	22	22	22

Formed: 1897

AYLESBURY UNITED

The Ducks

The main stand at the Buckingham Road Stadium.

Chairman: D W Pigott **President:** J Durban **Vice Chairman:** K T Arnold.
Secretary/Press Officer: Tony Graham c/o the club. (0296 88178 H / 436350 or 436525 B)
Manager: Steve Ketteridge **Coach:** TBA **Physio:** Mark Browes
Commercial Manager: Eric Norman.
Ground: The Stadium, Buckingham Road, Aylesbury HP20 2AQ (0296 436350/436525).
Directions: On A413 to Buckingham, just off ring road opposite Horse & Jockey PH. Arriving from Buckingham ground is on left - from all other directions follow Buckingham signs and ground on right. Half hour walk from Aylesbury rail and bus stations.
Capacity: 4,035 **Cover:** 891 **Seats:** 400 **Floodlights:** Yes **Metal Badges:** Yes
Club Shop: Yes, selling programmes, magazines, souvenirs, leisurewear. Contact secretary.
Colours: Green shaded quarters **Change colours:** Red & black stripes.
Newsline: 0891 446 824 **Midweek home matchday:** Tuesday
Club Sponsors: BMG **Reserve Team's League:** No reserve team.
Previous Leagues: Bucks Contiguous 1897-1903/ South Eastern 03-07/ Spartan 07-51/ Delphian 51-63/ Athenian 63-76/ Southern 76-88/ GMV Conference 88-89.
Previous Grounds: Printing Works Ground 1897-1935/ Sports Stadium, Wendover Rd (ground name later changed to The Stadium, Turnfurlong Lane) 35-85/ shared grounds 85-86.
Previous Name: Night School, Printing Works (merged in 1897).
Record Attendance: 6,000 v England 1988 *(at old ground: 7,500 v Watford, FA Cup 1st Rd 1951).*
Best FA Trophy season: Quarter-Final replay 80-81.
Best FA Cup season: 2nd Rd 88-89 89-90 91-92 (1st Rd 51-52 85-86 86-87 87-88 91-92).
League clubs defeated in FA Cup: Southend Utd 89-90.
Record Fees - Paid: £15,000 for Glenville Donegal (Northampton, 1990)
Received: £35,000 for Glenville Donegal (Maidstone Utd, 1991).
Players progressing to Football League: Ray Mabbutt (Bristol Rovers), Phil Barber (Crystal Palace 1986)
Clubhouse: Pub hours, but shut during matches. Function room available for hire (0296 436891). Bar snacks available.
Club Record Scorer: Cliff Hercules
Record Appearances: Cliff Hercules.
93-94 Captain: Paul Benning.
93-94 P.o.Y.: Matt Hayward.
93-94 Top scorer: Cliff Hercules.
Local Newspapers: Bucks Herald, Bucks Advertiser, Herald & Post.
Local Radio Stations: Three Counties Radio, Chiltern Radio, Fox FM, Mix 96.
Honours: Southern Lg 87-88 (Mids Div R-up 84-85, Sth Div R-up 79-80), Athenian Lg Div 2 R-up 67-68, Delphian Lg 53-54 (R-up 52-53, Lg Cup 59-60), Spartan Lg 08-09 (R-up 52-53, West Div 28-29 (R-up 45-46), Div 1 38-39 (R-up 34-35)), Berks & Bucks Snr Cup 13-14 85-86).

PROGRAMME DETAILS:
Pages: 32 **Price:** £1
Editor: Dave Gamage

AYLESBURY UNITED's 1993-94 CAMPAIGN

Date	Opponents	Comp.	Res	Gate	Goalscorers
21/08	**KINGSTONIAN**	DFL	3-6	634	Greene, Hercules, Benning
23/08	Wivenhoe Town	DFL	4-0	269	Hercules(2), Robinson, Hayward
28/08	Wokingham Town	DFL	3-0	359	Greene, Fleming, Lawford
31/08	**HENDON**	DFL	2-3	764	Greene, Lawford
04/09	**BROMLEY**	DFL	2-1	633	Greene, Blencowe
11/09	Marlow	DFL	0-1	495	
14/09	Brackley Town	B&B1	2-1	140	Hercules, Blencowe
18/09	**ENFIELD**	DFL	1-0	782	Hercules
21/09	Cheshunt	DLC1	2-1	326	Hercules(2)
02/10	Hitchin Town	DFL	1-5	556	Benning
05/10	**CARSHALTON ATH.**	DFL	3-0	455	Herclues, Fleming, Grenfell
09/10	Hayes	DFL	0-0	361	
12/10	**St ALBANS CITY**	DFL	1-2	596	Lawford
16/10	Dorking	DFL	4-1	250	Lawford(2), Sullivan, Hercules
23/10	**MARLOW**	FAC4q	1-2	926	Blencowe
26/10	**STEVENAGE BORO.**	DFL	0-1	673	
30/10	Harrow Borough	DFL	1-0	270	Hercules
06/11	**SUTTON UNITED**	DFL	1-2	583	Greene
13/11	Dulwich Hamlet	DFL	0-2	309	
16/11	**GRAYS ATHLETIC**	DLC2	1-4	295	Hercules
20/11	**YEADING**	DFL	1-1	340	Hercules
27/11	Nuneaton Borough	FAT3q	2-2	1,375	Stacey, Bashir
30/11	**NUNEATON BORO.**	FAT3qr	1-2	537	Hercules
04/12	**MOLESEY**	DFL	2-1	351	Langley(og), Blencowe
07/12	**BUCKINGHAM TOWN**	BSCsf(1)	2-1	136	Hayward, Hercules
11/12	Hendon	DFL	2-2	241	Guettouche, Fleming
18/12	**BASINGSTOKE T.**	DFL	4-4	415	Blencowe(2), Bashir, Hayward
27/12	Chesham United	DFL	4-1	1,465	Hercules(2), Blencowe, Beard
01/01	**MARLOW**	DFL	1-5	725	Blencowe
11/01	**BUCKINGHAM TOWN**	B&B1	1-0	300	Hercules
15/01	**WIVENHOE TOWN**	DFL	3-0	420	Blencowe, Bashir, Beard
29/01	**WOKINGHAM TOWN**	DFL	3-0	599	Bashir(2), West
01/02	Harrow Borough	CC2	1-2	152	West
05/02	Bromley	DFL	0-0	302	
12/02	**HAYES**	DFL	1-0	516	West
19/02	Enfield	DFL	0-4	683	
26/02	**DORKING**	DFL	2-0	733	McPherson, Blencowe
01/03	Abingdon Town	B&Bqf	0-0	195	
05/03	**St ALBANS CITY**	DFL	1-1	541	Bashir
08/03	**ABINGDON TOWN**	B&Bqfr	2-1	280	Hercules(2)
12/03	Carshalton Athletic	DFL	3-1	412	Grenfell, Hercules, Blencowe
19/03	**HITCHIN TOWN**	DFL	1-1	431	Bashir
23/03	Marlow	B&Bsf	1-1	438	Fleming
26/03	**HARROW BOROUGH**	DFL	0-1	555	
29/03	**MARLOW**	B&Bsfr	0-5	414	
02/04	Stevenage Borough	DFL	0-4	869	
04/04	**CHESHAM UNITED**	DFL	0-2	610	
09/04	Basingstoke Town	DFL	3-2	184	Hercules, Blencowe, Grenfell
11/04	Sutton United	DFL	1-3	380	Grenfell
16/04	**DULWICH HAMLET**	DFL	1-3	386	Blencowe
19/04	Kingstonian	DFL	1-2	397	Barton(og)
23/04	Yeading	DFL	2-1	164	Hercules, Stacey
30/04	**GRAYS ATHLETIC**	DFL	0-1	265	
03/05	Grays Athletic	DFL	0-2	155	
07/05	Molesey	DFL	2-1	145	McPherson, Blencowe
10/05	Buckingham Town	BSCsf(2)	0-2	140	

Key: DFL: Diadora League Premier Division, DLC: Diadora League Cup, CC: Carlsberg Cup, DFLS: Diadora League Championship Shield, FAC: F.A. Cup, FAT: F.A. Trophy, B&B: Berks & Bucks Senior Cup, BSC: Buckingham Senior Charity Cup.

SQUAD MEMBERS *(previous clubs listed in chronological order)*

GOALKEEPERS: Paul O'Reilly *(Dunstable, London Colney, St Albans, Hayes)*

DEFENDERS: Jason Hall *(Spurs, Portsmouth, Sing Tao(HK))*, **Kevin Day** *(Carnegie College, Worsbro. Bridge MW, Wycombe)*, **Keiron Sullivan** *(Banbury, Buckingham, Worcester, Kidderminster, VS Rugby)*, **Matthew Hayward** *(Aylesbury, Pitstone & Ivinghoe, Thame Utd)*, **Paul Benning** *(Hayes, Gosnells C.(Aust), Peterborough, Hayes, Hungerford, Chesham)*, **Phil Stacey** *(Leytonstone-Ilford, Camb. Utd, Walthamstow Ave., Bishop's Stortford, Epping, Enfield, Dagenham, Barnet, Slough)*.

MIDFIELD: Mark Mallinson *(Oxford C., Hungerford, Slough, Aylesbury, St Albans)*, **Faycal Guettouche** *(Algeria)*, **Justin Merritt** *(Watford)*, **Steve Heard** *(Camb. Utd, Silkeborge(Den), Rushden & Diamonds, Eynesbury R.)*, **Steve Grenfell** *(Spurs, Colchester, Bromley, Dagenham)*, **Mark Fleming** *(QPR, Brentford, Farnborough, Woking)*.

FORWARDS: Cliff Hercules *(Oving)*, **Paul Murray** *(Luton)*, **Keith Dirke** *(Youth Team)*, **Naseem Bashir** *(Reading, Slough, Chalfont St Peter, Chesham)*, **Gavin McPherson** *(Nottm Forest, St Albans, Barnet, Slough)*, **David Greene** *(Basildon, Woodford, Sawbridgeworth, Saffron Walden, Stevenage, Chelmsford, Slough, Billericay, Woking)*, **Jon Blencowe** *(Leicester C., Brackley, Long Buckby, Buckingham, Worcester, Buckingham)*.

1874 # BISHOP'S STORTFORD Blues

Bishop's Stortford celebrate their 1993-94 Diadora League Division One championship success.

Chairman: Gordon Lawrence **Vice-Chairman:** Mick Hancock **President:** B W A Bayford
Secretary: Jim Reynolds, 182 Fold Croft, Harlow CM20 1SN (0279 652531).
Manager: John Radford **Assistant Manager/Coach:** Ray Wickenden.
Physio: Micky Stevens **Press Officer:** Gareth Stephens (0279 813944).
Newsline: 0891 300109 **Commercial Manager:** John Radford.
Ground: George Wilson Stadium, Rhodes Ave., Bishop's Stortford CM23 3JN (0279 654140(club) 656538(office).
Directions: M11 jct 11, A120 towards town centre, right at crossroads into London Rd (A1184), right at mini-r'bout and cross railway bridge, right at next island (by garage), Rhodes Avenue is 2nd left (5-10 mins from M11). By rail: BR West Anglia Line (London Liverpool Str.-Cambridge) cross BR car park from main station entrance, over footbridge, thru 'maltings' area and 2nd left into South Rd, pass Rhodes Centre, Rhodes Avenue 1st right (5-10 mins walk from station).
Capacity: 6,000 **Cover:** 1,770 **Seats:** 270 **Floodlights:** Yes **Metal Badges:** Yes
Club Shop: Full stock inc. scarves, badges and other souvenirs. Massive stock of programmes and books etc. Catalogue available from shop manager Andy Stalley (0279 658536).
Cols: White & blue stripes/blue/blue **Change colours:** Yellow/blue/yellow. **Sponsors:** TBA
Previous Leagues: East Herts 1896-97 02-06 19-21/ Stansted & Dist. Lg 06-19/ Herts County 21-25 27-29/ Herts & Essex Border 25-27/ Spartan 29-51/ Delphian 51-63/ Athenian 63-73.
Prev. Grounds: Silver Leys 1874-1903/ The Laundry Field 03-19.
Midweek home matchday: Tuesday **Reserve Team's League:** Essex & Herts Border Comb.
Record Attendance: 6,000 v Peterborough United, F.A. Cup 2nd Rd 1972 & v Middlesbrough FA Cup 3rd Rd replay, 1983 (lost 1-2 after 2-2 draw).
Best FA Cup season: 3rd Rd replay (see above). 1st Rd 70-71 72-73 74-76 81-83 84-87.
League clubs betean in FA Cup: Reading 82-83.
Record win: 11-0; Nettleswell & Butntmill (H), Herts Junior Cup 2nd Rd 4/11/11; v Crown & Manor (H), Spartan Lg Div One 26/5/47; v Tufnell Park Edmonton (H), Delphian Lg 54-55.
Record defeat: 0-13 v Cheshunt (H), Herts Senior Cup 1st Rd 9/1/26.
Record Fees - Paid: £1,500 for Phil Hopkins (Walthamstow Avenue, 1984)
Received: £10,000 for Carl Hoddle (Leyton Orient, 1989)
Players progressing to Football Lge: Ted Sylvester (Clapton O.) 1911, AJ Thurley (Watford) 1927, Bryan Atkinson (Watford 1954), Roy Johnson (Chelsea) 1954, Peter Burridge (Crystal Pal.) 1956, Paddy Phelan (Southend) 1961, Mick Hollow (Orient 1962), Peter Phillips (Luton 1969), Terry Baker (Colchester) 1986, Tony Sorrell (Maidstone, Colchester, Barnet) 1988, Carl Hoddle (Leyton O., Barnet) 1989, Tom English (Colchester) 1989.
Clubhouse: Open matchdays and Mondays (bingo). Available for hire (weddings/functions). Rolls, crisps available - hot food on matchdays from tea-bar within ground. Clubroom also houses seven executive boxes available for hire per match or per season - further details from Commercial Manager.
Club Record Scorer: (Since 1929) Jimmy Badcock 123
Club Record Appearances: Phil Hopkins 543.
93-94 Captain: Phil Hopkins/ Billy Harrigan.
93-94 P.o.Y.: Andy Walker. **93-94 Top scorer:** Leo Fortune-West.
Local Press: B. Stortford Gazette, Herts & Essex Observer, Herald & Post.
Local Radio Stations: BBC Essex, Essex Radio, Breeze AM.
Honours: FA Tphy 80-81, FA Amtr Cup 73-74, Isthmian Lg Div 1 80-81 93-94 (Lg Cup 88-89, Full Mem. Cup 90-91), Prem. Inter Lg Cup 89-90, Athenian Lg 69-70 (R-up 66-67, Div 1 65-66, Div 2 R-up 64-65), Delphian Lg 54-55, Spartan Lg Div 2 (East) 31-32, London Snr Cup 73-74, Herts Snr Cup 32-33 58-59 59-60 63-64 70-71 72-73 73-74 75-76 86-87, E Anglian Cup 81-82, Herts Charity Cup 62-63 65-66 73-74 81-82 82-83 84-85 87-88, Herts Charity Shield 54-55, Herts I'mediate Cup(res) 93-94, Eastern F'lit Cup 84-85, Essex F'lit Cup 67-68, East Herts Lg 19-20, Stansted & D. Lg 19-20, Essex & Herts Border Comb(W) 81-82 88-89 (R-up(2) 92-94), Fred Budden Tphy R-up 78-79 90-91 92-93.

PROGRAMME DETAILS:
Pages: 40 **Price:** 80p
Editor: Dave Ryan
(0279 812725)

BISHOP'S STORTFORD's 1993-94 CAMPAIGN

Date	Opponents	Comp.	Res	Gate	Goalscorers
07/08	Royston Town	HCC1	6-0	106	Fortune-West(2), L Burns, Ingielewicz, Das(2)
21/08	Windsor & Eton	DFL	1-0	229	Fortune-West
24/08	**BARKING**	DFL	4-0	258	Das, L Burns, Fortune-West(2)
28/08	**BOSTON**	FACpr	4-0	364	Das, L Burns, Edmonds, Fortune-West
31/08	**CHALFONT St PETER**	DFL	4-0	321	L Burns(2), Ingielewicz, Hopkins
04/09	Worthing	DFL	1-0	332	Fortune-West
07/09	**St ALBANS CITY**	HCCqf	2-0	404	Scott, L Burns
11/09	**BURNHAM RAMBLERS**	FAC1q	2-0	479	Fortune-West, Ingielewicz
18/09	**BRAINTREE TOWN**	FAT1q	1-0	490	Fortune-West
21/09	Banstead Athletic	DLC1	6-0	246	Das, Edmonds, Ingielewicz(2), Fortune-West, L Burns *(played at home)*
25/09	Billericay Town	FAC2q	3-1	567	Fortune-West(2), Das
02/10	**RUISLIP MANOR**	DFL	3-0	461	Fortune-West(2), Edmonds
09/10	**CANVEY ISLAND**	FAC3q	0-1	921	
11/10	Purfleet	DFL	2-0	214	L Burns, Fortune-West
16/10	**BILLERICAY TOWN**	FAT2q	1-2	449	Das
19/10	**MAIDENHEAD UTD**	DFL	1-1	286	Fortune-West
23/10	**STAINES TOWN**	DFL	3-1	317	Fortune-West, Scott, Comerford
25/10	Croydon	DFL	4-1	85	Das(2), Scott, White
30/10	Berkhamsted Town	DFL	1-0	234	Das
02/11	**HITCHIN TOWN**	HSC1	3-0	353	Edmonds, Fortune-West(2)
06/11	**WEMBLEY**	DFL	3-1	383	Das, Hopkins, Comerford
09/11	Saffron Walden T.	EFC	2-2	313	Das, Fortune-West
16/11	Whyteleafe	DLC2	7-2	94	Scott, Fortune-West(3), Das, L Burns, Edmonds
20/11	**WHYTELEAFE**	DFL	5-1	341	Fortune-West, Ingielewicz, Das(2), L Burns
27/11	Leyton	DFL	1-0	151	Hopkins
30/11	**HAYES**	CC1	3-0	251	Das, Fortune-West, L Burns
04/12	**ABINGDON TOWN**	DFL	2-0	403	Own-goal, L Burns
11/12	Walton & Hersham	DFL	2-2	242	Das, Fortune-West
13/12	Stevenage Borough	EFC	0-1	266	
18/12	**BILLERICAY TOWN**	DFL	1-2	454	Das
21/12	**BOREHAM WOOD**	DFL	5-2	326	L Burns(2), Fortune-West(2), Walker
27/12	Heybridge Swifts	DFL	3-2	412	Ingielewicz, Fortune-West, Das
01/01	**UXBRIDGE**	DFL	1-2	512	T Burns
15/01	Barking	DFL	2-3	229	Edmonds, Das
17/01	Carshalton Athletic	DLC3	0-1	458	
22/01	**WINDSOR & ETON**	DFL	5-0	369	Ingielewicz(2), L Burns, Edmonds, White
25/01	Billericay Town	CC3	2-1	212	Comerford, Claridge
29/01	Chalfont St Peter	DFL	1-1	225	Comerford
05/02	**WORTHING**	DFL	2-0	394	Comerford, Fortune-West
08/02	**ROYSTON TOWN**	HSCqf	2-0	231	Das, Macciochi
12/02	Maidenhead United	BHL	1-1	209	Edmonds
17/02	**WALTON & HERSHAM**	DFL	1-0	385	Das
19/02	**PURFLEET**	DFL	2-3	360	Edmonds, Das
22/02	Yeading	CC3	1-0		Adamson
26/02	Stevenage Borough	HCCsf	0-2	221	
05/02	Boreham Wood	DFL	0-0	241	
08/03	Wembley	DFL	1-0	82	Fortune-West
12/03	**CROYDON**	DFL	9-1	330	Gunn(3), Comerford(2), Fortune-West(2), Das, Ingielewicz
15/03	**STEVENAGE BOR.**	HSCsf	0-4	194	
17/03	**SAFFRON WALDEN**	EFC	2-3	166	Hollamby, Baxter
19/03	Ruislip Manor	DFL	1-1	185	Fortune-West
22/03	**HENDON**	CCqf	1-1	242	L Burns *(lost 1-3 on penalties)*
26/03	**BERKHAMSTED T.**	DFL	3-0	324	Fortune-West, L Burns, Macchiochi
29/03	**TOOTING & MITCHAM**	DFL	2-2	286	Das, L Burns
31/03	**STEVENAGE BOR.**	EFC	1-2		Macchiochi
02/04	Staines Town	DFL	0-0	321	
07/04	**HEYBRIDGE Sw.**	DFL	0-0	357	
09/04	Billericay Town	DFL	0-0	371	
12/04	Tooting & Mitcham	DFL	1-0	184	Claridge
16/04	**BOGNOR REGIS T.**	DFL	1-0	363	Fortune-West
19/04	Uxbridge	DFL	1-0	146	Edmonds
23/04	Whyteleafe	DFL	1-0	195	Edmonds
30/04	**LEYTON**	DFL	2-2	612	Fortune-West, Claridge
02/05	Bognor Regis Town	DFL	0-0	280	
07/05	Abingdon Town	DFL	0-1	248	

SQUAD MEMBERS *(previous clubs listed in chronological order)*

GOALKEEPERS: Gavin King *(Cheshunt)*, **David Mallett** *(Leyton Orient, Leytonstone-I., Enfield, Dartford, Redbridge, Harlow)*

DEFENDERS: Billy Harrigan *(Cambridge Utd, B. Stortford, Walthamstow A., Leytonstone-I., Chesham)*, **Kevin Jordan** *(Spurs, Southend)*, **Andy Edmonds** *(Spurs, Enfield, Hendon, Dagenham, Enfield)*, **Phil Hopkins** *(Colchester, Chelmsford, Walthamstow Ave.)*, **Martin Sedgewick** *(Local Football)*, **Paul Baxter** *(Spurs, C. Palace, Leytonstone-Ilford, Enfield, Dagenham, Hendon, Leytonstone-Ilford, Boreham Wood)*

MIDFIELD: John Scott *(Sawbridgeworth)*, **Marc Das** *(Harlow, Grays Ath., Hertford, Hendon)*, **Nicky White** *(Youth Team)*, **Robbie Munn** *(Harlow)*, **Terry Burns** *(Cossor Sports, Ware, Harlow, Stevenage, Harlow)*, **Dave Macciochi** *(QPR, Brighton, Kingstonian, Dulwich, Whyteleafe)*

FORWARDS: Leo Fortune-West *(Tiptree Utd, Bishop's Stortford, Dagenham, Dartford, Bishop's Stortford, Hendon)*, **Stewart Ingielewicz** *(East Ham, Harlow, Dagenham, Billericay, Harlow)*, **Tony Comerford** *(West Ham)*, **Sean Adamson** *(Brighton Leyton-Wingate, Wealdstone, Saffron Walden)*, **Lee Burns** *(Sawbridgeworth, Harlow, Hertford, Stevenage, Bishop's Stortford, Stevenage, Harlow)*, **Andy Walker** *(Harlow, San Diego Sockers(US), Harlow, Grays, Boreham Wood, Harlow, Stevenage)*,.

BROMLEY

Formed: 1892 — The Lilywhites

Bromley's Trevor Aylott, who enjoyed a 530-appearance Football League career, scores the club's second goal in their home fixture against Dulwich Hamlet.

Photo - Paul Gardiner.

Chairman: M Perry **President:** G T Ransom, AM Inst BE, MHTTA
Secretary: Brian Traer, 43 Fairway, Pettswood, Orpington, Kent BR5 1EE (0689 820457).
Manager: George Wakeling **Asst Manager:** N/A **Coach:** N/A.
Press Officer: Ian Pettyfer **Physio:** J De Palma
Ground: Hayes Lane, Bromley, Kent BR2 9EF (081 460 5291).
Directions: 1 mile from Bromley South (BR). Buses 316, 146 and 119 pass ground. Junction 4 off M25, then A21 towards London.
Capacity: 8,500 **Cover:** 4,000 **Seats:** 2,000 **Floodlights:** Yes **Metal Badges:** Yes.
Club Shop: Yes.
Colours: White/black/white **Change colours:** All red
Previous Leagues: South London - 1894/ Southern 94-96/ London 96-98 99-1901/ West Kent 01-04/ Southern Suburban 04-07/ Kent 1898-99 11-14/ Spartan 07-08/ Isthmian 08-11/ Athenian 19-52.
Prev. Grounds: White Hart Field Cricket Ground, Widmore Rd (pre-1904)/ Plaistow Cricket Field 1904-37.
Midweek home matchday: Tuesday **Reserve Team's League:** Suburban
Record Attendance: 12,000 v Nigeria, 1950. **Newsline:** 0891 122 904.
Best FA Trophy season: Second Round 91-92.
Best FA Cup season: 2nd Rd replay v Scarborough 37-38, Lincoln 38-39, Watford 45-46.
Record Fees - Paid: Undisclosed **Received:** £50,000 for Jon Goodman (from Millwall, 1990).
Players progressing to Football League: Roy Merryfield (Chelsea), Stan Charlton (Arsenal 1952), Ron Heckman (Orient 1955), John Gregory (West Ham 1951), Bill Lloyd (Millwall 1956), Brian Kinsey (Charlton 1956), Harold Hobbs (Charlton & England), Matt Carmichael (Lincoln 1990), Leslie Locke (QPR 1956), Jon Goodman (Millwall).
Clubhouse: Open matchdays. Food available.
Club Record Goalscorer: George Brown 570 (1938-61)
Club Record Appearances: George Brown
93-94 Captain: Frank Coles.
93-94 P.o.Y.: Ollie Adeiji.
93-94 Top scorer: Pat Gordon.
Local Newspapers: Bromley Times (0474 363363).
Local Radio: Radio Kent, Bromley Hospital Radio, Bromley Local Radio.
Honours: FA Amateur Cup 10-11 37-38 48-49, Isthmian League(4) 08-10 53-54 60-61 (R-up 52-53 55-56 87-88, Div 1 R-up 79-80 85-86 90-91, Prince Phillip 5-a-side Cup 1979), Athenian League 22-23 48-49 50-51 (R-up 35-36), London League Div 2 1896-97, Spartan League 07-08, London Snr Cup 09-10 45-46 50-51, Kent Senior Cup 49-50 76-77 91-92, Kent Amateur Cup(12) 07-08 31-32 35-37 38-39 46-47 48-49 50-51 52-53 53-55 59-60.

PROGRAMME DETAILS:
Pages: 32 **Price:** 80p
Editor: John Self
(081 402 2391)

BROMLEY's 1993-94 CAMPAIGN

Date	Opponents	Comp.	Res	Gate	Goalscorers	
21/08	Hitchin Town	DFL	0-1	365		
24/08	**SUTTON UNITED**	DFL	1-4	367	Aylott	*(played at Dulwich Hamlet)*
28/08	**DORKING**	DFL	2-1	624	Gordon, Sharman	*(played at Dulwich Hamlet)*
31/08	Basingstoke Town	DFL	3-1	301	Raffington, Richards, Gordon	
04/09	Aylesbury United	DFL	1-2	633	Gordon	
11/09	**DULWICH HAMLET**	FAC1q	3-1	541	Aylott(2), Gordon	
14/09	**YEADING**	DFL	2-1	138	Richards, Aylott	*(played at Dulwich Hamlet)*
18/09	**MOLESEY**	FAT1q	0-2	365		
21/09	St Albans City	DLC1	1-2	232	Aylott	
25/09	**MARGATE**	FAC2q	0-3	343		
05/10	**ENFIELD**	DFL	1-2	268	Brown	*(played at Dulwich Hamlet)*
09/10	St Albans City	DFL	0-2	708		
12/10	**BROMLEY**	*DFL*	*2-2*	*202*	*Richards, Aylott*	*(match abandoned)*
16/10	**WIVENHOE TOWN**	DFL	6-0	302	Hamberger, Richards(3), Taylor	
18/10	Carshalton Ath.	DFL	1-2	545	Hamberger	
23/10	Wokingham Town	DFL	1-2	260	Bumstead	
26/10	**DOVER ATHLETIC**	KSC1	1-3	363	Aylott	
30/10	**KINGSTONIAN**	DFL	2-2	476	Taylor, Aylott	
06/11	**STEVENAGE BORO.**	DFL	1-2	472	Taylor	
13/11	Chesham United	DFL	0-5	631		
20/11	**HENDON**	DFL	3-3	307	Richards, Gordon, Raffington	
27/11	**HITCHIN TOWN**	DFL	0-0	329		
04/12	**GRAYS ATHLETIC**	DFL	0-2	255		
11/12	Yeading	DFL	3-2	179	Brown, Richards, Gordon	
14/12	Staines Town	DFL	1-3	214	Brown	
18/12	**MARLOW**	DFL	2-3	271	Brown, Coles	
27/12	Dulwich Hamlet	DFL	2-1	489	Brown, Antoine	
01/01	**BASINGSTOKE T.**	DFL	3-0	311	Brown(2), Gordon	
15/01	Sutton United	DFL	0-3	582		
18/01	**CROYDON**	CC2	3-1	177	Devine, Gordon, Antoine	
29/01	Dorking	DFL	3-0	287	Francis, Richards, Antoine	
02/02	Molesey	DFL	3-2	222	Francis(2), Gordon	
05/02	**AYLESBURY UTD**	DFL	0-0	306		
08/02	Leyton	LCC1	2-1	128	Gordon, Francis	
12/02	Harrow Borough	DFL	0-0	283		
19/02	**CARSHALTON ATH.**	DFL	0-2	422		
26/02	Wivenhoe Town	DFL	0-0	173		
01/03	Welling United	LCCqf	1-4	406	Richards	
05/02	**MOLESEY**	DFL	0-1	229		
09/03	Molesey	CC3	1-2	137	Rawlings	
12/03	Enfield	DFL	0-2	689		
19/03	**HAYES**	DFL	0-0	217		
21/03	Stevenage Borough	DFL	1-0	820	Antoine	
26/03	Kingstonian	DFL	0-3	554		
09/04	Marlow	DFL	4-3	271	Bumstead, Aylott, Antoine, Sharman	
12/04	**HARROW BOROUGH**	DFL	0-3	148		
16/04	**CHESHAM UNITED**	DFL	1-2	369	Gordon	
23/04	Hendon	DFL	1-2	191	Aylott	
26/04	**WOKINGHAM TOWN**	DFL	1-0	225	Gordon	
30/04	**St ALBANS CITY**	DFL	2-0	295	Gordon, White	
03/05	**DULWICH HAMLET**	DFL	3-2	398	Coates, Akers(og), Oakes	
07/05	Grays Athletic	DFL	2-3	235	Richards, Rawlings	

Key: DFL: Diadora League Premier Division, DLC: Diadora League Cup, CC: Carsberg Cup, FAC: F.A. Cup, FAT: F.A. Trophy, KSC: Kent Senior Cup, LCC: London Challenge Cup. Numbers after cup competitions denote rounds (r: replay, qf: Quarter-Final, sf: Semi-Final, f: Final. Numbers in brackets indicate legs, i.e. (1): 1st leg). Home fixtures are denoted by bold capitals, away matches by lower case. (p): penalty, og: Own goal.

SQUAD MEMBERS *(previous clubs listed in chronological order)*

GOALKEEPERS: Curtis Hayes *(Metrogas)*

DEFENDERS: Ian Rawlings *(Leyton Orient, Leyton-Wingate)*, **Ricky Antoine** *(Charlton)*, **Olu Adediji** *(Finchley, Bromley, Boreham Wood)*, **Keith Sharman** *(Clapton, Leyton Orient, Barking)*, **James Uvieghara** *(yth team)*, **John Raffington** *(Croydon, Carshalton, Epsom & E., Carshalton, Hendon, Sutton, Carshalton)*, **Steve Porter** *(Leyton Orient, Watford, Hornchurch, Collier R., Hornchurch, Aveley, Harlow, Dagenham & R., Purfleet)*

MIDFIELD: John Bumstead *(Chelsea, Charlton)*, **Elijah Bee** *(Leyton-Wingate)*, **Frank Coles** *(Charlton, Leytonstone-Ilford, Dagenham, Leytonstone-Ilford, Leyton-Wingate, Enfield)*, **Pat Gordon** *(Millwall, Leyton-Wingate)*, **Joe Francis** *(Millwall, Charlton, Epsom & E., Dartford, Canterbury, Erith, Welling, Erith)*

FORWARDS: Trevor Aylott *(Chelsea, Barnsley, Millwall, Luton, Crystal Pal., Bournemouth, Birmingham, Oxford Utd, Gillingham)*, **Sean Devine** *(Millwall)*, **Paul McMenemy** *(West Ham, Bromley, Margate)*, **Chris Hewitt** *(Old Bromleians)*, **Carl Richards** *(Dulwich, Enfield, Bournemouth, Birmingham, Peterborough, Blackpool, Enfield)*

1903 **CARSHALTON ATHLETIC** Robins

Carshalton Athletic FC 1993-94

Chairman: Andy Winters **Vice Chairman:** John Carpentiere **President:** Bill Cooper
Secretary: Vic Thompson, 11 Poulton Avenue, Sutton, Surrey SM1 3PZ (081 644 6402).
Manager: Billy Smith **Asst Manager:** Bobby Green **Coach:** Colin Turner
Press Officer: Martin Roper **Physio:** Ken Jones
Commercial Manager: John Carpentiere.
Ground: War Memorial Sports Ground, Colston Av, Carshalton SM5 2PW (081 642 8425).
Directions: Turn right out of Carshalton BR Station, and Colston Avenue is first left. Entrance 150 yards on right. London Transport bus 151 from Morden to Wrythe Green Lane.
Capacity: 8,000 **Cover:** 4,500 **Seats:** 240 **Floodlights:** Yes **Metal Badges:** Yes.
Club Shop: Yes, selling hats, scarves, T-shirts, programmes and various football souvenirs.
Colours: White (maroon trim)/maroon **Change colours:** Maroon/white.
Prev. Lges: Southern Suburban (pre-1911)/ Surrey Snr 22-23/ London 23-46/ Corinthian 46-56/ Athenian 56-73.
Previous Grounds: Wrythe Recreation Ground 1907-14/ Culvers Park 19-20.
Midweek home matchday: Monday **Reserve Team's League:** Suburban.
Club Sponsors: T C Cleaning.
Record Attendance: 7,800 v Wimbledon, London Senior Cup.
Best FA Trophy season: 3rd Rd 80-81 (lost 0-3 at home to Mossley (eventual Runners-up)).
Best FA Cup season: 2nd Rd 82-83, lost 1-4 at Torquay. (1st Rd 69-70 87-88).
Record win: 13-0 v Worthing, Loctite Cup Third Round 28/2/91.
League clubs defeated in FA Cup: None.
Record Fees - Paid: £2,000 for Jimmy Bolton, 1990.
Received: £15,000 for Curtis Warmington (Enfield).
Players progressing to Football League: Ernie Taylor (Newcastle, Blackpool, Manchester United), Billy Barragon (QPR), John McDonald (Notts County 1948), Frank George (Orient 1954), Thomas Williams (Colchester 1956), Alan Eagles (Orient 1957), Derek Razzell (QPR), Terry Stacey (Plymouth 1959), Roy Lunnes (Crystal Palace 1960), Les Burns (Charlton 1967), Ron Walker (Watford), Nobby Warren (Exeter), Gus Caesar (Arsenal), Darren Annon (Brentford) 1994, Ian Cox (Crystal Palace) 1994.
Clubhouse: Open every evening and lunchtime. Licenced bar, pool, darts, machines, discos on Saturday. Separate function hall (bookings taken). Food: sandwiches, rolls, burgers, hot dogs, teas, coffees and soft drinks. (081 642 8658).
Club Record Goalscorer: Jimmy Bolton
Club Record Appearances: Jon Raffington and Jon Warden.
93-94 Captain: Andy Riley.
93-94 P.o.Y.: Gary Bowyer.
93-94 Top scorer: Jimmy Bolton.
Club Newsline: 0891 446849.
Local Newspapers: Wallington & Carshalton Advertiser (668411), Carshalton Herald (6612221).
Local Radio Stations: Capital.
Hons: Isthmian League Div 2 Runners-up 76-77, Corinthian League 52-53 53-54, Surrey Senior League Runners-up 22-23, Surrey Senior Cup(3) 88-90 91-92, Surrey Senior Shield (Runners-up(2)), London Challenge Cup 91-92.

PROGRAMME DETAILS:
Pages: 14 **Price:** 80p
Editor: Roger Fear

CARSHALTON ATHLETIC's 1993-94 CAMPAIGN

Date	Opponents	Comp.	Res	Gate	Goalscorers
21/08	**ENFIELD**	DFL	0-3	614	
24/08	Kingstonian	DFL	2-0	538	Annon, Bolton
28/08	Wivenhoe Town	DFL	8-0	130	Bolton(5), Annon, Warden, Bowyer
30/08	**MARLOW**	DFL	2-1	351	Bolton, Warden
04/09	**HAYES**	DFL	2-0	462	Annon, Warden
11/09	**HAVANT TOWN**	FAC1q	2-0	371	Kane, Warden
18/09	**SUTTON UNITED**	DFL	1-0	1,262	Kane
20/09	**WIVENHOE TOWN**	DLC1	5-1		
25/09	**SHEPPEY UNITED**	FAC2q	5-1	474	Warden(2), Riley, Kane, Cox
28/09	Wokingham Town	DFL	4-0	245	Bolton, Warden, Kane, Bowyer
02/10	**HARROW BOROUGH**	DFL	2-1	495	Annon, Warden
05/10	Aylesbury United	DFL	0-3	455	
09/10	Basingstoke Town	FAC3q	3-1	417	Bolton, Richards, Annon
11/10	Stevenage Boro	DFL	4-2	1,066	Warden(2), Annon, Bolton
16/10	**CHESHAM UNITED**	DFL	1-1	752	Riley
18/10	**BROMLEY**	DFL	2-1	545	Riley, Bolton
23/10	Bashley	FAC4q	1-1	615	Riley
25/10	**BASHLEY**	FAC4qr	4-2	971	Beste(2), Bolton, Warden,
30/10	**DORKING**	DFL	1-2	500	Bolton
02/11	Dulwich Hamlet	DFL	1-2	222	Bolton
06/11	**GRAYS ATHLETIC**	DFL	3-0	422	Beste, Cooper, Bolton,
13/11	Barnet	FAC1	1-2	2,690	Annon
16/11	Tooting & Mitcham	DLC2	3-0		
20/11	**BASINGSTOKE TOWN**	DFL	2-0	425	Bolton, Cooper
27/11	Worthing	FAT3q	0-3		
30/11	Bognor Regis Town	CC1	2-2		*(won 4-1 on penalties)*
04/12	**YEADING**	DFL	2-0	377	Stevens, Priddle
11/12	Marlow	DFL	6-0	310	Warden(2), Cox, Beste(2), Annon
15/12	Molesey	SSC1	2-2		
18/12	**HENDON**	DFL	3-0	473	Annon, Kane, Beste
22/12	**MOLESEY**	SSC1r	0-2		
27/12	Sutton United	DFL	2-2	1,644	Bowyer, Bolton
01/01	**STEVENAGE BORO**.	DFL	2-0	1,244	Bowyer, Cuffie(og)
08/01	Grays Athletic	DFL	1-1	292	Bolton
12/01	Molesey	DFL	1-0	257	Riley
15/01	**KINGSTONIAN**	DFL	1-4	1,026	Cox
17/01	**BISHOP'S STORT.**	DLC3	1-0	458	
22/01	Hitchin Town	DFL	0-1	797	
25/01	Kingstonian	DLCqf	1-0		
29/01	**WIVENHOE TOWN**	DFL	4-3	527	Warden(2), Bolton, Cox
05/02	Hayes	DFL	3-3	341	Dear(og), Kane, Bolton
12/02	**WOKINGHAM TOWN**	DFL	1-0	504	Warden
19/02	Bromley	DFL	2-0	422	Beste, Cox
21/02	**SUTTON UNITED**	CC2	3-1	932	Bolton, Annon, Cox
26/02	Chesham United	DFL	1-2	1,011	Bolton
28/02	**CHERTSEY TOWN**	DLCsf(1)	0-3	638	
05/03	**DULWICH HAMLET**	DFL	0-1	466	
07/03	Purfleet	CC3	2-2		*(lost 7-8 on penalties)*
12/03	**AYLESBURY UTD.**	DFL	1-3	412	Bolton
15/03	Chertsey Town	DLCsf(2)	1-2	381	Warden
19/03	Harrow Borough	DFL	0-3	267	
26/03	Dorking	DFL	4-1	255	Bolton(3), Warden
02/04	**HITCHIN TOWN**	DFL	1-4	365	Fisher
09/04	Hendon	DFL	1-1	141	Bolton
23/04	Basingstoke Town	DFL	2-0	233	Bolton(2)
28/04	**St ALBANS CITY**	DFL	3-3	328	Bolton(3)
30/04	**MOLESEY**	DFL	0-1	304	
03/05	St Albans City	DFL	3-1	238	Richards(2), Egan
06/05	Enfield	DFL	1-1	485	Bower
07/05	Yeading	DFL	1-2	172	Fisher

Key: DFL: Diadora League Premier Division, DLC: Diadora League Cup, CC: (Diadora League) Carlsberg Cup, SSC: Surrey Senior Cup, FAC: F.A. Cup, FAT: F.A. Trophy. Number after cup competitions denote rounds (r: replay, qf: Quarter-Final, sf: Semi-Final, f: Final. Numbers in brackets indicate legs, i.e. (1): 1st leg). Home fixtures are denoted by bold capitals, away matches by lower case. (p): penalty, og: Own goal.

SQUAD MEMBERS *(previous clubs listed in chronological order)*

GOALKEEPERS: Les Cleevely *(Southampton, Crystal Palace, Wealdstone, Farnborough, Epson & Ewell)*

DEFENDERS: Gary Mitchell *(Carshalton, Croydon),* **Dave Stevens** *(Crystal Palace),* **Andy Fisher** *(Carshalton, Leatherhead, Molesey, Dorking, Dulwich),* **Stuart Lawson** *(Youth Team),* **Andy Riley** *(Malden Vale, Whyteleafe, Leatherhead),* **Kevin Fitzgerald** *(Dorking, Epsom & Ewell, Dorking),* **Sean Priddle** *(Wimbledon, Crewe, Exeter, Brentford, St. Albans, Harrow Boro., Southall, St. Albans, Sutton Utd).*

MIDFIELD: Gary Bowyer *(Crystal Palace, Carshalton, Whyteleafe, Bromley),* **Dean Park** *(Hayes),* **Gary Richards** *(Crawley, Leatherhead),* **Phil Dawson** *(Chipstead, Sutton Utd.),* **Dave Cooper** *(Wimbledon, Plymouth, Redbridge F., Crawley),* **John Egan** *(Walton & Hersham, Leatherhead, Whyteleafe, Molesey, Dorking, Dulwich, Molesey, Dulwich).*

FORWARDS: Conrad Kane *(Merstham, Dulwich, Bromley, Dulwich),* **Robin Beste** *(Chelsea, Dulwich, Warlingham),* **Jon Warden** *(Croydon, Tooting),* **Mark Edwards** *(Dulwich),* **Barry Ferdinand** *(Stevenage, Malden Vale, Whyteleafe),* **Jimmy Bolton** *(Spurs, Hillingdon Boro., Wimbledon, Farnborough, Tooting, Farnborough, Kiruna (Swe), Farnborough, Harrow Boro.).*

Formed: 1886

CHESHAM UNITED

The Generals

Chesham United 1993-94, with the trophies (Diadora League shield and trophy and the Berks & Bucks Senior Cup) won in 1992-93. Back Row (L/R): Ann Wheeler (Physio), Mark Dawber, Ian Mitchell, Andy Adebowale, Andy Lomas, Steve Bateman, Mickey Barnes, Darren Coleman, Chris Townsend, Andy York, Tony Hopkins, Dave Webley, Keith Power (Fitness Coach), Micky Gilchrist (Physio). Front: John Richardson, Gary Cobb, Naseem Bashir, Alan Randall (Assistant Manager), Tony Aplin (Chairman), Gerald Aplin (Manager, now Merthyr Tydfil), Barry Rake, Lee Costa, Garry Attrell.

President: Bill Wells **Chairman:** David Pembroke **Vice-Chairman:** Dennis Bone.
Secretary: David Stanley, 17 Old Vicarage Gdns, Markyate, St Albans, Herts AL3 9PW (0582 840707).
Manager: Paul Roberts **Coach:** Micky Gilchrist **Physio:** Ann Wheeler
Press Officer: Dennis Bone **Commercial Manager:** Ken Ambrose.
Ground: Meadow Park, Amy Lane, Amersham Road, Chesham HP5 1NE (0494 783964 - ground clubhouse. 0494 791608 - fax. 0891 884580 - match information service).
Directions: M25 junction 18, A404 to Amersham, A416 to Chesham - go down to r-about at foot of Amersham Hill, then sharp left. 10 mins walk from Chesham station (Metropolitan Line).
Capacity: 5,000 **Cover:** 2,500 **Seats:** 224 **Floodlights:** Yes **Metal Badges:** Yes
Club Shop: Yes. Open matchdays - Manager: Peter Annetts (0296 87615).
Colours: Claret & blue **Change colours:** Yellow & black. **Sponsors:** MFI.
Previous Leagues: Spartan 17-47/ Corinthian 47-63/ Athenian 63-73.
Midweek home matchday: Wednesday **Reserve Team's League:** N/A.
Record Attendance: 5,000 v Cambridge Utd, FA 3rd Rd 5/12/79.
Best FA Cup season: 3rd Rd as above (lost 0-2). Also 1st Rd 66-67 68-69 76-77 82-83.
Best FA Trophy season: 3rd Rd 92-93 (lost 1-3 at home to Sutton United).
Record Fees - Paid: Undisclosed (club policy)
Received: Undisclosed (club policy).
Players progressing to Football League: William Shipwright & Jimmy Strain (Watford 1953 & 55), Stewart Scullion (Charlton 1965), John Pyatt (L'pool 1967), Brian Carter (Brentford 1968), Kerry Dixon (Spurs 1978), Tony Curie (Torquay 1984).
Clubhouse: Open every evening & matchdays. Bar snacks. Available for hire (business training meetings, weddings etc).
Club Record Goalscorer: John Willis.
Club Record Appearances: Martin Baguley (600+).
93-94 Captain: Steve Bateman.
93-94 P.o.Y.: Mark Dawber.
93-94 Top scorer: Mark Dawber, Ian Mitchell, Dave Webley - 12 each.
Local Newspapers: Bucks Examiner (0494 792616), Bucks Advertiser (0895 632000), Bucks Free Press (0494 21212).
Local Radio Stations: Radio Chiltern (0582 666001).
Honours: FA Amtr Cup R-up 67-68, Isthmian Lg 92-93 (Div 1 90-91, Div 2 Nth 86-87, Associate Members Cup R-up 90-91, Charity Shield 93-94), Athenian Lg Div 1 Cup 63-64 68-69, Corinthian Lg R-up(2) 60-62 (Lg Cup 60-61), Spartan Lg(4) 21-23 24-25 32-33 (R-up 26-27 29-30 33-34), Berks & Bucks Snr Cup 21-22 25-26 28-29 33-34 47-48 50-51 64-65 66-67 75-76 92-93 (R-up 93-94).

PROGRAMME DETAILS:
Pages: 36 **Price:** £1.20
Editor: Secretary

CHESHAM UNITED's 1993-94 CAMPAIGN

Date	Opponents	Comp.	Res	Gate	Goalscorers
21/08	St Albans City	DFL	1-1	824	Barnes
25/08	**YEADING**	DFL	3-2	777	Banton(2), Webley
28/08	**GRAYS ATHLETIC**	DFL	2-1	764	Adebowale, Webley
01/09	Harrow Borough	DFL	4-0	549	Costa(2), Attrell, Banton
04/09	Sutton United	DFL	1-3	820	Webley
07/09	**MARLOW**	DFLS	4-1	427	Bashir(2), Rake, Mitchell
11/09	**St ALBANS CITY**	FAC1q	5-0	1,004	York, Webley, Mitchell(2), Cobb
15/09	**HITCHIN TOWN**	DFL	0-3	692	
18/09	**WIVENHOE TOWN**	DFL	5-1	618	Costa, Mitchell, Attrell, Banton(2)
25/09	**CHALFONT St PETER**	FAC2q	5-0	538	Banton(2), Rake, Webley, Own-Goal
28/09	Berkhamsted Town	DLC1	4-1	494	Dawber, Webley, Banton(2)
06/10	**HENDON**	DFL	2-1	694	Cobb, Attrell
09/10	Edgware Town	FAC3q	2-1	630	Dawber, Webley
12/10	**DULWICH HAMLET**	DFL	2-1	515	Dawber, Cobb
16/10	Carshalton Ath.	DFL	1-1	752	Webley
19/10	Basingstoke Town	DFL	3-2	320	Mitchell, Webley, Banton
23/10	**KIDDERMINSTER**	FAC4q	1-4	1,144	Dawber
26/10	**MARLOW**	DFL	1-3	628	Banton
30/10	Stevenage Borough	DFL	0-0	947	
06/11	Hayes	DFL	1-1	339	Webley
10/11	**WOKINGHAM TOWN**	DFL	3-0	478	Costa, Webley, Mitchell
13/11	**BROMLEY**	DFL	5-0	631	Mitchell(3), Jenkins, Coleman
16/11	Wokingham Town	DLC2	1-2	204	Webley *(Wokingham Town expelled)*
20/11	Enfield	DFL	1-0	886	Mitchell
27/11	Molesey	DFL	1-1	334	Mitchell
01/12	**St ALBANS CITY**	CC1	0-2	376	
04/12	Dorking	DFL	4-3	274	Dawber(2), Banton, York
11/12	**HARROW BOROUGH**	DFL	3-0	655	Adebowale, Mitchell, Dawber
15/12	**GRAYS ATHLETIC**	DLC3	3-2	269	Bateman, Rake, Richardson
18/12	Kingstonian	DFL	2-1	723	Mitchell, Dawber
27/12	**AYLESBURY UTD**	DFL	1-4	1,465	Costa
01/01	Hitchin Town	DFL	1-2	1,010	Lay(p), Catlin, Caesar(2), Blackman
03/01	**St ALBANS CITY**	DFL	0-0	871	
15/01	Yeading	DFL	2-0	385	Adebowale, Richardson
18/01	**BEACONSFIELD UTD**	B&B1	8-0	245	Banton(2), Dawber(3), Richardson, Cobb, Attrell
22/01	Sutton United	FAT1	0-2	1,027	
29/01	Grays Athletic	DFL	2-0	314	Bateman, Webley
05/02	**SUTTON UNITED**	DFL	1-0	917	Webley
12/02	Dulwich Hamlet	DFL	2-0	282	Adebowale, Richardson
19/02	**BASINGSTOKE T.**	DFL	2-1	624	Mitchell, Attrell
26/02	**CARSHALTON ATH.**	DFL	2-1	1,011	Mitchell, Dawber
01/03	Chalfont St Peter	B&Bqf	2-0	210	Coleman, Webley
05/03	Wokingham Town	DFL	0-2	336	
09/03	**MARLOW**	DLCqf	0-3	401	
12/03	Hendon	DFL	1-0	301	Dawber
16/03	**HAYES**	DFL	0-1	448	
19/03	**MOLESEY**	DFL	0-1	481	
23/03	**HUNGERFORD TOWN**	B&Bsf	2-0	248	Bateman, Costa
26/03	**STEVENAGE B.**	DFL	1-2	939	Webley
02/04	Marlow	DFL	2-0	590	Dawber(2)
04/04	Aylesbury United	DFL	2-0	610	Banton, Dawber
09/04	**KINGSTONIAN**	DFL	1-0	631	Mitchell
16/04	Bromley	DFL	2-1	369	Adebowale(2)
28/03	**ENFIELD**	DFL	2-3	888	Mitchell, Dawber
30/04	Wivenhoe Town	DFL	1-1	187	Attrell
02/05	MARLOW	B&Bf	0-1	782	*(played at Reading FC)*
07/05	**DORKING**	DFL	3-0	455	Barnes(2), Banton

Key: DFL: Diadora League Premier Division, DLC: Diadora League Cup, CC: Carlsberg Cup, DFLS: Diadora League Championship Shield, FAC: F.A. Cup, FAT: F.A. Trophy, B&B: Berks & Bucks Senior Cup.

SQUAD MEMBERS *(previous clubs listed in chronological order)*

GOALKEEPERS: Andy Lomas *(Eaton Bray, Arlesey, Baldock, Barnet),* **Rob Tenkorang** *(Fulham (A), Southall, Hendon, Finchley, Brook House, Wealdstone).*

DEFENDERS: Mickey Barnes *(Reading, Northampton, Basingstoke, Maidenhead Utd, Windsor, Barnet),* **Andrew Yorke** *(Exeter, Ebbw Vale, Merthyr),* **Darren Coleman** *(Forest Utd, Finchley, Edgware),* **Tony Hopkins** *(Chelsea, Bristol C., Euddevalle, Merthyr, Ebbw Vale, Aldershot, Hendon),*

MIDFIELD: Lee Costa *(Man Utd),* **Gary Cobb** *(Luton, Fulham),* **Mark Dawber** *(Virginia Water, Woking, Wycombe, Staines),* **John Richardson** *(Amersham, Chesham, Chalfont St Peter, Papatoetoe(NZ)),* **Ady Adebowale** *(Balls Park, Hertford, Bishop's Stortford),* **Jeff Hamlet** *(Wimbledon, Tooting, Crawley, Dulwich, Uxbridge, Southall, Uxbridge, Chesham, Maidenhead Utd., Uxbridge, Carterton, Thame Utd).*

FORWARDS: Mickey Banton *(Hellenic(SA), Windsor, Barnet, Chesham, Walton & Hersham),* **Ian Mitchell** *(Newport Co., Merthyr, Hereford),* **Barry Rake** *(Millwall, Slough),* **Darryl Franklin** *(Leeds Utd, Harrogate, Goole, Carlisle Utd, Chesham, Farsley C.),* **Gary Attrell** *(Britwell Hawks, Slough, Maidenhead Utd, Windsor, Farnborough, Windsor, Burnham, Marlow).*

Formed: 1893

DULWICH HAMLET

The Hamlet

Dulwich Hamlet's Gary Hewitt (left) concedes a penalty by bringing down Marlow forward Tim Buzaglo. Photo - Alan Coomes.

Chairman: Ian Woodley **Vice Chairman:** Glyn Beverley **President:** Tommy Jover
Secretary: John Hugh-Jones, Flat 8, Nell Cromer Court, 34-36 Hamlet Rd, Upper Norwood, London SE19 2AW.
Manager: Frank Murphy **Coach:** TBA **Physio:** Caroline Browne.
Press Officer: John Lawrence (071 733 6385) **Commercial Mgr:** Ian Woodley.
Ground: Champion Hill Stadium, Dog Kennel Hill, East Dulwich, London SE22 8BD (071 274 8707).
Directions: East Dulwich station, 200yds. Denmark Hill station, 10 mins walk. Herne Hill station then bus 37 stops near ground. Also buses 40 & 176 from Elephant & Castle, 185 from Victoria, 484 from Camberwell.
Capacity: 3,000 **Cover:** 1,000 **Seats:** 500 **Floodlights:** Yes **Metal Badges:** Yes
Club Shop: Yes, selling programmes, pennants, badges, scarves, baseball caps, replica shirts (by order only). Contact Mishi D Morath at club.
Previous Grounds: Woodwarde Road 1893-95/ College Farm 95-96/ Sunray Avenue 96-1902/ Freeman's Ground, Champion Hill 02-12/ Champion Hill (old ground) 1912-92/ Sandy Lane (groundshare with Tooting & Mitcham F.C.) 91-92.
Colours: Pink & blue stripes/blue/blue **Change colours:** Green & white stripes/green/green.
Club Sponsors: BCA Music Clubs.
Previous Leagues: Camberwell 1894-97/ Southern Suburban 1897-1900 01-07/ Dulwich 00-01/ Spartan 07-08.
Midweek home matchday: Tuesday **Former Name:** Camberwell
Reserve Team's League: Suburban.
Record Attendance: 20,744, Kingstonian v Stockton, FA Amateur Cup Final 1933 *(at refurbished ground: 744 v Hendon, 3/10/94).*
Best FA Cup season: 1st Rd replay 30-31 33-34. 1st Rd on 13 occasions; 25-31 32-38 48-49.
Record Fees - Paid: T Eames, G Allen **Received:** Emeka Nwajiobi (Luton).
Record win: 13-0 v Walton-on-Thames, 37-38.
Record defeat: 1-10 v Hendon, 63-64.
Players progressing to Football League: W Bellamy (Spurs), A Solly (Arsenal), J Moseley & E Tozer (Millwall), G Pearce (Plymouth), Gordon Jago (Charlton 1951), Ron Crisp (Watford 1961), James Ryan (Charlton 1963), Emeka Nwajiobi (Luton 1983), Andy Gray (Crystal Palace 1984), C Richards (Bournemouth), Phil Coleman (Millwall 1986), Andy Perry (Portsmouth 1986).
Clubhouse: Open 7 days a week, 3 bars. Function rooms and meeting room available for hire. Gymnasium, squash courts (071 274 8707).
Club Record Goalscorer: Edgar Kail 427 (1919-33)
Club Record Appearances: Reg Merritt 571 (50-66).
93-94 Captain: Lee Akers.
93-94 P.o.Y.: Gary Hewitt (Supporters'), Dave Coppin (Players').
93-94 Top scorer: Francis Vines 12.
Local Newspapers: South London Press (081 769 4444), S.E. London & Kentish Mercury (081 692 1122).
Honours: FA Amateur Cup 19-20 31-32 33-34 36-37, Isthmian League 19-20 25-26 32-33 48-49 (R-up(7) 21-22 23-24 29-31 33-34 46-47 58-59, Div 1 77-78), London Senior Cup 24-25 38-39 49-50 83-84 (R-up 05-06 07-08 20-21 27-28), Surrey Senior Cup(16) 04-06 08-10 19-20 22-23 24-25 27-28 33-34 36-37 46-47 49-50 57-59 73-75 (R-up(6) 11-12 31-33 37-38 50-51 67-68), London Chal. Cup R-up 91-92, London Charity Cup(12) 10-11(jt) 19-21 22-23 23-24(jt) 25-26 27-29 30-31(jt) 47-48 56-58, Surrey Senior Shield 72-73, Surrey Centen. Shld 77-78, Sth of the Thames Cup(4) 56-60, Southern Comb Cup 73-74, FA Trophy QF 79-80.

PROGRAMME DETAILS:
Pages: 36 **Price:** 70p
Editor: John Lawrence
(071 733 6385)

DULWICH HAMLET's 1993-94 CAMPAIGN

Date	Opponents	Comp.	Res	Gate	Goalscorers
21/08	**HAYES**	DFL	3-2	250	Murphy(2), Morris
23/08	Stevenage Boro	DFL	0-2	602	
28/08	Hendon	DFL	1-2	331	Murphy
31/08	**WOKINGHAM TOWN**	DFL	2-2	202	Murphy, Dickson
04/09	**MARLOW**	DFL	2-3	268	Murphy, Kerrins
11/09	Bromley	FAC1q	1-3	541	
13/09	Wivenhoe Town	DFL	4-3	149	Murphy(2), Powell, Thomas
18/09	**HASTINGS TOWN**	FAT1q	2-1	232	Murphy, Best
21/09	Grays Athletic	DLC1	2-4	142	
25/09	Hitchin Town	DFL	3-2	298	Fisher, Kerrins, Miller(og)
28/09	**SUTTON UNITED**	DFL	0-3	352	
02/10	**GRAY'S ATHLETIC**	DFL	2-3	182	Vines, Heffer(og)
05/10	Yeading	DFL	0-0	139	
12/10	Chesham United	DFL	1-2	515	Kerrins
16/10	Fisher '93	FAT2q	2-0	210	Beste, Hamilton
19/10	**ENFIELD**	DFL	2-2	303	Kerrins, Hamilton
30/10	Basingstoke Town	DFL	1-0	263	Vines
02/11	**CARSHALTON ATH**	DFL	2-1	222	Hewitt, Vines
06/11	Dorking	DFL	1-0	213	Beste
09/11	**MOLESEY**	DFL	1-0	174	Fowler
13/11	**AYLESBURY UNITED**	DFL	2-0	309	Beste, Kerrins
20/11	Harrow Borough	DFL	1-2	231	Vines
27/11	**GLOUCESTER CITY**	FAT3q	2-1	312	Egan, Vines
04/12	Kingstonian	DFL	0-3	589	
11/12	**WIVENHOE TOWN**	DFL	0-1	166	
14/12	**TOOTING & MITCHAM**	CC1	2-1		
27/12	**BROMLEY**	DFL	1-2	489	Leaburn
01/01	Wokingham Town	DFL	1-0	293	Kerrins
06/01	**DORKING**	DFL	1-1	279	Best
11/01	St. Albans City	DFL	3-4	481	Akers, Murphy, Hewitt
15/12	**STEVENAGE BORO**	DFL	0-2	338	
22/01	**KINGSTONIAN**	FAT1	1-2	487	Fisher
25/01	**WALTON & HERSHAM**	CC2	2-0		
29/01	**HENDON**	DFL	0-1	220	
05/02	Marlow	DFL	2-4	445	Collins, Smith
12/02	**CHESHAM UNITED**	DFL	0-2	282	
19/02	Molesey	DFL	0-0	241	
22/02	**KINGSTONIAN**	CC3	1-0		
26/02	**St ALBANS CITY**	DFL	1-2	273	Leaburn
05/03	Carshalton Athletic	DFL	1-0	466	Murphy
12/03	**YEADING**	DFL	1-1	170	Asaba
19/03	Grays Athletic	DFL	0-4	227	
22/03	Grays Athletic	CCqf	2-1	122	Leaburn, Best
26/03	**BASINGSTOKE TOWN**	DFL	1-1	206	Vines
29/03	Hayes	DFL	2-1	188	Akers, Asaba
02/04	Sutton United	DFL	3-0	660	Asaba(2), Vines
09/04	**HITCHIN TOWN**	DFL	0-0	185	
12/04	Hendon	CCsf	1-2	129	Leaburn
16/04	Aylesbury United	DFL	3-1	386	Vines, Asaba, Beste
23/04	**HARROW BORO**	DFL	1-2	235	Eaton
30/04	Enfield	DFL	0-3	681	
03/05	Bromley	DFL	2-3	398	Broderick, Vines
07/05	**KINGSTONIAN**	DFL	1-7	302	Beste

Key: DFL: Diadora League Premier Division, DLC: Diadora League Cup, CC: (Diadora League) Carlsberg Cup, FAC: F.A. Cup, FAT: F.A. Trophy. Number after cup competitions denote rounds (r: replay, qf: Quarter-Final, sf: Semi-Final, f: Final. Numbers in brackets indicate legs, i.e. (1): 1st leg).
Home fixtures are denoted by bold capitals, away matches by lower case. (p): penalty, og: Own goal.

SQUAD MEMBERS *(previous clubs listed in chronological order)*

GOALKEEPERS: John Power *(Limerick Utd, Limerick C., Kingstonian, Brentford, Farnborough, Sutton Utd.)*, **Colin Lewington** *(Erith, Gravesend, Chelmsford, Maidstone, Gravesend, Chatham, Corinthian, Dulwich, Chelmsford).*

DEFENDERS: Wayne Kerrins *(Fulham, Farnborough, Dulwich, Kingstonian)*, **Eddie Burns** *(Wimbledon)*, **Chris Dickson** *(Spurs), Brentford)*, **Dave Coppin** *(Carshalton Ath., Whyteleafe, Molesey)*, **Tony Finnigan** *(Barnet, Hendon)*, **Lee Akers** *(Dulwich, Bromley, Greenwich Boro., Bromley, Dulwich, Malden Vale, Dulwich, Croydon, Erith, Croydon, Tonbridge).*

MIDFIELD: Matt Kember *(Whyteleafe, Dulwich, Croydon)*, **Rodney Prosper** *(Croydon Ath. Horsham, Kingstonian, Tooting)*, **Matt Norris** *(Dulwich, Cray W., Croydon)*, **Peter Evans** *(Charlton, Croydon, Sutton Utd.)*, **Kevin Fowler** *(Arsenal (T.), Hendon, Dulwich, Molesey)*, **Kelvin Thomas** *(Bromley)*, **Gary Hewitt** *(Gateway, Erith, Dulwich, Hendon, Gravesend, Bromley, Margate, Bromley, Erith).*

FORWARDS: Frank Murphy *(Corby, Desborough, Kettering, Nuneaton Boro. Kettering, Barnet, Cray W., Kettering, Cray W.)*, **Jamie Kempster** *(Croydon)*, **Francis Vines** *(Thames Poly, Molesey, Kingstonian)*, **Lionel Best** *(Fisher Ath., Elms)*, **Glen Leaburn** *(Catford W., Croydon, Dorking, Croydon)*, **Trevor Collins** *(Ipswich, Colchester, Bury T., Stowmarket, Bury T. Wivenhoe)*, **Jamie Martin** *(Windsor)*, **Carl Asaba** *(Kingstonian).*

Formed: 1893

ENFIELD

The E's

The Enfield team that achieved an excellent 1-1 draw at Woking in the first-leg of the FA Challenge Trophy semi-finals. Back Row (L/R): Martin St Hilaire, Darren Collins, Andy Pape, Paul Turner, Greg Heald, Garry Britnell, Graham Roberts (Player-Manager, no longer with club). Front: Mark Pye, John Bailey, John Ridout, Martin Chester, Mark Hobson, Pat Ryan. *Photo - Dennis Nicholson.*

Chairman: A Lazarou **President:** T F Unwin.
Secretary: Alan Diment, 30 Apple Grove, Enfield, Middx EN1 3DD (081 363 6317).
Manager: George Borg **Coach:** Paul Siani/ Andy Pape.
Press Officer: Lee Harding **Physio:** Phil Seddon **Marketing Mgr:** Jonathon Moreland.
General Manager: Dee Curran. **Newsline:** 0891 122920.
Ground: The Stadium, Southbury Road, Enfield EN1 1YQ (081 292 0665).
Directions: At junction of A10 & A110. 800 yards from Southbury Road station. Buses from town centre.
Capacity: 8,500 **Cover:** 3,500 **Seats:** 820 **Shop:** Yes
Colours: White/blue **Change colours:** Blue (white & red trim)
Sponsors: Cable London Plc. **Record Gate:** 10,000 (10/10/62) v Spurs, floodlight opener.
Previous Leagues: Tottenham & Dist 1894-95/Nth Middx 96-1903/ London 03-13 20-21/Middx 08-12 19-20/ Athenian 12-14 21-39 45-63/Herts & Middx Comb 39-42/ Isthmian 63-81/ GMV Conference 81-90.
Previous Name: Enfield Spartans 1893-1900.
Metal Badges: £2 - special club centenary badge.
Previous Grounds: Baileys Field 1893-96/ Tuckers Field 96-1900/ Cherry Orchard Lane 1900-36.
Midweek matchday: Tuesday **Reserve Team's League:** Capital.
Best FA Cup season: 4th Rd replay 80-81 (lost 0-3 to Barnsley at Spurs (Att 35,244) after 1-1 draw).
League clubs beaten in F.A. Cup: Wimbledon, Northampton 77-78, Hereford, Port Vale 80-81, Wimbledon 81-82, Exeter 84-85, Orient 88-89, Aldershot 91-92.
Record Fees - Paid: For Gary Abbott (Barnet) **Received:** For Paul Furlong (Coventry City)
Players progressing to Football League: John Hollowbread & Peter Baker (Spurs 1952), Terry McQuade (Millwall 1961), Roger Day (Watford 1961), Jeff Harris (Orient 1964), Peter Feely (Chelsea 1970), Carl Richards (B'mouth 1980), Paul Furlong (Coventry 1991), Andy Pape (Barnet (1991).
Clubhouse: Starlight Suite. Bar open every lunch & evening. Snacks. Starlight nightclub, cabaret, dinner & dance.
Club Record Scorer: Tommy Lawrence **Club Record Appearances:** Steve King 617
93-94 Captain: Paul Turner. **93-94 P.o.Y.:** Greg Heald. **93-94 Top scorer:** Martin St Hilaire.
Local Press: Enfield Gazette (081 367 2345), Enfield Advertiser, Enfield Independent, Enfield Town Express.
Hons: FA Trophy 81-82 87-88, FA Amtr Cup R-up 66-67 69-70 (R-up 63-64 71-72), Alliance Premier League 82-83 85-86 (R-up 81-82, Lg Cup R-up 81-82), Isthmian Lg(7) 67-70 75-78 79-80 (R-up(7) 64-65 71-72 74-75 80-81 90-92 93-94, Lg Cup(2) 78-80 (R-up 91-92 93-94)), Athenian Lg(2) 61-63 (R-up 34-35), London Lg Div 1 11-12 (R-up 04-05 06-07, Middx Snr Cup(13) 13-14 46-47 61-62 65-66 68-71 77-81 88-89 90-91 (R-up(12) 10-11 20-21 47-48 51-52 57-60 62-63 66-67 72-73 75-76 84-85), London Snr Cup(6) 34-35 60-61 66-67 71-73 75-76 (R-up 63-64 67-68 70-71), Middx Lg (West) 09-10 (R-up 10-11), European Amtr Cup Winners Cup 69-70.

SQUAD MEMBERS *(previous clubs listed in chronological order)*

GOALKEEPERS: Gary McCann *(Fulham, Sutton)*, **Andy Pape** *(QPR, Ikast(Den), Crystal P., Charlton, Feltham, Harrow, Enfield, Barnet)*

DEFENDERS: Greg Heald *(Watford House Wdrs)*, **Lee Francis** *(Arsenal, Chesterfield)*, **Al-James Hannigan** *(Arsenal, Barnet, Harwich, Harlow, Marlow)*, **Micky Engwell** *(Southend, Chelmsford, Barking, Chelmsford, Chesham, Harrow)*, **Pat Jackman** *(Kingsbury, Leytonstone-I., B. Stortford, Dag. & Red., St Albans, Harrow, Chesham)*,.

MIDFIELD: Paul Hobson *(Burnley, Newcastle KB(Aust), St Albans)*, **Gary Britnell** *(Canvey I., Chelmsford, Dartford)*, **Mark Dalli** *(Watford, Boreham Wd)*, **Paul Turner** *(Arsenal, Camb., Utd, Farnborough)*, **Martin Chester** *(C. Palace, Crawley, Sutton, Dorking)*, **Mark Pye** *(West Ham, Nth Greenford, Harrow)*, **Pat Ryan** *(Newcastle Utd, Wrexham, B. Stortford, Takeley, B. Stortford, Chesham, Harrow)*

(squad continued on page 429)

PROGRAMME DETAILS:
Pages: 24 **Price:** £1
Editor: Lee Harding

ENFIELD's 1993-94 CAMPAIGN

Date	Opponents	Comp.	Res	Gate	Goalscorers
21/08	Carshalton Athletic	DFL	3-0	614	Collins(2), Hobson
24/08	**DORKING**	DFL	6-0	678	Hobson(3), St Hilaire, Turner, Collins
28/08	**HARROW BOROUGH**	DFL	2-0	810	Roberts, Bailey
31/08	Sutton United	DFL	1-1	889	Roberts
04/09	Grays Athletic	DFL	4-1	548	Sheringham(og), Bailey, Roberts, Hobson
11/09	**WELLING UNITED**	FAC1q	4-1	938	St Hilaire(2), Collins(2)
14/09	**BASINGSTOKE T.**	DFL	0-1	690	
18/09	Aylesbury United	DFL	0-1	782	
22/09	Cove	DLC1	5-1	225	Adams(2), Flemming(2), Hobson
25/09	**HEMEL HEMPSTEAD**	FAC2q	1-0	623	Flemming
28/09	**HITCHIN TOWN**	DFL	0-3	601	
02/10	**KINGSTONIAN**	DFL	3-0	702	Hobson, Green, Bailey
05/10	Bromley	DFL	2-1	268	Hobson, Bailey
09/10	Hornchurch	FAC3q	4-1	648	Collins, Ryan, Hobson, Greene
09/10	Marlow	DFL	1-2	454	Hannigan
19/10	Dulwich Hamlet	DFL	2-2	303	Greene, Collins
23/10	Wivenhoe Town	FAC4q	2-1	539	Greene, Collins
30/10	**WOKINGHAM TOWN**	DFL	1-0	651	Flemming
01/11	Wivenhoe Town	DFL	2-1	295	Hobson, Collins
06/11	**YEADING**	DFL	0-0	577	
13/11	**CARDIFF CITY**	FAC1	0-0	2,374	
16/11	Dorking	DLC2	4-1	187	Bailey, Ryan, Hobson, Greene
20/11	**CHESHAM UNITED**	DFL	0-1	886	
27/11	**CORBY TOWN**	FAT3q	2-1	414	St Hilaire(2)
30/11	Cardiff City	FAC1r	0-1	3,233	
04/12	**HENDON**	DFL	1-0	499	Francis
11/12	Basingstoke Town	DFL	2-1	349	Britnell, Cherry
14/12	Bognor Regis Town	DLC3	3-2	177	Collins(2), Whale
18/12	**STEVENAGE BORO.**	DFL	3-0	943	Collins(2), Bailey
21/12	**HAYES**	DFL	2-0	522	Collins(2)
27/12	St Albans City	DFL	1-2	1,538	Hobson
01/01	**SUTTON UNITED**	DFL	1-0	1,037	Collins
15/01	Dorking	DFL	3-1	391	Staples, Whale, Collins
18/01	**BRIMSDOWN ROVERS**	MSC1	1-0	233	Whale
22/01	**PURFLEET**	FAT1	2-0	703	St Hilaire, Collins
25/01	**SAFFRON WALDEN**	DLCqf	3-1	264	Pye, Whale, Turner
29/01	Harrow Borough	DFL	1-1	523	Britnell
01/02	**HENDON**	CC2	0-1	242	
05/02	**GRAYS ATHLETIC**	DFL	1-0	689	Bailey
08/02	Edgware Town	MSC2	4-5	200	Whale(2), Britnell, own-goal
12/02	Worthing	FAT2	1-1	838	Hobson
19/02	**AYLESBURY UTD**	DFL	4-0	683	Collins(2), Whale, Britnell
21/02	**WORTHING**	FAT2r	2-0	583	Whale, St Hilaire
26/02	Hayes	DFL	1-0	464	Whale
01/03	**WIVENHOE TOWN**	DFL	8-0	485	Collins(2), Cherry(2), Hobson(2), Bailey, Britnell
05/02	Bishop Auckland	FAT3	2-2	830	Hobson, St Hilaire
08/03	**BISHOP AUCKLAND**	FAT3r	2-1	890	Turner, Collins
12/03	**BROMLEY**	DFL	2-0	687	St Hilaire, Pye
15/03	Marlow	DLCsf(1)	1-1	283	St Hilaire
19/03	Kingstonian	DFL	2-1	663	Cherry, Britnell
22/03	Yeading	DFL	2-1	380	Hobson, Collins
26/03	Sutton United	FATqf	1-1	1,813	Anderson(og)
29/03	**SUTTON UNITED**	FATqfr	1-0	1,255	Roberts
04/04	**St ALBANS C.**	DFL	1-1	1,033	Hobson
07/04	**MARLOW**	DLCsf(2)	2-1	500	Britnell, Bailey
09/04	Stevenage Borough	DFL	1-0	1,905	St Hilaire
12/04	Hitchin Town	DFL	3-2	597	Collins(2), Hobson
16/04	Woking	FATsf(1)	1-1	3,841	Tucker(og)
19/04	Wokingham Town	DFL	1-1	319	Turner
23/04	**WOKING**	FATsf(2)	0-0	3,319	
26/04	WOKING	FATsfr	0-3	2,674	*(played at Wycombe Wanderers FC)*
28/04	Chesham United	DFL	3-2	888	Collins, Hobson, Pye
30/04	**DULWICH HAMLET**	DFL	3-0	681	Britnell, Roberts, Collins
02/05	CHERTSEY TOWN	DLCf	0-3		*(played at Hayes FC)*
04/05	**MARLOW**	DFL	0-0	460	
06/05	**CARSHALTON ATH.**	DFL	1-1	485	Collins
07/05	Hendon	DFL	2-0	385	Cherry(2)
09/05	Molesey	DFL	1-0	325	Cherry
11/05	**MOLESEY**	DFL	3-0	501	Bailey(2), Pye

Key: As for Hendon FC (page 437)

(squad continued from page 428):
FORWARDS: Darren Collins *(Petersfield, Northampton, Aylesbury)*, **Martin St Hilaire** *(Aveley, Chesham, Harlow, Harrow)*, **Robert Boyce** *(Youth Team)*, **Leroy Whale** *(Southampton, Rotherham, Basingstoke, Bashley)*, **Jon Bailey** *(Croydon, Dagenham)*, **David Fleming** *(Leyton)*, **John Ridout** *(Leyton Orient, Parmitarians, Harrow)*, **Richard Cherry** *(Gillingham, Colchester, Woodford, Barking, Grays, Redbridge F., Kingstonian, Hendon)*, **Mark Telfer** *(Enfield, Saffron Walden, Hertford)*.

Formed: 1890

GRAYS ATHLETIC

The Blues

Grays Athletic FC. Back Row (L/R): Billy Goldstone, Wayne Mitchell, Jim Sheringham, Winston Whittingham, Jason Walker, Paul Gothard, Danny Tripp, Steve Ward, R Forbes. Front: Phil Sammons, S Heffer, Dave Cusack, Ian Brown, S Baxter, Ian Durant, Andy Alexander.

Chairman: Frank Harris **Twin Managers:** Fred & Jeff Saxton
Secretary: Jeff Saxton, 216 Thundersley Park Road, South Benfleet, Essex SS7 1HP (0268 756964).
Asst Manager: Vince Craven **Physio:** Ted Cribb/Sandy Lawrence **Coach:** P Carey
Commercial Mgr: Bill Cherry **Press Officer:** Gordon Norman (04024 51733)
Ground: Recreation Ground, Bridge Road, Grays RM17 6BZ (0375 391649).
Directions: Seven minutes walk from Grays station - turn right round one way system, right into Clarence Road, and at end into Bridge Road. Bus No. 370. By road - A13 towards Southend from London, take Grays exit and follow signs to town centre, keep left on one-way system, continue up hill for about half a mile, turn right into Bridge Road, ground half mile on right.
Capacity: 4,500 **Cover:** 1,200 **Seats:** 300 **Floodlights:** Yes **Metal Badges:** Yes
Club Shop: Yes, selling official club history 'The First Hundred Years' (priced £6.95), club sweaters, T-shirts, replica shirts, mugs, scarves, ties, pennants, pens, key fobs, lapel badges, bookmarks, stickers, diaries. Contact Bill Grove (0875 391649).
Colours: Royal & white **Change colours:** All yellow.
Sponsors: Cory Environmental, London Advertising Centre Ltd, Harris Commercials, McDonalds.
Previous Leagues: Athenian 12-14 58-83/ London 14-24 26-39/ Kent 24-26/ Corinthian 45-58.
Midweek home matchday: Tuesday **Reserve Team's League:** Essex & Herts Border Comb.
Record Attendance: 9,500 v Chelmsford City, FA Cup Fourth Qualifying Round 1959.
Best FA Cup season: 1st Rd 51-52 88-89.
Record Fees - Paid: For Ian Durant (Canvey Island)
Rec'd: Undisclosed for Tony Witter (C. Palace) and Dwight Marshall (Plymouth 1991).
Players progressing to Football League: John Jordan (Spurs 1947), Ray Kemp (Reading 1949), Barry Silkman & Tony Banfield (Orient), Gary O'Reilly (Spurs), Wayne Entwhistle (Bury 1983), Michael Welch (Wimbledon 1984), Tony Witter (C Palace 1990), Dwight Marshall (Plymouth 1991).
Clubhouse: Bar, pool, darts, bar snacks available. Indoor sports hall, en-tout-cas surface 70' x 120' (0375 377753). Bar open every day.
Steward: Bill & Joe Diggery.
Club Record Goalscorer: Harry Brand 269 (1944-52)
Club Record Appearances: Phil Sammons, 563.
93-94 Captain: Jim Sheringham.
93-94 P.o.Y.: Steve Ward.
93-94 Top scorer: Winston Whittingham.
Local Newspapers: Thurrock Gazette (0375 372293)
Local Radio: BBC Essex, Radio Essex.
Hons: Isthmian Div 1 R-up 87-88 (Div 2 Sth 84-85, Lg Cup 91-92), Athenian Lg R-up 82-83 (Reserve Section R-up 58-59 (Cup R-up 59-60)), Corinthian Lg 45-46 (R-up 51-52 54-55 56-57, Lg Cup(2) 45-47, Mem. Shield(4) 45-47 77-78 79-80), L'don Lg 21-22 26-27 29-30 (R-up(4) 20-21 27-29 30-31, Lg Cup 36-37), Essex Snr Cup 14-15 20-21 22-23 44-45 56-57 87-88 93-94 (R-up(9) 19-20 23-24 25-26 52-55 57-58 65-66 88-89), East Anglian Cup 44-45 (R-up 43-44 54-55), Essex Thameside Tphy(6) 47-48 78-79 80-81 87-89 90-91 (R-up(7) 45-46 58-59 61-62 68-69 84-86 93-94), Essex Elizabeth Trophy 76-77 (R-up 65-66), Claridge Tphy 87-88 88-89, Mithras Cup 79-80, Essex Int Cup(3) 56-57 58-60 (Junior Cup 19-20 (R-up 58-59)), Essex & Herts Border Comb. East 87-88 (Ancillary Cup 78-79, Comb Cup 82-83), Fred Budden Tphy 86-87, Hornchurch Charity Cup 78-79 86-87, Neale Tphy 50-51, Ford Rate Tphy 83-84 85-86 87-88 (R-up 84-85 86-87).

PROGRAMME DETAILS:
Pages: 48 **Price:** 60p
Editor: Jeremy Mason
(0375 376428)

GRAYS ATHLETIC's 1993-94 CAMPAIGN

Date	Opponents	Comp.	Res	Gate	Goalscorers
21/08	**HENDON**	DFL	0-3	354	
25/08	Molesey	DFL	2-0	226	Whittingham(2)
28/08	Chesham United	DFL	1-2	764	Whittingham
31/08	**HAYES**	DFL	0-1	210	
04/09	**ENFIELD**	DFL	1-4	548	Kimble
11/09	**YEADING**	FAC1q	0-2	183	
18/09	Kingstonian	DFL	0-3	538	
21/09	**DULWICH HAMLET**	DLC1	4-2	142	Heffer, Walker(2), Mitchell
25/09	**MARLOW**	DFL	4-7	167	Forbes, Walker, Mitchell, Whittingham
27/09	Stevenage Borough	DFL	0-1	567	
02/10	Dulwich Hamlet	DFL	3-2	182	Goldstone(2), Mitchell
05/10	**BASINGSTOKE TOWN**	DFL	2-0	140	Mitchell, Walker
18/10	Dagenham & Redbridge	ESC2	3-1	280	Goldstone, Sammons, Sheringham
23/10	**ST ALBANS CITY**	DFL	0-1	310	
26/10	Romford	ETT1	3-1	228	Brown, Sammons, Mitchell
30/10	Sutton United	DFL	0-1	599	
06/11	Carshalton Athletic	DFL	0-3	422	
09/11	Hendon	DFL	1-2	195	Durant
13/11	**HITCHIN TOWN**	DFL	0-2	222	
16/11	Aylesbury United	DLC2	4-1	295	Mendy, Mitchell, Forbes, Carrez
20/11	Wokingham Town	DFL	0-3	201	
04/12	Bromley	DFL	2-0	255	Walker, Whittingham
11/12	**KINGSTONIAN**	DFL	0-3	249	
14/12	Chesham United	DLC3	2-3	269	Ward, Whittingham
18/12	Dorking	DFL	3-3	164	Durant(2), Whittingham
27/12	**WIVENHOE TOWN**	DFL	1-0	229	Walker
01/01	Hayes	DFL	3-1	294	Durant, Walker, Mitchell
08/01	**CARSHALTON ATH.**	DFL	1-1	292	Durant
15/01	**MOLESEY**	DFL	1-2	199	Mitchell
18/01	**HITCHIN TOWN**	CC2	2-1	110	Whittingham, Obebo
22/01	Farnborough Town	FAT1	1-1	521	Durant
25/01	**FARNBOROUGH T.**	FAT1r	2-0	277	Mitchell(2)
29/01	**CHESHAM UNITED**	DFL	0-2	314	
02/02	Harlow Town	ESCqf	3-1	58	Durant, Whittingham(2)
05/02	Enfield	DFL	0-1	689	
12/02	**BROMSGROVE R.**	FAT2	1-2	494	Goldstone
19/02	Marlow	DFL	1-3	224	Durant
26/02	**YEADING**	DFL	2-1	220	Whittingham, Durant
01/03	**LEYTON**	ESCsf	2-1	146	Mitchell, Whittingham
05/02	Harrow Borough	DFL	1-1	240	Mitchell
09/03	Harrow Borough	CC3	4-1	68	Wallace(2), Tripp, Whittingham
12/03	Basingstoke Town	DFL	0-0	217	
17/03	Hornchurch	ETTqf	1-0		Hamberger
19/03	**DULWICH HAMLET**	DFL	4-0	227	Whittingham(3), Wallace
22/03	**DULWICH HAMLET**	CCqf	1-2	122	Sheringham
26/03	**WOKINGHAM TOWN**	DFL	0-3	256	
29/03	**STEVENAGE BORO'**	DFL	1-2	251	Whittingham
02/04	St Albans City	DFL	3-5	347	Whittingham(2), Wallace
04/04	Wivenhoe Town	DFL	4-0	154	Walker, Cusack, Deadman, Alexander
09/04	**DORKING**	DFL	4-0	198	Wallace(3), Whittingham
12/04	Yeading	DFL	1-1	103	Goldstone
14/04	Billericay Town	ETTsf	2-1	180	Kimble, own goal
16/04	Hitchin Town	DFL	3-2	373	Wallace, Mitchell, Whittingham
19/04	**HARROW BOROUGH**	DFL	0-1	205	
25/04	**BILLERICAY TOWN**	ESCf	1-0		Whittingham *(at Dagenham & Redbridge FC)*
30/04	Aylesbury United	DFL	1-0	265	Durant
03/05	**AYLESBURY UTD**	DFL	2-0	155	Durant, Forbes
05/05	**SUTTON UNITED**	DFL	1-0	214	Sheringham
07/05	**BROMLEY**	DFL	3-2	235	Wallace(2), Sheringham
13/05	Canvey Island	ETTf	2-2		Durant, Wallace *(AET, lost 3-4 on penalties)*

Key: DFL: Diadora League Premier Division, DLC: Diadora League Cup, CC: Carlsberg Cup, FAC: F.A. Cup, FAT: F.A. Trophy, ESC: Essex Senior Cup, ETT: Essex Thameside Trophy. Numbers after cup competitions denote rounds (r: replay, qf: Quarter-Final, sf: Semi-Final, f: Final. Numbers in brackets indicate legs, i.e. (1): 1st leg). Home fixtures are denoted by bold capitals, away matches by lower case. (p): penalty, og: Own goal.

SQUAD MEMBERS *(previous clubs listed in chronological order)*

GOALKEEPERS: Paul Gothard *(Chelmsford City, Billericay Town)*, **Barrie Delf** *(Aston Villa, Southend Utd, Dartford)*, **Nathan Carey** *(Hertford)*

DEFENDERS: Billy Goldstone *(Barking, Woodford Town, East Ham Utd, Barking, Chelmsford City, Chesham Utd)*, **Andy Alexander** *(Brimsdown Rovers)*, **Ian Brown** *(Ards, Grays Athletic, Dartford)*, **Steve Ward** *(local football)*, **John Deadman** *(youth team)*, **Danny Tripp** *(Brentford, Dagenham & Redbridge)*, **Scott Baxter** *(Southend)*

MIDFIELD: Rodney Forbes *(Scunthorpe, Bridlington, SV Holzwickede(Germany))*, **Ian Durant** *(Canvey Island, Grays Athletic, Harlow Town)*, **John Deadman** *(yth team)*, **Wesley Mendy** *(Haringey, Brimsdown)*, **Gary Kimble** *(Charlton, Cambridge Utd, Doncaster, St Albans, Gillingham, Peterbrough, Dagenham & Redbridge, Hendon, Purfleet)*, **Phil Sammons** *(Dagenham, Tilbury, Walthamstow Avenue, Hornchurch)*, **Jason Walker** *(Wingate & Finchley)*, **Jimmy Sheringham** *(Dagenham, Billericay Town, Barking, Walthamstow Avenue, Barking, Grays Athletic, Dartford)*.

FORWARDS: Winston Whittingham *(Barkingside)*, **Danny Wallace** *(Hornchurch, Rainham Town, East Thurrock Utd)*, **Wayne Mitchell** *(Woodford Town, Hornchurch, Saffron Walden Town)*.

1933 # HARROW BOROUGH The Boro

The main stand at Harrow Borough's Earlsmead ground. *Photo - Martin Baker.*

Chairman: Martin Murphy **Vice Chairman:** Jim Ripley **President:** Jim Rogers
Secretary/Press Off.: Peter Rogers, 21 Ludlow Close, South Harrow, Middx HA2 8SR (081 248 8003).
Manager: Harry Manoe **Asst Manager:** Dave Kennedy **Physio:** Joe Parish.
Coach: Cliff Radley **Commercial Manager:** c/o the club.
Ground: Earlsmead, Carlyon Avenue, South Harrow, Middx HA2 8SS (081 422 5989/5221).
Directions: Underground to Northolt (Central Line) then 140 or 282 bus, or to South Harrow (Piccadilly Line) then 114 or H10. By road leave A40 at Target PH towards Northolt station (A312 north), left at lights, right at next island, ground 5th turning on right.
Capacity: 3,070 **Cover:** 1,000 **Seats:** 200 **Floodlights:** Yes **Metal Badges:** Yes.
Club Shop: Yes. Progs, scarves, badges, mugs, T-shirts, replica kits. Contact Bill Porter C/O The Club.
Colours: Red & white **Change colours:** Yellow & blue **Sponsors:** TBA.
Previous Leagues: Harrow & Dist 33-34/ Spartan 34-58/ Delphian 58-63/ Athenian 63-75.
Previous Ground: Northolt Road 33-34. **Previous Names:** Roxonian 1933-38/ Harrow Town 38-66.
Midweek home matchday: Wednesday **Best FA Cup season:** 2nd Rd 83-84 (1-3 at home to Newport Co).
Record Attendance: 3,000 v Wealdstone, F.A. Cup 1st Qualifying Round 1946.
Record Fees - Paid: To Dagenham for George Duck & Steve Jones
Received: £15,000 for Chris Hutchings (Chelsea)
Record win: 13-0 v Handley Page (A), Middlesex Snr Lg 18/10/41.
Rec. loss: 0-8 5 times: Wood Green T. (A) Middx Lge 14/9/40, Met Police (A) Spartan Lg 2/2/52, Briggs Spts (A) Spartan Lg 31/10/53, Hertford T. (A) Spartan Lge 24/4/53, Hendon (A) Middx Snr Cup 15/3/65.
Players progressing to Football League: Denis Russell (Arsenal 1946), Malcolm Lucas (Leyton Orient & Wales), Ron Shaw (Torquay 1947), Terry Eden (Raith Rovers 1948), Tom Carpenter (Watford 1950), Mike Bottoms (QPR 1960), Chris Hutchings (Chelsea 1980), Robert Holland (Crewe 1985), John Kerr (Portsmouth 1987), David Howell, Andy Pape & Eddie Stein (Barnet), David Byrne (Gillingham), Robert Rosario (Norwich), David Kemp (Crystal Palace), Mick Doherty (Reading), Dave Bassett (Wimbledon), Gary Borthwick (Bournemouth), Benny Laryea (Torquay).
Clubhouse: Open every day with normal licensing hours. Four bars, games room, varied entertainment venue for major sporting and social events. Hot and cold food available, buffets by prior request.
Club Record Scorer: Dave Pearce, 153
Club Record Appearances: Steve Emmanuel 522 (1st team only), Les Cunell 582, Colin Payne 557.
93-94 Captain: Jason Shaw. **93-94 P.o.Y.:** Neil Fraser.
93-94 Top scorer: Graham Westley 27.
Local Newspapers: Harrow Observer (081 427 4404).
Honours: Isthmian Lg 83-84 (Div 1 R-up 78-79), Athenian Lg Div 2 R-up 63-64, Spartan Lg R-up 57-58, Spartan Lg R-up 57-58 (Div 2 West 38-39 (R-up 37-38)), Middx Senior Cup 82-83 92-93, Harrow & Dist. Lg Div 1 R-up 33-34, Middx Charity Cup 79-80 92-93 (R-up 78-79), F.A. Trophy SF 82-83, F.A. Amateur Cup 2nd Rd 63-64.

SQUAD MEMBERS *(previous clubs listed in chronological order)*

GOALKEEPERS: David Hook *(Feltham, Hampton).*

DEFENDERS: David Bensted *(Brimsdown, Redbridge, Dartford),* **Tony Knight** *(Arsenal, Brisbane(Austr), Wealdstone, Harrow, Slough),* **Jason Court** *(St Albans, Chalfont, Boreham W., Hayes, Leverstock G., Hayes),* **Bob Booker** *(Bedmond, Brentford, Sheff. Utd, Brentford),* **Graham Pearce** *(Hillingdon, Barnet, Brighton, Gillingham, Brentford, Maidstone, Enfield, Kingstonian, Basingstoke).*

MIDFIELD: Andy Prutton *(Wormley, Cheshunt, Dartford),* **Jason Shaw** *(West Ham, Redbridge, Dartford),* **John Hurlock** *(Bedworth, Nuneaton, Altrincham, Droylsden),* **Daren Brown** *(Northwood, Hayes),* **Terry Benning** *(Watford, Brentford, Northwood, Tring T., St Albans, Hendon, Chesham, St Albans, Hayes).*

FORWARDS: Christian Metcalfe *(Chelsea),* **Lee Endersby** *(Brimsdown, Wembley),* **Neil Fraser** *(Harrow, Hayes),* **Graham Westley** *(QPR, Gillingham, Barnet, Wycombe, Kingstonian, Harlow, Enfield, Aylesbury).*

PROGRAMME DETAILS:
Pages: 28 **Price:** £1
Editor: Jim Rogers
(081 248 8003)

HARROW BOROUGH's 1993-94 CAMPAIGN

Date	Opponents	Comp.	Res	Gate	Goalscorers
04/08	**TOTTENHAM xi**	Fr.	3-4	540	Forrester, Hurlock, own-goal
07/08	**QUEENS PK RGRS xi**	Fr.	2-5	354	Fraser, Bensted
10/08	**LUTON TOWN xi**	Fr.	0-3	192	
14/08	Merthyr Tydfil	MMC	0-1		
17/08	**SOUTHALL**	Fr.	1-0		Fraser
21/08	**WOKINGHAM TOWN**	DFL	1-1	241	Fraser
24/08	Hayes	DFL	1-1	306	Westley
28/08	Enfield	DFL	0-2	810	
01/09	**CHESHAM UNITED**	DFL	0-4	549	
04/09	**KINGSTONIAN**	DFL	2-4	387	Westley(2)
11/09	**WEALDSTONE**	FAC1q	3-1	555	Shaw, own-goal, Westley
18/09	Uxbridge	FAT1q	2-1	225	Metcalfe, Pearce
25/09	**VIKING SPORTS**	FAC2q	6-0	185	Westley(2), Pearce, Bensted, Prutton, Hurlock
02/10	Carshalton Athletic	DFL	1-2	495	Bensted
06/10	**MOLESEY**	DFL	1-1	181	Westley
09/10	Chertsey Town	FAC3q	3-1	556	Westley, Court, Fraser
12/10	*Bromley*	*DFL*	*2-2*	*202*	*Westley, Emanuel (match abandoned)*
16/10	**BOREHAM WOOD**	FAT2q	0-0	233	
19/10	Boreham Wood	FAT2qr	2-1	122	Fraser, Prutton
23/10	VS Rugby	FAC4q	2-2	826	Fraser, Westley
27/10	**V.S. RUGBY**	FAC4qr	1-2	640	Westley
30/10	**AYLESBURY UTD**	DFL	0-1	269	
01/11	Ruislip Manor	DLC1	3-1		Emmanuel, Westley, Fraser
06/11	**BASINGSTOKE TOWN**	DFL	4-0	226	Emmanuel(2), Court, Fraser
10/11	**WIVENHOE TOWN**	DFL	3-0	219	Court, Westley(2)
13/11	Dorking	DFL	3-4	186	Westley(2), Fraser
16/11	Thame United	DLC2	4-4		Fraser(2), Prutton, Bensted
20/11	**DULWICH HAMLET**	DFL	2-1	233	Fraser(2)
23/11	Hendon	DFL	2-0	225	Emmanuel, Prutton
27/11	Wealdstone	FAT3q	2-2	364	Westley, Knight
01/12	**WEALDSTONE**	FAT3qr	3-0	557	Westley, Ripley(2)
04/12	**STEVENAGE BORO.**	DFL	1-0	450	Ripley
11/12	Chesham United	DFL	0-3	655	
15/12	**THAME UNITED**	DLC2r	3-3	143	Prutton(2), Metcalfe *(won 5-4 on pens)*
18/12	**St ALBANS CITY**	DFL	0-0	387	
21/12	Kingstonian	DLC3	1-6		Ripley
27/12	Yeading	DFL	0-2	353	
01/01	**HENDON**	DFL	2-1	470	Ripley(2)
08/01	Basingstoke Town	DFL	1-1	281	Emmaunuel
15/01	**HAYES**	DFL	3-3	391	Fraser(2), Metcalfe
19/01	**HENDON**	MSC1	0-1	161	*(match later declared null and void)*
22/01	**WORCESTER CITY**	FAT1	3-3	489	Fraser, Westley(2)
24/01	Worcester City	FAT1r	3-5	1,021	Bensted, Westley, Booker
29/01	**ENFIELD**	DFL	1-1	528	Prutton
01/02	**AYLESBURY UTD**	CC2	2-1	152	Hurlock, Westley
05/02	Kingstoniam	DFL	0-7	605	
09/02	**HENDON**	MSC1r	1-0	165	Prutton
12/02	**BROMLEY**	DFL	0-0	283	
19/02	Wivenhoe Town	DFL	3-2	151	Ripley, Shaw(2)
26/02	Hitchin Town	DFL	1-0	723	Shaw
01/03	Wokingham Town	DFL	1-0	195	Shaw
03/03	**STAINES TOWN**	MSCqf	2-3	146	Westley, Fraser
05/02	**GRAYS ATHLETIC**	DFL	1-1	240	Fraser
09/03	**GRAYS ATHLETIC**	CC3	1-4	68	Fraser
12/03	Molesey	DFL	0-0	190	
16/03	**HITCHIN TOWN**	DFL	1-1	170	Metcalfe
19/03	**CARSHALTON ATH.**	DFL	3-0	247	Hurlock, Fraser(2)
22/03	Sutton United	DFL	1-3	407	Fraser
26/03	Aylesbury United	DFL	1-0	555	Westley
02/04	**DORKING**	DFL	3-2	215	Knight, Endersby(2)
04/04	**YEADING**	DFL	1-0	302	Westley
06/04	**BRENTFORD**	MCC3	1-1	242	Westley *(won 7-6 on penalties)*
09/04	St Albans City	DFL	1-3	339	Westley
12/04	Bromley	DFL	3-0	148	Hurlock, Westley, Endersby
16/04	Marlow	DFL	1-0	310	Pearce
19/04	Grays Athletic	DFL	1-0	205	Court
21/04	Wembley	MCCqf	0-2		
23/04	Dulwich Hamlet	DFL	2-1	235	Bensted, Fraser
30/04	**MARLOW**	DFL	2-0	249	Prutton, Metcalfe
02/05	**SUTTON UNITED**	DFL	0-1	413	
07/05	Stevenage Borough	DFL	0-3	3,005	

Key: DFL: Diadora League Premier Division, DLC: Diadora League Cup, CC: Carsberg Cup, FAC: F.A. Cup, FAT: F.A. Trophy, MSC: Middlesex Senior Cup, MCC: Middlesex Senior Charity Cup, MMC: Merthyr Middlesex Charity Shield, Fr.: Friendly. Numbers after cup competitions denote rounds (r: replay, qf: Quarter-Final, sf: Semi-Final, f: Final. Numbers in brackets indicate legs, i.e. (1): 1st leg).
Home fixtures are denoted by bold capitals, away matches by lower case. (p): penalty, og: Own goal.

Formed: 1909

HAYES

The Missioners

The covered terracing at Church Road.

Chairman: Derek Goodall **Vice Chairman:** Vacant **President:** Les Lovering
Secretary: John Price, 18 Ickenham Court, West Ruislip, Middx HA4 7DJ (0895 631933).
Manager: Terry Brown **Asst Mgr:** Willy Wordsworth **Coach:** TBA
Press Officer: Trevor Griffith (0895 638013). **Physio:** Carl Ballard.
Commercial Manager: TBA **Sponsors:** McEwans Lager.
Ground: Townfield House, Church Road, Hayes, Middx UB3 2LE (081 573 4598).
Directions: M4 jct 3 onto Hayes bypass (The Parkway), A4020 to Hayes, 2nd major left turn (Church Rd), ground half mile on right. 1 mile from Hayes & Harlington (BR) - take bus H98 to Royal Oak pub. From Uxbridge tube station (Metropolitan line) take bus 207 to Adam & Eve pub opposite Church Rd.
Capacity: 9,500 **Cover:** 1,350 **Seats:** 450 **Floodlights:** Yes **Metal Badges:** Yes
Club Shop: Yes. Wide range of programmes (League and non-League). Replica kits, souvenirs, books and videos. Contact Lee Hermitage c/o Hayes F.C.
Cols: Red & white stripes/black/black **Change colours:** All blue
Prev. Lges: Local Lges 09-14/ Gt Western Suburban 19-22/ London 22-24/ Spartan 24-30/ Athenian 30-71.
Previous Ground: Botwell Common. **Previous Names:** Botwell Mission 1909-24.
Midweek home matchday: Tuesday
Reserve Team's League: Suburban (North).
Record Attendance: 15,370 v Bromley, FA Amateur Cup, 10/2/51.
Best FA Cup season: 2nd Rd replay 72-73. 1st Rd 13 times 27-28 31-32 33-34 38-39 46-47 64-65 72-74 87-92.
League clubs defeated in FA Cup: Bristol Rovers 72-73, Cardiff 90-91, Fulham 91-92.
Record Fees - Paid: £6,000 for Gary Keen (Hendon, 1990).
Received: £30,000 for Les Ferdinand (Queens Park Rangers, 1987).
Players progressing to Football League: Cyril Bacon (Orient 1946), Phil Nolan (Watford 1947), Dave Groombridge (Orient 1951), Jimmy Bloomfield (Brentford 1952), Derek Neale & Les Champelover (Brighton & Hove Albion 1956 & 57), Gordon Phillips (Brentford 1963, Robin Friday (Reading 1974), Les Smith (A Villa & England), Cyrille Regis (WBA 1977), Les Ferdinand (QPR & England) 1987, Derek Payne (Barnet, Southend) 1988.
Clubhouse: (081 573 0933). Sat 12-3 & 4.45-11pm. Midweek matchnights 6.30-11pm. Some cold snacks available. Dancehall. Steward: Fred Heritage
Club Record Scorer: Unknown.
Club Record Appearances: Reg Leather, 701
93-94 Captain: Andy Dear.
93-94 P.o.Y.:
93-94 Top scorer:
Local Newspaper: Hayes Gazette (0895 37161).
Local Radio Stations: Capital.
Honours: FA Amtr R-up 30-31 (SF 56-57), Isthmian Lg Cup R-up 78-79 80-81 87-88, Athenian Lg 56-57 (R-up 31-32 49-50), Spartan Lg 27-28 (R-up 25-26), Gt Western Suburban Lg(4) 20-24 (R-up 19-20), London Snr Cup 31-32 80-81 (R-up 36-37), Middx Snr Cup(8) 19-21 25-26 30-31 35-36 39-40 49-50 81-82, Middx Charity Cup (16 times), London Charity Cup 60-61, London Challenge Cup R-up 73-74, Middx Mnr Cup 11-12, FA Trophy QF 78-79, Premier Midweek f'lit Lge 75-76, Middx Premier Cup 86-87 87-88 88-89, Suburban Lg (Nth) 88-89 91-92 (Champions Cup 92-93).

PROGRAMME DETAILS:
Pages: 24 Price: 80p
Editor: Trevor Griffith
(0895 638013)

HAYES's 1993-94 CAMPAIGN

Date	Opponents	Comp.	Res	Gate	Goalscorers
21/08	Dulwich Hamlet	DFL	2-3	250	Thompson, Stevens
24/08	**HARROW BOROUGH**	DFL	1-1	306	Thompson
28/08	**HIT6HIN TOWN**	DFL	2-2	246	Riley, T Kelly
31/08	Grays Athletic	DFL	1-0	210	T Kelly
04/09	Carshalton Ath.	DFL	0-2	462	
11/09	**SUTTON UNITED**	DFL	1-8	365	Goodliffe
22/09	Bognor Regis T.	DLC1	0-2	240	
25/09	Wokingham Town	DFL	1-0	233	Pedlar
09/10	**AYLESBURY UTD**	DFL	0-0	361	
12/10	**YEADING**	DFL	0-1	296	
16/10	Marlow	FAT2q	1-1	260	Walton
19/10	**MARLOW**	FAT2qr	2-3	177	Goodliffe, T Kelly
23/10	**SLOUGH TOWN**	FAC4q	0-2	877	
26/10	Kingstonian	DFL	1-4	539	Riley
30/10	**WIVENHOE TOWN**	DFL	0-2	229	
02/11	Dorking	DFL	1-0	294	Catlin
06/11	**CHESHAM UNITED**	DFL	1-1	393	W Kelly
13/11	St Albans City	DFL	0-4	402	
20/11	**STEVENAGE BORO.**	DFL	1-3	356	W Kelly
27/11	Basingstoke Town	DFL	1-4	210	W Kelly
30/11	Bishop's Stortford	CC1	0-3	251	
04/12	**St ALBANS CITY**	DFL	2-1	320	G Boreham, Pedlar
11/12	Sutton United	DFL	1-0	599	Ross
14/12	**BROMLEY**	DFL	3-1	214	Ross(2), Pedlar
18/12	**MOLESEY**	DFL	3-0	261	Driscoll, T Kelly, Stevens
21/12	Enfield	DFL	0-2	522	
27/12	Hendon	DFL	2-0	283	W Kelly, Stevens
01/01	**GRAYS ATHLETIC**	DFL	1-3	294	Driscoll
15/01	Harrow Borough	DFL	3-3	382	Dear, Amissah, Driscoll
18/01	Marlow	DFL	3-4	486	Dear, Braithwaite, Stevens
22/01	**HENDON**	DFL	1-1	251	Dear
25/01	**POTTERS BAR TOWN**	MCC3	3-0	45	Pedlar, Stevens(2)
29/01	Hitchin Town	DFL	2-3	665	W Kelly(2)
02/02	Wealdstone	MSC1	1-2	191	Driscoll
05/02	**CARSHALTON ATH.**	DFL	3-3	341	Goodliffe, Braithwaite, Driscoll
12/02	Aylesbury United	DFL	0-1	516	
19/02	**DORKING**	DFL	3-2	229	Stevens(2), Pedlar
26/02	**ENFIELD**	DFL	0-1	464	
05/03	Yeading	DFL	3-2	335	Driscoll(2), Baker
12/03	**WOKINGHAM TOWN**	DFL	1-2	200	Stevens
16/03	Chesham United	DFL	1-0	448	Russell
19/03	Bromley	DFL	0-0	217	
26/03	Wivenhoe Town	DFL	6-0	133	Goodliffe, Pedlar(3), W Kelly, Stevens
29/03	**DULWICH HAMLET**	DFL	1-2	188	Baker
02/04	**KINGSTONIAN**	DFL	2-1	320	Pedlar, Rose
07/04	Staines Town	MCCqf	0-2	269	
09/04	Molesey	DFL	2-3	162	W Kelly, Pearce
16/04	**MARLOW**	DFL	2-0	292	Baker, W Kelly
23/04	Stevenage Borough	DFL	1-2	1,214	Pedlar
26/04	**BRENTFORD**	TEST	2-2	292	Knowles, Clarke
30/04	**BASINGSTOKE TOWN**	DFL	4-0	209	Pearce(2), Baker, Stevens

Key: DFL: Diadora League Premier Division, DLC: Diadora League Cup, CC: Diadora League Carlsberg Cup, DFLS: Diadora League Championship Shield, FAC: F.A. Cup, FAT: F.A. Trophy, MSC: Middlesex Senior Cup, MCC: Middlesex Charity Cup, TEST: Testimonial.
Numbers after cup competitions denote rounds (r: replay, qf: Quarter-Final, sf: Semi-Final, f: Final. Numbers in brackets indicate legs, i.e. (1): 1st leg).
Home fixtures are denoted by bold capitals, away matches by lower case. (p): penalty, og: Own goal.

SQUAD MEMBERS *(previous clubs listed in chronological order)*

GOALKEEPERS: Ian Chatfield *(Redhill, Chelsea).*

DEFENDERS: Warren Kelly *(Hemel Hempstead, St Albans),* **Vinny Murphy** *(Yeading),* **Micky Bennett** *(Harrow Boro., Burnham, Hounslow, Burnham),* **Jason Goodliffe** *(Brentford),* **Matt Catlin** *(Harefield Utd),* **Andy Dear** *(Wimbledon, Ronnskars(Fin), Leatherhead, Epsom & Ewell, Walton & Hersham, Kingstonian),* **Ian Waugh** *(Wealdstone, Chalfont St Peter),* **Dennis Parker** *(Rainham, Redbridge F., Barking, Bishop's Stortford, Woking, Bishop's Stortford).*

MIDFIELD: Roy Marshall *(Hillingdon, Uxbridge),* **Dean Hooper** *(Brentford, Marlow, Yeading, Marlow, Chalfont St Peter),* **Neal Stevens** *(Brook House),* **Freddie Amissah** *(Hampton, Fulham, Hampton),* **Gerry Solomon** *(Wealdstone, Hendon, Harrow Boro., St Albans, Enfield),* **Steve Baker** *(Spurs, Brentford, Brook House, Hayes, Southall, Yeading).*

FORWARDS: Lance Pedlar *(Ruislip Manor, Wembley, Hounslow, Wealdstone, Chelmsford, St Albans, Woking, Harrow Boro., Leatherhead),* **David Ross** *(St Albans, Wealdstone, St Albans),* **Tony Kelly** *(Wealdstone, Hillingdon, Harefield Utd, Hayes, Wealdstone),* **Lincoln Manderson** *(Leyton County, Dagenham, Redbridge F., Bishop's Stortford, Enfield, Harrow Boro.),* **David Pearce** *(Millwall, Wealdstone, Harrow Boro., Barnet, Dagenham, Wokingham, Kingstonian, Hayes, Kingstonian),* **Danny Butler** *(Belmont, Yeading, Hayes, Staines, Windsor).*

HENDON

Formed: 1908 Dons or Greens

Hendon's Richard Cherry watches his shot pass just the wrong side of the post in the FA Trophy defeat at the hands of Marlow at Claremont Road.

Photo - Paul Dennis.

Chairman: Elaine Green **Presidents:** Monty Hyams and Bobbie Butlin
Secretary: Graham Etchell, c/o Hendon FC.
Manager: Mick Browne **Asst Manager:** Ged Murphy **Coach:** Peter Lawrence
Press Officer: Secretary **Physio:** TBA.
Commercial Manager: John Finder.
Ground: Claremont Road, Cricklewood, London NW2 1AE (081 201 9494 (Fax: 081 9055966)).
Directions: From Brent Cross tube station (Northern Line) to the east take first left after flyover on North Circular - Claremont Rd is then left at 3rd mini-r'bout. From Golders Green station (Northern Line) take bus 226 or 102. From Cricklewood main line station, turn left out of station and Claremont Rd is first left - ground half mile down on right. Buses 102, 210, 226 and C11 pass ground.
Capacity: 8,000 **Cover:** 5,119 **Seats:** 381 **Floodlights:** Yes **Metal Badges:** Yes.
Club Shop: (Contact Pat Hunt 081 455 9185) Sells kit, bags, badges, pens, mugs, scarves, ties, programmes and other football souvenirs.
Cols: Green & white halves/white/green **Change colours:** Blue & black halves/black/black.
Previous Leagues: Finchley & Dist. 08-11/ Middx 10-11/ London 11-14/ Athenian 14-63.
Sponsors: Fender Guitars. **Previous Names:** Hampstead Town 08-33/ Golders Green 33-46.
Previous Grounds: Kensal Rise 08-12/ Avenue Ground, Cricklewood Lane 12-26.
Midweek matchday: Tuesday
Reserve Team's League: None. **Record Gate:** 9,000 v Northampton, FA Cup 1st Rd 1952.
Record win: 13-1 v Wingate (H), Middx Senior Cup 2/2/57.
Record defeat: 2-11 v Walthamstow Avenue (A), Athenian League 9/11/35.
Best F.A. Cup season: 3rd Rd replay 73-74 (lost 1-4 to Newcastle at Watford after 1-1 draw away). 1st Rd (15) 34-35 52-53 55-56 60-61 64-67 69-71 72-74 75-76 77-78 81-82 88-89.
League clubs defeated in F.A. Cup: Reading 75-76.
Record Fees - Paid: £4,500 for Martin Duffield (Enfield). **Received:** £30,000 for Iain Dowie (Luton).
Players progressing to Football League: Arnold Siegel (Orient 1946), William Dare (Brentford 1948), Roy Stroud (West Ham 1952), Miles Spector (Chelsea 1950), Jeff Darey (Brighton), Doug Orr (QPR 1957), Peter Shearing (West Ham 1960), Iain Dowie (Luton 1988), Peter Anderson (Luton), Jeff Harris (Orient), Phil Gridelet (Barnsley 1990), Gerry Soloman (Leyton Orient 1991), Junior Hunter & Micah Hyde (both Cambridge 93-94), Simon Clark (Peterborough 93-94).
Clubhouse: (081 455 9185 - contact Sally Brewster). Two bars and function hall open normal licensing hours 7 days a week. Hot & cold food, pool, darts, bingo, members club, satelite TV, entertainments. Available for private hire.
Club Record Goalscorer: Freddie Evans 176 (1929-35)
Club Record Apps: Bill Fisher 787 (1940-62).
93-94 Captain: Curtis Warmington.
93-94 P.o.Y.: Bob Dowie.
93-94 Top scorer: Gary Crawshaw.
Local Newspaper: Hendon Times (081 203 0411).
Local Radio Stations: Capital.
Hons: FA Amtr Cup 59-60 64-65 71-72 (R-up 54-55 65-66), European Amtr Champions 72-73, Isthmian Lg 64-65 72-73 (R-up 63-64 65-66 73-74, Lg Cup 76-77 (R-up 86-87), Full Members Cup 93-94), Premier Inter-League Cup R-up 86-87, Middx Lge 12-13 13-14, Athenian Lg 52-53 55-56 60-61 (R-up 28-29 32-33 47-48 48-49 51-52), London Lg Div 1 R-up 12-13 (Amtr Div 13-14), Finchley & Dist. Lg 10-11, London Snr Cup 63-64 68-69 (R-up 35-36 50-51 54-55 58-59 71-72), Middx Snr Cup(11) 33-34 38-39 55-56 57-58 59-60 64-65 66-67 71-74 85-86 (R-up 83-84), Middx Charity Cup(14) 21-22 26-27 35-36 44-48 53-54 56-57 75-77 78-79 84-85 87-88, FA Tphy 3rd Rd replay 76-77 77-78, London Intermediate Cup 64-65 72-73 75-76 79-80 (R-up 63-64 68-69), Middx Intermediate 64-65 66-67 72-73, Suburban Lg 92-93 (R-up 84-85).

PROGRAMME DETAILS:
Pages: 64 **Price:** £1
Editor: Secretary

HENDON's 1993-94 CAMPAIGN

Date	Opponents	Comp.	Res	Gate	Goalscorers
21/08	Grays Athletic	DFL	3-0	354	Cherry(2), Tripp(og)
24/08	**BASINGSTOKE T.**	DFL	6-0	239	Cherry(3), Ashenden, Stewart, Taylor
28/08	**DULWICH HANLET**	DFL	2-1	331	Crawshaw(2)
31/08	Aylesbury United	DFL	3-2	749	Ashenden, Crawshaw, Daly
04/09	St Albans City	DFL	0-0	728	
11/09	Gt Yarmouth Town	FAC1q	2-2	215	Daly, Taylor
14/09	**Gt YARMOUTH T.**	FAC1qr	4-2	232	Cherry, Crawshaw, Mason, Daly
18/09	**MARLOW**	FAT1q	1-2	247	Cherry
21/09	Boreham Wood	DLC1	2-3	125	Crawshaw, Taylor
25/09	**HEYBRIDGE SWIFTS**	FAC2q	5-2	171	Warmington, Cherry, Crawshaw, Mason, Taylor
28/09	**YEADING**	DFL	5-2	207	Clark(2), Crawshaw(3)
02/10	**STEVENAGE BORO.**	DFL	1-2	551	Blackman
06/10	Chesham United	DFL	1-2	694	Crawshaw
09/10	**CAMBRIDGE CITY**	FAC3q	0-1	382	
30/10	**HITCHIN TOWN**	DFL	2-4	323	Cherry, Taylor
06/11	Kingstonian	DFL	3-1	623	Kane(2), Cherry
09/11	**GRAYS ATHLETIC**	DFL	2-1	195	Kane, Cherry
13/11	**WOKINGHAM TOWN**	DFL	1-1	201	Cherry
20/11	Bromley	DFL	3-3	307	Clark, Crawshaw, Taylor
23/11	**HARROW BOROUGH**	DFL	0-2	225	
27/11	**DORKING**	DFL	3-1	184	Crawshaw(2), Taylor
04/12	Enfield	DFL	0-1	499	
11/12	**AYLESBURY UTD**	DFL	2-2	241	Blackman
18/12	Carshalton Athletic	DFL	0-3	473	
27/12	**HAYES**	DFL	0-2	283	
01/01	Harrow Borough	DFL	1-2	467	Crawshaw
15/01	Basingstoke Town	DFL	1-0	263	Heffer
19/01	Harrow Borough	MSC1	1-0	164	Blackman *(Match later declared null & void)*
22/01	Hayes	DFL	1-1	251	Polston
29/01	Dulwich Hamlet	DFL	1-0	220	Blackman
01/02	Enfield	CC2	1-0	242	Hardy
05/02	**St ALBANS CITY**	DFL	1-0	361	Polston
09/02	Harrow Borough	MSC1r	0-1	165	
12/02	Yeading	DFL	1-1	220	Blackman
16/02	Molesey	DFL	3-2	223	Ashdenden, Egbe, Blackman
19/02	**SUTTON UNITED**	DFL	0-1	358	
22/02	**UXBRIDGE**	CC3	1-0	66	Heffer
26/02	Marlow	DFL	1-2	445	Blackman
05/02	**WIVENHOE TOWN**	DFL	0-2	145	
12/03	**CHESHAM UNITED**	DFL	0-1	301	
19/03	Stevenage Borough	DFL	0-3	815	
22/03	Bishop's Stortford	CCqf	1-1	242	Warmington *(Hendon won 3-1 on penalties)*
26/03	Hitchin Town	DFL	0-0	497	
02/04	**MOLESEY**	DFL	2-0	183	Dowie, Dodman(og)
05/04	Sutton United	DFL	1-0	454	Anderson
09/04	**CARSHALTON ATH.**	DFL	1-1	141	Rutherford
12/04	**DULWICH HAMLET**	CCsf	2-1	129	Kelly, Heffer
16/04	Wokingham Town	DFL	2-0	224	Heffer, Hardy
18/04	**MARLOW**	DFL	0-1	153	
23/04	**BROMLEY**	DFL	2-1	191	Ashenden, Rutherford
26/04	Wivenhoe Town	DFL	4-0	146	Mason(2), Ashenden(2)
28/04	**KINGSTONIAN**	DFL	0-0	210	
30/04	Dorking	DFL	2-1	162	Warmington, Heffer
03/05	WOKINGHAM TOWN	CCf	2-1	494	Mason, Bourne *(played at Marlow FC)*
07/05	**ENFIELD**	DFL	0-2	385	

Key: DFL: Diadora League Premier Division, DLC: Diadora League Cup, CC: Carsberg Cup, FAC: F.A. Cup, FAT: F.A. Trophy, MSC: Middlesex Senior Cup. Numbers after cup competitions denote rounds (r: replay, qf: Quarter-Final, sf: Semi-Final, f: Final. Numbers in brackets indicate legs, i.e. (1): 1st leg).
Home fixtures are denoted by bold capitals, away matches by lower case. (p): penalty, og: Own goal.

SQUAD MEMBERS *(previous clubs listed in chronological order)*

GOALKEEPERS: Dave Root *(Launceston, Barking, Walthamstow Ave., Hendon, Eton Manor)*

DEFENDERS: Curtis Warmington *(West Ham, Thames Poly, Dulwich, Yeovil, Carshalton, Enfield,* **Lee Hunter** *(Colchester, Wigan, Wivenhoe),* **Mark Hill** *(Brentford, Wycombe, Maidstone, Slough),* **Andy Polston** *(Spurs, Brighton),* **Tommy Mason** *(Fulham, Brighton, Seattle Sounders(US), Dulwich, Taraque(NZ), Farnborough, Enfield)*

MIDFIELD: Bob Dowie *(Bishop Auckland, Hatfield, Cheshunt, Hertford, St Albans, Hendon, St Albans),* **Dennis Rodway** *(Charlton, Southend, Basildon),* **Steve Heffer** *(West Ham, Swindon, Southend, Grays),* **Robbie Bourne** *(Brimsdown, Finchley, Brimsdown, Boreham Wood),* **Dean Ross** *(local football),* **Mark Kane** *(Leyton Orient, Woodford, Walthamstow Ave., Woodford, Barking, Tampa Bay(US), Barking, Chelmsford, Enfield),* **Duncan Hardy** *(St Albans, Finchley, Cheshunt, Hendon, Cheshunt, Barnet, Bishop's Stortford,Hendon, Harrow, Stevenage, Sawbridgeworth)*

FORWARDS: Bradley Anderson *(Watford, Boreham Wood, St Albans, Stevenage, Hertford),* **Scott Anderson** *(Southend),* **Uche Egbe** *(Watford, Hendon, Wembley),* **Ian Rutherford** *(Luton, Crewe, Fleetwood, St Albans, Stafford, St Albans)*

Formed: 1928

HITCHIN TOWN

The Canaries

Hitchin Town 'keeper Peter Gleasure punches the ball clear during the fantastic 2-1 Christmas win away to deadly rivals Stevenage Borough.

Photo - Paul Dennis.

Chairman: Terry Barratt **Vice-Chairman:** Neil Jensen.
Secretary: Alan Sexton, 66 Nine Spring Ways, Hitchin, Herts SG4 9NU (0462 456003).
Manager: Andy Melvin **Asst Mgr:** Robin Wainwright **Coach:** Rob Johnson.
Press Officer: Neil Jensen (0462 454678) **Physio:** Peter Prince.
Clubcall Line: 0891 122 934 **Commercial Manager:** Mike Kitchener (0462 459628).
Ground: Top Field, Fishponds Road, Hitchin SG5 1NU (0462 459028-matchdays only).
Directions: On A505 near town centre opposite large green. 1 mile from Hitchin (BR).
Capacity: 4,000 **Cover:** 1,250 **Seats:** 500 **Floodlights:** Yes **Metal Badges:** Yes.
Club Shop: Yes, selling programmes, souvenirs etc. Contact Irvin Morgan.
Colours: Yellow/green/green **Change:** Black & white stripes/black/black.
Sponsors: Bristol & West Building Society.
Previous Lges: *Predecessors (Hitchin FC): South Eastern 01-08/ Spartan 09-11.* Spartan 28-39/ Athenian 45-63.
Midweek home matchday: Tuesday **Reserve Team:** No (youth team only).
Record win (in Isthmian League): 9-1 v Worthing (H), Division One, January 1991.
Record defeat (in Isthmian League): 0-10; v Kingstonian, 65-66; v Slough Town, 79-80. Both away.
Record Attendance: 7,878 v Wycombe Wanderers, FA Amateur Cup 3rd Rd 18/2/56.
Best FA Cup season: *Second Rd 1871-72 (Hitchin FC).* Second Round replay (v Swindon, lost 1-3 (A)) 1976-77, Second Rd (v Boston Utd, lost 0-1(A)) 73-74.
Record Fees - Paid: £2,000 for Ray Seeking (Potton United, July 1989)
Received: £5,750 for Steve Conroy (Kingstonian, December 1990).
Players progressing to Football League: Reg Smith (Millwall & England), Len Garwood (Spurs 1946), C J Walker, W Odell, S Foss, R Stevens, T Clarke, G Goodyear, L Harwood, P Burridge, Ray Kitchener (Chelsea 1954), D Bumstead, M Dixon, David Pacey (Luton 1956), Mike Dixon & Brian Whitby (Luton 1957), Keith Abiss (Brighton 1957), D Hille, G Ley, R Morton, L Payne (Newcastle & Reading), Micky Small (Brighton), Richard Nugent (Barnet).
Clubhouse: (0462 434483). Members bar, Function Hall (hireable). Open every day. Ample parking. Steward: Eamonn Watts.
Club Record Goalscorer (in one season): Eddie Armitage 84, 1931-32.
Club Record (Isthmian Lge) Appearances: Paul Giggle 950+ 67-88.
Club Record (Isthmian Lge) goals: Paul Giggle, 129.
93-94 Captain: Mark Burke.
93-94 P.o.Y./Top scorer: Steve Conroy, 23 Lge & Cup goals.
Local Papers: Hitchin Gazette/Hitchin Comet - Home Counties Newspapers (0727 866166), Hitchin Herald & Post (0727 846866) *But for up-to-date info contact Press Officer (above).*
Local Radio: Chiltern (0582 666001), Three Counties (0582 454748).
Hons: FA Amateur Cup SF 60-61 62-63, Isthmian League R-up 68-69 (Div 1 92-93), Spartan League 34-35, AFA Senior Cup 30-31, Herts Snr Cup(18-record) 1894-96 97-98 89-1900 02-03 04-05 09-10 30-32 33-34 37-39 40-41 42-43 61-62 69-70 74-77, London Senior Cup 69-70 (R-up 72-73), East Anglian Cup 72-73, Herts Charity Cup(16) 01-03 04-05 39-40 43-44 54-55 60-61 67-68 75-80, Herts I'mediate Cup(8) 39-40 46-47 48-49 56-57 60-62 67-69, Woolwich Trophy 82-83, Televised Sport International Cup 88-89 90-91, Southern Comb. Senior Floodlit Cup 90-91, FA Trophy 3rd Rd replay 76-77. Only Surviving FA founder member (1867).

PROGRAMME DETAILS:
Pages: 48 **Price:** 50p
Editor: Barry Swain

HITCHIN TOWN's 1993-94 CAMPAIGN

Date	Opponents	Comp.	Res	Gate	Goalscorers
21/07	**ARSENAL xi**	Fr.	2-0	691	Fisher, O'Keefe
24/07	**QUEENS PARK R. xi**	Fr.	3-4	304	Marshall, Ingram, Williams
31/07	**FULHAM**	Fr.	1-1	422	Ingram
03/08	**LEYTON ORIENT yth**	Fr.	3-1	236	McGonagle, Cosby, Bone
07/08	Buckingham Town	Fr.	0-2	98	
10/08	**CHELSEA xi**	Fr.	3-6	1,026	Hughes(2), Marshall
17/08	St Albans City	HCC1	3-4	314	McGonagle(2), Williams
21/08	**BROMLEY**	DFL	1-0	365	Johnson
24/08	Wokingham Town	DFL	0-2	264	
28/08	Hayes	DFL	2-1	246	McGonagle, Bone
31/08	**MOLESEY**	DFL	2-0	328	McGonagle, Scott
04/09	**WIVENHOE TOWN**	DFL	6-2	431	Conroy(3), Williams(3)
11/09	Dagenham & Redbridge	FAC1q	0-1	580	
15/09	Chesham United	DFL	3-0	692	Conroy(2), Williams
18/09	**BOREHAM WOOD**	FAT1q	0-2	366	
21/09	**UXBRIDGE**	DLC1	4-3	208	Cosby(2), Conroy, Miller
25/09	**DULWICH HAMLET**	DFL	2-3	298	Williams, Conroy
28/09	Enfield	DFL	3-0	601	Conroy(2), Williams
02/10	**AYLESBURY UTD**	DFL	5-1	556	Conroy, Thompson, McGonagle(2), Bone
05/10	Dorking	DFL	1-3	151	McGonagle
16/10	**KINGSTONIAN**	DFL	1-3	510	Cosby
23/10	**BASINGSTOKE T.**	DFL	1-0	398	Thompson
30/10	Hendon	DFL	4-2	323	Conroy(2), Williams(2)
02/11	Bishop's Stortford	HSC1	0-3	351	
06/11	**St ALBANS CITY**	DFL	1-3	821	Goodyear(og)
13/11	Grays Athletic	DFL	2-0	222	Williams, McGonagle
16/11	Kingstonian	DLC2	3-4	352	McGonagle, Marshall(2)
20/11	**SUTTON UNITED**	DFL	0-0	580	
23/11	Boreham Wood	CC1	3-1	152	Tighe, Marshall(2)
27/11	Bromley	DFL	0-0	329	
04/12	**MARLOW**	DFL	2-1	425	Williams, Scott
11/12	Molesey	DFL	2-1	193	Price, McGonagle
27/12	Stevenage Borough	DFL	2-1	2,489	Scott, Conroy
01/01	**CHESHAM UNITED**	DFL	2-1	1,019	Conroy(2)
15/01	**WOKINGHAM TOWN**	DFL	1-0	513	Conroy
18/01	Grays Athletic	CC2	1-2	152	Marshall
22/01	**CARSHALTON ATH.**	DFL	1-0	797	Conroy
29/01	**HAYES**	DFL	3-2	665	McGonagle(3)
05/02	Wivenhoe Town	DFL	7-0	264	Williams(2), Marshall(3), McGonagle, Miller
19/02	Kingstonian	DFL	5-3	659	Williams(2), McGonagle, Marshall(2)
26/02	**HARROW BOROUGH**	DFL	0-1	723	
01/03	Yeading	DFL	1-2	212	Shea
05/02	Basingstoke Town	DFL	3-1	278	Williams, McGonagle, Marshall
08/03	St Albans City	DFL	1-2	551	Williams
12/03	**DORKING**	DFL	2-3	582	McGonagle, Conroy
16/03	Harrow Borough	DFL	1-1	170	Conroy
19/03	Aylesbury United	DFL	1-1	431	Marshall
26/03	**HENDON**	DFL	0-0	497	
02/04	Carshalton Athletic	DFL	4-1	365	Marshall(2), Conroy(2)
04/04	**STEVENAGE BORO.**	DFL	1-3	2,503	Conroy
09/04	Dulwich Hamlet	DFL	0-0	185	
12/04	**ENFIELD**	DFL	2-3	597	Scott, Marshall
16/04	**GRAYS ATHLETIC**	DFL	2-3	373	Marshall(2)
23/04	Sutton United	DFL	0-2	602	
30/04	**YEADING**	DFL	4-2	256	Conroy, Bone, Marshall, Scott
07/05	Marlow	DFL	0-1	266	

Key: DFL: Diadora League Premier Division, DLC: Diadora League Cup, CC: Carlsberg Cup, FAC: F.A. Cup, FAT: F.A. Trophy, HCC: Herts Charity Cup, HSC: Herts Senior Cup, Fr.: Friendly. Numbers after cup competitions denote rounds (r: replay, qf: Quarter-Final, sf: Semi-Final, f: Final. Numbers in brackets indicate legs, i.e. (1): 1st leg).
Home fixtures are denoted by bold capitals, away matches by lower case. (p): penalty, og: Own goal.

SQUAD MEMBERS *(previous clubs listed in chronological order)*

GOALKEEPERS: Peter Gleasure *(Millwall, Northampton)*, **Duncan Payne** *(Welwyn GC)*

DEFENDERS: Jon Bone *(Luton, Hitchin, Baldock)*, **Steve Miller** *(Hitchin, St Albans, Stevenage, Vauxhall Mtrs)*, **Mark Burke** *(QPR, Luton)*, **Gavin Covington** *(Dunstable, Barnet, Hitchin, Wycombe)*, **Paul Price** *(Luton, Spurs, Minnesota Kicks(US) Swansea, Saltash Utd, Peterborough, Chelmsford, Wivenhoe, St Albans)*, **Steve Shea** *(Bedford, Edlesborough, St Albans, Stevenage, Chesham, Hitchin, St Albans, Harrow Boro., Staines, Hitchin, Harlow)*.

MIDFIELD: Mark McGonagle *(Luton, Baldock)*, **Shaun Marshall** *(Stevenage)*, **Rob Johnson** *(Bedford, Luton, Leicester C., Barnet)*, **Ian Scott** *(Luton, Aylesbury, St Albans)*, **Darren Thompson** *(Luton)*, **Sean Pearson** *(Langford, Hitchin, Wealdstone, Stevenage)*.

FORWARDS: Gary Williams *(Luton, Vauxhall Mtrs, Stevenage, Baldock)*, **Aaron Tighe** *(Luton)*, **Alan Cosby** *(Luton, Hendon, Hitchin, Barnet, St Albans, Chesham)*, **Stuart Brown** *(Luton, Slough)*, **Steve Conroy** *(Colchester, Hemel Hempstead, St Albans, Chesham, Hitchin, Kingstonian, Harrow Boro.)*.

Formed: 1885

KINGSTONIAN

The K's

Soloman Eriemo (right) of Kingstonian closes in on Hitchin's Steve Conroy during the Premier Division fixture at Kingsmeadow on 19th February.

Photo - Peter Lirettoc.

Chairman: G M Child **Vice Chairman:** David Gardener. **President:** J Webster.
Secretary: W R McNully, 71 Largewood Ave., Tolworth, Surbiton KT6 7NX (081 391 4552).
Manager: Richard Parkin **Asst Manager:** John Yemms **Coach:** Richard Parkin.
Press Officer: B P Frawley (081 541 5250) **Physio:** Gary Scott
Commercial Manager: Mrs A Dickinson (081 547 3336).
Ground: Kingsmeadow Stadium, Kingston Road, Kingston-on-Thames KT1 3PB (081 547 3335).
Directions: From town centre - Cambridge Rd on to Kingston Rd (A2043) to Malden Rd. From A3, turn off at New Malden and turn left on to A2043 - ground 1 mile on left. Half mile from Norbiton (BR), one mile from Kingston (BR). Bus 131 passes the ground.
Capacity: 9,000 **Cover:** 3,500 **Seats:** 690 **Floodlights:** Yes **Metal Badges:** Yes.
Club Shop: Sells programmes, shirts, pennants and other souvenirs. Contact Mrs Ann Dickinson (081 747 3336).
Cols: Red & white hoops/black/black **Change colours:** Black & white halves **Fanzine:** Yes.
Club Sponsors: Cherry Red Records.
Previous Lges: Kingston & Dist./ West Surrey/ Southern Suburban/ Athenian 1919-29.
Previous Names: Kingston & Surbiton YMCA 1885-87/ Saxons 87-90/ Kingston Wanderers 1893-1904/ Old Kingstonians 08-19.
Newsline: 0891 884 441. **Prev. Ground:** Various to 1921/ Richmond Rd 21-89.
Midweek home matchday: Tuesday **Reserve Team's League:** Suburban.
Record win: 15-1 v Delft, friendly 5/9/51 (competitive: 10-0 v Hitchin (H), Isthmian Lge 19/3/66).
Record defeat: 0-11 v Ilford (A), Isthmian Lge 13/2/37.
Record Attendance: 3,826 v Peterborough United, FA Cup First Round Proper 14/11/92. *At Richmond Road - 11,000 v Bishop Auckland, FA Amateur Cup 5/2/55.*
Best FA Cup season: 1st Rd replay 31-32 (after 2-2 draw at Luton lost 2-3 at home), 92-93 (after 1-1 draw v Peterborough lost 0-1 away). 1st Rd on three other occasions; 1926 (0-1 at Nunhead), 1930 (0-3 at Tunbridge Wells), 1933 (1-7 at home to Bristol City).
Record Fees - Paid: £10,000 for Richard Cherry (Redbridge Forest, 1991)
Received: £5,000 for Andy Duar (Hayes, 1992)
Players progressing to Football League: Carlo Nastri (Crystal Palace), Hugh Lindsay (Southampton 1965), Giles Still (Brighton 1979), David Byrne (Gillingham 1985), John Power (Brentford 1987).
Clubhouse: (081 547 3336) + banqueting centre, open seven days a week. Three fully licensed bars catering for up to 400 at any one time.
Club Record Goalscorer: Johnny Whig 295
Club Record Appearances: Micky Preston 555.
93-94 Captain: John Daly.
93-94 Player of the Year: Mark Underdown.
93-94 Top scorer: Jaime Ndah.
Local Newspaper: Surrey Comet (081 546 2261).
Local Radio Stations: County Sound.
Hons: FA Amtr Cup 32-33 (R-up 59-60), Isthmian Lg 33-34 36-37 (R-up 47-48 62-63, Div 1 R-up 84-85), Athenian Lg 23-24 25-26 (R-up 26-27), London Snr Cup 62-63 64-65 86-87 (R-up 23-24 25-26 30-31 46-47 83-84), Surrey Snr Cup(9) 25-26 30-32 34-35 38-39 51-52 62-64 66-67 (R-up 90-91).

PROGRAMME DETAILS:
Pages: 36 **Price:** £1
Editor: Mrs A Dickinson (081 547 3335)

KINGSTONIAN's 1993-94 CAMPAIGN

Date	Opponents	Comp.	Res	Gate	Goalscorers
21/08	Aylesbury Utd	DFL	6-3	634	Eriemo, Ndah, Akamoah, Kempton, Harlow, Wigmore
24/08	**CARSHALTON ATH.**	DFL	0-2	538	
28/08	**St ALBANS CITY**	DFL	0-1	624	
31/08	Yeading	DFL	3-2	332	Akamoah(2), Vines
04/09	Harrow Borough	DFL	4-2	385	Akamoah(2), Eriemo, Ndah
07/09	**DORKING**	DFL	2-2	463	Ndah, Eriemo
11/09	**ASHFORD TOWN**	FAC1q	2-1	396	Ndah(2)
14/09	Sutton United	DFL	1-2	918	Akamoah
18/09	**GRAYS ATHLETIC**	DFL	3-0	538	Ndah, Sugrue, Underdown
21/09	Aldershot Town	DLC1	4-0		
25/09	**BOGNOR REGIS TN**	FAC2q	1-1		Akamoah
28/09	Bognor Regis Tn	FAC2qr	6-1	450	Ndah(2), Wingfield (2), Harlow, Kempton
02/10	Enfield	DFL	0-3	702	
05/10	**WIVENHOE TOWN**	DFL	8-1	538	Braithwaite(2), Underdown(2), Ndah(2), Sugrue, Wingfield
09/10	Chatham Town	FAC3q	2-1	498	Harlow(2)
16/10	Hitchin Town	DFL	3-1	510	Underdown(2), Akamoah
23/10	**MET. POLICE**	FAC4q	0-1	689	
26/10	**HAYES**	DFL	4 1	530	Harlow(2), Ndah, Braitwaite
30/10	Bromley	DFL	2-2	476	Asaba(2)
06/11	**HENDON**	DFL	1-3	623	Kempton
13/11	Basingstoke Town	DFL	1-1	339	Wingfield
16/11	**HITCHIN TOWN**	DLC2	4-3	352	
20/11	**MARLOW**	DFL	1-1	539	Eriemo
27/11	Sittingbourne	FAT3q	2-1	1,248	Ndah, Harlow
04/12	**DULWICH HAMLET**	DFL	3-0	589	Ndah(2), Akuamoah
11/12	Grays Athletic	DFL	3-0	249	Russell, Sugrue, Akuamoah
14/12	Walton & Hersham	SSC1	0-2		
18/12	**CHESHAM UNITED**	DFL	1-2	723	Sugrue
21/12	**HARROW BOROUGH**	DLC3	6-1		
27/12	Molesey	DFL	1-1	714	Sugrue
01/01	**YEADING**	DFL	1-2	515	Ndah
11/01	**ABINGDON TOWN**	CC2	4-0		
15/01	Carshalton Athletic	DFL	4-1	1,026	Akamoah(2), Broderick(2)
22/01	Dulwich Hamlet	FAT1	2-1	705	Underdown(2)
25/01	**CARSHALTON ATH**	DLC4	0-1		
29/01	St Albans City	DFL	4-1	551	Underdown(3), Sugrue
01/02	Wokingham Town	DFL	3-1	297	Akamoah, Wingfield, Bradley(og)
05/02	**HARROW BOROUGH**	DFL	7-0	605	Wingfield(3), Asaba(2), Sugrue, Daly
12/02	**MERTHYR TYDFIL**	FAT2	0-2	853	
19/02	**HITCHIN TOWN**	DFL	3-5	659	Harlow, Asaba, Underdown
22/02	Dulwich Hamlet	CC3	0-1		
26/02	**WOKINGHAM TOWN**	DFL	5-0	515	Akamoah(2), Daly(2), Harlow
05/03	Stevenage Borough	DFL	1-4	909	Daly
08/03	Dorking	DFL	0-2	360	
12/03	Wivenhoe Town	DFL	1-1	237	Harlow
19/03	**ENFIELD**	DFL	1-2	663	Harlow
26/03	**BROMLEY**	DFL	3-0	554	Underdown, Harlow, Sugrue
02/04	Hayes	DFL	1-2	320	Underdown
04/04	**MOLESEY**	DFL	0-0	563	
09/04	Chesham United	DFL	0-1	631	
16/04	**BASINGSTOKE T.**	DFL	5-0	419	Wingfield(3), Ndah(2)
19/04	**AYLESBURY UTD**	DFL	2-1	397	Ndah, Wingfield
23/04	Marlow	DFL	3-3	405	Daly, Ndah, Underdown
28/04	Hendon	DFL	0-0	210	
30/04	**SUTTON UNITED**	DFL	0-2	765	
07/05	Dulwich Hamlet	DFL	7-1	302	Wingfield(4), Ndah(2), Sugrue

Key: DFL: Diadora League Premier Division, DLC: Diadora League Cup, CC: (Diadora League) Carlsberg Cup, SSC: Surrey Senior Cup, FAC: F.A. Cup, FAT: F.A. Trophy. Number after cup competitions denote rounds (r: replay, qf: Quarter-Final, sf: Semi-Final, f: Final. Numbers in brackets indicate legs, i.e. (1): 1st leg). Home fixtures are denoted by bold capitals, away matches by lower case. (p): penalty, og: Own goal.

SQUAD MEMBERS *(previous clubs listed in chronological order)*

GOALKEEPERS: Adrian Blake *(Walton & Hersham, Feltham, Yeading, Walton & Hersham).*
.gap 5
DEFENDERS: David Kempton *(Wimbledon, Napier City(NZ), Kiwi Utd(NZ), Walton & Hersham, Molesey, Ditton),* **John Finch** *(Chelsea, Leatherhead, Molesey, Dorking, Fulham),* **Lee Smart** *(Spurs, Brentford, Dag. & Red.),* **Phil Barton** *(Everton, Blackburn R., Bath, Morton, Arthurlie, Sutton Utd.),* **Andy Russell** *(Bracknell, Wycombe, Woking),* **Solomon Eriemo** *(Leytonstone-Ilford, Walthamstow A., Leyton-Wingate, Wealdstone),* **Darren Brodrick** *(Fulham).*

MIDFIELD: David Harlow *(Fulham, Farnborough),* **Neil Fewings** *(Kingstonian, Staines),* **Phil Wingfield** *(Walton & Hersham, Kingstonian, Walton & Hersham, Hayes),* **Mark Underdown** *(QPR, Staines, Sutton Utd.),* **Jon Daly** *(Crystal Palace, Croydon, Tooting, Croydon, Whyteleafe, Dulwich, Hendon).*

FORWARDS: Eddie Akamoah *(Carshalton),* **Jimmy Sugrue** *(Fulham),* **Jaimme Ndah** *(Crystal Palace, Croydon Ath., Horsham),* **Red Braithwaite** *(Fulham, Farnborough),* **Barry Blackman** *(Crystal Palace, Charlton, Uppsala(Swe.) Croydon, Edsbro (Swe.), Tooting, Yeovil, Wealdstone, Gloucester, Dulwich, Hendon).*

Formed: 1870

MARLOW

The Blues

Supporters join the players on Reading's Elm Park pitch to celebrate the Berks & Bucks Senior Cup victory, Marlow 1, Chesham United 0.

Photo - Piers Thompson, Maidenhead Advertiser.

Chairman: Michael Eagleton **Vice-Chairman:** Terry Staines **President:** Herbie Swadling.
Secretary: Terry Staines, 49 Sunnycroft, Downley, High Wycombe (0494 531580/473030).
Manager: Peter Foley **Coach:** Steve Hayward **Physio:** Sean Barker
Press Officer/Commercial Manager: Michael Eagleton (0628 486571).
Information Line (local call rates): 0628 477032).
Ground: Alfred Davis Memorial Ground, Oak Tree Road, Marlow SL7 3ED (0628 483970).
Directions: A404 to Marlow (from M4 or M40), then A4135 towards town centre. Turn right into Maple Rise (by ESSO garage), ground in road opposite (Oak Tree Rd). Half mile from Marlow (BR) station. Quarter mile from Chapel Street bus stops.
Capacity: 4,000 **Cover:** 600 **Seats:** 250 **Floodlights:** Yes **Metal Badges:** Yes
Club Shop: Yes, selling programmes, badges, ties, pens, videos etc.
Colours: Royal blue **Change colours:** Orange & black
Sponsors: Platts of Marlow.
Previous Leagues: Reading & Dist./ Spartan 1908-10 28-65/ Great Western Suburban/ Athenian 65-84.
Previous Name: Great Marlow.
Previous Grounds: Crown Ground 1870-1919)/ Star Meadow 19-24.
Midweek home matchday: Tuesday
Reserve Team's League: Suburban (West).
Record Attendance: 8,000; Slough Town v Wycombe Wanderers, Berks & Bucks Snr Cup Final, 1972. For Marlow game: 2,700 v Plymouth Argyle, FA Cup 1st Round 1993.
Best FA Cup season: Semi-Finals 1882. Also 3rd Rd 92-93 (lost 1-5 at Tottenham) and 1st Rd on 19 other occasions: 1871-85 86-88 92-93 1991-92 93-94.
Record Fees - Paid: £4,000 for Tim Buzaglo (Woking, 1993)
Received: £5,000 for Al-James Hannigan (Enfield, 1993).
Players progressing to Football League: Leo Markham (Watford 1972), Naseem Bashir (Reading).
Clubhouse: Open matchdays & most evenings. Snack bar open matchdays.
Club Record Goalscorer: Kevin Stone 31.
Club Record Appearances: Mick McKeown 500+.
93-94 Captain: David Lay
93-94 P.o.Y.: Trevor Baron.
93-94 Top scorer: David Lay.
Local Newspapers: Bucks Free Press (0494 521212), Maidenhead Advertiser (0628 771155), Evening Post (0734 575833).
Local Radio Stations: Eleven 70, Radio Berkshire, Radio 210
Honours: Isthmian Lg Div 1 87-88 (Div 2 South R-up 86-87, Lg Cup 92-93), Spartan Lg Div 1 37-38 (Div 2 West 29-30), Berks & Bucks Senior Cup 1880-81 82-83 84-85 85-86 87-88 88-89 89-90 93-94 96-97 98-99 99-1900 90-91 93-94, FA Trophy 1st Rd 1987-88 91-92, FA Vase 5th Rd replay 74-75.

PROGRAMME DETAILS:
Pages: 40 **Price:** £1
Editor: Paul Burdell/ John Addaway

MARLOW's 1993-94 CAMPAIGN

Date	Opponents	Comp.	Res	Gate	Goalscorers
21/08	Yeading	DFL	0-2	182	
24/08	**St ALBANS CITY**	DFL	4-2	315	Ferguson, Blackman(2), Lay
28/08	**BASINGSTOKE TOWN**	DFL	2-0	239	Lay, Buzaglo
30/08	Carshalton Athletic	DFL	1-2	515	Baron
04/09	Dulwich Hamlet	DFL	3-2	268	Lay(2(1p)), Ferguson
07/09	Chesham United	DFLS	1-4	821	Watkins
11/09	**AYLESBURY UTD**	DFL	1-0	495	Ferguson
18/09	Hendon	FAT1q	2-1	247	Caesar, Buzaglo
25/09	Grays Athletic	DFL	7-4	167	Lay(2(1p), Caesar(3), Buzaglo(2)
02/10	**DORKING**	DFL	2-1	384	Buzaglo, Watkins
04/10	Stevenage Borough	DFL	2-4	934	Regan, Caesar
09/10	**SUTTON UNITED**	DFL	3-2	485	Watkins, Lay, Anderson(og)
12/10	**ENFIELD**	DFL	2-1	582	Lay(2(1p))
16/10	**HAYES**	FAT2q	1-1	260	Catlin
19/10	Hayes	FAT2qr	3-2	270	Catlin(2), Lay
23/10	Aylesbury Utd	FAC4q	2-1	926	Lay, Watkins
26/10	Chesham United	DFL	3-1	628	Baron, Blackman, Buzaglo
30/10	**MOLESEY**	DFL	2-1	304	Lay, Watkins
02/11	**YEADING**	DLC1	2-0	332	Lay(p), Catlin
06/11	Wivenhoe Town	DFL	3-2	170	Ferguson, Lay, Buzaglo
13/11	**PLYMOUTH ARGYLE**	FAC1	0-2	2,700	
16/11	Wembley	DLC2	2-2	110	Lay(2)
20/11	Kingstonian	DFL	1-1	539	Nolan
23/11	**RUISLIP MANOR**	CC1	3-1	120	Nolan(3(2ps))
27/11	Gravesend & N'fleet	FAT3q	4-1	604	Regan, Watkins, Buzaglo, Caesar
30/11	**WEMBLEY**	DLC2r	2-1	190	Blackman, Watkins
04/12	Hitchin Town	DFL	1-2	425	Buzaglo
11/12	**CARSHALTON ATH.**	DFL	0-6	310	
14/12	Basingstoke Town	DLC3	1-1	205	Watkins
18/12	Bromley	DFL	3-2	287	Baron, Catlin, Blackman
27/12	**WOKINGHAM TOWN**	DFL	3-1	452	Baron, Catlin(2)
01/01	Aylesbury United	DFL	5-1	725	Lay(p), Catlin, Caesar(2), Blackman
04/01	**BASINGSTOKE TOWN**	DLC3r	3-2	208	Lay(p), Catlin, own-goal
08/01	**WIVENHOE TOWN**	DFL	3-1	358	Baron, Caesar(2)
11/01	**SLOUGH TOWN**	B&B1	1-0	461	
15/01	St Albans City	DFL	2-1	758	Baron, Catlin
18/01	**HAYES**	DFL	4-3	486	Lay(2), Baron, Russell(og)
29/01	Basingstoke Town	DFL	3-1	315	Caesar, Lay, Chewins(og)
05/02	**DULWICH HAMLET**	DFL	4-2	512	Caesar(2), Lay, Buzaglo
07/02	Worthing	FAT1	0-3	564	
09/02	**PURFLEET**	CC2	0-1		
16/02	Wycombe Wanderers	B&Bqf	3-1	1,060	Lay(2), Blackman
19/02	**GRAYS ATHLETIC**	DFL	3-1	224	Byrne, Lay, Watkins
26/02	**HENDON**	DFL	2-1	445	Blackman, Catlin
09/03	Chesham United	DLCqf	3-0		
12/03	**STEVENAGE BORO'**	DFL	0-0	1,020	
15/03	**ENFIELD**	DLCsf(1)	1-1	380	Buzaglo
19/03	Dorking	DFL	3-2	240	Caesar(2), Baron
23/03	**AYLESBURY UTD**	B&Bsf	1-1	438	Caesar
26/03	Molesey	DFL	1-1	193	Nolan
29/03	Aylesbury United	B&Bsfr	5-0	414	Baron, Lay(2), Caesar, Blackman
02/04	**CHESHAM UNITED**	DFL	0-2	590	
05/04	Wokingham Town	DFL	6-0	383	Baron(2), Lay, Cattlin(2), Blackman
07/04	Enfield	DLCsf(2)	1-2	500	Lay
09/04	**BROMLEY**	DFL	3-4	271	Lay(2), Glasgow
14/04	**HARROW BOROUGH**	DFL	0-1	310	
16/04	Hayes	DFL	0-2	292	
18/04	Hendon	DFL	1-0	153	Cattlin
20/04	Sutton United	DFL	2-2	418	Buzaglo, Nolan
23/04	**KINGSTONIAN**	DFL	3-3	405	Blackman, Baynes, Ferguson
28/03	**YEADING**	DFL	1-1	204	Blunden
30/04	Harrow Borough	DFL	0-2	252	
02/05	CHESHAM UNITED	B&Bf	1-0	782	Lay *(played at Reading FC)*
04/05	Enfield	DFL	0-0	460	
07/05	**HITCHIN TOWN**	DFL	1-0	266	Lay

Key: DFL: Diadora League Premier Division, DLC: Diadora League Cup, CC: Carlsberg Cup, DFLS: Diadora League Championship Shield, FAC: F.A. Cup, FAT: F.A. Trophy, B&B: Berks & Bucks Senior Cup.

SQUAD MEMBERS *(previous clubs listed in chronological order)*

GOALKEEPERS: Kevin Mitchell *(Reading, Egham T., Windsor & Eton, Woking, Leather, Slough T., Windsor & Eton)*, **Gary Lester** *(Chalfont St Peter, Wycombe Wdrs, Slough T., Chalfont St Peter)*.

DEFENDERS: Martin Malins *(Reading, Wokingham T.)*, **Steve Holmes** *(Blackburn Rovers, Enfield)*, **Stewart Mitchell** *(Gateshead, Hayes, Hendon, Slough T., Maidenhead U., Windsor & Eton, Woking, Basingstoke T.)*, **Dave Nolan** *(Hendon, Harrow B., Northwood)*, **Colin Ferguson** *(Reading, Maidenhead U., Burnham, Cookham Dean)*.

MIDFIELD: Kenny Glasgow *(Flackwell Hth, Marlow, Flackwell Hth, Marlow, Chalfont, Flackwell Hth, Marlow, Maidenhead, Burnham)*, **Garfield Blackman** *(Welwyn GC, Northwood)*, **Tony Dell** *(Marlow, Wycombe Wdrs, Slough T., Chesham U.)*, **John Caesar** *(Oakridge, Flackwell H.)*, **David Lay** *(Reading, Chesham U., Dunstable)*.

FORWARDS: Tim Buzaglo *(Weysiders, Woking)*, **Mark Watkins** *(Winslow U., Aylesbury U., St Albans City, Tring T., Harrow B., Tring T.)*, **Steve Baynes** *(Southampton, Maidenhead, Slough, Hillingdon, Windsor, Northwood, Maidenhead, Camberley, Flackwell Hth)*, **John Regan** *(Burnham, Kingstonian, Southall, Hayes, Chalfont St Peter, Wycombe Wdrs, Hounslow)*

MOLESEY

Formed: 1950 | The Moles

Molesey FC 1993-94. The club's most notable achievement in their first season of Premier Division football was reaching the First Round Proper of the FA Cup for the first time.

Photo - Eric Marsh.

Chairman: Martin Eede **President:** Fred Maynard
Secretary: John Chambers, 293 Walton Rd, West Molesey, Surrey KT8 0JN (081 979 4454).
Manager: John Rains **Physio:** Alan Brilliant **Coach:** Tony Rains.
Press Officer: Peter Bowers (c/o the clun).
Commercial Manager: Kevin Sweeny
Ground: 412 Walton Road, West Molesey, Surrey KT8 0JG (081 979 4823).
Directions: A3 from London to Hook, then A309 to Marquis of Granby pub, right to Hampton Court station, turn right for West Molesey, ground one mile on left.
Capacity: 4,000 **Cover:** 600 **Seats:** 400 **Floodlights:** Yes **Metal Badges:** Yes
Colours: White/black/black **Change colours:** Yellow/blue/yellow
Club Shop: Yes, contact John Chambers at the club.
Previous Leagues: Surrey Intermediate 53-56/ Surrey Snr 56-59/ Spartan 59-72/ Athenian 72-77.
Sponsors: Ivy Express Transport **Previous Name:** Molesey St Pauls 1950-53.
Midweek home matchday: Wednesday **Reserve Team's League:** Suburban.
Record Attendance: 1,255 v Sutton United, Surrey Senior Cup Semi-Final 1966.
Best FA Vase season: 6th Rd 81-82 **Best FA Trophy season:** 1st Rd replay 90-91.
Best FA Cup season: First Round Proper 93-94 (lost 0-4 at home to Bath City).
Record Fees - Paid: £500 for Chris Vidal (Leatherhead, 1988)
Received: £5,000 for Chris Vidal (Hythe Town, 1989).
Players progressing to Football League: John Finch (Fulham), Cyrille Regis (WBA, Coventry & England).
Clubhouse: Open every evening and weekend lunchtimes. 2 bars, discos, live artists, darts, bingo, pool.
Steward: John Chambers
Club Record Goalscorer: Michael Rose, 130
Club Record Appearances: Frank Hanley, 453
Local Radio: County Sound, Capital. **Local Newspapers:** Surrey Comet, Surrey Herald, Molesey News.
93-94 Captain: Steve Croad. **93-94 P.o.Y.:** David Pattulo. **93-94 Top Scorer:** Neil Pearson 26.
Honours: Isthmian Lg Div 1 R-up 92-93 (Div 2 South R-up 89-90, Lg Cup R-up 92-93), Surrey Senior Lg 57-58, (Lg Charity Cup 56-57), Spartan Lg R-up 59-60 (Lg Cup 61-62 (R-up 63-64)), Surrey Senior Shield R-up 74-75, Southern Combination Cup 90-91 93-94.

SQUAD MEMBERS *(previous clubs listed in chronological order)*

GOALKEEPERS: David Brace *(Fulham, Molesey, Walton Casuals)*

DEFENDERS: Roger Worrall *(Frinton Rovers, Croydon MO)*, **Clive Gartell** *(Epsom, Leatherhead, Molesey, Dulwich)*, **Richard Langley** *(Corinthian-Cas., Fulham, Kingstonian)*, **Dave Pattulo** *(Sheen Ath.)*, **Steve Croad** *(Addlestone, Hounslow, Carshalton, Farnborough, Yeading)*, **Lyndon Buckwell** *(Chelsea, Chessington, Epsom, Kingstonian)*, **Mark Dodman** *(Crystal Pal., Pretoria(SA), Leatherhead, Carshalton, Whyteleafe, Molesey, Dulwich)*, **Mark Harmsworth** *(Epsom, Hampton, Kingstonian, Hampton, Fisher, Hayes, Yeading, Walton & H., Yeading)*

MIDFIELD: Dave Rattue *(Molesey, Kingstonian, Leatherhead, Hampton, Whyteleafe)*, **Paul Harris** *(Whyteleafe, Tooting, Epsom, Molesey, Dulwich, Whyteleafe)*, **Gary Wilgoss** *(Whyteleafe, Carshalton, Dulwich)*, **Trevor McCoy** *(local football)*, **Peter Woods** *(Epsom, Kingstonian)*, **Paul Meredith** *(Cobham, Molesey, Tooting, Dorking, Banstead, Carshalton, Banstead, Epsom)*, **Benny Penfold** *(local football)*, **James Wenlock** *(Leatherhead)*, **Tony Borman** *(Crockenhill, Epsom, Croydon, Grays Ath., Whyteleafe, Leatherhead, Bromley, Whyteleafe)*, **Steve Emmanuel** *(Watford, Harrow, Staines, Harrow, Hayes, Chesham, Harlow, Maidenhead, Harrow)*

(continued opposite)

PROGRAMME DETAILS:
Pages: 26 **Price:** 80p
Editor: Peter Bowers
c/o the club

MOLESEY's 1993-94 CAMPAIGN

Date	Opponents	Comp.	Res	Gate	Goalscorers
21/08	Basingstoke Town	DFL	2-1	310	Winterhalter, Borman
25/08	**GRAYS ATHLETIC**	DFL	0-2	226	
28/08	**SUTTON UNITED**	DFL	0-0	561	
31/08	Hitchin Town	DFL	0-2	328	
04/09	Yeading	DFL	0-3	176	
11/09	Hastings Town	FAC1q	5-1	375	McCoy(2), Wilgoss, Pearson, White
15/09	**DORKING**	DFL	3-0	207	McCoy(2), Callaghan
18/09	Bromley	FAT1q	2-0	365	Wilgoss, Pearson
22/09	**NEWBURY TOWN**	DLC1	1-1		Callaghan
25/09	**CORINTHIAN**	FAC2q	2-0	138	Pearson(2)
06/10	Harrow Borough	DFL	1-1	178	McCoy
10/10	Greenwich Borough	FAC3q	4-0	280	Pearson(4) *(played at Bromley FC)*
16/10	**SITTINGBOURNE**	FAT2q	0-4	342	
19/09	Cobham	SSC2q	4-0		McKay(2), Pearson, Worrall *(played at home)*
23/10	**TOOTING & MITCHAM**	FAC4q	0-0	461	
26/10	Tooting & Mitcham	FAC4qr	2-1	702	Rattue, Worrall
30/10	Marlow	DFL	1-2	304	McCoy
02/11	Newbury Towm	DLC1r	3-2		Pearson(2), Rose
03/11	**CAMBERLEY TOWN**	SSC3q	4-1		Callaghan(2), White, Wilgoss
06/11	Wokingham Town	DFL	1-1	223	Pearson
09/11	Dulwich Hamlet	DFL	0-1	174	
13/11	**BATH CITY**	FAC1	0-4	913	
17/11	**STAINES TOWN**	DLC2	0-1	89	
20/11	Wivenhoe Town	DFL	4-3	184	Pearson(3), Wilgoss
27/11	**CHESHAM UNITED**	DFL	1-1	331	Pearson
30/11	Leatherhead	SSC4q	3-0		Callaghan, Pearson, Nelson
04/12	Aylesbury United	DFL	1-2	351	Pearson
11/12	**HITCHIN TOWN**	DFL	1-2	193	McCoy
15/12	**CARSHALTON ATH.**	SSC1	2-2		Rattue, Pearson
18/12	Hayes	DFL	0-3	261	
22/12	Carshalton Athletic	SSC1r	2-0		Pearson(2)
27/12	**KINGSTONIAN**	DFL	1-1	714	Pearson
01/01	Dorking	DFL	1-3	284	Borman
12/01	**CARSHALTON ATH.**	DFL	0-1	257	
15/01	Grays Athletic	DFL	2-1	199	Rice(2)
18/01	Malden Vale	SSCqf	3-1		McCoy(2), Callaghan
22/01	**BASINGSTOKE T.**	DFL	0-0	261	
26/01	**MAIDENHEAD UTD**	CC2	3-2	122	Rattue(2), Pearson
29/01	Sutton United	DFL	1-4	646	Langley
05/02	**BROMLEY**	DFL	2-3	222	Rattue, Rice
05/02	Yeading	DFL	0-0	161	
12/02	St Albans City	DFL	1-4	401	Newman
16/02	**HENDON**	DFL	2-3	223	Harris, Newman
19/02	**DULWICH HAMLET**	DFL	0-0	241	
26/02	**STEVENAGE BORO.**	DFL	1-2	431	Pearson
01/09	**WOKING**	SSCsf	0-3	925	
05/03	Bromley	DFL	1-0	224	Rose
09/03	**BROMLEY**	CC3	2-1	137	Rose(2)
12/03	**HARROW BOROUGH**	DFL	0-0	190	
16/03	**WOKINGHAM TOWN**	DFL	2-0	166	Pearson, Harris
19/03	Chesham United	DFL	1-0	481	Newman
22/03	St Albans City	CCqf	1-2	158	Pearson
26/03	**MARLOW**	DFL	1-1	193	Pattulo
30/03	**St ALBANS CITY**	DFL	2-1	237	Borman, Harris.
02/04	Hendon	DFL	0-2	183	
04/04	Kingstonian	DFL	0-0	563	
09/04	**HAYES**	DFL	3-2	162	Dodman, Rice, Newman
18/04	Stevenage Borough	DFL	2-4	1,004	Newman, Wilgoss
23/04	**WIVENHOE TOWN**	DFL	4-0	166	Croad, Borman, Pearson, Newman
30/04	**CARSHALTON ATH.**	DFL	1-0		Newman
07/05	**AYLESBURY UTD**	DFL	1-2	145	Brownlie
09/05	**ENFIELD**	DFL	0-1	325	
11/05	Enfield	DFL	0-3	501	
12/05	**STAINES TOWN**	SCCf	1-0	235	

Key: DFL: Diadora League Premier Division, DLC: Diadora League Cup, CC: Carsberg Cup, DFLS: Diadora League Championship Shield, FAC: F.A. Cup, FAT: F.A. Trophy, SSC: Surrey Senior Cup, SCC: Southern Combination Cup. Numbers after cup competitions denote rounds (r: replay, qf: Quarter-Final, sf: Semi-Final, f: Final. Numbers in brackets indicate legs, i.e. (1): 1st leg).
Home fixtures are denoted by bold capitals, away matches by lower case. (p): penalty, og: Own goal.

(continuation of squad)
FORWARDS: Micky Rose *(Dulwich, Crawley, Leatherhead, Carshalton)*, **Sean Rice** *(Ditton, Hampton)*, **Neil Pearson** *(Wimbledon, Dulwich)*, **Del Deanus** *(Spurs, Yeading)*, **Andre Forrester** *(Kingstonian)*, **Craig Orris** *(Wimbledon, Bromley, Kingstonian, Banstead, Bromley)*, **Steve Barwick** *(Hook, Sutton, Epsom, Walton & H.)*

PURFLEET

1985 | Fleet

Purfleet's Keith Barrett brings the ball clear of Martin St Hilaire during the FA Trophy First Round tie away to his former club Enfield.

Photo - Dennis Nicholson.

Chairman: Harry South **Vice Chairman:** Ken Worrall **President:** Keith Parker.
Secretary/Press Officer: Norman Posner, 1 Chase House Gdns, Hornchurch, Essex RM11 2PJ (0708 458301).
Manager: Gary Calder **Asst Manager:** Chris King **Coach:** Dennis Moore
Commercial Manager: Bob Andrews (0376 376602) **Physio:** Bob Johnson.
Ground: Thurrock Hotel, Ship Lane, Grays, Essex (0708 868901).
Directions: M25 or A13 to Dartford tunnel r'bout. Ground is fifty yards on right down Ship Lane. Nearest station is Purfleet, two miles from ground.
Capacity: 4,500 **Cover:** 1,000 **Seats:** 300 **Floodlights:** Yes
Club Shop: Yes, selling programmes and magazines. Contact Tommy South (0708 868901).
Colours: Green/yellow **Change colours:** Claret/blue.
Sponsors: John Joy Welding Ltd **Previous Names:** None.
Previous Grounds: None. **Previous League:** Essex Senior 85-89.
Midweek home matchday: Monday **Reserve Team's League:** Essex & Herts Border Combination.
Record Attendance: 950 v West Ham United, friendly 1989.
Best FA Cup season: Third Qualifying Rd 93-94 (lost 1-2 at home to Yeading).
Record win: 10-0 v Stansted (H) 86-87, v East Ham Utd (A) 87-88 (both Essex Senior League).
Record defeat: 0-5 v Kingsbury Town (H), Isthmian Lge Division One 89-90.
Players progressing to Football League: Paul Cobb (Leyton Orient).
Clubhouse: 10am-11pm every day. Snooker, squash, weights room, aerobics, a-la carte restaurant, steam room. Two bars, 56 bedroom hotel.
Steward: Tommy South.
Club Record Goalscorer: Terry Bellamy, 59.
Club Record Appearances: Colin McBride, 234.
93-94 Captain: Chris Blakesbrough.
93-94 P.o.Y.: Chris Blakesbrough.
93-94 Top scorer: Paul Cobb, 31.
Local Newspapers: Thurrock Recorder, Thurrock Gazette.
Local Radio Stations: Essex Radio, BBC Radio Essexx.
Hons: Isthmian Lg Div 2 91-92 (Div 1 R-up 93-94, Div 2 Nth R-up 88-89, Associate Members Tphy 91-92), Essex Snr Lg 87-88 (Lg Cup(2) 86-88), Stanford Charity Cup 87-88 (R-up 85-86).

PROGRAMME DETAILS:
Pages: 44 **Price:** 75p
Editor: Secretary

PURFLEET's 1993-94 CAMPAIGN

Date	Opponents	Comp.	Res	Gate	Goalscorers
21/08	**RUISLIP MANOR**	DFL	2-1		Cobb, Rees
24/08	Berkhamsted Town	DFL	5-1		Cobb(2), Brett(2), Barrett
28/08	Rainham Town	FACpr	5-1	92	Cobb(2), Spiteri, Blakebrough, Georgiou
31/08	Staines Town	DFL	1-0	289	Spiteri
04/09	**CROYDON**	DFL	2-4		Georgiou, Cobb
06/09	**LEYTON**	DFL	1-0		Cobb
11/09	Langford	FAC1q	4-1	114	Brett(2), Cobb, Matthews
18/09	Sudbury Town	FAT1q	3-3	352	Cobb(2), Donovan
20/09	**SUDBURY TOWN**	FAT1qr	3-0	191	Georgiou(2), Brett
25/09	Ruislip Manor	FAc2q	1-1	172	Cobb
27/09	**RUISLIP MANOR**	FAC2qr	1-0	97	Georgiou
02/10	Chalfont St Peter	DFL	2-1		Brett, Cobb
04/10	**HEYBRIDGE SWIFTS**	ESC1	1-4		Georgiou
09/10	**YEADING**	FAC3q	1-2	153	Cobb
11/10	**BISH. STORTFORD**	DFL	0-2	214	
16/10	Baldock Town	FAT2q	3-2	176	Brett(2), Rees
19/10	Tooting & Mitcham Utd	DFL	1-3		Cobb
23/10	Windsor & Eton	DFL	4-1		Jeyes, Rees, Cobb, Brett
30/10	**BARKING**	DFL	2-1		Cobb(2)
02/11	Sutton United	DLC1	0-2	291	
06/11	**MAIDENHEAD UTD**	DFL	1-0	72	Brett
08/11	**WORTHING**	DFL	1-1	117	Cobb
13/11	Abingdon Town	DFL	1-1		Brett
19/11	**WALTON & HERSH.**	DFL	0-0		
27/11	**HEYBRIDGE SWIFTS**	FAT3q	3-2	138	Donovan, Granger, Cobb
30/11	Boreham Wood	DFL	2-0		Cobb(2)
04/12	**BOGNOR REGIS T.**	DFL	2-0		Brett, Grainger
11/12	Leyton	DFL	1-2		Grainger
18/12	**UXBRIDGE**	DFL	0-3	85	
27/12	Billericay Town	DFL	2-2	402	Donovan, Houlding
01/01	**BOREHAM WOOD**	DFL	0-2		
08/01	Maidenhead United	DFL	1-1	166	Rees
15/01	**BERKHAMSTED T.**	DFL	1-1		Kimble
22/01	Enfield	FAT1	0-2	703	
29/01	**STAINES TOWN**	DFL	4-0	80	Brett(2), Cobb(2)
05/02	Croydon	DFL	4-1		Cobb(2), Brett, Jeyes
09/02	Marlow	CC2	1-0		Parratt
12/02	**TOOTING & MITCHAM**	DFL	1-0		Brett
19/02	Bishop's Stortford	DFL	3-2	360	Spiteri, Dickinson, Parratt
21/02	**WHYTELEAFE**	DFL	0-1		
26/02	Worthing	DFL	1-2	437	Jeyes
05/03	Heybridge Swifts	DFL	0-0		
07/03	**CARSHALTON ATH.**	CC3	2-2		Parratt, Jeyes *(won 8-7 on penalties)*
12/03	Whyteleafe	DFL	1-0		Cobb
15/03	Wembley	DFL	1-1		Spiteri
19/03	**CHALFONT St PETER**	DFL	1-0		Spiteri
21/03	**WOKINGHAM TOWN**	CCqf	1-1	112	Donovan *(lost 4-5 on penalties)*
26/03	Barking	DFL	3-0		Brett, Spiteri, Cobb
28/03	Ruislip Manor	DFL	3-2		Spiteri, Parratt, Sewell
02/04	**WINDSOR & ETON**	DFL	3-1		Blakebrough, Cobb, Richards
04/04	**BILLERICAY TOWN**	DFL	3-2	347	Richards, Cobb(2)
09/04	Uxbridge	DFL	2-1		Richards, Cobb
16/04	**ABINGDON TOWN**	DFL	4-0		Richards(2), Donovan, Parratt
19/04	Heybridge Swifts	DFL	0-0		
22/04	Walton & Hersham	DFL	2-2		Dickinson, Richards
30/04	**WEMBLEY**	DFL	0-0		
07/05	Bognor Regis Town	DFL	2-2		Spiteri, Rees

Key: DFL: Diadora League Division One, DLC: Diadora League Cup, CC: Carsberg Cup, FAC: F.A. Cup, FAT: F.A. Trophy, ESC: Essex Senior Cup. Numbers after cup competitions denote rounds (r: replay, qf: Quarter-Final, sf: Semi-Final, f: Final. Numbers in brackets indicate legs, i.e. (1): 1st leg).

SQUAD MEMBERS *(previous clubs listed in chronological order)*

GOALKEEPERS: Brian Smart *(Brechin, Rainham)*, **Kevin Foster** *(Chelmsford, Wealdstone, Dagenham & Redbridge, Chelmsford, Dagenham & R., Bishop's Stortford)*.

DEFENDERS: John Rees *(Aveley)*, **Ian Brooks** *(Collier R.)*, **Darren Houlding** *(Millwall Wdrs, Clapton, Aveley, Purfleet, Collier R.)*, **Graham Daly** *(Woodford, Walthamstow Av., Aveley)*, **Steve Dickinson** *(QPR)*, **Keith Barrett** *(Arsenal, Tottenham, Barking, Enfield, Wycombe, Redbridge, Dartford)*.

MIDFIELD: Jason Spiteri *(Clapton, Redbridge, Aveley)*, **Gary Keen** *(Chesham, St Albans, Hendon, St Albans, Hendon, Hayes, Hendon)*, **Lee Matthews** *(Southend Utd)*, **Tony Richards** *(West Ham, Barking)*, **Paul Donovan** *(Fulham, Dagenham)*, **Danny Smith** *(E Thurrock)*.

FORWARDS: Chris Blakebrough *(Hornchurch, Clapton, Hornchurch, Clapton, Redbridge, Aveley)*, **Paul Cobb** *(Purfleet, Leyton O.)*, **Alan Brett** *(Aveley, Purfleet, Aveley)*, **Nigel Jeyes** *(Dartford, Barking, Tilbury, Billericay, Basildon, Aveley)*, **George Georgiou** *(Leyton O., Enfield, Dagenham & R.)*, **Richard Newbery** *(Farnborough, Staines)*, **Bruce Sewell** *(Basildon, Collier R., Billericay, Ford, E Thurrock, Collier R.)*.

Formed: 1908

ST ALBANS CITY

The Saints

St Albans City pictured before their FA Trophy tie at Staines Town. *Photo - Eric Marsh.*

Chairman: Bernard Tominey **General Manager:** Allan Cockram **President:** Cllr Malcolm MacMillan
Secretary: Steve Trulock, 42 Heath Road, St Albans AL1 4DP (0727 834920).
Mgr: A Cockram/Martin Duffield **Physio:** Judith Monteith **Newsline:** 0891 664354
Press Off.: Dave Tavener (0582 401487) **Comm. Director:** Graham McDougall (0727 864296/866819).
Ground: Clarence Park, York Rd, St Albans, Herts AL1 4PL (0727 866819).
Directions: Turn left out of St Albans station - Clarence Park 200yds ahead across Hatfield Rd. By road from M25 (clockwise) - jct 21 to Noke Hotel island, straight on thru Chiswell Green towards St Albans, straight over 2 mini-r'bouts and one larger island, thru two sets of lights and right at island at far end of city centre (St Peters Str.) into Hatfield Rd, over 1 mini-r'bout, left at 2nd lights into Clarence Rd, ground on left. From M25 (anticlockwise), jct 22 onto A1081 towards city centre, 3rd exit at 2nd island, thru two lights, right at island just before Odeon into Alma Rd, right at lights, straight thru next 2 sets (road bends considerably) into Clarence Rd, ground on left.
Capacity: 6,000 **Cover:** 1,900 **Seats:** 904 **Floodlights:** Yes **Metal Badges:** Yes
Club Shop: Managed by Terry Edwards (0727 833685) and Ray Stanton. Large selection of club merchandise and League and non-League programmes. Magazines, videos etc. Shop merchandise managed by Leigh Page.
Cols: Blue & yellow stripes/blue/blue & yellow hoops. **Change cols:** Purple & white.
Previous Leagues: Herts County 08-10/ Spartan 08-20/ Athenian 20-23.
Midweek home matchday: Tuesday **Record Gate:** 9,757 v Ferryhill Ath., FA Amtr Cup QF 27/2/26.
Record win: 14-0 v Aylesbury United (H), Spartan League 19/10/12 (3 Aylesbury players turned up just before half-time - St Albans led 9-0 at the interval). **Record loss:** 0-11 v Wimbledon (H), Isthmian Lg 9/11/46.
Best FA Cup season: 2nd Rd replay 68-69 (lost 1-3 at Walsall after 1-1 draw), 80-81 (lost 1-4 at Torquay after 1-1 draw). Also 1st Rd 25-26 26-27 92-93. **League clubs defeated in FA Cup:** Brentford 24-25.
Record Fees - Paid: £5,000 for Martin Duffield (Sutton United, March 1992)
Rec.: £92,750 for Dean Austin (Southend 1990, + increments from subsequent move to Spurs).
Players progressing to Football League: Arthur Grimsdell (Spurs 1911), Ronnie Burke (Man Utd), John Meadows (W'ford 1951), Mike Rose (Charlton 1963), Joe Kinnear (Spurs 1965), John Mitchell (Fulham 1972), Allan Cockram (Brentford 1988), Dean Austin (Southend 1990), Tony Kelly (Stoke 1990), Michael Danzey (Cambridge 1992), Dean Williams (Brentford 1993).
Clubhouse: Tea bar within ground serves hot food. Clubhouse open matchdays and available for daytime and evening functions. Clubhouse manager, Ray McCord (0727 866819 or 837956).
Club Record Goalscorer: W H (Billy) Minter 368 (top scorer for 12 consecutive seasons 1920-32).
Club Record Appearances: Phil Wood 1,017 (63-84)
93-94 Captain: Allan Cockram + nine others.
93-94 P.o.Y.: Shaun Brett **93-94 Top scorer:** Steve Clark 33.
Local Newspapers: St Albans Observer, St Albans Review, St Albans Herald.
Local Radio Stations: BBC Radio Beds, Chiltern Radio.
Hons: Isthmian Lg 23-24 26-27 27-28 (R-up 54-55 92-93, Div 1 85-86, Div 2 R-up 83-84, Lg Cup R-up 89-90, Res. Sect. R-up 48-49 60-61 61-62), Athenian Lg 20-21 21-22 (R-up 22-23), Spartan Lg 11-12 (R-up 12-13, East Div 09-10), Herts Co. Lg 09-10 (West Div 08-09, Aubrey Cup(res) 61-62), London Snr Cup 70-71 (R-up 69-70), AFA Snr Cup 33-34 (R-up 30-31 32-33 34-35), E Anglian Cup 92-93, Herts Snr Cup(12) 24-25 28-29 34-35 43-44 46-47 50-51 54-57 65-66 67-69 (R-up 10-11 41-42 42-43 47-48 52-53 57-58 64-65 70-71 78-79 89-90), Herts Snr Tphy 86-87, Herts Charity Cup(25) 09-10 12-13 20-26 28-29 38-39 40-42 50-51 52-54 55-58 66-67 68-72 86-87 92-93 (R-up(18) 11-12 13-14 26-28 31-33 34-35 37-38 45-46 48-50 51-52 54-55 62-63 76-77 81-82 87-89), Mithras Cup 64-65 71-72 (R-up 76-77), Wycombe F'lit Cup(2) 68-70, St Albans Hosp Cup 45-46, Hitchin Centenary Cup 70-71 (R-up 71-72), Victory Cup 25-26 27-28, Liege Cup 26-27, Billy Minter Invit. Cup 90-91 91-92 92-93, FA Amtr Cup SF(4) 22-23 24-26 69-70, FA Tphy 2nd Rd 81-82 92-93. *Res.*: Wallspan Southern Comb. 82-83 (R-up 83-84, Lg Cup 87-88 (R-up 83-84)), Herts I'mediate Cup(8) 47-48 49-50 50-51 53-54 57-58 62-64 66-67, Herts Jnr Cup 13-14, Bingham Cox Cup 12-13, Herts Charity Shld 24-25 31-32 37-38 (R-up 23-24 30-31). *Youth*: South Co's Yth Lg 91-92, MBS Lg 88-89, Kermat Lg Cup 87-88, Southern Co's Yth Cup R-up 91-92, FA Yth Cup 2nd Rd 91-92.

PROGRAMME DETAILS:
Pages: 40 **Price:** £1.20
Editor: Ray Stanton
(0727 864182)

St ALBANS CITY's 1993-94 CAMPAIGN

Date	Opponents	Comp.	Res	Gate	Goalscorers
10/08	**BALDOCK TOWN**	EAC1	3-4	211	Clark(2), Ross
17/08	**HITCHIN TOWN**	HCC1	4-3	335	Cockram, Clark(3)
21/08	**CHESHAM UNITED**	DFL	1-1	824	Goodyear
24/08	Marlow	DFL	2-4	315	Duffield, Gurney
28/08	Kingstonian	DFL	1-0	624	Clark
31/08	**WIVENHOE TOWN**	DFL	9-1	424	Duffield(3), Clark, Bushay, Murphy, Cockram(3)
04/09	**HENDON**	DFL	0-0	728	
07/09	Bishop's Stortford	HCC2	0-2	404	
11/09	Chesham United	FAC1q	0-5	1,004	
14/09	Wokingham Town	DFL	3-1	331	Clark(2), Bushay
18/09	**STEVENAGE BORO.**	DFL	1-2	852	Bushay
21/09	**BROMLEY**	DLC1	2-1	232	Goodyear, Bushay
25/09	**SUTTON UNITED**	DFL	0-0	640	
02/10	Basingstoke Town	DFL	1-0	327	Bushay
09/10	**BROMLEY**	DFL	2-0	708	Pluckrose(2)
12/10	Aylesbury United	DFL	2-1	596	Clark, Pluckrose
23/10	Grays Athletic	DFL	1-0	310	Duffield
26/10	Hertford Town	HSC1	5-3	169	Clark(3), Bushay, Brett
30/10	**YEADING**	DFL	1-1	502	Clark
06/11	Hitchin Town	DFL	3-1	821	Duffield, Cockram, Bushay
13/11	**HAYES**	DFL	4-0	402	Brett, Clark, Bushay, Gurney
16/11	Leyton	DLC2	4-3	163	Gurney, Bushay(3)
27/11	Staines Town	FAT3q	3-0	321	Clark(2), Gurney
01/12	Chesham United	CC1	2-0	376	Bushay(2)
04/12	Hayes	DFL	1-2	320	Gurney
11/12	**WOKINGHAM TOWN**	DFL	2-0	465	Bushay, Pluckrose
14/12	Staines Town	DLC3	1-0	258	Cockram
18/12	Harrow Borough	DFL	0-0	387	
27/12	**ENFIELD**	DFL	2-1	1,530	Brett, Gurney
01/01	Wivenhoe Town	DFL	3-0	382	Duffield, Bushay, Clark
03/01	Chesham United	DFL	0-0	671	
11/01	**DULWICH HAMLET**	DFL	4-3	481	Clark(3), Bushay
15/01	**MARLOW**	DFL	1-2	758	Pluckrose
18/01	**BALDOCK TOWN**	HSC2	1-3	165	Clark
22/01	**MERTHYR TYDFIL**	FAT1	4-5	1,017	Pluckrose, Clark, Bushay, Brett
25/01	Chertsey Town	DLCqf	0-5	395	
29/01	**KINGSTONIAN**	DFL	1-4	551	Bushay
01/02	**LEYTON**	CC2	5-3	155	Pluckrose, Bushay(2), Zoricich, Murphy
05/02	Hendon	DFL	0-1	361	
12/02	**MOLESEY**	BHL	4-1	401	Cockram(2), Brett, Risley
19/02	Stevenage Borough	DFL	0-3	878	
22/02	**HEYBRIDGE Sw.**	CC3	3-3	112	Duffield, own-goal(2) *(won 4-3 on penalties)*
26/02	Dulwich Hamlet	DFL	2-1	273	Duffield, Clark
05/02	**AYLESBURY UTD**	DFL	1-1	541	Wilkinson
08/03	**HITCHIN TOWN**	DFL	2-1	551	Goodyear, Clark
12/03	Sutton United	DFL	1-4	740	Clark
15/03	Dorking	DFL	2-1	188	Wilkinson, Duffield
19/03	**BASINGSTOKE T.**	DFL	6-1	354	Clark(2), Duffield(2), Gurney, Wilkinson
22/03	**MOLESEY**	CCqf	2-1	158	Duffield, Bushay
26/03	Yeading	DFL	1-1	302	Clark
30/03	Molesey	DFL	1-2	237	Wilkinson
02/04	**GRAYS ATHLETIC**	DFL	5-3	347	Driscoll, Duffield(2), Clark, Pluckrose
04/04	Enfield	DFL	1-1	1,033	Clark
09/04	**HARROW BOROUGH**	DFL	3-1	339	Duffield(2), Brett
21/04	**WOKINGHAM TOWN**	CCsf	0-2	328	
23/04	**DORKING**	DFL	3-0	310	Clark, Pluckrose, Murphy
28/04	Carshalton Athletic	DFL	3-3	328	Risley, Clark, Driscoll
30/04	Bromley	DFL	0-2	295	
03/05	**CARSHALTON ATH.**	DFL	1-3	238	Cockram

Key: DFL: Diadora League Premier Division, DLC: Diadora League Cup, CC: Carsberg Cup, FAC: F.A. Cup, FAT: F.A. Trophy, EAC: East Anglian Cup, HCC: Herts Charity Cup, HSC: Herts Senior Cup. Numbers after cup competitions denote rounds (r: replay, qf: Quarter-Final, sf: Semi-Final, f: Final. Numbers in brackets indicate legs, i.e. (1): 1st leg).
Home fixtures are denoted by bold capitals, away matches by lower case. (p): penalty, og: Own goal.

SQUAD MEMBERS *(previous clubs listed in chronological order)*

GOALKEEPERS: Gary Westwood *(Ipswich, Reading, Wokingham)*

DEFENDERS: Dean Murphy *(Harpenden, Barnet, Wokingham),* **Clive Goodyear** *(Luton, Fulham, Ernest Borel(HK)),* **Erskine Smart** *(Arsenal, Watford, Kingsbury, Hendon, Enfield),* **Peter Risley** *(Hoddesdon, Ware, Bishop's Stortford, Dagenham),* **Chris Zoricich** *(Leyton Orient, Windsor & Eton),* **John Colfer** *(London Colney, Hitchin),* **Roy Edwards** *(Leyton-Wingate, Dagenham, St Albans, Stevenage, Dulwich, Aveley)*

MIDFIELD: Martin Duffield *(QPR, Enfield, Hendon, Sutton Utd),* **Allan Pluckrose** *(Falmouth, Torquay, SV Viktoria Goch(Ger), Aylesbury, Slough),* **Shaun Brett** *(Ware),* **Allan Cockram** *(Spurs, Bristol Rovers, Farnborough, St Albans, Brentford, Reading, Woking, Farnborough)*

FORWARDS: Steve Clark *(Stansted, Saffron Walden, Wivenhoe),* **Martin Gurney** *(St Albans, Harrow, Redbridge, Wokingham),* **Andy Driscoll** *(West Ham, Brentford, Yeading, Chertsey, Hayes),* **Trevor Wilkinson** *(Spurs, Enfield, Bogndal(Norway), Enfield, Hendon, St Albans, Hendon, Harlow).*

Formed: 1890

SLOUGH TOWN

The Rebels

Slough Town FC. Back Row (L/R): Kevin McGoldrick (Physio), Brian Lee, Steve Whitby, Ian Hazel, Paul Holland (released), Morrys Scott, Trevor Bunting, Lee Walker (released), Steve Scott (released), Andy Sayer, Stewart Bannister (Kitman). Front: Darren Hancock, Paul Manning (released), Mark Quamina (released), Mark Fiore, Les Briley (Manager, released), Colin Dutfield (released), Alan Dowson, Neal Stanley (released).

Chairman: A A Thorne **Vice-Chairman:** B A Thorne.
Secretary: Richard Hayward, c/o Slough Town FC.
Manager: Dave Russell **Asst Manager:** Laurie Craker.
Press Officer/Commercial Manager: Bob Green.
Ground: Wexham Park Stadium, Wexham Road, Slough, Berks SL2 5Q1 (0753 523358 Fax: 0753 516956).
Directions: From North: M25 J16 East London M40 J1 - South A412 through Iver Heath to George Green. 2nd set lights turn right by George PH, George Green. Church Lane 1 mile to end, then small roundabout, turn left, ground 1/4 mile on right. From East: M25 J15/M4 J5 to A4 West to Co-Op Superstore on right, A412 North (Uxbridge), dual carriageway to 4th set lights. Church Lane, then as from North. From South: If M25 then as from East. From Windsor A355 under M4 J6 to A4, turn right, pass Brunel Bus station on left, Tesco Superstore, also on left, then first left, Wexham Road, signposted Wexham Park Hospital, ground just over 1 mile on left. From West: If M4 J6 then as from South.
Capacity: 5,000 **Seats:** 390 **Cover:** 1,890 **Floodlights:** Yes.
Club colours: Amber/navy blue **Change colours:** All white
Record Attendance: 8,000 - Schoolboys u15 Final Slough v Liverpool - 1976
Club Shop: Yes, Contact John Linlow (0753 571710).
Previous Grounds: Dolphin Playing Fields, Chalvey Road Sports Ground, York Road Maidenhead 1920, Centre Sports Ground 1936-42.
Prev. Lges: Southern Alliance 1892-93/ Berks & Bucks 1901-05/ Gt Western Suburban/ Spartan 1920-39/ Herts & Middx 1940-45/ Corinthian 1946-63/ Athenian 1963-73/ Isthmian 1973-90/ Alliance Prem. (GMVC) 90-94.
Reserves' League: Suburban League
Midweek home matchday: Tuesdays
Record win: 17-0 v Railway Clearing House - 1921-22.
Record defeat: 1-11 v Chesham Town 1922
Record transfer fee: £18,000 for Colin Fielder from Farnborough - 1991
Record transfer fee received: £22,000 from Wycombe Wanderers for Steve Thompson - 1992
Past players who progressed to the Football League: Paul Barron, Dave Kemp, Roy Davies, Mickey Droy, Eric Young, Alan Paris, Tony Dennis.
Clubhouse: Rebels bar & Lounge bar open weekdays 7pm-11pm, weekends lunchtime/evenings. Banqueting hall for all types of functions. 25 bay golf driving range due to be opened.
1993-94 Captain: Alan Dowson.
1993-94 Top scorer: Morrys Scott.
1993-94 Player of the Year: Alan Dowson.
1993-94 Supporters' Player of the Year: Trevor Bunting.
Club record goalscorer: Terry Norris 85 - 1925/26
Record appearances: Terry Reardon 487 - 1964/81
Honours: FA Amateur Cup R-up 72-73; Spartan League R-up 20-21 21-22 31-32 32-33 38-39; Corinthian League 50-51 (R-up 45-46 46-47 55-56 56-57 57-58); Athenian League 67-68 71-72 72-73 (R-up 68-69, Div 1 64-65, League Cup 64-65 71-72 72-73); Isthmian League 80-81 89-90 (Div 2 R-up 73-74, League Cup 80-81 89-90); Berks & Bucks Senior Cup(9) 02-03 19-20 23-24 35-36 54-55 70-72 76-77 80-81.

PROGRAMME DETAILS:
Pages: 28 **Price:** £1
Ed.: John Linton/Eddie Marr

SLOUGH TOWN's 1993-94 CAMPAIGN

Date	Opponents	Comp.	Res	Gate	Goalscorers
21/08	Stalybridge Celtic	GMV	1-0	679	Stanley
24/08	**DOVER ATHLETIC**	GMV	1-0	1,074	Stanley
28/08	**HALIFAX TOWN**	GMV	2-0	1,170	Hazel, M Scott
30/08	Dagenham & Red.	GMV	0-1	1,371	
04/09	Kidderminster H.	GMV	0-0	1,009	
11/09	**STAFFORD RGRS**	GMV	3-0	907	M Scott(2), Stanley
18/09	Northwich Victoria	GMV	1-1	825	Stanley
21/09	**YEOVIL TOWN**	GMV	5-2	1,313	M Scott(3), Hazel, Fiore
25/09	Southport	GMV	0-1	1,224	
02/10	Gateshead	GMV	0-0	681	
09/10	**BATH CITY**	GMV	0-0	1,334	
12/10	**MERTHYR TYDFIL**	GMV	3-2	763	M Scott(2), Lewis(og)
16/10	Altrincham	GMV	0-2	578	
23/10	Hayes	FAC4q	2-0	877	M Scott, Fiore
30/10	**KIDDERMINSTER**	GMV	1-5	1,191	Walker
02/11	Bromsgrove Rovers	DC2	1-2	692	Fiore
06/11	**WITTON ALBION**	GMV	0-1	781	
13/11	**TORQUAY UNITED**	FAC1	1-2	2,371	M Scott
20/11	Macclesfield Town	GMV	2-2	1,033	M Scott(2)
27/11	**KETTERING TOWN**	GMV	0-2	1,122	
30/11	Bath City	GMV	0-3	541	
04/12	Dover Athletic	GMV	0-0	1,195	
11/12	**RUNCORN**	GMV	3-0	675	M Scott, Sayer(2)
18/12	Stafford Rangers	GMV	0-0	671	
27/12	Woking	GMV	1-2	2,913	Hazel
01/01	**DAGENHAM & R.**	GMV	3-1	975	Hancock, Watts, Fiore
08/01	Runcorn	GMV	2-3	563	Sayer, Hazel
11/01	Marlow	B&B1	0-1	461	
15/01	**STALYBRIDGE C.**	GMV	2-3	743	M Scott, Sayer
22/01	Billericay Town	FAT1	2-0	709	M Scott, Sayer
29/01	Telford United	GMV	1-4	833	M Scott
01/02	**WELLING UNITED**	GMV	1-1	650	Sayer
05/02	Merthyr Tydfil	GMV	1-5	430	Peters
12/02	Morcambe	FAT2	0-1	831	
19/02	Welling United	GMV	2-6	770	Sayer, Peters
05/03	Yeovil Town	GMV	2-0	2,021	Peters, Fiore
15/03	Kettering Town	GMV	0-2	1,434	
19/03	**TELFORD UTD**	GMV	0-0	575	
26/03	**NORTHWICH V.**	GMV	2-2	605	S Scott, Manning
02/04	Bromsgrove Rovers	GMV	1-0	752	Sayer
04/04	**WOKING**	GMV	0-0	1,433	
09/04	**MACCLESFIELD T.**	GMV	1-1	584	M Scott
14/04	**BROMSGROVE R.**	GMV	1-1	530	Alsford
16/04	Witton Albion	GMV	0-1	489	
23/04	**ALTRINCHAM**	GMV	0-2	674	
30/04	**SOUTHPORT**	GMV	0-0	663	
02/05	**GATESHEAD**	GMV	2-1	705	Lee, Hazel
07/05	Halifax Town	GMV	0-1	935	

Key: GMV: GM Vauxhall Conference, DC: Drinkwise (GM Vauxhall Conference) Cup, FAC: F.A. Cup, FAT: F.A. Trophy, B&B: Berks & Bucks Senior Cup. Numbers after cup competitions denote rounds (r: replay, qf: Quarter-Final, sf: Semi-Final, f: Final. Numbers in brackets indicate legs, i.e. (1): 1st leg).
Home fixtures are denoted by bold capitals, away matches by lower case. (p): penalty, og: Own goal.

SQUAD MEMBERS *(previous clubs listed in chronological order)*

GOALKEEPERS: Trevor Bunting *(Burnham, Wycombe, Marlow)*

DEFENDERS: Steve Bateman *(Hemel Hempstead, Everton, Harrow Borough, Chesham)*, **Graham Roberts** *(Southampton, Sholing Sports, Bournemouth, Portsmouth, Dorchester, Weymouth, Sours, Rangers, Chelsea, WBA, Enfield)*, **Trevor Baron** *(Marlow, Burnham, Chertsey T., Windsor & Eton, Slough T., Windsor & Eton, Woking, Marlow)*, **Alan Dowson** *(Millwall, Bradford C., Darlington)*, **Steve Whitby** *(Berkhamsted, Wycombe)*, **Darren Hancock** *(Charlton)*, **Paul McKay** *(Burnley)*, **Brian Lee** *(Millwall)*.

MIDFIELD: Neil Catlin *(Flackwell H., Maidenhead U., Flackwell H., Marlow, Flackwell H., Thame U., Marlow)*, **Mark Wojtowicz** *(Marlow)*, **Ian Hazel** *(Wimbledon, Maidstone, Bristol R.)*, **Mark Fiore** *(Wimbledon, Plymouth)*, **Steve Scott** *(QPR, Friska Viljor(Swe), Farnborough, Harrow, Hibernians(Malta))*

FORWARDS: Andy Sayer *(Wimbledon, Fulham, Leyton Orient)*, **Craig Osbourne** *(Wokingham, Chertsey, Burnham, Wokingham)*, **Brett Smith** *(Millwall)*, **Lee Walker** *(Millwall)*, **Morrys Scott** *(Swansea, Cardiff, Colchester, Southend, Plymouth, Northampton)*, **Mark West** *(West Ham, Reading, Wycombe)*, **Ansil Bushay** *(Marlow, Flackwell Hth, Beaconsfield, Chalfont, Marlow, Woking, St Albans)*

Formed: 1898 **SUTTON UNITED** The U's

Sutton United line up before the 4-1 victory over St Albans in March. Back Row (L/R): Larry Pritchard (Coach), Micky Cook, Ollie Morah, Nigel Golley, Dominic Feltham, Fitzroy McCaulsky, Paul Gates, Peter Byrne, Darren Anderson, Frank Dotson (Asst Manager), Keith Plum (Physio), Bill Webb (Kitman). Front: Steve Lunn, Simon Quail, David Jones, Paul Barrowcliff, Mark Costello, Steve Smart.

Chairman: David G Hermitage **Vice Chairman:** Bruce Elliott **President:** Andrew W Letts.
Secretary: Brian Williams, 49 Panmure Rd, Sydenham, London SE26 6NB (081 699 2721).
Manager: Alan Gane **Asst Manager/Physio:** Frank Dotson.
Press Officer: Tony Dolbear **Coach:** Larry Pritchard
Commercial Manager: Mike Baker.
Ground: Borough Sports Ground, Gander Green Lane, Sutton, Surrey SM1 2EY (081 644 5120/4440 Fax: 081 6445120).
Directions: Gander Green Lane runs between A232 (Cheam Road - turn by Sutton Cricket Club) and A217 (Oldfields Road - turn at 'Gander' PH lights). Ground opposite 'The Plough' 50 yards from West Sutton BR station. Bus 413 passes ground.
Capacity: 6,200 **Cover:** 1,800 **Seats:** 765 **Floodlights:** Yes **Metal Badges:** Yes.
Club Shop: Open on matchdays selling full range of souvenirs, match programmes, scarves, hats, replica kits. Mail orders accepted - contact Paul Hepburn via club.
Colours: Amber (chocolate trim) **Change colours:** White (chocolate trim). **Sponsors:** Securicor.
Previous Leagues: Sutton Junior/ Southern Suburban 10-21/ Athenian 21-63/ Isthmian 63-86/ GMVC 86-91.
Previous Names: Sutton Association, Sutton Guild Rovers (merged in 1898).
Midweek home matchday: Tuesday **Reserve Team's Lge:** Suburban. (Midweek: Capital).
Record Attendance: 14,000 v Leeds United, FA Cup 4th Rd 24/1/70.
Best FA Cup season: 4th Rd 69-70 88-89. Also 3rd Rd 87-88 93-94, 2nd Rd 81-82.
League clubs defeated in FA Cup: Aldershot, Peterborough 87-88/ Coventry City 88-89.
Record Fees - Paid: To Malmo FF for Paul McKinnon
Received: For Efan Ekoku (Bournemouth)/ Andy Barnes (Crystal Palace)
Players Progressing to Football Lge: M Robinson (C Palace), Charles Vaughan (Charlton 1947), Roy Hancox & Len Coules & Ray Colfar & Steven Galloway (C Palace 1950 & 51 & 58 & 84), T Barton (Fulham), Phil Woosnam (Orient 1955), Derek Gamblin (Portsmouth 1965), Mike Pentecost (Fulham 1966), John Faulkner (Leeds 1970), Mike Mellows (Reading 1970), Mick Fillery (Chelsea & QPR), Frank Cowley (Derby 1977), Paul McKinnon (Blackburn 1986), Ron Fearon (I'wich 1987), Paul Harding (Notts Co via Barnet), Efan Ekoku (Bournemouth 1991), Mark Golley (Maidstone), Andy Barnes (C Palace 1991), Paul Rogers (Sheff U 1992), Stuart Massey (C Palace 1992), Andy & Robert Scott (Sheff U 1993), Ollie Morah (Cambridge 1994).
Clubhouse: Open every day, normal pub hours, when sandwiches and hot meals are available. Halls and meeting rooms for hire.
Club Record Scorer: Paul McKinnon
Club Record Appearances: Larry Pritchard 781 (1965-84)
93-94 Captain: David Jones **93-94 Top scorer:** Ollie Morah.
93-94 P.o.Y.: Ollie Morah (Football Club), Fitzroy McCaulsky (Supporters Club), Steve Smart (Strikers Club).
Local Newspapers: Sutton Herald, Sutton Guardian.
Hons: Alliance Prem. Lg Bob Lord Trophy 90-91, FA Trophy R-up 80-81 (SF 92-93), FA Amtr Cup R-up 62-63 68-69 (SF 28-29 36-37 67-68), Isthmian Lg(3) 66-67 84-86 (R-up 67-68 70-71 81-82, Lg Cup(3) 82-84 85-86 (R-up 79-80), Loctite Cup 91-92), Athenian Lg 27-28 45-46 57-58 (R-up 46-47, Lg Cup 45-46 55-56 61-62 62-63, Reserve Section 61-62 (R-up 32-33)), Anglo Italian Semi-Pro Cup 1979 *1st British winners* (R-up 1980 1982), London Snr Cup 57-58 82-83, London Charity Cup 69-70 (R-up(3) 67-69 72-73), Surrey Snr Cup(12) 45-46 64-65 67-68 69-70 79-80 82-88 92-93 (R-up(9) 44-45 54-55 61-64 65-66 75-76 81-82 93-94), Surrey Prem. Cup(res) 82-83 92-93 93-94 (R-up 85-86 88-89), Surrey Intermediate Cup 66-67 71-72 78-79 81-82 (R-up 49-50 51-52 59-60 61-62 64-65 74-75), Surrey Jnr Cup R-up 09-10, Surrey Snr Charity Shield(3) 33-34 36-38 (R-up 21-22 23-24 30-31 34-35 38-39 59-60, Surrey Intermediate Charity Cup 31-32 (R-up 34-35 38-39), Dylon Charity Shield 1984 (R-up 1980 1982 1983 1985), Suburban Lg 74-75 77-78 78-79 81-82 83-84 84-85 85-86 91-92 (R-up 71-72 72-73 80-81 92-93, Lg Cup 80-81 (R-up 86-87)), Southern Youth Lg 86-87 87-88 88-89 (R-up 84-85 91-92, Lg Cup 86-87 (R-up 84-85 85-86 88-89)), Groningen Yth tournament 1983 1985 (R-up 1979 1981 1989 1991), John Ullman Invitation Cup 88-89.

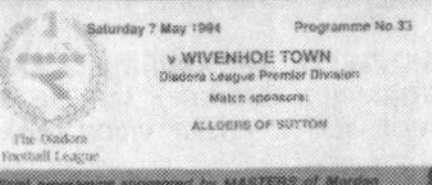

PROGRAMME DETAILS:
Pages: 48 **Price:** £1
Editor: Tony Dolbear

SUTTON UNITED's 1993-94 CAMPAIGN

Date	Opponents	Comp.	Res	Gate	Goalscorers
21/08	**STEVENAGE BORO.**	DFL	0-0	622	
24/08	Bromley	DFL	4-1	367	Golley(2), Smart, D Jones
28/08	Molesey	DFL	0-0	561	
31/08	**ENFIELD**	DFL	1-1	899	D Jones
04/09	**CHESHAM UNITED**	DFL	3-1	820	Morah, Thomas, D Jones
06/09	Stevenage Borough	DFL	2-3	936	Feltham, Thomas
11/09	Hayes	DFL	8-1	385	Feltham(3), Morah(3), Thomas(2)
14/09	**KINGSTONIAN**	DFL	2-1	918	D Jones, Morah
18/09	Carshalton Athletic	DFL	0-1	1,262	
25/09	St Albans City	DFL	0-0	640	
28/09	Dulwich Hamlet	DFL	3-0	352	D Jones(2), Morah
09/10	Marlow	DFL	2-3	485	D Jones, Morah
16/10	Basingstoke Town	DFL	0-0	395	
23/10	**MORETON TOWN**	FAC4q	0-0	804	
26/10	Moreton Town	FAC4qr	2-0	760	Newman(2)
30/10	**GRAYS ATHLETIC**	DFL	1-0	599	Newman
02/11	**PURFLEET**	DLC1	2-0	291	D Jones, Morah
06/11	Aylesbury United	DFL	2-1	583	D Jones, Byrne
13/11	**COLCHESTER UTD**	FAC1	4-3	3,051	Smart, Newman, Quail, Morah
17/11	**BOGNOR REGIS T.**	DLC2	1-3	156	Anderson
20/11	Hitchin Town	DFL	0-0	580	
22/11	Wivenhoe Town	DFL	3-0	165	Golley, Morah, McKinnon
30/11	**WORTHING**	CC1	5-1	281	Golley, Newman(2), Morah, Thomas
04/12	Torquay United	FAC2	1-0	3,414	D Jones
11/12	**HAYES**	DFL	0-1	599	
14/12	Whyteleafe	SSC1	3-0	193	Newman(2), Morah
18/12	Wokingham Town	DFL	1-0	379	Morah
27/12	**CARSHALTON ATH.**	DFL	2-2	1,644	D Jones, Anderson
01/01	Enfield	DFL	0-1	1,037	
08/01	Notts County	FA3	2-3	6,805	Barrowcliff, Smart
11/01	**DORKING**	DFL	3-0	485	D Jones, Morah, Lunn
15/01	**BROMLEY**	DFL	3-0	582	Quail, Lunn, Feltham
22/01	**CHESHAM UNITED**	FAT1	2-0	1,027	Morah, Feltham
29/01	**MOLESEY**	DFL	4-1	646	D Jones, Anderson, Feltham(2)
05/02	Chesham United	DFL	0-1	917	
12/02	**BATH CITY**	FAT2	6-1	1,188	Golley, Feltham(2), Morah(2), Barrowcliff
19/02	Hendon	DFL	1-0	358	Barrowcliff
21/02	Carshalton Athletic	CC2	1-3	932	D Jones
26/02	**BASINGSTOKE T.**	DFL	5-0	671	Gates, Golley, D Jones, Barrowcliff, Quail
05/03	**DOVER ATHLETIC**	FAT3	0-0	1,989	
08/03	Dover Athletic	FAT3r	3-2	2,207	D Jones(2), Morah
12/03	**St ALBANS CITY**	DFL	4-1	740	Barrowcliff(2), Morah(2)
14/03	Egham Town	SS2	3-0	159	Barrowcliff, Morah, Feltham
16/03	Crystal Palace	SSCsf	4-0	261	Morah(2), Feltham, Byrne
19/03	Yeading	DFL	0-0	302	
22/03	**HARROW BOROUGH**	DFL	3-1	407	Barrowcliff, Morah, Byrne
26/03	**ENFIELD**	FATqf	1-1	1,813	Morah
29/03	Enfield	FATqfr	0-1	1,255	
02/04	**DULWICH HAMLET**	DFL	0-3	660	
05/04	**HENDON**	DFL	0-1	454	
09/04	**WOKINGHAM TOWN**	DFL	1-0	473	Evans
11/04	**AYLESBURY UTD**	DFL	3-1	380	Feltham, Anderson, Morah
13/04	Dorking	DFL	3-1	300	Morah, Byrne, Evans
20/04	**MARLOW**	DFL	2-2	418	Morah, Feltham
23/04	**HITCHIN TOWN**	DFL	2-0	620	D Jones, Feltham
25/04	**YEADING**	DFL	1-1	363	D Jones
30/04	Kingstonian	DFL	2-0	765	Feltham, Morah
02/05	Harrow Borough	DFL	1-0	420	Morah
05/05	Grays Athletic	DFL	0-1	214	
07/05	**WIVENHOE TOWN**	DFL	5-0	565	Smart, Barrowcliff, Feltham, Morah, Golley
10/05	WOKING	SSCf	1-3	2,000	Feltham *(played at Kingstonian FC)*

Key: DFL: Diadora League Premier Division, DLC: Diadora League Cup, CC: Carlsberg Cup, DFLS: Diadora League Championship Shield, FAC: F.A. Cup, FAT: F.A. Trophy, SSC: Surrey Senior Cup. Numbers after cup competitions denote rounds (r: replay, qf: Quarter-Final, sf: Semi-Final, f: Final. Numbers in brackets indicate legs, i.e. (1): 1st leg).

SQUAD MEMBERS *(previous clubs listed in chronological order)*

GOALKEEPERS: Fitzroy McCaulsky *(Haringey Borough, Brimsdown R.)*, **Andy Harris** *(Youth Team)*

DEFENDERS: Nigel Golley *(C. Palace, Whyteleafe)*, **Billy Edwards** *(reserve team)*, **Giles Marchant** *(Wimbledon, Walton & Hersham)*, **Darren Anderson** *(Charlton, Aldershot, Slough)*, **Paul Gates** *(Whyteleafe, Chipstead)*, **Mark Costello** *(Youth Team)*, **Steve Steve Smart** *(Spurs, Barnet, Wealdstone)*

MIDFIELD: Gary Thomas *(Local Football)*, **Paul Underwood** *(Kingstonian)*, **Steve Lunn** *(Crystal Palace, Leatherhead, Dorking, Walton & Hersham, Dorking)*, **David Jones** *(Wimbledon), Epsom & Ewell, Kingstonian, Epsom & Ewell, Walton & Hersham, Staines)*, **Paul Barrowcliff** *(Brentford (J), Hendon, Finchley, Ruislip Manor. Hayes, Harrow Boro., St. Albans, Woking, Kingstonian, Ruislip Manor, Wycombe W.)*,

FORWARDS: Simon Quail *(Arsenal, Newmont Travel, Barking, Redbridge Forest, Dartford)*, **Micky Brown** *(Croydon, Dulwich, Tooting, Wealdstone, Bromley)*, **Zak Zakman** *(Three Bridges)*, **Richard Evans** *(Burnley, Wolves, Wokingham, Harrow, Windsor)*, **Dominic Feltham** *(Chelsea, Baltimore Blast(US))*, **Paul McKinnon** *(Chelsea, Woking, Malmo, Orebro, Tegs, Ryoden(HK), Slough)*, **Mark Watson** *(local football)*.

1896

WALTON & HERSHAM

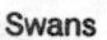

Walton & Hersham concede an early goal in their vital home fixture against Purfleet on Friday 22nd April. However, they fought back to draw 2-2, and both clubs were ultimately promoted from Division One behind champions Bishop's Stortford.

Photo - Eric Marsh.

Chairman: Nick Swindley **President:** W Bigmore.
Secretary: Gerry Place, 24 Stratton Road, Sunbury, Middx TW16 6PQ (0932 782414).
Manager: Neil Price **Asst Manager/Coach:** Chris McLaren
Press Officer: Brian Freeman (0932 560738) **Physio:** David Field
Commercial Manager: John Tickner.
Ground: Sports Ground, Stompond Lane, Walton-on-Thames (0932 245263-club, 247565-boardroom).
Directions: From North: Over Walton Bridge & along New Zealand Ave., down 1-way street and up A244 Hersham Road - ground 2nd right. From Esher: Down Lammas Lane then Esher Rd, straight over 1st r'bout, 4th exit at next r'bout (West Grove) 2nd left at end of Hersham Rd and Stompond Lane is half mile on left. Ten minutes walk fron Walton-on-Thames (BR). Bus 218 passes ground.
Capacity: 6,500 **Cover:** 2,500 **Seats:** 500 **Floodlights:** Yes **Metal Badges:** Yes.
Club Shop: Yes, open matchdays. Contact Rochard Old, c/o the club.
Colours: Red/white/black **Change colours:** Blue & black stripes/black/back.
Previous Leagues: Surrey Senior/ Corinthian 45-50/ Athenian 50-71.
Midweek home matchday: Tuesday **Reserve Team's League:** None.
Sponsors: TBA
Record win: 10-0 v Clevedon, FA Amateur Cup 1960.
Record Gate: 6,500 v Brighton, FA Cup First Round 73-74.
Best FA Cup season: 2nd Rd 72-73 (v Margate), 73-74 (v Hereford).
League clubs defeated in FA Cup: Exeter 72-73, Brighton 73-74.
Players progressing to Football League: Denis Pacey (Orient 1951), John Whitear (Aston Villa 1953), Andy McCulloch (QPR 1970), Mick Heath (Brentford 1971), Paul Priddy (Brentford 1972), Richard Teale (Queens Park Rangers 1973), Steve Parsons (Wimbledon 1977).
Clubhouse: (0932 245263). Open most nights. Bar, TV, darts, pool, refreshments on matchdays.
Club record scorer: Brian Jenkins.
Club record appearances: Terry Keen.
93-94 Captain: Mark Wilson.
93-94 P.o.Y. Justin Mitchell.
93-94 Top Scorer: Justin Mitchell 27.
Local Newspapers: Surrey Herald.
Local Radio Stations: County Sound.
Honours: FA Amateur Cup 72-73 (SF 51-52 52-53), Isthmian Lg R-up 72-73, Barassi Cup 73-74, Athenian Lg 68-69 (R-up 50-51 69-70 70-71, Lg Cup 69-70), Corinthian Lg(3) 46-49 (R-up 49-50), Premier Midweek F'lit Lg(3) 67-69 70-71 (R-up 71-72), Surrey Snr Cup 47-48 50-51 60-61 61-62 70-71 72-73 (R-up 46-47 51-52 59-60 69-70 71-72 73-74), London Snr Cup R-up 73-74, Southern Combination Cup 82-83 88-89 91-92, Surrey Combination Cup 49-50 91-92, John Livey Memorial Trophy 91-92.

PROGRAMME DETAILS:
Pages: 40 **Price:** £1.20
Editor: Brian Freeman/ Nick Swindley

WALTON & HERSHAM's 1993-94 CAMPAIGN

Date	Opponents	Comp.	Res	Goalscorers
21/08	**BERKHAMSTED T.**	DFL	2-1	Mitchell, Croxford
24/08	Bognor Regis Town	DFL	1-0	S Davidson
28/08	Cove	FACpr	1-2	L Davidson
31/08	Boreham Wood	DFL	0-0	
04/09	**WEMBLEY**	DFL	2-1	Clark Luwero
11/09	**UXBRIDGE**	DFL	1-0	Mitchell
14/09	**MALDEN VALE**	SCC	2-0	S Davidson, L Davidson
18/09	Fisher '93	FAT1q	0-1	
21/09	**ABINGDON TOWN**	DLC1	2-1	Elverson, L Davidson
28/09	Billericay Town	DFL	1-3	Clark
09/10	**CHALFONT St PETER**	DFL	1-0	Rutherford
16/10	Uxbridge	DFL	3-2	Mitchell, W Powell, Styles
19/10	**HEYBRIDGE SWIFTS**	DFL	2-1	Mitchell(2)
23/10	**ABINGDON TOWN**	DFL	1-3	Holt
26/10	**RUISLIP MANOR**	DFL	5-0	Mitchell(2), own-goal, Marchant, Clark
30/10	Maidenhead United	DFL	1-0	Mitchell
02/11	Leyton	DFL	1-5	Callaghan
06/11	Windsor & Eton	DFL	4-1	Gasson, Callaghan, Styles, L Davidson
13/11	**BARKING**	DFL	3-3	Mitchell, Styles, Callaghan
16/11	**WORTHING**	DLC2	0-1	
19/11	Purfleet	DFL	0-0	
30/11	Tooting & Mitcham Utd	SSC4q	4-1	Styles, Clark, L Davidson, Marchant
04/12	Croydon	DFL	4-1	Mitchell, Styles, Cowler, Gasson
11/12	**BISH. STORTFORD**	DFL	2-2	Croxford, Wilson
14/12	**KINGSTONIAN**	SSC1	2-0	Gasson, L Davidson
18/12	Worthing	DFL	0-1	
27/12	**TOOTING & MITCHAM**	DFL	1-1	Mitchell
15/01	**BGONOR REGIS T.**	DFL	3-0	L Davidson, Collins, Mitchell
19/01	Woking	SSC2	0-3	
22/01	Berkhamsted Town	DFL	3-2	Collins, Gasson, Mitchell
25/01	Dulwich Hamlet	CC2	0-2	
29/01	**BOREHAM WOOD**	DFL	3-1	Banton, L Davidson, Mitchell
08/02	**WHYTELEAFE**	DFL	2-1	Powell, own-goal
12/02	**LEYTON**	DFL	5-2	Banton(2), Collins(2), Mitchell
17/02	Bishop's Stortford	DFL	0-1	
19/02	Whyteleafe	DFL	4-1	Mitchell(3), Wilson
01/03	**STAINES TOWN**	DFL	1-1	Collins
05/03	Chalfont St Peter	DFL	1-1	Gasson
07/03	Ruislip Manor	DFL	1-0	Mitchell
12/03	**BILLERICAY TOWN**	DFL	1-2	Banton
15/03	Chipstead	SCC	1-2	Banton
19/03	Heybridge Swifts	DFL	2-1	Banton(2)
22/03	**WINDSOR & ETON**	DFL	3-1	own-goal, Mitchell(2)
26/03	**MAIDENHEAD UTD**	DFL	2-2	Banton(2)
02/04	Abingdon Town	DFL	3-0	Mitchell(3)
04/04	Tooting & Mitcham Utd	DFL	0-1	
09/04	**WORTHING**	DFL	1-2	G Powell
12/04	Wembley	DFL	1-1	Collins
16/04	Barking	DFL	2-4	Croxford, Mitchell
22/04	**PURFLEET**	DFL	2-2	Powell, Collins
30/04	Staines Town	DFL	0-0	
07/05	**CROYDON**	DFL	6-2	Mitchell(2), McKinnon(2), Croxford, Collins

Key: DFL: Diadora League Division One, DLC: Diadora League Cup, CC: Carlsberg Cup, FAC: F.A. Cup, FAT: F.A. Trophy, SSC: Surrey Senior Cup, SCC: Southern Combination Cup. Numbers after cup competitions denote rounds (r: replay, qf: Quarter-Final, sf: Semi-Final, f: Final. Numbers in brackets indicate legs, i.e. (1): 1st leg).

SQUAD MEMBERS *(previous clubs listed in chronological order)*

GOALKEEPERS: Trent Phillips *(Wimbledon, Staines, Camberley, Staines).*

DEFENDERS: Gary Powell *(Staines)*, **David Field** *(Staines, Camberley, Wealdstone)*, **Adie Cowler** *(Addlestone, Woking, Addlestone, Woking, Kingstonian)*, **John Gasson** *(Youth Team)*, **Steve Croxford** *(Windsor, Camberley, Maidenhead Utd)*, **Matt Elverson** *(Youth Team)*, **Steve Moss** *(Southampton, Woking, Camberley, Woking, Worthing, Carshalton, Basingstoke).*

MIDFIELD: Mark Wilson *(Feltham, Harrow Boro., Hampton, Feltham, Farnborough)*, **Ian White** *(Kingstonian, Molesey)*, **Stuart Davidson** *(Local Football)*, **Des Vartannes** *(Fulham, Aldershot, Farnborough, Cove)*, **Lee Davidson** *(Woking, Kingstonian)*, **Paul Clarke** *(Camb. Utd, St Albans)*, **David Holt** *(Kingstonian).*

FORWARDS: John Collins *(Cuffley, Dulwich, Wealdstone, Tooting)*, **Justin Mitchell** *(Youth Team)*, **Ashley Styles** *(Southend, Merstham)*, **Danny Adams** *(Watford, St Albans, Enfield, St Albans*, **Paul McKinnon** *(Woking, Sutton Utd, Malmo (Swe), Sutton Utd, Trelleborg (Swe), Sutton Utd, Teg(Swe), Sutton Utd, Blackburn R., Sutton Utd, Orebro(Swe), Sutton Utd, Slough, Sutton Utd).*

WOKINGHAM TOWN

Formed: 1875 — The Town

Wokingham Town pictured before taking on championship-chasing Stevenage Borough in an end-of-season fixture.
Photo - Eric Marsh.

Chairman: P Walsh **Vice Chairman:** R Croyden **President:** G Gale.
Secretary: John Aulsberry, 8 Paice Green, Wokingham RG11 1YN (0734 790441).
Manager: Roy Merryweather **Asst Manager:** Derek Cottrell **Coach:** Wayne Wanklin
Press Officer: John Ansell (0734 787699) **Physio:** Dave Lane
Commercial Manager: Roy Merryweather (0734 780253).
Ground: Town Ground, Finchampstead Road, Wokingham, Berks RG11 2NR (0734 780253).
Directions: Half mile from town centre on A321 (signed Camberley & Sandhurst) Finchampstead Rd - walk down Denmark Street to swimming pool and straight on onto Finchampstead Rd. Half mile from Wokingham (BR) - turn right out of station, walk along Wellington Rd to swimming pool, right into Finchampstead Rd - ground entrance on right immediately after railway bridge.
Capacity: 3,500 **Cover:** 1,500 **Seats:** 250 **Floodlights:** Yes **Metal Badges:** Yes.
Club Shop: Progs, scarves, magazines & club souvenirs. Contact Brian & Sue McKeown at club on matchdays.
Colours: Amber & black/black/black **Change colours:** Red/white/red.
Sponsors: Bulldog Service Station.
Previous Leagues: Reading & Dist./ Great Western Comb 07-54/ Metropolitan 54-57/ Delphian 57-59/ Corinthian 59-63/ Athenian 63-73.
Previous Grounds: Oxford Road 1875-1883/ Wellington Road 83-96/ Langborough Rd 96-1906.
Midweek home matchday: Tuesday **Reserve Team's Leagues:** Suburban, Capital.
Record Attendance: 3,473 v Norton Woodseats, FA Amateur Cup 57-58.
Best F.A. Cup season: 1st Rd replay 82-83 (lost 0-3 at Cardiff after 1-1 draw).
League clubs defeated in F.A. Cup: None.
Record Fees - Paid: £5,000 for Fred Hyatt (Burnham, 1990)
Received: £25,000 for Mark Harris (Crystal Palace, 1988).
Players progressing to Football League: Ian Kirkwood (Reading 1953), John Harley (Hartlepool 1976), Kirk Corbin (Cambridge 1978), Phil Alexander (Norwich 1981), Doug Hatcher (Aldershot 1983), Steven Butler & George Torrance (Brentford 1984), Mark Harris (Crystal Palace 1988), Gary Smart (Oxford 1988), Darren Barnard (Chelsea 1990), Paul Holsgrove (Luton Town 1991), Darron Wilkinson (Brighton) 1992.
Clubhouse: Mon-Sat 12-3 & 7-11pm (12-3 & 4.30-11pm Sat matchdays), Sun 12-2.30pm. Hot & cold food & snacks.
Club Record Goalscorer: Dave Pearce, 79.
Club Record Appearances: Dave Cox, 533.
93-94 Captain: Andy McKenzie
93-94 P.o.Y.: Russell Meara
93-94 Top scorer: Elliot Pearce, 10
Local Newspapers: Wokingham Times (782000), Wokingham News (Bracknell 20363), Reading Evening Post (55875).
Local Radio Stations: Radio 210.
Honours: Isthmian Lg R-up 89-90 (Div 1 81-82, Full Members Cup R-up 93-94), Berks & Bucks Snr Cup 68-69 82-83 84-85, Berks & Bucks Intermediate Cup 52-53, FA Tphy SF 87-88, FA Amtr Cup 4th Rd 57-58.

PROGRAMME DETAILS:
Pages: 32 **Price:** 80p
Editor: Mrs Anne Gale
(c/o the club)

WOKINGHAM TOWN's 1993-94 CAMPAIGN

Date	Opponents	Comp.	Res	Gate	Goalscorers
21/08	Harrow Borough	DFL	1-1	238	Hyatt
24/08	**HITCHIN TOWN**	DFL	2-0	264	Pearce, Walkington
28/08	**AYLESBURY UTD**	DFL	0-3	359	
31/08	Dulwich Hamlet	DFL	2-2	202	Pearce, Devereux
04/09	Dorking	DFL	3-1	287	Walkington(2), Morrisey
11/09	Dorcester Town	FAC1q	0-1	489	
14/09	**St ALBANS CITY**	DFL	1-3	331	Pearce
18/09	**MAIDENHEAD UTD**	FAT1q	1-0	275	Biggs
21/09	Met. Police	DLC1	4-3	76	Hampstead(2), McGrath, Hyatt
25/09	**HAYES**	DFL	0-1	233	
28/09	**CARSHALTON ATH.**	DFL	0-4	245	
02/10	Wivenhoe Town	DFL	2-3	175	Husband, Pearce
16/10	Abingdon Town	FAT2q	1-1	238	Husband
19/10	**ABINGDON TOWN**	FAT2qr	2-1	206	Devereux, Martin(og)
23/10	**BROMLEY**	DFL	2-1	260	Hampstead(2)
30/10	Enfield	DFL	0-1	651	
06/11	**MOLESEY**	DFL	1-1	223	Hyatt
10/11	Chesham United	DFL	0-3	478	
13/11	Hendon	DFL	1-1	201	Line
16/10	**CHESHAM UTD**	DLC2	2-1	204	Devereux, Frampton
20/11	**GRAYS ATHLETIC**	DFL	3-0	201	Line, Langley, Hurdwell
27/11	Waterlooville	FAT3q	0-3	233	
04/12	**BASINGSTOKE T.**	DFL	0-0	289	
11/12	St Albans City	DFL	0-2	465	
18/12	**SUTTON UNITED**	DFL	0-1	379	
27/12	Marlow	DFL	1-3	452	Aseh
01/01	**DULWICH HAMLET**	DFL	0-1	293	
15/01	Hitchin Town	DFL	0-1	513	
18/01	Basingstoke Town	CC2	1-1	127	Devereux *(Wokingham won 4-3 on penalties)*
22/01	Newport Pagnell	B&B1	0-3	175	
29/01	Aylesbury United	DFL	0-3	599	
01/02	**KINGSTONIAN**	DFL	1-3	297	Pearce
05/02	**DORKING**	DFL	3-1	209	Leather(2), Brennan(og)
12/02	Carshalton Ath.	DFL	0-1	504	
19/02	**YEADING**	DFL	1-2	182	Hampstead
22/02	**DORKING**	CC3	2-1	121	Hampstead, Langley
26/02	Kingstonian	DFL	0-5	515	
01/05	**HARROW BOROUGH**	DFL	0-1	195	
05/02	**CHESHAM UNITED**	DFL	2-0	336	Pearce, Hyatt
08/03	Yeading	DFL	3-1	151	Pearce(2), Hyatt
12/03	Hayes	DFL	2-1	300	Line, Hyatt
16/03	Molesey	DFL	0-2	166	
19/03	**WIVENHOE TOWN**	DFL	1-0	210	Biggs
21/03	Purfleet	CCqf	1-1	112	Langley *(Wokingham won 5-4 on penalties)*
26/03	Grays Athletic	DFL	3-0	256	Pearce, Duncan, Langley
05/04	**MARLOW**	DFL	0-6	383	
09/04	Sutton United	DFL	0-1	473	
11/04	Stevenage Boro.	DFL	0-1	836	
16/04	**HENDON**	DFL	0-2	224	
19/04	**ENFIELD**	DFL	1-1	319	Devereux
21/04	St Albans City	CCsf	2-0	228	Aseh, Devereux
26/04	Bromley	DFL	0-1	225	
30/04	**STEVENAGE B.**	DFL	0-1	619	
03/05	HENDON	CCf	1-2	494	Pearce *(played at Marlow FC)*
07/05	Basingstoke Town	DFL	2-1	222	McKenzie, Line

Key: DFL: Diadora League Premier Division, DLC: Diadora League Cup, CC: Carlsberg Cup, FAC: F.A. Cup, FAT: F.A. Trophy, B&B: Berks & Bucks Senior Cup. Numbers after cup competitions denote rounds (r: replay, qf: Quarter-Final, sf: Semi-Final, f: Final. Numbers in brackets indicate legs, i.e. (1): 1st leg).
Home fixtures are denoted by bold capitals, away matches by lower case. (p): penalty, og: Own goal.

SQUAD MEMBERS *(previous clubs listed in chronological order)*

GOALKEEPERS: Peter Scrivens *(Basingstoke, Camberley, Cobham, Wokingham, Hayes)*, **Russell Meara** *(Aylesbury)*.

DEFENDERS: Reg Leather *(Hayes, Hillingdon Boro., Woking, Hayes, Southall, Hayes, Leatherhead)*, **Iain Duncan** *(Leicester City, Thatcham, Basingstoke, Wealdstone, Windsor)*, **Simon Line** *(Crystal Palace, Brentford, Kingstonian, Chertsey)*, **Chris Tomlinson** *(Aldershot, Canterbury, Aldershot T.)*, **Jimmy Devereux** *(Aldershot, Basingstoke)*, **Jimmy Bradley** *(Wokingham, Staines)*, **Andy Mackenzie** *(Chesham, Hartley Wintney)*, **Darren Biggs** *(Aerostructures)*.

MIDFIELD: Freddie Hyatt *(Ruislip, Burnham)*, **Micky Hurdwell** *(Salisbury, Wokingham, Bracknell, Thatcham)*, **Nick Sheppard** *(Fleet)*, **Kevin Merryweather** *(Youth Team)*, **Jason Walkington** *(Southampton, Reading, Windsor, Basingstoke)*, **Giles Lee** *(Local Football)*.

FORWARDS: John Lawford *(Luton, Bishop's Stortford, Hayes, Aylesbury)*, **Elliott Pearce** *(Youth Team)*, **Tim Brooks** *(Wokingham, Camberley, Hungerford)*, **Mark Hampstead** *(Youth Team)*, **Stewart Husband** *(Youth Team)*, **Tommy Langley** *(Chelsea, QPR, Crystal Palace, AEk Athens(Gr), Coventry, Wolves, Aldershot, South China (HK), Exeter, Tampa Bay (USA))*.

YEADING

Formed: 1965 | The Dinc

Yeading's Lee Charles makes an acrobatic attempt to break the deadlock in the FA Cup First Round tie against Gillingham. Because it would have been too difficult to organise segregation at The Warren, Yeading borrowed the ground of near-neighbours Hayes to stage this their first ever match in the competition proper.
Photo - Francis Short.

Chairman: Phillip Spurden **Vice Chairman:** Steve Perryman **President:** Mr R Carter
Secretary/Press Officer: Peter Bickers, 140 Hercies Rd, Hillingdon, Middlesex (0895 811061).
Manager: Gordon Bartlett **Asst Manager:** Leo Morris **Coach:** Leo Morris.
Commercial Manager: Neil Roberts
Physio: Edward Cole.
Ground: The Warren, Beaconsfield Road, Hayes, Middx (081 848 7362/7369. fax: 081 561 2222).
Directions: Two miles from Hayes (BR) - take Uxbridge Road and turn right towards Southall, right into Springfield Road and then left into Beaconsfield Road. Bus 207 stops half mile from ground.
Capacity: 3,500 **Cover:** 1,500 **Seats:** 250 **Shop:** Planned **Metal Badges:** Yes
Colours: Red & black stripes/black/black **Change colours:** All white.
Sponsors: Heineken.
Previous Leagues: Hayes & District Yth/ Uxbridge/ S W Middx 1967-74/ Middx 74-84/ Spartan 1984-87.
Midweek home matchday: Tuesday **Reserve Team's League:** None.
Record Attendance: 3,000; v Hythe Town, FA Vase SF 1990; v Tottenham Hotspur, friendly.
Best FA Cup season: Third Qualifying Round 90-91.
Best FA Cup season: 1st Round replay 93-94 (lost 1-3 at Gillingham after 0-0 draw).
League clubs defeated in FA Cup: None.
Record Fees - Paid: **Received:** £45,000 for Andrew Impey (QPR).
Players progressing to Football League: Andrew Impey (QPR & England u-21).
Clubhouse: Open normal pub hours. Social Secretary: William Gritt.
Club Record Goalscorer: Dave Burt 327
Club Record Appearances: Norman Frape.
93-94 Captain: Jon Denton.
93-94 P.o.Y.: Phil Dicker.
93-94 Top scorer:
Local Newspapers: Hayes Gazette.
Honours: FA Vase 89-90, Isthmian League Div 2 Sth 89-90 (Div 1 R-up 91-92), Spartan League 86-87 (R-up 85-86, Senior Div R-up 84-85, League Cup 85-86 86-87), Middlesex Snr League(6) 71-73 74-76 81-82 83-84 (R-up 73-74 74-75 78-79, League Cup(6) 72-73 75-76 79-83), South West Middlesex League(2) 69-71, Middlesex Snr Cup 89-90 91-92, Middlesex Prem. Cup 80-81, Middlesex I'mediate Cup(5) 70-72 74-76 77-78, Middlesex Jnr Cup(4) 68-69 70-72 74-75, Uxbridge League 66-67, Middlesex Border League Cup 86-87 (AJA Cup 86-87), Suburban League Nth 87-88, Allied Counties Yth League 89-90 (League Cup 89-90).

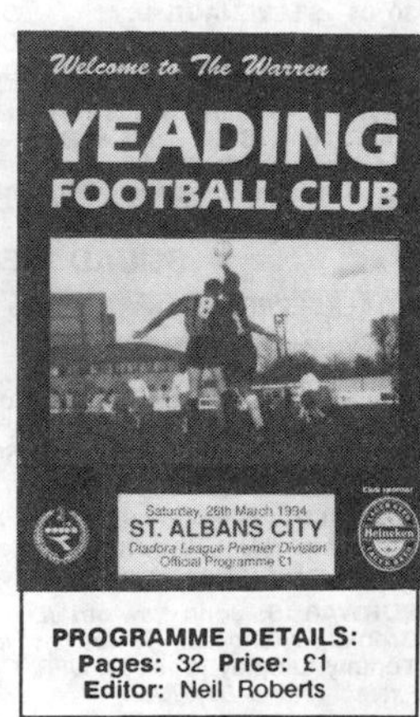

PROGRAMME DETAILS:
Pages: 32 **Price:** £1
Editor: Neil Roberts

YEADING's 1993-94 CAMPAIGN

Date	Opponents	Comp.	Res	Gate	Goalscorers
21/08	**MARLOW**	DFL	2-0	182	Charles, Hippolyte
25/08	Chesham United	DFL	2-3	777	Charles, Hippolyte
28/08	Stevenage Borough	DFL	1-4	506	Oatway
31/08	**KINGSTONIAN**	DFL	2-3	332	Sheldrick(2)
04/09	**MOLESEY**	DFL	3-0	176	Welsh, Hippolyte, Cordery
11/09	Grays Athletic	FAC1q	2-0	183	Hippolyte, Charles
14/09	Bromley	DFL	1-2	138	Cordery
18/09	Berkhamsted Town	FAT1q	1-1	105	Cordery
21/09	**BERKHAMSTED T.**	FAT1qr	2-0		Welsh, Charles
25/09	**KINGSBURY TOWN**	FAC2q	5-2	130	Charles(3), Welsh, Cassidy
28/09	Hendon	DFL	2-5	207	Warmington(og), Cassidy
05/10	**DULWICH HAMLET**	DFL	0-0	139	
09/10	Purfleet	FAC3q	2-1	153	Charles(2)
12/10	Hayes	DFL	1-0	296	Perry
16/10	**LEYTON**	FAT2q	1-1	107	Charles
19/10	Leyton	FAT2qr	3-1		Welsh, Sheldrick, Charles
23/10	Pershore Town	FAC4q	3-1	1,356	Welsh(2), Charles
30/10	St Albans City	DFL	1-1	502	Denton
02/11	Marlow	DLC1	0-2	332	
06/11	Enfield	DFL	0-0	577	
13/11	**GILLINGHAM**	FAC1	0-0	2,286	*(played at Hayes Football Club)*
20/11	Aylesbury United	DFL	1-1	340	Hippolyte
27/11	Billericay Town	FAT3q	0-2	283	
30/11	Gillingham	FAC1r	1-3	3,231	James
04/12	Carshalton Athletic	DFL	0-2	377	
11/12	**BROMLEY**	DFL	2-3	179	Cordery, Welsh
14/12	Berkhamsted Town	CC1	2-1		Hippolyte, Sheldrick
18/12	Wivenhoe Town	DFL	4-2	168	Ardren, Sheldrick, Perry, own-goal
27/12	**HARROW BOROUGH**	DFL	2-0	353	McIlvenna, Sheldrick
01/01	Kingstonian	DFL	2-1	515	McIlvenna, Sheldrick
04/01	**DORKING**	DFL	1-2	145	Welsh
15/01	**CHESHAM UTD**	DFL	0-2	385	
18/01	Wivenhoe Town	CC2	3-1		Hopson(2), Williams
22/01	**ASHFORD TOWN**	MSC1	6-0		Cordery, Dicker, Denton, Hippolyte(2), Hopson
25/01	**BASINGSTOKE T.**	DFL	3-1	122	Hippolyte(2), Sheldrick
29/01	**STEVENAGE BORO.**	DFL	0-2	403	
03/02	Northwood	MCC1	2-6		Godfrey(2)
05/02	Molesey	DFL	0-0	161	
08/02	Uxbridge	MSC2	0-4		
12/02	**HENDON**	DFL	1-1	220	Godfrey
19/02	Wokingham Town	DFL	2-1	182	Cordery, Welsh
22/02	**BISHOP'S STORT.**	CC3	0-1		
26/02	Grays Athletic	DFL	1-2	220	Croad
01/03	**HITCHIN TOWN**	DFL	2-1	212	Godfrey, Dicker
05/03	**HAYES**	DFL	2-3	335	Cuffie, Mulvaney
08/03	**WOKINGHAM TOWN**	DFL	1-3	151	Denton
12/03	Dulwich Hamlet	DFL	1-1	170	Godfrey
19/03	**SUTTON UNITED**	DFL	0-0	302	
21/03	**ENFIELD**	DFL	1-2	312	Godfrey
26/03	**St ALBANS C.**	DFL	1-1	302	Whiskey
02/04	Basingstoke Town	DFL	1-1	169	Oatway
04/04	Harrow Borough	DFL	0-1	302	
09/04	**WIVENHOE TOWN**	DFL	4-1	145	Godfrey(2), Sibanda, Hippolyte
12/04	**GRAYS ATHLETIC**	DFL	1-1	103	Cuffie
18/04	Dorking	DFL	3-4	63	Sibanda(2), Hippolyte
23/04	**AYLESBURY UTD**	DFL	1-2	164	Hippolyte
25/04	Sutton United	DFL	1-1	363	Hippolyte
28/04	Marlow	DFL	1-1	204	Sibanda
30/04	Hitchin Town	DFL	2-4	256	Sibanda, Miller(og)
07/05	**CARSHALTON ATH.**	DFL	2-1	172	Park, Sheldrick

Key: DFL: Diadora League Premier Division, DLC: Diadora League Cup, CC: Diadora League Carlsberg Cup, DFLS: Diadora League Championship Shield, FAC: F.A. Cup, FAT: F.A. Trophy, MSC: Middlesex Senior Cup, MCC: Middlesex Charity Cup. Numbers after cup competitions denote rounds (r: replay, qf: Quarter-Final, sf: Semi-Final, f: Final. Numbers in brackets indicate legs, i.e. (1): 1st leg).
Home fixtures are denoted by bold capitals, away matches by lower case. (p): penalty, og: Own goal.

SQUAD MEMBERS *(previous clubs listed in chronological order)*

GOALKEEPERS: Stuart McKenzie *(Hounslow, Southall, Hounslow, Harrow)*, **Matthew Fox** *(Yth team)*

DEFENDERS: Alan Ardren *(Hillingdon, Yeading, Ruislip, Yeading, Hayes)*, **Kyung-Hoon Park** *(South Korea)*, **Iain Williams** *(Chard, Plymouth, Yeovil, Bristol City, Yeovil, Borough Road College)*, **Phil Dicker** *(Brentford, Hanwell, Harrow, Southall, St Albans)*, **Mick Cuffie** *(Southall, Dunstable, Chelmsford, Dunstable, Hitchin, Dunstable, Baldock, Hayes, Stevenage)*

MIDFIELD: Jon Denton *(Hillingdon, Harefield, Hounslow)*, **Steve Cordery** *(Hayes, Maidenhead, Egham, Windsor, Chesham)*, **Johnson Hippolyte** *(Hounslow, Uxbridge, Chalfont, Wealdstone)*, **Earl Whiskey** *(Kingstonian, Hayes, Yeading, Leatherhead)*, **Keith James** *(Portsmouth, Slough, Walthamstow Ave., Hayes, Woking, Staines, Hayes, Southall, Yeading, Darking, Harrow*, **Charlie Oatway** *(yth team)*

FORWARDS: Hector Walsh *(Hive)*, **Anthony Sibanda** *(Cobh Ramblers, Collier Row, Hendon)*, **Kevin Godfrey** *(Leyton Orient, Plymouth, Brentford)*, **Paul Sheldrick** *(Fulham, Kingstonian)*, **Paul Mulvaney** *(Bracknell, Wycombe, Cheltenham, Bracknell, Woking, Cove, Maidenhead)*

DIVISION ONE 1993-94

	P	W	D	L	F	A	PTS
Bishop's Stortford	42	24	13	5	83	31	85
Purfleet	42	22	12	8	70	44	78
Walton & Hersham	42	22	11	9	81	53	77
Tooting & Mitcham	42	21	12	9	66	37	75
Heybridge Swifts	42	20	11	11	72	45	71
Billericay Town	42	20	11	11	70	51	71
Abingdon Town	42	20	10	12	61	50	70
Worthing	42	19	11	12	79	46	68
Leyton	42	20	8	14	88	66	68
Boreham Wood	42	17	15	10	69	50	66
Staines Town	42	18	9	15	85	56	63
Bognor Regis Town	42	15	14	13	57	48	59
Wembley	42	16	10	16	66	52	58
Barking	42	15	11	16	63	69	56
Uxbridge	42	15	8	19	57	58	53
Whyteleafe	42	15	6	21	71	90	51
Maidenhead United	42	12	13	17	52	48	49
Berkhamsted Town	42	12	9	21	65	77	45
Ruislip Manor	42	10	8	24	42	79	38
Chalfont St Peter	42	7	10	25	40	79	31
Windsor & Eton	42	8	7	27	47	94	31
Croydon	42	3	3	36	37	198	12

TOP SCORERS

	Lge	Cup	Tot
Leo Fortune-West (B. Stortford)	23	5	28
Justin Mitchell (Walton & Hersham)	27		27
Barry Popplewell (Leyton)	19	5	24

Below: *Bishop's Stortford, who won promotion back to the Premier Division taking the championship in some style. Back Row (L/R): Ray Wickenden (Asst Manager), Martin Sedgwick, Paul Baxter, Billy Harrigan, Lee Claridge, Gavin King, Leo Fortune-West, Dave Mallett, John Scott, Nicky White, Leroy Corbin, Kevin Jordan, Peter Fox (Physio). Front: Robbie Munn, Andy Edmonds, Andy Walker, Lee Burns, Phil Hopkins, John Radford (Manager), Mark Das, Stewart Ingielewicz, Terry Burns, Tony Comerford.*

RESULT CHART 1993-94

HOME TEAM	1	2	3	4	5	6	7	8	9	10	11	12	13	14	15	16	17	18	19	20	21	22
1. Abingdon	*	0-1	1-0	0-3	1-0	1-1	3-1	1-1	2-1	0-0	2-1	3-1	1-1	3-0	2-1	0-1	1-0	0-3	3-3	1-2	1-0	3-3
2. Barking	1-1	*	0-0	2-2	3-2	0-0	0-2	1-0	0-2	3-2	0-2	1-1	0-3	1-1	3-2	1-2	0-3	4-2	0-1	5-0	3-0	0-1
3. Berkhamsted	3-2	0-0	*	0-2	0-1	1-1	3-2	2-1	14-1	3-3	1-1	0-2	1-5	0-1	4-1	0-4	3-4	2-3	1-3	2-2	2-1	2-0
4. Billericay	5-0	1-0	1-1	*	0-0	1-0	0-0	3-4	3-0	0-4	3-4	3-2	2-2	6-1	0-5	0-1	2-0	3-1	0-1	3-4	1-1	0-0
5. Bishop's S.	2-0	4-0	3-0	1-2	*	1-0	5-2	4-0	9-1	0-0	2-2	1-1	2-3	3-0	3-1	2-2	1-2	1-0	3-1	5-1	5-0	2-0
6. Bognor Regis	1-0	1-2	4-2	0-1	0-0	*	2-2	4-1	8-0	1-2	3-2	2-1	2-2	1-0	3-1	1-1	1-0	0-1	0-4	4-1	0-1	0-0
7. Boreham Wd	1-1	2-3	0-0	1-1	0-0	0-0	*	0-1	10-0	2-1	1-2	2-0	0-2	3-1	1-1	2-1	1-0	0-0	0-0	1-0	2-2	3-1
8. Chalfont SP	0-1	1-1	0-2	1-3	1-1	0-0	1-1	*	4-0	1-1	0-6	0-2	1-2	0-2	0-5	2-1	1-2	1-1	2-1	0-1	3-0	0-3
9. Croydon	0-9	4-1	0-4	0-1	1-4	1-2	1-5	2-2	*	0-0	1-3	0-3	1-4	2-7	0-14	0-7	1-4	1-4	1-2	3-7	1-2	0-7
10. Heybridge	0-0	2-3	4-1	3-1	2-3	2-0	1-2	4-1	6-0	*	3-2	2-1	0-0	0-0	0-0	0-1	4-2	1-2	2-2	3-0	1-0	2-1
11. Leyton	2-3	0-2	1-3	0-2	0-1	2-1	1-1	3-2	3-1	1-2	*	1-1	2-1	2-0	5-3	0-1	4-0	5-1	4-1	6-1	3-3	1-1
12. Maidenhead	0-1	3-2	1-0	0-2	1-1	1-1	0-2.	3-1	4-0	1-0	0-1	*	1-1	1-2	0-1	1-1	0-0	0-1	0-0	4-0	4-1	1-2
13. Purfleet	4-0	2-1	1-1	3-2	0-2	2-0	0-2	1-0	2-4	0-0	1-0	1-0	*	2-1	4-0	1-0	0-3	0-0	0-0	0-1	3-1	1-1
14. Ruislip M.	0-2	2-2	1-2	1-1	1-1	2-0	1-2	1-2	0-0	1-2	1-0	3-1	2-3	*	0-6	3-0	0-0	0-1	2-0	0-2	1-2	2-1
15. Staines	0-0	1-3	2-0	1-1	0-0	0-2	1-1	2-0	3-0	0-1	2-3	3-1	0-1	4-0	*	3-0	4-2	0-0	3-2	1-0	2-0	2-1
16. Tooting	3-0	3-1	3-0	1-1	0-1	0-1	3-3	0-0	6-0	2-0	2-2	0-0	3-1	1-0	4-2	*	1-0	1-0	1-4	1-0	2-0	1-1
17. Uxbridge	1-0	2-2	6-0	0-1	0-1	2-2	4-2	2-1	3-1	0-1	1-2	0-0	1-2	0-0	2-0	0-2	*	2-3	0-3	0-0	2-1	1-1
18. Walton & H.	1-3	3-3	2-1	1-2	2-2	3-0	3-1	1-0	6-2	2-1	5-2	2-2	2-2	5-0	1-1	1-1	1-0	*	2-1	2-1	3-1	1-2
19. Wembley	4-5	3-0	3-0	3-2	0-1	0-1	1-2	1-0	7-0	0-1	1-1	0-2	1-1	2-0	0-2	0-1	2-0	1-1	*	1-4	1-4	2-4
20. Whyteleafe	0-1	1-4	2-1	0-0	1-1	2-4	1-2	3-2	6-1	3-2	1-2	1-3	0-1	6-2	3-3	2-0	0-2	1-4	1-1	*	2-1	3-2
21. Windsor	1-2	2-3	1-3	0-4	0-1	2-2	0-0	1-1	5-3	1-4	2-3	1-0	1-4	1-0	2-3	1-1	1-4	1-4	0-2	4-3	*	2-3
22. Worthing	0-1	3-0	1-0	1-2	0-1	1-1	2-1	4-1	5-0	2-3	2-1	2-2	2-1	6-0	0-1	0-0	5-1	1-0	0-0	5-1	2-0	*

Diadora (Isthmian) League Division One Ten Year Record

	84/5	85/6	86/7	87/8	88/9	89/0	90/1	91/2	92/3	93/4
Abingdon Town	-	-	-	-	-	-	-	6	6	7
Aveley	13	22	-	-	-	-	4	21	21	-
Barking	-	-	-	-	-	-	-	12	19	14
Basildon United	16	18	12	7	21	-	-	-	-	-
Basingstoke Town	-	-	-	-	2	-	-	-	-	-
Berkhamsted Town	-	-	-	-	-	-	-	-	-	18
Billericay Town	-	-	13	20	-	-	-	-	8	6
Bishop's Stortford	-	-	-	-	-	-	-	-	5	1
Bognor Regis Town	-	-	-	-	-	-	-	-	-	12
Boreham Wood	17	9	8	4	11	7	14	4	11	10
Bracknell Town	-	-	3	19	20	-	-	-	-	-
Bromley	8	2	-	-	-	-	2	-	-	-
Chalfont St Peter	-	-	-	-	16	11	11	13	18	20
Chesham United	4	20	-	18	14	10	1	-	-	-
Clapton	21	-	-	-	-	-	-	-	-	-
Collier Row	-	-	-	-	19	-	-	-	-	-
Croydon	-	-	-	-	-	17	17	18	17	22
Dorking	-	-	-	-	-	6	10	11	3	-
Dulwich Hamlet	-	-	-	-	-	-	12	3	-	-
Epsom & Ewell	-	-	20	-	-	-	-	-	-	-
Farnborough Town	1	-	-	-	-	-	-	-	-	-
Finchley	-	13	22	-	-	-	-	-	-	-
Grays Athletic	-	14	6	2	-	-	-	-	-	-
Hampton	9	5	11	9	17	19	-	-	-	-
Harlow Town	-	21	-	-	-	8	13	17	-	-
Hertford Town	22	-	-	-	-	-	-	-	-	-
Heybridge Swifts	-	-	-	-	-	-	18	19	16	5
Hitchin Town	-	-	-	-	4	4	5	8	1	-
Hornchurch	18	19	-	-	-	-	-	-	-	-
Kingsbury Town	-	-	7	14	8	22	-	-	-	-
Kingstonian	2	-	-	-	-	-	-	-	-	-
Leatherhead	3	15	10	10	12	20	-	-	-	-
Lewes	15	11	15	16	6	15	20	-	20	-
Leytonstone-Ilford	-	12	1	-	-	-	-	-	-	-
Leyton (-Wingate)	-	6	2	-	-	-	-	14	13	9
Maidenhead United	11	17	21	-	-	-	-	16	12	17
Marlow	-	-	-	1	-	-	-	-	-	-
Metropolitan Police	20	-	-	-	13	9	21	-	-	-
Molesey	-	-	-	-	-	-	8	10	2	-
Oxford City	14	4	17	12	-	-	-	-	-	-
Purfleet	-	-	-	-	-	21	-	-	4	2
Ruislip Manor	-	-	-	-	-	-	-	-	-	19
St Albans City	6	1	-	-	-	-	-	-	-	-
Southwick	-	-	4	11	15	3	19	-	-	-
Staines Town	10	8	14	5	1	-	-	-	-	11
Stevenage Borough	-	-	16	21	-	-	-	1	-	-
Tilbury	7	16	19	-	-	-	-	-	-	-
Tooting & Mitcham United	-	-	-	-	-	12	6	7	7	4
Uxbridge	-	7	9	17	9	18	16	15	15	15
Walthamstow Avenue	-	-	-	15	-	-	-	-	-	-
Walton & Hersham	12	10	18	8	7	5	7	9	10	3
Wembley	5	3	5	6	10	16	15	5	9	13
Whyteleafe	-	-	-	-	-	14	9	20	14	16
Windsor & Eton	-	-	-	-	-	-	-	-	-	21
Wivenhoe Town	-	-	-	-	5	1	-	-	-	-
Woking	19	-	-	3	3	2	-	-	-	-
Wolverton Town	-	-	-	22	-	-	-	-	-	-
Worthing	-	-	-	13	18	13	22	-	-	8
Yeading	-	-	-	-	-	-	3	2	-	-
No. of clubs competing	22	22	22	22	21	22	22	21	21	22

Formed: 1870

ABINGDON TOWN

Over The Bridge

Abingdon Town FC. Back Row (L/R): Keith Appleton (Coach), Brian House (Reserve Team Manager), Steve Hegarty, Martin Loakes, Kevin Connolly, Andy Martin, Ray Green, Carl Wilkins, John Ward, Aldrick Sutton, Paul Richardson, Robbie Carlisle, Martin Brown, Kurt Douglas, Ricky Gray (Kit Manager). Front: Allan Davies, Ray Stephens, Dave Ward, Roger Nichols (Assistant Manager), Keith Measor (Chairman), Darren Hickey (Captain), Craig Norcliffe (Vice-Chairman), Paul Lee (Manager), Kelvin Alexis, Gerry O'Loughlin, Kenny Campbell, Howard Kemp.
Photo courtesy of the Oxford & County Newspapers Group.

Chairman: Keith Measor **Vice Chairman:** Craig Norcliffe **President:** Dr Tim Reynolds
Secretary: Ted Quail, 107 Park Lane, Thatcham, Newbury, Berks RG13 4BH (0635 868967).
Manager: Paul Lee **Asst Manager:** Keith Appleton **Physio:** Ian Cummings.
Coach: Brian House **Press Officer:** Nick Quail (0235 832499)
Ground: Culham Road, Abingdon OX14 3BT (0235 555566-boardroom & press box, 521684-ground).
Directions: On A415 road to Dorchester-on-Thames half a mile south of town centre. Nearest rail station is Culham. Main line: Didcot Parkway or Oxford. Bus service from Didcot and London.
Capacity: 3,000 **Cover:** 1,771 **Seats:** 271 **Floodlights:** Yes **Metal Badges:** £2
Club Shop: Yes, selling programmes, magazines, scarves, badges.
Colours: Yellow & green **Change colours:** Blue & white.
Sponsors: Courage
Previous Name: Abingdon FC (amalgamated with St Michaels in 1899).
Previous Leagues: Oxford & District/ West Berks/ Reading Temperance/ North Berks/ Reading & District 1927-50/ Spartan 50-53/ Hellenic 53-88/ London Spartan 88-89.
Midweek home matchday: Tuesday **Reserve Team's League:** Suburban (West).
Record Attendance: 1,400 v Oxford City, FA Cup September 1960. (Crowds of over 5,000 in 20s and 30s).
Best FA Cup season: 4th Qualifying Rd 60-61 (lost 0-2 v Hitchin), 89-90 (0-3 at home to Slough), 92-93 (lost 1-2 at Merthyr Tydfil after 0-0 draw).
Best FA Vase season: 5th Round replay 89-90.
Players progressing to Football League: Maurice Owen (Swindon Town), George Buck (Stockport County & Reading), Sammy Chung (Reading, Norwich City, Watford & Wolverhampton Wanderers).
Clubhouse: (0235 521684). 7.30-11pm. 6pm matchdays. 12.30-2.30, 4-11 on Saturdays. Hot food on matchdays. Pool, darts, jukebox, canteen.
Club record appearances: John Harvey-Lynch.
93-94 Captain: Darren Hickey.
93-94 P.o.Y.: Andy Martin.
93-94 Top scorer: Liam Herbert.
Local Newspapers: Oxford Mail, Oxford Times, Abingdon Herald, South Oxon Guardian.
Honours: Berks & Bucks Senior Cup 58-59 (R-up 88-89 92-93), Isthmian League Div 2 (Sth) 90-91 (Associate Members Tphy R-up 90-91), London Spartan League 88-89 (League Cup SF 88-89), Hellenic League(4) 56-57 58-60 86-87 (R-up(3) 70-72 87-88, League Cup 57-58 70-71 81-82 (R-up 83-84 86-87), Div 1 75-76, Div 1 Cup 75-76, Res. Div(3) 69-71 86-87, Res. Div Cup 70-71 85-86, Res. Div Suppl. Cup 74-75), Oxford & District League(3) 1898-1901, Reading & District League 47-48, Berks & Bucks Jnr Cup 06-07, Abingdon Centenary Cup 58-59, Joan Lee Memorial Cup 69-70 70-71 86-87, Oxford I'mediate League (Reserves) 47-48, Newbury Graystoke Cup(Reserves) 93-94 (R-up 90-91).

PROGRAMME DETAILS:
Pages: 40 **Price:** 50p
Editor: Glenn Ford
(0865 891254)

Formed: 1992

ALDERSHOT TOWN

The Shots

Aldershot Town, who had another fabulous season winning a second consecutive promotion and reaching, at the first attempt, the Quarter-Finals of the FA Challenge Vase.

Photo - Eric Marsh.

Chairman: Terry Owens **President:** Arthur English
Club Secretary: Peter Bridgeman, 4 Shortheath Rd, Farnham, Surrey GU9 8SR (0252 725437. Fax: 0252 733659).
Company Secretary: Graham Brookland, c/o Aldershot Town FC.
Manager: Steve Wignall **Asst Manager:** Keith Baker **Coach:** Paul Shrubb
Physio: Ginge McAllister
Commercial Manager: Ian Crossley (0256 59313) **Club Newsline:** 0891 446 834.
Press Officer: Nick Fryer.
Ground: Recreation Ground, High Street, Aldershot, Hants GU11 1TW (0252 20211. Fax: 24347).
Directions: Ground situated on eastern end of High Street next to large multi-storey B.T. building. From M3 (jct 4) take A325 to Aldershot. After five miles at r'bout take 1st exit marked town centre (A323) into Wellington Ave. At Burger King r'bout take 2nd exit into High Street - ground on left, large car park adjacent. 5 mins walk from Aldershot (BR).
Capacity: 5,000 **Cover:** 4,500 **Seats:** 1,800 **Founded:** 1992. **Metal Badges:** Y
Cols: Red & blue stripes/red/blue **Change colours:** White & blue stripes/blue/blue.
Club Shop: Yes. Range of souvenirs, programmes, replica kits. Open matchdays or contact Bob Newell (0252 26829) for mail order.
Sponsors: Datrontech Plc **Players progressing to Football League:** N/A.
Previous Leagues: None. **Previous Name:** None.
Midweek home matchday: Tuesday **Reserve Team's League:** Suburban.
Record win: 7-0 v Gosport Borough (H), FA Vase Preliminary Round 2/10/93
Record defeat: 0-4 v Kingstonian (H), Isthmian League Cup 21/9/93.
Record Attendance: 5,961 v Farnborough Town, Hants Senior Cup SF 16/3/93. *Ground record: 19,138 Aldershot FC v Carlisle United, FA Cup 4th Rd replay 28/1/70.*
Record transfer fee paid: £1,000 to Camberley Town for Mark Watson, 1992.
Clubhouse: 7-11pm every evening and matchdays. Pool, darts, juke box, satellite TV Steward: Ian Turner c/o the club.
Club record scorer: Mark Butler 65.
Club record appearances: Mark Butler 102 (+4 sub).
93-94 Captain: Dave Osgood.
93-94 P.o.Y.: Steve Harris/ Keith Baker.
93-94 Top scorer: Mark Butler 35.
Local Newspapers: Aldershot News (0252 28221), Farnham Herald (0252 725224).
Local Radio: County Sound (203m m/w, 1476 khz), BBC Radio Surrey (104.6 fm), Radio 210 (210m m/w).
Hons: Isthmian Lge Div 3 92-93, Simpsonair Tphy 92-93, Skol Invitation Tphy 92-93, FA Vase QF 93-94, Hant Snr Cup SF 92-93.

PROGRAMME DETAILS:
Pages: 40 **Price:** £1
Editor: Karl Prentice/ Graham Brookland

Formed: 1880

BARKING

The Blues

Barking FC 1993-94. Back Row (L/R): Tony James (Coach), John Spencer (Trainer), David Thompson, Danny Gibson, Jimmy Tibbs, Brett Patience, Charles Wright, Darek Charles, Bert Hoyte, Jeff Wood, Mick Wetherall, Andy Meredith, John Knight (President), Roy Anderson. Front: Sean McCarthy, Chris Harvey, Mick Tarling, Tony Williams, Jamie McCabe, Tolo Mas, Robbie Gammons (captain), Perry Coney (Player-Manager).
Photo - Norman Dean.

Chairman: John Knight **Vice-Chairman/President:** John Ward.
Secretary: Roger Chilvers, 50 Harrow Rd, Barking, Essex IG11 7RA (081 591 5313).
Manager: Dennis Elliott **Asst Manager/Coach:** Tony James
Press Officer: Dave Blewitt **Physio:** Alan Jays **Comm Manager:** John Knight
Ground: Mayesbrook Park, Lodge Avenue, Dagenham RM8 2JR (081 595 6511).
Directions: Come off A13 on A1153 (Lodge Avenue), and ground 1 mile on left. Bus 162 from Barking station. Nearest tube station is Becontree.
Capacity: 4,200 **Cover:** 600 **Seats:** 200 **Floodlights:** Yes
Club Shop: Yes, selling programmes & magazines. Run by secretary and Norman Dean.
Colours: Royal (white pin stripes)/royal/royal.
Change colours: Yellow & green halves.
Kit Sponsors: K Sports.
Previous Leagues: London 1896-98 1909-26/ South Essex/ Athenian 23-52.
Previous Names: Barking Rovers, Barking Institute, Barking Woodville, Barking Town.
Previous Grounds: Eastbury Field, Vicage Field (until 1973).
Midweek home matchday: Tuesday
Record Attendance: (At Mayesbrook) 1,972 v Aldershot FA Cup 2nd Rd 1978.
Record win: 10-2 v Chelmsford City (A), FA Trophy, 11/11/78.
Record defeat: 0-8 v Marlow.
Best FA Cup season: 2nd Rd replay 81-82 (lost 1-3 at Gillingham after 1-1 draw). Also 2nd Rd 78-79 79-80 83-84, and 1st Rd 26-27 28-29 78-80.
League clubs defeated in FA Cup: Oxford Utd 79-80.
Record Fees - Paid: None over £1,000
Received: £6,000 for Alan Hull (Orient).
Players progressing to Football League: Don Colombo (Portsmouth 1953), Wally Bellet (Chelsea 1954), John Smith (Millwall 1956), Peter Carey (Orient 1957), Lawrie Abrahams (Charlton 1977), Kevin Hitchcock (Nottm Forest 1983), Dennis Bailey (Fulham 1986), Alan Hull (Orient 1987).
Clubhouse: 2 large bars, open daily 11am-11pm (Sundays Noon-11pm). Hot & cold food and drinks.
Club Record Goalscorer: Micky Guyton 135 (1924-30)
Club Record Appearances: Bob Makin 566
93-94 Captain: Alan Day.
93-94 P.o.Y.: Mick Tarlin.
93-94 Top scorer: Geoff Wood.
Local Newspapers: Dagenham & Barking, Barking & Dagenham Post.
Local Radio Stations: BBC Radio Essex.
Honours: FA Amateur Cup R-up 26-27, Isthmian Lg 78-79 (Lg Cup R-up 76-77), Athenian Lg 34-35 (R-up 24-25), London Lg 20-21 (Div 1 (A) 09-10), South Essex Lg Div 1 1898-99 (R-up 08-09, Div 2 1900-01 01-02 04-05 05-06), London Senior Cup 11-12 20-21 26-27 78-79 (R-up 19-20 75-76 79-80), Essex Senior Cup 1893-94 95-96 1919-20 45-46 62-63 69-70 89-90, Dylon Shield 79-80, Eastern Floodlit R-up 85-86, London Intermediate Cup 85-86.

PROGRAMME DETAILS:
Pages: 28 **Price:** 50p
Editor: Brad Robinson
(081 590 0934)

1896 **BASINGSTOKE TOWN** Stoke

The main stand at the Camrose Ground, Basingstoke.

Chairman: Gordon A Hill **Vice-Chairman:** Roger Bartlett **President:** Charles Foyle, Esq
Secretary/Press Officer: David Knight, 1 The Vale, Oakley, Basingstoke RG23 7LB (0256 781422)
Manager: Ernie Howe **Asst Manager:** R McCulloch **Physio:** Janet Darby.
Commercial Manager: Chris Richardson.
Ground: Camrose Road, Western Way, Basingstoke RG24 6HW (0256 25063).
Directions: Exit 6 off M3 and follow A30 west, ground off Winchester Road. Two miles from bus and rail stations.
Capacity: 6,000 **Cover:** 1,500 **Seats:** 840 **Metal Badges:** Yes
Colours: Blue & gold stripes **Change colours:** All white.
Sponsors: Basingstoke Press.
Previous Leagues: Hants 1900-40 45-71/ Southern 71-87.
Previous Ground: Castle Field 1896-1947.
Midweek home matchday: Tuesday **Reserve Team's League:** Suburban.
Club Shop: Yes, selling programmes, books, scarves, shirts etc. Contact Neil Tysoe.
Record Attendance: 4,091 v Northampton, FA Cup 1st Rd 1971.
Best FA Cup season: 2nd Rd 89-90 (lost 2-3 at home to Torquay). Also 1st Rd 71-72.
League clubs defeated in FA Cup: None.
Record win: 10-0 v Chichester City (H), FA Cup 1st Qualifying Round, September 1976.
Record defeat: 0-8 v Aylesbury United, Southern League, April 1979.
Record Fees - Paid: £4,750 for Steve Ingham (Gosport Borough)
Received: £6,750 for Steve Ingham (Bashley)
Players progressing to Football League: Tony Godfrey (Southampton 1958), John Neale (Exeter 1972), Mike Doherty (Reading 1982), Micky Cheetham (Ipswich 1988), Matt Carmichael (Lincoln), Tony Franklin (Exeter), Steve Welsh (Peterborough 1990).
Clubhouse: Open every day (including lunchtime)(0256 464353)
Steward: Cheryl Fox.
Club Record Goalscorer: Unkown
Club Record Appearances: Billy Coombs
93-94 Captain: Paul Chambers.
93-94 P.o.Y.: David Hawtin.
93-94 Top scorer: Paul Coombs 12.
Local Newspapers (+Tel.Nos.): Basingstoke Gazette (461131).
Local Radio Stations: Radio 210 (0734 413131)
Honours: Southern League Southern Div 85-86, Isthmian League Div 1 R-up 88-89, Hants League 67-68 69-70 70-71 (R-up 65-66 66-67 68-69, North Div 11-12 19-20), Hants Senior Cup 70-71 89-90

PROGRAMME DETAILS:
Pages: 40 **Price:** 80p
Editor: Michael Edwards

1895 **BERKHAMSTED TOWN** Lilywhites

BERKHAMSTED TOWN

Berkhamsted Town FC

Chairman: Bob Sear **Vice Chairman:** Brian McCarthy **President:** Dennis Wright
Secretary: Alan Dumpleton, 44 Woodlands Av., Berkhamsted, Herts HP4 2JQ (0442 863929).
Manager: Roy Butler **Coach:** Howard Cowley.
Press Officer: Grant Hastie **Physio:** Kevin Burke.
Commercial Manager: Jim Cleaver/ Bob Turnham.
Ground: Broadwater, Lower Kings Road, Berkhamsted, Herts HP4 2AA (0442 862815).
Directions: Adjacent to Berkhamsted station (Euston-Birmingham line). A41 to Berkhamsted town centre traffic lights, left into Lower Kings Road.
Capacity: 2,000 **Seats:** 120 **Cover:** 200 **Floodlights:** Yes **Founded:** 1895
Colours: White/black/black **Change:** Green & white halves. **Metal Badges:** Yes.
Club Shop: Old programmes and club scarves, ties, boot bags, and baseball hats available. See Graham Hastie.
Previous Ground: Sunnyside Enclosure 1895-1919/ Sports Ground 1919-83.
Previous Leagues: W Herts & Herts Co. 95-22/ Spartan 22-51 66-75/ Delphian 51-63/ Athenian 63-66 83-84/ London Spartan 75-83.
Midweek Matchday: Tuesday
Sponsors: C D Wright Electrical Wholesalers.
Reserve Team's League: Essex & Herts Border Combination.
Record Gate: 1,163 v Barnet, FA Cup 3rd Qual. Rd 1987.
Best FA Cup year: 3rd Qual Rd 87-88
Players progressing to Football League: Frank Broome, Maurice Cook, Keith Ryan (Wycombe).
Clubhouse: Open 7 days a week. Pool & darts.
Club Record Goalscorer:
Club Record Apps:
93-94 Captain: Ray Jeffery.
93-94 P.o.Y.: Gary Harthill.
93-94 Top scorer: Gary Harthill.
Local Press: Berkhamsted Herald, Berkhamsted Gazette.
Local Radio Stations: Chiltern Radio, Radio Beds.
Honours: Hertfordshire Senior Cup 52-53, London Spartan League 79-80 (Div 2 26-27), Herts Charity Shield 73-74 79-80 84-85 90-91 50-51(jt), Herts Senior County League Aubrey Cup 52-53, St Marys Cup(12), Apsley Senior Charity Cup(9), Wallspan Southern Combination 84-85 (Floodlit Cup 84-85).

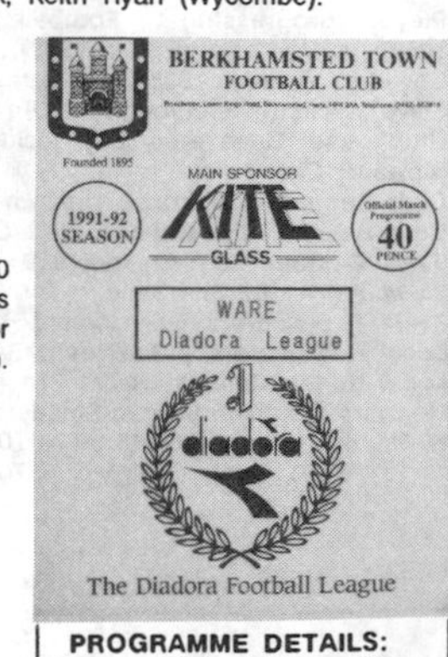

PROGRAMME DETAILS:
Pages: 32 (av.) **Price:** 70p
Editor: Bob Sear
(0442 864547)

Formed: 1880

BILLERICAY TOWN

The Town

Back Row (L/R): Tony Le Voi (Main Sponsors, Tony Le Voi Motors), Adrian West, Jason Lawes, Dave Roser, Leigh Hawkes, John Kendall (Manager), Adrian Smith, Paul Driscoll, Marc Sinfield, Pat Garrett (Coach), Ken Varney (Coach), 'Nobby' Brown (Coach), Derek Collyer (Tony Le Voi Motors). Front Mark Entwhistle, Greg Allen, Mark Keune, Steve Warner, Steve Munday, Ricki Finning, Paul Battram, Andy Skinner, Peter Williams (Physio).
Photo - Evening Echo.

Chairman: Brian Cornes **Vice C'men:** Roy Hassell/Terry Dennison **President:** Barry Spall
Secretary/Commercial Manager: Len Dewson, 14 Graham Close, Billericay, Essex CM12 0QW (0277 622375).
Manager: John Kendall **Coach:** Ken Varney **Asst Manager:** N/A
Press Officer: Phil Heady (0277 652226) **Physio:** Peter Williams.
Ground: New Lodge, Blunts Wall Road, Billericay CM12 9SA (0277 655177).
Directions: From Shenfield (A129) turn right at 1st lights then 2nd right. From Basildon (A129) proceed over 1st lights in town, then left at next lights and 2nd right. Half mile from Billericay (BR) station (London Liverpool Str.-Southend line). Ground 5 mins walk from buses 222, 251, 357, 255, 551.
Capacity: 3,600 **Seats:** 236 **Cover:** 1,140 **Founded:** 1880 **Metal Badges:** Yes
Colours: Royal/white/royal **Change colours:** Yellow/black/black
Club Shop: Yes, open matchdays for souvenirs, metal badges, old progs etc. Contact Steve Lewis (0277 625679).
Midweek Matches: Tuesday. **Previous Ground:** Archer Hall, Laindon (pre-1971)
Previous Leagues: Romford & Dist. 1890-1914/ Mid Essex 18-47/ South Essex Comb. 47-66/ Essex Olympian 66-71/ Essex Snr 71-77/ Athenian 77-79.
Sponsors: Tony Le Voi Motors, Grays **Reserves' Lge:** Essex & Herts Border Comb.
Best FA Cup year: 4th Qual Rd 77-78 **Best FA Vase year:** Winners
Record Gate: 3,841 v West Ham Utd, Floodlight opener 28/9/77. For competitive match: 3,193 v Farnborough Town, FA Vase SF 1st leg 13/3/76.
Record win: 11-0 v Stansted (A), Essex Senior League 5/5/76.
Record defeat: 3-10 v Chelmsford City (A), Essex Senior Cup 4/1/93.
Record Fees - Paid: Undisclosed.
Received: £22,500 (plus increments) for Steve Jones (West Ham, Nov. 1992).
Players progressing to Football League: Danny Westwood (QPR & Gillingham) 1975, Alan Hull, Danny Carter & Dave Cass (Orient) 1988, Dominic Ludden (Orient) 1992, Steve Jones (West Ham Utd) 1992.
Clubhouse: Open every evening 8-11pm (except Monday)(4-11pm Sat) and weekend lunchtimes noon-2pm. Discos, live entertainment, alcoves on ground floor and glass fronted viewing gallery on second.
Club Record Goalscorer: Fred Clayden 273
Club Record Appearances: John Pullen 418.
93-94 Captain: Marc Sinfield.
93-94 P.o.Y.: Andy Skinner.
Supporters' P.o.Y. 93-94: Mark Keune.
93-94 Top scorer: Paul Battram 28.
Local Press: Evening Echo (0268 522792), Billericay Gazette 0245 262421).
Local Radio: BBC Radio Essex (0268 522792), Essex Radio (0702 33311).
Hons: FA Vase (3 - a record) 75-77 78-79, Essex Snr Lg(3) 72-73 74-75 75-76 (R-up 71-72 73-74, Lg Cup(4) 71-74 76-77 (R-up 74-75), Challenge Cup 72-73), Isthmian Lg Div 2 79-80 (Div 1 R-up 80-81), Athenian Lg(2) 77-79 (Lg Cup 77-78), East Anglian Cup R-up 79-80 84-85, Essex Snr Cup 75-76 (R-up 85-86 93-94), Essex Snr Tphy 77-78 79-80, Essex Thameside Tphy 86-87 91-92 (R-up 90-91), Essex F'lit Tphy 77-78, Phillips F'lit Tphy 76-77, Rothmans Merit Award 1978.

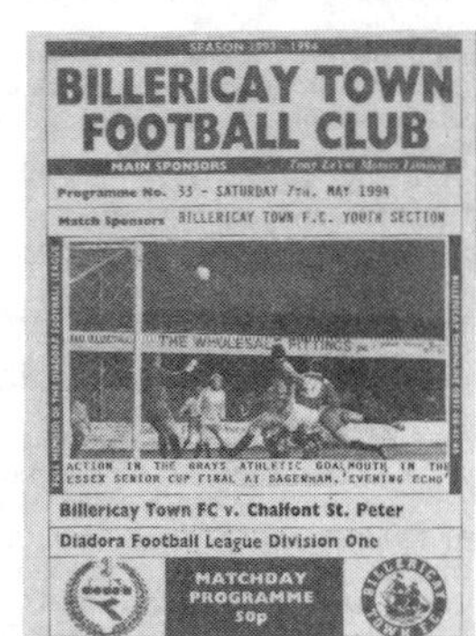

PROGRAMME DETAILS:
Pages: 40 **Price:** 50p
Editor: John Mapp
(0277 624087)

1883 BOGNOR REGIS TOWN The Rocks

Bognor Regis Town 1993-94.

Chairman: Mr J Pearce **Vice Chairman:** Mr M Rowland **President:** Mr S Rowlands
Secretary: Ted Brice, c/o The Club. (0243 864228(H)).
Manager: Mick Pullen **Asst Manager:** Neil Hider **Physio:** Steve Robinson
Press Officer: Martin Denyer **Comm. Manager:** Maurice Warner **Gen. Manager:** Jack Pearce
Ground: Nyewood Lane, Bognor Regis PO21 2TY (0243 822325).
Directions: West along seafront from pier, past Aldwick shopping centre, and right into Nyewood Lane.
Capacity: 6,000 **Cover:** 3,800 **Seats:** 243 **Floodlights:** Yes **Metal Badges:** Yes
Club Shop: Yes, selling programmes and normal club items.
Colours: White (green trim)/green/white **Change colours:** All yellow
Previous Leagues: West Sussex League 1896-1926/ Brighton, Hove & District League 26-27/ Sussex County League 27-72/ Southern League 72-81
Midweek home matchday: Monday **Reserve's League:** None.
Record Attendance: 3,642 v Swansea FA Cup 1st Rd replay, 1984.
Sponsors: Reynolds Furnishing Ltd, Bognor Regis.
Best FA Cup season: 2nd Rd 84-85 (lost 2-6 at Reading), 85-86 (1-6 at Gillingham), 88-89 (lost 0-1 at home to Cambridge). 1st Rd 72-73 86-87 87-88.
League clubs beaten in FA Cup: Swansea 84-85, Exeter 88-89.
Record Fees - Paid: None
Received: £10,500 for John Crumplin & Geoff Cooper (Brighton & Hove Albion, 1987) & Simon Rodger (Crystal Palace, 1989).
Players progressing to Football League: Ernie Randall (Chelsea 1950), John Standing (Brighton 1961), Andy Woon (Brentford 1972), John Crumplin & Geoff Cooper (Brighton 1987), Simon Rodger (Crystal Palace 1989).
Clubhouse: Open every night, matchdays and Sunday lunchtimes. Hot food available.
Club Record Goalscorer: Kevin Clements
Club Record Appearances: Mick Pullen, 886.
93-94 Captain: Chris Rustell.
93-94 P.o.Y.: Gary Sperry.
93-94 Top scorer: Marc Rice.
Local Newspapers (+Tel.Nos.): Bognor Regis Joural & Guardian (865421), Bognor Observer (864267), Brighton Argus (606799), Portsmouth News (64488).
Local Radio Stations: Radio Sussex, Ocean Sound, Radio Solent, Southern Sound.
Hons: Isthmian Lg Div 1 R-up 81-82, (Lg Cup 86-87), Southern Lg R-up 80-81 (Lg Cup R-up 80-81, Merit Cup 80-81), Sussex Lg 48-49 71-72 (R-up 38-39 51-52, Div 2 70-71, Invitation Cup 40-41 49-50 62-63 71-72), Brighton Lg R-up 26-27, W Sussex Lg(5) 20-25 (R-up 1896-97, 25-26), W Sussex Jnr Lg 10-11 13-14, Southern Co's Comb 78-79, Sussex Snr Cup(8) 54-56 79-84 86-87 (R-up 51-52 58-59 84-85), Sussex Prof. Cup 73-74, Sussex RUR Cup 71-72, Sussex I'mediate Cup 52-53, Littlehampton Hosp. Cup 29-30 33-34, Bognor Charity Cup(8) 28-29 30-31 32-33 37-38 47-48 58-59 71-73, Gosport War Mem. Cup(2) 81-83 (R-up 86-87), Snr Midweek F'lit Cup R-up 74-75, FA Amtr Cup 1st Rd 71-72, FA Tphy 1st Rd 80-81 90-91.

PROGRAMME DETAILS:
Pages: 36 **Price:** 60p
Editor: Maurice Warner
(0243 822325)

Formed: 1948

BOREHAM WOOD

The Wood

Boreham Wood goalkeeper Martin Taylor punches clear under pressure from two Bognor Regis forwards in the Division One fixture at Broughinge Road on 2nd October.

Photo - Andrew Relton.

Chairman: Phil Wallace **Vice Chairman:** A Perkins **President:** W F O'Neill.
Secretary: Bob Nicholson, 56 Newcombe Road, Shenley, Radlett, Herts WD7 9EJ (0923 856077).
Manager: Bobby Makin **Asst Manager:** Alan Carrington **Coach:** Micky Sparrow
Press Officer: John D Gill (081 998 6446) **Physio:** Dave Dickens
Ground: Meadow Park, Broughinge Road, Boreham Wood, Herts WD6 5AL (081 953 5097).
Directions: A1 towards London from M25, 1st turn off for Boreham Wood, head for town centre, into into Brook Rd at r'bout before town centre, Broughinge Rd is 1st left. 1 mile from Elstree & Boreham Wood station (Thameslink), then bus 292 or 107 to Red Lion (5 minutes walk).
Capacity: 3,500 **Cover:** 1,500 **Seats:** 250 **Floodlights:** Yes **Metal Badges:** Yes
Club Shop: Yes, selling old and new programmes, replica shirts, scarves, hats, magazines, club badges etc.
Colours: White/black/red **Change colours:** Red/red/black
Previous Leagues: Mid Herts 48-52/ Parthenon 52-57/ Spartan 56-66/ Athenian 66-74.
Previous Ground: Eldon Avenue 1948-63
Previous Names: Boreham Wood Rovers and Royal Retournez, amalgamated in 1948 to form the current club.
Midweek home matchday: Tuesday **Reserve Team's League:** Essex & Herts Border Comb.
Sponsors: L. & M. Foods/ Wansons/ Daly Markets.
Record Attendance: 2,500 v St Albans, F.A. Amateur Cup 70-71.
Best F.A. Cup season: 1st Rd replay (v Swindon) 77-78. Also 1st Rd (v Southend) 73-74.
Players progressing to Football League: Colin Franks (Watford & Sheff Utd), Charles Ntamark (Walsall).
Clubhouse: (081 953 5097). Holds 250, open normal pub hours. Hall available for hire. Sandwiches, filled rolls, hot pasties etc available.
Club Record Goalscorer: Micky Jackson 208
Club Record Appearances: Steve Waller 575
93-94 Captain: Barry Fox
93-94 Player of the Year: Dave Hatchett
93-94 Top scorer: Dominic Gentle
Local Newspapers: Boreham Wood Times, Watford Observer, Herts Advertiser.
Local Radio Stations: Chiltern Radio.
Honours: FA Amateur Cup 3rd Rd replay 70-71, FA Tphy 1st Rd replay 86-87, Isthmian Lg Div 2 76-77 (Yth Cup R-up 80-81), Athenian Lg 73-74 (Div 2 68-69, Div 1 R-up 69-70), Spartan Lg R-up 65-66, Herts Senior Cup 71-72 (R-up 66-67 74-75 79-80 87-88), Herts Junior Cup 51-52, Parthenon Lg 55-56 (R-up(2) 53-55 56-57, Herts Charity Shield 64-65, Herts Intermediate Cup 69-70, Herts Charity Cup(5) 80-81 83-84 85-86 88-90 (R-up 71-72 84-85 86-87 90-91 91-92 92-93), London Senior Cup R-up 89-90, London Intermediate Cup 70-71, Neale Trophy 69-70, Essex & Herts Border Comb 72-73 (Lg Cup 72-73, Western Div R-up 82-83 89-90), Mithras Cup 76-77, Middx Border Lg 81-82 (Lg Cup 79-80), Wallspan Floodlit 86-87.

PROGRAMME DETAILS:
Pages: 32 **Price:** 60p
Editor: J D Gill
(081 998 6446)

Formed: 1890

CHERTSEY TOWN

Curfews

Chertsey Town enjoyed a quite remarkable season winning both the Diadora League internal cups they contested, and finishing as runners-up to Newbury Town in the Division Two championship. Here Trevor Argrave cracks home a goal in the fixture against Lewes.

Photo - V Hardwick.

Chairman: David Rayner **Vice Chairman:** Chris Mason **President:** Cllr Chris Norman
Press Officer/Secretary: Chris Gay, 23 Richmond Close, Frimley, Camberley, Surrey GU16 5NR (0276 20745).
Manager: Jim Kelman **Asst Manager:** Steve Nicholls
Physio: Jean Lewis **Coach:** John Granville.
Commercial Manager: Brian Walker
Ground: Alwyns Lane, Chertsey, Surrey KT16 9DW (0932 561774).
Directions: Alwyns Lane is off Windsor Street at north end of shopping centre. 10 mins walk from Chertsey (BR). London Country bus.
Capacity: 3,000 **Seats:** 200 **Cover:** 400 **Floodlights:** Yes
Colours: Blue & white stripes/white/white **Change colours:** All red.
Club Shop: Yes (manager - Martin Gay 0276 20745) **Sponsors:** Data Express.
Previous Ground: The Grange (pre-World War 1)/ The Hollows (pre-1929).
Midweek Matchday: Tuesday
Previous Leagues: West Surrey (pre-1899)/ Surrey Jnr 1899-1920/ Surrey Intermediate 20-46/ Surrey Snr 46-63/ Metropolitan 63-66/ Gtr London 66-67/ Spartan 67-75/ London Spartan 75-76/ Athenian 76-84/ Isthmian 84-85/ Combined Counties 85-86.
Club Metal Badges: Yes, priced at £2
Youth Team's League: Southern Counties Youth League.
Record Gate: 2,150 v Aldershot, Isthmian Lge Division Two 4/12/93.
Best FA Cup year: 3rd Qualifying Rd 92-93 (lost 1-3 at home to Kingstonian).
Record win: 10-1 v Clapton (H), Isthmian Lge Division Three, 91-92.
Record defeat: 1-12 v Bromley (H), FA Cup Preliminary Rd, 82-83.
Players progressing to Football League: Rachid Harkouk (Crystal Palace, Queens Park Rangers & Notts County), Peter Cawley (Wimbledon 1987).
Clubhouse: Open weekday evenings and weekend lunchtimes.
Club Record Goalscorer: Alan Brown 54, 1962-63.
93-94 Captain: Paddy McCarthy.
93-94 P.O.Y.: Rory Gleeson.
93-94 Top scorer: Josh Price 33.
Local Press: Surrey Herald.
Hons: FA Vase QF 87-88 91-92, Isthmian League Cup 93-94 (Associate Members Trophy 93-94, Div 2 R-up 93-94, Div 3 R-up 91-92), Surrey Snr League 59-60 61-62 62-63 (League Cup 59-60 61-62), Combined Co's League R-up 85-86 (Concours Tphy 85-86), Surrey Snr Cup R-up 85-86, Spartan League & League Cup R-up 74-75.

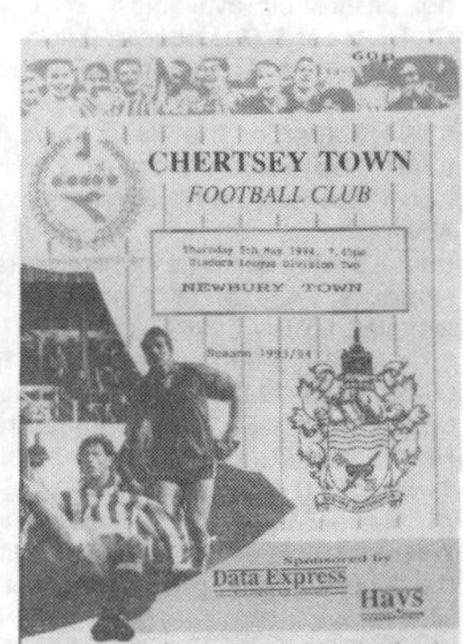

PROGRAMME DETAILS:
Pages: 32 **Price:** 60p
Editor: Secretary

Formed: 1880

DORKING

The Chicks

Dorking Player-Manager Steve Tutt has to take evasive action as Bromley's Pat Gordon effects a spectacular overhead kick. The Dorking player looking on is Tony Welch.

Photo - Paul Gardiner.

Chairman: Steve Lewis (Acting) **President:** Ingram Whittingham
Vice-Chairman: TBA
Secretary: Roger Brown, PO Box 136, Dorking RH4 2YP (0374 148383-mobile. Or Club No.).
Manager: Steve Tutt **Asst Manager:** Robin Lewis **Coach:** Ray Best
Press Officer: Secretary **Physio:** Alan Brilliant.
Ground: Meadowbank, Mill Lane, Dorking, Surrey RH4 1DX (0306 884112).
Directions: Mill Lane is off Dorking high street next to Woolworths and Marks & Spencers opposite the White Horse pub. Fork right in Mill Lane past the Malthouse pub. Half mile from both Dorking and Deepdene (BR) stations.
Capacity: 3,600 **Cover:** 800 **Seats:** 200 **Floodlights:** Yes **Metal Badges:** Yes
Club Shop: Yes, selling badges, scarves, programmes, books, anything!
Colours: Green & white hoops/white/white **Change colours:** All blue
Previous Ground: Prixham Lane (until 1953).
Previous Leagues: Surrey Senior 22-50 77-78/ Corinthian 50-63/ Athenian 63-74 78-80/ Southern 74-77.
Previous Names: Guildford & Dorking United (when club merged with Guildford in 1974)/Dorking Town 77-82.
Midweek home matchday: Tuesday **Reserve Team's League:** Suburban
Best FA Cup season: 1st Round Proper 92-93 (lost 2-3 at home to Plymouth Argyle).
Record Attendance: 4,500 v Folkestone Town, FA Cup 1st Qualifying Round 1955.
Record win: 7-0 v Barking, Isthmian League Division One, 31/10/92.
Players progressing to Football League: Steve Scrivens & John Finch (Fulham), Andy Ansah (Brentford 1989).
Clubhouse: Open matchdays, weekends and training nights. Hot & cold food on matchdays. Pool, bar billiards, widescreen TV, Fruit Machines.
Club Record Goalscorer: Andy Bushnell.
Club Record Appearances: Steve Lunn.
93-94 Captain: Tony Welch
93-94 P.o.Y.:
93-94 Top scorer:
Local Newspapers: Dorking Advertiser, Surrey Mirror.
Local Radio Stations: County Sound, Radio Surrey, Radio Mercury.
Honours: Isthmian League Div 2 Sth 88-89 (Full Members Cup R-up 92-93), Surrey Senior Cup R-up 1885-86 1989-90, Surrey Senior Shield(2) 58-60 (R-up 07-08 10-11 60-61), Surrey Senior League(4) 28-30 54-56 (R-up 51-52 53-54, League Cup 48-49 50-51 53-54, League Charity Cup(4) 48-49 53-54(jt), 54-56 (R-up(5) 28-30 46-47 50-51 77-78)), Gilbert Rice F'lit Cup 87-88 (R-up 89-90), Surrey I'mediate Cup 56-57 (R-up 54-55), Southern Comb. Challenge Cup 92-93, FA Trophy 2nd Rd 91-92, FA Vase 3rd Rd(3) 83-84 86-88.

PROGRAMME DETAILS:
Pages: 48+ **Price:** 80p
Editor: Secretary

Formed: 1880 **HEYBRIDGE SWIFTS** Swifts

HEYBRIDGE SWIFTS

The covered stand at Scraley Road.

Photo - James Wright.

Chairman: Michael Gibson **Vice Chairman:** Paul Wilkinson **President:** John Knight
Secretary: Dennis Fenn, 31 Saxon Way, Maldon, Essex CM9 7JN (0621 854798).
Manager: Garry Hill **Asst Manager:** Mick Loughton **Coach:** N/A
Press Officer: Tim Huxtable. **Physio:** Barry Anthony
Commercial Manager: Neil Foster.
Ground: Scraley Road, Heybridge, Maldon, Essex (0621 852978).
Directions: Leave Maldon on main road to Colchester, pass through Heybridge then turn right at sign to Tolleshunt Major (Scraley Road). Ground on right. Six miles from nearest station (Witham). By bus via Chelmsford and Maldon.
Capacity: 5,000 **Cover:** 200 **Seats:** 200 **Floodlights:** Yes **Metal Badges:** Yes
Club Shop: No, but club sweaters, enamel badges, old programmes sold on request.
Colours: Black & white stripes/black/black & white **Change colours:** All yellow.
Sponsors: Knight Contractors Ltd
Previous Leagues: North Essex/ South Essex/ Essex & Suffolk Border/ Essex Senior 1971-84.
Midweek home matchday: Tuesday **Reserve Team's League:** Essex & Herts Border Comb.
Record Attendance: 572 v Dartford, FA Cup 3rd Qualifying Rd 89-90.
Best FA Cup season: 4th Qualifying Rd 90-91 (lost 1-3 at Barnet).
League clubs defeated in FA Cup: None.
Best FA Trophy season: 2nd Rd Proper 92-93 (lost at Gateshead).
Record Fees - Paid: None **Received:** £12,000.
Players progressing to Football League: Simon Royce (Southend United).
Clubhouse: Two bars open every night. Games room, boardroom, kitchen (on matchdays).
Club Record Goalscorer: J Lamb 115
Club Record Appearances: H Askew 500+.
93-94 Captain: Warren May.
93-94 P.o.Y.: Steve Dowman.
93-94 Top scorer: Dave Matthews.
Local Newspapers: Maldon & Burnham Standard (0621 8522233).
Local Radio Stations: BBC Essex, Essex Radio.
Honours: Isthmian Lg Div 2 North 89-90, Essex Senior Trophy 81-82, Essex Senior Lg 81-82 82-83 83-84 (Lg Cup 82-83), JT Clarke Cup 82-83, Thorn EMI National Floodlit Competition R-up 82-83, Essex & Herts Border Combination R-up 88-89 90-91.

PROGRAMME DETAILS:
Pages: TBA **Price:** TBA
Editor: Peter Fenn
(0621 740878)

LEYTON

Formed: 1868 Lilywhites

Leyton FC 1993-94. *Photo - Harvey Lexton.*

Chairman: George Gross **President:** Laurie Aldridge
Joint Vice-Chairmen: Harry Stone/ David Ward.
Secretary: Mike Roberts, 168 Dawlish Drive, Ilford, Essex IG3 9EG (081 599 2384).
Manager: Peter McGillicuddy **Asst Manager:** Kevin Moran **Coach:** Paul Taylor
Press Officer: George Gross (0181 850 9082) **Physio:** Derek Bennett.
Commercial Manager: Chas E Gross (0181 850 9082).
Ground: Wingate-Leyton Stadium, 282 Lea Bridge Road, Leyton E10 7LD (0181 539 5405/6861).
Directions: Lea Bridge Rd is A104 - ground next to Hare & Hounds PH. Leyton (Central Line) thence bus 58 or 158 to Lea Bridge Rd. Clapton (BR) walk 100yds to Lea Bridge Rd r'bout buses 48 or 56 to ground. Blackhorse Road (Victoria Line), thence bus 158 to Lea Bridge Rd. Bus 48 runs direct to ground from London Bridge (BR) station.
Capacity: 1,500 **Cover:** 600 **Seats:** 200 **Floodlights:** Yes **Metal Badges:** Yes.
Club Shop: Sells programmes, pennants, scarves, badges etc. Contact Ian Wells c/o the club.
Colours: White/navy/white **Change colours:** All navy
Sponsors: ENCOM Cable TV & Telecommunications Ltd.
Previous Matlock Swifts 1889-1892/ Leyton 1892-1975/ Leyton-Wingate 1975-92.
Previous Leagues: Leyton & District Alliance/ South Essex/ Southern 05-11/ London 20-26/ Athenian 1927-82.
Midweek home matchday: Tuesday **Reserve Team League:** Essex & Herts Border Comb.
Record Attendance: 500 v Whickham, FA Vase 6th Rd 83-84 *(100,000 saw Leyton v Walthamstow Avenue, FA Amateur Cup final at Wembley, April 26th 1952).*
Record win: 10-2 v Horsham, 1982 **Record defeat:** 1-11 v Barnet, 1940.
Best FA Trophy season: Third Round 86-87.
Best FA Vase season: Sixth Round 83-84.
Best FA Cup season: 3rd Rd in 09-10, and 1st Rd on 15 other occasions.
League clubs defeated in FA Cup: Stockport 09-10, Merthyr Town 29-30.
Record Fees - Paid: £200 for Dwight Marshall (Hampton)
Received: £6,000 for T Williams (Redbridge Forest).
Players progressing to Football League: Charles Buchan (Sunderland) 1910, Casey (Chelsea) 1952, Ken Facey (Orient 1952), Mortimer Costello (Aldershot 1956), David Clark (Orient 1961).
Clubhouse: (081 539 5405). Open 11am-11pm Mon-Sat, 12-3 & 7-10.30pm Sun. Pool, darts, music, cribbage. No hot food - hot snacks are sold at tea bar on matchdays.
Club Record Goalscorer: Steve Lane 118
Club Record Appearances: Steve Hamberger 387.
93-94 Captain: Stuart McLean.
93-94 P.o.Y.: Tony Samuels.
93-94 Top scorer: Tony Samuels 29.
Local Press: Waltham Forest Guardian, Hackney Gazette
Local Radio Stations: LBC.
Honours: *Isthmian Lg Div 1 R-up 86-87 (Div 2 North 84-85), Essex Snr Tphy R-up 84-85, Thorn EMI National Floodlight Cup 84-85, FA Amateur Cup 26-27 27-28 (R-up 28-29 33-34 36-37 51-52), London Senior Cup 03-04 (R-up 33-34 37-38 45-46), London Charity Cup 34-35 36-37 (R-up 32-33 46-47 66-67 70-71), London Lg 23-24 24-25 25-26 (R-up 26-27, Lg Cup 56-57), Athenian Lg 28-29 65-66 66-67 76-77 81-82 (R-up 45-46 64-65 77-78, Div 2 Cup R-up 69-70), London Challenge Cup R-up 09-10 27-28, Essex Senior Cup 1896-97 97-98 99-1900 00-01 02-03 29-30 30-31 34-35, East Anglian Cup R-up 45-46 72-73, Essex Thameside Trophy 64-65 66-67 81-82 (R-up 63-64), Leyton & Dist. Alliance 1892-93 93-94, Sth Essex Lg 1895-96 96-97 99-1900.*

PROGRAMME DETAILS:
Pages: 32 **Price:** 75p
Editor: George Gross
(0181 850 9082 (tel + fax))

1869 **MAIDENHEAD UNITED** Magpies

Maidenhead United concede a goal to a fourteenth minute header from Chris Rustell in their home fixture against Bognor Regis Town on 14th September.

Photo - Andrew Relton.

Chairman: Jim Parsons **Vice Chairman:** Jon Swan **President:** Cliff West.
Secretary: Stan Payne, 14 Brookside, Honeycroft Hill, Uxbridge UB10 9NH (0895 236709).
Manager: John Watt **Asst Manager:** Derek Sweetman **Physio:** Jim Barrs.
Press Off.: John Swan (0628 473411) **Commercial Manager:** Roger Coombs (0628 337764).
Ground: York Road, Maidenhead, Berks SL6 1SQ (0628 24739).
Directions: From Maidenhead BR station proceed eastwards down Bell Street - ground 300yds along. From bus station, southwards down Bridge Avenue to York Road, turn right, ground 200yds on left. Large car park opposite ground entrance in York Road.
Capacity: 3,000 **Cover:** 900 **Seats:** 220 **Floodlights:** Yes **Metal Badges:** Yes
Club Shop: Yes, wide range of programmes and club souvenirs. Contact Mark Smith (0753 854674).
Cols: White & black stripes/black. **Change colours:** All blue. **Sponsors:** TBA.
Previous Name: Maidenhead, Maidenhead Norfolkians (club amalgamated in April 1919.
Previous Leagues: Southern 1894-1902/ West Berks 02-04/ Great Western Suburban 04-22/ Spartan 22-39/Great Western Combination 39-45/ Corinthian 45-63/ Athenian 63-73.
Previous Ground: Bond's Meadow 1870-1871.
Midweek home matchday: Tuesday **Reserve Team's League:** Suburban.
Record Attendance: 7,920 v Southall, FA Amateur quarter-final 7/3/36.
Best FA Cup season: Quarter Finals 1873-74 74-75 75-76.
Record win: 14-1 v Buckingham Town (H), FA Amateur Cup 6/9/52.
Record defeat: 0-14 v Chesham United (A), Spartan League 31/3/23.
Record transfer fee paid: £500 to Wycombe for Derek Harris, 1978.
Record fee received: £5,000 from Norwich for Alan Cordice, 1979.
Players progressing to Football League: Len Allum (Chelsea 1933), Derek Barley (Arsenal 1951), Roger Barrett (Grimsby 1958), Alan Cordice (Norwich 1979), Paul Priddy (Brentford 1972), David Kemp (Plymouth), Laurie Sanchez (Reading, Wimbledon), Eddie Kelsey, Jackie Palethorpe (Reading 1930), Benny Laryea, Roy Davies.
Clubhouse: Open some evenings & matchdays. Some hot food. Regular darts & pool matches.
Record Scorer: George Copas 270, 1924-35.
Record scorer in season: Jack Palethorpe 66, 1929-30.
Club Record Appearances: Bert Randall 532, 1950-64.
93-94 Captain: Kevin Stone. **93-94 P.o.Y.:** Trevor Roffey.
93-94 Top scorer: Paul Dadson, Kevin Stone 10.
Local Newspapers: Maidenhead Advertiser, Reading Evening Post.
Local Radio Stations: Radio 210, Star FM.
Hons: FA Amtr Cup SF 35-36, Isthmian Lg Div 2 Sth R-up 90-91 (Yth Cup R-up 77-78), Spartan Lg(3) 26-27 32-34 (R-up 28-29 30-31), Corinthian Lg 57-58 60-61 61-62 (R-up 58-59 59-60, Mem. Shield 56-57 61-62 (R-up(4) 48-49 50-51 59-61), Neale Cup 48-49 57-58 60-61, Res. Div 50-51 62-63), Gt Western Suburban Lg 19-20 (R-up 20-21), Berks & Bucks Snr Cup(16) 1894-96 1906-07 11-12 27-28 29-32 38-39 45-46 55-57 60-61 62-63 65-66 69-70 (R-up(11) 1881-82 92-94 97-98 1913-14 19-20 22-23 25-26 35-36 57-58 59-60), Berks & Bucks Benev. Cup(6) 30-31 36-37 39-40 58-69 60-61 (R-up 48-49 50-51), Mithras Cup R-up 63-64 66-67 68-69 78-79, Southern Comb. Cup R-up 81-82.

PROGRAMME DETAILS:
Pages: 36 **Price:** 60p
Editor: Andy Ross
(c/o The Club)

Formed: 1887

NEWBURY TOWN

The Town

Perhaps Newbury Town's most notable result in a terrific season was their 3-0 win at Division Two championship rivals Chertsey Town in the Second Round of the FA Vase on 20th November. They went on to reach the Quarter-Finals for the first time in their history. Here their American international forward Mike Masters surges past Chertsey defender Rory Gleeson.

Photo - Paul Dennis.

Chairman: John Holt **Vice Chairman:** TBA
Secretary: W Dent, 66 Volunteer Rd, Theale, Reading, Berks RG7 5DN (0734 323570).
Manager: Martin Deaner **Asst Manager:** R Mellor **Coach:** M Hicks
Press Officer: W Dent **Physio:** P Turner
Commercial Manager: H Wylie
Ground: Faraday Road, Newbury RG13 2AD (0635 40048-club, 36601-office).
Directions: A34 Robin Hood r'bout then A4 towards Reading, right at lights after 100 yards into Faraday Road. Ground at end.
Capacity: 2,500 **Seats:** 450 **Cover:** 450 **Floodlights:** Yes
Colours: Orange/white **Change colours:** Green & white
Club Shop: Yes **Metal Badges:** Yes
Midweek Matchday: Tuesday **Sponsors:** T.B.A.
Previous Leagues: Gt Western Suburban 04-27/ Hants 27-28/ Reading & Dist. 28-52/ Metropolitan 52-59/ Hellenic 59-82/ Athenian 82-83.
Previous Names: None **Previous Grounds:** None
Reserves' League: Suburban **Record Gate:** 2,300 Reading v Southampton, Hants Lg.
Best FA Cup year: Third Qualifying Round 80-81 (lost 1-4 to Farnborough).
Record Fees - Paid: £300 **Received:** £2,500
Nickname: Town.
Clubhouse: (0635 36601). Every night, Thurs-Sun lunchtimes. Two bars, function room, kitchen.
Players progressing to Football League: D McCartney (WBA), Darren Angell (P'smouth), Brett Angell (Southend), M Berry (Southampton), Ian Maidment (Reading).
93-94 Captain: Steve Kean
93-94 P.o.Y.: Club: Steve Richardson.
Players': Matthew McDonnell.
Supporters': Matthew McDonnell.
93-94 Top scorer: Matthew McDonnell.
Local Press: Newbury Weekly News, Newbury Evening Post.
Local Radio: Radio 210, Reading.
Hons: FA Vase QF 93-94 (5th Rd 79-80), Isthmian League Div 2 93-94, Athenian League 82-83, Berks & Bucks Senior Cup 1897-98 (Jnr Cup 1898-99 1900-01), Hellenic League 78-79 80-81 (League Cup 59-60 68-69), Metropolitan League Amtr Cup(6) 54-60, Newbury (Graystone Cup), Reading & District League(5), Hungerford Cup 88-89 89-90 90-91, Reading Town Senior Cup 31-32.

PROGRAMME DETAILS:
Pages: 12 **Price:** 40p
Editor: Secretary

Founded: 1938

RUISLIP MANOR

The Manor

Ruislip Manor's Martin Howard (right) challenges for the ball with Bobby Dennington of Tooting & Mitcham United in the April fixture at Sandy Lane.

Photo - Francis Short.

Chairman: Jim Klarfield **Vice Chairman:** Maurice Cuell **President:** J Barnett
Secretary: Mrs Avice Horne, 49 Evelyn Close, Whitton, Twickenham, Middx TW2 7BL (081 898 3581).
Match Secretary: Victor Klarfeld, 5 Brickwall Lane, Ruislip, Middx HA4 8JS (0895 633474).
Manager: Michael Schools **Asst Manager:** Alan Witham **Physio:** Marcia Ford.
Coach: Roger Goodhind/ Brian Pettifer.
Press Officer: Chris Pacey (081 459 9337) **Comm. Mgr:** James Klarfeld
Ground: Grosvenor Vale, off West End Road, Ruislip, Middx (0895 637487-office, 676168-boardroom - *this is also the club information line (charged) at normal rates rates which should be used especially when a game is in doubt*).
Directions: From London: A40 to Ruislip, turn off on A4180, right at r'bout into West End Rd, right into Grosvenor Vale after a mile and a half - ground at end. From Ruislip Manor station (Metropolitan Line) turn left out of station, then first right into Shenley Avenue, third left into Cranley Drive - ground 150 yds on left. E2 bus (Ealing Broadway-Ruislip Station) is only bus that passes top of Grosvenor Vale.
Capacity: 3,000 **Seats:** 175 **Cover:** 300 **Floodlights:** Yes **Metal Badges:** Yes
Colours: White/black/black **Change colours:** Yellow/blue/yellow.
Club Shop: Operated by Supporters Club. Sells metal badges, programmes, sweatshirts, coffee mugs, key-rings, pens, leisure tops, pennants, baseball caps, ties. Mr J Brennan, 119 Shenley Ave., Ruislip, Middx.
Midweek Matchday: Monday **Sponsors:** Light Years.
Reserve Team's League: Suburban (North).
Previous Leagues: Uxbridge 38-39/ Middx Snr 39-46/ London 46-58/ Spartan 58-65/ Athenian 65-84.
Previous Names: None. **Previous Ground:** Sidmouth Drive.
Record Gate: 2,000 v Tooting & Mitcham United, F.A. Amateur Cup 1962.
Best F.A. Cup year: Fourth Qualifying Round 90-91 (lost 2-5 at Halesowen Town).

Record transfer fee received: £6,000 for Dave Carroll (Wycombe Wanderers, July 1988).
Clubhouse: Mon-Fri noon-3.30 & 5.30-11pm, noon-3 & 7.30-10.30. Apart from normal range of beer, during football season there is real ale on hand pump. A catering mangeress does hot & cold meals before and after any match - menu ranges from steak, chips, peas to a ham sandwich.
Players progressing to Football League: Dave Carroll (via Wycombe Wanderers).
93-94 Captain: Peter Wilkins.
93-94 P.o.Y.: Chris Balls.
93-94 Top scorer: Martin Howard.
Local Press: Ruislip Northwood Gazette, All Sport Weekly
Hons: London Lg R-up 51-52 (Div 1 R-up 47-48), Isthmian Lg Div 2 R-up 92-93 (Associate Members Tphy 90-91), Athenian Lg Div 2 72-73, Middx Snr Cup SF(6), Middx Charity Cup R-up 90-91.

PROGRAMME DETAILS:
Pages: 32 **Price:** 60p
Editor: Victor Klarfeld
(0895 633474)

Formed: 1892

STAINES TOWN

The Swans

Staines Town - Middlesex Senior Cup and Senior Charity Cup winners 1993-94. *Photo - Eric Marsh.*

Chairman: Alan Boon **Vice Chairman:** Ken Williams **President:** Nigel Iggulden
Secretary: Steven Parsons, 3 Birch Green, Staines, Middx TW18 4HA (0784 450420).
Manager: Chris Wainwright **Asst Manager:** Keith Bristow **Physio:** Peter Judd
Commercial Mgr: Ken Williams **Press Officer:** Secretary + Stuart Moore (0784 421118)
Ground: Wheatsheaf Park, Wheatsheaf Lane, Staines TW18 2PD (0784 455988).
Directions: M25 jct 13 onto A30 Staines by-pass as far as Crooked Billett r'bout, town centre exit (A308) passing bus garage and under iron bridge where you turn left into South Street (1-way), pass central bus station then bear left into Laleham Rd, Wheatsheaf Lane 1km on right and ground 50m on left (large car park). From Staines Central (BR) station (linked to Waterloo, Reading, Windsor, Aldershot, Weybridge, Clapham Junction) turn right into Gresham Rd (crossing footbridge if coming from Egham or Windsor) and follow until turning left into Laleham Rd - Wheatsheaf Lane 1km on right. Buses 218, 518 and 767 pass Wheatsheaf Lane.
Capacity: 2,500 **Cover:** 850 **Seats:** 250 **Metal Badges:** £2.50
Colours: Old gold (blue trim)/blue/blue (old gold trim). **Change colours:** All white.
Club Shop: Souvenirs available from Harry Trim, 23 Grosvenor Rd, Staines, Middx TW18 2RN.
Previous Leagues: West London Alliance (pre-1900)/ West London/ West Middx (pre-1905)/ Gt Western Suburban 05-13 20-24/ Gt Western Comb/ Munitions Lg (World War 1)/ London Works (World War 1)/ Hounslow & District 19-20/ Spartan 24-35 58-71/ Middx Senior 43-52/ Parthenon 52-53/ Hellenic 53-58/ Athenian 71-73.
Previous Names: Staines Albany and St Peters Institute (merged) in 1905/Staines 05-18/Staines Lagonda 18-25/Staines Vale (pre-2nd World War).
Previous Grounds: Hammonds Farm, Linoleum Sports Grounds, Staines Moor, The Anglers Rest, Gorings Meadow, Shepperton Road (Laleham), Mill Mead (pre-1951).
Record Gate: 2,750 v Banco di Roma (Barassi Cup) 1975 *(70,000 saw 1st leg in Rome).*
Best FA Cup year: 1st Rd 84-85 (0-2 at Burton Alb) & 1879-80 (as St Peters Institute).
Midweek home matchday: Tuesday
Sponsors: Higgs & Hill Homes **Reserve team's league:** Suburban (since 1972).
Record win: 14-0 v Croydon (A), Isthmian League Division One 19/3/94. *Equals Isthmian League record winning margin, and is an overall Isthmian League record away win.*
Record defeat: 1-18 v Wycombe Wanderers (A), Great Western Suburban League 27/12/09.
Record Fees - Paid: Undisclosed for Richard Teale (Slough, August 1981)
Received: Undisclosed for Mark Dawber (Chesham, Dec. 1989).
Players progressing to Football League: Robert Bennett (Southend 1972), John Love (C Palace 1975), Peter Shaw (Charlton 1977), Eric Young (Brighton, W'don), Gordon Hill (M'wall, Man Utd, Derby, Wayne Stemp (Brighton), Martin Ferney (Fulham).
Clubhouse: Fully furnished clubhouse & function hall, open 7-11 matchdays and every evening. Rolls and other snacks available.
Club Record Goalscorer: Alan Gregory 122
Club Record Appearances: Dickie Watmore 840
93-94 Captain: John Crouch. **93-94 Top scorer:** Steve Beeks 26.
'Dick Watmore' & Players' P.o.Y. 93-94: Chris Wheatley.
Local Newspapers: Staines & Ashford News, Middx Chronicle.
Local Radio Stations: County Sound, LBC, GLR, Capital.
Hons: Isthmian Lg Div 1 74-75 88-89 (Div 2 74-75), Athian Lg Div 2 71-72 (Div 1 R-up 72-73), Spartan Lg 59-60 (R-up 71-72, Lg Cup 68-69 (R-up 70-71)), Hellenic Lg R-up 55-56 (Lg Cup R-up 53-54 55-56), Gt Western Suburban Lg Div 1 R-up 11-12 22-24 (Div 2 (Middx) 20-21), West London Alliance Div 1 1899-1900, West London Lg Div 1 00-01, West Middx Lg 04-05 (R-up 03-04), London Snr Cup R-up 76-77 80-81, Middx Snr Cup(6) 74-77 87-88 89-90 93-94 (R-up 09-10 32-33 79-80), Middx Snr Charity Cup 93-94, Middx Jnr Cup 01-02 03-04, Barassi Cup 1976, Southern Comb. Chall. Cup 64-65 66-67 68-69 (R-up 67-68 93-94), W Middx Cup 23-24, Staines Cottage Hosp Cup 24-25, Merthyr Middx Charity Shield 90-91, FA Amtr Cup 3rd Rd 23-24, FA Tphy 2nd Rd 2nd rep 76-77.

PROGRAMME DETAILS:
Pages: 44 **Price:** £1
Editor: Sec. + Stuart Moore (0784 421118)

1932 # TOOTING & MITCHAM UTD Terrors

Tooting & Mitcham United's Mark Tompkins brings the ball under control watched by Gary Bray of Ruislip Manor. Photo - Francis Short.

Chairman: John Buffoni **Vice Chairman:** Alan Simpson **President:** Cliff Bilham
Secretary: Roy Sisley, 23 Romney Road, Polegate, East Sussex BN26 6LH (0323 485716).
Manager: Trevor Ford **Coach:** Peter Shaw **Physio:** Danny Keenan
Press Officer: Secretary **Commercial Mgr:** John Pollard.
Ground: Sandy Lane, Mitcham, Surrey CR4 2HD (081 648 3248).
Directions: Tooting (BR) quarter mile. Sandy Lane is off Streatham Road near Swan Hotel.
Capacity: 8,000 **Cover:** 1,990 **Seats:** 1,990 **Floodlights:** Yes **Metal Badges:** Yes
Club Shop: Yes, selling souvenirs and confectionary, etc.
Colours: White & black **Change colours:** All red.
Sponsors: Claremont Coaches.
Previous Leagues: London 32-37/ Athenian 37-56.
Midweek home matchday: Tuesday **Reserve Team's League:** Suburban.
Record Attendance: 17,500 v QPR, FA Cup 2nd Rd 56-57.
Best FA Trophy season: 2nd Qualifying Rd Replay 71-72 81-82.
Best FA Amateur Cup season: 1st Rd replay 22-23.
Best FA Cup season: 4th Rd 75-76 (lost 1-3 at Bradford City). Also 3rd Rd 58-59, 2nd Rd 56-57 76-77, 1st Rd 48-49 50-51 63-64 74-75 77-78.
Record win: 11-0 v Welton Rovers, FA Amateur Cup 62-63.
Record defeat: 1-8 v Kingstonian, Surrey Snr Cup 66-67 & v Redbridge F. (H), Loctite Cup 3rd Rd 19/2/91.
League clubs defeated in FA Cup: Bournemouth & Boscombe Ath, Northampton 58-59, Swindon 75-76.
Record Fees - Paid: £9,000 for Dave Flint (Enfield)
Received: £10,000 for Herbie Smith (Luton).
Players progressing to Football League: Trevor Owen (Orient 1958), Dave Bumpstead (Millwall 1958), Paddy Hasty (Aldersot 1958), Walter Pearson (Aldershot 1961), Richie Ward & Alex Stepney (Millwall 1962 & 63), Vic Akers (Watford 1975), Paul Priddy (Wimbledon 1978), Carlton Fairweather & Brian Gayle (Wimbledon 1984).
Clubhouse: Open every evening and weekend lunchtimes. Wide variety of food available.
Club Record Goalscorer: Alan Ives 92 (1972-78)
Club Record Appearances: Danny Godwin 470.
93-94 Captain: Micky Stephens.
93-94 P.O.Y.: Ralph Cowan.
93-94 Top scorer: Mark Tompkins 24.
Local Newspapers: Mitcham News (081 672 1077), South London Press (081 769 4444), South London Guardian (081 644 4300).
Local Radio Stations: Capital.
Honours: Isthmian League 57-58 59-60 (Full Members Cup 92-93), Athenian League 49-50 54-55, London Challenge Cup R-up 59-60, Surrey Senior Cup 37-38 43-44 44-45 52-53 59-60 75-76 76-77 77-78, London Senior Cup 42-43 48-49 58-59 59-60 (R-up 43-44 44-45), South Thames Cup 69-70, Surrey Senior Shield 51-52 60-61 61-62 65-66.

PROGRAMME DETAILS:
Pages: 24 **Price:** 50p
Editor: Ian Bullock

Formed: 1871

UXBRIDGE

The Reds

Uxbridge FC 1993-94. Back Row (L/R): George Talbot (Manager), Lee Hanratty, Paul McCluskey, Gary Downes, Sean Dawson, Fergus Moore, Darren Smith, Mark Gill, Henry Tunbridge (Asst Manager), Ernie Kempster (Physio). Front: Bobby Roper (Player-Coach), Alan Gregory, Troy Birch, Jeremy Davies, Nicky Rider, Gerry Crawford.

Chairman: Alan Holloway **V. C'man/Jt Pres.:** Tom Barnard **Joint President:** Alan Odell.
Secretary: Graham Hiseman, 96 New Peachey Lane, Cowley, Uxbridge, Middx UB8 3SY (0895 237195).
Manager: George Talbot **Asst Mgr:** Henry Tunbridge **Coach:** Bobby Roper.
Press Officer: Andy Peart (0895 444946) **Physio:** Ernie Kempster
Ground: Honeycroft, Horton Road, West Drayton, Middx UB7 8HX (0895 445830).
Directions: From West Drayton (BR) turn right then 1st left (Horton Road). Ground 1 mile on left. From Uxbridge (LT) take 222, U3 or U5 bus to West Drayton station, then follow as above. By road, ground 1 mile north of M4 jct 4 taking road to Uxbridge and leaving by first junction and turning left into Horton Rd - ground 600yds on right.
Capacity: 5,000 **Cover:** 480 **Seats:** 201 **Floodlights:** Yes **Metal Badges:** Yes.
Club Shop: Yes, selling club badges, ties, pennants, mugs, T-shirts, jumpers, programmes (League & non-League), pens, key-rings etc. Contact secretary.
Colours: Red/white/red **Change colours:** All sky
Previous Leagues: Southern 1894-99/ Gt Western Suburban 1906-19 20-23/ Athenian 1919-20 24-37 63-82/ Spartan 37-38/ London 38-46/ Gt Western Comb. 39-45/ Corinthian 46-63.
Prev. Name: Uxbridge Town (23-45) **Prev. Grnds:** RAF Stadium 23-48/ Cleveland Rd 48-76.
Midweek home matchday: Tuesday **Reserve Team's League:** Suburban (North Division).
Record Attendance: 1,000 v Arsenal, floodlight opening 1981.
Best FA Trophy season: 1st Rd replay 88-89
Best FA Vase season: 4th Rd 83-84.
Best FA Cup season: 2nd Rd 1873-74. 1st Rd on three other occasions 1883-84 84-85 85-86.
Players progressing to Football League: William Hill (QPR 1951), Lee Stapleton (Fulham 1952), Gary Churchouse.
Clubhouse: (0895 443557). Large clubhouse with bar and dance hall. Open every evening and every lunchtime except Monday. Hot & cold snacks available on matchdays & at lunchtime. Opens at midday and 7pm (earlier for midweek evening games).
Club Record Scorer: Danny Needham, 125
Club Record Appearances: Roger Nicholls, 1054.
93-94 Captain: Gary Downes.
93-94 Top Scorer: Nicky Ryder.
93-94 P.o.Y.: Gary Downes.
93-94 Players' P.o.Y.: Troy Birch.
Local Newspapers (+Tel.Nos.): Middx Gazette (0895 58290).
Local Radio Stations: Capital, Greater London Radio.
Honours: FA Amateur Cup R-up 1897-98, London Challenge Cup 93-94, Isthmian League Div 2 South R-up 84-85 (League Cup R-up 85-86), Athenian League Cup R-up 81-82 (Div 2 Cup R-up 70-71, Reserve Section 69-70, Reserve Cup 68-69), Corinthian League 59-60 (R-up 49-50, League Memorial Shield 50-51 52-53), London League Western Div R-up 45-46, Middx Senior Cup 1893-94 95-96 1950-51, Middx Senior Charity Cup 07-08 12-13 35-36 81-82 (R-up 69-70 82-83 85-86), Allied Counties Yth League 92-93 (League Cup 86-87, League Shield 88-89 92-93).

PROGRAMME DETAILS:
Pages: 32-48 **Price:** 50p
Editor: A Peart/M Bodman (0895 444946/813445)

WEMBLEY

Formed: 1946 The Lions

Wembley FC 1993-94.

Chairman: Brian Gumm **Vice Chairman:** Eric Stringer **President:** Jim Bryan, BEM.
Secretary: Mrs Jean Gumm, 14 Woodfield Avenue, North Wembley, Middx HA0 3NR (081 908 3353).
Manager: Glen Charles **Assistant Manager:** Don Lucas.
Commercial Manager: Glen Charles
Press Officer: Richard Markiewicz (081 902 0541 - before 9pm).
Ground: Vale Farm, Watford Road, Sudbury, Wembley HA0 4UR (081 908 8169).
Directions: Sudbury Town (tube) 400 yds, or 10 mins walk from North Wembley (BR) station. Buses 18, 92, 245 & 182.
Capacity: 2,000 **Cover:** 350 **Seats:** 350 **Club Shop:** No **Metal Badges:** £2
Colours: Red & white **Change colours:** Yellow & black.
Sponsors: G & B Builders.
Previous Leagues: Middx 46-49/ Spartan 49-51/ Delphian 51-56/ Corinthian 56-63/ Athenian 63-75.
Midweek home matchday: Tuesday **Reserve Team's League:** Suburban (North).
Record Attendance: 2,654 v Wealdstone, FA Amateur Cup 52-53.
Best season in FA Cup: 1st Round Proper 1980-81 (lost 0-3 at Enfield).
Record win: 11-1 v Hermes, London Senior Cup 1963.
Record defeat: 0-16 v Chelsea, London Challenge Cup 59-60.
Record Fees - Paid: Nil **Received:** £10,000 for Gary Roberts (Brentford, 1981).
Players progressing to Football League: Ken Coote (Brentford 1949), Keith Cassells (Watford 1977), Mike O'Donague (Southampton 1979), A McGonigle (Olympiakos), Gary Roberts (Brentford 1980), Richard Cadette (Orient 1984).
Clubhouse: (081 904 8169). Open every night & weekend lunchtimes. Hot food on matchdays.
Club Record Goalscorer: Bill Handrahan 105 (1946-52)
Club Record Apps: Spud Murphy 505 (78-88).
93-94 Captain: Paul Shields.
Player of the Year: Steve Daly.
93-94 Top Scorer: Giuliano Grazioli.
Local Newspapers: Wembley & Harrow Observer.
Honours: FA Amateur Cup 2nd Rd 66-67 68-69, FA Tphy 1st Rd Proper 91-92, Middx Senior Cup 83-84 86-87 (R-up 55-56 68-69 78-79 87-88 91-92 92-93), Middx League 47-48 (League Cup 46-47), Middx Charity Cup 67-68(joint) 80-81(joint) 82-83 86-87 (R-up 83-84 87-88), Middx Invitation Cup 56-57, Athenian League R-up 74-75 (Div 1 R-up 67-68), Corinthian League Memorial Shield R-up 58-59, Delphian League R-up 55-56, Spartan League Div 1 West 50-51 (Dunkel Trophy 50-51(joint)), London Senior Cup R-up 55-56, Hitachi Cup SF 83-84, Suburban League North 85-86 (League Cup 84-85 (R-up 83-84)).

PROGRAMME DETAILS:
Pages: 28 **Price:** 50p
Editor: Richard Markiewicz
(081 902 0541 - before 9pm)

Formed: 1946

WHYTELEAFE

Leafe

Whyteleafe defend a corner as they lose 0-1 at home to promotion chasing Purfleet.
Photo - Brian Sandford.

President: A F Lidbury **Chairman:** Paul Owens **Vice-Chairman:** TBA
Secretary: Ian Robertson (0883 622096).
Manager: Paul Hinshelwood **Asst Manager/Coach:** Keith Wilkinson
Press Officer: Tony Lidbury (0883 622720)
Commercial Manager: Paul Owens.
Ground: 15 Church Road, Whyteleafe, Surrey CR3 0AR (081 660 5491).
Directions: Five minutes walk from Whyteleafe (BR) - turn right from station, and left into Church Road.
Capacity: 5,000 **Cover:** 200 **Seats:** 200 **Floodlights:** Yes **Metal Badges:** Yes
Colours: Green & white/green/white **Change colours:** Yellow/black/black
Sponsors: Sunday Sport.
Previous Leagues: Caterham & Edenbridge/ Croydon/ Thornton Heath & Dist./ Surrey Intermediate (East) 54-58/ Surrey Senior 58-75/ Spartan 75-81/ Athenian 81-84.
Midweek matchday: Tuesday **Reserve Team's League:** Suburban.
Record Attendance: 533.
Best FA Vase season: 5th Rd 80-81 85-86
Best FA Trophy season: 3rd Qualifying Rd 89-90
Best FA Cup season: Third Qualifying Round replay (lost 1-2 after 1-1 draw at Wokingham Town)
League clubs defeated in FA Cup: None.
Record Fees - Paid: £1,000 for Gary Bowyer (Carshalton)
Received: £25,000 for Steve Milton.
Players progressing to Football League: Steve Milton (Fulham).
Clubhouse: Open every lunchtime and evening. Hot and cold food, pool, darts, gaming machines.
93-94 Captain:
93-94 Player of the Year:
93-94: Clubman of the Year: Ian Robertson, secretary.
93-94 Top scorer:
Local Press: Croydon Advertiser.
Local Radio Stations:
Honours: Isthmian League Div 2 South R-up 88-89, Surrey Senior League 68-69 (League Cup R-up 68-69, League Charity Cup 71-72, Reserve Section 62-63 (Challenge Cup 62-63 (R-up 59-60), Surrey Senior Cup 68-69 (R-up 87-88), Surrey Premier Cup R-up 84-85, East Surrey Charity Cup 79-80 (R-up 76-77 77-78), Thornton Heath & Dist League 51-52 (League Cup 51-52, Div 4 R-up 51-52), Edenbridge Charity Cup 51-52, Caterham & Purley Hospital Cup 51-52, Surrey County Intermediate League East Section 1 55-56 Surrey Junior Cup R-up 51-52, Caterham & Edenbridge League Div 3 51-52, Borough of Croydon Charity Cup 56-57, Southern Yth League 89-90 (R-up 88-89, League Cup 88-89 89-90).

PROGRAMME DETAILS:
Pages: 36 **Price:** 70p
Editor: Tony Lidbury

WIVENHOE TOWN

Formed: 1925 The Dragons

Action from Wivenhoe Town's fixture at Carshalton Athletic. Their 3-4 defeat represented one of their better performances in a very difficult season.

Photo - Peter Lirettoc.

Chairman: Geoff Langsdon **Vice Chairman:** Dave Whymark **President:** Harry Welsh.
Secretary/Press Officer: Mike Boyle, 15 Daniell Drive, Colchester, Essex (0206 573223).
Manager: Phil Bloss **Asst Manager:**
Physio: Barry Wreford **Commercial Manager:** Phil Reeve.
Ground: Broad Lane Ground, Elmstead Road, Wivenhoe CO7 7HA (0206 823416).
Directions: Coming out of Colchester towards Clacton take first turning (right) towards Wivenhoe, first left and ground clearly visible on right at cross-roads. 1 mile from Wivenhoe (BR).
Capacity: 3,000 **Cover:** 1,300 **Seats:** 250 **Floodlights:** Yes **Metal Badges:** Yes
Club Shop: Yes, selling club scarves, key rings, pens, bobble hats, car stickers, metal badges, handbooks plus non-League and Football League programmes and magazines.
Colours: Royal/royal/white **Change colours:** Yellow/royal/yellow.
Previous Leagues: Brighlingsea & District 1927-50/ Colchester & East Essex 50-71/ Essex & Suffolk Border 71-79/ Essex Senior 79-86.
Previous Grounds: Spion Kop/ Broomfield/ Claude Watcham's Meadow/ Vine Farm/ Spion Kop/ Broomfield/ King George V Playing Fields/ Essex University.
Previous Name: Wivenhoe Rangers.
Midweek matchday: Tuesday **Reserve Team's League:** Essex & Herts Border Comb.
Record Attendance: 1,912 v Runcorn, FA Trophy 1st Rd, Feb 1990.
Best FA Cup season: 4th Qual Rd 89-90 (lost 2-3 at Halesowen Town), 93-94 (1-2 at home to Enfield).
Record Fees - Paid: N/A **Received:** £5,875 for Bobby Mayes (Redbridge Forest).
Record win: 18-0 v Nayland. **Record defeat:** 0-8 v Carshalton A. (H), Isthmian Lg 28/8/93.
Players progressing to Football League: Robert Reinelt (Gillingham) 1993.
Clubhouse: (0206 825380). Open normal pub hours.
Club Record Goalscorer: Paul Harrison, 258 goals in 350 games.
Club Record Appearances: Keith Bain, 536.
93-94 Captain: Christian McClean.
93-94 P.o.Y.: Nathan Munson.
93-94 Top scorer: Trevor Collins.
Local Newspapers: East Anglian Daily Times, Colchester Evening Gazette.
Local Radio Stations: BBC Radio Essex, Radio Orwell, BBC TV (Norwich).
Hons: FA Tphy 2nd Rd replay 89-90, FA Vase 5th Rd 82-83, Isthmian Lg Div 1 89-90 (Div 2 Nth 87-88), Essex Snr Lg R-up 79-80 81-82 85-86 (Harry Fisher Tphy 83-84 85-86), Essex & Suffolk Border Lg 78-79 (Div 1 72-73, Div 2 71-72, Lg Cup R-up(2) 75-77), Colchester & East Essex Lg 52-53 55-56 (R-up 70-71, Div 1 59-60 69-70, Div 2 R-up 68-69, Lg KO Cup 51-52 52-53 54-55 55-56 (R-up 59-60), Challenge Cup 52-53), Brighlingsea & Dist Lg Div 1 35-36 36-37 47-48 (R-up 37-38, Lg KO Cup 36-37 37-38 47-48, Challenge Cup 36-37), Essex Snr Tphy 87-88, Essex Jnr Cup R-up 55-56 78-79 (Group Finalists(3) 52-53 70-72), Amos Charity Cup(7) 36-38 51-56 (R-up 72-73), Stokes Cup(3) 48-49 52-54, Wivenhoe Charity Cup 52-53 68-69 73-74 78-79 (R-up 55-56 65-66 69-70 72-73), Cristal Monopole Cup 68-69 78-79 79-80 80-81 81-82 (R-up 65-66 67-68), Sidney James Mem. Tphy 69-70 (R-up 72-73), Tolleshunt D'Arcy Mem. Cup(3) 71-74 (R-up 70-71 77-78), Walton & District Charity Cup 73-74 78-79, Coggeshall Brotherhood Cup 80-81, Brantham Charity Cup R-up 82-83, Worthington Evans Cup 81-82 (R-up 80-81 85-86), Harwich Snr Cup R-up 84-85, Woodbridge Chal. Cup 91-92, Mat Fowler Shield 92-93 93-94.

PROGRAMME DETAILS:
Pages: 44 **Price:** £1
Editor: Mr M Boyle

Formed: 1886

WORTHING

The Rebels

Worthing FC 1993-94

Chairman: Beau Reynolds **Vice Chairman:** Ray Smith **President:** Monty Hollis.
Press Officer/Secretary: Alan Evans, 105 St Andrews Rd, Worthing, West Sussex BN13 1HR (0903 268253).
Manager: John Robson **Asst Manager:** TBA **Coach:** Jimmy Quinn
Physio: Jack Anderson **Press Officer:** Secretary.
Commercial Manager: Colin Hearsey.
Ground: Woodside Road, Worthing, West Sussex BN14 7HQ (0903 239575).
Directions: Follow A24 to town, at end of Broadwater Rd having gone over railway bridge, take 1st right into Teville Rd, take right into South Farm RD, 2nd left into Pavilion Rd, Woodside Rd is first right. Half a mile from Worthing (BR).
Capacity: 4,500 **Seats:** 450 **Cover:** 1,000 **Midweek matches:** Tuesday.
Colours: All red **Change colours:** All blue
Reserves' League: Unijet Sussex Res. Section.
Shop: Yes, selling T-shirts, sweatshirts, scarves, mugs, pens, progs (League & non-League), small pennants.
Previous Leagues: West Sussex/ Sussex County 20-48/ Corinthian 48-63/ Athenian 63-77.
Record Gate: 4,500 v Depot Battalion Royal Engineers, FA Amtr Cup 07-08.
Best FA Vase season: 5th Rd 78-79
Best FA Amateur Cup season: Quarter-Final replay 07-08.
Best FA Trophy season: 3rd Rd Replay 81-85
Best FA Cup year: 2nd Rd 82-83, lost 0-4 to Oxford Utd. Also 1st Rd 36-37.
Record Fees - Paid: £1,000 for Steve Guille (Bognor Regis Town, 1989).
Received: £7,500 for Tim Read (Woking, 1990).
Record defeat: 0-13 v Carshalton Athletic (A), Loctite Cup Third Round 28/2/91.
Clubhouse: Open two hours before kick-off and closes 11pm. Hot & cold food available.
Players progressing to Football League: Ken Suttle (Chelsea 1948), Alan Arnell & Fred Perry (Liverpool 1954), Craig Whitington (Scarborough, via Crawley Town) 1993.
Club Record Scorer: Mick Edmonds
Club Record Appearances: Geoff Raynsford
93-94 Captain: Steve Riley
93-94 Top scorer: Antoni Romasz
93-94 P.o.Y.: Steve Riley
Local Press: Evening Argus, Worthing Gazette & Herald.
Local Radio: Radio Sussex.
Hons: Isthmian Lg R-up(2) 83-85 (Div 1 82-83, Div 2 81-82 92-93), Athenian Lg Div 1 R-up 63-64 (Div 2 R-up 71-72, Lg Cup R-up 72-73, Mem. Shield 63-64), Sussex Snr Cup(19) 1892-93 1903-04 07-08 13-14 19-20 22-23 26-27 28-29 34-35 39-40 44-45 46-47 51-52 56-57 58-59 60-61 74-75 76-78, Sussex RUR Char. Cup(14) 03-04 06-08 09-10 13-14 19-20 22-23 26-27 33-34(jt) 41-42 44-45 48-49(jt) 52-54, Sussex Co. Lg(8) 20-22 26-27 28-29 30-31 33-34 38-40, W Sussex Lg(7) 1898-99 1903-04 06-08 09-10 12-14, Brighton Char. Cup(9) 29-31 34-35 62-63 69-71 73-74(jt) 80-82, Worthing Char. Cup(10) 11-12 25-27 30-31 32-35 37-39 64-65, AFA Invit. Cup 63-64 68-69 73-74 75-76 (Snr Cup R-up 36-37 46-47 48-49), Corinth. Lg Mem. Shield R-up 49-50 (Neale Tphy 58-59), Roy Hayden Mem. Tphy 1975(jt), 1977 1978, Don Morecraft Tphy 1972 1973 1976 1981 1982, Sussex F'lit Cup(2) 88-90, Sussex I'mediate Cup 34-35 64-65, Brighton Chal. Shield 29-30 31-32.

PROGRAMME DETAILS:
Pages: 32 **Price:** 60p
Editor: Secretary

DIVISION TWO 1993-94

	P	W	D	L	F	A	PTS
Newbury Town	42	32	7	3	115	36	103
Chertsey Town	42	33	3	6	121	48	102
Aldershot Town	42	30	7	5	78	27	97
Barton Rovers	42	25	8	9	68	37	83
Witham Town	42	21	10	11	68	51	73
Malden Vale	42	20	10	12	70	49	70
Thame United	42	19	12	11	87	51	69
Met. Police	42	20	9	13	75	54	69
Banstead Athletic	42	19	9	14	56	53	66
Aveley	42	19	5	15	60	66	62
Edgware Town	42	16	10	16	88	76	58
Saffron Walden	42	17	7	18	61	62	58
Hemel Hempstead	42	14	11	17	47	43	53
Egham Town	42	14	8	20	48	65	50
Ware	42	14	7	21	48	76	49
Hungerford Town	42	13	7	22	56	66	46
Tilbury	42	13	3	26	59	81	42
Hampton	42	12	5	25	42	70	41
Leatherhead	42	10	6	26	46	92	36
Lewes	42	8	10	24	38	85	34
Collier Row	42	7	8	27	37	88	29
Rainham Town	42	4	2	36	24	116	14

TOP SCORERS

	Lge	Cup	Tot
Matthew McDonnell (Newbury T.)	40	2	42
Mario Russo (Met. Police)	29	2	31
Mark Butler (Aldershot Town)	26	2	28
Scott McGleish (Edgware Town)	27	1	28
Lee Charles (Chertset Town)	20	8	28

Below: *Matthew McDonnell of Newbury Town, top-scorer in the Division, tries to find a way through two Chertsey Town defenders.*

Photo - Paul Dennis.

RESULT CHART 1993-94

HOME TEAM	1	2	3	4	5	6	7	8	9	10	11	12	13	14	15	16	17	18	19	20	21	22
1. Aldershot	*	2-1	1-2	1-0	1-1	1-0	3-0	3-2	3-0	2-0	3-1	1-0	4-0	1-2	3-1	1-0	2-0	1-0	0-0	2-0	4-0	1-0
2. Aveley	1-0	*	1-0	2-2	2-3	2-1	1-2	4-0	1-0	0-3	3-2	0-2	2-1	1-0	0-1	1-2	6-2	0-0	1-5	2-1	4-1	0-1
3. Banstead	0-0	2-2	*	0-3	4-3	2-0	1-3	1-0	2-0	0-0	3-2	3-0	1-0	1-1	0-1	0-1	4-1	0-2	3-1	3-1	1-0	1-1
4. Barton R.	0-1	2-0	1-0	*	1-0	3-0	5-4	4-1	1-1	0-0	2-0	1-0	4-0	0-2	1-0	0-0	3-0	0-1	2-2	2-0	3-2	0-3
5. Chertsey T.	3-2	3-2	4-0	3-2	*	10-2	1-1	0-0	2-0	5-1	4-2	6-2	5-0	3-0	5-1	3-2	4-0	5-2	5-0	1-0	3-0	5-1
6. Collier R.	1-3	1-2	2-3	1-0	2-3	*	2-2	3-1	0-1	0-1	1-1	2-1	0-0	0-3	2-2	0-3	0-2	3-2	3-2	0-3	1-3	0-2
7. Edgware	0-2	2-2	1-1	0-1	2-3	5-1	*	3-4	1-1	3-1	2-2	1-1	2-3	1-2	1-3	1-3	4-1	4-1	2-2	3-1	3-0	3-4
8. Egham T.	0-0	1-0	0-1	1-1	1-2	0-0	2-7	*	0-2	1-0	0-5	1-1	4-0	0-1	2-1	0-0	3-0	0-3	0-2	3-0	1-1	3-1
9. Hampton	0-3	4-0	2-1	0-1	0-2	2-1	1-2	0-1	*	1-1	1-0	2-3	1-1	1-4	0-1	1-1	2-0	0-3	0-3	1-2	3-1	0-5
10. Hemel H.	0-1	0-1	2-3	0-3	2-0	2-1	1-1	0-2	0-1	*	5-0	1-1	2-1	1-1	1-3	0-3	2-0	3-1	0-1	2-0	3-0	1-1
11. Hungerford	0-0	3-1	1-0	2-3	2-1	3-1	2-1	0-1	2-0	0-3	*	4-0	3-1	1-2	1-4	0-1	1-0	0-2	1-1	4-0	0-0	0-1
12. Leatherhead	0-5	2-3	1-2	0-2	1-5	0-1	0-2	2-0	1-0	0-1	2-0	*	1-0	1-0	2-1	3-6	6-0	0-1	0-8	0-0	0-2	1-2
13. Lewes	1-3	1-2	0-0	0-1	1-3	1-0	1-1	2-1	0-4	0-0	1-0	1-1	*	1-1	1-3	1-4	2-0	2-0	0-2	3-2	1-2	2-3
14. Malden V.	1-2	1-1	1-1	0-1	2-0	0-2	0-2	1-0	2-0	0-0	2-0	2-1	6-1	*	2-2	1-2	5-1	3-2	2-1	3-4	3-1	1-1
15. Met Police	1-3	5-1	1-3	1-1	0-1	2-0	0-2	0-3	2-1	0-0	5-1	5-0	4-2	1-1	*	1-1	0-1	2-1	0-0	4-1	0-0	1-1
16. Newbury	0-3	4-1	2-0	3-0	5-2	6-0	3-1	4-1	4-2	1-0	2-1	6-0	2-1	2-0	2-0	*	7-0	6-1	3-3	4-2	4-0	5-1
17. Rainham T.	1-2	0-1	1-4	0-4	0-3	1-1	1-2	0-3	0-3	1-0	0-3	0-4	0-0	1-7	1-2	1-2	*	3-0	1-6	2-3	0-5	0-1
18. Saffron WT	2-2	0-1	3-0	0-1	0-1	1-1	0-4	5-1	2-0	1-0	2-2	3-2	7-1	0-0	1-5	0-0	1-0	*	2-2	3-1	3-0	2-1
19. Thame U.	3-0	0-1	0-1	3-2	1-3	3-0	7-0	0-0	5-0	2-2	2-1	3-0	1-0	1-2	1-3	1-2	2-1	2-0	*	0-1	2-2	1-1
20. Tilbury	1-2	2-1	3-0	3-4	1-2	2-0	1-5	1-2	0-2	1-0	1-2	5-2	1-2	1-2	2-3	1-1	2-1	0-1	2-2	*	5-0	1-0
21. Ware	0-2	1-0	3-1	0-1	0-2	0-0	2-1	3-2	2-1	0-3	1-1	4-2	1-1	2-1	0-3	0-1	2-0	1-0	1-2	2-1	*	0-2
22. Witham T.	2-2	1-3	1-1	0-0	0-1	2-1	3-1	1-0	4-1	0-3	1-0	0-0	1-1	4-0	2-0	1-5	2-0	2-0	1-2	2-0	5-2	*

Diadora (Isthmian) League Division Two Ten Year Record

(See page 399 for clubs who only played in Div. 3 or Regionalised Div. 2)

(N - Denotes Division Two (North), S - Denotes Division Two (South))

	84/5	85/6	86/7	87/8	88/9	89/0	90/1	91/2	92/3	93/4
Aldershot Town	-	-	-	-	-	-	-	-	-	3
Aveley	-	-	5N	21N	9N	2N	-	-	-	10
Banstead Athletic	9S	11S	17S	21S	16S	11S	11S	14	13	9
Barton Rovers	15N	17N	7N	15N	8N	5N	10N	11	18	4
Berkhamsted Town	9N	10N	16N	4N	15N	17N	5N	18	3	-
Billericay Town	-	-	-	-	6N	15N	3N	3	-	-
Chertsey Town	19S	-	6S	6S	12S	13S	14S	-	7	2
Collier Row	-	-	9N	2N	-	8N	12N	-	-	21
Edgware Town	-	-	-	-	-	-	14N	-	11	11
Egham Town	6S	17S	14S	14S	10S	10S	3S	6	12	14
Hampton	-	-	-	-	-	-	12S	-	10	18
Harefield United	18N	18N	10S	13S	5S	12S	7S	19	21	-
Hemel Hempstead	14N	14N	20N	19N	12N	14N	9N	9	4	13
Hungerford Town	4S	13S	9S	8S	6S	9S	9S	10	19	16
Leatherhead	-	-	-	-	-	-	10S	4	14	19
Lewes	-	-	-	-	-	-	-	2	-	20
Malden Vale	-	-	-	-	-	15S	4S	15	6	6
Metropolitan Police	-	7S	7S	2S	-	-	-	7	5	8
Newbury Town	18S	4S	20S	18S	19S	7S	8S	22	9	1
Purfleet	-	-	-	-	2N	-	7N	1	-	-
Rainham Town	13S	13N	18N	16N	19N	21N	8N	16	20	22
Ruislip Manor	11S	19S	5S	9S	7S	4S	5S	5	2	-
Saffron Walden Town	5N	9N	11N	18N	20N	10N	11N	8	8	12
Southall	7S	8S	21S	16S	18S	6S	6S	20	22	-
Southwick	-	1S	-	-	-	-	-	21	-	-
Thame United	-	-	-	-	-	-	-	-	-	7
Tilbury	-	-	-	3N	17N	6N	17N	-	17	17
Ware	20N	15N	10N	6N	11N	13N	4N	17	15	15
Witham Town	-	-	-	7N	13N	20N	6N	13	16	5
Worthing	-	-	-	-	-	-	-	12	1	-
No. of clubs competing	20N	20N	22N	22N	22N	22N	22N	22	22	22
	19S	20S	21S	22S	21S	21S	22S			

AVELEY

Chairman: Tony Wallace **Vice C'man:** Bill Maddicks **President:** Ken Clay
Secretary: Ken Sutliff, 9 Westlyn Close, Rainham, Essex RM13 9JP (0708 555271).
Manager: Keith Newman **Asst Mgr/Coach:** John Kerslake
Press Officer: Alan Suttling **Physio:** Phil Hunter
Ground Address & Tel: 'Mill Field', Mill Road, Aveley, Essex RM15 4TR (0708 865940).
Directions: London - Southend A13, turn into Sandy Lane at Aveley. Rainham or Purfleet BR stations then bus No. 723 to the ground.
Capacity: 8,000 **Cover:** 400 **Seats:** 400 **Floodlights:** Yes **Founded:** 1927.
Club Shop: No **Metal Badges:** Yes
Colours: Royal blue/white/royal blue **Change colours:** All yellow.
Founded: 1927 **Club Sponsors:** Dagenham Motors.
Previous Leagues: Thurrock Combination 46-49/ London 49-57/ Delphian 57-63/ Athenian 63-73.
Midweek home matchday: Tuesday **Reserve Team's League:** Essex & Herts Border Comb.
Record Attendance: 3,741 v Slough Town, FA Amateur Cup 27/2/71.
Best F.A. Cup season: 1st Rd 70-71 (lost 0-1 to Yeovil).
League clubs defeated in F.A. Cup: None. **Record win:** 11-1 v Histon, 24/8/63
Record defeat: against Orient, Essex Thameside Trophy, 11/4/85.
Players progressing to Football League: David Case & Alan Hull (Orient), Alan Parkinson (Orient 1967), Yilmaz Orhan (W Ham 1972), Keith Day (Colchester 1984), Paul Williams (Charlton & Sheff Wed).
Clubhouse: Normal pub hours. All kinds of bar snacks and hot food.
Club Record Goalscorer: Jotty Wilks, 214 **Club Record Appearances:** Ken Riley, 422
Local Press: Thurrock Gazette (0375 372293). **Local Radio:** Radio Essex, Essex Radio.
93-94 Captain: M Loid. **93-94 Player of the Year:** G Waters. **93-94 Top scorer:** M Cole 14.
Honours: Isthmian Lg Div 2 (North) R-up 89-90 (Lg (AC Delco) Cup 89-90), London Lg 51-52 54-55 (R-up 55-56, Lg Cup 53-54), Delphian Lg R-up 57-58 (Lg Cup 61-62), Athenian Lg 70-71 (Div 2 R-up 68-69), Essex Junior Cup 47-48 48-49, Essex Thameside Trophy 79-80, Hornchurch Charity Cup 81-82 (R-up 83-84), East Anglian Cup 88-89, FA Amateur Cup QF 70-71, FA Tphy 3rd Qualifying Rd replay 74-75, FA Vase 3rd Rd 89-90.

BANSTEAD ATHLETIC

Chairman: Terry Molloy **President:**
Secretary: Gordon Taylor, 116 Kingston Avenue, North Cheam, Surrey SM3 9UF (081 641 2957).
Manager: Bobby Mapleson **Asst Mgr:** Michael Sorenson **Physio:** Kevin Taylor
Press Officer: Colin Darby **Commercial Manager:** Alan McIlvenna
Ground: Merland Rise, Tadworth, Surrey KT20 5JG (0737 350982).
Directions: Follow signs to Tattenham Corner (Epsom racecourse), then to Banstead Sports Centre. Ground adjacent to swimming pool. Half a mile from Tattenham Corner (BR). Bus 420 from Sutton stops outside ground. Also buses 406 & 727 from Epsom.
Capacity: 3,500 **Seats:** 250 **Cover:** 500 **Floodlights:** Yes **Founded:** 1944
Colours: Amber/black/black **Change colours:** Red & white **Nickname:** A's.
Programme: 28 pages, 50p **Editor:** Secretary **Club Shop:** No
Midweek Matchday: Tuesday **Previous Ground:** Tattenham Way Rec. 1944-50.
Previous Leagues: Surrey Int./Surrey Snr 49-65/ Spartan 65-75/ London Spartan 75-79/ Athenian 79-84.
Reserve Team's League: Suburban
Sponsors: PDM Marketing **Record Gate:** 1,400 v Leytonstone, FA Amateur 1953.
Best FA Cup year: 3rd Qual.Rd. 86-87
Record win: 12-0 v Reigate Priory **Record defeat:** 0-10 v St Albans City.
Players progressing to Football League: W Chesney & B Robinson (Crystal Palace).
Clubhouse: Mon-Sat noon-11pm, noon-2 & 7.30-11pm Sun. 2 bars, real ale, bar snacks.
Club Record Scorer: Harry Clark **Club Record Appearances:** Dennis Wall.
93-94 Captain: Steve Shaw **93-94 P.o.Y.:** Barry Laker **93-94 Top scorer:** Ian Kilpatrick 39
Local Press: Banstead Herald. **Local Radio Stations:**.
Hons: FA Vase QF 92-93, Surrey Snr Lg(6) 50-54 56-57 64-65 (R-up(5) 49-50 54-56 57-59, Lg Cup 57-58, Charity Cup 52-53 58-59), London Spartan Lg R-up 77-78 (Lg Cup(2) 65-67), Surrey Prem. Cup R-up 91-92, Surrey Snr Shield 55-56, Gilbert Rice F'lit Cup 81-82 86-87 (R-up(4) 82-86), Athenian Lg Cup(2) 80-82 (R-up 82-83 (SF 79-80)), Surrey Int. Lg(2) 47-49, Surrey Int. Cup 46-47 54-55, E. Surrey Charity Cup(4) 59-60 66-67 76-78 (R-up 79-80, I'mediate Sect. 75-76 (R-up 76-77), Jnr Sect. 81-82), Southern Comb. Cup R-up 69-70, Suburban Lg R-up 86-87.

Below: *Banstead celebrate inflicting a first-ever home league defeat on Aldershot.* *Photo - Eric Marsh.*

BARTON ROVERS

Chairman: R E Roberts **Vice Chairman:** A F Monks **President:** P Howarth.
Secretary: Owen Clark, 108 Manor Road, Barton-le-Clay, Bedford MK45 4NS (0582 882398).
Manager: Gordon Taylor **Asst Manager:** Paul Burgess **Coach:** TBA
Press Officer: N Rhodes (0582 881865) **Physio:** Roy Cullis.
Ground: Sharpenhoe Road, Barton-le-Clay, Bedford MK45 4SD (0582 882607).
Directions: M1 Jct 12, from London exit turn right, take 2nd right thru Harlington and Sharpenhoe. Ground on right entering village. 4 & a half miles from Harlington (BR), 6 miles from Luton (BR), good bus service from Luton.
Capacity: 4,000 **Seats:** 120 **Cover:** 1,120 **Floodlights:** Yes **Founded:** 1898
Colours: All blue **Change colours:** All red. **Club Shop:** No.
Programme: 36 pages, 50p **Editor:** Nick Rhodes (0582 881865) **Metal Badges:** Yes
Midweek Matchday: Tuesday **Kit Sponsors:** Linneys Sports **Nickname:** Rovers
Previous Grounds: Church Pitch 1898-1912/ Barton Cutting 1912/ Sharpenhoe Road 12-33/ Faldo Road 33-38/ Barton Rec. 46-75.
Reserves' Lg: Essex/Herts Border Comb **Previous Leagues:** Luton & Dist. 47-54/ Sth Midlands 54-79.
Record Gate: 1,900 v Nuneaton, FA Cup 4th Qual. Rd 1976. **Sponsors:** N/A.
Best FA Cup year: 1st Rd. 80-81 (lost 0-2 at Torquay United).
Record win: 17-1 v Flitwick Athletic (H), South Midlands Lge Division One 55-56.
Record defeat: 1-11 v Leighton United (H), South Midlands Lge Premier Division 62-63.
Record Fees - Paid: £1,000 for B Baldry (Hitchin Town, 1980).
Received: £1,000 for B Baldry (Bishop's Stortford, 1981).
Players progressing to Football Lge: Kevin Blackwell (Huddersfield, Torquay, Notts Co., Scarborough).
Clubhouse: Noon-3pm weekends (no football), noon-11pm (matchdays), 7-11pm weekdays. Real ale, hot & cold snacks, pool, darts, gaming machines.
Local Press: Luton News, Herald. **Local Radio:** Radio Chiltern, Radio Beds.
Record Scorer: Richard Camp 102, 1989-94. **Club Record Appearances:** Bill Goodyear 475, 1982-83.
93-94 Captain: Danny Turner **93-94 P.o.Y.:** Nick Chilvers **93-94 Top scorer:** Richard Camp 26.
Hons: FA Vase R-up 77-78 (SF 76-77 81-82, QF 75-76 78-79), S Mids Lg(8) 70-73 74-79 (R-up 67-68, Div 1 64-65 (R-up 55-56), Div 2 54-55, Lg Shld 57-58 60-61 68-69, Chal. Tphy(4) 71-72 74-75 77-79), Beds Snr Cup(5) 71-73 80-82 89-90 (R-up(3) 74-76 82-83 90-91, Prem. Cup R-up 81-82 83-84 88-89, I'mediate Cup 53-54), Luton & D. Lg Div 3 47-48, Nth Beds Charity Cup(6) 72-73 74-75 76-78 79-81 (R-up 70-71), Isth. Lg Assoc. Members Tphy R-up 92-93.

Barton Rovers. Back (L/R): Gordon Taylor (Mgr), Frank Geddes, Steve Hunt, Gordon Guile, Gary Turner, Graham Golds, Nick Chilvers, Andy Linsell, Neil Yates, Mick Clark (Physio), Owen Clark (Match Sec.). Front: Lee Cowley (Reserves' Mgr), Richard Camp, Tony McNally, Danny Turner (Captain), Brian Lalor, Paul Neufville.

BRACKNELL TOWN

Chairman: Dave Mihell **Vice Chairman:** Paul Broome **President:** Ian McGregor.
Secretary: Cliff McFadden, 15 Goodways Drive, Bracknell, Berks RG12 3AU (0344 52803).
Manager: Nick Collier **Asst Manager:** Ken Wilson **Coach:** Jeff Dennis
Press Officer: Robert Scully (0344 423749) **Physio:** Jeff Jones.
Ground: Larges Lane, Bracknell RG12 3AN (0344 412305).
Directions: Off A329 just before Met Office r'bout by Bracknell College, ground 200 yards. From Bracknell (BR)/bus station - right out of station, follow path over bridge, left down steps and follow cycle path ahead, after 300yds follow curve over footbridge, right and follow lane to end, left and ground on left after bend.
Capacity: 2,500 **Seats:** 150 **Cover:** 200 **Floodlights:** Yes **Founded:** 1896
Colours: All red **Change colours:** All blue **Nickname:** Robins
Programme: 32 pages, 50p **Editor:** Robert Scully (0344 423749) **Metal Badges:** Yes
Club Shop: Yes, selling metal badges, programmes, 'Team Talk' magazine, scarves, club sweaters, club ties. Contact Keith Smith c/o Bracknell Town FC.
Previous Grounds: None **Midweek Matchday:** Tuesday **Sponsors:** Panasonic
Previous Leagues: Great Western Comb./ Surrey Snr 63-70/ London Spartan 70-75.
Reserve's League: Suburban (west) **Record Gate:** 2,500 v Newquay, FA Amateur Cup 1971.
Best FA Cup season: 4th Qualifying Rd 1988 (lost 1-2 v Cheltenham Town).
Record win: 7-0 v Royston Town **Record defeat:** 0-9 v Royston & v Thame Utd.
Players progressing to Football League: Willie Graham (Brentford).
Clubhouse: Members' bar open 11am-11pm Mon-Sat, 12-3 & 7-10.30pm Sun. Function hall bookable.
Club Record Scorer: Richard Whithy **Club Record Appearances:** James Woodcock.
93-94 Captain: Tony Carter **P.o.Y:** Bobby Purser/Alan Henly (joint) **93-94 Top scorer:** Justin Day
Hons: Isthmian Lg Div 3 93-94 (Div 2 Sth R-up), Berks & Bucks Snr Cup R-up, Spartan Lg 82-83 (R-up(2)), Surrey Snr Lg 69-70 (Lg Cup 68-69 69-70).

CHALFONT St PETER

Chairman: David Pembroke **President:** Vacant.
Secretary: Mr Peter Court, 8 Lovel End, Chalfont St Peter, Bucks SL9 9NZ (0753 888583).
Press Officer: Malcolm Upton **Commercial Manager:** Ken Power.
Ground: The Playing Fields, Amersham Road, Chalfont St Peter SL9 7BQ (0753 885797).
Directions: A413 from Uxbridge (London) to Chalfont. Turn left 100 yds after 2nd major roundabout (between Ambulance station and Community Centre. Two miles from Gerrards Cross (BR), regular buses from Slough.
Capacity: 4,500 **Cover:** 220 **Seats:** 220 **Floodlights:** Yes **Metal Badges:** Yes.
Club Shop: Yes.
Colours: Red & green quarters/green/green **Change colours:** Yellow/blue/blue
Previous Leagues: Great Western Combination 1948-58/ Parthenon 58-59/ London 60-62/ Spartan 62-75/ London Spartan 75-76/ Athenian 76-84.
Midweek home matchday: Tuesday **Reserve Team's League:** Suburban
Record Attendance: 2,500 v Watford, benefit match 1985.
Best FA Cup season: 3rd Qualifying Rd 85-86 (wins over Banbury, King's Lynn and Barking).
League clubs defeated in FA Cup: None.
Record Fees - Paid: £750 to Chertsey (Steve Church, March 1989)
Players progressing to Football League: None.
Clubhouse: Open every evening, Saturday afternoons and Sunday lunchtimes.
Club Record Goalscorer: Unknown. **Club Record Appearances:** Colin Davies.
93-94 Captain: **93-94 P.o.Y.:** **93-94 Top scorer:**
Local Newspapers: Bucks Advertiser (0753 888333), Bucks Examiner, Bucks Free Press, Wycombe Midweek.
Local Radio Stations: Chilton Radio.
Honours: Isthmian Lg Div 2 87-88, Athenian Lg R-up 83-84 (Lg Cup 76-77 82-83), London Spartan Lg Div 2 75-76, Berks & Bucks Intermediate Cup 52-53, FA Tphy 3rd Qualifying Rd 89-90 91-92, FA Vase 4th Rd 87-88, Berks & Bucks Benevolent Cup 64-65.

CHESHUNT

Chairman: Mr Tony Wilson **Vice Chairman:** Mr Bill Moye **President:** Mr Roy Burt.
Secretary: Mrs Brenda Timpson, 82 T.olmers Rd, Cuffley, Potters Bar, Herts EN6 4JY (0707 874028).
Press Officer: Mr Fred Beer (0992 761138).
Manager: Gary Brooker **Assistant Manager:** Roland Cray.
Coach: Trevor Bailey **Physio:** Lou Dedman.
Ground: The Stadium, Theobalds Lane, Cheshunt, Herts (0992 26752).
Directions: M25 to junction 25, A10 nort towards Hertford past ground on right, turn back towards London at first traffic lights to enter. 400yds from Theobalds Grove BR station - turn left and left again for ground. Buses 279, 242, 715 and 310 to Theobalds Grove station.
Seats: 285 **Cover:** 600 **Capacity:** 2,500 **Floodlights:** Yes **Founded:** 1946.
Colours: Yellow/blue **Change colours:** All blue **Nickname:** Ambers
Programme: 20 pages, 50p **Editor:** Alan Timpson (0707 874028) **Club Shop:** No.
Midweek matchday: Tuesday **Prev. Ground:** Broomfield Lane 52-56. **Clubhouse:** Yes.
Sponsors: Lansing Linde Trifik **Reserve team's League:** None.
Previous Leagues: Athenian 19-20 21-31 64-77/ London 20-21 24-25 46-51 55-59/ Delphian 51-55/ Aetolian 59-62/ Spartan 62-64/ Isthmian 77-87.
Best FA Vase season: Qtr Final 81-82 **Best FA Cup season:** 4th Qual. Rd(4)
Record win: 11-1 v Hastings United (H), London League Premier Division 29/10/49.
Record defeat: 1-9 v Wolverton Town (A), Isthmian League Division (North) 21/2/87.
Record gate: 7,000 v Bromley, London Senior Cup 1947.
Record transfer fee paid: £250 for Tony Tillbrook (Boreham Wood, 1988).
Record transfer fee received: £1,500 for Andy Prutton (Dartford, 1989).
Players progressing to Football Lge: Ian Dowie, Steve Sedgeley.
Captain 93-94: Terry Hughes **Top Scorer 93-94:** Del Francois, 26. **P.o.Y. 93-94:** Mark Freeman
Hons: Athenian Lg 75-76 (R-up 73-74, Div 1 67-68, Div 2 R-up 65-66, Lg Cup 74-75 75-76), Spartan Lg 62-63 (Lg Cup 63-64 92-93 (R-up 89-90)), London Lg 49-50 (R-up 56-57, Div 1 47-48 48-49 (R-up 46-47), Div 1 Cup 46-47, Lg Cup R-up 58-59), Park Royal Cup 46-47), Isthmian Lg Div 2 R-up 81-82 (Div 3 R-up 93-94), Herts Snr Cup 23-24 (R-up 48-49 49-50 68-69 69-70 71-72 73-74), Herts Charity Cup 00-01 05-06 (R-up 70-71 74-75 80-81), Herts Charity Shield 46-47 65-66 (52-53 53-54 54-55 63-64 64-65), Herts Snr Centenary Tphy 91-92, East Anglian Cup 74-75 (R-up 75-76), Mithras Floodlit Cup 69-70 (R-up 75-76), London Charity Cup 73-74, Roy Bailey Tphy 90-91 93-94.

EDGWARE TOWN

Chairman: Mr M Flynn **President:** Mr V Deritis **Patron:** Russell Grant.
Secretary: Barry Boreham, 28 St Bridges Ave., Edgware, Middx HA8 6BS (081 952 1685).
Manager: Brian Rider **Coach:** Jim McGleish
Treasurer: T Donohue **Physio:** Gary Sadler MCSP
Press Officer: Brian Rider (081 907 6158)
Ground: White Lion Ground, High Street, Edgware HA8 5AQ (081 952 6799).
Directions: Turn left out of Edgware tube station (Northern Line), turn left again at crossroads and ground 300yds on right in Edgware High Street behind White Lion pub. Buses 32, 288 and 142.
Capacity: 5,000 **Seats:** 220 **Cover:** 1,500 **Floodlights:** Yes **Founded:** 1939
Colours: All green **Change colours:** All red
Programme: 16 pages, 50p **Programme Editor:** Kevin Brown (081 950 8065).
Reserve Team's League: Suburban **Metal Badges:** Planned. **Club Shop:** No
Previous Names: Edgware F.C. **Previous Grounds:** None. **Nickname:** Wares.
Midweek Matchday: Tuesday **Record Gate:** 8,500 v Wealdstone, FA Cup 1948.
Previous Leagues: Corinthian 46-63/ Athenian 64-84/ London Spartan 84-90.
Players progressing to Football League: Brian Stein (Luton), Dave Beasant (Wimbledon), Scott McGleish (Charlton 1994).
Clubhouse: Open nightly and Fri, Sat, Sun lunchtimes. Hot & cold food matchdays, cold food lunchtimes.
Steward: J Connell.
93-94 Captain: Seamus Finnerty **93-94 P.o.Y.:** Scott McGleish
93-94 Top scorer: Scott McGleish. **Club record appearances:** John Mangan.
Hons: FA Vase 5th Rd 91-92, Isthmian Lg Div 3 91-92, London Spartan Lg 87-88 89-90 (Lg Cup 87-88), Corinthian Lg R-up 53-54 (Memorial Shield 52-53 61-62), Athenian Lg R-up 81-82, Middx Snr Lg 40-41 41-42 42-43 43-44 44-45, Middx Snr Cup 47-48 (R-up 73-74 93-94), London Snr Cup R-up 47-48, Middx Border Lg Cup 79-80, Suburban Lg Div R-up 89-90.

Edgware Town FC 1993-94 *Photo - Gavin Ellis-Neville.*

CROYDON 1953 F.C.

Chairman: T W Fogarty **Vice Chairman:** J Langford.
Secretary: The Secretary, c/o Croydon FC (below).
Manager: Ken Jarvie/ Dickson Gill **Coach:** TBA
Ground: Croydon Sports Arena, Albert Road, South Norwood SE25 4QL (081 654 3462).
Directions: Train to East Croydon or Norwood Junction, then bus 12 to either Belmont or Dundee Road. Walk down either - ground at bottom. 5 mins walk from Woodside (BR).
Capacity: 8,000 **Cover:** 450 **Seats:** 450 **Club Shop:** Yes **Metal Badges:** £2.50
Colours: Sky blue/blue **Change colours:** All red **Sponsors:** TBA
Reserve Team's League: Suburban. **Previous Lges:** Surrey Snr 53-63/ Spartan 63-64/ Athenian 64-74.
Midweek home matchday: Monday **Previous Name:** Croydon Amateurs 1953-74.
Record Attendance: 1,450 v Wycombe, FA Cup 4th Qualifying Rd 1975.
Best FA Cup season: 2nd Rd replay 79-80 (lost 2-3 to Millwall after 1-1 draw).
Record Fees - Paid: Steve Brown
Received: Peter Evans (to Sutton Utd).
Players progressing to Football League: Alan Barnett (Plymouth 1955), Peter Bonetti (Chelsea), Leroy Ambrose (Charlton 1979), Steve Milton (Fulham - via Whyteleafe), Murray Jones (Crystal & Exeter - via Carshalton).
Clubhouse: (081 654 8555). Open every evening and lunchtime, holds 250, snacks available. Dancing, discos, bingo. Lounge bar available for private hire.
93-94 Captain: **Club Record Appearances:** Alec Jackson (400+)
Local Press: Croydon Advertiser (081 668 4111), Croydon Midweek Post, Croydon Times, Croydon Guardian.
Hons: FA Amateur Cup 3rd Rd 71-72, FA Tphy 2nd Rd(2) 81-83, Isthmian Lg Div 2 R-up 75-76, Surrey Snr Cup 81-82 (R-up 76-77), Surrey Prem Cup 86-87, Spartan Lg 63-64, Athenian Lg R-up 71-72 (Div 2 65-66 (R-up 70-71)), Surrey Snr Lg R-up 56-57 60-61 62-63 (Lg Cup 60-61, Charity Cup 53-54 62-63, Res Section 57-58), London Snr Cup R-up 78-79, Suburban Lg South 86-87 (Lg Cup(2)), Southern Yth Lg 85-86 (Lg Cup 85-86 87-88), Berger Yth Cup 78-79.

Photo opposite: *The courageous players who, despite receiving some horrific thrashings, fulfilled the fixtures of Croydon FC towards the end of the 1993-94 season.*

Photo - Dave West.

EGHAM TOWN

Chairman: Pat Bennett **Vice Chairman:** Peter Barnes **President:** Archie Doye
Secretary: Keith Thompson JP, 15a Clarence Str., Egham, Surrey TW20 9RL (0784 433277).
Manager: Mickey Byrne **Asst Manager:** Frank Sheridan **Physio:** Des Hunt.
Press Officer: Mark Ferguson (0932 783333) **Comm. Mgr:** Chris Thompson
Ground: Tempest Road, Pooley Green, Egham, Surrey TW20 9DW (0784 436466).
Directions: M25 jct 13, follow signs to Egham, under M25 at r'bout, left to end, left at mini-r'bout, over railway crossing, left to end (Pooley Green Rd), right, ground on right after 'Compasses' and 'Robin Hood' pubs. Bus 441 from Staines to Poolley Green. Forty mins walk from Egham (BR) station.
Capacity: 3,000 **Seats:** 230 **Cover:** 1,120 **Floodlights:** Yes **Founded:** 1877
Colours: White/blue/white **Change colours:** Yellow & blue **Reformed:** 1963.
Club Shop: Due to open 94-95 selling programmes. Contact Gareth Coates (0784 460182).
Programme: 12 pages, 60p **Editor:** Mark Ferguson (0932 783333) **Metal Badges:** £1.70
Midweek Matches: Tuesday. **Nickname:** Sarnies/Swans/Town. **Club Sponsors:** TBA
Previous Leagues: Hounslow & District 1896-1914/ Surrey Intermediate 19-22/ Surrey Senior 22-28 65-67/ Spartan 29-33 67-74/ Parthenon 64-65/ Athenian 74-77.
Previous Grounds: Anglers Rest 1877-1914/ Manorcroft Rd 19-26/ Vicarage Rd 26-27 28-39/ Green Lane 27-28.
Reserve Team's League: Suburban **Prev. Names:** Runnymede Rovers 1877-1905/ Egham FC 05-63.
Best FA Cup year: 4th Qual Rd 90-91 (lost 0-2 at Telford United.
Record Gate: 2,000 - Egham XI v Select XI, Billy King Memorial match 1981. Competitive: 1,400 v Wycombe Wanderers, FA Cup 2nd Qualifying Rd 1972.
Record Fees - Paid: £3,000 for Mark Butler, 1990.
Received: £4,000 for Mark Butler (Wycombe Wanderers, 1988).
Record win: 10-1 v Camberley, 81-82 **Record defeat:** 0-10 v Fisher Ath. (A), Parthenon League 64-65.
Clubhouse: (0784 435226) 7-11pm and weekend lunchtimes. Members bar, function hall and pool room.
Record Appearances: Dave Jones 850+. **Record Scorer:** Mark Butler 50 (91-92). Career record scorer too.
93-94 Captain: Various **93-94 Supporters' P.O.Y.:** Jason Day.
Players' P.O.Y. 93-94: Roland Pierre **93-94 Top scorer:** P Martin, I Bascombe, F Sheridan - 6.
Local Radio: County Sound. **Local Press:** Herald & News (0932 561111).
Hons: Isthmian Lg Associate Members Tphy R-up 91-92, Spartan Lg 71-72 (Lg Cup R-up 67-68), Athenian Lg R-up 75-76 (Div 2 74-75), Surrey Snr Cup R-up 91-92, Surrey Snr Lg 22-23 (Lg Charity Cup 22-23 (R-up 26-27 34-35)), Surrey Intermediate Lg 20-21, Surrey Intermediate Charity Cup 19-20 20-21 (R-up 26-27), North West Surrey Charity Cup 20-21, Egham Twinning Tournament 67-68 71-72 74-75 75-76 76-77 80-81, Southern Comb. Floodlit Cup 77-78 (R-up 83-84).

HAMPTON

Chairman: Robert Hayes **Vice Chairman:** Ken Gazzard **President:** Alan Simpson
Secretary: Adrian Mann, 30 Burniston Court, Manor Rd, Wallington, Surrey SM6 0AD (081 773 0858).
Manager: TBA **Assistant Manager:** TBA **Physio:** TBA
Press Officer: Les Rance **Commercial Manager:** Glen Hayler.
Ground: Beveree Stadium, Beaver Close, off Station Rd, Hampton TW12 2BX (081 941 4936-boardroom).
Directions: 5 mins walk along Station Rd from Hampton (BR) - half hourly service from London Waterloo via Clapham Junction, Wimbledon & Kingston. Buses 111 (Hampton-Heathrow) & 216 (Kingston-Staines) stop in Station Rd. 726 (Dartford-Kingston-Windsor) & 267 (Hammersmith-Hampton Court) stop in nearby Church Street. By road; A3 out of London, fork left (signed Staines/Esher/Sandown Pk) onto A243, A309 Staines exit to Hampton Ct at 'Scilly Isles' r'bout, left at r'bout after Hampton Ct Bridge onto A308, after 1 mile right into Church Str. (A311), left after White Hart after 200yds into High Str., Station Rd on right just before junction with A308. From M25; jct 12, M3 towards London, jct 1 for the A308 (Sunbury) and turn right under M'way onto A308 for Kingston & Hampton, continue past racecourse, left into Hampton High Str. just after waterworks (on right), Station Rd 1st left.
Capacity: 2,000 **Seats:** 200 **Cover:** 800 **Floodlights:** Yes **Founded:** 1920
Colours: Red & blue/white/blue **Change:** White/tangerine/tangerine. **Nickname:** Beavers
Club Shop: Yes, selling various club souvenirs and programmes. Contact Stefan Rance (081 898 1085).
Programme: 28 pages, 70p **Programme Editor:** Secretary **Metal Badges:** Yes
Midweek Matchday: Tuesday **Sponsors:** Saft-Nife Ltd.
Previous Leagues: Kingston & District 21-33/ South West Middx 33-59/ Surrey Snr 59-64/ Spartan 64-71/ Athenian 71-73.
Previous Names: None **Previous Grounds:** Hatherop Rec (until 1959).
Record win: 11-1 v Eastbourne United, Isthmian League Division Two (South), 91-92
Record defeat: 0-13 v Hounslow Town, Middlesex 62-63.
Reserve Team's League: Suburban **Record gate:** Unknown.
Best F.A. Cup year: 4th Qualifying Round 77-78 (lost 1-2 v Barnet).
Record Fees - Paid: £400 for Peter Shodiende (Hendon, 1981)
Received: £2,500 from APOP (Cyprus) for Ricky Walkes (June 1989).
Clubhouse: (081 979 2456). Lounge bar and Hall, open on matchdays and training nights. Hall available for hire.
Steward: Steve Penny.
Players progressing to Football League: Andy Rogers (Southampton, Plymouth, Reading), Dwight Marshall (Plymouth), Paul Rogers (Sheffield Utd).
Club Record Goalscorer: Peter Allen **Club Record Appearances:** Joe Andrews.
93-94 Top scorer: David Prior 10 **93-94 Captain & P.O.Y.:** Steve Cheshire
Local Newspapers: Middx Chronicle, Surrey Comet, Richmond & Twickemham Times, The Informer.
Hons: London Snr Cup(2) 86-88, Spartan Lg(4) 64-67 69-70 (R-up 67-68, Lg Cup(4) 64-68 (R-up(2) 68-70), Reserve Section 66-67 67-68, Reserve Cup 64-65 65-66 70-71), Surrey Snr Lg 63-64 (Lg Cup R-up 60-61, Reserve Cup 61-62), Middx Charity Cup 69-70 (R-up 68-69 71-72 89-90), Middx Snr Cup R-up 71-72 76-77, Athenian Lg Div 2 R-up 72-73, Southern Comb. Cup 68-69 71-72 76-77 81-82 83-84 85-86 (R-up 77-78 79-80), Middx Premier Cup(res) 92-93 (R-up 85-86 86-87), London I'mediate Cup(res) SF 64-65, Suburban Lg(Sth) R-up 85-86 (Lg Cup 85-86).

PHOTOS OPPOSITE

Top: Egham Town FC
Centre: Hampton FC
Foot: Hemel Hempstead FC
All Photos: Eric Marsh.

SAFT
NIFE

MFI

HEMEL HEMPSTEAD

Chairman: Mike Pearson **President:** R Doyle **Vice President:** Tom Abbott
Secretary: Denis Elkins, 119 Leys Rd, Hemel Hempstead, Herts HP3 9JX (0442 219749).
Manager: Pat Morrissey **Asst Manager:** Steve Ringrose **Coach:** Steve Ringrose
Press Officer: Secretary **Physio:** Chris Hewitt **Comm. Manager:** Mike Pearson.
Ground: Vauxhall Ground, Adeyfield Rd, Hemel Hempstead HP2 4HW (0442 242081-club, 259777-boardroom).
Directions: Euston to Hemel Hempstead Station. H2 or H3 bus to Windmill Rd, Longlands.
Capacity: 3,000 **Seats:** 100 **Cover:** Yes **Floodlights:** Yes **Founded:** 1885
Colours: All red **Change colours:** All blue
Club Shop: Yes **Metal Badges:** No **Sponsors:** TBA
Programme: 36 pages, 50p **Editor:** James Thrussell.
Midweek Matchday: Tuesday **Previous Leagues:** Spartan 22-52/ Delphian 52-63/ Athenian 63-77.
Previous Names: Apsley 1885-1947)/ Hemel H'stead Town (merged with Hemel H'stead Utd in 1947).
Previous Grounds: Crabtree Lane (til '71).
Reserve Team's League: Essex & Herts Border Combination **Nickname:** Hemel
Record Gate: 2,000 v Watford 1985 (at Crabtree Lane: 3,500 v Tooting, FA Amtr Cup 1st Rd 1962).
Best FA Cup year: Never past Qualifying Rounds.
Clubhouse: (0442 259777). 7-11pm weekends, noon-11pm weekends and Bank Holidays. Pool, darts. Bingo Tuesday. Race nights. Dancing Fri, Sat & Sun nights. Tea bar open matchdays; teas, soup, burgers, hot dogs.
Players progressing to Football League: Colin and Ernie Bateman (Watford).
Local Press: Hemel Gazette, Herald. **Local Radio:** Beds Radio.
Club Record Goalscorer: Dai Price **Club Record Apps:** John Wallace, 1012.
93-94 Captain: Neil Bartlett **93-94 P.o.Y.:** Lee Harvey **93-94 Top scorer:** Mark Barnard
Hons: Herts Snr Cup 05-06 07-08 08-09 25-26 61-62 65-66 91-92, Herts Charity Cup/Shield 25-26 34-35 51-52 63-64 76-77 83-84 (R-up 90-91), Spartan Lg 33-34, Herts Intermediate Cup 54-55 65-66 83-84, West Herts St Mary Cup 70-71 75-76 82-83 85-86 90-91 91-92, Athenian Lg Div 1 R-up 64-65 (Reserves Cup 65-66), Delphian Lg(reserves) 54-55 (Reserves Cup 54-55 61-62).

HUNGERFORD TOWN

Chairman: Ron Tarry **Vice Chairman:** Alan Richards **President:** Sir Seton Wills.
Secretary: Eric Richardson, 3 Windermere Way, Thatcham, Berks RG13 4UL (0536 868674).
Manager: Gerry Smith **Asst Manager:** Norman Matthews **Coach:** Dean Bailey
Press Officer: Michael Hall (0488 685241) **Physio:** Steve Puffet.
Ground: Town Ground, Bulpit Lane, Hungerford RG17 0AY (0488 682939-club, 684597-boardroom).
Directions: M4 jct 14 to A4, right and left at Bear Hotel, through town centre on A338, left into Priory Rd, second left into Bulpit Lane, over crossroads, ground on left. Three quarters of a mile from Hungerford BR station.
Capacity: 3,000 **Seats:** 130 **Cover:** 500 **Floodlights:** Yes **Founded:** 1886
Colours: White/blue/white **Change colours:** All red. **Metal Badges:** Yes
Club Shop: Yes. New badges available from Martin Wiltshire, 17 Sarum Way, Hungerford, Berks RG17 0LJ (0488 682218).
Programme: 24 pages, 40p **Editor:** Martin Wiltshire (0488 682218).
Club Sponsors: Below Stairs of Hungerford.
Midweek Matchday: Tuesday **Prev. Lges:** Newbury & D./ Swindon & D./ Hellenic 58-78.
Previous Names: None **Previous Grounds:** None.
Nickname: Crusaders. **Reserve Team's League:** Suburban (West)
Record Gate: 1,684 v Sudbury Town, FA Vase SF 1st leg 88-89 (20,000 v Modena in Italy 1981).
Record transfer fee paid: £4,000 for Joe Scott (Yeovil Town)
received: £3,800 for Joe Scott (Barnstaple Town).
Best FA Cup year: 1st Rd 79-80 (lost 1-3 at Slough Town).
Clubhouse: (0488 682939). Open every evening and lunchtimes including Sunday. 2 bars, dancehall, boardroom/committee room, darts, pool, fruit machines. Hot & cold snacks. Stewards: Bob & Sandra Ponsford.
Players progressing to Football League: Steve Hetzke (Reading, Blackpool, Sunderland), Bruce Walker (Swindon, Blackpool), Des McMahon (Reading), Brian Mundee (Bournemouth, Northampton), Darren Anderson.
Club Record Scorer: Ian Farr (200+) **Club Record Appearances:** Dean Bailey (approx 400)
93-94 Capt.: Warren Angell **93-94 P.o.Y.:** Neil Hugill **93-94 Top scorer:** Fred Austin 14
Local Press: Newbury Weekly News, Newbury Evening Post **Local Radio:** Berkshire Radio, Radio 210.
Hons: FA Vase SF 77-78 79-80 88-89, Berks & Bucks Snr Cup 81-82 (R-up 75-76 76-77), Hellenic Lg Div 1 70-71 (Prem Div Cup 77-78, Div 1 Cup 70-71, Benevolent Cup 60-61).

LEATHERHEAD

Photo opposite: *Leatherhead FC 1993-94. Photo - Eric Marsh.*

Chairman: G W Darby **Vice Chairman:** B Ashi **President:**
Secretary: Martyn Cole, 1 Elm Tree Ave., Esher, Surrey KT10 8JG (081 398 1751).
Manager: Paul Andrews **Assistant Manager:** **Coach:** Brian Stannard
Press Officer: G W Darby **Comm. Manager:** Paul Bentley **Physio:** Ted Richards.
Ground: Fetcham Grove, Guildford Rd, Leatherhead, Surrey KT22 9AS (0372 360151).
Directions: M25 jct 9 to Leatherhead; follow signs to Leisure Centre, ground adjacent. Half mile from Leatherhead (BR). London Country Buses 479 and 408 - ground opposite bus garage.
Capacity: 3,400 **Seats:** 200 **Cover:** 445 **Floodlights:** Yes **Founded:** 1946
Colours: All green **Change colours:** All yellow **Nickname:** Tanners
Programme: 20+ pages, 50p **Editor:** Bernard Edwards (0372 454573) **Club Shop:** No
Midweek Matchday: Tuesday **Record defeat:** 1-11 v Sutton United. **Record win:** Unknown
Previous Leagues: Surrey Snr 46-50/ Metropolitan 50-51/ Delphian 51-58/ Corinthian 58-63/ Athenian 63-72.
Reserve's League: Suburban (South) **Record Gate:** 5,500 v Wimbledon, 1976.
Best FA Cup year: 4th Rd 74-75 (lost 2-3 at Leic. City). Also 2nd Rd 75-76 76-77 78-79, 1st Rd 77-78 80-81.
League Clubs defeated in FA Cup: Colchester, Brighton 74-75/ Cambridge Utd 75-76/ Northampton 76-77.
Players progressing to Football League: Chris Kelly (Millwall), B Friend (Fulham), L Harwood (Port Vale), John Humphrey (Millwall).
Record Fees - Paid: £1,500 to Croydon (B Salkeld) **Rec'd:** £1,500 from Croydon (B Salkeld)
Clubhouse: Licensed bar open noon-11pm matchdays. Burgers, hot dogs, tea & coffee etc on matchdays.
Club Record Scorer: Not known **Club record appearances:** P Caswell.
93-94 Captain: Brian Stannard **93-94 P.o.Y. & Top Scorer:** M Joyner.
Local Radio: County Sound **Local Press:** Leatherhead Advertiser, Surrey Advertiser
Hons: Isthmian Lg Cup 77-78, Corinthian Lg 62-63, Athenian Ld Div 1 63-64, Surrey Snr Cup 68-69 (R-up 64-65 66-67 74-75 78-79), Surrey Snr Lg 46-47 47-48 48-49 49-50 (Lg Cup 49-50, Charity Cup 46-47 49-50), East Surrey Charity Cup 68-69 (R-up 67-68), Surrey Snr Shield 68-69, FA Amtr Cup SF 70-71 73-74 (QF 65-66 66-67 71-72), FA Tphy R-up 77-78, London Snr Cup R-up 74-75 77-78, Surrey Intermediate Cup, Southern Combination Cup 89-90.

MALDEN VALE

Chairman: Steve Pearce **President:** John Sladden.
Secretary: Andrew Pearce, 31 Ancaster Cres., New Malden, Surrey KT3 6BD (081 949 1475).
Manager: Ray Rembridge **Asst Mgr/Coach:** Bobby Green
Press Officer: Trevor Pearce **Commercial Manager:** Trevor Pearce.
Ground: Grand Drive, Raynes Park, London SW20 9NB (081 542 2193).
Directions: M25, jct 10, A3 towards London, turn off onto A298, right at 1st lights into Grand Drive, ground 200yds on left. Half mile from Raynes Park (BR). Buses 77a and 77c.
Capacity: 3,000 **Seats:** 180 **Cover:** 180 **Floodlights:** Yes **Founded:** 1967
Colours: Royal/royal/red **Change colours:** Green & white/green/green.
Club Shop: Yes. Programmes, badges, scarves, ties, jumpers. Contact Trevor Pearce (081 542 2193).
Programme: 10 pages, 50p **Programme Editor:** Andy Pearce
Midweek Matchday: Tuesday **Nickname:** The Vale.
Previous Leagues: Surrey Snr 77-78/ London Spartan 78-84/ Combined Counties 84-89.
Previous Name: None **Previous Grounds:** None.
Sponsors: None.
Reserve Team's League: Suburban **Rec. Gate:** 2,000 v Eastenders, Charity Match, 1991.
Best FA Cup year: Second Qualifying Rd 89-90 (lost 0-2 at Whyteleafe).
Clubhouse: Mon-Fri 6.30-11pm, Sat 12-11pm, Sun 12-3pm. Two bars, hot food.
Club Record Scorer: Martin Caller **Club Record Appearances:** David Stroud 1040, Trevor Pearce 940.
93-94 Captain: **93-94 P.o.Y.:** Mick Dalton **93-94 Top scorer:** Steve McKimm
Local Press: Surrey Comet, Morden Guardian, Wimbledon News. **Local Radio:** County Sounds.
Hons: London Spartan Lg 80-81 (R-up 83-84, Div 3 78-79 79-80, Lg Cup 80-81 83-84 (R-up 81-82 82-83)), Combined Co's Lg 84-85 (R-up 88-89, Concours Tphy 84-85 (R-up 85-86), Div 2 81-82), Surrey Snr Lg 77-78, Southern Combination Cup 78-79, Loctite Tphy QF 90-91.

Below: *Malden Vale FC pictured before their FA Vase tie at Aldershot Town.* *Photo - Eric Marsh.*

METROPOLITAN POLICE

Chairman: Paul Condon, QPM **Vice Chairman:** Terry Siggs OBE **President:** Paul Condon GPM
Secretary: Derek Alldridge MBE, 'Woodbeck', 3 Elmshorn, Epsom Downs, Surrey KT17 3PE (0737 50525).
Manager: Colin Rose **Coach:** John Cottam
Physio: Dick Pierce **Press Officer:** Cliff Travis (0932 782215).
Commercial Manager: Alan Dobson.
Ground: Metropolitan Police Sports Ground, Imber Court, East Molesey (081 398 7358).
Directions: From London: A3 then A309 to Scilly Isles r'bout, right into Hampton Court Way, left at 1st r'bout into Imber Court Rd - ground faces in 300yds. From M25 jct 10: A3 towards London for 1 mile, A307 through Cobham, left immediately after Sandown Park into Station Rd - ground 1 mile on left. Half mile from either Thames Ditton or Esher BR stations.
Capacity: 3,000 **Seats:** 297 **Cover:** 1,800 **Floodlights:** Yes **Founded:** 1919
Colours: All blue **Change colours:** All yellow **Nickname:** Blues.
Programme: 10 pages, 50p **Editor:** Chris Travis (0932 782215) **Club Shop:** No
Midweek Matchday: Tuesday **Club Sponsors:** McDonalds. **Metal Badges:** No
Previous Leagues: Spartan 28-60/ Metropolitan 60-71/ Southern 71-78.
Reserve Team's League: Suburban **Record Gate:** 4,500 v Kingstonian, FA Cup 1934.
Record win: 7-0 v Camberley, 1981 **Record defeat:** 1-11 v Wimbledon, 1956.
Best FA Cup year: 1st Rd 32-33 (0-9 at Northampton Town), 84-85 (0-3 at home to Dartford), 93-94 (0-3 at home to Crawley Town).
Clubhouse: (081 398 1267). Four bars, dancehall, cafeteria open 9am-11pm. Hot & cold food.
Club Record Scorer: Mario Russo **Club Record Appearances:** Pat Robert.
93-94 Captain: Mark Reed **93-94 P.o.Y & Top scorer:** Mario Russo.
Local Radio: County Sounds. **Local Press:** Surrey Comet, Surrey Herald.
Hons: Isthmian Lg Div 2 R-up 77-78 87-88, Spartan Lg 28-29 29-30 36-37 38-39 45-46 53-54 54-55 (R-up 47-48, Lg Cup 59-60 (R-up 57-58)), Middx Snr Cup 27-28, Surrey Snr Cup 32-33, Surrey Charity Shield 38-39, Metropolitan Lg Cup 68-69 (Amtr Cup 68-69 69-70), London Snr Cup R-up 34-35 40-41, Herts & Middx Comb. 39-40.

Metropolitan Police pictured at Lewes at the start of an epic FA Cup run to the First Round Proper.
Photo - Eric Marsh.

OXFORD CITY

Chairman: M Woodley **Vice Chairman:** R Holt **President:** M Harris.
Press Officer/Secretary: John Shepperd, 20 Howe Close, Wheatley, Oxford OX33 1SS (0865 872181).
Manager: Andy Thomas **Asst Manager:** Alan Thorne **Physio:** G Bowerman.
Ground: Court Place Farm, Marsh Lane, Marston, Oxford (0865 744493).
Directions: From London M40/A40, ring-road to North, take 1st slip road, follow signs to John Radcliffe hospital, ground on left after leaving flyover. From the north same ring-road.
Capacity: 2,000 **Seats:** 150 **Cover:** 150 **Floodlights:** Yes **Founded:** 1882
Colours: White & blue hoops **Change colours:** Red or green **Nickname:** City.
Programme: 60 pages, 50p **Programme Editor:** Secretary
Club Shop: To open at start of 1994-95 season.
Midweek Matchday: Tuesday **Sponsors:** Unipart OCM
Prev. Grnds: The White House 1882-1988/ Cuttleslowe Pk 1990-91/ Pressed Steel, Romanway, Cowley 91-93.
Prev. Lges: Isthmian 07-88/ South Midlands 90-93.**Record Gate:** 9,500 v Leytonstone, FA Amtr Cup 1950.
Best FA Cup year: Second Round 69-70 (lost 1-5 at home to Swansea Town).
Record Fees - Paid: £3,000 for S Adams (Woking) **Received:** £2,000 for P Dallaway (Witney Town).
Reserve Team's League: 'Minerva' South Midlands Reserve Section.
Players progressing to Football League: A Blakeman (Brentford 1946), C Holton (Arsenal 1950), K Savin (Derby 1950), E Wilcox (WBA 1948), R Adams (Blackpool 1948), A Jeffries (Brentford 1949), P James (Luton 1949), D Gordon (WBA 1947), V Mobley (Sheffield Wednesday 1963), J Varney (Hull 1950), P Lee (Hereford 1973), H Poole (Port Vale 1955), G Parker (Luton 1981), G McKeown (Arsenal 1984), D Meeson (Wolves 1952).
Record win: 9-0 v Harlow Town, Isthmian League 9/10/76.
Record defeat: 0-8 v Wycombe Wanderers, Isthmian League - date unknown.
Clubhouse: Open matchdays, most refreshments available.
Club Record Scorer: John Woodley **Club Record Appearances:** John Woodley.
93-94 P.o.Y.: Colin Fleet **93-94 Captain:** John Harvey-Lynch
Local Press: Oxford Mail **Local Radio:** BBC Radio Oxford, Fox FM.
Hons: FA Amateur Cup 05-06 (R-up 02-03 12-13), Isthmian Lg R-up 34-35 45-46 (Div 1 R-up 77-78), South Midlands Lg 92-93, Oxon Snr Cup(26).

SAFFRON WALDEN TOWN

Chairman: S Lander **Vice Chairman:** P Diggons.
Secretary: H J Harvey, 1 New Willow Cottage, Langley, Saffron Walden, Essex CB11 4RC (0799 550615).
Manager: Tony Mercer **Assistant Manager:** Bob Dodd **Coach:** Don Wiltshire.
Press Officer: Gary Phillips **Physio:** Peter White.
Ground: Catons Lane, Saffron Walden, Essex CB10 2DU (0799 22789).
Directions: In Saffron Walden High Street turn into Castle Street, left at T-junction, 1st left by Victory pub.
Capacity: 5,000 **Seats:** 500 **Cover:** 2,000 **Floodlights:** Yes **Founded:** 1872
Colours: Red/black/white **Change colours:** All yellow. **Nickname:** Bloods.
Programme: 24 pages, 50p **Editor:** Glyn Thomas (0799 521103) **Club Shop:** No
Midweek Matchday: Tuesday **Club Sponsors:** Tolly Cobbold. **Metal Badges:** No
Previous Leagues: Haverhill & Dist./ Stansted & Dist./ Cambridgeshire/ Nth Essex/ Herts Co./ Spartan 33-49 50-54/ Parthenon 49-50/ Essex Snr 71-74/ Eastern Co's 74-84.
Previous Grounds: None **Previous Names:** None. **Clubhouse:** No.
Record Gate: 6,000 v Rainham Ath., Essex Junior Cup Final 1926 (played at Crittals, Braintree).
Reserve Team's League: Essex & Herts Comb.
Best F.A. Cup year: Second Qualifying Round replay 84-85 (lost 1-2 at King's Lynn).
Club Record Scorer: John Tipputt **Club Record Appearances:** Les Page, 700+.
93-94 Captain: **93-94 P.o.Y.:** **93-94 Top scorer:**
Local Radio: Essex Radio, Radio Essex. **Local Press:** Saffron Walden Weekly News, Herald & Post.
Hons: Essex Snr Lg 73-74, Eastern Co's Lg 82-83, Spartan Lg Eastern Div 2 36-37, Essex Snr Tphy 82-83 83-84 84-85, Eastern F'lit Competition 91-92 (R-up 88-89, Nth Thames Group B 82-83), Essex Jnr Cup 1896-97 (R-up 25-26), Cambs Lg R-up 22-23, Essex & Herts Border Lg R-up 25-26(joint), Stansted & Dist. Lg 07-08 08-09 09-10 11-12 20-21 22-23 23-24, Haverhill & Dist. Lg 08-09 22-23 23-24 29-30 33-34.

THAME UNITED

Chairman: Jim Tite **Vice Chairman:** Paul K Smith
Secretary: Mr Paul K Smith, 18 Musgrave Rd, Chinnor, Oxon OX9 4PL (0844 354133).
Manager: Bob Pratley **Asst Manager:** Malcolm McIntosh **Physio:** Chris Perkins
Press Officer: Neil Crocker
Ground: Windmill Road, Thame, Oxon OX9 2DR (0844 213017).
Directions: Into Nelson Street from Market Square. 3 miles from Haddenham & Thame Parkway (BR). Nearest bus stop at Town Hall (half mile away).
Capacity: 2,500 **Seats:** 230 **Cover:** 400 **Floodlights:** Yes **Founded:** 1883
Colours: Red & black **Change colours:** Black & white **Club Shop:** No
Programme: 24 pages, 75p **Programme Editor:** Paul Smith (0844 354133).
Midweek Matchday: Tuesday **Sponsors:** Dayla Soft Drinks (Aylesbury).
Previous Leagues: Oxon Snr/ Hellenic 59-87/ Sth Midlands 87-91.
Previous Grounds: None **Previous Name:** Thame FC **Nickname:** United
Reserves' Lge: Suburban (West) **Record Gate:** 1,035 v Aldershot, Isthmian Div 2 4/4/94.
Record win: 9-0 v Bracknell, 31/10/92 **Record defeat:** 2-11 v Hungerford, FA Cup Prelim. Rd 1984.
Best FA Cup year: Third Qualifying Round 91-92 (lost 0-4 to Salisbury).
Clubhouse: Open every evening and weekend lunchtimes. Banquetting facilities for 200 (weddings, dinners, dances etc).
Record Scorer: Not known **Record appearances:** Steve Mayhew.
93-94 Captain: Kelly Lonergan **93-94 P.o.Y. & Top scorer:** Nigel Mott.
Local Radio: BBC Radio Oxford, Fox FM. **Local Press:** Oxford Mail, Thame Gazette, Bucks Free Press.
Hons: Isthmian Lg Div 3 R-up 92-93, Hellenic Lg 61-62 69-70 (Premier Div Cup(4)), Sth Mids Lg 90-91, Oxon Snr Cup 1894-95 05-06 08-09 09-10 75-76 80-81 92-93, Oxon Intermediate Cup 76-77 78-79 91-92, Oxon Charity Cup.

Thame United FC 1993-94. *Photo - Eric Marsh.*

TILBURY

Chairman: R Nash **Vice Chairman:** H McGill **President:** J B Wilson.
Secretary: M Southgate, 93 Falcon Avenue, Thames Hamlet, Grays, Essex (0375 377215).
Manager: Paul Armstrong **Asst Manager:** Roger Hutton
Comm. Manager: Paul Joynes. **Physio:** Roger Hutton **Press Officer:** Chairman
Ground: Chadfields, St Chad's Rd, Tilbury, Essex RM18 8NL (0375 23093).
Directions: BR from Fenchurch Street to Tilbury Town then bus 377 or 20 mins walk - right out of station, walk along Left Hand Road fork to town centre traffic lights, left into St Chads Rd, Chadfields 1 mile on left. By road; M25 (jct 30 or 31) - A13 Southend bound, Tilbury Docks turn off after 4 miles, Chadwell St Mary turn off (left) after another one and a half miles, left again after 400 metres, right at r'bout (signed Tilbury), right into St Chad's Rd after half mile, 1st right into Chadfields for ground.
Capacity: 3,500 **Seats:** 250 **Cover:** 1,000 **Floodlights:** Yes **Founded:** 1900
Colours: Black & white halves/black/black **Change colours:** All red.
Programme: Min 32 pages, 50p **Editor:** Lloyd Brown. **Club Shop:** No.
Midweek Matchday: Tuesday **Club Sponsors:** None. **Nickname:** Dockers
Previous Leagues: Grays & Dist. + Sth Essex (simultaneously)/ Kent 27-31/ London 31-39 46-50 57-62/ Sth Essex Comb. (war-time)/ Corinthian 50-57/ Delphian 62-63/ Athenian 63-73.
Previous Names: None
Previous Grounds: Green & Silley Weir Ground 1900-11/ Orient Field 19-38.
Reserve Team's League: Essex & Herts Border Comb.
Record Gate: 5,500 v Gorleston, FA Cup 4th Qual. Rd 19/11/49 (won 2-0).
Best FA Cup year: 3rd Rd Proper 77-78 (lost 0-4 at Stoke City). Also 1st Rd 49-50 (0-4 at Notts Co.)
Record transfer fee received: £2,000 for Tony Macklin (Grays Athletic, 1990); £2,000 for Steve Conner (Dartford, 1985)
Record win: 17-0 v No.9 Company Royal Artillery (H), South Essex League 4/10/02. In Senior Football; 13-2 v Chalfont National (A), London League 28/4/92.
Record defeat: 1-10 v Maidstone United (A), Corinthian League 4/9/62.
Clubhouse: Open every evening, all day Friday & Saturday, and Sunday lunchtimes. Pool, darts, TV, Function Hall. Hot and cold food available at most times.
Players progressing to Football League: L Le May, T Scannell, T Oakley, J Evans.
Club Record Scorer: Ross Livermore 305 (in 282 games, 1958-66).
Club Record Appearances: Nicky Smith 424 (1975-85).
93-94 Captain: Andy Swann **93-94 P.o.Y & Top Scorer:** Mark Phillips, 29 goals.
Local Radio: Essex Radio, BBC Essex. **Local Press:** Thurrock Gazette, Thurrock Recorder.
Hons: FA Amtr Cup QF, Isthmian Lg Div 1 75-76 (Div 1 Cup 74-75), Athenian Lg 68-69 (Div 2 62-63), London Lg 58-59 59-60 60-61 61-62 (Lg Cup 58-59 60-61 61-62 (R-up(3))), Delphian Lg 67-68 (Div 2 62-63), Essex Snr Cup 60-61 63-64 72-73 74-75 (R-up 46-47 47-48 69-70 71-72 78-79), Essex Professional Cup 75-76, Mithras Cup 72-73 75-76 76-77 78-79 (R-up 71-72 74-75), Essex Elizabethan Tphy 63-64 68-69 (R-up 55-56 59-60 64-65 67-68 70-71), Essex Floodlit Competition 68-69, Anglo-Italian Barassi Cup R-up 75-76, Essex Jnr Cup 08-09 24-25 (R-up 03-04), Stanford Charity Cup 62-63 92-93, Grays & Dist. Lg(numerous), Neale Trophy 65-66, Memorial Shield R-up 87-88.

WARE

Chairman: C T Hudson
Secretary: M L Rose, 12 The Green, Ware, Herts SG12 0QN (0920 464448).
Manager: Stuart Todd **Asst Mgr:** N/A
Physio: Frank Roberts **Coach:** John Godleman
Commercial Manager: N/A **Press Officer:** Cecil Hudson (0992 581862)
Ground: Buryfield, Park Road, Ware, Herts SG12 0AJ (0920 463247).
Directions: A10 off at junction A602 & B1001 signposted Ware, in Ware Park Road is on right behind 'Rank' factory. 1 mile from Ware (BR) station (Liverpool Street-Hertford East line).
Capacity: 3,000 **Seats:** 170 **Cover:** 600 **Floodlights:** Yes **Founded:** 1892
Colours: Blue & white stripes/blue/red **Change colours:** Amber/black **Metal Badges:** Yes.
Club Shop: Yes, open matchdays. Contact Robin Thirtle, 38 Page Hill, Ware, Herts SG12 0RZ (0920 468369).
Programme: 0 pages, 30p **Editor:** C T Hudson (0992 581862).
Midweek Matchday: Tuesday **Sponsors:** Charvill Bros Ltd.
Prev. Lges: East Herts/ North Middx & District 07-08/ Herts County 08-25/ Spartan 25-55/ Delphian 55-63/ Athenian 63-75.
Previous Names: None
Previous Grounds: Highfields/ Canons Park/ London Rd, Presdales Lower Park 1921-26.
Reserve Team's League: Essex & Herts Border Comb.
Record Gate: 2,500 v Arsenal XI 1974.
Record win: 10-1 v Wood Green Town **Record defeat:** 0-11 v Barnet.
Best FA Cup year: First Round Proper 68-69 (lost 1-6 to Luton Town). **Nickname:** Blues.
Clubhouse: Licensed bar open matchdays. Light snacks at refreshment bar.
Players progressing to Football League: Derek Saunders (Chelsea), Ken Humphrey (QPR).
Club Record Scorer: M Hibbert 229 **Club Record Appearances:** Gary Riddle 548.
Record Scorer in one season: George Dearman 98 (1926-27).
93-94 Top scorer: Damon Miles 20 **93-94 Captain & 93-94 P.o.Y.:** Jon Bridge.
Local Press: Herts Mercury, Herts Star (0920 554611), Herald & Post (0279 655225).
Hons: Herts Snr Cup 1898-99 03-04 06-07 21-22 53-54, Herts Charity Shield 26-27 56-57 58-59 62-63 85-86, Herts Charity Cup R-up 64-65 65-66 78-79 89-90, Spartan Lg 52-53 (Div 1 Sect.B 51-52, Div 2 Sect.A 26-27), Athenian Lg Div 2 Cup 65-66 72-73 (Div 2 Reserve Sect. 66-67 70-71), East Anglian Cup 73-74, Herts Co. Lg 08-09 21-22, East Herts Lg 04-05 06-07 (Lg Cup 06-07), Perry Cup 26-27 28-29 37-38 51-52 52-53 53-54 55-56, Dunkels Cup 52-53, Rolleston Cup 39-40 51-52.

WINDSOR & ETON

Chairman: Stephen Gillham **Vice-Chairman:** Fred Atkins **President:** Sir David Hill-Wood, Bt
Secretary: Peter Jackson, 9 Penwith Walk, Wych Hill Park, Woking, Surrey GU22 0JD (0483 715953).
Manager: John Clements **Asst Manager:** Alan Rowe **Coach:** TBA
Press Officer: Christopher Atkins (0344 885463) **Physio:** Des Hunt
Ground: Stag Meadow, St Leonards Road, Windsor, Berkshire SL4 3DR (0753 860656).
Directions: A332 from M4 junct 6. Left at r'bout (B3173), left into St Leonards Rd at lights on T-junction, ground 500 yards on right on B3022 opposite Stag & Hounds PH. 1 mile from town centre - pass available to St Leonards Rd. BR to Windsor Central station (from) Slough or Windsor Riverside (change at Staines from Waterloo).
Capacity: 4,500 **Cover:** 650 **Seats:** 400 **Floodlights:** Yes **Founded:** 1892
Club Shop: Yes, selling replica kit (to order), scarves, ties, badges, pennants and a selection of Football League and non-League programmes. Contact Michael Gregg.
Colours: Red (green trim)/red/red **Change colours:** White/black/black. **Nickname:** Royalists
Sponsors: Murex Welding Products. **Previous Ground:** Ballon Meadow 1892-1912.
Programme: 28 pages **Programme Editor:** Christopher Atkins (0344 885463).
Previous Leagues: Southern 1895-96/ West Berks/ Great Western Suburban 1907-22/ Athenian 22-29 63-81/ Spartan 29-32/ Great Western Comb/ Corinthian 45-50/ Metropolitan 50-60/ Delphian 60-63.
Midweek home matchday: Tuesday **Reserve Team's League:** Suburban (North)
Record Gate: 8,500 (Charity match). **League clubs defeated in FA Cup:** None.
Best FA Cup season: 2nd Rd replay 83-84. 1st Rd on seven occasions; 25-26 80-81 82-86 91-92.
Record Fees - Paid: £9,000 for Keith White (Slough Town).
Received: £45,000 for Michael Banton & Michael Barnes (Barnet).
Players progressing to Football League: Reg Dare (Southampton 1949), Steve Adams (Charlton 1979), Dave Barnett (Colchester 1988), Vic Woodley (Chelsea & England), Billy Coward (QPR, Walsall), Ken Groves (Preston), Dave Regis (Notts County)
Clubhouse: (0753 860656). Juke-box, Sky TV, licensed bar, darts, pool. Club available for parties & wedding receptions etc - contact Alan Baker on aforementioned number.
93-94 Captain: Kenny Cox **Record appearances:** Kevin Mitchell.
93-94 P.o.Y.: Mark Franks **93-94 Top scorer:** Michael Creighton.
Local Newspapers: Windsor & Eton Express, Windsor & East Berks Observer, Evening Post.
Hons: Isthmian Lg Div 1 83-84 (Div 2 R-up 82-83), Athenian Lg 79-80 80-81 (Lg Cup 79-80 (R-up 78-79 80-81), Div 2 Cup 63-64 (R-up 68-69)), Spartan Lg R-up 36-37 37-38 (Div 1 30-31), Metropolitan Lg R-up 53-54 (Lg Amtr Cup 51-52 52-53, Lg Cup 52-53 (R-up 53-54 54-55)), Gt Western Suburban Lg R-up 21-22, Berks & Bucks Snr Cup(11) 10-11 36-38 40-45 61-62 87-89 (R-up 07-08 24-25 26-27 38-39 46-47 62-63), Berks & Bucks Benev. Cup 35-36 37-38 46-47 62-63 (R-up 38-39 47-48 49-50), FA Amtr Cup 4th Rd 21-22, FA Vase SF 80-81 (QF 79-80), FA Tphy 3rd Rd 88-89.

WITHAM TOWN

Chairman: Mr A Marshall **Vice Chairman:** Reg Wright **President:** Mr B Olley.
Secretary: Reg Wright, 28 Mersey Rd, Witham, Essex CM8 1LJ (0376 512990).
Manager: Craig Johnson **Asst Mgr:** Dennis Pollock **Coach:** Gary Smith-Herzberg
Physio: Tony McCulloch **Press Officer:** Matthew Wright (0376 517018)
Ground: Spa Road, Witham, Essex CM8 1UN (0376 511198-lounge, 500146-reception, 520996-boardroom).
Directions: From Witham BR (network S.E.) station; through pub car park and follow road to Faulkbourne, at main r'bout turn left and ground is on the right. By road; Off A12 at Witham sign, left at 1st lights (Spinks Lane), right at end of road, follow road under railway bridge - ground 100yds on left.
Capacity: 2,000 **Seats:** 150 **Cover:** 150 **Floodlights:** Yes **Founded:** 1947
Colours: Red & black stripes/black/black **Change colours:** Green & yellow
Nickname: Town **Metal Badges:** No
Programme: 24 pages, 50p **Editor:** Matthew Wright (0376 517018) **Club Shop:** No.
Midweek Matchday: Tuesday **Reserve Team's League:** Essex & Herts Border Comb.
Previous Leagues: Mid Essex/ Essex & Suffolk Border/ Essex Senior 71-87.
Previous Names: None **Previous Ground:** None.
Record Gate: 800 v Billericay Town, Essex Senior League, May 1976.
Best FA Cup year: 2nd Qual. Rd 87-88 (v Gravesend), 88-89 (v B. Stortford), 89-90 (v Dartford).
Record transfer fee received: for Steve Tilson (Southend).
Record win: 7-0 v Southall 14/11/92 **Record defeat:** 1-6 v Saffron Walden 22/10/91.
Clubhouse: Three bars and large function room. Open every night and weekend lunctimes. Hot bar snacks and occasional a la carte dinners (max. seating 24). Darts, pool, table tennis teams.
Steward: Richard Green.
Players progressing to Football League: Steve Tilson (Southend).
Club Record Scorer: Colin Mitchell
Club Record Appearances: Keith Dent (16 years)
93-94 Top scorer: C J Emmanuel **93-94 Captain & P.o.Y.:** Graham Wood.
Local Press: Witham & Braintree Times, Essex Chronicle, East Anglian Daily Times.
Local Radio: BBC Essex, Essex Radio.
Hons: Essex Snr Lg 70-71 85-86 (R-up 84-85 86-87), Essex Snr Tphy 85-86 (R-up 88-89), FA Vase 5th Rd 85-86, Loctite Tphy SF 90-91.

DIVISION THREE 1993-94

	P	W	D	L	F	A	PTS
Bracknell Town	40	25	8	7	78	29	83
Cheshunt	40	23	12	5	62	34	81
Oxford City	40	24	6	10	94	55	78
Harlow Town	40	22	11	7	61	36	77
Southall	40	17	12	11	66	53	63
Camberley Town	40	18	7	15	56	50	61
Hertford Town	40	18	6	16	67	65	60
Royston Town	40	15	11	14	44	41	56
Northwood	40	15	11	14	78	77	56
Epsom & Ewell	40	15	9	16	63	62	54
Harefield United	40	12	15	13	45	55	51
Cove	40	15	6	19	59	74	51
Kinsbury Town	40	12	14	14	57	54	50
Feltham & H'slow	40	14	7	19	60	63	49
Leighton Town	40	12	11	17	51	64	47
East Thurrock U.	40	10	15	15	65	64	45
Clapton	40	12	9	19	51	65	45
Hornchurch	40	12	8	20	42	60	44
Tring Town	40	10	11	19	48	64	41
Flackwell Heath	40	9	11	20	44	83	38
Horsham	40	6	8	26	43	86	26

TOP SCORERS

	Lge	Cup	Tot
Tony Wood (Bracknell Town)	30	3	43
(inc. goals for Flackwell Heath)	*12*	*3*	
Mark Randall (Northwood)	21	3	24
David Whitehead (Hertford T.)	22	1	23

Below: *Bracknell Town - Division Three champions 1993-94.*

Photo - Eric Marsh.

RESULT CHART 1993-94

HOME TEAM	1	2	3	4	5	6	7	8	9	10	11	12	13	14	15	16	17	18	19	20	21
1. Bracknell Town	*	1-1	2-0	1-0	3-1	4-2	3-2	0-1	2-2	3-2	2-3	6-0	3-0	3-0	2-2	2-0	1-1	4-0	2-0	2-1	2-0
2. Camberley Town	0-1	*	1-1	2-0	5-1	4-0	0-0	2-0	2-0	1-1	0-1	3-1	3-0	3-1	1-1	0-0	1-0	2-1	1-0	3-1	3-1
3. Cheshunt	0-0	1-0	*	0-0	0-1	1-3	1-0	2-0	1-1	0-1	0-0	2-2	2-1	4-3	1-1	2-0	4-1	2-0	1-0	2-1	1-1
4. Clapton	1-0	2-0	1-3	*	1-1	3-2	2-0	4-2	1-1	1-1	2-3	3-1	0-2	2-1	1-1	3-0	0-1	1-3	3-0	0-1	4-0
5. Cove	0-3	1-0	0-2	4-3	*	2-1	2-5	2-2	5-1	0-0	2-0	1-2	4-1	2-1	1-4	5-2	3-3	1-2	2-0	5-2	1-0
6. East Thurrock	1-1	1-2	1-1	1-1	5-0	*	2-4	2-3	1-3	1-2	0-0	1-1	2-0	3-0	2-2	5-0	4-4	1-1	1-1	2-2	2-0
7. Epsom & Ewell	0-1	3-1	0-1	1-0	3-1	2-2	*	0-2	4-0	3-2	1-1	3-1	2-1	1-0	1-1	1-2	2-5	2-3	2-0	0-3	1-1
8. Feltham & H.	1-2	3-0	1-3	3-0	1-1	5-1	2-1	*	0-1	0-1	0-0	3-2	1-2	5-0	1-2	0-3	5-2	3-1	0-0	1-2	2-1
9. Flackwell Heath	1-0	1-0	0-0	1-1	0-0	1-5	2-2	2-1	*	1-4	1-2	1-2	0-1	1-1	1-4	1-1	1-5	1-4	1-2	0-2	1-4
10. Harefield Utd	0-1	1-0	1-3	1-1	1-0	0-0	0-1	2-2	1-1	*	2-3	0-0	2-0	1-0	1-0	0-1	2-2	1-5	1-1	1-1	1-3
11. Harlow Town	3-0	2-0	0-1	2-1	1-0	1-0	2-0	3-0	3-0	1-1	*	1-0	0-1	1-1	2-3	4-2	1-1	1-2	1-0	2-2	1-1
12. Hertford Town	1-0	2-1	0-2	5-1	1-2	3-2	4-2	3-0	3-1	1-2	2-3	*	0-2	4-2	2-3	1-1	1-0	2-1	0-2	1-1	1-0
13. Hornchurch	0-0	0-0	0-2	0-1	2-1	0-1	2-0	3-1	1-2	1-1	0-3	1-2	*	3-2	3-1	1-1	2-1	2-1	1-2	0-1	3-4
14. Horsham	0-6	0-5	1-1	3-0	3-1	3-1	2-5	1-3	1-3	0-1	0-2	0-1	1-1	*	0-0	3-2	3-1	1-2	0-0	1-3	1-2
15. Kingsbury Town	0-0	1-4	1-3	2-3	1-2	1-0	2-3	1-0	4-1	3-0	0-0	0-1	1-0	1-1	*	0-0	2-0	1-1	1-2	1-2	1-1
16. Leighton Town	1-2	4-0	1-4	2-1	4-0	2-3	2-1	2-1	1-3	5-0	1-3	2-0	0-0	2-0	1-0	*	2-2	1-3	0-0	1-1	1-1
17. Northwood	0-5	5-1	2-2	4-0	2-1	1-1	2-4	1-1	0-1	3-3	2-1	0-6	2-1	3-1	2-3	2-0	*	3-2	1-2	2-1	1-0
18. Oxford City	1-0	4-1	1-2	5-0	2-3	2-0	3-0	1-1	4-0	0-0	3-0	6-4	3-1	3-1	2-1	2-0	4-4	*	3-2	3-0	5-0
19. Royston Town	0-1	0-1	3-0	1-0	1-0	0-2	0-0	3-1	2-0	4-1	0-1	1-1	1-1	2-1	2-2	1-1	2-0	3-1	*	1-0	1-2
20. Southall	1-6	6-0	0-1	3-3	2-0	0-0	1-1	3-0	4-3	2-1	1-1	2-1	1-1	0-0	2-1	3-0	1-2	1-2	4-2	*	0-0
21. Tring Town	0-1	1-2	2-3	1-0	2-0	1-1	0-0	1-2	2-2	0-2	1-2	1-2	5-1	2-3	2-1	3-0	0-5	2-2	0-0	0-2	*

Diadora League Division Two/Three Ten Year Record

(N - Denoted Division Two (North), S - Denotes Division Two (South))

	84/5	85/6	86/7	87/8	88/9	89/0	90/1	91/2	92/3	93/4
Abingdon Town	-	-	-	-	-	3S	1S	-	-	-
Aldershot Town	-	-	-	-	-	-	-	-	1	-
Basildon United	-	-	-	-	-	7N	18N	-	-	-
Bracknell Town	8S	2S	-	-	-	19S	17S	17	16	1
Camberley Town	15S	16S	15S	19S	14S	17S	22S	15	18	6
Chalfont St Peter	7N	6N	8S	1S	-	-	-	-	-	-
Chertsey Town	19S	-	6S	6S	12S	13S	14S	2	-	-
Chesham United	-	-	1N	-	-	-	-	-	-	-
Cheshunt	12N	4N	22N	-	-	-	-	-	-	2
Clapton	-	19N	19N	13N	7N	12N	20N	20	17	17
Collier Row	-	-	9N	2N	-	8N	12N	10	3	-
Cove	-	-	-	-	-	-	19S	6	5	12
Dorking (Town)	12S	9S	3S	3S	1S	-	-	-	-	-
Eastbourne United	(see page 484 for Div.2 record)							21	-	-
East Thurrock United	-	-	-	-	-	-	-	-	8	16
Edgware Town	(see page 484 for Div.2 record)							1	-	-
Epsom & Ewell	-	-	-	5S	9S	14S	13S	9	15	10
Feltham	14S	10S	4S	4S	8S	18S	18S	-	-	-
Feltham & Hounslow Boro.	-	-	-	-	-	-	-	16	20	14
Finchley	2N	-	-	12N	3S	18N	21N	-	-	-
Flackwell Heath	8N	14S	16S	20S	13S	8S	16S	7	11	20
Grays Athletic	1S	-	-	-	-	-	-	-	-	-
Hampton	(see page 484 for Div.2 record)							4	-	-
Harefield United	-	-	-	-	-	-	-	-	-	11
Haringey Borough	19N	11N	3N	20N	-	-	-	-	-	-
Harlow Town	-	-	17N	5N	1N	-	-	-	-	4
Hertford Town	-	5N	15N	22N	10N	3N	15N	13	10	7
Heybridge Swifts	3N	3N	4N	9N	5N	1N	-	-	-	-
Hornchurch	-	-	14N	14N	16N	16N	19N	18	13	18
Horsham	10S	18S	13S	15S	20S	21S	15S	5	14	21
Kingsbury Town	17N	2N	-	-	-	-	13N	12	9	13
Leighton Town	-	-	-	-	-	-	-	-	4	15
Letchworth Garden City	10N	12N	6N	11N	21N	22N	-	-	-	-
Leyton-Wingate	1N	-	-	-	-	-	-	-	-	-
Maidenhead United	-	-	-	11S	17S	5S	2S	-	-	-
Marlow	13N	20S	2S	-	-	-	-	-	-	-
Molesey	3S	6S	19S	17S	4S	2S	-	-	-	-
Northwood	-A	-	-	-	-	-	-	-	6	9
Oxford City	-	-	-	-	-	-	-	-	-	3
Petersfield United	17S	12S	18S	22S	21S	20S	21S	14	19	-
Royston Town	11N	8N	21N	17N	18N	9N	16N	11	7	8
Southall	(see page 484 for Division Two record)									5
Stevenage Borough	4N	1N	-	-	4N	4N	1N	-	-	-
Thame United	-	-	-	-	-	-	-	8	2	-
Tilbury	(see page 484 for Div.2 record)							3	-	-
Tring Town	6N	7N	8N	10N	3N	19N	22N	19	12	19
Uxbridge	2S	-	-	-	-	-	-	-	-	-
Vauxhall Motors	-	16N	13N	8N	14N	11N	2N	-	-	-
Whyteleafe	5S	5S	12S	7S	2S	-	-	-	-	-
Wivenhoe Town	-	-	12N	1N	-	-	-	-	-	-
Woking	-	3S	1S	-	-	-	-	-	-	-
Wolverton Town	16N	20N	2N	-	22N	-	-	-	-	-
Yeading	-	-	-	10S	15S	1S	-	-	-	-
No. of clubs competing	20N	20N	22N	22N	22N	22N	22N	21	20	21
	19S	20S	21S	22S	21S	21S	22S			

BEDFORD TOWN

Chairman: Mike John **Vice Chairman:** D Donnelly **President:** Allen J Sturgess
Secretary: Barry Stephenson, 9 Aspen Ave., Bedford, Beds MK41 8BX (0234 342276).
Manager: Terry King **Asst Manager:** Andy Lloyd **Coach:** Neal Rodney
Physio: Paul Burstin **Press Officer:** David Donnelly (0234 359246).
Ground: Meadow Lane, Cardington, Beds.
Directions: On A603 Bedford to Sandy road. Come off A1 at Sandy following signs to Bedford - ground on right. From Bedford take Cardington Road out of town signposted Biggleswade and Sandy. An 'Eagles Special' bus picks up at various points in town and arrives at ground twenty minutes before kick-off, leaving fifteen minutes after game.
Capacity: 3,000 **Seats:** 100 **Cover:** 350 **Floodlights:** Yes **Founded:** 1908
Colours: Blue & white **Change Colours:** yellow & black **Reformed:** 1989.
Midweek Matchday: Tuesday **Sponsors:** Allen Sturges Travel **Nickname:** Eagles.
Club Shop: Yes, selling scarves, t-shirts, sweatshirts, mugs, badges, key-rings, programmes. Contact Bryan T Jefferies (0933 316255).
Previous Grounds: Allen Park, Queens Park, Bedford (park pitch) 1991-93. *(predecessors: London Rd/ Gasworks/ Queens Pk/ The Eyrie, Raleigh Street).*
Record Attendance: 3,000 v Peterborough Utd, ground opening 6/8/93. At Allen Park: 1,227 v Bedford Utd, South Midlands League Division One, 26/12/91. *(predecessors: 18,407 v Everton, FA Cup 4th Round 12/2/66).*
Previous Leagues: South Midlands 91-94 *(predecessors: Utd Co's 08-39/ Southern 46-82).*
Programme: 40 pages, 50p **Programme Editor:** Josie Meaney (0234 343239)
Record win: 9-0 v Ickleford & v Caddington
Record defeat: 1-5 v Toddington (Sth Mids Div. 1), 2-6 v Milton Keynes Boro. (Sth Mids Lge Cup).
Reserves' Lge: Sth Mids Lge Res. Div **Clubhouse:** Open matchdays. Bar meals and snacks.
Record transfer fee received: £15,000 for Bill Gardner (Southend) from predecessors, 1969.
Players progressing to Football League: Bill Gardner (Southend) 1969, Nicky Platnaeur (moved to Bristol Rovers when Bedford Town folded in 1977).
Captain 93-94: Jason Reed **Top Scorer & Player of the Year 93-94:** Jason Reed.
Club record scorer: Jason Reed **Club record appearances:** Vernon Pedley.
Hons: South Mids Lg 93-94 (Div 1 92-93, Floodlit Cup 93-94), Hinchingbrook Cup 93-94 *(predecessors: Southern Lg 58-59 (Div 1 69-70), Utd Co's Lg 30-31 32-33 33-34 (R-up 11-12 12-13 13-14 29-30 31-32 34-35 36-37), FA Cup 4th Rd 63-64 65-66, FA Tphy SF 74-75).*

CAMBERLEY TOWN

Chairman: Ian Waldren **Vice Chairman:** Gordon Foss **President:** Paul Prentice
Secretary: Keith Morgan, 5 Nairn Close, Frimley, Surrey GU16 5TA (0276 66512).
Manager: Paul Holden **Asst Manager:** Paul Xiberras **Coach:** Paul Holden
Press Officer: Andy Vaughan **Comm. Manager:** Andy Jennings **Physio:** Julia Richards.
Ground: Krooner Park, Krooner Road, off Frimley Rd, Camberley, Surrey GU15 2QP (0276 65392).
Directions: M3 Jct 4, follow signs to Frimley, follow B3411 towards Camberley, ground on left opposite 'The Standard' pub.
Capacity: 3,000 **Seats:** 195 **Cover:** 195 **Floodlights:** Yes **Founded:** 1896
Colours: Red (white trim)/red/red **Change colours:** All yellow **Metal Badges:** Yes.
Club Shop: Sells progs, scarves, shirts, bags, pullovers, ties, badges. Contact Andy Vaughan c/o the club.
Programme: 24 pages, 50p **Midweek Matchday:** Tuesday **Sponsors:** Zip Print
Previous Grounds: London Rd Rec 1898-1905 12-18/ Southwell Park Rd 05-09/ Martins Meadow 09-12.
Previous Leagues: Ascot & District/ West Surrey/ Aldershot Snr/ Surrey Snr 22-73/ Spartan 73-75/ Athenian 75-77 82-84/ Isthmian 77-82.
Previous Names: Camberley & Yorktown 1896-1946/ Camberley FC 46-67 when club merged with Camberley Wanderers.
Reserve's League: Suburban **Nickname:** 'Krooners', 'Reds' or 'Town'.
Record Gate: 3,500 v C. Palace, friendly 14/10/74. *Competitive: 2,066 v Aldershot, Isthmian Lge Div 3, 10/11/92.*
Best FA Cup year: 3rd Qual. Rd 78-79 **Record win:** 15-0 v Royal Engineers, friendly, 20/9/19.
Record defeat: 0-11 v Abingdon Town (A), Isthmian League Division Two (South) 25/8/90.
Clubhouse: Open matchdays and 2 evenings per week. Large bar and function hall, pool, darts. Local band on Fridays. Food available from burger bar on matchdays.
Captain 93-94: Paul Xiberras **Club record appearances:** Brian Ives.
93-94 P.o.Y.: Steve Spencer **93-94 Top scorer:** Tony Dixon and Steve Lloyd 15.
Local Press: Camberley News (0276 64444), Bracknell News (0344 56611).
Hons: FA Vase QF 85-86, Isthmian Lg Div 2 R-up 78-79, Surrey Snr Lg 30-31 31-32 32-33 (R-up 46-47 61-62, Lg Charity Cup 37-38 51-52 (R-up 31-32 36-37 54-55 72-73)), Surrey Snr Cup 78-79 (R-up 35-36), W. Surrey Lg 13-14 (R-up 12-13), Ascot & Dist Lg 03-04, Surrey Jnr Charity Cup R-up 08-09, Surrey Jnr Cup 1897-98 1909-10 (R-up 07-08), Aldershot Snr Lg 12-13 (Lg Charity Cup R-up 21-22), Southern Comb. Cup 80-81 (R-up 78-79 85-86 87-88).

Below: *Camberley Town FC 1993-94.*

CANVEY ISLAND

Chairman: W Overall **Manager:** Jeff King.
Secretary: Mrs Frances Roche, 56 Harvest Way, Canvey Island SS8 9RP (0268 698586).
Ground: Park Lane, Canvey Island (0268 682991).
Directions: A130 from A13 or A127 at Sadlers Farm r'bout, 1 mile right through town centre, first on right past old bus garage. Bus 3 or 151 from Benfleet (BR) to stop after Admiral Jellicoe (PH).
Seats: None **Cover:** 250 **Capacity:** 2,500 **Floodlights:** Yes **Founded:** 1926.
Colours: Yellow **Change cols:** Red **Record Gate:** 3,250 v Tiverton, FA Vase SF 27/3/93
Programme Editor: John Nash **Nickname:** Gulls.
Previous Lges: Southend & Dist./ Thurrock & Thameside Comb./ Parthenon/ Metropolitan/ Gtr London 64-71.
Best FA Cup season: Fourth Qualifying Round 93-94, lost 1-3 at Kettering Town.
Players progressing to Football League: Peter Taylor (Spurs, Crystal Palace & England).
Captain 93-94: Kevin Lee **Top Scorer 93-94:** Andy Jones 17.
Hons: FA Vase SF 92-93, Essex Snr Lg 86-87 92-93 (Lg Cup 83-84 92-93, Harry Fisher Memorial Trophy 93-94, Sportsmanship Award 83-84, Reserve Shield 91-92, Reserve Cup R-up 93-94), Essex Senior Trophy R-up 93-94, Essex Thameside Trophy 93-94, Gtr London Lg(2) 67-69 (Lg Cup 68-69).

CLAPTON

Chairman: Mike Fogg **Vice Chairman:** Pat Sweeney **President:** Mike Gliksten
Press Officer/Secretary: Bill Stockley, 6 Cheltenham Gardens, London E6 8DH (081 471 3055).
Manager: John Arnold **Asst Manager:** Gary Anderson **Coach:** B Balkwill
Commercial Manager: Micky Connolly **Physio:** P Kelly.
Ground: The Old Spotted Dog, Upton Lane, Forest Gate, London E7 9NP (081 472 0822).
Directions: BR to Forest Gate, tube to Plaistow (District Line), or bus 278 passes ground. Officials entrance in Upton Lane, spectator's in Disraeli Rd.
Capacity: 2,000 **Seats:** 200 **Cover:** 500 **Floodlights:** Yes **Founded:** 1878
Colours: Red & white stripes/black/black **Change colours:** Yellow/blue.
Club Shop: No **Sponsors:** None
Programme: 10 pages with admission **Programme Editor:** Secretary. **Metal Badges:** Yes
Previous Grounds: None **Midweek Matchday:** Tuesday **Nickname:** Tons
Previous Leagues: Southern 1894-96 (founder members)/ London 1896-97.
Reserves' Lge: Essex/Herts Border Com. **Record Gate:** 12,000 v Tottenham Hotspur, FA Cup 1898-99.
Best FA Cup year: 3rd Rd Proper 25-26 (lost 2-3 to Swindon at Upton Park).
League clubs defeated in FA Cup: Norwich City 1925-26.
Record defeat: 0-14 v Nottingham Forest (H), FA Cup 1st Rd 1890-91.
Players progressing to Football Lge: Numerous over past 116 years. Currently: Paul Williams (Crystal Palace), Gary Charles (Derby), Miguel de Souza (Birmingham).
Clubhouse: Open most evenings & match day. Light snacks available.
Club Record Goalscorer: Unknown **Club Record Appearances:** Dave Fahy.
93-94 Captain: Alan Bowers **93-94 P.o.Y.:** Simon Copping **93-94 Top scorer:** Tommy Williams
Hons: FA Amtr Cup 06-07 08-09 14-15 23-24 24-25 (R-up 04-05), Isthmian Lg 10-11 22-23 (R-up 05-06 07-08 09-10 24-25, Div 2 82-83), Essex Thames-side Tphy(2), FA Invitation Cup(2), London Snr Cup(2), London Charity Cup, Essex Snr Cup(4), First English team to play on the continent, beating a Belgian Select XI over Easter 1890.

Clapton FC 1993-94. *Photo - Bill Storey.*

COLLIER ROW

Chairman: Fred Mills **Vice Chairman:** George Rose **President:** Ron Walker.
Secretary: Ian Ansell, 120 Limes Ave., Limes Farm, Chigwell, Essex IG7 5LX (081 500 9778).
Manager: Don McGovern **Asst Manager:** Paul Downes **Coach:** Alan Marson
Press Officer: George Rose (0708 705611)
Ground: 'Sungate', Collier Row Rd, Collier Row, Romford, Essex (0708 722766).
Directions: A12 from London, left at Moby Dick (PH) traffic lights, right at next r'bout, ground entrance signposted 200 yards on right. London bus 247 passes ground.
Capacity: 2,000 **Seats:** 110 **Cover:** 200 **Floodlights:** Yes **Founded:** 1929
Colours: Red/black/black **Change colours:** All white **Nickname:** The Row
Club Shop: Yes, selling programmes, badges from non-league, League and foreign clubs, and a wide range of club souvenirs and a selection of sports books and video. Contact Ian Ansell (081 500 9778).
Res. Lge: Essex/Herts Border Comb. **Sponsors:** Allied Dunbar/Emerson Crane Hire
Programme: 20 pages, 50p **Editor:** Phil Sammons (0708 768845) **Metal Badges:** Yes
Midweek Matchday: Wednesday **Previous Leagues:** London Spartan 81-86.
Clubhouse: Yes, open normal pub hours **Record Gate:** 1,095 v Garforth Town, FA Vase 6th Rd 1987.
Record Defeat: 2-10 v Chertsey Town (H), Isthmian League Division Two 93-94.
Best FA Cup year: 1st Qualifying Rd replay 91-92, lost 0-1 v Purfleet (H) after 2-2 draw.
Record Scorer: Steve Thompson 158 **Club Record Appearances:** Graham Cole 278.
93-94 Captain: **93-94 P.o.Y:** Reg Gardiner.
Local Radio: Essex Radio, BBC Essex. **Local Press:** Havering Recorder/ Dagenham Post.
Hons: FA Vase SF 86-87 (QF 84-85), London Spartan Lg 83-84 85-86 (R-up 84-85, Senior Div 82-83, Lg Cup R-up 84-85), Isthmian Lg Div 2 North R-up 87-88, Knight Floodlit Cup R-up 89-90.

COVE

Chairman: Terry White **President:** Ron Brown
Secretary: Nick Stephens, 9 Hurst Rd, Hawley Estate, Farnborough, Hants (0252 542717).
Manager: Andy Leader **Asst Manager:** Steve Hibbins
Ground: Oak Farm, off Romayne Close, Cove, Farnborough, Hants GU14 8LB (0252 543615).
Directions: Farnborough (BR) 2 miles; right into Union Street, right at lights into Prospect Rd, left into West Heath Rd, right into Romayne close and follow signs to Cove FC. Or, M3 jct 4, follow A325 signed Aldershot & Farnham, right into Prospect Avenue (signposted Cove FC and Farnborough Town FC), then as above.
Capacity: 3,500 **Seats:** 75 **Cover:** 475 **Floodlights:** Yes **Founded:** 1897
Colours: Amber & black quarters **Change colours:** All red **Nickname:** None.
Club Shop: No, but club ties, badges and lighters are on sale in clubhouse.
Programme: 30 pages, 50p **Editor:** Graham Brown (0252 541152). **Metal Badges:** Yes
Previous Leagues: Aldershot Jnr/ Aldershot Intermediate 45-48/ Surrey Intermediate 48-71/ Surrey Snr 71-73/ Hants 74-81/ Combined Counties 81-90.
Midweek Matchday: Tuesday **Previous Grounds:** Cove Green 1897-1973/ Southwood Rd.
Reserve Team's League: Suburban **Record Gate:** 1,798 v Aldershot, Isthmian Lg Div 3, 1/5/93.
Sponsors: Oasis soft drinks **Best FA Cup year:** 1st Qual replay 91-92 (0-4 at Burgess Hill).
Record transfer fee paid: £250 for Nick Horton (Egham Town, 92-93).
Record win: 10-2 v Sway (H), 17/2/74. In Senior Football: 8-1 v Cobham (H), Comb. Co's Lg, 16/9/89.
Record defeat: 2-8 v Merrow (A), 17/1/69. In Senior Football: 1-6 v Hungerford (A), Isthmian Lg, 16/3/91.
Players progressing to Football League: Frank Broome, Maurice Cook.
Clubhouse: Mon-Fri 7-11pm, Sat noon-11pm, Sunday noon-3pm & 7-11pm. Juke box, pool, darts. Matchday hot food includes burgers, hot-dogs, chips, soup plus variety of sandwiches and other snacks.
Club Record Scorer: Nigel Thompson 164 **Record Appearances:** Nigel Thompson, 188 in four seasons.
93-94 Captain: John Cassidy **93-94 P.o.Y.:** Matt Murphy.
Hons: Surrey I'mediate Lg, Surrey Prem. Lg 49-50 52-53 53-54 63-64 67-68 (R-up 48-49 61-62 64-65, Lg Cup 59-60 60-61 69-70, Sportmanship Award 64-65 65-66 69-70, Reserve Section 59-60 60-61 61-62 64-65 (R-up 63-64 66-67 67-68 68-69), Reserve Cup 60-61 61-62), Combined Co's Lg Cup 81-82, Hants Lg Div 3 76-77 (Div 4 73-74, Div 2 R-up 77-78), Aldershot Snr Cup 71-72 77-78 79-80 90-91 91-92 (R-up 72-73), Southern Comb. Floodlit Cup 92-93, Aldershot Snr Shield 37-38 38-39 46-47 71-72, Aldershot Snr Lg 53-54 (Div 2 32-33 37-38 38-39, Div 2 Cup 50-51, Div 4 Cup 30-31).

EAST THURROCK UNITED

Chairman: Brian Grover **Vice Chairman:** Steve Wilson **President:** Len Firman
Secretary/Press Officer: Malcolm Harris, 14 Colne Valley, Upminster, Essex RM14 1QA (07082 28812).
Manager: Glen Case **Asst Manager:** Keith Reid **Coach:** Colin Reid
Physio: Paul Smith **Press Officer:** Malcolm Harris.
Ground: Rookery Hill, Corringham, Essex (0375 644166-club, 641009-boardroom).
Directions: A13 London-Southend, take 1014 at Stanford-le-Hope for two and a half miles - ground on left. Two miles from Stanford-le-Hope and Basildon BR stations.
Seats: 160 **Cover:** 360 **Capacity:** 3,000 **Floodlights:** Yes **Founded:** 1969.
Colours: Amber/black/black **Change colours:** Blue/white/white **Nickname:** Rocks
Programme: 24 pages, 50p **Editor:** Tony Smith (0268 292142) **Metal Badges:** Yes
Reserves' Lge: Essex/Herts Border Com. **Previous Name:** Corringham Social (pre-1969 Sunday side).
Club Shop: Sells programmes, badges, mags, scarves. Contact Dennis Sellick (0375 644166).
Record Gate: 947 v Trevor Brooking XI, May 1987. Competitive: 845 v Bashley, FA Vase 1989.
Prev. Lges: Sth Essex Comb./ Gtr London/ Metropolitan 72-75/ London Spartan 75-79/ Essex Snr 79-92.
Previous Grounds: Billet, Stanford-le-Hope 70-73 74-76/ Grays Athletic FC 73-74/ Tilbury FC 77-82/ New Thames Club 82-84.
Record win: 7-0 v Coggeshall (H) 1984 **Record defeat:** 0-9 v Eton Manor (A) 1982, both Essex Snr League.
Record Transfer Fee Paid: £2,000 + 10% of future fee for Greg Berry (Orient, 1989).
Players progressing to Football League: Greg Berry (Leyton Orient).
Clubhouse: Open all day seven days a week. Hot and cold snacks. Darts, pool, indoor bowls.
Local Radio: BBC Essex. **Local Press:** Thurrock Gazette/ Thurrock Recorder
Record Scorer: Graham Stewart 102 **Club Record Appearances:** Glen Case 600+.
93-94 Captain: Andy Innell **93-94 P.o.Y.:** Scott Harvey **93-94 Top Scorer:** Paul Barnett.
Honours: Metropolitan Lg Div 2 72-73, Essex Snr Lg R-up 88-89 (Lg Cup 88-89 91-92, Harry Fisher Mem. Tphy 83-84 90-91, Sportsmanship Award 81-82 86-87 89-89), Essex Snr Tphy R-up 91-92, Fred Budden Tphy R-up 89-90, Essex & Herts Border Comb. 89-90 (Lg Cup 89-90).

EPSOM & EWELL

Chairman: Peter Atkins **Vice Chairman:** Stella Lamont.
Secretary: David Wilson, 33 Delaporte Close, Epsom, Surrey KT17 4AF (0372 729817).
Manager: Adrian Hill **Coach:** John Wood **Physio:** Charlie Millard.
Press Officer: Stella Lamont (0737 356245) **Ground:** As Banstead Athletic FC.
Club Shop: No **Sponsors:** TBA **Nickname:** E's. **Founded:** 1917
Colours: Royal & white **Change colours:** All yellow.
Programme: 28/32 pages, 35p **Editor:** Stella Lamont (0737 356245).
Midweek Matches: Tuesday **Reserve Team's League:** Suburban
Previous Leagues: Surrey Snr 24-27 73-75/ London 27-49/ Corinthian 49-63/ Athenian 63-73 75-77.
Previous Names: Epsom Town (previously Epsom FC) merged with Ewell & Stoneleigh in 1960.
Previous Grounds: Horton Lane, Epsom 1925-26/ West Street, Ewell 26-93.
Best FA Cup year: 1st Rd Proper 33-34, lost 2-4 at Clapton Orient.
Best FA Vase year: Finalists 74-75 **Best FA Trophy year:** 2nd Rd Proper 81-82.
Record Gate: 5,000 v Kingstonian, FA Cup Second Qualifying Rd, 15/10/49.
Players progressing to Football League: Matt Elliott (Scunthorpe), Chris Powell (Southend), Paul Harding (Notts County, Birmingham), Murray Jones (Grimsby), Alan Pardew (Charlton), Mick Leonard (Chesterfield).
Clubhouse: Normal licensing hours, food available.
93-94 Captain: Ray Purvis **93-94 Top Scorer:** Nigel Webb 24.
93-94 P.o.Y.: Nigel Bennett **Reserves' P.o.Y. 93-94:** Greg Harfield.
Club Record Scorer: Tommy Tuite **Club Record Appearances:** Unknown.
Hons: FA Vase R-up 74-75, London Lg 27-28 (R-up 31-32 32-33 34-35 36-37 37-38), Corinthian Lg Memorial Shield 59-60 (R-up 51-52 56-57), Athenian Lg Div 2 R-up 75-76 (Lg Cup R-up 76-77, Div 2 Cup R-up 67-68), Isthmian Lg Div 2 77-78 (Div 1 R-up 83-84), Surrey Snr Lg 25-26 26-27 74-75 (R-up 73-74, Lg Cup 73-74 74-75, Charity Cup 26-27 (R-up 73-74), Res. Section 74-75, Res. Cup 75-76 (R-up 73-74)), Surrey Snr Cup 80-81 (R-up 28-29 53-54 83-84), Surrey Snr Shield 32-33 54-55, Surrey Intermediate Cup 29-30, Surrey Intermediate Charity Cup 57-58, Surrey Jnr Cup R-up 22-23, Surrey Yth Cup 33-34 (R-up 50-51), Southern Comb. Cup 79-80 (R-up 82-83 92-93), Southern Yth Lg (East) 91-92 (West) 93-94 (R-up 82-83 85-86, Lg Cup 91-92 (R-up 87-88)).

FELTHAM & HOUNSLOW BOROUGH

Chairman: W F P Seuke & S Das **President:** E J Pauling MBE, JP.
Secretary: Mrs Ann Wilson, 2 Farrier Close, Sunbury-on-Thames, Middx TW16 6NJ (0932 789492).
Manager: Bruce Butler **Physio:** Sarah Whitworth **Coach:** Bruce Butler
Press Officer: John Cronk (081 751 3663).
Ground: Feltham Arena, Shakespeare Avenue, Feltham, Middx TW14 9HY (081 890 6241-club, 6905/6119-ground). **Nb- the club have an artificial pitch.*
Directions: BR to Feltham then 5 mins walk through Glebelands Park. Buses 90, 285, 117, 237, H24 or H25 to Feltham station, or 116 to top of Shakespeare Avenue. By car; M3, M4, A312 Staines road towards Bedfont, second left is Shakespeare Avenue.
Capacity: 10,000 **Seats:** 750 **Cover:** 1,500 **Floodlights:** Yes **Founded:** 1991
Colours: Royal blue & red stripes/red/blue **Change colours:** Blue & white/blue/white.
Club Shop: No (old progs from Robert Healy, C/O the club) **Metal Badges:** No
Programme: 20 pages, 30p **Editor:** John Cronk (081 751 3663) **Nickname:** Borough.
Midweek Matchday: Wednesday **Reserve Team's League:** Suburban. **Sponsors:**
Previous Names: 1991 merger of Feltham FC and Hounslow FC. Feltham previously Tudor Park, Hounslow previously Hounslow Town.
Previous Grounds: Feltham: Rectory Fields, Glebelands, *Hounslow: Denbigh Road.*
Previous Leagues: Feltham: West Middx Sunday/ Staines & Dist./ Hounslow & Dist./ Surrey Snr 63-68/ Spartan 68-73/ Athenian 74-77. *Hounslow: West London/ West Middx/ London 1898-99 1927-29/ Gt Western Suburban/ Spartan 29-46/ Corinthian 46-55/ Athenian 55-76/ Southern 76-83 86-90/ Hellenic 83-86 90-91.*
Record Gate: 826 v Aldershot Town, Isthmian Lg Div 3, 19/9/92. *As Feltham FC: 1,938 v Hampton, Middx Snr Cup 1968 (Hounslow; 8,546 v Wycombe, FA Amtr Cup 53-54).*
Best FA Cup year: Preliminary Replay 91-92 (lost 0-4 at home to Burnham). *As Feltham FC: 3rd Qual Rd 77-78 (lost 1-4 to Tilbury) 82-83 (0-1 v Chesham). As Hounslow: 1st Rd Proper 55-56 (lost to Hastings United).*
Record Fees - Paid: Martin Tyler (Kingstonian) **Rec'd:** Rachid Harkouk (C Palace).
Clubhouse: Sun, Mon, Wed-Sat. 2 bars, dancehall available for hire. Pool, darts. **Steward:** P Bennett.
Players progressing to Football League: Rachid Harkouk (Crystal Palace, QPR, Notts Co), Andy Pape (QPR), Pat Gavin (Gillingham, Leicester), Bobby Wilson (Brentford), Tony Witter (Crystal Palace).
Club Record Scorer: Paul Clarke 130 **Club Record Appearances:** Paul Clarke 326.
Local Press: Middx Chronicle, Hounslow Feltham & Hanworth Times, Hounslow Borough Recorder.
Local Radio: Capital, Capital Gold, County Sounds.
Hons: Surrey Snr Lg R-up 65-66 (Lg Cup 65-66, Charity Cup 63-64 65-66), Southern Comb. Cup(2)(R-up(2)), Middx Summer Cup, Ashford Cup R-up. *Hounslow: FA Amtr Cup R-up 61-62 (SF 53-54), Hellenic Lg R-up 85-86 (Lg Cup 85-86), Gt Western Suburban Lg 24-25, Spartan Lg 45-46, West London Lg 1895-96, FA Vase 5th Rd 87-88.*

FLACKWELL HEATH

Chairman: D Smith **Vice Chairman:** W J Tapping **President:** Ken Crook
Secretary: Cyril Robinson, 5 Chapman Lane, Flackwell Heath, High Wycombe, Bucks HP10 9AZ (0628 526204).
Ground: Wilks Park, Heath End Rd, Flackwell Heath, High Wycombe, Bucks HP10 9EA (0628 523892).
Directions: M40 jct 4, follow A404 towards High Wycombe, 1st turning into Daws Hill Lane, continue for 2 miles until you see signs for the club, left into Magpie Lane, ground at rear of Magpie (PH). Bus 301 either from bus station or High Street near bottom of Crendon Street which comes from BR station. Ask for Oakland Way.
Capacity: 2,000 **Seats:** 150 **Cover:** Yes **Floodlights:** Yes **Founded:** 1907
Club Shop: No **Metal Badges:** No **Programme:** Yes **Editor:** Donna Burton (0628 520987).
Colours: Red/white/red **Change colours:** Yellow/black/yellow **Sponsors:** TBA
Midweek Matches: Tuesday. **Reserve Team's League:** Middx County
Record. win: 6-0 v Clapton & v Petersfield (both away) **Record defeat:** 0-6 v Royston (A).
Best FA Cup season: 2nd Qualifying Round replay 1990-91 (lost 0-3 at Grays after 2-2 draw).
Previous Leagues: Wycombe & District/ Gt Western Comb./ Hellenic 76-82/ Athenian 82-84.
Record Gate: 4,500 v Oxford U., charity game 1986 (competitive: 700 v Aldershot Town, 27/10/92).
Clubhouse: Open every night 6.30-11pm and before and after matches. Hot food in tea bar.
Club Record Scorer: Tony Woods **Club Record Appearamces:** Tony Woods.
Hons: Gt Western Combination 57-58 62-63, Hellenic Lg Div 1 R-up 76-77, Berks & Bucks Snr Cup SF 85-86.

HAREFIELD UNITED

Chairman: Mr Dave West **President:** Mr Ivor Mitchell
Secretary: Terry Devereux, 132 Organ Hall Rd, Boreham Wood WD6 4TL (081 207 0324).
Manager: Dave Finn **Assistant Manager:** Bill Dowd
Press Off.: Les Wiggins (0895 822254) **Physio:** Alan Carpenter, John Godfrey.
Ground: Preston Park, Breakespeare Rd, North Harefield, Middx UB9 6DG (0895 823474).
Directions: M25 jct 17, follow signs to Swakely corner then to Harefield A40. Denham (BR). Bus 347 from Watford.
Capacity: 2,000 **Seats:** 150 **Cover:** Yes **Floodlights:** Yes **Founded:** 1868
Colours: Red & white/black/red **Change colours:** Sky & navy.
Club Shop: No **Metal Badges:** Yes **Sponsors:**
Programme: 12-40 pages, 30p **Editor:** Eric Findall.
Midweek Matchday: Tuesday **Previous Leagues:** Uxbridge & Dist./ Gt Western Comb. 46-64/ Parthenon 64-68/ Middx 68-75/ Athenian 75-84.
Reserve Team's League: Suburban **Record Gate:** 430 v Bashley, FA Vase. **Nickname:** Hares.
Best FA Cup year: 2nd Qual. Rd replay 80-81 (lost 1-5 at Maidenhead), 86-87 (0-2 at Aylesbury).
Clubhouse: (0895 823474). Lunchtimes and evenings. Two bars, cold snacks (hot on matchdays).
Local Newspapers: Watford Observer, Harefield Gazette, Sports Weekly.
Local Radio: Hillingdon Hospital, Chiltern.
Hons: Middx Premier Cup 85-86, Athenian Lg R-up 83-84, Parthenon Lg 64-65 (Div 1 Cup 65-66), Middx Lg 66-67 68-69 69-70 70-71 (Lg Cup 66-67 68-69).

HARLOW TOWN

Chairman: Giorgio Di-Benedetto.
Secretary: Ron Bruce, 26 Monksbury, Harlow, Essex CM18 7TA (0279 431883).
Manager: Len Glover **Assistant Manager:** Bobby Kellard
Physio: Malcolm Roddy **Press Officer:** Colin Barratt (0279 651470).
Ground: Harlow Sports Centre, Hammarskjold Rd, Harlow CM20 2JF (0279 445319).
Directions: Near town centre, 10 mins walk from Harlow (BR) station.
Capacity: 10,000 **Cover:** 500 **Seats:** 400 **Floodlights:** Yes **Founded:** 1879.
Cols: Blue & black stripes/black/blue **Change colours:** White/black/white. **Nickname:** Hawks.
Programme: 28 pages, 50p **Editor:** Phil Tuson (0279 416743) **Club Shop:** No.
Previous Leagues: East Herts (pre-1932)/ Spartan 32-39 46-54/ London 54-61/ Delphian 61-63/ Athenian 63-73/ Isthmian 73-92/ inactive 92-93.
Previous Grounds: Harlow College, Marigolds 1919-22/ Green Man Field 22-60.
Midweek home matchday: Wednesday. **Reserve's League:** Essex & Herts Border Comb.
Record Attendance: 9,723 v Leicester, FA Cup 3rd Rd replay 8/1/80.
Best FA Cup season: 4th Rd 79-80 (lost 3-4 at Watford). Also 1st Rd 80-81 81-82.
League clubs defeated in FA Cup: Southend, Leicester 79-80.
Record win: 12-0 v Hertford Athletic (H), East Herts League 5/10/29.
Record defeat: 0-11 v Ware (A), Spartan League Division One (East) 6/3/48.
Players progressing to Football League: Jeff Wood (Charlton 1975), Neil Prosser (B'mouth 1980)
Club Record Goalscorer: Jeff Wood (45 in 88-89)
Club Record Appearances: Norman Gladwin (646 1949-70)
Clubhouse: Open daily 11am-11pm (10.30 Sundays). Three function rooms, hot & cold food, pool table, satellite TV, Childrens play area.
Local Press: Harlow Citizen (451698), Harlow Star (420333), Harlow Herald & Post (0279 655225).
Local Radio Stations: Essex Radio, BBC Essex.
Captain 93-94: Gary Seymour **P.O.Y. 93-94:** Micky Dingwall **Top Scorer 93-94:** Marc Salmon 15.
Honours: FA Amtr Cup 2nd Rd 72-73, FA Tphy 2nd Rd(2) 80-82, FA Vase 3rd Rd 88-89, Isthmian Lg Div 1 78-79 (R-up 82-83, Div 2 Nth 88-89, Yth Cup 77-78), Ath'n Lg Div 1 71-72, E Angl. Cup 89-90, Knight F'lit Cup R-up 87-88, Essex Snr Cup 78-79, Essex F'lit Competition R-up 71-72, London Lg Chal. Cup 59-60, Spartan Lg Cup 52-53, Epping Hosp. Cup(3) 46-49, Essex & Herts Border Comb Cup 75-76, Fred Budden Tphy 88-89 89-90, Chelmsford Yth Lg 86-87 (Lg Cup 86-87 87-88).

HERTFORD TOWN

President: Bernard Molloy **Chairman:** John Hedley **Vice Chairman:** Graham Wood.
Secretary: Stephen Hedley, 28 Cherry Tree Green, Hertford SG14 2HP (0992 587011).
Manager: Paul Reynolds **Asst Manager:** S Osgood **Coach:**
Press Officer: Graham Wood **Comm. Mgr:** Peter Slade **Physio:** Ray Price
Ground: Hertingfordbury Park, West Street, Hertford (0992 5837011).
Directions: Rail to Hertford Nth (from Moorgate) or Hertford East (Liverpool Str.); both 15 mins walk. Green Line bus to town centre then 10 mins walk. By road; off bypass heading east, turn off at Ford garage.
Capacity: 6,500 **Seats:** 200 **Cover:** 1,500 **Floodlights:** Yes **Founded:** 1908
Colours: All royal blue **Change colours:** All red
Club Shop: Club souvenirs available from Graham Showell, 5 Beehive Lane, Welwyn Garden City AL7 4BB.
Midweek Matches: Tuesday. **Nickname:** The Blues **Sponsors:** None
Previous Leagues: Herts Co./ Spartan 21-47 48-59/ Delphian 59-63/ Athenian 63-72/ Eastern Co's 72-73.
Programme: 28 pages, 30p **Programme Editor:** Graham Showell (0707 327859).
Reserve Team's League: Essex & Herts Border Comb.
Programme Editor: Graham Wood (assisted by Stephen Hendley/ Graham Showell).
Best FA Cup year: Fourth Qualifying Rd 73-74 (lost 1-2 at Hillingdon Borough).
Record Gate: 5,000 v Kingstonian, FA Amateur Cup 2nd Rd 55-56.
Players progressing to Football League: G Mazzon (Aldershot)
Clubhouse: Old clubhouse burnt down in 1992. New clubhouse due to open at start of 1994-95 season.
93-94 Captain: Jon Meakes **93-94 Top Scorer:** David Whitemead.
P.O.Y. 93-94: Bryan Hammatt **Club record appearances:** Robbie Burns.
Local Newspapers: Hertfordshire Mercury
Hons: Herts Charity Cup 72-73, Herts Snr Cup 66-67, Hertford Charity Shield 19-20 20-21 35-36 49-50 55-56 59-60, Eastern Co's Lg Cup 72-73, East Anglian Cup 62-63 69-70, Southern Co's Combination Floodlit Cup 93-94, Mithras Cup SF 85-86.

HORNCHURCH

Chairman: James Bradshaw **Vice Chairman:** K Nicholls.
Secretary: Mr Edward Harris, 13 Claremont Gdns, Upminster, Essex RM14 1DW (0402 227891).
Manager: Keith Newman **Asst Mgr & Coach:** John Kerslake
Press Officer: Robert Monger (0702 460539) **Physio:** D Edkins.
Commercial Manager: P O'Connor
Ground: The Stadium, Bridge Avenue, Upminster, Essex RM14 2LX (0402 220080).
Directions: Fenchurch Street to Upminster (BR) then 10 mins walk. Or tube to Upminster Bridge (LT), right outside station, 2nd right into Bridge Ave., ground 150yds on right. By road Bridge Avenue is off A124 between Hornchurch and Upminster. Buses 248, 348, 370, 373 from Romford or Upminster BR stations.
Capacity: 3,500 **Seats:** 300 **Cover:** 350 **Floodlights:** Yes **Founded:** 1923
Colours: White (red trim)/white/white **Change colours:** All sky.
Club Shop: Yes, selling programmes, handbooks, scarves, hats, souvenirs etc. Contact Ron Quantock, 120 The Avenue, Hornchurch, Essex RM12 4JC (0708 455529).
Programme: 16-20 pages with admission **Programme Editor:** F Hawthorn (0708 225451).
Midweek Matchday: Tuesday **Previous Ground:** Upminster Rec.
Previous Leagues: Romford 1925-38/ Spartan 38-52/ Delphian 52-59/ Athenian 59-75.
Previous Names: Hornchurch & Upminster (Upminster FC pre-1950s) merged with Upminster Wanderers in 1961.
Reserve Team's League: Essex & Herts Border Comb. **Nickname:** Urchins.
Sponsors: Premier Snacks **Record Gate:** 3,000 v Chelmsford, FA Cup 66-67.
Best FA Cup year: 4th Qualifying Rd 66-67, lost 0-4 at home to Chelmsford City.
Clubhouse: Mon-Fri 7.30-11pm, Sat noon-11pm, Sun noon-3pm. Bar snacks only (crisps, peanuts etc), but cafeteria open matchdays within ground.
Players progressing to Football League: D Armstrong (Millwall), R Lee (Charlton), Nicky Bissett (Brighton).
Local Press: Romford Recorder (0708 766044) **Local Radio:** Beds Radio.
Hons: Athenian Lg 66-67, Romford Lg(2), Essex Snr Cup R-up 86-87, Essex Jnr Cup, Essex Thamesside Tphy 84-85, F.A. Vase 5th Rd 74-75, Isthmian Yth Cup.

Henry Rios of Hertford (dark shirt) halts a run from Hornchurch's Lee O'Conner. *Photo - Rob Monger*

HORSHAM

Chairman: Maureen Smith **President:** G G Holtom
Secretary: Frank King, 51 Laughton Rd, Horsham, West Sussex RH21 4EJ (0403 64647).
Manager: Mark Dunk **Asst Manager:** None **Coach:**
Physio: Geoff Britton **Press Officer/Commercial Manager:** Pete Tanner (0403 252310).
Ground: Queen Street, Horsham RH13 5AD (0403 65787).
Directions: From Brighton Rd proceed into Queen Street towards town centre - ground entrance opposite Queens Head. 10 mins walk from Horsham (BR) station; along North Street past Arts Centre, fork left, left at lights, ground opposite Queens Head. Buses 107, 137, 2, 283 to Horsham Carfax then thru East Street under Iron Bridge and turn left.
Capacity: 4,300 **Seats:** 300 **Cover:** 1,800 **Nickname:** Hornets **Founded:** 1885
Colours: Amber/green/amber **Change colours:** All white.
Club Sponsors: Sun Alliance **Club Shop:** Yes. Contact Maurice Shevlin (0403 242863).
Programme: 40 pages, 65p **Editor:** Maurice Shevlin (0403 242863).
Midweek Matchday: Tuesday **Previous Ground:** Horsham Park.
Previous Leagues: W Sussex/ Sussex County 26-51/ Metropolitan 51-57/ Corinthian 57-63/ Athenian 63-73.
Reserve's Lge: Sussex Co. Res. sect. **Record Gate:** 8,000 v Swindon, FA Cup, November 1966.
Best FA Cup year: 1st Rd 47-48 (lost 1-9 at Notts County), 66-67 (lost 0-3 v Swindon).
Clubhouse: Normal licensing hours. Hot and cold snacks, dancehall, darts.
93-94 Captain: Mark Chaplain **93-94 P.o.Y.:** Martyn Patching **93-94 Top scorer:** Paul Harris 17.
Local Press: West Sussex County Times: Market Square, Horsham (0403 53371).
Hons: Sussex Snr Cup 33-34 38-39 49-50 53-54 71-72 73-74 75-76, Sussex RUR Charity Cup 1899-1900 30-31 31-32 33-34(jt with Worthing) 34-35 35-36 36-37 37-38(jt with Southwick) 45-46 48-49(jt with Worthing) 50-51 51-52 56-57, Sussex County Lg 31-32 32-33 34-35 35-36 36-37 37-38 46-47 (R-up 29-30 30-31 47-48 48-49, Lg Cup 45-46 46-47), Metropolitan Lg 51-52, Athenian Lg Div 2 72-73.

KINGSBURY TOWN

Chairman: Allan J Davies **Vice Chairman:** Paul Blackman.
Secretary: Peter Green, 57 Wembley Park Drive, Wembley, Middx HA9 8HE (081 902 1561).
Manager/Coach: Davin Finn **General Manager/Coach:** Peter Blain
Physio: Margaret Romer **Press Officer:** Allan Davies (0895 443761)
Ground: Silver Jubilee Park, Townsend Lane, Kingsbury, London NW9 0DE (081 205 1645-club, 5204-boardroom).
Directions: Underground to Kingsbury, cross road and take bus 183 to Townsend Lane (2 miles) - ground in far left-hand corner of Silver Jubilee Park.
Capacity: 4,000 **Seats:** 165 **Cover:** 250 **Nickname:** Kings **Founded:** 1927
Colours: Royal/white/royal **Change colours:** Yellow/navy/yellow.
Club Shop: Yes, selling club ties, pennants, metal badges - contact Allan Davies (0895 443761).
Programme: 16-20 pages, 50p **Editor:** Danny Armitt.
Midweek Matchday: Tuesday **Sponsors:** VPA Entertainment Technology.
Previous Leagues: Hellenic 27-30 (as Davis Sports)/ Willesden & District 30-43/ Middx Snr 44-47/ Parthenon 47-59/ Spartan 59-76 78-81/ Athenian 76-78 81-84.
Previous Name: Davis Sports **Reserve Team's League:** Suburban
Record win: 8-0 v Eastbourne U., 91-92. **Record Gate:** 1,300 v Wealdstone, FA Amateur Cup 1971.
Best FA Cup year: 3rd Qualifying Round 87-88 (lost 0-1 at home to Leytonstone-Ilford).
Record Fees - Paid: £500 **Received:** £600.
Clubhouse: (081 205 1645). Mon-Fri 7-11pm, Sat noon-11pm, Sun noon-2.30 & 7-10.30. Pool, darts, dancehall, food on matchdays.
Players progressing to Football League: Billy Dare (Brentford & West Ham, John Meadows, Dave Underwood, Dwight Marshall (Plymouth (via Grays Ath.)).
Club Record Appearances: Mick Coffey (goalkeeper).
P.o.Y. 93-94: Chris Simpson **Top Scorer & Captain 93-94:** Mark Ivers (18 goals).
Local Press: Harrow Observer, Willesden Chronicle, Allsport Weekly, Edgware & Finchley Times.
Hons: FA Vase 4th Rd 74-75, Isthmian Lg Div 2 Nth R-up 85-86, Spartan Lg Cup R-up 59-60 64-65, Parthenon Lg 51-52 (Prem Charity Cup 52-53 53-54, Snr Charity Cup 53-54), Middx Snr Cup R-up 88-89, Middx Charity Cup 85-86 (R-up 88-89), Middx Lg Charity Cup(3) 44-47, Willesden & Dist. Lg R-up 30-31 (Div 2 34-35).

Below: *Kingsbury Town 1993-94.*

LEIGHTON TOWN

Chairman: Bill Harrison **President:** Mike Hide.
Secretary: Alec Irvine, 12 Rowley Furrows, Linslade, Leighton Buzzard, Beds LU7 7SH (0525 376475).
Manager: Frank O'Brien **Physio:** George Lathwell
Commercial Manager: Richard Harding **Press Officer:** Ian McGregor (0525 370142).
Ground: Bell Close, Lake Street, Leighton Buzzard, Beds (0525 373311).
Directions: From bypass (A505) take A4146 (Billington Rd) towards Leighton Buzzard, straight over mini-r'bout & 1st left into car park - ground behind Camden Motors just before town centre. Half mile from Leighton Buzzard (BR) station. Buses from Luton, Aylesbury and Milton Keynes.
Capacity: 2,500 **Seats:** 155 **Cover:** 750 **Floodlights:** Yes **Founded:** 1885
Colours: Red & white **Change colours:** All blue **Nickname:** Reds.
Club Shop: Yes, selling badges, shirts, pennants, programmes, mugs.
Programme: 50p **Editor:** Ian McGregor (0525 370142). **Metal badges:** Yes.
Midweek Matchday: Tuesday **Sponsors:** Camden Motors.
Previous Leagues: Leighton & District/ South Midlands 22-24 26-29 46-54 55-56 76-92/ Spartan 22-53 67-74/ United Counties 74-76.
Previous Name: Leighton United **Previous Grounds:** None.
Reserve Team's League: South Midlands Lge Reserve Division. **Record win:** 7-2.
Record Gate: 1,522 v Aldershot T., Isthmian Lg Div 3, 30/1/93 **Record defeat:** 1-6.
Best FA Cup year: Third Qualifying Rounds 70-71, lost 1-2 at St Albans City.
Clubhouse: Normal licensing hours. Snack/refreshment bar on matchdays - full rang of hot snacks & drinks.
93-94 Captain: Paul Firth **93-94 P.o.Y.:** Ken Hollis **93-94 Top scorer:** Steven Drewe.
Local Press: Leighton Buzzard Observer/ The Herald/ The Citizen.
Local Radio: Three Counties Radio/ Radio Chiltern.
Hons: Sth Midlands Lg 66-67 91-92 (Lg Cup 90-91, O'Brien Tphy 90-91, Reserve Div 1 87 88 91-92, Reserve Div 2 76-77, Reserve Challenge Cup 93-94), Beds Snr Cup 26-27 67-68 68-69 69-70 92-93, Spartan Lg Div 2 23-24 27-28, Leighton & District Lg, Beds Intermediate Cup(res) 90-91, Beds Yth Cup 91-92 92-93, Chiltern Yth Lg Cup 93-94.

LEWES

Chairman: P Brook **President:** W D Carr, Esq
Secretary: Mr John Lewis, Marshlands, Kingston Rd, Lewes, East Sussex BN7 3NB (0273 472822).
Manager: Gary Allen **Asst Manager:** **Coach:**
Press Officer: **Commercial Manager:** **Physio:**
Ground: The Dripping Pan, Mountfield Road, Lewes BN7 1XN (0273 472574).
Directions: Two minute walk from Lewes (BR) - turn left out of station and left into Mountfield Road. Ground 100 yards on right.
Capacity: 5,000 **Cover:** 400 **Seats:** 400 **Nickname:** Rooks **Founded:** 1885
Metal Badges: Yes **Club Shop:** Yes.
Colours: Black & red hoops/black/red **Change colours:** Yellow/blue
Sponsors: Nico Construction Ltd **Record Gate:** 2,500 v Newhaven, Sussex County Lg 26/12/47.
Programme: 32 pages, 50p **Programme Editor:** Steve Kitchener (0273 475228).
Previous Leagues: Mid Sussex 1886-1920/ Sussex County 20-65/ Athenian 65-77.
Midweek home matchday: Tuesday **Reserve Team's League:** Sussex Co. reserve section.
Best FA Cup season: 4th Qualifying Rd (lost to Harwich & Parkeston)
Record Fees - Paid: **Received:** £2,500 for Grant Horscroft (Brighton)
Players progressing to Football League: *(to Brighton unless stated)* Don Bates (1950), Peter Knight (1964), Terry Stanley (1969), Colin Woffuden (1970), G Elphick & Steve Ford (Stoke 1981), Glen Geard, Grant Hrscroft (1987), J Hammond (Fulham), S Funnell, L Allen (Wimbledon), M Rice (Watford).
Clubhouse: (0273 472100). Bar, tea bar, pool, table tennis. **Steward:** P Brook.
Local Newspapers (+Tel.Nos.): Evening Argus, Sussex Express.
Local Radio Stations: BBC Radio Sussex, Southern Sound.
Honours: Isth. Lg Div 2 R-up 79-80 91-92, Ath'n Lg Div 1 69-70 (Div 2 67-68), Sussex Co. Lg 64-65 (R-up 24-25 33-34 58-59 63-64, Lg Cup 39-40), Mid Sussex Lg 10-11 13-14, Sussex Snr Cup 64-65 70-71 84-85 (R-up 79-80 82-83 87-88), Sussex Royal Ulster Rifles Charity Cup(3) 61-63 64-65, Gilbert Rice F'lit Cup 82-83 88-89, Neale Tphy 68-69, Sussex F'lit Cup 76-77 (SF 83-84), Southern Counties Comb Div 1 80-81, FA Tphy 1st Rd 82-83, FA Amtr Cup 2nd Rd 67-68, FA Vase 1st Rd 79-80.

Below: *Lewes FC 1993-94* *Photo - Eric Marsh.*

NORTHWOOD

Chairman: Andy Johnson **Vice Chairman:** Geoff Foster **President:** Lothar Hahn
Secretary: Steve Williams, 35 Evelyn Drive, Hatch End, Pinner, Middx HA5 4RL (081 428 1533 - home + fax).
Manager: John Walsh **Physio:** George Price
Coach: John Downey/John Toogood.
Commercial Mgr: Martin Ellis. **Press Officer:** Mick Russell (0923 827690)
Ground: Northwood Park, Chestnut Avenue, Northwood (0923 827148).
Directions: A404 (Pinner-Rickmansworth) - Chestnut Ave. on left by large grey iron railway bridge and Shell petrol station. Third of a mile from Northwood Hills station (Metropolitan Line) - turn right out of station to r'bout, left into Pinner Rd, left into Chestnut Ave. by Shell petrol station after 300yds. Buses 282 and H11 to Northwood Hills.
Capacity: 2,000 **Seats:** 150 **Cover:** 200 **Floodlights:** Yes **Founded:** 1907.
Colours: All red **Change colours:** Yellow & green **Midweek Matches:** Tuesday
Programme: 30 pages, 70p **Editor:** Alan Evans (081 566 2880) **Club Shop:** No
Reserve Team's League: Suburban **Sponsors:** IFS Freight Forwarding **Nickname:** Woods.
Previous Leagues: Harrow & Wembley 32-49/ Middx 49-78/ Hellenic 79-84/ London Spartan 84-92.
Previous Grounds: None. **Previous Names:** Northwood Town
Record Gate: 914 v Aldershot Town, Isthmian League Division Three, 16/1/93.
Best FA Vase year: 4th Rd 91-92. **Best FA Cup year:** Prel. Rd(4) 89-93.
Clubhouse: Weekends and most evenings from 6pm. Bar. Hot and cold food. Pool, darts, juke-box.
Players progressing to Football League: Gavin McGuire (Portsmouth).
Club Record Scorer: Garfield Blackman **Club Record Appearances:** Peter Lammin
93-94 Captain: Troy McAuliffe **93-94 P.o.Y & Top scorer:** Martin Randall.
Local Newspapers: Ruislip & Northwood Gazette, Allsport Weekly
Hons: Isthmian Lg Associate Members Cup 92-93, London Spartan Lg 91-92 (R-up 89-90, Lg Cup 89-90 91-92), Hellenic Lg Div 1 78-79 (Prem Div Cup R-up 81-82, Div 1 78-79), Middx Lg 77-78 (R-up 72-73 76-77, Div 1 R-up 71-72, Challenge Cup 74-75 76-77 77-78), Middx Snr Charity Cup R-up 93-94, Middx Snr Cup SF 91-92 92-93, Middx Jnr Cup 46-47 47-48 48-49, Harrow & Wembley Lg 31-32 32-33 33-34 34-35 35-36 36-37 46-47 47-48 48-49.

Northwood FC 1993-94. Back Row (L/R): George Price, Ray Bennett, Greg Phillips, Steve Matthews, Eddie Doyle (Physio), Eddie Coppinger, John Toogood (Coach), Rob Holland, Jason Delicata, Alan Merison (Manager). Front: Kevin Dobson, Lawrence Holmes, Steve Payton, Paul Rogan, Martin Randall, Troy McAuliffe.

SOUTHALL

Chairman: J J Loftus **President:** R E Fowler
Secretary: Maria Smith, 22 Barchester Rd, Harrow Weald, Middx HA3 5HH (081 863 6888).
Manager: TBA **Assistant Manager:** TBA **Coach:**
Press Officer: Chairnan **Physio:** George Richardson
Ground: Tring Town FC (see page 509). Southall will move to their own new ground in the next two years.
Ground directions & details: As Tring Town **Founded:** 1871
Colours: Red & white **Change colours:** Grey & white **Nickname:** Fowlers
Club Shop: No **Metal Badges:** No
Programme: 6 pages, 50p **Programme Editor:** Secretary **Record win:** 7-1
Midweek Matchday: Tuesday **Sponsors:** Longwood Builders **Record loss:** 0-8
Reserve Team's League: Middx County. **Record Gate:** 17,000 v Watford, FA Cup 3rd Rd 1935.
Previous Leagues: Southern 1896-1905/ Gt Western Suburban/ Herts & Middx/ Athenian 19-73.
Previous Grounds: Western Road 1871-1992/ Harefield Utd FC 92-94.
Previous Name: Southall & Ealing Borough 1975-80.
Best F.A. Cup year: 3rd Round 35-36 (lost 1-4 at home to Watford). Also 1st Rd 25-26 27-28 28-29 36-37 55-56.
League clubs defeated in FA Cup: Swindon Town 35-36.
Record Fees - Paid: **Received:** £5,000 for Alan Devonshire.
Players progressing to Football League: Alan Devonshire (West Ham), Gordon Hill (Millwall, Manchester Utd, Derby), Chris Hutchings (Chelsea, Brighton), Roger Joseph (Brentford), Les Ferdinand (QPR & England).
Clubhouse: Normal pub hours. Hot snacks available on matchdays.
Club Record Scorer: Steve Fraser **Record Appearances:** Hammid Harrak (from Youth team on).
Local Radio: Capital. **Local Press:** Ealing Gazette, Allsports Weekly.
Hons: FA Amtr Cup R-up 24-25 (SF 25-26 52-53), FA Vase R-up 85-86, Isthmian Lg Div 2 R-up 74-75, Gt Western Suburban Lg 12-13, Athenian Lg 26-27 (R-up 54-55), Middx Snr Cup(12) 07-08 10-11 11-12 12-13 22-23 23-24 24-25 26-27 36-37 44-45 53-54 54-55, Middx Charity Cup 10-11 11-12 13-14 22-23(jt with Botwell Mission) 23-24(jt with Botwell Mission) 27-28 36-37 51-52 68-69 83-84, London Snr Cup SF 35-36 84-85.

TRING TOWN

Chairman: Mr Roger Payne **President:** Mr G Smith.
Secretary: Mr Roger Payne, High Meadow Farm, Chivery, St Leonards, nr Tring (0296 630401).
Manager: Derek Mardle **Asst Manager:** Pat Lynch **Coach:** Pat Lynch
Physio: N/A **Press Officer:** Alan Lee **Commercial Mgr:** Secretary.
Ground: Pendley Sports Centre, Cow Lane, Tring, Herts HP23 5NS (0442 23075).
Directions: One mile from Tring centre on A41 - direct connection to M25 (jct 20) via new A41 bypass. One and a half miles from Tring (BR). Numerous buses from station and Watford-Aylesbury routes serve ground.
Capacity: 2,500 **Seats:** 200 **Cover:** 230 **Floodlights:** Yes **Founded:** 1904
Club Shop: No **Metal Badges:** No **Record win:** 12-0 **Record loss:** 1-9
Colours: Red/white/red **Change colours:** All blue. **Nickname:** Tee's.
Programme: 40p **Programme Editor:** Alan Lee.
Sponsors: Market Auto Centre.
Midweek Matchday: Monday **Reserve Team's League:** No reserve team.
Previous Leagues: Gt Western Combination/ Spartan 53-75/ Athenian 75-77.
Previous Names: None **Prev. Ground:** Tring Cricket Ground (40 yrs).
Record Attendance: 2,500 v West Ham United, friendly. Competitive game: 2,000 for Aylesbury United v Slough Town, FA Cup First Round replay, 1986.
Best FA Cup year: 3rd Qualifying Rd replay 84-85, lost 0-5 at Fisher after 1-1 draw.
Clubhouse: All licensing hours. Dancehall, pool, darts, kitchen.
Players progressing to Football League: Peter Gibbs (Watford).
Club Record Scorer: Gary Harthill **Club Record Appearances:** Gary Harthill.
93-94 Captain: Michael Thomas **93-94 P.o.Y.:** Isaac Fevrier. **93-94 Top scorer:** Chris Campbell.
Local Press: Bucks Herald, Tring Gazette, Watford Observer.
Local Radio: Chiltern, BBC Radio Bedford.
Hons: Spartan Lg 66-67, Herts Charity Shield (many times), Athenian Lg Div 2 R-up 76-77, Herts Snr Cup R-up.

Below: *Rupert Nelson lifts the ball over goalkeeper Lee Brown to put Hornchurch one up at Tring Town. However, the home side fight back to win 5-1.*

Photo - Robert Monger.

Compelling action from last season's Diadora Premier Division derby fixture between Marlow (dark shirts and shorts) and Aylesbury United at the Alfred Davis Memorial Ground.

Photo - Andrew Donnison.

HEREWARD SPORTS UNITED COUNTIES LEAGUE

FEEDER TO:
BEAZER HOMES LEAGUE

FOUNDED: 1895

Chairman: T N Bates

Hon. Secretary: R J Gamble, 8 Bostock Avenue, Northampton NN1 4LW.

ROTHWELL RETAIN THE CROWN

Rothwell Town retained the championship of the Hereward Sports United Counties League, the first side to win back-to-back Premier titles since Stamford in 1982. The Bones enjoyed a record breaking campaign. Their 105 points and 34 wins were new highs for the 99-year-old league, while their 114 league goals, matched by runners-up Stotfold, were new Premier Division bests. Add a second successive Benevolent Cup success, a Reserve Division One and Cup double and a second Manager of the Year award for long-serving boss Jack Murray, and Rothwell have few challengers for the accolade of 'Team of the Year'.

It wasn't a runaway title win for Rothwell. They needed to put together a fifteen match run without defeat to end the season to pull away from Stotfold, revitalised under former Arsenal player Ian Allinson, and 1992 champions Northampton Spencer whose fixture backlog eventually proved a hurdle too many to surmount. The Millers finished the season in third place, one ahead of near neighbours Cogenhoe who enjoyed their best-ever top flight campaign.

At the bottom of the table, Brackley occupied the basement place for a third successive season and, although they did record a couple of victories this time round, their goals against tally set new heights - 215 in 42 matches. Four managers during the season failed to turn the tide and the Saints will be looking to regroup in the Hellenic League next term. Also leaving the Premier Division are Daventry who have opted to return to Division One afer three years in the top flight, that despite finishing out of the relegation positions. Kempston finished next to bottom in the Premier with the lack of goal power the major problem at Hillgrounds. The Walnut Boys, none-the-less continue in membership of the top flight for next season.

In Division One, newcomers Vanaid, the first graduates of the League's feeder system, stormed to the championship seven points clear of perennial runners-up Higham, who took the runners-up medals for the fourth time in five seasons. Third place went to Olney, their best season since being demoted to Division One in 1980, while fourth placed ON Chenecks also enjoyed their best season in years.

Northampton Spencer's reward for another good season was Knockout Cup glory. They beat

Rothwell Town - Hereward Sports United Counties League champions 1993-94. Back Row (L/R): Dave Kenney, Dave McHutchison, Chris Munns, Shaun McPolin, Bernie Geoghegan, John Coe, Simon Munns, Kevin McDonald, Chris Lund, Barry Price, Adie Spencer. Centre: Dick Dighton (Goalkeeping Coach), Mark Southon (Programme Editor), Peter Cassell (Treasurer), Nigel Bates, Ryan Smythe, Glyn Davies, Neil Edwards, Chris Miller, Danny Liquorish, Andy Wright, Stewart Marshall, Grant Mawby, Graham Simmonds (First Team Assistant Manager), Bob Mullan (Youth Team Manager), Roger Barratt (Secretary), Jeremy Freestone (Vice-Chairman). Front: Mick Callaghan, Andy Pawluk (Joint Reserve Team Managers), Adrian Sheerin, Kevin Shoemake, Mike Bearcroft (both NPS, main club sponsors), Stuart Andrews (Chairman), Jack Murray (First Team Manager), Les Hornby, Kim Davies (Coach), Peter Bradley (Press Officer). Seated: Shaun Wills, Mark Humphrey, John Mason, Gary Chambers (Mascot), Paul Murphy, Tommy Manson.

Photo - Peter Barnes

Raunds 5-1 over two legs to take the silverware to Kingsthorpe Mill for a second time. The tournament saw Vanaid collect two Premier scalps while Higham, ON Chenecks and Whitworth also ousted top flight opposition.

Highlight of the season in outside competitions was Boston's run to the last four of the FA Chgallenge Vase, the first time in ten years that one of our clubs had progressed so far. Taunton spoilt the Poachers' Wembley dream but over the years this competition has thrown up a number of clubs who have overcome the disappointment of missing out at the final hurdle to book a Wembley place the season after. Perhaps 1994-95 will be Boston's year. In the FA Cup, Raunds reached the Third Round Qualifying where they lost 4-0 to Conference club Telford, the second consecutive season the Shopmates had reached this stage.

On the County Cup scene, Stotfold won the Bedfordshire Senior Cup for the first time in 29 years, beating Premier Division rivals Potton 2-1 to lift the trophy. Potton found some consolation in becoming joint winners of the Hunts Premier Cup when their scheduled final with Biggleswade was postponed and no alternative venue could be found. Northampton Spencer contested their second Northants Hillier Senior Cup final but were well beaten 5-0 by a rampant Rushden & Diamonds side at Nene Park, but the County's Junior Cup was won by Vanaid who pipped local rivals ON Chenecks 1-0 at the County Ground.

Having looked back briefly at the events of 1993/94, we now look forward to the new season which sees the league celebrate its Centenary. The occasion will be marked by a number of special events; a centenary dinner, a series of representative fixtures and the publication of a commemorative brochure. Joining us in this special season are Dunstable who have opted to leave the Beazer Homes League for financial reasons and a famous old name, St Neots Town. The loss of their ground a few seasons back saw the Saints leave the league but they reformed four years ago and have reeled off four successive Huntingdonshire League titles. A move to a fine new purpose-built stadium coupled with that on-field success has given them the chance to return to the Hereward Sports United Counties League.

Jeremy Biggs, Press Liaison Officer

1994 HEREWARD SPORTS UNITED COUNTIES LEAGUE REVIEW

(Available from September 1994 - Price: £3.25 inc. p. & p.)

The book contains club reviews, statistics, a club directory and dozens of team and action photos.

The Review is obtainable from Roger Gamble,
8 Bostock Avenue, Northampton NN1 4LW.
Cheques payable to the Hereward Sports United Counties League

GET ALL THE LEAGUE ACTION, PHONE

HEREWARD SPORTS
UNITED COUNTIES LEAGUE
NEWSLINE

0891 122 960

☎ 24 hours EVERY day ☎ Updated daily ☎ News from around the League
☎ Features, reviews and results ☎ The official **United Counties League** information service

Marketed by Sportslines (0386) 47302 Presented by Jeremy Biggs (0533) 702917

Calls cost 39p per minute cheap rate and 49p per minute at all other times.
Call costing correct at time of going to press.

PREM. DIVISION	P	W	D	L	F	A	PTS
Rothwell Town	42	34	3	5	114	38	105
Stotfold	42	31	5	6	114	48	98
N'pton Spencer	42	26	8	8	99	55	86
Cogenhoe United	42	25	6	11	93	55	81
Raunds Town	42	24	8	10	93	55	80
Mirrlees B'stone	42	21	8	13	83	60	71
Long Buckby	42	19	13	10	83	56	70
Boston	42	21	6	15	89	56	69
Eynesbury R.	42	18	13	11	104	63	67
Holbeach United	42	18	8	16	80	81	62
Stewarts & Lloyds	42	18	7	17	67	80	61
Potton United	42	16	9	17	74	65	57
Bourne Town	42	16	9	17	87	81	57
Spalding United	42	15	10	17	71	68	55
Newport Pagnell T.	42	14	11	17	52	64	53
Wellingborough T.	42	10	11	21	62	95	41
Desborough Town	42	12	5	25	70	105	41
Wootton Blue C.	42	11	7	24	65	86	40
Stamford	42	11	6	25	56	80	39
Daventry Town	42	10	5	27	47	95	35
Kempston Rovers	42	4	10	28	39	81	22
Brackley Town	42	2	4	36	41	216	10

Prem/Div 1 Fairplay Award: Higham/ON Chenecks
Reserve Divs Fairplay Award: Olney Town Res.

DIVISION ONE	P	W	D	L	F	A	PTS
N'pton Vanaid	34	22	7	3	109	32	73
Higham Town	32	20	6	6	89	25	66
Olney Town	32	19	5	8	81	28	62
ON Chenecks	32	18	6	8	67	32	60
St Ives Town	32	16	10	6	55	32	58
Whitworths	32	16	5	11	72	59	53
Ramsey Town	32	15	4	13	66	56	49
Blisworth	32	14	4	14	57	69	46
Bugbrooke St M.	32	13	4	15	66	65	43
Cottingham	32	12	4	16	54	67	40
Burton Park Wdrs	32	11	6	15	57	65	39
British Timken	32	11	5	16	40	57	38
Thrapston Venturas	32	11	4	17	56	62	37
Sharnbrook	32	11	3	18	54	91	36
Irchester United	32	9	5	18	32	77	32
Ford Sports	32	10	1	21	53	90	31
Harrowby United	32	2	5	25	40	141	11

Reserve Div 1 champions: Rothwell Town
Reserve Div 1 runners-up: Rushden & Diamonds
Reserve Div 2 champions: Bourne Town
Reserve Div 2 runners-up: Bugbrooke St Michaels
Reserve K.O. Cup winners: Rothwell Town
Reserve K.O. Cup runners-up: Raunds Town

RESULT CHART 1993-94

HOME TEAM	1	2	3	4	5	6	7	8	9	10	11	12	13	14	15	16	17	18	19	20	21	22
1. Boston	*	2-3	4-0	3-4	5-2	6-0	2-1	3-2	2-1	2-0	2-2	0-0	1-1	1-0	0-2	0-1	1-0	2-0	4-0	1-3	2-0	3-0
2. Bourne T.	1-3	*	13-0	1-3	2-0	4-1	5-5	1-4	3-3	0-2	3-2	2-1	3-1	1-0	2-1	1-3	1-2	0-2	4-0	2-2	3-3	2-2
3. Brackley T.	1-2	2-1	*	1-6	3-2	2-2	2-10	1-3	1-5	0-5	0-11	0-0	1-8	0-5	1-5	1-3	0-4	0-2	2-2	1-2	1-5	2-8
4. Cogenhoe	2-0	4-0	4-2	*	3-0	3-0	5-3	4-2	3-1	1-0	1-2	0-1	0-2	0-1	1-0	2-1	1-1	3-1	0-5	3-3	1-0	3-2
5. Daventry T.	1-5	0-6	5-0	0-3	*	1-2	0-3	3-2	1-0	1-2	2-0	0-2	0-0	0-3	0-3	1-3	4-2	3-1	2-3	0-1	1-5	1-0
6. Desborough	2-1	1-2	4-1	2-0	2-2	*	1-1	0-1	3-1	1-1	2-8	6-3	1-3	3-2	2-3	0-1	3-4	1-3	2-4	2-6	5-0	0-1
7. Eynesbury	1-1	2-2	10-0	1-1	3-0	6-0	*	4-0	2-1	1-1	1-1	0-1	4-1	2-0	2-2	1-2	0-1	1-3	0-1	1-2	0-1	1-0
8. Holbeach	0-5	2-1	10-0	1-1	1-0	5-1	3-3	*	1-0	2-1	4-0	3-2	2-5	1-1	1-2	3-3	6-3	1-0	0-0	1-2	3-1	2-2
9. Kempston	0-1	1-2	2-0	1-3	2-3	1-1	1-4	1-0	*	0-3	1-2	0-0	1-2	0-3	1-1	0-3	1-1	2-0	2-3	0-1	0-4	0-1
10. Long Buckby	1-1	5-3	9-3	0-2	0-1	2-1	3-3	1-1	2-0	*	0-0	1-0	2-1	6-2	2-2	0-2	1-1	1-0	4-0	1-2	3-3	2-1
11. Mirrlees B.	0-3	5-0	2-1	1-4	4-1	2-1	5-2	4-1	3-1	2-1	*	1-1	3-1	2-2	3-3	3-1	0-3	0-1	2-0	1-2	1-1	2-0
12. N'pt Pagnell	0-3	3-2	2-1	2-1	0-0	1-0	2-2	0-1	1-0	2-3	1-2	*	2-2	0-0	1-2	1-1	1-2	2-1	0-2	2-1	3-2	1-2
13. N. Spencer	2-1	3-1	7-0	0-0	2-1	2-0	2-3	3-2	3-2	3-3	1-0	3-2	*	2-1	1-2	5-2	3-1	2-1	3-0	3-1	6-3	1-0
14. Potton	2-1	1-3	7-1	0-5	5-1	4-0	3-3	0-1	2-0	1-1	1-1	3-1	1-1	*	1-0	1-3	1-2	2-0	1-1	1-6	4-1	2-1
15. Raunds T.	3-3	0-1	5-0	4-1	3-2	1-2	1-0	3-1	2-0	1-3	2-0	5-1	2-2	3-1	*	1-2	1-1	3-2	4-1	2-1	2-0	4-1
16. Rothwell	4-1	1-0	9-1	3-1	3-0	2-0	0-1	7-1	4-1	3-1	0-1	2-1	1-0	2-1	3-1	*	1-0	4-1	8-0	3-0	5-0	4-0
17. Spalding	4-1	2-2	3-1	2-1	2-2	4-1	2-3	0-1	1-1	1-1	0-1	1-1	0-2	2-0	1-3	2-3	*	1-0	2-0	1-2	6-0	2-2
18. Stamford	4-3	2-2	8-3	0-4	2-1	1-3	0-1	0-0	5-1	0-1	1-2	1-2	0-0	0-5	0-4	1-2	3-2	*	2-4	1-3	2-0	0-2
19. Stewart & L.	1-0	0-1	4-0	1-4	1-0	4-1	1-3	4-0	0-0	1-1	2-0	2-2	2-3	3-1	2-1	1-4	2-1	1-1	*	1-3	2-1	2-1
20. Storfold	2-0	2-0	6-0	3-1	0-0	3-0	1-5	6-2	2-2	2-4	4-0	3-0	2-1	2-0	4-0	1-1	6-1	3-1	5-1	*	4-0	3-0
21. Well'borough	3-2	1-1	3-3	1-1	2-3	1-5	2-2	2-1	1-1	0-1	1-0	1-3	1-4	1-1	0-2	0-2	1-0	1-1	2-1	1-4	*	5-1
22. Wootton BC	0-6	2-0	7-2	1-3	4-0	2-6	1-2	1-2	1-1	3-2	1-2	0-1	0-2	1-2	2-2	1-2	3-0	2-2	3-2	1-3	2-2	*

DIV. ONE RESULTS 1993-94	1	2	3	4	5	6	7	8	9	10	11	12	13	14	15	16	17
1. Bilsworth	*	1-5	4-1	0-3	3-1	3-2	4-1	0-5	3-1	1-2	1-3	2-2	1-1	2-1	1-2	0-5	1-0
2. British Timken	3-0	*	1-2	1-4	2-1	2-1	4-1	0-2	2-0	0-2	3-1	0-3	0-3	0-0	3-0	0-0	2-0
3. Bugbrooke St Michaels	2-2	2-0	*	3-1	4-1	2-3	6-2	0-6	5-0	2-6	1-1	1-2	1-4	1-1	3-3	2-0	0-3
4. Burton Park Wanderers	1-3	4-0	1-2	*	2-3	3-2	3-0	0-4	4-1	1-1	1-1	1-2	0-2	1-2	3-3	1-3	1-1
5. Cottingham	1-0	0-1	1-0	5-3	*	2-0	2-1	1-0	0-2	1-3	0-1	0-2	3-0	0-2	4-4	3-2	0-3
6. Ford Sports	8-0	2-0	4-2	4-2	1-5	*	3-1	1-3	3-1	1-6	0-7	0-3	2-1	3-0	0-4	1-2	1-3
7. Harrowby United	3-3	0-3	1-7	1-3	0-0	1-3	*	0-8	0-5	0-0	1-4	0-4	0-2	0-2	1-3	3-2	1-7
8. Higham Town	1-2	8-0	5-1	6-1	4-2	2-0	8-0	*	0-0	2-2	2-1	1-0	5-0	2-2	2-1	1-0	2-1
9. Irchester United	0-3	3-1	1-0	0-2	3-1	4-1	2-2	1-1	*	1-3	1-2	0-5	0-3	2-1	4-0	4-2	2-3
10. Northampton Vanaid	1-0	0-0	1-3	5-1	5-1	1-1	10-1	2-1	10-0	*	4-1	3-1	3-2	6-0	7-1	2-1	8-0
11. ON Chenecks	0-1	1-0	1-0	0-0	3-3	6-1	6-0	1-0	2-2	2-0	*	2-1	4-0	0-1	4-0	1-1	4-1
12. Olney Town	5-0	2-2	2-1	4-0	2-0	9-1	7-0	0-1	4-0	3-3	0-1	*	1-0	0-1	0-1	3-0	0-2
13. Ramsey Town	0-2	6-1	0-3	0-2	3-1	5-2	13-1	2-2	0-0	1-0	0-1	3-5	*	0-2	3-2	4-3	0-4
14. St Ives Town	2-0	2-1	1-3	1-1	2-0	5-1	8-2	2-2	2-0	1-1	1-0	0-0	0-0	*	4-0	4-0	2-3
15. Sharnbrook	3-11	2-0	4-3	0-1	2-4	2-1	5-1	0-3	2-1	0-6	0-2	0-4	1-2	0-2	*	2-1	3-2
16. Thrapston Venturas	2-3	2-1	3-1	1-5	2-3	1-0	2-2	1-0	6-0	1-2	3-2	0-3	1-2	1-1	4-2	*	2-2
17. Wellingborough Whitworths	2-0	2-2	0-2	4-1	5-5	2-0	2-3	1-0	4-1	1-4	3-2	2-2	3-4	0-0	4-2	3-1	*

MANAGER OF THE MONTH AWARDS 1993-94

Month	Premier Division	Division One
Aug/Sept.	Ian Allinson (Stotfold)	Dick Underwood (Vanaid)
October	Gary Sargent (N. Spencer)	Tony Pancoust (ON Chenecks)
November	Steve Blades (Mirrless B'stone)	Dick Underwood (Vanaid)
December	Dave Conlon (Cogenhoe Utd)	Vinny Keefe (Cottingham)
January	Jack Murray (Rothwell T.)	Tony Pancoust (ON Chenecks)
February	Steve Evans (Holbeach Utd)	Gary Savage (Higham Town)
March	Jack Murray (Rothwell T.)	Ian Lawson (Burton PW)
April/May	Jack Murray (Rothwell T.)	Ian Young (Whitworths)

Manager of the Year: Jack Murray (Rothwell Town)

PREMIER DIVISION - TEN YEAR RECORD

	84/85	85/86	86/87	87/88	88/89	89/90	90/91	91/92	92/93	93/94
Ampthill Town	20	14	21	-	-	-	-	-	-	-
APV Peterborough City	-	-	-	15	17	13	11	11	-	-
Arlesey Town	1	9	15	9	14	9	18	10	-	-
Baker Perkins							(See APV Peterborough City)			
Baldock Town	8	3	2	-	-	-	-	-	-	-
Boston	-	-	-	-	-	-	-	8	11	8
Bourne Town	10	17	20	21	20	4	1	4	8	13
Brackley Town	16	16	11	14	2	20	20	24	22	22
Buckingham Town	3	1	-	-	-	-	-	-	-	-
Burton Park Wanderers	-	-	-	-	-	17	22	-	-	-
Cogenhoe United	-	-	-	11	16	5	8	12	6	4
Daventry Town	-	-	-	-	-	-	-	14	5	20
Desborough Town	6	15	13	7	11	16	7	18	20	17
Eynesbury Rovers	17	20	17	16	12	21	3	7	9	9
Hamlet Stewarts & Lloyds							(See Stewarts & Lloyds)			
Holbeach United	18	10	8	20	3	1	13	23	19	10
Irthlingborough Diamonds	4	4	4	13	4	12	14	17	-	-
Kempston Rovers	-	-	16	19	19	22	15	15	15	21
Long Buckby	2	7	9	10	9	10	9	16	10	7
Mirrlees Blackstone	-	-	-	-	18	8	12	6	16	6
Newport Pagnell Town	12	21	-	-	-	-	-	-	14	15
Northampton Spencer	-	11	12	8	13	7	5	1	2	3
Potton United	7	6	1	4	1	14	4	13	4	12
Raunds Town	13	13	6	3	6	3	6	2	3	5
Rothwell Town	15	12	18	2	5	2	2	3	1	1
St Neots Town	19	18	19	18	-	-	-	-	-	-
Spalding United	-	-	7	1	-	-	-	21	13	14
Stamford	5	5	10	12	7	15	21	20	12	19
Stewarts & Lloyds (Corby)	11	2	5	6	15	11	17	9	7	11
Stotfold	14	19	3	5	10	6	10	5	17	2
Wellingborough Town	-	-	-	-	-	19	16	22	21	16
Wootton Blue Cross	9	8	14	17	8	18	19	19	18	18
No. of clubs competing	20	21	21	21	20	22	22	24	22	22

LEAGUE KNOCK-OUT CUP 1993-94

Preliminary Round

British Timkem *(removed)* Stewarts & Lloyds *w/o*
Ramsey Town v Cottingham 3-2*(aet)*
Daventry Town v Rothwell Town 3-2
Harrowby United v St Ives Town 0-6
Blisworth v Ford Sports 0-3
Northampton Vanaid v Wellingborough Town 2-0
Higham Town v Eynesbury Rovers 2-1

First Round

Stamford v Burton Park Wanderers 1-0
Thrapston Venturas v Raunds Town 1-5
Desborough Town v Bugbrooke St Michaels 2-0
Boston v Olney Town 3-0
Ford Sports v Brackley Town 1-2
Ramsey Town v Mirrlees Blackstone 1-5
Cogenhoe United v Potton United 1-2*(aet)*
Northampton Vanaid v Stewarts & Lloyds 2-1
Wellingborough Whitworths v Kempston 1-1,2-2*
Holbeach United v Stotfold 0-3
N'pton ON Chenecks v Wootton Blue Cross 3-2
Irchester United v Sharnbrook 1-4
St Ives Town v Newport Pagnell Town 1-4
Bourne Town v Long Buckby 1-0
Northampton Spencer v Higham Town 2-1
Spalding United v Daventry Town 4-1

Third Round

Northampton Spencer v Newport Pagnell 2-1
Stamford v Spalding United 3-2
Brackley Town v Boston 0-7*(Boston removed)*
Potton United v Sharnbrook 3-1
Mirrlees Blackstone v Raunds Town 2-2,0-4
N'pton Vanaid v Northampton ON Chenecks 6-0
Wellingborough Whitworths v Stotfold 0-4
Desborough Town v Bourne Town 1-2

Quarter-Finals

Stamford v Brackley Town 7-0
Northampton Vanaid v Potton United 1-2
Bourne Town v Raunds Town 1-5
Northampton Spencer v Stotfold 3-0

Semi-Finals

Raunds Town v Stamford 5-0
Northampton Spencer v Potton United 0-0,3-0

Final *(Two Legs)*:

Northampton Spencer 2 *(Calvert, McIlroy)*
Raunds Town 1 *(Carr)*
Spencer: Myers, Wilmott, Wilson, Francis, Jelley (Tansley), Gage, Arundel, Calvert, Heath, McIlroy, Smith.
Raunds: Morse, Field, M Smith (Foster), Bird, Boatswain, Carr, Giggs, P Smith, Keeble, Westley, McConnell.

Raunds Town 0
Northampton Spencer 3 *(McIlroy, Smith, Jelley)*
Raunds Town: Morse, Field (P Smith), McConnell, Bird, Boatswain (Foster), Carr, Pearce, M Smith, Keeble, Westley, Giggs.
Northampton Spencer: Myers, Wilmott, Wilson, Francis, Jelley, Gage, Arundel, Tansley, McIlroy (Heath), Belfon (O'Rourke), Smith.

* - Wellingborough Whitworths went through on away goals rule.

BENEVOLENT CUP 1993-94

Semi-Finals

Rothwell Town v Higham Town	3-1	Stotfold v Northampton Vanaid	0-1 *(aet)*

Final:

Rothwell Town 3 ***(McPolin, Wright, Mawby)***
Northampton Vainaid 0
Rothwell Town: Liquorish, Wright, Hornby (McHutchison), Humphrey, Bates, Sheerin, McDonald, Coe, McPolin, Davies, Murphy (Mawby).
Northampton Vanaid: Boughton, Finch, Corkram, Vigo, W Humphries (O'Riordan), Watson, Barrett, Sandy, Abrahams, P Humphries, Dore.

HEREWARD SPORTS

UNITED COUNTIES LEAGUE

NEWSLINE

0891 122 960

BE ON THE BALL FOR
LATEST NEWS
24 HOURS A DAY
7 DAYS A WEEK

INTERVIEWS
MATCH OF THE DAY
RESULTS & FIXTURES
UPDATED DAILY

0891 122 960

Calls cost 39p per minute cheap rate and 49p per minute at all other times.
Marketed by Sportslines (0386) 47302 or (0831) 464517
Call costing correct at time of going to press.

LEADING SCORERS 1993-94

PREMIER DIVISION	Club	League	KO Cup	Ben. Cup	Total
Dave Scotney	Bourne Town	39	2	-	41
Roy Boon	Stotfold	34	1	-	35
Shaun Keeble	Raunds Town	25	6	-	31
James Westley	Raunds Town	25	5	-	30
Mick Bennett	Stotfold	24	2	-	26
Sean McPolin	Rothwell Town	24	1	1	26
Steve Marshall *	Spalding United	24	1	-	25
Carl Smaller	Boston	21	4	-	25
Joey Martin #	Raunds Town	23	1	-	24
Jon Inwood	Wellingborough Town	23	-	-	23
Frank Belfon	Northampton Spencer	18	2	-	20
Kevin Lamb	Wootton Blue Cross	20	-	-	20
Paul Murphy	Rothwell Town	18	-	1	19
Tony Dunn	Mirrlees Blackstone	17	-	-	17
Steve Knibb	Cogenhoe United	17	-	-	17
Steve McIlroy	Northampton Spencer	13	4	-	17
Gary Walker	Eynesbury (including 2 for Stotfold)	17	-	-	17
Frank Atkins	Eynesbury (including 2 for Potton)	19	1	-	20
Dominic Genovese	Holbeach United	16	-	-	16
John McFarlane	Long Buckby	16	-	-	16
Ian Mann	Northampton Spencer	15	1	-	16
Ray Seekings	Potton United	13	3	-	16
Paul Sharp	Mirrlees Blackstone	16	-	-	16
Adrian Sheerin	Rothwell Town	14	1	1	16
Steve Forbes	Cogenhoe United	15	-	-	15
Darren King	Potton (including 1 for Kempston)	15	-	-	15
Brett McNamara	Stamford	15	-	-	15
Danny Reilly	Spalding United	15	-	-	15
Paul Smith	Northampton Spencer	13	2	-	15
Dave Botterill	Daventry (including 3 for Raunds)	12	2	-	14
Scott Kent	Holbeach United	14	-	-	14
Jason O'Connor	Holbeach United	14	-	-	14
Dave Brady	Newport Pagnell Town	11	2	-	13
Paul Cashin	Potton United	12	1	-	13
Fred McDonnell	Boston	11	2	-	13
Mark Mitchell	Bourne Town	13	-	-	13
Mark Schiavi	Bourne Town	13	-	-	13
Steve Scott	Eynesbury Rovers	13	-	-	13
Dave Torrance	Mirrlees Blackstone	12	1	-	13
Tony Calvert	Northampton Spencer	10	2	-	12
Tony Downes	Long Buckby	12	-	-	12
Grant Mawby	Rothwell Town	11	-	1	12
Danny Murphy	Stotfold	10	2	-	12

* - Includes 11 League, 1 KO Cup for Eynesbury Rovers
# - Includes 20 League, 1 KO Cup for Desborough Town

DIVISION ONE	Club	League	KO Cup	Ben. Cup	Total
Clive Woodland	Olney Town	33	-	-	33
Andy Evans	ON Chenecks	28	-	-	28
Dean Parkes	St Ives Town	24	3	-	27
Adam Sandy	Northampton Spencer	26	-	-	26
Roy Anderson	Northampton Vanaid	22	3	-	25
Jon Ogden	Higham Town	23	1	-	24
Steve Bendon *	Wellingborough Whitworths	22	-	-	22
Rod Hough	Ford Sports	17	1	-	18
Shay O'Riordan	Raunds Town	12	5	-	17
Derek Atkinson	Higham Town	16	-	-	16
Mark Hill	Bugbrooke St Michaels	16	-	-	16
Darren Frostwick	Burton Park Wanderers	15	-	-	15
Mark James	Thrapston Venturas	15	-	-	15
Tony Lambert	Northampton Vanaid	14	-	-	14

* - Includes 2 for Wellingborough Town

HAT-TRICKS 1993-94

PREMIER DIVISION

Seven Goals
Brett McNamara (Stamford) v Brackley 19/3/94

Six Goals
Tony Dunn (Mirrlees Blackstone) at Brackley 22/1/94
Gary Walker (Eynesbury) at Brackley 7/5/94

Five Goals
Mark Schiavi (Bourne Town) v Brackley 15/1/94
Dave Scotney (Bourne Town) v Brackley 15/1/94

Four Goals
James Westley (Raunds) v Newport Pagnell 21/8/93
Steve Marshall (Eynesbury) v N. Spencer 7/9/93
Tony Dunn (Mirrlees) at Desborough 27/11/93
Kevin Lamb (Wootton) v Brackley 18/12/93
Steve Scott (Eynesbury) v Brackley 2/4/94
Gary Walker (Eynesbury) v Brackley 2/4/94
Paul Cashin (Potton) at Stamford 9/4/94

Three Goals
Paul Smith (N. Spencer) v Stewart & L. 21/8/93
Roy Boon (Stotfold) at Potton 24/8/93
Mick Bennett (Stotfold) at Desborough 4/9/93
Sean McPolin (Rothwell) v Daventry 4/9/93
Shaun Keeble (Raunds) v Stamford 8/9/93
Roy Boon (Stotfold) v Holbeach 11/9/93
Dave Scotney (Bourne) v Wellingboro. 11/9/93
Steve Marshall (Eynesbury) at Stotfold 21/9/93
Mick Bennett (Stotfold) v Wellingboro. 12/10/93
Roy Boon (Stotfold) at Boston 23/10/93
Paul Murphy (Rothwell) at Holbeach 26/10/93
Mark Humphrey (Rothwell) v Brackley 30/10/93
Kevin McDonald (Rothwell) v Brackley 30/10/93
Paul Cashin (Potton) v Wellingboro. 6/11/93
Scott Kent (Holbeach) v Brackley 6/11/93
Jason O'Connor (Holbeach) v Brackley 6/11/93
Kevin Lamb (Wootton) v Brackley 9/11/93
Neil Worker (Cogenhoe) at Wootton 27/11/93
Sean McPolin (Rothwell) v Stewart & L. 4/12/93
Chris Goodchild (L. Buckby) v Brackley 3/1/94
Ian Shooter (Holbeach) at Bourne 3/1/94
Steve Forbes (Cogenhoe) at Brackley 8/1/94
John McFarlane (L. Buckby) v Potton 8/1/94
Sean McPolin (Rothwell) v Wellingboro. 8/1/94
Jon Inwood (Wellingboro.) v Wootton 29/1/94
Michael Smith (Wellingboro.) at Brackley 5/2/94
Dave Torrance (Mirrlees) v Bourne 12/2/94
Jason O'Connor (Holbeach) v Mirrlees 19/2/94
Mick Bennett (Stotfold) v Stewart & L. 5/3/94
Shaun Keeble (Raunds) v Cogenhoe 5/3/94
P J Hamill (S & L) at Kempston 8/3/94
James Westley (Raunds) at Brackley 8/3/94
Darren King (Potton) at Brackley 13/3/94
Shaun Walker (Boston) v Stewart & L. 15/3/94
Mark Mitchell (Bourne) v Eynesbury 19/3/94
Ian Mann (N'pton Spencer) v Holbeach 26/3/94
Carl Smaller (Boston) at Daventry 9/4/94
Danny Reilly (Spalding) v Boston 12/4/94
James Westley (Raunds) at Spalding 12/4/94
Roy Boon (Stotfold) v Mirrlees B. 16/4/94
Dave Scotney (Bourne) v Desboro. 16/4/94
Fred McDonnell (Boston) at Holbeach 21/4/94
Dave Scotney (Bourne) at Potton 23/4/94
Dave Scotney (Bourne) at Long Buckby 30/4/94

DIVISION One

Seven Goals
Dean Parkes (St Ives) v Harrowbyr 17/8/93

Five Goals
Stuart Kilby (Ramsey) v Harrowby 24/8/93
Andy Sandyn (Vanaid) v Irchester 9/10/93
Andy Sage (Olney) v Ford Spts 30/10/93

Four Goals
Mark James (Thrapston) v Irchester 14/8/93
Roy Anderson (Vanaid) v Whitworths 31/8/93
Roy Anderson (Vanaid) v Harrowby 4/9/93
Andy Evans (Chenecks) v Ford 25/9/93

Three Goals
Stuart Kilby (Ramsey) at Bugbrooke 14/8/93
Neil Tilley (Burton PW) v Ford 14/8/93
Dave Bonner (Ramsey) v Harrowby 24/8/93
Clive Woodland (Olney) v Blisworth 24/8/93
Jon Ogden (Higham) at Harrowby 28/8/93
Rod Hough (Ford) v Blisworth 31/8/93
Steve Christie (Higham) v Brit. Tim. 4/9/93
Adam Sandy (Vanaid) v Harrowby 4/9/93
Jon Ogden (Higham) at Bugbrooke 11/9/93
Dean Parkes (St Ives) v Thrapston 18/9/93
Neil Tilley (Burton PW) v Irchester 25/9/93
Mark Lawrence (Whitworths) at Harrowby 2/10/93
Jon Ogden (Higham) at Ford 2/10/93
Clive Woodland (Olney) v Burton PW 2/10/93
Paul Horton (Blisworth) at Burton PW 9/10/93
Steve Whitehead (Whitworths) v Sharnbrook 13/11/93
Steve Farthing (Sharnbrook) at Ford 4/12/93
Roy Anderson (Vanaid) at Ford 3/1/94
Steve Bendon (Whitworths) at Ford 22/1/94
Julian Barford (Chenecks) v Harrowby 29/1/94
Andy Evans (Chenecks) v Harrowby 29/1/94
Darren Frostwick (Burton PW) at Brit. T. 29/1/94
Rob Muir (Cottingham) at Sharnbrook 29/1/94
Clive Woodland (Olney) at Ford 29/1/94
Adam Sandy (Vanaid) at Cottingham 19/2/94
Derek Atkinson (Higham) v Harrowby 26/2/94
Steve Medlin (Higham) v Harrowbyr 26/2/94
Paul Horton (Blisworth) at Sharnbrook 5/3/94
Andy Evans (Chenecks) at Ford 26/3/94
Steve Bendon (Whitworths) at Ramsey 9/4/94
Jimmy Rogers (Cottingham) at Chenecks 23/4/94
Shay O'Riordan (Vanaid) v Sharnbrook 27/4/94.

LEAGUE KNOCKOUT CUP

Three goals
Mike McNamara (Mirrlees) at Ramsey 12/10/93
Shaun Keeble (Raunds) at Thrapston 23/10/93
Carl Smaller (Boston) at Brackley 27/11/93
Shay O'Riordan (Vanaid) v Chenecks 4/12/93
Simon Hyde (Stamford) v Brackley 26/2/94
James Westley (Raunds) v Stamford 22/3/94

1993-94 RESULTS ANALYSIS

	PREMIER DIVISION	DIVISION ONE
Biggest Home Win	Bourne 13, Brackley 0 *(15/1/94)*	Ramsey 13, Harrowby 1 *(24/8/93)*
Biggest Away Win	Brackley 0, Mirrlees 11 *(22/1/94)*	Sharnbrook 3, Blisworth 11 *(5/3/94)*
Highest Score Draw	Bourne 5, Eynesbury 5 *(19/2/94)*	3-3; six times
Highest Aggregate	Bourne 13, Brackley 0 *(15/1/94)*	Sharnbrook 3, Blisworth 11 *(5/3/94)*
Longest Unbeaten Run	15 games - Rothwell Town	22 games - Northampton Vanaid
" run without win	32 - Brackley Town	25 - Harrowby United
Most consecutive wins	10 - Rothwell Town	8 - Olney Town
Most consecutive draws	3 - Eynesbury/ Holbeach/ Wellingboro./Wootton BC	3 - St Ives Town
" " defeats	11 - Brackley Town	13 - Harrowby United
" " scoring games	25 - Stotfold	21 - ON Chenecks
" " without scoring	4 - Kempston Rovers	6 - Harrowby United
" " matches conceding	27 - Brackley Town	22 - Blisworth
" " not conceding	5 - Boston	6 - St Ives Town

PREMIER DIVISION CLUBS 1994-95

BOSTON TOWN

Chairman: Mick Vines **Vice Chairman:** J Rose. **Treasurer:** Ray Atkinson.
Secretary: A Crick, Daisy Cottage, Shore Rd, Freiston, Boston, Lincs PE22 0LU (0205 760162. Fax:760162).
Manager: Bob Don-Duncan **Asst Manager:** Shaughan Farrow. **Press Officer:** Peter Massam.
Ground: Tattershall Road, Boston, Lincs (0205 365470).
Directions: A52 Grantham - Sleaford, 2nd left into Brothertoft Road, Argyle Street to bridge, immediately over left into Tattershall Road, ground three quaters of a mile on left.
Capacity: 6,000 **Seats:** 450 **Cover:** 950 **Floodlights:** Yes **Founded:** 1963.
Programme: 32 pages, 25p **Programme Editor:** Andy Sandall **Club Shop:** No.
Club Colours: Blue & white **Change:** All white or all yellow **Nickname:** Poachers
Previous Ground: Mayflower. **Previous Name:** Boston FC, 1963-1994.
Midweek matchday: Tuesday
Reserves' League: None 94-95. **Record Gate:** 2,700 v Boston Utd, FA Cup 3rd Qual. Rd 1970.
Club Sponsors: Port of Boston. **Best FA Cup season:** 1st Rd Proper 76-77 (lost 1-3 at Barnsley)
Best FA Trophy season: Second Round 79-80 (lost 3-6 at Mossley after 0-0 draw).
Best FA Vase season: Semi-Finals 93-94 (lost 0-2 on aggregate to Taunton Town).
Previous Leagues: Lincs 63-65/ Central Alliance 65-66/ Eastern Co's 66-68/ Midland 68-82/ Northern Co's East 82-87/ Central Midlands 87-91.
Players progressing to Football League: Julian Joachim (Leicester City), Neil Mann (Hull City).
Clubhouse: Open every evening (except Sunday), matchdays and special functions. Bar & Executive Lounge. Darts & pool.
Captain 93-94: Derrick Nuttell **Club record scorer (in a season):** Carl Smaller 48, 1993-94.
Top Scorer 1993-94: Carl Smaller **Player of the Year 1993-94:** Carl Smaller/ Lee Cooper.
Honours: Midland Co's Lg 74-75 78-79 80-81 (Lg Cup 76-77), Lincs Snr 'A' Cup (5) 73-74 79-82 89-90 (Snr 'B' Cup 65-66), Central Mids Lg 88-89, Central Alliance 65-66, Lincs Lg 64-65, FA Vase SF 93-94.

BOURNE TOWN

Chairman: Geoff Charnock **Vice-Chairman:** Don Mitchell **President:** Ray Ferrer
Secretary/Press Officer: Don Mitchell, 55 West Rd, Bourne, Lincs PE10 9PS (0778 423382).
Manager: Mark Mitchell **Asst Manager:** Jimmy Jackson
Coach: Stuart Hodson **Physio:** Alan Todd.
Ground: Abbey Lawn, Abbey Road, Bourne, Lincs (0778 422292).
Directions: In market place take A151 Spalding Road, ground 500 yds on right. Public transport from Peterborough, Stamford and Grantham.
Capacity: 3,000 **Seats:** 300 **Cover:** 750 **Floodlights:** Yes **Founded:** 1883.
Programme: 24 pages, 40p **Editor:** Tony Gout (0778 425548) **Nickname:** Wakes
Colours: Maroon/sky/white **Change Colours:** White (maroon trim).
Midweek matchday: Wednesday **Club Shop:** Contact secretary for scarves, ties, badges.
Sponsors: Raymond Mays (Car Sales) **Record Attendance:** 3,000 v Chelmsford, FA Tphy 1970
Reserves' Lge: HSUCL Res Div 1 **Previous Ground:** Adjacent cricket field after WW2 until 1947.
Previous Leagues: Peterborough/ UCL 47-56/ Central Alliance 58-61/ Midland Counties 61-63.
Players to progress to Football League: Peter Grummit (Nottm Forest), Shaun Cunnington (Wrexham, Grimsby, Sunderland), David Palmer (Wrexham).
Local Press: Stamford Mercury, Lincs Free Press, Peterborough Evening Telegraph, Bourne Local.
Clubhouse details: Small, open matchdays and specific events. Food, confectionary available.
Captain 1993-94: Steve Appleby **Player of the Year 1993-94:** David Scotney.
Club record scorer & Top Scorer 93-94: David Scotley (43 league and 3 Cup goals 93-94).
Honours: Utd Co's Lg 68-69 69-70 71-72 90-91 (KO Cup 69-70, Benevolent Cup 90-91, Res Div 2 93-94), Lincs Snr 'A' Cup 71-72 (R-up 92-93), Central Alliance Division 1 South 59-60, Lincs Intermediate Cup 85-86.

COGENHOE UNITED

Chairman: Derek Wright **Vice Chairman:** Bob Earl **President:** Steve Brockwell
Sec./Press Off.: Mick Marriott, 14 Corn Kiln Close, Cogenhoe, Northants NN7 1NX (0604 890043).
Manager: Dave Conlon **Asst Manager:** Micky Donnelly **Physio:** Ian Blair.
Coach: Stuart Robertson **Commercial Manager:** Robert H Jones.
Ground: Compton Park, Brafield Rd, Cogenhoe, Northants (0604 890521).
Directions: Turn off A428 at Brafield-on-the-Green, first turn right to Cogenhoe or A45 to Billing Aquadrome. Carry on, take second Cogenhoe turn on left.
Capacity: 5,000 **Seats:** 100 **Cover:** 200 **Floodlights:** Yes **Founded:** 1967
Programme: 24 pages, 25p **Programme Editor:** Mick Marriott **Nickname:** Cooks.
Club Colours: Sky/navy **Change:** Red/black (or all white) **Club Shop:** No.
Midweek home matchday: Tuesday **Previous Ground:** Cogenhoe Village PF 1967-84.
Sponsors: Cogenhoe Dairy/ Ying Wa **Previous League:** Central Northants Combinatiom 1967-84.
Reserves' Lge: UCL Res. Div 1 **Record Gate:** 1,000 v Eastenders XI, Charity match 8/7/90.
Record win: 22-0 v Ravensthorpe, Central Northants Comb. Premier Division KO Cup, 79-80.
Record defeat: 0-6 v Yardley United, Central Northants Combination Division One, 1976-77.
Players to progress to Football League: Darren Bazeley (Watford 1989), Darren Harmon (Notts Co., Shrewsbury, Northampton 1989), Matt Murphy (Oxford Utd 1993), Gary Leonard (Northampton 1978).
Clubhouse: Open Tues-Fri 7-11pm, Sat noon-3 & 4-11pm, Sun noon-3 & 7-10.30pm. Crisps snacks etc. Hot food on matchdays.
Local Newspapers: Chronicle & Echo, Northants Evening Telegraph.
Club Captain 1993-94: Neil Heslop **Record scorer & appearance maker:** Tony Smith.
Top Scorer 93-94: Steve Knibb **Player of the Year 1993-94:** Darren Watts.
Hons: UCL Div 1 R-up 86-87 (Reserve Div 2 88-89), Daventry Charity Cup 91-92 (R-up 79-80), Central Northants Comb 80-81 82-83 83-84 (R-up 81-82, Prem Div Cup 82-83 (R-up 78-79), Div 1 Cup R-up 77-78, Charity Shield 82-83 83-84).

PHOTOS OPPOSITE:

Top: *Boston FC pictured before their FA Vase semi-final first-leg at Taunton.* *Photo - Eric Marsh*

Centre: *Bourne Town defenders Les Lawrence (9) and Mark Mitchell (6) contest a high ball during during the FA Cup Preliminary Round tie at Billericay Town.* *Photo - 'Evening Echo'.*

Foot: *Cogenhoe United, who enjoyed their highest-ever UCL finish in 1993-94.*

COGENHOE UNITED FOOTBALL CLUB

DESBOROUGH TOWN

Chairman: Bryan Walmsley **President:** Ernie Parsons.
Secretary: John Lee, 85 Breakleys Road, Desborough, Northants NN14 2PT (0536 760002).
Coach: George Wright **Commercial Manager:** Robert Bindley.
Ground: Waterworks Field, Braybrooke Rd, Desborough (0536 761350).
Directions: Half a mile west of A6 following signs for Braybrooke.
Capacity: 8,000 **Seats:** 250 **Cover:** 500 **Floodlights:** Yes **Founded:** 1896.
Programme: 48 pages with entry **Editor:** Robert Bindley
Club Colours: All blue **Change Colours:** All white.
Sponsors: Wincanton Transport/K Groves **Midweek matchday:** Tuesday **Nickname:** Ar Tarn
Record win: 10-1: v Huntingdon Utd (A) 1957 & v Stewarts & Lloyds (A) 1965, both Utd Co's Lge.
Record defeat: 11-0 v Rushden (A) 1934 **Record Attendance:** 8,000 v Kettering Town.
Record transfer fee received: £8,000 for Wakeley Gage, from Northampton Town.
Players progressing to Football League: Wakeley Gage (Northampton, Chester, Peterborough and Crewe), Jon Purdie & Campbell Chapman (Wolves), Andy Tillson (Grimsby, QPR & Bristol Rvrs).
Clubhouse details: Lounge & main hall, 2 bars, games room. Open every evening, weekend lunchtimes.
Local Newspapers: Evening Telegraph, Northants Post, Chronicle & Echo, Harborough Mail.
1993-94 Top Scorer: Joe Martin **Captain & Player of the Year 1993-94:** Gary Torrance.
Hons: Utd Co's (Prev. Northants) Lg 00-01 01-02 06-07 20-21 23-24 24-25 27-28 48-49 66-67 (R-up 02-03 10-11 19-20 22-23 79-80 (Div 2 10-11(Res) 28-29(Res) (R-up 09-10(Res) 26-27(Res) 51-52(Res)), KO Cup 77-78), Northants Snr Cup 10-11 13-14 28-29 51-52.

DUNSTABLE

Chairman: Bill Cameron **President:** Gerald Fox.
Secretary: Sandra Fenn, c/o Dunstable FC (0582 699696).
Manager: John Margerrison **Physio:** Alex Webber **Comm. Mgr:** Phil Elkington.
Ground: Creasey Park, Brewers Hill Road, Dunstable (0582 606691. fax: 606691).
Directions: Brewers Hill Road runs west from A505 at north end of Dunstable at large traffic island; turn right after 150 yds. 5 miles from Luton (BR), buses 67 and 70 (from Luton) pass 200 yds from ground.
Capacity: 10,000 **Cover:** 750 **Seats:** 500 **Floodlights:** Yes **Founded:** 1950
Programme: Yes **Programme Editor:** Bill Cameron **Club Shop:** Yes
Colours: All blue **Change colours:** All red. **Nickname:** The Blues
Midweek home matchday: Tuesday **Sponsors:** Fieldhouse & Husband. **Reserve Team:** No.
Previous Name: Dunstable Town. **Record Gate:** 6,000 v Manchester United, Friendly 1974.
Previous Leagues: Metropolitan 50-55 58-61 63-65/ Hellenic 55-58/ United Counties 61-63/ Southern 63-94.
Best FA Cup season: 1st Rd 56-67 (lost 1-3 at Margate).
Best FA Vase year: 2nd Rd 92-93 **Best FA Trophy year:** 3rd Qualifying Round 1972.
Record Fees - Paid: £1,500 for Stuart Atkins (Wycombe 1979)
Received: £20,000 for Kerry Dixon (Reading 1980).
Players progressing to Football League: Bill Garner (Southend, Chelsea), Keith Barber (Luton 1971), Kerry Dixon (Reading 1980), Laurie Ryan (C'bridge Utd).
Clubhouse: (0582 63800). Large clubroom and bar. Open evenings & matchdays.
93-94 Captain: Steve Georgiou **93-94 P.o.Y.:** Paul Lamb
Local Radio: Radio Beds, Chiltern. **Local Newspapers:** Dunstable Gazette, Herald, Citzen.
Honours: Southern Lg Div 1 Nth R-up 74-75, Hellenic Lg R-up 57-58, Beds Senior Cup 1895-96 1956-57 59-60 79-80 82-83 85-86 86-87 87-88 88-89, Beds Premier Cup 80-81 82-83.

EYNESBURY ROVERS

Chairman: Deryck Irons **President:** Bill Stephenson
Secretary/Press Officer: Deryck Irons, 12 Hadleigh Close, Bedford MK41 8JW (0234 268111).
Manager: Barry Cavilla **Asst Manager/Coach:** Dave Mountford.
Ground: Hall Road, Eynesbury, St Neots (0480 477449).
Directions: Approx 2 miles from A1, on South side of St Neots urban area, near Ernulf School.
Capacity: 3,000 **Seats:** 270 **Cover:** 270 **Floodlights:** Yes **Founded:** 1897
Programme: 24 pages, 30p **Editor:** Patrick Worrall **Club Shop:**
Colours: Royal blue & white **Change Colours:** All yellow. **Nickname:** Rovers.
Midweek matchday: Tuesday **Clubhouse:** Large bar, capacity 150, committee room
Sponsors: National Power/Terosons **Reserve Team's League:** United Counties Reserve Div. One.
Record Gate: 5,000 v Fulham 1953 **Previous Lges:** Sth Mids 34-39/ UCL 46-52/ Eastern Co's 52-63.
Best FA Vase year: 2nd Rd 85-86 88-89 **Best FA Cup year:** 4th Qual. Rd 54-55 (1-3 at Camb. Utd)
Players to progress to Football Lge: Chris Turner (P'boro, Luton, Cambridge), Denis Emery (P'boro)
Local Newspapers: Hunts Citizen, Cambridge Evening News, St Neots Weekly News.
Captain 93-94: Howard Keir **P.o.Y. 93-94:** Kevin Anderson **Top Scorer 93-94:** Gary Walker 15
Hons: UCL Div 1 76-77, Hunts Snr Cup(12) 13-14 46-47 48-51 54-55 56-57 69-70 84-85 90-93 (Prem. Cup 50-51 90-91, Scott Gatty Cup 35-36 56-57 84-85 89-90 (R-up 93-94(res)), Jnr Cup 21-22 26-27), Hinchingbrooke Cup(7) 46-47 48-52 57-58 66-67, Cambs Invit. Cup 61-62, E Anglian Cup R-up 90-91 91-92, S Mids F'lit Cup 90-91(Res).

HOLBEACH UNITED

President: John King **Chairman:** Francis Biggadyke
Sec: John Crunkhorn, The Old Nurseries, Bakers Corner, High Rd, Whaplode, Spalding PE12 6UA (0406 422540).
Mgr: Dominico Genovese/ Milton Graham **Ground:** Carters Park, Park Road, Holbeach (0406 24761).
Directions: Second left at traffic lights in town centre, 220 yds down road on left. From King's Lynn; sharp right at traffic lights.
Capacity: 4,000 **Seats:** 200 **Cover:** 450 **Floodlights:** Yes **Founded:** 1929.
Programme: 44 pages, 50p **Programme Editor:** Alan Wright **Club Shop:**
Colours: Old gold & black **Change Colours:** Blue & white **Nickname:** Tigers
Reserves' Lge: Peterborough **Clubhouse:** Large bar, lounge & kitchen, open every night.
Midweek matchday: Wednesday **Record Gate:** 4,094 v Wisbech 1954.
Sponsors: J F Buffham Transport/ Rings Quality Homes/ Anchor Produce '90.
Previous Leagues: Peterborough/ Utd Co's 46-55/ Eastern Co's 55-62/ Midland Co's 62-63.
Best FA Cup season: 1st Rd Proper 82-83 (lost 0-4 v Wrexham at Peterborough).
Best FA Tphy year: 2nd Qual 69-70 71-72 **Best FA Vase season:** 5th Rd 88-89 (lost 2-4 v Wisbech).
Local Newspapers: Lincs Free Press, Spalding Guardian, Peterborough Evening Telegraph.
93-94 Top Scorer: Dominic Genovese 16. **Player progressing to Football Lge:** Peter Rawcliffe (Lincoln).
Hons: UCL 89-90 (KO Cup 64-65 89-90, Benev. Cup), Lincs Snr Cup 'A'(3) 83-85 86-87 (Snr Cup 'B' 57-58)

KEMPSTON ROVERS

President: H Gilbert **Chairman:** Peter Burnage **Vice-Chairman/Comm. Mgr:** Ian Davis.
Press Officer/Secretary: Alan Scott, 26 King William Rd, Kempston, Bedford MK42 7AT (0234 854875).
Manager: Russell Shreeves **Assistant Manager:** Bobby Folds.
Ground: Hillgrounds Leisure, Hillgrounds Rd, Kempston, Bedford (0234 852346).
Directions: M1 jct 13, A421 to Kempston, Hillgrounds Rd is off the B531 main Kempston-Bedford road. Entrance to Hillgrounds Road is opposite Sainsburys on the B531 - ground can be found just over twi miles from Sainsburys entrance. British Rail to Bedford Thameslink/Midland then bus No.103 from Bedford town centre stops outside ground.
Capacity: 2,000 **Seats:** 100 **Cover:** 250 **Floodlights:** Yes **Founded:** 1884.
Programme: 36 pages, 40p **Programme Editor:** Alan Scott.
Colours: Red/white/black **Change Colours:** All yellow.
Nickname: Walnut Boys **Club record scorer:** Doug Jack.
Midweek matchday: Tuesday **Club Sponsors:** Kempston Bedding/ Dings Entertainment.
Record Attendance: unknown **Previous League:** Sth Mids 27-53.
Reserves's Lge: HUCL Res Div. **Club Shop:** No, but old programmes available from clubhouse.
Previous Grounds: Bedford Rd 1900s-1973/ Hillgrounds Road 74-86 *(three grounds in same road!).*
Players progressing to Football League: Ernie Fenn (WBA, Aston Villa), Matthew Woolgar (Luton 1994).
Clubhouse: Open 7-11pm every evening except Monday and weekend lunctimes noon-3pm. Sky TV, pool, fruit machines, hot pies & pasties.
Captain 1993-94: Peter Larkin **P.o.Y. 1993-94:** Martin Dazley **93-94 Top Scorer:** Dave Farrar 16.
Local Newspapers: Bedfordshire Times, Herald & Post.
Hons: Utd Co's Lg 73-74 (R-up 56-57 59-60 (Div 1 57-58 85-86, Div 2 55-56 (R-up 67-68), KO Cup 55-56 57-58 59-60 74-75 76-77), Beds Senior Cup 08-09 37-38 76-77 91-92 (R-up 92-93).

LONG BUCKBY

President: Alister Bruce **Chairman:** Ted Thresher
Secretary: Dave Austin, 6 Jubilee Close, Long Buckby NN6 7NP (0327 843286).
Manager: Mick Emms **Asst Manager:** Les Thurbon **Press Officer:** Dave Derrig
Ground: Station Rd, Long Buckby (0327 842682).
Directions: On Daventry - Long Buckby road. 400 yds from station (Northampton - Rugby line).
Capacity: 1,000 **Sseats:** 200 **Cover:** 200 **Floodlights:** Yes **Founded:** 1945
Programme: 16 pages **Programme Editor:** Dave Austin **Sponsors:** Ned.
Colours: All blue **Change colours:** Yellow & black **Nickname:** Bucks
Reserves' Lge: HSUCL Res Div 1 **Clubhouse:** Bar & concert room. Open matchdays.
Midweek matchday: Tuesday **Record Gate:** 750 v Kettering, Northants Snr Cup Final 1984.
Prev. Name: Long Buckby Nomads 1936. **Previous Lges:** Rugby & D./ Central Northants Comb. (pre-1968).
Best FA Vase season: 2nd Rd 85-86 **Best FA Cup season:** 1st Qualifying Rd 92-93..
Players progressing to Football League: Gary Mills (Nottingham Forest, Derby, Notts County, Leicester), Vince Overson (Burnley, Birmingham), Des Waldock (Northampton), Steve Norris (Scarborough, Carlisle, Halifax, Chesterfield).
Club Captain 1993-94: Simon Henry **Local Newspapers:** Chronicle & Echo, Daventry Weekly News.
93-94 Top Scorers: John McIlvane 16 **Player of the Year 1993-94:** Adrian Fuller.
Honours: UCL KO Cup 84-85 (UCL Div 2 70-71 71-72, Div 3 69-70, Div 2 KO Cup 71-72), Northants Snr Cup R-up.

MIRRLEES BLACKSTONE

Chairman: Bill Sewell **President:**
Secretary: Derek Hall, 67 Ringwood, South Bretton, Peterborough PE3 9SR (0733 332074).
Manager: Steve Blades **Press Officer:** Ian McGillivray
Ground: Lincoln Road, Stamford (0780 57835).
Directions: A6121 Stamford to Bourne road, 2nd left past MB works.
Capacity: 1,000 **Seats:** 100 **Cover:** Yes **Floodlights:** Yes **Founded:** 1920.
Programme: 20 pages, 20p **Editor:** Kevin Boor
Local Newspapers: Stamford Mercury, Herald & Post, Peterborough Evening Telegraph.
Club Colours: Blue & white **Change Colours:** Red & white.
Clubhouse details: Open evenings, lunchtimes & matchdays.
Sponsors: Dolpin Inn **Midweek matchday:** Tuesday **Nickname:** Stones
Record Gate: 700 v Glinton. **Record win:** 11-0 v Brackley, 22/1/94 (A Dunn 6 goals).
Previous Leagues: Peterborough Works/ Peterborough/ Stamford & District.
Previous Names: Rutland Ironworks/ Blackstone (until 1975).
Players to progress to Football League: Craig Goldsmith (Peterborough, Carlisle), Alan Neilson (Newcastle & Wales).
Captain 1993-94: S Hardy. **Player of the Year 1993-94:** I Pledger.
1993-94 Leading Scorer: P Sharp.
Club record scorer (in one game): A Dunn; 6 v Brackley Town, 22/1/94.
Hons: UCL Div 1 R-up 87-88 (Benevolent Cup R-up), Lincs Snr Cup 'A' 92-93.

NEWPORT PAGNELL TOWN

President: Ken Inch. **Chairman:** George Mackie
Secretary: John Anderson, 59 Willen Road, Newport Pagnell, Bucks MK16 0DE (0908 610440).
Manager: John Horsley/ Terry Ashton (joint). **Press Officer:** Barry Cook.
Ground: Willen Road, Newport Pagnell (0908 611993).
Directions: Adjacent to A442 Newport Pagnell by-pass.
Capacity: 2,000 **Seats:** 100 **Cover:** 100 **Floodlights:** Yes **Founded:** 1963.
Programme: 56 pages **Programme Editor:** Jim Bean **Club Shop:**
Clubhouse: Open every evening **Local Newspapers:** Milton Keynes Citizen.
Club colours: Green & white **Change colours:** Yellow & black **Nickname:** Swans
Best FA Vase year: 2nd Rd 84-85 **Previous Leagues:** Nth Bucks 63-71/ South Mids 71-73
Sponsors: Davenport Vernon **Prev. Grounds:** Bury Field Common/ Newport Pagnell Youth Club.
Captain 1993-94: Dave Abraham **Player of the Year 1993-94:** Gary Hartwell/ Sean Reedman.
93-94 Top Scorer: Dave Brady 13 **93-94 Leading Appearances:** Matt Quinn 40.
Hons: UCL Div 1 82-83 (R-up 91-92, Div 1 Cup 77-78), Daventry Charity Cup R-up 93-94.

NORTHAMPTON SPENCER

President: Barry Rumford **Chairman:** Graham Wrighting
Secretary: R Linnell, 53 Muscott Lane, Duston, Northampton (0604 751731).
Manager: Gary Sargent **Asst Manager:** Keith Bowen
Ground: Kingsthorpe Mill, Studland Rd, Northampton NN3 1NF (0604 718898).
Directions: Turn off Kingsthorpe Rd at traffic lights into Thornton Rd, 1st right into Studland Rd, ground at end.
Capacity: 2,000 **Seats:** 100 **Cover:** 350 **Floodlights:** Yes **Founded:** 1936
Programme: 40 pages, 40p **Programme Editor/Press Officer:** Andy Goldsmith
Colours: Yellow & green **Change Colours:** White & green **Nickname:** Millers
Midweek matchday: Tuesday **Clubhouse:** Lounge and bar, open normal licensing hours.
Club Sponsors: Doc Martens **Record Gate:** 800 v Nottm F., dressing-room opener 1993.
Previous Lge: Northampton Town 36-68 **Previous Name:** Spencer School Old Boys.
Reserves' Lge: HSUCL Res. Div. One **Prev. Grnds:** Dallington Park 1936-70, Duston High School 70-72.
Best FA Cup year: 1st Qual. Rd 93-94 **Best FA Vase year:** 4th Round 87-88 (lost 1-2 v Gresley Rovers)
Players to progress to Football League: Paul Stratford (Northampton), Wakeley Gage (Northampton, Chester, Peterborough, Crewe)
Local Newspapers: Chronicle & Echo, Northampton Post, Northants Advertiser.
Captain 1993-94: Paul Selley **Player of the Year 1993-94:**
93-94 Top Scorer: Frank Belfon 20 **1993-94 Leading Appearances:** Daryl Wilson 48.
Hons: United Counties Lg 91-92 (R-up 92-93, Div 1 84-85, KO Cup 88-89 93-94 (R-up 87-88), Benevolent Cup 91-92), Northants Snr Cup R-up 90-91 93-94.

POTTON UNITED

President: Peter Hutchinson. **Chairman:** Claude Munns
Secretary: Derek Inskip, 3 Bellevue Close, Potton, Beds SG19 2QA (0767 260355).
Manager: Ken Davidson **Asst Manager:** Alan Biley
Ground: The Hollow, Biggleswade Road, Potton (0767 261100).
Directions: Outskirts of Potton on Biggleswade Road (B1040). Three and a half miles from Sandy (BR). United Counties buses from Biggleswade.
Capacity: 2,000 **Seats:** 200 **Cover:** 250 **Floodlights:** Yes **Founded:** 1943
Programme: 48 pages, 50p **Pogramme Editor:** Ian Glashall **Club Shop:**
Club Sponsors: Darlows **Local Press:** Biggleswade Chronicle, St Neots Weekly News.
Colours: Blue & white **Change Colours:** All yellow **Nickname:** Royals
Midweek matchday: Tuesday **Clubhouse details:** Large (capacity for 100), opened 1985.
Reserves' Lge: HSUCL Res. Div. Two **Record Attendance:** 470 v Hastings Town, FA Vase 1989
Prev. Grnd: Recreation Grnd pre-1947 **Previous Lges:** Sth Mids 46-55/ Central Alliance 56-61
Best FA Trophy year: 3rd Qualifying Round 71-72 72-73.
Best FA Vase year: 5th Round 89-90 (lost 1-2 to Billericay Town).
Best FA Cup year: 3rd Qualifying Round 74-75 (lost 1-2 to Bedford Town).
Captain 1993-94: Dave Albone **Player of the Year 1993-94:** Darren Marsh.
93-94 Top Scorer: Ray Steerings 16 **93-94 Leading Appearances:** Mark Winwood 47.
Hons: Utd Co's Lg 86-87 88-89 (KO Cup 72-73, Benevolent Cup 88-89), Beds Snr Cup(5) 47-49 63-64 75-76 77-78 (R-up 93-94), Wallspan Floodlit Cup 87-88, Hinchingbrooke Cup 51-52 84-85 89-90 90-91 91-92, Hunts Premier Cup 89-90 91-92 93-94(joint), Beds I'mediate Cup 43-44, Southern Comb. Cup 92-93, Nth Beds Charity Cup(9) 58-60 65-67 70-72 85-86 87-88 89-90.

RAUNDS TOWN

Chairman: George Hagan **President:** R Woods
Secretary: Ian Brown, 4 Langham Rd, Raunds, Northants NN9 6LD (0933 623569).
Manager: Keith Burt **Asst Manager:** Glen Burdett
Ground: Kiln Park, London Road, Raunds, Northants NN9 6EQ (0933 623351).
Directions: Take Raunds turning at r'bout on A605 and ground is first left.
Capacity: 3,000 **Seats:** 100 **Cover:** 1,000 **Floodlights:** Yes **Founded:** 1896.
Prog.: 48 pages 30p (Wirral Club survey National Winner 1993 - Runner-up 1992 - UCL winner since 1989).
Press Officer & Programme Editor: Mick Jones
Colours: Red & black **Change Colours:** White. **Nickname:** Shopmates
Midweek matchday: Tuesday **Clubhouse:** On ground, open every day **Club Shop:** Yes.
Sponsors: Doc Martens **Reserve Team's League:** UCL Reserve Division One.
Record Attendance: 1,500 v Crystal Palace, ground opening 23/7/91.
Previous Leagues: Rushden & District, Central Northants Combination.
Previous Grounds: Greenhouse Field (until 1948), The Berristers (1948-91).
Best FA Cup season: Third Qualifying Round Rd 12-13 (lost 0-4 at Peterborough), 92-93 (0-4 at Nuneaton Borough), 93-94 (0-4 v Telford United).
Players to progress to Football League: Greg Downs (Norwich, Coventry, Birmingham, Hereford).
Local Newspapers: Northants Evening Telegraph, Wellingborough Post, Chronicle & Echo.
Captain 1993-94: Martin Lewis **1993-94 Leading Scorer:** Shaun Keeble.
Hons: UCL Div 1 82-83 (R-up 91-92, KO Cup 90-91 (R-up 83-84 93-94), Reserve Div 1 88-89 (R-up 86-87 87-88 89-90 90-91 91-92), Reserve KO Cup 84-85 88-89 93-94), Northants Snr Cup 90-91, Hunts Premier Cup R-up 92-93, Daventry Charity Cup R-up 83-84, Northants Jnr Cup 82-83 91-92(res) 92-93(res).

PHOTOS OPPOSITE:

Top: *Steve McIlroy fires home a last minute winner to give Northampton Spencer a vital 2-1 first-leg lead in the final of the Knock-Out Cup against Raunds Town.*
Photo - Neil Whittington.

Centre: *Kempston Rovers FC 1993-94.*

Foot: *Prolific scorer James Westley nets one of Raunds Town's three goals at home to to Potton United.*
Photo - Neil Whittington.

FOOTBALL CLUB

SPALDING UNITED

President: Brian Turner **Chairman:** Rod Quinton
Secretary: Howard Williamson, 26 Rembrant Way, Spalding, Lincs PE11 3HX (0775 711165).
Manger: Alan Day **Asst Manager:** Phil Ward **Press Officer:** Ray Tucker
Ground: Sir Halley Stewart Field, Winfrey Avenue, Spalding (0775 713328).
Directions: Town centre off A16, adjacent to bus station. 250 yds from Spalding (BR) station.
Capacity: 7,000 **Seats:** 350 **Cover:** 2,500 **Floodlights:** Yes **Founded:** 1921
Programme: 32 pages, 40p **Programme Editor:** Jack Grimwood **Club Shop:**
Colours: All blue **Change:** Red & black or all white **Nickname:** Tulips
Midweek matchday: Tuesday **Clubhouse details:** Open matchdays, and events.
Sponsors: A E Goodyear & Sons **Record Attendance:** 6,972 v Peterborough, FA Cup 1952.
Reserve Team's League: United Counties League Reserve Division Two.
Previous Leagues: Peterborough/ Utd Co's 31-55 68-78 86-88/ Eastern Co's 55-60/ Central Alliance 60-61/ Midland Co's 61-68/ Northern Co's (East) 82-86/ Southern 88-91.
Best FA Cup year: 1st Round 57-58 (1-3 at Durham City), 64-65 (3-5 at Newport County).
Best FA Trophy year: 2nd Qualifying Round 69-70 70-71 71-72 74-75 76-77 81-82.
Best FA Vase year: Quarter-Finals 89-90 (lost 1-3 to Guiseley).
Players progressing to Football League: Carl Shutt (Sheffield Wednesday, Bristol City, Leeds).
Local Newspapers: Lincs Free Press, Spalding Guardian, Peterborough Evening Telegraph.
Captain 1993-94: Paul Langford **Player of the Year 1993-94:** Paul Langford
Top Scorer 93-94: Danny Reilly 15 **Leading Appearances 1993-94:** Paul Langford 39.
Hons: Utd Co's Lg 54-55 74-75 87-88 (R-up 50-51 51-52 52-53 72-73 75-76, KO Cup 54-55), Northern Co's East Lg 83-84, Lincs Snr Cup 52-53, Lincs Snr 'A' Cup 87-88, Lincs Snr 'B' Cup 50-51, Evans Halshaw F'lit Cup 89-90.

STAMFORD

Chairman: Arthur Twiddy **Vice-Chairman:** Bill Warrington **Press Officer:** Stuart Gray
Secretary/Press Officer: Andrew Eason, 36 Queens Walk, Stamford, Lincs PE9 2QE (0780 54510).
Manager: Percy Freeman **Asst Manager:** Mike Brooks **Physio:** Richard Downs
Ground: Wothorpe Road, Stamford, Lincs (0780 63079).
Directions: Off A43 Kettering Rd, 1 mile east of A1. 200 yds from station.
Capacity: 5,000 **Seats:** 250 **Cover:** 1,250 **Floodlights:** Yes **Founded:** 1896
Programme: 32 pages, 50p **Prog. Editor:** Robin Peel (0733 233212) **Nickname:** Daniels
Club Shop: Wide range of Lge + non-Lge progs & club souvenirs. Contact Dave Salisbury (0780 52377)
Local Newspapers: Stamford Mercury, Peterborough Evening Telegraph, Herald & Post.
Club Colours: Red & navy **Change Colours:** All white
Sponsors: Jessups (Ford Dealers). **Midweek matchday:** Tuesday **Prev. Grounds:** None
Reserves' Lge: HSUCL Res Div **Record Gate:** 4,200 v Kettering, FA Cup Third Qual. Rd 1953.
Rec. win: 13-0 v P'boro. Res, UCL 29-30. **Record defeat:** 0-17 v Rothwell, FA Cup 27-28.
Previous Leagues: Peterborough/ Northants (UCL) 08-55/ Central Alliance 55-61/ Midland Co's 61-72.
Players to progress to Football League: Alan Birchenall (Chelsea, Crystal Palace, Leicester), Reg Chester (Aston Villa), Teddy Tye (Chelsea), Gerry Fell (Brighton, Southend, Torquay, York), Campbell Chapman (Wolves), Steve Collins (Peterborough), Keith Alexander (Grimsby, Stockport, Lincoln), Andy Tillson (Grimsby, QPR, Bristol Rovers), Brian Stubbs (Notts Co.), Domenico Genovese (Peterborough).
Clubhouse: Open matchdays, Sunday lunchtimes & evenings (bingo) plus midweek evenings for local pub league events, eg darts, cribbage, dominos. Food available matchdays - sandwiches, rolls etc.
Top Scorer 93-94: Brett McNamara **Captain & Player of the Year 1993-94:** Barry Hand.
Hons: FA Vase 79-80 (R-up 75-76 83-84), Utd Co's Lg 75-76 77-78 79-80 80-81 81-82 (KO Cup 51-52 75-76 79-80 81-82 85-86, Northants Lg 11-12, Lincs Snr 'A' Cup 78-79 82-83, Lincs Snr 'B' Cup 51-52 53-54, Hinchingbrooke Cup, William Scarber Mem. Cup 70-71 82-83 85-86 88-89 93-94, Stamford Chal. Cup 89-90, Lincs Jnr Cup 48-49.

STEWARTS & LLOYDS

Chairman: John Hamill. **Manager:** P J Hamill/ James Gillespie.
Secretary: Phil Mackay, 207 Rockingham Road, Kettering, Northants NN16 9JA (0536 410840).
Ground: Recreation Ground, Occupation Road, Corby (0536 401497).
Directions: On Occupation Rd at rear of Stewart & Lloyds Leisure Club, next to old Corby Town FC ground.
Capacity: 1,500 **Seats:** 100 **Cover:** 200 **Floodlights:** Yes **Year formed:** 1935
Club Colours: Yellow & blue **Change Colours:** Red & white **Nickname:** None
Programme: 8 pages with admission **Programme Editor/Press Officer:** Dave Foster
Clubhouse details: Licensed bar. **Local Press:** Northants Evening Telegraph
Midweek matchday: Tuesday **Previous Leagues:** Kettering Amateur
Previous Name: Hamlet Stewart & Lloyds (until 1992).
Players to progress to Football League: Andy McGowan (Northampton), Willie Graham (Brentford)
Hons: UCL R-up 85-86 (KO Cup, Div 1(2) 73-75, Div 1 Cup(2) 73-75, Div 2(Res) 76-77, Div 2 KO Cup(2) 75-77)
Captain 1993-94: Brian Ure **Player of the Year & Top Scorer 1993-94:** Dean McAlwane.
Record scorer: Joey Martin 46 (92-93) **1993-94 Leading Appearances:** Dean McAlwane 43, Brian Ure 43.

STOTFOLD

Chairman: Jerry Watson **Vice Chairman:** Graham Jarman **President:** Charles Hyde
Secretary: W Clegg, 12 Common Rd, Stotfold, Hitchin, Herts SG5 4BX (0462 730421).
Manager: Ian Allinson **Asst Manager:** Gordon Allinson
Physiotherapist: Keith Allinson **Press Officer:** Miss J Longhurst
Ground: Roker Park, The Green, Stotfold, Hitchin, Herts (0462 730765).
Directions: A507 from A1, right at lights, right at T-jct. A507 from Bedford via Shefford, left at lights, right at T-jct.
Capacity: 5,000 **Seats:** 50 **Cover:** 300 **Floodlights:** Yes **Nickname:** Eagles
Programme: 22 pages with entry **Programme Editor:** Keith Mayhew **Founded:** 1904.
Club Colours: Amber & black **Change Colours:** Sky blue **Reformed:** 1945.
Midweek matchday: Tuesday **Prev. Lges:** Biggleswade & D./ Nth Herts/ South Midlands 51-84.
Club Sponsors: Motorola **Record Attendance:** 1,000 v Letchworth Town, FA Amtr Cup.
Reserves' Lge: UCL Res Div One **Local Newspapers:** Comet, Biggleswade Chronicle.
Clubhouse details: Clubroom, bar, refreshment bar, dressing rooms, physio room.
Rec. scorer/Top scorer 93-94: Roy Boon **Record appearances:** Roy Boon/Dave Chellew.
Captain 1993-94: Gary Redmond **Player of the Year 1993-94:** Dave Chellew.
Hons: Utd Co's Lg R-up 93-94 (KO Cup R-up 91-92, Res Div 1 87-88), Sth Mids Lg 80-81 (R-up 55-56 57-58 58-59 59-60 63-64 65-66 77-78, Div 1 53-54, Chal. Tphy 81-82, Beds Snr Cup 64-65 93-94, Beds Premier Cup 81-82, Beds I'mediate Cup 58-59, Nth Beds Charity Cup 55-56 56-57 61-62 81-82 87-88 90-91, Beds Colts Lg 88-89.

Stamford AFC. Back Row (L/R): Steve Devonport, Simon Filipowicz, Chris Ray, Barry Hand, Shaun Greetham, Simon Hyde, Dennis Rhule, John Mann, Dave Smith. Front: Brett McNamara, Steve Chamberlain, Dave Parker-Meadows, Tim Spriggs, Ian Locke.

Photo - Andrew Eason.

WELLINGBOROUGH TOWN

President: Corville Brown. **Chairman:** Mike Namee
Secretary/Press Officer: Mike Walden, 5 Fernie Way, Wellingborough, Northants NN8 3LB (0933 279561).
Manager: Gordon Higgins
Ground: Dog & Duck, London Road, Wellingborough, Northants (0933 223536).
Directions: 200yds off A45 by-pass, by Dog & Duck PH. 1 mile from Wellingborough (BR).
Capacity: 5,000 **Seats:** 300 **Cover:** 500 **Floodlights:** Yes **Founded:** 1867
Programme: 20 pages **Programme Editor:** Secretary **Club Shop:**
Sponsors: Overstone Park School **Local Press:** Northants Evening Telegraph, Chronicle & Echo.
Club Colours: Blue & gold **Change Colours:** All red. **N'name:** Doughboys
Reserves' Lge: HSUCL Res. Div. Two **Clubhouse:** Full facilities. Open evenings & Sat lunchtimes.
Midweek matchday: Tuesday **Record Attendance:** 4,013 v Kettering Town.
Previous Leagues: Midland 1895-97 98-1901/ Southern 01-05 79-82/ Northants (Utd Co's) 19-34 36-56 61-68/ Central Alliance 56-61/ Metropolitan 68-70/ West Midlands Regional 70-71.
Players progressing to Football Lge: Phil Neal (N'hampton, L'pool & Eng.), Fanny Walden (Spurs & Eng.)
Record transfer fee paid: £50 for Barry Daldy (Corby Town)
Record transfer fee received: £1,200 for Frank Belfon (Rushden Town).
Best FA Cup season: 1st Round 28-29 (v Bristol Rovers) 65-66 (1-2 v Aldershot Town).
Best FA Trophy season: 1st Round 71-72 (lost 0-3 to Dartford after 1-1 and 0-0 draws).
Best FA Vase season: Preliminary Round 89-90 90-91 92-93 93-94.
Captain 1993-94: Tony West **Player of the Year 1993-94:** Peter Belfon
93-94 Top Scorer: Jon Inwood 23 **1993-94 Leading Appearances:** Jon Inwood 41.
Hons: Utd Co's Lg 10-11 62-63 64-65, Metropolitan Lge 69-70, Northants Snr Cup 1896-97 1901-02 02-03 33-34 47-48 49-50 81-82, Maunsell Cup 20-21 21-22.

WOOTTON BLUE CROSS

President: J Clarke. **Chairman:** D Peters
Secretary: Trevor Templeman, 81 Tickford Street, Newport Pagnell, Bucks MK16 9AW (0908 611053).
Manager: Ken Goodeve **Asst Manager:** Neil Simms.
Press Officer: Secretary
Ground: Weston Park, Bedford Road, Wootton (0234 767662).
Directions: Four miles south of Bedford on main road through village at rear of Post Office.
Capacity: 2,000 **Seats:** 50 **Cover:** 250 **Floodlights:** Yes **Founded:** 1887
Programme: 24 pages **Programme Editor:** Secretary. **Club Shop:**
Colours: Blue & white **Change:** All white or all yellow **Sponsors:** Marshall
Nickname: Blue Cross. **Reserve Team's League:** United Counties Reserve Div. Two.
Midweek matchday: Tuesday **Record Gate:** 838 v Luton, Beds Prem. Cup 1988.
Best FA Vase year: 3rd Rd 74-75 **Best FA Cup year:** 2nd Qual. Rd 50-51 (3-4 v Hitchin (H)).
Previous Leagues: Bedford & District/ South Midlands 46-55.
Previous Grounds: Recreation Ground, Fishers Field, Rose & Crown, Cockfield.
Players progressing to Football Lge: Tony Biggs (Arsenal).
Local Newspapers: Bedfordshire Times, Bedford Herald, Beds Express, Beds on Sunday.
Clubhouse details: Main hall, bar, darts, pool, bingo. Open every evening and weekend lunchtimes.
Captain 1993-94: **Player of the Year 1993-94:** Kevin Lamb.
93-94 Top Scorer: Kevin Lamb 20 **1993-94 Leading Appearances:** Kevin Lamb 40.
Hons: Utd Co's Lg Div 2 67-68 69-70 (KO Cup 82-83, Div 2 Cup 64-65), South Midlands Lg 47-48 (R-up 49-50), Beds Senior Cup 70-71, Hinchinbrooke Cup(5).

Wellingborough Town FC 1993-94. *Photo - Neil Whittington.*

DIVISION ONE CLUBS 1994-95

BLISWORTH

Chairman: Pete Edwards **President:** L Piggott.
Secretary: Terry Jeyes, 33 Buttmead, Blisworth, Northampton NN7 3DQ (0604 858750).
Manager: Phil Holding **Assistant Manager/Coach:** Steve Whelan.
Ground: Blisworth Playing Field, Courteenhall Road, Blisworth (0604 858024).
Directions: Courteenhall Road off A43.
Capacity: 1,000 **Seats/Cover:** No **Floodlights** No **Clubhouse:** Yes **Programme:** No.
Colours: Yellow & green **Change colours:** Red & black **Founded:** 1890.
Reserves' Lge: UCL Res. Div. 2 **Previous Lge:** Central Northants Combination 1978-87.
Captain 1993-94: Paul Smith. **Player of the Year 1993-94:** Dave Marell.
1993-94 Top Scorer: Paul Horton 9 **93-94 Leading Apps:** Mark Edwards, Neil Lovell, Paul Smith 30.
Hons: Northants Junior Cup 88-99 **Player progressing to Football Lge:** Dave Johnson (N'pton 83-84)

BRITISH TIMKEN

Chairman: John Hodkinson **Manager:** Kevin Simmonds **Asst Manager:** Dave Smith
Secretary: Gary Duff, 10 Oriel Row, Stefan Hill, Daventry, Northants NN11 4SP (0327 705362).
Ground: Braunston Road, Daventry, Northants (0327 301723).
Directions: A45 from Northampton to outskirts of Daventry, works entrance at top of Braunston Road.
Capacity: 2,500 **Seats:** 150 **Cover:** 150 **Floodlights:** No **Clubhouse:** Yes
Programme: 16 pages with admission. **Reserve Team's League:** Central Northants Comb.
Club colours: Red & black **Change colours:** Yellow & black. **Founded:** 1957.
Previous Name: British Timken Ath. **Previous League:** British Timken Athletic: Rugby & Dist. 57-61.
Best FA Vase season: Preliminary Round 76-77 77-78.
Captain 1993-94: Wayne Brown **Player of the Year 1993-94:** Darren Tann.
93-94 Top Scorer: Russell Brown 8 **1993-94 Leading Appearances:** Stefan Gunter 33.
Hons: British Timken Ath: UCL Div 1 62-63 (Div 1 KO Cup 75-76), Daventry Charity Cup 79-80. British Timken Duston: UCL Div 1 87-88 (Div 2 78-79, Benevolent Cup 87-88), Northants Snr Cup 54-55.

BUGBROOKE St MICHAELS

Chairman: John Curtis **President:** Jack Holt
Secretary: Roger Geary, 31 Kislingbury Rd, Bugbrooke, Northampton NN7 3QG (0604 831678).
Manager: Nick Verity **Asst Manager:** Tony Bonner. **Press Officer:** Rose Harris.
Ground: Birds Close, Gayton Road, Bugbrooke (0604 830707).
Directions: A45 Northampton to Daventry road, onto B4525 (Banbury Lane) at Kislingbury, left into Gayton Road, ground on left.
Capacity: 1,500 **Seats:** None **Cover:** Yes **Floodlights:** Yes **Founded:** 1929
Reserves' Lge: UCL Res. Div. 1 **Clubhouse:** Yes - normal licensing hours.
Programme: Eight pages. **Programme Editor:** Rose Harris **Nickname:** Badgers
Club colours: Blue & yellow **Change colours:** All green. **Record Gate:** 1,156
Previous Ground: School Close **Previous Lge:** Central Northants Combination 1952-87.
Players progressing to Football League: Kevin Slinn (Watford), Craig Adams (Northampton).
Club Sponsors: Church & Newman Builders.
Club Record Scorer: Vince Thomas **Club Record Appearances:** Jimmy Nord.
Captain 1993-94: Dale Williams **Player of the Year 1993-94:** Darren Andrews.
93-94 Top Scorer: Mark Hill 16 **1993-94 Leading Appearances:** Mark Hill 30.
Hons: Northants Jnr Cup 89-90, Central Northants Comb.(6) 68-72 76-77 85-86, UCL Res Div 2 R-up 93-94.

BURTON PARK WANDERERS

Chairman: Bernard Lloyd **Manager:** Ian Clarke
Secretary: David Haynes, 125 Churchill Way, Burton Latimer, Northants NN15 5RT (0536 724871).
Ground: Latimer Park, Polwell Lane, Burton Latimer (0536 725841).
Directions: Entering Burton Latimer, turn off A6 Station Rd and right into Powell Lane; ground on the right.
Capacity: 1,000 **Seats:** 100 **Cover:** 150 **Floodlights:** No **Founded:** 1961
Local Newspapers: Northants Evening Telegraph, Northants Post.
Colours: Yellow/green/black **Change Colours:** Red & black
Prog: 16 pages with entry **Nickname:** The Wanderers **Midweek matchday:** Tuesday
Previous Lge: Kettering Amateur **Record Attendance:** 253 v Rothwell, May 1989
Past Players to progress to Football League: Shaun Wills (Peterborough)
Honours: UCL Div 1 R-up, Benevolent Cup R-up

COTTINGHAM

Chairman: Mike Beadsworth **Manager:** Vinny Keefe **Asst Manager:** Jimmy Rogers
Secretary: Lindsay Brownlie, 30 Bancroft Rd, Cottingham, Market Harborough LE16 8XA (0536 771009).
Ground: Berryfield Rd, Cottingham (0536 770051).
Directions: One and a half miles from Corby on A427 turn right to Cottingham. At junction of B670 turn left; Berryfield Road 200 yds on right.
Capacity: 1,000 **Seats:** None **Cover:** Yes **Floodlights:** No **Programme:** No
Reserves' Lge: UCL Res. Div. 2 **Clubhouse:** Bar & changing rooms **Founded:**
Colours: Blue & black **Change colours:** Tangerine **Nickname:**
Previous Leagues: Market Harborough/ Kettering Amateur/ East Midlands Alliance.
Captain 1993-94: John Sneddon **Player of the Year 1993-94:** Danny Hamill.
93-94 Top Scorer: Jimmy Rogers 9 **1993-94 Leading Appearances:** John Sneddon 32.
Hons: UCL Div 1 R-up, Northants Jnr Cup **Sponsors:** Sportsworld-Pipeline Construction.

DAVENTRY TOWN

Chairman: Ray Humphries **Manager/Coach:** Mark Gwilliam **Asst Manager:** Jim Henderson
Secretary/Press Officer: Cliff Farthing, 45 The Fairway, Daventry, Northants NN11 4NW (0327 72149).
Ground: Elderstubbs Farm, Leamington Way, Daventry, Northants (0327 706286).
Directions: Adjacent to A45 by-pass at top of Staverton Road Sports Complex.
Capacity: 2,000 **Seats:** 250 **Cover:** 250 **Floodlights:** Yes **Founded:** 1886.
Programme: None **Local Newspapers:** Daventry Weekly Express, Herald & Post.
Colours: Black & white **Change colours:** All red. **Nickname:** None.
Midweek Matchday: Tuesday **Reserve Team's League:** Central Northants Comb.
Clubhouse: Large bar/kitchen **Record Attendance:** 350 v Ford Sports 1991.
Best FA Cup year: Prel. Rd 93-94 **Best FA Vase year:** Preliminary Rd 91-92 93-94.
Previous Leagues: Northampton Town (pre-1987)/ Central Northants Combination 87-89.
Players Progressing to Football League: Martin Aldridge (Northampton).
Captain 1993-94: Casey Waldock **Player of the Year 1993-94:** Andy Stoker.
93-94 Top Scorer: Dave Botterill 11 **1993-94 Leading Appearances:** Mark Gwilliam, Andy Stoker 42.
Hons: UCL Div 1(2) 89-91 (Lg Cup R-up 92-93, Highest Aggregate Cup), Northants Junior Cup 36-37 60-61 91-92.

FORD SPORTS

Chairman: Mel Knowles **Manager:** Russell Kennedy **Asst Manager:** Craig Everris.
Secretary: David Hirons, 53 Armull Cres., Daventry, Northants NN11 5AZ (0327 71461).
Ground: Royal Oak Way South, Daventry, Northants (0327 709219).
Directions: Enter Daventry on A45 or A361 and follow signs for Royal Oak Way
Capacity: 1,000 **Seats:** Yes **Cover:** Yes **Floodlights:** Yes **Founded:** 1968
Programme: 12 pages **Reserves' Lge:** UCL Res Div 2 **Clubhouse:** Yes
Colours: All red **Change colours:** Blue & red. **Nickname:** Motormen
Prev. Lge: Central Northants Comb **Player progressing to Football Lge:** Martin Aldridge (N'pton).
Captain 1993-94: Richard Green **P.O.Y. 1993-94:** Gordon Murdoch. **Sponsors:** Zurich.
93-94 Top Scorer: Rod Hough 18 **1993-94 Leading Appearances:** Rod Hough 33.
Hons: UCL Div 1 92-93 (Benevolent Cup R-up 92-93, Highest Aggregate Goalscoring Trophy 92-93).

HARROWBY UNITED

Chairman: Peter Beck **Manager:** Charlie Harvey **Coach:** Roy Walton
Secretary: Charlie Harvey, 64 Queensway, Grantham, Lincs NG31 9QD (0476 70255).
Ground: Harrowby Playing Fields, Harrowby Lane, Grantham (0476 590822).
Directions: From A1 take B6403, go past A52 roundabout, past Ancaster turn and take road to Harrowby. Continue into Grantham, ground on right opposite Cherry Tree public house.
Capacity: 1,500 **Seats:** 100 **Cover:** 150 **Floodlights:** No **Founded:** 1949.
Programme: 12 pages **Clubhouse:** Large bar open normal licensing hours.
Colours: Blue & white **Change colours:** Red & white. **Nickname:** Arrows.
Reserves' League: Grantham **Best FA Vase season:** Preliminary Round 91-92.
Previous Leagues: Grantham/ Lincs/ East Mids Regional Alliance (pre 1990).
Players progressing to Football League: Richard Liburd (Middlesbrough).
Captain 1993-94: Paul Weston **Player of the Year 1993-94:** Andy Sharpe.
93-94 Top Scorer: Graham Faust **1993-94 Leading Appearances:** Andy Sharpe 32.
Hons: Utd Co's Lg Div 1 91-92 (Benev. Cup R-up 91-92), Mids Regional All. 89-90 (Lg Cup 89-90), Lincs Snr 'B' Cup(2) 90-92.

HIGHAM TOWN

Chairman: Phil Palmer **Vice Chairman:** Robin James **President:** Robin James.
Secretary: Chris Ruff, 23 Queensway, Higham Ferrers NN10 8BU (0933 58862).
Manager: Gary Savage **Assistant Manager:** Alan Strickland
Coach: Kevin Roberts **Physio:** Keith Bates.
Ground: Recreation Ground, Vine Hill Drive, Higham Ferrers (0933 53751).
Directions: From Kettering 1st right on A6 after A45 junction to St Neots. From Bedford, 3rd left after entering town on A6 from Rushden. Higham is served by London-Bedford-Corby United Counties Coachlines, and United Counties local services Northampton-Raunds and Bedford-Kettering.
Capacity: 1,000 **Seats:** Nil **Cover:** 100 **Floodlights:** No **Founded:** 1895.
Programme: 12 pages with admission **Editor:** Secretary **Reformed:** 1920 & 1946
Colours: Sky/navy **Change colours:** Olive/white **Nickname:** Lankies.
Midweek home matches: Tuesday **Reserves' Lge:** UCL Reserve Div. **Sponsors:** Alpha Tankers
Previous Lges: Wellingborough 20-21/ Northants (now Utd Co's) 21-36/ Rushden 46-50.
Prev. Grnd: Duchy Farm Field 20-24 **Rec. Gate:** 5,700 v Chesterfield, FA Cup final qual. rd rep. 22-23.
Record win: 15-0 v Towcester Town (H), United Counties League Division One 3/4/93.
Record defeat: 0-12 v Kettering Town (A), United Counties League 8/2/36.
Past players progressing to Football League: Ernie Toseland (Coventry City 1928), George Webb (Manchester United 1936), Dave Ballard (Nottingham Forest 1958).
Clubhouse: Open during football season 8.30-11pm Tues, Thurs & Fri, from the end of Saturday games and noon-1.30pm Sundays. Light refreshments available after Saturday games.
Record scorer: Stuart Sinfield 136 **Record appearances:** Brian Harbour 485.
Captain 1993-94: Paul Redding **P.O.Y 1993-94:** John Sellers **1993-94 Top Scorer:** Ken Ogden 27
Hons: UCL Div 1 R-up 70-71 71-72 92-93 93-94, Northants Lg 21-22 22-23 (R-up 23-24 26-27), Northants Snr Cup 21-22 (R-up 30-31 32-33), Maunsell Premier Cup 22-23 33-34.

IRCHESTER UNITED

Chairman: Geoff Cotter **Manager:** Alan Ambridge.
Secretary: Perry Mayhew, 25 Finedon Street, Burton Latimer, Northants (0536 723341).
Ground: Alfred Street, Irchester (0933 312877).
Directions: Off Rushden Road to Wollaston Road, next to recreation ground.
Capacity: 1,000 **Seats:** None **Cover:** Yes **Floodlights:** No **Programme:** No
Colours: Black & yellow **Change colours:** White & claret **Clubhouse:** Yes
Reserves' Lge: UCL Res. Div. 2 **Previous Leagues:** Rushden & District 1936-69.
Best FA Cup year: Prel. Rd 34-35 **Best FA Vase year:** Preliminary Round 77-78.
Captain 1993-94: Roy Geeves **Player of the Year 1993-94:** Andy Toon.
93-94 Top Scorer: Dave Pocock 11 **1993-94 Leading Appearances:** Matt Tomkins 32.
Hons: Northants Lg Div 2 30-31 31-32, Northants Snr Cup 29-30 48-49 75-76, Rushden & District Lg 28-29 29-30 36-37 46-47 50-51 51-52 56-57.

NORTHAMPTON VANAID

Chairman: Rob Clarke **Manager:** Dick Underwood **Asst Manager:** Mick Calvert.
Secretary: Tony Loveday, 28 Rickyard Rd, The Arbours, Northampton NN3 3RR (0604 412502).
Ground: Fernie Fields, Moulton, Northampton (0604 670366).
Directions: R'bout at Lumbertub pub take turn to Moulton, 1st right signposted.
Capacity: 700 **Seats:** 100 **Cover:** Yes **Floodlights:** **Founded:** 1968
Programme: Yes **Programme Editor:** Tony Asker **Clubhouse:** Large bar. Hot food/bar meals
Colours: Blue/black/black **Change colours:** White & blue **Nickname:** Vans.
Prev. Lge: N'pton Town (pre-1993) **Reserves' Lge:** UCL Res Div 2 **Record Gate:** 78
Club Sponsors: Vanaid/ Crisis Couriers.
Captain 1993-94: Tim Agutter **Player of the Year 1993-94:** Nicky Cole.
Top Scorer 93-94: Adam Sandy 26 **Leading Appearances 93-94:** Adam Sandy, Kevin Ugo 36.
Honours: UCL Div 1 93-94 (Benevolent Cup R-up 93-94), Northants Jnr Cup 93-94, Northampton Town Lg 88-89 89-90.

NORTHAMPTON O.N. CHENECKS

Chairman: John Wilson **Manager:** Tony Pancoust.
Secretary: John Goodger, 74 Beech Avenue, Northampton NN3 2JG (0604 717224).
Ground: Billing Road, Northampton (0604 34045).
Directions: South ring road, exit A43 Kettering, left at lights, top of hill, ground 200 yds on right.
Capacity: 1,350 **Seats:** Yes **Cover:** Yes **Floodlights:** No **Founded:** 1946.
Prog.: 16 pages with entry **Reserves' Lge:** UCL Res Div 1 **Clubhouse:** Yes
Colours: White & blue **Change colours:** All red
Prev. Lge: N'pton Town (pre-1969) **Hons:** UCL Div 1 77-78 79-80, Northants Jnr Cup R-up 93-94
Captain 1993-94: **Player of the Year 1993-94:** Mark Tyrell.
93-94 Top Scorer: Andy Evans 28 **1993-94 Leading Appearances:** Mark Tyrell 32.

OLNEY TOWN

Chairman: Peter Shipton **Manager:** Alan Byron **Asst Manager:** Barry Simons
Secretary: Andrew Baldwin, 49 Midland Road, Olney, Bucks MK46 4BP (0234 711071)
Ground: East Street, Olney (0234 712227)
Directions: Enter Olney on A509 from Wellingborough, 100yds on left enter East St, ground 200 yds on left.
Capacity: 2,000 **Seats:** None **Cover:** Yes **Floodlights:** No **Prog.:** 32 pages
Club colours: White & black **Change colours:** Green & yellow. **Clubhouse:** Yes
Prev. Lges: Nth Bucks, Rushden & Dist. **Hons:** UCL Div 1 72-73, Berks & Bucks I'mediate Cup 92-93
Captain 1993-94: Paul Banks **Player of the Year 1993-94:** Clive Woodland.
1993-94 Leading Scorers: Clive Woodland (33 league + 2 Cup), Tommy Collins (17 league).
1993-94 Leading Appearances: Clive Woodland 31 (from 32), Paul Banks 31.

RAMSEY TOWN

Chairman: Ian Cooper **Vice-Chairman:** Syd Mortlock **President:** Albert Jones
Secretary: Mike Baldwin, 19 Slade Close, Ramsey, Cambs PE17 1LF (0487 814084).
Manager: Steve Jackson **Asst Manager:** Steve Long **Coach:** Simon Ward.
Physio: Danny Richardson **Press Officer:** Ian Cooper **Comm. Manager:** Hazel Dawson.
Ground: Cricketfield Lane, Ramsey, Huntingdon, Cambridgeshire PE17 1BG (0487 814218)
Directions: 100 yds off B1040 Ramsey to Warboys road.
Capacity: 1,000 **Seats:** None **Cover:** 50 **Floodlights:** Yes **Founded:**
Programme: 12 pages with admission **Editor:** Barry Colam (0487 812709) **Club Shop:** No.
Club colours: Amber & black **Change colours:** Red & white. **Nickname:** Rams
Sponsors: Burton Brothers Vauxhall **Previous Lge:** Peterborough & Dist. **Prev. Grounds:** None
Reserves' Lge: P'boro & Dist. **Honours:** UCL Div 1, Hunts Senior Cup(3).
Player progressing to Football Lge: Alec Chamberlain (Sunderland)
Clubhouse: Weekdays 6-11pm, Sat 11am-11pm, Sun noon-10.30pm.
Record scorer: Jim Barron **Record appearances & Top Scorer 93-94:** Stuart Kilby
Captain 1993-94: Steve Long **Player of the Year 1993-94:** Gary Richardson.

PHOTOS OPPOSITE

Top: *St Ives Town goalkeeper S Collins makes a fine reflex save to deny Roy Anderson, but his side still slip to a 0-6 defeat in this October 16th Division One fixture.*
Photo - Martin Wray

Centre: *Northampton ON Chenecks FC.*
Photo - Martin Wray

Top: *Andrew Bailey nets the winner in Olney Town's 2-1 home win over Bugbrooke St Michaels on a rain-swept New Year's Day.*
Photo - Neil Whittington.

St IVES TOWN

President: Ken Booth **Chairman:** Stewart White **Vice-Chairman:** Trevor Pryor.
Secretary: Jim Stocker, 23 Townsend Rd, Needingworth, St Ives, Cambs PE17 3SE (0480 492680).
Manager: Tony Coulson **Asst Mgr:** Warren Everdell **Coach:** Bob Broom.
Press Officer: Bob Sowter. **Comm. Manager:** Brian Reynolds **Physio:** Bob Money.
Ground: Westwood Rd, St Ives, Cambs (0480 63207).
Directions: From Huntingdon: A1123 thru Houghton, right at 2nd lighs into Ramsey Rd, after quarter mile turn right opp. Fire Station into Westwood Rd. From A604: Follow Huntingdon signs past 5 r'bouts, left into Ramsey Rd at lights then follow as above.
Capacity: 5,000 **Seats:** 130 **Cover:** 300 **Floodlights:** Yes **Founded:** 1887.
Programme: 8 pages **Editor:** Trevor Pryor (0480 497158) **Nickname:** Saints
Club colours: White & black **Change colours:** Blue & white. **Club Shop:** No.
Reserves' Lge: UCL Res Div 2 **Clubhouse:** Bar and entertainment room. Normal licensing hours.
Midweek home matchday: Tuesday **Record Gate:** 400 v Saffron Walden Town, FA Vase.
Previous Ground: Meadow Lane **Prev. Lges:** Cambs/ Central Amtr/ Hunts/ P'boro. & D. (pre-1985).
Best FA Vase year: 2nd Rd 89-89. **Best FA Cup year:** Prelim. Rd 50-51 (lost 2-5 at St Neots & Dist.)
Captain 1993-94: Cliff Miles **Player of the Year 1993-94:** Richard Ashton.
93-94 Top Scorer: Dean Parkes 27 **93-94 Leading Appearances:** Warren Everdell 34.
Honours: Hunts Snr Cup 00-01 11-12 22-23 25-26 29-30 81-82 86-87 87-88, Cambs Lg 22-23 23-24 24-25.

St NEOTS TOWN

Chairman: Bob Page **Press Officer:** Mike Birch.
Secretary: John Carroll, 95 St Neots Rd, Sandy, Beds SG19 1BP (0767 680709).
Manager: Guy Loveday **Asst Manager:** Tony McGovern**Coach:** Pete Brown.
Ground: Rowley Park, Cambridge Rd, St Neots, Cambs (0480 470012).
Directions: Through town centre, under railway bridge, 1st left.
Capacity: 3,000 **Seats:** TBA **Cover:** 250 **Floodlights:** Due **Founded:** 1879
Programme: Yes **Programme Editor:** Mike Birch **Nickname:** Saints
Reserves' Lge: UCL Res Div 2 **Clubhouse:** Built 1994. **Sponsors:** TBA
Club colours: Sky & navy **Change colours:** Blue & gold.
Previous Ground: Shortsands **Best FA Cup year:** 1st Rd 66-67 (lost 0-2 at Walsall).
Best FA Vase year: 3rd Rd 78-78 **Best FA Trophy year:** Second Qualifying Round 69-70 72-73.
Record Gate: 2,000 v Wisbech, 1966 **Previous Name:** St Neots & District 1879-1957.
Previous Lges: South Midlands 27-36 46-49/ United Counties 36-39 51-56 66-69 73-88/ Metropolitan 49-51 60-66/ Central Alliance 56-60/ Eastern Counties 69-73/ Huntingdonshire 90-94.
Captain 1993-94: John Carroll **Player of the Year 1993-94:** Jerry Green.
93-94 Top Scorer: Steve Gailbraith **Players progressing to Football Lge:** Frank Atkins (Cambridge).
Honours: Hunts Snr Cup(33), UCL 67-68 (KO Cup 67-68 68-69), Metropolitan Lg 49-50 (Lg Cup 79-80), South Midlands Lg 32-33, Huntingdonshire Lg 90-91 92-92 92-93 93-94.

SHARNBROOK

Chairman: Peter Butler **Manager:** Dick Williams **Asst Manager:** Roy Boulton
Secretary: Rob Stanton, 4 Towns End Rd, Sharnbrook, Beds (0234 782052).
Ground: Lodge Rd, Sharnbrook (0234 781080).
Directions: Second sign to Sharnbrook from Rushden on A6, under railway bridge, right at T-junction, left past church, right into Lodge Road.
Capacity: 1,000 **Seats:** None **Cover:** Yes **Floodlights:** No **Programme:** 12 pages
Colours: Claret & blue **Change colours:** Yellow & black. **Clubhouse:** Yes
Reserves' Lge: UCL Res Div 2 **Previous Leagues:** Bedford & District (pre-1968).
Hons: Beds I'mediate Cup 73-74 **Player progressing to Football Lge:** Matt Jackson (Luton, Everton)
93-94 Top Scorer: Alex McConville 8 **1993-94 Leading Appearances:** Steve Coverin 34.

THRAPSTON VENTURAS

President: Denis Barber **Chairman:** David Morson
Secretary: Derek Pickard, 9 Springfield Ave., Thrapston, Northants (0832 734102)
Manager: Gary Petts **Asst Manager:** Peter Wills. **Press Officer:** Mark James.
Ground: Chancery Lane, Thrapston, Northants (08012 732470).
Directions: Chancery Lane off A605 in town centre.
Capacity: 1,000 **Seats:** Yes **Cover:** Yes **Floodlights:** No **Founded:** 1960.
Programme: Yes **Programme Editor:** Mrs A J Petts **Prev. Lge:** Kettering Amtr (pre-1978)
Reserves' Lge: UCL Res Div 2 **Sponsors:** Thrapston Warehousing **Clubhouse:** Yes
Colours: Blue & white **Change colours:** All yellow **Nickname:** Venturas
Captain 1993-94: Lee Howard **Player of the Year 1993-94:** Paddy Lynch.
93-94 Top Scorer: Mark James 15
93-94 Leading Appearances: Simon Elbrow 31.
Honours: Northants Junior Cup 87-88, Kettering Amateur Lg 70-71 72-73 73-74 77-78.

WELLINGBOROUGH WHITWORTHS

Chairman: B Jarvis **Manager:** Ian Young **Asst Manager:** Martin Goodes.
Secretary: Ron Edwards, 15 James Rd, Wellingborough NN8 2LR (0933 227765).
Ground: London Road, Wellingborough, Northants (0933 227324).
Directions: Off London Road at Dog & Duck public house
Capacity: 700 **Seats:** None **Cover:** Yes **Floodlights:** No **Programme:** No
Colours: Blue & white **Change colours:** Green & white **Clubhouse:** Yes
Reserves' Lge: UCL Res Div 2 **Previous Leagues:** Rushden & Dist./ East Mids Alliance (pre-1985).
Captain 1993-94: Steve Grant **Player of the Year 1993-94:** Colin Ridgewas.
93-94 Top Scorer: Steve Benson 20 **1993-94 Leading Appearances:** Steve Grant 34.
Honours: Rushden & District Lg 76-77.

FEEDER TO:
BEAZER HOMES LEAGUE

President: D D Baker

Chairman: P C Wager

Vice-Chairman: E V Ward

Hon. Secretary: A R Vinter, The Smithy, The Square, Chilham, Canterbury, Kent CT4 8BY (0227 730884)

Champions in 1991-92, Herne Bay regained the Division One Championship in 1993-94 after completing an excellent season that saw them suffer only three League defeats and win the title by twenty five points from second placed Furness. The home record of nineteen wins and one defeat - that was against Tunbridge Wells - was second to none. Furness, one of the sides to defeat Herne Bay during the season, finished in a very creditable second place ahead of Chatham Town on goal difference with Thamesmead Town in fourth place.

At the foot of the table, Kent Police were left with the wooden spoon after completing a miserable season winning only once (that was in their last League match of the season against Darenth Heathside) and conceding an unfortunate 188 goals, 102 of those away from home. Darenth Heathside finished next to bottom after a poor season by their standards.

In Division two, Dover Athletic won the Championship by one point from the second placed club Herne Bay with Thamesmead Town in third place.

In the Divisional Cups, Ramsgate came from behind to beat Deal Town in the Final of the Division One Cup by two goals to one to retain the trophy they won the previous season, whilst in the Division Two Cup Dover Athletic completed the "double" when they beat Tonbridge in the Final. In the Kent Senior Trophy, Alma Swanley lifted the Cup by beating Folkestone Invicta in the Final but unfortunately they are no longer with us after their recent demise. In the Kent Intermediate Cup, Bromley beat Whitstable Town in the Final by four goals to one.

Nationally, Tunbridge Wells made good progress in the FA Vase whilst other clubs accounted for themselves well against tougher opponents in both Cup and Vase.

Ground improvements continue amongst the Winstonlead Kent League clubs and it is hoped in the near future that Sheppey United, who have been ground sharing with Faversham Town, will be returning "home" to a new venue. Dartford, who played at Cray Wanderers during the season, are now planning to share with Erith & Belvedere and, in the next few years, I'm sure they will be looking to return to their natural home.

Paul Rivers, Press Officer

Herne Bay - Winstonlead Kent League champions 1993-94. *Photo - Kentish Gazette.*

DIV. ONE	P	W	D	L	F	A	PTS
Herne Bay	40	33	4	3	102	26	103
Furness	40	23	9	8	94	37	78
Chatham Town	40	23	9	8	86	50	78
Thamesmead Town	40	21	11	8	93	47	74
Alma Swanley	40	22	8	10	90	50	74
Dartford	40	21	11	8	70	44	74
Beckenham Town	40	22	4	14	85	59	70
Corinthian	40	21	6	13	91	51	69
Ramsgate	40	20	6	14	90	67	66
Deal Town	40	18	8	14	102	73	62
Sheppey United	40	17	10	13	69	67	61
Folkestone Invicta	40	17	6	17	83	73	57
Faversham Town	40	14	6	20	68	80	48
Greenwich Borough	40	14	5	21	72	85	47
Whitstable Town	40	12	9	19	68	72	45
Tunbridge Wells	40	11	10	19	54	71	43
Cray Wanderers	40	11	9	20	37	65	42
Crockenhill	40	8	10	22	55	99	*33
Slade Green	40	8	7	25	42	87	31
Darenth Heathside	40	5	4	31	38	128	19
Kent Police	40	1	4	35	30	188	7

DIV. TWO	P	W	D	L	F	A	PTS
Dover Ath. Res.	24	17	4	3	56	15	55
Herne Bay Res.	24	17	3	4	51	25	54
Thamesmead Res.	24	13	6	5	53	27	45
Whitstable Res.	24	11	9	4	43	26	*41
Tonbridge AFC Res.	24	11	3	10	47	30	36
Hastings T. Res.	24	9	8	7	52	50	35
Folkestone I. Res.	24	8	5	11	44	51	29
Beckenham T. Res.	24	7	6	11	42	50	27
Chatham T. Res.	24	7	5	12	30	44	26
Deal Town Res.	24	7	1	16	26	62	22
Darenth H. Res.	24	5	6	13	31	43	21
Canterbury C. Res.	24	5	6	13	30	55	21
Ramsgate Res.	24	5	6	13	22	49	21

* - 1 point deducted

WINSTONLEAD KENT LEAGUE DIVISION ONE RESULT CHART 1993-94

HOME TEAM	1	2	3	4	5	6	7	8	9	10	11	12	13	14	15	16	17	18	19	20	21
1. Alma Swanley	*	1-0	1-1	0-2	1-1	5-0	5-3	1-1	3-2	2-0	5-0	0-3	6-0	0-2	6-0	2-1	0-3	2-0	0-3	3-0	0-3
2. Beckenham T.	2-1	*	1-1	2-1	5-0	0-0	6-2	0-4	1-3	2-0	2-1	1-1	5-1	2-1	7-2	2-3	0-1	2-0	3-2	3-1	2-1
3. Chatham Town	2-0	4-2	*	5-1	3-1	1-1	8-0	2-1	2-1	4-1	2-0	0-1	5-1	0-1	3-0	2-0	1-2	0-1	3-2	1-1	0-0
4. Corinthian	0-0	3-4	2-2	*	0-1	3-1	5-1	0-2	0-1	3-0	3-3	1-0	1-3	0-1	4-1	0-2	4-1	4-0	5-1	3-0	6-0
5. Cray Wanderers	0-1	1-0	0-2	2-2	*	0-0	2-1	1-2	2-1	1-0	1-2	1-2	0-1	0-1	2-0	1-1	0-2	1-0	1-1	1-1	1-1
6. Crockenhill	0-6	2-2	1-2	2-6	1-1	*	4-3	2-1	0-3	0-4	3-3	0-3	2-3	1-2	3-0	3-3	1-6	0-0	2-3	1-0	1-3
7. Darenth H'side	0-2	0-2	2-1	1-4	1-2	1-5	*	2-2	2-9	0-3	1-3	0-7	2-3	1-4	2-0	0-6	0-0	1-4	1-2	2-3	1-0
8. Dartford	2-3	2-0	0-2	0-0	1-0	4-1	1-0	*	2-2	2-1	0-0	1-2	2-1	0-0	1-1	1-0	3-1	6-1	0-4	4-4	2-2
9. Deal Town	1-1	0-4	2-3	1-2	6-2	7-2	1-1	0-1	*	6-0	2-2	2-4	5-2	2-2	5-2	2-1	2-2	4-1	1-4	2-1	2-1
10. Faversham Town	1-2	1-2	2-3	0-2	1-0	1-1	5-0	1-1	3-1	*	1-2	4-4	2-0	2-4	3-2	0-3	4-1	3-1	1-4	1-0	3-2
11. Folkestone Invicta	1-2	3-1	3-4	0-5	5-1	2-0	3-0	1-2	3-1	3-3	*	1-2	1-0	0-2	8-0	1-3	4-1	1-3	0-1	3-1	5-1
12. Furness	0-2	1-2	2-3	2-0	3-0	0-1	0-0	1-0	3-1	1-0	0-1	*	1-1	1-0	11-0	3-5	5-1	3-1	1-1	1-1	4-0
13. Greenwich Boro.	1-2	2-1	0-0	0-3	0-1	5-3	3-0	2-2	0-1	4-2	4-0	0-7	*	1-2	8-1	0-1	3-0	1-1	1-1	3-0	1-2
14. Herne Bay	3-1	2-1	5-0	3-0	3-1	2-0	6-0	2-1	4-2	1-0	2-1	1-0	3-0	*	5-0	4-0	4-1	5-0	2-1	2-3	4-0
15. Kent Police	0-4	2-6	0-4	1-2	2-4	1-1	2-1	0-4	1-5	1-2	1-7	1-6	1-9	0-7	*	1-5	2-2	0-3	1-7	2-2	0-5
16. Ramsgate	1-1	3-4	0-0	0-4	1-0	4-2	2-3	4-5	0-4	5-0	3-2	1-4	4-2	1-2	4-0	*	4-2	5-1	2-0	2-1	2-3
17. Sheppey United	2-2	1-0	3-2	2-1	4-1	2-3	4-0	0-3	2-2	3-1	3-0	2-2	0-3	0-3	5-1	1-0	*	1-0	1-1	0-0	1-0
18. Slade Green	2-6	1-2	0-2	2-2	0-1	0-2	0-1	0-1	1-5	2-3	2-3	1-1	1-0	2-2	3-0	1-3	2-2	*	1-4	0-0	1-5
19. Thamesmead T.	4-4	1-0	4-1	2-0	1-1	2-1	3-0	0-1	5-2	1-1	0-2	0-0	4-1	0-1	9-0	1-1	1-1	3-1	*	2-0	3-0
20. Tunbridge Wells	3-2	1-0	2-3	0-4	4-1	2-1	2-0	0-1	0-2	4-4	4-2	0-1	4-2	1-1	2-0	1-2	2-1	0-1	2-4	*	1-3
21. Whitstable Town	0-5	2-4	2-2	1-3	2-0	3-1	4-2	0-1	1-1	0-4	1-1	0-1	6-0	0-1	11-1	1-1	0-2	0-1	1-1	0-0	*

DIVISION TWO RESULT CHART 1993-94

HOME TEAM	1	2	3	4	5	6	7	8	9	10	11	12	13
1. Beckenham Town Res.	*	7-3	5-0	2-2	3-0	2-1	1-1	0-3	3-4	0-0	1-3	1-2	2-2
2. Canterbury City Res.	3-0	*	2-2	0-0	3-1	3-2	0-4	2-2	0-3	0-2	2-2	0-3	1-3
3. Chatham Town Res.	3-0	2-1	*	2-1	3-0	1-3	4-0	0-1	0-1	0-3	1-1	0-0	0-1
4. Darenth H. Res.	1-3	2-0	0-1	*	2-3	0-5	3-0	1-1	1-3	2-2	4-0	0-2	2-0
5. Deal Town Res.	3-1	1-2	3-2	0-1	*	0-2	2-5	0-5	1-3	1-1	0-1	1-0	0-4
6. Dover Ath. Res.	3-0	2-1	4-1	2-1	4-1	*	4-0	7-0	3-0	2-1	1-1	3-0	2-0
7. Folkestone Invicta Res.	1-2	7-2	4-1	0-0	4-1	0-1	*	3-1	2-3	0-0	3-2	2-3	1-4
8. Hastings T. Res.	2-2	1-1	3-1	3-2	0-3	2-2	11-2	*	1-1	5-1	1-2	4-3	1-1
9. Herne Bay Res.	3-0	1-0	1-1	4-1	1-3	1-0	2-1	2-1	*	6-0	1-0	2-0	1-1
10. Ramsgate Res.	1-4	1-1	2-2	1-0	0-1	0-1	2-1	3-0	1-3	*	0-1	1-7	0-2
11. Thamesmead T. Res.	6-1	5-1	2-0	4-2	4-0	0-0	2-2	8-0	0-3	3-0	*	1-0	1-1
12. Tonbridge AFC Res.	1-1	0-2	5-1	2-0	6-0	0-2	0-1	1-2	1-0	6-0	1-4	*	1-1
13. Whitstable T. Res.	2-1	2-0	1-2	3-3	5-1	0-0	0-0	2-2	4-2	1-0	2-0	1-3	*

DIVISION ONE CUP 1993-94

First Round

Dartford v Whitstable Town	1-2
Chatham Town v Thamesmead Town	0-1
Crockenhill v Slade Green	2-1
Folkestone Invicta v Kent Police	2-0
Faversham Town v Corinthian	1-2

Second Round

Greenwich Borough v Deal Town	1-2
Whitstable Town v Sheppey United	3-0
Tunbridge Wells v Folkestone Invicta	2-5
Ramsgate v Furness	3-1
Darenth Heathside v Cray Wanderers	0-4
Alma Swanley v Herne Bay	0-1
Thamesmead Town v Beckenham Town	3-2
Corinthian v Crockenhill	1-2

Quarter Finals

Deal Town v Cray Wanderers	7-2
Folkestone Invicta v Thamesmead Town	0-2
Whitstable Town v Herne Bay	2-1 *(aet)*
Ramsgate v Crockenhill	9-1

Semi-Finals (Two-legged)

Deal Town v Whitstable Town	3-0,0-0
Thamesmead Town v Ramsgate	1-4,2-1

Final: Ramsgate 2, Deal Town 1

DIVISION TWO CUP 1993-94

GROUP A.	P	W	D	L	F	A	PTS
Thamesmead Res.	4	3	1	0	14	4	10
Beckenham T. Res.	4	2	1	1	11	6	7
Darenth H. Res.	4	0	0	4	1	16	0

RESULTS	1	2	3
1. Beckenham Town Reserves	*	3-0	2-2
2. Darenth Heathside Reserves	0-5	*	1-5
3. Thamesmead Town Reserves	4-1	3-0	*

GROUP B.	P	W	D	L	F	A	PTS
Tonbridge Res.	4	2	1	1	9	10	7
Folkestone I. Res.	4	1	2	1	11	9	5
Hastings T. Res.	4	1	1	2	7	8	4

RESULTS	1	2	3
1. Folkestone Inv. Reserves	*	1-1	5-1
2. Hastings Town Reserves	4-2	*	1-2
3. Tonbridge AFC Reserves	3-3	3-1	*

GROUP C.	P	W	D	L	F	A	PTS
Herne Bay Res.	4	3	0	1	9	4	9
Whitstable Res.	4	2	0	2	5	5	6
Chatham T. Res.	4	1	0	3	3	8	3

RESULTS	1	2	3
1. Chatham Town Reserves	*	2-1	0-3
2. Herne Bay Reserves	3-1	*	2-1
3. Whitstable Town Reserves	1-0	0-3	*

GROUP D.	P	W	D	L	F	A	PTS
Dover Ath. Res.	6	6	0	0	27	0	18
Deal Town Res.	6	2	1	3	13	11	7
Ramsgate Res.	6	2	0	4	5	16	6
Canterbury Res.	6	1	1	4	6	24	4

RESULTS	1	2	3	4
1. Canterbury C. Reserves	*	2-2	0-7	2-1
2. Deal Town Reserves	4-1	*	0-2	6-0
3. Dover Ath. Reserves	8-0	4-0	*	2-0
4. Ramsgate Reserves	2-1	2-1	0-4	*

SEMI-FINALS (Two-legs):

Thamesmead Town Res. 0, Tonbridge Res. 0
Tonbridge Res. 1, Thamesmead Town Res. 0

Herne Bay Res. 3, Dover Athletic Res. 3
Dover Ath. Res. *(w/o)* Herne Bay Res. *(scr)*

FINAL:

Dover Atletic Reserves 4, Tonbridge AFC Res. 2

KENT LEAGUE DIVISION ONE TEN-YEAR RECORD

	84/5	85/6	86/7	87/8	88/9	89/0	90/1	91/2	92/3	93/4
Alma Swanley	11	1	3	12	6	5	8	5	5	5
Beckenham Town	4	15	15	8	17	12	14	14	9	7
Chatham Town	-	-	-	-	19	16	12	19	6	3
Corinthian	-	-	-	-	-	-	-	13	20	8
Cray Wanderers	5	14	10	7	7	18	2	18	17	17
Crockenhill	16	3	2	19	13	15	15	16	21	18
Danson (Bexley Borough)(Furness United)						*(see Furness)*				
Darenth Heathside	8	4	9	11	4	10	13	21	19	20
Dartford	-	-	-	-	-	-	-	-	-	6
Deal Town	12	18	16	16	2	4	5	3	4	10
Faversham Town	7	6	17	2	3	1	6	2	15	13
Folkestone Invicta	-	-	-	-	-	-	-	-	13	12
Furness	-	-	-	15	14	17	18	20	7	2
Greenwich Borough	6	7	1	1	16	6	17	9	16	14
Herne Bay	13	11	5	18	20	14	3	1	2	1
Hythe Town	2	12	11	5	1	-	-	-	-	-
Kent Police	15	9	18	6	12	11	19	11	18	21
Metropolitan Police (Hayes)	9	13	14	13	15	19	20	w/d	-	-
Ramsgate	17	8	4	10	9	20	10	10	12	9
Sheppey United	-	-	-	-	-	-	21	6	3	11
Sittingbourne	3	2	6	4	5	2	1	-	-	-
Slade Green	14	17	12	14	10	9	9	8	11	19
Thamesmead Town	-	-	-	-	-	-	-	17	8	4
Thames Polytechnic	-	10	13	17	18	13	16	15	-	-
Tonbridge AFC	-	-	-	-	-	-	3	4	1	-
Tunbridge Wells	1	5	7	9	11	7	11	12	14	16
Whitstable Town	10	16	8	3	8	8	7	7	10	15
Number of clubs	**17**	**18**	**18**	**19**	**20**	**20**	**21**	**22**	**21**	**21**

MANAGERS OF THE MONTH

Oct: Tommy Sampson (Herne B.)
Nov: John Adams (Chatham)
Dec: Jim Nokes (Deal Town)
Jan: Jim Nokes (Deal Town)
Feb: Lennie Lee (Ramsgate)
Mar: Todd Dowling (Corinthian)
Ap/May: Todd Dowling (Corinthian)

DIV. 2 TOP SCORERS

Lee Annett (Corinthian) 43
Dean Bowey (Thamesmead) 43
Karl Smith (Ramsgate) 40
Lee Bosson (Folkestone) 29
Wayne Barlow (Chatham) 27
Mark Wadhams (Deal) 26
Jonathon Lewis (Deal) 25
Glenn Payne (Thamesmead) 25
Mark Munday (Herne Bay) 24
Lee Garrett (Corinthian) 23

DIV. 2 TOP SCORERS

Liam Fox (Dover) 20
Danny Beal (Hastings) 17
Ian Walker (Herne B.) 16
Steve Rumball (Whitstable) 15
Jason Stephens (Whitstable) 13
Sean Pilbeam (Dover) 12

ALMA SWANLEY

(Resigned but, at time of going to press rumoured to have been readmitted. Ground as Furness FC)

BECKENHAM TOWN

Chairman: Les Chandler. **Vice Chairman:** B Hollaway.
Secretary: Peter Palmer, 107 Wentworth Rd, West Croydon, Surrey CR0 3HZ (081 689 2134).
Manager: Kevin Sugrue **Asst Manager/Press Officer:** Bob Chilvers (081 301 2624).
Ground: Eden Park Avenue, Beckenham, Kent (081 650 1066).
Directions: M25, A21 to Bromley then follow signs to Beckenham. Ground 1 mile west of town off A214, 2 mins walk from Eden Park (BR) station - trains from London Bridge. Bus 264.
Seats: 120 **Cover:** 120 **Capacity:** 4,000 **Floodlights:** Yes **Reformed:** 1971.
Colours: Red & white/red/white **Change Colours:** White/black/white **Nickname:** Reds.
Midweek matchday: Wednesday **Record Gate:** 692 v Greenwich Borough, League 1988.
Sponsors: F M Conway Ltd **Prev. Ground:** Stanhope Grove, Beckenham (60 yrs)
Previous Leagues: South East London Amtr 71-73/ Metropolitan 73-75/ London Spartan 75-82.
Programme: 8 pages, 50p **Programme Editor:** Bob Chilvers (081 301 2624)
Clubhouse: All day opening at weekends. Hot & cold food, teas, coffees, hotdogs, burgers, crusty rolls, bread pudding etc on matchdays. Bar and dance area. Pool tables and fruit machines.
Record Scorer: Ricky Bennett **Record appearances:** Lee Fabian.
Captain 93-94: Dave Eden **Club Shop:** Yes - contact secretary.
P.o.Y.: Jason Bragg **Top Scorer 93-94:** John Bull.
Hons: London Spartan Lg Cup R-up 77-78 78-79, Kent Snr Tphy R-up 81-82 93-94, Kent Lg Cup R-up 84-85 92-93 (Div 2 Cup R-up 90-91).

CANTERBURY CITY

Chairman: Geoff J Bradley **President:** V H Heslop.
Secretary/Press Officer: Keith J Smith, 7 Knight Ave., London Rd Est., Canterbury, Kent CT2 8PZ (0227 456116).
Manager: Willie Duncan **Asst Manager:** TBA **Coach:** Darren Hare.
Physio: Tony Pattenden **Commercial Mgr:** John Franks. **Press Off.:** David Morgan (0732 870633).
Ground: Kingsmead Stadium, Kingsmead Road, Canterbury CT2 7PH (0227 762220).
Directions: A28 out of city centre into Military Rd, left at first r-about into Tourtel Rd, straight over next r-about into Kingsmead Rd - stadium on right opposite Canterbury swimming pool. Half mile from Canterbury West (BR). Bus service 624 or 625 from Canterbury bus station - ask for Kingsmead crossroads.
Capacity: 5,000 **Cover:** 200 **Seats:** 200 **Floodlights:** Yes **Founded:** 1947.
Club Shop: Programmes, souvenirs, clothing etc. Contact secretary.
Colours: Navy/red/navy **Change:** Green & white/green/green **Nickname:** The City.
Programme: 24 pages, 50p **Programme Editor:** Secretary.
Sponsors: Shepherd Neame. **Previous Lges:** Kent 47-59/ Metropolitan 59-60/ Southern 60-94.
Previous Name: Canterbury Waverley **Previous Grounds:** Wincheap Grove, Bretts Corner 47-58.
Midweek home matchday: Wednesday **Reserve Team's League:** Winstonlead Kent Div 2
Record Attendance: 3,001 v Torquay, FA Cup 1st Rd 1964.
Record win: 10-0 v Deal Town (H), Southern League 30/1/65.
Record defeat: 0-9 v Corby Town (A), Southern League 16/9/63.
Best FA Cup season: 1st Rd 64-65 (lost 0-6 to Torquay), 68-69 (lost 0-1 to Swindon).
Record Fees - Paid: £2,000 for Graham Knight (Maidstone United)
Received: £2,000 for Dave Wiltshire (Gillingham).
Players progressing to Football League: Ron Gawler (Southend 1949), Arthur Hughes (Grimsby 1954), Arthur Nugent (Darlington 1956), John Richardson (Southport 1956), Tommy Horsfall (Cambridge Utd), Jimmy Murray (Wolves), Kenny Hill (Gillingham), Terry Norton (Brighton), Mark Weatherly (Gillingham), Pat Hilton (Brighton 1973), David Wiltshire (Gillingham 1974), Gary Pugh (Torquay 1984).
Clubhouse: Lounge bar open on matchdays. Snack bar sells burgers, hot-dogs, pies, chips, crisps, tea, coffee, soup and soft drinks.
Club Record Goalscorer: Allan Jones **Club Record Appearances:** John Carragher.
93-94 Captain: Joe Radford **93-94 Top scorer:** Julian Holmes 11.
Player of the Year 93-94: Paul Bagley **Supporters' Player of the Year 93-94:** Steve White.
Local Radio: Radio Kent, Invicta Radio **Local Newspapers:** Kentish Gazette (468181), Adscene (454545).
Honours: FA Trophy 2nd Rd replay 74-75, Kent Lg Cup 49-50 (Div 2 (Reserves) 90-91, Div 2 Cup (Reserves) 89-90), Kent Senior Cup 53-54, Kent Senior Trophy 79-80, Kent Intermediate Cup 73-74, Kent Messenger Trophy 74-75, Frank Norris Memorial Shield 88-89 89-90.

CHATHAM TOWN

Chairman: P Enright **President:**
Secretary: Brian Burcombe, 4 Hallwood Close, Parkwood, Rainham, Kent ME8 9NT (0634 363419).
Manager: John Adams **Asst Manager:**
Ground: Maidstone Road Sports Ground, Maidstone Road, Chatham, Kent (0634 812194).
Directions: M2, A229 Chatham turn-off, follow signs to Chatham, ground one and a half miles on right opposite garage. 1 mile from Chatham (BR).
Seats: 500 **Cover:** 1,000 **Capacity:** 5,000 **Floodlights:** Yes **Founded:** 1882.
Colours: Red & white hoops/black **Change Colours:** Yellow & green **Nickname:** Chats.
Midweek matchday: Tuesday **Record Gate:** 5,000 v Gillingham, 1980.
Sponsors: Topps Scaffolding **Previous Ground:** Great Lines, Chatham 1882-90.
Previous Lges: Southern (several spells)/ Aetolian 59-64/ Metropolitan 64-68/ Kent (Sev. spells).
Programme: 12 pages, 50p **Programme Editor:** Trevor Busby
Clubhouse: Matchdays and functions **Previous Names:** Chatham FC/ Medway FC (1970s).
Top Scorer 93-94: Wayne Barlow 27 **Hons:** Kent Lg(9) 1894-95 03-05 24-25 26-27 71-72 73-74 76-77 79-80 (R-up 02-03 23-24 25-26 70-71 74-75 80-81, Lg Cup 71-72 76-77 (R-up(3)), Thames & Medway Comb.(5) 1896-97 04-06 19-20 23-24, FA Cup QF (beat Nottm Forest 2-0 en route) 1888-89, FA Tphy 3rd Rd 70-71, Kent Snr Cup 1888-89 1904-05 10-11 18-19, Kent Snr Shield 19-20.

PHOTOS OPPOSITE: Top: *Beckenham Town FC. Back Row (L/R): R Chilvers, D Tucknott, M Kennedy, J Bull, L Fabian, P Gayle, J Moore, C Barrett, K Sugrue (Manager), P Palmer (Secretary). Front: G Asbury, M Moore, D Eden, R Bennett, W Kemp, K Randall.* *Photo - Dennis Nicholson.*
Centre: *Canterbury City FC. Back Row (L/R): Colin Rose (Reserve Physio), Tony Pattenden (Physio), Stuart Reed, Paul Neat, Paul Bagley, Darryl Griffiths, Julian Holmes, Bill Roffey (Player-Manager), Joe Radford, Willie Duncan (Reserve Manager). Front: Barry Gethin, Lee Ealham, Kevin Beale, Steve Talbot, Kevin Smart.*
Photo by courtesy of the Kentish Gazette.
Foot: *Chatham Town FC.* *Photo - Roger Turner.*

BECKENHAM TOWN F. C

Lehane Travel

CHATHAM TOWN FOOTBALL CLUB

CORINTHIAN

Chairman: R J Billings **Manager:** Tony Sitford
Secretary/Press Officer: Ken Bardoe, 18 Farmcroft, Gravesend, Kent DA11 7LT (0474 362609).
Ground: Gay Dawn, Valley Road, Fawkham, Nr Dartford, Kent DA3 8LZ (0474 707559/702335 fax:708431).
Directions: A2 off Longfield, take Fawkham Road - ground one mile on left. Or, A20 to Fawkham Green then ground one and a half miles on right. One and a quarter miles from Longfield (BR).
Seats: 134 **Cover:** 175 **Capacity:** 2,000 **Floodlights:** Yes **Founded:** 1972.
Colours: Green & white hoops/white **Change Colours:** Sky & white **Nickname:** None.
Midweek matchday: Tuesday **Record Gate:** 480 v Spurs, friendly 1979.
Clubhouse: Bar, cafeteria & restaurant **Reserves' Lge:** Wintonlead Kent Div 2 **Sponsors:** None
Programme: 12 pages, 30p **Players progressing to Football Lge:** Andy Hessenthaler (Watford).
Previous League: Southern 85-91. **Club Shop:** Yes - contact Jackie Heaver (0474 707559).
Record appearances: Gavin Tovey **Club record scorer & Top Scorer 93-94:** Lee Annett (34, 93-94)
Captain 93-94: Paul Garrett **P.o.Y. 93-94:** David Wright.
Hons: Essex AFA Snr Cup 82-83, Kent Snr Tphy 83-84 86-87 (I'mediate Cup(2) 89-91), Ft Lauderdale Tournament 84-85.

CRAY WANDERERS

President: Bill Faulkner **Chairman:** Bob Dell **Manager:** Eddie Davies
Secretary: Mr Kerry Phillips, 15 Watling Street, Bexleyheath, Kent DA6 7QJ (0322 554108).
Asst Manager: John Dunbar. **Coach:** Barry Simmonds **Press Off.:** Greg Mann (081 318 6888)
Ground: Oxford Road, Sidcup, Kent (081 300 9201).
Directions: Between Sidcup High Street and Footscray High Street; from A20 turn off for Footscray, left at lights, Oxford Rd is 3rd left. Three quarters of a mile from Sidcup (BR) station - Kentish bus 492 from Dartford and Sidcup station passes top of Oxford Rd - 30 mins service on Saturdays.
Seats: 106 **Cover:** 300 **Capacity:** 2,000 **Floodlights:** Due **Founded:** 1860.
Colours: Amber & black **Change Colours:** Claret & blue **Nickname:** Wands.
Midweek matchday: Tuesday **Record Gate:** 1,523 v Stamford, F.A. Vase QF 80-81.
Record win: 15-0 v Sevenoaks, 1894-95 **Record defeat:** 1-11 v Bromley, 20-21.
Sponsors: Brown & Tawse Ltd **Club Record Scorer:** Keith Collishaw, 272.
Programme: 16 pages, 50p **Editor:** Greg Mann (081 318 6888) **Club Shop:** No.
Previous Leagues: Kent Amtr/ West Kent/ Southern Suburban/ London 20-34 51-59/ Aetolian 59-64/ Gtr London 64-66/ Metropolitan 66-71/ London Metropolitan 71-75/ London Spartan 75-78.
Previous Grounds: Star Lane/ Tothills/ Twysden/ Fordcroft/ Grassmeade, St Mary Cray.
Clubhouse: Open pub hours (freehouse). Hot & cold food available.
P.o.Y. 93-94: Robert Welch **Captain & Top Scorer 93-94:** Ian Jenkins.
Hons: London Lg(2) 56-58 (Lg Cup 54-55), Aetolian Lg 62-63 (Lg Cup 63-64), Gtr London Lg 65-66 (Lg Cup(2) 64-66), Metropolitan Lg Cup 70-71 (Amtr Cup(2) 66-68), London Spartan Lg(2) 76-78, Kent Lg 01-02 80-81 (R-up 79-80 90-91, Lg Cup 83-84), Kent Snr Tphy 92-93, Kent Amtr Cup(4) 30-31 62-65.

CROCKENHILL

President: Mr H Miller **Chairman:** Alan Parkin **Vice-Chairman:** Brian Perfect
Sec.: Alan Cloke (0322 665804). **Commercial Manager:** Mike Floate (0322 668275).
Manager: Alan Whitehead **Asst Manager:** Glen Cooper **Coach:** Brian Crimmen.
Ground: 'Wested', Eynsford Road, Crockenhill, Kent (0322 662097).
Directions: Just off M25 junction 3, B2173 towards Swanley, left after 200yds into Wested Lane, ground 1 mile on right (Ord. Survey grid Ref: 516669 sheet 177). Just over a mile from Swanley (BR) station - trains from Victoria. Kentish Bus 477 to Crockenhill - at village shops turn left at T-juntion - ground 1 mile up narrow lane on left.
Seats: 200 **Cover:** 200 **Capacity:** 2,000 **Floodlights:** No **Founded:** 1946.
Cols: Red & white stripes/red/red **Change Colours:** All white **Nickname:** Crocks.
Programme: 8 pages + cover/ads **Programme Editor:** Mike Floate/ Bill Bamforth.
Midweek matchday: Tuesday **Reserve Team's League:** Sevenoaks & Dist. (Crockenhill Dundee).
Club Shop: To open September 1994, selling old programmes, club strip, scarves, pocket annuals, action photos, ground photos, framed photos of League grounds. Contact Mike Floate (0322 668275).
Record Gate: 800 v Maidstone, Kent Amtr Cup 1948. *3,500 at Raleys Field, Sevenoaks, for Sevenoaks Charity Cup final v Bromley Green in 1949. Crockenhill won 2-1.*
Prev. Lgs: Kent Amtr 46-59/ Aetolian 59-64/ Gtr London 64-68
Players prog. to Football Lge: Tony Cascarino (Gillingham) 1982, Steve Bruce (Gillingham via others) late 70s.
Clubhouse: Open matchdays, Sunday lunchtimes, many evenings. Wide range of food always available.
Captain 93-94: Mick Lear **Top Scorer & Player of the Year 93-94:** Mark 'Ginger' Twiner.
Hons: Kent Lg 82-83 (R-up 84-85), Kent Snr Tphy 80-81, Kent Jnr Cup R-up 48-49, West Kent Amtr Cup 56-57, Sevenoaks Charity Cup 48-49, Kent Amtr Lg 56-57 (R-up 54-55, Prem Div 53-54 (R-up 52-53), Div 1 48-49 (R-up 46-47), Snr Div Cup R-up 56-57, Div 1 Cup R-up 46-47).

DARENTH HEATHSIDE

Chairman/Mgr: Brian Smith. **Asst Mgr:** Clayton Hart. **Press Off.:** Martin Wiseman (0689 833083).
Secretary: A J Kingshott, 67 Avondale Rd, Bromley, Kent BR1 4HS (081 460 4834).
Coach: Brian Kinsey (ex-Charlton Athletic - over 400 League appearances).
Ground: The Heathside Club, Horton Road, South Darenth, Dartford, Kent (0322 863554).
Directions: Turn east off A225 (Dartford-Farningham) into Station Rd at brick railway bridge near Farningham Road BR station. Ground at bottom of Station Rd near large viaduct diagonally opposite 'The Sun'. Farningham Rd station (trains from London Victoria) is half mile away. Buses 14 & 15 from Dartford.
Seats: 140 **Cover:** 140 **Capacity:** 2,000 **Floodlights:** No **Founded:** 1951.
Colours: Blue/white **Change Colours:** All red **Nickname:** None.
Midweek matchday: Tuesday **Previous Name:** Heathside Sports.
Programme: 8 pages, 25p **Editor:** Martin Wiseman (0689 833083) **Sponsors:** Lea Brewer & Co.
Clubhouse: Open matcdays one and a half hours before kiv-off until about two and a half hours after match. Also open (bar from 9pm) Tuesday training nights. Hot & cold snacks available matchdays.
Prev. Lges: Local Lges (Dartford, Sidcup) 51-65/ Metropolitan 65-68/ Gtr London 68-71/ London Spartan 75-78.
Previous Grounds: Bexley Hospital 57-72, and various grounds at Bowne Rd, Bexley and Dartford Heath.
Record Gate: 900 v Jimmy Hill's International XI, club's Silver Jubilee match, 1976.
Record win: 9-1 v Riverside Sports, Kent Amateur Cup 71-72 (in Kent League: 7-0 v Ramsgate 80-81).
Record defeat: 0-8 twice; v Canvey Island, Gtr London Lge 69-70, & v Herne Bay, Kent Lge 92-93.
Players progressing to Football League: Ian Thompson (AFC Bournemouth).
Record Scorer (in one season): Dean Bowey 28 (89-90). **Record Appearances:** John Martinez 516.
Capt. 93-94: Danny Pedley **P.o.Y. 93-94:** Gary Preston **Top Scorer 93-94:** Ian Summers/ Lee Annett 9.
Hons: Kent Lg Cup R-up 80-81 85-86 (Div 2 Cup R-up 78-79), Kent Int. Cup 74-75 (Minor Cup 57-58 59-60 62-63).

DARTFORD

Chairman: Dave Skinner **Vice Chairman:** Dick Mace.
Secretary/Press Officer: Mike Brett-Smith, 83 Wellcome Ave., Dartford, Kent DA1 5JL (0322 277243).
Manager: Tony Durman **Asst Manager:** Alan Carrington **Coach:** Dave Wadhams.
Physio: Terry Skelton **Commercial Manager:** Steve Irving.
Ground: As Erith & Belvedere FC (see page 394). **Founded:** 1888
Colours: White/black/white **Change colours:** Red/white/red **Nickname:** Darts
Previous Leagues: Kent 1894-96 97-98 99-1902 09-14 21-26/ Southern 1896-98 99-1900 27-81 82-84 86-92/ GMV Conference 1981-82 84-86.
Programme: 28 pages, 60p **Programme Editor:** Secretary. **Reserve Team:** No.
Club Shop: Open matchdays. Progs, souvenirs, ties, handbooks, fanzines etc. Mail order; Norman Grimes (0322 271664 - evenings).
Sponsors: National Power. **Record Gate:** 11,004 v Leyton Orient FA Cup 1st Rd 48-49
Rec. win: 11-1 v Faversham, Kent Snr Cup. **Record defeat:** 0-10 v Guildford C., Southern Lge 1947.
Prev. Grounds: Brent Rec/ Lowfield Str./ Summers Meadow 1906-1914/ Watling Str. 21-92/ Cray Wdrs FC 93-94.
Best FA Cup season: 3rd Rd Proper 1935-36 (v Derby), 1936-37 (v Darlington).
League Clubs Defeated in FA Cup: Cardiff (1935), Exeter (1961) Aldershot (1968)
Record Fees: Paid: £6,000 for John Bartley (Chelmsford City, 1988)
Received: £25,000 for Andy Hesenthaler (from Watford, via Redbridge Forest)
Players progressing to Football Lge: Riley Cullum (Charlton 1947), Ted Croker (Charlton 1948), Frank Coombs (Bristol C. 1949), James Kelly (Gillingham 1951), Tom Ritchie (Grimsby 1958), Dave Underwood (Watford 1960), Derek Hales (Luton 1972), Archie Cross (Arsenal), Andy Hesenthaler (Watford via Redbridge F.).
Hons: Southern Lg(4) 30-32 73-74 83-84 (R-up(3) 80-81 87-89, Eastern Dib 30-31, Southern Div 80-81, Lg Cup(3) 76-77 87-89 (R-up 79-80 83-84 89-90), Championship Shield(3) 83-84 87-89), Kent Snr Cup(9) 30-33 34-35 47-48 69-70 72-73 80-88 (R-up 1893-94), Kent F'lit Cup(3) 64-66 70-71, Kent Lg Cup 24-25, Inter Lg Chal. 1974 (beat Boston Utd 5-3 on agg.), FA Trophy R-up 73-74.

Greenwich Borough's Vic Barton saves bravely at the feet of Dartford's Gary Julians. Photo - Keith Gillard.

DEAL TOWN

Chairman: John H Ullman **Vice-Chairman:** Bill Bennett.
Secretary: Mrs Ann Lewis, Silver Hill, Northbourne Rd, Mongeham, Deal, Kent CT14 0LF (0304 373918).
Manager: Jim Nokes **Asst Manager/Physio:** Dave Dadd
Coach: Joe Brayne **Commercial Mgr/Press Officer:** Dave Clements (0304 368776).
Ground: Charles Sports Ground, St Leonards Road, Deal, Kent (0304 375623).
Directions: A258 through Walmer, left into Cornwell Road, continue into Hamilton Road, veer left into Mill Rd, follow round to right into Manor Road, right into St Leonards Road, ground 100 yards on right. 1 mile from both Walmer and Deal BR stations. Local buses stop near ground.
Seats: 150 **Cover:** 500 **Capacity:** 2,000 **Floodlights:** Yes **Founded:** 1908.
Colours: Black & white hoops/white **Change Colours:** All yellow **Nickname:** Town.
Midweek matchday: Tuesday **Record Gate:** 4,000 v Billy Wright showbiz XI, Feb '61.
Reserves' Lge: Wintonlead Div 2 **Sponsors:** Carlsberg Tetley/ Deal Town Rangers.
Clubhouse: Matchdays & functions. Bar. Tea bar with hot & cold food.
Programme: 24 pages, 40p **Editor:** Dave Clements (0304 368776)
Club Shop: No, but back programmes are available from Colin Adams (0304 372784).
Previous Grounds: None **Player progressing to Football Lge:** Danny Wallace (Southampton)
Previous Leagues: Kent 09-59/ Aetolian 59-63/ Southern 63-66/ Gtr London 66-71
Record win: 11-1 v Tunbridge Wells (A), Kent League 20/2/93.
Record defeat: 0-10 v Tunbridge Wells (A), Kent League 6/5/86.
Record Scorer: Jim Nokes 129 **Club Record Appearances:** Alan Barton 503 (recent times).
Captain 93-94: Colin Gilmore **Top Scorer 93-94:** Paul Cureton **P.o.Y. 93-94:** Mark Wadhams 27.
Hons: Kent Lg 53-54 (R-up 88-89, Lg Cup 57-58 81-82 (R-up 93-94, SF 88-89 89-90), Kent Snr Tphy R-up 82-83 90-91, Gtr London Lg Cup 68-69, Aetolian Lg R-up 59-60.

FAVERSHAM TOWN

Chairman: Brian Mulherne **Vice-Chairman:** Richard Stebberds **President:** Mr R W B Neame
Secretary: K F Hammond, 8 Sherwood Close, Faversham, Kent ME13 7QS (0795 535612).
Manager: Hughie Stinson **Asst Manager:** Steve Wren **Physio:** Andy Potterton.
Coach: Bob Mason **Commercial Manager:** Chris Turner.
Ground: Shepherd Neame Stadium, Salters Lane, Faversham, Kent (0795 532738).
Directions: On A2 (Canterbury road) just west of town.
Seats: 350 **Cover:** 1,500 **Capacity:** 2,000 **Floodlights:** Yes **Founded:** 1901.
Colours: White/blue/red **Change Colours:** Red/white/blue **Nickname:** Town.
Midweek matchday: Tuesday **Record Gate:** 1,400 v Sheppey Utd, 1949.
Sponsors: Shepherd Neame Master Brewers
Previous Leagues: Aetolian 59-64/ Metropolitan 64-71/ Athenian 71-76.
Programme: 16 pages, 40p **Programme Editor:** John Barrett (0795 535500).
Reserves' Lge: Kent Lg Div 2 **Prev. Grounds:** Ashford Rd 1901-46/Gordon Square 46-58
Rec. win: 8-0 v Greenwich B., Aug'89 **Record defeat:** 0-9 v Sittingbourne, Jan '82.
Clubhouse: Open matchdays (Sat/Sun/Tues) Wed/Thurs. Snacks sold.
Club Record Scorer: Tony Rudd 43. **Club Record Appearances:** Bob Mason.
P.o.Y. 93-94: Scott Davenport **Captain & Top Scorer 93-94:** Bob Mason
Hons: Kent Lg 69-70 70-71 77-78 89-90 (R-up 87-88, Lg Cup 70-71 90-91 (R-up 82-83)), Kent Snr Tphy 76-77 77-78 (R-up 87-88 88-89), Kent Amtr Cup 56-57 58-59 71-72 72-73 73-74.

FOLKESTONE INVICTA

Chairman: Tony Guiver **President:** Wilfred Amory.
Secretary: Anthony Brough, 31 Stanley Rd, Folkestone, Kent CT19 4LQ (0303 277575).
Manager: Gary Stanliforth **Asst Manager:** Dennis Hunt **Coach:** Frank Barham.
Ground: The New Pavilion, Cheriton Road, Folkestine, Kent CT20 5JU (0303 57461).
Directions: On the A20 behind Presto foodstore, midway between Folkestone Central and Folkestone West BR stations.
Seats: 900 **Cover:** 3,500 **Capacity:** 4,000 **Floodlights:** Yes **Founded:** 1946.
Colours: Amber & black/black/black **Change Colours:** Red & white/white/red **Nickname:**
Midweek matchday: Tuesday **Previous Lges:** Kent County (pre-1991). **Sponsors:**
Rec. Gate: 1,211 v Brighton, friendly 26/9/91. *Ground record; 7,801 Folkestone v Margate, Kent Snr Cup 1958.*
Programme: 16 pages, 30p **Editor:** Neil Pitcher.
Clubhouse: Yes **Previous Ground:** South Rd, Hythe (pre-1991).
Top Scorer 93-94: Lee Bossom 29. **Hons:** Kent Lg Div 2 90-91.

FURNESS

Chairman: Alan Sutherland
Secretary/Press Officer: David Skeel, 3 Arbury House, Holmbury Park, Bromley, Kent BR1 2WG (081 464 8571).
Manager: Steve Brown **Physio:** Bob Pearson
Commercial Manager: Alan Simmonds.
Ground: Green Court Road, Crockenhill, Kent (0322 666120).
Directions: From junction of M25 & M20 follow signs for Swanley. Left at Crockenhill turning, then first right after motorway crossing. 500 yards from Swanley (BR).
Seats: 100 **Cover:** 200 **Capacity:** 1,500 **Floodlights:** No **Founded:** 1991.
Colours: All white **Change Colours:** All red or all blue **Nickname:** None.
Midweek matchday: Tuesday **Record Gate:** 350 v Newport IOW, FA Vase 1980.
Previous Names: Danson (Bexley Borough)(founded 1941) and Furness United merged in 1991. Danson Furness United 91-93.
Previous Grounds: Randell Down Road 41-53/ Eltham Road 53-60/ Crook Log, Brampton Road 60-92.
Prev. Lges: Sidcup & Dist./ S.E. London Amtr/ London Spartan 82-87. *Furness: Sth London Alliance (pre-1991).*
Club Sponsors: S H E Printers **Record win:** 11-0 v Kent Police, Kent Lge 93-94.
Programme: 12 pages, 50p **Editor:** Alan Sutherland (071 537 2817).
Clubhouse: Matchdays and functions **Player progressing to Football Lg:** Darren Adams (Cardiff 93-94).
Captain 93-94: Micky Cloke **Top Scorer 93-94:** Derek Reid.
P.O.Y. 93-94: Gary Ware **Hons:** Kent Lg R-up 93-94, SE Amteur Lg Cup R-up 60-61.

GREENWICH BOROUGH

President: T H M Edwaards **Chairman:** B Thompson.
Secretary: Ms Denise Richmond, 7 Castlecombe Rd, Mottingham, London SE9 4AU (081 851 4169).
Manager: Dave Waight **Asst Manager:** Doug Francis
Ground: Harrow Meadow, Eltham Green Rd, Eltham, London SE9 (081 850 3098).
Directions: South Circular (A205) to Yorkshire Grey pub, ground opposite. 1 mile from both Eltham and Kidbrooke BR stations.
Seats: 50 **Cover:** 50 **Capacity:** 2,500 **Floodlights:** Yes **Founded:** 1928.
Colours: Red & black **Change Colours:** Black & white **Nickname:** Boro.
Midweek matchday: Tuesday **Previous Ground:** Erith & Belvedere F.C. 1992-93.
Record Gate: 2,000 v Charlton, floodlight opening, 1978.
Record defeat: 0-8 v Faversham Town, August 1989.
Sponsors: Pelgary Ltd **Previous Name:** London Borough of Greenwich.
Previous Leagues: South London Alliance/ Kent Amateur/ London Spartan 77-84.
Programme: 8 pages, 20p **Programme Editor:** Denise Richmond. **Clubhouse:** Yes.
Hons: London Spartan Lg 79-80 (Lg Cup 82-83), Kent Lg 86-87 87-88 (Lg Cup 84-85 86-87), Kent Snr Tphy 84-85, FA Vase 5th Rd 89-90.

PHOTOS OPPOSITE:

Top: *Faversham Town's Bobby Mason heads just over the bar as his side win 1-0 at Cray Wanderers.*
Photo - Alan Coomes.

Centre: *Folkestone Invicta goalkeeper Ben Bryant punches the ball off the head of Glenn Payne during the 1-0 League Cup win over Thamesmead Town at Cheriton Road.*
Photo - Francis Short.

Foot: *Tony McKenzie of Furness outpaces Andrew Whittall during a 0-1 defeat at Corinthian.*
Photo - Alan Coomes.

RAY W DERERS FOOTBALL LUB

HERNE BAY

Chairman: M Todd **Vice Chairman:** R Todd. **President:** J Hodkinson
Secretary: S Connolly, 60 Ivanhoe Rd, Herne Bay, Kent CT6 6EQ (0227 363063).
Manager: Tom Sampson **Asst Manager:** Martin Farnie **Coach:** K Lissenden
Physio: J Hodkinson. **Commercial Manager:** Roy Twyman (0227 375774).
Press Officer: Roy Twyman/ Doug Smith.
Ground: Winch's Field, Stanley Gardens, Herne Bay, Kent (0227 374156).
Directions: Leave A299 at Herne Bay r'bout, 2nd left, 1st left. Half mile from Herne Bay (BR); down Station Approach (half mile), 1st right (Spencer Road), 2nd right.
Seats: 250 **Cover:** 2,000 **Capacity:** 5,000 **Floodlights:** Yes **Founded:** 1886.
Colours: Blue & white halves **Change Colours:** Red & black halves **Nickname:** The Bay.
Midweek matchday: Tuesday **Previous Ground:** Memorial Park 1886-1953.
Clubhouse: Open evenings and matchdays **Record Gate:** 2,303 v Margate, FA Cup 4th Qual. Rd 1970.
Sponsors: Waterways Caravan Park. **Reserve Team's League:** Kent League Division Two.
Previous Lges: Kent Amtr/ Thanet/ East Kent/ Kent 53-59/ Aetolian 59-64/ Athenian 64-74.
Programme: 36 pages, 50p **Editor:** Doug Smith/Roy Twyman **Club Shop:** Due.
Record win: 12-0; v Betteshanger CW Res. and Whitstable Res. (A), both Kent Div 2 55-56.
Record defeat: 0-9 v Hounslow, Athenian Lge 1973-74.
Record transfer fee received: £3,000 for Mark Munday (Gravesend) 1994.
Captain 93-94: Neil Brown **P.o.Y. 93-94:** Terry Martin **Top Scorer 93-94:** Mark Munday 33.
Hons: Kent Lg 91-92 93-94 (R-up 92-93, Div 2 62-63 63-64 (R-up 92-93(res) 93-94(res)), Lg Cup R-up 78-79, Div 2 Cup 53-54), Kent Snr Tphy 78-79, Kent Amtr Cup 57-58 (R-up 58-59 63-64 68-69 72-73), Aetolian Lg Div 2 62-63 63-64 (Lg Cup R-up 62-63, Div 2 Cup 62-63 63-64), Athenian Lg Div 2 70-71 (Lg Cup 66-67), Kent Amtr Lg Cup 53-54 54-55, Thames & Medway Comb. Cup R-up 61-62, FA Cup 4th Cup Qual. Rd 70-71 86-87.

KENT POLICE

Chairman: P Hermitage **President:** P Condon, Chief Constable.
Secretary: J C Bateman, Christmas Cottage, Lavender Square, Hawkhurst TN18 4DX (0622 681740).
Manager: Duncan McLachlan **Asst Mgr/Coach:** Staurt McFaden **Press Officer:** Secretry
Ground: Police H.Q., Sutton Rd, Maidstone, Kent (0622 690690).
Directions: Leave Maidstone on Hastings Road, then onto A274 to Rye Road.
Seats: 40 **Cover:** 60 **Capacity:** 3,000 **Floodlights:** No **Founded:** 1951.
Colours: Royal blue **Change Colours:** Blue & white **Nickname:** None.
Midweek matchday: Tues/Wed. **Record Gate:** Unknown.
Sponsors: **Previous League:** Kent Amateur.
Programme: 6 pages, £1 with entry **Programme Editor:** Secretary.
Record defeat: 0-11 v Furness, Kent Lge 93-94.
Clubhouse: Use HQ bar on matchdays. New changing room/ refreshment facilities adjacent to pitch.
Hons: Kent Lg R-up 69-70 (Lg Cup 69-70).

RAMSGATE

Chairman: R Lawson **Vice Chairman:** C Payne **President:** Mike Taylor.
Secretary/Press Officer: Tom Atkins, 8 Manston Rd, Ramsgate, Kent CT11 0RB (0843 595632).
Manager/Coach: Lennie Lee **Asst Manager:** Dave Bostock **Physio:** John Burroughs
Commercial Manager: Mick Beier (0304 820453).
Ground: Southwood Stadium, Prices Avenue, Ramsgate, Kent (0843 591662).
Directions: From London on A229, A253 into Ramsgate - left into Netherhill at r'bout, right into Ashburnham Rd, right into Southwood Rd. 15 mins walk from Ramsgate BR station; walk thru Warre Recreation Ground, along St Lawrence High Str., left at 'White Horse', follow Southwood Rd and turn right into Prices Avenue.
Seats: 400 **Cover:** 600 **Capacity:** 5,000 **Floodlights:** Yes **Founded:** 1946.
Colours: Yellow/green/green **Change Colours:** White/blue/blue **Nickname:** Rams.
Midweek matchday: Tuesday **Record Gate:** 5,200 v Margate, 56-57.
Sponsors: British Gas. **Reserve Team's League:** Winstonlead Kent Div. Two.
Programme: 30 pages **Editor:** Mick Beier (0304 820453) **Club Shop:** No.
Previous Name: Ramsgate Athletic **Previous Leagues:** Southern 59-75.
Record win: 9-1 v Crockenhill, Kent League Cup 22/1/94.
Clubhouse: Open matchdays & private functions. Two bars, two pool tables, darts. Hot & cold food on matchdays.
Club Record Scorer: Mick Williamson.
Top Scorer 93-94: Karl Smith 43 **Captain & P.o.Y. 93-94:** Scott Forbes
Hons: Kent Lg 49-50 55-56 56-57 (Lg Cup 48-49 92-93 93-94), Kent I'mediate Cup 54-55, Kent Snr Cup 63-64, Thames & Medway Cup 60-61, Kent Snr Shield 60-61, Kent Floodlit Tphy 69-70, Kent Snr Tphy(2) 87-89.

SHEPPEY UNITED

Chairman: Peter Sharrock **Manager:** Johnny Roseman.
Sec.: Mr Barry H Bundock, Dunedin, 104 Southsea Ave., Minster, Sheerness ME12 2NH (0795 876025).
Ground & Directions: As Faversham Town FC (see page 538). **Founded:** 1890.
Colours: Red & white/white **Change colours:** All blue
Midweek matchday: Tuesday **Nickname:** Islanders or Ites.
Previous Name: Sheppey Athletic. **Programme:** 20 pages, 40p
Previous Ground: Botany Road, St Georges Avenue, Sheerness (pre-1992).
Record Gate: 4,000 v Sittingbourne, Kent Senior Trophy 1927 (at Botany Road).
Previous Leagues: Southern 1894-1901 84-91/ Kent 01-27 32-59 72-84/ Aetolian 59-64/ Gtr London 64-65/ Metropolitan Lg 65-71.
Players progressing to Football League: E C Harper (England, Blackburn, Spurs, Preston).
Hons: Kent Lg(6) 05-07 27-28 72-73 74-75 78-79 (R-up 03-04 04-05 77-78 83-84, Lg Cup 75-76 78-79, Div 2(reserves) 32-33 84-85 (R-up 1894-95 1979-80)), Thames & Medway Comb. 08-09 12-13 22-23 25-26 28-29 55-56, Kent Amtr Cup 45-46 51-52, Kent Snr Shield 77-78, Kent Snr Cup R-up(3), Gtr London Lg 64-65, FA Cup 6th Qual. Rd 19-20, FA Tphy 1st Rd Proper 85-86.

PHOTOS OPPOSITE:

Top: *Kent Police keeper Steve Holpin cuts out a cross at home to Herne Bay.* *Photo - Paul Dennis.*

Centre: *Ramsgate FC - Winstonlead Kent League Cup winners 1993-94.* *Photo - Eric Marsh.*

Foot: *Micky Collins rolls in Dartford's third goal in a 3-1 win against Sheppey United.* *Photo - Keith Gillard.*

NBRIDGE FC

SLADE GREEN

President: William Dudley **Chairman:** Brian Smith. **Manager:** Tony Carley.
Secretary: Bruce Smith, 15 Gumping Rd, Orpington, Kent BR5 1RX (0689 858782).
Asst Mgr: Melvyn Phillips **Coach:** Peter Little **Physio:** Dave Austin.
Ground: The Small Glen, Moat Lane, Slade Green, Erith, Kent (0322 351077).
Directions: Off A206 between Erith & Dartford. 400 yards from Slade Green BR station. Buses 89 & B13.
Capacity: 3,000 **Seats:** 150 **Cover:** 400 **Floodlights:** Yes **Founded:** 1946.
Colours: White & green **Change Colours:** All yellow **Nickname:** The Green
Midweek matchday: Tuesday **Previous Name:** Slade Green Athletic 46-86.
Programme: 24 pages, with admission **Prog. Editor/Press Officer:** Robert Smith (0322 287982).
Previous Leagues: Dartford 46-52/ Kent Amateur 52-62/ Greater London 62-64.
Record Gate: 3,000 v Millwall, friendly 25/7/92.
Record win: 14-0 v Island Social, Kent Amtr Lge 1953.
Record defeat: 1-6; v Herne Bay, Kent Snr Cup 55-56; v Whitstable, Kent Lg 83-84; v Alma Swanley, Kent Lg 89-90; v Dartford, Kent Lg 26/12/93.
Players pogressing to Football League: Roy Dwight (Nottm Forest), Alan Clark (Charlton).
Club Record Scorer: Colin Dwyer **Club Record Appearances:** Colin Dwyer.
Captain 93-94: Graham Hill **Top Scorer 93-94:** Jason Head, 8 **P.o.Y. 93-94:** Colin Hart.
Hons: Kent Snr Tphy 91-92 (R-up 80-81), Kent Lg Cup 82-83, Kent Amtr Lg 52-53 60-61 (Lg Cup 60-61), Kent Intermediate Cup 61-62, Kent Benevolent Cup 46-47, West Kent 60-61 65-66, Dartford Lg R-up 48-49 (Lg Cup 47-48 (R-up 46-47)), Erith Hospitals Cup 46-47 48-49, Gtr London Lg R-up 68-69, Plumstead Challenge Cup 48-49.

THAMESHEAD TOWN

Chairman: Vacant **Vice Chairman:** Dave Jessop.
Secretary/Comm. Mgr: Paul Bayne, 9 Bayliss Ave., Thamesmead, London SE28 8NS (081 311 1276).
Manager: Mick Watts **Asst Manager:** Tony Pruce **Physio:** Stuart Bevis.
Coach: John Adams/Terry Hill **Press Officer:** Matthew Panting.
Ground: Bayliss Avenue, Thamesmead, London SE28 8NJ (081 311 4211).
Directions: From Abbey Wood (BR) north east along Harrow Manor Way, into Crossway at 3rd r'bout, Bayliss Av. is 3rd right (Bexley bus 272 stops in Crossway near Bayliss Av. By road: From Dartford tunnel A2 to London, exit Danson Interchange and follow signs for Thamesmead and Abbey Wood. From Blackheath tunnel exit on south side and follow signs to Woolwich, to Plumstead and then to Thamesmead.
Seats: 125 **Cover:** 125 **Capacity:** 400 **Floodlights:** Yes **Founded:** 1970.
Colours: Green & black **Change Colours:** All red **Nickname:** The Mead.
Sponsors: Courage Brewery **Reserves' Lge:** Winstonlead Kent D2 **Programmes:** Yes
Midweek home matchday: Tues/Thurs **Previous Ground:** Meridian Sports Ground, Charlton.
Clubhouse: Mon-Fri 6-11pm, Sat 12-11pm, Sun 12-3 & 7-10.30pm. Double bar, lounge, dance-floor, children's games room, video machines, hot & cold food.
Record win: 9-0 v Kent Police, Kent League 19/4/94.
Prev. Lge: London Spartan 80-91. **Record Gate:** 400 v Wimbledon, ground opening 1988.
Caprain 93-94: Philip Miles **Club record appearances:** Delroy D'Oyley.
Top Scorer 93-94: Dean Bowey 47 **Player of the Year 93-94:** Terry Malin.
Hons: Spartan Lg Div 3 79-80 (Lg Cup 84-85 86-87, I'mediate champs 85-86), Kent I'mediate Cup 83-84. 4 promotions, and 9 trophies (inc London FA and Kent FA Cups) in progress thru Spartan I'mediate Divs, 1980-87.

Thamesmead Town goalkeeper Steve Allen manages to push the ball over the bar despite a challenge from Paul Hobbs of Chatham Town, and his side go on to record a 4-1 home in this May Bank Holiday morning fixture. *Photo - Alan Coomes.*

PHOTOS OPPOSITE: **Top:** *Slade Green FC.* *Photo - Robert Smith.*
Centre: *Deal Town FC.* *Photo - Richard Brock.*
Foot: *Darenth Heathside FC.* *Photo - Alan Coomes.*

TUNBRIDGE WELLS

Chairman: R J Bonny **Vice Chairman:** P C Wager.
Secretary: P C Wager, 46 Mereworth Rd, Tunbridge Wells, Kent TN4 9PL (0892 524182).
Manager: Mark Higgs **Asst Manager:** Tony Atkins **Coach:** Roger Pitchfork
Press Officer: R Bonny (0892 531898). **Commercial Mgr:** Norman Sales.
Ground: Culverden Stadium, Culverden Down, Tunbridge Wells, Kent TN4 (0892 520517).
Directions: Leaving town on main Tonbridge road (A26), turn left opposite 'Red Lion' pub - ground half mile. 1 mile from Tunbridge Wells Central (BR). Served by any Tunbridge Wells-Tonbridge bus - alight at St Johns.
Seats: 350 **Cover:** 1,000 **Capacity:** 5,000 **Floodlights:** Yes **Founded:** 1886.
Club Shop: Yes, selling programmes, badges etc. **Reformed:** 1967.
Colours: Red & white **Change Colours:** Yellow/blue **Nickname:** Wells.
Midweek matchday: Tuesday **Record Gate:** 967 v Maidstone United, FA Cup 1969.
Sponsors: Private Patients Plan. **Clubhouse:** Open matchdays and as required.
Programme: 16 pages, 30p **Programme Editor:** Secretary.
Prev. Names: None. *predecessors: T. Wells FC 1886-1910 47-50/ T. Wells Rgrs 03-09 63-67/ T. Wells Utd 51-62.*
Previous Grounds: Down Lane 1906/ Combley Park 06-10/ Swiss Cottage 06-14/Down Farm 19-39/ St Johns 47-50/ Eridge Road 50-51.
Record win: 10-0 v Deal (H), May'86 **Record defeat:** 1-11 v Deal Town (H), 20/2/93.
Record Scorer: John Wingate 151 **Club Record Appearances:** Tony Atkins 410.
Captain 93-94: Rick Pedelty **P.o.Y. 93-94:** Lloyd Stephens.
Top Scorer 93-94: Peter Manktelow 12, Rashid Short 10.
Hons: Kent Lg 84-85 (R-up 68-69, Lg Cup 74-75 77-78 85-86 87-88), Kent Snr Tphy R-up 85-86 91-92.

Tunbridge Wells FC 1993-94.

Photo - Richard Brock.

WHITSTABLE TOWN

Chairman: Joe Brownett **Vice Chairman:** Peter Dale **President:** George Gifford.
Secretary: Mrs Sylvia J Davis, 5 Old Bridge Rd, Whitstable, Kent CT5 1RJ (0227 265646).
Manager: Wayne Godden **Asst Manager:** John Crabbe **Physio:** Andy Harman
Press Officer: Darryl Harman **Commercial Manager:** Trevor Myhill (0227 277297).
Ground: Belmont Road, Belmont, Whitstable, Kent (0227 266012).
Directions: From Thanet Way (A299), left at Tescos r'bout and down Millstrood Rd - ground at bottom of road, 400yds from Whitstable (BR) station. Car park at Grimshall Rd entrance.
Capacity: 2,000 **Cover:** 1,000 **Seats:** 500 **Floodlights:** Yes **Founded:** 1885.
Colours: Red/white/red **Change colours:** Yellow/black
Midweek matchday: Tuesday **Nickname:** 'Oystermen', 'Reds', or 'Natives'.
Sponsors: D & J Tyres
Club Shop: Yes, selling old programmes and club souvenirs. Contact Trevor Myhill (0227 277297).
Programme: 48 pages, 50p **Programme Editor:** Trevor Myhill (0227 277297).
Record win: 18-0 v Greenstreet (H), Faversham & District Lge 20-21.
Record defeat: 0-10 v Sittingbourne (A), FA Cup 1st Qualifying Round 1962-63.
Record Gate: 2,500 v Gravesend & Northfleet, FA Cup 3rd Qualifying Rd, 19/10/87.
Clubhouse: Social & recreation purposes, open all matchdays. Bar. Hot food & drinks at tea-bar.
Prev. Names: Whitstable Utd (pre-1886)/ Whitstable Swifts 93-95/ Whitstable Town 95-1905/ Whitstable FC 08-66.
Prev. Grnds: Saddleston's Field 1885-94/ Westmeads (Cromwell Rd) 94-95/ Joy Lane 95-1908/ Church Rd 08-09.
Prev. Lges: E. Kent 1897-1909/ Kent 09-59/ Aetolian 59-60/ Kent Amtr 60-62 63-64/ Seanglian 62-63/ Gtr London 64-67/ Kent Premier 67-68 (also in New Brompton, Thanet and Faversham & Dist. Lges over the years).
Top Scorer 93-94: Gary Pullen **Captain & Player of the Year 93-94:** Geoff Record.
Club record scorer: Barry Godfrey **Club record appearances:** Frank Cox 429 (1950-60).
Hons: Kent Lg Div 2 27-28 33-34 49-50 (Lg Cup 79-80 (R-up 89-90 91-92)), Kent Amtr Lg East 60-61, Kent Amtr Cup 28-29, Kent Snr Tphy R-up 78-79 89-90 92-93, Gtr London Lg Cup R-up 65-66, Kent Amtr Cup 28-29, Kent Midweek Lg Cup 92-93.

JEWSON WESSEX LEAGUE

FEEDER TO:
BEAZER HOMES LEAGUE

President: Jack Barter

Chairman: Alf Peckham **Vice-Chairman:** Cyril Hurlock

Hon. Secretary/Treasurer: Norman Cook, 5 Holmsley Court, Bartley Meadows, Totton, Southampton SO4 2JF (0703 865464)

WIMBORNE TOWN BACK ON TOP

The number of clubs competing in the First Division increased to twenty-three. Andover dropped down from the Beazer Homes League due to the heavy cost of travelling, Petersfield Town was reformed from Petersfield United who dropped out of the Diadora League, and Downton were promoted from the Hampshire League, replacing releged Romsey Town. However, after playing just one game, Sholing Sports lost their ground and were therefore unable to take any further part. Consequently fixtures were disrupted and were even more severely affected by what surely must have been the wettest season for a long time. We experienced water-logged pitches as early as the end of September and were continually plagued with the problem right through to mid-April. With the co-operation of everyone concerned we managed to complete the programmes on schedule apart from just one fixture which was played on Monday 9th May 1994.

Wimborne Town reclaimed the First Division championship as early as 20th April when they won at Downton, and went on to amass 107 points and a winning margin of eighteen points. Interest was therefore focused on the battle for the runners-up spot. Thatcham had their sights set on promotion to the BHL and needed the runners-up spot to be considered, but a dreadful finish in which they managed just one point from their last four games meant that they could only finish in a disappointing fourth place. Andover took second place in fine style, scoring 137 goals in the process, and would have pushed Wimborne much closer but for a poor spell of form in January when the heavy pitches were at their worst. Andover also boasted the League's leading goalscorer in Gary Lewis with a massive total of 46. The rest of the pack could not keep pace, but three marksmen did well in joint second place with 27 goals each; Ian Laing of Thatcham, Jason Lovell of Wimborne and John Smith of Fleet.

The reigning champions AFC Lymington lost the services of their main strikeforce and were unable to find adequate replacements. Their defensive record was the best in the League, and a strong finish pushed them up into third position. Gosport Borough were always in the leading group, but a poor end to the campaign - three defeats in the last five games - saw them drop to fifth place. Fleet Town enjoyed their best season in the Wessex League, finishing sixth, but it could have been even better but for a disappointing finish.

Wimborne Town completed a magnificient double by winning the Jewson Wessex League Cup when they trounced Thatcham Town 7-0 at Andover FC. Havant Town Reserves followed suit by

Wimborne Town - Jewson Wessex League champions 1993-94. *Photo - Eric Marsh.*

winning the Combination double. In the final of the Jewson Wessex Combination Cup, staged at BAT FC, they defeated Bemerton Heath Harlequins Reserves 2-0.

The Manager of the Month Award was once again sponsored by Millbrook Furnishing Industries, and we thank Mr Ted Croll for his continued interest and generous support. Wimborne Town's double success reflected the fact that their manager Kevin Mulkern won this award on three occasions, but following close behind was Andover's Ken Cunningham-Brown who scooped the award twice. The other winners were Trevor King (Horndean), Roger Sherwood (Gosport Borough) and Cliff Huxford (Brockenhurst).

Portsmouth RN received the award for the "Best Programme" and are to be congratulated on their first award within the Wessex League. Perhaps they can follow this up with a success on the field

Our congratulations go to all clubs who represented the League so ably in the FA Competitions, notably Wimborne Town, who reached the fifth round of the FA Vase and Wimborne Town and Andover for reaching the third qualifying round of the FA Cup. Special mention also to AFC Lymington for winning the Russell Cotes Cup in the all Wessex League final against Gosport Borough.

Lenny Wolfe preserved his unbeaten run in charge of the Wessex League Representative Team. During such a wet winter it was a credit to clubs and players that we managed to fit in two games. The first was a good performance against the Hampshire FA Senior Squad which, incidentally, consisted almost entirely of Wessex League players, and we ran out 4-2 winners. This was followed by a much tougher fixture against the Unijet Sussex County League where we fought back from a 2-0 deficit to earn a 2-2 draw.

It was decided by the Joint Liaison Committee that Cowes Sports be promoted to the Wessex League from the Hampshire League for season 1994-95 and that Whitchurch United, the bottom club in the Wessex League in season 1993-94 be placed in the Hampshire League for the ensuing season. There were no other applications to join the League so we will be operating with 22 clubs in the First Division. In my opinion this is the maximum number to effectively administer a Division and if we ever have a greater number than this I feel that a restructuring of the League must be given serious consideration. Whitchurch United Reserves drop out of the Combination Division and withdrawals were received from Petersfield Town Reserves, Newport IOW Reserves, and Havant Town Reserves, although the latter club decided to reapply. There were no other applications for the Combination Division.

All clubs have one more year to erect a 150 seater stand and/or lay hard standing around the whole of the pitch. Any club not meeting these requirements will be refused entry into the League for season 1995/96. Clubs can still make application for a loan of up to £2000 from the League to assist with these improvements and clubs are urged to take advantage of the grant scheme run by the Football Trust.

Norman Cook, Secretary

First Division	P	W	D	L	F	A	PTS
Wimborne Town	42	34	5	3	126	41	107
Andover	42	27	8	7	137	48	89
AFC Lymington	42	27	5	10	73	33	86
Thatcham Town	42	25	7	10	96	51	82
Gosport Borough	42	23	10	9	87	55	79
Fleet Town	42	21	9	12	82	48	72
Bemerton Hth Harl.	42	19	11	12	72	56	68
Brockenhurst	42	17	12	13	70	64	63
BAT Sports	42	17	10	15	66	66	61
Christchurch	42	15	13	14	55	58	58
Bournemouth	42	16	6	20	67	78	54
Ryde Sports	42	14	10	18	61	77	52
Portsmouth RN	42	13	10	19	59	78	49
East Cowes Vics	42	14	7	21	78	114	49
Eastleigh	42	12	12	18	47	54	48
Downton	42	12	10	20	59	82	46
Horndean	42	13	6	23	56	95	45
Petersfield Town	42	11	7	24	64	96	40
Aerostructures	42	11	6	25	41	84	39
Swanage T. & H.	42	10	7	25	53	89	37
AFC Totton	42	9	9	24	43	90	36
Whitchurch United	42	4	2	29	51	96	35

Top Scorers:
46 - G Lewis (Andover). 27 - I Laing (Thatcham), J Lovell (Wimborne), J Smith (Fleet). 26 - G Joseph (Gosport). 24 - J Gomershall (Andover). 22 - M Turner (Wimborne). 21 - J O'Rourke (East Cowes), D Ross (Swanage). 18 - D McBride (Bournemouth). 17 - M Barrett (Gosport), J Hervey (Lymington). 16 - R Maynard (Bemerton).

Combination	P	W	D	L	F	A	PTS
Havant Town Res.	36	25	8	3	115	34	83
Bashley Res.	36	22	6	8	88	40	72
Waterlooville Res.	36	19	9	8	80	59	66
Downton Res.	36	19	4	13	71	46	61
Wimborne T. Res.	36	18	5	13	82	50	59
AFC Lym'ton Res.	36	17	7	12	74	51	58
Newport IOW Res.	36	16	10	10	77	62	58
Eastleigh Res.	36	16	5	15	69	72	53
AFC Totton Res.	36	15	6	15	80	64	51
Bournemouth Res.	36	15	6	15	66	78	51
Aerostruct. Res.	36	15	5	16	56	60	50
Bemerton HH Res.	36	13	10	13	58	49	49
Gosport B. Res.	36	13	7	16	61	80	46
Christchurch Res.	36	12	8	16	50	64	*43
Petersfield T. Res.	36	11	7	18	64	106	40
BAT Spts Res.	36	11	6	19	53	74	*38
Horndean Res.	36	10	6	20	57	86	*35
Whitchurch U. Res.	36	11	2	23	48	93	35
Brockenhurst Res.	36	3	5	28	37	118	14

* - 1 point deducted

Top Scorers:
23 - S Jones (Downton). 22 - B Cooper (Newport). 21 - A Bundy (Bashley). 19 - D Milkins (Waterlooville), D Tasker (AFC Totton). 17 - D Blenman (Wimborne), R Semark (Havant).

FIRST DIVISION RESULT CHART 1993-94

HOME TEAM	1	2	3	4	5	6	7	8	9	10	11	12	13	14	15	16	17	18	19	20	21	22
1. AFC Lym'ton	*	2-0	2-0	3-5	1-0	2-0	2-3	4-1	1-1	1-1	5-1	0-1	2-0	0-0	1-0	4-0	1-0	3-1	3-0	4-1	3-0	0-1
2. AFC Totton	0-5	*	0-0	0-3	1-0	1-4	1-0	2-1	0-0	0-5	3-2	0-0	1-1	3-0	4-2	0-5	7-1	0-2	0-0	0-5	1-0	1-2
3. Aerostruct.	1-3	1-1	*	0-5	2-6	2-1	1-0	2-3	3-0	0-2	0-3	1-1	1-2	0-2	1-3	2-0	2-2	1-0	2-0	1-2	2-0	1-3
4. Andover	0-3	5-0	10-1	*	4-2	2-2	3-4	7-0	0-0	1-1	10-0	5-1	0-1	3-1	2-0	2-0	1-1	4-0	5-0	3-1	3-0	1-4
5. BAT Sports	1-2	2-1	2-0	1-1	*	0-3	0-0	1-1	2-2	2-1	6-3	2-1	0-3	0-0	0-0	4-3	3-2	4-0	1-1	1-1	2-0	3-1
6. Bemerton	0-4	2-2	1-0	0-2	1-0	*	0-0	0-0	0-1	9-2	1-2	0-0	1-1	0-1	2-0	7-2	4-2	0-4	3-1	0-2	4-1	3-2
7. Bournemouth	1-1	2-1	2-3	1-0	3-0	2-3	*	2-2	1-0	5-0	4-3	2-2	1-6	1-1	1-2	2-3	1-2	1-2	0-1	0-2	2-1	1-3
8. Brockenhurst	1-3	1-0	0-0	1-6	3-1	0-0	2-0	*	0-0	1-2	3-5	2-1	1-0	2-3	4-0	2-0	0-0	2-0	0-0	3-2	5-2	1-2
9. Christchurch	0-3	2-0	1-2	1-3	1-1	5-0	1-3	1-2	*	1-0	1-1	4-3	1-1	0-4	1-0	0-1	0-2	0-0	2-1	2-1	0-1	2-1
10. Downton	0-1	3-2	0-1	0-5	1-2	0-4	3-4	0-1	1-4	*	2-3	0-0	1-1	0-1	0-1	2-2	1-3	3-1	2-2	0-6	1-1	0-1
11. East Cowes	2-3	1-1	1-0	0-3	5-1	0-2	4-1	1-3	1-2	2-3	*	1-4	2-2	1-6	5-0	2-2	2-1	2-0	1-1	2-3	3-0	1-7
12. Eastleigh	0-1	2-0	0-0	0-4	1-0	0-0	5-0	3-0	1-0	1-1	3-0	*	0-3	0-1	0-1	2-0	0-0	0-1	0-0	2-4	3-0	1-2
13. Fleet Town	2-0	2-0	1-0	2-2	5-0	3-4	0-2	4-3	1-0	0-1	6-2	0-0	*	4-1	5-3	1-0	3-0	3-0	4-0	0-1	2-1	0-3
14. Gosport	1-0	3-2	3-0	1-4	2-3	0-0	3-1	2-1	3-3	0-1	5-3	2-1	2-0	*	1-3	6-2	0-0	1-1	3-1	0-0	5-2	1-1
15. Horndean	1-0	3-0	1-0	3-3	0-1	1-1	1-2	2-2	2-3	0-2	2-4	0-2	2-2	0-4	*	3-1	1-0	4-3	1-0	2-4	2-3	2-2
16. Petersfield	0-1	1-2	1-3	1-7	2-4	1-0	1-2	0-2	3-0	1-4	1-1	5-2	0-3	1-3	3-1	*	1-1	6-0	3-2	0-4	2-1	1-2
17. P'mouth RN	2-1	2-0	1-0	2-0	2-3	2-3	3-2	0-0	1-2	3-3	2-0	3-2	1-0	3-8	3-2	2-2	*	1-2	4-1	0-2	0-2	0-4
18. Ryde Spts	0-1	5-2	3-0	1-2	0-0	0-2	3-1	1-1	2-2	1-0	1-1	4-1	1-1	2-2	2-1	1-1	1-1	*	5-1	1-5	3-2	1-2
19. Swanage	2-1	1-0	4-2	1-3	1-0	1-2	0-2	0-4	2-2	0-2	1-2	3-0	0-4	1-3	7-1	5-1	5-1	3-1	*	1-2	1-2	1-8
20. Thatcham	2-1	1-1	3-0	1-3	1-0	2-2	2-1	1-1	1-2	4-3	6-1	0-0	4-1	0-1	7-1	1-1	2-1	4-0	3-0	*	1-0	1-4
21. Whitchurch	0-4	5-2	4-2	3-3	2-4	0-1	2-3	1-6	2-4	1-2	0-2	0-1	2-1	2-1	0-2	1-3	2-1	1-4	1-0	2-1	*	0-1
22. Wimborne	1-1	6-1	5-1	4-2	2-1	3-0	3-1	3-2	1-1	3-3	7-0	2-0	2-1	3-0	7-0	2-1	2-1	5-1	3-1	3-0	3-1	*

COMBINATION RESULT CHART 1993-94

HOME TEAM	1	2	3	4	5	6	7	8	9	10	11	12	13	14	15	16	17	18	19
1. AFC Lymington Res.	*	1-0	1-0	0-1	0-0	2-1	2-1	3-3	0-2	1-0	1-0	1-2	1-3	6-1	4-0	1-0	6-1	7-0	7-3
2. AFC Totton Res.	8-1	*	1-3	1-2	1-2	1-1	3-0	4-1	1-1	4-2	5-1	3-2	1-1	3-2	3-2	1-6	0-1	5-0	2-0
3. Aerostructures Res.	0-0	1-1	*	3-2	1-2	1-0	2-3	1-2	1-0	2-0	1-2	3-0	2-3	3-2	1-4	8-1	0-2	1-4	0-2
4. BAT Sports Res.	1-3	2-2	1-1	*	0-2	0-0	7-3	5-1	1-2	1-3	1-4	3-2	0-3	1-3	1-1	1-5	1-2	3-0	0-1
5. Bashley Res.	1-0	3-1	0-1	6-0	*	1-1	4-1	3-0	4-2	3-2	4-0	3-0	1-2	2-2	1-2	7-0	0-3	4-0	0-7
6. Bemerton HH Res.	1-1	2-0	2-1	2-1	0-2	*	5-0	4-0	5-0	0-3	1-2	4-2	1-3	1-1	1-1	3-0	0-0	2-3	1-3
7. Bournemouth Res.	0-3	2-1	1-3	1-4	1-3	0-0	*	3-1	4-0	2-1	2-2	1-1	3-2	2-2	2-0	4-1	0-0	2-0	2-1
8. Brockenhurst Res.	1-3	1-2	0-3	0-4	0-6	2-1	1-3	*	1-4	0-3	3-4	0-4	0-2	0-1	0-3	4-4	0-3	0-3	0-7
9. Christchurch Res.	1-1	4-0	0-1	0-0	0-3	2-1	0-3	3-2	*	2-0	2-1	0-4	0-3	2-3	2-0	1-1	1-1	1-2	1-3
10. Downton Res.	2-1	3-0	8-0	3-0	1-0	0-2	2-2	1-1	3-2	*	2-1	0-1	0-2	3-0	0-4	1-0	2-0	0-1	2-0
11. Eastleigh Res.	2-1	2-6	1-1	1-3	1-3	1-3	3-1	6-1	1-2	0-5	*	0-2	1-1	3-1	2-2	2-0	3-1	3-1	0-2
12. Gosport Boro. Res.	1-5	1-1	2-2	1-0	0-3	1-2	2-7	2-0	2-2	2-0	2-0	*	1-1	3-0	1-5	6-2	4-0	0-3	2-2
13. Havant Town Res.	2-0	0-1	3-0	1-1	4-3	5-1	3-1	8-2	3-0	1-3	4-0	6-0	*	2-2	5-0	10-0	3-3	6-0	0-0
14. Horndean Res.	1-1	2-1	3-0	3-1	1-3	0-3	0-2	4-1	2-3	0-2	0-4	1-0	2-2	*	2-3	4-2	0-3	1-2	0-9
15. Newport IOW Res.	2-0	3-2	1-0	7-1	1-1	2-2	5-1	3-3	1-4	3-3	2-2	1-4	0-3	3-2	*	0-0	3-0	2-1	5-2
16. Petersfield T. Res.	5-4	0-7	2-3	2-1	0-5	2-2	3-2	5-1	2-2	1-4	2-3	5-1	0-5	4-3	0-0	*	2-2	0-3	2-1
17. Waterlooville Res.	1-1	4-3	3-1	5-0	1-1	2-1	6-1	2-2	2-1	3-3	2-3	6-1	1-3	2-5	3-1	2-0	*	3-1	3-1
18. Whitchurch Utd Res.	1-3	2-3	0-3	0-1	3-1	0-2	1-3	0-3	1-0	0-3	2-6	2-2	2-7	3-1	2-5	2-3	2-3	*	1-1
19. Wimborne Town Res.	3-2	3-2	1-2	0-2	1-1	4-0	4-0	1-0	1-1	4-1	0-2	6-0	1-3	1-0	1-0	0-2	3-4	3-0	*

WESSEX LEAGUE CUP 1993-94

First Round (2 legs, aggregate scores)
AFC Totton v BAT Sports 5-4
Andover v AFC Lymington 2-0
Brockenhurst v Portsmouth Royal Navy 4-1
Gosport Borough v Christchurch 7-3
Ryde Sports .v Whitchurch United 7-2
Thatcham Town v Horndean 9-2

Second Round (2 legs, aggregate scores)
Bemerton Heath v Bournemouth 8-2
Brockenhurst v AFC Totton 2-0
Eastleigh v Andover 1-1*(E win on away gls)*
Fleet Town v East Cowes Vics 4-3
Gosport Borough v Petersfield Town 7-0
Swanage v Downton 3-3*(Swanage on pens)*
Thatcham Town v Aerostructures 6-0
Wimborne Town v Ryde Sports 3-1

Quarter-Finals (2 legs, aggregate scores)
Bemerton Heath Harlequins v Eastleigh 3-2
Gosport v Brockenhurst 3-3*(G on away gls)*
Thatcham Town v Swanage Town & Hers. 4-2
Wimborne Town v Fleet Town 3-2

Semi-Finals (2 legs, aggregate scores)
Thatcham Town v Bemerton Heath H. 3-1
Wimborne Town v Gosport Borough 8-1

Final *(at Andover FC)*
Wimborne Town v Thatcham Town 7-0

WESSEX COMBINATION CUP 1993-94

First Round
Bournemouth Res v Horndean Res 1-2
Havant Town Res v Christchurch Res 1-1
Replay: Christchurch Res v Havant Res. 0-6

Second Round
Aerostructutes Res v Bemerton Res 0-5
AFC Totton Res v AFC Lymington Res 0-5
Bashley Res v Downton Res 0-3
BAT Sports Res v Waterlooville Res 4-3
Eastleigh Res v Bournemouth Res 0-2
Gosport Boro. Res v Wimborne Res 1-2
Newport IOW Res v Whitchurch Utd Res 4-2
Petersfield Town Res v Havant Town Res 1-2

Quarter-Finals
AFC Lymington Res v Bemerton Hth Res 0-4
BAT Sports Res v B'mouth Res 3-3,0-5
Downton Res v Havant Town Res 0-1
Wimborne Town Res v Newport IOW Res 3-2

Semi-Finals
Bemerton Hth Res v Bournemouth Res 2-1
Wimborne Town Res v Havant Town Res 0-2

Final *(at BAT Sports FC)*
Havant Town Res v Bemerton Hth H. Res 2-1

WESSEX LEAGUE FIRST DIVISION RECORD (SINCE FORMATION)

	86/7	87/8	88/9	89/0	90/1	91/2	92/3	93/4
Aerostructures Spts & Soc.	-	13	10	12	16	9	12	19
AFC Lymington	-	-	5	5	9	2	1	3
AFC Totton	3	8	14	6	14	17	16	21
Andover	-	-	-	-	-	-	-	2
Bashley	1	1	1	-	-	-	-	-
BAT Sports	-	-	-	3	8	16	18	9
Bemerton Heath Harlequins	-	-	-	8	18	8	3	7
Bournemouth	15	10	12	10	3	6	7	11
Brockenhurst	17	18	16	17	7	12	10	8
Christchurst	-	5	13	15	15	13	13	10
Downton	-	-	-	-	-	-	-	16
East Cowes Victoria Athletic	-	9	8	13	13	14	20	14
Eastleigh	8	12	9	14	12	10	9	15
Fleet Town	-	-	-	18	10	11	8	6
Folland Sports (see Aerostructures)								
Gosport Borough	-	-	-	-	-	-	5	5
Havant Town	5	2	2	11	1	-	-	-
Horndean	14	14	11	16	20	18	11	17
Lymington Town	10	19	-	-	-	-	-	-
Newport Isle of Wight	4	4	3	2	-	-	-	-
Petersfield Town	-	-	-	-	-	-	-	18
Portals Athletic	12	-	-	-	-	-	-	-
Portsmouth Royal Navy	13	16	17	19	17	19	17	13
Romsey Town	16	3	7	1	4	4	21	-
Road Sea Southampton	2	-	-	-	-	-	-	-
Ryde Sports	-	-	-	-	11	7	6	12
Sholing Sports	9	7	15	9	19	15	19	w/d
Steyning Town	11	17	-	-	-	-	-	-
Swanage Town & Herston	-	-	-	-	2	5	14	20
Thatcham Town	6	11	4	7	6	3	4	4
Wellworthy Athletic	7	15	-	-	-	-	-	-
Whitchurch United	-	-	-	-	-	-	15	22
Wimborne Town	-	6	6	4	5	1	2	1

AEROSTRUCTURES SPORTS & SOCIAL CLUB

Chairman: Al Tritten **Manager:** Steve Beck **Gen. Mgr:** Nigel Kent
Secretary: Matthew Newbold, 40 Westwood Close, Hamble, Southampton, Hants SO31 4LG (0703 453600).
Ground: Folland Park, Kings Avenue, Hamble (0703 452173).
Directions: M27 junction 8, then B3397 to Hamble. One and a half miles from Hamble (BR); turn right out of station, proceed for one mile then turn right into Queens Avenue. Ground 50 yards on right.
Midweek Matches: Tues (1st team), Wed (Res) **Previous Name:** Folland Sports (pre-1990).
Colours: White/white/red **Change colours:** Red/black/white. **Floodlights:** Yes
Record defeat: 1-10 v Andover (A), Wessex League 93-94.
Clubhouse: 300 capacity social club. Tennis, bowls, hockey.
Honours: Hants Lg Div 3 80-81 (Div 4 79-80), Hants Intermediate Cup 79-90, Southampton Snr Cup(4).

ANDOVER

Chairman: K Cunningham-Brown **Vice-Chairman:** M C Burford **President:** R Coleman
Secretary: Mrs Elsy Ardolino, The Coach House, The Holt, Tangley, Andover, Hants SP11 0RY (0264 70656).
Manager: Ken Cunningham-Brown **Asst Manager:** Mike Burford
Coach: Frank Gregon **Physio:** Terry Carr.
Ground: Portway Stadium, West Portway Industrial Estate, Andover SP10 3LF (0264 333052).
Directions: On western outskirts - follow any sign to Portway Industrial estate. Approx 2 miles from station.
Capacity: 3,000 **Cover:** 250 **Seats:** 250 **Floodlights:** Yes **Founded:** 1883.
Programme: 20 pages, 50p **Club Shop:** No. **Metal Badges:** Yes.
Colours: Red & black shirts/black/red **Change cols:** Tangarine/white/tangarine **Nickname:** The Lions.
Sponsors: Hospital Saving Association.
Prev. Lges: Salisbury & D./ Hants 1896-98 99-1901 02-62/ Southern 1898-99 1971-93/ Western 1962-71.
Previous Name: Andover Town **Previous Ground:** The Walled Meadow (until 1989).
Midweek home matchday: Tuesday **Reserve Team's League:** None (2 youth sides).
Record Gate: 1,100 v Leicester, ground opening. *(3,484 v Gillingham at Walled Meadow, previous ground).*
Record win: 10-0 v East Cowes Victoria Athletic (H), Wessex League 93-94.
Best FA Trophy season: 3rd Qualifying Rd 69-70 70-71.
Best FA Vase season: Fourth Round 93-94 (lost 1-3 at Falmouth Town)
Best FA Cup season: 1st Rd 62-63 (lost 0-1 to Gillingham).
Record Fees - Paid: £8,000 for Roger Emms (Newbury)
Received: £6,000 for Jeremy Stagg (Bashley).
Players progressing to Football League: Keith Wilson (Southampton 1959), Nigel Spackman (B'mouth 1980), Colin Court (Reading 1981), A Kingston (Southampton), P Brown (Southampton, Walsall), Emeka Nwajiobi (Luton).
Clubhouse: As a pub, but available for private functions.
Club Record Scorer: T Randall 73 **Club Record Appearances:** P Pollard 469
Captain 93-94: K O'Leary **P.o.Y. 93-94:** Mark Belbin **Top Scorer 93-94:** Gary Lewis.
Honours: Wessex Lg R-up 93-94, Western Lg R-up 69-70 70-71, Hants Lg 13-14 24-25 33-34 44-45 48-49 50-51 61-62 (R-up 42-43, Northern Div 13-14, Div 2 R-up 37-38, Combination (reserves) 87-88), Salisbury & Dist Lg 1894-95 95-96 96-97 99-1900 03-04 07-08 12-13, Hants Senior Cup 48-49 50-51 55-56 64-65, Russell Cotes Cup 23-24 31-32 37-38 44-45 52-53 58-59 60-61 61-62, Pickfords Cup 50-51, Hants Intermediate Cup 59-60 60-61, Hants Junior Cup 19-20 (R-up 1893-94 1910-11 12-13), May Lg 1899-00 00-01 01-02 07-08 08-09.

B.A.T. SPORTS

Chairman: Mr D Batt **Manager:** Sean Mallon.
Secretary: D Saich, 32 Salcombe Cres., Totton, Southampton SO4 3FP (0703 860797).
Ground: BAT Sports Ground, Southern Gdns, off Ringwood Road, Totton (0703 862143).
Directions: Into centre of Totton, proceed up Ringwood Rd past small r'bout, 2nd left into Southern Gardens. Half mile from Totton (BR), bus X2 (Southampton-Bournemouth).
Seats: 12-15 **Cover:** 50 **Capacity:** 3,000 **Floodlights:** Yes **Founded:** 1925
Midweek Matches: Tuesday **Colours:** Blue & white halves/blue/white **Change:** All red.
Programme: 8-10 pages, 30p **Best FA Vase year:** Extra-Preliminary Rd 91-92
Clubhouse: Normal licensing hrs, all day for members' sports facilities. Darts, pool, juke box. Hot & cold snacks.

BEMERTON HEATH HARLEQUINS

Chairman: George Parker **President:** Peter Say.
Secretary: D J Heather, 31 Hollows Close, Salisbury, Wilts SP2 8JU (0722 32600).
Manager: Steve Slade **Physio:** Andy Nash **Coach:** Gary Cross
Ground: Western Way, Bemerton Heath, Salisbury, Wilts (0722 331925).
Directions: Turn off A36 Salisbury-Bristol Rd at Skew Bridge (right turn if coming out of Salisbury), 1st left into Pembroke Rd for half mile, 2nd left along Western Way - ground quarter mile at end. 40 mins walk from Salisbury (BR) station. Bus 351 or 352 from city centre stops at junction of Pembroke Rd/ Western Way.
Clubhouse: Yes **Seats:** 50 **Cover:** 350 **Floodlights:** Yes **Founded:** May 1989
Previous Names: Bemerton Athletic, Moon FC & Bemerton Boys; all merged in 1989.
Previous Leagues: B'ton Ath.: Salis. & Wilts Comb., Moon: Salis. & Andover Sunday, B'ton Boys: Mid Wilts.
Cols: Black & white **Change colours:** Amber/white/white **Nickname:** Quins **Prog.:** 32 pages, 50p
Midweek Matches: Tuesday **Record Gate:** 480 v Bognor, FA Cup 2nd Qual Rd 1992.
Captain 93-94: **Top Scorer 93-94:**
P.o.Y. 93-94: **Club record appearances:** Keith Richardson.
Hons: Wilts Snr Cup 92-93. *Wilts Lg(3) as Bemerton Athletic*

BOURNEMOUTH

Chairman: V C Dominey **Vice Chairman:** J B Wood **President:** D Nippard
Secretary: W G Johnston, 25 Edward Rd, Bournemouth BH11 8SX (0202 511767).
Manager: Alex Pike **Asst Manager:** Nick Jennings **Coach:** Chris Weller
Physio: Irvin Brown **Comm. Manager:** Alex Pike **Press Officer:** Mark Willis.
Ground: Victoria Park, Winton, Bournemouth, Dorset (0202 515123).
Directions: Any bus to Wimborne Road, Winton. 2 miles from Bournemouth Central (BR).
Seats: 250 **Cover:** 250 **Capacity:** 3,000 **Floodlights:** Yes **Founded:** 1875.
Colours: All red **Change colours:** All yellow **Nickname:** Poppies.
Programme: 58 pages, 50p **Programme Editor:** Mark Willis **Club Shop:** No.
Sponsors: Chapel Carpets **Midweek Matches:** Tuesday **Prev. Lge:** Hants.
Previous Ground: Dene Park 1888-90 **Local Newspaper:** Evening Echo. **Rec. Gate:** Unknown
Reserves' Lge: Jewson Wessex Comb. **Record fee rec.:** £1,500 for Chike Onourah (Wimborne 93-94)
Previous Names: Bournemouth Rovers 1875-88/ Bournemouth Dene Park 1888-90.
Clubhouse: Open daily 7-11pm, Sandwiches & hot snacks (burgers, chips etc).
Captain 93-94: Peter Howard **Top Scorer 93-94:** Darren McBride.
P.o.Y. 93-94: Peter Howard **Club record scorer:** B Head
Hons: Hants Lg 13-13 21-22, B'mouth Snr Cup 66-67 89-90, Texaco F'lit Cup R-up 91-92, Hant I'mediate Cup 49-50 69-70, Hants Yth Cup 54-55 57-58 67-68.

Bournemouth 'Poppies' FC.

BROCKENHURST

Chairman: Bob Philpott **Manager:** Cliff Huxford.
Secretary: Mr D Chandler, 300 Salisbury Road, Totton, Southampton SO4 3LZ (0703 862957)
Ground: Grigg Lane, Brockenhurst, Hants (0590 23544).
Directions: 400 yds from Brockenhurst station, just off main shopping area.
Seats: 200 **Cover:** 300 **Capacity:** 2,000 **Floodlights:** Yes **Founded:** 1898
Midweek Matches: Tues (Wed reserves) **Clubhouse:** Every evening plus Tues, Sat & Sun lunchtimes.
Colours: Blue & white stripes/white/blue **Change colours:** All red.
Programme: 12 pages, 20p, **Editor:** C Fisher **Prev. League:** Hants 24-26 47-86
Hons: Hants I'mediate Cup 61-62, B'mouth Snr Cup 60-61, Hants Lg 75-76 (R-up 73-74 79-80, Div 2 70-71 (R-up 60-61), Div 3 59-60), F.A. Amateur Cup 2nd Rd 73-74.

CHRISTCHURCH

President: Gerald Page **Chairman:** Cliff Taylor **Vice Chairman:** Brian Farmer
Secretary: Mrs D Page, 89 Parkway Drive, Bournemouth BH8 9JS (0202 304996).
Manager: Alan Bryant **Asst Manager:** Steve Hudspith.
Physio: Brian Finch **Press Officer:** Dennis James.
Ground: Christchurch Sporting Club, Hurn Bridge, Avon Causeway, Christchurch (0202 473792).
Directions: A338 from Ringwood, turn off signed Hurn Airport on left. Before Airport use mini roundabout & take exit signed to Sopley and ground is immediately on the right. 3 miles from Christchurch (BR).
Seats: 15 **Cover:** 50 **Capacity:** 2,000 **Floodlights:** Yes **Founded:** 1885
Midweek Matches: Wednesday **Previous League:** Hampshire.
Sponsors: Franklin Transport **Previous Ground:** Barrack Rd Recreation Ground (until 1984).
Colours: All royal blue (white trim) **Change colours:** All yellow **Nickname:** Priory
Programme: 16 pages, 25p **Programme Editor:** John Whiting/Pete Gardner.
Clubhouse: Normal pub hours. Cooked food at lunchtimes.
Players progressing to Football Lge: Jody Craddock (Cambridge Utd 1993), Dan West (Aston Villa, 1994).
Captain 93-94: Steve Joyce **Top Scorer 93-94:** Steve Hudspith.
P.o.Y. 93-94: Lee Naylor **Club record appearances:** John Haynes.
Honours: Hants Jnr Cup 1892-93 1911-12 20-21, Hants Int. Cup 86-87, Pickford Cup 1991, Hants Lg Div 2 37-38 47-48 85-86 (Div 3 56-57), B'mouth Snr Cup(5) 56-57 59-60 67-70, B'mouth Page-Croft Cup 93-94.

COWES SPORTS

Chairman: Ray Sleep. **Manager:** Dale Young.
Secretary: Mr W G Murray, 53 Park Rd, Cowes, Isle of Wight PO31 7LY (0983 294445).
Ground: Westwood Park, Reynolds Close, off Park Rd, Cowes, Isle of Wight (0983 293793).
Directions: Take Park Road out of Cowes centre. Reynolds Close is a right turn half mile up hill.
Capacity: **Seats:** Yes **Cover:** Stand **Floodlights:** Yes **Founded:**
Cols: Blue & white stripes/black/blue **Change colours:** All red
Honours: Hampshire Lg 93-94. **Previous League:** Hampshire (pre-1994)
Best FA Cup season: Fourth Qualifying Round replay 57-58 (lost 1-4 at Trowbridge after 2-2 draw).

DOWNTON

Chairman: Trevor Halski. **Sec.:** R Hillman, 15 Moot Gdns, Downton, nr Salisbury SP5 3LG (0725 20815)
Ground: Brian Whitehead Sports Ground, Wick Lane, Downton (0725 22162).
Directions: Travelling south from Salisbury on A338 turn right into Wick Lane opposite turn for Downton village centre - ground quarter mile on left.
Colours: All red **Change colours:** All blue. **Previous League:** Hants (pre-1993).

EAST COWES VICTORIA ATHLETIC

President: A Woolford. **Chairman:** M Diash **Vice-Chairman:** M Everett.
Secretary: L Bray, 57 Grange Rd, East Cowes, I.O.W. PO32 6DY (0983 200276).
Ground: Beatrice Avenue Ground, East Cowes, I.O.W. (0938 297165).
Mgr: L Cade/D Ohren **Coach:** D Ohren **Physio:** D Allan.
Directions: From the ferry: 1 mile from town centre on lower main road to Newport or Ryde, near Whippingham Church adjacent to Osborne Middle School.
Seats: 200 **Cover:** 400 **Capacity:** 4,000 **Floodlights:** Yes **Founded:** 1968.
Midweek Matches: Wednesday **Sponsors:** IOW Group '90 **Club Shop:** No.
Previous Names: East Cowes Victoria (founded 1888) merged with East Cowes Athletic in 1968.
Previous Leagues: (E.C. Vics): I.O.W. 1898-19 21-47/ Hants 14-21 47-87.
Record win: 9-0 v Brading (A), Hants Lg 86-87. **Rec. defeat:** 0-10 v Andover (A), Wessex Lg 93-94.
Colours: Red & white stripes/black/white **Change colours:** Blue. **Nickname:** Vics.
Programme: 14 pages, 30p **Programme Editor:** Darren Dyer (0983 297488).
Reserves' League: Isle of Wight. **Record Gate:** 2,000 v Poole Town, FA Cup 1954
Midweek matchday: Wednesday **Clubhouse:** Open matchdays/most evenings. Crisps/confectionary sold.
Player progressing to Football League: Gareth Williams (Aston Villa, via Gosport Borough, 1987).
Top Scorer 93-94: J O'Rourke **Club record appearances:** Joe Reed.
Captain 93-94: S Ellsbury **P.o.Y. 93-94:** S Lawton.
Hons: (as East Cowes Vics pre-'68): Wessex Lg Cup 87-88, IOW Snr Gold Cup(7) 79-80 81-86 88-89, Hants Lg 85-86 86-87 (Div 2 52-53 82-83, Div 3 63-64 71-72, Div 3 West 47-48), IOW Lg 1898-99 99-1900 30-31 34-35 78-79 82-83 86-87 87-88 (Div 2 1898-99 1904-05 06-07, Div 3 28-29 32-33, Comb Div 2 87-88 90-91), IOW Chal. Cup(13) 1899-1902 19-20 47-48 50-53 80-81 84-85 87-88 90-92, IOW Mem. Cup 19-20 32-33 82-83 87-88 90-91, Brooklyn Cup 86-87 87-88 89-90 91-92, IOW Charity Cup 23-24 25-26, IOW Centenary Cup 89-90 91-92.

EASTLEIGH

Chairman: Mr A G Froud **President:** Derik Brooks.
Secretary: Mr R G Kearslake, 10 Binsey Close, Millbrook, Southampton, Hants SO16 4AQ (0703 779545).
Manager: Don Gowans **Asst Manager:** Mark Barber **Physio:** Derek Browning.
Press Officer: Mrs D Gowans **Commercial Manager:** John Pothecary (0962 713685).
Ground: 'Ten Acres', Stoneham Lane, North Stoneham, Eastleigh SO5 3HT (0703 613361).
Directions: M27 to Jct 5, to r'bout - exit marked Stoneham Lane, ground on left but carry on to r'bout and come back down Stoneham Lane, turning right opposite Concord Club. Ground 400 yds on left. Three quarters of a mile from Southampton Parkway (BR). Bus 48 (Southampton-Winchester) to Stoneham Church stop.
Seats: 150 **Cover:** 210 **Capacity:** 4,300 **Floodlights:** Yes **Founded:** 1946.
Midweek home matches: Tuesday **Prev. Lges:** Southampton Jnr & Snr 46-59/ Hants 50-86.
Colours: All royal blue **Change colours:** Yellow & emerald **Nickname:** None.
Programme: 32 pages with admission **Programme Editor:** John Pothecary **Club Shop:** No.
Rec. Gate: 2,500 v S'pton, f'light opener 30/9/75. **Prev. Names:** Swaythling Ath. 46-73/ Swaythling 73-80
Previous Grounds: Southampton Common 46-47/ Walnut Avenue, Swaythling 47-75.
Clubhouse: Licence 11am-11pm Mon-Sat plus Sundays. Extensive facilities for weddings, parties, skittles and seminars. All catering undertaken.
Record win: 12-1 v Hythe & Dibden, home 11/12/48 **Record defeat:** 0-11 v Austin Spts, away 1/1/47.
Club record scorer: Johnny Williams, 177 **Club record appearances:** Ian Knight, 611.
Hons: FA Vase 4th Rd 90-91, Wessex Lg Cup R-up 91-92, Hants Lg Div 2 69-70 (R-up 54-55 60-61 62-63 64-65(Res), Div 3(W) 50-51 53-54 70-71(Res), Comb.(Res) 86-87)), Hants Midweek F'lit Cup 78-79, Soton Snr Lg(W) 49-50 (R-up 51-52(Res), Div 1 56-57(Res) 57-58(Res)), Russell Cotes R-up 76-77 80-81 89-90, Hants I'mediate Cup 50-51 56-57(Res) 74-75(Res)(R-up 73-74(Res)), Soton Snr Cup(Res) 74-75 78-79 87-88 (R-up(8) 55-56 57-59 60-61 66-67 71-72 80-81 87-88), Soton Jnr Lg Div 2 47-48(Res), Reg Mathieson Tphy(Res) 74-75 78-79 87-88.

FLEET TOWN

Chairman: Anthony Cherry **Vice Chairman:** Bob Worthington **President:** Les Hocking
Secretary: Mr Spencer Lunt, 156 Kings Road, Fleet, Hants GU13 9DT (0252 615303).
Manager: Colin Sturgess **Assistant Manager:** Jess Bone
Coach: Joe Roach **Physio:** Steve Hyde
Ground: Calthorpe Park, Crookham Road, Fleet, Hants (0252 623804).
Directions: M3 jct 4A, into Fleet past BR station to town centre. Ground clearly marked at Oatsheaf pub crossroads.
Seats: 200 **Cover:** 250 **Capacity:** 2,000 **Floodlights:** Yes **Founded:** 1890.
Midweek Matches: Wednesday **Sponsors:** Hart Dist Council **Nickname:** Blues
Colours: Navy & sky **Change colours:** White & red
Programme: 20 pages **Programme Editor:** Secretary.
Club Shop: To open 1994-95 **Clubhouse:** Yes. Hot & cold food served.
Reserves' League: Suburban **Previous Lges:** Hants/ Athenian/ Combined Co's/ Chiltonian.
Record win: 7-0 **Record transfer paid:** £1,500 to Farnborough, 1991.
Club Record Scorer: Mark Frampton **Club record appearances:** Steve Hodge/ Paul Dear.
Captain 93-94: David Wells **Top Scorer 93-94:** John Smith.
Hons: Wessex Lg Cup R-up 92-93, Hants Lg Div 2 R-up 61-62 (Div 1 R-up 60-61), Aldershot Snr Cup 92-93, Simpsonair Challenge Shield 1993, Hants Yth Lg Div 3 92-93.

Fleet Town pictured after beating Aldershot Town on penalties to win the pre-season Simpsonair Shield. Photo - Dave West.

GOSPORT BOROUGH

Chairman: I T Hay **President:** W J Adams.
Secretary: B V Cosgrave, 2 Cavanna Close, Rowner, Gosport PO13 0PE (0329 314117).
Manager: Roger Sherwood **Asst Manager:** Paul Smith **Coach:** Tommy Hare
Physio: Dave Topliss **Commercial Director:** Roger Barrell
Ground: Privett Park, Privett Road, Gosport, Hants (0705 583986).
Directions: M27 junct 11, then A32 Fareham to Gosport, at Brockhurst r-about (after about 3 miles) right into Military Road passing thru H.M.S. Sultan, left into Privett Road at next r-about, ground 300 yds on left signed 'Privett Park Enclosure'. 2 miles from Portsmouth Harbour (BR) or Fareham (BR).
Capacity: 5,000 **Cover:** 650 **Seats:** 500 **Floodlights:** Yes **Founded:** 1944.
Prog.: 20 pages, 50p **Editor:** Ian Hay (0329 314601) **Club Shop:** No **Metal Badges:** Yes
Colours: Yellow/blue/blue **Change colours:** Blue/white/red. **Sponsors:** Eurokit
Midweek matchday: Wednesday **Prev. Lges:** Portsmouth 44-45/ Hants 45-78/ Southern 78-92
Previous Name: Gosport Borough Athletic **Record Gate:** 4,770 v Pegasus, FA Amtr Cup 1951.
Nickname: The Boro' **Previous Grounds:** None.
Reserve Team's League: Wessex Combination.
Best FA Trophy year: 1st Rd 88-89 **Best FA Amateur Cup year:** 3rd Rd 47-48 66-67
Best FA Vase year: 6th Rd rep 77-78 **Best FA Cup year:** 4th Qual. Rd 80-81 (lost to Windsor & Eton).
Record Fees - Paid: £6,000 for Sandy Baird (Basingstoke Town, 1990)
Received: £30,000+ for Gareth Williams (Aston Villa, 1987).
Record win: 14-0 v Cunliffe-Owen, Hampshire Lg Div 1 45-46.
Record defeat: 0-9 twice; v Newport, Hants Lg Div 1 47-48. v Gloucester (A), Southern Lg Prem Div 89-90.
Players progressing to Football League: Peter Harris (P'smouth, N'castle & Scotland), B Sherwood, D Dimmer, S Berry, Ron Blackman (Reading 1947), Richard Pearson (P'smouth 1949), Albert Mundy & Mike Barnard (P'smouth 1951), Peter Smith (G'ham 1954), Alan Grant (Brighton 1956), Brian Gibbs (B'mouth 1957), Gary Juryeff (P'smouth), Robert Carroll (Brentford 1986), Gareth Williams (A Villa 1988).
Clubhouse: (0705 583986). Open matchdays from 1.30pm Saturday, 6.30pm Wednesday. Refreshment hut sells hot food and drinks.
Record Scorer: Richie Coulbert 192 **Record Appearances:** Tony Mahoney 764.
93-94 Captain: Andy Williams **93-94 P.o.Y.:** Gary Payne **93-94 Top scorer:** Gary Joseph
Local Newspapers: Portsmouth Evening News, Southampton Evening Echo.
Honours: Wessex Lg Cup 92-93, Southern Lg Div 1 South R-up 84-85, Hants Lg 45-46 76-77 77-78 (Div 3 (Reserves) 70-71 75-76), Portsmouth Lg R-up 44-45, Hants Senior Cup 87-88, Russell Cotes Cup R-up 93-94, Hants Intermediate Cup 70-71, Portsmouth Senior Cup 61-62 69-70 70-71 93-94, South West Counties Pratten Challenge Cup 77-78.

HORNDEAN

Chairman: Mr J Knight **President:** Ron Coldrick
Vice Chairman: John Knight **Treasurer:** Rosmarie Crouch.
Secretary: Mrs Gladys Berry, 74 Five Heads Road, Horndean PO8 9NZ (0705 591698).
Manager: Trevor King.
Ground: Five Heads Park, Five Heads Road, Horndean (0705 591363).
Directions: 8 miles north of Portsmouth, just off A3. Five Heads Road is a turning off main road. 2 miles from Rowlands Castle (BR).
Seats: 50 **Cover:** 200 **Capacity:** 3,200 **Floodlights:** Yes **Founded:** 1887
Midweek Matches: Wednesday **Nickname:** Deans.
Previous Ground: Horndean Rec. 1887-1969.
Colours: Red/black/red **Change colours:** Green & white/green/green.
Programme: 16 pages, with admission **Programme Editor:** Derek Usher
Record Gate: 1,560 v Waterlooville, Victory Cup April 1971.
Best FA Cup season: 1st Qualifying Round replay 1982-83 (lost 2-3 at Eastbourne Utd after 1-1 draw).
Best FA Vase season: 1st Round 85-86 88-89.
Clubhouse: Open every evening plus Sat & Sun lunctimes
Honours: Hants Div 2 79-80 (Div 3 75-76, Div 4 74-75), Portsmouth Senior Cup 75-76 79-80 (R-up 86-87, Portsmouth Lg 69-70 70-71 71-72, Wessex Lg Cup R-up 86-87, Portsmouth Jnr Cup 64-65, South East Counties Floodlit Cup R-up 92-93.

(A.F.C.) LYMINGTON

Chairman: John Mills **Vice Chairman:** Ian Snook **President:** Howard Wilkinson
Secretary: John Osey, 9 Samphire Close, Lymington Meadows, Lymington, Hants SO41 9LR (0590 676995).
Manager: Derek Binns **Asst Manager:** Robbie Ingrem **Coach:** Eric Corlett.
Physio: Glynne Osey **Commercial Manager:** Richard Millbery.
Press Officer: John Mills (0590 682830).
Ground: Lymington Sports Ground, Southampton Road, Lymington (0590 671305).
Directions: M27 jct 1, follow signs (A337) to Lymington via Lyndhurst and Brockenhurst, ground on left (signposted) 250yds after 2nd set of lights on entering town. 1 mile from Lymington Town BR station.
Seats: 200 **Cover:** 200 **Capacity:** 3,000 **Floodlights:** Yes **Founded:** 1988
Midweek Matches: Monday **Record Gate:** 1,098 v Southampton, stand opening 1989.
Colours: Red & black hoops/black/red **Change colours:** Yellow/green/green. **Nickname:** Linnets
Programme: 32 pages, 40p **Editor:** John Mills (0590 682830). **Sponsors:** TBA
Reserve Team's League: Wessex Combination.
Club Shop: Yes, selling scarves, ties, enamel badges, car stickers, programmes (League & non-League). Contact Stephen Jones (0590 676040).
Previous Name: Lymington Town (until 1988 when the club merged with Wellworthy Athletic).
Previous Ground: Ampress Ground (Wellworthy Athletic), until 1988 merger.
Previous Lges: Lymington Town: Hants/ Wessex. Wellworthy: Bournemouth/ Hants/ Wessex.
Best FA Cup season: 3rd Qualifying Rd 92-93 (lost 0-1 at home to Cheltenham Town).
Record win: 11-1 v Romsey Town (H), Wessex League 9/11/92.
Record defeat: 0-8 v Basingstoke Town (A), Hampshire Senior Cup 10/4/90.
Clubhouse: Sat 2-7pm and training and match nights. Rolls, hot pies.
Club Record Scorer: David Perrett 107 **Club Record Appearances:** Glen Limburn 317 (out of poss. 320)
Captain 93-94: Glen Limburn **P.o.Y. 93-94:** Dave Jenman **Top Scorers 93-94:** Jason Hervey.
Honours: Wessex Lg 92-93 (R-up 91-92, Lg Cup 88-89, Comb.(res) 92-93), Hants Snr Cup R-up 89-90, Texaco Cup 91-92, Bournemouth Snr Cup 92-93, Russell Cotes Cup 93-94 (R-up 91-92 92-93), Pickford Cup R-up 92-93. As Lymington Town: Russell Cotes Cup 35-36, Bournemouth Snr Cup 83-84 (R-up 69-71 84-85), Hants Lg Div 3 67-68 (Div 2 R-up 83-84), Pickford Cup 52-53. As Wellworthy Athletic: Bournemouth Snr Cup 87-88 (R-up 53-54), Hants Intermediate Cup 56-57 84-85, Pickford Cup 84-85, Bournemouth Lg 84-85, Hants Lg Div 3 R-up 85-86.

PETERSFIELD TOWN

Chairman: Peter De Sisto.
Secretary: M Nicholl, 49 Durford Rd, Petersfield, Hants GU31 4ER (0730 261735).
Manager: Gary Stevens **Asst Manager:**
Ground: Love Lane, Petersfield, Hants (0730 262177).
Directions: On A3 circulatory system. 10 mins walk from Petersfield BR station heading towards London.
Seats: 135 **Cover:** 385 **Capacity:** 4,000 **Floodlights:** Yes **Reformed:** 1993
Midweek Matches: Monday **Previous Leagues:** None
Colours: Red, green & white stripes/white/red **Change cols:** White/blue/white
Club Sponsors: Tradeline Windows **Club Shop:** No.
Programme: T.B.A. **Clubhouse:** Yes.
Record Gate: 1,500 - Gary Stevens All-Stars v Aston Villa, Tony Barton memorial match 10/11/93.
Hons: None. **Best F.A. Cup season:** Not entered to date.

PORTSMOUTH ROYAL NAVY

Chairman: Mr J Molloy, OBE.
Secretary: Mr S Carter, 2 Sedgewick Close, Gosport, Hants PO13 9RB (0705 619917).
Manager: Paul Spinks/ D Reid **Coach:** G Young **Physio:** G Bramble
Ground: RN Stadium, Burnaby Road, (West) Portsmouth (0705) 822351 Ext. 24235).
Directions: From Portsmouth Harbour (BR), turn right onto The Hard, pass under the rail bridge and turn left into Park Road, after approx 200yds take 1st right into Burnaby Road. Entrance to ground via main gate of HMS Temeraire.
Seats: 500 **Cover:** 500 **Capacity:** 1,500 **Floodlights:** Yes **Founded:** 1962
Midweek Matches: Monday **Prev. Ground:** Victory Stadium 1962-87. **Nickname:** Sailors.
Colours: Royal/white/royal **Change colours:** All red **Club Shop:** No.
Prog.: 32 pages, voted Jewson Wessex 'Programme of the Year' 93-94. Free with entry - additional copies 50p.
Previous Lge: Hampshire 1962-86 **Club Sponsors:** Peter Adams Financial Services.
Reserve Team's League: Portsmouth & District.
Clubhouse: Open 1 and a half hrs before k.o. and 2 hrs after game on matchdays and by arrangement only.
Captain 93-94: Mick Travers **Top Scorer 93-94:** John Oliver **P.o.Y. 93-94:** John Sturt
Hons: Russell-Cotes Cup 67-68, Basingstoke Lg Div 2, Hants Lg Div 2 67-68 77-78 80-81.

RYDE SPORTS

President: John Keynes **Chairman:** Mr S Rann
Secretary: Raymond Fleming, Glenmead, Chilton Lane, Brighstone, Ryde, Isle of Wight PO30 4DR (0983 740113).
Manager: Dennis Probee **Asst Manager:** Tony Newman.
Physio: Tom Kennedy **Commercial Manager:** Mark Firmin (0983 812906).
Ground: Smallbrook Stadium, Ashey Rd, Ryde (0983 812906).
Directions: From the Pier Head follow directions to the Royal Isle of Wight Hospital, carry on past the hospital turning left at the Partlands Hotel - ground is one mile along Ashey Road. Not served by public transport.
Seats: 450 **Cover:** 1,500 **Capacity:** 5,000 **Floodlights:** 246 lux **Founded:** 1888.
Midweek Matches: Wednesday **Previous League:** Hants.
Colours: Red/white/red **Change colours:** White/blue/blue. **Metal Badges:** Yes.
Programme: 20 pages, 50p. **Editor:** Mark Firmin (0983 812906) **Nickname:** The Reds.
Previous Ground: Partlands (pre-1990). **Club Sponsors:** Wight Sports/ Hoevertravel.
Reserves' League: Isle of Wight **Record Gate:** 3,100 v Aston Villa 17/12/90.
Best FA Vase season: Prel. Rd 90-91 **Best FA Cup season:** 3rd Rd Proper 35-36.
Players pogressing to Football League: Roy Shiner (Sheff Wed), Keiron Baker & Kevin Allen (Bournemouth). *(Also Wally Hammond played for Ryde before achieving fame in cricket).*
Clubhouse: Open everyday. 2 bars, function suite, balcony overlooking stadium, restaurant, fitness centre, gym, treatment room.
Club shop: Yes, selling old & new programmes, metal badges, scarves & pennants, sportswear.
Captain 93-94: Shaun Flux **Current longest-serving player:** Terry Pawling.
Top Scorer 93-94: Lee Dixon **Player of the Year 93-94:** Andy Rayner.
Honours: Hants Lg 1899-00 25-26 89-90 (Div 2 88-89, Div 3 64-65), Hants Snr Cup(8) 1899-00 03-04 25-26 34-39, IOW Gold Cup(7) 26-27 46-47 48-49 55-56 61-64, IOW Snr Challenge Cup 1898-99, IOW Gold Cup(7) 26-27 46-47 48-49 55-56 61-64, IOW Challenge Cup 27 28 80 81, P'mouth Snr Cup 1899-00 00-01 05-06 19-20 53-54 66-67 89-90, IOW Charity Cup(7) 18-22 44-47, Ryde & Dist Cup 89-90, Westwood Cup 84 85, IOW Lg 20-21 (Div 2 80-81), Memorial Cup 93-94.

Ryde Sports FC

SWANAGE TOWN & HERSTON

President: Mayor of Swanage **Chairman:** Leonard Marsh
Secretary: Mrs H Ibbs, 8 Steppes, Langton Matravers, Swanage, Dorset BH19 3EY (0929 423570).
Manager: Mr A McManus **Coach:** Mr B Benjafield
Physio: Mr P Stockley **Press Officer:** Mr C Smith (0929 426362).
Ground: Days Park, off De Moulham Road, Swanage, Dorset (0929 424633).
Directions: A351 to Swanage, turn left onto sea front, 2nd left into Seaward Rd, 1st right into De Moulham Rd, through north beach car park into ground. Bus no. 21 from Poole stops in Seaward Rd 200yds from ground.
Seats: 150 **Cover:** 150 **Capacity:** 2,000 **Floodlights:** Yes **Founded:** 1898.
Midweek Matches: Tuesday **Previous Lge:** Dorset Comb./ Western 84-91.
Colours: White/black/black. **Change colours:** Blue/yellow/blue. **Club Shop:** No.
Programme: Yes **Editor:** Mr D Ibbs (0929 423570) **Previous Grounds:** None.
Nickname: Swans **Prev. Name:** Swanage (merged with Herston late 60s)
Reserves' League: Dorset Combination.
Clubhouse: Open match days & special functions organised by local organisations. Hot snacks + usual pub cold snacks available.
Club record scorer: Alan Fooks **Club record appearances:** Alan Fooks.
Hons: Western Lg Div 1 88-89, Wessex Lg R-up 90-91, Dorset Snr Cup 89-90, Mark Frowde Cup 89-90.

THATCHAM TOWN

Chairman: Mr A E Hyde **President:** Dave Quaintance
Secretary: Mr P W Woodacre, 19 Hartmead Rd, Thatcham, Berks RG13 4LS (0635 868203).
Manager: Des McMahon **Press Off:** Phil Liles (0635 66018) **Coach:** Dave Cox
Ground: Waterside Park, Crookham Rd, Thatcham, Berks (0635 862016/873912).
Directions: 2 mins walk from from Thatcham BR station.
Seats: 300 **Cover:** 300 **Capacity:** 3,000 **Floodlights:** Yes **Founded:** 1896
Midweek Matches: Tuesday **Best FA Vase season:** QF 88-89
Colours: Blue & white stripes/blue/blue **Change colours:** White/white/red
Programme: 28 pages, 40p **Programme Editor:** Dave Ware
Previous Grounds: Station Rd 51-52/ Lancaster Close 52-92.
Record Gate: 600 v Fulham, floodlight opening (at Lancaster Close).
Clubhouse: Open every evening & weekend lunchtimes. **Hons:** Wessex Lg Cup(2) 90-92 (R-up 93-94)

(A.F.C.) TOTTON

Chairman: Mr Richard Vowles **Vice Chairman:** Mr P Maiden **President:** Mr D Maton.
Secretary: Mrs S Benfield, 35 Fishers Rd, Totton, Southampton SO4 4HW (0703 865421).
Manager: Eddie Harper **Asst Manager/Coach:** TBA
Commercial Mgr: Mr E Ffister **Press Officer:** Mr P Chilcott (0703 860453).
Ground: Testwood Park, Testwood Place, Totton, Southampton (0703 868981).
Directions: 5 mins walk from Totton station. Turn off r'bout in Totton centre into Library Rd, then 1st left & 2nd rd.
Seats: 200 **Cover:** 250 **Capacity:** 2,500 **Floodlights:** Yes **Founded:** 1886
Record Gate: 600 v Windsor & Eton, F.A. Cup 4th Qualifying Rd 82-83.
Sponsors: Burger Rack **Midweek Matches:** Wednesday
Cols: Blue & white halves/blue/blue **Change colours:** Red/white/red **Nickname:** Stags.
Club Shop: No **Programme:** 30 pages with admission
Previous Name: Totton FC (until merger with Totton Athletic in 1979).
Previous League: Hants 1886-1986 **Previous Grounds:** Downs Park/ Mayfield Park.
Clubhouse: Open for matches and training sessions. Burgers, sandwiches, tea, coffee, biscuits etc available.
Captain 93-94: **Top Scorer 93-94:**
P.o.Y. 93-94:
Hons: Hants Lg(2)

WIMBORNE TOWN

Chairman: Mr B Maidment **Vice Chairman:** Mr P Goulding **President:** Sir Michael Hanham, Bart
Secretary: Mr K Holloway, 1 Laburnum Close, Ferndown, Dorset BH22 9TX (0202 892795).
Manager: Billy Elliott **Asst Manager:** TBA
Physio: S Edwards **Press Officer:** S Churchill.
Ground: Cuthbury, Cowgrove Road, Wimborne, Dorset BH21 4EL (0202 884821).
Directions: Wimborne to Blandford Road, behind Victoria Hospital.
Seats: None **Cover:** 400 **Capacity:** 3,250 **Floodlights:** Yes **Founded:** 1878
Midweek Matches: Tuesday **Club Sponsors:** Ryan Homes. **Nickname:** Magpies
Record Gate: 3,250 v Bamber Bridge, FA Vase Semi Final 2nd Leg, 28/3/92.
Cols: Black & white stripes/black/black **Change colours:** Green & white/white/gree & white.
Programme: 36 pages, 50p **Programme Editor:** Secretary
Club Shop: Yes, selling programmes, hats, scarves, t-shirts, replica kit, pens, metal badges.
Best FA Vase season: Winners **Best FA Cup season:** 1st Rd Proper 82-83.
Previous Leagues: Dorset/ Western 81-86.
Record win (in Wessex Lg): 8-0 v Eastleigh 91-92 & v Romsey Town 92-93.
Record defeat (in Wessex Lg): 2-6 v Thatcham Town 91-92.
Record transfer fee paid: £5,500 for J P Lovell (Bashley, 1992).
Record fee received: £6,000; for J P Lovell (Bashley, 1989) & for Tommy Killick (Dorchester, 1993).
Clubhouse: Evenings 7-11pm, Sat noon-11pm, Sun noon-3 & 7-10.30pm. Bar. Skittle alley.
Captain 93-94: **Top Scorer 93-94:** Jason Lovell 27.
P.o.Y. 93-94: **Club Record Scorer:** G Manson 50, 1980-81.
Honours: FA Vase 91-92, Wessex Lg 91-92 93-94 (R-up 92-93, Lg Cup 93-94 (R-up 90-91)), Hants Snr Cup SF 89-90, Dorset Lg Div 1(2) 80-81 81-82 (R-up 38-39 72-73, Div 2 31-32 34-35 36-37 (R-up 35-36), Lg Cup R-up(4) 72-74 80-82), Dorset Snr Cup(4) 80-82 85-86 91-92, Mark Frowde Cup 92-93, Dorset Snr Amateur Cup 36-37 63-64, Dorset Jnr Cup 31-32 36-37 (R-up 13-14 34-35), Dorset Minor Cup 12-13, Dorset Jnr Amateur Cup(4) 34-36 38-39.

Below: *Tommy Killick fires a powerful right-foot shot past Waterlooville skipper Duncan Burns during Wimborne's narrow FA Cup Third Qualifying Round defeat at the hands of the BHL Premier Division side. A couple of months later Killick was to transfer to Dorset's other Magpies - Dorchester Town - for a club record transfer fee.*
Photo - Paul Dennis.

GREAT MILLS LEAGUE

WESTERN LEAGUE

FEEDER TO:
BEAZER HOMES LEAGUE

President: S G Priddle
Chairman: S G Priddle

Vice-Chairman: R J Webber

Treasuer: Mrs Joan Ellis

Hon. Secretary: M E Washer, 16 Heathfield Rd, Nalisea, Bristol BS19 1EB (0275 851314)

This time last year I was stating that it would be difficult to surpass the events of our successful Centenary Year. Little did one realise that this season would come very close to doing just that. Pride of place must inevitably go to Taunton Town for their valiant effort to win the FA Vase Final at Wembley. For those of us present that day, and particularly for those who had watched Tiverton the year before, this was a particularly hard pill to swallow, for all the inconsistencies, fortunes and drama that this great game provides, were all wrapped up in one match. Let us hope that we do not emulate Dundee United in their record for the quest to win the Scottish Cup..

On the League front, congratulations were due to Tiverton Town who were very worthy Champions and proved that good quality football always prevails in the end. To their League success they added the Les Phillips and Devon St Lukes Cups for a significant treble. If runners-up Taunton Town wanted some solace, it came from their Reserves who won both the Combination League and Cup.

At the bottom we saw that relegation for Minehead and Exmouth Town, both strong sides in the past, and for both now is the time to retrench the basis to ensure a future that will be sound. No one club is exempt from the vagaries of football and fortune.

In the First Division, promotion came to both Barnstaple Town and Bridport. Indeed Barnstable had a hard but successful year; they were only two rounds away from the First Round proper of the FA Cup, losing at Weymouth in a very close game.

At the bottom of the League we sadly lost Ottery St Mary to the Devon County League and Radstock Town to the Somerset League. The latter considered themselves unfortunate in that, like Melksham Town the year before, others passed them in a final dash from behind. This perhaps proves how tight a division it is nowadays with the Pyramid leagues below waiting for chances to take over. This year the League is welcoming Bridgwater Town to its ranks after a few years away from us, and also the Wiltshire League has provided us with Melksham Town and Amesbury Town, who must hope that they emulate the strong impact made by Pewsey Vale in their first season with us, and providing the top goal-scorer in the League for good measure.

Last but not least, we must pay tribute to sponsors Great Mills, not only for their continued support in this the thirteenth year, but also for affirming that by increasing the total amount for distribution to Clubs. In the tight economical world of today, this is a tremendous gesture which is much appreciated by everyone in the League. Once again there is motivation for everyone for next season - dare we hope that next season is just as exciting as this one just gone?

Finally, congratulations to our chairman Stan Priddle, who at the recent AGM was granted the Presidency of our League. This does not mean we are losing him from the job of chairman, but it does ensure that we shall retain the advice and experience of someone who never misses seeing every club in a season, and thus ensures that regular contact and opinions are always in mind. That is what gave us the strong foundation for our League, and will maintain that base in the future.

Maurice Washer, Secretary

Tiverton Town - Premier Division Champions and Les Phillips Cup winners 1993-94.

PREM. DIV.	P	W	D	L	F	A	PTS
Tiverton Town	34	31	3	0	125	22	96
Taunton Town	34	26	2	7	98	38	80
Mangotsfield Utd	34	19	6	9	75	40	63
Paulton Rovers	34	18	7	9	55	42	61
Saltash United	34	18	6	10	67	36	60
Torrington	34	16	10	8	66	46	58
Liskeard Athletic	34	16	5	13	66	46	53
Chippenham Town	34	14	7	13	58	51	49
Bideford	34	13	8	13	60	69	*44
Odd Down Ath.	34	10	12	12	59	58	42
Crediton United	34	10	8	16	42	65	38
Westbury United	34	9	9	16	40	61	36
Bristol Mnr Farm	34	11	3	20	51	71	36
Calne Town	34	8	9	17	50	76	33
Frome Town	34	9	6	19	33	61	33
Elmore	34	8	8	18	51	83	32
Exmouth Town	34	6	4	24	35	93	22
Minehead	34	6	3	25	38	105	**15

* - 3 points deducted

DIV. ONE	P	W	D	L	F	A	PTS
Barnstaple Town	38	26	8	2	107	39	89
Bridport	38	24	7	7	90	46	79
Brislington	38	23	8	7	73	35	77
Pewsey Vale	38	20	11	7	84	47	71
Keynsham Town	38	21	7	10	80	50	70
Clyst Rovers	38	16	15	7	68	50	63
Backwell United	38	18	8	12	64	45	62
Welton Rovers	38	16	10	12	73	53	58
Devizes Town	38	16	10	12	64	61	58
Chard Town	38	16	9	13	48	51	57
Ilfracombe Town	38	16	8	14	70	42	56
Bishop Sutton	38	12	14	12	58	48	50
Glastonbury	38	14	8	16	68	66	50
Larkhall Athletic	38	12	7	19	52	69	43
Warminster Town	38	8	11	19	47	57	35
Wellington	38	9	6	23	51	92	33
Dawlish Town	38	9	5	24	46	125	32
Heavitree United	38	8	7	23	47	90	31
Radstock Town	38	8	6	24	44	73	30
Ottery St Mary	38	2	5	31	37	132	11

COMBINATION	P	W	D	L	F	A	PTS
Taunton T. Res.	26	21	2	3	104	22	65
Tiverton T. Res.	26	21	0	5	100	28	63
Elmore Res.	26	15	6	5	83	27	51
Crediton Utd Res.	26	15	6	5	75	33	51
Heavitree Utd Res.	26	13	3	10	73	60	42
Exmouth Town Res.	26	13	3	10	47	61	42
Wellington Res.	26	10	4	12	58	49	34
Barnstaple T. Res.	26	10	4	12	57	57	34
Torrington Res.	26	9	7	10	37	53	34
Chard Town Res.	26	9	5	12	31	43	32
Ottery St M. Res.	26	8	3	15	50	83	27
Clyst Rovers Res.	26	5	6	15	29	65	21
Minehead Res.	26	5	2	19	32	108	17
Dawlish T. Res.	26	2	1	23	29	116	7

LES PHILLIPS CUP 1993-94

First Round
Exmouth Town 2, Chard Town 1
Torrington 2, Elmore 0
Chippenham Town 0, Brislington 1
Larkhall Ath. 0, Mangotsfield United 5
Bristol Manor Farm 1, Devizes Town 2
Backwell United 3, Keynsham Town 1

Second Round
Exmouth Town 0, Taunton Town 5
Saltash United 2, Torrington 5
Wellington 0, Barnstaple Town 2
Dawlish Town 2, Minehead 1
Clyst Rovers 2, Crediton United 5
Heavitree United 2, Bideford 1
Ottery St Mary 1, Tiverton Town 10
Liskeard Athletic 3, Ilfracombe Town 0
Paulton Rovers 2, Bridport 0
Warminster Town 4, Calne Town 2
Pewsey Vale 9, Devizes Town 0
Radstock Town 2, Odd Down 5
Bishop Sutton 2, Frome Town 0
Glastonbury 3, Welton Rovers 0
Backwell United 1, Westbury United 0
Brislington 5, Mangotsfield United 4

Third Round
Liskeard Athletic 2, Odd Down 1
Barnstaple Town 2, Warminster Town 1
Backwell United 2, Tiverton Town 6
Crediton United 0, Bishop Sutton 3
Taunton Town 5, Torrington 1
Heavitree United 0, Paulton Rovers 2
Glastonbury 2, Dawlish Town 0
Pewsey Vale 0, Brislington 2

Quarter-Finals
Bishop Sutton 0, Tiverton Town 2
Brislington 3, Paulton Rovers 1
Glastonbury 1, Taunton Town 3
Barnstaple Town 1, Liskeard Athletic 3

Semi-Finals
Brislington 0, Tiverton Town 3
Liskeard Athletic 0, Taunton Town 1

Final *(at Dawlish Town, Sat May 14th)*:
Tiverton Town 4 *(Everett, Smith 2, Scott)*
Taunton Town 1 *(Durham)*

Combination Cup Final *(at Crediton, Wed 11th May)*:
Taunton T. Reserves 5, Barnstaple Town Reserves 1

Taunton Town FC, who suffered the bitter disappointment of finishing as runners-up in the League, League Cup and FA Vase. Back Row (L/R): Tom Harris (Chairman), Alan Walsh, Andy Perrett, Nigel Jarvis, Kevin Thaws, Kevin Maloy, Dean Radford, Nicky Hendy, Keith Graddon, Tony Rutland (Vice-Chairman), Terry Rowles (Manager). Front: David Jenkins (Asst Manager), Damon Palfrey, Andy Payne, Paul West, Jamie Ward, Dave Ewens (Captain), John Durham, Wayne Morris, Peter Hatch (Physio). Mascot: Ryan Perrett.

GREAT MILLS WESTERN LEAGUE PREMIER DIVISION RESULT CHART 1993-94

HOME TEAM	1	2	3	4	5	6	7	8	9	10	11	12	13	14	15	16	17	18
1. Bideford	*	1-4	5-0	1-2	3-2	2-0	1-1	2-2	3-2	2-5	1-4	2-1	1-1	0-0	3-0	0-4	2-0	4-3
2. Bristol Manor Farm	3-0	*	1-3	0-2	3-0	2-3	5-1	2-0	2-5	1-3	1-4	0-4	1-2	1-4	2-5	0-2	0-3	1-1
3. Calne Town	3-1	2-0	*	5-3	2-1	1-2	2-1	1-4	2-3	1-2	0-0	1-2	0-2	0-3	1-4	2-4	0-1	0-0
4. Chippenham Town	0-1	3-0	2-3	*	0-0	7-2	0-2	2-0	1-0	2-0	6-2	2-2	1-1	0-3	2-2	1-3	2-2	3-0
5. Crediton United	3-1	2-4	3-3	3-0	*	0-5	1-1	3-2	0-2	1-0	1-1	1-3	0-2	2-1	4-0	0-3	0-1	2-1
6. Elmore	3-3	0-2	2-2	1-3	1-1	*	1-3	1-2	1-5	2-2	3-2	1-1	1-4	0-3	1-6	0-6	1-2	4-0
7. Exmouth Town	2-2	0-3	3-2	0-4	1-3	1-2	*	2-0	1-2	0-1	2-0	1-3	0-1	0-4	0-2	0-5	0-3	1-1
8. Frome Town	3-1	1-1	1-4	1-2	0-1	1-0	2-1	*	0-3	3-2	2-1	0-1	0-0	0-3	0-1	0-3	0-4	0-2
9. Liskeard Athletic	2-1	0-1	7-1	0-1	2-0	1-4	3-2	4-1	*	0-1	1-0	2-1	1-1	1-3	1-3	0-3	1-1	5-1
10. Mangotsfield United	6-0	3-0	4-1	1-0	1-1	2-0	5-0	1-1	4-1	*	6-1	2-2	2-3	4-1	0-2	1-2	3-2	0-1
11. Minehead	2-1	1-2	0-5	0-1	0-2	2-0	6-5	0-4	1-5	1-4	*	1-2	0-1	0-2	0-4	2-6	1-6	1-1
12. Odd Down Athletic	2-2	3-0	0-0	3-1	1-1	6-2	1-3	1-1	2-0	0-2	11-1	*	0-2	0-5	1-5	2-2	1-1	1-2
13. Paulton Rovers	0-1	3-2	3-0	1-1	3-1	0-2	3-0	2-0	2-1	0-3	1-3	3-2	*	1-2	2-1	0-3	2-2	1-2
14. Saltash United	1-2	2-1	1-1	4-0	2-1	2-2	3-0	1-1	2-1	0-0	6-0	1-1	0-2	*	1-2	0-1	0-1	1-0
15. Taunton Town	3-2	5-0	4-0	1-1	3-0	4-1	4-0	2-0	2-0	4-0	3-0	4-0	3-1	2-1	*	1-3	1-4	4-0
16. Tiverton Town	4-1	6-2	3-0	2-1	9-1	0-0	5-0	4-0	0-0	3-2	5-0	4-0	4-0	6-2	5-1	*	5-0	5-0
17. Torrington	1-2	2-2	2-2	3-1	3-0	2-2	6-0	3-0	0-3	1-2	2-0	1-1	2-2	2-1	1-6	1-3	*	1-0
18. Westbury United	0-4	1-2	0-0	2-1	1-1	3-1	7-1	0-1	2-2	1-1	3-1	2-0	0-3	1-3	1-4	1-2	0-0	*

DIVISION ONE RESULT CHART 1993-94

HOME TEAM	1	2	3	4	5	6	7	0	9	10	11	12	13	14	15	16	17	18	19	20
1. Backwell United	*	1-1	0-0	1-3	0-0	2-1	0-1	3 0	1-1	4 3	2-2	0-2	0-3	4-3	3-1	2-2	1-2	1-0	2-1	5-0
2. Barnstaple Town	0-2	*	3-3	6-0	2-1	4-1	4-4	3-1	7-3	2-0	3-0	2-1	2-2	3-1	5-0	2-2	5-0	1-0	2-0	3-2
3. Bishop Sutton	1-2	0-0	*	2-3	4-0	0-2	1-3	3-1	1-1	0-1	4-0	1-0	2-2	0-1	5-2	2-0	1-1	4-1	0-2	2-2
4. Bridport	1-0	2-1	0-0	*	1-2	2-0	2-0	4-0	2-0	2-0	4-0	1-0	0-0	2-1	5-0	4-0	4-0	2-0	6-2	0-0
5. Brislington	2-1	1-1	0-1	4-1	*	3-0	4-0	3-0	4-1	3-1	4-1	0-0	0-0	3-0	3-2	0-1	3-1	2-1	2-1	4-0
6. Chard Town	1-0	0-4	2-0	1-4	2-2	*	2-1	3-2	2-4	1-4	3-0	0-0	2-1	0-0	3-1	0-0	3-0	1-0	1-0	1-1
7. Clyst Rovers	0-0	3-1	1-1	1-1	0-4	2-0	*	2-2	1-0	2-0	1-0	1-1	3-4	1-1	5-0	2-2	1-1	0-0	4-2	2-2
8. Dawlish Town	0-8	1-2	2-1	1-4	2-2	1-1	0-5	*	0-4	2-4	1-1	1-5	4-3	2-0	2-0	2-1	3-1	1-3	3-1	0-8
9. Devizes Town	1-3	1-3	1-1	3-1	0-1	1-2	3-2	4-1	*	2-1	1-0	0-1	4-2	0-3	3-1	3-2	2-1	2-0	2-2	1-1
10. Glastonbury	0-4	1-1	2-0	4-4	0-0	2-1	1-1	1-2	2-0	*	1-1	1-0	1-3	1-2	7-5	3-4	1-0	1-1	6-0	1-2
11. Heavitree United	0-1	0-3	1-4	0-2	1-5	2-3	1-4	4-2	2-2	2-5	*	2-4	2-4	2-2	3-2	1-4	1-0	2-0	2-0	3-1
12. Ilfracombe Town	2-1	0-2	1-1	2-3	3-0	2-0	0-0	5-0	5-2	2-0	1-1	*	0-1	0-0	6-0	0-1	4-1	2-0	3-2	2-1
13. Keynsham Town	1-1	0-2	2-2	1-3	3-1	1-2	0-2	1-2	0-2	3-1	1-2	2-0	*	6-2	4-1	2-0	2-1	2-1	4-0	1-0
14. Larkhall Athletic	2-3	0-5	1-0	1-3	0-4	0-1	2-3	5-1	2-0	4-0	1-2	3-1	2-6	*	1-1	1-1	1-4	1-1	4-1	0-1
15. Ottery St Mary	1-0	0-4	0-3	0-7	0-1	1-1	1-4	2-0	0-2	0-5	2-2	0-3	1-3	1-2	*	2-6	0-3	0-4	1-4	2-4
16. Pewsey Vale	3-2	1-4	4-0	3-2	3-0	1-1	2-3	13-0	1-1	1-1	2-0	4-2	0-0	1-0	1-1	*	3-0	2-0	0-0	2-1
17. Radstock Town	4-0	0-3	0-0	4-0	1-2	0-3	0-0	5-1	2-2	0-1	2-1	3-2	0-1	0-1	2-2	1-2	*	0-1	1-4	0-2
18. Warminster Town	0-1	3-4	1-3	1-1	0-2	1-1	2-2	3-0	0-0	3-1	3-1	1-1	1-2	1-2	5-2	1-2	3-1	*	1-1	2-2
19. Wellington	0-2	1-4	2-4	2-2	0-1	1-0	0-1	2-2	2-3	1-3	2-1	0-7	1-5	1-0	5-2	1-5	2-1	1-1	*	3-1
20. Welton Rovers	0-2	1-3	1-1	3-2	0-0	1-0	3-0	5-1	1-1	1-1	4-1	3-1	0-1	3-0	6-0	0-2	4-1	3-1	3-1	*

Barnstaple Town - Division One champions 1993-94. Back Row (L/R): Martin Nicholls, Craig Rice, Bobby Hancock, Ian Baker, Phil Lloyd, Peter Copeland, Richard Hill. Front: Alan Chapman, Paul Parkin, David Slade, Richard Andrews (Mascot), Mark Richards, Gary Kember, Steve Murch.

Photo - Richard Brock.

END OF SEASON STATISTICS
ATTENDANCES

PREMIER DIVISION

Club	Total	Ave.	200+ gates
Bideford	2130	125	2
Bristol Manor Farm	1035	61	1
Calne Town	1467	86	
Chippenham Town	1709	100	1
Crediton United	2169	128	1
Elmore	1917	113	1
Exmouth Town	1732	102	1
Frome Town	1216	71	
Liskeard Athletic	2125	124	4
Mangotsfield Utd	3012	177	5
Minehead	1510	89	2
Odd Down	1177	69	
Paulton Rovers	2053	121	
Saltash United	2109	124	3
Taunton Town	8010	471	17
Tiverton Town	7953	468	17
Torrington	1702	100	1
Westbury Utd	1694	100	
Total (306 recorded)	**43543**	**142**	**56**

Top Scorers (League only)
Kevin Smith (Tiverton) 34
Andy Perrett (Taunton) 29
Mark Saunders (Tiverton) 29
Phil Everett (Tiverton) 28

FIRST DIVISION

Club	Total	Ave.	200+ gates
Backwell United	1480	78	1
Barnstaple Town	2854	168	1
Bishop Sutton	1736	91	2
Bridport	3734	197	8
Brislington	1506	79	
Chard Town	774	41	
Clyst Rovers	1167	61	
Dawlish Town	905	48	
Devizes Town	1072	56	
Glastonbury	1009	53	
Heavitree United	770	41	
Ilfracombe Town	1981	104	1
Keynsham Town	1185	62	
Larkhall Athletic	828	44	
Ottery St Mary	718	38	
Pewsey Vale	2400	126	3
Radstock Town	1195	63	
Warminster Town	2667	140	1
Wellington	1398	74	
Welton Rovers	172	91	1
Total (380 recorded)	**31102**	**82**	**18**

Top Scorers
B Flippance (Pewsey Vale) 49
D Bryant (Ilfracombe Town) 25
S Day (Keynsham Town) 25
D Walkey (Bridport) 25
D Roberts (Clyst Rovers) 25

Highest Attendances
2854 - Taunton Town v Tiverton Town *(7/3/94)*
1947 - Tiverton Town v Taunton Town *(13/4/94)*
925 - Elmore v Tiverton Town *(27/12/93)*
904 - Tiverton Town v Westbury United *(16/4/94)*
720 - Tiverton Town v Elmore *(1/4/94)*
546 - Tiverton Town v Liskeard Athletic *(28/4/94)*
475 - Crediton United v Tiverton Town *(22/4/94)*
460 - Saltash United v Liskeard Athletic *(27/12/93)*
438 - Tiverton Town v Mangotsfield Utd *(12/2/94)*
415 - Taunton Town v Elmore *(14/3/94)*

No. of players registered: 1,909 (92-93: 2,061 91-92: 2,054 90-91: 2,0407).
Transfers Actioned: 201 (92-93: 241 91-92: 232 90-91: 194 89-90: 241 88-89: 206).

Ilfracombe Town defender Richard Pitt just manages to avoid a lunging tackle watched by team-mate Richard Pickard during the Division One fixture at Bishop Sutton on Sunday 6th February. This match, played in the kind of atrocious weather conditions that typified the 1993-94 Great Mills League season, had to be abandoned at 0-0 after 63 minutes when Ilfracombe captain Steve West suffered a broken leg.

Photo - Dave West.

GREAT MILLS WESTERN LEAGUE PREMIER DIVISION TEN YEAR RECORD

	84/5	85/6	86/7	87/8	88/9	89/0	90/1	91/2	92/3	93/4
Barnstaple Town	13	17	11	12	9	18	20	–	–	–
Bideford	2	3	6	10	16	16	12	4	14	9
Bristol City Reserves	3	9	3	7	–	–	–	–	–	–
Bristol Manor Farm	6	11	5	8	6	12	14	16	13	13
Calne Town	–	–	–	–	–	–	–	–	–	14
Chard Town	11	21	22	–	15	15	16	18	19	–
Chippenham Town	7	5	9	20	12	13	17	14	16	8
Clandown	14	14	20	22	–	–	–	–	–	–
Clevedon Town	17	10	12	13	11	10	11	2	1	–
Crediton United	–	–	–	–	–	–	–	–	–	11
Dawlish Town	16	8	14	15	19	14	9	13	20	–
Devizes Town	22	–	–	–	–	–	–	–	–	–
Elmore	–	–	–	–	–	–	–	9	12	16
Exmouth Town	4	1	2	6	2	5	19	17	11	17
Frome Town	18	13	19	18	17	20	13	19	15	15
Liskeard Athletic	10	2	4	1	4	2	8	12	18	7
Mangotsfield Utd	8	6	10	3	18	3	1	8	5	3
Melksham Town	9	16	18	21	–	–	–	–	–	–
Minehead	12	12	21	19	21	–	–	11	17	18
Odd Down Athletic	–	–	–	–	–	–	–	–	–	10
Ottery St Mary	–	–	–	–	–	–	18	21	–	–
Paulton Rovers	5	19	16	14	8	11	10	10	8	4
Plymouth Argyle Reserves	15	20	7	4	5	7	3	6	10	–
Radstock Town	–	–	17	16	14	19	21	–	–	–
Saltash United	1	4	1	2	1	8	6	5	3	5
Shepton Mallet Town	21	22	–	–	–	–	–	–	–	–
Swanage Town & Herston	–	–	–	11	10	9	–	–	–	–
Taunton Town	20	7	8	9	3	1	7	7	4	2
Tiverton Town	–	–	–	–	–	4	4	3	2	1
Torquay United Reserves	–	–	–	–	–	–	–	–	9	–
Torrington	–	15	15	17	20	17	2	15	6	6
Welton Rovers	–	–	–	–	13	21	15	20	–	–
Westbury United	–	–	–	–	–	–	–	–	7	12
Weston-super-Mare	19	18	13	5	7	6	5	1	–	–
No. of Clubs	**22**	**22**	**22**	**22**	**21**	**21**	**21**	**21**	**20**	**18**

GREAT MILLS WESTERN LEAGUE DIVISION ONE TEN YEAR RECORD

	84/5	85/6	86/7	87/8	88/9	89/0	90/1	91/2	92/3	93/4
Backwell United	7	6	9	10	9	2	16	12	8	7
Barnstaple Town	–	–	–	–	–	–	–	17	9	1
Bath City Reserves	13	11	3	4	15	18	12	4	–	–
Bishop Sutton	–	–	–	–	–	–	–	13	13	12
Bridport	–	–	–	–	3	4	6	9	10	2
Brislington	–	–	–	–	–	–	–	8	4	3
Calne Town	–	–	19	13	4	12	3	7	2	–
Chard Town	–	–	–	2	–	–	–	–	–	10
Clandown	–	–	–	–	14	13	14	18	–	–
Clyst Rovers	–	–	–	–	–	–	–	–	6	6
Crediton United	–	–	–	–	–	–	10	3	3	–
Dawlish Town	–	–	–	–	–	–	–	–	–	17
Devizes Town	–	14	6	6	5	10	8	20	12	9
Elmore	14	15	14	18	20	14	2	–	–	–
Glastonbury	12	18	22	19	19	19	21	14	16	13
Heavitree United	11	10	21	16	11	11	20	22	11	18
Ilfracombe Town	21	19	20	15	8	3	9	10	18	11
Keynsham Town	8	16	13	7	10	8	13	6	7	5
Larkhall Athletic	10	5	7	5	1	6	19	15	17	14
Melksham Town	–	–	–	–	12	9	15	21	21	–
Minehead	–	–	–	–	–	20	1	–	–	–
Odd Down Athletic	22	21	12	14	6	5	4	11	1	–
Ottery St Mary	9	7	11	9	13	1	–	–	19	20
Pewsey Vale	–	–	–	–	–	–	–	–	–	4
Portway-Bristol	1	1	2	–	–	–	–	–	–	–
Radstock Town	6	2	–	–	–	–	–	16	20	19
Swanage Town & Herston	4	8	1	–	–	–	–	–	–	–
Tiverton Town	17	13	16	3	2	–	–	–	–	–
Torquay Utd Reserves	–	–	–	–	–	–	7	2	–	–
Torrington	2	–	–	–	–	–	–	–	–	–
Warminster Town	19	22	10	11	18	15	18	5	5	15
Wellington	5	12	18	12	7	17	11	19	15	16
Welton Rovers	16	17	8	1	–	–	–	–	14	8
Westbury United	20	20	15	8	16	7	5	1	–	–
Weymouth Reserves	18	9	17	–	–	–	–	–	–	–
Wimborne Town	3	4	5	–	–	–	–	–	–	–
Yeovil Town Reserves	15	3	4	17	17	16	17	–	–	–
No. of Clubs	**22**	**22**	**22**	**19**	**20**	**20**	**21**	**22**	**21**	**20**

PREMIER DIVISION CLUBS 1994-95

BARNSTAPLE TOWN

President: Wilf Harris **Chairman:** Vic Hamilton-Philip **Vice Chairman:** Peter Woodhams.
Secretary: Gordon Lavercombe, 1 Haldene Terrace, Yeo Vale, Barnstaple, Devon EX32 7AQ (0271 79481).
Manager: Bryan Hill **Asst Manager:** Paul Hillier **Physio:** Dr Amir Arslenagic
Coach: Paul Hillier **Commercial Manager:** Roy Smith.
Ground: Mill Road, Barnstaple, North Devon (0271 743469).
Directions: A361 towards Ilfracombe (from M5 Jct 26), in Barnstaple follow A361 Ilfracombe signs, second left after crossing small bridge is Mill Road.
Seats: 250 **Cover:** 1,000 **Capacity:** 5,000 **Floodlights:** Yes **Year Formed:** 1906
Colours: Red & white **Change colours:** All yellow **Nickname:** Barum.
Sponsors: N T Shapland & Petter **Prev. Lges:** Nth Devon, Devon & Exeter, S. Western
Prev. Grounds: Town Wharf (Pre 1920's); Highfield Rd, Newport (until 1935), Pilton Pk, Rock Pk.
Previous Name: Barnstaple Ship Yard **Rec. Gate:** 6,200 v Bournemouth, FA Cup 1st Rd, 1954
Programme: 40 pages, 50p **Programme Editor:** David Priscott (0271 328316).
Midweek Matches: Tuesday **Local Press:** N. Devon Journal Herald **Club Shop:** No.
Reserve Team's League: Great Mills Combination.
Record win: 12-1 v Tavistock (H), FA Cup Third Qualifying Round 1954.
Record defeat: 1-10 v Mangotsfield United (A), Western League Premier Division 90-91.
Record transfer fee paid: £4,000 for Joe Scott (Hungerford Town, 1980).
Record transfer fee received: £6,000 for Ian Doyle (Bristol City).
Clubhouse: Full license. Bar snacks. **Club record appearances:** Trevor Burnell
Past players progressing to Football League: Len Pickard (Bristol Rovers 1951), John Neale (Exeter 1972), Barrie Vassallo (Torquay 1977), Ian Doyle (Bristol City 1978), Ryan Souter (Swindon 1994), Jason Cadie (Reading 1994).
Captain 93-94: Mark Richards **Top Scorer & P.o.Y. 93-94:** Martin Nicholls 34.
Hon: Western Lg 52-53 79-80 (R-up 80-81 81-82, Div 1 49-50 93-94, Merit Cup 74-75 83-84 84-85, Combination 92-93), FA Cup 1st Rd replay 51-52, Devon Professional Cup 62-63 64-65 67-68 69-70 71-72 72-73 74-75 76-77 77-78 78-79 79-80 80-81, Devon Lg, Devon St Lukes Cup 87-88, Devon Snr Cup 92-93, Devon Youth Cup 48-49 51-52.

BIDEFORD

President: C C Prust **Chairman:** J McElwee
Secretary: Mr Ron Ackland, Korna House, Shebbear, North Devon EX21 5RU (0409 281451).
Manager: Peter Buckingham **Coach:** G Waldron.
Ground: The Sports Ground, Kingsley Road, Bideford (0237 274974).
Directions: A361 for Bideford - ground on right as you enter the town.
Seats: 120 **Cover:** 1,000 **Capacity:** 6,000 **Floodlights:** Yes **Founded:** 1946
Colours: All red **Change colours:** All blue. **Nickname:** Robins
Previous Name: Bideford Town **Prev. Lges:** Devon & Exeter 47-49/ Western 49-72/ Southern 72-75
Prev. Ground: Hansen Ground (1 season) **Record Gate:** 6,000 v Gloucester C., FA Cup 4th Qual. Rd 1960
Programme: 32 pages, 50p **Programme Editor:** A U Kelly.
Midweek Matchday: Wednesday. **Club record appearances:** Derek May 528.
Record win: 16-0 v Soundwell 50-51 **Record defeat:** 0-10 v Bristol City 51-52.
Players progressing to Football League: Shaun Taylor (Swindon Town).
Clubhouse: 'Robins Nest' - on ground. Open lunchtimes and evenings, snacks and bar menu available. Manager: Mrs Sue Tyrell.
Record scorer: Peter Drule 190 **Record appearances:** Derek May 527.
Players' P.o.Y. 93-94: Gary Bedler **Captain, Top Sorer & P.o.Y. 93-94:** Kevin Nancekivell.
Hons: Western Lg 63-64 70-71 71-72 81-82 82-83 (Div 1 51-52, Div 3 49-50, Lg Cup 71-72 84-85, Alan Young Cup 64-65 69-70, Merit Cup 68-69, Subsidiary Cup 71-72), Devon Snr Cup 79-80, Devon St Lukes Cup 81-82 83-84 85-86 (R-up 86-87 91-92 93-94), FA Cup 1st Rd 64-65(replay) 73-74 77-78 81-82.

Bideford FC - Devon St Lukes College Cup runners-up 1993-94.

BRIDPORT

President: B Williams **Chairman:** D Fowler
Secretary: Keith Morgan, 95 Orchard Crescent, Bridport DT6 5HA (0308 25113).
Manager/Coach: Geoff Joy **Asst Manager/Physio:** Alan Newey.
Ground: The Beehive, St Mary's Field, Bridport, Dorset (0308 23834).
Directions: Take West Bay road from town centre, turn right immediately before Palmers Brewery.
Seats: 200 **Cover:** 400 **Capacity:** 2,000 **Floodlights:** Yes **Founded:** 1887
Cols: Red & black/black/red & black **Change:** Blue & white/white/blue & white **Nickname:** Bees
Midweek Matches: Wednesday **Reserve Team's League:** Dorset Combination.
Programme: 32 pages, 30p **Programme Editor:** John Hallett (0308 868795).
Club Shop: Yes, selling programmes, jerseys, ties etc. Contact John Hallett (above).
Club Sponsors: TBA **Previous Grounds:** Pymore (pre 1930s); Crown Field (pre 1953)
Previous Leagues: Perry Street/ Western 61-84/ Dorset Combination 84-88.
Record transfer fee received: £2,000 for Tommy Henderson. **Record fee paid:** £1,000 for Steve Crabb.
Record Attendance: 1,150 v Exeter City, 1981; 3,000 v Chelsea, at Crown, 1950
Clubhouse: Yes, open matchdays and for functions. Hot and cold snacks available.
Captain 93-94: Derek Walker **Club record scorer (in a season):** Eric Hoole 36.
Top Scorer 93-94: Derek Walker 29 **Player of the Year 93-94:** Derek Walker.
Hons: Western Lg Cup 70-71 72-73 77-78 (R-up 76-77, Div 1 R-up 93-94, Merit Cup 69-70 71-72 73-74); FA Vase 5th Rd 88-89; Dorset Comb.(3) 85-88 (Lg Cup 86-87 87-88); Dorset Snr Cup(8) 63-64 69-71 75-76 78-81 87-88; Dorset Snr Amtr Cup(6) 48-50 54-55 56-57 70-72; W. Dorset Chal. Bowl 07-08; Perry Str. Lg 22-23; Mark Frowde Cup 76-77 88-89

BRISTOL MANOR FARM

President: Fred Wardle **Chairman:** Laurie West **Vice Chairman:** Brian Bartlett.
Press Officer/Secretary: John Coles, 33 Jubilee Cres., Mangotsfield, Bristol BS17 3BB (0272 563075).
Manager: Chris Rex **Asst Mgr:** Barry Fry/Terry Hooper **Physio:** Alan Williams.
Coach: Darren Rowe **Commercial Manager:** Steve Price (0272 826952).
Ground: 'The Creek', Portway, Sea Mills, Bristol BS9 2HS (0272 683571).
Directions: M5 jct 18 (Avonmouth Bridge), follow A4 for Bristol - U-turn on dual carriageway by Bristol & West sports ground and return for half mile on A4 - ground entrance is down narrow lane on left (hidden entrance). Near to Sea Mills station (BR Temple Meads-Severn Beach line).
Seats: 84 **Cover:** 350 **Capacity:** 2,000 **Floodlights:** Yes **Year Formed:** 1964
Colours: Red/black/black **Change colours:** White/red/red **Nickname:** The Farm
Prev. Name: Manor Farm O.B. 1964-68 **Prev. Lges:** Bristol Suburban 64-69/ Somerset Snr 69-77.
Previous Grounds: None **Record Attendance:** 500 v Portway, Western Lg 1974.
Programme: 28 pages, 40p **Editor:** Steve Price (0272 826952) **Club Shop:** No.
Club Sponsors: Wardle Fencing. **Reserve team's League:** Somerset Senior.
Players progressing to Football League: Ian Hedges (Newport) 88-89, Gary Smart (Bristol Rovers).
Clubhouse: Lounge bar, entertainments, skittle alley, bar meals. Open every night and lunchtime Sat & Sun.
Record win: 8-2, away to Frome, 2/9/84 **Record defeat:** 1-8, away to Exmouth, 5/5/86.
Record transfer fee paid: Nil **Received:** £3,000 for Nicky Dent (Yeovil Town, 1989).
Club record scorer: Chris Rex, 222 **Club record appearances:** Paul Williams, 812.
Captain 93-94: Peter Hall **P.o.Y. 93-94:** Dean Smart **Top Scorer 93-94:** Nicky Scarrett.
Hons: Western Lg Div 1 82-83, Glos Tphy 87-88, Glos Amtr Cup 89-90, Somerset Snr Lg Div 1 (Lg Cup, Div 2).

CALNE TOWN

President: Fred Rutty **Chairman:** David Heath **Vice Chairman:** N/A
Press Officer/Secretary: Laurie Drake, 22 Falcon Rd, Calne, Wilts SN11 8PL (0249 814471).
Manager: Mike Leeson **Coach:** Terry Connor.
Ground: Bremhill View, Lickhill Rd., North End, Calne (0249 816716).
Directions: Entering town from Bristol, keep left all the way taking slip road to North End, off main Swindon Road.
Seats: 78 **Cover:** 250 **Capacity:** 2,500 **Floodlights:** Yes **Founded:** 1887.
Colours: White/black/white **Change colours:** Yellow/blue/yellow **Nickname:** Lilywhites
Midweek Matches: Wednesday **Sponsors:** Nightfreight **Club Shop:** No.
Programme: 16 pages, 50p **Programme Editor:** Mr Laurie Drake (0249 814471).
Previous League: Wilts Co. (pre-1986) **Record Gate:** 1,100 v Swindon, Friendly 25/7/1987.
Prev. Names: Calne Town (est. 1886)/ Harris Utd - clubs merged/ Calne & Harris Utd - 1920-67.
Reserves' League: Wilts Co. Lge **Prev. Ground:** Anchor Road Rec. 1887-1967.
Record win: 10-0 v Heavitree (H) **Record defeat:** 1-5 v Minehead (A).
Clubhouse: Mon-Fri 7-11pm, Sat-Sun 12-11pm. Filled rolls, hot food, tea, coffee, sweets etc.
Club record scorer: Robbie Lardner **Club record appearances:** Gary Swallow, 259.
Captain 93-94: Andy Davies **Top Scorer 93-94:** Jamie Rowe **P.o.Y. 93-94:** Mark Brown.
Hons: Western Lg Div 1 R-up 92-93, Wilts Snr Cup 12-13 34-35 84-85 (R-up 1893-94 94-95 1911-12 49-50), Wilts Lg 33-34 ('Ghia' Cup 80-81 85-86, Div 2 79-80, Div 3 85-86, Div 4 81-82).

CHIPPENHAM TOWN

President: G W Terrell **Chairman:** D S Webb **Vice-Chairman:** R G Terrell.
Secretary: Mr A L Wimble, 31 Southmead, Chippenham, Wilts SN14 0RT (0249 655361).
Manager: Jeff Evans **Assistant Manager:** Mike Ford.
Coach: Andy Black **Physio:** Paul Christopher/ John Palmer.
Press Officer: Roy Brookes **Commercial Manager:** Richard Terrell
Ground: Hardenhuish Park, Bristol Road, Chippenham (0249 650400).
Directions: M4 jct 17, A429 into Chippenham, follow signs for Trowbridge/Bath until r'bout, left onto A420 into town, ground 400yds on left. 5 mins walk from railway station on main A420 Bristol Road.
Seats: 100 **Cover:** 300 **Capacity:** 4,000 **Floodlights:** Yes **Year Formed:** 1873
Midweek matches: Wednesday **Sponsors:** Supreme Video/ Shoestrings Food Services.
Club colours: All blue **Change colours:** Yellow/black. **Nickname:** None.
Previous Grounds: Westmead, Lowden, Little George Lane, Malmesbury Rd
Previous Lges: Hellenic, Wilts Snr, Wilts Prem. **Record Gate:** 4,800 v Chippenham Utd, Western Lg, 1951.
Programme: 32 pages, 50p **Programme Editor:** Sandie Webb (0249 653142)
Clubhouse: Oppen matchdays. Food sold **Club Shop:** Sells programmes. Contact Roger Lewis (0249 650400).
Record scorer: Dave Ferris **Record appearances:** Ian Monnery.
Captain, Player of the Year and Top Scorer 93-94: Richard Lardner.
Hons: FA Cup 1st Rd 51-52, Western Lg 51-52 (Div 1 80-81, Div 2 52-53(Res) 80-81), Wilts Shield/Snr Cup/Snr Lge.

CREDITON UNITED

Chairman: D J Blanchflower **Vice Chairman:** C R Gillard **President:** W J Ash.
Secretary: Brian Maunder, 39 Geneva Close, Exeter, Devon EX2 4NH (0392 411592).
Manager: Trevor Atkins **Assistant Manager:** Brian Maunder **Coach:** Tony Kellow.
Treasurer: D Job **Commercial Manager:** Tony Kellow (0392 214659).
Ground: Lord's Meadow Sports Centre, Crediton (0363 774671-club, 777930-commercial dept.).
Directions: A337 to Crediton from Exeter, right onto A3072 (signposted Tiverton) at White Hart Hotel, turn right into Commercial Rd for Lord's Meadow Ind. Est.- Sports Centre car park 250 metres on left.
Seats: 150 **Cover:** 150 **Capacity:** 2,000 **Floodlights:** Yes **Founded:**
Club colours: Blue/black/black **Change colours:** Amber/white/blue. **Club Shop:** No.
Midweek Matches: Wednesday **Previous Lge:** Devon & Exeter (pre-1990)
Sponsors: Graphic.
Hons: Devon & Exeter Lg 87-88 (R-up 88-89, Harry Wood Trophy 88-89, Snr Div 1 62-63 66-67, Jnr Div 3 48-49(jt) 49-50, Snr Div 2b(res) 70-71, Snr Div 3(res) 86-87, Jnr Div 3(res) 56-57, I'mediate Div 3('A') 91-92, I'mediate Div 4 R-up('B') 92-93, I'mediate Div 5 R-up('B') 91-92), East Devon Snr Cup 33-34, Okehampton Challenge Cup 72-73 74-75, Whitbread Flowers Cup 78-79, Bill Rees Trophy 86-87, Geary Cup(res) 84-85 86-87, Liddon Cup('A') 84-85 86-87.

ELMORE

Chairman: A J Cockram **Vice Chairman:** A Davey **President:** None.
Secretary: L F Tapp, Patrona, Calverleigh, Tiverton, Devon EX16 8BE.
Manager: Ken Freeman **Asst Manager:** S Downs **Coach:** Eamonn Collins.
Physio: R Ruffles. **Commercial Manager:** K Sharland (0884 242842).
Ground: Horsdon Park, Tiverton, Devon EX16 4DE (0884 252341).
Directions: M5 Jct 27, A373 towards Tiverton, leave at 1st sign for Tiverton & Business Park, ground 500yds on right.
Seats: 200 **Cover:** 300 **Capacity:** 3,000 **Floodlights:** Yes **Founded:** 1947
Midweek matches: Tuesday **Club Sponsors:** Ken White Signs.
Colours: Green & white **Change colours:** Red/black/black **Nickname:** Eagles.
Previous Leagues: Devon & Exeter 47-74/ South Western 74-78.
Previous Grounds: None **Record Gate:** 1,271 v Tiverton, Western Lg 27/12/92.
Programme: 12 pages, 30p **Editor:** Mrs Freeman (0884 242842)
Club Shop: Yes, selling clothing, kit, programmes, memorabilia. Contact Mr K Sharland (0884 242842).
Record win: 17-0 **Record defeat:** 2-7
Clubhouse: 11am-11pm Mon-Sat, 12-3 & 7-10.30pm Sat. Full canteen service - hot & cold meals & snacks.
Captain 93-94: A Skinner **Top Scorer 93-94 & Club record scorer:** Mark Seatherton.
P.o.Y. 93-94: A Skinner. **Club record appearances:** P Webber.
Hons: East Devon Snr Cup 72-73 75-76, Western Lg Cup 90-91 (Div 1 R-up 90-91, Prem Div Merit Cup R-up 91-92, Div 1 Merit Cup 86-87 89-90 90-91), Devon St Lukes Cup R-up 90-91, Devon Snr Cup 87-88, Devon Intermediate Cup 60-61, Football Express Cup 60-61, Devon & Exeter Lg Div 2A 73-74 86-87(res)(Div 1A 76-77(res)), Devon Yth Cup 77-78.

FROME TOWN

President: Mr C W Norton **Chairman:** Mr G Norris **Vice Chairman:** Mr A Castle
Secretary: Mrs S J Merrill, 56 Nightingale Ave., Frome, Somerset BA11 2VW (0373 473820).
Manager: Phil Morris **Asst Manager:** T Bull **Press Officer:** Steve Jupp.
Ground: Badgers hill, Berkeley Road, Frome (0373 453643).
Directions: Locate "Vine Tree Inn", Bath Road; ground 100 yds from Inn (1 mile from town centre and Frome BR station).
Seats: 250 **Cover:** 800 **Capacity:** 5,000 **Floodlights:** Yes **Founded:** 1904
Colours: All red **Change colours:** White/black/black **Nickname:** Robins.
Previous Grounds: None **Previous League:** Wilts Premier **Club Shop:** No.
Programme: 30 pages, 50p **Programme Editor:** Secretary
Sponsors: Woodman Furniture **Record Gate:** Unknown.
Midweek home matchday: Wednesday **Reserve team's League:** Somerset Senior.
Clubhouse: Evenings & weekends. Cold food only.
Captain 93-94: **Top Scorer 93-94:**
P.o.Y. 93-94:
Hons: Western Lg 78-79 (Div 2 19-20, Div 2 R-up 54-55, Lg Cup 79-80 82-83, Merit Cup 82-83, Alan Young Cup 79-80, Subsidiary Cup 59-60), FA Cup 1st Rd 54-55, Somerset Premier Cup 66-67 68-69 82-83, Wilts Premier Lg 62-63, Western Co's F'lit Cup 83-84, Somerset Snr Cup 32-33 33-34 50-51, Somerset Snr Lg 06-07 08-09 10-11 (Div 1(res) 90-91, Div 3(res) 85-86, Lg Cup(res) 91-92).

LISKEARD ATHLETIC

President: **Chairman:** David Hick **Vice Chairman:** Dave Rawlings
Secretary: Adrian Wilton, Martina, Dawes Close, Dobwalls, Liskeard, Cornwall PL14 6JD (0579 20980).
Manager: Jimmy Hargreaves **Asst Manager/Coach:** Alan Gillett.
Commercial Manager: Alan Mayne (0579 343593).
Ground: Lux Park, Liskeard, Cornwall (0579 42665).
Directions: Take Tavistock Road (A390) from town centre, after 1/2 mile turn left on St Cleer Road (following signs to Lux Park Sports Complex) and the ground is 200 yards on left. Half mile from Liskeard BR station.
Seats: 100 **Cover:** 300 **Capacity:** 2,000 **Floodlights:** Yes **Year Formed:** 1889
Club colours: All blue **Change colours:** All green **Nickname:** Blues.
Previous Leagues: East Cornwall Premier, Plymouth & District, South Western 66-79.
Midweek matchday: Tuesday **Players progressing to Football Lge:** Bradley Swiggs.
Programme: 10 pages, 30p **Editor:** Commercial Manager. **Club Shop:** No.
Record win: 8-1 **Record defeat:** 1-6 **Record transfer fee received:** £1,000.
Sponsors: Jollys soft drinks/ Robin Wotton Electrical/ Gilbert Outfitters.
Clubhouse details: (0579 342665) Normal licensing hours. Hot & cold food available.
Captain 93-94: **Top Scorer & P.o.Y. 93-94:**
Club record scorer: Not known **Club record appearances:** Brian Bunney, 500+.
Hons: South Western Lg 76-77 78-79 (R-up 75-76 77-78; Lg Cup 76-77 78-79) Western Lg 87-88 (R-up 85-86 89-90, Merit Cup 80-81); Cornwall Snr Cup 04-05 83-84 84-85 85-86 88-89 89-90 (R-up 70-71 75-76 76-77 78-79); Cornwall Charity Cup 21-22 79-80, Cornwall Jnr Cup 05-06 13-14 26-27; SW Pratten Cup 78-79; E Cornwall Prem RAOB Cup 67-68, Plymouth & Dist. Lg 60-61 (Div 1 59-60 (R-up 54-55 73-74), Div 2 76-77(Res)), Victory Cup 60-61, Charity Cup 59-60), E Cornwall Prem. Lg (Reserves) 84-85 92-93 (Lg Cup 88-89).

MANGOTSFIELD UNITED

President: Mr A J Hill **Chairman:** Mr R Davis **Vice Chairman:** Mr P Selway
Secretary: Mr R Gray, 105 Chiltern Close, Warmley, Bristol BS15 5UW (0272 616523).
Mgr: Graham Bird/David Payne **Physio:** J Cummings **Press Officer:** Secretary
Ground: Cossham Street, Mangotsfield, Bristol BS17 3EW (0272 560119).
Directions: M4 jct 19, M32 jct 1; A4174 marked Downend, through lights, over double mini-r'bout to Mangotsfield, left by village church onto B4465 signposted Pucklechurch, ground quarter mile on right. From central Bristol take A432 thru Fishponds, Staple Hill, to Mangotsfield and turn right by village church onto B4465. From Bath/Keynsham follow A4175, right at island at Willsbridge onto A431, then rejoin A4175 at next island (Cherry Garden Hill) to Bridge Yate, straight over double mini-r'bout and take 1st left, right into Carsons Rd after 1 mile and follow to Mangotsfield village & turn right by church onto B4465.
Seats: 300 **Cover:** 800 **Capacity:** 2,500 **Floodlights:** Yes **Founded:** 1950
Colours: Maroon & sky **Change colours:** All white **Nickname:** The Field
Players to progress to Football League: G.Megson, S.White, G.Penrice, P.Purnell, N.Tanner, M.Hooper.
Previous Leagues: Bristol & District 50-67/ Avon Premier Combination 67-72.
Record Gate: 2,386 v Bath City, FA Cup 77-78
Programme: 32 pages, 50p. **Programme Editor:** Bob Smale (0272 401926).
Club Shop: Yes. Contact Ron Loftus (0272 756510), David Smale (0272 662246) or Bob Smale.
Clubhouse: Open 11am-11pm. Snacks - hot food on matchdays. Lounge bar for official functions etc.
Sponsors: Aaron Roofing Supplies
Midweek home matchday: Tuesday **Reserve team's League:** Somerset Senior.
Top Scorer4: Martyn Grimshaw **Captain & Player of the Year 93-94:** Denis McCoy.
Hons: Western Lg 90-91 (Lg Cup 73-74 (R-up 86-87) Div 1 R-up 82-83); Somerset Prem. Cup 87-88 (R-up 88-89); Glos Snr Cup 68-69 75-76; Glos FA Trophy 84-85 86-87 90-91 93-94; Hungerford Invitation Cup 74-75; Rothmans National Cup R up 77 78, Hanham Invitation Charity Cup 84-85 85-86, Somerset Snr Lg(Reserves) Div 2 75-76 (Div 3 74-75), Somerset Comb. Cup 74-75, Glos Yth Shield 81-82 84-85 (R-up 82-83), Somerset Floodlit Yth Lg 81-82 82-83 83-84 84-85 87-88, Somerset Yth Shield 76-77.

ODD DOWN ATHLETIC

President: P A L Hill **Chairman:** Dave Loxton **Vice Chairman:** Mike Wilkins
Secretary: Mike Mancini, 36 Caledonian Rd., East Twerton, Bath BA3 2RD (0225 423293).
Manager: Paul Gover.
Ground: Combe Hay Lane, Odd Down, Bath (0225 832491).
Directions: On main Bath/Exeter road - leaving Bath turn left into Combe Hay Lane opposite Lamplighters Pub. 40 mins walk from Bath (BR).
Seats: 160 **Cover:** 250 **Capacity:** 1,000 **Floodlights:** Yes. **Founded:** 1901
Colours: White/black/black **Change colours:** Green/white/green
Programme: 12 pages with admission **Programme Editor:** Secretary **Club Shop:** No.
Sponsors: Streamline Coaches **Prev. Lges:** Wilts Premier, Bath & District, Somerset Senior
Midweek Matches: Tuesday **Reserve Team's League:** Somerset Senior
Record win: 11-1 v Minehead (H), Western League Premier Division 19/3/94.
Clubhouse: Yes, open noon-3 & 7-11pm. Hot & cold food available.
Record Scorer: Joe Matano 89 **Record appearances:** L Burns and T Ridewood, both 291.
Captain 93-94: Terry Mancini **Player of the Year 93-94:** Simon Charity.
Top Scorer 93-94: M Godwin 16 **Hons:** Western Lg Div 1 92-93, Somerset Snr Cup 91-92.

PAULTON ROVERS

President: Mr T Pow **Chairman:** Mr D Bissex **Vice Chairman:** Mr D Carter
Secretary: Mr J E Pool, 111 Charlton Park, Midsomer Norton, Avon BA3 4BP (0761 415190).
Manager: Dave King **Physio:** John Pool.
Commercial Manager: K Simmons. **Press Officer:** D Bissex (0761 412463)
Ground: Athletic Ground, Winterfield Road, Paulton (0761 412907).
Directions: Leave A39 at Farrington Gurney (approx 15 miles south of Bristol), follow A362 marked Radstock for two miles, left at junction B3355 to Paulton, ground on right. Bus services from Bristol and Bath.
Seats: 138 **Cover:** 200 **Capacity:** 5,000 **Floodlights:** Yes **Founded:** 1881
Colours: White/maroon/maroon **Change colours:** All yellow **Nickname:** Rovers.
Midweek matches: Tuesday **Previous Leagues:** Wilts Premier/ Somerset Snr.
Previous Grounds: Chapel Field/ Cricket Ground/ Recreation Ground 1946-48.
Record Gate: 2,000 v Crewe, FA Cup, 1906-07
Programme: 20 pages, 30p **Programme Editor:** D Bissex (0761 412463).
Club Shop: Old programmes available - contact Chairman.
Clubhouse: 3 bars, lounge, skittle alley, dance hall. Capacity 300. Catering facilities.
Club Sponsors: Plaza Truro/ Design Windows/ Berkley Coaches.
Reserves' League: Somerset Snr. **Club record appearances/P.o.Y. 93-94:** Mike Deeks.
Club record scorer: D Clark.
Captain 93-94: Greg Taylor **Top Scorer 93-94:** D Clarke.
Hons: Western Lg Div 2 R-up 1900-01, Somerset Snr Cup 00-01 02-03 03-04 07-08 08-09 09-10 34-35 67-68 68-69 71-72 72-73 74-75, Somerset Snr Lg 00-01 03-04 04-05 70-71 71-72 72-73 73-74
Local Newspapers: Bath Evening Chronicle, Bristol Evening Post, Western Daily Post.

SALTASH UNITED

President: P Skinnard **Chairman:** M Howard **Manager:** Chris Harrison
Secretary: C D Phillips, 85 Lakeview Close, Tamerton Foliot, Plymouth PL5 4LT (0752 705845).
Ground: Kimberley Stadium, Callington Road, Saltash, Cornwall (0752 845746).
Directions: First left after crossing Tamar Bridge, through town centre, at top of town fork right at mimi r'bout, ground 400 yds ahead on left.
Seats: 250 **Cover:** 250 **Capacity:** 3,000 **Floodlights:** Yes **Year Formed:** 1947
Club colours: All red **Change:** Black & white stripes/black/black **Nickname:** The Ashes
Previous Leagues: Cornwall Snr/ South Western 51-59 62-76/ East Cornwall Premier 59-62.
Programme: 20 pages, 30p **Programme Editor:** TBA
Midweek Matches: Wednesday **Local Newspapers:** Western Evening Herald, The Cornish Times.
Clubhouse: Club attached to stand and caters for dancing and club activities.
Hons: Cornwall Snr Lg 49-50 50-51, Western Lg 84-85 86-87 88-89 (R-up 83-84 87-88, Lg Cup 86-87 87-88 (R-up 88-89), Div 1 76-77, Merit Cup 79-80 87-88), Sth Western Lg 53-54 75-76 (R-up 52-53 73-74 74-75, Lg Cup 51-52 69-70 73-74), Cornwall Snr Cup 50-51 74-75 81-82 87-88 90-91.

TAUNTON TOWN

Chairman: T F Harris **Vice Chairman:** A J Rutland. **Treasuer:** Joan Ellis
Secretary: The Secretary, C/O the club (see below).
Manager: Terry Rowles **Asst Manager:** David Jenkins. **Physio:** Peter Hatch
Ground: Wordsworth Drive, Taunton, Somerset TA1 2HG (0823 278191).
Directions: Leave M5 Jct 25, follow signs to town centre, at 2nd set of lights turn left into Wordsworth Drive; ground on left. 25 mins walk from Taunton (BR); turn left out of station and follow road right through town centre bearing left into East Reach. Follow road down and turn right into Wordsworth Drive shortly after Victoria pub.
Seats: 250 **Cover:** 1,000 **Capacity:** 4,000 **Floodlights:** Yes **Year Formed:** 1947
Midweek matches: Monday **Club Sponsors:** Taunton Cider Co. **Nickname:** Peacocks
Club colours: Sky blue & claret/claret/sky blue
Change colours: Yellow/blue/yellow. **Record Gate:** 2,960 v Torquay, Western Lg, 1958
Record win: 12-0 v Dawlish Town (A), FA Cup Preliminary Rd, 28/8/93.
Record defeat: 0-8 v Cheltenham Town (A), FA Cup 2nd Qualifying Rd, 28/9/91.
Previous Grounds: Several prior to 1953. **Reserve Team's League:** Great Mills Combination.
Newsline: 0891 122 901 **Previous Lges:** Western 54-77/ Southern 77-83.
Programme: 28 pages, 50p **Programme Editor:** Tom Harris.
Club Shop: Yes, selling club souvenirs; hats, scarves etc.
Best FA Cup season: 1st Rd Proper 81-82 (lost 1-2 at Swindon Town).
Best FA Trophy season: 1st Rd Proper 80-81 (lost 1-5 v Hendon at Queens Park Rangers).
Best FA Vase season: Finalists 93-94.
Clubhouse: Social club to accommodate 300, full bar facilities, separate bar & hall for private functions.
Players progressing to Football League: Charlie Rutter (Cardiff), Stuart Brace (Southend & Grimsby).
Record appearances: Tony Payne **Record scorer** (in a season): Reg Oram 67.
Captain 93-94: Dave Ewens **P.o.Y. & Top Scorer 93-94:** Andy Perrett, 62 goals
Hons: FA Vase R-up 93-94, Western Lg 68-69 89-90 (R-up 93-94, Les Phillips Cup R-up 93-94, Alan Young Cup 73-74 75-76(jt with Falmouth), Charity Challenge Cup 49-50 50-51), Somerset Snr Lg 52-53, Somerset Prem. Cup R-up 82-83 89-90 92-93.

TIVERTON TOWN

President: Dan McCauley **Chairman:** Gordon Anderson **Vice-Chairman:** Dave Wright
Secretary: Ramsay Findlay, 35 Park Road, Tiverton, Devon EX16 6AY (0884 256341).
Manager: Martyn Rogers **Asst Manager:** John Owen
Physio: Alan Morgan **Press Officer:** Sid Chorley.
Ground: Ladysmead, Bolham Road, Tiverton, Devon EX16 8SG (0884 252397).
Directions: M5 Jct 27, west towards Tiverton on A373, continue to end of dual carriageway and turn left at r'about; ground entrance 300yds on right alongside BP petrol station.
Seats: 300 **Cover:** 700 **Capacity:** 3,000 **Floodlights:** Yes **Year Formed:** 1920
Colours: Amber/amber/black **Change:** All white (black facings) **Nickname:** Tivvy.
Programme: 24 pages, 50p **Programme Editor:** James Wade (0823 278878)
Club Shop: Programmes, metal badges, scarves, hats etc available. Contact James Wade (0823 278878).
Previous League: Devon & Exeter **Previous ground:** The Elms, Blundell Road 1920-39
Clubhouse: Lunctimes, evenings. All day Sat during the season. 3 bars. Food (burgers, hot dogs, chips etc).
Players progressing to Football League: Jason Smith (Coventry City, 1993).
Midweek matches: Wednesday **Record Gate:** 2,602 v Canvey Island, FA Vase SF 20/3/93.
Captain 93-94: Hedley Steele **Top Scorer:** Kevin Smith.
P.o.Y. 93-94: Phil Everett.
Hons: FA Vase R-up 92-93 (QF 93-94), FA Cup 1st Rnd 90-91 (lost 2-6 at Aldershot) 91-92 (lost 0-5 at Barnet); Western Lg 93-94 (R-up 92-93, Les Phillips Cup 92-93 93-94, Amateur Trophy 77-78 78-79, Div 1 R-up 88-89), Devon St Lukes Cup 90-91 91-92 92-93 93-94 (R-up 89-90), Devon & Exeter Lg 51-52 66-67 70-71 84-85; Devon Snr Cup 55-56 65-66; East Devon Snr Cup 35-36 37-38 52-53 55-56 60-61 62-63 66-67; North Devon Charity Cup 72-73 86-87

TORRINGTON

President: Frank Morris **Chairman:** TBA
Sec./Press Officer: Robert T Dymond, Flat 4, 26 South Street, Torrington, Devon EX38 8AB (0805 23569).
Manager: John Hore **Asst Manager:** Nigel Menhenick **Physio:** Owen Cooke.
Ground: Vicarage Field, School Lane, Great Torrington (0805 22853).
Directions: (From North, Barnstaple, Exeter, South Molton) In town centre turn left by parish church, turn right at swimming pool, ground behind swimming pool. Good parking. Red Bus from Bideford and Barnstaple (nearest BR station). Bus stop 300yds from ground.
Seats: None **Cover:** 2,000 **Capacity:** 4,000 **Floodlights:** Yes **Year Formed:** 1908
Midweek Matches: Wednesday **Club Sponsors:** Bideford Tool **Club Shop:** No.
Cols: Green & white hoops/white/white **Change colours:** Blue & white stripes/navy/blue.
Programme: 32 pages, 30p **Programme Editor:** Secretary & Rachel Hutchings.
Previous Grounds: None **Nickname:** Torrie or Supergreens **Record win:** 18-0.
Previous Leagues: North Devon/ Devon & Exeter/ South Western 77-84.
Clubhouse: Weekdays 7-11pm, Sat 11am-11pm, Sun 12-3 & 7-10.30pm. Two bars. Light snacks available. New kitchen and offices being built to open 1993-94.
Local Newspapers: North Devon Journal, Bideford Gazette
Record transfer fee paid: Nil **Received:** £3,000 for Dave Walter (Yeovil Town).
Captain 93-94: **Top Scorer 93-94:**
P.o.Y. 93-94:
Club record scorer: Trevor Watkins, 254 **Club record appearances:** Nigel Reed, 450+.
Hons: Western Lg R-up 90-91 (Lg Cup R-up 91-92, Div 1 R-up 84-85, Merit Cup 91-92), South Western Lg R-up 80-81 82-83 (Lg Cup 80-81), Devon Cup, Devon & Exeter Lg & Cup double, various local cup wins inc. Torridge Cup 92-93.

WESTBURY UNITED

Chairman: Philip Alford **Vice Chairman:** Bert Back **President:** George Nicholls.
Secretary: Ernie Barber, 7 Farleigh Close, Westbury, Wilts. BA13 3TF (0373 822117).
Manager/Coach: Steve Gay **Asst Manager:** N/A. **Physio:** Lee Webb
Press Officer: Paul Lusty **Commercial Manager:** Tom Lawrence.
Ground: Meadow Lane, Westbury (0373 823409).
Directions: In town centre, A350, follow signs for BR station, Meadow Lane on right (club signposted). Ten mins walk from railway station (on main London-South West + South Coast-Bristol lines).
Seats: 150 **Cover:** 150 **Capacity:** 3,500 **Floodlights:** Yes **Year Formed:** 1921
Colours: Green/white/green **Change colours:** Red/black/red.
Midweek Matches: Tuesday **Prev. Leagues:** Wilts Comb./ Wilts Co. (pre-1984)
Nickname: White Horsemen **Previous Ground:** Redland Lane (pre-1935).
Programme: 16 pages, 30p **Programme Editor:** Eli Manasseh (0373 826754).
Club Shop: Yes. Shirts, scarves, hats, badges and various programmes.
Sponsors: Wheelers Electrical **Reserve Team's league:** Trowbridge League.
Record Gate: 4,000 v Llanelli, FA Cup 1st Rd 1937 (match was on Littlewoods coupon!).
Players progressing to Football League: John Atyeo (Bristol City and England).
Clubhouse: Evenings 7-11pm, Fri, Sat & Sun lunctimes 12-3pm.
Top Scorer 93-94: Steve Davis **Captain & P.o.Y. 93-94:** Graham Underhill.
Honours: Western Lg Div 1 91-92, Wilts Senior Cup 31-32 32-33 47-48 51-52, Wilts Combination, Wilts Lg 34-35 37-38 38-39 49-50 50-51 55-56, Wilts Premier Shield R-up 92-93.

Paulton Rovers pictured before their excellent FA Vase win at Croydon Athletic. *Photo - Gavin Ellis-Neville.*

Saltash United FC. Back Row (L/R): Mark Gammon, Eddie Shapland, Steve Kidd, Dave Walter, Trace Norton, Paul Wilmot, Darren Willis. Front: Lee Cansfield, Steve Pugh, Tony Ginter, Andy Wright, Paul Sidley, Paul Edwards. *Photo - Richard Brock.*

DIVISION ONE CLUBS 1993-94

AMESBURY TOWN

President: Mr S Dunford **Chairman:** Mr P Taylor
Secretary: Mrs N Chalmers, 43 Coltsfoot Close, Amesbury SP4 7NP (0980 624101).
Manager: D Graham **Asst Manager:** N Stewart **Press Officer:** A Holman
Ground: Amesbury Recreation Ground, Amesbury, Wiltshire (0980 623489).
Directions: Amesbury is nine miles north of Salisbury from where there is an excellent bus service. Turn left at Lloyds bank, cross bridge, left at road corner into recreation ground.
Colours: Blue/white **Change colours:** All red **Floodlights:** Yes
Previous Name: Amesbury FC **Prev. Lgs:** Salisbury & D., Wilts (pre-'94) **Programme:** Yes.
Midweek home matches: Tuesday **Sponsors:** Amesbury Motorcare/Dunford Removals.
Top Scorer 93-94: D Coker **Player of the Year:** M Byrne. **Clubhouse:** No.
Captain 93-94: P Thorne. **Hons:** Wilts Senr Cup 93-94, Wilts Lg R-up 93-94.

BACKWELL UNITED

President: Bill Roberts **Chairman:** Chris Strong **Vice-Chairman:** Jeff Summers.
Secretary: Bill Coggins, 34 Westfield Road, Backwell, Bristol BS19 3ND (0275 463424).
Manager: Adrian Britton **Asst Manager:** Mike Kelly **Physio:** Ian Pinkney
Coach: Andy Eisentrager **Press Officer:** Peter Higgins.
Commercial Manager: Dick Cole (0275 463627).
Ground: Recreation Ground, Backwell, Avon (0275 462612).
Directions: Near centre of Backwell on main A370 Bristol to Weston-super-Mare road. Buses from Bristol or Weston, or 20 mins walk from Nailsea & Backwell (BR) station; turn right out of station, right at traffic lights (half mile), ground quarter mile on right just past car sales.
Seats: None **Cover:** 150 **Capacity:** 1,000 **Floodlights:** Yes **Founded:** 1911.
Club colours: All red **Change colours:** All sky **Nickname:** Reds.
Programme: 20 pages, 25p. **Editor:** Dick Cole (0275 463627) **Club Shop:** No.
Midweek Matches: Tuesday **Club Sponsors:** C W Jones Carpets.
Previous Grounds: Two in Backwell prior to 1939. Club reformed in 1946.
Previous Lges: Clevedon & Dist/ Bristol Church of England/ Bristol Surburban (pre 1970)/ Somerset Snr 70-83
Record attendance: 400 v Robinsons, Somerset Lg, Easter Monday 1982
Record win: 8-0 v Dawlish Town (A), Western League Division One 4/12.93.
Record defeat: 2-6 v Tiverton Town (H), Les Phillips Cup QF 1/2/94.
Clubhouse: Open 6-11pm weekdays, 12.30-11pm Sat. Filled rolls, crisps, nuts chocolate available.
Record scorer: Steve Spalding **Record appearances:** Wayne Buxton.
Top Scorer 93-94: Steve Spalding **Player of the Year 93-94:** Craig Owen.
Honours: Somerset Snr Lg 77-78 79-80 80-81 81-82 82-83 (Lg Cup 82-83 (R-up 79-80) Div 1 72-73); Somerset Snr Cup 81-82; SW Co.'s Sutton Transformer Cup 81-82

BISHOP SUTTON

Chairman: Bob Redding **Vice Chairman:** Roy Penney **President:** Bob Redding.
Secretary: Mr Roy Penney, 33 Ridgway Lane, Whitchurch, Bristol BS14 9PN (0275 541392).
Manager: TBA **Physio:** T Tucker.
Comm. Mgr: G Williams. **Press Officer:** Alex Thomas.
Ground: Lake View, Wick Road, Bishop Sutton (0275 333097).
Directions: On A368 at rear of Butchers Arms pub – Ground signposted on left entering village from the West.
Seats: None **Cover:** 200 **Capacity:** 1,500 **Floodlights:** No **Founded:** 1977.
Cols: All blue **Change colours:** All red. **Sponsors:** Harlequin Motor Centre.
Midweek Matches: Tuesday **Previous Ground:** Adjacent cricket field **Nickname:** Bishops.
Prev. Leagues: Weston & Dist. Yth/ Bristol & Avon/ Somerset Snr (pre 1991) **Club Shop:** No.
Programme: 10 pages, £1 with entry **Reserve team's League:** Somerset Senior.
Record win: 15-0 v Glastonbury Res. **Record Gate:** 400 v Bristol City, friendly.
Players progressing to Football Lge: David Lee (Chelsea), S Williams (Southampton), J French (Bristol Rovers), I Harvey (Swindon Town).
Clubhouse: Open matchdays. Rolls, pies and usual pub food available.
Captain 93-94: Lee Scadding **Top Scorer 93-94:** Darren Pool **P.O.Y. 93-94:** A Hawkins.
Hons: Somerset Snr Lg R-up 89-90 (Div 1 83-84 (R-up 81-82), Div 2 82-83), Bristol & Avon Lg 80-81 (Div 2 79-80), Somerset Jnr Cup 80-81, Weston Yth Lg 77-78, Chew Valley KO Cup 83-84, Mid-Somerset Lg(Res) R-up 82-83 (Div 3 81-82).

BRISLINGTON

President: C Elston **Chairman:** Paul Bishop **Vice-Chairman:** P K Brake
Secretary: F G Durbin, 52 Arlington Road, St Annes, Bristol BS4 4AJ (0272 777169).
Manager: Jamie Patch **Asst Manager:** Mike Richarson **Physio:** Art Rowland/Dave Gould
Ground: Ironmould Lane, Brislington, Bristol (0272 778531).
Directions: Four miles out of Bristol on main A4 to Bath – turn left up lane opposite Garden Centre
Seats: None **Cover:** 100 **Floodlights:** No **Club Shop:** No **Nickname:** Bris.
Colours: Red/black/red **Change colours:** Blue & white
Previous ground: Victory Park **Previous League:** Somerset Senior (pre-1991).
Reserve's League: Somerset Senior **Best FA Vase year:** 3rd Rd 89-90 (lost 2-3 at Abingdon T.)
Midweek matches: Wednesday **Club Sponsors:** Trade Windows.
Programme: 50p **Editor:** Reg Mockeridge (0272 643294). **Clubhouse:** On ground, open matchdays.
Hons: Somerset Snr Cup 92-93 (R-up 93-94), Somerset Snr Lge, Les Phillips Cup SF 93-94.

BRIDGWATER TOWN '84

Chairman: Keith Setter. **Sec:** Miss S A Wright, 37 Kidsbury Road, Bridgwater TA6 7AQ (0278 421189)
Ground: Fairfax Park, Fairfax Road, Bridgwater (0278 446899 - matchdays only).
Directions: M5 jct 23, follow signs to Glastonbury (A39), turn right for Bridgwater (A39), turn left for Bridgwater College (Parkway), ground half mile on right; enter through college. One mile from Bridgwater (BR).
Seats: Yes **Cover:** Yes **Floodlights:** No **Clubhouse:** No **Founded:** 1984.
Colours: Red/black or white/red **Change colours:** Blue/blue or white/blue.
Reserve's League: Somerset Senior **Prev. Lge:** Somerset Snr (pre-1994) **Programme:** Yes.
Top Scorer 93-94: Matt Lazenby **Hons:** Somerset Snr Cup 93-94, Somerset Snr Lge 90-91 91-92.

CHARD TOWN

President: John Smith **Chairman:** Brian Beer **Vice Chairman:** Roy Goodland.
Secretary/Press Off.: Colin Dunford, 27 Manor Gardens, Ilchester, Yeovil, Somerset BA22 8LE (0935 841217).
Manager: Bob Russell **Coach:** Peter Smith.
Physio: Andy Williams **Commercial Manager:** Fred George.
Ground: Town Ground, Zembard Lane, Chard (04606 61402).
Directions: 150 yards from the town centre, off Combe Street. 8 miles from Crewkerne BR station.
Seats: None **Cover:** 200 **Capacity:** 1,500 **Floodlights:** Yes **Founded:** 1920
Colours: Cherry red/navy **Change colours:** Sky/maroon **Nickname:** Robins.
Previous Grounds: None **Prev. Lges:** Somerset Snr 20-24 48-75/ Perry Street 25-48.
Programme: 24 pages with entry **Programme Editor:** Secretary. **Sponsors:** RV Lock
Midweek matches: Wednesday **Reserve Team's League:** Great Mills Combination.
Captain 93-94: Dave Linney **Clubhouse:** Matchdays & most evenings. Snacks served
P.o.Y. 93-94: Wayne Behan **Top Scorer 93-94:** Andy Bell 9.
Hons: Som. Snr Lg 49-50 53-54 59-60 67-68 69-70 (Lg Cup 61-62 71-72 76-77); Western Lg Div 1 R-up 83-84 87-88 (Merit Cup 82-83, Comb. Cup(Res) 91-92 (R-up 92-93)); Som. Snr Cup 52-53 66-67; S W Co's Cup 88-89

CLYST ROVERS

President: Mr P W Brown **Chairman:** Malcolm Hale **Vice Chairman:** Colin Dadson
Secretary: John Edwards, Lamorna, Pinn Lane, Pinhoe, Exeter EX1 3RF (0392 68633).
Manager: Sammy Kingdom **Asst Manager:** Mike Follett **Physio:** Bill Wreford.
Press Officer: Sammy Kingdom **Commercial Manager:** Mr Bob Hookway (0884 259975).
Ground: Waterslade Park, Clyst Honiton, Devon (0884 259152).
Directions: A30 following signs for Exeter Airport. Coming from Exeter take 1st right after airport turning (ground signposted) up narrow 200yds past Duke of York Pub.
Seats: 130 **Cover:** 300 **Capacity:** 3,000 **Floodlights:** Yes **Founded:** 1926.
Colours: Blue & white **Change colours:** Red & black **Reformed:** 1951.
Midweek Matches: Wednesday **Previous Grounds:** Fair Oak 1926-44.
Previous Leagues: Exeter & District 26-44 51-66/ Exeter & District Sunday 67-82/ South Western 81-92.
Programme: 32 pages, 30p **Editor:** Ray Dack (0392 215075) **Nickname:** Rovers.
Club Shop: Yes - new for 1993-94. Programmes, souvenirs etc.
Sponsors: Vantage Pharmacy, Paignton **Record Gate:** 768 v Tiverton, Devon St Lukes final 11/5/93.
Record win: 6-0 v Heavitree United, 1993. **Record defeat:** 0-12 v Torpoint, Sth Western Lge, Oct 1990.
Clubhouse: Open one and a half hours before kick off and after game. Excellent food available.
Hons: Devon St Lukes Cup R-up 92-93, Western Lg Cup SF 92-93.

DAWLISH TOWN

President: Bob Webster **Chairman:** Phil Aylines **Vice-Chairman:** Peter Burridge
Secretary: Graham Jones, 133 Kingsdown Cres., Dawlish, Devon EX7 0HB (0626 866004).
Manager: Peter Gartrell **Assistant Manager:** Ian Hill.
Ground: Sandy Lane, off Exeter Road, Dawlish (0626 863110).
Directions: Approx 1 mile from centre of town, off main Exeter road (A379).
Seats: 200 **Cover:** 200 **Capacity:** 2,000 **Floodlights:** Yes **Founded:** 1889
Cols: Green & white/white/green & white **Change colours:** Blue & white/blue/blue & white.
Previous League: Devon & Exeter. **Previous Ground:** Barley Bank 1875-1900
Record defeat: 0-18 v Clevedon (A), Western League Premier Division 92-93.
Record Gate: 1,500 v Heavitree Utd, Devon Prem. Cup Q-Final
Programme: 34 pages, 30p **Programme Editor:** Roy Bolt.
Midweek home matchday: Tuesday **Clubhouse:** Open nightly, situated in car park opposite ground.
Hons: Western Lg Cup 80-81 83-84, Devon Premier Cup 69-70 72-73 80-81, Devon Snr Cup 57-58 67-68, Devon St Lukes Cup 82-83 (R-up 81-82), FA Vase Quarter Finals 86-87.

DEVIZES TOWN

Chairman: B Taylor **Manager:** A Stevens
Secretary: Chris Dodd, 69 Broadleas Park, Devizes, Wilts SN10 5JG (0380 726205).
Ground: Nursteed Road, Devizes. (0380 722817).
Directions: Off Nursteed Road (A342 signposted Andover); leaving town ground on right opposite Eastleigh Rd.
Seats: 370 **Cover:** 400 **Capacity:** 2,500 **Floodlights:** Yes **Founded:** 1883
Cols: Red & white stripes/black/black **Change colours:** Green & white/white/white
Previous Ground: London Rd (pre 1946) **Previous Name:** Southbroom (until early 1900s)
Previous Leagues: Wilts Comb./ Wilts Premier.
Hons: Wilts Snr Cup 07-08 49-50 56-57 57-58 58-59 60-61 61-62 62-63 65-66 67-68 70-71 71-72 73-74 78-79.

EXMOUTH TOWN

President: Mr Brian Bradley **Chairman:** Mr P Marshall **Vice Chairman:** Mr John Dibsdall
Secretary: Mr D J Richardson, 44 Whitchurch Ave., Exeter EX2 5NT (0392 430985).
Manager: Graham Weeks. **Assistant Manager:** N/A **Physio:** Julian Bennett
Press Officer: John Dibsdall **Commercial Manager:** Terry Chapman (0395 279085).
Ground: Southern Road, Exmouth (0395 279085 (Office)).
Directions: On right side of main Exeter to Exmouth road (A376). Half mile from Exmouth (BR) station.
Seats: 100 **Cover:** 250 **Capacity:** 2,500 **Floodlights:** Yes **Year Formed:** 1933
Colours: Royal & white **Change colours:** Yellow & white.
Nickname: 'Town' or 'Blues' **Previous Lge:** Devon & Exeter 1933-73.
Programme: 36 pages, 30p **Editor:** Terry Chapman (0395 279085)
Midweek home matchday: Tuesday **Reserves' League:** Gt Mills Comb. **Sponsors:** None.
Previous Grounds: Maer Cricket Field 33-38 48-64; Raleigh Park, Withycombe 38-39
Club Shop: Yes. Selection of non-League programmes (up to 20,000 in stock) and other club sounvenirs.
Record Gate: 2,395 v Liverpool XI, friendly in 1987.
Record win: 8-1 v Bristol Manor F., 1986 **Record defeat:** 0-10 v Tiverton (A), Devon St Lukes Cup QF 16/2/94.
Clubhouse: Open every night and weekend lunchtimes. Snacks available.
Captain 93-94: Keith Pitman **Top Scorer 93-94:** Shane Powell **P.o.Y. 93-94:** Paul Gidley
Club Record Scorer: Mel Pym, 117 **Record Appearances:** Keith Sprague, Geoff Weeks 410 (Western Lg)
Hons: FA Vase SF 84-85; Western Lg 83-84 85-86 (R-up 86-87 88-89; Lg Cup 88-89; Div 1 R-up 81-82; Sportmanship Tphy 86-87 92-93); Devon Prem Cup 70-71 79-80; Devon St Lukes Cup(3) 84-85 88-90; Devon Snr Cup 50-51; E Devon Snr Cup 50-51 82-83; Harry Wood Mem. Cup 81-82; Exmouth Chal. Cup(7) 64-67 68-69 70-72 73-74

GLASTONBURY

President: Mr L R Reed **Chairman:** Keith Harmon **Treasurer:** Mr K Snook.
Vice President: Mr R Burns **Press Off.:** Les Heal (0458 832037) **Manager:** Simon White.
Secretary: David McCartney, 3 Pound Close, Glastonbury BA6 9LG (0458 831701).
Ground: Abbey Moor Stadium, Godney Road, Glastonbury, Somerset (0458 831460).
Directions: At bottom of town centre take Northload Street, first right after crossing bridge, ground immediately on right.
Seats: Nil **Cover:** 300 **Capacity:** 1,500 **Floodlights:** Yes **Founded:** 1890.
Colours: Old gold/black/old gold **Change colours:** White/white/orange **Nickname:** None
Programme: 24 pages, 30p **Prog. Editor:** Les Heal (0458 832037).
Sponsors: Masterglaze
Midweek Matches: Wednesday **Previous Leagues:** Bristol & District, Bristol Suburban
Previous Ground: Abbey Park (Pre-1982). **Record Gate:** 3,892 v Exeter City, FA Cup 1st Rd 25/11/52
Record win: 10-0; v Paulton Rovers (H) 27/3/48; v Portland Utd (H) 13/1/51, both Western League.
Record defeat: 0-9 v Wellington (H), Western League Division One 7/1/89.
Record scorer: Jim Allaway 42 **Record appearances:** Brian Mortimer 496.
Captain 93-94: Neil Seymour **Clubhouse:** Yes, on ground. Hot snacks from tea bar on matchdays.
Top Scorer 93-94: Dominico Cinicola **Sportsman of the Year 93-94:** Richard Smith.
Hons: Western Lg 48-49 50-51 69-70 (R-up 47-48 51-52, Lg Cup 65-66 (SF 83-84), Alan Young Cup 67-68 (jt with Minehead) 70-71); Somerset Professional Cup 37-38 48-49; Somerset Snr Cup 35-36; Somerset Charity Cup 32-33; Somerset Jnr Cup 12-13 13-14; Somerset Lg 49-50 50-51

HEAVITREE UNITED

President: Mr E Drew **Chairman:** Mr B Conoway **Vice Chairman:** Mr K Carpenter
Secretary: Mr A S Kitson, 13 Tuckfield Close, Wonford, Exeter EX2 5LR (0392 72027).
Manager/Coach: Bill Ring **Asst Manager:** D Bray **Physio:** R Channing.
Ground: Wingfield Park, East Wonford Hill, Exeter, Devon (0392 73020).
Directions: Leave M5 at Exeter Granada Services, follow signs for City Centre/ Heavitree for approx. 3 miles and ground is situated on left at top of East Wonford Hill.
Seats: 150 **Cover:** 150 **Capacity:** 500 **Floodlights:** No **Founded:** 1885.
Colours: All royal (yellow trim) **Change colours:** White & black stripes **Nickname:** Heavies.
Programme: 20 pages, 20p **Editor:** Dave Jeffery (0392 73020) **Club Shop:** No.
Prev. Ground: Heavitree Park (pre-1950) **Previous Lges:** Exeter & Dist./ Devon & Exeter.
Club Sponsors: Refuge Assurance **Record Gate:** 350 v Exeter City, friendly 1989.
Midweek home matchday: Tuesday
Record win: 6-0 v Ilfracombe Town **Record defeat:** 0-13 v Larkhall Athletic.
Clubhouse: 12am-12pm daily. Wide range of matchday hot food.
Club record scorer: John Laskey **Club record appearances:** Alan Kingdom.
Hons: Exeter & Dist Lg 46-47 51-52 (Snr Div 2 56-57 59-60 60-61 67-68), Devon & Exeter Lg 70-71 76-77, Devon Snr Cup 46-47 60-61 70-71, E Devon Snr Cup 46-47 70-71 76-77, Wheaton Tphy 87-88.

ILFRACOMBE TOWN

Chairman: TBA **Vice-Chairman:** Des Lee **President:** TBA
Secretary/Press Officer: Tony Alcock, 2 Worth Road, Ilfracombe, North Devon EX34 9JA (0271 862686).
Manager: Dave Sheehan **Asst Manager:** Alan Ray.
Coach: Steve West **Physio:** Paul Jaggers.
Ground: Marlborough Road, Ilfracombe, Devon (0271 865939).
Directions: A361 to Ilfracombe, 1st right in town after lights, follow Marlborough Rd to top, ground on left.
Seats: None **Cover:** 450 **Capacity:** 2,000 **Floodlights:** Yes **Founded:** 1902
Colours: Blue & white **Change colours:** Coral & purple **Nickname:** Bluebirds
Record attendance: 3,000 v Bristol City, Ground opening, 2/10/24 **Club Shop:** No.
Previous Names: Ilfracombe FC 02-09/ Ilfracombe Utd 09-14/ Ilfracombe Comrades 14-20.
Previous Grounds: Shaftesbury Field/ Brimlands/ Killacleave (all pre-1924).
Previous Leagues: North Devon 04-14 20-22 60-84/ East Devon Premier 22-31/ Exeter & District 32-39 46-49/ Western 49-59/ South Western League (Reserves) 53-54.
Programme: 8 pages, 40p **Editor:** Peter Bidgood (0271 864756) **Sponsors:** TBA
Player progressing to Football Lge: Jason Smith (Coventry via Tiverton)
Midweek home matchday: Tuesday **Reserve team's League:** North Devon.
Record win: 10-0 v Chipping Sodbury, 51-52.
Record defeat: 0-8 v Odd Down (A), Western League Division One, 92-93.
Clubhouse: Every night 7-11pm and weekend lunchtimes. Hot & cold meals on matchdays.
Club record scorer: Paul Jenkins **Club record appearances:** Bobby Hancock 363.
Top Scorer 93-94: Kevin Bryant **Captain & P.o.Y. 93-94:** Kevin Bryant
Hons: East Devon Premier Lg 25-26 28-29 29-30, North Devon Senior Lg, North Devon Premier Lg 66-67 70-71 81-82 82-83, Western Lg Div 2 R-up 52-53.

KEYNSHAM TOWN

President: K Dowling **Chairman:** Colin Smith.
Secretary: Adrian Summers, 8 Wells Close, Whitchurch, Bristol BS14 0PD (0275 835761).
Manager: John Ellener **Physio:** A Weaver
Press Officer: D Brassington **Commercial Manager:** L Dowling.
Ground: Crown Field, Bristol Road, Keynsham (0272 865876).
Directions: A4 from Bristol to Bath, ground on left before entering village opposite Crown Inn. Bus service every 30 mins from Bristol passes ground. 10 mins walk from Keynsham BR station.
Seats: 120 **Cover:** 500 **Capacity:** 2,000 **Floodlights:** Yes **Founded:** 1895
Colours: Yellow/blue **Change colours:** White **Nickname:** K's.
Previous Grounds: The Hams 1886-1910; Gaston 1910-25; Park Road 25-30; Charlton Rd 30-39.
Record Gate: 3,000 v Chelsea, floodlight opening 88-89. Competitive: 2,160 v Saltash, Amateur Cup, Oct 1952.
Previous Leagues: Bristol District, Bristol Comb., Bristol Premier, Somerset Snr.
Programme: 32 pages, 25p **Editor:** Brian Pratt (0275 835219) **Club Shop:** No.
Sponsors: Ace Building Services (Bristol) Ltd.
Clubhouse: Evenings & before & after games. Sunday lunch. Snacks.
Midweek home matchday: Monday **Reserve team's League:** Somerset Senior.
Captain 93-94: Steve Clarke **Top Scorer:** Sean Day **P.o.Y. 93-94:** Jamie Boulton.
Hons: Somerset Lg Div 1 77-78; Somerset Snr Cup 51-52 57-58; GFA Jnr Cup 25-26, Somerset & Avon (South) Premier Cup 79-80 (SF 93-94), FA Cup 4th Qualifying Rd.

LARKHALL ATHLETIC

President: A J Rhymes **Chairman:** A J Grace **Manager:** Gerald Rich
Secretary: Mervyn Liles, 9 Eastbourne Ave., Claremont Rd., Bath BA1 6EW (0225 319427).
Ground: "Plain Ham", Charlcombe Lane, Larkhall, Bath (0225 334952).
Directions: A4 from Bath, 1 mile from city centre turn left into St Saviours Rd. In Larkhall square fork left, and right at junction, road bears into Charlcombe Lane. Ground on right as lane narrows.
Seats: None **Cover:** 50 **Capacity:** 1,000 **Floodlights:** No **Founded:** 1914
Colours: All royal blue **Change colours:** All red **Nickname:** Larks.
Previous League: Somerset Snr **Midweek Matches:** Tuesday
Hons: Som. Snr Cup 75-76, Som. Snr Lg, Western Lg Div 1 88-89 (Div 1 Merit Cup(4) 83-86 87-88(jt with Yeovil Res).

MELKSHAM TOWN

President: H J Goodenough **Chairman:** M J Harris
Secretary: Mr P R Macey, 30 Wellington Square, Bowerhill, Melksham SN12 6QX (0225 706876).
Ground: The Conigre, Melksham (0225 702843).
Directions: Just off main square at back of town car park.
Capacity: 3,000 **Seats:** Due **Cover:** 1,500 **Floodlights:** Yes **Founded:** 1876.
Colours: Old gold/black/black. **Change colours:** Green/white/green.
Previous Leagues: Wiltshire 1894-1974 93-94/ Western 74-93.
Previous Grounds: Challymead/ Old Brighton Road Field.
Record Gate: 2,821 v Trowbridge Town, FA Cup 57-58.
Clubhouse: Inside ground, open every evening & weekend lunchtimes.
Hons: Wilts Lg 03-04 93-94 (R-up 24-25 29-30 59-60 67-68 68-69 71-72), Western Lg Div 1 79-80, Wilts Snr Cup 03-04 69-70 77-78 (R-up 57-58 67-68 68-69), Wilts Shield 80-81 81-82 84-85 (R-up 86 87), FA Amateur Cup 1st Rd 68-69.

MINEHEAD

President: A C Copp **Chairman:** David Gaydon
Secretary: Thomas Smith, Marley's, Martlett Road, Minehead TA24 5QE (0643 703698).
Manager: Steve Gummer **Coach:** Peter Dunne.
Ground: The Recreation Ground, Irnham Road, Minehead, Somerset (0643 704989).
Directions: Entering town from east on A39 turn right into King Edward Road at Police station, first left into Alexandra Rd and follow signs to car park; ground entrance within. Regular buses to Minehead from Taunton, the nearest railhead.
Seats: 250 **Cover:** 700 **Capacity:** 3,500 **Floodlights:** Yes **Founded:** 1889.
Club colours: All blue **Change colours:** All yellow **Nickname:**
Programme: 24 pages, 20p **Editor:** Secretary.
Midweek Matches: Wednesday **Record Gate:** 3,600 v Exeter City, FA Cup 2nd Rd, 17/12/77.
Prev. Lges: Somerset Snr/ Southern 72-83. **Record defeat:** 1-11 v Odd Down (A), Western Lg Prem Div 19/3/94.
Hons: Southern Lg R-up 76-77 (Div 1 Sth 75-76, Merit Cup 75-76), Western Lg R-up 66-67 71-72 (Div 1 90-91, Alan Young Cup 67-68 (jt with Glastonbury), Somerset Premier Cup 60-61 73-74 76-77.

PEWSEY VALE

President: **Chairman:** M Britten **Manager:** K Franklin.
Secretary: Mrs Barbara Flippance, 17 Slater Rd, Pewsey SN9 5EE (0672 63665).
Ground: Recreation Ground, Ball Rd, Pewsey (0672 62990).
Directions: On entering Pewsey from A345, at the Market Place proceed to end of High Street and turn right into Ball Rd, entrance to ground on right opposite pub. BR to Pewsey station.
Seats: **Cover:** Yes **Capacity:** **Floodlights:** No **Year Formed:**
Colours: White/blue/white **Change colours:** Red/black/red.
Previous Lge: Wilts Co. (pre-1993). **Previous Name:** Pewsey Y.M. (until late 1940s).
Midweek home matchday: Wednesday **Hons:** Wiltshire County League 92-93.

WARMINSTER TOWN

President: Bob Peaty **Chairman:** Colin Ball **Vice-Chairman:** Bob Pitman.
Secretary: Dave Carpenter, Cley View, 46 Upper Marsh Rd, Warminster, Wilts BA12 9pn (0985 212198).
Manager: Derek Wesley **Assistant Manager:** Peter Russell.
Ground: Weymouth Street, Warminster, Wilts BA12 0985 217828).
Directions: Take A350 for Weymouth from lights at centre of town - ground on left at brow of hill.
Seats: 75 **Cover:** 150 **Capacity:** 2,000 **Floodlights:** No **Founded:** 1878
Cols: Red & black stripes/black/black **Change:** All sky **Nickname:** Red & blacks
Previous Grounds: None **Previous League:** Wiltshire
Record Gate: 1,500 for Ladies International, England v Wales, mid-1970s.
Programme: 24 pages, 30p **Editor:** Chris Finch (0985 217326) **Club Shop:** No.
Sponsors: Lyons **Clubhouse:** Opened 22/7/94. Evenings/matchdays/as required
Midweek home matchday: Wednesday **Reserve team's League:** Wilthsire.
Captain: Paul Newman **P.o.Y. 93-94:** Gary Peters **Top Scorer 93-94:** Adie McHugh
Hons: Wilts Snr Cup 1900-01 02-03 10-11 (R-up 09-10 26-27 32-33 53-54); Wilts Prem. Lg 56-57; Wilts Jnr Cup R-up 21-22 27-28 55-56 58-59; Central Wilts Lg 08-09

WELLINGTON

President: Alan Shire **Chairman:** Selwyn Aspin **Vice-Chairman:** Ken Bird.
Secretary: Tony Brown, 6 Courtland Rd, Wellington, Somerset TA21 8ND (0823 662920).
Manager: Iain Blake **Asst Manager:** Graham Aspin **Physio:** Ken Pearson.
Ground: Wellington Playing Field, North Street, Wellington, Somerset (0823 664810).
Directions: At town centre traffic lights turn into North St., then first left by Fire Station into the public car park that adjoins the ground.
Seats: None **Cover:** 200 **Capacity:** 3,000 **Floodlights:** Yes **Founded:** 1892
Cols: Coral (purple & white trim)/pple/pple **Change colours:** Blue & claret stripes/blue/blue
Midweek Matches: Tuesday **Previous Leagues:** Taunton Saturday, Somerset Senior
Reserves' Lge: Combination **Club Sponsors:** A J Shire/ Somerset Care (Wellington).
Programme Editor: Jeff Brown **Players progressing to Football Lge:** Nick Jennings (Plymouth).
Record Scorer: Ken Jones **Top Scorer 93-94:** Terry Coppin.
Captain 93-94: Ian Jackson **Player of the Year 93-94:** Darren Knowling.
Hons: Western Lg Div 1 R-up 80-81 (Merit Cup 91-92), Somerset Snr Lg Div 1 R-up, Rowbarton & Seward Cup.

WELTON ROVERS

Chairman: Roy James
Secretary: Geoff Baker, 6 Longfellow Road, Westfield, Radstock, Bath BA3 3YZ (0761 413742).
Manager: Alan O'Leary **Asst Manager:** John Goss.
Physio: John Carver **Commercial Manager/Press Officer:** John Churchill.
Ground: West Clewes, North Road, Midsomer Norton, Somerset (0761 412097).
Directions: A367 Bath to Radstock – right at lights at foot of hill onto A362, ground on right.
Seats: 300 **Cover:** 300 **Capacity:** 2,400 **Floodlights:** Yes **Year Formed:** 1887
Colours: Green & white/white/white **Change colours:** Royal blue. **Nickname:** Rovers.
Previous Grounds: None **Previous Leagues:** None **Club Shop:** No.
Record Gate: 2,000 v Bromley, FA Amateur Cup 1963
Programme: 12 pages, 25p **Programme Editor:** S Paget
Club Sponsors: J J Saunders
Midweek home matchday: Monday **Reserve team's League:** Somerset Senior.
Clubhouse: 7.30-11pm daily, Sat matchdays 1.30-2.45pm, Sun noon-2pm.
Captain 93-94: Mick Bartlett **Top Scorer 93-94:** Trevor O'Neill 22.
P.o.Y. 93-94: Mark Evans **Club record scorer:** Ian Henderson, 51
Hons: Western Lg 11-12 64-65 65-66 66-67 73-74 (Div 1 59-60 87-88; Amateur Cup 56-57 57-58 58-59 59-60; Alan Young Cup 65-66 66-67 67-68(joint)); Somerset Snr Cup 06-07 11-12 12-13 13-14 19-20 24-25 25-26 60-61 61-62 62-63, Somerset I'mediate Cup 77-78, Somerset Jnr Cup 06-07(joint) 24-25 30-31, WBC Clares City of Wells Cup 78-79.

Bruising action as Devizes (stripes) win 4-0 at troubled Dawlish on September 4th. *Photo - Martyn Hillstead*

MIDLAND FOOTBALL ALLIANCE

FEEDER TO:
BEAZER HOMES LEAGUE

President: Neville Jeynes

Vice-Presidents: Roger Goadby, Gordon Cutler

Chairman: Pat Fellows **Vice-Chairman:** Mark Lycett

Hon. Secretary: Ken H Goodfellow,
11 Emsworth Grove, Kings Heath, Birmingham B14 6HY
(021 624 3186)

Press Liaison Officer: David Jenkin (0203 662711)

EXCITING NEW DAWN

The Midland Football Alliance is in its first season, and will feed into the Beazer Homes (Southern) League. The twenty founder member clubs have been drawn equally (ten clubs each) from the Midland Combination and West Midlands (Regional) League. These two competitions will now serve as feeders to the Midland Football Alliance.

BARWELL

Chairman: David Laing **Vice Chairman:** Roger Goadby.
Secretary: Mrs C J Blackhouse, 39 Ploughmans Drive, Shepshed, Leics (0509 508917).
Manager: David Callow **Asst Manager:** Paul Shackleton
Physio: Viv Coleman. **Press Officer:** Mervyn Nash.
Ground: Kirkby Rd, Barwell, Leics (0455 843067).
Directions: M42 jct 10 (Tamworth Services), A5 towards Nuneaton, sharp left signed Market Bosworth after 11 miles (400m after Longshoot Motel), left for Barwell at 3rd island (3 miles), right onto B581 after half mile to Barwell centre (1 mile), turn left opposite Nat West bank and immediately right into Kirkby Rd - entrance to Barwell Spts & social Club 400m on right. From M69 jct 1 take B4109 towards Hinckley, right at lights after one and a half miles into Brookside, at end after 1 mile left onto Burbage Rd, left signed Leicester (A47) at 2nd lights, after Rugby Club take next left for Barwell, half mile to town centre - over mini-r'bout and Kirkby Rd is 50yds on right. BR to Hinckley station - bus station is 200yds away via Station Rd - take Leicester bus and Barwell is 1st village en route (two and a half miles)
Capacity: 2,500 **Seats:** 140 **Cover:** 750 **Floodlights:** Yes **Founded:** 1992.
Colours: Yellow/green/yellow **Change colours:** Black & white stripes/black/black.
Previous Names: Barwell Athletic F.C., Hinckley F.C. - amalgamated in 1992.
Previous Ground: Barwell Athletic: None. Hinckley: groundshare at Hinckley Athletic (pre-1992).
Previous Lges: Midland Combination 92-94. *Barwell Ath.: Leics Senior. Hinckley: Central Midlands 86-88.*
Programme: 36 pages, 50p **Editor:** Alan Mason (Curzon Publications - 0533 625354).
Club Sponsors: Cleartherm **Midweek home matchday:** Tuesday
Nickname: Canaries. **Clubhouse:** Evenings & lunchtimes. Snacks available.
Captain 93-94: **Top Scorer 93-94:** Scott Kempin
P.o.Y. 93-94:
Club record scorer: Joey Aitchison **Club record appearances:** Kevin Johnson.
Hons: Barwell Athletic: Leics Snr Lg Tebbutt Brown Cup 91-92.

BOLDMERE St MICHAELS

Manager: Alan Parsons
Secretary: D Green, 4 Blandford Ave., Castle Bromwich, Birmingham B36 9HX (021 7475 404).
Ground: Church Road, Boldmere, Sutton Coldfield (021 373 4435).
Directions: A38 & A5127 from City towards S. Coldfield, left at Yenton lights onto A452 (Chester Rd), Church Rd is 6th turning on the right. 400yds from Chester Road (BR).
Capacity: 2,500 **Seats:** 100 **Covered:** 100 **Floodlights:** Yes **Nickname:** Mikes.
Colours: White/black/black **Change Colours:** All yellow (black trim) **Founded:** 1882
Midweek matches: Tues/Thurs **Previous Leagues:** West Mids 49-63/ Midland Combination 63-94.
Programme: 28 pages, 30p **Programme Editor:** Dave Tolley (021 382 7130)
Clubhouse: Bar & lounge, every evening and four lunchtimes
Hons: Birmingham AFA 36-37, Birmingham AFA Snr Cup, Birmingham Jnr Cup, FA Amtr Cup SF 47-48, AFA Snr Cup 47-48, Central Amtr Lg 48-49, Midland Comb.(3) 85-86 88-90 (Challenge Cup 77-78 89-90, Tony Allden Memorial Cup 78-79 88-89 91-92, Challenge Trophy 86-87).
Players who progressed to Football League: John Barton (Everton, Derby County), Kevin Collins (Shrewsbury), Jack Lane (Birmingham City, Notts Co.), John Lewis (Walsall), Don Moss (Cardiff, C Palace), Harry Parkes (Aston Villa), Wally Soden (Coventry).

BOLEHALL SWIFTS

President: Mr Dennis Baker **Chairman:** Mr G Mulvey **Vice-Chairman:** Mr W Gould.
Secretary: Mr John Boyce, 99 Falcon, Wilnecote, Tamworth, Staffs B77 5DW (0827 261428).
Manager Gary Brown **Asst Manager:** R Brown **Coach/Physio:** B Davis
Commercial Mgr: Mr D James **Press Officer:** Mr L Bretherton/ Mr W Gould (0827 64530).
Ground: Rene Road, Bolehall, Tamworth (0827 62637).
Ground: A51 signs south to Bolebridge island, left under railway arches into Amington Rd, 4th left into Leedham Ave, fork right into Rene Rd, ground on right by school. From Tamworth BR station walk up Victoria Road for three quarters of a mile and catch No.3 or No.6 mini-bus to Bolehall. Alight at Leedham Avenue or Rene Road and follow as above.
Capacity: 2,000 **Seats:** 500 **Cover:** 600 **Floodlights:** Yes **Founded:** 1953
Midweek matches: Wednesday **Reserves' League:** None **Nickname:** Swifts
Colours: White/black/black **Change Colours:** All green **Club Shop:** No.
Programme: 16 pages, 50p **Editor:** Mr W Gould (0827 64530).
Previous Leagues: Sutton Lge/ Staffs County 74-80/ Midland Combination 80-94.
Previous Grounds: None **Club Sponsors:** Grahams Coaches.
Record win: 7-1 v Mile Oak Rovers & Youth, Ernie Brown Memorial Cup semi-final 30/4/93.
Record defeat: 0-8 v Solihull Borough (A), Birmingham Senior Cup Second Round replay 27/11/91.
Clubhouse: Large Social Club - 2 rooms. Open every evening (7-11) and lunchtimes. Entertainment Saturday nights. Cobs and crisps etc available.
Record Scorer: Billy Oughton **Record appearances:** Duane Mellors 196.
Captain 93-94: Conroy Gordon **Top Scorer 93-94:** Dean Albrighton **P.o.Y. 93-94:** Dave Wassell
Hons: Midland Combination Div 2 84-85 (Challenge Vase 84-85, Presidents Cup Runners-up 85-86), Fazeley Charity Cup 84-85 (Runners-up 85-86), Ernie Brown Memorial Cup Runners-up 89-90 90-91 91-92 92-93 93-94, Jack Mould Cup Runners-up 85-86.

BRIERLEY HILL TOWN

Chairman: Peter Lawrenson **Vice-Chairman:** Terry Baker.
Secretary/Press Officer: D G Dew, 148 King William Street, Amblecote, Stourbridge DY8 4EP (0384 376902).
Manager: Richard Gwinnett **Asst Manager:** Steve Scott **Coach:** Chris Conway.
Ground: The Dell Sports Stadium, Bryce Rd, Pensnett, Brierley Hill, West Mids (0384 77289).
Directions: At lights in the Brierley Hill High Street turn into Bank Street by Police Station. Proceed over bridge into Pensnett Road, ground three quarters of a mile on left Paddy's Garage. Main entrance 120yds in Bryce Road.
Seats: 300 **Cover:** 300 **Capacity:** 5,000 **Floodlights:** Yes **Founded:** 1955
Colours: Blue **Change colours:** Yellow **Club Shop:** No.
Programme: 20 pages, 50p **Programme Editor:** Secretary
Previous Name: Oldswinford F & SC 1955-93.
Previous Leagues: Kidderminster (eight seasons)/ Staffs County (South)(seven seasons)/ West Midlands Regional (pre-1994).
Previous Grounds: Field Lane/ Wollescote Park/ Swinford Common, Stourbridge 56-58/ South Road, Stourbridge 58-75/ Cottage Street (Brierley Hill Alliance FC) 75-77/ South Road, Stourbridge.
Club Sponsors: Various **Record Gate:** 800 v Wolverhampton Wdrs, friendly.
Midweek matchday: Mon or Wed. **Nickname:** Lions.
Record transfer fee paid: Nil **Received:** From Wolves for Neil Edwards.
Clubhouse: Open Mon, Wed & Fri. Hot foods & drinks on matchdays - Best hot dogs in the Midlands!
Captain 93-94: Adrian Ibbetson **Top Scorer 93-94:** Mark Ellis.
Hons: West Midlands (Regional) League Prem. Div Cup Runners-up 84-85 (Div 1 80-81 (Div 1 Cup 80-81)).

CHASETOWN

Chairman: G Rollins **Vice Chairman:** A Purcell **President:** A Scorey.
Secretary: J T Bacon, 67 Hill St., Chasetown, Walsall WS7 8XU (0543 672642).
Manager: Graham Smith **Asst Manager:** Benny Brown **Coach:** N/A
Physio: E Highfield. **Commercial Mgr/Press Officer:** David M Shelton (0543 682222).
Ground: The Scholars, Church Street, Chasetown (0543 682222/684609).
Directions: Follow Motorways M5, M6 or M42 and follow signs for A5. A5 to White Horse Road/Wharf Lane, left into Highfields Rd (B5011), left into Church Street at top of hill, ground at end just beyond church. Buses B94 or B95 from Walsall.
Seats: 112 **Cover:** 250 **Capacity:** 2,000 **Floodlights:** Yes **Founded:** 1954.
Colours: All blue **Change cols:** Red & black/black/black. **Nickname:** Scholars
Programme: 26 pages, 50p **Programme Editor:** David Shelton (0543 682222)
Club Shop: Yes, selling jumpers, sweatshirts, T-shirts, programmes, ties, enamel badges, bannerettes, pens, key fobs, sports bottles. Contact David Shelton (0543 682222).
Prev. Grnd: Burntwood Rec Cte (pre'83) **Previous Name:** Chase Terrace Old Scholars 54-72.
Reserves' Lge: West Midlands **Record Gate:** 659 v Tamworth, FA Cup 2nd Qualifying Rd 1/10/88.
Previous Leagues: Cannock Yth 54-58/ Lichfield & Dist. 58-61/ Staffs Co. 61-72/ West Midlands (Regional) 72-94.
Club Sponsors: Aynsley Windows **Midweek home matchday:** Tuesday
Record win: 14-1 v Hanford (H), Walsall Senior Cup 17/10/92.
Record defeat: 1-8 v Telford United Reserves, West Mids (Regional) Lge Division One.
Clubhouse: Mon-Fri 7.30-11pm, Sat 11.30am-11pm, Sun 8-10.30pm. Basic snacks, but club caterers available on request.
Club record scorer: T Dixon 164 **Club record appearances:** A Cox 469 (+15 sub).
Captain 93-94: David Langston **Top Scorer 93-94:** Tony Dixon 22 **P.o.Y. 93-94:** Jon Rose.
Hons: West Midlands (Regional) League Runners-up 90-91 92-93 (League Cup 89-90 90-91, Div 1 77-78 (Runners-up 73-74 74-75 75-76 80-81 82-83), Div 1 Cup Runners-up 80-81 82-83, Div 2 Runners-up 87-88, Div 2 Cup Runners-up 86-87), Walsall Senior Cup 90-91 92-93, Staffs Senior Cup Runners-up 91-92.

HALESOWEN HARRIERS

Secretary: Brian P Beasley, 69 Bower Lane, Quarry Bank, West Mids DY5 2DU (0384 62124).
Manager: Derek Beasley **Asst Manager:** Rod Brown
Coach: Trevor Argent **Physio:** D Bowen.
Ground: Hayes Park, Park Rd, Colley Gate, Halesowen (0384 896748. Club Newsline: 0891 66 42 52).
Directions: On A458 Birmingham to Stourbridge Road (B'ham 10 miles, Stourbridge 4 miles) - main bus route. M5 Jct 3 (towards Kidderminster), right at 1st island (towards Dudley), turn left at island (towards Stourbridge), straight over next island then 3 miles to ground on left-hand side, 200yds past Park Lane. Just over a mile from Lye BR station.
Seats: 350 **Cover:** 500 **Capacity:** 4,000 **Floodlights:** Yes **Founded:** 1961
Colours: White **Change colours:** Sky. **Club Shop:** No.
Programme: 24-28 pages **Editor:** The Editor, HHFC (0384 896741).
Sponsors: A Page (Building Merchants) **Previous Leagues:** Festival (Sunday)/ West Midlands (pre-1994).
Previous Grounds: Birmingham parks 61-70/ Halesowen Town FC 70-84 (both whilst in Sunday football).
Record Gate: 750; friendlies v Walsall and Wolves in 1985. Competitive; 450 v Lye, Lge 1988.
Nickname: Lilywhites **Midweek home matchday:** Tuesday or Wednesday.
Record win: 12-1 v Lichfield & v Malvern Town, 1986.
Record defeat: 2-8 v Frickley Athletic (A), F.A. Cup 2nd Qualifying Rd 26/9/92.
Record transfer fee paid: £750 to Oldswinford for L Booth, 1991.
Clubhouse: Open every evening (possibly every lunchtimes from July '93). Limited range of hot ssnacks, but full cold snack kitchen.
Captain 93-94: Steve Brain **P.o.Y. 93-94:** Paul Waddington **Top Scorer 93-94:** Ian Perry
Hons: West Mids Lg Div 1 85-86 (Div 2 84-85, Div 2 Cup 84-85), Inter City Bowl 67-68 68-69, Festival Lg(5)(R-up(9)), FA Sunday Cup SF 79-80, Midland Sunday Cup, Birmingham Sunday Cup.

HINCKLEY ATHLETIC

Chairman: M Voce **Vice Chairman:** R Mayne **President:** D Loakes.
Secretary: Mr J Colver, 19 Edinburgh Rd, Earl Shilton, Leics LE9 7HP (0455 841452).
Manager: John Hanna **Asst Manager:** B Nally **Coach:** F Harrison
Physio: P Miller **Comm. Manager:** G Farmer **Press Officer:** A Gibbs.
Ground: Middlefield Lane, Hinckley. Leics (0455 613553).
Directions: A47 Coventry Road towards Hinckley. Keep on Inner Ring Road to lights at top of Upper Bond Street at junction of Ashby Road/Derby Road. Turn left and ground is at the bottom of Middlefield Lane. Two miles from Hinckley (BR).
Seats: 300 **Cover:** 1,000 **Capacity:** 5,000 **Floodlights:** Yes **Founded:** 1889
Club colours: Red/black/red **Change colours:** All blue **Club Shop:** No.
Programme: 36 pages, 50p **Editor:** A Mason (0553 891899).
Reserves' Lge: West Midlands **Previous Ground:** Hollywell Lane, London Rd (pre'40)
Previous Leagues: Leicestershire & Northants/ Leicestershire Senior/ Birmingham Combination 14-39 47-54/ West Midlands (Regional) 54-59 64-94/ Southern 63-64.
Previous Names: Hinckley AFC, Hinckley Town, Hinckley United.
Best FA Cup season: 2nd Rd Proper 54-55 (lost 1-2 at Rochdale), 62-63 (2-7 at Queens Pk Rgrs).
Best FA Trophy season: 1st Qualifying Rd 69-70 72-73 73-74.
Best FA Vase season: 76-77 77-78 78-79 89-90 93-94.
Record Gate: 5,410 v Nuneaton Borough, Birmingham Combination 26/12/49.
Players progressing to Football League: John Allen (Port Vale).
Club Sponsors: Vend Fabrics **Midweek home matchday:** Tuesday **Nickname:** Robins.
Clubhouse: Social club with lounge, games room, and concert room. Open each evening, Sunday lunch and matchdays. Hot & cold food available (0455 615012).
Record Scorer: M Hodgkins **Record appearances:** S Markham.
Captain 93-94: Mark Orton **Top Scorer 93-94 & P.o.Y. 93-94:** M Hodgkins.
Hons: Leics Snr Cup 1899-1900 00-01 09-10 82-83, Leics Snr Lg 1896-97 97-98 99-1900 08-09 09-10 13-14, Birmingham Comb. 23-24 26-27 (R-up 22-23), West Mids (Reg.) Lg R-up 82-83, Birmingham Snr Cup 54-55(jt with Brush Sports), Leics Challenge Cup 57-58 58-59 59-60 60-61 61-62 67-68.

Hinckley Athletic FC. Back Row (L/R): Bill Nally, Martin Bewell, Steve Markham, Sven Sinden, Mark Orton, Tommy Shevlin, Michael Love, Dean Curry, Alex Irvine, John Hanna (Manager). Front: Mark Hodgkins, Paul Green, Gareth Williams, Russell Dodds, Dave Stringer, Darren Dickson, Fred Harrison (Coach).

Photo - Keith Clayton.

KNYPERSLEY VICTORIA

Chairman: A Farr **Vice Chairman:** P Leese **President:** G Quinn.
Secretary: P H Freeman, 30 Caton Crescent, Milton, Stoke-on-Trent ST6 8XQ (0782 543123).
Manager: Robert Horton **Asst Mgr:** Eric Mountford **Coach:** Eric Mountford
Physio: N Gregory **Press Officer/Commercial Manager:** J A Shenton (0782 517962).
Ground: Tunstall Road, Knypersley, Stoke-on-Trent, (0782 522737/ 513304).
Directions: M6 Jct 15 join A500, 4th exit, pick up A527, follow through Tunstall, Chell, to Biddulph. Ground is situated on A527 just before Biddulph. From M6 jct 18 follow signs to Holmes Chapel then Congleton, A527 o Biddulph, continue thru lights, ground on left. Bus 61 Congleton-Tunstall passes ground.
Seats: 200 **Cover:** 200 **Capacity:** 1,200 **Floodlights:** Yes **Founded:** 1969.
Colours: Claret/claret/blue **Change Colours:** White/blue/white **Nickname:** The Vics.
Previous Grounds: None **Record Gate:** 1,100 v Pt Vale, friendly 1989.
Programme: 30-36 pages, 50p. **Editor:** J A Shenton (0782 517962) **Sponsors:** TBA
Club Shop: No, but club badges obtainable from J A Shenton (number above).
Previous Leagues: Leek & Moorlands 69-78/ Staffs Co. (North) 78-83/ Staffs Senior 83-90/ West Midland (Regional) 90-94.
Record fee received: Nil **Record transfer fee paid:** £1,000 M Biddle (Congleton, 1993)
Midweek home matchday: Tues/Thurs **Reserve team's League:** Staffs Senior (Biddulph Victoria).
Record win: 10-0 v Clancey Dudley, West Midlands (Regional) League Division One 90-91.
Record defeat: 0-9 v Meir KA, Staffordshire Senior League.
Clubhouse: Open from 1pm on Saturdays and 7pm weekdays. Burgers, hot dogs, crisps etc served from tea-bar at games.
Club record scorer: J Burndred **Club record appearances:** M Gosling, 450.
P.o.Y. 93-94: David Smallcross **Top Scorer & Player of the Year 93-94:** John Burndred.
Hons: West Mids Lg Div 1 92-93, Staffs Snr Lg 84-85 (Lg Cup 84-85 85-86), Staffs Co. Lg R-up 79-80, Staffs FA Vase 83-84 86-87, Sentinel Cup 86-87, Leek & Moorlands Lg 72-73 (Div 2 71-72).

OLDBURY UNITED

Chairman: Roger Fennell **Vice Chairman:** Ken Harris.
Secretary: Tom Hood, 112 Brook Road, Oldbury, Warley, West Mids B68 8AD (021 522 7737).
Manager: Jeff Allard **Asst Mgr:** Kevin Hadley **Physio:** Tony Dandy
Press Officer: Martin Scott **Commercial Manager:** Eddie Winkett.
Ground: The Cricketts, York Road, Rowley Regis, Warley, West Midlands (021 559 5564).
Directions: M5 jct 2, follow Blackheath & Halesowen signs, first left at lights and fourth left into York Road (turning before motorway flyover), ground 200yds on left. One and a half miles from Sandwell & Dudley and Rowley Regis BR stations. Bus 404 from West Bromwich, Oldbury and Blackheath.
Seats: 300 **Cover:** 1,000 **Capacity:** 3,000 **Floodlights:** Yes **Founded:** 1958
Cols: All blue (white flashes/trim) **Change colours:** All yellow (blue flashes/trim)
Previous Names: Queens Colts 58-62/ Whiteheath Utd 62-65. **Nickname:** Cricketts
Record Gate: 2,200 v Walsall Wood, Walsall Snr Cup Final 1982.
Prev. Lges: Oldbury 58-62/ Warwick & W Mids All. 62-65/ Worcs (later Midland) Comb. 65-82/ Southern 82-86.
Previous Grounds: Brittana Park 61-63/ Newbury Lane (Oldbury Stadium) 63-78.
Players progressing to F'ball Lge: C Gordon, L Conoway, J Scott, R O'Kelly, G Nardiello, Dakin, T Reece.
Programme: 24 pages, 50p **Programme Editor:** Secretary
Club Shop: No, but club metal badges, polo shirts and jumpers can be obtained from secretary.
Midweek home matchday: Tuesday **Club Sponsors:** Beswick Paper Group, Oldbury.
Record win: 10-1 v Blakenall **Record defeat:** 1-9 v Moor Green.
Record transfer fee paid: Nil **Received:** £10,000 for Colin Gordon (Swindon, 1985).
Clubhouse: Mon-Fri 7.30-11pm, Sat-Sun 12-2.30 (12-11pm Sat matchdays). Hot dogs, pies, burgers, cobs and hot drinks available from kitchen on matchdays only.
Hons: West Mids Lg 92-93, Staffs Snr Cup 87-88, Midland Comb. R-up 78-79 (Presidents Cup 72-73(res), Div 3 R-up 82-83(res), Chal. Vase 82-83(res)), Walsall Snr Cup 82-83, B'ham Snr Amtr Cup, Oldbury Lg Div 2 61-62, Worcs Snr Urn 86-87, Sandwell Charity Cup 86-87.

PAGET RANGERS

Chairman: R R Ruddick **Vice-Chairman:** Cliff Cockerill **President:** Ron Timmings
Secretary: Ian T Price, 24 Biddulp Court, Braemar Rd, Sutton Coldfield, West Mids B73 6LN (021 355 7072).
Manager/Physio: Eddie Caulfield **Assistant Manager:** Paul Edwards.
Press Officer: Chris Inman **Commercial Manager:** Ian Price.
Ground & Directions: As Sutton Coldfield Town *(see page 384)*
Colours: Gold/black/gold **Change colours:** All red **Founded:** 1938
Programme: Yes **Programme Editor:** W Dudley **Nickname:** The "P's"
Previous Grnd: Pype Hayes Park 38-46/ Springfield Rd, Warmley 46-93.
Record Gate: 2,000 v A Villa, F'light opening 1971.
Record win: 24-1 v Evesham Town (A), Central Amateur League Knock-Out Cup 26/11/49.
Club Shop: No, but metal badges available from chairman or secretary.
Previous Leagues: Birmingham Suburban/ Central Amateur/ Midland Combination 50-81/ Southern 86-88/ West Midlands (Regional) 88-94.
Players progressing to Football League: John Gittens (Southampton for £10,000).
Captain 93-94: Gary Williams **Top Scorer 93-94:** Ian Paul 19.
Player of the Year 93-94: Gary Price (goalkeeper).
Hons: West Mids Lg R-up 91-92 (Lg Cup 91-92), Midland Comb.(6) 59-61 69-71 82-83 85-86 (R-up 77-78, Lg Cup 59-60 66-67, Div 1 Cup 70-71, Div 3 82-83(res)), B'ham Jnr Cup 51-52, Walsall Snr Cup 85-86.

Photo Opposite: *Paget Rangers pictured at their borrowed home. Back Row (L/R): Carl Hancel, Ian Paul, Sean Dunne, Neil Moroney, Gary Price, Craig Darkes, Richard Brown, Brendan McCarthy. Centre: Paul Vanes (Committee), Derek Culling (Physio), John Capaldi, Bob Whittingham, Jason Darkes, Gary Williams (Club Captain), Gary Edmonds, Stuart Tucker (Captain), Alan Hunt, Paul Edwards (Assistant Manager). Front: Eddie Caulfield (Manager), Cliff Cockerill (Vice-Chairman), Peter Plevey (Trustee), Ron Timmings (President), Bob Ruddick (Chairman), George Brain (Committee), Peter Kearney (Committee).*

PERSHORE TOWN '88

Chairman: Mr A Bradstock **Vice Chairman:** Mr C Scarrett.
Secretary: Mr A J Barnett, 8 Croft Cottages, Cropthorne, Nr Pershore, Worcs WR10 3LX (0386 860243).
Manager: Colin Shepherd **Asst Manager:** Kenneth Gwynne.
Press Officer: Mr C Millward. **Physio:** Rick Harber/Mark Palfrey
Commercial Manager: Mr C Milward/ Mr S Sefton.
Ground: King George XI Playing Fields, High Street, Pershore, Worcs (0386 556902).
Directions: M5 jct 7, A44 to Pershore (8 miles) cross 1st lights in Pershore, at 2nd lights turn left & fold road round into King Georges Way, ground immediately on left.
Seats: 120 **Cover:** 120 **Capacity:** 4,000 **Floodlights:** Yes **Founded:** 1988.
Colours: Blue & white/blue/blue **Change colours:** Yellow/green/yellow.
Previous Grounds: None **Previous League:** Midland Combination 90-94.
Prev. Names: Formed by the 1988 amalgamation of Pershore Utd, Pershore Rec Rovers & Pershore Bulletts.
Programme: 20 pages, 50p **Editor:** Mr T S Conway (0386 554390)
Club Shop: No, but club ties, jumpers, sweatshirts & jackets and various programmes are available.
Reserves' Lge: Mids Comb Res Div. **Midweek home matchday:** Tuesday **Nickname:** The Town
Best FA Cup season: 4th Qualifying Round 93-94 (lost 1-3 to Yeading).
Best FA Vase season: Preliminary Rd 92-93 (lost 0-1 at Stewarts & Lloyds).
Record Gate: 1,356 v Yeading, FA Cup 4th Qualifying Round 23/10/93.
Record win: 10-0 v Ledbury Town, Robert Biggart Memorial Cup semi-final, May 1992.
Record defeat: 1-4 v Stapenhill (H), Midland Combination Challenge Cup SF 92-93.
Record transfer fee paid: Undisclosed for Simon Judge (Worcester City, 93-94).
Record fee received: Undisclosed for Simon Judge (Worcester, 92-93).
Clubhouse: Bar open Tue-Thur 7.30-11pm, Fri 2-6 & 7.30-11pm, Sat noon-11pm, Sun noon-3 & 7-10.30pm. Coffee, tea, soup, hot pies and rolls available during matches. Abbey Suite function room available for bookings.
Record scorer: Simon Judge 63 **Record appearances:** Ian Aldington, 192 + 5 sub.
Captain 93-94: Ian Aldington **Top Scorer 93-94:** Simon Judge 23.
Players' P.o.Y. 93-94: Gary Aldington **Supporters' P.o.Y. 93-94:** Ian Aldington.
Hons: Midland Combination 93-94 (Div 2 89-90), Worcs Jnr Cup 90-91, Robert Biggart Cup(2) 90-92 (R-up 89-90), Worcs Snr Urn R-up 92-93, Jack Mould Cup 90-91, Alfred Terry Cup 90-91, Martley Hosp. Cup('A') 90-91, Pershore Hosp. Cup(Res) 92-93 93-94, Evesham Hosp. Minor Cup R-up('A') 93-94.

ROCESTER

Chairman: Mr D Hill
Secretary: Mr Gilbert Egerton, 23 Eaton Road, Rocester, Uttoxeter, Staffs ST14 5LL (0889 590101).
Manager: Brian Beresford **Asst Mgr:** Keith Milner **Reserves' Mgr:** Mick Collins
Press Officer: Ian Cruddas (0889 564173).
Ground: The Rivers Field, Mill Street, Rocester, Uttoxeter, Staffs (0889 590463).
Directions: From A50 r'bout adjoining Little Chef restaurant at Uttoxeter take B5030 towards Rocester and Alton Towers, right into Rocester village after 3 miles over narrow bridge, in village centre bear right at sharp left-hand bend into Mill Str., ground 500yds on left just past former cotton mill.
Seats: 200 **Cover:** 500 **Capacity:** 4,000 **Floodlights:** Yes **Founded:** 1876
Colours: Amber/black/black **Change colours:** All sky blue **Nickname:** Romans
Programme: 32 pages, 50p **Programme Editor:** Ian Cruddas (0889 564173).
Club Shop: Yes, selling mostly programmes and a few Rocester souvenirs. Contact Ian Cruddas (0889 564173).
Record Transfer Fee Paid: £1,000 for Paul Ede (from Burton Albion, September 1989).
Record Transfer Fee Received: £8,000 for Tony Hemmings (from Northwich Victoria, March 1991).
Players progressing to Football League: George Shepherd (Derby County), Mark Sale (Birmingham).
Record Gate: 1,026 v Halesowen Town, FA Vase 4th Rd January 1987 (at Leek Town FC).
Previous Lges: Ashbourne/ Leek & Moorland/ Cheadle & Distrist/ Uttoxeter Amateur/ Stafford 53-57/ Staffs County Nth 57-84/ Staffs Senior 84-87/ West Mids 87-94.
Reserves' Lge: West Midlands **Previous Ground:** Mill Street, Rocester (early 1900s-1987).
Midweek home matchday: Tuesday **Sponsors:** H.K.B. Steels Ltd, Tipton.
Record win: 14-0 (twice) **Record defeat:** 0-9.
Players progressing to Football League: Bert Carpenter (Manchester Utd), Joe Carpenter (Brighton), George Shepherd (Derby), Mark Sale (Birmingham, Torquay), Tony Hemmings (Wycombe (via Northwich)).
Clubhouse: On matchdays (normal licensing hours) and other special events. Hot drinks and snacks during games.
Club record scorer: Mick Collins **Club record appearances:** Peter Swanwick.
Captain 93-94: Nigel Simms **Top Scorer 93-94:** Cory Johnson **P.o.Y. 93-94:** Paul Ede.
Hons: West Mids Lg R-up 89-90 (Div 1 87-88, Div 1 Cup 87-88), Staffs Snr Lg(2) 85-87, Staffs FA Vase 85-86 87-88.

RUSHALL OLYMPIC

Chairman: John Burks **Vice Chairman:** Trevor Westwood **President:** Brian Greenwood.
Secretary: Peter Athersmith, 46 Blakenall Lane, Leamore, Walsall (0922 711735).
Manager: Joey Nugent **Asst Manager:** Ron Tranter **Coach:** John Capaldi.
Physio: Eddie Judge **Press Officer:** Darren Stockall (0922 379153).
Ground: Dales Lane, off Daw End Lane, Rushall, Nr Walsall (0922 641021).
Directions: From Rushall centre (A461) take B4154 signed Aldridge. Approx., 1 mile on right, directly opposite Royal Oak Public House, in Daw End Lane. Ground on right. Two miles from Walsall (BR) station.
Seats: 200 **Cover:** 200 **Capacity:** 2,500 **Floodlights:** Yes **Founded:** 1951
Colours: Amber/black/black **Change colours:** White/red/red **Nickname:** Pics.
Programme: 36 pages **Editor:** Darren Stockall (0922 379153) **Sponsors:** WM Print
Reserves' Lge: West Mids (Reg.) **Record Gate:** 2,000 v Leeds Utd Old Boys, charity match 1982.
Previous Grounds: Rowley Place 51-75/ Aston University 76-79.
Previous Leagues: Walsall Amateur 52-55/ Staffs County (South) 56-78/ West Midlands (Regional) 78-94.
Players progressing to Football League: Lee Sinnott (Watford), Lee Palin (Aston Villa, Nottingham Forest, Bradford City), Stuart Watkiss (Walsall).
Midweek home matchday: Tuesday **Record transfer received:** £1,500 for Steve Taylor (Bromsgrove).
Record win: 7-1 **Record defeat:** 0-6 v Bilston, FA Vase.
Clubhouse: Excellent bar/lounge, kitchen, adjoining large refreshment facilities. Bar open every night 8-11pm, Saturday matchdays before and after game, Sunday noon-2.30pm.
Top Scorer: David Battison **Player of the Year 93-94:**
Record scorer: Graham Wiggin **Record appearances/Captain 93-94:** Alan Dawson (400+ apps).
Hons: West Mids League Div 1 79-80, Walsall Amtr League Div 1 55-56 (Div 2 52-53, Snr Cup 54-55 55-56, Jabez Cliff Cup 55-56), Staffs Co. League Div 1 60-61 61-62 62-63 64-65 (Div 2 56-57), Walsall Charity Cup 52-53, Walsall Chal. Cup 54-55 56-57, Walsall Memorial Charity Cup 55-56 56-57 57-58 58-59 59-60 60-61 61-62, W Preston Chal. Cup 56-57, Cannock & Dist. Charity Cup 56-57, Wednesbury Snr Cup 58-59 59-60 60-61, Sporting Star Cup 59-60 60-61 (joint) 64-65 65-66 67-68, J W Edge 62-63 66-67, Walsall Snr Cup 64-65, Lichfield Charity 64-65 66-67, Staffs Yth Cup 81-82.

SANDWELL BOROUGH

Manager: Paul Molesworth. **Founded:** 1918.
Secretary: Ken Jones, 19 Henn Drive, Princes End, Tipton, West Mids DY4 9NN (021 557 9429).
Ground: Oldbury Sports Centre, Newbury Lane, Oldbury (021 552 1759).
Directions: Follow A4123 Birmingham-Wolverhampton Rd, past island at jnt 2 M5, after half mile turn left into Newbury Lane and stadium is on the right. 2 miles from Sandwell & Dudley (BR).
Capacity: 3,000 **Seats:** 200 **Cover:** 600 **Floodlights:** Yes **Nickname:** Trees
Midweek matches: Wednesday **Previous Grnd:** Londonderry, Smethwick 18-81
Colours: Green & white stripes/green/green **Change Colours:** Amber & black
Record Gate: 950 v Halesowen T., FA Cup 1987
Programme: 12 pages 25p **Programme Editor:** R Unitt.
Previous Leagues: Birmingham Suburban/ Central Amateur/ Worcs (Midlands Combination) 48-88 90-94/ Southern 88-90.
Previous names: Smethwick Town, Smethwick Highfield, Ashtree Highfield
Clubhouse: Licensed bar overlooking pitch. Open everyday
Players who have progressed to Football League: Andy Micklewright (Bristol Rov, Bristol City, Swindon, Exeter), Gary Bull (Southampton, Cambridge Utd)
Hons: Midland Combination Challenge Cup Runners-up(5) 49-50 51-53 67-68 74-75, Challenge Trophy Runners-up 88-89, Pres. Cup 79-80 (Runners-up 76-77), Div 2 Runners-up 79-80), Birmingham Jnr Cup.

SHEPSHED DYNAMO

Chairman/Comm. Mgr: Paul Mitchell **Vice Chairman:** Mr M Clayton.
Secretary: Mr Peter Bull, 17 Welland Rd, Barrow-on-Soar, Leicestershire LE12 8NA (0509 413338).
Manager: Mark O'Kane **Assistant Manager:** John Ramshaw.
Physio: John Watterson **Press Officer:** Maurice Brindley (0509 267922)
Ground: The Dovecote, Butthole Lane, Shepshed, Leicestershire (0509 502684).
Directions: M1 junction 23, A512 towards Ashby, right at first lights, right at garage in Forest Street, right into Butthole Lane opposite Black Swan. Five miles from Loughborough (BR).
Capacity: 5,000 **Cover:** 1,500 **Seats:** 209 **Floodlights:** Yes **Founded:** 1890
Colours: Black & white **Change colours:** All green **Nickname:** Raiders.
Previous Leagues: Leicestershire Senior 07-16 19-27 46-50 51-81/ Midland Counties 81-82/ Northern Counties (East) 82-83/ Southern 83-88/ Northern Premier 88-93.
Previous Grounds: Ashby Road (pre-1897)/ Little Haw Farm.
Previous Names: Shepshed Albion 1890-1975 91-94/ Shepshed Charterhouse 75-91.
Midweek home matchday: Tuesday **Record Attendance:** 1,672. **Club Shop:** TBA
Best FA Vase season: Semi-Finalists 78-79.
Best FA Trophy season: 1st Rd Replay 85-86 89-90.
Best FA Cup season: 1st Rd 82-83 (lost 1-5 at Preston North End).
Rec. fee paid: £2,000 for Doug Newton **Received:** £10,000 for John Deakin.
Players progressing to Football League: Neil Grewcock (Burnley 1984), Gordon Tucker (Huddersfield 1987), Devon White (Bristol Rovers 1987), John Deakin (Birmingham City).
Clubhouse: Accomodates 120 in main room, 50 in others.
Club Record Scorer: Jeff Lissaman **Club Record Appearances:** Austin Straker 300.
Honours: Southern League Midland Division Runners-up 83-84, Northern Counties (East) League 82-83 (League Cup 82-83), Midland Counties League 81-82 (League Cup 81-82), Leicestershire Senior League 10-11 20-21 78-79 79-80 80-81 (Runners-up 21-22, Div 2 53-54 65-66 77-78, Div 2 Cup 77-78), Leicestershire Senior Cup 77-78 79-80 81-82 83-84 84-85 85-86 87-88, FA Vase SF 78-79, Loughborough Charity Cup 92-93.

SHIFNAL TOWN

Chairman: Mr D Adams **Vice Chairman:** Mr R Owen **President:** Mr R Arnold
Secretary: Mr D Groucott, 4 Idsall Cres., Shifnal, Shropshire, TF11 8ES (0952 402255).
Manager/Coach: Ken Jones **Asst Manager:** S Frisby
Physio: W Grainger **Press Officer:** Mr G Davies (0952 460326).
Ground: Phoenix Park, Coppice Green Lane, Shifnal, Shropshire.
Directions: M54 jct 3, A41 towards Newport, 1st left for Shifnal (3 miles), in Shifnal take 1st right, and sharp right again up Coppice Green Lane, ground 800yds on left past Idsall School. 1 mile from Shifnal BR station.
Seats: 104 **Cover:** 300 **Capacity:** 3,000 **Floodlights:** Yes **Founded:** 1964
Colours: Red/white/black **Change colours:** Yellow/green **Nickname:** None.
Midweek home matchday: Wednesday **Previous Grounds:** Admirals Park 80-85
Previous Leagues: Wellington (East Dist.) 64-69/ Shropshire County 69-77 85-93/ West Midlands 77-85/ Midland Combination 93-94.
Reserves' League: None at present **Record win:** 10-1 v Malvern, 82-83 **Record loss:** 1-6
Programme: 18 pages, 50p **Programme Editor:** G Davies (0952 460326).
Club Shop: No, but club items for sale include sports shirts, jumpers, scarves, bobble hats, ties, metal badges. Contact Secretary.
Sponsors: Associated Cold Stores & Transport Ltd.
Record Gate: 1,002 v Bridgnorth Town, F.A. Vase 3rd Rd 83-84 (at Admirals Park).
Clubhouse: Not on ground but in Newport Rd, Shifnal. Open Mon-Fri 7.30-11pm, noon-11pm Sat matchdays, noon-2.30 & 7.30-11pm Sat non-matchdays, Sun noon-3 & 7.30-11pm.
Captain 93-94: Mark Rix **Top Scorer 93-94:** John Powell 34.
P.O.Y. 93-94: John Powell **Club record scorer:** Steve Kelly 35.
Hons: West Mids Lg 80-81 81-82 (Div 1 78-79), Shropshire Snr Cup 80-81 90-91 92-93.

STAPENHILL

Chairman: Bob Hutchinson **Vice Chairman:** Ken Hulland **President:** Bill Wilkinson.
Secretary: Peter Regent, 22 Grasmere Close, Stapenhill, Burton-on-Trent DE15 9DS (0283 340583).
Manager: Eric Avens **Asst Mgr:** Dale Hutchinson **Physio:** Ken Hulland.
Coach: Dale Hutchinson **Press Officer:** Secretary.
Ground: Edge Hill, Maple Grove, Stapenhill, Burton-on-Trent (0283 62471).
Directions: Three miles from Burton on A444 Measham Rd, turn right (coming from Burton) at Copperhearth Public House into Sycamore Rd, Maple Grove is 5th left. 3 miles from Burton-on-Trent (BR) - use buses 22, 23, 38 from opposite station.
Capacity: 2,000 **Seats:** 50 **Covered:** 200 **Floodlights:** Yes **Founded:** 1947.
Midweek matches: Wednesday **Record Gate:** 2,000 v Gresley, Derbys Snr Cup final 88-89.
Colours: Red/white/red **Change Colours:** Blue/white/blue **Nickname:** Swans.
Programme: 12 pages, 30p **Programme Editor:** **Club Shop:** No..
Reserves' Lge: Midland Comb. **Previous League:** Leics Snr 58-89/ Midland Combination 89-94.
Previous Name: Stapenhill Waterside Community Centre.
Sponsors: K C Hulland Builders **Clubhouse:** In ground. Pub hours. Matchday tea bar.
Record win: 11-0 v Alcester Town (H), Midland Combination Premier Division, 1992-93.
Record defeat: 0-7 v Bridgnorth Town, FA Vase.
Record scorer: Brian Beresford 123 **Record appearances:** Ian Pearsall 172.
Captain 93-94: Dave Carlin **Top Scorer 93-94:** Richard Walker 23 **P.o.Y. 93-94:** Peter Thompson
Hons: Midland Combination R-up 92-93 (Div 1 89-90, Challenge Cup 92-93 93-94), Leics Snr Lg 59-60 86-87 88-89 (Tebbutt Brown Cup(2) 87-89), Leics Snr Cup 69-70 86-87, Derby Snr Cup R-up 88-89 91-92.

STRATFORD TOWN

President: Sir W Lawrence **Chairman:** G Cutler **Vice-Chairman:** M Powlett.
Secretary: P W Gardner, 17 Trevelyan Crescent, Stratford-upon-Avon, Warks CV37 9LL (0789 268432).
Manager: S Dixon **Physio:** N Dixon **Commercial Mgr:** J Carruthers.
Ground: Masons Road, off Alcester Road, Stratford-upon-Avon, Warks (0789 297479).
Directions: Follow Alcester/Worcester A422 signs from town centre - Masons Rd is 1st right afterrailway bridge. 400 yards from Stratford-on-Avon (BR) station. Local buses for West Green Drive.
Capacity: 2,000 **Seat/Cover:** 200 **Floodlights:** Yes **Nickname:** The Town **Founded:** 1944
Midweek Matches: Tuesday **Clubhouse:** Open every nights but Sunday **Club Shop:** No.
Colours: Tangerine/black/tangerine **Change Colours:** White/white/black
Programme: 20 pages, 50p **Reserves' League:** Midland Comb. Reserve Division.
Previous Name: Stratford Town Amateur **Prev. Lgs:** W Mids 57-70/ Mid Com. 70-73 75-94/ Hellenic 70-75.
Sponsors: Porters Precision Products **Record Gate:** 484 v A. Villa, Birmingham Snr Cup, Oct 1984
Players who have progressed to Football League: Martin Hicks (Charlton, Reading, Birmingham), Roy Proverbs (Coventry, Bournemouth, Gillingham), Richard Landon (Plymouth Argyle (via Bedworth Utd)).
Captain 93-94: Dave Roberts **P.o.Y. 93-94:** Andy Beechey **Top Scorer 93-94:** John Mitchell.
Hons: Midland Comb 56-57 86-87 (Chal. Cup 86-87 88-89 (R-up 55-56), Chal. Vase 81-82, Jack Mould Tphy 81-82, Tony Allden Mem. Cup 86-87, B'ham Snr Cup 62-63.

WEST MIDLANDS POLICE

President: Chief Constable R Hadfield OBE **Manager:** Colin Brookes/Mark Fogarty
Chairman: Asst Chief Constable D G Ibbs MBE **Vice Chairman:** Superintendent M Male.
Secretary: B H Nunn, 98 Griffins Brook Lane, Bournville, Birmingham B30 1QG (021 476 5223).
Press Officer: Tony Pearson. **Commercial Manager:** John Black.
Ground: Police Spts Ground, 'Tally Ho', Pershore Road, Edgbaston, Birmingham B5 7RN (021 472 2944).
Directions: 2 miles south west of city on A441 Pershore Road. Ground is on the left 50yds past Priory Road lights (Warks County Cricket Ground). 3 miles from Birmingham New Street (BR) - buses 41, 45 & 47 from city.
Capacity: 2,500 **Seats:** 224 **Covered:** 224 **Floodlights:** Yes **Founded:** 1974
Midweek matches: Tues/Thurs. **Reserve Team's League:** Midland Combination.
Programme: 16 pages, 50p **Editor:** K Horrigan (021 626 4020x6100) **Club Shop:** No.
Cols: Red & black stripes/black/black **Change Cols:** Yellow/green/green. **Record win:** 9-3
Record Gate: 1,072 v Sudbury Town, FA Vase QF 29/2/92. **Record defeat:** 1-10.
Previous Names: Birmingham City Police (founded 1938), West Mids Constabulary - merged in 1974.
Previous Leagues: B'ham Wednesday 28-38/ Mercian 46-53/ B'ham Works 53-69/ Midland Combination 74-94.
Clubhouse: Complex of 3 bars including snooker room, ballroom, kitchen. Hot & cold food. Open all day.
Captain 93-94: S Hopcroft **P.O.Y. 93-94:** N Hornby **Top Scorer 93-94:** G Hussey.
Hons: FA Vase QF 91-92, Mids Comb 90-91 (R-up 93-94, Chal. Cup 74-75 (R-up 85-86)), Tony Allden Mem. Cup 75-76 (R-up 91-92), B'ham Jnr Cup, Worcs Snr Urn 84-85 90-91 91-92 (R-up 81-82 85-86), National Police Cup(12) 61-65 66-67 69-70 73-76 80-81 87-88 91-92 (R-up(7) 67-68 70-72 76-78 88-89 93-94), Aston Villa Cup 60-61 64-65 65-66.

WILLENHALL TOWN

President: Jack **Chairman:** L D Crutchley **Vice Chairman:** G L Mills.
Secretary: Barry Hall, 10 Mills Meadow Close, Willenhall, West Midlands WV12 5YE (0922 409017).
Manager: Chris Robinson **Asst Manager:** Brian Fox **Coach:** Darren Wright
Physio: John Porter **Commercial Manager:** D MacMillan.
Ground: Noose Lane, Willenhall, West Midlands (0902 605132-club, 636586-office).
Directions: Noose Lane is off the main A454 Walsall to Wolverhampton road. 3 miles from jct 10 (M6) - follow signs for Wolverhampton for 2 miles and turn right into Neachells Lane at 'Neachells' pub, first right into Watery Lane and left at island into Noose Lane - ground 200yds on left. Two and a half miles from Wolverhampton (BR). Buses 525, 526, 529.
Seats: 324 **Cover:** 500 **Capacity:** 5,000 **Floodlights:** Yes **Founded:** 1953
Colours: All red **Change colours:** Yellow & green **Nickname:** Reds
Programme: 40 pages, 50p **Editor:** Keith Badger (0902 636586).
Midweek home matchday: Monday. **Club sponsors:** TPB Motors (Wednesfield).
Record win: 11-0 **Record defeat:** 1-6.
Reserves' lge: Staffs Co.(Sth) **Record transfer fee received:** £5,000.
Record transfer fee paid: £2,000 for Gary Stevens (Cheltenham Town, 1981).
Record Gate: 3,454 v Crewe Alexandra, FA Cup 1st Rd 1981.
Previous Leagues: Wolverhampton Amateur/ Staffs County/ West Mids 75-82 91-94/ Southern 82-91.
Previous Grounds: Farmers Field, Spring Lane 53-55/ Memorial Park 55-74/ Marstons Spts Grd 74-75.
Club Shop: Yes, selling programmes (past & present), replica kit, badges, *Team Talk* magazine.
Players progressing to Football League: Sean O'Driscoll (Fulham & Bournemouth), Joe Jackson (Wolves), Stuart Watkiss (Wolves & Walsall), Tony Moore (Sheff Utd), Andy Reece (Bristol Rovers).
Clubhouse: Open Mon-Thurs 12-3 & 7-11pm, Fri-Sat 11am-11pm, Sun 12-2 & 7-10.30pm. Pies, cobs, crisps etc available.
Club record scorer: Gary Matthews **Club record appearances:** Gary Matthews.
Captain 93-94: Darren Wright **P.o.Y. 93-94:** Ada Fitzhugh **Top-scorer 93-94:** Gary Piggott.
Hons: FA Vase R-up 80-81, West Mids Lg 78-79 (Div 1 75-76, Prem. Div Cup 79-80, Div 2 Cup 78-79(res)), Birmingham Snr Cup R-up 82-83, J W Hunt Cup 73-74.

The definitive BUSINESS MAGAZINE for the football industry.

Unlike all other football magazines available today, *Football Management* is the only publication that covers all commercial and business issues relevant to the successful running of a modern day club.

Published bi-monthly, *Football Management* is essential reading for every club administrator and commercial manager regardless of club status or league standing.

This invaluable publication is available to readers of the non-League directory at a special price of £15 for eight issues. To find out more telephone 0705 822122 or send a cheque to the following address.

Portman Publishing and Communications Limited
16 Long Acre Court, Hampshire Street, Portsmouth PO1 5LJ.

THE INDEPENDENT BUSINESS JOURNAL OF THE FOOTBALL FRATERNITY

WEST MIDLANDS (REGIONAL) LEAGUE

FEEDER TO:
MIDLAND ALLIANCE

Hon. Secretary: Neil Juggins,
14 Badgers Lane, Blackwell, Bromsgrove.

ILKESTON WIN EXCITING TITLE RACE

Once again the destination of the Premier Division Championship was left undecided until the closing days of the season, this having been the norm for the recent seasons.

Rocester were the early pace-setters and they headed the table until January, after which they faded and ultimately finished 6th. Reigning champions Oldbury United then took over at the top, closely followed by Blakenall, Stourport Swifts and Ilkeston Town, the Derbyshire club having several games in hand. These eventually proved decisive for Ilkeston who reached the top in the closing days of the season, aided by victories over both Blakenall and Stourport, to take the championship for the first time (and just two years after taking the Division One title). To cap an excellent season Ilkeston then went on to complete the double (the first for 6 years) by defeating Paget Rangers in the league cup final.

Elsewhere in this section Alvechurch Sports, formed from the ashes of the former Alvechurch club, were also amongst the early pace-setters, but financial problems cropped up and the club folded in mid-season. Down at the bottom, Cradley Town and West Bromwich Town fought to avoid the re-election places, West Brom comfortably claiming bottom spot after failing to win a game since 6th November when they won at Stourport, of all places. That defeat ultimately cost Stourport the championship and they had to settle for the Keys Cup.

Newcomers Stafford Town made an immediate impact by leading Division One early on. However, a fixture backlog allowed Gornal Athletic to take over early in the new year. Gornal were still top at the conclusion of their fixtures but Stafford, though trailing by 16 points, still had 7 games to play and they made sure of the title with a game to spare.

Cannock Chase suffered an early season suspension which left them rooted to the bottom due to fixtures being unplayed, but they finished safely towards the middle of the table by the season's end. Gornal Sports moved to the ground of former league club Bilston United and changed their name accordingly, whilst Cheslyn Hay was the club that ended up being cast adrift at the bottom.

The other honours in this section went to Wolverhampton United, making a record 4th appearance in the Division One League Cup Final. Their 3-0 victory came at the expense of a Lichfield club making its first Final appearance in 18 years of trying.

The newly constituted reserve division was probably not surprisingly won by Rushall Olympic Reserves, last season's Division 2 champions. For good measure they also won their league cup group, which required a further 12 games due to the clubs being split into 2 groups during the early stages, but were then unexpectedly beaten by lowly Tividale Reserves (runners-up in the other group), who in turn were beaten by Hinckley Athletic Reserves in the final.

The youth section was, as expected, dominated by the professional clubs, Birmingham City completing a league and cup double and suffering just one defeat in the whole season.

The League's clubs picked up their usual share of honours in external competitions. Stourport Swifts retained the Worcestershire Senior Urn whilst Wolverhampton United recorded their first cup final success for several years in the Birmingham County FA Vase. Ludlow Town were successful in the Shropshire Cup for the first time since joining the league in 1979, whilst Rushall Reserves were Walsall Challenge Cup winners for the 3rd time in 4 seasons.

Progress in the national competitions was again rather disappointing. Only Pelsall Villa got as far as the Second Qualifying Round of the FA Cup, losing 2-1 to Pershore. Pelsall were also one of just two clubs to progress beyond the second round of the FA Vase. They fell 4-2 to Halstead in the 3rd round but pride of place this season went to Hinckley Athletic who reached the 5th round before losing to Newbury.

The best performance of all was that of Wednesfield who reached the final of the Staffs Senior Cup for the first time. Unfortunately their game against Macclesfield Town of the GMVC has been held over until next season.

Pre-season had seen the first major structural change since the introduction of a third division back in 1976, with clubs in Divisions One and Two being re-arranged into two sections, one for reserve sides, the other for non-reserve sides. Events on the field, however, tended to be rather overshadowed by the spectre of the Midland Alliance which finally came into existence after much debate. The outcome of this was that the WMRL has undergone the biggest mass exodus of clubs in its 105 year history, with ten of the Premier Division sides joining a similar number from the Midland Combination in the new organisation. It was the choice of clubs that caused the most heated debate, for ground facilities were the major consideration allied to a restriction of no more than ten clubs to be selected from the WMRL in order not to decimate the league completely. Consequently the likes of Blakenall and Stourport Swifts, who would have made the grade easily on playing standards, were overlooked. To compound the matter the majority of Combination clubs selected had arguably inferior ground facilities but were given time to rectify the matter.

In all the WMRL have lost 20 sides from last season's competition. In addition to the 10 clubs elected to the Midland Alliance, Ilkeston Town have been elected to the Southern League, whilst Alvechurch Sports (in mid-season) and West Bromwich Town have disbanded and three reserve sides have been dispensed with. The other three sides have tranferred to the Midland Combination.

As a consequence of this the league have undergone a major restructuring, with the remaining clubs being divided between the Premier and First Divisions. The basic criteria was the availability of floodlights and there proved to be sufficient clubs to accommodate this due to the number of ground-sharing arrangements. So all clubs with floodlit grounds have been placed in the Premier Division, with the remaining clubs going into Division One. This is probably not the ideal scenario (Bilston United and Manders, for instance, both finished near the bottom of Division One last time round) but was the most practical solution and definitely preferable to, say, having a small number of clubs with a restricted programme or having to play each other 3 or 4 times. One unfortunate outcome was that the presence of Moxley Rangers and Wolverhampton Casuals in Division One meant their respective reserve sides had to retire from the competition. Conversely, Bilston United, Gornal Athletic, Ludlow Town and Tividale have taken advantage of the shake up by installing floodlights in order to gain promotion, three years after the introduction of the floodlighting rule resulted in Tividale being demoted and Ludlow being denied promotion due to the lack of appropriate facilities. Other clubs to benefit from late changes were Rushall Olympic, who took Ilkeston's place in the Alliance after they were excluded from the original ten clubs selected, and Stafford Town who sorted out a ground-sharing arrangement with Stafford Rangers to claim the Premier Division place they had earned on the field but seemed likely to be denied off it.

Finally, it is fitting that mention should be made of two servants of the WMRL who resigned from their positions after 22 years of service. Ken Goodfellow joined the management committee in 1972 and later acted as Assistant Secretary for a season, Fixtures Secretary for three and had been Secretary since 1981. Olive Etheridge has generated the league's results service since 1972 and has been Administrative Assistant since 1986.

Steve Carr, League Historian

PREM. DIV.	P	W	D	L	F	A	PTS
Ilkeston Town	38	25	6	7	102	43	81
Stourport Swifts	38	24	7	7	83	37	79
Oldbury United	38	23	9	6	85	42	78
Blakenall	38	23	8	7	78	45	77
Paget Rangers	38	21	5	12	79	43	68
Knypersley Victoria	38	19	8	11	75	60	65
Rocester	38	20	4	14	83	63	64
Hinckley Athletic	38	18	7	13	77	58	61
Chasetown	38	18	6	14	51	57	60
Pelsall Villa	38	16	8	14	70	78	56
Willenhall Town	38	15	8	15	73	60	53
Wednesfield	38	13	11	14	65	63	50
Halesowen Harriers	38	15	5	18	63	66	50
Darlaston	38	12	12	14	61	74	48
Lye Town	38	10	10	18	43	67	40
Brierley Hill T.	38	11	5	22	56	83	38
Rushall Olympic	38	10	7	21	53	76	*34
Westfields	38	7	7	24	58	92	28
Cradley Town	38	4	10	24	42	104	22
West Bromwich T.	38	3	3	32	37	123	12

* - 3 points deducted
Alvechurch Sports withdrew - record expunged

DIV. ONE	P	W	D	L	F	A	PTS
Stafford Town	40	32	2	6	109	52	98
Gornal Athletic	40	30	4	6	92	35	94
Tividale	40	26	5	9	96	48	83
Ludlow Town	40	21	7	12	70	39	70
Walsall Wood	40	19	10	11	71	40	67
Bloxwich Strollers	40	20	3	17	101	68	63
Wolves United	40	18	8	14	89	70	62
Tipton Town	40	19	5	16	68	67	62
Malvern Town	40	18	8	14	73	74	62
Ettingshall HT	40	16	10	14	70	71	58
Wolves Casuals	40	17	5	18	73	63	56
Hill Top Rangers	40	14	11	15	66	72	53
Lichfield	40	14	12	14	66	60	*50
Great Wyrley	40	13	9	18	63	85	48
Cannock Chase	40	12	11	17	60	84	47
Donnington Wood	40	11	10	19	50	54	43
Manders	40	11	10	19	54	70	43
Bilston United	40	11	10	19	54	91	43
Moxley Rangers	40	8	5	27	47	81	29
Wem Town	40	8	5	27	46	116	29
Cheslyn Hay	40	5	4	31	32	110	19

* - 4 points deducted

RESERVE DIV.	P	W	D	L	F	A	PTS
Rushall O. Res.	24	22	1	1	75	20	67
Rocester Res.	24	16	5	3	73	31	53
Lye Town Res.	24	13	3	8	59	44	42
Hinckley Ath. Res.	24	10	7	7	50	33	37
Pelsall Villa Res.	24	9	6	9	50	47	33
Wolves Casuals Res.	24	9	6	9	41	47	33
Oldbury Utd Res.	24	10	3	11	42	49	33
Chasetown Res.	24	10	3	11	47	41	*30
Halesowen H. Res.	24	7	8	9	43	53	29
Walsall Wood Res.	24	8	1	15	33	52	25
Tividale Res.	24	6	5	13	33	47	23
Cradley Town Res.	24	4	8	12	28	47	20
Moxley Rgrs Res.	24	2	4	18	15	78	10

* - 3 points deducted

YOUTH DIV.	P	W	D	L	F	A	PTS
Birmingham C. Yth	26	23	2	1	95	16	71
Hereford Utd Yth	26	21	1	4	118	41	64
Hinckley Town Yth	26	18	4	4	66	23	58
Lye Town Yth	26	15	4	7	56	35	49
Oldbury Utd Yth	26	12	3	11	48	54	39
Hinckley Ath. Yth	26	10	4	12	61	67	34
Blakenall Yth	26	11	1	14	51	63	34
Redditch U. Yth	26	10	3	13	44	56	33
Boldmere SM Yth	26	9	4	13	58	69	31
Pelsall Villa Yth	26	9	3	14	57	72	30
Wednesfield Yth	26	7	7	12	39	56	28
Brierley HT Yth	26	5	5	16	39	69	20
Chasetown Yth	26	5	5	16	41	81	20
Darlaston Yth	26	4	0	22	31	102	12

WEST MIDLANDS LEAGUE PREMIER DIVISION RESULT CHART 1993-94

HOME TEAM	1	2	3	4	5	6	7	8	9	10	11	12	13	14	15	16	17	18	19	20	21
1. Alvechurch Sports	*	3-1	2-0	*	1-1	*	*	*	*	*	2-2	*	*	*	*	3-0	*	5-0	*	0-2	*
2. Blakenall	*	*	3-0	3-1	1-0	1-0	3-1	3-0	2-3	2-2	1-0	0-0	1-3	2-0	3-2	0-0	3-1	1-3	2-1	2-0	1-1
3. Brierley Hill Town	*	0-2	*	1-2	1-2	4-3	1-3	1-1	0-2	5-0	0-0	0-3	0-0	1-2	0-3	2-0	0-4	0-0	4-0	1-3	0-0
4. Chasetown	*	2-5	2-4	*	4-1	0-0	1-0	2-2	1-2	1-0	1-3	3-4	1-0	3-1	0-0	2-0	0-2	0-0	4-0	1-0	1-0
5. Cradley Town	*	1-5	0-5	1-2	*	0-0	2-2	0-2	0-3	0-3	0-0	0-2	1-3	2-3	2-3	2-1	0-3	0-2	2-1	1-8	3-3
6. Darlaston	3-1	0-4	0-2	3-1	1-1	*	1-0	2-1	3-3	1-3	3-2	2-2	1-1	3-1	0-3	2-3	1-4	2-5	8-1	3-2	1-3
7. Halesowen H.	1-3	1-5	4-0	2-0	2-1	1-2	*	0-1	3-0	0-2	2-1	4-2	1-1	3-3	1-4	2-2	1-3	2-4	3-2	2-0	2-2
8. Hinckley Athletic	1-0	3-3	6-2	1-0	3-0	2-2	3-0	*	3-2	4-1	1-0	1-2	3-0	0-2	1-1	1-2	1-1	1-2	6-1	4-2	3-2
9. Ilkeston Town	2-0	3-1	8-0	0-1	8-0	3-1	2-4	2-0	*	1-1	2-0	0-1	2-1	4-1	5-0	2-0	1-0	3-1	6-0	3-3	2-1
10. Knypersley Vic.	*	1-0	4-0	1-0	1-1	5-1	1-0	4-1	2-1	*	5-4	3-1	1-5	2-2	0-1	2-1	2-2	0-2	4-2	6-1	2-3
11. Lye Town	*	1-1	0-5	1-1	0-0	2-2	3-2	3-1	2-2	2-0	*	1-1	0-3	0-2	2-1	0-2	2-3	0-0	3-1	0-1	1-6
12. Oldbury United	*	2-3	5-0	7-1	2-0	1-1	1-3	3-1	2-3	0-0	3-0	*	3-2	3-0	3-2	3-0	0-1	4-1	3-2	1-0	1-1
13. Paget Rangers	*	1-2	3-2	1-2	3-2	4-0	2-0	0-1	0-1	4-1	1-0	0-0	*	2-1	1-3	3-1	1-2	3-0	6-0	3-0	1-0
14. Pelsall Villa	0-1	2-4	3-4	3-0	4-3	0-1	1-0	1-3	1-1	3-1	4-2	1-1	1-1	*	1-3	2-1	1-7	4-3	2-1	4-2	0-3
15. Rocester	*	2-1	4-1	0-2	8-1	0-2	0-3	1-4	0-2	1-1	4-1	0-1	1-3	5-1	*	3-1	0-0	2-1	4-2	6-2	2-4
16. Rushall Olympic	*	2-3	2-1	0-1	3-1	2-3	3-1	1-7	0-4	2-3	0-2	1-2	2-4	1-1	0-3	*	1-1	0-1	2-1	3-2	4-4
17. Stourport Swifts	*	3-0	1-0	5-0	0-1	3-0	2-0	1-0	3-3	0-1	1-1	0-1	4-2	2-2	2-0	3-2	*	2-0	1-2	2-0	4-3
18. Wednesfield	*	1-1	1-3	1-1	4-4	1-1	0-1	3-0	1-5	1-3	1-2	2-2	0-4	2-2	3-0	1-1	1-2	*	4-1	4-0	2-0
19. West Bromwich T.	*	1-1	1-4	2-3	3-2	1-1	2-4	1-2	0-5	1-5	0-1	0-6	0-2	0-3	3-5	0-5	0-3	0-2	*	3-1	0-2
20. Westfields	1-2	1-2	5-2	0-1	2-2	1-1	3-1	4-2	1-2	1-1	0-1	1-4	1-4	2-3	2-4	1-1	4-3	2-2	0-0	*	0-2
21. Willenhall Town	*	0-1	1-0	1-3	3-3	1-3	0-2	1-1	3-1	3-1	4-0	2-3	2-1	0-2	1-2	0-1	0-2	4-3	2-1	5-0	*

NB. Alvechurch Sports withdrew. Record expunged and show above for interest only.

WEST MIDLANDS LEAGUE DIVISION ONE RESULT CHART 1993-94

HOME TEAM	1	2	3	4	5	6	7	8	9	10	11	12	13	14	15	16	17	18	19	20	21
1. Bilston United	*	0-7	2-1	4-0	0-1	3-3	1-3	3-4	2-5	1-1	0-0	1-3	1-1	2-0	2-1	1-0	0-3	0-1	5-3	2-1	1-0
2. Bloxwich Strollers	9-1	*	3-2	2-1	1-2	1-0	1-1	1-4	4-0	2-1	0-1	3-0	3-0	4-3	4-1	4-1	0-2	1-0	1-2	2-0	0-1
3. Cannock Chase	2-1	4-4	*	3-0	0-2	1-1	1-3	2-3	2-2	1-1	1-1	2-1	1-1	2-1	3-1	1-1	1-2	2-2	3-2	0-2	2-1
4. Cheslyn Hay	1-0	0-10	0-1	*	2-1	0-5	1-4	0-1	0-3	0-0	1-1	0-4	1-2	1-3	1-3	6-2	0-2	0-2	0-2	0-3	0-1
5. Donnington Wd	0-1	0-4	1-3	2-1	*	1-0	1-3	5-0	0-0	1-1	0-1	0-1	4-0	3-0	2-3	1-2	0-2	1-0	4-1	2-2	0-1
6. Ettingshall HT	1-1	3-2	2-2	3-0	3-2	*	2-0	2-0	1-2	2-1	2-4	1-1	1-0	2-1	1-3	1-2	0-4	0-4	3-1	1-1	4-6
7. Gornal Athletic	4-0	4-0	3-0	4-1	1-0	2-3	*	3-1	1-0	8-1	1-0	2-1	4-3	3-1	0-2	3-2	4-2	4-0	4-0	2-1	4-2
8. Great Wyrley	1-1	5-2	2-1	1-0	2-2	1-0	0-2	*	1-1	1-1	0-3	5-0	5-4	2-1	2-3	2-2	1-3	0-2	3-0	1-1	1-3
9. Hill Top Rangers	2-2	1-5	2-1	6-3	0-0	5-3	0-0	5-2	*	4-1	1-4	2-5	2-0	2-1	0-1	2-1	1-2	3-0	1-1	0-0	2-2
10. Lichfield	1-1	5-1	0-1	1-0	2-1	0-2	1-2	1-1	2-1	*	0-2	6-0	3-1	4-0	2-3	0-1	3-1	0-3	6-1	1-0	2-2
11. Ludlow Town	3-2	0-2	2-0	1-0	2-2	1-2	0-0	3-1	0-1	1-1	*	3-4	5-1	1-0	0-2	1-0	0-2	4-1	4-1	0-1	5-0
12. Malvern Town	2-1	3-1	4-2	1-1	1-0	3-3	0-1	5-0	2-1	2-0	2-1	*	1-1	3-1	2-3	0-5	2-0	1-1	0-3	2-5	6-3
13. Manders	2-0	1-2	5-2	1-3	1-1	0-1	0-1	1-2	0-0	1-1	1-1	2-2	*	1-0	3-1	4-1	2-6	0-0	6-0	2-1	1-2
14. Moxley Rangers	1-2	3-2	4-1	2-0	1-3	1-2	1-3	1-1	5-1	1-4	0-2	1-1	3-0	*	2-4	0-3	2-1	1-3	2-0	0-0	1-2
15. Stafford Town	8-0	5-1	1-1	4-2	2-1	5-1	2-2	4-1	3-2	0-2	2-1	2-1	0-2	3-1	*	3-1	5-2	2-1	4-0	5-1	2-1
16. Tipton Town	3-3	1-0	3-5	2-1	1-1	3-2	1-1	1-0	0-1	2-2	1-0	3-0	2-0	2-0	2-3	*	0-3	2-1	4-1	2-3	2-1
17. Tividale	1-0	3-2	9-0	4-0	0-0	0-0	1-0	4-3	1-0	4-0	1-6	4-0	2-0	0-0	1-2	2-3	*	0-2	5-3	2-1	1-1
18. Walsall Wood	0-0	4-1	1-1	5-2	2-0	2-2	1-0	5-1	2-0	1-2	0-2	0-0	0-0	5-0	1-2	2-1	0-0	*	4-1	4-0	4-1
19. Wem Town	1-2	0-7	2-1	1-1	2-0	0-2	0-2	1-1	3-3	2-1	0-1	2-1	0-2	1-0	0-4	1-2	2-9	1-1	*	2-3	1-2
20. Wolves Casuals	4-2	1-0	6-0	1-2	4-2	3-1	1-3	3-1	6-0	1-4	2-1	0-2	0-1	4-1	0-4	3-0	0-2	0-3	8-1	*	1-2
21. Wolves United	7-3	2-2	0-1	6-0	1-1	2-2	0-1	3-0	4-2	1-1	1-2	2-4	5-1	2-2	1-2	3-1	2-3	2-1	4-1	1-0	*

WEST MIDLANDS LEAGUE RESERVE DIVISION RESULT CHART 1993-94

HOME TEAM	1	2	3	4	5	6	7	8	9	10	11	12	13
1. Chasetown Res.	*	4-1	0-4	1-1	4-2	4-1	8-1	4-3	0-1	1-3	2-1	0-2	0-2
2. Cradley Town Res.	0-3	*	2-2	0-2	2-2	0-1	3-4	1-2	2-1	1-4	1-1	1-0	0-3
3. Halesowen Harr. Res.	3-1	4-1	*	2-2	0-2	3-0	2-1	4-2	2-2	1-2	2-0	2-3	2-2
4. Hinckley Ath. Res.	1-1	0-0	9-0	*	3-2	1-0	1-3	6-0	2-2	1-3	1-2	7-0	2-0
5. Lye Town Res.	1-5	2-1	2-2	5-1	*	5-1	2-1	2-0	1-3	1-3	1-2	7-3	5-3
6. Moxley Rgrs Res.	0-4	0-0	2-1	0-1	0-2	*	0-3	3-6	0-3	0-6	2-2	1-4	0-2
7. Oldbury United Res.	2-0	0-2	0-0	4-2	1-1	5-0	*	0-2	2-6	1-3	2-1	4-2	3-2
8. Pelsall Villa Res.	0-2	1-1	3-3	1-1	1-2	6-0	2-1	*	2-2	1-1	6-2	2-0	0-0
9. Rocester Res.	3-1	2-0	2-2	4-2	3-1	7-0	4-0	6-2	*	1-2	2-2	4-1	5-3
10. Rushall Olympic Res.	3-0	3-1	6-1	1-0	3-1	6-1	3-0	4-1	2-1	*	4-1	2-1	4-2
11. Tividale Res.	2-1	1-1	6-1	0-1	1-3	0-0	0-3	1-2	1-3	0-2	*	1-0	5-2
12. Walsall Wood Res.	3-0	1-1	2-0	1-2	0-2	0-2	2-0	1-0	0-3	0-4	4-1	*	1-3
13. Wolves Casuals Res.	1-1	4-0	1-0	1-1	1-5	1-1	1-1	0-5	1-3	2-1	1-0	3-2	*

WEST MIDLANDS LEAGUE YOUTH DIVISION RESULT CHART 1993-94

HOME TEAM	1	2	3	4	5	6	7	8	9	10	11	12	13	14
1. Birmingham City Yth	*	1-0	5-0	3-0	2-0	3-1	6-0	3-1	8-0	2-1	3-0	5-0	3-0	3-2
2. Blakenall Yth	0-6	*	3-2	2-0	5-1	4-0	2-4	2-4	0-1	0-2	0-1	6-0	4-3	0-2
3. Boldmere St Mich. Yth	3-3	4-2	*	5-5	5-1	1-3	2-3	4-0	0-2	3-2	4-0	2-4	3-3	0-4
4. Brierley Hill T. Yth	0-3	2-3	1-2	*	2-2	3-2	0-2	3-0	0-4	1-1	1-2	3-3	2-1	1-2
5. Chasetown Yth	0-1	0-2	2-1	4-3	*	4-0	0-6	2-2	1-3	1-5	1-1	2-3	0-2	0-3
6. Datlaston Yth	0-5	2-4	1-3	1-2	1-3	*	2-11	0-2	0-1	1-6	2-4	5-3	1-2	1-0
7. Hereford United Yth	2-1	8-1	6-2	4-1	13-2	12-0	*	5-0	2-1	3-1	2-3	5-4	5-1	9-1
8. Hinckley Ath. Yth	1-5	7-1	3-3	5-1	3-3	3-1	0-1	*	0-3	2-3	5-1	1-5	4-2	3-3
9. Hinckley Town Yth	1-1	2-1	4-1	4-0	3-0	8-0	2-2	5-0	*	1-2	3-0	4-1	3-0	1-3
10. Lye Town Yth	1-3	3-1	3-1	3-1	3-2	3-0	0-3	5-1	0-0	*	2-1	2-1	0-2	1-1
11. Oldbury Utd Yth	0-4	3-1	1-0	5-1	4-2	2-5	2-3	3-5	0-1	4-1	*	2-0	2-1	1-2
12. Pelsall Villa Yth	1-5	3-4	5-1	4-2	3-2	6-1	4-2	2-5	0-5	0-0	0-1	*	1-3	2-1
13. Redditch Utd Yth	2-4	1-1	2-4	2-4	1-2	4-0	2-1	1-0	1-4	0-4	2-2	2-1	*	3-1
14. Wednesfiels Yth	0-7	1-2	1-2	0-0	4-4	3-1	1-4	0-4	0-0	0-2	3-3	1-1	0-1	*

PREMIER DIVISION CUP 1993-94

First Round

Cradley Town v Pelsall Villa	2-1	Blakenall v Rushall Olympic	3-2
Willenhall v Alvechurch Sports	4-3	Knypersley Victoria v Chasetown	1-3
Rocester v Stourport Swifts	3-0		

Second Round

Cradley Town v Blakenall	0-1	West Bromwich Town v Ilkeston Town	1-5
Darlaston v Lye Town	1-2	Westfields v Brierley Hill Town	2-0
Oldbury United v Willenhall Town	2-3	Wednesfield v Chasetown	3-2
Halesowen Harriers v Paget Rangers	2-6	Hinckley Athletic v Rocester	1-1,3-1

Quarter Finals

Blakenall v Ilkeston Town	2-4	Westfields v Lye Town	0-3
Wednesfield v Willenhall Town	1-2	Paget Rangers v Hinckley Athletic	1-1,2-0

Semi-Finals (Two-legged)

Ilkeston Town v Lye Town	3-2,2-2	Paget Rangers v Willenhall Town	3-2,4-2

Final: Ilkeston Town 2, Paget Rangers 0

DIVISION ONE CUP 1993-94

First Round

Wolverhampton Casuals v Hill Top Rangers	2-0	Lichfield v Cannock Chase	2-1
Bloxwich Strollers v Tividale	2-1	Tipton Town v Cheslyn Hay	8-0
Walsall Wood v Gornal Athletic	3-0		

Second Round

Wolverhampton Casuals v Lichfield	1-2	Malvern Town v Ludlow Town	0-0,1-4
Stafford Town v Moxley Rangers	5-0	Ettingshall Holy Trinity v Bloxwich Strollers	1-2
Manders v Tipton Town	0-2	Walsall Wood v Great Wyrley	3-1
Donnington Wood v Wem Town	4-1	Wolverhampton United v Bilston United	3-1

Quarter Finals

Ludlow Town v Lichfield	1-1,0-1	Stafford Town v Bloxwich Strollers	5-2
Walsall Wood v Tipton Town	1-0	Donnington Wood v Wolverhampton United	1-2

Semi-Finals (Two-legged)

Lichfield v Stafford Town	2-0,2-3	Wolverhampton Utd v Walsall Wd	2-1,3-4*(aet)*,3-2*(aet)*

Final: Wolverhampton United 3, Lichfield 0

RESERVE DIVISION CUP 1993-94

GROUP A.	P	W	D	L	F	A	PTS
Rushall Olympic	12	8	2	2	29	10	26
Hinckley Athletic	12	7	2	3	30	14	23
Chasetown	12	6	3	3	23	21	21
Wolves Casuals	12	5	3	4	23	24	18
Rocester	12	5	1	6	22	19	16
Pelsall Villa	12	4	3	5	18	23	15
Walsall Wood	12	0	0	12	8	42	0

RESULTS	1	2	3	4	5	6	7
1. Chasetown	*	2-1	1-1	2-1	0-7	3-0	1-0
2. Hinckley A.	3-1	*	1-0	3-1	1-1	4-0	5-2
3. Pelsall V.	4-2	1-2	*	3-0	1-4	4-1	0-4
4. Rocester	1-1	2-0	5-0	*	1-2	2-1	2-3
5. Rushall O.	0-2	2-1	0-0	2-0	*	3-1	1-2
6. Walsall Wd	1-6	0-7	2-3	1-2	0-3	*	0-1
7. Wolves Cas.	2-2	2-2	1-1	1-5	1-4	4-1	*

GROUP B.	P	W	D	L	F	A	PTS
Lye Town	10	6	3	1	29	16	21
Tividale	10	5	2	3	24	19	17
Halesowen Harriers	10	4	3	3	29	24	15
Oldbury United	10	4	2	4	18	21	14
Cradley Town	10	3	2	5	17	24	11
Moxley Rangers	10	2	0	8	17	30	6

RESULTS	1	2	3	4	5	6
1. Cradley T.	*	3-3	1-3	4-1	0-2	0-3
2. H'owen Harr.	5-1	*	1-2	2-1	2-5	5-2
3. Lye Town	2-2	2-2	*	4-1	1-2	5-2
4. Moxley R.	2-3	3-5	2-4	*	3-1	3-1
5. Oldbury	1-2	2-2	1-4	3-1	*	1-1
6. Tividale	2-1	3-2	2-2	3-0	5-0	*

SF: Hinckley Athletic Res. 1, Lye Town Res. 0

SF: Rushall Olympic Res. 0, Tividale Res. 1

Final: Hinckley Athletic Reserves 2, Tividale Reserves 0

YOUTH DIVISION CUP 1993-94

First Round

Lye Town Yth v Blakenall Yth	0-1	Pelsall Villa Yth v Brierley Hill Town Yth	5-1
Redditch Utd Yth v Birmingham City Yth	0-5	Hinckley Athletic Yth v Chasetown Yth	5-3
Hereford Utd Yth v Hinckley Town Yth	2-1	Boldmere St Michaels Yth v Oldbury Utd Yth	2-2,1-3
Darlaston Yth	bye	Wednesfield Yth	bye

Quarter Finals

Blakenall Yth v Wednesfield Yth	2-1	Hinckley Athletic Yth v Pelsall Villa Yth	0-0,3-4
Birmingham City Yth v Oldbury Utd Yth	1-1,6-1	Hereford United Yth v Darlaston Yth	11-1

Semi-Finals (Two-legged)

Blakenall Yth v Pelsall Villa Yth	1-3,1-3	Birmingham City Yth v Hereford United Yth	4-2,1-1

Final: Birmingham City Youth 6, Pelsall Villa Youth 0

PREMIER DIVISION CLUBS 1994-95

BLAKENALL

President: J Bridgett **Chairman:** P Langston **Vice-Chairman:** D Cotterill
Secretary: David Birch, 64 Wimperis Way, Great Barr, Birmingham B43 7DF (021 360 3574).
Manager: Bob Green **Asst Manager:** Graham Callaghan **Coach:** Brian Taylor
Commercial Mgr: Jeff Husted **Press Officer:** Russell Brown (0902 787853).
Ground: Red Lion Ground, Somerfield Rd, Bloxwich, Walsall, West Mids (0922 405835).
Directions: M6 jct 10, follow signs for Walsall centre. At 1st lights turn left (about 200yds from Motorway junction) into Bloxwich Lane. Keep following this lane to the 'T' junction and turn right into Leamore Lane, at this island turn left into Somerfield Road. Ground is approx. 400yds on the right.
Seats: 250 **Cover:** 250 **Capacity:** 2,500 **Floodlights:** Yes **Founded:** 1946.
Colours: Blue & white stripes/blue/blue **Change colours:** All red **Nickname:** Lions.
Clubhouse: Yes **Midweek home matchday:** Tuesday.
Programme: 52 pages **Programme Editor:** Russell Brown (0902 787853).
Previous Leagues: Bloxwich Comb./ Staffs County/ Midland Comb. 60-79.
Record transfer fee received: £10,000 for Darren Simkin (Wolverhampton Wanderers, 1992).
Captain 93-94: Mark Wakefield **Top Scorer 93-94:** Mark Tolley, 17
Hons: West Midlands (Regional) Lg 88-89, Midland Comb. 76-77, Walsall Snr Cup (6)

BILSTON UNITED

Secretary: Stephen Parsonage, 16 Stanton Avenue, Woodsetton, Dudley, West Mids DY1 3RR (0902 676598).
Ground: Rooker Avenue, Parkfields, Bilston, West Midlands.
Directions: Follow New Birmingham Road (A4123) towards Wolverhampton. After crossing A4039 fork right into Dixon Street, Rooker Avenue is 5th right.
Capacity: **Seats:** None **Cover:** Yes **Floodlights:** Yes **Founded:** 1979.
Colours: All red **Change colours:** White/black/black
Previous Name: Gornal Sports 1979-1994.
Previous Ground: Gornal Athletic FC (pre-1994).
Hons: W Mids Lg Div 2 R-up 91-92.

BLOXWICH STROLLERS

Secretary: George A Llewellyn, 7 Birchover Road, Walsall WS2 8TU (0922 614595).
Manager: Leigh Taylor **Assistant Manager:** Gavin Stanton.
Ground & Directions: As Blakenall FC (see above).
Colours: White/red/red **Change colours:** All yellow **Founded:** 1888.
Programme: Yes **Programme Editor:** Neil Morris.
Previous Leagues: Walsall/ Birmingham Combination 13-32/ West Mids 52-55/ Bloxwich Combination/ West Mids Metropolitan/ Staffs Co. (Sth)/ Midland Combination (pre-1988).
Previous Grounds: The Red Lion (originally)/ T P Riley Community Centre, Lichfield Rd (pre'87).
Previous Name: Little Bloxwich Strollers **Top Scorers 93-94:** Ricky Watson & Jason Marsden.
Hons: Birmingham Comb. 24-25 (R-up 22-23), West Mids Lg Div 2 R-up 92-93 (Div 2 Cup R-up 92-93), Staffs Co. Lg Sth, Edge Cup, Lg Shield 84-85, Walsall Challenge Cup 92-93, Walsall Charity Cup, Staffs Jnr Cup, Walsall Lg.

Below: *Bloxwich Strollers FC. Back Row (L/R): Leigh Taylor (Manager), Gavin Stanton (Assistant Manager), Jason Marsden, Wayne Edwards, Ricky Watson, Mark Bentley, Phil Hollingworth, Craig Sorrill, Scott Piper, Colin Smith. Front: Roy Holden, Bryan Brown, Pat Hall, Darrol Sherwood, Mary Perry, Neil Gould.*

CRADLEY TOWN

Chairman: Roger Holden **Vice Chairman:** R Kurtain **President:** W Forrest
Secretary: T Hetheridge, c/o Cradley Town FC
Manager: Steve Daniels **Asst Manager:** T Hetheridge **Coach:** W Mole.
Physio: S Ward **Comm. Manager:** A Jones **Press Off.:** A Hills (0384 69585)
Ground: Beeches View, Beeches View Avenue, Cradley, Halesowen, Cradley Heath (0384 69904).
Directions: M5 jct 3, take A456, right at 2nd island, left into Rosemary Rd after Fox Hunt pub, Landsdown Rd, Dunstall Rd, left at T-junction, left again at next T-junction (Beeches Rd East), 1st left (Abbey Rd), right at end, ground 50yds on left. Nearest BR station is Cradley Heath.
Seats: 200 **Cover:** 1,500 **Capacity:** 3,000 **Floodlights:** Yes **Founded:** 1944.
Colours: Red & black **Change colours:** Yellow & green **Nickname:** Lukes
Previous Name: Albion Haden United **Previous Grounds:** None.
Previous Leagues: Metropolitan/ Brierley Hill/ Kidderminster/ West Mids Amtr/ Midland Comb. 71-82.
Programme: 20 pages, 50p **Programme Editor:** Paper Plane **Club Shop:** No.
Club Sponsors: TBA **Record Gate:** 1,000 v Aston Villa, friendly.
Midweek home matchday: Tuesday **Reserve team's League:** West Mids Lge Division Two.
Record win: 9-1 v Wolverhampton United (H), West Midlands League 1990.
Record defeat: 0-8 v Ilkeston Town (A), 1993.
Record transfer fee paid: £1,000 for Darren Marsh (Oldswinford, 1992).
Received: £20,000 for John Williams (Portsmouth, 1991).
Players progressing to Football Lge: Alan Nicholls (Plymouth (via Cheltenham)), John Williams, Jon Ford, Andy McFarlane (all Swansea), Duane Darby (Torquay).
Club record scorer: Jim Nuggent **Clubhouse:** Open all day every day. Food available.
Captain 93-94: John Street **Club record apearances:** R J Hayward.
Top Scorer 93-94: C Marriott **P.o.Y. 93-94:** Mark Blake.
Hons: West Mids Lg Div 1 90-91, Midland Comb. Div 2 72-73 (R-up 75-76 77-78, Presidents Cup 74-75 75-76, Invitation 72-73), Metropolitan Lg 70-71, Wednesbury Charity Cup 90-91, Dudley Guest Hosp. Cup 71-72 72-73 75-76 90-91.

DARLASTON

Chairman: Alan Schofield **Vice-Chairman:** Tom Reaney.
Secretary: Andrew Hickman, 31 Willenhall Street, Darlaston WS10 8NE (021 568 7514).
Manager: Jimmy McMorran. **Assistant Manager:** Colin Johnson.
Press Officer: Neil Chambers **Commercial Manager:** Craig Davies.
Ground: City Ground, Waverley Rd, Darlaston (021 526 4423).
Directions: M6 Jct 10, onto A454 towards Willenhall, left at lights outside 'Lane Arms' into Bentley Rd North, follow down hill and over rail and canal bridges to traffic lights. Cross over the lights into Richards Street and along into Victoria Rd, 1st right into Slater Street and ground on left but entrance is next left in Waverley Rd.
Seats: Yes **Cover:** Yes **Capacity:** **Floodlights:** Yes. **Founded:** 1874
Colours: Blue & white stripes/blue/blue **Change colours:** All yellow **Nickname:** Blues.
Prev. Lges: Junior leagues (inc Wednesbury League) pre-1908/ B'gham Comb. 08-11 28-54/ W Mids 11-28.
Midweek home matches: Tuesday **Club Sponsors:** Metafin Holdings
Club Shop: Might open for season 1994-95
Reserves' Lge: West Mids Div 1 **Clubhouse:** On ground, open matchdays. Hot/cold drinks/snacks.
Programme: Yes **Programme Editor:** Dave Stevenson (021 526 2465).
Players progressing to Football League: Jack Burkett (Nottingham Forest), Andy McFarlane (Swansea City).
Captain 93-94: Nigel Hopkins **Top Scorer 93-94:** Simon Archer **P.o.Y. 93-94:** Iqbal Patel
Hons: West Mids Lg Div 1 89-90 (R-up 91-92 92-93, Div 1 Cup Cup 89-90), Birmingham Snr Cup 72-73, Birmingham Vase 90-91 91-92, Birmingham Jnr Lg 07-08, Birmingham Comb. 10-11 37-38 45-46 (Tillotson Cup 36-37 37-38 38-39 45-46), Keys Cup 11-12), Wednesbury Lg(5) 1896-1901.

ETTINGSHALL HOLY TRINITY

Chairman: TBA **Vice-Chairman:** David Caddick **President:** David Gadd.
Secretary: Graham Mills, 27 Ashen Close, Sedgley, Dudley, West Mids DY3 3UZ (0902 662222).
Manager: Joe Owen **Asst Manager:** Dave Downing. **Coach:** Graham Mills.
Ground: As Willenhall Town FC (see page 578). **Founded:** 1920.
Colours: Green/white **Change colours:** Yellow/blue **Nickname:** Trins.
Previous League: Wednesbury Church & Chapel (early 1900s)/ Bilston Youth (1950s)/ Wolverhampton & District Amateur (1960s)/ Staffs County (South).
Previous Grounds: Compton Park (4 years)/ Bilston Town FC 89-92/ Aldersley Stadium 92-94.
Programme: Yes **Programme Editor:** Geoff Little (0902 883121).
Midweek home matchday: Wednesday **Club Sponsors:** Direct Batteries/ DKB Electric.
Record win: 13-0 v Chubbs Sports, Hunt Cup.
Captain 93-94: Mark Walker **Top Scorer 93-94:** Gary Chalk.
Hons: West Mids Lg Div 1 Cup R-up 85-86 (Div 2 R-up 84-85, Sporting Award 85-86), Staffs Co. Lg R-up 82-83 (Lg Shield 82-83 83-84, Ike Cooper Cup 82-84 83-84, Sporting Club Award 81-82), Wolverhampton & District Amateur Lg 80-81 (Div 1 65-66, Div 2 64-65, Div 1/2 Cup 64-65 65-66, A H Oakley Cup 80-81), J W Hunt Cup 82-83 83-84 (R-up 79-80), Wolverhampton Cup 83-84 (R-up 82-83).

GORNAL ATHLETIC

Chairman: Ken Taylor
Secretary: Paul Westwood, 18 The Close, Lower Gornal, Dudley DY3 2JY (0902 664209).
Manager: John Gwinnell **Coach:** Ian Clark/ Ross Hill.
Reserves' Manager: Ian Davies **Commercial Manager:** Martin Wedgebury.
Ground: Garden Walk Stadium, Lower Gornal, Dudley, West Midlands (0384 252285).
Directions: From Dudley take A459 to Sedgley past the Burton Rd Hospital. 1st on left at the Green Dragon public house on the B4175 (Jews Lane). Follow the road until you come to the Old Bull's Head, turn left into Rednall Road, 2nd left to Garden Walk.
Seats: 100 **Cover:** 500 **Capacity:** 3,000 **Floodlights:** Yes **Founded:** 1945.
Colours: Yellow/green/yellow **Change colours:** All sky **Club Shop:** No.
Previous Name: Lower Gornal Ath. **Previous Lge:** Midland Comb. 51-63 **Nickname:** Peacocks
Sponsors: Jasper Steels **Reserve Team's League:** West Mids (Regional) Lge Res. Div.
Record transfer fees received: £1,500 for Gary Bell and for George Andrews both to Cardiff City, 1965.
Captain 93-94: Ross Hill **P.o.Y. 93-94:** David Brookes **Top Scorer 93-94:** Dean Cadman.
Hons: West Mids Lg Div 1 R-up 83-84 (Div 1 Cup 92-93), Birmingham Vase 91-92.

HILL TOP RANGERS

Chairman: Mr J Scott **Sec.:** Mr Paul Allen, 14 Queen Street, Wednesbury, West Midlands WS10 7PT.
Manager: Paul Allen **Asst Manager:** Dave Scott **Coach:** Karl Freeth.
Physio: J Scott **Press Officer:** Mrs S Allen.
Ground: Darlaston FC (see page 584). **Founded:** 1980.
Colours: Yellow/black/yellow **Change Colours:** Red/navy/red **Club Shop:** No.
Previous Grounds: The Jesson 1980/ Hydes Rd 81-84/ Red House Park 84-87/ Darlaston FC 87-93/ Hadley Stadium, Sandwell 93-94.
Previous Leagues: West Bromwich & Dist. 80-84/ West Mids Metropolitan 84-86/ Mercian FA 86-88.
Programme: With entry, or 50p **Programme Editor:** Secretary
Midweek home matchday: Tuesday **Record Gate:** 165 v Darlaston, W Mids Lg Div 1 12/4/94.
Record win: 15-0 v Ham Baker 7/1/84 (Cup) & v Minworth 18/10/86 (League).
Record defeat: 1-9 v West Bromwich Athletic 28/11/81 (Cup match, West Brom a Div higher).
Players progressing to Football League: Andy Pearce (Coventry City, Sheffield Wednesday via Stourbridge and Halesowen Town).
Clubhouse: Inside ground. Hot food from Sportsmans Bar. Snacks (crisps, chocolate) and hot and cold drinks available from tea bar at top of ground.
Top Scorer 93-94: Stuart Clark **Captain & P.o.Y. 93-94:** Paul Rushton.
Club record scorer: Dean Cadman 175 **Club record appearances:** Dave Scott 399.
Hons: West Midlands (Regional) Lg Div 2 89-90, West Midlands Metropolitan Lg R-up 85-86, Mercian FA 86-87, West Bromwich District Charity Cup.

LUDLOW TOWN

Chairman: A Cade **Sec.:** Miss K Evans, Riddings Park, Riddings Road, Ludlow, Shropshire SY8 1HZ.
Manager: Graham Swinbourne **Asst Manager:** Bob Bodenham **Coach:** John Roe.
Ground: The Riddings, Riddings Road, Ludlow, Shropshire (0584 875103).
Directions: From Kidderminster road A4117; straight over r'bout into Henley Rd, 2nd left into Sandpits Rd, follow road for a quarter mile until road bears round to the left into Ridding Road - ground immediately on right.
Seats: No **Cover:** 150 **Floodlights:** Yes **Clubhouse:** Yes **Programme:** No
Cols: Red (white pin stripes)/black/black (red tops) **Change colours:** Royal blue/white/royal
Previous League: Kidderminster.
Hons: Wes Mids Lg Div 1 Cup 90-91, Shropshire County Challenge Cup 93-94, Presteigne-Otway Cup 90-91.

LYE TOWN

Chairman: Geoff Ball **President:** Geoff Ball **Manager:** Ian Cole
Secretary: Mrs Audrey Ball, 79 Aretha Close, Crestwood Park, Kingswinford, West Mids DY6 8SW (0384 839216).
Asst Manager: Dave Beasley **Coach:** Alan Moore **Physio:** Harry Hill.
Ground: Stourbridge Road, Lye (0384 422672).
Directions: On A458 Birmingham-Stourbridge road about 400yds after lights/crossroads at Lye. From M5 jct 3 take road marked Kidderminster as far as lights at bottom of Hagley Hill, right at island, 3rd turn off at next island, 3rd turn off at crossroads/lights, left, ground about 400yds on left. Quarter mile from Lye (BR).
Seats: 100 **Cover:** 600 **Capacity:** 5,000 **Floodlights:** Yes **Founded:** 1930.
Colours: White/red/red **Change Colours:** All sky **Nickname:** Flyers.
Programme: 24 pages, 40p **Programme Editor:** Dave Liley
Clubhouse: Yes (0384 822672). **Previous Leagues:** Midland Combination 31-39.
Record Gate: 6,000 v Brierley Alliance. **Hons:** West Mids Lg R-up 76-77 78-79 79-80 80-81 (Prem. Div Cup 75-76), Midland Comb. 35-36 (R-up 32-33 34-35 37-38), B'ham Snr Cup R-up 80-81.

MALVERN TOWN

Chairman: R C Tandy **President:** R H Mann **Manager:** Martyn Day
Secretary: G F Knapper, 27 Alexandra Lane, Malvern, Worcs WR14 1JF (0684 574861).
Ground: Langland Stadium, Langland Avenue, Malvern, Worcs (0684 574068).
Directions: From Worcester take main road to Malvern. When reaching Malvern turn left at 1st lights into Pickersleigh Ave., follow to Langland Arms Pub on left, left into Madresfield Rd, 2nd left into Langland Ave., ground 100yds on right. 1 mile from Malvern (BR).
Seats: 140 **Cover:** 310 **Capacity:** 4,000 **Floodlights:** Yes **Founded:** 1947.
Colours: Claret & blue/white/sky **Change colours:** White/black/claret.
Prog: 12 pages 20p (special matches) **Programme Editor:** Dave Liley
Clubhouse: 2 bars, large dance area **Previous League:** Midland Comb. 55-79.
Hons: Worcester/ Midland Comb. 55-56. **Record Gate:** 1,221 v Worcester, FA Cup

Below: *The stand at Malvern's Langland Stadium.* *Photo - Kerry Miller.*

MANDERS

Chairman: Colin Greatrix **Sec:** Barry Hall, 10 Miles Meadow Close, Willenhall WV12 5YE (0922 409017).
Manager: Tom Stokes **Asst Manager:** Martin Eccleston **Physio:** Eddie Edwards.
Ground & Directions: Wednesfield FC (see page 588) **Founded:** 1935.
Colours: White/red/red **Change colours:** Green/black/black **Reformed:** 1988.
Nickname: Paintmen. **Prev. Grnds:** Cannock Rd Spts Grnd/ Ashmore Park/ Wednesfield High Sch.
Prev. Lge: Wolverhampton Works **Clubhouse:** Normal licensing hrs (maybe shut Wed. evening).
Honours: West Mids Lg Div 2 Cup 92-93, JW Hunt Cup(3), Wolverhampton Charity Cup 76-77 79-80 83-84.

PELSALL VILLA

Chairman: C V Dolphin **Vice Chairman:** J H Gough **President:** B J Hill
Secretary: Gareth J Evans, 72 St Pauls Crescent, Pelsall, Walsall WS3 4ET (0922 693114).
Manager: Reg Priest **Asst Manager:** None **Coach:** M Rawlins
Press Officer: B J Hill **Commercial Manager:** C V Dolpin. **Physio:** R New
Ground: The Bush, Walsall Rd, Heath End, Pelsall, Walsall (0922 682018 or 692748 matchdays only).
Directions: M6 jct 7 marked A34 B'gham. Take A34 towards Walsall to 1st island, turn right (marked Ring Road), cross two islands. At large island at bottom of hill take last exit marked Lichfield, up hill, cross next island to lights. Continue to next set of lights and turn left (B4154 Pelsall). Go over railway bridge to Old Bush pub on right (next to Pelsall Cricket and Sports Club).
Seats: Yes **Cover:** 624 **Capacity:** 2,000 **Floodlights:** Yes **Reformed:** 1961.
Colours: Red & black/white or black/white or black
Change colours: Blue & white/black or white/black or white.
Programme: 52 pages, 50p **Programme Editor:** Secretary
Club Shop: Yes, selling scarves, ties, badges, rosettes, footballs, notebooks, pens, Pelsall Villa footballer and varied programmes. Contact M Miller (0922 684498).
Previous Grounds: None **Previous League:** Staffs County (South) 61-81.
Club Nickname: Villians **Record Gate:** 1,800 v Aston Villa 28/11/91.
Midweek home matchday: Monday **Reserve's League:** West Mids Reserve Division.
Record win: 7-0 v Westfields **Rec. defeat:** 1-7; v Gresley; v Stourport (H), WML 29/1/94.
Record transfer fee paid: £800 for Dean Walters (Blakenall, 1992).
Received: £2,000 for Phil Wood (Halesowen, 1993).
Best FA Cup season: 3rd Qualifying Rd 92-93 (lost 2-4 at Gainsborough Trinity).
Best FA Vase season: 5th Rd 92-93 (lost 0-1 at Buckingham Town).
Clubhouse: Mon-Fri 7.30-11pm, Sat noon-11pm, Sun noon-3 & 7.30-10.30pm. Hot & cold meals.
Captain 93-94: Kevin Gough **Top Scorer & P.O.Y. 93-94:** Dean Walters.
Club record scorer: Kevin Gough 182 **Club record appearances:** Kevin Gough 388.
Hons: West Mids Lg Div 1 Cup 88-89 (R-up 89-90, Div 2 Cup R-up 83-84, Youth Div Cup R-up 93-94), Walsall Snr Cup R-up 89-90 92-93, Wednesbury Charity Cup 67-68 68-69 69-70 73-74 88-89 89-90 (R-up 66-67 70-71 72-73 87-88 90-91 92-93 93-94), D Stanton Shield(2) 73-75 (R-up 75-76), Sporting Star Cup 76-77 (R-up 61-62), Staffs Co. (Sth) Lg R-up 68-69 (Div 1(res) 83-84, Prem Div Tphy(res)89-90), Rugeley Charity Cup 78-79 (R-up 69-70), Bloxwich Charity Cup(2) 81-83, Staffs Jnr Cup 68-69, Cannock Chase Charity Cup 63-64, Edge Cup 83-84, Ike Cooper Tphy R-up 89-90.

STAFFORD TOWN

President: T Logan **Chairman:** A Bowers.
Secretary: Mrs Debbie Curtis, 16 Canberra Drive, Stafford (0785 46554).
Manager: Chris Curtiss **Press Officer:** David Howard (0785 222686).
Ground: As Stafford Rangers FC (see page 202).
Programme: 28 pages, 50p **Editor:** David Howard (0785 222686) **Founded:** 1974
Colours: All red **Change colours:** All blue.
Nickname: Reds or Town **Previous Names:** Stafford Town 74-90/ Stafford MSHD 90-92.
Prev. Grnds: Silkmore Lane 74-77/ Burton Manor Spts Grnd 77-88/ Riverway 88-91/ Rowley Park Stadium 91-94.
Previous Leagues: Staffs County (North) 74-77 82-84/ Midland Combination 77-82/ Staffs Senior 84-93.
Midweek home matches: Mon/Wed **Club Shop:** No - just old programmes available.
Record win: 14-0 v Leek CSOB (H), Staffs Senior League 8/10/88.
Captain 93-94: Neale Kirkland **Top Scorer 93-94:** Steve Goodwin, 37.
Hons: WMRL Div 1 93-94, Staffs Snr Lg R-up 91-92, Midland Comb. Div 2 78-79, Staffs Vase 84-85 92-93 (R-up 87-88), Bourne Sports Trophy 84-85, Walsall Senior Cup SF 91-92.

STOURPORT SWIFTS

Chairman: Chris Reynolds **Vice Chairman:** Trevor Roberts **President:** Roy Crowe.
Secretary: John McDonald, 65 Princess Way, Stourport-on-Severn (0299 822088).
Coach: John Holmes. **Joint Managers:** Phil Mullen/ Pat Lynch
Physio: John Kane. **Commercial Manager:** Peter Longmore.
Press Officer: Dave Watts (0299 823349).
Ground: Walshes Meadow, off Harold Davis Drive, Stourport-on-Severn (0299 825188).
Directions: Follow one-way system through Stourport sign posted Sports Centre. Go over River Severn Bridge, turn left into Harold Davies Drive. Ground is at rear of Sports Centre. Nearest rail station is Kidderminster.
Seats: 320 **Cover:** 200 **Capacity:** 2,000 **Floodlights:** Yes **Founded:** 1882.
Colours: Black & gold/black/black **Change colours:** All Red **Nickname:** Swifts.
Previous Grounds: Bewdley Rd/ Moor Hall Park/ Feathers Farm/ Olive Grove/ Hawthorns.
Previous Leagues: Kidderminster/ Worcester/ Midland Combination.
Programme: 40 pages, 50p **Editor:** Dave Watts (0299 823349) **Club Shop:** No.
Club Sponsors: T. & J. Joinery **Record Gate:** 4,000 v Birmingham, charity match.
Midweek home matchday: Tuesday **Reserve team's League:** Kidderminster. **Record win:** 10-0
Clubhouse: Clubhouse open matchdays. Hot snacks available. Licensed bar. **Record defeat:** 1-7
Club record scorer: Norman Laker **Club record appearances:** Vaughan Little.
Captain 93-94: Nigel Laker **Top Scorer 93-94:** Simon Marsh **P.o.Y. 93-94:** Trevor Kerby
Hons: West Mids Lg Div 1 R-up 87-88 (Premier Div Cup 92-93, Div 2 Cup R-up 82-83), Worcs Snr Urn 92-93 93-94, Worcestershire Infirmary Cup 93-94.

PHOTOS OPPOSITE:
Top: *Tividale FC. Photo - Maurice Dunning.*
Centre: *Pelsall Villa on the defensive during last season's home fixture against Paget.*
Foot: *Westfields FC.*

TIVIDALE

Chairman: Don Ashton **President:** Lord Peter Archer.
Secretary: D Aston, 18 Hollies Rd, Tividale, Warley, West Mids B69 1SX (0384 239206).
Manager: Terry Jones **Asst Mgr:** Kevin Mullinder **Coach:** M Dunning/A James.
Physio: J Cotton/K Nicklin **Commercial Manager:** Terry Jones (0902 25800).
Press Officer: T Clark. **Newsline:** 0891 66 42 52.
Ground: The Beeches, Packwood Rd, Tividale, Warley, West Midlands B69 1UL (0384 211743).
Directions: Dudley Port Station to Burnt tree, left towards Birmingham, ground 1 mile on right. Or, M5 jct 2, follow Dudley signs A4123, after approx 2 miles turn left into Regent Rd and left again into Elm Terraces, first left into Birch Crescent. Packwood Rd is second left - ground at end of cul-de-sac.
Seats: 200 **Cover:** 1,000 **Capacity:** 3,500 **Floodlights:** Yes **Founded:** 1954
Colours: Yellow **Change colours:** Red **Nickname:** Dales
Prog.: 40 pages, £1.75 inc entry/raffle **Programme Editor:** Robert Shinfield (0384 241154).
Previous Lges: Handsworth & District 56-60/ inactive 60-62/ West Mids Alliance 62-66.
Previous Ground: City Road. **Record Gate:** 2,400 v Telford United, FA Cup.
Club Sponsors: Richmond Insurance **Players progressing to Football Lge:** G Hughes, L May.
Midweek home matchday: Tuesday **Reserve team's League:** Div. Two. **Club Shop:** No.
Record transfer fee paid: Nil **Received:** £3,000 for Leroy May (Hereford, 1993).
Clubhouse: Mon-Fri 8-11pm, Sat 12-11pm, Sun 12-3 & 8-10.30. Cobs, rolls, sandwiches available.
Hons: W Mids Lg Div 1 72-73 (Prem. Div Cup 76-77, Div 1 Cup 72-73), Wednesbury Charity Cup 76-77.

WALSALL WOOD

Manager: Michael Speake
Secretary: Cliff Mycock, 11 Brock Close, Walsall Wood, Walsall WS9 1ND (0543 373180).
Ground: Oak Park, Lichfield Rd, Walsall (0543 361084).
Directions: Off A461 Walsall-Lichfield Rd, 4 miles from Walsall town centre and 100yds south of junction with A4152 Aldridge-Brownhills. If travelling via M6/M5 exit motorway at jct 7 (Post House) and continue on A34 towards Walsall before joining A4148 which connects with the A461. 4 miles from Walsall (BR) station - regular buses pass ground.
Capacity: 3,000 **Seats:** 400 **Cover:** 400 **Floodlights:** Yes **Founded:** 1928.
Colours: Red/black/red **Change colours:** All blue **Programme:** Y
Previous Grounds: None **Previous Leagues:** Mids Comb. 51-92/ Staffs Snr 92-93.
Previous Names: Walsall Wood, Walsall Sportsco merged in 1982 to form Walsall Borough. Name later reverted.
Record Gate: 800 v Aston Villa, 1980.
Clubhouse: Evenings, matchdays and Sunday lunchtimes. Darts, pool, juke box. Hot snacks on matchdays.
Hons: Midland Comb. 51-52 (R-up 53-54 54-55 57-58 58-59 60-61, Lg Cup 54-55 60-61 (R-up 56-57 58-59)), B'ham Jnr Cup 76-77. *Walsall Sportsco: Mids Comb. Lg Cup 79-80.*

WEDNESFIELD

Chairman: R Thomas **Vice Chairman:** J Massey
Secretary: James Highfield, 6 Soberton Close, Wednesfield, West Mids WV11 2QX (0902 724771).
Manager/Coach: Ken Hall **Asst Manager:** TBA **Physio:** M Andrews
Commercial Mgr: D Clayton **Press Officer:** J Massey (0902 781819).
Ground: Cottage Ground, Amos Lane, Wednesfield, Wolverhampton (0902 735506).
Directions: From Wolverhampton on the A4124 Wednesfield Rd. Stay on road right through Wednesfield until island. Leave island at first exit (Wood End Rd), left after about 200yds into Amos Lane. Ground is on right, approx. 400yds along. 3 miles from Wolverhampton BR station. Bus 559 to Wood End or 560 to Red Lion.
Seats: 148 **Cover:** 250 **Capacity:** 1,000 **Floodlights:** Yes **Founded:** 1961.
Colours: Red & white stripes/black/black **Change colours:** Green & yellow stripes/green/yellow
Programme: 50p **Programme Editor:** TBA **Club Shop:** No.
Record Gate: 480 v Burton Albion, FA Cup 1981.
Previous Ground: St Georges PF 61-76 **Previous Name:** Wednesfield Social 61-89.
Previous League: Wolverhampton & District Amateur 61-76.
Club Sponsors: Ansells **Midweek home matchday:** Tuesday **Nickname:** Cottagers.
Clubhouse: Evenings 7-11pm. Food (burgers, chips etc) on 1st team matchdays.
Hons: West Mids Lg Div 1 76-77 (R-up 77-78), Staffs Senior Cup finalists 93-94.

WESTFIELDS

Chairman: Steven Knight **Vice Chairman:** Roy Williams **President:** Denis Hartland
Sec./Press Off./Comm. Mgr: Andy Morris, 17 Fayre Oaks Green, Kings Acre, Hereford HR4 0QT (0432 264711).
Manager: Gary Stevens **Asst Manager:** Sean Edwards **Coach:** Phil Dean
Ground: Thorn Lighting, Holme Lacy Rd, Rotherwas, Hereford (0432 268131, club-410548).
Directions: Proceed 1 mile south from Hereford on A49, left in Home Lacy Rd at Broadleys Inn, proceed 1 mile to Thorn Lighting Rotherwas, ground on the right on Rotherwas Ind. Estate. 2 miles from Hereford (BR).
Seats: 100 **Cover:** 200 **Capacity:** 2,000 **Floodlights:** Yes **Founded:** 1966
Colours: Maroon & sky **Change colours:** Sky & white
Previous Grounds: Widemarsh Common 66-73/ King George Playing Fields 73-74.
Previous Leagues: Herefordshire Sunday 66-74/ Herefordshire 72-74/ Worcester & Dist. 74-77.
Programme: 16 pages, 30p **Programme Editor:** Secretary **Club Shop:** No.
Club Sponsors: Hereford Times **Record Gate:** 1,057 v Hereford Utd, t'monial 1980.
Midweek home matchday: Tuesday **Reserve team's League:** Herefordshire.
Record win: 11-0 v Coventry Sporting **Record defeat:** 0-7 v Pelsall Villa.
Record transfer fee paid: Nil **Received:** £4,000 for Alex Sykes (Mansfield, 1992).
Nickname: The Fields. **Clubhouse:** Evenings 7-11pm, matchdays 12-11pm. Bar snacks.
Players progressing to Football League: Alex Sykes (Mansfield 1992), Gary Bowyer (Nottingham Forest 1989), John Layton (Hereford United 1974).
Captain 93-94: Danny Corner **Top Scorer 93-94:** Paul Burton 46
P.o.Y. 93-94: Marc Priday.
Club record scorer: Brian Preece **Club record appearances:** Phil Powell/ Mark Tabb.
Hons: West Mids Lg Div 1 86-87 (Div 2 R-up 83-84 (Div 2 Cup 79-80 83-84))), Herefordshire Snr Cup 85-86 88-89 91-92 (Yth Cup 92-93), Kington Chall. Cup 83-84 85-86 86-87 89-90, Kington Invitation Cup 84-85 85-86 86-87, Presteigne Ottway Cup 78-79 81-82 84-85 93-94, Worcs Jnr Cup 79-80, Wye Guild Cup 74-75 77-78, Hereford Sunday Lg 75-76 76-77 (Div 1 71-72, Div 2 76-77, Div 3 75-76, Prem Div Cup 75-76 76-77, Div 1 Cup 73-74 74-75, Div 3 Cup 72-73), Smart Brown Cup 67-68.

West Midlands League Premier Division Ten Year Record

	84/5	85/6	86/7	87/8	88/9	89/0	90/1	91/2	92/3	93/4
Alvechurch Sports	-	-	-	-	-	-	-	-	9	w/d
Armitage	19	20	19	-	-	-	-	-	-	-
Atherstone United	3	3	1	-	-	-	-	-	-	-
Bilston Town	2	-	-	-	-	-	-	-	-	-
Blakenall	18	15	20	12	1	4	14	4	12	4
Brereton Social	14	10	14	-	-	-	-	-	-	-
Brierley Hill Town	10	14	17	18	19	18	18	19	17	16
Chasetown	16	17	9	5	9	10	2	5	2	9
Cradley Town	-	-	-	-	-	-	-	14	16	19
Darlaston	-	-	-	-	-	-	4	-	-	14
GKN Sankey	11	7	11	16	-	-	-	-	-	-
Gresley Rovers	8	2	4	4	2	3	1	1	-	-
Halesowen Harriers	-	-	7	6	3	9	10	10	15	13
Halesowen Town	1	1	-	-	-	-	-	-	-	-
Harrisons	-	4	10	11	12	12	-	-	-	-
Hinckley Athletic	9	8	8	10	14	6	5	15	14	8
Hinckley Town	-	-	-	-	7	1	-	-	-	-
Ilkeston Town	-	-	-	-	-	-	7	-	6	1
Knypersley Victoria	-	-	-	-	-	-	-	-	-	6
Lye Town	12	6	13	3	8	5	9	9	19	15
Malvern Town	17	12	6	7	10	13	21	16	-	-
Millfields (see West Bromwich Town)										
Oldbury United	-	-	2	2	6	8	3	7	1	3
Oldswinford F & SC (see Brierley Hill Town)										
Paget Rangers	-	-	-	-	4	11	17	2	3	5
Pelsall Villa	-	-	-	-	-	-	15	12	11	10
Rocester	-	-	-	-	11	2	11	6	4	7
Rushall Olympic	13	11	12	9	5	14	12	8	7	17
Shifnal Town	20	13	-	-	-	-	-	-	-	-
Stourport Swifts	-	-	-	-	21	15	13	3	5	2
Tamworth	7	9	5	1	-	-	-	-	-	-
Tipton Town	5	19	18	15	20	21	22	-	-	-
Tividale	6	16	15	13	13	19	20	-	-	-
Wednesfield (Social)	4	5	3	8	16	7	6	17	8	12
West Bromwich Town	-	-	-	-	18	20	8	13	10	20
Westfields	-	-	-	14	17	17	19	18	18	18
Willenhall Town	-	-	-	-	-	-	-	11	13	11
Wolverhampton Casuals	-	-	-	-	15	16	16	-	-	-
Wolverhampton United	15	18	16	17	-	-	-	-	-	-
No. of clubs competing	20	20	20	18	21	21	21	19	19	20

Gornal Athletic - Division One runners-up 1993-94.

DIVISION ONE CLUBS 1994-95

CANNOCK CHASE

Chairman: Peter Lomas **Vice Chairman:** P Walsgrove **President:** W Longmore
Secretary: Mark Clementson, 79 Stafford Rd, Huntington, Cannock, Staffs WS12 4NU (0543 425418).
Manager: Alan Dennison.
Ground: West Cannock Spts Centre, Bradbury Lane, Hednesford WS12 4EP (0543 422141).
Directions: From Cannock take A34 towards Stafford, right into Pye Green Rd half mile from town centre (park and Leisure Centre on left), thru 2 sets of lights across island, after 3 miles right into Broadhurst Green, ground 1 mile down hill on right.
Seats: None **Cover:** 50 **Capacity:** 2,000 **Floodlights:** No **Founded:** 1968.
Colours: White/black/red **Change Colours:** Red/red/black **Nickname:** The Prog
Programme: Yes **Editor:** Peter Lomas (0543 570118) **Club Shop:** No.
Previous Leagues: Cannock Chase 68-76/ Mid Staffs 76-78/ Staffs Co. (Sth) 78-84/ Staffs Snr 84-86.
Previous Grounds: Hednesford Park 68-79/ Heath Hayes F.C. (goundshare) 79-80.
Club Sponsors: Betaprint Press Ltd **Midweek home matchday:** Wednesday
Club record scorer: Keith Kelly **Club record appearances:** P Walsgrove 800.
Clubhouse: Open matchdays. **Hons:** W Mids Lg Div 1 Cup R-up 91-92.

CHASETOWN RESERVES *(see page 572)*

CRADLEY TOWN RESERVES *(see page 584)*

DARLASTON RESERVES *(see page 584)*

GOODYEAR

Secretary: Mr Donnelly, 49 Ecclestone Road, Ashmoor Park, Wolverhampton WV11 2QG (0902 865230).
Ground: Adjacent to Aldersley Stadium, Aldersley Road, Tettenhall, Wolverhampton.
Directions: From central Wolverhampton take A41 (Tettenhall Rd) for just over a mile, right into Lower Str., right into Aldersley Rd, ground at end past stadium. From M54 jct 2, A49 towards Wolverhampton, right into Oxley Moor Rd and follow signs to Aldersley Stadium.
Capacity: **Seats:** None **Cover:** None **Floodlights:** No **Founded:**
Previous League: Wolverhampton Works League (pre-1994).

GORNAL ATHLETIC RESERVES *(see page 584)*

GREAT WYRLEY

President: F Titley **Chairman:** Colin Misra. **Press Officer:** Roy Smith.
Secretary: Dennis Holford, 79 Broadstone Ave., Leamore, Walsall WS3 1JA (0922 493423).
Manager: Fred Dinham **Asst Mgr:** Phil Whitehouse **Coach:** Ron Evans
Ground: Hazelbrook Ground, Hazel Lane, Gt Wyrley (0922 410366).
Directions: A34 thru Gt Wyrley until you get to Star Public House, left into Hazel Lane. Ground is on the left. **N.B.** Please park on tarmac ground at side of ground.
Seats: No **Cover:** Yes **Floodlights:** No **Programme:** Yes **Founded:** 1960.
Colours: Red/black/black **Change Colours:** All blue
Programme: 12 pages, 20p **Programme Editor:** Colin Misra.
Clubhouse: On ground, with kitchen. Open Tues 7.30-10.30pm, Fri-Sat 7.30-11pm, Sun 8.30-10.30pm.
Captain 93-94: Tony Ryan **Player of the Year 93-94:** John Roache.
Top Scorer 93-94: Simon Reach **Hons:** West Mids Lg Div 2 82-83.

HINCKLEY ATHLETIC RESERVES *(see page 573)*

LICHFIELD

Chairman: C Clarke
Secretary: M Cohen, 5 Mesnes Green, Lichfield, Staffs WS14 9AB (0543 255497).
Ground: Shortbutts Lane, Lichfield, Staffs (0543 262246)*******Important Note: Possible groundshshare at Hednesford Town. Spectators should check before travelling*******.
Directions: From A5 proceed to island at A5127 Birmingham Rd, right into Shortbuts Lane, ground on left approx. 300 yds after railway bridge.
Seats: No **Cover:** Yes **Floodlights:** No **Clubhouse:** Yes **Founded:** 1966.
Colours: All royal blue **Change colours:** All red **Programme:** Yes
Hons: WMRL Div 1 Cup R-up 93-94, Walsall Chal. Cup 66-67, Lichfield Charity Cup.

MORDA UNITED

Manager: Colin Turner **Chairman:** G Davies
Secretary: W M Clarke, 50 Langland Rdy, Oswestry, Shropshire (0691 661985).
Ground: Weston Road, Morda, Oswestry, Shropshire.
Directions: Morda is on B5069 south of Oswestry. At crossroads take road to east (Weston), left opp. Drill pub (Weston Lane), ground 400yds on left. Nearest station is Gobowen. Oswestry-Welshpool buses pass thru Morda.
Capacity: **Seats:** 120 **Cover:** 180 **Floodlights:** No **Founded:** 1976
Colours: Yellow/blue **Change colours:** Red/black
Programme: Yes **Programme Editor:** Secretary.
Clubhouse: Yes, on ground **Previous League:** Mid-Wales (pre-1994).
Hons: Mid-Wales Lg R-up 92-93 (Lg Cup 93-94, Summer Cup 1992).

MOXLEY RANGERS

Chairman: C Aldritt **Sec.:** P Whitehouse, 4 Golf Lane, Bilston, West Ms WV14 6RF (0902 459089).
Ground: Darlaston Community Sports & Social Club, Hall Street, Darlaston (021 526 5217).
Directions: M6 jct 10, A454 Wolverhampton Rd towards Bilston, approx. 2 miles to island, round island towards Bilston, 1st left into Darlaston Lane, over canal bridge, 2nd left into Hall Str., ground 50yds on right.
Colours: All red **Change:** Black & white/black/black **Clubhouse:** Yes **Founded:** 1966.

OLDBURY UNITED RESERVES *(see page 574)*

PELSALL VILLA RESERVES *(see page 586)*

ROCESTER RESERVES *(see page 575)*

RUSHALL OLYMPIC RESERVES *(see page 576)*

TIPTON TOWN

President: W Powell **Chairman:** H C Hackett **Vice Chairman:** D Fisher.
Press Officer/Secretary: John A Cross, 1 Moreton Close, Tipton, West Mids DY4 0DG (021 556 3566).
Manager: Dave Edwards **Physio:** John Pope **Coach:** Mel Perry.
Commercial Manager: Steve Mills.
Ground: Tipton Recreation & Community Centre, Wednesbury Oak Rd, Tipton (021 556 5067/ 502 5534).
Directions: M5 jct 2, A4123 towards Dudley/ Wolverhampton turning right at junction with A4037 - ground on right adjacent to Dales (ASDA) superstore about 2 miles further on. From M6 jct 9 take A461 through Wednesbury and proceed to Ocker Hill, Tipton, turning right at island towards Wolverhampton, next left at lights after half a mile - ground 50yds on left. On 245 bus route.
Seats: 150 **Cover:** 150 **Capacity:** 2,000 **Floodlights:** No **Formed:** 1948
Cols: Black & white stripes/black/red **Change colours:** Blue/white/white **Nickname:** None
Previous Grounds: Jubilee Park 48-66/ Lee, Howl & Co. Ltd Works Ground 66-70.
Prev. Lge: Wolverhampton Amateur 48-66. **Record Gate:** 1,300 v Wolves, friendly 1/8/88.
Programme: 24 pages, 50p **Programme Editor:** Secretary **Club Shop:** No.
Sponsors: Status Systems/ Tipton & Coseley
Midweek home matchday: Wednesday **Reserve team's League:** Staffs County (South).
Record win: 8-0 v Cheslyn Hay (H), WML Division One Cup 93-94.
Record defeat: 2-12 v Bilston Town, Walsall Senior Cup.
Record transfer fee paid: Nil **Received:** £1,000 for Steve Bull (West Brom.).
Clubhouse: Open noon-11pm. Hot meat pies, microwave meals, cold sandwiches available.
Club record scorer: Graham Lappage **Club record appearances:** Mick Henley, 600.
Captain: Carl Davis **P.o.Y. 93-94:** Wayne Thornton
Top Scorer 93-94: Darren Smith, Errol Johnson - both 11.
Hons: West Midlands Lg Div 1 83-84 (R-up 76-77, Div 1 Cup 83-84), Birmingham Challenge Vase 86-87, Wednesbury Senior Charity Cup 74-75 75-76 79-80 80-81.

TIVIDALE RESERVES *(see page 588)*

WEM TOWN

Chairman: G Sage
Secretary: Mrs Beverley Hoyle, 24 Coseley Ave., Telford Estate, Shrewsbury SY2 5UP (0743 358818).
Ground: Bowensfield, Wem, Salop (0939 33287).
Directions: M54 jct A42 for Newport and Whitchurch, in Newport take the B5062 to High Ercall, then B5063 to Shawbury and Wem. Entering Wem carry on to T-junction, right under rail bridge. Continue to T-junction by church, right, then left turning for Whitchurch opposite the White Lion, continue for a quarter mile and turn left at the Hawkestone Pub into Pyms Rd; ground 2nd left.
Seats: No **Cover:** Yes **Floodlights:** No **Clubhouse:** No **Founded:** 1921.
Colours: All sky **Change colours:** White/black/black **Programme:**

WOLVERHAMPTON CASUALS

Chairman: G Jones **President:** Clive Hammond **Manager:** Horace Crutchley
Secretary: Michael J Green, 63 St Philip's Ave., Pennfields, Wolverhampton WV3 7GD (0902 333677).
Ground: Brinsford Lane, Coven, Wolverhampton (0902 782314).
Directions: Onto M54 from M6 North, at jct 2 turn right (A449 to Stafford). Ground half a mile, turn right into Brinsford Lane. 2 miles from Billbrooke (BR). Stafford-Wolverhampton buses pass ground.
Seats: 50 **Cover:** 50 **Capacity:** 2,000 **Floodlights:** No **Founded:** 1896
Colours: Green/white/green **Change colours:** White/black/white
Programme: 28 pages, 30p **Programme Editor:** G Smith
Previous Name: Staffs Casuals (pre-1981) **Previous Ground:** Aldersley Stadium.
Clubhouse: Bar and snacks, open Tues, Wed, Thurs, Sat, Sun & alternative Mon.
Players progressing to Football League: David Heywood (Wolves).
Prev. Lges: B'gham AFA, W'hampton Amtr **Hons:** W Mids Lg Div 1 R-up(3) 85-88 (Div 1 Cup 85-86).

WOLVERHAMPTON UNITED

Chairman: T Pritchard **Manager:** Micky Ward.
Secretary: Philip Taylor, 15 Burbage Close, Fallings Park, Wolverhampton WV10 9YG (0902 725513).
Ground: Prestwood Rd Spts Centre, Prestwood Rd West, Wednesfield (0902 730881).
Directions: Situated between Nos. 44 and 46 Prestwood Rd West, approached by way of a drive between the two houses. From Wolverhampton centre Ring Road, follow round to Stafford Str. (A449), join Cannock Rd (A460), after 1 mile bear right into Victoria Road, cross over into Thorneycroft Lane/Prestwood Rd West - ground on right 200yds from pedestrian crossing.
Seats: 200 **Cover:** Yes **Programme:** Yes **Clubhouse:** Yes **Founded:** 1976.
Colours: Old gold/black/gold **Change colours:** Red & black/Black/Red
Hons: WMRL Div 1 Section B 76-77 (R-up 81-82, Div 1 Cup 76-77 81-82 93-94), Birmingham Co. Vase 93-94.

Youth Division 1994-95: *Birmingham City, Bilston United, Birstall United, Blakenall, Boldmere St Michaels, Brierley Hill Town, Chasetown, Cradley Town, Darlaston, Hinckley Ath., Hinckley Town, Ludlow Town, Lye Town, Oldbury Utd, Pelsall Villa, Redditch Utd, Stourport Swifts, Wednesfield.*

SKOL MIDLAND FOOTBALL COMBINATION

FEEDER TO:
MIDLAND ALLIANCE

Treasurer: L W James JP
Secretary: Norman Harvey

PERSHORE BOW OUT OF WITH THE CHAMPIONSHIP

Pershore Town are the Premier Division Champions after a stunning end of season run that saw them pull in a number of games in hand to overhaul their rivals. The title was not clinched until they beat Meir KA in their final match of the season.

Their excellent run in the FA Cup where they reached the Fourth Qualifying Round, and severe problems with their pitch, meant they were trailing from the start of the season. Shepshed Albion set off at a fine pace and threatened to run away with the title, but off-field problems saw them fall away to finish fourth.

Runners-up were West Midlands Police who had looked favourites to win the league until their form failed them in the last month. Further heart-break came in the National Police Cup where they lost to Devon & Cornwall in the final at Home Park. Shifnal Town were always on the fringe of things all season but ultimately their home form let them down.

The Challenge Cup will provide a question for the quiz buffs - who lost 3-2 to Stratford Town in the Quarter-Final but still won the Challenge Cup Final? The answer - Stapenhill who retained the Cup after a 1-0 win at Bromsgrove Rovers thanks to a goal from Richard Walker just before half-time, that proved enough to sink Boldmere St Michaels. Meir KA also collected silverware beating Ball Haye Green 2-0 to lift the Staffs Vase.

In Division One, West Midlands Fire Service proved the team to beat as they lifted a League and Cup double by five points from Handrahan Timbers. The Firemen defeated Badsey Rangers 1-0 in the Final of the Presidents Cup and followed that by winning the Fire Service Midland Cup, beating Derbyshire 2-0.

For Timbers it was a season that promised much but ended in a triple heartbreak as they were League runners-up and also were beaten in the finals of the Birmingham County Vase and the JW Hunt Cup.

Hams Hall delighted their supporters by beating Gresley Rovers Reserves 4-1 in the final of the Fazeley Charity Cup, Colletts Green were winners of the Worcester Junior Cup and Solihull Borough Reserves won the Smedley Crooke Cup to bring silverware into the Combination.

Division Two proved to be a triumph for the clubs who joined at the start of the season. Massey Ferguson proved to be the best team in the Division with just one defeat in 41 Combination League and Cup ties, scoring 137 goals in their 36 league games, to end up 15 points clear of early leaders

Pershore Town - Skol Midland Combination champions 1993-94. Front left to right: N Annis, R Walker, A Brant, W Barnes, S Judge, M Langford, M Rivers, G Aldington, D McCormick, S Barber, I Aldington (Captain), M Davis. Kneeling: H Rawle.

Jaguar-Daimler who also had a fine season. Thimblemill Rec. split the Coventry clubs to finish third from Sphinx and GPT. In the Challenge Vase, as already mentioned, Massey Ferguson beat Swift PP 2-1 in an entertaining game.

The new 3rd Division title went down to the final game of the season as Albright & Wilson clinched the title to hold off the fast finishing Continental Star by two points. Earlier in the season Blackheath Electrodrives had posed the main threat to the title, leading the table for a couple of months, only for Continental Star to move up to runners-up in the final two weeks of the season. To complete a fine first season in the Combination, Star reached the final of the Challenge Urn, only to lose 4-1 to Bilston Community College.

The highly competitive Reserve Division saw Hednesford Town lead the table only once, when it counted after their final game after a magnificent end of season run, to pip Bromsgrove Rovers. For much of the season it looked as though the title was destined for Nuneaton Borough or Gresley Rovers but both fell away to finish third and fifth respectively. The Challenge Trophy Final saw another side defeated in an earlier round reach the Final. Hednesford Town had lost to Tamworth who had fielded an ineligible player. The Lambs were removed from the competition but, unlike with Stapenhill, there was no happy ending as Burton Albion recorded a 2-1 win in an excellent advert for this most competitive league.

There was also success for Reserve Division clubs in outside cups. Tamworth's second string won the Ernie Brown Cup, Gresley Rovers Reserves won the Derbyshire Divisional Cup South, Hednesford Town Reserves triumphed in the Sandwell Charity Cup and Pershore Town Reserves won the Pershore Hospitals Cup. Bromsgrove Rovers Reserves also went down narrowly to Stourport Swifts' first team in the Final of the Worcester Senior Urn.

Despite enjoying a most competitive season all round, it is off the field events that have made most headlines. The newly formed Midland Alliance has taken no less than ten sides from the Combination Premier Division, all of whom were to be floodlit by the start of 1994/95 season, leaving the Division very light on clubs with the facilities required for promotion. It is anticipated that the league will run with fewer teams in each Division next season. This will reduce the early kick-off games at the start and end of the season.

The Combination has lost two fine officers this season. Chairman Lewis Wathen resigned this year and also 'Mr Combination' himself - Les James - has stepped down from the position of secretary of the League after 37 years to be replaced by Fixture Secretary Norman Harvey. Fortunately his expertise will not be lost completely as he remains as League Treasurer. I am sure everyone will join me in wishing Les good health and our best wishes in the future.

Next season will be a tough one for the Combination, but the league continues to attract clubs and will soon once again be a force to be reckoned with.

Steve Davies

PREM. DIVISION	P	W	D	L	F	A	PTS
Pershore Town	42	25	13	4	84	35	88
West Mids Police	42	25	10	7	95	49	85
Shifnal Town	42	25	8	9	112	35	83
Shepshed Albion	42	23	10	9	87	47	79
Boldmere St Mich.	42	22	7	13	74	54	73
Northfield Town	42	20	9	13	83	65	69
Studley BKL	42	19	11	12	91	76	68
Wellesbourne	42	18	11	13	78	60	65
Stratford Town	42	19	8	15	73	56	65
Meir KA	42	17	11	14	101	78	62
Stapenhill	42	17	11	14	77	55	62
Barwell	42	18	8	16	69	61	62
Sandwell Borough	42	15	14	13	82	71	59
Bolehall Swifts	42	17	7	18	61	77	58
Knowle	42	12	13	17	63	67	49
Bloxwich Town	42	14	6	22	65	108	48
Coleshill Town	42	10	15	17	53	72	45
Kings Heath	42	11	9	22	65	99	42
Highgate United	42	12	6	24	58	98	42
Chelmsley Town	42	8	9	25	55	94	33
Ansells	42	5	11	26	43	109	26
Mile Oak Rovers	42	2	9	31	32	135	15

DIVISION ONE	P	W	D	L	F	A	PTS
W Mids Fire Serv.	36	25	5	6	86	35	80
Handrahan Timbers	36	22	9	5	72	44	75
Solihull B. Res.	36	21	5	10	95	55	68
Kenilworth Town	36	20	8	8	77	38	68
Colletts Green	36	19	8	9	76	46	65
Olton Royale	36	19	6	11	64	43	63
Sherwood Celtic	36	16	12	8	68	41	60
Shirley Town	36	16	7	13	63	65	55
Hams Hall	36	15	3	18	66	65	48
Kings Norton ex-S.	36	11	11	14	60	65	44
Southam United	36	11	11	14	45	54	44
Upton Town	36	11	11	14	49	64	44
Monica Star	36	13	2	21	52	74	41
Becketts Sporting	36	11	6	19	49	83	39
Badsey Rangers	36	10	7	19	43	61	37
Polesworth Nth W.	36	10	4	22	54	78	34
Barlestone St Giles	36	10	3	23	58	84	33
Dudley Sports	36	7	11	18	53	84	32
Wilmcote	36	8	5	23	54	105	29

DIVISION TWO	P	W	D	L	F	A	PTS
Massey Fergusson	36	30	5	1	137	27	95
Jaguar-Daimler	36	25	5	6	103	41	80
Thimblemill Rec	36	24	5	7	79	31	77
Sphinx	36	23	7	6	96	49	76
GPT (Coventry)	36	21	7	8	75	49	70
Holly Lane	36	18	8	10	91	63	62
Fairfield Villa	36	16	7	13	61	38	55
Swift PP	36	14	7	15	64	54	49
Burntwood	36	13	7	16	61	84	46
Rugby Town	36	11	10	15	65	67	43
Archdales	36	12	7	17	60	85	43
Studley BKL Res.	36	12	5	19	57	73	41
Alvis SGL	36	10	10	16	36	56	40
Enville Athletic	36	11	5	20	59	81	38
Coleshill T. Res.	36	9	7	20	41	81	34
Ledbury Town '84	36	8	7	21	66	100	31
Sutton C'field Res.	36	7	10	19	53	87	31
Meir KA Res.	36	9	2	25	46	117	29
Earlswood Town	36	5	7	24	29	96	22

DIVISION THREE	P	W	D	L	F	A	PTS
Albright & Wilson	30	22	4	4	91	30	70
Continental Star	30	22	2	6	99	35	68
Blacheath Elect.	30	21	2	7	86	38	65
Bilston Comm. C.	30	19	5	6	96	40	62
W Mids Police Res.	30	18	5	7	84	48	59
Alveston	30	17	4	9	98	53	55
Mitchells & But.	30	16	6	8	102	57	54
Wellesbourne Res.	30	15	7	8	86	47	52
Stapenhill Res.	30	14	6	10	62	48	48
Ansells Res.	30	12	5	13	58	61	41
Kenilworth T. Res.	30	9	3	18	59	82	30
Wilmcote Res.	30	7	7	16	34	84	28
Park Rangers	30	6	4	20	68	98	22
Enville Ath. Res.	30	3	4	23	30	106	13
Dudley Spts Res.	30	2	6	22	34	110	12
B'stone St G. Res.	30	1	2	27	16	166	5

RESERVE DIV.	P	W	D	L	F	A	PTS
Hednesford T. Res.	34	24	3	5	109	44	75
Bromsgrove R. Res.	32	23	5	4	118	44	74
Nuneaton B. Res.	32	23	4	5	88	29	73
Kidderminster Res.	32	23	1	8	90	38	70
Gresley R. Res.	32	18	5	9	101	60	59
Halesowen T. Res.	32	16	6	10	82	61	54
Burton Albion Res.	32	15	3	14	72	60	48
Redditch Utd Res.	32	14	6	12	62	69	48
Tamworth Res.	32	11	7	14	65	81	40
Bridgnorth T. Res.	32	12	4	16	55	89	40
Barwell Res.	32	11	3	18	53	82	36
Stratford T. Res.	32	10	4	18	59	81	34
Leicester U. Res.	32	8	6	18	45	78	30
Atherstone U. Res.	32	6	10	16	43	67	28
VS Rugby Res.	32	7	6	19	44	83	27
Pershore T. Res.	32	6	3	23	40	101	21
Boldmere SM Res.	32	5	4	23	43	101	19

PREMIER DIVISION RESULT CHART 1993-94

HOME TEAM	1	2	3	4	5	6	7	8	9	10	11	12	13	14	15	16	17	18	19	20	21	22
1. Ansells	*	1-1	4-4	0-3	1-2	2-2	0-2	2-2	1-1	1-1	1-2	0-1	1-5	1-0	2-2	1-3	0-6	0-5	1-3	2-4	0-1	1-4
2. Barwell	5-0	*	2-1	0-2	0-1	1-0	1-0	1-2	2-1	0-2	2-2	3-2	1-1	1-2	2-1	0-0	1-0	2-2	4-2	0-1	3-0	2-0
3. Bloxwich	0-2	5-4	*	3-1	1-3	1-2	3-0	3-1	2-3	0-4	2-2	2-1	0-3	0-3	3-3	1-0	0-4	0-4	2-3	2-0	4-1	3-3
4. Boldmere	5-0	2-0	3-0	*	2-1	2-0	0-0	2-0	5-0	4-1	1-4	4-1	0-2	1-0	3-3	4-0	0-6	3-0	1-1	4-1	2-1	0-2
5. Bolehall	5-3	0-3	0-3	2-1	*	4-2	3-3	0-2	2-4	2-1	1-2	1-0	2-1	0-3	4-1	1-4	0-6	0-4	2-0	4-1	2-2	0-3
6. Chelmsley	1-2	0-2	0-1	1-2	0-3	*	1-3	1-3	2-0	2-2	2-4	7-2	1-4	0-0	7-2	1-1	1-7	1-4	0-2	2-2	0-2	0-0
7. Coleshill	1-0	0-1	0-0	1-3	1-1	3-2	*	0-1	1-1	1-1	1-1	5-0	2-5	0-0	1-2	3-0	1-3	1-1	0-5	2-2	1-0	0-2
8. Highgate	3-2	2-4	5-0	2-3	0-2	1-3	2-1	*	2-1	1-2	1-2	2-0	0-0	0-5	1-0	3-3	1-5	1-4	0-1	3-3	1-2	0-4
9. Kings Heath	1-2	4-3	2-1	0-0	2-1	1-2	2-2	2-2	*	2-3	1-5	6-1	1-2	0-0	2-0	1-1	0-3	4-4	0-1	3-2	1-2	1-3
10. Knowle	2-2	0-2	2-1	1-1	0-1	2-2	0-4	2-0	7-1	*	1-0	5-0	2-5	1-2	1-3	0-3	0-2	1-0	1-1	1-2	1-1	2-2
11. Meir KA	5-2	2-4	9-1	2-1	0-0	1-2	3-0	4-1	2-1	3-1	*	9-0	1-2	1-2	3-4	3-5	0-4	2-2	2-0	3-4	2-3	0-3
12. Mile Oak R.	0-1	1-1	0-1	1-2	1-2	0-2	0-2	1-2	1-2	1-1	3-3	*	0-0	0-4	1-1	0-2	0-5	2-2	1-1	0-6	3-2	0-3
13. Northfield	3-0	1-1	2-4	4-0	4-1	1-0	3-1	1-1	3-1	1-5	0-3	6-1	*	1-1	1-3	4-1	0-0	3-1	1-1	1-3	1-3	2-2
14. Pershore	2-1	2-0	4-1	0-0	3-1	2-0	3-4	3-2	4-0	3-2	2-2	5-2	3-0	*	0-0	0-0	2-0	1-4	2-1	3-1	1-1	3-1
15. Sandwell	0-0	4-2	2-2	3-0	0-0	1-1	8-0	3-1	2-0	1-0	2-2	7-1	1-3	1-1	*	1-0	3-2	1-2	1-2	3-0	2-2	2-3
16. Shepshed	3-1	4-1	10-0	0-2	1-0	3-0	3-1	0-1	4-1	0-0	4-0	6-0	3-1	1-2	4-3	*	1-0	3-2	0-1	1-1	2-0	1-1
17. Shifnal	4-0	3-1	0-2	2-3	2-3	5-1	1-1	6-0	6-0	1-2	2-2	0-0	2-0	1-1	2-0	0-1	*	3-0	3-1	1-1	1-0	1-1
18. Stapenhill	1-1	2-0	0-2	3-0	1-1	4-0	1-1	1-0	4-0	1-1	2-2	2-1	1-2	0-2	3-1	0-1	0-1	*	0-1	1-1	1-0	1-2
19. Stratford	2-0	1-3	5-1	1-1	0-0	6-2	0-0	6-2	1-3	1-0	1-0	8-0	3-0	0-2	1-2	0-2	2-2	2-1	*	2-1	1-4	0-2
20. Studley	4-0	1-1	2-0	3-1	3-2	3-1	2-0	4-2	1-4	3-1	4-2	2-2	4-2	2-2	1-1	2-2	1-6	2-3	2-0	*	1-2	2-3
21. Wellesbourne	1-1	3-2	5-1	1-0	3-0	1-1	3-1	5-1	4-4	4-1	1-2	3-1	3-0	1-1	2-2	1-1	1-2	2-1	1-2	1-2	*	1-1
22. WM Police	7-1	1-0	4-2	1-0	3-1	2-0	2-2	4-1	3-1	0-0	2-2	7-0	1-2	0-3	3-0	3-1	1-2	1-2	2-1	0-4	3-2	*

DIV. ONE RESULTS

DIV. ONE RESULTS	1	2	3	4	5	6	7	8	9	10	11	12	13	14	15	16	17	18	19
1. Badsey Rangers	*	0-4	1-2	1-1	2-1	1-3	2-3	2-2	2-2	2-0	3-0	2-1	0-1	4-1	0-2	1-1	0-2	1-0	7-1
2. Barlestone St Giles	2-0	*	3-2	2-5	0-4	1-2	2-7	0-3	2-0	4-2	0-3	4-0	1-1	2-3	2-4	3-3	1-4	0-2	3-1
3. Becketts Sporting Club	3-2	3-2	*	0-4	3-0	3-0	1-1	0-2	0-3	1-2	2-2	1-0	0-3	2-2	0-5	0-1	2-1	3-3	2-1
4. Colletts Green	1-1	1-0	1-3	*	3-2	4-1	0-1	0-2	3-1	6-1	2-0	2-1	0-3	2-1	2-2	0-0	0-0	0-1	4-1
5. Dudley Sports	0-0	1-3	5-2	0-4	*	2-2	2-2	1-4	3-2	0-1	0-1	4-3	3-3	1-1	0-4	2-2	1-1	0-4	6-3
6. Hams Hall	4-1	3-1	6-0	3-1	2-3	*	1-2	2-3	2-3	2-2	1-2	2-1	0-2	0-2	0-3	1-2	3-2	2-5	1-2
7. Handrahan Timbers	2-0	1-1	3-1	5-1	1-0	1-4	*	3-2	4-1	3-2	2-1	2-1	2-0	0-2	2-0	3-0	0-1	1-1	1-1
8. Kenilworth Town	3-0	4-0	5-1	1-1	3-0	1-0	0-2	*	1-1	2-0	1-1	4-1	0-0	3-0	7-2	3-1	2-0	1-3	4-1
9. Kings Norton Ex-Service	2-0	3-1	1-2	0-0	4-0	4-0	1-1	2-2	*	4-3	0-0	4-3	0-3	2-3	1-2	0-0	4-1	0-1	1-1
10. Monica Star	0-2	4-2	2-1	2-1	4-0	1-4	2-0	2-3	2-4	*	0-3	1-1	0-1	1-2	3-1	0-4	1-3	0-2	1-0
11. Olton Royale	0-1	3-2	5-3	3-2	2-1	1-0	0-1	4-0	2-2	1-0	*	1-0	3-2	1-1	1-2	0-1	5-0	0-1	8-2
12. Polesworth Nth Warwick	1-2	2-0	3-1	0-6	3-3	1-2	1-2	1-0	3-1	1-3	0-2	*	1-0	2-4	3-4	3-2	1-0	4-2	2-4
13. Sherwood Celtic	3-1	1-0	2-2	0-1	4-4	1-1	1-1	1-1	1-1	3-1	3-0	2-1	*	4-0	1-3	2-1	4-0	0-0	6-2
14. Shirley Town	2-0	1-4	0-2	2-3	1-1	1-3	1-2	2-1	3-0	0-1	0-3	5-2	1-0	*	1-1	1-1	3-3	2-1	3-2
15. Solihull Boro. Res.	6-1	2-1	2-0	0-2	5-1	0-2	6-1	1-0	2-3	4-1	3-0	1-1	5-1	7-1	*	2-3	4-5	1-1	4-0
16. Southam United	2-0	5-0	1-1	1-1	2-0	1-2	1-4	0-2	1-1	1-3	0-1	1-0	0-0	0-4	1-3	*	2-2	0-2	2-1
17. Upton Town	1-0	1-0	0-0	1-2	0-0	1-3	1-3	1-1	1-0	3-1	1-1	0-1	1-1	0-2	2-2	2-0	*	1-9	3-0
18. West Mids Fire Service	1-1	3-0	6-0	2-4	3-1	3-2	2-2	2-0	5-0	1-0	2-1	0-1	4-3	2-1	4-0	3-0	2-1	*	3-1
19. Wilmcote	1-0	0-5	3-1	2-6	0-1	1-0	1-1	0-4	5-2	2-3	2-3	4-4	0-5	2-4	1-0	1-2	3-3	2-0	*

DIV. TWO RESULTS

DIV. TWO RESULTS	1	2	3	4	5	6	7	8	9	10	11	12	13	14	15	16	17	18	19
1. Alvis SGL	*	3-1	0-1	0-0	3-0	0-4	1-0	0-3	2-3	0-0	1-2	0-3	4-0	1-1	1-1	2-1	2-1	0-3	0-2
2. Archdale '73	4-1	*	1-1	1-3	1-0	3-2	2-1	1-3	3-2	0-3	2-2	0-6	6-2	1-0	0-0	1-0	3-5	1-1	1-5
3. Burntwood	0-0	6-3	*	8-0	2-0	2-1	4-1	1-0	0-1	2-3	3-1	1-7	1-4	4-0	2-8	3-0	1-1	1-4	0-2
4. Coleshill Town Reserves	1-1	2-2	2-3	*	4-3	1-4	0-1	3-0	0-4	2-2	2-0	0-3	5-1	2-2	1-3	0-1	1-0	0-4	0-1
5. Earlswood Town	0-0	0-1	2-1	1-1	*	1-0	1-1	2-1	0-8	1-2	2-1	0-8	1-3	1-1	1-1	0-2	0-4	1-2	0-3
6. Enville Athletic	1-2	0-1	0-3	3-0	2-1	*	1-6	0-2	4-2	0-6	7-1	0-5	4-1	0-1	2-3	1-1	4-1	1-4	1-5
7. Fairfield Villa	2-1	4-0	5-1	0-0	0-0	5-1	*	2-0	1-1	0-1	2-0	0-2	2-0	0-2	0-1	2-1	4-0	2-2	0-2
8. GPT (Coventry)	2-0	3-3	5-0	2-0	3-1	4-1	0-0	*	3-2	2-1	4-2	1-6	2-1	1-0	1-2	3-0	4-2	1-0	3-3
9. Holly Lane	6-0	4-1	0-3	4-0	2-1	4-2	1-0	4-4	*	2-0	6-3	1-3	4-3	2-2	1-4	2-2	0-0	1-0	2-3
10. Jaguar-Daimler	3-1	4-2	3-0	6-0	1-1	1-1	5-2	0-2	3-2	*	5-0	2-2	8-1	1-2	5-1	4-1	5-2	3-0	1-0
11. Ledbury Town	1-1	3-2	3-0	2-3	2-1	2-3	0-4	1-1	3-4	1-2	*	2-2	4-1	2-2	2-2	1-4	6-0	0-4	0-0
12. Massey Fergusson	3-0	3-5	8-0	3-1	6-1	2-0	1-1	2-0	3-1	4-0	5-1	*	9-1	3-1	2-0	6-1	3-1	1-1	1-1
13. Meir KA Reserves	1-2	2-1	1-1	1-2	0-1	1-2	0-8	2-4	1-1	0-5	1-5	1-4	*	1-0	0-3	0-4	1-0	3-1	0-2
14. Rugby Town	1-3	3-1	4-2	3-1	5-1	2-2	0-1	1-1	2-2	0-3	6-2	2-3	3-4	*	1-4	4-2	2-2	2-2	1-3
15. Sphinx	2-0	4-2	5-1	1-0	6-0	1-3	1-0	0-0	2-1	4-1	5-0	1-4	7-1	4-3	*	5-0	4-1	3-4	2-1
16. Studley BKL Reserves	0-3	1-2	1-1	4-0	5-2	0-0	2-1	2-3	2-4	1-3	6-2	0-4	2-3	2-0	1-1	*	0-4	2-1	1-0
17. Sutton Coldfield T. Res.	0-0	1-1	1-1	3-1	7-0	2-2	0-1	1-5	1-1	1-8	0-6	0-3	1-3	0-2	5-2	0-5	*	0-0	1-1
18. Swift PP	1-1	2-1	1-1	1-3	4-1	2-0	3-0	1-2	1-3	1-2	4-1	0-4	4-1	2-4	1-2	2-0	1-3	*	0-1
19. Thimblemill REC	2-1	3-1	6-0	3-0	3-1	3-0	1-2	2-0	2-3	0-1	3-2	0-3	4-0	1-0	1-1	3-0	4-2	3-0	*

Prem. Div. Top Scorer: Steve Bott (Meir KA) 40 **Div. One Top Scorer:** Junior McKeon (Shirley) 32
D2 Top Scorer: Michael Marshall (Massey F.) 38 **Div. Three Top Scorer:** Roger Stafford (Blackheath) 39
Reserve Division Top Scorer: Mick Taplin (Gresley Rovers Reserves) 21

DIV. THREE RESULTS

DIV. THREE RESULTS	1	2	3	4	5	6	7	8	9	10	11	12	13	14	15	16
1. Albright & Wilson	*	6-1	3-0	12-0	2-1	3-2	1-1	1-0	4-0	7-3	3-1	2-1	2-0	7-0	3-0	2-2
2. Alveston	3-3	*	2-0	9-0	2-2	4-1	2-3	6-1	5-0	6-0	3-1	4-1	5-6	4-1	1-3	2-0
3. Ansells Reserves	1-4	3-0	*	3-0	1-4	1-3	2-5	2-1	2-1	0-4	2-1	3-0	0-1	0-1	5-1	2-1
4. Barlestone St Giles Reserves	2-2	0-8	0-4	*	0-6	0-4	0-2	1-1	3-0	1-8	1-9	0-5	1-5	0-3	1-4	0-1
5. Bilston Community College	3-1	6-3	2-1	4-0	*	1-2	1-3	3-1	4-0	3-1	6-4	2-0	7-2	1-1	3-3	0-0
6. Blackheath Electrodrives	1-0	2-1	0-0	8-0	1-2	*	2-0	7-1	6-0	3-0	6-0	3-0	2-0	2-1	2-6	4-1
7. Continental Star	1-0	4-1	3-0	12-0	3-1	1-0	*	10-0	5-1	5-0	2-5	5-4	2-0	1-2	3-2	2-0
8. Dudley Sports Reserves	1-3	1-4	0-3	2-1	0-4	2-4	1-11	*	0-0	0-0	2-6	5-2	0-6	1-4	1-2	1-1
9. Enville Athletic Reserves	0-2	2-5	4-5	3-1	0-1	1-4	1-3	1-1	*	3-1	2-3	1-1	2-2	2-1	0-3	0-1
10. Kenilworth Town Reserves	1-4	1-1	0-5	4-2	0-4	1-3	2-3	4-1	12-2	*	2-0	2-0	1-2	0-0	1-5	4-1
11. Mitchells & Butlers	1-4	0-0	8-2	13-0	2-1	5-1	0-0	4-2	5-0	6-0	*	5-3	2-2	1-1	2-1	9-2
12. Park Rangers	1-4	1-5	5-5	9-0	1-7	2-6	1-3	4-3	5-0	3-5	2-3	*	0-3	4-3	1-6	5-2
13. Stapenhill Reserves	0-1	0-2	2-1	7-0	1-2	0-3	2-1	3-3	2-1	2-0	5-2	2-1	*	4-2	1-2	1-1
14. Wellesbourne Reserves	3-0	4-2	0-0	7-0	3-2	1-1	3-0	8-1	7-0	6-0	2-2	5-2	0-0	*	1-4	7-1
15. West Midlands Police Reserves	0-1	1-2	2-2	8-1	2-2	3-1	1-0	3-1	7-1	2-1	0-2	4-4	1-1	4-3	*	2-0
16. Wilmcote Reserves	0-4	0-5	3-3	3-1	0-11	1-2	0-5	2-0	5-2	2-1	0-0	1-1	1-0	1-6	1-2	*

RES. DIV. RESULTS

RES. DIV. RESULTS	1	2	3	4	5	6	7	8	9	10	11	12	13	14	15	16	17	18	19
1. Atherstone Utd Res.	*	2-2	1-2	1-2	2-6	0-4		1-1	0-2	0-4	0-0	1-1	1-3	3-0	1-1		2-1	0-2	0-1
2. Barwell Reserves	1-1	*	1-2	3-0	0-2	3-1		0-6	0-1	0-2	1-3	6-1	0-3	5-0	2-1	3-3	2-0	3-2	2-2
3. Boldmere St Mich. Res.	1-2	2-3	*	1-2	2-2	1-2		2-2	1-4	0-3	4-7	2-3	1-3	2-1	2-2		3-0	2-4	1-3
4. Bridgnorth Town Res.	2-2	4-2	7-0	*	2-4	0-9		6-1	0-4	1-8	0-3	4-2	1-3	2-1	3-3	3-2	2-2	1-1	3-1
5. Bromsgrove Rovers Res.	4-3	15-0	7-1	0-1	*	5-1	7-0	1-4	1-1	3-0	1-0	3-2	2-1	9-0	5-2		5-1	6-3	4-1
6. Burton Albion Res.	3-0	3-1	1-0	0-2	2-3	*		1-4	3-3	0-3	2-3	1-0	2-1	3-1	0-2		7-1	1-0	7-1
7. Evesham United Res.	1-2		2-1				*												
8. Gresley Rovers Res.	5-0	4-3	5-0	8-0	3-2	1-2		*	4-2	2-2	0-2	5-1	1-1	3-1	5-1		4-4	5-1	3-1
9. Halesowen Town Res.	1-1	4-2	2-0	8-0	0-7	5-2		5-3	*	0-1	0-2	5-1	1-1	5-1	3-0		2-3	2-5	3-2
10. Hednesford Town Res.	4-4	4-0	4-2	7-0	5-2	1-1		2-1	2-1	*	2-3	4-1	3-2	6-1	3-2	2-2	9-1	4-0	9-0
11. Kidderminster Harr. Res.	1-3	2-1	2-0	3-2	2-3	4-0		1-0	3-1	5-0	*	5-1	0-2	9-2	7-2		3-1	4-1	5-0
12. Leicester Utd Res.	3-1	0-2	3-1	0-1	1-1	0-3		1-3	1-1	1-2	1-0	*	0-4	5-0	3-1		1-1	2-2	2-1
13. Nuneaton Borough Res.	1-0	4-1	8-0	2-0	1-2	2-1		4-2	2-2	3-0	2-0	4-1	*	1-2	4-1		4-0	4-1	0-0
14. Pershore Town Res.	1-1	2-1	1-2	2-1	1-1	3-2		3-1	3-2	1-4	0-2	2-2	1-5	*	1-2		0-4	2-3	1-2
15. Redditch Utd Res.	3-2	3-2	5-0	1-0	0-6	3-1		4-1	1-2	3-2	3-2	3-2	0-1	3-0	*		2-1	4-4	2-1
16. Shepshed Albion Res.														0-0	3-1	*	3-1		
17. Stratford Town Res.	6-2	0-1	1-1	2-1	0-2	4-1		1-4	4-5	3-4	1-2	0-1	2-4	5-3	2-1		*	0-1	3-0
18. Tamworth Res.	2-5	6-2	5-2	3-1	1-3	1-1		4-5	3-2	0-4	0-4	4-1	1-6	3-2	0-0		0-1	*	1-1
19. VS Rugby Res.	0-1	0-1	5-3	2-4	1-1	2-5		1-5	2-3	1-3	2-1	5-1	0-2	2-1	1-1		2-4	1-1	*

N.b. *Shepshed Albion and Evesham Utd both withdrew. Playing records expunged, but shown for interest.*

CHALLENGE CUP 1993-94

First Round
Boldmere St Michaels v Coleshill Town 1-0
Kings Heath v Barwell 2-5*(aet)*
Knowle v Mile Oak Rovers & Youth 2-1
Polesworth North Warwick v West Mids Police 1-7
Upton Town *(w/o)* Alcester Town *(scr)*
Handrahan Timbers v Stapenhill 0-3
Kings Norton Ex-Service v Chelmsley Town 1-0*(aet)*
Pershore Town v Southam United 5-4*(aet)*
Bolehall Swifts v Shepshed Albion 1-2*(aet)*

Second Round
Barlestone St Giles v Highgate United 2-7
Colletts Green v Barwell 2-0
Meir KA v Kings Norton Ex-Service 0-3
Northfield Town v Studley BKL 4-1
Shifnal Town v Dudley Sports 3-0
Stapenhill v Badsey Rangers 4-0
Upton Town v Shepshed Albion 0-2*(aet)*
West Midlands Police v Sandwell Borough 3-1
Bloxwich Town v Becketts Sporting Club 2-4
Hams Hall v Pershore Town 0-3
Monica Star v Olton Royale 2-1
Sherwood Celtic v Ansells 0-1
Shirley Town v Knowle 3-5*(aet)*
Stratford Town v Kenilworth Town 1-1,2-0
Wellesbourne v West Midlands Fire Service 2-1
Wilmcote v Boldmere St Michaels 0-2

Third Round
Ansells v Highgate United 4-3
Colletts Green v Kings Norton Ex-Service 0-1
Pershore Town v Stratford Town 0-1
Wellesbourne v Knowle 0-2
Becketts SC v Shifnal Town *(played at Shifnal)* 1-6
Monica Star v Northfield Town 0-5
Stapenhill v Shepshed Albion 6-3
West Mids Police v Boldmere St Michaels 3-3,0-1

Quarter-Finals
Ansells v Boldmere St Michaels 0-4
Shifnal Town v Kings Norton Ex-Service 9-0
Northfield Town v Knowle 3-2
Stratford T. v Stapenhill 3-2*(aet, Stratford expelled)*

Semi-Finals
Stapenhill v Shifnal Town 2-1
Northfield Town v Boldmere St Michaels 2-3

Final *(at Bromsgrove Rovers FC)*: Stapenhill 1, Boldmere St Michaels 0

PRESIDENTS CUP 1993-94

First Round
Barlestone St Giles v Solihull Boro. Res. 1-3
Hams Hall v Dudley Sports 2-0
Colletts Green v Sherwood Celtic 4-1*(aet)*
Polesworth North Warwick v Monica Star 2-1

Second Round
Colletts Green v Badsey Rangers 1-2
Kenilworth Town v Southam United 1-2
Olton Royale v Handrahan Timbers 3-1
Wilmcote v Upton Town 1-2
Becketts v Hams Hall *(played at Hams H.)* 3-1*(aet)*
Kings Norton Ex-Servicemen v Shirley Town 4-0
Polesworth North Warwick v Solihull Boro. Res. 1-5
West Mids Fire Service *(w/o)* Alcester Town *(scr)*

Quarter-Finals
Kings Norton Ex-Service v Upton Town 2-0
Solihull Borough Reserves v Becketts SC 2-0
Olton Royale v Badsey Rangers 0-1
Southam United v West Midlands Fire Service 0-1

Semi-Finals
Badsey Rangers v Kings Norton Ex-Service 1-0
West Mids Fire Service v Solihull Boro. Res. 2-1

Final *(at Knowle FC)*: West Midlands Fire Service 1, Badsey Rangers 0

CHALLENGE VASE 1993-94

First Round

Archdales v Massey Fergusson 0-4
Meir KA Reserves v Burntwood 1-0
Fairfield Villa v Rugby Town 4-2

Second Round

Burntwood v Alvis SGL 1-0*(aet)*
GPT (Coventry) v Sphinx 1-0
Ledbury Town v Earlswood Town 4-2
Swift PP v Holly Lane 4-1
Enville Athletic v Coleshill Town Reserves 0-3
Jaguar-Daimler v Massey Ferguson 1-4*(aet)*
Studley BKL Reserves v Fairfield Villa 1-0
Thimblemill REC v Sutton Coldfield T. Reserves 3-0

Quarter-Finals

GPT (Coventry) v Ledbury Town 7-0
Swift PP v Burntwood 6-1
Studley BKL Reserves v Massey Ferguson 0-1
Thimblemill REC v Coleshill Town Reserves 3-0

Semi-Finals

Thimblemill REC v Massey Ferguson 0-3
GPT (Coventry) v Swift PP 1-1,1-1*(aet, 2-4 pens)*

Final *(at Jaguar-Daimler FC)*: Massey Ferguson 2, Swift PP 1

CHALLENGE URN 1993-94

First Round

Albright & Wilson v Barlestone St Giles Res. 14-0
Ansells Reserves v Park Rangers 3-1
Blackheath Electrodrives v Stapenhill Res. 3-0
Kenilworth Town Res. v Enville Ath. Res. 5-0
Alveston v Wilmcote Reserves 5-0
Bilston Community College v Wellesbourne Res. 3-1
Continental Star v Dudley Spts Reserves 7-0
W Mids Pol. Res. v Mitchells & Butlers 0-0,2-3*(aet)*

Quarter-Finals

Alveston v Bilston Community College 3-6
Kenilworth T. Res. v Blackheath Electrodrives 4-3
Ansells Reserves v Albright & Wilson 0-2
Mitchells & Butlers v Continental Star 1-6

Semi-Finals

Bilston Community College v Kenilworth Res. 5-0
Continental Star v Albright & Wilson 1-0

Final *(at Stratford Town FC)*: Bilston Community College 4, Continental Star 1

CHALLENGE TROPHY 1993-94

First Round

Boldmere St Michaels Res. v Gresley R. Res. 1-0
Redditch Utd Reserves v VS Rugby Reserves 2-1
Bromsgrove Res. v Kidderminster H. Res. 1-1,6-1

Second Round

Atherstone Utd Res. v Barwell Res. 0-2
Burton Albion Reserves v Bridgnorth T. Res. 6-2
Pershore Town Reserves v Leicester Utd Res. 1-7
Halesowen Town Res. *(w/o)* Evesham U. Res. *(scr)*
Boldmere SM Reserves v Nuneaton B. Res. 0-4*(ab)*,1-3
Hednesford T. Reserves v Bromsgrove R. Res. 3-0
Stratford T. Res. v Tamworth Reserves 2-2,2-5
Redditch U. Res. *(w/o)* Shepshed Albion Res. *(scr)*

Quarter-Finals

Barwell Reserves v Nuneaton Boro. Reserves 0-3
Halesowen T. Res. v Redditch Utd Reserves 1-2*(aet)*
Burton A. Reserves v Leicester Utd Reserves 3-1
Hednesford Res. v Tamworth Res. 1-2*(T'worth expelled)*

Semi-Finals

Nuneaton Borough Res. v Burton Albion Res. 1-2
Redditch Utd Res. v Hednesford Town Reserves 0-1

Final *(at Gresley Rovers FC)*: Burton Albion Reserves 2, Hednesford Town Reserves 1

PREMIER DIVISION CLUBS 1994-95

ALVECHURCH VILLA

Chairman: **Vice-Chairman:** **President:**
Secretary: D Lawrence, 9 Rufford Close, Alcester, Warwickshire B49 6EE (0789 7694595).
Ground: Lye Meadow, Redditch Rd, Alvechurch, Worcs (021 445 2929).
Directions: M42 jct 2, left for Alvechurch (A441) at 1st island, pass right thru Alvechurch - ground on left half mile after village. 10 mins walk from Alvechurch BR station. Birmingham-Redditch buses pass ground.
Seats: TBA **Cover:** Yes **Capacity:** 3,000 **Floodlights:** No **Founded:** 1994
Colours: TBA **Change colours:** TBA
Previous Name: None *(predecessors, Alvechurch FC, founded 1929, folded in 1992. All italicised historical entries below apply to this previous club).*
Previous Grounds: None *(predecessors: The Meadows (pre-1957)).*
Previous Leagues: None *(predecessors: Midland Comb. 61-73/ West Mids 73-78/ Southern 78-92).*
Club Sponsors: TBA **Record Gate:** *1,600 v Enfield, FA Amtr Cup 1964.*
Nickname: The Church. **Midweek home matchday:** TBA
Record win: *7-1 v Redditch Utd* **Record defeat:** *1-8 v Halesowen Town.*
Record transfer fee paid: *£3,000 for Peter Gocan (Worcester City)*
Received: *£28,000 for Andy Comyn (Aston Villa, 1990).*
Best FA Cup year: Not entered to date *(predessors: 3rd Rd 73-74 beating Exeter en route. Also 1st Rd 71-72).*
Players progressing to Football League: *Derek Newman (Southampton 1964), John Mason (Peterborough 1966), Colin Brazier (Wolves 1975), Ron Green (Walsall 1977), Richard Kelly (Walsall 1979), Sean O'Driscoll (Fulham 1979), Alan Smith (Leicester 1982 (now Arsenal & England)), Neil Cusack (Leicester 1987), David Kelly (Walsall 1982), Brian Palgrave (Walsall 1984), Andy Comyn (Aston Villa 1990).*
Club record scorer: *Graham Allner* **Club record appearances:** *Kevin Palmer.*
Hons: *Southern Lg 80-81 (Midland Div R-up 81-82, Lg Cup 82-83, Championship Match 80-81), West Mids Lg 73-74 74-75 75-76 76-77 (R-up 77-78, Lg Cup 73-74 74-75 77-78, Midland Comb. 62-63 64-65 66-67 71-72 (R-up 63-64 65-66 66-67 68-69 72-73, Lg Cup 64-65 65-66 67-68 68-69 71-72), Worcs Snr Cup 72-73 73-74 76-77, B'gham Snr Amtr Cup 73-74, B'gham Jnr Cup 65-66 67-68, Border Counties F'lit Cup 75-76.*

ANSELLS

Manager: Bernard Cronin
Secretary: J Cronin, 32 Whittleford Grove, Castle Bromwich, Birmingham B36 9SL (021 747 9925).
Ground: Ansells Sports Club, Aldridge Rd, Perry Barr, Birmingham (021 356 4296).
Directions: Coming from city centre Aldridge Rd is a right turn (just before Perry Barr stadium) off the main Birmingham to Walsall road. Ground entrance almost immediately on right.
Capacity: TBA **Seats:** No **Cover:** Yes. **Floodlights:** No
Previous League: Birmingham Works (pre-1992).
Clubhouse: Large Social Club.
Hons: Midland Combination Div 2 92-93, Birmingham Works Lg (numerous occasions).

BLOXWICH TOWN

President: M M Ross **Chairman:** C S Sanghera/ A S Bain.
Secretary: S Clarke, 10 Sandhill Str., Bloxwich, Walsall WS3 2JH (0922 492463).
Manager: M Folland/P Knox **Coach:** Jim Skidmore.
Physio: D McGuire **Commercial Manager:** K Jones.
Ground: Abbey Park, Glastonbury Crescent, Bloxwich, Walsall. (0922 77640)
Directions: A34 Walsall-Bloxwich, then west onto A4124. Ground 2-3 miles on right, s.p. Mossley Estate.
Capacity: 1,000 **Seats:** 200 **Covered:** 400 **Floodlights:** Yes **Nickname:** Kestrels
Midweek Matches: Tues/Thurs **Previous Name:** Bloxwich FC. **Founded:** 1977.
Colours: Blue/white/blue **Change Colours:** Grey & white diamonds/red/red.
Programme: 16 pages 20p **Programme Editor:** R S Badesha **Club Shop:** No.
Sponsors: Romak Leisurewear
Record defeat: 1-9 v Meir KA (A), Mids Comb. 1/1/94.
Players progressing to Football League: Martin O'Connor (Crystal Palace & Walsall).
Captain 93-94: P Hall **Top Scorer 93-94:** M Sparrock.
Hons: Bloxwich Comb.(2), Staffs Co. Lg Div 1, Walsall Snr Cup R-up 86-87, Invitation Cup 89-90, Midland Combination Div 1 89-90, Alan Peck Cup (3).

CHELMSLEY TOWN '94

Manager: Bill Cox.
Secretary: M Redfern, 51 Imperial Road, Coleshill, Warks B46 1HG (0675 466531).
Ground: The Pavilion, Coleshill Road, Marston Green, West Midlands (021 779 5400).
Directions: A452 Chester Rd towards N.E.C., right into Coleshill Heath Rd, right into Coleshill Rd (s.p. Marston Green). Ground on right (s.p. Chelmsley Hospital). 10 mins walk from Marston Green (BR).
Capacity: 2,500 **Seats:** 50 **Cover:** 200 **Floodlights:** No **Founded:** 1927
Midweek matches: Tuesday **Prev. Lges:** Handsworth/ B'ham Yth O.B./ Mercian.
Colours: Sky & white stripes/sky/sky **Change Colours:** Yellow/black/black
Programme: 24 pages 30p **Programme Editor:** Terry Stanners
Previous Name: Christchurch (pre 1969) **Previous Ground:** Coleshill Hall Hospital, Selly Oak
Clubhouse: One room bar and clubroom **Record Gate:** 3,000 v A Villa Old Stars, charity game.
Players who have progressed to Football League: Bob Peyton (Port Vale)
Hons: B'ham Yth Committee Champions & B'ham Vase R-up 90-91, Handsworth Lg, Mercian Lg(3), Mids Comb 87-88 (Presidents Cup 77-78, Invitation Cup 77-78 87-88).

COLESHILL TOWN

Manager: Robert Nimmons **Founded:** 1894.
Secretary: G Phillips, 49 Circus Ave., Chelmsley Wood, Birmingham B37 3NG (021 770 9513).
Ground: Pack Meadow, Packington Lane, Coleshill, Birmingham B46 3JQ (0675 63259).
Directions: A446 to A4117 towards Coleshill, Packington Lane forks from A4117, south of village and ground is 150 yds on right. M6 jct 4, 1 mile away.
Capacity: 3,000 **Seats:** 50 **Cover:** 50 **Floodlights:** Yes **Nickname:** Coalmen.
Midweek matches: Tues/Thurs **Record Gate:** 1,000.
Colours: All maroon **Change Colours:** Green/white/green
Clubhouse: Bar open 7 nights a week. Bar manager resident. **Programme:** 30p, **Editor:** Mavis Gordon
Players who have progressed to Football League: Gary Shaw (Aston Villa, Walsall)
Hons: Mercian Lg 75-76, Walsall Snr Cup 82-83 (R-up 83-84), Midland Comb. R-up 83-84 (Div 2 69-70 (R-up 74-75), Invitation Cup 1970, Presidents Cup R-up(2) 67-69).

HANDRAHAN TIMBERS

Chairman: E J Smith **President:** W J Handrahan
Secretary: Stuart Fereday, 93 Millfield Cres., Kidderminster (0562 820385).
Manager: Mitchell Woods **Asst Manager:** Phillip McNally
Press Officer: E J Smith (0384 295394).
Ground: The Mile Flat Sports Ground, Mile Flat, Wallheath, Kingswinford, West Mids (0381 484755).
Cover: 200 **Seats:** 40 **Floodlights:** No **Nickname:** Timbers **Founded:** 1982.
Colours: Red/black/red **Change colours:** Sky/navy/navy **Club Shop:** No.
Previous Grounds: None **Previous Leagues:** Staffs County Lg (South) 82-86.
Programme: Occasionally **Clubhouse:** Teas only. **Record win:** 9-0
Sponsors: W J Handrahan & Son **Midweek home matchday:** Wednesday **Record defeat:** 0-6.
Captain: Roy Moran **Top Scorer 93-94:** Paul Baker.
Club record scorer: Paul Baker **Club record appearances:** Jonathan Role.
Hons: Midland Combination Div 1 R-up 93-94, Birmingham Challenge Vase R-up 93-94, Wednesbury Charity Cup 91-92, J W Hunt Cup 92-93 (R-up 93-94).

HIGHGATE UNITED

Chairman: T G Bishop **Treasurer:** F H Drennan **Founded:** 1947.
Secretary: G Read, 23 Southam Rd, Hall Green, Birmingham B28 8DQ (021 777 1786).
Manager: TBA **Assistant Manager:** TBA
Physio: Garry Bishop **Press Officer:** N C Sawyer.
Ground: The Coppice, Tythe Barn Lane, Shirley, Solihull B90 1PH (021 744 4194).
Directions: A34 from City through Shirley, fork right B4102 (Tanworth Lane), half mile then right into Dickens Heath Rd, then first right and the ground is on the left. 100yds from Whitlocks End (BR).
Capacity: 5,000 **Seats:** 250 **Covered:** 750 **Floodlights:** Due 1995
Colours: All red **Change Colours:** All white **Nickname:** The Gate.
Midweek matches: Tuesday **Record Gate:** 4,000 v Enfield, FA Amateur Cup QF 1967.
Programme: 28 pages, 40p **Programme Editor:** Terry Bishop (0676 22788).
Clubhouse: Members Club open Tues, Wed, Thurs, Sat & Sun. Light refreshments available at weekends.
Players progressing to Football League: John Gayle (W'ledon), Keith Leonard (A Villa, P Vale), Geoff Scott (Leic.)
Captain 93-94: Graham Wark **P.o.Y. 93-94:** Mark Page **Top Scorer 93-94:** Garry Annard.
Hons: Midland Comb.(3) 72-75 (Div 2 66-67 68-69 71-72, Lg Cup(5) 72-74 75-77 84-85 (R-up 78-79 92-93), Presidents Cup 70-71 85-86), Tony Allden Mem. Cup 74-75, Invit. Cup 68-69 71-72 85-86, West Mids All. 63-64, Birmingham Snr Cup 73-74 (SF 91-92).

KINGS HEATH

Manager: Barry Hancocks **Founded:** 1964.
Secretary: Dennis Ellis, 2 Willsbridge Covert, Druids Heath, Birmingham B14 5YD (021 625 6019)
Ground: Triplex Sports Ground, Eckershall Road, Kings Norton (021 422 1087).
Previous Names: Horse Shoe FC/ Kings Heath Amateur.
Cols: Gold shadow stripes/black/gold **Change Colours:** All red **Nickname:** The Kings
Programme: 12 pages **Programme Editor:** M Kite
93-94 Top Scorer: Mark Averill 32. **Previous Ground:** Shirley Town (pre-1994).
Players progressing to Football League: Geoff Scott (Stoke, Leicester, Birmingham).
Hons: Midland Combination Div 1 R-up 92-93 (Div 2 R-up 82-83, Presidents Cup R-up 79-80 81-82 92-93), Birmingham Challenge Vase R-up 86-87.

KNOWLE

Manager: Gerry Clarke **Assistant Manager:** Stan Tims **Founded:** 1926.
Secretary: Ray Gardner, 11 Runcorn Close, Chelmsley Wood, Birmingham B37 6QX (021 770 9273).
Ground: Hampton Rd, Knowle, Solihull (0564 779807). **Directions:** A41 Warwick Rd from City, left at Wilsons Pub into Hampton Rd, ground 200 yds on right. 1 mile from Dorridge (BR). Buses from Solihull.
Capacity: 3,000 **Seats:** 72 **Cover:** 200 **Floodlights:** No **Nickname:** Robins.
Midweek matches: Wednesday **Record Gate:** 1,000 in FA Vase 1980.
Programme: 20 pages, 25p **Editor:** Dave Radburn
Colours: Red/white/red **Change Colours:** Yellow/black/yellow
Previous Name: Knowle North Star 80-87 **Previous Ground:** Bentley Heath Village
Clubhouse: Seating for 60, tea bar **Previous Lges:** Birmingham Yth O.B./ Birmingham Alliance.
Players who have progressed to Football League: Guy Russell (Birmingham City)
Hons: B'gham Jnr Cup R-up 70-71, FA Vase QF 81-82, Midland Combination Div 2 R-up 68-69.

MEIR K.A.

President: John Whitfield **Chairman:** Des Reaney **Vice Chairman:** Michael McDonnel.
Secretary: Stanley Tooth, 29 Colclough Road, Meir, Stoke-on-Trent ST3 6DH (0782 310145).
Manager: Des Reaney **Asst Manager:** Terry Lees **Coach:** Terry Lees.
Press Officer: Graham Birks **Commercial Manager:** Huw Smalley (0889 562008).
Ground: Stanley Park, Hilderstone Road, Meir Heath, Stoke-on-Trent (0455 613553)
Directions: M6 jct 14, A34 to Stone, A520 from Stone, right (B5066) at Meir Heath, ground on right. 2 miles from Blythe Bridge (BR).
Capacity: 5,000 **Seats:** 400 **Cover:** 1,000 **Floodlights:** Due **Founded:** 1976.
Colours: Old gold/black/black **Change colours:** All blue. **Nickname:** Kings.
Previous Ground: Normacot Rec. **Previous Name:** Station Shoulder of Mutton.
Programme: 24 pages 50p **Programme Editor:** Steve Osborne
Midweek home matchday: Wednesday **Club Sponsors:** John Whitfield & Sons.
Previous Leagues: Staffs Alliance/ Staffs Snr 84-92.
Record win: 9-0 v Mile Oak Rovers (H), Midland Combination 15/1/94 **Record loss:** 1-5
Clubhouse: Built in 1982, open matchdays. Hot food.
Club Record Scorer: W J Anderson **Club Record Appearances:** David Preston, 500+
P.o.Y. 93-94: Alan Hope **Top Scorer 93-94:** Steve Bott 40
Hons: Staffs Snr Lg 91-92, Staffs FA Vase 93-94.

NORTHFIELD TOWN

Chairman: Eric Rough **Manager:** Tom Owens **Founded:** 1966.
Secretary: Monty Patrick, 38 Pensford Rd, Northfield, Birmingham B31 3AG (021 475 2057).
Ground: Shenley Lane, Selly Oak, Birmingham B29 (021 478 3900).
Directions: A38 from City, past Selly Oak, opposite Woodlands/Royal Orthopaedic Hospital turn right into Whitehill Lane, right at end into Shenley Lane. Ground on right. One and a half miles from Northfield (BR).
Capacity: 3,500 **Seats:** None **Cover:** Yes **Floodlights:** No **Nickname:** The Cross
Midweek Matches: Tues/Thurs **Clubhouse:** Brick built clubhouse. (021 478 3870).
Colours: Yellow/blue/yellow **Change Colours:** Blue & yellow/blue
Record Gate: 3,300, Charity match, 1967 **Programme:** 24 pages 25p, **Editor:** Eric Rough.
Previous Names: Allens Cross/ Cross Castle Utd/ Northfield Town Amateur/ Northfield FC.
Previous League: Midland Combination.
Players who have progressed to Football League: Clive Whitehead (WBA), Colin Brazier (Wolves, Walsall), Mark Rees (Walsall), Carlton Palmer (WBA, Sheffield Wed)
Hons: Midlands Comb. 61-62 75-76 (Div 2 61-62(res) 63-64, Chal. Cup 56-57 (R-up 63-64 86-87), Presidents Cup 61-62 80-81), Tony Allden Mem. Cup 1977, Birmingham Snr Amtr Cup 74-75, Lord Mayor of Birmingham Charity Cup R-up 92-93, Birmingham Jnr Cup 1958, 1962, Birmingham Co. Yth Cup(3) 69-72, Worcs Co. Yth Cup(4).

OLTON ROYALE

Manager: Derek Attwood. **Founded:** 1969.
Secretary: Brian D Fox, 26 Claines Road, Northfield, Birmingham B31 2EE (021 475 4465).
Ground: Bay Tree Farm, Middle Lane, Wythall, Near Birmingham (0564 826612).
Colours: All red **93-94 Top Scorer:**
Previous Name: West Heath United (1969-93).
Hons: Midland Combination Div 2 R-up 84-85, Smedley Crooke Charity Cup 92-93.

SHERWOOD CELTIC

Manager: Mark Foggerty. **Founded:** 1982
Secretary: Mark Askey, 96 Newborough Road, Shirley, Solihull B90 2HF (021 603 7622).
Ground: As Knowle FC (page 598) **Colours:** Gold/green/gold **Programme:** Yes
Previous Ground: Becketts Farm, Wythall (pre-'92) **Hons:** Fazeley Charity Cup R-up 92-93.

SHIRLEY TOWN

Manager: Pete Sysum.
Secretary: N Charles, 40 Daberry Field, Kings Heath, Birmingham B14 6RX (021 443 2922).
Ground: Shirley Stadium, Tile House Lane, Shirley, Solihull (021 744 1560).
Directions: A34 B'gham to Shirley, right onto B4025 towards Shirley (BR) - ground one and a half miles on left.
Colours: All red **Previous League:** B'ham Comb. 35-38. **Founded:** 1926
Top Scorer 93-94: Junior McKeon 32 **Hons:** Midland Combination Division 2 R-up 92-93.

STUDLEY B.K.L.

Chairman: D Robinson **Vice-Chairman:** Alec James **President:** N/A
Secretary: Gary Shepherd, 38 Lightoak Close, Walk Wood, Redditch, Worcs B97 (0527 546639).
Manager: John Adams **Assistant Manager:** Alan Scarfe.
Physio: Derrick Mutton **Press Officer:** Dave Chiswell.
Ground: 'Beehive', BKL Spts Ground, Abbeyfields, Birmingham Rd, Studley, Warks (0527 24780).
Capacity: **Seats:** None **Cover:** Yes **Floodlights:** No **Founded:** 1971.
Colours: Sky/navy/navy **Change colours:** White/red **Nickname:** Bees.
Sponsors: BKL Fittings **Previous Name:** BKL Works
Clubhouse: Yes, on ground **Reserve Team's League:** Skol Midland Combination Division Two.
Programme: 30p **Ed.:** Alec James, 14 Eldersfield Close, Churchill, Redditch B98 9NG
Previous League: Redditch & South Warwickshire Sunday Combination 71-87.
Top Scorer 93-94: Mark Witton **Captain 93-94 & Club record appearances:** Lee Adams.
P.o.Y. 93-94: Ian Donegan **Club Record Scorer:** Kevin Rowlands.
Hons: Midland Comb. Div 1 91-92 (Chal. Cup R-up 91-92, Presidents Cup R-up 91-92, Div 2 Cup 87-88), Smedley Crooke Charity Cup 90-91 91-92.

UPTON TOWN

Chairman: John Cook **Vice Chairman:** Bill Jones **President:** Steve Goode.
Secretary/Press Officer: Don Roberts, 6 Gardens Close, Upton-on-Severn, Worcs WR8 0LT (0684 593439).
Manager: Alan Kealy **Assistant Manager:** Reg Wood
Coach: M Lowe **Physio:** A Pugh.
Commercial Manager: Les Wadley.
Ground: Malvern Town FC (see page 585) **Founded:** 1904
Colours: Green & white **Change:** Red & black stripes **Nickname:** Emeralds
Programme: 16 pages, 50p **Editor:** Graham Hill (0905 351653) **Club Shop:** No.
Sponsors: D.G. Car & Van Hire **Prev. Ground:** Old Street, Upton-on-Severn (pre'92)
Previous Leagues: Malvern 04-71/ Worcester & Dist. 72-85/ Kidderminster 85-88.
Midweek home matchday: Tuesday **Record Gate:** 350 v Colletts Green, Mids Comb. Div 1, 7/4/94.
Record win: 13-1 **Record defeat:** 0-17.
Clubhouse: Evenings 7.30-11pm, Saturday matchdays 12.30-11pm. Food (hamburgers etc), tea, coffee, squash available on matchdays.
Captain 93-94: John Hayes **Top Scorer 93-94:** Carl Hobbs 15 **P.o.Y. 93-94:** Mark Walker
Club record scorer: Paul Buckley **Club record appearances:** Keith Aingel.
Hons: Midland Combination Div 2 89-90 (Jack Mould Tphy 89-90, Presidents Cup R-up 89-90), Worcs Jnr Cup 73-74 88-89 (R-up 74-75), Worcs Minor Cup 24-25 86-87.

WELLESBOURNE

Chairman: Mr C Keyes **Manager:** Stuart Dixon. **Asst Manager:** Allan Stacey.
Secretary: R Burns, 32 St Peters Rd, Wellesbourne, Warks CV36 9PD (0789 840301).
Ground: The Sports Field, Loxley Close, Wellesbourne (0789 841878).
Seats: 80 **Cover:** 100 **Floodlights:** No **Nickname:** Bourne **Founded:** 1932.
Programme: 30 pages, 80p **Programme Editor:** Mr A Mason **Club Shop:** No.
Colours: All blue **Change colours:** Yellow/black/black **Sponsors:** Various
Midweek home matchday: Tuesday **Previous Leagues:** Covenrty & North Warks/ Stratford Alliance.
Previous Grounds: None **Reserve Team's League:** Midland Combination Division Three
Clubhouse: Open all day matchdays. Sandwiches, crisps, drinks, tea, coffee available.
P.o.Y. 93-94: Mick Clements **Captain & Top Scorer 93-94:** Nick Keaney.
Hons: Midlands Comb. Div 1 92-93 (Presidents Cup 91-92, Invitation Cup 92-93 93-94.

WEST MIDLANDS FIRE SERVICE

Chairman: Mr R Jefferies **President:** Chief Fire Officer.
Secretary: Mr J Clarke, 51 Stonebury Ave., Eastern Green, Coventry CV5 7FW (0203 467997).
Manager: Ian Green **Asst Manager:** Clive Mason.
Ground: 'The Glades', Lugtrout Lane, Solihull (021 705 8602).
Directions: M42 jct 5, A45 towards B'ham Airport, leave at next junction and at island take 1st exit (Catherine de Barnes Lane) - ground half mile on left. Nearest station is Birmingham International. No buses pass ground.
Seats: None **Cover:** 150 **Floodlights:** No **Club Shop:** No **Founded:** 1947
Colours: All red **Change colours:** White/navy/navy **Previous Grounds:** None.
Previous Leagues: Birmingham AFA (pre-1986).
Programme: 12 pages, 25p **Editor:** J Kempson (0922 408464)
Sponsors: Contract Fire Sytems Ltd **Record defeat:** 1-14 v West Heath United.
Midweek home matchday: Tues/Thurs **Nickname:** None.
Clubhouse: No. **Club record appearances:** Brian Farrell.
Captain 93-94: **Top Scorer 93-94:** **P.O.Y. 93-94:**
Hons: Midland Combination Div 1 93-94 (Div 2 87-88, Presidents Cup 93-94, Jack Mould Trophy 87-88), Fire Services National Cup 89-90, Fire District Cup 90-91.

MIDLAND COMBINATION PREMIER DIVISION 10-YEAR RECORD

	84/5	85/6	86/7	87/8	88/9	89/0	90/1	91/2	92/3	93/4
Alcester Town	-	-	-	-	-	-	-	13	20	-
Ansells	-	-	-	-	-	-	-	-	-	21
Armitage '90	-	-	-	-	-	-	-	2	1	-
Ashtree Highfield	(see Sandwell Borough)									
Barlestone St Giles	-	-	-	-	-	-	-	17	19	-
Barwell	-	-	-	-	-	-	-	-	11	12
Bloxwich Town	-	5	16	19	-	7	15	20	18	16
Boldmere St Michaels	4	1	4	2	1	1	12	9	8	5
Bolehall Swifts	-	-	20	12	11	8	16	10	9	14
Chelmsley Town	-	-	-	-	13	13	18	15	16	20
Coleshill Town	17	11	18	7	16	16	8	12	7	17
Evesham United	13	13	13	5	3	3	3	1	-	-
Highgate United	6	12	9	17	10	11	9	4	17	19
Hinckley	-	-	-	-	9	12	10	19	-	-
Hurley Daw Mill	14	14	-	-	-	-	-	-	-	-
Kings Heath	18	20	15	10	12	15	13	18	-	18
Kings Norton Ex-Service	-	-	-	-	-	-	21	-	-	-
Knowle (North Star)	20	16	14	14	14	18	14	16	10	15
Leamington	-	-	-	15	-	-	-	-	-	-
Meir KA	-	-	-	-	-	-	-	-	13	11
Mile Oak Rovers & Youth	1	-	-	-	-	19	17	21	14	22
New World	5	15	-	-	-	-	-	-	-	-
Northfield Town	16	4	6	9	6	2	6	11	12	6
Paget Rangers	3	2	2	-	-	-	-	-	-	-
Pershore Town	-	-	-	-	-	-	-	6	4	1
Polesworth North Warwick	7	9	11	16	15	14	20	-	-	-
Princes End United	-	-	12	8	4	9	19	-	-	-
Racing Club Warwick	10	10	3	1	2	-	-	-	-	-
Sandwell Borough	12	19	10	3	-	-	4	5	5	13
Shepshed Albion	-	-	-	-	-	-	-	-	-	4
Shifnal Town	-	-	-	-	-	-	-	-	-	3
Shirley Town	-	-	-	-	18	-	-	-	-	-
Smethwick Highfield	(see Sandwell Borough)									
Solihull Borough	2	7	7	11	17	10	2	-	-	-
Southam United	19	17	17	-	-	-	-	-	-	-
Stapenhill	-	-	-	-	-	4	7	8	2	10
Stratford Town	9	6	1	4	7	5	5	14	3	9
Streetley Celtic	-	-	-	-	-	20	-	-	-	-
Studley BKL	-	-	-	-	-	-	-	-	15	7
Studley Sporting	15	18	19	-	-	-	-	-	-	-
Walsall Borough/Wood	17	11	8	8	13	8	17	11	7	-
Wellesbourne	-	-	-	-	-	-	-	-	-	8
West Midlands Police	8	3	5	6	5	6	1	3	6	2
Wilmcote	-	-	-	18	-	-	-	-	-	-
No. of clubs competing	20	20	20	19	18	20	21	21	20	22

DIVISION ONE CLUBS 1994-95

BADSEY RANGERS

Chairman: A Stallard **Vice Chairman:** G Brooks **President:** A W Sparrow.
Secretary: M J Loram, 39 Synehurst, Badsey, Evesham, Worcs WR11 5UI (0386 832040).
Manager: Alex Ogg **Asst Manager:** Max Green **Comm. Mgr:** Mrs L Rogers
Ground: Badsey Recreation Ground, Sands Lane, Badsey, Evesham (0386 830867).
Directions: B4035 from Evesham to Badsey (2 miles), right into Synehurst by Lloyds Bank, thru village, left into School Lane after 'Wheatsheaf', next right into Willersey Rd, Sands Lane is 1st left - ground at end on left. Bus service negligable
Seats: 50 **Cover:** 250 **Capacity:** 3,000 **Floodlights:** No **Founded:** 1890
Cols: Red & black stripes/black/black **Change colours:** Tangerine/white/tangerine.
Previous Grounds: Aldington Pastures, Aldington, Evesham 1890-1920.
Prev. Lges: N Cotswold & Vale of Evesham 1893-1902/ Worcester (time out in Stratford All. and Central Amtr) 03-89.
Programme: 20 pages, 50p **Programme Editor:** Mrs L Rogers (0386 49602).
Club Shop: No, but a small book published to celebrate club centenary in 1990 is available for £3.50 from club the club secretary. It is a historical record of the club.
Record Gate: 2,500 v Evesham United, Worcester Infirmary Cup final 1949.
Sponsors: Goodalls (Vauxhall) **Record win:** 24-0 v Essex House 4/10/02 **Record defeat:** 3-19
Clubhouse: Tea bar sells tea, coffee, soup, confectionary, rolls, crisps, pies, pasties, hot-dogs etc.
Captain 93-94: G Cowley **Top Scorer 93-94:** J Gregory **P.o.Y. 93-94:** S Hands.
Hons: Mids Comb. Div 1 R-up 91-92 (Div 2 90-91, Presidents Cup R-up 93-94), Jack Mould Tphy R-up 91-92 *(plus scores of local competition honours that are all listed in the official club history (see note above).*

BARLESTONE St GILES

Mgr: John Farrington **Sec.:** T Wentworth, 3 Rush Close, Newbold Verdon, Leicester LE9 9LX (0455 822602).
Ground: Barton Road, Barlestone, Nuneaton. **Nickname:** Saints.
Colours: Gold/black/black **Previous League:** Leics Snr (until 1991)

BILSTON COMMUNITY COLLEGE

Chairman: Mr Earl Laird **Manager:** Brian Waldron.
Secretary: J Calloway, 4 Mervyn Rd, Bradley, Bilston, West Midlands WV14 8DF (0902 491799).
Ground: Bilston Town FC *(see Beazer Homes League section)*
Colours: All navy **Change:** Green & gold/green. **Programme:** No.
Previous Lge: Staffs Co. (Sth) (pre-1993) **Prev. Ground:** Springvale S & S, Millfields Rd, Bilston (pre-1993).
Hons: Midland Comb. Chall. Urn 93-94, Staffs Co. (Sth) Lg(4) 89-93, J W Hunt Charity Cup 90-91.

COLLETTS GREEN

President: T Perkins **Chairman:** G Robinson. **Manager:** A Green
Secretary: A Perkins, 3 Mark Close, Malvern, Worcestershire WR14 1LW (0684 567762)
Assistant Manager: S Humphries **Coach/Physio:** D Ilsley.
Ground: Victoria Park, Malvern **Directions:** A few minutes walk from Malvern Link (BR) station.
Seats: None **Cover:** Yes **Floodlights:** No **Club Shop:** No **Nickname:** The Green
Colours: All green **Change colours:** All white **Clubhouse:** No.
Prev. Name: Three Nuns (pre-1992) **Prev. League:** Worcester Sunday (pre-1992).
Reserves' League: None **Club Sponsors:** C T Phipps/ P S Tools/ R Green Painting.
Programme: Yes, 50p **Players progressing to Football League:** None.
Record win: 8-1 v Archdales (H), Midland Combination Division Two 92-93.
Rec. loss: 1-4; v Handrahan Timbers (A), Mids Comb. Div 1 93-94; v Monica Star (A), Mids Comb. Div 2 92-93.
Record scorer: P Slade **Record appearances/ Captain 93-94:** M Lowe.
P.o.Y. 93-94: A Morrison **Top Scorer 93-94:** Philip Slade 33.
Hons: Midland Combination Challenge Vase 92-93, Worcs Junior Cup 93-94 (R-up 92-93).

DUDLEY SPORTS

Chairman: J Forrest **Vice Chairman:** M Webster **President:** H Bradney
Secretary: Mrs Joan Forrest, 39 Smallshire Way, Wordsley, West Mids DY8 4XQ (0384 378558).
Manager: P Checketts **Asst Manager:** A Sharp **Coach:** M Webster
Physio: D Hemmings **Press Officer/Commercial Manager:** Steve Lawrence.
Ground: High Ercal Avenue, Brierley Hill, West Mids (Brierley Hill 571260).
Directions: Just off A461 Dudley-Stourbridge Rd; coming from S'bridge, left after Silver Lane P.O.
Seats: None **Cover:** 200 **Capacity:** 2,000 **Floodlights:** No **Founded:** 1978
Colours: Red/black/red **Change colours:** All blue **Club Shop:** No.
Previous League: Birmingham Works **Sponsors:** R's Tool Hire **Nickname:** Pie Men
Programme: 12 pages, 50p **Programme Editor:** Steve Lawrence (0384 230123)
Midweek home matchday: Tuesday **Record Gate:** 700 v Polesworth, B'ham Vase Oct '89.
Record win: 10-1 v Alcester Town **Record defeat:** 1-6 v Badsey Rangers.
Clubhouse: Open weekday evenings 7-11pm, all day Sat, Sun 12-2 & 7-10.30pm. Large club with function room and snooker rooms. Hot food available.
Captain 93-94: **Top Scorer 93-94:** Paul Shinton.
Club record scorer: Paul Shinton **Club record appearances:** John Pearson.
Hons: Birmingham Works Lg 80-81, Midland Combination Presidents Cup 90-91, Bass Cup, W.B.A. Shield, Black & White Cup, Aston Villa Shield.

G.P.T. (COVENTRY)

President: K Nylor **Chairman:** B Olsen.
Secretary: P Scanlon, 61 Norton Hill, Wyken, Coventry, West Mids CV2 3AX (0203 616576).
Manager/Coach: John Moore **Physio:** Suffolk Clinic **Commercial Mgr:** D Cooper
Ground: GEC Sports Ground, Allard Way, Copsewood, Coventry.
Capacity: **Seats:** 120 **Cover:** 240 **Floodlights:** No **Founded:** 1960
Colours: Blue & white **Change colours:** All red **Nickname:** G's.
Midweek home matchday: Tuesday **Reserves' Lge:** Coventry Alliance **Nickname:** G's.
Programme: Yes, £1 with admission **Previous League:** Coventry Alliance (pre-1993).
Clubhouse: Open normal pub hours. Sandwiches available.
Captain 93-94: S Rammell **Top Scorer 93-94:** I Evatt.

HAMS HALL

President: E J Parkes **Chairman:** A S Lakin.
General Mgr/Press Officer: Bob Ringrose, 6 Holly Drive, Hurley, Atherstone, Warks CV9 2JY (0827 872747).
Manager: Colin Middleton **Asst Manager:** Alan Adey
Physio: N/A **Commercial Manager:** Phil Haseley.
Ground: Hams Hall Generating Station, Lea Marston, Sutton Coldfield B76 0BG (0675 463223).
Directions: M42 jct 9, A446 signed Coleshill, Water Orton & M6, 1st left main gate of power station. Rail to Water Orton BR station.
Seats: None **Cover:** 700 **Capacity:** 2,000 **Floodlights:** No **Founded:** 1930
Colours: White/black/black **Change colours:** Sky & navy **Nickname:** Powermen
Previous Grounds: None. **Previous Lges:** Sutton Amtr 32-79/ Mercian FA 79-89.
Programme: 24 pages, free **Programme Editor:** Press Officer **Club Shop:** No.
Club Sponsors: Powergen **Rec. Gate:** 800 - A. Villa Shield 1986 (at Villa Park)
Midweek home matchday: Wednesday
Clubhouse: Open after matches and Monday, Wednesday & Saturday evenings. Fresh cobs available.
Club record scorer: Ken Taylor 166 **Club record appearances:** Arthur Lakin 363.
Top Scorer 93-94: Neil Pitkin 28 **Captain & Player of the Year 93-94:** Craig Smith.
Hons: Midland Combination Div 2 R-up 91-92, Jack Mould Trophy 92-93, Ernie Brown Cup 92-93, Walsall Challenge Cup 88-89, Fazeley Charity Cup 92-93 93-94, Mercian Lg Aston Villa Shield 85-86. Many honours in Sutton Amateur Lg.

JAGUAR-DAIMLER

Secretary: R Marnell, 119 Beake, Radford, Coventry, West Mids CV6 3BE (0203 599474).
Ground: Jaguar Sports & Social Club, Middlemarch Rd, Coventry.
Nickname: Jags.
Previous League: Coventry Alliance (pre-1993).
Honours: Midland Combination Div 2 R-up 93-94.

KENILWORTH TOWN

Manager: John Clark **President:** Bernard Jones. **Founded:** 1936
Secretary: Richard Brooks, 33 Suncliffe Drive, Kenilworth, Warks CV8 1FH (0926 57728).
Ground: Gypsey Lane (off Rouncil Lane), Kenilworth, Warks (0926 50851).
Seats: No **Cover:** Yes **Club Shop:** No **Floodlights:** No **Programme:** 50p
Cols: Blue & white halves/white/blue **Previous Name:** Kenilworth Rangers (pre-1992).
Midweek home matchday: Tuesday **Previous Grounds:** Scott Road/ Glasshouse Lane.
Sponsors: Davies Bakery, Kenilworth **Clubhouse:** Open matchdays. Hot food available.
Record win: 17-0 v Bubbenhall, Coventry & North Warks Lge Prem Div 25/2/89
Captain 93-94: Simon Kerr **93-94 Top Scorer:** Richard Hamer.
Hons: Birmingham Challenge Vase 92-93.

KINGS NORTON EX-SERVICEMEN

President: M T Hickey **Founded:** 1982
Sec: Andy Wright, 29 Tarrington Court, Hawkesley, Birmingham B33 9TG (021 4459 8986).
Ground: Highgate Utd FC (see Premier Division section).
Colours: All blue **Change colours:** Yellow/green/green.
Programme Editor: S Jesic **Previous Ground:** Becketts Farm, Wythall.
Hons: Midland Comb. Div 2 R-up 85-86 (Presidents Cup 92-93, Challenge Vase R-up 84-85), Solihull Charity Cup R-up 84-85, Smedley Crooke Charity Cup 87-88 (R-up 89-90).

MASSEY-FERGUSON

Manager: Frank McDermott
Secretary: C Richards, 20 Winchat Close, Binley, Coventry, West Midlands CV3 2FE (0203 458695).
Ground: Massey-Ferguson Sports Ground, Banner Lane, Tile Hill, Coventry.
Previous League: Coventry Alliance (pre-1993).
Top Scorer 93-94: Michael Marshall **Honours:** Midland Comb. Div 2 93-94 (Chall. Vase 93-94)

MONICA STAR

Manager: Tony Carter **Founded:** 1977.
Secretary: A Rourke, 35 Fairlands, Yardley, Birmingham B26 2DT (021 789 6695).
Ground: As Chelmsley Town (see Premier Division). **Colours:** Red/black/red
Prev. Ground: The Glades, Lugtrout Lane, Solihull (pre-'92) **Top Scorer 93-94:**

POLESWORTH NORTH WARWICK

Manager: David Wright.
Secretary: E Guild, 43 Station Road, Polesworth, Tamworth, Staffs B78 1BG (0827 893690).
Ground: North Warwick Sports Ground, Hermitage Hill, Tamworth Road, Polesworth (892482).
Seats: 50 **Capacity:** 1,000 **Floodlights:** No **Founded:** 1966 **Nickname:** Poles
Colours: Green & white hoops/green/yellow **Change colours:** Tangerine & black
Previous League: Mercian. **Clubhouse:** Bar, tea room and refreshments.
Hons: Midland Combination Challenge Cup 83-84 (Presidents Cup(2) 82-84), Birmingham Jnr Cup 83-84, Ernie Brown Cup 91-92.
Players progressing to Football League: Dave Tunnicliffe (Birmingham City).

SOUTHAM UNITED

Chairman: N Srmstrong **Vice-Chairman:** T Frost.
Secretary: R J Hancocks, 18 Warwick Road, Southam, Leamington Spa CV33 0HN (0926 813483).
Manager: Dave Draper **Asst Manager:** Dave Sharpe **Physio:** Barry Cramp
Ground: Banbury Road Ground, Southam, Leamington Spa (0926 812091).
Directions: On righthand side of A423 Banbury Road heading south from Southam.
Capacity: 2,000 **Seats:** 50 **Cover:** 100 **Floodlights:** No **Nickname:** Saints
Colours: Yellow/black/black **Change:** Red & white stripes/red/red **Club Shop:** No.
Programme: Av. 50 pages, 50p **Programme Editor:** Mrs A Hancocks.
Prev. Lge: Coventry & North Warks **Record Gate:** 1,500 v Coventry City, friendly 1990.
Midweek matchday: Tues or Thurs. **Reserve Team's League:** Coventry & District.
Sponsors: B & M Sleeper Coaches **Player progressing to Football Lge:** Stephen Bicknell (Leicester).
Record win: 10-0 v Studley **Record defeat:** 1-7 v Kings Heath.
Clubhouse: Open every evening and matchdays. Hot pies, rolls, tea & coffee available at matches.
Captain 93-94: Nigel Shanahan **Club record scorer & appearance-maker:** Bob Hancocks.
Top Scorer 93-94: John Angove **Player of the Year 93-94:** Mark Calcutt.
Hons: Mids Comb. Div 3 80-81 (Div 2 R-up 82-83, Chal. Vase 80-81).

SPHINX

Manager: Billy Hollywood.
Secretary: G Newey, 18 Brierley Rd, Henley Green, Coventry, West Mids CV2 1RS (0203 603659).
Ground: Sphinx Sports Ground, Sidderley Ave., Stoke Aldermoor, Coventry.
Previous League: Coventry Alliance (pre-1993).

WILMCOTE

Manager: Martin Skipp **Founded:** 1971.
Secretary: Mrs Jennifer Smith, 2 Wavensmere Cottage, Wootten Wawen, Solihull B95 6BS (0564 794552).
Ground: The Patch, Wilmcote Men's Club, Aston Cantlow Road, Wilmcote, Stratford (0789 297895).
Directions: Wilmcote signs off A34, right at T-junction opposite garage; ground on right.
Seats: No **Cover:** Yes **Clubhouse:** Yes **Programme:** No **Nickname:** Cote.
Colours: Yellow/green/yellow **Previous League:** Stratford Alliance.
Players progressing to Football League: Steve Mardinbrow (Coventry City), John Smith (WBA).

DIVISION TWO CLUBS 1994-95

ALBRIGHT & WILSON

Secretary: Mrs J Haven, 16 Springfield Lane, Rowley Regis, Warley, West Midlands B65 8PS (0384 211465).
Ground: Albright & Wilson Spts Club, Tat Bank, Oldbury, Warley (021 552 1048).
Directions: A4034 Oldbury Road from M5 jct 2; right at island along A457 Smethwick Road, second right into Stone Street and continue to Tat Bank.
Colours: All sky **Change colours:** Gold/black/black **Founded:** 1935.
Previous League: West Midlands (Regional) (pre-1993).
Honours: Midland Comb. Div 3 93-94.

ALVIS S.G.L.

Manager: Adrian Newbury.
Secretary: D A Leslie, 9 Stephenson Close, Milverton, Leamington Spa CV32 6BS (0926 336700).
Ground: Alvis Spts & Social Club, Green Lane, Finham, Coventry.
Previous League: Coventry Alliance (pre-1993).

ALVESTON

Secretary: P Beese, 36 Bishops Close, Stratford-upon-Avon, Warks CV37 9ED (0789 267966).
Ground: Home Guard Club, Main Street, Tiddington, Stratford-upon-Avon.
Previous League: Stratford Alliance (pre-1993).

ARCHDALES '73

Manager: Martin Stephens **Colours:** Red/white/red **Founded:** 1934
Secretary: R T Widdowson, 33 Mayfield Avenue, Worcester WR3 8LA (0905 27866).
Ground: Windermere Drive, Worcester (0905 51410) **Nickname:** Dales

BLACKHEATH ELECTRODRIVES

Chairman: Mr G Ellison **Vice Chairman:** Tony Brookes
Secretary/Press Officer: Mr Tito Martire, 10 Marshwood Croft, Halesowen B62 0EZ (021 422 3449).
Manager: Bob Homer. **Assistant Manager:** Tony Brookes.
Ground: Electrodrives Sports Ground, Cakemore Road, Rowley Regis, Warley (021 559 1500).
Directions: A4123 towards Birmingham from M5 jct 2, right at 'Hen & Chickens' (B4169) - ground half mile on left 100 yds before works entrance in Cakemore Rd.
Seats: Nil **Cover:** Nil **Capacity:** 2,000 **Floodlights:** No **Formed:** 1920.
Colours: All red **Change colours:** All blue **Nickname:** "G's"
Sponsors: Blackheath Electrodrives. **Previous Lges:** Birmingham Works 20-88/ West Midlands 88-93.
Programme: No **Club Shop:** No **Previous Name:** Blackheath Electromotors (pre-1992)
Midweek home matchday: Wednesday **Reserve team's League:** Kidderminster.
Record win: 11-0 v Smethwick **Record defeat:** 1-7 v Cheslyn Hay.
Clubhouse: Nearby. Snack bar on ground.
Captain 93-94: Mark Lovatt **Top Scorer & P.o.Y. 93-94:** Roger Stafford.
Club record scorer: Paul Birch **Club record appearances:** Mark Lovatt.

BURNTWOOD

Manager: Martin Daley
Secretary: Mr Yeomans, 28 Beacon Drive, Rolleston-on-Dove, Burton-on-Trent DE13 9EN (0253 520030).
Ground: Memorial Institute, Rugeley Rd, Burntwood.

COLESHILL TOWN RESERVES *(see page 597)*

CONTINENTAL STAR

Secretary: Noel O'Donnell, 4 Fern Rd, Erdington, Birmingham B24 9DE (021 354 2277).
Ground: Magnet Centre, Park Approach, Erdington, Birmingham.
Previous League: Birmingham Works (pre-1993).
Hons: Midland Comb. Div 3 R-up 93-94 (Chal. Urn R-up 93-94).

EARLSWOOD TOWN

Chairman: Jim Jones **Vice-Chairman:** John Sharpe **President:** R Taylor.
Secretary: Keith Addis, 16 Ansley Close, Matchborough East, Redditch B98 0AX (0527 526454).
Manager/Coach: Mark Clifton **Assistant Manager:** John Ashford.
Commercial Mgr: Dave McKeever **Press Officer:** Jim Jones (021 745 3397)
Ground: Malthouse Lane, Earlswood, near Solihull (05646 703989).
Directions: M42 jct 3 (A435), follow signs for Foreshaw Heath, right at T-junction after three quarters of a mile, left at sign for Terrys Green after three quarters of a mile, ground half mile on right. Or A34 from Birmingham, right for Earlswood at Calenders restaurant, right into Springbrook Lane (just past Earlswood Garage) after 5 and a half miles, left at end, ground on left. Train to 'The Lakes' station - ground adjacent.
Seats: None **Cover:** 100 **Capacity:** 1,000 **Floodlights:** No **Founded:** 1968
Colours: Red/black/red **Change:** Green & yellow/green/green **Nickname:** Earls
Previous League: Mercian. **Previous Ground:** Lady Lane, Earlswood 68-75.
Programme: 20 pages, 50p **Programme Editor:** Emma Jones.
Club Shop: Yes. Club programmes, enamel badges etc available. Contact John Sharpe (021 444 7979).
Club Sponsors: Earlswood Garage **Record Gate:** 500 v Aston Villa Old Stars, charity game 1991.
Midweek home matchday: Wednesday **Clubhouse:** Open matchdays. Bar snacks + fresh sandwiches.
Reserve Team's League: Redditch & South Warks Combination.
Captain 93-94: Garry Sealey **P.o.Y. 93-94:** Mickey Moore (goalkeeper).

ENVILLE ATHLETIC

Manager: David Pell **Colours:** All sky blue **Founded:** 1890
Secretary: Ms M Mackin, 36 Dudley Walk, Goldthorn Park, West Midlands WV4 5HD (0902 337729).
Ground: Hall Drive Ground, Hall Drive, Enville, Stourbridge (Kinver 872368).
Reserve Team's League: Kidderminster & District.
Clubhouse: Yes **Cover:** No **Hons:** B'ham Co. FA Vase QF 91-92.

FAIRFIELD VILLA

Chairman: P Eades **Vice Chairman:** J Rea **President:** L J Hill.
Secretary/Press Officer: C W Harris, 7 Churchill Road, Catshill, Bromsgrove B61 0PE (0527 831049).
Manager/Coach: Cliff Hughes **Physio:** S Kings/ C Waldron.
Ground: Recreation Ground, Stourbridge Road (B4091), Fairfield, Bromsgrove (0527 77049).
Directions: M5 jct 4, A491 towards Stourbridge, at next island take B4091 into village, ground three quarters of a mile on left.
Capacity: 500 **Seats:** None **Floodlights:** No **Founded:** 1902 **Reformed:** 1959
Colours: Red & black **Change colours:** All blue **Nickname:** Villa.
Previous Grounds: None **Previous Lges:** Bromsgrove 59-69/ Kidderminster 70-84.
Sponsors: Richards Packages **Club Shop:** No **Programme:** No.
Clubhouse: Evenings 8-11pm, matchdays, Sun noon- & 8-10.30pm. Sandwiches available.
Club record scorer: K Downing **Club record appearances:** J Peplow.
Captain 93-94: K Pedlingham **Top Scorer 93-94:** Phil Cotterill **P.o.Y. 93-94:** D Tudge/I Green
Hons: Bromsgrove Lg 69-70, Kidderminster Lg 81-82 83-84, Malvern Invitation Cup 77-78, Worcs Junior Cup 77-78, Smedley Crooke Charity Cup R-up 91-92 93-94.

HOLLY LANE '92

Chairman: Tom Keogh **Vice Chairman:** Harry Parks **President:** George Harvey.
Secretary: R G Ashton, 19 Grange Road, Erdington, Birmingham B24 0DG (021 350 2352).
Manager: Derek Stevens **Asst Manager:** TBA **Coach:** Paul Snowball.
Press Officer: Neil Cleaver.
Ground: Holly Sports & Social Centre, Holly Lane, Erdington, Birmingham B24.
Seats: None **Floodlights:** No **Founded:** 1992 **Programmes:** Yes **Club Shop:** No.
Colours: Yellow/green **Change colours:** yellow/black **Nickname:** The Lane.
Previous League: Birmingham Works (as Holly Lane Sports & Social) 90-92.
Record win: 15-0 v Sutton Coldfield Town Reserves (A), Midland Comb. Div 2 11/12/93.
Record defeat: 3-7 v Studley BKL Reserves (A), Midland Combination Div 2 7/4/93.
Midweek home matchday: Thursday **Clubhouse:** Open all day Saturday, snacks available.
Programme: 12 pages, 50p **Editor:** Derek Stevens (021 523 3776) **Sponsors:** None
Capt. & P.o.Y. 93-94: Michael Brewster **Top Scorer 93-94:** David McMahon/Lionel Foster.
Club record scorer: Lionel Foster **Club record appearances:** Derek Hill.
Hons: Birmingham Works Lg Div 5 90-91, Birmingham City Shield 90-91, Sports Argus Cup 91-92.

LEDBURY TOWN '84

Chairman: Mr C Bloise **Vice Chairman:** Mr D Skyers **President:** Mr C Hutchings
Secretary: Mrs J Phillips, The Newtons, Much Marcle, Ledbury (0531 84382).
Directions: By foot, New Street bears off the bottom of Ledbury High Street - ground half mile on left. However, there is no vehicular access so exit by-pass at 2nd r'bout (coming from M50 and the south) - ground on right.
Manager: Ralph Tyler. **Ground:** New Street, Ledbury.
Seats: 50 **Cover:** 50 **Capacity:** 200 **Floodlights:** Yes **Founded:** 1966
Colours: Black & white **Change colours:** Blue & black
Programme: Twelve pages, £1 with admission.
Sponsors: Hills of Ledbury **Clubhouse:** Yes, on ground.

RICHMOND SWIFTS

Chairman: M Rowley **Vice-Chairman:** S Sanders.
Secretary: Tony Moogan, 6 George Arthur Rd, Saltley, Birmingham B8 1LW (021 328 9720).
Manager: Pat Foley **Assistant Manager:** Peter Dunbavin.
Coach: Morris Gittens **Commercial Manager/Press Office:** Fred Evans
Ground: Triplex Sports Ground, Eckershall Road, Kings Norton (021 422 1087).
Seats: None **Cover:** None **Floodlights:** No **Founded:** 1994 **Nickname:** Nomads
Colours: White (red trim) **Change colours** Blue (white trim).
Programme: Yes, for 94-95 **Midweek home matchdays:** Tuesday.
Previous Names: Swift Personalised Products (founded 1979)/ Richmond Amateurs - clubs merged in 1994. All historical entries below pertain to Swift PP except those *italicised.*
Previous League: Birmingham Works. *Richmond Amateurs: Birmingham AFA, pre-1994.*
Sponsors: Swift Personalised Products/ BGR Financial Consultants.
Previous Grounds: Shirley Town FC (pre-'92)/ Wythall Park, Silver Street, Wythall (Wythall FC) 92-93/ Alvechurch FC 93-94 (pre-Xmas)/ British Gas Sports Ground, Woodacre Rd, Erdington 93-94.
Record win: 6-0 v Burntwood, 93-94 **Record defeat:** 0-6 v Archdales, 92-93.
Capt. & P.o.Y. 93-94: S Brown **Club Record Scorer/ Top Scorer 93-94:** A Dunkley (21, 93-94).
Hons: Midland Combination Challenge Vase R-up 93-94, Kings Norton Lg Divs 1 + 2 and Lg Cup, Mercian Lg Div 1, Birmingham Works Lg, Birmingham Jnr Cup R-up.

RUGBY TOWN

President: John Dean **Chairman:** Paul Moss **Manager:** Barry Collinson.
Secretary: B Sewell, 38 Barn Road, Rugby, Warwickshire CV21 1JZ (0788 571738).
Ground: East Warwickshire College *(*** N.B. The club will probably be on a new ground for 94-95 ****).*
Previous Names: Rugby Town/ Rugby Irish - clubs merged in 1992.
93-94 Captain: J Whiteside **Previous League:** Coventry & North Warwick 1992-93.

STUDLEY B.K.L. RESERVES *(see page 599)*

THIMBLEMILL R.E.C.

Manager: Peter Gardiner **Programme:** Yes **Founded:** 1964.
Secretary: G M Houten, 68 Gower Road, Lapal, Halesowen, West Mids B62 9BT (021 442 3357).
Ground: Thimblemill Recreation, Thimblemill Road, Smethwick, Warley (021 429 2459).
Colours: White (blue trim)/white/navy blue
Hons: Midland Combination Challenge Vase R-up 92-93 (Challenge Cup QF 91-92).

DIVISION THREE CLUBS 1994-95

ANSELLS RESERVES *(see page 597)*

BARLESTONE St GILES RESERVES *(see page 601)*

BIRCHFIELD SPORTS

Secretary: T Howell, 32 Arbor Gate, Shire Oak, Walsall, West Midlands WS9 9ZF (0543 452041).
Ground: British Gas Sports Ground, Woodacre Rd, Erdington (021 373 1018).
Colours: Blue/white/blue **Previous Names:** Swan Spts/ Newtown Utd - clubs merged 1994.
Previous Lges: Swan Sports - Birmingham Works (pre-1994)/ Newtown Utd - Black County Alliance (pre-1994).

BROWNHILLS TOWN

Chairman: Alan Payne **Manager:** Tim Wall **Founded:** 1957
Secretary: Mr C Kelly, School House, St Marks Rd, Shire Oak, Brownhills (0543 374193)
Physio: Steve Hughes **Trainer:** Paul Gibson.
Ground: Jubilee Park, Hanney Hay Rd, Hammerwich, Brownhills.
Directions: A5 Watling Street from Cannock towards Lichfield, thru lights by Chasewater Amusement Park, Hanney Rd 1st left after next lights.
Cover: No **Capacity:** 800 **Floodlights:** No **Programme:** 32 pages, 25p
Cols: Sky & white stripes/royal/sky **Change colours:** Red & white/red
Cloubhouse: Hospitality lounge only **Previous League:** Staffs County League (South) pre-1994.
Hons: Staffs Co. (Sth) Lg Div 1 R-up 91-92 (Lge Shield R-up 91-92), Cannock Charity Cup 90-91.

CADBURY ATHLETIC

Secretary: J Peckham, 35 Maurice Rd, Kings Heath, Birmingham B14 6DL (021 444 2594).
Ground: Bournville Recreation Ground, Bournville Lane, Bournville, Birmingham.
Cols: Blue & white halves **Previous Leagues:** None **Founded:** 1994.

CHESLYN HAY

Chairman: Gordon Cross **Vice-Presidents:** Larry Lazenby, Jim Randall. **Founded:** 1984.
Secretary: Mr Ivor Osborne, 16 Littlewood Lane, Cheslyn Hay, Walsall WS6 7EJ (0922 414755).
Manager: Carl Oulton. **Assistant Manager:** Richard Cross.
Physio: Bill Cox **Press Officer:** Dave Ellis.
Ground: As Great Wyrley FC (see West Midlands League section).
Programme: Yes **Editor:** Dawn Cox (0922 408678) **Club Shop:** Not yet **Nickname:** The Hay
Colours: Orange/white/orange **Change:** Blue & white stripes/blue/blue.
Previous Grounds: Lucas Sports 84-88/ Rushall Community Centre 88-89/ Cheslyn Hay Rec. 89-90/ Harrison MW ground (on opposite side of Hazel Lane) 90-91.
Previous Leagues: Bloxwich Comb. 84-88/ Staffs County (South) 88-90/ West Midlands (Regional) 90-94.
Midweek home matchday: Tuesday **Record Gate:** 126 v Gt Wyrley, West Mids Lge Div One 26/3/94.
Record win: 8-1 v Mitchells & Butlers Reserves, 14/1/89.
Record defeat: 0-10 v Bloxwich Strollers (H), West Midlands (Regional) Lge 9/10/93.
Club Sponsors: Pro-Clean **Clubhouse:** Open evenings & matchdays.
Club record scorer: Gary Osborne, 52 **Club record appearances:** Gary Osborne, 290.
Captain 93-94: Dave Gibson **Top Scorer 93-94:** Scott Hydon, Dave Gibson.
P.o.Y. 93-94: Ian Hawkins, Darren Pemberton. **Hons:** Bloxwich Comb. Lg Cup 86-87 87-88.

DUDLEY SPORTS RESERVES *(see page 601)*

ENVILLE ATHLETIC RESERVES *(see page 604)*

KINGS HEATH RESERVES *(see page 598)*

MITCHELLS & BUTLERS

Chairman: L Linford **Manager:** T Malanaphy.
Secretary: Mr Ian R Burford, 141 Cape Hill, Smethwick, West Mids B66 4SH (021 565 2143).
Asst Manager: P Walsh **Coach:** M Shaw **Physio:** J McGowan.
Ground: City Road, Edgbaston, Birmingham (021 420 1576/429 2469(club)).
Directions: From Birmingham City centre follow Broad Street down Five Ways island, go under island into Hagley Rd, right into Sandon Rd after approx one and a half miles, right at 1st lights into City Road. From M5 jct 1, left at 2nd island onto A457, after 3rd set of lights 1st right into Shenstone Road, right at 'T' junction into City Road - ground entrance 100 yds on left. Buses 82, 87, 88 & 89 from Birmingham centre - alight at Summerfield Park and take 1st left into City Road.
Seats: Nil **Cover:** 50 **Capacity:** 500 **Floodlights:** No **Founded:** 1871
Colours: Navy & sky **Change colours:** All red **Nickname:** Brewers.
Previous Grounds: Winson Street 1877/ The Oval, Cape Hill 1888.
Previous Names: Birmingham St George/ Mitchells St George.
Previous Leagues: Football Alliance/ Birmingham Works (pre-1985).
Programme: No **Club Shop:** No. **Club Sponsors:** V.T. Plastics/ Stevetone.
Record win: 13-0 v Barlestone St Giles Reserves, Midland Combination Division Three 11/12/93.
(Recent) Record Gate: 450 v Birmingham City, friendly.
Midweek home matchday: Tuesday **Reserve team's League:** Staffs Co. (South).
Captain 93-94: **Top Scorer & P.o.Y. 93-94:**
Club record scorer: R Cox/ D Jessop. **Clubhouse:** Open after matches. Cold food available.
Hons: Staffs Chal. Cup twice (including 1-0 win over West Brom in final at Stoke in 1888), WBA Shield 82-83 83-84, B'ham Wks Lg Div 1 82-83 (Div 4(res) 82-83), M & B Cup 82-83, Sandwell Charity Cup 84-85.

MOXLEY RANGERS RESERVES *(see page 590)*

PARK RANGERS

President: Dennis Gallear. **Chairman:** Bernard Leishenring
Secretary: Peter Worwood, 3 Speedwell Close, Aldridge, West Mids WS9 0DL (0922 56385).
Manager: Frank Beglin **Commercial Mgr:** Nick Willis (0384 74374).
Press Officer: Mike Bullock (0384 74528).
Ground: Tividale Community Centre, Lower City Road, Tividale, Warley, West Mids (021 544 8332).
Directions: A4123 towards Dudley from M5 jct 2; Lower City Road is on right opposite 'Huntsman' pub and ground is signposted 300yds on right. 126 bus from Dudley or Birmingham. Nearest BR station is Dudley Port.
Seats: None **Cover:** No **Capacity:** 1,000 **Floodlights:** No **Founded:** 1968
Cols: Red & white stripes/black/red **Change colours:** Yellow/black/black. **Reserve team:** No.
Previous Leagues: West Midlands Metropolitan/ Staffs County (South)/ West Mids (Regional) 91-93.
Programme: 28 pages, free **Editor:** Mike Bullock (0384 74528) **Club Shop:** No.
Sponsors: Aldridge Electrical **Midweek home matchday:** Tuesday
Record win: 11-1 v Bearwood Am. **Record defeat:** 0-9 v Bloxwich Strollers.
Nickname: Salamanders **Clubhouse:** Yes. Food for special matches only.
Captain 93-94: Richard Beeton **Top Scorer 93-94:** Rob Hingley.
P.O.Y. 93-94: Robin Wall **Club record scorer:** Pat Hoban.
Hons: Albion Shield 68-69, West Mids Metropolitan Lg Div 1 North 70-71, Jennings Invitation Cup 73-74, Ike Cooper Cup 90-91.

STUDLEY UNITED

Secretary: J Suval, 29 Humbleton Close, Lodge Park, Redditch, Worcs B98 7LT (0527 525455).
Ground: Abbey Stadium, Redditch.
Colours: Sky/white **Previous League:** Stratford Alliance (pre-1994).
Honours: Stratford Alliance Nursing Home Cup 93-94.

WELLESBOURNE RESERVES *(see page 599)*

WEST MIDLANDS POLICE RESERVES *(see page 577)*

WILMCOTE RESERVES *(see page 603)*

WOLVERHAMPTON CASUALS RESERVES *(see page 591)*

ESSEX SENIOR LEAGUE (Est. 1971)

FEEDER TO:
DIADORA LEAGUE

President: David Pond, FCA

Chairman/Publicity Officer: Robert Errington

Vice-Chairman: Vernon Sitch

Treasurer: Margaret Errington

Secretary: David Wingrove, 8 Oak Place, North Weald, Epping, Essex CM16 6JJ (0992 522147)

BASILDON UNITED IN DOUBLE SUCCESS

In an extremely successful year for the League in outside competitions, domestic honours were achieved by Basildon United with Vic Elson's lads winning the League and Challenge Cup in his first season as Manager.

A League record was achieved by Canvey Island who ventured further than any team previously in the FA Cup, going down 1-3 to Kettering of the GMV Conference in the Fourth Qualifying Round after wins over Boston United and Bishop's Stortford in earlier rounds. Their fantastic success over the past two years culminated in acceptance to the Diadora League, and we wish them every good wish in the future which has seen previous Senior League clubs still reaping reward for their endeavours.

Another honour for Canvey was the Essex Thameside Trophy - again a first for the League. They also kept the flag flying longer than any other club in the FA Vase, though Ford United can look back on being one of the most difficult hurdles for Diss Town on their Wembley adventure. The Motormen played host to Moscow Dynamo in the mid-season and were League runners-up. Their season, one of the best for years saw, more silverware in the magnificant shape of the London Senior Cup when they defeated Hanwell to lift the trophy - the first time, once again, for a Senior League Club.

Sawbridgeworth Town won the Hertfordshire Senior Trophy and were League Cup runners-up. All clubs in Essex and Sawbridgeworth, in Herts, now look forward to competing in their County Senior Cup competitions rather than the Trophy and this is partly down to the excellent standards of Senior football and Grounds one can expect in the Essex Senior League.

Brentwood started on their new ground in October, and Maldon Town left their's after 41 years at Fambridge Road with a brand new stadium being built for the new season. They will also be managed by Ben Embery who moves over from Great Wakering Rovers, a club that impressed many

Basildon United - Senior League champions and League Cup winners 1993-94. Photo - Robert Errington.

clubs in the FA Vase with their superb catering and "feasts" after home ties!

All Officers continue the good work of the League with the only constitutional changes being in the Reserve League which finds Stansted Reserves being replaced by Eton Manor Reserves.

One of the most universally popular awards last season was that for 'Secretary of the Year' with "Mr East Ham" Reuben Gane applauded for his hard work in running every section of the club in such an admirable way. Another unique honour went to Hullbridge Sports who won the Sportsmanship Award for the third successive season, whilst the oddest achievement went to Scot Ardley at Stansted FC who was not only the Leading Reserve goalscorer with 33 but his first team's leading scorer as well, with 6! He won the Trophy for the overall top league scorer. Reward for the island of Canvey's second senior side, Concord Rangers, came in the form of first place in the Wirral Programme Awards for our League with their programme edited by Paul Norton-Ashley.

Robert Errington, Chairman

LEAGUE TABLES 1993-94

SEN. SECTION	P	W	D	L	F	A	PTS
Basildon United	30	21	7	2	64	18	70
Ford United	30	20	6	4	64	16	66
Canvey Island	30	19	5	6	50	22	62
Romford	30	16	6	8	52	37	54
Gt Wakering R.	30	16	5	9	69	40	53
Bowers United	30	14	6	10	40	44	48
Brentwood	30	13	6	11	49	43	45
Sawbridgeworth	30	13	6	11	46	40	45
Concord Rangers	30	11	7	12	50	41	40
East Ham United	30	10	8	12	46	54	38
Maldon Town	30	11	3	16	38	46	36
Eton Manor	30	8	2	20	37	74	26
Southend Manor	30	6	7	17	42	65	25
Burnham Ramblers	30	7	4	19	32	55	25
Hullbridge Spts	30	5	7	18	30	74	22
Stansted	30	4	7	19	28	68	19

RES. SECTION	P	W	D	L	F	A	PTS
Gt Wakering Res.	24	17	3	4	76	22	54
Sawbridgeworth Res.	24	14	3	7	51	27	45
Brentwood Res.	24	13	5	6	50	30	44
Balsildon U. Res.	24	12	6	6	52	41	42
Hullbridge S. Res.	24	12	5	7	49	29	41
Burnham R. Res.	24	12	3	9	50	45	39
Southend Mnr Res.	24	11	3	10	33	60	36
Stansted Res.	24	11	1	12	55	58	34
Bowers Utd Res.	24	6	7	11	37	38	25
Canvey Is. Res.	24	7	4	13	29	40	25
Maldon Town Res.	24	7	2	15	45	53	23
Concord Rgrs Res.	24	6	5	13	27	56	23
Brightlingsea Res.	24	2	5	17	26	81	11

SENIOR SECTION RESULTS

	1	2	3	4	5	6	7	8	9	10	11	12	13	14	15	16
1. Basildon United	*	1-0	0-1	4-0	0-0	3-1	3-1	5-2	0-0	2-1	7-0	2-1	1-1	1-1	1-1	1-0
2. Bowers United	0-1	*	3-1	2-1	0-2	0-7	3-4	4-1	0-2	2-1	3-0	2-1	1-0	1-0	1-0	3-2
3. Brentwood	0-3	0-1	*	3-0	1-2	0-1	2-2	5-1	0-0	1-4	4-1	2-1	3-2	0-3	3-2	1-1
4. Burnham Ramblers	0-2	1-1	1-0	*	1-4	1-4	2-1	0-1	0-1	1-2	3-0	3-1	2-3	1-0	2-5	0-0
5. Canvey Island	0-1	0-0	1-2	2-1	*	1-0	3-1	4-0	1-0	2-0	1-1	4-1	1-1	0-0	6-1	3-0
6. Concord Rangers	1-3	0-0	0-1	3-1	0-1	*	0-0	3-0	1-3	1-1	1-0	2-0	0-1	5-0	0-0	0-0
7. East Ham United	0-1	1-1	3-1	1-0	0-1	1-1	*	0-1	0-4	2-1	3-1	1-0	0-2	0-0	5-3	7-4
8. Eton Manor	0-3	1-2	3-3	0-3	0-2	2-4	1-1	*	0-1	2-1	1-2	2-1	2-1	3-2	2-3	1-3
9. Ford United	2-2	5-0	2-0	0-0	2-0	5-0	6-1	3-2	*	2-0	4-0	0-0	0-1	1-0	3-2	4-0
10. Great Wakering Rovers	0-3	5-2	1-2	4-1	4-2	2-1	2-3	5-0	1-1	*	6-1	2-0	1-0	2-2	8-0	3-1
11. Hullbridge Sports	0-5	1-1	1-3	1-3	2-0	2-2	3-2	6-1	0-2	0-1	*	0-0	1-4	0-4	0-0	1-1
12. Maldon Town	0-1	2-1	0-2	3-2	2-4	2-0	2-1	2-0	2-0	1-1	2-1	*	1-4	4-1	1-0	2-0
13. Romford	0-2	1-0	1-1	4-1	1-0	3-2	1-1	2-1	0-3	2-3	1-1	1-0	*	1-0	4-1	1-0
14. Sawbridgeworth Town	1-3	1-2	2-0	1-0	0-1	5-3	1-0	2-1	2-1	2-2	4-0	2-1	4-3	*	1-0	3-0
15. Southend Manor	1-1	2-2	1-1	1-0	0-1	1-2	5-3	1-4	1-2	1-2	4-0	2-5	2-2	2-0	*	0-2
16. Stansted	2-3	0-2	0-6	1-1	0-1	2-5	0-0	0-2	0-5	0-3	1-4	3-0	2-4	2-2	1-0	*

RES. SECT. RESULTS	1	2	3	4	5	6	7	8	9	10	11	12	13
1. Basildon U. Res	*	0-0	4-1	2-2	2-2	2-1	2-0	2-0	1-0	4-4	2-0	5-0	1-3
2. Bowers Utd Res	0-1	*	0-0	7-0	1-3	1-2	2-2	0-2	1-1	2-1	0-2	1-2	4-0
3. Brentwood Res	2-1	0-0	*	10-0	3-1	1-2	3-0	2-0	1-1	3-1	1-0	0-1	3-4
4. Brightlingsea Res	2-2	1-0	1-4	*	1-2	3-0	3-4	0-7	0-3	2-3	2-2	1-2	1-5
5. Burnham Rblrs Res	4-2	1-3	0-1	4-2	*	4-2	3-4	1-3	2-2	2-1	4-3	5-0	5-4
6. Canvey Island Res	2-1	0-2	1-2	1-1	0-1	*	0-0	1-4	2-0	3-2	0-1	0-0	5-0
7. Concord Rangers Res	0-2	3-3	0-3	1-1	2-1	3-0	*	1-3	0-5	3-2	0-0	0-1	2-3
8. Gt Wakering Res.	2-2	3-3	1-1	9-1	3-1	4-0	6-0	*	0-1	2-0	3-1	5-1	3-0
9. Hullbridge Spts Res	2-4	1-4	1-0	3-1	1-1	2-1	3-0	1-2	*	3-0	2-2	6-0	6-1
10. Maldon Town Res	7-1	5-1	3-4	1-0	0-1	0-0	0-1	1-3	3-2	*	2-4	4-0	2-1
11. Sawbridgeworth T. Res	4-0	2-0	4-0	4-0	1-0	3-0	2-0	2-1	0-1	3-0	*	1-2	2-5
12. Southend Manor Res	1-6	4-2	3-3	2-1	3-0	0-5	3-1	0-5	0-1	2-1	1-5	*	2-2
13. Stansted Res	2-3	2-0	1-2	3-0	1-2	3-1	5-0	0-5	3-1	6-2	1-3	0-3	*

LEAGUE CHALLENGE CUP

First Round

Bowers United v Maldon Town	0-1 *(aet)*	Great Wakering Rovers v Hullbridge Sports	6-0
East Ham United v Burnham Ramblers	1-2	Basildon United v Concord Rangers	1-0
Eton Manor v Romford	1-6	Canvey Island v Ford United	0-6
Brentwood v Southend Manor	5-2	Stansted v Sawbridgeworth Town	0-2

Quarter-Finals

Burnham Ramblers v Basildon United	1-3	Maldon Town v Great Wakering Rovers	6-3
Brentwood v Sawbridgeworth Town	2-4 *(aet)*	Romford v Ford United	2-1 *(aet)*

Semi-Finals (Two Legs)

Romford v Sawbridgeworth	0-1 *(R'fd expelled)*	Maldon Town v Basildon United	0-3,0-4

Final *(at Burnham Ramblers FC, Saturday 30th April. Attendance: 162)*:
Basildon Utd 3 *(Taylor 18, Kean 35, Wren 49)*, **Sawbridgeworth Town 0**
Basildon: Stephen Mead, Wayne Martin, Mark Wagner, Jeff Short, Cliff Moorcraft, Russell Kean, Burgess Pocock, Greg Hunt, Paul Wren, John Taylor, Jimmy Hammond. Subs: Jason Coles, Graham Stewart. *Sawbridgeworth:* Jeff Wood, Keith Culverhouse, David Lawrence, Dave Williams, Lol Stapleton, Richard Head, Andy Lewis, Gary Dance, Gary Meadows, Chris Quinn, Richard Stapleton. Subs: Lol Staplton & Ally Hollison.
Referee: John Wiffen (Chelmsford). *Linesmen:* Ken Brown (Rayleigh), Alan Locker (Canvey Island).

HARRY FISHER MEMORIAL TROPHY 1993-94

Quarter-Finals

Bowers United v Canvey Island	1-2	Concord Rangers v East Ham United	2-1
Eton Manor v Hullbridge Sports	0-1	Stansted v Southend Manor	4-0

Semi-Finals

Canvey Island v Concord Rangers	0-0,2-0	Hullbridge Sports v Stansted	1-0,2-4

Final *(at East Ham United FC, Monday 2nd May. Attendance: 203)*:
Canvey Island 4 *(Wiseman 23, Jones 32, McDonald 70, Own-Goal 60)* **Stansted 1** *(Ardley 57)*
Canvey: Gary Harrold, Micky Doyle, Luis Harvey, Tony Mercer, Steve Porter, Kevin Lee, Allen Jacobs, Steve Wiseman, John Potter, Andy Jones, Andy McDonald. Subs: Jamie Wallace, Mark Dziadulewicz. *Stansted:* Sean O'Neill, Richard Smith, Matthew Nash, Scott Cole, Steve Loomes, John Cooper, Richie Taylor, Rod Stringer, Scott Ardley, Keith Wills, Ian Das. Subs: Graham Crisp, Jimmy Cramer.

Right: *Harry Fisher Junior presents Kevin Lee, captain of Canvey Island, with the Harry Fisher Memorial Cup. Photo - Robert Errington.*

SENIOR SECTION TOP-SCORERS:

21 - Paul Flack (Gt Wakering);
19 - John Baptiste (Ford);
17 - Andy Jones (Canvey), Barry Rainbird (Basildon);
16 - Gary Caldon (Maldon), David Stittle (Brentwood);
15 - Richard Stapleton (Sawbridgeworth);
14 - Howard Mackler (Gt Wakering), Steve Card (Bowers);
13 - Sean Adams (Romford);
12 - Len Cook (Brentwood), Cornel Dobbs (East Ham);
11 - Neil Ramsay & Spencer Bush (Gt Wakering), Micky Ross (Romford);
10 - Paul Wren (Bowers);
9 - Steve Knott (Concord);
8 - Mark Dorado (Maldon), Martin Hatcher (Burnham), Martyn Lawrence (Southend M.), Tony O'Keefe (East Ham), Steve Stott (Eton M.), John Taylor (Basildon).

RESERVE DIVISION CUP 1993-94

First Round

Stansted Res v Burnham Ramblers Res	4-4,1-2	Hullbridge Res v Southend Manor Res	2-2,3-2
Sawbridgeworth T. Res v Maldon T. Res	4-1	Great Wakering R. Res v Brentwood Res	5-1

Quarter-Finals

Basildon United Res v Canvey Island Res	1-2	Burnham Ramblers Res v Hullbridge Spts Res	2-3
Sawbridgeworth Res v Brightlingsea Res	4-0	Concord Rangers Res v Great Wakering R. Res	2-1

Semi-Finals

Sawbridgeworth Res v Concord R. Res	2-1,1-1	Canvey Island Res v Hullbridge Spts Res	3-0,0-1

Final *(at Bowers United FC, Monday 9th May, Attendance: 100)*:
Canvey Island Reserves 0, Sawbridgeworth Town Reserves 0 *(aet. Sawbridgeworth won 4-2 on pens.).*
Canvey: Steve Norton-Ashley, Cliff McDonald, Warren Bryant, Richard Thacker, Dave Tiley, John Hood, Keith Brown, Colin Hubbard, Chris Budd, David Jenkins, Martin Gibbs. Subs: Wayne Franklin, Neil McDonal. *Sawbridgeworth:* Danny Green, Chris Webb, Terry Blanchard, Steve Smith, Steve Hastler, John Wicks, Lol Stapleton, Adam Woodrow, Nicky Kemp, Wardle. Subs: Hobbs.

RESERVE DIVISION SHIELD 1993-94

First Round

Southend Manor Res v Stansted Rangers	1-2

Semi-Finals

Bowers Utd Res v Brentwood Res	1-0,1-4*(aet)*	Stansted Res v Maldon Town Res	2-1,0-2

Final *(at Basildon United FC, 18th April, Attendance: 87)*:
Maldon Town Reserves 1 *(Holloway 45)*, **Brentwood Reserves 0**
Maldon: Read, Stone, Cutchey, Arnold, Kerr, Cornwall, Read, Debell, Holloway, Collins, Tokeley. *Brentwood:* McCayna, Stiles, Walker, Butcher, Pether, Bird, Dackombe, Turner, Holmes, Lloyd, Robertson. Sub: Handley.

RESERVE SECTION TOP-SCORERS:
33 - Scott Ardley (Stansted Reserves); 30 - Clive Syrett (Gt Wakering Reserves); 18 - Gary Lloyd (Brentwood Reserves); 15 - Graham Shaw (Burnham Reserves); 13 - P Holmes (Brentwood Reserves); 12 - Jarvis (Hullbridge Reserves); 11 - Holloway (Maldon Reserves); 10 - Kemp (Sawbridgeworth Reserves); 9 - Gordon (Bowers Reserves); 8 - Game (Sawbridgeworth Reserves), Harris (Gt Wakering Reserves), Kelynack (Hullbridge Reserves).

FACTS & FEATS

Best Run: Basildon United: 10 wins out of 10 from 28th August to 27th November, and unbeaten (13 wins, 3 draws) from 21st August until 29th January.

Biggest home win: Great Wakering Rovers 8, Southend Manor 0 - Monday 27th December.
Biggest away win: Bowers United 0, Concord Rangers 7 - Saturday 20th November.

Five goals in a game: By Clive Syrett of Great Wakering Reserves v Brentwood Reserves, League Cup.

BASILDON UNITED

President: Mr J Oakes **Chairman:** Mr Mr Carter **Vice-Chairman:** Mr R Douch
Secretary: Trevor Thomas, 100 Littlecroft, South Woodham Ferrers, Essex CM3 5GQ (0245 323645).
Manager: Vic Elson **Asst Manager:** M Rothon
Press Officer: P Crowhurst (0268 545290)
Ground: Gardiners Close, Gardiners Lane, Basildon, Essex SS14 3AW (0268 520268).
Directions: A176 off Southend arterial (A127), left at r'bout into Cranes Farm Road, proceed to end of duel carriageway, left at lights, Gardiners Close is 1st left (Football Club signed). Two and a half miles from Basildon BR station.
Seats: 400 **Cover:** 1,000 **Capacity:** 2,000 **Floodlights:** Yes **Founded:** 1963.
Colours: Amber & black stripes **Change:** Sky & navy **Sponsors:** Beesbar
Previous Name: Armada Sports **Previous Ground:** Grosvenor Park 63-69.
Previous Leagues: Grays & Thurrock/ Gtr London 68-70/ Essex Snr 70-80/ Athenian 80-81/ Isthmian 81-91.
Reserves' Lge: Essex Snr Res Div. **Record Gate:** 4,000 v West Ham, ground opening 11/8/70
Programme: 16 pages, 30p **Editor:** P Crowhurst (0268 545290). **Club Shop:** No.
Midweek Matches: Tuesday **Clubhouse:** Open lunchtimes, evenings, weekends. Hot food sold.
Players progressing to Football League: Jeff Hull (Colchester), Alan Hull (Orient), David Matthews & Steve Tilson (Southend), Jonathan Gould (Coventry City), Ken Charlery (Watford), Steve Jones (West Ham (via Billericay)).
Captain 93-94: Wayne Martin **Top Scorer 93-94:** Barry Rainbird. **P.o.Y. 93-94:** J Short/S Mead.
Hons: Isthmian Lg Div 2 83-83, Essex Snr Lg(5) 76-80 93-94 (Lg Cup 77-78 93-94, Reserve Cup 92-93), Essex Senior Trophy 78-79.

BOWERS UNITED

Chairman: P Felham **Manager:** Steve Wheeler
Secretary: E D Brown, 92 Quilters Straight, Fryerns, Basildon, Essex SS14 2SJ (0268 521201).
Ground: Crown Avenue, off Kenneth Rd, Pitsea, Basildon (0268 555583).
Directions: Turn into Rectory Rd from Old London Rd (B1464) at Pitsea Broadway into Kenneth Rd, right at top into Crown Avenue. One and a quarter miles from Pitsea (BR). Bus 523 to Rectory Rd, Bowers Guild.
Seats: 200 **Stand:** Yes **Capacity:** 2,000 **Floodlights:** Yes **Founded:** 1946.
Colours: Red & black **Change colours:** Blue/white/white.
Previous Ground: Gun Meadow, Pitsea.
Previous Leagues: Thurrock & Thameside Comb./Olympian. **Clubhouse:** Open every night.
Players progressing to Football League: Steve Tilson (Southend Utd).
Record Gate: 1,800 v Billericay Town, FA Vase. **Midweek Matches:** Wednesday.
Top Scorer 93-94: Steve Card.
Hons: Thurrock & Thameside Comb. 58-59/ Essex Snr Lg 80-81 (Div 1 Cup 90-91, Harry Fisher Mem. Tphy 91-92, Reserve Div R-up 92-93).

BRENTWOOD

Chairman: K J O'Neale **Manager:** Derek Stittle
Secretary: C Harris, 56 Viking Way, Brentwood, Essex CM15 9HY (0277 219564).
Ground: Brentwood Centre, Doddinghurst Rd, Brentwood, Essex.
Directions:
Cover: Yes **Seats:** **Capacity:** **Floodlights:** **Founded:** 1955.
Colours: Sky & navy**Change colours:** All yellow **Programme:** Free with admission
Previous Names: Manor Ath. 55-70/ Brentwood Ath. 70-72. **Nickname:** Blues
Previous Grounds: King George, Hartswood/ 'Larkins', Ongar (pre-1992)/ East Ham Utd FC 1992-94.
Previous Leagues: Romford & District/ Sth Essex Combination/ London & Essex Border/ Olympian.
Top Scorer 93-94: David Stittle.
Hons: Olympian Lg Cup 67-68, Essex Intermediate Cup 76-77, Essex Lg Cup 75-76 78-79 90-91 (Reserve Shield R-up 93-94).

Below: *Brentwood No.3 Jeff Holmes closes in on Colin Wood during one of the first league fixtures to be played at the Brentwood Centre - a goalless draw with Ford United on March 12th.*

Photo - Martin Wray.

BURNHAM RAMBLERS

President: R J Cole, Esq. **Chairman:** Gordon Brasted **Vice-Chairman:** Ron Hatcher
Secretary: Gordon Brasted, 6 Ramblers Way, Burnham-on-Crouch, Essex CM0 8LR (0621 782785).
Manager: Alan Gemmell **Asst Manager:** Paul Bolton **Physio:** Cyril Tennant
Press Officer: Secretary **Commercial Manager:** Jack Frost.
Ground: 'Leslie Field', Springfield Rd, Burnham-on-Crouch CM0 8TE (0621 784383).
Directions: On B1010 from South Woodham Ferrers, turn right half mile before town. 15 mins from Burnham (BR).
Seats: 300 **Stand:** Yes **Capacity:** 5,000 **Floodlights:** Yes **Founded:** 1900
Colours: Royal blue **Change colours:** Red
Programme: 36 pages, 40p **Programme Editor:** Ron Bush (0621 783706).
Nickname: Ramblers **Record Gate:** 1,500.
Midweek matches: Tuesday. **Previous Lges:** N Essex/ Mid-Essex/Olympian/ SE Essex
Reserves' Lge: Essex Snr Div 1 **Previous Grounds:** Wick Rd, Millfields/ Saltcourts (orig.)
Players progressing to Football League: I Woolf (West Ham) 1911, Gordon Brasted (Arsenal) 1953, John Warner (Colchester) 1990.
Clubhouse: Open Mon-FRi 7-11pm, Sat noon-3 & 5-11pm, Sun noon-3 & 7-9.30pm. Hot meals & snacks available.
Captain 93-94: Tony Wilkin **P.O.Y. 93-94:** Gordon English **Top Scorer 93-94:** Gary Shaw.
Hons: Olympian Lg 65-66, Essex I'mediate Cup R-up 81-82, Essex Snr Lg Cup R-up 86-87 89-90 (Reserve Cup 89-90 (R-up 92-93), Reserve Shield R-up 90-91).

CONCORD RANGERS

President: Albert Lant **Chairman:** Grant Beglan **Manager:** C Crerle/Alan Howard
Secretary: Robert Fletcher, 76 Eastwood Rd, Rayleigh, Essex SS6 7JP (0268 770885).
Ground: Thames Road, Canvey Island (0268 691780). **Midweek Matches:** Tuesday.
Seats: No **Capacity:** 1,500 **Cover:** Yes **Floodlights:** Yes **Founded:** 1967.
Colours: Yellow/blue **Change colours:** Blue
Club Sponsor: Aspect Contracts. **Prev. Lges:** Southend & D. All./ Essex I'mediate (pre-1991)
Programme: 10 pages, 50p **Programme Editor:** Paul Ashley (0268 698491).
Previous Ground: Waterside. **Record Gate:** 1,500 v Lee Chapel North, FA Sunday Cup 89-90
Clubhouse: Evenings & weekends. **Record win:** 7-0 v Bowers Utd (A), Essex Snr Lge 20/11/93.
Top Scorer 93-94: Steve Knott **Captain & Player of the Year 93-94:** Wayne Howard.
Hons: Essex I'mediate Lg Div 2 & Lg Cup, Southend Alliance, Wirral Programme Award 93-94.

EAST HAM UNITED

Chairman: E H Whatmough
Mamager/Secretary/Comm. Mgr: Reuben Gane, 108 Beccles Drive, Barking IG11 9HZ (081 594 7861).
Physio: Barry O'Keeffe **Press Officer:** Roland Clooge **Coach:** Harry Cripps
Ground: Ferndale Spts Grnd, East Ham Manorway, Beckton E6 4NG (071 476 5514).
Directions: East Ham Manorway - Cyprus Place - Beckton off A13 Newham Way from east or west. Nearest tube is East Ham thence bus 101 to ground.
Seats: 150 **Cover:** 300 **Capacity:** 2,500 **Floodlights:** Yes **Founded:** 1933.
Colours: Green, white & gold **Change colours:** Gold/green **Programme:** Yes.
Previous Lges: Spartan, Metropolitan **Previous Name:** Storey Ath. 1933-53 **Nickname:** Hammers.
Clubhouse: Evenings & weekends. **Midweek Matchday:** Tuesday
Record Gate: 4,250 - East Ham (inc George Best) v West Ham, friendly 15/2/76 at Terrance McMillan Stadium. 2,400 v Sutton United, FA Amateur Cup 14/11/53.
Previous Ground: Whitebarn Lane (previous East Ham Utd, formed 1880 and played in Sth Essex Lge) 1892-1914/ Tilletss Farm 1933-46.
Players progressing to Football League: Lee Holmes (Brentford 1972), Miguel de Souza (Birmingham City 1988 via Charlton Athletic).
Record scorer: David Norris **Record appearances:** Ken Bowhill, 1964-84.
Captain, Top Scorer & Player of the Year 1993-94: Cornel Dobbs.
Hons: Metropolitan Lg, FA Vase QF, Essex Snr Tphy 76-77, Gtr London Lg Cup 69-70, London Jnr Cup 46-47, Bob Murrant Memorial Trophy 93-94, Carpathian Charity Cup 93-94.

Right: *East Ham United pictured after winning the Carpathian Charity Cup. This cup was formed in 1992-93 by East Ham United to aid homeless children and poor villages in Romania. The competition is a one-off invitation cup final, and this year East Ham beat Barking 2-1. Pictured in the photo are: Back (L/R): Roy Humphries, Reuben Gane (Manager), Tony O'Reilly, Troy Spicer, Roy Lawley, Derek Burnett, Simon Ayaoge, John Charlton, Tony O'Keeffe, Gary Douglas. Centre: Richard Gane, Dave Reilly. Front: Mark Robson (Charlton Athletic/East Ham fan), Cornel Dobbs, Jamie Brownlow.*

ETON MANOR

Chairman: D McCann.
Secretary: George E Whiting, 69 John Walsh Tower, Montague Rd., Leytonstone E11 3ET (081 558 3594).
Manager: A Jones **Coach:** C Drane **Physio:** F Rose.
Ground: ******* *At Roding Lane, Buckhurst Hill (081 504 9937). The ground is being brought up to 'senior' standard, but in the meantime the club will probably play all home games at Stansted FC (see below). Spectators should phone the club secretary (evenings only) or Stansted FC to check match information.* *********
Colours: Sky & navy **Change colours:** All yellow **Nickname:** The Manor
Midweek Matches: TBA **Reserves' League:** Ilford & Dist. **Founded:** 1901
Programme: 12 pages with entry **Programme Editor:** Secretary
Record Gate: 600 v Leyton Orient, opening of floodlights at Roding Lane.
Previous Grounds: Wildness, Hackney/ GUS Sports Ground, Clapton/ Walthamstow Avenue FC/ Norwegian Ground, Barking.
Previous Name: Wilderness Leyton.
Previous Leagues: London 33-59/ Aetolian 59-64/ Greater London 64-69/ Metropolitan 69-75.
Clubhouse: Evenings (except Mondays), matchdays & Sunday mornings. Bar snacks.
Club record scorer: Dave Sams **Top Scorer 93-94:** S Stott, B Walker (joint)
Captain 93-94: Mark Downes **Player-of-the-Year 93-94:** Lee Leather.
Hons: Essex Snr Cup R-up 37-38, London Lg 33-34 37-38 52-53 53-54 (R-up 48-49 57-58, Lg Cup 55-56 (R-up 46-47 54-55)), Greater London Lg 64-65, Essex Intermediate Cup 64-65, London Intermediate Cup R-up 33-34 66-67, Essex Snr Lg Sportsmanship Award 75-76 (Div 1 Cup 90-91, Reserve Div 76-77, Reserve Div Cup 91-92).

FORD UNITED

Chairman: J M Rowe **Vice-Chairman:** Phil Kershaw **President:** Stuart J Harmer
Secretary: K D Dobson, 14 Thornbush, Lee Chapel North, Basildon, Essex SS15 5HW (081 526 1453).
Manager: John Bennett **Asst Manager:** Melvyn Attwell **Press Officer:** Dave Pringle
Ground: Ford Spts & Soc. Club, Rush Green Rd., Romford (0708 745678). **Directions:** On the A124 (Rush Green road) on left going towards Hornchurch. 2 miles from Romford (BR). Buses 173, 175 87, 106, 23.
Seats: 800 **Cover:** Yes **Capacity:** 2,500 **Floodlights:** Yes **Founded:** 1958
Colours: All royal blue **Change:** Yellow/red/yellow. **Nickname:** Motormen
Programme: Yes **Programme Editor:** Colin Mynott (0268 281002).
Previous Names: Briggs Sports (founded 1934) & Fords Sports (founded 1934) merged in 1958.
Previous Grnd: Victoria Rd (now Dagenham & Redbridge FC) **Prev. Lges:** Spartan, Aetolian, Metropolitan
Reserve Team's League: Essex & Herts Border Combination.
Players progressing to Football League: Les Allen (Spurs), Mick Flanagan (QPR, Charlton, Crystal Palace), Jim Stannard (Fulham, Southend, Millwall), Nicky Hammond (Arsenal, Swindon), Laurie Abrahams (Charlton), Doug Barton (Reading, Newport).
Record Gate: 58,000 Briggs Sports v Bishop Auckland, at St James Park, Newcastle, FA Amateur Cup.
Clubhouse: 4 bars, 2 dance halls, tea bar, snooker room.
Captain 93-94: Paul Evans **Club record appearances:** Roger Bond.
Top Scorer 93-94: Ken Baptiste **Player of the Year 93-94:** Terence Beck.
Hons: FA Amateur Cup SF 53-54, London Snr Cup 55-56 56-57 93-94, Essex Snr Trophy 90-91 91-92, Essex Snr Cup 39-40 49-50 50-51 51-52, Spartan Lg 49-50 50-51 55-56 56-57 57-58, London Lg 36-37 38-39, Essex Elizabethan 59-60 60-61 70-71, Gtr London Lg 70-71, Essex Snr Lg 91-92 (R-up 93-94, Lg Cup 85-86, Sportsmanship Award 77-78 79-80 80-81), Essex & Herts Border Comb.(res) 93-94 (Lg Cup 93-94).

GREAT WAKERING ROVERS

President: Eddie Ellis **Chairman:** Trevor Lovell **Vice-Chairman:** Barry Beadle.
Secretary: Roger Sampson, 37 Lee Lotts, Gt Wakering, Southend-on-Sea, Essex SS3 0HA (0702 218794).
Manager: Kevin Maddocks **Assistant Manager:** Eddie Nash.
Physio: John Lattimer **Comm. Manager/Press Officer:** Nobby Johnson (0702 611964).
Ground: Burroughs Park, Little Wakering Hall Lane, Gt Wakering, Southend-on-Sea SS3 0HQ (0702 217812).
Directions: 4a bus from Shoeburyness (BR), 4a or 4b from Southend - alight at British Legion in Gt Wakering alongside which runs Little Wakering Hall Lane. A127 past Southend signposted Gt Wakering. In Gt Wakering, half mile past large Esso garage is along High Street is Little Wakering Hall Lane, ground 250 yds along on left.
Seats: 150 **Cover:** 300 **Capacity:** 1,500 **Floodlights:** Yes **Founded:** 1919
Cols: Green & white stripes/white/green **Change cols:** Red & yellow/red/red **Nickname:** Rovers
Programme: 24-32 pages, 50p **Editor:** Nobby Johnson (0702 611964) **Club Shop:** Not yet
Midweek Matchday: Tuesday **Reserves' Lge:** Essex Snr Res sect. **Sponsors:** TBA
Previous Ground: Gt Wakering Rec. **Record Gate:** 500 v Leyton Orient, friendly 18/7/92.
Previous Leagues: Southend & District 19-81/ Southend Alliance 81-89/ Essex Intermediate 89-92.
Players progressing to Football League: Les Stubbs (Southend, Chelsea) 1947, Jackie Bridge (Southend Utd) 1948, Kevin Maddocks (Maidstone Utd).
Record win (in Senior Football): 8-1 v Southend Manor (H), Essex Snr Lge 27/12/93.
Record defeat (in Senior Football): 3-6 v Maldon Vale (A), Essex Snr Lge 26/3/94.
Clubhouse: Self built with new extension this season to increase capacity to 225. Open weekday evenings, Sat 11am-11pm, Sun noon-3 & 7.30-10.30pm. Hot meals, snacks, rolls, tea, coffee available matchdays.
Captain 93-94: Howard Mackler **P.o.Y. 93-94:** Neil Ramsay **Top Scorer 93-94:** Paul Flack.
Hons: Essex I'mediate Cup 91-92, Essex I'mediate Lg Div 2 91-92 (Div 3 90-91, Lg Cup 91-92), Southend Charity Shield 90-91 91-92, Essex Snr Lg Reserve Section 93-94 (Wirral Programme Award 92-93).

HULLBRIDGE SPORTS

Chairman: Brian Lloyd **Manager:** Mark Lloyd
Secretary: Mrs G Adams, Hullbridge Spts & Social Club, Lower Rd, Hullbridge, Essex SS5 6BJ (0702 230420).
Ground: Lower Road, Hullbridge, Essex SS5 6BJ (0702 230420).
Directions: Turn into Rawreth Lane from A130 (left if arriving from Chelmsford), down to mini-r'bout, left, across next mini-r'bout, up hill, ground signed on right just past garage.
Seats: No **Cover:** Yes **Capacity:** **Floodlights:** No **Founded:** 1945
Colours: Royal blue & white/white/blue **Change colours:** White/black.
Midweek matches: Tues/Thursday. **Prog. Editor:** Mrs Lynne Ward. **Sponsor:** Thermo Shield
Prev. Grounds: Pooles Lane Rec. **Prev. Lges:** Southend & Dist./ Alliance/ Essex I'mediate
Clubhouse details: Lounge bar, function hall with bar & changing rooms - set in 16 acre land.
Top Scorer 93-94: Keith Pullen 7.
Honours: Essex Intermediate Snr Div Cup 87-88, Southend & District Lg Div 1 65-66 (Div 2 51-52, Div 3 56-57), French Cup 51-52, Essex Snr Lg Sportsmanship Award 91-92 92-93 93-94.

Darren Southgate scores one of Ford United's six goals at home to East Ham. *Photo - Richard Brock.*

MALDON TOWN

Chairman: TBA **Manager:** Ben Embery. **Secretary:** Ms Toni Morrant.
Ground: *New ground for 1993-94 - no details received from club.*
Founded: 1946. **Previous Lges:** Eastern Counties, Essex & Suffolk Border.
Colours: Blue & white hoops **Change colours:** Red & white hoops **Programme:** Yes
Top Scorer 93-94: Gary Caldon 16. **Previous Ground:** Fambridge Road (pre-1994).
Hons: Essex Snr Lg 84-85 (Sportsmanship Award 88-89, Reserve Shield 93-94), Essex & Suffolk Border Lg 55-56 (Cup 64-65), Essex Intermediate Cup 51-52, Tolleshunt D'Arcy Cup 93-94.

ROMFORD

President: Roy Mills **Chairman:** Dave Howie **Vice-Chairman:** Steve Gardener.
Secretary: Bob Knightley, 7 Tulip Close, Harold Hill, Romford, Essex RM3 8BX (0708 374900).
Manager: Lyndon Lynch. **Asst Mgr:** Paul Turnpenny **Coach:** Phil O'Reilly
Physio: Allem Hyde **Press Officer:** Andy Adams (0708 347781).
Ground: As Hornchurch FC (see Diadora Lge section) **Founded:** 1929 **Reformed:** 1992.
Colours: Gold/blue/gold **Change colours:** Blue/gold/blue **Nickname:** The Boro
Programme: 24 pages, 50p **Editor:** Ian Howitt
Club Shop: Yes, selling replica shirts, scarves, hats, enamel badges, programmes etc. Contact Barry Quantrill, 11 Easedale Drive, Elm Park, Hornchurch.
Previous Grounds: Brooklands Sports Ground *(original club).* **Midweek Matchday:** Tuesday.
Record Gate: 2,005 v Arsenal Celebrity XI, 28/5/92. **Sponsors:** Romford Recorder
Previous Leagues: None *(Original club: London 29-31/ Athenian 31-39/ Isthmian 45-59/ Southern 59-78)*
Record win: 6-1 v Eton Manor (A), Essex Senior League Cup 16/10/93.
Record defeat: 0-5 v Halstead Town (A), Essex Senior Trophy 28/9/93.
Clubhouse: Licensed bar plus refreshment room serving hot & cold drinks, burgers, hotdogs, snacks etc.
Local Newspapers: Romford Recorder, Post, Yellow Advertiser, Observer.
Record scorer: Shaun Adams 17 **Record appearances/P.o.Y. 93-94:** Roy Drake, 78 appearances.
Captain 93-94: John Simmonds **Top Scorer 93-94:** Shaun Adams 17.
Hons: None *(Original club: FA Amtr Cup R-up 48-49, Southern Lg 66-67 (Div 1 R-up 59-60), Athenian Lg 35-36 36-37 (R-up 38-39), Essex Snr Cup 31-32 33-34 37-38 46-47, Essex Thameside Tphy 51-52 55-56 57-58).*

Below: *Romford FC. Back Row (L/R): Lee Faulkner, Lee Murcott, Roy Drake, Gary Osborne, Steve Brock, John Burrows, Lyndon Lynch (Manager). Front: Terry Venton, Paul Turnpenny, Andy Priest, Mark Brett, Paul King, Shaun Adams.*

Photo - Bob Knightley.

SAWBRIDGEWORTH TOWN

Chairman: Geoff Moore **Manager:** Don Watters
Secretary: Mr H T Annis, 15 Tunmeade, Harlow, Essex CM20 3HS (0279 425865).
Ground: Crofters End, West Road, Sawbridgeworth (0279 722039). **Nickname:** Robins.
Directions: Three quarters of a mile from station; up Station Road then West Road.
Seats: No **Capacity:** 1,500 **Cover:** 250 **Floodlights:** Yes **Founded:** 1890.
Colours: Red & black **Change colours:** Blue
Programme Editor: Ron Alder (0279 722360) **Previous Leagues:** Essex Olympian, Spartan 36-53.
Previous Grounds: Hyde Hall/ Pishiobury/ Hand & Crown.
Record Gate: 610 v Bishop's Stortford. **Top Scorer 93-94:** Richard Stapleton 15
Hons: Essex Olympian Lg 71-72, Essex Snr Lg R-up 92-93 (Harry Fisher Mem. Cup 87-88, Lg Cup R-up 92-93 93-94, Reserve Div 91-92 92-93 (R-up 93-94), Reserve Shield R-up 92-93), Herts Snr Tphy 90-91 93-94 (R-up 92-93), Herts Charity Shield 92-93, Uttlesford Charity Cup 92-93, Herts Intermediate Cup R-up 93-93(reserves).

SOUTHEND MANOR

Chairman: John Hughes **Vice-Chairman/Commercial Manager:** G Cops.
Secretary: Dave Kittle, 15 Seymour Rd, Hadleigh, Benfleet, Essex SS7 2HB (0702 559581)
Manager: Dave Cox **Physio:** John Threadgold **Coach:** Dick Gray
Press Officer: Dave Cox (0268 527202).
Ground: Southchurch Park Arena, Lifstan Way, Southend-on-Sea. (0702 615577)
Directions: A127 then A1159 for 1 mile turn right at second r-about at Rusty Bucket PH, due south for 1 mile - ground on right near sea front.
Seats: 500 **Cover:** Yes **Capacity:** 2,000 **Floodlights:** Yes **Founded:** 1955
Colours: Yellow, red & black **Change colours:** Black & white **Nickname:** The Manor
Programme: 10 pages, 50p **Programme Editor:** Dave Cox (0268 527202).
Sponsors: Reeder Glazing **Midweek Matchday:** Wednesday
Reserves' Lge: Essex Snr Res. Div. **Record Gate:** 1,521 v Southend Utd, 22/7/91, floodlight opener.
Previous Leagues: Southend Borough Combination, Southend Alliance
Clubhouse: Open every evening **Previous Grounds:** Victory Spts/ Oakwood Rec.
Captain 93-94: Danny Saggers **Top Scorer 93-94:** Martyn Lawrence.
Hons: Essex Snr Trophy 92-93, Essex Intermediate Cup 78-79, Essex Snr Lg 90-91 (Lg Cup 87-88, ESL Challenge Cup 89-90, Harry Fisher Mem. Tphy 90-91 92-93 (R-up 91-92)).

STANSTED

President: P Cunningham **Chairman:** Terry Shoebridge
Secretary: P A G Heal, 28 Mountfitchet Rd, Stansted CM24 8NW (0279 812053)
Manager: Bob Dodd/Tony Mercer **Asst Manager:** Alan Mitchell **Coach:** Micky Leslie.
Ground: Hargrave Park, Cambridge Road, Stansted (0279 812897).
Directions: B1383 north of Bishops Stortford on west side of Cambridge Rd. Stansted (BR) - 1/2 mile
Seats: 200 **Cover:** Yes **Capacity:** 2,000 **Floodlights:** Yes **Founded:** 1902
Cols: Blue & black/black/blue **Change:** Yellow & green/gree/green **Programme:** Yes
Midweek home matches: Tuesday. **Record attendance:** 828 v Whickham (FA Vase 83-84).
Prev. Lges: Spartan, London, Herts Co. **Previous Grounds:** Greens Meadow/Chapel Hill
Reserves' League: None 94-95 **Clubhouse:** Open matchdays to 11pm. Sandwiches available.
Top Scorer 93-94: Scott Ardley **Captain & Player of the Year 93-94:** Rod Stringer.
Honours: FA Vase 83-84, Essex Snr Lg 83-84 (Lg Cup 83-84, Harry Fisher Mem. Tphy 82-83 84-85 (R-up 92-93 93-94), Reserve Shield 92-93), East Anglian Cup 83-84, Courage Eastern Floodlight Comp 83-84.

RESERVE DIVISION CONSTITUTION 1994-95: Basildon United, Bowers United, Brentwood, Brightlingsea United, Burnham Ramblers, Canvey Island, Concord Rangers, Eton Manor *(new, replacing Stansted)*, Great Wakering Rovers, Hullbridge Sports, Maldon Town, Sawbridgeworth Town, Southend Manor.

The impressive Trophy table at the Essex Senior League Presentation Dance. *Photo - Robert Errington.*

HELLENIC LEAGUE (Est. 1953)

FEEDER TO:
BEAZER HOMES LEAGUE

Chairman: N A S Matthews

Press Officer: T Cuss

Secretary: M J Jenkins,
Leamington Drive, Faringdon, Oxon SN7 7JZ (0367 240042)

MORETON TOWN ENJOY A FABULOUS SEASON

After the previous season's near miss during which they waited until June 12th 1993 to play their last fixture, Moreton made no mistakes taking the Premier Division Championship by a clear margin of 12 points. The second place challenge was very much closer with Shortwood, Banbury, Wantage and Fairford all fighting hard for the runners-up spot which was finally taken by the former. Moreton Town completed a League and Cup double by winning the Premier Division Challenge Cup defeating Gloucestershire neighbours Cirencester Town.

The Division One title was fought out between Carterton, Pegasus Juniors and Highworth. Carterton secured the championship in the last week of the season with victory over Pegasus Juniors, who themselves overhauled long-time leaders Highworth by winning their final fixture. Wootton Bassett overcame Pegasus to win the Division One Challenge Cup, but this was at the second attempt, the first match having ended in a goalless draw.

Swindon Supermarine took the Reserve Section Honours with Carterton Town Runners-up, whilst North Leigh defeated Abingdon United in the Reserve Section Challenge Cup Final.

Our Representative side played just one game this season, against the Army Football Association, and we recorded one of our best victories for many years defeating the visitors to Cirencester Town FC by 2 goals to 1.

Moreton Town reached the Fourth Qualifying Round of the FA Cup losing in a replay to Sutton United. Indeed the First Round proper might well have been accessible, only a goal-line clearance in the final minutes of the first game thwarting the visiting Moreton side. Milton United and North Leigh reached the Second Round of the FA Vase, whilst in county cups we had representatives in most finals without achieving the ultimate aim; in the Berks & Bucks Senior Trophy Abingdon United were Runners Up; in the Goucestershire Trophy Moreton Town achieved a similar position; Pegasus Juniors emulated this in the Herefordshire Senior Cup; in the Oxfordshire Intermediate Cup Carterton Town Reserves finished second; in the Wiltshire Senior Cup Swindon Supermarine were defeated finalists. Banbury United had a successful run in the Birmingham Senior Cup overcoming Kings Heath and West Bromwich Albion before bowing out to Walsall.

Our Season has sadly seen the death of Vice-President Ronald Chard and Vice-Chairman Ray Barlow together with a number of club representatives. Although not in the best of health, Ray Barlow had guided the Ground Grading Committee through their given task of inspecting all Premier Division clubs and their facilities before October 30th 1993 which resulted in all Clubs receiving a Schedule of mandatory requiremnts for Ground Grading purposes. All Clubs in the Premier Division will now have floodlight facilities for the forthcoming Season.

Trevor Cuss, Press Liasison Officer

Moreton Town - Hellenic League champions 1993-94.

PREM. DIV.	P	W	D	L	F	A	PTS
Moreton Town	34	25	6	3	74	21	81
Shortwood United	34	21	6	7	66	48	69
Banbury United	34	18	9	7	74	44	63
Wantage Town	34	18	9	7	68	38	63
Fairford Town	34	18	7	9	76	51	61
Cinderford Town	34	17	6	11	57	39	57
Bicester Town	34	17	6	11	64	48	57
S'don Supermarine	34	16	6	12	64	42	*51
Rayners Lane	34	13	7	14	64	53	46
Tuffley Rovers	34	14	4	16	60	53	46
Milton United	34	13	6	15	59	68	45
Abingdon United	34	12	8	14	60	57	44
Cirencester Town	34	12	4	18	53	62	40
North Leigh	34	10	9	15	60	58	39
Almondsbury Town	34	10	7	17	38	61	37
Headington Amtrs	34	7	11	16	43	77	32
Wollen Sports	34	4	6	24	34	95	18
Kintbury Rangers	34	2	1	31	17	126	17

* - 3 points deducted

DIV. ONE	P	W	D	L	F	A	PTS
Carterton Town	34	21	8	5	82	27	71
Pegasus Juniors	34	21	6	7	86	44	69
Highworth Town	34	20	8	6	58	30	68
Lambourn Sports	34	17	10	7	65	38	61
Bishops Cleeve	34	17	8	9	79	54	59
Hallen	34	16	10	8	62	50	58
Easington Sports	34	15	9	10	66	49	54
Wallingford Town	34	14	11	9	74	54	53
Wootton Bassett T.	34	15	8	11	65	57	53
Cheltenham Saras	34	14	9	11	63	50	51
Ardley United	34	12	11	11	59	50	47
Kidlington	34	10	8	16	52	68	38
Purton	34	10	7	17	52	74	37
Cirencester United	34	8	7	19	50	81	31
Didcot Town	34	9	2	23	49	97	29
Yarnton	34	8	4	22	43	85	**26
Clanfield	34	4	9	21	32	75	21
Letcombe Sports	34	6	3	25	26	80	21

* - 3 points deducted

RESERVE DIV.	P	W	D	L	F	A	PTS
Supermarine Res.	24	18	3	3	90	27	57
Carterton Res.	24	18	2	4	68	32	56
Fairford Res.	24	17	3	4	63	23	54
Headington Res.	24	17	3	4	73	39	54
Highworth T. Res.	24	14	5	5	60	34	47
Cheltenham S. Res.	24	15	1	8	59	38	46
Bicester Town Res.	24	12	7	5	67	37	43
Abingdon Utd Res.	24	12	6	6	62	42	42
North Leigh Res.	24	13	2	9	55	36	41
Easington S. Res.	24	11	5	8	40	30	38
Cirencester T. Res.	24	11	4	9	42	29	37
Almondsbury Res.	24	9	6	9	47	43	33
Wallingford T. Res.	24	8	8	8	59	45	32
Wantage Town Res.	24	9	3	12	52	49	30
Kidlington Res.	24	9	3	12	52	49	30
Cirencester U. Res.	24	8	6	10	43	54	30
Wollen Sports Res.	24	9	3	12	49	61	30
Banbury Utd Res.	24	8	3	13	39	47	27

Moreton Town and Witney Town withdrew - records expunged

PREMIER DIVISION CHALLENGE CUP 1993-94

First Round
Almondsbury 2, Abingdon United 1
Bicester Town 2, Wollen Sports 3

Second Round
Moreton United 3, Milton United 1
Wollen Sports 2, Almondsbury Town 0
Wantage Town 1, Fairford Town 3
Headington Amateurs 0, North Leigh 0
r: North Leigh 2, Headington Amateurs 1
Tuffley Rovers 2, Cirencester Town 3
Swindon Supermarine 4, Kintbury Rangers 0
Shortwood United 2, Rayners Lane 0
Banbury United 3, Cinderford Town 0

Quarter-Finals
Moreton Town 2, Wollen Sports 0
Fairford Town 2, North Leigh 1
Cirencester Town 4, Swindon Supermarine 1
Shortwood United 3, Banbury United 1

Semi-Finals (Two-Legged)
Moreton Town 1, Fairford Town 1
Fairford Town 0, Moreton Town 1
Cirencester Town 4, Shortwood United 1
Shortwood United 2, Cirencester Town 1

Final *(at Fairford Town)*:
Moreton Town 2, Cirencester Town 1

DIVISION ONE CHALLENGE CUP 1993-94

First Round
Lambourn Sports 1, Cheltenham Saracens 0
Wootton Bassett Town 2, Kidlington 2
r: Kidlington 1, Wootton Bassett Town 2

Second Round
Bishops Cleeve 0, Carterton Town 1
Didcot Town 1, Wootton Bassett Town 3
Easington Sports 2, Highworth Town 0
Clanfield 0, Letcombe 1
Purton 0, Ardley United 3
Hallen 3, Cirencester United 1
Lambourn Sports 7, Wallingford Town 1
Pegasus Juniors 6, Yarnton 3

Quarter-Finals
Easington Sports 2, Letcombe 1
Carterton Town 2, Wootton Bassett Town 3
Ardley United 3, Hallen 1
Pegasus Juniors 3, Lambourn Sports 2

Semi-Finals (Two-Legged)
Pegasus Juniors 5, Ardley United 1
Ardley United 0, Pegasus Juniors 1
Easington Sports 1, Wootton Bassett Town 2
Wootton Bassett Town 2, Easington Sports 1

Final *(at Cirencester Town)*:
Pegasus Juniors 0, Wootton Bassett Town 0

Replay *(at Shortwood United)*:
Wootton Bassett Town 3, Pegasus Juniors 2

RESERVE SECTION CHALLENGE CUP 1993-94

First Round
Abingdon Utd Res. 9, Clanfield Res. 0
Almondsbury Town Res. 4, Highworth T. Res. 1
Witney Town Res. 5, Ardley Utd Res. 1
Fairford Town Res. 5, Wantage Town Res. 0
Yarnton Res. 3, Cheltenham Saras Res. 5
Headington Amtrs Res. 5, Kidlington Res. 0
Moreton Town Res. 5, Cirencester T. Res. 1
Wollen Spts Res. 9, Kintbury Rgrs Res. 0
Cirencester T. Res. 0, Milton Utd Res. 1
Wallingford T. Res. 6, Didcot T. Res. 1
North Leigh Res. 3, Swindon Supermarine Res. 2

Second Round
Abingdon United Res. 3, Almondsbury Res. 2
Banbury Utd Res. 2, Witney Town Res. 0
Letcombe Res. 0, Fairford Town Res. 3
Milton Utd Res. 2, Headington Amtrs Res. 4
Cheltenham Saras Res. 3, Wallingford Res. 0
Wollen Spts Res. 1, Moreton Town Res. 2
Carterton T. Res. 4, Bicester Town Res. 1
Easington Spts Res. 0, North Leigh Res. 3

Quarter-Finals
Banbury Utd Res. 2, Abingdon Utd Res. 3
Fairford Town Res. 4, Headington A. Res. 2
Cheltenham Saras Res. *(w/o)* Moreton Town Res. *(scr)*
Carterton T. Res. 3, North Leigh Res. 1
(Carterton expelled for fielding ineligible player)

Semi-Finals (Two-Legged)
Fairford Town Res. 2, Abingdon Utd Res. 3
Abingdon Utd Res. 2, Fairford Town Res. 0
Cheltenham Saras Res. 1, North Leigh Res. 2
North Leigh Res. 4, Cheltenham Saras Res. 2

Final *(at Fairford Town)*:
North Leigh Reserves 5, Abingdon United Reserves 0

HELLENIC LEAGUE PREMIER DIVISION RESULT CHART 1993-94

HOME TEAM	1	2	3	4	5	6	7	8	9	10	11	12	13	14	15	16	17	18
1. Abingdon United	*	1-0	0-0	1-2	0-1	7-0	0-2	2-4	3-0	2-2	0-5	3-2	3-1	2-3	1-1	0-2	0-1	7-2
2. Almondsbury Town	1-1	*	4-3	1-1	3-0	1-1	2-2	1-0	3-1	2-1	1-4	2-0	0-6	0-1	2-2	1-0	0-2	1-1
3. Banbury United	4-2	2-0	*	2-1	2-1	2-0	0-2	8-1	3-1	3-1	2-4	3-1	2-0	3-1	1-1	2-3	2-2	4-1
4. Bicester Town	3-0	4-0	3-3	*	0-2	1-4	1-4	2-0	2-1	2-1	2-2	1-3	5-1	8-0	1-0	3-1	1-1	2-0
5. Cinderford Town	3-1	0-1	2-1	4-1	*	5-1	1-0	0-1	3-0	1-0	0-0	5-1	3-2	4-0	0-2	1-1	0-2	2-1
6. Cirencester Town	2-4	1-0	1-0	0-1	3-0	*	5-2	2-2	3-0	1-0	1-2	1-0	2-2	1-2	0-2	2-3	1-2	8-2
7. Fairford Town	2-2	5-2	0-4	2-0	3-0	0-2	*	2-2	4-0	3-4	0-2	1-4	3-2	3-0	2-1	3-2	3-1	1-1
8. Headington Amateurs	2-4	0-0	1-1	2-2	0-5	2-1	1-1	*	4-2	2-2	0-0	2-2	0-3	1-2	1-5	3-2	1-5	3-0
9. Kintbury Rangers	0-1	1-3	0-2	0-4	1-1	0-1	0-3	1-4	*	0-4	0-2	0-2	1-4	1-3	2-1	0-4	1-4	3-2
10. Milton United	0-0	4-1	1-3	1-0	3-1	1-2	1-4	2-1	5-0	*	1-2	2-2	0-1	1-4	2-1	2-3	4-2	5-1
11. Moreton Town	1-0	2-1	2-0	3-0	2-1	4-0	2-2	3-0	5-0	2-0	*	5-0	2-1	2-3	1-0	3-0	1-2	3-0
12. North Leigh	2-2	3-1	1-1	4-2	1-3	1-0	2-3	4-0	10-0	1-2	0-0	*	0-2	1-1	1-2	2-2	0-2	4-0
13. Rayners Lane	1-1	3-0	3-4	0-2	0-0	4-2	0-5	3-0	8-0	3-0	0-1	1-1	*	2-2	2-0	2-1	2-3	0-0
14. Shortwood United	1-0	3-1	0-0	2-0	1-1	2-1	2-1	3-1	5-0	1-1	2-1	2-1	3-1	*	6-0	4-5	1-1	1-0
15. Swindon Supermarine	1-2	2-0	0-2	0-1	1-3	3-3	2-0	1-1	6-1	4-0	0-1	2-1	2-0	3-0	*	2-0	3-1	3-1
16. Tuffley Rovers	2-0	0-2	0-1	1-2	1-0	2-1	1-3	4-0	8-0	0-2	1-1	0-1	1-2	1-0	1-3	*	2-0	5-2
17. Wantage Town	2-3	2-0	0-0	2-2	3-2	1-0	0-0	1-1	6-0	2-2	1-2	3-0	3-1	0-1	1-1	3-1	*	1-0
18. Wollen Sports	2-5	2-1	3-4	0-2	0-1	2-0	2-5	1-0	3-0	1-2	0-2	2-2	1-1	0-4	1-7	0-0	0-4	*

HELLENIC LEAGUE DIVISION ONE RESULT CHART 1993-94

HOME TEAM	1	2	3	4	5	6	7	8	9	10	11	12	13	14	15	16	17	18
1. Ardley United	*	3-0	1-3	2-2	1-0	3-0	3-4	1-1	2-2	1-2	3-0	1-1	4-0	2-4	3-2	2-2	3-0	3-1
2. Bishops Cleeve	1-1	*	1-1	3-2	4-0	5-0	3-1	0-2	1-1	4-0	4-0	1-1	6-2	1-1	4-2	2-2	1-4	3-1
3. Carterton Town	2-0	2-1	*	1-1	3-0	2-0	5-0	1-1	4-0	0-1	0-1	1-2	0-0	5-2	2-1	1-1	1-2	6-2
4. Cheltenham Saracens	4-1	1-4	1-2	*	4-3	3-0	2-0	2-3	2-0	2-3	2-1	1-1	3-1	0-0	1-1	3-2	2-2	0-2
5. Cirencester United	1-3	2-3	2-2	1-3	*	3-3	3-1	2-0	1-2	0-3	2-1	1-3	3-0	2-3	1-1	2-2	1-3	1-1
6. Clanfield '85	1-1	3-1	0-3	1-1	0-0	*	0-1	1-2	1-2	0-3	3-3	0-2	3-4	2-1	1-2	1-1	0-2	2-1
7. Didcot Town	2-1	4-6	0-2	0-3	2-2	4-0	*	0-2	0-2	0-1	0-2	0-4	2-0	1-8	3-4	0-7	6-3	4-1
8. Easington Sports	1-1	3-4	1-2	4-1	5-2	3-3	5-0	*	0-1	0-3	6-1	2-0	4-1	1-2	1-2	1-1	1-4	2-1
9. Hallen	1-2	3-0	0-4	1-1	4-2	3-1	2-4	1-1	*	0-0	0-4	1-2	2-0	2-2	4-2	2-2	2-2	4-0
10. Highworth Town	1-1	1-1	0-3	1-0	3-0	6-0	5-2	1-1	0-1	*	2-2	1-1	1-0	1-0	3-1	1-1	0-1	1-1
11. Kidlington	2-1	1-4	2-2	1-0	0-2	3-1	2-1	0-0	0-2	0-2	*	2-3	0-0	1-2	2-3	1-1	2-1	1-0
12. Lambourn Sports	1-1	1-0	1-1	5-1	5-1	1-0	2-0	0-1	1-1	0-1	4-2	*	3-0	2-3	5-0	0-0	0-0	6-0
13. Letcombe	1-2	0-3	0-3	0-4	0-2	2-0	5-2	1-3	1-4	0-2	1-0	0-5	*	0-2	1-1	1-2	2-0	2-0
14. Pegasus Juniors	0-2	3-1	0-4	0-1	4-0	1-1	4-1	2-0	3-0	2-3	3-1	4-0	1-0	*	5-1	2-1	4-2	9-1
15. Purton	2-1	1-3	0-3	0-0	1-3	1-1	0-1	4-2	2-3	1-2	2-2	2-2	2-0	0-1	*	1-4	4-0	2-1
16. Wallingford Town	2-0	0-2	0-8	2-3	2-1	2-0	3-0	1-3	0-2	3-1	7-4	8-0	4-0	2-2	4-2	*	2-0	2-1
17. Wootton Bassett Town	1-1	4-1	3-2	0-6	8-1	0-1	3-1	2-2	2-2	1-0	2-2	0-1	4-1	1-1	1-2	3-1	*	3-1
18. Yarnton	3-2	1-1	0-1	2-1	1-3	3-2	2-2	1-2	1-1	0-3	2-6	1-0	3-0	2-5	4-0	2-0	0-1	*

HELLENIC LEAGUE PREMIER DIVISION TEN YEAR RECORD

	84/5	85/6	86/7	87/8	88/9	89/0	90/1	91/2	92/3	93/4
Abingdon Town	11	4	1	2	-	-	-	-	-	-
Abingdon United	6	7	6	4	3	3	7	6	15	12
Almondsbury (Picksons)(Town)	10	17	-	-	-	7	10	3	6	15
Banbury United	-	-	-	-	-	-	8	10	11	3
Bicester Town	14	15	14	10	6	6	3	9	9	7
Bishops Cleeve	-	-	-	16	10	16	14	18	-	-
Carterton Town	-	-	-	-	-	-	12	17	-	-
Cinderford Town	-	-	-	-	-	-	-	5	5	6
Cirencester Town	-	-	-	-	-	-	-	2	4	13
Clanfield	18	-	-	-			-	-	-	-
Didcot Town	17	-	-	5	8	15	4	7	18	-
Fairford Town	8	13	15	8	4	5	2	11	12	5
Headington Amateurs	-	-	-	-	-	12	5	12	13	16
Hounslow	5	3	2	-	-	-	9	-	-	-
Kintbury Rangers	-	-	-	-	15	8	11	14	14	18
Maidenhead Town	13	18	-	-	-	-	-	-	-	-
Milton United	-	-	-	-	-	-	1	4	3	11
Moreton Town	2	9	8	12	7	13	17	16	2	1
Morris Motors	9	14	7	14	-	-	-	-	-	-
Newport AFC	-	-	-	-	-	1	-	-	-	-
North Leigh	-	-	-	-	-	-	-	-	-	14
Pegasus Juniors	-	11	12	17	5	9	15	13	17	-
Penhill				(See Swindon Athletic)						
Rayners Lane	12	6	13	13	13	11	13	15	10	9
Ruislip Park	-	-	-	-	-	18	-	-	-	-
Sharpness	4	1	5	7	2	4	-	-	-	-
Shortwood United	1	2	3	3	11	2	6	1	7	2
Supermarine	3	5	11	15	14	17	-	-	-	-
Swindon Athletic	-	-	9	6	9	10	16	8	-	-
Swindon Supermarine	-	-	-	-	-	-	-	-	8	8
Thame United	16	10	17	9	-	-	-	-	-	-
Tuffley Rovers	-	-	-	-	-	-	-	-	-	10
Viking Sports	-	-	4	11	17	-	-	-	-	-
Wallingford Town	15	12	16	18	16	-	-	-	-	-
Wantage Town	7	16	18	-	12	14	18	-	16	3
Wollen Sports	-	-	-	-	-	-	-	-	1	17
Yate Town	-	8	10	1	1	-	-	-	-	-
No. of clubs competing	18	18	18	18	17	18	18	18	18	18

PREMIER DIVISION CLUBS 1994-95

ABINGDON UNITED

Chairman: P Evans **Vice-Chairman:** A White **President:**
Secretary: Terry Hutchinson, 41 Austin Place, Dunmore Farm Estate, Abingdon, Oxon OX14 1LT (0494 452559).
Manager: K Stopps **Asst Manager:** R Hayward **PHysio:** A Wise
Coach: John Blackmore. **Press Officer:** W Fletcher (0235 520255.
Ground: Northcourt Road, Abingdon OX14 1PL (0235 520255).
Directions: From north (Oxford) leave A34 at Abingdon north sign and Northcourt Rd is 1st major turning after r'bout. From South, East or West leave Abingdon on A4183 and turn left into Northcourt Rd after 1 mile. 2 miles from Redley (BR)
Seats: 52 **Cover:** 120 **Capacity:** 2,000 **Floodlights:** Yes **Founded:** 1946
Colours: Yellow/blue/yellow **Change colours:** White/red/white. **Nickname:** The U's
Reserves' Lge: Hellenic Res section **Previous league:** North Berks **Prev. Grnds:** None
Programme: 30p **Programme Editor:** W Fletcher, ACJI (0235 20255).
Midweek home matchday: Tuesday **Record Gate:** 500 v Abingdon T., Berks & Bucks Snr Cup 1989-90.
Clubhouse: Two bars, food available. Open normal pub hours every day.
Top Scorer 93-94: S Brierty **Club record appearances:** D Webb.
Captain 93-94: D Miles **Player of the Year 93-94:** S Bloomfield.
Honours: N Berks Lg 53-54 (Lg Cup R-up 53-54, Charity Shield 52-53), Hellenic Div 1 R-up 76-77 81-82 (Lg Cup R-up 89-90, Div 1 Cup 65-66 81-82 (R-up 66-67, Reserve Cup R-up 93-94), Berks & Bucks Snr Cup R-up 83-84, Berks & Bucks Snr Tphy R-up 93-94.

ALMONDSBURY TOWN

Secretary: D W Winstone, 4 St Michaels Close, Winterbourne, Bristol BS17 1NS (0454 773771).
Ground: Oaklands Park, Almondsbury, Bristol (0454 612220/201343).
Directions: Adjacent to M5 junction 16 - follow A38 Thornbury - ground first left. 4 miles from Bristol Parkway (BR). County bus services to Thornbury, Stroud and Gloucester.
Seats: None **Cover:** No **Capacity:** 2,000 **Floodlights:** Yes **Founded:** 1897
Colours: Blue/white/blue **Change colours:** Red/black/black.
Record Gate: Hellenic Cup Final replay 89-90.
Previous Leagues: Bristol Weslyan/ Bristol Suburban/ Bristol Premier Comb./ Glos Co.
Previous Names: Almondsbury/ Almondsbury Greenway/ Almondsbury '85/ Almondsbury Picksons.
Previous Ground: Almondsbury Rec. (until 1986). **Programme:** 20 pages 25p
Nickname: Almonds. **Clubhouse:** 7 days, all sports, refreshments, function room, entertainment, skittles.
Hons: FA Vase R-up 78-79 (SF 77-78), Glos Co. Lg(4) 76-78 79-81 (R-up 75-76 81-82), GFA Chal. Tphy 78-79 (R-up 80-81), Avon Prem. Comb. 74-75, Glos Snr Amtr Cup 87-88, Hellenic Lg 83-84 (R-up 82-83, Lg Cup(2) 83-85).

BANBURY UNITED

Chairman: J Breslin **Vice Chairman:** N/A **President:** N/A
Secretary: D K Jesson, 'Wychwood House', 3 Winchester Close, Banbury OX16 8FB (0295 257262).
Manager: Wallie Hastie **Asst Manager:** Ian Bowyer **Coach:** Phil Houghton.
Physio: John Source **Commercial Mgr:** Alan Glazier **Press Officer:** Barry Worsley.
Ground: The Stadium, off Station Rd, Banbury, Oxon (0295 263354).
Directions: M40 jct 11, follow signs for Banbury then BR station, turn right down narrow lane before entering station forecourt; eastern end of town.
Seats: 240 **Cover:** 800 **Capacity:** 6,500 **Floodlights:** Yes **Founded:** 1933
Colours: White/blue/blue **Change colours:** Blue/white/red **Reformed:** 1965
Previous Name: Banbury Spencer. **Club Sponsors:** J B Motors. **Nickname:** Puritans.
Prev. Lges: Banbury Jnr 33-34/ Oxon Snr 34-35/ Birmingham Comb. 35-54/ W. Mids 54-66/ Southern 66-90.
Record Attendance: 7,160 v Oxford City, FA Cup 3rd Qualifying Round, 30/10/48.
Best FA Cup season: 1st Rd replay 73-74 (Also 1st Rd 47-48 61-62 72-73).
Reserves' Lge: Hellenic Res. section **Best FA Trophy year:** 3rd Rd 70-71 73-74.
Midweek matches: Tuesday.
Clubhouse: Match days & week-ends. Mid-week on hire. Hot food available during aftermatches.
Record transfer fee paid: £2,000 for Phil Emsden (Oxford Utd, Jan 1980)
Record transfer fee received: £20,000 Kevin Wilson (Derby, December 1979)
Programme: 24 pages 50p **Editor:** Barry Worsley (0295 255536)
Club Shop: Yes. Programmes, mugs, ties, sweaters, badges. Contact Barry Worsley (0295 255536).
Players progressing to Football League: Ollie Kearns (Reading), Kevin Wilson & Richard Pratley (Derby), Mick Kearns & Terry Muckleberg (Oxford), Martin Singleton (Coventry).
Record win: 12-0 v RNAS Culham, Oxon Snr Cup 45-46.
Record defeat: 2-11 v West Bromwich Albion 'A', Birmingham Comb. 38-39.
Club record scorer: Dick Pike (1935-48), Tony Jacques (65-76) - both 222.
Captain 93-94: Martin Singleton **Club record appearances:** Dave Matthews.
P.o.Y. 93-94: Dean Hill **Top Scorer 93-94:** Jody McKay 23.
Honours: Oxon Snr Cup 78-79 87-88 (R-up 35-36 48-49 82-83 86-87 88-89 92-93), Birmingham Comb. R-up 47-48, Oxon Prof. Cup 52-53(jt) 70-71(jt) 72-73 77-78 79-80(jt), Hellenic Lg Cup R-up 91-92, Birmingham Snr Cup R-up 48-49 59-60 (SF 46-47), Oxon Snr Lg 34-35 39-40 47-48(res), Banbury Jnr Lg 33-34, Oxon Charity Cup 34-35 (R-up 39-40), Banbury Charity Cup 34-35, Banbury Gold Cross Cup R-up 34-35, Tillotson Cup 46-47 (R-up 45-46), Oxon Hosp. Cup 46-47 (R-up 45-46), Oxon Benev. Cup R-up 77-78 80-81 82-83, Daventry Charity Cup 88-89 89-90, Smiths Mem. Cup 68-69 69-70 (R-up 66-67 67-68), Hitchin Centenary Cup 68-69 (R-up 67-68), Leamington Jnr Cup 50-51 51-52, Leamington & Dist. Lg(res) 51-52, Leamington Charity Cup 51-52, Warks Comb. R-up 57-58 60-61 (Presidents Cup R-up 60-61), Midland Floodlit Cup 67-68, Prem. Midweek F'lit Lg R-up 73-74, Shaw & Kilburn F'lit Lg 77-78, Northants Snr Yth Lg Cup 91-92, Wallspan Comb. 85-86.

Photo opposite: *Banbury United FC. Back Row (L/R): Dave Bristow, Matthew Reynolds, Andy Swan, Neil Sole, Andy Poole, Ian Bowyer, Jody McKay, Dean Hill. Front: Mark Coleman, John Dunham, Darren Reynolds, Paul Warrington, Phil Houghton.*
Photo - Courtesy of the Banbury Guardian.

BICESTER TOWN

Chairman: Terry Williams **Vice Chairman:** Bill Hammond **President:** Mike Staniford.
Secretary/Press Officer: Phil Allen, 38 Bassett Avenue, Bicester OX6 7TZ (0869 252125).
Manager: Kevin Leach. **Physio:** Ray Huntley **Coach:** Steve Silman
Ground: Sports Ground, Oxford Rd, Bicester (0869 241936)
Directions: From Oxford; past Tescos on outskirts of Bicester - ground on right. From Aylesbury; turn left at first island on outskirts of Bicester onto bypass, right at next island, pass Tescos & ground on right.
Seats: 250 **Cover:** 550 **Capacity:** **Floodlights:** Yes **Founded:** 1876
Colours: Red & white stripes/black/red **Change:** Yellow/black/yellow.
Previous Lge: Oxon Senior **Reserve team's league:** Hellenic Lge Reserve Division.
Programme: With admission **Programme Editor:** Secretary
Nickname: Foxhunters **Previous Name:** Slade Banbury Road (pre-1923).
Clubhouse: One bar **Record Gate:** 955 v Portsmouth, floodlight inauguration 1/2/94.
Captain 93-94: Matthew Cresswell **P.o.Y. & Top Scorer:** Brian Flannery.
Hons: Hellenic Lg 60-1 77-78 (Lg Cup 90-91 (R-up 92-93), Div 1 76-77).

BRACKLEY TOWN

Chairman: Kim Golding **President:** Miss C Billingham
Secretary: Don Webb, 32 Bridge Str., Brackley, Northants NN13 5EW (0280 704780).
Manager: Don Watts **Asst Manager:** Chris Possinger. **Press Officer:** Pat Ashby
Ground: St James Park, Churchill Way, Brackley, Northants (0280 704077).
Directions: Churchill Way, east off A43, south end of town
Capacity: 3,500 **Seats:** 400 **Cover:** 50 **Floodlights:** Yes **Founded:** 1890.
Colours: Red, black & white **Change Colours:** All yellow **Nickname:** Saints
Programme: No **Midweek matchday:** Tuesday
Local Newspapers: Brackley Advertiser, Banbury Guardian, Herald & Post.
Clubhouse details: Lounge & main hall. Open all week
Record Attendance: 600 v Kettering, Northants Senior Cup 1989
Previous Leagues: Banbury & District/ North Bucks/ Hellenic 77-83/ United Counties 83-94.
Previous Grounds: Banbury Road, Manor Road, Buckingham Road (upto 1974).
Players to progress to Football League: Jon Blencowe (Leicester)
Hons: UCL 88-89 (Div 1 83-84), N'hants Snr Cup R-up, Buck'ham Charity Cup, Hellenic Lg Div 1 Cup 82-83.

CARTERTON TOWN

President: Mr G Fox **Chairman:** Mr R Stephens **Vice-Chairman:** Mr G Maxwell
Secretary/Physio: Mr R Stephens, 40 Shillbrook Avenue, Carterton, Oxfordshire (0993 843135).
Manager: A Thorne **Asst Manager:** A Dore **Press Officer:** T Sherwood.
Ground: Kilkenny Lane, Carterton, Oxfordshire (0993 842410)
Directions: Enter Swinbrook Rd which off the Burford-Carterton road, proceed into Kilkenny Lane (one track road), ground car park 200yds on left before sharp corner. Hourly buses to Carterton from Oxford.
Seats: 50 **Cover:** 100 **Capacity:** 1,500 **Floodlights:** Yes **Founded:** 1922
Colours: Yellow/blue/yellow **Change colours:** All blue **Reformed:** 1946/1983
Previous Leagues: Witney & District **Record Gate:** 600 v Oxford Utd, Oxon Snr Cup 93-94.
Programme: 20 pages with admission **Programme Editor:** Jenny Maxwell (0993 841301).
Sponsors: Morlands Brewery **Reserve Team's League:** Hellenic Reserve section.
Midweek home matches: Wednesday. **Club record goalscorer:** Tim Dorrington.
Clubhouse: Lounge & fully licensed bar open every day 7.30-11pm, Sat & Sun noon-2pm, Sat 4-6pm. Snacks & meals available.
Top Scorer 93-94: Tim Dorrington **Captain & Player of the Year 93-94:** Andy Henry.
Hons: Oxon Junior Shield 85-86, Oxon Snr Cup R-up 90-91, Witney & Dist. Lg 65-66 (Div 1 84-85 76-77), Hellenic Lg Div 1 89-90 93-94 (Reserve Div 1989-90 (R-up 93-94)), Oxon Intermediate Cup R-up 93-94(res.)

CINDERFORD TOWN

Chairman: A Saunders **Vice Chairman/Press Officer:** A Peacey **President:** S Watkins.
Secretary: C Warren, 9c Tusculum Way, Mitcheldean, Glos GL17 0HZ (0594 543065).
Manager: Tim Harris **Coach:** Denzil Brizland **Physio:** Keith Marfell.
Ground: The Causeway, Hilldene, Cinderford, Glos (0594 22039).
Directions: From Gloucester take A40 to Ross-on-Wye, then A48 - Chepstow. In 10 miles turn right at Elton garage onto A4151 signed Cinderford, thru Littledean, up steep hill, right at crossroads, second left into Latimer Rd. Ground 5 mins walk from town centre.
Seats: 250 **Cover:** 1,000 **Capacity:** 3,500 **Floodlights:** Yes **Founded:** 1922.
Club colours: White (red trim) **Change colours:** Gold & black **Nickname:** Town.
Record Attendance: 4,850 v Minehead, Western League, 1955-56.
Previous Leagues: Western 46-59/ Glos Northern Snr 60-62/ Warwickshire Combination 63-64/ West Midlands 65-69/ Gloucestershire County 70-73 85-89/ Midland Comb. 74-84.
Programme: 28 pages, with entry **Editors:** Chris Warren/ Graham Bevan.
Club Shop: Souvenirs: Club badges (£2), ties, mugs etc. Programme exchanges welcome - contact secretary.
Midweek home matchday: Wednesday **Reserve's League:** Glos. Northern Senior.
Clubhouse: Open every day. 2 bars, kitchen, 2 skittle alleys, darts, dancehall, committee room.
Captain 93-94: **Top Scorer 93-94:**
P.o.Y. 93-94:
Hons: Hellenic League Div 1 90-91, Glos Northern Senior League Div 1 38-39 60-61 (Runners-up(6) 35-37 61-63 66-67 80-81), Nth Glos League Div 1 38-39 60-61, Glos Senior Amtr Cup (Nth)(6) 49-50 54-56 68-69 70-71 76-77 (Runners-up 34-35 57-58 80-81), Western League Div 2 56-57, Warwickshire Comb. 63-64, W Mids League Prem Div Cup 68-69, Glos Jnr Cup (Nth) 80-81, Midland Comb. 81-82, Glos Co. League Runners-up 69-70 71-72 73-74; Glos F.A. Tphy Runners-up 92-93.

CIRENCESTER TOWN

President: Alec Hibberd **Chairman:** Robin Thompson
Secretary: Brian Davis, 97 Golden Farm Rd, Cirencester, Glos GL7 1DG (0285 654274).
Ground: The Stadium, Smithsfield, Chesterton Lane, Cirencester (0285 645783).
Directions: Follow By-pass towards Bristol. The ground is signposted on the left approx quarter of a mile from town. 3 miles from Kemble (BR).
Seats: None **Cover:** 200 **Capacity:** 1,500 **Floodlights:** Yes **Founded:** 1870
Colours: Red & black/black/red **Change colours:** All blue.
Record Attendance: 1,200 in 1968 FA Amateur Cup. **Clubhouse details:** Open 5 nights
Hons: GFA Senior Amtr Cup 79-80, GFA Challenge Trophy Runners-up 91-92, Hellenic League Runners-up 91-92 (Div 1 73-74 (Runners-up 90-91), Div 1 Cup 90-91).

FAIRFORD TOWN

President: B W Wall **Chairman/Press Officer:** M B Tanner
Secretary: M J Cook, "Bow Wow" Down Ampney, Cirencester GL7 5QU (0793 751240).
Ground: Cinder Lane, Fairford, Cirencester (0285 712071).
Manager: Paul Richardson **Asst Manager:** Gerry Kelly.
Physio: T Williams **Commercial Manager:** E Howard.
Directions: Entering Fairford on A417 from Lechlade turn left down Cinder Lane 150yds after 40mph sign. From Cirencester on same road, follow thru village and turn right down Cinder Lane 400yds after Railway Inn. Buses from Swindon, Lechlade and Cirencester.
Seats: None **Cover:** 50 **Capacity:** 2,000 **Floodlights:** Yes **Founded:** 1891
Colours: Red/white/red **Change colours:** White/blue/blue **Nickname:** Town.
Previous Leagues: Cirencester & District (pre-1946)/ Swindon & District 46-70.
Previous Grounds: None **Record Gate:** 1,500 v Swindon Town, friendly 18/7/92.
Programme: 20 pages with admission **Programme Editor:** Chairman **Club Shop:** No.
Club Sponsors: Jewson **Midweek home matchday:** Wednesday
Record win: 9-0 v Moreton T. **Record defeat:** 0-9 v Sharpness.
Reserve Team's League: Hellenic Reserve section.
Clubhouse: Open each evening, weekend lunches & before and after all games
Captain 93-94: John Hathaway **Top Scorer 93-94:** Chris Panter.
P.o.Y. 93-94: Martin Gullis **Club record scorer:** Pat Toomey.
Hons: Glos Challenge Trophy 79-80 (Runners-up 82-83), Hellenic League Runners-up 78-79 79-80 90-91 (Premier Div Cup 78-79, Div 1 71-72, Div 1 Cup 71-72), Glos Jnr Cup 62-63, Swindon & Dist League 64-65 68-69.

HIGHWORTH TOWN

President: Alan Vockins **Chairman:** Darren Robbins **Vice Chairman:** Clive Webb.
Secretary: Fraser Haines, 16 Blandford Mews, Highworth, Swindon SN6 7BQ (0793 861838).
Manager/Coach: Rohan Haines **Asst Manager:** Tony Garland
Physio: Steven Luker **Commercial Manager/Press Officer:** David Evans.
Directions: Enter on A361 from Swindon, past Simpsons Garage, straight over island, next sharp left into Green by Vet's Surgery - ground & car park 60yds on left next to Sports Hall.
Seats: 50 **Cover:** 250 **Capacity:** 2,000 **Floodlights:** Yes **Founded:** 1894.
Colours: Red & white stripes **Change colours:** All blue **Club Shop:** No.
Programme: 16 pages, 60p **Editor:** George Ranson (Shrivenham 782808).
Prev. Lges: Wilts/Swindon & Dist. **Club Sponsors:** Smart Movers.
Midweek home matchday: Wednesday **Reserves' Lge:** Hellenic Reserve Div. **Nickname:** Worthians
Record win: 12-0 v Beeches, Arthur Shipway Cup 1992.
Record defeat: 2-8 v Milton United, Hellenic League Division One, 1987.
Record Gate: 300 v Swindon Supermarine, Wiltshire Senior quarter-final, 1994.
Clubhouse: Sat 12-2.30 & 4.30-11pm. Mon, Wed & Fri 7-11pm. Rolls & Hot food.
Record scorer: Kevin Higgs **Record appearances:** Rod Haines.
Top Scorer 93-94: Edward Gordon **Captain & Player of the Year 93-94:** Darren Hale.
Hons: Wilts Senior Cup 63-64 72-73 (Runners-up 88-89), Hellenic Div 1 Cup 88-89, Arthur Shipway Cup 88-89 93-94, Swindon & District League 63-64 64-65 65-66 68-69.

KINTBURY RANGERS

President: P Adamson **Chairman:** D Palmer.
Secretary: A K Plank, 26 Kennet Road, Kintbury, Newbury RG15 0XW (0488 58460).
Mgr/Coach/Physio: Howard Dim **Assistant Manager:** Andy Head
Commercial Manager/Press Officer: Colin Godfrey (0635 874209).
Ground: Recreation Ground, Inkpen Road, Kintbury (0488 57001).
Directions: Turn off A4 (signed Kintbury) between Newbury/Hungerford. 2nd left after level crossing into Inkpen Road, entrance 200yds on right by Jubilee Centre. Half mile from Kintbury (BR).
Seats: None **Cover:** No **Capacity:** 1,000 **Floodlights:** Yes **Founded:** 1890
Cols: Amber/black **Change colours:** White/blue **Nickname:** Rangers **Reformed:** 1943.
Reserves' Lge: Hellenic Res. sect. **Previous Leagues:** Newbury District/ Nth Berks.
Programme: 16 pages, 50p **Programme Editor:** Colin Godfrey (0635 874209)
Rec. Gate: 400 v Newport AFC, 1990. **Clubhouse:** Open nightly 7.30-11. Hot/cold meals matchdays.
Captain 93-94: Paul Byrne **Club record appearances:** Nigel Llewellyn.
Top Scorer 93-94: Jemer Parish **Player of the Year 93-94:** Kenny Rogers.
Hons: Nth Berks Lg 77-78 81-82, Hellenic Lg Div 1 R-up 87-88, Berks & Bucks I'mediate Cup 60-61 (R-up 87-88).

MORETON TOWN

President: Lord Dulverton **Chairman:** Phil Gould **Vice-Chairman:** Ian Honour.
Secretary/Comm. Manager: A C Honour, 28 Evenlode Gdns, Moreton-in-Marsh, Glos GL56 0JF (0608 651392
Manager: Nick Jordan. **Asst Manager/Coach:** Andy Semke
Physio: Vince Saunders **Press Officer:** Colin Hancox.
Ground: London Road, Moreton-in-Marsh, Glos GL56 0HN (0608 650861).
Directions: On main Oxford - Worcester road A44. Half mile from Moreton (BR).
Seats: 50 **Cover:** 200 **Capacity:** 3,000 **Floodlights:** Yes **Founded:** 1908.
Colours: White/navy/white **Change colours:** Blue/white/blue
Programme: 40 pages, 50p **Programme Editor:** TBA.
Nickname: Lilywhites **Previous Leagues:** Cheltenham/ Mid Cotswold
Record Gate: 1,100 v Newport, 1963. **Clubhouse:** Open every night & all day weekends.
Midweek home matchday: Wednesday **Club Sponsors:** Abbotts Builders.
Players progressing to Football League: Simon Brain (Hereford, via Cheltenham).
Best FA Cup season: 4th Qualifying Round replay 93-94 (lost 0-2 after 0-0 draw at Sutton United).
Top Scorer 93-94: Steve Yates **Captain & Player of the Year 93-94:** Sean Whelan.
Hons: Biggart Cup 69-70 (R-up 84-85), Hellenic Lg 73-74 75-76 82-83 93-94 (R-up 74-75 75-76 81-82 83-84 84-85 92-93, Premier Division Cup 82-83 92-93 93-94), Glos Challenge Trophy 80-81 81-82 85-86 (R-up 84-85 93-94), Beighton Floodlit Cup 92-93 93-94.

NORTH LEIGH

President: Mrs C Smith **Chairman:** Mr B Norton **Vice Chairman:** C Cadwallader/ P Palfreyman.
Secretary: Mr P J Dix, 8 Windmill Close, North Leigh, Nr Witney, Oxon OX8 6RP (0993 881199).
Manager/Coach: Mr P Townsend **Asst Manager:** Mr P King
Physio: Mr R Keen **Press Officer:** Barry Norton (0993 881777).
Ground: Eynsham Hall Park Sports Ground, North Leigh, nr Witney, Oxon (0993 881427).
Directions: Ground is situated off A4095 Witney to Woodstock road 3 miles east of Witney. Entrance to ground is 300yds east of Main Park Entrance.
Seats: 100 **Cover:** 200 **Capacity:** 2,000 **Floodlights:** Yes **Founded:** 1908
Colours: Sky/navy **Change colours:** All orange **Nickname:** None.
Previous Grounds: None **Previous Leagues:** Witney & District 08-89.
Programme: 20 pages, £1 with entry **Midweek home matches:** Wednesday **Club Shop:** No.
Club Sponsors: Various **Clubhouse:** Bar open matches. Snacks available.
Club record scorer: P Coles **Club record appearances:** P King.
Hons: Hellenic Lg Div 1 R-up 92-93 (Res. Cup 93-94), Oxon Jnr Shield 56-57 83-84, Oxon Charity Cup 84-85 88-89, Witney & D. Lg(13) 50-57 84-90 (Lg Cup(10) 47-48 51-52 53-55 56-57 81-82 85-89), Oxon Yth Cup 93-94, Oxon Yth u-17 Lg & Cup 93-94.

PEGASUS JUNIORS

President: P S Hill **Chairman:** R W Pasley
Secretary: K Gladwib, 69 Hampton Dene Road, Hereford HR1 1UX (0432 353549).
Manager: D Bragg **Commercial Manager:** K Bishop.
Ground: Hereford Leisure Centre, Holmer Road, Hereford.
Directions: Leisure centre signposted from city centre on A49 Leominster road.
Seats: None **Cover:** None **Capacity:** **Floodlights:** Yes **Founded:** 1955
Programme: 20p **Programme Editor:** D.Llewellyn **Clubhouse:** 48 Stowens Street.
Cols: Red/white/red **Change colours:** All white **Previous Leagues:** Hereford/Worcester
Previous Grounds: Hereford Utd FC/ Essex Arms Spts Ground, Widemarsh Str.
Hons: Herefordshire Snr Amtr Cup 71-72, Herefordshire Co. Chal. Cup(5) 81-83 84-85 87-88 89-90 (R-up 93-94), Worcs Snr Urn 85-86, Hellenic Lg Div 1 84-85 (R-up 93-94, Div 1 Cup R-up 93-94).

SHORTWOOD UNITED

President: Hugh Robinson **Chairman:** Peter Webb **Vice C'man:** Chris Rivers, Stan Grant
Sec./Press Off.: Mark Webb, 1 The Bungalow, Shortwood, Nailsworth, Stroud, Glos GL6 0SD (0453 833204).
Manager: Steve Hurn **Asst Manager:** TBA **Coach:** Roger Smith
Physio: Adrian Brown **Commercial Manager:** Keith Sheppard.
Ground: "Meadow Bank", Shortwood, Nailsworth, Gloucestershire (0453 833936).
Directions: In Nailsworth turn into Spring Hill then first left. Continue past shop and and keep left past "Britannia" (signposted Shortwood) - continue to end for ground. 4 miles from Stroud (BR).
Seats: 50 **Cover:** 150 **Capacity:** 5,000 **Floodlights:** Yes **Founded:** 1900
Colours: All red **Change:** All blue **Nickname:** The Wood.
Prev. Grnd: Table Land, Wallow Green **Prev. Lges:** Stroud/ Glos Northern Snr/ Glos Co.
Record Attendance: 1,000 v Forest Green Rovers, FA Vase 5th Rd 81-82. **Club Shop:** No.
Programme: 18 pages, 30p **Programme Editor:** Keith Sheppard **Record win:** 11-0
Sponsors: Richard Lacey Insurance **Midweek home matchday:** Wednesday **Record defeat:** 0-9
Reserves' Lge: Glos Northern Snr **Rec. transfer fee received:** Paul Tester (Cheltenham, 80-81).
Clubhouse: Mon-Sat 7-11pm, Sun noon-12 & 7-10.30pm. Crisps etc in bar, hot food kitchen on matchdays.
Captain 93-94: Nick Ackland **Club record scorer & record appearances:** Peter Grant.
Top Scorer 93-94: Rob Cook. **P.O.Y. 93-94:** Gary Marshall **Honours** *(listed overleaf)*

Shortwood United Honours *(carried over from page 621)*: Glos Co. Lg 81-82 (R-up 80-81), Glos Tphy 83-84 91-92 (R-up 79-80), Hellenic Lg 84-85 91-92 (R-up 85-86 89-90 93-94, Div 1 R-up 83-84, Div 1 Cup 83-84), Hungerford Merit Cup, Glos Snr Amtr Cup 85-86 (R-up 79-80), Stroud Charity Cup 91-92 92-93 93-94, Stroud Lg 27-28 (Div 2 26-27 64-65(res), Div 3 25-26 49-50(res) 62-63(res)), Glos Northern Snr Lg R-up 67-68 91-92(res)(Div 2 62-63 80-81(res) 90-91(res)), Arthur Shipway Cup 78-79 79-80.

SWINDON SUPERMARINE

Secretary: Eric Stott, 43 Stanier Street, Swindon, Wilts SN1 5QU (0793 521301).
Ground: Highworth Road, South Marston, Swindon (0973) 824828
Directions: On A361 Swindon/Highworth road, adjoining Marston Industrial Estate. 6 miles from Swindon (BR) - buses in direction of Highworth, Fairford & Lechdale. If lost ask for Vickers Sports Ground.
Seats: 75 **Cover:** 120 **Capacity:** 1,000 **Floodlights:** Yes **Founded:** 1992.
Colours: White/blue/blue **Change colours:** All red **Programme:** Yes
Previous Names: Supermarine (prev. Vickers Armstrong 46-81), Swindon Athletic (prev. Penhill Yth Centre 70-84/ Penhill 84-84-89) amalgamated in 1992.
Previous Leagues: Supermarine: Wilts, *Swindon Athletic: Wilts/ Swindon & District.*
Previous Ground: Supermarine: Vickers Airfield (until mid-1960s), *Swindon Ath.: Merton 70-84/ 'Southbrook', Pinehurst Road 84-92.*
Hons: Wilts Snr Cup R-up 93-94, Hellenic Lg Reserve Section 93-94. As Supermarine: Wilts Snr Cup 85-86 (R-up 74-75 84-85), Hellenic Div 1 R-Up 82-83 (Res Section West R-up 84-85 (Challenge Cup 83-84), Wilts Comb Snr 75-76, Swindon & District Lg Div 3 55-56, Dr Elliott Cup(5), Faringdon Thursday Memorial Cup(3). *Swindon Ath.: Wilts Snr Cup 82-83 86-87 89-90 (R-up 83-84 85-86 90-91), Hellenic Lg Div 1 85-86 86-87, Wilts Co. Lg 82-83 83-84).*

TUFFLEY ROVERS

President: A E Wathen **Chairman:** T Newport **Vice Chairman:** R Craddoc.
Secretary: D M Williams, 10 Byron Avenue, Gloucester GL2 6AF (0452 305776).
Manager: A Ireland **Asst Manager:** J Common
Ground: Glevum Park, Lower Tuffley Lane, Gloucester (0452 504905).
Directions: Follow Gloucester city ring-rd to r'bout signed M5 South & Bristol, take 4th exit signed Hempsted & city centre, after 200yds turn right (McDonalds on corner) into Lower Tuffley Lane, ground 400yds on left.
Seats: 50 **Cover:** Yes **Capacity:** **Floodlights:** Yes **Founded:** 1929
Colours: Claret/blue **Change colours:** All white **Nickname:** None
Previous Grounds: Stroud Rd, Gloucester/ Randwick Park, Tuffley. **Club Shop:** No.
Previous Leagues: Stroud/ Glos Northern Senior/ Glos County (pre-1991).
Programme: approx 10 pages with entry **Editor:** Mr A Purdy, 43 Ermin Park, Brockworth.
Club Sponsors: Ermin Plant **Reserve team's League:** Stroud League.
Clubhouse: 800 yds from ground. Open before & after matches, and normal pub hours at other times. Snacks.
Captain 93-94: C Medcroft **Top Scorer 93-94:** W Organ **P.o.Y. 93-94:** A Pritchett.
Hons: Hellenic Lg Div 1 92-93 (Div 1 Cup 92-93), Glos Co. Lge 90-91, Glos Snr Amtr Cup 87-88, Stroud Lg 72-73, Glos Northern Snr Lg 87-88 (Div 2 79-80).

Carterton Town's R Irvine (right) evades a challenge as the Division champions-elect win 3-0 at Clanfield.
Photo - Gavin Ellis-Neville.

DIVISION ONE CLUBS 1994-95

ARDLEY UNITED

Secretary: The Secretary, c/o Ardley United FC, The Playing Fields, Ardley, near Oxford.
Ground: Playing Fields, Ardley. **Colours:** All red **Change colours:** White/navy/navy
Prev. Lge: Oxon Snr (pre-1993) **Hons:** Oxon Snr Lg R-up 92-93 (Pres. Cup R-up 90-91 91-92).

BISHOPS CLEEVE

President: D Billingham **Chairman:** J Davies
Secretary: Phil Tustain, 7 Dale Walk, Bishops Cleeve, Glos GL52 4PR (0242 674968).
Ground: Stoke Rd, Bishops Cleeve (084267 6752). **Directions:** 3 miles north of Cheltenham on A435. 3rd left in village into Stoke Rd - ground on right. 4 miles from Cheltenham (BR); served by Cheltenham to Tewkesbury buses.
Seats: None **Cover:** 50 **Capacity:** 1,500 **Floodlights:** No **Founded:** 1892.
Colours: Green/silver/silver **Change colours:** Green/black/yellow.
Prev. Lges: Cheltenham, Nth Glos **Prev. Grnds:** The Skiller (pre-1913), Village Field (pre-1950)
Record Gate: 1,000 v Cardiff City, clubhouse opening.
Clubhouse: Full facilities, bar, dance area **Honours:** Hellenic Lg Cup R-up 90-91.

CHELTENHAM SARACENS

Chairman: J Utteridge **Manager:** Gary Bryan.
Secretary: R Attwood, 179 Arle Road, Cheltenham GL51 8LJ (0242 515855).
Asst Manager: C Elsworthy **Coach:** John Caskton **Physio:** Ted Critchley
Press Officer: Terry Coates (0242 520499).
Ground: Petersfield Park, Tewkesbury Road, Cheltenham (0242 589134).
Directions: 1 mile from Cheltenham centre on A4019 Tewksbury Road (next to B & Q) - 1st left over railway bridge, 1st left and follow service road.
Seats: None **Cover:** 100 **Capacity:** 2,000 **Floodlights:** No **Founded:** 1964.
Colours: All blue **Change colours:** All red **Club Shop:** No **Nickname:** Saras.
Prog.: 20 pages, 50p (Ed: Secretary) **Previous League:** Cheltenham 1964-86. **Prev. Grnds:** None
Reserve Team's League: Hellenic Reserve section.
Players progressing to Football League: Steve Cotterill (Wimbledon, Bournemouth) 1988, Keith Knight (Reading) 1989.
Hons: Glos Snr Cup 91-92. **Clubhouse:** 2 mins away at 16-20 Swindon Rd, Cheltenham.
Captain 93-94: Phil Webb **Top Scorer 93-94:** Clive Shatford **93-94 P.o.Y.:** Richard Alder

CIRENCESTER UNITED

President: A Day **Chairman:** J Austin **Vice Chairman:** B Meredith
Secretary/Press Officer: G Varley, 95 Valley Rd, Cirencester, Glos GL7 2JW (0285 657836).
Manager: G Mitchell **Asst Mgr:** B Muir **Coach:** A Smith **Physio:** B Dorey
Ground: Four Acres P.F., Chesterton Lane (0285 651726).
Directions: Dual carriageway towards Bristol, under footbridge, first left after Cirencester Town F.C., ground 200yds on left hand side.
Seats: None **Cover:** No **Programme:** Yes **Floodlights:** No **Founded:** 1970
Colours: White/red/red **Change colours:** Green & yellow **Nickname:** Herd.
Previous Grounds: None **Previous Name:** The Herd (pre-1990)
Previous Leagues: Cirencester & District (4 years)/ Cheltenham (8 years).
Programme: 16 pages, 50p **Editor:** N Warriner (0285 656187) **Club Shop:** No.
Sponsors: D G Sunner (Builders)
Clubhouse: Training nights & matchdays. Rolls & sundries available.
Club record scorer: M Day **Club record appearances:** A Smith.
Hons: Glos Snr Amtr Cup R-up 86-87 89-90, Cirencester Lg 72-73 74-75 (Div 2(3) 71-73 74-75, Lg Cup 74-75, Res. Cup 74-75), Cheltenham Lg 76-77 83-84 (Div 2 75-76, Lg Cup 83-84 (R-up 86-87), Snr Charity Cup 86-87), Stroud Charity Cup 86-87 (Section A 82-83 83-84), Arthur Shipway Cup 86-87 (R-up 87-88 92-93), Fairford Hospital Cup R-up(4) 83-85 90-91 92-93.

CLANFIELD

President: B Wallis **Chairman:** B Court
Secretary: J Osborne, 70 Lancut Road, Witney, Oxon OX8 5AQ (0993 771631).
Manager: G Lock **Asst Manager/Physio:** C Harding
Ground: Radcot Road, Clanfield, Oxon (0367 81314)
Directions: On A4095 8 miles west of Witney & 4 miles east of Faringdon on south side of Clanfield. Buses from Witney - contact Thames Transit for details.
Seats: No **Cover:** 300 **Capacity:** 2,000 **Floodlights:** No **Founded:** 1890
Prev. Grnds: None **Prev. Lges:** Nth Berks/ Witney & Dist. **Clubhouse:** Every evening & Sat/Sun lunch
Colours: Red & blue/blue/red **Change colours:** Blue/white/blue **Nickname:** Robins
Programme: 8 pages, with admission **Editor:** Secretary **Club Shop:** No.
Sponsors: Morelands Brewery **Reserves' Lge:** Hellenic League Reserve section.
Captain 93-94: Peter Burborough **Top Scorer 93-94:** Peter Osborne 9 **P.o.Y. 93-94:** Terry Moss.
Hons: Oxon Jnr Shield 32-33, Oxon I'mediate Cup 67-68, Witney & Dist. Lg 66-67 (Div 1 65-66, Div 2 64-65), Hellenic Lg Div 1 69-70 (Premier Div Cup 72-73, Div 1 Cup 69-70 85-86), Jim Newman Mem. Tphy 83-84 87-88, Faringdon Thursday Memorial Cup 69-70 71-72.

DIDCOT TOWN

President: Bryan Gough **Chairman:** Jim Charman **Manager:** Larry Hill
Secretary: J A Gardner, 8 Green Close, Didcot OX11 8TE (0235 813884).
Ground: 58 Station Road, Didcot (0235 813212). **Clubhouse:** Every evenings and Sunday lunchtimes.
Directions: Midway down Station Rd, Didcot, on right quarter mile from Railway Station towards town centre.
Seats: None **Cover:** 200 **Capacity:** 5,000 **Floodlights:** No **Founded:** 1907
Colours: Red/white/red **Change colours:** All blue
Prev. Lges: Hellenic 53-57/ Metropolitan 57-63. **Nickname:** Railwaymen.
Record Attendance: 2,000 v Wycombe Wanderers, Berks & Bucks Senior Cup 1953.
Programme: 50p **Programme Editor:** Ian Miller.
Honours: Hellenic Lg 53-54 (Lg Cup 1965-66 66-67, Div 1 76-77, Div 1 Cup 76-77).

EASINGTON SPORTS

President: Bob Turnbull **Chairman:** Terry Horley
Secretary: G Lines, 28 Orchard Way, Banbury, Oxon OX16 0HA (0295 254762).
Manager: Philip Lines **Asst Manager:** Bryan Robinson **Press Officer:** R Johnson.
Ground: Addison Road, Easington Estate, Banbury, Oxon (0295 257006).
Directions: From Oxford A423. After passing under flyover on the outskirts of Banbury take first turning left into Grange Road then third right into Addison Rd. Ground at top on left. One and a half miles from Banbury (BR).
Seats: 50 **Cover:** 100 **Capacity:** 1,000 **Floodlights:** No **Founded:** 1946
Cols: Red & white stripes/white/white **Change colours:** White & blue halves/blue/blue.
Programme: Yes, 25p **Record Gate:** 300 v Witney Town, Oxon Snr Cup 1956
Previous Ground: Bodicote. **Prev. Lges:** Banbury Jnr/ Oxon Snr/ Warkwick Combination.
Reserves' Lge: Hellenic Res. section **Clubhouse:** Changing rooms, showers, bar facilities and food.
Captain 93-94: Karlton Stratford **Top Scorer 93-94:** Darren Deeley.
Honours: Oxon Snr Cup R-up, Oxon Intermediate League & Cup, Oxon Snr Lg.

ENDSLEIGH

Secretary: N Toplis, 136 Stratton Heights, Cirencester, Glos GL7 2RL (0285 643104).
Ground: Cheltenham Town FC *(see page 326)*
Colours: Blue/blue/white **Change colours:** Yellow/blue/white.
Previous Ground: The Folley, Swindon Road, Cheltenham (pre-1993)
Previous League: Glos Northern Snr (pre'93)/ Gloucestershire County 93-94.
Hons: Glos Co. Lg R-up 93-94, Glos Northern Snr Lg 92-93 (Div 1 91-92).

HALLEN

Chairman: Mr Roy Toye **Manager:** Gary Bell.
Secretary: C Jones, 67 Meadowland Rd, Henbury, Bristol BS10 7FW (0272 508572).
Ground: Hallen Playing Fields, Moorhouse Lane, Hallen, Nr Bristol (0272 504610).
Directions: M5 jct 17, A4018 to Henbury r'bout, right, right again at junction, next right to Station Road, left into Avonmouth Road at r'bout. One mile to Hallen, ground first left, then right into lane to ground.
Seats: No **Cover:** No **Clubhouse:** Yes **Programme:** No **Founded:** 1949
Colours: All blue **Change Colours:** Green & white stripes/green/green
Previous Names: Lawrence Weston Athletic (80's), Lawrence Weston Hallen (pre-1991).
Prev. Grnd: Kings Weston (early 1980's) **Previous League:** Glos County (pre-1993) **Record Gate:** 250
Hons: Glos County Lg 92-93, Glos Snr Trophy 92-93.

HEADINGTON AMATEURS

President: John Dunne **Chairman:** Donald Light **Vice Chairman:** Paul Sammons.
Secretary: C Barrett, 7 Holland Place, Wood Farm, Oxford (0865 750828).
Manager: Andy Sinnott **Physio:** Chris Gillick **Press Officer:** Andy Sinnott.
Ground: Barton Rec., Barton Village Road, Barton, Oxon (0865 60489).
Directions: From Green Rd r'bout, Headington, (on A40) take Barton/Islip exit (1st exit coming from Witney, last coming from London), turn left into North Way, follow road for half mile - ground at bottom of hill on left.
Seats: None **Cover:** None **Floodlights:** No **Founded:** 1949. **Nickname:** A's.
Colours: All red **Change:** All blue **Midweek home matchday:** Wednesday **Record win:** 5-0
Previous Leagues: Oxford City Junior 49-66/ Oxford Senior 67-88. **Record defeat:** 1-6.
Programme: 8 pages, £1 with entry **Editor:** Stan Hawkswood (0865 65546) **Club Shop:** No.
Sponsors: Oxford Marquees **Previous Ground:** Romanway, Cowley (pre-1990).
Reserves' Lge: Hellenic Res. sect. **Player progressing to Football Lge:** James Light (Oxford) 1970s.
Record win: 6-0 v Carterton (H) 1991 **Record defeat:** 1-8 v Banbury United (A), February 1994.
Clubhouse: Open Tues & Thurs 6-11pm, Sat matchdays 4.45-11pm. Rolls, chips, burgers, hot dogs, sweets etc.
Captain 93-94: Keith Drackett **Top Scorer 93-94:** Russell Vircavs.
Club record scorer: Tony Penge **Club record appearances:** Keith Drackett.
Hons: Oxon Snr League(4) 72-74 75-77 (R-up 71-72 74-75 77-78 81-82 84-85, Div 1 68-69, Presidents Cup(2) 72-74 (R-up 71-72 77-78 84-85)), Oxon Charity Cup 75-76 (Intermediate Cup 88-89), Hellenic League Div 1 R-up 87-88 (Res. Sect. 92-93, Res. Cup 91-92).

KIDLINGTON

President: Colin Rosser **Chairman:** A F Grose **Manager:** Ken Fagan
Secretary: A Canning, 6 Meadow View, Kidlington, Oxford OX5 1HQ (08675 7726).
Commercial Manager: J Nicholl **Ground:** Yarnton Rd, Kidlington, Oxford (08675 5628).
Directions: From Kidlington r'bout (junction of A4260 & A34) A423 north to Kidlington; after 1st lights take 2nd left (Yarnton Road), ground is 200yds on the left.
Colours: Yellow/blue/yellow **Change colours:** All green **Floodlights:** No
Programme: 20 pages, 20p **Programme Editor:** M A Canning **Founded:** 1920
Previous League: Oxon Snr 47-54. **Clubhouse:** Two bars open after matches
Honours: Oxon Snr Lg 53-54 (R-up 47-48), Hellenic Lg Cup 74-75 (R-up 68-69 73-74 74-75, Div 1 R-up 63-64 78-79), Oxon Intermediate Cup 52-53 84-85 (R-up 68-69 73-74 74-75), FA Vase 5th last sixteen 76-77.

LAMBOURN SPORTS

President: N L Fraser **Chairman:** A J Moyle **Vice Chairman:** E O'Neilly
Secretary: C G Bettison, 13 Mill Lane, Lambourn, Berks RG16 7YP (0488 72320).
Manager: Don Rogers.
Ground: Bockhampton Rd, Lambourn, Berks (0488 72214).
Directions: From Lambourn Church take Newbury St, then 1st right into Station Rd, left at T junction into Bockhampton Rd, ground on left.
Seats: **Cover:** 150 **Capacity:** 2,000 **Floodlights:** No **Founded:** 1889
Colours: Red & white stripes/red/red **Change colours:** All blue **Programme:** 12 pages
Reserve Team's League: North Berks.
Previous Leagues: Newbury & Dist. 11-51/ Swindon & Dist. 51-61/ Hellenic 61-72/ Nth Berks 72-77.
Clubhouse: Bars, lounge, dancehall, billard room, kitchen, open 7 nights, Saturdays from 4pm
Captain 93-94: Tony Dyer **Club record scorer:** Stan Fisher, 600 1st team, 634 in total
Top Scorer 93-94: Mark Smith **Player of the Year 93-94:** Dave Guthrie.
Hons: Berks & Bucks Intermediate Cup 61-62 79-80, Hellenic Lg Div 1 81-82 (R-up 61-62, Div 1 Cup 61-62 79-80).

Easington Sports FC. Back Row (L/R): B Robinson (Asst Manager), P Hickman, N Sullivan, J Thorne, L Perkins, W McDowell, T Fowler. Front: M Coleman, D Deeley, K Stratford (Captain), D White, R Green, M Mortell.

Didcot Town FC. *Photo - Gavin Ellis-Neville.*

Lambourn Sports FC. *Photo - Gavin Ellis-Neville.*

LETCOMBE SPORTS

President: G Oliver **Chairman:** D Stock **Vice-Chairman:** D Davies.
Secretary: Mr D Williams, 8 Larkdown, Wantage OX12 8HE (0235 764130).
Manager: TBA **Commercial Manager:** R Stock.
Ground: Bassett Road, Letcombe Regis, Wantage, Oxon (02357 68685).
Directions: B4507 Swindon road from Wantage, left for Letcombe Regis, follow road thru Letcombe Regis; ground on right on far side of village.
Seats: No **Cover:** No **Floodlights:** No **Nickname:** None **Founded:** 1960.
Colours: All yellow **Change colours:** All white **Prev. Grounds:** None
Sponsors: Autotype/ D McDowell **Previous Lges:** North Berks 60-90/ Chiltonian 90-93.
Programme: 6 pages, £1 with entry **Programme Editor:** Secretary **Club Shop:** No.
Reserves' Lge: Hellenic Res. sect. **Clubhouse:** Open evenings except Monday. Rolls & hot food sold.
Local Press: Oxford Mail/ Wantage Herald.
Record scorer: R Taylor **Record appearances:** P Davies.
Top Scorer 93-94: F Dorrian **Captain & Player of the Year 93-94:** P Belcher.
Hons: Chiltonian Lg Div 1 90-91, North Berks Lg 89-90 (Lg Cup 87-88, War Memorial Cup 89-90, A G Kingham Cup 89-90.

MILTON UNITED

President: Mr J Cannon **Chairman:** Mr K Tull **Vice-Chairman:** Mr P Mitchell
Secretary: Maldwyn James, 45 Whitehorns Way, Drayton, Abingdon OX14 4LH (0235 531789).
Manager: Neil Allen **Asst Manager:** Kevin Jones **Coach:** Paul Biddle/Chris Russell
Physio: John Belcher **Press Officer:** David Jones (0235 816376)
Ground: The Sportsfield, High Street, Milton, Abingdon, Oxon (0235) 832999
Directions: Use A34 bypass approx 10 miles north of M4 jct.13 & 10 miles south of Oxford. Leave A34 at Milton Hill roundabout and follow signs to Milton Park Est. After roundabout follow road over railway bridge, take 1st left, ground immediately on left.
Capacity: **Seats:** None **Cover:** None **Floodlights:** No **Founded:** 1926
Colours: Claret & sky/sky/sky **Change cols:** All white or all sky **Club Shop:** No.
Sponsors: Morlands Brewery **Record Gate:** 500 v Almondsbury Picksons, Hellenic Lg 90-91.
Programme: Yes **Programme Editor:** David Taylor (0235 816376).
Midweek matchday: Tues/Wed **Reserve Team's League:** Hellenic League Reserve section.
Club record scorer: Nigel Mott **Clubhouse:** On ground, open matchdays.
Top Scorer 93-94: Alan Osborne **Player of the Year 93-94:** Paul Thomas.
Hons: Hellenic Lg 90-91 (Div 1 89-90), Nth Berks Lg(4) 85-86 87-89 (R-up 84-85 86-87, Lg Cup(3) 84-86 88-89, Div 2 80-81, Charity Shield(4) 84-86 87-89 (R-up 82-83), Nth Berks War Mem. Cup(3) 83-85 87-88, Berks & Bucks I'mediate Cup 90-91.

PURTON

President: Graham Price **Chairman:** Alan Eastwood **Vice Chairman:** N Jones.
Secretary: Nick Webb, 4 Glevum Close, Purton, Swindon, Wilts SN5 9HA (0793 770242).
Manager: S Paish.
Ground: The Red House, Purton (0793 770262 - Saturday afternoons only).
Directions: Purton is on B4041 Wootton Bassett to Cricklade Road. Ground near village hall.
Seats: **Capacity** **Cover:** **Floodlights:** No **Founded:** 1923
Colours: Red/white/red **Change colours:** Blue & black.
Programme: 40 pagesp **Programme Editor:** Alan Eastwood (0793 694036).
Clubhouse: Open after matches **Sponsors:** Courtoulds.
Captain 93-94: I Jones **Top Scorer & P.o.Y. 93-94:** Mark Collier.
Hons: Wilts Lg 48-49 85-86 (Div 2 83-84, Div 3 86-87), Wilts Snr Cup(6) 38-39 48-49 50-51 54-55 87-89, Wilts Yth Cup 77-78 85-86 88-89, Fairford Hosp. Cup(3) 87-89 93-94.

RAYNERS LANE

Chairman: Dave Blewitt **President/Commercial Mgr:** Tom Lynn (081 868 4671).
Secretary: Tony Pratt, 4 Stirling Close, Cowley, Uxbridge, Middx UB8 2BA (0895 233853).
Manager/Coach/Press Officer: Don Durkin (0753 889502) **Asst Mgr:** Richard Hedge.
Ground: Tithe Farm Social Club, 151 Rayners Lane, South Harrow, Middx (081 866 9659).
Directions: Right from Rayners Lane Station, 1st left (Rayners Lane), grnd on right. By road: off A40 at Polish War Memorial junction (1st after Northolt aerodrome), left into A4180 (West End Rd), right into Station Approach, right into Victoria Rd at lights, over r'bout, 2nd left after next lights (Rayners Lane) - grnd half mile on left.
Seats: 32 **Cover:** 50 **Capacity:** 1,000 **Floodlights:** No **Founded:** 1933
Colours: Yellow/green **Change colours:** Red/black **Nickname:** The Lane
Sponsors: A & J Bull **Previous Lges:** Parthenon/ Spartan/ Middx.
Programme: 28 pages **Editor:** Tom Lynn (081 8684671) **Club Shop:** No.
Record Attendance: 550 v Wealdstone, Middx Senior Cup, 1983.
Clubhouse: 2 bars, open all day matchdays. Also tea bar.
Midweek home matchday: Tuesday **Reserve team's League:** Middx County Lge.
Captain 93-94: Gerry Hynes **Top Scorer 93-94:** Tony Verni.
P.o.Y. 93-94: **Club record appearances:** Paul Abell.
Hons: Hellenic Lg 82-83 (Div 1 Cup 1980-81), Middx Lg Cup 71-72, Middx Premier Cup 83-84 (R-up 72-73), Harrow Wembley & Dist. Lg 39-40 40-41 44-45 (Lg Cup 41-42 43-44 44-45), Parthenon Lg 50-51 (R-up 52-53, Lg Cup 48-49 52-53 56-57), Middx Summer Cup 1991, West Middx Midweek Lg 36-37.

PHOTOS OPPOSITE:

Top: *Carterton Town FC - Hellenic League Division One champions.*
Photo - Gavin Ellis-Neville.

Centre: *P Sherwood fires in a shot during Carterton Town's 3-0 derby win at Clanfield during the Christmas Holiday.*
Photo - Gavin Ellis-Neville.

Foot: *Clanfield '85 FC. Back Row (L/R): B Court (Chairman), A Howard, D Ashby, S McPherson, S Miller, C Farmer, T Collins, C Wheeler, P Bennett. Front: N Hughes, P Carpenter, P Osborne, G Lock (Manager), P Woolford, J Court.*

CARTERTON
TYRE
SERVICES

WALLINGFORD TOWN

President: K A J Lester **Chairman:** A M Brannan **Vice Chairman:** G Lee.
Secretary: R Nobes,. 41 Alnatt Ave., Wallingford, Oxon OX10 8PJ (0491 836619).
Manager: L Hill **Physio:** Jimmy Coster.
Press Officer: R May (0491 837391).
Ground: Wallingford Sports Trust, Hithercroft Rd, Wallingford, Oxon (0491 35044).
Directions: From town centre - south on A329 out of 1-way system, 100yds right into St Johns Road after r'bout at Green Tree pub, fork left at Plough pub into Hithercroft Rd, ground 200yds on right before new r'bout on new ring-rd. From Didcot - turn right at new r'bout on ring-rd, ground on left at next r'bout. 2 miles from Cholsey (BR). Buses from Reading and Oxford to town centre.
Seats: No **Cover:** 500 **Capacity:** 1,500 **Floodlights:** No **Founded:** 1922
Club colours: Red & black hoops/black/black **Change colours:** Gold
Programme: 16 pages with admission **Editor:** R May (0491 837391) **Club Shop:** No.
Nickname: The Town **Previous Ground:** The Bull Croft 1922-78.
Previous Lge: Reading & Dist. (pre-1953) **Rec. Gate:** 1,000 v Wycombe, Berks & Bucks S.C. 1982
Players progressing to Football League: John Dreyer (Oxford United 1985).
Sponsors: Rich's Cafe American **Midweek home matchday:** Wednesday
Record win: 15-1 v Lambourn (A), 1960s **Record defeat:** 0-8 v Carterton (H), Hellenic Lg Div 1 93-94.
Record transfer fee paid received: £2,000 from Oxford on signing John Dreyer in 1976 - not a transfer.
Clubhouse: Weekdays 7.30-11pm, Sat noon-2 & 4-11pm, Sun noon-2 & 7-10.30pm. Rolls available Saturday.
Captain 93-94: T Mason **Reserve Team's League:** Hellenic Reserve section.
Top Scorer 93-94: S Wood 35 **P.o.Y. 93-94:** M Carrigan
Record Scorer S Wood 105 **Hons:** Hellenic Lg 68-69 (Premier Division Cup 58-59).

WANTAGE TOWN

President: Ernie Smart **Chairman:** D O'Brien **Vice-Chairman:** A Willis.
Secretary: J T Bolton, 15 Broadmarsh Close, Grove, Wantage, Oxon (0235 764223).
Manager: Gary Ackling **Asst Manager:** Kevin O'Hanlon
Commercial Manager: Andy Wells (0235 767291).
Ground: Alfredian Park, Manor Park, Wantage, Oxon (0235 764781).
Directions: Take Hungerford Road from Wantage, ground signposted on right oppsite recreation ground.
Seats: 50 **Cover:** 300 **Capacity:** 1,500 **Floodlights:** No **Founded:** 1892
Colours: Green & white **Change colours:** All white. **Record Gate:** 1,800
Programme: 28 pages, 50p **Programme Editor:** Andy Wells (0235 767291).
Midweek Matchday: Wednesday **Club Sponsors:** J I R H (Builder).
Club Shop: No, but various items (badges, club history, ties) available from Commercial Manager).
Prev. Lges: Swindon & Dist. 1901-12 30-35 47-56/ North Berks 12-22 38-40 46-47/ Reading & D. 22-30 35-38.
Prev. Grnd: Challow Park (pre-1922) **Clubhouse:** Mon-Fri 7.30-11pm, Sat noon-2.30, 4-7pm.
Record win: 11-1 v Amersham Town (A), Hellenic League 60-61.
Record defeat: 0-14 v Thame United (A), 20/1/62.
Past players progressing to Football League: Roy Burton and Colin Duncan (both Oxford United).
Record Scorer: A Rolls **Top Scorer 93-94:** Karl Little, 21.
Captain 93-94: John Culley **Player of the Year 93-94:** Jeb Ciampoli.
Hons: Hellenic Lg R-up 81-82 (Div 1 80-81 (R-up 69-70 87-88 91-92), Div 1 Cup R-up 91-92), Oxon Snr Cup 82-83, Berks & Bucks Intermediate Cup 54-55, Swindon & District Lg 07-08 33-34 52-53 55-56.

WOOTTON BASSETT TOWN

Chairman: Alan Blyth
Sec./Press Officer: Mr R Carter, 14 Blackthorn Close, Wootton Bassett, Swindon, Wilts SN4 7JE (0793 851386).
Manager: Micky Woolford **Asst Manager/Coach:** Kev Moloney.
Ground: Gerard Buxton Sports Ground, Rylands Way, Wootton Bassett, Swindon (0793 853880).
Directions: M4 jnct 16 to Wootton Bassett (A3102), left at 2nd r'bout (Prince of Wales pub on right), 2nd left into Longleaze (just after Mobil garage) and Rylands Way is 3rd right by shops, ground 100yds on right. Coming from Calne/Devizes proceed thru town centre and turn right into Longleaze after Shell petrol station on right - Rylands Ave. is 3rd left. Coming from Malmesbury take last exit off r'bout by Prince of Wales pub and Longleaze is 2nd left.
Seats: None **Cover:** 350 **Capacity:** 4,000 **Floodlights:** Due **Founded:** 1882
Colours: Blue & white hoops **Change colours:** Yellow/green. **Nickname:** None.
Programme: 12 pages, free **Programme Editor:** T.B.A. **Club Shop:** No.
Previous Grounds: None **Record Gate:** 2,505 v Swindon T., friendly 20/7/91.
Sponsors: Cathy Moore Recruitment **Previous Leagues:** Wilts (pre-1988). **Record win:** 11-2
Midweek home matchday: Tue/Wed **Reserve team's League:** Wiltshire. **Record defeat:** 0-9
Clubhouse: Open every matchdays, usual opening hours. Usual type of bar food available together with filled rolls. Tea & coffee available over bar. Matchday refreshments - teas, coffees, soups with light snacks.
Record scorer: Brian (Toby) Ewing **Record appearances:** Steve Thomas.
Hons: Hellenic Lg Div 1 Cup 89-90 93-94, Wilts Lg 87-88 (Div 2 84-85, Subsidiary Cup 78-79), Wilts Snr Cup R-up 02-03 03-04 87-88, Ghia Snr 83-84, Ghia Jnr Cup R-up 88-89, FA Amateur Cup QF 26-27.

YARNTON

Chairman: M C Warner **Vice Chairman:** A Oliver **President:** TBA
Secretary: B G Harris, 28 Orpwood Way, Abingdon OX14 5PX (0235 526621).
Manager: A Bunting **Asst Manager:** K Fisher **Press Off.:** A Stiff
Ground: Little Marsh, Green Lane, Yarnton, Oxon (0865 842037).
Directions: North of Oxford on A44 - head for Woodstock/Evesham. Ground situated behind The Grapes pub. Entrance on right before roundabout. Oxford-Woodstock buses stop near ground, Oxford-Kidlington stop 30mins walk from ground.
Seats: None **Cover:** None **Capacity:** Unknown **Floodlights:** No **Founded:** 1947
Colours: Blue **Change colours:** White. **Club Shop:** No.
Previous Grounds: None **Previous Lges:** Witney & Dist. 47-80/ Oxon Snr 80-91.
Programme: 12 pages, £1 with admission **Record Gate:** 150 v Kidlington. **Clubhouse:** No.
Midweek home matchday: Tuesday **Sponsors:** Woodstock Felt Roofing & Red Lion, Yarnton
Hons: Oxford Jnr Shield 76-77, Witney & Dist. Lg Div 2 72-73 (Supplementary Cup 65-66), Oxon Snr Lg Div 1 80-81 (Ben Turner Cup 90-91), Oxon Jnr Chal. Cup 56-57 72-73, Fred Ford Mem. Cup 76-77, Burford Spts Cup 76-77.

SPARTAN LEAGUE

FEEDER TO:
DIADORA LEAGUE

FOUNDED: 1974
(Merger of the London League (founded 1896) & the Spartan League (1907)

Presidents: K G Aston, JP

Chairman: B Stallard

Hon. Secretary: D Cordell, 44 Greenleas, Waltham Abbey, Essex (0992 712428)

The season closed with Willesden (Hawkeye) improving on last season's high position by winning the Premier Division championship from Croydon Athletic by two points.

Considering the weather of the previous season it was hoped that, with fewer clubs in the Premier Division, there would be no backlog of fixtures at the end of the season, but the weather again played a major part in the smooth running of the fixtures. Whereas in the previous season there was only one major weather problem, this year there were several. Because of this, a few clubs had some catching up to do at the end.

Willesden lost only three games and managed a goal difference of +52, whilst Croydon Athletic claimed a +81 goals difference and improved considerably on the previous year's finish of 11th. St Margaretsbury, celebrating their Centenary, finished third thus maintaining their strong influence in the League since joining from the Herts Senior County League. The biggest disappointment was the showing of Brimsdown Rovers, Runners-up in 1991-92 and champions in 1992-93 but only a lowly 14th position in 1993-94.

The loss of Cheshunt to the Isthmian League (though they have won promotion to Division Two at the first attempt), and the move by Eltham Town out of Senior football, reduced the Division down at the start of the season. Unfortunately, St Andrews having to close during the season reduced the numbers yet again. There seems to be shortage of clubs coming up, either because they cannot meet the new Senior Status standards or because of the lack of funds. Next season a further three clubs, all of whom fall into the catergories mentioned, will not be playing in the Premier Division.

The League Cup final finished in a 1-1 draw after extra-time between Hanwell Town and Wellesden. The replay will be at the beginning of next season. Mention must be made of Hanwell Town who made their third consecutive appearance in the London Senior Cup Final but failed to add to their previous two wins.

The League kept up its strong showing in the London Intermediate Cup when Clapton Villa beat Walthamstow Trojans after a drawn game. In winning the Trophy, Clapton Villa became the seventh successive Spartan club to win the Trophy. Clapton Villa were also runners up to Lewisham Elms in Division One. In the London Junior Cup, the League provided both finalists when Walthamstow St Marys beat STC Ivor Grove.

Basil Stallard, Chairman

PREM. DIV.	P	W	D	L	F	A	PTS
Willesden (H'eye)	36	26	7	3	77	25	85
Croydon Athletic	36	26	5	5	118	37	83
St Margaretsbury	36	23	5	8	77	48	74
Hillingdon Borough	36	21	7	8	86	45	70
Tower Hamlets	36	22	3	11	91	59	69
Corinthian-Casuals	36	19	6	11	82	44	63
Walthamstow Pen.	36	17	7	12	69	60	58
Waltham Abbey	36	16	5	15	50	52	55
Brook House	36	16	3	17	64	68	51
Hanwell Athletic	36	15	3	18	60	57	48
Cockfosters	36	13	9	14	55	52	48
Haringey Borough	36	14	6	16	45	58	*42
Barkingside	36	11	8	17	65	87	41
Brimsdown Rovers	36	11	4	21	37	50	37
Beaconsfield Utd	36	9	9	18	49	89	36
Nth Greenford Utd	36	10	4	22	40	71	34
Beckton United	36	9	5	22	60	116	*26
Southgate	36	6	5	25	47	90	23
Amersham Town	36	5	5	26	42	106	20

* - 6 points deducted

DIV. ONE	P	W	D	L	F	A	PTS
Lewisham Elms	30	22	4	4	98	28	70
Clapton Villa	29	17	4	8	78	42	55
Old Roan	30	16	7	7	61	39	55
Metrogas	30	17	5	8	73	45	#53
Woolwich Town	30	16	7	7	66	36	#52
Ilford	30	15	4	11	69	53	49
Craven	30	14	5	11	75	64	47
Metpol (Chigwell)	30	13	8	9	54	53	47
Leyton County	28	14	4	10	54	45	46
Cray Valley	30	10	5	15	51	79	35
Bridon Ropes	30	9	6	15	58	64	33
Walthamstow Troj.	27	8	7	12	48	56	31
Catford Wanderers	30	5	12	13	44	62	27
AFC Eltham	30	6	7	17	53	90	25
Woodford Town	29	4	5	20	44	93	17
SE Olympic	29	2	6	21	41	118	*11

* - 1 point deducted
# - 3 points deducted

RESERVE DIV.	P	W	D	L	F	A	PTS
Willesden (H.) Res.	14	11	1	2	50	17	34
Walt. Trojans Res.	14	9	3	2	56	24	30
Waltham Abb. Res.	14	8	2	4	39	21	26
Woolwich T. Res.	14	7	1	6	37	26	22
Cray Valley Res.	14	4	3	7	17	32	15
SE Olympic Res.	14	4	2	8	35	50	14
Metpol (Chig). Res.	14	2	3	9	18	45	9
Catford Wdrs Res.	14	2	3	9	11	48	9

DIV. TWO	P	W	D	L	F	A	PTS
Tottnham Wine	14	12	1	1	61	17	37
STC Ivor Grove	14	11	1	2	40	20	34
Walt. St Marys	14	8	2	4	40	24	26
Classic Inter	14	7	2	5	46	45	23
Singh Sabha	14	5	2	7	32	38	*16
Lewisham District	14	3	3	8	33	39	12
Leyton Co. Res.	14	3	1	10	28	36	10
Ollerton	14	1	0	13	26	87	3

PREMIER DIVISION RESULT CHART 1993-94

HOME TEAM	1	2	3	4	5	6	7	8	9	10	11	12	13	14	15	16	17	18	19	20
1. Amersham Town	*	2-0	1-1	1-1	0-1	2-1	0-1	1-5	2-2	1-8	0-1	0-1	0-1	1-5	2-3	4-4	2-3	0-2	1-4	1-2
2. Barkingside	5-1	*	4-4	3-4	1-4	2-1	1-1	2-1	4-4	0-5	1-2	3-1	1-1	2-1	6-2	6-1	4-3	2-2	1-2	0-3
3. Beaconsfield United	0-5	1-1	*	5-5	0-2	1-3	2-1	0-3	1-0	1-0	3-3	4-2	1-2		1-2	3-2	0-3	0-3	1-5	0-3
4. Beckton United	1-3	1-2	2-3	*	0-3	3-2	3-6	2-4	1-8	2-4	2-1	1-1	0-3		0-5	2-6	3-7	2-1	1-5	0-2
5. Brimsdown Rovers	1-0	0-2	0-1	0-1	*	0-1	0-2	0-1	0-3	2-1	2-3	0-2	1-1		0-2	4-1	1-0	2-1	2-4	0-2
6. Brook House	2-0	3-2	3-1	1-3	2-1	*	2-0	0-5	2-4	0-2	6-2	1-4	3-0	1-1	5-4	2-0	6-1	1-1	2-3	0-2
7. Cockfosters	7-3	5-0	2-0	2-2	0-0	2-2	*	0-5	0-1	1-1	2-1	1-2	1-3	3-0	0-2	3-0	1-2	4-0	1-1	1-1
8. Corinthian-Casuals	9-1	2-0	1-1	2-1	2-0	3-0	0-0	*	3-2	4-1	4-0	0-2	0-1	5-0	3-2	2-0	3-0	1-0	1-2	2-3
9. Croydon Athletic	6-1	2-0	7-1	6-0	1-1	5-0	3-1	2-1	*	3-0	4-0	3-1	5-0	4-1	3-1	4-0	1-4	4-0	2-1	0-0
10. Hanwell Town	3-0	3-1	1-2	2-3	3-2	2-1	0-1	1-0	2-1	*	1-4	2-1	1-1	3-2	3-1	1-1	1-2	1-2	2-3	3-4
11. Haringey Borough	1-0	1-1	0-0	3-0	2-1	0-1	2-0	0-0	0-5	0-2	*	1-0	1-0		0-0	1-1	1-3	3-0	3-1	1-5
12. Hillingdon Borough	9-0	4-1	5-0	6-2	2-0	0-1	1-0	2-2	3-3	3-1	3-2	*	1-0		2-2	5-1	4-0	1-1	5-2	0-2
13. North Greenford Utd	1-2	2-1	3-2	2-1	1-2	0-0	0-1	2-6	1-7	0-1	0-2	0-1	*	0-0	0-1	1-5	0-5	1-4	1-2	1-2
14. St Andrews	3-4		0-3	2-2		0-1	1-1	2-5		0-0	0-3			*	0-1			1-0	2-4	
15. St Margaretsbury	3-0	7-1	1-0	5-1	1-1	3-2	2-1	2-2	1-3	2-0	2-0	3-1	1-0		*	2-0	2-1	2-1	3-1	0-2
16. Southgate Athletic	2-1	0-3	1-1	0-3	2-1	3-4	2-3	2-1	0-3	4-1	0-1	2-4	0-3	1-2	1-2	*	2-4	0-2	1-1	0-1
17. Tower Hamlets	7-4	8-0	2-2	3-0	1-0	3-0	3-1	5-0	1-3	2-0	2-1	1-3	0-2	6-3	2-2	5-2	*	3-0	3-1	1-0
18. Waltham Abbey	1-1	0-1	4-1	2-3	3-2	2-1	2-3	3-2	0-1	1-0	3-1	0-1	2-1		0-1	1-0	2-0	*	1-0	0-4
19. Walthamstow Pennant	1-0	2-1	3-4	2-2	0-1	2-1	0-0	2-0	1-6	0-2	2-1	2-2	3-2		2-3	3-1	5-1	1-1	*	0-1
20. Willesden (Hawkeye)	6-0	2-2	4-1	5-1	2-0	0-2	3-0	2-2	3-1	2-0	1-0	1-1	4-3	3-1	1-0	2-0	0-0	1-2	0-0	*

St Andrews withdrew - record expunged & shown above for interest only

SENIOR CHALLENGE CUP 1993-94

First Round

Haringey Borough v Brook House 1-0
Hillingdon Borough v Brook House 4-2*(aet)*
Beaconsfield United v Walthamstow Pennant 2-0
Willesden (Hawkeye) v St Margaretsbury 4-0

Second Round

Hanwell Town v Barkingside 2-1*(aet)*
St Andrews v Corinthian-Casuals 0-2
Tower Hamlets v Brimsdown Rovers 3-2
Hillingdon Borough v Amersham Town 5-1
Cockfosters v Beaconsfield United 3-0
Croydon Athletic *(w/o)* Waltham Abbey *(scr)*
Haringey Borough v Southgate 3-0
Willesden (Hawkwye) v North Greenford United 1-0

Quarter-Finals

Hanwell Town v Cockfosters 6-3*(aet)*
Tower Hamlets v Haringey Borough 2-0
Corinthian-Casuals v Croydon Athletic 1-2
Hillingdon Borough v Willesden (Hawkeye) 0-1

Semi-Finals

Tower Hamlets v Willesden (Hawkeye) 1-2
Hanwell Town v Croydon Athletic 0-0,1-0

Final: Willesden (Hawkeye) 1, Hanwell Town 1 *(aet, replay held over to 1994-95)*

SPARTAN PREMIER DIVISION LEAGUE TEN-YEAR RECORD

	84/5	85/6	86/7	87/8	88/9	89/0	90/1	91/2	92/3	93/4
Abingdon Town	-	-	-	-	1	-	-	-	-	-
Amersham Town	11	15	10	15	13	19	10	16	20	19
Barkingside	-	-	12	9	5	8	2	6	16	13
Beaconsfield Utd	9	6	16	11	18	17	13	14	13	15
Beckton United	15	13	13	13	19	10	14	18	21	18
Brimsdown Rovers	3	5	3	5	7	14	7	2	1	14
BROB Barnet	17	-	-	-	-	-	-	-	-	-
Bromley Athletic (see Eltham Town)										
Brook House	-	-	-	-	-	11	12	4	14	9
Burnham	1	-	-	-	-	-	-	-	-	-
Cheshunt	-	-	-	4	6	4	4	8	3	-
Cockfosters	-	-	-	-	-	-	-	12	8	11
Collier Row	2	1	-	-	-	-	-	-	-	-
Corinthian-Casuals	16	-	14	17	16	5	5	9	2	6
Crown & Manor	-	11	9	16	20	-	-	-	-	-
Croydon Athletic	-	-	-	10	2	13	15	10	11	2
Danson (Bexley Borough)	12	12	15	-	-	-	-	-	-	-
Edgware Town	14	7	4	1	4	1	-	-	-	-
Eltham Town	-	-	-	-	17	18	18	19	18	-
Hanwell Town	5	9	11	6	11	12	8	7	5	10
Haringey Borough	-	-	-	-	-	6	6	3	15	12
Hillingdon Borough	-	-	-	-	-	-	16	13	17	4
North Greenford United	-	-	-	-	14	15	17	17	19	16
Northwood	6	8	7	12	3	2	3	1	-	-
Pennant (see Walthamstow Pennant)										
Redhill	7	3	2	7	-	-	-	-	-	-
St Andrews	-	-	-	-	-	-	-	-	9	w/d
St Margaretsbury	-	-	-	-	-	-	-	-	6	3
Southgate (Athletic)	-	-	5	2	8	3	11	15	22	17
Southwark Borough	-	-	-	3	9	-	-	-	-	-
Swanley Town	13	16	-	-	-	-	-	-	-	-
Thamesmead Town	-	-	-	-	15	16	19	-	-	-
Thatcham Town	4	4	-	-	-	-	-	-	-	-
Tower Hamlets	-	-	-	-	-	-	-	-	10	5
Ulysses	-	-	17	-	-	-	-	-	-	-
Waltham Abbey	8	10	6	14	12	9	9	11	12	8
Walthamstow Pennant	10	14	8	8	10	7	1	5	7	7
Wandsworth & Norwood (see Croydon Athletic)										
Willesden (Hawkeye)	-	-	-	-	-	-	-	-	4	1
Yeading	-	2	1	-	-	-	-	-	-	-
No. of Clubs competing	17	16	17	17	20	19	19	19	22	19

PREMIER DIVISION CLUBS 1994-95

AMERSHAM TOWN

Chairman: Raymond Jones **Vice Chairman:** Mike Gagahan **President:** Graham Taylor
Secretary: Richard Phillips, 16 Cameron Rd, Chesham, Bucks HP5 3BS (0494 484469).
Manager: Steve Simmons **Coach:** Oscar Ringsell
Commercial Mgr/Press Officer: David Rake (0844 290176).
Ground: Spratley's Meadow, School Lane, Amersham (0494 727428). **Directions:** A413 London to Aylesbury road, right into Mill Lane at end of Amersham old town, left into School Lane at top of Hill Lane, ground on left 200yds past school. 1 mile from Amersham Station - BR & underground Metropolitan Line.
Seats: None **Cover:** No **Capacity:** 1,500 **Floodlights:** No **Founded:** 1890
Previous Leagues: Wycombe & Dist. Comb./ Aylesbury & Dist./ Chesham/ Gt Western Suburban 20-23/ Spartan 23-53 61-62/ Hellenic 53-61 62-72.
Record Gate: 2,000 v Aston V., centenary match 1990 (at Chesham).
Colours: Black & white stripes/black/black
Change colours: Tangerine/black/black
Previous Ground: Barn Meadow (pre-1920).
Midweek home matches: Tuesday **Reserve's League:** Middx Co. **Nickname:** Magpies.
Programme: With admission **Editor:** David Rake (0844 290176) **Club Shop:** No.
Clubhouse: Open matchdays. Bar facilities. Teas, coffees and light snacks (+ Jess Pearce's rock cakes!).
Captain 93-94: **93-94 P.o.Y.:** **Top Scorer 93-94:**
Hons: Hellenic League 63-64 (Runners-up 64-65 65-66, Div 1 62-63, League Cup 53-54), London Spartan League Runners-up 79-80, St Marys Cup 89-90 (Runners-up 90-91), Berks & Bucks Jnr Cup 22-23 (Snr Cup SF 79-80 80-81), Wycombe Challenge Cup 23-24.

BARKINGSIDE

President: A Smith **Chairman:** K Harris.
Secretary/Press Officer: N A Ingram, 45 Cheneys Rd, Leytonstone, London E11 3LL (081 555 1447).
Manager: W Reed **Asst Manager:** G Barnard **Physio:** A Bevan
Ground: Oakside, Station Road, Barkingside, Ilford, Essex (081 550 3611). **Club Shop:** No.
Directions: From London A12 Eastern Avenue to Green Gate, left into Hurns Rd to Barkingside, right into Craven Gardens, right again Carlton Drive leading to Station Road, under bridge and ground entrance on right. Adjacent to Barkingside station (Central Line), 3 miles from Ilford station (BR). Bus 169 to Craven Gardens.
Seats: 60 **Cover:** 60 **Capacity:** 1,000 **Floodlights:** Yes **Founded:** 1898.
Previous Leagues: Ilford & Dist. 1898-1925 44-47/ Ilford Minor 25-44/ Sth Essex 47-48/ Walthamstow 48-50/ London 50-64/ Gtr London 64-71/ Metropolitan-London 71-75.
Previous Grounds: Fulwell Cross PF 1898-1921/ Clayhall Rec 21-29/ Hainault PF 29-33/ Barkingside Rec 33-57.
Cols: Blue & white hoops/white/blue **Change colours:** All Red **Sponsors:** Directa
Programme: 12 pages with admission **Programme Editor:** J Brown (081 500 5125).
Midweek home matchday: Tuesday
Reserve's lge: Ess. & Herts Border Comb**Record Gate:** 957 v Arsenal Res., London League 1957.
Clubhouse: Saturdays 1pm-midnight, midweek matchnights 6.30-11pm. Rolls, hotdogs, hamburgers.
1993-94 Captain: R O'Brien **1993-94 P.o.Y.** J Harris/ C Dobson **1993-94 Top-scorer:** S Kent
Hons: South Essex League Runners-up 46-47, London League Runners-up 49-50 (League Cup 55-56 (Runners-up 52-53 62-63)), Ilford Fest. Cup 51-52, Romford Char. Cup 51-52, Gtr London League 64-65, London Spartan League Runners-up 90-91 (Harry Sunderland Shld 83-84 (Runners-up 84-85).

BEACONSFIELD S.Y.C.O.B.

President: T Keylock **Chairman:** Edward Fletcher. **Manager:** Ian Dare.
Secretary: Mr Paul Hughes, 14 Fairfield Lane, Farnham Royal, Bucks SL2 3BX (0753 643883).
Ground: Holloways Park, Slough Road, Beaconsfield, Bucks (0494 676868).
Directions: M40 (Jct 2), 1st exit to A355. Club 100yds on right. One and a miles from Beaconsfield (BR). Bus 441 Slough/ High Wycombe.
Seats: None **Cover:** 60 **Capacity:** 1,000 **Floodlights:** Yes **Founded:** 1994.
Colours: White/black/black **Change colours:** Sky & white stripes/white/sky.
Previous Name: Beaconsfield Utd (founded 1921)/ Slough Youth Club Old Boys (1941). Clubs merged 1994.
Previous Leagues: Beaconsfield United: Wycombe & District/ Maidenhead. *Slough YCOB: Windsor, Slough & District/ East Berks/ Chiltonian (pre-1994).*
Previous Grounds: *Slough YCOB: Hatmill Community Centre, Burnham Lane, Slough (pre-1994).*
Best FA Vase season: Beaconsfield: 1st Rd 83-84 85-86 87-88.
Record Gate: 300; Beaconsfield United v Chesham United, Berks & Bucks Snr Cup 1985.
Local Press: Bucks Advertiser, Bucks Free Press, Slough Observer, Slough Express, Maidenhead Advertiser.
Clubhouse: Open evenings and matchdays. Bar, Committee Room, Hall, Kitchen, Changing Room
Hounours: *Slough YCOB: Chiltonian League Rup 93-94 (League Cup 92-93), Slough Town Cup Runners-up 91-92.*

BRIMSDOWN ROVERS

Chairman/Secretary: Graham Dodd, 57 Roundmoor Drive, Cheshunt, Herts EN8 9HU (0992 826820).
Ground: Goldsdown Road, Enfield, Middlesex (081 804 5491).
Directions: BR from Liverpool Street to Brimsdown (half mile away but not open Saturdays) or Southbury Road. By road off Green Street, itself off Hertford Road (A1010). Buses 191 or 307.
Seats: None **Cover:** 50 **Capacity:** 1,000 **Floodlights:** Yes **Founded:** 1948.
Previous Leagues: Northern Suburban **Previous Name:** Durham Rovers/ Brimsdown FC
Colours: Black & white stripes/black (white if floodlit)/black (white floodlit)
Change colours: All yellow
Best FA Vase season: 2nd Rd rep. 84-85
Best FA Cup season: 3rd Qual. replay 91-92
Record Gate: 412 v Chesham Utd, FA Cup 3rd Qual. Rd 12/10/91.
Clubhouse: Large lounge & clubroom, games room & stage. 3 bars (300 capacity)
Hons: Spartan League 92-93.

BROOK HOUSE

President: G Waddock **Chairman:** M Ralph **Vice-Chairman:** B Crump.
Secretary: Mr Barry Stone, 53 St Marys Rd, Hayes, Middlesex UB3 2JP (081 848 4798).
Manager: Dermot Jackson **Assy Manager:** Frank Lutt **Press Officer:** Frank Lamb.
Ground: Farm Park, Kingshill Avenue, Hayes, Middlesex (081 845 0110).
Directions: From London or North Circular Road: A40 Western Avenue to Target roundabout, turn left towards Hayes (A312), over White Hart r'bout towards Hayes, turn right at traffic lights in to Kingshill Avenue, ground 1 mile on right. Nearest BR station is Hayes & Harlington, then bus 90 or 195 to Brook House pub. Nearest tube is Northolt (central line), then bus to ground.
Seats: None **Cover:** 75 **Capacity:** 250 **Floodlights:** Yes **Founded:** 1974
Colours: Blue & white stripes/blue/blue **Change:** Green & white stripes/green/green
Programme: 10 pages, £1.50 with entry **Programme Editor:** Frank Lamb **Club Shop:** No
Midweek home matchday: Monday **Reserve Team's League:** Middlesex County
Best FA Cup year: 1st Qual. Rd 93-94. **Best FA Vase year:** Prelim. Rd 90-91 91-92 93-94.
Players progressing to Football League: Neil Shipperley (Brook House).
Clubhouse: Open weekdays 7-11pm, Sat noon-11pm, Sun noon-3 & 7-10.30pm
Top Scorer 93-94: S Walker **Captain & Player of the Year:** Fergus Rushe.

COCKFOSTERS

Chairman: Frank Brownlie **Vice Chairman:** Ken Harris **President:** Vic Bates
Secretary: Graham Bint, 15 Chigwell Park, Chigwell, Essex IG7 5BE (081 500 7369).
Manager: Derek Townsend **Asst Manager:** Billy Roche **Coach:** Les Picking
Physio: Derek Carlisle **Press Off.:** Frank Brownlie **Comm. Mgr:** Alan Simmons
Ground: Cockfosters Sports Ground, Chalk Lane, Cockfosters, Barnet (081 449 5833).
Directions: Ground on A111. M25 Jct 24 (Potters Bar), take A111 signed Cockfosters - ground 2 miles on right. Adjacent to Cockfosters underground station (Picadilly Line). Bus 298 to Cockfosters station.
Seats: None **Cover:** 50 **Capacity:** 1,000 **Floodlights:** No **Founded:** 1921.
Colours: All Red **Change colours:** All White **Nickname:** Fosters
Previous Grounds: None **Previous Name:** Cockfosters Athletic
Previous Leagues: Wood Green & District 21-46/ Northern Suburban 46-66/ Herts Snr Co. 66-91.
Record Gate: 408 v Saffron Walden, Herts Senior County Lg 68-69.
Programme: 12 pages, £1 with entry **Editor:** Alan Simmons (081 440 7998) **Club Shop:** No.
Midweek home matchday: Tuesday **Reserve team's League:** Middx County.
Record win: 10-1 v Rickmansworth T. **Record defeat:** 2-7 v Leggatts Old Boys (both 1968)
Players progressing to Football League: Justin Gentle (Luton, Colchester).
Clubhouse: 7-11pm Tues & Thurs, 4-11pm Sat, noon-3pm Sunday. Hot and cold food on matchdays.
Top Scorer 93-94: Justin Harris, 20 **Sponsors:** Waivis Plastil Engineering Co. Ltd
Captain 93-94: Graham Poulton **P.o.Y. 93-94:** Graham Lee.
Club record scorer: Peter Benham **Club record appearances:** Bob Davis (500+).
Hons: London Intermediate Cup 70-71 89-90, Herts Snr Co. Lg 78-79 80-81 83-84 (R-up 82-83 84-85, Aubrey Cup 78-79 84-85 (R-up 70-71 77-78)), Herts Intermediate Cup 78-79 (R-up 71-72 73-74 74-75), Northern Suburban Lg 61-62 (R-up 50-51 65-66, Div 1 49-50 60-61 (R-up 46-47 48-49)), F.A. Vase 2nd Rd 91-92.

CORINTHIAN CASUALS

President: Sir Maurice Coop **Chairman:** D G Harrison **Manager:** Roger Steer.
Secretary: Mr Brian Wakefield, 5 Martingales Close, Ham Common, Richmond, Surrey (081 940 9208).
Ground: King George's Field, Hook Rise, South Tolworth, Surrey KT6 7NA (081 397 3368).
Directions: A3 to Tolworth r'bout (The Toby Jug). Hook Rise is slip road immediately after the Toby Jug pub. Turn left under railway bridge after a quarter mile - ground immediately on right. Half mile from Tolworth (BR); turn left, continue to Toby Jug, then as above. K2 Hoppa bus from Kingston passes ground.
Seats: 126 **Cover:** 250 **Capacity:** 1,700 **Floodlights:** Yes **Founded:** 1939.
Previous Leagues: Isthmian 39-84 **Reserve Team's League:** Suburban.
Previous Names: Casuals (founded 1883), Corinthians (founded 1882) merged in 1939.
Previous Grounds: Many, including The Oval, Wimbledon Park Stadium, Tooting & Mitcham Utd FC, Molesey FC.
Colours: White/navy/navy **Change colours:** Chocolate & Pink/navy/navy
Programme: 24-48 pages, £1 **Best FA Cup season:** 1st Rd replay 85-86.
Players progressing to Football League: Andy Gray, Tony Finnegan, Alan Pardew to Crystal Palace.
Clubhouse: Evenings, matchdays, Sunday lunchtimes. Darts, pool, hot & cold snacks on matchdays.
Captain 93-94: Trevor Waller **P.o.Y. 93-94:** Bruce Martin **Top Scorer 93-94:** Cliff West.
Hons: FA Am. Cup R-up 55-56 (SF 56-57), Spartan Lg R-up 92-93 (Lg Cup R-up 91-92), L'don Snr Cup R-up 91-92.

CROYDON ATHLETIC

Chairman: Keith Tuckey **Vice Chairman:** Ken Fisher.
Secretary: Tony Peck, 60 Cheviot Road, West Norwood, London SE27 0LG (081 670 2556).
Manager: Martin Caller **Asst Manager:** Colin Sunborg **Physio:** Micky Reed.
Coach: Roy Davies **Press Officer:** Clive Thompson
Ground: NFC Sports, off Mayfield Road, Thornton Heath (081 684 4951).
Directions: From Norbury follow London Rd towards Croydon, turn right into Headcorn Rd, left into Silverleigh Rd, right into Mayfield Crescent, right into Mayfield Rd, left at end and follow road/path to ground. One mile from Norbury (BR). Buses 109, 154.
Seats: 120 **Cover:** 130 **Capacity:** 3,000 **Floodlights:** Yes **Founded:** 1986.
Colours: Maroon & white **Change colours:** All white **Nickname:** Rams.
Prev. Names: Wandsworth FC (est 1948), Norwood FC (est 1947) merged 1986/ Wandsworth & Norwood 86-90.
Previous Grounds: Norwood FC - Lloyds Park 1961-81, Wisley R.H.S. 77-88/ Wandsworth FC - Morfax (Fisher Athletic's original ground) 82-86.
Best FA Vase season: 3rd Rd 93-94 **Best FA Cup season:** 1st Qual. Rd Rep. 89-90
Record Gate: 400 **Reserve Team's League:** Suburban (South)
Programme: 38 pages, 50p **Programme Editor:** Secretary
Club Shop: Club badges, baseball hats, programmes available. Contact Mr Brian Byles at ground.
Club Sponsors: TCS Media **Midweek home matchday:** Tuesday
Record win: 8-1 v Beckton United (A), October 1993. **Record defeat:** 1-9 v Yeading 86-87.
Clubhouse: Open matchdays (inc Reserve & Youth) and Sun noon-3pm, Tues & Thurs & Fri 7-11pm, Sat noon-11pm. Bar, pool, canteen, darts, dominoes. Hot & cold snacks, tea & coffee.
Top Scorer 93-94: Mark Fremington **Captain & P.o.Y.:** Hughie Mann.
Club record scorer: Graham Edginton **Club record appearances:** Graham Edginton/ Paul Gall.
Hons: London Spartan Lg R-up 88-89 93-94 (Reserve Div R-up 88-89, Reserve Cup 88-89), London Snr Cup R-up 91-92, Southern Youth Lg 92-93.

Amersham Town FC. *Photo - Martin Wray.*

Barkingside FC. *Photo - Richard Brock.*

Croydon Athletic - Spartan League runners-up 1993-94. *Photo - Dave West.*

HANWELL TOWN

Chairman/Press Officer: Bob Fisher **President:** Sam Kelso **Manager:** Roy Nairn
Secretaryr: J A Wake, 38 Warwick Ave., South Harrow HA2 8RD (081 422 1048).
Asst Manager: Arthur Rowlands **Physio:** Roy Tyler **Coach:** Tim Soutar
Ground: Reynolds Field, Perivale Lane, Perivale, Greenford, Middx (081 998 1701).
Directions: A40 Oxford road from London, exit B456 for Ealing, ground on corner of junction approached immediately via left turn into Perivale Lane. 3rd of a mile from Perivale tube station (central line).
Seats: None **Cover:** 200 **Capacity:** 2,000 **Floodlights:** Yes **Founded:** 1948
Previous Grounds: Local parks. **Previous Leagues:** Middx/ Middx County **Club Shop:** No.
Colours: Black & white stripes **Change colours:** All red. **Nickname:** The Town
Reserves' Lge: Middx County **Record Gate:** 600 v Spurs, Floodlight opening October 1989.
Midweek home matchday: Wednesday **Record fee received:** £2,000 for Pat Gavin (Gillingham, 1990).
Record defeat: 0-6. **Record win:** 10-0 v Brook House, Spartan Lge
Programme: 16 pages, 50p **Editor:** Julie Soutar, C/O The club.
Clubhouse: Saturday matchdays 2-11pm, Wednesdays 6-11pm, Non-matchdays 7.30-11pm.
Captain 93-94: Ray Duffy **Top Scorer & Player of the Year 93-94:** Ricky Denny, 45 goals.
Club record scorer: Tony Pickering **Club record appearances:** Phil Player, 20 seasons, 617 games.
Hons: London Spartan Lg 83-84 (Lg Cup finalists 93-94, London Snr Cup 91-92 92-93 (R-up 93-94), Middx Charity Cup R-up 92-93.

HARINGEY BOROUGH

Chairman: Michael O'Hallaron **Vice-Chairman:** T O'Connell.
Secretary: Neville K Watson, 42 Roslyn Road, South Tottenham, London N15 5ET (081 809 0824).
Ground: Coles Park, White Hart Lane, Wood Green N22 (081 881 9184).
Directions: Wood Green (Picadilly Line). BR (Eastern Region) to White Hart Lane, W3 bus passes ground A105 or A10 from Nth. Circular to Wood Green.
Seats: 280 **Cover:** Yes **Capacity:** 2,500 **Floodlights:** Yes **Founded:**
Previous Leagues: London 07-14/ Isthmian 19-52 84-88/ Spartan 52-54/ Delphian 54-63/ Athenian 63-84.
Previous Names: Edmonton/ Tufnell Park/ Tufnell Park Edmonton/ Edmonton & Haringey.
Cols: Tangerine & black/black/black **Change colours:** Yellow & black/black/black.
Clubhouse: Open 7 days a week

HILLINGDON BOROUGH

Secretary: Graham Bundy, 43 Heatherwood Drive, Hayes, Middlesex UB4 8TN (081 845 7355).
Manager: John Morris **Asst Manager:** John Toogood **Coach:** Dave Silman.
Physio: Dave Pook **Commercial Mgr:** Ken Rogers **Press Officer:** John Mason.
Ground: Middlesex Stadium, Breakspear Road, Ruislip, Middx HA4 7SB (0895 639544).
Directions: From A40 take B467 (signed Ickenham), left at 2nd r'bout into Breakspear Rd South, right after 1 mile by Breakspear pub - ground half mile on left. Nearest station is Ruislip. Bus U1 passes ground.
Seats: 150 **Cover:** 150 **Capacity:** 1,500 **Floodlights:** Yes **Founded:** 1990
Midweek Matches: Wednesday **Sponsors:** Airport Motor Radiator Co. **Nickname:** Boro.
Colours: White/blue/blue **Change colours:** Red & white stripes/white/red.
Programme: 20 pages **Editor:** John Mason (081 868 7551) **Club Shop:** No.
Clubhouse: Mon-Fri 7.30-11pm, Sat lunchtimes (functions in evening), Sun lunchtime & 7.30-10.30pm.
Reserve team's League: Suburban. **Received:** £1,000 for Craig Johnson (Wealdstone).
Record win: 9-0 v Amersham Town (H), Spartan League Premier Division 93-94.
Record defeat: 0-8 v Newport AFC
Captain 93-94: Phil Heggie **Top Scorer & P.o.Y. 93-94:** Marker Lester, 35 goals.

St MARGARETSBURY

Chairman: T I Blacktin **President:** R L Groucott
Secretary: M Naeem, 2 Kingfisher Close, Stanstead St Margarets, Herts (0920 870972).
Manager: Kelvin Hart **Asst Manager:** Colin Richards **Coach:** Ian Priest
Physio: Derek Ridgewell.
Ground: Station Road, Stanstead St Margarets, Nr Ware, Herts (0920 870473).
Directions: Harlow/Chelmsford exit from A10 to A414, take B181 at Amwell after 300yds towards Stanstead Abotts - ground quarter mile on right. 300yds from St Margaretsbury BR station (Liverpool Str.-Hertford East line).
Seats: 60 **Cover:** 60 **Capacity:** 1,000 **Floodlights:** No **Founded:** 1894
Colours: Red & black **Change colours:** All white **Nickname:** The Bury.
Previous Grounds: Mill Field, Stanstead Abbotts pre-1962.
Previous Leagues: East Herts/ Hertford & Dist./ Waltham & District 47-48/ Herts Co. 48-92.
Programme: 16 pages, £1.50 with entry **Editor:** Jane Free (0920 870431)
Club Shop: No, but Centenary Brochure available from J Smith, 97 Lampits, Hoddesdon, Herts (cheques for £6 (inc p&p) payable to St Margaretsbury FC).
Midweek home matchday: Tuesday **Sponsors:** Universal Office Automation, Hertford.
Reserves' Lge: Hertford & Dist. **Record Gate:** 327 v Wisbech Town, FA Vse 3rd Round 14/12/85.
Record win: 15-1 v Sun Sports (H), Herts Senior County League Division Two, 1948-49.
Record defeat: 0-9 v Herts Police (H), Herts Senior County League Division One 11/11/89.
Clubhouse: Bar open 7-11pm + Sat noon-2, Sun noon-3pm. Bar snacks available.
Captain 93-94: Paul Letts **Top Scorer 93-94:** Barry White 16 **P.o.Y. 93-94:** Russell Ling.
Hons: Herts Snr Centenary Tphy 92-93, Herts County Lg Div 2 48-49 (Div 3 78-79, Aubrey Cup 48-49 71-72, Reserve Div 1 82-83 86-87, Reserve Cup 84-85 86-87 87-88), Waltham & Dist Lg 46-47.

PHOTOS OPPOSITE:

Top: *Hanwell Town, finalists in both the London Senior and Spartan League Cups. Back Row (L/R): Arthur Rowlands, Roy Tyler, Dave Mangan, Paul Paull, Mick Ford, Ashley Fairbrother, Roy Nairn, Paul Riordan, Derek Franklin, Richard Natswell, Nigel Hutchinson, John Bivens, Tim Soutar. Front: Danny Thompson, Rob Williams, Phil Player, Sam Kelso, Ray Duffy, Rob Fisher, Ricky Denny, Billy Beeston, Francis Siziba.*

Centre: *P Holmes of Hillingdon Borough takes on Darren Wilson as his side lose 1-3 at St Margaretsbury.* *Photo - Martin Wray.*

Foot: *St Margaretsbury FC.* *Photo - Martin Wray.*

UMBRO

TOWER HAMLETS

Chairman: Roy Manning **Vice Chairman:** Ray Gipson.
Sec./Comm. Mgr: John Westwood, 69 Chadbourn Est., Chadbourn St., Poplar, London E14 6QP (071 515 9830).
Manager: Henry Carter **Asst Manager:** Kevin Gray
Press Officer: Ray Gipson **Physio:** Howard Cooper
Ground: Mile End Stadium, Rhodeswell Road, London E14 (081 980 1885).
Directions: From Blackwall tunnel left into East India Dock Rd to Commercial Rd, right (Burdett Road), ground on left. From Mile End tube (Dist. Line); 3rd left out of station (Canal Rd) keep right of fork - ground on left.
Capacity: 5,000 **Cover:** 300 **Seats:** 300 **Floodlights:** Yes **Club Shop:** No
Programme: 12 pages, £1 with entry (Editor: Darren Gallery 071515 9830) **Founded:**
Colours: Blue/white/white **Change colours:** Yellow/blue/yellow
Club Nickname: Tipples **Club Sponsors:** Alexio Roofing.
Midweek matchday: Wednesday **Record win:** 22-0 **Record defeat:** 0-8
Previous Name: KGP Tipples **Record Gate:** Unknown.
Previous Leagues: Clapton Stoke Newington/ South West Essex/ Eastern Suburban
Previous Grounds: Burgess Rd 79-85/ Victoria Park 85-86.
Record Fees - Paid: None **Received:** Tracksuits from Charlton for Danny Warden.
Clubhouse: Open 2 hours before kick-off and 3 hours after selling rolls and pies etc. New clubhouse being built, hopefully now open.
Club Record Scorer: Darren Gallery **Club Record Appearances:** Darren Gallery.
Honours: Spartan Lg Div 1 89-90 (Div 2 88-89), London Intermediate Cup 88-89 90-91 (R-up 91-92).

WALTHAM ABBEY

Chairman: Phil Morris **President:** John King
Secretary: Mr David Hodges, 45 Eagle Close, Abbeyfields, Walham Abbey, Essex EN9 3NA (0992 651594).
Manager: Denis Tekel **Asst Manager:** Joe Collins.
Ground: Capershotts, Sewardstone Road, Waltham Abbey, Essex (0992 711287).
Directions: Just off M25 jct 26. Waltham Cross (BR Eastern Region) station three miles distant. 242 Bus.
Seats: None **Cover:** 100 **Capacity:** 2,000 **Floodlights:** Yes **Founded:** 1948.
Cols: Green & white hoops/white/green **Change:** Red & black hoops/red/red. **Nickname:** The Abbey
Previous Leagues: Northen Suburban **Midweek matchday:** Wednesday
Rec. Gate: 1,800 v Spurs, charity game **Reserve's Lge:** Essex & Herts Border Combination
Previous Names: W. Abbey Utd/ W. Abbey Beechfield
Programme: 8 pages, £1.50 with entry **Editor:** David Hodges (0992 652594) **Club Shop:** No.
Best FA Cup season: Prel. Rd 90-91 **Best FA Vase season:** Prel. Rd 87-88 88-89 89-90
Clubhouse: 7-11pm Mon-Fri, 11am-11pm Sat, noon-3pm Sun. Cold snacks, pool, darts.
Captain 93-94: Ray Simpson **Top Scorer 93-94:** **P.o.Y. 93-94:**
Club record scorer: Paul Holloway **Club record appearances:** Colin Winter.

WALTHAMSTOW PENNANT

Chairman: R Wren **Vice Chairman:** C Dowsett **President:** M Holmwood.
Secretary: Bert Hepburn, 57 Rowan Ave., Chingford E4 8QT (081 531 5238).
Manager: J Smith **Asst Manager:** C Rufus **Physio:** G Stiles
Press Officer: J Solkhon **Commercial Manager:** J Clark.
Ground: Wadham Lodge, Brookscroft Road, Walthamstow, London E7 (081 527 2444).
Directions: North Cirular Road to Crooked Billet, turn into Chingford Road, Brookscroft Road first turning on left. Walthamstow Central tube (Victoria Line) one mile away, then buses W21 or 256.
Seats: 200 **Cover:** 200 **Capacity:** 1,000 **Floodlights:** Yes **Founded:** 1966
Colours: White/blue/blue **Change colours:** Yellow/green/yellow **Club Shop:** No.
Previous Name: Pennant **Record win:** 9-1 **Record defeat:** 1-8.
Previous Leagues: South West Essex 66-74/ Metropolitan London 74-83.
Record Gate: 860 v Leyton Orient, Floodlight opening 1989.
Midweek matchday: Wednesday **Reserve's League:** Essex & Herts Border Comb.
Programme: £1.50 with admission **Programme Editor:** J Clark (081 527 5034).
Best FA Vase season: 5th Rd 90-91 **Best FA Cup season:** 1st Qual. Rd 89-90 90-91 91-92
Clubhouse: Bars open before and after all matches. Pool, darts. Teas & rolls on matchdays.
Hons: London Spartan Lg 90-91 (Lg Cup 88-89 90-91), S.W. Essex Lg 72-73 (Jnr Cup 68-69, Intermediate Cup 69-70, Snr Cup 70-71), London Jnr Cup 73-74.

WILLESDEN HAWKEYE

Chairman: Mr Rodney Gooden **Vice Chairman:** Mr Hugh Harrison **President:** Mr Roy Forbes-Allen
Secretary: Mr Clifton Jackson, Flat 1 Vale Farm House, 76 Watford Rd, Sudbury, Middx HA0 3HG (081 908 2664).
Manager: Carl Stewart **Physio:** Linval Sayles **Coach:** Patrick Allen.
Press Officer: Livon Houslin **Commercial Manager:** Roy Forbes-Allen.
Ground: Linford Christie Stadium (formally West London Stadium), Du Cane Rd, London W12 (081 749 5505).
Directions: A40 to White City, right at underpass into Scrubs Lane, 1st left into Du Cane Rd, stadium behind Hammersmith Hospital. Nearest tube White City or East Acton.
Seats: 300 **Cover:** 300 **Capacity:** 1,000 **Floodlights:** Yes **Founded:** 1984
Colours: Yellow/black/black **Change Colours:** Red & white/red/red **Club Shop:** No.
Previous Name: Hawkeye (Willesden) **Prev. Lges:** London West End/ Middx Co. **Nickname:** Hawks.
Reserves' Lge: Spartan Res. Div **Prev. Ground:** Willesden Spts Centre, Donnington Rd (pre-1992).
Programme: Yes **Sponsors:** Marlin House Trading Company Ltd (Dragon Stout)
Nickname: Hawks. **Record Gate:** 100 v Staines, Middx Snr Cup 20/1/93.
Midweek home matchday: Wednesday **Clubhouse:** Matchday cafeteria on site. Bar due 93-94.
Club record scorer: Conley Hall **Club record appearances:** Ruben Kildare.
Captain 93-94: George Green **Top Scorer 93-94:** Dave Kellman
P.o.Y. 93-94: Brian Smikle **Hons:** Spartan Lg 93-94 (Div 1 91-92, Lg Cup finalists 93-94).

PHOTOS OPPOSITE:

Top: *Tower Hamlets FC* *Photo - Gavin Ellis-Neville.*

Centre: *Waltham Abbey FC. Back Row (L/R): Everns Liburd, Andy Reynolds, Micky Joyce, Chris Reynolds, Neil Tilley, Martin Coomber, Colin Winter, Tony Manning, Robert Woolston. Front: Howard Darby, Denis Tekel (Manager), Stephen Shaw, Stuart Johnson, Ray Simpson (Captain), Sam Obeney, Joe Collins (General Manager).* *Photo - Gavin Ellis-Neville.*

Foot: *Walthamstow Pennant score a late free-kick winner at home to Barkingside.* *Photo - Richard Brock.*

ALEXIO
ROOFING

DIVISION ONE CLUBS 1994-95

BECKTON UNITED

Chairman: L Lees.
Secretary: K Mann, Oulton Crescent, Barking, Essex IG11 9HF (081 591 8402).
Ground: East Ham, Manor Way, London E6, near Industrial Park (071) 476 4857
Directions: A13 from City or Essex, Nth Circular Rd from Middlesex. From A13 turn into Manor Way by Beckton flyover. By rail, East Ham (Underground). Buses from East Ham or North Woolwich.
Seats: None **Cover:** 150 **Capacity:** 1,000 **Floodlights:** No **Founded:** 1966.
Previous Name: Ceevor FC **Previous Grounds:** None.
Colours: Navy & white/navy/navy **Change colours:** Orange/navy/navy
Clubhouse: None; adjacent pub used **Best FA Vase season:** 3rd Rd 85-86.

BRIDON ROPES

Chairman: David Coulstock.
Secretary: Richard Clements, 3 Fenwick Close, Woolwich, London SE18 4DD (081 244 1167).
Ground: Meridian Sports Ground, Charlton Park Lane, Charlton SE7 (081 856 1923).
Directions: Take Central London exit from Blackwall Tunnel, left at r'bout into Shooters Hill Rd, 6th left into Charlton Park Lane, ground on right. BR to Woolwich Arsenal station.
Cols: Blue & white halves/blue/blue **Change Colours:** All red.

CATFORD WANDERERS

Chairman: John Hassett.
Secretary: Mark Heywood, 25b Ardgowan Rd, Catford, London SE6 1AJ (081 244 9818).
Ground & Directions: Beckenham Hill Road, Catford SE6 (081 698 1259). From Bromley Road turn into Beckenham Hill Rd at Sainsbury Homebase. Ground behind Homebase. Beckenham Hill (BR).
Cols: Black & white stripes/black/black **Change Colours:** Red & black hoops/black/black.

CLAPTON VILLA

Chairman: G Kendrick
Secretary: J B Singh, 28 Abbotsfield Rd, Goodmayes, Ilford, Essex IG3 9SL (081 599 5244).
Ground & Directions: Wadham Lodge Sports Centre, Wadham Road, London E17 (081 527 3064). A406 exit from Crooked Billet r'bout into Wadham Rd - Sports Centre on left. BR to Highams Park or Walthamstow Central.
Colours: Red & white stripes/white/white **Change Colours:** Sky/maroon/blue.
Previous Ground: Douglas Eyre Sports Centre, Walthamstow (pre-1994).
Honours: Spartan Lg Div 1 93-94 (Div 2 91-92, Benevolent Cup 90-91).

CRAVEN

Chairman: W Green.
Secretary: Danny Day, 23 Chudleigh Crescent, Ilford, Essex IG3 9AT (081 590 4471).
Ground & Directions: Jenkins Lane, Barking (081 594 8442). 200 yds east from junction of A406 (North Circular) and A13 (Newham Way) on A13. Barking (BR).
Colours: Sky/royal/royal. **Change Colours:** Yellow/green/green.

CRAY VALLEY

Chairman: P Williams.
Secretary: S W Chapman, 60 Bradenham Ave., Welling, Kent DA16 2JG (081 304 5387).
Ground & Directions: STC Ivor Grove, New Eltham (081 850 2057). A20 from London to Fiveways junction, left into Southwood Road, left at lights, Ivor Grove on left - ground at end. From Eltham High Street turn into Footscray Rd (A211) then right into Ivor Grove. New Eltham (BR).
Colours: Black & jade/black/black **Change:** Blue & maroon blue stripes/sky/black.

LEWISHAM ELMS

Secretary: Clinton Rhule, 6 Waddon Close, Croydon CR0 4JT (081 680 6893).
Ground & Directions: Elm Lane, Catford Hill, London SE6 (081 311 3123). One minute from South Circular. Catford Bridge (BR).
Colours: Red & white stripes/navy **Change:** Red & black/black/blue
Previous Name: Elms FC (pre-1992). **Honours:** Spartan Lg Div 1 93-94.

Lewisham Elms - Spartan League Division One champions 93-94. Back Row (L/R): Paul McMonagle, Barry Thomas, Winston Dean, Ian Austin, Jimmy Lindsay, Darren Green, Steve Judge. Front: John Farley, Troy Morrison, Charlie Ansah, Derek Aboagye, Anthony Bennett, Joe O'Connor.

Photo - Richard Brock.

Beckton United - who drop out of the Premier Division for 1994-95.

Bridon Ropes FC - Back (L/R): L Potter (Asst Mgr), S Pettengell, J Tallis, R Doherty, V French, S Edwards, B Onumalk, L Adams, R Clements (Mgr). Front: G Platt, M Merdjan, A Robins, S Donovan, M Larouche, G Austin.

Cray Valley FC. Front Row (L/R): P Williams (Manager), P James, M Doyle, D White, R Constable, P Martin, T Martin, M Anson. Front: E Mustapha, S Chapman, P Troke, C Meech, A Lopateugi, R Nelson.

All Photos - Richard Brock.

LEYTON COUNTY

Chairman: Michael Mignott.
Secretary: Kirt Kirwan, 120 Malvern Road, Leytonstone, London E11 3DL (081 539 9210).
Ground: Walthamstow Pennant FC (see page 636).
Colours: White/blue/blue **Change Colours:** Yellow/blue/yellow
Previous Ground: Crawley Road, Leyton E10 (pre 1994).

METPOL CHIGWELL

Chairman: Mr P Mathias.
Secretary: Bernie Hunt, 134 Stanley Avenue, Gidea Park, Romford RM2 5DA (0708 701322).
Ground & Directions: Met Police Sports Ground, High Road, Chigwell, Essex (081 500 2735 or 500 1017). A113 Chigwell Road off North Circular (A406), left at mini r-about for just over a mile. Club on left after junction with Chigwell Rise. Tube to Chigwell or Buckhurst Hill (Central Line).
Cols: White & black stripes/black/black **Change:** All yellow.

OLD ROAN

Chairman: P Osborne.
Secretary: Ian Stuart Daniels, 24 Waldeck Road, Dartford, Kent DA1 1UA (0322 220165).
Ground & Directions: Roan School Playing Fields, Kidbrooke Park Road, London SE12 (081 856 1915). At start of A20. Kidbrooke (BR) or buses 21 and 22.
Colours: Blue/black/black **Change Colours:** All red

TOTTENHAM WINE

Chairman: Mr G William.
Secretary: Mr Lindsay Boyaram, 33 Adlington Close, off Ploughman Close, Edmonton N18.
Ground & Directions: As Woodford FC (see Division Two).
Colours: Gold/blue/white **Change Colours:** Blue & white/blue/white.
Honours: Spartan Lg Div 2 93-94.

WALTHAMSTOW TROJANS

Secretary: Troy Townsend, 54 Grove Park Ave., Chingford, London E4 8SS (081 527 7911).
Ground & Directions: Ive Farm Arena, Villiers Close, Leyton E10 (081 539 6352). From Lea Bridge Road turn into Church Road, then after half a mile right into Villiers Close. Leyton (tube - Central Line).
Cols: Red (navy pin stripes)/navy/navy **Change Colours:** White (navy pin stripes)/navy/navy.

WALTHAMSTOW TROJANS

Secretary: Troy Townsend, 54 Grove Park Ave., Chingford E4 8SS (081 527 7911).
Ground & Directions: Ive Farm Arena, Villiers Close, Leyton E10 (081 539 6352). From Lea Bridge Road turn into Church Road, then after half a mile right into Villiers Close. Leyton (tube - Central Line).
Colours: All sky **Change Colours:** All amber
Honours: London Intermediate Cup R-up 93-94.

WOODFORD TOWN

Chairman: Stephen Robertson.
Secretary: Mr W Robertson, 2 Humphrey Close, Clayhill, Ilford, Essex IG5 0RW (081 550 6680).
Ground & Directions: As East Ham United FC (see page 611).
Colours: Royal & white/black/black **Change Colours:** White & black stripes/white/white.

WOOLWICH TOWN

Chairman: Philip Legg.
Secretary: J R Kelly, 88 Hook Lane, Welling, Kent DA16 2DP (081 303 8977).
Ground & Directions: As Greenwich Borough FC (see page 538).
Colours: Thick red & blue stripes/black/black **Change:** Yellow/black/black.
Previous Ground: Flamingo Park, Sidcup. (Pre-1994).

Below: *Woolwich Town FC, pictured before a home game at their shared ground in Eltham Green Road. Back Row (L/R): J Dunning (Coach), D Griffin, D Garner, S Knibbs, C Clark, D Jolly, G Taylor, M Clark, T Branch, A Putnam (Manager). Front: E Ninaokobia, J Rainey, D Skinner, A Stuart, S Cook, A Muskett.*

Photo - Richard Brock.

SPARTAN LEAGUE DIVISION ONE TEN-YEAR RECORD

	84/5	85/6	86/7	87/8	88/9	89/0	90/1	91/2	92/3	93/4
AFC Eltham	-	-	-	-	-	-	-	-	8	14
AFC Millwall	-	-	-	-	12	5	2	-	-	-
Barkingside	6	5	-	-	-	-	-	-	-	-
Brent	11	11	-	-	-	-	-	-	-	-
Bridon Ropes	-	-	-	-	-	-	-	-	-	11
BROB Barnet	-	3	11	-	-	-	-	-	-	-
Bromlet Athletic (see Eltham Town)										
Brook House	-	-	-	-	6	-	-	-	-	-
Catford Wanderers	-	4	6	1	3	9	11	14	13	13
Chingford	1-	12	10	-	-	-	-	-	-	-
Chingdord Town Wanderers	-	-	-	-	-	-	-	-	12	-
Clapton Villa	-	-	-	-	-	-	-	-	3	2
Corinthian-Casuals	-	1	-	-	-	-	-	-	-	-
Craven	-	-	-	-	-	-	-	4	2	7
Cray Valley	-	-	-	-	-	-	-	8	9	10
Crown & Manor	1	-	-	-	-	-	-	-	-	-
Elms (see Lewisham Elms)										
Eltham Town	-	-	7	4	-	-	-	-	-	-
Hackney Downs Athletic	-	-	-	2	5	7	-	-	-	-
Ilford	-	-	-	-	13	16	8	-	-	6
KGP Tipples (see Tower Hamlets Tipples)										
Lewisham Elms	-	-	-	-	-	-	-	3	6	1
Leyton County	-	-	-	-	-	-	7	7	5	9
Metrogas	-	-	-	-	2	4	6	5	1	4
Metpol (Chigwell)	-	-	13	11	14	13	12	9	10	8
Newmont Travel	-	-	-	-	1	3	-	-	-	-
North Greenford United	4	9	14	6	-	-	-	-	-	-
Old Roan	-	-	9	8	7	8	9	11	4	3
Penhill Standard	9	6	12	12	16	15	15	-	-	-
Pennant (see Walthamstow Pennant)										
Phoenix Sports	-	-	8	9	10	14	14	13	-	-
REMA (Charlton)	-	-	-	-	11	10	-	-	-	-
Royal Arsenal Sp.R.A.	12	13	15	13	-	-	-	-	-	-
Royal George	-	-	-	-	8	2	3	10	-	-
Sangley Sports	-	-	-	-	-	-	1	-	-	-
South East Olympic	-	-	-	-	-	-	-	-	14	16
Southgate Athletic	-	2	-	-	-	-	-	-	-	-
Southwark Borough	8	10	1	-	-	-	-	-	-	-
Swanley Town	-	-	2	10	9	12	10	12	15	-
Thamesmead Town	-	-	3	3	-	-	-	-	-	-
Thames Polytechnic	3	-	-	-	-	-	-	-	-	-
Tower Hamlets Tipples	-	-	-	-	-	1	4	2	-	-
Ulysses	5	8	-	7	15	11	13	-	-	-
Walthamstow Trojans	-	-	5	5	4	6	5	6	7	12
Wandsworth & Norwood	7	7	4	-	-	-	-	-	-	-
Willesden (Hawkeye)	-	-	-	-	-	-	-	1	-	-
Woodford Town	-	-	-	-	-	-	-	-	-	15
Woolwich Town	-	-	-	-	-	-	-	-	11	5
Yeading	2	-	-	-	-	-	-	-	-	-
No. of Clubs competing	13	13	15	13	16	16	15	14	15	16

DIVISION TWO CLUBS 1994-95

CHINGFORD UNITED

Chairman: Mr Martin Kane.
Secretary: Mrs J Cleaver, 33 Aragon Close, Hainault, Ilford, Essex IG6 2TQ (081 501 1770).
Ground & Directions: Newgate Street, Chingford E4 6JB. Left at Woodford High Road traffic lights, right into Chingford Lane opposite Wheelwrights pub, right into Chingdale Rd, forward into Newgate Street, ground on right. Nearest station is Hyams Park.
Colours: Red & white stripes/red/red & white **Change:** Black & white stripes/black/black.

CLASSIC INTER

Chairman: T Smith.
Secretary: Lloyd Joseph, 27 Benson Ave., East Ham, London E6 3EE (081 552 3132).
Ground: Kingfisher Sports Ground, Billett Road, Walthamstow E17. Into Billett Rd at Crooked Billet r'bout off North Circular (A406).
Colours: Blue & white/blue/white **Change colours:** White/black/white.
Previous Ground: Ive Farm Sports Ground, Leyton (pre-1994).

HUNTSMAN

Chairman: Mr H Howard.
Secretary: Keith R Boanas, Kent House Tavern, Thesiger Road, Penge, London SE20 7NQ (081 778 5696).
Ground & Directions: Huntsman Sports, Manor Way, Blackheath SE3 (081 852 3602). Lee Road from Blackheath - Manor Way on left hand side before Lee Green crossroads. Via Lewisham to Lee Green - left at lights then 3rd right. Via Sutcliffe Park to Lee Green, right at lights then 3rd right into Manor Way. Nearest stations are Lee Green and Blackheath.
Colours: Yellow/royal/yellow **Change Colours:** Berry red/navy/berry red.

LEYTON COUNTY RESERVES *(details opposite)*

MERIDIAN

Chairman: Peter Page.
Secretary: Lenny Andrews, Meridian Sports & Social Club, Charlton Park Lane, Charlton SE7 (081 857 8247).
Ground: As Bridon Ropes FC (see page 638).
Colours: Red/black/black **Change Colours:** Yellow/black/black.

METPOL CHIGWELL RESERVES *(see page 640)*

SINGH SABHA

Chairman: Mr H S Lakhan
Secretary: Mr R S Boparai, 28 Abbotsford Rd, Goodmayes, Ilford, Essex IG3 9SL (081 599 5044).
Ground & Directions: As Clapton Villa *(see page 638).*
Colours: All white **Change colours:** Red/white/white.

SOUTH EAST OLYMPIC

Chairman/Secretary: D Wilson, 74 Shrofford Road, Bromley BR1 5PF (081 698 1192).
Ground & Directions: As Huntsman FC *(see page 641).*
Colours: Green/navy/green **Change Colours:** White/black/red.

SOUTHWARK '94

Chairman: Anthony Faweh.
Secretary: Mr John R Stancombe, 106 RNIB Garrow House, 190 Kensal Rd, North Kensngton, London W10 5BN (081 673 4010).
Ground & Directions: Southwark Park, Hawkstone Rd, Surrey Quays, London SE16 (071 231 9442). From Rotherhithe Tunnel (A101) left at r'bout into Lower Rd (A200), right into Hawkstone Rd (A2208) and park entrance on right. From A2 take Deptford Church Street (A2209) and left into Creek Rd/Evelyn Street (A200), at Surrey Quays left into Hawkstone Rd - ground on right.
Colours: Sky & chocolate/chocolate/sky **Change colours:** Green/white/green

WALTHAMSTOW St MARYS

Chairman: E A Kelly
Secretary: Nick Adams, Shambledon Chase, 58 Crouch Hill, London N4 4AH (071 263 1530).
Ground & Directions: Drapers Field, Gordon Rd, Leyton E15. Lea Bridge Rd (A104) to Leyton High Rd, right into Cranbourne, 1st left into Gordon Rd - Drapers Field at end. Tube to Leyton (Central Line).
Colours: Red/black/red **Change colours:** Sky/white/sky.
Honours: London Junior Cup 93-94.

WALTHAMSTOW TROJANS RESERVES *(see page 640)*

WILLESDEN (HAWKEYE) RESERVES *(see page 636)*

WOODFORD

Chairman: Mr Bruce Rossdale.
Secretary: Ray Cheek, 50a Richmond Crescent, Highams Park, London E4 9RU (081 527 4958).
Ground & Directions: 267/269 Snakes Lane, Woodford, Essex IG1 7JJ (081 506 0023). Dartford Tunnel via Gants Hill into Eastern Avenue onto North Circular A406 (M11 intersection) into Woodford New Road. Eastern Avenue A12 to 'Charlie Browns' r'bout Woodford, Broadmead Rd.
Colours: Yellow/green/green **Change colours:** Red/black/black.

WOOLWICH TOWN RESERVES *(see page 640)*

An excellent action shot showing Laroche of Bridon Ropes clearing spectacularly during his side's 2-2 draw at Old Roan in Division One.

Photo - Richard Brock.

CARLING NORTH WEST COUNTIES LEAGUE

FEEDER TO:
NORTHERN PREMIER LEAGUE

FOUNDED: 1982

President: Canon J R Smith, MA

Chairman: J E Hinchliffe

Treasurer: K H Dean

Secretary: M Darby, 87 Hillary Road, Hyde, Cheshire SK14 4EB (061 368 6243).

ATHERTON L.R. RETAIN THE CROWN

The start of the 1993-94 season saw the North West Counties League flying under a different banner but still under the sponsorship of Bass Breweries. At the request of Bass, the brand name of Carling was adopted and the League became known as The Carling North West Counties League.

In Division One, Atherton Laburnum Rovers once again took the Championship title and, after the disappointment of last season when they were unable to progress into the Northern Premier League due to their facilities not being up to NPL standards, the end of the 1993/94 Season saw them in a much better position. With the many ground improvements now having been carried out, including the erection of an impressive all-steel stand, 'Rovers' have now achieved their goal and 1994/95 will see them progressing up the Football Pyramid into the NPL. It has certainly been a truly historic year for the club who, under the management of Dave Morris, reached the Semi-Finals of the FA Vase, beating 'favourites' Aldershot Town along the way, and they also ended up as runners-up in the Tennents Floodlit Trophy. At the League's Presentation Evening in June Dave, Morris' achievements were duly acknowledged when he was named 'Manager of the Year' in Division One.

In Division Two, Haslingden completed their first year in the CNWCL by lifting the Division Two title but, due to their facilities not reaching First Division standards, were unable to go forward for promotion. Haslingden's Manager, Geoff Dean, was named 'Manager of the Year' in Division Two and their prolific goalscorer Jimmy Clarke won the Player of the Year Award in Division Two.

The Division Two runners-up, North Trafford who also won the Lamot Pils Trophy and the Reserve Division, have been promoted to Division One along with third-placed Holker Old Boys, both having worked long and hard on their grounds and facilities to achieve the necessary standards.

For their first season back in the North West Counties League, Rossendale United took the Runners-up spot in the First Division and also lifted the Carling League Challenge up beating St Helens Town by the only goal of the final.

At the bottom end of the scale in Division One there was a battle against relegation fought out between Flixton and Skelmersdale United, both ending on equal points but Flixton, having the poorer goal difference, now face the 'big drop' into the Second Division.

In Division Two, K Chell and Squires Gate finished in the bottom two placings but only Squires

Atherton Laburnum Rovers - Carling North West Counties League Division One champions 1993-94. Back Row (L/R): Gerry Luska (Coach), Jeremy Lord, Andy Feeley, Dave Liptrot, Andy Hills, Lee Unsworth, Rob Holgate, Tony Pemberton, Paul Kirwan. Front: Keith Ingham, Paul Burrows, Dave Morris (Manager), Jim Evans (Captain), Mike Southern, Stuart Humphries. *Photo - Steve Allen.*

Gate went forward for re-election at the Annual General Meeting and were duly accepted, as sadly we saw the demise of Staffordshire-based club K Chell. One other club in the Second Division has also disbanded, namely Ellesmere Port Town.

At the AGM, Warrington-based club Tetley Walker applied for Membership of the League and were unanimously accepted by all Member Clubs. For the forthcoming season the League will comprise of 22 Clubs in the First Division and 16 Clubs in the Second Division.

Other Clubs who have earned themselves honours this term are as follows: St Helens Town (Finalists in the Carling League Challenge Cup and Runners-up in the Reserve Division), Bootle (won the Tennents Floodlit Trophy), Darwen (won the Reserve Division Challenge Cup just beating Maghull on penalties), Maghull (Finalists in the Reserve Division Challenge Cup and Finalists in the Lamot Pils Trophy. They also won the Liverpool Challenge Cup), Newcastle Town (won the Walsall Senior Cup), Clitheroe (won the East Lancs Floodlit Trophy).

Other presentations that were made at the Dinner Dance and Presentation Evening, held at the Palace Hotel, Buxton, included The Fair Play Awards, sponsored by REALCO EQUIPMENT, and introduced for the first time this season. In Division One the Fair Play Award went to Clitheroe, and in Division Two to Squires Gate. John Giblin of Nantwich Town was named 'Player of the Year' in Division One.

The Programme of the Year Awards were as follows: St Helens Town - Best Programme Overall; Bradford Park Avenue - Winner in Division One; Atherton Collieries - Winner in Division Two

Away from the playing side, and a presentation of a cut glass engraved goblet was made to Bill Heywood who has now been made a Life Member of the League. Bill has served as a Representative on the Management Committee since the North West Counties League was formed in 1982.

The 13th Season of the Carling North West Counties League kicked off on the 13th August, with two of the Member Clubs flying under different banners. Westhoughton Town have reverting back to their previous name of Daisy Hill, whilst North Trafford will be known simply as Trafford.

Irene Davies, League Newsletter Editor.

DIV. ONE	P	W	D	L	F	A	PTS
Atherton LR	42	25	13	4	83	34	88
Rossendale Utd	42	25	9	8	76	46	84
Burscough	42	22	13	7	107	50	79
Nantwich Town	42	22	11	9	80	54	77
Eastwood Hanley	42	22	11	9	75	52	77
Bootle	42	21	10	11	77	61	73
Penrith	42	20	11	11	62	44	71
Blackpool Rovers	42	19	10	13	64	57	67
Clitheroe	42	19	9	14	75	58	66
Kidsgrove Ath.	42	16	10	16	70	61	58
St Helens Town	42	14	13	15	60	55	55
Prescot AFC	42	14	13	15	46	47	55
Maine Road	42	14	13	15	58	64	55
Newcastle Town	42	14	10	18	66	67	52
Bradford Park Ave.	42	12	12	18	54	79	48
Darwen	42	12	8	22	38	61	44
Glossop Nth End	42	12	8	22	58	86	44
Salford City	42	11	10	21	50	67	43
Chadderton	42	10	8	24	49	85	38
Bacup Borough	42	9	9	24	57	85	36
Skelmersdale Utd	42	8	8	26	55	92	32
Flixton	42	9	5	28	35	90	32

Top Scorers (League + Cup = Total): S Pennington (St Helens) 27 + 18 = 45, S O'Neill (Bootle) 28 + 13 = 41, G Martindale (Burscough) 29 + 7 = 36, D Liptrot (Atherton LR) 20 + 11 = 31, J Scarlett (Nantwich) 14 + 14 = 28, K Johnstone (Blackpool Rovers) 22 + 5 = 27, K Bates (Eastwood Hanley) 21 + 4 = 25, B Livesey (Bacup) 18 + 6 = 24, S Morgan (Glossop) 14 + 10 = 24, S Parker (Atherton) 14 + 10 = 24, D Emmett (Rossendale) 17 + 7 = 24, P Hulme (Eastwood Hanley) 19 + 4 = 23, B Knowles (Bootle) 15 + 6 = 21, T Fyfe (Penrith) 14 + 6 = 20, P James (Newcastle) 14 + 6 = 20, M McDonough (Burscough) 12 + 8 = 20, B Welsh (Rossendale) 12 + 8 = 20, J Penman (Clitheroe) 16 + 3 = 19, J Giblin (Nantwich) 15 + 4 = 19, A Russell (Burscough) 15 + 3 = 18, A Kamars (Kidsgrove & K Chell) 18 + 0 = 18, G Young (Clitheroe) 9 + 8 = 17, M Heys (Clitheroe) 9 + 7 = 16, K Vincent (Bootle) 6 + 10 = 16.

DIV. TWO	P	W	D	L	F	A	PTS
Haslingden	34	26	5	3	117	39	83
North Trafford	34	24	2	8	95	36	74
Holker Old Boys	34	23	3	8	75	40	72
Stantondale	34	20	8	8	88	45	68
Castleton Gabriels	34	19	6	9	55	46	63
Nelson	34	16	8	10	75	52	56
Atherton Collieries	34	15	9	10	58	40	54
Maghull	34	15	8	11	70	46	53
Ellesmere Pt Town	34	14	8	12	62	63	50
Formby	34	12	11	11	59	50	47
Oldham Town	34	13	6	15	61	68	45
Cheadle Town	34	11	9	14	69	62	42
Blackpool Mechs	34	10	5	19	50	69	35
Westhoughton T.	34	9	3	22	53	100	30
Ashton Town	34	7	8	19	42	91	29
Irlam Town	34	8	4	22	41	73	28
K Chell	34	4	6	24	35	97	18
Squires Gate	34	1	0	24	20	108	12

Top Scorers (League + Cup = Total): J Clarke (Haslingden) 39 + 7 = 46, G Peyton (Nelson) 36 + 8 = 44, L Cooper (Maghull) 24 + 16 = 40, G Dodd (Stantondale) 22 + 14 = 36, B Cooper (Stantondale) 26 + 9 = 35, S Parry (Haslingden) 20 + 4 = 24, R Brierley (Cheadle) 20 + 1 = 21, S Caley (Westhoughton) 20 + 1 = 21, P Meachin (Ellesmere Port) 14 + 7 = 21, B Roberts (Maghull) 14 + 5 = 19, C Small (North Trafford) 13 + 6 = 19, C Roach (Oldham) 17 + 1 = 18, A Morris (Ashton) 14 + 2 = 16, C Wilson (North Trafford) 13 + 3 = 16, G Vaughan (North Trafford) 12 + 4 = 16.

RESERVE DIV.	P	W	D	L	F	A	PTS
Nth Trafford Res.	32	22	6	4	96	34	72
St Helens T. Res.	32	20	7	5	83	34	67
Maghull Res.	32	19	7	6	70	32	64
Holker OB Res.	32	16	8	8	64	34	56
Salford City Res.	32	17	5	10	66	45	56
B'pool Mechs Res.	32	17	5	10	65	48	56
Atherton Col. Res.	32	15	9	8	69	45	54
Kidsgrove A. Res.	32	17	2	13	74	52	53
Haslingden Res.	32	16	5	11	56	52	53
Chadderton Res.	32	14	5	13	75	80	47
Rossendale U. Res.	32	14	5	13	64	71	47
Darwen Res.	32	12	4	16	55	64	40
Maine Road Res.	32	8	9	17	51	70	27
Prescot AFC Res.	32	7	6	19	41	66	27
Ashton Town Res.	32	7	2	23	37	89	23
Oldham Town Res.	32	4	5	23	43	103	17
Squires Gate Res.	32	2	4	26	26	116	10

DIVISION ONE RESULT CHART 1993-94

HOME TEAM	1	2	3	4	5	6	7	8	9	10	11	12	13	14	15	16	17	18	19	20	21	22
1. Atherton LR	*	1-0	2-0	3-1	4-0	0-1	4-1	4-4	1-1	2-1	2-1	3-1	1-0	1-1	2-2	1-0	0-0	4-0	1-2	0-0	4-1	1-0
2. Bacup Bor.	0-0	*	0-1	2-3	1-3	2-2	0-2	0-2	0-1	0-1	2-1	5-2	0-4	1-3	2-1	1-2	2-1	1-1	1-2	0-4	3-3	5-2
3. B'pool Rvrs	0-3	1-3	*	1-2	1-1	0-1	4-2	1-3	3-0	2-0	1-0	2-1	2-2	1-1	1-4	0-1	2-2	1-1	1-1	1-1	1-2	0-1
4. Bootle	3-3	1-1	0-1	*	5-1	4-2	3-0	3-1	1-1	0-2	2-0	5-3	3-1	2-2	0-2	0-0	2-1	0-2	0-1	0-1	4-0	2-3
5. B'ford PA	2-4	2-4	2-6	1-1	*	2-2	2-1	2-3	4-1	0-0	2-1	4-1	3-2	1-2	3-1	1-1	0-0	0-0	3-0	2-0	1-4	0-0
6. Burscough	0-1	4-3	4-1	0-2	1-1	*	1-1	1-1	4-0	1-1	4-0	8-0	2-2	3-0	9-3	1-2	2-2	1-2	5-1	3-2	4-2	4-0
7. Chadderton	0-5	3-0	1-3	1-2	1-2	0-2	*	1-2	1-2	1-1	0-2	2-1	0-5	1-3	0-2	0-3	2-0	0-0	2-3	1-1	1-1	4-4
8. Clitheroe	1-1	3-1	1-2	7-0	1-1	0-3	3-0	*	2-2	4-0	0-0	0-1	1-0	0-1	2-1	6-3	0-2	1-2	1-4	3-1	2-0	1-0
9. Darwen	2-1	3-0	1-2	1-2	2-0	0-0	0-0	0-1	*	0-3	2-0	1-0	1-3	1-1	1-3	1-2	1-0	0-1	0-3	2-1	0-2	3-1
10. E'wood Han.	2-1	3-1	2-1	5-3	2-0	1-0	0-1	4-3	2-0	*	3-3	3-1	3-2	3-0	1-1	2-2	7-1	2-1	0-0	1-3	1-1	2-0
11. Flixton	1-4	0-5	0-2	1-3	1-0	0-5	0-1	1-1	0-1	1-2	*	0-3	2-1	0-3	0-7	1-1	1-0	0-0	0-4	2-1	1-0	5-1
12. Glossop NE	0-3	1-1	1-2	1-1	3-1	3-0	1-2	1-0	1-0	2-2	3-0	*	1-3	0-1	1-2	3-3	0-6	1-1	0-2	1-0	2-1	4-3
13. Kidsgrove	2-3	3-0	2-4	0-2	4-0	1-2	2-1	0-2	1-0	1-3	2-0	2-1	*	1-1	0-0	5-1	1-0	0-0	1-2	2-0	1-0	1-1
14. Maine Road	1-4	1-1	0-1	1-1	1-1	1-6	1-2	1-0	1-1	1-3	0-2	2-2	1-2	*	1-0	1-3	0-1	0-0	2-1	1-2	3-1	5-2
15. Nantwich T.	1-2	1-0	1-1	4-0	0-2	3-3	1-0	3-2	2-1	3-2	3-1	1-0	1-1	1-1	*	0-2	1-1	4-2	1-0	2-2	2-0	1-2
16. Newcastle	0-1	1-3	3-0	1-2	1-1	1-1	4-1	2-3	1-3	0-0	2-0	4-5	1-1	1-2	1-4	*	0-1	1-2	1-2	2-1	3-0	1-1
17. Penrith	1-1	1-0	0-2	2-2	1-0	0-3	1-1	0-0	2-0	3-0	5-1	3-1	3-0	3-1	1-0	3-2	*	0-1	4-2	1-0	2-0	2-1
18. Prescot	0-2	4-0	1-2	0-1	2-0	2-2	4-1	0-1	1-1	1-2	2-1	2-3	1-2	1-2	0-1	1-0	0-2	*	0-2	1-1	0-0	1-0
19. Rossendale	0-0	1-1	1-1	0-0	1-0	0-3	3-2	2-1	1-0	2-1	4-1	0-0	5-1	3-2	1-1	1-3	3-0	4-0	*	3-1	1-1	2-1
20. St Helens	0-0	2-0	2-4	1-3	5-0	0-1	3-2	3-2	2-0	1-1	2-0	3-1	2-2	1-1	0-2	2-1	1-1	1-1	1-3	*	1-1	3-0
21. Salford	0-0	5-1	1-2	0-2	2-3	1-2	4-5	0-0	2-0	0-1	1-2	2-1	3-2	1-0	1-2	0-1	0-0	0-3	2-1	1-1	*	1-0
22. Skelmersdale	1-3	2-4	0-0	1-4	6-0	2-2	0-1	2-4	3-1	2-0	3-2	0-0	2-2	2-5	2-4	3-2	0-3	0-1	0-2	0-1	1-3	*

North West Counties Division One 10-Year Record

	84/5	85/6	86/7	87/8	88/9	89/0	90/1	91/2	92/3	93/4
Accrington Stanley	15	11	2	-	-	-	-	-	-	-
Ashton United	-	-	-	-	17	9	3	1	-	-
Atherton Laburnam Rovers	-	-	-	17	14	14	18	11	1	1
Bacup Borough	-	-	-	-	-	-	14	14	15	20
Bamber Bridge	-	-	-	-	-	-	-	-	2	-
Blackpool Mechanics	-	-	-	-	-	-	-	-	22	-
Blackpool Rovers	-	-	-	-	-	-	-	4	12	8
Bootle	14	15	5	13	9	11	13	18	-	6
Bradford Park Avenue	-	-	-	-	-	-	-	17	6	15
Burscough	3	9	12	10	10	17	-	-	10	3
Caernarfon Town	2	-	-	-	-	-	-	-	-	-
Chadderton	-	-	-	-	-	18	-	-	3	19
Clitheroe	-	1	3	3	12	5	15	9	7	9
Colne Dynamoes	-	-	-	1	-	-	-	-	-	-
Colwyn Bay	-	-	-	4	4	3	2	-	-	-
Congleton Town	10	2	11	-	-	-	-	-	-	-
Curzon Ashton	6	8	19	-	-	-	-	-	-	-
Darwen	-	-	-	7	5	6	16	10	17	16
Eastwood Hanley	5	3	14	-	-	-	4	3	18	5
Ellesmere Port & Neston	-	-	-	6	11	-	-	-	-	-
Fleetwood Town	8	5	8	-	-	-	-	-	-	-
Flixton	-	-	-	-	7	12	7	8	11	22
Formby	17	20	-	14	18	-	-	-	-	-
Glossop (North End)	16	18	20	18	-	-	-	-	16	17
Great Harwood Town	-	-	-	-	-	-	-	2	-	-
Irlam Town	-	6	18	-	-	-	-	-	-	-
Kidsgrove Athletic	-	-	-	-	-	-	-	-	20	10
Kirkby Town (See Knowsley United)										
Knowsley United	-	-	4	9	2	2	1	-	-	-
Lancaster City	19	-	-	-	-	-	-	-	-	-
Leek Town	9	7	16	-	-	-	-	-	-	-
Leyland Motors	11	12	13	11	8	13	12	-	-	-
Maine Road	-	-	-	-	-	-	9	16	19	13
Nantwich Town	-	-	-	-	-	7	11	12	13	4
Netherfield	18	17	17	-	-	-	-	-	-	-
Newcastle Town	-	-	-	-	-	-	-	-	5	14
Penrith	20	16	9	-	-	-	17	6	14	7
Prescot AFC	13	19	-	12	15	10	6	5	4	12
Prescot Cables (see Prescot A.F.C.)										
Radcliffe Borough	1	14	15	-	-	-	-	-	-	-
Rossendale United	-	-	10	2	1	-	-	-	-	2
St Helens Town	12	10	6	5	3	8	8	15	8	11
Salford (City)	-	-	-	15	16	16	19	-	9	18
Skelmersdale United	-	-	-	16	13	15	10	7	21	21
Stalybridge Celtic	4	4	1	-	-	-	-	-	-	-
Vauxhall GM	-	-	-	-	-	4	5	13	-	-
Warrington Town	-	-	-	8	6	1	-	-	-	-
Winsford United	7	13	7	-	-	-	-	-	-	-
No. of clubs competing	20	20	20	18	18	18	19	18	22	22

DIVISION TWO RESULT CHART 1993-94

HOME TEAM	1	2	3	4	5	6	7	8	9	10	11	12	13	14	15	16	17	18
1. Ashton Town	*	1-1	3-2	0-3	0-4	1-3	2-2	4-5	0-3	2-4	2-2	4-2	2-2	3-0	0-5	0-0	2-4	4-0
2. Atherton Col.	6-0	*	1-0	1-1	1-2	1-1	0-0	1-4	1-2	4-0	2-1	1-0	0-3	1-2	2-1	5-0	2-2	2-2
3. B'pool Mechs	4-2	0-1	*	1-0	2-1	1-3	0-1	0-6	0-1	0-1	1-2	0-2	0-0	2-0	3-3	9-0	3-3	4-0
4. Castleton Gab.	5-0	0-3	2-0	*	2-0	1-1	1-1	0-6	3-4	3-0	2-1	2-0	3-1	0-5	1-4	2-0	2-0	3-2
5. Cheadle Town	1-0	0-2	7-1	2-3	*	3-0	5-2	2-6	0-1	2-1	1-1	1-3	3-3	0-2	3-2	6-0	1-1	1-1
6. Ellesmere Pt T.	4-1	0-3	3-2	1-2	2-2	*	2-1	3-2	2-4	1-0	2-0	3-3	1-3	3-2	3-2	2-0	2-2	3-1
7. Formby	1-1	2-1	0-1	2-1	2-1	2-3	*	2-2	0-1	2-1	3-0	0-3	4-1	1-3	3-3	5-0	2-2	3-0
8. Haslingden	7-0	2-0	3-1	1-1	4-2	3-3	0-0	*	2-0	6-1	10-0	3-1	1-1	4-1	4-0	5-3	3-2	3-0
9. Holker OB	0-0	2-2	2-0	0-1	2-1	3-1	2-1	2-4	*	5-0	5-0	1-3	3-1	2-4	2-0	3-0	0-2	7-0
10. Irlam Town	1-3	0-2	3-0	1-2	1-1	2-2	0-3	0-1	1-2	*	0-1	3-2	0-6	0-2	5-0	2-2	1-3	1-3
11. K Chell	0-1	3-1	1-3	1-3	2-2	2-1	0-0	1-2	1-2	0-3	*	1-4	1-5	1-2	0-3	2-0	2-5	1-3
12. Maghull	2-0	1-2	4-1	1-2	0-0	2-0	1-1	2-0	1-3	3-1	6-2	*	1-1	2-3	1-1	1-1	0-1	4-2
13. Nelson	2-0	0-0	2-1	1-1	4-1	4-1	1-1	5-1	1-0	3-0	3-0	2-4	*	0-3	4-3	3-0	2-3	4-0
14. North Trafford	8-0	5-0	7-1	2-0	4-1	0-0	3-0	0-4	0-1	3-1	3-0	1-1	5-2	*	2-0	3-0	1-2	2-1
15. Oldham Town	2-0	1-2	3-2	0-1	1-1	2-1	1-4	0-5	0-2	0-0	4-1	1-0	2-1	0-5	*	4-1	2-2	5-1
16. Squires Gate	2-2	0-6	0-1	0-0	0-6	0-4	3-0	1-5	2-2	0-1	1-1	1-1	2-3	0-9	0-1	*	0-7	0-0
17. Stantondale	3-0	1-1	1-1	0-1	6-0	2-0	4-2	0-1	4-3	3-2	7-2	0-1	2-0	0-1	3-1	3-1	*	4-2
18. Westhoughton T.	1-2	1-0	2-3	2-3	0-6	4-1	1-6	0-2	2-3	1-4	4-2	1-8	3-1	3-2	3-4	4-0	3-2	*

10-Year Record

10-Year Record	84/5	85/6	86/7	87/8	88/9	89/0	90/1	91/2	92/3	93/4
Ashton Town	-	-	-	10	17	10	15	17	16	15
Ashton United	4	14	3	1	-	-	-	-	-	-
Atherton Collieries	-	-	-	8	11	8	18	13	9	7
Atherton L.R.	10	11	17	-	-	-	-	-	-	-
Bacup Borough	-	-	-	22	9	2	-	-	-	-
Bamber Bridge	-	-	-	-	-	-	4	1	-	-
Blackpool Mechanics	-	-	12	15	16	3	5	3	-	13
Blackpool Wren Rovers	6	3	4	3	4	4	2	-	-	-
Bootle	-	-	-	-	-	-	-	-	2	-
Bradford Park Avenue	-	-	-	-	-	-	3	-	-	-
Burnley Bank Hall	-	-	-	-	-	-	-	-	10	-
Burscough	-	-	-	-	-	-	9	4	-	-
Castleton Gabriels	-	-	-	-	-	-	11	8	6	5
Chadderton	8	6	7	13	3	-	12	11	-	-
Cheadle Town	-	-	-	12	14	6	7	9	12	12
Clitheroe	1	-	-	-	-	-	-	-	-	-
Colne Dynamoes	9	7	8	-	-	-	-	-	-	-
Colwyn Bay	-	5	5	-	-	-	-	-	-	-
Daisy Hill (see Westhoughton United)										
Darwen	16	15	6	-	-	-	-	-	-	-
Droylsden	5	10	1	-	-	-	-	-	-	-
Ellesmere Port & Neston	18	13	10	-	-	-	-	-	-	-
Ellesmere Port Town	-	-	-	-	-	-	-	-	4	9
Flixton	-	-	-	2	-	-	-	-	-	-
Ford Motors	12	17	-	17	-	-	-	-	-	-
Formby	-	-	11	-	-	12	17	5	8	10
Glossop	-	-	-	-	13	14	8	6	-	-
Great Harwood Town	7	8	15	14	7	5	1	-	-	-
Haslingden	-	-	-	-	-	-	-	-	-	1
Holker Old Boys	-	-	-	-	-	-	-	15	15	3
Irlam Town	2	-	-	-	-	-	-	-	18	16
K Chell	-	-	-	-	-	-	-	-	14	17
Kidsgrove Athletic	-	-	-	-	-	-	14	10	-	-
Kirkby Town (see Knowsley United)										
Knowsley United	-	1	-	-	-	-	-	-	-	-
Lancaster City	-	12	13	-	-	-	-	-	-	-
Maghull	-	-	-	6	8	7	13	16	1	8
Maine Road	-	-	-	5	2	1	-	-	-	-
Nantwich Town	11	18	-	21	5	-	-	-	-	-
Nelson	-	-	-	16	-	-	-	-	17	6
Newcastle Town	-	-	-	4	6	13	6	2	-	-
Newton	-	-	-	20	18	16	-	-	-	-
North Trafford	-	-	-	-	-	-	-	-	7	2
Oldham Town	-	-	16	11	15	9	16	12	3	11
Padiham	17	-	-	19	12	11	-	-	-	-
Prescot Cables	-	-	14	-	-	-	-	-	-	-
Rossendale United	14	2	-	-	-	-	-	-	-	-
Salford City	15	16	18	-	-	-	-	7	-	-
Skelmersdale United	13	9	9	-	-	-	-	-	-	-
Squires Gate	-	-	-	-	-	-	-	14	13	18
Stantondale	-	-	-	-	-	-	-	-	5	4
Vauxhall GM	-	-	-	7	1	-	-	-	-	-
Warrington Town	3	4	2	-	-	-	-	-	-	-
Westhoughton Town	-	-	-	18	10	15	10	18	11	14
Whitworth Valley	-	-	-	9	-	-	-	-	-	-
No. of clubs competing	18	18	18	22	18	16	18	18	18	18

CARLING LEAGUE CHALLENGE CUP 1993-94

First Round

Atherton Collieries v Ellesmere Port Town 2-0
Castleton Gabriels v Cheadle Town 1-1,3-0
Holker Old Boys v Irlam Town 3-2
North Trafford v Westhoughton Town 4-0
Blackpool Mechanics v Maghull 1-2
Haslingden v K Chell 8-0
Nelson v Ashton Town 5-1
Oldham Town v Stantondale 0-5

Second Round

Burscough v Atherton Collieries 2-2,4-2
Bradford Park Avenue v Castleton Gabriels 6-4
Flixton v Darwen 1-1,2-0
Glossop North End v Nelson 2-5
Kidsgrove Athletic v Maine Road 0-2
North Trafford v Chadderton 1-0
Prescot AFC v Newcastle Town 2-0
Salford City v St Helens Town 1-2
Blackpool Rovers v Holker Old Boys 2-2,3-1*(aet)*
Clitheroe v Squires Gate 8-0
Formby v Skelmersdale United 0-1
Haslingden v Bacup Borough 0-1
Nantwich Town v Eastwood Hanley 1-1,1-2
Penrith v Maghull 1-1,4-4*(Penrith won on pens)*
Rossendale United v Atherton Laburnum Rovers 3-0
Stantondale v Bootle 4-3

Third Round

Blackpool Rovers v Bacup Borough 2-1
Nelson v Rossendale United 2-2,1-4
Penrith v Flixton 0-0,0-1
Skelmersdale United v Clitheroe 1-5
Burscough v Maine Road 1-1,1-3*(aet)*
North Trafford v Bradford Park Avenue 1-1,6-0
St Helens Town v Eastwood Hanley 1-1,2-1
Stantondale v Prescot AFC 5-0

Quarter-Finals

Flixton v Blackpool Rovers 2-2,0-1
St Helens Town v Clitheroe 3-2
Maine Road v Rossendale United 0-1
Stantondale v North Trafford 2-0

Semi-Finals (Two Legs)

St Helens Town v Blackpool Rovers 2-1,3-1
Rossendale United v Stantondale 3-0,3-0

Final *(at Bury FC, Monday 2nd May)*: Rossendale United 1, St Helens Town 0

Rossendale United - Carling League Challenge Cup winners 1993-94. *Photo - John L Newton.*

TENNENTS FLOODLIT TROPHY 1993-94

First Round (Two Legs, Away Goals rule applicable)

Blackpool Rovers v Clitheroe 0-4,1-4
Chadderton v Bradford Park Avenue 1-0,2-1
Eastwood Hanley v Kidsgrove Athletic 1-2,1-2
Glossop North End v Bacup Borough 1-1,2-1
Bootle v Skelmersdale United 3-1,2-4
Darwen v Penrith 0-2,2-2
Ellesmere Port Town v Nantwich Town 0-3,0-4
Haslingden *(scr)* Salford City *(w/o)*

Second Round

Burscough v Newcastle Town 2-1
Flixton v Clitheroe 1-1,3-1
Kidsgrove Athletic v Bootle 0-3
Atherton LR *(bye)*
Chadderton v St Helens Town 4-3
Holker Old Boys v Penrith 1-2
Salford City v Glossop North End 4-3
Nantwich Town *(bye)*

Quarter Finals

Burscough v Flixton 3-0
Penrith v Atherton Laburnum Rovers 1-3
Chadderton v Nantwich Town 3-3,0-2
Salford City v Bootle 1-4

Semi-Finals (Two Legs)

Burscough v Bootle 1-1,1-3
Nantwich Town v Atherton Laburnum Rovers 1-3,2-3

Final *(at Skelmersdale Utd FC, Thursday 28th April)*: Bootle 2, Atherton LR 1

LAMOT PILS TROPHY (DIVISION TWO) TROPHY 1993-94

Preliminary Round

Ashton Town v Irlam Town 5-0
Nelson v Haslingden 2-5

First Round

Ashton Town v Stantondale 1-4
Ellesmere Port Town v K Chell 1-1,2-1
Haslingden v Castleton Gabriels 3-0
Blackpool Mechanics v Atherton Collieries 3-3,0-3
Formby v Maghull 2-2,1-6
North Trafford v Cheadle Town 2-0

Quarter-Finals

Atherton Collieries v Maghull 0-2
Haslingden v Oldham Town 3-3,3-0
Ellesmere P. v Stantondale 2-2,3-3 *(EP on away goals)*
Holker Old Boys v North Trafford 1-1,0-2

Semi-Finals (Two Legs)

Ellesmere Port Town v Maghull 1-2,2-7
Haslingden v North Trafford 2-3,0-6 *(both games played at North Trafford)*

Final *(at Skelmersdale Utd FC, Wednesday 4th May)*: North Trafford 3, Maghull 1

RESERVE DIVISION CUP 1993-94

Preliminary Round

Blackpool Mechs Res. v Ashton Town Res. 2-1

First Round

Atherton Collieries Res. v Squires Gate Res. 7-0
Chadderton Res. v Maghull Res. 1-3
Holker Old Boys Res. v Rossendale Res. 3-1
Oldham Town Res. v Darwen Res. 3-3,1-3
Blackpool Mechs Res. v North Trafford Res. 0-0,1-2
Haslingden Res. v Salford City Res. 1-3
Kidsgrove Ath. Res. v Prescot AFC Res. 3-1
Maine Road Res. v St Helens Town Res. 3-1

Quarter-Finals

Atherton Coll. Res. v Salford City Res. 3-1
Maghull Res. v Maine Road Res. 2-0
Kidsgrove Res. v Darwen Res. 1-1 *(K'grove withdrew)*
North Trafford Res. v Holker OB Res. 1-0

Semi-Finals

Atherton C. Res v Darwen Res *(at Salford)* 0-1
Maghull Res. v N. Trafford Res *(at St Helens)* 2-1

Final *(at Atherton Collieries FC, Tuesday 10th May)*: Maghull Res. 1, Darwen Res. 1 *(Darwen won 4-3 on pens)*

DIVISION ONE CLUBS 1994-95

BACUP BOROUGH

President: W Shufflebottom **Chairman:** W Heywood **Vice Chairman:** D Whatmough
Secretary: F Manning, 10 Warwick Street, Haslingden, Rossendale, Lancs BB4 5LR (0706 221886).
Manager: TBA **Asst Manager:** TBA **Commercial Mgr:**
Ground: West View, Cowtoot Lane, Blackthorn, Bacup, Lancashire (0706 878655).
Directions: From M62, M66 onto A681 through Rawtenstall to Bacup centre, left onto A671 towards Burnley, after approx 300 yds right (immed. before the Irwell Inn) climbing Cooper Street, right into Blackthorn Lane then first left into Cowtoot Lane to ground.
Seats: 500 **Cover:** 1,000 **Capacity:** 3,000 **Floodlights:** Yes **Founded:** 1875
Colours: Black & white stripes/black/black **Change colours:** All red
Previous league: Lancs Comb. 03-82. **Midweek Matches:** Tuesday.
Previous Name: Bacup FC. **Previous Grounds:** None
Programme: 12 pages, 30p **Editor:** D Whatmough (0706 875041) **Club Shop:** Not yet
Club Sponsors: Hoover Ltd **Record Gate:** 4,980 v Nelson 1947 **Nickname:** The Boro
Clubhouse: Open matchdays and private functions (for which buffets can be provided). Pies and sandwiches on matchdays.
Captain 93-94: **P.o.Y. 93-94:** **Club record scorer:** Jimmy Clarke
Hons: Lancs Jnr Cup 10-11 (R-up 22-23 74-75), Lancs Comb. 46-47 (Lg Cup R-up 46-47 80-81, NW Co's Lg Div 2 R-up 89-90.

BLACKPOOL (WREN) ROVERS

Chairman: J Nolan **Manager:** John Dodd.
Secretary: Paul Kimberley, 34 Priory Gate, South Shore, Blackpool, Lancs FY4 2QE (0253 349853).
Ground: Bruce Park, School Road, Marton, Blackpool, Lancs (0253 760570).
Directions: M6 to M55, leave at Jct 4, left onto A583, sharp right at 1st lights (Whitehill Rd)., follow signs for Airport. Ground approx 1.5 miles on right. 6 miles from Blackpool North (BR).
Seats: 250 **Cover:** 750 **Capacity:** 1,000 **Floodlights:** Yes **Founded:** 1936
Record Gate: 1,011 v Manchester City, floodlight opener October 1991.
Colours: All red **Change colours:** All blue
Programme: 20 pages, 20p **Programme Editor:** P Kimberley **Club shop:** No
Clubhouse: Open matchdays only **Midweek matches:** Tuesday.
Previous Name: Wren Rovers **Prev. Lges:** Blackpool Amtr, West Lancs, Lancs Comb. 72-82.
Hons: W Lancs Lg 69-70 70-71 (Lg Cup(2)), Lancs FA Shield 69-70 70-71, Lancs Comb. 78-79 80-81 (R-up 77-78, Lg Cup 78-79, Bridge Shield 76-77).

BOOTLE

Chairman: TBA **Manager:** Tommy Fagan
Secretary/Press Officer: Paul Carr, 58 Orchard Hey, Old Roan, Bootle, Merseyside L30 8RY (051 474 0153).
Ground: Bucks Park, Northern Perimeter Road, Netherton, Bootle, Merseyside L30 7PT (051 520 0645).
Directions: At end of M57 & M58 follow signs to Bootle/All Docks. Turn right at next lights by Police station. Entrance 150 yds on right. 300 yds from Old Roan statiom. Bus 55 (150yds from ground), 302 341 345 350 (350yds).
Seats: 400 **Cover:** 1,400 **Capacity:** 5,000 **Floodlights:** Yes **Founded:** 1953
Record Gate: 750 v Carshalton Athletic, FA Trophy 2nd Rd 31/1/81.
Colours: All blue **Change colours:** All yellow **Nickname:** Bucks
Previous Grounds: Edinburgh Park 1953-73, Orrell Mount Park 1973-78.
Previous leagues: Liverpool Shipping, Liverpool County Comb., Lancs Comb. 74-78, Cheshire Co. 78-82.
Previous Name: Langton 1953-73 **Club Sponsors:** Jawbone Tavern **Club Shop:** No.
Programme: 32 pages, 50p **Programme Editor:** Secretary
Clubhouse: Yes. Normal pub hours. Darts & pool.
Midweek home matchday: Tuesday **Reserve team's League:** Liverpool Co. Combination.
Record win: 9-1 v Glossop (H), North West Counties League 8/2/86
Record defeat: 1-8 v Accrington Stanley (A), North West Counties League 19/2/83.
Players progressing to Football League: Graeme Worsley (Shrewsbury Town 1989).
Capt./P.o.Y (joint) 93-94: Lee Royle **Top Scorer & P.o.Y. (joint) 93-94:** Steve O'Neill (41 goals)
Local Newspapers: Bootle Times **Club record appearances:** Peter Cumiskey (almost 400).
Hons: North West Counties League Div 2 Runners-up 92-93 (Floodlit Trophy 93-94), Liverpool Challenge Cup 64-65 75-76 78-79, Liverpool Amtr Cup 65-66 67-68 73-74, Lancs Amtr Cup 69-70, Liverpool County Combination 64-65 65-66 67-68 68-69 69-70 70-71 71-72 72-73 73-74, George Mahon Cup 66 67 67-68 68-69 69-70 72-73 73-74, Lancs Combination 75-76 76-77 (League Cup 75-76), Cheshire County League Div 2 78-79.

BRADFORD PARK AVENUE

Chairman: R Robinson **President:** C Atkinson.
Secretary: A Sutcliffe, 2 Glenlee Rd, Bradford, West Yorks BD7 2QA (0274 576460).
Manager: Gordon Rayner **Asst Manager:**
Physio: D Stordy **Press Officer:** T R Clapham.
Ground: Batley Rugby Taverners Club, Mount Pleasant, Batley WF17 7NL (0924 470062).
Directions: M62 Jct 27, onto M62 towards Huddersfield, follow signs to Batley R.L.F.C.
Seats: 500 **Cover:** 500 **Capacity:** 5,000 **Floodlights:** Yes **Reformed:** 1988
Midweek Matches: Tuesday **Record Gate:** 1,740 v Leeds Utd, pre-season 1989
Colours: White/green/white **Change colours:** Amber/black/red **Nickname:** Avenue
Programme: 32 pages, 60p **Club Shop:** Yes - contact G Sawyer (0274 607780).
Clubhouse: Run by rugby club, open matchdays. Tea bar, snacks.
Previous Leagues: West Riding County Amtr 88-89, Central Mids 89-90.
Prev. Grounds: Manningham Mills, Bradford 88-89/ Bramley R.L.F.C., McLaren Field, Bramley, Leeds 89-93.
Record win: 6-0 v Penrith (A) 92-93 **Record defeat:** 0-6 v Gainsborough Town (A) 89-90.
Club record scorer: Darren Wardman **Club record appearances:** Rohan Eli
Captain 93-94: Tony Pearson **Top Scorer 93-94:**
P.o.Y. 93-94:
Hons: West Riding Snr Cup 90-91 **Best FA Cup year:** 2nd Qual. Rd 92-93 (0-2 at Accrington)

BURSCOUGH

President: John Mawdsley **Chairman:** Frank Parr **Vice Chairman:** Stuart Heaps
Secretary/Press Officer: Stan Strickland, 109 Redgate, Ormskirk, Lancs L39 3NW (0695 574722).
Manager: Russ Perkins **Assistant Manager:** Bob Howard
Physio: Rod Cottam **Commercial Manager:** Mark Parr (0704 896243).
Ground: Victoria Park, Mart Lane, Burscough, Ormskirk, Lancs L40 0SD (0704 893237).
Directions: M6 Jct 27, follow signs thru Parbold A5209, right into Junction Lane (signed Burscough & Martin Mere) to lights, right onto A59 from Ormskirk to Burscough Village, 2nd left over canal bridge into Mart Lane to ground. Half a mile from Burscough Bridge BR station (Wigan-Southport line). Slightly further from Burscough Junction (Ormskirk-Preston line).
Seats: 220 **Cover:** 1,000 **Capacity:** 3,000 **Floodlights:** Yes **Founded:** 1946
Colours: Green/white/white **Change colours:** All white **Nickname:** Linnets
Programme: 36 pages, 50p **Editor:** Mark Parr (0704 896243) **Club Shop:** No
Midweek Matches: Tuesday **Best FA Cup season:** 1st Rd 59-60 77-78 79-80 80-81.
Previous Grounds: None **Record Gate:** 3,500 v Crewe Alexandra, FA 1st Rd 1959
Previous Leagues: Liverpool County Comb. 46-53, Lancs Comb. 53-70, Cheshire Co. 70-82.
Club Sponsors: Blueline Taxis **Reserve team:** None.
Record win: 10-0 v Cromptons Recreation, Lancashire Combination 1947.
Record defeat: 1-9 v Rossendale United (A), North West Counties League Division One 88-89.
Record transfer fee paid: Undisclosed for Arthur Green (Burton Albion, 1948).
Record transfer fee received: £10,000 for Gary Martindale (Bolton Wanderers, March 1994).
Players progressing to Football League: Louis Bimpson (Liverpool 1953), Bill Parker (Liverpool 53-54), Billy Pilson (Stoke 53-54), Arthur Green (Huddersfield), Ken Waterhouse (Preston), Kenny Spencer (Everton), Frank Gamble (Derby 1980), Tony Rigby (Bury), Shaun Teale (Aston Villa), Liam Watson (Preston), Kevin Formby (Rochdale 1994), Gary Martindale (Bolton 1994).
Clubhouse: 'Barons Club' (privately owned, access from outside ground). Mon-Thurs 7-11pm, Fri 4-11pm, Sat 1-11pm, Sun noon-3 & 7-10.30pm. No food. John Smiths & Websters beers.
Captain 93-94: Tony Quinn **Top Scorer & Joint P.o.Y. 93-94:** Gary Martindale.
Joint P.o.Y. 93-94: Alex Russell **Club record scorer:** Wesley Bridge, 73 in 1947-48.
Hons: Cheshire County League Runners-up 70-71 (League Cup 74-75 (Runners-up 73-74)), Liverpool Senior Non-League Cup 71-72, Lancs Combination 55-56 69-70, Lancs Jnr Cup 47-48 49-50 66-67, North West Counties League 82-83 (League Cup 92-93 (Runners-up 91-92), Challenge Shield 82-83), George Mahon Cup 47-48, Liverpool County Combination 49-50 (Div 2 53-54), Liverpool Challenge Cup 47-48 51-52, Liverpool Senior Cup Runners-up 92-93, Bill Tyrer Memorial Trophy 1990.

CHADDERTON

President: Derek Glynn **Chairman:** Harry Mayall **Vice Chairman:** N/A
Secretary: David Ball, 9 Roxbury Avenue, Salem, Oldham, Lancs OL4 5JE (061 678 9624).
Manager: Peter Evans **Asst Manager:** TBA
Coach: TBA **Physio:** Roy Houghton **Press Officer:** Secretary
Ground: Andrew Street, Chadderton, Oldham, Lancs (061 624 9733).
Directions: M62 Jct 20, A627(M) to Oldham. Motorway then becomes dual carriageway. Turn left at first major traffic lights A669 (Middleton Road), then first left opposite 'Harlequin' P.H. into Burnley Street - Andrew Street 2nd left. 1 mile from Oldham Werneth (BR), buses 458 & 459 (Oldham-Manchester) stop at the Harlequin.
Seats: 200 **Cover:** 700 **Capacity:** 2,500 **Floodlights:** Yes **Founded:** 1947
Best Gates: 1,500 v Guinness Exports 1969 & 1,257 v Oldham Athletic, pre-season friendly 1991.
Colours: Red & white/white/red **Change colours:** All yellow **Nickname:** Chaddy
Programme: 28-32 pages **Programme Editor:** Secretary **Sponsors:** S W Foam.
Club Shop: No, but ties, mugs, pens, coasters, key rings, car stickers etc are on sale in clubhouse. Contact Dave Greaves (061 624 9733).
Midweek Matches: Wednesday **Clubhouse:** Matchdays only. Hot & cold snack during & after games
Players progressing to Football League: David Platt (Crewe, Aston Villa, Bari, Juventus, Sampdoria), John Pemberton (Crewe, Crystal Palace, Sheffield Utd, Leeds), Graham Bell (Oldham, Preston), Paul Hilton (Bury, West Ham), Don Graham (Bury).
Previous Leagues: Oldham Amateur, Manchester Amateur, Manchester 64-80, Lancs Comb. 80-82
Previous Grounds: None **Reserves' Lge:** Carling NWCL Reserve Division.
Captain 93-94: Paul Bowler **P.o.Y. 93-94:** Brian Hilton
Top Scorer 93-94: Dave Chadwick 12 **Club Record Appearances:** Billy Elwell 750+ (1964-90).
Hons: Oldham Amateur League Cup 54-55, Manchester Amateur League 62-63 (North Div 55-56), Manchester Prem Cup R-up 82-83 (Challenge Tphy 71-72 (R-up 72-73)), Manchester League Div 1 66-67 (Div 2 64-65, Gilgryst Cup. 69-70, Murray Shield 65-66), Lancs Comb. Cup R-up 81-82, Alfred Pettit & Hulme Celtic Cup 61-62, Nth West Co's Floodlit Tphy R-up 92-93 (Reserve Div 85-86 (R-up 90-91), Reserve Cup 91-92 (R-up 90-91)), Manchester Yth Cup 59-60 (R-up 60-61).

CLITHEROE

Chairman: S Rush **President:** Jer Aspinall
Secretary/Press Officer: Colin Wilson, 4 Moss Street, Clitheroe, Lancs BB7 1DP (0200 24370).
Mgr: Denis Underwood/Gary Butcher **Coach:** Harry Lighbown **Physio:** Keith Lord.
Ground: Shawbridge, Clitheroe, Lancs (0200 23344).
Directions: M6 jct 31, A59 to Clitheroe (17 miles), at 4th r'bout left into Pendle Rd, after 1 mile ground is just before 'The Bridge Inn' on the right. 11 miles from Blackburn BR station.
Seats: 200 **Cover:** 750 **Capacity:** 4,000 **Floodlights:** Yes **Founded:** 1877
Midweek home matchday: Monday **Record Gate:** 1,600 v Atherstone Utd, FA Vase 82-83.
Colours: Blue & white stripes/blue **Change colours:** All red **Club Shop:** No.
Reserves' League: East Lancs **Previous Lges:** Blackburn & Dist./Lancs Comb. 03-04 05-10 25-82.
Prev. Ground: Upbrooks (pre-1900) **Clubhouse:** Open during matches. Snacks available.
Previous Name: Clitheroe Central 1877-1914.
Programme: 12 pages, 40p **Programme Editor:** Ian Rimmer
Record transfer fee received: £400 for Ray Woods (Leeds United).
Players progressing to Football League: Ray Woods (Leeds 1950), Chris Sims (Blackburn 1960).
Record Scorer: Don Francis **Record appearances:** Lindsey Wallace.
Top Scorer 93-94: John Penman **Captain & Player of the Year 93-94:** Lee Sculpher.
Local Newspapers: Clitheroe Advertiser, Citizen, Lancs Evening Tele.
Hons: Lancs Comb. 79-80 (League Cup 34-35), Lancs Challenge Tphy 1892-93 1984-85, NW Co's League 85-86 (Div 2 84-85, Div 3 83-84, Div 1 Fair Play Award 93-94), East Lancs Floodlit Trophy 93-94.

DARWEN

President: E Devlin **Chairman:** M Elsworth
Secretary: Lynn Atkinson, 58 Harwood Str., Darwen, Lancs BB3 1PD (0254 761755).
Manager: Ian McGarry **Asst Manager:** Brian Gardner **Physio:** Mick Sharples
Ground: Anchor Ground, Anchor Road, Darwen, Lancs (0254 705627).
Directions: A666 Blackburn/Bolton road, 1 mile north of Darwen town centre, turn right at Anchor Hotel, ground 100 yds on left. One and a half miles from Darwen (BR), bus 51 to Anchor Hotel.
Seats: 250 **Cover:** 2,000 **Capacity:** 4,000 **Floodlights:** Yes **Founded:** 1875
Previous Ground: Barley Bank. **Record Gate:** 9,000 v Luton, FA Cup 1909
Colours: Red & white/white/red **Change colours:** All blue
Prev. Lges: Football Alliance 1889-91, Football Lg 91-99, Lancs Lg 99-03, Lancs Comb. 03-75, Ches. Co. 75-82.
Programme: 20 pages, 20p **Programme Editor:** N Walsh **Club Shop:** No
Sponsors: Prince Moran **Reserve Team's League:** North West Co's Reserve Division.
Clubhouse: Matchday only. **Best FA Cup season:** Semi Finals
Midweek Matches: Wednesday **Local Newspapers:** Darwen Advertiser, Lancs Eve. Tele.
Captain 93-94: Martin Atkinson **P.o.Y. 93-94:** Mark Walsh **Top Scorer 93-94:** Nigel Yates
Hons: NW Co's League 82-83 (Res. Div Cup 93-94), Lancs League 01-02, Lancs Comb. 30-31 31-32 72-73 74-75 (League Cup 29-30 30-31 74-75, Lancs Jnr Cup 72-73, George Watson Tphy 72-73, Lancs FA Yth Cup 74-75, Lancs F'lit Tphy 89-90.

PHOTOS OPPOSITE:

Top: *Keith Vincent tries an acrobatic shot during his side's 2-1 win at Darwen on October 23rd.* *Photo - Rob Ruddock.*

Centre: *Clitheroe FC.* *Photo - John L Newton.*

Foot: *Clitheroe's Bursnell evades a couple of challenges as his side go down 0-1 at Glossop North End on the opening day of the season.* *Photo - Colin Stevens.*

CLITHEROE FOOTBALL CLUB

EASTWOOD HANLEY

Chairman: Geoff Eccleston **Vice Chairman:** **President:** Gerald Littlehales
Secretary: John L Reid, 2 Northam Rd, Sneyd Green, Stoke-on-Trent, Staffs ST1 6DA (0782 279062).
Manager: Jimmy Wallace **Asst Mgr/Coach:** Michael Bates **Physio:** Graham Plant
Commercial Mgr: Richard Marsh **Press Officer:** Geoff Eccleston (0782 47187).
Ground: Berryhill Fields, Trentmill Rd, Hanley, Stoke-on-Trent, Staffs (0782 274238).
Directions: M6 Jct 16, A500 to 2nd r'bout (about 10 miles), turn left (under bridge), left again onto A52 (signed Leek), cross A50 after 1 mile, after a further quarter mile turn right into Trentmill Rd (Ray Booth Cars). From south; M6 jct 15, follow A500 past Stoke City F.C., then follow as above from r'bout. One mile from Stoke-on-Trent (BR).
Seats: 250 **Cover:** 1,500 **Capacity:** 3,500 **Floodlights:** Yes **Founded:** 1946
Record Gate: 5,000 v Stoke City (Brooks Bros Testimonial) 1978
Colours: All blue **Change:** Yellow/black/yellow **Nickname:** Blues.
Previous Leagues: Mid-Cheshire, Manchester, West Midlands (Regional) 68-78, Cheshire County 78-82, North West Counties Lg 82-87, Northern Premier 87-90.
Programme: 32 pages, 35p **Editor:** Geoff Eccleston (0782 47187) **Club Shop:** No
Previous Names: Eastwood (Hanley added to contrast with Town), Trent Rovers (incorporated in 1982).
Players progressing to League: Melia Alecksic (Spurs), Maurice Doyle (QPR).
Clubhouse: Open matchdays. Refrestment bar open matchdays.
Midweek home matchday: Tuesday **Reserve team:** None.
Record win: 11-2 v Manchester University (A), Manchester League Cup.
Record defeat: 1-9 v Alvechurch, West Midlands (Regional) League, 1964.
Record transfer fee paid: Nil **Received:** £1,300 for Steve Norris (Leek Town).
Top Scorer 93-94: **Captain & P.o.Y. 93-94:**
Record scorer: A Tunstall 84 (63-64) **Record appearances:** Mick Astley, 1968-78.
Hons: Manc. Lg Gilgryst Cup 67-68, Staffs Snr Cup 85-86, Staffs FA Vase 81-82.
Local Newspapers: Evening Sentinel, S-o-T Herald & Post.

GLOSSOP NORTH END

Chairman: P Heginbotham **President:** C T Boak
Secretary: P Hammond, 15 Longmoor Road, Simmondley, Glossop, Derbys SK13 9NH (0457 863852).
Manager: Ged Coyne **Asst Manager:** Tommy Martin **Physio:** TBA.
Commercial Manager: Mike Perkin. **Press Officer:** Secretary.
Ground: Arthur Goldthorpe Stadium, Surrey Street, Glossop, Derbys (0457 855469).
Directions: A57 (Manchester-Sheffield) to Glossop town centre, turn into Shrewsbury Street, follow to top of the hill, left at T-junction for ground. 700 yds from Glossop (BR). Buses 236 & 237 from Manchester.
Seats: 209 **Cover:** 509 **Capacity:** 2,374 **Floodlights:** Yes **Founded:** 1886
Cols: Blue & white stripes/blue/red **Change colours:** All gold. **Nickname:** Hillmen.
Programme: 32 pages, 40p **Editor:** Mr P Heginbotham (061 439 3932).
Reserve's Lge: North Western Alliance. **Club Shop:** Sells progs + souvenirs (Dave Crooks 0457 855884).
Midweek Matches: Tuesday **Sponsor:** Davis Blank Furniss Solicitors.
Previous Names: Glossop North End 1886-1898/ Glossop FC 1898-1992.
Previous Leagues: Midland 1896-98/ Football Lge 1898-1915/ Manchester Lge 15-56 66-78/ Lancs Combination 56-66/ Cheshire County 78-82.
Record Attendance: 10,736 v Preston North End, FA Cup 1913/14
Record transfer fee paid: £3,000 for Andy Gorton (Lincoln City, 1989).
Record transfer fee received: £3,000 for Andy Gorton (Oldham Athletic, 1990).
Players progressing to Football League: Jimmy Rollands (Rochdale), Ray Redshaw (Wigan Athletic).
Clubhouse: Licensed bar. Hot & cold drinks and pies etc on matchdays.
Top Scorer 93-94: Neil Brown **Captain & Player of the Year 93-94:** Steve Morgan.
Hons: Nth West Co's Lg Lamot Pils Trophy 90-91, Manchester Lg 27-28 (Gilgryst Cup 22-23 29-30 34-35 74-75), Football Lg Div 2 R-up 1898-99, FA Amateur Cup QF 08-09.

HOLKER OLD BOYS

President: R Brady **Chairman:** Ron Moffatt **Vice Chairman:** Ray Sharp.
Secretary: Allan Wilson, 56 Fairfield Lane, Barrow-in-Furness, Cumbria LA13 9AL (0229 822983).
Manager: Des Johnson **Asst Manager:** Jim Capstick **Coach:** Jim Ballantyne.
Physio: Mark Hetherington **Comm. Manager:** Ged Woods **Press Officer:** John Taylor
Ground: Rakesmoor Lane, Howcoat, Barrow-in-Furness, Cumbria (0229 828176).
Directions: M6 Jct 36, A590 to Barrow-in-Furness, on entering Barrow, continue across r'bout, 2nd right (Dalton Lane) to top of road, right into Rakesmoor Lane, ground on right.
Seats: 220 **Cover:** 500 **Capacity:** 2,500 **Floodlights:** Yes **Founded:** 1936
Colours: Green/white **Change colours:** Blue/red **Nickname:** Cobs.
Midweek Matches: Wednesdays **Club Sponsors::** Kitchen Design Studio.
Previous Leagues: North Western/ Furness Premier/ West Lancs 70-91.
Previous Grounds: None.
Programme: 8 pages, 30p **Rec. Gate:** 400 v Emlyn Hughes All Stars **Club Shop:** No.
Record win: 12-0 **Record defeat:** 1-8 v Newcastle T. (H) 91-92.
Clubhouse: Weekdays 8-11pm, Sat noon-11pm, Sunday normal licensing hours. Pies & peas on matchdays.
Top Scorer 93-94: Mike Ballantyne **Captain & P.o.Y. 93-94:** Mike Ballantyne
Club record scorer: Dave Conlin **Hons:** W Lancs Lg 86-87, Lancs Junior Shield 88-89 90-91.

KIDSGROVE ATHLETIC

Chairman: D Stringer **Manager:** Peter Ward.
Secretary: Barry Brereton, Field View, 9 Moreton Close, Werrington, Staffs ST9 0PH (0782 303850).
Ground: Clough Hall, Hollinwood Road, Kidsgrove, Stoke-on-Trent, Staffs (0782 782412).
Directions: M6 Jct 16, A500 towards Stoke, 2nd junction onto A34 towards Manchester, turn right at 1st set of lights into Cedar Ave., 2nd right into Lower Ash Rd., and 3rd left into Hollinwood Road to ground.
Seats: Yes **Cover:** Yes **Capacity:** **Floodlights:** Yes **Year Formed:** 1952
Cols: Blue & white **Record Gate:** 538 **Clubhouse:** Yes **Midweek Home Matches:** Tuesday
Prev. Leagues: Staffs Co./ Mid Cheshire (pre-1991). **Record Gate:** 538
Hons: Mid Cheshire Lg 70-71 78-79 86-87 87-88 (R-up 68-69 85-86, Lg Cup 67-68 69-70 85-86 (R-up 84-85 86-87)), Staffs Co. FA Vase 78-79 88-89, Sentinel Cup 66-67 76-77 84-85 (R-up 58-59 78-79 79-80 83-84), Leek Cup 84-85, Hanley Cup 65-66.

MAINE ROAD

Chairman: Mr R Meredith **President:** Mr F G Thompson.
Secretary: Mr K Hunter, 157 Aston Ave., Fallowfield, Manchester M14 7HN (061 226 9937).
Manager: Mr D Barber **Coach:** Mr R Meredith **Physio:** Ms J Carter.
Press Officer: Mr P Randall
Ground: Manch. Co. FA Grnd, Brantingham Rd., Chorlton-cum-Hardy, Manchester M21 1TG (061 862 9619).
Directions: M63 Jct 7, A56 towards City Centre, right onto A5145, onto A6010 to Chorlton, through lights (ignore pedestrian lights), left at next lights into Withington Rd, left into Brantingham Rd, ground 400 yds on left. Manchester A-Z ref. 100/6B. 2 miles from Stretford (Metrolink(tram)), 3 miles from Piccadilly and Victoria (BR). Buses 85, 102, 103, 168, 188, 276, 277.
Seats: 200 **Cover:** 700 **Capacity:** 2,000 **Floodlights:** Yes **Founded:** 1955
Colours: All blue **Change:** All yellow **Nickname:** Blues **Midweek home matchday:** Tuesday
Prev. Name: City Supporters Rusholme **Rec. Gate:** 875 v Altrincham, FA Cup 2nd Qual. Rd 29/9/90.
Sponsors: Surface Engineers **Reserve Team's League:** NW Co's Lge Reserve Division.
Prev. Grnds: Hough End PF 55-73/ Ward Street O.B. 73-75/ Tootal Spts Ground 75-79/ Leesfield 79-80.
Previous Leagues: Rusholme Sunday 55-66/ Manchester Amtr Sunday 66-72/ Manchester 72-87.
Programme: 48 pages, 50p **Editor:** Mr R Price (061 442 7269) **Souvenir Shop:** None
Best FA Vase year: 2nd Rd 89-90 91-92 **Best FA Cup year:** 2nd Qual. 2nd replay 92-93.
Rec. win: 15-0 v Little Hulton 2/9/86 **Record defeat:** 6-10 v Old Altrinchamians 22/9/79.
Clubhouse: Before/during/after games. Refreshment bar sells hot & cold drinks, pies, crisps, confectionary.
Top scorer 93-94: Tim Crane 9 **Captain & P.o.Y 93-94:** Ian Walker.
Record scorer: John Wright 140 **Record appearances:** Robin Gibson 382.
Hons: Manc. Prem. Lg(4) 82-86 (R-up 86-87, Div 1 73-74, Div 2 72-73, Gilgryst Cup(2) 82-84 (R-up(2) 85-87), Murray Shield(2) 72-74), Manc. Prem. Cup 87-88 (Chal. Cup(4) 82-83 84-87, I'mediate Cup(2) 75-77, Amtr Cup 72-73), NW Co's Lg Div 2 89-90 (R-up 88-89).

NANTWICH TOWN

President: J Davies **Chairman:** A Pye
Secretary: A J Birtwistle, 16 Lyceum Way, Crewe, Cheshire CW1 3YF (0270 258751).
Manager: Clive Jackson. **Asst Manager:** John Brydon.
Coach: John Brydon **Physio:** Keith Leigh.
Ground: Jackson Avenue, off London Road, Nantwich, Cheshire (0270 624098).
Directions: M6 Jct 16, A500 for Nantwich (about 8 miles), continue on A52 over railway crossing (London Rd), first right into Jackson Avenue. From Chester take A51. 3 miles from Crewe (BR).
Seats: 150 **Cover:** 555 **Capacity:** 1,500 **Floodlights:** Yes **Founded:** 1894
Club Sponsors: Intercare **Record Gate:** 2,750 v Altrincham, Cheshire Senior Cup 66-67.
Colours: Green/white **Change colours:** All yellow. **Nickname:** Dabbers
Midweek matchday: Wednesday. **Previous Name:** Nantwich FC (pre 1973)
Programme: 18 pages, 50p **Programme Editor:** Che Kerrin (0270 624098).
Reserves' League: Crewe & Dist. **Club Shop:** Yes (contact Che Kerrin at above no.).
Record transfer fee paid: N/A **Record fee received:** £2,500 (P Mayman, Northwich).
Clubhouse: Every night except Sunday 8pm-11pm. Hot pies available.
Previous Leagues: Shropshire & Dist./ The Combination 1892-94 1901-10/ Lancs Comb. 12-15/ Cheshire Combination 19-38/ Manchester/ Mid-Cheshire/ Cheshire County 68-82.
Top scorer 93-94: John Scarlett **Club Record Scorer:** Gerry Duffy, 42 in 61-62.
Captain 93-94: Adrian Dunn **Player of the Year 93-94:** Dave Pullar.
Hons: Cheshire Co. Lg 80-81 (R-up 00-01), Ches. Snr Cup 32-33 75-76 (R-up 1898-99 13-14 29-30), Ches. Jnr Cup 1895-96 (R-up 1890-91 96-97), Manc. Lg R-up 66-67 (Gilgryst Cup R-up 67-68), Crewe & Dist Cup 97-98 98-99 01-02 61-62 (R-up 1889-90 90-91 04-05 51-52 60-61), The Combination R-up 02-03, Crewe Amtr Comb. 46-47, Shropshire & Dist Lg R-up 1891-92, Mid Ches. Lg 63-64 (R-up 61-62 64-65, Lg Cup 61-62 63-64 (R-up 64-65)), Ches. Amtr Cup 63-64 (R-up 61-62), Ches. Jnr Cup 1895-96 (R-up 90-91 96-97), Mid Ches. Cup 48-49.

NEWCASTLE TOWN

Chairman: Mr J W Walker **Vice-Chairman/President:** Mr K H Walshaw.
Secretary: John F Cotton, 293 Weston Road, Weston Coyney, Stoke-on-Trent, Staffs ST3 6HA (0782 333445).
Manager: Alan Sides **Asst Manager:** Glyn Chamberlain **Coach:** David Buckley.
Physio: Colin Spencer **Comm. Manager:** Cliff Saut **Press Officer:** Barry Shenton.
Ground: 'Lyme Valley Parkway Stadium', Lilleshall Road, Clayton, Newcastle-under-Lyne, Staffs (0782 662351).
Directions: M6 jct 15, A500 for Stoke, left at r'bout A519 for Newcastle, right at 2nd r'bout into Stafford Ave., 1st left into Tittensor Road to ground. 3 miles from Stoke-on-Trent (BR).
Seats: 300 **Cover:** 1,000 **Capacity:** 4,000 **Floodlights:** Yes **Founded:** 1986
Midweek Matches: Tuesday **Club Sponsors:** Henleys Ford
Previous Names: Parkway Hanley (founded 1964, later Clayton Park/ Parkway Clayton)/ Newcastle Town (founded 1980) - clubs merged in 1986.
Record Attendance: 3,586 v Stoke City, friendly August 1991. *Competitive: 577 v Gresley Rovers, FA Vase 4th Rd 18/1/92. Parkway Clayton: 2,620 v Stoke City, 1964.*
Colours: Royal/royal/red **Change colours:** All yellow **Nickname:** Castle.
Programme: 40 pages, 50p **Editor:** Peter Tindall (0260 28093)
Club Shop: Yes, selling programmes, enamel badges, replica shirts etc. Contact secretary.
Previous Lges: Hanley & Dist. Sunday/ North Staffs Sunday/ Potteries & Dist. Sunday/ Newcastle/ Staffs Co./ Mid Cheshire.
Previous Grounds: Hanley Park 64-79/ Northwood Lane, Clayton 79-85.
Record win: 7-0 v Blackpool Mechanics, 8-1 v Holker Old Boys.
Record defeat: 0-5 v Eastwood Hanley (A).
Reserve Team: Parkway Clayton, Midland League.
Players progressing to Football League: Carl Beeston, Graham Shaw, Paul Ware, Dave Ritchie, Darren Hope.
Clubhouse: On ground, open Saturday matchdays noon-7.30pm and midweek 5-11pm. Hot and cold food always available.
Rec. scorer: Shaun Wade 64 (Lge only) **Record appearances:** Philip Butler 200 (in NWCL only).
Captain 93-94: Ken Lawton **Top Scorer 93-94:** Paul James 22 **P.o.Y. 93-94:** Steve Griffiths
Hons: Nth West Co's Lg Div 2 R-up 91-92 (Floodlit Tphy 92-93, Lamot Pils Tphy 91-92), FA Vase 5th Rd 91-92, Mid Cheshire Lg 85-86 (R-up 86-87, Div 2 82-83 90-91(res), Lg Cup 84-85), Walsall Snr Cup 93-94, Newcastle Mayor's Charity Cup 89-90, Staffs FA Vase R-up 92-93(res), Midland Sunday Cup 85-86 86-87 (R-up 84-85 87-88), Potteries & Dist Sunday Lg 84-85 85-86 (Lg Cup 84-85 85-86), Staffs Sunday Cup 79-80 (R-up 86-87), Leek Cup 87-88, Sentinel Sunday Cup 84-85, Sentinel u-18 Shield 86-87 (R-up 93-94), Staffs Yth u-18 Cup 88-89 92-93 93-94 (R-up 86-87, u-16 86-87), Wirral programme award (for NWCL) 88-89 91-92 92-93 93-94 (Div 2 87-88 88-89 90-91 91-92).

PENRITH

Chairman: D Johnson **Vice Chairman:** M Robson
Secretary: W Brogden, 47 Folly Lane, Penrith, Cumbria CA11 8BU (0768 62551).
Manager: Stuart Rome **Physio:** Barry Graham.
Press Officer: J Bell (0768 63898) **Commercial Manager:** Stuart Rome.
Ground: Southend Road Ground, Penrith, Cumbria (0768 663318).
Directions: M6 Jct 40, onto dual carriageway to Appleby & Scotch Corner, turn off at next r'bout approx half a mile into Penrith, follow A6 into town, take 1st left for ground. Three quarters of a mile from Penrith (BR).
Seats: 200 **Cover:** 1,000 **Capacity:** 4,000 **Floodlights:** Yes **Founded:** 1894
Colours: Blue/white/blue **Change colours:** All red **Nickname:** Blues.
Previous leagues: Carlisle & Dist., Northern 48-82, NW Co's 82-87, Northern Prem. 87-90
Programme: 24 pages, 50p **Editor:** Mr J Bell (0768 63898) **Club Shop:** No
Players progressing to Football League: K Sawyers, G Fell, G Mossop (all Carlisle).
Best FA Cup season: 2nd Rd 81-82 **League Clubs beaten in FA Cup:** Chester 81-82.
Midweek Matches: Wednesday **Record Gate:** 4,000 v West Auckland, 1961.
Record transfer fee paid: £750 for A Carruthers (Netherfield)
Record transfer fee received: £1,000 for B Brown (Queen of the South)
Previous Grounds: None.
Reserve team: None **Sponsors:** Titteringtons Holidays
Record win: 13-2 v Parton Utd **Record defeat:** 0-13 v Bishop Auckland.
Clubhouse: Open Thurs-Fri 9.30pm-2am, Sat 2-6pm & 9.30pm-2am, Wed match nights 6.30-10.30pm.
Club record scorer: C Short **Club record appearances:** Ray Thornton.
Captain 93-94: Alan Batey **Top Scorer & Player of the Year 93-94:** Tony Fyfe.
Local Press: Cumberland & Westmorland Herald, Cumberland News.
Hons: Northern Lg R-up 61-62, NW Co's Lg R-up 83-84, Cumberland Snr Cup 60-61 61-62 62-63 63-64 64-65 65-66 70-71 72-73 74-75 80-81.

PRESCOT A.F.C.

President: Mr B F Taylor **Chairman:** Ted Mercer **Vice Chairman:** Arthur Creegan
Secretary: Mr G H Hayward, 38 Central Ave., Prescot, Merseyside L34 1NB (051 430 6762).
Manager: Joe Gibiliru **Asst Manager:** Lee Madin
Commercial Manager: John Richards (0744 57613).
Ground: 'Sandra Park', Hope Street, Prescot, Knowsley, Merseyside (051 430 0507).
Directions: M62 Jct 7, A57 to Prescot town centre (3 miles), right into Hope Street. Three quarters of a mile from Prescot (BR). Buses 10, 10A, 10C from Liverpool & Wigan.
Seats: 400 **Cover:** 2,000 **Capacity:** 8,000 **Floodlights:** Yes **Founded:** 1884
Record Gate: 8,122 v Ashton National, 1932 **Metal Badges:** Yes.
Colours: Gold/black/black **Change colours:** All red **Nickname:** Tigers.
Previous Names: Prescot Athletic/ Prescot Cables 46-65 80-90/ Prescot Town 65-80.
Previous Leagues: Liverpool Co. Comb./ Lancs Comb. 1897-98 18-20 27-33 36-67/ Ches. Co. 33-36 78-82/ Lancs Lg 01-02/ Mid Cheshire 67-78.
Programme: 30 pages, 40p **Programme Editor:** S Richards **Club Shop:** No
Midweek Matches: Tuesday **Best FA Cup season:** 2nd Rd 57-58 59-60
Clubhouse: Refreshment bar, open matchdays/evenings for hot & cold refreshments.
Hons: Lancs Comb. 56-57 (Lg Cup 47-48), Ches. Co. Lg 78-79, Mid Ches. Lg 76-77, L'pool Non-League Cup(4) 51-53 58-59 60-61, L'pool Chal. Cup(6) 27-30 48-49 61-62 77-78, Lancs Int. Cup 1895-96, George Mahon Cup 23-24 25-27 36-37, Lord Wavertree Cup 65-66.

ROSSENDALE UNITED

Chairman: Tony Saunders **Vice-Chairman:** W Carleton **President:** Clifford Barcoft.
Secretary/Press Officer: Hughie Cairney, 9 Cloister Drive, Darwen, Lancs BB3 3JX (0254 773642).
Manager: Brent Peters **Asst Manager:** Simon Holding **Physio:** Syd Parkinson
Ground: Dark Lane, Newchurch, Rawtenstall, Rossendale, Lancs (0706 215119).
Directions: M66, then A682 to Rawstenstall, keep left around r'bout past library until Bishop Blaize pub, right into Newchurch Road (past market), after a mile turn right into Staghills Road - through estate to ground (half mile). Buses 32 or 33 from Rawtenstall (to Todmorden, Edgenride or Burnley) stop at ground.
Capacity: 4,000 **Cover:** 1,000 **Seats:** 400 **Floodlights:** Yes **Founded:** 1898
Club Shop: Yes, selling programmes, magazines, metal badges, souvenirs. Contact Ian Turtle (0706 227027).
Colours: Blue & white/white/blue **Change colours:** Yellow (blue sleeves)/blue/yellow
Previous Leagues: North East Lancs Comb./ Lancs Comb. 1898-99 1901-70/ Central Lancs 1899-1901/ Cheshire County 70-82/ North West Counties 82-89/ Northern Premier 89-93.
Previous Grounds: None **Nickname:** Stags
Midweek home matchday: Wednesday **Record Attendance:** 3,400 v Shrewsbury, FA Cup 75-76.
Sponsors: Carlsberg Tetley **Reserve Team's League:** Carling NWCL Reserve Division.
Programme: 36 pages, 50p **Programme Editor:** Bill Haworth.
Best FA Cup season: 2nd Rd 71-72 (1-4 v Bolton at Bury FC). Also 1st Rd 75-76 (0-1 at home to Shrewsbury Town).
Record win: 10-0 v Wigan Rovers, Lancs Combination 69-70.
Record defeat: 0-14 v Morecambe, Lancs Comination 67-68.
Record Fees - Paid: £3,000 for Jimmy Clarke (Buxton, 1992)
Received: £1,500 for Dave O'Neill (Huddersfield Town, 1974).
layers progressing to Football League: Tommy Lawton, Geoff Smith (Bradford City 1952), Edmund Hartley & William O'Loughton (Oldham 1956 & 60), Colin Blunt (Burnley 1964), Fred Eyre (Bradford PA 1969), Dave O'Neill (Huddersfield), Carl Parker (Rochdale 1992).
Clubhouse: Evenings & matchdays. Hot snacks. Snooker room. Pool, darts, satellite TV, concert room.
Club Record Goalscorer: Bob Scott **Club Record Appearances:** Johnny Clarke 770, 1947-65.
93-94 Captain: Wayne Haworth **93-94 P.o.Y.:** Duncan McFadyen
93-94 Top scorer: Darren Emmett **Local Radio Stations:** Red Rose, Radio Lancashire.
Local Newspapers: Rossendale Free, Lancs Evening Telegraph, Rossendale Herald & Post, Rossendale Mail.
Honours: North West Counties Lg 88-89 (R-up 87-88 93-94, Div 2 R-up 85-86, Lg Cup 93-94, Champions Trophy R-up 93-94), Lancs Comb 26-27 (R-up 54-55, Lg Cup 28-29, Div 2 56-57), Cheshire County Lg 70-71 (R-up 71-72 73-74, Lg Cup 73-74), Lancs Junior Cup (ATS Challenge Tphy) 11-12 72-73 (R-up 27-28), Central Lancs Lg 1900, Lancs Floodlit Cup 70-71 71-72 73-74, FA Vase 5th Rd 86-87 88-89, FA Tphy 2nd Rd 81-82.

Penrith FC. Back Row (L/R): S Rome (Manager), T Fyfe, S Ripley, P Penwick, S Bellas, G Milne, S Gate, J Henderson. Front: L Armstrong, S Hudson, M Gardner, A Batey (Captain), P Simpson, P Harbach.
Photo - John L Newton.

St HELENS TOWN

President: Mr J Jones. **Chairman/Press Officer:** J Barrett
Secretary: W J Noctor, 95 Sutton Park Drive, Marshalls Cross, St Helens WA9 3TR (0744 816182).
Manager: James McBride **Asst Manager:** Derek McClatchey **Coach:** John Neary
Ground: Town Ground, Houghton Road, Sutton, St Helens, Merseyside (0744 812721).
Directions: M62 Jct 7, at r'bout take 5th exit (St Helens linkroad, A570) for 3 miles, at 3rd r'bout take exit for Sutton, at next r'bout take 1st exit to lights, follow road to right, down Robins Lane, straight on to Station Rd, at crossroads (station on right) straight across into Leonard Street, right at t-junction, ground on right. Buses 121, 122, 5D, 41, 6 to St Helens Junction.
Seats: 200 **Cover:** 550 **Capacity:** 4,400 **Floodlights:** Yes **Founded:** 1901
Colours: Blue/white/blue **Change colours:** All yellow **Reformed:** 1946
Record Gate: 4,000 v Manchester City, Bert Trautmann transfer match, April 1950.
Previous Leagues: Lancs Comb. 03-14 49-75/ Liverpool County Combination 49-74/ Cheshire County 74-82.
Programme: 24 pages, 40p **Editor:** John McKiernan (0744 815726) **Nickname:** 'Town'
Club Shop: Yes, selling badges, scarves, pennants, non-League and League publications - contact secretary.
Midweek Matches: Wednesday **Local Newspapers:** Reporter, Star, Leader,Echo.
Previous Grounds: Park Road 01-52/ City Road 52-53.
Reserve team's League: North West Counties League Reserve Division.
Record win: 10-4 v Everton 'B' 1952 **Record loss:** 1-8 v Liverpool Res., L'pool Snr Cup 1950.
Players progressing to Football League: Bert Trautmann, John Connelly, John Quinn, Mike Davock, Billy Foulkes, Dave Bamber, Bryan Griffiths, Mark Leonard, Joe Paladino.
Record appearances: Alan Wellens. **Clubhouse:** Weekdays 8-11pm, Saturday matchdays 2-6.30pm.
Top Scorer 93-94: Steve Pennington 45 **Captain & Player of the Year 93-94:** John O'Neill.
Hons: FA Vase 86-87, North West Counties Lg Cup R-up 93-94 (Res Div R-up 93-94), George Mahon Cup 49-50, Lancs Comb. 71-72 (Div 2 50-51, Lg Cup R-up 70-71), Liverpool Snr Cup R-up 76-77, Lancs Jnr Cup R-up 66-67, Bass Charrington Cup 72-73, St Helens Comb. Hosp. Cup Winners & R-up.

St Helens Town. Back (L/R): James McBride (Manager), Steve Hockenhull, Steve Pennington, Jamie Fahey (now Horwich), Neil Weaver, Ian Langton, Derek McClatchey, William Davies, John Neary (Sponge Man). Front: Steve Cannon, Terry Hoey, Glenn Walker (now Horwich), Gary Lowe, Stuart Phoenix (now Horwich), Neil Shaw.
Photo - Richard Brock.

SALFORD CITY

Chairman: Harold Brearley **Manager:** Syd Whyte. **Asst Manager:**
Secretary: Geoff Doyle, 4 Beech Avenue, Irlam, Manchester M30 6TF (061 775 5159).
Press Officer: Ged Carter **Commercial Manager:** Mike Hilditch.
Ground: Moor Lane, Kersal, Salford, Manchester (061 792 6287).
Directions: M62 jct 17, A56 Bury New Road to Manchester, continue thro' 4 sets of lights, right into Moor Lane, 1st left into Neville Road to ground. 4 miles from Manchester Victoria (BR). Buses 96, 139, 94, 95 to Moor Lane.
Seats: 260 **Cover:** 600 **Capacity:** 8,000 **Floodlights:** Yes **Founded:** 1940
Midweek Matches: Tuesday **Record Attendance:** 3,000 v Whickham FA Vase 1981
Colours: Tangerine/black/black **Change colours:** Blue & white stripes/blue/blue.
Prev. Names: Salford Central 40-63/ Salford Amateurs 1963 until merger with Anson Villa/ Salford FC.
Previous Ground: Crescent, Salford **Previous Leagues:** Manchester 63-80/ Cheshire Co. 80-82.
Programme: 24 pages, 50p **Programme Editor:** Secretary **Nickname:** Ammies.
Clubhouse: Open matchdays only. Hot snacks.
Captain 93-94: **Top Scorer 93-94:** **P.o.Y. 93-94:**
Hons: Lancashire Amateur Cup 72-73 74-75 76-77, Manchester Senior Cup(4) 73-77, Manchester Challenge Cup(3) 73-76, Manchester Lg(4) 74-77 78-79 (Div 1 68-69, Open Tphy 75-76, Murray Shield 68-69), Manchester I'mediate Cup. *As Anson Villa: Manchester Lg Div 2 62-63 (Open Tphy 77-78(res)).*

SKELMERSDALE UNITED

Chairman: D Tomlinson **Vice Chairman:** T Garner.
Secretary/Press Officer: Peter McQueen, 71 Carfield, Skelmersdale WN8 9DR (0695 21101).
Manager: Jimmy Williams **Asst Manager/Physio:** Kevin Melling.
Coach: Peter Smith **Commercial Manager:** Ralph Martin.
Ground: White Moss Park, White Moss Road, Skelmersdale, Lancs (0695 22123).
Directions: M58 Jct 3, at 2nd r'bout take 3rd exit towards Skelmersdale, continue for approx 1 mile, ground on the right. 4 miles from Ormskirk (BR).
Seats: 250 **Cover:** 1,000 **Capacity:** 10,000 **Floodlights:** Yes **Founded:** 1882
Record Gate: 7,500 v Slough FA Amateur Cup 1967
Colours: Blue/white/white. **Change colours:** All yellow **Nickname:** Skemmers
Previous Leagues: Liverpool County Combination, Lancashire Combination 1891-93 03-07 21-24 55-68 76-78, Cheshire County 68-71 78-82, Northern Premier 71-76.
Previous Ground: Sandy Lane 1882-1958.
Programme: 20 pages, 50p **Programme Editor:** Team effort **Club Shop:** No
Club Sponsors: Tamcos Training **Reserve team:** None.
Record transfer fee received: £10,000 for Russell Payne (Liverpool, 1990).
Clubhouse: None, but matchday food bar sells hot drinks, soup, hot pies & pasties etc.
Best FA Cup year: 1st Rd 67-68 (0-2 at Scunthorpe), 68-69 (0-2 at Chesterfield), 71-72 (0-4 at Tranmere).
Midweek Matches: Tuesday **Local Press:** Ormskirk & Skelmersdale Advertiser.
Captain 93-94: **Top Scorer 93-94:**
Hons: FA Amateur Cup 70-71 (R-up 66-67), Ches. Co. Lg(2) 68-70 (Jubilee Cup 69-70), Liverpool Co. Combination 10-11 13-14 14-15 19-20 38-39 39-40 45-46 50-51 51-52 53-54, Lancashire Combination Div 2 55-56, Liverpool Challenge Cup 11-12 13-14 19-20 20-21 38-39 39-40 45-46 46-47, Lancashire Amateur Shield 07-08, George Mahon 24-25 34-35 39-40 51-52 54-55, Lancashire F'lit Cup 69-70, Lancashire Jnr Cup(3) 14-15 69-71, Ashworth Cup 70-71, Barassi Anglo-Italian Cup 70-71, Liverpool Non-League Cup(2) 73-75, North West Co's Lg Cup R-up 82-83 (Reserve Cup 83-84).

TRAFFORD

Chairman: J Ackerley **Vice Chairman:** D Brown **President:** K Illingworth.
Secretary: Graham Foxall, 62 Grosvenor Road, Urmston M41 5AQ (061 746 9726).
Manager: David Law **Coach:** Wilhelm Johannessen **Asst Mgr:** John Ferguson.
Physio: **Press Officer:** Richard Kedzior (061 860 5917).
Ground: Shawe View, Shawe Rd, off Chassen Road, Flixton, Urmston, Manchester M31.
Directions: M63 jct 4, B5158 towards Urmston, 1st exit at island, right into Moorside Rd at next lights, 2nd exit at next island, sharp left at next lights, 1st right into Pennybridge Lane (next to Bird-i'th-Hand pub), car park 100yds on left - ground adjacent.
Capacity: 2,500 **Seats:** 222 **Cover:** 732 **Floodlights:** Yes **Founded:** 1990
Colours: All white **Change Colours:** All red. **Nickname:** The North
Previous Name: North Trafford 90-94 **Previous Lge:** Mid-Cheshire 90-92. **Prev. Grnds:** None
Programme: 24 pages, 50p **Editor:** Richard Kedzior (061 860 5917) **Club Shop:** No.
Sponsors: Illingworth Developments/ Joe Brown (Building Contractors) Ltd.
Record Gate: 220 v Northwich Vics, friendly Aug 92.
Midweek home matchday: Tuesday **Reserves' Lge:** NW Co's Res Div **Clubhouse:** Yes.
Record win: 10-0 v Haslingden St Mary's (A), Lancs Amateur Shield Second Round 12/10/91.
Record defeat: 0-6 v Oldham Town (H), North West Counties League Division Two 13/3/93.
Player progressing to Football League: Anthony Vaughan (Ipswich) 1992.
Club record scorer: Tony Jones 53 **Club record appearances:** Peter Jones 103.
Top Scorer 93-94: Colin Small 21 **Captain & Player of the Year 93-94:** Mike Dunphy.
Hons: North West Co's Lg Lamot Pils Trophy 93-94 (Div 2 R-up 93-94, Reserve Div 93-94), Mid-Cheshire Lg Div 2 R-up 90-91.

DIVISION TWO CLUBS 1994-95

ASHTON TOWN

President: W Pomfrett **Chairman:** G Messer **Manager:** Norman Hickson
Secretary: C G Ashcroft, 8 Mason Close, Ashton-in-Makerfield, Wigan WN4 8SD (0942 717565).
Ground: Edge Green Street, Ashton-in-Makerfield, Wigan WN4 8SY (0942 719168).
Directions: M6 Jct 23, A49 to Ashton-in-M. Right at lights onto A58 towards Bolton. After 3/4 mile turn right at 'Rams Head' P.H. into Golbourne Rd. After 200 yds right into Edge Green Str. Ground at end.
Record Gate: 600 v Accrington 76-77 **Best FA Vase season:** Prelim. Rd 84-85 **Founded:** 1965
Cols: Red (white pin stripe)/red/red **Change colours:** All sky blue **Floodlights:** No
Previous Leagues: Warrington, Lancs Comb. 03-11 71-78, Ches. Co. 78-82.
Midweek Matches: Tuesday **Hons:** Warrington Lg Guardian Cup.

ATHERTON COLLIERIES

Chairman: A P Delooze **Vice Chairman:** W Shaw **President:** J Fielding
Secretary/Press Officer: C Neill, 40 Winmarleigh Gdns, Pennington, Leigh (0942 679255/886600).
Manager: Steve Walton **Asst Manager:** I Lamb **Coach:** R Hough
Physio: Trevor Ball **Commercial Manager:** D Pratano.
Ground: Alder House, Alder Street, Atherton, Gt Manchester (0942 884649).
Directions: M61 Jct 5, follow sign for Westhoughton, left onto A6, right onto A579 (Newbrook Rd/Bolton Rd) into Atherton. *(From M61 jct 4, left, right onto A6 after 80yds, left down Newbrook Rd at 1st lights).* At lights next to Atherton town hall turn left into High Str., 2nd left into Alder St. to ground. Quarter mile from Atherton Central (BR).
Seats: 300 **Cover:** 1,000 **Capacity:** 2,500 **Floodlights:** Yes **Founded:** 1916
Cols: Black & white stripes/black/black. **Change colours:** All red. **Nickname:** Colls
Reserves' Lge: CNWCL Res Div **Record Gate:** 3,300 in Lancs Combination, 1920's
Midweek Matches: Tuesday **Club Sponsors:** L & I Eaton
Club Shop: Yes, selling replica shirts, programmes, enamel badges, key-rings. Contact Secretary.
Programme: 40 pages, 50p **Editor:** Secretary *(CNWCL Div 2 Programme of the Year, 93-94)*
Previous Lges: Bolton Comb. 20-50 52-71, Lancs Comb. 50-52 71-78, Cheshire Co. 78-82.
Players progressing to Football League: J Parkinson (Wigan), Russell Beardsmore (Manchester Utd).
Clubhouse: Open Mon-Fri 7-11pm, Sat 11am-11pm, Sun noon-3 & 7-10.30pm. Hot & cold food on matchdays.
Captain 93-94: S Wallace **P.O.Y.:** D Owen **Top Scorer 93-94:** K Daley.
Hons: NW Co's. Lg Div 3 86-87, Bridge Shield 85-86, Lancs Jnr Shield 19-20 22-23 41-42 45-46 56-57 64-65.

BLACKPOOL MECHANICS

Chairman: Thomas Baldwin **Vice Chairman:** John Sanderson **President:** Peter Sutton
Sec./Press Off./Physio: William Singleton, 'Circular Quay', 36 Colwyn Ave., Blackpool FY4 4EU (0253 768105).
Manager: John Betmead **Asst Manager:** Joe Hulme.
Coach: Stephen Parkinson **Commercial Manager:** Jim Taylor.
Ground: Back Common Edge Rd, Blackpool, Lancs (0253 761721).
Directions: M6 to M55, follow Airport signs. Left at r'bout along A583 (Preston New Rd) to lights, right into Whitehill Rd, becomes School Road, to lights. Straight over main road & follow signs for Blackpool Mechanics F.C. to ground. Rail to Blackpool North - then bus 11c from Talbot Road bus station (next to rail station) and alight at Shovels Hotel, Common Edge Rd.
Seats: 250 **Cover:** 1,700 **Capacity:** 2,000 **Floodlights:** Yes **Founded:** 1947
Club colours: All green **Change colours:** All blue **Nickname:** Mechs
Programme: 10 pages, 50p **Editor:** Steve Goss (0253 43946) **Metal Badges:** Yes
Midweek home matchday: Tuesday **Club Sponsors:** Yates Wine Lodge, Talbot Rd, Blackpool.
Club Shop: Yes, Managed by Steve Goss (142 Clifton Drive, South Shore, Blackpool (0253 43946). Ties, sweaters, old programmes, metal badges.
Prev. Ground: Stanley Pk 47-49 **Record Gate:** 1,200 v Morecambe, Lancs Comb, August 1968
Previous Leagues: Blackpool & Fylde Combination, West Lancs, Lancs Comb. 62-68.
Clubhouse: Match days, training nights. Dancehall. Matchday food: pie & peas, hot dogs, hamburgers, hot pot.
Captain, Top Scorer & P.o.Y. 93-94:
Hons: Lancs Comb. R-up 74-75 (Bridge Shield 72-73, George Watson Tphy 75-76), NW Co's. Lg Div 3 85-86, W Lancs Lg 60-61 62-63 (R-up 59-60), Fylde & Dist Lg 53-54 56-57 (R-up(3) 54-56 57-58, Div 2 50-51, Lg Cup 52-53 57-58 (R-up 55-56 58-59)), Bannister Cup 52-53 56-57 (R-up(3) 55-56 57-59), Evening KO Cup 61-62, B'pool & Dist Amtr Lg Brackwell Cup R-up(2) 57-59, Lancs Jnr Shield 57-58 60-61 (R-up 54-55), Richardson Cup(2) 60-62, B'pool Co-op Medal 54-55 60-61. Nederlands Cuttrale Sportsbond Festival: Den Haag Cup R-up 53-54, Dordrecht R-up 55-56, Rotterdam R-up 59-60.

CASTLETON GABRIELS

Chairman: T E Butterworth **Vice Chairman:** R Butterworth.
Secretary: David Lord, 34 Fairway, Castleton, Rochdale OL11 3BU (0706 522719).
Manager: Gary Broadbent **Assistant Manager:** Neil Mills.
Coach: Neil Mills **Press Officer:** David Lord (0706 522719).
Ground: Butterworth Park, Chadwick Lane, off Heywood Rd., Castleton, Rochdale (0706 527103).
Directions: M62 Jct 20, A6272M to r'bout. Left towards Castleton (A664 Edinburgh Way) to next r'bout, keeping Tesco Superstore to the left, take 1st exit to next r'bout, take 2nd exit into Manchester Rd (A664), after just under mile turn right at 'Top House' P.H. into Heywood Rd., to end & ground on right.
Seats: 250 **Cover:** 500 **Capacity:** 1,500 **Floodlights:** Yes **Founded:** 1924
Colours: Blue/navy blue/blue. **Change colours:** Red/white/red. **Nickname:** Gabs.
Prev. Name: St Gabriels (pre-1960s) **Previous Ground:** Park pitches/ Springfield Pk 1960s-81.
Previous Leagues: Rochdale Sunday Schools 24-84/ Manchester 84-89.
Record Gate: 640 v Rochdale, pre-season friendly 1991. Competitive: 450 v Bamber Bridge 86-87, Lancs Shield
Programme: 28 pages, 50p **Editor:** David Lord (0706 523972) **Club Shop:** No.
Club Sponsors: Dale Mill **Reserve Team's League:** Rochdale Alliance.
Record win: 6-0 v Westhoughton Town (A), North West Counties League Division Two 23/11/91.
Record defeat: 0-6 v Formby (H), North West Counties League Division Two 5/3/93.
Players progressing to Football League: Dean Stokes (Port Vale) 1992.
Clubhouse: Open seven nights a night and all day Saturday. Pie & peas and sandwiches available matchdays (pie & peas only at Reserve matches).
Midweek home matchday: Tuesday **Club record scorer:** Tom KcKenna 16, season 1991-92.
Capt. 93-94: Gary Broadbent **P.o.Y. 93-94:** Jason Smart **Top Scorer 93-94:** Warren Miles 14.
Hons: Manc. Lg 86-87 (Murray Shield 86-87), Nth West Co's Lg Cup SF 91-92.

CHEADLE TOWN

President: Freddie Pye **Chairman:** Chris Davies **Vice-Chairman:** Clive Williams
Secretary: Susan Burton, 2 Lavington Ave., Cheadle, Stockport, Cheshire SK8 2HH (061 491 2190).
Manager: Clive Rothel **Physio:** John Hornbuckle
Press Officer: Chris Davies (061 428 2510).
Ground: Park Road Stadium, Park Road, Cheadle, Cheshire SK8 2AN (061 428 2510).
Directions: M63 Jct 11, follow signs towards Cheadle, Park Road half mile on left. 1 mile from Gatley (BR), buses from Stockport.
Seats: 300 **Cover:** 300 **Capacity:** 2,500 **Floodlights:** Yes **Founded:** 1961
Midweek Matches: Wednesday **Record Gate:** 760 v Stockport County, August 1993.
Colours: All White **Change colours:** All blue.
Programme: 20 pages, 25p **Editor:** Chris Davies (061 428 2510) **Club Shop:** No
Reserves' Lge: NW Alliance **Clubhouse:** Open every night. Food available.
Previous Grounds: Hyde United 5yrs, Glossop 3yrs
Previous Lges: Manc. (pre 1987). **Previous Name:** Grasmere Rovers 1961-83
Record win: 7-1 v Blackpool Mechanics (H), North West Counties League Division One, October 1993.
Players progressing to Football League: Ashley Ward (Crewe), Steve Bushell (York).
Club record scorer: Peter Tilley **Club record appearances:** John McArdle
Captain 93-94: Martin Randles **P.o.Y. 93-94:** John Doyle **Top Scorer 93-94:** Russell Brierley.
Hons: Manchester Lg Div 1 79-80 (R-up 80-81 81-82), Manchester Amtr Cup 79-80, Manchester Challenge Cup R-up(3) 79-82, Derbys Cup 80-81 (R-up 81-82).

Photo opposite: *Cheadle Town pictured before their away game at Westhoughton Town on 17th August. Photo - Colin Stevens.*

DAISY HILL

Chairman: D Haworth **Manager:** Jimmy Hulton.
Secretary: Bob Naylor, 8 Bailey Fold, Westhoughton, Bolton, Lancs BL5 3AH (0942 813720).
Asst Mgr/Physio: Gary Bradley **Coach:** Tony Riley **Press Officer:** Chris Casey.
Ground: New Sirs, St James Street, Westhoughton, Bolton, Lancs (0942 818544).
Directions: M61 Jct 5, A58 (Snydale Way/Park Road) for 1.5 miles, left into Leigh Road (B5235) for 1 mile, right fork into village then left. Straight forward between Church and School into St James Street. Ground 250 yds on the left. Half mile from Daisy Hill (BR).
Seats: 200 **Cover:** 250 **Capacity:** 2,000 **Floodlights:** No **Founded:** 1894
Colours: All royal blue. **Change:** Red & black stripes/black/black **Reformed:** 1951
Programme: Yes **Club Shop:** No, but past programmes are available.
Previous Name: Westhoughton Town **Midweek Matches:** Tuesday
Reserves' Lge CNWL Res Div. **Previous Grounds:** Various - being researched
Clubhouse: Open normal licensing hours during any football activity. Snacks on matchdays.
Record Attendance: 2,000 v Horwich RMI, Westhoughton Charity Cup final May 1980.
Previous Leagues: Westhoughton/ Bolton Comb./ Lancs Combination. 78-82.
Players progressing to Football League: Barry Butler (Chester City via Atherton LR).
Captain 93-94: Rob Sawyer **Record scorer/appearances:** Alan Roscoe, 300 goals. 450 games.
Top Scorer 93-94: Simon Casey 21 **Player of the Year 93-94:** Mark Ford.
Hons: Bolton Comb. 62-63 72-73 75-76 77-78 (Lg Cup(4) 59-60 61-62 71-73), Lancs Shield 61-62 71-72 86-87.

FLIXTON

President: Councillor F H Eadie **Chairman:** Mr J Mitchell.
Secretary: John Fradley, 14 Highbury Ave., Flixton, Manchester (061 747 0552).
Manager: Brian Griffin **Asst Manager:** Alan Heathcote **Coach:** David Higgs
Press Off.: Trevor Entwistle **Commercial Manager:** David Trow.
Ground: Valley Road, Flixton, Manchester M31 2RQ (061 748 2903).
Directions: M63 Jct 3, B5214 (signed Urmston), follow Trafford General Hosp. signs, at 4th r'bout take 3rd exit (Woodbridge Rd), ground at top. One and a quarter miles from Flixton BR station (trains from Manchester Oxford Rd) - turn right out of station onto Flixton Rd, left after quarter mile into Woodsend Rd, at r'bout after quarter mile take 2nd exit into Woodbridge Rd - ground at top. Take any bus from Manchester Picadilly bus station to Flixton and alight at Flixton Red Lion.
Seats: 200 **Cover:** 600 **Capacity:** 2,000 **Floodlights:** Yes **Founded:** 1960.
Record Gate: 1,145 v Manchester Utd 1989-90, Inauguration of Floodlights
Colours: Blue & white stripes/white/blue **Change colours:** All yellow **Nickname:** Flixs
Previous leagues: South Manchester & Wythenshawe 60-63/ Lancs & Cheshire 63-73/ Manchester 73-86.
Programme: 36 pages, 50p **Editor:** Graham Foxall (061 746 9726) **Club Shop:** Not yet
Best FA Cup season: 1st Qualifying Round replay 91-92 (lost 1-2 at Mossley after 1-1 draw).
Best FA Vase season: 3rd Rd 91-92
Midweek Matches: Tuesday **Reserves' League:** North Western Alliance.
Record win: 7-1 v Daisy Hill 86-87 **Record defeat:** 1-10 v Knowsley Utd 90-91.
Clubhouse: Open daily 1-3 & 7.30-11pm. Sandwiches available most evenings.
Club Record Scorer: Gary McDonald **Club Record Appearances:** John Mitchell/ Stan Matthews.
Capt. 93-94: **P.o.Y. 93-94:**
Top Scorer 93-94:
Hons: NW Co's Lg Div 2 R-up 87-88 (Div 3 R-up 86-87, Div 3 Cup SF 86-87, Res. Chal. Cup 87-88 90-91 (R-up 88-89 89-90 91-92 92-93), Res. Div East 89-90, Res. Div Sth 92-93), Manc. Lg R-up 78-79 81-82 85-86 (Div 1 77-78, Div 2(res) 82-83 85-86, Open Tphy 80-81), Lancs Amtr Cup 79-80 (R-up 80-81), Manc. Chal. Tphy 83-84 (R-up(2) 84-86), Manc. Prem. Cup R-up 86-87 91-92, Manc. Amtr Cup R-up 88-89.

FORMBY

Chairman: Chris Welsh **Sec:** B G Prescott, 5 Abbotts Way, Formby, Merseyside L37 6DR (0704 879857).
Manager: Peter Hennerty **Assistant Manager:** Mike Scott.
Coach: Billy Buck **Physio:** Keith Johnson
Commercial Manager/ Press Officer: Paul Lawler (0704 878409).
Ground: Brows Lane, Formby, Merseyside (07048 72603).
Directions: A565 Liverpool-Southport, turn for Formby at lights opposite Di-it-All DIY into Altcar Rd, fork left at junction to r'bout (opposite Blundell Arms Hotel), take 2nd exit then sharp left into Duke Street, 1st right into Elbow Lane, ground entrance 50yds on left. Half a mile from Formby (BR), buses from Formby & Southport stations.
Seats: 200 **Cover:** 500 **Capacity:** 2,000 **Floodlights:** No **Founded:** 1919
Midweek Matches: Wednesday. **Record Gate:** 2,500 v Oldham, FA Cup 1st Rd 24/11/73
Colours: Yellow/blue/yellow **Change:** White/black/black **Nickname:** Squirrels
Programme: 25 pages, 30p **Editor:** Paul Lawler (0704 878409)
Club Shop: Yes, stocking programmes, enamel badges and other souvenirs. Contact Paul Lawler (0704 878409).
Best FA Cup season: 1st Rd 73-74 (lost 0-2 at home to Oldham Athletic).
Previous Leagues: Liverpool Co. Comb. 19-68/ Lancs Comb. 68-71, Ches. Co. 71-72.
Record win: 11-1 v Earle (H) 18/10/52 **Record defeat:** 0-10 v Irlam Town (H) 18/1/86.
Record transfer fee paid: Unknown **Received:** £1,000 for Geoff Twentyman (Chorley).
Clubhouse: Social club and offices sadly destroyed in fire in September 1990, and as yet unreplaced. However, matchday refreshment bar stocks hot food & drinks.
Hons: Liverpool Co. Comb. 48-49 (R-up 51-52 52-53 64-65, George Mahon Cup 64-65 67-68 (R-up 55-56 56-57), Liverpool Senior Cup 77-78 (R-up 84-85, Challenge Cup 52-53 63-64 67-68 (R-up 64-65), Amtr Cup(3) 29-30 47-49), Lancs Amtr Cup 34-35.

HASLINGDEN

Manager: Geoff Dean.
Secretary: Brian Mella, 6 Bridge End Close, Helmshore, Rossendale (0706 226398)
Ground: Ewood Bridge, Manchester Rd, Haslingden, Lancs (0706 217814).
Directions: From South: M66 Blackburn/Clitheroe exit, left at r'bout past Woolpack Hotel, sharp left at bottom of hill - ground 100yds on right. From North; M6 Jct 31, A59 to Blackburn, take ring-road at Moat House Hotel and follow signs to M65, leave M65 at jct 8 and follow signs for Bury, follow dual-c'way for about 5 miles and leave at Todmorden exit, right at lights, straight across r'bout by Woolpack Hotel, then follow as above.
Seats: **Cover:** **Capacity:** **Floodlights:** Yes **Founded:** 1969
Colours: Tangerine/black/tangerine **Record Gate:** 551 v Blackburn, August 1993.
Midweek Matches: Tuesdays **Previous Leagues:** West Lancashire (pre-1993)
Hons: North West Co's Lg Div 2 93-94, West Lancs Lg Div 2 80-81 (R-up 92-93, Presidents Cup 71-72 80-81 92-93).

IRLAM TOWN

Chairman: K A Marsh **Vice Chairman:** E Keiller.
Secretary: Stuart Law, 6 Brabham Mews, Swinton, Manchester M27 3HH (061 728 1065).
Manager: Stuart Parker **Press Officer:** D W Murray
Ground: Silver Street, Irlam (061 775 5599).
Directions: M6 jct 21 then east on A57 - Silver Street is opposite the Sports pub after five and a half miles. Or, M63 jct 2 and west on A57 for two and a half miles - turn right after Nags Head (PH). 1 mile from Irlam (BR).
Capacity: 3,000 **Cover:** 500 **Seats:** 250 **Floodlights:** Yes **Club Shop:** No
Colours: All gold **Change colours:** Red & black. **Floodlights:** Yes
Programme: 28 pages, 50p **Programme Editor:** D W Murray
Prev. Lges: Manc. (until 1978)/ Cheshire Co. 78-82/ Nth West Co's 82-87/ Northern Prem. 87-92.
Midweek matchday: Tuesday **Record Gate:** 2,000 v Man Utd, f'light opening 1986.
Record Fees - Paid: **Received:** £8,000.
Players progressing to Football League: Tony Caldwell (Bolton Wanderers), Tony Jarvis (Oldham Athletic 1986), Graham Leishman (Mansfield Town 1988).
Clubhouse: Lounge, vault, kitchen, dressing rooms, committee.
Local Newspapers: Advertiser, Manchester Evening News.
Local Radio: Piccadilly, Key 103. **Sponsors:** P M Communications, M L Electro Optics.
Hons: FA Vase 5th Rd 81-82, FA Amateur Cup 1st Rd 70-71, North West Counties Div 2 R-up 84-85, Manchester Lg 73-74 (R-up 76-77, Gilgryst Cup 73-74), Manchester Premier Cup 84-85 (R-up 78-79 81-82 87-88). *Reserves: Manchester Amateur Cup 81-82, North West Counties Lg Reserve Div 83-84 (Lg Cup 82-83 85-86), Northern Combination 88-89 (Lg Cup 87-88 88-89 89-90).*

MAGHULL

Chairman: Les Jacques **Vice Chairman:** G Fisher **President:** M Latham.
Secretary: Danny Sherlock, 14 Alexander Drive, Lydiate, Merseyside L31 2NJ (051 526 2306).
Manager: Arthur McCumiskey **Coach:** Tommy Barry **Physio:** T Kidman.
Comm. Manager: Ron Young **Press Officer:** Andy Boyd (051 526 2715).
Ground: Old Hall Field, Hall Lane, Maghull, Merseyside (051 526 7320).
Directions: M57 or M58 to end (Switch Island), A59 towards Preston (Northway) to lights at Hall Lane, turn right following signs for Maghull Station. Ground 200 yds on the left. Half mile from Maghull (Merseyrail).
Seats: None **Cover:** 75 **Capacity:** 500 **Floodlights:** No **Founded:** 1921
Colours: Blue & red stripes **Change colours:** All yellow
Programme: 40 pages, 50p **Programme Editor:** Press Officer **Club Shop:** No.
Midweek Matches: Tuesday **Record Gate:** 500 v Marine, L'pool Chal. Cup 1982/83
Sponsors: Northway Taxis **Previous Ground:** Pimbley Recreation Ground 1921-59.
Previous Leagues: I Zingari/ Liverpool Co. Comb./ Lancs Comb. 72-78/ Cheshire Co. 78-82.
Clubhouse: Fully licenced clubhouse & lounge open matchdays and midweek. Hot & cold food available.
Reserves' Lge: NWCL Res Div. **Club record scorer & appearance-maker:** Bobby Prince.
Captain 93-94: Billy Roberts **Top Scorer 93-94:** Lee Cooper.
Hons: Liverpool Co. Amtr Cup 34-35 58-59, Liverpool Co. Chal. Cup 79-80 80-81 85-86 93-94, Lancs FA Amtr Cup 49-50, Lancs Comb. Cup 77-78, Liverpool Co. Comb. 66-67, North West Co's Lg Div 2 92-93 (Res. Div Cup R-up 93-94).

NELSON

Chairman: T A M Beckett **Vice-Chairman:** A Barness.
Secretary: C R King, 2 King Edward Terrace, Barrow Road, Nelson, Lancashire BB9 8NJ (0282 616394)
Manager: Nigel Coates. **Assistant Manager:** P Rigby.
Ground: Victoria Park, Lomesway, Nelson, Lancs (0282 63820).
Directions: M65 jct 13, 1st left (A6068), 2nd left (B6249 for Nelson), 2nd right signed Lomeshaye Village to ground.
Capacity: **Seats:** 60 **Cover:** 200 **Floodlights:** No **Nickname:** Blues
Colours: Blue & white stripes **Change colours:** White/red
Midweek home matchday: Wednesday **Reserve Team's League:** North West Co's Reserve Div.
Previous Leagues: Lancashire 1889-98 1900-01/ Football League 1898-1900/ Lancashire Combination 01-16 46-82/ Nth West Counties 82-88/ West Lancashire 88-92.
Clubhouse: Bar open matchdays
Hons: Lancs Lg 1895-96 (R-up 97-98), Lancs Comb. 1949-50 51-52 (R-up 47-48 50-51 60-61, Lg Cip 49-50 50-51 59-60, Bridge Shield 75-76, George Watson Tphy 78-79, Div 2 R-up(res) 47-48 51-52), Lancs Jnr Cup 07-08 54-55, FA Cup 2nd Rd Proper 30-31(replay) 50-51 (1st Rd 32-33 51-52 53-54).

OLDHAM TOWN

Chairman: K Hughes **Manager:** Harold Hazard.
Secretary: William John O'Neil, 72 Broadbent Rd, Watersheddings, Oldham OL1 4HY (061 628 8788).
Ground: Whitebank Stadium, Whitebank Rd, Hollins, Oldham, Lancs OL8 3JH (061 624 2689).
Directions: M62 jct 18, M66 to Heaton Pk, right on to A576, left at 2nd lights on to A6104, follow Victoria Ave. on to Hollinwood Ave. under bridge to T-junction, right then 1st left at Roxy Cinema, follow Hollins Rd for one & a half miles to Fire Station, left on to Elm Rd and follow to next left, Whitebank Rd on left.
Seats: **Cover:** Yes **Capacity:** **Floodlights:** No **Founded:** 1964
Record Gate: 250 v Mossley, Manchester Premier Cup 1987/88 (at Nordens Road).
Colours: Blue/white/blue. **Midweek Matches:** Wednesday
Programme: 16 pages, 25p **Programme Editor:** M Kirfoot.
Previous Grounds: National Park/ Nordens Roads (pre-1994).
Clubhouse: Open evenings and matchdays.
Prev. Names: Dew Construction/ Oldham Dew. **Prev. Lges:** Manch. Amtr/ Lancashire Comb. 81-82.

SQUIRES GATE

Chairman: Brian Addison **Vice President:** Brian Addison.
Secretary: John Maguire, 2 Squires Court, Cairn Grove, Blackpool, Lancs FY4.
Manager: Paul Arnold **Assistant Manager:** John Chippendale.
Ground: School Road, Marton, Blackpool, Lancs (0253 798584).
Directions: M6 to M55 jct 4, left onto A583, right at 1st lights (Whitehall Rd) follow signs for airport. Ground approx. one and a half miles on right.
Seats: 2 rows **Cover:** One side **Capacity:** **Floodlights:** No **Formed:** 1948
Colours: All royal **Midweek Matches:** Tuesday **Prog.:** 20 pages **Clubhouse:** Yes
Prev. Lges: W. Lancs (pre-1991) **Hons:** W. Lancs Lg Div 2 80-81 (Richardson Cup 86-87).

STANTONDALE

President: Ken Wood **Chairman:** Roy Grundy **Vice-Chairman:** Mike Shiels
Secretary: Ken Baker, 10 Haymans Green, Maghull, Merseyside L31 6DA (051 526 4041).
Mgr/Press Off.: Tommy Lawson **Asst Manager:** Garry Britton **Coach:** Eric Warren
Ground: Leisure Time Club, Orrell Lane, Bootle, Merseyside L20 (051 525 2115).
Directions: M57 to M58 to end at Switch Island, follow signs to Bootle and Docks (A5063) Dunnings Bridge Rd to r'bout, left into Netherton Way, take lefthand lane at lights into Orrell Lane, ground on left next to M.F.I.
Colours: Green/silver/white **Midweek home matchdays:** Tuesday **Floodlights:** No
Colours: All green **Change colours:** **Founded:** 1986
Sponsors: Charlotte Sports **Previous League:** Liverpool County Combination (pre-1992).
Programme: 28 pages, 50p **Programme Editor:** Garry Britton (0695 23090) **Clubhouse:** Yes.
Captain 93-94: Steve Walmsley **Top scorer 93-94 & Club record scorer:** Graham Dodd.
Player of the Year 93-94: Paul Diamond.
Hons: NW Co's Lg Lamot Pils Cup 92-93, Liverpool County Comb. 90-91 (Div 2 87-88, George Mahon Cup R-up 90-91), Liverpool Jnr Cup 90-91 (R-up 88-89), Liverpool Challenge Cup 91-92, McEwans Lager Cup 91-92, Lord Wavertree Cup R-up 87-88.

TETLEY WALKER

President: J Sixsmith **Chairman:** R Fisher
Secretary: B Gleave, 8 Cossack Ave., Orford, Warrington, Cheshire WA2 9PB (0925 659559).
Manager I Kinsey **Asst Manager:** R Fisher
Physio: P Cowell **Press Officer:** B McLaughlin.
Ground: Tetley Walker Club, Long Lane, Orford, Warrington, Cheshire WA2 9PB (0925 634904).
Ground: From M62 follow signs to Warrington town centre on A49. After about one and a half miles turn left at 2nd r'bout (next to Coachmans pub), ground about 500yds on left. Rail to Warrington Central station then taxi - fare about £2 from station to ground.
Capacity: **Seats:** 40 **Cover:** 150 **Floodlights:** No **Founded:** 1974
Midweek matches: Tuesday **Reserves' Lge:** Warrington & D. **Nickname:** Walkers
Colours: White/red **Change Cols:** Maroon & sky stripes **Club Shop:** Not yet.
Programme: Average 10 pages **Programme Editor:** Mr P Cowell (0925 573063).
Previous League: Warrington & District 1974-94.
Previous Grounds: None **Clubhouse:** Open noon-midnight. Food includes sandwiches & pies.
Record win: 10-1 v Grappenhall Sports (A), Guardian Cup 1992-93.
Record appearances: Ray Arnold **Top Scorer 93-94:** Tony Plant, 36.
Captain 93-94: Stephen Roberts **Player of the Year 93-94:** Stephen Roberts.
Hons: Warrington & Dist. Lg 86-87 93-94 (R-up 85-86 92-93, Guardian Cup 84-85 85-86 93-94 (R-up 86-87)).

Billy Roberts celebrates the first of his hat-trick of goals for Maghull against the now defunct K Chell.
Photo - Rob Ruddock.

Tony Flanagan, of League leaders Haslingden, leaves Paul Salanki stranded in a 6-0 win at Blackpool Mechanics.
Photo - Alan Watson.

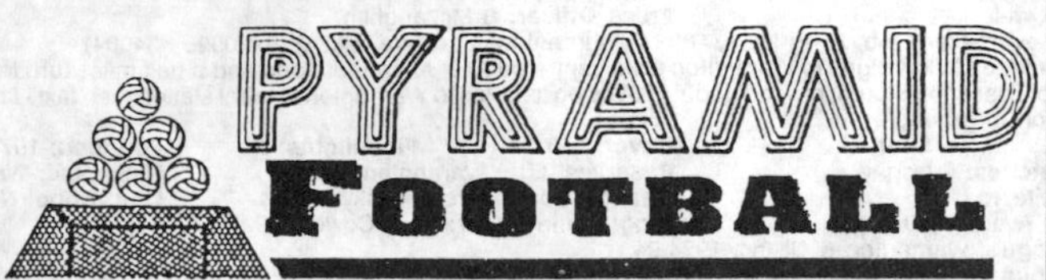

The Magazine for Non-League Fans By Non-League Fans

Po Box 553, London N2 8LJ

Each issue of Pyramid Football contains:

*** All the news from more than 20 leagues**

*** Features on clubs, personalities and programme collecting**

*** Details of teams changing leagues and moving to new grounds**

*** Photographs of Non-League grounds**

*** Readers' letters, attendance figures, etc.**

*** All the Non-League fixtures for each day are broadcast on our Fixtures Telephone Line**

Ring - 0891 66 45 60 (24 hours)

Calls cost 39p per minute cheap rate & 49p per minute at all other times

The 1994/5 subscription rate is £6.50 for three issues

For your subscription send a cheque/postal order to:

Pyramid Football, PO Box 553, London N2 8LJ

NB: Those who subscribe after the season has started will receive the relevant back issues.

Editor: Tony Incenzo.

UNIJET SUSSEX COUNTY LEAGUE

FEEDER TO:
BEAZER HOMES LEAGUE

FOUNDED: 1920

President: P S Strange

Chairman: P R Bentley

Vice-Chairman: L Ralph

Treasurer: F I D Ralph

Secretary: P Wells, 37 Bewley Road, Angmering BN16 4JL (0903 771146).

WICK LIGHT THE WAY

In the senior divisions, Division One comprised 20 teams for the first time, with Division Two 18. The former was achieved by relegating only Midhurst & Easebourne from the previous season, Eastbourne Town gaining a reprieve, while promoting the top three from Division Two; Crowborough Athletic, Stamco and East Grinstead. Withdean and Storrington replaced Seaford Town and Haywards Heath Town in Division Two. Division Three was expanded to 16 teams, Buxted gaining a reprieve while Ferring dropped back to the Unijet West Sussex League, with Sunallon from that League, Edwards Sports from the Crawley League and Lingfield from the Unijet Mid-Sussex League joining as the champions of their respective Leagues, the latter re-joining after four seasons in their feeder League.

Division One was won by Wick, many people's favourite throughout the season, in scoring a total of 111 League goals and accumulating 97 points from the 114 available. Whitehawk were runners-up some 16 points adrift, and Langney Sports a further 8 points away, but in turn having a minimum ten point gap ahead of all others. Bexhill Town and Chichester City occupied the last two places, with the former only just failing to make a last ditch attempt for safety.

Division Two was won by Shoreham, completing the 'double', with closest rivals Southwick taking the runners-up spot. Midhurst & Easebourne United for the second consecutive season filled a relegation spot, accompanied by Little Common Albion. Their places will be taken by Bosham, atoning for the previous season's third place, and Lingfield, back into senior football after an eight year absence, and after only one season back in Division Three. The positions appropriate for relegation were filled by Shinewater Association and Franklands Village, but they will retain their status within this League.

It is interesting to note that Franklands Village finished the season averaging more than a point per march with 31 from their 30 matches, and a goal difference of only minus 13. It led to some

Wick - Unijet Sussex County League champions 1993-94. *Photo - Eric Marsh.*

discussion regarding the possibility of potential promotees being involved in play-offs with those filling the relegation spots, but the availablity of grounds at the end of the season enters into the practicalities of such a situation. On May 7th, the final Saturday of the season, no fewer than 5 teams in both Division 2 and 3 were fighting to avoid relegation, an indication of the relative strengths of those Divisions.

For those with statistical interests, no fewer than 436 matches involving teams from within the senior League's six Divisions fell victim to postponement. From September through to May, excessive rain made groundmen's lives impossible, with only a handful of matches played in the second round of the SCFA Intermediate Cup on October 9th. On Saturday November 20th, a full League Fixture List was played, but the next Saturday on which such an event re-occurred was not until April 23rd. Inevitably, this led to much congestion at the end of the season, but the last League fixtures were completed on Wednesday 11th May, only 3 days after the original planned final date.

The League Challenge Cup, a new trophy to be named as the John O'Hara Cup to commemorate our previous Patron and President, was won by Whitehawk defeating Wick in the final at Burgess Hill by a 4-0 scoreline. The Division Two Cup was won by Shoreham, 2-1 victors at Southwick over last season winner's Lancing, and the Division Three Cup Final played at, Horsham YMCA, saw Ifield defeat Forest by 4 goals to 2, in front of a crowd of over 250.

P R Bentley, Chairman

Man of the Match and hat-trick scorer Simon Pierce with the John O'Hara League Cup after Whitehawk's 4-0 win against Wick at Burgess Hill Town on Good Friday.

Photo - Eric Marsh.

DIVISION ONE 1993-94

	P	W	D	L	F	A	PTS
Wick	38	31	4	3	111	30	97
Whitehawk	38	25	6	7	74	43	81
Langney Sports	38	22	7	9	84	59	73
Peacehaven & T.	38	16	15	7	71	37	63
Pagham	38	18	9	11	77	51	63
Hailsham Town	38	18	8	12	72	61	62
Burgess Hill T.	38	17	9	12	75	55	60
Newhaven	38	17	19	12	79	67	60
Stamco	38	16	7	15	77	59	55
Arundel	38	15	9	14	66	57	54
Oakwood	38	14	9	17	56	64	49
Three Bridges	38	12	9	17	68	84	45
Littlehampton T.	38	11	11	16	58	62	44
Portfield	38	12	7	19	60	90	43
East Grinstead	38	10	13	15	39	69	43
Crowborough A.	38	10	7	21	62	88	37
Eastbourne Town	38	10	7	21	41	73	37
Ringmer	38	11	3	24	50	93	36
Bexhill Town	38	0	6	23	53	82	33
Chichester City	38	5	9	24	47	96	24

Manager of the month awards

Aug	Ray McCarthy (Burgess Hill T.)
Sept	Mike Rogers (Newhaven)
Oct	Norman Cairns (Wick)
Nov	Butch Reeves (Whitehawk)
Dec	Micky Reed (Stamco)
Jan	Butch Reeves (Whitehawk)
Feb	Peter Cherry (Langney Sports)
Mar	Norman Cairns (Wick)
Apr/May	Mark Bennett (Arundel)

Manager of the Season:
Norman Cairns (Wick)

LEADING SCORERS (League matches only)

Paul Boxall (Littlehampton) 30
Adie Miles (Pagham) 24
Rod Wood (Wick) 23
Mark Vickers (Pagham) 23
Steve Guille (Wick) 22
Terry Withers (Wick) 22

Roy Hayden Trophy: Wick 2, Peacehaven 1
Norman Wingate Trophy: Peacehaven 2, Pagham 1

DIVISON ONE RESULTS 1993-94

HOME TEAM	1.	2	3	4	5	6	7	8	9	10	11	12	13	14	15	16	17	18	19	20
1. Arundel	*	1-1	0-2	2-0	4-1	1-2	0-2	1-2	1-3	2-2	3-0	0-0	2-2	1-0	1-0	3-1	1-1	1-2	1-0	1-0
2. Bexhill Town	1-3	*	0-3	5-2	3-3	1-2	3-0	1-3	3-4	2-0	0-3	0-2	1-9	0-0	1-2	0-2	2-5	1-4	3-2	1-2
3. Burgess Hill Town	0-1	0-0	*	4-1	3-1	2-2	4-2	0-0	0-3	4-1	2-2	2-3	2-1	1-2	2-2	6-0	1-2	4-0	3-2	1-1
4. Chichester City	0-3	2-1	0-4	*	2-2	5-0	3-1	2-2	1-3	1-1	2-6	1-3	1-3	2-2	3-4	0-0	2-1	1-1	0-1	0-2
5. Crowborough Ath.	2-3	0-2	0-1	7-1	*	0-2	2-0	5-0	1-3	1-1	1-1	3-0	1-1	1-4	4-2	0-4	3-1	3-1	1-0	1-2
6. East Grinstead	4-3	2-1	2-4	1-1	1-1	*	0-0	1-2	1-1	2-0	1-1	1-1	2-2	1-3	0-1	1-1	0-5	2-1	0-4	0-5
7. Eastbourne Town	0-3	0-1	1-3	4-0	0-1	1-0	*	0-1	0-0	2-2	3-0	2-1	2-3	1-0	1-1	2-1	0-3	5-3	1-1	0-8
8. Hailsham Town	1-0	1-0	4-3	5-2	4-0	1-1	0-2	*	2-2	1-3	5-2	4-1	2-0	1-1	4-0	5-0	3-1	2-0	1-2	2-1
9. Langney Sports	5-2	1-0	3-1	4-2	2-1	4-0	5-0	2-0	*	0-0	6-1	4-0	0-0	2-1	2-2	1-0	1-2	1-0	1-2	1-7
10. Littlehampton Town	1-4	2-0	1-1	1-0	1-2	1-2	1-4	3-1	1-3	*	2-2	1-2	5-1	0-0	4-3	5-0	2-0	3-4	0-2	3-2
11. Newhaven	4-0	5-4	0-1	1-1	4-2	4-0	2-2	2-0	1-2	4-0	*	2-0	2-2	1-1	2-2	5-0	3-0	3-2	1-4	0-2
12. Oakwood	0-5	2-3	2-3	2-0	3-1	1-0	1-0	2-2	1-3	2-2	2-3	*	1-0	0-0	3-0	4-0	0-1	2-2	5-1	0-3
13. Pagham	2-1	3-0	3-1	2-0	1-1	1-1	2-1	2-1	3-2	2-1	2-0	4-1	*	0-3	5-1	7-0	0-1	6-0	0-1	1-1
14. Peacehaven & Tels.	1-1	1-1	2-2	1-2	5-1	4-1	3-0	4-4	8-0	1-1	3-2	2-0	0-0	*	4-0	4-0	4-3	1-0	1-1	1-2
15. Portfield	2-1	1-1	0-2	2-1	5-1	2-0	3-0	0-2	0-4	1-0	1-2	2-4	0-1	1-2	*	4-2	4-1	2-1	2-3	1-2
16. Rinmger	2-3	2-1	1-0	4-2	4-2	0-1	2-0	2-1	2-1	0-1	1-2	2-4	1-2	1-2	6-3	*	0-3	3-3	2-6	0-1
17. Stamco	3-3	4-5	2-0	3-1	5-2	0-1	0-0	2-0	1-1	1-1	3-0	2-0	4-0	0-0	10-1	0-2	*	0-3	1-1	2-3
18. Three Bridges	4-4	1-4	1-1	2-2	4-2	1-1	3-1	1-1	4-1	0-5	2-4	1-0	2-0	2-0	3-3	3-1	3-0	*	1-2	1-4
19. Whitehawk	3-1	2-0	4-1	1-0	2-1	1-1	4-1	3-1	3-2	1-0	4-0	2-1	3-2	0-0	0-0	1-0	3-2	2-1	*	1-2
20. Wick	0-0	1-0	3-1	5-1	6-1	2-0	3-0	7-1	5-1	2-0	1-2	0-0	3-2	1-0	5-0	4-1	3-2	6-1	3-1	*

Sussex County League Division One Ten Year Record

	84/5	85/6	86/7	87/8	88/9	89/0	90/1	91/2	92/3	93/4
Arundel	5	9	1	12	16	16	8	11	12	10
Bexhill Town	-	-	-	-	-	-	15	16	11	10
Burgess Hill Town	8	7	11	9	5	4	6	6	14	7
Chichester City	-	13	15	-	-	-	-	15	16	20
Crowborough Athletic	-	-	-	-	-	-	-	-	-	16
East Grinstead	-	-	-	-	-	-	-	-	-	15
Eastbourne Town	3	3	5	4	15	15	16	12	17	17
Hailsham Town	14	11	14	6	4	13	13	8	10	6
Hastings Town Reserves	9	-	-	-	-	-	-	-	-	-
Haywards Heath Town	-	-	3	7	13	12	14	18	-	-
Horsham YMCA	11	15	13	16	-	-	-	-	-	-
Lancing	12	10	10	13	12	17	-	-	-	-
Langney Sports	-	-	-	-	10	3	3	2	4	3
Littlehampton Town	2	6	6	14	7	2	1	3	7	13
Midhurst & Eastbourne	15	14	16	-	-	-	-	-	18	-
Newhaven	-	-	-	-	-	-	-	10	6	8
Oakwood	-	-	-	-	17	-	9	14	8	11
Pagham	-	-	-	1	1	8	4	4	2	5
Peacehaven & Telscombe	10	5	7	8	8	5	2	1	1	4
Portfield	7	8	12	15	18	-	-	-	13	14
Redhill	-	-	-	-	11	18	-	-	-	-
Ringmer	13	16	-	-	-	10	12	9	15	18
Seaford Town	-	-	-	-	-	11	17	-	-	-
Selsey	-	-	-	11	9	14	18	-	-	-
Shoreham	-	12	8	10	14	9	11	17	-	-
Stamco	-	-	-	-	-	-	-	-	-	9
Steyning Town	1	1	-	-	-	-	-	-	-	-
Three Bridges	6	2	4	2	2	7	7	7	9	12
Whitehawk	4	4	2	5	3	6	10	13	5	2
Wick	16	-	9	3	6	1	5	5	3	1
No. of clubs competing	16	16	16	16	18	18	18	18	18	20

3

DIVISION TWO 1993-94

	P	W	D	L	F	A	PTS
Peacehaven & Tel.	34	25	4	5	68	28	79
Southwick	34	24	8	4	64	26	74
Hassocks	34	20	6	8	78	38	66
Redhill	34	20	5	9	89	51	65
Lancing	34	18	9	7	63	37	63
Horsham YMCA	34	17	7	10	45	42	58
Selsey	34	15	9	10	66	51	54
Mile Oak	34	14	6	14	70	63	48
Sidley United	34	14	6	14	72	77	48
Worthing United	34	13	7	14	55	59	46
Eastbourne United	34	12	8	14	58	64	44
Saltdean United	34	13	5	16	55	67	44
Withdean	34	11	5	18	50	72	38
Steyning Town	34	8	5	21	47	84	29
Broadbridge Heath	34	7	7	20	45	70	28
Storrington	34	6	8	20	45	72	26
Midhurst & E'bne	34	8	2	24	40	94	26
Little Common A.	34	6	7	21	29	74	25

Manager of the month awards

Aug	Nick Greenwood/Pete Liddell (Hassocks)
Sept	John Sears/Paul Duffell (Redhill)
Oct	Brian Donnelly (Shoreham)
Nov	Cyril Jeanes (Sidley United)
Dec	Micky Fogden (Southwick)
Jan	Nick Greenwood/Pete Liddell (Hassocks)
Feb	Dave Kew (Selsey)
Mar	Brian Donnelly (Shoreham)
Apr/May	Nick Greenwood/Pete Liddell (Hassocks)

Manager of the Season:
Brian Donnelly (Shoreham)

LEADING SCORERS (League matches only)

Kevin Bevis (Sidley) 30
Robert Kitchen (Hassocks) 24
Neil Roberts (Mile Oak) 22
Steve Gurney (Lancing) 21

DIVISON TWO RESULTS 1993-94

HOME TEAM	1	2	3	4	5	6	7	8	9	10	11	12	13	14	15	16	17	18
1. Broadbridge Heath	*	2-0	1-3	2-2	0-2	0-0	0-2	4-3	1-2	0-0	1-2	0-4	1-2	0-4	6-2	0-0	2-0	2-2
2. Eastbourne United	2-3	*	0-1	2-0	0-0	2-1	3-2	2-3	2-2	1-0	0-1	0-2	2-1	1-0	3-2	1-1	1-1	4-2
3. Hassocks	1-0	2-2	*	2-0	4-1	3-0	6-0	1-2	2-4	3-0	4-0	0-4	3-3	1-2	3-0	1-1	2-0	2-1
4. Horsham YMCA	3-2	5-1	1-1	*	0-1	2-1	7-1	3-1	2-1	2-2	1-4	1-1	2-2	0-1	2-1	2-1	6-0	0-1
5. Lancing	3-0	1-1	2-1	0-2	*	0-0	2-1	1-0	1-1	2-1	2-2	0-1	7-3	1-1	1-0	2-0	2-0	3-1
6. Little Common Albion	0-0	3-7	3-1	1-4	1-4	*	2-0	0-4	0-2	2-1	0-2	1-2	1-2	0-0	1-3	1-0	1-4	3-1
7. Midhurst & Easebourne	0-4	0-2	1-6	0-4	0-4	2-0	*	3-1	0-5	2-1	1-1	0-1	0-2	0-3	6-0	2-1	1-1	0-2
8. Mile Oak	5-1	6-0	1-4	1-1	2-5	7-1	1-2	*	3-2	2-0	1-0	1-2	1-3	2-2	1-0	2-4	3-2	2-3
9. Redhill	3-2	4-1	1-3	1-3	1-1	9-0	2-1	4-1	*	3-0	1-1	0-1	4-2	3-2	1-2	5-3	4-1	3-0
10. Saltdean United	3-2	2-0	1-4	1-2	2-1	0-0	3-1	3-2	3-5	*	1-1	1-1	4-0	2-4	3-0	2-0	1-3	2-1
11. Selsey	4-2	6-1	0-2	0-1	1-0	2-1	5-2	0-0	2-2	6-1	*	2-0	1-3	1-2	0-1	3-1	1-4	1-3
12. Shoreham	2-1	1-0	1-0	2-1	2-3	3-1	2-1	0-1	5-1	4-1	0-2	*	4-2	0-0	4-1	6-0	3-1	1-1
13. Sidley United	1-1	2-3	1-3	4-2	2-1	0-0	6-4	1-3	3-2	3-1	3-3	0-1	*	1-1	3-1	6-1	2-3	3-1
14. Southwick	3-0	1-0	2-0	2-0	0-0	1-0	3-2	4-0	1-0	5-1	3-1	3-0	3-0	*	4-1	3-1	1-1	10-0
15. Steyning Town	3-1	3-3	0-3	0-0	1-5	4-2	3-0	1-4	1-3	1-3	0-4	1-3	5-2	1-1	*	2-2	2-3	3-2
16. Storrington	0-2	2-2	0-0	0-1	3-1	1-2	1-2	2-2	0-3	4-5	1-3	0-2	5-1	0-1	1-1	*	5-1	2-1
17. Withdean	1-0	0-4	2-5	0-3	2-3	1-0	5-1	1-1	1-3	0-1	2-2	1-2	1-3	2-0	3-1	1-2	*	2-1
18. Worthing United	6-2	2-1	1-1	3-0	1-1	0-0	5-0	1-1	0-2	0-3	2-2	0-1	2-0	2-1	1-0	3-1	3-0	*

Sussex County League Division Two Ten Year Record

	84/5	85/6	86/7	87/8	88/9	89/0	90/1	91/2	92/3	93/4
Albion United	13	6	-	-	-	-	-	-	-	-
Bexhill Town	16	-	3	2	6	1	-	-	-	-
Bosham	-	7	8	14	11	13	9	16	-	-
Broadbridge Heath	-	-	-	-	9	9	8	11	15	15
Chichester City	2	-	-	4	5	3	2	-	-	-
Crowborough Athletic	-	-	-	12	13	7	13	9	1	-
East Grinstead	6	5	4	11	14	-	-	14	3	-
East Preston	-	-	-	-	-	-	-	17	-	-
Eastbourne United	-	-	-	-	-	-	-	-	16	11
Ferring	8	8	7	10	10	15	-	-	-	-
Franklands Village	10	15	15	-	-	10	16	-	-	-
Hassocks	5	11	11	-	12	-	-	-	8	3
Haywards Heath Town	7	3	-	-	-	-	-	-	19	-
Horsham Y.M.C.A.	-	-	-	-	8	5	3	6	6	6
Lancing	-	-	-	-	-	-	7	15	4	5
Langney Sports	-	-	-	1	-	-	-	-	-	-
Lingfield	12	16	-	-	-	-	-	-	-	-
Little Common Albion	-	-	6	6	12	14	11	12	13	18
Midhurst & Easebourne	-	-	-	8	3	12	12	2	-	17
Mile Oak	-	-	-	-	-	-	-	-	9	8
Newhaven	15	12	10	13	7	11	1	-	-	-
Oakwood	-	10	5	3	-	2	-	-	-	-
Pagham	3	2	1	-	-	-	-	-	-	-
Portfield	-	-	-	-	-	4	5	1	-	-
Redhill	-	-	-	-	-	-	4	4	12	4
Ringmer	-	-	14	5	2	-	-	-	-	-
Saltdean United	-	-	-	-	-	8	14	13	17	12
Seaford Town	-	-	9	9	1	-	-	8	18	-
Selsey	11	13	2	-	-	-	-	7	11	7
Shoreham	1	-	-	-	-	-	-	-	7	1
Sidley United	9	4	16	-	-	-	15	10	14	9
Southwick	-	-	-	-	-	-	-	-	10	2
Stamco	-	-	-	-	-	6	10	3	2	-
Steyning Town	-	-	-	-	-	-	-	-	-	14
Storrington	4	9	13	7	4	16	-	-	-	
Wick	-	1	-	-	-	-	-	-	-	-
Wigmore Athletic	14	14	12	15			(see Worthing United)			
Withdean	-	-	-	-	-	-	-	-	-	13
Worthing United (see also Wigmore Athletic)							6	5	5	10
No. of clubs competing	16	16	16	15	14	16	16	17	19	18

DIVISION THREE 1993-94

	P	W	D	L	F	A	PTS
Bosham	30	19	5	6	69	33	62
Lingfield	30	18	5	7	62	33	59
East Preston	30	14	6	10	60	46	48
Ifield	30	13	8	9	68	48	47
Sunallon	30	12	8	10	58	48	44
Seaford Town	30	13	4	13	36	37	43
Hurstpierpoint	30	12	6	12	55	51	42
Forest	30	12	6	12	51	62	42
St Francis Hosp.	30	10	7	13	50	44	37
Buxted	30	10	6	14	51	67	36
Sidlesham	30	9	9	12	49	66	36
Lindfield Rgrs	30	9	8	13	45	43	35
Haywards Hth T.	30	10	5	15	39	54	35
Edwards Sports	30	7	13	10	46	60	34
Shinewater Assn	30	9	6	15	39	53	33
Franklands Village	30	7	10	13	40	53	31

Manager of the month awards

Aug Dave Shearing (Seaford Town)
Sept Malcolm Roberts (Sunallon)
Oct Richie Reynolds (Bosham)
Nov Richie Reynolds (Bosham)
Dec Graham Powell (Forest)
Jan John Finneran (East Preston)
Feb Ali Rennie (Ifield)
Mar Dennis Moore (Lingfield)
Apr/May Ken Swallow (Lindfield Rgrs)

Manager of the Season:
Ritchie Reynolds (Bosham)

LEADING SCORERS (League matches only)
Danny Bryan (Hurstpierpoint) 23
Ifield (Des Lyons) 19
Ian Cole (East Preston) 18

DIVISON THREE RESULTS 1993-94

HOME TEAM	1	2	3	4	5	6	7	8	9	10	11	12	13	14	15	16
1. Bosham	*	1-1	0-3	4-0	5-0	3-1	6-0	4-1	2-2	2-1	2-1	5-1	1-0	1-0	1-1	2-1
2. Buxted	1-2	*	0-5	1-1	3-0	4-1	3-1	4-0	1-7	2-3	1-1	2-3	2-3	3-1	5-5	1-7
3. East Preston	1-1	3-2	*	2-2	3-0	0-0	4-1	1-3	2-1	4-1	0-1	3-2	3-0	3-4	1-2	3-1
4. Edwards Sports	1-5	2-0	2-2	*	1-3	3-4	0-2	0-1	3-3	2-1	1-6	0-0	0-3	4-1	2-0	2-0
5. Forest	2-1	5-2	1-3	2-2	*	2-1	3-4	3-2	0-3	2-1	4-1	1-1	1-4	1-1	4-2	2-0
6. Franklands Village	1-2	0-1	2-2	2-2	2-2	*	0-2	1-0	5-2	0-3	0-3	2-0	2-0	3-3	1-2	2-2
7. Haywards Heath Town	0-3	0-1	1-3	3-0	3-1	1-1	*	0-1	0-5	2-1	1-1	0-1	0-2	2-1	3-3	2-0
8. Hurstpierpoint	3-3	2-2	1-5	1-1	3-1	0-1	2-1	*	4-2	0-1	4-1	0-1	2-1	2-1	10-0	1-4
9. Ifield	0-1	2-0	4-1	1-1	4-4	4-0	1-0	5-5	*	1-0	2-0	2-4	1-1	0-0	2-1	2-0
10. Lindfield Rangers	2-1	1-1	4-0	4-4	1-2	3-3	1-1	0-0	3-0	*	0-1	2-2	5-0	1-0	2-3	0-3
11. Lingfield	3-1	2-0	2-1	3-1	3-1	3-2	1-3	4-3	3-2	0-0	*	1-0	2-1	5-2	4-1	1-1
12. St Francis Hospital	0-2	2-3	3-0	L/W	3-1	0-3	2-1	0-1	0-0	0-0	2-4	*	2-1	2-0	1-2	2-2
13. Seaford Town	2-0	0-2	2-0	2-2	0-1	0-0	1-0	0-1	2-0	1-0	1-0	2-1	*	0-1	1-1	3-2
14. Shinewater Association	0-2	1-2	3-1	1-4	3-0	2-0	1-2	3-2	2-1	2-1	1-1	2-1	0-1	*	1-1	2-2
15. Sidlesham	1-5	4-0	0-2	2-2	0-1	3-1	1-1	0-0	2-5	1-2	3-0	1-1	2-1	2-0	*	2-3
16. Sunallon	3-1	2-1	1-1	1-1	1-1	0-0	4-2	1-0	1-4	3-1	2-4	1-3	3-1	3-0	4-1	*

Sussex County League Division Three Ten Year Record

	84/5	85/6	86/7	87/8	88/9	89/0	90/1	91/2	92/3	93/4
A.P.V. Athletic	-	7	10	7	-	-	-	-	-	-
Bexhill Town	-	2	-	-	-	-	-	-	-	-
Bosham	2	-	-	-	-	-	-	-	3	1
Broadbridge Heath	8	14	8	3	-	-	-	-	-	-
Buxted	-	-	-	-	-	12	12	11	13	10
Cooksbridge	11	13	4	6	12	-	-	-	-	-
Crowborough Athletic	7	9	2	-	-	-	-	-	-	-
East Grinstead	-	-	-	-	-	5	3	-	-	-
East Preston	10	3	6	12	13	8	2	-	12	3
Eastbourne Rangers	12	8	11	-	-	-			-	-
Edwards Sports	-	-	-	-	-	-	-	-	-	14
Falcons	-	-	-	-	5	-	-	-	-	-
Ferring	-	-	-	-	-	-	9	8	14	
Forest	-	-	-	-	6	9	7	12	5	8
Franklands Village	-	-	-	8	3	-	-	10	10	16
Hassocks	-	-	-	9	8	4	6	1	-	-
Haywards Heath Town	-	-	-	-	-	-	-	-	-	12
Hurstpierpoint	14	11	12	5	9	6	13	6	6	7
Ifield	13	6	5	2	11	13	1	4	7	4
Langney Sports	5	4	1	-	-	-	-	-	-	-
Leftovers Sports	-	15	13	10	14	10	11	14	-	-
Lindfield Rangers	-	-	-	-	-	-	-	7	9	12
Lingfield	-	-	14	14	16	-	-	-	-	2
Midway	4	12	3	1	15	-	-	-	-	-
Mile Oak	-	-	-	4	10	3	5	2	-	-
Oakwood	1	-	-	-	-	-	-	-	-	-
Rottingdean	-	-	-	-	-	7	8	13	-	-
St Francis Hospital	15	-	-	-	-	-	-	-	8	9
Saltdean United	3	5	9	11	1	-	-	-	-	-
Seaford Town	6	1	-	-	-	-	-	-	-	6
Shinewater Association	-	-	-	-	-	-	-	-	11	15
Sidlesham	-	-	-	-	-	-	-	3	4	11
Sidley United	-	-	-	13	4	2	-	-	-	-
Stamco	-	-	-	-	2	-	-	-	-	-
Storrington	-	-	-	-	-	-	10	9	2	-
Sunallon	-	-	-	-	-	-	-	-	-	5
Town Mead	-	-	-	-	-	11	-	-	-	-
Westdene	9	10	7	-	-	-	-	-	-	-
Withdean	-	-	-	-	-	14	4	5	1	-
Worthing United	-	-	-	-	7	1	-	-	-	-
No. of clubs competing	15	15	14	14	16	14	13	14	14	16

DIVISION ONE CLUBS 1994-95

ARUNDEL

Chairman: Michael Peters **Vice Chairman:** S Brennan.
Secretary/Press Officer: Peter Wells, 37 Bewley Road, Angmering BN16 4JL (0903 771146).
Manager: Mark Bennett **Assistant Manager:** S Bates.
Ground: Mill Road, Arundel (0903 882548). **Directions:** A27 from Worthing to Arundel town centre, 1st right into Mill Road, ground thru large car park (on right). 1 mile from Arundel (BR).
Seats: 100 **Cover:** 200 **Capacity:** 2,200 **Floodlights:** 206 lux **Founded:** 1889
Colours: Red/white/red **Change colours:** All yellow **Nickname:** Mulletts
Programme: 8 pages, free **Programme Editor:** Secretary **Sponsors:** None
Midweek matchday: Tuesday. **Record Gate:** 2,200 v Chichester, League 67-68
Previous Lge: West Sussex 1896-1975 **Previous Grounds:** Castle Park/ Station Rd Ground.
Players progressing to Football League: John Templeman (Brighton & Hove Albion 1966).
Reserves' Lge: Sussex Co. Res Div (W) **Record win:** 13-0 v Horsham YMCA (H), Sussex Lg Div 1 21/12/85.
Clubhouse: 2 bars, kitchen, toilets, telephone, pool, darts, Sky TV. Normal pub hours. No food.
Record Scorer: Paul J Bennett **Record appearances:** 537, Paul Bennett (goalkeeper).
Captain 93-94: S Bates **Player of the Year:** R Hellen.
93-94 Top Scorer: Paul J Bennett 23 **Local Press:** Arun Gazette
Hons: Sussex County Lg 57-58 58-59 86-87 (Lg Cup 86-87, Div 2 Cup 76-77, Reserve Section 78-79, Reserve Section Cup 78-79, Merit Table winners 80-81, Sussex Fives 1984 1987), Sussex RUR Charity Cup 68-69 72-73 78-79 79-80, Sussex Jnr Cup 07-08, West Sussex Lg (Reserves) 70-71 (Malcolm Simmonds Cup 70-71).

BURGESS HILL TOWN

President: Jack Lake **Manager:** Ray McCarthy **Chairman:** Jim Collins.
Secretary: David McKechnie, 20 Junction Rd, Burgess Hill RH15 0JD (0444 241790).
Ground: Leylands Park, Burgess Hill, West Sussex RH15 8AW (0444 242429).
Directions: Wivelsfield Station (BR out of Victoria), turn right, first left, ground on right.
Seats: 100 **Cover:** Yes **Capacity:** 2,000 **Floodlights:** Yes **Founded:** 1882
Colours: Yellow/black/black **Change colours:** All red **Club badges:** No
Programme: Yes **Midweek matchday:** Tuesday **Admission:** £2 **Nickname:** Hillians
Record Gate: 600 v Carshalton A., FA Cup 3rd Qual. 1981. **Sponsors:** Park Cameras
Local Press: Mid Sussex Times **Clubhouse:** Bar & social facilities. Tea bar.
Captain 93-94: Mark Nye **93-94 Top Scorer:** Lee Isaac.
Hons: Sussex County Lg 75-76 (Div 2 74-75, Lg Cup 73-74 79-80 (R-up 90-91), Div 2 Cup 73-73, Reserve Section 76-77 77-78 91-92, Reserve Sect. East 77-78 82-83 84-85, Reserve Cup 82-83, Yth Sect. West 91-92, Sussex Fives 1980), Mid-Sussex Lg 00-01 03-04 39-40 46-47 56-57 (Div 2 03-04(res), Div 3 20-21 36-37, Div 4(res) 56-57, Montgomery Cup 39-40 56-57, Mowatt Cup 45-46, Sussex Snr Cup 1883-84 84-85 85-86, Sussex RUR Charity Cup R-up 91-92, Sussex I'mediate Cup 76-77, Sussex Jnr Cup 1889-90, Sussex Yth Cup 91-92.

Below: *Burgess Hill top-scorer leads a Portfield defender a merry dance.* *Photo - Graham Cotterill.*

CROWBOROUGH ATHLETIC

President: Mr Peter Taylor **Chairman:** Mr Barry Sykes
Secretary: Roddy Harman, 3 Shirley Cottage, Woodbury Park Ave., Tunbridge Wells, Kent (0892 545765).
Manager: Roger Crouch **Press Officer:** Peter Crisp (0892 655470).
Ground: Alderbrook Recreation Ground, Fermor Road, Crowborough (0892 661893).
Directions: Turn east off A26 at Crowborough. Cross traffic lights, through High Street, right into Croft Rd, continue into Whitehall Rd and Fermor Rd, Alderbrook is second right after mini-r'bout.
Seats: None **Cover:** 200 **Capacity:** 1,000 **F'lights:** Due 93-94 **Founded:** 1894
Colours: White/navy/navy **Change colours:** Red & yellow **Nickname:** Crows.
Programme Editor: Peter Crisp (0892 655470) **Sponsors:** Blackden Enterprises Ltd.
Previous League: Brighton **Clubhouse:** Bar facilities & tea bar on matchdays
Midweek Matchday: Wednesday **Local Press:** Kent & Sussex Courier. **Club badges:** No.
93-94 Top Scorer: Darren Longley 20 **Record Gate:** 439 v Stamco, Sussex Co. Lge Div 2 1/5/93.
Hons: Sussex Co. Lg Div 1 92-93 (Div 2 Cup 77-78, Div 3 R-up), Sussex Intermediate Cup 86-87.

EASTBOURNE TOWN

Chairman: Roger Addems **Manager:** Pete Roberts.
Secretary: Roger Cooper, 81 St Philips Ave., Eastbourne, East Sussex BN22 8LY (0323 734426).
Ground: The Saffrons, Compton Place Road, Eastbourne, East Sussex (0323 23734).
Directions: Turn south west off A22 into Grove Road (opposite BR station). Ground quarter mile on right.
Seats: 100 **Cover:** Yes **Capacity:** 3,000 **Floodlights:** No **Founded:** 1882
Colours: Yellow/blue/blue **Changes:** White & black/white/white **Nickname:** 'Bourne'
Programme Editor: Sid Myall (0323 728096) **Admission:** £1.50/80p
Previous Leagues: Southern Amtr 07-46/ Corinthian 60-63/ Athenian 63-76.
Record Gate: 7,378 v Hastings U. 1953 **Prev. Ground:** Devonshire Park 1881-85 **Metal Badges:** Yes
Sponsors: Eastbourne Car Auctions **Local Press:** Eastbourne Gazetté & Herald Chronicle
Prev. Name: Eastbourne FC (pre-1970) **Clubhouse:** Fully licensed bar. Board room. Tea bar.
93-94 Top Scorer: Roger Mayall 14.
Hons: Sussex County Lg 76-77, Sussex Snr Cup(12) 1889-91 93-95 98-1901 02-03 21-22 31-33 52-53, Sussex RUR Charity Cup 32-33 47-48 49-50, Southern Amtr Lg(2), AFA Snr Cup 21-22 24-25 (R-up 22-23 23-24), AFA Invitation Cup 69-70 (R-up 56-57 68-69 70-71).

EAST GRINSTEAD

President: Peter Paice **Chairman:** Peter Cadman **Vice-Chairman:** Nada Waugh.
Secretary: Gary Bullen, 4 Churchfields, Nutley, East Sussex TN22 3NA (0825 713138).
Manager: Mark Arnold **Coach:** Peter Ransom/Roy Crouch **Physio:** Andy Peppercorn.
Comm. Mgr: Tracey Francis **Press Officer:** Bruce Talbot (0293 543809).
Ground: East Court, East Grinstead (0342 325885).
Directions: A264 Tunbridge Wells road (Moat Road) until mini-r'bout at bottom of Blackwell Hollow, turn immediately right by club sign then 1st left, ground 200yds down lane past rifle club on right.
Seats: None **Cover:** 400 **Capacity:** 3,000 **Floodlights:** Yes **Founded:** 1890
Colours: Amber & black **Change colours:** All sky **Nickname:** Wasps
Programme: Ave 36 pages, 50p **Programme Editor:** Press Officer **Metal Badges:** Yes
Club Shop: Badges (£2.50), club history (£2), scarves (£5), mugs (£2) available from tea bar on matchdays or via post - contact Press Officer.
Sponsors: Rydon Construction. **Record Gate:** 2,006 v Lancing, FA Amateur Cup 8/11/48
Midweek Matchday: Wednesday. **Reserves Team's League:** Sussex County Reserve Div. (East).
Previous Leagues: Mid-Sussex 1900-15 35-37/ Sussex County 20-32/ Southern Amateur League 32-35.
Previous Grounds: West Street Cricket Ground (pre-1963)/ King George's Field 63-68.
Players progressing to Football League: Tony Charman (Spurs), David Stripp (Arsenal).
Clubhouse: Open 1.30-10.30 matchdays (6-11 midweek matches). Available for hire. Darts, pool, satellite TV. Hot food available Saturdays, rolls etc available at midweek matches.
93-94 Top Scorer: Steve Norris **Local Press:** East Grinstead Observer.
P.o.Y. 93-94: Kevin Robbins **Club record appearances:** Guy Hill in 19 seasons - 1977-94.
Hons: Sussex RUR Charity Cup 74-75, Sussex Co. Lg Invitation Cup 51-52, Sussex Jnr Cup (jointly) 07-08, Sussex Youth Cup 86-87, Southern Amtr Lg Snr Div 3 31-32, Mid-Sussex Lg(6)(Lg Cup(7)), Brighton Lg(3)(Lg Cup(3)).

HAILSHAM TOWN

President: M W Walker **Chairman:** Dave Challinor **Manager:** Steve Richardson.
Secretary/Press Officer: Derek York, 59 Anglesey Avenue, Horsebridge, Hailsham BN27 3BQ (0323 848024).
Ground: The Beaconsfield, Western Road, Hailsham, East Sussex (0323 840446).
Directions: A22 to Arlington Road, turn east, then left into South Road - left into Diplocks Way until Daltons. Four miles from Polegate (BR - Brighton-Eastbourne line); regular bus service from Eastbourne.
Seats: None **Cover:** 300 **Capacity:** 2,000 **Floodlights:** Yes **Founded:** 1885
Colours: Yellow & green **Change colours:** Red **Nickname:** None
Programme: Yes **Programme Editor:** Secretary **Admission:** £2
Previous League: E Sussex, Southern Comb. **Previous Ground:** Western Rd Rec.
Record Gate: 1,350 v Hungerford, FA Vase Feb '80 **Metal Badges:** No.
Clubhouse: Hot and cold snacks. Open every evening, matchdays and Sundays, tea bar.
Local Press: Hailsham Gazette, Eastbourne Herald, Sussex Express
Midweek matchday: Wednesday. **93-94 Top Scorers:**
Hons: FA Vase 5th Rd 88-89, Sussex County Lg Div 2 R-up 80-81, Southern Co's Comb. 74-75, Sussex RUR Charity Cup, Sussex I'mediate Cup, Hastings Snr Cup, Sussex Jnr Cup, E Sussex Lg Cup, Hailsham Charity Cup.

LANGNEY SPORTS

President: Mr J Stonestreet **Chairman:** Mr Len Smith **Mgr:** Peter Cherry
Secretary: Mrs Myra Stephens, 7b Erica Close, Langney, Eastbourne, East Sussex BN23 8BT (0323 766050).
Physio: S Courtney **Commercial Manager:** M Grimer.
Ground: Priory Lane, Eastbourne, East Sussex (0323 766265).
Directions: A22 to Polegate, A27 to Stone Cross, right onto B32104 to Langney Shopping Centre, then left and first right. One mile from Pevensey & Westham (BR). Buses from Eastbourne.
Seats: None **Cover:** 200 **Capacity:** 1,000 **Floodlights:** Yes **Founded:** 1966
Colours: All red **Change:** Sky & navy stripes/navy **Nickname:** None
Midweek Matchday: Tuesday
Programme: Yes **Editor:** Mike Spooner (0323 461003)
Club Shop: To open 1994-95 **Record Gate:** 1,000+ v Crystal Palace, f'light opener 90-91.
Sponsors: Nobo Group Plc. **Previous League:** Eastbourne & Hastings
Record win: 10-1 v Haywards Heath Town, Sussex County League Division One 11/4/92.
Record defeat: 0-8; v Sheppey United (A), FA Vase Preliminary Rd 9/10/93; v Peacehaven Telscombe (A), Sussex County Lg Division One 9/11/93.
Previous Grounds: Princes Park, Wartling Rd, Eastbourne/ Adjacent pitch.
Clubhouse: Open every evening & lunchtime with adjoining sports hall, board room, matchday tea bar.
Local Press: Eastbourne Gazette & Herald
Record scorer: Nigel 146 **Record appearances:** Steve Dell 325.
P.o.Y. 93-94: Darren Baker **93-94 Top Scorer & Captain:** Mick Green.
Hons: Sussex Co. Lg R-up 91-92 (Div 2 87-88, Lg Cup 89-90, Div 3 86-87, Div 3 Cup 86-87, 5-aside comp. 1990), Sussex I'mediate Cup 85-86, Eastbourne Challenge Cup 85-86 86-87.

LITTLEHAMPTON TOWN

President: Ian Cunningham **Chairman:** B Suter **Mgr:** Kevin Hotston
Secretary/Press Officer: Mark Warren, 49 Oakcroft Gardens, Littlehampton, West Sussex.
Ground: The Sportsfield, St Flora's Road, Littlehampton (0903 713944).
Directions: 10 minutes walk from Littlehampton station (BR) - turn left along Terminus Rd, continue through High Street and Church Rd to junction with St Flora's Rd (left).
Seats: 260 **Cover:** 260 **Capacity:** 4,000 **Floodlights:** Yes **Founded:** 1894
Colours: All gold **Change:** Blue/whitewhite **Nickname:** Marigolds
Programme Editor: Mr C Scrimshaw (0903 713466) **Local Press:** Littlehampton Gazette
Record Gate: 4,000 v Northampton, FA Cup 1st Rd Proper 90-91 **Sponsors:**
Midweek Matches: Tuesday **Club metal badges:** Yes **Admission:** £1.50
Clubhouse: Sportsman (Private Club). Separate board room & tea bar.
93-94 Top Scorer: Paul Boxall 18.
Hons: FA Vase SF 90-91, FA Cup 1st Rd 90-91, Sussex Co. Lg 90-91 (Lg 58-59(jt with Shoreham) 75-76 76-77 84-85 90-91 (R-up 91-92)), Sussex Snr Cup 73-74 (R-up 90-91).

NEWHAVEN

President: **Chairman:** M Godden **Manager:** M Rosers
Secretary: F D Dixon, 39 Southdown Avenue, Peacehaven, East Sussex BN10 8RX (0273 585514).
Ground: Fort Road, Newhaven, East Sussex (0273 513940).
Directions: A275 from Lewes, or A259 coast rd, to Newhaven 1-way system. 1 mile from Newhaven Town (BR).
Seats: 50 **Cover:** Yes **Capacity:** 4,000 **Floodlights:** Yes **Founded:** 1887
Colours: All red **Change colours:** Yellow/green **Nickname:** Dockers
Programme: Yes **Editor:** Mike Taylor (0273 515232) **Admission:** £1.50 **Metal Badges:** No
Previous Leagues: None (founder members of SCFL) **Previous Name:** Newhaven Town.
Record Gate: 3,000 **Previous Ground:** None (Lewes FC temporarily 90-91)
Midweek Matchday: Tuesday **Clubhouse:** Being redeveloped **Sponsors:** Sealink.
Local Press: Evening Argus, Sussex Express
Captain 93-94: Matthew Wiltshire **93-94 Top Scorer:** Andy Blythe 28.
Hons: Sussex County Lg 53-54 (Div 2 71-72 90-91, Invitation Cup 48-49, Lg Cup R-up 92-93, Reserve Section East R-up 92-93), Sussex Snr Cup R-up 53-54, Sussex RUR Charity Cup 93-94.

OAKWOOD

President: TBA **Chairman:** A T Bridges
Secretary: Gerry Martin, 'Singlegate', Tinsley Green, Crawley RH10 3NS (0293 882400).
Manager: Alan Gould **Asst Mgr:** Dudley Christensen **Coach:** Neil Blackwell
Physio: Tim Wheelhouse **Press Officer:** Simon Milham (0293 615043).
Ground: Tinsley Lane, Three Bridges, Crawley, West Sussex (0293 515742).
Directions: From A23 to Gatwick, take 1st set of lights into Manor Royal, pass next lights, over r'bout to warehouse marked Canon, turn right signposted Oakwood. Last clubhouse down lane. Two miles north of Three Bridges (BR).
Seats: 20 **Cover:** Yes **Capacity:** 3,000 **Floodlights:** Yes **Founded:** 1966
Colours: Red/white/red **Change colours:** White/blue/white **Nickname:** Oaks
Programme: 24 pages, 50p **Editor:** Simon Milham (0293 615043) **Club Shop:** No.
Previous Ground: Park pitches. **Previous Lgs:** Crawley & Dist., Southern Co's Comb.
Record Gate: 367 **Midweek Matchday:** Tuesday **Metal Badges:** Yes
Sponsors: Linden Plc. **Reserve Team's League:** Sussex County Reserve section.
Clubhouse: Pool tables, multidart boards, large bar area. Board room & tea bar.
Record appearances: Peter Brackpool **Local Press:** Crawley Observer, Crawley News
Captain 93-94: Steve Breach **93-94 Top Scorer:** Lee Mobsby **P.o.Y. 93-94:** Billy Bower.
Hons: Sussex Snr Cup R-up 92-93, Sussex Co. Lg Div 2 R-up 89-90 (Div 2 Cup 89-90, Div 3 84-85), Southern Comb. Cup 83-84.

PAGHAM

Chairman: I Baker **Vice-Chairman:** D Abburon **President:** A Peirce
Secretary/Press Officer: Mr Eric G Nunn, 8 West Drive, Aldwick, Bognor Regis PO21 4LY (0243 262879).
Manager/Coach: G Peach **Asst Manager:** P Gilbert **Comm. Manager:** A Dixon
Ground: Nyetimber Lane, Pagham, West Sussex (0243 266112).
Directions: Turn off A27 Chichester by-pass (signposted A259 Pagham). Ground in village of Nyetimber. Three miles from Bognor (BR). Buses 260 & 240.
Seats: 200 **Cover:** 200 **Capacity:** 2,000 **Floodlights:** Yes **Founded:** 1903
Colours: White/black/black **Change colours:** Yellow/green **Nickname:** Lions.
Midweek Matchday: Tuesday **Reserve Team's League:** Unijet Sussex Co. Reserve Div.
Programme: 12 pages, 50p **Programme Editor:** Secretary **Club Shop:** No.
Record Gate: 1,200 v Bognor, 1971. **Sponsors:** Nyetimber Mazda.
Previous Grounds: None **Previous Leagues:** Chichester 1903-50/ West Sussex 50-69.
Record win: 10-1 v Seaford Town (A), Sussex County League Division Two, 1970.
Record defeat: 0-7 v Newport IOW (H), FA Amateur Cup, mid-1970s.
Clubhouse: Bar open to members and visitors matchdays and some evenings. Hot food, pool, darts, satellite TV. Tea bar.
Local Press: Bognor Observer **Club Record Scorer:** Mark Vickers/ R Deluca.
93-94 Top Scorer: Mark Vickers 43 **93-93 Captain & Player-of-the-Year:** C Young.
Hons: Sussex Co. Lg R-up 80-81 87-88 88-89 92-93 (Div 2 78-79 86-87, Lg Cup 88-89, Div 2 Cup 71-72 85-86, Res. Sect. West 80-81, Res Sect. Cup 80-81, Res Section Cup 77-78 80-81 87-88 88-89 90-91), Sussex F'lit Cup R-up 88-89, Sussex RUR Charity Cup 88-89 (R-up 93-94), West Sussex Lg 65-66 68-69 69-70, Malcolm Simmonds Cup 67-68, Sussex I'mediate Cup 66-67.

PEACEHAVEN & TELSCOMBE

President: Mr W Parris **Chairman:** Mr Jim Edwards **Mgr:** P Edwards
Secretary/Press Officer: Mr Keith Parris, 12 Abbey Close, Peacehaven, E. Sussex BN10 7SD (0273 585173).
Ground: Piddinghoe Avenue, Peacehaven, East Sussex (0273 582471).
Directions: Arriving from Brighton on A259, cross r'bout and Piddinghoe Avenue is next left after 2nd set of lights - ground at end. From Newhaven Piddinghoe Avenue is first right after first set of lights. Three miles from Newhaven (BR). Peacehaven is served by Brighton to Newhaven and Eastbourne buses.
Seats: None **Cover:** 250 **Capacity:** 3,000 **Floodlights:** Yes **Founded:** 1923
Colours: White/black/black **Change colours:** All sky **Nickname:** The Tye
Programme: Yes **Programme Editor:** Secretary
Local Press: Evening Argus/ Sussex Express
Record Gate: 1,420 v Littlehampton, League 11/5/91. **Sponsors:** Brighton & Newhaven Fish Sales.
Previous Ground: Telscombe Tye **Previous Leagues:** Lewes/ Brighton
Previous Names: Peacehaven Rangers merged with Telscombe Tye in 1923/ Peacehaven & Telscombe Cliffs (for one season only in early 1980's).
Midweek Matches: Wednesday **Metal badges:** No **Admission:** £1.50
Clubhouse: Bar open evenings and weekends, pool darts, hot and cold food available. Tea bar.
93-94 Top Scorer: Mark Taylor 13.
Hons: Sussex Co. Lg 78-79 81-82 82-83 91-92 92-93 (R-up 77-78 80-81 90-91, Lg Cup 91-92 92-93, Div 2 R-up 75-76, Div 2 Cup 75-76, Norman Wingate Tphy 82-83 91-92 92-93 93-94, Hayden Tphy 82-83 92-93, Div 2 Invitation Cup 69-70, Res. Sect. 83-84 92-93 (R-up 91-92), Res Sect. Cup 81-82 83-84 85-86 86-87 87-88, Res Sect East R-up 90-91), Sussex Snr Cup R-up 81-82 93-94, Sussex RUR Charity Cup 77-78 81-82 92-93 (R-up 80-81 89-90 90-91), Brighton Charity Cup 91-92 92-93, Vernon Wentworth 91-92 92-93, FA Cup 4th Qual. Rd 90-91, FA Vase 5th Rd 92-93.

Below: *Peacehaven & Telcombe pictured before the Sussex Senior Cup final.* *Photo - Gavin Ellis-Neville.*

PORTFIELD

Manager: Joe Laidlaw **President:** C Nowell **Chairman:** T Rustell
Secretary: Mr J Dowling, 00 St James Square, Chichester, West Sussex PO19 4NZ (0243 797044).
Ground: Church Road, Portfield, Chichester, West Sussex PO19 4HN (0243 779875)
Directions: A27 from Arundel to Chichester, take road to signposted city centre then 1st left (Church Rd) after supermarket r'bout. 1 mile from Chichester (BR).
Seats: 8 **Cover:** 200 **Capacity:** 2,000 **Floodlights:** Yes **Founded:** 1896
Colours: Amber/black/black **Change colours:** All white **Nickname:** Field.
Programme Editor: TBA **Admission:** £1.50 & £1 **Metal Badges:** No.
Record Gate: Unknown **Midweek Matchday:** Tuesday
Clubhouse: 2 bars, pool, snooker, seating for 100, dance floor, darts, boardroom. Ta bar sells hot/cold food.
Previous League: West Sussex. **Local Press:** Chichester Observer
Previous Grounds: Downers (until 1952)/ Florence Road (until 1959).
Sponsors: Wadham Kenning. **93-94 Top Scorer:** Sean Forry 14.
Hons: Sussex Co. Lg Div 2 72-73 83-84 91-92 (Div 2 Cup 70-71 72-73, Reserve Sect. Cup 91-92, 5-aside comp. 1991), W Sussex Lg 46-47 48-49 (Malcolm Simmonds Cup 46-47), Sussex Jnr Cup 45-46, Benevolent Cup 46-47.

RINGMER

President: Sir G Christie **Chairman:** Richard Soan
Secretary: Pam Howard, 66 Springett Avenue, Ringmer BN8 5HD (0273 813818).
Manager: B Smith **Press Officer:** Alan Harper (0323 764263)
Ground: Caburn Pavillion, Anchor Field, Ringmer (0273 812738).
Directions: Turn into Springett Avenue opposite Ringmer village green. Anchor Field first left. Five miles from Lewes (BR).
Seats: 100 **Cover:** Yes **Capacity:** 1,000 **Floodlights:** Yes **Founded:** 1906.
Colours: Sky & navy blue **Change colours:** All yellow **Nickname:** None
Programme: Yes **Editor:** Alan Harper (0323 764263) **Admission:** £2 **Club ties:** Yes.
Previous League: Brighton **Previous Names:** None. **Metal Badges:** No
Record Gate: 1,200 in FA Cup **Previous Grounds:** None.
Midweek Matchday: Tuesday **Clubhouse:** 2 bars, function room, boardroom, tea bar.
Local Press: Sussex Express **93-94 Top Scorer:** Syd Harman 20.
Hons: FA Cup 1st Rd Proper 70-71 (lost 0-3 at Colchester Utd), Sussex Co. Lg 70-71 (Div 2 68-69, Div 2 Invitation Cup 66-67, Res. Sect. 80-81, Res. Sect. East 79-80 80-81 (R-up 89-90), Yth Section 87-88, Yth Section East 87-88), Sussex Snr Cup 72-73 (R-up 80-81), Sussex Jnr Cup 25-26.

SHOREHAM

President: Mr Alf Bloom **Chairman:** Mr John Bell.
Secretary: Mr Glen Hilton, 67 Test Rd, Sompting, West Sussex BN15 0EP (0903 763024).
Manager: B Donnelly **Press Officer:** Mr Michael Wenham (0273 596009).
Ground: Middle Road, Shoreham-by-Sea, West Sussex (0273 454261).
Directions: Half mile from Shoreham-by-Sea (BR) - east across level crossing, up Dolphin Road, ground 150yds on right. Or, A27 to Southlands Hospital - south down Hammy Lane, left at end, ground opposite.
Seats: 20 **Cover:** 1 stand **Capacity:** 1,500 **Floodlights:** Yes **Founded:** 1892
Colours: Blue & white **Change colours:** Red & white **Nickname:** Musselmen
Programme: Yes **Editor:** Mr M Wenham (0273 596009) **Admission:** £1.50
Previous League: West Sussex **Midweek Matchday:** Wednesday **Metal Badges:** No
Record Gate: 1,342 v Wimbledon (floodlight opening 1986).
Sponsors: Len German Wholesalers. **Previous Ground:** Buckingham Park (pre-1970)
Local Press: Shoreham Herald **Clubhouse:** Seats 70. Bar, pool, darts, tea bar.
93-94 Top Scorer: Tobi Hitchison 17.
Hons: Sussex Co. Lg 51-52 52-53 77-78 (R-up 34-35, Div 2 61-62 76-77 84-85 93-94, Div 2 Cup 74-75 82-83, Invitation Cup 57-58), Sussex Snr Cup 01-02 05-06, Sussex F'lit Cup R-up 89-90, Sussex RUR Charity Cup 02-03 05-06, Vernon Wentworth Cup 86-87.

SOUTHWICK

Chairman: Roy Pollard **Vice-Chairman:** Dave Cook **President:** Dr D W Gordon, MBBS Dr.COG
Secretary: Peter Hallett, 10 Hawkins Close, Shoreham-by-Sea, West Sussex BN43 6TL (0273 594349).
Manager/Coach: Russell Bromage **Assistant Manager:** Chris White/ Ray Westgate.
Coach: Russell Brommage **Press Officer:** Paul Symes (0273 594142).
Ground: Old Barn Way, off Manor Hall Way, Southwick, Brighton BN43 4NT (0273 591744).
Directions: Five minutes walk from either Fishergate or Southwick BR stations. By A27 from Brighton take 1st left after 'Southwick' sign to Leisure Centre. Ground adjacent.
Seats: 220 **Cover:** 1,220 **Capacity:** 3,500 **Floodlights:** Yes **Founded:** 1882
Colours: Red & black stripes/black/red **Change Colours:** Yellow/red/red **Sponsors:** Ninex.
Record Gate: 3,200 v Showbiz side 1971 **Midweek matchday:** Tuesday **Metal Badges:** Yes.
Programme: Yes **Editor:** Paul Symes (0273 594142) **Reserves' Lge:** Sussex Co. Res **Previous Leagues:** West Sussex 1896-1920/ Sussex County 20-52 54-84/ Metropolitan 52-54/ Combined Counties 84-85/ Isthmian 85-92. **Previous Grounds:** Croft Avenue/ The Green/ Oldfield Crescent.
Players progressing to Football League: Charles & William Buttenshaw (Luton 1948).
Best FA Cup season: 1st Rd Proper 74-75 (lost 0-5 at AFC Bournemouth). **Nickname:** Wickers
Best FA Amtr Cup season: 3rd 28-29 **Best FA Vase season:** 3rd Rd 79-80 85-86
Local Newspaper: Evening Argus (0273 606799), Shoreham Herald (0273 455104), Adur Herald.
Clubhouse: Weekdays noon-3 & 6-11pm, all day Saturday, normal hrs Sunday. Members bar & boardroom with bar. Snacks on matchdays from tea bar.
Captain 93-94: David Willis **P.o.Y. 93-94:** Matthew Atkins **93-94 Top Scorer:** Tony Ropke.
Hons: Isthmian Lg Div 2 Sth 85-86, Sus. Co. Lg 25-26 27-28 29-30 47-48 68-69 74-75 (R-up(9) 23-24 28-29 36-37 39-40 70-71 76-77 78-80 82-83, Lg Cup 77-78, Div 1 Invit. Cup 65-66, Div 2 R-up 65-66), Combined Co's Lg R-up 84-85, Sus. Snr Cup 1896-97 1910-11 12-13 24-25 27-28 29-30 30-31 36-37 47-48 67-68, Sus. RUR Charity Cup(10) 1896-97 08-09 10-11 24-26 27-30 37-38 76-77, W. Sus. Lg 1896-97 97-98 1908-09 10-11, Sus. Jnr Cup 1891-92.

STAMCO

Chairman: Leon Shepperdson **Vice-Chairman:** Terry Hewham **President:** Mrs K Shepperdson
Secretary: Alan Ramsay, 8 Montgomery Rd, Hastings, East Sussex TN35 4LA (0424 712395).
Manager: Micky Reed **Physio:** Peter Butcher **Coach:** Brian Collins
Commercial Mgr: Neil Cranham **Press Officer:** John Corneleus (0424 753242).
Ground: The Firs, Elphinstone Road, Hastings, East Sussex (0424 434755).
Directions: Adjacent to Hastings Town FC - see Beazer Homes League section for directions.
Seats: 50 **Cover:** 250 **Capacity:** 1,500 **Floodlights:** Yes **Founded:** 1971
Colours: Blue/white/blue **Change colours:** White/blue/white **Metal Badges:** Yes.
Programme: 60 pages, 50p **Editor:** Peter High (0424 431482) **Nickname:** None
Sponsors: TBA **Prev. Grounds:** Council pitches 71-76/ Pannel Lane, Pett 1971-93.
Record Gate: 520 v Peacehaven & Telscombe, Sussex County League Division One 25/8/93. At old ground: 527 v Hastings Town, Sussex Senior Cup Second Round 92-93.
Previous Leagues: Southern Counties Combination/ East Sussex/ Hastings.
Midweek Matchday: Tuesday or Wednesday.
Record win: 10-1 v Portfield (H), Sussex County League Division One 4/12/93.
Record defeat: 2-6 v Pagham (A), Sussex RUR Charity Cup 22/1/94.
Clubhouse: Licensed bar open normal pubhours. Hot foof from tea bar.
Local Newspaper: Hastings Observer. **Club record appearances:** Gary Cawkill.
Captain 93-94: Ian Menzies **Club Record Scorer:** Dean Kewley
93-94 Top Scorer: Dean Kewley **Player-of-the-Year 93-94:** Brian McDermott.
Hons: Sussex Co. Lg Div 2 R-up 92-93 (Div 2 Cup R-up 89-90 90-91, Div 3 R-up, Div 3 Cup R-up, Reserve Section East 92-93), Hastings Snr Invitation Cup 89-90, Hastings Intermediate Cup 79-80 81-82 82-83 85-86 86-87 87-88.

THREE BRIDGES

President: Mr Jim Steele **Chairman:** Mr O'Brien
Secretary: Mr Martin Clarke, 18 Mannings Close, Pound Hill, Crawley RH10 3TX (0293 883726).
Manager: Mr Bobby Nash **Press Officer:** Mr Alf Blackler
Ground: Jubilee Field, Three Bridges, Crawley, West Sussex (0293 530540).
Directions: 200yds from Three Bridges (BR) - towards Crawley town centre.
Seats: None **Cover:** 400 **Capacity:** 3,500 **Floodlights:** Yes **Founded:** 1901
Colours: Amber & black **Change colours:** All white **Nickname:** Bridges
Programme: Yes **Editor:** Mark Stacy (0293 885864) **Admission:** £1.50
Previous Lgs: Mid Sussex/ Redhill & District **Previous Grounds:** None.
Record Gate: 2,000 v Horsham, 1948 **Midweek Matchday:** Tuesday **Metal Badges:** No
Clubhouse: Bar, dance floor, pool, darts **Sponsors:** Auto Body Care
93-94 Top Scorer: Andrew West 18. **93-94 Captain:** John Malthouse
Local Press: Crawley Observer, Crawley News
Hons: Sussex Co. Lg R-up 85-86 87-88 88-89 (Div 2 54-55, Invitation Cup 70-71, Div 2 Invitation Cup 62-63), Sussex RUR Charity Cup 82-83.

WHITEHAWK

President: Ron Wiltshire **Chairman/Comm. Mgr:** Ken Powell **Vice-Chairman:** David Powell
Secretary: John Rosenblatt, 25 Arundel Street, Brighton BN2 5TH (0273 680322).
Manager: Butch Reeves **Asst Manager:** Vic Standen **Coach:** Paul Hubbard.
Ground: The Enclosed Ground, East Brighton Park (0273 609736).
Directions: Follow Brighton seafront road towards Newhaven, turn inland (Arundel Road) opposite Marina, 3rd right into Roedean Road, 1st left into Wilson Avenue. Three miles from Brighton (BR); take Newhaven, Eastbourne or Saltdean bus to Marina, then as above.
Seats: None **Cover:** 500 **Capacity:** 3,000 **Floodlights:** Yes **Founded:** 1945
Colours: All red **Change colours:** All blue **Nickname:** Hawks
Midweek Matchday: Wednesday
Programme: £2 with admission **Programme Editor:** Tony Kelly (0273 698203)
Local Press: Evening Argus **Sponsors:** Brighton Co-operative Society.
Record Gate: 2,100 v Bognor Regis Town, FA Cup 4th Qualifying Rd replay 88-89.
Clubhouse: Licensed bar, pool, darts. Board room. Tea bar.
Previous League: Brighton Hove & Dist. **Previous Grounds:** None **Metal Badges:** No
Previous Name: Whitehawk & Manor Farm Old Boys (until 1958).
93-94 Top Scorer: Simon Pierce **Captain & Player of the Year 93-94:** Russell Gunn
Club record scorer: Billy Ford **Club record appearances:** Ken Powell 1,103.
Hons: Sussex Co. Lg 61-62 63-64 83-84 (Div 2 67-68 80-81, Lg Cup 82-83 93-94, Invitation Cup 60-61 69-70, Div 2 Cup 80-81), Sussex Snr Cup 50-51 61-62, Sussex RUR Charity Cup 54-55 58-59 90-91, Sussex I'mediate Cup 49-50, Sussex Jnr Cup 48-49 51-52, Brighton Charity Cup 51-52 59-60 61-62 82-83 87-88 88-89, Worthing Charity Cup 82-83, FA Vase 5th Rd 93-94.

WICK

Chairman/Manager: Norman Cairns **Vice-Chairman:** John Burnett **President:** M Hood
Secretary: C N Little, 4 Leeward Rd, Littlehampton, West Sussex BN17 6PG (0903 721962).
Asst Manager: Carl Stabler **Press Officer:** Thomas Cairns (0903 501857)
Ground: Crabtree Park, Coomes Way, Wick, Littlehampton, West Sussex (0903 713535).
Directions: A27 to Crossbush, left at Howards Hotel, after 1 mile cross level crossing, turn left into Coombes Way next to Locomotive PH - ground at end. One and a half miles from Littlehampton (BR).
Seats: 50 **Cover:** 200 **Capacity:** 2,000 **Floodlights:** Yes **Founded:** 1892
Colours: Red & black **Change colours:** Green & white
Programme: Yes **Editor:** Les Page (0903 260837) **Local Press:** Littlehampton Gazette.
Record Gate: 900. **Sponsors:** T.B.A. **Nickname:** Wickers
Prev. Grounds: Southfields Rec. **Previous League:** West Sussex **Metal Badges:** No.
Midweek Matches: Tuesday **Clubhouse:** First floor. Capacity 120. Tea bar.
Admission: £2 (£1 OAP/child) **Reserve Team's League:** Unijet Sussex Co. Reserve Div.
Captain 93-94: Steve Welman **93-94 Top Scorer:** Steve Guille.
Hons: Sussex Snr Cup 92-93, Sussex Co. Lg 89-90 93-94 (Lg Cup 87-88 (R-up 93-94), Div 2 81-82 85-86, Div 2 Cup R-up 81-82, Norman Wingate Tphy 88-89 90-91, Res. Sect West 87-88 90-91, Sussex 5-aside R-up 85-86), Sussex RUR Charity Cup 89-90, Gilbert Rice F'lit Cup R-up 80-81 81-82, Sussex Jnr Cup 59-60, Brighton Charity Cup 85-86.

Wick's Paul Williams (left) tussles with Simon Edwards of Whitehawk during the league leaders surprise 0-4 defeat in the final of the John O'Hara League Cup.

Photo - Roger Turner.

DIVISION TWO CLUBS 1994-95

BEXHILL TOWN

President: Barry Woodcock **Chairman:** Peter Eastham **Manager:** J Lambert
Secretary: Mr E N Hughes, 5 Badgers Way, Hastings, East Sussex TN34 2QD (0424 427967).
Ground: The Polegrove, Brockley Rd, Bexhill-on-Sea, East Sussex (0424 220732).
Directions: At Little Common r'bout take 3rd exit to Cooden Sea Rd, left into Cooden Drive for one and a half miles, Brockley Rd on the right. Three quarters of a mile from Bexhill Central (BR).
Seats: 250 **Cover:** 250 **Capacity:** 2,000 **Floodlights:** No **Founded:** 1926
Colours: Green & white **Change colours:** Black & white **Nickname:** Green Machine
Previous Name: Bexhill Town Athletic.
Programme: Yes **Programme Editor:** Mr G Sully **Admission:** £1.50/£1/50p
Record Gate: 2,000 **Clubhouse:** New clubroom and bar facilities
Local Press: Bexhill Observer **93-94 Top Scorer:** Neil Phillips 16.
Hons: Sussex Co. Lg 56-57 65-66 (Invit. Cup 55-56), Sussex RUR Char. Cup 57-58 73-74, Hastings Challenge Cup 93-94, Sussex Midweek Cup 25-26.

BOSHAM

President: D G Phillips **Chairman:** M Maiden **Manager:** R L Collyer
Secretary: R D Probee, 39 Arnold Way, Bosham, West Sussex PO18 8NJ (0243 572570).
Ground: Walton Lane, Bosham, West Sussex PO18 8QF (0243 574011).
Directions: Half mile from Bosham (BR) - walk south down station road, over A27 r'bout, left at T-junction, ground entrance 50 yds on left.
Seats: None **Cover:** 50 **Capacity:** 2,000 **Floodlights:** No **Founded:** 1901
Colours: Red/white/red **Change colours:** White/black/white **Nickname:** Robins
Programme: Yes **Programme Editor:** Secretary **Admission:** None **Metal Badges:** No
Previous Leagues: Chichester & Dist Jnr/ Chichester & Bognor/ Chichester & Dist./ West Sussex
Midweek Matchday: Tuesday. **Sponsors:** None.
Clubhouse: Lounge bar, open evenings & weekends. Tea bar.
93-94 Top Scorer: Gary Wheatcroft 15.
Local Press: Portsmouth News, Chichester Observer.
Hons: Sussex Co. Lg Div 3 93-94 (R-up 84-85, Div 3 Cup 84-85 (R-up 92-93), Reserve Sect. West R-up 92-93), Sussex Jnr Cup 55-56, West Sussex Lg 77-78 (Div 2 56-57), Chichester & Dist. Jnr Lg 06-07, Chichester & Bognor Lg 11-12 12-13 (Lg Cup 11-12), Chichester & Dist. Lg 53-54 55-56, Chichester Charity Cup 55-56.

BROADBRIDGE HEATH

President: G W Manketelow **Chairman:** K Soames **Manager:** J Laker
Secretary: Andy Crisp, 19 Church Rd, Broadbridge Heath, Horsham, West Sussex RH12 3LD (0403 252273).
Ground: Broadbridge Heath Sports Centre, Wickhurst Lane, Horsham (0403 65871).
Directions: Alongside A24, Horsham north/south bypass.
Seats: 300 **Cover:** 300 **Capacity:** 1,300 **F'lights:** Not full **Founded:** 1919
Colours: All royal blue **Change colours:** All red **Nickname:** Bears
Programme: Yes **Editor:** G Street (0403 240596) **Admission:** £1 **Metal badges:** No
Previous Leagues: Horsham, West Sussex, Southern Co's Comb. **Record Gate:** 240
Clubhouse: Bar. Kitchen serving meals, pool, darts, social club etc. **Sponsors:** Badgers
Midweek matches: Tue or Wed **Local Press:** West Sussex County Times.
93-94 Top Scorer: Alan Simpson 11 **Prev. Ground:** Guildford Rd, Broadbridge Heath.

CHICHESTER CITY

President: G Redford **Chairman:** T Wallis
Secretary: J F Hutter, 28 Stockbride Gdns, Donnington, Chichester, West Sussex PO19 2QT (0243 785839).
Manager/Coach: Eamonn Collins **Assistant Manager:** Shaun Tetley **Physio:** Wally Lightfoot
Press Officer: T Wallis (0705 464438).
Ground: Oaklands Park, Chichester (0243 785978).
Directions: Half mile north of city centre adjacent to Festival Theatre. Turn into Northgate car park from Oaklands Way and entrance is beside Tennis and Squash club. 1 mile from Chichester (BR) - walk north through city centre.
Seats: 50 **Cover:** 500 **Capacity:** 2,500 **Floodlights:** No **Founded:** 1873
Colours: White/black/black **Change colours:** All red **Nickname:** Lilywhites
Midweek home matchday: Tuesday. **Reserve Team's League:** Sussex County Reserve section.
Programme: Yes **Editor:** T Wallis (0705 464438) **Club Shop:** No
Prev. Name: Chichester FC (pre-1960) **Record Gate:** 2,500 v Dorchester, FA Cup 1960
Local Press: Chichester Observer **Previous Lgs:** Chichester/ West Sussex 1886-1920
Previous Grounds: New Park Rec. 1873-81/ Priory Park 1881-1956.
Best FA Cup year: 1st Round Proper 60-61 (lost 0-11 at Bristol City).
Record win: 11-0 v East Grinstead, Sussex County League Division One 1968.
Record defeat: 0-11 v Bristol City, FA Cup 1st Round 1960-61.
Record transfer fee received: £700 for Tom Pegler (Bognor Regis Town) 1993.
Clubhouse: Licensed, open matchdays and some evenings. Tea bar & boadroom.
Club record scorer: David Green **Club record appearances:** Neal Holder.
Captain 93-94: Neil Drinkwater **93-94 Top Scorer:** Peter Kearvell **P.o.Y. 93-94:** Lee Preston.
Hons: Sussex Co. Lg(5) 59-61 67-68 72-73 79-80 (R-up(4) 50-51 61-62 65-67, Invitation Cup 47-48 54-55 56-57 63-64, Div 2 R-up 84-85 90-91, Div 2 Cup 84-85 87-88 90-91, PG Cunningham Sportsmanship Trophy 82-83), Sussex Snr Cup 25-26, Sussex RUR Charity Cup 60-61(jt with Brighton & HA) 63-64, Sussex I'mediate Cup 67-68, West Sussex Lg (reserves) 66-67 (Div 1 45-46), Chich. Charity Cup 73-74, G C Hillier Mem. Tphy 1984+85+88+89+90, Coronation Cup 1989+90, Simmonds Cup 46-47 49-50 64-65 66-67, Sussex Yth Cup 88-89, Sussex Yth Lg (West) 88-89 89-90.

EASTBOURNE UNITED

President: Andrew Curry **Chairman:** Mr M Howell **Vice-Chairman:** Mr S Dorling
Secretary: Margaret Gygax, 63 Middleton Drive, Eastbourne, East Sussex BN23 6HD (0323 735672).
Manager: T Wood **Press Officer:** Steve Dorling (0323 724541).
Ground: The Oval, Channel View Rd, Eastbourne, East Sussex (0323 269989).
Directions: To seafront and turn left. Turn left into Channel View Rd at Princess Park and ground 1st right. 2 miles from Eastbourne (BR).
Seats: 160 **Cover:** 160 **Capacity:** 3,000 **Floodlights:** Yes **Founded:** 1894
Colours: White/black/black **Change colours:** All tangerine **Nickname:** The "U's"
Programme: 36 pages **Editor:** Steve Dorling (0323 724541) **Metal Badges:** Yes
Record Gate: 11,000 at Lynchmere **Previous Ground:** Lynchmere
Prev. Name: Eastbourne Old Comrades **Reserve Team's League:** Sussex County Res. Div. (East).
Previous Leagues: Sussex Co. 21-28 35-56/ Metropolitan 56-64/ Athenian 64-77/ Isthmian 77-92.
Sponsors: Plan-a-Head **Clubhouse:** Bar, lounge, dancefloor, stage, tea bar, board room.
Midweek Matchday: Tuesday **Local Press:** Eastbourne Gazette + Herald, Evening Argus
Players progressing to Football League: B Salvage, T Funnell, M French.
Captain 93-94: Neil Ivemy **93-94 Top Scorer:** Steve Loughton.
Hons: Sussex Co. Lg 54-55, Sussex Snr Cup(5) 60-61 62-64 66-67 68-69 (R-up 89-90), Sussex RUR Charity Cup 55-56, Metropolitan Lg Cup 60-61, Athenian Lg Div 2 66-67 (Div 1 R-up 68-69), Sussex I'mediate Cup 65-66 68-69.

HASSOCKS

President: Maurice Boxall **Chairman:** Jim Goodrum
Secretary: Bob Preston, 65 Oak Hall, Burgess Hill, West Sussex RH15 0DA (0444 245695).
Manager: Nick Greenwood/ Peter Liddell **Press Off.:** Paul Elphick (0444 454492) **Physio:** Norman Dodds
Ground: The Beacon, Brighton Rd, Hassocks (0273 846040)
Directions: Off A273 Pyecombe-Burgess Hill 300yds south of Stonepound crossroads (B2116) to Hurstpierpoint or Hassocks.
Seats: None **Cover:** 100 **Capacity:** **Floodlights:** No **Founded:** 1902
Colours: Red/white/red **Change colours:** All yellow.
Programme: Yes **Editor:** Paul Elphick (0444 454492) **Admission:** £1.50 **Metal Badges:** No.
Previous Leagues: Mid Sussex/ Brighton Hove & Dist./ Southern Co's Comb. **Nickname:** Robins
Record Gate: 340 v Bognor Regis Town, Sussex Senior Cup 92-93. *At previous ground: 400 v Nottingham University, AFA Snr Cup January 1978.*
Midweek Matchday: Wednesday **Clubhouse:** Clubroom, bar, kitchen.
Sponsors: Benwood Copiers **Local Press:** Burgess Hill Times, Evening Argus
93-94 Top Scorer: Robbie Kitchen **Previous Ground:** Adastra Park, Hassocks (pre-1992).
Captain 93-94: Adam Booth **Player of the Year 93-94:** Stuart Agate.
Hons: Sussex County Lg Div 3 91-92 (Res. Sect. East R-up 92-93), Southern Counties Comb. 76-77 (Lg Cup 79-80), Brighton Hove & Dist. Lg 71-72, Sussex Intermediate Cup 74-75 (R-up 80-81), Mid-Sussex Snr Cup R-up 93-94(reserves), Mid-Sussex Lg Div 7 93-94('B' team).

HORSHAM Y.M.C.A.

President: Gordon Head **Chairman:** John Cashman **Manager:** John Suter
Secretary/Press Off.: Bill Bower, 5 Patching Close, Ifield, Crawley, West Sussex RH11 0ES (0293 533831).
Ground: Gorings Mead, Horsham, West Sussex (0403 252689).
Directions: At end of lane at rear of Horsham FC (see page 506). Half mile from Horsham (BR).
Seats: 100 **Cover:** 200 **Capacity:** 800 **Floodlights:** Yes **Founded:** 1898
Colours: White/black/red **Change colours:** All red **Nickname:** "YM's"
Programme: Yes **Editor:** B Denyer (0403 741401) **Metal Badges:** No (ties + jumpers)
Record Gate: 600 v Horsham, FA Cup **Previous Ground:** Lyons Field, Kings Rd **Admission:** £1.50
Clubhouse: Bar, kitchen, main hall, bar, committee room.
Previous League: Horsham & District/ Brighton Hove & District/ Mid Sussex.
Sponsors: Principal Copiers/ Swift Surveying Services Ltd. **Midweek Matchday:** Tuesday
Local Newspaper: West Sussex County Times **93-94 Top Scorer:** Paul Crimmen 10.
Hons: Sussex Co. Lg Div 2 65-66 82-83 (Lg Cup 81-82, Invitation Cup 66-67 67-68, Div 2 Invitation Cup 59-60 61-62, Reserve Section West R-up).

LANCING

President: R G Steele **Chairman:** R J Brown
Secretary: J Chisnall, 15 Orchard Way, Lancing, West Sussex BN15 9ED (0903 763048).
Manager: G Russell **Physio:** Malcolm Stuart.
Commercial Manager: John Vallis **Press Officer:** John Rea (0903 761142).
Ground: Culver Road, Lancing, West Sussex (0903 764398).
Directions: Third turning left north of Lancing station (BR).
Seats: 350 **Cover:** 350 **Capacity:** 2,400 **Floodlights:** Yes **Founded:** 1941
Colours: Yellow/blue/yellow **Change colours:** All red **Nickname:** Yellows
Programme: Yes **Editor:** John Rea (0903 761142) **Sponsors:** Churchill Windows.
Previous Name: Lancing Athletic **Previous Ground:** Croshaw Rec, Sompting.
Local Press: Lancing Herald, Evening Argus.
Previous League: Brighton Hove & Dist. **Metal Badges:** No.
Record Gate: 2,591 v Tooting, FA Amtr Cup 22/11/47. At Culver Road: 2,340 v Worthing 25/10/52.
Midweek Matches: Wednesday **Clubhouse:** Run by Sussex F.A. Tea bar **Admission:** £1.50p
Captain 93-94: Mark Burt **93-94 Top Scorer:** Paul Burchell.
Hons: Sussex Co. Lg R-up 49-50 64-65 (Div 2 57-58 69-70 (R-up 82-83), Div 2 Cup 81-82 92-93, Invitation Cup), Sussex RUR Charity Cup 65-66, Brighton Lg 46-47 47-48, Sussex Intermediate Cup 46-47, Brighton Charity Cup 83-84 84-85 86-87.

LINGFIELD

Chairman: M Tomsett **Manager:** D Moore. **Coach:** T Charman.
Secretary: K Munns, 109 Saxbys Lane, Lingfield, Sussex RH7 6DP (0343 833735).
Ground: Godstone Rd, Lingfield (0342 834269). **Midweek matches:** Tues or Wed.
Seats: None **Cover:** 250 **Clubhouse:** Yes **Capacity:** 1,000 **Floodlights:** Yes
Colours: Scarlet & amber stripes/black/yellow **Prev. Lges:** Sussex County/ Mid-Sussex
Captain 93-94: I Tomsett **Top Scorer 93-94:** C Lilley.
Hons: Mid-Sussex Lg 92-93, Sussex Co. Lg Div 3 R-up 93-94 **Player of the Year 93-94:** C Desir

MILE OAK

Manager: Tony Gratwicke **Chairman:** R A Kearly **President:** D Bean
Secretary: C D Brown, 19 The Crescent, Southwick, West Sussex BN42 4LB (0273 591346).
Ground: Mile Oak Recreation Ground, Graham Avenue, Mile Oak (No telephone).
Directions: From A27 take Mile Oak Road or Locks Hill & Valley Road to Chalky Road, ground 500yds on right along Graham Avenue which runs up valley from centre of Chalky Road.
Seats: None **Cover:** Yes **Capacity:** **Floodlights:** No **Founded:** 1960
Colours: All tangerine **Change colours:** All white **Nickname:** The Oak
Programme: Yes **Editor:** C Tew (0273 881696) **Admission:** £1.50 **Metal Badges:** No
Previous Leagues: Southern Counties Combination/ Brighton Hove & District
Record Gate: 175 **Previous Ground:** Victoria Rec., Portslade.
Midweek Matchday: Tuesday **Clubhouse:** Mile Oak Pavillion; Hall and tea bar.
Sponsors: Lancing Glass Works Ltd **93-94 Top Scorer:** Neil Roberts 22
Local Press: Brighton Evening Argus, Shoreham Herald
Hons: Sussex Co. League Div 3 Runners-up 91-92 (Div 2 Cup Runners-up 92-93), Southern Counties Combination 86-87, Brighton Hove & District League 80-81, Vernon Wentworth Cup 85-86, Sussex Intermediate Cup Runners-up 88-89.

REDHILL

President: Malcolm Chatfield **Chairman:** John Park. **Vice-Chairman:** Brian Thomas
Secretary: Mr Neil Hoad, 'Braeside', 2b Earlswood Rd, Redhill, Surrey RH1 6HE (0737 766726).
Manager: Ray Purvis **Asst Manager:** Peter Burdett **Coach:** Doug Harmer
Physio: John Costick **Press Officer:** Ian Austen.
Ground: Kiln Brow, Three Arch Road, Redhill, Surrey (0737 762129).
Directions: On left hand side of A23, two and a half miles south of Redhill.
Seats: 100 **Cover:** 100 **Capacity:** 3,100 **Floodlights:** Yes **Founded:** 1894
Cols: Red & white stripes/white/red **Change colours:** White/black. **Metal Badges:** Yes
Club Shop: Yes, selling badges, sweatshirts, mugs, hats, scarves, pennants, teddy bears, key rings, car stickers, combs, pens, pencils, programmes etc. Contact Spencer Mitchell, 21 Colebrook Rd, Redhill RH1 2BL (0737 780634).
Record Gate: 1,200 v Crystal Palace & All Star XI, Brian Medlicott Testimonial 1989
Programme: 36 pages, 50p **Editor:** Eric Lee (0737 760708)
Nickname: Reds/Lobsters **Midweek home matchday:** Tuesday.
Sponsors: Pink's Gym. **Reserve Team's League:** Suburban League (South).
Previous Leagues: East West Surrey/ Spartan 09-10/ Southern Suburban/ London 21-23/ Athenian 23-84.
Local Newspaper: Surrey Mirror & The Independent.
Previous Grounds: Memorial Sports Ground, London Road 1894-1986.
Record win: 9-0; v Crown & Manor (H), London Spartan League 3/10/87; v Little Common Albion (H), Sussex County League Division Two 25/9/93.
Record defeat: 1-7 v Peacehaven & Telscombe (H), Sussex County League Cup 9/2/93.
Clubhouse: Social club, bar, canteen, board room, club shop, tanoy, toilets.
Club record scorer: Steve Turner 109 **Club record appearances:** Brian Medlicott 766.
Captain 93-94: Mark Endsleigh **93-94 Top Scorer:** David Fry **P.o.Y. 93-94:** Steve Smith.
Hons: FA Amtr Cup SF 25-25, FA Cup 1st Rd 57-58, Athenian League 24-25 83-84 (League Cup 69-70 70-71), Surrey Snr Cup 28-29, Gilbert Rice F'lit Cup 80-81, Sussex County League Div 2 Cup 91-92, Southern Co's Comb. Cup 90-91.

SALTDEAN UNITED

Chairman: Mike Walker **President:** Jim Bower
Secretary: I S Fielding, 40 Rowan Way, Rottingdean, Brighton BN2 7FP (0273 304995).
Manager: G Green **Asst Manager:** Martin Langley **Physio:** Mandy Carr
Coach: Dennis Maskell **Press Officer:** Julian Appleton.
Ground: Hill Park, Combe Vale, Saltdean, Brighton (0273 309898).
Directions: A259 coast road east from Brighton to Saltdean Lido, left into Arundel Drive West, and Saltdean Vale to bridle path at beginning of Combe Vale. Club 200yds along track.
Seats: 50 **Cover:** Yes **Capacity:** 2,000 **Floodlights:** No **Founded:** 1967
Colours: Red & black **Change colours:** Blue & yellow **Nickname:** Tigers
Programme: Yes **Editor:** T Clarke (0273 309898) **Admission:** £1.50 **Metal Bagdes:** No.
Record Gate: 250 **Previous Grounds:** None **Sponsors:** Sunley
Clubhouse: Licensed bar, lounge, juke box, video games, board room, tea bar.
Previous League: Brighton Hove & Dist. **Local Press:** Brighton Evening Argus.
Captain 93-94: Steve Eke **93-94 Top Scorer:** Phil Treagus.
P.o.Y. 93-94: Micky Brown **Hons:** Sussex Co. League Div 3 88-89.

SELSEY

Chairman: Derek Longworth **Manager:** D Kew/ G Peach **President:** Roy Glew
Secretary: Mr D C Lee, 29 Malthouse Cottages, West Wittering, Chichester, West Sussex PO20 8QJ (0243 513788).
Press Officer: Mr P Emms. **Ground:** High Street Ground, Selsey, Chichester, West Sussex (0243 603420)
Directions: B2145 from Chichester to Selsey, turn right by Fire Station. Regular buses from Chichester.
Seats: 50 **Cover:** Yes **Capacity:** 2,250 **Floodlights:** Yes **Founded:** 1923
Colours: Blue/white/blue **Change colours:** White/red/red **Metal Badges:** No
Programme Editor: Mrs D Hayers (0243 604013) **Admission:** £1.50 **Nickname:** Blues
Midweek Matchday: Wednesday **Record Gate:** 750-800 v Chichester or Portfield, 1950's
Clubhouse: Bar, hospitality room, lounge, toilets, kitchen. **Sponsors:** Allslade Welding & Fabrications Ltd
Local Newspapers: Chichester Observer, Evening Argus, Portsmouth Evening News.
93-94 Top Scorer: Neil Darnley 18 **Previous Leagues:** Chichester & Dist./ West Sussex.
Hons: Sussex Co. League Runners-up 89-90 (Div 2 63-64 75-76 (Runners-up 86-87), Div 2 Cup 86-87 (Runners-up 84-85), Div 2 Invitation Cup 63-64, Sussex 5-aside 88-89), Sussex Snr Cup Runners-up 63-64, Sussex I'mediate Cup 58-59, Sussex Jnr Cup(Reserves) 76-77, West Sussex League 54-55 55-56 57-58 58-59 60-61 (Malcolm Simmonds Cup 55-56 56-57 57-58 58-59).

SIDLEY UNITED

President: Tibby Adams **Chairman/Press Off.:** Peter Snow (0424 210974)
Manager: Steve Johnson **Secretary:** Jasper Yevell, 3 Mendip Gdns, Hastings, E. Sussex (0424 433951).
Ground: Gullivers Sports Ground, North Road, Glovers Lane, Sidley, Bexhill-on-Sea (0424 217078).
Directions: From Brighton on A259 to Bexhill bypass traffic lights, left into London Road, continue into Sidley, right into Glovers Lane and 1st left into North Road. One mile from Bexhill (BR).
Seats: None **Cover:** 150 **Capacity:** 1,500 **Floodlights:** No **Founded:** 1906
Colours: Royal & sky blue **Change colours:** All red **Nickname:** Blues
Programme: Yes **Editor:** Mr Peter Snow (0424 210974) **Admission:** £1.20 (50p OAP)
Previous Leagues: East Sussex/ Hastings & District **Metal Badges:** Yes
Record Gate: 1,300 in 1959 **Previous Grounds:** None. **Sponsors:** J Burke
Midweek Matchday: Tues/ Weds **Clubhouse:** Large bar area & function room. Tea bar.
93-94 Top Scorer: Kevin Bevis 30 **Local Press:** Bexhill Observer, Bexhill News
Hons: Suss. Co. Lg Div 2 58-59 64-65 (Div 2 Invit. Cup 57-58), Suss. I'mediate Cup 47-48, Suss. Jnr Cup 24-25.

STEYNING TOWN

President: R Head **Chairman:** I Kennett
Secretary: Mrs H Ellis, 1 Breach Close, Steyning, West Sussex BN44 3RZ (0903 816495).
Manager: B Paine **Asst Manager:** T Hatchett **Coach:** C Hutchings.
Ground: The Shooting Field, Steyning, West Sussex (0903 812228).
Directions: A27 east then A283 turn off - town centre turning at r'bout, right into Church Street, straight into Church Lane, straight into Shooting Field, ground on left by Grammar School. Bus 10 from Shoreham-by-Sea BR station stops at end of road.
Seats: None **Cover:** 400 **Capacity:** 2,000 **Floodlights:** Yes **Club Shop:** No.
Colours: Red/white/red **Change colours:** All blue **Founded:** 1900
Midweek home matchday: Wednesday **Record Gate:** 1,100 v Halesowen Town, FA Vase QF 84-85.
Previous Leagues: Sussex County 64-86/ Wessex 86-88/ Combined Counties 88-93.
Programme: 28 pages, 50p **Programme Editor:** B Owen (0403 253371).
Record win: 15-0 v Battle, 1968 **Record defeat:** 1-11 v Littlehampton Town, 1991.
Record transfer fee paid: Nil **Received:** £1,000 for Paul Walker (Wokingham, 1989).
Clubhouse: Tues-Fri 7-11pm, Sat 12-3 & 4.30-11pm, Sun 12-3 & 7-10.30pm. Snacks available.
Top Scorer 93-94: Julian Durrand 10.
Club record scorer: D Deans, 42 **Club record appearances:** N Manvell, 800.
Hons: FA Vase QF 84-85, Sussex Snr Cup 85-86 88-89, Sussex Co. Lg 84-85 85-86 (Lg Cup 77-78 83-84 85-86, Div 2 Invitation Cup 65-66, Reserve Section West 88-89), Sussex RUR Charity Cup 79-80, Vernon Wentworth Cup 33-34, Sussex Jnr Cup 01-02 37-38.

STORRINGTON

President: D Medhurst **Chairman:** A Massimo.
Secretary: K Dalmon, 4 End Cottages, Storrington Rd, Amberley, Arundel, West Sussex BN18 9LX (0798 831887).
Manager: A Massimo/ F Massimo **Press Officer:** T Brookes.
Ground: Recreation Ground, Pulborough Road, Storrington (0903 745860).
Directions: Turn west on A283 (off A24). Ground opposite pond to the west of the village
Seats: None **Cover:** Yes **Nickname:** Swans **Floodlights:** No **Founded:** 1920
Colours: All blue **Change colours:** White/navy/navy
Programme: Yes **Editor:** TBA **Previous Leagues:** Worthing/ W Sussex.
Previous Grounds: None **Sponsors:** The White Horse, The Square, Storrington
Clubhouse: Clubroom with bar, dressing rooms & toilets
Local Newspapers: Chanctonbury Herald, Horsham County Times.
93-94 Top Scorer: Eamonn Searle 12 **Hons:** Sussex Co. Lg Div 3 R-up 92-93, Worthing Lg(3).

WITHDEAN

Chairman: Keith Turrell **Vice-Chairman:** Rob Ketcher **President:** Graham Spicer
Secretary: Dave J Gunstone, 285 Brighton Rd, Lancing, West Sussex BN15 8JR (0903 750083).
Manager: Derek Tharme. **Assistant Manager:** Stan Hunt.
Ground: Withdean Stadium, off Valley Drive, Brighton (0703 551638).
Directions: Off main London - Brighton road.
Seats: 1,000 **Cover:** Due **Capacity:** 10,000 **Floodlights:** No **Founded:** 1984.
Colours: Red/blue/blue **Change Colours:** All white **Metal Badges:** No.
Programme Editor: Dave Bull **Clubhouse:** Pub on ground **Club Shop:** No.
Previous Ground: Council pitch. **Previous Leagues:** Brighton Hove & District
Midweek Matchday: **Local Newspaper:** Brighton Evening Argus
93-94 Top Scorer: Dave Agnew **Player of the Year 93-94:** Colin Wood.
Sponsors: Express Computers Consultants Ltd.
Hons: Sussex Co. Lg Div 3 92-93 (Div 3 Cup 91-92).

WORTHING UNITED

President: Ken Higson **Chairman:** Mr L Newbon
Secretary: Mr Malcolm Gamlen, 1 Westbourne Ave., Worthing, West Sussex BN14 8DE (0903 263655).
Manager: Mr Brian Woolmer **Press Officer:** Mr Brian Woolmer.
Ground: Beeches Avenue, Lyons Way, Worthing, West Sussex (0903 234466).
Directions: From west on A27, Beeches Avenue is 4th left past Barn Hill r'bout. From east take 2nd left past lights at Downlands Hotel and proceed to Beeches Avenue - go to and follow concrete road to cap park.
Seats: 100 **Cover:** 500 **Capacity:** 1,000 **Floodlights:** No **Founded:** 1988
Colours: Sky & white **Change colours:** All white **Nickname:** None
Programme: Yes **Editor:** N Woolmer (0903 772698) **Sponsors:** Tinsley Robor.
Previous Names: Wigmore Athletic (founded 1948) merged with Southdown in 1988.
Previous Leagues: **Previous Grounds:** Harrison Road, Worthing.
Midweek Matches: **Record Gate:** 180 v Northwood, FA Vase 3rd Rd 91-92.
Clubhouse: Bar (capacity 80), refreshment facilities (tea bar). **Metal badges:** Yes
Admission: £1.50 (75p OAP & children).
Local Newspapers: Worthing Herald. **93-94 Top Scorer:** Steve Gurney 12
Hons: *As Wigmore Athletic prior to 1988.* Sussex Co. Lg Challenge Cup 74-75 (Invitation Cup 59-60, Div 2 52-53, Div 2 Invitation Cup 59-60, Div 3 89-90, Reserve Section West 92-93, 5-aside comp. R-up 1993), Sussex Jnr Cup 49-50.

DIVISION THREE CLUBS 1994-95

BUXTED

President: C S Winter **Chairman:** K Isted
Secretary: P J Durrant, 'Haven', Station Rd, Isfield, East Sussex TN22 5XB (0825 750449).
Mgr/Press Off.: P Neal **Asst Manager:** G Lucas **Comm. Manager:** K Miles.
Ground: Buxted Recreation Ground, Framfield Road, Buxted (0825 812431).
Directions: A272 to Buxted, under rail bridge, first right into Framfield Rd opposite Buxted Inn, ground 250 yds on right. Railway station with hourly service 500yds from ground.
Seats: None **Cover:** No **Floodlights:** No **Founded:** 1918 **Nickname:** The Bux.
Previous Grounds: None **Colours:** Red & black halves/black/black & red
Reserves' Lge: Mid-Sussex **Change colours:** Blue & white stripes/blue/blue
Programme: 16 pages, 30p **Editor:** Ken Isted (0825 763593) **Club Shop:** No.
Sponsors: Crowson Fabrics **Midweek home matchday:** Tuesday.
Previous Leagues: Hailsham/ Brighton Hove & District (pre-1982)/ Mid Sussex 82-89.
Record win: 32-0 v Kings Head (Cuckfield), Lewes & District Sunday League.
Clubhouse: Pavillion with social area and bar, Tea bar. Open from one hour before kick-off until 11pm. Food: Pies, chips, crisps, peanuts, chocolate bars.
Local Newspapers: The Courier, Sussex Express
Captain 93-94: Keith West **93-94 Top Scorer:** Lee Wooden 15 **P.o.Y. 93-94:** Paul Divall
Honours: Mid-Sussex Lg 86-87 88-89, Brighton Lg R-up 77-78, Montgomery Cup 83-84 84-85 88-89.

EAST PRESTON

President: Greg Stanley **Chairman:** Dennis Cooper **Vice-Chairman:** Don Pryke.
Secretary: Keith Freeman, 41 Ambersham Cres., East Preston, West Sussex BN16 1AJ (0903 771158).
Manager: John Finneran **Assistant Manager:** Ian Cole.
Coach: Adie Cooper **Physio:** Natasha Finneran.
Ground: Roundstone Rrecreation Ground, East Preston, West Sussex (0903 776026).
Directions: Less than a mile from Angmering (BR) station. A259 from Worthing to Roundstone Hotel (6 miles), turn south over railway crossing, left past Centurion garage, right into Roundstone Drive.
Seats: None **Cover:** 40 **Capacity:** **Floodlights:** No **Reformed:** 1966
Colours: White/black/black **Change:** Green/sky/sky **Nickname:** None
Programme: Yes, six pages **Editor:** Mick Miles (0903 787615) **Sponsors:** Focus DIY
Previous Lges: Worthing/ W Sussex **Reserve Team's League:** Unijet Sussex Co. Res. Div (West).
Clubhouse details: 4 dressing rooms. Licensed bar open Tues-Fri evenings, Sat noon-3pm, Sun noon-3 & 7-11pm. Kitchen serves light refreshments on matchdays.
Captain 93-94: Robert Leggett **Local Press:** Littlehampton Gazette.
Top Scorer 93-94: Ian Cole 38 **Player of the Year 93-94:** Gary Standing.
Hons: Sussex Co. Lg Div 3 83-84 (R-up 90-91, Div 3 Cup 87-88 (R-up 89-90)), West Sussex Lg 77-78 80-81 81-82 82-83 (Malcolm Simmonds Cup 80-81 82-83, Div 2 Sth 81-82, Div 3 Sth 79-80, Div 5 Sth 82-83, Chichester Cup 87-88, Div 4 Cup 86-87, Boreham Tphy 77-78 90-91 (R-up 93-94)), Vernon Wentworth Cup 80-81 89-90, Worthing Lg 67-68 (Div 2 68-69(res), Benev. Tphy 66-67 68-69), Worthing Charity Cup 68-69.

EDWARDS SPORTS

Chairman: M Weever **Manager:** Chris Lenson.
Secretary: Mr McQueenie, 119 Trefoil Cres., Crawley RH11 9EY (0293 549666).
Ground: Edwards Sports Ground, Ifield, Crawley.
Directions: Follow signs to Ifield off A23, over mini-r'bout to Ifield Ave., 3rd left into Ifield Green.
Seats: None **Cover:** Yes **Prev. Lge:** Crawley & Dist. (pre-1993) **Floodlights:** No
Colours: Red & black/black/black **Hons:** Crawley & D. Lg 92-93. **Top Scorer 93-94:** Paul Gurd 14.

FOREST

Chairman/Press Officer: Graham Powell (0403 273169).
Secretary: Mrs Gill Holtquist, 2 Woodside, Horsham, West Sussex RH13 5UF (0403 267154).
Manager: Colin Johnson **Physio:** Rob Nevins.
Ground: Roffey Sports Social Club, Spooners Road, Roffey, Horsham, West Sussex (0403 210223).
Directions: Spooners Rd off main Crawley Rd, approx 100yds from the Fitzalian Arms heading towards Crawley.
Seats: No **Cover:** 250 **Capacity:** 1,000 **Floodlights:** No **Founded:** 1958
Colours: All blue & white **Change colours:** Green/yellow **Metal Badges:** No.
Programme: Yes **Programme Editor:** Graham Powell (0403 273169)
Previous Leagues: Crawley/ Southern Co's Comb./Mid-Sussex **Reserves' Lge:** West Sussex
Local Newspapers: West Sussex County Times. **Previous Ground:** Forest Boys School.
Sponsors: Roffey Sports & Social Club **Record Gate:** Unknown. **Nickname:** None
Clubhouse: 2 large bars/ snooker room (3 tables)/ bar billiards/ darts/ pool/ board room/ tea bar.
Record Scorer: Neil Liley 195 **Club Record Appearances:** Colin Johnson 373.
Captain 93-94: Danny Lucas **P.o.Y. 93-94:** Grahame Funnell **93-94 Top Scorers:** Micky Fairs 15.
Hons: Mid-Sussex Lg 87-88 (Montgomery Cup 87-88), Horsham Floodlit Cup 83-84 84-85, Mid-Sussex Snr Charity Cup 76-77 84-85 85-86 86-87 89-90, Sussex I'mediate Cup 87-88, Crawley Lg 76-77 (Div 1 64-65 73-74, Div 3 63-64 68-69, Crawley Charity Shield 67-68 75-76, Crawley Jubilee Cup 76-77).

FRANKLANDS VILLAGE

President: J Rutherford **Chairman:** P Gaston
Secretary: Mr N J Worsfold, Flat 3, 5 Sydney Rd, Haywards Heath, West Sussex RH16 1QQ (0444 415331).
Manager: P Batchelor **Press Officer:** Mr R Collins.
Ground: Hardy Memorial Playing Fields, Franklands Village, Haywards Heath, West Sussex (0444 440138).
Directions: A272 H. Heath to Uckfield road, left at Birch Service Station which leads down to the village.
Seats: No **Cover:** 400 sq ft. **Capacity:** N/A **Floodlights:** No **Founded:** 1956
Colours: All royal blue **Change colours:** Gold & black **Nickname:** None.
Programme: Yes **Editor:** Mrs L Worsfold (0444 416475) **Midweek Midweek:** Wednesday
Previous Leagues: Mid Sussex/ Crawley/ Brighton Hove & District/ Southern Counties Combination.
Clubhouse details: Franklands Village Social Club. Bar, function room, pool, snooker room, games room, committe room, darts, television, tea bar.
Previous Grounds: None **Record Gate:** 500 **Admission:** N/A **Metal Badges:** No
Local Newspapers: Mid Sussex Times. **93-94 Top Scorer:** Mark Ormandroyd 15 **Sponsors:** Abacus.
Hons: Brighton Lg 76-77 78-79, Sussex Co. Lg Div 3 R-up (Div 3 Cup 88-89 92-93), Southern Co's Comb. 82-83, Mid-Sussex Charity Cup 79-80 80-81 82-83 88-89, Sussex Intermediate Cup 88-89.

HAYWARDS HEATH TOWN

Manager: Grant Paskins **President:** Tony Lander **Chairman:** Alan Jenkins.
Secretary: Stan Barnes, 'Fairfields', London Rd, Hassocks, West Sussex BN6 9NE (0444 235192).
Ground: Hanbury Park Stadium, Allen Road, Haywards Heath, West Sussex (0444 412837).
Directions: A272 to Haywards Heath town centre. At Sussex r'bout, north on B2078 (Hazelgrove Road), first right into New England Road, 4th right into Allen Road which leads to ground. 1 mile from Haywards Heath (BR).
Seats: 490 **Cover:** 490 **Capacity:** 5,000 **Floodlights:** Yes **Founded:** 1888
Colours: White (blue trim)/blue/blue **Change colours:** All yellow **Nickname:** Bluebells
Programme: Yes **Editor:** Pat Bucknell (0444 457726) **Admission:** £1.50 **Sponsors:**
Previous Leagues: Mid Sussex/ Metropolitan 52-61. **Metal Badges:** No.
Previous Grounds: Muster Green/ Haywards Heath Recreation Ground/ Victoria Park.
Previous Names: Haywards Heath Junior/ Haywards Heath Excelsoir/ Haywards Heath FC 1895-1988.
Record Gate: 4,000 v Horsham, Metropolitan League, 1952.
Local Newspaper: Mid Sussex Times **Clubhouse:** Bar, small dance floor, pool.
93-94 Top Scorer: Simon Ellis/ Martin Smith - 10 each.
Hons: Sussex Snr Cup 57-58, Sussex RUR Charity Cup 66-67 74-75 75-76, Sussex Co. League 45-46 49-50 50-51 69-70 (R-up 74-75, League Cup 72-73), Mid Sussex League 11-12 19-20 22-23 23-24 24-25, Montgomery Cup 19-20 22-23 24-25.

HURSTPIERPOINT

President: **Chairman:** W Marchant **Manager:** Steve Chambers
Secretary/Press Officer: Paul John, 16 Church Close, Burgess Hill, West Sussex RH15 8EZ (0444 247183).
Manager: Simon Marchant **Coach:** Roger Chapman **Physio:** Mike Yaxley
Ground: The Pavilion, Fairfield Recreation Ground, Cuckfield Rd, Hurstpierpoint, Sussex (0273 834785).
Directions: At Hurst crossroads (mini r'bout) proceed north into Cuckfield Rd (B2117) for 1km. Entrance to ground between houses Nos 158 & 160.
Seats: None **Cover:** No **Floodlights:** No **Nickname:** The Point **Founded:** 1886
Colours: Blue & black stripes/blue/blue **Change:** Yellow/green/yellow.
Programme: 8 pages **Editor:** Matthew Bosher (0273 835290) **Midweek Matchday:** Tuesday
Previous Leagues: Mid Sussex/ Brighton Hove & District/ Southern Counties Combination.
Sponsors: Picket & White. **Reserve Team's League:** Mid-Sussex.
Record win: 10-0 v Sidlesham, Sussex County League Division Three 18/12/93.
Clubhouse: Facilities for refreshments including licenced premises and tea bar.
Local Newspapers: Mid Sussex Times, West Sussex County Times **Metal Badges:** No
Record scorer: Mark Stafford **Record appearances:** David Packham
Captain 93-94: Timothy Stevens **Top scorer & Player of the Year 93-94:** Danny Bryan (31 goals)

IFIELD

President: Brian Crossley **Chairman:** Bert Morton
Secretary: Rob Anderson, 15 Sissinghurst Close, Pound Hill, Crawley, West Sussex RH10 7FX (0293 886215).
Manager: Ali Rennie **Assistant Manager:** Robbie Bicker.
Physio: Ron Parsons **Press Officer:** Geoff Thornton.
Ground: Ifield Green, Rusper Rd, Ifield, Crawley (0293 536569).
Directions: From Ifield BR station follow Ifield Drive, 2nd left into Rudgwick Rd, turn right, ground 600 yds on left.
Seats/Cover: No **Capacity:** 1,000 **Nickname:** Villagers **Floodlights:** No **Founded:** 1950.
Colours: Red & white/black/black **Change colours:** Blue & white/black **Metal Badges:** No
Programme: 24 pages, free **Editor:** Geoff Thornton (0293 531911)
Midweek Matchday: Wednesday **Sponsors:** AM Turnham, Building Contractor.
Previous Grounds: None **Previous Leagues:** Redhill 50-53/ Crawley & Dist. 53-84
Reserves' Lge: West Sussex **Record Gate:** 117 v Edwards Spts, Sussex Co. Lge Div 3 20/4/94.
Record win: 14-0 v Lavant (H), Sussex Intermediate Cup Second Round, 26/9/92.
Record defeat: 1-7 v Worthing United (A), Sussex County League Division Three, 26/8/89.
Clubhouse: Open 7-11pm evenings and noon-11pm matchdays. Snacks & rolls available. Pool, darts, Sky TV.
Local Press: Crawley News, Crawley Observer
Record Scorer: Des Lyons 158 **Record appearances:** Steve Corbett 525.
Captain 93-94: Mark Russell **P.o.Y. 93-94:** Keith Cook **93-94 Top Scorer:** Des Lyons 38.
Hons: Sussex County League Div 3 90-91 (Div 3 Cup 93-94), Mid-Sussex Snr Cup 73-74, Crawley League 73-74, Crawley Senior Cup 83-84.

LITTLE COMMON ALBION

Chairman/Manager: K E Cherry **President:** Councillor Ivor Brampton.
Secretary: Mrs M Cherry, 11 Bidwell Avenue, Bexhill-on-Sea, East Sussex TN39 4DB (0424 217191).
Ground: Little Common Rec., Pear Tree Lane, Little Common, East Sussex (0424 35861)
Directions: A259 from Brighton.
Seats: None **Cover:** 250 **Capacity:** **Floodlights:** No **Founded:** 1960
Colours: Claret & blue **Change colours:** White & blue **Nickname:** Common
Programme: Yes **Editor:** Chas Tibbutt (0424 713757) **Admission:** £1.50 **Metal Badges:** No.
Record Gate: 251 **Clubhouse:** Bar, clubroom, tea bar **Midweek Matchday:** Wednesday
Local Newspapers: Bexhill Observer **Previous League:** East Sussex
Sponsors: D Scotcher. **93-94 Top Scorer:** Tyson Bennett 7.
Hons: East Sussex League(2) 75-77 (League Cup 76-77), Hastings Intermediate Cup 76-77, Hawkhurst Challenge Cup 75-76 76-77, Sussex Minor Cup 75-76, Sussex County League PG Cunningham Sportsmanship Award 92-93.

LINDFIELD RANGERS

Manager: Mr Dave Richardson **Chairman:** Squadron Ldr B F Ryan **President:** N Fisk
Secretary: Mr P Fisk, Dormer Cottage, 64 Oathall Rd, Haywards Heath (0444 412112).
Press Officer: R Tilford (0825 763737). **Ground:** Underhill Lane, Clayton, East Sussex.
Directions: A23 from Brighton to Pycombe Garage, right onto Burgess Hill Rd, at bottom of Pycombe Hill turn right into ground.
Seats: None **Cover:** No **Nickname:** None **Floodlights:** No **Founded:** 1983.
Colours: Red/white/red **Change colours:** Blue & white hoops **Metal Badges:** No
Programme: **Midweek Matchday:** **Sponsors:** Trident Copiers.
Previous Leagues: Crawley & District/ Mid Sussex (pre-1991).
Previous Ground: Hickmans Lane, Lindfield. **Clubhouse:** Tea bar.
93-94 Top Scorer: Richard Tilford **Hons:** Mid Sussex Lg 90-91

MIDHURST & EASEBOURNE

Chairman: Pat Perry **President:** Andy Robertson.
Secretary: Ted Dummer, 14 Nine Acres, June Lane, Midhurst, West Sussex GU29 9EP (0730 813887).
Manager: Stuart Groves **Assistant Manager:** Wayne Hyde.
Press Officer: Rex Lane (0730 812839).
Ground: Rotherfield, Dodsley Lane, Easebourne, Midhurst, West Sussex (0730 816557)
Directions: Ground one mile out of Midhurst on London Road (A286) opposite BP Garage. Ample car parking. Buses pass ground every hour.
Seats: 60 **Cover:** 200 **Capacity:** 800 **Floodlights:** No **Founded:** 1946
Colours: All royal blue **Change colours:** Red/black/black **Nickname:** None
Programme: 8 pages, free **Editor:** Secretary **Club Shop:** No.
Reserves' Lge: Sussex Co. Res. sect. **Record Gate:** 300 in local Gingell Cup, 1989.
Clubhouse: Clubhouse with canteen and bar. Open matchdays & training nights only.
Previous Grounds: None **Sponsors:** Frankform International.
Local Press: Midhurst & Petworth Observer. West Sussex Gazette
Previous Leagues: West Sussex 46-79/ Southern Co's Combination 79-81.
Players progressing to Football League: Colin Gibson (Aston Villa, Man Utd, Leicester).
P.o.Y. 93-94: Adrian Holden **Captain & Top Scorer 93-94:** Michael Steele.
Hons: Sussex Co. Lg Div 2 R-up 81-82 91-92 (Div 2 Cup 88-89), Southern Co's Comb. Div 2 80-81 (Chal. Cup 80-81), W Sussex Lg 67-68 76-77 79-80 (Div 1 55-56 62-63 64-65, Malcolm Simmonds Cup 59-60 73-74 77-78 79-80, Bareham Tphy 70-71), Sussex I'mediate Cup(5) 54-57 62-63 77-78.

St FRANCIS HOSPITAL

President: Brian Pate **Chairman:** Phil Gaffney **Vice-Chairman:** Vic Stevens.
Secretary: Mr E Toner, 3 Catkin Way, Haywards Heath, West Sussex RH16 5TU (0444 457798).
Manager: Glenn Morgan **Asst Mgr:** Claudio Sutherland **Coach:** Craig Stewart.
Physio: Jimmy McQ. **Press Officer:** Glenn Morgan (0444 454016).
Ground: 'Downsview', Princess Royal Hospital, Haywards Heath, West Sussex RH16 4EZ.
Directions: Entering Haywards Heath from any direction follow signs to Princess Royal Hospital. On entering PRH follow signs to Sports Complex - football pitch is behind swimming pool. Buses on the hour from Haywards Heath station.
Seats: None **Cover:** None **Capacity:** 600 **Floodlights:** No **Founded:** 1890.
Colours: Green & white **Change:** Blue & black stripes/blue/blue **Nickname:** Saints
Previous Grounds: None **Local Newspaper:** Mid-Sussex Times. **Metal badges:** No
Programme: 12 pages, 50p **Editor:** Glenn Morgen (0444 454016) **Club Shop:** No
Sponsors: Murphys Irish Stout **Previous Lges:** Brighton/ Sussex County/ Mid Sussex (pre-1992).
Reserves' Lge: Mid-Sussex **Record Gate:** 240 in a Sussex Co. Div 3 fixture, December 1993.
Record win: 15-0 v Kingstonians, Brighton League 1982.
Record defeat: 0-11 v Franklands Village, 1980.
Record transfer fee: Four barrels of Guinness.
Clubhouse: Very active clubhouse 200yds from ground open daily 7-11pm. Food on Saturdays after matches. Pool, darts, snooker, table tennis, bowls, hockey, tennis, swimming pool and drama section which includes most of the football team.
Club record scorer: Simon Hatton **Club record appearances:** Jim Sheils (retired).
Captain 93-94: Steve King **P.o.Y. 93-94:** Paul Strangeman **Top Scorer 93-94:** Tim Dunne.
Hons: Sussex Intermediate Cup R-up, Mid-Sussex Senior Charity Cup.

SEAFORD TOWN

President: J V Tanner **Chairman:** Fred Gillman **Mgr:** Dave Shearing.
Secretary: Mick Webster, 113 Lexden Drive, Seaford, East Sussex BN25 3JF (0323 899218).
Ground: Crouch Gardens, East Street, Seaford, East Sussex (0323 892221).
Directions: Enter Seaford on A259 and turn into Warwick Road (opposite Library), continue into East Street. Ground along Crouch Lane (by phone box). Third of a mile from Seaford (BR).
Seats: 50 **Cover:** 50 **Capacity:** 1,000 **Floodlights:** No **Founded:** 1889
Colours: All red **Change colours:** All blue **Metal Badges:** No. **Nickname:** Town
Programme: Yes **Editor:** Secretary **Sponsors:** TBA **Previous Name or Grounds:** None.
Previous Leagues: Sussex 01-02/ Mid-Sussex 02-52/ Sussex County 52-78/ Southern Counties Combination/ Brighton Hove & District.
Midweek Matches: Tuesday **Record Gate:** 800 v Brighton & HA 16/8/89.
Clubhouse: Tea Bar, Licensed bar. Pool, darts **Admission:** £1
Local Newspapers: Seaford Gazette, Sussex Express.
93-94 Top Scorer: Anthony Mills.
Hons: Sussex Co. Lg Invitation Cup 58-59 (Div 2 88-89 (R-up 63-64), Div 3 85-86, Div 3 Cup 85-86), Sussex Jnr Cup 09-10, Brighton Lg Div 1 80-81, Sussex RUR Charity Cup R-up 73-74, Montgomery Cup 35-36 38-39.

SHINEWATER ASSOCIATION

President: A Rose **Chairman:** S Courtney **Vice-Chairman:** J Pinyoun
Secretary: B Dowling, 79 Harebeating Drive, Hailsham, East Sussex BN27 1JE (0323 442488).
Manager: A Walsh **Physio:** P Fear.
Press Officer: A Holman **Commercial Manager:** G Pinyoun.
Ground: Shinewater Lane, Milfoil Drive, North Langney, Eastbourne, East Sussex.
Directions: A27, B2104 to Eastbourne at Stone Cross, under railway bridge, 1st left Larkspur Drive, 1st left Milfoil Drive, 3rd left Shinewater Lane.
Seats: None **Cover:** None **N'name:** The Shine **Capacity:** 2,000 **Floodlights:** No
Colours: Sky/navy/navy **Change colours:** All yellow **Admission:** None
Programme: 24 pages, 50p **Programme Editor:** Secretary **Metal Badges:** Yes.
Previous Grounds: None **Previous Leagues:** East Sussex. **Sponsors:** Trimseal
Record Gate: 110 v St Francis Hospital, Sussex County League Division Three 26/4/94.
Record win: 13-4 Eastbourne Challenge Cup 26/11/93.
Record defeat: 1-6 v Tenterden & St Michaels 10/4/91.
Local Press: Eastbourne Herald, Eastbourne Gazette.
Clubhouse: Open matchdays 10am-10pm. Breakfast, pies, hotdogs, burgers.
Record Scorer: S Pettitt **Record appearances:** C Dowling, 128.
Top Scorer 93-94: G Osborne **Player of the Year:** G Smith.
Captain 93-94: G Holder. **Hons:** E Sussex Lg 91-92, Eastbourne Chal. Cup 91-92 93-94.

SIDLESHAM

Manager: P Cleverley **President:** Cyril Cooper **Chairman:** Roy Parker
Secretary: Mr Peter Turner, 14 Ashurst Close, North Bersted, Bognor Regis PO21 5UJ (0243 867970).
Ground: The Recreation Ground, Sidlesham, West Sussex (0243 641538). **Directions:** Signposted Hunston/Selsey (B2145) - from r'bout travel south towards Selsey for four miles; ground on right between houses.
Seats: None **Cover:** 100 **Nickname:** None **Floodlights:** Yes **Reformed:** 1946.
Colours: Yellow & green stripes/black/black **Change colours:** All blue
Programme: Yes **Editor:** Mr Patrick Phillips (0243 603028) **Previous Grounds:** None.
Midweek Matchday: Wednesday
Local Press: Chichester Observer **Previous Leagues:** West Sussex (pre-1991).
Clubhouse: Large bar, separate function room, snooker room, board room, tea bar (food).
Metal Badges: No **Sponsors:** TBA **Record Gate:** 120 **93-94 Top Scorer:** Christopher Walder 11.
Hons: Sussex Co. Lg Div 3 Cup 91-92, Malcolm Simmonds Cup 78-79 90-91, Sussex I'mediate Cup 90-91.

SUNALLON

Manager: M Roberts **Chairman:** B Goring.
Secretary: D Roberts, 6 Foxley Chase, Horsham, West Sussex RH12 4AX (0403 260033).
Ground: Meadowlands, North Heath Lane, Horsham, West Sussex (0403 253814).
Directions: Into Horsham on Warnham Rd, left at lights, over mini-r'bout into North Heath Lane, ground on left. Twenty minutes walk from Horsham BR station.
Seats: None **Cover:** None **Floodlights:** No **Clubhouse:** Yes **Programme:** Yes
Colours: Yellow/blue/blue **Top Scorer 93-94:** Dean Lewis 14.
Hons: West Sussex Lg 92-93. **Previous Leagues:** West Sussex (pre-1993)

DIVISION ONE ATTENDANCES 1993-94

HOME TEAM	1	2	3	4	5	6	7	8	9	10	11	12	13	14	15	16	17	18	19	20	total
1. ARUNDEL	*	49	57	56	61	60	46	57	87	135	55	40	44	57	51	59	65	61	117	210	1367
2. BEXHILL	68	*	110	108	88	85	140	170	153	114	60	62	86	40	72	80	445	85	82	77	2125
3. BURGESS HT	90	123	*	133	75	136	156	115	116	134	79	46	77	159	81	117	105	185	100	210	2237
4. CHICHESTER	42	70	75	*	60	65	65	80	80	225	85	95	85	95	125	50	80	65	85	120	1627
5. CROWBORO.	84	90	99	80	*	125	97	130	108	117	85	82	92	180	95	83	170	110	92	88	2007
6. E GRINSTEAD	65	154	155	62	183	*	168	178	100	103	147	218	120	96	38	100	65	79	103	125	2259
7. EASTBNE T.	98	96	110	97	130	154	*	355	385	105	170	70	110	110	103	120	235	108	103	85	2744
8. HAILSHAM	157	196	350	283	269	226	295	*	785	152	204	258	282	289	209	247	214	190	195	325	5128
9. LANGNEY	176	130	173	90	130	147	360	620	*	135	100	180	120	127	160	145	300	200	170	244	3707
10. L'HAMPTON	280	75	66	120	124	105	105	305	152	*	173	63	177	143	146	120	110	105	134	232	2739
11. NEWHAVEN	100	100	80	60	140	110	100	230	100	80	*	100	90	250	90	140	150	100	85	200	2305
12. OAKWOOD	50	90	144	50	95	70	76	110	66	60	42	*	50	53	56	76	60	263	100	70	1582
13. PAGHAM	80	60	130	140	80	150	50	110	40	84	100	75	*	35	100	98	140	73	110	210	1865
14. PEACEHAVEN	85	107	178	84	91	139	141	242	164	131	209	100	103	*	102	206	159	99	276	189	2807
15. PORTFIELD	60	40	60	230	43	35	35	60	45	130	36	48	59	36	*	54	42	35	40	75	1163
16. RINGMER	95	75	117	58	141	125	101	134	178	73	103	65	62	33	70	*	78	91	98	92	1809
17. STAMCO	120	142	53	46	96	58	265	322	98	119	60	142	49	520	98	57	*	55	51	194	2545
18. THREE BRIDGES	28	35	59	64	183	114	89	34	56	73	83	164	62	110	38	68	95	*	134	87	1576
19. WHITEHAWK	106	70	200	100	100	110	106	100	75	150	60	100	46	200	75	100	120	150	*	200	2168
20. WICK	110	93	125	83	85	65	120	120	102	150	110	80	160	105	124	90	150	60	175	*	2107

Highest Gate: 785 - Hailsham Town v Langney Sports. **Highest Average:** 270 - Hailsham Town.

DIV. 2 GATES	1	2	3	4	5	6	7	8	9	10	11	12	13	14	15	16	17	18	total
1. B'BDGE HTH	*	43	35	78	42	53	87	43	63	35	32	70	28	65	82	85	45	35	923
2. EASTBNE UTD	58	*	43	93	74	62	59	123	109	142	62	56	146	65	62	42	59	45	1302
3. HASSOCKS	62	70	*	75	95	109	117	63	137	42	123	112	55	92	172	80	103	70	1577
4. HORS. YMCA	127	65	51	*	69	41	69	46	96	46	40	170	43	80	78	65	53	81	1222
5. LANCING	57	70	65	60	*	83	83	62	49	69	61	124	54	96	82	120	88	172	1365
6. L. COMMON	40	86	40	20	26	*	30	60	25	30	30	45	120	60	30	23	30	80	775
7. MIDHURST	80	50	70	120	40	60	*	70	70	70	80	100	80	50	70	60	50	60	1180
8. MILE OAK	48	120	78	66	54	78	53	*	70	60	52	181	48	165	62	40	125	42	1342
9. REDHILL	120	115	77	63	127	98	80	106	*	105	90	180	102	127	101	80	80	120	1772
10. SALTDEAN	55	65	101	73	52	76	85	72	105	*	60	95	95	130	89	48	110	84	1395
11. SELSEY	66	62	105	70	90	45	85	70	81	65	*	87	49	55	60	55	55	81	1189
12. SHOREHAM	52	94	90	33	79	30	60	44	75	37	47	*	57	578	60	61	35	120	1552
13. SIDLEY U.	87	181	[illegible]	117	111	199	80	128	104	143	110	104	*	114	97	110	87	89	1865
14. SOUTHWICK	134	179	160	141	266	116	91	141	87	160	135	520	97	*	105	50	116	142	2640
15. STEYNING	52	35	30	43	40	60	48	35	30	25	50	86	28	65	*	85	30	50	797
16. STORRINGTON	62	35	68	100	48	36	44	51	100	70	75	126	82	84	30	*	47	80	1118
17. WITHDEAN	40	12	52	35	14	12	12	22	23	27	15	64	14	36	30	20	*	16	444
18. WORTHING U.	40	68	85	46	80	43	46	60	63	33	92	65	47	88	55	53	65	*	1029

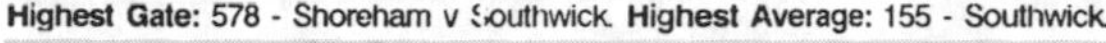

Highest Gate: 578 - Shoreham v Southwick. **Highest Average:** 155 - Southwick.

Langney Sports FC. Back Row (L/R): P Andrews, S Courtney, J Morley, M Jones, S Worman, M Cooke, M Green, G Callingham, S Colbran, J O'Neil, P Cherry (Manager). Front: D Wild, P Stevens, D Ashworth, D Baker, D Cooke, S Dell, J Boyd, T Fever, S Parks. Photo - Roger Turner.

DIV. TWO MERIT TABLE

Awards: 1st: £300 2nd: £200 3rd: £100

Win (W) = +5pts
Win by 5 or more goals (F) = +5pts
No goals against (N) = +5pts
Clean games - no cautions/sent-off (C) = +5pts
Cautions (B) = -5pts Sendings-off (S) = -20pts

	W	F	N	C	B	S	PTS
Wick	155	45	75	155	-35	-20	375
Stamco	80	20	60	165	-25	0	300
Whitehawk	125	5	55	135	-75	0	245
East Grinstead	50	50	0	25	160	-40	195
Burgess Hill Town	85	5	50	130	-75	0	195
Hailsham Town	90	15	50	130	-60	-40	185
Pagham	90	20	40	130	-60	-40	180
Peacehaven & Tel.	80	10	65	130	-60	-60	165
Three Bridges	60	0	25	135	-65	0	155
Arundel	75	5	55	125	-95	-20	145
Ringmer	55	5	30	125	-75	0	140
Langney Sports	110	15	60	105	-115	-40	135
Eastbourne Town	50	5	45	120	-75	-40	105
Oakwood	70	5	50	120	-80	-60	105
Crowborough Ath.	50	10	25	125	-70	-40	100
Littlehampton Town	45	55	15	40	-110	-105	95
Bexhill Town	45	10	30	125	-85	-40	85
Chichester City	25	5	10	130	-80	-20	70
Portfield	60	5	25	125	-60	-100	55
Newhaven	85	15	35	90	-150	-80	-5

DIV. TWO MERIT TABLE

Awards: 1st: £300 2nd: £200 3rd: £100

Win (W) = +5pts
Win by 5 or more goals (F) = +5pts
No goals against (N) = +5pts
Clean games - no cautions/sent-off (C) = +5pts
Cautions (B) = -5pts
Sendings-off (S) = -20pts

	W	F	N	C	B	S	PTS
Southwick	110	10	80	125	-60	-20	245
Horsham YMCA	85	15	35	140	-40	0	235
Hassocks	100	15	60	125	-50	-20	230
Mile Oak	70	15	35	140	-30	-20	210
Worthing United	65	10	40	130	-45	0	200
Redhill	100	20	35	115	-70	-20	180
Shoreham	125	10	65	95	-75	-60	160
Lancing	90	15	55	100	-85	-20	155
Withdean	55	5	15	125	-50	0	150
Midhurst & E'bourne	40	5	15	130	-50	0	140
Broadbridge Heath	35	5	40	120	-45	-20	135
Little Common A.	30	0	45	125	-45	-20	135
Sidley United	70	10	10	110	-75	-20	105
Selsey	75	15	30	95	-120	0	95
Saltdean United	65	5	40	90	-105	-20	75
Storrington	30	10	10	90	-95	0	45
Steyning Town	40	5	15	90	-115	-20	15
Eastbourne United	60	5	30	70	-130	-40	-5

DIV. THREE MERIT TABLE

Awards: 1st: £200 2nd: £100 3rd: £50

Win (W) = +5pts
Win by 5 or more goals (F) = +5pts
No goals against (N) = +5pts
Clean games - no cautions/sent-off (C) = +5pts
Cautions (B) = -5pts Sendings-off (S) = -20pts

	W	F	N	C	B	S	PTS
Lingfield	90	10	30	125	-25	0	230
Sunallon	60	5	20	125	-25	-20	165
St Francis Hosp.	50	0	35	125	-25	-20	165
Hurstpierpoint	60	10	35	120	-45	-20	160
Ifield	65	20	50	90	-60	-20	145
Haywards Heath T.	50	0	20	115	-45	0	140
Lindfield Rangers	45	5	40	120	-30	-40	140
Edwards Sports	35	0	20	115	-40	0	130
East Preston	70	10	30	95	-70	-20	115
Bosham	95	25	45	60	-115	0	110
Franklands V.	35	10	40	115	-45	-60	95
Shinewater Assoc.	45	0	20	100	-55	-40	70
Forest	60	5	15	100	-60	-60	60
Seaford Town	65	0	50	70	-105	-40	40
Buxted	50	5	25	80	-100	-40	20
Sidlesham	45	5	20	65	-125	-40	-30

P.G. CUNNINGHAM SPORTSMANSHIP TROPHY

Club	%
Burgess Hill Town	76.32
Wick	76.32
Broadbridge Heath	75.59
Peacehaven & Telscombe	75.26
Stamco	74.74
Little Common Albion	74.71
Sidley United	74.71
Eastbourne Town	73.95
Hassocks	73.82
Mile Oak	73.24
Southwick	73.24
Rinmger	73.16
Crowborough Athletic	72.89
Hailsham Town	72.37
Arundel	72.10
Bexhill Town	71.58
East Grinstead	71.05
Three Bridges	71.05
Eastbourne United	70.88
Horsham YMCA	70.88
Midhurst & Easebourne	70.59
Pagham	70.53
Lancing	70.29
Redhill	70.29
Worthing United	70.29
Oakwood	70.26
Saltdean United	70.00
Portfield	69.74
Storrington	69.71
Withdean	69.71
Chichester City	69.21
Littlehampton Town	68.95
Whitehawk	68.95
Shoreham	68.53
Steyning Town	67.65
Selsey	64.41
Langney Sports	63.95
Newhaven	61.32

DIV. THREE SPORTSMANSHIP

Club	%
Lingfield	80.00
Forest	77.30
Edwards Sports	75.67
Franklands Village	74.33
Lindfield Rangers	74.33
Sunallon	74.00
St Francis Hospital	73.33
Hurstpierpoint	72.33
Seaford Town	71.67
Shinewater Association	71.67
Haywards Heath Town	71.00
Ifield	70.33
Bosham	68.00
East Preston	67.67
Buxted	66.00
Sidlesham	58.33

RESERVE SECTION

PREM. DIV.	P	W	D	L	F	A	PTS
Peacehaven Res.	28	20	5	3	77	22	65
Stamco Res.	28	17	4	7	55	29	55
L'pton Town Res.	28	14	6	8	59	37	48
Portfield Res.	28	14	5	9	58	56	47
Burgess Hill Res.	28	13	4	10	52	42	44
Horsham YMCA Res.	28	13	4	11	62	47	*43
Ringmer Res.	28	12	7	9	44	44	43
Worthing Utd Res.	28	12	4	12	52	65	*40
Worthing Res.	28	10	8	10	60	53	*38
Hassocks Res.	28	11	4	13	46	57	37
Pagham Res.	28	10	6	12	44	59	36
Langney Spts Res.	28	9	4	15	71	64	31
Bosham Res.	28	6	9	13	40	63	27
Wick Res.	28	5	8	15	35	69	23
Newhaven Res.	28	3	3	22	36	84	*12

* - points adjusted

RES. DIV. (EAST)	P	W	D	L	F	A	PTS
Whitehawk Res.	26	18	6	2	78	24	60
Hailsham T. Res.	26	17	2	7	57	39	53
Crowborough Res.	26	17	1	8	85	38	52
Lewes Res.	26	14	9	3	62	27	51
Eastbourne T. Res.	26	12	6	8	51	41	42
E Grinstead Res.	26	10	7	9	41	34	*37
Sidley Utd Res.	26	10	7	9	45	39	37
Little Com. Res.	26	9	6	11	45	54	33
Bexhill T. Res.	26	8	6	12	31	53	*30
Haywards H. Res.	26	9	3	14	34	65	30
Saltdean U. Res.	26	8	0	18	48	65	*24
Seaford T. Res.	26	6	5	15	36	61	23
Franklands V. Res.	26	5	6	15	30	54	21
Eastbne Utd Res.	26	5	4	17	22	70	19

* - points adjusted

RES. DIV. (WEST)	P	W	D	L	F	A	PTS
Southwick Ress	26	17	4	5	72	26	55
Oakwood Res.	26	15	9	2	59	28	54
Chichester Res.	26	14	4	8	55	30	46
Mile Oak Res.	26	13	5	8	52	37	44
Arundel Res.	26	13	4	9	50	44	43
Steyning T. Res.	26	14	0	12	47	43	42
Broadbdge H. Res.	26	11	5	10	51	54	38
Midhurst & E. Res.	26	10	5	11	57	51	35
Lancing Res.	26	9	6	11	38	38	33
Shoreham Res.	26	10	3	13	41	48	33
Selsey Res.	26	9	5	12	41	50	32
East Preston Res.	26	10	1	15	35	46	31
Withdean Res.	26	9	2	15	29	54	29
Storrington Res.	26	1	1	24	23	100	4

RESERVE PREM. DIV. RESULTS	1	2	3	4	5	6	7	8	9	10	11	12	13	14	15
1. Bosham Reserves	*	0-3	0-3	1-0	2-0	4-2	3-2	1-1	0-0	1-1	3-0	2-3	3-3	1-6	2-3
2. Burgess Hill Town Reserves	2-1	*	0-2	1-3	2-0	2-2	5-1	2-3	2-6	2-4	1-2	0-1	5-1	4-0	4-2
3. Hassocks Reserves	2-1	0-3	*	1-5	1-0	1-2	1-0	3-2	0-4	2-2	2-1	1-1	1-1	1-5	3-3
4. Horsham YMCA Reserves	3-1	1-1	4-0	*	1-3	4-3	W-L	1-1	1-2	1-2	2-3	1-3	2-1	0-1	5-1
5. Langney Sports Reserves	4-0	1-1	0-4	1-6	*	3-4	5-1	6-2	0-1	3-1	2-5	1-2	1-2	1-4	7-2
6. Littlehampton Town Reserves	2-2	1-1	1-2	6-1	2-1	*	6-1	1-0	1-1	4-2	0-0	2-0	2-0	0-1	3-2
7. Newhaven Reserves	2-2	1-0	4-0	1-4	1-8	1-2	*	3-4	1-4	1-4	5-1	0-6	2-3	2-2	0-1
8. Pagham Reserves	1-0	1-2	1-4	2-2	1-5	1-0	5-2	*	1-1	1-2	0-0	3-1	6-3	2-0	3-1
9. Peacehaven & Telscombe Reserves	10-1	0-2	2-1	0-2	5-2	1-0	2-0	3-1	*	3-0	1-1	1-1	6-0	6-0	3-0
10. Portfield Reserves	2-2	1-0	2-1	2-1	1-6	2-1	6-1	4-0	1-2	*	3-2	1-0	1-3	3-3	1-4
11. Ringmer Reserves	3-1	1-2	2-1	1-4	1-0	3-2	2-0	0-1	2-1	1-1	*	2-0	1-1	1-0	1-1
12. Stamco Reserves	1-1	1-1	3-1	4-1	3-2	0-1	1-0	5-0	0-2	3-1	2-1	*	3-1	2-0	4-0
13. Wick Reserves	0-2	1-3	1-5	0-3	2-2	0-3	1-1	3-0	1-3	1-3	2-2	0-3	*	3-3	1-0
14. Worthing Reserves	3-3	3-0	5-3	3-3	2-2	L-W	5-1	1-1	0-1	6-3	2-5	2-0	0-0	*	2-3
15. Worthing United Reserves	1-0	2-1	2-0	2-1	5-5	0-6	1-2	3-0	1-6	1-2	4-0	1-2	3-0	2-1	*

RES. DIV. (EAST) RESULTS	1	2	3	4	5	6	7	8	9	10	11	12	13	14
1. Bexhill Town Reserves	*	1-2	L-W	2-2	5-1	W-L	0-1	2-2	1-3	0-2	L-W	2-1	1-1	3-2
2. Crowborough Athletic Reserves	9-1	*	3-0	1-2	9-1	5-0	3-1	2-3	1-1	2-1	3-0	6-1	2-1	2-3
3. East Grinstead Reserves	4-0	1-3	*	1-3	1-1	3-0	2-2	5-0	0-0	5-0	1-0	5-0	4-0	1-1
4. Eastbourne Town Reserves	1-1	2-0	3-1	*	2-1	8-0	2-0	0-1	1-2	1-2	3-2	1-0	1-1	2-2
5. Eastbourne United Reserves	0-1	0-1	0-0	2-5	*	1-0	0-3	1-0	0-3	1-1	0-4	1-3	4-0	0-6
6. Franklands Villages Reserves	0-0	0-6	1-0	3-1	5-0	*	0-2	1-2	0-0	2-3	2-3	2-3	0-0	1-1
7. Hailsham Town Reserves	2-0	4-2	4-0	1-1	1-0	3-2	*	2-3	5-3	7-0	3-2	2-1	3-1	1-2
8. Haywards Heath Town Reserves	1-3	0-4	1-0	1-2	2-0	3-1	0-1	*	0-6	3-3	6-3	0-7	0-0	2-4
9. Lewes Reserves	0-0	3-1	2-2	4-1	2-2	1-1	1-2	1-0	*	1-1	2-1	7-1	7-1	0-0
10. Little Common Albion Reserves	3-1	2-5	0-1	1-4	3-1	5-1	1-4	7-0	2-3	*	0-2	0-0	0-0	2-3
11. Saltdean United Reserves	3-4	2-7	2-3	4-1	2-3	1-4	4-1	3-1	0-3	1-2	*	3-5	1-2	0-1
12. Seaford Town Reserves	0-1	3-2	1-1	1-1	0-1	1-3	0-2	0-1	0-3	0-3	5-3	*	0-3	1-1
13. Sidley United Reserves	5-2	0-1	2-0	6-1	2-1	2-1	7-0	4-0	1-2	1-1	1-2	2-2	*	0-2
14. Whitehawk Reserves	8-0	5-3	5-0	1-0	9-0	0-0	2-0	3-2	3-3	5-0	3-0	5-0	1-2	*

RES. DIV. (WEST) RESULTS	1	2	3	4	5	6	7	8	9	10	11	12	13	14
1. Arundel Reserves	*	2-1	1-0	5-3	1-1	1-3	4-2	1-1	1-2	4-1	2-5	2-1	4-0	2-1
2. Broadbridge Heath Reserves	2-1	*	1-3	3-0	0-0	2-5	1-5	0-5	3-2	3-0	0-6	6-1	4-0	5-2
3. Chichester City Reserves	2-0	3-3	*	5-0	2-0	2-0	4-0	1-1	1-2	4-0	0-2	2-5	5-1	4-0
4. East Preston Reserves	2-1	0-1	1-0	*	0-1	2-1	2-0	1-2	0-2	0-3	0-1	2-0	3-2	2-0
5. Lancing Reserves	2-0	1-2	2-2	4-2	*	1-1	1-3	1-1	4-0	0-2	1-3	2-3	5-0	1-2
6. Midhurst & Easebourne Reserves	2-3	1-1	3-0	4-2	1-3	*	0-1	0-1	1-1	2-1	2-2	2-1	10-2	0-1
7. Mile Oak Reserves	2-2	3-3	1-3	1-0	4-2	3-0	*	1-1	4-1	3-1	0-2	3-1	4-1	0-1
8. Oakwood Reserves	1-1	4-1	2-1	3-1	0-0	2-3	1-1	*	3-0	3-1	1-3	4-2	4-1	2-0
9. Selsey Reserves	2-1	2-1	1-2	1-3	5-1	1-1	0-3	2-2	*	3-1	1-1	0-1	4-1	2-2
10. Shoreham Reserves	2-3	1-0	0-2	2-1	1-2	1-3	1-1	2-2	3-2	*	1-0	1-2	4-1	3-1
11. Southwick Reserves	3-4	1-1	1-1	2-1	1-0	8-2	1-0	1-4	2-3	3-0	*	0-2	2-0	3-0
12. Steyning Town Reserves	1-2	2-0	2-3	1-4	2-1	2-1	4-0	1-2	1-0	0-1	0-4	*	2-0	4-1
13. Storrington Reserves	1-2	2-4	0-3	0-2	0-1	4-7	0-4	1-5	5-2	1-1	0-9	0-5	*	0-3
14. Withean	1-0	2-3	1-0	1-1	0-1	4-2	0-3	1-2	2-0	2-7	0-6	0-1	1-0	*

Left: *Eastbourne Town FC. Back Row (L/R): Peter Roberts (Manager), Richard Hughes, Mark Norman, Nick Barden, Dave Winterton, Stuarts Addems, Darren Smith, Ian Williams. Front: Wayne Pettigrew, Simon Hynes, Colin Hopgood, Jimmy Chater, Mark Van Den Bossche, Chris Pennington. Photo - Dave West.*

UNIJET SUSSEX COUNTY LEAGUE YOUTH SECTION

WORTHING'S CLEAN SWEEP

The 1993-94 season saw under-18s football in Sussex dominated by Worthing FC, although the general standard was very high.

The Unijet Sussex County League has run a Youth Section for thirteen years. It is open to the under-18 side of any full or associate member of the league. All games are played on the senior side's ground, which means that many of the youth teams get the opportunity to play under floodlights on a regular basis, although most fixtures are contested on Sunday mornings.

This last season saw 23 teams enter sides, competing in East and West sections. Worthing won the West Section with a 100% record, although they were chased for most of the season by Worthing United and Mile Oak especially. The latter fell away badly in the closing stages when they were playing two games a week because of their tremendous cup run.

In the East Section, Bexhill Town and Eastbourne Town had a tremendous battle which went right to the last week. In the end, Eastbourne's huge fixture backlog told on them, and Bexhill Town won their first East Section title, with an amazing 100 goals from only 20 games.

In the championship play-off, Bexhill performed well below their ability and in the end were well beaten (5-1) by Worthing in a match played at Eastbourne Town's ground.

The following Thursday night, in front of over 200 spectators at Whitehawk's ground, Worthing completed the double by beating Mile Oak 3-1. However, the score-line does not reflect the closeness of this encounter. Mile Oak, in their first season in the County Youth League, went ahead after just four minutes with a goal from Justin Simmons. Worthing were lucky to go in at half-time only one goal behind. However, they came back with renewed enthusiasm, and the words of manager Elwyn Rees must still have been ringing in their ears when they levelled the score after just two minutes of the second-half with a goal from Dean Lever. Normal time ended with no further goals, and so the game entered extra-time, and in the end Worthing's greater fitness told with goals from Damien Dunford and Ben Milford. The match had been a fine example of the quality of both football and sportsmanship seen throughout the County League during the season.

The League continues to attract more and more teams as sides realise that in the current economic climate their future lies with developing their own players. Thirty sides have signed up for 1994-95, and they will all be striving for some of the success that Worthing enjoyed.

Groundhoppers are always most welcome at Youth Section games, and although I cannot promise a programme I can assure you of a warm welcome and some good quality football.

Stephen Wood, Youth Section Secretary.

WEST SECTION	P	W	D	L	F	A	PTS
Worthing	22	22	0	0	96	7	66
Worthing United	22	15	1	6	68	36	46
Steyning Town	22	14	2	6	65	40	44
Storrington	22	13	4	5	59	44	43
Mile Oak	22	13	2	7	54	31	41
Broadbridge Heath	22	12	0	10	57	53	36
Wick	22	11	1	10	50	41	34
Southwick	22	10	2	10	43	47	32
Selsey	22	6	1	15	22	58	19
Littlehampton T.	22	5	1	16	29	67	16
Bosham	22	2	0	20	20	113	6
Midhurst & E'bne	22	1	2	19	22	48	5

EAST SECTION	P	W	D	L	F	A	PTS
Bexhill Town	20	17	2	1	100	16	53
Eastbourne Town	20	14	5	1	68	23	47
Hassocks	20	13	1	6	51	42	40
Lewes	20	12	1	7	53	32	37
Burgess Hill T.	20	10	3	7	51	25	33
Newhaven	20	8	5	7	33	29	29
Ringmer	20	7	2	11	43	43	23
Seaford Town	20	5	4	11	43	49	19
Whitehawk	20	2	5	13	26	60	11
Hailsham Town	20	2	5	13	26	69	11
St Francis Hosp.	20	3	1	16	11	117	10

Worthing FC u-18s - Unijet Sussex County League Youth Section champions and League Cup winners 1993-94.

FEDERATION BREWERY NORTHERN LEAGUE

FEEDER TO:
NORTHERN PREMIER LEAGUE

FOUNDED: 1889
(The World's Second Oldest League)

President: Ernest Armstrong, PC.

Chairman: A Clark.

Hon. Secretary: A Golightly IPFA, 85 Park Road North, Chester-le-Street, Co.Durhum DH3 3SA (091 388 2056)

The papers, even the *Financial Times*, have been full of the Northern League all year. "Northern League set for major gains", "Northern League sweeps to victory" and so forth. Whatever the story, the Northern League has come out of it well.

Sadly, this is not the world's second oldest football league - proud and unprejudiced in the North-East of England - but a right wing political party in Italy. They only have four or five other parties, a porn actress MP, the occasional dictator and a few thousand Mafiosi to worry about. We, infinitely worse, have the godfathers of the Non-League Pyramid.

The Egyptians, good builders, would never have let this pyramid off the ground. Bad democrats, they'd probably now like what they see.

Whatever its egalitarian intentions, the Pyramid has fast become a one way street, and for many leagues below the second or third level it seems downhill all the way. Slaves to the system, we worry not just about the mechanics - will we, and many others, EVER gain a club by relegation? - But about the motives.

Yet while we will return shortly to this jerry-built monolith, it is dangerous (and all too easy) to become obsessed by it. Obsession is not paralysis, however. Away from the Pyramid's insidious shadow the Northern League (English version) remains buoyant, innovative, progressive and proud. We play good football, too.

Perhaps the season's highlight was Billingham Synthonia's run to an FA Trophy quarter-final replay, losing by the odd goal to Woking, the eventual winners. Two Conference sides and another from the NPL Premier Division had fallen en route, Synners recording a Northern League club's 50th national competition victory over a side from Conference level since re-organisation in 1974.

Still, however - this pesky Pyramid again - there are those who seek sedulously to deny our first division clubs their 20-year place in the FA Trophy. Letters have been written, levers pulled, ears bent. Ultimately the decision is the FA's, a position complicated because Arthur Clark - the League's

Durham City FC - Federation Brewery Northern League Champions 1993-94. Back Row (L/R): David Race, John Reach, Michael Connor, Peter Bragan, Neil Shotton, Dave Callaghan, Derek Ord. Front: Perry Briggs, Arthur Graham, Michael Taylor, Mark Ferguson. *Photo - Richard Brock.*

uniquely dedicated chairman - is also chairman of the FA Trophy committee. Though his own position is invidious, those slanderers who creep round seeking whomsoever they can destroy should be assured that there is no more upright nor honest man in football. Let someone else in the FA, therefore, tell the rug pullers to mind their own bloody business.

We started the season recovering from what became known as the "Whitby Town Affair" and ended it with yet more rule book brandishing. Durham City became champions, only their second trophy of any sort since leaving the Third Division North in 1927, but were denied promotion through the Pyramid because their new ground wasn't able to meet NPL deadlines. The riverside Ferens Park, home since 1950, had nostalgically been vacated at the end of April. However unfortunate for Durham, it seems to us that the NPL acted within its own rules - there can be regret, but no argument. City, meanwhile, will start this season ground-sharing with Chester-le-Street.

Blyth Spartans, league leaders for much of the season by the length of an FA agenda, gain unexpected promotion from second place. They go both with our blessing and with our thanks for 30 years distinguished league membership during which they won the championship ten times. Most, however, will remember the Spartans for the epic adventures of 1977-78, when they reached an FA Cup fifth round replay and men like Alder, Clarke, Shoulder, Houghton and Carney became household names. In 1993-94 Spartans also won the Northumberland Senior Cup, comfortably beating Newcastle United reserves in the semi-final, but lost 2-0 to Northallerton Town in the League Challenge Cup final. They will be no less formidable in the NPL. Guisborough Town won the North Riding Senior Cup for the third successive season.

Hartlepool Town and Morpeth Town, champions respectively of the Vaux Wearside League and McEwans Northern Alliance, join our second division next season on promotion through the Pyramid. Hartlepool, unable to find a suitable home in their own backyard, will ground-share with Ferryhill Athletic - 20 miles away. Though a majority of clubs at the League annual meeting was unhappy with the arrangement, an FA appeal sensibly ruled in Town's favour.

Morpeth Town were accepted on a unanimous vote and come with a quickly developing ground, a reputedly millionaire chairman and very high hopes. We wish both newcomers well.

Brandon United and Stockton, who hope next season to have moved to their own impressive new stadium, are relegated from the first division. Bedlington Terriers, free scoring champions, Peterlee and Prudhoe are promoted from the second.

Sadly, a sporting tragedy, we lose South Bank. Founded in 1868 and the oldest football club north of York, the Bankers were the League's only surviving founder member. Three times League champions, three times Amateur Cup finalists, once winners, the Teesside club had played at Normanby Road throughout their NL career. A series of arson attacks and other criminal acts that began in 1991 had destroyed their facilities, and a bitter dispute with the insurers drags on.

Seven league deadlines for some kind of restoration were met with promises and inaction. At the 1993 annual meeting the club's membership was suspended for 12 months in the hope that a year of grace might spur salvation. Nothing whatever happened, except that planning permission for commercial development was gained for the Normanby Road site. Correspondence was ignored, the club's only communication coming on the afternoon of the 1994 meeting. Their fate was quick, wretched and inevitable though one day we hope to welcome them back.

For several years South Bank had played an early season game against the League champions for the Craven Cup, named in memory of Charles Craven, the Darlington solicitor whose initiative was chiefly responsible for the League's formation. The Craven Cup will now become a knock-out competition for second division clubs.

There is much else that gives cause for optimism. The Tyneside based Federation Brewery, providers of the House of Commons' best beer, has renewed its generous sponsorship. Quaser, the sportswear company, is likely more heavily to invest in its backing of the league's sportsmanship awards, underlining our committment to fair play. Our relationships with the Northern Alliance and the Wearside League, the FBNL feeders, are a model (and an example) of what a true sporting fraternity should be; our administration remains admirable.

In spite of everything, we continue to love and enjoy our football up north and the Groundhoppers weekend, coming up to its fourth Easter, now has a reputation both nationally and internationally as a reflection of that spirit. It has become a joyful reunion of genuine football fans - and also, it might reasonably be added, a guarantee of rotten weather. We hope for clemency, and still more visitors, from April 14-16 1995. *Northern Ventures Northern Gains*, the League magazine, is also much praised - not least by the editor, who'd never win the shrinking violet class at Chelsea flower show. For the sixth successive season it remains at 30p.

But the spirit of the Northern League, and its success, is much more about the unsung heroes - the men and women whose indomitable enthusiasm and endless efforts sustain senior Non-League football often in the face of extraordinary adversity. Next Easter's groundhoppers will spend Saturday evening in Washington's wonderful new clubhouse, rebuilt despite the most fearsome obstacles after yet another arson attack. They will spend Friday evening at Ashington, another former Third Division North club that last season came close to having its life support machine switched off. Now the Colliers are reinvigorated. The Charlton brothers, local lads made pretty canny, are joint presidents and the sleeves rolled up town hums with offers of help.

Our visitors will see new floodlights at Bedlington and Shotton Comrades, new facilities at Prudhoe, progress almost everywhere.

Yet though we do not - cannot - stand still, it seems that others forever move the finishing tape. Reallity is just one of the victims, integrity sometimes another, of a devil take the hindmost system that seems too often to confuse football with rat race.

Most of us up here believe firmly in the true principles of the Pyramid. We also hold firm to the adage that what comes up must come down. Perhaps that also applies to that jerry-built monolith.

Mike Amos, British Regional Sports Journalist of the Year 1994.

DIVISION ONE	P	W	D	L	F	A	PTS
Durham City	38	23	11	4	88	39	80
Blyth Spartans	38	22	7	9	81	37	73
Seaham Red Star	38	20	10	8	70	40	70
Whitby Town	38	17	14	7	90	57	65
Guisborough T.	38	17	12	9	71	41	63
Northallerton T.	38	18	7	13	68	39	61
Tow Law Town	38	18	6	14	70	58	60
Murton	38	17	8	13	63	65	59
Shildon	38	17	6	15	59	54	57
Billingham Syn.	38	15	9	14	57	45	54
Dunston Feds	38	15	9	14	72	69	54
Consett	38	15	6	17	67	70	*48
Ferryhill Ath.	38	11	8	19	61	81	41
Newcastle Blue S.	38	11	8	19	44	65	41
Hebburn	38	12	5	21	55	93	41
Eppleton CW	38	11	7	20	52	76	40
Chester-le-Street	38	13	5	20	64	74	**38
West Auckland	38	10	8	20	49	89	28
Brandon United	38	9	6	23	45	94	33
Stockton	38	9	8	21	46	86	*32

DIVISION TWO	P	W	D	L	F	A	PTS
Bedlington Terriers	36	28	5	3	114	36	89
Peterlee Newtown	36	23	9	4	77	27	78
Prudhoe East End	36	21	9	6	72	36	72
Evenwood Town	36	22	4	10	78	47	70
Easington Colliery	36	20	7	9	77	40	67
Billingham Town	36	21	3	12	88	49	66
Crook Town	36	18	8	10	80	58	62
Norton & Stockton	36	18	7	11	72	70	61
Darlington CS	36	18	2	16	65	68	56
Whickham	36	16	7	13	71	64	*52
Washington	36	14	5	17	67	72	47
Esh Winning	36	12	7	17	50	72	43
Langley Park SSC	36	12	5	19	55	67	41
Shotton Comrades	36	9	9	18	61	84	36
Alnwick Town	36	10	7	19	50	69	*34
Willington	36	9	3	24	48	90	30
Ashington	36	8	3	25	46	100	*24
Ryhope CA	36	7	3	26	37	94	**18
Horden Colliery W.	36	3	3	30	35	100	12

* = 3pts deducted ** = 6 pts deducted

DIVISION ONE RESULT CHART 1993-94

HOME TEAM	1	2	3	4	5	6	7	8	9	10	11	12	13	14	15	16	17	18	19	20
1. Billingham Synthonia	*	0-1	2-1	0-2	2-1	6-1	1-2	1-3	0-1	1-2	1-0	1-1	2-1	0-2	0-3	2-1	1-1	1-1	3-0	0-0
2. Blyth Spartans	3-1	*	5-0	2-0	4-0	2-0	1-2	1-1	3-0	4-0	2-1	1-2	2-1	0-2	1-2	2-0	4-1	3-1	2-2	3-1
3. Brandon Utd	0-6	2-1	*	1-1	3-2	0-4	1-5	1-2	3-2	0-2	2-3	0-2	2-0	0-1	0-3	1-4	1-1	0-1	2-4	3-3
4. Chester-le-Street	1-0	1-7	5-0	*	3-1	3-3	0-2	2-4	1-0	3-2	2-0	1-3	1-0	1-4	0-1	0-2	5-0	6-0	3-0	1-3
5. Consett	1-1	0-4	6-1	3-0	*	2-1	0-3	1-3	4-0	1-1	1-1	1-2	0-1	1-0	2-3	2-1	2-1	0-3	1-5	1-1
6. Dunston FB	1-1	3-1	1-1	1-1	2-0	*	3-0	0-1	1-2	0-0	4-5	3-2	2-0	2-2	0-2	1-1	3-1	3-1	5-0	2-2
7. Durham City	2-3	0-0	3-0	4-2	2-4	3-0	*	0-0	3-0	1-1	2-1	2-0	1-1	1-1	4-2	2-1	5-1	1-1	5-1	0-0
8. Eppleton	1-6	2-2	2-2	3-1	1-0	2-3	2-3	*	0-3	1-0	1-2	1-1	0-1	1-3	3-1	1-3	0-0	0-1	0-2	2-2
9. Ferryhill	0-0	1-1	1-2	0-1	1-3	1-2	1-1	4-0	*	0-3	2-1	5-2	3-0	0-3	0-0	2-1	2-2	0-1	1-1	2-4
10. Guisborough	3-0	1-1	4-0	4-1	1-1	3-2	0-1	3-0	3-1	*	5-0	5-2	1-0	1-1	1-1	1-0	1-1	3-1	2-2	1-1
11. Hebburn	1-1	2-5	0-4	2-1	2-7	3-0	1-2	4-3	0-2	2-0	*	0-1	0-3	2-0	1-8	0-4	4-2	0-1	1-1	2-3
12. Murton	0-0	0-2	3-1	4-3	0-5	1-0	1-4	1-3	1-1	2-1	4-1	*	2-2	4-3	0-0	3-2	0-2	2-1	4-0	2-1
13. Newcastle Blue Star	2-0	1-1	1-2	2-1	2-2	2-3	3-0	3-1	2-0	2-1	2-2	1-5	*	0-3	0-1	1-1	0-4	3-2	1-3	0-3
14. Northallerton	1-2	0-1	0-2	4-2	3-0	3-0	0-0	0-1	1-1	3-0	7-0	1-2	2-0	*	0-0	3-0	2-0	1-0	0-2	3-2
15. Seaham Red Star	0-1	1-2	3-0	1-1	2-4	3-1	1-1	2-0	7-2	3-2	0-0	3-0	0-0	3-2	*	1-0	4-2	0-1	2-0	1-1
16. Shildon	1-0	3-1	1-3	1-1	0-1	1-1	0-5	2-1	1-0	0-5	4-1	1-1	3-1	1-0	3-0	*	1-0	2-1	1-0	2-2
17. Stockton	4-3	0-2	3-0	4-3	2-3	1-3	1-3	2-1	0-2	0-4	0-1	1-0	1-1	1-1	0-2	1-6	*	0-4	2-0	0-5
18. Tow Law Town	0-3	2-0	3-1	3-1	3-0	4-1	2-4	5-1	4-0	0-2	1-4	1-1	1-0	3-2	1-1	4-1	5-1	*	0-1	2-2
19. West Auckland	0-3	0-4	2-2	1-2	3-4	0-3	1-8	3-2	0-3	2-2	2-1	1-0	0-4	0-4	0-1	2-1	2-3	3-3	*	3-3
20. Whitby Town	0-2	1-0	2-1	2-1	2-0	6-7	1-1	5-2	5-1	0-0	3-4	4-2	7-0	3-0	4-2	1-2	0-0	4-2	1-0	*

DIV. TWO RESULTS	1	2	3	4	5	6	7	8	9	10	11	12	13	14	15	16	17	18	19
1. Alnwick Town	*	1-0	1-2	1-3	1-4	0-2	1-2	2-1	2-1	3-1	1-1	1-0	1-1	1-2	3-2	3-0	2-2	2-3	0-0
2. Ashington	2-3	*	2-6	1-2	0-2	0-5	1-2	1-1	2-3	2-1	0-4	1-4	0-3	1-2	1-1	2-0	1-0	1-1	3-0
3. Bedlington	3-1	4-0	*	2-3	2-1	4-2	2-1	4-0	2-1	4-0	5-0	4-1	1-2	1-1	3-0	5-2	4-1	5-1	4-1
4. Billingham Town	1-0	1-2	2-3	*	3-2	1-0	0-4	4-1	3-1	2-1	3-1	1-2	1-2	1-1	2-0	3-1	1-3	2-0	0-0
5. Crook Town	3-3	2-1	2-2	3-3	*	1-2	0-3	1-0	2-3	7-0	3-0	0-0	0-0	2-1	2-0	4-4	2-2	2-0	2-3
6. Darlington CS	2-0	2-3	0-7	3-2	2-2	*	1-0	1-3	0-5	2-0	1-3	3-1	0-1	0-2	4-0	2-1	2-3	3-2	0-1
7. Easington Coll.	1-3	7-0	0-0	4-2	5-2	1-2	*	3-1	2-0	2-0	1-1	2-3	1-2	2-0	2-1	2-1	3-2	0-0	2-0
8. Esh Winning	1-1	5-1	0-5	2-6	0-4	2-3	0-5	*	2-1	2-1	2-3	2-0	2-3	0-2	2-1	2-2	1-0	3-2	2-0
9. Evenwood Town	3-1	3-2	1-0	3-1	0-2	4-1	3-2	0-0	*	5-0	3-2	3-1	0-0	1-1	1-0	2-0	2-1	0-2	3-1
10. Horden CW	0-2	4-2	1-3	0-5	0-2	0-2	2-3	1-2	1-2	*	0-2	0-0	0-1	1-3	1-4	1-1	3-6	1-2	1-4
11. Langley Park	1-0	7-1	0-3	0-4	2-3	1-2	0-0	0-0	1-0	1-2	*	2-4	0-2	2-0	3-1	2-1	1-2	1-4	1-0
12. Norton & Stockton	3-2	2-3	1-6	0-7	1-2	3-2	1-0	3-2	2-2	3-2	5-2	*	0-0	2-1	2-1	6-3	2-2	4-2	3-0
13. Peterlee Newtown	1-1	4-0	2-2	1-0	3-1	4-0	1-1	3-1	4-0	1-0	3-0	3-3	*	1-1	4-0	2-3	2-0	1-2	3-1
14. Prudhoe EE	2-1	5-2	1-3	2-0	3-0	3-1	2-1	1-1	2-0	1-1	1-1	2-0	3-0	*	5-0	2-2	4-1	1-0	1-0
15. Ryhope CA	2-1	2-1	2-5	0-5	1-4	2-0	0-3	1-0	1-0	2-4	1-3	0-1	0-4	0-6	*	1-2	3-3	0-4	6-1
16. Shotton Comrades	3-2	4-3	0-0	0-4	0-4	2-5	0-0	2-2	2-5	3-2	0-1	2-0	1-3	1-3	1-1	*	2-1	3-5	6-0
17. Washington	5-1	1-2	0-1	0-3	5-0	0-3	3-4	3-0	0-5	4-2	2-1	2-4	0-5	5-1	1-0	1-0	*	0-0	3-1
18. Whickham	4-1	3-0	1-3	0-6	2-3	2-2	3-3	0-2	1-6	4-1	1-0	2-4	1-0	1-1	6-0	1-1	3-0	*	3-1
19. Willington	2-1	3-2	2-4	3-1	1-4	2-3	0-3	2-3	1-3	6-0	3-2	1-1	0-5	0-3	4-1	2-5	1-3	1-3	*

NORTHERN LEAGUE CUP 1993-94

First Round

Consett v Shildon 2-5
Murton v Ashington 3-0
Alnwick Town v Easington Colliery 0-2
Whickham v Bedlington Terriers 1-4
Esh Winning v Newcastle Blue Star 0-3
Langley Park S & S United v Tow Law Town 0-8
Billingham Town v Chester-le-Street Town 0-1

Second Round

Willington v Stockton 2-7
Northallerton Town v Washington 5-2
West Auckland v Chester-le-Street Town 5-6
Hebburn v Darlington Cleveland Social 4-3
Easington Colliery v Dunston Fed. Brewery 1-3
Billingham Synthonia v Ryhope Comm. Assn 8-0
Brandon United v Newcastle Blue Star 2-0
Evenwood Town v Blyth Spartans 1-2
Seaham Red Star v Whitby Town 2-1
Prudhoe v Tow Law 1-1 *(Tow Law won on penalties)*
Shildon v Durham City 4-2
Murton v Norton & Stockton Ancients 5-0
Eppleton Colliery Welfare v Crook Town 2-0
Shotton v Horden CW 1-1 *(Shotton won on penalties)*
Bedlington Terriers v Ferryhill Athletic 4-1
Guisborough Town v Peterlee Newtown 2-0

Second Round

Northallerton Town v Tow Law Town 5-3
Hebburn v Murton 3-8
Billingham Synthonia v Shotton Comrades 4-1
Blyth Spartans v Guisborough Town 2-1
Chester-le-St. v Shildon 2-3 *(Shildon won on pens)*
Dunston Federation Brewery v Eppleton CW 5-3
Brandon United v Bedlington Terriers 2-1
Stockton v Seaham Red Star 2-0

(continued overleaf)

Quarter-Finals *(continued from page 687)*

Northallerton Town v Shildon	1-0	Murton v Dunston Federation Brewery	0-2
Blyth Spartans v Stockton	3-0	Billingham Synthonia v Brandon United	0-1

Semi-Finals

Brandon United v Blyth Spartans	1-2	Northallerton Town v Dunston Federation Brewery	2-0

Final: Northallerton Town 2, Blyth Spartans 0

Northern League Division One Ten Year Record

	84/5	85/6	86/7	87/8	88/9	89/0	90/1	91/2	92/3	93/4
Alnwick Town	-	-	-	-	-	8	19	-	-	-
Bedlington Terriers	-	2	20	-	-	-	-	-	-	-
Billingham Synthonia	12	19	-	3	1	1	4	5	2	10
Billingham Town	-	20	-	-	5	19		-	-	-
Bishops Auckland	1	1	2	6	-	-	-	-	-	-
Blyth Spartans	2	4	1	1	9	9	3	6	4	2
Brandon United	-	8	12	10	7	18	17	15	15	19
Chester-le-Street Town	8	7	16	18	19	-	-	-	9	17
Consett	15	13	13	20	-	6	5	9	10	12
Crook Town	16	9	17	17	20	-	-	-	-	-
Dunston Federation Brewery	-	-	-	-	-	-	-	-	-	11
Durham City	-	-	-	-	14	17	20	-	6	1
Easington Colliery	-	-	10	15	13	20	-	17	18	-
Eppleton Colliery Welfare	-	-	-	-	-	-	-	-	-	16
Ferryhill Athletic	14	18	18	14	8	13	8	16	17	13
Gretna	6	11	7	7	3	2	1	1	-	-
Guisborough Town	-	-	-	5	4	7	2	4	3	5
Hartlepool United Reserves	-	10	15	-	-	-	-	-	-	-
Hebburn	-	-	-	-	-	-	-	-	16	15
Horden Colliery Welfare	17	-	-	-	-	-	-	-	-	-
Langley Park	-	-	-	-	-	-	-	19	-	-
Murton	-	-	-	-	-	-	13	2	8	8
Newcastle Blue Star	-	-	4	2	6	4	10	13	13	14
Northallerton Town	-	-	-	-	-	-	9	8	11	6
North Shields	5	12	6	9	18	-	-	-	-	-
Peterlee Newtown	9	6	19	-	-	-	16	12	19	-
Ryhope Community Assoc.	10	15	14	19	-	-	-	-	-	-
Seaham Red Star	-	-	-	-	16	10	11	11	5	3
Shildon	18	-	-	12	17	14	14	18	-	9
South Bank	3	3	8	16	15	16	12	7	20	-
Spennymoor United	11	14	3	11	11	11	-	-	-	-
Stockton	-	-	-	-	10	5	18	-	7	20
Tow Law Town	4	5	9	8	2	3	7	10	14	7
West Auckland Town	-	-	-	-	-	-	-	14	12	18
Whickham	-	-	-	-	-	15	15	20	-	-
Whitby Town	7	16	11	13	12	12	6	3	1	4
Whitley Bay	13	17	5	4	-	-	-	-	-	-
No. of Clubs	18	20	20	20	20	20	20	20	20	20

Division Two Record

	84/5	85/6	86/7	87/8	88/9	89/0	90/1	91/2	92/3	93/4
Alnwick Town	14	10	7	6	2	-	-	9	9	15
Ashington	10	8	10	15	5	13	12	12	8	17
Bedlington Terriers	2	-	-	7	7	9	11	19	17	1
Billingham Sythonia	-	-	1	-	-	-	-	-	-	-
Billingham Town	4	-	4	4	-	-	5	7	4	6
Brandon United	1	-	-	-	-	-	-	-	-	-
Chester-Le-Street Town	-	-	-	-	-	5	16	3	-	-
Consett	-	-	-	-	1	-	-	-	-	-
Crook Town	-	-	-	-	-	6	13	8	18	7
Darlington C(B)(S)	8	18	16	14	16	12	10	18	11	9
Darlington Reserves	16	15	-	-	-	-	-	-	-	-
Dunston Federation Brewery	-	-	-	-	-	-	-	5	1	-
Durham City	5	4	13	3	-	-	-	2	-	-
Easington Colliery	-	2	-	-	-	-	3	-	-	5
Eppleton Colliery Welfare	-	-	-	-	-	-	-	-	2	-
Esh Winning	11	20	17	5	15	20	7	11	13	12
Evenwood Town	15	17	14	16	17	7	6	17	6	4
Guisborough Town	-	3	2	-	-	-	-	-	-	-
Hartlepool United Reserves	3	-	-	-	-	-	-	-	-	-
Hebburn	-	-	-	-	-	15	4	4	-	-
Horden Colliery Welfare	-	13	18	11	8	16	19	15	19	19
Langley Park Welfare	9	12	19	12	13	4	2	-	20	13
Murton	-	-	-	-	11	1	-	-	-	-
Newcasite Blue Star	-	1	-	-	-	-	-	-	-	-
Northallerton Town	12	16	12	9	9	2	-	-	-	-
Norton & Stockton Ancients	13	9	8	10	14	18	9	13	12	8
Peterlee Newtown	-	-	-	8	6	3	-	-	-	2
Prudhoe East End	-	-	-	-	4	8	8	6	5	3
Ryhope Community Assoc.	-	-	-	-	10	11	14	10	10	18
Seaham Red Star	6	6	9	2	-	-	-	-	-	-
Shildon	-	19	3	-	-	-	-	-	3	-
Shotton Comrades	18	14	15	18	20	17	15	14	14	14
Stockton	-	7	6	1	-	-	-	1	-	-
Washington	-	-	-	-	18	10	17	16	15	11
West Auckland Town	17	5	5	17	12	19	1	-	-	-
Whickham	-	-	-	-	3	-	-	-	7	10
Willington	7	11	11	13	19	14	18	20	16	16
No. of Clubs	18	20	19	18	20	20	19	20	20	19

DIVISION ONE CLUBS 1994-95

BEDLINGTON TERRIERS

Chairman: Robert Cox **Press Officer:** Eric Young (0670 829196)
Secretary: Eric Young, 6 Millbank Place, Bedlington, Northumberland NE22 5AT (0670 829196).
Manager: Keith Perry **Assistant Manager:** Steven Locker.
Coach: Tony Lowery **Physio:** John Nicholson.
Ground: Welfare Park, Park Rd., Bedlington, Northumberland (0670 825485).
Directions: Into Bedlington, turn left at 'Northumberland Arms' on Front Street, then second right, ground on right after 100 yds.
Seats: 40 **Cover:** Yes **Capacity:** 1,500 **Floodlights:** Yes **Year Formed:** 1949
Midweek Matches: Wednesday **Previous Leagues:** Northern Alliance.
Colours: Red/black **Change colours:** All blue **Souvenir Shop:** No
Programme: 40 pages, 50p
Clubhouse: Open every evening, 11-11pm Sat. & Sun lunch. Pool, darts etc.
Record win: 9-0 v Ashington (A), Northumberland Senior Cup 93-94.
Record Attendance: 1,013 v Blyth Spartans, Northern Lg 85-86.
Previous Names: Bedlington Mechanics 49-53/ Colliery Welfare 53-56/ Mechanics 56-61/ Bedlington United 61-65/ Bedlington Colliery 65-68/ Bedlington Town 68-74.
Captain: Kevin Harmison **Club record scorer:** Ian Donaldson.
P.o.Y. 93-94: Graeme McCabe **Top Scorer 93-94:** Steven Brown, Mark Cameron - 24 each.
Hons: Northern League Div 2 94-95 (R-up 84-85), Northern Alliance 66-67 (R-up 67-68 69-70 71 72, Lg Cup 57-58 66-67 69-70 81-82.

BILLINGHAM SYNTHONIA

Chairman: Mr Harry Davies **Vice Chairman:** Mr Peter Lax **President:** Mr Dennis Rickards
Sec./Press Officer: Graham Craggs, '2' Ribble Close, Billingham, Cleveland TS22 5NT (0642 535856).
Manager: Stuart Coleby **Physio:** Tony Hetherington **Coach:** Lenny Gunn
Ground: The Stadium, Central Avenue, Billingham, Cleveland (0642 552358).
Directions: Turn off A19 onto A1027 signposted Billingham, Norton (this applies from either north or south), continue straigh on along Central Avenue, ground on left opposite office block. By rail; ground 1 mile along Cowpen Lane from Billingham (BR).
Seats: 370 **Cover:** 370 **Capacity:** 1,970 **Floodlights:** Yes **Founded:** 1923
Club colours: Green/white/green. **Change colours:** All blue **Club Shop:** No.
Midweek Matches: Wednesday **Previous League:** Teesside (1923-War).
Programme: 12 pages (+ads), 50p **Editor:** Harry Davies (0642 560445) **Souvenir Shop:** No.
Rec. Gate: 4,200 v Bishop Auck. 6/9/58. **Clubhouse:** 200yds across car park. Normal club hours.
Best FA Trophy season: Quarter-final replay 93-94 (lost 1-2 after 1-1 draw at Woking).
Best FA Cup season: 1st Rd 48-49 51-52 56-57 57-58 87-88 89-90.
Prev. Ground: Belasis Lane 23-58 **Previous Name:** Billingham Synthonia Recreation
Players progressing to Football League: Peter Atkinson & Ken Harrison (Hull 1947), Ernie Wardle & John Murray (M'boro 1948 & 49), Richard Mulvaney (Blackburn 1964), Mike Hodgson (Hartlepool 1964), David Hockaday (Blackpool 1975), Terry Gaffney (Hartlepool 1977), Aidan Davidson (Notts County 1988).
Nickname: Synners **Club Sponsors:** Billingham Arms Hotel.
Club record scorer: Tony Hetherington **Club record appearances:** Andy Harbron.
Captain 93-94: Tony Lynch **Top Scorer 93-94:** Charlie Butler **P.o.Y. 93-94:** Gary Popple
Honours: Northern Lg 56-57 88-89 89-90 (R-up 49-50 50-51*(No goals conceded at home; P 13, W 12, D 1, L 0; F 44, A 0)* 51-52, Lg Cup 51-52 87-88 89-90, Div 2 86-87), Teesside Lg 36-37 (Lg Cup 34-35 38-39), Durham Challenge Cup 88-89 90-91, North Riding Snr Cup 66-67 71-72 78-79, North Riding Amateur Cup 38-39 56-57 62-63 63-64, FA Amateur Cup 4th Rd 48-49, FA Tphy QF replay 93-94.

Billingham Synthonia, the Northern League's FA Trophy flag-flyers, pictured before their vital 2-1 home win against Brandon United on Easter Saturday. Back Row (L/R): Tommy Connor, Richie Allen, Andy Harbron, Tony Lynch, Gary Popple, David O'Gorman, Charlie Butler, Tommy Cashley (Physio). Front: Barney Malone, Sean O'Brien, Paul Roberts, Craig Blyth, Andrew Banks, Lenny Darkes, Geoff Lilley.

Photo - Richard Brock.

CHESTER-LE-STREET TOWN

Chairman: John Tomlinson **Vice Chairman:** Jack Thornback **President:** John Holden.
Secretary: Melvin Atkinson, 1 St Marys Close, Chester-le-Street, Co Durham DH2 3EG (091 388 3664).
Manager: John Lang **Asst Mgr/Coach:** Peter Stronach **Physio:** Billy Jacobson.
Commercial Manager: Paul Days **Press Officer:** Jack Thornback (091 3883554).
Ground: Moor Park, Chester Moor, Chester-le Street, County Durham (091 3883363).
Directions: Ground lies approx 2 miles south of town on A167 (C.-le-S. to Durham road). Regular buses from C.-le-S. and Durham pass ground. Railway station 2 miles distant in town centre.
Seats: 200 **Cover:** 500 **Capacity:** 2,000 **Floodlights:** Yes **Founded:** 1972
Midweek Matches: Tuesday **Shop:** No, but old programmes available from editor.
Cols: Blue & white hoops/white/white **Change colours:** All yellow.
Programme: 32 pages, 30p **Programme Editor:** Press Officer **Nickname:** Cestrians
Clubhouse details: Open matchdays, Wed, Thurs & Sun. Wed/Thurs 7-10.30pm, Sun 12-2pm, midweek matches 6.30-10.30pm, Sat 12-10.30pm.
Previous Names: Garden Farm 1972-78.
Record win: 8-0 v Billingham T., FA Vase Preliminary Rd 6/10/84.
Record defeaat: 1-7 v Curzon Ashton, FA Vase Third Rd, 12/12/92.
Previous Leagues: Newcastle City Amtr 72-75/ Washington 75/ Wearside 77-83.
Previous Grounds: Ravensworth Welfare, Low Fell 72-73/ Riverside Pk 73-78/ Sacriston Welfare 78-79.
Record Gate: 473 v Barrow, FA Cup 83-84 (3,000 for Sunderland v Newcastle, Bradford appeal match 1985).
Players progressing to Football League: Dave Atkinson (Sunderland 1986), Peter Ward (Huddersfield 1987).
Captain & P.o.Y. 93-94: **Top Scorer 93-94:**
Club record scorer: Colin Howey, 50 **Club record appearances:** Brian Wray, 148.
Hons: Northern Lg Div 2 83-84, Wearside Lg 80-81 (R-up 82-83), Monkwearmouth Cup 80-81 81-82, FA Vase 4th Rd 91-92, Washington Lg, Durham Minor Cup, Washington AM Cup.

CONSETT

Chairman: F Lemon **Vice Chairman:** I Hamilton. **President:** D McVickers
Secretary: Peter McClean, 11 Cohort Close, Ebchester, Consett, Co. Durham DH8 0PG (0207 562712).
Manager: Colin Carr **Physio:** Joe Darroch **Press Officer:** TBA
Ground: Belle Vue Park, Ashdale Road, Consett, County Durham (0207 503788)
Directions: Quarter of mile north of town centre - along Medomsley Rd, left down Ashdale Rd, ground 100m yards on left. Follow signs for Sports Centre and Baths. Buses 745, 711 & 772 from Newcastle, 719, 765 from Durham. w signs for Sports Centre and Baths, about 800 yds from town centre.
Seats: 400 **Cover:** 1,000 **Capacity:** 4,000 **Floodlights:** Yes **Founded:** 1899
Colours: Red/black/red **Change colours:** Sky blue/dark blue/sky blue
Previous Leagues: Northern Alliance 19-26 35-37/ North Eastern 26-35 37-58 62-64/ Midland 58-60/ Northern Counties 60-62/ Wearside 64-70.
Programme: 16 pages, 30p **Programme Editor:** Colin French **Souvenir Shop:** No
Record Gate: 7,000 v Sunderland Reserves, first match at Belle Vue, 1950. **Nickname:** Steelmen
Clubhouse: Matchdays, and evenings on request. Darts & pool.
Best FA Cup season: 1st Rd 58-59 (lost 0-5 at Doncaster Rovers).
Previous Grounds: Vicarage Field (pre-1948)/ Leadgates Eden Colliery 48-50.
Players progressing to Football League: Tommy Lumley (Charlton), Alan Ellison (Reading), Laurie Cunningham (Barnsley), Jimmy Moir (Carlisle), Jackie Boyd (West Bromwich Albion).
Hons: North Eastern Lg 39-40 (Div 2 26-27, Lg Cup 50-51(jt) 53-54), Durham Challenge 47-48 49-50 58-59 60-61 68-69 (R-up 76-77 89-90), Northern Lg R-up 76-77 (Div 2 88-89, Lg Cup 78-79 80-81), Northern Counties Lg 61-62, Sunderland Shipowners Cup 67-68, Monkwearmouth Charity Cup 67-68, Wearside Lg R-up 68-69 69-70, FA Trophy 2nd Rd 78-79.
Local Newspapers: Journal, Northern Echo, Consett Advertiser. **Midweek Matches:** Wednesday

DUNSTON FEDERATION BREWERY

Chairman: John Thompson **Vice-Chairman:** Fred Fowles **President:** Norman Rippon.
Secretary: Bill Montague, 12 Dundee Close, Chapel House, Newcastle-upon-Tyne NE5 1JJ (091 2672250).
Manager: Peter Quigley **Asst Manager:** Steve Kendal **Physio:** Glen Martin.
Press Officer: Secretary **Commercial Secretary:** Malcolm James.
Ground: Federation Park, Wellington Road, Dunston, Gateshead (091 493 2935).
Directions: Dunston/Whickham exit off A1(M), ground 400 yds north along Dunston Rd on left. 1 mile from Dunston or Metrocentre stations. Numerous buses from Gateshead & Metrocentre stop outside ground.
Seats: 80 **Cover:** 200 **Capacity:** 2,000 **Floodlights:** Yes **Founded:** 1975
Colours: All blue (white trim) **Change:** Racing green/white. **Nickname:** The Fed
Programme: 28 pages, 30p **Editor:** Ian McPherson (091 420 5583) **Souvenir Shop:** No
Previous Ground: Dunston public park 75-86
Previous Leagues: Northrn Amtr 75-80/ Northern Combination 80-87/ Wearside 87-91.
Record Attendance: 1,550 - Sunderland Shipowners Cup Final 1/4/88.
Previous Names: Whickham Sports/ Dunston Mechanics Sports.
Best F.A. Vase season: Quarter-Finals 92-93 (lost 0-2 at Gresley Rovers).
Best F.A. Cup season: 3rd Qualifying Rd 92-93 (lost 0-3 to Northallerton Town).
Sponsors: Federation Brewery **Clubhouse:** Matchdays only. Hot & cold snacks, darts, pool.
Midweek home matchday: Tuesday **Reserve team:** None.
Record win: 11-0 v Willington (A), Northern League Division Two, 1992-93.
Record defeat: 1-6 v Billingham Synthonia (A), Northern Division One, 1993-94.
Club record scorer: Paul King **Club record appearances:** Paul Dixon.
Captain 93-94: Tom Ditchburn **Top Scorer 93-94:** Ian Mulholland.
P.o.Y. 93-94: David Guthrie.
Hons: Northern Lg Div 2 92-93, Northern Amtr Lg 77-78 (R-up 76-77 78-79, Lg Cup 77-78 78-79 (R-up 75-76), Lg Shield 78-79 79-80), Wearside Lg 88-89 89-90 (R-up 90-91, Lg Cup 90-91), Northern Comb. 86-87 (R-up 80-81 83-84 85-86, Lg Cup 83-84 86-87 (R-up 80-81 84-85 85-86)), Sunderland Shipowners Cup 87-88, Durham County Tphy 81-82 (R-up 83-84 85-86, Minor Cup 79-80 (R-up 78-79)), Gateshead Charity Cup 77-78 80-81, Heddon Homes Cup 80-81.

DURHAM CITY

Chairman: Dennis Kerry **Vice Chairman:** A Thompson **President:** G Newton.
Secretary: T Derrick, 63 Staneway, Felling, Gateshead NE10 8LS (091 469 6935).
Manager: B Cruddas **Asst Manager/Coach:** T Harrison
Physio: Joanne Dowson **Commercial Manager:** D Willis.
Press Officer: Secretary.
Ground: TBA (to groundshare at Chester-le-Street Town at start of 94-95 season).
Directions: TBA
Seats: **Cover:** **Capacity:** **Floodlights:** Yes **Founded:** 1918
Colours: Yellow/blue/yellow **Change colours:** Red/black/red. **Reformed:** 1949.
Programme: 30 pages **Editor:** Dave Asberry (091 386 6469) **Souvenir Shop:** No
Clubhouse details: Mon - Fri 7-11pm & Sat 12-6 & 7-11pm (closed Sunday). **Nickname:** City
Previous Leagues: Victory 18-19/ North Eastern 19-21 28-38/ Football League 21-28/ Wearside 38-39 50-51.
Prev. Grounds: Garden House Park 18-21/ Holliday Park 21-38/ Ferens Park 49-94. *Nb club disbanded in 1938.*
Record Attendance: 6,000 v Tranmere Rovers, FA Cup 2nd Rd 56-57 *(at Ferens Park).*
Best FA Cup season: 2nd Rd 25-26 57-58 (Also 1st Rd 27-28 55-56).
Players progressing to Football League: Harry Houlahan (Newcastle 1951), Derek Clark (Lincoln 1951), Leo Dale & David Adamson (Doncaster 1954 & 70), Stan Johnstone (Gateshead 1954), Dennis Coughlan (Barnsley 1957), John Wile (Sunderland 1966), Brian Taylor (Coventry 1968), Paul Malcolm (Rochdale 1984).
Midweek Matches: Wednesday. **Local Press:** Northern Echo, Sunderland Echo, Evening Chronicle.
Club Sponsors: Key Windows **Club record appearances:** Joe Raine, 552.
Captain 93-94: Billy Irwin **P.o.Y. 93-94:** Dave Race (keeper) **Top Scorer 93-94:** Michael Taylor, 29.
Hons: Northern Lg 93-94 (R-up 70-71, Div 2 R-up 30-31 91-92), FA Vase QF 87-88, Durham Benevolent Bowl 55-56, FA Amtr Cup 2nd Rd rep. 57-58, FA Tphy 1st Rd 83-84, Durham Challenge Cup R-up(2).

Andy Whitmore of Eppleton Colliery Welfare (dark strip) heads clear under pressure from Durham City's Mark Ferguson. Eppleton did exceptionally well to hold the run-away league leaders to a goalless draw in this Easter Monday fixture, Durham's last-ever game at Ferens Park. *Photo - Gavin Ellis-Neville.*

EPPLETON COLLIERY WELFARE

Chairman: Ralph Lawson **Vice Chairman:** Mr R D Tate **President:** Mr F Hartis.
Secretary: Mr K Browell, 9 Willis Street, Hetton-le-Hole DH15 9AE (091 526 0080).
Manager: Stephen Johnson **Asst Manager:** Gerry Hogan **Physio:** Ted Collinson.
Commercial Mgr: David Gardner **Press Officer:** Secretary.
Ground: Eppleton Welfare Park, Park View, Hetton-le-Hole, Tyne & Wear (091 5261048).
Directions: Situated behind Front Street Post Office & directly behind Hetton swimming baths, Hetton-le-Hole on A182. Buses 194, 535, 231, X5, X94 in Front Street. 8 miles from Durham BR statio; buses 154 and 254 from Durham.
Seats: 50 **Cover:** 500 **Capacity:** 2,500 **Floodlights:** Yes **Founded:** 1929.
Colours: White (blue/black trim)/blue/blue **Change:** Yellow/green/yellow.
Record Attendance: 2,300 v Emlyn Hughes All-Stars, July 1992. Competitive: 1,250 - Monkwearmouth Charity Cup Final 1987-88.
Previous Grounds: None **Previous Names:** None (merged with Natcobos, early 70's).
Previous Leagues: Wearside 51-65 74-92/ Houghton & District 65-74.
Programme: 16 pages, 20p **Editor:** Fred Berry (091 584 2452) **Nickname:** Welfare
Club Shop: Club sweaters, polo shirts, metal lapel badges available - contact David Gardiner (091 526 5543).
Club Sponsors: Citibank Life
Midweek home matchday: Wednesday **Reserve team's League:** None.
Clubhouse: Bar & lounge on ground. Normal opening hours. Whitbread beers.
P.o.Y. 93-94: Graham Wood **Captain & Top Scorer 93-94:** Paul Bryson
Hons: Northern Lg Div 2 R-up 92-93, Wearside Lg 90-91 91-92 (Lg Cup 74-75 78-79 87-88, Sunderland Shipowners Cup 47-48 85-86 90-91 (R-up 91-92), Monkwearmouth Charity Charity Cup 89-90 90-91 91-92), Durham Challenge Cup 89-90.

FERRYHILL ATHLETIC

Chairman: B Campbell **Vice Chairman:** W Walker **President:** Forster.
Secretary: Ralph Carr, 23 Morrison Terrace, Ferryhill Station, Co. Durham DL17 9DQ (0740 652437).
Manager: P Mulcaster **Asst Manager:** M Crowe **Coach:** G Hartley.
Press Officer: Secretary **Physio:** V Chapman/ M Mulcaster.
Ground: Darlington Road, Ferryhill, County Durham (0740 651937).
Directions: Ground on main A167 (old A1) Darlington-Durham road, on left coming from south. United buses 722 & 723 (Newcastle-Darlington) pass ground.
Seats: 400 **Cover:** 400 **Capacity:** 6,000 **Floodlights:** Yes **Founded:** 1921.
Colours: Amber & black quarters **Change colours:** Red & white stripes/white/white.
Midweek Matches: Tuesday **Previous Leagues:** Palatine 21-23. **Nickname:** Latics.
Record Attendance: 13,000 v Bishop Auckland, FA Amateur Cup.
Record win: 18-0 v Skinningrove Works (H), FA Cup First Qualifying Rd 26/9/53.
Previous Name: Dean Bank Villa. **Best F.A. Cup season:** 1st Rd 35-36 53-54.
Players progressing to Football League: William Marsh (Barsley 1947), Richard Steel (Bristol City 1953), Alex Greenwood (Chelsea 1953), John Edgar & John Peverell (Darlington 1954 & 59), Roland Horney (Blackburn 1963), John Pearson (Hartlepool 1967).
Programme: TBA **Midweek home matchday:** Tuesday **Club Shop:** No.
Clubhouse: Opens 7pm Mon-Fri, 7pm Sat (1pm matchdays), Sun 12-3 & 7pm Sundays.
Captain 93-94: **Top Scorer 93-94:**
Honours: Northern Lg 37-38 47-48 57-58 (R-up 23-24), Durham Challenge Cup 23-24 70-71, Durham Benevolent Cup 53-54 56-57 61-62, Durham Amateur Cup 21-22, FA Amateur Cup 4th Rd 25-26 63-64, FA Trophy 2nd Qualifying Rd replay 81-82 89-90 90-91.
Local Newspapers: Northern Echo

Ferryhill's Ged Hartley leaves Graham Williams of Guisborough on the deck, but his side slip to a 0-3 defeat. *Photo - Dave West.*

GUISBOROUGH TOWN

Chairman: John Newton **Vice Chairman:** Keith Watson **President:** Vacant
Secretary: Keith Smeltzer, 55 Thames Ave., Guisborough, Cleveland TS14 8AR (0287 638993).
Manager: Mike Hodgson **Asst Manager:** Bob Dewhirst **Coach:** Alec Smith.
Physio: Bobby Veart **Press Officer:** John Newton.
Ground: King George V Ground, Howlbeck Rd, Guisborough, Cleveland (0287 636925).
Directions: From west: bear left at 2nd set of lights, left into Howlbeck Rd after quarter mile, ground at end. Buses from Middlesbrough.
Seats: 100 **Cover:** 400 **Capacity:** 3,500 **Floodlights:** Yes **Founded:** 1973.
Colours: Red & white **Change colours:** Yellow **Nickname:** Priorymen
Previous Leagues: Middlesbrough & District/ South Bank/ Northern Alliance 77-80/ Midland Counties 80-82/ Northern Counties (East) 82-85.
Programme: 32 pages, 40p **Programme Editor:** Les Crossman (0642 473478).
Club Shop: Yes, selling clothing etc. Contact Bob & Gladys Hall (0287 635769).
Club Sponsors: Bells Stores. **Midweek home matchday:** Wednesday
Reserve Team's League: Vaux Wearside.
Record Gate: 3,112 v Hungerford, FA Vase SF, 1980 *(at Middlesbrough FC - 5,990 v Bury, FA Cup 1st Rd 1988).*
Best FA Cup season: First Round Proper 1988-89 (lost 0-1 to Bury).
Rec. win: 6-0 v Ferryhill & v Easington **Record defeat:** 0-4 v Billingham Synthonia.
Clubhouse: Evenings & weekends. Darts & pool. Hot & cold snacks and drinks from kitchen on matchdays.
Players progressing to Football League: Frank Harrison (Middlesbrough 1982), Mark Foster (Leicester 1983).
Local Newspapers: Middlesbrough Evening Gazette, Northern Echo.
Record scorer: Mark Davis 551 **Record appearances:** Mark Davis 323.
Captain 93-94: Trevor Smith **P.o.Y. 93-94:** Neal Grannycombe **Top Scorer 93-94:** Mark Davis 25
Hons: FA Vase R-up 79-80, Northern Lg Cup 87-88 (Div 2 R-up 86-87), Northern Alliance 79-80 (R-up 78-79, Lg Cup 78-79), North Riding Senior Cup 89-90 90-91 91-92 92-93 93-94, FA Trophy 1st Rd replay 90-91.

Ferryhill Athletic - who completed a second consecutive 'great escape' from relegation in 1993-94.
Photo - Dave West.

HEBBURN

Chairman: J Hunter **Vice-Chairman:** B Errington
Secretary: Mr Lawrence Appleby, 49 Heaton Park Court, Heaton, Newcastle-upon-Tyne NE6 5PR (091 276 6965)
Manager: Tony Robinson **Assistant Manager/Coach:** Peter Harrison.
Commercial Manager: George McHugh. **Press Officer:** Alan Armstrong (091 430 0078).
Ground: Hebburn Sports & Social, Club Ground, South Drive, Hebburn (091 483 5101).
Directions: On the main road through the town about 1 mile from railway station. Hebburn lies on the Metroline - excellent bus service from Heworth Metro.
Seats: 20 **Cover:** 200 **Capacity:** 2,000 **Floodlights:** Yes **Founded:** 1912
Colours: Yellow & black stripes/black/black **Change colours:** Red/red/blue
Programme: 24 pages, 30p **Programme Editor:** John Diamond **Souvenir Shop:** No
Midweek Matches: Wednesday **Sponsors:** Forrest Caterers **Nickname:** Hornets.
Previous Grounds: None **Previous Names:** Reyrolles/ Hebburn Reyrolles (pre-1988).
Previous Leagues: Jarrow & Dist. Jnr 12-14/ South Shields Comb. 19-22/ Tyneside Comb. 22-27/ Tyneside 27-39/ Northern Comb. 41-44 45-59/ North Eastern 44-45 59-60/ Wearside 60-89.
Best FA Vase season: 2nd Round 91-92.
Best FA Cup season: 2nd Qualifying Rd replay 89-90 (lost 0-3 at South Bank).
Record win: 10-1 **Record defeat:** 3-10.
Record Gate: 503 v Darwen, FA Cup Preliminary Round replay 7/9/91.
Clubhouse details: Open 7-11pm weekdays, Sat 11am-1pm, Sun noon-2.30pm. Pool, darts etc.
Capt. 93-94: Les Tatum **Top Scorer 93-94:** Stuart Wright **Record scorer:** Keith Carter
Hons: Shields Gazette Cup 91-92, Wearside Lg 66-67 (Monkwearmouth Charity Cup 68-69), Durham Challenge Cup 42-43 91-92, Tyneside Lg 38-39, Northern Comb. 43-44, Gateshead Charity Cup 35-36 37-38, Palmer Hospital Cup 27-28, Hebburn Aged Miners Cup 35-36, Heddon Homes Cup 42-43, Hebburn Infirmary Cup 35-36 36-37 37-38 38-39.

MURTON

Chairman: J T Pratt **Vice Chairman:** J Hudson **President:** John Hellens.
Secretary: J C Gardner, 74 Winds Lonnen, Murton, County Durham SR7 9TG (091 526 3449).
Manager: Jeff Cranson **Asst Mgr:** Brian Burlinson **Coach:** Richie Madden.
Physio: Vince Symmonds **Press Officer:** Willie Grogan **Commercial Mgr:** T Carr.
Ground: Recreation Park, Church Lane, Murton, County Durham (091 517 0814).
Directions: Exit A19 onto B1285 heading west into Murton - Church Lane on left opposite catholic church.
Seats: 100 **Cover:** 320 **Capacity:** 3,500 **Floodlights:** Yes **Founded:** 1904
Colours: White (red trim) **Change colours:** Red/black/red **Nickname:** Gnashers
Previous Grounds: Fatton Pasture 04-28.
Previous Names: Murton Red Star 04-28/ Murton Colliery Welfare 28-88.
Previous Leagues: Wearside 13-46 51-88/ North East Counties 46-51.
Past players progressing to Football League: Numerous.
Programme: 12 pages, 30p **Programme Editor:** Stuart Upperton **Club Shop:** No.
Club Sponsors: John Hellyns **Midweek home matchday:** Wednesday
Record Gate: 3,500 v Spennymoor Utd, Durham Challenge Cup 1951.
Record win: 17-1 v Thornley **Record defeat:** 0-14 v South Shields (H).
Clubhouse: 'The International' 300 yards from ground on B1285. Normal pub hours. Restaurant upstairs. Function room for 100. Open plan downstairs with horse shoe bar. Matchday snacks at ground.
Club record scorer: **Club record appearances:** Robert Welch 500 (1962-78).
Hons: Northern Lg Div 2 89-90, Wearside Lg 28-29 36-37 59-60 (Lg Cup 58-59 70-71), Sunderland Shipowners Cup 59-60 69-70 70-71, Monkwearmouth Charity Cup 21-22 28-29 34-35 35-36 63-64 70-71 87-88, Durham Chall. Cup 92-93, Durham Jnr Cup 50-51.

NORTHALLERTON TOWN

Chairman: John Farndane **Vice Chairman:** Ian Bolland **President:** Dennis Cope
Secretary: Mr Ken Homer, 28 Aysgarth Grove, Romanby, Northallerton, North Yorks DL7 8HY (0609 779686).
Manager/Coach: Archie Stevens **Physio:** John Murray
Comm. Mgr: Les Hood (0609 774580) **Press Officer:** Ian Bolland (0609 776900).
Ground: Ainderby Rd, Romanby, Northallerton, North Yorks (0609 772418).
Directions: Leave A1 at Leeming Bar (A684) follow signs to Northallerton, approaching town take B1333 signed Romanby - ground 250yds on left. Three quarters of a mile from Northallerton BR station - local bus from town centre (one and a half miles) passes ground.
Seats: 150 **Cover:** 500 **Capacity:** 3,000 **Floodlights:** Yes **Founded:** 1893
Colours: Black & white/black/black **Change colours:** Yellow/blue/yellow. **Nickname:** Town
Previous Leagues: Allertonshire (now defunct)/ Vale of Mowbray (defunct)/ Ripon & Dist./ Teesside/ North Yorks (defunct)/ Darlington & Dist./ Harrogate & Dist.
Programme: 16 pages, 50p **Previous Ground:** Bluestone Ground (pre-1975).
Shop: Sells replica kit, scarves, rosettes, progs, badges. Mike Walker (0609 780835)/Les Hood (774580).
Club Sponsors: TBA **Record Gate:** 671 v Farnborough, FA Tphy 3rd Rd 20/2/93.
Midweek home matchday: Wednesday **Best FA Cup year:** 4th Qual. Rd 92-93, lost 1-3 at Accrington
Best FA Trophy year: 3rd Round 92-93 (lost 1-3 at home to Farnborough Town).
Record win: 7-0 v Willington (A) **Record defeat:** 2-7 v Easington (A), both Northern Lg Div 2.
Prev. Name: Northallerton Alliance. **Reserve Team's League:** Vaux Wearside.
Clubhouse: Mon-Fri 7.30-11pm, Sat noon-7.30pm, Sun 12-2 & 7.30-10.30pm.
Players progressing to Football League: Andy Toman (Hartlepool, Darlington, Scarborough).
Local Newspapers: Northern Echo, Darlington & Stockton Times, North Yorks News.
Captain 93-94: Lee Wasden **P.o.Y. & Top Scorer 93-94:** John Wood.
Club record scorer: John Woods **Club record appearances:** Lee Wasden.
Hons: Northern Lg Cup 93-94 (Div 2 R-up 89-90), North Riding Snr Cup R-up 83-84, Harrogate & Dist. Lg, Richmond Cup, Bedale Cup, Millbank Cup, Orde Powlett Cup, Harrogate Invitation Cup, Alverton Trophy.

PETERLEE NEWTOWN

President: David Brown **Chairman:** Brian Hall **Vice-Chairman:** Bill Burnett.
Press Officer/Secretary: Danny Cassidy, 23 Melbury Str., Seaham, County Durham SR7 7NF (091 581 4591).
Manager: Tommy Smith **Asst Manager:** Eddie Freeman **Physio:** Ron Lamdrel.
Ground: Eden Lane, Peterlee, County Durham (091 586 3004). **Directions:** From town centre Fire Station, turn left into Edenhill Rd, then right into Robson Ave. Left at the next junction and ground is on the right.
Seats: 50 **Cover:** 200 **Capacity:** 6,000 **Floodlights:** Yes **Year Formed:** 1976
Colours: Sky/navy/sky **Change colours:** Yellow/black/yellow **Club Shop:** No.
Programme: 10 pages, 30p **Programme Editor:** Secretary
Sponsors: Artix Ltd **Previous lges:** Northern Alliance 76-79/ Wearside 79-82.
Clubhouse details: Open normal licensing hours. Sandwiches etc available.
Nickame: Newtowners. **Rec. Gate:** 2,350 v Northern, Hillsborough Fund match 1989.
Midweek Matches: Wednesday. **Local Press:** Hartlepool Mail, Sunderland Echo, Northern Echo.
Best FA Cup season: 4th Qual. Rd replay 85-86 (lost 0-1 at home to Whitby after 2-2 draw).
Players progressing to Football Lge: Keith Fairless (Scarborough) 1986, Brian Honour (Hartlepool) 1988).
Club record scorer: Keith Fairless **Club record appearances:** Keith Bendelow.
Capt. 93-94: Stephen Routledge **P.o.Y. 93-94:** Stuart Dawson **Top Scorer 93-94:** Chris Hall.
Honours: Northern Lg Div 2 82-83, North Eastern F'lit League, 4th Qual Rd FA Cup

PRUDHOE TOWN

Chairman: George Bell **Manager:** Terry Hunter **Asst Manager:** Kenny Barton
Secretary: Brian Tulip, 12 Orchard Close, Prudhoe NE42 5LP (0661 833169).
Physio: Ernie Goodfellow **Press Officer:** D Noble.
Ground: Kimberley Park, Broomhouse Road, Prudhoe, Northumberland NE42 5EH (Tel/Fax: 0661 835900).
Directions: Approach Prudhoe along A695, turn right at 'Falcon' Inn, 200 yds down Eastwood Rd., turn left into Broomhouse Rd., ground on right.
Seats: 150 **Cover:** Yes **Capacity:** 5,000 **Floodlights:** Yes **Founded:** 1959
Cols: Royal & white hoops/royal/white **Change:** White & blue chevrons/navy/sky.
Programme: 8 pages, 20p **Programme Editor:** J Smith **Nickname:** Citizens
Midweek Matches: Wednesday **Clubhouse:** Open every evening plus Sat/Sun lunchtimes
Prev. Lges: Hexham & Dist 59-69/ Newcastle & Dist 69-71/ Northern Comb./ Northern Amtr/ Northern All. 84-88.
Sponsors: Swinton Insurance **Record Gate:** 2,500 v Blyth, Northumberland Snr Cup 1981.
Previous Names: Ovington 1969-75/ Prudhoe East End 75-94.
Previous Grounds: Farm field, Ovington 59-68/ Mickley Welfare 68-69.
Captain 93-94: Mick Lee **Top Scorer 93-94:** David Fothergill **P.o.Y. 93-94:** Allen Myhill.
Hons: Hexham & Dist. Lg 68-69 (Lg Cup 68-69), Newcastle & Dist. Lg 69-70 70-71 (Lg Cup 69-70, Charity Shield 69-70 70-71), Northern Comb. 79-80, Northerm Amtr Lg 71-72, Clayton Charity Cup 68-69, Northumberland Minor Cup 78-79, Northumberland Benevolent Bowl 79-80, Heddon Homes Charity Cup 81-82.

Right: *Prudhoe striker Ian Phillips lofts the opening goal into the net during the second-half of the 2-0 win at Darlington Cleveland Social on Easter Sunday.*
Photo - Dave West.

R.T.M. NEWCASTLE

Chairman: Tom Brown **Vice-Chairman:** Brian Mordue.
Secretary/Press Off.: Jim Anderson, 7 Whitbeck Rd, Statyford, Newcastle-upon-Tyne NE5 2XA (091 274 3941).
Manager/Coach: Rob Carney **Assistant Manager:** S Carney **Physio:** Michael Hayley
Ground: Wheatsheaf Sports Ground, Woolsington, Newcastle-upon-Tyne (091 286 0425).
Directions: From central station follow airport signs for 7 miles - ground next to Wheatsheaf Hotel on left, approximately 800yds before airport. Callerton Parkway metro station is 400yds from ground.
Seats: 300 **Cover:** 300 **Capacity:** 2,000 **Floodlights:** Yes **Founded:** 1930
Colours: Blue & white/white/blue **Change colours:** All red **Nickname:** 'Star'
Previous Grounds: None **Previous Names:** Blue Star 30-86/ Newcastle Blue Star 86-94.
Club Sponsors: RTM **Reserve Team's League:** None.
Previous Leagues: Newcastle Business Houses 32-38/ North East Amateur/ Tyneside Amateur/ Northern Combination/ Wearside 75-85.
Past players progressing to Football League: Ian Crumplin & Tony Robinson (Hartlepool 1976 & 1986), Barry Dunn (Darlington 1979), Ian McInerney (Huddersfield Town 1988).
Programme: 12 pages, 30p **Programme Editor:** Brian Mordue (091 267 9698).
Midweek home matchday: Monday **Record Gate:** 1,800 v Almondsbury Greenway, FA Vase SF 77-78.
Club Shop: Yes - open matchdays. **Clubhouse:** Matchdays only. Hotdogs, soup, sandwiches available.
Best FA Cup season: 1st Rd 84-85 (lost 0-2 at York C.).
Best FA Trophy season: Quarter-finals 88-89 (lost 1-4 at home to Telford United).
Captain 93-94: P Gibson **Club record appearances & record scorer:** Ian Crumplin.
Top Scorer 93-94: S Pidgeon **Player-of-the-Year 93-94:** P O'Hagan.
Hons: FA Vase 77-78 (SF 81-82), FA Trophy QF 88-89, Northern Lg R-up 87-88 (Lg Cup 85-86 (R-up(1)), Div 2 85-86), Wearside Lg 73-74 75-76 82-83 83-84 84-85 (R-up 74-75 77-78 79-80, Lg Cup 76-77 79-80 80-81 82-83 83-84, Sunderland Shipowners Cup 82 83 84 85, Monkwearmouth Charity Cup 74-75 79-80 82-83 88-89, Northern Comb. 62-63 68-69 (Lg Cup 66-67 71-72), Northumberland Snr Cup 76 77 82 83 85-86 87-88 (R-up 74-75 78-79 80-81, Minor Cup 64-65), J R Cleator Cup 86-87.

Peter Gibson of Blue Star, now RTM Newcastle, beats of two Seaham defenders. *Photo - Dave West.*

SEAHAM RED STAR

Chairman: Bryan C Mayhew **Vice Chairman:** Reg Atkinson **President:** Michael English.
Secretary: John McBeth, 29 Frederick Street, Seaham, County Durham SR7 7HX (091 581 5712).
Manager: Chris Copeland **Asst Manager:** Paul Walker.
Physio: Allan Jackson **Press Officer:** John Campbell (091 581 4308).
Ground: Seaham Town Park, Stockton Road, Seaham, County Durham (091 581 2540).
Directions: From Tyne Tunnel: A19 Teeside approx 8 miles; B1404 Seaham slip road, left at top of slip road. Right at traffic lights & first left past school into ground.
Seats: 60 **Cover:** 200 **Capacity:** 4,000 **Floodlights:** Yes **Year Formed:** 1973
Colours: Red & white/red/red **Change colours:** All blue **Nickname:** The Star
Previous Leagues: Sunday football/ Houghton & District 73-74/ Northern Alliance 74-79/ Wearside 79-83.
Programme: 20 pages **Editor:** David Copeland (091 581 8514) **Club Shop:** No.
Clubhouse details: New clubhouse. Mon-Sat 11am-11pm, Sun 12-2, 7-10.30pm. Large function room, snooker, pool, Restuarant & Bars.
Record Attendance: 1,500 v Guisborough, Wearside Lg/ v Sunderland, floodlight opener 1979.
Previous Name: Seaham Colliery Welfare Red Star 78-87.
Previous Grounds: Deneside Recreation Recreation Park 73-75/ Vane Tempest Welfare 75-78.
Players progressing to Football League: Bobby Davison (Huddersfield 1980), Nigel Gleghorn (Ipswich 1985), Billy Stubbs (Nottm Forest 1987), Paul Nixon (Bristol Rovers (1989), Mick Smith (Hartlepool).
Local Newspapers: Sunderland Echo, Journal, Northern Echo, Football Echo, Washington Times.
Midweek home matchday: Wednesday **Reserve team's League:** Banks Youth League.
Club record scorer: Tom Henderson **Club record appearances:** Michael Whitfield.
Hons: Northern Lg Cup 92-93, Phillips F'lit Tphy 78-79, Durham Chal. Cup 79-80, Wearside Lg 81-82 (Lg Cup 81-82, Div 2 R-up 87-88, Monkwearmouth Charity Cup R-up 79-80), FA Vase 5th Rd 78-79, FA Tphy 2nd Rd 89-90.

SHILDON

Chairman: Bill Aisbitt **Vice Chairman:** George Elliott **President:** John Atkinson.
Secretary: Mike Armitage, 22 Hambleton Ct, Byerley Park, Newton Aycliffe, Co. Durham DL5 7HR (0325 316322).
Manager: Ray Gowan **Asst Manager:** Phil Owers **Physio:** Jimmy Smalls
Press Officer: Secretary **Ground:** Dean Street, Shildon, County Durham (0388 773877).
Directions: In the town centre one mile from BR station and 300yds from Darlington-Bishop Auckland bus stop (Hippodrome stop).
Seats: 400 **Cover:** 500 **Capacity:** 4,000 **Floodlights:** Yes **Founded:** 1890
Club colours: All red **Change colours:** Green & black or all blue.
Programme: 28 pages, 30p **Editor:** Neil Bennett (0325 332310) **Souvenir Shop:** No
Clubhouse details: Open every evening 7.30-11pm (open earlier on matchnights), 1pm onwards on Satrurday matchdays. Bar, pool & darts.
Previous Leagues: Auckland & District 1892-96/ Wearside 96-97/ North Eastern 07-32.
Record Attendance: 13,000 - Leeholme v Perkinsville, schoolboys game, 1920s. For Shildon game; 11,000 Shildon v Ferryhill Athletic, Durham Senior Cup 1922.
Previous Name: Shildon Town 1890-94/ Shildon Utd 94-1900/ Shildon Athletic 00-23.
Best FA Cup season: 2nd Rd 36-37. Also 1st Rd 27-28 29-30 34-35 36-37 55-56 59-60 61-62.
Record win: 13-1 Tow Law Town (H), Northern League 10/3/34.
Record defeat: 0-12 v Whitley Bay (A), Northern League 26/8/61.
Players progressing to Football League: Ken Whitfield (Wolves 1947), James Smith (Chelsea 1951), Mike Peacock & Philip Shute (Darlington 1960 & 84), Kevin Stonehouse (Blackburn 1979).
Local Newspapers: Northern Echo **Midweek Matches:** Wednesday
Club Sponsors: Atkinsons Stairs **Club Nickname:** Railwaymen.
Club record appareances: Bryan Dale **Club record scorer:** Jack Downing, 61 (1936-37).
Captain 93-94: Bryan Liddle **P.o.Y. 93-94:** Charlie Walton **Top Scorer 93-94:** Nigel Bolton.
Honours: Northern Lg 33-34 34-35 35-36 36-37 39-40 (R-up 32-33 38-39, Lg Cup 33-34 34-35 37-38 38-39 39-40 52-53), Durham Challenge Cup 07-08 25-26 71-72, Durham Amateur Cup 01-02 02-03, Durham Benevelopment Bowl 24-25, FA Trophy 3rd Qualifying Rd 74-75, FA Amateur Cup 4th Rd 58-59, FA Vase 1st Rd 86-87.

Shildon suffered a heavy 0-5 home defeat against Durham City on Good Friday. Here the experienced John Reach (extreme right) opens the visitors' account.

Photo - Alan Watson.

TOW LAW TOWN

Chairman: Harry Hodgson **Press Officer:** Secretary
Secretary: Bernard Fairbairn, 3 Coppice Walk, Mowden Park, Darlington, County Durham DL3 9DP (0325 350743).
Manager: Stuart Leeming **Assistant Manager:** Michael Haley
Ground: Ironworks Road, Tow Law, Bishop Auckland (0388 731443).
Directions: Just of High Street in Tow Law town centre.
Seats: 200 **Cover:** 300 **Capacity:** 6,000 **Floodlights:** Due **Founded:** 1890
Colours: Black & white stripes/black/black & white **Change colours:** Red & white
Previous leagues: None **Programme:** None **Club Shop:** Yes
Clubhouse: Every evening 8.30 -10.30. **Record Gate:** 5,500 v Mansfield Town, FA Cup 1967.
Best FA Cup season: 2nd Rd replay 67-68. Also Competition Proper 68-69 84-85 89-90.
League Clubs defeated in F.A. Cup: Mansfield Town 67-68. **Nickname:** Lawyers.
Players progressing to Football League: Reuben Cook & Ralph Guthrie (Arsenal 1951 & 53), Gordon Hughes & Terry Melling & Chris Waddle (Newcastle 1956 & 65 & 80), Eric Johnstone & Kevin Dixon (Carlisle 1963 & 83), Keith Adamson (Barnsley 1966), Tom Henderson (Bradford PA 1969), Vincent Chapman (Huddersfield 1988).
Hons: Rothmans National Cup 1977, Northern Lg 23-24 24-25 (R-up 28-29 88-89, Lg Cup 73-74, Rothmans Overseas Cup 76-77), Durham Chal. Cup 1895-96, Durham Amtr Cup 1892-93, FA Amtr Cup 3rd Rd rep. 70-71, FA Tphy 2nd Rd rep. 82-83.
Local Newspapers: Northern Echo **Midweek Matches:** Tuesday

WEST AUCKLAND TOWN

Chairman: Mr Norman Ayton **Vice Chairman:** Mr L Nevison **President:** Mr B Hathaway
Sec./Press Officer: Allen Bayles, 11 Edith Terrace, West Auckland, Co. Durham DL14 9JT (0388 833783).
Manager: Alan Gates **Assistant Manager:** Roger Wicks **Coach:** Eric Gates
Commercial Manager: Dave Buckingham.
Ground: Darlington Road, West Auckland, County Durham (0388 834403).
Directions: Leaving West Auckland take A68 - ground on right before leaving the village. On bus route via Bishop Auckland from Newcastle or Darlington.
Seats: 250 **Cover:** 250 **Capacity:** 3,000 **Floodlights:** Yes **Founded:** 1892
Midweek Matches: Tuesday **Prev. Names:** St Helens Utd (1919 only)/ West Auck. Town.
Colours: All white **Change colours:** Tangerine/red/red. **Nickname:** West.
Sponsors: Fenwick Transport/ Southfield Builders/ Hath-away Roofing. **Souvenir Shop:** No.
Previous League: Auckland & District.
Clubhouse: None - use local Working Men's Club five mins walk away (Thomas Lipton Trophy on display within). On ground reception room for visiting officials and snack bar selling teas, coffees, soup, pies, burgers etc.
Record Attendance: 6,000 v Dulwich Hamlet, F.A. Amateur Cup 58-59.
Best FA Cup season: 1st Rd 58-59 61-62
Players progressing to Football League: None.
Record win: 11-0 in Durham Co. Cup **Record defeat:** 0-10 v Stanley United.
Top Scorer 93-94: Paul Adamson **Captain & P.o.Y. 93-94:** Robin Gill.
Club record scorer: George Brown **Club record appearances:** Alan Porter, 10 seasons.
Hons: FA Amtr Cup R-up 60-61 (QF 59-60), Northern Lg 59-60 60-61 (Div 2 90-91, Lg Cup 59-60 62-63 (R-up 48-49 61-62 63-64)), Durham Challenge Cup 63-64, Durham Benevolent Cup 62-63, FA Trophy 3rd Rd 77-78, Sir Thomas Lipton Trophy (First World Cup!) 1909 1911.

Mark Wheldon of West Auckland has a shot blocked by Chester-le-Street's Paul Clark (hoops).
Photo - Alan Watson.

WHITBY TOWN

Chairman: G Manser **President:** Don Dunwell.
Secretary: Charles T Woodward, 31 Castle Rd, Whitby, North Yorks YO21 3NQ (0947 602312).
Manager: R H 'Bob' Scaife **Asst Manager:** L Scott **Physio:** I Jackson.
Press Officer: Secretary **Commercial Manager:** G Manser (0947 83382).
Ground: Turnbull Ground, Upgang Lane, Whitby, North Yorks (0947 604847).
Directions: Take A174 road from town centre. Ground on offside travelling towards Sandsend.
Seats: 200 **Cover:** 400 **Capacity:** 4,000 **Floodlights:** Yes **Founded:** 1926
Colours: All royal blue **Change colours:** All white **Previous Lges:** None
Programme: 22 pages, 40p **Editor:** G Manser (0947 83382)
Souvenir Shop: Yes, contact secretary.
Record Attendance: 4,000 v Scarborough, North Riding Snr Cup 18/4/65
Nickname: Seasiders. **Prev. Name:** Whitby Utd (pre-1950)
Best F.A. Cup season: 2nd Rd 83-84 (0-1 at Wigan).
Football League Clubs defeated in F.A. Cup: Halifax Town 83-84.
Players progressing to Football League: Malcolm Poskett (Hartlepool, Brighton, Watford, Sammy Kemp (Huddersfield), Jimmy Mulvaney (Hartlepool, Barrow, Stockport), Bobby Veart (Hartlepool), Derek Hampton & Trevor Smith & John Linacre & Phil Linacre (Hartlepool), Mark Hine (Grimsby).
Midweek Matches: Wednesday **Local Newspapers:** Whitby Gazette, Northern Echo.
Club Sponsors: Arnott Insurance **Record win:** 11-2 v Cargo Fleet Wks, 1950
Rec. defeat: 3-13 v Willington, 24/3/28. **Clubhouse:** Mon-Fri 7-11pm, Sat 12-11pm, Sun 12-2 & 7-10.30.
Club record scorer: Paul Pitman **Club record appearances:** Derek Hampton.
Captain 93-94: S Corden **P.o.Y. 93-94:** J Scott **Top Scorer 93-94:** Phil Linacre 39
Honours: FA Amtr Cup R-up 64-65, FA Tphy QF 83-84, Northern Lg 92-93 (R-up 27-28 33-34 67-68 81-82 82-83, Lg Cup 28-29 63-64 69-70 76-77 84-85), Rothmans Overseas Cup 75-76 77-78), Nth Riding Snr Cup 83-84 84-85 87-88 90-91.

DIVISION TWO CLUBS 1994-95

ALNWICK TOWN

Chairman: J Draycott **Press Officer:** Secretary
Secretary: R Miller, 31 York Cres., Alnwick, Northumberland NE66 1RL (0665 605118).
Manager: D Clark **Assistant Manager:** Dave Williamson.
Ground: St James' Park, Alnwick, Northumberland (0665 603162).
Directions: 35 miles north of Newcastle on A1, take the slip road to Alnwick, then first left. At roundabout turn left, ground is then on your left.
Seats: 100 **Cover:** 200 **Capacity:** 2,500 **Floodlights:** Yes **Founded:** 1879
Colours: Black & white stripes/black/black **Change colours:** All yellow
Reserve Team's League: North Northumberland **Sponsors:** TBA.
Previous Leagues: North Northumberland/ East Northumberland/ Northern Alliance 36-39 46-64 65-82/ Durham Central 64-65.
Programme: 20 pages, 25p **Programme Editor:** **Souvenir Shop:**
Previous Leagues: Northern Alliance 35-39 46-64 64-82.
Record Attendance: 600 v Bedlington Terriers, Northern Alliance 1971.
Previous Names: Alnwick United Services/ Alnwick United.
Best FA Cup season: 3rd Qual. Rd 51-52 (3-4 at Blyth), 57-58 (4-6 at Easington Colliery).
Players progressing to Football League: George Turnbull (Grimsby 1950), Brian Pringle (1973).
Honours: Northern Lg Div 2 R-up 88-89, Northern Alliance 37-38 62-63 63-64 65-66 67-68 68-69 69-70 70-71 71-72 (R-up 59-60 61-62 66-67 72-73, Lg Cup 61-62 65-66 67-68 68-69 70-71, Subsidiary Cup 80-81), Durham Central Lg Cup 64-65, Northumberland Benevolent Bowl 86-87, Northumberland SNR Cup R-up 61-62, Northumberland Amtr Cup 71-72, FA Trophy 3rd Qualifying Rd 90-91.
Midweek Matches: Tuesday **Local Press:** Northumberland Gazette.

ASHINGTON

Chairman: Ray Graham **Press Officer:** Brian Bennett (0670 856606)
Secretary: D Peary (0670 816564).
Ground: Portland Park, Ashington NE63 9XG (0670 812240).
Directions: 200 yds north at traffic lights in centre of town.
Seats: 350 **Cover:** 2,200 **Capacity:** 4,000 **Floodlights:** Yes **Year Formed:** 1883
Midweek Matches: Wednesday
Club colours: Black & white stripes/black/black **Change colours:** All red
Programme: Yes, 20p **Programme Editor:** C Sanderson
Clubhouse: Normal licensing hours. **Record Gate:** 13,199 v Rochdale, FA Cup 2nd Rd 9/12/50.
Previous Leagues: Northern Alliance 1892-93 1902-14 69-70/ Football League/ North Eastern 14-21 29-58 62-64/ Midland 58-60/ Northern Counties 60-62/ Wearside 64-65/ Northern Premier 68-69.
Nickname: The Colliers. **Best FA Cup season:** 3rd Rd 26-27.
League Clubs defeated in F.A. Cup: Halifax Town 50-51.
Past players progressing to Football League: Tony Lowery (Mansfield), Les Mutrie (Colchester), R Cummins (Aberdeen, Newcastle).
Hons: FA Amateur Cup SF 73-74, Northumberland Snr 20-21 32-33 38-39 49-50 55-56 56-57 61-62 66-67 79-80, Northumberland Challenge Bowl 12-13 21-22 22-23 23-24 25-26 33-34, Midland Lg 58-59, North Eastern Lg Cup 33-34(jt with Sunderland Reserves) 39-40 (Div 2 26-27(Res)), Northern Alliance 13-14 24-25(Res) 39-40(Res) 55-56(Res) (R-up 05-06 10-11 11-12 22-23(Res) 54-55(Res) 56-57(Res), Lg Cup 47-48(Res)).

Right: *Gary Crawley goes close for Norton & Stockton Ancients during their 2-1 win at basement club Ashington in January.*
Photo - Alan Watson.

BILLINGHAM TOWN

Chairman: Mr G A Maxwell **Presdent:** Mr F Cook, MP
Secretary: Thomas Donnelly, 36 Cumberland Crescent, Billingham, Cleveland TS23 1AY (0642 555332).
Manager: Trevor Arnold **Assistant Manager:** Joe Roddy
Ground: Bedford Terrace, Billingham, Cleveland. (0642 560043)
Directions: Leave A19 on A1027 (signed Billingham). Turn left at 3rd roundabout, over bridge 1st left, then 1st left again to ground.
Seats: 250 **Cover:** 250 **Capacity:** 3,000 **Floodlights:** Yes **Founded:** 1967
Colours: All royal (white trim) **Change colours:** All red
Programme: 28 pages, 40p. **Editor:** Alex Matthews (0642 586570) **Souvenir Shop:** No
Clubhouse: Open matchdays. Hot & cold food.
Previous Lges: Stockton & Dist. 68-74/ Teesside 74-82.
Record Attendance: 1,500 v Manchester City, FA Youth Cup 1985.
Midweek Matches: Tuesday **Previous Ground:** Mill Lane (pre-1974).
Reserves' Lge: Teesside **Previous Name:** Billingham Social Club (pre-1982).
Nickname: The Social. **Best FA Cup season:** 1st Round Proper 1955-56.
Players progressing to Football League: Gary Pallister (Middlesbrough & Manchester Utd), Gerry Forrest (Southampton), Dave Robinson (Halifax), Tony Barratt (Hartlepool), Mark Hine (Grimsby & Darlington), Tony Hall (Middlesbrough), Graham Hall (Arsenal).
Record scorer: Paul Rowntree 100 **Record appearances:** Darren Marsh, 250 in Northern League.
Captain 93-94: Darren Marsh. **Top Scorer & Player of the Year 93-94:** Paul Rowntree.
Honours: Durham Amateur Cup 76-77 77-78, Teesside Lg 77-78 81-82, Nth Riding Snr Cup R-up 76-77 81-82, Stockton & Dist. Lg(3).

BRANDON UNITED

Chairman: Neil Scott **Vice Chairman:** Norman Green **President:** Terry Jacques
Sec./Press Off.: Brian Richardson, 108 Braunespath Estate, New Brancepeth, Durham DH7 7JF (091 373 1304).
Manager: Terry Harrison **Asst Mgr:** Brian Mulligan
Coach: John Carey **Physio:** Bev Dougherty
Ground: Welfare Ground, rear of Commercial Street, Brandon, Durham (091 378 2957).
Directions: A690 - 3 miles west of Durham City. Buses 49 & 49A from Durham.
Seats: 60 **Cover:** 300 **Capacity:** 4,060 **Floodlights:** Yes **Founded:** 1972.
Colours: All red **Change colours:** All blue.
Previous Lges: Durham & Dist. Sunday 68-77/ Northern All. 77-80/ Northern Amtr 80-81/ Wearside 81-83.
Programme: 40 pages, 30p. **Editor:** Keith Nellis (091 378 0704) **Souvenir Shop:** No
Clubhouse: Open every day, lunch & evening. Pool & juke box. Entertainment at weekends.
Best FA Cup season: 1st Rd replay 88-89 (lost to Doncaster). Also 1st Rd 79-80.
League Clubs defeated in FA Cup: None.
Record Gate: 2,500, FA Sunday Cup SF. **Previous Name:** Rostrons 72-74.
Nickname: United **Club Sponsors:** Shildon Sawmills.
Players progressing to Football League: Bryan Liddle & Dean Gibb (Hartlepool 1984 & 86), Paul Dalton (Manchester Utd 1988), Neil Richardson (Rotherham).
Local Newspapers: Newcastle Journal, Northern Echo. **Midweek Matches:** Wednesday
Record win: 10-0 v Stobswood Welfare (H), Northern Alliance 24/3/78.
Record defeat: 0-9 v Murton (H), Northern Lge 28/11/92.
Top Scorer 93-94: Gary Forbes **P.o.Y. 93-94:** Derek McRae.
Club record scorer: Tommy Holden **Club record appearances:** Derek Charlton.
Hons: FA Sunday Cup 75-76, FA Vase QF 82-83 83-84, Northern Lg Div 2 84-85 (Lg Cup R-up 92-93), Northern All.(2) 77-79 (R-up 79-80, Lg Cup 77-78 79-80 (R-up 78-79)), Sunderland Shipowners Cup 81-82, Durham Co. Sunday Cup 73-74 75-76 76-77, FA Tphy 3rd Qual. Rd 87-88 89-90, Durham & Dist Sunday Lg(4) 73-77 (Div 2 69-70, Div 3 68-69), Staffieri Cup 75-76.

Right: Gary Forbes of Brandon United nutmegs Billingham Synthonia's David O'Gorman.
Photo - Gavin Ellis-Neville.

CROOK TOWN

Chairman: Wilf Dobinson **Vice-Chairman:** Brian Humphreys **President:** Herbert Hutchinson.
Secretary: William Hall, 17 Wareham Way, Sunnybrow, Crook, County Durham DL15 0NG (0388 745195).
Manager: Alan Shoulder **Physio:** Ken Taylor.
Comm. Manager: Billy Penman **Press Officer:** Alan Stewart (0388 766780).
Ground: Millfield Ground, West Road, Crook, County Durham (0388 762050).
Directions: 400 yds west of town centre on Wolsingham Road (A689). Nearest BR station is Bishop Auckland (5 miles). Buses 1A & 1B from Bishop Auckland or X46 & X47 from Durham.
Seats: 400 **Cover:** 1,150 **Capacity:** 9,000 **Floodlights:** Yes **Year Formed:** 1889
Colours: Amber/black/black **Change colours:** White/blue/red
Nickname: Black & Ambers **Reserve Team's League:** Crook & District.
Programme: 24 pages, 50p **Programme Editor:** Allan Wood (0661 852068).
Club Sponsors: NMC (UK) Ltd **Previous Name:** Crook Colliery Welfare 1943-1949.
Prev. Lges: Auckland & District 1894-96/ Northern 1896-28 29-30/ Durham Central 28-29/ North Eastern 30-36.
Record Attendance: 17,500 v Walton & Hersham, FA Amateur Cup quarter-final 24/12/52.
Midweek Matches: Wednesday **Club Shop:** Enamel badges/replica shirts available from club.
Best FA Vase season: 2nd Rd 93-94 **Best FA Trophy season:** 3rd Round replay 76-77.
Best FA Cup season: 3rd Rd (v Leicester) 31-32. 2nd Rd four times. 1st Rd ten times.
Record win: 12-0 v South Bank - both home & away within seven days (5/4/58 & 12/4/58) - all 24 goals conceded by the same goalkeeper. Both Northern League matches.
Record defeat: 0-11 v Bishop Auckland (A), Northern League 17/12/38.
Players progressing to Football League: J Kasher (Sunderland), Monty Wilkinson (Newcastle) 1927, Jack Alderson (Crystal Palace), Tom Poskett (Grimsby 1928), Colin Cook (Chesterfield) 1932, Tommy Ward (Sheff Wed 1937), Roy Stephenson (Burnley 1949), Patrick Henson (WBA 1950), Norman Douglas (Chelsea 1952), John Coatsworth (Gateshead 1957), Robert Dixon (Arsenal 1957), Ken Grant (Gateshead 1958), Seamus O'Connell (Carlisle 1958), Mike Tracey (Luton 1959), Frank Clark (Newcastle 1962), Ken Bowron (Berwick 1963), Arnold Coates (Queen of the South 1963), Peter Garbutt (Carlisle 1964), Ray Snowball (Darlington 1964), Wilson Hepplewhite (Carlisle 1965), Chris Neal (Darlington 1967), Malcolm Crosby (Aldershot 1971), Alan Little (Aston Villa 1973), Terry Turnbull (Hartlepool 1976), Gary Whetter (Darlington 1986).
Clubhouse details: Open 7-11 each evening plus matchdays. Pool, darts, satellite TV.
Record Scorer: Ronnie Tompson 118, 1952-62
Record appearances: Jimmy McMillan 505, 1951-68 (plus a record four FA Amateur Cup winner's medals).
Captain 93-94: Wayne Brown **Top Scorer:** Craig Warburton 15 **P.o.Y. 93-94:** Ian McGraghan
Honours: FA Amtr Cup 00-01 53-54 58-59 61-62 63-64 (SF 48-49 57-58 59-60), Northern Lg 14-15 26-27 52-53 58-59 62-63 (R-up 24-25 46-47 53-54 54-55 55-56 63-64 64-65, Lg Cup 36-37 45-46 60-61 (R-up 25-26 54-55 58-59 62-63)), Durham Challenge Cup 26-27 31-32 54-55 59-60, Durham Benevolent Bowl 13-14 19-20 21-22 25-26 54-55, FA Trophy 2nd Rd 76-77. *Twelve players capped by England at Amateur International level.*

DARLINGTON CLEVELAND SOCIAL

Chairman: S Guy **President:** D Morrison/ W Stephenson.
Secretary/Press Officer/Commercial Manager: B Pickering (0325 461907).
Manager: Roger Wicks **Coach:** Nick Day/ Steve Wright **Physio:** Kevin Reece.
Ground: Neasham Road, Darlington (0325 469735).
Directions: From Darlington BR station turn left and follow Park Lane. At bottom turn left into Parkside, ground on left. Leave A1 at A66, follow Darlington by-pass and turn right into Neasham Rd at 3rd island - follow to ground. Or, leave A1 on A167 and follow to town centre, turn left following signs for station, at 2nd r'bout turn left into Parkgate, right at next r'bout following signs for Neasham, after 1 mile turn between social club and public house into Geneva Lane (ground).
Seats: None **Cover:** 700 **Capacity:** 3,000 **Floodlights:** Yes **Founded:** 1903
Colours: All yellow **Change colours:** Black & white stripes
Programme: New for 93-94, 50p **Programme Editor:** Secretary
Midweek Matchday: Wednesday **Club Sponsors:** To be determined by draw.
Clubhouse details: Normal social club hours. No food - canteen open matchdays in ground.
Previous Leagues: Local works league 03-62/ Darlington & Dist. 62-81/ Northern Alliance 81-83.
Nickname: The Bridge. **Record Gate:** 2,500 v Darlington, friendly
Players progressing to Football League: Jeff Wealands (Birmingham City, Manchester United).
Youth team's Lge: Banks Northern Yth **Previous Name:** Darlington Cleveland Bridge 1903-1993.
Honours: Northern Alliance 82-83, North Riding Challenge Cup 81-82, Northern Region County Cup 82-83, Darlington & Dist. Lg (5) - over twenty local cups in Darlington & Dist.

EASINGTON COLLIERY

Chairman: F Wellburn **Vice-Chairman:** Charlie Dodds.
Secretary: Tom Goodrum, 8 Oswald Terrace, Easington Colliery, Peterlee SR8 3LB (091 527 0737)
Manager: Lol Jones **Asst Mgr/Coach:** Kenny Charlton **Physio:** Davy Smith.
Press Officer: Alan Purvis **Commercial Manager:** Fred Wellburn (091 586 9986).
Ground: Easington Colliery Welfare Ground, CW Park, Easington, Co Durham. (091 527 3047)
Directions: A19 Easington turn-off, B1284 thru Easington till Black Diamond PH (next to zebra crossing), turn right for ground.
Seats: 20 **Cover:** 450 **Capacity:** 2,450 **Floodlights:** Yes **Founded:** 1913
Midweek Matches: Tuesday **Nickname:** The Colliery. **Sponsors:** None.
Cols: White & green stripes/green/green **Change colours:** Yellow/black/yellow **Reserves:** None.
Programme: No **Programme Editor:** N/A. **Club Shop:** No
Clubhouse details: Normal licensing hours. Pies, soup and sandwiches available.
Previous Leagues: Wearside 13-37 39-64 73-88.
Record Attendance: 4,500 v Tranmere Rovers, FA Cup 1st Round 1955.
Prev. Name: Easington Colliery Welfare. **Best FA Cup season:** 1st Round Proper 1955-56.
Players progressing to Football League: Ron Greener (Newcastle 1951), Frank Wayman (Darlington 1957), John Langridge (Hartlepool 1982).
Record win: 7-0 v Ashington (H), Northern League Division Two 93-94.
Record defeat: 2-8 v Blyth Spartans (A), Northern League Division One 1988.
Captain & P.o.Y.: 93-94: G Gofton **Top Scorer 93-94:** T Garside.
Club record scorer: D Howard **Club record appearances:** D Howard.
Honours: Northern Lg Div 2 R-up 85-86, Wearside League 29-30 31-32 32-33 47-48 48-49 (R-up 28-29 46-47 73-74, Lg Cup 32-33 45-46 61-62), Monkwearmouth Cup 30-31 47-48 75-76, Sunderland Shipowners Cup 74-75 79-80, FA Trophy 2nd Qualifying Rd replay 88-89, FA Vase 4th Rd replay 82-83.

ESH WINNING

Chairman: Charles Allen Ryan **Vice Chairman:** Anthony Clarney **President:** Jack Lumsden
Secretary/Press Officer: Mr R Hinds, 158 Norburn Park, Witton Gilbert, Co. Durham DH7 6SQ (091 371 0204).
Manager: Douglas Robson **Physio:** Barry Wainwright. **Comm. Mgr:** Dave Greener.
Ground: West Terrace, Waterhouses, Durham (091 373 3872).
Directions: Durham to Ushaw Moor, to Esh Winning; ground 1 mile further at Waterhouses.
Seats: 160 **Cover:** 160 **Capacity:** 3,500 **Floodlights:** Yes **Year Formed:** 1967
Midweek Matches: Tuesday **Club Sponsors:** Lumsden & Carroll.
Colours: Green & yellow halves/green/green. **Change colours:** All orange.
Programme: 20 pages, 50p **Programme Editor:** Harold Wharton **Souvenir Shop:** No
Previous Grounds: None **Prev. Lges:** Durham & Dist Sunday/ Northern Alliance 81-82.
Nickname: 'Esh' **Previous Names:** Esh Winning Pineapple (pre-1982).
Clubhouse: Open daily. Snacks served **Record Gate:** 900 v Liverpool Fantail, FA Sunday Cup 1982.
Best FA Cup season: 2nd Qualifying Rd 90-91 (lost 1-3 at home to Spennymoor).
Best FA Vase season: 2nd Round 83-84.
Record win: 9-0 v Langley Park (H) **Record defeat:** 0-8 v Dunston FB (A).
Record transfer fee paid: Nil **Received:** £400 for Derek Middleton (Easington Colliery).
Top Scorer 93-94: Paul Ward **Captain & P.o.Y. 93-94:** Peter Colledge
Club record scorer: Ray Pegg 27 **Club record appearances:** Paul Hewitson 40.
Honours: Durham & District Sunday Lg 78-79 79-80, Durham County Sunday Cup R-up 78-79, Staffieri Cup 74-75, Guards Cup 72-73, North Durham Youth Lg 93-94.

EVENWOOD TOWN

Chairman: Gordon Nicholson **Press Officer:** Secretary **President:** N Colegrove.
Secretary: Jim Coates, 19 Wellgarth, Evenwood, Bishop Auckland, Co Durham DL14 9QU (0388 833035).
Manager: Dr Graeme Forster. **Press Officer:** H T Carnall.
Ground: Welfare Ground, Stones End, Evenwood, County Durham (0388 832281).
Directions: In village centre by Sports & Social club in Stones Rd.
Seats: 32 **Cover:** 200 **Capacity:** 3,500 **Floodlights:** Yes **Founded:** 1890
Sponsors: C A Roofing **Midweek Matches:** Wednesday **Programme:** None
Club colours: All blue **Change:** Red (white sleeves)/white/red (white hoops).
Nickname: The Wood. **Clubhouse:** Open lunch & evening every day.
Best FA Cup season: 1st Rd 1936. **Record Gate:** 9,000 v Bishop Auckland, FA Amtr Cup 1931.
Previous Leagues: Barnard Castle & District 1893-94/ Auckland & District 1894-96 1903-04 08-23 28-31/ Wear Valley 1896-99 1904-06 24-25/ Gauntlett Valley 06-07/ South Durham 27-28.
Captain 93-94: Graham Cook. **Players progressing to Football Lge:** Too numerous to record.
Top Scorer 93-94: I Moxon **Player of the Year 93-94:** Graham Cook, S Bates (joint).
Hons: Northern Lg 48-49 69-70 70-71 (Lg Cup 35-36), Durham Challenge Cup 69-70.

Paul Gates of Darlington CS hits a shot against Stuart Brackley of Prudhoe. *Photo - Gavin Ellis-Neville.*

Esh Winning FC.

Evenwood Town FC.

HARTLEPOOL TOWN

Chairman/Treasurer: Robert Lupton
Secretary/Press Officer: Gordon Thornton, 14 Regency Drive, Hartlepool TS25 1LX (0429 266527).
Ground & Directions: As Ferryhill Athletic FC (see page 692).
Colours: Red/white/red **Change colours:** Blue & black/white/black.
Previous Name: Greatham Mayfair (pre-1991)
Previous Leagues: Hartlepool/ Teesside/ Wearside 88-94.
Previous Ground: Mayfair Park, Mayfair Centre, Tees Road, Seaton Carew (pre-1993).
Honours: Wearside Lg R-up 91-92 92-93 93-94 (Shipowners Cup 91-92 (R-up 92-93)).

HORDEN COLLIERY WELFARE

Chairman: J McCoy **Press Officer:** Secretary
Secretary: Robert Wood, 29 Morpeth Str., Horden, Peterlee, County Durham SR8 4BE (091 586 8802).
Ground: Welfare Park Ground, Park Road, Horden, Peterlee, County Durham (091 518 0248)
Directions: A19 to Peterlee, signposted from there.
Seats: 300 **Cover:** 400 **Capacity:** 4,500 **Floodlights:** Yes **Reformed:** 1980
Midweek Matches: Tuesday **Programme:** 10 pages, 20p **Nickname:** Colliers
Colours: Red (white trim)/red/red **Change colours:** Blue/black/blue
Clubhouse: Normal licensing hours. Hot & cold snacks, darts, pool.
Previous Lges: Wearside 07-35 63-75/ N. Eastern 35-58 62-64/ Midland (Co's) 58-60/ Northern Co's 60-62.
Best FA Cup year: 2nd Rd 38-39 (2-3 at home to Newport Co.). Also 1st Rd 25-26 52-53 53-54 54-55 81-82.
Previous Names: Horden Athletic. **Record Attendance:** 8,000 - FA Cup 1937.
Players progressing to Football League: Paul Dobson (Hartlepool United).
Hons: Durham Challenge Cup 35-36 63-64 80-81 81-82, Durham Benevolent Cup 33-34, Wearside Lg 11-12 12-13 13-14 33-34 64-65 67-68 69-70 70-71 71-72 72-73 (Lg Cup 33-34 49-50, Monkwearmouth Charity Cup 12-13 23-24 32-33 69-70 72-73, Sunderland Shipowners Cup 65-66 72-73), North Eastern Lg 37-38 63-64 ('Non-Reserve' Medal 50-51).

Right: *Horden defender Tony Taylor (No. 2) closes in on Whickham striker Paul Crake during a 1-2 home defeat.*
Photo - Dave West.

LANGLEY PARK S. & S. UNITED

Chairman: C Fairless **President:** Bobby Robson.
Secretary: G M Freeman, 35 Kidd Ave., Sherburn Village, Durham DH6 1JR (091 372 1960).
Manager: Vic Hillier **Press Officer:** Secretary
Ground: Welfare Ground, Low Moor Road, Langley Park, Durham (091 373 1526).
Directions: A691 Durham to Consett. First left after Witton Gilbert, signed Langley Park. Turn right in town centre, ground quarter of a mile on right. Frequent buses from Durham.
Seats: 30 **Cover:** 500 **Capacity:** 3,000 **Floodlights:** No **Reformed:** 1973
Midweek Matches: Tuesday
Club colours: All blue **Change colours:** White/navy/navy OR All yellow
Programme: 30+ pages, 20p. **Programme Editor:** Jeff Dover **Club Shop:** No
Clubhouse: Open every evening, plus Sat & Sun lunch & directly after match on matchdays.
Previous Leagues: Durham & District Sunday/ Durham City & District.
Previous Name: Rams Head (pre-1983) as Sunday side.
Best FA Cup season: 2nd Qualifying Rd replay 90-91 (lost 0-1 at home to Easington Colliery).
Hons: FA Sunday Cup 76-77, Northern Lg Div 2 R-up 90-91, Staffieri Cup 74-75 76-77 77-78 78-79 80-81, Durham & Dist Lg JW Morgan Mem. Cup 82-83, Durham & Dist. Sunday Lg 78-79 (Lg Cup 76-77 78-78 79-80), FA Vase 2nd Rd 85-86 90-91.

MORPETH TOWN

Chairman: K B Beattie **Press Officer:** R Griffiths (0670 516533).
Secretary: W Hollan, 7 North Leech, Lancaster Park, Morpeth (0670 511086).
Manager/Coach: B Penfold **Ground:** Craik Park, Morpeth Common, Morpeth.
Directions: Morpeth signs off A1 onto A197, take B6524, right at Mitford sign, right after 1 mile into ground next to Morpeth Common.
Colours: Yellow/black **Change colours:** Red (white trim)
Previous Ground: Storey Park, Morpeth (pre-1992).
Previous League: Northern Alliance (pre-1994).
Hons: Northern Alliance 83-84 93-94 (R-up 37-38 65-66 73-74 81-82 84-85, Challenge Cup 38-39 85-86 93-94 (R-up 36-37 62-63 73-74)).

NORTON & STOCKTON ANCIENTS

Chairman: Richard Scott **President:** Dennis Swales.
Secretary: Steve Clarkson, 4 South Way, Norton, Stockton-on-Tees, Cleveland TS20 2TQ (0642 534524)
Press Officer: Brian Symons (0642 585836).
Ground: Station Road, Norton, Stockton-on-Tees, Cleveland (0642 530203).
Directions: Norton village 2 miles from Stockton centre, turn into Station Road on outskirts of village.
Seats: 200 **Cover:** Yes **Capacity:** 2,000 **Floodlights:** No **Year Formed:** 1959
Midweek Matches: Wednesday
Cols: Amber (black trim)/black/amber **Change colours:** White with amber trim
Nickname: Ancients **Previous Name:** Norton & Stockton Cricket Club Trust.
Programme: 12 pages with entry **Programme Editor:** Richard Scott
Clubhouse details: Full bar facilities, 150 yds from ground.
Previous Leagues: Teesside (pre-1982).
Record Attendance: 1,430 v Middlesbrough, Friendly 1988.
Best F.A. Cup season: First Qualifying Rd(4) 88-89 90-93.
Hons: Northern Lg Cup 81-82.

Gary Cawley of Norton & Stockton Ancients bursts through the Washington defence. *Photo - Alan Watson.*

RYHOPE COMMUNITY ASSOCIATION

Chairman: D Lawson **Vice Chairman:** R Baines **President:** A Clark.
Sec./Press Officer: Eric Dryden, 3 Maclyn Close, Moorside, Sunderland, Tyne & Wear SR3 2SY (091 528 8358).
Manager: John Oliver **Asst Mgr:** Mick Clark **Coach:** Ralph Wright
Physio: Bill Todd **Commercial Manager:** D Lawson
Ground: Meadow Park, Ryhope, Sunderland (091 523 6555).
Directions: From Sunderland follow signs for A19 south - ground adjacent to Cherry Knowle Hospitals in Ryhope.
Seats: 150 **Cover:** 200 **Capacity:** 2,000 **Floodlights:** Yes **Founded:** 1960
Midweek Matches: Tuesday **Record Gate:** 2,000 v Newcastle, friendly 1982.
Colours: Red & white stripes **Change colours:** All blue **Nickname:** Ryes
Programme: 40 pages, 50p **Editor:** D Lawson (091 567 799) **Club Shop:** No.
Sponsors: Lawson Freight **Clubhouse:** Open matchdays. Hot dogs, burgers, beverages.
Previous Leagues: Seaham & District/ Houghton & District/ Northern Alliance 78-82.
Players progressing to Football League: Kevin Todd (Newcastle United).
Record transfer received: £2,000 (from Newcastle for Kevin Todd, 1983).
Record win: 15-0 **Record loss:** 0-8
Record appearances: Paul Carr **Club Record scorer & Top Scorer 93-94:** Ian Lawson.
Captain 93-94: Alfie Bell **Player of the Year 93-94:** Glen Moan.
Hons: Northern Alliance Lg Cup 80-81, Northern Lg Div 2 83-84, Banks Yth League & Cup double 92-93.

SHOTTON COMRADES

Chairman: Mr J Maddison **Vice Chairman:** Mr M Taylor **President:** Mr G Taylor.
Secretary/Press Officer: Mr W Banks, 6 Syston Close, Chilton Moor, Fencehouses, Houghton-le-Spring, Tyne & Wear DH4 6TB (091 385 5361).
Manager: J Maddison **Asst Manager:** W Constantine. **Physio:** I Riley.
Coach: I Riley/J Purvis **Commercial Manager:** Mr T Robinson.
Ground: Shotton Recreational Ground, Station Road, Shotton Colliery, Co. Durham (091 526 2859).
Directions: A19 to Peterlee to Shotton, right at War Mem. t-junction, follow round 800yds, ground on right.
Seats: 80 **Cover:** 400 **Capacity:** 1,700 **Floodlights:** No **Year Formed:** 1973
Colours: Black & white halves/black/black **Change colours:** All orange.
Club Sponsors: T.B.A. **Midweek home matches:** Wednesday **Nickname:** Coms
Programme: 12 pages, 20p **Programme Editor:** Mr E A Jones **Club Shop:** No
Previous Leagues: Peterlee Sunday 74-76/ Houghton & District 76-80/ Northern Alliance 80-83.
Previous Grounds: None **Record Attendance:** 1,726 v Dennis Waterman XI.
Best FA Cup season: 2nd Qualifying Rd 85-86 (lost 0-2 at home to Wingate). **Clubhouse:** No.
Reserves' Lge: Banks u-19 Yth **Record transfer received:** £500 for G Gudlip (Shildon)
Rec. win: 8-0 v Bedlington Ter. (H), '92 **Rec. defeat:** 1-7 v Brandon Utd (A), F.A. Cup Prel. Rd 91-92.
Captain & P.o.Y. 93-94: J Cudlip **Top Scorer 93-94:** David Belwood
Record scorer: Keith Willets 50 **Record appearances:** J Cudlip.
Hons: Houghton & District Lg 78-79 (Lg Cup(2)), Northern Alliance Lg Cup SF, Hetton Charity Cup 78-79, Peterlee Sunday Lg 75-76 (Div 2 74-75), FA Vase 1st Rd 86-87 90-91, Durham Challenge Cup QF 78-79 (Minor Cup QF 78-79).

WASHINGTON

Chairman: Billy Blevins **Press Officer:** John Hurst (091 438 4513).
Secretary: George Abbott, 14 Grosvenor Street, Southwick, Sunderland SR5 2DG (091 549 1384).
Ground: Albany Park, Spout Lane, Concord, Washington (091 417 7779).
Directions: Ground situated behind the cinema opposite bus station.
Seats: 25 **Cover:** Yes **Capacity:** 3,000 **Floodlights:** No **Founded:** 1949
Colours: All red **Change colours:** All blue **Midweek Matches:** Wednesday
Programme: 8 pages, 10p **Programme Editor:** Mr Bull (091 4164618) **Club Shop:** No
Clubhouse: Open normal licensing hours, with live entertainment, pool etc. **Nickname:** Mechanics
Previous Leagues: Washington Amateur/ Northern Alliance 67-68/ Wearside 68-88.
Previous Ground: Usworth Welfare Park **Record Gate:** 3,800 v Bradford Park Avenue, FA Cup 1970.

STOCKTON

Chairman: Alan Ruddy **Commercial Manager:** Peter Morris (0642 760779)
Secretary/Press Officer: John M Smith, 71 Rimswell Road, Fairfield, Stockton-on-Tees, Cleveland TS19 7LE (0642 584593).
Manager: Alan Robinson **Asst Mgr:** Peter Morris **Coach:** Peter May/Michael Watson
Ground: Teesdale Park, Acklam Road, Thornaby, Stockton-on-Tees TS19 8TZ (0642 606803).
Directions: A19 to Thornaby turn off, ground half mile on right. One mile from Thornaby BR station. Any Stockton-Middlesbrough bus - stop at Acklam Rd, Thornaby.
Seats: 20 **Cover:** 200 **Capacity:** 5,000 **Floodlights:** Yes **Year Formed:** 1980
Club colours: Red & black stripes/black/red **Change colours:** All sky.
Previous Leagues: Stockton & District 80-81/ Wearside 81-85.
Reserves' Lge: Teesside **Previous Names:** Stockton Cricket Club 65-80.
Previous Grounds: Grangefield Youth & Community Centre, Stockton 80-82/ Tilery Sports Centre 82-83.
Programme: 24 pages, 30p **Programme Editor:** Secretary **Souvenir Shop:** No.
Midweek Matches: Tuesday. **Local Newspapers:** Northern Echo, Evening Gazette.
Clubhouse: 200+ seater social club with concert room, pool/games room and bar. Open every night and Sunday lunchtimes and all day Saturday. Sandwiches available in bar, canteen in ground sells pies, burgers, soup, drinks etc.
Best FA Cup season: 4th Qual. Rd replay 92-93 (lost 1-2 at home to Blyth after 1-1 draw).
Record Attendance: 3,000 v Middlebrough, pre-season friendly August 1986.
Club Sponsors: Intertractor **Record win:** 10-0 v Evenwood (H), Div 2 91-92.
Capt. 93-94: Michael Sell **P.o.Y. 93-94:** Paddy Woods **Club record appearances:** Michael Watson.
Hons: Northern Lg Div 2 87-88 91-92, Nth Riding Co. Cup 85-86, FA Vase 2nd Rd, FA Tphy 1st Rd.

WHICKHAM

Chairman: Robert Ferriday **Manager:** Billy Hodgson **Press Officer:** Secretary
Secretary: Mr M A McIntyre, 43 Duckpool Lane, Whickham, Newcastle upon Tyne, Tyne & Wear NE16 4TE (091 488 4644).
Ground: Glebe Ground, Rectory Lane, Whickham (091 488 3054).
Directions: A692 (Consett) from A69. Left at r'bout signed Consett/Whickham. Up hill and right at mini-r'bout. Continue along & turn left into Rectory Lane (by Lloyds Bank) for about 500 yds, clubhouse on right.
Seats: 100 **Cover:** Yes **Capacity:** 4,000 **Floodlights:** Due **Founded:** 1944
Colours: Black & white stripes/black/black **Change colours:** All white
Previous Leagues: Derwent Valley -55/ Northern Comb. 55-57 59-74/ Tyneside Amtr 57-59/ Wearside 74-88.
Programme: 20p **Midweek Matches:** Wednesday **Souvenir Shop:** No
Clubhouse: Mon-Fri. 12-3 & 7-11, Sat.11-11, Sun. 12-2, 7.30-11
Record Gate: 3,165 v Windsor & Eton, F.A. Vase SF 1981.
Prev. Ground: Rectory Rec. Field **Best F.A. Cup season:** 1st Qual. 89-90 (0-1 at Nth Shields)
Players progressing to Football League: Nigel Walker (Newcastle 1977), David Norton (Hartlepool 1981), Mike Carroll (Chesterfield 1981).
Honours: FA Vase 80-81, Wearside Lg 77-78 87-88 (R-up 80-81 84-85, Lg Cup 86-87, Monkwearmouth Charity Cup 76-77, Sunderland Shipowners Cup 77-78 80-81), Northern Comb. 69-70 72-73 73-74 (Lg Cup 60-61 73-74).
Local Newspapers: Newcastle Journal, Sunday Sun, Evening Chronicle

WILLINGTON

Chairman: Desmond Ayre **Vice-Chairman:** Bob Nichols **President:** Don Warner
Secretary/Press Officer: Mr R H Nichols, 34 Stephenson Cres., Willington, Co. Durham DL15 9PF (0288 745297).
Manager: Malcolm Smith **Asst Manager:** David Brand **Physio:** Kevin Stonehouse.
Ground: Hall Lane, Hall Lane Estate, Willington, County Durham (0388 746221).
Directions: Willington is on A690 seven miles west of Durham city and 2 miles east of Crook. Off main through road at 'The Black Horse Tavern' corner turn into Commercial Street, then into Hall Lane after 100yds. Northern Bus Co. operates a service through Willington from Crook or Durham city. Bond Bros Bus Transport operates a service from Bishop Auckland.
Seats: 350 **Cover:** 400 **Capacity:** 7,000 **Floodlights:** Yes **Founded:** 1906.
Colours: Blue & white stripes/blue/blue **Change colours:** Yellow/green/yellow.
Programme: 20 pages, 20p **Programme Editor:** Secretary
Club shop: Pending opening. In the meantime, Secretary can supply club badges, old programmes and *Northern Ventures* League magazine.
Midweek Matches: Wednesday **Previous Leagues:** Auckland & Dist. 1906-11.
Nickname: Blue & Whites **Reserve Team's League:** None.
Record Attendance: 10,000 v Bromley, FA Amateur Cup 2nd Rd 24/1/53.
Best FA Cup season: 1st Rd replay 73-74 (lost 1-6 at Blackburn after 0-0 draw). Also 1st Rd 45-46 50-51.
Prev. Grnd: West End Ground 1906-11. **Previous Names:** Willington Temperance 1906-11.
Record win: 13-3 v Whitby (H), 1928 **Record defeat:** 0-11 v Dunston (H), 5/9/92 - both Northern Lge.
Record transfer fee paid: £250 for Dominic Dimambro (Whitby Town) 1990.
Record transfer fee received: £550 for Dominic Dimambro (Whitby Town) 1988.
Players progressing to Football League: George Tweedy (Grimsby) 1933, Andy Graver (Newcastle) 1947, Brian Ronson (Fulham) 1953, Martin Burleigh (Newcastle) 1969. *All 'keeper except Graver (centre forward).*
Clubhouse: Open evenings 7-11pm at Saturday matchdays 1-11pm. Bar facilities. Tea shop on matchdays.
Record scorer: John 'Boxer' Taylor, 55-69. **Club record appearances:** Stan Rutherford, 1947-61.
Captain 93-94: Mark Blunt **Top Scorer 93-94:** Simon Andrews **P.o.Y. 93-94:** Brett Cummings.
Hons: FA Amateur Cup 49-50 (R-up 38-39, SF 27-28), Northern League 13-14 25-26 29-30 (R-up 12-13 57-58 75-76, League Cup 24-25 25-26 27-28 56-57 30-31 31-32 48-49 74-75), FA Trophy 3rd Rd 75-76, Durham Benevolent Cup 48-49 50-51 57-58.

WEARSIDE LEAGUE

FOUNDED: 1892

FEEDER TO:

FEDERATION BREWERY NORTHERN LEAGUE

President: J C Thomas

Chairman: P J Maguire

Hon Secretary & Treasurer: Bill Robson,
12 Deneside, Howden-le-Wear, Crook, Co. Durham DL15 8JR

THIRD TIME LUCKY FOR HARTLEPOOL TOWN

Hartlepool Town, after missing out on the League Championship in the previous two seasons, at last came good to clinch the title at the third attempt, and so qualified for promotion via the Pyramid to Division Two of the FB Northern League.

With a repeat of the last two years, the destination of the championship in both divisions of the league was not decided until the very last week of the season. Hartlepool Town, despite a late attack of nerves, took the Division One title at the expense of Marske United, while Washington Nissan booked their return to the higher flight in a nail-biting finish which saw them overcoming the challenge of North Ormesby Sports.

South Shields, after the disappointment of not gaining promotion to the Northern League, found that they were unable to match their good run from the previous year. They only finished in fourth place while their hopes were further dashed as they went down in the finals of the League and Monkwearmouth Cups at the hands of Silksworth and Marske United respectively.

In the Sunderland Shipowners Cup, Herrington CW put aside their indifferent form of previous years to upset the form book with a convincing 2-0 win over Jarrow Roofing.

Nissan rounded off what was their best season since joining the League to retain the Division Two Cup following a rousing final win over Cumbrians Marchon, who in 1994-95 will play under the name of Whitehaven Amateurs.

Clubs from Division Two again featured well in the League's domestic cup competitions with Birtley Town and Hebburn DT reaching the semi-final stages of the League Cup.

On the County Cup scene sides from the League had a very disappointing year with only Washington Glebe and Brinkburn CA making any appreciable showing in the Durham Trophy while all others went out at an early stage in their respective competitions.

On the question of the Pyramid, the League is now firmly committed to membership of the North East Section of the System. With the member clubs looking for automatic promotion and relegation to be in place between the league and the FB Northern League by the end of 1994-95 season, sides in Division One have been given until the end of April 1995 to bring their grounds up to the required standard or face automatic relegation to Division Two of the Vaux Wearside League.

Therefore at next year's Annual General Meeting a system of adjustment between Divisions One and Two will be implemented to bring the League up to the required 50% minimum standard stipulated by the Northern League. The subject of the extension of the Pyramid below Division Two of the League has again been put on hold for a further season. Following a meeting with the Football Association, County Football Associations and the Teesside and Washington Leagues, the member clubs decided that the Vaux Wearside League should carry out a series of advisory inspections of the grounds and facilities of those Leagues wishing to join the Pyramid before making a final decision on the future of the System below the VWL at next year's AGM.

Next season will see three new clubs taking part in Division Two. Harton & Westoe CW were elected as Associate Members at the Annual General Meeting with Prudhoe Swinton and Hartlepool United Reserves joining at the July Extraordinary General Meeting to bring the complement of teams in Division Two up to fifteen. With the promotion of Hartlepool Town via the Pyramid, and the resignation of Newton Aycliffe in mid-season, the bottom two clubs in Division One, Wolviston and Jarrow, retained their status, the section being retained at eighteen clubs with the promotion of Nissan and North Ormesby from Division Two.

The leading goalscorers in the two divisions of the league were Steve Harkus of South Shields (44 goals) and Richard Salt of Northallerton Town Supporters (28 goals).

Bill Robson, Secretary.

DIV. ONE	P	W	D	L	F	A	PTS
Hartlepool Town	32	23	6	3	93	27	75
Marske United	32	25	2	5	97	25	74
Jarrow Roofing	32	20	7	6	79	34	67
South Shields	32	18	7	7	79	44	61
Silksworth	32	16	3	13	53	50	51
Kennek Roker	32	14	8	10	55	49	50
Ryhope CW	32	12	6	14	55	74	42
Windscale United	32	11	8	13	74	72	41
Cleadon SC	32	11	7	14	47	68	40
Herrington CW	32	11	5	16	68	72	38
Hartlepool BWOB	32	11	5	16	56	64	38
Annfield Plain	32	10	8	14	47	57	38
North Shields	32	11	5	16	61	80	38
Cleator Moor C.	32	10	4	18	49	85	34
Boldon CA	32	8	6	18	43	70	30
Wolviston	32	6	8	18	46	82	26
Jarrow	32	5	5	22	38	87	20

DIV. TWO	P	W	D	L	F	A	PTS
Nissan	32	27	2	3	88	34	83
North Ormesby	32	25	6	1	102	16	81
Hebburn DT	32	21	4	7	78	37	67
Birtley Town	32	19	6	7	74	34	63
Washington Glebe	32	19	6	7	85	50	63
Stanley United	32	18	5	9	66	46	59
SS County Kitchens	32	16	5	11	70	53	53
Northallerton TS	32	16	3	13	69	61	51
Marchon	32	15	5	12	73	42	50
Guisboro. Priory	32	12	4	16	68	63	37
Murton Inter.	32	10	6	16	64	71	36
Fulwell Myers	32	9	4	19	41	71	31
Wingate Mall	32	7	6	19	46	76	27
Tradelink	32	7	4	21	48	95	25
Newcastle City	32	6	7	19	40	91	25
Usworth Village	32	2	6	24	24	94	12
Esh Winning Alb.	32	1	5	26	29	122	8

VAUX WEARSIDE LEAGUE DIVISION ONE RESULT CHART 1993-94

HOME TEAM	1	2	3	4	5	6	7	8	9	10	11	12	13	14	15	16	17	18
1. Annfield Plain	*	1-2	1-0	0-3	1-3	2-4	3-0	2-2	1-2		2-0	2-1	3-2	1-2	3-3	0-1	1-3	0-2
2. Boldon Community Assoc.	1-2	*	5-2	1-2	1-4	3-1	2-0	1-1	0-2	7-0	2-0	1-3	0-2	3-3	0-3	2-0	1-1	1-1
3. Cleator Moor Celtic	1-2	3-4	*	1-1	2-3	4-5	2-1	3-2	1-7		3-1	3-1	2-4	3-1	2-2	2-1	2-0	1-4
4. Hartlepool Boys Welfare OB	2-3	0-2	4-1	*	1-1	4-0	2-0	2-4	0-3	4-2	1-5	4-1	2-6	0-3	1-1	0-0	4-1	4-2
5. Hartlepool Town	1-1	3-0	5-0	3-0	*	5-2	3-1	1-0	0-2		5-0	2-3	2-0	2-1	5-2	4-0	5-0	4-0
6. Herrington Colliery Welf.	2-1	5-1	2-2	2-3	1-2	*	4-3	1-3	0-2	4-2	2-2	1-3	0-1	4-0	2-3	4-4	2-1	5-2
7. Jarrow	0-1	3-2	3-1	2-2	0-5	3-2	*	0-2	1-3	4-0	2-2	1-4	1-4	1-2	0-3	0-4	0-5	3-2
8. Jarrow Roofing	1-1	4-0	2-0	4-3	1-1	3-1	3-1	*	1-1		6-0	2-0	5-1	5-0	2-1	2-0	6-2	3-0
9. Marske United	4-0	2-1	4-0	2-0	0-0	3-2	6-0	0-1	*	3-0	16-0	1-0	0-4	7-0	2-1	6-1	3-0	7-1
10. Newton Aycliffe	0-5	2-4	1-2		1-3					*		0-3	2-4		0-1	0-3	3-5	3-3
11. North Shields	1-1	3-3	7-1	2-1	1-5	1-5	2-2	1-0	3-0	4-2	*	1-2	1-2	2-0	0-1	0-1	2-1	4-2
12. Silksworth	2-1	3-2	1-2	2-1	1-0	1-0	3-0	0-2	0-1		0-2	*	1-2	1-1	0-1	3-0	3-3	2-0
13. South Shields	3-3	4-0	3-0	1-0	0-1	0-1	3-0	1-1	3-4		3-2	2-2	*	1-3	2-2	6-1	4-1	3-0
14. South Shields Cleadon SC	0-3	2-0	1-0	3-1	2-2	0-0	0-3	3-1	0-2		2-6	1-3	0-3	*	0-2	0-0	2-2	2-3
15. Sunderland Kennek Roker	1-1	4-0	1-1	1-3	0-4	2-0	2-0	2-1	1-0	6-0	2-0	2-4	0-3	1-1	*	2-3	1-4	2-2
16. Sunderland Vaux Ryhope	3-2	0-0	6-0	3-1	0-6	6-4	4-3	3-6	0-2	2-2	1-0	3-1	1-1	0-3	1-2	*	4-1	2-2
17. Windscale United	2-2	4-1	1-3	3-1	3-3	1-3	2-2	0-1	3-2	7-3	4-2	5-0	3-3	4-6	2-0	7-2	*	5-2
18. Wolviston	3-0	2-1	0-1	1-4	1-3	1-1	2-2	2-2	0-1	4-1	2-8	1-2	2-2	2-3	0-4	2-0	0-0	*

NB - Newton Aycliffe withdrew. Playing record expunged, but shown for curiosity's sake.

DIV. TWO RESULTS 1993-94	1	2	3	4	5	6	7	8	9	10	11	12	13	14	15	16	17
1. Birtley Town	*	8-0	5-1	0-2	2-1	5-0	3-0	0-1	0-1	3-0	2-0	3-1	1-0	3-0	1-2	0-2	2-0
2. Esh Winning Albion	2-2	*	1-5	1-2	0-3	0-3	1-1	3-7	2-9	0-0	1-3	0-2	1-4	1-2	1-3	0-3	0-4
3. Guisborough Priory	1-1	4-0	*	3-1	3-0	0-4	2-3	2-3	0-2	1-3	2-4	0-0	7-1	0-0	1-0	1-2	3-5
4. Hebburn DT	2-0	3-0	2-2	*	1-6	3-2	3-0	3-2	1-3	3-2	0-0	2-0	3-1	1-0	6-2	3-0	5-0
5. Marchon	1-2	6-1	2-0	3-1	*	5-0	7-0	4-1	0-1	3-1	0-3	2-0	3-0	3-3	0-4	0-0	1-0
6. Murton International	2-2	4-1	2-5	1-4	1-1	*	0-0	5-2	0-5	1-3	1-3	2-2	1-3	5-1	0-1	2-4	5-1
7. Newcastle City	1-3	6-1	2-1	0-6	4-3	1-3	*	0-1	0-6	1-5	0-5	2-4	5-2	3-1	0-1	0-5	1-1
8. Northallerton Town Supporters	2-4	4-0	4-1	1-0	1-2	1-1	2-1	*	0-2	1-0	1-2	4-0	2-0	2-1	2-2	0-1	4-1
9. North Ormesby	1-1	8-1	4-2	0-0	2-1	3-1	3-0	5-0	*	4-0	1-2	4-0	4-1	4-0	3-0	4-0	3-0
10. South Shields County Kitchens	0-3	3-3	2-1	0-2	2-0	4-0	2-2	3-2	0-0	*	1-0	2-0	2-4	4-0	3-4	1-2	5-2
11. Stanley United	0-0	1-0	0-3	2-3	1-0	2-0	6-0	3-2	0-6	2-2	*	7-3	3-1	2-1	1-4	0-2	2-2
12. Sunderland Fulwell Myers	0-2	5-1	1-3	0-1	3-1	5-0	1-1	1-6	0-4	1-2	1-2	*	3-1	2-0	0-3	0-3	1-0
13. Sunderland Tradelink	0-4	1-5	2-5	0-10	0-8	0-2	1-1	1-1	0-2	1-5	1-3	3-1	*	1-1	4-2	0-1	7-2
14. Usworth Village	2-5	3-0	0-4	1-2	0-3	0-1	2-2	1-2	0-5	1-6	1-1	1-1	1-5	*	0-5	0-6	0-3
15. Washington Glebe	4-4	1-1	4-1	3-1	1-1	2-2	6-1	4-2	1-1	1-2	2-1	1-2	3-1	3-0	*	5-2	3-1
16. Washington Nissan	4-1	8-0	3-2	2-1	3-2	2-1	2-1	5-2	1-1	4-1	2-0	3-1	2-1	6-1	2-5	*	1-0
17. Wingate Mall	1-2	4-1	0-3	0-0	1-1	0-2	2-1	2-4	1-1	1-4	1-5	5-0	1-1	3-0	1-6	1-2	*

LEAGUE CUP 1993-94

Preliminary Round

Sunderland Kennek Roker v Boldon CA 2-0
Wingate Mall v Washington Nissan 1-2
Sunderland Vaux Ryhope v Stanley United 3-4

First Round

Birtley Town v Murton International 4-1
Usworth Village v Northallerton Supporters 1-6
Hartlepool BWOB v South Shields 1-2
Washington Nissan v Hartlepool Town 1-4
Annfield Plain v Herrington Colliery Welf. 6-1
Jarrow v Newcastle City 4-0
North Shields v Washington Glebe 1-2
Silksworth v Cleator Moor Celtic 4-2
Sunderland Tradelink v Marchon 3-0
S. Shields Cleadon SC v County Kitchens Brink. 1-3
Stanley United v Wolviston 3-3,1-2
Sunderland Fulwell Myers v Marske United 0-3
Jarrow Roofing v Windscale United 4-2
Hebburn DT v Esh Winning Albion 6-0
Newton Aycliffe v Guisborough Priory 2-1
North Ormesby v Boldon Community Assoc. 2-2,2-0

Second Round

Birtley Town v Sunderland Tradelink 7-0
South Shields v Wolviston 3-1
Annfield P. v Jarrow Roofing Boldon CA 1-1,2-1
Washington Glebe v Newton Aycliffe 0-1
Northallerton Sup. v County Kitchens Brinkburn 1-0
Hartlepool Town v Marske United 1-0
Jarrow v Hebburn DT 0-3
Silksworth v North Ormesby 2-0

Quarter-Finals

South Shields v Hartlepool Town 4-2*(aet)*
Annfield Plain v Hebburn DT 0-1*(aet)*
Birtley Town v Northallerton Town Supporters 3-2
Newton Aycliffe *(scr)* Silksworth *(w/o)*

Semi-Finals

Birtley Town v South Shields 2-3
Hebburn DT v Silksworth 0-3

Final: Silksworth 2, South Shields 0

DIVISION TWO CUP 1993-94 **Preliminary Round**

Fulwell Myers v County Kitchens Brinkburn 0-3

First Round

Murton International v Esh Winning Alb. 4-5*(aet)*
Hebburn DT v Guisborough Priory 3-2
Sunderland Tradelink v Washington Nissan 0-3
Northallerton Supporters v Wingate Mall 4-4,3-0
Birtley Town v Marchon 0-2
Stanley United v County Kitchens Brinkburn 1-2
Washington Glebe v Usworth Village 1-0
North Ormesby v Newcastle City 1-0

Quarter-Finals

Esh Winning Albion v Marchon 1-3
Washington Nissan v Washington Glebe 1-0
Hebburn DT v County Kitchens Brinkburn 1-0
Northallerton Supporters v North Ormesby 1-0

Semi-Finals

Marchon v Hebburn DT 5-3*(aet)*
Washington Nissan v Northallerton Town Supp. 1-0

Final: Washington Nissan 2, Marchon 0

SUNDERLAND SHIPOWNERS' CUP 1993-94 **Preliminary Round**

Sunderland Kennek Roker v Windscale 1-3
Boldon Community Assn v Vaux Ryhope CW 0-2
North Ormesby v South Shields 1-1,3-5*(aet)*

Second Round

Washington Nissan v Hartlepool BWOB 0-4
Northallerton Supporters v Guisboro. Priory 2-0
Newcastle City v Sunderland Fulwell Myers 0-1
Hartlepool Town v South Shields 4-3
Sun. Vaux VRCW v Jarrow Roofing BCA 5-6*(aet)*
Birtley Town v Jarrow 1-0
Usworth Village v County Kitchens Brinkburn 0-3
Marske United v Hebburn DT 1-0
Esh Winning Albion v Windscale 0-1
Wolviston v Sunderland Tradelink 4-2
Herrington CW v Cleadon Social Club 2-1
Cleator Moor Celtic v Silksworth 2-3
Murton International v Stanley United 2-3
Annfield Plain v North Shields 2-1
Wingate Mall v Newton Aycliffe 1-3
Washington Glebe v Marchon 9-1

Second Round

Hartlepool BWOB v Windscale 0-0,0-4
Sunderland Fulwell Myers v Herrington CW 1-2
Jarrow Roofing Boldon CA v Stanley United 3-1
Co. Kitchens Brinkburn v Newton Aycliffe 5-2
Northallerton Town Supporters v Wolviston 3-0
Hartlepool Town v Silksworth 3-0
Birtley Town v Annfield Plain 1-2
Marske United v Washington Glebe 6-0

Quarter-Finals

Windscale v Northallerton Town Supporters 2-1
Jarrow Roofing Boldon CA v Annfield Plain 4-1
Herrington CW v Hartlepool Town 2-1
County Kitchens Brinkburn v Marske United 1-3*(aet)*

Semi-Finals

Windscale v Herrington Colliery Welfare 0-2
Jarrow Roofing Boldon CA v Marske Utd 3-3,2-1

Final *(at Jarrow Roofing Boldon CA FC, Fri 1st April)*: Jarrow Roofing Boldon CA 0, Herrington CW 2

VAUX WEARSIDE LEAGUE DIVISION ONE TEN YEAR RECORD

	84/5	85/6	86/7	87/8	88/9	89/0	90/1	91/2	92/3	93/4
Annfield Plain	9	4	1	18	13	7	3	5	6	12
Blackhall Colliery Welfare	-	-	-	12	17	-	-	-	-	-
Boldon Community Association	13	16	13	15	8	4	4	6	8	15
Clarke Champions	16	15	18	16	16	-	-	-	-	-
(S. Shields) Cleadon Social Club	-	-	-	-	-	-	-	8	9	9
Cleator Moor Celtic	-	-	-	-	11	12	8	12	13	14
Coundon Three Tuns	3	1	8	2	15	6	14	-	-	-
Darlington Railway Athletic	-	-	-	-	-	-	-	14	-	-
Dawdon Colliery Welfare	18	17	10	8	14	13	10	-	-	-
Dunston Federation Brewery	-	-	-	9	1	1	2	-	-	-
Easington Colliery	8	-	-	-	-	-	-	-	-	-
Eppleton Colliery Welfare	5	10	6	3	2	2	1	1	-	
Gateshead Reserves	14	8	20	-	-	-	-	-	-	-
Greatham Mayfair Centre					(See Hartlepool Town)					
Hartlepool Boys Welfare Old Boys	-	-	5	17	9	9	17	-	-	11
Hartlepool Town	-	-	-	-	-	-	12	2	2	1
Hebburn (formerly Reyrolles)	19	13	15	7	5	-	-	-	-	-
Herrington Colliery Welfare	-	-	17	19	10	14	16	13	14	10
Jarrow	-	-	-	-	-	-	-	-	-	17
Jarrow Roofing Boldon CA	-	-	-	-	-	-	-	-	4	3
Marske United	-	7	7	6	6	8	6	4	5	2
Murton Colliery Welfare	12	2	2	4	-	-	-	-	-	-
Newcastle Blue Star	1	-	-	-	-	-	-	-	-	-
Newcastle (ex-NEI) Bohemians	-	-	-	-	-	15	13	16	-	-
Newton Aycliffe	17	11	16	13	7	3	9	9	12	w/d
(Washington) Nissan	-	-	-	-	-	-	18	-	-	-
North Shields	-	-	-	-	-	-	-	-	-	13
Reyrolles						(See Hebburn)				
Roker				(See Sunderland (IFG)(Kennek) Roker)						
Ryhope Colliery Welfare	6	18	14	20	-	-	-	-	-	-
Sporting Club Vaux				(See Sunderland Vaux Ryhope CW)						
Silksworth	-	-	-	-	-	-	-	-	3	5
South Shields	4	12	9	5	4	5	5	3	1	4
Stockton EDC	20	-	-	-	-	-	-	-	-	-
Sunderland (IFG)(Kennek) Roker	15	14	12	14	12	10	7	11	7	6
Sunderland Vaux Ryhope CW	-	-	-	-	3	11	11	10	11	7
Usworth Village	-	-	-	-	-	-	-	15	-	-
Washington	10	6	11	11	-	-	-	-	-	-
Whickham	2	3	4	1	-	-	-	-	-	-
Windscale	-	-	-	-	-	-	-	-	15	8
Wingate	7	9	19	-	-	-	-	-	-	-
Wolviston	-	-	-	-	-	-	15	7	10	16
No. of clubs competing	**20**	**18**	**20**	**20**	**17**	**15**	**18**	**16**	**15**	**17**

MONKWEARMOUTH CHARITY CUP 1993-94

Preliminary Round

Sth Shields Cleadon SC v Nth Shields	1-1,0-2	Murton International v Jarrow Roofing Boldon CA	2-5
Newcastle City v South Shields	0-8		

First Round

Sunderland Tradelink v Wingate Mall	2-1	Herrington Colliery Welfare v Marske United	1-2
Washington Glebe v Birtley Town	2-1	Silksworth v Usworth Village	4-0
Hebburn DT v North Shields	2-0	Boldon Community Association v Newton Aycliffe	5-1
Jarrow v Marchon	2-0	Stanley United v Northallerton T. Supporters	4-2
Jarrow Roofing BCA v Annfield Plain	2-1	Sunderland Vaux Ryhope CW v Fulwell Myers	2-1
Guisborough Priory v Wolviston	3-2	South Shields Co. Kitchens v North Ormesby	1-2
Hartlepool BWOB v Hartlepool Town	0-2	Esh Winning Albion v Sunderland Kennek Roker	2-4
South Shields v Washington Nissan	2-1	Windscale v Cleator Moor Celtic	4-3

Second Round

Sunderland Tradelink v Marske United	1-3	Washington Glebe v Silksworth	1-3
Hebburn DT v Boldon Community Assn	2-0	Jarrow v Stanley United	3-2
Jarrow Roofing BCA v Vaux Ryhope CW	5-1	Guisborough Priory v North Ormesby Sports	0-1
Hartlepool Town v Kennek Roker	2-1 *(aet)*	South Shields v Windscale	5-0

Quarter-Finals

Marske United v Silksworth	4-1	Hebburn DT v Jarrow	1-0
Jarrow Roofing Boldon CA v North Ormesby	1-0	Hartlepool Town v South Shields	0-1 *(aet)*

Semi-Finals

Marske United v Hebburn DT	5-1	Jarrow Roofing Boldon CA v South Shields	2-3

Final *(at South Shields FC, Mon 4th April)*: South Shields 0, Marske United 3

DIVISION ONE CLUBS 1994-95

ANNFIELD PLAIN

Chairman: J H Barrett **Press Officer:** F Ross, 15 Northgate, Annfield Plain.
Sec./Treasurer: Marshall Lawson, 24 Northgate, Anfield Plain, Stanley, Co. Durham DH9 7UY (0207 235879).
Manager: D Longstaff **Ground:** Derwent Park, Annfield Plain.
Directions: On A693 road to Consett, 200 yds west of junction with A6067. Ground behind new housing estate. 6 miles from Durham (BR). Buses from Sunderland, Newcastle & Durham.
Seats: 20 **Cover:** 200 **Capacity:** 6,000 **Floodlights:** No **Founded:** 1890.
Colours: Claret/white/claret **Change colours:** All blue.
Programme: 16 pages, 20p **Record Attendance:** 7,200 v Southport, FA Cup 28-29.
Previous Names: Annfield Plain Celtic. **Local Press:** Newcastle Journal.
Previous Leagues: North Eastern 25-58 62-64/ Northern Alliance 02-25 58-60.
Past players progressing to Football League: A Graver (Lincoln), N Wilkinson (York), K Smith (Blackpool), J Hather (Aberdeen).
Honours: Wearside Lg 84-85 (Monkwearmouth Charity Cup 92-93), FA Cup 1st Rd 26-27 28-29 64-65, Durham Challenge Cup 52-53, Northern Alliance 19-20, Harelaw Snr Cup 35-36, North Eastern Lg Cup 46-47.

BOLDON COMMUNITY ASSOCIATION

Chairman: R A O Shepherd. **Vice Chairman:** G Smith **President:** A Brewster.
Sec./Press Off./Commercial Mgr: George Pollard, 126 Horsley Hill Road, South Shields (091 4546821).
Manager: Bill Newham **Asst Manager:** P Quinn **Coach:** Tommy Frazer.
Treasurer: A Bell **Physio:** G Meston/ R Fenwick
Ground: Boldon Community Association, North Road, Boldon Colliery.
Directions: A19 to junction with A184 Sunderland/Newcastle. Follow signs to Boldon Asda stores, then to North Road Social Club (SHACK). Ground behind. 800 yds from East Boldon (BR). Buses 533, 531, 319, 528.
Seats: 100 **Cover:** 400 **Capacity:** 3,500 **Floodlights:** No **Founded:** 1892.
Colours: Green & yellow halves **Change:** Red (white sleeves)/black **Programme:** No.
Record Attendance: 1,550 v Stockton, Durham Challenge Cup 1934. **Nickname:** Villa.
Previous Names: Boldon Villa (reformed in 1946)/ Boldon Colliery Welfare 50-76.
Prev. Grnds: Station Rd/ Colliery Rd **Prev. Lges:** None (Boldon Villa: Sth Tyne Alliance)
Clubhouse: Matchdays only. Bar snacks
Club Sponsors: Tyne Dock Engineering Co., South Shields.
Midweek home matchday: Mon or Wed **Reserve team:** None.
Captain 93-94: **Top Scorer 93-94:**
P.o.Y. 93-94:
Club record scorer: Darran Palmer **Club record appearances:** Peter Quinn.
Hons: Wearside Lg 52-53 54-55 74-75 (Lg Cup 67-68 72-73 75-76, Monkwearmouth Charity Cup 57-58 71-72, Shipowners Cup 62-63 71-72 75-76 76-77 78-79 88-89).

CLEATOR MOOR CELTIC

Chairman: R Doyle **Press Officer:** Secretary
Secretary: Pat McGrath, 105 Birks Road, Cleator Moor, Cumbria CA25 5HS (0946 811488).
Ground: Birks Field, Birks Road, Cleator Moor, Cumbria (0946 812476).
Directions: A66 to Bridgefoot, A595 for Barrow at Hensingham, left to Cleator Moor after 2 miles, left approaching town centre to Birks Road, club 200 yds on left. 5 miles from Whitehaven (BR).
Seats: No **Cover:** 500 **Capacity:** 2,000 **Floodlights:** No **Founded:** 1908.
Colours: Green & white/white/white **Change colours:** All green
Record Attendance: 3,100 v Penrith 1950 (12,212 v Tranmere at Workington, FA Cup 1st Rd 1950).
Previous Ground: The Celtic Field 08-59
Previous Leagues: West Cumberland/ Carlisle & Dist. (pre'88).
Past players progressing to Football League: Billy Elliott & Pat Fitzsimmons (Preston), Joe Kennedy (West Bromwich Albion), Charlie Woods & Paul Tynan (Ipswich Town)
Honours: FA Cup 1st Rd 50-51, West Cumberland Lg(51).

HARTLEPOOL BOYS WELFARE OLD BOYS

Chairman: Glen Thompson **Press Officer/Treasurer:** George Lester (0429 275327).
Secretary: Tom Harvey, 59 Wansbeck Gdns, Hartlepool TS26 9JH (0429 264753).
Manager: Jimmy Costello **Asst Manager:** Wilf Constantine **Physio:** Tony Metcalfe.
Ground: Grayfields Enclosure, Jesmond Road, Hartlepool.
Directions: Leave A19 on A179 signed Hartlepool, right for Throston Grange at 1st r'bout, left at 1st lights into Jesmond Road, ground 400yds on left.
Seats: None **Cover:** No **Capacity:** **Floodlights:** No **Founded:** 1952.
Colours: All white **Change colours:** All yellow. **Nickname:** None.
Previous Grounds: None **Prev. Lges:** Hartlepool Church/ Hartlepool & Dist./ Teesside.
Reserve team: None **Local Press:** Hartlepool Mail.
Players progressing to Football League: A Walsh (Middlesbrough, Darlington, Bristol City).
Programme: 10 pages, 50p **Programme Editor:** Secretary **Club Shop:** No.
Midweek home matchday: Monday **Clubhouse:** No.
Captain 93-94: **Top Scorer 93-94:**
P.o.Y. 93-94:
Hons: FA Vase 3rd Rd, Wearside Lg Div 2 92-93, Hartlepool Church Lg(2)(Lg Cup(3)), Hartlepool Mem. Shield, Durham Amateur Cup 64-65 73-74 (Minor Cup 60-61 (R-up 64-65)), Hartlepool & Dist. Lg(3)(Lg Cup(3)), Horden Aged Miners Cup, Wingate Aged Miners Cup, Teesside Lg 73-74 85-86(R-up(3)).

HERRINGTON COLLIERY WELFARE

Chairman: Paul Foster **Treasurer:** W Oxenden.
Secretary/Press Officer: Mel Speding, 12 Lodore Court, Doxford Park, Sunderland (091 520 0881).
Ground: Welfare Park, New Herrington.
Directions: Situated on B1286 between the Board Inn and Herrington Burn. Behind New Herrington W.M.C.
Colours: Black & white/black/black & white **Change:** Grey & black/grey/grey.
Previous Leagues: Washington Amateur 76-89. **Founded:** 1920 **Reformed:** 1976.
Hons: Monkwearmouth Charity Cup 09-10 10-11 31-32, Sunderland Shipowners Cup 93-94 (R-up 89-90), NCB National 5-aside 1975.

JARROW

Chairman: Dave Wiscombe **Treasurer:** Gavin Bainbridge.
Secretary/Press Officer: Calum McAuley, 109 Bamburgh Avenue, South Shields (091 4555924).
Ground: Perth Green Community Centre.
Directions: From A19 or A1(M) follow drections to South Shields, right onto John Reid Road. First slip road onto Brockley Whinns Estate, follow road past Red Hackle pub, third left left onto Inverness Road, then right into Perth Green Community Centre.
Colours: All yellow **Change:** All green **Founded:** 1980.
Prev. Names: Unionist FC/ Benson Perth Green. **Prev. Lges:** Sth Tyne 80-87/ Washington 87-91.
Hons: Sth Tyne Lg & Lg Cup, Washington Lg R-up 89-90 (Lg Cup 90-91, Aged Peoples Tphy R-up 90-91), Gateshead Charity Cup 90-91, Durham Tphy R-up 90-91.

JARROW ROOFING BOLDON C.A.

Chairman: Brian Marshall **Press Officer:** Rose McLoughlin.
Vice-Chairman/Secretary/Manager: Richard McLoughlin, 8 Kitchener Terrace, Jarrow NE32 5PU (091 4899825).
Coach: Kevin Arnott **Physio:** Fred Corner.
Ground: Adjacent to Boldon CA (above).
Seats: 150 **Cover:** 800 **Capacity:** 3,500 **Floodlights:** No **Founded:** 1987.
Colours: Blue & white **Change colours:** Claret & blue
Programme: 20 pages, free with entry **Editor:** Brian Marshall (091 455 1190) **Club Shop:** No.
Sponsors: Jarrow Roofing Co. **Record Gate:** 500 v South Shields **Nickname:** Roofing.
Midweek home matchday: Mon/Wed **Previous Leagues:** Mid-Tyne/ Tyneside Amtr 88-91.
Clubhouse: Open most nights and weekend lunchtimes. Chips, hotdogs, burgers etc available from tea bar on matchdays.
Captain 93-94: Colin Myers **Club record scorer & Top Scorer 93-94:** Michael Haley.
P.o.Y. 93-94: Kevin Arnott **Club record appearances:** Kevin Gibson.
Hons: Wearside Lg Div 2 R-up 91-92 (Sunderland Shipowners Cup R-up 93-94), Tyneside Amtr Lg R-up 90-91 (Chal. Shield 90-91 (R-up 89-90), Bill Dixon Cup 90-91), Mid-Tyne Lg 87-88, Fred Giles Cup R-up 87-88, Gateshead Charity Cup SF 90-91.

MARSKE UNITED

President: Raymond Jarvis **Chairman/Press Off.:** John Hodgson **Vice Chairman:** John Corner.
Secretary: Ian Rowe, 2 Cliff Cres., Loftus, Saltburn, Cleveland TS13 4RY (0287 644606).
Manager: Allan Marples **Asst Manager:** Barry Sill **Coach:** Charlie Bell
Physio: Barry Schollay **Commercial Mgr:** Don Willan **Treasurer:** Mrs Pat Hodgson.
Ground: Mount Pleasant, Mount Pleasant Ave., Marske-by-Sea, Redcar (0642 471091).
Directions: From A19 take A174 exit marked Yarm, Teesport, Redcar, Whitby and head east towards Teesport and Redcar, continue on A174 and enter Marske by A1040 or A1084. In town square right into Southfield Road, and right again to ground. 300 yds from Marske BR station - trains from Darlington via Middlesbrough.
Seats: 40 **Cover:** 50 **Capacity:** 2,000 **Floodlights:** No **Founded:** 1956.
Colours: Yellow/blue/white **Change:** Blue/white/blue. **Nickname:** Codheads
Previous Ground: None. **Record Gate:** 950 v Sunderland, friendly 1983.
Midweek home matchday: Wednesday **Previous Lges:** Cleveland/ Sth Bank & Dist./ Teesside 76-85.
Past players progressing to Football League: Peter Beagrie (Middlesbrough, Stoke City, Sheffield United, Everton, England 'B'), Dave Logan (Mansfield Town, Scarborough), Tony Butles (Gillingham).
Programme: 32 pages with entry **Programme Editor:** John Hodgson (0642 484006).
Club Shop: Club scarves, ties and sweaters available - contact Mrs P Hodgson (0642 484006).
Club Sponsors: Arnott Insurance **Reserve team's League:** Teesside Alliance.
Record win: 16-0 **Record defeat:** 3-9.
Clubhouse: Open every night and weekend lunchtimes. Food served after all games.
Club record scorer: Chris Morgan **Club record appearances:** John Hodgson.
Local Press: Sunday Sun/ Northern Echo/ Middlesbrough Evening Gazette.
Honours: North Riding County Cup 84-85, Teesside Lg 80-81 84-85, Wearside Lg R-up 93-94 (Lg Cup 92-93 (R-up 88-89), Monkwearmouth Charity Cup 93-94).

NORTH ORMESBY SPORTS

Chairman: Geoffrey Cane **Treasurer:** Martin Gibb **Manager:** Gary Stirland
Secretary/Press Off.: Peter Livingstone, 5 Guisborough Rd, Thornaby, Cleveland TS17 8EE (0642 614019).
Asst Manager: Mark Foster. **Coach:** Mark Puttick **Physio:** Geoffrey Cane.
Ground: Vicarage Playing Fields, Ormesby Rd, Middlesbrough (0609 772418).
Directions: Bus No.17 (every 12 mins) from M'boro bus station to Old Vic pub. By road, A19, A66 M'boro, A172 to r'bout, left on to A1085, right at Buccaneer Hotel lights (filter lane), grnd 300yds on right behind Old Vic.
Capacity: 1,000 **Seats:** None **Cover:** No **Floodlights:** No **Founded:** 1993.
Cols: Black & red halves/black/black **Change:** Yellow/green/yellow. **Nickname:** Doggy
Prev. Grounds/Leagues: None **Record Gate:** 426 v South Shields, Shipowners Cup 14/8/93.
Midweek home matchday: Wednesday **Club Shop:** Planned for proposed new ground.
Programme: 20 pages, 50p **Programme Editor:** David Canning.oneline 2
Record win: 9-2 v Esh Winning Albion (A), Wearside League Division Two 11/12/93.
Record defeat: 3-5 v South Shields (A), Sunderland Shipoweners Cup Preliminary Round replay 4/9/93.
Clubhouse: Adjacent pub - the Old Vic - used for after-match refresments. Open 11am-11pm.
Captain 93-94: Stephen Smith **Top Scorer 93-94/Club record scorer:** Stephen Parkes, 18.
P.o.Y. 93-94: Andrew Doddy **Club record apps:** Mark Foster 45. **Hons:** VWL D2 R-up 93-94.

NORTH SHIELDS

Chairman: Alan Neasham. **Press Officer:** Raymond Laidlaw (091 257 3271).
Secretary: Robert D Wilkinson, 72 Albatross Way, The Links, Blyth NE24 3QH (0670 352237).
Manager: Robert Wears **Coach:** Brian Latty
Physio: Alan Stokoe **Commercial Manager:** Michael Harris.
Ground: Swallow Sports Ground, Kings Road North, Rising Sun, Wallsend.
Directions: From Tyne Tunnel; A19 northbound, left at 1st r'bout onto A1058 coast road, 3rd exit, right at bottom of slip road, 1st left, right after 500yds where road bears left after next crossroads, ground 500yds on right. From west; Thru Newcastle onto A1052 coast road, 2nd exit to r'bout, 2nd exit and continue parallel to coast road, road bears left, when road bears right turn left (straight on), ground 500yds on right after next crossroads.
Capacity: 2,000 **Seats:** **Floodlights:** No **Nickname:** New Robins **Reformed:** 1992
Colours: All red **Change colours:** Sky/navy/navy **Sponsors:** Metroland
Programme: 40 pages, 50p **Editor:** Kenneth Green (091 257 9044) **Previous Lges:** None
Previous Grounds: Appleby Park, August 1992 - January 1993/ Percy Main Amateurs FC Jan '93 - May '93.
Record win: 8-2 v Wolviston (A), Wearside League Division One 13/11/93.
Record defeat: 0-16 v Marske United (A), Wearside Lague Division One 20/4/94.
Clubhouse: Open every night 7.30-11pm and weekends 11am-3pm. Food for matchdays and private functions.
Top Scorer 93-94: Michael Sloanes 21 **Club Record Scorer & Captain 93-94:** John Capewell (22 goals).
P.o.Y. 93-94: Dave Hodgson **Club Record Appearances:** Anthony Howarth & Martin Swales, 53.
Hons: Wearside Lg Div 2 R-up 92-93.

SILKSWORTH

Chairman: Jeff Eltringham **Treasurer:** Anthony Stubbs
Secretary/Press Officer: John Cumiskey, 21 Symington Gdns, Silksworth (091 5283098).
Ground: Silkworth Welfare Park **Directions:** Behind Lord Seaham Public House, Blind Lane, Silksworth. 3 miles from Sunderland (BR), bus 133 to Vicarage Court from Sunderland centre.
Seats: No **Cover:** None **Capacity:** 1,600 **Floodlights:** No **Founded:**
Colours: All white **Change colours:** All red. **Reformed:** 1988.
Players progressing to Football League: Bobby Gurney (Sunderland).
Hons: Wearside Lg 26-27 57-58 (Div 2 91-92, Lg Cup 51-52 59-60 93-94, Monkwearmouth Charity Cup 19-20 51-52, Shipowners Cup 53-54, Div 2 Cup 91-92).

SOUTH SHIELDS

Chairman: John Rundle **Vice Chairman:** George Scott **President:** Dick Butler.
Secretary/Press Officer: David Fall, 50 Basil Way, South Shields NE34 8UD (091 536 6809).
Manager: Peter Feenan **Physio:** John Watson **Comm. Mgr:** M McGuire
Ground: Filtrona Park, Shaftesbury Avenue, Simonside Industrial Estate, South Shields NE34 9PH.
Directions: A1(M), A194(M) to S. Shields, A194 town centre road for 5 miles, ignore A1300 (Sunderland & coast), turn left at next lights beside Co-op store into Simonside Ind. Est. (Shaftesbury Ave.), ground at bottom on right.
Seats: None **Cover:** 200 **Capacity:** 2,000 **Floodlights:** Yes **Founded:** 1974
Colours: Claret/blue/white **Change:** Black/white **Nickname:** Mariners
Prev. Lge: Northern Alliance 74-76. **Prev. Ground:** Jack Clarke Park 74-92.
Rec. Gate: 400 v Hartlepool T., Shipowners Cup final 3/5/93. *At prev. ground: 1,500 v Brigg, FA Vase 1975.*
Clubhouse: 2 function suites. Kitchen. **Local Press:** Shields Gazette/ Newcastle Journal.
Programme: 20p **Programme Editor:** Steve Leonard
Midweek home matchday: Wednesday **Club Shop:** Yes, selling hats, scarves etc. Contact secretary.
Captain 93-94: Paul Thompson **Top Scorer & P.o.Y. 93-94:** Steve Harkus.
Hons: FA Vase QF 75-76, Northern All. 74-75 75-76, Wearside Lg 76-77 92-93 (Monkwearmouth Cup 86-87 (R-up 93-94), Lg Cup R-up 82-83 83-84 93-94, Shipowners Cup 92-93 (R-up 83-84)), Durham Chal. Cup 76-77.

SOUTH SHIELDS CLEADON SOCIAL CLUB

Chairman: Gordon Ferries **Vice-Chairman/Press Off./Manager:** David Wood (091 4554607).
Secretary: Mr Charlie Appleby, 49 Tynedale Rd, South Shields (091 454 5724).
Asst Manager: Steve Duguid **Commercial Manager:** Joan Wood
Coach: Andy Wilkinson **Ground:** Jack Clarke Park, South Shields.
Directions: Enter South Shields on A194 to r'bout taking you on to A1300 John Reid Rd. 2nd left at 3rd r'bout into King George Rd then Sunderland Road, right at lights into Grosvenor Rd then then left into Horsly Hill Rd. Ground on right behind indoor bowls centre. Three quarters of a mile from Chichester Metro station.
Capacity: 400 **Seats:** 25 **Cover:** 75 **Floodlights:** No **Founded:** Early 60s
Colours: White & black **Change:** Claret **Club Shop:** No
Midweek home matches: Wednesday **Sponsors:** Cleadon & Dist. Soc. Club **Nickname:** The Club
Previous Leagues: Shields & Dist. 64-67/ South Tyne 67-73/ Washington Amtr 73-89.
Prev. Grnds: Harton Welf./ Metupa Pk **Record Gate:** 300 v South Shields, VWL Div 1 26/12/92.
Player progressing to Football League: Ian Hamilton (Darlington) 1980.
Record win: 16-0 v Chester-le-Street Reserves, Washington League 25/4/88.
Record defeat: 0-8 v Marske United, Wearside League Division One 25/8/93.
Clubhouse: Cleadon SC, Fulwell Av., S. Shields. Normal pub hrs except Sat. All types of sandwiches etc.
Captain 93-94: Mark Harrison **P.o.Y. 93-94:** Micky Bainbridge **Top Scorer 93-94:** Justin Perry.
Hons: W'side Lg Div 2 90-91, Shields & D Lg, W'gton Lg 77-78 84-85, Durham Cup, various local cups pre-1990.

SUNDERLAND KENNEK ROKER

Chairman: J Broadbent **Press Officer:** Secretary **Treasurer:** Les Dodd.
Secretary: Tom W Clark, 55 Vicarage Close, New Silksworth SR3 1BQ (091 5211242).
Ground: As Silksworth (see above). **Record Attendance:** Unknown. **Founded:** 1940.
Colours: Red & white stripes/black/black **Change:** Sky/navy/navy.
Previous Names: Roker Methodists/ Roker/ Roker Zanussi/ Sunderland Roker/ Sunderland I.F.G. Roker.
Local Press: Sunderland Echo.
Players progressing to Football League: Paul Rutherford (Newcastle).
Hons: Wearside Lg Cup 91-92 (Shipowners Cup 89-90 (R-up 80-81), Monkwearmouth Charity Cup R-up 80-81).

SUNDERLAND RYHOPE COLLIERY WELFARE

Chairman: R E Forster **Press Officer:** Secretary **Treasurer:** I Mankin.
Secretary: Trevor Whitehead, 6 Byron Walk, Gateshead (091 477 2065).
Ground: Ryhope Recreation Park, Ryhope Street, Ryhope, Sunderland (091 521 2843).
Directions: Take A19 (3 miles south of Sunderland centre) to Ryhope village, at Village Green turn into Evelyn Terrace/Ryhope Street and carry on up bank past Presto's for 600 yds - ground appears on left. 3 miles from Sunderland Central (BR), bus every 10 minutes from Sunderland centre.
Seats: No **Cover:** No **Capacity:** 1,000 **Floodlights:** Yes **Founded:** 1988.
Colours: All blue **Change colours:** Red & white/black/red.
Previous Names: Ryhope Colliery Welfare (founded 1898, previously Ryhope Villa) merged with Sporting Club Vaux (founded in 1968 as Monkwearmouth, later Bishopwearmouth, South Hetton) in 1988/ Sunderland Vaux Ryhope Colliery Welfare 88-93.
Previous Grounds: Sporting Club Vaux: Glenesk Road (pre-1988).
Previous Leagues: Sporting Club Vaux: Tyne & Wear/ North Eastern Amateur.
Record Gate: 2,000; Ryhope Colliery Welfare v Workington, FA Cup 1967.
Players progressing to Football League: Alan Harding (Lincoln, Darlington, Hartlepool), Kenny Ellis (Hartlepool, Darlington, Belgian clubs), Kenny Mitchell (prof. Icelandic club), Robert Malt (Leeds), Brian Smiles (Chelsea), Ron Robinson (Ipswich, Leeds), Nigel Staddington (Doncaster, Sunderland).
Honours *(Sporting Club Vaux hons italicised)* Wearside Lg 61-62 62-63 63-64 65-66 (Lg Cup 63-64 77-78), Durham Challenge Cup 77-78, Monkwearmouth Charity Cup 09-10 65-66 66-67, Sunderland Shipowners Cup 61-62 *86-87*, FA Cup 1st Rd Proper 67-68, FA Vase 1st Rd 81-82.

WASHINGTON NISSAN

Chairman: Colin Dodge **Press Officer:** Secretary
Secretary: Harry English, 159 Alston Crescent, Seaburn Dene, Sunderland SR6 8NF (091 5487194)
Manager: Stan Fenwick **Assistant Manager/Top Scorer 93-94:** Keith Robertson.
Coach: Darren Ward **Treasurer:** Tom Dixon
Ground: Nissan Spts Complex.
Directions: Northwards along A1 (M) use A690 (sign post Sunderland) to connect with A19, travel north on A19, after passing the A1231 turn off the plant is on the left. Go past plant and follow signs for 'Nissan Offices'. Southwards along A19 and leave A19 at signpost for 'Nissan Offices'.
Colours: All blue **Change colours:** All red **Founded:** 1988
Midweek home matchdays: Wednesday
Clubhouse: Open Mon-Fri 5-11pm, Sat 11am-11pm, Sun noon-3 & 7-10.30pm
Captain 93-94: Nigel Saddington **Player of the Year 93-94:** Gary Wright.
Hons: Wearside Lg Div 1 93-94 (Lg Cup R-up 91-92, Div 2 Cup 92-93 93-94), Nissan European Tphy 88-89 90-91 92-93.

WINDSCALE

Chairman: R Napier **Press Officer:** Secretary **Treasurer:** A Barwise
Secretary: Geoff Turrell, 65 Leathwaite, Loop Road South, Whitehaven, Cumbria CA28 7UG (0936 62229)
Ground: Falcon Field, Egremont. **Directions:** A66 to Bridgefoot, A595 for Barrow, at bottom of hill approaching Egremont take 3rd turn off island (signed) Smithfield/ Gillfoot, ground in centre of housing estate
Colours: White/black/black **Change:** Royal & white stripes/royal/white
Previous Lges: West Cumberland Snr/ Derwent Valley/ Furness Premier. **Founded:** 1950
Hons: Furness Snr Cup 85-86 **Previous Names:** Windscale Rovers/ Windscale United.

WOLVISTON

Chairman: Eddie Poole **Vice Chairman:** Derek Stockton **President:** Bob Smith
Sec./Press Officer: Keith Simpson, 14 Lodore Grove, Acklam, Middlesbrough TS5 8PB (0642 823734).
Manager: John Johnson **Asst Manager:** Kevin Smith **Coach:** Alan Lucas
Physio: Jonathan Baker.
Ground: Metcalfe Way, Wynyard Road, Wolviston, Billingham, Cleveland TS22 5NE.
Directions: Situated on Wynyard Road between Thorpe Thewles and Wolviston. From A19 onto A689 into Wolviston village, take Wynyard Road heading towards Thorpe Thewles, ground on left before Sir John Halls Estate. Or, from A1(M) to Stockton direction, turn left at Thorpe Thewles along Wynyard Road, ground on right after Sir John Halls Estate. All public transport to Billingham town centre just under one mile from ground.
Seats: None **Cover:** 200 **Capacity:** 2,000 **Floodlights:** No **Founded:** 1910
Colours: Royal/white/royal **Change:** Scarlet/white/scarlet. **Nickname:** Wolves
Prev. Name: Wolviston St Peters 10-46 **Prev. Lges:** Stockton & Dist. 46-82/ Teesside 82-88.
Previous Grounds: Greenwood Rd, Billingham (5 years)/ Billingham Community Centre (10 years).
Programme: 8 pages, 20p **Editor:** Secretary or Ben Foreman (0642 550352).
Sponsors: R.C.I. Industrial Cleaners **Rec. Gate:** 500 v Middlesbrough 27/7/93 **Club Shop:** No.
Midweek home matchday: Wednesday **Reserve team's League:** Stockton & District.
Record win: 13-0 v Ministry of Defence FC **Record defeat:** 1-8 v South Shields
Clubhouse: Licensed bar. Tea room. Lounge. Hot & cold meals, sandwiches, crisps, soft drinks. Open 11am-11pm on matchdays.
Players progressing to Football League: Peter (Pike) Atkinson (Grimsby), David Hockaday (Blackpool, Swindon), Ken McCue (Blackpool), Kenny Lowe (Hartlepool), Laurie Duff (Leicester).
Club record scorer: Bob Easby 54 **Club record appearances:** Bob Easby 300+.
Captain 93-94: Colin Stott **Top Scorer 93-94:** Peter Simpson 20 **P.O.Y. 93-94:** Gary Murray.
Hons: Wearside Lg Div 2 89-90 (Lg Cup R-up 92-93), Teesside Lg R-up 84-85 (R T Raine Cup 86-87), Durham FA Trophy R-up 89-90, Stockton & District Lg 73-74 75-76 76-77 (Lg Cup 72-73 74-75 77-78, Lg Charity Cup 79-80).

DIVISION TWO CLUBS 1994-95

BIRTLEY TOWN

Chairman: J Heslington **Vice-Chairman:** J Grainger.
Secretary/Press Officer: Richard Barrett, 16 Coldstream, Ouston, Chester-le-Street DH2 1LQ (091 410 7395).
Manager: Barry Fleming **Asst Manager:** David Smith
Coach: Malcolm Thompson **Commercial Manager:** Ray Stafford.
Ground: Birtley Sports Complex.
Directions: (From Durham) Off A1(M) signpsted for Chester-le-Street, take 2nd turn off r-bout signed Birtley, take last turn off next r-bout (still signed Birtley), after one and a half miles take 1st left after AEI Cables - ground at rear of sports complex.
Seats: None **Cover:** None **Capacity:** **Floodlights:** No. **Founded:** 1890
Cols: Green & white stripes/white/white **Change colours:** Red/blue/red. **Reformed:** 1986
Previous League: Northern Alliance. **Previous Ground:** Birtley Welfare Ground, 1986-1994.
Midweek home matches: Wednesday **Club Sponsors:** C & C Coachworks **Club Shop:** No
Reserves' Lge: None **Clubhouse:** Matchdays only. Not licensed.
Programme: 32 pages, 25p **Programme Editor:** D Smith, 25 Penshaw View, Birtley.
Record Gate: 400 v South Shields, League Cup semi-final 93-94.
Record win: 7-0 v Sunderland Tradelink, Wearside League Cup 93-94.
Record defeat: 1-4 v Nissan, Wearside League Division Two 93-94.
Record appearances: Barry Fleming **Record scorer & Top Scorer 93-94:** Billy Davidson 25.
Captain 93-94: Alan Pearson **P.o.Y. 93-94:** Neil Pick.
Hons: Wearside Lg 45-46 (Lg Cup 35-36), Northern Alliance 23-24 (R-up 13-14).

CHILTON MOOR

Press Off./Treasurer/Sec.: Steven Cullen, 302 Leechmere Rd, Tunstall, Sunderland SR2 9DF (091 5226164).
Ground: Houghton Complex.
Directions: A690 for Durham from A19, A182 slip road for Washington town centre, 1st left at next r'bout, 1st right, 2nd left to Leyburn Grove.
Colours: Red/black/black **Change colours:** All sky.
Previous Names: David Brown FC/ Mountain Daisy 85-87/ Castle View 87-90/ Usworth Village 90-94.
Previous Leagues: Wearside Apprentices/ Wearside Comb. 72-79/ North Eastern Amtr 79-88/ Washington 88-90.
Hons: Wearside Comb. R-up 78-79, GHB Eltringham Tphy 85-86, North Eastern Amtr Lg 87-88.

GUISBOROUGH PRIORY

Founded: 1993 *(Reserve side of Guisborough Town - see page 692)*

HARTLEPOOL UNITED RESERVES

President: E Leadbitter, MP **Chairman:** C Gibson **Vice-Chairman:** A Bamford.
Secretary: The Secretary, c/o Hartlepool United FC.
Ground: The Victoria Ground, Hartlepool, Cleveland TS24 8BZ (0429 272584).
Directions: From North: A1, A19 then A179 to Hartlepool, right at crossroads into Clarence Rd for ground. From South: A1, A19 then A689 to town centre then bear right into Clarence Rd. BR to Hartlepool Church Street station.
Colours: Sky & navy **Changes:** All yellow or All siver grey.
Previous Leagues: Wearside (pre-1982)/ Northern 82-87/ Midland Senior 87-94.
Honours: Wearside Lg 79-80 (Lg Cup 71-72, Monkwearmouth Charity Cup 73-74, Sunderland Shipowners Cup 23-24 32-33).

MURTON INTERNATIONAL

Chairman: Mr T Pratt **Vice-Chairman:** D Simpson.
Sec./Press Off.: John Collings, 7 Station Rd South, Murton, Seaham, Co. Durham SR7 9RS (091 526 4906).
Manager: Eddie Guy **Physio:** Graham Beaghan. **Founded:** 1992
Ground: As Murton (see page 693).
Cols: All white **Change colours:** All red **Previous Leagues:** None.
Programme: No. **Club Shop:** No. **Previous Grounds:** None. **Nickname:** The Nash
Midweek home matchday: Wednesday.
Record win: 8-0 v Northern Co's (A) **Record defeat:** 3-9 v Hylton Castle, both Durham Tphy Sep '93
Club record scorer: Jason Lennox **Club record appearances:** Tony Metcalfe.
Captain 93-94: John Vine **Top Scorer 93-94:** Dean Rowell **P.o.Y. 93-94:** Mark Reeves.

NEWCASTLE CITY

Chairman: Kami Kundi **Press Officer:** Tom McClements/ Shindi Dhugga.
Secretary: Satinder Dhugga, 15 Casteway, Dinnington, Newcastle-upon-Tyne NE13 7LS (091 661 821506).
Treasurer: Dav Mattu **Ground:** Broadway East, Gosforth.
Directions: A1 turning off at Gosforth, Fawdon, follow signs for Fawdon leading to Kingston Park Rd, pass 1 set of lights, left at mini-r'bout, 1st left to ground. Through town over Tyne Bridge take Gosforth turn off, thru Gosforth High Street, pass ASDA (on right), main r'bout, left at Broadway West, ground 400yds on right.
Colours: Yellow/blue/yellow **Change:** Blue/blue/yellow **Founded:** 1993.

NORTHALLERTON TOWN SUPPORTERS

Secretary: Trevor Arnold, 55 Ullswater Drive, Acklam, Middlesbrough TS5 7DJ (0642 823923).
Ground: As Northallerton Town (see page 694). **Founded:** 1992
Colours: Black & white stripes/black/black **Change colours:** All yellow

PRUDHOE SWINTON

Founded: 1994 *(Reserve side of Prudhoe Town - see page 694)*

SOUTH SHIELDS BRINKBURN C.A.

Chairman: Barry Raper **Press Officer:** Graham Carlton (091 456 2835).
Secretary: Martin Lynn, 261 Sunderland Rd, South Shields (091 455 5145)
Manager/Coach: G Charlton **Treasurer:** Dean Apes.
Ground: Brinkburn Comprehensive School, Harton Lane, South Shields.
Directions: A19, left filter for South Shields, right at 1st r'bout onto A194, 200yds right onto John Reid Rd (A1300), 2 miles to 3rd r'bout, 1st left after r'bout into Temple Park Rd to Grey Hen pub, left into Harton Lane, ground 150yds on left - concealed entrance.
Colours: Red/navy/red **Change colours:** All blue
Previous Name: South Shield County Kitchens Brinkburn (pre-1994).
Prev. Lge: Northern Alliance (pre-1993) **Hons:** Northern Alliance Amateur Cup R-up 91-92.

SOUTH SHIELDS HARTON & WESTHOE COLLIERY WELFARE

Chairman: **Founded:**
Secretary: Mr D Key, 3 Tarragon Way, South Shields, Tyne & Wear NE34 8TA (091 536 7432).
Ground:
Colours: **Change:**

STANLEY UNITED

President: A Westgarth **Vice-President:** B Waiting.
Secretary/Manager/Commercial Manager/Press Officer/Treasurer: J V Kirkup, 9 Brookes Rise, Regents Green, Langley, Durham DH7 8XY (091 3780921)
Physio: J Burn. **Asst Manager/Coach:** K Finnegan
Ground: High Road, Stanley, near Crook (nicknamed Hill Top Ground).
Directions: From Teeside on A689 to Bishop Auckland and onto Crook, turn left at Market Place then first right for Tow Law to Billy Row and Stanley, right at top of bank then first left, ground is 250 yards on left. From Tyneside and Sunderland; to Durham city onto A690 westbound thru Langley Moor, thru Brancepeth Village, turn right onto Oakenshaw/Tow Law road for approx. 3 miles, turn right at junction, after half a mile turn right opposite Post Office in Stanley after half mile, ground is 250 yards on left
Seats: None **Cover:** 300 **Capacity:** 3,000 **Floodlights:** No **Founded:** 1890.
Colours: Red & white stripes/black/red **Change colours:** Sky/navy/navy **Nickname:** The Nops
Programme: Yes, new for 94-95 **Programme Editor:** K Finnegan (091 410 0046).
Previous Name: Stanley Nops 1880-1890. **Record Gate:** 5,000 v Leytonstone, FA Amtr Cup QF, 1920.
Previous Leagues: Mid-Durham/ Crook & District/ South Durham Alliance (all pre-1910)/ Northern 10-36 45-74/ Durham Central 36-45/ Durham City & Dist. 74-88.
Players progressing to Football League: Geoff Strong (Liverpool, Arsenal), Tommy Cummins (Burnley), Dickie Dale & Eli Ashurst (Birmingham), Jackie Brown & John Wilkinson (York), Gordon Bradley & Fred Batty (Bradford PA), Archie Brown (Sunderland), Jackie Howarth (Chelsea, Aldershot), John Birbeck (Norwich), Alan Ball (Queen of the South), Dickie Smart Exeter, Bill McKay (Bolton), Ed Holmes (Barnsley).
Club Shop: No, but club jerseys, polo shirts and training tops available from secretary.
Sponsors: Company Cars Direct **Clubhouse:** Open matchdays. Fast food & light refreshments.
Midweek home matchday: Mon/Wed **Reserve team:** None.
Record transfer fee paid: Nil **Received:** Undisclosed for Geoff Strong (Arsenal, 1958).
Capt. 93-94: Dave Edwards **Top Scorer 93-94:** Dave Edwards/Graeme Kendal **P.o.Y. 93-94.** Keith Burn.
Major Honours: Northern Lg 45-46 61-62 63-64 (R-up 62-63, Lg Cup 46-47 57-58 61-62), FA Cup 1st Rd 53-54, FA Amtr Cup SF 19-20, Durham Challenge Cup 41-42, Durham Amtr Cup 00-01 05-06, Wearside Lg John McGrath Mem. Tphy (Fair-Play award) 92-93. *Club champions of all league entered except Wearside Lge.*

SUNDERLAND SPORTING CLUB FULWELL

President: John Holtan **Chairman:** Bob Craggs **Vice Chairman:** Colin Dagg.
Press Off./Secretary: Alan Morton, 44 Hartside Rd, Nookside, Sunderland SR4 8BD (091 528 3270)
Manager: Ian Peary **Asst Manager:** Mark Harrison **Coach:** Tommy Middlemist
Physio: Ben Wattling (Neepha Ltd) **Comm. Mgr:** Janette Morton
Ground: Northumbria Centre, Washington, Tyne & Wear.
Directions: From A19 take A1231 to Washington, A195 for District 12, right at 3rd r'bout, ground on left.
Seats: No **Cover:** None **Floodlights:** No **Capacity:** 2,000 **Founded:** 1985.
Colours: Blue & white stripes **Change:** Red & white stripes **Nickname:** None.
Programme: 32-40 pages, 50p **Editors:** Bob Craggs/Janette Morton **Clubhouse:** No.
Club Shop: Yes, selling tracksuits, pennants, blazer badges, ski hats, scarves, programmes etc. Contact Bob Craggs (091 565 4095).
Record win: 11-0 v Sandmills 1987 **Sponsors:** Myers Plumbing & Heating Ltd
Record defeat: 0-7 v Stanley Utd 1993 **Previous Ground:** Monkwearmouth School 85-91.
Midweek home matchday: Monday **Previous League:** Wearside Combination 87-91.
Previous Names: R & J Carpets/ Sunderland Flo-Gas Fulwell (pre-'93)/ Sunderland Fulwell Myers 93-94.
Club Newsline: 0891 333097 **Reserve Team's League:** Wearside Combination.
Record gate: 428 v West Barns, Dunbar - Anglo-Scottish Elizabethan Cup final 29/8/93.
Record Scorer: Robert Johnson 85-94 **Club record appearances:** Christopher Holtan.
Captain 93-94: Christopher Holtan **Top Scorer & Player of the Year 93-94:** Robert Johnson.
Hons: Anglo-Scottish Elizabethan Cup 1993, Wearside Combination 90-91 (Div 2 R-up 89-90, Div 3 R-up 88-89), Jollies Cup 88-89, J S Pears Memorial Trophy 88-89 89-90, CEFAS Div 2 88-89.

WASHINGTON GLEBE WELFARE

Chairman: Frank Lanaghan **Press Officer:** Secretary
Secretary: Robert Robson, 24 Talbot Close, Glebe, Washington NE38 7RH (091 4151893).
Treasurer: Graham Thirlaway **Ground:** Washington Glebe Welfare.
Directions: A1 them A19, A1231 into Washington, 3rd exit road (signed Gateshead A195), turn for District 9 at r'bout, right for Washington Village at next r'bout, right at 1st T-jnct., pitch 200 yds on right.
Colours: Blue & white **Change colours:** All red.

WHITEHAVEN AMATEURS

Chairman: Neil Fennell **Press Officer:** Secretary
Secretary: Ian Green, 57 Glenridding Walk, Whitehaven, Cumbria (0946 62149)
Manager: Ian Green **Assistant Manager:** Ian Atkins.
Ground: Albright & Wilson, Whitehaven Works
Directions: From A66 (from Carlisle via Cockermouth or M6 jct 40) turn on to A595 to Whitehaven. Follow 'Town Centre' A5094 then 'St Bees' B5345 thru one-way system, past supermarkets, fork right up hill at junction signed 'Sandwith and Marchon Works', ground on right of main road beyond works at top of hill. Two miles from Bransty (BR).
Seats: None **Cover:** 50 **Capacity:** 1,000 **Floodlights:** No **Founded:** 1957
Colours: Blue/black/blue **Change colours:** Red/white/red
Previous Leagues: West Cumberland/ Carlisle & District/ Cumberland.
Previous Names: Haig Colliery/ Marchon (pre-1994).
Clubhouse: Works Social Club 1 mile away. Normal pub hours.
Programme: Occasionally issued **Top Scorer/P.o.Y. 93-94:** Kevin Henderson
Club Sponsors: Company (A & W).
Honours: Cumberland Cup 90-91, County League 87-88 88-89, Wearside Lg Div 2 Cup R-up 93-94.

WINGATE

Chairman: Joe Bannister **Press Officer:** Ray Morton
Secretary: Richard Hayes, 40 Tyrone Road, Fairfield, Stockton on Tees TS19 7JW (0642 588900).
Treasurer: John Malcolm **Ground:** Welfare Park, Wingate
Directions: From North A19 to A181 junct, South A19 to A179 junct. From Durham A181; to B1280, Front Street, Wingate turn right at Queens Head Public House. Ground 400 yards ahead through Market Crescent.
Colours: Red/white/red **Change colours:** Sky/navy/sky.
Previous Names: Wingate St Marys, Wingate Wanderers merged in 1967 to form Wingate FC. This club then merged with Billingham Cassel Mall in 1992 to form Wingate Mall FC. Name reverted to Wingate in 1994.
Previous Leagues: Hartlepool & Dist. *(St Marys & Wanderers)*/ Wearside 67-87/ Auckland & Dist. 87-88. *Billingham Cassel Mall: Teesside (pre-1992).*
Hons: Wearside Lg R-up 78-79 (Lg Cup 69-70 (R-up 78-79), Div 2 Cup R-up 92-93), Monkwearmouth Charity Cup 77-78 83-84, Shipowners Cup R-up 67-68 78-79), Durham Chal. Cup R-up 73-74, J V Madden Cup 92-93, FA Cup 3rd Qual. Rd. *Cassel Mall: Teesside Lg 91-92.*

South Shields attack during their crucial Vaux Wearside League Division One clash at home to leaders Hartlepool Town on 15th January. However, the visitors win 1-0 and go on to clinch the title and promotion.
Photo - John Diamond.

COURAGE BEST SCOTCH NORTHERN ALLIANCE

FOUNDED: 1890

FEEDER TO: FEDERATION BREWERY NORTHERN LEAGUE

President: Sir John Hall (Newcastle United FC) **Chairman:** R M Griffiths

Press Officer: Bill Gardner, 12 Coronation Road, Sunniside, Newcastle upon Tyne NE16 5NR (091 4883422).

SECOND TITLE FOR MORPETH TOWN

Morpeth Town last won the Premier Division championship ten years ago and, after going close in 1992-93 when finishing in fourth place, they continued their recent improvement by taking the 1993-94 title at the expense of runners-up Carlisle City who pressed them hard right up to the penultimate game of the season.

Morpeth crowned a highly successful season by also claiming the League Cup, beating Ponteland United 4-0 in the final replay at Newton Park, Heaton Stannington.

Three clubs were involved in the Division One title race but Benfield Park and Hebburn Reyrolle were finally shaken off by eventual champions Amble Town. Amble have now claimed the Division Two and Division One titles in successive seasons and also added the Division One Combination Cup to their trophy cupboard. Runners-up Benfield Park were promoted into the Premier Division on the basis of their final league position and their excellent ground which is still being developed.

Ashington Hirst were Division Two champions after building up an unbeaten away record which spanned two league seasons. Runners-up Orwin New Winning also claimed the Northumberland Minor Cup by beating Amble in the final. The Wallsend-based club has made tremendous strides since finishing second from bottom in their first Alliance season in 1992-93.

Ponteland United of the Premier Division were once again great ambassadors for the Alliance in the FA Vase. Before their third round 2-0 extra-time defeat by Oadby Town, Ponteland had beaten Shotton Comrades, Alnwick Town, Seaton Delaval and Liversedge.

Bill Gardner, Press Officer

PREM. DIV.	P	W	D	L	F	A	PTS
Morpeth Town	30	25	2	3	86	27	77
Carlisle City	30	22	3	5	73	33	69
Ponteland United	30	18	5	7	80	43	59
Seaton Delaval Am.	30	16	7	7	61	37	55
West Allotment C.	30	17	3	10	74	48	54
Gillford Park	30	13	7	10	56	31	46
Walker	30	14	3	13	64	57	45
Spittal Rovers	30	13	5	12	40	44	44
Winlaton Hallgarth	30	12	6	12	58	50	42
Seaton Terrace	30	12	6	12	49	47	42
Longbenton	30	11	6	13	60	53	39
Westerhope	30	11	3	16	40	55	36
Blyth Kitty Brew.	30	8	3	19	39	76	27
Haltwhistle CP	30	6	5	19	38	51	*20
Heaton Stannington	30	4	4	22	38	117	16

* - 3 points deducted.

TOP SCORERS

John Moscrop (Morpeth) 32
Ian Chater (Ponteland) 29

DIV. ONE	P	W	D	L	F	A	PTS
Amble Town	28	21	4	3	100	29	67
Benfield Park	28	19	6	3	84	20	63
Reyrolle	28	20	3	5	84	34	63
Swalwell	28	16	6	6	67	40	54
Dudley Welfare	28	12	7	9	51	55	43
Ryton	28	13	4	11	45	52	43
St Columbas	28	13	6	9	62	47	*42
Hexham Swinton	28	10	7	11	48	46	37
Newbiggin CW	28	9	9	10	57	49	36
Percy Main	28	11	2	15	53	80	35
Bohemians	28	9	4	15	51	67	31
Procter & Gamble	28	7	4	17	34	76	25
Northern Co's	28	7	4	17	45	72	*22
Wylam	28	6	1	21	35	86	19
Forest Hall	28	2	3	23	20	83	9

* - 3 points deducted. Percy Rovers' record expunged as they failed to complete their fixtures.

TOP SCORERS

Robert Pile (Amble) 19
Colin Scandal (Hexham) 15

DIV. TWO	P	W	D	L	F	A	PTS
Ashington HP	28	23	4	1	126	38	73
Orwin New Winning	28	20	4	4	91	49	64
Shankhouse	28	18	4	6	93	25	58
Heddon Institute	28	17	2	9	73	41	53
Newcastle Univ.	28	15	2	11	56	58	47
Marden Athletic	28	16	1	11	70	56	*46
Highfields	28	14	3	11	67	47	45
Stobswood	28	14	2	12	68	48	44
DHSS	28	14	5	9	60	62	*44
Norgas	28	11	2	15	52	83	35
Monkseaton KOSA	28	7	6	15	45	59	27
Durham Rangers	28	8	3	17	53	83	27
Shilbottle CW	28	6	4	18	32	62	22
Northern Electric	28	5	1	22	36	82	16
Wallsend Rising S.	28	0	1	27	19	148	1

* - 3 points deducted. Swalwell Crowley resigned just prior to start of season.

TOP SCORERS

Peter Jennings (Shankhouse) 48
Dave McKenzie (Ashington HP) 27

PREMIER DIVISON RESULTS 1993-94

HOME TEAM	1	2	3	4	5	6	7	8	9	10	11	12	13	14	15	16
1. Blyth Kitty Brewster	*	0-3	0-3	1-7	3-0	4-1	0-1	2-3	0-3	2-1	2-0	0-3	4-1	0-4	1-5	1-2
2. Carlisle City	4-1	*	0-0	1-0	1-4	3-0	1-3	4-0	3-2	0-0	2-2	1-5	6-1	3-1	3-0	1-2
3. Carlisle Gillford Park	9-0	1-2	*	1-2	5-0	6-0	1-3	1-3	0-1	2-2	3-1	0-1	2-2	1-0	3-1	4-1
4. Haltwhistle Crown Paints	4-1	0-1	0-1	*	0-2	1-1	1-1	1-4	0-1	1-1	0-2	0-1	6-1	0-4	3-0	0-0
5. Heaton Stannington	0-1	2-5	2-2	2-1	*	0-4	4-6	3-3	1-5	2-3	2-3	0-14	1-2	1-4	1-5	0-2
6. Longbenton	4-1	0-5	2-0	2-1	13-0	*	0-1	0-3	1-1	1-6	3-1	5-1	0-0	2-3	0-1	1-1
7. Morpeth Town	2-0	1-0	1-0	6-0	4-0	4-0	*	2-2	3-2	1-2	1-0	3-2	3-0	1-2	3-1	4-0
8. Ponteland United	3-0	1-3	0-0	2-0	5-2	3-0	3-5	*	2-3	2-5	2-1	3-1	11-2	4-0	1-1	0-2
9. Seaton Delaval Amateurs	1-1	1-4	2-0	1-0	5-1	1-2	0-2	1-1	*	3-2	2-1	1-1	5-1	2-2	3-1	2-2
10. Seaton Delaval Seaton Terr.	0-0	0-1	0-0	1-0	5-1	1-4	0-3	0-2	0-2	*	3-1	3-1	3-2	1-3	2-0	2-2
11. Spittal Rovers	2-1	0-3	0-3	3-2	6-2	1-1	1-0	0-3	0-0	1-0	*	1-1	1-0	0-1	2-1	3-2
12. Walker	3-2	1-2	2-1	3-2	1-2	1-0	1-3	1-3	2-0	2-4	1-1	*	3-0	2-0	0-1	2-0
13. Wark	2-4	1-3	0-2	1-3	1-1	0-9	1-9	0-4	1-5	2-2	0-3	3-4	*	1-2	2-0	0-6
14. West Allotment Celtic	3-2	2-4	1-2	4-2	3-2	1-1	2-3	1-2	2-1	3-0	1-2	9-1	6-0	*	3-3	4-2
15. Westerhope	0-3	4-1	0-1	1-0	0-0	0-2	1-4	2-1	0-3	2-0	0-1	4-2	3-2	0-1	*	1-7
16. Winlaton Hallgarth	2-2	0-3	2-2	2-2	5-0	2-1	0-3	0-4	1-2	3-1	2-0	3-1	7-2	3-2	0-2	*

DIVISION ONE RESULT CHART 1993-94

HOME TEAM	1	2	3	4	5	6	7	8	9	10	11	12	13	14	15
1. Amble Town	*	6-0	2-1	3-2	2-2	4-1	3-0	3-0	3-2	5-0	3-0	8-0	1-1	1-4	5-1
2. Dudley Welfare	0-3	*	2-0	1-1	4-3	1-1	1-1	0-0	0-2	1-1	3-1	1-0	0-1	1-4	3-2
3. Forest Hall	0-9	1-2	*	6-1	1-2	1-5	0-1	2-4	0-6	0-2	0-1	3-3	0-2	1-2	0-1
4. Gateshead Northern C.	1-2	2-4	2-1	*	3-1	0-3	2-3	2-2	0-3	5-3	2-3	1-2	2-2	1-3	3-1
5. Gosforth Bohemians	1-4	4-6	2-0	1-2	*	0-6	1-1	1-1	2-5	1-1	4-3	4-2	1-0	1-3	4-0
6. Hebburn Reyrolle	2-0	1-0	10-0	4-0	2-1	*	3-1	3-2	0-0	1-0	2-2	2-1	4-2	1-3	8-2
7. Hexham Swinton	0-1	2-3	3-0	1-2	4-1	1-5	*	3-1	1-3	0-1	2-2	1-1	3-0	0-4	2-1
8. Newbiggin CW	1-6	1-2	7-0	2-3	2-1	0-1	3-3	*	1-1	2-1	2-0	3-0	2-1	1-1	2-3
9. Newcastle Benfield Pk	1-1	3-1	1-1	6-1	2-1	0-1	2-0	1-1	*	2-1	2-0	11-0	6-0	0-1	3-0
10. Nth Shields Columbas	1-4	8-2	0-0	2-0	2-1	5-3	2-1	1-1	1-4	*	1-0	4-4	5-3	4-0	3-0
11. Percy Main	0-6	1-0	1-2	4-3	2-3	0-5	1-6	2-10	1-9	1-5	*	4-2	6-0	2-3	5-0
12. Proctor & Gamble	1-3	1-1	1-0	2-1	2-3	2-1	0-1	3-2	0-4	1-0	0-2	*	0-2	3-2	0-2
13. Ryton	1-0	1-3	3-0	1-0	1-0	2-5	0-0	3-1	0-1	4-4	3-4	3-0	*	2-1	2-0
14. Swalwell	3-3	3-3	7-0	3-3	5-1	2-0	1-5	0-0	1-1	1-0	1-2	3-1	2-3	*	1-0
15. Wylam	3-9	1-6	1-0	3-0	1-4	2-4	2-2	2-3	1-3	0-4	1-3	4-2	1-2	0-3	*

DIVISION TWO RESULT CHART 1993-94

HOME TEAM	1	2	3	4	5	6	7	8	9	10	11	12	13	14	15
1. Ashington Hurst Prog.	*	4-1	5-1	2-2	1-1	3-2	2-2	14-0	7-3	3-4	5-2	1-0	3-0	2-1	9-0
2. Gateshead Durham R.	4-6	*	1-4	2-1	1-5	0-0	3-1	1-0	2-4	1-7	0-0	1-4	1-2	4-3	6-4
3. Heddon Institute	3-4	1-0	*	3-1	2-5	4-1	2-0	2-3	0-3	3-1	5-1	1-1	2-1	4-1	4-1
4. Highfields	1-4	4-1	2-0	*	3-0	0-0	5-1	0-4	6-1	2-3	3-0	0-4	4-3	1-2	12-0
5. Marden Athletic	2-4	2-0	2-4	3-1	*	1-0	0-1	4-2	0-3	1-4	3-0	1-4	1-0	0-5	5-1
6. Monkseaton KOSA RH	0-1	3-5	0-1	1-3	1-7	*	2-2	1-3	0-4	1-3	3-0	0-5	1-1	1-1	9-1
7. Newcastle DHSS	0-8	5-4	1-0	2-2	4-1	0-5	*	1-0	4-1	2-2	6-0	0-4	5-3	0-2	6-2
8. Norgas United	1-5	5-4	0-12	1-2	3-2	1-3	1-4	*	0-3	0-3	4-3	5-2	0-2	0-4	8-1
9. Newcastle University	1-6	3-0	2-1	4-3	2-6	3-1	2-2	1-0	*	0-3	1-0	0-2	1-0	1-2	5-0
10. Orwin New Winning	2-2	3-3	1-1	1-3	3-7	4-1	3-0	4-1	2-1	*	4-3	0-4	2-0	5-3	5-1
11. Northern Electric	1-7	2-1	1-2	2-1	1-3	0-2	0-2	2-4	1-3	0-3	*	2-4	3-4	1-3	5-0
12. Shankhouse	1-3	6-1	0-2	2-1	5-0	0-0	1-2	0-0	4-0	3-4	3-0	*	8-0	4-0	14-0
13. Shilbottle Colliery W.	1-3	3-0	0-2	0-1	0-2	4-3	1-3	0-0	1-1	0-3	1-4	0-3	*	1-3	2-0
14. Stobswood Welfare	2-7	1-3	2-0	0-1	1-2	1-2	5-0	1-2	4-1	3-4	5-0	1-1	2-1	*	6-0
15. Wallsend Rising Sun	0-5	0-3	1-7	1-2	0-4	1-2	1-4	2-4	1-2	0-8	0-2	0-4	1-1	0-4	*

LEAGUE CUP 1993-94

First Round (Division One clubs exempt)

Northern Electric v Ashington Hirst Progress. 0-7
Carlisle Gillford Park v Spittal Rovers 3-1
Wark v Norgas United 0-1
Seaton Delaval Amateurs v Heddon Institute 5-4
Stobswood Welfare v Highfields United 2-0
Newcastle DHSS v Blyth Kitty Brewster 1-2
Longbenton v Marden Athletic 7-2
Morpeth Town *(bye)*
Winlaton Hallgarth v West Allotment Celtic 3-2
Carlisle City v Walker 3-1
Seaton Delaval Seaton Terrace v Newcastle Univ. 0-1
Wallsend Rising Sun v Westerhope 0-12
Orwin New Winning v Shilbottle Colliery Welfare 8-1
Heaton Stannington v Gate. Durham Rangers 3-4
Haltwhistle Crown Paints v Shankhouse 3-0
Monkseaton KOSA Robin Hood v Ponteland Utd 1-4

Second Round

Amble Town v Wylam 8-1
Carlisle City v Ryton 9-1
Orwin New Winning v Westerhope 1-2
Percy Rovers v Longbenton 1-5
Winlaton Hallgarth v Stobswood Welfare 7-2
Morpeth Town v 6ewcastle Benfield Park 1-0
Carlisle Gillford Park v Ponteland United 2-3
Hebburn Reyrolle v Dudley Welfare 4-2
Blyth Kitty Brewster v Haltwhistle Crown Paints 1-0
Newcastle University v Newbiggin Central Welfare 5-2
Gate. Durham Rgrs v North Shields St Columbas 4-3
Swalwell v Hexham Swinton 3-1
Procter & Gamble v Ashington Hirst Progressive 2-3
Norgas United v Seaton Delaval Amateurs 0-4
Forest Hall v Gosforth Bohemians 1-3
Gateshead Northern Counties v Percy Main 2-1

Third Round

Amble Town v Ponteland United 0-4
Swalwell v Carlisle City 2-4
Morpeth Town v Winlaton Hallgarth 5-3
Westerhope v Gosforth Bohemians 4-0
Gateshead Northern Co's v Gate. Durham Rgrs 0-1
Seaton Delaval Amateurs v Blyth Kitty Brewster 2-1
Newcastle University v Ashington Hirst Progressive 1-3
Hebburn Reyrolle v Longbenton 2-0

Quarter-Finals

Morpeth Town v Carlisle City 2-1
Westerhope v Gateshead Durham Rangers 2-1
Seaton Delaval Amateurs v Ponteland United 0-4
Hebburn Reyrolle v Ashington Hirst Progressive 4-1

Semi Finals

Morpeth Town v Westerhope 4-2
Hebburn Reyrolle v Ponteland United 1-4

Final *(at Heatington Stannington FC)*: Morpeth Town 1, Ponteland United 1 *(aet)*
Replay *(at Heatington Stannington FC)*: Morpeth Town 4, Ponteland United 0

PREM. DIV. 10-YR RECORD	84/5	85/6	86/7	87/8	88/9	89/0	90/1	91/2	92/3	93/4
Blyth Kitty Brewster	-	-	-	-	-	-	-	11	14	13
Carlisle City	13	9	16	-	-	-	-	-	3	2
Carlisle Gillford Park	-	-	-	-	-	-	11	3	7	6
Dudley Welfare	1	11	12	6	12	15	-	-	-	-
Dunston Tyne Sports	-	1	2	15	4	13	-	-	-	-
Forest Hall	8	12	8	5	10	3	5	12	16	-
Gateshead Tyne					(see Dunston Tyne)					
Gorforth St Nicholas	14	14	4	3	-	-	-	-	-	-
Haltwhistle Crown Paints	15	-	-	-	-	12	13	9	9	14
Heaton Stannington	-	-	13	7	6	8	3	14	12	15
Longbenton	-	-	-	-	-	-	-	-	-	11
Morpeth Town	2	3	3	9	9	10	12	13	4	1
Newbiggin Colliery Welfare	-	-	-	12	5	4	8	16	-	-
Percy Main Amateurs	12	13	11	11	13	6	15	-	-	-
Ponteland United	4	10	5	13	8	5	9	10	8	3
Prudhoe East End	3	2	7	2	-	-	-	-	-	-
Seaton Delaval Amateurs	5	8	15	8	3	1	4	4	1	4
Seaton Terrace	7	7	10	1	1	9	2	6	5	10
Spittal Rovers	-	-	-	-	-	-	-	5	11	8
Stobsood Welfare	10	16	-	-	15	-	-	-	-	-
Swalwell	-	-	14	14	7	11	6	15	-	-
Walker	-	-	-	-	-	-	7	2	6	7
Wallsend Town	9	15	-	-	-	-	-	-	-	-
Wark	-	-	-	-	11	14	14	8	13	16
West Allotment Celtic	6	5	1	4	2	2	1	1	2	5
Westerhope Hillheads	-	-	-	-	-	-	10	7	15	13
Wigton	11	6	9	10	14	7	-	-	-	-
Winlaton Hallgarth	-	-	-	-	-	-	-	-	10	9
Winlaton Queens Head	-	4	6	-	-	-	-	-	-	-
No. of clubs competing	15	16	16	15	15	15	15	16	16	16

PREMIER DIVISION CLUBS 1994-95

BLYTH SEAHORSE

Chairman: G Allen **Manager/Coach:** P Johnson
Secretary/Press Officer: J Norris, 28 Dene View Drive, Cowpen Estate, Blyth (0670 352940).
Ground: Tynedale High School, Blyth.
Directions: Coming north on Spine Rd take slip road signed Kitty Brewster Ind. Est., take right exit & follow signs, 1st left after mini-r'bout, school half mile on right.
Colours: Blue & maroon/maroon **Change colours:** All blue.
Prev. Name: Blyth Kitty Brewster (pre-'94) **Hons:** Northern All. Div 1 90-91 (Div 2 88-89, Lg Cup R-up 90-91).

CARLISLE CITY

Chairman: G Walker **Manager/Coach:** D Iveson/ W Armstrong.
Secretary/Press Officer: J Ewbanks, 16 Lansdown Cres., Stanwix, Carlisle (0228 34623).
Ground: The Sheep Mount.
Directions: B6264 Brampton-Carlisle road (not A69) direst to Hardwick Circus, keep in righthand lane at r'bout and take far exit (Workington), dual c'way down hill (Carlisle Castle on right), where road intersects double back on yourself and take turning before castle, left and follow down hill, bear left as road divides, over to sports field.
Colours: All sky **Change colours:** White/red **Hons:** Northern All. R-up(5) 75-78 79-80 93-94 (Div 1 91-92, Chal. Cup 75-76 93-94 (R-up 76-77), Comb. Cup 91-92).

CARLISLE GILLFORD PARK

Chairman: R Wilson **Manager/Coach:** R Rutherford.
Secretary: J Carr, 7 Blackwell Rd, Currock, Carlisle CA2 4AB (0228 26449).
Ground: Gillford Park, Carlisle (0228 26649).
Directions: A69 to Rose Hill r'bout, straight over & 2nd left into Eastern Way, 1 mile to lights, left, 1st right Petrill Bank Rd, right at bridge, ground 200yds up this road.
Colours: All red **Change colours:** White (black pin-stripe)/black.

HALTWHISTLE CROWN PAINTS

Chairman: J Jackson) **Manager/Coach:** TBA
Secretary: R Skeet, 14 Westgate, Haltwhistle (0434 320703/ 321271).
Press Off.: M Tyers (0434 320234) **Ground:** South Tyne Park, Haltwhistle.
Directions: A69 to Haltwhistle, off Main Rd at sign for Hadrian Works, under rail bridge. Parking at Crown Paints car park.
Colours: All royal blue **Change colours:** Black & white.

HEATON STANNINGTON

Chairman: W Pitt **Manager/Press Off./Coach:** J Anderson (091 410 9757).
Secretary: J R Groundsell, 73 Cleveland Gdns, High Heaton, Newcastle (091 266 7464).
Ground: Newton Park, Newton Rd, High Heaton, Newcastle.
Directions: From Newcastle; left at 'Corner House' pub lights into Newton Rd, left at r'bout for 30yds, ground on right behind shops. From South Gosforth; into Freeman Rd, pass Freeman Hosp., left at next r'bout, ground 250yds on left.
Cols: White/black/white **Change colours:** Red/white **Hons:** Northern All. Chal. Cup R-up 88-89.

LONGBENTON

Chairman: J Fawcett **Manager/Coach:** P Rudd.
Press Officer/Secretary: G Minto, 43 Elizabeth Cres., Dudley, Cramlingham NE23 7AJ (091 250 1581).
Ground: Burradon Recreation Centre. **Directions:** From south: from r'bout at Sth Gosforth to r'bout at Killingworth on A189, left to Cramlingham, right at next r'bout, left at mini-r'bout into Burradon. From north: A189 to Annitsford, left to Burradon, ground behing houses.
Colours: White/black **Change colours:** Red/white.
Hons: Northern All. Div 1 92-93 (Div 2 R-up 89-90, Combination Cup 92-93).

NEWCASTLE BENFIELD PARK

Chairman: J Rowe **Manager:** T Sword
Secretary: K Morpeth, 126 Weldon Cres., High Heaton, Newcastle-upon-Tyne NE7 7JD (091 281 8465).
Coach: D McDonald **Press Officer:** R Graham (091 274 5305).
Ground: Benfield Park.
Directions: From Newcastle take 2nd exit after Corner House pub, right into Benfield Rd, ground on left in school grounds.
Colours: Black & white stripes/black **Change colours:** All blue.
Honours: Northern Alliance Div 1 R-up 93-94.

PONTELAND UNITED

Chairman: F W Smith **Manager:** P Lowery **Coach:** W Charlton
Press Officer/Secretary: L McMahon, 1 Wardle Drive, Annitsford, Cramlingham (091 250 0463).
Ground: Ponteland Leisure Centre, Ponteland (0661 25441).
Directions: Left at lights entering Ponteland from Newcastle, ground 100m on left at Castle Ward Spts Centre.
Seats: None **Cover:** None **Capacity:** 3,500 **Floodlights:** No **Founded:** 1900.
Colours: Black & white stripes/black **Change colours:** Blue & red stripes.
Record Gate: 3,500 v Blyth Spartans, 1982-83.
Hons: Northern Alliance Lg Cup R-up 91-92 92-93 93-94 (Chal. Cup R-up 84-85 90-91 93-94).

SEATON TERRACE AMATEURS

Chairman: T Ashburn **Manager:** K Scott
Secretary: V Donnelly, 6 Hollymount Square, Bedlington (0670 829464).
Coach: B Phillips **Press Officer:** K Scott (0670 714105)
Ground: Wheatridge Park, Seaton Delaval.
Directions: A189 from Newcastle, at Annitsford r'bout A190 to Seaton Delaval, left at r'bout entering village, ground 450yds on right next to Deal Garage and behind Market Garden. 3 miles from Cramlington BR station. Bus 363 from Newcastle passes ground.
Seats: None **Cover:** 200 **Capacity:** 6,000 **Floodlights:** No **Founded:**
Colours: White/red **Change colours:** All blue
Previous Names: Seaton Delaval Amateurs/ Seaton Delaval Seaton Terrace - clubs merged 1994.
Previous Ground: Seaton Terrace: Bates Welfare (pre-1994).
Record Gate (Seaton Delaval Amateurs): 6,000 in 1926.
Hons: Seaton Delaval Amateurs: Northern All. 89-90 92-93 (R-up 20-21, Chall. Cup 88-89 92-93). *Seaton Terrace: Northern All. 87-88 88-89 (Lg Cup 90-91, Chal. Cup 86-87 91-92).*

SPITTAL ROVERS

Chairman: G Johnson **Manager/Coach:** W Young.
Secretary: D Burglass, 7-13 Wheatfield Place, Edingburgh EH11 3PE (031 3135235).
Press Officer: G Burn (0289 305835) **Ground:** Shieldfield Park, Berwick-on-Tweed.
Directions: A1 to r'bout signposting Berwick, follow to r'bout at Sports Centre, straight over, left immediately after after railway bridge up Shieldfield Terrace, ground 200yds on right.
Colours: Black & white stripes/black/red **Change colours:** Red/black.
Honours: Northumberland Bowl 93-94.

WALKER

Chairman: R T McClellan **Manager/Coach:** T Welsh.
Sec./Press Officer: Mr B Mulroy, 31 Dalton Cres., Byker Walk, Newcastle-upon-Tyne NE6 2DA (091 263 4237).
Ground: Monkchester Recreation Ground. **Directions:** From City: Shields Rd to Union Rd, to Welbeck Rd, into Monkchester Rd, left into pitch (between houses) opposite Norbury Grove.
Club colours: White/black/black. **Change colours:** Green/green/black.
Hons: Northern Alliance Div 1 R-up 89-90.

WARK

Chairman: D Chrisholm **Manager:** K Glendinning **Coach:** J Wright
Secretary/Press Officer: J Armstrong, 12 St Michaels Mount, Wark, Hexham (0434 230382).
Ground: Wark Spts Field, Wark, Hexham (0434 230359).
Directions: Enter Wark, right at filling station over river bridge, turn right and ground is on right.
Club colours: Blue/white **Change colours:** Yellow/white.

WEST ALLOTMENT CELTIC

Chairman: J Mather **Manager/Coach:** D Taylor.
Secretary: J T Jackson, 4 Rosewood Crescent, Seaton Sluice, Whitley Bay (091 237 0416).
Press Officer: A Smailes (091 253 2172). **Ground:** Backworth Miners Welfare (091 268 1048).
Directions: From Newcastle, Old Coast Rd (A189) to Sth Gosforth, A191 to Holystone r'bout, A186 to mini r'bout at Shiremoor, left (B1322), ground 1 mile on left, entrance opp. Backworth Soc. Club. 2 miles Shiremoor Metro.
Seats: None **Cover:** None **Capacity:** 800 **Floodlights:** No **Founded:** 1928.
Colours: Black & white stripes/black **Change colours:** All blue.
Previous Ground: Farm Ground 1928-68. **Hons:** Northern Alliance 86-87 90-91 91-92 (R-up 88-89 89-90 92-93, Lg Cup 92-93, Challenge Cup 84-85 90-91), Northumberland Senior Bowl 92-93.

WESTERHOPE

Chairman: J Loan **Manager/Coach:** S Armstrong.
Secretary: J Loan, 17 Greystead Close, Chapel Park, Newcastle-upon-Tyne NE5 1SR (091 267 9132).
Press Officer: B Patterson (091 264 5211).
Ground: Cowgate Tavern Sports Ground, Ponteland Rd, Newcastle-upon-Tyne.
Directions: Kenton turn off A1, over Kenton r'bout & next 2 r'bouts, ground on right behind Co-op dairy.
Colours: White/white/blue **Change colours:** Sky & navy.
Hons: Northern All. Div 1 89-90. **Previous Ground:** Riverside Park, Newburn (pre-1993).

WINLATON

Chairman: TBA **Manager/Coach:** K Rides.
Secretary/Press Officer: G S Batey, 6 Wylam View, Winlaton (091 414 7970).
Ground: Shiblon Park, Blaydon. **Directions:** From north, over new A1 bridge to 1st slip road, take Swalwell and Consett road to r'bour, Blaydon Baths car park and ground 400yds on right.
Colours: White/navy/navy **Change colours:** All red.
Previous Name: Winlaton Hallgarth (pre-1994).
Hons: Northern All. Lg Cup 91-92 (Div 1 R-up 91-92, Comb. Cup R-up 91-92).

DIVISION ONE CLUBS 1994-95

AMBLE TOWN

Chairman: E Reynolds **Press Officer:** R Prouse (091 284 3711).
Secretary: R Falkous, 30 George Street, Amble, Morpeth, Northumberland NE65 0DW (0665 711041).
Manager/Coach: R Gibbard. **Ground:** Amble Welfare Park, Acklington Rd, Amble
Directions: From Ashington or Morpeth; north on A1068 entering Amble past industrial est. on right, over zebra crossing 100yds turn left before Masons Arms, follow as if you are going out of Amble. New Hassal Housing estate on right, turn left opp. Coquet High School car park. Pitch adjacent.
Colours: All tangerine **Change colours:** All blue.
Hons: Northern Alliance(5) 54-55 56-57 58-61 (Div 1 93-94, Div 2 92-93, Challenge Cup 54-55 60-61 (R-up 37-38 59-60), Combination Cup 93-94).

ASHINGTON HIRST PROGRESSIVE

Chairman: J S Evans **Press Officer:** A Johnson (0670 816464).
Secretary: G Gibbons, 41 Hawthorn Road, Ashington (0670 815218).
Manager/Coach: G Gibbons.
Ground: Ashington High School, Green Lane, Ashington.
Directions: From Spine Rd, Ashington turn off at Woodhorn, A197 at next 2 r'bouts, left at next r'bout, at end turn right, then left down Park Rd, school 500yds on right.
Colours: Yellow/green **Change colours:** Red/white
Hons: Northern Alliance Div 2 93-94 (Amateur Cup 91-92).

DUDLEY WELFARE

Chairman: R Ord **Manager/Coach:** J Scragg.
Secretary: A Ord, 33 Front Street, Annitsford, Cramlingham, Northumberland NE23 7RQ (091 250 0262).
Press Officer: Secretary **Ground:** Duldley Welfare.
Directions: From Tyne Tunnel follow A1 to Moor Farm r'bout, A1 Morpeth road then 1st slip road, left at junction, ground on left opp. Owen Pugh. From Newcastle follow main Morpeth road as far as Seaton Burn flyover, take A1 in southerly direction (signed Tyne Tunnel), 1st slip road to r'bout then follow signs to Dudley and as above.
Colours: Green/white/green **Change colours:** Blue/white.
Hons: Northern Alliance 84-85 (R-up 83-84, Chal. Cup 83-84 (R-up 82-83)).

FOREST HALL

Chairman: B Lofthouse **Manager/Coach:** TBA
Secretary: G Willis, 4 Lythe Way, Benton, Newcastle-upon-Tyne NE12 8LP (091 215 1226).
Press Officer: Secretary **Ground:** Procter & Gamble Spts, Great Lime Rd, Forest Hall.
Directions: From West Moor, east along Great Lime Rd towards Whitley Bay, ground on north side 150yds past Musketeer pub. A1 (Morpeth road) from Tyne Tunnel, left towards next at r'bout with A191 Whitley Bay road, right onto Great Lime Rd, ground on north side just under a mile.
Colours: All red **Change colours:** Black & white stripes
Hons: Northern All. Chal. Cup R-up 89-90.

GATESHEAD NORTHERN COUNTIES

Manager/Coach: J Hetherington **Press Officer:** Secretary
Secretary/Chairman: A Skelton, 101 Tebay Drive, Denton Burn, Newcastle-upon-Tyne NE5 2XH (091 275 0228).
Ground: Wardley Welfare, Felling.
Directions: From Gateshead International Stadium to Heworth r'bout, across, left at slip road at Wardley Black Bull after 1km. A194, left at top of slip road, second right after 250m, ground 800m on right.
Colours: White/blue **Change colours:** All blue.

GOSFORTH BOHEMIAN

Chairman/Press Officer: J Bell (091 268 3306) **Manager/Coach:** P Rowntree.
Secretary: B Dale, 118 Newton Road, Newcastle (091 281 1403)
Ground: Benson Park, Brunton Park Estate, Gosforth
Directions: Turn off Great North Road after passing Gosforth Rugby Club into Polwarth Drive. 2nd left into Layfield Road then 1st right into South Ridge Ground 50 yards on left (concealed entrance between houses)
Colours: Red & white/black **Change colours:** All blue **Founded:** 1893.
Hons: Northern Alliance Div 2 R-up 92-93.

HEBBURN REYROLLE

Chairman: F Hopkins **Manager/Coach:** V Pearson.
Secretary: G Taylor, 29 Crawley Ave., Hebburn NE31 2LT (091 483 4537).
Press Officer: A Graham. **Ground:** Hebburn Sports Ground, Victoria Road West, Hebburn. Alternative ground: South Tyneside College, Mill Lane, Hebburn.
Directions: From Newcastle along Felling by-pass, Heworth r'bout take Hebburn/Jarrow road, ground two and a half miles on left. College ground as above, but from Newcastle ground approx. 2 miles on right. From Tunnel ground approx. two and a half miles on left.
Colours: Red/black **Change colours:** Royal blue/blue.
Hons: Northern All. Seymour Cup R-up 92-93.
Previous Name: Hebburn N.E.I. Reyrolle (pre-1993).

HEXHAM SWINTON

Chairman: D Tiffin **Press Officer:** P Rutherford (0434 606161 ex4288)
Secretary: D Tiffin, 8 Valebrook, Hexham, Northumberland NE46 2BQ (0434 604573).
Manager/Coach: D Soulsby **Ground:** Wentworth Park, Hexham.
Directions: A69 to Hexham r'bout, left towards Hexham, follow to mini-r'bout, straight over and 1st left into car park. Ground opposite Hexham BR station (Carlisle-Newcastle line).
Colours: All red **Change colours:** White/black or red.

NEWBIGGIN CENTRAL WELFARE

Chairman: H Callan **Manager/Coach:** W Robson.
Press Officer/Secretary: W Cooper, 33 Spital Crescent, Newbiggin (0670 854941).
Ground: Newbiggin Central Welfare, Newbiggin. **Directions:** Enter Newbiggin from Spine Road towards town centre. After 2nd zebra crossing ground on right after 200 yds just before school entrance.
Colours: White & blue/blue **Change colours:** Red/black/black
Hons: Northern Alliance Chal. Cup R-up 46-47 88-89 (Div 1 R-up 92-93).

NEWCASTLE PROCTER & GAMBLE

Chairman: B Hazeldine **Manager/Coach:** B Hudson.
Press Officer/Secretary: T Hutchinson, 13 Maud Terrace, West Allotment, Whitley Bay, Tyne & Wear (091 270 1795).
Ground: Longbenton Community High School.
Directions: From Newcastle, Benton Rd to Four Lane Ends metro station, continue to 2nd r'bout, right into Goathland Ave., ground and school at end.
Colours: Red & blue/blue **Change colours:** All red.
Hons: Northern Alliance Div 2 90-91.

NORTH SHIELDS St COLUMBAS

Chairman: N Hooper **Manager/Coach:** J Wall.
Secretary: A J Baird, 23 Balkwell Ave., North Shields, Tyne & Wear NE29 7JN (091 258 0833).
Press Off.: D Wall (091 253 0992) **Ground:** Appletree Pk, Preston Ave., North Shields.
Directions: Coast road to Tynemouth swimming baths, right to North Shields, 2nd left after school into Preston Ave., ground on left after Rugby Club.
Colours: All white **Change colours:** Green & yellow stripes/green.
Hons: Northern Alliance Seymour Cup (Combination Cup R-up 92-93).

ORWIN ROSEHILL

Chairman: A Gilroy **Manager/Coach:** N Bains.
Secretary: S J Pattinson, 37 North Terrace, Wallsend, Tyne & Wear NE28 6PZ (091 263 9172).
Press Off.: B Burn (091 263 1248) **Ground:** Lightfoot Stadium, Walker, Newcastle-upon-Tyne.
Directions: Travelling from Newcastle towards Whitley Bay on coast road, take C127 slip road in Benfield Rd to Wharrier Street. Ground on left - look for the big 'Dome'.
Colours: Blue & black stripes/black **Change colours:** Yellow & green/green.
Previous Names: New Winning (Wallsend)(pre-1993)/ Orwin New Winning (Wallsend) 93-94.
Previous Ground: Wallsend Sports Centre (pre'94)
Previous Lge: South East Northumberland (pre-1992)
Honours: Northern Alliance Div 2 R-up 93-94, Northumberland Minor Cup 93-94.

PERCY MAIN AMATEURS

Chairman: E Beasley **Mgr/Coach/Press Off.:** P Rogerson (091 258 3924)
Secretary: G Marsh, 32 Selkirk Way, Chirton Park, North Shields, Tyne & Wear (091 258 0202).
Ground: St John's Green, Percy Main.
Directions: Nth Shield road from Tyne Tunnel past Duke of Wellington, 2nd left after half mile, ground on right. From North and West turn off coast road at Formica factory, right down Norham Rd to Percy Main Social Club, road to Percy Main Village at r'bout, after half mile left at St John's Terrace. Ground on left past church.
Colours: Claret & blue/blue **Change colours:** Red & white/black.
Hons: Northern Alliance 80-81 81-82 (R-up 82-83, Lg Cup 71-72, Chal. Cup R-up 79-80 86-87).

RYTON

Chairman: H Taylor **Manager:** A Patterson. **Coach:** C Dixon
Secretary: L Robson, 31 Park View Gdns, Runhead, Ryton (091 413 7628).
Press Officer: C Dixon (091 413 5447)
Ground: Clara Vale Recreation Ground.
Directions: Thru Ryton to Crawcock crossroads, right 50yds down road, right at T-junction, entering Clara Vale ground is signposted.
Colours: Blue & black stripes/black **Change colours:** Orange/black.

SWALWELL

Chairman: T Todd **Manager/Coach:** M Falcus.
Secretary: S Sibbald, 33 Affleck Street, Gateshead NE8 1QR (091 477 0064).
Press Officer: T E Todd (091 460 5171).
Ground: Avenue Ground, Hexham Road, Swalwell.
Directions: From Newcastle cross river by Redbeugh Bridge, take A69 (Western bypass) for 3 miles, 1st left after Metro Centre. Right at r'bout, after half mile ground on right just past Fewsters and opposite Blaydon Rugby Club.
Colours: Red & white/black **Change colours:** All blue
Hons: Northern Alliance Lg Seymour Cup 92-93.

WYLAM

Chairman: TBA **Manager/Coach:** R Whinham.
Secretary: J Wilson, 5 David Terrace, Crawcock, Tyne & Wear NE40 4DF (091 413 4795).
Press Officer: G Bowmer (0661 852035). **Ground:** Wylam Playing Fields.
Directions: From Newcastle, A69 Hexham road to Wylam turn, into village, left opp. bus shelter by Black Bull heading towards Fox & Hounds. Pitch opposite.
Colours: Red & blue stripes **Change colours:** Yellow/black/white.
Hons: Div 2 R-up 90-91.

SECOND DIVISION CLUBS 1994-1995

ALNWICK AYDON FOREST

Chairman: J Athey **Press Officer:** M Belisle (0665 604443).
Secretary: D Lowes, 14 Cornhill Estate, Alnwick, Northumberland NE66 1RX (0665 510874).
Manager/Coach: D Lowes. **Ground:** As Alnwick Town FC (see page 698).
Colours: Maroon & sky/sky **Change colours:** Black & white stripes/black.
Previous League: North Northumberland (pre-1994).

HEDDON INSTITUTE

Chairman: A Smith **Manager/Coach:** B Tailford.
Secretary: N A D Anderson, 14 Aquila Drive, Heddon on the Wall (0661 853136)
Press Officer: N A D Anderson (0661 853136).
Ground: Throckley Welfare, Throckley
Directions: A69 Newcastle take Throckley exit, turn left at roundabout approx. quarter mile, right into Poplar Street, ground at end. Bus No. X82 and X83 from Eldon Centre, Newcastle to Throckley.
Colours: Maroon & blue **Change colours:** All blue.

HEXHAM BORDER COUNTIES

Chairman: F McKie. **Manager/Coach/Press Officer:** Arnie White (0434 608300).
Secretary: A Leetham, 27 Peth Head, Hexham, Northumberland NE46 1 HQ (0434 605784).
Ground: Wentworth Park, Hexham, Northumberland.
Directions: Travelling on the A69 Hexham bypass, take the Hexham slip road and go over the Tyne Bridge. Go straight over mini-r'bout and take 1st left into Wentworth car-park - ground adjacent to Wentworth Leisure Centre.
Colours: Red & black stripes/white **Change colours:** Blue/white. **Founded:** 1989.
Previous Name: Hexham Town 89-93 **Previous League:** Hexham & North Tyne 89-94.
Hons: Hexham & Nth Tyne Lg 92-93 93-94 (Lg Cup 93-94 (R-up 92-94), Clayton Charity Cup 92-93 (R-up 93-94).

HIGHFIELDS UNITED BERWICK

Chairman: B Weatherburn **Manager/Coach/Press Officer:** S Roughead (0289 308162).
Secretary: B Dytor, 43 Newfields, Berwick-on-Tweed (0289 305342).
Ground: Pier Field, Berwick-on-Tweed.
Directions: A1 to Berwick centre, right down High Str., keep right of Town Hall, right into Hide Hill, left at bottom into Silver Str., straight over staggered crossroads, follow road along river bank to clifftops carpark.
Colours: Yellow & blue/blue **Change colours:** Blue & white/blue.
Previous Name: Highfield United (pre-1994).

MARDEN ATHLETIC

Chairman: TBA **Manager/Coach:** M Hunt.
Secretary/Press Officer: F Hunt, 50 Kingston Drive, Whitley Bay, Tyne & Wear NE26 1JJ (091 252 7300)
Ground: Monkseaton High School, Monkseaton, Whitley Bay, Tyne & Wear.
Directions: From Coast Road from Newcastle to Tynemouth, look for Tynemouth Swimming Baths and turn left at r'bout, proceed to r'bout at Foxhunters pub and right, left at next r'bout, school ground 150 yards on left.
Colours: White & blue stripes/blue **Change colours:** Black & white hoops/black.
Previous Grounds: Churchill Playing Fields, Whitley Bay (pre-1993)/ Valley Garden School, Monkseaton 93-94.

MONKSEATON K.O.S.A. ROBIN HOOD

Chairman: P LePatourel **Manager/Coach:** K Birrell
Secretary: R A Woods, 15 Rayleigh Drive, Wideopen, Newcastle-upon-Tyne (091 236 2988).
Press Officer: D Gill (091 274 8595).
Directions: From Newcastle Coast Road to Tynemouth Swimmming Baths, left at r'bout and proceed to r'bout at Foxhunters Pub, turn right at this roundabout and left at next r'bout. School ground is 150 yards on left
Colours: Yellow/green/yellow **Change colours:** Green/black.

NEWCASTLE D.H.S.S.

Chairman: R G Blenkinsopp **Press Officer:** M Carr (091 225 6733).
Secretary: L Procter, 4 Alcombe Crescent, Red House Farm Estate, Newcastle-upon-Tyne (091 285 3320).
Manager/Coach: J Atkinson **Ground:** Darsley Park, Longbenton.
Directions: Bus or Metro to Four Lane Ends, Benton. Grounds half mile along Old Whitley Rd towards coast.
Colours: All red **Change colours:** Sky/navy. **Previous Lge:** Tyneside Amateur (pre-1992).

NEWCASTLE NORGAS UNITED

Chairman: M Grant **Press Officer:** P Benson (091 268 5100).
Secretary: M Hopper, 18 Thirlmere Close, Killingworth, Newcastle-upon-Tyne (091 268 2658)
Manager/Coach: M Grant **Ground:** Whitley Park, Whitley Road, Benton.
Directions: Bus or Metro to Four Lane Ends, Benton, park half mile along Old Whitley Rd on right (towards coast).
Colours: White/black/black **Change colours:** Green/white/white.

NEWCASTLE UNIVERSITY

Secretary/Press Officer: L Melville, 131 Wingrove Gardens, Fenham, Newcastle-upon-Tyne (091 273 5814).
Chairman/Manager/Coach: T Cross. **Ground:** Cochrane Park, Newcastle-upon-Tyne.
Directions: From Newcastle, left off coast road at 1st slip road after Corner House pub, right at next r'bout into Etherstone Ave., ground 400yds on left.
Colours: Blue/black/blue **Change colours:** Red/black/red.

OTTERBURN

Chairman: R Stephen **Manager/Coach:** M Corbett.
Secretary: J Cowans, Greenchesters Farm, Otterburn, Northumberland (0830 520471).
Press Officer: B Stoker (0830 520418). **Ground:** Sports Centre Ground, Otterburn, Northumberland.
Directions: Travelling north on the A696 from Ponteland, turn right in the village of Otterburn and proceed towards the RTC Sports Centre.
Colours: Yellow/blue **Change colours:** Red/black.
Previous Leagues: Hexham & North Tyne/ North East Amateur 92-94.
Honours: Hexham & North Tyne League 90-91 91-92.

RUTHERFORD NEWCASTLE

Chairman: A Gardiner **Manager/Coach:** J Tate.
Secretary: S Coxon, 6 Hollydene, Kibblesworth, Gateshead NE11 0NR (091 410 9604).
Press Officer: S Armstrong (091 482 4080)
Ground: Farnacres, Lobley Hill, Gateshead, Tyne & Wear.
Directions: Travelling either north or south on A1, take slip road onto the A692 Consett Rd at Lobley Hill r'bout. Take 1st left up the bank after r'bout, turning into Beechwood Gdns, then take 4th left into Pinewood Gdns. Travel the full length of this road and then turn right on to the Old Church Rd - ground 100yds on right.
Colours: Red & black stripes/black **Change colours:** Blue/white
Previous League: North East Amateur (pre-1994)

SHANKHOUSE

Chairman: F Dobson **Manager/Coach:** K Schooling
Press Officer/Secretary: S Ramsey, 6 Brinkburn Avenue, Cramlington (0670 715943).
Ground: Bates Welfare, Seaton Delaval (formerly Seaton Terrace FC ground).
Directions: Entering Seaton Delaval on A190 from Annitsford and Newcastle, turn right at r'bout into village. Ground approx half mile on right adjacent to road.
Colours: Yellow/blue **Change colours:** Red & blue/blue
Previous Ground: East Hartford Welfare (pre-1994).
Hons: Northern Alliance 1892-93 (R-up 95-96, Amateur Cup 93-94), Northumberland Snr Cup 1885-86(joint) 86-87 90-91 92-93 93-94 94-95 (Minor Cup 1992-93).

SHILBOTTLE COLLIERY WELFARE

Chairman: G Brown **Manager/Coach:** I Ford.
Press Off./Secretary: P Andrucci, 7 Kiln Lonnen, Shilbottle, Alnwick NE66 2UR (0665 575488).
Ground: Shilbottle Welfare Ground.
Directions: A1 north, right turn 3 miles south of Alnwick and follow signs to Shilbottle.
Colours: Green/white/green **Change colours:** White/black/black
Previous Leagues: Northern Alliance 46-54/ North Northumberland 54-93.
Hons: North Northumberland Lg 91-92 (R-up 92-93, Anderson Cup 92-93).

STOBSWOOD WELFARE

Chairman/Press Officer: J W Rutherford (0670 790110).
Secretary: I Service, 41 Elizabeth Street, Widdrington, Morpeth NE61 5NW (0670 790110 - messages).
Manager/Coach: N Gibbard **Ground:** Stobswood Welfare (0670 790609).
Directions: A1 to Morpeth, turn right over bridge and follow road to Widdrington, left at Karva Woodcraft, right after 300 yds, ground at bottom.
Colours: Yellow/black **Change colours:** Red/blue
Hons: Northern All. Div 2 R-up 88-89 (Chal. Cup 82-83 (R-up 83-84)).

THROCKLEY & DISTRICT SOCIAL CLUB

Chairman: A Martin **Manager/Coach:** M Murray.
Secretary: A Finlay, West Denton Park, Newcastle-upon-Tyne NE15 8UU (091 267 6493).
Press Officer: S Oliver (091 267 4100).
Ground: Newburn Leisure Centre, Grange Road, Newburn.
Directions: From A1 travel west along A69 to Throckley. Leave at the Throckley slip road and travel south through Throckley and into Newburn. The Leisure Centre is on the North Bank of the Tyne just upstream from Newburn Bridge.
Colours: White & navy/navy **Change colours:** Emerald green/green.
Previous League: Newcastle District Welfare (pre-1994).

WALKER LEDWOOD FOSSE

Chairman: W Callanan **Manager/Coach:** T Lunn.
Secretary: K Slade, 59 Moorland Cres., Walkergate, Newcastle-upon-Tyne NE6 4AT (091 276 1519)
Press Officer: H Dale (091 266 5122)
Ground: Miller's Dene, Walkergate, Newcastle-upon-Tyne.
Directions: Miller's Dene Fosseway from Newcastle, travel through Byker to the r'bout at the top of Shields Rd, turn right & continue to next r'bout, left at B & Q store & continue down Fosseway. The ground is the second one down the Fosseway past Fire Station on left.
Colours: All white **Change colours:** Red & blue stripes.
Previous League: Tyneside Amateur (pre-1994).
Honours: Tyneside Amateur Lg 92-93 (R-up 93-94, Bill Dixon Memorial Cup 92-93 93-94, Jack Bowman Trophy 93-94).

WHEELCROFT

Chairman: J Markwell **Manager:** N Young **Coach:** M Turner.
Secretary: N Young, 35 Seaton Close, Wardley, Gateshead NE10 8SF (091 438 4024)
Press Officer: M Thornton (091 438 2704)
Ground: As Gateshead Northern Counties (page 719).
Colours: Black & silver/black **Change colours:** All blue
Previous Name: Gateshead Durham Rangers (pre-1994).
Previous League: South East Northumberland (pre-1993).

Leicester City Bought...1
Aldershot Town Bought...1

Big club or small... this is probably the best £30 your club can spend on Chris Meredith's

"Guide to Successfully Marketing a Football Club"

As featured on BBC Local Radio Stations...
An excellent publication that helps clubs increase commercial income by marketing direct to businesses.
●Attracting new sponsors & advertisers ●Running a successful lottery operation ●New income generating ideas ● Plus much, much more!

Copies can be obtained by sending a cheque for £30.00 made payable to C.O. Meredith 19, Worlds End Hill, Bracknell, Berks RG12 3XH

TIMBER & BUILDING MATERIALS

JEWSON EASTERN COUNTIES LEAGUE

FEEDER TO:
BEAZER HOMES LEAGUE

FOUNDED: 1935

President: Derek I Needham

Treasurer: Bruce A Badcock

Secretary: Colin Lamb,
3 Land Close, Clacton-on-Sea, Essex CO16 8UJ (0255 436398)

WROXHAM COMPLETE HAT-TRICK

After a gripping championship race, Wroxham just edged out Halstead Town and Newmarket Town to retain the Jewson Eastern Counties League championship. It was, incredibly, the club's third consecutive title - their third in only five seasons in the Premier Division - and was all the more commendable because the Yachtsmen had been handicapped by a late start to the season owing to a Norfolk FA suspension.

Division One saw oustanding success for two well-supported Suffolk clubs, Hadleigh United and Woodbridge Town, who occupied the two promotion positions with a healthy gap over third-placed Warboys Town. The championship went to Hadleigh, but Woodbridge Town enjoyed the distinction of winning the League Cup beating Premier Division Chatteris Town in the final.

It was an exceptional year for the Jewson Eastern Counties League in outside competitions. County Cup successes were enjoyed by Chatteris Town, Halstead Town, Somersham Town, Newmarket Town, Woodbridge Town and Fakenham Town, but the ultimate honour went to Diss Town - fourth-placed in the Premier Division - who took 8,000 fans to Wembley and brought home the FA Challenge Vase.

Wroxham - Jewson Eastern Counties League champions 1993-94.

JEWSON EASTERN COUNTIES LEAGUE TABLES 1993-94

PREM. DIVISION	P	W	D	L	F	A	PTS
Wroxham	42	28	7	7	92	41	91
Halstead Town	42	26	6	8	112	49	90
Newmarket Town	42	26	8	8	82	48	86
Diss Town	42	24	10	8	95	48	82
Stowmarket Town	42	21	6	15	70	59	69
Wisbech Town	42	19	11	12	61	44	68
Sudbury Wanderers	42	19	10	13	75	59	67
Felixstowe Town	42	18	12	12	65	47	66
Lowestoft T.	42	19	7	16	62	62	64
Haverhill Rovers	42	18	9	15	71	61	63
Harwich & Park.	42	16	13	13	72	63	61
Chatteris Town	42	16	9	17	52	65	57
Cornard United	42	15	10	17	68	72	55
Tiptree United	42	14	9	19	64	72	51
Watton United	42	13	8	21	47	75	47
Gt Yarmouth T.	42	12	9	21	50	60	45
Fakenham Town	42	10	13	19	51	81	43
Soham Town Rgrs	42	10	10	22	69	103	40
March Town Utd	42	9	11	22	39	70	38
Histon	42	8	12	22	48	87	36
Gorleston	42	8	9	25	43	77	33
Norwich United	42	8	7	27	49	94	31

FIRST DIVISION	P	W	D	L	F	A	Pts
Hadleigh Utd	34	27	4	3	96	30	85
Woodbridge Town	34	25	5	4	100	31	80
Warboys Town	34	22	5	7	56	31	71
Sudbury T. Res.	34	22	3	9	102	49	69
Mildenhall Town	34	16	4	14	69	59	52
Downham Town	34	15	7	12	52	43	52
Somersham Town	34	14	8	12	65	57	50
Brightlingsea Utd	34	15	5	14	54	53	50
Stanway Rovers	34	14	6	14	59	57	48
Ipswich Wanderers	34	14	5	15	66	57	47
Ely City	34	11	12	11	49	51	45
Cambridge C. Res.	34	12	4	18	61	68	40
Clacton Town	34	10	9	15	46	63	39
Bury Town Res.	34	10	7	17	58	91	37
Brantham Athletic	34	9	6	19	59	90	33
Long Sutton Ath.	34	6	10	18	46	76	28
Swaffham Town	34	6	5	23	33	91	23
Thetford Town	34	3	5	26	28	102	14

E.C.L. PREMIER DIVISION RESULT CHART 1993-94

HOME TEAM	1	2	3	4	5	6	7	8	9	10	11	12	13	14	15	16	17	18	19	20	21	22
1. Chatteris	*	4-0	0-3	3-1	1-4	1-3	1-1	0-6	2-5	1-1	2-2	1-0	0-3	3-1	2-1	5-1	1-3	3-0	1-1	3-0	1-0	0-1
2. Cornard	1-3	*	1-1	1-0	0-0	2-1	2-1	3-1	1-1	2-5	3-2	1-2	2-2	2-4	5-1	4-3	2-4	0-2	1-1	0-2	1-0	1-2
3. Diss	3-0	2-2	*	3-1	3-0	1-1	3-1	0-0	3-2	3-3	2-0	4-1	4-1	0-2	1-1	3-0	0-1	4-2	6-0	5-0	1-2	3-1
4. Fakenham	0-1	2-2	2-4	*	1-4	3-0	0-2	2-2	3-2	2-0	3-1	3-1	0-0	2-2	2-0	2-4	0-4	1-1	1-1	2-3	2-1	1-4
5. Felixstowe	1-2	1-1	1-1	0-1	*	2-1	0-0	1-0	2-3	2-2	4-0	3-0	6-0	0-2	1-0	2-2	3-1	1-1	0-3	3-2	1-0	2-2
6. Gorleston	1-0	1-2	0-1	0-0	1-2	*	1-2	2-5	0-2	0-2	1-1	1-2	1-1	0-4	0-1	0-2	3-3	1-1	2-3	2-3	1-2	1-3
7. Gt Yarmouth	1-0	2-1	0-1	1-0	1-1	0-1	*	1-3	5-1	0-2	2-2	0-1	0-1	1-4	1-2	4-0	3-0	1-3	2-2	3-0	1-1	0-1
8. Halstead	2-0	1-1	3-2	5-0	0-1	4-0	5-0	*	2-2	3-1	3-1	3-2	4-3	3-1	7-0	4-1	1-0	2-1	2-0	3-1	1-2	2-3
9. Harwich	1-1	1-3	3-2	2-0	1-1	1-1	3-1	3-4	*	3-0	5-0	1-1	0-0	2-1	1-1	2-0	2-1	1-2	1-1	2-2	1-1	0-3
10. Haverhill	0-1	0-2	3-0	3-0	0-2	2-1	2-3	1-3	1-0	*	4-1	2-1	0-1	1-0	2-1	3-2	6-1	4-0	1-0	1-1	4-0	0-1
11. Histon	1-0	3-1	1-1	2-2	1-0	0-1	1-1	1-2	1-0	2-2	*	0-4	0-0	1-4	2-5	3-1	1-2	1-5	1-1	2-3	1-0	3-1
12. Lowestoft	3-0	1-0	2-2	2-1	0-0	1-0	1-1	0-2	3-3	0-0	4-1	*	3-0	0-2	2-1	0-2	1-0	1-3	2-1	3-1	0-1	1-0
13. March TU	1-2	0-2	1-3	5-0	0-3	0-2	0-0	0-5	0-1	1-1	1-1	1-2	*	0-0	4-0	0-1	2-0	0-3	1-1	1-0	1-4	0-1
14. Newmarket	1-0	0-4	0-2	0-0	2-2	4-1	3-0	2-2	1-0	2-0	4-2	3-1	1-0	*	1-0	2-2	2-1	3-2	1-0	1-0	4-1	6-3
15. Norwich U.	1-1	1-0	1-1	0-1	0-2	1-0	0-3	1-4	1-4	1-2	1-1	2-4	6-1	1-3	*	3-1	2-5	0-3	3-6	2-0	0-3	1-3
16. Soham TR	1-2	3-2	1-2	1-2	1-3	4-4	1-0	2-2	2-2	5-4	2-3	0-3	3-1	2-2	2-2	*	0-4	0-2	0-2	2-2	1-2	3-10
17. Stowmarket	3-0	0-2	2-1	3-3	3-0	2-0	0-2	0-3	0-3	1-1	1-0	1-1	4-0	3-2	2-1	2-1	*	1-1	2-1	2-1	1-0	1-2
18. Sudbury W.	4-0	2-0	3-0	2-2	2-1	1-2	1-0	1-0	5-0	0-4	1-0	3-5	2-1	0-2	2-2	1-1	2-0	*	2-3	0-1	3-0	1-1
19. Tiptree U.	2-3	4-1	1-6	5-1	3-1	1-2	2-1	1-2	0-3	4-0	2-0	3-0	0-2	1-2	2-0	0-4	0-3	1-1	*	0-1	0-0	1-4
20. Watton Utd	0-0	1-5	1-5	1-1	1-0	1-1	3-2	1-5	0-2	1-1	3-1	3-1	0-2	0-1	2-0	0-3	0-1	1-0	0-1	*	3-3	0-1
21. Wisbech T.	0-0	2-2	1-2	2-0	2-0	0-1	1-0	2-1	1-0	4-0	1-1	3-0	0-0	0-0	3-1	2-2	3-2	6-2	3-1	2-0	*	0-0
22. Wroxham	1-1	3-0	0-1	1-1	0-2	4-1	3-0	3-0	4-0	3-0	2-0	3-0	2-1	3-0	2-1	5-0	0-0	2-2	3-2	0-2	1-0	*

DIV. ONE RESULTS	1	2	3	4	5	6	7	8	9	10	11	12	13	14	15	16	17	18
1. Brantham Athletic	*	6-1	2-3	0-3	0-2	0-3	2-3	1-4	0-5	2-1	5-1	2-3	1-2	3-2	6-2	0-0	0-1	0-5
2. Brightlingsea United	3-0	*	3-1	0-1	1-1	1-3	0-1	1-1	1-1	0-1	2-1	2-1	6-1	3-2	1-0	3-0	2-4	0-3
3. Bury Town Reserves	1-3	2-0	*	4-0	1-0	1-6	3-2	0-4	1-1	2-2	2-4	2-4	1-2	0-4	4-2	4-0	0-4	1-1
4. Cambridge City Reserves	1-7	1-2	9-2	*	3-0	1-0	3-2	1-2	1-4	2-1	3-2	2-2	0-3	1-3	5-1	2-1	0-1	2-4
5. Clacton Town	4-1	2-2	2-3	0-0	*	1-3	1-0	1-2	1-0	1-1	1-4	1-1	0-0	3-4	1-0	3-1	1-1	0-4
6. Downham Town	2-2	0-1	4-2	2-1	3-0	*	1-2	0-1	4-2	1-0	1-0	0-1	1-1	2-2	1-1	0-0	0-1	1-2
7. Ely City	1-1	0-2	3-2	1-4	1-1	0-1	*	2-3	2-0	2-2	1-2	1-1	2-0	3-2	3-2	1-1	1-1	1-1
8. Hadleigh United	4-2	3-1	4-2	5-1	3-1	3-1	0-0	*	4-3	6-0	0-1	3-0	5-1	2-1	6-1	5-0	2-1	1-1
9. Ipswich Wanderers	0-1	0-2	4-2	1-1	2-0	0-0	2-3	1-1	*	3-1	1-4	4-0	2-0	2-3	3-0	2-1	1-4	1-4
10. Long Sutton Athletic	1-1	1-1	2-2	1-0	5-4	2-0	1-1	1-5	3-5	*	4-0	2-2	1-1	1-2	1-2	4-3	1-3	2-3
11. Mildenhall Town	3-1	4-3	0-0	2-1	2-3	0-1	1-2	0-3	3-2	8-1	*	1-4	1-1	0-4	1-1	4-1	0-2	0-1
12. Somersham Town	1-1	3-1	5-2	2-1	0-0	1-3	1-1	0-2	3-2	1-0	1-2	*	3-2	2-4	4-1	8-1	0-2	1-2
13. Stanway Rovers	1-3	0-1	2-3	2-4	4-2	2-0	0-0	0-1	2-1	3-1	1-2	4-0	*	0-5	8-1	3-0	1-0	5-2
14. Sudbury Town Reserves	9-2	4-1	10-0	3-2	4-1	1-0	5-2	2-0	1-2	5-1	1-4	1-1	2-2	*	3-1	2-0	0-1	2-1
15. Swaffham Town	2-2	1-5	1-4	2-1	1-2	1-3	1-1	0-4	1-2	1-0	1-1	0-3	0-1	2-1	*	3-1	1-0	0-5
16. Thetford Town	4-1	0-1	0-0	0-0	1-3	2-4	0-4	0-4	1-5	3-1	0-9	1-4	2-3	0-2	1-0	*	0-1	1-4
17. Warboys Town	3-1	2-1	3-1	3-2	1-2	1-1	2-0	2-1	1-0	0-0	0-1	2-1	1-0	2-5	3-0	2-1	*	1-1
18. Woodbridge Town	9-0	2-0	0-0	3-2	2-1	7-0	2-0	1-2	1-2	1-0	4-1	2-1	3-1	2-1	4-0	10-1	3-0	*

JEWSON SPORTSMANSHIP TROPHY 1993-94: Sudbury Wanderers.
(previous winners: 88-89: Brantham Athletic, 89-90: Lowestoft Town, 90-91: Woodbridge Town, 91-92: Woodbridge Town, 92-93: Woodbridge Town).

JEWSON FAIR PLAY TROPHY 1993-94: Hadleigh United.
(previous winners: 91-92: Stowmarket Town, 92-93: Thetford Town).

PHOTOS OPPOSITE:

Top: *Warboys Town defender Simon Burton times his tackle perfectly to dispossess Thetford's Chris Bray.*

Centre: *Soham Town Rangers forward Darren Theobald bursts through during his side's home defeat against Stowmarket Town.*

Foot: *Stowmarket Town goalkeeper Darren Holden is beaten from the spot by Newmarket Town's Salvatore Maiorana (out of picture) - a goal that put the 'Jockeys' on top of the table in April.*

All photos - Martin Wray.

CARTER

JEWSON EASTERN COUNTIES LEAGUE CUP 1993-94

Preliminary Round *(Attendances in parentheses)*

Brantham Ath. v Mildenhall Town *(61)*	3-0	Gorleston v Wroxham *(134)*	0-1*(aet)*
Gt Yarmouth T. v Long Sutton A. *(75)*	6-0	Haverhill Rovers v Swaffham Town *(83)*	5-0
Newmarket T. v Halstead T. *(135)*	3-2	Tiptree Town v Warboys Town *(41)*	0-1

First Round

Bury Town Res. v Newmarket Town *(129)*	0-3	Chatteris Town v Brantham Athletic *(52)*	3-1
Diss Town v Cornard United *(196)*	5-0	Fakenham Town v Ely City *(154)*	5-1
Gt Yarmouth v Sudbury Town Res. *(72)*	3-1	Hadleigh Utd v Clacton Town *(123)*	4-0
Haverhill Rovers v Histon *(106)*	1-0	Lowestfoft Town v Downham Town *(113)*	0-2
Norwich U. v Camb. C. Res. *(35 & 46)*	1-1,1-4	Somersham Town v Warboys Town *(116)*	2-1
Stowmarket Town v Felixstowe Town *(114)*	2-1	Sudbury Wanderers v Stanway Rovers *(56)*	6-0
Thetford v Wisbech *(150)*	0-8*(Wisbech expelled)*	Watton United v Brightlingsea Utd *(55)*	0-1
Woodbridge Town v Soham Town Rgrs *(133)*	1-0	Wroxham v Harwich & Parkeston *(135)*	2-3

Second Round

Cambridge City Reserves v Thetford *(43)*	4-1	Chatters T. v Sudbury Town Reserves *(40)*	1-0*(aet)*
Hadleigh Town v Haverhill Rovers *(124)*	3-0	Harwich & Parkeston v Gt Yarmouth Town *(157)*	2-1
Newmarket Town v Downham Town *(93)*	6-0	Somersham Town v Fakenham Town *(42)*	1-2
Stowmarket v Diss Town *(125 & 225)*	3-3,0-1	Woodbridge Town v Brightlingsea Utd *(62)*	2-1

Quarter-Finals

Fakenham v Chatteris Town *(147 & 66)*	2-2,1-2	Newmarket Town v Cambridge City Res. *(159)*	3-0
Hadleigh United v Diss Town *(159)*	2-1*(aet)*	Harwich & Parkeston v Woodbridge *(107)*	1-2*(aet)*

Semi-Finals

Chatteris Town v Hadleigh United *(128)*	2-1	Newmarket Town v Woodbridge Town *(166)*	0-1

Final *(at Sudbury Wanderers FC, 13/4/93)*: Woodbridge Town 2, Chatteris Town 0 *(att: 206).*

Great Yarmouth Town's captain, John Scott, fires in a fierce shot against Harwich & Parkeston.

Photo - Gavin Ellis-Neville.

JEWSON EASTERN LEAGUE ATTENDANCES 1993-94

Club	Games	Total	Ave	Best Gate 93-94	
Chatteris Town	30	2,173	72	169	(16/5 - League v. Diss)
Cornard United	28	2,320	83	214	(27/12 - League v. Sudbury Wdrs)
Diss Town	28	10,712	383	1,731	(19/3 - FA Vase v. Atherton LR)
Fakenham Town	26	4,412	170	388	(12/2 - Norf. Snr Cup v Diss)
Felixstowe Town	28	2,288	82	151	(27/10 - League v. Tiptree)
Gorleston	24	3,033	126	248	(4/4 - League v. Gt Yarmouth)
Gt Yarmouth Town	26	3,013	116	330	(27/12 - League v. Gorleston)
Halstead Town	35	8,167	233	900	(9/10 - FA Cup v. Dagenham)
Harwich & Parkeston	31	4,963	160	275	(26/10 - E Ang Cup v. Colchester)
Haverhill Rovers	27	2,448	91	197	(1/3 - Suff Prem C v. Newmarket)
Histon	26	1,935	74	161	(1/3 - Camb. Cup v. Wisbech)
Lowestoft Town	28	4,389	157	301	(8/2 - League v. Wroxham)
March Town Utd	26	2,853	110	220	(25/1 - League v. Wisbech)
Newmarket Town	27	3,260	121	302	(14/9 - FA Cup v. Chelmsford)
Norwich United	23	1,590	69	143	(9/4 - League v. Diss)
Soham Town Rgrs	29	4,074	140	312	(14/4 - League v. Newmarket)
Stowmarket Town	26	2,508	96	269	(30/4 - League v. Diss)
Sudbury Wanderers	25	2,615	105	263	(8/3 - League v. Halstead)
Tiptree United	28	1,880	67	118	(22/1 - League v. Halstead)
Watton United	25	2,213	89	220	(1/1 - League v. Wroxham)
Wisbech Town	29	7,657	264	406	(11/12 - FA Vase v. Collier R.)
Wroxham	25	4,443	178	834	(26/4 - League v. Diss)
Division One					
Brantham Athletic	24	1,650	69	160	(19/1 - Suff Snr v. Woodbridge)
Brightlingsea Utd	19	1,707	90	178	(27/12 - League v. Clacton)
Bury Town Reserves	19	1,892	102	197	(26/10 - Sf Snr v. Sudbury Res)
Cambridge C. Reserves	19	755	40	68	(6/5 - League v. Hadleigh)
Clacton Town	22	1,334	61	110	(15/1 - League v Hadleigh)
Downham Town	17	1,104	65	98	(26/8 - League v. Swaffham)
Ely City	20	1,164	58	159	(27/4 - Soham CC v Mildenhall)
Hadleigh Utd	27	4,109	152	507	(27/4 - League v. Woodbridge)
Ipswich Wdrs	20	1,738	87	335	(4/4 - League v. Woodbridge)
Long Sutton Ath.	21	991	47	92	(4/9 - FA Vase v Gt Wakering)
Mildenhall Town	19	1,501	79	125	(1/1 - League v. Hadleigh)
Somersham Town	25	1,301	52	116	(16/10 - League v. Warboys)
Stanway Rovers	21	1,090	52	156	(10/5 - League v. Hadleigh)
Sudbury Town Reserves	18	1,751	97	237	(9/10 - League v. Bury Res.)
Swaffham Town	18	1,273	71	170	(14/9 - League v. Mildenhall)
Thetford Town	20	1,735	87	150	(16/10 - Lge Cup v. Wisbech)
Warboys Town	25	2,192	88	170	(27/12 - League v. Somersham)
Woodbridge Town	24	2,746	114	256	(27/12 - League v. Ipswich W.)

The above includes Jewson League and League Cup matches and, where notified, FA Cup, FA Vase, East Anglian Cup, Eastern Floodlit Competition and County Cup ties.

PREMIER DIVISION - TEN YEAR RECORD

	84/85	85/86	86/87	87/88	88/89	89/90	90/91	91/92	92/93	93/94
Braintree Town	1	6	2	2	2	3	2	-	-	-
Brantham Athletic	16	16	19	20	17	8	19	17	21	-
Brightlingsea Utd	-	-	-	-	-	-	-	20	22	-
Bury Town	9	4	3	-	-	-	-	-	-	-
Chatteris Town	15	19	15	7	19	21	21	19	16	12
Clacton Town	17	22	12	12	18	20	12	21	-	-
Colchester U. Res.	7	2	7	14	-	-	-	-	-	-
Cornard United	-	-	-	-	-	-	8	3	4	13
Diss Town	-	-	-	-	-	-	-	-	5	4
Ely City	18	20	22	22	20	-	-	-	-	-
Fakenham Town	-	-	-	-	-	-	-	-	7	17
Felixstowe Town	14	12	17	17	11	13	13	13	9	8
Gorleston	11	13	18	18	10	5	17	12	10	21
Gt. Yarmouth Town	3	3	6	4	5	6	18	14	11	16
Halstead Town	-	-	-	-	-	14	3	9	15	2
Harwich & Parkes.	21	17	14	13	14	4	5	6	6	11
Haverhill Rovers	20	14	13	10	7	15	4	8	14	10
Histon	8	10	21	5	6	7	10	15	20	20
Lowestoft Town	4	11	9	8	12	18	9	11	17	9
March Town Utd.	6	7	4	1	4	9	15	10	18	19
Newmarket Town	19	21	16	15	16	17	20	7	3	3
Norwich United	-	-	-	-	-	-	-	4	8	22
Soham Town Rangers	12	18	20	21	21	-	-	-	-	18
Stowmarket Town	10	8	10	19	8	11	11	2	13	5
Sudbury Town	2	1	1	3	1	1	-	-	-	-
Sudbury Wanderers	-	-	-	-	-	-	-	-	-	7
Thetford Town	22	15	23	16	9	2	14	22	-	-
Tiptree United	13	5	5	11	15	19	16	16	12	14
Watton United	-	-	8	9	13	16	6	18	19	15
Wisbech Town	5	9	11	6	3	10	1	5	2	6
Wroxham	-	-	-	-	-	12	7	1	1	1
Teams Competing	**22**	**22**	**23**	**22**	**21**	**21**	**21**	**22**	**22**	**22**

PREMIER DIVISION STATISTICS

LEAGUE STATISTICS				1993-94 STATISTICS	
Club	**Season Joined**		**Championships or Best Placing**	**Leading Appearances League & Lge. Cup**	**Leading Goalscorers League & Lge. Cup**
Chatteris	1966/67	28	3rd - 1968	48 - * Steve Hudson 45 - Mark Southwell 41 - Steve Bedford 39 - Julian Young	12 - Julian Young 11 - Steve Hudson 7 - Steve Bedford
Cornard Utd	1989/90	5	3rd - 1992 Div 1 1990	37 - Micky Stratton 36 - Gary Clarke - Richard Schultz - Andy Smiles	9 - Andy Smiles 8 - Micky Stratton 7 - Scott Young
Diss Town	1988/89	5	4th - 1994 Div 1 1992	46 - * Paul Hartle 44 - Gary Smith - Robert Woodcock 43 - Robert Musgrave	16 - Steve Miles 12 - Paul Warne 11 - Kelly Barth 10 - Paul Gibbs
Fakenham Town	1988/89	6	7th - 1993 Div 1 runners-up 1992	46 - * Kevin Topping 44 - Shaun Drake 42 - Richard Dye 40 - Mark King	13 - Paul Reeve - Kevin Topping 7 - Richard Dye
Felixstowe	1976/77	18	8th - 1983 & 1994	43 - * Nicky Barker - * Tony Gayfer 42 - Shaun Curtis - Micky Smith	16 - Shaun Curtis 10 - Tony Gayfer 9 - Aaron Howell
Gorleston	1935/36 1969/70	18 25	1953, 1973 1980, 1981	43 - Paul Cooper 39 - Andy Gee - Steve King 38 - Dean Bamment	8 - Paul Cooper 6 - Steve King 5 - Russell Carter - Colin Danby
Gt Yarmouth	1935/36	52	1969	48 - * Mark Vincent 44 - Steve Foyster 42 - David Hatch - Luke Price	19 - Peter Monro 6 - Mark Vincent 5 - Shaun Bunker - Gary Durrant
Halstead	1988/89	6	2nd - 1994 Div 1 runners-up 1988/89	41 - Dave Streetley 38 - Gary Skeggs 36 - Brian Devereaux	26 - John Kemp 14 - Andy Smiles 13 - Brian Devereaux - Kevin Rayson - Dave Streatley
Harwich	1935/36 1938/39 1984/85	2 19 10	1935 (Jt)	42 - Darren Scoulding - Brendan Tuck 37 - Gary Hudson - Micky Johnson	20 - Brendan Tuck 9 - Micky Johnson 6 - Lee Abrehart
Haverhill	1964/65	30	1979	42 - Neil Farlie 41 - Andy Ince 38 - Lee Fish - Andy Salter	20 - Andy Ince 18 - Alistair Suddery 7 - Dave Brown - Steve Martin
Histon	1965/66	29	4th - 1975	35 - Nick Foulkes - Paul Shadrack 33 - Kevin Seagrave 28 - Nacer Relazani	7 - Nigel Foster - Paul Shadrack 6 - Gary Haylock
Lowestoft	1935/36	52	1936, 1938 1963, 1965-68 1970-71, 1978	43 - * Tony Gill - Stephen Wade 42 - Cameron Smith 41 - Jason Burman	12 - Micky Chapman 11 - Matthew Barbrook - Cameron Smith
March Town	1954/55	40	1988	43 - * Tony O'Donovan 42 - John Gilson 37 - Stuart Mason 36 - Mark Wales	8 - Stuart Mason 5 - Steve Bailey 4 - Martin Bradley
Newmarket	1937/38 1959/60	8 35	2nd - 1967	47 - * Matt Eden - * Colin Vowden 45 - Andy Morton 44 - Jerry Rose	19 - Matt Eden 18 - Jerry Rose 11 - Martin Pammenter 10 - Salvatore Maiorana
Norwich United	1989/90	5	4th - 1992 Div 1 Winners 1991	44 - * Tim Sayer 37 - Richard Hatch 35 - Eugine Dunford - John Edridge	7 - Andrew Ellis 6 - John Randall 5 - Martin Moy

PREMIER DIVISION STATISTICS - CONTINUED

LEAGUE STATISTICS				1990-91 STATISTICS	
Club	Season Joined		Championships or Best Placing	Leading Appearances League & Lge. Cups	Leading Goalscorers League & Lge. Cups
Soham T. Rgrs	1963/64 1993/94	26 1	18th - 1994 Div 1 runners-up 1993	44 - * Darren Theobald 42 - Andy Bullett 40 - Phil Coulsen 38 - David Braybrooke	24 - Darren Theobald 17 - Andy Bullett 5 - Kevin Rogers
Stowmarket	1952/53	42	2nd - 1992	45 - * Melvyn Aidiss - * Roger Aldiss 44 - Marvin Hall - Steve Gayfer	14 - Marvin Hall 12 - David King 11 - Paul Southgate
Sudbury Wdrs	1993/94	1	7th - 1994 Div 1 champions 1993	43 - Chris Rose 41 - Steve Day 38 - Darren Pratt - Andrew Fenwick	15 - Adam Crofton 12 - Steve Day - Darren Pratt
Tiptree	1979/80	15	1982	41 - Judd Coe - Andy Jackson 39 - Gary Nash 37 - Chris Guy - Nicky Lee	23 - Lee Sonnex 12 - Judd Coe 7 - Chris Guy
Watton	1986/87	8	8th - 1987	43 - * Mark Bond 41 - Mark Blockwell - Paul Jarvis	11 - Mark Blockwell 5 - Alan Wiles 4 - Peter Blackmuir - Steve Rumbelow - Chris Watts
Wisbech	1950/51 1970/71	2 24	1972 & 1977 & 1991	44 - * Mark Ovendale 41 - Andy Stewart 40 - Dave Massingham 39 - Martin Lindsay	16 - Chris Carey 10 - Dave Massingham 9 - Martin Lindsay
Wroxham	1988/89	7	1992, 1993 & 1994	44 - * Mark Crowe 43 - Ryan Lemmon 41 - Adrian Harris	34 - Scott Snowling 19 - Jon Rigby 12 - Stuart Larter

* - Denotes ever-present in Jewson League/ Jewson League Cup.

LEADING SCORERS 1993-94

Premier Division

34 - Scott Snowling (Wroxham)
26 - John Kemp (Halstead Town)
24 - Darren Theobald (Soham Town Rgrs)
23 - Andy Smiles (Halstead/Cornard Utd)
- Lee Sonnex (Tiptree United)
20 - Andy Ince (Haverhill Rovers)
20 - Brendan Tuck (Harwich & P.)
19 - Matt Eden (Newmarket Town)
- Peter Monro (Great Yarmouth)
- Jon Rigby (Wroxham)
18 - Jerry Rose (Newmarket Town)
- Alistair Suddery (Haverhill)
17 - Adrian Bullett (Soham T. Rgrs)
16 - Chris Carey (Wisbech T.)
- Shaun Curtis (Felixstowe)
- Stephen Miles (Diss Town)

Division One

25 - Paul Keys (Hadleigh Utd)
- Steve McKenna (Bury Town Reserves)
24 - Andy Orvis (Sudbury Town Reserves)
23 - Dave Hubbick (Woodbridge Town)
22 - Wayne Bond (Stanway Rovers)
- Donnie Davis (Hadleigh United)
21 - Martin Bennett (Woodbridge T.)
- Robbie Cooke (Warboys Town)
16 - Spencer Breeze (Ipswich Wdrs)
- Lee Sharp (Mildenhall Town)
15 - Ian Boon (Somersham Town)
- Dave Claxton (Hadleigh Utd)
- John Stace (Clacton Town)

Individual Scoring Feats:

6 goals: Dave Hubbick (Woodbridge) 20/11/93 v. Thetford Town.
: John McLean (Cambridge City Res.) 29/3/94 v. Bury Town Res.
4 goals: Peter Monro (Gt Yarmouth) 18/9/93 v. Long Sutton *(League Cup)*
: Stuart Larter (Wroxham) 21/9/93 v. Soham Town Rangers.
: Scott Snowling (Wroxham) 20/10/93 v. Soham Town Rangers.
: Scott Snowling (Wroxham) 2/11/93 v. Fakenham Town.
: Neil Kennedy (Mildenhall Town) 27/12/93 v. Thetford Town.
: Andy Orvis (Sudbury Town Res.) 5/3/94 v. Stanway Rovers.
: Neil Pope (Cambridge City Res.) 12/3/94 v. Swaffham Town.
: Lee Sonnex (Tiptree United) 12/3/94 v. Fakenham Town
: Julian Hazell (Harwich & Parkeston) 15/3/94 v. Histon.
: John Kemp (Halstead Town) 12/4/94 v. Gorleston.
: Alistair Suddery (Haverhill Rovers) 16/4/94 v. Wisbech Town.

There were a total of 60 hat-tricks recorded during the season 1993-94, 21 in the Premier Division, and 29 in Division One. Steve McKenna (Bury Town Reserves) and Paul Keys (Hadleigh United) both hit three.

MONTHLY AWARDS 1993-94

Month	Premier Division Club of the Month	Division One Club of the Month	Good Conduct
Aug/Sept	Diss Town	Sudbury Town Res.	Clacton Town
October	Halstead Town	Woodbridge Town	Hadleigh United
November	Great Yarmouth Town	Hadleigh United	Sudbury Wanderers
December	Wroxham	Ipswich Wanderers	Cambridge City Res.
January	Newmarket Town	Hadleigh United	Wroxham
February	Sudbury Wanderers	Thetford Town	Woodbridge Town
March	Wisbech Town	Warboys Town	Haverhill Rovers
April	Halstead Town	Woodbridge Town	Diss Town

Diss Town - FA Vase winners 1993-94. Back Row (L/R): Mal Mundey (Assistant Manager), Paul Hartle, Paul Gibbs, Robert Woodcock, Jason Carter, Ian Manning, John Musgrove (Coach). Centre: Chris Clements, Paul Warne, Stephen Miles, Jason Fletcher, Robert Musgrave, Tom Casey. Front: Kelly Barth, Phil Mortimer, Gary Smith (Captain), Bill Punton (Manager), Martin Woolsey, Phil Bugg, Peter Mendham.

Soham Town Rangers FC *Photo - Eric Marsh.*

PREMIER DIVISION CLUBS 1994-95

CHATTERIS TOWN

Chairman: A Parish **President:** J Chambers **Manager:** Lester Kent/ Dave Simmons
Secretary: Anthony Summers, 41 The Elms, Chatteris, Cambs PE16 6JN (0354 692062).
Ground: West Street, Chatteris (0354 692139).
Directions: Entering Chatteris on A141 from Huntingdon turn right into West Street after by-pass roundabout.
Seats: 250 **Cover:** 400 **Capacity:** 2,000 **Floodlights:** Yes **Founded:** 1920.
Colours: All white **Change colours:** Red & black **Nickname:** Lillies.
Previous League: Peterborough **Midweek Matches:** Wednesday **Pennants:** Yes.
Clubhouse details: Bar & tea bar. **Record Gate:** 2,000 v March Town Utd, League 5/5/88.
Programme: 12 pages, 20p **Previous Ground:** First Drove
Matchday food & drink: Tea, coffee, cold drinks, confectionary, burgers, hotdogs, sandwiches, soup, rolls.
Players progressing to Football League: Andy Rogers (Reading, Southend, Plymouth), Dave Gregory (Plymouth).
Honours: Eastern Counties Lg Cup 67-68, Peterborough Premier Lg(3).

CORNARD UNITED

President: Len Hodgson **Chairman:** Ivan Cocker **Vice-Chairman:** David Nickells
Secretary: Richard Powell, 14 North Rise, Great Cornard, Sudbury, Suffolk CO10 0DE (0787 371671).
Manager: Clive Hesketh **Physio:** Ron Saddington **Comm. Mgr:** Dave Hill.
Ground: Blackhouse Lane Sportsfield, Great Cornard, Suffolk (0787 376719).
Directions: Left off r'bout on A134 coming from Ipswich/Colchester into Sudbury, follow signs for Country Park - ground is immediately opposite along Blackhouse Lane
Seats: 250 **Cover:** 500 **Capacity:** 2,000 **Floodlights:** Yes **Founded:** 1964.
Colours: Blue/white **Change colours:** All white. **Club Shop:** No.
Previous Grounds: Cornard Rec 64-71/ Great Cornard Upper School 71-85.
Prev. Lges: Sudbury Sunday 64-65/ Bury St E. & Dist. 65-72/ Colchester 71-78/ Essex & Suffolk Border 78-89.
Record Attendance: 509 v Leyton Orient, friendly 9/8/93. Competitive: 330 v Sudbury Town, Eastern Floodlit League 4/2/92.
Midweek Matches: Wednesday **Sponsors:** Brooks Transport **Nickname:** Ards.
Programme: 16 pages **Programme Editor:** TBA
Local Newspaper: Suffolk Free Press. **Reserve Team's League:** Essex & Suffolk Border.
Record win: 18-2 v St Peters House, Colchester League 14/9/72.
Record defeat: 4-10 v Finningham, Bury League 7/2/68.
Clubhouse details: Open matchdays & Sunday lunchtimes. Food available.
Matchday food & drink: Tea, coffee, cold drinks, confectionary, hotdogs, burgers, soup, sandwiches, rolls.
Captain 93-94: Mick Stratton. **Club Record Scorer & Top Scorer 93-94:** Andy Smiles.
P.o.Y. 93-94: Adrian Hunt Press. **Club record appearances:** Malcolm Fisher.
Honours: Eastern Co's Lg Div 1 89-90 (Lg Cup R-up 92-93), Essex & Suffolk Border Lg 88-89 (Lg Cup 88-89), Suffolk Snr Cup 89-90, Suffolk Jnr Cup R-up 84-85.

DISS TOWN

Chairman: Des Tebble **President:** R A Gooderham **Treasurer:** Noel Mullenger.
Secretary: Mr Richard Upson, Bamburgh House, Brewers Green Lane, Diss, Norfolk IP22 3QP (0379 642923).
Manager: Bill Punton **Asst Manager:** Mal Mundey
Coach: John Musgrove **Physio:** Mick Mundey.
Ground: Brewers Green Lane, Diss (0379 651223).
Directions: Just off B1066 Diss-Thetford road, near Roydon School. One and a half miles from Diss (BR).
Seats: 280 **Cover:** Yes **Capacity:** 2,500 **Floodlights:** Yes **Founded:** 1888.
Colours: Tangerine/navy/tangerine **Change colours:** White/navy/tangerine. **Pennants:** Yes.
Previous Leagues: Norwich & District/ Norfolk & Suffolk 35-64/ Anglian Combination 64-82.
Midweek Matches: Tuesday **Previous Ground:** Roydon Road 1886-1982.
Record Gate: 1,731 v Atherton LR, FA Vase SF 1st leg 10/3/94 **Nickname:** Tangerines.
Programme: 10 pages, 30p **Programme Editor:** G Enderby
Sponsors: Diss Fasteners **Reserve Team's League:** Anglian Combination.
Club Shop: Yes, selling replica shirts, hats, scarves, old programmes, pennants, mugs, t-shirts.
Clubhouse details: Open evenings (except Sunday), Sat/Sun lunchtimes, and matchdays.
Matchday food & drink: Tea, coffee, cold drinks, confectionary, burgers, hotdogs, soup, rolls.
Players progressing to the Football League: Alec Thurlow (Man City), Mervyn Cawston (Norwich), Trevor Whymark (Ipswich), Clive Stafford (Colchester).
Captain 93-94: Garry Smith **Top Scorer 93-94:** Steve Miles **P.o.Y. 93-94:** Jason Carter.
Honours: FA Vase 93-94 (QF 91-92), Eastern Co's Lg Div 1 91-92, Anglian Comb. 76-77 78-79 (R-up 74-75, Div 1 67-68 73-74, Lg Cup 67-68 79-80 81-82), Norfolk & Suffolk Lg R-up 55-56 (Applegate Cup 56-57 57-58(joint)(R-up 55-56)), Norfolk Snr Cup 74-75, Norfolk Jnr Cup 1891-92.

FAKENHAM TOWN

Chairman: Tony Fisher **President:** B E Woodhouse **Manager:** Nolan Keeley
Secretary: E V Linnell, 40 Warren Avenue, Fakenham, Norfolk NR21 8NP (0328 855445).
Press Officer: J Cushion **Commercial Manager:** R Lane.
Ground: Barons Hall Lawn, Norwich Road, Fakenham (0328 862939).
Directions: Adjacent to Police Station in Norwich Road.
Seats: 80 **Cover:** 300 **Capacity:** 1,500 **Floodlights:** Yes **Founded:** 1884.
Colours: Amber & black **Change colours:** Red & white **Club Shop:** Yes.
Midweek Matchday: Tuesday. **Sponsors:** English Garages **Nickname:** Ghosts.
Previous Grounds: Hempton Green 1884-89/ Star Meadow 89-1907
Previous Leagues: North Norfolk 1884-1910/ Norwich & District 10-35/ Norfolk & Suffolk 35-64/ Anglian Combination 64-87.
Reserves' League: Anglian Comb. **Record Gate:** 1,000 v Norwich City, floodlight inauguration.
Clubhouse details: Bar, colour TV and pool table.
Matchday food & drink: Tea, coffee, cold drinks, confectionary, soup.
Programme: 32 pages (Barnes Print), 20p **Local Newspapers:** Fakenham & Wells Times.
Players progressing to the Football League: Nolan Keeley (Scunthorpe & Lincoln).
Captain 93-94: Kevin Topping **P.o.Y. 93-94:** Trevor Marshall **Top Scorer 93-94:** Paul Reeve.
Hons: Norfolk Snr Cup(5) 70-71 72-74 91-92 93-94, Eastern Co's Lg Div 1 R-up 91-92, Anglian Comb. Cup 78-79.

FELIXSTOWE TOWN

Chairman: Dave Ashford **President:** TBA **Manager:** Paul Adams.
Secretary: Norman Howlett, 139 Ashcroft Rd, Ipswich, Suffolk (0473 749137).
Ground: Dellwood Avenue, Felixstowe (0394 282917).
Directions: A45 to Felixstowe. Turn right at 3rd r'bout then 1st left - ground 100 yds on left. 5 mins from Felixstowe (BR) and town centre.
Seats: 200 **Cover:** 200 **Capacity:** 2,000 **Floodlights:** Yes **Founded:** 1890.
Colours: Red/white & black **Change:** Blue & white/black **Nickname:** Seasiders.
Prev. Leagues: Essex & Suffolk Border/ Ipswich & Dist. **Midweek Matches:** Wednesday
Record Attendance: 1,500 v Ipswich Town, floodlight inauguration 25/1/91.
Programme: 16 pages, 30p **Programme Editor:** P Griffiths.
Clubhouse details: Bar, snack bar, TV, darts, pool table. **Local Newspaper:** East Anglia Daily Times.
Matchday food & drink: Tea, coffee, cold drinks, confectionary, hotdogs, burgers, soup, rolls.
Honours: Suffolk Senior Cup 66-67 74-75. **Club Shop:** Yes **Enamel Badges & Pennants:** Yes.

GREAT YARMOUTH TOWN

Chairman: Colin Smith **President:** Derek Needham **Manager:** Mel Antcliffe.
Secretary: Michael Capon, 16 Orchard Way, Fleggburgh, Gt Yarmouth, Norfolk NR29 3AY (0493 369530).
Ground: Wellesey Recreation Ground, Wellesey Road (0493 842936).
Directions: Just off Marine Parade, 200 yds north of Britannia Pier. Half a mile from Vauxhall (BR).
Seats: 500 **Cover:** 2,100 **Capacity:** 3,600 **Floodlights:** Yes **Founded:** 1897.
Colours: Amber & black/black **Change colours:** White/blue **Nickname:** Bloaters.
Previous Leagues: Norfolk & Suffolk **Midweek Matches:** Tuesday **Club Shop:** No.
Record Attendance: 8,944 v Crystal Palace, FA Cup 1st Rd 52-53. **Pennants:** Yes
Record Victory: 13-0 v Cromer, FA Cup 1st Qualifying Rd 52-53. **Prog.:** 20 pages, 50p
Clubhouse details: (0493 8443373). Dancehall, Committee Room, darts, pool.
Matchday food & drink: Tea, coffee, cold drinks, confectionary, hotdogs, burgers, soup, sandwiches, rolls.
Local Newspapers: Yarmouth Mercury (844201), Eastern Football News (Norwich 283111).
Players progressing to the Football League: Roy Hollis (Norwich), Mel Blyth & Nolan Keeley (Scunthorpe), Steven Davy (West Ham), Kevin Ready (Aston Villa), Gary Butcher (Blackburn).
Honours: Eastern Co's League 68-69 (Runners-up 56-57 67-68 77-78 78-79, League Cup 37-38 74-75 80-81), East Anglian Cup(3), Norfolk Snr Cup(12)(Runners-up(22)), Norfolk Premier Cup(twice shared), Norfolk & Suffolk League 13-14 26-27 27-28, FA Vase SF 82-83, FA Cup 2nd Rd(2)(1st Rd(1)), Anglian Comb. Cup 65-66(res), E Anglian League 56-57(res).

HADLEIGH UNITED

President: H Claireaux, Esq **Chairman:** S R King **Vice-Chairman:** Peter Vardon
Secretary: Alvin H Jarrad, Waterworks Cottages, Raydon, Ipswich, Suffolk IP7 5LF (0473 311798).
Manager: Alan Dilloway. **Assistant Manager:** Donnie Davis.
Physio: Mick Klipalo **Press Officer:** Terry Adams.
Ground: Millfield, Duke Street, Hadleigh, Suffolk (0473 822165).
Directions: Turn off A12 approx halfway between Ipswich & Hadleigh. Take B1070 & follow signs to Hadleigh. Duke Street is off the High Street - turn left by Library.
Seats: 250 **Cover:** 500 **Capacity:** 3,000 **Floodlights:** Yes **Founded:** 1892.
Colours: White/navy/white **Change colours:** All yellow
Programme: 12 pages, 50p **Programme Editor:** Simon King (0473 827134).
Reserves' Lge: Essex & Suff. Border **Player progressing to Football Lge:** Perry Groves (Arsenal).
Midweek Matches: Tuesday. **Prev. Lge:** Suffolk & Ipswich (prev. Ipswich & D.)(pre-1991).
Sponsors: Partridge Coaches **Previous Grounds:** Grays Meadow, Ipswich Roa.
Record Gate: 507 v Woodbridge Town, Jewson Eastern Counties League Division One 27/4/94.
Record win: 6-0 v Long Sutton (H) 16/4/94.
Record defeat: 1-7 v Fakenham Town (A) 4/1/92.
Nickname: Brettsiders. **Clubhouse:** Open matchdays, Fridays & Sunday lunchtimes.
Matchday food & drink: Tea, coffee, cold drinks, confectionary, soup, hotdogs, beefburgers.
Captain 93-94: Carl David **P.O.Y. 93-94:** Steve Buckle **Top Scorer 93-94:** Paul Keys 31.
Honours: Ipswich & Dist./Suffolk & Ipswich League 53-54 56-57 73-74 76-77 78-79 (Mick McNeil League Cup 76-77 80-81 81-82 86-87)), Suffolk Senior Cup 68-69 71-72 82-83.

HALSTEAD TOWN

Chairman: Michael Gage **Vice-Chairman:** D Hume **President:** Mr E J R McDowell
Secretary: Michael Gage, 3 Bois Hall Gdns, Halstead, Essex CO2 2HX (0787 475110).
Manager: Keith Martin **Asst Manager:** I Phillips **Physio:** B Dunster.
Ground: Rosemary Lane, Halstead, Essex (0787 472082).
Directions: A131 Chelmsford to Braintree - follow signs to Halstead. In Halstead, 1st left after Police Station, then 1st right, and first left to ground.
Seats: 492 **Cover:** 500 **Capacity:** 2,000 **Floodlights:** Yes **Founded:** 1879.
Colours: White & black **Change colours:** Red & white
Previous Lges: Nth Essex/ Halstead & Dist./ Haverhill/ Essex & Suffolk Border/ Essex Snr 80-88.
Previous Grounds: Three Gates 1879-1948, Coggeshall Pieces, Ravens Meadow, King George Playing Field.
Record Attendance: 4,000 v Walthamstow Avenue, Essex Senior Cup 1949.
Clubhouse details: Open evenings and matchdays. **Programme:** 30p **Editor:** D Osborne.
Matchday food & drink: Tea, coffee, cold drinks, confectionary, burgers, hotdogs, sandwiches, rolls.
Players progressing to the Football League: Steve Allen (Wimbledon Physio).
Midweek Matches: Tuesday **Local Newspaper:** Halstead Gazette.
Captain 93-94: G Skeggs **Top Scorer & Player of the Year 93-94:** J Kemp.
Hons: Eastern Co's League Runners-up 93-94 (Div 1 Runners-up 89-90), Essex Senior Trophy 93-94, Knight Floodlit Cup Runners-up 90-91, Essex & Suffolk Border League(3) 57-59 77-78 (Runners-up 49-50 54-55 60-61, League Cup(4) 57-59 73-74 93-94(res), Div 1(res) 93-94), Essex Snr League Cup Runners-up 79-80, Essex Jnr Cup 01-02 46-47 (Runners-up 00-01).

HARWICH & PARKESTON

Chairman: Paul Revell **Vice-Chairman:** Alan Preston **President:** J Whitmore
Secretary: Graham Firth, 24 Glebe Close, Wix, Essex CO11 2SD (0255 870805).
Manager: Martin Head **Assistant Manager:** Don James.
Physio: Mick Jeffries **Press Officer:** Carl Allan
Ground: Royal Oak, Main Road, Dovercourt, Harwich (0255 503649).
Directions: On main road into Dovercourt. 600 yds from Dovercourt (BR).
Seats: 350 **Cover:** 1,000 **Capacity:** 5,000 **Floodlights:** Yes **Founded:** 1877.
Colours: Black & white stripes/black **Change colours:** Yellow **Nickname:** Shrimpers.
Previous Lges: Eastern Co's 35-37 38-64/ Essex County 37-38/ Athenian 64-73 83-84/ Isthmian 73-83.
Midweek Matches: Tuesday **Previous Ground:** Phoenix Field, Seafront.
Record Attendance: 5,649 v Romford, FA Amateur Cup 4th Rd 19/3/38. **Club Shop:** Yes
Newsline: 0898 664 250. **Pennants & Enamel Badges:** Yes
Clubhouse details: Open every day. Dances, bingo, darts, pool, function room.
Matchday food & drink: Tea, coffee, cold drinks, confectionary, hotdogs, burgers, soup.
Players progressing to the Football League: I Gillespie (C Palace, Ipswich), G Waites, K Sanderson, Ian Brown (Bristol City 1991).
Prog.: 20 pages, 30p (Ed.: A Schooler) **Local Paper:** Harwich & Manningtree Standard.
Reserve Team's League: Essex & Suffolk Border Prem. Div.
Captain 93-94: Gary Hudson **Top Scorer & Player of the Year 93-94:** Brendan Tuck (28 goals)
Player Honours: FA Amateur Cup R-up 1898-99 1952-53, FA Vase QF 90-91, Eastern Counties Lg 35-36(joint)(Lg Cup 35-36 36-37), Essex County Lg 37-38, Athenian Lg Div 1 R-up 65-66 (Div 2 64-65, Lg Cup 64-65), Essex Senior Cup 1898-99 1936-37, Essex Senior Trophy 89-90, AFA Senior Cup 35-36 36-37, Worthington Evans Cup 80-81.

HAVERHILL ROVERS

Chairman: Ray Esdale **President:** N Haykock
Secretary: C Davies, 8 Helions Park Avenue, Haverhill, Suffolk CB9 8BL (0440 705472).
Manager: Roger Staples. **Asst Mgr/Coach:** N Farlie **Physio:** S Goodall.
Press Officer: Ray Esdale
Ground: Hamlet Croft, (0440 702137).
Directions: Centre of Haverhill.
Seats: 200 **Cover:** 200 **Capacity:** 3,000 **Floodlights:** Yes **Founded:** 1886.
Colours: All red **Change colours:** All yellow **Prev. League:** Essex & Suffolk Border.
Record Attendance: 1,537 v Warrington Town, FA Vase QF 86-87. **Nickname:** Rovers.
Midweek Matches: Tuesday **Programme:** 24 pages, 30p (**Editor:** R Esdale)
Clubhouse details: Open matchdays and functions.
Matchday food & drink: Tea, coffee, cold drinks, confectionary, burgers, hotdogs.
Local Paper: Haverhill Echo. **Players progressing to the Football League:** R Wilkins (Colchester).
Honours: Eastern Co's Lg 78-79 (Lg Cup 64-65), E & S Border Lg 62-63 63-64, East Anglian Cup 90-91.

HISTON

Chairman: Gareth Baldwin **President:** G P Muncey **Manager:** Tom Finney
Secretary: Debbie Cook, 5 Caxton Lane, Foxton, Cambridgeshire CB2 6SR (0223 872126).
Ground: Bridge Road, Impington, Cambridge (0223 232301).
Directions: Leave A45 northern Cambridge bypass on B1049 (signposted Histon and Cottenham). Ground half a mile on right. 5 miles from Cambridge (BR). Bus No. 104.
Seats: 250 **Cover:** 200 **Capacity:** 2,250 **Floodlights:** Yes **Founded:** 1904.
Colours: Red (white stripes)/red/black **Change colours:** All blue.
Previous Leagues: Cambridgeshire 04-48/ Spartan 48-60/ Delphian 60-63/ Athenian 63-65.
Midweek Matches: Tuesday **Previous Name:** Histon Institute 04-51.
Programme: 16 pages, 50p **Prog. Editor:** Kevin Woollard.
Record Gate: 2,400 v K. Lynn, FA Cup. **Local Newspaper:** Cambridge Evening News.
Clubhouse details: Bar/lounge open Tues-Sun evenings, Sun lunctimes and matchdays.
Matchday food & drink: Tea, coffee, cold drinks, confectionary, soup, rolls.
Honours: Eastern Co's Lg Cup 90-91, Cambridge Invitation Cup 77-78 79-80 (R-up 50-51 52-53 53-54), Spartan Lg Div 1 (East) 50-51, Cambs Chal. Cup, Cambs Lg Section 'A'.

LOWESTOFT TOWN

Chairman: Roy Harper **Vice-Chairman:** Rex Butcher **President:** W Yates
Secretary: Terry Lynes, 156 Denmark Road, Lowestoft, Suffolk NR32 2EL (0502 564034).
Manager: Micky Chapman **Press Officer:** Michael Pearce.
Ground: Crown Meadow, Love Road, Lowestoft (0502 573818).
Directions: Just off A12, 10 mins walk from Lowestoft (BR).
Seats: 466 **Cover:** 500 **Capacity:** 4,000 **Floodlights:** Yes **Founded:** 1890.
Colours: Blue & white **Change colours:** Yellow/red/yellow **Nickname:** Blues.
Prev. Lge: Norfolk & Suffolk 1897-1935 **Midweek Matches:** Tuesday **Metal Badges:** Yes
Programme: 20 pages, 30p **Programme Editor:** Secretary
Club Shop: Yes, selling programmes, badges, scarves, pennants, pens, key-rings, mugs. Contact Dave Brooks (0502 531998).
Reserves' Lge: Anglian Combination **Record Attendance:** 5,000 v Watford, FA Cup 1st Rd 9/12/67.
Record win: 19-0 v Thetford Town (H), Eastern Counties League.
Players progressing to Football League: Eddie Spearitt (Ipswich 1965), Nigel Cassidy (Norwich 1967), Richard Money (Scunthorpe 1973), Graham Franklin (Southend 1977).
Club Sponsors: John Grose **Clubhouse details:** Pub hours
Matchday food & drink: Tea, coffee, cold drinks, confectionary, hotdogs, burgers, soup.
Record Scorer: M Tooley 383 **Record appearances:** C Peck 629.
Captain 93-94: Cameron Smith **Top Scorer 93-94:** Micky Chapman 19
P.o.Y. 93-94: Matthew Barbrook
Honours: Eastern Co's Lg(8) 35-36(joint) 37-38 62-63 64-65 67-68 69-71 77-78 (Lg Cup(7) 38-39 54-55 65-67 68-69 75-76 83-84), Norf. & Suffolk Lg(8) 1897-99 1900-04 28-29 30-31, Suffolk Prem. Cup(5) 66-67 71-72 74-75 78-80, Suffolk Snr Cup(10) 02-03 22-24 25-26 31-32 35-36 46-49 55-56, E Anglian Cup(10), FA Cup 1st Rd 26-27 38-39 66-67 77-78, Anglian Comb. (Reserves) 77-78 79-80 (Lg Cup 76-77), E Anglian Lg (Reserves) 57-58 63-64.

MARCH TOWN UNITED

Chairman: Geoff Allen **President:** D Wilkinson **Manager:** Tony Godden.
Secretary: C R Woodcock, 24 Grounds Avenue, March, Cambs PE15 9BG (0354 54817).
Ground: GER Sports Ground, Robin Goodfellows Lane, March (0354 53073).
Directions: 5 mins from town centre, 10 mins from BR station.
Seats: 500 **Cover:** 2,000 **Capacity:** 4,000 **Floodlights:** Yes **Founded:** 1885.
Club colours: Yellow/blue **Change colours:** Blue & black stripes/white.
Previous Ground: The Avenue (prior to 1946). **Nickname:** Hares
Previous Leagues: Peterborough/ Isle of Ely/ Utd Co's 48-54.
Midweek Matches: Tuesday **Record Gate:** 7,500 v King's Lynn, FA Cup 1956.
Clubhouse: On ground, seating 150. **Programme:** 30p **Prog. Editor:** S Snell c/o Secretary
Matchday food & drink: Tea, coffee, cold drinks, soup, sandwiches, rolls.
Local Newspapers: Cambs Times, Fenland Advertiser, Peterborough Evening Telegraph.
Honours: Eastern Co's Lg 87-88 (Lg Cup 60-61), Utd Co's Lg 53-64, FA Cup 1st Rd 53-54 (lost to Brentford) 77-78 (to Swindon), Cambs Invitation Cup 54-55, East Anglian Cup 53-54(jt with Barking).

NEWMARKET TOWN

Chairman: K Sheppard **President:** M J Nicholas **Manager:** David Pinkowski.
Secretary: Mr Eddie Leafhead, 56 Churchill Court, Rowley Drive, Newmarket CB8 0JZ (0638 669503).
Ground: Cricketfield Road, off New Cheveley Road, Newmarket (0638 663637).
Directions: 400 yds from Newmarket (BR) - turn right into Green Road, right at crossroads New Cheveley Road - ground at top on left.
Seats: 200 **Cover:** 150 **Capacity:** 3,000 **Floodlights:** Yes **Founded:** 1877.
Colours: Yellow/navy/blue **Change:** Red/black/red **Nickname:** Jockeys.
Previous Name: Newmarket FC. **Prev. Grounds:** The Severals 1877-78/ Sefton Lodge 1878-85
Prev. Lges: Bury Snr/ Ipswich Snr/ Essex & Suffolk Border/ Utd Co's 34-37/ Eastern Co's 37-52.
Record Attendance: 2,701 v Abbey Utd (now Cambridge Utd), FA Cup 1st Qualifying Rd 1/10/49.
Best F.A. Cup year: 4th Qualifying Rd 92-93 (lost 0-2 at home to Hayes).
Midweek Matches: Tuesday **Clubhouse details:** Matchdays only.
Programme: 30p **Programme Editor:** G Eales.
Matchday food & drink: Tea, coffee, cold drinks, confectionary, burgers, hotdogs, soup, sandwiches, rolls.
Players progressing to the Football League: Mick Lambert (Ipswich), M Wright (Northampton), G Tweed (Coventry), R Fuller (Charlton).
Honours: Suffolk Snr Cup 34-35 93-94, Cambs Invitation Cup 58-59, Cambs Challenge Cup 21-22 26-27, Cambs Snr Lg, 19-20, Ipswich Snr Lg 30-31 31-32 32-33 33-34, Peterborough Lg 57-58.

SOHAM TOWN RANGERS

Chairman: C J Murfitt **President:** J Mann
Secretary: Wendy Gammon, 32 Broad Piece, Soham, Cambs CB7 5EL (0353 722139).
Manager: Andrew Parker **Asst Manager:** Richard Goodjohn **Coach:** Mick Drury
Ground: Julius Martins Lane, Soham, Cambs (0353 720732).
Directions: A142 between Newmarket and Ely - Julius Martins Lane.
Seats: 200 **Cover:** 1,500 **Capacity:** 2,000 **Floodlights:** Yes **Founded:** 1947.
Colours: Green/white **Change colours:** Blue/yellow/black **Nickname:** Town or Rangers.
Previous Lges: Peterborough & Dist. **Record Gate:** 3,000 v Pegasus, FA Amateur Cup 1963.
Sponsors: CJ Murfitt/ N & C Glass **Previous Ground:** Soham Rangers: Brook Street 1919-47.
Reserves' Lge: Cambs Prem. B. **Previous Names:** Soham Town and Soham Rgrs merged in 1947.
Programme: With admission **Programme Editor:** Graham Eley.
Midweek Matchday: Wednesday **Clubhouse:** General bar, Stud Bar, Lounge Bar.
Local Newspapers: Ely Standard, Newmarket Journal, Cambridge Evening News.
Captain 93-94: Phil Hubbard **Top Scorer & Player of the Year 93-94:** Darren Theobald.
Hons: Eastern Co's Lg Div 1 R-up 92-93, P'boro. Lg(3), *6-0 win v renowned Pegasus in '63 Amtr Cup.*

STOWMARKET TOWN

Chairman: John Kerry **Vice-Chairman:** Peter Banham **President:** Ron Crascall
Secretary: Andy Horrex, 29 Windermere Rd, Stowmarket, Suffolk (0449 674184).
Manager: Trevor Wardlaw **Assistant Manager:** Paul Davis.
Physio: John Chandler **Commercial Manager:** Colin Davies.
Ground: Green Meadows Stadium, Bury Road, Stowmarket (0449 612533).
Directions: About 800 yds from Stowmarket BR station - turn right at 1st lights and head out of town over r'bout into Bury Road - ground on right.
Seats: 200 **Cover:** 450 **Capacity:** 2,000 **Floodlights:** Yes **Founded:** 1883.
Colours: Old gold & black **Change colours:** Red & black **Nickname:** Stow
Midweek Matches: Wednesday **Reserves' Lge:** Essex & Suffolk Border **Metal Badges:** Yes.
Programme: 20 pages, 30p **Programme Editor:** Peter & Mark Banham (0449 676506).
Club Shop: Open at all 1st team games selling progs (Lge & non-Lge), metal badges, replica shirts, scarves, key fobs, car stickers, sweat-shirts, club jumpers. Contact John Gillingham, 23 Windermere Rd, Stowmarket IP14 1LD (0449 674507).
Previous Leagues: Ipswich & Dist./ Essex & Suffolk Border 25-52.
Previous Grounds: The Cricket Meadow, where the club played for 101 years up to the start of 84-84 season.
Record Gate: 1,200 v Ipswich Town, friendly July 1994. At Cricket Meadow: 3,800 v Romford, FA Amtr Cup 1st Rd 15/12/51.
Previous Names: Stowupland Corinthians/ Stowmarket Corinthians/ Stowmarket FC
Local Press: East Anglian, Bury Free Press
Clubhouse: Bar open 7pm onwards Mon-Fri, and at weekend lunchtimes.
Matchday food & drink: Tea, coffee, cold drinks, confectionary, hotdogs, burgers, soup, sandwiches, rolls, ice cream, cream cakes.
Players progressing to Football League: Craig Oldfield (Colchester), Les Tibbott, Ted Phillips & Brian Klug (Ipswich).
Captain 93-94: Dave King **P.o.Y 93-94:** Marvin Hall **Top Scorer 93-94:** John Wilcock
Honours: Eastern Co's Lg R-up 91-92, Suffolk Premier Cup(4), Suffolk Snr Cup(10), Suffolk Jnr Cup.

SUDBURY WANDERERS

Chairman: N Smith **President:** **Manager:** Mick Mills.
Secretary: Brian Tatum, 4 Beaconsfield Close, Sudbury, Suffolk CO10 6JR (0787 375840).
Ground: Brundon Lane, Sudbury, Suffolk (0787 376213).
Directions: From Sudbury centre follow Halstead/Chelmsford signs for about 1 mile. Take 1st right after railway bridge at foot of steep hill, and 1st right after sharp lefthand bend.
Seats: 200 **Cover:** 150 **Capacity:** 2,500 **Floodlights:** Yes **Founded:** 1958
Midweek Matchday: Tuesday **Prog.:** With entry **Colours:** Yellow
Nickname: Wanderers
Record Attendance: 248 v Woodbridge Town, Jewson Eastern Counties League Division One 20/4/93.
Clubhouse: Matchdays/ training nights. **Matchday food & drink:** Hot & cold drinks, confectionary.
Hons: Eastern Counties League Div 1 92-93, Ess. & Suff. Border League(2) 89-91 (Runners-up 88-89), Suffolk Snr Cup 90-91.

TIPTREE UNITED

Chairman: Frederick Byles **President:** Len Foakes **Manager:** Steve Sutton.
Secretary/Press Officer: Peter G Fidge, 77 Chelmer Road, Chelmsford, Essex CM2 6AA (0245 353667).
Ground: Chapel Road, Tiptree, Essex (0621 815213).
Directions: Enter town on B1023 - Chapel Road is left at second crossroads, ground 200yds on left. 3 miles from Kelverdon (BR). Served by Eastern National Colchester to Maldon bus.
Seats: 150 **Cover:** 300 **Capacity:** 2,500 **Floodlights:** Yes **Founded:** 1933.
Club colours: All red **Change colours:** All white. **Nickname:** Strawberries.
Midweek Matchday: Tuesday. **Previous Lges:** Essex & Suffolk Border/ Essex Snr 78-84
Record Attendance: 1,210 v Spurs, floodlight inauguration Dec 1990.
Programme: 30 pages, 30p **Programme Editor:** Secretary
Sponsors: S Smith (Transport) **Reserves' Lge:** Essex & Herts Comb. **Club Shop:** No.
Local Newspapers: Colchester Evening Gazette, Essex County Standard.
Clubhouse details: Large bar, two snooker tables, pool, darts, netball, badminton, pigeon club, bingo. Dance hall seats 180, small hall seats 60. Open daily 7-11pm (all day Fri & Sat) and noon-2.30, 7-10.30 Sun.
Captain 93-94: Gary Nash **Top Scorer 93-94:** Lee Sonnex **P.o.Y. 93-94:** R Willsher.
Honours: Essex Snr Tphy 80-81, Eastern Counties League 81-82 (League Cup 81-82 84-85), Essex Snr League Runners-up 75-76 77-78, Harwich Charity Cup(4).

WATTON UNITED

Chairman: Dick Jessup **Vice-Chairman:** Phil Scott **President:** Malcolm Warner.
Secretary: Tim Warner, 9 Spinney Close, Beech Rd, Beetley, Dereham, Norfolk NR20 4TB (0362 860016).
Manager: Chris Watts/ Steve Bunting **Physio:** M Kay.
Commercial Manager: Committee **Press Officer:** R Wordon
Ground: Dereham Road, Watton, Norfolk (0953 881281).
Directions: On A1075 towards Dereham about half a mile from junction with B1108.
Seats: 50 **Cover:** 150 **Capacity:** 2,000 **Floodlights:** Yes **Founded:** 1888.
Club colours: All white **Change colours:** Green/black/green **Nickname:** Brecklanders.
Midweek Matchday: Tuesday. **Previous Lges:** East Anglian/ Anglian Combination.
Club Sponsors: Style Windows **Record Gate:** 1,200 v Norwich City, floodlight inauguration 1985.
Programme: 25p **Programme Editor:** Robin Wordon **Club Shop:** No.
Clubhouse: Watton 881281. **Reserve Team's League:** Anglian Combination.
Matchday food & drink: Tea, coffee, cold drinks, confectionary, burgers, soup, sandwiches, rolls.
Players progressing to Football League: Chris Watts (Norwich), Robert Taylor (Leyton Orient, Brentford).
Captain: Tim Warner **P.o.Y. 93-94:** Mark Bond **Top Scorer 93-94:** Mark Brockwell 21
Honours: Anglian Combination 66-67 67-68 85-86 (League Cup 66-67 69-70).

WISBECH TOWN

Chairman: M E Davis **President:** J W A Chilvers **Vice Chairman:** A Buchan.
Secretary: M E Davis, Ely House, 158 Lynn Rd, Wisbech, Cambs PE13 3EB (0945 583567).
Manager: J Gallagher/ K Rudd **Newsline:** 0898 446 887.
Ground: Fenland Park, Lerowe Road, Wisbech, Cambs (0945 584176).
Directions: On Lerowe Road, a right turn off the A47 Lynn Road. Twenty minutes walk from town centre. Irregular bus services to Wisbech from Peterborough or March.
Seats: 258 **Cover:** 3,000 **Capacity:** 7,500 **Floodlights:** Yes **Founded:** 1920.
Club colours: Red/white **Change colours:** Blue/white **Nickname:** Fenmen.
Previous Lges: Peterborough/ Utd Counties 35-50/ Eastern Counties 50-52/ Midland 52-58/ Southern 58-70.
Previous Grounds: Wisbech Park 20-21/ Waisoken Rectory 21-22/ Harecroft Road 22-47.
Record Attendance: 8,004 v Peterborough United, Midland League 25/8/57. **Metal Badges:** Yes.
Midweek Matchday: Tuesday. **Clubhouse:** Open every day **Pennants:** Yes.
Programme: 36 pages, 40p **Programme Editor:** Secretary **Club Shop:** Yes.
Matchday food & drink: Tea, coffee, cold drinks, confectionary, burgers, hotdogs, soup, sandwiches, rolls.
Players progressing to Football League: Chris Watts and Robert Taylor (both Norwich City).
Honours: FA Cup 2nd Rd 57-58 (1st Rd(5) 45-46 58-60 64-66), FA Vase SF 84-85 85-86, Southern League Div 1 61-62, Utd Counties League(4) 46-48 49-50 61-62(reserves)(Runners-up 48-49, League Cup 35-36 (Runners-up 46-47)), Midland League Runners-up 57-58, Eastern Counties League 71-72 76-77 90-91 (Runners-up 70-71 73-74 83-84 92-93, League Cup 50-51 70-71 71-72 (Runners-up 73-74 76-77 86-87), Cambs Invitation Cup(8) 52-53 55-56 57-58 74-76 81-83 91-92, East Anglian Cup 87-88 (Runners-up 40-41 48-49), Peterborough League 24-25 27-28 28-29 31-32 32-33, Peterborough Snr Cup 32-33 76-77 89-90.

WOODBRIDGE TOWN

Chairman: K Dixon **President:** J Coates
Secretary: Ralph Coxall, 5 Orchard Close, Woodbridge, Suffolk IP12 1LD (0394 387839).
Manager: Dave Simmons **Assistant Manager:** Neil Thatcher.
Press Officer: Mick Banthorpe **Commercial Manager:** Ivan Rattle.
Ground: Notcutts Park, Seckford Hall Road, Woodbridge, Suffolk (0394 385308).
Directions: Turning into Woodbridge off last r'bout from Lowestoft, or 1st r'bout from Ipswich. Take 1st turning left and 1st left again. Drive to ground at end of road on left.
Seats: 50 **Cover:** 200 **Capacity:** Unknown **Floodlights:** Yes **Founded:** 1885.
Colours: Black & white stripes/white/white **Change colours:** Blue/white/blue.
Previous Ground: Kingston PF **Nickname:** The Bridge or Woodpeckers.
Midweek Matches: Wednesday **Previous Leagues:** Suffolk & Ipswich
Reserves' League: Suff. & Ipswich **Record Gate:** 3,000 v Arsenal, floodlight opener 2/10/90.
Sponsors: Posh Windows & Doors **Local Newspapers:** East Anglian Daily Times.
Programme: 36 pages, 20p **Programme Editor:** K Dixon
Clubhouse details: Visitors bar, lounge bar, function hall.
Matchday food & drink: Tea, coffee, cold drinks, confectionary, hotdogs, soup, burgers, sandwiches, rolls. Also small cooked meals after match.
Captain 93-94: Simon Fryatt **Top Scorer 93-94:** David Hubbick.
Honours: Suffolk Senior Cup(4), Eastern Counties Lg Cup 93-94.

WROXHAM

Chairman: T Jarrett **President:** L King
Secretary/Press Officer: Chris Green, 24 Keys Drive, Wroxham, Norfolk NR12 8SS (0603 783936).
Manager: Bruce Cunningham **Asst Manager:** Keith Robson **Coach:** John Waters.
Physio: G Christmas **Commercial Manager:** Tom Jarrett.
Ground: Trafford Park, Wroxham, Norfolk (0603 783583).
Directions: Arriving from Norwich turn left at Castle PH and keep left to ground. Two and a half miles from Hoveton (BR). Buses 722, 724 and 717.
Seats: 50 **Cover:** 250 **Capacity:** 2,500 **Floodlights:** Yes **Founded:** 1892.
Club colours: Blue/white **Change colours:** Jade/black. **Nickname:** Yachtsmen.
Midweek Matchday: Tuesday. **Reserves' Lge:** Anglian Comb. **Club Shop:** No.
Programme: 20 pages with entry **Programme Editor:** Ray Bayles (0603 403555).
Previous Leagues: Norwich City/ East Anglian/ Norwich & Dist./ Anglian Comb. 64-88.
Previous Grounds: Norwich Road/ The Avenue/ Keys Hill (all pre-1947).
Record Attendance: 1,011 v Wisbech Town, Eastern Counties League Premier Division 16/3/93.
Record win: 15-2 v Thetford Town (H), Eastern Counties League Premier Division 17/1/92.
Record defeat: 1-24 v Blofield (A), Norwich & District League, early 1960s.
Players progressing to Football League: Matthew Metcalf (Brentford) 1993.
Local Newspapers: North Norfolk, Eastern Football (Norwich 28311).
Clubhouse details: Bar, pool, darts, carpet bowls etc.
Matchday food & drink: Tea, coffee. cold drinks, confectionary, burgers, hotdogs, soup, sandwiches, rolls.
Club record scorer: Matthew Metcalf **Club record appearances:** Mark Halsey.
Captain 93-94: Stu Larter **P.o.Y. 93-94:** Adrian Harris **Top Scorer 93-94:** Scott Snowling
Honours: Eastern Co's Lg 91-92 92-93 93-94 (Lg Cup 92-93 (R-up 90-91), Div 1 88-89), Norfolk Snr Cup 92-93, Anglian Combination (5)(Lg Cup(6)).

DIVISION ONE CLUBS 1994-95

BRANTHAM ATHLETIC

Chairman: Alan Clarke **President:** D White **Manager:** Graham Warren.
Secretary: Dave Baldwin, 20 Brooklands Road, Brantham, Essex CO11 1RP (0206 392757).
Ground: B.A.S. Club, New Village, Brantham, Manningtree, Essex (0206 392506).
Directions: Leave A12 at B1070 junction signposted Manningtree. Ground just off A137.
Seats: 100 **Cover:** 200 **Capacity:** 1,500 **Floodlights:** Yes **Founded:** 1887.
Colours: Blue & white **Change colours:** Red & black **Pennants:** Yes.
Midweek Matches: Wednesday **Previous League:** Essex & Suffolk Border.
Programme: 24 pages, 25p **Record Gate:** 1,500 v VS Rugby, FA Vase 5th Rd 82-83.
Clubhouse details: Open daily, licensing hours. 2 bars, dancing, snooker, pool, refreshments.
Matchday food & drink: Tea, coffee, cold drinks, confectionary, burgers(after), chips(after), soup, rolls.
Honours: Suffolk Senior Cup, Essex Border Lg(4), Essex & Suffolk Border League Cup(2), Suffolk Premier Cup, Jewson Sportsmanship Award 88-89.

BRIGHTLINGSEA UNITED

Chairman: Graham Steady **Manager:** Frank Thompson.
Secretary: H J Beere, 108 Regent Road, Brighlingsea, Essex CO7 0NZ (0206 303122).
Ground: North Road, Brightlingsea, Essex (0206 304199).
Directions: B1027 Colchester-Clacton, B1029 from Thorrington Cross - follow Church Road into town, left into Spring Road, left into Church Road. Nearest station; Colchester then bus 78 to Brighlingsea.
Seats: 50 **Cover:** 250 **Capacity:** 2,000 **Floodlights:** Yes **Club Shop:** Yes.
Colours: Red/white **Change colours:** All blue **Nickname:** Oystermen.
Previous Leagues: Tendring Hundred, Essex & Suffolk Border, Essex Senior 1972-90.
Midweek Matches: Wednesday **Record Gate:** 1,200 v Colchester, friendly 68-69.
Programme: 24 pages, 30p **Prog. Editor:** M Cole (0206 304430) **Founded:** 1887
Clubhouse details: Open matchadays and all evenings bar Sunday.
Matchday food & drink: Tea, coffee, cold drinks, confectionary, hotdogs, sandwiches, rolls.
Local Newspapers: Essex County Standard, Evening Gazette.
Honours: Essex Snr Lg 88-89 89-90 (Harry Fisher Mem. Tphy 89-90 (R-up 88-89), Lg Cup R-up 78-79), Eastern Co's Lg Div 1 R-up 90-91, Essex & Suffolk Border Lg Prem. Div Cup 71-72, Harwich Charity Cup 87-88, Worthington Evans Cup 76-77 77-78 78-79.

BURY TOWN RES. *(see page 392)* CAMBRIDGE CITY RES. *(see page 322)*

CLACTON TOWN

Chairman: Fred Lawrence **President:** R Manning **Manager:** Jimmy Minter/Steve Wright.
Secretary: George Betts, 15 Hill Rd, Gt Clacton, Essex CO15 4EN (0255 474427).
Ground: The Rushgreen Bowl, Rushgreen Road, Clacton-on-Sea (0255 432590).
Directions: A133 to Clacton, at r'bout right into St Johns Rd, 4th left Cloes Lane, 3rd right Rushgreen Rd, ground approximately half mile on right. From B1027 take main Jaywick turn off (Jaywick Lane), then 2nd left (after about a mile) into Rushgreen Rd. Ground 400 yds. 2 miles from Clacton (BR), buses 3, 5 or 5a to Coopers Lane/Rushgreen Rd.
Seats: 200 **Cover:** Yes **Capacity:** 2,500 **Floodlights:** Yes **Founded:** 1892.
Colours: Royal blue **Change colours:** All red **Club Shop:** Yes
Previous Grounds: Clacton Stadium, Old Road 06-87/ Gainsford Av (temp). **Metal Badges:** Yes.
Midweek Matches: Tuesday **Pennants:** Yes.
Record Attendance: 3,505 v Romford, FA Cup 1st Qualifying Rd 1952 (at Old Road).
Previous Leagues: Eastern Co's 35-37 38-58/ Southern 58-64.
Programme: 40 pages, 30p **Local Paper:** Clacton Gazette **Nickname:** Seasiders.
Clubhouse details: Licensed club. Open 7-11pm Mon-Sat, 12-3pm Sat-Sun.
Matchday food & drink: Tea, coffee, cold drinks, confectionary, burgers, hotdogs, soup, rolls.
Players progressing to Football League: Vivian Woodward (Spurs, Chelsea, England), Mick Everitt (Arsenal, Northampton), Christian McLean (Bristol Rovers).
Captain 93-94: Jimmy Minter
Honours: Southern Lg Div 1 59-60, Eastern Co's Lg R-up 36-37 53-54 64-65 74-75 (Lg Cup 73-74), East Anglian Cup 53-54, Worthington Evans Cup 56-57 67-68 74-75, FA Cup 1st Rd (v Southend) 60-61.

DOWNHAM TOWN

Chairman: John Fysh **President:** T G Barker **Manager:** Kevin Bunn.
Secretary: B Connor, 02, Bungalow, Windsor Street, Downham Market, Norfolk PE38 9EG (0366 383179).
Ground: Lynn Road, Downham Market, Norfolk (0366 388424).
Directions: One and a quarter miles from Downham Market (BR) - continue to town clock, turn left and ground is three quarters of a mile down Lynn Road.
Seats: None **Cover:** Yes **Capacity:** 1,000 **Floodlights:** Yes **Founded:** 1881.
Colours: Red & white **Change colours:** Yellow/navy **Nickname:** Town
Midweek Matches: Tuesday **Previous Leagues:** Peterborough
Record Attendance: 292 v Diss Town, Jewson League Division One 1991/92.
Clubhouse: Open matchdays **Programme:** By Barnes Promotions, with entry
Matchday food & drink: Tea, coffee, cold drinks, confectionary, hotdogs, burgers, soup, sandwiches, rolls.
Honours: P'boro Lg(5) 62-63 73-74 78-79 86-88, Norfolk Senior Cup 63-64 65-66 (R-up(3) 66-69).

ELY CITY

Chairman: Roger Pauley **President:** Doug Unwin **Manager:** Steve Clark.
Secretary: Derek Oakey, 37 Fordham Road, Soham, Nr Ely, Cambs CB7 5AH (0353 722141).
Ground: Unwin Sports Ground, Downham Road (0353 662035).
Directions: A10 Ely by-pass turn off for Downham. 3 miles (approx) from Ely (BR).
Seats: 150 **Cover:** 350 **Capacity:** 1,500 **Floodlights:** Yes **Founded:** 1885
Colours: All red **Change colours:** Sky/royal **Nickname:** Robins **Metal Badges:** Yes.
Previous Lges: Peterborough/ Central Alliance 58-60. **Midweek Matches:** Tuesday
Record Gate: 260 v Soham, Eastern Co's Lg Div 1, 12/4/93. *At old ground: 4,260 v Torquay, FA Cup 56-57*
Clubhouse details: Open matchdays **Local Press:** Ely Standard (0353 667831). **Programme:** 20p
Matchday food & drink: Tea, coffee, cold drinks, confectionary, hotdogs, burgers, sandwiches, rolls.
Hons: Cambs Snr Cup 47-48, Eastern Co's Lg R-up 69-70 (Lg Cup 79-80), FA Cup 1st Rd 56-56 (2-6 v Torquay).

GORLESTON

Chairman: A Norton **President:** J Jones **Manager:** Paul Tong.
Secretary: Kevin Antcliffe, 62 Englands Lane, Gorleston, Gt Yarmouth, Norfolk NR31 6BE (0493 668475).
Ground: Emerald Park, Woodfarm Lane, Gorleston, Great Yarmouth (0493 602802).
Directions: On Magdalen Estate - follow signs to Crematorium, turn left and follow road to ground. Five and a half miles from Great Yarmouth Vauxhall (BR).
Seats: 100 **Cover:** 5,000 **Capacity:** 5,000 **Floodlights:** Yes **Founded:** 1884.
Colours: Green & white **Change colours:** All white. **Nickname:** Greens.
Prev. Ground: Recreation Ground. **Prev. Leagues:** Norfolk & Suffolk/ Anglian Comb.
Midweek Matchday: Tuesday. **Record Gate:** 4,473 v Orient, FA Cup 1st Rd 29/11/51.
Prog.: 30p (Ed.: D Benson) **Clubhouse:** Bar, colour TV, pool table, darts, snacks.
Matchday food & drink: Tea, coffee, cold drinks, confectionary, burgers, hotdogs, soup, rolls.
Past players progressing to the Football League: Billy Bailey (Wolves & England), Dave Stringer (Norwich), R Carter (Aston Villa), D Carter (Man City), A Brown (Charlton, S Morgan (Cambridge).
Honours: Eastern Co's Lg 52-53 72-73 79-80 80-81 (R-up 82-83, Lg Cup 55-56 (R-up 91-92)), Norf. Snr Cup(13)(R-up(24)), Anglian Comb. 68-69, Norf. & Suf. Lg(7) 20-21 25-26 29-30 31-35, E Anglian Lg 52-53(res.).

IPSWICH WANDERERS

Chairman: J Barker **President:** **Manager:** Brian Swift.
Secretary: Keith Bassett, 15 Heathercroft Road, Ipswich, Suffolk IP1 6QG (0473 748458).
Ground: Humberdoucey Road, Ipswich, Suffolk (0473 728581).
Directions: A12 north of Ipswich Rushmere Golf Club. Players Road into Humberdovey Lane.
Seats: None **Cover:** Yes **Capacity:** 2,000 **Floodlights:** Yes **Founded:** 1983.
Colours: Blue/blue/white **Change colours:** Red & black/red/red.
Nickname: Wanderers. **Club Sponsors:** Car Glass & Trim.
Previous Leagues: Little David Sunday **Previous Names:** Loadwell Ipswich.
Midweek Matches: Wednesday **Record Gate:** 335 v Woodbridge, ECL Div 1 4/4/94.
Programme: With admission **Clubhouse details:** Bar, refreshments.
Matchday food & drink: Tea, coffee, cold drinks, confectionary, burgers, hotdogs, sandwiches, rolls.
Captain 93-94: G Hart **Local Press:** East Anglian Daily Times, Evening Star.
Top Scorer 93-94: S Breeze **Player of the Year 93-94:** J Clarke.

KING'S LYNN RESERVES *(see page 375 for full details)*

LONG SUTTON ATHLETIC

Chairman: P Batterham **Vice-Chairman:** P Childs **President:** V W Day
Secretary: Simon Caney, 6 The Paddocks, Kingsgate, Geoney, Lincs.
Manager: J Lowery.
Ground: London Road, Long Sutton, Spalding, Lincs (0406 364208).
Directions: On left hand side of old A17 entering village from Wisbech or King's Lynn.
Seats: None **Cover:** 100 **Capacity:** 1,000 **Floodlights:** Yes **Founded:** 1922.
Colours: Black & white stripes/black **Change colours:** Green/yellow/green **Nickname:** Magpies
Previous League: Peterborough. **Prev. Name:** Long Sutton Town 1922-55. **Programme:** 25p
Record Gate: 537 v Grimsby, friendly. **Clubhouse:** Open matchdays. Licensed bar. Hot food.
Matchday food & drink: Tea, coffee, cold drinks, pies, pasties, sandwiches.
Midweek Matchday: Tuesday. **Club Sponsors:** D A Rollins Electrical.
Local Press: Wisbech Standard, Spalding Guardian, Lincs Free Press.
Top Scorer 93-94: Nicky Scott **Club record scorer:** Michael Wayman.
Captain 93-94: Shaun Flatt **Player of the Year 93-94:** Martin Sharman.
Honours: Lincs Junior Cup 85-86 (R-up 87-88), Lincs 'B' Snr Cup 88-89, TSLB Challenge Cup 88-89.

MILDENHALL TOWN

Chairman: B Brigden **President:** J E Butcher **Manager:** Mark Goldsack.
Secretary: B W Hensby, 14 Sanderling Close, Mildenhall, Suffolk IP28 7LF (0638 715772).
Ground: Recreation Way, Mildenhall, Suffolk (0638 713449).
Directions: Next to swimming pool/car, quarter of a mile from town centre.
Seats: None **Capacity:** 2,000 **Midweek Matchday:** Tuesday **Founded:** 1890.
Club colours: Amber/black **Change colours:** All white **Nickname:** Town or yellows.
Previous Leagues: Bury & District/ Cambs Lg 2B, 1B & Premier.
Record Attendance: 350 v Norwich City, friendly 22/7/89.
Programme: Free with admission **Editor:** D Isaac **Clubhouse:** Open matchdays & functions.
Matchday food & drink: Tea, coffee, cold drinks, confectionary, sandwiches, rolls.
Local Newspapers: Bury Free Press, Newmarket Journal, Cambridge Evening News.
Honours: Suffolk Junior Cup 1899-1900.

NORWICH UNITED

Chairman: John Hilditch **Vice-Chairman:** J Cubitt **President:** Michael Miles
Secretary: M G Alexander, The Orchard, High Street, Mundesley, Norfolk (0263 721943).
Manager: Peter Self **Comm. Manager:** J Cubitt **Physio:** Mike Chapman.
Ground: Plantation Road, Blofield, Norwich, Norfolk NR13 4PL (0603 716963).
Directions: Half a mile from Blofield village - coming from Norwich on Yarmouth Road turn left in Blofield at Kings Head pub and follow to Plantation Rd (ground on right after bridge over bypass). Half-hour walk Brundall BR (Norwich-Yarmouth line).
Seats: 100 **Cover:** 1,000 **Capacity:** 3,000 **Floodlights:** Yes **Founded:** 1903.
Club colours: Yellow & blue **Change colours:** All red **Metal Badges:** Yes
Programme: 24 pages, 50p **Programme Editor:** Secretary **Pennants:** Yes
Midweek Matches: Tuesday **Previous Leagues** Anglian Comb. **Nickname:** Planters.
Previous Ground: Gothic Club, Heartsease Lane, Norwich (until end of 90-91).
Record Attendance: 401 v Wroxham, League match, 2/10/91.
Clubhouse details: All facilities. **Local Newspaper:** Eastern Counties Newspapers.
Matchday food & drink: Tea, coffee, cold drinks, confectionary, hotdogs, burgers, soup, sandwiches, rolls.
Club record scorer: Not known **Club record appearances:** Tim Sayer.
Captain 93-94: Tim Sayer **Top Scorer 93-94:** Andy Ellis **P.o.Y. 93-94:** TBA
Honours: Eastern Co's Lg Div 1 90-91 (R-up 89-89, Lg Cup 91-92), Anglian Combination 88-89.

SOMERSHAM TOWN

Chairman: David Hardy **Vice-Chairman:** Ian Camplejohn **President:** Jack Marjason
Secretary: John Lyon, 'Molineux' 1 Asplins Avenue, Needingworth, Huntingdon PE17 3SX (0480 464411).
Manager: Norman Hudson **Coach:** Dave Lill **Physio:** Alan Magnus
Press Officer: Dave Hardy (0487 840441) **Commercial Mgr:** Norman Ward (0487 840181).
Ground: West End Ground, St Ives Road, Somersham, Cambs (0487 843384).
Directions: On A604 St Ives to Somersham on right as you enter town.
Seats: None **Cover:** 200 **Capacity:** 1,500 **Floodlights:** Yes **Founded:** 1893.
Colours: All old gold**Change colours:** Sky/maroon/sky **Midweek matchday:** Tuesday.
Previous League: Peterborough & Dist. **Record Gate:** 538 v Norwich City, floodlight inauguration 19/11/91.
Programme: 76 pages, 30p **Programme Editor:** Dave Hardy (0487 840441)
Sponsors: T S Frozen Foods **Clubhouse:** Open Friday, Sat/Sun lunchtimes.
Nickname: Westenders **Reserve Team's League:** Kershaw Cambridgeshire Premier A.
Matchday food & drink: Tea, coffee, cold drinks, confectionary, rolls.
Local Newspapers: Hunts Post, Cambs News, Citizen Express, St Ives Weekly.
Captain & Top Scorer 93-94: Ian Boon **Record scorer & appearance-maker:** Terry Butcher
Player-of-the-Year 93-94: Ian Magnus and Ian Boon (joint).
Honours: Hunts Snr Cup 72-73 93-94, Peterboro Snr Cup 84-85, Hinchingbrooke Cup 53-54, Cambs Lg Premier B Div 93-94(reserves).

Right: *Loyal to the bitter end! Despite a shocking season, propping up the rest of the Jewson League, Thetford Town supporters still find something to shout about.*
Photo - Martin Wray.

STANWAY ROVERS

Chairman: Mr D J Clark **President:** Colin Henson.
Secretary: Richard Degville, 5 Old Heath Road, Colchester, Essex CO1 2ES (0206 792599).
Manager: Peter Barlow **Asst Manager:** Dave Reynolds **Physio:** John Chandler
Ground: 'Hawthorns', New Farm Road, Stanway, Colchester, Essex (0206 578187).
Directions: Take turn off marked Stanway off A12. Turn right and go over flyover to Tollgate r'bout, 1st right into Villa Rd, after 25 yards turn left into Church Rd, 200 yards on left into New Farm Rd, ground 400 yards on left. Nearest BR station is Colchester North.
Seats: None **Cover:** 200 **Capacity:** 1,500 **Floodlights:** Yes **Founded:**
Colours: Yellow/black/black **Change colours:** Green/white/red **Nickname:** Rovers.
Reserves' Lge: Essex & Suff. Border **Record Gate:** 156 v Hadleigh, ECL Division One 10/7/94.
Club Shop: Club pennants, ties sold **Prev. Lges:** Colchester & E Essex/ Essex & Suff. Border (pre-1992).
Previous Ground: Stanway Secondary School, Winstree Road (20 years).
Programme: 12 pages, 50p **Programme Editor:** Secretary
Midweek matchday: Tuesday. **Local Press:** Essex County Standard, Evening Gazette.
Sponsors: Collier & Catchpole/Tarmac Roadstone Ltd.
Record win: 8-1 v Swaffham Town (H), Eastern Counties League Division One 26/3/94.
Record defeat: 2-8 v West Bergholt (A), Essex & Suffolk Border League Premier Division, 1992.
Players progressing to Football League: Andy Farrell (Colchester, Burnley).
Clubhouse: 6.45-11pm evenings, noon-11pm Sats. Rolls, sandwiches, soup, tea, coffee etc available matchdays.
Captain 93-94: Ian Edwards **P.O.Y. 93-94:** Danny King **Top Scorer 93-94:** Wayne Bond
Honours: Essex Intermediate Cup R-up 89-90 90-91, Essex & Suffolk Border Lg R-up 91-92 (Div 1 86-87, Div 2 81-81 85-86), Essex Junior Cup R-up 74-75 (QF 73-74).

SUDBURY TOWN RESERVES *(see page 354 for full details)*

SWAFFHAM TOWN

Chairman: R Goldsmith **President:** **Manager:** Barry Cook.
Secretary: David Ward, 2 Princes Street, Swaffham, Norfolk PE37 7BX (0760 722516).
Ground: Shoemakers Lane, Swaffham, Norfolk (0760 722700).
Seats: None **Cover:** **Capacity:** 2,000 **Floodlights:** Yes **Founded:** 1892.
Colours: Black & white stripes/black/black. **Change:** Yellow/black/yellow.
Nickname: Pedlars
Midweek Matchay: Tuesday. **Previous Leagues:** Dereham, Anglian Combination
Record Attendance: 250 v Downham Town, Jewson Eastern Co's League Cup 3/9/91.
Clubhouse details: Open Tuesday, Thursday, Saturday & Sunday lunchtimes & evenings.
Matchday food & drink: Tea, coffee, cold drinks, confectionary, rolls (occasionally).
Programme: 36 pages, 30p **Hons:** Norfolk Snr Cup(2), Anglian Comb. 89-90 (Div 1 88-89).

THETFORD TOWN

Chairman: M Bailey **Vice-Chairman:** T Goban **Press Officer:** Mick Burgess.
Secretary: John Wordley, 4 Claxton Close, Thetford, Norfolk IP24 1BA (0842 762530).
Manager: John Dennis **Coach:** Stuart Williams **Comm. Mgr:** Ray Grant.
Ground: Mundford Road, Thetford, Norfolk (0842 766120).
Directions: Turn off bypass (A11) at A143 junction - ground 800yds towards Thetford.
Seats: 400 **Cover:** 400 **Capacity:** 2,000 **Floodlights:** Yes **Founded:** 1884.
Colours: Claret/blue **Change:** Sky & navy checks **Prev. Grnds:** None
Previous Leagues: Norfolk & Suffolk **Midweek Matches:** Tuesday **Club Shop:** No.
Reserves' Lge: Anglian Comb. **Local Press:** Thetford & Watton Times, Bury Free Press.
Programme: 48 pages, 30p **Programme Editor:** Graham Mills (0480 385425).
Club Sponsors: Ray Powell **Clubhouse details:** Bar, teas, refreshments, light meals.
Matchday food & drink: Tea, coffee, cold drinks, confectionary, hotdogs, burgers, sandwiches, rolls.
Record Gate: 394 v Diss Town, Norfolk Snr Cup 20/1/91.
Players progressing to Football League: Dick Scott (Norwich City, Cardiff City), Kevin Seggie (Leeds United), Simon Milton (Ipswich Town).
P.O.Y. 93-94: Marcus Bier **Captain & Top Scorer 93-94:** Clive Denniss.
Honours: Eastern Co's Lg R-up 89-90, Norfolk & Suffolk Lg 54-55, Norfolk Snr Senior Cup 47-48 90-91.

WARBOYS TOWN

Chairman: Trevor Chamberlain **President:** G C Bowd **Manager:** Robbie Cook.
Secretary: R O England, 39 High Street, Warboys, Huntingdon PE17 2TA (0487 822312).
Ground: Sports Field, Forge Way, off High Street, Warboys, Cambs (0487 823483).
Directions: Access through Forge Way, half way along south side of High Street.
Seats: None **Cover:** 200 **Capacity:** 2,000 **Floodlights:** Yes **Founded:** 1885.
Colours: Red/white **Change colours:** Blue & maroon/blue **Nickname:** Witches.
Midweek Matches: Tuesday
Previous Leagues: Peterborough & District 46-48 56-88/ Utd Co's 50-56/ Huntingdonshire 48-50.
Record Attendance: 500 v Ramsey Town, Hunts Senior Cup Semi Final.
Programme: 12 pages, 20p **Programme Editor:** M England
Local Newspaper: Hunts Post (0480 411481).
Clubhouse: Bar, lounge, function hall. Open every evening & Sunday lunchtime. Various entertainments.
Matchday food & drink: Tea, coffee, cold drinks, confectionary, sandwiches, rolls.
Past Players progressing to Football League: Alex Chamberlain (Ipswich, Everton, Colchester).
Honours: Utd Co's Lg Div 2 R-up 54-55, P'boro Lg R-up(2) 59-60 61-62, P'boro Snr Cup 63-64, Hunts Snr Cup 26-27 28-29 31-32 32-33 (R-up 92-93), Hunts Scott Gatty Cup 30-31. Reserves: Hunts Benevolent Cup 57-58, Hunts Junior Cup 24-25 27-28 52-53, Hunts Lower Junior Cup 75-76 77-78.

Warboys Town FC. Back Row (L/R): Mike Higgins, Simon Burton, Mark Cooper, Gary Hooke, Mike Matthews, Simon Mead, Stuart Trueblood. Front: James McCallum, Mark Nightingale, Andy Tuffs, Steve Phillips, Robert Sullivan. Photo - Martin Wray.

Thetford Town FC. Back Row (L/R): Stuart Williams (Asst Manager), Martin Freudi, Lee Brooks, Colin Grant, Chris Tucker, Clive Dennis, Chris Woodrow, Marcus Bier, John Dennis (Manager). Front: Neil Quincey, Chris Bray, Peter Smith, George Parmain, Mark Holsey, Sean Anger.

Photo - Martin Wray.

PARASOL COMBINED COUNTIES LEAGUE

FOUNDED: 1922 (as the Surrey Senior League)

FEEDER TO:
DIADORA LEAGUE

Chairman: Dennis Pollard

Hon. Secretary: A R Ford,
Pennings Cottage, Aldershot Rd,
Guiildford GU3 3AA (0483 67284)

PEPPARD REPEAT 1993 'DOUBLE'

The season started promisingly with twenty-one clubs in membership, the highest number ever and three more than in the previous season. However, as the League officers had feared, this number meant pressure on the number of fixtures and, coupled with the spell of bad weather, it resulted in fixtures continuing until June 1st. Problems also arose when it was discovered that Peppard Football Club's new pitch in Reading was under-size - they were forced to return to their former ground after strenuous efforts by Reading Borough Council failed to remedy the situation.

Despite all the upheaval, however, Peppard went on to win both the Premier Division and Reserve Section as they had done the previous season, their first in the League, but did even better this time by winning both the Premier and Reserve Section Challenge Cups and the League Vase. What was partcularly pleasing was that all the success was achieved whilst, at the same time, winning the award for the best disciplinary record in the League.

In outside competitions, Peppard reached the final of the Oxfordshire Senior Cup and the semi-final of the Intermediate Cup. Newcomers Eton Wick were also successful in retaining the Berks & Bucks County Senior Trophy.

At the end of the season, Frimley Green were relegated and replaced by Netherne, who have been promoted as champions of the Surrey County Premier League. Ditton have resigned and Virgina Water and Farleigh Rovers were not re-elected at the Annual General Meeting. All three of these clubs are likely to be competing in the Surrey League this coming season. As a result, the League now reverts to eighteen clubs and, with Ash United and Ashford Town hoping to have floodlights in operation very shortly, it is anticipated that there will be much less fixture congestion in the forthcoming season.

Dennis Pollard, Chairman

Peppard FC - Parasol Combined Counties League champions 1993-94. *Photo - Eric Marsh.*

PREM. DIV.	P	W	D	L	F	A	PTS
Peppard	40	35	2	3	128	33	107
Ashford Town	40	31	4	5	102	37	97
Eton Wick	40	20	9	11	97	57	69
Cranleigh	40	20	9	11	89	73	69
Chipstead	40	19	11	10	79	54	68
DCA Basingstoke	40	19	11	10	78	61	68
Ash United	40	18	9	13	84	72	63
Westfield	40	17	11	12	56	42	62
Virginia Water	40	18	7	15	74	68	61
Sandhurst Town	40	17	9	14	65	63	60
Cobham	40	15	7	18	69	70	52
Farleigh Rovers	40	12	13	15	72	77	49
Bedfont	40	10	16	14	47	47	46
Godalming & Gfd	40	11	13	16	50	62	46
Hartley Wintney	40	12	8	20	61	90	44
Viking Sports	40	11	8	21	58	77	41
Merstham	40	9	11	20	54	90	38
Farnham Town	40	10	8	22	47	87	38
Horley Town	40	10	6	24	54	105	36
Ditton	40	8	9	23	55	97	33
Frimley Green	40	3	9	28	40	107	18

RESERVE DIV.	P	W	D	L	F	A	PTS
Peppard Res.	38	31	2	5	117	29	95
Farleigh R. Res.	38	24	8	6	101	62	80
Ashford T. Res.	38	21	12	5	80	46	75
Cobham Res.	38	19	10	9	67	43	67
Eton Wick Res.	38	19	9	10	85	60	66
Viking S. Res.	38	18	8	12	88	63	62
Virginia Wtr Res.	38	18	8	12	65	59	62
Bedfont Res.	38	18	7	13	63	50	61
Ash Utd Res.	38	15	8	15	71	69	53
DCA B'stoke Res.	38	15	7	16	58	61	52
Merstham Res.	38	15	6	17	69	74	51
Hartley Win. Res.	38	14	9	15	65	77	51
Godalming Res.	38	12	9	17	56	62	45
Sandhurst T. Res.	38	12	7	19	57	77	43
Horley Town Res.	38	10	12	16	64	71	42
Ditton Res.	38	11	6	21	48	97	39
Westfield Res.	38	9	11	18	37	52	38
Cranleigh Res.	38	8	6	24	61	109	30
Frimley Gn Res.	38	6	7	25	34	82	25
Farnham T. Res.	38	6	6	26	38	81	24

PREMIER DIVISION RESULT CHART 1993-94

HOME TEAM	1	2	3	4	5	6	7	8	9	10	11	12	13	14	15	16	17	18	19	20	21
1. Ash United	*	0-3	0-3	3-1	2-1	3-1	2-2	5-1	2-4	4-2	2-1	3-0	3-0	1-0	5-0	7-3	2-5	2-3	3-1	0-0	0-0
2. Ashford T.(Mx)	4-2	*	0-0	3-1	2-0	3-2	1-2	1-1	1-3	2-0	2-0	6-2	1-0	1-0	6-0	2-1	5-0	2-1	3-1	1-0	1-0
3. Bedfont	3-0	0-1	*	2-0	2-2	1-3	2-3	0-0	1-1	2-2	1-1	1-0	0-1	3-3	0-1	1-1	0-1	0-2	1-1	0-1	0-2
4. Chipstead	1-1	0-2	1-0	*	4-5	2-3	1-3	2-2	2-1	2-1	4-0	3-1	3-0	5-1	3-0	1-0	1-0	2-1	1-0	3-1	1-0
5. Cobham	3-1	0-4	3-1	2-4	*	3-1	0-1	2-0	3-0	0-1	3-0	6-0	2-2	1-2	6-0	1-2	1-1	1-3	3-1	0-1	2-4
6. Cranleigh	2-2	0-4	2-2	0-4	1-1	*	1-1	3-2	2-2	0-2	5-0	2-0	1-0	5-1	3-0	6-1	2-6	1-5	3-0	2-4	3-2
7. DCA Basingstoke	1-3	1-3	2-1	2-1	2-2	1-2	*	3-0	2-2	5-3	4-3	1-1	3-2	3-0	3-0	2-2	2-4	0-2	3-1	5-2	0-3
8. Ditton	3-2	0-3	0-3	1-1	0-1	1-2	3-2	*	0-1	2-0	1-1	3-1	0-1	2-3	3-3	5-2	0-4	1-3	0-1	2-0	0-1
9. Eton Wick	0-2	0-2	1-2	1-1	8-1	2-3	3-1	3-1	*	5-2	4-0	1-0	2-2	7-2	11-1	2-1	0-1	3-1	1-0	1-3	2-0
10. Farleigh Rovers	6-2	3-2	1-1	1-1	0-0	0-4	1-2	2-2	4-4	*	3-0	W-L	3-1	2-0	2-1	0-0	2-4	3-2	1-4	2-4	2-2
11. Farnham Town	1-1	0-2	1-0	0-6	4-1	1-1	0-0	1-2	3-2	5-4	*	3-1	2-1	4-0	2-1	2-3	0-3	1-1	0-7	1-3	1-0
12. Frimley Green	1-2	1-7	1-1	2-3	0-1	1-6	1-3	3-3	1-3	0-3	1-5	*	2-2	1-4	3-2	1-3	0-5	2-4	1-1	1-1	3-1
13. Godalming & G.	1-1	2-2	4-0	0-0	1-2	0-2	0-0	3-2	2-1	1-1	3-0	1-1	*	0-4	1-0	2-0	0-5	1-0	6-1	0-0	0-0
14. Hartley Wintney	1-2	1-1	1-1	2-2	2-4	0-1	1-3	2-1	0-3	1-4	2-0	4-0	2-1	*	0-1	6-1	0-2	0-2	3-2	2-0	2-2
15. Horley Town	1-4	0-3	2-4	2-1	2-1	5-2	2-2	2-2	3-3	1-1	1-0	2-1	2-3	2-2	*	5-1	1-2	1-2	2-0	2-3	1-2
16. Merstham	1-3	1-4	0-1	2-2	3-2	2-2	1-2	1-4	0-0	2-2	1-0	1-2	1-0	1-1	3-0	*	0-5	3-3	3-3	2-2	0-1
17. Peppard	2-2	7-1	1-0	2-1	4-0	4-0	1-0	9-1	2-0	2-1	4-0	W-L	2-1	6-1	5-0	2-1	*	3-0	2-0	6-1	2-1
18. Sandhurst T.	1-3	0-4	2-2	0-1	2-1	1-1	1-5	W-L	0-1	2-2	0-0	1-1	2-2	2-2	3-1	2-1	3-2	*	2-0	1-2	2-0
19. Viking Sports	4-2	1-2	1-1	3-3	2-1	2-5	1-1	2-1	0-5	2-1	1-1	2-2	1-0	1-2	1-2	5-0	1-4	0-2	*	3-1	1-0
20. Virgina Water	2-2	2-4	0-2	2-2	0-1	1-3	2-0	2-1	2-3	0-0	4-3	2-1	6-1	6-1	3-1	0-1	1-6	8-1	2-0	*	3-0
21. Westfield	1-0	2-1	0-0	2-2	0-0	1-1	0-0	6-2	1-1	3-2	2-0	5-0	2-2	4-0	3-1	1-0	1-2	1-0	1-0	1-0	*

Chipstead's Mark Endacott gets a helping hand as his side push forward at home to Eton Wick.
Photo - Dennis Nicholson.

LEAGUE CHALLENGE CUP 1993-94

First Round

Ash United v Cobham	1-0	Ditton v Viking Sports	1-3*(aet)*
Eton Wick v Frimley Green	0-1	Farleigh Rovers v Horley Town	3-1
Sandhurst Town v Merstham	3-3,2-1		

Second Round

Ash United v Viking Sports	2-1	Cranleigh v Ashford Town (Middx)	3-5
Farleigh Rovers v Peppard	0-5	Godalming & Guildford v DCA Basingstoke	0-1
Hartley Wintney v Frimley Green	2-1	Sandhurst Town v Chipstead	0-3
Virginia Water v Farnham Town	4-1	Westfield v Bedfont	0-1

Quarter-Finals

Ash United v Bedfont	1-0*(aet)*	Ashford Town (Middx) v Chipstead	3-1
Hartley Wintney v Peppard	1-2	Virginia Water v DCA Basingstoke	2-2*(aet)*,1-0

Semi-Finals

Ashford Town (Middx) v Virginia Water	2-0	Peppard v Ash	1-0*(abandoned after 40 mins)*,3-2*(aet)*

Final *(at Woking FC)*: Peppard 2, Ashford Town (Middx) 1

The captains Peppard and Ashford pictured before the first of their two domestic final meetings.
Photo - Eric Marsh.

CHALLENGE VASE 1993-94

First Round

Bedfont v Ash United	3-1	Eton Wick v Virginia Water	5-2
Frimley Green v Hartley Wintney	1-1,0-3	Merstham v Westfield	1-2
Sandhurst Town v Godalming & Guildford	0-3		

Second Round

Chipstead v Bedfont	2-3	Cranleigh v Ditton	3-0
Farleigh Rovers v Ashford Town (Mx)	1-1,2-3	Farnham Town v DCA Basingstoke	1-3
Godalming & Guildford v Eton Wick	2-4*(aet)*	Hartley Wintney v Westfield	2-3
Peppard v Horley Town	4-2	Viking Sports v Cobham	0-3

Quarter-Finals

Bedfont v Westfield	2-1	Cranleigh v Cobham	1-3
DCA Basingstoke v Ashford Town (Middx)	0-3	Peppard v Eton Wick	1-0

Semi-Finals

Cobham v Ashford Town (Middx)	0-1	Peppard v Bedfont	3-1

Final *(at Woking FC)*: Peppard 1, Ashford Town (Middx) 0

RESERVE SECTION SECTION CHALLENGE CUP 1993-94

First Round

Cobham Res v Sandhurst Town Res	5-1	Merstham Res v Ditton Reserves	1-0*(both expelled)*
Viking Spts Res v Hartley Wintney Reserves	5-1	Virginia Wtr Res v Horley Res	2-0*(both expelled)*

Second Round

Ashford Town Res v Frimley Green Reserves	1-0	Cobham Reserves *(w/o)* Virginia Water Reserves	
DCA Basingstoke Res. v Bedfont Reserves	3-2	Eton Wick Reserves v Cranleigh Reserves	2-3
Farleigh Rovers Res v Ash United Reserves	2-1	Godalming & Guildford Reserves *(w/o)* Merstham Res	
Viking Sports Res v Peppard Reserves	0-4	Westfield Res v Farnham Town Reserves	1-2

Quarter-Finals

Cobham Reserves v Cranleigh Reserves	3-0	DCA Basingstoke Reserves v Farleigh R. Reserves	1-4
Farnham T. Res. v Ashford Town Reserves	2-3	Godalming & G. Res v Peppard Reserves	3-5*(aet)*

Semi-Finals

Cobham Reserves v Peppard Res	0-9	Farleigh R. Reserves v Ashford T. Reserves	2-1*(aet)*

Final *(at Egham Town FC)*: Peppard Reserves 5, Farleigh Rovers Reserves 0

PARASOL (COMBINED COUNTIES) LEAGUE TEN YEAR RECORD

	84/5	85/6	86/7	87/8	88/9	89/0	90/1	91/2	92/3	93/4
Ashford Town (Middx)	–	–	–	–	–	–	5	6	3	2
Ash United	5	3	1	13	10	4	8	9	6	7
B.A.e. Weybridge					(See Weybridge Town)					
Bedfont	–	–	–	11	12	16	7	8	12	13
Chertsey Town	–	2	–	–	–	–	–	–	–	–
Chipstead	–	–	4	7	4	1	2	3	2	5
Chobham	13	12	12	15	18	18	–	–	–	–
Cobham	17	8	11	4	11	8	10	4	17	11
Cove	18	13	13	12	17	3	–	–	–	–
Cranleigh	12	17	16	16	15	17	15	7	10	4
DCA Basingstoke	–	–	–	–	–	–	–	–	13	6
Ditton F. & S.C.	–	–	–	–	–	–	–	5	18	20
Eton Wick	–	–	–	–	–	–	–	–	–	3
Farleigh Rovers	11	15	14	14	8	9	6	11	16	12
Farnham Town	10	5	2	3	5	6	1	1	–	18
Fleet Town	19	19	–	–	–	–	–	–	–	–
Frimley Green	14	18	15	17	16	13	9	13	15	21
Godalming (Town)(& Guildford)	9	10	7	5	13	10	13	17	9	14
Hartley Wintney	16	11	8	10	7	11	14	15	8	15
Horley Town	15	16	9	9	9	14	16	18	14	19
Malden Town	6	6	10	6	14	5	3	2	w/d	–
Malden Vale	1	4	3	8	2	–	–	–	–	–
Merstham	3	7	6	2	3	2	4	14	4	17
Peppard	–	–	–	–	–	–	–	–	1	1
Sandhurst Town	–	–	–	–	–	–	17	19	7	10
Southwick	2	–	–	–	–	–	–	–	–	–
Steyning Town	–	–	–	–	6	7	12	10	11	–
Viking Sports	–	–	–	–	–	–	–	12	5	16
Virginia Water	7	14	18	–	–	–	–	–	–	9
Westfield	8	9	17	18	19	15	11	16	19	8
Weybridge Town	4	1	5	1	1	12	–	–	–	–
No. of Clubs	**19**	**19**	**18**	**18**	**19**	**18**	**17**	**19**	**19**	**21**

Wooden-spoonists Frimley Green, who sadly leave the Parasol Combined Counties League this summer, relegated under the Pyramid system. They will now play their football in the Surrey Intermediate (Western) League.
Photo - Eric Marsh.

Reserve Division Constitution 1994-95: Ash United, Ashford Town, Bedfont, Cobham, Cranleigh, DCA Basingstoke, Eton Wick, Farnham Town, Godalming & Guildford, Hartley Wintney, Horley Town, Merstham, Netherne, Peppard, Sandhurst Town, Viking Sports, Westfield.

ASHFORD TOWN (MIDDX)

President: E Britzman **Chairman:** R Parker **Vice Chairman:** Alan Pingham.
Secretary: A B J Constable, 30 Marlborough Rd, Ashford, Middx TW15 3QA (0784 244515).
Manager: Dave Kent **Asst Manager:** TBA
Physio: D Hanks **Press Secretary:** D Baker
Ground: Short Lane, Stanwell, Staines, Middx (0784 245908).
Directions: M25 jct 13, A30 towards London, 3rd left at footbridge after Ashford Hospital crossroads - ground signposted after quarter of a mile on right down Short Lane. Two miles from Ashford (BR) and Hatton Cross (tube) stations. Bus route 116.
Seats: None **Cover:** 75 **Capacity:** 2,000 **Floodlights:** Due **Year Formed:** 1964
Colours: Tangerine & white **Change colours:** All blue **Nickname:** Ash Trees
Programme: 20 pages, 50p **Programme Editor:** Secretary
Club Shop: No, but secretary always willing to swap any non-Lge progs for old Ashford progs.
Previous Leagues: Hounslow & Dist. 64-68/ Surrey Intermediate 68-82/ Surrey Premier 82-90.
Midweek matchday: Tuesday **Previous Ground:** Clockhouse Lane Rec.
Sponsors: Gildas Morris & Co Builders **Record Gate:** 750 v Brentford, friendly 29/7/86.
Record win: 11-2 v Pyrford, 12/2/83 **Record defeat:** 0-7 v Tolworth, 3/12/83.
Clubhouse: Open 7 days a week. Refreshments always available - hot food on matchdays. Fruit machine, patio and barbecue, boardroom.
Club record scorer: Andy Smith **Club record appearances:** Alan Contable 650.
Captain 93-94: Micky Scott **Top Scorer 93-94:** Lee Holman **P.o.Y. 93-94:** Ian Miles
Hons: Combined Co's Lg R-up 93-94 (Chall. Cup R-up 92-93 93-94, Lg Vase Cup R-up 91-92 93-94), Surrey Intermediate Lg, Surrey Prem. Cup 89-90, Middx Prem. Cup R-up 89-90.

Below: *Ashford Town (Middx) - Parasol League runners-up 1993-94.* *Photo - Eric Marsh.*

ASH UNITED

President: Mrs B Wallman **Chairman:** R J Atkins
Secretary: Mr Alan Haberle, 30 Longfield Rd, Ash, nr Aldershot, Hants GU12 6NA (0252 20385).
Ground: Youngs Drive, off Shawfield Rd, Ash, Nr Aldershot (0252 20385).
Directions: A323 towards Ash, left into Shawfield Rd, right into Ash Church Rd, right at crossroads into Shawfield Rd. 1 mile from both Ash and Ash Vale BR stations.
Seats: None **Cover:** Overhang **Capacity:** 1,500 **Floodlights:** No **Founded:** 1911
Colours: Green/red/green **Change colours:** All blue
Programme: 36 pages, 50p with admission. Editor: Gareth Watmore.
Midweek Matchday: Tuesday **Previous Ground:** Ash Common Rec. 70-71
Previous Leagues: Surrey Snr, Aldershot Snr

BEDFONT

President: Jack Newman **Vice Pres.:** F Nichols/W Feltz **Chairman:** Alan Hale.
Vice Chairman: K Stone.
Secretary: Tom Fountain, 23 Sherborne Rd, Bedfont, Middlesex TW14 8ES (081 384 3730).
Manager: Alan Humphries **Coach:** Cliff Williamson.
Asst Manager: Bob Barnes **Physio:** Paul Donworth.
Ground: The Orchard, Hatton Rd, Bedfont, Middx (081 890 7264).
Directions: Turn down Faggs Rd opposite Hatton Cross (Picadilly Line) station on Great South Western Rd (A30), then sharp right into Hatton Rd. Ground opposite Duke of Wellington pub.
Seats: None **Cover:** 50 **Capacity:** **Floodlights:** Yes **Founded:** 1968.
Colours: Yellow/blue/blue **Change colours:** Claret & blue stripes.
Previous Names: Bedfont Institute (founded 1900), Bedfont Rangers (founded 1950) and Fairholme United (founded 1953) all merged in 1968. Club later merged with Interharvester (1973) and Bedfont Eagles (1988).
Previous Ground: Bedfont Rec. **Midweek matchday:** Tuesday.
Clubhouse: Yes.
Programme: 28 pages, 50p. Editors: Alan Humphries (0932 563548) and Colin McNeill (081 384 8410).
Captain 93-94: Cairon Dixon.
Hons: Combined Counties Lg Chall. Vase 92-93 (Reserve Div R-up 88-89, Reserve Cup R-up 89-90, Grant McClennan Yth Cup 91-92), Middx Lg 73-74 76-77 (Div 1(res) 71-72 78-79 79-80, Div 1 Cup 71-72 78-79 79-80), Surrey Premier Lg 84-85 86-87, Middx Intermediate Cup 69-70 76-77, International Contois Tournament 1992, Liege Euromann Tournament 1989, Harold Clayton Cup 90-91, Hounslow & Dist. Lg Div 1(res) 86-87.

CHIPSTEAD

President: B Nicholls **Chairman:** Keith Rivers
Secretary: K Allsopp, 51 Lakers Rise, Woodsterne, Banstead, Surrey SM7 3JX (0737 359989).
Manager: John Sears **Coach:** Paul Duffield.
Ground: High Road, Chipstead, Surrey (0737 553250).
Directions: Brighton Road northbound, left into Church Lane, left into Hogcross Lane, right into High Road. One and a half miles from Chipstead (BR).
Seats: 30 **Cover:** 100 **Capacity:** 2,000 **Floodlights:** Yes **Founded:** 1906
Midweek matchday: Tuesday.
Colours: Green/white/green **Change cols:** Yellow/yellow/white **Programme:** 44 pages
Previous Leagues: Surrey Intermediate 62-82/ Surrey Premier 82-86 **Nickname:** Chips
Hons: Surrey Premier Lg R-up 82-83 83-84 85-86 (Lg Cup 82-83 84-85 85-86), Combined Co's Lg 89-90 (R-up 90-91 92-93, Lg Cup 86-87 90-91 92-93, Elite Class Cup R-up 89-90, Reserve Section Cup 92-93).

COBHAM

Chairman: E Strange
Secretary: Gerry Petit, 149 Bridge Rd, Chessington, Surrey KT9 2RT (081 397 0433).
Ground: Leg O'Mutton Field, Downside Bridge Rd, Cobham, Surrey (0932 865959).
Directions: A307 (Portsmouth Road) towards Leatherhead, right into Between Streets, right into Downside Rd then right opposite car park. Two miles from Cobham & Stoke D'Abernon (BR).
Seats: None **Cover:** No **Capacity:** 2,000 **Floodlights:** No **Founded:** 1892
Colours: All red **Change colours:** Yellow/blue/blue.
Midweek matchday: Wednesday.
Previous League: Surrey Senior. **Previous Grounds:** Cobham Rec.
Programme: FA Vase matches only **Record Gate:** 2,000 v Showbiz team, charity match 1975.

CRANLEIGH

Chairman: Roy Kelsey **Vice Chairman:** Trevor Moor **President:** Alan Pavia.
Secretary: Mark Edwards, 42 Finnart Close, Weybridge, Surrey (0932 856716).
Manager: Tom Kelsey **Asst Manager:** TBA **Coach:** Jackie Graham
Ground: Snoxall Playing Fields, Knowle Lane, Cranleigh (0483 275295).
Directions: A281 from Guildford towards Horsham, at Shalford take B2128 to Cranleigh High Street, right opposite Onslow Arms into Knowle Lane, ground half mile on left. Public transport: Guildford (BR) then bus 273 or 283.
Seats: None **Cover:** No **Capacity:** 450 **Floodlights:** No **Founded:** 1893.
Colours: Blue/blue/yellow **Change colours:** Grey/black. **Nickname:** Cranes.
Record Gate: 450 v C Palace, friendly 1989. Competitive: 285 v Hailsham, F.A. Vase 3rd Rd 12/12/92.
Sponsors: R W Coupe - Est. Agents **Clubhouse:** Licensed bar. Hot food on matchdays.
Programme: £1 with admission **Editor:** Peter Slater (0483 894248) **Club Shop:** No.
Midweek home matchday: Tuesday **Rec. win:** 9-1 v Merstham, Dan-Air Elite Class Cup QF 91-92
Previous League: Surrey Intermediate.
Captain 93-94: Gary Wells **Top Scorer 93-94:** Chris Lamboll.
Hons: West Sussex County Times Cup 92-93, F.A. Vase 3rd Rd 92-93.

D.C.A. BASINGSTOKE

Chairman: M A Davis **Vice Chairman:** K R W Haystaff **President:** K J Dudley
Secretary: D J Brand, 128 Stratfield Rd, Oakridge, Basingstoke, Hants RG21 2SA (0256 57309).
Manager: Alec Walker **Asst Manager:** Alan Tait/ Mark Gardener.
Ground: Whiteditch Playing Field, Sherbourne Rd, Basingstoke, Hants (0256 844866).
Directions: From Basingstoke BR station, turn right out of main entrance towards Chapel Hill, continue past Rising Sun pub, right into Sherbourne Rd, ground 800yds up on right.
Seats: None **Cover:** None **Capacity:** Unknown **Floodlights:** No. **Founded:** 1971
Colours: Navy & sky **Previous Name:** Soldiers Return. **Programmes:** No.
Previous Grounds: None **Prev. Lges:** North Hants/ Hants (pre-'92) **Club Shop:** No.
Midweek home matchday: Tuesday **Clubhouse:** Approx. one mile from ground.
Clubhouse: Evenings 7-11pm, matchdays 12-11pm. Bar snacks.
Captain 93-94: **P.o.Y. 93-94:**
Hons: Hants Lg Div 2 88-89 (Div 1 R-up 90-91), Basingstoke Snr Cup 83-84 87-88 90-91, North Hants Lg 87-88, North Hants Snr Cup 87-88 88-89 (R-up 90-91).

ETON WICK

Vice-Chairman: Bob Cannon. **President:** Lionel Jarratt **Chairman:** Joe Bussey
Secretary: Mr Lionel E Jarratt, 1 Colenorton Cres., Eton Wick, Windsor SL4 6N (0753 865010).
Coach: Frank Carter. **Manager:** Jim Hartridge **Asst Manager:** Bob Cannon.
Physio: Mick Turner **Press Officer:** Joe Bussey
Ground: Haywards Mead, Eton Wick, Windsor (0753 852749).
Directions: Windsor Rd Slough under M4 m'way to r'bout, 1st exit to lights at Eton College, turn right - club one and a half miles on left in Eton Wick. BR to Windsor & Eton.
Seats: None **Cover:** No **Capacity:** 1,500 **Floodlights:** No **Founded:** 1881.
Colours: Amber/black **Change colours:** All white **Club Shop:** No.
Programme: Yes, for donations **Programme Editor:** Joe Bussey (0753 859493).
Midweek matchday: Tues/Thurs **Local Press:** Slough Windsor Observer/ Express
Reserves' League: Combined Co's Reserve Division.
Previous Lges: Windor Slough & Dist. (pre-'91)/ Chiltonian 91-93.
Clubhouse: Open Mon-Fri noon-2.30 & 7-11pm, Sat noon-11pm, Sun noon-3 & 7-10.30pm. Full range of hot & cold food and drinks available.
Captain 93-94: Jim Hartridge **P.o.Y. 93-94:** Mark Anderson **Top Scorer 93-94:** Micky Foulkes
Hons: Chiltonian Lg 92-93 (Div 1 91-92, Lg Cup R-up 91-92, Res Div 2 91-92), Slough Town Snr Cup 52-53 68-69 70-71 76-77 83-84 85-86 86-87 91-92 92-93 (Jnr Cup 86-87 92-93), Berks & Bucks Snr Trophy 92-93 93-94 (Intermediate Cup 91-92, Jnr Cup 86-87), Windsor, Slough & D. Lg 74-75 86-87 (Lg Cup 79-80, Res. Lg Cup 78-79 85-86 87-88), Maidenhead Norfolkian Cup 65-66.

FARNHAM TOWN

Chairman: N Harrington **President:** J Butters.
Secretary: Ms A Young, 106 St Peters Gdns, Wrecclesham, Surrey (0252 735432).
Manager: Scotty Green **Asst Manager:** **Coach:**
Press Officer: **Commercial Mgr:** **Physio:**
Ground: Memorial Ground, Babbs Mead, West Street, Farnham, Surrey (0252 715305).
Directions: Take A325 (West Street) at junction with A31 Farnham by-pass, then first right. From Farnham (BR), left into Station Hill, left into Union Rd, round Downing Street, left into West Street and Babbs Mead is 3rd left.
Capacity: 2,000 **Seats:** None **Cover:** 150 **Floodlights:** Yes **Founded:** 1921
Colours: Claret & sky stripes/sky/claret **Change colours:** All yellow **Club Shop:** No
Programme: Yes **Editor:** **Metal Badges:**
Previous Name: Farnham Star **Previous Grounds:** Farnham Park.
Previous Leagues: Surrey Intermediate/ Surrey Snr 47-71/ Spartan 71-75/ London Spartan 75-80/ Combined Counties 80-92.
Midweek Matchday: Tuesday **Sponsors:** Frazer Freight.
Record Gate: 500 v Kingstonian, Surrey Snr Cup 1960. **Nickname:**
Reserve Team's League: **Best FA Cup year:** Never past Qualifying Rounds
Clubhouse: Yes **Local Press:** Farnham Herald.
Hons: Combined Counties Lg 90-91 91-92 (Challenge Tphy 91-92 (R-up 89-90).

Farnham Town FC. *Photo - Eric Marsh.*

GODALMING & GUILDFORD

President: W Kyle **Chairman:** Mike Palmer **Vice-Chairman:** C J Keen
Secretary: Mrs Jane Phillips, 135 Manor Rd, Stoughton, Guildford, Surrey GU2 6NR (0483 571372).
Mgr: John Hollis/Micky Wollen **Asst Manager:** Angelo Balbato.
Physio: Ron Lucas **Press Officer:** Secretary.
Ground: Weycourt, Meadrow, Godalming, Surrey (0483 417520).
Directions: A3100 from Guildford - carry on past Godalming Rugby Club and ground on right just after Burmah garage. Coming out of Godalming on A3100, ground on left by Leather Bottle pub. Three quarters of a mile from Farncombe BR station.
Seats: Yes **Cover:** 200 **Capacity:** 1,500 **Floodlights:** 276 lux **Programme:** Yes
Colours: Green/amber **Change colours:** All yellow. **Founded:** 1971
Club Shop: Not at present **Midweek matchday:** Tuesday/Thursday. **Nickname:** The Weys
Previous Leagues: Surrey Intermediate 71-78/ Surrey County Senior 78-79.
Previous Ground: Broadwater Park, Farncombe 71-73
Previous Names: Godalming & Farncombe 71-80/ Godalming Town 80-92.
Record Gate: 600+ - Ex-Guildford City XI v Ex-Football Lg XI, Tony Burge benefit, 1991.
Sponsors: Chapples Wine Bar (Reserves: JMG Electrical Services, Youth: Jordains Garage).
Record win: 11-2 v Fleet Town. **Players progressing to Football Lge:** John Humphreys (Millwall)
Clubhouse: Open Tues & Thurs evenings and matchdays. Hot & cold drinks and snacks, chocolate & crisps.
Record scorer: Paul Hampshire 123 **Record appearances:** Andy Metcalfe 287 (111 goals).
Hons: Combined Co's Lg 83-84 (Challenge Trophy 82-83, Reserve Challenge Cup 91-92 (R-up 92-93)), Surrey Intermediate Lg Premier Division Cup 71-72.

HARTLEY WINTNEY

President: D Gorsky **Chairman:** W Mitchell
Secretary: Miss Julie Martin, 127 Hearsey Gardens, Blackwater, nr Camberley, Hants GU17 0ET (0252 878526).
Ground: Memorial Playing Fields, Green Lane, Hartley Wintney, Hants (0251 263586).
Directions: A30 west through Camberley, left at parade of shops at beginning of village then sharp right - ground on right. Two miles from Winchfield (BR).
Seats: None **Cover:** No **Capacity:** 2,000 **Floodlights:** No **Founded:** 1897
Colours: Tangerine/black/tangerine **Change colours:** White/blue/blue **Programme:** Yes
Previous Leagues: Basingstoke/ Aldershot **Nickname:** The Row
Midweek matchday: Tuesday.

HORLEY TOWN

Chairman: Mr S Munday **Vice Chairman:** Mr G McLaren **President:** Mr K Pritchard
Secretary: Mr P C Freeman, Long Acre, 140 Balcombe Rd, Horley, Surrey RH6 9DS (0293 784368).
Manager: Laurence Gearey **Coach:** Peter Heyne **Physio:** Philip Sparkes.
Ground: The Defence, Smallfield Rd, Horley, Surrey (0293 786075).
Directions: From Horley (BR) station turn right down Station Approach, left into The Grove, over traffic lights into Smallfield Rd - ground 1 mile on left down Smallfield Rd.
Seats: None **Cover:** 100 **Capacity:** 1,000 **Floodlights:** Yes **Founded:** 1898
Colours: Claret & blue/claret/blue **Change colours:** Sky/navy/navy **Programme:** 50p
Midweek matchdays: Tuesday **Prev. Ground:** Gasworks Grnd, Balcombe Rd (pre 1948)
Prev. Lges: Redhill & D. 45-49/ Surrey Int. 49-72/ Surrey Snr 72-78/ London Spartan 78-81/ Athenian 81-84.
Sponsors: Carter Thorne Carpets **Record Gate:** 1,000 v Spurs, pre-season friendly 1983
Record win: 10-0 v Lion Sports 1978 **Record defeat:** 0-10 v Southwick 1985 **Club Shop:** No.
Reserves' Lge: Comb Co's Res Div
Player progressing to Football Lge: Nicky Forster (Gillingham, Brentford) 1992.
Clubhouse: Evenings 7-11pm, weekend lunchtimes. Hot food on matchdays only.
Captain 93-94: Jimmy Mahoney **Top Scorer & Player of the Year 93-94:** Dave Forster
Club record scorer: Ian Peters **Club record appearances:** Dave Jupp.
Hons: Surrey Snr Lg 76-77 (Charity Cup 76-77 77-78), Surrey Intermediate (Eastern) Lg Cup 66-67.

MERSTHAM

President: Stan Baker **Chairman:** Geoff Taylor **Vice Chairman:** Steve D'Arcy.
Secretary: Mrs Sheila Williams, 33 Lymden Gdns, Reigate, Surrey (0737 245877).
Manager: Joe McElligott **Asst Manager:** Martin Rosser **Coach:** Allan Cook.
Physio: Carl Burke **Press Officer:** Roger Peerless.
Ground: Merstham Rec., Weldon Way, Merstham, Redhill, Surrey (0737 43279).
Directions: Leave Merstham village (A23) by School Hill, take 5th right (Weldon Way), clubhouse and car park 100m on right. Ground also accessible from Albury Rd (2nd right off School). 10 mins walk from Merstham (BR); down School Hill, under railway bridge, fork left then right into Albury Road, ground entrance half way down on left.
Seats: 100 **Cover:** 100 **Capacity:** 2,000 **Floodlights:** Yes (177 lux)
Colours: Amber & black **Change colours:** Silver grey **Founded:** 1892.
Club Sponsors: Whitbread **Midweek home matchday:** Tuesday
Record win: 11-0 **Record defeat:** 1-9
Previous Leagues: Redhill & Dist./ Surrey Co. S.E. I'mediate/ Surrey Snr 64-78/ London Spartan 78-85.
Previous Grounds: Merstham Weir/ Merstham Lime Works (pre-1920s).
Clubhouse: Across adjacent footpath. Open daily (am & pm). Snacks available.
Hons: Combined Co's Lg R-up 87-88 89-90 (Elite Class Cup 89-90 (R-up 90-91), Reserve Section 90-91), London Spartan Lg 79-89 (Lg Cup 79-80), Surrey Snr Lg 71-72, Surrey Snr Charity Cup 79-80, East Surrey Charity Cup 80-81, Surrey I'mediate Lg 52-53.

NETHERNE

President: Noel Duffy **Chairman:** Steve Clark
Secretary: Mike West, 17 Gladwell Rd, Bromley, Kent BR1 4DA (081 402 0753).
Manager Alan Worrall **Asst Manager:** Colin Worrall **Coach:** Bob Rumble.
Press Officer: Bob Rumble **Commercial Mgr:** Bob Rumble
Ground: Netherne Sports Club, Woodplace Lane, Hooley, Coulsdon, Surrey CR5 1YE (0737 552064).
Ground: One mile from end of M32. Turn right off Brighton Rd into Woodplace Lane, follow up hill for about half a mile, ground on left. Approx 20 mins walk from Coulsdon South (BR) station.
Capacity: **Seats:** None **Cover:** 50 **Floodlights:** No **Founded:** 1968
Colours: Blue & black stripes **Change Colours:** All maroon
Club Shop: To open 95-96 season **Reserve Team's League:** Combined Co's Reserve Division.
Programme: 24 pages, 50p **Editor:** Steve Clark (0737 552200).
Previous Leagues: Croydon Saturday 68-76/ Surrey Eastern Intermediate 76-79/ Surrey South Eastern Intermediate 79-89/ Surrey County Premier 89-94.
Prev. Grounds: Higher Drive, Purley 68-77/ Sparrows Den, West Wickham 78-83/ Mollison Drive, Wallington 83-85.
Record win: 7-3 v Limpsfield Blues, 1982 **Record defeat:** 1-8 v Springfield Hospital.
Clubhouse: Open matchdays with hot food available over bar. Outside tea also available with hot food.
Record Scorer: Michael Rumble 350 **Record appearances:** Steve Parker 500.
Captain 93-94: Andy Munslow **Top Scorer & Player of the Year 93-94:** Andy Munslow, 20 goals.
Hons: Surrey Co. Prem. Lg 93-94 (Lg Cup 92-93), Surrey South Eastern Intermediate Comb. 88-89.

Below: *Parasol League newcomers Netherne FC.*

Eton Wick's Colin Landeg (right) prepares to take on Tony Jackson of Merstham. Photo - Francis Short.

The Ditton 'keeper clutches the ball as a Cobham forward prepares to pounce. Photo - Dennis Nicholson.

Westfield FC. Photo - Eric Marsh.

PEPPARD

Chairman: C F Clayton **President:** V F Clayton
Vice-Chairman/Sec.: Reece Pigden, 9 Newfield Rd, Sonning Common, Reading, Berks RG4 9TB (0734 723445).
Manager: Graham Haddrell **Asst Manager:** A Grover **Physio:** Austin Rogers.
Ground: Bishopswood Sports Centre, Horsepond Rd, Sonning Common, nr Reading (0734 712265).
Directions: Bus services 137 or 138 to Peppard Post Office then 1st left into Horespond Rd - ground 800yds on left. Junction 8/9 of **M4**, proceed to Henley. Straight over lights in town and contine for 3 miles until B481, left towards Sonning Common/Reading, after just over a mile take right fork at foot of steep hill towards Kidmore End, Cane End & Woodcote. Straight over next crossroads and ground on left after half a mile.
Seats/Cover: None **Capacity:** 2,000 **Floodlights:** No **Founded:** 1903 **Nickname:** Pepps
Colours: All red **Change colours:** Sky/navy **Club Shop:** No.
Previous Lges: Reading & Dist. 64-87/ Chiltonian 87-92/ Combined Counties 92-93.
Previous Names: Sonning Common Peppard (Peppard FC merged with Sonning Common FC in 1984 - name reverted to Peppard FC in 1990).
Previous Grounds: Peppard Common 03-85/ Palmer Park, Reading (most of 1993-94 season).
Programme: Ave. 52 pages, 50p **Editor:** Reece Pigden (0734 723445) - 9th in 93-94 Wirral Survey.
Midweek matchday: Tuesday **Sponsors:** Business Moves.
Reserves' Lge: Comb. Co's Res section **Clubhouse:** Normal bar hrs matchdays. Tea bar/snacks available.
Local Newspapers: Reading Chronicle, Reading Evening Post, Henley Standard
Local Radio: Radio 210, Radio Oxford, Radio Berks.
Club record scorer: Jim Aberdein **Club record appearances:** Ray Will.
Captain 93-94: Kim Watkins **Top Scorer 93-94:** Andy Shildrick 51 **P.o.Y. 93-94:** Matthew Webb
Hons: Combined Co's Lg 92-93 93-94 (Lg Cup 93-94, Lg Vase 93-94, Res. Div 92-93 93-94, Res. Cup 93-94), Chiltonian Lg(2) 90-92 (R-up 89-90, Lg Cup(4) 87-89 90-92), Reading & Dist. Lg(7) 74-75 77-78 79-82 84-85 86-87, Oxon Snr Cup 79-80 81-82 (R-up 89-90 93-94), Oxon I'mediate Cup(3) 74-76 92-93(res), Reading Snr Cup(6) 79-82 89-92, Wycombe Snr Cup 91-92, Reading Jnr Cup 60-61 81-82(res) 87-88(res).

SANDHURST TOWN

Chairman: M Shields
Secretary: J E Parker, 24 Florence Rd, College Town, Camberley, Surrey GU15 4QD (0276 32308).
Manager: Tony O'Connor **Coach:** Steve Atkins.
Ground: Memorial Ground, Yorktown Rd, Sandhurst (0252 873767).
Directions: A30 westwards through Camberley, right at r-bout with traffic lights, past superstore turning right, left at next r'bout. Ground next to Town & Council offices and Community Sports Centre.
Seats: None **Cover:** No **Floodlights:** No **Programme:** Yes **Nickname:** Fizzers
Colours: Red/black/black **Change colours:** All gold **Metal Badges:** Yes
Midweek matchday: Tuesday.
Previous Leagues: Reading & Dist./ East Berks/ Aldershot Snr 79-84/ Chiltonian 84-90.
Captain 93-94: **Top Scorer 93-94:**
Hons: Combined Co's Lg Chal. Vase R-up 92-93 (Reserve Chal. Cup R-up 91-92), Chiltonian Lg R-up 86-87, Aldershot Snr Lg R-up 83-84.

VIKING SPORTS

President: Roy Bartlett **Chairman:** Gary Yost **Manager:** Glyn Owen.
Secretary: John Bennett, 6 Bridge House, Boston Manor Rd, Brentford TW8 9LH (081 568 9047).
Asst Manager: Tony Waugh **Coach:** Andy Waddock **Physio:** Eric Neal.
Ground: Avenue Park, Western Avenue, Greenford, Middx (081 578 2706).
Directions: On London-bound carriageway of A40, 300 yds before Greenford flyover and slip road to A4127. 12 mins walk from Greenford (Central Line) station - turn right out of station and to A40 and turn right - ground quarter mile on right.
Seats: 50 **Cover:** 100 **Capacity:** 400 **Floodlights:** Yes **Founded:** 1945
Colours: Tangerine **Change colours:** Sky/maroon **Nickname:** Vikings.
Programme: 12 pages, 20p **Editor:** Andy Evans (081 991 1930) **Club Shop:** No.
Clubhouse: Open every evening except Sunday. Hot & cold snacks on matchdays.
Midweek matchday: Tuesday **Record Gate:** 180 v Lambourn, Hellenic Lg 1982
Prev. Lge: Middx 70-80/ Hellenic 80-91 **Prev. Grounds:** Churchfield (pre-1965) **Metal Badges:** Yes.
Players progressing to Football League: Gordon Bartlett (Portsmouth), Alan Devonshire (West Ham).
Club Sponsors: Measham Self-Drive **Club Record Scorer:** Frank Healy, 43.
Record win: 8-0 v Aldermaston, 1986 **Record defeat:** 1-7 v Bicester Town, 1988.
P.o.Y. 93-94: Jon Durkan **Captain & Top Scorer 93-94:** Roy Oatway
Hons: Hellenic Lg Div 1 85-86 (Div 1 Cup R-up 90-91).

WESTFIELD

Chairman: K Moody **Manager:** John Martin.
Secretary: Mr Philip Arthur-Worsop, 10 Martin Way, Woking, Surrey (0483 715659).
Ground: Woking Park, Kingfield, Woking, Surrey (no telephone).
Directions: Adjacent to Woking FC (see GMV Conference section).
Seats: None **Cover:** No **Capacity:** 1,000 **Floodlights:** No **Programme:** No
Colours: White/blue/blue **Change colours:** All yellow. **Clubhouse:** Yes.
Previous League: Surrey Co. Snr.

NORTHERN COUNTIES (EAST) LEAGUE

FEEDER TO:
NORTHERN PREMIER LEAGUE

FOUNDED: 1982
(Amalgamation of Yorkshire League (founded 1920) and the Midland League (founded 1889))

President: H F Catt.

Chairman: C Morris.

Treasurer: G A Freeman.

Hon. Secretary: B Wood, 6 Restmore Ave., Guiseley, Leeds LS20 9DG (0943 874558)

STOCKSBRIDGE WIN THRILLING TITLE RACE

As champions of the Central Midlands League, Arnold Town rejoined the NCEL and local pundits were keen to see if they could emulate Lincoln United and Hucknall Town by progressing straight through to the top division.

Many clubs were the victims of the severe weather resulting in a very distorted and uneven fixture list. With the disparity in the number of fixtures played, the eventual destination of the Premier Division title was very uncertain in the period to Christmas with Maltby MW, Sheffield and Brigg in contention. Stocksbridge entered the race in the New Year when they occupied second place. Followers of Thackley will know that over the years they have always tended to produce a good defence, and this season was remarkable in that just eleven goals were conceded in the club's last eighteen matches - very definitely a contributory factor in their eventual final position. There is no doubt all championship contenders have periods of ascendancy and depression - every sort of emotion was evident to clubs on the final day of the campaign, though.

The season before it had all depended on goal difference for Spennymoor to snatch the

Arnold Town - Northern Counties (East) League Division One champions 1993-94. Back Row (L/R): John Bartlett (Asst Manager), Pete Catling, Lee Walshaw, Steve Hare, Gavin Ottewell, Seamus McDonagh, Steve Odell, Kris Maddison, Mark Goodwin (Captain), Neil Waters, Iain McCulloch (Manager). Front: Peter Fletcher, Gary Simpson, Craig Maddison, Chris Freestone, Chris White, David Taylor (Ilkeston Town), Simon Richmond, Andy Elliott.
Photo courtesy of T Bailey Forman Newspapers.

championship from Pickering, but on the morning of this season's May 7th there were four clubs on seventy-one points with three of them realistic winners of the title. To add spice to the contest, Eccleshill needed a win at home to Stockbridge to help their struggle against relegation, whilst Thackley were at bottom club Winterton and Lincoln United were away at Belper.

With Lincoln United managing only a 1-1 draw at Belper, the initiative switched to either Thackley or Park Steels. Despite a vital goal by Thackley's Stuart Taylor (the Division's leading scorer), a 1-0 victory at Winterton left the Bradfordians anxiously wondering whether their neighbours, Eccleshill, could defeat their main rivals. It was not to be, as Stocksbridge hung on to win 1-0 and take the title from Thackley. Stocksbridge's expected move up to the NPL has not materialised, though. Despite, playing their part in the final countdown, both Eccleshill and Winterton are relegated to Division One. All Premier Division clubs should be congratulated for helping to produce a memorable championship race.

In Division One, newcomers Arnold proved the strength of their squad by losing just two matches until mid-February, and this undoubtedly provided the platform for their eventual success. Pressed by both Hatfield Main and, in earlier days, Garforth Town, there were other promotion hopefuls emerging in Hallam, Louth United and Yorkshire Amateurs. Hatfield ended their campaign early, however, and were left hoping they could hold on to a promotion place. It didn't happen. Arnold themselves stuttered a little in the run-in but finally took the championship by two points from Hallam, who made up for their considerable disappointment of the previous season by hanging on to second place. In the end, Hatfield Main slipped to fourth place behind Louth, so, just as in the 1992-93 season, the new entrants from the CML proved formidable opponents. Immingham and Brodsworth finished at the bottom of the Division and had to formally apply for re-election.

Two unfortunate problems concerned the same club - Selby Town. It was necessary to deduct six points from their total for player registration irregularities, and they were the first senior team for some time to fail to fulfil a fixture. A bright spot for them was their mid-season form which lifted them from bottom position to fifth-from-bottom.

Often the Reserve Division championship has tended to be dominated by the invited reserve teams of NPL clubs and, after a 1992-93 title win by Guiseley, it was they and Emley who made the early running. Also prominent were Thackley and Eccleshill Reserves. With just three defeats all season and a heavy programme of matches at the end, Guiseley took the title, again, by six points from runners-up Eccleshill who helped to lift the gloom of their first team's relegation. Emley ended the season in third place but one club may wish their record was not the subject of comment here - Tadcaster Albion Reserves with a mammoth 125 goals conceded! With ground problems evident at Nethermoor during last season's wet weather, champions Guiseley Reserves will be unable to take up the invitation extended to the four invited Reserve Teams of NPL clubs.

Our League Cup provided its usual crop of interesting results in the early rounds; Lincoln United 8 Liversedge 0; Pontefract Collieries. 0 Yorkshire Amateur 1; Louth 5 Winterton 3; amongst some to mention. The Semi-Finals provided wins by the odd goal for Hucknall and Thackley against North Ferriby and Lincoln United respectively to set up an intriguing final at Ossett Town's ground. It was a chance for Thackley to make amends for their slip in the title race but their Nottinghamshire opponents had other ideas. Two early goals set the pattern for Hucknall who took the Cup with a 4-1 win. Certainly well deserved on the night, but surprising given Thackley's defensive record.

The President's Cup reached its climax at Brigg's ground when Lincoln United recorded a 2-1 win over Pontefract. Strikes by Tony Simmons and Gerard Creane were enough to give Lincoln the initiative as Darren Sheridan's goal for Pontefract proved too late. League President, Frank Catt, presented his cup to Lincoln's captain, Steve Carter, at the end of their successful cup run.

Guiseley Reserves had a double triumph by taking the Reserve Division Cup by 3-0 to add to their championship success. An unfortunate Pontefract Collieries own-goal gave Guiseley an early second-half lead, and two further goals sealed the tie at Ossett Albion's ground. At least Pontefract had the distinction of providing two NCE cup finalists. The three clubs which hosted our Finals are thanked here for their efforts on the League's behalf.

A look at National Competitions indicated a relatively early demise for our clubs in the FA Cup, though North Ferriby United did earn a replay at Chorley in the Third Qualifying Round before going out 2-1. Clubs realistically have a much better chance of progressing in the FA Vase and we did merit six clubs in the Third Round. Thackley lost after a replay in Round Four whilst Belper went one better to reach Round Five. Their opponents were Taunton who went on to reach the Final, and a 3-1 defeat for the Christ Church Meadow outfit did not really reflect their good play.

After bemoaning lack of County Cup success last, our clubs did much better this year. Pickering's first appearance in the North Riding Senior Cup final, at Whitby against former NCE club Guisborough, did not bring success but was a notable achievement. However, Sheffield defeated NPL Division One side Worksop in the Sheffield & Hallam Senior Cup played at Hillsborough. After a 1-1 scoreline had failed to seperate the sides at the end of extra-time, our team took the trophy 6-5 on penalties. Another Cup Final played on a FL ground was the East Riding Senior Cup - this time at Boothferry Park, Hull. A narrow 1-0 victory was Hall Road Rangers' reward against local side Sculcoates Amateurs. Brigg surprisingly played their Lincolnshire Senior 'A' Cup Final on their own ground which probably helped them to a 5-2 victory over Lincoln United.

Looking ahead to next season, we are all very sad that Stocksbridge have not been able to take up a promotion position in the NPL, so our Premier Divivion will not receive a demoted club. It will again operate with 20 clubs whilst Division One will have an additional club in Blidworth Welfare from the CML. The Reserve Division will be made up of the same teams as last season with the exception of Armthorpe Welfare Reserves and Guiseley Reserves.

Barry Wood, Secretary

PREM. DIV.	P	W	D	L	F	A	PTS
Stocksbridge PS	38	23	5	10	82	39	74
Thackley	38	21	11	6	57	32	74
Lincoln United	38	21	9	8	82	44	72
Sheffield	38	22	5	11	69	49	71
Brigg Town	38	18	8	12	77	54	62
Pickering Town	38	17	10	11	76	61	61
Maltby MW	38	18	6	14	77	62	60
Ossett Albion	38	16	12	10	73	59	60
Nth Ferriby Utd	38	18	5	15	57	43	59
Armthorpe Welfare	38	14	15	9	55	42	57
Liversedge	38	17	4	17	63	65	55
Glasshoughton Welf.	38	13	11	14	51	58	50
Denaby United	38	13	7	18	66	66	46
Hucknall Town	38	13	5	20	48	65	44
Belper Town	38	12	7	19	57	75	43
Ossett Town	38	10	11	17	43	71	41
Pontefract Colls	38	10	10	18	52	71	40
Ashfield United	38	9	8	21	50	85	35
Eccleshill United	38	8	9	21	44	75	33
Winterton Rgrs	38	6	4	28	40	103	22

DIV. ONE	P	W	D	L	F	A	PTS
Arnold Town	28	20	1	7	88	34	61
Hallam	28	18	5	5	64	26	59
Louth United	28	17	4	7	72	38	55
Hatfield Main	28	17	4	7	61	33	55
Yorks Amateur	28	16	4	8	51	25	52
Garforth Town	28	15	6	7	39	28	51
Rossington Main	28	12	4	12	43	47	40
Worsbrough Bdge	28	11	3	14	49	47	36
Harrogate Railway	28	10	5	13	47	56	35
Hall Road Rgrs	28	9	6	13	57	63	33
Selby Town	28	10	5	13	44	66	*29
Tadcaster Albion	28	8	2	18	38	73	26
RES Parkgate	28	6	5	17	43	69	23
Immingham Town	28	6	5	17	33	76	23
Brodsworth MW	28	3	5	20	26	74	14

* - 6 points deducted

RESERVE DIV.	P	W	D	L	F	A	PTS
Guiseley Res.	32	24	5	3	117	36	77
Eccleshill Res.	32	22	5	5	100	51	71
Emley Res.	32	19	10	3	97	38	67
Thackley Res.	32	17	8	7	71	41	59
Ossett Albion Res.	32	17	3	12	91	64	54
Pontefract C. Res.	32	17	2	13	64	68	53
Farsley Celtic Res.	32	16	7	9	67	55	*51
Yorks Amtr Res.	32	11	12	9	59	60	45
Glasshoughton Res.	32	14	3	15	58	80	45
Armthorpe Res.	32	11	6	15	70	76	39
Liversedge Res.	32	10	4	18	63	71	34
Harrogate T. Res.	32	9	7	16	43	65	34
Garforth T. Res.	32	8	6	18	46	80	30
Hall Road Rd Res.	32	7	8	17	63	73	29
Brodsworth Res.	32	6	9	17	36	67	27
Ossett T. Res.	32	7	6	19	45	81	27
Tadcaster A. Res.	32	3	7	22	41	125	16

* - 4 points deducted

PREMIER DIVISION RESULT CHART 1993-94

HOME TEAM	1	2	3	4	5	6	7	8	9	10	11	12	13	14	15	16	17	18	19	20
1. Armthorpe Welfare	*	2-0	3-5	0-0	0-0	2-1	0-1	3-0	0-1	2-2	1-1	2-1	2-1	3-0	2-0	4-0	4-0	0-1	0-1	1-0
2. Ashfield United	2-2	*	0-1	0-7	1-0	6-3	1-1	3-0	1-4	4-1	1-5	1-1	1-3	0-1	4-3	2-2	1-2	1-2	2-0	3-1
3. Belper Town	0-1	3-1	*	2-0	1-5	1-2	4-1	1-3	1-1	4-0	2-1	1-0	1-3	1-1	2-5	4-1	1-2	2-1	2-2	3-4
4. Brigg Town	3-1	3-1	1-3	*	2-4	4-1	3-1	1-1	1-3	1-2	0-0	0-0	4-3	4-3	1-2	3-5	0-1	1-0	3-2	1-1
5. Denaby United	3-3	2-1	1-0	0-0	*	1-1	1-2	1-1	0-2	1-1	1-1	0-2	2-3	1-3	5-4	2-3	6-1	1-2	2-4	9-0
6. Eccleshill United	1-2	0-1	1-0	2-1	0-2	*	1-1	1-4	2-1	1-3	0-4	0-0	3-3	0-0	2-3	4-1	2-3	0-1	0-3	3-1
7. Glasshoughton Welf.	1-1	1-1	1-1	0-1	2-1	1-1	*	2-0	2-2	2-1	1-3	0-2	4-2	5-1	3-3	1-0	0-2	1-1	1-1	2-1
8. Hucknall Town	1-1	0-2	3-2	3-5	0-2	2-0	0-2	*	0-2	2-4	1-2	0-1	0-1	2-3	2-2	2-1	1-0	1-0	1-2	4-2
9. Lincoln United	1-3	3-1	4-0	3-2	9-0	3-2	2-0	1-0	*	2-4	3-0	1-1	1-1	3-0	1-0	5-0	1-2	2-1	3-0	7-1
10. Liversedge	1-0	4-1	1-0	0-0	3-0	2-0	2-0	4-0	1-2	*	0-2	3-1	1-4	3-1	1-2	2-1	1-2	1-3	0-2	5-1
11. Maltby Miners Welf.	2-2	2-0	4-2	1-4	3-2	4-0	1-2	4-1	1-1	3-2	*	0-0	2-5	0-1	1-2	3-0	0-1	2-0	2-1	1-2
12. North Ferriby Utd	1-1	3-1	4-0	2-1	1-3	0-1	3-1	0-1	3-1	6-1	2-1	*	3-0	3-2	1-2	2-0	0-3	1-0	1-2	3-1
13. Ossett Albion	1-1	1-1	1-1	0-0	3-0	2-0	2-3	2-1	3-2	3-0	5-3	0-1	*	1-1	3-3	1-3	1-1	1-1	0-0	2-1
14. Ossett Town	1-1	0-0	1-1	1-5	1-2	2-1	1-0	1-1	1-2	3-1	4-1	0-3	2-3	*	0-0	1-2	0-1	0-5	1-1	1-0
15. Pickering Town	4-1	2-2	4-0	1-2	1-0	1-1	2-1	0-1	2-2	3-1	1-3	3-2	3-1	5-0	*	2-1	1-1	3-3	0-3	1-0
16. Pontefract Collieries	1-1	5-1	5-1	0-2	1-0	1-1	1-2	1-3	0-0	0-0	1-4	0-1	2-2	1-1	1-0	*	1-1	0-2	2-2	2-0
17. Sheffield	3-1	3-0	1-2	1-2	0-2	2-2	4-2	3-0	3-2	1-3	4-0	2-0	0-2	3-0	3-0	2-3	*	4-3	1-1	4-1
18. Stocksbridge Park S.	0-0	7-0	3-0	3-1	4-1	4-0	2-0	2-3	2-2	1-0	5-2	3-1	2-1	3-0	2-0	4-2	0-2	*	0-1	3-0
19. Thackley	1-1	1-0	1-0	0-0	4-0	2-1	2-0	1-0	2-1	3-0	1-2	1-0	3-1	1-1	1-1	0-0	1-0	2-3	*	1-0
20. Winterton Rangers	0-1	3-2	2-2	1-6	2-3	1-3	1-1	0-3	1-1	1-2	1-6	2-1	0-2	2-3	1-5	3-2	2-0	0-3	0-1	*

DIV. ONE RESULTS	1	2	3	4	5	6	7	8	9	10	11	12	13	14	15
1. Arnold Town	*	4-2	1-2	4-1	0-2	4-1	0-4	3-1	2-1	5-1	4-0	4-1	3-0	3-2	1-2
2. Brodsworth Miners W.	0-5	*	0-0	2-3	0-2	1-3	1-2	1-1	0-1	1-2	3-1	1-3	1-0	2-0	0-6
3. Garforth Town	1-4	2-0	*	4-2	0-3	5-0	1-0	2-1	0-4	0-0	1-0	0-1	1-0	2-2	2-0
4. Hall Road Rangers	1-4	5-0	1-4	*	0-3	3-1	1-3	5-1	1-2	3-1	2-1	1-1	0-2	1-2	2-2
5. Hallam	1-2	2-2	4-1	5-3	*	3-1	1-1	4-0	4-2	2-0	2-3	1-1	5-1	3-0	1-1
6. Harrogate Railway Ath.	1-7	4-3	1-0	3-2	0-1	*	2-0	1-1	0-1	1-1	3-3	3-0	4-1	1-2	0-2
7. Hatfield Main	2-2	5-0	1-3	4-2	1-0	0-1	*	3-1	0-3	4-1	2-0	3-3	5-0	0-0	0-3
8. Immingham Town	1-3	2-2	0-3	2-2	2-0	3-2	1-6	*	1-4	3-1	2-2	3-1	0-2	0-1	1-0
9. Louth United	2-1	3-1	2-2	0-0	0-3	1-1	1-2	6-2	*	3-1	2-3	6-1	4-1	5-1	2-1
10. RES Parkgate	0-5	2-0	0-1	1-1	1-2	5-5	2-3	4-1	2-4	*	4-2	2-2	3-2	1-4	1-2
11. Rossington Main	2-1	4-1	0-1	3-3	0-2	2-1	0-2	2-1	1-0	3-2	*	1-1	2-1	0-1	0-1
12. Selby Town	0-9	1-0	1-0	4-5	0-3	2-1	1-2	0-1	1-6	3-1	3-1	*	2-4	3-4	2-1
13. Tadcaster Albion	0-1	2-0	0-0	3-6	1-1	0-4	2-3	7-1	0-5	2-1	1-4	1-4	*	2-1	3-2
14. Worsbrough Bdge MW	2-6	8-1	0-1	0-1	0-2	1-2	0-3	4-0	1-1	4-0	0-2	0-2	7-0	*	2-1
15. Yorkshire Amateur	1-0	1-1	0-0	1-0	3-2	2-0	1-0	5-0	5-1	1-3	0-1	2-0	3-0	2-0	*

LEAGUE CUP 1994-95

First Round

Brodsworth Miners Welfare v Hatfield Main 3-2
Garforth Town v Arnold Town 3-2
RES Parkgate v Rossington Main 2-8

Second Round

Belper Town v Ashfield United 1-0
Eccleshill United v Thackley 0-5
Glasshoughton Welfare v Brodsworth MW 1-0
Hallam v Tadcaster Albion 1-0

(continued overleaf)

(League Cup, continued from page 753)

Harrogate Railway Athletic v Hall Road Rgrs 3-2
Lincoln United v Liversedge 8-0
Maltby Miners Welfare v Pickering Town 0-3
North Ferriby United v Selby Town 3-2
Ossett Town v Armthorpe Welfare 1-3
Stocksbridge Park Steels v Rossington Main 3-1
Hucknall Town v Sheffield 4-1
Louth United v Immingham Town 1-0
Worsborough Bdge Miners Welfare v Brigg Town 1-3
Ossett Albion v Garforth Town 3-2
Pontefract Collieries v Yorkshire Amateur 0-1
Winterton Rangers v Denaby United 2-1

Third Round

Belper Town v Stocksbridge Park Steels 0-2
Glasshoughton Welfare v Lincoln United 1-1,0-2
Louth United v Winterton Rangers 5-3
Thackley v Armthorpe Welfare 4-3
Brigg Town v Ossett Albion 1-2
Hucknall Town v Pickering Town 2-0
North Ferriby United v Hallam 2-1
Yorkshire Amateur v Harrogate Railway Athletic 2-0

Quarter-Finals

Hucknall Town v Louth United 3-1
Stocksbridge Park Steels v Lincoln United 0-4
Ossett Albion v Thackley 1-1,1-2
Yorkshire Amateur v North Ferriby United 0-2

Semi-Finals

Hucknall Town v North Ferriby United 2-1
Lincoln United v Thackley 0-1

Final: Hucknall Town 4, Thackley 1

PRESIDENT'S CUP 1993-94

First Round

Armthorpe Welfare v Immingham Town 0-0,2-0
Ashfield United v Maltby Miners Welfare 1-2
Eccleshill Utd v Pontefract Collieries 1-2
Hatfield Main v RES Parkgate 5-2
North Ferriby United v Ossett Albion 3-1
Rossington Main v Lincoln United 0-2
Winterton Rangers v Yorkshire Amateur 3-1
Arnold Town v Hallam 1-0
Belper Town v Denaby United 1-0
Harrogate Railway Athletic v Ossett Town 3-2
Louth United v Hucknall Town 1-4
Pickering Town v Thackley 3-2
Stocksbridge Park Steels v Brigg Town 0-2

Second Round

Arnold Town v Sheffield 2-2,1-0
Brigg Town v Harrogate Railway Athletic 3-1
Hatfield Main v Winterton Rangers 4-0
North Ferriby United v Liversedge 0-3
Belper Town v Pontefract Collieries 0-2
Glasshoughton Welfare v Lincoln United 2-2,2-4
Maltby Miners Welfare v Hucknall Town 1-1,1-4
Pickering Town v Armthorpe Welfare 0-1

Quarter-Finals

Arnold Town v Liversedge 4-2
Lincoln Unuted v Hucknall Town 5-3
Hatfield Main v Brigg Town 2-1
Pontefract Collieries v Armthorpe Welfare 1-0

Semi-Finals

Arnold Town v Lincoln United 2-4
Pontefract Collieries v Hatfield Main 2-1

Final: Lincoln United 2, Pontefract Collieries 1

Eventual champions Stockbridge Park Steels (dark shirts) put visiting St Helens Town in a mix during a Preliminary Round FA Cup tie on Sunday 29th August. The match had to be played on a Sunday because the Yorkshire side's facilities are shared with cricket - the very reason why the club were unable to take up the Northern Premier League place their championship would normally have earned. *Photo - Colin Stevens*

Northern Counties (East) Premier Division Ten Year Record

	84/5	85/6	86/7	87/8	88/9	89/0	90/1	91/2	92/3	93/4
Alfreton Town	4	6	1	–	–	–	–	–	–	–
Appleby Frodingham	16	18	–	–	–	–	–	–	–	–
Armthorpe Welfare	–	–	12	2	11	7	9	13	19	10
Arnold	7	1	–	–	–	–	–	–	–	–
Ashfield United	12	7	5	–	–	8	12	2	11	18
Belper Town	1	9	15	16	10	12	13	11	13	15
Bentley Victoria	15	14	14	–	–	–	–	–	–	–
Boston	17	17	19	–	–	–	–	–	–	–
Bridlington Town	–	–	10	4	3	1	–	–	–	–
Bridlington Trinity	9	19	17	13	16	4	–	–	–	–
Brigg Town	–	–	18	15	14	10	5	8	6	5
Denaby United	6	11	6	3	6	3	15	3	7	13
Eastwood Town	2	5	13	–	–	–	–	–	–	–
Eccleshill United	–	–	–	–	–	–	–	17	9	19
Emley	8	2	4	1	1	–	–	–	–	–
Farsley Celtic	–	8	2	–	–	–	–	–	–	–
Glasshoughton Welfare	–	–	–	–	–	–	–	19	18	12
Grimethorpe Miners Welfare	–	–	–	9	15	17	–	–	–	–
Guisborough Town	5	–	–	–	–	–	–	–	–	–
Guiseley	3	3	16	7	5	11	1	–	–	–
Hallam	–	–	–	10	12	14	–	–	–	–
Harrogate Railway Athletic	–	–	–	12	8	5	7	18	20	–
Harrogate Town	–	–	9	–	–	–	–	–	–	–
Hatfield Main	–	–	–	11	2	2	–	–	–	–
Heanor Town	18	15	–	–	–	–	–	–	–	–
Hucknall Town	–	–	–	–	–	–	–	–	–	14
Ilkeston Town	13	20	–	–	–	–	–	–	–	–
Lincoln United	–	–	–	–	–	–	–	–	–	3
Liversedge	–	–	–	–	–	–	–	14	14	11
Long Eaton United	–	4	11	14	13	–	–	–	–	–
Maltby Miners Welfare	–	–	–	–	–	–	6	7	4	7
Mexborough Town	19	–	–	–	–	–	–	–	–	–
North Ferriby United	–	–	3	6	4	6	4	4	3	9
North Shields	–	–	–	–	–	2	2	1	–	–
Ossett Albion	–	–	–	17	17	16	14	10	8	8
Ossett Town	–	–	–	–	–	–	8	12	12	16
Pickering Town	–	–	–	–	–	–	–	–	2	6
Pontefract Collieries	14	12	8	8	7	13	16	16	17	17
Sheffield	–	–	–	–	–	9	–	6	15	4
Spalding United	11	16	–	–	–	–	–	–	–	–
Spennymoor United	–	–	–	–	–	–	3	5	1	–
Stocksbridge Park Steels	–	–	–	–	–	–	–	–	16	1
Sutton Town					*(see Ashfield United)*					
Thackley	10	10	7	5	9	15	11	9	5	2
Winterton Rangers	–	–	–	–	–	–	10	15	10	20
No. of Clubs	19	20	19	17	17	18	16	19	20	20

PREMIER DIVISION CLUBS 1994-95

ARMTHORPE WELFARE

Chairman: Alan Bell **Vice Chairman:** James Houston
Secretary: Eric Cottam, 'Roydean', Whiphill Lane, Armthorpe, Doncaster DN3 3JP (0302 832514).
Manager: Carl Leighton **Asst Manager:** John McKeown **Coach:** Steve Taylor.
Physio: Joey Johnson **Comm. Manager:** Peter Camm **Press Officer:** Sharon Morgan.
Ground: Welfare Ground, Church Str., Armthorpe (0302 833674-Welfare, 0302 831247-Club No.).
Directions: From north: Turn left at main r'bout in centre of Doncaster, straight across next r/about on to Wheatley Hall Rd. Right at Mines Rescue Station, go to top of hill on to Armthorpe Rd. From south: M18 jct 4, on to A630, left at r'bout then proceed to next r'bout and turn right. Ground 400yds on left behind Plough Inn. Two and a half miles from Doncaster (BR). Buses A2, A3 & 181 pass ground.
Formed: 1926 **Disbanded:** 1974 **Reformed:** 1976
Seats: 200 **Cover:** 400 **Capacity:** 2,500 **Floodlights:** Yes **Nickname:** Wellie.
Midweek matches: Tuesday **Record Att.:** 2,000 v Doncaster R., Charity match 85-86
Colours: White/navy/white **Change colours:** Navy/white/navy **Club Shop:** No.
Programme: 24 pages **Editor:** Miss Sharon Morgan (0302 834475).
Previous League: Doncaster Senior **Club Sponsors:** Houston Transport.
Local Paper: Doncaster Evening Star **Clubhouse:** No. Wheatsheaf Hotel used after matches.
Record win: 7-0 **Record defeat:** 1-7
Club record scorer: Martin Johnson **Club record appearances:** Gary Leighton.
Club honours: Northern Co's East Lg R-up 87-88 (Lg Cup R-up 91-92, Div 1 R-up 83-84, East Central Div 1 84-85); Doncaster & Dist. Lg 82-83 (Div 1 81-82, Div 2 79-80, Div 3 78-79; Lg Cup 79-80 80-81 81-82 82-83; Challenge Cup 82-83); West Riding Chall. Cup 81-82 82-83; Goole & Thorne Dist. Cup 82-83

ARNOLD TOWN

President: Alan Croome **Chairman:** David Law. **Vice-Chairman:** Ivan Long.
Secretary: Steve Shout, 11 Newholme Drive, Wilford, Nottm NG3 5QD (0602 815390).
Manager: Iain McCullóch **Asst Mgr:** Peter Moody/John Bartlett
General Manager: Ray O'Brien **Physio:** John Bartlett **Res. Manager:** Jim Batey.
Comm. Manager: Tom Cross **Press Officer:** Martin Williams (0602 598759).
Ground: King George V Playing Fields, Gedling Rd, Arnold, Nottm (0602 263660).
Directions: From Nth M1 jct 26, B6004 (Stockhill Lane) 3 miles to A60 (White Hart pub on left), right at A60, immediate left (St Albans Rd), thru lights by Sainsburys, left at rear of Sainsburys, ground on right adjacent to market. From A1(M)/A614/A60 to lights (White Hart on right), 1st left thru lights, St Albans Rd then as above. From Nottm ring-road left into A60, right into Nottingham Rd after quarter mile to lights at Sainsburys, right then as above. Four miles from Nottingham Midland BR station. Buses 53, 55, 59 pass ground, buses 25, 26, 40 56, 57, 58 within 100yds.
Capacity: 3,400 **Seats:** 150 **Cover:** 950 **Floodlights:** Yes **Founded:** 1989
Midweek matches: Tuesday **Sponsors:** Mapperley Sports **Nickname:** Eagles
Cols: Yellow (blue pin stripes)/blue/yel. **Change Colours:** All white (blue trim) **Supporters' Club:** Yes.
Programme: 40 pages, 50p **Editor:** Mark Butler (0602 795396)
Club Shop: Opened September 1994 selling progs, scarves, badges, jumpers, pennants, key fobs, car stickers, mugs, *Team Talk* magazine. Programme swaps welcome. Contact Ken Baker (0602 204650).
Prev. Names: Arnold FC (founded 1928 as Arnold St Marys) merged with Arnold Kingswell (founded 1962) 1989.
Previous Grounds: Calverton Road Rec. 28-57/ Church Lane 57-62. *Kingswell: Nottingham Rd 62-89.*
Previous Leagues: Central Midlands 89-93. *Arnold FC: Notts Alliance (pre-war)/ Central Alliance 55-63/ Midland 63-82/ Northern Co's East 82-86/ Central Mids 86-89. Kingswell: Notts Youth/ Notts Amateur/ Notts Spartan/ East Midlands Regional (pre'76)/Midland 76-82/ Northern Co's East 82-86/ Central Midlands 86-89.*
Record Gate: 3,390; Arnold FC v Bristol Rovers, FA Cup 1st Rd, 9/12/67.
Reserves' Lge: Midland Reg. All. **Player progressing to Football League:** Devon White.
Record win: 9-0 v Selby Town (A), Northern Counties (East) League Division One 21/8/93.
Record defeat: 0-5 v Lincoln United, FA Vase Preliminary Round replay 9/10/91.
Record transfer fee paid: Nil **Rec'd** (Arnold FC): £2,000 for Devon White (Lincoln C., 1985).
Clubhouse: Licensed bar open matchdays & training night. Hot/cold drinks/food from tea-bar on matchdays.
Local Press: Nottm Evening Post & Football Post (0602 482000), Nottm Weekly Post & Recorder (0602 461222), Nottm Herald & Post (0602 481300).
Local Radio: Radio Nottm, Radio Trent (GEM AM), Nottm Hospital Radio.
Captain 93-94: Mark Goodwin **Top Scorer 93-94:** Chris Freestone 41 (33 league).
Players' P.o.Y. 93-94: Gavin Ottewell **Manager's P.o.Y 93-94:** Steve Hare.
Supporters' P.o.Y.: Christ Freestone.
Record scorer: Richard Johnson 71 **Record appearances:** Richard Johnson 156.
Hons (as Arnold FC + Arnold Town FC): Central Mids Lg 92-93 (R-up 88-89, Lg Cup 87-88 (R-up 90-91), Floodlit Cup 89-90); Northern Co's East Lg 85-86 (R-up 83-84, Div 1 93-94); Notts Snr Cup 60-61 64-65 65-66 68-69 70-71 92-93 (R-up 69-70 75-76 76-77 84-85); FA Cup 1st Rd replay 77-78; Central Alliance 62-63; FA Tphy 2nd Rd replay 71-72; Midland Co's Lg R-up 70-71 75-76 (Lg Cup 74-75 (R-up 80-81)). *Arnold Kingswell: Midland Co's Lg Div 1 79-80 (R-up 75-76 78-79 81-82, Lg R-up 75-76 76-77), Notts Snr Cup R-up 79-80 81-82.*

ASHFIELD UNITED

President: Frank Haynes MP **Chairman:** John E B Martin **Vice-Chairman:** Roy Gregory
Secretary: Frank Granger, Hawthorn Cottage, New Street, South Normanton DE55 2BS (0773 510066).
Manager: Bud Evans **Asst Manager:** Dave Moxon **Coach:** Darrel Bailey
Physio: Ken Peck **Press Officer:** Peter Bough **Comm. Mgr:** Secretary.
Ground: Lowmoor Road, Kirkby-in-Ashfield, Notts (0623 752181).
Directions: M1 jct 28, A38 towards Mansfield, at 4th lights turn right onto B6021 (s.p. Kirkby-in-Ashfield). After half mile turn right at lights into Lowmoor Rd immediately after crossing railway lines. Ground half mile on left next to Lowmoor Inn. Nearest rail station is Alfreton & Mansfield Parkway - 3 miles.
Seats: 250 **Cover:** 500 **Capacity:** 8,000 **Floodlights:** Yes **Founded:** 1885.
Club Shop: Yes (contact Peter Bough).
Prev. Name: Sutton Town 1885-1992 **Midweek matches:** Tuesday **Nickname:** Snipes
Club colours: Claret & blue **Change colours:** All white
Programme: 60 pages, 60p **Programme Editor:** Peter Bough
Sponsors: Home Brewery Co. **Reserve Team's League:** Midlands Regional Alliance.
Previous leagues: Notts & District, Notts & Derbys, Midland Comb., Derbys Senior, Central Comb., Notts Alliance, Central Alliance, Midland League, NE Counties, Northern Premier.
Prev. Grnds: Dog & Duck 1885-97/ New Cross 98-1919/ Avenue Ground 19-39/ Skegby MW 49-51/ Prestic Rd 51-77.
Record attendance: 1,562 v Leeds United, floodlight opening, 1980. *At Priestic Rd: 6,000 v Peterborough Utd, 1958. At The Avenue: 8,000 v Reading, FA Cup 1933.*
Local newspapers: Mansfield Chad **Captain 93-94:** R Flint **Player of the Year 93-94:** D Burrows.
Honours: Notts Snr Cup 08-09 12-13 13-14 23-24 55-56 57-58 59-60 61-62 62-63 63-64 67-68 69-70 71-72 72-73 73-74 74-75 76-77; Notts & Dist Lg 05-06 06-07; Derby Snr Lg 30-31 31-32 32-33; Central Alliance 50-51; Northern Co. East Lg R-up 91-92 (Lg Cup 85-86); Mansfield Charity Cup 1892-93 05-06 23-24; Sutton Charity Cup 29-30 30-31 31-32; Byron Cup 30-31 31-32; FA Cup 2nd Rnd 1933-34

BELPER TOWN

President: Alan Benfield **Chairman:** Phil Varney **Manager:** Martin Rowe.
Secretary: Mr D Laughlin, Lorne Cottage, Hagg Lane, Fritchley, Derbys DE5 2HJ (0773 856556).
Asst Manager: Mick Williamson **Press Officer:** D R Laughlin/S Wilton
Ground: Christ Church Meadow, Bridge Street, Belper (0773 825549).
Directions: From M1 North, Jnct. 28 onto A38 towards Derby, turn off at A610 (s.p. Ripley/Nottingham), then 4 exit at roundabout towards Ambergate. At junction with A6 (Hurt Arms Hotel) left to Belper. Ground on right past traffic lights. 400 yards from Belper (BR).
Seats: 200 **Cover:** 1,500 **Capacity:** 6,000 **Floodlights:** Yes **Year formed:** 1883
Club colours: Gold/black/gold **Change colours:** Sky & white **Nickname:** Nailers
Midweek matches: Tuesday **Programme:** 24 pages, 40p, **Editor:** David Laughlin.
Rec. Gate: 3,600 v Ilkeston, 1951 **Prev. Lges:** Central Alliance 57-61/ Midland Co's 61-82
Clubhouse details: Bar (Tetley and Castlemaine). Hot & cold food.
Prev. Ground: Acorn Ground (pre-1951) **Local newspapers:** Derby Evening Telegraph, Belper News
Captain: Mark Townsend.
Honours: Midland Counties Lg 79-80, Central Alliance League 1958-59, N. Counties East League 1984-85, Derbys Snr Cup 58-59 60-61 62-63 79-80, FA Cup 1st Round Proper 1887-88 (4th Qual. Rnd 1964-65), FA Vase 5th Rd 93-94.

Armthorpe Welfare (dark shorts) attack during their 1-1 draw at Ossett Town. *Photo - Barry Lockwood.*

Ashfield's Scott Warden takes evasive action as Belper's John Bookbinder lets fly. *Photo - Tony Gregory.*

Belper Town FC. *Photo - David Robinson.*

BRIGG TOWN

President: B Robins **Chairman:** H Williams **Manager:** Ralph Clayton
Secretary: R B Taylor, 'Highfield House', Barton Rd, Wrawby, Brigg, South Humbs DN20 8SH (0652 652284).
Coach: John Kaye **Commercial Manager:** H Williams
Ground: The Hawthorns, Hawthorn Avenue, Brigg (0652 652767).
Directions: From M180 Scunthorpe East, A18 through Brigg leaving on Wrawby Rd, left into East Parade/Woodbine Ave, follow houses on right into Hawthorn Ave. One mile from Brigg (BR).
Seats: 250 **Cover:** 2 Stands **Capacity:** 4,000 **Floodlights:** Yes **Year formed:** 1864
Colours: Black & white stripes/black/black **Change colours:** Orange shirts
Programme: 16 pages **Programme Editor:** Secretary **Nickname:** Zebras
Previous Leagues: Lindsey/ Lincs 48-76/ Midland Counties 76-82
Previous Grounds: Manor House Convent, Station Rd (pre 1939); Brocklesby Ox 1939-59
Clubhouse: Licensed club open matchdays **Rec. Gate:** 2,000 v Boston U. 1953 (at Brocklesby Ox).
Honours: Northern Co's East Lg Presidents Cup R-up 91-92 92-93, Lincs Lg 49-50 53-54 73-74 75-76 (Div 1 68-69 69-70 70-71 71-72, Lg Cup 49-50 65-66 68-69 69-70 72-73); Mids Co's Lg 77-78 (Lg Cup 77-78), Lincs 'A' Snr Cup 75-76 76-77 93-94, Lincs 'B' Snr Cup 54-55 56-57 66-67 68-69 84-85.

DENABY UNITED

President: Alan Wilson **Chairman:** Joe Cooper **Gen. Manager:** Dennis Hobson
Secretary: Mrs B Norton, 2 Castle Grove Terrace, Low Rd, Conisborough DN12 3EA (0709 864042).
Manager: David Lloyd **Asst Manager:** TBA **Physio:** Frank Tingle.
Ground: Tickhill Square, Denaby Main, Doncaster (0709 864042).
Directions: From Conisbrough take first left in Denaby along Wadworth St. From Mexborough take first right after Reresby Arms, left on to Bolton St. then left on to Wheatley Street. Rail to Conisbrough.
Seats: 250 **Cover:** 350 **Capacity:** 6,000 **Floodlights:** Yes **Year formed:** 1895
Clubhouse: None. **Midweek matches:** Tuesday or Wednesday **Sponsors:** various
Colours: Red & white/red/red **Change colours:** Yellow/green/yellow **Nickname:** None.
Programme: 48 pages 35p **Programme Editor:** David Green (0709 862319)
Reserves' League: None **Previous Ground:** Denaby Recreation Ground 1895-1912.
Previous Leagues: Sheffield Association 1900-02 15-18 19-20 40-45/ Midland 02-13 20-40 45-60 61-65/ Doncaster & District 18-19/ Central Alliance 60-61/ Yorks 65-82.
Record attendance: 3,801 v Oldham Athletic, FA Cup 1st Rnd Proper 15/11/58
Record win: 20-0 v Shirebrook Colliery (A), Central Alliance 60-61.
Record transfer fee paid: £350 for Kevin Deakin (Mossley, 1984).
Record transfer fee received: £5,000 for Jonathan Brown (Exeter, 1990).
Players progressing to Football League: Jack Barker (Derby & England), Keith Burkinshaw (Liverpool 1953), Andy Barnsley (Rotherham 1985), Chris Beaumont (Rochdale 1988), Jonathan Brown (Exeter 1990).
Local newspapers: South Yorks Times, Doncaster Free Press.
Captain 93-94: Andy Cracknell **Top Scorer 93-94:** Rob Spotswood 23 **P.o.Y. 93-94:** Lee Myers.
Honours: Yorks Lg R-up 67-68 (Div 2 R-up 66-67, Div 3 R-up 81-82, Lg Cup 71-72); Northern Counties East Div 1 South R-up 83-84; Midland Lg R-up 07-08; Sheffield & Hallamshire Snr Cup 32-33 35-36 86-87; Thorn EMI Floodlight Competition R-up 83-84; Sheffield Association Lg 40-41; Mexborough Montague Cup 14-15.

Denaby United FC. Back Row (L/R): David Sharpe, Craig Loftus, Martin Barnfield, Steve Myles, David Middleton, Rob Spotswood, Alan Maguire, Lee Myers, Mark License, Frank Tingle (Physio). Front: Ian Smith, Marcus Brameld, Bud Evans (Manager, now Ashfield United), David Porter (93-94 Kit Sponsor), Wilf Race (now manager of Denaby & Cadeby MW), Tony Holgate, Phil Watkin.

GLASSHOUGHTON WELFARE

President: R Rooker **Chairman:** Mr G Day
Secretary: E Jones, 'Marrica', Westfields Ave., Cutsyke, Castleford W10 5JJ (0977 556257).
Manager: Mr Wayne Day **Asst Manager/Coach:** Mr M Ripley.
Ground: Glasshoughton Welfare, Leeds Rd, Glasshoughton, Castleford (0977 518981).
Directions: M62 junct. 31 or 32 towards Castleford. From exit 32 the road comes into Glasshoughton. From exit 31 turn right at 2nd roundabout at Whitwood Tech. College. Ground is on left in Leeds Road. Car park on ground. 1 mile from Castleford (BR).
Club colours: All blue **Change colours:** All yellow
Seats: None **Covered:** 250 **Capacity:** 2,000 **Floodlights:** Yes **Founded:** 1964
Record Att.: 300 v Bradford C – F'light opening 1990
Previous Name: Anson Sports 1964-76 **Previous Ground:** Saville Park 1964-76
Previous League: West Yorkshire **Clubhouse:** Bar & refreshment facilities.
Programme: 20 pages, 20p **Programme Editor:** Mr G Day.

HALLAM

Chairman: A Scanlan **Vice Chairman:** A Cooper **President:** T Stones.
Secretary: G L Holland, 34 Standon Cres., Sheffield S9 1PP (0742 490428).
Manager: G Kenny **Physio:** J Beachell **Press Off.:** M Radford
Ground: Sandygate, Sandygate Road, Crosspool, Sheffield S10 (0742 309484).
Directions: A57 Sheffield to Glossop Rd, left at Crosspool shopping area signed 'Lodge Moor' on to Sandygate Rd. Ground half mile on left opposite Plough Inn. 51 bus from Crucible Theatre.
Seats: None **Cover:** 200 **Capacity:** 2,000 **Floodlights:** Yes **Year formed:** 1860
Nickname: Countrymen **Club Sponsors:** H.I.S. & Umbro Int. Ltd.
Colours: Blue/white/blue **Change colours:** All red
Programme: 8 pages with entry **Editor:** Mark Radford (0742 434529). **Club Shop:** No.
Midweek Matches: Wednesday **Previous leagues:** Yorkshire 52-82.
Record Gate: 2,000 v Hendon, FA Amtr Cup 3rd Rd 1959. (13,855 v Dulwich at Hillsborough, FA Amtr Cup 1955).
Clubhouse: Licensed bar and meals in Plough Inn opposite. Hot & cold snacks in ground for matches.
Record win: 7-0 v Hatfield Main (H) 92-93, & v Kiveton Park (H) 69-70.
Rec. loss: 0-7 v Hatfield Main (A) 88-89 **Local Press:** Star, Green'Un, Sheffield Telegraph.
Players progressing to Football League: Sean Connelly to Stockport County, 1992-93.
Club record scorer: A Stainrod 46 **Club record appearances:** P Ellis 500+.
Captain 93-94: S Sidebottom **Top Scorer 93-94:** S Bergara 14 **P.o.Y. 93-94:** I McMillan
Hons: Northern Counties (East) League Div 1 Runners-up 90-91 93-94, Yorkshire League Div 2 60-61 (Runners-up 56-57), Sheffield & Hallamshire Snr Cup 50-51 61-62 64-65 67-68.

HUCKNALL TOWN

President: Andy Stewart **Chairman:** John Coleman **Vice-Chairman:** J Beharall
Secretary: Brian Scothern, 95 Brookfield Ave., Shortwood Estate, Hucknall, Notts NG15 6FF (0602 634208).
Manager: Edward Mullane **Assistant Manager:** John H Coleman
Coach: Paul Smalley **Physio:** Ken Burton.
Ground: Watnall Road, Hucknall, Notts NG15 7LP (0602 641292).
Directions: M1 jct 27, A608 to lights, right onto A611 to Hucknall, right at r'bout (new by-pass), over next r'bout, right at next r'bout into Watnall Rd - ground entrance on right. From M1 jct 26 follow Nottm signs to lights on island, left onto A610, right at Three Ponds Pub onto B600 towards Watnall, 200 yds past Queens Head turn right signed Hucknall, follow over motorway and past Rolls Royce - ground on left. 7 miles from Nottingham (BR) - bus 344.
Capacity: 2,000 **Seats:** 240 **Cover:** 1,100 **Floodlights:** Yes **Founded:** 1946.
Colours: Yellow/black/red **Change colours:** White/black or red/black or red.
Midweek home matches: Tuesday **Club Shop:** Matchdays only - contact secretary.
Programme: 30 pages, 50p **Programme Editor:** Simon Matters. **Nickname:** Town.
Prev. Ground: Higham Park 46-54 **Clubhouse:** Every night and weekend lunchtimes
Previous Name: Hucknall Colliery Welfare (until closure of pit in 1988).
Previous Leagues: Bulwell & Dist. 46-59 60-65/ Central Alliance 59-60/ Notts Spartan 65-70/ Notts Alliance 70-89/ Central Midlands 89-92.
Sponsors: Doff-Portland **Record Gate:** 1,305 v Macclesfield, FA Cup 2nd Qual 26/9/92.
Reserve Team's League: Midlands Regional Alliance.
Local Newspapers: Hucknall & Bulwell Dispatch/ Nottm Evening Post/ Nottm Football Post.
Captain 93-94: John Chamberlain **P.o.Y. 93-94:** David Kent **Top Scorer 93-94:** Mark Nangle 21.
Hons: Northern Counties (East) League Div 1 Runners-up 92-93 (League Cup 93-94), Central Midlands League(2) 89-91 (Runners-up 91-92, League Cup(3) 89-92), Notts Alliance(4) 76-78 87-89 (League Cup 78-79, Div 1 72-73, Div 2 70-71, Intermediate Cup 72-73); Notts Snr Cup 84-85 90-91 (Runners-up 83-84 85-86 87-88 89-90); FA Vase Quarter-Finals 85-86.

LINCOLN UNITED

President: A Simpson **Chairman:** K Roe **Vice Chairman:** P Morley
Secretary/Press Officer: Keith Weaver, 22 Grainsby Close, Lincoln LN6 7QF (0522 531832).
Manager: Gary Goddard **Asst Manager:** Gerard Creane **Coach:** John Wilkinson.
Physio: Anthony Adams **Commercial Manager:** Roy Parnham.
Ground: Ashby Avenue, Hartsholme, Lincoln (0522 690674).
Directions: From Newark A46 onto Lincoln relief road (A446), right at 2nd r'bout for Birchwood (Skellingthorpe Rd), go for 1 mile passing lake and Country Park, 1st right 10yds after 30mph sign into Ashby Ave., ground entrance 200 yds, opposite Old Peoples home. From north proceed along A57 via Saxilby until reaching A46 Lincoln Relief Road - continue on this and turn left at r'bout signed Birchwood then as above. 3 miles from Loncoln Central (BR).
Capacity: 1,750 **Seats:** 150 **Covered:** 250 **Founded:** 1938 **Floodlights:** Yes
Colours: All white **Change Colours:** All yellow **Nickname:** United
Programme: 40 pages, 50p **Editor:** John Wilkinson (0522 788880)
Club Shop: No, but old programmes on sale on matchdays - contact secretary.
Clubhouse: Open every day normal licensing hours. Matchday snack bar - hot & cold food & drinks.
Prev. Lges: Lincs 45-48 60-67/ Lincoln 48-60/ Yorkshire 67-82/ Northern Co's East 82-86/ Central Midlands 82-92.
Prev. Grounds: Skew Bridge (1940's)/ Co-op Spts Ground (til mid-60's)/ Hartsholme Cricket Grnd (til '82).
Previous Name: Lincoln Amateurs (until an ex-professional signed in 1954).
Record Gate: 1,200 v Crook Town, FA Amateur Cup 1st Rd Proper, 1968.
Best FA Cup season: First Round Proper 91-92 (lost 0-7 at Huddersfield Town).
Club Sponsors: Hykeham Forum Supplies/ City Tyre Experts.
Midweek home matchday: Tuesday **Reserve team's League:** Lincolnshire.
Record win: 10-0 v Winterton **Record defeat:** 0-7 v Heanor Town, 1989.
Record transfer fee paid: £250 for Dean Dye (Sutton Town, July 1990) - only player ever bought.
Record transfer fee received: £3,000 for Dean Dye (Charlton Athletic, July 1991).
Captain 93-94: **Top Scorer 93-94:**
Record scorer: Terry Nelson 175 **Record appearances:** Brian Davies 436.
Local Newspapers: Lincolnshire Echo, Lincoln Standard.
Hons: Northern Co's (E) League Div 1 92-93 (Div 1 Sth 82-83, Div 2 85-86, Presidents Cup 93-94), Yorkshire League 70-71 73-74 (League Cup 70-71), Lincolnshire League 63-64, Lincolnshire Snr 'A' Cup 72-73 85-86 (Runners-up 91-92 93-94, 'B' Cup 63-64 70-71), Central Midlands League 91-92 (Wakefield Cup 90-91), Evans Halshaw Floodlit Cup Runners-up 92-93, Lincolnshire I'mediate Cup(7) 67-73 80-81.

LIVERSEDGE

Chairman: Bob Gawthorpe **Manager:** Colin Penrose **Asst Mgr:** Stuart Harrison
Secretary/Press Officer: Michael Balmforth, 5 Victoria Rd., Gomersal, Cleckheaton BD19 4RG (0274 862123).
Ground: Clayborn Ground, Quaker Lane, Hightown Rd, Cleckheaton, West Yorks (0274 862108).
Directions: M62 jct 26, A638 into Cleckheaton, right at lights on corner of Memorial Park, through next lights & under railway bridge, 1st left (Hightown Rd) and Quaker Lane is approx quarter mile on left and leads to ground. From M1 jct 40, A638 thru Dewsbury and Heckmondwike to Cleckheaton, left at Memorial Park lights then as above. Buses 218 & 220 (Leeds-Huddersfield) pass top of Quaker Lane.
Seats: None **Cover:** 750 **Capacity:** 2,000 **Floodlights:** Yes **Founded:** 1910
Colours: Blue & black **Change colours:** All yellow **Nickname:** Sedge
Programme: 28 pages, 30p **Programme Editor:** Secretary **Club Shop:** No
Midweek Matches: Tuesday **Reserves' Lge:** NCEL Res. Div. **Sponsors:** Various
Previous Leagues: Spen Valley/ West Riding County Amateur 22-72/ Yorkshire 72-82.
Previous Ground: Primrose Lane, Hightown. **Clubhouse:** Matchdays, Tues, Thursday. Pool, TV. Pies + crisps
Players progressing to Football League: Garry Briggs (Oxford), Martin Hirst (Bristol City).
Local Press: Yorkshire Evening Post, Telegraph & Argus, Spen Valley News, Spenbrough Guardian.
Hons: West Riding Co. Chal. Cup 48-49 51-52 69-70; West Riding County Cup 89-90; North Counties East Lg Div 1 R-up 89-90 (Div 2 R-up 88-89); West Riding Co. Amtr Lg(6) 23-24 25-27 64-66 68-69 (Lg Cup 57-58 64-65).

MALTBY MINERS WELFARE

President: H Henson **Chairman:** G McCormick **Vice Chairman:** M Richardson
Secretary: Mr S P Mallender, 109 Sycamore Avenue, Bramley, Rotherham, Sth Yorks S66 0PA (0709 549958).
Manager: Gary Waller **Asst Mgr:** Richard Moon **Physio:** T Morris
Press Off.: N Dunhill (0709 815676). **Commercial Mgr:** A Marshall (0302 743518).
Ground: Muglet Lane, Maltby (0709 812462 (match days)). **Directions:** Exit M18 at junct with A631. Two miles into Maltby, right at crossroads at Queens Hotel corner on to B6427. Ground 3/4 mile on left. Bus 101 from Rotherham stops at ground. Bus 287 from Sheffield to Queens Hotel, then follow as above.
Seats: 150e **Cover:** 300 **Capacity:** 2,000 **Floodlights:** Yes **Reformed:** 1972
Sponsors: Jack Green Sports **Midweek home matchday:** Tuesday. **Clubhouse:** No
Record Gate: 1,500 v Sheffield Wed., friendly June 91-92. Competitive: 940 v Thackley, Yorks Lg Cup 77-78.
Colours: White/black/white **Change colours:** Yellow/blue/yellow **Nickname:** Miners
Programme: 12 pages, 50p **Editor:** Nick Dunhill (0709 815676) **Club Shop:** No
Previous name: Maltby Main **Prev. lges:** Sheff. Co. Snr/ Yorks 73-82. **Record win:** 6-0
Players progressing to Football Lge: Michael Williams (Sheff Wed) 91-92. **Record defeat:** 2-5
Top Scorer 93-94: Russ Evans **Captain & P.o.Y. 93-94:** Russ Evans.
Hons: Sheffield & Hallamshire Snr Cup 77-78, Northern Counties East Lg Presidents Cup 92-93 (SF 90-91), Mexborough Montague Cup 76-77 80-81 90-91, Yorks Lg R-up 77-78, Sheffield Wharncliffe Cup 80-81.

NORTH FERRIBY UNITED

President: Brian Thacker **Chairman:** Jeff Frank **Vice Chairman:** Brian Sievewright
Secretary: Stephen Tather, 16 Peasholme, Heads Lane, Hessle, E Yorks HU13 0NY (0482 642046).
Manager: Peter Daniel **Asst Mgr:** Richard Woomble **Coach/Physio:** TBA
Press Officer: Roy Wallis **Commercial Manager:** Barry Johnson.
Ground: Grange Lane, Church Road, North Ferriby HU14 3AA (0482 634601).
Directions: Main Leeds-Hull road A63 or M62, North Ferriby is 8 miles west of Hull. Into North Ferriby, thru village past the Duke of Cumberland Hotel, right down Church Rd, ground half mile on left. One mile from North Ferriby (BR).
Seats: 250 **Cover:** 1,000 **Capacity:** 5,000 **Floodlights:** Yes **Founded:** 1934.
Colours: Green/white **Change colours:** Maroon/sky **Nickname:** United
Midweek home matches: Tuesday **Sponsors:** Sentry Alarms **Club Shop:** No
Programme: 32 pages, 50p **Programme Editor:** Jeff Frank (0482 634601).
Previous leagues: East Riding Church/ East Riding Amateur/ Yorks 69-82.
Reserves' Lge: E Riding Amtr **Record Gate:** 1,800 v Tamworth, FA Vase Semi-Final, 1989
Record win: 8-0 v North Newbald, East Riding Senior Cup 1992.
Record defeat: 1-7 v North Shields, Northern Counties (East) League Premier Division 1991.
Record transfer fee received: £3,000 for Tim Hotte (Hull City, 1988).
Players progressing to Football League: Tim Hotte (Hull) 1988, Ian Ironside (Halifax) 1988, Darren France, Dean Windass & Mick Matthews (Hull) 1991.
Local newspapers: Hull Daily Mail **Clubhouse details:** Bar, lounge, TV, pool - open every night
Club record scorer: Stuart McKenzie **Club record appearances:** Richard Woomble, 1974-94.
Captain 93-94: Dave Levesley **P.o.Y. 93-94:** Paul Newman **Top Scorer 93-94:** Stuart McKenzie 32
Hons: FA Vase SF 88-89 (QF 89-90, 5th Rd 87-88); Yorkshire Lg R-up 75-76 (Lg Cup 74-75, Div 2 70-71), Northern Co's East Div 1 85-86 (Lg Cup R-up) 90-91, Presidents Cup 90-91, Div 1 (North), R-up 82-83, Reserve Div R-up 90-91); East Riding Snr Cup 70-71 76-77 77-78 78-79 90-91; East Riding Church Lg 37-38.

OSSETT ALBION

President: Miss Helen Worth **Chairman:** N A Wigglesworth **Vice-Chairman:** S B Garside.
Secretary: David Chambers, 109 South Parade, Ossett, West Yorks WF5 0EB (0924 276004).
Manager: Jimmy Martin **Asst Manager:** George Grouse **Coach:** Peter Eaton.
Commercial Mgr: D Riley **Physio:** John Hirst **Press Officer:** N Wigglesworth (0924 275630).
Ground: Dimple Wells, Ossett (0924 273618-club, 0924 280450-ground (matchday only)).
Directions: M1 jct 40. Take Wakefield road, right at Post House Hotel down Queens Drive. At end right then second left down Southdale Rd. At end right, then first left down Dimple Wells (cars only). Coaches take second left following the road for 200yds bearing left twice. Four miles from both Wakefield and Dewsbury BR stations. Buses 116 and 117.
Seats: 200 **Cover:** 500 **Capacity:** 3,000 **Floodlights:** Yes **Founded:** 1944
Reserves' Lge: NCEL Res Div **Midweek matches:** Tuesday **Nickname:** Albion
Colours: Old gold/black/black **Change colours:** All white **Sponsors:** Arco.
Programme: 44 pages, 50p **Programme Editor:** N Wigglesworth (0924 275630).
Club Shop: Yes, selling lapel badges, pennants, programmes etc. Contact chairman.
Previous Ground: Fearn House **Record Gate:** 1,200 v Leeds Utd, floodlight opening 1986.
Record win: 12-0 v British Ropes (H), Yorkshire League Division Two 6/5/59.
Record defeat: 2-11 v Swillington (A), West Yorkshire League Division One 25/4/56.
Previous Lges: Heavy Woollen Area 44-49/ West Riding Co. Amtr 49-50/ West Yorks 50-57/ Yorks 57-82.
Clubhouse: 3 bars + function room, open 7 days per week - catering available.
Players progressing to Football League: Gary Brook (Newport, Scarborough, Blackpool) 1987, Ian Ironside (Barnsley, Middlesbrough, Scarborough) 1980.
Local Press: Wakefield Express *(continued opposite)*

Liversedge FC. Back Row (L/R): Peter Crowther, Sean Twohig, Mark Woffendin, Simon O'Hara, Dean Rayne, Karl Milner, Andy Yates. Front: Andy Payne, John Hendrick, Mick Oddy, Paul Smith, Karl Gray, Mark Wilkinson.

North Ferriby United FC. Back Row (L/R): Dave Robinson (Asst Manager), Stuart McKenzie, Paul Newman, Mark Tennison, Ged Stead, Mick Trotter, Dave Levesley, Billly Heath, Peter Daniel (Manager). Front: Steve Robinson, Richard Twigger, Darren Wildridge, Alan Ward, Daniel O'Neill (Mascot), Shane Milner, Phil Devaney.

(Ossett Albion details continued from page 760)

Club record appearances: Peter Eaton - 800+ in 22 years.
Club record scorer: John Balmer.
Captain 93-94: Shaun Joyce
Top Scorer & P.o.Y. 93-94: John Balmer (44 goals).
Hons: Yorks Lg 74-75 (R-up 59-60 61-62, Lg Cup 75-76, 76-77, Div 2 78-79, 80-81 (R-up 58-59)); Northern Co. East Div 1 86-87 (Lg Cup 83-84); West Yorks Lg 53-54 55-56 (Div 2 52-53, Lg Cup 52-53); West Riding County Cup 64-65 65-66 67-68; Wheatley Cup 56-57 58-59

Right: *John Balmer, Ossett Albion's club record scorer and Player of the Year.*

OSSETT TOWN

President: John Carter **Chairman:** Graham Firth **Vice Chairman:** G Froggett
Secretary: Frank Lloyd, 27 Park Close, Mapplewell, Barnsley S75 6BY (0226 382415).
Manager: Wayne Day **Asst Manager:** David Ingham **Coach:** Steve Carter
Press Officer: Bruce Saul **Commercial Manager:** David Coxhill.
Ground: Ingfield, Prospect Road, Ossett, Wakefield WF5 8AN (0924 272960).
Directions: M1 jct 40, B6129 to Ossett, left into Dale Street, left again at lights opposite bus station on ring road, ground on left. Nearest stations Dewsbury or Wakefield Westgate - both three miles from. Buses 116, 117, 126 and 127 from Wakefield, buses 116, 126 and 127 from Dewsbury, buses 117, 118 or 216 from Leeds.
Seats: 360 **Cover:** 650 **Capacity:** 4,000 **Floodlights:** Yes **Founded:** 1936
Colours: All red **Change colours:** All sky **Midweek matches:** Tuesday
Programme: 12 pages, 50p **Programme Editor:** Bruce Saul
Club Shop: Yes, selling programmes, sweaters, badges, hats. Contact club.
Sponsors: Action Stations **Record Gate:** 2,600 v Manchester Utd, friendly 1988
Clubhouse: Fri & Sun lunctimes, all day Sat & every evening. Hand-pulled beer. Pie/peas, chips, soup from tea bar.
Local Press: Dewsbury Reporter **Previous Leagues:** Leeds 36-39/ Yorkshire 45-82.
Prev. Ground: Fern House (pre-1958) **Record fee received:** £1,350 for Derek Blackburn (Swansea 1957).
Reserves' Lge: NCEL Reserve Div. **Record defeat:** 0-7 v Easington Colliery, FA Vase 8/10/83.
Record win: 10-1 v Harrogate RA (H), Northern Co's (East) Lge Premier Division 27/4/93.
Players prog. to Football Lge: Arnold Kendall/Ron Liversedge/Gary Chapman (B'ford C) 1949/56/88, Derek Blackburn (S'sea) 1957, Simon Lowe (Barnsley) 1983, Mick Norbury (Scarboro.) 1989, Mike Williams (Sheff W.) 1990.
P.o.Y. 93-94: Gareth Dodd. **Captain 93-94 & Club record appeances:** Steve Worsfold.
Top Scorer 93-94: Tommy Graham 5 **Club Record Scorer:** Dave Leadbeater.
Hons: W Riding Co. Cup 58-59 81-82, NECL Cup 89-90 (Div 2 88-89, Res Div 88-89, Res. Cup(2) 87-89).

PICKERING TOWN

President: S P Boak **Chairman:** M T Jones **Vice Chairman:** A Dunning
Secretary/Press Officer: Mr K W Sales, 'Glen-Keith', 4 Northway, Pickering, North Yorks YO18 8NN (0751 473348).
Manager: Nigel Tate **Assistant Manager/Physio:** Michael Hudson
Coach: Shaun McGinty **Commercial Manager:** B Wood.
Ground: Recreation Club, Mill Lane (off Malton Rd), Pickering, North Yorkshire (0751 473317).
Directions: A169 from Malton, 1st left past Police Station and B.P. garage into Mill Lane, ground 300yds on right.
Seats: 100 **Cover:** 500 **Capacity:** 2,000 **Floodlights:** Yes **Founded:** 1888
Midweek home matches: Tuesday **Club Sponsors:** Flamingoland **Nickname:** Pikes
Programme: 32 pages, 50p **Programme Editor:** Secretary. **Club Shop:** Not yet
Colours: Royal/white/royal **Change colours:** Yellow/blue.
Reserves' Lge: York & Dist. **Record Gate:** 1,412 v Notts County, friendly, August 1991.
Previous leagues: Beckett/ York & District/ Scarborough & District/ Yorkshire 72-82.
Clubhouse: Open 1.30pm for Saturday games, 6pm for midweek games. Various beers. Food available from Football Club Kitchen at half-time and after games.
Players progressing to Football League: Chris & Craig Short (both Scarborough & Notts County).
Local Press: Pickering Gazette & Herald, Yorkshire Evening Press, Mercury, Scarborough Evening News.
Hons: NCEL R-up 92-93 (Div 2 1987-88, Div 1 R-up 91-92), Yorks Lg Div 3 73-74, North Riding Snr Cup R-up 93-94, North Riding County Cup 90-91.

PONTEFRACT COLLIERIES

President: R Blatherwick **Chairman:** Anthony Dunwell, JP **Vice Chairman:** D Walker
Secretary: Sid Mason, 16 Harefield Rd, Pontefract, West Yorks WF8 2HX (0977 707756).
Manager: Paul Dooler **Asst Mgr:** Fred Bennett **Coach:** Dave Cope.
Physio: Roy Muggleton **Press Officer:** Barry Bennett (0977 682593).
Ground: Skinner Lane, Pontefract, West Yorkshire (0977 702180).
Directions: M62 jct 32 towards Pontefract. Left at traffic lights opposite Racecourse entrance (travelling through Pontefract follow Racecourse/Leeds signs to traffic lights and turn right) - ground past Territorial Army unit. 1 mile from Monkhill (BR). All Leeds and Castleford buses stop near ground.
Seats: 100 **Cover:** 400 **Capacity:** 2,000 **Floodlights:** Yes **Founded:** 1958
Midweek home matches: Tuesday **Reserves' Lge:** NCEL Reserve Div. **Nickname:** Colls
Sponsors: John Betts Quality Used Cars **Previous leagues:** West Yorkshire 58-79/ Yorkshire 79-82.
Colours: White/blue/blue **Change colours:** All yellow **Club Shop:** No
Programme: 8 pages, 30p **Programme Editor:** Barry Bennett (0977 682593).
Local Press: Pontefract/Castleford Express **Record attendance:** 1,000 v Hull City – floodlight opening 1985.
Players progressing to Football League: David Penney to Derby County, 1985.
Clubhouse: Fully licensed. Hot & cold snacks. Open one and a half hours before any game, and after games with hours to suit demand.
Club Record Scorer: Martin Brock **Club Record Appearances:** John Brown
Captain 93-94: Steve Whitelam **P.o.Y. 93-94:** Dean Limb **Top Scorer 93-94:** Martin Brock.
Hons: Northern Co's East Lg Div 1 83-84 (Div 2 R-up 82-83, Floodlit Comp 87-88 88-89); Yorks Lg Div 3 81-82; West Riding Co. Cup R-up 87-88 90-91; Embleton Cup 82-83 86-87; Castleford FA Cup 82-83 86-87; West Yorks Lg.

SHEFFIELD

Chairman: Alan Methley **Vice Chairman:** Paul Wilder. **President:** John Green
Secretary: Stephen Hall, 24 Crofton Ave., Sheffield S6 1WF (0742 344553).
Manager: Kenny Johnson **Asst Manager:** Andy Morley **Coach:** Andy Jackson
Press Officer: Alan Methley **Commercial Manager:** John Green.
Ground: Sheffield International Stadium (Don Valley), Worksop Rd, Sheffield S9.
Directions: M1 jct 33, dual c'way towards city centre, take 2nd exit (A57), right at bottom of slip road, continue to lights at bottom of hill, right at lights then left at rear of Morrisons supermarket, follow road and stadium entrance and car park is on right just after low bridge. Rotherham buses from city centre pass ground.
Seats: 25,000 **Cover:** 13,000 **Capacity:** 25,000 **Floodlights:** Yes **Founded:** 1856.
Colours: Red/black/black **Change colours:** All blue. **Nickname:** The Club.
Programme: Average 16 pages, 50p **Editor:** B Willis (0742 392423). **Club Shop:** No.
Previous league: Yorks 49-82 **Club Sponsors:** Daily Star **Reserve Team:** No.
Prev. grounds: Abbeydale Park, Dore (pre-'89)/ Sheffield Amat. Spts Club, Hillsborough Park 89-91.
Clubhouse: No. **Record Gate:** 2,000 v Barton Rovers, FA Vase SF 76-77.
Midweek matchday: Wednesday **Player progressing to Football Lge:** Richard Peacock, Hull 93-94.
Capt. 93-94: Greg Mitchell **Top Scorer 93-94:** Richard Bainbridge **P.o.Y. 93-94:** Jimmy Flynn.
Hons: FA Amtr Cup 03-04, FA Vase R-up 76-77, NCEL Cup 93-94 (Div 1 88-89 90-91), Yorks Lg Div 2 76-77.

STOCKSBRIDGE PARK STEELS

President: C D Sedgwick **Chairman:** A Bethel **Vice-Chairman:** M Grimmer.
Secretary: Michael Grimmer, 48 Hole House Lane, Stocksbridge, Sheffield S30 5BP (0742 886470).
Manager: Mick Horne **Asst Manager:** Trevor Gough.
Physio/Press Officer: Geoff Littlewood (0742 463328).
Commercial Manager: Andrew Horsley (0742 883867).
Ground: Bracken Moor Lane, Stocksbridge, Sheffield (0742 882045).
Directions: M1 jct 35a from south, 36 from north, A616 to Stocksbridge (A6102 from Sheffield – on arriving at Stocksbridge turn left into Nanny Hill under the Clock Tower and continue up the hill for about 500 yds - ground on left.
Seats: 450 **Cover:** 700 **Capacity:** 3,500 **Floodlights:** Yes **Founded:** 1986
Colours: Yellow/blue **Change colours:** All blue **Nickname:** Steels
Midweek matches: Tuesday **Sponsors:** St Christophers **Metal badges:** £2
Programme: With admission **Editor:** Geoff Littlewood (0742 463328)
Prev. Ground: Stonemoor 49-51 52-53 **Record Gate:** 2,000 v Sheffield Wed., Floodlight opening Oct '91.
Reserves' Lge: Whitbread Co. Snr **Prev. Names:** Stocksbridge Works, Oxley Park; clubs merged in 1986.
Previous Leagues: Sheffield Amateur/ Sheffield Association/ Yorkshire 49-82.
Club Shop: No, but badges, mugs and scarves on sale.
Players progressing to Football League: Peter Eustace (Sheffield Wednesday) 1960 *(from Stocksbridge Works)*, Lee Mills (Wolverhampton Wanderers) 1992.
Record fee received: £15,000 for Lee Mills (Wolves, 1992).
Local newpapers: Sheffield Trader, Green'un, The Star
Clubhouse: Open seven days (lunchtime & evenings). No food, but separate food bar open for matches.
Captain 93-94: Craig Chadburn **Top Scorer 93-94:** Trevor Jones.
Player of the Year 93-94: Paul Nasim, John Fletcher, Andy Carney.
Hons: Northern Co's East Lg 93-94 (Div I 91-92, Lg Cup SF 92-93, Presidents Cup SF 91-92), Sheffield & Hallamshire Snr Cup 51-52 92-93 (SF 93-94), Yorks Lg 51 52 54 55 55 56 56 57 57 58 61-62 62-63 (R-up 60-61, Div 2 50-51 64-65, Div 3 70-71 74-75 (R-up 78-79), Lg Cup 61-62).

THACKLEY

President: Maurice Selby **Chairman:** John Myers **Manager/Coach:** Warren Rayner
Secretary: Stewart Willingham, 3 Kirklands Close, Baildon, Shipley, West Yorks BD17 6HN (0274 598589).
Asst Manager: Jan Kudelinitzky **Physio:** Maurice Atkinson/ John Waller.
Treasurer: Paul Clark **Press Officer:** Jamie Scott (0274 611520).
Ground: Dennyfield, Ainsbury Avenue, Thackley, Bradford (0274 615571).
Directions: On main Leeds/Keighley A657 road, turn off at Thackley corner which is 2 miles from Shipley traffic lights and 1 mile from Greengates lights. Ainsbury Avenue bears to the right 200yds down the hill. Ground is 200yds along Ainsbury Avenue on the right. 3 miles from Bradford Interchange (BR), one and a half miles from Shipley (BR). Buses to Thackley corner (400 yds).
Seats: 100 **Cover:** 300 **Capacity:** 3,000 **Floodlights:** Yes **Founded:** 1930.
Colours: Red & white/white/red **Change colours:** All white
Midweek matches: Tuesday
Programme: 28 pages, 30p **Programme Editor:** Secretary
Club Shop: Yes. Programmes, souvenirs. Metal badges available - £2.50 + s.a.e. Contact Jamie Scott (0274 61152).
Previous leagues: Bradford Amateur, W. Riding County Amateur, W. Yorks, Yorks 67-82.
Record Att.: 1,500 v Leeds Utd 1983 **Previous name:** Thackley Wesleyians 1930-39.
Sponsors: Aprodite Shipping. **Best FA Vase year:** 5th Rd 80-81 (0-2 v Whickham).
Players progressing to Football League: Tony Brown (Leeds, Doncaster, Scunthorpe, Rochdale), Ian Ormondroyd (Bradford City, Aston Villa, Derby, Leicester).
Clubhouse details: Hot & cold snacks on matchdays. Open Tues-Sunday evenings, matchdays and weekend lunchtimes. Boardroom, committee room, dancefloor, darts, pool, gaming machines.
Local Press: Bradford Telegraph & Argus, Bradford Str, Aire Valley Target.
Captain 93-94: Warren Fletcher **Top Scorer 93-94:** Stuart Taylor 48.
Hons: Northern Co's (East) Lg R-up 93-94 (Lg Cup R-up 93-94), Yorks Lg Div 2 73-74, West Yorks Lg 66-67, West Riding Co. Amtr Lg 57-58 58-59 59-60, West Riding Co. Cup 73-74 74-75, West Riding Co. Chal. Cup 63-64 66-67, Bradford & Dist. Snr Cup(10) 38-39 49-50 55-56 57-60 65-67 78-79 87-88.

Thackley - Northern Counties (East) League runners-up 1993-94. *Photo - Colin Stevens.*

DIV. 1 10-YEAR RECORD	84/5	85/6	86/7	87/8	88/9	89/0	90/1	91/2	92/3	93/4
Armthorpe Welfare	1C	–	–	–	–	–	–	–	–	–
Arnold Kingswell	8S	–	–	–	–	–	–	–	–	–
Arnold Town	–	–	–	–	–	–	–	–	–	3
Blidworth Welfare	15S	–	–	–	–	–	–	–	–	–
Borrowash Victoria	2S	7	–	–	–	–	–	–	–	–
Bradley Rangers	3N	10	5	5	15	–	–	3	w/d	–
Bridlington Town	5N	6	–	–	–	–	–	–	–	–
Brigg Town	2C	12	–	–	–	–	–	–	–	–
Brodsworth Miners Welfare	–	–	–	–	–	–	–	15	13	15
Collingham & Linton	16N	–	–	–	8	10	–	–	–	–
Eccleshill United	–	–	–	7	7	7	5	–	–	–
Farsley Celtic	1N	–	–	–	–	–	–	–	–	–
Frecheville Community	16S	–	–	10	13	11	–	–	–	–
Fryston Colliery Welfare	16C	–	–	–	–	–	–	–	–	–
Garforth Town	9N	–	11	14	6	6	6	11	9	6
Glasshoughton Welfare	–	–	–	–	–	–	11	–	–	–
Graham Street Prims	14S	–	–	–	–	–	–	–	–	–
Grimethorpe Miners Welfare	10C	–	12	–	–	–	–	–	–	–
Hallam	9S	–	6	–	–	–	2	5	3	2
Hall Road Rangers	14N	–	–	–	–	–	–	6	8	10
Harrogate Railway Athletic	4N	14	4	–	–	–	–	–	–	9
Harrogate Town	2N	3	–	–	–	–	–	–	–	–
Harworth Colliery Institute	5S	8	–	–	–	–	–	–	–	–
Hatfield Main	5C	11	3	–	–	–	8	16	11	4
Hucknall Town	–	–	–	–	–	–	–	–	2	–
Immingham Town	–	–	–	9	9	9	–	9	12	14
Kimberley Town	16S	–	–	–	–	–	–	–	–	–
Kiveton Park	12S	–	14	11	10	8	–	–	–	–
Lincoln United	11S	–	–	–	–	–	–	–	1	–
Liversedge	8N	–	–	–	–	2	3	–	–	–
Long Eaton United	1S	–	–	–	–	–	–	–	–	–
Louth United	–	–	–	–	–	–	–	–	–	3
Maltby Miners Welfare	11C	–	9	3	4	5	–	–	–	–
Mexborough Town	–	13	16	15	11	15	13	–	–	–
North Ferriby United	7N	1	–	–	–	–	–	–	–	–
Oakham United	13S	–	–	–	–	–	–	–	–	–
Ossett Albion	4C	5	1	–	–	–	–	–	–	–
Ossett Town	8C	–	–	–	–	3	–	–	–	–
Phoenix Park	12N	–	–	–	–	–	–	–	–	–
Pickering Town	11N	–	–	–	5	14	4	2	–	–
Pilkington Recreation	6C	16	10	13	16	–	–	–	–	–
RES Parkgate	9C	–	15	4	12	12	9	8	5	13
Retford Rail	4S	–	–	–	–	–	–	–	–	–
Rossington Main	–	–	–	–	–	–	–	7	7	7
Rowntree Mackintosh	6N	4	2	2	2	1	–	–	–	–
Selby Town	13N	–	–	–	–	–	7	13	14	11
Sheffield	6S	2	17	8	1	–	1	–	–	–
Staveley Works	7S	–	7	12	–	–	–	–	–	–
Stocksbridge Park Steels	–	–	–	–	–	–	–	1	–	–
Stocksbridge Works	14C	–	–	–	–	–	–	–	–	–
Tadcaster Albion	17N	–	–	–	–	–	–	12	6	12
Thorne Colliery	7C	–	–	–	–	–	–	–	–	–
Wombwell Town	15C	–	–	–	–	–	–	–	–	–
Woolley Miners Welfare	3C	9	13	6	3	4	–	–	–	–
Worsborough Bridge MW & A.	13C	–	–	–	–	–	–	10	10	8
York Railway Institute	10N	–	8	1	14	13	10	14	–	–
Yorkshire Amateur	15N	–	–	–	–	–	–	4	4	5
Yorkshire Main	12C	–	–	–	–	–	12	–	–	–
No. of Clubs	**17N 16S/16C**	**16**	**18**	**16**	**16**	**16**	**13**	**16**	**14**	**15**

(C - Div 1 Central, N - Div 1 North, S - Div 1 South (S)

DIVISION ONE CLUBS 1994-95

BLIDWORTH WELFARE

President: Ray Hilton **Chairman:** Harry Cassells **Vice-Chairman:** TBA
Secretary: Bill Deakin, 220 Brick Kiln Lane, Mansfield, Notts NG19 6LR (0623 29033).
Manager: Andy Brown **Asst Manager:** John Miller **Coach:** Shaun Hird.
Comm. Manager: Chris Jukes **Press Officer:** Pete Craggs, 21 Pecks Hill, Mansfield.
Ground: Welfare Ground, Mansfield Rd, Blidworth, Mansfield (0623 798724).
Directions: On B6020, Rainworth side of Blidworth. From M1 jct 27 take A608 to Kirby and Annesley Woodhouse, at lights follow A611 to Kirby then take B6020 through Ravenshead to Blidworth - thru village and ground at top of hill on right. From A1 follow A614 and A617 to Rainworth, left at lights then 1st right on to B6020 to Blidworth - ground on left at top of hill. Served by Mansfield-Nottingham buses.
Capacity: 3,000 **Seats:** 200 **Cover:** 700 **Floodlights:** Yes **Reformed:** 1980.
Programme: 32 pages, 50p **Editor:** Pete Craggs **Club Shop:** No.
Colours: All green **Change colours:** All yellow **Nickname:** Hawks
Midweek home matchdays: Wednesday **Record Gate:** 400 v Shirebrook Colliery, league 89-90.
Previous Grounds: None. **Prev. Lges:** Notts All. 80-82/ NCEL 82-86/ Centrals Mids 86-94.
Record win: 6-0 v Harworth Colliery Institute (H), League Cup 91-92.
Record defeat: 0-11 v Sheffield Aurora (A), Central Midlands League 90-91.
Clubhouse: Welfare Social Club built 199. Normal matchday hours.
Club record scorer: Andy Locker **Club record appearances:** Dave Colley.
Captain 93-94: Steve Giles **P.O.Y. 93-94:** Simon Challenger **Top Scorer 93-94:** Ian Dudley

BRODSWORTH WELFARE

Chairman: Mr J Yorke **Press Officer:** Mr J Mounsey
Secretary: Mr K Medcalf, 3 Farm Court, Adwick-le-Street, Doncaster DN6 7AP (0302 723749).
Manager: Neil Harle **Asst Manager:** **Physio:** J Bedford.
Ground: Welfare Ground, Woodlands, Nr. Doncaster (0302 728380). **Directions:** Adjacent to the old Great North Rd (A638), 3 miles north of Doncaster at Woodlands. Ground entrance approx 30 yds into Welfare Rd. Left turn into Car Park. Regular bus service from North Bridge Bus Station, Doncaster.
Seats: No **Cover:** 250 **Capacity:** 3,000 **Floodlights:** No **Founded:** 1912
Colours: TBA **Change colours:** TBA **Club Shop:** No **Nickname:** Brody
Previous Name: Brodsworth Main **Previous Leagues:** Doncaster Snr/ Sheffield/ Yorks.
Midweek home matchday: Tuesday **Programme:** 8 pages, compiled by committee.
Record fee paid: Nil **Record fee received:** From Wolves for Barry Stobart, 1960.
Clubhouse: No. Matchday drinks and snacks at Foresters Arms Hotel, off Doncaster Rd in Woodlands.
Hons: Yorks Lg 24-25, Donc. & Dist. Lg 84-85 (Lg Cup 85-86, Div 2 78-79, Div 2 Cup 78-79), Sheffield Jnr Cup 83-84, Mexborough Montagu Cup 91-92 92-93.

ECCLESHILL UNITED

Chairman: Keith Firth **Press Officer:** Bill Rawlings (0274 635753).
Secretary: Lewis N Dixon, 61 Mount St., Eccleshill, Bradford BD2 2JN (0274 638053).
Manager: Barry Gallagher **Physio:** Gordon McGlynn
Ground: Plumpton Park, Kingsway, Wrose, Bradford BD2 1PN (0274 615739).
Directions: M62 jct 26 onto M606, right on Bradford Ring Road A6177, left onto A650 for Bradford at 2nd r'bout. A650 Bradford Inner Ring Road onto Canal Rd, branch right opposite Woodheads Builders Merchants into Kings Rd, fork right after 30mph sign to junction with Wrose Rd, across junction - continuation of Kings Rd, 1st left onto Kingsway - ground 200 yds on roght. 2 miles from Bradford (BR). Buses 686 or 687 for Wrose.
Seats: 225 **Cover:** 225 **Capacity:** 2,225 **Floodlights:** Yes **Year Reformed:** 1948
Midweek matches: Wednesday **Reserves' Lge:** NCE Res. Div. **Nickname:** Eagles
Colours: Blue & white stripes **Change colours:** All yellow
Programme: 24-28 pages, 50p **Programme Editor:** Raymond Maule (0274 662428).
Previous Ground: Myers Lane **Record Gate:** 600 v Bradford City 90-91.
Previous Name: Eccleshill FC **Previous Lges:** Bradford Amateur/ West Riding County Amateur.
Record win: 7-1 v Yorkshire Main (H), Northern Counties (East) League Division Two 86-87.
Rec. defeat: 0-6; v Rossington M. (A), NCEL Cup 2nd Rd 92-93; v Gt Harwood T. (A), FA Cup Prelim. Rd 91-92.
Club Shop: Yes, selling pennants, enamel badges, old programmes, mugs etc. Contact Roy Maule Snr, 25 Third Avenue, Bradford Moor, Bradford (0274 662428).
Players progressing to Football League: Terry Dolan (Huddersfield, Bradford PA, Bradford City).
Clubhouse: Open normal licensing hours. Bar, lounge, games room, kitchen (hot & cold snacks), committee room
Captain 93-94: Barry Gallagher **Top Scorer 93-94:** Lal Corbally.
Club record scorer: Paul Viner. **Club record appearances:** Paul Viner.
Local newspapers: Bradford Telegraph & Argus, Bradford Star Free Press.
Honours: Northern Counties East Div 2 R-up 86-87 (Reserve Div 86-87 89-90 (R-up 87-88 93-94)); Bradford Amtr Lg Cup 61-62; Bradford & Dist. Snr Cup 84-85; Bradford & Dist. FA Snr Cup 85-86; West Riding County Amateur Lg 76-77

GARFORTH TOWN

President: Norman Hebbron **Chairman:** Stephen Hayle.
Secretary: Paul Bracewell, 24 Coupland Rd, Garforth, Leeds LS25 1AD (0532 863314).
Manager/Coach: Paul Dooley **Asst Manager:** Fred Bennett **Physio:** Ken Mills
Commercial Mgr: Mike Fullerton **Press Officer:** Kevin Strangeway (0532 866500).
Ground: Brierlands Lane, Aberford Road, Garforth, Leeds (0532 864083). **Directions:** From South/East/North, A642 from A1 to Garforth, ground one and a half miles on left over brow of hill. From South West, M62 jct 30, A642 to Garforth (A63 to Garforth from Leeds), thru Garforth on A642, ground on right 1 mile on from lights just past junior school and Indian restaurant. Buses 18 & 83 from Leeds, alight at East Garforth Post Office - ground 500yds on right walking away from Garforth. By rail to Garforth (Leeds-York) line - cross over bridge to Safeways side and ground just under 1 mile down road.
Seats: None **Cover:** 100 **Capacity:** 2,000 **Floodlights:** No **Founded:** 1965
Cols: Red (navy stripe)/navy/red **Change colours:** Green & white stripes/green/green
Prog.: 28 glossy pages, 50p **Editor:** Kevin Strangeway (0532 866500) **Nickname:** Miners
Club Shop: Open before & during matches selling non-League and Football League programmes.
Sponsors: Clarks of Wakefield **Previous lges:** Leeds Sunday Comb./ West Yorks/ Yorks 78-82.
Clubhouse: Matchdays & training nights. **Previous names:** Miners Arms 64-78, Garforth Miners 78-79
Midweek home matches: Tuesday **Record attendance:** 817 v Leeds, friendly 1987
Record win: 7-0 v Immingham Town (H), Northern Counties (East) League Division One 1991-92.
Record defeat: 1-7 v Lincoln United (A), Northern Counties (East) League Division One 1992-93.
Club record scorer: Vinnie Archer **Club record appearances:** Philip Matthews (1982-93).
Hons: FA Vase QF 85-86; Northern Co's East Lg Div 2 R-up 85-86; Yorks Lg Div 3 R-up 79-80, Barkston Ash Snr Cup 80-81 84-85 85-86 86-87 92-93.

HALL ROAD RANGERS

Chairman: R Smailes **Vice Chairman:** J Urbanowiez **Manager:** Pete Smith
President/Secretary: E Richardson, 35 Hall Road, Hull, Nth Humbs HU6 8QW (0482 43781).
Asst Mgr: Peter Smethurst **Press Officer:** Ray Bamforth **Comm. Mgr:** R Smailes.
Ground: Dene Park, Dene Close, Beverley Rd, Dunswell, Nr Hull (0482 850101). **Directions:** Hull-Beverley road (A1079 and A1174). Dunswell is first village from the Hull boundary. Entrance to ground on A1174 is 20 yds past large r/about and opposite Dunswell Village road sign. Four & a half miles from Hull (BR).
Seats: 50 **Cover:** 750 **Capacity:** 1,200 **Floodlights:** Yes **Founded:** 1959.
Colours: Blue & white hoops/blue/blue **Change colours:** Green & white hoops
Previous ground: Hull Co-Op (until 1968) **Record Gate:** 350 v Hull City XI, August '91.
Programme: 12 pages, 30p **Programme Editor:** Mrs Sue Smith (0482 437402)
Club Shop: Yes, selling badges, scarves, hats, sweatshirts, t-shirts, mugs.
Midweek Matches: Wednesday **Reserves' Lge:** NCEL Res Div. **Nickname:** Rangers.
Local Press: Hull Daily Mail **Previous Leagues:** East Riding/ Yorks 68-82.
Players progressing to Football Lge: Gerry Ingram (Blackpool, Sheff Wed).
Clubhouse: Open all week for drinks and snacks. Bar snacks. Snooker, pool, darts.
Captain 93-94: Paul Osborne **Top Scorer & Player of the Year 93-94:** Harry Cardwell.
Record Scorer: G James **Record Appearances:** G James.
Hons: Northern Co's East Lg Div 2 90-91, Yorks Lg Div 3 72-73 79-80, East Riding Snr Cup 72-73 93-94.

HARROGATE RAILWAY ATHLETIC

President: J Robinson **Chairman:** C Robinson
Secretary: W D Oldfield, 80 Stonefall Ave., Harrogate, Nth Yorks HG2 7NP (0423 888941).
Manager: G Shepherd **Coach:** P Williamson **Physio:** J Tope
Press Officer/Programme Ed.: C Dinsdale (0423 521815) **Commercial Mgr:** C W Robinson (0423 880022).
Ground: Station View, Starbeck, Harrogate (0423 885539).
Directions: A59 Harrogate to Knaresborough road. After approx 1.5 miles turn left just before railway level crossing. Ground is 150 yds up the lane. Adjacent to Starbeck (BR). Served by any Harrogate to Knareborough bus.
Seats: None **Cover:** 600 **Capacity:** 3,000 **Floodlights:** Yes **Founded:** 1935
Club colours: All red **Change:** White & blue hoops **Nickname:** The Rail
Midweek home matchday: Wednesday **Rec. Gate:** 1,400; 1962 FA Amtr Cup **Sponsors:** T.B.A.
Club Shop: Yes, selling programmes, pennants, badges etc. Contact K Dinsdale (0423 521815).
Previous leagues: West Yorkshire/ Harrogate District/ Yorkshire 55-73 80-82.
Clubhouse: Games, TV room, lounge, open normal public house hours every day. Hot food.
Top Scorer 93-94: **Captain & P.o.Y. 93-94:**
Hons: Northern Co's (East) Lg Cup 86-87 **Local Press:** Yorkshire Post, Harrogate Herald & Advertiser.

HATFIELD MAIN

President: G Bailey **Chairman:** A Jones **Vice Chairman:** B Keenan
Secretary: Mr Bruce Hatton, 92 Ingram Rd, Dunscroft, Doncaster, Sth Yorks DN7 4JE (0302 841648).
Manager: John Reed **Asst Manager:** John Kirk **Coach:** Darryl Pugh.
Physio: Tommy Kirk. **Commercial Manager:** Barry Speakman.
Ground: Dunscroft Welfare Ground, Dunscroft, Doncaster, Sth Yorks (0302 841326).
Directions: From Doncaster (A18) Scunthorpe Rd to Dunsville, left at Flarepath Hotel down Broadway. Ground half mile on right. Half mile from Stamforth & Hatfield (BR). Buses every fifteen minutes from Doncaster.
Seats: None **Cover:** 600 **Capacity:** 4,000 **Floodlights:** Yes **Founded:** 1936.
Programme: 25 pages, 50p **Editor:** Tony Ingram (0302 842795) **Club Shop:** No.
Colours: All white **Change:** Red & white stripes/red/red **Nickname:** The Main
Previous League: Yorkshire 55-82. **Clubhouse:** Full licensing hrs. Hot/cold drinks/snacks.
Hons: West Riding Co. Cup. **Record transfer fee received:** £1,000 for Mark Hall (York C.)
Record Gate: 1,000 v Leeds, A Jones testimonial. Competitive: 750 v Bishop Auckland, FA Amtr Cup
Midweek home matchday: Tuesday **Reserve team's League:** Doncaster Senior.
Club Sponsors: K Greenall.
Players progressing to Football League: Mark Atkins (Scunthorpe, Blackburn), Mark Hall (York).
Captain 93-94: Gary Kay **Top Scorer 93-94:** Shaun Lanagham, Jason Miller (both 16).
P.o.Y. 93-94: Shaun Lanagham **Club record appearances:** Lal Dutt.

IMMINGHAM TOWN

President: N/A **Chairman:** Alan Wilson **Manager:** TBA
Secretary: Terry Paul, 28 Anglian Way, Market Rasen, Lincs LN9 3RP (0673 843654).
Ground: 'Woodlands', Woodlands Avenue, Immingham, South Humberside (0469 75724).
Directions: M180 & A180 – 1st exit to Immingham. Straight on at r/about, through lights and right at next r/about. Entrance on right between ATS Tyres and Lectec Services. 3 miles from Habrough (BR). Buses from Grimsby.
Seats: None **Cover:** 100 **Capacity:** 2,000 **Floodlights:** Yes **Founded:** 1912.
Colours: Maroon & sky **Change:** White/black/white **Reformed:** 1945 & 69
Previous Grounds: Spring Street 12-15 (when 1st club folded)/ Pelham Rd 45-52 (2nd club folded).
Previous Leagues: Lincs 12-13 48-52 70-86/ Bennett Lge 14-15/ Grimsby & D. 13-14 45-48 69-70.
Reserves' League: None **Record Gate:** 950 v Sheffield United, floodlight opening, April 1992.
Programme: 24 pages, 50p **Editor:** Rob Holt (0469 573292) **Club Shop:** No.
Midweek home matchday: Tuesday **Club Spnsors:** None **Nickname:** Pilgrims
Record win: 9-2 v Old Lincolnians (H), Lincolnshire League Division Two, 1971-72.
Record defeat: 0-8 v Pickering Town (A), Northern Counties (East) League Division One, 1991-92.
Clubhouse: Open every evening & matchdays. Hot & cold food.
Club record scorer: Roy Gladwell **Club record appearances:** Unknown at present.
Captain 93-94: Various **Top Scorer 93-94:** Trevor Crawford, 16.
Hons: Lincs Snr 'B' Cup 73-74 80-81 (R-up 81-82 82-83 83-84), Lincs Lg Supplementary Cup 71-72 86-87 (Chal. Cup 83-84 84-85, Div 2 Cup R-up(res) 76-77, Tom Fox Cup 83-84, Bill Allison Cup(res) R-up 86-87), Lins Cup-Winners Cup 70-71, Lambert Cup 72-73 74-75, Grimsby & D. Lg 46-47 70-71 (R-up 45-46 47-48, Div 3 R-up 46-47, Telegraph Snr Cup 45-46 46-47(joint)(R-up 47-48), Wilson Cup 45-46 46-47 (R-up 47-48), War Memorial Cup 46-47 71-72(res), Kelly Cup 47-48 46-47(joint), Bellamy Cup 47-48 (R-up 46-47)), Grimsby Suppl. Cup 86-87.

LOUTH UNITED

President: Mr C Hounsome **Chairman:** Mr G Horton.
Secretary/Press Officer: Mr P Smith, 84 Scartho Road, Grimsby, South Humberside DN33 2BG (0472 879356).
Manager: Peter Lea **Asst Manager:** Martin Teanby **Coach:** Brian Casey
Club Manager: Jim Bloomer **Commercial Manager:** TBA **Physio:** Kenny Vincent.
Ground: Park Avenue, Louth, Lincs (0507 607351).
Directions: A16 To Louth Market Place, exit via Eastgate/Eastfield Rd, to 1st junction, past Fire Station.
Capacity: 4,000 **Seats:** None **Cover:** 400 **Founded:** 1947 **Floodlights:** Yes
Midweek matches: Tuesday **Club Sponsors:** R.G.B. Packaging, Grimsby.
Programme: 50p **Editor:** Albany Jordan (0507 607570) **Club Shop:** No
Colours: All royal blue **Change Colours:** Red & black stripes **Sponsors:** TBA
Reserves' League: Lincolnshire **Record Gate:** 3,200 v Derby Co., friendly, October 1990.
Previous Grounds: None **Previous Names:** Merger of Louth Nats & Louth Town.
Record transfer fee received: £10,000 for Martyn Chalk (Derby County, 1990).
Previous Leagues: Lincs 47-75 82-88/ Midland Co's Lg 76-82/ Central Midlands 88-93.
Players progressing to Football League: Terry Donovan (Grimsby), Paul Bartlett (Derby), Brian Klug (Ipswich), Glen Cockerill (Lincoln, Watford, Southampton), Peter Rawcliffe (Grimsby), Peter Green (Grimsby), Martyn Chalk (Derby).
Clubhouse: Weekdays 6.30-11.45pm, Sat noon-11.45pm. Full bar facilities. Snacks: filled rolls, crisps, nuts etc.
Record Scorer: Peter Rawcliffe 39 **Record Apperances:** Gary Smith 476.
Top Scorer 93-94: Allan Cooper 31 **Captain 93-94:** Steve Newby **P.o.Y. 93-94:** Shaun Hawkey
Hons: Lincs Lg 72-73 86-87 85-86 (Div 1 57-58 66-67 67-68, Lg Challenge Cup 73-74 86-87, Lg Charity Cup 55-56 56-57 67-68, Lg Supplementary Cup 85-86), Central Mids Lg Cup R-up 92-93 (F'lit Cup R-up 91-92), Lincs Snr 'A' Cup 77-78 (Snr'B' Cup(res) 91-92).

PARKGATE

President: T L Dabbs **Chairman:** A T Dudill **Vice Chairman:** R Goodwin
Secretary: Bruce Bickerdike, 2 Cardew Close, Rawmarsh, Rotherham S62 6LB (0709 522305 (tel & fax)).
Manager: Alan Stringer **Asst Manager:** Paul Greaves **Physio:** P Sheffield.
Press Officer: Bruce Bickerdike (0709 522305).
Ground: Roundwood Sports Complex, Green Lane, Rawmarsh, Rotherham (0709 523471).
Directions: From Rotherham A633 to Rawmarsh. From Doncaster A630 to Conisbrough, then A6023 through Swinton to Rawmarsh. Ground at Green Lane – right from Rotherham, left from Conisbrough at the Crown Inn. Ground 800yds on right
Seats: 300 **Cover:** 300 **Capacity:** 1,000 **Floodlights:** Yes **Founded:** 1969
Colours: White/black/white **Change colours:** All sky.
Nickname: The Gate or The Steelmen.
Midweek matches: Tuesday **Club Sponsors:** Rotherham Engineering Steels.
Programme: 20 pages, 50p **Editor:** Bruce Bickerdike (0709 522305) **Club Shop:** No.
Previous Name: BSC Parkgate (until mid-eighties)/ RES Parkgate (pre-1994).
Previous leagues: Rotherham Association/ Whitbread County Senior/ Yorkshire 74-82
Record attendance: v Worksop 1982
Clubhouse: Licensed bar, 2 lounges, including dance floor. Open until 10.30pm Mon-Thurs & Sun, 11pm Fr-Sat. Meals available lunchtime Wed-Sat.
Local Newspapers: Star/ Green'Un/ Rotherham Advertiser/ Sth Yorks Times/ Dearne Valley Weekender.

ROSSINGTON MAIN

President: K Melvin **Chairman:** Mr S Tagg **Commercial Mgr:** G Shaw
Secretary: Mr Malcolm Day, 3 Coronach Way, Rossington, Doncaster DN11 0RL (0302 863516).
Manager/Coach: Mr D Carlin **Asst Mgr/Coach:** Mr S Downing
Ground: Welfare Ground, Oxford St, Rossington, Doncaster (0302 865524).
Directions: Enter Rossington and go over the railway crossings. Pass the Welfare Club on right, Oxford Street is next right - ground is at bottom. 8 miles from Doncaster (BR).
Seats: 200 **Cover:** 500 **Capacity:** 1,200 **Floodlights:** Yes **Founded:** 1925
Colours: All blue **Change colours:** All white. **Midweek matches:** Tuesday
Programme: 32 pages, 50p **Programme Editor:** Mr S Tagg.
Prev. Lges: Yorks/ Central Mids. **Record attendance:** 1,200 v Doncaster Rovers (date unknown).
Clubhouse: Rossington Miners Welfare **Local Newspapers:** Village Life - own newspaper.
Club honours: Central Mids Lg Prem. Div 84-85 (Prem. Div Cup 84-85, Div 1 Cup 83-84).

Despite the brave effort of Rossington Main 'keeper Gary Copley, Peter Coyne scores an FA Cup goal for Rossendale.
Photo - Colin Stevens.

SELBY TOWN

President: R Coultish **Chairman:** J Vause **General Mgr:** B Wilkes
Secretary: Mr J A Storey, Cobblecroft, Hardenshaw Lane, Camblesforth, York YO8 8JA.
Manager: Ian Hope **Asst Manager:** J Storey **Coach:** B Walker.
Ground: Flaxley Road Ground, Richard Street, Selby, North Yorkshire YO8 0BN.
Directions: From Leeds, left at main traffic lights in Selby down Scott Rd. then 1st left into Richard St. From Doncaster go straight across main traffic lights into Scott Road then 1st left. From York right at main traffic lights into Scott Rd, and 1st left. 1 mile from Selby (BR).
Seats: 100 **Cover:** 750 **Capacity:** 5,000 **Floodlights:** Yes **Founded:** 1911
Club colours: All white **Change colours:** All red.
Programme: 12 pages, 30p **Programme Editor:** M Fairweather (0757 705376).
Nickname: The Robins **Main Sponsors:** Irwin & Co Builders
Prev. League: Yorkshire (1920-82) **Prev. ground:** Bowling Green, James St. 1920-51
Past players to progress to Football League: Numerous
Best FA Cup performance: Second Round Proper 1954-55
Best FA Vase performance: Preliminary Round 1989-90
Record attendance: 7,000 v Bradford Park Avenue (FA Cup 1st Rnd 1953-54)
Clubhouse: Bar at ground open first and second team matchdays
Midweek Matches: Wednesday **Local Newspaper:** Selby Times.
Club honours: Yorkshire Lg 32-33 34-35 35-36 52-53 53-54 (R-up 24-25 25-26 27-28 28-29 30-31 31-32 50-51 55-56, Div 3 R-up 74-75, Lg Cup 37-38 53-54 54-55 62-63); Northern Co. East Div 2 R-up 89-90; West Riding Snr Cup 37-38; West Riding Co Cup 27-28 48-49; West Riding Chall. Cup 34-35 35-36

TADCASTER ALBION

Chairman: Mike Burnett **President:** Lord Edward Stourton. **Manager:** Ken Payne.
Secretary: Mrs A J Burnett, 6 Beech Grove House, Ouston Lane, Tadcaster LS24 8DP (0937 832802).
Ground: The Park, Ings Lane, Tadcaster. 0937 832844
Directions: From West Riding and South Yorks, turn right off A659 at John Smith's Brewery Clock. From East Riding turn left off A659 after passing over river bridge and pelican crossing (New Street).
Cols: Red (white trim)/white/red **Change colours:** White/black/black
Programme: 20 pages. **Programme Editor:** L West.

WINTERTON RANGERS

President: J W Hiles **Chairman:** D Waterfall **Vice Chairman:** A Smith
Secretary/Press Officer: G Spencer, 2 Dale Park Ave., Winterton, Scunthorpe, Sth Humbs DN15 9UY (0724 732039).
Manager: Mick Wild **Asst Manager/Coach:** Kev Rooney
Ground: West Street, Winterton, Scunthorpe, South Humberside (0724 732628).
Directions: From Scunthorpe take A1077 Barton-on-Humber road for 5 miles. On entering Winterton take second right (Eastgate), third left (Northlands Road) and first right (West Street). Ground 200yds on left
Seats: 200 **Covered:** 200 **Capacity:** 3,000 **Floodlights:** Yes **Founded:** 1930
Colours: White/navy/white **Change colours:** All red **Nickname:** Rangers
Midweek home matches: Wednesday **Sponsors:** Ledgerwood Motors **Club Shop:** No.
Programme: 28-36 pages, 50p **Programme Editor:** M Fowler (0724 732628).
Previous Grounds: Watery Lane 1930-48. **Best FA Vase year:** QF 76-77
Best FA Cup year: 4th Qualifying Rd replay 76-77 (lost 2-3 at Droylsden after 3-3 draw).
Previous League: Scunthorpe & Dist. 45-65/ Lincs 65-70/ Yorkshire 70-82.
Record attendance: 1,200 v Sheffield Utd – Official opening of floodlights, October 1978.
Record transfer fee received: £5,000 for Henry Smith (Leeds United, 1979).
Clubhouse: Open matchdays & evenings Mon-Sat, hot & cold food available on matchdays. Pool and snooker rooms.
Local Press: Scunthorpe Evening Telegraph
Players progressing to Football League: Henry Smith (Leeds, Hearts), Keith Walwyn (Chesterfield, York, Carlisle), Rick Greenhough (Chester, York)
Captain 93-94: **P.o.Y. 93-94:** **Top Scorer 93-94:**
Hons: Lincs Jnr Cup 47-48 61-62; Lincs Snr 'B' Cup 69-70; Yorks Lg 71-72 76-77 78-79 (Lg Cup 80-81); Northern Co's East Lg Div 2 89-90; Scunthorpe Lg & Cup many times; Philips National F'light 6-aside 76-77.

WORSBROUGH BRIDGE M.W. & ATHLETIC

Chairman: Mr J Wright **Press Officer:** Mr A Wright (0226 243418).
Secretary: D Smith, 18 Shield Avenue, Worsbrough Bridge, Barnsley, S. Yorks S70 5BQ (0226 243418).
Manager: K Paddon **Asst Manager:**
Ground: Park Road, Worsbrough Bridge, Barnsley (0226 284452).
Directions: On the A61 Barnsley-Sheffield road two miles south of Barnsley, 2 miles from M1 jnt 36 opposite Blackburns Bridge. Two and a half miles from Barnsley (BR). Yorkshire Traction run buses every 10 mins thru Worsbrough Bridge.
Seats: 175 **Cover:** 175 **Capacity:** 2,000 **Floodlights:** Due **Founded:** 1921
Colours: All red **Change colours:** Yellow/blue **Reformed:** 1947
Record attendance: 2,300 v Blyth Spartans, FA Amateur Cup 1971
Previous Leagues: Barnsley 52-61/ County Snr 62-70/ Yorks 71-82. **Prog:** 20 pages, 20p
Hons: Northern Co's East Lg Div 1 R-up 90-91 (Div 3 R-up 85-86), Sheffield Snr Cup R-up 72-73, County Snr Lg 65-66 69-70 (R-up 62-63, Lg Cup 65-66), Barnsley Lg 52-53 58-59 59-60 (Lg Cup 56-57 58-59 (R-up 53-54)), Beckett Cup 57-58.

YORKSHIRE AMATEUR

President: Rayner Barker **Chairman:** William Ellis
Secretary: Brian Whaley, 50 Moseley Wood Walk, Leeds LS16 7HG (0532 679806).
Manager: Malcolm White **Asst Mgr:** Steve Jeffery **Coach:** Brian Richardson
Physio: Terry Davies **Commercial Manager:** Chas Sharman (0532 628499).
Ground: Bracken Edge, Sycamore Avenue, Leeds LS8 4DZ (0532 624093).
Directions: From South M1 to Leeds, then A58 Wetherby Road to Fforde Green Hotel, left at lights and proceed to Sycamore Ave. (on right). From East A1 to Boot & Shoe Inn then to Shaftesbury Hotel, turn right into Harehills Lane, then to Sycamore Avenue. Two and a half miles from Leeds (BR). Buses 2, 3 & 20 from Briggate to Harehills Ave.
Seats: None **Cover:** 160 **Capacity:** 1,550 **Floodlights:** Yes **Founded:** 1919.
Colours: White/blue/red **Change colours:** All red **Nickname:** Ammers.
Midweek Matches: Tuesday **Previous ground:** Elland Road 1919-20
Sponsors: Bridge Electrical **Record Gate:** 4,000 v Wimbledon, FA Amateur Cup QF 1932.
Programme: 8 pages, 30p **Programme Editor:** Chas Sharman (0532 628498)
Club Shop: Yes, selling sweat shirts, ties, badges, caps, scarves. Contact W Ellis (0405 839990).
Previous League: Yorks 20-24 30-82.
Players progressing to Football League: Gary Strodder & Stuart Naylor (WBA), Peter Swan (Leeds), Brian Deane (Doncaster, Sheffield United, Leeds).
Clubhouse: Bar, tea bar, games room, lounge. Every night 8.30-11pm, Sat matchdays noon-11pm, Sun lunchtime noon-3pm.
Local Newspapers: Yorkshire Post/ Yorkshire Evening Post/ North Leeds Advertiser.
Captain 93-93: Brian Hill **Top Scorer 93-94:** Gary Jackson **P.o.Y. 93-94:** Paul Lowrey.
Hons: FA Amtr Cup SF 31-32, West Riding Co. Cup(3), Yorks Lg 31-32 (Div 2 58-59 (R-up 52-53 71-72), Div 3 77-78, Lg Cup 32-33), Leeds & Dist. Snr Cup.

RESERVE DIVISION CONSTITUTION 1994-95

Brodsworth MW Res.
Eccleshill Utd Res.
Emley Res.
Farsley Celtic Res.
Garforth Town Res.
Glasshoughton Welf. Res.
Hall Road Rangers Res.
Harrogate Town Res.
Liversedge Res.
Ossett Albion Res.
Ossett Town Res.
Pontefract Colls Res.
Tadcaster Albion Res.
Thackley Res.
Yorkshire Amateur Res.

JOHN SMITH'S BITTER CENTRAL MIDLANDS LEAGUE

FEEDER TO:
The Northern Counties (East) League

President: L Nowicki

Chairman: F A Harwood

Secretary: F A Harwood,
103 Vestry Rd, Oakwood, Derby.

Public Relations Officer: Stan Wilton, 'Haven Holme', 57 Main Road, Smalley, Ilkeston, Derbyshire, DE7 6DS.

The John Smith's Bitter CML enjoyed another excellent season with the Supreme Division championship eventually finding its way to Derbyshire for the first time - but only just. Glapwell is in the North-East corner of the county on the borders with both Yorkshire and Nottinghamshire.

For much of the season it was a three cornered-title race between Glapwell, who did not get off to the best possible start, Gedling Town and Kiveton Park. Then Oakham United appeared on the scene to threaten and latterly, after a magnificent run in the Sheffield & Hallamshire FA Senior Cup, came Staveley Miners Welfare.

At the death it was Oakham and Staveley who pushed the hardest and Oakham who gained the runners-up spot ahead of Kiveton Par,k whose magnificent first season in the top flight was recognised with third place.

Oakham, it might be said, were the League's "Bridesmaids". Not only did they finish up second in the League, but it was also a position they held in both the John Smith's Bitter League Cup and the Wakefield Floodlit Cup. The former competition was a triumph for Heanor Town, a team who threatened so much and at the end of the day achieved some reward for what, by their standards, was a poor season. The League runners-up position twelve months earlier, on goal difference to Arnold Town, looked to be the springboard to Heanor's first championship success for 35 years, but a change of manager and playing staff midway through the campaign left them in mid-table. Their 2-0 success over Oakham in the League Cup Final at Mansfield Town's Field Mill ground at least brought some silverware to the Town Ground.

Field Mill was also the venue for the Wakefield Cup Final and a game between the champions and the runners-up. Disappointed Oakham completed their 'set' of runners-up medals by losing a thrilling game to Glapwell, and Glapwell's own achievements were supplemented by a place in the semi-final of the Derbyshire Senior Challenge Cup, losing out 1-0 to Northern Premier League Matlock Town in a replay at Causeway Lane.

The Premier Division title looked to be going nowhere but South Normanton Athletic from day one of the season. Then Athletic hit a dreadful patch in January and February, despite recording a ground record attendance for their League Cup tie against Heanor Town. Norton Woodseats took over the helm and Nuthall and Thorne Colliery pushed hard. Norton Woodseats became the last unbeaten side in the League, but eventually they suffered a mini loss of form, and, although South Normanton recovered, it was a jubilant Nuthall who completed an easy 4-1 home win over Mickleover Royal British Legion in their last game of the season to become 'Rags to Riches'

Glapwell FC - John Smith's Bitter Central Midlands League champions 1993-94. *Photo - Martin Wray.*

championship paraders. Last season Nutall had to apply for re-election to the League - now they are on the verge of improving their Basil Russell Playing Fields ground to play in the Supreme Division.

South Normanton Athletic and Norton Woodseats will also be promoted if they can satisfy the League's Ground Grading Committee that their grounds are up to scratch.

Thorne Colliery will not be too disappointed with their first season in the League at just missing out on promotion. Their consolation was in finishing higher in the table than their neighbours and arch-rivals Askern Welfare. And Thorne brought into the League with them a touch of what can be done and a fine example to all. They did not have one home game postponed during the season and, as the League Council feel that sometimes clubs are a little hasty in attempting to call off games, Thorne's example was a boost to us all.

Askern Welfare achieved something approaching a remarkable feat. During the course of the season they scored 73 goals, 67 of which came from their deadly twin strikeforce of Mark Illman and Tony Hattersley!

Mickleover Sports enjoyed a good season, and like their cross-city (Derby) rivals Derby Carriage & Wagon (Reckitts) were disappointed to miss out on a possible promotion place. But Sports, in particular, might have found the amount of work required on their magnificent new sports complex a touch too much to have guaranteed their promotion.

Off the field, the League made enormous strides in consolidating their position within the Northern Pyramid, considerably strengthening their ties with the Northern Counties (East) League. In this respect, Blidworth Welfare, the only suitable applicant, have been recommended for promotion next season. A umber of clubs applied for entry into the League for the 1994-95 season at the AGM, including Case Sports, Killamarsh Athletic, Holbrook Miners Welfare.

The last word must be on a high note; pity poor Shardlow St James who battled throughout much of the season taking pasting after pasting ..... but they battled on ..... and on. Their first point of the season duly arrived on the last Saturday in December, their first win a couple of months later, and ..... low and behold, they end the season with two magnificent home victories. Great credit to Shardlow for sticking to their guns.

Stan Wilton, Public Relations Officer.

SUPREME DIV.	P	W	D	L	F	A	PTS
Glapwell	32	22	7	3	75	25	73
Oakham United	32	20	4	8	62	39	64
Kiveton Park	32	17	10	5	71	34	61
Staveley MW	32	16	9	7	76	39	57
Gedling Town	32	16	8	8	61	41	56
Priory (Eastwood)	32	13	12	7	51	38	51
Blidworth Welfare	32	15	3	14	51	39	48
Borrowash Victoria	32	11	12	9	51	43	45
Heanor Town	32	12	7	13	49	54	43
Shirebrook Town	32	12	5	15	51	57	41
Rossington	32	12	4	16	56	76	40
Sheffield Aurora	32	9	8	15	50	61	35
Long Eaton Utd	32	7	11	14	40	57	32
Harworth CI	32	8	8	16	49	85	32
Nettleham	32	9	4	19	28	63	31
Sandiacre Town	32	8	4	20	49	73	28
Kimberley Town	32	4	6	22	34	80	18

Top Scorers: David Waller (Glapwell) 28, Terry Griffin (Harworth) 22, Brendan Yates (Oakham) 21, Alan Wells (Staveley) 20, Lee Edwards (Priory) 19, Robert Nelson (Rossington) 19, Graham Millington (Heanor) 17, Michael Bradley (Gedling) 14, Gary Briscoe (Sandiacre) 14, Ian Dudley (Blidworth) 14, Russell Roddis (Borrowash) 14, Leslie Harris (Kiveton Park) 13, Gary Weston (Long Eaton) 13.

DIV. ONE	P	W	D	L	F	A	PTS
Nuthall	28	20	4	4	63	27	64
Sth Normanton Ath.	28	20	1	7	84	31	61
Norton Woodseats	28	18	5	5	72	37	59
Thorne Colliery	28	16	4	8	59	34	52
Askern Welfare	28	16	3	9	73	43	51
Mickleover Sports	28	15	4	9	54	38	49
Derby CW (Reckitts)	28	11	8	9	51	39	41
Radford	28	11	8	9	50	43	41
Newhall United	28	9	8	11	42	50	35
Biwater	28	9	5	14	48	54	32
Derby Rolls Royce	28	8	6	14	53	57	30
Mickleover RBL	28	8	6	14	28	40	30
Stanton Ilkeston	28	5	3	20	29	65	18
Blackwell MW	28	4	5	19	29	64	17
Shardlow St James	28	3	4	21	17	130	13

Top Scorers: Mark Illman (Askern) 35, Tony Hattersley (Askern) 32, Barry Spence (Thorne Colliery) 21, Stephen Brown (Mickleover Sports) 20, Paul Fountain (Radford) 18, Michael Bott (South Normanton Athletic) 17, Peter Green (South Normanton Athletic) 17, Simon Barlow (Biwater) 16, Steven Carruthers (Nuthall) 16, Neil Hall (Newhall United), 13, Steve Leary (Norton Woodseats) 13, Michael Wilson (Radford) 13.

RES. PREM. DIV.	P	W	D	L	F	A	PTS
Arnold Town Res.	26	18	5	3	76	26	59
Shirebrook Res.	26	16	7	3	76	28	55
Norton W'seats Res.	26	14	7	5	61	36	49
Borrowash V. Res.	26	13	7	6	59	27	46
Priory (E'wood) Res.	26	13	7	6	52	28	46
Hucknall T. Res.	26	11	8	7	40	33	41
Blidworth W. Res.	26	11	3	12	45	43	36
Kimberley T. Res.	26	10	4	12	46	47	34
Glapwell Res.	26	10	3	13	47	61	33
Oakham Utd Res.	26	9	5	12	56	53	32
Derby CW (R.) Res.	26	6	5	15	31	52	23
Biwater Res.	26	6	4	16	38	68	22
M'over RBL Res.	26	6	3	17	21	66	21
Stanton Ilk. Res.	26	4	2	20	31	111	14

Top Scorers: James Brownlee (Arnold) 24, Steve Hill (Shirebrook) 24, Christopher Smith (Priory) 16, Tony Edge (Norton Woodseats) 15, Ryan Pollard (Priory) 15, Stephen Bull (Arnold) 13, Darren Telford (Blidworth) 11, Lee Widowson (Oakham) 10.

RES. DIV. ONE	P	W	D	L	F	A	PTS
Nuthall Res.	18	13	2	3	44	18	41
Rossington Res.	18	11	3	4	65	27	36
Derby RR Res.	18	11	1	6	46	23	34
Gedling Town Res.	18	10	6	2	62	30	*33
Sandiacre T. Res.	18	7	5	6	40	37	26
Mickleover S. Res.	18	8	1	9	37	37	25
Long Eaton U. Res.	18	7	2	9	36	54	23
Radford Res.	18	5	4	9	25	52	19
Harworth CI Res.	18	3	2	13	24	61	11
Shardlow SJ Res.	18	0	4	14	24	64	4

* - 3 points deducted

Top Scorers: Michael Abonyi (Rossington) 17, Richard Anderson (Nuthall) 14, Steve Warner (Mickleover Sports) 14, Leighton Lee (Rossington) 13, Neil Furber (Derby Rolls Royce) 11, Steve McArdle (Gedling Town) 11, Steve Taylor (Sandiacre Town) 11, N Marshall (Radford) 10.

SUP. DIV. RESULTS	1	2	3	4	5	6	7	8	9	10	11	12	13	14	15	16	17
1. Blidworth Welfare	*	1-1	2-0	0-1	2-0	4-2	2-1	0-0	3-0	1-0	2-0	2-3	1-3	4-1	1-3	0-1	3-0
2. Borrowash Victoria	2-1	*	2-0	1-1	3-4	0-0	4-1	0-0	2-0	3-0	0-3	0-0	3-0	1-1	1-1	3-0	2-2
3. Gedling Town	3-0	1-1	*	2-1	3-1	0-1	2-1	1-1	1-1	2-1	3-0	1-3	5-1	3-0	2-1	1-1	0-0
4. Glapwell	1-0	5-1	2-2	*	5-1	4-1	5-0	2-2	3-0	5-0	2-3	4-1	2-0	2-1	0-1	3-1	3-2
5. Harworth Colliery I.	1-4	0-1	0-5	0-1	*	3-5	1-1	1-1	1-1	0-1	0-0	3-3	1-5	2-0	2-1	4-6	3-3
6. Heanor Town	1-2	3-2	1-1	0-3	1-2	*	2-0	3-2	2-0	1-2	1-3	2-0	0-2	3-1	6-2	1-0	0-4
7. Kimberley Town	1-2	1-3	2-1	0-2	2-2	1-1	*	0-2	0-4	1-0	2-2	1-3	2-3	3-1	3-2	1-2	0-2
8. Kiveton Park	2-0	2-1	3-1	0-0	10-0	2-2	5-2	*	0-0	2-0	3-2	2-1	2-2	1-0	1-2	4-2	2-2
9. Long Eaton United	1-3	0-0	2-4	0-2	5-2	2-2	6-1	0-4	*	0-4	0-4	1-1	3-1	1-0	3-3	0-3	2-1
10. Nettleham	2-1	0-2	1-2	0-1	1-2	0-0	0-0	1-4	0-0	*	0-3	1-0	0-3	3-1	1-0	2-1	0-3
11. Oakham United	2-1	1-0	1-3	2-2	2-1	2-0	2-0	2-6	3-2	3-0	*	1-0	4-1	2-1	2-0	1-0	3-0
12. Priory (Eastwood)	3-2	1-1	1-1	0-0	2-1	0-0	1-1	0-2	1-2	3-0	2-0	*	3-1	3-3	4-1	2-1	2-2
13. Rossington	2-5	4-3	2-3	0-2	2-3	2-0	3-1	1-4	1-1	3-3	3-2	0-3	*	1-2	2-1	2-0	0-7
14. Sandiacre Town	0-2	1-3	1-3	0-4	2-3	4-3	4-2	2-0	1-1	1-3	2-1	1-3	5-1	*	3-1	2-3	2-1
15. Sheffield Aurora	0-0	2-2	2-0	2-3	3-3	1-3	4-2	0-1	1-0	5-2	1-4	0-0	0-3	3-2	*	5-0	0-3
16. Shirebrook Town	1-0	3-1	0-3	1-3	1-2	3-1	2-0	2-1	1-0	5-0	1-1	0-1	1-1	3-3	2-2	*	1-2
17. Staveley Miners Welf.	1-0	4-2	5-2	1-1	3-0	0-1	5-1	2-0	2-2	5-0	0-1	1-1	4-1	4-1	0-0	5-3	*

PREMIER DIV. RESULTS	1	2	3	4	5	6	7	8	9	10	11	12	13	14	15	16
1. Askern Welfare	*	2-3	7-0	2-0	0-2	13-0	0-3	3-1	1-1	1-0	2-3	4-0	9-1	2-3	2-0	1-0
2. Biwater	1-4	*	2-1	1-0	2-6	5-1	2-2	1-1	4-0	1-2	0-1	2-1	7-0	0-2	3-0	1-3
3. Blackwell Miners Welfare	3-4	2-2	*	0-1	2-1	2-1	0-1	2-1	0-4	2-2	1-6	1-2	1-1	0-1	1-3	0-3
4. Derby Carriage & Wagon	0-2	1-1	1-0	*	2-2		0-0	1-1	2-2	2-7	2-1	0-3	13-0	0-2	2-0	2-1
5. Derby Rolls Royce	4-0	3-3	1-1	2-3	*		1-1	2-1	5-0	1-6	2-3	1-1	3-0	0-2	2-0	0-2
6. Kingston *(record expunged)*			0-3			*	1-4	0-1	1-4	1-3			4-0	1-6	4-2	3-4
7. Mickleover Royal British L.	2-0	1-2	2-3	2-5	1-0		*	2-0	2-1	0-1	1-1	1-2	3-1	0-2	0-0	1-2
8. Mickleover Sports	3-2	1-0	2-1	2-1	1-1	4-0	2-0	*	4-1	2-3	0-2	1-2	9-0	0-5	2-0	3-1
9. Newhall United	2-2	4-3	2-2	0-4	2-0	5-0	2-0	0-1	*	0-0	0-2	2-2	4-0	2-0	3-1	2-2
10. Norton Woodseats	1-6	2-1	2-0	2-1	3-2		2-0	1-1	3-2	*	1-1	4-0	8-1	4-2	3-0	3-0
11. Nuthall	0-2	2-0	1-0	2-1	6-4	9-0	4-1	1-2	2-0	0-0	*	2-0	2-0	2-1	3-1	1-0
12. Radford	4-4	4-3	3-1	1-1	3-1		0-0	1-2	1-2	3-0	0-1	*	8-0	0-2	1-0	1-1
13. Shardlow St James	0-5	3-1	0-2	0-0	3-2		1-0	0-5	0-0	0-6	0-7	3-3	*	0-8	0-7	2-3
14. South Normanton Athletic	5-0	4-0	3-2	0-2	6-1		4-0	3-1	4-0	5-1	2-4	3-1	7-0	*	4-0	1-4
15. Stanton Ilkeston	0-3	1-2	3-1	1-2	0-3	3-0	0-2	2-4	1-3	1-5	2-2	0-0	2-0	3-1	*	1-6
16. Thorne Colliery	1-3	1-0	3-0	2-2	3-1	5-0	2-0	0-1	2-1	2-0	2-1	1-3	5-1	2-2	5-0	*

RES. PREM. RESULTS	1	2	3	4	5	6	7	8	9	10	11	12	13	14
1. Arnold T. Res.	*	3-3	1-0	3-0	3-1	3-1	0-1	2-2	5-1	2-1	1-0	1-1	2-3	8-1
2. Biwater Res.	1-5	*	2-3	2-0	1-0	0-2	3-3	3-4	0-2	2-0	1-0	0-3	1-3	3-1
3. Blidworth Res.	1-5	1-0	*	1-2	1-2	3-1	2-0	2-3	3-0	5-4	1-2	3-2	3-3	1-2
4. Borrowash Res.	1-4	5-1	2-3	*	2-0	4-0	1-2	1-2	1-1	3-2	9-2	0-0	0-0	10-0
5. Derby CW(R) Res.	1-0	1-1	1-0	0-4	*	1-1	1-1	3-1	0-1	2-3	1-1	2-2	1-5	6-1
6. Glapwell Res.	1-4	7-3	2-0	2-3	3-1	*	4-5	2-1	3-2	0-3	3-0	1-0	1-6	2-4
7. Hucknall Res.	0-4	3-3	0-0	0-1	1-0	1-3	*	0-1	4-0	2-3	2-1	0-0	2-1	3-1
8. Kimberley	1-2	1-0	1-2	0-0	2-4	2-0	0-1	*	2-0	1-2	1-3	2-1	0-5	2-2
9. M'over RBL Res.	0-5	0-1	1-0	0-5	1-0	0-0	1-2	0-5	*	1-1	1-4	0-4	1-3	6-1
10. Norton Wood. Res.	1-1	3-1	2-1	0-0	7-1	1-1	0-0	3-1	2-0	*	3-1	3-0	2-2	7-3
11. Oakham Utd Res.	1-5	6-1	1-2	0-2	3-0	6-0	0-5	3-3	9-1	2-2	*	0-2	0-0	3-1
12. Priory (E'wood) Res.	1-2	6-2	0-0	1-1	2-0	5-0	1-0	2-1	1-0	4-0	2-2	*	1-0	5-1
13. Shirebrook T. Res.	2-2	2-1	3-1	1-1	3-1	3-1	2-2	4-1	5-0	0-2	4-1	3-0	*	9-0
14. Stanton Ilk. Res.	0-3	4-2	1-6	0-1	2-1	1-6	0-0	0-6	0-2	0-4	0-5	4-6	1-4	*

RES. DIV. 1 RESULTS	1	2	3	4	5	6	7	8	9	10
1. Derby Rolls Royce Reserves	*	2-2	3-0	5-0	0-1	5-1	1-0	1-0	2-0	5-3
2. Gedling Town Reserves	2-1	*	4-1	1-2	3-1	0-0	11-1	2-2	5-1	4-4
3. Harworth C.I. Reserves	1-3	1-6	*	1-4	+-2	0-1	4-5	0-4	3-8	3-1
4. Long Eaton Utd Res.	0-4	1-5	9-1	*	3-2	1-3	3-0	4-3	1-0	2-2
5. Mickleover S. Reserves	1-2	2-4	3-4	7-2	*	0-5	3-0	0-2	2-1	3-1
6. Nuthall Reserves	2-0	4-0	4-0	2-0	3-2	*	4-1	1-1	1-2	4-1
7. Radford Reserves	2-0	2-2	0-0	3-1	0-2	2-1	*	0-9	3-3	3-0
8. Rossington Reserves	3-1	3-5	1-0	11-1	5-2	1-2	4-1	*	2-2	4-3
9. Sandiacre Town Reserves	3-2	2-2	2-2	3-1	1-1	0-2	3-1	2-5	*	5-2
10. Shardlow St James Res.	2-9	0-4	1-2	1-1	0-3	2-4	1-1	0-5	0-2	*

LEAGUE CUP 1994-95

Preliminary Round

Derby C & W (Reckitts) v Norton Woodseats 2-2,0-1

First Round

Askern Welfare v Mickleover RBL 3-1
Blidworth Welfare v Sheffield Aurora 4-0
Gedling Town v Heanor Town 3-3,2-3
Mickleover Sports v Stanton Ilkeston 0-1
Nuthall v Derby Rolls Royce 0-4
Priory (Eastwood) v Glapwell 1-4
Shardlow St James v Nettleham 0-4
Staveley Miners Welfare v Sandiacre Town 1-0
Biwater v Kiveton Park 1-1,0-3
Borrowash Victoria v Thorne Colliery 2-1
Kingston v Radford 0-2
Newhall United v Blackwell Miners Welfare 2-3
Oakham United v Kimberley Town 3-2
Rossington v Long Eaton United 0-1
Shirebrook Town v Norton Woodseats 3-1
South Normanton Athletic v Harworth CI 5-1

Second Round

South Normanton Athletic v Heanor Town 0-4
Glapwell v Kiveton Park 1-4
Stanton Ilkeston v Radford 2-3
Nettleham v Borrowash Victoria 0-1
Blackwell Miners Welfare v Derby Rolls Royce 0-1
Oakham United v Long Eaton United 3-1
Shirebrook Town v Blidworth Welfare 1-1,4-1
Askern Welfare v Staveley Miners Welfare 1-2

Quarter-Finals

Heanor Town v Staveley Miners Welfare 1-1,2-1
Borrowash Victoria v Kiveton Park 0-2
Derby Rolls Royce v Radford 1-2
Shirebrook Town v Oakham United 2-5

Semi-Final *(at Kimberley Town FC)*
Heanor v Radford 0-0*(aet, 7-6 on pens)*

Semi-Final *(at Glapwell FC)*
Oakham United v Kiveton Park 1-0*(aet)*

Final *(at Mansfield Town, Thurs 12th May)*: Heanor Town 2, Oakham United 0

WAKEFIELD FLOODLIT CUP 1993-94

GROUP A.	P	W	D	L	F	A	PTS
Blidworth Welfare	6	2	3	1	10	6	9
Nettleham	6	2	3	1	8	5	9
Sheffield Aurora	6	2	2	2	10	11	8
Staveley MW	6	1	2	3	3	9	5

RESULTS	1	2	3	4
1. Blidworth Welfare	*	1-1	5-0	2-0
2. Nettleham	0-0	*	1-1	1-2
3. Sheffield Aurora	4-1	1-4	*	0-0
4. Staveley Miners Welfare	1-1	1-1	0-4	*

GROUP B.	P	W	D	L	F	A	PTS
Gedling Town	4	3	1	0	15	4	10
Shirebrook Town	4	0	3	1	2	8	3
Borrowash Victoria	4	0	2	2	2	7	2

RESULTS	1	2	3
1. Borrowash Victoria	*	1-4	0-0
2. Gedling Town	3-1	*	7-1
3. Shirebrook Town	0-0	1-1	*

GROUP C.	P	W	D	L	F	A	PTS
Oakham United	4	2	2	0	14	5	8
Heanor Town	4	1	1	2	14	12	4
Harworth CI	4	1	1	2	9	20	4

RESULTS	1	2	3
1. Harworth Colliery Institute	*	4-3	2-2
2. Heanor Town	8-3	*	2-4
3. Oakham United	7-0	1-1	*

GROUP D.	P	W	D	L	F	A	PTS
Glapwell	6	3	0	1	7	4	9
Priory (Eastwood)	6	2	1	1	6	4	7
Kimberley Town	6	0	1	3	2	7	1

RESULTS	1	2	3
1. Glapwell	*	2-0	2-0
2. Kimberley Town	1-2	*	1-3
3. Priory (Eastwood)	3-1	0-0	*

Quarter-Finals

Oakham United 2, Shirebrook Town 2
Shirebrook Town 1, Oakham United 2
Blidworth Welfare 0, Priory (Eastwood) 5
Gedling Town 1, Heanor Town 2
Glapwell 3, Nettleham 1

Semi-Finals

Oakham 2, Priory (Eastwood) 0 *(at Staveley MW)*
Glapwell 1, Heanor Town 1 *(at Blidworth) - Glapwell won 4-2 on penalties*

Final *(at Mansfield Town FC, Thurs 17th May)*:
Glapwell 2, Oakham United 1

RESERVE DIVISIONS CUP 1993-94

Preliminary Round

Gedling Town Res. v Kimberley Town Res. 1-2
Long Eaton Utd Res. v Mickleover Spts Res. 1-4
Borrowash Vic. Res. v Shirebrook Town Res. 4-1
Glapwell Res. v Mickleover RBL Res. 7-1
Hucknall Town Res. v Arnold Town Res. 3-2
Stanton Ilkeston Res. v Oakham United Res. 1-11
Priory (Eastwood) Res. v Shardlow St James Res. 5-2
Nuthall Res. v Norton W. Res. 2-2,0-3*(both expelled)*

First Round

Glapwell Res. *(bye)*
Radford Res. v Oakham United Res. 1-2
Priory (Eastwood) Res. v Hucknall Town Res. 2-1
M'over S. Res. v Ross'ton Res. 0-0*(both expelled)*
Blidworth Welfare Res. v Biwater Res. 2-5
Derby CW(R) Res. v Harworth Colliery I. Res. 1-1,2-1
Borrowash V. Res. v Sandiacre Town Res. 3-1
Derby Rolls Royce Res. v Kimberley Town Res. 1-3

Quarter-Finals

Derby C & W (Reck.) Res. v Biwater Res. 4-1
Oakham Utd Res. v Glapwell Res. 1-3
Priory (Eastwood) Res. v Kimberley Town Res. 3-2
Borrowash Victoria Res. *(bye)*

Semi-Final *(at Borrowash Victoria FC)*
Derby C & W (Reck.) Res. v Glapwell Res. 1-0

Semi-Final *(at Oakham United FC)*
Borrowash V. Res. v Priory (Eastwood) Res. 2-1

Final *(at Moorways Stadium, Derby, Mon 23rd May)*: Borrowash Res. 1, Derby Carriage & Wagon Res. 0 *(aet)*

KEN MARSLAND TROPHY 1993-94

GROUP A.	P	W	D	L	F	A	PTS
Derby RR Res.	8	5	1	2	19	10	16
Mickleovers S. Res.	8	5	1	2	17	13	16
Nuthall Res.	8	4	2	2	23	12	14
Rossington Res.	8	2	2	4	15	16	8
Harworth CI Res.	8	0	2	6	12	35	2

RESULTS	1	2	3	4	5
1. Derby RR Res.	*	3-0	1-2	3-0	5-1
2. Harworth CI Res.	2-3	*	0-2	4-4	0-0
3. Mickleover Spts Res.	2-2	6-2	*	1-3	2-0
4. Nuthall Res.	1-2	7-1	4-0	*	3-0
5. Rossington Res.	2-0	10-3	1-2	1-1	*

GROUP B.	P	W	D	L	F	A	PTS
Gedling T. Res.	8	6	1	1	28	7	19
Sandiacre T. Res.	8	5	1	2	16	8	16
Long Eaton Res.	8	4	1	3	16	17	13
Radford Res.	8	2	2	4	15	19	8
Shardlow SJ Res.	8	0	1	7	11	35	1

RESULTS	1	2	3	4	5
1. Gedling Res.	*	2-0	2-2	0-1	0-10
2. Long Eaton Res.	2-4	*	4-2	1-0	2-1
3. Radford Res.	1-2	1-2	*	2-2	3-2
4. Sandiacre Res.	0-1	3-1	3-1	*	3-2
5. Shardlow SJ Res.	0-7	4-4	2-3	0-3	*

Final *(at Borrowash Victoria FC, Thurs 10th May)*:
Gedling Town Res. 2, Derby Rolls Royce Res. 1

Action from the Easter Monday Supreme Division fixture between Nettleham and Staveley Miners Welfare at the former's neat Mulsanne Park ground.

Photo - Dave West.

SUPREME DIVISION CLUBS 1994-95

BORROWASH VICTORIA

Chairman: Ian Anderson **Vice Chairman:** Peter Erwin.
Sec./Press Officer: Ian Collins, 30 Margreave Road, Chaddesden, Derby DE21 6JD (0332 678016).
Manager/Coach: Peter McGurk **Asst Manager:** Graham Walker **Physio:** Stewart Worthington
Ground: Asterdale Club, Borrowash Road, Spondon, Derby (0332 668656).
Directions: M1 jct 25, A52 towards Derby, 3rd left off by-pass into Borrowash Rd, ground 400 yds on left. 2 miles from Spondon (BR). Nottingham to Derby buses pass nearby.
Capacity: 5,000 **Seats:** No **Covered:** 500 **Floodlights:** Yes **Founded:** 1911
Midweek matches: Tuesday **Prev. Grnd:** Dean Drive, B'wash 11-84 **Reformed:** 1963.
Colours: Red/white/black **Change Colours:** All yellow **Nickname:** Vics.
Programme: 16 pages, 50p **Editor:** Secretary.
Club Shop: No, but club ties, pens, pencils and key rings are available - contact secretary.
Record Gate: 2,000 v Nottingham Forest, floodlight opening 22/10/85.
Prev. Lges: Derby Sunday School & Welfare 52-57/ Derby Comb./ Midland 79-82/ Northern Co's East.
Club Sponsors: Derwent Print. **Clubhouse:** Normal pub hours. Hot & cold food.
Record win: 11-1 **Record defeat:** 3-8
Club record scorer: Paul Acklam **Club record appearances:** Neil Kellogg.
Captain 93-94: Steve Weightman **P.o.Y. 93-94:** Richard Miles **Top Scorer 93-94:** Russell Roddis.
Hons: Northern Co's East Lg Div 1 Sth 83-84 (R-up 84-85, Div 2 Sth R-up 82-83), Derby Comb. 77-78 (R-up(10) 65-66 68-74 75-77 78-79, Lg Cup 68-69 75-76 (R-up 63-64 66-67), Midland Co's Lg Div 80-81 (Div 1 Cup 80-81), Derbys Snr Cup R-up 90-91, Derbys Div. Cup 73-74 (R-up 70-71 72-73), Central Midlands Lg B E Webbe Cup R-up 88-89 (Reserves Cup 93-94), FA Cup 3rd Qual. Rd 91-92.

GEDLING TOWN

Chairman: R A Ash **President:** P M Robinson.
Secretary: Roland Ash, 80 Portland Drive, Carlton, Nottingham NG14 5PZ (0602 670047).
Manager: Dave Sands/ Cameron Holroyd **Physio:** Pete Tyas
Doctor: Alan Scott **Commercial Manager:** Dave Sands.
Ground: 'Riverside Ground', rear Ferry Boat Inn, Stoke Inn, Stoke Biddulph, Gedling, Nottm (0602 770258).
Directions: From Notts County F.C., A612 towards Southwell for 2 miles to Burton Joyce, Station Rd, then Stoke Lane. Ground rear of Ferry Boat Inn.
Capacity: 2,000 **Seats:** None **Cover:** 500 **Floodlights:** Yes **Founded:** 1989.
Colours: Red/black/red **Change colours:** Yellow/blue/yellow **Nickname:** None.
Previous Grounds: None **Previous Leagues:** Notts Amateur.
Programme: 32 pages, 50p **Programme Editor:** Secretary **Club Shop:** No.
Midweek home matchday: Wednesday **Sponsors:** Barrett Homes/ P R Scaffolding Ltd.
Record win: 5-0 **Clubhouse:** Matchdays only. Hot & cold food. Licensed bar.
Record scorer: Darren Terry **Record appearances:** G Watson.
Top Scorer 93-94: Michael Bradley 14. **Record Gate:** 250 v Arnold, Wakefield F'lit Tphy 92-93.
Hons: Central Mids Lg Div 1 90-91 (Premier Div R-up 91-92, Wakefield Floodlit Trophy 92-93, Ken Marsland Cup(Res.) 93-94), Notts Amtr Lg 89-90 (Snr Cup R-up 89-90).

GLAPWELL

Secretary: Steven Brown, 2 Carter Lane West, Shirebrook, Mansfield NG20 8NA (0623 743661).
Manager: Dave Waller
Ground: Hall Corner, Park Ave., Glapwell, Chesterfield, Derbyshire (0623 812213).
Directions: A617 towards Mansfield from M1 jct 29, left at Young Vanish Inn after 2 miles, ground 100yds on right. From Mansfield on A617, right at Glapwell crossroads after 5 miles, ground 100 yds on right.
Colours: Black & white stripes/black/black **Change colours:** Red/black/black.
Floodlights: Yes **Midweek home matches:** Wednesday
Programme: 16 pages, 30p **Programme Editor:** Brian Caton.
Top Scorers 93-94: David Waller 28, Andrew Womble 11, Willie Gamble 10.
Hons: Central Midlands Lg 93-94 (Floodlit Cup 93-94), Derbyshire Senior Cup SF 93-94.

A Glapwell forward is denied by a superb tackle from Sean Smith of Sandiacre. *Photo - Martin Wray.*

A Glapwell defender makes a desperate clearance during the closing moments of the 2-1 win over Sandiacre. Photo - Martin Wray.

HARWORTH COLLIERY INSTITUTE

Chairman: Paul Wilson **Vice-Chairman:** N/A **President:** Bert Fielding.
Secretary: Tom Brogan, 30 Lindsey Road, Harworth, Doncaster, Sth Yorks DN11 8QH (0302 750132).
Manager: Alan Needham **Asst Manager:** Terry Griffin **Physio:** David Butler.
Commercial Mgr: Steve Tucker **Press Officer:** Mark Hickling (0302 744569)
Ground: Recreation Ground, Scrooby Rd, Bircotes, Doncaster (0302 750614).
Directions: Off A1(M) at Blyth, head towards Bawtry for approx 2 miles, take third left, ground in village at top of hill on left. Or, from Doncaster to Bawtry then head for A1(M) and turn left after caravan site - ground at top of hill.
Capacity: 2,000 **Seats:** None **Cover:** 500 **Founded:** 1931 **Floodlights:** Yes
Colours: All red **Change Colours:** White & blue. **Nickname:** Reds.
Programme: 44 pages, 40p **Editor:** Steve Owen (0302 750322). **Club Shop:** No.
Midweek matches: Wednesday **Reserve Team's League:** Gainsborough & District.
Previous Grounds: None **Record Gate:** 350 v Congleton, FA Cup 1st Qual. Rd 1988.
Previous Lges: Doncaster Senior/ Sheffield County Senior/ Yorkshire 46-50 77-82/ Northern Co's (East).
Players progressing to Football League: Billy Griffin (Sheffield Wednesday) 1957, Graham Cawthorne (Grimsby Town) 1979), Lee Butler (Lincoln City) 1986.
Clubhouse: Open most night, Sat afternoon & evening & Sun lunchtime. Sandwiches available. Matchdays & Sunday lunchtimes. Darts, pool, food
Captain 93-94: Dave Blagg **Club record appearances:** Robert Needham.
Top Scorer 93-94: Terry Griffin **Player of the Year 93-94:** Dave Blagg.
Hons: Wharncliffe Charity Cup 62-63 74-75, Central Midlands League 87-88 (Runners-up 86-87, Challenge Cup 86-87 87-88, F'lit Cup 91-92 (Runners-up 89-90)), Sheffield Senior League 64-65 74-75, Sheffield & Hallamshire Senior Cup SF 87-88

HEANOR TOWN

Secretary: Keith Costello, 45 Stainsby Avenue, Heanor, Derbyshire DE75 7EL (0773 719446).
Manager: Bobby Sykes
Ground: The Town Ground, Mayfield Avenue, Heanor (0773 713742/715815).
Directions: North: M1 (J27), A608. South: M1 (J26), A610-A608
Capacity: 3,500 **Seats:** 200 **Cover:** 800 **Founded:** 1883 **Floodlights:** Yes
Programme: 20 pages, 30p **Programme Editor:** Secretary **Clubhouse:** Yes
Midweek matches: Wednesday **Record Gate:** 6,411 v Carlisle, FA Cup 1958.
Colours: White/black/blue **Change Colours:** All red
Previous Name: Heanor Athletic **Top Scorer 93-94:** Graham Millington 17.
Previous League: Midland Co's 1894-97 98-1900 26-28 61-72 74-82/ Central Alliance 21-25 47-61/ West Midlands (Regional) 72-74/ Northern Co's League East 82-86.
Hons: Central Midlands League Cup 93-94 (Runners-up 86-87 92-93, B E Webbe Removals Cup 88-89), West Midlands Reg. League Runners-up 72-73; Midland Co's League Runners-up 65-66 67-68; Derbys Senior Cup(9) 1892-94 1946-47 65-69 70-71 78-79; FA Cup 1st Rd 58-59 63-64.

KIMBERLEY TOWN

Chairman: George Giddens **Vice Chairman:** Reg Izzard **President:** R J Penney.
Secretary: Horace Hibbert, 62 Eastwood Road, Kimberley, Nottingham NG16 2HZ (0602 383382).
Manager: Julian Garmston **Asst Manager:** Brian Harrison
Press Officer: Gary Jayes **Commercial Manager:** Carl Parkin.
Ground: Stag Ground, Nottingham Road, Kimberley (0602 382788).
Directions: Through Nuthall from M1 jct 26 to Kimberley, ground entrance 150 yds after Stag Inn. 6 miles from Nottingham (BR). Trent Buses R11, R12, R13, 357 & 358 all stop outside ground.
Seats: None **Cover:** 150 **Capacity:** 2,500 **Floodlights:** Yes **Founded:** 1948
Colours: Blue/white/blue **Change colours:** White/black/white **Nickname:** Stags.
Previous Grounds: None **Prev. Name:** Kimberley YMCA, 1948-56.
Reserves' Lge: CML Res Div 1 **Record Gate:** 1,122 v Eastwood, Midland Co's Lg April 76.
Previous Leagues: Notts Amateur 48-55/ Central Alliance 55-66/ East Midlands 66-71/ Midland Counties 71-80/ Northern Counties (East) 80-86.
Programme: 20 pages, 20p **Programme Editor:** TBA **Club Shop:** No.
Midweek home matchday: Tuesday **Clubhouse:** Matchdays and evenings, snacks available.
Record win: 8-1 (opponents not known) **Record defeat:** 1-9 v Bridlington Trinity (H), NCEL 4/5/81.
Record transfer fee paid: Nil **Received:** £2,000 for Andy Hill (Derby, Sept '81).
Captain 93-94: Julian Garmston **Top Scorer & Player-of-the-Year 93-94:** Paul Fletcher
Club record scorer: Graham Cutts **Club record appearances:** Dennis Froggatt.
Hons: Notts Amateur Lg Div 1 54-55, Central Alliance Div 2 R-up 57-58.

Kimberley's Chris Browne (right) surges past Chris Simpson in the 1-3 Bank Holiday defeat at Rossington.
Photo - Martin Wray

KIVETON PARK

Secretary/Prog. Editor: John Holden, 184 Wales Road, Kiveton Park, Sheffield S31 8RF (0909 779508).
Manager: Brian Mellon **Assistant Manager:** Glyn Reeves
Ground: Hard Lane, Kiveton Park, Sheffield (0836 690873).
Directions: Follow Worksop signs from M1 exit 31, left down Goosecar Lane after a quarter mile, over crossroads and ground is 200 yds on the right before rail bridge.
Capacity: 2,000 **Seats:** 200 **Floodlights:** Due 94-95 **Founded:** Early 1900s
Colours: Claret/sky/claret **Change colours:** Black & white stripes/black/black
Programme: 24 pages, 50. **Midweek home matchday:** Tuesday
Hons: Yorks Lg Div 2 77-78 **Prev. Lges:** Yorks 63-82/ Northern Co's East 82-91.
Top Scorers 93-94: Leslie Harris 13, David Bright 11.

LONG EATON UNITED

Chairman: J C Fairley **Vice Chairman:** M Reynolds.
Secretary: Michael Raven, 71 Stanton Rd, Sandiacre, Nottingham NG10 5EQ (0602 393947).
Manager: J Fairley Jnr/ B Webster **Coach:** J Fairley Jnr.
Physio: J Hopkins **Commercial Manager:** A Spray.
Press Officer: G W Whitehead (0332 872849).
Ground: Grange Park, Station Road, Long Eaton, Nottingham (0602 735700).
Directions: From Nottingham, A52 to r'bout by 'Bardills Garden Centre', left onto B6003 to t-junction & lights, right into Station Rd, ground opposite Speedway Stadium. From M1 jct 25, A52 signed Nottingham, right onto B6003 at 1st r'bout then as above. 2 miles from Long Eaton (BR).
Seats: None **Cover:** 500 **Capacity:** 5,000 **Floodlights:** No **Founded:** 1956
Colours: All blue **Change:** Yellow/green/black. **Nickname:** Blues.
Previous Name: Long Eaton Town. **Record Gate:** 2,000 - 1973 FA Cup.
Previous Leagues: Central Alliance 59-61/ Midland Co's 61-82/ Northern Co's East 82-89.
Programme: 16-20 pages, 30p **Previous Grounds:** None. **Club Shop:** No.
Midweek home matchday: Tuesday **Sponsors:** M C Builders/ Railway Inn, Long Eaton.
Record transfer fee received: £5,000 for Anton Lambert (Scunthorpe), £3,000 for Garry Birtles (Nottm Forest).
Clubhouse: Open matchdays one hour either side of kick-off. Hot & cold drinks, confectionery, sausage rolls, burgers etc.
Top Scorer 93-94: Gary Weston 13. **Club Record Scorer:** Gary Weston 32, Graham Walker 32.
Hons: Derbys Snr Cup 64-65 75-76, Midland Co's Lg R-up 76-77, Central Alliance Div South 58-59, Northern Co's (East) Div 1 South 84-85.

NETTLEHAM

Secretary: John Wilson, 21 Chaucer Drive, Lincoln LN2 4LN (0522 530566).
Manager: Ian Musson **Ground:** Mulsanne Park, Field Close, Nettleham (0522 750007).
Directions: A46 approx. 3 miles north of Lincoln, right at Brown Cow Pub, proceed past Church 2nd turning on right.
Colours: All blue **Colours:** Red (white trim)/red/red **Floodlights:** Yes.
Midweek home matches: Tuesday **Programme:** 48 pages, 50p (Editor: Colin Benton).
Top Scorer 93-94: James Rainey 6.
Hons: Central Mids Lg Premier Division Cup R-up 87-88, Village Tphy, Nursing Cup, Kelly Read Cup, Blankney Hunt Cup, Lincoln & Dist. Amtr Cup R-up, Joe Miller Tphy(2).

OAKHAM UNITED

Chairman: Mr L Tagg **Manager:** Paul Elrick. **Press Officer:** Stuart Lee.
Secretary: Gary Leivers, 84 Mansfield Rd, Skegby, Sutton-in-Ashfield, Notts NG16 3EN (0623 517038).
Ground: Mansfield Hosiery Mills, Mansfield Rd, Sutton-in-Ashfield, Notts (0623 552376).
Directions: From M1 junction 28, A38 for Mansfield, ground half mile past Sutton on left. A617 from Mansfield towards M1. 3 miles from Alfreton/Mansfield Parkway (BR).
Capacity: 2,000 **Seats:** None **Cover:** 350 **Founded:** 1969 **Floodlights:** Yes
Colours: White/navy/white **Change Cols:** Yellow/green/yellow **Club Shop:** No.
Midweek matches: Tuesday **Previous Lges:** Midland Co's/ Northern Co's East
Programme: 28 pages, 30p **Programme Editor:** Secretary.
Club Sponsors: Major Oak Securities, Ashfield Concrete.
Record Gate: 500 v Sutton Town, Midland Counties League 79-80.
Player progressing to Football Lge: Dion Dublin (Cambridge, Man Utd).
Clubhouse: Every evening and weekend lunchtimes. Darts, pool, meals and hot snacks on matchdays.
Top Scorer 93-94: Brendan Yates **Player of the Year 93-94:** Neil Campion (goalkeeper).
Hons: Midland Co's Div 1 Lg Cup 79-80 (Div 1 R-up 79-80), Central Mids Lg R-up 93-94 (Lg Cup R-up 93-94, Floodlit Trophy R-up 93-94).

PRIORY (EASTWOOD)

Secretary: Steve Wadsley, 3 Wainfleet Close, Ilkeston, Derbyshire DE7 9HR (0602 300422).
Manager: Kevin Smith
Ground: Birnam Park, off Eastwood By-Pass, Eastwood, Nottingham (0836 749883).
Directions: M1 junction 26 to Langley Mill, ground on left
Capacity: 2,000 **Seats:** 200 **Cover:** 200 **Founded:** 1967 **Floodlights:** Yes
Midweek matches: Tuesday **Prog.:** 20 pages, 30p (Ed.: Reg Forde) **Clubhouse:** No.
Colours: Red/black/black **Change Colours:** Yellow/white/white
Previous League: Notts Amtr/ Central Alliance/ East Mids Regional Alliance.
Top Scorers 93-94: Lee Edwards 19, Nigel Gillott 8, Kevin Smith 7.
Club honours: Central Mids Lg Prem. Div 88-89 (Div 1 R-up 87-88), East Mids Regional Alliance Div 1, Notts Intermediate Cup 90-91(reserves).

ROSSINGTON

Chairman: Mr K Spencer
Sec./Press Off.: Ian Wilson, The Wickets, 3 Hollin Close, Rossington, Doncaster DN11 0XX (0302 867221).
Joint Managers: Mr I Wilson, Mr G Mountford. **Physio:** G Murden.
Commercial Manager: G Shaw.
Ground: Welfare Ground, West End Lane, Rossington, Doncaster (0302 868272).
Directions: From south: M18 jct 1, A631 to Bawtry via Maltby/Tickhill, 1 mile out of Tickhill take B6463 to Rossington. From north: A638 out of Doncaster towards Bawtry, 4 miles from Racecourse to Rossington. In Rossington take road to colliery, over level crossing, ground on right after Sports Centre. 6 miles from Doncaster (BR) - buses run every 15 mins from Southern Bus Station (journey time 25 mins) - ground 5 mins walk from terminus.
Seats: None **Cover:** 200 **Capacity:** Unknown **Floodlights:** No **Founded:** 1990
Colours: Red/black/navy **Change colours:** White/black/sky **Club Shop:** No.
Previous Ground: Station FC: Tornedale School Field 73-85 (still used by Sunday & Youth sides).
Previous Leagues: Station FC: Bentley 73-79/ Donc. Snr 80-85. Haslam Sports: Local Sunday football.
Previous Names: Station Hotel 73-82/ Station 82-89. Merged with Haslam Sports/ Rossington Haslam 89-90.
Programme: 40+ pages, £1 with entry **Programme Editor:** Secretary **Club Shop:** No.
Sponsors: Rossington Hall Investments **Record Gate:** 234 v Emley, Sheffield Snr Cup 12/12/92.
Reserves' Lge: CML Res Div **Midweek home matchday:** Wednesday **Nickname:** The Locals
Record win: 14-1 (Sheff. Jnr Shield) **Record defeat:** 0-7 v Staveley MW (H), CML Supreme Div 12/3/94).
Players progressing to Football League: David Moss (Doncaster & Chesterfield via Worksop).
Clubhouse: Evenings & matchdays. Sandwiches, rolls, satellite TV, pool
Club record scorer: Tommy Henderson **Club record appearances:** Tommy Henderson.
Captain 93-94: Colin Holvey **Top Scorer 93-94:** Robert Nelson 19 **P.o.Y. 93-94:** Nigel Feirn
Hons: Central Mids Lg Div 1 87-88 (Prem Div R-up 92-93, Div 1 Cup R-up 86-87 87-88, Res. Div 1 Cup 87-88, Res Div 1 R-up 93-94, Res. Div 2 Champs Cup R-up 86-87), Doncaster Snr Lg Div 2 R-up 85-86 (Div 1 Cup R-up 85-86), Sheffield & Hallamshire Jnr Shield 83-84, Bentley Lg 77-78 78-79 (Lg Shield 74-75 78-79).

PHOTO OPPOSITE:
Rossington pictured before their 3-1 home win over Kimberley Town at the Welfare Ground on 4th April 1994.
Photo - Martin Wray.

SANDIACRE TOWN

President: None **Chairman:** Les Fountain.
Secretary: Mel Williams, 38 Pasture Road, Stapleford NG9 8GL (0602 392415).
Manager: Mick Rodgers **Asst Manager:** Ged Le Blond **Coach:** Mike Rose
Physio: Les Fountain **Press Officer:** A Walker. **Commercial Manager:** J Thornhill.
Ground: St Giles Park, Stanton Road, Sandiacre, Nottingham NG10 5EP (0602 392880).
Directions: M1 jct 25, follow signs to Sandiacre passing Post House Hotel on right, straight over crossroads into Rushy Lane and towards Stanton, 1st right after 1000yds into Stanton Rd, ground at bottom after another 1000yds. Trent buses from Nottingham to Derby alighting at Sandiacre Market Place - from traffic lights go along Town Street (canal on your right) eventually past Comet (on right) then left into Church Street, follow to Stanton and ground is 200yds on right (total distance half mile).
Seats: None **Cover:** 250 **Capacity:** 2,000 **Floodlights:** Due **Founded:** 1978
Cols: Red/navy/red **Change:** All sky **Reformed:** 1991
Prev. Grounds: Kilburn Welfare 93-94 **Prev. Lge:** Midlands Regional Alliance. **Sponsors:** None
Programme: 44 pages, 50p **Programme Editor:** Secretary **Club Shop:** No.
Reserves' Lge: CML Res. Div. **Midweek home matchday:** Tuesday **Nickname:** Saints.
Record win: 12-0 v Ilkeston Reserves **Record defeat:** 0-4 v Eastwood Town Reserves.
Clubhouse: Members club open 8-11pm daily, Sunday lunchtimes, and from 4.40pm Saturday matchdays. Cobs, crisps etc - mobile cafe provides hot food (burgers, hot dogs, peas) and hot & cold drinks on matchdays.
Record scorer: Mark Robinson 56 **Record appearances:** Mark Robinson 62.
Top Scorer 93-94: Gary Briscoe 14 **Captain & Player of the Year 93-94:** Ged Le Blond.
Hons: Central Mids Lg Premier Div 92-93 (Lg Cup 92-93), Midlands Regional Alliance 91-92.

SHEFFIELD AURORA

President: P W F Wilson **Chairman:** G A Harper.
Secretary: D Brown, 139 Whitehill Rd, Brinsworth, Rotherham, Sth Yorks S60 5JQ (0709 363878).
Manager: John Eastwood **Coach:** S Berresford **Physio:** A Atkinson.
Press Officer: G B Stirling **Commercial Manager:** P Cresswell.
Ground: Aurora Sports & Social Club, Bawtry Rd, Brinsworth, Rotherham S60 5ND (0709 372613).
Directions: M1 jct 34 (Meadowhall), exit island onto A631 Bawtry Rd, ground 1 mile on right. Buses from Sheffield; 24 to Maltby or 19 to Brinsworth.
Capacity: 2,000 **Seats:** None **Cover:** 300 **Floodlights:** Yes **Founded:** 1964.
Colours: White/blue **Change Colours:** All red **Nickname:** Aurora
Previous Grounds: None **Previous Lges:** Matchard/ Whitbread Co. Senior.
Previous Name: Crookes **Rec. Gate:** 650 v Worksop, Sheffield Snr Cup 90-91
Programme: 10 pages, 50p **Programme Editor:** P Cresswell **Club Shop:** No.
Club Sponsors: Aurora Plc **Midweek home matchday:** Tuesday or Friday.
Record win: 11-0 v Blidworth (H), Central Mids Lg 90-91 **Record defeat:** 1-6
Clubhouse: Normal licensing hours. Snacks and buffets available.
Club record scorer: S Marshall **Club record appearances:** John Eastwood.
Captain 93-94: **Top Scorer 93-94:** Paul Dodd 10.
Hons: Centrals Midlands Lg Wakefield Floodlit Cup 90-91, Sheffield & Hallamshire Snr Cup R-up 85-86, Hatchard Lg Div 1 83-83, Whitbread Co. Snr Lg 83-84 (Lg Cup 85-86).

PHOTOS OPPOSITE

Top: *South Normanton Athletic - Premier Division runners-up 1993-94.*

Foot: *Staveley Miners Welfare FC. Back Row (L/R): Daryn Evans, Kevin Wragg, Mick Collins, Gary Weighill, Carl Fuller, Phil Greaves, Andy Knowles, Ady Wells. Front: David Tromans (Manager), Mick Hoskins, Darren Vernon, Lee Vernon, Steve Botchett, Steve Shipp, John Seels, Mick Holden.*

SHIREBROOK TOWN

Chairman/Press Officer: Mr T Rowbottom
Secretary: Mr S P Wall, 26 Carter Lane West, Shirebrook, Mansfield, Notts NG20 8NA (0623 747638).
Manager: Neil Moore **Assistant Manager:** Graham Charlesworth.
Ground: BRSA Ground, Langwith Rd, Mansfield (0623 742535).
Directions: M1 jct 29, A617 to Mansfield, 2.5 miles, B6407 Shirebrook, through town to Langwith Rd. Bus 81 from Chesterfield or 23 from Mansfield.
Capacity: 2,000 **Seats:** None **Cover:** 400 **Floodlights:** Yes **Founded:** 1985
Cols: Red & black stripes/black/red **Change Colours:** All blue
Prev. Name: Shirebrook Colliery 85-93 **Record Gate:** 2,200 v Mansfield, floodlight opening 10/10/91
Programme: 28 pages, 50p **Programme Editor:** K Easom (0623 747603).
Midweek home matches: Tuesday **Clubhouse:** No.
Club Sponsors: Topline Windows **Record transfer received:** £4,000 for G Castledine (Mansfield 1991)
Record win: 8-1 v Nettleham (H), Central Midlands League Supreme Division 3/4/93.
Record defeat: 0-7 v Newhall United (A), Derbyshire Senior Cup 8/10/88.
Record Scorer: S Hill **Record appearances:** P Hayes 165, 1985-89.
Captain 93-94: G Tennant **Top Scorer 93-94:** David Thacker/ Richard Burns, 9 each.
P.o.Y. 93-94: G Quincey. **Hons:** Central Midlands League Reserve Prem Div 93-94.

SOUTH NORMANTON ATHLETIC

Chairman: Terry Ball **Vice C'man:** Jim Wright **President:** Monsieur A Thibaudeau.
Secretary: Steve Phillips, 59 Derby Rd, Swanwick, Derbyshire DE55 1AB (0773 603895).
Manager: Graham Brentnall **Asst Manager:** Clive Churm.
Coach: Terry Ball **Physio:** Terry Hodson.
Press Off.: Kev Miles (0773 510925)
Commercial Manager: Andy Smithurst (0773 510925).
Ground: South Normanton Miners Welfare Ground, Lees Lane, South Normanton, Derby (0773 581491, club-811396).
Directions: B6019 from from M1 exit 28, right after 1 mile (in South Normanton) at Mobil garage into Market Street, after quarter mile turn left immediately after The Clock pub into Lees Lane, ground at bottom. Half hour's walk from Alfreton & Mansfield Parkway BR station.
Seats: None **Cover:** 500 **Floodlights:** Due **Nickname:** Athletic **Founded:** 1980
Colours: Yellow/blue/blue **Change colours:** White/red/red **Sponsors:** Exchem Plc
Midweek home matchdays: Wednesday **Reserve Team's League:** None
Programme: Average 60 pages, 50p **Programme Editor:** Kevin Miles (0773 510925).
Club Shop: Yes, with a good stock of progs, magazines, badges. Also ties, jumpers. Contact Kev Miles (above)
Previous Leagues: Alfreton & District Sunday 80-87/ Mansfield Sunday 87-90.
Record win: 8-0; v Retford Rail (A), CML Div 1 3/11/90; v Shardlow St James (A), CML Premier Div 2/10/93; v Shardlow St James (H), Derbyshire Senior Cup 1st Round 9/10/93.
Record defeat: 1-7 v Sandiacre Town (H), CML Premier Division 30/1/93.
Record Gate: 409 v Heanor Town, Central Midlands League Cup Second Rd 1/1/94.
Clubhouse: Open matchdays 11am-11pm and Wednesdays 6.30-11pm. Matchday refreshments from tea bar include pie & peas, soups etc.
Record scorer: Peter Green 31 **Record apps:** Dave Vallance 132 (Sat only), Mick Kane 286 (overall)
Captain 93-94: Clive Churm **P.o.Y. 93-94:** Gary Bennett **Top Scorer 93-94:** Peter Green, 20
Hons: Central Mids Lg Prem Div R-up 93-94, Alfreton & Dist. Sunday Lg 86-87 (Div 2 83-84, Div 3 R-up 80-81, Suppl. Shield 84-85, W L Screen Bowl 86-87), Mansfield Sunday Lg Prem. Div Cup 88-89 (Div 1 R-up 87-88).

STAVELEY MINERS WELFARE

Chairman: Henry Ireson **Vice-Chairman:** Phil White.
Secretary: John Wilmot, 12 Winster Rd, Staveley, Chesterfield, Derbyshire S43 3HZ (0246 476875).
Manager: David Tromans **Asst Manager:** David Pugh **Physio:** Dominic Gage/Neil Gilliver
Comm. Mgr: Tom Rowland **Press Officer:** Andy Knowles (0246 272325).
Ground: Inkersall Road, Staveley, Chesterfield, Derbyshire (0246 471441).
Directions: M1 jct 30, follow A619 Chesterfield - Staveley is 3 miles from jct 30. Turn left at GK Garage in Staveley town centre into Inkersall Rd - ground 200yds on right at side of Speedwell Rooms. Frequent buses (47, 70, 72, 75, 77) from Chesterfield stop in Staveley town centre - 3 mins walk to ground.
Capacity: 5,000 **Cover:** 200 **Seats:** 200 **Floodlights:** Yes **Founded:** 1989
Cols: Blue & black halves/black/black **Change cols:** Yellow/blue/yellow **N'name:** The Welfare
Midweek home matches: Wednesday. **Prev. Lgs:** Chesterfield & D. Amtr 89-91/ County Snr 91-93.
Programme: 16 pages, 30p **Programme Editor:** Tony Barnes (0246 474448).
Previous Grounds: None **Record Gate:** 280 v Stocksbridge, Sheffield Snr Cup 22/1/94.
Sponsors: Autoworld Garage **Reserve Team's League:** Central Midlands Lge Reserve Div.
Club Shop: Yes. Sells numerous programmes. Contact Craig Cousins (0246 475068).
Record win: 14-0 v Abbeydale (A), County Senior League Division Two 31/10/92.
Record defeat: 0-5 v Stocksbridge Park Steels (A), Sheffield & Hallamsire Senior Cup 9/11/91.
Clubhouse: The Staveley Miners Welfare, 500yds from ground, is open before and after games.
Club record scorer: Paul Nicholls **Club record appearances:** Shane Turner.
Captain 93-94: Mick Hoskins **Top Scorer 93-94:** Ady Wells.
Player of the Year 93-94: Rob Atkin/ Carl Fuller (joint).
Hons: County Snr Lg Div 2 92-93 (Div 3 91-92), Chesterfield & D. Amtr Lg R-up 89-90 90-91 (Byron (Lge) Cup 89-90 (R-up 90-91)).

PREMIER DIVISION CLUBS 1994-95

ASKERN MINERS WELFARE

Secretary: Miss Lynn Sudworth, 12 Marlborough Rd, Askern, Doncaster DN6 0LN (0302 712814).
Ground: Doncaster Road, Askern, Doncaster (0302 700957).
Directions: A1/A639 Pontefract. Follow sign for Askern/Campsall. At T-junction right. Left at Anne Arms, right at Supersave, ground on right.
Floodlights: No **Colours:** White (black stripes)/white/black
Midweek home matches: Tuesday or Thursday
Programme: 20 pages, 50p **Programme Editor:** Ron Poundall.
Top Scorers 93-94: Tony Hattersley 32, Mark Illman 35.

BIWATER

President: B W S Nuttall, MBE JP **Chairman:** P Owen **Vice Chairman/Asst Mgr:** A Bramley
Secretary: Alan Kilcline, 4 Deerpark Crescent, Wingerworth, Chesterfield S42 6XF (0246 276707).
Manager/Coach: Phil Tingay **Physio:** D Stoppard
Press Officer: D Jones **Commercial Manager:** R Haney.
Ground: John's Street, off Market Street, Clay Cross. **Directions:** A61 Chesterfield-Derby road, turn onto A6175 (signed M1) in Clay Cross Centre, then north into Brassington Street and follow to ground.
Seats: None **Cover:** 150 **Capacity:** **Floodlights:** No **Reformed:** 1952
Colours: Red/white/red **Change colours:** Blue/black/black. **Nickname:** The Works
Previous Grounds: None **Previous Name:** Clay Cross Works 1952-1988.
Prev. Lges: Ripley & Dist./ Chesterfield & Dist./ Sutton & Skegby/ Matlock & Dist./ East Mids/ Derbys Snr.
Programme: 50p **Programme Editor:** P Owen **Club Shop:** No.
Club Sponsors: Biwaters Plc **Record Gate:** 364 v Matlock, Derbyshire Snr Cup.
Midweek matchday: Mon or Wed **Clubhouse:** Open matchdays only.
Club record scorer: G Simpson **Club record appearances:** Bobby Wilks 350.
Captain 93-94: **Top Scorer 93-94:** Simon Barlow 16.
Hons: FA Vase QF, Central Midlands Lg Premier Div 79-80 (Div 1 83-84, Div 1 Cup 88-89 (R-up 89-90), Reserve Div 1 88-89 (R-up 91-92)). *Plus virtually every major honour in above Leagues.*

BLACKWELL MINERS WELFARE

Chairman: Mr M Bunning **Vice-Chairman:** Mr C Bunning.
Secretary: Julian Riley, 22 Glinton Ave., Blackwell, Alfreton, Derbys DE55 5HD (0773 862411).
Manager: Steve Woodward **Asst Mgr/Coach:** Phil Burnham **Physio:** Eric Eyley.
Ground & Directions: Welfare Ground, Primrose Hill, Blackwell, Derbyshire DE55 5JE. (0773 811295). A38 towards Mansfield from M1 jct 38, left onto B6406 after half a mile, left after a mile, ground on left.
Capacity: 600 **Seats:** 50 **Cover:** 50 **Floodlights:** No **Reformed:** 1974.
Cols: Red & white stripes/red/red **Change colours:** All silver grey. **Club Shop:** No.
Midweek home matchdays: Wednesday **Previous Lge:** Sutton & Skegby 74-78. **Clubhouse:** No.
Programme: 28 pages, 50p **Programme Editor:** Secretary
Sponsors: B & B Travel **Record Gate:** 289 v South Normanton Athletic, 1993-94.
Club record scorer: Julian Riley **Club record appearances:** Derrick Hopkinson.
Captain 93-94: Peter Maltby **Top Scorer 93-94:** Julian Riley, 15.
Honours: Central Mids Lg Senior Div 84-85 (Central Div R-up 85-86, Senior Div Cup 84-85, Div 1 Cup 87-88), Derbyshire Jnr Cup 77-78 82-83 83-84 (R-up 76-77), Derbyshire Divisional Cup 85-86.

CASE SPORTS

Secretary: D W Henderson, 18 King George's Road, New Rossington, Doncaster, South Yorkshire DN11 0PR (0302 865027).
Ground & Directions: TBA

CLIPSTONE WELFARE

Secretary: Barry Clarke, 40 Church Road, Clipstone, Mansfield, NG21 9DG (0623 640829).
Ground & Directions: Clipstone Lido Ground (0632 655674). B6030 from Mansfield, on left entering Clipstone.
Colours: Black & red stripes/black/red
Previous League: Notts Alliance (pre-1994).
Hons: Notts Snr Cup 85-86 93-94, Notts Alliance 72-73 73-74 74-75 92-93 93-94 (Lg Cup 72-73 73-74 74-75 93-94 (R-up 92-93)), Notts I'mediate Cup 55-56.

DERBY CARRIAGE & WAGON (RECKITTS)

Chairman: Laurie Astle **Joint Presidents:** Bill Steadman, Mick Allen.
Secretary: David Wright, 6 Athol Close, Sinfin, Derby DE24 9LZ (0332 756833).
Manager: Stewart Woodings **Coach:** Mick Bentley **Physio:** Mick Ward.
Ground: Carriage & Wagon Welfare, Longbridge Lane, off Ascot Drive, Derby (0332 571376).
Directions: M1 jct 25, A52 towards Derby, A5111 Raynesway (ring-road) for about 3 miles, right at 1st island (A6 - city centre), left at 2nd island into Ascot Drive, Longbridge Lane 1st right after filling station, ground at bottom.
Seats: None **Cover:** None **Capacity:** 600 **Floodlights:** No **Founded:** 1935
Colours: Yellow/navy/navy **Change colours:** Blue/yellow/yellow **Nickname:** The Wagon
Sponsors: Reckitt & Colman **Reserves' Lge:** CML Res Prem. **Prev. Grounds:** None
Previous Leagues: Derby Amtr/ Derby Comb./ Derbys Snr/ Central Alliance/ East Mids Regional.
Programme: 32 pages, 40p **Editor:** Caroline Murphy (0332 664502) **Club Shop:** No.
Midweek home games: Mon or Wed **Clubhouse:** Normal hours. Hot pies etc available.
Captain 93-94: Lee Astle **Top Scorer 93-94:** Frank Hopka **P.o.Y. 93-94:** Matt Johnson.
Hons: Central Alliance 77-78, East Mids Regional Lg R-up 83-84 (Div 1 81-82), Central Mids Lg Premier Div R-up 85-86 (Premier Div Cup R-up 85-86, Div 1 Cup 89-90 (R-up 90-91), Prem Div Sportsmanship Cup 85-86, Reserve Div 1 R-up 92-93, Reserves' Cup R-up 93-94), Derby Floodlit Cup R-up 85-86, Derby Divisional Cup (Sth) R-up 83-84.

DERBY ROLLS ROYCE

Secretary: Michael Lomax, 47 Cleveland Avenue, Caddesden, Derby DE2 6SB (0332 664183).
Manager: D Tice **Ground:** Rolls Royce Rec. Society, Moor Lane, Derby (0332 249167).
Directions: Derby ringroad, Osmaston Park Road, Moor Lane; ground adjacent to Swimming Baths.
Cols: Blue & white stripes/blue/blue **Change:** Black & white stripes/black/black
Floodlights: No **Midweek home matchday:** Wedneshay
Programme: 8-12 pages, 50p **Programme Editor:** Paul McCracken.
Top Scorers 93-94: Andy Mellor 11, Paul Boyce 9.
Hons: Central Mids Lg Ken Marsland Cup(Res.) R-up 93-94.

HOLBROOK MINERS WELFARE

Secretary: Michael Turner, Shyloh, 68 Wormwells Lane, Ripley, Derbyshire DE5 8JB (0773 746851).
Ground: Carters Lane, Holbrook (adjecent to Miners Welfare in centre of village).
Clubhouse: Miners Welfare, open normal licensing hours.
Previous League: Midlands Regional Alliance (pre-1994).

KILLAMARSH ATHLETIC

Secretary: Philip Bright, 17 Marrison Drive, Killamarsh, Sheffield, South Yorkshire SY31 8HF (0742 482763).
Ground & Directions: TBA
Presvious League: Chesterfield (pre-1994).

MEXBOROUGH ATHLETIC (OAKHOUSE)

Secretary: Nev Wheeler, 15 Holmshore Drive, Sheffield, South Yorkshire S13 8UJ (0742 694142).
Ground: Mexborough Athletic Club, Hampden Rd, Mexborough (0709 586479).
Directions: Just off A6023 Conisborough-Mexborough road opposite Police Station. Half mile from Mexborough BR station.
Capacity: 1,500 **Seats:** 150 **Cover:** 150 **Floodlights:** No
Previous League: County Snr (pre-1994) **Previous Name:** Sheffield Oakhouse (pre-1994)
Ground record attendance: 1,800 - Mexborough Town (now defunct) v Scarborough, FA Trophy 1973.

MICKLEOVER ROYAL BRITISH LEGION

President: A N Waplington **Chairman:** Ron Curd.
Secretary: Ray Taylor, 15 Inglwood Avenue, Mickleover, Derby DE3 5RT (0332 515047).
Manager: Alan Feathertone **Assistant Manager:** Dave Mann.
Ground: Ypres Lodge, Western Rd, Mickleover (0332 513548).
Colours: Tangerine/black/black **Midweek home matchday:** Tuesday **Founded:** 1945
Nickname: Legionnaires.
Previous Leagues: Derbys Sunday/ East Mids/ Derby Premier. **Floodlights:** No.
Previous Grounds: Ypres Lodge 45-91/ Gresley Rovers FC 91-92/ Belper Town FC 92-93.
Programme: 36 pages, 30p **Programme Editor:** Michael Mouse Snr.
Captain 93-94: Anthony Clark **Top Scorer 93-94:** Mark Ashwell 9.
Hons: Centrals Mids Lg Premier Div 89-90 90-91 (R-up 88-89, Lg Cup 88-89 89-90, Reserve Lg Cup 82-83 (R-up 88-89 92-93), Res Div 1 Cup R-up 88-89), East Mids Lg 80-81, Derbys Divisional Cup South 80-81.

MICKLEOVER SPORTS

Secretary: Derek Hewitt, 1 Milton Close, Mickleover, Derbyshire DE3 5QN (0332 515295).
Ground: Mickleover Sports Ground, Station Rd, Mickleover, Derby (0332 521167).
Midweek matchdays: Tuesday **Colours:** Red & black stripes/black/red.
Programme: 28 pages **Programme Editor:** Tony Shaw **Floodlights:** No.
Top Scorers 93-94: Stephen Brown 20, Kevin Joyce 11.

NEWHALL UNITED

Chairman: Sid Gutteridge **Manager:** TBA **Physio:** Melvyn Mole & Bob Evans.
Secretary: David Wain, 26 Willow Drive, Newhall, Swadlincote, Derbys DE11 0NW (0283 225188).
Ground: Hewfields Ground, St Johns Drive, Newhall, Swadlincote (0283 551029).
Directions: Turn off A50 (Burton to Ashby-de-la-Zouch) down into Newhall at Chesterfield Arms, to bottom and turn right into Main Street. Left at Lamb Inn into Oversetts Rd, 2nd right into John Street, left into St Johns Drive, ground on left.
Seats: 80 **Cover:** 400 **Capacity:** 2,000 **Floodlights:** Due 93-94.
Colours: Scarlet & navy halves **Change colours:** All white. **Nickname:** Blues
Programme: 24 pages, 25p **Programme Editor:** Nigel Tilley (0283 211207)
Club Sponsors: Ernie Watkins Builders **Record Gate:** 2,000 v Burton Albion, FA Cup.
Midweek home matchday: Wednesday **Previous Leagues:** Central Alliance/ E Mids Regional.
Clubhouse: Brand new. Brick built out of proceeds of landsale. **Club Shop:** No.
Captain 93-94: Nigel Steele **P.O.Y. & Top Scorer 93-94:** Neil Hall.
Club record scorer: John Wain, 349 **Club record appearances:** John Wain, 510.
Hons: Derbys Prem. Lg 73-74 78-79 (Lg Cup 72-73), Bass Vase 73-74, Mavis Marsland Bowl R-up 91-92.

NUTHALL

President: Bill Smith **Chairman:** A Farmer **Vice Chairman:** R Naylor.
Secretary: Tony Benniston, 117 Broad Lane, Brinsley, Nottm NG16 5BU (0773 712350).
Manager/Coach: G Webster **Asst Mgr:** M Cook **Physio:** A Gunn.
Press Officer: K Robinson **Commercial Manager:** J Heading.
Ground & Directions: Basil Russell Playing Fields, Maple Drive, Nuthall, Nottingham (0602 384765). M1 jct 26/ A610 southbound left southbound, right northbound.
Seats: None **Cover:** 50 **Floodlights:** No **Founded:** 1976 **Nickname:** Larks
Colours: Sky/navy/sky **Change colours:** All yellow.
Previous Grounds: None **Previous Leagues:** East Midlands Regional.
Programme: 30 pages, 50p **Editor:** Mr P Taylor (0602 507071) **Club Shop:** No.
Clubhouse: Open matchdays. Food & drinks from one hour prior to kick-off.
Club record scorer: J Paxton **Club record appearances:** L Wild.
Captain 93-94: **Top Scorers 93-94:** Steven Carruthers 21, Kevin Simms 9.
Hons: Central Mids Lg Snr Div 84-85 (Prem Div 93-94, Prem Div Cup R-up 84-85, Div 1 Cup SF 89-90, Res Div 1 93-94), East Mids Regional Lg 82-83 83-84 (R-up 79-80 80-81, Div 1 R-up 78-79, Lg Cup 81 82 (R up 70 80 83 84)), Notts Intermediate Cup 79-80 (Snr Cup SF 84-85, Jnr Cup R-up 78-79 (SF 79-80), Minor Cup 82-83), Central Alliance Div 1 R-up 79-80.

RADFORD

Secretary: Chris Daykin, 22 Balmoral Grove, Hucknall, Nottm.
Manager: Terry Lack **Ground:** Radford Road, Radford, Nottm (0602 423250).
Directions: A610 Alfreton Road, left just into Bobbersmill Road, ground at top on right.
Cols: Claret & blue/blue/blue **Change:** White/black/black **Floodlights:** No
Midweek home matchdays: Tuesday **Programme:** 16 pages, 30p (Editor: Secretary).
Previous name: Radford Olympic. **Hons:** Derbys Prem. Lg Div 1 R-up 84-85.
Top Scorers 93-94: Paul Fountain 18, Michael Wilson 13.

SHARDLOW St JAMES

President: D Irving **Chairman:** D Spencer **Vice-Chairman:** G Proudler
Secretary: S R Symcox, 22 West End Drive, Shardlow, Derby DE7 2GY (0332 792733).
Manager: M Spooner **Asst Manager:** Ray Foulds **Physio:** Richard Foulds
Coach: A Smith/J Wain **Press Officer:** A Lindsay (0332 572085).
Commercial Manager: I Potter. **Ground:** The Wharf, Shardlow, Derby.
Directions: A6 Derby/Leicester, 6 miles out of Derby at Shardlow take next left after Shardlow church (on right), ground 100yds on left.
Colours: Sky/navy/sk **Club Sponsor:** Mr D Irving. **Nickname:** Saints
Prev. Lges: Derby Amtr/ Derby Welf./ Derby Snr/ Derby Prem./ Cen. Mids/ Midland Regional Alliance.
Previous Grounds: Coronation Field, Shardlow/ Willn Lane, Shardlow.
Programme: 20 pages, 50p **Editor:** A Lindsay (0332 572085) **Club Shop:** No.
Nickname: Saints **Clubhouse:** No **Floodlights:** No.
Club record scorer: W Shaw **Club record appearances:** W Shaw.
Captain 93-94: Richard Foulds **Top Scorer 93-94:** Ian Wright 5.
Hons: Central Mids Lg Div 1 R-up 84-85 (Div 1 Cup R-up 84-85), Mids Regional Alliance 90-91 (Lg Cup 90-91, Div 1 89-90, Jnr Cup 89-90), Derbyshire Divisional Cup (Sth) R-up 90-91, Derbyshire Premier Lg Premier Div Cup 78-79 (Snr Div Cup 73-74, Reserve Div R-up 80-81, Reserve Div Cup 79-80), Derby & District Comb. Div 2 70-71 (Div 5 68-69 (R-up 67-68), Div 3 Cup 69-70, Div 5 Cup 68-69).

STANTON (ILKESTON)

Secretary: Steven Hurst, 32 Bennett Str., Long Eaton, Nottingham NG10 4RA (0602 730229).
Manager: Martin Cooper.
Ground & Directions: Hallam Fields Sports Ground, Stanton Club, Hallam Fields, Nr Ilkeston, Derbys (0602 323244). From South, M1 (J25) to Nottm, 1st r-about turn left. From North, M1 (J26), Ilkeston, through to to Hallam Fields.
Capacity: 2,000 **Seats:** None **Cover:** 300 **Floodlights:** No **Founded:** 1921.
Cols: Blue & white stripes/blue/blue **Change Colours:** Yellow/black/blue
Programme: 28 pages, 50p **Programme Editor:** Graham Barksby.
Previous Leagues: Central Alliance 55-58/ Derbyshire Premier/ East Mids Regional Alliance.
Previous Name: Stanton Works. **Midweek home matchday:** Tuesday
Top Scorer 93-94: Paul Smith.
Hons: Central Mids Lg Prem. Div 85-86 86-87 (Prem. Div Cup 85-86).

THORNE COLLIERY

Secretary: Glyn Jones, Democratic Club & Institute, Southfield Rd, Thorne, Doncaster DN8 5NS (0405 816329).
Ground: Miners Welfare Ground, Southfield Rd, Thorne, Doncaster.
Cols: Blue & white stripes/blue/blue **Prev. Lge:** Doncaster Snr (pre-1993) **Floodlights:** No.
Programme Editor: Secretary **Midweek home matchday:** Wednesday
Top Scorer 93-94: Barry Spence 21.

Dave Waller, who enjoyed a career in professional football with Shrewsbury Town, Crewe Alexandra and Chesterfield, starred for Glapwell during their championship winning season of 1993-94 in the Central Midlands League. Here he shakes off his marker during the 2-1 home win over Sandiacre Town on Easter Bank Holiday Monday.

Photo - Martin Wray.

minerva®

SOUTH MIDLANDS LEAGUE

FEEDER TO:
DIADORA LEAGUE
FOUNDED: 1922.

President: A G Joyce.

Chairman: P Burns.

Hon. Secretary: M Mitchell, 26 Leighton Court,
Dunstable, Beds LU6 1EW (Dunstable 667291)

THE EAGLES FLY HIGHEST

Bedford Town, one of the most famous names in the history of non-League football, made a significant step in their quest to emulate the achievements of their illustrious predecessors when they became champions of the Minerva South Midlands League last season. Coming just three seasons after their reformation, their efforts have assured them of promotion to the Diadora League Division Three in 1994-95.

Their success was never in doubt as they headed the table from the opening day in August, right through a season which was disrupted by wet weather. They eventually claimed the title with a 12 point margin over closest challengers, Luton Old Boys. The Eagles thus became the first club since Shefford Town in 1983-84 to win the Division One and Premier Division titles in consecutive seasons.

The Eagles set the pace from the start of the campaign, and with a total of eight different clubs occupying second place at various times during the season, none of them were able to make a serious challenge for the title. At one stage Bedford Town held a lead of over 20 points over their closest challengers! A sequence of 15 consecutive league victories ended in February, and it was to be another month before they were to suffer their first defeat at the hands of Biggleswade Town. Biggleswade themselves enjoyed another successful season finishing in the top three for the third time in four seasons.

Jason Reed, of champions Bedford Town, towers above the Biggleswade defence during a fixture at the New Eyrie, the new ground that was inaugurated at the start of the 1993-94 campaign.

Photo - Martin Wray.

At the foot of the table, Milton Keynes, who rose from the ashes of the dufunct Milton Keynes Borough, spend almost the whole of the season occupying the bottom position, but gained a reprieve when it was decided not to relegate any clubs at the end of the season.

The first-ever winners of the newly formed Senior Division were Toddington Rovers who were also celebrating their centenary season. Rovers ended the season with an unbeaten away record in the league. They moved to the top of the table in October and remained there for the rest of the season lifting the title nine points ahead of runners-up London Colney. The Hertfordshire side ended their season on a high note gaining maximum points from their last seven matches including 11-0 and 9-0 victories in the final week of the season!.

The climax of the season proved to be a disappointment for Risborough Rangers, after they had remained in the top two until 9th April, they won only two of their final 11 games and finally slipped to sixth place. Pitstone & Ivinghoe, like their Premier Division counterparts Milton Keynes, spent almost the entire season anchored to the bottom of the table and also escaped relegation at the end of the campaign.

Stony Stratford Town were the top goalscorers in the Minerva South Midlands League with a total of 108 in 30 matches. They clinched the Division One title 11 points ahead of runners-up Delco. Both clubs gaining promotion to the Senior Division this season. Stony Stratford suffered their only away defeat in their final game of the season, and enjoyed a spell of 27 league matches without defeat. In keeping with the other two divisions, the destiny of the championship was never much in doubt once they climbed to the top spot in mid October.

At the bottom of the table, Sandy Albion struggled once more and never moved from the foot of the table from Christmas until the end of the season, a period which saw them win only once. They went on to concede over 100 goals by the end of the campaign.

In the League's various cup competitions, there was a surprise in the Challenge Trophy sponsored by O'Brien Butchers. For the first time since the knock-out competition was first contested back in 1955, no Premier Division club was represented in the Final. The winners were Senior Division runners-up London Colney who defeated Division One newcomers Houghton Town 2-0 in the final at Harpenden. On their respective routes to the final, five Premier Division sides fell to their 'giant-killing' feats. London Colney's victims included favourites Bedford Town, while the previous season's winners, Biggleswade Town were elimintated by Houghton in one of the biggest shocks of the competition.

The early stages of the three divisional cup competitions were played on a group basis to determine the qualifiers for the knock-out phases. The eventual winners were: Arlesey Town (O'Brien Butchers Premier Division Cup), Toddington Rovers (Senior Division Cup) and Stony Stratford Town (Division One Cup). Toddington and Stony Stratford therefore achieved their respective league and cup 'doubles'.

In the national cup competitions, the SML had mixed fortunes last season. None of the League's seven entrants in the FA Cup went beyond the 1st Qualifying Round, but Arlesey Town enjoyed a magnificent season in the FA Vase where they reached the 6th Round before losing 3-2 at home to Boston. Arlesey were just minutes away from a famous victory leading 2-1, but conceded two late goals in a thrilling encounter at Lamb Meadow.

There was only little joy for SML clubs in County Cup competitions. London Colney lifted the Herts Charity Shield winning the all SML final against Hoddesdon Town. In another all SML clash, Delco defeated Houghton Town 3-1 to win the Beds Intermediate Cup. Oxford City Reserves completed a hat-trick of County cup successes for the SML when they defeted Carterton 8-0 in the Oxfordshire Intermediate Cup Final.

In the reserve team competitions, Hatfield Town, Division 1B champions, defeated Division 1A champions Toddington Rovers in the play-off to decide their championship. De-Havilland won the Division 2 title, while Leighton Town denied Barton Rovers' attempt to win the Reserve Challenge Trophy for a fourth successive season when they defeated them by the only goal of the final at Letchworth.

Minerva Footballs will once again be sponsoring the SML in 1994/95. Their support is appreciated together with that of O'Brien Butchers who last season sponsored cup competitions for a tenth successive season.

The 1994-95 season sees a number of familiar names missing from the SML's ranks for various reasons. Bedford Town have gained promotion to the Diadora League, while five other clubs will not be competing this season: Ashcroft, Milton Keynes County, Sandy Albion, Shefford Town and Shenley & Loughton. The SML welcomes six new members including the Royston Town who return after ten seasons, together with Dunstable Old Boys who join the Premier Division. Joining Division One are Abbey National (MK), Bow Brickhill, Clifton Old Boys, and Kents Athletic.

Paul Gardner, League Historian & Statistician.

PREMIER DIV.	P	W	D	L	F	A	PTS
Bedford Town	30	22	5	3	94	26	71
Luton Old Boys	30	19	2	9	61	47	59
Biggleswade Town	30	16	5	9	48	36	53
Welwyn GC	30	14	5	11	43	44	47
Brache Sparta	30	13	7	10	47	36	46
Arlesey Town	30	12	8	10	54	49	44
Wingate & Finchley	30	13	5	12	45	44	44
Hoddesdon Town	30	11	10	9	42	33	43
Langford	30	12	7	11	54	50	43
Hatfield Town	30	13	4	13	57	54	43
Harpenden Town	30	11	7	12	38	38	40
Shillington	30	10	5	15	42	47	35
Buckingham Ath.	30	9	2	19	51	76	29
Potters Bar Town	30	7	7	16	35	60	28
Letchworth GC	30	8	4	18	39	75	28
Milton Keynes	30	5	7	18	31	66	22

SENIOR DIV.	P	W	D	L	F	A	PTS
Toddington Rvrs	26	21	4	1	78	25	67
London Colney	26	18	4	4	82	28	58
Totternhoe	26	15	5	6	66	39	50
Shenley/Loughton	26	13	5	8	38	31	44
Shefford Town	26	11	8	7	50	38	41
Risborough Rgrs	26	12	5	9	49	40	41
Winslow United	26	12	4	10	55	58	40
Leverstock Green	26	11	4	11	41	34	37
Ampthill Town	26	9	4	13	38	47	31
Tring Athletic	26	8	6	12	37	47	30
Bedford United	26	6	6	14	47	67	24
The 61 FC (Luton)	26	6	5	15	35	56	23
New Bradwell St P.	26	4	2	20	20	63	14
Pitstone & Ivinghoe	26	3	4	19	25	88	*10

* - 3 points deducted

DIV. ONE	P	W	D	L	F	A	PTS
Stony Stratford	30	23	5	2	108	34	74
Delco	30	20	3	7	68	40	63
Houghton Town	30	20	2	8	67	38	62
Flamstead	30	17	2	11	63	47	53
Walden Rangers	30	15	6	9	69	45	51
De Havilland	30	15	4	11	65	65	49
Ashcroft	30	14	6	10	54	48	48
Cranfield United	30	13	3	14	66	58	42
Scot	30	12	5	13	57	63	41
Eaton Bray	30	11	6	13	53	56	39
Caddington	30	11	6	13	39	57	39
Potters Bar Crus.	30	11	3	16	76	72	36
Emberton	30	11	3	16	53	69	36
Mercedes-Benz	30	7	7	16	40	62	28
MK County	30	5	2	23	30	75	17
Sandy Albion	30	3	1	26	29	108	10

PREMIER DIVISON RESULTS 1993-94

HOME TEAM	1	2	3	4	5	6	7	8	9	10	11	12	13	14	15	16
1. Arlesey Town	*	3-1	1-1	1-1	4-1	2-0	1-1	1-0	2-0	4-0	2-4	4-0	2-2	1-1	1-2	2-0
2. Bedford Town	0-0	*	1-2	4-0	5-0	1-1	5-0	1-1	1-0	3-1	7-0	5-2	4-0	7-1	5-2	2-0
3. Biggleswade Town	4-1	2-3	*	2-2	4-3	1-0	2-0	1-3	1-3	2-0	3-0	0-1	4-2	2-0	1-0	1-1
4. Brache Sparta	3-1	1-3	2-0	*	3-0	1-1	1-2	1-1	0-2	6-0	1-2	2-0	1-2	2-1	1-1	1-2
5. Buckingham Athletic	6-2	1-3	1-1	1-3	*	0-2	1-3	0-2	2-4	5-1	2-1	3-0	3-3	3-2	1-0	2-3
6. Harpenden Town	1-2	1-1	1-0	0-1	2-1	*	1-1	0-2	2-0	1-0	0-1	6-1	1-0	1-1	2-3	0-1
7. Hatfield Town	4-0	0-2	1-2	1-4	5-1	3-0	*	1-0	3-3	7-4	1-2	2-2	2-1	1-0	2-4	3-0
8. Hoddesdon Town	3-1	1-2	2-0	3-2	4-1	1-1	1-3	*	1-1	1-0	1-1	3-0	1-1	0-0	1-3	1-1
9. Langford	3-1	1-4	0-0	1-2	1-0	5-1	4-2	2-2	*	2-5	1-1	4-1	1-3	0-2	2-0	1-2
10. Letchworth Garden City	3-1	0-7	0-1	1-0	2-1	1-1	1-4	1-1	2-2	*	3-2	0-1	0-0	3-2	0-2	2-1
11. Luton Old Boys	3-1	2-1	4-3	1-0	6-1	0-3	2-1	1-0	2-1	4-2	*	5-2	4-0	1-2	0-2	5-3
12. Milton Keynes	2-2	0-3	2-3	0-1	1-2	0-2	2-1	0-2	2-3	5-3	1-2	*	0-0	1-1	1-0	0-0
13. Potters Bar Town	0-3	4-4	0-1	1-2	1-4	2-1	5-1	1-0	0-2	0-3	0-3	2-1	*	0-3	1-2	1-3
14. Shillington	1-2	0-2	1-2	1-2	3-1	4-1	0-2	2-4	1-2	1-0	1-0	2-2	2-0	*	0-1	0-2
15. Welwyn Garden City	2-2	0-4	0-2	1-1	1-3	1-3	1-0	2-0	3-1	3-0	1-0	1-1	2-2	0-3	*	3-2
16. Wingate & Finchley	0-4	0-3	1-0	0-0	4-1	1-2	2-0	2-0	2-2	5-1	1-2	2-0	0-1	2-4	2-0	*

SENIOR DIV. RESULTS	1	2	3	4	5	6	7	8	9	10	11	12	13	14
1. Ampthill Town	*	3-1	2-1	0-2	3-0	5-2	0-3	0-0	1-1	1-2	2-6	0-2	2-3	1-2
2. Bedford United	0-1	*	0-0	2-2	3-1	8-0	6-1	2-5	1-5	2-7	1-3	1-1	1-2	1-2
3. Leverstock Green	4-0	1-0	*	1-3	7-0	3-1	2-1	0-0	1-3	0-1	1-1	2-1	1-0	2-4
4. London Colney	4-2	11-0	2-0	*	3-1	5-2	3-1	2-2	2-1	0-1	4-1	0-0	2-3	8-2
5. New Bradwell St Peter	0-2	1-3	1-3	0-2	*	0-1	0-4	2-3	0-4	1-3	1-2	0-1	1-1	2-1
6. Pitstone & Ivinghoe	2-2	2-2	0-4	0-4	1-2	*	0-5	0-4	1-2	0-4	0-5	0-3	0-0	2-1
7. Risborough Rangers	0-1	2-2	0-1	0-4	2-1	6-1	*	0-0	0-1	0-0	1-1	3-2	5-2	5-2
8. Shefford Town	0-3	4-2	4-1	0-1	2-0	2-0	1-1	*	3-0	0-2	2-2	2-0	5-1	5-4
9. Shenley & Loughton	1-0	1-2	2-0	0-9	2-0	4-0	0-2	0-0	*	0-1	0-0	4-0	1-0	2-0
10. Toddington Rovers	4-0	5-1	2-3	3-2	2-2	5-0	5-2	5-0	3-1	*	4-3	3-1	2-0	2-2
11. Totternhoe	2-1	0-2	4-3	1-0	4-0	1-5	0-1	3-2	3-0	1-1	*	3-2	4-0	6-1
12. Tring Athletic	2-1	1-1	0-0	2-2	1-2	6-1	0-2	3-1	0-1	1-4	0-5	*	3-2	1-1
13. The 61 FC (Luton)	0-2	3-1	#	1-2	0-2	2-2	4-0	0-0	1-1	2-5	3-4	3-4	*	1-3
14. Winslow United	3-3	3-2	2-0	2-3	3-0	3-2	1-2	4-3	1-1	0-2	2-1	3-0	3-1	*

DIV. ONE RESULTS	1	2	3	4	5	6	7	8	9	10	11	12	13	14	15	16
1. Ashcroft	*	1-1	1-0	1-1	0-2	3-2	2-1	3-2	1-2	2-0	2-2	4-3	4-0	4-1	1-3	4-0
2. Caddington	3-1	*	2-1	1-0	4-3	3-1	#	1-1	0-2	3-0	0-1	2-1	3-1	3-3	0-4	0-4
3. Cranfield United	2-2	3-1	*	2-0	3-6	3-2	0-3	0-2	1-2	5-0	3-3	2-0	2-1	5-1	0-5	1-2
4. De Havilland	2-2	4-2	1-1	*	1-4	4-0	5-1	5-4	2-2	2-1	2-1	3-1	5-1	2-1	1-6	0-4
5. Delco	3-0	3-1	6-0	2-4	*	2-1	3-2	2-0	0-2	3-1	1-1	3-1	4-2	0-0	0-1	0-4
6. Eaton Bray	0-1	0-0	2-1	1-5	1-1	*	2-0	3-0	1-0	3-0	5-2	2-2	6-0	2-3	0-3	0-0
7. Emberton	1-3	1-1	1-4	6-3	1-2	1-1	*	1-3	2-4	#	2-1	2-5	3-0	4-3	1-5	2-2
8. Flamstead	3-0	3-2	2-3	4-2	2-3	2-1	3-1	*	4-0	3-1	1-2	3-1	3-0	2-0	0-2	1-1
9. Houghton Town	2-4	0-1	1-0	2-0	0-2	1-2	1-0	4-2	*	3-1	4-2	8-1	1-0	4-2	3-0	3-2
10. Milton Keynes County	0-3	3-0	0-3	#	#	2-3	0-2	1-2	0-2	*	3-2	2-8	4-1	2-4	1-5	1-1
11. Mercedes Benz	0-1	2-1	4-2	2-4	0-3	1-5	0-1	1-2	0-1	1-1	*	0-4	1-1	0-1	1-4	1-1
12. Potters Bar Crusaders	3-2	7-0	3-8	3-2	0-2	6-0	2-3	1-2	2-5	2-1	2-3	*	4-0	0-0	1-1	4-0
13. Sandy Albion	3-0	0-1	0-7	0-3	0-3	0-4	4-6	0-2	2-7	1-2	0-1	1-4	*	2-3	2-6	4-2
14. Scot	1-1	4-2	1-3	1-2	3-1	6-1	2-4	1-0	2-0	1-2	1-1	3-2	1-3	*	1-2	0-6
15. Stony Stratford Town	2-1	1-1	3-1	7-0	5-3	1-1	6-1	4-1	0-0	5-1	3-2	3-1	11-0	1-3	*	6-3
16. Walden Rangers	3-0	2-0	1-0	2-0	0-1	3-1	2-0	1-4	2-1	5-0	1-2	5-2	5-0	2-4	3-3	*

- points awarded

Bruising action from Bedford Town's 4-1 Christmas win at neighbours Langford in the Premier Division.
Photo - Jon Weaver.

CHALLENGE TROPHY 1993-94

First Round
Luton Old Boys 2, Hoddesdon Town 1
De Havilland 2, Harpenden Town 3
Ampthill Town 1, Caddington 0
Potters Bar Town 0, Bedford United 1
Pirton *(scr)* v Langdord *(w/o)*
Leverstock Green 0, Shillington 1
Stony Stratford Town 2, Welwyn GC 4
London Colney 4, Milton Keynes County 1
Tring Athletic 4, Scot 2
Wingate & Finchley 1, Delco 2
Flamstead 1, Hatfield Town 2
Buckingham Athletic 1, Brache Sparta 2
Sandy Albion 2, Houghton Town 6
Winslow United 3, New Bradwell St Peter 2
Potters Bar Town 1, Shefford Town 0

Second Round
Biggleswade Town 2, Potters Bar Town 1
Risborough 3, Emberton 2 *(after 2-2 draw)*
The 61 FC 1, Harpenden Town 4
Luton Old Boys 2, Tring Athletic 1
Milton Keynes 4, Pitstone & Ivinghoe 0
Shenley & Loughton 4, Winslow United 3
Letchworth Garden City 0, Brache Sparta 2
Houghton Town 6, Walden Rangers 3
Shillington 2, Cranfield United 0
London Colney 2, Bedford United 1
Hatfield Town 0, Toddington Rovers 2
Mercedes-Benz 1, Eaton Bray 5
Bedford Town 7, Totternhoe 1
Ashcroft 1, Welwyn Garden City 0
Ampthill Town 0, Arlesey Town 4
Langford 4, Delco 2

Third Round
Brache Sparta 3, Arlesey Town 1
Milton Keynes 0, Risborough Rangers 2
London Colney 4, Harpenden Town 2
Eaton Bray 2, Bedford Town 3
Luton Old Boys 1, Houghton Town 6
Shenley & Loughton 4, Toddington Rovers 2
Biggleswade 2, Shillington 1 *(after 2-2 draw)*
Ashcroft 0, Langford Town 4

Quarter-Finals
Shenley & Loughton 2, Langford 1
Bedford Town 6, Risborough Rangers 2
London Colney 1, Brache 0 *(after 0-0 draw)*
Houghton 4, Biggleswade 3 *(after 1-1 draw)*

Semi-Finals (two legs)
London Colney 0 + 2, Bedford Town 0 + 1
Shenley & L. 2 + 1, Houghton Town 3 + 2

Final: London Colney 2, Houghton Town 0

PREMIER DIVISION CUP

Group A	P	W	D	L	F	A	PTS
Norwich City Res.	6	4	2	0	14	5	14
Arlesey Town	6	2	4	0	17	8	10
Letchworth GC	6	1	2	3	7	18	5
Harpenden Town	6	0	2	4	5	12	7

Group B	P	W	D	L	F	A	PTS
Brache Sparta	6	4	2	0	11	6	14
Luton Old Boys	6	3	3	0	19	11	12
Buckingham Ath.	6	1	1	4	9	16	4
Milton Keynes	6	0	2	4	7	13	2

Group C	P	W	D	L	F	A	PTS
Biggleswade Town	6	3	2	1	17	11	11
Hatfield Town	6	2	3	1	15	14	9
Welwyn GC	6	2	3	1	14	13	9
Langford	6	1	0	5	7	15	3

Group D	P	W	D	L	F	A	PTS
Potters Bar Town	6	3	2	1	7	4	11
Hoddesdon Town	6	2	2	2	11	8	8
Shillington	6	2	2	2	9	10	8
Wingate & Finchley	6	2	0	4	6	11	6

Quarter-Finals
Bedford Town 1, Luton Old Boys 0
Brache Sparta 1, Arlesey Town 2 *(aet)*
Hoddesdon 1, Biggleswade 0 *(after 0-0 draw)*
Potters Bar Town 2, Hatfield Town 3

Semi-Finals
Hoddesdon Town 0, Arlesey 1 *(after 1-1 draw)*
Bedford Town 1, Hatfield Town 2 *(aet)*

Final: Arlesey Town 2, Hatfield Town 0

SENIOR DIVISION CUP

Group A	P	W	D	L	F	A	PTS
Leverstock Green	12	8	2	2	27	8	26
Tring Athletic	12	8	1	3	26	15	25
London Colney	12	6	3	3	33	12	21
Totternhoe	11	5	3	3	22	22	18
Risborough Rgrs	10	3	4	3	19	19	13
Pitstone & Iv.	11	1	1	9	11	37	4
The 61 FC	12	1	0	9	13	38	3

GROUP B.	P	W	D	L	F	A	PTS
Toddington Rvrs	11	9	2	0	28	8	29
Winslow United	12	7	1	4	23	17	22
Shenley & L'ton	10	4	3	3	20	16	15
Bedford United	12	3	4	5	15	21	13
Ampthill Town	11	3	2	6	21	26	11
Shefford Town	11	4	1	6	17	24	*10
New Bradwell SP	11	2	1	8	11	23	7

* - 3 points deducted

Final: Toddington Rovers 4, Leverstock Green 1

DIVISION ONE CUP

Group A	P	W	D	L	F	A	PTS
De Havilland	6	5	1	0	19	6	6
Potters BC	6	3	2	1	12	10	11
Walden Rangers	6	2	1	3	8	8	7
Sandy Albion	6	0	0	6	4	19	0

Group B	P	W	D	L	F	A	PTS
Caddington	6	4	1	1	12	4	13
Ashcroft	5	2	2	1	9	7	8
Eaton Bray	5	1	2	2	4	6	5
Flamstead	4	0	1	3	2	10	1

Group C	P	W	D	L	F	A	PTS
Houghton Town	5	3	2	0	18	5	11
Cranfield United	5	2	1	2	7	9	7
Scot	6	1	2	3	8	18	5
Delco	4	1	1	2	8	9	4

Group D	P	W	D	L	F	A	PTS
Stony Stratford	6	3	2	1	21	8	11
Emberton	5	2	1	2	10	10	7
Mercedes-Benz	5	0	5	0	7	7	5
MK County	6	1	2	3	9	22	5

Semi-Finals
De Havilland 0, Stony Stratford Town 1
Caddington 1, Houghton Town 3 *(aet)*

Final: Stony Stratford Town 5, Houghton Town 3

South Midlands League Premier Division Ten Year Records

	84/5	85/6	86/7	87/8	88/9	89/0	90/1	91/2	92/3	93/4
Arlesey Town	–	–	–	–	–	–	–	–	3	6
Ashcroft Co-Op	14	16	–	–	–	–	–	–	–	–
Bedford Town	–	–	–	–	–	–	–	–	–	1
Biggleswade Town	–	–	–	15	15	5	3	3	7	3
Brache Sparta	16	–	–	–	16	14	18	7	2	5
Buckingham Athletic	–	–	–	–	–	–	–	18	17	13
Cranfield Utd	–	14	12	16	–	–	–	–	–	–
Eaton Bray Utd	3	1	8	11	–	–	–	–	–	–
Electrolux	–	–	–	8	14	8	10	–	–	–
Harpenden Town	–	–	–	–	–	–	7	12	10	11
Hatfield Town	–	–	–	–	–	–	–	–	5	10
Hoddesdon Town	7	9	3	5	5	4	9	6	6	8
Knebworth	4	6	15	17	–	–	–	–	–	–
Langford	–	15	13	3	1	16	13	10	14	9
Leighton Town	13	3	9	6	10	3	4	1	–	–
Letchworth Gdn City	–	–	–	–	–	–	6	14	11	15
Leverstock Green	–	–	–	–	–	–	–	8	9	–
Luton Old Boys	–	–	–	–	–	–	–	–	16	2
Milton Keynes Borough	–	10	4	11	18	12	19	2	12	–
Milton Keynes	–	–	–	–	–	–	–	–	–	16
New Bradwell St Peter	12	7	14	12	11	11	17	19	22	–
Oxford City	–	–	–	–	–	–	–	9	1	–
Pirton	9	11	8	13	12	13	14	16	21	–
Pitstone & Ivinghoe	–	–	–	–	8	1	16	15	18	–
Potters Bar Town	–	–	–	–	–	–	–	11	13	14
Selby	10	1	1	2	3	–	–	–	–	–
Shefford Town	3	5	16	10	17	19	–	–	–	–
Shillington	6	13	2	1	4	7	5	4	8	12
61 FC (Luton)	8	4	7	7	7	15	15	20	20	–
Thame United	–	–	–	–	2	2	1	–	–	–
Totternhoe	–	–	6	4	9	6	11	13	15	–
Vauxhall Motors	2	–	–	–	–	–	–	–	–	–
Waterlows (Dunstable)	15	–	–	–	–	–	–	–	–	–
Welwyn Garden City	11	2	10	9	6	10	12	17	19	4
Welwyn Garden Utd	–	–	–	–	–	18	–	–	–	–
Wingate (Finchley)	–	–	–	–	–	–	8	5	4	7
Winslow United	5	12	5	14	13	17	20	21	–	–
Wolverton AFC	–	–	–	–	–	9	2	w/d	–	–
No. of Clubs	**16**	**16**	**16**	**17**	**18**	**19**	**20**	**21**	**22**	**16**

South Midlands League Senior (Division One until 93-94) Ten Year Records

	84/5	85/6	86/7	87/8	88/9	89/0	90/1	91/2	92/3	93/4
Ampthill Town	–	–	–	–	–	–	–	9	13	9
Ashcroft (Co-Op)	–	–	6	8	4	5	5	1	12	–
Bedford Town	–	–	–	–	–	–	–	4	1	–
Bedford United	–	–	–	–	–	10	10	3	3	11
Biggleswade Town	10	8	2	–	–	–	–	–	–	–
Brache Sparta	–	9	9	2	–	–	–	–	–	–
Buckingham Athletic	–	1	11	9	2	4	1	–	–	–
Caddington	–	–	4	3	3	3	6	19	9	–
Cranfield United	6	–	–	–	7	6	14	10	17	–
De Havilland	–	–	–	–	–	–	–	–	20	–
Delco (Products)	–	–	–	12	8	13	7	7	15	–
Electrolux	7	3	1	–	–	–	–	–	–	–
Emberton	–	–	–	–	–	–	–	18	18	–
Flamstead	–	–	–	–	–	–	8	16	19	–
Harpenden Town	13	4	12	11	12	1	–	–	–	–
Ickleford	14	11	10	13	5	14	11	11	22	–
Langford	3	–	–	–	–	–	–	–	–	–
Leverstock Green	–	–	–	–	–	–	–	–	–	8
London Colney	–	–	–	–	–	–	–	–	2	2
Luton Old Boys	–	–	–	–	–	–	–	2	–	–
Millford Villa	–	–	14	–	–	–	–	–	–	–
Milton Keynes Borough	1	–	–	–	–	–	–	–	–	–
Milton Keynes Town	–	–	–	6	–	–	–	–	–	–
Milton Keynes United	8	12	7	–	–	–	–	–	–	–
Mowlem	2	–	–	–	–	–	–	–	–	–
New Bradwell St Peter	–	–	–	–	–	–	–	–	–	13
Oxford City	–	–	–	–	–	–	3	–	–	–
Pitstone & Ivinghoe	11	5	5	1	–	–	–	–	–	14
Potters Bar Crusaders	–	–	–	–	–	–	4	14	8	–
Risborough Rangers	–	–	–	–	–	15	17	8	4	6
Sandy Albion	12	10	13	10	10	16	18	13	16	–
Shefford Town	–	–	–	–	–	–	13	17	11	5
Shenley & Loughton	–	–	–	–	–	8	2	5	5	4
Stony Stratford Town	–	–	–	5	11	7	16	20	14	–
The 61 FC (Luton)	–	–	–	–	–	–	–	–	–	12
Toddington Rovers	–	–	–	–	–	12	15	6	6	1
Totternhoe	5	2	–	–	–	–	–	–	–	3
Tring Athletic	–	–	–	–	9	9	12	12	10	10
Walden Rangers	9	7	3	4	6	11	9	15	21	–
Welwyn Garden United	4	6	8	7	1	–	–	–	–	–
Wingate	–	–	–	–	–	2	–	–	–	–
Winslow United	–	–	–	–	–	–	–	–	7	7
No. of Clubs	**14**	**12**	**14**	**13**	**12**	**16**	**18**	**20**	**22**	**14**

PREMIER DIVISION CLUBS 1994-95

ARLESEY TOWN

Chairman: John Milton **Vice-Chairman:** Scott Geekie **President:** Maurice Crouch.
Secretary: John Albon, 13 St Johns Rd, Arlesey, Beds SG15 6ST (0462 731318).
Manager: Robbie O'Keefe **Asst Manager:** Phil Cavaner **Coach:** Colin Cardines
Physio: Jim Anderson.
Ground: Lamb Meadow, Hitchin Rd, Arlesey (0462 731448).
Directions: On main road thru village. From Hitchin, ground 200 yds past Biggs Wall on left.
Press Officer & Programme Editor: Tony Smith
Capacity: 8,000 **Seats:** 120 **Cover:** 1,000 **Floodlights:** Yes **Founded:** 1891.
Programme: Yes, 50p **Programme Editor:** Pete Brennan (0462 834455).
Colours: Sky & navy **Change Colours:** All yellow **Nickname:** Blues.
Midweek matchday: Tuesday **Record Gate:** 2,000 v Luton Res, Beds Snr Cup 1906
Sponsors: Milcutt Goldstar **Previous Ground:** Bury Meadow 1919-39.
Reserve Team's League: Southe Midlands League Reserve Division.
Prev. Lges: Biggleswade & Dist./ Beds Co. (S. Mids) 22-26 27-28/ Parthenon/ London 58-60/ Utd Co's 33-36 82-92.
Players to progress to Football League: Roland Legate (Luton), Pat Kruse (Brentford, Leicester)
Clubhouse: Members bar & function room. Open daily 6-11.30, Sat noon-11.30, Sin noon-2.30 & 6-11.30.
Captain 93-94: Gary Marshall **Local Press:** Biggleswade Chronicle, Hitchin Gazette.
Top Scorer 93-94: Sean Glasgow **Player of the Year 93-94:** John Hawkins, Nigel Cardines.
Hons: Utd Co's Lg 84-85 (KO Cup), Sth Mids Lg 51-52 52-53 (Chal. Cup 79-80, Prem Div Cup 93-94, Championship Shield 64-65, F'lit Cup), Beds Snr Cup 65-66 78-79, FA Vase QF 93-94.

Arlesey Town - Premier Division Cup winners 1993-94. Back Row (L/R): M Playford, E Marshall, P Tansley, N Cardines, J Hawkins, Z Flanagan, D Lelliott, D Craig, E James. Front: T Kelly, S Mullins, S Gyalog, D Howell, S Glasgow, N Reed. Photo - Richard Brock.

BIGGLESWADE TOWN

Chairman: M Jarvis **Vice Chairman:** N/A **President:** R Dorrington.
Secretary: G Arkwright, 21 Willsheres Road, Biggleswade, Beds SG18 0BU (0767 316992).
Manager: K Davidson **Physio:** R Ashcroft.
Ground: 'Fairfield', Fairfield Road, Biggleswade, Beds (0767 312374).
Directions: A1 North r'bout, left immediately after metal bridge into car park. 10 mins walk from Biggleswade (BR).
Capacity: 2,400 **Seats:** 250 **Cover:** 400 **Floodlights:** Yes **Founded:** 1874
Colours: All green **Change:** Blue/blue/white **Nickname:** Waders
Record Gate: 2,000 **Club Sponsors:** The Meat Shop. **Club Shop:** No.
Previous Leagues: Biggleswade & Dist. 02-20/ Bedford & Dist. 09-12/ Utd Co's (prev. Northants Lg) 20-39 51-55 63-80/ Spartan 46-51/ Eastern Co's 55-63.
Previous Name: Biggleswade & District. **Clubhouse:** Open all matchdays. Filled rolls available.
Programme: 56 pages, with admission (extra copies available 50p each).
Players progressing to Football League: Darran Hay (Cambridge United) 1994.
Clubhouse: Open all matchdays. Filled rolls available. Refreshment hut sells hotdogs, teas, coffees, snacks.
Captain 93-94: D Beddall **Top Scorer 93-94:** Darran Hay.
Hons: Sth Mids Lg 23-24 (Div 1 52-53, Lg Cup 92-93, Prem. Div Tphy 91-92), Beds Snr Cup 02-03 07-08 46-47 51-52 61-62 62-63 66-67 73-74, Beds Premier Cup 22-23 27-28, Nth Beds Charity Cup 07-08 09-10 22-27 33-34(joint) 49-50 52-53 54-55 57-58 62-63 64-65 67-68 68-69 73-74 91-92, Utd Co's Lg Cup 63-64 73-74, Hunts Premier Cup 92-93 93-94(joint), Hinchingbrooke Cup 03-04 92-93, Jess Piggott Trophy 87-88 89-90 91-92 92-93.

BRACHE SPARTA

Chairman: Mr Roy Standring **President:** Mr Doug Smith.
Secretary: Mr Maurice Raymond Franklin, 62 Katherine Drive, Dunstable LU5 4NU (0582 661177).
Manager: Mr Kevin Millett. **Physio:** C E Jones.
Ground: Foxdell Spts Ground, Dallow Rd, Luton LU1 1UP (0582 20751).
Directions: Left off A505 to Dunstable into Chaul Lane at r'bout. Proceed across new relief road - ground entrance adjacent to Foxdell Junior School.
Cover: 100 **Seats:** 25 **Capacity:** 400 **Floodlights:** Yes **Founded:** 1960
Colours: White/navy/white **Change Colours:** All royal **Nickname:** None.
Midweek home maches: Wednesday **Previous League:** Luton & Dist.
Previous Grounds: Crawley Green Road, Luton (public park)/ Hitchin Town FC (groundshare 93-94).
Programme: 30 pages, £1 **Club Sponsors:** A & E Engineering.
Clubhouse: Open daily noon-3 & 7.30-11pm. Light snacks, rolls, sandwiches, burgers, chips, tea, coffee etc available.
Top Scorer 93-94: Robbie O'Keefe **Club Record Scorer:** Pat Walsh
Hons: SML R-up 92-93 (Div 1 R-up 83-84 87-88, Lg Cup R-up 75-76 80-81 92-93, Prem Div Cup R-up 91-92, Res. Div 2 R-up 75-76, Res. Cup R-up 87-88), Luton & D. Lg 67-68 69-70 70-71 71-72, William Pease Trophy 66-67 67-68 70-71 71-72, Beds Intermediate Cup 71-72 (R-up 68-69 70-71), Beds Jnr Cup 82-83, Leighton Chal. Cup R-up 69-70.

BUCKINGHAM ATHLETIC

Chairman: Mr Ron Ackerman **President:** Mr Malcolm Macillop. **Manager:** Malcolm East.
Secretary: Peter Hinson, 12 Badgers Way, Buckingham MK18 1AY (0280 816212).
Ground: Stratford Fields, Stratford Rd, Buckingham (0280 816945).
Directions: From Milton Keynes take the A422 Stony Stratford-Buckingham road – ground on left just before town centre. From Aylesbury, turn right at 1st r-about, across 2nd r-bout, left at 3rd – ground at bottom of hill on left.
Capacity: 1,500 **Seats:** No **Cover:** 200 **Floodlights:** Yes **Founded:** 1933
Colours: All sky **Change Cols:** Red & white/white/red **Nickname:** Swans
Midweek home matchday: Wednesday **Previous Leagues:** North Bucks/ Hellenic.
Programme: 10 pages, 50p
Hons: Sth Mids Lg Div 1 85-86 90-91 (R-up 88-89, Div 1 Cup 90-91), Nth Bucks Lg 84-85 (Lg Cup 83-84, Lg Shield 60-61), Berks & Bucks Jnr Cup 65-66, Buckingham Charity Cup 69-70 71-72.

DUNSTABLE OLD BOYS

Secretary: Gerry Butler, 78 Park Street, Luton, Beds LU1 3ET (0582 23373)
Ground & Directions: As Dunstable FC *(see page 520).*
Cols: Red (navy & yellow hoops)/red/red **Change colours:** Blue/white/blue.
Prev. Name: Luton Old Boys (pre-1994) **Previous Ground:** Chaul End Lane, Luton.
Programme: Yes **Programme Editor:** Alan Garner (0582 492998).
Hons: South Midlands Lg R-up 93-94 (Premier Div Trophy 92-93, Div 1 Trophy 91-92, Div 2 R-up 91-92)

HARPENDEN TOWN

Chairman: Alan King **Manager:** Steve Woolfrey.
Secretary: Stephen Whiting, 169 Grove Rd, Harpenden, Herts AL5 1SY (0582 761600).
Ground: Rothamsted Park, Amenbury Lane, Harpenden (0582 715724). **Directions:** A1081 to Harpenden. Turn left/right at George Hotel into Leyton Road. Turn left into Amenbury Road, then left again (50yds) into 'Pay and Display' car park - the club entrance is signposted thru car park to opposite corner.
Capacity: 1,500 **Seats:** 25 **Cover:** 100 **Floodlights:** Yes **Founded:** 1891
Colours: Yellow/blue/blue **Change Colours:** Blue/yellow/yellow **Nickname:** The Town
Previous Grounds: None **Previous Name:** Harpenden FC 1891-1908.
Programme: With admission **Programme Editor:** Alan King (0582 455643).
Midweek home matchday: Tuesday **Previous Leagues:** Mid-Herts/ Herts County.
Hons: Sth Mids Lg 61-62 64-65 (Championship Shield 67-68, Lg Cup 70-71, Div 1 89-90, Prem Div Tphy 89-90, Reserve Div 89-90), Herts Co. Lg 11-12 49-50 51-52 53-54 (Aubrey Cup 20-21 28-29 50-51 51-52), Mid-Herts Lg 09-10 20-21, Pratt Cup 06-07 08-09 10-11, Herts Jnr Cup 01-02 09-10 11-12 20-21 25-26, Herts I'mediate Cup 52-53, Herts Charity Shield 07-08, Bingham Cox Cup 1896-97 1902-03 09-10 20-21.

HATFIELD TOWN

Chairman: Terry Edwards **Vice Chairman:** Peter Robinson **President:** Edward Rowley.
Secretary: Mrs Vivien Doctor, 1 Cloverland, Hatfield, Herts AL10 9ED (0707 269545).
Manager: Malcolm Doctor **Asst Manager:** Darryl Holmes.
Coach: Laird Budge **Physio:** Chris Berks.
Ground: Gosling Sports Park, Stanborough, Welwyn Garden City (0707 331056). **Directions:** A1(M) jct 4 to r'bout, 1st exit A6129 towards Stanborough Lakes, right at next r'bout, ground 800 yds on right.
Capacity: 3,000 **Seats:** 50 **Cover:** 1,000 **Floodlights:** Yes **Founded:** 1989
Colours: Blue/white/blue **Change Colours:** All red **Nickname:** Town
Previous Ground: Roe Hill Playing Fields, Briars Lane, Hatfield (pre-1992).
Midweek matchday: Wednesday **Prev. Lges:** Mids Herts/ Herts Co. Snr (pre'92)
Programme: 20 pages, £1 with entry **Editor:** Terry Edwards (0707 278319) **Club Shop:** No.
Record Gate: 350 v Welwyn Garden City, South Midlands League Premier Division 27/1/93.
Record win: 10-2 v Wingate & Finchley (A), FA Vase Preliminary Round 1/10/93.
Record loss: 1-6 v Totternhoe, South Midlands League Premier Division 92-93.
Clubhouse: Sat 4.30-11pm, Wed 7-11pm. Hot & cold snacks.
Top Scorer 93-94: Darren Collins **Captain & Player-of-the-Year 93-94:** Fintan Carrick.
Club record scorer: Eamonn Rogers **Club record appearances:** Gary Durbridge.
Hons: South Mids Lg Premier Div Cup R-up 93-94, Herts Co. Snr Lg 91-92 (Div 1 90-91, Div 2 89-90).

HODDESDON TOWN

President: Peter Haynes **Chairman:** Mr Elmer Elliott **Deputy Chairman:** Roger Merton.
Secretary: Mike Malone, 23 Chadwell, Ware, Herts SG12 9JY.
Manager: Ray Greenall **Asst Manager:** Jim Briggs **Coach:** John Walton.
Comm. Mgr: Elmer Elliott **Press Officer:** Roger Merton (0992 441410).
Ground: 'Lowfield', Park View, Hoddesdon, Herts (0992 463133).
Directions: A10, A1170 and follow signs to town centre until left-hand fork signposted Broxbourne, right at 1st mini r-about into Cock Lane and 1st right is Park View. Ground on 200yds left opposite Park Rd. Nearest BR station is Broxbourne.
Capacity: 3,000 **Seats:** 250 **Cover:** 250 **Floodlights:** Yes **Founded:** 1879
Midweek home matchday: Tuesday **Nickname:** Lilywhites/ Lowfielders **Club Shop:** No.
Colours: White/black/white **Change Colours:** All yellow.
Record Gate: 3,500 v West Ham, friendly 1975.
Previous Grounds: Mancers Field 1879-99/ Essex Rd Arena 1953-54.
Previous Leagues: East Herts 1896-1908 11-21/ Herts Co. 08-25/ Nth Middx District 10-22/ Spartan 25-75/ London Spartan 75-77/ Athenian 77-84.
Reserves' Lge: Essex/Herts Border Com. **Player progressing to Football League:** Mickey Droy (Chelsea).
Programme: 72-100 pages 60p **Programme Editor:** Mrs Jane Sinden (0767 631297).
Record win: 20-0 v Croxley, Herts Challenge Cup SF 1888-89.
Record defeat: 0-15 v Enfield (A), FA Cup Second Qualifying Round 1959-60.
Clubhouse: Bar and well-stocked tea bar with hot food open at every game.
Captain 93-94: Jeff Cross **Club record appearances:** Stuart Parker 553.
Top Scorer 93-94: Gary Cummings 21 **Club record scorer:** H W (Bert) Haynes approx 600, 1918-33.
Player of the Year 93-94: David Wilson **Players' Player of the Year 93-94:** Jeff Cross.
Hons: FA Vase 74-75 (1st winners), Sth Mids Lg Lg Cup 85-86 86-87 91-92 (Premier Div Tphy R-up 92-93), Spartan Lg 70-71 (R-up(3) 71-74, Div 1 35-36, Div 2 'B' 27-28, Lg Cup(2) 70-72), Herts Snr Cup(3) 1886-88 89-90, Herts Charity Shield(4) 47-48 70-72 78-79, Herts Snr Centenary Tphy 86-87, Sth Mids Floodlit Cup 89-90 (R-up 92-93), Waltham Hospital Cup 27-28, Perry Charity Cup(7), East Anglian Cup Group finalists 92-93.

LANGFORD

Chairman: Ian Chessum **Vice Chairman:** Mick Quinlan **President:** Ted Rutt.
Secretary: Frank Woodward, 2 North Lane, Gamlingay, Sandy, Beds SG19 3NT (0767 51022).
Manager: Pete Hayes **Asst Mgr:** Eric Cumberbatch **Coach:** Mick Kerry.
Press Officer: Secretary **Commercial Manager:** Vacant.
Ground: Forde Park, Langford Road, Henlow SG16 6AF (0426 816106). *Freehold purchased Feb 1992.*
Directions: Halfway between Langford and Henlow on A6001 Hitchin to Biggleswade road. Bus 177 on main Hitchin-Biggleswade route stops right outside ground.
Capacity: 4,000 **Seats:** 100 **Cover:** 250 **Floodlights:** Yes **Founded:** 1910.
Cols: Red & white **Change Colours:** Blue &white **Previous Lge:** Bedford & Dist. (pre-'51).
Record Gate: 450 v Q.P.R., 75th Anniversary and clubhouse opening, 22/8/85.
Previous Grounds: The Leys 10-37/ Bulls Meadow 37-53/ Langford Plyaing Field 53-84.
Programme: 38 pages, £1.75 with entry **Editor:** Keith Mayhew (0462 314767)
Club Shop: Scarves, lapel badges and programmes available. Contact secretary.
Sponsors: Fine Stamps Ltd, A.H. Printers **Midweek home matchday:** Tuesday **Nickname:** Reds.
Record transfer fee paid: Nil **Rec'd:** Undisclosed for Ian Phelan (Bedford T., Sept '91).
Clubhouse: Weekday evenings, matchdays 11am-11pm, Sun 12-3pm. Hot food on matchdays only. Function room with private bar available for hire.
Capt. 93-94: Glen Swain **Top Scorer 93-94:** Barry Dellar 22 **P.o.Y. 93-94:** David Drury.
Hons: S Mids Lg 88-89 (Lg Cup 73-74 75-76, Prem. Div Tphy 88-89, O'Brien Div 1 Tphy 84-85), N Beds Charity Cup 27-28 30-31 69-70 75-76 86-87 92-93 93-94, Bedford & Dist. Lg 30-31 31-32 32-33, Bedford I'mediate Cup 68-69, Hinchingbrooke Cup 72-73.

Langford FC. *Photo - Dave West.*

LETCHWORTH GARDEN CITY

Chairman: John McNeilliey **President:** Anthony Burrows **Manager:** Mick Clements.
Secretary: R Austin, 22 St Katherines Close, Ickleford, Herts SG5 3XS (0462 457811).
Ground: Baldock Road, Letchworth, Herts SG6 2GN (0462 684691).
Directions: Jct 9 (A6141) off A1M straight over large r-about, right at next r-about, ground on right. From Luton (A505) thru Hitchin, ground 3 miles after Hitchin. 2 miles from Letchworth (BR).
Capacity: 3,200 **Cover:** 400 **Seats:** 200 **Floodlights:** Yes **Founded:** 1906
Colours: Blue/white **Change Colours:** All red
Programme: 24 pages, 50p **Midweek matchday:** Tuesday **Nickname:** Bluebirds.
Previous Name: Garden City/ Letchworth Ath./ Letchworth Town
Previous Grounds: Letchworth Corner/ Garth Rd/ Cashio Lane.
Previous Leagues: Herts Co. 06-07/ Biggleswade 07-08/ Nth Herts 08-22/ S Mids 22-23 24-29/ Spartan 29-56/ Athenian 63-77/ Isthmian 77-90.
Players progressing to Football League: Imre Varadi, Keith Larner.
Hons: Herts Lg 11-12, Spartan Lg 29-30 35-36 51-52, Delphian Lg 57-58, Athenian Lg 74-75 (Mem. Shield 65-66 66-67), Herts Snr Cup 12-13 35-36 51-52, Herts Charity Shield 22-23 47-48 87-88 91-92, East Anglian Cup 76-77, Woolwich Cup 81-82, Hitchin Cup 81-82.

MILTON KEYNES

Chairman: John Wisson **President:** None.
Secretary: Mr Neasham Galloway, 22 Bascote, Tinkersbridge MK6 3DW (0908 608275).
Manager: Alan Blackman **Asst Manager:** Riki Barry **Physio:** John Butcher
Press Officer: Dave Popejoy **Commercial Manager:** Morrell Maison.
Ground: Manor Fields, Bletchley, Milton Keynes (0908 375256)
Directions: Old A5 to Fenny Stratford, about 500yds on left go over bridge opposite Belvedere Nursuries into Manor Fields - ground on right.
Capacity: 3,000 **Seats:** 160 **Cover:** 1,000 **Floodlights:** Yes **Founded:** 1993.
Colours: Yellow/blue/yellow **Change Colours:** Blue/white/white **Nickname:** None.
Programme: 16 pages, 40p **Programme Editor:** **Club Shop:** No.
Clubhouse: Two bars. Upstairs bar open every evening. Function hall available for hire. Snack available.
Previous Grounds: None **Previous Leagues:** None.
Previous Names: None. **Record Gate:** 250 v Bedford Town, S. Mids Lge 30/4/94.
Midweek home matchday: Tuesday **Reserves' Lge:** Minerva Sth Mids Reserve Div 1A.
Record win: 4-0 v Pitstone & Ivinghoe (H), Sth Mids Lge Challenge Trophy 12/10/93.
Record defeat: 1-6 v Harpenden Town (A), South Midlands League Premier Division 11/9/93.
Record scorer: Andy McCabe **Record appearances:** Paul Joyce.
Top Scorer 93-94: Andy McCabe **Captain 93-94:** Bernie McConnell **Hons:** None.

POTTERS BAR TOWN

Chairman: John Robinson **Vice Chairman:** Vacant **President:** Bert Wright
Secretary: Peter Waller, 26 Queen Annes Grove, Bush Hill Park, Enfield, Middx EN1 2JR (081 360 7859).
Manager: John Harding **Asst Manager:** Richard Hinde **Physio:** Vacant
Press Off.: Richard Brassett **Commercial Manager:** Frank Bentley.
Ground: Parkfield Centre, The Walk, Potters Bar, Herts EN6 1QN (0707 654833).
Directions: M25 jct 24, enter Potters Bar along Southgate Rd (A111), at 1st lights right into the High St (A1000), half mile left into The Walk, ground 200 yds on right (opp. Potters Bar Cricket Club). BR to to Potters Bar - The Walk is directly opposite station - ground half mile up hill on left.
Capacity: 2,000 **Seats:** 25 **Cover:** 100 **Floodlights:** Yes **Founded:** 1960
Cols: Red & royal stripes/royal/royal **Change colours:** White/red/red
Previous Leagues: Barnet & Dist. 60-65/ Nth London Comb. 65-68/ Herts Snr Co. 68-91.
Previous Names: Mount Grace Old Scholars/ Mount Grace (Potters Bar) until 1991.
Record Gate: 387 v Barnet, floodlight opener 8/12/93. Competitive: 200 v Cockfosters, Herts Snr Co. Lge.
Previous Grounds: None. **Nickname:** The Grace.
Programme: 16 pages, £1 **Programme Editor:** Robert Brassett (081 443 0442).
Club Shop: Scarves, ties and old programmes from Robert Brassett, 24b Cranborne Parade, Milton Lane, Potters Bar EN6 3BA (081 443 0442).
Sponsors: Welwyn Design Contracts/ Black Cat Video/ Cask & Stillage/ Fed. of Middx Spts/ Pubali Tandoori Restaurant.
Midweek matchday: Tues or Wed. **Best FA Vase season:** Third Round, 90-91.
Record win: 19-0 v Arkley, North London Combination 27/2/65.
Record defeat: 1-9 v Rolls Royce Engines, Herts County Aubrey Cup 10/1/70.
Players progressing to Football League: Keith Bertschin (Birmingham, Ipswich, Stoke, Barnet etc).
Clubhouse: Sat 12.30-11pm, Sun noon-3pm, Tues & Thurs 7.30-11pm, midweek matchnights 6-11pm.
Club record scorer: Micky Gray 269 **Club record appearances:** Mick Holson 708 (60-89).
Captain 93-94: Steve Newby **Top Scorer 93-94:** Mark Trossell **P.o.Y. 93-94:** Neil Garrett
Hons: Herts Co. Lg 90-91 (Div 1 73-74 81-82, Aubrey Cup 90-91 (R-up 87-88, Div 3(res) 73-74, Reserve Div 2 88-89, Reserve Div 1 R-up 89-90, Reserve Cup R-up 75-76), Herts I'mediate Cup 73-74, Barnet & Dist. Lg R-up 64-65 (Div 1 61-62, Div 2 R-up(res) 62-63, Div 3('A') 62-63), Barnet Jnr Cup 61-62, Nth L'don Comb. 67-68 (Div 1(res) 67-68, Div 2 R-up 65-66), Barnet Charity Cup 63-64 (R-up 64-65 68-69 70-71(res)), Potters Bar Charity Cup 76-77, Herts Snr Centenary Tphy SF 91-92, Herts Charity Shield SF 74-75 75-76, Sth Mids Lg Res Div 2 91-92, Mid-Herts Lg Div 1 R-up('A') 92-93 (Div 2('A') 87-88, Div 2 Cup('A') 84-85 87-88 (R-up 83-84 86-87), Div 4 R-up('B') 85-86, Reserve Shield('B') R-up 83-84), Mid-Herts Jnr Charity Shield('B') 76-77, Herts Co. Yth u-18 Cup 93-94.

ROYSTON TOWN

Chairman: Tony Moulding **Vice-Chairman:** Bernard Brown **President:** Bill Cosgrove
Secretary/Press Officer: Trevor Glasscock, 14 Goodwood Rd, Royston, Herts SG8 9TF (0763 244580).
Manager: Tony Galvin **Asst Mgr:** Kevin Rowark **Coach:** Kevin Rowark
Physio: Brian O'Flanaghan **Commercial Manager:** John Penny.
Ground: Garden Walk, Royston, Herts SG8 7HP (0763 241204).
Directions: From Baldock, A505 to Royston bypass, right at 2nd island onto A10 towards London, 2nd left is Garden Walk; ground 100 yds on left. From A11, exit 10 turning left onto A505, left at 1st island, 2nd left is Garden Walk. Ten mins walk from Royston (BR).
Capacity: 4,000 **Seats:** 300 **Cover:** 300 **Floodlights:** Yes **Founded:** 1875
Colours: White/black/black **Change colours:** Red/white/white **Metal Badges:** Yes
Shop: Badges, old progs, clubs scarves available from club officials **Nickname:** Crows.
Programme: 16 pages, 30p **Editor:** Bernard Brown (0763 243969).
Midweek Matchday: Wednesday **Sponsors:** ABA Consultants.
Previous Leagues: Buntingford & Dist. 18-28/ Cambs 28-50/ Herts Co. 50-59 62-77/ Sth Mids 59-62 77-84/ Isthmian 84-94.
Previous Names: None **Previous Grounds:** Newmarket Rd, Baldock Rd, Mackeral Hall.
Record Gate: 876 v Aldershot, 13/2/93 **Reserve Team's League:** Essex & Herts Border Comb.
Record win: 13-2 v Addult, 78-70 **Record loss:** 0-9 v Bromley & v Stevenage Borough.
Best FA Cup year: Second Qualifying Round 59-60 (lost 0-9 at Barnet), 89-90 (lost 0-3 at Bromley).
Clubhouse: Mon-Thurs 7-11pm, Fri 11am-3 & 7-11pm, Sat 11am-3 & 4-11pm, Sun noon-3pm. Large hall. Darts, pool, discos and live bands. **Steward:** Mr & Mrs P Nesbitt.
Players progressing to Football League: John Smith (Spurs).
Club Record Scorer: Trevor Glasscock 289 (1968-82) **Club Record Appearances:** Fred Bradley 713.
93-94 Capt.: John Moulding **93-94 P.o.Y.:** Simon Dobson **93-94 Top scorer:** Paddy Butcher.
Local Radio: Radio Cambridgeshire, Radio Bedfordshire, Chiltern Radio.
Local Press: Royston Crow (0763 245142), Cambridge Evening News (0223 358877).
Hons: Herts Co. Lg 76-77 (Div 1 69-70 76-77), Sth Mids Lg R-up 79-80 (Div 1 78-79, Chall. Cup R-up 78-79, Res Div 1 79-80 (Div 2 78-79), Res Section Tphy R-up 82-83), Herts Charity Shield 81-82 89-90 (R-up 78-79 88-89), Creake Shield 20-21, Cambs Lg Div 2 29-30, Herts Intermediate Cup 88-89 (R-up 89-90), Nth Herts Lg 4 Cup 78-79 79-80 (Div R-up 82-83, Div 3 R-up 81-82, Div 4 R-up 79-80) Televised Spts Lg 88-89 (F'lit Cup 89-90), Chiltern Yth Lg 89-90 (Lg Cup R-up 86-87 88-89 90-91, Southern Comb. Res. F'lit Cup 91-92, Greg Cup R-up 90-91.

SHILLINGTON

Chairman: Stan Burgdine **President:** Brian Bowles.
Secretary: Aubrey J Cole, 32 Greenfields, Shillington, Hitchin, Herts SG5 3NX (0462 711322).
Manager: Paul Stephens **Physio:** Noel Lewis **Press Officer:** Paul Stephens.
Ground: Playing Fields, Greenfields, Shillington, Hitchin SG5 3NX (0462 711757).
Directions: From Luton: A6 to Barton-le-Clay (by-pass), left at r'bout to Shillington via Higham Gobion. From Hitchin or Bedford turn off at 'Bird in Hand', Henlow Camp signposted Shillington. Five miles from Hitchin (BR).
Capacity: 600 **Seats:** 50 **Cover:** 100 **Floodlights:** Yes **Formed:** 1946.
Colours: White/red/red **Change Colours:** All yellow.
Midweek matchdays: Tuesday **Record Gate:** 600 v Baldock Town.
Previous Lge: Luton & Dist. 1946-54 **Previous Ground:** Parsonage Lane.
Programme: £1 with admission. **Programme Editor:** Paul Stephens (0582 561418).
Clubhouse: Open every evening and weekend lunctimes. Rolls available on matchdays.
Hons: Sth Mids Lg 87-88 (R-up 64-65 86-87, Lg Cup 82-83 (R-up 64-65 65-66 84-85 91-92), Div 1 80-81 (R-up 75-76), Prem Div Tphy 87-88, Reserve Div 2 65-66, Reserve Shield/Tphy 68-69 79-80, Reserve Div R-up 80-81, Reserve Div 1 R-up 84-85 86-87 88-89), Beds Snr Cup R-up 63-64 64-65 (Jnr Cup 76-77), Barton Invitation Cup R-up 68-69 71-72, Houghton Regis Chall. Cup 85-86, Napier Electric Sportsmanship award 78-79.

WELWYN GARDEN CITY

Chairman: John Newman **Manager:** Pat Maslen
Secretary: Richard Dunning, 38 Cowper Road, Welwyn Garden City, Herts AL7 3LS (0707 334536).
Press Officer: Keith Browne. **Physiotherapist:** Arthur Wood/ Derek Carlisle.
Ground: Herns Lane, Welwyn Garden City (0707 328470).
Directions: From A1 follow signs for industrial area. Take one-way system opposite Avdel Ltd (signed Hertford B195), take 2nd exit off one-way system. Ground 400 yards on left. One and a half miles from Welwyn GC (BR).
Capacity: 1,500 **Seats:** 40 **Cover:** 120 **Floodlights:** Yes **Founded:** 1921
Cols: Maroon & blue/white/maroon **Change Colours:** Yellow/blue/yellow
Midweek Matches: Tuesday **Club Shop:** Yes **Metal Badges:** Yes **Nickname:** Citizens.
Programme: 24 pages, 50p **Programme Editor:** Keith Browne (0707 251854).
Clubhouse: Open every night and weekend lunchtimes. Members Bar, function Hall. Steward: Ron Baird.
Record Gate: 600 v Welwyn Garden United.
Previous Ground: Springfields **Previous Lges:** Spartan/ Metropolitan/ Gtr London
Best FA Vase year: 1st Rd 86-87. **Best FA Cup year:** Prel. Rd replay 89-90.
Local Newspapers: Welwyn & Hatfield Times, Welwyn & Hatfield Herald & Post.
Hons: Herts Snr Centenary Tphy 84-85 (R-up 88-89), Herts Charity Shield 27-28 86-87 87-88 (R-up 48-49), Sth Mids Lg 73-74 (R-up 85-86, Div 1 69-70 81-82, Lg Cup R-up 74-75 81-82 88-89, Reserve Cup 85-86).

WINGATE & FINCHLEY

Chairman: Peter Rebak **Vice Chairman:** L Black **President:** H Whidden.
Secretary: Malcolm Graves, 28 Wise Lane, Mill Hill, London NW7 2RE (081 959 3825).
Manager: Martin Burt **Asst Manager:** Jeff Bookman **Coach:** Jeff Bookman.
Physio: Amos Shanaan **Comm. Manager:** Steven Jacobs **Press Off.:** Simon Martindale.
Ground: Bill Masters Stadium, Summers Lane, Finchley, London N12 (081 446 0906)
Directions: North Circular (A406) to jct with High Road Finchley (A1000), go north and Summers Lane is 200 yards on right - parking for 80 cars. Tube to East Finchley Station (Northern Line) and then 263 bus to Summers Lane. Buses 263 and and 17.
Capacity: 8,500 **Seats:** 500 **Cover:** 500 **Floodlights:** Yes **Founded:** 1991
Colours: Blue/white/blue **Change Colours:** All red **Nickname:** Blues
Programme: 24 pages, 50p **Editor:** Marc Morris (081 346 6215) **Club Shop:** No.
Club Sponsors: Levy Gee
Record Gate: 9,555 - Finchley v Bishop Auckland, F.A. Amateur Cup QF 49-50.
Midweek home matchday: Tuesday **Reserve's Lge:** Essex & Herts Border Comb. (West)
Record win: 9-0, Wingate v Sarratt, Herts County League Division One, 20/4/85.
Record defeat: 0-5, Wingate v Tudor Corinthians, Herts County League Division One, 13/4/85.
Clubhouse: Open during matches. Also tea-bar selling most refreshments.
Club record scorer: Marc Morris 578 **Club record appearances:** Marc Morris 587 (1975-93).
Previous Names: Wingate (founded 1946), Finchley (founded late 1800s) merged in 1991.
Previous Grounds: Finchley FC: Long Lane 1874-84/ Green Man 84-94/ Woodhouse Lane 94-99/ Swan & Pyramids 99-1901/ Fallow Court 01-21/ Station Meadow 21-29. Wingate: Wingate Stadium 46-75/ Brickfield Lane, Arkley 75-91.
Prev. Lges: Finchley: London 02-12 14-1523-25 30-39/ Athenian 12-14 29-30 45-73/ Isth'n 73-91. Wingate: Middx 46-52/ London 52-62/ Delphian 62-63/ Athenian 63-75/ Barnet Yth, Hendon & Dist. Sunday 75-84/ Herts 84-89.
Hons: Finchley: London Snr Cup, London Charity Cup, FA Amtr Cup SF, Athenian Lg 53-54 (R-up 63-64 65-66), London Lg 36-37 (R-up 35-36, Div 2 06-07(jt with Enfield), Lg Cup 34-35, Park Royal Cup 37-38). Wingate: Middx Lg(2)(R-up(1), Lg Cup), London Lg R-up(2)(Lg Cup(1)), Middx Snr Cup SF, FA Vase QF 74-75, Athenian Lg Div 2 69-70, Herts Co. Lg Div 1 84-85 (Aubrey Cup 85-86), Herts I'mediate Cup 84-85, Herts Snr Tphy 86-87, Sth Mids Lg Div 1 R-up 89-90 (Lg Cup SF 89-90), Barnet Yth Lg 75-76, Pete Morrison Cup 82-83 83-84 (R-up 79-80 84-85), Hendon & Dist. Int. Div 79-80.

Gary Cummins, Hoddesdon Town's second most prolific goalscorer of all time, receives a memento from club chairman Elmer Elliott to mark his 250th goal for the club. Gary has also played 423 games in the Lilywhites' colours. Photo - Colin Sinden.

SENIOR DIVISION CLUBS 1994-95

AMPTHILL TOWN

Chairman: Richard Brown **President:** Gary Williams.
Secretary: Eric Turner, 34 Dunstable Street, Ampthill, Beds MK45 2JT (0525 403128).
Manager: Neil Rodney. **Ground:** Woburn Road, Ampthill (0525 404440)
Directions: From Ampthill Town Centre follow signs to Woburn then 1st right into Ampthill Park.
Capacity: 1,500 **Seats:** 30 **Cover:** 400 **Floodlights:** No **Founded:** 1888.
Colours: Yellow/red/red **Change Colours:** Blue/black/black **Nickname:** Town
Previous Grounds: None **Previous Lges:** S Mids 51-65/ Utd Co's 65-91.
Midweek home matchday: Tuesday **Programme:** 16 pages, 50p with admission.
Hons: Sth Mids Lg 59-60 (C'ship Shield 58-59 59-60), North Beds Charity Cup 84-85.

BEDFORD UNITED

Chairman: John Cleverley **Vice Chairman:** Jim McMullen **President:** D Rostron
Secretary: Mick Jozwiak, 6 Tunstall Walk, Goldington, Bedford MK41 0AF (0234 342435).
Manager: Bob Bell **Assistant Manager:** Trevor Barnett
Coach: Colin Hoyland **Press Officer:** Jim McMullem.
Ground: Hillgrounds, Kempston.
Directions: M1 jct 13, A421 to Bedford, follow signs to Kempston at 1st r'bout, 2nd r'bout keep left, 3rd r'bout turn right, Hillgrounds is 1st left, ground half mile on left.
Capacity: 1,000 **Seats:** 25 **Cover:** 100 **Floodlights:** No **Founded:** 1957
Colours: White/blue/blue **Change cols:** Red & white/red/red **Nickname:** United
Midweek home matches: Tuesday **Clubhouse:** Open matchdays. Hot/cold snacks/drinks available.
Programme: 24 pages, £1 **Programme Editor:** Geoff Seagrave (0234 856117).
Club Sponsors: Grant Thornton **Reserve Team's League:** South Midlands Lge Reserve section.
Prev. Lge: Bedford & Dist. (pre'89) **Previous Name:** Printers Diemer-Reynolds (pre'72)
Previous Ground: Fairhill, Clapham Rd (pre'93).
Record Gate: (at Fairhill) 852 v Bedford Town, South Midlands League Division One 26/12/92.
Record scorer: Brian Fibbs **Record appearances:** Simon Fordham.
Top Scorer 93-94: Paul Conway **Captain & Player of the Year:** Mark Jozwiak.
Hons: Bedford & Dist Lg Premier Division & Division One, County Junior Cup, Biggleswade KO Cup, Butchers Cup(2), Britania Cup, Bedford Charity Cup.

DELCO

Chairman: Paul Shepherd **President:** N Lee **Manager:** S Howarth.
Secretary: Terry E Owen, 29 Elm Park Close, Houghton Regis, Dunstable, Beds LU5 5PN (0582 863273).
Ground: Delco Chassis Sports Ground (0582 695668)
Directions: On main A5 Trunk Rd to the north of Dunstable. Ground entrance is approximately 100yds south of traffic lights at Chalk Cutting.
Capacity: 2,000 **Seats:** 30 **Cover:** 80 **Floodlights:** No **Founded:** 1934.
Colours: Red/white/red **Change Colours:** Blue/white/blue. **Nickname:** None
Programme: 12 pages, 50p **Midweek home matchday:** Tuesday
Record Gate: 432 v Bedford Town. **Previous Ground:** AC Delco Spts Ground.
Previous League: Luton & South Beds Dist./ Hellenic 69-73.
Previous Names: AC Sphinx 46-52/ AC Delco 52-85/ Delco Products 85-93.
Hons: South Midlands Lg Div 1 R-up 93-94, William Pease Tphy R-up, SOS Allen Cup, Luton News Cup(3), Luton Lg Invitation Cup(2), Lorman Cup(4).

LEVERSTOCK GREEN

President: L Bolino **Chairman:** R Saville
Secretary: S D Robinson, 11 Connaught Close, Hemel Hempstead, Herts HP2 7AB (0442 65734)
Manager: M Vipond **Asst Manager:** D Edwards **Press Officer:** R Barter
Ground: Pancake Lane, Leverstock Green, Hemel Hempstead (0442 246280).
Directions: From M1 leave at A4147 to 2nd r-about. 1st exit to Leverstock Green, Pancake Lane is on left 300 yrds past the 'Leather Bottle' pub.
Seats: 25 **Cover:** 100 **Floodlights:** No **Founded:** 1907 **Nickname:** The Green.
Previous Leagues: West Herts (pre-1950)/Herts County 50-91.
Colours: Green & white/black/green **Change Colours:** Green & black/white/black
Programme: 24 pages, 50p **Clubhouse:** Yes.
Top scorer 93-94: Dean Pearce **P.o.Y. 93-94:** David Hindle/ Tim Healey (joint winners).
Players progressing to Football League: Dean Austin (Tottenham Hotspur).
Hons: South Midlands Lg Snr Div Cup R-up 93-94, Herts Centenary Tphy R-up 91-92, Herts Charity Shield R-up 91-92, Frank Major Tphy 1991.

LONDON COLNEY

Chairman: K Hull **Vice Chairman:** M Chick **President:** I Holt.
Secretary: W G Gash, 8 Whitehorse Lane, London Colney, Herts AL2 1JX (0727 823192).
Manager: S Seabrook/ H Wright **Physio:** T Brown **Press Officer:** S Buchanan.
Ground: Gotslandswick, London Colney (0727 22132).
Directions: From London Colney r'bout (junction of A414/A1081) take A414 towards Watford, after layby (300yds) turn left (hidden turning marked 'Sports Ground') and follow around to gates. Three miles from St Albans (BR). Buses 84 & 358.
Capacity: 1,000 **Cover:** 100 **Seats:** 30 **Floodlights:** No **Founded:** 1907.
Colours: All royal **Change Colours:** Yellow/black/yellow **Nickname:** Blueboys
Programme: £1 with entry **Previous Lges:** Mid Herts 1907-54/ Herts Co. 07-92.
Club Sponsors: Heath Construction **Previous Ground:** Whitehorse Lane 07-75.
Clubhouse: Open after games. Hot food available.
Hons: Sth Mids Lg Snr Div R-up 93-94 (Challenge Trophy 93-94, Div 1 R-up 92-93, Res. Div 1 92-93), Herts Co. Lg 56-57 59-60 86-87 88-89 (R-up 57-58 58-59, Aubrey Cup 21-22 22-23 56-57 58-59 81-82, Res. Div 1 87-88 88-89 89-90 91-92, Res. Cup 62-63 89-90 91-92 (R-up 70-71)), Herts Centenary Tphy 89-90 (R-up 90-91), Herts I'mediate Cup 58-59 74-75 82-83, Herts Charity Shield 61-62 (R-up 59-60), Herts Jnr Cup 54-55, Mid Herts Lg 91-92(res) (Div 1 22-23 53-54 54-55 89-90(res), Div 2 19-20 48-49, Div 3 81-82(res), Bingham Cox Cup 20-21 53-54 89-90(res) (R-up 91-92(res))), Mid Herts Benevolent Cup 27-28 29-30 48-49 (Benevolent Shield 51-52 52-53 53-54 54-55, Charity Cup 48-49), St Albans Playing Fields Cup 62-63 73-74 75-76 80-81, Frank Major Tphy 74-75 75-76.

NEW BRADWELL St PETER

Chairman: Mr J E Haynes **Vice-Chairman:** Mr K Felce **President:** Mr J P Booden.
Secretary: Mr L Smith, 47 Rowle Close, Stantonbury, Milton Keynes MK14 6BJ (0908 319522).
Manager: Mr J Gunn **Press Officer:** Mr P Smith.
Ground: Recreation Ground, Bradwell Road, New Bradwell, Milton Keynes MK13 7AT (0908 313835)
Directions: From M1 Jnt 14 go towards Newport Pagnell, left at 1st r-about into H3 (A422 Monks Way). Over 5 r-abouts, right at 6th island into V6 (Grafton St.), go right the way round (back on yourself) 1st island, 1st left, left at T-Junct, ground half mile on left (before bridge).
Nickname: Peters **Seats:** 30 **Cover:** 100 **Floodlights:** No **Founded:** 1902
Colours: Maroon & blue stripes/maroon/maroon
Change: Green & yellow halves/green/green.
Previous Name: Stantonbury St James (predecessors were New Bradwell St James)/ Stantonbury St Peters (until merger with New Bradwell Corinthians in 1946).
Previous Grounds: Red Bridge (pre-1947)/ Mutual Meadow, Newport Rd.
Previous League: North Bucks **Club Sponsors:** The Manulife Group.
Programme: 32 pages, £1 with entry **Editor:** Mr K Felce (0908 312210).
Midweek home matchday: Wednesday
Clubhouse: Members only (a member can sign in 2 guests). Open every evening and weekend lunchtimes. No food available.
Captain 93-94: Gary Kerrigan **Top Scorer 93-94:** Patrick Booden **P.O.Y. 93-94:** Adrian Keating.
Hons: Sth Mids Lg Div 1 76-77 83-84 (Reserve Div 2 R-up 76-77), Nth Bucks Lg 12-13 13-14 39-40 (R-up 48-49, Div 3 69-70, Div 3 Shield 69-70), Leighton Challenge Cup(5), Stantonbury Cup 84-85, Milton Keynes Referees Challenge Cup 84-85, Berks & Bucks Minor Cup 51-52. *Predecessors (New Bradwell St James): Nth Bucks Lg(5) 1896-1901, Berks & Bucks Jnr Cup 00-01, Berks & Bucks Snr Cup R-up 01-02.*

PITSTONE & IVINGHOE

Chairman: Harry Bowden **President:** R Adlem
Secretary: David Hawkins, 26 Glebe Close, Pitstone, Leighton Buzzard, Beds LU7 9AZ (0296 661456).
Manager: Mark Roberts **Assistant Manager:** Martin Butcher.
Physio: Ken McParland **Press Officer:** R Adlemr.
Ground: Pitstone Recreation Ground, Vicarage Road, Pitstone, Bucks (0296 661271)
Directions: Tring Rd from Dunstable, turn right for Ivinghoe, and continue through to Pitstone r-about; ground left then right. From Aylesbury - left at 'Rising Sun' in Aston Clinton, keep on that road to Pitstone r'bout; ground right then right. Bus 61 from Luton or Aylesbury. Nearest BR stations are Tring or Cheddington.
Cover: 100 **Seats:** 25 **Capacity:** 500 **Floodlights:** No **Founded:** 1958
Colours: Red & black stripes/black/black **Change Colours:** Blue/blue/white.
Midweek home matches: Tuesday **Previous Leagues:** Aylesbury/ West Herts/ Dunstable Alliance.
Previous Grounds: None **Previous Name:** Ivinghoe & Pitstone.
Programme: 16 pages £1 with admission **Programme Editor:** R Adlem (0296 668663).
Record gate: 350 v Leighton Town, South Midlands League Premier Division 1/1/93.
Clubhouse: Open after every match 3.30pm until late. Rolls, crisps nuts etc available.
Top Scorer 93-94: Philip Wilson 7.
Hons: Sth Mids Lg 89-90 (Div 1 87-88, Lg Cup 88-89, Div 1 Cup 87-88, Reserve Div 2 R-up 85-86), Dunstable Alliance 73-74 75-76 76-77, Dunstable Premier Cup 74-75 76-77, Reading Jnr Cup 76-77 (R-up 75-76), Aspley Snr Cup 68-69, Aspley Jnr Cup 66-67, West Herts Chal. Cup 58-59, Marworth Cup 67-68, Roseberry Cup 67-68, Berks & Bucks Jnr Cup R-up 79-80(reserves).

RISBOROUGH RANGERS

Chairman: C Makepeace
Secretary: Derrick J Wallace, 42 Ash Rd, Princes Risborough, Bucks HP27 0BQ (0844 345179)
Manager: Dave Dunsworth **Asst Manager:** Mark Avery **Physio:** Ken Sheppard
Ground: Windsor's, Horsendon Lane, Princes Risborough (08444 274176)
Directions: Rear of Princes Risborough BR Station (Chiltern Line). A4010 from Aylesbury thru Princes Risborough, fork right onto A4009, left by thatched cottage, over railway bridge, immediate right ground 150 yds on right.
Capacity: 2,000 **Seats:** 25 **Cover:** 100 **Floodlights:** No **Founded:** 1971
Colours: Red & white **Change Colours:** Blue & white
Programme: 20+ pages, £1 with entry **Editor:** D Freeman (0844 274852) **Club Shop:** No.
Midweek home matchday: Tuesday. **Clubhouse:** Yes. Snacks available matchdays.
Previous League: Wycombe & Dist. **Record Gate:** 1,200 v Showbiz XI.
Club Sponsors: Systems 3R **Reserve Team's League:** South Midlands Reserve Div.
P.O.Y. 93-94: Andy Peel **Captain 93-94/Club record appearances:** Mark Avery.
Top Scorer 93-94: Mark Leslie **Club record scorer:** Craig Smith.
Hons: Berks & Bucks Jnr Cup 85-86, Wycombe & District Lg Div 2 85-86 (Div 3 84-85).

THE 61 F.C. (LUTON)

Chairman: S Ledwidge **Vice Chairman:** M Haynes **President:** G B Mapp.
Secretary/Manager: R Everitt, 44 Somersby Close, Luton LU1 3XB (0582 485095).
Asst Manager: P Miller **Physio:** D Everitt **Comercial Mgr:** M Haynes
Ground: Kingsway, Beverley Road, Luton, Beds. (0582 582965)
Directions: M1 jct 11, A505 to Luton centre, right at 1st island, 1st left, Beverley Rd is 3rd left, entrance in Beverley Rd, exactly 1 mile junction 11. All Luton to Dunstable buses pass ground - alight at Beech Hill Bowling Club. One mile from both Leagrave and Luton BR stations.
Capacity: 2,500 **Cover:** 150 **Seats:** 100 **Floodlights:** No **Formed:** 1961
Colours: Sky/royal/royal **Change:** Red/black/red **Nickname:** Two Blues
Previous Grounds: None **Previous Leagues:** Luton & District 61-72/ Hellenic 72-73
Club Sponsors: CB Security **Record Gate:** 265 v Selby, SML Tphy final 1st leg, 16/4/88.
Programme: 8 pages **Programme Editor:** Secretary **Club Shop:** No.
Midweek home matchday: Wednesday **Player progressing to Football Lge:** Peter Gleasure (Millwall) 1976
Clubhouse: Open every evening and weekend lunchtimes. Hot and cold snacks.
Club record scorer: Sandor Simon **Club record appearances:** Roger Smith 620.
Captain 93-94: Pat Miller **Top Scorer 93-94:** Nick Abraham 17.
P.O.Y. 93-94: Sean Ledwidge **Hons:** Beds Snr Cup 83-84.

STONY STRATFORD TOWN

Chairman: R Gustafson **Manager:** Perry Mercer
Secretary: Maurice J Barber, 26 Boundary Cres., Stony Stratford, Milton Keynes MK11 1DF (0908 567930).
Ground: Sports Ground, Ostlers Lane, Stony Stratford (0908 562267)
Directions: From Dunstable old A5, Watling Street, on approaching Bletchley continue on A5 loop road (Hinkley) to end of dual c'way to A422/A508 r'bout. First exit, thru lights, 2nd right into Ostlers Lane. From M1 jct 13 pick up A421 and join A5 (Hinkley) and proceed as above.
Capacity: 500+ **Seats:** None **Cover:** No **Floodlights:** No **Reformed:** 1953
Previous Leagues: North Bucks & Dist./ Northampton Combination.
Colours: Sky/navy/navy **Change Colours:** Red/black/red
Programme: 10 pages, £1 with entry **Midweek matchday:** Tuesday.
Players progressing to Football Lge: George Henson (Northampton (in 1929)), Wolves, Swansea, Bradford PA & Sheffield Utd).
Honours: Sth Mids Lg R-up 70-71 71-72 (Div 1 93-94, Div 1 Cup 93-94).

Dean Mercer heads home for Stony Stratford Town in the Division One Cup final against Houghton Town. The goal made it 3-3, and the divisional champions went on to complete a League and Cup 'double' by winning 5-3.
Photo - Neil Whittington.

TODDINGTON ROVERS

Chairman: Hugh Geddes **Vice Chairman:** Brian Horne **President:** Peter Turner.
Secretary: Tony H Simmonds, 5 Manor Road, Toddington, Nr Dunstable, Beds LU5 6AH (0525 872786).
Manager: Steve Loasby **Asst Manager:** Alan Loeasby **Coach:** Roger King.
Physio: John Cullen **Press Officer:** Colin Bryson.
Ground: Recreation Ground, Luton Road, Toddington, Nr Dunstable, Beds.
Directions: 1 mile to Toddington village centre from M1, take on-way street signposted Luton, ground 150yds on left. From A5 to Toddington via Knebworth, turn right in village centre, left after 200yds into Luton Road.
Seats: No **Cover:** 100 **Nickname:** Rovers **Floodlights:** No **Founded:** 1894
Colours: Black & white stripes **Change Colours:** Red & black stripes/black/black
Previous Name: Toddington Star. **Prev Grnds:** Alma Farm, Dropshort 47 64. **Club Shop:** No.
Midweek home matchday: Tuesday **Prev. Lg:** Luton & S Beds & D. 1894-1988. **Nickname:** Rovers
Programme: 36 pages, 75p (includes admission & raffle) **Editor:** Secretary
Sponsors: O'Neill Plant Hire **Record Gate:** 160 v Silsoe, Luton & D. Lg 26/1/23.
Record win: 11-0 v Luton St Marys 1981 **Record defeat:** 0-9 v Bidwell 1957
Clubhouse: Tea room available at ground. Club use Toddington Social & Services Club 600 yds available - cold food always available after matches.
Club record scorer: David Ashby **Club record appearances:** George Stewart, 1050.
Hons: South Midlands Lg Snr Div 93-94 (Snr Div Cup 93-94), Luton & District South Beds Lge R-up 57-58 58-59 63-64 (Div 1 29-30 30-31 31-32, Div 2 28-29 47-48, Div 3 26-27 47-48, Div 4 25-26), Luton News Cup R-up 80-81, Leighton Chall. Cup R-up 58-59, Beds Jnr Cup 30-31, Beds Intermediate Cup R-up 57-58 58-59 62-63. SML Awards - Special Award 89-90, Napier English Electric Sportsmanship Tphy 91-92, Best Prog. & Secretary of the Year 92-93.

TOTTERNHOE

Chairman: Jim Basterfield **Vice Chairman:** John Power **President:** Alf Joyce.
Secretary: Jim Basterfield, 41 Park Avenue, Totternhoe, Dunstable, Beds LU6 1QF (0582 667941)
Manager: Alex Butler **Assistant Manager:** Paul Simmonds
Coach: Graham Dibsdall **Physio:** Roy Mackerness.
Ground: Totternhoe Recreation Ground, Dunstable (0582 606738).
Directions: Turn off the main Dunstable to Tring Road B489. Ground on right as you enter the Totternhoe. Five miles from Leighton Buzzard (BR), 7 miles from Luton. Bus 61 Luton-Aylesbury.
Capacity: 1,000 **Seats:** 30 **Cover:** 200 **Floodlights:** No **Founded:** 1906
Colours: All red **Change Colours:** Blue & white hoops/blue/blue
Record Gate: 300 v Luton Town, clubhouse opening 13/10/82
Previous Grounds: None **Previous League:** Luton & Dist. (pre-1958).
Programme: 16 pages, 80p with entry **Club Sponsors:** Building Conservations **Club Shop:** No.
Midweek home matchday: Tuesday **Club Nickname:** Totts.
Record win: 11-0 v Commill Cars, 1961 **Record defeat:** 0-11 v Sandy Albion, 1963.
Clubhouse: Open evenings 8pm, Saturday after games, Sunday lunchtime. Sweets, confectionary, tea, coffee, soups at matches.
Club record scorer: John Waites, 48 **Club record appearances:** John Binding, 631.
Hons: Sth Mids Lg Div 1 61-62 (R-up 68-69 85-86), Beds Snr Cup R-up 69-70 86-87 91-92, Beds I'mediate Cup 77-78 (R-up 81-82), Luton & Dist. Lg 57-58.

TRING ATHLETIC

Chairman: Paul Nichols **President:** Paul Nichols
Secretary: Ralph Griffiths, 42 Bedgrove, Aylesbury, Bucks HP21 7BD (0296 26425).
Manager: Mick Eldridge **Asst Manager:** Ray Brimson **Coach:** Richard Vincent.
Physio: Jean Adams.
Ground: Miswell Lane, Tring, Herts.
Directions: Through Tring on main road towards Aylesbury, right just after Anchor PH into Miswell Lane, pitch approximately 500yds on right opposite Beaconsfield Road. Tring railway station is several miles outside town, but ground can be reached by bus or taxi.
Seats: 25+ **Cover:** 100+ **Floodlights:** No **Founded:** 1958 **Nickname:** Athletic
Colours: Red & black **Change colours:** green. **Sponsors:** Heygates
Prev. Name: Tring Athletic & Youth. **Prev. Grnd:** Pendley Spts Centre (Tring Town FC) 89-92.
Programme: 36 pages, 50p **Programme Editor:** Secretary **Club Shop:** No.
Midweek matchday: Wednesday **Previous League:** West Herts 58-88.
Rec. win: 10-2 v Ickleford (A) 10/4/93 **Record defeat:** 2-7 v Buckingham Ath. (H) 1/10/82.
Players progressing to Football League: Peter Gibbs (Watford 'keeper in late seventies).
Clubhouse: Bar, open matchdays, training nights & Sunday lunchtimes. Crisps & filled rolls available.
Captain 93-94: Grant Mosley **Top Scorer 93-94:** Danny Glass **P.o.Y. 93-94:** Danny Glass/ 'T' Rice
Club record scorer: Ian Butler **Club record appearances:** Alan Sheppard.
Hons: West Herts Lg R-up 72-73 (Lg Cup 65-66, Div 1 61-62 64-65 65-66 (R-up 71-72 85-86), Div 2(res) 71-72 (R-up 62-63), Div 3 R-up 83-84, Reserve Cup 72-73), Apsley Snr Cup R-up 71-72 87-88, Marsworth Cup(res) 72-73, Apsley Jnr Cup(res) R-up 93-94.

Tring Athletic FC.

WINSLOW UNITED

Chairman: J B Robins **Manager:** L Lamb.
Secretary: David F Ward, 29 Avenue Rd, Winslow, Buckingham MK18 3DH (0296 713202).
Ground: Winslow Recreation Ground, Elmfields Gate, Winslow (0296 713057)
Directions: A413 from Aylesbury to Winslow, in High Street turn right into Emerald Gate, ground 100yds on left opposite car park. From Milton Keynes take A421 to Buckingham, turn left thru Gt Horwood to Winslow, turn left off High Street into Emerald Gate.
Capacity: 2,000 **Seats:** 25 **Cover:** 100 **Floodlights:** Yes **Founded:** 1891.
Colours: Yellow/blue/blue **Change Colours:** Red/black/black **Club Shop:** No.
Record Gate: 720 v Aylesbury Utd, Berks & Bucks Snr Cup.
Previous Grounds: None **Previous Leagues:** Leighton/ North Bucks.
Programme: 16 pages, £1 with entry **Editor:** J Robins (0296 714206).
Midweek home matchday: Tuesday
Clubhouse: Open every eveining except Wednesday. Full weekend opening. Youngers beers. Various snacks on matchdays.
P.o.Y. 93-94: **Captain & Top Scorer 93-94:**
Club record scorer: B McConnell
Hons: Sth Mids Lg R-up 75-76 (Div 1 74-75), Berks & Bucks Jnr Cup 67-68, Buckingham Charity Cup 29-30 32-33 66-67 67-68 73-74 74-75 77-78 79-80 81-82, Stantonbury Charity Cup 67-68 73-74 78-79 82-83 83-84 85-86, Leighton Challenge Cup 92-93.

DIVISION ONE CLUBS 1994-95

ABBEY NATIONAL (M.K.)

Secretary: Michael Burnside, 32 Falcon View, Greens Norton, Northants NN12 8BT (0327 352095).
Ground: Loughton Sports & Social Club, Linceslade Grove, Loughton, Milton Keynes (0908 690668)
Directions: From M1 Jct 14 follow H6, Childs Way for 5 miles until V4 Watling Way (Knowlhill r-about), right to Loughton r-about, right along H5 Portway – 1st right Linceslade Grove. From old A5 (Watling Street) turn right at Great Holm Fire Station onto H5 Portway, 1st right into Paynes Drive then 1st left into Linceslade Grove.
Capacity: 550 **Cover:** 40 **Seats:** 25 **Floodlights:** No **Founded:** 1947.
Cols: Black & white stripes/black/black **Change Colours:** Black & red stripes/white/black.
Programme: Yes **Midweek home matchday:** Doug Sinclair (0525 376952).
Previous League: North Bucks & District (pre-1994).
Previous Ground: MK Sports Club, Wroughon-on-the-Green (pre-1994).

BOW BRICKHILL

Secretary: Dennis Hatton, 17 Watling Street, Bletchley, Milton Keynes MK2 2BU (0908 648529).
Ground: Rushmere Close, Bow Brickhill (0860 627089 - mobile).
Directions: M1 Jct 13, thru Aspley Guise to Woburn Sands then on to Bow Brickhill - right into Rushmere Close in village centre.
Colours: Red (blue stripe)/blue/blue **Change Colours:** All blue.
Previous League: Bedford & District (pre-1994).
Honours: Bedford & District League Div 4 92-93 (Aubrey Tingley Memorial Cup 93-94).

CADDINGTON

Chairman: Peter Spowage **Hon. President:** David Pleat **Manager:** Leigh Glenister
Secretary: Fred Rook, 44 Clifford Crescent, Luton, Beds LU4 9HR (0582 580453).
Ground: Caddington Recreation Club, Manor Road, Luton (0582 450151).
Directions: On entering village turn into Manor Road (adjacent to shops and village green), proceed 500 metres: Clubhouse and ground on left side next to Catholic Church.
Capacity: Unknown **Seats:** Not yet **Cover:** Due **Floodlights:** No **Founded:** 1971.
Colours: Red & black/black/red **Change:** Blue (broad white stripe)/blue/blue.
Programme: No **Record Gate:** 150 v Barton Rvrs, Beds Snr Cup.
Prev. Names: Five Oaks/ The Oaks **Prev. Lge:** Luton & Sth Beds Dist. **Nickname:** The Oaks
Prev. Grnd: Stockwood Public Park **Midweek home matchday:** Tuesday or Thursday.
Players progressing to Football League: Paul Kerling to professional football in Holland.
Hons: Beds Intermediate Cup 85-86 92-93, Luton & Sth Beds Dist. League 84-85 (League Cup 84-85), William Pease Cup 83-84.

CLIFTON OLD BOYS

Secretary: Richard Puckey, 99 Millstream Close, Hitchin, Herts SG4 0DB (0462 453125).
Ground: Luton Regional Sports Centre, St Thomas Rd, Stopsley, Luton, Beds (0582 402493)
Directions: Leave Luton on A505 towards Hitchin, left at Jansell House r'bout, right at Stopsley War Memorial into St Thomas Rd - ground entrance 400yds on right.
Colours: Red (white sleeves)/red/red **Change Colours:** Yellow (blue trim)/blue/blue.

CRANFIELD UNITED

Chairman: Roger Thompson **Vice Chairman:** Jim Brandon **President:** Mick Johnson.
Secretary: Paul Kilcoyne, 10 Springfield Way, Cranfield, Bedford MK43 0JN (0234 751492).
Manager: Trevor Evans **Asst Manager:** Ray Perry **Coach:**
Ground: Crawley Road, Cranfield, Bedford MK43 0AA (0234 751444)
Directions: M1 jct 13 – A5140 to Bedford, 100 yds turn left, follow signposts to Cranfield, through village, left into Mill Rd, left into Crawley Rd, ground on left after houses. From Bedford – A5140, right at Marston Morteyne r'bout 'Little Chef', left at T-junction into village, left into Crane Way, continue to ground on left.
Capacity: 3,000 **Seats:** 50 **Cover:** 150 **Floodlights:** Yes
Founded: 1904
Cols: Red & white stripes/red/red **Change:** Red & blue multi-col./sky/sky **Nickname:** United
Previous Leagues: Bedford & Dist. 04-32 61-76/ North Bucks 33-48/ South Midlands 49-60.
Previous Grounds: Various local pitches.
Clubhouse: Open every evening and weekend lunchtimes. Bingo Mondays. Tea/rolls available most weekends, hot food for special events. Parking for sixty cars.
Programme: 16 pages with admission **Sponsors:** Vision 'Bourne End' Ltd **Club Shop:** No.
Midweek home matchday: Wednesday
Record win: 13-0 v Woburn (H), 8/1/72 **Record defeat:** 1-11 v Bletchley (H), 11/1/56.
Club record scorer: Mick Johnson 500+ **Club record appearances:** Mick Johnson 900+.
Captain 93-94: Chris Hyde **Top Scorer 93-94:** Clint Ledger **P.o.Y. 93-94:** Andy Jones
Hons: South Mids League Div 2 50-51 (Div 1 Runners-up 51-52, Cove Tphy Runners-up 85-86, Sportsmanship Award 77-78 85-86), Bedford & Dist. League Runners-up 74-75 (Div 1 67-68), Beds Snr Cup Runners-up 51-52, Stantonbury Cup 87-88, Beds Charity Cup Runners-up 64-65, Hinchingbrooke Cup Runners-up 92-93, Aubrey Tingay Cup Runners-up 1976, Beds Jnr Cup Runners-up 49-50, Beds Minor Cup 35-36, North Bucks Chall. Shield 48-49, Nth Bucks League Div 2 35-36.

DE HAVILLAND

Chairman: M J Hollis **Manager:** P Long.
Secretary: Roy Ridgway, 85 Garden Ave., Hatfield, Herts AL10 8LH (0707 267327).
Ground: Comet Way, Hatfield (0707 263204/ 262665).
Directions: From south leave A1(M) at Hatfield turn, A1001 to Birchwood r'bout, 1st exit into car park. From north leave A1(M) at Welwyn G.C., A1001 to Birchwood r'bout and 4th exit into car park.
Capacity: **Seats:** None **Cover:** No **Floodlights:** No **Founded:** 1934.
Colours: Blue & white/blue/red **Change colours:** Red/red/black **Nickname:** DH
Programme: Sometimes, 30p **Previous League:** Herts Snr Co. (pre-1992)

EATON BRAY

Chairman: Derek Jackson **President:** Roy Bennett **Manager:** Paul Reeves.
Secretary: Mark Holmes, 3 Alfred Str., Dunstable, Beds LU5 4HZ (0582 605204).
Ground: The Rye, Eaton Bray (0582 221443).
Directions: Follow A5 thru Dunstable past A.C. Delco, left onto Leighton Buzzard bypass, 1st left and follow signs to Eaton Bray, turn right 500yds ground on right.
Capacity: **Seats:** None **Cover:** 30 **Floodlights:** No **Founded:** 1989.
Cols: White (blue stripe)/blue/white **Change Colours:** Sky/navy/white. **Nickname:** None
Programme: 16 pages, 50p **Midweek home matchday:** Thursday

EMBERTON

Chairman/Secretary: R L Dugdale, 9 Stone Court, West Lane, Emberton, Nr Olney, Bucks MK46 5ND (0234 711004).
Manager: P York **Assistant Manager:** R Goodman
Coach: C Beard/N Bunker
Ground: Hulton Drive, Emberton, Nr Olney, Bucks.
Directions: M1 jct 14 to Newport Pagnell, right onto A422 at 1st r'bout straight on north towards Olney. Emberton lies before Olney. Turn left at 2nd turning into village and 1st right Hulton Drive. Buses from Northampton, Bedford and Milton Keynes.
Capacity: 400 **Seats:** No **Cover:** No **Floodlights:** No **Reformed:** 1968
Colours: Maroon/white **Change colours:** Navy/white **Nickname:** Rams
Previous Ground: Clifton Reynes (10yrs). **Previous Lges:** Rushden & Dist. 66-85/ East Northants 85-91.
Programme: 12 pages, £1 with entry **Programme Editor:** Secretary **Club Shop:** No.
Sponsors: Dugdale Builders **Record Gate:** 180 v Bedford T., Sth Mids Lg Div 1.
Midweek home matchday: Wednesday **Reserve Team's League:** South Midlands Lge Reserve Div.
Clubhouse: Matchdays. Tea, coffee, soft drinks, confectionary.
P.o.Y. 93-94: W Botham **Top Scorer 93-94:**
Club record scorer: D Maloney 54 **Club record appearances:** R L Dugdale.
Hons: E Northants Lg 90-91 (R-up 86-87, Lg Cup 90-91), Rushden & Dist. Lg 84-85 85-86 (Lg Cup 84-85, Jnr Shield 79-80), Nth Bucks Lg Div 3 37-38, Haynes Tphy 69-70, Hamblin Cup 90-91, Stantonbury Cup R-up 92-93 (SF 91-92).

FLAMSTEAD

Chairman: Mr Alan Morrice **Manager:** Tony Dumingan
Secretary: Mrs Susan Hayward, Greenways, Old Watling Str., Flamstead, St Albans, Herts AL3 8HN (0582 841213).
Ground: Friendless Lane, Flamstead, St Albans, Herts (0582 841307).
Ground Directions: From Dunstable Town Centre travel south on A5 Trunk Road towards the M1. Follow for approximately 3 miles then turn right opposite Hertfordshire Moat House Hotel. Ground and parking approximately half a mile on the corner of the first right turn.
Seats: None **Cover:** None **Floodlights:** No **Founded:** 1962. **Nickname:** None
Colours: White/red **Change Colours:** Orange/black
Programme: 4 pages, 25p **Midweek home matchday:** Tuesday.
Previous League: Luton & South Beds District.

HOUGHTON TOWN

Chairman: D McMorrow **Manager:** P Rowe.
Secretary: Desmond Stewart, 9 Grove Rd, Houghton Regis, Dunstable, Beds LU5 5PD (0582 864286).
Ground: Houghton Town Associated Club, Park Rd North, Houghton Regis (0582 866128)
Directions: M1 jct 11, head towards Dunstable, right at island into Poynters Rd, straight over next island keeping left at small r'bout onto Park Rd North - ground on left 10yds before pelican crossing.
Capacity: **Seats:** None **Cover:** No **Floodlights:** No **Founded:** 1993
Colours: All blue **Change Colours:** All red
Programme: £1 with entry **Midweek home matchday:** Tuesday.
Honours: South Midlands Lg Challenge Trophy R-up 93-94 (Div 1 Cup R-up 93-94).

KENTS ATHLETIC

Secretary:
Ground:
Previous League: Bedford & District (pre-1994).

MERCEDES BENZ

Chairman: Martin Parlett **President:** Nigel Wells
Sec.: Bob Flight, Mercedes (UK) Ltd, Mercedes Benz Centre, Tongwell, Milton Keynes MK15 8BA (0604 764433).
Manager: Stuart Collard **Assistant Manager:** Nick Hamper.
Coach: Kevin England **Physio:** Nick Booth.
Ground: The Barn, Pannier Place, Downs Barn, Milton Keynes, Bucks (0908 245158).
Directions: M1 jct 14, A509 for Milton Keynes, right onto H5 Portway at 1st island, right onto V9 Overstreet at 3rd island, 1st left into Downs Barn Boulevard, 2nd left into Pannier Place, ground at top of hill.
Capacity: 300 **Cover:** No **Seats:** None **Floodlights:** No **Founded:** 1967.
Colours: All royal blue **Change Colours:** All white **Nickname:** Blues.
Programme: 16 pages, 50p **Programme Editor:** Secretary **Club Shop:** No.
Previous Leagues: Milton Keynes Sunday/ North Bucks & District (pre'93).
Midweek home matches: Wednesday **Previous Ground:** Willen Rd, Newport Pagnell.
Sponsors: Mercedes-Benz (UK) Ltd **Reserve team's league:** South Midlands Reserve Div.
Past players progressing to Football League: Michael Peters (Wycombe Wanderers 1991).
Record win: 24-2 v Milton Keynes Saints, Berks & Bucks Junior Cup First Round 16/10/93.
Record defeat: 1-8 v Greenleys, Milton Keynes Sunday League Cup First Round 22/11/87.
Clubhouse: Not on ground, but the Mercedes-Benz Sports & Social Club is situated one mile from the ground and is open normal licensing hours.
Record scorer: Stuart Collard 128 **Record appearances:** Stuart Collard 197.
Captain 93-94: Tony Deeble **P.o.Y. 93-94:** Adam Peach **Top Scorer 93-94:** Micky Green 35.
Hons: Nth Bucks Lg Div 1 90-91 (Premier Div Cup 92-93, Intermediate Tphy 91-92), Daimler-Benz Austrian International Tournament R-up 1990.

PHOTOS OPPOSITE

Top: *Hoddesdon Town FC. Back Row (L/R): Ray Greenall (Manager), Lee Browne, Paul Robbins, Gary Cummins, Stuart Parker, Chris Westphal, Glenn Swaby, John Walton (Coach), Jim Briggs (Asst Manager). Front: Martin Payne, Jaffa Ibrahim, Pablo Ardiles, Jeff Cross (Captain), Adam Clarke, Mel Musa, David Wilson.* *Photo - Colin I Sinden.*

Centre: *Sandy Albion FC, who sadly revert to the Bedford & District League for 1994-95 having played in the SML since 1958.* *Photo - Dave West.*

Foot: *Darek Jozwiak nets from close-range for Bedford United in a 3-1 Senior Division home win against New Bradwell St Peter.* *Photo - Gordon Whittington.*

Herald

B.S.G.

POTTERS BAR CRUSADERS

Chairman: Steve Sandford **President:** John Metselaar **Manager:** Clive Eldridge.
Secretary: Linda Eldridge, 169 Ashwood Road, Potters Bar, Herts EN6 2QE (0707 646059).
Asst Mgr/Coach: Bob Lee **Physio:** Steve Sandford
Press Officer: Robert Cavallini (0707 650543).
Ground: Furzefield Centre, Mutton Lane, Potters Bar (0707 650764) *(Synthetic pitch).*
Directions: A1(M)/M25 to Bignalls Corner, follow signs to South Mymms, right into A111 (Mutton Lane). King George V playing fields 1 mile on the left. (Next to Furzefield Centre).
Capacity: 400 **Seats:** None **Cover:** Due 94-95 **Floodlights:** Yes **Founded:** 1948
Colours: Blue & white **Change Colours:** Yellow (blue trim) **Nickname:** Crusaders
Programme: 30-40 pages, 50p **Editor:** Robert Cavallini (0707 650543) **Club Shop:** No.
Midweek home matchday: Tuesday. **Reserve Team's League:** South Midlands Lge Reserve section.
Previous Grounds: Wrotham Park 51-54/ Parkfield School 54-57/ King George V Playing Fields 57-90.
Previous Leagues: Barnet & Dist. 51-59/ Northern Suburban 59-71/ Herts Senior County County 71-90.
Record Gate: 1,000 v ITV World of Sport XI 27/4/75 (lost 1-2).
Record win: 16-0; v New Barnet (H) 4/12/54; v Vale Utd 'A' (A) 21/11/53. Both Barnet & D. Lge Div 1.
Record defeat: 0-12 v London Colney (A), Herts Senior County League Premier Division 16/4/88.
Clubhouse: Open daily 5.30-11pm, noon-11pm Saturdays, noon-3pm Sundays.
Record scorer: Peter A Clarke 241 **Record appearances:** Dave Gamester 1000+.
Top Scorer 93-94: Mark Abrey 18 **Captain & Player of the Year 93-94:** Steve Carter.
Honours: Herts Co. Lg Div 1 R-up 83-84 (Aubrey Cup SF 73-74, Reserve Cup R-up 84-85), Northern Suburban Lg R-up 63-64 69-70 (Div 1 R-up 59-60 62-63, Div 2 R-up 70-71 71-72, Res. Div 66-67 (R-up 62-63)), Barnet Lg 58-59 (R-up 57-58, Div 1 54-55, Div 2 R-up 55-56 60-61), Herts I'mediate Cup R-up 76-77 (Jnr Cup SF 60-61), Potters Bar Charity Cup 59-60 62-63 63-64 65-66 67-68 78-79 79-80 81-82 82-83 84-85 (R-up 60-61 61-62 64-65 70-71 74-75 77-78 80-81 87-88 89-90), Barnet Cup 69-70 (R-up 57-58), Barnet Charity Cup 58-59, Barnet Jnr Cup 54-55 (R-up 53-54 59-60), Mid-Herts Lg(Res.) Div 2 84-85 (Div 3 78-79, Div 2 Cup 81-82, Div 3 Cup R-up 78-79).

SCOT

Chairman: Brian Greengrass **Manager:** Peter Soper (Reserves: John McConnell).
Secretary: Thomas Hallford, 32 Browning Cres., Bletchley, Milton Keynes MK3 5AU (0908 640365).
Ground: Selbourne Ave., Bletchley, Milton Keynes (0908 372057).
Directions: Main roads to Bletchley then A421 Buckingham road, at Glen Garage right into Newton Rd, 2nd left into Selbourne Ave., through railway bridge to bottom of road.
Capacity: **Seats:** None **Cover:** No **Floodlights:** No **Founded:** 1968.
Colours: Blue (black stripe)/black/blue **Change Colours:** All white
Prev. Grnd: Tattenhoe Lane, Bletchley **Prev. Lges:** Nth Bucks & Dist./ Aylesbury & Dist.
Programme: Yes **Midweek home matches:** Wednesday **Nickname:** Scots.
Previous Names: None **Hons:** Nth Bucks & Dist. Lg 91-92.

WALDEN RANGERS

Chairman: Mr M I Garrett **Manager:** Cliff Bailey.
Secretary: Irene Oodian, 9 Garfield Court, Handcross Rd, Luton, Beds LU2 8JZ (0582 483090).
Ground: Breachwood Green Rec., Chapel Rd, Breachwood Green, Herts (0438 833332).
Directions: From Luton Airport roundabout (Eaton Green Rd)(away from Vauxhall/ IBC direction) take country road to Breachwood Green (2 miles). From Hitchin on A602, take country road to Preston (6 miles to Breachwood Green).
Floodlights: No **Founded:** 1966
Colours: Blue/white/blue **Change Colours:** Red/black/red

Paul Daniels of Potters Bar Town (No.6) shows some magical control during the first-half of a remarkable 4-4 draw at home to Bedford Town in the Premier Division on 26th February.

Photo - Martin Wray.

AMATEUR FOOTBALL ALLIANCE

Secretary: W P Goss,
55 Islington Park Street,
London N1 1QB (071 359 3493).

The AFA Rep. XI which beat Oxford University 3-0 at Iffley Road on Wednesday 20th October. Back Row (L/R): Forbes Chapman (Norsemen - Manager), Grant White (Duncombe Sports), Gary Burawick (Winchmore Hill), Derek Broadley (South Bank Poly), Peter Watson (Old Tenisonians), Steve Carnana (London University), Gary Casey (Winchmore Hill), M Brown (Bank of England - Physio). Front: Richard Burdett (Parkfield), Adam Dince (Crouch End Vampires), Barry McGuinness (Old Meadonians), Neil Linter (West Wickham), Paul Feeley (South Bank Poly), John McDonagh (Bank of England - Captain), Clive Berry (Norsemen), Ron Broom (Barclays Bank).
Photo - James Wright.

A.F.A. SENIOR CUP 1993-94 First Round

Old Foresters v Old Suttonians	1-2
Hadley v Ulysses	0-2
Bank of England v Old Westhameians	4-0
Old Chigwellians v Old Salesians	5-0
Norsemen v Old Isleworthians	5-2
Fulham Compton OB v Cardinal Manning OB	1-6
Crouch End Vampires v Broomfield	3-1
Merton v Wake Green	2-3
National Westminster Bank v Cuaco	6-1
South Bank Poly v Ryl Bank of Scotland	11-0
Old Woodhouseians v BBC	4-2
Baltic Exchange v Old Colfeians	0-5
Old Addeyians v Glyn Old Boys	0-6
Old Hamptonians v Nottsborough	1-4
Albanian v Old Minchendenians	4-5
Old Bealonians v Old Aloysians	1-2
Old Owens v Old Malvernians	5-0
Winchmore Hill v Old Esthameians	2-2,0-1*(aet)*
West Wickham v Latymer Old Boys	3-0
Old Latymerians v Old Tollingtonians	4-2*(aet)*
Midland Bank v Parkfield	1-2
Ealing Association v Brentham	8-0
Bourneside v Old Kingsburians	2-2*(aet)-B.scr.*
Civil Service v Lensbury	4-1
Old Parkonians v Old Finchleians	3-1*(aet)*
Nottinghamshire v Old Stationers	1-1,1-3
Old Grammarians v Old Parmiterians	1-0
Lancing Old Boys v Old Ignatians	0-7
Old Southallians v Silhill	0-6
Old Actonians Association v Old Vaughanians	3-0
Old Tenisonians v Alleyn Old Boys	2-0
Old Meadonians v Polytechnic	0-4

Second Round

Old Stationers v Parkfield	2-1
Bank of England v Old Colfeians	4-0
Old Latymerians v Ulysses	2-0
West Wickham v Old Minchendenians	2-1*(aet)*
Ealing Association v Cardinal Manning OB	4-3
Wake Green v Glyn Old Boys	2-0*(aet)*
South Bank Poly v Old Esthameians	3-0
Nottsborough v Civil Service	3-3,0-1
Crouch End Vampires v Old Kingburians	2-1
Old Grammarians v Silhill	3-2*(aet)*
Old Aloysians v Old Owens	4-0
Old Chigwellians v Old Parkonians	0-0,0-0*(1-3 pens)*
National Westminster Bank v Polytechnic	2-3
Old Actonians Association v Old Suttonians	1-2
Norsemen v Old Ignatians	0-2
Old Woodhouseians v Old Tenisonians	2-1

Third Round

Old Suttonians v Old Ignatians	0-2
Crouch End Vampires v Old Grammarians	4-1
Old Woodhouseians v South Bank Poly	1-4
West Wickham v Old Aloysians	3-1
Polytechnic v Bank of England	3-1
Ealing Association v Old Latymerians	0-1
Old Parkonians v Wake Green	2-1
Old Stationers v Civil Service	1-3

Quarter-Finals

Polytechnic v Old Parkonians	2-0
Civil Service v Old Ignatians	0-1
West Wickham v South Bank Polytechnic	0-1
Crouch End Vampires v Old Latymerians	1-0

Semi-Finals

Crouch End Vampires v Polytechnic	2-0
Old Ignatians v South Bank Polytechnic	2-1*(aet)*

Final: Crouch End Vampires 3, Old Ignatians 1

OTHER AMATEUR FOOTBALL ALLIANCE CUP FINAL RESULTS

W.E. GREENLAND MEMORIAL
Old Etonians 2, Hill Samuel 1

A.F.A. ESSEX SENIOR
Old Chigwellians 2, Old Parkonians 1

A.F.A. MIDDLESEX SENIOR
Civil Service 1, E Barnet Old Grammarians 0

A.F.A. SURREY SENIOR
Nat West Bank 2, South Bank Poly 1 *(aet)*

A.F.A. INTERMEDIATE
Carshalton Res. 1, Old Hamptonians Res. 0

A.F.A. ESSEX INTERMEDIATE
Old Parmiterians Res. 4, Old Highburians Res. 1

A.F.A. KENT INTERMEDIATE
Lloyds Bank Res. 2, Colonial Mutual 0

A.F.A. SURREY INTERMEDIATE
Nat West Bank Res. 5, Temple Bar 2

A.F.A. MIDDLESEX INTERMEDIATE
Old Ignatians Res. 4, Polytechnic Res. 0

A.F.A. JUNIOR
Civil Service 'A' 3, Winchmore Hill 'A' 0

A.F.A. MINOR
Old Esthameians 'B' 3, South Bank Poly 'C' 0

SENIOR NOVETS
Lloyds Bank 'C' 1, Old Suttonians 'C' 0

INTERMEDIATE NOVETS
Old Salvatorians 'D' 4, Norsemen 'D' 2

JUNIOR NOVETS
Old Parmiterians 1th 3, Nat West Bank "B" 2

VETERANS
Winchmore Hill Vets 5, Old Chigwellians Vets 3

OPEN VETERANS
Port of London Authority V. 1, Toby Veterans 0

SOUTHERN AMATEUR LEAGUE

FIRST DIVISION	P	W	D	L	F	A	PTS
South Bank Poly	22	15	4	3	49	23	34
Crouch End Vamps	22	9	11	2	39	24	29
Norsemen	22	9	6	7	40	30	24
Civil Service	22	10	4	8	36	41	24
Nat West Bank	22	9	5	8	42	28	23
Old Actonians A.	22	11	1	10	35	32	23
Old Esthameians	22	7	8	7	38	34	22
Winchmore Hill	22	8	4	10	31	34	20
Midland Bank	22	8	4	10	32	44	20
West Wickham	22	4	10	8	34	40	18
Carshalton	22	7	4	11	37	49	18
Lensbury	22	4	1	17	30	64	9

SECOND DIVISION	P	W	D	L	F	A	PTS
East Barnet OG	22	16	4	2	59	22	36
Old Latymerians	22	14	4	4	48	27	32
Polytechnic	22	12	4	6	54	30	28
Old Stationers	22	12	3	7	50	36	27
Alexandra Park	22	9	8	5	61	38	26
Lloyds Bank	22	9	6	7	34	31	24
Old Parkonians	22	8	5	9	35	33	21
Old Bromleians	22	8	5	9	41	47	21
Kew Association	22	8	3	11	44	46	19
Broomfield	22	7	5	10	41	46	19
Southgate Olympic	22	2	2	18	24	93	6
Ibis	22	0	5	17	22	64	5

Reserve Section
Div 1: 12 teams, won by Old Esthameians
Div 2: 12 teams, won by Old Parmiterians
Div 3: 12 teams, won by Old Salesians

3rd Teams Section
Div 1: 12 teams, won by Nat West Bank
Div 2: 12 teams, won by Old Parmiterians
Div 3: 12 teams, won by Crouch End Vampires

THIRD DIVISION	P	W	D	L	F	A	PTS
Old Parmiterians	22	14	5	3	58	17	33
Old W'minster Citiz.	22	14	5	3	56	29	33
Cuaco	22	14	3	5	68	33	31
Bank of England	22	12	6	4	50	28	30
Barclays Bank	22	12	5	5	52	27	29
Brentham	22	9	5	8	49	49	23
Old Lyonians	22	9	4	9	51	41	22
Alleyn Old Boys	22	7	5	10	40	55	19
Old Salesians	22	6	6	10	43	45	18
Merton	22	5	3	14	36	56	13
Reigate Priory	22	2	3	17	27	80	7
Ryl Bank of Scot.	22	2	2	18	19	89	6

4th Teams Section
Div 1: 12 teams, won by Old Stationers
Div 2: 12 teams, won by Old Parmiterians
Div 3: 12 teams, won by Old Parkonians

5th Teams Section
Div 1: 10 teams, won by Nat West Bank
Div 2: 10 teams, won by Old Parmiterians
Div 3: 10 teams, won by O Westmin. Citizens

6th Teams Section
Div 1: 10 teams, won by Civil Service
Div 2: 9 teams, won by West Wickham
Div 3: 8 teams, won by Lloyds Bank

7th Teams Section
Div 1: 9 teams, won by Winchmore Hill
Div 2: 9 teams, won by Old Stationers

8th Teams Section
Div 1: 7 teams, won by Old Parmiterians
Div 2: 6 teams, won by Barclays Bank

9th & 10th Teams Sections
Div 1: 12 teams, won by Old Parmiterians 9th

The Southern Amateur League Representative XI 1993-94. *Photo - Gavin Ellis-Neville.*

SOUTHERN OLYMPIAN LEAGUE

DIVISION ONE	P	W	D	L	F	A	PTS
Parkfield	18	11	4	3	56	30	26
Witan	18	11	3	4	45	25	25
Old Owens	18	11	3	4	44	27	25
Nottsborough	18	8	5	5	34	22	21
Old Grammarians	18	9	2	7	46	33	20
Wandsworth Boro.	18	7	1	10	34	37	15
Mill Hill Village	18	6	3	9	26	41	15
St Marys College	18	5	4	9	27	46	14
Old Bealonians	18	5	3	10	27	44	13
Old Finchleians	18	2	2	14	27	61	6

DIVISION TWO	P	W	D	L	F	A	PTS
Southgate County	20	15	3	2	56	18	33
Ulysses	20	11	6	3	44	20	28
UCL Academicals	20	11	5	4	59	27	27
Albanian	20	10	4	6	51	36	24
Hadley	20	11	1	8	41	28	23
Duncombe Sports	20	8	5	7	43	35	21
Old Fairlopians	20	10	1	9	40	54	21
Ealing Association	20	6	2	12	53	60	14
Cor.-Casuals 'A'	20	6	2	12	40	54	14
Poligons	20	5	4	11	46	61	14
Old Monovians	20	0	1	19	13	93	1

DIVISION THREE	P	W	D	L	F	A	PTS
Hale End Ath.	20	15	4	1	54	20	34
Hon. Artillery Co.	19	13	3	3	53	21	29
Old Woodhouseians	20	9	7	4	51	31	25
Bourneside	16	10	2	4	49	43	22
BBC	19	8	5	6	43	27	*19
Old Colfeians	20	8	2	10	39	45	18
City of London	20	5	8	7	34	40	18
Westerns	20	5	5	10	43	57	15
Birkbeck College	20	6	3	11	27	43	13
Pegasus (Inner Tple)	20	2	5	13	29	55	9
H'stead Heathens	19	3	2	14	25	65	8

Intermediate Section
Div 1: 10 teams, won by Albanian Res
Div 2: 11 teams, won by Witan Res
Div 3: 10 teams, won by Hale End Ath. Res
Div 4: 11 teams, won by London Airways Res

DIVISION FOUR	P	W	D	L	F	A	PTS
London Welsh	14	12	0	2	60	14	28
Brent	14	9	2	3	50	18	20
Fulham Compton OB	14	10	0	4	48	26	20
Centymca	14	4	4	6	34	21	25
Inland Revenue	14	8	2	10	39	40	18
Mayfield Athletic	14	8	2	10	48	49	18
London Airways	14	7	3	10	42	52	*17
Economicals	14	1	0	13	15	77	*2

* - 2 points deducted

Junior Section
Div 1: 10 teams, won by Old Finchleians 'A'
Div 2: 10 teams, won by Mill Hill Village 'A'
Div 3: 9 teams, won by Mill Hill Village 'B'
Div 4: 10 teams, won by Albanian 'C'

Minor Section
Div A: 10 teams, won by UCL Academicals 'B'
Div B: 10 teams, won by Albanian 'D'
Div C: 9 teams, won by London Welsh 'A'
Div D: 10 teams, won by Mayfield Ath. 'B'
Div E: 6 teams, won by Old Finchleians 'F'
Div F: 9 teams, won by Fulham Compton OB 'C'
Veterans: 6 teams, won by Tansley Vets

Senior Challenge Bowl: Parkfield
Senior Challenge Shield: Old Owens
Intermediate Chal. Cup: Old Owens Res
Intermediate Chal. Shield: Nottsborough Res
Junior Challenge Cup: Old Owens 'A'
Junior Challenge Shield: BBC 'A'
Mander Cup: UCL Academicals 'B'
Mander Shield: City of London 'B'
Burntwood Trophy: Old Finchleians 'C'
Burntwood Shield: BBC 'C'
Thomas Parmiter Cup: City of London 'D'
Thomas Parmiter Shield: Parkfield 'D'
Veterans' Challenge Cup: Albanian Vets
Veterans' Chal. Shield: Old Finchleians Vets

ARTHURIAN LEAGUE

ARTHUR DUNN CUP FINAL:
OLD CHIGWELLIANS 2, OLD SALOPIANS 2
replay: OLD CHIGWELLIANS 5, OLD SALOPIANS 2

Junior League Cup Final:
Old Carthusians Res. 1, Old Harrovians Res. 0

PREM. DIVISION	P	W	D	L	F	A	PTS
Lancing Old Boys	16	9	6	1	38	19	24
Old Chigwellians	16	10	3	3	41	10	23
Old Carthusians	16	10	2	4	41	24	22
Old Brentwoods	16	8	1	7	34	37	17
Old Etonians	16	6	3	7	22	22	15
Old Malvernians	16	4	6	6	24	29	14
Old Reptonians	16	6	1	9	27	35	13
Old Cholmeleians	16	5	3	8	27	34	*11
Old Salopians	16	0	3	13	25	61	3

DIVISION ONE	P	W	D	L	F	A	PTS
Old Wellingburians	18	14	1	3	70	19	29
Old Aldenhamians	18	14	1	3	67	26	29
Old Foresters	18	14	2	2	61	25	*28
Old Bradfieldians	18	9	2	7	43	44	20
Old Harrovians	18	9	1	8	59	42	19
Old Haileyburians	18	8	1	9	38	40	17
Old Witleians	18	6	2	10	40	52	14
Old Wykehamists	18	5	0	13	37	53	10
Old Ardinians	18	3	1	14	23	89	10
Old Westminsters	18	1	3	14	29	77	5

DIVISION TWO	P	W	D	L	F	A	PTS
Old Cholmel. Res.	16	12	3	1	50	21	27
Old Carthus. Res.	16	10	3	3	38	29	23
Old Chigwel. Res.	16	7	5	4	53	37	19
Old Chigwel. 'A'	16	6	4	6	35	40	16
Old Reptonians Res.	16	4	5	7	29	34	13
Old Etonians Res.	16	5	2	9	44	43	12
Old Foresters 'A'	16	6	2	8	36	46	*12
Old Salopians Res.	16	4	3	9	21	39	11
Old Brentw. Res.	16	4	1	11	28	45	9

DIVISION THREE	P	W	D	L	F	A	PTS
Old Aldenham. Res.	16	11	1	4	57	36	23
Lancing OB Res.	16	10	2	4	46	27	22
Old Wellingb. Res.	16	6	6	4	28	30	18
Old Harrovians Res.	16	7	3	6	32	27	17
Old Malvern. Res.	16	7	3	6	36	34	17
Old Cholmelians 'A'	16	6	4	6	31	30	16
Old Westminst. Res.	16	5	4	7	33	39	14
Old Cholmelians 'B'	16	5	3	8	35	37	13
Old Eastbournians	16	0	4	12	20	58	4

* - 2 points deducted

Derrik Moore Veterans' Cup:
Old Brentwoods Vets 2, Old Carthusians Vets 1

Div. 4 - 8 teams, won by Old Etonians 'A'
Div. 5 - 7 teams, won by Old Brentwoods 'B'

LONDON BANKS F.A. *(League merged in London Financial FA - see overleaf)*

Challenge Cup: Lensbury Res. 2, Lloyds Bank 0
Senior Cup: Coutts 1, Morgan Guaranty 0
Senior Plate: Goldman Sachs 5, Salomon Bros 1
Minor Cup: Nat West 'D' 2, Lloyds Bank 'C' 0
Junior Cup: Nat West "A" 2, Citibank Res 1
Junior Plate: Union Bank Switz 3, Chase Manhattan 0
Veterans' Cup: Midland Bank 3, Lensbury 1
Sportsmans Cup: Morgan Guaranty 3, Kleinwort Benson 0

REPRESENTATIVE MATCHES
Daily Telegraph Cup: Utd Banks 3, Stock Exchange 1

Royal Marines 1, United Banks 2
United Banks 2, Old Boys League 1

Royal Marines 4, London Banks 2
London Banks 2, London Insurance FA "B" 2

LONDON FINANCIAL F.A. *(inaugural season)*

DIVISION ONE	P	W	D	L	F	A	PTS
Coutts	18	15	1	2	92	18	31
Liverpool Victoria	18	13	1	4	76	28	27
Credit Suisse	18	11	3	4	47	27	25
Temple Bar	18	8	3	7	51	33	19
Kleinwort Benson	18	7	3	8	50	57	17
Hill Samuel IM	18	7	3	8	34	42	17
Sun Alliance	18	6	2	10	32	48	14
Colonial Mutual	18	5	2	11	27	52	12
Granby	18	3	3	12	30	69	9
Salomon Brothers	18	2	5	11	23	88	9

DIVISION TWO	P	W	D	L	F	A	PTS
Bank America	18	14	2	2	55	14	30
Hong Kong Bank	18	13	2	3	60	25	28
Chemical Bank	18	13	1	4	76	29	27
Citibank	18	12	2	4	50	26	26
Eagle Star	18	8	3	7	48	49	19
Bardhill	18	6	3	9	32	33	15
Allied Irish Bank	18	4	4	10	29	49	12
Noble Lowndes	18	2	5	11	22	51	9
Bowring	18	3	2	13	26	69	8
Temple Bar Res.	18	2	2	14	46	61	6

DIVISION THREE	P	W	D	L	F	A	PTS
Morgan Stanley Int.	20	17	2	1	109	28	36
Sedgwick	20	16	2	2	95	25	34
Coutts Res.	20	13	1	6	60	42	27
Polytechnic 'A'	20	10	4	6	66	49	24
Nat West Bank 'A'	20	10	1	9	59	49	21
Union Bank Switz	20	9	2	9	48	47	20
Gaflac	20	8	2	10	35	57	18
Goldman Sachs	20	7	1	12	29	24	15
Granby Res.	20	5	2	13	37	105	12
Liverpool Vic. Res.	20	4	3	13	41	84	11
Temple Bar 'A'	20	0	2	18	25	94	2

Div 4: 11 teams, won by Morgan Guaranty
Div 5: 10 teams, won by ANZ Banking Group
Div 6: 9 teams, won by British Gas Bromley

Sportsmanship Trophy: ANZ Banking Group

LONDON INSURANCE F.A.

(League merged in London Financial FA)

Chal. Cup: Liverpool Vic. 5, Temple Bar 3 *(aet)*
Charity Cup: Liverpool Victoria 1, Granby 0
Junior Cup: Sedgwick 9, Sun Alliance Res. 2
Minor Cup: Cuaco 'C' 2, Temple Bar 'C' 1
W A Jewell Mem. Tphy (5-aside): Temple Bar
W A Jewell Mem. Tphy (5-aside) R-up: Granby

REPRESENTATIVE MATCHES:

London Insurance FA 2, Southern Olympian Lge 2
London Insurance FA 1, British Insurance Inst 4
Southern Amtr Lge "B" 3, London Insurance FA 1
United Hospitals 1, London Insurance FA 3
Old Boys League 2, London Insurance FA 1
London Banks Lge 2, London Insurance FA "B" 2

Below: *The London Insurance Representative XI that lost 1-2 to the Old Boys League on 17th February. Photo - Gavin Ellis-Neville.*

CIVIL SERVICE LEAGUE

PREM. DIVISION	P	W	D	L	F	A	PTS
Enery	18	13	2	3	49	27	41
War Office	18	11	2	5	62	27	35
New Scot Y Comets	18	10	3	5	42	23	33
Chelsea Exiles	17	11	1	5	44	40	*31
Diplomatic Service	18	8	3	7	29	28	27
Fingerprint Office	18	5	5	8	34	38	+23
Customs & Excise	16	6	4	6	37	34	22
Lambeth Bdge Hse	18	5	2	11	40	54	+20
Broadway Central	18	6	1	10	41	47	*16
Royal Householod	18	1	1	16	19	79	4

Mount Pleasant SSC - withdrew from League
* - 3 points deducted   + - 3 points awarded
Top Scorer: Tony Lewis (War Office) 25

DIVISION ONE	P	W	D	L	F	A	PTS
Agricola	21	18	3	0	83	25	57
FC Sparta Centrals	21	17	1	3	77	16	52
Cabinet Off/Treasury	21	14	1	6	76	45	43
Customs & Ex. Res.	21	7	4	10	50	44	25
NSY Comets Res.	21	6	2	13	34	59	20
War Office Res.	21	5	4	12	35	78	19
Energy Res.	21	4	2	15	24	71	14
Newlands Pk Rgrs	21	3	3	15	26	67	12

Top Scorer: Martin Joliffe (FC Sparta Centrals) 35

Coronation Cup: New Scotland Yard Comets beat FC Sparta Centrals 4-3 on penalties after a 0-0 draw.
Nalgo Cup: Energy 2, Customs & Excise 0
McKenzie Cup: Lambeth Bridge Hse 6, Energy Res. 1

Founder Cup: Enery Res. 2, Customs & E. Res. 0
Charles Adams Fairplay Tphy: FC Sparta Centrals)
Bob Spicer (6-aside) Tphy: Chelsea Ex. 7, Energy 6 *(aet)*

THE OLD BOYS LEAGUE

PREMIER DIVISION	P	W	D	L	F	A	PTS
Old Ignatians	20	14	4	2	54	19	32
Cardinal Manning	20	13	3	4	50	26	29
Old Meadonians	20	13	2	5	45	16	28
Glyn Old Boys	20	9	5	6	38	28	23
Old Aloysians	20	7	6	7	34	28	20
Old Hamptonians	20	8	4	8	35	41	20
Chertsey O Sales.	20	9	2	9	32	41	20
Old Tenisonians	20	6	4	10	21	32	16
Old Danes	20	4	5	11	28	49	13
Old Wilsonians	20	4	2	14	20	46	10
Old Tiffinians	20	4	1	15	21	52	9

SENIOR DIV. ONE	P	W	D	L	F	A	PTS
O Tenison. Res.	18	13	2	3	33	16	28
Clapham Old Xav.	18	12	2	4	47	32	26
Pheonix Old Boys	18	9	6	3	43	27	24
Old Isleworthians	18	9	2	7	38	35	20
Old Edmontonians	18	6	5	7	37	39	17
Latymer Old Boys	18	7	2	9	36	34	16
Old Salvatorians	18	6	3	9	25	25	15
Old Suttonians	18	6	3	9	35	37	15
Old Wokingians	18	5	5	9	25	35	14
Enfield Old Gram.	18	2	1	15	17	56	5

SENIOR DIV. TWO	P	W	D	L	F	A	PTS
Old Kingsburians	20	14	2	4	70	20	30
Shene Old Gramm.	20	14	2	4	55	30	30
Old Vaughanians	20	12	3	5	58	30	27
Mill Hill Co. OB	20	11	4	5	59	39	26
Old Tollingtonians	20	9	2	9	45	35	20
Old Minchendenians	20	8	3	9	38	47	19
Old Ingnatians Res.	20	8	1	11	41	54	17
Old Mead. Res.	20	7	3	10	31	44	17
Old Southallians	20	5	4	11	44	63	14
John Fisher OB	20	4	3	13	32	68	11
Leyton County OB	20	4	1	15	29	72	*7

* - 2 points deducted

SENIOR DIV. 3	P	W	D	L	F	A	PTS
Old Manorians	20	16	4	0	62	15	36
Old Camdenians	20	12	6	2	39	20	30
Old Highburians	20	7	6	7	46	39	20
Chorleywood Danes	20	6	8	6	44	39	20
Old Hampt. Res.	20	9	2	9	30	32	20
Phoenix OB Res.	20	6	7	7	46	42	19
Old Greenfordians	20	7	3	10	37	46	17
Old Alpertonians	20	6	5	9	29	49	17
Old Addeyans	20	6	4	10	47	46	16
Old Dorkinians	20	6	3	11	29	49	15
Old Aloysians Res.	20	3	4	13	25	57	10

I'mediate Div Nth: 12 teams, won by Latymer OB Res.
I'mediate Div Sth: 12 teams, won by Glyn OB Res.
Div 1 Nth: 10 teams, won by Old Camdenians Res
Div 1 Sth: 11 teams, won by Old Tiffinians Res
Div 1 W: 11 teams, won by Mill Hill County OB Res.
Div 2 Nth: 8 teams, won by London Hospital OB
Div 2 Sth: 11 teams, won by Old Sedcoians Res
Div 2 W: 11 teams, won by Old Vaughanians 'A'
Div 3 Nth: 9 teams, won by Latymer OB 'B'
Div 3 Sth: 11 teams, won by Old Strandians
Div 3 W: 10 teams, won Old Magdalenians
Div 4 Nth: 9 teams, won by O Edmontonians 'B'
Div 4 Sth: 11 teams, won by Clapham O Xaverians 'B'
Div 4 W: 11 teams, won by Old Southallians 'A'
Div 5 Nth: 9 teams, won by Davenant Wdrs Old Boys
Div 5 Sth: 9 teams, won by Old St Mary's Res.
Div 5 W: 9 teams, won by Old Salvatorians 'D'
Div 6 Nth: 9 teams, won by Old Egbertians 'A'
Div 6 Sth: 9 teams, won by Old Tiffinians 'C'
Div 6 W: 10 teams, won by Old Southallians 'B'
Div 7 Nth: 9 teams, won by Old Wood Green OB 'B'
Div 7 Sth: 10 teams, won by Old Addeyans 'B'
Div 7 W: 10 teams, won by Phoenix Old Boys 'C'
Div 8 Nth: 9 teams, won by Queen Mary Col. OB Res
Div 8 Sth: 10 teams, won by Chertsey O Salesians 'D'
Div 8 W: 9 teams, won by Phoenix Old Boys 'D'
Div 9 Sth: 8 teams, won by Wilsonians 'E'
Div 9 W: 7 teams, won by Old Salvatorians 'H'

LONDON OLD BOYS' CUPS

Senior:
Old Meadonians 2, Old Hamptonians 1

Intermediate:
Old Parmiterians Res. 3, Latymer OB Res. 3
Latymer OB Res. 2, Old Parmiterians Res. 1

Junior:
Old Meadonians 'A' 2, Old Parmiterians Res. 1

Minor:
Old Salvatorians 'B' 1, O Minchendenians 'B' 0

Novets:
Old Parmiterians 'B' 4, Albanian 'C' 3

Drummond Cup:
Old Salvatorians 'D' 4, Old Actonians Assn 'D' 0

Nemean Cup:
Old Vaughanians 'F' 3, Old Salvatorians 'E' 2

Veterans' Cup:
Old Woodvillians Vets 2, Old Owens Vets 0

STOCK EXCHANGE REP. MATCHES

Stock Ex. FA 0, Essex Sunday Corinthians 2
Stock Exchange FA 4, United Hospitals 1
United Banks 3, Stock Exchange FA 1
Stock Ex. 4, Independent Sunday League 4
Stock Exchange 0, London Legal League 2
Southern Amtr Lge "B" 3, Stock Ex. FA 0
Stock Ex. FA 1, South Essex Sunday Lge 6

Annual European Tournament - Amsterdam
Stock Exchange FA 0, Paris Bourse 1
Stock Exchange FA 4, Dusseldorf Bourse 5

Below: *The Old Boys League Representative XI which beat the London Insurance FA 2-1 on 17th February. Photo - Gavin Ellis-Neville.*

LONDON LEGAL LEAGUE

DIVISION ONE	P	W	D	L	F	A	PTS
Wilde Sapte	18	10	8	0	43	24	28
Slaughter & May	18	12	2	4	51	31	26
Grays Inn	18	11	2	5	59	31	24
Pegasus (Inner Tple)	18	8	5	5	47	31	21
Herbert Smith	18	8	1	9	39	39	17
Freshfields	18	7	2	9	37	46	16
Linkaters & Paines	18	6	4	8	35	54	16
Cameron Markby H.	18	5	4	9	45	44	14
Clifford Chance	18	4	4	10	28	33	12
Allen & Overy	18	2	2	14	31	82	6

League Challenge Cup:
Grays Inn 3, Watson Farley & Williams 0

Weavers Arms Cup:
Nabarro Nathanson 3, Gouldens 0

DIVISION TWO	P	W	D	L	F	A	PTS
Nabarro Nathanson	18	15	1	2	53	17	31
DJ Freeman & Co	18	11	4	3	44	30	26
Lovell White Durrant	18	11	1	6	42	28	23
Gouldens	18	6	6	6	39	39	18
Stephenson Harwood	18	8	1	9	39	39	17
Taylor Joynson Gar.	18	7	2	9	29	29	16
Simmons & Simmons	18	6	2	10	39	41	14
Norton Rose	18	6	2	10	20	35	14
Macfarlanes	18	4	3	11	20	39	11
Titmuss/Sainer/Webb	18	5	0	13	26	54	10

DIVISION THREE	P	W	D	L	F	A	PTS
Watson Farley & W.	18	14	3	1	61	18	31
SJ Berwin	18	12	3	3	71	38	27
Rosling King	18	12	1	5	59	39	25
Baker & McKenzie	18	9	5	4	55	30	23
Denton Hall	18	10	3	5	44	26	23
Beachcroft Stanleys	18	8	2	8	44	22	18
McKenna & Co.	18	6	3	9	37	47	15
Richards Butler	18	5	2	11	28	56	12
Mishcon de Reya	18	1	1	16	21	69	3
Rowe & Maw	18	1	1	16	24	79	3

MIDLAND AMATEUR ALLIANCE

DIVISION ONE	P	W	D	L	F	A	PTS
Sherwood Amateurs	20	15	5	0	73	22	35
Lady Bay	20	14	3	4	89	30	31
Old Elizabethans	20	11	4	5	62	19	26
Magdala Amateurs	20	11	4	5	57	43	26
Derbyshire Amateurs	20	8	3	9	39	50	19
Bassingfield	20	6	6	8	49	53	18
Peoples College	20	7	3	10	35	51	17
Brunts Old Boys	20	8	1	11	36	54	17
Old Bemrosians	20	4	4	12	34	60	12
Kirton BW	20	3	4	13	27	79	10
Nottinghamshire	20	2	5	13	20	60	9

Senior Cup winners: Old Bemrosians
Challenge Trophy: Old Elzabethans
HB Poole Trophy: Sherwood Amateurs
Intermediate Cup: Sherwood Amtrs 'A'
Minor Cup: Old Elizabethans 'A'
Supplementary Cup: Tibshelf OB Res.

DIVISION TWO	P	W	D	L	F	A	PTS
FC Toton	20	13	3	4	48	28	29
Magdala Ams Res.	20	12	4	4	48	29	28
Ilkeston Electric	20	12	3	5	54	42	27
Chilwell	20	10	4	6	46	39	24
Old Elizabeth. Res.	20	8	7	5	61	46	23
Nottm Un. Postgrads	20	9	5	6	46	46	23
Woodborough Utd	20	7	3	10	49	51	17
Sherwood Amtrs Res	20	5	6	9	48	48	16
Tibshelf Old Boys	20	7	1	12	38	61	15
County Nalgo	20	3	5	12	32	48	11
Beeston OB Assn	20	2	3	15	51	54	83

Div 3: 12 teams, won by Keyworth AFC
Div 4: 10 teams, won Derbys Amtrs Res.
Division 2 Challenge Cup: Magdala Amtrs Res.
Division 3 Challenge Cup: Keyworth AFC
Division 4 Challenge Cup: Derbys Amtrs 'A'

UNIVERSITY of LONDON INTER-COLLEGIATE LEAGUE

PREMIER DIV.	P	W	D	L	F	A	PTS
Royal Holloway	14	10	1	3	51	23	21
Goldsmiths College	14	9	2	3	32	22	20
University College	14	9	0	5	44	18	18
King's College	14	8	0	6	24	20	16
L'don Sch of Econ.	14	6	1	7	27	33	13
Q.Mary Westfield	14	5	2	7	28	27	12
Imperial College	14	4	2	8	25	45	10
St George HM Sch.	14	0	2	12	15	57	2

Challenge Cup Final:
Royal Holloway College 1, King's College 0

DIVISION ONE	P	W	D	L	F	A	PTS
Univ. Coll. Res.	18	15	3	0	52	12	33
Ryl Free Hos. MS	18	11	2	5	43	23	24
Ryl Holloway Res.	18	10	2	6	50	28	22
Ch.X/W'minster HMS	18	8	2	8	31	36	18
UMDS	18	8	1	9	29	30	17
Kings Col. HMS	18	8	1	9	32	37	17
St Barthol. HMS	18	7	1	10	31	37	15
Un. Coll/Middx HMS	18	6	2	10	24	36	14
Imperial Col. Res.	18	4	2	12	28	52	10
St Mary's HMS	18	4	2	12	19	49	10

DIVISION TWO	P	W	D	L	F	A	PTS
Q. Mary W'fld Res.	16	11	4	1	68	28	26
LSE Res.	16	12	1	3	56	20	25
Univ. College 'A'	16	8	5	3	38	34	21
Ryl Holloway 'A'	16	8	4	4	31	17	20
L'don Ryl Med. Col.	16	8	2	6	52	41	18
King's College Res.	16	5	2	9	40	37	12
Sch Slav/Eur. Stud.	16	4	4	8	28	37	12
Ryl Sch of Mines	16	3	0	13	13	66	6
King's College 'A'	16	1	2	13	18	63	4

DIVISION THREE	P	W	D	L	F	A	PTS
Goldsmith's C. Res.	17	13	3	1	51	21	29
Imperial Coll. 'A'	18	11	3	4	69	40	25
Univ. College 'B'	18	8	4	6	50	31	20
QM Westfield 'A'	18	7	4	7	46	42	18
Ryl Vetinary Coll.	18	7	3	8	49	53	17
St Geo. HMS Res.	17	7	2	8	22	40	16
LSE 'A'	18	6	3	9	42	46	15
Goldsmith's C. 'A'	17	4	6	7	28	43	14
Ryl Free HMS Res.	17	5	2	10	36	53	12
Imperial Coll. 'B'	18	5	0	13	36	58	10

NB: HMS - Hospital Medical School

Div 4: 10 teams, won by Royal Holloway 'B'
Div 5: 9 teams, won by Queen Mary Westfield 'C'
Div 6: 8 teams, won by Royal Holloway 'C'

UNIV. of LONDON REP. XI RESULTS 93-94

Ulysses	lost 1-4
Old Boys League	lost 0-3
Southern Amateur League	lost 2-4
United Hospitals	drew 2-2
Royal Navy XI	lost 0-5
Arthurian League	drew 1-1
Royal Air Force XI	drew 2-2
London Legal League	won 3-2
Arny Crusaders	won 2-1
Southern Olympian League	lost 1-2
Metropolitan Police	lost 1-3
Cambridge University	won 3-1
Middlesex County FA XI	drew 1-1
AFA	won 4-1
Crystal Palace XI	lost 0-2
Oxford University	lost 0-2

AVON (SOUTH) & SOMERSET F.A.

Secretary: Mrs H Marchment,
30 North Road, Midsomer Norton, Bath, Avon BA3 2QQ (0761 410280).

PREMIER CUP 1993-94

First Round

Glastonbury v Radstock Town	3-2	Welton Rovers v Paulton Rovers	1-0

Second Round

Minehead *(scr.)* Weston-super-Mare *(w/o)*		Mangsotsfield United v Bristol Rovers Reserves	0-6
Chard Town v Keynsham Town	2-2,0-2	Frome Town v Yeovil Town	0-6
Welton Rovers v Taunton Town	3-3,0-7	Bristol City Reserves v Odd Down	3-0
Wellington v Glastonbury	1-4	Clevedon Town v Bath City	0-2

Quarter-Finals

Weston-super-Mare v Yeovil Town	1-3	Bristol City Reserves v Bath City	1-3
Glastonbury v Keynsham Town	0-3	Bristol Rovers Reserves v Taunton Town	3-0

Semi-Finals

Keynsham Town v Bristol Rovers Reserves	1-2	Bath City v Yeovil Town	1-0

Final. First Leg *(Thurs 21st April, at Bath City FC)*: Bath City 3, Bristol Rovers Res. 2
Second Leg *(Tues 3rd May, at Bath City FC)*: Bath City 2, Bristol Rovers Reserves 2

OTHER COUNTY FINALS 1993-94

Senior Cup *(at Paulton Rovers FC, Mon 2nd May)*: Bridgwater Town 1, Brislington 0
Sunday Junior Cup: Crown Inn 2, Bridgwater YMCA 1 *(aet)*
Durnford Cup: Bridgwater Sunday League 1, Perry Street League 0

COLBORNE TROPHIES SOMERSET SENIOR LEAGUE (Est. 1890)

President: O H Baker.
Chairman: F R Neal.
Secretary: C Rose, Sutley House,
Pilton, Shepton Mallet BA4 4BL (0749 89767).

Having come to the end of another season, the League now reaches another milestone in it's history. No longer will there be lengthy 'constitution' meetings with a long queue of hopeful Junior clubs seeking a break into the Senior ranks. This May, 16 clubs were represented to fill two positions. In keeping with previous years, the club seeking re-election was successful whilst the vacancy has been filled by Weston & District League side Cleeve West Town who are situated between Weston and Bristol.

Next year will see the expansion of the Pyramid System to Junior Leagues. Moving in the upward direction, Bridgwater Town '84 will compete in the Great Mills League next season, whilst one of Somerset's oldest clubs - Radstock Town - will take their place. One other departure from the

Street FC - Somerset Senior League Division Three champions 1993-94. *Photo - Tim Lancaster.*

Premier Division will be Avon & Somerset Constabulary (due to internal policy), having competed in that Division since 1982.

Portishead, after 20 odd years, became the 36th Club to have it's name engraved on the Premier Division Trophy as Champions. In true championship style they lost just two of their last 16 matches, and at one stage played 630 minutes (seven matches) without conceding a goal.

Their Runners-up, Bridgwater Town had an exceptional season, carrying off the League Cup by 9-8 in penalties after a goal-less 120 minutes against neighbours Clevedon Town Reserves. To round off the season, they re-gained their hold on the County Senior Challenge Cup, defeating Great Mills League Brislington 1-0 in the Final.

Last season's Champions Long Sutton experienced their poorest season as did their neighbours Shepton Mallet and Castle Cary, finishing in the bottom half of the division.

After just one season in Division One, Longwell Green Abbotonians and Weston St John return to the Premier Division, the former rounding off their programme undefeated in their last 13 matches. Winscombe were their own worst enemies; had they won just three of their fifteen drawn matches they would have been amongst the promoted, but had to settle for 6th place. At the other end, Larkhall Athletic Reserves and Frome Town Reserves were left stranded at the bottom.

In Division Two there was a tense finish as the top two, Odd Down and Keynsham Cricketers, met in the final match of the season, but Odd Down's victory saw them go up as champions of the division with the Cricketers and Churchill. These two are inseparable as they moved up from Division Three together last season. The latter had a remarkable run from 4th September to 19th March (20 games) unbeaten. A sad season for Mendip AFC Wells saw them relegated for the second successive season.

Turning to the Third Division, Street - one of the founder members of the League - took over the leadership from Glastonbury Reserves when the two met on Boxing Day, and never looked back, and after two years they gained a place in the higher Division, and will be joined by Clandown, Clutton and Westland United Reserves. But, spare a thought for Glastonbury who held top spot until Christmas and finally missed promotion by one position for the third year running. Don't mention local derbies in Glastonbury. Of their matches with neighbours Wells City, Street and Shepton Mallet they only managed one victory, two draws and three defeats. To rub salt into the wound, they were second highest goalscorers to Street with 101, and jointly with Clandown they conceeded fewer goals - 33.

Luck as well as goals play a part in this great sport. Perhaps those who lost out last season will have their turn in 1994-5.

Les Heal, League Life Member.

PREM. DIV.	P	W	D	L	F	A	PTS
Portishead	34	25	5	4	72	22	80
Bridgwater Town	34	18	10	6	85	38	64
Clevedon T. Res.	34	20	3	11	75	44	63
Burnham United	34	17	6	11	75	59	57
Imperial United	34	17	6	11	61	52	57
Peasedown Athletic	34	16	8	10	88	67	56
Clevedon United	34	15	8	11	68	60	53
Fry Club	34	15	7	12	62	53	52
Avon/Som. Police	34	14	9	11	57	62	51
Westland United	34	13	9	12	63	60	48
Shepton Mallet T.	34	12	8	14	71	59	44
Shirehampton	34	10	14	10	51	50	44
Long Sutton	34	11	8	15	68	80	41
Mangotsfield Res.	34	11	7	16	60	71	40
Brislington Res.	34	12	2	20	52	58	38
Bristol MF Res.	34	10	7	17	56	66	37
Castle Cary	34	5	5	24	40	92	20
Weston-s-M. Res.	34	1	6	27	29	139	*8

* - 1 point deducted

DIV. TWO	P	W	D	L	F	A	PTS
Odd Down A. Res.	34	22	10	2	84	32	76
Keynsham Cricketers	34	22	7	5	84	41	73
Churchill Club '70	34	21	6	7	70	34	69
Timsbury Athletic	34	19	8	7	81	50	65
Watchet Town	34	17	8	9	56	35	59
Blackbrook	34	17	7	10	78	45	58
Backwell Utd Res.	34	15	8	11	61	41	53
Paulton Rvrs Res.	34	14	7	13	63	60	49
Tunley Athletic	34	14	4	16	61	73	46
Long Ashton	34	12	7	15	41	49	43
Cheddar	34	9	11	14	45	65	38
Clevedon Utd Res.	34	9	7	18	39	58	34
Imperial Bristol	34	9	7	18	36	70	34
Welton Rvrs Res.	34	7	12	15	38	53	33
St George E-in-G.	34	8	9	17	36	54	33
Mendip Wells	34	9	7	18	36	70	*33
Wrington-Redhill	34	6	9	19	30	66	27
Weston St J. Res.	34	6	6	22	44	85	24

* - 1 point deducted

DIV. ONE	P	W	D	L	F	A	PTS
Longwell Gn Abbot.	34	20	10	4	78	39	70
Weston St Johns	33	20	7	5	59	38	67
Wells City	34	18	9	7	59	35	63
Bridgwater T. Res.	34	17	11	6	82	38	62
Stockwood Green	34	18	5	11	57	35	59
Winscombe	34	14	15	5	48	29	57
Portishead Res.	34	16	9	9	59	45	57
Nailsea United	34	13	4	17	46	46	43
Hengrove Athletic	34	12	6	16	57	61	42
Keynsham T. Res.	34	12	6	16	54	60	42
Saltford	34	9	14	11	48	53	41
Bishop Sutton Res.	34	11	8	15	44	56	41
Dundry Ath. '82	34	10	7	17	51	81	37
Congresbury	34	9	9	16	49	57	36
Ilminster Town	34	10	5	19	40	61	35
Robinsons	34	7	11	16	43	58	32
Larkhall Ath. Res.	34	8	7	19	50	66	31
Frome Town Res.	33	7	5	21	40	89	*25

* - 1 point deducted

DIV. THREE	P	W	D	L	F	A	PTS
Street	34	25	4	5	106	37	79
Clandown	34	23	6	5	92	33	75
Westland Utd Res.	34	24	4	6	98	40	*76
Clutton	34	22	8	4	78	35	74
Glastonbury Res.	34	22	5	7	101	33	71
Wells City Res.	34	18	7	9	86	45	61
Fry's Club Res.	34	13	9	12	74	57	48
Banwell	34	14	6	14	65	70	48
Yatton Athletic	34	13	7	14	54	73	*45
Temple Cloud	34	12	5	17	57	63	41
Nailsea Town	33	15	5	13	76	83	#41
Nailsea Utd Res.	34	10	7	17	47	69	37
Shepton Mallet Res.	33	10	5	18	64	90	**33
Farleigh Sports	34	8	6	20	54	93	30
Worle	34	7	7	20	55	88	28
Hengrove Ath. Res.	34	6	7	21	57	101	25
Robinsons Res.	34	4	7	23	40	104	*18
Imperial Bris. Res.	34	4	5	25	29	116	*16

* - 1 point deducted # - 9 points deducted

SOMERSET SENIOR LEAGUE PREMIER DIVISION RESULT CHART 1993-94

HOME TEAM	1	2	3	4	5	6	7	8	9	10	11	12	13	14	15	16	17	18
1. Avon & Somerset Constab.	*	4-1	1-0	0-4	2-1	2-1	3-1	3-1	1-1	1-5	2-2	1-2	1-3	3-1	1-0	1-2	2-2	5-1
2. Bridgwater Town '84	0-0	*	2-0	1-1	1-1	1-1	3-1	0-0	6-0	5-1	1-1	3-1	1-1	5-2	1-1	1-0	1-1	10-0
3. Brislington Reserves	4-0	0-1	*	1-2	3-4	3-1	1-2	1-2	1-2	2-0	3-0	2-0	0-4	1-4	0-4	1-1	2-0	2-0
4. Burnham United	4-2	1-7	1-5	*	2-2	4-1	1-2	1-3	2-1	2-2	3-4	0-2	0-2	3-1	2-1	6-0	0-2	8-1
5. Bristol Manor Farm Reserves	0-2	0-8	2-0	0-1	*	3-0	1-3	0-1	2-2	0-3	2-2	6-0	1-3	2-3	2-3	0-0	3-1	7-0
6. Castle Cary	0-1	0-5	5-1	0-0	2-3	*	0-2	1-4	1-0	4-2	1-5	2-2	2-5	1-5	3-1	1-5	1-3	2-2
7. Clevedon Town Reserves	1-1	1-0	1-2	4-2	1-2	4-1	*	6-1	2-1	1-1	5-1	3-2	0-1	5-0	1-2	1-0	1-2	0-2
8. Clevedon United	5-1	2-2	2-1	2-4	3-0	3-1	1-1	*	3-2	0-1	0-0	4-1	0-1	3-1	1-5	1-4	4-1	6-0
9. Fry's Club	4-2	5-1	1-0	1-1	0-0	1-0	1-3	2-2	*	4-1	4-2	2-1	0-2	2-3	0-1	1-1	1-1	5-0
10. Imperial United	0-2	1-2	3-0	0-1	4-0	2-1	2-1	0-0	2-1	*	3-2	3-2	0-2	2-1	1-0	1-1	3-0	3-2
11. Long Sutton	2-3	2-3	1-8	1-3	1-0	5-1	2-3	4-0	1-2	2-1	*	1-4	2-1	4-4	1-1	2-2	4-2	5-1
12. Mangotsfield Utd Reserves	1-1	0-1	2-0	2-3	6-0	0-0	0-3	0-5	0-1	1-3	4-1	*	3-3	2-2	1-6	2-0	0-1	2-2
13. Portishead	1-1	1-0	5-0	1-0	2-0	3-0	2-0	4-0	1-2	0-1	0-1	2-2	*	2-1	1-0	1-1	3-0	3-0
14. Peasedown Athletic	6-2	1-4	1-0	2-2	2-1	2-1	2-0	7-3	3-0	2-2	4-0	1-2	2-3	*	3-2	1-1	0-0	2-0
15. Shepton Mallet Town	1-2	1-2	3-2	1-4	1-2	6-2	1-5	2-2	1-2	1-1	0-4	5-2	1-3	2-2	*	2-1	3-2	1-1
16. Shirehampton	1-0	2-0	0-3	3-2	2-2	3-0	0-3	0-0	3-2	4-1	6-0	2-4	0-1	4-4	0-0	*	0-0	1-1
17. Westland United	2-2	4-2	1-1	1-2	2-1	3-1	2-1	3-0	0-3	4-2	1-1	2-5	0-2	1-5	2-2	4-0	*	7-1
18. Weston-super-Mare Reserves	2-2	1-4	0-1	1-4	0-6	1-2	2-6	0-4	3-6	1-4	0-2	0-2	0-3	2-8	0-10	1-1	1-5	*

SOMERSET SENIOR LEAGUE DIVISION ONE RESULT CHART 1993-94

HOME TEAM	1	2	3	4	5	6	7	8	9	10	11	12	13	14	15	16	17	18
1. Bishop Sutton Reserves	*	3-2	2-1	3-5	3-1	2-2	1-2	1-1	0-0	0-1	2-0	1-3	1-1	0-2	0-1	1-1	1-3	1-1
2. Bridgwater Town Reserves	0-1	*	2-1	2-2	9-1	2-1	5-0	3-1	3-0	1-2	0-0	2-2	1-0	4-0	1-1	2-2	2-2	0-0
3. Congresbury	2-1	1-1	*	0-0	1-3	2-2	0-1	1-2	2-2	0-5	1-3	1-2	3-1	1-1	2-1	3-7	0-1	1-1
4. Dundry Athletic '92	2-3	1-5	3-6	*	3-1	0-3	2-0	1-3	3-2	2-2	1-6	1-0	3-3	4-2	0-3	1-0	1-2	1-2
5. Frome Town Reserves	2-1	0-5	2-2	0-1	*	1-2	1-2	2-0	1-3	1-3	0-0	2-3	2-2	3-1	0-1	2-1	2-4	1-4
6. Hengrove Athletic	1-1	1-1	2-0	1-1	7-2	*	1-2	0-1	5-2	2-3	1-4	0-1	1-0	1-3	0-1	2-3	3-2	2-1
7. Ilminster Town	1-2	1-3	1-3	4-0	1-2	1-2	*	1-1	2-1	2-1	0-1	3-1	2-4	1-1	1-0	1-1	0-1	0-3
8. Keynsham Town Reserves	0-1	6-3	0-1	5-0	6-0	1-3	3-2	*	2-1	1-4	0-2	2-3	4-2	3-3	1-0	1-2	1-1	2-3
9. Larkhall Athletic Reserves	3-2	1-3	2-4	1-0	2-2	4-1	1-0	7-0	*	2-3	3-0	0-1	2-2	2-2	0-1	0-1	0-2	0-0
10. Longwell Green Abbotonians	2-1	0-0	2-2	2-0	4-1	3-1	8-2	0-0	2-2	*	3-2	2-1	3-0	0-0	3-0	2-3	6-0	0-0
11. Nailsea United	2-1	2-3	1-2	3-2	0-1	1-3	0-1	1-2	3-1	1-2	*	0-1	2-0	4-2	1-0	1-3	0-1	0-0
12. Portishead Reserves	4-1	2-2	1-1	5-0	3-1	3-1	2-0	2-1	3-0	1-2	1-1	*	2-3	2-1	3-2	0-1	0-0	1-2
13. Robinsons	1-2	0-4	2-1	1-1	2-2	0-1	3-1	0-0	4-1	3-3	1-0	3-3	*	0-2	0-1	0-0	0-1	1-2
14. Saltford	0-0	0-5	1-2	1-1	5-0	4-3	2-2	3-0	1-2	1-1	2-0	1-1	2-1	*	1-1	2-2	1-0	1-1
15. Stockwood Green	1-2	2-1	3-2	3-1	3-1	6-1	4-1	2-1	4-1	0-1	1-2	3-1	1-0	3-0	*	6-2	0-2	0-0
16. Wells City	1-2	0-1	3-0	5-1	2-0	1-0	1-1	1-0	1-0	2-1	0-2	0-0	0-1	2-0	0-0	*	1-1	3-1
17. Weston St Johns	3-1	0-3	4-0	0-2		1-1	2-1	4-1	2-0	4-1	4-1	5-1	3-1	1-0	3-2	0-4	*	0-0
18. Winscombe	4-0	2-1	2-0	3-5	3-0	1-0	4-0	0-2	4-2	1-1	1-0	0-0	1-1	0-0	0-0	0-1	1-1	*

SOMERSET SENIOR LEAGUE DIVISION TWO RESULT CHART 1993-94

HOME TEAM	1	2	3	4	5	6	7	8	9	10	11	12	13	14	15	16	17	18
1. Blackbrook	*	3-0	0-2	2-0	2-1	7-3	0-0	0-2	3-0	0-2	3-2	1-0	0-4	3-1	3-1	3-1	1-1	2-2
2. Backwell United Reserves	1-2	*	5-0	1-0	1-2	0-2	2-1	4-0	2-2	1-4	1-1	2-1	4-0	3-3	0-0	3-0	1-1	1-1
3. Cheddar	2-0	0-3	*	0-1	0-1	4-0	0-4	0-1	1-1	1-1	0-1	0-0	1-1	3-0	2-5	4-3	4-2	1-1
4. Clevedon United Reserves	1-5	1-6	1-1	*	1-4	2-0	2-2	0-0	4-0	1-1	2-1	0-2	3-0	1-2	0-1	0-0	0-4	2-0
5. Churchill Club '70	0-0	1-0	4-2	5-1	*	0-1	2-3	4-1	5-0	1-4	4-1	3-1	2-0	4-0	1-0	2-1	4-0	2-0
6. Imperial Bristol	0-3	0-2	1-0	2-1	0-0	*	1-3	2-2	1-3	0-2	1-1	0-0	2-2	1-1	0-2	1-4	2-1	3-0
7. Keynsham Cricketers	2-1	3-0	6-1	5-0	2-2	3-0	*	3-3	6-0	1-4	3-2	4-3	2-2	3-1	3-0	2-0	5-0	2-1
8. Long Ashton	3-3	0-0	0-1	2-0	0-4	0-1	0-2	*	0-2	0-5	2-0	1-1	0-2	6-2	0-1	2-4	2-1	0-0
9. Mendip AFC Wells	0-11	3-2	2-2	2-0	1-3	3-0	2-5	0-1	*	1-3	0-2	0-1	1-2	3-2	0-1	1-2	2-0	3-0
10. Odd Down Ath. Reserves	2-1	0-1	2-1	0-0	2-1	2-1	1-2	1-0	3-0	*	2-2	4-0	2-2	4-1	1-0	2-2	3-0	3-0
11. Paulton Rovers Reserves	1-3	0-2	1-3	3-1	2-3	6-0	3-0	2-1	2-2	1-5	*	3-0	1-1	2-0	3-0	1-0	4-2	5-0
12. St George Easton-in-Gordano	1-0	0-1	1-1	2-1	1-1	3-0	1-2	0-2	1-1	3-1	1-1	*	1-2	4-4	0-2	3-1	1-1	1-0
13. Timsbury Athletic	3-2	4-2	8-2	1-3	1-1	3-1	2-0	1-0	2-0	1-1	5-1	5-1	*	2-1	2-2	5-1	5-2	0-3
14. Tunley Athletic	3-2	0-4	5-1	1-0	0-1	1-3	2-0	2-4	4-3	2-4	2-0	4-1	2-1	*	3-2	1-0	3-1	1-2
15. Watchet Town	1-1	1-0	0-0	1-0	4-0	3-1	1-1	0-1	1-2	2-2	7-1	1-0	3-1	2-2	*	1-1	1-0	5-1
16. Welton Rovers Reserves	1-3	0-0	2-3	0-5	0-0	1-1	1-1	0-1	1-1	1-1	1-1	2-0	0-2	2-0	3-0	*	1-0	1-1
17. Weston St John Reserves	2-2	1-2	2-2	2-6	2-0	3-2	1-2	1-0	2-2	1-6	1-3	0-2	3-5	1-3	0-4	2-1	*	4-0
18. Wrington-Redhill	0-6	1-4	0-0	0-0	0-2	2-3	0-1	0-4	4-0	1-1	2-3	2-0	1-4	0-2	0-1	0-0	4-0	*

SOMERSET SENIOR LEAGUE DIVISION THREE RESULT CHART 1993-94

HOME TEAM	1	2	3	4	5	6	7	8	9	10	11	12	13	14	15	16	17	18
1. Banwell	*	0-1	3-1	4-1	3-2	0-3	4-2	1-0	1-2	5-2	5-1	3-1	2-2	2-1	0-5	0-5	2-2	2-2
2. Clandown	3-0	*	1-1	4-0	1-0	2-1	8-0	4-0	6-2	0-0	1-0	3-0	3-0	1-0	3-1	1-3	4-1	4-0
3. Clutton	2-0	3-1	*	4-1	3-1	3-2	4-0	4-0	2-0	4-1	7-1	2-0	1-3	1-0	3-2	1-0	1-1	2-1
4. Farleigh Sports	2-2	2-3	0-3	*	2-1	0-6	4-4	3-2	0-3	3-4	2-2	1-2	1-4	0-1	2-1	0-3	5-2	3-1
5. Frys Club Reserves	4-1	0-1	1-1	3-0	*	3-0	2-2	4-0	3-3	3-0	6-0	1-1	0-2	1-1	2-3	1-1	4-2	1-1
6. Glastonbury Reserves	3-1	2-2	0-0	4-1	3-0	*	2-1	6-0	4-0	7-0	4-0	4-0	0-1	5-1	0-0	0-1	8-0	3-0
7. Hengrove Athletic Reserves	3-3	2-2	2-5	2-3	2-2	1-4	*	3-1	2-4	4-1	2-0	6-0	0-4	1-4	1-6	0-1	1-1	0-3
8. Imperial Bristol Reserves	3-2	1-2	1-7	0-4	1-4	0-3	3-1	*	1-0	3-3	0-0	0-5	0-7	0-4	0-6	3-9	5-1	0-1
9. Nailsea Town	1-3	1-1	2-1	4-1	4-0	3-8	3-4	1-1	*	3-2	2-1		1-2	0-5	4-2	1-3	5-1	3-2
10. Nailsea United Reserves	2-0	4-2	1-1	2-0	1-2	1-2	4-0	0-0	2-6	*	3-0	2-3	0-6	1-0	0-1	0-0	1-1	1-2
11. Robinsons Reserves	2-0	0-11	1-2	1-1	3-5	2-2	2-2	6-0	3-0	0-1	*	5-0	0-2	1-4	1-5	1-1	2-4	0-2
12. Shepton Mallet T. Reserves	2-5	1-4	1-2	3-3	2-3	3-1	5-4	1-0	4-4	0-2	3-1	*	3-3	6-2	1-1	3-4	2-1	2-5
13. Street	3-0	3-2	5-1	5-3	2-1	3-0	2-1	7-0	0-2	2-1	9-1	4-2	*	4-0	0-2	0-1	8-1	0-0
14. Temple Cloud	2-2	1-3	1-1	1-0	2-3	2-4	1-2	2-0	5-0	2-0	4-1	0-4	3-3	*	3-1	0-1	2-1	1-1
15. Wells City Reserves	1-3	2-1	1-1	3-2	2-2	1-1	6-0	4-1	8-2	2-1	1-1	3-0	0-1	2-0	*	6-2	0-0	3-5
16. Westland United Reserves	2-1	2-2	0-1	7-1	2-0	1-3	6-1	6-1	5-0	2-0	7-0	5-1	2-5	3-2	1-0	*	5-0	2-3
17. Worle	1-2	1-2	0-3	2-2	3-2	0-2	1-0	2-2	2-3	1-2	4-1	3-2	1-3	0-2	1-2	0-2	*	11-0
18. Yatton Athletic	1-3	0-3	1-1	0-1	2-7	0-4	3-1	3-0	1-1	2-2	2-0	3-1	2-1	2-1	0-3	2-3	1-3	*

PREMIER DIVISION CLUBS 1994-95

BRIDGWATER TOWN '84 RESERVES (see page 566)

BRISLINGTON RESERVES (see page 566)

BURNHAM UNITED

Chairman: Stuart Taylor
Secretary: Mr A Laurence, 23 Rosewood Close, Burnham-on-Sea TA8 1HG (0278 786264).
Ground: Burnham Road Playing Field, Cassis Close, Highbridge.
Directions: Follow Burnham signs from Highbridge town centre - ground on right of Burnham Road. Highbridge (BR) station served by Taunton-Bristol Temple Meads stopping service. Bus 21 from Taunton.
Colours: All red **Change colours:** All blue.

CLEVEDON TOWN RESERVES (see page 393)

CLEVEDON UNITED

Chairman: Alan Rides.
Secretary: Andy Locker, 8 Runnymead, Clevedon, Avon BS21 5EN (0275 343425).
Ground: Coleridge Vale PF, Coleridge Vale Road, Clevedon.
Directions: M5 jct 20, straight over r'bout, ground through 'Pay & Display' car park opposite supermarket.
Cols: Red, white & black/black/black **Change colours:** Blue/black/black

FRY CLUB

Chairman: P Wilkins.
Secretary: P Hardidge, 26 Berenda Drive, Longwell Green, Bristol BS15 6YX (0272 327153).
Ground: Cadbury Schweppes, Somerdale, Keynsham, Bristol (0272 861235)
Directions: On A4175, outside Keynsham BR station in Somerdale factory complex.
Colours: Red/white/white **Change colours:** Blue/white/white.

IMPERIAL UNITED

Chairman: Chris Holloway.
Secretary: John Harvey, 7 Hencliffe Rd, Stockwood, Bristol BS14 8AP (0275 839711).
Ground: Imperial Athletic Club, West Town Lane, Knowle, Bristol (0272 777210).
Directions: A37 south of Bristol, left into West Town Lane (signed Stockwood and Brislington), ground opposite next mini r'bout. Buses 54 and 57 from Bristol Temple Meads (BR).
Colours: All navy **Change colours:** All white.

LONG SUTTON

Chairman/Secretary: R Sams, Brookside, Crowds Lane, Long Sutton, Langport TA10 9NR (0485 241395).
Ground: Recreation Ground, Long Sutton.
Directions: Ground entrance on south side of A372 about three miles east of Langport. Bus 54, Taunton-Yeovil.
Colours: Red/black/red. **Change colours:** Yellow/black/red.

LONGWELL GREEN ABBOTONIANS

Chairman: D Jones.
Secretary: R G Threader, 6 Little Dowles, Cadbury Heath, Bristol BS15 5AW (0272 670306).
Ground: Community Association, Shellards Rd, Longwell Green.
Directions: From Bristol; A4175 Keynsham to Willsbridge, left up steep hill (Willsbridge Hill), across r'bout, right fork into Shellards Road, ground on right behind Community Centre.
Colours: All royal blue. **Change colours:** White/white/black.

MANGOTSFIELD UNITED RESERVES (see page 563)

PEASEDOWN ATHLETIC

Chairman: Mrs G Young.
Secretary: R E Clark, 33 Hillcrest, Peasedown St John, Bath BA2 8JL (0761 434006).
Ground: Miners Welfare Field, Church Road, Peasedown St John (0761 437319 - Cricket Club).
Directions: On west side of A367 Bath-Radstock road just south of Peasedown St John, near Red Post Inn.
Colours: Blue/white/blue **Change:** Orange/black/black. **Previous Name:** Peasedown Miners Welfare.

PORTISHEAD

Chairman: Martin Hatfield.
Secretary: Terry McKenna, 4 Glebe House, Glebe Rd, Portishead, nr Bristol BS20 9QJ (0275 848648).
Ground: Bristol Road Playing Fields, Portishead (0275 847136).
Directions: M5 jct 19, A369 towards Portishead, left at r'bout, ground on left after right hand bend.
Colours: White/black/red **Change colours:** All blue.

RADSTOCK TOWN

President: Mr D Curtis **Chairman:** Ron Rendall **Vice Chairman:** Dave Gregory
Secretary: Mr Ron Rendall, 32 Huish Court, Writhlington, Radstock, Avon BA3 3LR (0761 435573).
Manager: Nigel Bryant **Asst Manager:** Steve Paget.
Ground: Southfield, Frome Hill, Radstock (0761 435004).
Directions: From Radstock centre take A362 for Frome, up hill and turn right before Fromeway Inn and right again into ground car park. Rail to Bath BR station, then bus.
Seats: 150 **Cover:** 150 **Capacity:** 2,000 **Floodlights:** Yes **Year Formed:** 1895
Cols: Red & black quarters/black/red **Change:** Blue & white halves/blue/blue **Nickname:** Rads.
Midweek Matches: Wednesday **Record Gate:** 2,000 v Yeovil, FA Cup, 1937
Previous Leagues: Somerset Senior/ Wilts County/ Western 04-10 20-59 79-94.
Programme: 16 pages, 20p **Programme Editor:** Secretary
Club Shop: Sells lapel badges, key fobs, non-league programmes, club ties. Contact secretary.
Clubhouse details: Two bars, skittle alley and darts. Open Fri-Sat 7-11pm (2-11pm Sat during season), Sun noon-3 & 7-10.30pm. Matchday tea hut sells hot & cold snacks & drinks.
Captain 93-94: Dennis Mullings **P.O.Y. & Top Scorer 93-94:** John Morgan.
Honours: Somerset Snr Lg 27-28 28-29 76-77 78-79 (Div 1 72-73), Somerset Snr Cup(13 - a record) 1895-96 1905-06 27-28 29-30 31-32 36-37 38-39 59-60 63-64 65-66 73-74 82-83 84-85), Western Lg Div 1 R-up 85-86.

SHEPTON MALLET TOWN

Chairman: F Farran. **Sec.:** K J Hurrell, 3 Buckland Rd, Shepton Mallet BA4 5TQ (0749 344037).
Ground: Playing Fields, Old Wells Rd, West Shepton, Shepton Mallet (07490 344609).
Directions: Into town centre and follow signs for Eye Hospital. Ground behind.
Colours: Black & white **Change colours:** All green **Floodlights:** Yes.

SHIREHAMPTON

Chairman: Michael Wiltshire
Secretary: Keith Hawkins, 7 Windcliffe Crescent, Lawrence Weston, Bristol BS11 0JU (0272 828664).
Ground: Recreation Ground, Penpole Lane, Shirehampton, Bristol (0272 235461).
Directions: M5 jct 18, B4054 into Lower High Street, left into Penpole Lane. Ground half mile on left at top of hill. Half mile from Shirehampton (BR).
Colours: Red & white/red/red **Change colours:** Black & white/black/red.

WELLS CITY

Chairman: D House.
Secretary: S Parfitt, 7 Walnut Tree Close, Wookey Hole Rd, Wells (0749 670657).
Ground: The Athletic Ground, Rowdens Rd, off Glastonbury Rd, Wells (0749 672228).
Directions: Rowdens Road is a right turn off the A39 entering Wells from Glastonbury (the south).
Colours: Navy/white/navy **Change colours:** All white.

WESTLAND UNITED

Chairman: Chris Ham.
Secretary: Chris Ham, 9 Kilve, Dunster Cres., Oldmixon, Weston-super-Mare BS24 9ED (0934 814358).
Ground: Westland Sports Club, Winterstoke Road, Weston-super-Mare (0934 632037).
Directions: As Weston-super-Mare FC (see page 405) then continue up Winterstoke Road - ground quarter mile on right.
Colours: White/blue/white **Change colours:** Red/blue/red.

WESTON St JOHN

Chairman: P Trapani.
Secretary: Bob Flaskett, 12 Kennford Tamar Rd, Worle, Weston-super-Mare BS22 0LE (0934 515260).
Ground: Coleridge Road, Bourneville Estate, Weston-super-Mare (0934 622456).
Directions: As for Weston-super-Mare FC (see page 405) then proceed up Winterstoke Road, right into Byron Road, left into Coleridge Road, ground on left.
Colours: All maroon **Change colours:** All red.

DIVISION ONE CLUBS 1994-95

BISHOP SUTTON RESERVES (see page 566)

BRISTOL MANOR FARM RESERVES (see page 561)

CASTLE CARY

Chairman/Secretary: Mr R Osmond, 6 West Park, Castle Cary BA7 7DB (0963 350104).
Ground: Donald Pither Memorial Field, Ansford Rd, Castle Cary (0963 51538).
Directions: In village follow signs for car park - ground entrance opposite. One mile from Castle Cary station (main line from London Paddington).
Colours: All red. **Change colours:** All blue.

CHURCHILL CLUB '70

Chairman: R Blatherwick.
Secretary: Neil Hickman, Dolberrow, New Road, Churchill, Bristol BS19 5NW (0934 852858).
Ground: Recreation Field, Ladymead Lane, Churchill.
Directions: A38 south from Bristol. Ladymead Lane on right just before Churchill traffic lights.
Colours: Sky/claret. **Change colours:** All royal blue.

CONGRESBURY

Chairman: S Hayett.
Secretary: Dr Chris Sherwin, Flat 3, The Precint, Brinsea Rd, Congresbury, Bristol BS19 5JG (0934 876083).
Ground: Broadstone Playing Fields, Stonewell Lane, Congresbury (0934 832150)
Directions: A38 south from Bristol, take B3133 for Congresbury at Lower Langford. Entering Congresbury turn left immediately before Post Office, bear right, ground at end of narrow lane.
Colours: All white. **Change colours:** Red/black/black.

DUNDRY ATHLETIC

Chairman: Bill Hunt.
Secretary: Steve Saunders, 74 Meadowside Drive, Whitchurch, Bristol BS14 0NS (0275 830085).
Ground: Dundry Playing Fields, Crabtree Lane, Dundry (0272 645536)
Directions: A38 south from Bristol (signed Airport), left for Dundry half mile after motel, ground unmissable in village.

HENGROVE ATHLETIC

Chairman: S Docherty.
Secretary: Robert Watkins, 4 Rowberrow St Giles Estate, Whitchurch, Bristol BS14 0AD (0275 834944).
Ground: Norton Lane, Whitchurch, Bristol (0275 832894).
Directions: A37 south from Bristol, through Whitchurch, right into Norton Lane just after humped-back bridge, ground half mile on left.
Colours: Green/white/green **Change colours:** Blue/black/blue.

ILMINSTER TOWN

Chairman: Len Cole.
Secretary: Colin Williams, 58 Herne Rise, Ilminster TA19 0HJ (0460 54577).
Ground: Recreation Ground, Ilminster (0460 57456)
Directions: In town centre turn into Ditton Street, turn right at petrol station, ground on left.
Colours: Navy & sky/navy/navy **Change colours:** White (black trim)/black/black.

KEYNSHAM CRICKETERS

Chairman: Steven Wakefield.
Secretary: Mrs G Spicer, 123 Queens Rd, Keynsham, Bristol BS18 2NU (0272 867414).
Ground: Manor Road Playing Field, Keynsham, Bristol.
Directions: A4175 into Keynsham, straight over 1st mini-r'bout, left at 2nd, down Bath Hill, over double mini-r'bout and next r'bout into Wells Way, left fork into Manor Road, ground on right.
Colours: Green & yellow **Change colours:** Black & white.

KEYNSHAM TOWN RESERVES (see page 568)

NAILSEA UNITED

Chairman: David Williams.
Secretary: John Hobbs, 4 Kingston Rd, Nailsea, Bristol BS19 2RD (0275 855432).
Ground: Grove Sports Grove, Old Church, Nailsea (0275 856892)
Directions: M5 jct 20, B3130 through Tickenham to Nailsea High Street. Bear right, ground on south side of town clearly signposted Grove Sports Centre. One mile from Nailsea & Backwell (BR).
Cols: Red & black stripes/black/black **Change colours:** All green.

ODD DOWN ATHLETIC RESERVES (see page 563)

PORTISHEAD RESERVES (see page 810)

ROBINSONS

Chairman: David J Webb.
Secretary: David K Palmer, 57 Headley Park Rd, Bristol BS13 7NJ (0272 649251).
Ground: Robinson Athletic Club, St Johns Lane, Bedminster, Bristol (0272 664183)
Directions: From Bristol Temple Meads follow Wells road (A37), right at lights by YMCA, across two mini r'bouts, ground 400 yards on left behing Engineers Arms. Ten minutes walk from Bedminster (BR).
Cols: White & black stripes/black/black **Change colours:** Red or white/black/black.

SALTFORD

Chairman: D Pratt
Secretary: C A Wheeler, 10 Orland Way, Longwell Green, Bristol BS15 6XX (0225 324670).
Ground: Norman Road Playing Fields, Saltford (0225 873725)
Directions: A4 Bristol to Bath. Turn off into Norman Road in Saltford.
Colours: All blue **Change colours:** Red/black/black.

STOCKWOOD GREEN

Chairman: P Beacham.
Secretary: R Llewellin, 9 Warren Gardens, Stockwood, Bristol BS14 8TL (0275 833460).
Ground: Old Knowle Cricket Club, Stockwood Lane, Bristol.
Directions: As Imperial United (page 810) but continue up Sturminster Road. At top of hill turn right, then left into Stockwood Lane. Ground on sharp bend on right.
Colours: All navy **Change colours:** Red & white stripes/red/red.

WESTON-SUPER-MARE RESERVES (see page 405)

WINSCOMBE

Chairman: A Poolman
Secretary: R S Liddiard, 2 Ash Close, Winscombe BS25 1HT (0934 843396).
Ground: Recreation Ground, The Lynch, Winscombe (0934 842720 - Cricket Club).
Directions: A38 south from Bristol, turn right for Winscombe at Sidcot, left at sharp bend, ground at end.
Colours: All royal blue **Change colours:** All red **Floodlights:** Yes.

DIVISION TWO CLUBS 1994-95

BACKWELL UNITED RESERVES (see page 566)

BLACKBROOK

Chairman: B Rowlinson.
Secretary: R D Pepperell, 6 Sherford Terrace, Taunton TA1 3SE (0823 282892).
Ground: Blackbrook Pavillion, Blackbrook Way, Taunton (0823 333435)
Directions: M5 jct 25 and head for Taunton centre, left at 1st lights (Creech Castle Hotel junction), left at sharp right-hand bend into Ilminster Rd and follow signs to Sports Centre. Regular shuttle bus from town centre.
Colours: Green & white. **Change colours:** All blue.

CHEDDAR

Chairman: Steve Chivers
Secretary: Mark Higginbottom, 2 Mewswell Drive, Cheddar BS27 3LL (0934 744102).
Ground: Bowdens Park, Wells Road, Cheddar.
Directions: Ground on south side of A371 on eastern fringe of Cheddar.
Cols: Yellow & black/black/black **Change colours:** All royal blue **Floodlights:** Yes.

CLANDOWN

Chairman: Terry Gillard
Secretary: Rachel Robinson, Alpine House, Farrington Rd, Paulton, Bristol BS18 5LW (0761 416410).
Ground: Thynne Field, Clandown, Radstock (0761 434274)
Directions: Half mile out of Radstock off A367 towards Bath - turn left at top of steep hill.
Cols: Black & white stripes/black/black **Change colours:** All red **Floodlights:** Yes.

CLEVEDON UNITED RESERVES (see page 810)

CLUTTON

Chairman: R D Drury. **Ground:** Warwick Fields, Upper Bristol Road, Clutton
Secretary: S M Elias, 9 Greyfield View, Temple Cloud, Bristol BS18 5DL (0761 453503).
Directions: Ground behind Warwick Arms on right of A37 south from Bristol.
Colours: Blue/white/blue **Change colours:** Orange/white/white.

FROME TOWN RESERVES (see page 562)

IMPERIAL BRISTOL

Chairman: Chris Backwell. **Ground & Directions:** As Imperial United (see page 810)
Secretary: Mike Jones, 41 Cadogan Rd, Hengrove, Bristol BS14 8TF (0272 715743).
Colours: Yellow/blue/white. **Change colours:** All blue.

LARKHALL ATHLETIC RESERVES (see page 569)

LONG ASHTON

Chairman: Angus Bell.
Secretary: Pete Thorne, 8 Coombe Rd, Nailsea, Bristol BS19 2HS (0275 852300).
Ground: Long Ashton Recreation Ground, Keedwell Hill, Long Ashton.
Directions: M5 jct 19, A369 towards Bristol, at r'bout follow B3128 to Long Ashton, left into village, ground right up Keedwell Hill.
Cols: Blue & yellow/blue/blue **Change colours:** Green & white/black/black.

PAULTON ROVERS RESERVES (see page 563)

St GEORGE EASTON-IN-GORDANO

Chairman: Chris Flanagan.
Secretary: Mrs Glenis Jones, 29 Newsome Ave., Pill, Bristol BS20 0DW (0275 372875).
Ground: Court Hay, Easton-in-Gordano.
Directions: M5 jct 19, A369 towards Bristol into Easton-in-Gordano village, left into St Georges Hill which joins Priory Road, ground on left.
Colours: Red/white/red **Change colours:** All white.

STREET

Chairman: D Snook.
Secretary: L Clark, 6 Chichester Rd, Street BA16 0QX (0458 45869)
Ground: Tannery Field, Middlebrooks, Street (0458 45987).
Directions: Near Millfields School.
Colours: Green/white **Change colours:** Blue/white.

TIMSBURY ATHLETIC

Chairman: Jack Hasell.
Secretary: Martyn Sage, 3 Newmans Lane, Timsbury, Bath BA3 1JA (0761 471290).
Ground: Recreation Field, North Road, Timsbury.
Directions: As for Tunley (following page) but continue into Timsbury. Ground at crossroads by Cricket Club.
Colours: Sky/navy/navy **Change colours:** Yellow/black/red.

TUNLEY ATHLETIC

Chairman: R Doel.
Secretary: G Caslake, 84 Critchell Rd, Frome BA11 4HW (0373 467921).
Ground: Tunley Recreation Centre.
Directions: A367 Bath-Radstock road, turn right onto B3155, through Tunley, ground on right.
Cols: Royal & black stripes/black/royal **Change colours:** Green & white or Red & black.

WATCHET TOWN

Chairman: J Perkins.
Secretary: Mike Clausen, 41 Kingsland, Watchet TA23 0UE (0984 631773).
Ground: The Memorial Ground, Doniford Road (0984 631041).
Directions: On coast road, east of town, signposted Playing Fields.
Colours: Red/black/black **Change colours:** Yellow/black/black.

WELTON ROVERS RESERVES (see page 570)

WESTLANDS SPORTS RESERVES (see page 811)

DIVISION THREE CLUBS 1994-95

BANWELL

Chairman: J Gooding.
Secretary: C C Gibbons, 76 Blackthorn Gardens, Worle, Weston-super-Mare, Avon BS22 0SA (0934 512903).
Ground: Riverside Ground, Riverside, Banwell.
Directions: A38 south from Bristol, right onto A368 at Churchill, into Banwell village, right in village centre, left, ground entrance concealed on right just before row of houses heading out of village.
Colours: Red/white/red **Change colours:** Blue & yellow/blue/yellow.

CLEEVE WEST TOWN

Ground: King George V Playing Fields, Cleeve, near Bristol.
Secretary: Mr Paul Turnbull, 3 Crewkerne Close, Nailsea BS19 2FS (0275 858528).
Previous League: Weston-super-Mare & District (pre-1994).

FARLEIGH SPORTS

Chairman: A P Mills.
Secretary: D Griffiths, 149 Newland Rd, Withywood, Bristol BS13 9DT (0272 465196).
Ground: Ironmould Lane Brislington
Directions: On opposite side of lane from Brislington FC (see page 566).
Previous Ground: Farleigh Hospital, Flax Bourton (pre-1993).
Colours: Blue & white/black/black **Change colours:** Green & white.

FRY CLUB RESERVES (see page 810)

GLASTONBURY RESERVES (see page 568)

HENGROVE ATHLETIC RESERVES (see page 811)

IMPERIAL BRISTOL RESERVES (see page 812)

MENDIP WELLS

Chairman: R Padfield.
Secretary: N W Church, 48 Mount Pleasant Ave., Wells BA5 2JQ (0749 674347).
Ground: Old Frome Road, Wells. HQ: Britannia Inn (0749 672033).
Directions: From Wells city centre follow signs to Mendip Hospital. Ground on right immediately after golf course.
Cols: Yellow (blue trim)/blue/blue **Change colours:** Blue & red stripes/black/blue.

NAILSEA TOWN

Chairman: Philip Reed. **Ground:** Fryth Way, Causeway View, Nailsea
Secretary: Colin Garraway, 50 Crows Grove, Bradley Stoke North, Bristol BS12 0DA (0454 201499).
Colours: All white **Change colours:** All blue.

NAILSEA UTD RESERVES, ROBINSONS RESERVES (see page 812)

SHEPTON MALLET RESERVES (see page 810)

TEMPLE CLOUD

Chairman: Peter Bowden.
Secretary: Mr S Coles, 3 Downsway, Paulton, Bristol BS18 5XE (0761 412420)
Ground: Camley Playing Fields, Temple Inn Lane, Temple Cloud.
Directions: A37 south from Bristol, left into Temple Lane at Temple Inn, ground on right.
Cols: Sky & navy diamonds/navy/navy **Change colours:** All yellow.

WELLS CITY RESERVES, WESTON St JOHN RESERVES (see page 811)

WORLE

Secretary: D Brne, 44 Beach Rd, Kewstoke, Weston-super-Mare BS22 9UU (0934 625585).
Ground: Worle Recreation Ground, Station Road, Worle. **Directions:** A370 from Bristol to Worle, ground on right at junction with Station Road.
Cols: Black & white stripes/black/black **Change colours:** Red/black/black.

WRINGTON-REDHILL

Chairman: Timothy Bush.
Secretary: B D Bull, 4 Church Rd, Redhill, Bristol BS18 7SQ (0934 862027).
Ground: Recreation Ground, Silver Street, Wrington. **Directions:** A38 south from Bristol, right towards Wrington at foot of steep hill after airport, ground in Wrington village.
Colours: All yellow **Change colours:** Green/black/black.

YATTON ATHLETIC

Chairman: J Coombes. **Ground:** 'Hangstone', Stowey Road, Yatton.
Secretary: A Coombes, 29 Court Ave., Yatton BS19 4EP (0934 833997).
Colours: All maroon **Change colours:** All sky.

YEOVIL & DISTRICT LEAGUE

FOUNDED: 1903

PREM. DIV.	P	W	D	L	F	A	PTS
Martock United	20	17	0	3	87	23	51
Bishop's Caundle	20	17	3	1	61	24	51
Henstridge	20	14	2	4	93	32	44
Wincanton Town	20	12	1	7	54	45	37
Ilchester	20	7	5	8	41	39	26
Long Sutton Res.	20	8	2	10	30	38	26
Milborne Port	20	6	3	11	41	51	21
Bradford Abbas	20	5	2	13	29	60	17
Stoke	20	4	4	12	39	55	16
Somerton	20	4	3	13	38	77	15
Langport Town	20	3	1	16	21	88	10

DIV. ONE	P	W	D	L	F	A	PTS
Tintinhull	22	19	1	2	78	23	58
Westland Spts Res.	22	18	2	2	102	27	56
Baltonsborough	22	13	2	7	68	37	41
Ash Rovers	22	10	4	8	53	53	34
Bruton Town	22	10	3	9	51	36	33
Sherborne T. Res.	22	11	0	11	41	38	33
Masons Arms	22	9	4	9	42	40	31
Chilthorne Dormer	22	9	4	9	49	64	31
Westland Assoc.	22	9	3	10	48	52	30
St Crispin	22	3	3	16	37	91	12
Milborne Pt Res.	22	3	3	16	22	78	12
Trinity	22	3	1	18	30	79	10

DIV. TWO	P	W	D	L	F	A	PTS
Keinton Mandeville	22	20	1	1	107	36	61
Castle Cary Res.	22	18	2	2	68	27	56
AFC Camel	22	13	3	6	73	41	42
Wincanton Res.	22	12	0	10	63	55	36
Henstridge Res.	22	9	5	8	52	48	32
Templecombe	22	10	2	10	46	45	32
St Crispin Res.	22	8	1	13	46	73	25
Somerton Res.	22	7	2	13	39	66	23
Normalair	22	6	3	13	38	52	21
Odcombe	22	6	2	14	55	84	20
Ilchester Res.	22	5	5	12	31	62	20
Corinthians	22	3	4	15	27	56	13

DIV. THREE	P	W	D	L	F	A	PTS
Martock Utd Res.	20	15	3	2	45	19	48
Street Res.	20	13	3	4	58	18	42
Stoke Res.	20	12	1	7	61	37	37
Charlton Athletic	20	10	4	6	55	41	34
Baltonsboro. Res.	20	10	3	7	41	46	33
Ansford Rovers	20	8	3	9	52	51	27
Tintinhull Res.	20	8	1	11	47	39	25
Milborne Port 'A'	20	6	1	13	32	62	19
Langport T. Res.	20	5	3	12	31	72	18
Yetminster	20	4	5	11	36	48	17
Spartans	20	4	3	13	30	54	15

DIV. FOUR	P	W	D	L	F	A	PTS
Bish. Caund. Res.	24	21	1	2	112	25	64
Kingsbury	24	20	1	3	116	33	61
Wessex	24	15	0	9	75	42	45
Yeovil Rangers	24	13	3	8	78	59	42
Templecombe Res.	24	12	5	7	58	47	41
Bradford Res.	24	11	3	10	70	75	36
Chilthorne Res.	24	10	3	11	70	75	33
Normalair Res.	24	10	3	11	52	65	33
Pen Mill	24	10	0	14	71	80	30
Yetminster Res.	24	8	3	13	58	88	27
Keinton Mand. Res.	24	6	3	15	60	75	21
Yeovil Saints	24	5	2	17	46	94	17
Charlton United	24	1	1	22	29	134	4

DIV. FIVE	P	W	D	L	F	A	PTS
Pitney	22	16	4	2	72	22	52
Montacute	22	15	3	4	75	33	48
Westland Colts	22	13	4	5	76	39	43
Wincanton Colts	22	11	5	6	61	57	38
Pen Mill Res.	22	10	5	7	63	55	35
Corinthians Res.	22	9	5	8	44	43	32
Ansford Rvrs Res.	22	8	5	9	58	71	29
Royal Oak	22	7	6	9	49	35	27
Preston Rangers	22	8	1	13	50	76	25
Barn Lane	22	5	6	11	60	65	21
AFC Camel Res.	22	3	3	16	38	78	12
Odcombe Res.	22	3	1	18	28	80	10

Youth Division Champions:
Under-16s (12): Centaur
Under-15s Div. 1 (7): Galmington
Under-15s Div. 2 (6): Codford Youth
Under-14s Div. 1 (6): Westland
Under-14s Div. 2 (8): Pen Mill 'B'

YEOVIL SUNDAY LEAGUE (Est. 1975)

DIV. ONE	P	W	D	L	F	A	PTS
Sun Inn	20	17	2	1	94	23	53
Royal Oak Rgrs	20	16	0	4	105	35	***45
Bradford Sports	20	13	3	4	77	47	*41
Swan	20	11	2	7	59	57	*35
Nether Compton	20	9	1	10	58	60	28
Westminster	20	9	1	10	56	61	28
Wagtail	20	9	2	9	70	78	**27
FC Kingston	20	7	3	10	61	61	24
Brewers Arms	20	6	2	12	50	65	20
King William	20	3	1	16	48	83	10
Westfield Wdrs	20	1	1	18	38	141	4

* - 1 point deducted

Lower Division Champions:
Div. 2 (12): Bell Inn Yeovil
Div. 3 (8): Hambridge Hammers
Div. 4 (12): Langport

WESTON-s.-MARE SUNDAY L.(Est. 1975)

DIV. ONE	P	W	D	L	F	A	PTS
Slipway Inn	16	12	2	2	85	39	26
Bedford Restaurant	16	10	4	2	60	40	24
The Heron	16	8	1	7	57	50	17
Tropicana	16	8	2	6	46	54	*16
Nicks Bar	16	7	0	9	58	54	14
AMS Sports	16	6	2	7	40	42	14
Madisons	16	4	5	6	46	51	13
Moorland Rebels	16	5	2	9	55	68	12
Walter Lawrence	16	1	2	13	34	83	4

* - 2 points deducted

Lower Division Champions:
Div. 2 (9): Charley Browns.
Div. 3 (8): Kewstoke United

Cup Finals:

KO Cup: Madisons 3, Tropicana 1
Franks Bar Cup: Slipway Inn 8, Madisons 0
Glyn Vaughan Memorial Shield: Charley Browns 3, Weston Cricket Club 2
Keith Seabright Memorial Shield: Farmhouse Royals 3, Weston Crusaders 2

Sporting Awards:

Div. 1: Nicks Bar **Div. 2:** Plough Inn
Div. 3: Weston Crusaders.

Top Scorer (Lge games): Brian Dudley (Weston Cricket Club) 38

Clevedon United, of the Somerset Senior League Premier Division. *Photo - Tim Lancaster.*

Street attack the Clandown goal during the top-of-the table Senior League Division Three clash. Street won 3-2 to clinch the title, but both these former Western League clubs were eventually promoted.
Photo - Tim Lancaster.

Palace Court FC, of the Blackmore Vale Sunday League Divisiom Two. Back Row (L/R): Claire Taylor (Chairperson), Pete Lancaster, Mike Brown, Andy Mitchell, Danny Pardew, Simon Case, Glen Riggs, Mark Case, Anthea Lancaster (Secretary). Front: Tim Lancaster (Manager), Will Pope, Richard Bryant, Andy Dawe (Captain), Kevin Jutson, Jon Cooper, Darren Boulton. *Photo - Mike Floate.*

R B SERVICES MID-SOMERSET LEAGUE (Est. 1950)

PREM. DIV.	P	W	D	L	F	A	PTS
Mells & Vobster	20	19	0	1	72	15	38
Chew Magna	20	13	3	4	61	32	29
Farmborough	20	10	5	5	48	32	25
High Littleton	20	10	4	6	50	37	24
Peasedown MYCOR	20	9	5	6	41	30	23
Belrose	20	10	2	8	50	48	22
Frome Collegians	20	7	6	7	38	27	20
Publow & Pensford	20	4	6	10	33	51	14
Evercreech Rovers	20	5	3	12	34	48	13
Stratton Rovers	20	2	3	15	33	95	7
Stoke Rovers	20	1	3	16	28	73	5

DIV. ONE	P	W	D	L	F	A	PTS
Coleford Athletic	20	17	2	1	90	28	36
Meadow Rangers	20	15	2	3	67	30	32
Dundry Ath. Res.	20	11	4	5	53	36	26
Saltford Res.	20	11	3	6	53	46	25
Mells & Vobs. Res.	20	8	6	6	51	55	22
Clutton Res.	20	8	1	11	38	52	17
Timsbury Ath. Res.	20	5	6	9	40	45	16
Sportshouse	20	5	5	10	50	56	15
Chilcompton	20	6	2	12	36	53	14
Norton Hill	20	3	4	13	35	54	10
Temple Cloud Res.	20	2	3	15	20	78	7

DIV. TWO	P	W	D	L	F	A	PTS
P'down MYCOR Res.	26	18	4	4	78	33	40
Littleton Sports	26	18	3	5	67	34	39
Welton Rovers 'A'	26	15	6	5	81	29	36
Tunley Ath. Res.	26	15	6	5	70	40	36
Mendip Wells Res.	26	11	7	8	68	48	29
Chew Magna Res.	26	12	5	9	60	47	29
Pilton United	26	12	5	9	61	56	29
Clapton	26	11	4	11	58	51	26
Purnells Sports	26	8	8	10	55	64	24
Frome Coll. Res.	26	9	3	14	58	67	21
Evercreech R. Res.	26	6	6	14	50	71	18
Saltford 'A'	26	7	3	16	51	73	17
Farrington Gurney	26	7	3	16	40	83	17
Interhound	26	1	1	24	26	127	3

DIV. THREE	P	W	D	L	F	A	PTS
Waterside	24	21	1	2	106	34	43
Oakhill	24	17	3	4	73	34	37
Farmborough Res.	24	13	3	8	49	42	29
Dundry Ath. 'A'	24	11	6	7	60	41	28
Welton Rovers 'B'	24	11	6	7	49	45	28
Chew Magna 'A'	24	11	5	8	48	41	27
Belrose Res.	24	9	7	8	52	36	25
P'down MYCOR 'A'	24	9	6	9	50	49	24
P'down St John Rvrs	24	6	7	11	46	57	19
Stoke Rovers Res.	24	7	5	12	41	52	19
Chilcompton Res.	24	8	3	13	48	71	19
Welton Arsenal	24	2	3	19	18	64	7
Pilton Utd Res.	24	3	1	20	31	105	7

TAUNTON & DIST. SATURDAY LGE

DIV. ONE	P	W	D	L	F	A	PTS
Sydenham Rangers	20	16	2	2	76	31	34
Wyvern	20	14	1	5	52	24	29
Bishops Lydeard	20	12	1	7	70	38	25
British Cellophane	20	8	7	5	50	40	23
Westonzoyland	20	10	2	8	58	34	22
Priorswood Utd	20	7	7	6	27	31	21
Middlezoy Rovers	20	9	2	9	44	57	20
Hulan United	20	6	8	6	40	29	20
Nether Stowey	20	5	2	13	36	71	12
Highbridge Town	20	3	5	12	28	70	11
Spaxton	20	0	3	17	16	72	3

DIV. TWO	P	W	D	L	F	A	PTS
Victoria Inn	22	19	2	1	84	17	40
Club Rangers	22	14	3	5	59	30	31
Hinkley Point	22	12	4	6	63	47	28
British Rail	22	13	0	9	75	50	26
Priorswood Utd Res.	22	12	2	8	54	49	26
Watchet Town Res.	22	9	4	9	38	44	22
Bish. Lydeard Res.	22	8	3	11	54	64	19
Alcombe Rovers	22	8	2	12	55	55	18
Knight Rangers	22	8	2	12	51	54	18
British Cello. Res.	22	5	4	13	40	66	14
Dulverton Town	22	4	4	14	29	84	12
Norton Fitzwarren	22	3	4	15	29	71	10

DIV. THREE	P	W	D	L	F	A	PTS
Porlock	20	13	2	5	84	35	28
Redgate	20	12	4	4	79	36	28
Staplegrove	20	13	2	5	63	38	28
Taverners	20	10	4	6	61	41	24
Middlezoy R. Res.	20	9	4	7	43	41	22
Rockwell Green	20	7	5	8	54	55	19
Bridgwater T. 'A'	20	7	5	8	49	53	19
Marketeers	20	7	5	8	47	63	19
Avimo Eagles	20	5	5	10	48	62	15
Alcombe Rvrs Res.	20	5	3	12	46	78	13
Williton	20	2	1	17	22	94	5

DIV. FOUR	P	W	D	L	F	A	PTS
Civil Service	22	15	3	4	91	40	33
Hemyock	22	12	8	2	71	38	32
North Petherton	22	14	2	6	76	40	30
Wyvern Res.	22	8	8	6	58	52	24
Tone Vale Hosp.	22	9	5	8	52	54	23
British Rail Res.	22	7	8	7	61	50	22
Wembdon Cricketers	22	8	5	9	47	44	21
Williton Wanderers	22	7	7	8	51	53	21
Staplegrove Res.	22	7	3	12	50	71	17
Crown Dynamos	22	7	2	13	43	71	16
Quantock Pride	22	4	6	12	49	88	14
Highbridge T. Res.	22	4	3	15	49	97	11

DIV. FIVE	P	W	D	L	F	A	PTS
Blackbrook Res.	22	17	3	2	96	16	37
Shepherds Wed.	22	17	0	5	97	31	34
Creech '93	22	14	5	3	88	30	33
Stogursey Greyhnds	22	16	1	5	80	34	33
Haygrove	22	13	3	6	85	62	29
Exmoor Rangers	22	12	2	8	102	68	26
Porlock Res.	22	9	3	10	75	56	21
Brit. Cellophane 'A'	22	7	4	11	47	64	18
Spaxton Res.	22	6	2	14	47	102	14
Linden	22	6	1	15	36	70	13
Sampford Blues	22	1	1	20	19	121	3
Nether Stowey Res.	22	1	1	20	16	134	3

CUP FINALS:

Lge KO Cup: Bishops Lydeard 1, Sydenham Rgrs 0
Seward Mem. Cup: Taverners 3, Blackbrook Res. 1
Rowbarton Charity Cup: Sydenham Rangers 1, Victoria Inn 0
Gardner Security Trophy: Competition abandoned due to the persistent wet weather.

DON BIDGOOD BRIDGWATER & DISTRICT SUNDAY LGE (Est. 1966)

DIV. ONE	P	W	D	L	F	A	PTS
Bridgwater YMCA	16	15	0	1	59	16	30
Blake Old Boys	16	10	2	4	62	30	22
Commercial Inn	16	8	2	6	42	33	18
RO Phoenix	16	8	2	6	30	30	18
Berrow Athletic	16	8	0	8	35	52	16
Mansion House	16	6	3	7	41	45	15
Cavaliers	16	6	1	9	39	39	13
Ashcott	16	4	3	9	32	49	11
Coasters	16	0	1	15	25	70	1

Lower Division Champions:
Div. 2 (11): Tiger Old Boys
Div. 3 (16): Wembdon

Cup Finals:
Bill Brown KO Cup: B'water YMCA 1, Mansion Hse 0
Dave Hobbs League Cup: Bridgwater YMCA 2, Blake Old Boys 1
Danny Markall Mem. Referees Cup: Chilton Wanderers 6, Nether Stowey 0
Tom Bell Trophy: Cavaliers 4, Commercial 2

BLACKMORE VALE SUNDAY LEAGUE

FOUNDED: 1914

DIV. ONE	P	W	D	L	F	A	PTS
Henstridge	16	16	0	0	87	20	32
Templecombe	16	12	1	3	57	38	23
Stour Provost	16	11	0	5	62	34	22
Country Club	16	10	1	5	50	31	21
Child Okeford	16	7	2	7	43	43	16
Sturminster Newton	16	6	1	9	32	43	13
Iwerne Minster	16	2	1	13	29	64	5
Kings Arms	16	2	1	13	19	55	5
Shaston	16	2	1	13	23	79	5

Lower Division Champions:
Div. 2 (14): Half Moon **Div. 3** (13): Sherborne

BEDFORDSHIRE F.A.

Secretary: Peter D Brown,
19 Lambs Close, Dunstable LU5 4QA (0582 668013).

SENIOR CUP 1993-94

Preliminary Round

Ampthill Town v Dunstable	1-2
Bedford Town v Potton United	2-5
Stotfold v Barton Rovers	3-1
Shillington v Toddington Rovers	2-0

First Round

Totternhoe v Kempston Rovers	4-0
Bedford United v Leighton Town	0-2
Wootton Blue Cross v Luton Old Boys	0-3
Stotfold v Shillington	3-0
Brache Sparta v Biggleswade Town	1-0
Potton United v Langford	2-0
61FC (Luton) v Shefford Town *(at Brache Sparta)*	1-2
Dunstable v Arlesey Town	4-1

Quarter-Finals

Brache Sparta v Dunstable	1-2
Stotfold v Totternhoe	2-1*(aet)*
Leighton Town v Shefford Town	1-1,1-0
Luton Old Boys v Potton United	2-2,2-4*(aet)*

Semi-Finals

Stotfold v Dunstable *(at Barton Rovers)*	3-1
Potton United v Leighton Town *(at Langford)*	2-1

Final *(Mon 9th May, at Arlesey Town FC)*: Potton United 2, Stotfold 1

BEDFORD & DISTRICT LEAGUE (Est. 1904)

Secretary: Mr G B Snelson,
19 Bamburgh Drive, Bedford MK41 8JP (0234 344417).

PREM. DIV.	P	W	D	L	F	A	PTS
Dunton	24	20	2	2	97	28	42
Biggleswade United	24	18	4	2	66	18	40
GF Meltis	24	18	2	4	76	30	38
Eaton Socon	24	15	3	6	55	29	33
Wilshamstead	24	14	1	9	65	47	29
Cotton End Utd	24	10	2	12	59	57	22
Clapham & Oakley S.	24	9	4	11	46	48	22
Elstow Abbey	24	8	3	13	43	57	19
Bromham United	24	7	5	12	49	68	19
Arlesey Social	24	5	7	12	39	56	17
Woburn	24	8	0	16	41	69	16
Ickwell & Old Warden	24	4	2	18	34	75	10
Marston Shelton Rvrs	24	2	1	21	32	120	5

Constitution for 94-95: *Bedford Telephones, Biggleswade Utd, Bromham Utd, Caldecote, Clapham & Oakley Sports, Cotton End, Dunton, Eaton Socon, Elstow Abbey, GF Meltis, Henlow Italians, Ickwell & OW, Wilshamstead, Woburn.*

DIV. ONE	P	W	D	L	F	A	PTS
Caldecote	26	19	4	3	96	29	42
Henlow Italians	26	15	6	5	70	28	36
Bedford Telephones	26	16	2	8	79	40	34
Riseley Sports	26	15	3	8	65	36	33
Hunting Athletic	26	11	8	7	56	50	30
Bedford NE Avenue	26	10	7	9	55	70	27
Stevington	26	11	4	11	70	73	26
Campton	26	10	6	10	36	43	26
Brickhill Tigers	26	9	6	11	48	48	24
Wootton United	26	10	3	13	46	62	23
Lidlington Utd SC	26	9	2	15	63	80	20
Moggerhanger	26	7	4	15	35	66	18
Rushden Rangers	26	4	6	16	36	80	14
Ickwell & OW Res.	26	4	3	19	28	78	11

94-95: *Bedford NE Ave., Biggleswade Utd Res., Brickhill Tigers, Campton, Hunting Ath., Kempston Town, Lidlington, Marston Shelton Rvrs, Moggerhanger, Riseley Spts, Sandy Albion, Stevington, White Horse, Wootton Utd.* (continued overleaf)

Caldecote FC - Bedford & District League Division One champions 1993-94. *Photo - Dave West.*

DIV. TWO	P	W	D	L	F	A	PTS
White Horse	26	19	4	3	91	35	42
Biggleswade U. Res.	26	16	7	3	68	29	39
Kempston Town	26	16	6	5	68	41	36
Bedford SA	26	13	5	8	65	48	31
Wilshamstead Res.	26	13	4	9	62	56	30
Henlow	26	13	4	9	44	54	30
USACLI	26	10	8	8	69	54	28
Blunham	26	12	2	12	57	66	26
Ryl Oak Kempston	26	10	4	12	68	60	24
St Cuthberts	26	7	6	13	48	67	20
Renhold United	26	4	7	15	37	69	15
Westoning	26	6	3	17	52	85	15
Pheasant	26	4	6	16	43	68	14
Ampthill Athletic	26	4	6	16	36	76	14

94-95: *Bedford Eagles, Bedford SA, Blunham, Caldecote Res., Henlow, Ickwell & OW Res., Renhold Utd, Rushden Rgrs, St Cuthberts, Sandy Town, The Bell (Queens Park), USACLI, Wilshamstead Res.*

DIV. THREE	P	W	D	L	F	A	PTS
The Bell (Queens Pk)	24	17	4	3	78	36	38
Caldecote Res.	24	14	7	3	63	38	35
Sandy Town	24	10	8	6	62	34	28
Tempsford	24	12	4	8	53	52	28
Bow Brickhill	24	11	5	8	77	49	27
Bromham Utd Res.	24	9	8	7	60	62	26
Gt Barford (1988)	24	11	3	10	57	42	25
Clapham & Oak. Res.	24	10	4	10	69	58	24
Potton Town	24	10	4	10	47	43	24
Corinthians	24	7	5	11	40	46	20
Eaton Socon Res.	24	5	5	14	37	62	15
Biggleswade T. 'A'	24	6	3	15	40	68	15
Marston Shelton Res	24	3	1	20	36	129	7

94-95: *Ampthill Ath., Biggleswade T. 'A', Bromham Utd Res., Clapham & Oakley Res., Clifton, Corinthians, Cranfield Village, Duke Inn Spts, Eaton Socon Res., Great Barford, Pheasant, Potton Town, Sandy Albion Res., Westoning.*

DIV. FOUR	P	W	D	L	F	A	PTS
Clifton	26	19	6	1	78	26	44
Duke Inn Spts	26	20	3	3	92	22	43
Cranfield Village	26	18	5	3	82	25	41
Hunting Ath. Res.	26	13	4	9	59	41	30
Westoning Res.	26	12	5	9	64	54	29
Dunton Res.	26	12	4	10	59	57	28
Elstow Abbey Res.	26	11	5	10	76	66	27
Kempston Athletic	26	11	3	12	52	48	25
Renhold Utd Res.	26	11	3	12	63	71	25
Sandy Town Res.	26	8	7	11	44	54	23
Campton Res.	26	6	7	13	35	66	19
Roxton	26	5	5	16	45	83	15
Bedford Albion	26	3	2	21	37	107	8
Lidlington U. Res.	26	1	5	20	29	95	7

94-95: *Biggleswade Utd 'A', Campton Res., Dunton Res., Elstow Abbey Res., Haynes, Hunting Ath. Res., Kempston Ath., Kempston T. Res., Marston Shelton Res., North Park Rgrs, Sandy T. Res., Turvey, Wootton Utd Res.*

DIV. FIVE	P	W	D	L	F	A	PTS
Haynes	26	21	4	1	92	25	46
Wootton Utd Res.	26	20	3	3	78	25	43
Henlow Ital. Res.	26	18	4	4	76	37	40
Turvey	26	14	4	8	73	41	32
Kempston T. Res.	26	11	7	8	65	45	29
Golden Lion	26	11	5	10	52	46	27
Potton Town Res.	26	11	3	12	73	73	25
Woburn Res.	26	11	1	14	56	64	23
Cople Sports	26	9	4	13	39	57	22
Bow Brickhill Res.	26	6	6	14	41	65	18
Moggerhanger Res.	26	5	7	14	37	73	17
Brickhill Utd	26	8	1	17	37	84	17
Rushden Rgrs Res.	26	6	4	16	39	67	16
Black Horse Wootton	26	4	1	21	35	89	9

94-95: *Bedford Albion, Black Horse Wootton, Blunham Res., Brickhill Utd, Cople Sports, Golden Lion, Lidlington Utd SC Res., Moggerhanger Res., Olympus Sports, Potton Town Res., Rushden Rgrs, Sandy Town 'A', Woburn Res.*

BEDFORD & DIST. LGE CUP FINALS:

Britannia Cup: Biggleswade United 4, GF Meltis 0
Aubrey Tingley Memorial Cup: Bow Brickhill 3, White Horse 1
Diamond Jubilee Cup: Clifton 3, Cranfield Village 1 *(aet)*

MICHAEL R PETERS BEDFORD & DIST. SUNDAY LGE

FOUNDED: 1962

Craddock Plastic Prem. Div.

	P	W	D	L	F	A	PTS
Queensmen	22	15	4	3	68	28	34
Meltis	22	17	0	5	77	39	34
B'ford Young Indians	22	14	6	2	56	23	34
B'ford West Indians	22	14	4	4	68	32	32
Griffin	22	11	4	7	53	49	26
Fox & Duck Sports	22	8	5	9	33	48	21
Biggleswade Liberal	22	8	4	10	35	33	20
Gamlingay Eagles	22	7	4	11	36	46	18
Gamlingay OB	22	6	4	12	34	56	16
Ryl Oak (Caldecote)	22	4	5	13	43	52	13
Carlton/Pavenham U.	22	3	2	17	28	74	8
Clapham Groomsmen	22	4	0	18	26	76	8

Lower Division Champions:
Bedford Bed Centre D1 (13): Cranfield Utd (Sunday)
Keyline D2 (13): Bluebell Casuals
Lee Roofing D3 (11): Saracens Head
T R Metals D4 (13): Oakley Rangers
Modplan D5 (12): The Pheasant (Sunday)
Bedford Mobile Communication D6: The Red Lion (Wilstead)

CHEF & BREWER LUTON SUNDAY LEAGUE

FOUNDED: 1987

DIV. ONE	P	W	D	L	F	A	PTS
Purley Tavern	18	14	1	3	79	28	43
Lea Spts Stopsley	18	13	3	2	68	23	42
Dunst. First & Last	18	10	1	7	50	34	31
AFC Barn Owl B	18	9	2	7	68	53	29
Hightown	18	8	4	6	73	45	28
First & Last Utd	18	7	2	9	54	45	23
Meds	18	7	1	10	52	57	22
Luton Dukes	18	7	1	10	36	41	22
AFC Oakley Res.	18	4	2	12	34	110	14
Bridge Tavern	18	2	1	13	30	108	7

Lower Division Champion:
Div. 2 (9): AMC United

Cup Finals:
T T Trophies League Cup: One Nation 3, AMC Utd 2
Luther Blissett Invitation Cup: Hightown 1, Lea Sports Stopsley Reserves 0
Steve Smith Memorial Trophy: One Nation 2, AFC Barn Owl B 1

BERKS & BUCKS F.A.

Established: 1878

Secretary: W J Gosling,
15a London Street, Faringdon, Oxon SN7 8AG (0367 242099).

SENIOR CUP 1993-94

First Qualifying Round *(void for season 1993-94)*

Second Qualifying Round

Burnham v Windsor & Eton	2-0	Newport Pagnell Town v Flackwell Heath	4-3
Buckingham Town v Newbury Town	2-0	Beaconsfield United *(w/o)* Milton Keynes Borough *(scr)*	
Thatcham Town v Kintbury Rangers	9-0	Chalfont St Peter v Maidenhead United	1-0

First Round

Hungerford Town v Bracknell Town	4-3	Beaconsfield v Chesham Utd *(at Chesham Utd)*	0-8
Reading v Abingdon Town	0-4	Marlow v Slough Town	1-0*(aet)*
Thatcham Town v Wycombe Wanderers	1-4	Aylesbury United v Buckingham Town	1-0
Newport Pagnell Town v Wokingham Town	3-0	Chalfont St Peter v Burnham	3-3,1-0

Quarter-Finals

Chalfont St Peter v Chesham United	0-2	Hungerford Town v Newport Pagnell Town	2-0
Abingdon Town v Aylesbury United	0-0,0-1	Wycombe Wanderers v Marlow	1-3

Semi-Finals

Marlow v Aylesbury United	1-1,5-0	Chesham United v Hungerford Town	2-0

Final *(at Reading FC, Monday 2nd May)*: Marlow 1, Chesham United 0

OTHER COUNTY FINALS 1993-94

Senior Trophy *(at Marlow FC, Sat 16th April)*: Eton Wick 6, Abingdon United 3 *(aet)*
Intermediate Cup: *won by Mortimer FC.*

Mortimer FC - Berks & Bucks Intermediate Cup winners 1993-94. *Photo - Peter Toft.*

CHARRINGTON CHILTONIAN LEAGUE

Chairman: Mr D Newell
Treasurer: Mr R G Woolman
Hon. Secretary: Mr R A Lipscombe,
31 Broughton Avenue, Aylesbury,
Bucks HP20 1NN (0296 394781).

LONG-TIME LEADERS CAUGHT ON THE LINE

A very successful campaign culminated with Holmer Green winning their last game to take the Premier Division title after Slough YCOB had lead the table for most of the season. Slough YCOB finished as runners-up with Stocklake in third place. Slough Irish Society, in their first season, won the First Division championship, with Chalfont Wasps as runners-up followed in third place by Slough Heating.

In the Reserve Divisions, winners of Division One were Slough YCOB followed by Reading Town and Iver. In Division Two, the winners were Wallingford United followed by Stokenchurch in runners-up position and Chinnor in third place.

This year's League Cup final was played at Chalfont St Peter between Finchampstead and Martin Baker. This season Finchampstead gained success with a comfortable win. In the Reserve League Cup final, played at Chalfont in the morning, Slough YCOB comfortably beat Iver.

In outside cup competitions the League had success in the Wycombe Senior Cup, Slough Town Senior Cup, Slough Town Junior Cup and the Marsworth Reserve Cup, competitions won respectively by Holmer Green, Slough Irish, Iver Reserves and Stocklake Reserves.

To give Division One clubs extra games, a Subsidiary Cup was arranged, and Wallingford United beat Iver in the final at Prestwood.

During the season, the League have had discussions with the Parasol Combined Counties with regards to a possible link-up. The meeting, on 9th June 1994, indicated that the Sub Committee should continue with more detailed discussions.

Let's hope the next twelve months see the League continue to develop, and good luck to all clubs, new and old.

R A Lipscombe, League Secretary

Holmer Green - League champions 1993-94. *Photo - Gavin Ellis-Neville.*

PREM. DIV.	P	W	D	L	F	A	PTS
Holmer Green	26	17	7	2	65	20	58
Slough YCOB	26	18	3	5	67	29	57
Stocklake	26	14	3	9	46	31	45
Binfield	26	13	5	8	45	34	44
Finchampstead	26	13	4	9	46	38	43
Wooburn Athletic	26	12	6	8	53	53	42
Brill United	26	11	4	11	52	43	37
Reading Town	26	10	5	11	50	64	35
Henley Town	26	9	6	11	47	58	33
Martin Baker Spts	26	9	5	12	42	41	32
Wraysbury	26	7	10	9	44	55	31
Broadmoor Staff	26	6	4	16	47	69	22
Prestwood	26	6	4	16	30	56	22
Penn & Tylers Gn	26	1	6	19	21	64	9

RES. DIV. ONE	P	W	D	L	F	A	PTS
Slough YCOB Res.	24	17	4	3	90	37	55
Reading T. Res.	23	13	8	2	63	28	47
Martin Baker Res.	24	14	4	6	72	47	46
Iver Res.	23	14	3	6	80	39	45
Finchampstead Res.	24	13	6	5	68	37	45
Holmer Green Res.	24	10	5	9	65	48	35
Wooburn Ath. Res.	24	8	6	10	64	78	30
Binfield Res.	24	7	4	13	43	74	25
Drayton Wdrs Res.	24	7	4	13	39	73	25
Prestwood Res.	24	7	1	16	42	82	22
Penn & TG Res.	24	7	0	17	40	64	21
Stocklake Res.	24	5	6	13	30	55	21
Henley Town Res.	24	6	3	15	44	78	21

DIV. ONE	P	W	D	L	F	A	PTS
Slough Irish Soc.	20	16	1	3	68	24	49
Chalfont Wasps	20	14	2	4	67	32	44
Slough Heating	20	10	3	7	47	32	33
Denham United	20	10	3	7	42	41	33
Vansittart Wdrs	20	9	4	7	53	26	31
Drayton Wanderers	20	8	4	8	39	28	28
Iver	20	7	4	9	48	47	25
Wallingford Utd	20	7	4	9	41	46	25
Stokenchurch	20	8	1	11	40	47	25
Chinnor	20	5	6	9	42	42	21
Hazells	20	0	0	20	7	129	0

RES. DIV. TWO	P	W	D	L	F	A	PTS
Wallingford U. Res.	18	10	2	6	53	29	32
Stokenchurch Res.	18	10	2	6	31	25	32
Slough Heating Res.	18	8	4	6	45	42	28
Slough Irish Res.	18	8	3	7	54	40	27
Vansittart Res.	18	9	0	9	39	37	27
Chalfont Wasps Res.	17	8	3	6	33	35	27
Chinnor Res.	17	8	2	7	33	34	26
Broadmoor S. Res.	18	7	4	7	46	43	25
Brill Utd Res.	18	5	5	8	36	50	20
Denham Utd Res.	18	2	3	13	24	59	9

PREMIER DIVISION RESULT CHART 1993-94

HOME TEAM	1	2	3	4	5	6	7	8	9	10	11	12	13	14
1. Binfield	*	2-2	4-1	3-0	1-2	0-0	2-1	2-1	1-0	3-1	0-2	2-0	2-2	1-3
2. Brill United	8-0	*	3-1	0-1	6-2	2-2	3-2	1-0	1-3	1-2	1-2	1-0	2-5	2-2
3. Broadmoor Staff	0-1	1-2	*	2-1	2-1	1-7	1-2	2-3	5-1	10-4	2-5	3-1	0-1	3-3
4. Finchampstead	1-3	4-1	1-0	*	0-1	2-2	0-4	4-0	4-1	3-1	1-4	3-1	2-0	1-3
5. Henley Town	1-4	3-2	0-0	2-1	*	0-1	1-1	3-0	0-2	4-2	3-5	3-1	2-2	2-2
6. Holmer Green	1-0	2-0	6-0	2-3	2-0	*	2-0	3-1	1-1	0-1	1-1	1-0	3-0	2-2
7. Martin Maker Sports	0-0	1-3	5-1	1-1	5-1	1-3	*	2-0	2-0	5-2	0-4	1-2	2-2	1-3
8. Penn & Tylers Green	1-2	1-3	0-0	1-1	4-4	0-8	1-2	*	1-1	1-2	1-3	2-3	1-2	0-0
9. Prestwood	0-4	0-4	0-2	1-1	3-3	1-2	1-0	2-0	*	2-0	0-1	3-4	1-3	0-1
10. Reading Town	2-2	0-0	4-4	1-2	1-3	3-3	2-1	4-1	3-2	*	3-2	W-L	1-1	5-0
11. Slough Yth Club OB	2-0	4-1	3-1	0-1	2-0	0-2	4-0	5-0	5-0	3-0	*	2-3	3-2	3-0
12. Stocklake	1-0	1-0	3-0	0-1	4-1	0-2	0-0	2-0	3-0	3-1	1-1	*	5-1	4-1
13. Wooburn Athletic	2-1	2-1	3-2	4-3	2-1	0-5	1-3	2-0	3-2	3-4	5-0	1-3	*	2-2
14. Wraysbury	0-5	0-2	5-3	0-4	3-4	1-2	1-0	1-1	2-3	5-1	1-1	1-1	2-2	*

DIV. ONE RESULTS	1	2	3	4	5	6	7	8	9	10	11
1. Chalfont Wasps	*	4-2	2-3	2-0	9-1	4-3	2-2	0-1	2-0	3-1	3-1
2. Chinnor	1-3	*	2-2	1-0	9-1	0-0	3-3	2-3	2-3	0-0	3-0
3. Denham United	1-0	3-2	*	2-1	7-1	2-4	0-2	2-2	0-4	3-0	1-2
4. Drayton Wanderers	3-4	3-1	0-0	*	8-0	1-1	1-0	2-4	1-0	0-2	3-3
5. Hazells	0-10	1-3	1-6	0-5	*	L-W	0-7	0-6	0-5	0-8	0-5
6. Iver	2-3	4-1	10-3	1-2	7-2	*	0-5	0-2	6-2	2-2	3-3
7. Slough Heating	2-0	2-2	1-4	0-4	5-0	2-0	*	0-2	3-1	0-1	0-3
8. Slough Irish Society	2-6	5-2	0-1	4-2	12-0	6-0	2-4	*	8-0	1-0	2-1
9. Stokenchurch	3-4	1-1	2-0	1-0	7-0	1-3	2-3	0-2	*	0-1	3-1
10. Vansittart Wanderers	3-5	1-3	0-1	1-1	6-0	4-1	5-1	0-1	9-1	*	6-0
11. Wallingford United	1-1	3-2	5-1	1-2	4-0	2-1	0-5	2-3	1-4	3-3	*

RES. DIV. ONE RESULTS	1	2	3	4	5	6	7	8	9	10	11	12	13
1. Binfield Res.	*	1-0	2-2	2-1	4-3	1-4	1-3	2-1	2-4	1-7	0-2	1-1	1-1
2. Drayton Wdrs Res.	1-0	*	0-7	2-1	2-2	3-5	2-2	2-0	3-2	2-2	0-2	4-1	6-2
3. Finchampstead Res.	5-0	3-1	*	5-0	1-3	1-4	3-0	3-0	6-0	2-2	1-1	4-2	3-3
4. Henley Town Res.	3-1	2-1	1-3	*	3-3	2-1	3-5	4-6	2-4	1-1	2-3	4-2	3-3
5. Holmer Green Res.	8-2	10-4	0-1	4-0	*	4-3	2-2	2-0	5-0	4-2	1-4	6-1	0-0
6. Iver Res.	6-1	4-0	4-1	5-0	3-1	*	1-2	8-1	3-0		6-3	6-0	4-5
7. Martin Baker Res.	5-2	3-0	3-3	4-0	0-4	1-3	*	4-1	6-1	3-4	2-1	1-0	11-3
8. Penn & TG Res.	0-1	6-0	1-4	5-3	2-1	0-2	0-3	*	2-1	1-3	0-2	3-1	2-4
9. Prestwood Res.	0-13	5-1	1-3	3-1	3-1	4-1	3-3	0-3	*	1-5	1-3	2-3	3-4
10. Reading Town Res.	2-0	4-0	2-1	11-0	1-0	1-1	3-1	4-1	1-3	*	2-2	1-1	W-L
11. Slough YCOB Res.	12-1	7-2	6-4	2-0	7-0	3-3	2-0	5-2	W-L	1-1	*	5-1	12-3
12. Stocklake Res.	0-1	1-1	0-0	0-2	1-1	2-0	2-3	2-1	1-0	2-2	3-1	*	1-3
13. Wooburn Athletic Res.	3-3	1-2	1-2	2-6	2-0	3-3	3-5	3-2	10-1	0-2	2-4	3-2	*

RES. DIV. TWO RESULTS	1	2	3	4	5	6	7	8	9	10
1. Brill United Res.	*	4-4	5-4	2-1	2-0	1-1	3-5	0-0	5-3	2-7
2. Broadmoor Staff Res.	1-1	*	3-5	0-1	3-0	4-3	3-5	3-0	4-1	2-0
3. Chalfont Wasps Res.	3-1	2-2	*	0-3	2-2	2-2	0-7	3-0	0-1	1-0
4. Chinnor Res.	5-1	2-5		*	6-2	1-3	0-0	0-0	3-2	2-1
5. Denham United Reserves	2-2	0-5	0-4	4-1	*	2-2	4-1	1-3	1-3	1-2
6. Slough Heating Reserves	1-3	5-1	6-0	1-3	5-1	*	0-7	3-1	3-1	5-2
7. Slough Irish Society Res.	4-3	5-2	0-2	0-3	6-2	4-4	*	2-3	0-2	4-3
8. Stokenchurch Reserves	1-0	4-2	0-2	4-0	4-1	0-1	W-L	*	3-1	1-3
9. Vansittart Wdrs Reserves	4-1	3-0	2-3	4-2	2-1	3-0	4-2	0-3	*	2-3
10. Wallingford Utd Reserves	4-0	2-2	1-0	5-0	6-0	6-0	2-2	3-4	3-1	*

LEAGUE CUP

First Round

Henley Town v Chalfont Wasps	2-1	Iver v Wooburn Athletic	4-2
Brill United v Binfield	1-1,0-1	Drayton Wanderers v Slough Irish Society	2-3
Finchampsted v Denham United	4-2	Slough Youth Club Old Boys v Wraysbury	3-1
Stocklake v Wallingford Wanderers	4-2	Holmer Green v Chinnor	5-1
Prestwood v Stokenchurch	5-0		

Second Round

Henley Town v Iver	7-2	Binfield v Slough Irish Society	2-1*(aet)*
Finchampstead v Slough YC Old Boys	3-2	Vansittart Wanderers v Stocklake	1-3
Slough Heating v Broadmoor Staff	0-2	Penn & Tylers Green v Martin Baker Sports	1-2
Holmer Green v Prestwood	1-0	Reading Town *(bye)*	

Quarter-Finals

Henley Town v Binfield	0-1	Reading Town v Finchampstead	0-2
Stocklake v Broadmoor Staff	3-0	Martin Baker Sports v Holmer Green	2-2,2-1

Semi-Finals

Binfield v Finchampstead *(at Broadmoor)*	0-1	Stocklake v Martin Baker Spts *(at Prestwood)*	0-1

Final *(at Chalfont St Peter FC)*: Finchampstead 3, Martin Baker Sports & Social 0

Martin Baker's M Nevin (No.8), and grounded goalkeeper J Mason, are unable to prevent Holmer Green equalising during the League Cup quarter-final on 26th March. However, their side recorded a 2-1 away win in the replay.
Photo - Gavin Ellis-Neville.

RESERVES CUP

First Round

Martin Baker Res. v Chinnor Res.	4-0	Finchampstead Res. v Holmer Green Res.	2-1
Binfield Res. v Slough YCOB Res.	4-5	Henley T. Res. v Slough Heating Res.	3-1
Broadmoor Staff Res. v Wallingford Res.	3-1*(aet)*	Stokenchurch Res. v Drayton Wdrs Res.	3-4*(aet)*
Vansittart Wdrs Res. v Slough Irish Res.	1-9		

Second Round

Martin Baker Res. v Finchampstead Res.	3-2	Reading Town Res. v Slough YCOB Res.	2-3
Wooburn Ath. Res. v Denham Utd Res.	8-2	Prestwood Res. v Slough Heating Res.	4-2
Chalfont Wasps Res. v Broadmoor S. Res.	1-1,2-4	Iver Res. v Penn & Tylers Green Res.	1-0
Drayton Wdrs Res. v Slough Irish Res.	2-0	Stocklake Res. *(bye)*	

Quarter-Finals

Martin Baker Res. v Slough YCOB Res.	0-2	Wooburn Ath. Res. v Prestwood Res.	6-5*(aet)*
Stocklake Res. v Broadmoor Staff Res.	0-1	Iver Res. v Drayton Wanderers Res.	0-0,4-3

Semi-Finals

Slough YCOB v Wooburn *(at Penn & Tylers)*	4-2	Broadmoor Res. v Iver Res. *(at Chalfont Wasps)*	2-3

Final *(at Chalfont St Peter FC)*: Slough Youth Club Old Boys Reserves 2, Iver Reserves 1.

Reserve Division One Constitution 1994-95: Binfield Reserves, Drayton Wanderers Reserves, Finchampstead Reserves, Holmer Green Reserves, Iver Reserves, Martin Baker Sports Reserves, Penn & Tylers Green Reserves, Prestwood Reserves, Reading Town Reserves, Stokenchurch Reserves, Wallingford United Reserves, Wooburn Athletic Reserves.

Reserve Division Two Constitution 1994-95: Brill United Reserves, Broadmoor Social Reserves, Chalfont Wasps Reserves, Denham United Reserves, Henley Town Reserves, Old Paludians Reserves, Slough Heating Reserves, Stocklake Reserves, Vansittart Wanderers Reserves, Wraysbury Reserves.

PREMIER DIVISION CLUBS 1994-95

BINFIELD

Chairman: Paul Hammerstone **Manager:** TBA
Secretary: Paul Hammerstone, 3 Knox Green, Binfield, Berks RG12 5HZ (0344 427179).
Ground: Stubbs Hill, Binfield, Berks. **Directions:** From A329 (Bracknell-Wokingham) by Shoulder of Mutton PH, take St Mark's Rd into village which leads into Terrace Rd South and North then at t-junction with Church Lane by All Saints Church, turn right & Stubbs Hill 1st left.
Seats: Yes **Cover:** Yes **Programme:** Sometimes **Founded:** 1892.
Colours: All red **Change colours:** All blue.
Local Press: Bracknell News/ Times. **Sponsors:** Churchill Financial Consultants.
Prev. League: Reading & Dist. (pre-1987). **Clubhouse:** Kitchen, bar, lounge, changing rooms, showers.
Hons: Chilt. Lg R-up 91-92 (Div 1 89-90, Lg Cup R-up 89-90), Rdng Snr Cup R-up 91-92, Gt Western Comb. 46-47.

BRILL UNITED

Chairman: Mr S Shipperley **Manager:** TBA
Secretary: Mr D Nappin, 68 Windmill Str., Brill, Aylesbury, Berks HP18 9TJ (0844 237292).
Ground: Brill Recreation Ground, Church Street, Brill, Aylesbury, Bucks (0844 237388).
Directions: Church Street is immediately behind Red Lion pub in village centre.
Seats: No **Cover:** No **Sponsors:** Sun Inn, Brill **Founded:** 1890.
Cols: Black & white stripes/black/black **Change colours:** All red. **Programme:** No
Prev. Leagues: Oxon Snr/ Lord Jersey. **Clubhouse:** Bar, on ground.
Hons: Chilt. Lg Cup 86-87 (Div 1 R-up 90-91) **Local Press:** Oxford Mail, Bucks Herald, Thame Gazette.

BROADMOOR SOCIAL

Chairman: Mr J W Sheppard **Manager:** Mr P Long.
Secretary: Mr M A Roberts, 14 Hone Hill, Sandhurst, Camberley, Surrey (0252 879513).
Ground: Cricket Field Grove, Broadmoor Est., Crowthorne, Berks (0344 772612). **Founded:** 1896.
Directions: Off M4 at A329(M) for Bracknell, follow signs to Crowthorne, first left after r'bout, Brookers Garage, ground on right at top of hill
Seats: No **Cover:** Yes **Programme:** Yes
Colours: Red/white/white. **Change colours:** Green/black.
Local Press: Reading Evening Post, Reading Chronicle, Crowthorne/ Wokingham News.
Previous League: Reading Senior. **Previous Name:** Broadmoor Staff (pre-1994)
Clubhouse: Broadmoor Staff Club. **Hons:** Chiltonian Lg Div 1 92-93.

CHALFONT WASPS

Chairman: T J Hooker **Manager:** TBA
Secretary: S Paget, 29 Lower Rd, Chalfont St Peter, Bucks SL9 9AL (0753 885604).
Ground: Playing Fields, Bowstridge Lane, Chalfont St Giles HP8 4DF (0494 875050).
Directions: Turn off A413 (Aylesbury-Uxbridge), thru village, first left into Bowstridge Lane after shops, quarter mile up lane turn right into Crossley by small green - ground directly ahead thru gates.
Seats: No **Cover:** Yes **Programme:** No **Clubhouse:** Yes **Founded:** 1922.
Colours: Amber & black **Change colours:** Red/white.
Prev. League: Wycombe & District **Local Press:** Bucks Free Press, Bucks Examiner.
Sponsors: TDK Motor Company. **Honours:** Chiltonian Lg Div 1 R-up 93-94.

FINCHAMPSTEAD

Chairman: Mr Mike Husk **Manager:** Mr Mick Shaw.
Secretary: Mr R Bradley, 37 Alpha Rd, Chobham, Surrey GU24 8NE (0276 855367).
Ground: Memorial Ground, Finchampstead (0734 732890). **Directions:** From Wokingham on A321, right onto B3016 to Greyhound pub, right onto B3348, ground 200yds on right.
Seats: No **Cover:** No **Programme:** Yes **Founded:** 1952.
Prev. League: Reading & Dist. **Clubhouse:** Club bar, sports bar, changing facilities.
Colours: Blue & white stripes/blue **Change colours:** All red.
Local Press: Wokingham Times/ Wokingham News/ Reading Evening Post.
Hons: Chiltonian Lg 87-88 (R-up 92-93, Lg Cup 93-94 (R-up 88-89 92-93)).

HENLEY TOWN

Chairman: Mr A R Bryan **Manager:** TBA
Secretary: Mr A Kingston, 50 Birdhill Ave., Reading, Berks RG2 7JU.
Ground: The Triangle Ground, Mill Lane, Henley-on-Thames, Oxon (0491 576463).
Directions: Leave Henley town centre on Reading Road (A4155), Mill Lane 1 mile on left before garage with car wash on corner - turn right into car park after 200yds. 10 mins walk from BR station.
Seats: No **Cover:** No **Prog.:** 25p (Editor: Tony Kingston) **Founded:** 1871.
Colours: White/black/black **Change colours:** Blue & red stripes/black.
Sponsors: Bear Systems **Clubhouse:** Bar & function room.
Prev. Lges: Reading & Dist/ Spartan 31-52/ Gt Western Comb. 52-57/ Hellenic 57-71/ Ercol Snr.
Local Radio: Radio 210, Radio Oxford **Local Press:** Henley Standard, Reading Evening Post.
Hons: Oxon Snr Cup 03-04 10-11 12-13 13-14 46-47 (R-up 19-20 34-35), Hellenic Lg Div 1 63-64 67-68 (Benev. Cup 62-63 (R-up 61-62)), Spartan Lg Div 1 36-37 (Div 2 33-34), Ercol Snr Lg 78-79, Chiltonian Lg Div 1 87-88, Wycombe Snr Cup 78-79, Reading Snr Cup 78-79, Oxon Charity Cup 04-05 13-14 36-37 62-63 (R-up 02-03 09-1034-35 47-48), Bradley Charity Cup 38-39, Henley Hosp. Charity Cup(15)(R-up(7)).

HOLMER GREEN

Chairman: TBA **Manager:** Barry Hedley.
Secretary: Mr P W Scholes, The Brambles, Penfold Lane, Holmer Green, Bucks HP15 6XS (0494 713867).
Ground: Holmer Green Sports Association, Watchet Lane, Holmer Green, Bucks (0494 711485).
Directions: From High Wycombe on A404 Amersham road, left at Hazlemere towards Gt Missenden, follow for one and a half miles (ignoring sign for Holmer Green), ground on left 100yds before 'Mandarin Duck'.
Seats: No **Cover:** No **Sponsors:** D & E Moulds. **Founded:** 1908.
Colours: Green/white **Change colours:** Blue/red.
Programme: Yes **Previous League:** Ercol Senior.
Local Press: Bucks Free Press. **Clubhouse:** 2 bars open daily. Function room, hot food.
Hons: Chiltonian Lg 84-85 85-86 93-94 (Res Div 1 92-93, Res Cup 92-93), Wycombe Snr Cup 91-92 93-94 (Jnr Cup R-up(res) 92-93).

Home goalkeeper J Mason watches in despair as his fumble directs the ball into the Martin Baker Sports net putting visitors Holmer Green 2-1 up in this League Cup quarter-final

Photo - Gavin Ellis-Neville.

Martin Baker Sports & Social FC 1993-94.

Photo - Gavin Ellis-Neville.

MARTIN BAKER SPORTS & SOCIAL

Chairman: Mr B Gray **Manager:** Mr K Sibley.
Secretary: W Wright, Hillside Cottage, Tilehouse Lane, Denham, Bucks UB9 5DD (0895 832977).
Ground: Martin's Field, Tilehouse Lane, Denham, Bucks (0895 833077).
Directions: Tilehouse Lane is second left on A412 from A40 (not M40!) London-Oxford route. Travelling from Watford, entrance is 150yds up Tilehouse Lane on right between houses.
Seats: No **Cover:** No **Programme:** Yes **Founded:** 1961.
Colours: White/navy **Change colours:** Yellow/royal.
Previous League: London Commercial.
Clubhouse: Bar, with refreshments available.
Local Press: Uxbridge Gazette/ Slough Observer/ All Sport Weekly.
Sponsors: Martin Baker Sports & Social Club.
Hons: Chiltonian Lg Cup R-up 93-94, Wycombe Snr Cup R-up 92-93

PRESTWOOD

Chairman: M White **Manager:** C McDaid.
Secretary: Mr G Stansbury, 31 Colne Rd, High Wycombe, Bucks (0494 521792).
Ground: Prestwood Sports Centre, Honor End Lane, Prestwood, Great Missenden, Bucks (0240 65946).
Directions: From Chequers pub in village centre, ground 1 mile on left down road signed Gt Hampden.
Seats: No **Cover:** No **Programme:** Yes **Founded:** 1934.
Colours: Claret & sky/white **Change colours:** Sky/white.
Local Press: Bucks Free Press/ Bucks Herald.
Clubhouse: On ground. **Prev. League:** Princes Risborough 34-36/ Wycombe 36-84.
Prev. Grnd: Prestwood Common (pre'80) **Hons:** Wycombe Lg 51-52 81-82 (Div 1 36-37).

READING TOWN

Chairman: Mr N Milne **Manager:** Mr R Ford.
Secretary: M Chatfield, 11 Goddard Close, Shinfield Village, Reading, Berks RG2 9DR.
Ground: Reading Town Spts Ground, Scours Lane, Tilehurst, Reading, Berks (0734 453555).
Directions: Out of Reading on Oxford road (A329), past Battle Hosp. Scours Lane 1st right after r'bout.
Seats: Yes **Cover:** Yes **Programme:** Yes **Sponsors:** None **Founded:** 1963.
Colours: Black & red halves/black **Change colours:** Sky/white.
Previous Names: Reading Garage/ I.T.S. Reading Town.
Prev. Leagues: Reading & District. **Prev. Ground:** Kings Meadow Rd, Reading (pre'92).
Clubhouse: Yes **Local Press:** Reading Chronicle/ Reading Evening Post.
Honours: Chiltonian Lg Res Div 1 R-up 93-94.

STOCKLAKE

Chairman: Mr Bob Hogg **Manager:** Mr P Harvey.
Secretary: Mr Tom Exton, 116 Narbeth Drive, Aylesbury, Bucks HP20 1PZ (0296 415780).
Ground: Stocklake Sports & Social Club, Hayward Way, Aylesbury, Bucks (0296 23324).
Directions: In Aylesbury join A41 Bicester road, right into Jackson Way at last r'bout leaving Aylesbury, 2nd left is Haywards Way - ground at end.
Seats: No **Cover:** No **Programme:** Yes **Sponsors:** TBA **Founded:** 1966.
Colours: Coral (blue stripe)/purple **Change colours:** All red.
Prev. Lges: Aylesbury Dist./ Wycombe Snr **Clubhouse:** Bar, tea bar, games room, private bar.
Local Press: Bucks Herald/ Bucks Advertiser.
Hons: Chiltonian Lg R-up 90-91, Marsworth Reserves Cup 93-94.

WOOBURN ATHLETIC

Chairman: Mr A R Nash **Manager:** Mr J Austin.
Secretary: Mr B Nash, 10 Philip Drive, Flackwell Heath, Bucks HP10 9JB (0628 523293).
Ground: Wooburn Park, Town Lane, Wooburn Green, Bucks (0628 819201/520772).
Directions: Turn off A4094 Loudwater-Maidenhead road down behind Wooburn church, left at T-junct, ground entrance straight ahead at right-hand bend in road.
Seats: No **Cover:** No **Sponsors:** Carlsberg. **Founded:** 1897.
Colours: Red & white/red **Change colours:** Green/white **Programme:** Yes.
Local Press: Bucks Free Press/ Star/ Maidenhead Advertiser
Prev. Lge: Wycombe Ercol Senior **Clubhouse:** Wooburn WMC, 16 The Green, Wooburn Green.
Hons: Chiltonian Lg Div 1 R-up 92-93, Wycombe Snr Cup 92-93, Maidenhead Jnr Cup(res) 92-93.

WRAYSBURY-COOPERS

Chairman: Mr D W Hammond **Manager:** C Sherlock.
Secretary: Mr J Rice, 77 Grange Way, Iver, Bucks (0753 652780).
Ground: Memorial Ground, Wraysbury, Bucks (0784 482155).
Directions: From M4 jct 5 follow signs to Datchet (B376), then Horton, then Wraysbury - left at George Hotel into The Green - ground and parking at end.
Seats: No **Cover:** No **Programme:** No **Founded:** 1902.
Colours: Green & white **Previous Name:** Coopers Payen.
Prev. League: Slough Windsor & Dist. **Clubhouse:** One minute walk from pitch.
Local Press: Slough Observer/ Windsor & Eton Espress.
Hons: Chiltonian Lg 86-87 88-89 89-90 (Lg Cup R-up 85-86 86-87 87-88 90-91, Reserves Cup R-up 92-93).

Wraysbury FC *Photo - Gavin Ellis-Neville*

Slough Youth Club Old Boys - runners-up in the Premier Division in 1993-94 having held the lead for much of the season. For 1994-95 they have merged with Spartan League side Beanconsfield United, and will play under the name of Beaconsfield & Slough Youth Club Old Boys.

Photo - Gavin Ellis-Neville.

DIVISION ONE CLUBS 1994-95

BEACONSFIELD & SLOUGH Y.C.O.B. RESERVES *(see page 631)*

DENHAM UNITED

Chairman: Gerry Spencer **Manager:** Gary Marks (reserves: John Osborne).
Secretary: Colin Stevens, 18 The Dene, West Molesey, Surrey KT8 2HL (081 783 0433).
Ground: Oxford Road, Denham, Bucks (0895 238717).
Directions: Entering Uxbridge on A4020, ground is quarter mile on left after Denham roundabout.
Seats: No **Cover:** No **Programme:** Yes **Sponsors:** None **Founded:** 1905.
Colours: Blue & white/blue **Change colours:** Red/blue.
Local Press: Berks & Bucks Advertiser, Uxbridge Gazette.
Prev. Lgs: Uxbridge & Dist./ W. Middx **Clubhouse:** Licensed bar, changing rooms and social area.

DRAYTON WANDERERS

Chairman: Mike Ash **Manager:** Roger Poulter.
Secretary: D Reader, 36 Shenley Ave., Ruslip Manor, Middx HA4 6BX (0895 675121).
Ground: Cowley Rec., Cowley High Rd, Cowley, Nr Uxbridge.
Directions: One and a half miles south of Uxbridge (follow signs for Heathrow/West Drayton) opposite Grand Union pub.
Seats: No **Cover:** No **Programme:** Yes **Clubhouse:** No **Founded:** 1964.
Colours: Black & white stripes/black **Change colours:** Claret/white.
Sponsors: Browne's Mini-Buses.
Prev. League: West Middx. **Previous Name:** Uxbridge Town (mid 80s-1992).
Hons: Chilt. Lg Div 1 85-86 **Local Press:** West Drayton & Uxbridge Gazette.

IVER

Chairman: Mr R Rankin **Manager:** Mr M Hodges.
Secretary: Mr S Law, 59 Grange Way, Iver, Bucks SL0 9NT (0753 819780).
Ground: Lee Barton, High Street, Iver, Bucks (0753 651248).
Directions: A412 from Slough or Denham to Iver Heath (Crooked Billet r'bout), Wood Lane turning Iver, left at mini-r'bout, 2 miles to Iver High Street, 2nd right past school (on left) - Lee Barton to club car park.
Programme: Yes **Founded:** 1946.
Colours: Coral & navy stripes/navy **Change colours:** White & blue halves/blue.
Prev. Lge: Windsor Slough & Dist. **Clubhouse:** Members bar with full facilties.
Sponsors: AK Designs **Local Press:** Slough Observer/ Slough Express.
Honours: Chiltonian Lg Res. Div Cup R-up 93-94, Slough Town Jnr Cup (Res.) 93-94.

OLD PALUDIANS

Secretary: D Aslett, 14 Cornwall Close, Eton Wick, Windsor, Berks SL4 6NB (0628 31176).
Ground: Stanley Jones Field, Berry Hill, Taplow, near Maidenhead (0628 21745).
Directions: A4 (Bath Road) from Slough towards Maidenhead, right at B476 towards Taplow, ground on right behind Dumb Bell pub and City Ford Garage.
Colours: Sky/navy **Change colours:** Maroon/white.

PENN & TYLERS GREEN

Chairman: Mr A Prowse **Manager:** Mr D Russell.
Secretary: Mr R Dalling, 28 Baring Rd, Beaconsfield, Bucks HP9 2NE (0494 671424).
Ground: French School Meadow, Elm Road, Penn, Bucks (0494 815346).
Directions: Entrance on B474 Beaconsfield-Hazlemere road, almost opposite Horse & Groom pub.
Seats: No **Cover:** No **Programme:** Yes **Founded:** 1905.
Colours: Blue & white stripes/blue. **Change colours:** Yellow/white.
Local Press: Bucks Free Press.
Prev. League: Wycombe Senior **Clubhouse:** Bar, 4 dressing rooms, 3 sets of showers.

QUARRY NOMADS

Secretary: K Dalton, 58 Pitts Rd, Headington, Oxon (0865 65332).
Ground: St Margarets Road, Headington, Oxford.
Directions: On reaching Oxford's Green Rd r'bout (McDonalds on left), turn left towards Cowley, right at lights then 1st left, thru village, ground is 1st cross road.
Colours: Black & white stripes/black **Change colours:** Red & white stripes/white.
Previous League: Oxfordshire Senior (pre-1994)

SLOUGH HEATING

Chairman: P Healey **Manager:** TBA.
Secretary: J Lake, 1 Hardymead Court, Kingsmead Rd, Loudwater, Bucks HP11 1JS (0494 464147).
Ground: Farnham Park (0753 666252).
Seats: No **Cover:** No **Programme:** No **Founded:** 1923
Colours: Red/black **Change colours:** White/black.
Previous Lge: East Berks (pre'93) **Local Press:** Slough Observer/ Slough Express.

STOKENCHURCH

Chairman: Mr D Errington **Manager:** Mr R Thorne/ Mr M Dowding.
Secretary: Mrs B K Hunt, 'Deneholme', 4 Lowes Close, Stokenchurch, Bucks HP14 3TN (0494 482535).
Ground: Longburrow Park, Stokenchurch, Bucks HP14 3TQ (0494 482703).
Directions: From A40 High Wycombe/ Oxford Rd turn either just before or after Kings Arms Hotel. 100yds on behind hotel is Royal Oak pub - Park Road is down right hand side as you look at pub.
Seats: No **Cover:** No **Programme:** Yes **Founded:** 1886.
Colours: Green & white/black/black **Change colours:** Orange/black.
Clubhouse: Fleur-de-Lys **Local Press:** Bucks Free Press/ Star.
Prev. Lges: Wycombe Comb./ Reading & Dist./ Hellenic 53-73.
Sponsors: Teal Furniture **Hons:** Hellenic Lg R-up 56-57, Chilt. Lg Res Div 2 R-up 93-94.

VANSITTART WANDERERS

Secretary: A Ball, 124 Long Readings Labe, Britwell, Slough, Berks SL2 1QB (0753 550470).
Ground: Slough Grammar School, Lascelles Rd (0753 522892).
Directions: Thru Slough on A4 heading east, past Co-op r'bout, right into Lascelles Rd - School on right.
Seats: No **Cover:** No **Programme:** No **Founded:** 1989
Colours: White & sky/black **Change colours:** Navy/white.
Prev. Lge: E Berks (champs 92-93) **Local Press:** Slough Observer/ Slough Express.

WALLINGFORD UNITED

Chairman: Mr E L Townsend **Manager:** Mr D Graham.
Secretary: Mr E Gniadek, 17 Offas Close, Benson, Wallingford, Oxon OX10 6NR (0491 838540).
Ground: Bull Croft, Wallingford, Oxon (0491 837173).
Directions: Enter Wallingford over Wallingford Bridge from Crawmarsh, straight over lights in town centre, right at mini-r'bout by Cross Keys pub, ground 100 metres on right - parking opposite in Blackstone Upper School lay-by.
Seats: No **Cover:** Yes **Programme:** Yes **Sponsors:** Vantage **Founded:** 1934.
Colours: Red & white/red **Change colours:** Green/white.
Local Press: Wallingford Herald/ Reading Ev. Post.
Prev. League: Reading & Dist. **Clubhouse:** No (use adjacent Cross Keys pub).
Honours: Chiltonian Lg Res Div 2 93-94.

CHESHAM SUNDAY LEAGUE

FOUNDED: 1967

PREM. DIV.	P	W	D	L	F	A	PTS
Iyax '61	16	12	2	2	56	19	38
Gatecrashers	16	11	2	3	44	22	35
Pioneer	16	9	2	5	43	29	29
Oldens	16	7	2	7	42	42	23
Martin Baker	16	6	3	7	24	30	21
Chesham Nomads	16	6	2	7	30	39	20
Eldorado	16	5	2	9	33	39	17
Missenden	16	4	3	9	28	46	15
Ashley Green	16	2	1	13	22	56	7

Lower Division Champions:
Div. 1 (10): Iyax '61 Reserves
Div. 2 (10): Amersham '92
Div. 3 (9): Belmont
Div. 4 (19): Nightingales

League Cup: Gatecrashers
Subsidiary Cup: Chalfont Saints
Junior Invitation Cup: St Josephs

READING FOOTBALL LEAGUE (Est. 1989)

President: Leon Summers.

Chairman: John Dell.

Deputy Chairman: Mark Rozzier.

Secretary: David Jeanes, 6 Hawkesbury Drive, Fords Farm, Calcot, Reading RG3 5ZP (0734 413926).

Once again the Senior section of the League was hotly contested, with Mortimer eventually taking the title for the first time. They also won the Berks & Bucks Intermediate Cup. The runners-up spot was challenged right up to the final matches of the season, with Reading Exiles eventually edging out South Reading.

The Berkshire Trophy Centre Senior Cup was played at Elm Park (courtesy of Reading Football Club) and, in a highly competitive match, saw South Reading beat Woodley Yeoman 3-1.

The annual representative match against the Oxfordshire Senior League for the Slevin Trophy, was played in November. This year it was played at the new Oxford City ground, with Oxfordshire just taking the honours 2-1.

During the season four players registered with the League were selected to represent the County FA.

Philip Lewis, Minutes Secretary

SENIOR DIV.	P	W	D	L	F	A	PTS
Mortimer	20	17	2	1	57	16	53
Reading Exiles	20	13	3	4	56	14	42
South Reading	20	13	2	5	57	27	41
Marlow United	20	13	2	5	42	33	41
Cookham Dean	20	11	4	5	49	32	37
Checkendon	20	7	2	11	36	49	23
Forest	20	6	4	10	33	37	22
West Reading	20	5	3	12	30	51	18
Woodley Yeoman	20	4	4	12	31	58	16
Reading Old Blues	20	4	1	15	36	70	13
REME	20	2	3	15	25	65	9

PREM. DIV.	P	W	D	L	F	A	PTS
AFC Maidenhead	20	15	4	1	49	25	49
Theale	20	12	4	4	52	38	40
Old Prestonians	20	12	2	6	53	30	38
Reading University	20	12	1	7	60	34	37
Ibis	20	11	1	8	54	34	34
Richfield Rovers	20	9	1	10	55	37	28
Tilehurst	20	7	6	7	39	33	27
Berkshire CS	20	7	3	10	39	47	24
Earlbourne	20	7	2	11	39	47	23
CS Reading	20	3	2	15	30	76	11
Thames Vale	20	1	2	17	13	82	5

D1 KENNET	P	W	D	L	F	A	PTS
Sutton Exiles	22	17	3	2	79	29	54
Cox Green	22	16	1	5	87	27	49
Pangbourne	22	15	2	5	63	27	47
Rabsons Rovers	22	14	3	5	63	30	45
Reading Exiles Res.	22	11	4	7	42	38	37
Cantley Manor	22	9	6	7	46	32	33
Cookham Dean Res.	22	8	3	11	32	36	27
Emmbrook	22	8	3	11	53	64	27
SRCC	22	7	1	14	48	65	22
Wargrave	22	6	2	14	32	62	20
West Reading Res.	22	4	2	16	25	91	14
Englefield	22	1	2	19	19	88	5

D1 THAMES	P	W	D	L	F	A	PTS
SEB	20	13	4	3	81	37	43
Forest Res.	20	13	3	4	53	32	42
Mortimer Res.	20	11	5	4	57	24	38
Shinfield	20	11	2	7	45	31	35
Frilsham & Y.	20	10	4	6	58	42	34
Finchampstead 'A'	20	9	3	8	41	45	30
Unity	20	8	3	9	47	43	27
Ibis Res.	20	8	2	10	37	43	26
Royal Mail	20	5	1	14	21	72	16
Sonning	20	3	3	14	20	54	12
Nettlebed United	20	4	0	16	23	60	12

D2 KENNET	P	W	D	L	F	A	PTS
Sonning Common	22	15	3	4	67	38	48
Westwood	22	14	4	4	61	25	46
Forest 'A'	22	13	5	4	49	30	44
Goring	22	13	4	5	68	28	43
Woodley	22	14	1	7	65	40	43
Bucklebury	22	11	2	9	55	41	35
Hurst	22	10	2	10	41	55	32
Marlow Utd Res.	22	8	3	11	54	53	27
Theale Res.	22	7	3	12	38	53	24
Newtown Henley	22	6	4	12	45	52	22
Berks CS Res.	22	4	3	15	38	72	15
British Telecom.	22	0	0	22	26	120	0

D2 THAMES	P	W	D	L	F	A	PTS
Roundhead	22	20	1	1	76	17	61
Peppard 'A'	22	17	0	5	81	30	51
Richfield R. Res.	22	12	4	6	58	40	40
Rifle Volunteer	22	13	0	9	63	55	39
Reading YMCA	22	11	3	8	62	60	36
Woodley Yeo. Res.	22	10	1	11	56	54	31
RBC Sweatshop	22	8	4	10	49	53	28
Compton	22	8	2	12	53	61	26
Rabsons R. Res.	22	8	2	12	34	49	26
REME Apprentice	22	6	3	13	54	79	21
Tilehurst Res.	22	3	4	15	33	64	13
Henley Wanderers	22	3	2	17	42	99	11

D3 KENNET	P	W	D	L	F	A	PTS
Lower Earley	20	17	1	2	85	29	52
Caversham Park V.	20	16	4	0	67	14	52
Rides United	20	11	2	7	76	40	35
Highmoor	20	9	5	6	60	44	32
Westwood Res.	20	9	2	9	44	51	29
Earlbourne Res.	20	8	3	9	47	48	27
Pangbourne Res.	20	7	3	10	43	51	24
Emmbrook Res.	20	7	1	12	44	72	22
Hurst Res.	20	5	2	13	29	62	17
SEB Res.	20	4	3	13	47	68	15
Calcot	20	3	2	15	35	98	11

D3 THAMES	P	W	D	L	F	A	PTS
Pegasus	22	18	4	0	126	14	58
Reading Univ. Res.	22	13	6	3	52	30	45
Reading OB Res.	22	13	3	6	55	40	42
AFC M'head Res.	22	10	5	7	61	39	35
Englefield Res.	22	8	6	8	49	67	30
Twyford	22	9	1	12	50	69	28
Crowthorne	22	7	5	10	47	57	26
Old Preston. Res.	22	7	5	10	40	53	26
Ibis 'A'	22	8	2	12	44	63	26
Sonning SC	22	6	6	10	66	66	24
Wargrave Res.	22	4	5	13	29	71	17
Reading Town 'A'	22	3	4	15	29	79	13

D4 KENNET	P	W	D	L	F	A	PTS
Cox Green Res.	20	16	1	3	65	18	49
Whycliffe	20	15	2	3	63	24	47
Pincents Manor	20	13	3	4	69	49	42
ARM	20	12	1	7	66	44	37
AFC Southcote	20	11	2	7	60	41	35
Frilsham & Y. Res.	20	8	2	10	42	63	26
South End	20	8	1	11	32	45	25
Bucklebury Res.	20	6	1	13	37	52	19
Woodley Town Res.	20	4	4	12	41	62	16
ILM Social Club	20	5	1	14	34	66	16
Ibis 'B'	20	2	2	16	25	70	8

SENIOR DIVISION RESULT CHART 1993-94

HOME TEAM		1	2	3	4	5	6	7	8	9	10	11
1.	Checkendon Sports	*	1-4	1-6	0-2	0-3	2-1	0-1	5-1	0-3	5-1	2-1
2.	Cookham Dean	2-4	*	0-0	1-1	0-1	3-0	0-0	4-0	2-1	3-1	5-0
3.	Forest Old Boys	1-1	1-1	*	0-1	0-1	1-0	0-2	5-2	0-3	1-2	4-2
4.	Marlow United	3-2	2-3	2-1	*	0-3	2-1	1-2	3-2	3-2	2-1	1-4
5.	Mortimer	6-1	2-3	6-2	2-2	*	5-0	2-1	3-1	1-0	3-2	8-0
6.	REME Aborfield	2-2	2-9	1-1	2-5	1-3	*	0-4	4-2	1-3	1-3	1-4
7.	Reading Exiles	3-0	7-0	1-2	3-1	0-1	0-0	*	4-0	1-1	3-0	8-1
8.	Reading Old Blues	1-5	3-2	3-4	0-5	1-3	1-2	2-7	*	4-6	1-1	5-0
9.	South Reading	5-3	3-1	3-1	2-3	0-1	5-1	2-1	4-1	*	4-1	3-1
10.	West Reading	2-0	2-4	2-1	2-3	1-2	4-3	1-3	1-3	0-6	*	1-1
11.	Woodley Yeoman	1-2	1-2	3-2	L-W	1-1	6-2	0-5	2-3	1-1	2-2	*

PREMIER DIVISION		1	2	3	4	5	6	7	8	9	10	11
1.	AFC Maidenhead	*	2-1	5-3	2-1	4-1	1-0	4-3	4-2	W-L	2-2	2-2
2.	Berkshire County Sports	1-2	*	9-0	1-3	W-L	0-1	3-10	1-2	W-L	1-1	2-1
3.	CS Reading	0-2	7-2	*	3-5	0-5	1-1	1-6	1-2	3-0	0-3	0-5
4.	Earlbourne	0-0	1-2	4-2	*	0-3	1-7	1-2	1-2	1-1	1-2	5-3
5.	Ibis	3-2	2-3	6-2	3-2	*	4-1	2-1	L-W	6-0	1-3	2-2
6.	Old Prestonians	3-5	5-4	5-1	5-1	1-0	*	1-2	4-2	W-L	5-0	3-1
7.	Reading University	1-2	0-3	7-0	1-2	4-2	3-2	*	W-L	7-1	2-2	3-0
8.	Richfield Rovers	1-3	3-2	3-1	1-3	1-3	0-1	1-3	*	15-1	6-1	1-2
9.	Thames Vale	0-5	3-3	0-2	0-5	2-3	1-6	1-3	1-10	*	1-4	W-L
10.	Theale	0-1	4-1	5-2	3-2	5-4	2-2	1-0	3-1	6-1	*	3-2
11.	Tilehurst	1-1	0-0	1-1	4-0	1-4	1-0	5-2	2-2	3-0	3-2	*

DIV. 1 (KENNET)		1	2	3	4	5	6	7	8	9	10	11	12
1.	Cantley Manor	*	0-0	0-1	2-2	5-0	1-2	1-1	0-0	3-1	3-3	1-2	2-0
2.	Cookham Dean Reserves	3-0	*	1-3	1-2	6-0	1-4	0-1	2-0	2-1	0-2	W-L	3-0
3.	Cox Green	0-3	2-0	*	4-0	2-0	0-1	2-3	8-1	6-1	3-3	4-1	7-2
4.	Emmbrook Sports Club	5-1	2-3	0-7	*	3-3	1-5	4-1	0-3	5-2	2-7	2-1	3-4
5.	Englefield	0-3	0-2	1-9	0-2	*	0-5	0-3	0-8	1-4	1-7	3-4	0-0
6.	Pangbourne	1-2	5-1	0-5	5-2	6-0	*	2-1	3-1	5-3	1-2	0-0	2-4
7.	Rabsons Rovers	5-1	3-1	3-1	2-1	6-3	0-1	*	1-1	2-2	1-2	6-0	5-0
8.	Reading Exiles Reserves	1-0	2-0	0-2	6-6	4-0	1-1	2-1	*	3-0	0-3	1-0	W-L
9.	South Reading CC	3-6	3-2	3-5	2-4	2-1	1-0	2-4	0-1	*	0-3	1-3	5-3
10.	Sutton Exiles	2-2	4-2	3-1	2-0	3-2	1-3	1-3	4-1	4-2	*	5-1	8-0
11.	Wargrave	0-2	1-1	0-8	2-7	1-0	0-3	3-4	4-2	1-5	1-5	*	6-0
12.	West Reading Reserves	0-8	1-1	1-7	1-0	3-4	0-8	0-7	3-4	1-5	0-5	2-1	*

DIV. 1 (THAMES)		1	2	3	4	5	6	7	8	9	10	11
1.	Finchampstead 'A'	*	3-3	2-5	W-L	0-2	W-L	6-2	4-4	2-1	0-1	0-4
2.	Forest Old Boys Reserves	2-1	*	0-2	1-0	2-1	5-1	1-0	2-6	0-0	9-0	3-2
3.	Frilsham & Yattendon	2-4	3-6	*	5-5	2-2	6-1	1-2	2-2	1-0	5-1	1-2
4.	Ibis Reserves	2-4	2-3	1-2	*	1-0	2-1	2-1	2-1	3-2	2-3	3-1
5.	Mortimer Reserves	8-2	1-2	1-1	1-2	*	3-0	2-0	9-3	3-1	2-2	4-3
6.	Nettlebed United	2-3	0-2	1-3	3-2	0-5	*	3-2	1-4	0-2	2-1	1-4
7.	Royal Mail	0-5	0-6	3-5	3-2	1-5	2-0	*	1-7	0-2	2-0	0-0
8.	SEB (Reading)	3-1	4-1	4-1	5-0	0-0	6-1	12-0	*	3-1	6-1	2-0
9.	Shinfield	3-2	0-1	4-3	2-2	0-1	3-1	5-1	6-4	*	4-2	3-0
10.	Sonning	0-1	2-2	0-3	3-1	2-2	0-1	0-1	2-3	0-2	*	0-3
11.	Unity	1-1	4-2	1-5	2-3	0-5	5-4	8-0	2-2	2-4	3-0	*

DIV. 2 (KENNET)		1	2	3	4	5	6	7	8	9	10	11	12
1.	Berks County Spts Reserves	*	5-0	0-1	3-3	1-2	2-5	4-2	1-7	1-3	2-4	1-4	3-6
2.	British Telecom	1-6	*	0-4	2-6	0-12	1-2	1-7	1-8	1-5	2-9	1-9	0-3
3.	Bucklebury	5-0	7-2	*	3-1	2-3	1-1	3-1	6-1	1-3	5-2	1-7	1-4
4.	Forest Old Boys 'A'	2-0	5-2	2-1	*	1-1	0-1	3-2	1-1	4-2	4-3	0-2	1-0
5.	Goring United	4-1	2-0	2-2	1-0	*	9-1	0-2	1-2	2-2	9-0	4-2	4-3
6.	Hurst	3-0	7-3	2-4	0-1	1-5	*	1-3	2-1	2-6	0-2	0-1	0-6
7.	Marlow United Reserves	7-0	6-4	1-3	1-3	2-1	0-1	*	2-2	3-5	3-3	2-5	5-2
8.	Newtown Henley	2-2	5-3	1-3	2-2	3-2	2-3	0-1	*	2-4	0-2	W-L	1-2
9.	Sonning Common	2-2	W-L	2-1	0-3	3-1	1-2	4-1	4-1	*	4-0	4-0	3-5
10.	Theale Reserves	2-3	W-L	2-0	1-3	L-W	1-3	1-1	3-1	1-3	*	0-1	0-3
11.	Westwood United	6-1	3-1	2-0	1-1	0-0	2-2	3-2	5-2	1-1	4-0	*	3-1
12.	Woodley Town	1-0	9-1	2-1	1-3	0-3	4-2	4-0	2-1	4-6	2-2	1-0	*

DIV. 2 (THAMES)		1	2	3	4	5	6	7	8	9	10	11	12
1.	Compton	*	5-1	0-4	1-1	5-1	3-4	3-1	3-2	1-4	2-5	2-1	4-5
2.	Henley Wanderers	3-4	*	1-4	2-3	2-5	0-3	0-6	2-3	2-5	2-14	4-0	1-8
3.	Peppard 'A'	5-2	6-2	*	5-2	8-0	4-0	2-4	4-1	4-2	1-3	5-0	9-2
4.	RBC (Nalgo) Sweatshop	1-4	3-3	1-3	*	2-1	4-1	4-4	3-1	3-4	0-1	3-2	2-3
5.	REME Apprentices	5-2	5-5	1-6	2-6	*	6-1	1-2	1-4	1-5	2-7	6-1	2-4
6.	Rabsons Rovers Reserves	2-5	4-2	0-1	0-2	2-1	*	1-3	1-2	1-3	1-0	1-1	2-1
7.	Reading YMCA	3-1	4-2	1-0	1-1	8-8	2-1	*	1-3	1-4	0-4	5-3	2-4
8.	Richfield Rovers Reserves	3-0	5-1	2-4	3-0	1-1	1-1	5-2	*	6-2	1-4	1-1	3-0
9.	Rifle Volunteer	1-0	2-3	0-2	4-2	3-0	4-3	3-6	3-4	*	1-4	3-1	2-4
10.	Roundhead	2-1	4-0	3-0	2-1	2-0	4-1	2-0	3-1	4-2	*	2-1	0-0
11.	Tilehurst Reserves	4-4	3-4	0-3	5-2	1-2	0-1	0-4	2-2	2-4	0-3	*	3-2
12.	Woodley Yeoman Reserves	3-1	3-0	3-1	1-3	2-3	0-3	8-2	1-4	1-2	0-3	1-2	*

DIV. 3 (KENNET)		1	2	3	4	5	6	7	8	9	10	11
1.	Calcot Community Assoc.	*	0-7	3-5	6-6	0-6	1-6	2-7	0-5	1-6	2-1	7-1
2.	Caversham Park	3-2	*	1-1	5-0	4-1	8-1	2-0	2-0	3-1	3-2	3-0
3.	Earlbourne Reserves	3-2	0-2	*	1-4	0-1	0-4	2-2	4-2	0-2	2-2	1-2
4.	Emmbrook Reserves	7-1	0-7	1-2	*	1-0	2-0	1-13	3-2	2-5	5-0	4-0
5.	Highmoor	1-1	1-1	1-5	5-3	*	10-0	1-6	1-1	4-3	2-3	8-3
6.	Hurst Reserves	1-0	0-2	2-3	2-0	3-3	*	0-1	3-2	1-3	1-7	0-2
7.	Lower Earley	9-1	2-5	5-4	6-1	2-0	5-0	*	3-1	3-1	3-2	3-1
8.	Pangbourne Reserves	4-1	1-2	4-2	3-1	1-5	3-2	1-5	*	3-1	3-1	1-2
9.	Rides United	10-0	0-5	3-4	6-0	3-3	4-1	1-2	3-3	*	7-3	7-1
10.	SEB (Reading) Reserves	3-4	1-1	1-6	3-2	3-5	1-1	3-6	8-1	0-8	*	2-4
11.	Westwood United Reserves	7-1	1-1	4-2	5-1	1-2	5-1	0-2	2-2	1-2	2-1	*

DIV. 3 (THAMES)		1	2	3	4	5	6	7	8	9	10	11	12
1.	AFC Maidenhead Reserves	*	5-3	0-2	2-2	2-1	1-1	14-1	0-2	0-0	4-4	4-1	6-1
2.	Crowthorne	2-0	*	0-4	3-4	0-2	1-1	2-2	1-5	1-5	5-2	2-1	8-1
3.	Englefield Reserves	3-1	3-3	*	6-1	5-0	2-4	L-W	1-1	0-1	2-2	6-1	2-2
4.	Ibis 'A'	1-4	2-1	5-2	*	1-6	0-5	4-1	2-5	1-3	1-2	1-2	6-0
5.	Old Prestonians Reserves	0-4	1-3	2-2	1-1	*	0-5	W-L	1-3	1-1	3-3	5-2	2-2
6.	Pegasus	4-0	1-1	24-0	8-0	8-1	*	9-1	6-1	6-2	5-1	8-1	8-0
7.	Reading Town 'A'	0-4	4-0	4-1	0-3	1-2	0-7	*	3-3	L-W	2-5	2-5	3-3
8.	Reading Old Blues Res.	2-0	4-3	5-2	2-1	1-0	0-5	2-2	*	2-0	3-2	1-2	4-0
9.	Reading Univ. Reserves	3-3	6-2	0-2	4-3	1-0	0-0	3-1	2-1	*	2-2	5-0	1-0
10.	Sonning Sports Club	0-1	3-3	10-1	3-5	2-6	1-4	3-2	3-5	1-4	*	3-1	3-3
11.	Twyford	1-3	1-2	1-3	3-0	4-3	0-4	9-0	1-0	4-4	1-11	*	3-1
12.	Wargrave Reserves	5-3	0-1	0-0	L-W	2-3	1-4	W-L	4-3	0-5	3-0	1-6	*

DIV. 4 (KENNET)		1	2	3	4	5	6	7	8	9	10	11
1.	AFC Southcote	*	5-1	1-0	0-4	5-0	6-3	7-0	0-3	4-1	3-2	7-0
2.	ARM	3-2	*	1-3	2-3	7-2	3-1	8-1	1-7	1-0	1-4	4-2
3.	Bucklebury Reserves	3-3	2-4	*	2-3	1-6	2-1	5-1	2-4	3-2	2-5	3-2
4.	Cox Green Reserves	4-3	3-3	L-W	*	5-0	3-0	W-L	1-3	3-0	1-2	5-0
5.	Frilsham & Yattendon Res.	2-6	0-1	3-0	1-6	*	4-2	0-9	6-1	3-1	1-2	1-0
6.	Ibis 'B'	0-3	0-6	2-0	1-3	2-4	*	5-2	2-2	1-2	0-8	1-1
7.	ILM Social Club	1-2	0-9	3-2	1-8	5-1	2-0	*	2-4	3-0	0-3	2-2
8.	Pincents Manor	2-1	1-4	3-2	0-3	6-6	4-2	5-2	*	2-0	3-3	5-4
9.	South End	1-1	2-1	4-3	0-4	L-W	5-1	1-0	2-4	*	3-1	3-1
10.	Whycliffe	2-1	4-1	1-0	0-3	2-0	7-0	3-0	3-1	6-1	*	3-1
11.	Woodley Town Reserves	9-0	2-5	3-2	0-3	2-2	3-1	1-0	3-9	3-4	2-2	*

DIV. 4 (THAMES)		1	2	3	4	5	6	7	8	9	10	11	12
1.	Caversham Park Reserves	*	2-4	1-2	1-3	1-4	0-7	L-W	0-4	1-1	1-3	1-3	2-6
2.	Checkendon Spts Reserves	2-2	*	2-3	3-1	9-0	2-3	4-4	2-5	3-3	2-4	3-2	3-7
3.	Gladstone	7-2	3-1	*	5-2	3-0	4-0	2-4	0-4	6-0	3-1	1-1	1-3
4.	Goring United Reserves	1-4	2-1	1-3	*	5-0	5-1	0-7	2-5	6-1	5-0	2-1	1-2
5.	Highmoor Reserves	1-1	2-5	L-W	1-1	*	1-2	1-5	1-2	4-1	0-3	2-2	2-3
6.	Lower Earley Reserves	5-1	3-0	3-3	2-3	1-2	*	6-0	1-3	3-1	1-4	4-2	1-7
7.	Marlow United 'A'	2-2	4-2	2-0	3-1	2-1	4-2	*	1-3	10-1	1-2	3-2	7-1
8.	Rockwell Collins	3-2	2-1	0-1	3-1	5-1	2-0	2-3	*	1-2	1-1	6-0	0-5
9.	Shinfield Reserves	3-4	1-2	3-3	2-1	5-2	3-3	2-3	0-6	*	4-3	2-5	3-5
10.	Sonning Common Reserves	5-3	2-0	L-W	3-0	3-1	6-0	4-3	2-3	2-0	*	2-0	0-2
11.	Thameside	5-2	3-1	2-3	1-1	6-2	2-1	6-0	0-3	2-2	6-7	*	1-8
12.	Whitley Rovers	7-1	5-0	6-1	3-0	11-0	3-0	4-4	3-0	12-0	4-2	6-0	*

CLUB DIRECTORY

A.F.C. MAIDENHEAD

Secretary: Mrs D Saunders, 12 Crescent Court, 113 Crescent Rd, Reading RG1 5SJ (0734 261390).
Ground: Claires Court School, Approach Rd, Taplow (opposite Taplow Station).
Colours: Green/white/green **Reserves colours:** Red/black/black

A.F.C. SOUTHCOTE

Secretary: Noel O'Reilly, 254 Gainsborough Rd, Southcote, Reading RG3 3BP (0734 566032).
Cols: Red & blue stripes/royal/royal **Ground:** Prospect Park, Liebenrood Road, Reading.

A.R.M. ATHLETIC

Secretary: Mark Grigg, 36 Derwent Close, Shinfield, Reading RG2 8PZ (0734 755065).
Colours: Blue/navy/white. **Ground:** Lower Whitley Rec, Basingstoke Rd, Reading.

BERKSHIRE COUNTY SPORTS

Secretary: Mark Harris, 41 Kerris Way, Earley, Reading RG6 2UW (0734 861015).
Grnd: Berkshire Co. Spts Club, Sonning Lane, Sonning. **Cols:** All white *(Reserves: All blue).*

BRITISH TELECOM

Secretary: Andy Townsend, 7a Castle Cres., Reading RG1 6AQ (0734 573751).
Ground: Palmer Park, Wokingham Rd, Reading.
H.Q.: British Telecom Sports & Social Club, 14 London Rd, Reading RG1 5AD (0734 872390)
Colours: White & black stripes/black/black **Reserves colours:** All royal.

BUCKLEBURY

Secretary: Richard Morris, East View, Broad Lane, Upper Bucklebury, Reading (0635 865484).
Ground: Lower Rec. Ground, Bucklebury. **H.Q.:** The Blade Bone Inn, Bucklebury (0734 712326).
Colours: White/black/black **Reserves colours:** Blue/white/blue

CALCOT COMMUNITY ASSOCIATION

Secretary: Mrs A Vasey, 3 Barclay Rd, Calcot, Reading RG3 7EL (0734 411132).
H.Q.: Calcot CA, Highview, Calcot **Ground:** Calcot Rec., Highview, Calcot.
Colours: Blue & white/blue/blue **Change colours:** White/green/green.

CANTLEY MANOR

Secretary: Nicholas Patterson, 11 Chatton Close, Lower Earley, Reading RG6 4DY (0734 876032).
Ground: Cantley Park, Milton Rd, Wokingham (0734 793188 - HQ (Penguin & Vulture)).
Cols: Black & white stripes/black/white **Change colours:** Sky & white/maroon/maroon.

CAVERSHAM PARK

Secretary: Neil Spiker, 9 Jordan Close, Caversham Park Village, Reading RG4 0PN (0734 478467).
Grnd: Clayfield Copse, Caversham Park **Cols:** Red & black/black/black (Res: Red/black/black)

CHECKENDON SPORTS

Secretary: Ernie Smith, 10 Emmens Close, Checkendon, Reading RG8 0TU (0491 681575).
H.Q.: Four Horses, Checkendon, Reading RG8 0QS (0491 680325)
Ground: Checkendon PF **Colours:** White/royal/white (Res: Green/black/green).

COMPTON

Secretary: Mick Pinfold, 11 Manor Cres., Compton, Newbury RG16 0NR (0635 578521).
Ground: Burrell Rd Rec., Compton.
Colours: Royal/white/royal **H.Q.:** The Pavilion, Burrell Rd, Compton.

COOKHAM DEAN

Secretary: Rory Gavin, 14 Northfield Rd, Maidenhead SL6 7JP (0628 32997)
Ground: Alfred Major Rec., Hillcrest Ave., Cookham Rise, Maidenhead.
H.Q.: 0628 819423 **Cols:** Red & black/black/red. **Res. cols:** Red & black hoops/black/red

COX GREEN

Secretary: Mrs Janet Gilbert, 6 Anstey Place, Burghfield Common RG7 3NQ (0734 835473).
Ground: Desborough Pk, The Croft, Norden Rd, Maidenhead.
Cols: Green & white/black/black **Reserves' colours:** Green/black/black.

CROWTHORNE SPORTS

Secretary: Russell Shaw, 1 Froxfield Down, Forest Park, Bracknell RG12 3YB (0344 488437)
Ground: Morgan Rec., Wellington Rd, Crowthorne
Colours: White/black/black **H.Q.:** Crowthorne Social Club, Wellington Rd.

C.S. READING

Secretary: Bob Davies, 54 Balmore Drive, Caversham, Reading RG4 8NN (0734 571608).
Ground & HQ: RCSSA Club, James Lane, Burghfield.
Colours: Yellow/blue/yellow **Change colours:** White & red/red/red.

EARLBOURNE

Secretary: Paul Sheppard, 48 Harvard Close, Woodley, Reading RG5 4UJ (0734 699908).
Ground: Woodford Park, Haddon Drive, Woodley, Reading RG5 4LY (0734 690356).
Cols: Black & blue stripes/black/black **Res. colours:** Black & red stripes/black/black.

EMMBROOK SPORTS CLUB

Secretary: Glyn Webb, 1 Toutley Close, Emmbrook, Wokingham RG11 1JH (0734 788967).
Ground: Emmbrook Sports Ground, Lowther Road, Emmbrook, Wokingham (0734 780209).
Cols: Royal & white hoops/royal/royal **Res. cols:** All royal. (Alt: (both teams) all yellow).

ENGLEFIELD

Secretary: Mark Smyth, 19 Trelawney Drive, Tilehurst, Reading RG3 5WQ (0734 410485).
Ground: Englefield SC, Englefield Str., Englefield (off A4 Theale-Pangbourne road).
Colours: Red/red/red & white **Res. cols:** Red/white/red (Alt (both): All white.

FINCHAMPSTEAD 'A' *(details as 1st team - see Chiltonian League)*

FOREST OLD BOYS

Secretary: Bob Hulett, 10 Ramsbury Drive, Earley, Reading RG6 2RT (0734 663514).
Colours: Yellow & blue/blue/blue. **Ground:** Woodford Pk, Haddon Drive, Woodley (0734 690356).

FRILSHAM & YATTENDON

Secretary: Brian Cannons, 2 Squash Court Cottage, Yattendon, Newbury RG16 0XT (0635 201357).
Ground: Frilsham PF, Frilsham Common, Frilsham, nr Hermitage.
H.Q.: Yattendon Social Club, Yattendon Village Hall (0635 201847).
Colours: Blue/white/red **Reserves colours:** Blue & white/white/red.

GLADSTONE

Secretary: Mike Stagg, 5 Vine Cres., Reading RG3 3LT (0734 507678). **Grnd:** As AFC Southcote (above)
HQ: Horncastle Pub, Bath Rd, Reading. **Colours:** Yellow & green/green/green.

GORING UNITED

Secretary: Peter Jones, Bywater, Icknield Rd, Goring-on-Thames RG8 0DE (0491 872809).
Ground: Gardiners Recreation Ground, Upper Red Cross Rd, Goring.
H.Q.: Goring Social Club, High Street, Goring (0491 873105).
Cols: Yellow & green/green/yellow **Reserves colours:** Blue/black/black.

HENLEY WANDERERS

Secretary: Robin Bishop, 3 Stirling Close, Caversham Park Village, Reading RG4 0SH (0734 470029).
Cols: Yellow (royal trim)/royal/royal **Ground:** Mill Lane Spts Centre, Reading Rd, Henley-on-Thames.

HIGHMOOR

Secretary: Chris Gallimore, 240 Wensley Rd, Coley Park, Reading, RG1 6ED (0734 578289).
Ground: Highmoor Athletic Ground, Highmoor, Henley, Oxon.
Colours: All blue *(Reserves: Red & black/black/red)*.

HURST

Secretary: Mrs S Hicks, Rosevale, School Rd, Hurst RG10 0DR (0734 341541).
Ground: Hinton Rd, Hurst, Reading. **Cols:** Tangerine/black/black *(Reserves: All royal).*

IBIS

Secretary: Tony McGrath, 25 Luscombe Close, Caversham, Reading RG4 0LG (0734 478161).
Ground: IBIS Sports Club, Scours Lane, Reading RG3 6AY (0734 424130).
Cols: Blue & white stripes/black/black **Reserves colours:** Maroon & blue/blue/maroon.
'A' cols: Red & black stripes/black/black **'B' colours:** Yellow/blue/white.

I.L.M. SOCIAL CLUB

Secretary: Richard Smith, 3 Parthia Close, Katesgrove Lane, Reading RG1 2NQ (0734 502422).
Ground: Bulmershe Court, Woodlands Ave., Woodley, Reading. **Cols:** Blue/blue/white
H.Q.: Hays Distribution, Theale, Reading RG7 4HN (0734 303636). **Reserves cols:** Green/grey/white.

LOWER EARLEY

Secretary: Mr S Price, 50 Faygate Way, Lower Earley, Reading RG6 4DA (0734 864227).
Ground: Laurel Park, Marefield, Lower Earley (groundsman: 0734 875147).
H.Q.: Bearwood Social Club, Bearwood Rd, Winnerish (0734 782953)
Colours: All maroon **Res. cols:** All sky (Alt (both teams): Royal/white/white).

MAIDEN SOCIAL

Secretary: Tim Hancock, 54 Cannock Way, Lower Earley, Reading (0734 753235).
Colours: All royal **Ground:** Cintra Park, Cintra Ave., Reading.
H.Q.: Maiden Place Social Club, Maiden Place, Lower Earley (0734 268872).

MARLOW UNITED

Secretary: Jayne Flint, 17 Stapleton Close, Marlow, Bucks (0628 474490).
H.Q.: Bank of England PH, Dean Street, Marlow
Ground: Gossmore Park, Gossmore Lane, Marlow.
Colours: Blue/black/navy **Res. cols:** Blue/white/blue *('A': Red/white/red).*

MORTIMER

Secretary: Steve Dell, 30 Croft Rd, Mortimer, nr Reading RG7 3TS (0734 333821).
Colours: Amber/black/black **Grnd:** Alfred Palmer Mem. P.F., West End Rd, Mortimer.

NETTLEBED UNITED

Sec: Pauline Mutch, 7 Fernhurst Rd, Calcot, Reading RG3 7EA (0734 417988). **Colours:** All sky
Grnd: Recreation Grnd, Watlington Rd, Nettlebed, Henley-on-Thames. **Reserves cols:** White/navy/navy.

NEWTOWN HENLEY

Secretary: Mrs M Grant, 6 Peppard Lane, Henley-on-Thames, Oxon RG9 1NJ (0491 576457).
Ground: Harpsden Village, Nr Henley-on-Thames, Oxon (Parking at Harpsden Hall).
Cols: Green & white hoops/white/white **Res. colours:** Black & white stripes/black/black.

OLD PRESTONIANS

Secretary: Mr P J Curran, 5 New Bright Street, Holybrook Est., Reading RG1 6QQ (0734 574034).
Grnd: Presentation College, 63 Bath Rd, Reading *(entry via Southcote Lane)*(0734 572861/581709).
Cols: Blue & red stripes/blue/blue **Res. colours:** Black & white stripes/black/black.

PANGBOURNE

Secretary: Mr T McAllister, 2 Aston Ave., Pangbourne, Reading (0734 842104).
H.Q.: Pangbourne WMC (0734 842426) **Ground:** Thames Ave. Rec., Pangbourne.
Colours: All blue **Reserves colours:** All blue (Alt: all red).

PEGASUS

Secretary: Barry Hoy, 24 Hadleigh Rise, Caversham Park Village, Reading RG4 0RW (0734 476434).
HQ: White Horse, Emmer Green **Ground:** Emmer Green Rec. Ground.
Cols: Red & white halves/red/red **Change colours:** Sky/black/black.

PEPPARD 'A' *(details as page 750)*

PINCENTS MANOR

Secretary: Caroline Price, 20 Kernham Drive, Westwood Fields, Tilehurst, Reading RG3 6GB (0734 418055).
HQ: Pincents Manor Golf & Country Club, Pincents Lane, Calcot.
Cols: Maroon & royal/royal/royal. **Ground:** Holybrook Linear Park, Charrington Way, Calcot.

R.B.C. (NALGO) SWEATSHOP

Secretary: Andy Winterbottom, 258 Kidmore Rd, Reading RG4 7NE (0734 472566).
H.Q.: Civic Offices, Civic Cte, Reading (390448/412) **Grnd:** Palmer Pk, Wokingham Rd, Reading
Colours: Blue & white hoops/black/blue **Change cols:** Gold/black/black.

RABSON ROVERS

Secretary: Peter Parker, 103a Belmont Rd, Reading RG3 2UT (0734 585892).
Ground: Rabson Recreation Ground, Northumberland Ave., Reading.
H.Q.: South Reading Leisure Centre, Northumberland Ave., Reading (0734 864910).
Colours: Red/white/red. **Change colours:** Blue/white/red.

READING EXILES

Secretary: M J Aust, 24 Aylsham Close, Tilehurst, Reading RG3 4XG (0734 421453).
Ground: Holme Park Spts & Soc. Club, Sonning-on-Thames (0734 691305). (Opp. Reading Cricket Club).
Cols: Royal & white stripes/royal/royal **Res. cols:** Navy & white stripes/navy/navy

READING OLD BLUES

Secretary: Frank Glasspool, 17 Wyndham Cres., Woodley, Reading RG5 3AY (0734 692800).
Ground: Sol Joel Playing Field, Church Rd, Earley, Reading.
HQ: Reading Blue Coat School, Holme Park, Sonning, Reading.
Colours: Yellow/navy/yellow *(Reserves: Sky/white/white).*

READING TOWN 'A'

Ground: Prospect Park, Liebenrood Rd, Reading *(other details as Chiltonian Lge entry).*

READING UNIVERSITY

Secretary: Jason Wood, Reading Univ. Students Union, PO Box 230, Whiteknights, Reading (0734 351905).
HQ: Spts Fed. Office, Students Union, PO Box 230, Whiteknights, Reading RG6 2AZ (0734 86022x220).
Colours: Maroon/blue/blue **Grnd:** Athletics Pavilion, Reading Univ., Whiteknights.

READING Y.M.C.A.
Secretary: Wilf Fewtrell, 56 Waldeck Str., Reading RG1 2RE (0734 873593).
Ground: Christchurch Meadows, George Street, Caversham, Reading.
Cols: Red & black stripes/black/black **H.Q.:** Marlborough House, Parkside Rd, Reading RG1

R.E.M.E. ARBORFIELD
Secretary: Peter Davies, 73 Chestnut Cres., Shinfield, Reading RG2 9HA (0734 884107).
Ground: Sports Pavilion, Biggs Lane, Princess Marina College, Arborfield (entrance thru College).
HQ: School of Electronic Engineering, Biggs Lane, Arborfield.
Cols: Blue & yel./yel./blue **Res. cols:** Black & orange/blue/blue **'A' cols:** Red/white/red

RICHFIELD ROVERS
Secretary: Nigel Sawyer, 37 Brayford Rd, Reading RG2 8LT (0734 873613).
Ground: As Lower Earley (above) **HQ:** Wallingford Arms, Caroline Str., Reading (0734 575272)
Colours: All red **Reserves colours:** Yellow/blue/yellow.

RIDES UNITED
Secretary: Mark Watchorn, 27 Ringwood, Great Hollands, Bracknell RG12 8YG (0344 411561).
Ground: Rides Community Centre, Gorse Ride North, Finchampstead (0734 732852).
Colours: Red/blue/white **Change colours:** Blue/sky/blue.

RIFLE VOLUNTEER
Secretary: Roy Martin, 23 Kent Close, Woosehill, Wokingham RG11 9AN (0734 891887).
Ground: Elizabeth Rd, Wokingham, Berks (off Norreys Ave.)
Colours: Green & black stripes/black/green & black

ROCKWELL COLLINS
Secretary: Steven Fahy, 4 Haddon Drive, Woodley, Reading RG5 4LU (0734 261111).
Ground: As Reading Old Blues (above) **Colours:** Yellow/green/yellow.
HQ: Rockwell Collins UK Ltd, Sutton Business Park, Reading.

ROUNDHEAD
Secretary: Eric Wise, 63 St Saviours Rd, Reading RG1 6EJ (0734 588426).
Ground: Coley Park, St Saviours Rd, Coley, Reading.
HQ: Roundhead Pub, Wensley Rd, Reading (0734 588426).
Colours: Green & white/white/red.

ROYAL MAIL
Secretary: Reg Leadbetter, 27 Strathy Close, Tilehurst, Reading RG3 2PP (0734 425217)
Ground: Cintra Park, Cintra Ave., Reading. **Cols:** Blue (red & white diamonds)/blue/blue
H.Q.: RPOSSC, 6 Richfield Ave., Reading (0734 568157). **Change colours:** All red

St BARTHOLOMEWS
Secretary: G Douglas, 26 Finch Rd, Maiden Erleigh, Reading RG6 2JU (0734 665091).
Ground: Sol Joel Playing Field, Church Rd, Earley, Reading.
Colours: Blue/white/blue **Change colours:** Red/black/red.

S.E.B. (READING)
Secretary: Philip Lewis, 21 Kent Rd, Reading RG3 2EJ (0734 575206).
HQ: Southern Electric Social Club, Vastern Rd, Reading.
Colours: Green & yellow/green/green **Grnd:** Christchurch Meadow, George St., Caversham, Rdg.

SHINFIELD
Secretary: Simon Gray, 15 Hawkesbury Drive, Fords Farm, Calcot, Reading RG3 5YZ (0734 443480)
Ground: Millworth Lane, Shinfield, Reading. **Colours:** All claret *(Reserves: All red)*.

SONNING
Secretary: Mrs Valerie Backhouse, 35 Pound Lane, Sonning, Reading RG4 0XD (0734 697009).
Grnd: The Pavilion, King George VI Mem. PF, Pound Lane, Sonning. **Colours:** Red/white/red.

SONNING COMMON
Secretary: Sue Evans, 287 Gosbrook Rd, Caversham, Reading RG4 8DX (0734 476646).
Ground: Peppard Cricket Club, Peppard Common, Stoke Row Rd, Peppard.
HQ: Red Lion, Peppard Common (0491 628329).
Cols: Red & black stripes/black/red **Reserves colours:** Red & white/white/red.

SONNING SPORTS
Secretary: Steven Freeman, 55 Francis Str., Reading RG1 2QB (0734 500017).
Ground: Palmer Park, Wokingham Rd, Reading. **Colours:** Orange/white/orange.

SOUTH END
Secretary: David Dawson, 24 Gosbrook Rd, Caversham, Reading RG4 8BS (0734 462057).
Ground: Bradfield Cricket Club, Heath Rd, Bradfield, Berks.
Colours: Black & white stripes/black/black.

SOUTH READING
Secretary: Terry Darlow, Four Horseshoes PH, 177 Basingstoke Rd, Reading RG2 0HX (0734 871604).
G: Whitley Wood, Rec., Basingstoke Rd, Reading **HQ:** 4 Horsehoes (see sec.) **Cols:** Red/black/black.

SOUTH READING C.C.
Secretary: Mike Gardner, 23 Buckland Rd, Reading RG2 7ST (0734 862859).
Colours: Orange/black/black **Ground & HQ:** As Rabson Rovers (above)

SUTTON EXILES
Secretary: Michael Charles, 32 Eastwood Rd, Woodley, Reading RG5 3PY (0734 448130).
Cols: Green & white/white/white **Ground:** Cintra Park, Cintra Avenue.
HQ: Mexifoods Ltd, Great Lea Farm, Three Mile Cross, Reading RG7 1LJ (0734 885472).

THAMESIDE
Secretary: Chris Francis, 23 Coventry Rd, Reading RG1 3ND (0734 664630).
H.Q.: Cellulair, Bennet Rd, Reading (0734 861961).
Colours: White/blue/mauve **Ground:** As Reading Town 'A' (above)

THAMES VALE
Secretary: Mrs N Croshaw, 114 Severn Way, Tilehurst, Reading RG3 4HU (0734 429452).
Colours: Green & white **Ground:** As Reading Town 'A' (above)

THEALE

Secretary: Chris Sheppard, 11 Carron Close, Tilehurst, Reading RG3 4DS (0734 412859).
Ground: Englefield Rd. Rec., Theale **H.Q.:** Crown Inn, Theale, Reading RG7 5DG (0734 302310).
Cols: Red & black stripes/black/black **Res. colours:** Blue & black stripes/black/black.

TILEHURST

Secretary: Pat Durkin, 83 Chichester Rd, Tilehurst, Reading RG3 4XJ (0734 422350).
Ground: Victoria Rec. Ground, Kentwood Hill, Tilehurst, Reading.
Cols: Black & white stripes/black/black **Res. cols:** Red/black/black.

TWYFORD & RUSCOMBE

Secretary: Miss M Bradbury, 4 Pennfields, Ruscombe, Twyford RG10 9BD (0734 345229).
Colours: Sky/navy/sky **Ground:** Loddon Hall Rd Rec., Twyford (0734 345268)

UNITY

Secretary: Richard Weekes, 65 Liverpool Rd, Reading RG1 3PN (0734 263227).
Ground: As SEB Reading (above). **HQ:** After Dark Club, London Street, Reading.
Colours: Amber/black/black (Alt: Yellow & red stripes/red/red).

WALLINGFORD RENEGADES

Secretary: David White, 14 Fludger Close, Wallingford, Oxon OX10 9BP (0491 834360).
Ground: Aston Tirrold Recreation Ground, Chalk Hill, Aston Tirrold, Oxon.
Colours: Grey/red/red **Change colours:** TBA.

WARGRAVE

Secretary: Andy Dearing, 4 Longfield House, Longfield Rd, Twyford RG10 9AN (0734 343065).
Ground: Wargrave Recreation Ground, Recreation Rd, Wargrave.
HQ: The Greyhound, High Street, Wargrave (0734 402556).
Colours: White/royal/royal **Reserves' colours:** All royal.

WEST READING

Secretary: Mrs Susan Porton, 6 Hampstead Court, Grovelands Rd, Reading RG3 2QQ (0734 504034).
Ground: Bensheaf Meadow Community Park, Calcot, Reading
Colours: Amber/black/black & amber **HQ:** Spread Eagle Pub, Norfolk Rd, Reading

WESTWOOD UNITED

Secretary: Mrs Penny Brodie, 58 Devonshire Gdns, Tilehurst, Reading RG3 6FP (0734 424329).
Ground: Cotswold Sports Centre, Downsway, Tilehurst, Reading.
H.Q.: Westwood Club, Downsway, Tilehurst, Reading (0734 429865)
Cols: Red & white/black/black **Change colours:** Yellow/blue/blue.

WOODLEY TOWN

Secretary: Mark Rozzier, 23 Welford Rd, Woodley, Reading RG5 4QS (0734 693235).
Ground: As Woodley Yeoman (below) **Cols:** Blue & white halves/royal/white.
Reserves' colours: Navy, white & emerald/navy/navy.

WOODLEY YEOMAN

Secretary: Mrs D Ballard, 68 Howth Drive, Woodley, Berks RG5 3EG (0734 662289).
Ground: Woodford Park, Haddon Drive, Woodley, Berks RG5 4LY (0734 690356).
Previous Name: Woodley Arms (pre-1993).
Colours: Green/white/white **Reserves colours:** Red & black stripes/black/black.

WYCLIFFE

Secretary: David Bolton, 2 Clements Close, Spencers Wood, Reading RG7 1HT (0734 883829).
Ground: Holme Park, Sonning Lane, Sonning.
HQ: Wycliffe Baptist Church, Church Kings Road, Reading (0734 666521).
Colours: Orange/white/white.

'READING EVENING POST' READING SENIOR CUP 1993-94

First Round

Wallingford United v West Reading	3-1	Henley Town v Didcot Casuals	4-2
Harwell v Old Prestonians	2-1	Benson v Forest Old Boys	2-4
Earlsbourne United v Reading Town	0-5	Theale v Stokenchurch	4-1
Faringdon Town v Binfield	0-5	Ibis v Peppard Reserves	3-3*(4-3 on penalties)*

Second Round

South Reading v Broadmoor Staff	2-3	Reading Town v Woodley Yeoman	5-3
AEA v Reading Exiles	0-9	Mortimer v Wallingford United	8-0
Drayton Wanderers v Ibis	0-4	Henley Town v Theale	4-0
Harwell v Forest Old Boys	2-0	Binfield v Finchampstead	0-2

Quarter-Finals

Finchampstead v Ibis	6-1	Reading Town v Henley Town	1-0
Mortimer v Harwell	2-3	Broadmoor Staff v Reading Exiles	3-2

Semi-Finals

Harwell v Finchampstead	0-0*(5-4 on pens)*	Broadmoor Staff v Reading Town	1-2

Final: Harwell 4, Reading Town 3 *(after extra-time)*

NORTH BERKS LEAGUE

FOUNDED: 1909

DIV. ONE	P	W	D	L	F	A	PTS
Saxton Rovers	26	21	4	1	104	14	46
Harwell	26	21	2	3	68	16	44
Drayton	26	19	2	5	59	44	40
Great Shefford	26	16	4	6	76	31	36
Berinsfield	26	10	4	12	69	64	24
Didcot Casuals	26	10	4	12	53	59	24
Faringdon Town	26	11	2	13	46	55	24
Woodcote	26	10	2	14	54	71	22
Botley United	26	9	4	13	32	53	22
Marcham	26	9	3	14	39	59	21
Sutton Courtenay	26	6	6	14	46	64	18
AEA	26	5	7	14	37	55	17
Grove Rangers	26	7	3	16	41	72	17
Benson	26	3	3	20	35	70	9

DIV. TWO	P	W	D	L	F	A	PTS
* Radley	24	17	4	3	82	28	38
* Saxton R. Res.	24	17	4	3	73	26	38
Steventon	24	14	6	4	49	29	34
Blewbury	24	13	4	7	61	48	30
Long Wittenham	24	14	1	9	68	32	29
Appleton	24	10	6	8	54	45	26
Shrivenham	24	11	2	11	61	45	24
Hanney United	24	9	4	11	46	45	22
Benson Lions	24	9	2	13	38	46	20
Wootton & DS Utd	24	7	4	13	36	45	18
Uffington United	24	6	3	15	36	77	15
Hagbourne United	24	5	4	15	26	64	14
Challow United	24	2	0	22	25	125	4

* - Saxton won title after play-off

DIV. THREE	P	W	D	L	F	A	PTS
Dorchester	24	21	1	2	75	15	43
Gt Shefford Res.	24	18	2	4	94	27	38
Warborough	24	16	1	7	67	48	33
Botley Res.	24	15	1	8	69	28	31
Stanford	24	12	3	9	61	52	27
Grove Rgrs Res.	24	10	2	12	50	53	22
Ardington	24	11	0	13	38	65	22
Lambourn Spts Res.	24	9	2	13	54	44	20
Radley Res.	24	8	4	12	60	73	20
Drayton Res.	24	8	3	13	32	48	19
Lg Wittenham Res.	24	7	3	14	42	63	17
AEA Res.	24	6	1	17	34	78	13
Shrivenham Res.	24	3	1	20	22	115	7

DIV. FOUR	P	W	D	L	F	A	PTS
Childrey United	26	21	5	0	131	21	47
Thatcham Town 'A'	26	18	2	6	92	31	38
Coleshill	26	18	2	6	102	50	38
Buckland	26	18	2	6	87	35	38
Faringdon T. Res.	26	17	3	6	100	30	37
Harwell Res.	26	15	5	6	120	30	35
Sutton Court. Res.	26	12	4	10	59	48	28
Didcot Cas. Res.	26	11	4	11	70	60	26
Woodcote Res.	26	8	4	14	57	79	20
Steventon Res.	26	8	3	15	41	60	19
Wootton & DS Res.	26	8	1	17	41	85	17
AEA 'A'	26	4	3	19	28	121	11
Stanford Res.	26	2	5	19	21	101	9
Challow Res.	26	0	1	25	15	203	1

DIV. FIVE	P	W	D	L	F	A	PTS
Kingston & South.	28	23	3	2	124	25	49
Blewbury Res.	28	21	3	4	115	39	45
Marcham Res.	28	17	5	6	94	48	39
Ardington Res.	28	15	5	8	75	57	35
Hanney Utd Res.	28	16	3	9	61	53	35
Dorchester Res.	28	12	7	9	64	59	31
Buckland Res.	28	12	4	12	52	60	28
Coleshill Res.	28	11	4	13	65	71	26
Faringdon Town 'A'	28	12	2	14	50	58	26
Benson Res.	28	9	4	15	73	84	22
Childrey U. Res.	28	9	4	15	49	73	22
Micro Focus	28	9	2	17	40	59	20
Uffington Res.	28	7	5	16	43	95	19
Hagbourne Res.	28	7	2	19	32	81	16
Warborough Res.	28	2	3	23	41	116	7

Cup Finals:
North Berks Cup: Harwell 2, Great Shefford 0
Charity Shield: Harwell 1, Saxton Rovers 0
League Cup: Thatcham 'A' 1, Sutt. Courtenay Res. 0
War Memorial Cup: Childrey Utd 3, Warborough 1
Kingham Cup: Botley Res. 2, Saxton R. Res. 1 *(aet)*
Allnatt Cup: Drayton 3, Berinsfield 2

HAYES & GILES INSURANCE EAST BERKS LEAGUE

DIV. ONE	P	W	D	L	F	A	PTS
Spital Old Boys	18	13	2	3	58	30	28
CBS (Bracknell)	18	13	2	3	49	33	28
Running Horse	18	10	4	4	51	30	24
Old Windsor F/WMC	18	10	2	6	50	37	22
Condors '24	18	9	2	7	35	26	20
Singh Sabha (Slough)	18	7	3	8	33	41	17
Bracknell Boys Club	18	5	5	8	40	45	15
Chalvey (WMC) Spts	18	7	1	10	44	54	15
Windsor Gt Park	18	2	3	13	21	55	7
Windsor & Eton CC	18	0	4	14	18	48	4

DIV. TWO	P	W	D	L	F	A	PTS
AC Maidenhead	22	19	2	1	87	28	40
Slough YCOB Res.	22	17	3	2	90	36	37
Iver Heath Rovers	22	13	2	7	72	49	28
Holyport	22	10	6	6	69	43	26
Braywick Rovers	22	11	4	7	55	46	26
Running Horse Res.	22	11	3	8	54	51	25
Prince of Wales	22	11	2	9	57	45	24
ICI (Slough)	22	9	1	12	63	59	19
Cippenham United	22	6	3	13	41	49	15
Slough Laurencians	22	5	2	15	38	85	12
Condors '94 Res.	22	3	2	17	32	86	8
Maidenhead Wdrs	22	1	2	19	21	102	4

DIV. THREE	P	W	D	L	F	A	PTS
Egham Royals	18	12	0	6	60	28	24
Slough Ryl Mail	18	10	3	5	50	30	23
Hewlett Packard	18	10	3	5	45	34	23
Waltham St Lwarence	18	9	3	6	55	34	21
Cippenham Sports	18	10	1	7	44	47	21
Iver Hth Rvrs Res.	18	8	1	9	46	55	17
Chalvey (WMC) Res.	18	6	3	9	37	49	15
BMW	18	6	1	11	28	41	13
Spital OB Res.	17	5	2	10	32	51	12
Slough Heating Res.	17	3	3	11	18	46	9

DIV. FOUR	P	W	D	L	F	A	PTS
Eton Town	18	13	1	4	77	30	27
Furze Platt	18	11	1	6	54	32	23
Jealotts Hill	18	10	3	5	48	35	23
Fromme Frais	18	9	2	7	51	43	20
Henley YMCA	18	9	2	7	42	39	20
Iver Res.	18	9	2	7	42	41	20
Bracknell Saints	18	7	1	10	51	53	15
Met. Office	18	7	1	10	41	44	15
Slough Laur. Res.	18	4	2	12	35	65	10
ICI (Slough) Res.	18	2	3	13	20	79	7

DIV. FIVE	P	W	D	L	F	A	PTS
Pheasant (Burnham)	17	17	0	0	90	18	34
Mercian United	18	11	3	4	57	37	25
Bracknell BC Res.	18	9	4	5	54	42	22
Ascot United	18	7	5	6	51	42	19
Front Line	18	6	5	7	44	45	17
Crane Sports	18	6	4	8	45	47	16
Slough Heat. 'A'	18	6	2	10	31	49	14
Hewlett Pack. Res.	17	5	4	8	31	50	14
Windsor & ECC Res.	18	4	3	11	35	49	11
Holyport Res.	18	2	2	14	28	87	6

DIV. SIX	P	W	D	L	F	A	PTS
KS Gryf	20	14	3	3	82	33	31
Holyport 'A'	20	13	2	5	68	39	28
Cippenham S. Res.	20	12	4	4	59	35	28
Running Horse 'A'	20	13	2	5	55	40	28
Waltham St L. Res.	20	10	6	4	65	44	26
Alcan	20	8	4	8	42	41	20
Britwell Chick. Ranch	20	7	2	11	32	53	16
Met. Office Res.	20	6	3	11	31	58	15
Patmoor Strikers	20	5	1	14	37	72	11
Hurley	20	4	2	14	31	59	10
Braywick R. Res.	20	0	7	13	22	50	7

Presidents Cup Final:
Hewlett Packard 2, Waltham St Lawrence 1

HIGH WYCOMBE SUNDAY COMBINATION

FOUNDED: 1967

PREM. DIV.	P	W	D	L	F	A	PTS
Hedsor Social	22	20	1	1	105	19	41
Lane End Utd	22	19	1	2	100	21	39
Wooburn Park	22	11	4	7	53	43	26
Chinnor Exiles	22	12	1	9	66	49	25
Bank of England	22	11	3	8	57	41	25
Pandect	22	12	1	9	59	48	25
Foresters	22	8	4	10	63	48	20
Hithercroft	22	9	2	11	58	63	20
King George V	22	7	5	10	39	61	19
Chinnor Sports	22	7	1	14	61	57	15
Rose & Crown	22	2	3	17	26	101	7
Black & Decker	22	0	2	20	16	152	2

Lower Division Champions:
Div. 1 (11): Bat & Ball
Div. 2 (11): Hughenden Valley
Div. 3 (12): Green Dragon
Div. 4 (13): Masons Arms
Div. 5 (14): Widmer End

OBSERVER INDUSTRIAL SUNDAY LEAGUE

FOUNDED: 1963

PREM. DIV.	P	W	D	L	F	A	PTS
Slough Irish	22	18	1	3	89	27	37
Sara Lee	22	14	3	5	77	48	31
Cippenham Sports	22	12	4	6	45	40	28
Iver Spts & Social	22	11	2	9	47	38	24
Langley Tavern	22	11	2	9	56	51	24
Nacional	22	10	3	9	45	45	23
AC Carpenters	22	10	2	10	40	47	22
KS Gryf	22	7	4	11	34	48	18
Old Paludians	22	7	4	11	25	40	18
Phoenix Old Boys	22	8	1	13	50	69	17
Slough Heating	22	3	5	14	29	50	11
ICI Dulux	22	5	1	16	41	65	11

Lower Division Champions:
Div. 1 (10): Swans
Div. 2 (10): Printers Devil
Div. 3 (10): Red Lion
Div. 4 (12): Langley Old Boys Res.

Challenge Cup Final *(at Wycombe Wdrs, 8th May)*: Hedsor Social 5, Bank of England Reserves 2

SLOUGH TOWN CHALLENGE CUP 1993-94

First Round
Windsor & Eton CC v Martin Baker Reserves 0-5
Slough Heating v Windsor Great Park 6-0
Eton Wick Reserves v Singh Sabha Slough 4-0

Second Round
Slough Laurencians v Martin Baker Res. 0-5
Old Paludians v Vansittart Wanderers 1-3
Slough Youth Club OB v Slough Heating 3-0
Condors '94 v ICI (Slough) 4-3
Chalvey v Eton Wick Reserves 1-4
Iver v Slough Irish 1-4
Beaconsfield United Res. v Wraysbury 0-6
Spital Old Boys v Phoenix Old Boys 3-1

Quarter-Finals
Slough Irish v Vansittart Wanderers 6-1
Spital OB v Slough Youth Club Old Boys 0-10
Martin Baker Reserves v Eton Wick Reserves 2-0
Wraysbury v Condors '94 4-2

Semi-Finals
Martin Baker Reserves v Slough Irish 0-1
Wraysbury v Slough Youth Club OB 1-1*(aet)*,0-6

Final *(at Slough Town FC, att: 750)*: Slough Irish 2, Slough Youth Club Old Boys 0

STANTONBURY CHARITY CUP 1993-94

The 'Stantonbury Hospital Cup', as it was first called, was founded in 1920 by the Stantonbury Hospital Fund Committee with all profits from the football competition, together with those of the Stantonbury Carnival, going to the Northampton General Hospital. The competition gained its present name in 1948 when the National Health Scheme came into being and the Hospital Fund ceased. The first final was won by Wolverton Town who beat Newport Autos 2-1 at the Red Bridge Field, New Bradwell, before a large crowd on May 12th, 1921.

First Round
Winslow United v Emberton 3-4
Hanslope v Newport Pagnell *(at N'port Pag.)* 0-2
Stony Stratford Town v Old Bradwell United 15-0
Sherington v Deanshanger 3-3*(at N'port Pag.)*,0-4

Semi-Finals (Two-legged)
Newport Pagnell v Emberton 1-0,1-1*(at N'port P.)*
Stony Stratford Town v Deanshanger Ath. 4-1,6-1

Final *(at The Park, Wolverton, Sun 8th May)*: Newport Pagnell Town 2, Stony Stratford Town 1

Newport Pagnell Town pictured after their Stantonbury Charity Cup victory. *Photo - Richard Brock.*

BIRMINGHAM F.A.

Secretary: M Pennick FFA,
Ray Hall Lane, Great Barr, Birmingham B43 6JF (021 357 4278).

SENIOR CUP 1993-94

First Round

Coleshill Town v West Bromwich Town 0-3
Banbury United v Kings Heath 4-0
Burton Albion v Solihull Borough 4-0
Northfield Town v Sandwell Borough 1-0
Evesham Utd v Paget Rgrs 1-1,0-0*(7-6 pens)*
Tamworth v Brierley Hill Town 1-0
Rocester v Sutton Coldfield Town 1-3
Darlaston v Halesowen Harriers 4-3
Oldbury United v Bolehall Swifts 0-1
Cradley Town v Worcester City 2-2,2-0
Mile Oak Rovers & Youth v Highgate United 2-2,1-2
Wednesfield v Stourbridge 2-4
Redditch United v Halesowen Town 1-1,2-4
Boldmere St Mich. v Atherstone 2-2,0-0*(4-1 pens)*

Second Round

Cradley Town v Bolehall Swifts 2-0
Burton Albion v Coventry City 1-0
Moor Green v Knowle 4-0
West Bromwich Town v Walsall 0-1
Hednesford Town v Darlaston 1-0
Banbury United v West Bromwich Albion 2-1
Halesowen Town v West Midlands Police 2-1
Racing Club Warwick v Northfield Town 4-4,1-2
Bedworth United v Highgate United 3-2
Birmingham City v Lye Town 4-0
Evesham United v Tamworth 1-3
Stratford Town v Wolverhampton Wanderers 1-0
Aston Villa v Willenhall Town 2-2,3-2
Dudley Town v Stourbridge 1-1,3-2
Boldmere St Michaels v VS Rugby 1-2
Nuneaton Borough v Sutton Coldfield Town 2-1

Third Round

Moor Green v Cradley Town 6-1
Aston Villa v Halesowen Town 2-0
Burton Albion v Bedworth United 1-0
Dudley Town v Hednesford Town 1-3
VS Rugby v Northfield Town 0-0,0-1
Stratford Town v Birmingham City 1-1,1-2
Walsall v Banbury United 1-1,2-1*(aet)*
Nuneaton Borough v Tamworth 2-0

Quarter-Finals

Aston Villa v Hednesford Town 1-2
Burton Albion v Birmingham City 1-3
Walsall v Northfield Town 2-1
Moor Green v Nuneaton Borough 6-1

Semi-Finals

Birmingham City v Walsall 1-1,1-3
Hednesford Town v Moor Green 3-1

Final *(at Hednesford Town FC, Tues 26th April)*: Hednesford Town 0, Walsall 3. Scorers: Lillis, Peer & Marsh.

LORD MAYOR of BIRMINGHAM'S CHARITY CUP 1993-94

First Round

Moor Green v Highgate United 2-1
Boldmere St Michaels v Solihull Borough 1-4
Paget Rangers v West Midlands Police 2-4
Sutton Coldfield Town v Northfield Town 2-0

Semi-Finals

Sutton Coldfield Town v Moor Green 2-1
West Midlands Police v Solihull Borough 0-3

Final *(at Moor Green FC, Mon 9th May)*: Solihull Borough 1, Sutton Coldfield Town 0

OTHER COUNTY FINALS:

Challenge Vase *(at Willenhall Town)*: Wolverhampton United 3, Handrahan Timbers 2
Junior Cup *(at Nuneaton Borough)*: Triumph 3, Sutton United 1
Sunday Challenge Cup *(at Ray Hall Lane, BCFA Hq)*: Lodge Cottrell 2, Dulwich 0 *(after 0-0 draw at Sutton Coldfield Town)*
Sunday Challenge Vase *(at Sutton Coldfield Town)*: Cradley Olympic 2, JF Kennedy 0
Sunday Junior Cup *(at Sutton Coldfield Town)*: Rover Sports 5, Delta 2
Minor Challenge Cup *(at Ray Hall Lane)*: Shenley Radford 3, Bedworth Trent Valley 1
Youth Cup *(at Ray Hall Lane)*: Stratford Town 1, Hednesford Town 0
W.H.L. Harrison Shield *(at Ray Hall Lane)*: Leamington & Dist. Sunday Lge 3, Tamworth Sunday Lge 1
Campbell Orr Shield *(at Ray Hall Lane)*: 'Mitchells & Butlers' Coventry Alliance XI 2, Birmingham AFA XI 1

STRATFORD-UPON-AVON ALLIANCE

FOUNDED 1896

JOURNAL PREM.	P	W	D	L	F	A	PTS
Henley Forest	22	17	3	2	62	30	54
Long Compton Rvrs	22	14	4	4	54	30	46
Badsey United	22	14	3	5	60	37	45
FISSC	22	13	4	5	59	28	43
Studley United	22	12	4	6	51	31	40
Bidford Boys Club	22	10	2	10	42	36	32
Alcester Keys	22	7	2	13	33	49	23
Inkberrow	22	6	5	11	22	42	23
Bretforton OB	22	6	3	13	25	50	21
Broadway United	22	6	2	14	41	58	20
Claverdon Old Boys	22	6	1	15	27	55	19
Alveston Res.	22	4	1	17	20	50	13

HERALD D1	P	W	D	L	F	A	PTS
Cattani	20	17	2	1	86	15	53
Inter Murphys	20	14	1	5	69	36	43
Recreation Rovers	20	13	2	5	53	41	41
Duke	20	11	5	4	50	35	38
Salford Priors	20	9	3	8	51	39	30
Quinton	20	7	3	10	34	51	24
Halfords	20	7	1	12	38	60	22
Henley Forest Res.	20	6	3	11	35	64	21
Moreton Morrell	20	5	3	12	24	52	18
Welford	20	4	2	14	36	52	14
Blockley Sports	20	2	5	13	35	66	11

WHITBREAD D2	P	W	D	L	F	A	PTS
Talbot	24	20	1	3	77	32	61
Wickhamford Sports	24	16	3	5	86	48	51
Leamington Vict.	24	15	5	4	77	30	50
FISSC Res.	24	14	3	7	65	34	45
Bidford Boys Res.	24	14	3	7	76	51	45
Badsey Utd Res.	24	13	4	7	71	39	43
Alcester Bear	24	12	2	10	80	62	38
Arrow Valley Soc.	24	11	4	9	70	49	37
Bretforton OB Res.	24	9	6	9	73	58	33
Henley Forest 'A'	24	6	3	15	39	81	21
Shipston Engineering	24	5	2	17	32	82	17
Long Compton Res.	24	1	2	21	25	103	5
Quinton Res.	24	1	0	23	24	126	3

Cup Finals:

Hospital Cup: Bretforton Sports OB 2, FISSC 1
Nursing Home Cup: Studley Utd 2, Henley Forest 1
Prem. Div. Cup: Badsey Utd 2, Bretforton Spts OB 0
Div. One Cup: Cattani 2, Welford 0
Div. Two Cup: Arrow Valley beat Alcester Bear 5-3 on penalties after a 4-4 draw.

HOTEL & CATERERS SPORTS ASSOC. (MIDLANDS)

	P	W	D	L	F	A	PTS
Jewel in the Crown	18	15	1	2	71	14	31
Wedgnock Inn	18	14	1	3	61	21	29
Wilmcote AFC '92	18	10	2	6	46	34	22
Home Bakery	18	9	2	7	49	29	20
Galileo	18	7	5	6	38	30	19
Stratford Albion	18	7	3	8	31	34	17
Tramway Rovers	18	6	3	9	38	44	15
Leamington Soc. C.	18	5	3	10	20	46	13
Nenplas	18	4	2	12	22	56	10
Tiddington	18	1	2	15	17	85	4

Cup Finals:

Association Shield: Wedgnock Inn 4, Jewel in Crn 3
De Vere Cup: Wedgnock I. 1, Jewel 0 *(after 3-3 draw)*

BIRMINGHAM & DISTRICT WEDNESDAY AMATEUR F.A.

FOUNDED: 1900

Once a three-division set-up, the association last season had just five teams. "The league started off when early closing was pretty much universal, though now it's much more difficult to find teams who can play on Wednesday afternoons", league President Dave Whitton told the *Birmingham Chronicle.*

	P	W	D	L	F	A	PTS
Hunters Moon	13	12	0	1	105	22	24
WM Market Traders	11	6	2	3	42	24	14
Midlands United	10	4	2	4	41	29	10
Goodyear Wingfoot	9	1	0	8	34	50	2
Small Heath Wed.	9	1	0	8	13	110	2

Golden Cross records expunged from League

Full 1993-94 results

Hunters Moon 3, Goodyear Wingfoot 2
Midlands United 2, Hunters Moon 6
Goodyear Wingfoot 1, Midlands United 5
Hunters Moon 4, West Mids Market Traders 2
Small Heath Wednesday 1, Midlands United 15
Small Heath Wednesday 0, Hunters Moon 6
Midlands United 3, West Mids Market Traders 3
Goodyear Wingfoot 1, Hunters Moon 10
West Mids Market Traders 10, Small Heath Wed. 1
Hunters Moon 6, Midlands United 1
Golden Cross 1, West Mids Market Traders 3
Goodyear Wingfoot 1, West Mids Market Traders 9
Midlands United 6, Small Heath Wednesday 1
Hunters Moon 16, Small Heath Wednesday 2
West Mids Market Traders 3, Midlands United 1
Midlands United 2, West Mids Market Traders 2
West Mids Market Traders 0, Hunters Moon 6
Goodyear Wingfoot 1, Hunters Moon 10
Small Hth Wednesday 2, West Mids Market Traders 1
Small Heath Wednesday 3, Hunters Moon 19
West Mids Market Traders 5, Goodyear Wingfoot 0
Goodyear Wingfoot 2, West Mids Market Traders 3
Hunters Moon 12, Small Heath Wednesday 3
Hunters Moon 5, Midlands United 1
Goodyear Wingfoot 1, Midlands United 5
West Mids Market Traders 4, Hunters Moon 2
Goodyear Wingfoot 25, Small Heath Wednesday 0

DUDLEY & CRADLEY HEATH SUNDAY LEAGUE

FOUNDED: 1910

PREMIER DIV.	P	W	D	L	F	A	PTS
Woodside United	20	17	3	0	91	19	37
Dudley Labour	20	17	1	2	86	31	35
Wollescote Villa	20	10	3	7	41	32	23
Tavern	20	10	2	8	41	31	22
Malt Shovel	20	10	1	9	42	50	21
Roebuck	20	9	2	9	44	32	20
Albron	20	10	0	10	42	40	20
Homark	20	7	3	10	44	52	17
Rose & Crown	20	5	4	11	41	62	14
Wrens Nest	20	2	3	15	27	77	7
C. Plough	20	2	0	18	24	97	4

Lower Division Champions:
Div. 1 (9): Railway Rangers
Div. 2 (11): Sporting Club
Div. 3 (10): Sedgley Red Lion
Div. 4 (11): Dock & Iron
Div. 5 (14): Waterloo Sports

Cup Finals:

Dudley Guest Cup: Woodside Utd 4, Washington 0
Joe Stanton Trophy: Dudley Labour 4, Railway Rangers 0
Thornleigh Freight Cup: Lower Gornal RBL 3, Coseley White Lion 2
Prem Div Cup: Woodside Utd 4, Wollescote Villa 0
Div 1 Cup: Railway Rgrs 2, Tenth Lock 1 *(aet)*
Div 2 Cup: Baggeridge Social 4, Old Hill Castle 0
Div 3 Cup: Colley Gate Talbot beat Castle Hill 5-4 on penalties after a 2-2 draw
Div 4 Cup: Hatfield Rangers 3, Dock & Iron 1
Div 5 Cup: Wordsley Lions beat Fox Tavern 3-2 on penalties after a 1-1 draw.
Sec. of the Year: Derek Alldritt (Tavern Olympic)

BIRMINGHAM & DISTRICT A.F.A.

PREM. DIV.	P	W	D	L	F	A	PTS
Wake Green Amtrs	26	17	5	4	81	25	39
Sutton United	26	17	5	4	63	26	39
Old Wulfrunians	26	17	4	5	71	46	38
Dunlop Sports	26	10	11	5	45	34	31
Walsall Phoenix	26	12	5	9	62	48	29
Smethwick Hall OB	26	8	10	8	39	41	26
Kynoch IMI	26	9	7	10	54	46	25
GEC Avery	26	10	4	12	59	72	24
Silhill	26	8	7	11	39	54	23
Parkfield Amateurs	26	7	6	13	50	62	20
Handsworth GSOB	26	7	6	13	48	71	20
Tamworth QEOB	26	7	5	14	38	72	19
Colinthians	26	5	7	14	43	68	17
Wythall Richmond	26	4	6	16	31	58	14

DIV. ONE	P	W	D	L	F	A	PTS
Village	24	18	2	4	62	26	38
Holly Lodge	24	16	5	3	78	46	37
Bickenhill	24	12	5	7	59	51	29
Shirley Athletic	24	12	3	9	63	38	27
Sutton United Res.	24	12	3	9	51	43	27
Penncroft	24	11	5	8	51	47	27
Wake Gn Am. Res.	24	11	4	9	62	44	26
West Hagley	24	9	7	8	53	42	25
Britannia OB	24	8	6	10	52	50	22
Causeway United	24	9	3	12	52	57	21
Univ. Barbarians	24	6	7	11	25	52	19
Scammell	24	2	7	15	37	64	11
St Francis Xavier	24	1	1	22	24	109	3

DIV. TWO	P	W	D	L	F	A	PTS
Old Nortonians	26	17	3	6	79	28	37
Elmdon Sports	26	16	4	6	86	40	36
Transaction	26	13	7	6	67	54	33
Wake Gn Am. 'A'	26	13	6	7	65	49	32
Collins	25	12	7	6	88	55	31
T'worth QEOB Res.	25	13	3	9	76	63	29
FC Milan	26	9	10	7	50	42	28
Welwyn	26	12	3	11	65	70	27
Ajax United	26	7	9	10	51	49	23
Sutton United 'A'	26	7	9	10	46	63	23
H'sworth GSOB Res.	26	8	6	12	60	67	22
Cresconians	26	6	2	18	42	90	14
West Mids Travel	25	5	4	16	50	117	14
Midland Bank	25	4	3	18	29	67	11

DIV. THREE	P	W	D	L	F	A	PTS
New Fullbrook	26	20	4	2	80	29	44
Silhill Res.	26	19	5	2	79	31	43
Brit Telecom Spts	26	17	6	3	73	38	40
Yardley Optical Snrs	26	15	8	3	85	41	38
CG Selley Oak	26	13	4	9	72	59	30
Bartley Green OB	26	13	4	9	74	67	30
Old Wulfrun. Res.	26	9	8	9	57	45	26
Barclays Bank	26	7	8	11	49	49	22
Britannic Assurance	26	7	4	15	45	64	18
Lloyds Bank	26	5	6	15	38	69	16
Sparkbrook Elim	26	4	7	15	55	85	15
Digby Amateurs	26	7	1	18	39	86	15
Somers Sports	26	5	4	17	65	105	14
Colinthians Res.	26	4	5	17	36	79	13

DIV. FOUR	P	W	D	L	F	A	PTS
Dunlop Spts Res.	26	22	1	3	128	41	45
Cradley Castings	25	16	7	2	70	35	39
W'sall Phoenix Res.	26	15	5	6	73	43	35
Parkfield Amtrs Res.	26	10	8	8	45	55	28
Silhill 'A'	25	11	4	10	60	49	26
Northfield Juniors	26	9	8	9	51	52	26
West Hagley Res.	26	10	4	12	58	64	24
College	26	8	7	11	54	59	23
St Phillips GSOB	26	9	5	12	69	86	23
Cresconians Res.	26	8	6	12	46	67	22
H'sworth GSOB 'A'	26	8	5	13	55	70	21
Tudor Webasto	26	8	2	16	47	67	18
Bantry Rovers	26	5	8	13	44	76	18
Handsworth Wood	26	4	6	16	44	80	14

DIV. FIVE	P	W	D	L	F	A	PTS
Engine White Star	24	19	4	1	97	34	42
GEC Avery Res.	24	15	4	5	76	41	34
Sutton Utd 'B'	24	14	6	4	65	38	*32
Yardley Grange	24	13	3	8	56	37	29
Keaps	24	12	5	7	54	43	29
Shirley Ath. Res.	24	11	3	10	51	41	25
Village Res.	24	8	6	10	51	57	22
Old Nortonians Res.	24	5	9	10	40	50	19
Britannia OB Res.	24	9	1	14	50	75	19
Wake Gn Amtrs 'B'	24	7	4	13	51	66	18
Welwyn Res.	24	7	4	13	44	60	18
Old Wulfrun. 'A'	24	5	5	14	43	70	15
T'worth QEOB 'A'	24	2	4	18	40	106	8

* - 2 points deducted

DIV. SIX	P	W	D	L	F	A	PTS
Perryfields Lincoln	24	19	3	2	101	29	41
Colmore Rovers	24	17	3	4	97	33	37
Old Wulfrun. 'B'	24	15	6	3	87	38	36
Severn Trent Water	24	15	3	6	69	37	33
Wood Wanderers	24	14	3	7	67	43	31
Silhill 'B'	24	11	5	8	71	56	27
Hansworth Wd Res.	24	12	3	9	77	67	27
Sutton United 'C'	24	9	5	10	59	66	23
Holly Lodge 'B'	24	6	4	14	52	61	16
Colinthians 'A'	24	5	3	16	52	80	13
Britannic As. Res.	24	6	1	17	49	116	13
Cresconians 'A'	24	2	4	18	27	102	8
Rowley	24	2	3	19	22	102	7

DIV. SEVEN	P	W	D	L	F	A	PTS
Silhill 'C'	24	18	2	4	96	39	38
B Telecom Res.	24	17	2	5	74	26	36
Settlement	24	16	3	5	80	41	35
Solihull Gas	24	14	3	7	77	51	31
Manchester Wdrs	24	12	4	8	68	47	28
Holly Lodge OB	24	12	4	8	67	49	28
Wake Gn Am. 'C'	24	12	2	10	84	69	26
Digby Amtrs Res.	24	8	5	11	58	59	21
Britannia OB 'A'	24	10	1	13	57	83	21
Sparkbrook El. Res.	24	7	2	15	53	73	16
Walsall Phoenix 'A'	24	7	2	15	43	90	16
Aston '76	24	5	1	18	37	100	11
H'sworth GSOB 'B'	24	2	1	21	33	100	5

DIV. EIGHT	P	W	D	L	F	A	PTS
Village 'A'	24	17	5	2	90	31	39
Dynamo Brandhall	24	17	2	5	84	39	36
Lloyds Bank Res.	24	15	3	6	67	30	33
College Res.	24	13	5	6	67	47	31
Sutton Utd 'D'	24	12	4	8	58	48	28
Old Nortonians 'A'	24	12	3	9	48	39	27
St Francis X. Res.	24	11	1	12	72	56	23
Silhill 'D'	24	8	3	13	44	60	19
Holly Lodge 'A'	24	7	5	12	66	91	19
Wake Gn Amtrs 'D'	24	5	5	14	32	55	15
Walsall Phoenix 'B'	24	3	9	12	36	76	15
Old Wulfrun. 'C'	24	5	4	15	43	66	14
Colinthians 'B'	24	5	3	16	32	92	13

DIV. NINE	P	W	D	L	F	A	PTS
GEC Avery 'A'	20	15	3	2	103	26	33
Parkfield Amtr 'A'	20	13	4	3	85	33	30
Rubery Athletic	20	12	3	5	50	26	27
Shirley Ath. 'A'	20	11	4	5	45	36	26
Colmore Rvrs 'A'	20	9	5	6	53	42	23
Engine WS Res.	20	10	2	8	67	48	22
Cresconians 'B'	20	7	3	10	45	77	17
H'sworth GSOB 'C'	20	7	0	13	62	90	14
Village 'B'	20	6	1	13	50	56	13
Dy. Brandhall Res.	20	3	3	14	33	83	9
Walsall Phoenix 'C'	20	3	0	17	20	96	6

CORONATION SUNDAY LEAGUE & ALLIANCE

PREM. DIV.	P	W	D	L	F	A	PTS
Kenwick Dynamo	22	18	2	2	75	18	38
Leefal	22	17	3	2	54	17	37
Kingshurst	22	12	5	4	47	28	31
Bournville Warriors	22	11	6	5	50	29	28
Sheldon Heath Soc.	22	8	6	8	38	41	22
Bordesley Rovers	22	9	1	12	39	60	19
Bell Marston Green	22	7	4	11	37	44	18
Wychall Sports	22	9	2	12	46	55	18
Farthings	22	7	4	11	30	39	18
St Gerrards	22	6	6	10	33	50	18
Olton Royale	22	3	4	15	29	48	10
Bromford Colts	22	2	3	17	32	91	7

Lower Division Champions:
Prem. Div. 1 (11): Richmond
Div. 1 (9): Aztec International
Div. 2 (10): Dovecote United
Div. 3 (11): Rio Saints
Div. 4 (11): Athletic Castle Vale
Alliance 1 (12): Greenlands Social
Alliance 2 (12): Marston Green Social
Alliance 3 (12): Silhill Rangers
Alliance 4 (12): Bournville Celtic
Alliance 5 (11): Lea Hall Brit. Legion

First Personnel Coronation Cup: Leefal
First Personnel Cor. Cup R-up: Kingshurst
Keeley Cup: Leefal
Keeley Cup R-up: Bournville Warriors
George Tomlinson Cup: FC Roma
George Tomlinson Cup R-up: HIM United
Sandells Snr Cup: Hare & Hounds Rednal 'A'
Sandells Senior Cup R-up: Rio Saints
Jim Walsh Cup: Rio Saints
Jim Walsh Cup R-up: Hare & Hounds Rednal 'A'
JR Computers Alliance Cup: Gallery
JR Computers All. Cup R-up: Marston Green
Delmar Cup: Marston Green Social
Delmar Cup R-up: Saltney Lions
Sid Houlders Cup: Marston Green Social
Sid Houlders Cup R-up: Farthings 'B'
Trevor Thornton Cup: Lea Hall Brit. Legion
Trev. Thorn. Cup R-up: Hare/Hounds Rednal 'B'
Celebration Disco Shield: Bournville Celtic
Cel. Disco Shld R-up: Lea Hall Brit. Legion

BEACON SUNDAY LEAGUE

FOUNDED: 1978

PREMIERSHIP	P	W	D	L	F	A	PTS
East Park Rangers	18	15	2	1	79	20	32
Fordhoves A.	18	14	0	4	54	39	28
Vicarage	18	10	3	5	37	33	23
Bentley	18	10	0	8	53	51	20
Wrottesley Arms	18	6	3	9	37	31	15
Pear Partridge	18	5	5	8	27	42	15
Claregate Wdrs	18	5	4	9	37	52	14
Woodcross Spread E.	18	5	3	10	23	44	13
Bescot United	18	5	3	10	27	51	13
Heath Town	18	3	1	14	18	29	7

Lower Division Champions:
Div. 1 (10): Sedgley Cabin
Div. 2 (12): Longacres
Div. 3 (11): Pear Tree

CENTRAL WARWICKSHIRE OVER-35's LEAGUE

FOUNDED: 1979

PREM. DIV.	P	W	D	L	F	A	PTS
Baldwin & Williams	14	12	1	1	51	12	25
Club Sporting	14	7	3	4	46	16	17
Farthings OB	14	7	2	5	27	35	16
Folly Lane OB	14	6	3	5	25	27	15
Kings Heath Vets	14	5	3	6	28	38	13
Painted Lady	14	4	2	8	19	29	10
Sher Khan	14	4	2	8	31	43	10
Co-op Tennis	14	3	0	11	16	43	6

Lower Division Champions:
Div. 2 (9): Kynoch

Cup Finals:
Open Cup: Club Sporting 1, Baldwin & Williams 0
W H Richards Mem. Cup: Kynoch 3, Kings Hth Vets 2
Supplementary Competition Play-off: Kings Heath Veterans 7, St Philips Veterans 5

Hill Top Rangers FC. The Midlands senior non-League scene has experienced a great upheaval this summer with the formation of the new Midland Football Alliance. Hill Top Rangers were one of the beneficaries, taking one of the ten places that became vacant in the Premier Division of the West Midlands (Regional) League.

CAMBRIDGESHIRE F.A.

Secretary: R E Rogers,
20 Aingers Road, Histon, Cambs CB4 4JP.

INVITATION CUP 1993-94

First Round

March Town United v Ely City	2-4	Soham Town Rgrs v Chatteris	3-3,1-1*(aet)*,1-3
Wisbech Town v Philips UK	3-0	Histon v Cambridge City	5-2

Semi-Finals

Histon v Wisbech Town	0-1	Chatteris Town v Ely City	2-1

Final *(at March Town Utd FC, 6th April)*: Chatteris Town 3, Wisbech Town 1 *(att: 43)*

CHALLENGE CUP 1993-94

Preliminary Round

TSB Rangers v Whittlesford United 2-3

First Round

Whittlesey United v Haddenham Rovers	6-3	Bebden v Haslingford	4-2
Gamlingay v Cherry Hinton	2-4	Great Shelford v Histon Reserves	3-1
Philips UK v Bluntisham Rangers	3-2	Chatteris Town Reserves v West Wratting	1-1,1-2
Linton Granta v Whittlesford United	3-1	Collenham United v Over Sports	1-2
Levrington v March Town Utd Res.	1-1,2-1	Steeple Bumstead v Foxton	2-2,3-2
Meanea United v Fulbourn Institute	1-4	Soham Town Rgrs Res. v Newmarket T. Res.	3-3,0-4
Somersham Town Reserves v Longstanton	2-7	Waterbeach v Bassingbourn	2-2,2-1
Godmanchester v Wisbech Town	3-1	Sawston Rovers *(bye)*	

Second Round

Levrington Sports v West Wratting	3-0	Linton Granta v Newmarket Town Reserves	2-3
Cherry Hinton v Godmanchester	4-2	Philips UK v Waterbeach	0-2
Over Sports v Great Shelford	2-1	Fulbourn Institute v Longstanton	2-0
Sawston Rovers v Steeple Bumpstead	4-0	Debden v Whittlesey United	4-2

Quarter-Finals

Waterbeach v Newmarket Town Reserves	3-1	Fulbourn Institute v Over Sports	3-1
Levrington Sports v Cherry Hinton	4-2	Debden v Sawston Rovers	2-0

Semi-Finals

Fulbourn Institute v Debden	3-1	Levrington Sports v Newmarket Town Reserves	2-1

Final *(at Ely City FC, Sat 7th May)*: Levrington Sports 2, Fulbourn Institute 0

OTHER COUNTY FINALS:

Sunday Challenge Cup: Howard Mallett 3, Anchor 1
Sunday Centenary Cup: Papworth 3, Poplar Farm 2

KERSHAW CAMBRIDGESHIRE LEAGUE

PREMIER A	P	W	D	L	F	A	PTS
Foxton	28	20	4	4	98	44	64
Steeple Bumpstead	28	20	3	5	52	29	63
Waterbeach	28	16	6	6	52	44	54
Cherry Hinton	28	16	3	9	46	47	51
Great Shelford	28	15	5	8	58	42	50
Philips UK	28	13	8	7	57	39	47
Godmanchester	28	10	6	12	42	53	36
Over Sports	28	9	8	11	48	47	35
Longstanton	28	7	9	12	38	49	30
West Wratting	28	9	3	16	41	56	30
Gamlingay	28	7	8	13	44	48	29
Fulbourn	28	7	8	13	41	47	29
Bassingbourn	28	7	8	13	35	59	29
Linton Granta	28	6	7	15	48	60	25
Haslingfield	28	3	4	21	47	83	10

DIV. 1A	P	W	D	L	F	A	PTS
Comberton United	24	18	4	2	76	31	58
Gt Shelford Res.	24	17	3	4	82	33	54
Cherry Hinton Res.	24	13	5	6	48	48	44
Balsham	24	10	6	8	42	32	36
Camb. Univ. Press	24	11	3	10	48	45	36
Linton Res.	24	9	8	7	54	49	35
Thurlow	24	9	5	10	46	44	32
Gamlingay Res.	24	7	5	12	37	43	26
Schering	24	8	2	14	44	64	26
Abington United	24	7	4	13	41	47	25
Fulbourn Res.	24	7	4	13	33	56	25
Eternit	24	7	2	15	35	62	23
Hardwick	24	6	3	15	43	75	21

PREMIER B	P	W	D	L	F	A	PTS
Somersham T. Res.	28	17	7	4	67	40	58
Newmarket T. Res.	28	16	9	3	74	41	57
Sawston Rovers	28	15	7	6	78	42	52
Bluntisham	28	12	8	8	74	48	44
Whittlesford	28	14	2	12	64	65	44
Soham T. Rgrs Res.	28	11	10	7	52	44	43
Histon Res.	28	12	6	10	49	51	42
Haddenham	28	9	9	10	50	42	36
Debden	28	9	9	10	59	57	36
Over Sports Res.	28	10	6	12	45	54	36
Cottenham United	28	9	3	16	51	88	30
TSB Rangers	28	9	5	14	47	47	29
Philips UK Res.	28	8	3	17	48	70	27
Steeple Bump. Res.	28	5	8	15	41	77	23
Earith United	28	6	4	18	33	72	22

DIV. 1B	P	W	D	L	F	A	PTS
Girton United	24	19	2	3	80	23	59
Mildenhall T. Res.	24	17	2	5	74	33	53
Papworth	24	14	5	5	62	32	47
Ely City Res.	24	12	6	6	56	56	42
Fordham	24	11	6	7	63	54	39
Soham United	24	11	3	10	50	59	36
Wicken Amateurs	24	10	3	11	62	58	33
Milton	24	7	7	10	55	47	28
Willingham	24	8	4	12	57	58	28
Barton Mills	24	4	11	9	28	42	23
St Ives T. Res.	24	5	7	12	44	56	22
Burwell	24	6	3	15	55	88	21
Littleport Town	24	1	3	20	27	107	6

(tables continued overleaf)

DIV. 2A	P	W	D	L	F	A	PTS
Waterbeach Res.	22	15	4	3	53	26	49
Ashdon Villa	22	15	3	4	55	28	48
West Wratting Res.	22	15	4	4	68	26	46
Great Chishill	22	14	4	4	61	26	46
Fowlmere	22	9	4	9	53	36	31
Sawston United	22	9	3	10	52	41	30
Debden United	22	8	3	11	41	57	27
Duxford United	22	6	4	12	43	61	22
Thurlow Res.	22	7	1	14	39	84	22
Litlington Ath.	22	6	2	14	25	56	20
Melbourn	22	6	1	15	26	57	19
Philips UK 'A'	22	6	1	15	31	49	16

DIV. 2B	P	W	D	L	F	A	PTS
West Row	24	21	1	2	99	33	64
Camden United	24	19	1	4	55	26	58
Hemingford United	24	14	6	4	77	44	48
Godmanchester Res.	24	14	2	8	55	40	44
Warboys Town Res.	24	11	2	11	43	40	35
Little Downham	24	11	1	12	38	35	34
Napp Sports	24	10	3	11	45	45	33
Bluntisham Res.	24	10	3	11	38	41	33
Swavesey	24	9	3	12	52	50	30
Longstanton Res.	24	7	4	13	39	64	25
Lode	24	7	2	15	38	59	23
Isleham United	24	5	3	16	31	68	18
Eastern Gas	24	1	3	20	18	83	6

DIV. 3A	P	W	D	L	F	A	PTS
Cherry Hinton 'A'	20	15	1	4	57	27	46
Orwell	20	14	2	4	64	30	44
Mott McDonalds	20	12	3	5	70	34	39
Sawton Rovers Res.	20	11	4	5	56	29	37
Bassingbourn Res.	20	11	2	7	38	29	35
Comberton Utd Res.	20	10	2	8	48	39	32
Haslingfield Res.	20	9	4	7	42	36	31
Whittlesford Res.	20	5	6	9	36	43	21
Fulbourn 'A'	20	3	4	13	33	68	13
Papworth Res.	20	2	3	15	29	65	9
TSB Res.	20	2	1	17	13	86	7

DIV. 3B	P	W	D	L	F	A	PTS
Camb. UP Res.	22	19	0	3	85	27	57
Somersham T. 'A'	22	15	1	6	60	33	46
Stretham	22	12	5	5	54	37	41
Milton Res.	22	12	3	7	59	38	39
Cottenham U. Res.	22	10	4	8	52	40	34
West Row Res.	22	9	2	11	49	50	29
Haddenham R. Res.	22	8	5	9	48	59	29
Coleridge	22	8	3	11	49	53	27
Dullingham	22	8	2	12	50	55	26
Earith Utd Res.	22	8	1	13	34	63	25
Sutton United	22	5	5	12	33	52	20
Camden Res.	22	1	3	18	27	93	6

Below: *Steeple Bumpstead FC - Kershaw Cambridgeshire League runners-up 1993-94.*
Photo - Martin Wray.

DIV. 4A	P	W	D	L	F	A	PTS
Interoyston	24	20	2	2	82	31	62
Foxton Res.	24	14	8	2	67	34	50
Barrington	24	13	4	7	49	29	43
Castle Camps	24	13	3	8	59	43	42
Tally Ho Trumpington	24	12	3	9	48	44	39
Ashdon Villa Res.	24	11	4	9	43	38	37
Linton 'A'	24	11	3	10	55	39	36
Saffron Rangers	24	11	1	12	56	54	34
Sawston White Lion	24	10	4	10	38	41	34
Abington Res.	24	9	2	13	39	56	29
Elmdon	24	6	2	16	44	54	20
Harston	24	3	6	15	28	69	15
Fowlmere Res.	24	1	2	21	18	94	5

DIV. 4B	P	W	D	L	F	A	PTS
St Ives Town 'A'	24	18	3	3	71	31	57
Soham United Res.	24	15	4	5	79	38	49
Marshalls Sports	24	14	2	8	70	38	44
Fulbourn Hospital	24	12	6	6	64	40	42
Mepal Sports	24	12	5	7	45	35	41
Ely City 'A'	24	12	4	8	51	42	40
Bottisham Sports	24	8	8	8	47	43	32
Fordham Res.	24	8	3	13	36	58	27
Willingham Res.	24	7	5	12	39	56	26
Milton 'A'	24	8	2	14	43	80	26
Ltle Downham Res.	24	6	4	14	48	70	22
Littleport T. Res.	24	6	3	15	44	63	21
Wilbraham	24	4	3	17	20	63	15

DIV. 5A	P	W	D	L	F	A	PTS
Schering Res.	24	18	4	2	65	24	58
Sawston Utd Res.	24	16	6	2	73	23	54
Newport Veterans	24	17	1	6	75	39	52
Great Chesterford	24	13	5	6	69	37	44
Gt Chishill Res.	24	12	5	7	52	40	41
Elsworth Sports	24	12	2	10	64	51	38
Barton	24	11	2	11	55	45	35
Duxford Res.	24	10	3	11	51	53	33
Litlington Res.	24	9	4	11	40	48	31
Melbourn Res.	24	8	4	12	43	66	28
Barrington Res.	24	3	4	17	35	65	13
Sawston WL Res.	24	3	4	17	14	68	13
Castle Camps Res.	24	2	0	22	20	97	6

DIV. 5B	P	W	D	L	F	A	PTS
Newmarket SC	24	21	2	1	113	30	65
Mildenhall Town 'A'	24	17	1	6	82	39	52
Napp Sports Res.	24	14	5	5	69	37	47
Hemingford Res.	24	13	5	6	76	37	44
Over Sports 'A'	24	13	4	7	61	35	43
Girton United Res.	24	13	2	9	65	54	41
Hardwick Res.	24	9	2	13	50	69	29
Barton Mills Res.	24	6	7	11	32	44	25
Camb. Uni. P. 'A'	24	6	5	13	39	63	23
Isleham Utd Res.	24	7	1	16	38	63	22
Coleridge Res.	24	6	1	17	42	101	19
Sutton Utd Res.	24	5	4	15	28	100	19
Lode Res.	24	5	3	16	30	53	18

Newmarket Town Reserves - Premier 'B' runners-up 1993-94. Back Row (L/R): T Phillips (Trainer), G Chilvers, J Portlock, B Phillips, S Rutherford, G Bugg, M Hateley, R Conway, A Free (Asst Manager). Front: M Wallace, J Grimster, J Campbell, G Grainger, S Warner, P Cole (Manager).

Philips UK, who had a disappointing season after their championship success of 1992-93

Soham Town Rangers Reserves. Back Row (L/R): C Cooke, C Hood (Captain), M Ogden, S Saby, C Boneham, R Goodjohn, S Sizer (Manager). Front: J Bedford, M Wells, S Day, G Purdey, P Braybrooke, L Pyle.

All Photos - Martin Wray.

PETERBOROUGH & DISTRICT LEAGUE

Hon. Secretary: M J Croson,
44 Storrington Way, Werrington,
Peterborough PE4 6QP.

ESTABLISHED 1902

PREM. DIV.	P	W	D	L	F	A	PTS
Ortonians	30	23	5	2	78	26	74
Perkins Sports	30	18	7	5	86	37	61
Moulton Harrox	30	16	7	7	69	37	55
Eye United	30	16	7	7	75	47	55
Deeping Rangers	30	15	3	12	53	54	48
Pinchbeck United	30	12	5	13	50	56	41
Hotpoint	30	11	7	12	57	50	40
Stamford Belvedere	30	11	7	12	61	79	40
Thomas Cook	30	9	11	10	61	56	38
Leverington Spts	30	9	8	13	55	56	35
Oundle Town	30	9	8	13	58	63	35
Whittlesey United	30	9	7	14	41	64	34
Wisbech Town Res.	30	8	7	15	42	62	31
March T. Utd Res.	30	7	8	15	31	65	29
Alconbury	30	6	10	14	48	72	28
Chatteris T. Res.	30	5	5	20	20	68	20

DIV. ONE	P	W	D	L	F	A	PTS
Outwell Swifts	30	21	7	2	85	30	70
Ortonians Res.	30	18	8	4	84	33	62
Kings Cliffe	30	20	1	9	87	55	61
Perkins Spts Res.	30	16	6	8	66	38	54
Brotherhoods Spts	30	16	4	10	61	56	52
Pearl Assurance	30	15	4	11	75	50	49
Manea United	30	14	7	9	62	46	49
Thomas Cook Res.	30	13	3	14	58	63	42
Stilton United	29	13	2	14	72	60	41
Ryhall United	30	12	2	16	64	78	38
Holbeach U. Res.	30	11	4	15	45	61	37
Deeping Rgrs Res.	30	10	3	17	51	65	33
ICA Juventus	29	8	8	13	37	46	32
Pinchbeck Utd Res.	30	8	3	19	35	76	27
Thurlby United	30	6	6	18	47	96	24
Newage	30	2	4	24	38	114	10

Below: *Wayne Woods, captain of Outwell Swifts, receives the championship trophy from League Vice-President Richard Senior.*

Photo - Martin Wray.

DIV. TWO	P	W	D	L	F	A	PTS
Ketton	26	16	6	4	60	32	54
Deeping Rgrs 'A'	26	14	9	3	63	31	51
March T. Utd 'A'	26	15	3	8	63	52	48
Leverington S. Res.	26	13	6	7	65	39	45
Crowland Town	26	13	6	7	64	48	45
Gedney Hill	26	12	3	11	51	42	39
Stamford Bel. Res.	26	11	5	10	49	50	38
Sawtry	26	11	5	10	49	51	38
Ramsey Town Res.	26	8	5	13	46	46	29
Oundle Town Res.	26	8	5	13	52	61	29
Whittlesey U. Res.	26	7	7	12	43	48	28
Glinton United	26	7	5	14	28	45	26
Doddington Utd	26	7	3	16	35	71	24
Peterborough Rvrs	26	5	2	19	39	91	17

DIV. THREE	P	W	D	L	F	A	PTS
Eye United Res.	28	25	1	2	104	35	76
Pearl Assur. Res.	28	17	4	7	77	40	55
Moulton Harrox Res.	28	14	5	9	63	57	47
Hotpoint Res.	28	13	4	11	67	50	43
Oakham Town '91	28	13	3	12	84	58	42
Hereward Old Boys	28	11	8	9	50	53	41
Silver Jubilee	28	11	6	11	79	73	39
Throney	28	11	6	11	75	82	39
Bell Walsoken	28	10	9	9	54	63	39
Thomas Cook 'A'	28	11	5	12	64	55	38
March St Marys	28	9	7	12	47	79	34
Alconbury Res.	28	9	4	15	45	64	31
Thurlby Utd Res.	28	9	3	16	54	82	30
Newage Res.	28	6	8	14	37	63	26
Stilton Utd Res.	28	2	5	21	37	83	11

DIV. FOUR	P	W	D	L	F	A	PTS
Whittlesey B Star	30	19	6	5	84	43	63
Outwell Swifts Res.	30	19	6	5	82	45	63
Ryhall Utd Res.	30	19	5	6	99	43	62
Chatteris Town 'A'	30	20	2	8	84	53	62
Fairleede Spt Man.	30	18	2	10	74	43	56
Pearl Assurance 'A'	30	15	4	11	77	61	49
Hereward OB Res.	30	12	7	11	76	83	43
Leverington S. 'A'	30	12	7	11	50	60	43
Parson Drove	30	13	2	15	59	67	41
Torney Res.	30	11	4	14	70	73	37
Glinton Utd Res.	29	8	8	14	53	63	32
Manea United Res.	30	8	5	17	50	75	29
Oakham T. '91 Res.	30	7	7	16	60	83	28
Wimblington	30	7	4	19	46	88	25
Sawtry Res.	29	7	3	19	46	83	24
Doddington U. Res.	30	6	4	20	44	91	22

DIV. FIVE	P	W	D	L	F	A	PTS
Langtoft United	22	19	3	0	106	15	60
Brotherhoods Res.	22	17	3	2	70	15	54
Deeping R. Res.	22	13	3	6	67	33	42
Kings Cliffe Res.	22	14	0	8	69	43	42
Sutton Bridge	22	13	0	9	61	37	39
March BRAZA	22	12	2	8	51	38	38
Crowland Town Res.	22	11	1	10	49	48	34
Silver Jubilee Res.	22	9	0	13	58	69	27
March St Marys Res.	22	7	0	15	43	73	21
Ketton Res.	22	7	0	15	44	78	21
Gorefield	22	3	1	18	24	86	10
Wisbech C W House	22	0	1	21	20	127	1

Senior Cup winners: Perkins Sports
Challenge Cup: Kings Cliffe
Jnr Cup: Hotpoint Res. **Minor Cup:** Langtoft U.

PHOTOS OPPOSITE *(all by Martin Wray)*

Top: *Ortonians - League Champions 93-94. Back (L/R): Graham Norris, Neale Chinery, Alan Bird, Neil Hursthouse, Mick Shortland, Lee Davison. Front: Mick Graham, Simon Fletcher, Mick Talbot, Darren French, John McLeod.*

Centre: *Outwell Swifts - Division One Champions.*

Foot: *Eye Utd FC. Back: P Foskett (Trainer), C Goldsmith, P Lilley, J Winters, L Peacock, G Richardson, D English, A Barker, S Hurry (Mgr). Front: P McCrudden, S Laws, P Johnson, R Blake, M Jeary.*

PETERBOROUGH & DISTRICT LEAGUE CLUB DIRECTORY

ALCONBURY
Secretary: Mrs S Glover, 16 Rockingham Road, Sawtry, Hunts PE17 6SQ (0487 832095).
Ground: Alconbury Sports & Social Club, Gt. North Road, Alconbury. **Colours:** Gold/Black.

BELL (WALSOKEN)
Secretary: Keith Williams, 22 Guild Road, Wisbech Cambs PE13 3UL (0945 64564)
Ground: Barton Road, Wisbech **Colours:** All red.

BROTHERHOOD SPORTS
Secretary: T Bannister, 19 Scalford Drive, Dogsthorpe, Northants PE1 4XQ (0733 890045).
Ground: Peterborough Sports & Leisure, Lincoln Road. **Colours:** White & Blue.

CHATTERIS TOWN RESERVES
Secretary: Tony Summers, 41 The Elms, Chatteris, Cambs PE16 6JN (0354 692062).
Ground: West Street, Chatteris. **Colours:** White & Sky Blue.

CROWLAND TOWN
Secretary: Jackie Atkinson, 4 The Chase, Crowland, Lincs PE6 0LN (0733 211431).
Ground: Snowden Field, Thorney Road, Crowland. **Colours:** Red & White.

DEEPING RANGERS
Secretary: Jon Sandall, 11 Curlew Walk, Market Deeping, Lincs PE6 8RY (0778 346006).
Ground: Outgang Road, Market Deeping **Colours:** Claret & Blue.

DODDINGTON UNITED
Secretary: D Bamford, 9 Church Lane, Doddington, Cambs PE15 0TA (0354 740026).
Ground: Hospital Road, Doddington. **Colours:** Red & Red.

EYE UNITED
Secretary: P Mitchell, 9 Little Johns Close, Peterborough, Northants PE3 9AS (0733 261586).
Ground: Lindisfarne Road, Eye. **Colours:** Green & White.

FAIRLEEDE
Secretary: P. Buddle, 81 West Street, Chatteris, Cambs PE16 6HR (0345 693710).
Ground: Fairway, Chatteris. **Colours:** Orange.

GEDNEY HILL
Secretary: David Barfoot 'Conifers', Shepeau Stow, Whaplode Drove Spalding PE12 0UQ. (0406 330619).
Ground: North Road, Gedney Hill. **Colours:** Navy & Sky Blue.

GLINTON UNITED
Secretary: S Pateman, 8 Sheridan Road, Peterborough, Northants PE1 3LQ (0733 348049.
Ground: Rectory Lane, Glinton. **Colours:** Claret & Blue.

GOREFIELD
Secretary: Edward Grange, 155 Broadgate, Sutton St. Edmund, Spalding, Lincs PE12 0LT (0945 700628).
Ground: Wolf Lane, Gorefield. **Colours:** Red.

HEREWARD OLD BOYS
Secretary: Russell Lowe, 54 Ellingham Avenue, March, Cambs PE15 9TE (0404 51835).
Ground: Estover Road, or Neale Wade School, March. **Colours:** Blue & Black.

HOLBEACH UNITED RESERVES
Secretary: John Crunkhorn, The Old Nurseries, Barbers Corner, High Road, Whaplode, Spalding Lincs PE12 6OA (0406 22540).
Ground: Carters Park. **Colours:** Old Gold & Black.

HOTPOINT
Secretary: A Andrews, 3 Faringdon Close, Peterborough, Hunts PE1 4RR (0733 342897).
Ground: Celta Road. **Colours:** Sky Blue.

I.C.A./JUVENTUS
Secretary: Carmine Salerno, 77 Garton End Road, Peterborough, Hunts PE1 4EZ (0733 53280).
Ground: Fletton Avenue. **Colours:** Blue & White.

KETTON
Secretary: Alan Pearce, 11 Capendale Close, Ketton, Leics PE9 3RU (0780 721163).
Ground: Pit Lane, Ketton, nr Stamford **Colours:** Red & White.

KINGS CLIFFE UNITED
Secretary: Mrs C A Lattimore, 72 Wood Road, Kings Cliffe, Peterborough PE8 6XF (0780 470538)
Ground: Middle School, Kings Cliffe. **Colours:** Red & Navy.

LANGTOFT UNITED
Secretary: Jane Woodthorpe, 16 East End, Langtoft, Lincs PE6 9LP (0733 347253)
Ground: Langtoft Sports Ground. **Colours:** Black & White.

LEVERINGTON SPORTS
Secretary: Neville Missin, 12 Gorefield Road, Leverington, Wisbech, Cambs PE13 5BB (0945 582234).
Ground: Church Road, Leverington. **Colours:** Yellow & black.

MANEA UNITED
Secretary: Philip Hawes, 25 Station Road, Manea, Cambs PE15 0JA (0354 680355).
Ground: Park Road, Manea. **Colours:** Green & Black.

MARCH BRAZA
Secretary: Roger Money, 147 Cavalry Drive, March, Cambs PE15 9OP (0354 56550).
Ground: Braza Playing Field, Elm Road, March. **Colours:** Blue & Blue.

MARCH St MARY
Secretary: P. Mason, 58 Hereward Street, March, Cambs PE15 8LZ (0354 51735).
Ground: Estover Road, March. **Colours:** Red & Blue.

MARCH TOWN UNITED RESERVES

Secretary: C R Woodcock, 24 Grounds Avenue, March, Cambs PE15 9BG (0354 54817).
Ground: Estover Road. **Colours:** Yellow/Blue & Blue

MOULTON HARROX

Secretary: Jeremy Hudson, 12 Breda Court, Aalsmeer Rise, Spalding Lincs (0775 762773).
Ground: Broad Lane, Moulton. **Colours:** Gold & Black.

NEWAGE

Secretary: Terry Brookes, 38 Parkfield Road, Ryhall, Stamford, Lincs PE9 4ER (0780 51407).
Ground: Empingham Road. **Colours:** Blue & Blue.

OAKHAM TOWN '91

Secretary: Philip Hitchens, Dolben Lodge, Ranksborough Hall, Langham, Leics (0572 722984).
Grnd: Vale of Cathos Coll., Cold Overton Rd, Oakham. **Colours:** Yellow & Green.

ORTONIANS

Secretary: Peter Spridgeon, 79 Granville Ave., Northborough, Hunts PE6 9DE (0778 342011).
Ground: Bushfields Sports Centre. **Colours:** Blue.

OUNDLE TOWN

Secretary: M W Smith, 5 Bassett Place, Oundle, Peterborough, Northants PE8 4BT (0832 272013).
Ground: Station Road, Oundle. **Colours:** Black & White Stripes.

OUTWELL SWIFTS

Secretary: D Luckett, Monterrey, Basin Road, Outwell, Wisbech, Cambs PE14 8TQ (0945 773012).
Ground: The Nest, Wisbech Rd, Outwell. **Colours:** Blue & White Halves.

PARSON DROVE '92

Secretary: Mrs A Richardson, 12 Station Avenue, Murrow, Wisbech, Cambs (0945 700404).
Ground: Main Road, Parson Drove. **Colours:** White & Navy.

PEARL ASSURANCE

Secretary: R Young, 11 Holmes Way, Paston, Peterborough, Northants PE4 7XZ (0733 576461).
Ground: Woodlands, Splash Lane, Castor. **Colours:** Yellow.

PERKINS SPORTS

Secretary: J Canty, 25 Sherbourne Road, Peterborough, Northants (0733 54883).
Ground: Oxney Road, Peterborough. **Colours:** Blue.

PETERBOROUGH ROVERS

Secretary: Mrs M J Starkey, 18 Wisbech Road, Thorney, Peterborough, Northants PE6 0SB (0733 270836).
Ground: Fulbrige Road, Peterborough. **Colours:** Blue/White & Black.

PINCHBECK UNITED

Secretary: C Clow, 2 Milestone Lane, Pinchbeck, Spalding Lincs PE11 3XX (0775 680330).
Ground: Knight Street, Pinchbeck. **Colours:** Red & Black.

Pinchbeck United FC. Back Row (L/R): T Dames, F Gent, P Howard, M Sargeant, D Whisker, G Harrison, S Moore. Front: C Woolsey, P Blackburn, S Foster, T Maltby. *Photo - Martin Wray.*

RAMSEY TOWN RESERVES

Secretary: M J Baldwin, 19 Slade Close, Ramsey, Huntingdon PE17 2RN (0487 814084).
Ground: Cricket Field Lane, Ramsey, PE17 1BG. **Colours:** Yellow & Black.

RYHALL UNITED

Secretary: R A Young, 17 Cliff Crescent, Stamford, Lincs PE9 1AG (0780 62552x384).
Ground: Meadows Playing Field, Ryhall. **Colours:** Blue & White.

SAWTRY

Secretary: Alan Vallance, 7 Abbey Close, Sawtry, Huntingdon PE17 5UG (0487 834734).
Ground: Greenfields, Straight Drove, Sawtry or Gidding Road, Sawtry.
Colours: Amber & black.

SILVER JUBILEE
Secretary: Nigel Frith-Robinson, 105 Langley, Bretton, Peterborough, Northants PE3 8QD (0733 264544).
Ground: Bretton Woods. **Colours:** Red & Black.

STAMFORD BELVEDERE
Secretary: K Rawlins, 25 Lancaster Road, Stamford, Lincs PE9 1LJ (0708 62577).
Ground: Queen Eleanor School, Green Lane, Stamford. **Colours:** Amber & Black.

STILTON UNITED
Secretary: Mrs Pam Gibbs, 29 Manor Road, Stilton, Peterborough PE7 3XA (0733 241201).
Ground: Darke Memorial Playing Field, Stilton. **Colours:** Blue.

SUTTON BRIDGE UNITED
Secretary: David Earth, 58 St. Mathews Drive, Sutton Bridge, Lincs PE12 9RJ (0406 350667).
Ground: Memorial Park, Sutton Bridge. **Colours:** Red & Black Stripes.

THOMAS COOK
Secretary: Sean Gallagher, 12 Lingwood Park, Longthorpe, Peterborough PE3 6RX (0733 330400).
Ground: Thorpe Wood, Peterborough. **Colours:** Red & Black.

THORNEY
Secretary: P J Chelton, 4 Woburn Drive, Thorney, Peterborough, Cambs PE6 0SN (0733 270578).
Ground: The Park, Thorney. **Colours:** Amber & Black.

THURLBY
Secretary: A Pfleiderer, 4 Park View, Thulby, Lincs PE10 0EU (0778 393739).
Ground: Lawrence Park, Thurlby. **Colours:** White & Blue.

WALNUTS SPORTS
Secretary: Mr A Spink (0945 585691).
Ground: Gordon Fendyck School, Wisbech. **Colours:** Blue & Yellow.

WHITTLESEY BLUE STAR
Secretary: I Medcalf, 77 Fountains Place, Eye, Cambs PE6 7XX (0733 223589).
Ground: Manor Leisure Centre, Station Rd, Whittlesey. **Colours:** Sky Blue & Claret

WHITTLESEY UNITED
Secretary: T G Bass, 23 Horsegate, Whittlesey, Cambs PE7 1JD (0733 203078).
Ground: Manor Field, Station Road, Whittlesey. **Colours:** Royal Blue

WIMBLINGTON
Secretary: Michael Boyden, 30 Eaton Estage, Wimblington, Cambs PE15 0QE (0354 740342).
Ground: The Park Wimblington. **Colours:** Royal Blue.

WISBECH CARPET WAREHOUSE
Secretary: Alan Milton, Star Cottage, Sutton St. James, Spalding, Lincs PE12 0SR (094585 371).
Ground: Spalding Castle Sports Centre. **Colours:** White & Blue

WISBECH TOWN RESERVES
Secretary: G B Roseberry, Gaywood, Friday Bridge Rd, Elm, Wisbech, Cambs PE14 0AT (0945 860791).
Ground: Fenland Park, Lerowe Road, Wisbech. **Colours:** All Red.

INTER SPORT PETERBOROUGH & DIST. SUNDAY COMBINATION

FOUNDED: 1969

DIV. ONE	P	W	D	L	F	A	PTS
L T Athletic	16	14	2	0	73	16	44
Peter Pan	16	9	4	3	55	29	31
Broadgate	16	8	3	5	39	33	27
Aragon	16	8	1	7	46	34	25
Redring Electric	16	6	3	7	40	43	21
Crown	16	5	5	6	39	42	20
Swiss Cottage	16	6	1	9	36	65	19
Railway	16	3	1	12	26	61	10
Monarch	16	2	2	12	29	60	8

Lower Division Champions:
Div. 2 (13): McCains
Div. 3 (13): L T Athletic Res.
Div. 4 (14): New Dimensions

Hereward Sports Divs 1 & 2 Cup: L T Athletic
Hereward Sports Cup R-up: McCain
McCain Divs 3 & 4 Cup: Thomas Cook
McCain Cup R-up: Peterborough Railway

CAMBRIDGE & DISTRICT SUNDAY LEAGUE

Frank Holland Senior Div.

	P	W	D	L	F	A	PTS
Sawston Keys	16	14	2	0	82	18	44
Bar Hill	16	10	4	2	65	14	34
Italcomb	16	9	3	4	59	30	30
Howard Mallett	16	9	1	6	42	38	28
Swaffham United	16	7	2	7	39	42	23
Newnarket Albion	16	5	4	7	22	37	19
Girton Eagles	16	5	3	8	31	47	18
Fordham Crown Rgrs	16	3	1	12	30	67	10
Fulbourn Athletic	16	0	0	16	46	90	*-3

* - 3 points deducted

Lower Div. Champs (Play-offs, eg 1A v 1B, used):
Div. 1A (9): Anchor *(won play-off 3-2)*
Div. 1B (10): Babraham
Div. 2A (11): Witchford
Div. 2B (10): Cambridge Cosmos *(won play-off 2-0)*
Div. 3A (11): Freshfield Utd
Div. 3B (11): Schering Rovers *(won play-off 6-3)*
Div. 4A (10): Poplar Farm
Div. 4B (10): Papworth *(won play-off 2-1)*
Div. 5A (10): NCI Musketeers *(won play-off 8-0)*
Div. 5B (10): Kneesworth

Cup Finals:
Porters Dawson Lge Cup: Bar Hill 2, Sawston Keys 0
De Niro's Jnr Cup: Metals Research 2, Tankard U. 0
VB Trophies Lower Junior Cup: NCI Musketeers 1, Schering Rovers 0

MICK McNEIL CAMBRIDGESHIRE SUNDAY ALLIANCE

DIV. ONE	P	W	D	L	F	A	PTS
Brookfields	20	16	2	2	95	28	34
Fen Ditton	20	15	3	2	92	37	33
Jollyboys	20	12	2	6	50	35	26
Chishill Athletic	20	10	5	5	49	43	25
Ickleton	20	9	2	9	55	50	20
IDA Darwin	20	6	5	9	38	46	17
Carlton	20	6	4	10	43	68	16
Academicals	20	4	7	9	34	45	15
Chem. Labs	20	5	4	11	44	56	14
Reed	20	5	3	12	36	80	13
Oakington	20	3	1	16	28	76	7

Lower Division Champions:
Div. 2 (11): Three Horseshoes

Lge Cup Final: Fen Ditton 2, Brookfields 0 *(aet)*

CHANNEL ISLANDS

THE SEASON'S REVIEW

by REX BENNET, GUERNSEY EVENING PRESS & STAR

SYLVANS WIN GUERNSEY TITLE FOR FIRST TIME

Disappointingly for the Guernsey FA who were celebrating their Centenary, Jersey dominated the inter-island competitions in the Channel Islands' 1993-94 season. But the achievement of the season was that of Guernsey club Sylvans who won the championship of their island's premier league, the Priaulx, for the first time in their 72 year history.

Guernsey FA President Alec Le Noury presents the Priaulx Cup to Sylvans captain Joel Avery.

They accomplished the feat with a very young side - most of the players were in their youth team the previous term - and, ultmately, in dramatic circumstances. Northerners, who had beaten them 3-0 on three occasions in league and cup matches, were odds-on favourites to regain the title when they visited St Peter's for the final Priaulx game of the season because, the previous weekend, they had knocked Vale Recreation out of the running with a decisive 5-2 away win over them. But things went wrong for North from the start. They had their goalkeeper sent off early on for a professional foul - Sylvans scored from the resultant penalty - and, after changing ends two goals in arrears, lost two of their midfield players with serious injuries and had to play the final 35 minutes with only nine men.

The upshot was that Sylvans cruised to a 4-1 win, with their Paul Gallienne completing a hat-trick, and finished three points ahead of Vale Rec and four ahead of North at the top of the table. Sylvans' success, right royally celebrated in the west of the island, was a triumph for manager Colin Renouf, a star of the St Martin's side which won the title a record nine seasons in succession in the 1960s/70s

Guerney's Sylvans, with manager Colin Renouf (left) celebrate the 4-1 win over Northerners which made them the island's champions for the first time in their 72-year history.

and whose team included his two sons, midfielders Jan and Lee.

The club's supporters naturally turned out in force for the Upton Park Cup match against Jersey champions First Tower United at The Track in Guernsey but, despite a brave effort, their young side lost 1-0 to a goal scored by Tower's Richard Muddyman just before half time.

Jersey also won the Muratti Cup in the islands' 'Home International' competition. They rewrote the record book in routing gallant little Alderney 18-0 at Springfield Stadium - Alderney's previous worst defeat had been 12-0 at Guernsey's hands in 1978 - and then, also playing at home, beat Guernsey 3-1 in the final. Kevin Le Tissier gave Guernsey the lead early in the second-half but Jersey proceeded to win with two goals by official man-of-the-match Simon Petulla, who notched his second, and the game's clincher, from the penalty spot, and one by new cap Nick de Jesus. It was a disappointing first Muratti final for Guernsey's new manager, Colin Fallaize, and the result put Jersey two wins ahead of Guernsey in the series which began way back in 1905.

In the build-up to the final, Jersey lost 3-0 away to Aldershot Town and Guernsey were beaten 2-0 by Newport AFC at Gloucester. Guernsey played an FA XI - England's semi-professional side - in Guernsey as part of their Centenary celebrations and did well to hold the strong visiting team to 1-3, scoring first through Carl Le Tissier, brother of Southampton and England's Matthew. They also took part in a triangular tournament with a Middlesex County FA representative side and the Royal Navy and came out on top, beating Middlesex 4-1 and the Navy 3-2.

Guernsey's Centenary Year was, unfortunately, marred by a weekend's strike by the island's referees who downed whistles in protest at the reduction, from 17 months to 12 months, of a suspension imposed on a player found guilty of assaulting a referee in a local 3rd XI cup tie. It was the first time such action had ever been taken by the refs, but the weekend's full programme of 11 matches went ahead with volunteers, including retired referees, standing in for the official arbiters.

The year was also blemished by the fact that, towards the end of the Vale Recreation-First Tower United Jeremie Cup Final which Vale won 1-0, Vale captain Chris Dyer was head-butted in the face by Brian McGovern of the visiting side. McGovern was subsequently suspended for five and a half months by the Jersey FA, fined £200, and ordered to pay Dyer £200 compensation when he appeared before Guernsey's Magistrate's Court. It was the first time a player had ever appeared before the court on a charge relating to an on-the-field offence.

Jersey also beat Guernsey at Under-21 and Under-18 level (4-1 and 1-0) and their Under-18 champions, St Ouen, won the 'Junior Upton' for the first time in beating Guernsey's Northerners 3-2 after extra-time. Guernsey's Under-15 schoolboys beat their counterparts 2-1, however, to maintain their remarkable record of not having lost on Jersey soil since 1972.

It was a memorable season for Sylvans' 18-year-old centre-half John Nobes because, in addition to helping his club to their first Priaulx League title, he was capped by Guernsey at both senior and youth level and was also voted the island's Footballer-of-the-Year by his fellow players.

Jersey's Player-of-the-Year was attacking left-back Ian Daly of St Paul's - the original club of Blackburn Rovers' Graeme Le Saux who, like Guernsey's Matt Le Tissier, is now an England Cap.

Rex Bennet

Paul Gallienne (right) wheels away in triumph after completing his hat-trick in Sylvans' Priaulx League title-clinching win over Northerners.

CHESHIRE F.A. (Est. 1878)

Secretary: A Collins,
The Cottage, Hartford Moss Rec Centre,
Winnington, Northwich CW8 4BG (0606 871166)

CHESHIRE BUILDING SOCIETY SENIOR CUP 1993-94

First Round

Congleton Town v Ellesmere Port Town 4-4,2-3

Second Round

Altrincham v Macclesfield Town	0-1	Colwyn Bay v Stalybridge Celtic	4-1
Ellesmere Port Town v Nantwich Town	0-5	Runcorn v Hyde United	2-1
Vauxhall v Northwich Victoria	3-4*(aet)*	Warrington Town v General Chemicals	2-1

Quarter-Finals

Nantwich Town v Runcorn	1-3	Macclesfield T. v Colywn Bay	7-1*(Macc. expelled)*
Winsford United v Northwich Victoria	0-6	Warrington Town v Witton Albion	2-1

Semi-Finals (two-legged)

Colwyn Bay v Northwich Victoria	0-0,2-3	Warrington Town v Runcorn	0-0,0-2

Final *(at Witton Albion FC, Mon 2nd May)*: Northwich Victoria 1, Runcorn 0

CHESHIRE BUILDING SOCIETY SENIOR AMATEUR CUP 1993-94

First Round

Ashville v Styal	3-1	Littlemoor v Newton Athletic	6-2
Middlewich Athletic v General Chemicals	0-2	Patington Village v Shell (Wirral)	0-7
Mond Rangers v Stork	2-0		

Second Round

Mellor v Broadheath Central	1-5	Blacon Athletic v Bromborough Pool	0-10
Wilmslow Albion v Alsager	2-0	Mersey Royal v Stockport Georgians	2-3*(aet)*
Knutsford v Grove United	2-0	Willaston v Upton Athletic Association	2-1
Hazel Grove v West Kirby	0-1	Old Stoconians v Gatley	3-0
Lymm v Shell	5-3*(aet)*	St Werburghs v Woodley SC	1-5
Old Stopfordians v Bramhall	2-5	Blacon Youth Club v Cheadle Town	1-3*(aet)*
Winnington Park v Moreton	4-3	Crewe Rolls Royce v Frodsham United	2-5
Chester Nomads v BICC Helsby	1-3	Cheadle Heath Nomads v Linotype	1-0
AFC Zeneca v Old Altrinchamians	0-3	Bollington Athletic v General Chemicals	3-0
Atlantic v Mond Rangers	0-5	Littlemoor v Christleton	4-6
Manor Athletic v Barnton	2-0	Poynton v Cheadle Hulme	0-2
MANWEB v Newton (Wirral)	2-3	Ashville v Dukinfield Town	1-1,1-2

Third Round

Newton v Woodley SC	2-1	Bramhall v Capenhurst	0-0,0-2
Cheadle Heath Nomads v Manor Athletic	1-0	Heswall v Bromborough Pool	2-5
Cammell Laird v Malpas	4-0	BICC Helsby v Disley Amateurs	0-2
Vauxhall Motors v Broadheath Central	2-1	Frodsham United v Dukinfield Amateurs	1-4
Lymm v Bollington Athletic	0-7	Dukinfield Town v Mond Rangers	6-2
Old Stoconians v Willaston	1-2	Chistleton v Old Altrinchamians	3-2
Stockport Georgians v Knutsford	2-0	West Kirby v Winnington	3-3,2-1
Cheadle Town v Cheadle Hulme	6-1	Wilmslow Albion v Poulton Victoria	0-2

Fourth Round

Bromborough Pool v Cammell Laird	2-6	Dukinfield Amateurs v Cheadle Heath Nomads	0-4
Stockport Georgians v Disley Amateurs	0-3	Cheadle Town v Poulton Victoria	1-2*(aet)*
Newton v Willaston	2-1	West Kirby v Bollington Athletic	0-2*(aet)*
Dukinfield Town v Christleton	3-1*(aet)*	Vauxhall v Capenhurst	2-1

Quarter-Finals

Newton v Cammell Laird	1-4	Bollington Athletic v Cheadle Heath Nomads	2-1
Disley Amateurs v Poulton Victoria	1-3	Vauxhall v Dukinfield Town	4-1

Semi-Finals

Cammell L. v Poulton V. *(at Vauxhall 8/3/94)*	1-0	Vauxhall v Bollington *(at Warrington T. 9/3/94)*	2-4

Final *(at Chester City FC, Fri 29th April)*: Cammell Laird 3, Vauxhall 2

OTHER COUNTY FINALS 1993-94

Sunday Challenge Cup *(at Vauxhall FC, Sun 24th April)*: Pilot 1, Oaklands BG 0
Minor Cup *(at Christleton FC, Sun 20th March)*: Halebarns United 2, Northwich Town 0
Youth Cup *(at Christleton FC, Sun 6th March)*: Ashville Youth 4, Warrington Town 0

CARLSBERG-TETLEY WEST CHESHIRE LEAGUE

President: K Halsall
Treasurer: R Prescott
Hon. Secretary: L Bullock, 8 Cambridge Rd, Bromborough, Wirral L62 7JA (051 334 3545)

After another busy season a number of clubs have covered themselves in glory, but the supreme accolade goes to Cammell LAird. Not only have they achieved the first championship double of winning Divisions 1 and 2 for over 30 years, but they also retained the Cheshire Building Society County Amateur Cup, completed a hat trick of Pyke Cup successes, and opened the campaign by lifting the Bill Weight Trophy.

Laird's main challengers for what was a remarkable 15th title in 20 seasons were Bromborough Pool and Vauxhall Motors. With just over a month remaining Vauxhalls appeared to be in the driving seat. However, two defeats inflicted by the eventual champions helped push them into third place with Bromborough Pool, whose style of play won many admirers, finishing as runners up.

The Amateur and Pyke cups were gained in the space of four days and in each final Lairds had to fight back from being two goals down. For the third successive season the County Amateur Cup final was contested by Carlsberg Tetley West Cheshire clubs with Lairds overcoming Vauxhalls 3-2, while Shell, after holding a 3-1 lead, were overturned 5-3 in the Pyke Cup.

To complete a notable league double the Lairds Reserves outfit just pipped Poulton Victoria Reserves to win Division Two. Vics were to also lose out in the West Cheshire Bowl final going down by the odd goal in three to Mond Rangers. Further success came Monds' way when winning the Castlemaine Shoot Out Ttophy complete with 36 gallons of the sponsor's beer, and they also provided the League's Player-of-the-Year in striker Paul Howard.

The Wirral Senior Cup was lifted by Poulton Victoria who gained a solitary goal final victory over holders Capenhurst, while underdogs Ashville Reserves had an extra-time win over Cammell Laird Reserves in the Wirral Amateur Cup final. Other member clubs achieving district honours were General Chemicals (Runcorn Senior Cup) and Christleton who achieved a Chester double when their sides collected the Chester Senior and Challenge Cups between them.

The League's Representative Side achieved an unprecidented hat-trick of victories in the Cooper Smith Challenge Cup contested against the Green Insulation Mid-Cheshire League. Goals from Ian Cooke (Cammell Laird) and Gareth Drury (Vauxhalls) helped to secure a 2-1 victory.

A new feature this season, initiated by Carlsberg Tetley, was a Manager of the Month award which provided a great deal of interest, and their Club of the Year award (along with a cheque for £200) went to Manor Athletic who proved to have the best discipline and aministration record throughout the season.

The George Law Trophy, which goes to the club doing most to enhance the reputation of the League, went, not surprisingly, to Cammell Laird. This completed a trememdous campaign for a club who had started their trophy collecting back in August when winning the Bill Weight Trophy.

Ray Concliffe, Hon. Publicity Officer

Poulton Victoria FC - Wirral Senior Cup winners 1993-94. *Photo - Colin Stevens.*

DIV. ONE	P	W	D	L	F	A	PTS
Cammell Laird	30	23	2	5	100	37	48
Bromborough Pool	30	22	3	5	91	35	47
Vauxhall	30	21	1	8	64	35	43
Poulton Victoria	30	17	7	6	68	32	41
Capenhurst	30	18	4	8	56	39	40
Heswall	30	18	3	9	70	47	39
Christleton	30	12	8	10	49	36	32
Merseyside Police	30	11	8	11	57	58	30
Stork	30	10	6	14	52	68	26
Mersey Royal	30	8	7	15	41	53	23
Shell	30	10	3	17	41	70	23
Moreton	30	8	7	15	41	76	23
Ashville	30	9	4	17	43	65	22
Newton	30	8	4	18	42	81	20
Gen. Chemicals	30	6	3	21	29	65	15
Upton Ath. Assoc.	30	3	2	25	27	74	8

DIV. TWO	P	W	D	L	F	A	PTS
Cammell Ld Res.	34	25	3	6	104	41	53
Poulton Vics Res.	34	24	4	6	98	45	52
Mond Rangers	34	22	6	6	100	42	50
Vauxhall Res.	34	23	3	8	85	48	49
Christleton Res.	34	20	7	7	75	54	47
West Kirby	34	13	8	13	46	49	34
Blacon Youth Club	34	12	7	15	67	85	31
Heswall Res.	34	13	5	16	68	87	31
Manor Athletic	34	12	6	16	75	81	30
Capenhurst Res.	34	12	6	16	57	74	30
Mersey Police Res.	34	10	9	15	60	67	29
Mersey Royal Res.	34	12	5	17	50	59	29
Shell Res.	34	10	8	16	60	72	28
Ashville Res.	34	11	6	17	47	65	28
Rivacre Rossfield	34	11	3	20	56	83	25
Brombor. Pool Res.	34	7	10	17	68	91	24
Stork Res.	34	8	5	21	46	79	21
Willaston	34	8	5	21	38	78	21

CARLSBERG TETLEY WEST CHESHIRE LEAGUE DIVISON ONE RESULTS 1993-94

HOME TEAM	1	2	3	4	5	6	7	8	9	10	11	12	13	14	15	16
1. Ashville	*	1-1	0-2	0-3	2-2	1-0	0-3	2-2	2-0	1-3	3-0	0-1	2-3	1-3	1-0	0-1
2. Bromborough Pool	3-1	*	2-1	2-2	5-2	4-0	1-1	2-1	2-3	2-1	2-0	1-0	4-2	4-0	3-1	5-1
3. Cammell Laird	3-2	0-3	*	1-1	2-1	3-0	1-4	2-2	5-1	9-0	5-0	3-2	2-1	5-1	2-3	2-0
4. Capenhurst	2-1	2-5	2-5	*	3-0	2-0	3-2	1-0	1-4	1-1	3-0	0-2	3-2	3-1	2-0	2-1
5. Christleton	0-1	3-2	1-5	0-1	*	1-1	1-1	1-0	2-2	1-2	1-1	0-0	2-0	0-0	3-2	3-0
6. General Chemicals	3-1	2-4	0-2	1-5	0-5	*	0-3	1-2	0-4	0-1	2-4	1-3	1-2	1-0	2-0	0-1
7. Heswall	5-7	2-0	1-3	1-0	0-4	3-0	*	1-1	1-3	5-2	3-0	1-2	5-0	3-0	2-1	1-4
8. Mersey Royal	1-1	3-2	0-4	0-3	0-2	2-2	1-2	*	1-3	1-4	2-0	0-2	1-2	3-2	3-0	2-1
9. Merseyside Police	2-3	0-6	5-3	3-0	1-2	0-2	0-2	2-2	*	2-1	2-2	1-1	1-2	3-3	2-1	2-3
10. Moreton	1-2	0-7	1-6	0-1	1-0	2-0	1-3	4-4	1-1	*	1-0	1-2	2-7	3-3	2-2	0-3
11. Newton	3-1	2-5	1-2	3-2	0-4	1-2	2-3	1-2	2-2	2-2	*	0-7	4-2	2-7	1-0	1-3
12. Poulton Victoria	3-1	0-4	0-2	1-1	1-1	4-1	3-5	1-0	3-1	6-0	5-2	*	5-0	3-1	3-0	1-2
13. Shell	3-0	1-6	0-4	0-1	0-5	2-1	1-2	2-1	0-2	0-0	0-3	1-1	*	2-2	1-2	2-1
14. Stork	5-4	1-2	0-6	0-2	2-0	0-0	4-2	1-4	1-3	3-2	0-2	1-1	2-1	*	4-2	1-4
15. Upton Athletic Association	1-2	0-1	2-7	1-3	0-2	1-5	1-3	1-0	1-1	0-1	2-3	0-4	1-2	0-2	*	1-2
16. Vauxhall	6-0	2-1	1-3	2-1	1-0	2-1	1-0	1-0	3-1	2-1	6-0	1-1	4-0	0-2	5-1	*

DIVISION TWO RESULTS	1	2	3	4	5	6	7	8	9	10	11	12	13	14	15	16	17	18
1. Ashville Reserves	*	1-3	2-2	3-2	2-0	2-3	6-1	3-3	1-0	1-0	0-2	3-1	0-2	0-2	0-1	2-4	2-3	1-1
2. Blacon Youth Club	0-2	*	6-3	2-4	1-1	1-1	4-1	3-2	4-1	5-1	1-1	2-3	4-0	1-1	6-1	0-5	1-2	6-1
3. Bromborough Pool Reserves	0-1	1-1	*	1-2	4-4	1-5	1-3	2-2	2-1	3-2	3-3	0-0	4-2	2-4	4-3	1-2	1-2	3-3
4. Cammell Laird Reserves	3-0	10-0	3-1	*	2-0	1-0	6-6	5-1	5-0	2-1	4-1	0-0	1-0	4-3	2-0	3-1	2-0	5-0
5. Capenhurst Reserves	2-1	7-1	2-1	3-5	*	2-3	3-0	4-0	0-0	2-1	0-3	0-5	1-1	1-2	3-2	2-1	0-3	2-0
6. Christleton Reserves	0-2	0-0	4-1	1-0	3-0	*	7-0	0-0	3-2	5-5	1-1	0-2	2-0	3-1	3-1	1-4	1-1	3-1
7. Heswall Reserves	3-0	4-3	4-0	1-2	2-0	2-3	*	1-4	0-1	0-0	3-2	1-6	4-4	2-1	7-1	3-2	0-2	3-0
8. Manor Athletic Reserves	3-0	1-2	8-1	0-4	1-4	2-4	1-2	*	4-1	3-2	0-7	3-4	6-1	1-1	3-2	1-3	0-2	5-2
9. Mersey Royal Reserves	1-1	5-0	1-0	1-2	0-3	0-2	3-2	3-1	*	0-5	3-2	1-2	1-2	3-1	5-1	0-1	5-0	0-0
10. Merseyside Police Reserves	6-1	0-0	1-8	1-0	1-3	2-3	1-1	6-2	1-1	*	0-3	1-6	3-1	1-3	0-0	1-3	3-0	2-0
11. Mond Rangers	5-0	8-1	0-1	1-1	2-0	8-2	5-1	3-1	2-0	1-1	*	4-3	7-3	4-2	6-1	2-3	2-0	3-0
12. Poulton Victoria Reserves	3-4	2-4	4-4	3-0	9-2	5-0	6-1	2-2	3-0	3-0	1-2	*	2-0	3-1	1-0	4-2	1-0	2-0
13. Rivacre Rossfield	3-1	4-2	2-1	1-7	4-1	4-2	5-3	0-1	0-1	0-3	1-2	1-2	*	1-4	3-1	2-5	1-1	1-2
14. Shell Reserves	3-1	3-0	3-3	2-6	3-3	0-0	2-0	1-5	3-5	2-2	0-1	1-3	1-2	*	4-1	2-7	0-0	0-2
15. Stork Reserves	0-2	2-0	3-1	2-1	1-1	0-2	2-3	2-3	2-1	1-1	0-1	5-1	2-0	2-2	*	2-2	1-3	1-2
16. Vauxhall Reserves	1-0	2-3	3-2	3-2	2-0	1-3	2-1	1-1	1-0	0-2	3-1	0-3	2-0	2-1	3-1	*	5-1	0-0
17. West Kirby	1-1	4-0	2-2	0-4	6-0	0-2	1-1	2-0	2-2	2-1	1-1	1-2	2-5	1-0	0-1	0-1	*	1-0
18. Willaston	1-1	1-0	3-4	2-4	2-1	2-3	1-2	1-5	1-2	2-3	1-4	0-1	2-0	0-1	3-1	1-8	1-0	*

S Connolly of Bromborough Pool skips past Poulton Victoria's N Ormes. *Photo - Colin Stevens.*

CARLSBERG-TETLEY WEST CHESHIRE LEAGUE CLUBS 1994-95

(Divisional Constitutions unchanged from 1993-94).

ASHVILLE

Chairman: Kenny Baker
Secretary: Eddie Parker, 26 Mere Heath, Moreton, Wirral L46 3SH (051 678 0745).
Ground & Directions: Villa Park Cross Lane, Wallasey Village, Wallasey (051 638 2127). Cross Lane is off Leasowe Road, entrance behind Wallesey Rugby Club. Merseyrail to Wallesey Village - cross road to Mosslands Drive, School Lane on right, ground under bridge.
Colours: White/black/black. **Founded:** 1949

BLACON YOUTH CLUB

Chairman: Peter Barnes
Secretary: Colin Lawson, 54 Adelaide Road, Blacon, Chester CH1 5SZ (0244 375508).
Ground & Directions: Cairns Crescent Playing Fields, Blacon, Chester. Parkgate Road to the Ben Whitehouse Garage, approach new island, 3rd exit into Blacon, along Blacon Avenue to Parade Shops (RHS), left opposite, 1st right, Western Avenue 2nd right, Melbourne Road, 1st right, Cairns Crescent. Buses 1,2,2a,2e to Blacon from Chester bus station.
Colours: Black & white stripes/black/black **Founded:** 1964

BROMBOROUGH POOL

Chairman: Arthur Margerison
Secretary: Alan Pringle, 3 Willow Grove, Moreton, Wirral L46 0TU (051 677 0065).
Ground & Directions: The Green, South View Road, Bromborough Pool (051 645 3476). A41 from Ellesmere Port and Chester to Bromborough. Into Dock Road at Port Sunlight Works, past Fire Station, left into Pool Village, 1st right down Village Green - pavilion on far left of green. Buses C1,C3,C4 from Chester - alight at Bromborough Pool Lane. 41 MPTE from Birkenhead.
Cols: All blue (white pinstripe) **Sponsors:** Ocean Software **Founded:** 1884

CAMMELL LAIRD

Chairman: Arthur Parker
Secretary: Ray Steele, 46 Croft Avenue, Bromborough, Wirral L62 2BR (051 334 8998).
Ground & Directions: Kirklands, St Peters Road, Rock Ferry, Birkenhead (051 645 5991). A41 New Chester Road to Rock Ferry - turn down Proctor Road - ground behind Crosville Bus Station.
Colours: All blue **Sponsors:** MET ARC **Founded:** 1900

CAPENHURST

Chairman: Dave Kilfoyle
Secretary: Roger Knight, 8 Wenlock Gardens, Great Sutton, South Wirral L66 2QZ (051 355 5736).
Ground & Directions: Capenhurst Sports Ground, Capenhurst Lane, Capenhurst (051 339 4101). A41 Birkenhead/Chester road to Capenhurst lights, down Capenhurst Lane, over railway, past BNLF factory, ground on right. Crosville bus C1 to Capenhurst lights on A41. Train to Capenhurst (Wirral Line).
Founded: 1952 **Colours:** Claret & sky **Sponsors:** BNF/Urenco Capenhurst Atlantic Communcations

CHRISTLETON

Chairman: Ron Mayers
Secretary: Kenneth Price, 35 Canadian Avenue, Hoole, Chester CH2 3HQ (0244 313513).
Ground & Directions: Little Heath, Christleton (0244 332153). Turn off A51 Chester/Northwich road at sign to Littleton and Christleton - follow road to pond on the left and turn left. Bus from Chester to Christleton.
Colours: Red/black/red **Covered:** Yes **Founded:** 1966
Sponsors: Kidsons Impey Chester Motor Auctions.

GENERAL CHEMICALS

Chairman: Michael Jaques
Secretary: Roy Nickson, 44 York Street, Runcorn, Cheshire WA7 5BA (0928 576632).
Ground & Directions: ICI (Weston) Club, Sandy Lane, Weston Point, Runcorn. M56 to Runcorn Expressway - take Castner Kellner turn off. 1 mile from Runcorn (BR). Bus to Weston Point.
Previous Name: Castner Kellner **Covered Accomdation:** 100 **Floodlights:** Y
Colours: Navy & white stripes **Sponsors:** O'Hares Electrical **Founded:** 1958

HESWALL

Chairman: Ernie Wakelam
Secretary: Jake Horan, 13 Reedville, Bebington, Wirral L63 2HS (051 644 0459).
Ground & Directions: Gayton Park, Brimstage Road, Heswall, Wirral (051 342 7523). From Birkenhead; Barnston Road, left into Brimstage Road, then first right. From Chester; Chester High Road to Gayton r-bout, Brimstage Rd then 1st right. From West Kirkby; Telegraph, left at Gayton r-bout then 1st right. 1 mile from Heswall Hills (BR).
Colours: Yellow/blue/yellow **Rec. Gate:** 1,000 v Sheff. Wed. 7/8/87 **Founded:** 1891

MANOR ATHLETIC

Chairman: Tony Bell
Secretary: Stewart Galtress, 3 Centurion Close, Meols, Wirral L47 7BZ (051 632 3211).
Ground & Directions: Unilever Sports Ground, Bromborough. A41 Chester New Road to Candy (Kelvinator) factory, left (from Birkenhead) into Old Hall Road, 1st right. Buses to Green Lane, Bromborough.
Colours: White/black/red **Sponsors:** Vavoline Oil Company **Founded:** 1968

MERSEY ROYAL

Chairman: Tony Nelson **Secretary:** Billy Morris, 28 Charlwood Close, 3rd Avenue, Manor Green, Beechwood, Birkenhead L43 9XF (051 678 7161).
Ground & Directions: As Manor Athletic (above).
Colours: Red & white/red/red **Sponsors:** Hanks Construction **Founded:** 1946
Prevvious Ground: Valley Road, Bidston, Birkenhead (pre-1992).

MERSEYSIDE POLICE

Chairman: Pat Carraghan.
Secretary: Eddie McGrath, 36 Gaywood Court, St Nicholas Rd, Blundellsands L23 6XN.
Ground & Directions: Fairfield Sports Ground, Prescot Road, Liverpool L7 0JD (051 228 2352). From city travel via Kensington towards Old Swan, into Prescot Road - ground on corner with Fairfield Street. One and a half miles from Limestreet (BR).
Colours: Maroon/maroon/sky **Sponsors:** Davies & Co, surveyors **Founded:** 1885
Record Attendance: 1,500 v Kent Police, National Police Final 22/5/73.

MOND RANGERS

Chairman: Roy Roberts
Secretary: John Worthington, 5 Bellingham Drive, Runcorn WA7 4XN (0928 567477).
Ground & Directions: Ground-share at General Chemicals FC (see preceding page).
Colours: Sky/blue/blue. **Club Sponsors:** Comid Engineering **Founded:** 1967

MORETON

Chairman: Ray Navarro
Secretary: Tony Heffernan, 30 Appleton Drive, Upton, Wirral L49 1SJ (051 678 5973).
Ground & Directions: 73 Upton Road, Moreton, Wirral (051 677 3235). M53 jct 2, follow signs to Moreton - ground quarter mile on right. MPTE bus 3 passes ground.
Colours: Red/navy/navy **Sponsors:** Fluid Power Services **Founded:** 1900

NEWTON

Chairman: Fred Sherlock
Secretary: Alan Dabner, 41 St David Road, Claughton, Birkenhead L43 8SW (051 652 5648).
Ground & Directions: Millcroft, Frankby Road, Greasby, Wirral (051 677 8382). M53 to West Kirby, left at lights, right at lights at Upton Cross, ground 3 miles on left in Frankby Road. MPTE bus 96 from Birkenhead Woodside passes ground, MPTE 78 terminus 3 mins walk.
Colours: Yellow/blue/white **Sponsors:** Cory Bros Shipping **Founded:** 1933

POULTON VICTORIA

Chairman: Tom Quinn
Secretary: H Deery, 15 Dorset Drive, Irby, Wirral L61 8SX (051 648 2903).
Ground & Directions: Victoria Park, Rankin Street, Wallesey (051 638 3559). Wallesey Docks signs off M53, right into Limelin Lane by Vics Club, Rankin Street 6th left. Buses 10 & 11 to Gorsey Lane from Birkenhead. 20 mins from Birkenhead North (BR).
Colours: All royal blue **Club Sponsors:** Windsors (Wallesey) **Founded:** 1935
Previous Ground: Wallace Park 1935-72

RIVACRE ROSSFIELD

Chairman: Dorian Harvey
Secretary: K R Hornby, 310 Chester Road, Whitby, Ellesmere Port L66 2NY (051 356 1695).
Ground & Directions: Rivacre Sports & Social Club, Rivacre Road, Overpool, Ellesmere Port (051 355 2574). From lights at junction of Rossmore and Overpool Roads (cemetery gates), proceed down Rivacre Road - club on right. Crosville buses C3 & C4 to Overpool Cemetery.
Colours: Tangerine/black/black **Club Sponsors:** Rivacre Social Club **Founded:** 1954

SHELL

Chairman: Roy Jones
Secretary: Joseph Davies, 35 Glencoe Road, Great Sutton, South Wirral L66 4NA (051 339 0652).
Ground & Directions: Chester Road, Whitby, Ellesmere Port (051 355 2704/2364). A5117 turn right at 3rd island coming from M53 jct 10 (4th coming from jct 10); club on right. All buses to Ellesmere Port (BR), or C3 from Chester.
Colours: Red/blue/blue **Sponsors:** Portions Control Ltd **Founded:** 1924

STORK

Chairman: Keith Formston.
Secretary: Steve Carter, 7 Elm Rd, Bebington, Wirral L63 8PF (051 645 6697).
Ground & Directions: Unilever Sports Ground Bromborough *(see Manor Athletic - page 907)*.
Colours: All green **Sponsors:** The Village Leisure Hotel **Founded:** 1920

UPTON ATHLETIC ASSOCIATION

Chairman: Peter Upton
Secretary: Barry Gaulton, St Marks Crescent, Whitby, Ellesmere Port L66 2XD (051 330 1504).
Ground & Directions: Cheshire County Council Sports & Social Club, Plas Newton Lane, Chester CH2 1PR (0244 318167). At end of M53, right, right at A41 r'bout (signed Zoo), 1st right into Mannings Lane, ground 100yds on left.
Colours: All blue **Founded:** 1964

VAUXHALL MOTORS

Chairman: Tony Woodley
Secretary: Steve McInerney, 12 Merton Rd, Gt Sutton, South Wirral L66 2SW (051 356 0941).
Ground & Directions: Vauxhall Sports Ground, Rivacre Road, Ellesmere Port (051 327 2115). Turn into Hooton Green off A41 at Hooton crossroa, left at 'T' junction, right at next 'T' junction, ground 100 yds on right.
Colours: Sky/navy/sky **Club Sponsors:** James Edwards **Founded:** 1963
Floodlights: Y

WEST KIRBY

Chairman: Ken Raine.
Secretary: Mrs Carole Paisey, 80a Banks Road, West Kirby L48 0RE (051 625 6936).
Ground & Directions: Marine Park, Greenbank Road, West Kirby (051 625 7734). From Concourse, West Kirby, along Orrysdale Road and Anglesey Road into Greenbank Road.
Colours: White/blue/blue **Club Sponsors:** Don Walker Insurance **Founded:** 1895

WILLASTON

Chairman: Martin Collins
Secretary: Harvey Rushton, 31 Moss Close, Willaston, South Wirral L62 2XQ (051 327 7419).
Ground & Directions: Recreation Ground, Neston Road, Willaston, South Wirral. Off A41 at Hooton crossroads, along Hooton Road and through Willaston; ground on right behing Primary School.
Colours: All white **Founded:** 1962

WEST CHESHIRE LEAGUE, AND OTHER LOCAL CUPS 1993-94

PYKE CUP

First Round

General Chemicals v Vauxhall	3-1	Newton v Upton Athletic Association	1-3
Moreton v Poulton Victoria	1-4	Stork v Christleton	0-2
Mersey Royal v Shell	0-1	Heswall v Merseyside Police	2-3
Bromborough Pool v Ashville	6-2	Cammell Laird v Capenhurst	6-2

Quarter-Finals

Cammell Laird v Poulton Victoria	4-3	General Chemicals v Merseyside Police	2-3
Bromborough Pool v Christleton	1-2	Shell v Upton Athletic Association	4-1

Semi-Finals

Christleton v Cammell Laird	1-2	Shell v Merseyside Police	1-0

Final: Cammell Laird 5, Shell 3

BILL WEIGHT MEMORIAL TROPHY

Semi-Finals

Christleton v Cammell Laird	1-2	Merseyside Police v Blacon Youth Club	0-2

Final: Cammell Laird 2, Blacon Youth Club 2 *(Cammell Laird won 3-1 on penalties)*

WIRRAL SENIOR CUP

First Round

Ashville v Moreton	4-2	Willaston v Heswall	2-1
Poulton Victoria v Stork	2-0	Shell v Bromborough Pool	1-4
Newton v Vauxhall	0-3		

Quarter-Finals

Willaston v Poulton Victoria	0-3	Mersey Royal v Cammell Laird	1-3
Capenhurst v Vauxhall	1-0	Ashville v Bromborough Pool *(disqualified)*	0-1

Semi-Finals

Capenhurst v Ashville	1-0	Poulton Victoria v Cammell Laird	2-0

Final: Poulton Victoria 1, Capenhurst 0

CASTELMAINE XXXX COMPETITION

Semi-Finals (Divisional Winners)

Manor Athletic v Shell	0-3	Merseyside Police v Mond Rangers	3-5

Final: Mond Rangers 4, Shell 3

WEST CHESHIRE LEAGUE BOWL

First Round

Manor Athletic v Shell	4-0	Cammell Laird v Poulton Victoria	2-4*(aet)*

Second Round

Rivacre Rossfield v Blacon Youth Club	5-2	Vauxhall v Merseyside Police	5-2
Mersey Royal v Manor Athletic	2-3	Poulton Victoria v Christleton	4-1
Willaston v Bromborough Pool	3-1	Ashville v Stork	2-3
Capenhurst v Mond Rangers	0-1	West Kirby v Heswall	5-2

Quarter-Finals

Stork v Willaston	0-1	West Kirby v Mond Rangers	1-2
Rivacre Rossfield v Vauxhall	1-2	Manor Athletic v Poulton Victoria	0-1

Semi-Finals

Vauxhall v Mond Rangers	0-1	Willaston v Poulton Victoria	0-2

Final: Mond Rangers 2, Poulton Victoria 1

WIRRAL AMATEUR CUP

Second Round

Ashville v Capenhurst	4-2	Mersey Ferries v West Kirby	0-3
Shell v Heswall	3-1	Rivacre Rossfield v Willaston	1-3
Manor Athletic v Moreton	6-4	Newton v Bromborough Pool	1-5
Stork v New Brighton	2-3	Poulton Victoria v Cammell Laird	1-4

Quarter-Finals

Ashville v West Kirby	2-0	Shell v Willaston	0-0,2-1
Manor Athletic v Bromborough Pool	3-2	New Brighton v Cammell Laird	1-3

Semi-Finals

Ashville v Manor Athletic	3-2	Cammell Laird v Shell	3-1

Final: Ashville 3, Cammell Laird 2 *(aet)*

CHESTER DISTRICT F.A. SENIOR CUP

Semi-Finals

Blacon Youth v Manweb	2-1	Christleton v St Werburghs	3-1

Final: Christleton 2, Blacon Youth Club 1 *(aet)*

CHESTER DISTRICT F.A. CHALLENGE CUP

Final: Christleton Reserves 4, Deva Social 1

RUNCORN DISTRICT F.A. CUP

Semi-Finals

Mond Rangers v Bridge Athletic	0-2	Helsby BI v General Chemicals	1-7

Final: General Chemicals 2, Bridge Athletic 0

REPRESENTATIVE FIXTURE: West Cheshire League 2, Mid-Cheshire League 1

GREEN INSULATION MID-CHESHIRE LEAGUE (Est. 1948)

President: W Salt, Esq.
Chairman: R Atherton, Esq.
Vice Chairman: J A Walton, Esq.
Treasurer: T B Riley, Esq.
Hon. Secretary: E B Davies,
34 Ryebank Road, Firswood, Manchester M16 0FP (061 881 5732).

The 1993-94 season will be remembered for the prolonged wet weather responsible for many postponed fixtures - including replays in cup ties, the league lost a total of 94 games. Fixtures were completely wiped out on three Saturdays.

Despite these problems the championship race was exciting, although at one time it looked to be all over when in mid-October Linotype were 12 points clear of Chorlton Town, the team that eventually finished as runners-up. Linotyupe had a disastrous second half of the season whilst Chorlton continued a great run to overtake the Altrincham side in April. A see-saw developed at the top, with these two sides changing places over the last four weeks. Chorlton's last game of the season, against the previous year's champions, saw their title aspirations disappear with Grove United winning by the odd goal, and so the champions, who had led the division for seven months, were Linotype.

The Second Division saw Bollington Athletic win the title after staying in the top three all season. Runners-up were Bramhall who, despite a huge back-log of fixtures, eventually won enough points to take them back into Division One.

The League Cup competition saw some giant-killers at work in the early rounds, but Grove United won the Cup proving to good for a revitalised Barnton.

In the Division Two Cup, Beeches Reserves played some attractive football to overcome Bramhall, who were probably feeling the strain of a tough end of season programme, to take the Cup.

Bollington Athletic kept the league's colours flying in the Cheshire Amateur Cup but, although beaten, were not disgraced in a closely fought semi-final.

This season's inter-league fixture with neighbours West Cheshire was spoilt by high winds and, as far as we were concerned, the two goals that we were beaten by. Nevertheless the league side put up a great performance and if chances had been taken there would have been a different winner.

E B Davies, Hon. Secretary

Linotype FC - Green Insulation Mid-Cheshire League champions 1993-94.

DIV. ONE	P	W	D	L	F	A	PTS
Linotype	30	21	7	2	66	18	70
Chorlton Town	30	21	5	4	96	39	68
Grove United	30	20	5	5	68	28	65
The Beeches	30	18	8	6	75	50	56
Rylands	30	16	7	7	56	36	55
Garswood United	30	13	11	6	71	52	50
Barnton	30	14	7	9	60	43	49
Broadheath Central	30	11	9	10	57	54	42
Knutsford	30	10	10	10	80	58	40
Poynton	30	11	6	13	51	50	39
Malpas	30	9	5	16	50	78	32
Winnington Park	30	8	5	17	45	86	29
Whitchurch Alport	30	7	6	17	46	54	27
Middlewich Athletic	30	5	7	18	43	62	22
Wilmslow Albion	30	4	4	22	27	104	16
Hanley Town	30	1	4	25	28	108	7

DIV. TWO	P	W	D	L	F	A	PTS
Bollington Ath.	32	24	2	6	88	41	74
Bramhall	32	19	8	5	84	34	65
Linotype Res.	32	18	6	8	68	41	60
AFC Zeneca	32	17	8	7	75	51	59
Warrington T. Res.	32	16	6	10	68	43	54
Styal	32	15	6	11	75	57	51
Chorlton T. Res.	32	15	5	12	78	58	50
Pilkington	32	12	10	10	67	48	46
Littlemoor	32	12	9	11	74	60	45
Garswood U. Res.	32	12	7	13	65	64	43
The Beeches Res.	32	13	4	14	68	77	43
Poynton Res.	32	10	6	16	54	78	36
Grove Utd Res.	32	10	4	18	53	79	34
Lostock Gralam	32	11	1	20	66	96	34
Alsager	32	8	9	15	67	66	33
Rylands Res.	32	9	6	17	52	81	33
Wilmslow A. Res.	32	1	3	28	37	165	6

DIVISION ONE CLUBS 1994-95

BARNTON

Chairman: William Perrin **Manager:** Mike Alcock/ Steve Moore.
Secretary: Peter Stanley, 10 Westfield Grove, Barnton, Nr Northwich, Cheshire CW8 4QB (0606 782305).
Ground: Townfield, Townfield Lane, Barnton.
Directions: Turn off A553 (Northwich-Runcorn) at Beech Tree Inn in Barnton village into Beech Lane. Right at T-junction with Townfield Lane - ground 200yds on left.
Colours: Black & white stripes/black/black **Change Colours:** Amber/black/amber.

(THE) BEECHES

Chairman: Gordon Rigby **Manager:** D Corrigan.
Secretary: David Corrigan, 7 Burrows Avenue, Haydock, St Helens WA11 0DE (0744 572273).
Ground: Beechams Social Club, Sutton Rd, St Helens (0744 25906).
Directions: Approach from Widnes on A570, right at lights after St Helens Hospital into Sutton Rd, right at next lights, ground 200yds on left.
Colours: All blue **Change Colours:** Claret & blue/claret/claret

BOLLINGTON ATHLETIC

Chairman: A Deery **Manager:** Michael McKernan.
Secretary: Anthony Holmes, 79 Parkgate Rd, Macclesfield, Cheshire SK11 7SZ (0625 615044).
Ground: Recreation Ground, Bollington.
Directions: Turn off A523 (Macclesfield-Stockport) at 1st sign for Bollington. Follow for one and a half miles to Dog & Partridge, left into Adlington Rd, ground 100yds on right.
Colours: Jade & silver/silver **Change Colours:** Tangerine/black.

BRAMHALL

Chairman: M Cruse **Manager:** Mark Weaver.
Secretary: Bernard Johnson, 25 Bean Leach Rd, Hazel Grove SK7 4LD (061 456 2542).
Ground: Lumb Lane, Bramhall.
Directions: Centre of Bramhall take Lumb Lane (pizza shop on corner), grnd 300yds on right behind village club.
Colours: Red/black/black **Change Colours:** Yellow/blue/blue (All blue:Res)

BROADHEATH CENTRAL

Chairman: J Tighe **Manager:** Michael Merry.
Secretary: David Murphy, 10 Green Drive, Timperley, Altrincham WA15 6JW (061 980 1925).
Ground: Viaduct Rd, Broadheath, Altrincham. **Directions:** One and a half miles north of Altrincham on A56 Manchester Road; turn right immediately after B & Q and Halfords. A-Z ref. 2D 79.
Colours: Black & red stripes/black/black **Change Colours:** All blue.

CHORLTON TOWN

Chairman: Ronald Anderson **Manager:** I R Jarratt
Secretary: Jim Calderbank, 9 Trafford Drive, Timperley, Altrincham WA15 6ET (061 969 1156).
Ground: Longford Stadium, Longford Park.
Directions: A-Z ref. P58 4C. From M63 take A56 Chester Road towards Manchester, right into Edge Lane shortly after passing under M63, left into Ryebank Rd after a few hundred yds, ground 400yds on left.
At the time of going to press, it was rumoured that Chorlton may move the ground of Winnington Park FC who have folded this summer. Ground: Moss Farm, Northwich (0606 79987). Directions: A559 towards Chester, 1 mile outside Northwich turn left into Moss Rd which leads to Moss Farm.
Cols: Black & red stripes/white/white (Blue & black stripes/black/black:Res) **Change Colours:** All white.

GARSWOOD UNITED

Chairman: D Finnegan **Manager:** A Aspinall.
Secretary: John Richards, 359 Elephant Lane, Chatto Heath, St Helens WA9 5HF (0744 851569).
Ground: Simms Lane Ends, Garswood Road, Garswood, Nr Wigan (0744 892258).
Directions: A580 towards Liverpool, right into Liverpool Rd (A58), left into Garswood Rd (signposted Garswood), follow round, left at triangle, upto crossroads, straight ahead, entrance 100yds on left.
Colours: Blue & white stripes/blue/blue **Change Colours:** All red.

GROVE UNITED

Chairman: J J Murphy **Manager:** S Crowther.
Secretary: Mark Boothby, 68 Deneside Cres., Hazel Grove, Cheshire SK7 4NU (061 456 7610).
Ground: Half Moon Lane, Alfreton Rd, Offerto/ Lisburne Lane, Stockport.
Directions: Lisburne Lane is a continuation of Cherry Tree Lane off the A6 or Dialstone Lane. M56 jct 13, 4th exit at r'bout A626, at 2nd lights after one and a half miles turn right at Golden Hind pub.
Colours: Red/black/black **Change Colours:** All blue.

KNUTSFORD

Chairman: Richard Walker **Manager:** Kenneth Harrison
Secretary: Michael Binnie, The Bungalow, 145 Manchester Rd, Wilmslow SK9 2JN (0625 537909).
Ground: Manchester Road, Knutsford.
Directions: Situated on Knutsford to Altrincham & Warrington road.
Colours: Red/white (All blue:Res) **Change Colours:** All blue (White or red:Res)

LINOTYPE

Chairman: G Smith **Manager:** K Gardner
Secretary: Graham Fothergill, 11 St Marys Rd, Sale, Cheshire M33 1SB (061 969 4999).
Ground: British Airways Club, Clay Lane, Timperley, Altrincham (061 980 7354).
Directions: Clay Lane off Thorley Lane. Off A560 Altrincham-Stockport road (Timperley, Altrincham). corner.
Colours: White/black/red **Change Colours:** Red & black/black/black.

MALPAS

Chairman: Peter Downey **Manager:** Bernard Lloyd.
Secretary: Bernard Lloyd, 15 Springfield Avenue, Malpas, Cheshire SY14 8QD (0948 860812).
Ground: Malpas & District Sports Club, Oxheys, Wrexham Rd, Malpas, Cheshire (0948 860662).
Directions: On arrival in Malpas, up Church Str., carry on into Wrexham Rd, right into ground which is signposted.
Colours: Red/blue/red **Change Colours:** All blue.

MIDDLEWICH ATHLETIC

Chairman: B Fletcher **Manager:** P McAleer.
Secretary: Brian Longley, 16 Northway, Holmes Chapel CW4 7EF (0477 373310).
Ground: Seddon Str., Middlewich **Directions:** St Michaels Way to Webb Street, Seddon Street on left.
Colours: Red/white/red **Change Colours:** All blue.

POYNTON

Chairman: J Malam **Manager:** C Nicholson (I Cook: Reserves).
Secretary: Paul Burch, 24 Brooklands Avenue, Poynton, Cheshire SK12 1HZ (0625 871205).
Ground: London Rd North, Poynton (0625 875765). **Directions:** On main A523 between Macclesfield and Hazel Grove, approx 300yds from Poynton village centre traffic lights.
Colours: Red/black/black **Change Colours:** White & blue/blue/blue.

RYLANDS

Chairman: Fredrick Bibby **Manager:** T Selby.
Secretary: Ian Finchett, 31 Elizabeth Drive, Padgate, Warrington WA1 4JQ (0925 816911).
Ground: Gorsey Lane, Warrington (0925 35700). **Directions:** M6 jct 21, A57 to Warrington, through two sets of lights, right at the Chevvies Rock'n Roll Cafe, carry straight on, ground on right.
Colours: Maroon & grey/maroon/grey **Change Colours:** All yellow.

WHITCHURCH ALPORT

Chairman: J Jackson **Manager:** P Wainwright.
Secretary: Andrew Mitchell, 8 Mill Cottages, Grindley Brook, Whitchurch, Salop SY13 4QH (0948 6150).
Ground: Yockings Park, Whitchurch, Shropshire. **Directions:** To lights on A41 main through road, left up Talbot Street to Ready Mix concrete plant; ground 200yds further on left.
Colours: Red & white stripes/black/black **Change:** Yellow/green/yellow.

WILMSLOW ALBION

Chairman: Geoff Thornton **Manager:** Rob O'Connor (Winnie Montrose: Reserves).
Secretary: John Smith, 3 Holly Farm House, Isherwood Rd, Carrington, Urmston M31 4BH.
Ground: Oakwood Farm, Styal Rd, Styal, Wilmslow (0625 535823).
Directions: M56 jct 6, A538 towards Wilmslow, 1st left for Styal (Altrincham Rd) after Airport tunnel, and procced to T-junction passing Styal FC and Ship Inn - ground 2nd left opposite Quarry Bank Mill. A-Z ref 982A.
Colours: Yellow/blue/yellow **Change Colours:** All blue.

DIVISISION TWO CLUBS 1994-95

ALSAGER

Chairman: Kevin Dean **Manager:** P Clegg.
Secretary: John Dykes, 7 Dairylands Rd, Church Lawton, Stoke-on-Trent ST7 3FU (0270 877722).
Ground: The Town Ground, Wood Park, Alsager.
Directions: M6 jct 16, A500 towards Stoke, turn left for Alsager after half mile, follow lane to lights, in village centre turn right into Lawton Rd, 3rd left Moorhouse Avenue, 2nd right Woodland Court, ground entrance on righthand corner.
Colours: Black & white/black/black **Change Colours:** Blue/black/black.

CHEADLE HEATH NOMADS, CHESTER NOMADS *(both new clubs)*

LITTLEMOOR

Chairman: Frank Morris **Manager:** Frank Sanders.
Secretary: Stanley McQuarrie, 46 Bramhall Lane, Stockport SK2 6HZ (061 429 66394).
Ground: Ward Street, St Marys Way, Stockport.
Directions: M63 jct 13 onto St Marys Way - ground 4th on left 1 mile on right. A-Z ref 74 4C.
Colours: Black & white stripes/black/black **Change:** Blue/white/blue.

LOSTOCK GRALAM

Chairman: D Washburn **Manager:** G Knop.
Secretary: Andy Hough, 44 Shelley Ave., Wincham, Northwich, Cheshire CW9 6PH (0565 733383).
Ground: Slow & Easy Hotel, Manchester Rd, Lostock Gralam, Northwich.
Directions: M6, A556 signed Chester, right at island after 4 miles onto Manchester Rd, Slow & Easy Hotel 1 mile on right - ground behind.
Cols: Sky & white stripes/white/blue **Prev. Lges:** Mid-Cheshire/ Crewe & Dist. (R-up 92-93)

PILKINGTON RECREATION

Chairman: G Barlow **Manager:** J Dawson.
Secretary: Dave Johnson, 4 Darent Rd, Haydock, Merseyside WA11 0HH (0744 34734).
Ground: Ruskin Drive, St Helens (0744 22893).
Directions: M6 jct 23, A580, left at 3rd lights, continue to Hope Anchor pub, right into Bishop Rd, continue to halt sign, follow road around to Ruskin Rd (2nd left). Ground in Ruskin Rd.
Colours: Green & yellow/green/green **Change Cols:** Maroon & grey/maroon/maroon & grey.

STYAL

Chairman: Ben Hurren **Manager:** D Wyatt.
Secretary: Alan Jones, 1 Oak Brow Cottages, Altrincham Rd, Styal, Wilmslow SK9 4JE (0625 530270).
Ground: Altrincham Road, Styal (0625 529303). **Directions:** From M56 take A538 towards Wilmslow, 1st left after tunnel, before the Valley Lodge Hotel, ground two miles up on left.
Colours: Amber & yellow/red/white **Change Colours:** All blue.

(A.F.C.) ZENECA

Chairman: David Black **Manager:** Glyn H Ingham.
Secretary: Neal Roberts, 18 Chatsworth Ave., Macclesfield, Cheshire SK11 7DB (0625 617718).
Ground: I.C.I. Cals Social Centre, Alderley Park (0625 512902).
Directions: From A537 (Knutsford-Macclesfield) turn left at Monks Heath traffic lights (jct with A34). 1st right after 200yds in Matthews Garden Centre, immediate right, then left and follow road to Sports Centre.
Colours: All royal blue **Change Colours:** Red & black/black/red.
Previous Name: ICI Pharmaceuticals (pre-1993).

This Division also includes Reserve sides of: The Beeches, Bollington Ath., Chorlton Town, Garswood U., Grove U., Linotype, Knutsford, Poynton, Rylands, Warrington Town and Whitchurch Alport.

MID-CHESHIRE SUNDAY LGE

FOUNDED: 1966

PREM. DIV.	P	W	D	L	F	A	PTS
Egerton BC	18	14	1	3	48	16	29
Dragon Athletic	18	13	3	2	44	16	29
Roebuck	18	11	4	3	42	21	26
Oaklands BG	18	10	3	5	46	24	23
Liverpool SC	18	10	2	6	57	26	22
Golden Lion	18	6	2	10	30	45	14
FC Salter	18	6	3	9	42	43	*13
Pockets	18	3	5	10	20	45	11
Greenbank	18	2	5	11	26	56	*7
Kings Lock	18	1	0	17	17	80	*0

* - 2 points deducted

Lower Division Champions:
Div. 1 (12): Stanley Arms
Div. 2 (11): Oddfellows D.
Div. 3 (12): Holt Lloyd

Cup Finals:
League Cup: Dragon Athletic 2, Liverpool SC 1
Mid-Cheshire FA Sun. Cup: Roebuck 2, FC Salter 1

CREWE REGIONAL SUNDAY LGE

FOUNDED: 1965

PREM. DIV.	P	W	D	L	F	A	PTS
Malpas	18	14	2	2	53	18	30
Willaston White Star	18	13	1	4	51	27	27
Haslington Villa	18	12	2	2	45	28	26
The Star	18	9	4	5	44	35	22
Betley	18	10	1	7	54	43	21
Verdin & Weston U.	18	8	1	9	39	39	17
Wybunbury	18	6	3	9	48	39	15
Cumberland Arms	18	4	2	12	33	58	10
Widdowson	18	3	1	14	29	60	7
Faddiley	18	2	1	15	22	57	5

Lower Division Champions:
Div. 1 (12): Vickers
Div. 2 (13): ABB Transportation

Cup Finals:
Prem. Div: Verdin & Weston Utd 4, Haslington V. 0
Chronicle Trophy: Verdin & Weston 2, Haslington 1
Div. 1 Cup: Willaston Villa 3, Wrenbury 1
Div. 2 Cup: Dysart Arms 2, ABB Transportation 1
Crewe FA Sun. Cup: Haslington V. 3, Verdin & W. 2
Crewe FA Sunday Vase winners: ABB Transportation

Garswood United of the Green Insulation Mid-Cheshire League. Back Row (L/R): Steve Connor (Matthew Brown PLC, main sponsors), Denis Smith (Chairman), Charlie West (Asst Manager), Mark Kelly, Paul Dixon, Andy Cunliffe, Paul Fillingham, Phil Spibey, Dave Aspinall, Alan Aspinall (Manager), John Cox (Treasurer). Front: Gary Darbyshire, Adrian Riley, Jimmy Woodyer (Captain), Jeff Mosley, John Eaves, Steve McMurtry.

Karl Thomas (centre) of Runcorn wrestles with Darren Tinson during the Cheshire Building Social Senior Cup final at Witton Albion's Wincham Park. Northwich Victoria won the final by its only goal.

Photo - Keith Clayton.

CORNWALL F.A.

Secretary: J M Ryder,
Penare, 16 Gloweth View, Truro, Cornwall TR1 3JZ.

SENIOR CUP 1993-94

First Round

Foxhole Stars v Penryn Athletic 3-3,1-3
Helston Athletic v Callington Town 2-2,0-2

Second Round

Illogan RBL v St Ives Town 0-4
Camelford v Bude 0-3
St Breward v Sticker 0-4
St Agnes v Callington Town 0-3
RNAS Culdrose v Pendeen Rovers 4-0
Perranwell v Padstow United 3-2
St Dennis v Ludgvan 1-0

Third Round

Bude v Penryn Athletic 0-2
Launceston v Penzance 5-1
Mousehole v Wadebridge Town 0-2
Newquay v RAF St Mawgan 7-1
Riviera Coasters v Callington Town 3-3,0-5
St Just v Perranwell 1-0
Sticker v St Blazey 1-1,0-3
Falmouth Town v Bodmin Town 0-2
Bugle v RNAS Culdrose 1-1,2-1
Millbrook v Mullion 1-2
Nanpean Rovers v Truro City 0-2
Porthleven v Liskeard Athletic 0-0,0-1
St Ives Town v St Austell 1-1,0-6
Saltash United v St Dennis 3-0
Tintagel v Roche 2-2,0-3
Torpoint Athletic v Marazion Blues 16-0

Fourth Round

St Just v Launceston 0-4
Torpoint Athletic v Mullion 5-0
Bodmin Town v St Blazey 4-1
Liskeard Athletic v Newquay 3-1
Saltash United v Bugle 6-1
Wadebridge Town v St Austell 4-1
Truro City v Roche 7-0
Callington Town v Penryn Athletic 1-3

Quarter-Finals

Torpoint Athletic v Liskeard Athletic 1-1,1-4
Saltash United v Penryn Athletic 4-1
Truro City v Launceston 1-1,4-2
Wadebridge Town v Bodmin Town 0-1

Semi-Finals

Bodmin Town v Truro City *(at Newquay)* 2-0
Liskeard Ath. v Saltash United *(at Bodmin Town)* 2-1

Final *(at St Austell FC, Sat 23rd April)*: Liskeard Athletic 2, Bodmin Town 1

OTHER COUNTY FINALS:

Junior Cup *(at Newquay FC)*: Biscovey 2, Troon 0
Sunday Cup *(at Truro City FC)*: Penryn Athletic 2, Probus 0

JEWSON SOUTH WESTERN LEAGUE (Est. 1951)

President: Mr Tony Jewells **Chairman:** Mr Tristan Scott

Secretary: Mr Melvyn Goodenough,
Rose Cottage, Milton Damerel,
Holsworthy, Devon EX22 7DH (0409 261402)

	P	W	D	L	F	A	PTS
Bodmin Town	34	26	2	6	103	27	80
Newquay	34	24	8	2	92	33	80
Truro City	34	25	4	5	98	31	79
Falmouth Town	34	20	10	4	75	43	70
Launceston	34	19	7	8	86	43	64
Porthleven	34	16	6	12	71	66	54
Torpoint Athletic	34	14	10	10	67	59	52
St Austell	34	14	6	14	71	57	48
Holsworthy	34	13	9	12	44	50	48
Tavistock	34	13	7	14	70	69	46
St Blazey	34	12	9	13	76	59	45
Mullion	34	11	6	17	56	77	39
D & C Police	34	8	10	16	54	70	34
Appledore/BAAC	34	8	8	18	44	75	32
Millbrook	34	6	7	21	48	86	25
Wadebridge Town	34	6	5	23	34	94	23
Penzance	34	5	6	23	54	107	21
Okehampton Argyle	34	3	6	25	19	116	15

Top Scorers:
A Waddell (Bodmin) 43,
M Damerell (Truro) 29,
S Wherry (Truro) 27,
J Burrows (Porthleven) 24,
S O'Brien (Penzance) 24.

Bodmin Town completed the 'double' taking the championship on goal difference from Newquay and thrashing holders Truro City in the League Cup final. It was their second championship success having previously taken the title in 1990-91, but it was their first League Cup success having been beaten finalists in 1977-78 and 1988-89.

Bodmin also appeared in the final of the Cornwall Senior Cup where they were narrowly defeated by Liskeard Athletic of the Great Mills Western League. Tavistock reached the final of the Devon Premier Cup where they lost to Stoke Gabriel of the Westward Developments Devon County League, but Devon & Cornwall Police won the British Police Cup defeating West Midlands Police at Home Park, Plymouth. Torpoint enjoyed a successful run in the FA Vase before being beaten by Diss Town, the eventual winners.

Holsworthy were awarded the League's Sporting Trophy, narrowly ahead of newcomers Okehampton Argyle, whilst Porthleven clinched 'Best Kept Ground' award and John Short from Wadebridge was the top marked referee.

Mel Goodenough, Hon. Secretary

JEWSON SOUTH WESTERN LEAGUE RESULT CHART 1993-94

HOME TEAM	1	2	3	4	5	6	7	8	9	10	11	12	13	14	15	16	17	18
1. Appledore/BAAC	*	0-2	0-2	1-2	1-1	1-3	2-3	4-2	1-5	2-2	4-1	2-2	2-1	2-0	0-2	0-0	1-3	4-2
2. Bodmin Town	5-0	*	4-0	4-0	0-1	0-3	2-0	2-1	0-2	4-0	8-2	7-0	5-0	5-2	6-0	1-2	0-0	2-0
3. Devon/Cornwall Police	0-1	3-3	*	1-2	3-5	0-3	2-0	2-3	1-1	8-0	2-3	0-2	1-3	2-5	2-2	1-5	1-1	1-0
4. Falmouth Town	1-1	3-2	2-1	*	3-0	1-1	3-1	3-0	2-2	3-0	3-1	0-6	3-1	5-4	3-1	2-3	3-2	5-0
5. Holsworthy	1-0	0-4	2-4	0-0	*	1-4	2-1	4-0	1-1	2-0	1-0	2-0	0-0	1-3	3-3	0-0	1-2	4-0
6. Launceston	3-1	1-3	1-1	1-1	1-0	*	3-1	6-2	0-1	7-0	5-2	6-2	2-1	2-4	2-3	2-0	0-3	3-3
7. Millbrook	2-2	1-2	2-2	0-3	0-1	1-2	*	2-1	0-1	3-0	5-2	1-2	2-0	1-6	1-4	0-1	1-5	1-1
8. Mullion	1-1	0-1	1-1	0-3	4-1	1-5	7-1	*	0-3	2-0	3-0	0-3	1-3	1-1	2-1	3-3	2-2	3-1
9. Newquay	3-2	2-4	1-0	2-0	5-0	1-1	3-2	1-1	*	7-0	5-3	5-0	1-0	4-3	4-2	1-1	2-1	6-2
10. Okehampton Argyle	0-0	0-6	0-5	0-0	2-2	0-5	3-1	0-2	0-1	*	1-1	1-0	0-6	1-4	0-1	1-4	1-8	0-0
11. Penzance	7-1	1-3	0-0	1-4	1-1	1-1	1-1	0-3	1-7	1-2	*	2-5	3-0	0-4	2-2	3-1	0-4	3-1
12. Porthleven	3-2	3-1	2-2	0-0	1-0	2-1	4-2	0-2	1-1	2-0	6-2	*	0-3	2-2	3-1	4-1	2-4	3-1
13. St Austell	3-1	0-2	1-2	0-3	0-1	2-0	4-4	4-1	0-0	6-2	6-3	4-1	*	3-1	1-5	3-0	3-4	3-0
14. St Blazey	0-1	0-3	3-0	1-1	1-1	1-2	1-1	3-0	1-3	6-0	6-2	1-1	3-1	*	2-2	0-0	2-3	0-1
15. Tavistock	2-0	0-2	4-1	3-3	1-2	0-4	8-0	5-2	1-2	3-0	5-3	1-5	2-2	3-0	*	1-2	0-4	2-1
16. Torpoint Athletic	7-2	0-4	1-1	2-2	1-0	0-4	2-2	5-1	0-2	8-3	3-0	4-2	0-5	2-2	0-0	*	1-0	7-1
17. Truro City	4-0	0-1	6-0	1-2	3-1	1-0	2-1	4-0	2-1	3-0	3-2	3-1	1-1	2-1	4-0	4-0	*	3-0
18. Wadebridge Town	0-2	0-5	1-2	0-4	1-2	2-2	2-4	2-4	0-6	3-0	1-0	2-1	1-1	1-3	2-1	2-1	0-6	*

JEWSON SOUTHERN LEAGUE CUP 1993-94

Preliminary Round
Torpoint Athletic v St Blazey 1-1,3-1
Okehampton Argyle v Millbrook 0-1

First Round
Appledore/BAAC v D & C Police 2-2,0-5
Truro City v Penzance 4-0
Falmouth Town v Wadebridge Town 4-0
St Austell v Launceston 4-0
Millbrook v Porthleven 6-1
Torpoint Athletic v Newquay 2-2,1-0*(aet)*
Tavistock v Holsworthy 2-2,0-1
Bodmin Town v Mullion 3-0

Quarter Finals
D & C Police v Bodmin Town *(at Bodmin)* 0-3
St Austell v Truro City 1-2
Millbrook v Falmouth Town 1-0
Torpoint Athletic v Holsworthy 3-1

Semi-Finals
Bodmin Town v Millbrook *(at St Blazey)* 2-0
Truro City v Torpoint Athletic *(at Bodmin Town)* 3-1

Final *(at Newquay FC)*: Bodmin Town 5, Truro City 0

JEWSON SOUTH WESTERN LEAGUE TEN YEAR RECORD

	84/5	85/6	86/7	87/8	88/9	89/0	90/1	91/2	92/3	93/4
Appledore/Bideford AAC	7	14	14	12	18	11	9	7	10	14
Bodmin Town	18	4	5	4	3	3	1	5	2	1
Bugle	1	5	12	20	15	5	8	3	–	–
Clyst Rovers	11	11	10	19	14	8	14	6	–	–
Devon & Cornwall Police	–	–	–	–	–	–	–	16	12	13
Falmouth Town	6	1	1	2	2	1	3	1	6	4
Holsworthy	19	20	18	17	17	17	16	11	7	9
Launceston	15	19	17	13	5	7	15	15	4	9
Millbrook	5	3	3	5	10	6	11	14	15	15
Mullion	–	–	–	–	–	–	–	–	9	12
Newquay	3	2	8	1	4	4	4	2	3	2
Newton Abbot	10	10	9	11	13	–	–	–	–	–
Oak Villa	–	–	–	16	11	–	–	–	–	–
Okehampton Argyle	–	–	–	–	–	–	–	–	–	18
Penryn Athletic	–	15	–	–	–	–	–	–	–	–
Penzance	17	17	19	15	16	15	17	18	11	17
Plymouth Civil Service	13	–	–	–	–	–	–	–	–	–
Portleven	–	–	–	–	–	16	13	8	13	6
St Austell	16	8	6	6	12	13	5	13	17	8
St Blazey	2	9	2	3	2	2	2	9	5	11
Tavistock	12	16	16	18	9	9	12	17	8	10
Teignmouth	14	18	13	10	–	–	–	–	–	–
Torpoint Athletic	9	12	15	14	8	14	6	10	16	7
Torquay United Res	–	13	7	9	–	–	–	–	–	–
Truro City	8	6	11	8	6	10	7	4	1	3
Wadebridge Town	4	7	4	7	7	12	10	12	14	16
No. of Clubs	**19**	**20**	**19**	**20**	**18**	**17**	**17**	**18**	**17**	**18**

APPLEDORE-BIDEFORD A.A.C.

President: B Brennan **Chairman:** M Lane **Vice-Chairman:** B Taylor
Secretary: Eddie Nichols, 14 Alexandra Terrace, Bideford EX39 2PL (0237 475493).
Manager: M Stevens **Asst Manager:** J Lamont **Coach:** D Barrett.
Ground: Marshford, Churchill Way, Appledore, North Devon (0237 477099)
Directions: Before Appledore, on right of A386 approaching village.
Capacity: **Seats:** None **Cover:** 100 **Floodlights:** No **Founded:** 1978
Colours: All yellow **Change colours:** All blue. **Nickname:** Fishermen
Programme: Yes, with admission **Clubhouse:** Open when required **Club Shop:** No.
Reserves' Lge: North Devon **Prev. Lges:** Nth Devon/ Devon & Exeter **Prev. Grounds:** None
Midweek home matchday: Tuesday **Player progressing to Football Lge:** Mark Edworthy (Plymouth)
Record win: 9-1 v Torpoint (H) **Record defeat:** 1-10 v Falmouth (A), both South Western League.
Club record scorer: Mark Stevens **Club record appearances:** S Sluman
Captain 93-94: D Dark **P.O.Y. 93-94:** C Armstrong **Top Scorer 93-94:** D Downing
Honours: Devon Premier Cup 83-84.

BODMIN TOWN

Chairman: Mr A J Gynn **Vice-Chairman:** Mr C Hooper **President:** Mr R Flowerdew
Secretary: Martin Mullis, 24 Jubilee Terrace, Bodmin PL31 2QE (0208 77685).
Manager: Dudley Barry **Asst Manager:** Brian Shannon **Physio:** Jim Brewer
Commercial Manager: Mrs Sheila Chapman
Ground: Priory Park (0208 78165) - Just off town centre in large park complex, at rear of town car park.
Capacity: **Cover:** Grandstand **Seats:** Yes **Floodlights:** Yes **Founded:** 1889
Colours: Amber & black/black **Change colours:** All sky
Programme: 20 pages, 30p **Programme Editor:** Secretary **Club Shop:** No.
Sponsors: Gynn Construction **Nickname:** Black & Ambers
Midweek home matchday: Tuesday **Reserve team's League:** East Cornwall Premier.
Record win: 14-1 v Bugle (H), South Western Lg Cup 88-89.
Clubhouse: Mon-Thurs 6-11pm, Fri-Say noon-11pm, Sun noon-3 & 7-10.30pm. Bar snacks available most times.
Captain 93-94: Paul Mildon **Top Scorer 93-94:** Andy Woodell 47 **P.o.Y. 93-94:** Chris Hawke
Honours: South Western Lg 90-91 93-94 (R-up 92-93, Lg Cup 93-94 (R-up 77-78 88-89)), Cornwall Snr Cup R-up 93-94, Cornwall Charity Cup 86-87 89-90.

DEVON & CORNWALL POLICE

Chairman: Mr Brian Hart **Vice Chairman:** Vacant **President:** Mr J Evans.
Secretary: Mr Steve Bennett, C/O Police Station, Budshead Way, Crownhill, Plymouth PL6 5HT (0752 691227).
Manager: Jon Hillson/Gordon Nisbet **Asst Manager:** Steve Spear **Physio:** Dave Cook
Coach: Dave Cook **Commercial Manager:** Alan Eva.
Ground: Mill Bay Park, Plymouth **Clubhouse:** No. Matchdays tea bar sells light snacks.
Directions: Ground in West Hoe Road behind the 'Pavilions' leisure centre complex on Union Street (City Centre). Less than a mile from both main bus and railway stations.
Seats: No **Cover:** No **Capacity:** 2,000 **Floodlights:** No **Founded:** 1967.
Colours: All blue **Change colours:** All yellow **Nickname:** None.
Programme: 28 pages, with admission **Programme Editor:** Garry Kitchen **Club Shop:** No.
Previous Leagues: None **Previous Grounds:** Various prior to 1991-92.
Sponsors: Intercounty Distribution
Midweek home matchday: Tuesday **Reserve team:** None.
Record win: 10-0 v Peel Centre, at Middlemoor, Exeter, Southern Counties Police Cup 1990-91.
Record defeat: 0-6 v Truro City (A), South Western League 27/11/93.
Record Gate: 750 v West Mids Police, National Police Cup final 12/5/94 - at Home Park Plymouth. At Millbay Park; 168 v Bodmin Town, South Western League 6/10/91.
Current Players with Football League experience: Gordon Nisbet (WBA, Hull, Plymouth, Exeter), George Torrance (Brentford), Gerry Nardiello (Shrewsbury, Cardiff, Torquay), Graeme Kirkup (Exeter).
Club record scorer: Wayne Arthur **Club record appearances:** Wayne Arthur/Steve Spear (joint).
Captain 93-94: Steve Spear **Top Scorer 93-94:** Chris Hayfield **P.O.Y. 93-94:** Wayne Arthur
Hons: Devon Premier Cup 92-93, National Police Cup 93-94, South Western Lg Cup R-up 91-92, South West Co's Police Cup(5) 87-88 90-92 93-94, Falfield Police Cup(12) 69-72 73-75 76-77 78-79 80-81 85-86 87-89 91-92 (R-up 75-76 77-78 79-80 90-91), Wirral Programme Award for South Western Lg 91-92 92-93.

FALMOUTH TOWN

Chairman: Malcolm Newland **Vice Chairman:** Paul Ashburn **President:** Seb Coe.
Secretary: Mike Rowe, 15 Chestnut Close, Falmouth, Cornwall (0326 319163).
Manager: Ray Nicholls **Asst Manager:** Dave Ball.
Coach: Keith Barker **Press Officer:** Mike Odgers (0209 715766).
Ground: Bickland Park, Bickland Vale, Falmouth, Cornwall (0326 375156).
Directions: Follow A39 to Tregoniggie Industrial Estate - will pass ground on left. One and a half miles from Penmere Halt (BR) on Falmouth-Truro branch line. Bus service from town centre.
Seats: 300 **Cover:** 1,200 **Capacity:** 6,000 **Floodlights:** Yes **Founded:** 1946.
Colours: Amber/black **Change colours:** Blue/white. **Club Shop:** TBA
Previous Grounds: Ashfield 46-50/ Union Corner Rec 50-57.
Record Gate: 6,300 v Oxford United, FA Cup 1st Round 3/11/62.
Previous Leagues: Cornish Snr 50-51/ South Western 51-74/ Western 74-83.
Record win: 13-0 v Penzance (A), South Western League Cup 3/10/64.
Record defeat: 1-8 v Torpoint Athletic (A), South Western League 22/5/68.
Best FA Cup season: 1st Round 62-63 (lost 1-2 v Oxford United) 67-68 (lost 2-5 at Peterborough Utd).
Best FA Vase season: Quarter-Final replay 86-87 (lost 0-1 after 1-1 draw at St Helens Town).
Best FA Trophy season: 2nd Round proper 77-78.
Nickname: Town **Club Sponsors:** Stralfors/ Diadora.
Programme: 16 pages, 30p **Programme Editor:** Mike Odgers (0209 715766)
Midweek home matchday: Tues/Wed **Reserve team's League:** Jollys Cornwall Comb.
Players progressing to Football League: Roy Carter (Hereford 1975), Joe Scott (Bournemouth 1978), Tony Kellow (Exeter 1976), John Hodge (Exeter 1991).
Record transfer fee received: £12,000 for Tony Kellow (Exeter City 1976).
Clubhouse: Mon-Fri 7-11pm, Sat 12-11pm, Sun 12-3 & 7-10.30pm. Meals available.
Record Scorer: Joe Scott 198, 1972-78 **Record Appearances:** Keith Manley 580 (approx), 1970-83.
Captain 93-94: Dave Gardner **Top Scorer 93-94:** Glyn Hooper, 23
Hons: Cornish Snr Cup(10) 61-62 64-66 67-68 70-71 73-74 75-79 (R-up(7) 66-67 72-73 81-83 89-92), Western Lg(4) 74-78 (Lg Cup 74-75, Alan Young Cup 74-75 75-76 77-78(joint)), South Western Lg(12) 61-62 65-66 67-68 70-74 85-87 88-90 91-92 (R-up 58-59 64-65 69-70 87-88, Lg Cup(9) 57-59 61-63 67-68 70-71 85-86 90-92 (R-up(5) 59-60 71-72 86-88 92-93)), Pratten Cup 73-74, Cornwall Charity Cup 59-60, Cornwall Comb.(res) 83-84 (Supplementary Cup 93-94 (R-up 90-91)).

HOLSWORTHY

Manager: Terry Andrews. **Assistant Manager:** Peter England.
Secretary: Ray Latty, 13 Victoria Square, Holsworthy, Devon EX22 6AA (0409 253529).
Ground: Upcott Field (0409 254295) **Nickname:** Magpies **Cover:** Yes **Floodlights:** No.
Programme: 8 pages, £1 with entry **Editor:** Terry Irewin.
Colours: Black & white/black/black **Change colours:** Gold/white/gold. **Nickname:** Magpies
Record defeat: 1-9 v St Blazey (A), SWL 88-89 **Hons:** Devon Snr Cup 53-54 (Prem. Cup 71-72 76-77)

LAUNCESTON

Chairman: D Redstone **Vice Chairman:** D Heard **President:** D Viggers.
Secretary: Chris Martin, 3 Tavistock Road, Launceston, Cornwall PL15 9HA (0566 776175).
Manager: Roger Fice **General Manager:** Keith Ellacott.
Physio: D James **Ground:** Pennygillam, Launceston (0566 773279)
Directions: Follow signs to Pennygillam Industrial Est., just off main A30 - ground 400yds on left.
Programme: Yes **Seats:** 150 **Cover:** 150 **Floodlights:** Yes **Nickname:** Clarets
Cols: Claret & blue **Change:** Sky **Midweek matchday:** Tues/Wed **Club Shop:** No.
Sponsors: D Viggers Coal **Reserve team's League:** Plymouth & Dist.
Clubhouse: Open after every game. Bar meals.
Hons: S. Western Lg R-up 84-85, Cornish Snr Cup 1899-1900 00-01 82-83 (R-up 92-93, Charity Cup R-up 88-89).

MILLBROOK

President: Mrs E Weekes **Chairman:** Mr J Weekes **Vice Chairman:** Mr K Townsend.
Secretary: Murray Hyslop, 14 St Andrews Street, Millbrook, Cornwall PL10 1BE (0752 823271).
Manager: Mr J Bennett **Asst Manager:** Mr S Matthews **Press Officer:** Mr W Linney.
Ground: Mill Park, Millbrook, Cornwall (0752 822113)
Directions: From Torpoint Ferry - 3 miles to Antony on A374, fork left, after 1 mile turn left again and follow B3247 to Millbrook (3 miles), take road marked 'Town Centre Southdown', right at mini-r'bout after quarter mile, ground clearly visible. From Tamar Bridge - follow signs for Torpoint, 2 miles after Polbathic take right turning marked Millbrook, 5 miles to Millbrook then proceed as above.
Capacity: **Seats:** None **Cover:** 200 **Floodlights:** Yes **Founded:** 1973.
Colours: Black & white **Change colours:** Red/black/black **Nickname:** The Brook
Prev. Ground: Insworke Pk (14yrs) **Prev. Lges:** Plymouth Comb.(8yrs)/ Plymouth & Dist.(6yrs).
Programme: 20 pages, 10p **Editor:** Mr J Weekes (0752 822637) **Club Shop:** No.
Club Sponsors: Plymouth Boat Cruises Ltd.
Midweek home matchday: Tuesday **Reserve team's League.** Plymouth & District.
Clubhouse: Weekdays 7-11pm, Sat 11am-11pm, Sun noon-3 & 7.30-10.30. Hot food (chips, burgers etc) available during and after matchdays.
Top Scorer 93-94: **P.o.Y. 93-94:**
Club record scorer: Unknown **Club record appearances:** John Horne 215.
Hons: South Western Lg R-up 81-82, Cornwall Snr Cup R-up 83-84 (Charity Cup 84-85, Jnr Cup 75-76), Plymouth & District Lg 80-81 (Div 1 R-up 76-77).

MULLION

President: Derek Wilkes **Chairman:** Clive Biddick **Vice Chairman:** Anthony Meagor.
Secretary: Stewart Colin Westwood, 4 St Mellans Terrace, Mullion, Helston, Cornwall TR12 7EH (0326 240991).
Manager: Alan Carey **Coach:** Clive Moakes **Comm. Mgr:** Peter Butler.
Press Officer: Secretary **Physios:** Norman Carey/ Mick Letford.
Ground: Clifden Parc, Mullion (0326 240676)
Directions: Leave Helston on A3083 signed Lizard, at Mullion Holiday Park turn right onto B3296 signed Mullion Cove, thru Mullion 1-way system and continue on B3296, take 1st right after cricket field (on left), right again after 100yds - ground 50yds on left. Helston-Lizard bus passes ground.
Capacity: 2,200 **Seats:** None **Cover:** 100 **Floodlights:** No **Founded:** 1902.
Colours: Red & blue stripes **Change colours:** All white. **Nickname:** Gulls.
Previous Leagues: Helston & Dist. 02-18/ Cornwall County 18-48/ Cornwall Snr 48-56/ Falmouth & Helston 56-69/ Cornwall Comb. 69-92.
Previous Grounds: Garro Lane/ The Commons
Club Sponsors: West Bromwich Building Society.
Record Gate: 1,550 v Helston, Cornwall County League, 33-34.
Prog.: 30 pages **Editor:** Secretary **Club Shop:** Yes - contact Beau Meagor (0326 240044).
Midweek home matchday: Tuesday **Reserve team's League:** Cornwall Combination.
Record win: 16-0 v Tideford (H), Cornwall Snr Cup 86-87.
Record defeat: 0-5 v Torpoint Athletic (A), Cornwall Senior Cup 93-94.
Clubhouse: Normal licensing hours. Darts, pool. Hot & cold snacks and meals after matches.
Captain 93-94: Alan Carey **Top Scorer 93-94:** Ian Pattison.
P.o.Y. 93-94: Steve Tunnicliffe **Club record scorer & appearances:** Andrew Harry.
Hons: Cornwall Comb.(3) 85-86 90-92 (R-up(4) 80-83 86-87, Lg Cup(2) 90-92 (R-up 88-89), Suppl. Cup 85-86), Evely Cup 90-91 91-92.

NEWQUAY

President: J L Parker **Chairman:** A Kendall **Vice-Chairman:** B Blears.
Secretary: Brian Biggin, 8 Mitchell Ave., Newquay TR7 1BN (0637 875623).
Mgr/Coach: Graham Nicholls **Asst Manager:** Andy Mattock **Physio:** Ross McOnie
Ground: Mount Wise, Newquay (0637 872935)
Directions: Half mile from Newquay BR station - follow 1-way system for 2 miles - ground signed on left just before Windsor Hotel. By road, turn right at mini r-bout following signs for beach (not town centre), left on to 1-way system, then as above.
Seats: 250 **Cover:** 500 **Capacity:** 4,000 **Floodlights:** Yes **Founded:** 1890.
Colours: Red & white stripes **Change colours:** Sky & navy
Nickname: Peppermints
Prev. Names: Newquay 1890-1903/ N'quay One & All 03-12/ N'quay Utd 20-27/ N'quay Rovers 27-37.
Previous Leagues: West Cornwall/ Plymouth & District 21-27/ Cornish Senior 31-51.
Previous Grounds: JIB Field 1890-1912/ Tregunnel, Ennors Meadow, Lusty Glaze 1912-22.
Programme: 16 pages, 30p **Programme Editor:** Secretary **Club Shop:** No
Clubhouse details: 7-11pm weekdays, noon-11pm Sat, noon-3 & 7-10pm Sun. Cold snacks available.
Players progressing to Football League: Chris Morris (Sheffield Wednesday, Celtic & Eire), David Philp (Plymouth Argyle), Kevin Miller (Exeter City).
Club Sponsors: Studs Sports **Reserve Team's League:** Cornwall Combination.
Captain 93-94: Nigel Rowe **P.o.Y.: 93-94:** Andrew Street **Top Scorer 93-94:** Alan Lenton.
Hons: FA Vase 3rd Rd 90-91, Cornish Snr Cup 34-35 52-53 54-55 56-57 91-92 (R-up(9) 05-07 08-09 25-26 33-34 35-36 57-58 69-70 84-85), S. Western Lg(7) 58-60 77-78 79-80 81-82 83-84 87-88 (R-up 57-58 85-86 93-94, Lg Cup 55-56 88-89 (R-up(4) 56-58 79-81), Cornish Charity Cup(13) 06-07 08-09 53-56 57-59 62-63 69-70 74-75 76-78 88-89 (R-up(9) 07-08 20-21 56-57 60-61 73-74 75-76 81-82 84-86), W. Cornwall Lg 06-07 (R-up(2) 07-09), Cornish Snr Lg Herald Cup 34-35 (R-up(7) 33-34 35-36 49-51 55-57 58-59).

OKEHAMPTON ARGYLE

Chairman: Mr J Domaille, OBE **President:** Mr G Maddaford
Secretary: Colin Beer, 76 North Street, Okehampton, Devon (0837 52989).
Manager: Ollie Burton **Assistant Manager:** Trevor Watkins.
Press Officer: Alan King **Commercial Manager:** Peter Carter.
Ground: Simmons Park, Okehampton, Devon.
Directions: From town centre follow signs to Swimming Pool - ground behind at top end of park.
Seats: None **Cover:** Yes **Programme:** Yes **Floodlights:** No **Founded:** 1929
Colours: All blue **Change colours:** All red **Nickname:** Argyle.
Previous Grounds: None **Previous Lges:** West Devon 29-32/ Devon & Exeter 32-93.
Prog.: 32 pages, £1.20 with entry **Programme Editor:** Michael Drew. **Club Shop:** No
Club Sponsors: Okehampton Times **Record Gate:** Yes, on ground.
Reserves' League: North Devon **Clubhouse:** Under construction.
Captain 93-94: T Watkins **Top Scorer & P.o.Y. 93-94:** A Windser
Hons: Devon Jnr Cup 46-47, West Devon Lg 31-32 (Start Cup 31-32), Devon & Exeter Lg 47-48 (Bill Rees Sportsmanship Shield 90-91 91-92), Football Express Cup 52-53.

PENZANCE

President: Len Stanbury **Chairman:** Jim Dann
Secretary: Brian Harris, Hillview Cottage, Canonstown, Hayle TR27 6ND (0736 740062).
Manager: Roger Toms **Coach:** T.B.A. **Trainer:** Ken Prowse.
Ground: Penlee Park (0736 61964) **Floodlights:** Yes **Seats:** Yes **Founded:** 1888.
Directions: Seafront road past harbour, after amusement arcade turn right at r'bout (Alexander Rd), ground second right. Fifteen minutes walk from Penzance (BR); directions as above.
Colours: Black & white/black/black **Change colours:** All blue **Nickname:** Magpies.
Clubhouse: Yes **Reserve team's league:** Cornwall Comb.
Captain 93-94: **Top Scorer 93-94:** S O'Brien 24.
Players progressing to Football League: Gerry Gazzard (Brentford), Tony Kellow (Exeter).
Hons: Cornish Snr Cup 1892-93 95-96 97-98 98-99 1903-04 07-08 47-48 60-61 72-73 80-81 (R-up 1896-97 99-1900 00-01 04-05 48-49 49-50 54-55 56-57 74-75), South Western Lg 55-56 56-57 74-75 (Lg Cup R-up 60-61), Cornwall Charity Cup 47-48 48-49 (R-up 21-22 63-64), Cornwall Snr Lg Div 2 57-58 (Div 2 Cup 53-54 54-55), Cornwall Comb. R-up 65-66 (Lg Cup 69-70 (R-up 81-82)), Cornwall Jnr Cup (West) 03-04 04-05 05-06 07-08 09-10.

PORTHLEVEN

President: Mr W O Allen **Chairman:** Mr W Tearney **Vice Chairman:** Mr L Williams
Secretary: Keith Downing, 27 Gibson Way, Porthleven, Helston TR13 9AN (0326 561160).
Manager: Charlie Coombes **Coach:** Paul Christie **Comm. Mgr:** Mr V James.
Ground: Gala Parc, Mill Lane, Porthleven (0208 574754).
Directions: Arriving from Penzance on A394, B3304 into Porthleven, ground on left immediately before town. Coming from Helston on B3304 ground on right as you exit town. Buses from Helston and Penzance.
Capacity: **Seats:** None **Cover:** Yes **Floodlights:** No. **Programme:** 20p
Colours: Amber/black **Change colours:** All blue **Nickname:** Fishermen
Previous Leagues: West Penwith/ Cornwall Snr/ South Western 66-77/ Cornwall Combination 77-89.
Reserves' Lge: Cornwall Comb. **Previous Grounds:** Treza Downs/ Sunset Farm.
Clubhouse: Mon-Fri 7-11pm, Sat 11am-8pm, Sun 11am-3 & 7-10.30pm. Full food menu.
P.o.Y. 93-94: **Top Scorer 93-94:** J Burrows 24.
Hons: Sth Western Lg R-up 72-73, Cornwall Comb.(6) 59-60 63-64 65-67 78-79 88-89 (Lg Cup(6) 62-63 64-66 83-85 86-87, Suppl. Cup 88-89 91-92(res)), Cornwall Charity Cup 70-71, Cornwall Snr Cup R-up 68-69, George Evely Cup 64-65 65-66 83-84 86-87, West Penwith Lg, Penzance Hosp. Cup, Penzance Charity Cup.

St AUSTELL

Chairman: Rog Pope **Asst Chairman:** Derek Silk
Secretary: Peter Beard, 24 Alexandra Rd, St Austell, Cornwall PL25 4QP (0726 64138).
Manager: Glyn Avery **Asst Manager:** Colin Bunney **Physio:** N McKenna
Ground: Poltair Park (0726 77099). **Directions:** 5 mins walk north of St Austell (BR).
Seats: 200 **Cover:** 300 **Capacity:** 8,000 **Floodlights:** No **Founded:** 1890.
Colours: White/black/black **Change colours:** Blue/black/blue.
Previous Leagues: Rocky Park (1890s) **Record Gate:** 15,000 v Penzance, Senior Cup 1949.
Hons: South Western Lg 68-69 (R-up(4) 63-64 65-66 71-73, Lg Cup 64-65 71-73 87-88 (R-up 52-53 68-69 70-71 89-90)), Cornish Snr Cup(11) 11-14 33-34 38-39 45-47 63-64 68-69 71-72.

St BLAZEY

Vice Chairman: Mr P Clemow. **President:** Mr O Rowe **Chairman:** Mr H Cooke
Secretary/Press Officer: Mike Newcombe, 29 Par Green, Par, Cornwall PL24 2AF (0726 815964).
Manager: Terry Andrews **Coach:** David Pearce **Physio:** Richy Brown
Ground: Blaise Park, Station Road, St Blazey (0726 814110).
Directions: A390 Liskeard-St Austell road, turn into Station Road at lights in St Blazey village; ground 100 yards on left. One and a half miles from Par (BR).
Seats: 200 **Cover:** 700 **Capacity:** 3,500 **Floodlights:** Yes **Founded:** 1896.
Colours: Green/black **Change colours:** All white **Nickname:** Saints
Previous Leagues: Bodmin & Dist. 07-14 20-26/ St Austell & Dist. 14-20/ Cornwall County 27-29/ Cornwall Snr 31-33 46-51/ Plymouth & Dist. 29-31 37-39.
Programme: 24 pages, 30p **Editor:** S Paynter (0726 813150) **Club Shop:** No.
Sponsors: Express Joinery **Record Gate:** 6,500 v St Austell, Cornwall Snr Cup 48-49.
Midweek home matchday: Tues/Wed **Reserve team's League:** East Cornwall Premier.
Record win: 15-0 v Tavistock (H) and v Nanpean Rovers (A).
Record defeat: 0-14 v Wadebridge Town (A)
Clubhouse: Weekdays 11am-3pm & 7-11pm, Sat 11am-11.45pm, Sun noon-2.30 & 7.11pm. Bar snacks.
Players progressing to Football League: Nigel Martyn (Bristol Rovers, Crystal Palace & England).
Club record scorer: B Tallamy **Club record appearances:** W Isbell.
Captain 93-94: K Cook **P.o.Y. 93-94:** A Philp **Top Scorer 93-94:** Gary Marshall
Hons: SWL(6) 54-55 57-58 62-64 80-81 82-83 (R-up(9) 51-52 55-57 61-62 84-85 86-87 88-91, Lg Cup 53-54 56-57 66-67(joint) 81-82 86-87 (R-up 61-62 63-64 82-83 84-85 90-91)), Cornish Snr Cup 35-36 49-50 53-54 55-56 57-58 59-60 62-63 86-87, Cornish Charity Cup 35-36 56-57 83-84, Cornwall Snr Lg Cup (Herald Cup) 35-36 48-49.

TAVISTOCK

President: Mr G Worth **Chairman:** Mr R A Fenner **Vice Chairman:** Mr D R D Pethick
Secretary: Philip Lowe, 1 Bainbridge Court, Colebrook, Plympton, PL7 4HH (0752 335273).
Manager: Steve Metters **Asst Manager:** T.B.A. **Coach:** Alan Gillett.
Physio: Les Mewton **Press Officer:** Chairman.
Ground: Langsford Park, Crowndale Rd, Tavistock (0822 614447)
Directions: A386 from Plymouth, left after Ford garage into Crowndale Rd, ground half mile on left.
Capacity: 2,000 **Seats:** 200 **Cover:** 200 **Floodlights:** Yes **Founded:** 1888.
Colours: Black & red/black/red **Change colours:** Blue & white or yellow & white
Prev. Lge: Plymouth & Dist. 06-52 **Previous Grounds:** Green Lane/ Sandy Park (pre-1940).
Programme: 32 pages, with entry **Programme Editor:** Secretary **Club Shop:** No.
Sponsors: Dave Carter Spts, Plymouth **Record Gate:** 5,000 v Calstock, Bedford Cup final 1952.
Midweek home matchday: Tuesday **Reserve team's League:** Plymouth & District.
Nickname: 'Tavy' or 'Lambs' **Record win:** 10-0 v Penzance (A), South Western Lg 91-92.
Record transfer fee paid: Nil **Received:** £1,000 for Neil Langman (Plymouth, Sept '53).
Players progressing to Football League: Peter Langman (Plymouth, 1951), Neil Langman (Plymouth, 1953).
Clubhouse: Open all day Saturday and evenings 6.30-10.30 or 11pm. Hot & cold food. Darts, pool, Sky T.V.
Captain 93-94: **Top Scorer 93-94:**
P.o.Y. 93-94: **Club record appearances:** A Pethick 1,000+.
Hons: Devon Premier Cup 90-91 (R-up 93-94), Devon Snr Cup 1889-90 1968-69 77-78 81-82, South Western Lg Cup 68-69 (R-up 76-77 83-84), Bedford Cup on numerous occasions.

TORPOINT ATHLETIC

Manager: Phil Cardew
Secretary: Vic Grimwood, 43 Henerdon Heights, Plympton PL7 3EY (0752 81344).
Ground: Mill Field (0752 812889)
Directions: Bear left from Torpoint ferry, ground down hill on left after half a mile.
Clubhouse: Yes **Programme:** Yes **Seats:** Yes **Cover:** Yes **Floodlights:** No
Colours: Gold & black stripes/black/black **Change colours:** All white.
Previous League: Plymouth & District League.
Record win: 16-0 v Marazion Blues (H), Cornwall Senior Cup 3rd Rd 93-94.
Best FA Vase season: 4th Round 93-94 (lost 0-3 at home to Diss Town, eventual winners).
Hons: South Western Lg 64-65 66-67 (Lg Cup R-up 65-66), Cornish Snr Cup 1896-97 1905-06 06-07 08-09 09-10 19-20 28-29 32-33.

Torpoint Athletic FC, pictured before their sensational 6-2 FA Vase win at Tunbridge Wells.
Photo - Francis Short.

TRURO CITY

Manager: Steve Massey
Secretary: Ray Rowe, 5 Alverton Gardens, Truro, Cornwall TR1 1JA (0872 70684).
Ground: Treyew Road, Truro, Cornwall (0872 78853) **Seats:** Yes **Floodlights:** Yes.
Directions: On A39 by-pass south of city. 10 mins walk from BR station; up hill and left at junction.
Colours: Red & black/black/black **Change colours:** Yellow/red/red.
Top Scorer 93-94: Steve Wherry 20 **Reserve Team's League:** Cornwall Combination.
Hons: South Western Lg 60-61 69-70 92-93 (R-up 54-55 62-63 66-67 67-68 70-71, Lg Cup 59-60 66-67(joint) 92-93 (R-up 54-55 58-59 67-68 93-94)), Cornish Snr Cup 1894-95 1901-02 02-03 10-11 23-24 26-27 27-28 37-38 58-59 66-67 69-70, Cornish Charity Cup 19-20 28-29 29-30 30-31 49-50 64-65 80-81, Cornish Snr Lg 31-32 32-33, Cornwall Comb. Supplementary Cup 92-93(res).

WADEBRIDGE TOWN

Manager: Steve Cudmore.
Secretary: Barry Cudmore, 3 Marine Terrace, Wadebridge, Cornwall PL27 7AJ (0208 813826).
Ground: Bodieve Park (0208 812537) **Seats:** Yes **Cover:** Ample **Floodlights:** No
Directions: At junction of A39 and B3314 to east of Wadebridge. **Nickname:** Bridgers.
Colours: Red/red/white **Change colours:** All blue.
Reserve Team's League: East Cornwall Premier.
Hons: South Western Lg R-up 68-69 78-79 79-80 (Lg Cup 74-75 75-76 77-78 79-80 84-85 (R-up 62-63 69-70 81-82, Cornish Snr Cup 79-80, Cornish Charity Cup 26-27 33-34 51-52 63-64 72-73 75-76 81-82 84-85.

CORNISH GUARDIAN
EAST CORNWALL PREMIER LEAGUE

FINAL TABLE	P	W	D	L	F	A	PTS
Liskeard Ath. Res.	34	30	3	1	121	38	63
Roche	34	26	5	3	122	33	57
Nanpean Rovers	34	25	2	7	118	36	52
St Dennis	34	19	5	10	104	67	43
Bodmin Town Res.	34	19	4	11	91	55	43
Sticker	34	17	7	10	107	67	41
Saltash Utd Res.	34	19	2	13	89	53	40
Callington	34	15	9	10	84	65	39
Bugle	34	14	9	11	63	58	37
St Blazey Res.	34	14	7	13	105	86	35
Bude	34	14	3	17	60	67	31
St Breward	34	13	5	16	78	92	31
Camelford	34	11	8	15	52	55	30
Foxhole Stars	34	9	5	20	49	89	23
Padstow United	34	7	7	20	58	112	21
Wadebridge T. Res.	34	5	3	26	28	109	13
Riviera Coasters	34	4	4	26	35	135	12
Tintagel	34	1	0	33	29	176	2

LEAGUE CUP WINNERS: Nanpean Rovers
LEAGUE CUP RUNNERS-UP: Liskeard Ath. Res.

GEORGE EVELY CUP
(ECPL Cup winners v Cornwall Comb. Cup winners)
Nanpean Rovers 3, Perranwell 1

BUDE

Ground: Broadclose (behind school off Broadclose Hill) **Secretary:** A Clark (0288 353974)
Clubhouse: Yes **Cover:** No **Colours:** Royal Blue

BUGLE

Ground: Molinnis (0726 851123) **Secretary:** T Riedling (0208 73293)
Ground: Turn off A391 St Austell-Bodmin road into Molinnis (right turn just after Bugle centre if coming from St Austell). 5 mins walk from Bugle BR station (Par-Newquay line) - head towards village and turn left into Molinnis.
Cover: Yes **Seats:** Yes **Clubhouse:** Shut **Floodlights:** No
Colours: White & black **Previous League:** South Western 1955-92.
Hons: South Western Lg 84-85 (Lg Cup 83-84), Cornish Snr Cup 51-52.

CALLINGTON

Ground: Callington Community School **Secretary:** P Brown (0566 833851)
Directions: Callington school is on right hand side of A388 travelling north of town towards St Austell. Inside school ground keep left for club's pitch.
Clubhouse: No **Programme:** No **Cover:** No **Colours:** Blue.
Hons: League Cup R-up 90-91. **Previous League:** Plymouth & Dist. Lg (pre-1990).

FOXHOLE STARS

Ground: Goverseth PF, Goverseth Rd **Secretary:** S Smith (0726 66895)
Directions: South on B3279 from Nanpean, ground entrance signed on right entering Foxhole.
Clubhouse: Yes, newly built **Cover:** No **Colours:** Black & white
Hons: Lg Cup 90-91

NANPEAN ROVERS

Ground: Victoria Park **Secretary:** A Craddock (0726 823543)
Directions: Ground entrance on left as you travel north through village centre on B3279.
Clubhouse: Yes **Programme:** Yes **Cover:** Yes **Seats:** No.
Colours: Amber and Black **Previous League:** South Western.

PADSTOW UNITED

Ground: Jury Park, Wadebridge Rd, Padstow **Secretary:** S Alcock (0841 533476)
Ground Directions: On right hand side of A389 about one mile before Padstow.
Clubhouse: No **Programme:** No **Cover:** No **Colours:** Green.
Hons: Supplementary Cup 88-89.

RIVIERA COASTERS

Ground: St Austell FC (page 798) **Secretary:** G Rowett (0726 64476) **Colours:** Green

ROCHE

Ground: Trezaise Rd, Roche **Secretary:** D Roach (0208 831866)
Ground Directions: On right-hand side of B3274 as you enter Roche from St Austell direction.
Clubhouse Yes **Programme:** No **Cover:** No **Colours:** Red
Hons: ECPL R-up 93-94 (Lg Cup R-up 92-93, Supplementary Cup R-up 88-89).

St BREWARD

Ground: Brake Park, St Breward **Secretary:** Mrs Kay (0208 850030)
Colours: Red & black stripes **Cover:** Yes **Clubhouse:** No.

St CLEER

Ground: Rec. Field, St Cleer (nr Liskeard) **Secretary:** I Savigar (0579 340374)

St DENNIS

Ground: Boscawen Park, St Dennis **Secretary:** P Searle (0726 63280)
Directions: Coming north on B3279 turn left in St Dennis village centre by Boscawen Hotel.
Clubhouse: Yes **Cover:** No **Colours:** Amber & black
Hons: East Cornwall Lg 87-88 (Lg Cup R-up 88-89).

STICKER

Ground: Ennis Farm, St Stephen Rd, Sticker **Secretary:** G Phillips (0726 61299)
Directions: Take road for St Stephens) in Sticker village. Ground half mile on right opposite farm.
Clubhouse: No **Cover:** Yes

The League also contains the Reserve sides of: Bodmin Town (page 863), Liskeard Athletic (page 562), St Blazey (page 865), Saltash United (page 563), and Wadebridge Town (page 866).

JOLLY'S CORNWALL COMBINATION

FINAL TABLE	P	W	D	L	F	A	PTS
Penryn Athletic	36	30	5	1	115	18	65
Mullion Res.	36	24	9	3	118	38	57
Truro City Res.	36	25	3	8	111	47	53
Perranwell	36	23	6	7	92	33	52
RNAS Culdrose	36	19	9	8	80	38	47
St Ives Town	36	18	10	8	64	38	46
Pendeen Rovers	36	20	5	11	85	55	45
Portleven Res.	36	18	5	13	86	67	41
Falmouth T. Res.	36	18	3	15	79	48	39
Newquay Res.	36	15	5	16	75	62	35
Mousehole	36	14	6	16	49	82	34
Helston Athletic	36	13	7	16	74	71	33
St Just	36	12	8	16	49	65	32
St Agnes	36	13	2	21	66	78	28
Ludgvan	36	8	4	23	38	80	*22
RAF St Mawgan	36	7	7	21	41	79	*21
Penzance Res.	36	7	5	24	39	110	19
Illogan RBL	36	5	4	27	34	88	4
Marazion Blue	36	0	1	35	11	204	1

* - points adjusted

LEAGUE CUP FINAL *(at Falmouth Town FC)*:
Perranwell 7, Porthleven Reserves 0

SUPPLEMENTARY CUP FINAL *(at Porthleven FC)*
(Cup for League Cup 1st Round losers)
Falmouth Town Reserves 2, RNAS Culdrose 2
Replay: Falmouth Town R. 3, RNAS Culdrose 0

GEORGE EVELY CUP
(ECPL Cup winners v Cornwall Comb. Cup winners)
Nanpean Rovers 3, Perranwell 1

HELSTON ATHLETIC

Ground: Kellaway Parc, Clodgy Lane (0326 573742) **Secretary:** B Dunstan (0326 573358)
Ground Directions: On A394 Helston bypass, on right coming from Falmouth.
Clubhouse: Yes **Programme:** No **Cover:** Yes; clubhouse overhang **Colours:** Royal Blue
Hons: Cornish Senior Cup 36-37, Champ 64-65 87-88 **Reserves:** Falmouth-Helston Lg.

ILLOGAN R.B.L.

Ground: Oxland Park (0209 216488) **Secretary:** S Harrison (0209 211046)
Ground Directions: Turn right for Illogan off Camborne to Redruth road. Ground on right down Richards Lane.
Clubhouse: Yes **Programme:** No **Cover:** Stand **Colours:**
Hons: Champs 70-71 71-72 73-74, Runners-up 69-70 72-73 **Reserves:** W C'wall Mining Lg.

LUDGVAN

Ground: Fairfield (0736 740774) **Secretary:** M Brownfield (0736 740603)
Ground Directions: Turn right off A30 for Ludgvan Leaze (after Crowlas). Ground on right.
Clubhouse: Village Hall **Programme:** Yes **Cover:** Yes **Colours:** Yellow and green
Formed: 1960 **Reserves:** West Penwith League
Hons: League Cup 82-83, Eveley Cup 1983, Penzance & Dist Charity Cup 89-90, West Cornwall Hosp Cup 89-90

MARAZION BLUES

Ground: Trevenner (0736 711020) **Secretary:** T Whitford (0736 711095)
Ground Directions: Through Marazion village and turn up Shop Hill opposite Fire Engine Pub.
Clubhouse: Community Centre **Programme:** No **Cover:** Yes **Colours:** All Blue
Floodlights: Installed during 1990-91 **Reserves:** West Penwith Lg.

MOUSEHOLE

Ground: Trungle Park, Paul **Secretary:** R Walke (0736 50483)
Ground Directions: In Paul village, 1 mile inland from Mousehole. **Formed:** 1922-23
Clubhouse: Yes **Programme:** Yes **Cover:** Yes **Colours:** Green & white hoops **Nickname:** Seagulls
Hons: Runners-up 85-86, League Cup 75-76, Evely Cup 1976 **Reserves:** West Penwith Lg.

PENDEEN ROVERS

Ground: Borlaise Park (0736 788274) **Secretary:** D Trezise (0736 788274)
Ground Directions: B3306 St Ives to St Just road. Ground immediately on left down road to Pendeen Lighthouse.
Clubhouse: Yes **Programme:** Yes **Cover:** No **Colours:** Amber and Black **Reserves:** West Penwith Lg.

PENRYN ATHLETIC

Ground: Kernick, Kernick Rd (0326 75182) **Secretary:** M Young (0326 374098)
Ground Directions: Turn off A394 at sign for Kernick Industrial estate. Ground on right on road into town.
Clubhouse: Yes **Programme:** No **Cover:** Yes **Cols:** Red & Black stripes **Reserves:** Falmouth-Helston Lg.
Previous League: South Western 85-86.
Hons: Champs 80-81 81-82 82-83 84-85 86-87 89-90 92-93 (R-up 83-84 88-89), League Cup 87-88 88-89 (R-up 90-91), Evely Cup 88-89.

PERRANWELL

Ground: Perran-Ar-Worthal PF **Secretary:** I Arnold (0209 219406)
Ground Directions: On Falmouth to Truro branch-line, or by road 1 mile off A39 (turn right at Perranaworthal).
Clubhouse: No **Cover:** Yes **Colours:** Royal Blue
Hons: Champs 76-77, R-up 75-76 92-93, Lg Cup 92-93 93-94. **Reserves:** Falmouth-Helston Lg.

R.A.F. ST MAWGAN

Ground: St Eval **Secretary:** S Jessup (0841 540202)
Ground Directions: Follow signs for St Eval from St Columb Major. Ground in village on the right.
Clubhouse No **Programme:** No **Cover:** No **Nickname:** The Airmen **Colours:** Blue and white quarters
Hons: Supplementary Cup runners-up 88-89.

R.N.A.S. CULDROSE

Grnd: Spts Field, RNAS Culdrose, Helston (0326 574121x7167) **Sec.:** PT Office (0326 574121x2404)
Ground Directions: On A3083 Helston to Lizard Road, on right just before turning to St Keverne.
Hons: Lg Cup R-up 92-93, Supplementary Cup R-up 93-94 **Reserves:** Falmouth-Helston Lg.

St AGNES

Ground: Enys Park, West Polperro (0872 553673) **Secretary:** J Stenning (0872 552657)
Ground Directions: On cliffs to the north-west of the village.
Clubhouse: Yes **Programme:** Yes **Nickname:** Aggie **Colours:** White/Black
Reserves: Falmouth-Helston Lg.

St IVES TOWN

Ground: The Saltings, Lelant **Secretary:** Miss B Quick (0736 794435).
Ground Directions: Adjacent to Lelant Saltings BR station (St Erth-St Ives line) or fifteen mins walk from St Erth main line station. By road, turn off A30 for St Ives onto A3074, right at 1st island and left into 'Merlins' theme park - ground car park at end.
Clubhouse: No **Cover:** Yes **Colours:** Blue **Reserves:** Mining Div Lg. **Prev. Lge:** Mining Div Lg.

St JUST

Ground: Lafrowda Park **Secretary:** T Addicoate (0736 7875)
Ground Dirctions: In village take Cape Cornwall Road. First left, left again and ground at end of terrace.
Clubhouse: Yes **Cover:** Yes **Nickname:** The Tinners **Reserves:** West Penwith Lg. **Programme:** Yes
Hons: Champs 61-62, Runners-up 62-63 63-64 73-74 74-75 76-77, Supplementary Cup R-up 92-93.

TROON

Ground: Grouter Park **Secretary:** Mrs T Penberthy (0209 713538)
Dirctions: South thru Troon from Camborne, turn left exiting the village - ground quarter mile down lane on right.
Previous Lge: Falmouth-Helston (pre-1994) **Hons:** Cornwall Jnr Cup.

See also the Jewson South Western League section for details of Falmouth Town, Mullion, Newquay, Penzance, Porthleven and Truro City who all field their Reserve sides in the Jollys Combination.

ARKINS & ASHTON PLYMOUTH & DISTRICT LEAGUE (Est. 1905)

PREMIER DIV.	P	W	D	L	F	A	PTS
Plymouth Command	30	22	3	5	121	53	60
Tavistock Res.	30	20	4	6	113	42	64
Prince Rock	30	18	5	7	118	69	59
Woodland Fort	30	17	6	7	96	59	57
Marjons	30	17	6	7	103	70	57
Millbrook Res.	30	14	7	9	70	51	49
Brixton AFC	30	15	3	12	77	80	48
Hooe St John	30	12	7	11	84	64	43
Plym. Civil Service	30	13	4	13	68	79	43
Plymstock Utd Res.	30	12	6	12	65	68	42
Wessex Rangers	30	10	6	14	74	84	36
Old Suttonians	30	9	5	16	68	99	32
Dynamo Villa	30	8	6	16	61	90	30
Torpoint Ath. Res.	30	7	8	15	52	85	29
Launceston Res.	30	5	2	23	44	112	17
Weston Mill OV Res.	30	2	0	28	41	152	6

Leading scorers: 40 - Flain (Marjons); 37 - Bennett (Hooe); 35 - Holdroyd (Plymouth Command); 30 - Smith (Plymouth Command); 28 - Webb (Tavistock), Pluckrose (Old Suttonians); 25 - Evans + Fice (Woodland Fort); 22 - Jackson (Prince Rock); 19 - King (Wessex); 18 - Roberts (Tavistock); 16 - Smith (Tavistock), Dann (Prince Rock); 15 - Harding (Prince Rock), Anderson (Launceston), 14 - Weaving (Prince Rock); 13 - Roach (Old Suttonians), Love (Dynamo Villa), Trudgeon (Marjons); 12 - Mahoney (Weston Mill), Cross (Prince Rock), Cornish (Plymouth CS).

DIV. ONE	P	W	D	L	F	A	PTS
Vospers	24	19	3	2	106	33	60
Elburton Villa Res.	24	18	3	3	86	27	57
Dobwalls	24	13	4	7	63	52	43
Prince Rock YC	24	14	1	9	56	51	43
Satellite Sports	24	11	6	7	59	50	39
Callington T. Res.	24	11	5	8	49	42	38
Bere Alston Utd	24	10	6	8	73	56	36
AFC Rangers	24	9	7	8	51	42	34
Green Waves	24	10	3	11	56	52	33
Saltash Town	24	7	3	14	48	67	24
DML	24	4	2	18	34	90	14
Old Sutton. Res.	24	4	0	20	28	102	12
Ivybridge T. Res.	24	2	5	17	27	72	11

Leading Scorers: 30 - Treble (Dobwalls); 28 - Green (Green Waves); 24 - Richards (AFC Rangers); 21 - Sherriff (Vospers); 19 - Morgan + Spear (Vospers); 15 - Seldon (Elburton); 14 - Collins + Lunnon (Vospers), Ellicott (Prince Rock YC), Noonan (Satellite); 13 - Kendall (Satellite), Croft (Saltash); 11 - Ridgeway (Bere Alston), Hamley (Elburton); 10 - Rawlinson (Bere Alston), Powell (Elburton).

DIV. TWO	P	W	D	L	F	A	PTS
City Social SC	22	17	3	2	85	44	54
Ply. Parkway Res.	22	16	3	3	93	51	51
Marjons Res.	22	13	3	6	66	35	42
Polperro	22	12	1	9	57	42	37
Hooe St John Res.	22	10	3	9	60	58	33
Challenger Tyres	22	10	3	9	47	48	33
YMCA Rangers	22	8	6	8	64	61	30
Tavistock 'A'	22	7	4	11	52	59	25
Prince Rock YC Res.	22	6	4	12	50	67	22
Plym. Electricity	22	5	3	14	40	71	18
West Park PO	22	3	6	13	33	64	15
Roborough	22	4	3	15	32	81	15

Leading Scorers: 21 - Goldstone (Parkway), Widger (Marjons); 20 - Pusiak (Prince Rock YC), Leonard (Parkway); 18 - Moore (City Social), Wassall (YMCA), Journeaux (Hooe); 16 - Pearse (Parkway); 15 - Faulkner (Polperro); 14 - Dan (Polperro), Libby (YMCA); 13 - Ching (Hooe); 12 - Prior (Challenger Tyres), Moore (Hooe), Jordan (Marjons); 11 - Elliott (Tavistock), McFerran (City Social); 10 - Whitfield (YMCA), Andreas (Roborough).

DIV. THREE	P	W	D	L	F	A	PTS
Wessex Rgrs Res.	24	19	3	2	101	30	60
Sherwood	24	18	4	2	96	32	58
Kingstamerton CA	24	18	1	5	83	37	55
Swingletree	24	17	2	5	73	27	53
Lee Moor	24	12	3	9	60	61	39
Ker Street SC	24	10	5	9	67	66	35
Falstaff Wanderers	24	10	1	13	52	67	11
Calstock	24	8	4	12	54	62	28
Stoke Climsland	24	7	5	12	45	72	26
New Park Athletic	24	6	6	12	38	68	24
First & Last	24	4	6	14	30	59	18
Plym. International	24	2	4	18	20	76	10
Cardinal United	24	0	6	18	38	100	6

Leading Scorers: 31 - Berry (Sherwood); 30 - Jones (Ker Street); 28 - Truscott (Swingletree); 21 - Hendy (Wessex); 19 - Rowe (Wessex), Drew (Sherwood); 18 - Phillips (Lee Moor), Deacon (Kingstamerton); 17 - Bolton (Sherwood); 15 - Beal (New Park), Crocumbe (Swingletree), Corbyn (Kingstamerton); 13 - Willmott (Wessex), Simmonds (Wessex); 12 - Spurr (Calstock), Travers (Lee Moor); 11 - Dickson (Falstaff), Wadland (Stoke Climsland).

DIV. FOUR	P	W	D	L	F	A	PTS
Swingletree Res.	26	21	4	1	142	31	67
Kingstamerton Res.	26	20	3	3	128	36	63
Millbay Colts	26	19	2	5	117	61	59
Horrabridge Rgrs	26	18	2	6	132	51	56
Varley Trophies	26	16	0	10	82	71	48
Toshiba	26	13	7	6	74	41	46
Gunnislake	26	13	5	8	76	64	44
Famous Firkin	26	12	3	11	84	74	39
Trafalgar Hotel	26	6	5	15	48	89	23
Devon Tors	26	6	4	16	41	89	22
Vine Hotel	26	5	3	18	63	108	18
New Park Ath. Res.	26	4	5	17	46	107	17
Abakon	26	4	1	21	37	154	13
Bullpoint Rangers	26	0	6	20	37	129	6

Leading Scorers:
61 - Stephens (Swingletree); 35 - Goldsmith (Kingstamerton); 34 - Thompson (Swingletree); 33 - Goldsmith (Toshiba); 31 Rowlands (Gunnislake); 30 - Joce (Millbay Colts); 29 - Lawrence (Millbay Colts); 26 - Bowen (Horrabridge); 25 - Gaden (Horrabridge); 24 - White (Kingstamerton); 22 - Clay (Varley); 17 - Braddon (Firkin); 16 - Hann (Horrabridge); 15 - Aldore (Horrabridge); 13 - Clevatt (Vine Hotel), Buckley (Trafalgar); 12 - Halifax + Tallis (Firkin).

All internal cup competitions were abandoned because of the wet weather.

NB. *This League is, of course, primarily a Devon League, but it does include a large minority of Cornish clubs.*

FALMOUTH-HELSTON LEAGUE

DIV. ONE	P	W	D	L	F	A	PTS
Falmouth Athletic	26	22	2	2	141	20	46
Penryn Ath. Res.	26	22	1	3	96	25	45
Troon	26	19	4	3	81	30	42
Hayle	26	15	3	8	63	61	33
Mawnan	26	12	6	8	64	44	30
Constantine	26	13	4	9	65	63	30
Perranporth	26	11	5	10	50	63	27
Wendron	26	10	6	10	72	54	26
Duchy	26	10	4	12	70	55	24
Truro City 'A'	26	6	6	14	48	81	18
Helston Ath. Res.	26	6	4	16	45	71	16
St Day	26	5	5	16	38	78	15
Perranwell Res.	26	0	5	21	29	107	5
Lanner	26	1	3	22	31	137	5

Percy Stephens Cup: Falmouth Athletic
Percy Stephens Cup r-up: Mawnan
Lockhart Cup: Falmouth Athletic
Lockhart Cup r-up: Wendron

DIV. TWO	P	W	D	L	F	A	PTS
Penryn Ath. 'A'	30	26	2	2	139	20	54
Falmouth Ath. Res.	30	21	4	5	114	32	46
Ruan Minor	30	20	5	5	69	40	45
Mawgan	30	19	4	7	96	54	#44
Lizard	30	19	4	7	104	43	42
Duchy Res.	30	16	4	10	106	78	*34
Hayle Res.	30	15	1	14	69	78	#33
Truro GWRSA	30	14	2	14	89	58	30
Wendron Res.	30	12	6	12	74	60	30
Mawnan Res.	30	10	6	14	72	65	26
Helston Ath. 'A'	30	12	1	17	64	80	25
Perranport Res.	30	10	3	17	50	92	23
Constantine Res.	30	9	5	16	59	60	*21
Mabe	30	5	1	24	48	111	11
Cury	30	4	0	26	42	152	8
Lanner Res.	30	1	0	29	27	212	2

* - 2 points deducted # - 2 points awarded

Barker Bowl: Penryn Athletic 'A'
Barker Bowl r-up: Ruan Minor
League Cup: Truro GWRSA
League Cup r-up: Hayle Reserves
Wheatley Cobb Cup: Falmouth Ath. Reserves
Wheatley Cobb Cup r-up: Helston Athletic 'A'

ONE & ALL SPORTS MINING DIVISION LEAGUE

DIV. ONE	P	W	D	L	F	A	PTS
Chacewater	28	22	4	2	106	27	48
Trelander	28	19	4	5	105	38	42
Gulval	28	17	6	5	103	47	40
Halsetown	28	14	10	4	44	20	38
Carharrack	28	13	7	8	70	55	33
Camborne Town	28	12	6	10	66	60	30
Troon Res.	28	11	6	11	80	56	28
RNAS Culdrose Res.	28	13	0	15	51	52	26
St Ives T. Res.	28	8	9	11	44	60	25
Trispen	28	9	5	14	60	92	23
Goonhavern	28	9	5	14	43	75	23
St Newlyn East	28	9	4	15	52	63	22
Holman SC	28	8	6	14	55	67	22
Illogan RBL Res.	28	8	2	18	35	75	18
St Agnes Res.	28	0	2	26	15	122	2

DIV. TWO	P	W	D	L	F	A	PTS
Trelawney	24	21	1	2	130	23	43
Rosudgeon-Kennegy	24	21	1	2	90	30	43
Camborne Sch of M.	24	14	4	6	81	54	32
Castle United	24	13	4	7	55	45	30
Chacewater Res.	24	13	3	8	74	57	29
Frogpool-Cusgarne	24	9	8	7	59	50	26
Holman SC	24	9	4	11	54	58	22
Camborne Rovers	24	9	3	12	63	64	21
Trispen Res.	24	8	4	12	48	88	20
Truro GWRSA	24	5	5	14	57	54	15
Threemilestone SC	24	6	2	16	50	106	14
St Ives Town 'A'	24	4	3	17	34	75	11
St Newlyn E. Res.	24	3	0	21	31	121	6

DIV. THREE	P	W	D	L	F	A	PTS
Cubert	20	16	1	3	76	31	33
Gulval Res.	20	14	2	4	63	29	30
Gwinear Churchtown	20	11	2	7	45	39	24
Carharrack Res.	20	8	5	7	43	46	21
Camborne Town Res.	20	8	4	8	45	43	20
Redruth United	20	9	2	9	51	54	20
St Day Res.	20	9	2	9	48	38	20
Rosudgeon-K. Res.	20	7	5	8	49	62	19
Goonhavern Res.	20	8	2	10	42	45	18
Redruth Dynamo	20	3	4	13	31	50	10
Frogpool-Cus. Res.	20	2	1	17	26	82	5

Devon & Cornwall Police, of the Jewson South Western League, pictured before their historic victory over West Midlands Police in the National Police Cup final at Home Park, Plymouth. Back Row (L/R): Chris Ormand, Peter Small, Dave Ford, Adrian Street, Dave Cortes, Gordon Nisbet, Graeme Kirkup, Nick Taylor. Front: Chris Hayfield, George Torrance, Adam Spear (Mascot), Steve Spear, Wayne Arthur, Dave Street.

CUMBERLAND F.A.

Secretary: R Johnson,
72 Victoria Rd, Workington, Cumbria CA14 2QT (0900 603979).

SENIOR CUP 1993-94

First Round

Carlisle City v Braithwaite	8-0	Mirehouse v British Steel	1-0
Windscale United v Sporting Club	3-0	Marchon Reserves v Silloth	4-1
Parton United v Keswick	1-4	Workington v Marchon	2-0
Carlisle Gillford Park v Egremont St Marys	4-1	Langwathby v Whitehaven Miners Welf. Reserves	2-3

Second Round

Abbeytown v Whitehaven Miners Welfare	3-1	Alston Town v Museum	2-3
Gretna v Penrith United	7-2	Workington v Carlisle City	4-2
Longtown v Cleator Moor Celtic	1-0	Albert v Greystoke	3-2
Mirehouse v Marchon Reserves	2-1	Cumbria Police v Whitehaven Rangers	9-0
FC Copeland v St Bees	3-1	Wetheriggs v Northbank	3-4
Kirkoswald v Carlisle United Reserves	0-3	Wigton v Windscales United	0-3
Wigton Harriers *(w/o)* Joiners Arms *(scr)*		Whitehaven Miners Reserves v Aspatria Spartans	2-3
Carlisle Gillford Park v Penrith	1-0	Windscales v Keswick	4-0

Third Round

Museum v Mirehouse	3-1	Cumbria Police v Carlisle Gillford Park	1-3
Aspatria Spartans v Longtown	3-2	Windscales v Northbank	8-0
Albert v Workington	0-7	FC Copeland v Wigton Harriers	0-5
Gretna v Abbeytown	2-1	Carlisle United Reserves v Windscales	4-2

Quarter-Finals

Aspatria Spartans v Workington	0-8	Carlisle United Reserves v Wigton Harriers	6-0
Windscales United v Gretna	0-7	Carlisle Gillford Park v Museum	2-0

Semi-Finals

Gretna v Workington	3-1	Carlisle United Reserves v Carlisle Gillford Park	2-1

Final *(at Gretna FC, Thurs 5th May)*: Gretna 3, Carlisle United Reserves 0

OTHER COUNTY FINALS

Sunday Cup *(Sun 8th May)*: Queens Arms 1, Magpie 0
Under-16 Cup *(Tues 10th May)*: Ex-Servicemen 3, Penrith 0 *(after 1-1 draw on Tues 26th April)*
Under-14 Cup *(Wed 4th May)*: Castletown 2, Cleator Moor Celtic 1
Under-12 Cup *(Wed 18th May)*: Seaton 4, Marchon 1
Under-10 Cup *(Sun 15th May)*: St Edmunds 3, Upperby 0

Gretna pictured after their convincing win against Carlisle United Reserves in the Senior Cup final.
Photo - Alan Watson.

CARLISLE & DISTRICT LEAGUE

FINAL TABLE	P	W	D	L	F	A	PTS
Abbeytown	22	21	0	1	71	14	42
Northbank	22	13	4	5	61	34	30
Longtown	22	11	7	4	55	29	29
Museum	22	11	5	6	70	36	27
Wigton	22	12	5	7	52	39	27
Carlisle City Res.	22	10	3	9	46	50	23
Gillford Park Res.	22	8	4	12	45	60	20
Whitehaven Miners	22	8	1	13	57	64	17
Silloth	22	7	3	12	47	55	17
Wigton Harriers	22	5	4	13	51	69	14
Sporting Museum	22	6	1	15	42	72	13
Aspatria Spartans	22	2	1	19	30	105	6

LGE CUP FINAL: Abbeytown 1, Northbank 0

CLUB DIRECTORY 1994-95

ABBEYTOWN

Secretary: G Mattinson, 17 Golf Terrace, Silloth (32316).
Ground: Abbeytown Recreation Ground **Colours:** Red & black.

ASPATRIA SPARTANS

Secretary: J W Pattinson, 67 Lawson Str., Aspatria (20733)
Ground: St Mungos Park, Aspatria **Colours:** T.B.A.

CARLISLE CITY RES., GILLFORD PARK RES. *(see Courage Northern Alliance section)*

LONGTOWN

Secretary: R Boguszynski, 27 Esk Str., Longtown (Longtown 825)
Ground: Lochinvar School **Colours:** Blue

MUSEUM

Secretary: J Earl, 56 Crummock Str., Carlisle (28019)
Ground: Richardson Street, Carlisle. **Colours:** Red.

NORTHBANK

Secretary: W Martin, 26 Jackson Rd, Houghton, Carlisle (31226).
Ground: Keenan Park **Colours:** Red.

SPORTING MUSEUM

Secretary: M Pearson, 38 Hillary Grove, Carlisle (512311)
Ground: Richardson Street, Carlisle **Colours:** Green

SILLOTH

Secretary: S Hart, 10 Skiddaw Str., Silloth (31817).
Ground: Eden Street, Silloth. **Colours:** Blue.

WHITEHAVEN MINERS SOCIAL

Secretary: M Morton, 35 Criffel Rd, Parton, Whitehaven (695658)
Ground: Rec. Ground (Whitehaven 65421)(next to Rugby League ground) **Colours:** Red

WIGTON

Secretary: J Hetherington, 40 South End, Wigton (42955)
Ground: Barton Laws **Colours:** Black & white stripes

WIGTON HARRIERS

Secretary: G Johnston, 34a King Str., Wigton (45155)
Ground: Barton Laws **Colours:** White

CARLISLE CITY SUNDAY LEAGUE

FOUNDED: 1963

DIV. ONE	P	W	D	L	F	A	PTS
Nenthead	22	18	3	1	82	27	39
Pirelli	22	17	1	4	79	35	35
WM Club	22	15	3	4	66	43	33
Howard Arms	22	11	4	7	50	44	26
Arroyo	22	10	4	8	67	53	24
Joiners	22	9	3	10	53	45	21
Magpie	22	9	2	11	51	59	20
Belle Vue	22	8	2	12	50	56	18
Museum	22	5	3	14	38	72	13
Howard Rangers	22	5	2	15	36	60	12
Eskdale Thistle	22	4	5	13	40	67	*11
Wrestlers	22	3	4	15	34	85	10

* - 2 points deducted

Lower Division Champions:
Div. 2 (13): Kirkbridge
Div. 3 (14): Upperby MI

League Cup Final: Nenthead 4, WM Club 0

DERBYSHIRE F.A.

Secretary: K Compton,
The Grandstand, Moorways Stadium,
Moor Lane, Derby DE2 8FB (0332 361422)

SENIOR CUP 1993-94

First Round

Biwater v Shirebrook Town	1-2
Glapwell v Stanton Ilkeston	11-0
Sth Normanton Athletic v Shardlow St James	8-0
Borrowash Victoria v Newhall United	0-2
Sandiacre Town v Rocester *(at Rocester)*	0-2
Derby C. & Wagon (Reck.) v Long Eaton Utd	2-1
Derby Rolls Royce v Glossop North End	1-8
Heanor Town v Mickleover Royal British Legion	4-1
Meir KA v Mickleover Sports	4-1
All others *(byes or exemptions)*	

Second Round

Glossop North End v Shirebrook Town	1-1,3-1
Glapwell v Heanor Town	2-0
Derby C & W (Reckitts) v Blackwell MW	6-0
South Normanton Athletic v Newhall United	2-0
Rocester v Meir KA	2-3
All others *(byes or exemptions)*	

Third Round

South Normanton Athletic v Glapwell	0-1
Belper Town v Buxton	1-1,1-2
Stapenhill v Meir KA	1-2
Ilkeston Town v Derby Carriage & Wagon (Reck.)	2-1

Quarter-Finals

Glossop North End v Alfreton Town	0-2
Gresley Rovers v Buxton	1-0
Glapwell v Ilkeston Town	2-1*(aet)*
Matlock Town v Meir KA	4-0

Semi-Finals

Glapwell v Matlock Town	0-0,0-1
Gresley Rovers v Alfreton Town	2-1

Final. 1st leg *(Wed 4th May, attendance 437)*: Matlock Town 0, Gresley Rovers 1
Final. 2nd leg *(Tues 10th May, attendance 847)*: Gresley Rovers 3, Matlock Town 1

OTHER COUNTY FINALS

Divisional Cup (South): Gresley Rovers Reserves 2, Ilkeston Town Reserves 1

Gresley Rovers FC - Derbyshire Senior Cup winners 1993-94.

Photo - Eric Marsh.

MIDLANDS REGIONAL ALLIANCE (Est. 1985)

Details kindly supplied by David Robinson

PREMIER DIV.	P	W	D	L	F	A	PTS
Normanton Athletic	30	22	4	4	76	31	70
Ilkeston Town Res.	30	21	6	3	67	23	69
Belper Town Res.	30	17	4	9	77	43	55
Belper United	30	16	7	7	69	40	55
Mackworth United	30	17	4	9	81	59	55
Eastwood T. Res.	30	15	5	10	72	53	50
Brailsford	30	14	6	10	67	47	48
Slack & Parr	30	13	8	9	52	50	47
Ripley Town	30	11	7	12	67	60	40
Rowsley '86	30	8	12	10	46	51	36
Butterley Brick	30	11	3	16	65	74	36
Matlock United	30	10	3	17	47	61	33
Riddings St James	30	7	3	20	41	89	24
Holbrook Miners W.	30	5	8	17	52	87	23
Alfreton Town Res.	30	5	6	19	47	88	21
Ashfield Utd Res.	30	4	2	24	27	97	14

DIV. ONE	P	W	D	L	F	A	PTS
Selston	26	21	2	3	77	18	65
Holbrook St Mich.	26	20	3	3	82	27	63
West Hallam	26	18	4	4	51	24	58
Kirk Hallam Castle	26	16	7	3	62	33	55
Littleover Ivanhoe	26	15	4	7	56	30	49
Matlock Utd Res.	26	9	6	11	51	60	33
Draycott	26	10	3	13	41	51	33
Swanwick Pen. Rd	26	9	4	13	47	53	31
Gotham United	26	9	3	14	40	51	30
Mackworth Utd Res.	26	7	5	14	40	63	26
Ripley Town Res.	26	6	5	15	37	66	23
New Eastwood	26	6	4	16	39	84	22
Brailsford Res.	26	6	1	19	49	60	19
Slack & Parr Res.	26	3	3	20	32	84	12

DIV. TWO	P	W	D	L	F	A	PTS
Belper Utd Res.	26	20	4	2	110	21	64
Ripley Town Res.	26	18	2	6	82	37	56
Petersham United	26	18	1	7	81	30	55
Holbrook SM Res.	26	14	6	6	64	43	48
Holbrook MW Res.	26	12	5	9	73	48	41
Brailsford 'A'	26	11	7	8	69	48	40
Swanwick PR Res.	26	12	4	10	58	61	40
Derby Arms	26	11	6	9	67	53	39
Rolls Royce & Ass.	26	10	6	10	64	51	36
Ridding St J. Res.	26	7	5	14	48	82	26
Draycott Res.	26	6	6	14	63	93	24
New Eastwood Res.	26	5	5	16	51	81	20
Ilkeston Mitre	26	4	3	19	32	106	15
Cotmanhay	26	3	2	21	45	153	11

Challenge Cup winners: Normanton Athletic
Junior Cup winners: Littleover Ivanhoe

Season 1993-94, in the Premier Division at least, belonged to Normanton Athletic. The long time pace-setters in the League, they finally finished with a League and Cup double as they totally demolished Brailsford in the Challenge Cup Final. However, a slight hiccup in the run-in, and a winning streak in the second-half of the season by Ilkeston Town Reserves - the like of which took Matlock United to the championship in the previous season - saw Normanton under threat as the season went into its final phase. Ilkeston's winning run ended with a draw, while Normanton scored seven to win their match and the title.

Ilkeston Town Reserves were very much the bridesmaids in this season. A good run in the Derbyshire Divisional Cup (South) saw them reach the final only to loose 2-1 to Gresley Rovers Reserves. Normanton Athletic, the holders of that competition, saw their hopes of a remarkable treble perish when Holbrook St Michaels beat them. The Saints, incidentally, found themselves cast in the role of another of the season's almost teams. True, they did gain promotion from Division One but only as runners-up to Selston who beat Holbrook on their own pitch, holding that advantage right up until the tape.

Holbrook then finished as runners-up in the Junior Cup, Littleover Ivanhoe scoring the only goal of the final to defeat them. Nor were the Saints able to capitalise on their cup victory over Normanton. The very next round saw their exit, as indeed it did after they had defeated Belper Town, the defending champions, in the Belper Nursing Cup.

Actually it was a good season for Belper clubs for not only did the Town Reserves finish third and United fourth in the Premier Division, but Belper United Reserves stormed to the Division Two title, eight points clear of Ripley Town 'A' in second place and with a goal difference of 89. Added to which Dave Rees, Secretary of Belper United, was voted the League's Secretary of the Year.

Petersham United were the third team involved in the battle for the Division Two title, and for most of the season they looked the favourites, particularly when they inflicted one of only two defeats on Belper United Reserves. However, the last two weeks of the season saw the top teams all playing each other and, with Belper United gaining revenge for that earlier defeat, Petersham found the skids had been put under their game with the result that they dropped vital points, ultimately slipping into third spot.

At the other end of the table, Holbrook MW and Riddings St James appeared to be in a battle to avoid relegation right from the off, Holbrook facing the prospect of being relegated for the second successive season. In the event, both avoided finishing in either of the two bottom spots with some crucial wins in the final matches. This left Alfreton Town Reserves and Ashfield United Reserves in the two botton places. The latter were victims of wholesale defections by their first team squad which produced promotion for their reserves but left the team as a whole sadly under strength at times. Alfreton, too, had their problems with their trainer suffering a touch-line heart attack during one match.

Early season, New Eastwood seemed certain to be relegated from Division One, but a remarkable revival after the New Year saw them clamber up the table if only to third from bottom. This left Brailsford Reserves and Slack & Parr Reserves, newly promoted last season, in the bottom two places.

Cotmanhay, as in previous seasons, finished near the foot of Division Two, one place lower than last season in fact when New Eastwood Reserves propped them up. New Eastwood Reserves moved up two places with Ilkeston Mitre providing the filling in the sandwich. Cotmanhay did score more goals than before though, but sadly let more in at the other end of the park. They are to be congratulated though for their sporting approach to the game and for the way they continued to field a full side in the wake of some rather heavy defeats.

The two cup competitions went more or less with form but did produce one memorable tie when Draycott almost came back from a 7 goal deficit to surprise Selston, the latter holding on for a 7-6 victory in the end.

The big plus factor to emerge from the season was a general increase in attendances. Indeed on several notable occasions teams from this League actually had more spectators watching their matches than teams in allegedly higher standard competitions.

David Robinson

Midlands Regional Alliance Prem. Div. Constitution 93-94 *(Grounds & Secretaries italicised)*: **Arnold Town Reserves** (see page 756), **Belper Town Reserves** (see page 756), **Belper United** *(Alton Manor, Nailers Way, Belper. David Rees 0332 881635)*, **Brailsford** *(Osmaston Polo Ground, Osmaston, nr Ashbourne. George Smith 0335 60831)*, **Butterley Brick** *(Waingroves Brickworks, Peasehill Rd, Ripley. M Boam 0773 715277)*, **Eastwood Town Reserves** (see page 298), **Holbrook St Michaels** *(Holbrook Park, Mellors Lane, Holbrook, Derby. Paul Roberts 0332 882600)*, **Hucknall Town Reserves** (see page 759), **Ilkeston Town Reserves** (see page 374), **Mackworth United** *(Derby Tertiary College, Prince Charles Ave., Mackworth, Derby. Paul Spray 0332 517321)*, **Matlock Town Reserves** (see page 276), **Matlock United** *(Cavendish Park, Matlock. Barry Jamieson 0629 564414)*, **Normanton Athletic** *(Alvaston Park, Meadow Lane, Alvaston, Derby (0332 571221). David Cooper 0332 767875)*, **Ridding St James** *(The Park, West Str., Riddings, Derbyshire (Leabrook 607907). Vickie Newey 0773 853358)*, **Ripley Town** *(Nottingham Rd, Ripley. Sandra Inglesant 0773 748528)*, **Rowsley '86** *(Rowsley Rec. Nigel Burston 0246 851609)*, **Selston** *(Selston Parish Hall, Mansfield Rd, Selston. Louise Warnock 0773 863120)*, **Slack & Parr** *(Long Lane, Kegworth, Derby (0509 674206). Roy Withers 0602 726170)*.

Division One Constitution 93-94:
Alfreton Town Reserves (see page 290), **Ashfield Utd Reserves** (see page 756), **Belper United Reserves**, **Brailsford Reserves**, **Cromford** *(Cromford Meadows)*, **Draycott** *(Hopwell Ground, Draycott, Derby. John Capps 0332 873451)*, **Gotham United** *(Memorial PF, Nottingham Rd, Gotham. Allan Pearson 0602 830581)*, **Kirk Hallam Castle** *(East Mids Electricity Spts Ground, High Lane East, West Hallam (0602 329982). C Trueman 0602 322280)*, **Littleover Ivanhoe** *(King George V PF, off Carlisle Ave., Littleover, Derby (0332 766076). P J Glover 0332 772514)*, **Matlock Utd Reserves**, **Newark Town**, **New Eastwood** *(Codnor Miners Welfare. John Walters 0602 458449)*, **Ripley Town Reserves**, **Slack & Parr Reserves**, **Swanwick Pentrich Road** *(Highfield Rd, Swanwick. Brian Kerry 0773 749704)*, **West Hallam** *(Beech Lane Rec, West Hallam. Mark Johnson 0602 445086)*.

Division Two Constitution 93-94:
Brailsford 'A', **Bridge Inn (Ilkeston)**, **Cotmamhay** *(Pavilion PF, Cotmanhay, Ilkeston. Steven Hufton 0602 303486)*, **Derby Arms** *(TBA, John Draper 0773 762747)*, **Draycott Res.**, **Holbrook St Michaels Res.**, **Ilkeston Mitre** *(as Cotmanhay (above). Marion Thornley 0602 321199)*, **New Eastwood Res.**, **Petersham United** *(West Park, Long Eaton. Tony Yates 0602 463691)*, **Ripley Town 'A'**, **Rolls Royce & Associates** *(Rolls Royce Sports Ground, Merrill Way, Allenton. Paul A Hutsby 0773 740208)*, **Selston Res.**, **Sutton AFC**, **Swanwick Pentrich Road Res.**.

Belper United FC. *Photo - David Robinson.*

DERBY SENIOR LGE (Est. 1892)

Two-up two-down promotion-relegation system.

PREM. DIV.	P	W	D	L	F	A	PTS
Little Eaton	22	16	4	2	82	21	36
Ockbrook	22	13	5	4	83	42	31
Melbourne Dynamo	22	13	4	5	64	37	30
Santos	22	12	5	5	63	39	29
Alfreton Athletic	22	10	4	8	52	52	24
Allenton Athletic	22	8	8	6	31	32	24
Stanley Common	22	8	3	11	55	75	19
Park Tavern	22	6	6	10	44	51	18
Grenville Athletic	22	7	4	11	44	54	18
Aston	22	6	5	11	49	61	17
Allestree	22	5	4	13	38	70	14
Castle Donnington	22	1	2	19	19	91	4

Prem. Div. Cup: Allestree 3, Little Eaton 2
Frank Andrew Mem. Tphy: Qualcast 1, Ockbrook 0

DIV. ONE	P	W	D	L	F	A	PTS
Tutbury Hawthorn	20	15	3	2	70	30	33
Alvaston & Boulton	20	15	2	3	61	17	32
AC Rolls Royce	20	13	4	3	65	27	30
Hemington	20	10	6	4	58	43	26
Qualcast	20	11	3	6	64	51	25
Smalley Villa	20	9	3	8	51	48	21
Belper St John	20	5	4	11	32	47	14
Findern	20	7	0	13	39	60	14
Sermatech	20	5	1	14	47	61	11
Meadows	20	4	2	14	34	67	10
Sudbury Park	20	1	2	17	34	104	4

DIV. TWO	P	W	D	L	F	A	PTS
Ambergate	22	16	3	3	100	47	35
Concorde United	22	15	4	3	86	43	34
Little Eaton Res.	22	14	4	4	72	36	32
Aston Res.	22	13	3	6	61	28	29
Spa Inn	22	10	6	6	56	42	26
Belper St J. Res.	22	11	4	7	52	38	26
Punjab United	22	8	2	12	42	48	18
Thorntons	22	6	6	10	44	60	18
Qualcast Res.	22	6	4	12	42	79	16
Allestree Res.	22	5	3	14	36	66	13
Bargate Rovers	22	4	4	14	38	66	12
Kirk Hallam Utd	22	2	1	19	31	107	5

DIV. THREE	P	W	D	L	F	A	PTS
Melbourne Dyn. Res.	24	21	2	1	95	24	44
Liversage Arms	24	20	2	2	114	20	42
Rolls Royce	24	16	3	5	83	31	35
Alvaston & B. Res.	24	15	3	6	68	41	33
Derventio	24	11	5	8	72	54	27
Shipley	24	10	3	11	60	77	23
Wagon & Horses	24	10	2	12	63	60	22
AC Rolls Royce Res.	24	8	3	13	60	57	19
St Marys	24	8	3	13	40	89	19
Christians	24	8	2	14	47	62	18
Bargate Rvrs Res.	24	5	3	16	36	82	13
Castle Donn. Res.	24	5	0	19	36	90	10
Ambergate Res.	24	3	1	20	20	107	7

Lower Div. Cup Finals:
Div. 1: Hemington bt Qualcast on pens after 2-2 draw
Div. 2: Concorde Utd 4, Aston Res. 0
Div. 3: Liversage Arms 5, Rolls Royce 2

CHESTERFIELD & DISTRICT

MANSFIELD BITTER SUNDAY LEAGUE (Est. 1966)

J Construction Alma Cup (Divs 1, 2 & 3):
Winners: Brampton Rovers
Runners-up: Killamarsh Juniors

DIV. ONE	P	W	D	L	F	A	PTS
Woolley Moor	24	15	5	4	55	34	35
KSPO	24	14	6	4	55	36	34
Three Horseshoes	24	14	3	7	57	47	31
Eckington West End	24	15	0	3	57	40	30
Hasland Park Rgrs	24	10	7	7	55	46	27
Staveley MW	24	11	4	9	54	35	26
Due Lea	24	11	3	10	42	38	25
Holmesfield	24	9	4	11	53	60	22
Brampton Rovers	24	8	4	12	51	46	20
Killamarsh Juniors	24	9	2	13	28	35	20
Hyde Park	24	5	7	12	36	60	17
Kelstedge	24	4	5	15	46	81	13
Wingerworth	24	5	2	17	32	63	12

Mansfield Cup (Divs 4, 5 & 6):
Winners: Newbold WMC
Runners-up: New Inn Newton

Chatsworth Cup (Divs 7, 8 & 9):
Winners: Somersall Rangers
Runners-up: Barlborough Miners Welfare

Hutson Cup (Divs 10, 11 & 12):
Winners: Hady Miners Welfare
Runners-up: Travellers Rest County

Woolley Moor - Chesterfield & District Sunday League champions 1993-94. Back Row (L/R): Billy Auld, Keith Buckley, Ian Carline, Mick Boam, Andy Greenhough (Manager), Phil Rowley, Mick Eades, Adrian Cowlishaw, Dave Corcoran, Eric Germany. Front: Graham Greaves, Adam Carline, Stuart Auld, Stuart Herd, Nigel Bailey, Ian Cooke, Pete Maltby.

KSPO - Chesterfield & District Sunday League runners-up 1993-94. Back Row (L/R): Gary Grafton, Phil Tingay, Neil Hardy, Paul Gould, Joe Bolton, Keith Edwards, Kevin Hardy. Front: Roger Cutt, John Gould, Dean Hollis, Shaun Oldfield, Kevin Lee.

DEVON F.A.

Secretary: C T Squirrell, 51a Wolborough Street, Newton Abbot TQ12 1JQ (0626 332077)

St LUKES COLLEGE CUP 1993-94

First Round

Barnstaple T. v Clyst R.	3-1 *(B'taple expelled)*	Dawlish Town v Exmouth Town	1-5
Ilfracombe Town v Crediton United	1-5	Ottery St Mary v Torrington	1-5

Quarter-Finals

Crediton United v Clyst Rovers	0-2	Tiverton Town v Exmouth Town	10-0
Bideford v Elmore	1-0	Heavitree United v Torrington	0-5

Semi-Finals

Torrington v Tiverton Town	0-1	Clyst Rovers v Bideford	1-2

Final *(at Bideford FC, Mon 2nd May)*: Bideford 0, Tiverton Town 1

PREMIER CUP 1993-94

Fourth Round

Budleigh Salterton v Tavistock	0-3	Plymouth Command v Dartmouth United	2-0
Ivybridge Town v Hooe St John	1-3	Prince Rock v Upton Athletic	0-3
Kingsteignton Athletic v St Martins	3-1	Stoke Gabriel v Plymstock United	1-0
Upton Vale v Devon & Cornwall Police	0-4	Newton Abbot Spurs v Buckfastleigh Rangers	1-0

Quarter-Finals

Kingsteignton Athletic v Stoke Gabriel	1-6	Plymouth Command v Upton Vale	2-3
Newton Abbot Spurs v Tavistock	1-7	Devon & Cornwall Police v Hooe St John	4-1

Semi-Finals

Upton Athletic v Stoke Gabriel	2-2,1-4	Devon & Cornwall Police v Tavistock	1-2

Final *(at Torquay United FC, Tues 15th March)*: Stoke Gabriel 4, Tavistock 2

Stoke Gabriel, Devon Premier Cup winners 1993-94, celebrate their semi-final win over Upton Athletic. Photo - Richard Brock.

OTHER COUNTY FINALS 1993-94

Senior Cup *(at Elmore FC, Thurs 21st April)*: Cheriton Fitzpaine 3, Barnstaple Town Reserves 1
Intermediate Cup *(at Crediton Utd FC, Tues 26th April)*: Combined '89 5, Mortehoe & Woolacombe 0
Sunday Senior Cup *(at Tavistock FC, Sun 20th March)*: Torquay Civil Service 3, Mountbatten 2 *(aet)*
Sunday Supplementary Cup *(at Brixham Utd FC, Sun 10th April)*: Steambridge 3, 100 Club 0
Midweek Cup *(at Newton Abbot Spurs FC, Wed 23rd March)*: Wakeham Builders 3, Rolle College 2
Youth Cup *(at Newton Abbot FC, Sat 17th April)*: Budleigh Salterton 2, Weston Mill Oak Villa 1
Under-16 Cup *(at Plymouth Argyle FC, Fri 16th April)*: Weston Mill Oak Villa 2, Kitto Magpies 1
East Devon Senior Cup *(at Topsham Town FC, Sun 8th May)*: Willand Rovers 4, Buckland Athletic 3

WESTWARD DEVELOPMENTS DEVON COUNTY LEAGUE

Chairman: Brian Williams.
Vice-Chairman: William Smale.
Treasurer: Barry Widdicombe.
Hon. Secretary: Roger Lowe, Panorama, Lamerton, Tavistock, Devon PL19 8SD (0822 613516).

From the start of the season, Newton Abbot began to stride away from the rest, and with only one defeat up to the 25th game, surprisingly they then lost three games in succession, and Stoke Gabriel were in with a chance to overtake them. However, because of their successful cup runs (and the wet weather), Stoke Gabriel had just too many games to catch up, and had to settle for the runners-up place to the champions, Newton Abbot.

Plymouth Parkway and Weston Mill Oak Villa battled it out for third place, with Parkway winning against WMOV in the very last game of the season. The Bass Cup was deservedly won by Alphington who beat Willand Rovers 2-1 in an exciting final played at Cullompton. Willand Rovers have now twice been runners-up in the Bass Cup.

The League was proud that Stoke Gabriel won the Devon Premier Cup, beating Tavistock, from the Jewson South Western League, 4-2 in the final at Plainmoor, Torquay. All agreed that this was the best and most exciting Premier Cup Final seen for many years.

The coming season begins the operation of the FA Pyramid System with Ottery St Mary being relegated to the County League from the Great Mills Western League Division One.

Roger Lowe, League Secretary.

FINAL TABLE	P	W	D	L	F	A	PTS
Newton Abbot	30	23	3	4	122	28	72
Stoke Gabriel	30	19	6	5	85	37	63
Plymouth Parkway	30	19	4	7	71	44	61
Weston Mill OV	30	16	7	7	71	38	55
Willand Rovers	30	16	6	8	70	58	54
NT Paignton	30	16	4	10	81	54	32
Buckfastleigh Rgrs	30	17	1	12	59	50	52
Plymstock United	30	14	4	12	52	51	46
Alphington	30	11	8	11	65	61	41
Elburton Villa	30	12	3	15	54	55	39
Teignmouth	30	9	4	17	46	79	31
Cullompton Rgrs	30	7	7	16	49	68	28
Newton St Cyres	30	7	5	18	38	86	26
Ivybridge Town	30	7	5	18	39	95	26
Chagford	30	6	5	19	52	70	23
Topsham Town	30	4	4	22	23	95	13

TOP SCORERS (LGE & BASS CUP):
G Ross (Newton Abbot) 33
A Cussack (Weston Mill OV) 30
A Pike (Newton Abbot) 28
D Stocker (Stoke Gabriel) 23
C Acton (Willand Rovers) 21

BASS CUP 1993-94

First Round
Alphington 3, Newton St Cyres 1
Cullompton Rgrs 0, Weston Mill Oak Villa 5
Elburton Villa 2, Stoke Gabriel 7
Newton Abbot 1, Chagford 2
NT Paignton 1, Buckfastleigh Rangers 4
Plymouth Parkway 5, Ivybridge Town 1
Topsham Town 0, Teignmouth 0
Teignmouth 2, Topsham Town 1
Willand Rovers 2, Plymstock United 0

Quarter-Finals
Buckfastleigh Rangers 1, Alphington 3
Chagford 1, Willand Rovers 2
Teignmouth 4, Plymouth Parkway 2
Weston Mill Oak Villa 4, Topsham Town 4
Stoke Gabriel 1, Weston Mill Oak Villa 5

Semi-Finals
Willand 4, Teignmouth 2 *(at Topsham Town)*
Alphington 2, Weston Mill 1 *(at Ivybridge Town)*

Final *(at Cullompton, Mon 2nd May)*:
Alphington 2, Willand Rovers 1

Newton Abbot FC - Westward Developments Devon County League champions 1993-94. Photo - James Wright.

ALPHINGTON

Secretary: Keith Phare, 23 Sussex Close, Exeter EX4 1LP (0392 58636).
Ground: The Chronicles, Church Road, Alphington (0392 79556)
Cover: Yes **Clubhouse:** Yes **Floodlights:** No **Programme:** Yes
Colours: Amber/black/black **Change colours:** Blue & black/white/blue.
Previous League: Devon & Exeter. **Hons:** Devon County Lg Cup 93-94.

BUCKFASTLEIGH RANGERS

Secretary: Mrs J Voisey, 61 Oaklands Park, Buckfastleigh TQ11 0AP (0364 42446).
Ground: Ducks Pond Playing Fields, Buckfastleigh, Devon
Directions: On east side of 3380, just off main A38, to south of Buckfastleigh village centre.
Cover: No **Clubhouse:** Yes **Floodlights:** Yes.
Previous League: South Devon.
Colours: All green **Change colours:** Red & blue/blue/blue
Hons: Devon County Lg 92-93.

CHAGFORD

Secretary: Ken Vincent (0647 433648).
Ground: Padley Common, Chagford.
Colours: Royal & sky stripes/navy/sky **Change colours:** All white.
Previous League: South Devon.

CULLOMPTON RANGERS

Chairman: D Clode **Vice Chairman:** M Scott **President:** L Bourne
Secretary: K Norman, 78 Langlands Rd, Cullompton (0884 33539).
Manager/Coach: Ray Pratt **Asst Manager:** M Scott.
Ground: Speeds Meadow, Duke Street, Cullompton, Devon.
Directions: M5 jct 28, head for town centre, turn left, through thru town centre for 1 mile, left into Meadow Lane, past sports centre, right at T-junction, left after 100yds and follow signs.
Seats: None **Cover:** 100 **Capacity:** **Floodlights:** No **Founded:** 1943
Colours: Red & black **Change colours:** Royal blue **Nickname:** Rangers
Previous League: Devon & Exeter 43-92 **Previous Grounds:** Station Drive/ Court Drive/ Exeter Rd.
Programme: 10 pages, £1 with entry **Programme Editor:** Secretary **Club Shop:** No.
Club Sponsors: Manor House Hotel **Reserve team's League:** Devon & Exeter.
Player progressing to Football League: Richard Pears (Exeter City) 1992-93.
Clubhouse: Licensed bar open nightly at 8pm, after matches and Sunday lunctimes. Basket meals. Half-time tea.
Top Scorer 93-94: Ray Pratt **Captain & P.o.Y. 93-94:** Rob Broomfield.
Hons: Devon & Exeter Lg 61-62 63-64 (Snr Div 59-60 78-79, Int Div 1 R-up 93-94(res), Jnr Div 3 49-50 59-60(res)), East Devon Snr Cup 83-84, Devon Premier Cup R-up 84-85, Axminster Hosp. Cup 92-93, Golesworthy & Grange Cup(res) 92-93 93-94.

ELBURTON VILLA

Secretary: Mr P Wilmott, 5 Gara Close, Elburton, Plymouth PL9 8UN (0752 401750).
Ground: Haye Road, Elburton, Plymouth.
Cover: **Floodlights:** No **Clubhouse:** No **Tea Bar:** Yes **Programme:** Yes.
Colours: Red & black/red & black/ white & red (black hoop)
Change colours: Grey & white/grey/grey.
Previous League: Plymouth & Dist.

IVYBRIDGE TOWN

Secretary: Garfield Goodwin, 36 Longland Close, Plympton, Plymouth PL7 3HD (0752 344364)
Manager: Brian Howard **Asst Manager:** Garth Goodwin.
Ground: Erme Playing Fields, Ivybridge (0752 892584). **Previous League:** Plymouth & Dist.
Directions: Coming from Plymouth on A38 take Ivybridge turn, double back over A38 and take 1st left - ground entrance quarter mile on right after Industrial Estate.
Cover: No **Floodlights:** No **Clubhouse:** Yes **Tea Bar:** Yes **Programme:** No
Colours: Green/white/green **Change colours:** Navy & white/navy/navy

NEWTON ABBOT

President: Mr S Riddler **Chairman:** Mr R Flaherty **Vice Chairman:** Mr J Hazlewood
Secretary: Mr R Perkins, 21 Prospect Terrace, Newton Abbot, Devon (0626 61596).
Managers: D Kendal/I Sanderson
Ground: The Playing Fields, Coach Rd, Newton Abbot (0626 335011).
Directions: Half mile off the Torquay Road leading to Newton Abbot centre, past Ford Park tennis courts.
Seats: None **Cover:** No **Capacity:** **Floodlights:** No **Founded:** 1964
Colours: White/black/black **Change colours:** Yellow or Red **Nickname:** None.
Previous Names: Newton Dynamos/ Newton Abbot Dynamos.
Previous Grounds: Centrax Sports Field (for 24 years).
Previous Leagues: South Devon Minor 64-66/ South Devon 66-77 89-92/ South Western 77-89.
Programme: 24 pages, £1 with entry **Programme Editor:** J Hazlewood **Club Shop:** No.
Club Sponsors: M Hoare
Midweek home matchday: Wednesday **Reserve team's League:** South Devon.
Clubhouse: Open Fri evenings & weekend lunchtimes & evening. Variety of food available.
Captain 93-94: **Top Scorer 93-94:** G Ross 33.
Hons: Devon Co. Lg 93-94 (R-up 92-93, Lg Cup 92-93), Herald Cup 72-73 74-75 75-76 (R-up 73-74), Devon Prem. Cup R-up 82-83 87-88 (Snr Cup R-up 90-91, I'mediate Cup R-up 74-75), Sth Devon Lg R-up 72-73 (Div 1 87-88 (R-up 71-72), Div 2 70-71 85-86 (R-up 69-70), Div 3 84-85, Div 4 75-76 80-81, Div 5 R-up 79-80), Div 6 R-up 78-79 91-92, Div 7 89-90, Jnr Div 2 68-69, Jnr Div 3 67-68, Charity Shield R-up 73-74 75-76 76-77, Les Bishop Cup 74-75 75-76 80-81 (R-up 68-69), Ronald Cup 69-70 81-82 82-83, Greenaway Cup 79-80 (R-up 71-72), Clive Olney Cup 88-89 (R-up 89-90), Torbay Comb. Div 2 76-77, Tyrone Power Cup R-up 75-76, Dahl Cup 75-76 (R-up 64-65), W Treeby Cup 92-93(res), Sth Western Lg Sporting Tphy 86-87.

NEWTON St CYRES

Chairman: Kelvyn Baker **Vice Chairman:** David Holman **President:** John Harris
Secretary: Roger Dymond, 12 New Estate, Newton St Cyres, Devon (0392 851719).
Manager: Kevin Skinner **Physio:** Ray Wright
Ground: The Recreation Ground, Station Rd, Newton St Cyres, Devon (0392 851546).
Directions: A377 from Exeter towards Crediton, on reaching Newton Cyres proceed to village centre, and turn right (signposted BR station) - ground half mile on right. Trains to Exeter Central station or buses from Exeter coach station.
Seats: None **Cover:** None **Capacity:** 550 **Floodlights:** No **Founded:** 1956
Colours: Red & white/white/red **Change:** Blue & white/blue/blue **Nickname:** Saints
Previous Grounds: None **Previous Leagues:** Devon & Exeter 56-92.
Programme: 6-8 pages, 50p **Programme Editor:** T.B.A **Club Shop:** No.
Sponsors: De Paula Spts/ Quickes **Reserve team's League:** Devon & Exeter.
Clubhouse: Mon-Fri 8-11pm, Sat 4.30-11pm, Sun noon-2 & 7-11pm. Food available after Saturday matches - burgers, chips, pasties etc.
Club record scorer: Dave Newbery **Club record appearances:** Kelvyn Baker.
Hons: Devon Premier Cup 88-89 (Snr Cup 74-75, I'mediate Cup 72-73), Devon & Exeter Lg 88-89 (Lg Cup 88-89), East Devon Snr Cup 88-89 89-90 90-91 92-93.

NORTHERN TELECOM PAIGNTON

Chairman/Press Officer/Secretary: J Sargent (0803 854551) **Vice Chairman:** J O'Connor
Manager: E Kelly **Asst Manager:** D Newton **Coach:** W Young
Physio: P Gabriel **Commercial Manager:** John Foster (0803 521878)
Ground: Long Road, Paignton (0803 57062).
Directions: From Newton Abbot follow signs to Brixham, right into Long Rd at N/T factory - pitch 100yds on right.
Seats: None **Cover:** None **Capacity:** 2,000 **Floodlights:** No **Founded:** 1968
Colours: Red/black/black **Change colours:** All blue **Nickname:** None
Previous Name: S.T.C. Paignton 68-92 **Previous League:** South Devon 68-92. **Prev. Grounds:** None
Programme: £1 with admission **Editor:** John Foster (0803 521878) **Club Shop:** No.
Club Sponsors: Bass **Record Gate:** v Southampton, 1992 - new changing rooms opening.
Clubhouse: Yes. Wide range of food. **Reserve team's League:** South Devon
P.o.Y. 93-94: **Club record appearances:** Steve Carpenter.
Hons: Herald Cup 87-88 89-90 (R-up 91-92), Sth Devon Lg Div 1 R-up 78-79 (Div 2 75-76, Div 3 74-75 88-89(res), Div 4 73-74), Devon Premier Cup R-up 89-90, Bell Cup 87-88 88-89, Devon Yth Cup 89-90.

OTTERY St MARY

President: H F Pinney **Chairman:** D Priest **Manager:** D Pook
Secretary: Brian Barnden, 37 Eastlands, Hemyock, Cullompton, Devon EX15 3QP (0823 680981).
Ground: Washbrook Meadows, Butts Road, Ottery St Mary, Devon EX11 1EL (0404 813539).
Directions: From main town square, turn left following road around church, 2nd right into Butts Rd. Or, B3177 to Ottery from A30 Honiton by-pass - ground on left past Otter workshops.
Seats: 120 **Cover:** 120 **Capacity:** 2,000 **Floodlights:** Yes **Year Formed:** 1911
Colours: Yellow (blue trim)/royal/royal **Change colours:** All white. **Nickname:** The Otters
Record Gate: 2,500 v Nottm F., 1985 **Prev. Lges:** Devon & Exeter/ South Western 74-76/ Western 76-94.
Programme: 36 pages, 20p. **Programme Editor:** Ray Dack
Midweek Matches: Wednesday **Clubhouse details:** On ground, open Mon-Sat 7-11, Sun noon-2pm.
Captain 93-94: Micky Turner **Player of the Year 93-94:** Kevin Beaver.
Hons: East Devon Snr Cup, Devon & Exeter Lg, Western Lg Div 1 89-90

PLYMOUTH PARKWAY

Chairman: G Baggott **Commercial Manager:** R Hamilton.
Secretary: S Cadmore, 25 Dudley Gdns, Plymouth, Devon PL6 5PE (0752 782661).
Joint Manager: K Pond **Joint Manager:** G Baggott **Physio:** V Easterbrook
Ground: Parkway Sports Club, Tamar Vale, Ernesettle Lane, Ernesettle, Plymouth (0752 363080).
Directions: Ernesettle exit off A38, follow signs to Ernesettle Ind. Est. - ground halfway down steep hill.
Seats: None **Cover:** 50 **Capacity:** **Floodlights:** Yes **Founded:** 1987
Colours: Yellow/royal **Change colours:** Tangerine/black **Nickname:** Parkies
Previous Name: E.A.F. Plymouth 87-93. **Previous Lge:** Plymouth & Dist. 87-92 **Prev. Grounds:** None
Programme: 10-12 pages, £1 with entry **Programme Editor:** Secretary **Club Shop:** No.
Sponsors: Bee Clear **Reserve team's League:** Plymouth & District.
Record win: 22-0 **Record defeat:** 0-8
Clubhouse: Open 11am-3 & 7-11pm, and all day Saturdays. Hot food & drinks available.
Captain 93-94: M Young **Top Scorer 93-94:** M Goldstone.
P.o.Y. 93-94: D Horswell **Club record appearances:** Paul Mapstone ('keeper) 173.
Hons: Plymouth & Dist. Lg Div 2 90-91 (Div 4 Cup 88-89 (R-up 91-92(res)), Div 3 Cup R-up 89-90 84).

PLYMSTOCK UNITED

Chairman: J Cain **Vice Chairman:** J Challen **President:** R Burroughs
Secretary: A Demuth, 35 Treveneague Gdns, Manadon, Plymouth PL2 3SX (0752 782807).
Manager: Tim Halford **Asst Manager:** Des Hill
Commercial Mgr: Allen Stone **Press Officer:** John George (0752 335011).
Ground: Deans Cross, Plymstock, Plymouth, Devon (0752 406776).
Directions: Local bus service to Plymstock Broadway.
Seats: None **Cover:** No **Floodlights:** No **Club Shop:** No. **Founded:** 1946
Colours: Red/white/red **Change colours:** Gold/black/gold **Nickname:** Reds.
Previous Grounds: None **Previous Leagues:** Plymouth & District (pre-1992).
Programme: 20 pages, 50p - voted best in League **Editor:** John George (0752 335011)
Sponsors: J G Business Machines **Clubhouse:** Normal bar hours. Hot food to order.
Midweek home matchday: Tues/Thurs **Reserve team's League:** Plymouth & Dist.
Record win: 15-0 v Bere Alston **Rec. defeat:** 4-7 v Newton St Cyres, Devon Prem. Cup 89-90
Captain 93-94: Tony Cawse **Top Scorer 93-94:** Matt Jarvis **P.o.Y. 93-94:** TBA
Club record scorer: Unknown **Club record appearances:** A Demuth 350 approx, 1980-92.
Hons: Plymouth & Dist Lg 66-67 74-75 84-85 (R-up 75-76 76-77 90-91), Devon Snr Cup R-up 87-88, Victory Cup 67-68 74-75 78-79 86-87 (R-up 62-63 69-70 71-72 76-77 77-78 83-84).

STOKE GABRIEL

Chairman: John Banks **Vice Chairman:** Ken Rogers.
Secretary: Mr B Prowse, 269 Teignmouth Rd, St Marychurch, Torquay TQ1 4RT (0803 327930).
Manager: John Cudlipp **Assistant Manager:** Trevor Massey.
Ground: G J Churchward Mem. Grnd, Broadley Lane, Stoke Gabriel
Directions: Turn right into Broadley Lane just before Four Crosses crossroads approaching from Paington.
Seats: None **Cover:** No **Capacity:** **Floodlights:** No **Founded:** 1910.
Previous Lge: Sth Devon (pre-1992) **Reserve Team's League:** South Devon.
Colours: All blue **Change colours:** All yellow.
Previous Ground: Farmers fields prior to 1981.
Clubhouse: Headquarters in Victoria & Albert Inn. Tea bar on ground.
Top Scorer 93-94: D Stocker 23.
Hons: Devon Premier Cup 93-94 (R-up 91-92), Devon County Lg R-up 93-94, Torbay Herald Cup 83-84 88-89, South Devon Lg 87-88 88-89 (Belli Cip 90-91), Torbay Youth Cup 92-93 (R-up 86-87).

TEIGNMOUTH

President: Mr K Mason **Chairman:** Mr V Pond **Vice-Chairman:** Ms L Parie
Secretary: Mr P Crawford, 6 Higher Brimley, Teignmouth, TQ14 8JS (0626 772108).
Manager: G Bedford **Asst Manager:** N/A **Physio:** N/A
Ground: Coombe Valley, Lower Combe Lane, Teignmouth, Devon (0626 776688).
Directions: From Newton Abbot: Turn left into Mill Lane 100yds past lights at Shaldon Bridge, right after 100yds into Fourth Ave., 2nd right, car park down hill on left. From Exeter: Turn right (past cemetary) into Higher Combe Lane, 1st left down Deer Park Ave., right at bottom & follow road round to left, turn right & right again - ground down hill on left. Rail to Teignmouth (BR).
Seats: None **Cover:** 1,500 **Club Shop:** No **Floodlights:** No **Founded:** 1946
Colours: White/black/black **Change colours:** Coral & mauve **Nickname:** Teigns
Previous Grounds: None **Previous Leagues:** Sth Devon 46-82 89-92/ Sth Western 82-89.
Programme: No **Sponsors:** Simply Affordable
Reserve team's League: South Devon. **Clubhouse:** Mon-Fri 5-11pm, Sat noon-11, Sun noon-2 & 7-10.30
Record win: 5-1; v Topsham (H) 14/11/92; v Plymstock Utd (A) 5/9/92 - both Devon Co. Lge.
Record defeat: 0-9 v Weston Mill Oak Villa (A), Devon County League 11/5/94.
Top Scorer 93-94: Simon Webster **Captain & Player of the Year 93-94:** Wayne Randall.
Club record scorer: Simon Webster **Club record appearances:** Joe Dunn 520.
Hons: Torbay Herald Cup 58-59 79-80 80-81, Sth Western Lg Cup R-up 85-86, Sth Devon Lg Div 1 85-86(res) 89-90, Devon County Lg Cup SF 93-94.

TOPSHAM TOWN

Secretary: Mr D G Marks, 66 Gloucester Rd, Exeter EX4 2EE (0392 58896).
Ground: Coronation Field, Exeter Road, Topsham (0392 873678).
Cover: Yes **Seats:** No **Clubhouse:** Yes **Floodlights:** No **Programme:** Yes
Cols: Blue & black stripes/blue/blue **Change colours:** White/black/white
Previous League: Devon & Exeter.

WESTON MILL OAK VILLA

Secretary: Mr R Carpenter, 11b St Eval Place, Ernsettle, Plymouth PL5 2RN (0752 364037).
Ground: WMOV Sports Ground, Ferndale Rd, Weston Mill, Plymouth (0752 363352).
Cover: No **Floodlights:** No **Clubhouse:** Yes **Tea Bar:** Yes **Programme:** Yes
Colours: All green **Change colours:** Blue/black/black
Previous Name: Oak Villa **Previous League:** Sth Western 87-89/ Plymouth & Dist.
Previous Ground: Tamar Spts & Social Club, Ernesettle (whilst in South Western League).
Record win: 9-0 v Teignmouth (H), Devon County League 11/5/94.
Top Scorer 93-94: Adie Cussack 30 **Hons:** Devon County Lg Cup SF 93-94

WILLAND ROVERS

Chairman: M Mares **Vice Chairman:** R Jones **President:** J Spearing
Secretary/Press Officer: A L Jarrett, 2 College Court, Uffculme, Cullompton EX15 3EQ (0884 841210).
Manager: Mike Howe **Coach:** Peter Rogers **General Mgr:** Mike Mitchell
Ground: Silver Street, Willand, nr Cullompton, Devon (0884 33885).
Directions: Ground situated on east side of B3181, halfway between M5 jcts 27 & 28. 2 miles from Tiverton Parkway BR station. Regular buses from Exeter via Cullompton.
Seats: 200 **Cover:** 200 **Capacity:** 1,000 **Floodlights:** Yes **Founded:** 1946
Colours: White/black/black **Change colours:** All blue **Nickname:** Rovers
Previous Grounds: None **Previous Lges:** Tiverton & Dist. 46-58/ Devon & Exeter 58-92.
Programme: 8 pages, with admission **Programme Editor:** Secretary **Club Shop:** No.
Club Sponsors: Pearl Assurance **Record Gate:** 500 v Newton Abbot, League, 22/8/92.
Midweek home matchday: Wednesday **Reserve team's League:** North Devon.
Clubhouse: Open Sat 11am-2pm & 4.30-11pm, weekday evenings & Sun lunchtime. Food available.
Record scorer: Adrian Gladstone-Smith **Club record appearances:** Mike Mitchell.
Top Scorer 93-94: Chris Acton **Captain & Player of the Year 93-94:** Steve Guppy.
Hons: Devon Snr Cup 85-86 (I'mediate Cup 66-67), Devon Co. Lg Cup R-up 92-93 93-94, Exeter & Dist. Lg Snr Div 1 70-71 (Jnr Div 1 67-68, Jnr Div 2 64-65, Jnr Div 3 65-66, Premier Lg Cup 79-80), East Devon Snr Cup 72-73 91-92 93-94.

DEVON & EXETER LEAGUE

Details kindly supplied by Nigel Davis

PREM. DIV.	P	W	D	L	F	A	PTS
Exeter City Res.	28	23	4	1	121	34	73
Budleigh Salterton	28	23	0	5	95	38	69
University	28	17	5	6	84	36	56
Exeter CS	28	17	4	7	83	38	55
Buckland Athletic	28	16	5	7	74	48	53
Feniton United	28	13	1	14	54	69	40
Chelston	28	11	4	13	52	64	37
St Martin's	28	11	3	14	67	72	36
Exmouth Amateurs	28	7	8	13	49	51	29
Clyst Valley	28	9	2	17	51	76	29
Beer Albion	28	8	5	15	35	71	29
Sidmouth Town	28	7	6	15	51	85	27
Honiton Town	28	6	7	15	51	81	25
Culm United	28	8	1	19	37	95	25
Lapford	28	6	1	21	48	94	19

SENIOR 1	P	W	D	L	F	A	PTS
Cheriton Fitzpaine	26	18	5	3	113	42	59
Exeter St Thomas	26	17	4	5	82	28	55
Morchard Bishop	26	15	5	6	78	40	50
Budleigh Sal. Res.	26	15	4	7	84	37	49
Westexe Rovers	26	13	6	7	66	45	45
Pinhoe	26	14	2	10	73	53	44
East Budleigh	26	14	2	10	79	75	44
Dawlish Town 'A'	26	12	5	9	62	64	41
Sidbury United	26	12	3	11	56	43	39
Lympstone	26	10	3	13	53	64	33
Bickleigh	26	6	6	14	53	68	24
Wonford	26	7	3	16	45	84	24
London & Manch.	26	2	2	22	28	111	8
Offwell & Widworthy	26	2	0	24	32	150	6

SENIOR 2	P	W	D	L	F	A	PTS
Exeter CS Res.	26	18	5	3	74	36	59
Dunkeswell Rovers	25	15	5	5	53	31	50
Tedburn St Mary	26	15	4	7	69	43	49
University Res.	26	14	1	11	77	53	43
Hatherleigh Town	26	13	4	9	62	58	43
Rockbeare Rockets	26	10	8	8	57	45	38
Bampton	26	10	7	9	47	41	37
Colyton	26	10	6	10	56	65	36
Woodbury	26	9	6	11	70	86	33
Village Inn	26	9	3	14	58	69	30
Newtown	26	9	3	14	35	50	30
Exmouth Am. Res.	25	8	4	13	49	66	28
Littleham	26	6	7	13	39	54	25
Exeter St T. Res.	26	2	3	21	33	82	9

SENIOR 3	P	W	D	L	F	A	PTS
Dawlish Villa	28	21	3	4	72	21	66
Witheridge	28	19	1	8	104	44	58
North Tawton	28	17	5	6	58	39	56
Halwill	28	16	1	11	68	49	49
Broadclyst	28	13	4	11	56	49	43
Seaton Town	28	12	4	12	61	62	40
Bradninch	28	12	4	12	44	51	40
Dawlish Town 'B'	28	13	4	11	62	71	40
Chulmleigh	28	10	4	14	47	69	34
Bow AAC	28	10	2	16	53	62	32
Sidmouth T. Res.	28	10	5	13	57	70	32
Kentisbeare	28	9	5	14	44	66	32
Honiton Town Res.	28	9	3	16	49	62	30
Northlew	28	6	5	17	54	74	23
Lympstone Res.	28	6	4	18	44	84	22

I'MEDIATE 1	P	W	D	L	F	A	PTS
Alphington Res.	26	25	1	0	126	24	76
Cullompton R. Res.	25	18	5	3	95	32	59
Buckland Ath. Res.	26	17	2	7	101	46	53
Newton St Cy. Res.	26	16	3	7	104	47	51
Pinhoe Res.	26	16	2	8	99	40	50
Winkleigh	26	13	3	10	82	69	42
Sidbury Res.	26	10	4	12	51	43	34
Westexe R. Res.	26	9	6	11	64	63	33
University 'A'	26	8	6	12	63	85	30
Tipton St John	26	8	4	14	52	70	28
South Zeal Utd	26	8	1	17	62	94	25
Folly Gate	26	7	3	16	66	74	24
St Mark's	26	5	4	17	54	108	19
Culmstock	26	0	0	26	24	238	0

I'MEDIATE 2	P	W	D	L	F	A	PTS
Wonford Res.	28	21	5	2	102	45	68
Gardeners Arms	28	19	4	5	106	37	61
Crediton Utd 'A'	28	18	5	5	114	51	59
Silverton	28	16	4	8	81	59	52
Awliscombe	28	15	5	8	63	53	50
St Martin's Res.	28	12	2	14	75	58	38
Feniton Utd Res.	28	11	4	13	70	62	37
Culm United Res.	28	11	2	15	74	88	35
Newtown Res.	28	9	5	14	54	76	32
Dunkeswell Res.	28	8	7	13	48	69	31
Tedburn SM Res.	28	9	3	16	46	88	30
Newton Poppleford	28	9	3	16	52	102	30
E Budleigh Res.	28	8	4	16	47	65	28
Woodbury	28	8	4	16	44	79	28
Payhembury	28	5	5	18	49	93	20

I'MEDIATE 3	P	W	D	L	F	A	PTS
Thorverton	26	22	1	3	110	38	67
Cheriton Fitz. Res.	25	18	1	7	85	36	55
Morchard Bis. Res.	26	16	4	6	96	52	52
Beer Albion Res.	26	15	4	7	74	49	49
Bickleigh Res.	26	14	3	9	93	57	45
Colyton Res.	26	13	5	8	56	51	44
Crediton Utd 'B'	26	12	6	8	75	73	42
Crescent	26	12	2	12	78	94	38
University 'B'	26	11	2	13	74	76	35
YMCA	26	10	1	15	78	73	31
Clyst Valley Res.	26	8	4	14	48	69	28
Queens Head	26	8	1	17	60	74	25
Sandford	26	4	2	20	47	118	14
Offwell & W. Res.	26	0	2	24	25	139	2

I'MEDIATE 4	P	W	D	L	F	A	PTS
Crescent Res.	28	21	4	3	84	32	67
Tap & Barrel	28	20	1	7	114	49	61
Upottery	28	18	7	3	91	41	61
Bradninch Res.	28	18	2	8	90	55	56
Winkleigh Res.	28	15	3	10	76	59	48
Medical Sickness	28	14	6	8	73	59	48
Rockbeare R. Res.	28	14	5	9	59	54	47
Witheridge Res.	28	12	3	13	74	68	39
Dawlish Villa Res.	28	9	6	13	56	59	33
Lapford Res.	28	8	8	12	64	78	32
Seaton T. Res.	28	9	0	19	52	82	27
Newton Pop. Res.	28	8	3	17	54	101	27
Halwill Res.	28	6	8	14	48	72	26
Hatherleigh Res.	28	5	6	17	49	78	21
St Mark's Res.	28	1	2	25	38	135	5

I'MEDIATE 4	P	W	D	L	F	A	PTS
Bickleigh 'A'	24	18	2	4	92	32	56
Bampton Res.	25	17	2	5	93	44	53
Honiton Town 'A'	24	14	4	6	77	56	46
Exmouth Amtrs 'A'	24	13	5	6	68	28	44
Sampford Peverell	24	11	5	8	83	51	38
Kenisbeare Res.	24	11	3	10	59	54	36
Newton St Cy. 'A'	24	11	2	11	60	56	35
Broadclyst Res.	24	9	1	14	57	69	28
Awliscombe Res.	24	8	3	13	48	66	27
Tipton St J. Res.	24	8	2	14	46	85	26
Silverton Res.	24	6	6	12	54	94	24
Nth Tawton Res.	24	6	2	16	42	83	20
Bow AAC Res.	24	4	3	17	28	89	15

PREMIER DIVISION CLUBS 1994-95

BEER ALBION

Secretary: Roger Hoare, 'Petercot', Clapps Lane, Beer, Seaton EX12 3HQ (0297 22146).
Ground: Furzebrake, Stovar Long Lane (0297 24324) **Colours:** Sky/sky/navy.

BUCKLAND ATHLETIC

Secretary: Mrs Christine Holmes, 65 The Avenue, Newton Abbot TQ12 2DB (0626 69345).
Ground: Homers Lane, Kingsteignton (0626 62602) **Colours:** Yellow/black/black.

BUDLEIGH SALTERTON

Secretary: Nick Pannell, 33 Armytage Rd, Budleigh Salterton EX9 6SD (0395 445877).
Ground: Greenway Lane, Budleigh S. (0395 443850) **Colours:** All red.

CHELSTON

Secretary: Mr R Doble, 56 Teignmouth Rd, Torquay, Devon TQ1 4ET (0803 329359).
Ground: Armada Way, Nut Bush Lane, Chelston, Torquay **Cols:** White & black/black/black

CHERITON FITZPAINE

Secretary: A J Cummings, 36 Winchester Ave., Exwick, Exeter EX4 2DJ (0392 78639).
Ground: White Cross, Cheriton Fitzpaine (0363 366511) **Colours:** Red/white/white.

CLYST VALLEY

Secretary: J M Luscombe, 94 Rivermead Rd, Exeter EX2 4RL (0392 56631).
Ground: Exmouth Rd, Clyst St Mary **Colours:** Blue/white/blue.

CULM UNITED

Secretary: Mr J Turner, 80 Highfield Terrace, Uffculme, nr Cullompton EX15 3EW (0884 840187).
Grnd: Magelake Meadow, Uffculme (0884 841831) **Colours:** Blue & white/blue/blue.

EXETER CIVIL SERVICE

Secretary: Mr A Dewar, 5 Guys Road, Exwick, Exeter EX4 2AN (0392 214544).
Ground: Foxhayes, Exwick (0392 73976) **Colours:** Royal & black stripes/black/black.

EXMOUTH AMATEURS

Secretary: John Ingham, 47 Evergreen Close, Exmouth EX8 4AR (0395 278144).
Ground: Warren View Spts Ground, Halsdon Ave. **Colours:** Yellow/black/black.

FENITON UNITED

Secretary: Mel J Mead, Leigh Hill Farmhouse, Ashill, Cullompton EX15 3LY (0884 840397).
Ground: Station Rd PF, Feniton (0404 850835) **Colours:** White/navy/navy.

HONITON TOWN

Secretary: Paul Winser, 8 West View Terrace, Honiton EX14 8LY (0404 44493).
Grnd: Mountbatten Pk, Ottery Moor Lane (0404 42543) **Cols:** Tangerine & black/black/tang. & black.

LAPFORD

Secretary: John Burrows, 11 Barris, Lapford, Crediton EX17 6PT (0363 83358).
Grnd: Edgerly Cross, Edgerly Lane, Lapford (0363 83128) **Colours:** Green/green/white.

MORCHARD BISHOP

Sec: Charles Parkhouse, 10 Old Rectory Gdns, Morchard Bishop, Crediton EX17 6PF (0363 877263).
Ground: Wood Lane PF, Morchard Bishop, Crediton (0363 877342) **Cols:** Sky/navy/sky.

St MARTINS

Secretary: Mrs G Brown, 9 Crockwells Rd, Exminster, Exeter EX6 8DH (0392 832067).
Ground: Minster Park, Exminster Hosp. (0392 823909) **Colours:** Red/black/black.

SIDMOUTH TOWN

Secretary: Neil T Anthony, 155 Manstone Ave., Sidmouth EX10 9TH (0395 577782).
Grd: Manstone Rec, Manstone Lane, Sidmouth (0395 577087) **Colours:** Red/white/red.

UNIVERSITY of EXETER

Sec: J L Tink, Univ. Athletic Union, Cornwall House, St Germans Rd, Exeter EX4 6TG (0392 79852).
Ground: Gras Lawn, Barrack Rd, Exeter (0392 71897) **Cols:** Green & white stripes/black/black.

SENIOR DIVISION ONE CLUBS 1994-95

BICKLEIGH

Secretary: A C Dascombe, Meadhayes Farm, Cadeleigh, Tiverton EX16 8HN (0884 855253).
Grnd: Horsdon Pk, Tiverton (Res & 'A': Happy Meadow, Bickleigh) **Cols:** Tangerine & black/black/tang.

DUNKESWELL ROVERS

Secretary: Mrs Marion Broom, Orchard View, Dunkeswell, Honiton EX14 0QH (0404 891377).
Ground: near Highfield Garage, Dunkeswell, Honiton **Colours:** All blue.

EAST BUDLEIGH

Secretary: Chris Pratt, Flat 3, 70 Belmont Rd, Exeter EX1 2HQ (0392 76555).
Ground: Vicarage Rd Rec, East Budleigh **Colours:** Blue (white pin-stripe)/blue/blue.

EXETER St THOMAS

Secretary: Geoff Turner, Flat B, 19 Old Vicarage Rd, St Thomas, Exeter EX2 9BJ (0392 424950).
Ground: Heath Barton Childrens Centre, Beacon Heath **Colours:** Red/black/red.

HATHERLEIGH TOWN

Sec: Frank W Nutt, Old Police Station, South Str., Hatherleigh, Okehampton EX20 3JB (0837 810338).
Ground: Okehampton Rd Spts Field, Hatherleigh (0837 810346) **Cols:** Navy & sky stripes/navy/sky.

LYMPSTONE

Secretary: Chris Gooding, 51 Rosebery Rd, Exmouth EX8 1SQ (0395 265707).
Ground: C.T.C. Royal Marines, Lympstone **Colours:** White/black/red.

PINHOE

Secretary: Arthur G Hitchcock, 2 Parkers Close Lane, Pinhoe, Exeter EX1 3TA (0392 461858).
Grnd: Station Field, Pinn Lane, Pinhoe, Exeter (0392 461294) **Colours:** Yellow/black/black.

SIDBURY UNITED

Secretary: M Baker, 44 Sidford High Street, Sidford, Sidmouth EX10 9SL (0395 515983).
Grd: Byes Lane Rec, Sidford, Sidmouth (0395 579257) **Colours:** Maroon/sky/maroon.

TEDBURN ST MARY

Secretary: Miss Karen M Wood, Two Gates, Tedburn St Mary, Exeter EX6 6AY (0647 61454).
Ground: Lords Meadow, Crediton. **Colours:** All red.

WESTEXE ROVERS

Secretary: A I Butt, 2 Narrow Lane, Tiverton EX16 5EJ (0884 253651).
Ground: Westexe Recreation Ground, Tiverton **Colours:** Yellow/royal/royal.

This Division also contains the Reserve sides of: Budleigh Salterton, Dawlish Town, Exeter Civil Service, University of Exeter.

SENIOR DIVISION TWO CLUBS 1994-95

BAMPTON

Secretary: D P Penney, 7 Ford Rd, Bampton, Tiverton, Devon EX16 9LW (0398 331675).
Ground: Watchet Rd Rec, Bampton, Tiverton **Colours:** All blue.

BROADCLYST

Secretary: Mrs Christine O'Reilly, 123 Beacon Lane, Exeter EX4 8LT (0392 439160).
Ground: Broadclyst Recreation Ground **Colours:** Yellow/red/red.

COLYTON

Secretary: R P Turner, 7 Mount View, Colyton EX13 6RH (0297 553657).
Ground: Chantry Bridge, Road Green **Cols:** Red & white stripes.

DAWLISH VILLA

Secretary: T H Else, 11 Mount Lea Close, Dawlish EX7 9EP (0626 862892).
Ground: Starcross Rec, Generals Lane, Dawlish **Cols:** Sky & white stripes/black/black

HALWILL

Secretary: David Trout, Bercot, 5 Pine View Close, Halwill Junction, Beaworthy EX21 5XL (0409 221316).
Ground: Halwill Junction, Beaworthy **Colours:** All white.

NEWTOWN

Secretary: Paul A G Kennard, 41 Mayflower Ave., Pennsylvania, Exeter EX4 5DS (0392 52426).
Ground: Grace Road, Marsh Barton (0392 50300) **Colours:** Blue & maroon/maroon/blue.

NORTH TAWTON

Secretary: Miss J Simons, 3 Gostwyck Close, North Tawton EX20 2HR (0837 82368).
Ground: Wordens, Exeter Street, North Tawton **Cols:** Red & blue stripes/red/red.

OFFWELL & WIDWORTHY

Secretary: Mrs R Fowler, Woodway, Offwell, Honiton, EX14 9RY (0404 831652).
Ground: Offwell Recreation Ground (0404 831713) **Colours:** Green & yellow/green/green.

ROCKBEARE ROCKETS

Secretary: Lionel J Hawkins, 2 Lazenby Rd, Wilmcombe, Tiverton EX16 4AF (0884 256601).
Ground: opposite Rockbeare Village Hall **Colours:** Red/black/black.

SEATON TOWN

Secretary: B R Adams, 12 Queen Str., Seaton EX12 2NY (0297 23473).
Ground: Hillymead, Colyford Rd, Seaton **Cols:** Green/white/green & white.

VILLAGE INN

Secretary: Paul S Richards, 14 Oakfield Rd, St Thomas, Exeter EX4 1BA (0392 221715).
Ground: Flower Pot Fields, Exwick, Exeter (entrance by Okehampton Rd rail bridge) **Cols:** All sky.

WITHERIDGE

Secretary: Miss Nicola Brooke, 9 Fore Str., Witheridge, Tiverton EX16 8AT (0884 860594).
Ground: Witheridge Spts Field (behind Fire Station) **Colours:** Yellow/blue/yellow.

WONFORD

Secretary: R G Johns, Ground Floor Flat, 4 Chestnut Avenue, Exeter EX2 6DH (0392 494954).
Ground: Wonford Sports Centre, Exeter **Colours:** Gold/black/gold.

WOODBURY SALTERTON

Secretary: Derek Raddon, 132 Briar Cres., Wonford, Exeter EX2 6DR (0392 73447).
Ground: Honey Lane, Woodbury Salterton **Colours:** White/navy/navy.

SENIOR DIVISION THREE CLUBS 1994-95

BOW A.A.C.

Secretary: Mrs Angela Pengelly, 58 Godfrey Gdns, Bow, Crediton EX17 6HT (0363 82533).
Ground: Bow Village PF, Bow, Credition **Colours:** White (red trim)/red/red.

BRADNINCH

Secretary: Mrs C Acton, 8 Bilbie Close, Cullompton, Devon EX15 1LG (0884 32010).
Ground: Keynsham Ave., Bradnich (0392 881353) **Colours:** All yellow.

CHULMLEIGH

Secretary: Mrs Sue Fewings, 4 Beacon Rise, Chulmleigh EX18 7BP (0769 80402).
Ground: Leigh Road PF, Chulmleigh **Colours:** Green/red/red.

KENTISBEARE

Secretary: David Goff, Fenbeare, Kentisbeare, Cullompton EX15 2BW (0884 6597).
Ground: Rectory Park, Kentisbeare, Cullompton **Colours:** Emerald & white/emerald/emerald.

LITTLEHAM

Secretary: Roger Halliday, 9 Mountbatten Close, Exmouth EX8 4DJ (0395 274018).
Ground: Rolle College PF, Douglas Ave., Exmouth **Colours:** Yellow & green/green/yellow

This Division also contains the Reserve sides of: Alphington, Buckland Ath., Cullompton Rgrs, Dawlish Town

('A' team), Exeter St Thomas, Exmouth Amateurs, Newton St Cyres, Sidmouth Town, Topsham Town.

INTERMEDIATE DIVISION ONE CLUBS 1994-95

AWLISCOMBE

Secretary: Mr L W Layzell, Lelamarie, Awliscombe, Honiton, Devon EX14 0PP (0404 42308).
Ground: Greenway Lane, Awliscombe, Honiton **Colours:** Amber & black.

GARDENERS ARMS

Secretary: Mrs Mary Alford, 142 Burnthouse Lane, Exeter EX2 6NB (0392 438578).
Ground: Pitch 1, Wonford Fields, Exeter **Colours:** Green & yellow.

NORTHLEW

Secretary: Mrs L Adams, Kimwood, Northlew, Okehampton EX20 3PB (0409 221619).
Ground: Kimber **Colours:** Red & white/red/red.

SILVERTON

Secretary: Anthony Parry, 10 Coach Rd, Silverton, Exeter EX5 4JL (0392 860055).
Ground: Coach Rd Rec, Silverton, Exeter **Colours:** Green/black/black.

SOUTH ZEAL UNITED

Secretary: Mrs S E Collins, 6 Cross Meadow, Spreyton EX17 5DX (0647 723505).
Ground: South Zeal Rec (next to Post Office) **Colours:** Green/black/green.

TIPTON ST JOHN

Secretary: Alan Diprose, Flat 1, Roseland Court, Heavitree, Exeter EX1 2TJ (0392 79799).
Ground: Tipton St John Playing Fields **Colours:** Yellow/blue/blue.

WINKLEIGH

Secretary: G Boll, 8 Prospect Way, Lapford, Crediton EX17 6QB (0363 83152).
Ground: Winkleigh Recreation Field **Colours:** All red.

This Division also contains the Reserve sides of: Crediton Utd, Honiton Town, Lympstone *('A' team)*, Pinhoe, University *('A' team)*, Westexe Rovers, Wonford.

INTERMEDIATE DIVISION TWO CLUBS 1994-95

FOLLY GATE & INWARDLEIGH

Secretary: Mrs A Chastey, Roseann, Folly Gate, Okehampton EX20 3AF (0837 53121).
Grnd: Folly Gate Pleasure Grounds, Okehampton **Colours:** White/black/black.

NEWTON POPPLEFORD

Secretary: Mrs Lin Wallen, Exeter Inn, High Str., Newton Poppleford, Sidmouth EX10 0EG (0395 68295).
Ground: Back Lane PF, Newton Poppleford, Sidmouth **Colours:** Green & white hoops/white/green.

ST MARKS

Secretary: R Westcott, 21 North Ave., Heavitree, Exeter EX1 2DU (0392 438684).
Ground: King George V PF, Countess Wear, Exeter **Colours:** All white.

THORVERTON

Secretary: L Jones, Ivy Cottage, Thorverton, Exeter EX5 5NH (0392 861064).
Ground: Raddon Rd Rec, Thorverton, Exeter **Cols:** White (blue trim)/blue/blue.

This Division also contains the Reserve sides of: Beer Albion, Bickleigh, Cheriton Fitzpaine, Colyton, Culm Utd, Dunkeswell Rovers, Feniton Utd, Morchard Bishop, Newtown, St Martin's, Tedburn St Mary.

INTERMEDIATE DIVISION THREE CLUBS 1994-95

CRESCENT

Secretary: Peter Lovell, Sunnyholme, Shillingford St George, Exeter EX2 9QL (0392 832308).
Ground: Grace Road, Marsh Barton **Cols:** Yellow & green/green/green.

MEDICAL SICKNESS SOCIETY

Secretary: Chris Frankum, Pynes Hill House, Rydon Lane, Exeter EX2 5SP (0392 449279).
Ground: Pynes Hill, Rydon Lane, Exeter **Colours:** Maroon/sky/maroon.

OAKWOOD (previously Exeter YMCA)

Secretary: Ray W Shepherd, 4 Thompson Rd, Exeter EX1 2UB (0392 217313).
Ground: Exwick PF, Exwick, Exeter **Colours:** Blue & black stripes/black/black.

PAYHEMBURY

Secretary: Andrew Pearcey, 26 Hillside, Payhembury, Honiton EX14 0HB (0404 84449).
Ground: Victoria Dairy Farm, Payhembury, Honiton **Cols:** Black & white stripes/black/black.

TAP & BARREL

Secretary: Wayne Thornton, 61 Milton Rd, Burnthouse Lane, Exeter EX2 6DB (0392 422293).
Ground: Wonford Sports Centre, Exeter **Cols:** Red & black stripes/black/black.

UPOTTERY

Secretary: Martyn P Richards, Turf Moor, 3 Ashleigh Rd, Honiton EX14 8TD (0404 41450).
Ground: Brookfield, Aller Hill, Upottery. **Colours:** All red.

WOODBURY

Secretary: Mrs J Gooding, 21 New Way, Woodbury Salterton, Exeter EX5 1PW (0395 232452).
Ground: Woodbury Salterton Playing Fields **Colours:** Red/black/black.

This Division also contains the Reserve sides of: Bradninch, Clyst Valley, Crediton Utd *('A' team)*, East Budleigh, Rockbeare Rockets, University *('B' team)*, Winkleigh, Witheridge.

INTERMEDIATE DIVISION FOUR CLUBS 1994-95

CULMSTOCK

Secretary: S W Thresher, 4 Hunters Way, Culmstock, Cullompton EX15 3HJ (0884 840100).
Ground: The Hams, Culmstock, Cullompton **Colours:** All blue.

EXETER ART & DESIGN, LORD'S XI, PRIORY *(new clubs)*

SANDFORD

Secretary: A J Wright, Hillside, Sandford, Crediton EX17 4NH (0363 773264).
Ground: Sandford Recreation Ground **Colours:** All green.

This Division also contains the Reserve sides of: Bampton, Bickleigh *('A' team)*, Crescent, Dawlish Villa, Exxmouth Amateurs *('A' team)*, Honiton Town *('A' team)*, Lapford, Newton Poppleford, Offwell & Widworthy, Seaton Town.

INTERMEDIATE DIVISION FIVE CLUBS 1994-95

SAMPFORD PEVERELL

Secretary: Mrs J Hills, 67 Boobery, Sampford Peverell, Tiverton EX16 7BS (0884 820459).
Ground: Whitnage Rd, Sampford Peverell, Tiverton **Cols:** Amber & black/black/black.

This Division also contains the Reserve sides of: Awliscombe, Bow AAC, Broadclyst, Chulmleigh, Cullompton Rgrs *('A' team)*, Halwill, Hatherleigh Town, Kentisbeare, Newton St Cyres *('A' team)*, North Tawton, St Mark's, Silverton, Thorverton, Tipton St John.

MOD-DEC WINDOWS SOUTH DEVON LEAGUE

President: M W Benney, Esq. **Chairman:** E O Benney.
Hon. Secretary: W G L Parker,
23 Higher Coombe Drive, Teignmouth (7745277)

It was a difficult season because of the bad weather throughout November, December and January. This resulted in the season being extended in order to complete the games and enable the presentation of the League Trophies at the League's Annual Dinner on 19th May.

Hele Rovers won the prestigous **Herald Cup** beating Bovey Tracey in the final, whilst the winners of the various divisional cups were: **Belli Cup** - Winners: Upton Athletic, R-up: Kingsteignton Athletic, **Dartmouth Cup** - Winners: Liverton United, R-up: Newton '66, **Lidstone Cup** - Winners: Harburtonford, R-up St Marychurch, **Clive Olney Cup** - Winners: Moretonhampstead Reserves, R-up: Watcombe United, **Bill Treeby Cup** - Winners: Hele Rovers Reserves, R-up: Newton Abbot Reserves, **Les Bishop Cup** - Winners: Buckfastleigh Rangers 'A', R-up: NT Paignton Saints, **Ivor Andrews Cup:** Winners: Bishopsteignton Reserves, R-up: Brixham Utd Reserves.

W G L Parker, Hon. Secretary

Premier Division	P	W	D	L	F	A	PTS
Newton A. Spurs	30	24	5	1	85	17	53
Upton Athletic	30	22	3	5	86	31	47
Dartmouth YMRC	30	18	7	5	76	38	43
Dartmouth United	30	12	11	7	54	41	35
Brixham Villa	30	13	8	9	46	37	34
Kingsteignton A.	30	14	3	13	59	50	31
Waldon	30	12	6	12	58	68	30
Bovey Tracey	30	12	5	13	50	52	29
Dartington United	30	10	7	13	52	48	27
Newton Town	30	11	4	15	49	74	26
Stoke Gabriel Res.	30	7	9	14	38	60	23
Newton Rangers	30	9	4	17	54	61	22
Hele Rovers	30	8	6	16	38	46	22
Upton Vale	30	6	10	14	34	70	22
Teign Village	30	9	4	17	37	81	22
Walls Blake Bearne	30	4	6	20	29	71	14

Division One	P	W	D	L	F	A	PTS
Brixham Town	26	24	1	1	110	25	49
Brixham United	26	19	5	2	77	25	43
Newton Abbot '66	26	17	5	4	75	41	39
Victoria Rgrs	26	9	9	8	58	59	27
Kingskerswell	26	12	2	12	73	60	26
Paignton Town	26	9	8	9	52	46	26
Liverton United	26	8	10	8	40	36	26
Newton Spurs Res.	26	9	6	11	52	43	24
Galmpton United	26	8	7	11	64	61	23
South Brent	26	6	9	11	58	59	21
Chelston Res.	26	8	4	14	40	77	20
Ipplepen Athletic	26	6	7	13	36	69	19
Upton Ath. Res.	26	6	5	15	37	65	17
Windsor United	26	0	4	22	22	128	4

Division Two	P	W	D	L	F	A	PTS
Loddiswell	26	19	5	2	85	23	43
Babbacombe Cor.	18	20	3	3	85	36	43
Totnes Town	26	18	3	5	55	27	39
Kingsteignton Res.	26	17	3	6	77	50	37
Buckfastleigh Res.	26	16	3	7	73	34	35
NT Paignton Res.	26	12	6	8	76	45	30
Dartington U. Res.	26	11	1	14	46	61	23
Beesands Rovers	26	8	6	12	39	52	22
Harbertonford	26	9	3	14	42	72	21
Moretonhampstead	26	9	1	16	46	70	19
Galmpton Utd Res.	26	5	4	17	37	75	14
Newton Rgrs Res	26	5	4	17	32	70	14
St Mary & Tq Gram.	26	5	3	18	35	70	13
Foxhole United	26	5	1	20	36	79	11

Division Three	P	W	D	L	F	A	PTS
Tq Christians-in-S.	26	19	4	3	86	20	42
Combined '89	26	20	2	4	86	35	42
Ashburton	26	17	1	8	71	45	35
Newton '66 Res.	26	15	4	7	72	52	34
Dartmouth U. Res.	26	15	1	10	50	44	31
Ilsington Villa	26	11	5	10	71	66	27
Brixham Villa Res.	26	11	4	11	60	50	26
Bishopsteignton	26	10	6	10	54	65	26
Churston Ferrers	26	8	8	10	58	59	24
Chudleigh Ath.	26	8	5	13	69	58	21
D'mouth YMRC Res.	26	8	3	15	54	72	19
Paignton Villa	26	7	2	17	46	91	16
Dittisham United	26	5	5	16	59	100	15
Kingskerswell Res.	26	2	2	22	41	120	6

Division Four	P	W	D	L	F	A	PTS
Babbacombe Rgrs	24	23	1	0	135	24	47
Teignmouth Res.	24	20	1	3	86	41	41
Buckfastleigh 'A'	24	18	3	3	108	31	39
WBB Res.	24	13	4	7	56	53	30
Newton T. Res.	24	11	4	9	60	58	26
Staverton & Lan.	24	9	5	10	55	51	23
Thurlestone SM	24	7	8	9	56	59	22
NT P'ton Saints	24	9	3	12	48	62	21
Kellaton United	24	8	2	14	42	79	18
Newton United	24	6	5	13	39	69	17
Channings Wood	24	5	3	16	45	84	13
Paignton United	24	2	6	16	29	81	10
Centrax	24	2	1	21	29	96	5

Division Five	P	W	D	L	F	A	PTS
Victoria R. Res.	26	20	0	6	66	25	40
Newton Abb. Res.	26	18	3	5	95	30	39
Broadhempston Utd	26	17	4	5	98	50	38
Hele Rovers Res.	26	16	5	5	83	43	37
Newton Villa	26	14	3	9	93	55	31
Waldon Res.	26	15	1	10	70	67	31
Chagford Res.	26	11	5	10	69	59	27
Meadowbrook Res.	26	11	3	12	55	63	25
South Brent Res.	26	10	3	13	64	67	23
Liverton Utd Res.	26	8	3	15	38	61	19
Bovey Tracey Res.	26	8	3	15	57	87	19
Torbay Gents	26	7	3	16	54	78	17
Ipplepen Ath. Res.	26	8	1	17	53	105	17
Foxhole U. Res.	26	0	1	25	34	139	1

Division Six	P	W	D	L	F	A	PTS
Brixham U. Res.	26	23	3	0	108	16	49
Combined '89 Res.	26	20	4	2	103	19	44
Totnes Town Res.	26	17	6	3	65	21	40
B'steignton Res.	26	15	5	6	75	47	35
Abbotskerswell	26	14	7	5	71	45	35
East Allington	26	11	5	10	58	55	27
Teign Villa Res.	26	9	3	14	49	67	21
Harburtonford Res.	26	7	7	12	47	69	21
Dartington Hall	26	7	7	12	55	79	21
Bradley Villa	26	6	5	15	45	89	17
Ashburton Res.	26	6	5	15	54	99	17
B'combe Cor. Res.	26	5	3	18	58	109	13
B'combe Rgrs Res.	26	5	2	19	54	86	12
Paignton V. Res.	26	5	2	19	48	89	12

Division Seven	P	W	D	L	F	A	PTS
Watcombe United	26	22	2	2	111	29	46
Brixham T. Res.	26	21	2	3	96	30	44
Loddiswell Res.	26	19	1	6	107	41	39
Chudleigh A. Res.	26	15	6	5	83	45	36
M'hampstead Res.	26	15	2	9	59	37	32
Riviera Spurs	26	10	7	9	68	55	27
Newton Utd Res.	26	10	3	13	57	76	23
Paignton Utd Res.	26	7	6	13	54	67	20
Centrax Res.	26	7	6	13	46	81	20
Stav. & Lan. Res.	26	8	4	14	53	90	20
Beesands R. Res.	26	8	3	15	44	78	19
Sth Brent Extras	26	5	5	16	42	89	15
Sidekicks	26	5	4	17	46	83	14
Barton United	26	3	3	20	36	101	9

PREMIER DIVISION CLUBS 1994-95

BOVEY TRACEY
Secretary: Mr Allen Cowell, 22 South View, Bovey Tracey TQ13 9AQ (0626 834564).
Ground: Bovey Tracey Rec, Millmarsh Park **Colours:** Green/red/red.

BRIXHAM TOWN
Secretary: Paul Collier, 15 Holwell Rd, Brixham TQ5 9NE (0803 882280).
Ground: Furzeham Green, Brixham **Colours:** Blue.

BRIXHAM UNITED
Secretary: Mark Buley, 6 Rea Barn Rd, Brixham TQ5 9DU (0803 858872).
Ground: Wall Park, Wall Park Road, Brixham **Cols:** White & blue/blue/white

BRIXHAM VILLA
Secretary: J W L Harris, 47 Great Rea Rd, Brixham TQ5 9SW (0803 856671).
Ground: St Mary's Park, Brixham **Colours:** All white.

DARTINGTON UNITED
Secretary: John Easterbrook, 4 Paignton Rd, Stoke Gabriel TQ9 6SW (0803 782789.
Ground: Dorothy Elmhirst Mem. Ground, Dartlington **Cols:** Blue & black stripes/black/blue

DARTMOUTH UNITED
Secretary: Mr Colin Saint, 9 Grenville Close, Dartmouth TQ6 9UU (0803 834654).
Ground: Longcross **Colours:** White & black.

DARTMOUTH Y.M.R.C.
Secretary: Mr Gordon Coote, 6 Mill Cres., Dartmouth TQ6 9TQ (0803 834545).
Ground: Coronation Park, Dartmouth **Colours:** Red & black.

HELE ROVERS
Secretary: Mrs Julie Shapter, 7 Beechfield Place, Barton, Torquay TQ2 8HX (0803 324194).
Ground: Barton Downs **Colours:** Grey/red/black.

KINGSTEIGNTON ATHLETIC
Secretary: Mr J R Bibbings, Meadow View, Wear Farm, Bishopsteignton TQ14 9PX (0626 770734).
Ground: Broadpark, Broadway Rd, Kingsteignton **Colours:** Red/white/red.

NEWTON ABBOT SPURS
Secretary: Mr Mark Hayman, Haymans Newsagents, Dolpin Squ., Bovey Tracey TQ13 9AL (0626 832505).
Ground: Recreational Trust Centre, Marsh Rd, Newton Abbot **Cols:** White & blue hoops/blue/blue

NEWTON RANGERS
Secretary: Mr Roger Poultney, Belfield Rd, Paignton TQ3 3UZ (0803 552740).
Ground: Forches Cross **Colours:** All blue.

NEWTON TOWN
Secretary: Miss M Howard, 64 Ridgway Rd, Aller Park, Newton Abbot TQ12 4LS (0626 69213).
Ground: Denbury PF **Colours:** Yellow/red.

STOKE GABRIEL RESERVES *(see page 881)*

UPTON ATHLETIC
Secretary: Mr A J Bastow, 63 Western Rd, St Marychurch, Torquay TQ1 4RJ (0803 327134).
Ground: Cricketfield Road **Colours:** Green/white

UPTON VALE
Secretary: Mr H Kelly, 14 Upton Rd, Torquay TQ1 4AG (0803 313067).
Ground: Cricketfield Road **Colours:** Blue & white.

WALDON ATHLETIC
Secretary: Mr M Browne, 50 Shirburn Rd, Torquay TQ1 3JL (0803 313179).
Ground: Windmill Hill, top Audley Ave., Torquay **Colours:** Claret & blue.

DIVISION ONE 1994-95

BABBACOMBE CORINTHIANS
Secretary: Tony Bowden, 14 Peasland Rd, Watcombe Park, Torquay TQ2 8NY (0803 312176).
Ground: Stoodley Knowle (pitch one) **Colours:** Claret & blue

CHELSTON RESERVES *(see page 883)*

GALMPTON UNITED
Secretary: Mr M Collins, 45 Penwill Way, Paignton (0803 526366).
Ground: Galmpton & Churston War Mem. PF **Colours:** Green & black.

IPPLEPEN ATHLETIC
Secretary: Dave Crimp, 41 Pembroke Rd, Paignton TQ3 3UR (0803 553186).
Ground: Ipplepen Village PF **Colours:** Yellow/green/yellow.

KINGSKERSWELL
Secretary: Mr G Gaisford, Lymington Rd, Torquay TQ1 4AU (0803 326186).
Ground: The Playing Field, Kingskerswell **Colours:** Blue/navy/blue.

LIVERTON UNITED
Secretary: Don Pady, 3 Priory Ave., Kingskerswell TQ12 5AQ (0803 873015).
Ground: Halford, Liverton **Colours:** Sky & black.

LODDISWELL
Secretary: Mr R Alston, 1 Little Reeds, Loddiswell TQ7 4QH (0548 550855).
Ground: Loddiswell PF **Colours:** Black & green.

NEWTON ABBOT '66
Secretary: Mr Stuart Tucker, Devonia, 41 Fore Street, Bishopsteignton TQ14 9QR (0626 7799738).
Ground: Osborne Park **Colours:** Sky/navy/sky.

NEWTON ABBOT SPURS RESERVES *(see page 887)*

PAIGNTON TOWN
Secretary: David G D Faux, 24 Collingwood Rd, Paignton TQ4 5PG (0803 522940).
Ground: Clennon Valley **Colours:** Red & black/black/black.

SOUTH BRENT
Secretary: Keith Anderson, 1/2 Fore Str., South Brent TQ10 9BQ (0364 73352).
Ground: Palstone Park **Colours:** Orange/black.

TEIGN VILLAGE
Secretary: Mr G J Beer, 59 Teign Village, Bovey Tracey TQ13 9QT (0626 852605).
Ground: **Colours:** Scarlet & black

VICTORIA RANGERS
Secretary: Mrs J Stone, 13 Barnfield Close, Galmpton, Brixham TQ5 0LY (0803 843160).
Ground: Northern Telecom (top pitch), Long Rd, Paignton **Colours:** Yellow/navy/navy.

WATTS BLAKE BEARNE
Secretary: Mr Colin Freestone, 11 Jubilee Rd, Newton Abbot TQ12 1LB (0626 65886).
Ground: Addbrook Farm, Kingsteignton **Colours:** Yellow/blue/yellow.

DIVISION TWO CLUBS 1994-95

ASHBURTON
Secretary: Mrs J White, Victoria Inn, North Str., Ashburton TQ13 7QH (0364 652402).
Ground: Chuley Rd, Ashburton **Cols:** Amber & black/red/red.

BEESANDS ROVERS
Secretary: Mr Bill Bajley-Lewis, 44 Rack Park Rd, Kingsbridge TQ7 1DQ (0548 852974).
Ground: Beesands Cellars **Colours:** Amber/black.

COMBINED '89
Secretary: Mr D Stowers, 40b Cavern Rd, Torquay TQ1 1NS (0803 290223).
Ground: King George V PF, Torquay **Colours:** Black & blue stripes.

HARBERTONFORD
Secretary: Mr S Jane, 1 Mill Meadow, Harbertonford, nr Totnes TQ9 7SZ (0803 732479).
Ground: The Hams, Harbertonford **Colours:** Yellow/green/green.

MORETONHAMPSTEAD
Secretary: Miss J Shears, 7 Bowring Mead, Moretonhampstead TQ13 8NP (0647 40244).
Ground: Wadley Brook, Moretonhampstead **Colours:** Amber & black.

TORQUAY CHRISTIANS IN SPORT
Secretary: Mr F C Stapleton, 14 Brunel Ave., Watcombe, Torquay, Devon TQ2 8NW (0803 314222).
Ground: King George V PF, Watcombe, Torquay **Colours:** Green & yellow/black.

TOTNES TOWN
Secretary: Mr Nick Elford, 47 Westonfields, Bridgetown, Totnes TQ9 5QX (0803 862632/863370).
Ground: Borough Park, Totnes **Colours:** Blue/white/white.

Plus the Reserve sides of: Buckfastleigh Rangers *(see page 879)*, Dartington United, Galmpton United, Kingsteignton Ath., Newton Rangers, Northern Telecom Paignton *(see page 880)*, Upton Athletic.

DIVISION THREE CLUBS 1994-95

BABBACOMBE RANGERS
Secretary: Mrs Sylvia Cuss, 1 Avon Rd, Shiphay, Torquay TQ2 7LB (0803 613161).
Ground: Stoodly Knowle **Colours:** Yellow & black.

BISHOPSTEIGNTON UNITED
Secretary: Mr D Laughton, 5 Buckeridge Rd, Teignmouth TQ14 8NU (0626 776992).
Ground: Humber Park, Bishopsteignton **Colours:** All blue.

CHUDLEIGH ATHLETIC
Secretary: G Doble, 33 New Exeter Str., Chudleigh TQ13 0DA (0626 852981).
Ground: Kate Brook, Chudleigh **Colours:** Claret & blue/white/blue.

CHURSTON FERRERS
Secretary: Philip Worrall, 8 Burton Villa Close, Brixham TQ5 9JB (0803 853408).
Ground: Brixham Community College **Colours:** White/navy.

FOXHOLE UNITED
Secretary: Mr A R Barker, 62 Barnfield Rd, Paignton TQ3 2JU (0803 554112).
Ground: Belfield Park, Belfield Rd, Brixham **Colours:** All sky.

ILSINGTON VILLA
Secretary: Mr K Leaman, 22 Mellons Close, Bradley Valley, Newton Abbot TQ12 1YF (0626 53852).
Ground: Alston Cross, nr Ashburton **Colours:** Blue/white/blue.

PAIGNTON VILLA

Secretary: Mr R G McDonald, 3 St Johns Place, Braddons Hill West, Torquay TQ1 1BH (0803 215392).
Ground: Whiterock, Paignton **Colours:** Claret & blue.

St MARYCHURCH & TORQUAY GRAMMARIANS

Secretary: Mr Eddie B Finnemore, 37 Cavern Rd, Ellacombe, Torquay TQ1 1NS (0803 211877).
Ground: Torquay Boys Grammar School **Colours:** All green.

Plus the Reserves sides of: Brixham Villa, Buckfastleigh Rgrs *('A' team)*, Dartmouth United, Dartmouth YMRC, Newton Abbot '66, Teignmouth *(see page 881).*

DIVISION FOUR CLUBS 1994-95

BROADHEMPSTON UNITED

Secretary: Mr John Bailey, Apple Cottage, Dean Prior, Buckfastleigh TQ11 0LY (0364 423344).
Ground: Headlands, Broadhempston **Colours:** Sky/navy/navy.

CHANNINGS WOOD

Secretary: Mr W Walker, 9 Haywain Close, Edginswell, Torquay TQ2 7SG (0803 615238).
Ground: HM Prison, Channings Wood, Denbury, Newton Abbot **Colours:** Orange/blue.

DITTISHAM UNITED

Secretary: Mr D Allen, 6 Galmpton Glade, Galmpton, Brixham TQ5 0LU (0803 842949).
Ground: The Meadow **Colours:** Green/black.

KELLATON UNITED

Secretary: Mr B D Thuel, 18 Higher Park, East Prawle, Kingsbridge TQ7 2DB (0548 51297).
Ground: East Prawle **Colours:** All yellow

NEWTON UNITED

Secretary: S Down, 14 Prospect Terrace, Newton Abbot TQ12 2LL (0626 64256).
Ground: Bakers Park, Newton Abbot **Colours:** Purple & white stripes/purple/purple.

NORTHERN TELECOM PAIGNTON SAINTS

Secretary: Mrs D L Edwards, 10 Summerlands Close Summercombe, Brixham TQ5 0EA (0803 857324).
Ground: Long Rd, Paignton **Colours:** Red & navy/navy/navy & red.

STAVERTON & LANDSCOVE

Secretary: Mr Tony Lewis, Little Orchard, 3 Dornafield Close, Ipplepen, Newton Abbot TQ12 5SN (0803 813089).
Ground: Staverton Rec. **Colours:** All orange.

THURLESTONE & SOUTH MILTON UNITED

Secretary: Mrs E Seccombe, 5 Hazel Close, Kingsbridge TQ7 1VA (0548 857765).
Ground: Opposite Thurlestone Village Hall **Colours:** Yellow/blue.

Plus the Reserve sides of: Hele Rovers, Kingskerswell, Newton Town, Watts Blake Bearne.

DIVISION FIVE CLUBS 1994-95

CENTRAX

Secretary: Mr A P Maiden, Monkswell Park, Ilsham Marine Drive, Torquay TQ1 2PH (0803 211448).
Ground: Centrax Sports Field, Newton Abbot **Colours:** Blue & black/blue

MEADOWBROOK ATHLETIC

Secretary: Mrs Shirley Hard, 4 Priory Drive, Totnes TQ9 5HU (0803 864139).
Ground: Dartington **Colours:** Green & white stripes/green.

NEWTON VILLA

Secretary: Mr M G Branch, 139 East Street, Newton Abbot TQ12 2LQ (0626 51964).
Ground: Decoy Park **Colours:** Red & blue halves/blue/red.

PAIGNTON UNITED

Secretary: Chris Pine, 99 Occombe Valley Rd, Paignton TQ3 1QT (0803 555900).
Ground: White Rock, Paignton **Colours:** Sky & white stripes/navy/navy.

TORBAY GENTLEMEN

Secretary: Mr David Vernon, 8 Gibson Rd, Paignton TQ4 7AG (0803 846053).
Ground: Easterfield Lane **Colours:** Red & black stripes/black/black.

Plus the Reserves sides of: Bishopsteignton, Bovey Tracey, Brixham Utd, Chagford *(see page 879)*,Combined '89, Liverton United, South Brent, Totnes Town, Waldon Athletic.

DIVISION SIX CLUBS 1994-95

ABBOTSKERSWELL

Secretary: Mr R H Woodmore, 18 Barnfield Terrace, Abbotskerswell, TQ12 5PD (0626 62688).
Ground: Bakers Park, Abbotskerswell **Colours:** Orange & black.

BRADLEY VILLA

Secretary: Kevin Robins, 90 Barton Drive, Newton Abbot TQ12 1YU (0626 335308).
Ground: Decoy Lake, Newton Abbot **Cols:** White & black stripes/black/black

DARTINGTON HALL

Secretary: Mr Stephen Hamilton, 22 Parkers Way, Bridgetown, Totnes (0803 866393).
Ground: Foxhole, Dartington Hall **Cols:** White & black stripes/black/black

EAST ALLINGTON UNITED

Secretary: Mrs G C Weekes, 5 Vineyard Terrace, East Allington, Totnes TQ9 7QZ (0548 52411).
Ground: Rectory Rd, E Allington, Totnes **Cols:** Orange & black/black/orange & black

WATCOMBE UNITED

Secretary: Mrs L M Hooper, 28 Crownhill Park, Torquay TQ2 5LW (0803 201125).
Ground: King George V PF, Watcombe, Torquay **Colours:** Navy & sky.

Plus the Reserves sides of: Ashburton, Babbacombe Corinthians, Brixham Town, Chudleigh Ath., Harbertonford, Ipplepen Ath., Loddiswell, Moretonhampstead, Teign Village.

DIVISION SEVEN CLUBS 1994-95

BARTON UNITED

Secretary: Mr Michael Mussson, 55 Upton Hall, Torquay (0803 325949).
Ground: **Cols:** Yellow (black trim)/black/black

LANGDON

Secretary: Mr Neil Graham, 95 Coombe Vale Rd, Teignmouth TQ14 9EN (0626 776600).
Ground: **Cols:** Red & black stripes/black/black

RIVIERA SPURS

Secretary: Tony Hele, 43 Second Ave., Daison, Torquay, TQ1 4JD (0803 324132).
Ground: Windmill Hill pitch 2, Torquay **Colours:** Red & navy halves/red/navy.

Plus the Reserve sides of: Babbacombe Rgrs, Beesands R., Newton Utd, Paignton Utd, Paignton Villa, South Brent *(Extras)*, Torquay Christians in Sport, Watcombe United.

Upton Athletic - runners-up in the South Devon League for the past two seasons. Back Row (L/R): Rod Turner, Gerry Passmore, James Eustice, Brian McManus, Gary Passmore, Keith Fenner, Paul Corderoy, Tony Carter, Rod Bastow. Front: Peter Bastow (Manager), Craig Bastow, Steve Eustice (Captain), Ian Bastow, Colin Bastow, Ian Phillips, Stuart Baker (Trainer). Photo - Richard Brock.

Upton Athletic goalkeeper Gary Passmore cannot prevent Stoke Gabriel scoring their fourth, and clinching, goal in the Devon Premier Cup semi-final replay at Watts Blake Bearne. Photo - Richard Brock.

BIDEFORD TOOL NORTH DEVON LEAGUE

President: Mr A S Beer.
Chairman: Mr W Smale.
Vice Chairman: Mr G Shapland.
Hon. Secretary: H W Bartlett, 20 Granville Avenue, Yeo Vale, Barnstaple EX32 7AH (43415).

PREM. DIVISION	P	W	D	L	F	A	PTS
Bradworthy United	34	25	6	3	95	24	81
Appledore Res.	34	23	7	4	96	45	76
Willand Rvrs Res.	34	19	6	9	113	80	63
Morwenstow	34	20	2	12	88	64	62
Combe Martin	34	18	6	10	109	61	60
Fremington Fox.	34	16	7	11	86	53	55
Braunton	34	16	6	12	78	64	54
Chittlehampton	34	15	5	14	78	71	50
Holsworthy	34	12	8	14	62	76	44
Dolton Rangers	34	13	5	16	52	81	44
Parkhead	34	12	7	15	52	76	43
Shamwickshire	34	11	9	14	77	80	42
RAF Chivenor	34	13	3	18	68	80	42
Putford	34	11	5	18	53	84	38
Bideford Res.	34	10	6	18	51	82	36
Ilfracombe T. Res.	34	8	8	18	50	78	32
Barnstaple AAC	34	8	3	23	54	101	27
Topsham T. Res.	34	5	3	26	28	90	18

Divisional Cup Final:
Appledore & BAAC Res. 2, Dolton Rgrs 0

94-95 Constitution: Appledore/BAAC Reserves, Bradworthy Utd, Braunton, Chittlehampton, Combe Martin, Dolton Rgrs, Fremington Foxhounds, Holsworthy Reserves, Ilfracombe Town Reserves, Kilkhampton *(new side, joining from Kingsley League)*, Morwenstow, Parkhead, Putford, Shamwickshire, South Molton, Torrington Admirals *(formerly Admiral Vernon)*, Torrington Reserves, Willand Rovers Reserves

SENIOR DIV.	P	W	D	L	F	A	PTS
Anchor	28	23	0	5	125	44	69
South Molton	28	20	2	6	100	48	62
Admiral Vernon	28	18	5	5	84	38	59
Northam Lions	28	15	4	9	64	58	49
Golden Lion	28	15	4	9	57	54	49
Shebbear	28	15	1	12	56	57	46
Bradworthy U. Res.	28	12	4	12	62	57	40
Fremington Res.	28	12	3	13	59	52	39
Hartland	28	11	5	12	48	59	38
North Molton	28	9	4	15	40	71	31
Bratton Fleming	28	8	6	14	46	77	30
Lynton & Lynmouth	28	7	5	16	66	97	26
Bell Athletic	28	7	3	18	49	78	24
Combe Martin Res.	28	6	4	18	42	83	22
Okehampton A. Res.	28	6	2	20	56	81	20

Divisional Cup Final:
South Molton 4, Bell Athletic 1

94-95 Constitution: Appledore/BAAC 'A', Barnstaple AAC, Bell Athletic, Bradworthy Utd Reserves, Bratton Fleming, Bridgerule *(new club, runners-up in Kingsley League 93-94)*, Combe Martin Reserves, Fremington Foxhounds Reserves, Golden Lion, Hartland, Lynton & Lynmouth, North Molton, Northam Lions, Rolle Quay *(formerly Anchor)*, Shapland, Shebbear.

INT. DIV. ONE	P	W	D	L	F	A	PTS
Shapland	22	18	1	3	102	34	55
Appledore 'A'	22	17	0	5	95	34	51
Mortehoe & W.	22	14	2	6	99	41	44
Torrington 'A'	22	14	1	7	80	62	43
Ilfracombe T. 'A'	22	11	4	7	71	45	37
Clovelly	22	10	3	9	60	46	33
South Molton Res.	22	10	1	11	45	62	31
Swimbridge	22	9	0	13	54	71	27
Parkhead Res.	22	6	4	12	52	79	22
Dolton Res.	22	6	1	15	44	84	19
Anchor Res.	22	4	2	16	41	88	14
Okehampton A. 'A'	22	3	1	18	42	139	10

Divisional Cup Final:
Shapland 2, Mortehoe & Woolacombe 0

94-95 Constitution: AFC Barum, Clovelly, Dolton Rgrs Reserves, Georgeham & Croyde, Ilfracombe Town 'A', Merton, Mortehoe & Woolacombe, Okehampton Argyle Reserves, Parkhead Reserves, Rolle Quay Reserves, South Molton Reserves, Swimbridge, Torrington Colts, Westward Ho!.

INT. DIV. TWO	P	W	D	L	F	A	PTS
AFC Barum	24	19	2	3	114	26	59
Westward Ho!	24	18	3	3	83	29	57
Georgeham/Croyde	24	17	5	2	96	29	56
Merton	24	13	4	7	65	43	43
Golden Lion Res.	24	9	7	8	49	38	34
Admiral Vern. Res.	24	10	4	10	46	49	34
Shamwickshire Res.	24	10	1	13	54	88	31
Buckland Brewer	24	8	5	11	37	52	29
Hartland Res.	24	8	3	13	40	74	27
Chittlehampton Res.	24	5	6	13	38	55	21
RAF Chivenor Res.	24	5	5	14	40	70	20
Northam Lions Res.	24	6	0	18	51	85	18
Lynton & L. Res.	24	4	3	17	37	112	15

Divisional Cup Final:
Westward Ho! 3, AFC Barum 1

94-95 Constitution: Braunton Former Pupils *(new club)*, Buckland Brewer, Chittlehampton Reserves, Chivenor, Golden Lion Reserves, Hartland Reserves, Landkey, Lynton & Lynmouth Reserves, Northam Lions Reserves, Okehampton Argyle 'A', Putford Reserves, St Mary's, Shamwickshire Reserves, Torrington Admirals Reserves

INT. DIV. THREE	P	W	D	L	F	A	PTS
Putford Res.	22	15	2	5	77	36	47
St Mary's	22	14	2	6	73	41	44
Landkey	22	13	2	7	78	50	41
Barnst. AAC Res.	22	13	2	7	48	39	41
Shapland Res.	22	12	2	8	71	55	38
High Bickington	22	11	3	8	54	65	36
AFC Barum Res.	22	9	3	10	65	69	30
B'staple Riverside	22	8	5	9	68	59	29
Georgeham Res.	22	8	4	10	41	49	28
Brunswick Wharf	22	7	2	13	59	59	23
Bratton Fleming Res.	22	5	1	16	37	71	16
Shebbear Res.	22	2	2	18	35	114	8

Divisional Cup Final:
Barnstaple AAC 3, Bratton Fleming 1

94-95 Constitution: AFC Barum Reserves, Barnstaple AAC Reserves, Barnstaple Riverside, Bratton Fleming Reserves, Braunton Reserves, Braunton Former Pupils Reserves, Georgeham & Croyde Reserves, High Bickington, Inter Cleos *(new club)*, North Molton Reserves, Shapland Reserves, Shebbear Reserves, Westward Ho! Athletic *(new club)*, Woolsery *(returning from Kingsley League)*.

BETA PLYMOUTH SUNDAY LGE

DIV. ONE	P	W	D	L	F	A	PTS
Victory Inn	18	17	0	1	61	27	34
Underhill MBS	18	15	0	3	69	29	30
Gleasons	18	12	1	5	85	50	25
Dingle Cleaning Ctrs	18	8	4	6	76	60	20
Leigham Hawks	18	9	1	6	60	54	19
Waterloo Inn	18	8	3	7	45	40	19
WEST	18	7	0	11	34	60	14
Michael Draper & Co	18	4	1	13	39	58	9
VIC Rangers	18	3	0	15	28	70	6
Holbeton Spurs	18	2	0	16	28	77	4

Lower Division Champions:
Div. 2 (14): Marnic FC
Div. 3 (13): Hilliers FC

Cup Winners (/Runners-up)
Geoff Dawkins Lge Cup: Underhill MB (Gleasons)
Plym. Sound FM Cup: Waterloo Inn (Leigham Hawks)
Timothy Chal. Cup: SecuriGuard (The Woodlands)
Key Transport Cup: Satellite Spts (Prince Regent)
Div 1 Cup: Victory Inn (Underhill MB)
Div 2 Cup: Marnic (Hellerman Electric)
Div 3 Cup: Hilliers (Indian Inn)

Most Sporting Team Awards
Div 1: Holbeton Spurs
Div 2: SecuriGuard
Div 3: Sports Press Spurs

Sportsman Trophy (most 'Man of the Match Awards'):
N Roberts (Gleasons)

BRIDGE MOTORCYCLE CENTRE EXETER & DIST. SUNDAY LGE

FOUNDED: 1966

DIV. ONE	P	W	D	L	F	A	PTS
Horse & Groom	22	20	0	2	85	29	60
Barley Mow	22	16	2	4	74	23	50
Sawyers	22	14	2	6	73	45	44
Exmouth Rangers	22	14	0	8	66	45	42
Eagle Tavern	22	12	2	8	65	49	38
Kings Arms	22	10	2	10	58	66	32
V Soldier	22	8	1	13	43	72	25
Rennes	22	9	1	12	81	68	*24
Mitre	22	6	2	14	49	72	20
Royal Oak	22	6	2	14	38	77	*16
Bridford	22	5	0	17	48	85	15
Green Gables	22	3	4	15	39	88	13

* - 4 points deducted

Lower Division Champions:
Div. 2 (13): 100 Club
Div. 3 (14): Amory Amateurs
Div. 4 (14): Bishop Blaize
Div. 5 (14): Athletico Devonport
Div. 6 (13): Cheriton Fitzpaine

KO Cup winners: Barley Mow
Jim Howard Cup: St Martins

Devon's outstanding team of the 1993-94 - Tiverton Town - pictured here after defeating Taunton Town 4-1 at Dawlish to win the Great Mills Western League Les Phillips Cup, thus completing a 'treble' of trophies. Back Row (L/R): Neil Saunders, Steve Hynds, Hedley Steele, Mark Saunders, John Owen, Kevin Smith, Martyn Grimshaw, Alan Morgan (Physio), Steve Daly. Front: Ian Nott, Matthew Scott, Lee Annunziata, Martyn Rogers (Manager, partly concealed with Cup), Paul Edwards, Gary Carpenter, Phil Everett.

Photo - Nigel Davis.

DORSET F.A.

Secretary: P S Hough, County Ground,
Blandford Close, Hamworthy, Poole BH15 4BF (0202 682375).

SENIOR CUP 1993-94

First Round

Hamworthy Engineering v Sherborne Town	2-1	Sturminster Newton Utd v Flight Refuelling	1-2
Hamworthy Utd v Gillingham Town	1-0	Bournemouth Spts v Holt United	2-2,3-1
Wareham Rangers v Shaftesbury	4-3	Verwood Town v Blandford United	1-1,1-2
Weymouth Sports v Parley Sports	1-0		

Second Round

Bournemouth Sports v St Pauls (Jersey)	1-3	Hamworthy Engineering v Flight Refuelling	2-1
Weymouth v Dorcester Town	0-1	Bridport v Wareham Rangers	2-0
Hamworthy United v Poole Town	0-2	Wimborne Town v Blandford United	5-0
Northerners (Guernsey) v Swanage T & H.	5-2	Weymouth Sports v Portland United	0-3

Quarter-Finals

Wimborne Town v Poole Town	2-4	St Pauls (Jersey) v Hamworthy Engineering	3-0
Bridport v Portland United	1-0	Norrtherners (Guernsey) v Dorchester Town	1-5

Semi-Finals

Bridport v Dorchester Town	0-1	St Pauls (Jersey) v Poole Town	0-0,0-4

Final *(at Swanage Town & Herston FC, Tues 19th April)*: Dorchester Town 1, Poole Town 0

OTHER COUNTY FINALS:

Senior Trophy *(at Bridport FC, Thurs 21st April)*: Broadmayne 3, Dorchester YMCA 2 *(aet)*

Hamworthy Engineering - Dorset Combination champions 1993-94. In only their second season in the Combination, Engineering topped the table from start to finish and eventually took the title by five points from reigning champions Westland Sports.

Photo - Tim Lancaster.

DORSET COMBINATION (Founded 1957)

President: A P Humphries, Esq.
Vice Presidents: T Coll, T W Scorah, D Walters
Chairman: E Maidment, Esq.
Hon. Secretary: G A Theobald, Esq.,
41 South Road, Corfe Mullen, Wimborne BH21 3HZ (0202 697994).
Press Officer: T W Scorah (0202 699650).

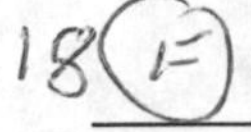

FINAL TABLE	P	W	D	L	F	A	PTS
Hamworthy Eng.	38	29	6	3	111	37	93
Westland Sports	38	29	1	8	112	39	88
Portland United	38	26	5	7	99	39	83
Sherborne Town	38	26	3	9	95	44	81
Weymouth Sports	38	19	7	12	75	61	64
Blandford United	38	18	7	13	60	50	61
Bridport	38	18	6	14	72	68	60
Poole Town Res.	38	18	8	12	77	59	*59
Bournemouth Spts	38	18	4	16	87	64	58
Sturminster Newton	38	13	12	13	46	44	51
Hamworthy United	38	16	3	19	81	96	51
Weymouth Res.	38	11	12	15	76	83	45
Swanage T&H Res.	38	13	6	19	76	86	45
Flight Refuelling	38	11	10	17	52	61	43
Gillingham Town	38	12	4	22	58	74	40
Shaftesbury	38	9	9	20	52	75	36
Parley Sports	38	10	5	23	63	121	35
Dorchester T. Res.	38	9	6	23	61	113	*30
Wareham Rangers	38	7	7	24	36	78	28
Holt United	38	6	3	29	35	132	21

* - 3 points deducted

HAMWORTHY ENGINEER TITLE-WINNING OPPORTUNITY

After making an excellent Combination debut in 1992-93, Hamworthy Engineering were always favourites to take the title, and this they duly did, topping the table for virtually the entire campaign. A late spurt by the out-going champions, Westland Sports of Yeovil, saw them finish in second place ahead of Portland United, who bid a fond farewell to their historic ground at Grove Corner this summer.

To compensate for losing their grip on the championship, Westland at least had the consolation of retaining the Combination Cup. They beat near neighbours Sherborne Town by the odd goal in five in a thrilling final at Shaftesbury, thus making it three win out of three in the final having previously lifted the Cup in 1984 and last season.

As well as reaching the Combination Cup final, Sherborne Town again did the Combination proud in the FA Vase, recording notable victories over Jewson Wessex clubs BAT and Horndean before bowing out in a replay to Channel Islanders First Tower United.

There are no changes to the Combination membership this summer; an application to join by Dorset League champions Allendale was unsuccessful, so the bottom two teams - Holt United and Wareham Rangers - are re-elected.

A very small price to pay for a club who scored 111 league goals in 1993-94. You know what you can do with your Carling FA Premiership and its inflated prices.

Photo - Tim Lancaster.

COMBINATION CUP 1993-94

First Round

Bournemouth Sports v Gillingham Town	3-5	Holt United v Parley Sports	3-4
Sturminster Newton v Poole Town Reserves	2-0	Weymouth Sports v Hamworthy Engineering	3-1

Second Round

Blandford Utd v Swanage T & H Reserves	0-1	Dorchester Town Reserves v Bridport Reserves	0-2
Hamworthy Engineering v Shaftesbury	5-2	Parley Sports v Sturminster Newton United	0-2
Portland United v Flight Refuelling	4-1	Sherborne Town v Weymouth Sports	1-1,1-0
Wareham Rangers v Gillingham Town	3-4*(aet)*	Weymouth Reserves v Westland Sports	0-2

Quarter Finals

Gillingham Town v Sherborne Town	2-3*(aet)*	Hamworthy Engineering v Westland Sports	1-4*(aet)*
Sturminster Newton v Portland United	1-0	Swanage T & H Reserves v Bridport Reserves	2-1

Semi-Finals

Sturminster Newton v Sherborne Town	0-1	Swanage Town & Herston Res. v Westland Spts	0-1

Final *(at Shaftesbury FC, Tues 17th May)*: Westland Sports 3, Sherborne Town 2

Weymouth Sports, who enjoyed a very good inaugural season in the Combination. Who would bet against them emulating Hamworthy Engineering and winning the title in their second year?

Photo - Tim Lancaster.

Sherborne Town's Dave Mann (stripes) tries to get past a Sturminster Newton defender, but his side slip to a 0-3 home defeat in this local derby at the Terrace.

Photo - Tim Lancaster.

DORSET COMBINATION CLUBS 1994-95

BLANDFORD UNITED

Chairman: G Pike
Secretary: David Upshall, 18 Ramsbury Court, Ramsbury Gdns, Blandford Forum, Dorset DT11 7UL (0258 456125).
Ground: Recreation Ground, Park Lane, Blandford Forum, Dorset. (HQ Tel: 0258 456374).
Colours: Royal/white/royal **Change colours:** All red
Cover: No **Programme:** Yes **Clubhouse:** No

BOURNEMOUTH SPORTS CLUB

Chairman: T Bloor.
Secretary: Andy Carr, 260 West Way, Broadstone, Poole BH18 9LL (0202 691949).
Ground: Chapel Gate, East Parley, Christchurch, Dorset BH23 6BD (0202 581933).
Colours: Gold/black/black **Change colours:** All sky
Cover: No **Programme:** Yes **Clubhouse:** Yes

BRIDPORT RESERVES *(see page 561)*

DORCHESTER TOWN RESERVES *(see page 332)*

FLIGHT REFUELLING

Chairman: B White.
Secretary: Harry W Doyle, 27 Fairview Cres., Broadstone, Poole BH18 9AP (0202 698393).
Ground: Merley Park, Merley, Wimborne, Dorset (0202 885773).
Colours: Sky/navy/navy **Change colours:** All yellow
Cover: No **Programme:** Yes **Clubhouse:** Yes

GILLINGHAM TOWN

Chairman: E Murphy.
Secretary: David J Ayles, 37 Sylvan Way, Bay Road, Gillingham SP8 4EQ (0747 822065).
Ground: Hardings Lane, Gillingham (0747 823673).
Cols: Tangerine & black/black/black **Change colours:** Blue/navy/blue
Cover: Yes **Programme:** Yes **Clubhouse:** Yes

HAMWORTHY ENGINEERING

Chairman: M Robson.
Secretary: Ray Willis, 52 Heckford Rd, Poole BH15 2LY (0202 677063).
Ground: Hamworthy Rec. Club, Magna Rd, Canford Magna, Wimborne, Dorset BH21 3AE (0202 881922).
Colours: All green **Change colours:** White & blue stripes/navy/navy
Cover: No **Programme:** No **Clubhouse:** Yes

HAMWORTHY UNITED

Chairman: M Squire
Secretary: Roy Mitchener, 68 St Mary's Rd, Poole, Dorset BH15 2LL (0202 676128).
Ground: The County Ground, Blandford Close, Hamworthy, Poole, Dorset (0202 674974).
Colours: Maroon & sky/sky/maroon **Change colours:** Green & black stripes/black/black
Cover: Yes **Floodlights:** Yes **Programme:** Yes **Clubhouse:** Yes

HOLT UNITED

Chairman: H Richardson.
Secretary: Simon Dean, Broomhill Farm House, White Sheet Rd, Broomhill, Wimborne BH21 7AR (0202 840046).
Ground: Petersham Lane, Gaunts Common, Holt, Wimborne, Dorset (0258 840379).
Colours: Red & white/white/red **Change colours:** Yellow/green/yellow
Cover: No **Programme:** No **Clubhouse:** Yes

PARLEY SPORTS

Chairman: O Williams.
Secretary: Russell Digby, 1a Allens Rd, Upton, Poole BH16 5BT (0202 623632).
Ground: Parley Sports Club, Christchurch, West Parley, Bournemouth, Dorset (0202 573345).
Colours: Yellow/blue/yellow **Change colours:** Blue/yellow/blue
Cover: No **Programme:** No **Clubhouse:** Yes

POOLE TOWN RESERVES *(see page 400)*

PORTLAND UNITED

Chairman: R Carlyle.
Secretary: David M Camp, 23 Four Acres, Weston, Portland DT5 2LG (0305 821816).
Ground: *New ground for 1994-95*
Colours: Blue/blue/red **Change colours:** Red & white/white/blue.
Cover: Yes **Programme:** Yes **Clubhouse:** Yes

SHAFTESBURY

Chairman: P Humphries.
Secretary: Miss Alison Charlton, 33 St Rumbolds Rd, Shaftesbury SP7 8NE (0747 54584).
Ground: Cockrams, Coppice Street, Shaftesbury (0747 53990).
Colours: Red/black/red **Change colours:** All green
Cover: Yes **Floodlights:** Yes **Programme:** No **Clubhouse:** Yes

SHERBORNE TOWN

Chairman: I Shipper.
Secretary: Roger V Woolmington, 23 Harbour Rd, Sherborne DT9 4AL (0935 813048).
Ground: Raleigh Grove, The Terrace Playing Fields, Sherborne (0935 816110).
Colours: Black & white stripes/black/black **Change colours:** All tangerine
Cover: Yes **Programme:** Yes **Clubhouse:** Yes

STURMINSTER NEWTON

Chairman: R Clarke.
Secretary: David Walters, 44 Filbridge Rise, Sturminster Newton, Dorset DT10 1BP (0258 472381).
Ground: Ricketts Lane, Sturminster Newton, Dorset. (HQ (RBL) Tel: 0258 472437).
Colours: Red/black/black **Change colours:** All blue
Cover: Yes **Programme:** Yes **Clubhouse:** No

DURHAM F.A.

Secretary: J R Walsh,
'Codeslaw', Ferens Park, Durham DH1 1JZ (091 384 8653).

COMMERCIAL UNION COUNTY CHALLENGE CUP 1993-94

First Qualifying Round

Sunderland Vaux Ryhope v Darlington CS	2-1

Second Qualifying Round

Peterlee Newtown v Annfield Plain	2-0
West Auckland Town v Stanley United	2-1
Wolviston v Crook Town	1-4
Sunderland Vaux Ryhope CW v Esh Winning	6-2
Easington Colliery v Whickham	3-0
Jarrow Roofing Boldon CA v Newton Aycliffe	3-0
Sunderland Kennek Roker v Dunston Feds	1-3
Norton & Stockton Ancients v Ryhope CA	8-3
Shotton Comrades v Hartlepool Boys Welfare OB	1-3
Boldon Community Assoc. v Herrington CW	0-1
Ferryhill Athletic v Washington	5-0
South Shields v Seaham Red Star	4-0
Brandon United v Washington Nissan	2-4
Silksworth v Hebburn DT	4-1
Willington v Shildon	1-6
Langley Park S & S Utd v Esh Winning Albion	3-0

First Round

Dunston Federation Brewery v Evenwood T.	2-1
Hebburn v Langley Park S & S United	2-1
Sunderland Vaux Ryhope v Hartlepool Town	0-1
Eppleton Coll. Welfare v Easington Colliery	4-2
Shildon v West Auckland Town	4-0
Crook Town v Sth Shields Cleadon SC	3-3,2-0
Chester-le-Street Town v Murton	5-2
Silksworth v Horden Colliery Welfare	4-2
Bishop Auckland v Ferryhill Athletic	3-0
Peterlee Newtown v Tow Law Town	5-2
Hartlepool Boys Welfare OB v Washington Nissan	0-2
Herrington Colliery Welfare v Spennymoor United	0-4
Durham City v Billingham Synthonia	2-4
Jarrow Roofing Boldon Community A. v Consett	0-2
Norton & Stockton Ancients v Cockfield	1-4
Billingham Town v South Shields	2-1

Second Round

Silksworth v Bishop Auckland	1-5
Hartlepool Town v Crook Town	3-0
Consett v Cockfield	2-1
Billingham Synthonia v Spennymoor United	2-3
Shildon v Eppleton Colliery Welfare	4-2
Chester-le-Street Town v Peterlee Newtown	2-0
Dunston Federation Brewery v Billingham Town	0-1
Washington Nissan v Hebburn	0-2

Quarter-Finals

Consett v Shildon	1-2
Bishop Auckland v Hartlepool Town	2-1
Spennymoor United v Billingham Town	8-3
Hebburn v Chester-le-Street Town	5-2

Semi-Finals

Shildon v Spennymoor United	0-4
Bishop Auckland v Hebburn	6-1

Final: Spennymoor United 2, Bishop Auckland 2
Replay: Spennymoor United 3, Bishop Auckland 2 *(aet)*

OTHER COUNTY FINALS:

Minor Cup *(at Billigham Town FC, Thurs 21st April)*: Hartlepool BW Seniors 3, Darlington Simpson Rolling Mills 0
Sunday Cup *(at Horden Colliery Welfare, Sun 24th April)*: Stockton Roseworth 2, Sunderland Humbledon Plains Farm 1 *(aet)*
Youth Cup U-18 *(at Spennymoor Utd, Thurs 14th April)*: Trimdon Juniors 3, Esh Winning Juniors 0
Youth Minor Cup *(at Eppleton CW, Sun 17th April)*: Stockton West End beat Gateshead Redheugh Boys Club 4-3 on penalties after a 2-2 draw.

Hartlepool Lion Hotel, who did the County proud in reaching the final of the FA Sunday Cup.
Photo - Paul Dennis.

TYNESIDE AMATEUR LEAGUE

FOUNDED: 1949

	P	W	D	L	F	A	PTS
Simonside Soc. Club	18	17	1	0	77	21	52
Walker Ledwood F.	18	12	3	3	74	27	39
Shieldfield Inn	18	10	3	5	65	35	33
N'castle Univ. 'A'	18	8	2	8	53	43	26
Jarrow Lad	18	7	4	7	40	53	25
Wallsend Cooksons	18	5	6	7	33	48	21
Jarrow Roofing County	18	5	3	10	44	55	18
DHSS Wanderers	18	4	4	10	27	47	16
Lindisfarne Athletic	18	5	0	13	35	56	15
Wallsend Athletic	18	3	2	13	34	77	11

Tommy Heslop Player of the Year Trophy: Tom Savage (Lindisfarne Athletic)
Matt Docherty Leading Scorer Trophy: Jimmy Gibson (Simonside Social Club) - 22 goals.
Harry Gibson Sportsmanship Trophy: Newcastle University 'A'

Cup Finals:

Challenge Shield *(at Gateshead FC 18/4/94)*:
Shieldfield Inn 2, Newcastle University 'A' 1
Bill Dixon Mem. Cup *(at Heaton Stannington FC 5/5/94)*:
Walker Ledwood Fosse 5, Simonside Social Club 1
Jack Bowman Trophy *(at Heaton Stannington FC 11/5/94)*:
Walker Ledwood Fosse 3, Shieldfield Inn 1
Tusz-Coleman Trophy *(at Whitley Bay FC 25/3/94)*:
Royal Engineers beat Tyneside Amateur League XI 8-7 on penalties after a 2-2 draw.
Thames & Tyne Cup *(at Heaton Stannington FC 7/5/94)*:
Tyneside Amtr Lge XI 4, West Middx Comb. XI 3

The Tyneside Amateur League has now merged with the North Eastern Amateur League and is operating as the Tyneside & North Eastern Amateur League.

THORPE INSURANCE TYNE & WEAR LEAGUE

	P	W	D	L	F	A	PTS
The Grange	24	20	1	3	109	33	61
Rolls Royce	24	18	2	4	101	30	56
Freeman Hospital	24	15	5	4	91	53	*47
The Fort	24	14	3	7	78	63	45
Crown Photography	24	14	2	8	79	57	44
Weardale House	24	11	6	7	74	53	39
East Northumbria	24	11	5	8	55	74	*35
Bartrams Liquormart	24	8	6	10	51	56	30
Crown Low Fell	24	9	2	13	73	76	*26
Ivy House	24	7	2	15	54	81	23
251 Field Ambulance	24	3	3	18	34	97	12
Cleadon New Ship	24	2	5	17	36	85	11
Dunsfords	24	3	0	21	33	110	9

* - 3 points deducted

Cup Finals:

League Cup: Freeman Hosp. 5, Weardale House 0
John Lockey Mem. Tphy: Crown Pho. 4, Fort 2
Thorpe Insurance Cup: Freeman H. 2, Weardale H. 1
Mason Cup: East Northumbria 4, Crown Low Fell 2

EMERGENCY SERVICES LEAGUE

	P	W	D	L	F	A	PTS
Stockton Police	18	15	2	1	56	15	32
Durham North Pol.	18	16	0	2	72	29	32
Sunderland Police	18	11	3	4	53	30	25
Darlington Police	18	11	2	5	53	22	24
Durham HQ Police	18	4	6	8	38	54	14
Durham Fire	18	6	1	11	38	43	13
Middlesbrough Pol.	18	5	3	10	27	40	13
East Durham F&R	18	5	1	12	42	57	11
Hartlepool Police	18	2	6	10	21	44	10
Cleveland East Pol.	18	3	0	15	15	81	6

Championship Match (teams on level pts play-off): Stockton Police 6, Durham North Police 5

Cup Finals:

League Cup: Durham North Police 3, Sunderland Police 2 *(aet)*
Wanless/McConnell Shield: Stockton Police 7, Durham HQ Police 3

DARLINGTON & DISTRICT LEAGUE

FOUNDED: 1893

DIV. A.	P	W	D	L	F	A	PTS
Moore Lane SC	24	19	3	2	70	17	41
Stillington WMC	24	18	4	2	76	33	40
Eastbourne YC	24	18	3	3	87	40	39
Archdeacon	24	11	7	6	63	49	29
Darlington GSOB	24	12	4	8	47	39	28
T & W Branksome	24	11	6	7	53	47	28
Albert Hill WMC	24	9	5	10	47	54	23
Hole-in-the-Wall Ath.	24	8	4	12	50	52	20
Glaxo	24	6	5	13	42	64	17
Hurworth Grange	24	6	2	16	50	84	14
D'ton Railway Ath.	24	5	3	16	53	68	13
Richmond T. Hall Hot.	24	4	1	19	34	78	9
Hogans	24	4	3	17	38	85	*9

* - 2 points deducted

DIV. B.	P	W	D	L	F	A	PTS
East End WMC	26	22	2	2	84	26	46
AFC Flymo	26	20	4	2	105	33	44
Weymouth PO	26	19	2	5	76	38	40
Elders	26	15	6	5	79	52	36
Shildon United	26	14	3	9	74	52	31
College SU	26	12	6	8	68	48	30
Bowater	26	13	4	9	61	55	30
Brown Trout	26	11	5	10	63	56	27
Rise Carr Hotel	26	8	3	15	66	81	19
RAC Darlington	26	6	6	14	49	63	18
Builders Arms	26	6	5	15	37	64	17
Hope Inn	26	2	5	19	21	78	9
DGSOB Res.	26	3	3	20	26	102	9
Torrington	26	3	2	21	47	108	8

Cup Finals:

Lge Chall. Cup: Stillington WMC 2, Shildon Utd 0
Moss & Campbell Cup: Stillington WMC beat Moore Lane SC 4-2 on penalties after a 1-1 draw & extra-time
Walter Stones Trophy: Richmond Town Hall Hotel 4, Eastbourne YC 3
B Div Trophy: AFC Flymo 4, Elders 1 *(aet)*
B Div Secondary Cup: AFC Flymo 2, Shildon Utd 1
Invitation Trophy: Richmond THH 2, T & W Branksome 1 *(aet)*

NORTH EAST CHRISTIAN FELLOWSHIP LEAGUE

	P	W	D	L	F	A	PTS
Chowdean Chapel	18	18	0	0	115	24	54
Ryton CP	18	13	2	3	71	32	41
Heaton Hearts	18	13	1	4	55	32	40
Crossroads	18	12	0	6	66	32	36
Beacon Lough BC	18	12	0	6	64	39	36
Emmanuel Yarm	18	10	3	5	65	43	33
Bethshan	18	10	0	8	69	62	30
St Georges Fatfield	18	9	3	6	53	30	30
Whitley B. Churches	18	9	2	7	58	44	29
Bethany	18	9	1	8	80	43	28
Jesmond Parish Ch.	18	9	1	8	49	49	28
Ryton Croft Park	18	7	3	8	43	46	24
Chester-le-Str. YF	18	7	1	10	36	39	22
Consett Meth. Ch.	18	6	1	11	39	78	19
Chowdean Christians	18	5	2	11	26	54	17
Heworth Christian F.	18	4	3	11	26	60	15
Athenians Christian	18	4	1	13	27	75	13
Westgate Road BC	18	1	2	15	27	123	5
Stakeford Colliers YF	18	0	0	18	18	82	0

PHOTOS OPPOSITE:

Top: *Ferryhill Black Bull FC, Hathaway Auckland & District League.* *Photo - Dave West.*

Centre: *Sunderland SC Fulwell, Vaux Wearside League.*

Top: *Darlington Caledonians FC, Hathaway Auckland & District League.* *Photo - Dave West.*

FLO GAS

MAIDEN CASTLE LEAGUE

(DURHAM UNIV. ATH. UNION)

The Maiden Castle League involves all the colleges in Durham University together with Houghall, the local agricultural college and university staff. Due to the appalling weather, it proved impossible to complete a full fixture programme, so it was decided that a points average would be taken, with a proviso that at least fifteen fixtures had been played. Therefore Hatfield A did not win the First Division, but had their points total divided by fifteen rather than the thirteen games they had played.

The Athletic Union also run a Trophy Competition, although the rules of participation are slightly different to the Maiden Castle League. Instead of a complete ban on all members of the university teams (competing in the UAU competition), second and third team players are permitted to represent their college providing they have played for the first team on fewer than five occasions. This year the competition was won by Hild/Bede who beat Castle (University College) 1-0 in the final.

Nick Dunham, DUAU Secretary

DIV. ONE	P	W	D	L	F	A	Ave.
Mildert A.	18	14	2	2	65	27	2.44
Castle A.	16	11	3	2	52	23	2.25
Hatfield A.	13	11	0	2	46	18	2.20
Collingwood A.	15	10	0	5	39	23	2.00
Staff	10	8	2	0	47	10	1.73
Grad. Society	18	8	0	10	32	60	1.33
Aidan's A.	15	5	4	6	35	30	1.27
Houghall	18	5	4	9	41	56	1.06
Hild/Bede A.	17	3	2	12	27	57	0.65
Trevelyan A.	18	2	2	14	28	65	0.44
Chad's	18	1	1	16	19	62	0.22

Top Scorer: T Thompson (Staff) 20

DIV. TWO	P	W	D	L	F	A	Ave.
Cuthbert's A.	17	15	1	1	72	19	2.71
Mildert B.	21	15	2	4	70	21	2.24
Grey A.	19	13	3	3	52	23	2.21
Castle B.	20	13	4	3	80	40	2.15
Aidan's B.	17	10	5	2	82	28	2.06
Collingwood B.	19	7	3	9	46	55	1.26
John's	17	6	3	8	43	52	1.24
Cuthbert's B.	17	5	1	11	48	79	0.94
Grey B.	16	4	2	10	33	73	0.88
Hild/Bede B.	16	2	1	13	18	64	0.44
Trevelyan B.	20	0	6	14	29	81	0.30
Hatfield B.	17	0	5	12	29	72	0.29

JUSTSPORT DURHAM & DISTRICT SUNDAY LEAGUE

FOUNDED: 1967

PREM. DIV.	P	W	D	L	F	A	PTS
Framwellgate Moor	22	17	2	3	86	26	53
Sherburn WMC	22	16	5	1	84	28	53
Relton Terrace WMC	22	14	2	6	71	41	44
Peterlee Cath. Club	22	13	4	5	54	36	43
Ferryhill WMC	22	12	3	7	59	38	*36
Byers Green WMC	22	7	4	11	50	71	25
Sacriston WMC	22	9	1	12	50	72	*25
Shiney Row	22	7	2	13	47	65	23
Hetton Change Is.	22	6	5	11	42	68	23
West Cornforth Vic.	22	6	3	13	39	63	21
Jasprint Biddick Inn	22	6	3	13	38	54	*18
Belmont WMC	22	1	2	19	20	77	5

* - 3 points deducted

Lower Division Champions:
Div. 1 (12): Fishburn WMC
Div. 2 (11): Newton Hall
Div. 3 (12): Brasside
Div. 4 (11): Leamside Three Horse Shoes
Div. 5 (12): Dog & Gun
Div. 6 (12): Bankhead Wanderers

Racing Promotions Staffieri Cup: Peterlee CC
Staffieri Cup R-up: Ferryhill WMC
Moor Coachworks Lg Cup: Framwellgate Moor WMC
League Cup R-up: Sherburn Village WMC
Ramside Cup: Framwellgate Moor WMC
Ramside Cup R-up: Hollymere
Durham City AFC Supp. Guards Cup: Lambton Arms
Guards Cup R-up: Sedgefield
Russell Office Systems Presidents Cup: Hollymere
Presidents Cup R-up: Osborne WMC
Solar Glass Hedgeley Fair-Play Award: Meadowfield City

DARLINGTON & DIST. SUNDAY MORNING INVITATION LEAGUE

FOUNDED: 1993

	P	W	D	L	F	A	PTS
Stooperdale	21	15	3	3	68	42	33
Springfield Ath.	21	13	2	6	93	73	28
Coundon AGL	21	12	2	7	74	47	26
AFC Brinkburn	21	12	2	7	73	49	*24
Jack Horners	21	8	4	9	63	78	20
Calor	21	7	6	8	55	72	20
Golden Cock	21	3	3	15	50	70	9
Coundon Bull Ox	21	1	4	16	39	84	6

* - 2 points deducted

Cup Finals:
League Cup: Stooperdale 4, Springfield Ath. 3
SKS Trophy: AFC Brinkburn beat Coundon AGL 5-3 on penalties after a 1-1 draw.

EAST RIDING F.A.

Secretary: D R Johnson,
52 Bethune Ave., Hull HU4 7EJ.

SENIOR CUP First Round

Ideal Standard v Odeon 1-3
North Ferriby United v Bulmans 0-1
Westella Shopacheck v Kingston 2-1
Rudston United v Haltemprice 0-2
Malet Lambert YC *(w/o)* Bridlington Town *(scr)*

Second Round

Haltemprice v Dairycoates 3-2
Hilltop v Reckitts 1-5
Cavalier Club v Hull City 0-4
Odeon v Westella Shopacheck 2-3
Hall Road Rangers v Cottingham Sports Club 3-0
Schultz YC *(w/o)* Bulmans *(scr)*
Malet Lambert YC v Hotal Paragon 5-1
Sculcoates Amateurs v Hedon United 3-0

Quarter-Finals

Haltemprice v Hall Road Rangers 1-2
Schultz YC v Malet Lambert YC 0-1
Hull City v Sculcoates Amateurs 0-1
Westella Shopacheck v Reckitts 2-3

Semi-Final *(at Hall Rd Rgrs FC, Tues 19th April)*
Sculcoates Amateurs v Reckitts 2-1

Semi-Final *(at Northern Foods FC, Wed 20th April)*
Hall Road Rangers v Malet Lambert YC 7-1

Final *(at Hull City FC, Mon 9th May)*: Hall Road Rangers 1, Sculcoates Amateurs 0

Hall Road Rangers celebrate the East Riding Senior Cup success.

SENIOR COUNTRY CUP First Round

Driffield El v Olympia Station 2-3
Full Measure v Ward FC 4-5
Beverley Old Grammarians v Filey Town 1-2
Hornsea United v Holme Rovers Reserves 4-2
Nafferton Royals v Brandesburton 2-3
Howden Amateurs v Greyhound 0-2
Hunmanby United v Flamborough 1-4
Mkt Weighton U. v Bridlington Labour Soc. 2-1
Middleton Rovers v Hutton Cranswick 4-1
Charles Dickens *(scr)* North Newbald *(w/o)*
Leconfield *(w/o)* Rudston United Reserves *(scr)*
Shiptonthorpe v North Cave 0-4
Quay United v Withernsea 5-2
Little Driffield v Viking Panthers 1-5
Pocklington Sports v Stamford Bridge 0-0,3-1
Holme Rovers *(bye)*

Second Round

Quay United v Flamborough AFC 2-1
Pocklington Town v Holme Rovers 2-0
Brandesburton v North Newbald 0-1
Viking Panthers v North Cave 2-7
Market Weighton United v Olympia Station 1-1,1-5
Hornsea Town v Ward FC 2-3
Middleton Rovers v Leconfield 0-3
Filey Town v Greyhound 1-0

Quarter-Finals

Leconfield v Filey Town 1-2
Olympia Station v Pocklington Town 1-0
North Cave v Ward FC 1-2
Quay United v North Newbald 4-1

Semi-Final *(at Wilberfoss FC, Tues 12th April)*
Ward FC v Olympia Station 2-0

Semi-Final *(at Hunmanby Utd FC, Thurs 14th April)*
Filey Town v Quay United 7-2*(Filey expelled)*

Final *(at Hunmanby United FC, Mon 2nd May)*: Ward FC 5, Quay United 0

OTHER COUNTY FINALS

Intermediate Cup *(at Northern Foods FC, Thurs 5th May)*: Youngs FC 1, Anlaby United 0
Junior Cup *(at Hall Road Rgrs FC, Tues 3rd May)*: COGS 3, Crown Sovereign 1
Qualifying Cup *(at Hall Road Rgrs FC, Thurs 28th April)*: Smith & Nephew Res. 2, Sutton Fields SBCA 1
Intermediate Country Cup *(at Leconfield FC, Tues 10th May)*: Fulford Utd 4, Filey Town Res. 1
Junior Country Cup *(at Ward FC, Sherburn, Wed 27th April)*: Leconfield Res. 4, Norton United 0
Qualifying Country Cup *(at Rudston Utd FC, Wed 4th May)*: Mermaid 2, Revelstoke Reserves 1
Midweek Cup *(at Hall Road Rgrs FC, Tues 26th April)*: Wyke College 2, Endyke Hotel 1
Frank Varey & Dr J Lilley Youth Cup *(at Hull City FC, Thurs 5th May)*: Sculcoates Amtrs 4, Leconfield 0
Youth Cup *(at Hall Road Rgrs FC, Tues 17th May)*: St Andrews 1, Springhead Boys u-16 0

EAST RIDING COUNTY LEAGUE

President: W A Piercy.

Chairman: C Bodsworth.

Treasurer: R Waudby.

Hon. Secretary: D Simmons, 24 Gorton Road, Willerby, North Humberside HU10 (0482 658998).

The season proved to be a triumph for two clubs in particular, one a long-standing established outfit and the other a new club.

Sculcoates Amateurs have their roots in the earlier years of the century, and enjoyed probably their greatest season ever. The club clinched the Premier Division championship for the third successive year and completed a clean sweep with the H E Dean and the League Senior Cups. Further glory came their way when they reached the final of the County Senior Cup where they lost narrowly to NCEL side Hall Road Rangers (Haltemprice and Westella Shopacheck also reached the quarter-final stages of this competition). Sculcoates' dominance threatens to be a long-term prospect as their youthful Reserve XI won the Second Division title as well as retaining the Dr Lilley Cup (the ERCFA's premier youth competition).

Viking Safeway had a successful start to their tenure in the League following their creation as a splinter from Woodlands AFC. The Vikings gained a place in the Premier Division at the first attempt by winning the Division One title in some style. They proved that they will be an asset to the top flight by removing a number of Premier sides from the cups. Not unlike Sculcoates, they seem have secured future success by the creation of an excellent Reserve team founded on youth - the younger Vikings also gained promotion by pipping Westella Shopacheck 'A' for the Fourth Division crown.

The only trophies to escape these two clubs were both claimed by Third Division clubs. After losing successive relegation battles, Beverley Town have arrested their decline in fine style to claim the Division Three title, whilst Anlaby Amateurs Reserves took the H Robinson Cup - a competition won by their first team the two previous years.

Dave Simmons, Hon. General Secretary

Premier Division	P	W	D	L	F	A	PTS
Sculcoates Am.	24	18	6	0	80	10	42
North Cave	24	16	4	4	60	21	36
Woodlands	24	11	8	5	44	29	30
Westella Shopa.	24	10	8	6	56	26	28
Leconfield	24	9	10	5	54	35	28
Haltemprice	24	10	7	7	47	35	27
Holme Rovers	24	10	5	9	41	42	25
Beverley OG	24	9	5	10	42	37	23
Mkt Weighton U.	24	7	6	11	32	55	20
Cavalier	24	7	5	12	35	35	19
Rudston United	24	5	8	11	36	55	18
Howden Arms	24	7	0	17	35	69	14
North Newbald	24	0	2	22	17	130	2

Division One	P	W	D	L	F	A	PTS
Viking Safeway	18	16	1	1	61	16	33
Hodgson	18	14	1	3	62	25	29
Gilberdyke Utd	18	13	2	3	63	23	28
Anlaby United	18	10	3	5	59	26	23
Westella S. Res.	18	7	2	9	27	42	16
North Cave Res.	18	7	1	10	29	41	15
Thorngumbald	18	5	2	11	41	66	12
Easington United	18	5	1	12	53	64	11
Brandesburton	18	4	1	13	32	41	9
Holme Rvrs Res.	18	1	2	15	18	101	4

Division Two	P	W	D	L	F	A	PTS
Sculcoates Res.	22	14	4	4	61	29	32
Skidby Millers	22	11	8	3	73	27	30
Hook Amateurs	22	12	4	6	71	49	28
Holmpton United	22	8	7	7	38	42	23
Haltemprice Res.	22	7	9	6	33	38	23
Aldbrough Utd	22	9	5	8	39	46	23
Long Riston	22	10	3	9	51	65	23
Royal Oak	22	6	6	10	50	55	18
Bransholme Ath.	22	5	8	9	50	59	18
Anlaby Amateurs	22	7	3	12	41	61	17
Beverley OG Res.	22	7	2	13	43	48	16
Walton Club	22	4	5	13	39	70	13

Division Three	P	W	D	L	F	A	PTS
Beverley Town	24	18	2	4	118	24	38
Leconfield Res.	24	17	1	6	71	30	35
Tickton.	21	16	3	5	74	45	35
Walkington	24	14	2	8	58	40	30
Anlaby Am. Res.	24	11	7	6	55	43	29
Riston Bay Horse	24	12	5	7	49	39	29
Barkers	24	11	6	7	54	40	28
Howden Amtrs Res.	24	10	5	9	74	47	25
Mkt Weighton Res.	24	7	4	13	39	55	18
Thorngumbald Res.	24	8	1	15	41	77	17
Leven Mbrs Club	24	5	4	15	47	78	14
Holme Rvrs 'A'	24	3	2	19	29	116	8
Hornsea Old Boys	24	1	4	19	28	103	6

Division Four	P	W	D	L	F	A	PTS
Viking S. Res.	20	17	1	2	85	20	35
Westella S. 'A'	20	14	4	2	73	27	32
Grovehill Amtrs	20	14	2	4	73	36	30
Skidby M. Res.	20	13	3	4	47	33	29
Nth Newbald 'A'	20	10	2	8	36	42	22
Molescroft Rgrs	20	5	3	12	30	49	13
Howden Amtrs 'A'	20	5	3	12	43	64	13
Long Riston Res.	20	4	5	11	29	54	13
Little Weighton	20	3	5	12	32	52	11
Brandesburton Res.	20	5	1	14	29	52	11
Mkt Weighton 'A'	20	5	1	14	23	71	11

PREM. DIV. RESULTS		1	2	3	4	5	6	7	8	9	10	11	12	13
1.	Beverley Old Gramm.	*	2-1	2-1	0-3	0-2	0-0	1-3	0-3	11-2	1-1	0-1	1-4	1-0
2.	Cavalier	1-0	*	0-1	1-2	3-1	1-2	0-1	0-5	3-0	6-0	1-4	0-2	1-1
3.	Haltemprice	2-2	0-1	*	2-2	1-0	2-2	5-3	2-0	6-2	0-0	0-3	2-2	2-2
4.	Holme Rovers	1-0	0-1	1-2	*	5-2	2-5	2-0	0-5	5-1	1-0	1-3	0-3	1-2
5.	Howden Amateurs	0-7	1-0	1-0	2-3	*	1-6	1-2	1-2	5-1	2-1	1-3	2-5	1-2
6.	Leconfield	0-0	6-0	1-3	3-3	7-1	*	2-0	2-6	1-1	4-1	0-0	3-0	3-3
7.	Mkt Weighton United	1-5	0-0	3-0	1-1	0-1	3-1	*	1-3	2-1	2-2	0-6	0-0	0-3
8.	North Cave	6-1	3-0	2-1	3-0	4-0	0-0	5-3	*	5-2	1-0	2-3	1-0	0-0
9.	North Newbald	0-1	0-12	0-7	0-4	0-6	0-4	1-4	0-1	*	2-2	0-7	0-10	2-5
10.	Rudston United	0-2	2-2	0-4	1-2	6-1	2-1	2-2	3-3	3-1	*	0-5	3-2	1-2
11.	Sculcoates Amateurs	1-1	0-0	4-0	4-1	1-0	5-0	9-0	0-0	7-0	6-1	*	4-1	1-1
12.	Westella Shopacheck	2-0	1-0	1-1	1-1	6-2	0-0	1-1	1-0	12-1	2-2	0-0	*	0-1
13.	Woodlands	2-4	1-1	1-3	0-0	4-1	1-1	3-0	1-0	7-0	1-3	0-3	1-0	*

DIV. ONE RESULTS		1	2	3	4	5	6	7	8	9	10
1.	Anlaby United	*	2-0	5-0	0-4	1-1	8-2	4-1	2-2	1-3	1-2
2.	Brandesburton	1-7	*	3-5	0-2	1-2	3-3	4-0	1-2	0-3	0-2
3.	Easington United	0-3	3-1	*	2-2	4-5	11-0	1-3	3-8	2-7	3-1
4.	Gilberdyke	2-1	1-0	3-0	*	3-5	9-2	2-1	7-1	1-2	5-0
5.	Hodgson AFC	1-2	2-1	7-1	4-3	*	5-1	2-0	6-0	1-3	6-2
6.	Holme Rovers Reserves	1-8	1-8	0-8	0-8	0-5	*	0-1	5-4	1-5	0-3
7.	North Cave	0-4	2-1	3-2	1-1	2-5	3-0	*	6-3	0-5	4-1
8.	Thorngumbald	2-7	1-5	5-3	3-5	0-2	3-0	2-1	*	0-6	2-2
9.	Viking Safeway	2-2	1-0	4-2	1-2	1-0	7-0	3-1	3-2	*	4-1
10.	Westella Shopacheck Res.	2-1	2-3	4-3	0-3	0-3	2-2	1-0	2-1	0-1	*

DIV. TWO RESULTS		1	2	3	4	5	6	7	8	9	10	11	12
1.	Aldbrough United	*	1-0	2-4	3-3	1-1	0-1	2-2	3-2	2-1	0-2	0-6	5-2
2.	Anlaby Amateurs	3-0	*	1-5	2-6	0-2	2-1	0-4	3-2	4-4	2-4	1-5	4-4
3.	Beverley Old Gramm. Res.	1-2	1-2	*	4-2	0-2	2-1	0-4	6-0	0-1	0-3	1-3	3-1
4.	Bransholme	0-0	0-4	4-2	*	3-4	2-2	0-2	6-8	0-3	1-1	1-1	3-5
5.	Haltemprice	0-0	2-1	0-0	1-2	*	2-2	1-2	0-0	1-6	0-4	3-3	1-0
6.	Holmpton United	1-4	3-1	2-0	1-1	2-0	*	4-4	0-4	1-1	2-0	1-1	2-1
7.	Hook Amateurs	4-3	1-1	6-2	4-8	1-2	5-3	*	3-4	6-1	1-2	5-3	6-0
8.	Long Riston	2-1	2-3	2-1	0-6	1-5	3-0	4-1	*	5-5	0-2	0-7	3-1
9.	Royal Oak	1-3	3-1	1-0	1-1	1-1	4-5	3-4	2-3	*	1-4	1-1	3-1
10.	Sculcoates Amtrs Reserves	7-0	6-2	5-4	1-1	4-0	1-2	2-3	3-4	3-2	*	1-1	2-1
11.	Skidby Millers	2-3	4-0	2-2	8-0	2-2	2-0	1-1	5-0	5-2	0-2	*	6-1
12.	Walton Club	1-4	1-4	2-5	2-0	3-3	2-2	3-2	2-2	4-3	2-2	0-5	*

DIV. THREE RESULTS		1	2	3	4	5	6	7	8	9	10	11	12	13
1.	Anlaby Amtrs Res.	*	1-1	1-3	7-0	1-1	3-1	1-4	3-3	4-3	1-1	3-1	1-2	1-0
2.	Barkers	1-1	*	0-7	2-0	3-1	2-2	2-1	1-3	2-2	1-2	5-1	1-4	1-1
3.	Beverley Town	1-2	4-2	*	10-0	8-0	6-1	1-1	12-2	8-1	4-1	4-0	1-2	6-1
4.	Holme Rovers 'A'	2-6	1-6	0-10	*	3-3	0-3	3-6	1-2	0-3	0-4	1-0	2-4	2-4
5.	Hornsea Old Boys	1-5	0-5	0-7	2-3	*	2-9	0-1	1-7	0-8	1-3	3-5	0-6	2-3
6.	Howden Amtrs Res,	2-5	2-2	2-1	13-1	2-4	*	4-0	3-1	1-1	2-2	10-0	2-2	1-4
7.	Leconfield	6-0	0-3	1-3	3-0	5-0	1-0	*	2-1	4-0	1-3	4-0	4-3	1-3
8.	Leven Mambers Club	1-1	0-5	1-7	8-3	3-3	0-3	1-4	*	1-3	0-0	3-0	1-4	0-4
9.	Market Weighton Utd	2-0	0-2	1-1	1-2	3-0	1-0	1-5	3-2	*	2-2	1-6	0-3	0-3
10.	Riston Bay Horse	1-2	2-1	1-6	6-1	3-0	2-1	0-2	5-0	1-0	*	2-3	1-5	2-3
11.	Thorngumbald	1-2	1-2	2-1	6-0	3-1	2-4	0-8	3-2	2-1	1-1	*	2-9	0-3
12.	Tickton	3-2	2-1	2-4	3-3	2-2	4-3	0-3	5-4	2-1	2-3	2-1	*	3-1
13.	Walkington	2-2	2-3	0-3	4-1	5-1	1-3	1-4	2-1	4-1	0-1	5-1	2-0	*

DIV. FOUR RESULTS		1	2	3	4	5	6	7	8	9	10	11
1.	Brandesburton Reserves	*	1-5	2-3	1-0	4-1	3-1	1-4	1-3	0-2	1-3	0-1
2.	Groveill Amateurs	3-1	*	5-1	3-0	6-0	4-3	2-1	3-0	3-5	3-4	3-3
3.	Howden Amateurs 'A'	8-0	0-8	*	5-3	4-0	2-3	1-2	1-2	1-3	1-13	2-8
4.	Little Weighton	1-5	1-3	2-2	*	1-1	4-0	3-0	2-1	2-2	0-1	0-6
5.	Long Riston	2-3	1-6	1-1	3-3	*	0-1	3-3	2-1	3-2	2-4	2-4
6.	Market Weighton U. 'A'	0-0	2-6	1-5	3-2	0-3	*	4-3	1-6	0-2	0-7	0-6
7.	Molescroft Rangers	1-0	1-3	1-0	2-2	1-2	2-3	*	1-4	1-1	1-6	0-3
8.	North Newbald Res.	1-0	3-1	3-2	3-2	0-0	2-0	2-0	*	2-4	0-7	0-0
9.	Skidby Millers Reserves	3-1	2-5	3-1	3-0	3-2	3-1	0-5	2-0	*	4-3	1-1
10.	Viking Safeway Reserves	4-2	6-0	2-2	3-1	3-0	4-0	2-0	7-0	0-2	*	3-1
11.	Westella Shopacheck 'A'	6-3	1-1	2-1	5-3	4-1	7-0	7-1	6-3	2-0	0-3	*

H E DEAN CUP 1993-94

Preliminary Round

Bransholme Athletic v Riston Bay Horse	2-1	Leven Members Club v Anlaby United	0-8
Hornsea Old Boys v Grovehill Amateurs	1-2	Cavalier Club v Beverley Town	2-1

First Round

Haltemprice v Hodgsons	3-2	Barkers v Walton Club	2-8
Rudston United v Walkington	5-0	Anlaby Amateurs v Cavalier	0-2
Market Weighton Utd v Skidby Millers	2-4	Gilberdyke United v Beverley Old Grammarians	3-0
Howden Amateurs v Grovehill Amateurs	5-1	Anlaby United *(w/o)* Black Prince Royals *(scr)*	
Woodlands v Royal Oak	5-3	Brandesburton v Long Riston	2-1
Hook Amateurs v Holme Rovers	2-5	Westella Shopacheck v Thorngumbald	5-1
Molescroft Rangers v Viking Safeway	0-5	Bransholme Athletic v Sculcoates Amateurs	0-6
North Newbald v North Cave	1-3	Easington United v Leconfield	0-2

Second Round

Skidby Millers v Sculcoates Amateurs	0-5	Brandesburton v Anlaby United	2-1
Gilberdyke United v Viking Safeway	1-2	Howden Amateurs v Holme Rovers	0-4
Haltemprice v Walton Club	7-1	Leconfield v North Cave	1-1,3-0
Woodlands v Westella Shopacheck	0-1	Rudston United v Cavalier Club	1-4

(continued overleaf)

Quarter-Finals *(H E Dean Cup continued)*

Westella Shopacheck v Leconfield 3-1
Cavalier Club v Haltemprice 1-0
Brandesburton v Viking Safeway 1-3
Sculcoates Amateurs v Holme Rovers 8-0

Semi-Finals

Viking Safeway v Westella Shopacheck 3-1
Cavalier Club v Sculcoates Amateurs 2-0

Final: Sculcoates Amateurs 6, Viking Safeway 2

LEAGUE SENIOR CUP 1993-94 First Round

Woodlands v Holme Rovers 5-2
Howden Amtrs v Beverley Old Grammarians 0-4
North Newbald v Cavalier Club 2-1
Leconfield v Market Weighton United 2-0
Westella Shopacheck v Rudston United 1-0

Quarter-Finals

North Cave v Beverley Old Grammarians 2-1
Leconfield v North Newbald 6-0
Sculcoates Amateurs v Haltemprice 3-0
Westella Shopacheck v Woodlands 2-1

Semi-Finals

Leconfield v Sculcoates Amateurs 0-2
North Cave v Westella Shopacheck 1-0

Final: Sculcoates Amateurs 3, North Cave 0

LEAGUE JUNIOR CUP 1993-94 First Round

Easington United v Walton Club 8-1
North Cave Reserves v Holmpton United 1-1,2-1
Black Prince Ryls *(w/o)* Beaver *(scr)*
Thorngumbald v Aldbrough 9-3
Hodgsons v Long Riston 3-2
Westella Shopacheck Res. v Brandesburton 1-2
Anlaby Amateurs v Royal Oak 4-3
Beverley Old Grammarians v Hook Amateurs 0-3

Second Round

Bransholme Athletic v Anlaby Amateurs 3-0
Sculcoates Res. *(w/o)* Black Prince Ryls *(scr)*
Anlaby United v North Cave Reserves 3-2
Hook Amateurs v Holme Rovers Reserves 5-1
Haltemprice Reserves v Brandesburton 2-5
Easington United v Skidby Millers 3-0
Viking Safeway v Gilberdyke United 5-1
Thorngumbald v Hodgsons 5-3

Quarter-Finals

Easington United v Hook Amateurs 4-0
Thorngumbald v Brandesburton 4-2
Sculcoates Amateurs Reserves v Anlaby Utd 1-3
Bransholme Athletic v Viking Safeway 2-3

Semi-Finals

Anlaby United v Thorngumbald 1-0
Viking Safeway v Easington United 2-1

Final: Viking Safeway 4, Anlaby United 3

H ROBINSON CUP 1993-94 First Round

Tickton v Long Riston Reserves 8-0
Howden Amtrs 'A' *(w/o)* Holme Rovers 'B' *(scr)*
Molescroft Rangers v Hornsea Old Boys 3-0
Beverley Town v Leven Members Club 3-0
Riston Bay Horse v Howden Amateurs Res. 1-4
Viking Safeway Res. v Westella S. Res. 4-2
Mkt Weighton Utd Res. v Leconfield Res. 0-2
Brandesburton Reserves v Barkers 1-3
Mkt Weighton Utd 'A' v North Newbald Res. 1-3

Second Round

Viking Safeway Res. v Howden Amtrs Res. 0-4
Skidby Millers Res. v Walkington 1-4
Holme Rovers 'A' v Anlaby Amtrs Reserves 1-2
Little Weighton v Molescroft Rangers 2-4
Beverley T. Reserves v Leconfield Reserves 2-1
North Newbald Res. v Tickton 2-4
Howden Amtrs 'A' v Grovehill Amateurs 2-3
Thorngumbald Reserves v Barkers 1-0

Quarter-Finals

Howden Amateurs Res. v Grovehill Amtrs 5-2
Thorngumbald Reserves v Tickton 3-3,1-4
Walkington v Beverley Town 0-3
Molescroft Rangers v Anlaby Amateurs Res. 1-4

Semi-Finals

Howden A. Res. v Tickton 2-0*(Howden expelled)*
Anlaby Amateurs Reserves v Beverley Town 5-3

Final: Anlaby Amateurs Reserves 3, Tickton 2

PREMIER DIVISION CLUBS 1994-95

BEVERLEY OLD GRAMMARIANS

Secretary: Nick Gutteridge, 212 Goddard Ave., Hull (0482 446548).
Ground: Grammar School, Queensgate, Beverley **Colours:** Red & black/black.

CAVALIER CLUB

Secretary: Dave Marshall, 12 Isledane, Orchard Park, Hull HU6 9DZ (0482 806053)
Ground: Pitch 2, Oak Road PF, Hull **Colours:** Green & yellow stripes.

HALTEMPRICE

Secretary: Keith Failey, 77 Beech Rd, Ellhoughton, HU15 1JY (0482 666994)
Ground: King George V PF, Beverley Rd, Kirkella **Colours:** Blue & white.

HODGSONS A.F.C.

Secretary: Steve Bruce, 47 Queensmead, Beverley HU17 8PQ (0482 868633)
Ground: Beverley Leisure Centre, Flemingate, Beverley **Colours:** Yellow & blue.

HOLME ROVERS

Secretary: Paul Harrison, 4 Hawthorn Drive, Holme-on-Spalding Moor, York YO4 4AP (0430 861140)
Ground: Village Hall, High Str., Holme-on-Spalding Moor **Colours:** White & blue/blue.

LECONFIELD

Secretary: Peter Todd, 9 Melbourne Square, Leconfield (0964 550529)
Ground: Miles Lane, Leconfield **Colours:** Yellow/green

MARKET WEIGHTON UNITED

Secretary: Stephen P Denness, Holly Tree Farm, Holme-on-Spalding Moor, York YO4 4HE (0430 860413)
Ground: Goodmanham Rd, Market Weighton **Colours:** Green & white.

NORTH CAVE

Secretary: Cliff Robson, 6 Blanshards Lane, North Cave HU15 2LN (0430 422071)
Ground: Church Street PF, North Cave **Colours:** Blue/white.

RUDSTON UNITED

Secretary: R W Overfield, 18 Eastgate, Rudston, Driffield YO25 0UX (0262 420397).
Ground: Burton Fleming Rd PF, Rudston **Colours:** All blue.

SCULCOATES AMATEURS

Secretary: Tony Exton, 9 32nd Avenue, Hull HU6 9SD (0482 802600)
Ground: Pitch No.1 Oak Rd Playing Fields, Hull **Colours:** Black & white.

VIKING SAFEWAY

Secretary: J Pheasnt, 27 Ullswater Grove, Goole DN14 6JR (0405 765456)
Ground: West Park or Western Rd, Goole **Colours:** Blue & white

WESTELLA & WILLERBY

Secretary: Roger Wauby, 3 Lawson Close, Walkington, Hull HU17 8TR (0482 870868)
Colours: Black & white stripes/white
Ground: Hull & ER Ath. Club, Chanterlands Ave., Hull *('A' team: As Haltemprice (above))*

WOODLANDS

Secretary: Raymond Kinder, 46 Victoria Str., Goole DN14 5EX (0405 768826)
Ground: Parkside School, Western Rd, Goole **Colours:** Orange/purple.

DIVISION ONE CLUBS 1994-95

ANLABY UNITED

Secretary: Steve Smith, 12 Hawkshead Green, Malham Ave., Hull HU4 7SZ (0482 562925).
Ground: King George V PF, Beverley Rd, Hull **Colours:** Red & black.

BRANDESBURTON

Secretary: Kevin Atkinson, 35 Reeds Way, Brandesburton YO25 8S (0964 543807)
Ground: Catwick Lane, Brandesburton **Colours:** Black & amber stripes.

EASINGTON UNITED

Secretary: Mrs Judith Foster, 5 Humber Lane, Patrington, Hull HU12 0PJ.
Ground: Low Farm, Easington **Colours:** Navy & sky/sky.

HOOK AMATEURS

Secretary: Kevin Young, 'Mandavale', High Str., Hook, Goole DN14 5NY (0405 760322)
Ground: Church Lane, Hook **Cols:** Green & gold or black & white

HOWDEN AMATEURS

Secretary: Brian Stevens, 15 Derwent Ave., Howden, nr Goole DN14 7AJ (0430 431185)
Ground: Ashes Park, Playing Field, Howden **Colours:** Red & black.

SKIDBY MILLERS

Secretary: Ron Leveridge, 121 Main Str., Skidby, Cottingham, Hull HU16 5TX (0482 847289)
Ground: Skidby PF, Manor Garth, Skidby **Colours:** Red & white.

SOUTH CAVE UNITED

Secretary: Norman Elliott, 41 Church Str., South Cave, Brough HU15 2EP (0430 422577)
Ground: Church Street, South Cave **Colours:** Orange/blue.

THORNGUMBALD

Secretary: Arthur Brummit, 9 Bridge Bungalows, Burstwick, Hull HU12 9JS (0964 622271)
Ground: Plumtree Rd, Thorngumbald **Colours:** White & navy stripes.

This Division also includes the reserve sides of: Holme Rovers, North Cave, Sculcoates Amtrs.

DIVISION TWO CLUBS 1994-95

ALDBROUGH UNITED

Secretary: David Barnes, 2 Nottingham Rd, Aldbrough, Hull HU11 4RJ (0904 527547)
Ground: Hornsea Road, Aldbrough **Colours:** Black & red stripes/black.

ANLABY AMATEURS

Secretary: Ray Harteveld, 14a Pease Court, High Street, Hull HU1 1NG (0482 589254)
Ground: As Haltemprice (Premier Div.) **Colours:** Yellow & blue

BEVERLEY TOWN

Secretary: Terry Brocklehurst, 10 Waterside Rd, Beverley HU17 0PP (0482 871336)
Ground: Beverley Leisure Centre, Flemingate, Beverley **Colours:** Sky & claret stripes.

BRANSHOLME ATHLETIC

Secretary: Alan Clark, 187 Sutton Rd, Hull HU6 7DP (0482 802449)
Ground: Bude Rd, Bransholme **Colours:** Red & white.

HOLMPTON UNITED

Secretary: Wayne Christie, 20 Garrick Close, Pocklington YO4 2YX (0759 306796)
Ground: Welwick Rd, Patrington **Colours:** Green & black stripes.

LONG RISTON

Secretary: Harry Grimston, 14 Riseway, Long Riston, Hull HU11 5JN (0964 562053).
Ground: Main Street, Long Riston **Colours:** Red/white.

NORTH NEWBALD

Secretary: Ken Smith, 13 Church Mount, North Newbald, York YO4 3SY (0430 827438)
Grnd: South Newbald Rd PF, North Newbald **Colours:** Yellow & red.

ROYAL OAK

Secretary: Jim Calvert, c/o Royal Oak Pub, Cartwright Ave., Beverley HU17 8LX (0482 862416)
Ground: Central Avenue, Beverley. **Colours:** Blue & white stripes

TICKTON

Secretary: Alan Hayton, 54 Churchfields, Tickton, Beverley HU17 9RQ (0964 542040)
Ground: Playing Fields, Main Str., Tickton, Beverley **Colours:** White & blue

This Division also includes the reserve sides of: Beverley OG, Haltemprice.

DIVISION THREE CLUBS 1994-95

BARKERS

Secretary: Michael Shipley, 38 Eastgate, Beverley HU17 0DT (0482 865520).
Grnd: Beverley Leisure Centre, Flemingate, Beverley **Colours:** Claret/black.

LEVEN MEMBERS' CLUB

Secretary: Tim Pearson, 55 East Str., Leven, Beverley HU17 5NG (0964 542597)
Ground: Leven PF, North Street, Leven. **Colours:** Maroon.

RISTON BAY HORSE

Secretary: John Carlill, Joiners House, Main Street, Long Riston HU11 5JP (0964 562245)
Ground: King George V PF, Cottingham **Colours:** Claret & blue.

WALKINGTON

Secretary: Martin Davey, 30 West End Rd, Walkington, Beverley, HU17 8SX (0482 871020)
Ground: Beech View, Walkington, Beverley. **Colours:** Blue & white.

WALTON CLUB

Secretary: S Holbrook, 60 Patterdale Rd, Spring Bank West, Hull HU5 5AR (0482 509888).
Ground: King George V, Beverley Rd, Kirkella **Colours:** Blue & white.

This Division also includes the reserve sides of: Anlaby Amtrs, Howden Amtrs, Market Weighton Utd, South Cave Utd, Thorngumbald, Viking Safeway.

DIVISION FOUR CLUBS 1994-95

BOOTHFERRY RANGERS

Secretary: Nick Rhodes, 19 Lowfield Rd, Anlaby HU10 7BP (0482 651545).
Ground: Sydney Smith School, First Lane, Anlaby **Colours:** Red & black stripes/black.

GROVEHILL AMATEURS

Secretary: Colin Conman, 191 Holmechurch Lane, Beverley HU17 0QE (0482 864500)
Ground: Longcroft School, Burton Rd, Beverley **Colours:** Orange/black.
Previous Name: Sloop (pre-1993).

HORNSEA OLD BOYS

Secretary: Barry Senior, 123 Cliff Rd, Hornsea HU18 1JB (0964 533289).
Ground: Hornsea School, Eastgate, Hornsea **Colours:** Red/black.

LITTLE WEIGHTON

Secretary: Stephen Christmas, 4 The Close, Little Weighton HU20 3XA (0482 841366).
Ground: White Gap Road, Little Weighton **Colours:** Yellow & green.

MARINER'S ARMS

Secretary: Mark Leak, 128 Main Street, Etton HU17 7AX (0430 810451).
Ground: Black Mill, Beverley, Westwood **Colours:** Yellow & blue/blue.

MOLESCROFT RANGERS

Secretary: Roy Ritson, 20 Hargreave Close, Beverley HU17 7BG (0482 862723)
Ground: Longcroft School, Burton Rd, Beverley **Cols:** Blue & black stripes/black

REAL M.C.K.

Secretary: Crescencio Rodriguez, 12 Waveney Rd, Longhill Estate HU8 9ES (0482 712744)
Ground: Bude Road, Bransholme **Colours:** Blue/red.

This Division also includes the reserve sides of: Brandesburton, Holme Rovers ('A'), Howden Amtrs ('A'), Long Riston, Market Weighton Utd ('A'), North Newbald, Skidby Millers.

LINLEY HAULAGE
KINGSTON-UPON-HULL SUNDAY LEAGUE **FOUNDED:** 1951

PREM. DIV.	P	W	D	L	F	A	PTS
B & A Scaffolding	20	16	4	0	62	18	36
Brighams	20	15	2	3	56	29	32
New Inn	20	11	5	4	46	25	27
Chalk Lane	20	11	4	5	61	29	26
Swanfield	20	11	2	7	48	33	24
Northwood	20	7	3	10	30	42	17
Viking	20	5	5	10	35	44	15
Settingdyke YC	20	5	5	10	35	55	15
St Peters	20	5	3	12	26	52	13
Lord Nelson	20	3	4	13	18	53	10
Keyingham	20	1	3	16	25	62	5

Lower Division Champions:
Div. 1 (12): W Simpsons
Div. 2 (11): West Lee Youth Club
Div. 3 (10): Chalk Lane 'B'
Div. 4 (12): Malet Uni Flo
Div. 5 (12): Falcon
Div. 6 (12): Cottingham
Div. 7 (12): Gower Rangers
Div. 8 (12): Newbridge Carpets
Div. 9 (12): Lambwath Juventus
Div. 10 (11): Holderness Casuals
Div. 11 (12): Stadium Developments
Div. 12 (12): Craven
Div. 13 (12): AFC Randles
Div. 14 (12): Elloughton
Div. 15 (12): Skippers
Div. 16 (12): City Ensign
Div. 17 (12): Waterloo Rangers
Div. 18 (11): Priory Rangers
Div. 19 (12): Appollo
Div. 20 (11): FC Hudsons

Cup Winners:
'Munro' Senior Cup: Swanfield
'Hostick' Intermediate Cup: Mill Lane Utd
'Halford' Intermediate Cup: AFC Randles
'Linley Haulage' Junior Cup: Skippers

Sporting Award: Bilton Vipers (Div. 9)

ENGLISH SCHOOLS F.A.

Chief Executive: M R Berry, 4a Eastgate St., Stafford ST16 2NQ (0785 51142).

Contributor to Non-League Directory: Mike Simmonds, 19 The Spinney, Bulcote, Burton Joyce, Nottingham NG14 5GX (0602 313299).

THE INTERNATIONAL SEASON - Under 18

The England Schools Under 18 squad, chosen as it is from the relatively small percentage of population still in full-time education, had another good season, bearing in mind that five of the six opponents choose from the whole age cohort and frequently field young professional players.

The highlight was undoubtedly the match against Holland at Carrow Road, Norwich, when the visitors fielded their full Youth side preparing for their UEFA campaign. Goals from Lester and Bates, and an excellent defensive display, brought England a 2-1 victory. The squad also retained the Centenary Shield, played this season in Berne, with 3-0 successes against both Wales and Switzerland, and will be hoping for a hat-trick when the tournament is staged in England in 1994-95.

The Under 18's broke new ground with their tour to Austria and Slovakia. A 1-1 draw with the former was well deserved, but against Slovakia England never recovered from the shock of conceding a first minute goal and could not match a team containing several players appearing regularly in the country's professional League.

RESULTS

ENGLAND 1 *(Stevens(p))*, FRANCE 2
(at Gillingham FC, 2nd March)

ENGLAND 3 *(Lester(2), Stevens(p))*, WALES 0
(Centenary Shield, in Berne, 27th March)

SWITZERLAND 0, ENGLAND 3 *(Smith, Lester, Stevens(p))*
(Centenary Shield, in Berne, 31st March)

AUSTRIA 1, ENGLAND 1 *(Bates)*
(in Gloggnitz, 19th April)

SLOVAKIA 4, ENGLAND 0
(in Bratislava, 21st April)

ENGLAND 2 *(Lester, Bates*, HOLLAND 1
(at Norwich City FC, 3rd May)

APPEARANCES

Kelvin Arterton (Kent) 3
Lee Crane (Cambridgeshire) 3
Paul Bates - Captain (Kent) 6
Mark Scott (Durham) 6
Andrew Duncan (Durham) 5 (+ 1 sub)
David Challinor (Cheshire) 6
Dean Smith (Northumberland) 6
Mark Pinch (Sussex) 6
Jack Lester (South Yorkshire 6
Jamie Waters (Wiltshire) 3 (+2)
Richard Fidler (South Yorkshire 2 (+4)
Shaun Stevens (Berkshire) 5 (+1)
Sam Aiston (Northumberland) 4 (+2)
Matthew Taylor (Devon) 1 (+3)
Robert Gough (Devon) 3 (+2)
Dale Band (Cornwall) 1 (+3)

CENTENARY SHIELD

	P	W	D	L	F	A	PTS
England	2	2	0	0	6	0	4
Wales	2	1	0	1	1	3	2
Switzerland	2	0	0	2	0	4	0

GOALS

Lester 4
Stevens 3 (3 penalties)
Bates 2
Smith 1

England Schools' Under 18 Squad 1993-94. Back Row (L/R): Frank Melia (Physio), Mark Scott, Sam Aiston, Dean Smith, Lee Crane, Peter Amos (Manager), Kelvin Arterton, Andrew Duncan, David Challinor, Shaun Stevens, Paul Brackwell (Assistant Manager). Front: Paul Bates, Dale Band, Robert Gough, Richard Fidler, Mark Pinch, Jack Lester, Matthew Taylor, Jamie Waters.

THE INTERNATIONAL SEASON - Under 15

The England Schools' international side had a record-breaking season, becoming the first team to win all their games since the international season was extended beyond the Home Countries 38 years ago. Not only did this mean that they regained the Victory Shield, the Home International Championship, but also won both their matches in Germany for the first time and completed a Wembley 'double' - something which had not happened since 1988.

The season began with two victories over Wales and Northern Ireland but, in view of past records, that was to be expected. A comforable 3-0 win over Switzerland still did not satisfy the doubters but, when a 1-0 success in Holland was followed by a similar scoreline to clinch the Victory Shield in Scotland, they began to change their tune. They were eventually convinced when, after 14 visits, England won both matches in Germany, a 3-2 win in front of 65,000 at the Olympic Stadium in Berlin being followed by an easier success at Cottbus in the former East Germany.

Anti-climax seemed possible when Massac put France 1-0 ahead in the final match at Wembley. Although Bunn equalised soon after the interval, the chance of a 100% record seemed to be slipping away until, in the last minute, to the delight of the squad and supporters, Mark Platts curled in a 25 yard free-kick for the winner.

RESULTS

ENGLAND 2 *(Brach(2))*, WALES 0
(Victory Shield, at Coventry C. FC, 11th Feb.)

ENGLAND 5 *(Branch(2), Wilson(2), Marshall)*, NORTHERN IRELAND 1
(Victory Shield, at Sunderland FC, 25th Feb.)

ENGLAND 3 *(Gower(2), Wilson)*, SWITZERLAND 0
(Walkers Crisps Cup, at Wembley 12th March)

HOLLAND 0, ENGLAND 1 *(Gower)*
(in Appingedam, 9th April)

SCOTLAND 0, ENGLAND 1
(Victory Shield, in Cumbernauld, 5th May)

GERMANY 2, ENGLAND 3 *(Gower, Bunn, Wilson)*
(in Berlin, 17th May)

GERMANY 1, ENGLAND 3 *(Branch, Wilson, Gower)*
(in Cottbus, 19th May)

ENGLAND 2 *(Bunn, Platts)*, FRANCE 1
(Walker Crisps Int. Shield, at Wembley, 11th June)

VICTORY SHIELD

	P	W	D	L	F	A	PTS
England	3	3	0	0	8	1	6
Northern Ireland	3	2	0	1	4	6	4
Scotland	3	1	0	2	3	3	2
Wales	3	0	0	3	0	5	0

APPEARANCES

Luke Weaver (Barnet SFA) 5
John O'Toole (Sefton/FA School) 3
Elliott Dickman (Derwentside/FA School) 6 (+1)
Neil Clement (Solihull/FA School) 8
John Curtis - Captain (Nuneaton/FA School) 8
Mark Perry (Ealing SFA) 6 (+1)
Luke Staton (Worksop & Retford) 5
Mark Gower (Havering/FA School) 8
John Marshall (Bournemouth/FA School) 7
Mark Platts (Sheffield SFA) 8
Mark Wilson (Scunthorpe/FA School) 4 (+3)
Michael Branch (Liverpool/FA School) 8
Thomas Culshaw (Liverpool/FA School) 3 (+2)
Jody Morris (Surrey/FA School) 3 (+2)
Andrew Sullivan (Aldershot SFA) 1 (+4)
James Bunn (Enfield SFA) 4 (+3)

GOALS:

Lester 4, Wilson 5, Branch 5, Gower 5, Bunn 3, Marshall 1, Platts 1

Below: *England Schools' Under 15 Squad 1993-94. Back Row (L/R): Andrew Sullivan, Elliott Dickman, Mark Wilson, John Owens (Manager), Mike Dickinson (Physio), Mark Perry, Mark Platts. Centre: Jody Morris, Michael Branch, James Bunn, Thomas Culshaw, Steve Avory (Manager), John Marshall, Mark Gower, Neil Clement. Front: John O'Toole, John Curtis (Captain), Tony Cryer (Chairman), Luke Staton, Luke Weaver.*

English Schools' F.A. British Gas Trophy 1993-94

First Leg	Second Leg
27th April, at Ashton United FC	7th May, Sheffield United FC
Tameside 1-1 Sheffield	Sheffield 3-0 Tameside

Sheffield won 3-1 on aggregate.

Sheffield's victory in the premier schools' competition was their ninth since it began in 1905 and conslidated their hold on second place in the overall honours' list behind Liverpool.

Their win was not without its problems as Tameside, in uncharted waters as they had never previously progressed beyond the last eight, defended capably in the first-leg and then went ahead with five minutes remaining. Well marshalled by Steven Morris, they restricted Sheffield to few chances, and when the visitors lost their England striker, Mark Platts, through injury, they must have feared the worst. Five minutes from time, this was confirmed when David Wills broke clear on the right and his good cross was swept in by Chris Woods to give Tameside their narrow first-leg advantage.

The return match at Bramall Lane could have resembled a "wake" as Sheffield United had been relegated from the Premier League earlier that day. The city's schools' side provided some consolation as first Carl Smith equalised midway through the first-half, and then-second half efforts from captain David Capper and Mark Platts brought them their 3-1 aggregate victory.

Sheffield's route to the final

Round 1	Bye		
Round 2	Wakefield	(H)	9-0
Round 3	Blackburn	(H)	3-1
Round 4	West Tyne	(H)	6-0
Round 5	E. Northumberland	(H)	4-3
Round 6	North Leicestershire	(H)	5-0
S-Final	Bradford	(A)	1-0

Tameside's route to the final

Round 1	Mid-Cheshire	(A)	9-1
Round 2	Preston	(H)	7-1
Round 3	Coventry	(A)	4-2
Round 4	Nottingham	(H)	2-1
Round 5	Manchester	(A)	3-0
Round 6	Basildon	(H)	1-1
Replay	Basildon	(A)	3-2
S-Final	Cambridge	(H)	1-0

Winners Sheffield Schools' FA (above) and runners-up Tameside SFA (below). *Photos - Ron Lane.*

E.S.F.A. ADIDAS COUNTY CHAMPIONSHIPS

Apart from the two international sides, the two national County Championships provide the highest level of schools' football for the best players in the country. Both are sponsored by Adidas and organised in a similar way with Regional winners meeting in the national stages. The only difference between the Under 19 and the Under 16 Championships is that the latter spreads over two seasons.

E.S.F.A. ADIDAS UNDER-19 COUNTY CHAMPIONSHIP

Final

14th May, at Wigan Athletic FC

Middlesex 2-0 Merseyside

Middlesex Squad: Simon Hughes, Darren Hendy, Robert Thomas, Paul Hammett, Paul Page, Michael Shaw, Peter Sogbodjor, Kieron Gallagher, Daniel Abela, Gary Boreham, Joe House, Ben Hodson, Danny Draper, Rene Street, Daniel Oriot, Jon Campbell, Alex Pinket.

Merseyside Squad: John Carriage, Colin O'Donnell, Ian Milby, Neil Davies, Peter Spellman, Joe Donnelly, Vincent O'Brien, Adam Williams, Chris Rimmer, Eddie McCullough, Joe Dunford, Phil Cantwell, Stephem Hughes, Carl Tierney, Stephen Sullivan, Leigh Williams.

Middlesex's route to the final

	Surrey	(A) 2-0
	Sussex	(H) 2-0
	Inner London - *awarded match*	
Reg. Final	Bedfordshire	2-1
Nat. SF	West Midlands	3-1

Merseyside's route to the final

	Cheshire	(H) 1-0
	Cheshire	(A) 2-0
	Gtr Manchester	(H) 1-2
	Gtr Manchester	(A) 3-0
	Lancashire	(H) 3-3
	Lancashire	(A) 2-3
Reg. Final	South Yorkshire	(A) 2-0
Nat. SF	Devon	(H) 2-0

Middlesex - ESFA Adidas under-19 County Champions 1993-94. Back Row (L/R): R Page, I Bath (Manager), D Draper, R Street, A Pinket, J Campbell, B Hodson, S Hughes, P Page, J House, A Peel, O Williams. Front: P Sogbodjor, D Abela, P Hammett, K Gallagher, G Boreham, R Thomas, D Henry, M Shaw, D Oriot.

E.S.F.A. ADIDAS UNDER-16 COUNTY CHAMPIONSHIP

Final

10th November, at Southend United FC

Esssex 2-1 Nottinghamshire

Essex, making their seventh appearance in the final in the eleven years of the competition's existence, won the trophy for the fourth time. Nottinghamshire, making their first-ever appearance in at national final, took the lead after 30 minutes through Ian Robinson, but two goals from England Schools' under-15 international Lee Hodges gave Essex a 2-1 half-time lead which they held throughout a goalless second period.

Essex's route to the final

	Middlesex	(H) 5-0
	Kent	(H) 2-0
	Surrey	(A) 4-0
	Sussex	(H) 3-1
	Buckinghamshire	(A) 7-2
SE Co's SF	Hertfordshire	(H) 2-1
SE Co's F	Inner London	(A) 3-3
Replay	Inner London	(H) 1-0
Nat. SF	Merseyside	(H) 4-2

Nottinghamshire's route to the final

	Lincolnshire	(H) 7-0
	Humberside	(H) 3-1
	Northamptonshire	(A) 1-0
	Leicestershire	(H) 1-1
	Derbyshire	(A) 0-3
Mids SF	Staffordshire	(H) 2-1
Mids Final	Leicestershire	(A) 4-0
Nat. SF	Devon	(A) 2-0

E.S.F.A. Individual Schools' Competitions 1993-94

Individual schools competitions at local and county level provide the 'grass roots' football for an estimated 250,000 players involved in English Schools' FA activities throughout the season. Four of these are continued at national level to produce a national champion.

English Schools' Mars Under 19 Championship

Chesterfield Col. (Derbyshire) 1-1 South-East 6th Form Col., Benfleet (Essex).
Played at Chesterfield FC, May 16th

The Mars Trophy was shared for the second season in a row after this 1-1 draw in a match which came to an exciting second-half climax. Sean Lowe put the home side ahead after ten minutes when he headed in a long throw from his captain Craig Myhill. South-East Essex mounted a strong second-half rally and it was no more than they deserved when Neil Harris hooked in a volley with 15 minutes remaining. Both sides went close to a winner, but a shared Trophy was probably the best outcome.

ROUTES TO THE FINAL

Chesterfield College

Rd 1 v Barnsley Col. (S Yorks)	(A) 1-1
Replay	(H) 2-1
Rd 2 v Jack Hunt Sch., Peterboro.	(A) 4-2
Rd 3 v Telford Col. (Shropshire)	(H) 2-0
Rd 4 v De la Salle High Sch.,	(H) 0-0
Replay Liverpool	(A) 4-3(aet)
Semi-final v Longlands Col., Middlesbrough	(H) 2-2
Replay	(A) 6-4

S E Essex 6th Form College

Rd 1 v St Dominic's, Harrow	(A) 5-0
Rd 2 v Hemel Hempstead School	(A) 3-0
Rd 3 v Wilson's GS, Wallington	(A) 5-2
Rd 4 v Vandyke Upper Sch., L.Buzzard	(A) 3-1
Semi-final v Eastbourne 6th Form College	(H) 2-0

English Schools' Under 16 Championship

Barking Abbey School (Essex) 2-2 St Theodore's School, Burnley (Lancs)
Played at Dagenham & Redbridge FC, May 7th

Barking Abbey became the third Essex School in twenty years to win the under-16 Individual Schools' final. A fine all-round side which conceded only two goals, scoring fourteen, en route to the final, Barking Abbey, after a slow start, controlled the game scoring two second-half goals through Terry May and Matthew Bird.

Barking Abbey School

Rd 1 v Mildenhall School	(A) 2-0
Rd 2 v Hewett Sch. (Norfolk)	(A) 3-0
Rd 3 v Denefield (Berks)	(A) 4-0
Rd 4 v Hazelwich (Sussex)	(H) 2-0
S-f v Brampton Mnr (Essex)	(H) 3-2

St Theodore's RC School

Rd 1 v Cockermouth (Cumbria)	(A) 4-1
Rd 2 v Houghton Kepier (Durham)	(A) 2-0
Rd 3 v Brinsworth (Sth Yorks)	(H) 2-1
Rd 4 v Campion High (Merseyside)	(A) 3-3
Replay	(A) 1-1(4-3 on penalties)
S-f v Shenley Court (W Mids)	(A) 2-1

English Schools' McDonalds Under 12 5-a-sides

Over 17,000 pupils took part in the McDonalds five-a-sides which reached their climax at the Aston Villa Leisure Centre on April 23rd when twelve area champions competed for the national title.

Semi-Finals

St Wilfrid's School (South Shields) 5, Windsor High School (Salford) 2
Hadrian Park Middle School (Wallsend) 4, St Augustine's School (London) 1

Final: Hadrian Park Middle School 4, St Wilfrid's School 1

English Schools' Monster Munch Cup (Under 11, 6-a-side)

The four sides which competed at Wembley in the semi-finals and final of the Monster Munch Cup were the survivors of over 8,000 schools who set out on the road to the national stadium in September.

Final: Cavendish Primary School, Hull 4, Howard Middle School, Bury St Edmunds 1
3rd/4th Play-off: Courthouse Junior Sch. (Maidenhead) 2, Thorp Hesly Junior School (Rotherham) 1

English Schools' Monster Munch 'Sevens'

The semi-finals and final of this new competition for Primary representative sides took place at Wembley Stadium on 12th March.

Semi-Finals: Newbury 3, Derby 0 — Liverpool 3, Tower Hamlets 0

Final: Liverpool 1, Newbury 0 — **3rd/4th Play-off:** Derby 1, Tower Hamlets 0

NON-LEAGUE FOOTBALL RESULTS MAGAZINE

The Country's Longest Running National Non-League Football Monthly Magazine

Nearing its Fifteenth Year, BNLF is by far the most established and up to-date for Tables and Results each month covering the whole of the non-league Pyramid, including Scotland & Wales. Continually published since 1981 it has proven track record second to none Regularly features over 50/60 Tables, All the COUNTY FA SENIOR CUP draws & results, plus regular up-dates & news snippets.

INCLUDING ALL THE F A CUP, TROPHY & VASE, SCOTTISH JUNIOR CUP, WELSH CUP & TROPHY, DRAWS & RESULTS THROUGHOUT THE SEASON

MIDLANDS / SOUTH WEST / NORTH EAST
SOUTH EAST / NORTH WEST

Are You Missing Out ?
Stay on the Ball with The BNLF. 1994-95 Subscription £16-00

August to June Inc. Start your subscription when you like, The seasons back issues available if required.

Previous Seasons issues also available - Send your Name & address Now To;-

THE BUREAU OF NON-LEAGUE FOOTBALL
173,LEYTONSTONE ROAD,LONDON, E15 1LH.

FOUNDED 1882

ESSEX F.A.

Secretary: T Alexander,
31 Mildmay Rd, Chelmsford CM2 0DN (0245 357727)

SENIOR CUP

First Round

Dagenham & Redbridge v Collier Row	6-4
Hornchurch v Rainham Town	3-2
Aveley v Colchester United	6-1
Purfleet v Heybridge Swifts	1-4
Witham Town v Southend United	1-6
Barking v Tilbury	1-2

Second Round

Braintree Town v Chelmsford City	1-1,0-2
Southend United v Heybridge Swifts	2-1
Wivenhoe Town v Billericay Town	0-5
Leyton Orient v Tilbury	2-1
Harlow Town v Hornchurch	2-0
Saffron Walden v Aveley	3-0*(Saffron Walden expelled)*
East Thurrock United v Leyton	2-4
Dagenham & Redbridge v Grays Athletic	1-3

Quarter-Finals

Aveley v Chelmsford City	3-5*(aet)*
Leyton v Southend United	7-0
Harlow Town v Grays Athletic	1-3
Leyton Orient v Billericay Town	1-2

Semi-Finals

Billericay Town v Chelmsford City	2-1
Grays Athletic v Leyton	2-1

Final *(at Dagenham & Redbridge FC, Mon 25th April)*: Grays Athletic 1, Billericay Town 0

SENIOR TROPHY

First Round

Barkingside v Clacton Town	1-4
Basildon United v Stansted	1-0
Halstead Town v Romford	5-0
Tiptree United v Hullbridge Sports	3-2
Bowers United v Eton Manor	1-0
Stanway Rvrs v Brightlingsea Utd	1-1*(aet)*,3-1
Maldon Town v Brentwood	0-1

Second Round

Bowers United v Southend Manor	5-2
Canvey Island v Basildon United	1-0
Halstead Town v Clacton Town	2-1
Concord Rangers v Brentwood	1-3*(ae)*
Harwich & Parkeston v Gt Wakering R.	2-2*(aet)*,4-2
East Ham United v Tiptree United	0-2
Walthamstow Pennant v Stanway Rovers	2-1
Ford United v Burnham Ramblers	3-0

Quarter-Finals

Bowers United v Halstead Town	0-4
Walthamstow Pen. *(scr)* Harwich & Parkeston	*(w/o)*
Tiptree United v Ford United	2-4
Canvey Island v Brentwood *(at Brentwood)*	4-2

Semi-Finals

Canvey Island v Harwich & Parkeston	2-0
Halstead Town v Ford United	4-2

Final *(At Braintree Town FC, Tues 19th April)*: Halstead Town 2, Canvey Island 0

OTHER COUNTY FINALS:

Intermediate Cup *(11/4/94)*: Kelvedon Hatch 2, South Woodham Ferrers 1

Victorious Kelvedon Hatch players, led by captain Brian Powell (right), receive the Essex Intermediate Cup. Photo - Richard Brock.

ESSEX THAMES-SIDE

CHALLENGE TROPHY

There were two withdrawals for season 1993/94 viz Purleet and Eton Manor, the latter following their loss of senior status, and we welcomed four clubs - Barking, Bowers United, East Thurrock United and Romford - into the Competition. East Thurrock and Barking actually drew each other in the First Round, the men from Corringham being victorious after extra-time, and the other matches in this Round produced victories for Walthamstow Pennant, Canvey Island and Aveley, who had an excellent 5-3 away victory over Southend Manor with Jimmy Ablitt notching a hat-trick for the Millers.

First Round

Walthamstow Pennant 2, Burnham Rambers 0
East Thurrock Utd 2, Barking 1 *(aet)*
Canvey Island 2, Bowers United 0
Southend Manor 3, Aveley 5

The Second Round saw these four winners joined by the remaining twelve clubs including the holders, Leyton, and last year's runners-up Rainham Town. The latter narrowly lost at home to Aveley whilst Leyton crashed out of the Competition losing 4-3 on penalties at Basildon United, this after 120 minutes football had produced one goal and a host of near misses apiece. The other two "Diadora League" versus "Essex Senior League" ties saw honours even, Grays winning an excellent match at Romford by 3-1 whilst Ford United were victorious by the same score after extra-time at hosts Tilbury. Both London Spartan League clubs bowed out of this season's competition in this round, Barkingside losing narrowly 2-1 at home to East Thurrock, whilst Walthamstow Pennant lost 5-0 at Canvey Island after extra-time. Andy Jones netted four goals for the Islanders, this after the first 90 minutes had failed to produce any score! Another amazing scoreline was recorded at Billericay Town where the home side beat Chelmsford City 9-1, Steve Warner bagging a hat-trick. The remaining fixture of the round produced a match typical of the Competition with Hornchurch finally overcoming neighbours Collier Row 4-3 after 90 exhilerating minutes of cup-tie football.

Second Round

Rainham Town 0, Aveley 1
Basildon Utd 1, Leyton 1 *(4-3 on penalties)*
Hornchurch 4, Collier Row 3
Canvey Island 5, Walthamstow Pennant 0 *(aet)*
Romford 1, Grays Athletic 3
Billericay Town 9, Chelmsford City 1
Tilbury 1, Ford United 3 *(aet)*
Barkingside 1, East Thurrock United 2

The four Quarter-Finals were all closely fought matches as might be expected. Grays Athletic needed an extra half an hour before overcoming Hornchurch by a single goal, whilst old adversaries Basildon United and Billericay Town clashed at Gardiners Close, the visitors making the short journey home with a 2-0 victory under their belts. The two remaining fixtures resulted in notable Diadora scalps for Canvey Island and Ford United who beat Aveley 1-0 and East Thurrock United (4-1 after extra-time) respectively.

Quarter-Finals

Hornchurch 0, Grays Athletic 1 *(aet)*
Ford United 4, East Thurrock United 1 *(aet)*
Basildon United 0, Billericay Town 2
Aveley 0, Canvey Island 1

A place in the final for an ESL club was guaranteed when the Semi-Final draw paired Canvey Island with Ford United and the two remaining Diadora sides, Billericay Town and Grays Athletic, together. Once again two closely fought matches ensued, with Canvey Island eventually overcoming Ford United with two second-half goals, and Grays triumphant at Billericay by the odd goal in three - ironically an own goal.

Semi-Finals

Canvey Island 2, Ford United 0
Billericay Town 1, Grays Athletic 2

The Competition records of the two finalists could not have been more different. Grays Athletic were competing in their sixth final in ten years, winning on three occasions (1988, 1989 and 1991) to add to their earlier victories in 1948 and 1981. Canvey Island on the other hand were in their first final, having entered the competition for the first time in 1987, their previous best being a Semi-Final place in season 1991/92. Irrespective of who won, both clubs had already achieved notable feats with Canvey Island battling through from the First Round and Grays reaching the final despite being drawn away from home in every round (including, of course, the final!)

The final tie at Canvey Island was played on the eve of the FA Cup Final, and a crowd of over 600 saw the home side take a deserved two goal first-half advantage before the visitors showed their power and experience battling back to level matters and take the match into extra-time. The extra 30 minutes was end-to-end stuff with many exciting moments but sadly no goals and so we proceeded to the dreaded penalty shoot-out. Grays' hopes of adding the Thames-side Trophy to the Essex Senior Cup they had already won were severely dented when they missed both their opening kicks and, although Canvey also missed a kick, it seemed inevitable that Andy Jones, the leading scorer in the Competition with 6 goals, in true "Roy of the Rovers" fashion, should be left with the task of winning the trophy for the minnows, which he duly did.

Dave Bowman, Secretary

Final *(at Canvey Island FC, Fri 13th May)*

Canvey Island 2, Grays Athletic 2
(Canvey Island won 4-3 on penalties)

ESSEX INTERMEDIATE LEAGUE

FOUNDED:
1966 (as the Essex Olympian League)

President: P K Byford

Chairman: C W Rand

Hon. Secretary: R F Hurrell, 102 Falmouth Road, Springfield, Chelmsford, CM1 5JA (0245 256922)

The season was dominated by two clubs who took the majority of the honours available to them. Firstly, our congratulations to Kelvedon Hatch for achieving the highest accolade at our level by winning the Essex Intermediate Cup over another of our clubs, South Woodham Ferrers, who with Writtle and Rayleigh Town made up the Semi-Finals; for the first time, all four clubs represented came from the same League. We also had Hatfield Peverel and SC Henderson in the Quarter-Finals.

Kelvedon Hatch also achieved our Senior Division One Championship for the first time, having been runners-up on two previous occasions, but lost their hold on the Senior Division's Cup to Writtle. Not to be outdone, their Reserve team won a close match over Barnston in the Reserve Divisions Cup Final. Congraulations also to Writtle who having reached the Semi-Final of the Essex Intermediate Cup reversed the tables and won the Senior Division Cup for the first time since appearing as runners-ups in our first ever Cup Final in 1967 and again in 1973. They also finished runners-up in Senior Division One and won the Bill Spurgeon Cup in another close game with Hatfield Peverel. Their Reserves reached the final of the Essex Junior Cup, narrowly losing on penalties, but with excellent consistency retained the Reserve Division One Championship.

After two seasons, Takeley returned to Senior Division One as Champions of Senior Division Two accompanied by still-climbing Broomfield who have made the jump form 3rd to 1st Divisions in consecutive seasons. Ongar Town picked themselves up after 3 seasons in Division 3 to become Champions and, in only their 2nd season with us Clavering, gain promotion as runners-up.

South Woodham Ferrers continued their progress after the previous season's Reserve Division 2 championship by finishing runners-up in Reserve Division 1; an excellent performance. Clavering Reserves have accomplished the same success as Broomfield as, after promotion last season, they are champions of Reserve Division 2 moving up in consecutive years. Caribbean improved on last season to finish as Runners-up. Barnston have had their best season to date; having lost narrowly in the Reserve Cup Final they put that behind them, got the extra points from games in hand, and triumphed as Champions of Reserve Division 3, with Broomfield, not to be outdone by their seniors, gaining promotion as runners-up.

Congratulations go to Great Baddow for retaining the Burnham Charity Cup and to Herongate for their first success in the Southend Charity Shield. Our Clubs featured in many other Charity Cup Finals, but had to take second best on these occasions.

At our Annual Presentation Dinner, Bob Tyler of Barnston was a popular winner of the Clubman of the Year Award, Dave Ball of Ekco, Club Linesman of the Year, Steve Andow first recipient of the Referee of the Year Award donated by Emmelle Sports, and Stambridge Reserves won the Sportsmanship Cup. Alan Taylor of White Notley was the Leading Goalscorer of the Year

Phil Coultard, Publicity Secretary.

Writtle FC - Senior Division Cup winners 1993-94. Back Row (L/R): Phil Chript (Manager), Dave Candler, Colin Hill, Gavin Rock, Jimmy Wright, Peter Locke, Mick Clark. Front: Dean Bishop, Pip Baker, Lee Reading, Barry Roberts, Kevin Adams, John Potter.

Photo - Richard Brock.

Senior Div. 1	P	W	D	L	F	A	PTS
Kelvedon Hatch	24	17	5	2	62	21	39
Writtle	24	15	7	2	55	20	37
Standard (Harlow)	24	16	2	6	64	41	34
Hatfield Peverel	24	14	2	8	53	31	30
S Woodham Ferrers	24	10	6	8	54	51	26
Rayleigh Town	24	9	5	10	41	39	23
Herongate Ath.	24	8	5	11	23	33	21
Stambridge	24	8	3	13	33	48	19
Essex Police	24	8	3	13	35	52	19
Old Chelmsfordians	24	7	4	13	34	55	18
Benfleet	24	5	7	12	32	50	17
Harold Wood Ath.	24	5	5	14	32	53	15
Runwell Hospital	24	6	2	16	31	55	14

Senior Div. 2	P	W	D	L	F	A	PTS
Takeley	26	19	3	4	52	22	41
Broomfield	26	16	7	3	55	22	39
SC Henderson	26	17	4	5	80	37	38
Sandon Royals	26	14	8	4	56	44	36
Doddinghurst	26	12	5	9	56	44	29
B. Stfd Swifts	26	12	5	9	49	48	29
Rayleigh Athletic	26	10	7	9	54	53	27
Mountnessing	26	8	7	11	36	48	23
White Notley	26	6	9	11	32	46	21
Ekco Sports	26	9	3	14	46	62	21
Danbury Trafford	26	6	8	12	44	54	20
Barnston	26	6	5	15	38	57	17
Shell Club	26	6	4	16	31	45	16
Basildon Town	26	3	3	20	35	89	9

Senior Div. 3	P	W	D	L	F	A	PTS
Ongar Town	22	18	1	3	89	20	37
Clavering	22	18	2	4	59	30	34
Springfield	22	14	4	4	60	37	32
Hutton	22	12	6	4	62	20	30
Caribbean IS	22	10	5	7	50	37	25
Great Baddow	22	7	9	6	50	38	23
AFC Cressing	22	7	3	12	60	54	17
Ramsden	22	7	3	12	44	54	17
Galleywood	22	7	3	12	37	67	17
Eppingsale	22	5	3	14	30	67	13
Brentwood Manor	22	4	2	16	23	61	10
Upminster	22	4	1	17	32	103	9

Reserve Div. 1	P	W	D	L	F	A	PTS
Writtle Res	24	18	3	3	69	22	39
SW Ferrers Res	24	16	5	3	54	23	37
O Chelms. Res	24	14	4	6	55	29	32
Herongate Res	24	14	4	6	56	32	32
Sandon Ryls Res	24	12	3	9	46	35	27
Kelvedon H. Res	24	10	7	7	39	35	27
Stanard (H) Res	23	11	4	8	64	38	26
Benfleet Res	24	7	8	9	30	35	22
Rayleigh T. Res	23	9	3	11	32	34	21
Harold Wd A. Res	24	6	6	12	37	40	18
Runwell H. Res	24	5	3	16	26	67	13
Shell Club Res	24	4	1	19	21	70	9
Takeley Res	24	3	1	20	26	96	7

Reserve Div. 2	P	W	D	L	F	A	PTS
Clavering Res	22	17	2	3	58	26	36
Caribbean Res	22	16	1	5	56	30	33
Springfield Res	22	12	4	6	40	29	28
BS Swifts Res	22	10	6	6	45	28	26
SC Henderson Res	22	10	5	7	46	37	25
Essex Police Res	22	10	2	10	41	37	22
Mountnessing Res	22	9	1	12	40	48	19
Ramsden Res	22	8	2	12	32	40	18
Ekco Spts Res	22	7	3	12	37	46	17
Dod'hurst Res.	22	7	3	12	34	51	17
Brentwood M. Res	22	6	3	13	37	43	15
Stambridge Res	22	2	4	16	18	69	8

Reserve Div. 3	P	W	D	L	F	A	PTS
Barnston AFC Res	26	17	5	4	71	33	39
Broomfield Res	26	17	5	4	71	37	39
White Notley Res	26	16	4	6	72	46	36
Hatfield P. Res	26	13	7	6	55	37	33
Galleywood Res	26	14	3	9	48	38	31
AFC Cressing Res	26	14	2	10	68	56	30
Hutton Res	26	11	8	7	49	47	30
Ongar Town Res	26	10	3	13	52	49	23
Rayleigh Ath. Res	26	9	4	13	40	45	22
Eppingsale Res	26	10	2	14	46	62	22
D. Trafford Res	26	9	2	15	47	60	20
Basildon T. Res	26	6	5	15	41	61	17
Upminster Res	26	4	3	19	45	89	11
Gt Baddow Res	26	5	1	20	40	75	11

SENIOR DIV. 1 RESULTS	1	2	3	4	5	6	7	8	9	10	11	12	13
1. Benfleet	*	1-1	3-2	1-1	0-2	0-2	4-4	0-3	0-0	1-2	1-2	3-2	3-3
2. Essex Police	2-1	*	4-0	1-0	1-1	1-4	0-3	1-3	4-3	7-2	1-1	1-3	1-4
3. Harold Wood Athletic	2-2	2-1	*	2-1	0-0	0-4	2-4	3-2	1-1	1-2	3-0	1-2	1-5
4. Hatfield Peverell	2-0	3-0	4-2	*	1-0	4-0	4-1	1-0	5-3	1-3	3-1	7-2	0-1
5. Herongate Athletic	2-2	0-2	1-0	0-1	*	0-1	2-1	1-0	2-3	3-2	2-3	1-0	0-1
6. Kelvedon Hatch	4-1	3-0	3-0	3-0	3-0	*	3-1	3-0	2-1	2-2	3-1	4-0	0-0
7. Old Chelmsfordians	1-0	4-1	1-3	0-4	0-0	0-4	*	0-4	2-0	2-5	0-0	1-1	1-7
8. Rayleigh Town	3-2	3-1	3-3	1-0	1-2	1-3	1-2	*	3-2	1-1	0-0	0-1	1-1
9. Runwell Hospital	0-1	0-1	2-1	0-3	1-2	2-1	3-2	0-2	*	2-4	0-2	0-2	1-5
10. South Woodham Ferrers	6-1	5-1	1-1	1-4	2-2	1-1	1-0	2-4	1-3	*	3-2	2-6	3-3
11. Stambridge	1-3	3-2	2-1	4-0	3-0	0-3	1-2	2-1	1-2	1-3	*	2-3	0-2
12. Standard (Harlow)	1-2	3-0	3-1	3-2	4-0	3-3	4-2	8-4	4-1	1-0	6-1	*	1-3
13. Writtle	2-0	0-1	2-0	2-2	1-0	3-3	1-0	0-0	4-1	1-0	4-0	0-1	*

SENIOR DIV. 2 RESULTS	1	2	3	4	5	6	7	8	9	10	11	12	13	14
1. Barnston	*	2-1	4-1	2-2	2-1	0-1	2-2	2-4	2-2	0-2	1-2	2-3	3-6	2-1
2. Basildon Town	2-3	*	1-5	0-4	0-0	2-2	4-1	3-2	3-7	0-2	3-5	1-7	0-2	0-1
3. Bishop's Stortford Swifts	2-1	3-0	*	0-0	2-1	1-2	2-5	0-0	2-1	0-3	2-1	1-1	1-2	1-1
4. Broomfield	1-1	4-0	5-2	*	2-2	1-0	3-1	0-1	8-1	0-0	3-2	2-1	0-3	4-1
5. Danbury Trafford	4-1	2-0	1-4	0-1	*	2-1,	1-3	1-1	2-4	0-3	3-2	2-4	0-1	1-1
6. Doddinghurst Olympic	0-0	6-1	4-2	0-2	2-2	*	5-1	4-2	1-3	3-3	4-1	3-4	1-0	3-0
7. Ekco Sports	4-0	5-3	1-2	1-3	1-5	2-3	*	6-2	2-1	0-3	W-L	1-6	0-2	2-0
8. Mountnessing	0-3	5-1	2-1	0-3	2-2	0-1	1-1	*	2-1	0-2	2-0	4-2	0-2	0-0
9. Rayleigh Athletic	3-1	2-2	2-3	0-0	3-2	0-2	3-1	2-2	*	4-1	1-0		2-4	2-2
10. Sandon Royals	2-1	7-3	3-3	1-3	3-3	4-3	1-1	2-0	0-0	*	2-1	2-2	2-0	4-1
11. Shell Club	2-1	3-2	2-4	0-1	2-2	1-0	2-3	0-2	0-1	0-1	*	0-0	1-2	1-1
12. Sporting Club Henderson	1-0	6-2	5-2	2-1	6-2	5-1	4-0	5-1	2-3	2-1	3-0	*	0-1	3-0
13. Takeley	4-0	4-1	0-2	1-1	2-0	2-1	W-L	3-0	2-1	3-1	1-1	2-2	*	0-2
14. White Notley	4-2	4-1	0-1	0-1	1-3	3-3	3-2	1-1	3-3	1-1	0-2	1-0	0-3	*

SENIOR DIV. 3 RESULTS	1	2	3	4	5	6	7	8	9	10	11	12
1. AFC Cressing	*	8-1	5-3	2-3	1-1	4-1	4-3	0-3	1-3	1-3	0-5	4-2
2. Brentwood Manor	3-2	*	0-1	0-4	1-1	1-3	3-0	0-1	0-4	3-0	0-1	2-2
3. Caribbean Inter Sports	2-2	3-1	*	2-3	2-1	3-0	3-3	2-2	1-3	5-1	2-0	2-0
4. Clavering	2-1	4-0	2-1	*	1-2	2-0	3-2	2-1	3-1	3-0	2-3	7-0
5. Eppingsale	2-9	3-0	1-0	0-4	*	3-2	1-1	0-6	1-8	2-3	1-3	2-3
6. Galleywood	4-0	2-1	2-5	1-0	2-1	*	0-8	1-1	0-7	2-6	1-2	1-2
7. Great Baddow	1-1	4-0	0-0	1-2	2-1	7-1	*	2-2	1-6	2-2	3-0	2-5
8. Hutton	4-1	4-0	2-0	2-2	4-1	1-2	0-0	*	2-0	6-0	1-1	7-0
9. Ongar Town	6-0	4-1	2-2	4-2	4-0	7-0	0-1	3-2	*	2-1	5-0	5-1
10. Ramsden	5-1	4-1	1-5	3-4	5-1	1-1	2-2	0-3	0-3	*	0-1	5-1
11. Springfield	3-2	6-2	4-1	1-1	5-0	4-4	2-2	3-2	0-5	2-1	*	7-0
12. Upminster	4-11	0-4	2-5	2-3	1-5	1-7	0-3	0-6	1-7	3-1	2-7	*

RESERVE DIV. 1 RESULTS	1	2	3	4	5	6	7	8	9	10	11	12	13
1. Benfleet Res.	*	0-0	2-4	2-3	0-0	1-0	1-1	2-3	1-0	2-3	1-1	2-1	5-3
2. Harold Wood Ath. Res.	1-1	*	0-0	2-3	2-1	1-1	4-0	0-0	2-0	0-1	2-3	6-3	1-4
3. Herongate Athletic Res.	1-1	4-0	*	1-0	5-1	4-0	2-0	4-3	4-1	0-0	2-0	W-L	0-1
4. Kelvedon Hatch Res.	0-3	2-2	3-1	*	1-1	1-0	1-3	1-4	7-1	3-1	1-2	W-L	1-3
5. Old Chelmsfordians Res.	0-2	4-2	2-1	2-2	*	5-3	7-0	2-1	1-0	1-2	3-2	2-1	2-0
6. Rayleigh Town Res.	0-0	3-2	2-3	2-1	2-1	*	1-0	2-0	1-0	L-W	0-4	5-0	1-2
7. Runwell Hospital Res.	0-1	1-0	2-4	1-1	0-5	4-2	*	0-3	1-3	0-2	0-5	5-0	2-3
8. Sandon Royals	2-1	2-0	5-0	0-3	0-1	2-1	2-2	*	6-2	0-2	2-3	4-2	0-0
9. Shell Club Reserves	0-0	1-4	1-6	L-W	0-1	0-2	0-2	0-4	*	1-3	2-1	3-1	0-6
10. Sth Woodham Ferrers Res.	2-1	2-1	2-1	0-0	1-1	3-0	7-1	L-W	6-0	*	3-3	3-2	0-1
11. Standard (Harlow) Res.	4-0	3-2	1-1	2-3	0-1		7-0	0-1	8-1	1-1	*	10-3	2-6
12. Takeley Res.	1-0	1-3	0-6	1-1	0-1	0-4	2-1	2-1	2-5	3-8	0-2	*	0-7
13. Writtle Res.	4-1	W-L	5-2	1-1	2-0	0-0	4-0	5-1	1-0	1-2	3-0	7-1	*

RESERVE DIV. 1 RESULTS	1	2	3	4	5	6	7	8	9	10	11	12
1. Bishop's Stfd Swifts Res.	*	0-0	4-2	2-3	2-0	4-1	3-1	1-1	1-0	1-1	1-1	8-0
2. Brentwood Manor Res.	2-4	*	3-6	1-3	2-3	1-1	5-1	2-4	2-5	1-2	4-1	4-1
3. Caribbean Inter Spts Res.	2-0	W-L	*	5-3	1-2	4-2	2-1	2-0	3-1	0-3	5-0	4-0
4. Clavering	1-1	2-1	1-2	*	2-1	W-L	2-1	2-0	4-2	5-1	1-0	3-2
5. Doddinghurst Res.	1-4	1-2	1-3	0-3	*	4-2	0-4	3-5	3-3	3-0	1-5	1-2
6. Ekco Sports Res.	4-1	2-1	0-2	0-4	5-0	*	0-3	0-1	4-1	0-0	3-2	1-1
7. Essex Police Res.	1-2	2-1	1-1	0-6	0-2	5-0	*	6-2	2-0	1-1	W-L	4-2
8. Mountnessing Res.	1-4	0-1	0-2	1-0	1-3	1-5	1-3	*	1-0	3-1	1-4	7-0
9. Ramsden Res.	3-0	2-3	2-0	1-2	2-2	3-1	W-L	1-4	*	0-2	3-0	W-L
10. Springfield Res.	W-L	1-0	2-3	2-3	0-1	3-2	3-1	3-0	4-1	*	2-2	5-0
11. SC Henderson Res.	1-1	2-1	4-1	2-2	1-0	4-0	4-3	4-2	2-0	2-3	*	3-1
12. Stambridge Res.	2-1	0-0	0-6	1-6	2-2	1-4	0-1	1-4	0-2	0-1	2-2	*

RESERVE DIV. 3 RESULTS	1	2	3	4	5	6	7	8	9	10	11	12	13	14
1. AFC Cressing Res.	*	0-3	3-1	1-1	5-2	5-0	1-2	5-0	2-1	0-4	1-4	1-0	5-6	3-2
2. Barnston Res.	3-2	*	2-0	0-2	0-1	2-0	3-1	3-2	0-1	5-3	3-0	3-3	8-2	1-1
3. Basildon Town Res.	1-6	1-3	*	1-5	3-1	1-3	1-2	5-0	1-1	1-2	2-2	3-4	4-3	2-4
4. Broomfield Res.	2-1	3-1	2-1	*	3-1	3-0	2-1	1-1	5-3	4-3	4-1	2-2	9-1	1-1
5. Danbury Trafford Res.	0-2	2-4	0-4	3-1	*	1-2	0-2	7-0	2-3	2-5	2-4	W-L	0-1	2-6
6. Eppingsale Res.	2-4	1-6	1-2	1-0	2-3	*	0-1	4-2	2-2	1-3	1-5	1-0	5-3	2-3
7. Galleywood Res.	0-3	2-2	4-1	0-3	3-2	3-2	*	4-0	2-1	3-3	1-0	0-1	2-2	1-0
8. Great Baddow Res.	5-7	0-3	2-0	L-W	0-2	1-3	0-4	*	4-2	0-1	4-2	L-W	2-1	0-4
9. Hatfield Peverell Res.	5-1	0-0	1-1	4-2	1-1	2-1	0-2	4-2	*	5-0	0-0	3-2	4-1	1-3
10. Hutton Res.	1-1	1-1	1-1	2-3	0-5	2-2	2-1	3-1	0-0	*	3-1	2-1	W-L	3-3
11. Ongar Town Res.	4-1	1-2	4-1	1-3	4-1	1-2	2-1	6-1	1-3	1-1	*	0-1	4-1	1-2
12. Rayleigh Athletic Res.	0-1	0-2	0-0	5-3	1-2	0-4	1-2	2-3	0-2	3-0	1-0	*	3-3	0-2
13. Upminster Res.	3-4	4-7	1-2	1-1	2-3	0-3	3-2	W-L	1-3	0-3	0-2	3-4	*	0-3
14. White Notley	4-1	0-2	4-1	1-4	2-2	5-1	3-2	W-L	1-3	2-1	7-1	3-6	6-3	*

ESSEX INTERMEDIATE LEAGUE CUP 1993-94

First Round

AFC Cressing v Stambridge	0-4	Broomfield *(w/o)* Maldon St Marys *(scr)*	
Eppingsale v Barnston	1-3	Sporting Club Henderson v Galleywood	7-0
Kelvedon Hatch v Herongate Athletic	5-4	Clavering v Great Baddow	2-1
Benfleet v Shell Club	5-2	Ongar Town v Harold Wood Athletic	1-2

Second Round

Danbury Trafford v Upminster	9-0	Ramsden v Springfield	1-0
Sandon Royals v Standard (Harlow)	1-3	Stambridge v White Notley	2-2,3-1
Broomfield v Barnston	4-1	Sporting Club Henderson v Bish. Stortford Swifts	6-2
South Woodham Ferrers v Rayleigh Town	8-1	Mountnessing v Kelvedon Hatch	0-1
Rayleigh Athletic v Hatfield Peverell	2-1	Clavering v Old Chelmsfordians	1-4
Hutton v Doddinghurst Olympic	1-3	Runwell Hospital v Benfleet	4-0
Ekco Sports v Brentwood Manor	3-2	Takeley v Basildon Town	2-2,1-2
Writtle v Harold Wood Athletic	0-0,5-1	Caribbean International Sports v Essex Police	2-3

Third Round

Danbury Trafford v Ramsden	3-4	Standard v Stambridge	1-1,0-0*(4-5 on pens)*
Broomfield v Sporting Club Henderson	0-1	South Woodham Ferrers v Kelvedon Hatch	2-3
Rayleigh Athletic v Old Chelmsfordians	0-4	Doddinghurst Olympic v Runwell Hospital	4-1
Ekco Sports v Basildon Town	6-0	Writtle v Essex Police	4-1

Quarter-Finals

Ramsden v Stambridge	2-1	Sporting Club Henderson v Kelvedon Hatch	1-3
Old Chelmsfordians v Doddinghurst Olympic	2-0	Ekco Sports v Writtle	0-4

Semi-Finals

Ramsden v Kelvedon Hatch	1-5	Old Chelmsfordians v Writtle	1-2

Final *(at Braintree Town FC, 14/4/94)*: Writtle 4, Kelvedon Hatch 2

ESSEX INTERMEDIATE RESERVES' CUP 1993-94

First Round

Broomfield Res. v Basildon Town Res.	5-3	Clavering Res. v Great Baddow Res.	8-1
Hatfield Peverell Res. v Ongar Town Res.	3-1	Barnston Res. v Ekco Sports Res.	4-0
Stambridge Res. v Old Chelmsfordians Res.	1-2	Brentwood Manor Res. v White Notley Res.	0-2
Takeley Res. v Rayleigh Athletic Res.	4-2	Caribbean Res. v South Woodham Ferrers Res.	3-2

Second Round

Essex Police Res. v Danbury Trafford Res.	7-2	Ramsden Res. v Bishop's Stfd Swifts Res.	3-2
Rayleigh Town Res. v Broomfield Res.	1-2	Clavering Res. v Hatfield Peverell Res.	2-1
Barnston Res. v Eppingsale Res.	3-0	AFC Cressing Res. v Runwell Hospital Res.	2-4
Standard Res. v Old Chelmsfordians Res.	1-0	SC Henderson Res. v White Notley Res.	4-6

(continued overleaf)

Mountessing Res. *(w/o)* Maldon St M. Res. *(scr)*		Benfleet Res. v Sandon Royals Res.	3-1
Takeley Res. v Kelvedon Hatch Res.	0-2	Upminster Res. v Galleywood Res.	2-1
Shell Club v Harold Wood Athletic Res.	3-5	Doddinghurst Res. v Caribbean IS Res.	3-0
Writtle Res. v Herongate Athletic Res.	0-1	Springfield Res. v Hutton Res.	5-2

Third Round

Ramsden Res. v Essex Police Res.	0-3	Barnston Res. v Runwell Hospital Res.	3-2
Broomfield Res. v Clavering Res.	1-2	Standard (Harlow) Res. v White Notley Res.	2-1
Mountnessing v Benfleet	1-5*(Benfleet expelled)*	Kelvedon Res. v Upminster Res.	2-0
Harold Wood Ath. Res. v Doddinghurst Res.	3-0	Herongate Athletic Res. v Springfield Res.	4-2

Quarter-Finals

Essex Police Res. v Clavering Res.	0-1	Barnston *(w/o)* Standard (Harlow) *(scr)*	
Mountnessing Res. v Kelvedon Hatch Res.	0-5	Harold Wood Ath. Res. v Herongate Athletic Res.	0-1

Semi-Finals

Barnston Res. v Clavering Res.	6-1	Kelvedon Hatch Res. v Herongate Athletic Res.	3-2

Final *(at Kelvedon Hatch FC, 27/4/94)*: Kelvedon Hatch 3, Barnston Reserves 2

SENIOR DIVISION ONE CLUBS 1994-95

BENFLEET

Chairman: M Bumpus **Manager:** D Dady.
Secretary: J Hunt, 29 Stell Ave., South Woodham Ferrers, Chelmsford CM3 5GH (0245 328622).
Ground: The Club House, Woodside Extension, Manor Rd, Benfleet, Rayleigh (0268 743957).
Colours: All sky **Change colours:** Green/black/green.

BROOMFIELD

Chairman: A Browning **Manager:** C Harrison.
Secretary: C M Blackboro, 69 Wallasea Gdns, Springfield, Chelmsford CM1 5JY (0245 251481).
Ground: The Angel Meadow, Main Road, Broomfield, Chelmsford.
Colours: Red & black stripes/black/black **Change colours:** White/black/black.

ESSEX POLICE

Chairman: J A Dickinson **Manager:** D C Murthwaite.
Secretary: K S Bevell, 68 The Fairway, Leigh-on-Sea, Essex SS9 4QS (0702 522936).
Ground: Police H.Q. (rear of Training School), Kingston Ave., Chelmsford (0245 267267).
Cols: Blue & white stripes/blue/red **Change colours:** White/blue/red.

HATFIELD PEVEREL

Chairman: R Windibank **Manager:** C Wallington.
Secretary: C L Ballard, 3 Laburnum Way, Hatfield Peverel, Chelmsford CM3 2LP (0245 380132).
Ground: Strutt Memorial Field, Maldon Road, Hatfield Peverel.
Colours: Red/black/black **Change colours:** Green/black/black.

HERONGATE ATHLETIC

Chairman: T Ardley **Manager:** R Roser.
Secretary: B Sweeting, 64 Greenshaw, Brentwood CM14 4YH (0277 218190).
Ground: Adjacent to 77 Billericay Rd, Herongate, Brentwood CM13 3PU (0277 811260).
Colours: Yellow/black/yellow **Change colours:** Red/white/white.

KELVEDON HATCH

Chairman: D L Hughes **Manager:** R Bluck.
Secretary: R Balcombe, 22 Teesdale Rd, Leytonstone, London E11 1NQ (081 989 4977).
Ground: New Hall, School Rd, Kelvedon Hatch, Brentwood CM15 0DH (0277 372153).
Colours: All red **Change colours:** All blue.

OLD CHELMSFORDIANS

Chairman: M McNally **Manager:** C Eve.
Secretary: D Chandler, 8 Trotwood Close, Chelmsford CM1 4UZ (0245 442804).
Ground: Lawford Lane, Roxwell, Chelmsford CM1 2NS (0245 420442).
Colours: Red & black stripes/black/black **Change colours:** White/black/black.

RAYLEIGH TOWN

Chairman: A G Mason **Manager:** D Clarke.
Secretary: D H Medlock, 53 Hamilton Gdns, Hockley SS5 5BX (0702 203340).
Ground: London Road, Rayleigh (0268 784001) (on north side of A129 just west of Rayleigh).
Colours: White/blue/blue **Change colours:** Blue/white/white.

SOUTH WOODHAM FERRERS UNITED

Chairman: J Oliver **Manager:** K Pope.
Secretary: J Bird, 3 Gandalfs Ride, South Woodham Ferrers, Chelmsford CM3 5WX (0245 324139).
Ground: William de Ferrers Centre, Trinity Square. **Prev. Grnd:** Saltcoats Pk, Ferrers Rd (pre-'93).
Colours: All blue **Change colours:** Red/white/red.

STAMBRIDGE

Chairman: R Shepheard **Manager:** G Hawes.
Secretary: A Hines, 62 Eanshall Ave., Prittlewell, Southend-on-Sea SS2 6NU (0702 330534).
Ground: Rochford Rd, Great Stambridge, Rochford SS4 2AX (0702 258988).
Cols: Gold (black trim)/black/gold & black **Change cols:** Blue & white stripes/black/gold & black.

STANDARD (HARLOW)

Chairman: B Rye **Manager:** P Bull.
Secretary: J Gotobed, 33 Whitewaits, Harlow CM20 3LL (0279 422799).
Ground: Standard Spts Ground, London Rd, Maypole Corner, Harlow (0279 417750).
Colours: White (green trim)/green/white **Change colours:** Green & white hoops/white/green.

TAKELEY

Chairman: M C Ellis **Manager:** S Farndon.
Secretary: P Flawn, 13 Venmore Drive, Dunmow CM6 1HN (0371 872540).
Ground: Station Road, Takeley (adjacent to old railway bridge).
Colours: Sky/black/black **Change colours:** Green & white hoops/green/green.

WRITTLE

Chairman: E R Gallacher **Manager:** P Thrift.
Secretary: S M Turner, 39 Patching Hall Lane, Chelmsford CM1 4BT (0245 354896).
Ground: Playing Fields, Paradise Rd, Writtle, Chelmsford CM1 3HW (0245 420332).
Colours: White/black/black **Change colours:** Blue/black/black.

SENIOR DIVISION TWO CLUBS 1994-95

BARNSTON A.F.C.

Chairman: R Walbanke **Manager:** W Williams
Secretary: R Tyler, 52 Watts Close, Barnston, Dunmow CM6 1LT (0371 872017).
Ground: High Easter Road, Barnston, Dumow CM6 1LZ.
Colours: All royal **Change colours:** Yellow/royal/royal.

BISHOP'S STORTFORD SWIFTS

Chairman: P J Hunt **Manager:** J Brace.
Secretary: P L Kitson, 18 Park Rd, Stansted CM24 8PB (0279 813107).
Ground: Silver Leys, Hadham Rd (A1250), Bishop's Stortford, Herts CM23 1MP (0279 658941).
Colours: All red **Change colours:** All blue.

CLAVERING

Chairman: T K Oliver **Manager:** P Isherwood.
Secretary: P A Flack, 7 Longley, Langley, Saffron Walden (0799 550428).
Ground: Jubilee Field Green, Clavering, Saffron Walden.
Colours: White (black trim)/black/black **Change colours:** Green/black/green.

DANBURY TRAFFORD

Chairman: R N Ellis **Manager:** D Chaplin.
Secretary: S A Rose, 'Shalamar', Struan Ave., Stanford-le-Hope SS17 8DG (0375 670160).
Ground: Eves Corner, Danbury, Chelmsford (0245 414515).
Colours: All royal **Change cols:** Claret (blue pin-stripe)/claret/claret

EKCO SOCIAL & SPORTS

Chairman: R E Westley **Manager:** I Ness.
Secretary: M Lupton, 105 Vardon Drive, Leigh-on-Sea SS9 3SJ (0702 715521).
Ground: Thornford Gdns, Prittlewell, Southend-on-S. (0702 351641-off., 347602-clubhouse). On A1159.
Colours: Yellow (green trim)/green/yellow **Change colours:** White (green trim)/green/yellow.

HAROLD WOOD ATHLETIC

Chairman: A Adams **Manager:** N Meekings.
Secretary: P Jones, 61 Juniper Way, Harold Wood RM3 0YQ (071 638 2323).
Ground: Harold Wood Recreation Park, Harold View, Harold Wood, Romford (0708 34882).
Colours: Claret & blue halves/claret/claret **Change colours:** White/claret/claret.

MOUNTNESSING

Chairman: D Pegram **Manager:** D Brooks.
Secretary: K Gough, 302 Roman Rd, Mountnessing, Brentwood CM15 0TZ (0277 354835).
Ground: Warley Playing Fields, The Drive, Warley, Brentwood.
Colours: Red & black stripes/black/black **Change colours:** White/black/black.

ONGAR TOWN

Chairman: R C Salmon **Manager:** T McManus.
Secretary: D V Jolly, 1 High Street, Great Bardfield CM7 4RF (0371 810897).
Ground: Love Lane Sports Ground, High Street, Ongar CM5 9BL (0277 363838).
Colours: All red **Change colours:** All blue.

RAYLEIGH ATHLETIC

Chairman: M Jupe **Manager:** P Keys.
Secretary: M Jupe, Poplar Lodge, Rayleigh Ave., Eastwood, Leigh-on-Sea SS9 3DN (0702 528136).
Ground: King George Playing Fields, Webster Way, Rayleigh SS6 8JQ.
Cols: Gold, black & white/black/black **Change colours:** Silver grey/black/black.

RUNWELL HOSPITAL

Chairman: K G Bowles **Manager:** R Saveall.
Secretary: B Hyde, 5 Redgate Close, Wickford SS11 8NG (0268 767509).
Ground: Runwell Hospital, Runwell Chase, Wickford SS11 7QE (0268 562967).
Colours: Yellow/blue/yellow **Change colours:** All green.

SANDON ROYALS

Chairman: I Marshall **Manager:** R Colman.
Secretary: D J Hamilton, 8 Douglas Close, Galleywood, Chelmsford CM2 8YD (0245 74694).
Ground: Sandon Sports Ground.
Prev. Name: Gt Baddow Ryl Engineers **Prev. Grnd:** Springfield Hall Pk, Arun Close, Springfield (pre'93)
Colours: Royal/white/royal **Change colours:** Red/white/royal.

SPORTING CLUB HENDERSONS

Chairman: A Day **Manager:** B A Smith.
Secretary: T Cooper, 62 Portchester Rd, Billericay CM12 0UQ (0277 659232).
Ground: Kenilworth Ave., Harold Park, Romford RM3 9NE (0402 342256).
Colours: White/red/red **Change colours:** Red or blue/red/red.

WHITE NOTLEY

Chairman: D Cleal **Manager:** P Reade.
Secretary: D McKinley, 2 Ridlands Close, Tye Green, Cressing, Braintree CM7 8JD (0376 348820).
Ground: Oak Road, Faulkbourne, Witham (0376 519864).
Colours: Blue/white/blue **Change colours:** White (green pinstripe)/green/green.

SENIOR DIVISION THREE CLUBS 1994-95

BASILDON TOWN

Chairman: P Cole **Manager:** T Braney.
Secretary: D Lovell, 16 Poley Rd, Stanford-le-Hope SS17 0JJ (0375 679999).
Ground: Eversley Rd Rec., Crest Avenue, Pitsea, Basildon (0268 583076).
Cols: Blue (white trim)/blue/blue **Change colours:** White (red trim)/white/red.

BRENTWOOD MANOR

Chairman: K O'Neale **Manager:** D Platt.
Secretary: C Harris, 56 Viking Way, Pilgrims Hatch, Brentwood CM14 9HY (0277 219564).
Ground: Larkins Playing Field, Ongar Road, Pilgrims Hatch, Brentwood CM15 9JB (0277 210464)
Colours: All blue **Change colours:** All amber.

(A.F.C.) CRESSING

Chairman: R Crane **Manager:** L Straiton.
Secretary: T Hammond, 125 Rayne Rd, Braintree CM7 7QD (0376 347519).
Ground: Cressing Spts & Social Club, Jeffrey Rd, Tye Green, Cressing, Braintree (0376 45521).
Cols: White/black/black (red tops) **Change colours:** Yellow/black/yellow.

EPPINGSALE

Chairman: J H Corner **Manager:** A Moretto
Secretary: I H Corner, 26 Rushkin Ave., Waltham Abbey EN9 3BP (0992 768696).
Ground: Stonards Hill P.F., Tidys Lane, Epping.
Colours: All sky **Change colours:** White/black/red.

GALLEYWOOD

Chairman: D Wilson **Manager:** D Blundell
Secretary: I M Gordon, 86 Keene Way, Galleywood, Chelmsford CM2 8NR (0245 492640).
Ground: Clarkes Field, Slades Lane, Galleywood, Chelmsford (on east side of B1007).
Colours: Orange/black/black **Change colours:** All sky.

GREAT BADDOW

Chairman: J Cooper **Manager:** J Clark.
Secretary: R W Royce, 50 Watchouse Rd, Galleywood, Chelmsford CM2 8PT (0245 264950).
Ground: Gt Baddow Rec., Baddow Rd, Chelmsford (0245 75899).
Colours: White/maroon/maroon **Change colours:** Blue/blue/white.

HUTTON

Chairman: J Hall **Manager:** P Garrett.
Secretary: L Rayner, 5 Surman Cres., Hutton, Brentwood (0277 225519).
Ground: Polo Fields, Hall Green Lane, Brentwood (0277 262257).
Colours: Yellow & green stripes/green/yellow **Change:** Red/black/red & white

ILFORD

Secretary: Michael Foley, 21 South Park Drive, Essex IG3 9AA (081 599 8950).
Ground: Cricklefield Stadium, Ilford. **Previous League:** Spartan (pre-1994).

RAMSDEN

Chairman: J Hodges **Manager:** D Moody.
Secretary: S H Howett, 63 Wainwright Ave., Hutton, Brentwood CM2 7EJ (0277 217022).
Ground: Nursery Sports Ground, Downham Rd, Ramsden Heath, Billericay.
Colours: White (maroon trim)/maroon/maroon **Change colours:** Red/white/red.

SHELL CLUB

Chairman: K Thorogood **Manager:** TBA.
Secretary: A C Gaskin, 13 Balmoral Ave., Corringham SS17 7PB (0375 641898).
Ground: Shell Club, Springhouse Rd, Corringham SS17 7QT (0375 673100).
Colours: Green & yellow/green/green **Change colours:** Blue & white/red/red.

SPRINGFIELD

Chairman: G Wilson **Manager:** C Rice.
Secretary: N Digby, 578 Linnet Drive, Tile Kiln, Chelmsford CM2 8AW (0245 350260).
Ground: Pollards Meadow, Church Lane, Springfield, Chelmsford CM1 5SF (0245 492441).
Cols: Sky (navy trim)/black/black **Change colours:** White (red trim)/red/red.

UPMINSTER

Chairman: S Hudson **Manager:** P Adams.
Secretary: J Hatton, 35 Norfolk Rd, Romford RM2 5XH (0402 442041).
Ground: Upminster Hall Playing Fields, Hall Lane, Upminster (0222 20320).
Colours: Grey/black/black **Change colours:** All red.

Reserve Division One 1994-95: Benfleet, Clavering, Harold Wood Ath., Herongate Ath., Kelvedon Hatch, Old Chelmsfordians, Rayleigh Town, Runwell Hosp., Sandon Royals, Sth Woodhams Ferrers Utd, Springfield, Standard, Writtle.
Reserve Division Two 1994-95: Barnston, Bishop's Stortford Swifts, Broomfield, Ekco, Essex Police, Mountnessing, Ramsden, Shell Club, Sporting Club Henderson, Takeley, White Notley.
Reserve Division Three 1994-95: AFC Cressing, Basildon Town, Brentwood Manor, Danbury Trafford, Eppingscale, Galleywood, Gt Baddow, Hatfield Peverel, Hutton, Ongar Town, Rayleigh Ath., Stambridge, Upminster.

PHOTOS OPPOSITE

Top: *South Woodham Ferrers United. Back Row (L/R): Kieron Smith, Kevin Bridge, Glen Melposs, Richard Farrell, Keith Pope, David Groom, Steven Hopkins, Steve Oliver, Jeremy Clayton, Paul Bowers, Fred Clayton (Joint-Manager). Front: Kevin Anderson (Manager), Wayne Palmer, Bill Glibbery, Neil Howard, Steven Cornwell, Ian Harris, Micky Dean, Keith Wallis.*

Photo - Richard Brock.

Centre: *Hutton FC.*

Photo - Gavin Ellis-Neville.

Foot: *Ilford FC, who have switched from the Spartan League*

Photo - Gavin Ellis-Neville.

SPALL

LEKO ENGINEERING

MID-ESSEX LEAGUE

PREM. DIV.	P	W	D	L	F	A	PTS
Weir House	20	17	1	2	60	24	52
Tillington Hotspur	20	14	3	3	54	16	45
Heybridge Sports	20	12	2	6	57	29	38
Boreham	20	8	5	7	44	34	29
Delafield	20	8	5	7	34	47	29
Terling Villa	20	6	6	8	33	32	24
Braintree & Bocking	20	7	3	10	42	53	24
Southminster	20	7	2	11	28	52	23
Beacon Hill Rovers	20	5	5	10	39	51	20
Writtle Victoria	20	4	3	13	28	67	15
Roxwell	20	4	1	15	31	45	13

Prem D. Cup Final: Weir House 2, Heybridge Spts 1

Dave Strachan Cup Final:
Tillingham Hotspur 6, Hullbridge Sports 'A' 2

DIV. ONE	P	W	D	L	F	A	PTS
Marconi Athletic	22	16	3	3	76	36	51
Shenfield	22	15	3	4	52	23	48
EEV	22	13	6	3	59	35	45
St Margarets	22	13	3	6	68	28	42
Estric	22	11	1	10	48	37	34
Outwood Common	22	9	4	9	41	62	31
Stock United	22	9	3	10	39	39	30
Boreham Res.	22	7	2	11	35	67	23
O Chelmsfordians 'A'	22	6	4	12	38	53	22
Writtle 'A'	22	6	3	13	32	45	21
Harold Wood	22	6	3	13	42	66	21
Burnham Rblrs 'A'	22	2	3	17	23	62	9

Div 1 Cup Final: Marconi Ath. 5, Estric 2

DIV. 2 (top two)	P	W	D	L	F	A	PTS
Shelley Royales	24	20	2	2	107	24	62
Margaretting Rvrs	24	15	5	4	73	30	50

D2 Cup Final: Margaretting R. 1, Shelley Ryls 0

DIV. 3 (top two)	P	W	D	L	F	A	PTS
Charrington Spts	20	15	4	1	60	21	49
Hullbridge Spts 'A'	20	12	3	5	53	29	39

Div 3 Cup Final: Abridge 4, Rainsford 3

DIV. 4 (top two)	P	W	D	L	F	A	PTS
Benfleet Amtrs	26	20	2	4	76	34	62
Woodham Athletic	24	19	4	3	89	27	61

D4 Cup Final: Heybridge S. Res. 4, Benfleet Amtrs 2

DIV. 5 (top two)	P	W	D	L	F	A	PTS
Tillingham H. Res.	24	19	2	3	101	31	59
Hannakins Farm	24	14	5	3	69	30	47

D5 Cup Final: Hannakins Farm, Shenfield Res.

DIV. 6 (top two)	P	W	D	L	F	A	PTS
Springfield	26	20	3	3	120	37	63
Margaretting R. Res.	26	18	4	4	93	41	58

D6 Cup Final: Springfield 4, Shelley R. Res. 0

VETERANS' DIV.	P	W	D	L	F	A	PTS
Herongate Ath.	12	12	0	0	55	4	36
Writtle Victoria	12	9	1	2	34	15	28
Hutton	12	7	1	4	41	26	22
AFC Cressing	12	5	0	7	30	44	15
Hannakins Farm	12	3	0	9	19	43	9
Shelley Royales	12	3	0	9	18	50	9
Burnham Ramblers	12	2	0	10	19	34	6

COLCHESTER & EAST ESSEX LEAGUE

PREM. DIV.	P	W	D	L	F	A	PTS
Kirby United	18	13	3	2	49	15	42
University	18	12	2	4	55	17	38
Eight-a-Green	18	12	2	4	51	30	38
Birch Park	18	11	2	5	46	21	35
Tollesbury	18	9	2	7	52	29	29
Weeley Res.	18	7	2	9	33	48	23
Nayland	18	6	5	8	38	41	20
Colchester Hotspur	18	6	0	12	28	35	18
Stoke-in-Nayland	18	6	0	12	28	60	18
Colchester Lathel	18	0	0	18	14	97	0

DIV. ONE	P	W	D	L	F	A	PTS
Feering United	22	17	2	3	68	30	53
Paxmans EE	22	14	7	1	72	31	49
Colne Engaine	22	13	4	5	43	27	43
Cosmos	22	10	5	7	49	35	35
Riverside	22	9	4	9	46	49	31
Clarendon	22	9	3	10	63	70	30
AFC Layer	22	6	9	7	48	46	27
Dragoon	22	6	8	8	49	50	26
Harwich Rangers	22	7	3	12	50	63	24
University Res.	22	5	5	12	32	54	20
Oyster	22	3	9	10	33	53	18
Little Clacton	22	2	3	17	30	71	9

DIV. TWO	P	W	D	L	F	A	PTS
West End Res.	22	15	3	4	72	40	48
Castle BB	22	13	5	4	65	42	44
Colchester Police	22	12	4	6	73	53	40
St Oysth Res.	22	11	7	4	64	50	40
Doverston	22	12	2	9	60	43	38
Foxash Social Res.	22	10	7	5	51	39	37
Royal London Res.	22	7	5	10	52	52	26
Earls Colne Res.	22	6	5	11	51	73	23
Donyland Swifts	22	6	4	12	54	65	22
Cinque Port	22	5	3	14	33	55	18
Gt Bentley Res.	22	3	8	11	35	66	17
Oyster Res.	22	4	3	15	35	71	15

DIV. THREE	P	W	D	L	F	A	PTS
White Hall	22	20	2	0	94	18	62
Ardleigh United	22	16	4	2	72	29	52
Paxmans EE Res.	22	13	6	3	52	36	45
University 'A'	22	11	1	10	57	50	34
Weeley 'A'	22	9	6	7	73	56	33
Charter House	22	8	5	9	58	62	29
Camulodunum	22	7	7	8	50	43	28
Tollesbury Res.	22	6	5	11	54	63	23
Coggeshall Res.	22	6	5	11	35	52	23
Wormingford Res.	22	5	2	15	31	61	17
Stoke-by-Nay. Res.	22	4	2	16	38	73	14
Bradfield Res.	22	2	5	15	29	84	11

DIV. FOUR	P	W	D	L	F	A	PTS
Walton Town Res.	26	19	4	3	93	30	61
Clacton Town 'A'	26	18	4	4	117	42	58
Mistley Utd 'A'	26	16	3	7	57	39	51
Cosmos Res.	26	14	4	8	84	75	46
Five Bells	26	14	2	10	70	63	44
Severalls Res.	26	13	4	9	84	59	43
Birch Park Res.	26	11	9	6	64	50	42
Mustang	26	12	4	10	72	62	40
Bures United Res.	26	9	3	14	57	58	30
Feering Utd Res.	26	8	4	14	46	75	28
Woods	26	6	5	15	62	100	23
Eigh-a-Green Res.	26	5	5	16	31	68	20
Ardleigh Utd Res.	26	5	4	17	44	83	19
Little Clacton Res.	26	3	3	20	39	99	12

THURROCK THAMES-SIDE

COMBINATION (Est: 1880s)

FINAL TABLE	P	W	L	D	F	A	PTS
New Tilbury Cal. C.	18	15	1	2	101	31	47
Flint Street Club	18	14	1	3	82	26	45
Old Kingstonians	18	12	4	2	60	25	38
Batters	18	9	5	4	50	35	31
Torchbearer	18	8	7	3	62	41	27
Cranrock Rovers	15	5	7	3	40	54	18
East Tilbury Dyn.	18	5	11	2	40	66	17
Fairmeade Ath.	17	4	13	0	26	60	12
Admiral Jellicoe	12	3	9	0	12	40	9
Exmouth United	17	0	16	1	9	97	1

League Cup: Flint Street
League Cup R-up: Batters
St John Ambulance Cup: New Tilbury Calcutta Club
St John Ambulance Cup R-up: Old Kingstonians

POPE & SMITH

CHELMSFORD SUNDAY LEAGUE

FOUNDED: 1962

PREM. DIV.	P	W	D	L	F	A	PTS
Melbourne United	20	15	1	4	46	19	31
Ongar United	20	12	4	4	52	28	28
Cherry Tree Spts	20	9	5	6	36	35	23
CKS Templar	20	8	4	8	38	38	20
Little Waltham	20	8	4	8	39	49	20
Woodham Town	20	7	5	8	39	29	19
Writtle	20	9	1	10	49	53	19
Gt Baddow Kings Hd	20	7	3	10	40	43	17
Highfield Victoria	20	5	6	9	40	43	16
Priory Sports	20	7	1	12	30	50	15
Redstones	20	5	2	13	39	61	12

Lower Division Champions:
Div. 1 (11): Danbury
Div. 2 (11): Hutton
Div. 3 (10): Westbeech Wanderers
Div. 4 (10): Worbouys
Div. 5 (10): Great Baddow Kings Head Res.
Div. 6 (10): Danbury Res.

Cup Finals:
Prem Div: Melbourne United 3, Ongar United 1
Div. 1: Danbury 4, Longmeads Manor 0
Div. 2: Hutton 1, Little Waltham Res. 0
Div. 3: Whitbread Sports 2, Writtle Res. 1
Div. 4: Worbouys 3, Nags Head Wanderers 2
Div. 5: Terling Social 1, Margaretting S & S 0
Div. 6: Chelmsford SC Res. 1, Roxwell Rvrs 0
John Coward Chal.: Melbourne U. 3, Ongar U. 2 *(aet)*
Peter Gillott Reserves' Chal.: Cherry Tree Sports Res. 3, Great Baddow Kings Head Res. 2
Charity Shield: Ongar United 5, Priory Spts 0

SMALLCOMBE SPORTS THURROCK ASSOCIATION SUNDAY LEAGUE

PREM. DIV.	P	W	D	L	F	A	PTS
Scruttons	16	13	2	1	39	9	28
Attreed Sports	16	10	1	5	28	22	21
Beechcroft	16	8	3	5	28	21	19
Stifford Clays Soc.	16	7	3	6	18	16	17
Oaks	16	7	2	7	22	26	16
Ultimate	16	5	4	7	24	28	14
Ockendon M & S	16	4	3	9	24	35	11
Worlds End	16	4	3	9	22	34	11
St Ives	16	3	1	12	18	32	7

Lower Division Champions:
Div. 1 (11): Grays Athletic Colts
Div. 2 (11): Pegasus
Div. 3 (12): Cricketers
Div. 4 (12): Belhus Park Royals
Div. 5 (12): Proctor
Div. 6 (11): Lynster

Cup Finals:
Prem. Div.: Scruttons 3, Worlds End 1
Div. 1: Belhus Park Athletic 2, Archer 1
Div. 2: Pegasus 3, Davidsons 0
Div. 3: Rabbitts 6, Fen 0
Div. 4: Belhus Park Royals 2, Woodview 1
Div. 5: Proctor 5, Shell Club 1
Div. 6: Optimist 4, Waljohns 0
Senior Benev. Cup: Scruttons 4, Worlds End 0
Junior Benev. Cup: Proctor 2, Shell Club 0

VANGE SUNDAY LEAGUE

FOUNDED: 1968

PREM. DIV.	P	W	D	L	F	A	PTS
Winston	16	12	0	4	47	22	36
Rettendon	16	11	2	3	40	14	35
C Z '81	16	9	4	3	46	21	31
Crouch Nomads	16	8	4	4	42	31	28
Scotia	16	6	4	6	35	35	22
Greeves	16	6	1	9	38	39	19
Rackets	16	4	2	10	37	54	14
Courage	16	3	4	9	29	50	13
Mopsies Park	16	1	3	12	17	65	6

Lower Division Champions:
Div. 1 (8): Tristar
Div. 2 (11): Ceekay Sports
Div. 3 (10): Proline

Cup Finals:
Challenge Cup: Winston 4, Geeves 0
Benevolent Cup: CZ '81 2, Linford Wdrs 1 *(aet)*
Prem. Div. Cup: CZ '81 4, Rettendon 0
Div. 1 Cup: Tristar 1, Linford Wanderers 0
Div. 2 Cup: Ceekay 2, Laindon 0
Div. 3 Cup: Prolines 4, Crays Hill 0
Sportsmanship Trophy: Hodgson

BARKING & DISTRICT SUNDAY LEAGUE

FOUNDED: 1971

PREM. DIV.	P	W	D	L	F	A	PTS
Byron Red Star	20	14	4	2	52	14	32
Blakehall	20	12	3	5	55	34	27
Cosmopolitan	20	12	2	6	32	20	26
Newbury Pk Rgrs	20	11	2	7	50	34	24
Southchurch Utd	20	10	4	6	42	32	24
Hornchurch Wasps	20	9	5	6	40	25	23
Morfdown Elect	20	9	2	9	33	41	20
London City	20	7	4	9	31	40	18
Fairview Rangers	20	8	0	12	41	43	16
Lakeview	20	2	2	16	35	66	6
Nightingale	20	2	0	18	18	78	4

Lower Division Champions:
Div. 1 (11): Holloway
Div. 2 (10): Warmington Rovers
Div. 3 (12): Becontree Manor

Cup Finals:
Lge Cup: Cosmopolitan 1, Byron Red Star 0 *(aet)*
Prem Div Cup: Fairview Rgrs 4, Cosmopolitan 3 *(aet)*
Div. 1 Cup: Lacey Wanderers 3, Keo 1
Div. 2 Cup: Morsefield 1, Plaistow Sporting 0
Div. 3 Cup: Rotary 4, Becontree Manor 2 *(aet)*

SOUTH ESSEX SUNDAY LEAGUE

PREM. DIV.	P	W	D	L	F	A	PTS
Rush Green SC	22	15	6	1	81	23	51
Wanstead Wandos	22	14	3	5	62	35	45
Debden Sports	19	10	5	4	54	30	35
Billet Uplands	21	10	4	7	48	43	34
Cranbrook United	19	8	6	5	54	44	30
Queens Athletic	22	8	4	10	36	40	28
LITA Sports	21	6	8	7	33	46	26
Guardian United	20	6	6	8	38	46	24
Barn Sports	20	5	8	7	32	36	23
Sentinel	22	7	2	13	43	65	23
Goldstar	22	4	3	15	28	69	15
Cricketers Hollywood	22	2	7	13	28	57	13

Lower Division Champions:
Div. 1 (10): Supra
Div. 2 (11): Glenfield
Div. 3 (13): Valetta

BOBBY SWIFT BOOKMAKERS

CLACTON & DISTRICT SUNDAY LEAGUE

FOUNDED: 1967

PREM. DIV.	P	W	D	L	F	A	PTS
Clacton Harlequins	16	13	1	2	51	16	*27
FC Spartak	16	12	2	2	65	28	26
More Sports	16	8	3	5	67	43	19
Cosmos Sporting	16	8	2	6	42	31	18
West Wing	16	6	5	5	41	45	17
Napier Royals	16	6	2	8	39	44	14
Gunfleet Old Boys	16	4	4	8	33	38	**12
Sunday Shrimpers	16	5	0	11	37	58	10
St Osyth	16	0	1	15	23	93	1

* - 4 points awarded

Lower Division Champions:
Div. 1 (10): Inter Hotspur
Div. 2 (11): Sunday Shrimpers Res.
Div. 3 (8): Spooner United
Div. 4 (12): Litchfield Rangers

ESSEX SUNDAY COMBINATION

FOUNDED: 1937

PREM. DIV.	P	W	D	L	F	A	PTS
Coach & Horses	12	7	2	3	40	23	23
St Peters	12	5	6	1	28	12	21
Nacanco	12	5	3	4	31	30	18
Manor House	12	4	4	4	17	30	16
Ton	11	4	2	5	20	20	14
Ford Utd Supp.	11	2	6	3	17	16	12
Stragas	12	1	3	8	8	30	6

Withdrawn - New Beckton, Scala, Star Albion

Lower Division Champions:
Prem. Div. (10): Lacey Hand
Div. 1 (8): Pretoria Seniors
Div. 2 (8): Cardinals
Div. 3 (9): Sultan
Div. 4 (8): Taverners
Div. 5 (7): Gateways

Cup Winners (Runners-up)
C White Cup: Coaches & Horses (Nacanco)
Milton Cup: Rainham WMC (Castleton)
Morfey Cup: Pretoria Snrs (Eastern Rangers)
J Lizziemore Cup: POW Sports (Cardinals)
Beitler Cup: Sultan (Dagenham Westside)
T Evans Cup: Taverners (Vernon)
J Hoy Cup: Gatesways (Singleton Rangers)
Premier Cup: Coach & Horses (Pretoria Snrs)
McDougall Cup: Sultan (Dagenham Westside)
Simister Cup: Pegstonians (Gateways)
Endeavour Cup: St Peters

Secretary of the Year: K White (London Fire B.)
Linesman of the Year: R Fenton (Barking Rgrs)
Referee of the Year: K Barker

SOUTHEND

SUNDAY LEAGUE

FOUNDED: 1964

PREM. DIV.	P	W	D	L	F	A	PTS
Rayleigh Town	16	12	3	1	52	21	27
Oakwood Sports	16	12	2	2	51	22	26
Hockley Brit. Leg.	16	9	1	6	47	26	19
Spartek	16	8	1	7	43	41	17
Trinity	16	7	3	6	27	28	17
Lodge Athletic	16	4	3	9	26	46	11
Hadleigh Town	16	4	2	10	27	44	10
Progress Rovers	16	4	2	10	22	49	10
Catholic United	16	2	3	11	32	50	7

* - 4 points awarded

Lower Division Champions:
Div. 1 (11): Rochford Sports
Div. 2 (11): South Benfleet United
Div. 3 (12): Lodge Athletic Reserves
Div. 4 (12): Rayleigh Olympiads
Div. 5 (12): Oakwood Sports Reserves
Div. 6 (12): Kingston Athletic
Div. 7 (10): Salford
Div. 8 (10): Bellevue Wanderers

Cup Finals
Lge Cup Section A: Rayleigh T. 1, Oakwoos Spts 0
Lge Cup Sections B & C: Abandoned due to weather
Lge Cup Section D: Salford 5, Malpin Utd Res. 3
Charity Cup Sec. A: Spartek 1, Thundersley Rvrs 0
Charity Cup Sec. B: Kings Field Cas. 4, Salford 2
Charity Cup Sec. C: Oakwood Sports Reserves 3, Hullbridge Sports Reserves 1

BRAINTREE & NORTH ESSEX SUNDAY LEAGUE

PREM. DIV.	P	W	D	L	F	A	PTS
Bocking	14	11	1	2	50	10	34
CFC Braintree	14	11	1	2	55	21	34
Boars Head	14	6	2	2	30	31	20
Western Arms	14	5	3	6	25	33	18
Swan Hotel	11	5	2	7	27	44	17
Feering	11	4	4	6	31	34	16
Crittall	14	4	3	7	22	35	15
Stebbing	14	1	2	11	13	48	5

GLOUCESTERSHIRE F.A.

Secretary: E J Marsh, 46 Douglas Road, Horfield, Bristol BS7 0JD (0272 519435)

SENIOR CHALLENGE CUP 1993-94

The Senior Challenge Cup is for Conference and Beazer Homes League clubs, plus the winner of the previous season's Trophy if they wish and their facilities are adedequate. Newport were drawn at home in the final, making Gloucester City the away team on their own ground! Newport's win meant that the Cup left Gloucestershire for the first time since it was first contested in 1936-37.

First Round

Cheltenham Town v Gloucester City *(att: 449)* 0-1

Semi-Finals

Yate Town v Newport AFC *(att: 111)* 0-1

Forest Green Rovers v Gloucester *(att: 281)* 2-3*(aet)*

Final *(at Gloucester City FC, 12th April)*: Newport AFC 1, Gloucester City 0

CHALLENGE CUP 1993-94

The Challenge Trophy is for clubs from the Great Mills, Hellenic, Gloucestershire County and Somerset Senior Leagues (Premier Division clubs only in the latter case).

First Round

Almondsbury Town v Mangotsfield United 0-5
Cirencester Town v Tuffley Rovers 1-0
Fairford Town v DRG 3-2
Moreton Town v Cirencester United 6-0
Patchway Town v Henbury Old Boys 3-0
St Marks CA v Winterbourne United 0-1
Shirehampton v Bishops Cleeve 0-2
Smiths Athletic v Totterdown Athletic 1-1,2-1
Cinderford v Bristol MF 0-0,1-1*(1-3 on pens)*
Ellwood v Endsleigh 5-0
Hallen v Cheltenham Saracens 1-1,2-2*(2-3 on pens)*
Old Georgians v Dowty Dynamoes 3-0
Pucklechurch Spts v Longwell Green Abbotonians 1-2
St Philips Marsh Adult School v Campden Town 2-0
Shortwood United v Harrow Hill 7-2
Wotton Rovers v Cadbury Heath 2-1

Second Round

Cirencester Town v Bishops Cleeve 4-0
Ellwood v Mangotsfield United 1-3
Moreton Town v Old Georgians 3-1
Winterbourne Utd v St Philips MAS 0-2
Cheltenham Saras v Longwell Green Abbotonians 1-0
Fairford Town v Shortwood United 3-0
Patchway Town v Smiths Athletic 2-2,2-0
Wotton Rovers v Bristol Manor Farm 1-3

Quarter-Finals

Cirencester Town v Moreton Town 0-2
Patchway T. v Fairford *(at Fairford)* 1-3
Bristol MF v Cheltenham Saras *(at Chelt. Saras)* 0-1
Mangotsfield Utd v St Philips Marsh Adult School 3-1

Semi-Finals

Mangotsfield United v Cheltenham Saras 3-1 *(at Yate Town FC, 2nd March)*
Moreton Town v Fairford Town 2-0 *(at Cirencester Town FC, 16th March)*

Final *(at Forest Green Rovers FC, Mon 2nd May)*: Mangotsfield Utd 3, Moreton Town 1 *(aet)*

OTHER COUNTY FINALS 1993-94

Below the Trophy, the competitions are split into North and South for adult competitions.

Senior Amateur Cup (S) *(at Cadbury Heath FC, 3rd May)*: Pucklechurch Sports Reserves 3, Stoke Gifford United 1 *(after 0-0 draw at Yate Town FC 19/4/94)*.
Senior Amateur Cup (N) *(at Gloucester City FC, 27th April)*: Shortwood Utd Reserves 2, King's Stanley 0
Junior Cup (S) *(at Mangotsfield Utd FC, 6th April)*: DRG Reserves 4, Old Cothamians 1
Junior Cup (N) *(at Cirencester Town FC, 26th April)*: St Marks CA Reserves 2, Tetbury Town 1 *(aet)*
Intermediate Cup (S) *(at Stapleton FC, 9th May)*: Crest Allies 4, Westerleigh Sports 3 *(after 2-2 draw at Sun Life FC, 21/4/94)*
Intermediate Cup (N) *(at Shortwood Utd FC, 28th April)*: Hardwicke Reserves 2, Down Ampney 0
Minor Cup (S) *(at Almondsbury Town FC, 28th April)*: NSC Reserves 4, Hilton Rangers 3 *(NSC Reserves fielded ineligible players - competition declared void)*
Minor Cup (N) *(at Frampton United FC, 3rd May)*: Ramblers Reserves 1, Arlingham 0
Primary Cup (S) *(at Bitton FC, 25th April)*: Oldlands 'A' 3, Hillfield Old Boys 'A' 0
Primary Cup (N) *(at Bishops Cleeve FC, 25th April)*: Hatherley Rangers 3, Tewkesbury Town Youth 1 *(after 1-1 draw also at Bishops Cleeve (19/4/94) and extra-timwe)*
Sunday Premier Cup (S) *(at Yate Town FC, 24th April)*: St Joseph's 4, Lebeq Tavern Courage 0
Sunday Premier Cup (N) *(at Tuffley Rovers FC, 1st May)*: Brockworth Nomads 1, Brockworth Parish 0
Sunday Intermediate Cup (S) *(at Sun Life FC, 17th April)*: Bromley Heath Old Boys 3, Fortfield 1
Sunday Intermediate Cup (N) *(at Harrow Hill FC, 17th April)*: Customade 5, Windsor Drive 2
Sunday Minor Cup (S) *(at Sun Life FC, 1st May)*: Bell Rhabits Reserves 3, Old Georgians Cricketers 2 *(after 2-2 draw also at Sun Life FC, 10/4/94)*
Sunday Minor Cup (N) *(at Brimscombe & Thrupp FC, 15th May)*: Stow Town 3, Cleeve Wanderers 2 *(after 4-4 draw also at Brimscombe & Thrupp FC, 8/5/94)*
Youth Shield *(at Yate Town FC, 5th May)*: Hallen 4, Mangotsfield United 1
John Kennedy Cup (under-16s) *(at Gloucester City FC, 4th May)*: Hucclecote CA 2, Robinswood 1
Wilk Osborne Cup (under-14s) *(at Stonehouse Freeway FC, 2nd May)*: Downend United 1, Robinswood 0
Alec Buckland Cup (under-12s) *(at Hallen FC, 12th May)*: Downend United 2, Windsor Drive CA 1 *(aet)*
Under-16 Inter-League *(at Stapletonn FC, 16th May)*: Gloucester 3, Bristol & Avon 1
Under-14 Inter-League *(at Frampton Utd FC, 27th April)*: Stroud & District 3, Gloucester 2
Under-12 Inter-League *(at Mangotsfield Utd FC, 26th April)*: Bristol Junior 5, Cheltenham Minor 2

(Details kindly supplied by Colin Timbrell, GFA Historian)

GLOUCESTERSHIRE COUNTY LEAGUE (Est. 1968)

Chairman: A C Barrett.

Vice-Chairman: J D Hart.

Treasurer: P T McPherson.

Hon. Secretary: D J Herbert, 8 Fernhurst Rd, St George, Bristol BS5 7TQ (0272 517696)

CADBURY HEATH LEAVE IT LATE

St Philips Marsh Adult School threw the championship wide open by defeating Cabdury Heath 1-0 at home, leaving the title to be decided over the last two games. The last day of the season saw Cabury Heath requiring a point or Endsleigh requiring three points to take the title. St Philips MAS, who had been in contention all season, travelled to Wotton Rovers and a win by 1-0 was not enough to take the runner-up place. Endsleigh were away to local rivals St Marks CA and finished with a 3-1 win to claim the second spot. Cadbury Heath finished in championship form by defeating Stapleton 3-0 at home to lift the title. Cadbury Heath have won the championship on four previous occasions, the last time being the 1973/74 season, and they have finished runners-up on three previous occasions.

Relegated club Dowty Dynamos gained their first and only win of the season at the 24th attempt; 4-1 at home against Stapleton. Campden Town, the other relegated club, were unable to complete their fixtures and the league table was incomplete as they struggled to raise a side away to Stapleton.

In the JJ Bailey Cup, the League XI took on the South Wales Amateur League at Ton Pentre, finishing worthy winners 2-1. This followed the success of the 1-0 win against the GFA XI Representative side. Unfortunately, because of the weather and backlog of fixtures, the JJ Bailey Cup could not be completed.

D J Herbert, Secretary

FINAL TABLE	P	W	D	L	F	A	PTS
Cadbury Heath	34	24	5	5	68	28	77
Endsleigh	34	23	5	6	78	27	74
St Philips MAS	34	23	4	7	66	22	73
Ellwood	34	18	9	7	67	34	63
Henbury Old Boys	34	18	8	8	67	41	62
Patchway Town	34	16	11	7	67	35	59
Harrow Hill	34	16	5	13	73	42	53
Totterdown Ath.	34	15	7	12	63	56	52
DRG	34	15	5	14	54	50	50
Old Georgians	34	14	6	14	46	53	48
Pucklechurch Spts	34	13	8	13	41	51	47
St Marks CA	34	13	7	14	50	47	46
Wotton Rovers	34	13	3	18	56	56	42
Smiths Athletic	34	11	9	14	50	56	42
Stapleton	33	8	5	20	34	69	29
Winterbourne Utd	34	7	6	21	42	70	27
Campden Town	33	2	4	27	27	116	10
Dowty Dynamos	34	1	3	30	30	126	6

Top Scorers: P Turnbull (Ellwood) 23, M Brown (Ellwood) 18, P Bartley (Henbury) 17, I Day (Cadbury Heath) 17, C Brain (Harrow Hill) 16, I Wilde (Old Georgians) 15, L Nash (St Philips MAS) 14, I Shephard (Wotton) 14, C Ferretti (Totterdown) 13, M Blake (Harrow Hill) 12, M Preddy (St Marks) 12.

SPORTSMANSHIP SHIELD

Marks are awarded to clubs by their opponents.

Dowty Dynamoes	122
Pucklechurch Sports	119
Campden Town	118
Wotton Rovers	117
DRG	114
Harrow Hill	114
Henbury Old Boys	113
Cadbury Heath	112
Ellwood	110
St Marks CA	109
St Philips Marsh Adult School	109
Smiths Athletic	109
Totterdown Athletic	108
Patchway Town	106
Old Georgians	105
Endsleigh	104
Stapleton	97
Winterbourne United	94

GLOUCESTERSHIRE COUNTY LEAGUE RESULT CHART 1993-94

HOME TEAM	1	2	3	4	5	6	7	8	9	10	11	12	13	14	15	16	17	18
1. Cadbury Heath	*	2-1	2-0	3-0	2-0	0-0	3-0	2-1	0-2	1-1	2-0	1-0	2-0	2-0	3-0	2-0	4-3	1-1
2. Campden Town	2-2	*	4-0	0-1	0-5	2-2	0-5	1-2	1-1	0-3	0-2	0-3	1-2	2-6	0-5	2-6	3-1	0-6
3. Dowty Dynamos	1-6	2-2	*	1-2	2-6	0-3	1-3	1-6	0-4	0-4	3-3	1-4	0-7	3-4	4-1	1-6	2-2	0-1
4. DRG	1-2	4-2	4-2	*	2-0	0-0	4-0	1-2	0-0	1-2	6-1	1-2	0-4	3-3	2-0	1-2	2-0	4-2
5. Ellwood	1-1	5-0	4-1	4-1	*	1-0	0-1	1-0	2-2	0-1	0-0	3-3	0-3	2-0	5-0	2-3	2-0	3-2
6. Endsleigh	0-2	8-0	2-0	3-1	2-3	*	2-1	4-2	2-1	2-1	6-0	3-1	0-2	0-0	4-1	1-1	2-0	3-0
7. Harrow Hill	0-1	8-0	5-0	4-2	2-3	0-2	*	0-1	6-0	1-1	4-0	2-1	2-4	3-0	9-0	0-0	1-0	1-2
8. Henbury Old Boys	1-2	6-0	2-1	0-1	0-2	1-0	1-1	*	0-0	2-2	4-1	1-1	2-0	2-1	5-1	2-0	2-1	3-3
9. Old Georgians	1-4	5-1	3-1	1-3	1-2	0-2	2-0	0-1	*	1-4	1-1	3-0	1-0	1-3	2-1	2-0	3-2	0-2
10. Patchway Town	3-2	4-0	4-0	0-2	1-1	0-1	2-3	1-2	4-0	*	0-0	0-0	2-1	0-0	1-1	2-3	7-0	2-0
11. Pucklechurch Sports	2-0	5-0	1-0	2-0	1-0	0-6	1-1	0-0	0-1	1-2	*	1-1	1-2	2-0	2-1	1-3	1-0	4-1
12. St Marks CA	0-2	2-0	1-0	3-0	1-1	1-3	1-1	1-2	0-1	0-2	2-1	*	0-2	0-1	4-1	0-2	2-1	3-1
13. St Philips Marsh Adult Sch.	1-0	1-0	3-0	1-0	0-1	1-0	2-0	4-0	0-0	1-1	0-0	1-2	*	3-1	3-0	2-1	3-0	4-0
14. Smiths Athletic	1-3	4-1	3-2	1-1	1-1	1-2	2-0	2-2	0-1	1-2	1-3	2-1	0-3	*	0-0	2-3	2-1	1-2
15. Stapleton	0-2		6-0	0-2	0-2	2-4	3-1	0-0	1-0	1-2	2-0	1-4	2-1	2-2	*	0-1	1-0	0-1
16. Totterdown Athletic	0-4	3-1	4-0	1-0	1-1	1-5	1-2	3-4	3-4	1-1	0-2	2-2	1-2	2-3	0-0	*	3-1	3-2
17. Winterbourne United	4-1	2-1	6-1	1-1	0-0	1-3	0-3	0-6	4-1	3-3	2-1	1-3	2-2	0-0	0-1	1-2	*	2-1
18. Wotton Rovers	1-2	3-0	8-0	0-1	0-3	0-1	0-3	3-2	3-1	3-2	0-1	3-1	0-1	1-2	3-0	1-1	0-1	*

GLOUCESTERSHIRE COUNTY LEAGUE CLUBS 1994-95

BROADWELL AMATEURS

Secretary: G Hurcombe, 15 Bessemer Close, High Nash, Coleford, Glos GL16 8HH (0594 834630).
Ground: The Hawthorns, Poolway Road, Broadwell, near Coleford (0594 837347).
Directions: B4228 to Coleford then B4028 out of Coleford, B4226 into Broadwell - ground on right.
Colours: Claret & blue/claret/blue **Change colours:** Gold/black/black
Prev. Lge: Glos Northern Snr (pre-1994) **Honours:** Glos Northern Snr Lg 93-94 (R-up 92-93).

CADBURY HEATH

Secretary: C Thomas, 73 Ridgeway Rd, Fishponds, Bristol BS16 3ED (0272 518097).
Ground: 'Springfield', Cadbury Heath Rd, Warmley, Bristol (0272 675730).
Directions: A420 from Bristol through Kingswood, across new r'bout, right into Tower Rd North, past school, right into Cadbury Heath Rd, ground immediately on right down alley.
Colours: Red/black/black (red tops) **Change Colours:** Yellow/black/black.
Hons: Glos Co. Lg 70-71 71-72 72-73 73-74 93-94 (R-up 74-75 90-91 91-92), Glos Amtr Cup Sth(3), FA Vase QF.

D.R.G.

Secretary: J A Jacobs, 80 The Meadows, Hanham, Bristol BS15 3PB (0272 611845).
Ground: 'Shortwood', Carsons Road, Mangotsfield, Bristol (0272 560390).
Directions: M4 jct 19 onto M32, off at jct 1 onto A4174 follow signs for Downend then Mangotsfield. Continue through town, road becomes Carsons Road, ground on right after factory.
Seats: None **Cover:** No **Capacity:** 1,000 **Clubhouse:** Yes **Founded:** 1962
Colours: Maroon & blue stripes/maroon/maroon **Change Colours:** Yellow/maroon/maroon
Previous Name: R.W.P. (pre-1986) **Previous Ground:** St Johns Lane 62-66. **Clubhouse:** Yes.
Record Gate: 500 v Pucklechurch Sports, Bristol Combination 1/4/86.

ELLWOOD

Secretary: R J Cole, 64 Allaston Rd, Lydney, Glos, GL15 5ST (0594 844395).
Ground: Bromley Rd, Ellwood, Coleford, Glos (0594 832927).
Directions: B4234 to Parkend then B4431 up hill to next crossroads, turn left - ground half mile on left.
Colours: All royal blue **Change Colours:** Red/royal blue/royal blue

HARROW HILL

Secretary: R C Beckett, 'Sunny View', Bridge Rd, Harrow Hill, Drybrook, Glos GL17 9ST (0594 543390).
Ground: Larksfield Rd, Harrow Hill, Drybrook, Glos (0954 543873).
Directions: A40 from Gloucester for for seven miles, left onto A4136 and continue for eight miles to Harrow Hill, right into Trinity Road near Church, right into Larkfield Road after half a mile, ground on right.
Seats: No **Cover:** Yes **Capacity:** 2,000 **Clubhouse:** Yes **Founded:** 1932
Colours: Blue/claret/sky **Change Colours:** Yellow/claret/blue.
Record Gate: 500-600, local cup, 1960s.
Best FA Vase season: 1st Rd 88-89 **Hons:** Glos Northern Snr Lg(4) 63-65 71-72 81-82.

HENBURY OLD BOYS

Secretary: C B Barron, 126 Charlton Rd, Westbury-on-Trym, Bristol BS10 6NL (0272 504002).
Ground: Arnall Drive Playing Fields, Henbury, Bristol (0272 590475). **Founded:** 1962
Directions: M5 jct 17, down Cribbs Causeway, into Station Road, left into Henbury Rd, ground on left.
Colours: Amber & black/black/black **Change Colours:** Blue/black/black.
Hons: Avon Combination 82-83 (Lg Cup 83-84), Glos Snr Amtr Cup South, Fry Club Cup 92-93.

OLD GEORGIANS

Secretary: D M Latcham, 87 Vicarage Rd, Whitehall, Bristol BS5 9AQ (0272 556292).
Ground: St George's School PF, Johnsons Lane, Whitehall, Bristol (0272 516888).
Directions: M32 jct 2, left, left, right at lights, right behind Kings Head. Buses 6 or 7 from central Bristol. One mile from Stapleton Road (BR).
Seats: None **Cover:** No **Capacity:** 1,500 **Clubhouse:** Yes **Founded:** 1905.
Colours: Sky (navy sleeves)/navy/navy **Change Colours:** Red/navy/red
Record Gate: 770 v Stansted, FA Vase QF 4/3/84. **Manager:** Brian Tufton.
Hons: Glos Co. Lg 82-83 84-85 (R-up 83-84 92-93), Glos Chal. Tphy, Glos Snr Amtr Cup Sth, FA Vase QF 83-84.

OLDLAND

Secretary: R Hamblin, 152 Stockwood Lane, Stockwood, Bristol BS14 8TA (0275 835203).
Ground: Castle Road, Oldland Common, Bristol.
Directions: A4175 from Kingswood to Keynsham, pass Dolphin pub, next left by Post Office.
Colours: Blue & white/blue/blue **Previous League:** County of Avon Premier Comb. (pre-1994).
Hons: Avon Premier Combination 93-94.

PATCHWAY TOWN

Secretary: R Stewart, 22 Arlingham Way, Patchway, Bristol, BS12 5NQ (0272 792983).
Ground: 'Scott Park', Coniston Rd, Patchway, Bristol (0272 691203)
Directions: M5 jct 16, A38 towards Bristol, right into Coniston Road, ground signposted Scott Park.
Colours: Black & white stripes/black/black **Change Colours:** All royal blue
Hons: Glos County Lg 91-92

PUCKLECHURCH SPORTS

Secretary: R B Savage, 54 Shortwood Rd, Pucklechurch, Bristol BS17 3RN (0272 373972).
Ground: Pucklechurch Recreation Ground, Pucklechurch, Abson (0275 822102).
Directions: M32 jct 1 follow A4174 through Downend to Mangotsfield, left signposted Pucklechurch, continue to village, turn right, ground on left.
Seats: No **Cover:** None **Clubhouse:** Yes **Prog:** 32 pages,40p **Editor:** M Dowse.
Colours: Green/white/green **Change Colours:** All white.
Hons: Avon Comb. 77-78 78-79 87-88 (Div 2 66-67, Lg Cup 77-78 78-79 87-88), Glos Jnr Cup 65-66 82-83, Bristol & District Lg 72-73.

St MARKS C.A.

Secretary: W Pember, 11 Linworth Rd, Bishops Cleeve, Cheltenham, Glos GL52 4PF (0242 673800).
Ground: Dowty Arle Court Sports Ground, Hatherley Lane, Cheltenham (0242 525515).
Directions: In Cheltenham follow signs for GCHQ. Ground adjacent. **Clubhouse:** Yes
Colours: Royal blue/royal blue/red **Change Colours:** Red with white hoop/royal blue/red
Prev. Ground: Cheltenham Town FC **Hons:** Glos Northern Snr Lg 74-75 78-79 83-84.

St PHILIPS MARSH ADULT SCHOOL

Secretary: T R Green, 35 Braienkridge Rd, Brislington, Bristol BS4 3SW (0272 770530).
Ground: John Harvey Sports Ground, Norton Lane, Whitchurch, Bristol (0272 837271).
Directions: A37 south from Bristol, through Whitchurch, right into Norton Lane just after humped back bridge. Ground first right.
Seats: No **Cover:** No **Clubhouse:** Yes **Programme:** Yes **Founded:**
Colours: White/black/black **Change Colours:** Red & white/red/red.

SMITHS ATHLETIC

Secretary: P H Jurd, 11 Shawgreen Lane, Prestbury, Cheltenham, Glos GL52 3BS (0242 529188).
Colours: All royal blue **Change Colours:** All red.
Hons: Glos Northern Snr Lg 91-92 **Previous League:** Glos Northern Snr (until 1992).

STAPLETON

Secretary: M Dodd, 108 Downend Rd, Fishponds, Bristol BS16 5BH (0272 400544).
Ground & Directions: Frenchay Park Playing Field, Frenchay, Bristol. M32 jct 1, A4174, follow signs to Frenchay Hospital - ground opposite. Or M32 jct 2, follow signs for Frenchay through Stapleton, ground on left.
Seats: No **Cover:** No **Clubhouse:** Yes **Programme:** Yes **Founded:** 1932.
Colours: All burgundy **Change Colours:** White/white/purple.

TOTTERDOWN P.O.B.

Secretary: Mrs G V Salter, 65 Novers Park Drive, Knowle, Bristol BS4 1RH (0272 632720).
Ground: City & Port of Bristol Sports Ground, Nibley Rd, Shirehampton, Bristol.
Directions: 5 mins walk from Shirehampton (BR) station (Temple Meads-Severn Beach line).
Colours: Red/navy/black **Change Colours:** Yellow/blue/yellow.
Prevous Names: Totterdown Ath., Port of Bristol - clubs merged 1994. *Notes below apply to Totterdown.*
Prev. Lge: Bristol & Suburban (pre'93) **Hons:** Bristol & Suburban Lg R-up 92-93.
Previous Ground: Bristol & West Indian Cricket Ground, Gordon PF, Gordon Rd, Whitehall, Bristol (pre-1994).

WINTERBOURNE UNITED

Secretary: J Lloyd, 31 Park Avenue, Winterbourne, Bristol BS17 1NH (0454 775841).
Ground: Parkside Ave. Rec., Winterbourne, Bristol. - Behind school, just beyond shops in Winterbourne.
Seats: No **Cover:** Yes **Clubhouse:** Yes **Previous Lge:** Avon Comb. (until 1992)
Colours: White/red/red **Change Colours:** Blue & white stripes/blue/blue

WOTTON ROVERS

Secretary: M P Excell, 94 Bearlands, Wotton-under-Edge, Glos. GL12 7SB (0453 845178).
Ground: Synwell Playing Field, Synwell Lane, Wotton-under-Edge (0453 842929).
Directions: From Wotton war memorial down hill and follow Synwell Lane. Ground on left.
Seats: None **Cover:** No **Capacity:** 2,000 **Clubhouse:** Yes **Founded:** 1959.
Colours: White (multi-col.)/white/red **Change Colours:** White/white/red
Record Gate: 2,000 **Programme:** 20 pages, 50p
Previous Names: Synwell Rovers (pre-1959)/ Wotton-under-Edge FC.

COUNTY OF AVON PREMIER COMBINATION

(Established 1957)

Hon. Secretary: Vernon Windell,
89 St Peters Rise, Headley Park, Bristol BS13 7NA.

PREM. DIV.	P	W	D	L	F	A	PTS
Oldland	32	25	3	4	90	27	53
Bitton	32	24	3	5	84	23	51
Highridge United	32	22	3	7	63	41	47
Hanham Athletic	32	20	6	6	71	36	46
Sea Mills Park	32	15	6	11	76	54	37
Hambrook	32	16	4	12	74	56	36
Shaftesbury Crusade	32	11	10	11	58	57	32
Thornbury Town	32	14	3	15	60	52	31
Longwell Green Spts	32	10	8	14	56	57	28
Sun Life	32	8	12	12	55	62	28
Hillfields OB	32	11	6	15	59	71	28
Bristol Union	32	10	7	15	43	62	27
Nicholas Wanderers	32	11	3	18	50	58	25
Spartak Downend	32	11	5	16	69	91	*25
Iron Acton	32	9	7	16	56	78	25
Olveston United	32	6	9	17	31	59	21
Bristol St George	32	0	3	29	22	131	3

* - 2 points deducted

DIV. ONE	P	W	D	L	F	A	PTS
Hartcliffe	26	20	4	2	70	30	44
Bristol 5 OB	26	19	4	3	85	26	42
Frampton Athletic	26	20	2	4	81	22	42
Lawrence Rovers	26	11	5	10	60	59	27
Pucklechurch Res.	26	11	5	10	39	47	27
Archway St Philips	26	7	9	10	41	45	23
Bristol University	26	8	6	12	37	49	22
Shirehampton Res.	26	7	8	11	41	58	22
Patchway T. Res.	26	7	7	12	45	50	21
St Philips MAS Res.	26	8	4	14	41	60	20
Henbury OB Res.	26	9	2	15	38	72	20
Chipping Sodbury	26	7	5	14	45	66	19
Staple Hill	26	6	6	14	38	64	18
Hallen Res.	26	6	5	15	43	56	17

Grounds *(Addresses italicised)*:
Archway St Phillips *(Iron Mould Lane, Brislington)*, Barr Utd *(BAWA Ground, Southmead Rd)*, Bitton *(Bitton Rec.)*, Bristol 5 OB *(St George Sch)*, Bristol St George *(Butler Mem., Whiteway Rd)*, Bristol Union/Univ. *(Univ. PF, Coombe Lane)*, Chipping Sodbury *(The Ridings)*, Frampton Ath. *(Beesmoor Rd, Frampton Cotterell)*, Hambrook *(Whiteshill Common, Moorend Lane)*, Hanham Ath. *(Vicarage Rd)*, Hillfields OB *(Thicket Ave., Fishponds)*, Iron Acton *(Sunnyside Lane, Iron Acton)*, Lawrence Rvrs *(Lawrence Weston PF)*, Longwell Green Spts *(Shellards Rd, Longwell Gn)*, Nicholas Wdrs *(Dundridge PF)*, Olveston Utd *(The Plain, Old Down, Tockington)*, Sea Mills Park *(Sea Mills Rec.)*, Shaftesbury Crusade *(Landseer Ave., Lockleaze)*, Spartak Downend *(Whitchurch)*, Staple Hill *(Blackhorse Rd, Mangotsfield)*, Sun Life *(Cribbs Causeway)*, Thornbury Town *(Munday PF, Kington Lane)*.

BRISTOL & SUBURBAN LEAGUE

(Established 1894)

BOSLEY CUP FINAL *(at Avonmouth FC, Wed 11th May)*:
Broad Plain House Old Boys 2, Glenside Hospital Social Club 1

Premier Division	P	W	D	L	F	A	PTS
Broad Plain Hse OB	30	24	4	2	118	18	52
Yate Town Res.	30	21	7	2	90	32	49
Avonmouth	30	23	2	5	82	29	48
Nat West Court	30	17	5	8	48	33	39
St Aldhelms	30	18	2	10	73	44	38
Exeter United	30	17	3	10	61	47	37
Plough & Windmill U.	30	14	6	10	69	58	34
Stoke Gifford Utd	30	14	5	11	55	50	33
TDR Dynamo	30	12	3	15	58	68	27
Glenside Hosp SC	30	9	7	14	69	72	27
Almondsbury	30	10	4	15	69	72	25
Old Georgians Res.	30	9	3	18	54	76	21
Bristol Telephones	30	7	4	19	44	68	18
Filton Athletic	30	7	3	20	31	93	17
Lockleaze	30	3	5	22	39	114	11
Avon Fire Brigade	30	3	1	26	32	102	7

Premier Div. Two	P	W	D	L	F	A	PTS
Tytherington Rocks	28	25	2	1	110	22	52
Southmead Athletic	28	18	5	5	103	57	41
Cadbury Hth Res.	28	15	5	8	66	35	35
Almass	28	13	4	11	62	48	30
Ridings Heath	28	11	7	10	51	50	29
CTK Southside	28	13	2	13	73	58	28
Alveston Down Spts	28	10	7	11	42	52	27
Imperial Saints	28	10	7	11	43	71	27
Teyfant Athletic	28	12	2	14	48	51	26
Potterswood	28	9	5	14	56	71	23
Fishponds Old Boys	28	9	5	14	55	70	23
Portway Bristol	28	10	3	15	56	75	23
Rolls Royce OB	28	9	4	16	40	66	20
Port of Bristol	28	8	4	16	36	93	20
Hartcliffe OB	28	6	4	18	49	72	16

Division One	P	W	D	L	F	A	PTS
Old Cothamians	30	23	4	3	136	38	50
BC Timbers	30	24	2	4	103	38	50
Exeter United Res.	30	18	5	7	82	51	41
EP Somerdale Utd	30	17	3	10	95	71	37
St Aldhelms Res.	30	15	6	9	76	53	36
Avonmouth Res.	30	14	5	11	86	72	33
Wanderers	30	14	4	12	68	68	32
Thrissells Nomads	30	11	9	10	70	51	31
Imperial Utd Res.	30	11	6	13	50	77	28
Avon Dynamo BAWA	30	9	7	14	60	73	25
Bristol North West	30	10	5	15	56	82	25
Nat. Smelting Co.	30	9	5	16	55	65	23
Patchway Nth End	30	7	8	15	45	76	22
Glenside Hosp. Res.	30	7	6	17	35	80	20
Ashton Rangers	30	8	2	20	36	72	18
Old Georgians 'A'	30	3	3	24	34	119	9

Division Two	P	W	D	L	F	A	PTS
Totterdown A. Res.	30	22	6	2	109	38	50
Almondsbury Safeway	30	17	9	4	89	42	43
ICI Severnside	30	18	4	8	87	50	40
Sun All. Phoenix	30	14	9	7	74	38	37
Bristol Crusaders	30	13	8	9	71	47	34
Raysfield	30	14	6	10	68	60	34
Little Stoke SC	30	14	5	11	67	53	33
Whitchurch	30	13	5	12	53	61	31
Horfield Old Boys	30	13	1	16	73	77	27
Broad Plain H. Res.	30	10	5	15	78	77	25
Oldbury-on-Severn	30	10	4	16	67	90	24
Frenchay Hosp. SC	30	10	4	16	47	72	24
Bristol St And.	30	9	3	18	64	96	21
Clifton Rangers	30	8	3	19	60	101	19
Pt of Bristol Res.	30	6	7	17	44	93	19
Corinthian Spts	30	7	5	18	47	103	19

Division Three	P	W	D	L	F	A	PTS
Stoke Gifford Res.	32	24	5	3	99	38	53
Crest Allies	32	22	4	6	92	54	48
London Life	32	21	5	6	107	42	47
Old Georgians 'B'	32	19	7	6	106	57	45
Lockleaze Sports	32	18	5	9	68	49	41
Old Cothamians Res.	32	17	6	9	72	49	40
Hengrove Old Boys	32	17	4	11	77	71	38
De Veys	32	17	1	14	71	55	35
Stockwood Gn Res.	32	15	5	12	72	57	35
P & W United Res.	32	13	5	14	60	75	31
Nat W. Court Res.	32	11	5	16	61	95	27
Fromeside	32	8	7	17	37	61	23
Tytherington R. Res.	32	7	6	19	54	74	20
Fishponds OB Res.	32	6	8	18	45	82	20
Parson Street OB	32	5	5	22	47	97	15
Bristol Tel. Res.	32	5	5	22	36	93	15
Portway Brist. Res.	32	4	3	25	42	97	11

Division Four	P	W	D	L	F	A	PTS
Brislington 'A'	30	22	4	4	85	21	48
Bristol Corinthians	30	22	4	4	108	57	48
Nat Smelting Res.	30	21	5	4	75	41	47
St Annes Town	30	20	5	5	82	30	45
Almondsbury Res.	30	14	5	11	66	44	33
H & J Sports	30	13	8	9	67	48	33
Southmead A. Res.	30	13	3	14	56	73	29
Sefton Park	30	13	2	15	67	66	28
Exeter United 'A'	30	8	8	14	50	59	24
Avonmouth 'A'	30	10	4	16	58	68	24
Imperial Saints Res.	30	8	7	15	53	75	23
Brandon Sports	30	9	3	18	46	76	21
Hengrove Ath. BC	30	8	4	18	54	83	20
Avon D. BAWA Res.	30	7	6	17	45	79	20
Frenchay H. Res.	30	8	3	19	47	82	19
AFC Universal	30	6	5	19	43	103	17

Division Five	P	W	D	L	F	A	PTS
Hartcliffe OB Res.	26	18	4	4	78	32	40
EP Somerdale Res.	26	19	1	6	80	47	39
Bristol Crus. Res.	26	16	3	7	71	47	35
Broad Plain H. 'A'	26	14	4	8	74	43	32
Almondsbury 'A'	26	15	1	10	57	60	31
Wanderers Res.	26	14	1	11	63	49	29
Ridings High Res.	26	13	2	11	68	50	28
Whitchurch Res.	26	10	5	11	57	58	25
Clifton Rgrs Res.	26	10	2	14	47	55	22
ICI Severnside Res.	26	8	4	12	69	73	20
Avon Fire B. Res.	26	8	3	15	40	69	19
Filton Ath. Res.	26	6	5	15	48	65	17
Glenside Hosp. 'A'	26	6	4	16	34	72	16
Ltle Stoke SC Res.	26	4	3	19	49	115	11

Division Six	P	W	D	L	F	A	PTS
Potterswood Res.	28	24	2	2	96	31	50
Sun. A. Phoenix Res.	28	21	2	5	106	29	44
St Annes T. Res.	28	17	3	8	73	49	37
Alveston DS Res.	28	16	4	8	100	52	36
Thrissells N. Res.	28	12	3	13	83	71	27
London Life Res.	28	11	5	12	62	72	27
Brist. St And. Res.	28	10	6	12	51	75	26
Corinthian Spts Res.	28	10	3	15	63	75	23
Pt of Bristol 'A'	28	9	5	14	46	65	23
Parson Str. OB Res.	28	10	3	15	44	77	23
Lockleaze Spts Res.	28	10	3	15	64	105	23
Fishponds OB 'A'	28	6	10	12	51	64	22
Wanderers 'A'	28	8	6	14	37	60	22
Nat Smelting 'A'	28	8	5	15	73	73	21
Oldury-on-Sev. Res.	28	6	4	18	38	89	16

GLOUCESTERSHIRE NORTHERN SENIOR LEAGUE (Est. 1922)

President: H J Morgan.
Vice-President: A D Bushell.
Chairman: R Davis.
Vice-Chairman: E J George.
Hon. Secretary: W N Pember, 11 Linworth Rd, Bishops Cleeve, Cheltenham GL52 4PF (673800).

The Pyramid in Gloucestershire is functioning efficiently. Northern Senior League champions Broadwell Amateurs are promoted to the County League with relegated Dowty Dynamoes making the reverse journey. Within the Northern Senior League, the Stonehouse Freeway, Ellwood Reserves and Yate Town 'A' are all promoted from Division Two, with Cam Bulldogs, Coleford United and Hilldene Athletic relegated. Under the Pyramid system the champions of the Cheltenham, Stroud and North Gloucestershire Leagues (Crescent United, Eastcombe and Harrow Hill Reserves) are all promoted to Division Two. ICI Fibres are relegated.

DIV. ONE	P	W	D	L	F	A	PTS
Broadwell Amtrs	30	19	10	1	67	25	48
Brockworth	30	19	7	4	85	32	45
Dursley Town	30	16	8	6	54	29	40
Viney St Swithins	30	15	9	6	67	42	39
Hardwicke	30	14	11	5	56	37	39
Kings Stanley	30	15	7	8	52	31	37
Shortwood Utd Res.	30	14	8	8	69	43	36
Lydbrook Athletic	30	14	5	11	70	61	33
Longford	30	14	3	13	59	59	31
Sharpness	30	12	5	13	62	61	29
Frampton United	30	12	3	15	68	60	27
Berkeley Town	30	9	8	13	40	63	26
Worrall Hill	30	8	2	20	31	62	18
Cam Bulldogs	30	5	5	20	31	83	*13
Hilldene Athletic	30	2	5	23	38	106	9
Coleford United	30	3	2	25	33	88	8

* - 2 points deducted

DIV. TWO	P	W	D	L	F	A	PTS
Stonehouse Freeway	26	16	5	5	56	30	37
Ellwood Res.	26	17	3	6	54	29	37
Yate Town 'A'	26	16	4	6	75	38	36
Lydney Town	26	17	2	7	56	32	36
Charfield	26	15	5	6	47	27	35
Nuclear Electric	26	12	5	9	41	42	29
Taverners	26	10	8	8	50	45	28
Brimscombe/Thrupp	26	8	8	10	33	36	24
Vikings	26	6	10	10	50	57	22
Bibury	26	7	6	13	47	57	20
Longlevens	26	5	8	13	21	45	18
Gala Wilton	26	6	4	16	30	67	16
Newent Town	26	4	7	15	23	55	15
ICI Fibres	26	3	5	18	16	39	11

The records of Cinderford Town Reserves and Yorkley were deleted following their withdrawal.

FOREST GREEN ROVERS SUPPORTERS CLUB TROPHY 1993-94

First Round

Nuclear Electric v Newent Town	3-0
Brockworth v Longlevens	4-0
Viney St Swithens v Coleford United	3-0
Frampton United v GALA Wilton	6-1
Hardwicke v Dursley Town	1-0
Stonehouse Freeway v ICI Fibres	3-1
Lydney Town v Worrall Hill	2-0
Yate Town 'A' v Cam Bulldogs	5-1
Yorkley v Lydbrook Athletic	1-3
Longford v Shortwood United Reserves	0-3
Charfield v Vikings	3-2
Hilldene Athletic v Cinderford Town Reserves	0-2
Ellwood Reserves v Broadwell Amateurs	0-2
Taveners v King's Stanley	1-1*(K Stanley on pens)*
Brimscombe & T. v Bibury	1-1*(Bibury on pens)*
Sharpness v Berkeley Town	3-1

Second Round

Bibury v Nuclear Electric	1-4
Brockworth v Viney St Swithens	2-1
Broadwell Amateurs v Vikings	4-0
King's Stanley v Sharpness	5-1
Lydbrook Athletic v Hardwicke	2-1
Stonehouse Freeway v Shortwood Utd Reserves	3-2
Cinderford Town Reserves v Yate Town 'A'	3-1
Frampton U. v Lydney	3-3*(Lydney on pens)*

Quarter-Finals

Nuclear Electric v Brockworth	0-3
Broadwell Amateurs v Lydney Town	1-0
Lydbrook v Kin's Stanley	5-5*(K Stanley on pens)*
Cinderford T. Reserves v Stonehouse Freeway	1-7

Semi-Finals

Broadwell Amateurs v Brockworth	0-2
Stonehouse Freeway v King's Stanley	2-0

Final: Brockworth 2, Stonehouse Freeway 0 *(aet)*

FIRST DIVISION CLUBS 1994-95

BERKELEY TOWN

Secretary: Alan Dimery, 22 Jubilee Rd, Dursley, Glos GL11 4ES (Dursley 542981).
Colours: Green & yellow stripes/green **Change colours:** All blue.
Ground: Station Rd, Berkeley.

BROCKWORTH

Secretary: Andrew Bracewell, 10 Boverton Drive, Brockworth, Glos GL3 4DB (0452 610160).
Colours: White/black **Change colours:** Amber/black.
Ground: Mill Lane, Brockworth (0452 862556).
Hons: Glos Northern Snr Lg Div 1 92-93 (Lg Cup 92-93), Cheltenham Lg 91-92.

DOWTY DYNAMOS

Secretary: C J Brown, 25 Courtenay Street, Cheltenham, Glos GL50 4LR (0242 511117).
Ground: As St Marks CA *(see Gloucestershire County League section)*
Colours: Blue & white **Change Colours:** Red/blue/blue
Previous Lge: Glos County 91-94 **Prev. Name:** Alstone Dynamos 47-79 **Founded:** 1947
Hons: Glos Nthn Snr Lg 90-91, Cheltenham Lg R-up 88-89 (Div 2 76-77 79-80), Winchcombe Cup 89-90 (R-up 90-91).

DURSLEY TOWN

Secretary: P James, 8 Meadow Vale, Tilsdown, Dursley, Glos GL11 6HJ (0453 547413).
Colours: Red/black **Change colours:** All blue.
Ground: Recreation Ground, Kingshill Road, Dursley, Glos.

ELLWOOD RESERVES *(see Gloucestershire County League section)*

FRAMPTON UNITED

Secretary: H G Tudor, 'Ad Extremum', Frampton-upon-Severn, Glos GL2 7EA (0452 740224).
Colours: Royal & white stripes **Change colours:** All white.
Ground: Bell Field, Frampton-on-Severn

HARDWICKE

Secretary: A J King, 25 Elmsgrove Road East, Hardwicke, Glos GL2 6PY (0452 728603).
Colours: All white **Change colours:** All yellow.
Ground: Green Lane, Hardwicke (0452 720587).

KINGS STANLEY

Secretary: R K Bassett, 8 Guildings Way, Kings Stanley, Stonehouse, Glos GL1 3LF (0453 824012).
Colours: Maroon & royal blue. **Change colours:** Black & white.
Ground: Marling Close, Kings Stanley (0453 828975).

LONGFORD

Secretary: T Godwin, 2 Abbotts Cottage, Sandhurst, Gloucester GL2 9NW (0452 730727).
Colours: Sky/navy. **Change colours:** Red & white stripes.
Ground: Longford Playing Fields, Longford Lane.

LYDBROOK

Secretary: J A Price, 'Wobage', Fourth Avenue, Greytree, Ross-on-Wye HR9 7HR (0989 63788).
Colours: Black & white. **Change colours:** Blue.
Ground: Reeds, Lower Lydbrook.

SHARPNESS

Secretary: J Thomas, 69 Oldminster Rd, Sharpness, Nr Berkeley, Glos GL13 9UR (0453 811397).
Colours: Red/white **Change colours:** All white or all blue.
Ground: Berkeley Vale Community School.

SHORTWOOD UNITED RESERVES *(see Hellenic League section)*

STONEHOUSE FREEWAY

Secretary: M Smith, 2 The Cottage, The Cross, Eastington, Stonehouse, Glos GL10 3AB (0453 824214).
Colours: Black & white hoops/black **Change colours:** White/black.
Ground: Oldends Lane, Stonehouse, Glos.

VINEY St SWITHINS

Secretary: A R Thomas, 'Ravenscoft', 28 Allaston Rd, Lydney, Glos GL15 5ST (0594 843634).
Colours: Red/black **Change colours:** Blue/white.
Ground: Viney St Swithins Sports & Social Club, Viney Hill (0594 510658).

WORRALL HILL

Secretary: B Wadley, 9 Hillside Terrace, Joys Green, Lydbrook, Glos GL17 9DY (0594 860587).
Colours: All red **Change colours:** All blue.
Ground: Worrall Hill, Lydbrook, Glos (0594 860532).

YATE TOWN 'A' *(see page 527)*

SECOND DIVISION CLUBS 1994-95

BIBURY

Secretary: P W Brown, 43 Pheasant Way, Cirencester GL7 1BJ (0285 655169).
Colours: Red/black **Change colours:** Blue/black.
Ground: Aldsworth Rd, Bibury.

BRIMSCOMBE & THRUPP

Secretary: B F Roberts, 16 Berrells Rd, Tetbury, Glos GL8 8ED (0666 502545).
Colours: White/navy **Change colours:** All navy.
Ground: The Meadow, London Rd, Brimscombe, Nr Stroud, Glos.

CAM BULLDOGS

Secretary: J R Jewitt, 58 Woodview Rd, Dursley, Glos GL11 5SE (0453 548879).
Colours: All yellow **Change colours:** Red/green.
Ground: Cam Sports Club, Everlands, Cam (0453 546736).

CHARFIELD

Secretary: P Kirby, 209 Dovecote, Yate, Bristol BS17 4PF (0454 316266).
Colours: Red/navy **Ground:** Charfield Memorial Hall (0454 260204).

COLEFORD UNITED

Secretary: T Smith, 3A Lower Palmers Flat, Coalway, Coleford, Glos GL16 7LT (0594 834791).
Colours: White/black **Change colours:** Red/black.
Ground: King George V Playing Fields, Victoria Rd, Coleford.

CRESCENT UNITED

Secretary: Brian Lester, 93 Millham Rd, Bishops Cleeve, Cheltenham, Glos (0242 676929).
Colours: All green **Ground:** Whaddon Road Recreation Ground, Cheltenham.
Honours: Cheltenham Lg 93-94.

EASTCOMBE

Secretary: John Pollard, Newholme, Middle Hill, Chalford Hill, Stroud, Glos (Stroud 884704).
Colours: Gold **Ground:** The Rec., Eastcombe **Honours:** Stroud & Dist. Lg 93-94.

G.A.L.A. WILTON

Secretary: T R Onions, 19 Teddington Gdns, Gloucester GL4 9RL (0452 612420).
Colours: Old gold/black **Change colours:** Yellow/blue.
Ground: Gala Club, Fairmile Gardens, Tewkesbury Rd, Gloucester (0452 524447).

HARROW HILL RESERVES *(see Gloucestershire County League section)*

HILLDENE ATHLETIC

Secretary: Gary Sleeman, 26 Forest View, Buckshaft Rd, Cinderford, Glos GL14 3DP (0594 822950).
Colours: Sky blue. **Change colours:** Red.
Ground: Miners Welfare Ground, Barleycorn Square, off Station Street, Cinderford.

LONGLEVENS

Secretary: W G Davis, 28 Simon Road, Longlevens, Gloucester GL2 0TP (0452 422450).
Colours: Red/white **Change colours:** Yellow/white.
Ground: The Pavilion, Longford Lane, Longlevens, Gloucester (0452 308152).

LYDNEY TOWN

Secretary: R A Sansom, 17 Woodland Rise, Lydney, Glos GL15 5LH (0594 843210).
Colours: White/navy **Change colours:** Yellow/navy.
Ground: Lydney Recreation Trust Ground (0594 844523).

NEWENT TOWN

Secretary: John Jones, 1 West View, Newent, Glos GL18 1TE (0531 821465).
Colours: Orange & blue & white/blue **Change colours:** All red.
Ground: Wildsmith Meadow, Gloucester Rd, Newent, Glos (0531 821509).

NUCLEAR ELECTRIC

Secretary: P L Nurden, 52 Gambier Parry Gdns, Gloucester GL2 9RD (0452 411506).
Colours: Yellow/green **Change colours:** All red.
Ground: ICI Sports Ground, Green Street, Brockworth (0452 371040).

TAVERNERS

Secretary: David Burton, 41 Fairmead, Cam, Dursley GL11 5JR (0453 548000).
Colours: Blue **Change colours:** White.
Ground: Recreation Ground, High Street, Hawkesbury Upton, Avon.

VIKINGS (STROUD)

Secretary: A R Brown, 1 St Lawrence Rd, Barnwood, Gloucester GL4 7QR (0452 615446).
Colours: Orange & white. **Change colours:** Claret & blue.
Ground: Birds Eye Walls Sports & Social Club, Hammonds Way, Barnwood, Gloucester.

BRISTOL DOWNS LEAGUE **FOUNDED:** 1905

DIV. ONE	P	W	D	L	F	A	PTS
Clifton St Vincents	26	22	2	2	89	28	46
Clifton Rockets	26	21	2	3	78	16	44
Sneyd Park	26	20	2	4	64	22	42
DDAS	26	17	6	3	93	26	40
The Mont	26	11	8	7	37	33	30
Ceramic Palace	26	10	9	7	40	34	29
West Town Utd	26	9	4	13	44	70	*20
KGC Panels	26	8	4	14	42	74	20
Retainers	26	8	3	15	27	48	19
Pump House	26	6	4	16	45	67	16
Torpedo	26	6	4	16	41	82	16
Europa Stars	26	7	1	18	32	62	15
St Judes YC	26	5	5	16	40	76	15
Tebby	26	4	2	20	22	58	10

DIV. TWO	P	W	D	L	F	A	PTS
Sneyd Park Res.	26	18	5	3	78	32	41
Fruit Displays	26	19	2	5	71	25	40
Clifton Rock. Res.	26	18	3	5	66	34	39
DDAS Res.	26	18	3	6	86	36	38
Clifton St V. Res.	26	14	5	7	84	47	33
Southmead United	26	15	1	10	83	58	31
Conham Rangers	26	9	6	11	63	61	24
Glenvic Sports	26	9	5	12	54	57	23
Ryl Mail Drivers	26	7	8	11	48	67	22
Portland Old Boys	26	8	3	15	47	70	19
KE Warmley	26	8	2	16	55	71	18
Luccombe Garage	26	5	4	17	33	71	14
Europa Saints Res.	26	3	6	17	29	99	12
Stowells CP	26	2	6	18	34	102	10

* - 2 points deducted

Norman Hardy Cup: Clifton Rock. (R-up: Europa Sts)

DIV. THREE	P	W	D	L	F	A	PTS
R & J Transport	26	15	6	5	63	38	36
Penpole Inn	26	15	5	6	70	42	35
Bristol Leisurewear	26	14	6	6	72	52	34
Torpedo Res.	26	12	7	7	65	54	31
Sneyd Park 'A'	26	9	8	9	53	52	26
Courage Olympic	26	11	4	11	52	58	26
The Mont Res.	26	11	3	12	69	61	25
Davison Printers	26	9	7	10	46	44	25
Clifton St V. 'A'	26	10	5	11	44	48	25
St Judes YC Res.	26	8	7	11	53	62	23
DDAS 'A'	26	8	4	14	50	56	20
Retainers Res.	26	7	6	13	45	60	20
Cotswool Old Boys	26	7	5	14	56	71	19
Broad Plain	26	7	5	14	57	99	17

DIV. FOUR	P	W	D	L	F	A	PTS
Cotham Old Boys	26	22	3	1	96	26	47
Sneyd Park 'B'	26	20	2	4	85	33	42
Broad Plain Res.	26	18	2	6	111	33	38
KGC Panels Res.	26	17	4	5	82	42	38
Pump House Res.	26	15	4	7	95	49	34
Conham Rgrs Res.	26	15	2	9	52	41	32
Davison Prin. Res.	26	11	2	13	59	55	24
Bristol Deaf	26	10	3	13	60	73	23
Torpedo 'A'	26	9	4	13	62	61	22
St Andrews	26	10	2	14	56	69	22
Tebby Res.	26	7	2	17	37	81	16
Clifton St V. 'B'	26	5	1	20	26	102	11
C & C Tyres	26	3	4	19	49	101	10
West Town U. Res.	26	2	1	23	26	120	*3

* - 2 points deducted

All Saints Cup: Sneyd Park 'A' (R-up: Bristol Deaf)

BRISTOL & AVON LEAGUE

FOUNDED: 1910

PREM. DIV.	P	W	D	L	F	A	PTS
Brimsham Green	24	17	3	4	110	33	37
Bristol MBS Spts	24	16	4	4	105	25	36
Allmass Spts Res.	24	16	1	7	96	56	33
Brislington CC	24	13	5	6	78	50	31
Keynsham Town 'A'	24	14	3	7	72	44	31
Cross Hands	24	12	2	10	53	57	26
Ashton Gate OB	24	9	7	8	55	47	25
Lawrence Rvrs 'A'	24	8	5	11	43	63	21
Crockerne P.	24	6	5	13	31	57	17
Somerdale Rangers	24	6	5	13	27	69	17
AEK Sports	24	6	4	14	37	90	16
Avdon Athletic	24	4	3	17	40	96	11
Hartcliffe CC Utd	24	4	3	17	33	89	11

DIV. ONE	P	W	D	L	F	A	PTS
Henbury OB 'B'	30	27	1	2	137	31	55
Greyfriars Ath. 'A'	30	20	7	3	64	28	47
Brislington Ath.	30	18	6	6	86	44	42
Oldland 'B'	30	18	5	7	86	45	41
Totterdown A. Res.	30	16	6	8	84	55	38
Brimsham Gn Res.	30	15	6	9	69	59	36
Winterbourne D'gons	30	13	8	9	82	59	34
St Nicholas Res.	30	14	3	13	75	69	31
Hartcliffe 'A'	30	11	5	14	76	80	27
Oil Sports	30	11	5	14	52	64	27
Wick Athletic	30	10	5	15	58	73	25
Broad Plain HYC	30	11	3	16	73	102	25
Wolseley United	30	7	3	20	58	85	17
Bristol Five BC	30	6	2	22	63	133	14
Sun Life 'B'	30	4	4	22	36	95	12
Quest Cleaning Res.	30	2	5	23	30	123	9

CRISTIE STROUD & DIST. LGE

FOUNDED: 1902

DIV. ONE	P	W	D	L	F	A	PTS
Eastcombe	30	20	7	3	63	21	47
Upton St Leonards	30	21	3	6	92	45	45
Tufflet Rvrs Res.	30	20	3	7	103	56	43
Whitminster	30	18	6	6	69	39	42
Tetbury Town	30	15	8	7	71	42	38
King's Stanley Res.	30	13	8	9	59	53	34
Whiteshill Utd	30	13	7	10	76	47	33
Randwick	30	12	6	12	66	55	30
Ebley	30	10	6	14	50	70	26
Wotton Rvrs Res.	30	10	5	15	56	63	25
Slimbridge	30	7	11	12	53	69	25
Coaley Rovers	30	9	7	14	41	59	25
Uley	30	9	5	16	62	75	23
Thornbury T. Res.	30	8	5	17	53	69	21
Brimscombe/T. Res.	30	7	6	17	41	82	*19
Longlevens Res.	30	0	3	27	20	130	*2

DIV. TWO	P	W	D	L	F	A	PTS
Uplands United	30	25	1	4	108	52	51
Dusley Town Res.	30	20	9	1	102	30	49
Kingswood	30	19	4	7	69	33	42
Hillesley United	30	18	5	7	87	53	*40
AC Horton (1972)	30	16	4	10	96	62	36
Longford Res.	30	14	2	12	76	73	32
Minchinhampton	30	13	5	12	71	71	31
Frampton Utd Res.	30	10	10	10	50	50	30
Oakridge	29	12	6	12	49	52	30
Laurentian Life	30	11	3	16	73	81	25
Leonard Stanley	30	11	1	18	46	69	23
Alkerton Rgrs	30	8	6	16	51	63	22
Tibberton United	29	9	4	17	66	96	22
Whiteshill Utd Res.	30	5	8	17	40	35	18
Cam Bulldogs Res.	30	6	3	21	39	105	15
Berkeley Town Res.	30	5	3	22	34	82	13

DIV. THREE	P	W	D	L	F	A	PTS
Horsley United	28	20	5	3	101	50	45
Stonehouse F. Res.	28	18	6	4	86	45	42
Hardwicke Res.	28	18	5	5	99	40	41
Ramblers	28	17	6	5	93	55	40
Nuclear Elect. Res.	28	12	8	8	59	50	32
Tuffley Rvrs 'A'	28	13	5	10	72	52	31
Charfield Res.	28	11	9	8	51	41	**29
Shipton Moyne	28	10	8	10	67	58	28
Taverners Res.	28	12	1	15	58	57	25
Shurdington Rvrs	28	9	7	12	59	63	25
Woodchester	28	9	6	13	63	81	24
Gloucester CS	28	7	5	16	54	77	*18
Glevum United	28	7	2	19	51	101	16
Cashes Green	28	5	4	19	45	98	14
Uley Res.	28	2	3	23	40	130	7

DIV. FOUR	P	W	D	L	F	A	PTS
Nympsfield	26	22	3	1	88	24	47
Dursley Town 'A'	26	17	3	6	78	35	37
Vikings Res.	26	17	3	6	75	37	37
Slimbridge Res.	26	13	7	6	79	44	33
Chalford	26	15	3	8	66	48	33
Thornbury T. 'A'	26	12	3	11	73	65	27
Whitminster Res.	26	11	4	11	44	42	26
Bensons	26	10	4	12	70	59	24
Wotton Rvrs 'A'	26	8	7	11	52	57	23
Minchinhampton Res.	26	9	4	13	58	56	22
ICI Fibres Res.	26	11	0	15	55	62	22
Longlevens 'A'	26	6	3	17	35	95	15
Randwick Res.	26	4	3	19	37	124	11
Coaley Rvrs Res.	26	2	3	21	35	97	7

DIV. FIVE	P	W	D	L	F	A	PTS
Ramblers Res.	28	21	5	2	95	43	47
Upton St L. Res.	28	18	8	2	83	40	44
Arlingham Res.	28	17	5	6	94	40	39
NSSC Res.	28	19	1	8	82	50	39
Kingswood Res.	28	15	4	9	65	46	34
Price Walker	28	14	4	10	90	49	32
Ebley Res.	28	14	4	10	67	59	32
Eastcombe Res.	28	14	3	11	67	55	31
Slimbridge 'A'	28	12	5	11	57	55	29
Wickwar United	28	8	5	15	50	68	21
Tetbury Town Res.	28	9	3	16	47	67	21
Oakridge Res.	28	5	8	15	45	64	18
Laurentian L. Res.	28	6	2	20	38	90	14
Reeves United	28	5	3	20	45	94	13
Uley 'A'	28	2	2	24	37	142	6

DIV. SIX	P	W	D	L	F	A	PTS
Sharpness Res.	26	23	1	2	96	20	47
Parkside United	26	18	1	7	101	45	37
Horsley Utd Res.	26	15	4	7	88	45	34
Stonehouse F. 'A'	26	13	5	8	74	60	31
Old Barnwoodians	26	13	3	10	79	60	29
Woodchester Res.	26	10	7	9	56	72	27
Uplands Utd Res.	26	10	6	10	53	51	26
Shurdington R. Res.	26	11	4	11	64	69	26
Eagle Star 'B'	26	8	6	12	49	53	22
Leonard Stan. Res.	26	9	2	15	51	72	20
Alkerton Rgrs Res.	26	7	6	13	44	67	20
North Nibley	26	8	2	16	54	73	18
Gloucester CS Res.	26	6	4	16	51	93	*15
Berkeley Town 'A'	26	5	1	20	34	114	11
LDS - *withdrew*	5	2	0	3	9	14	11

DIV. SEVEN	P	W	D	L	F	A	PTS
Thornbury T. 'B'	26	21	1	4	105	48	43
NSSC Res.	26	17	3	6	81	44	37
Pressboard	26	14	6	6	80	38	34
Chalford Res.	26	14	5	7	53	32	33
Shipton Moyne Res.	26	11	8	7	47	35	30
Newcomers	26	11	6	9	54	51	28
Sherston T. Res.	26	11	5	10	80	57	27
Cashes Green Res	26	12	3	11	55	52	27
Hillview Rgrs	26	9	5	12	50	63	23
Renishaw	26	6	8	12	46	63	20
Bensons Res.	26	8	4	14	47	70	20
Dursley Town 'B'	26	7	5	14	50	65	19
FC Westrip	26	6	3	17	27	77	15
Glevum United Res.	26	2	4	20	38	118	8

* - 1 point deducted

New teams for 1994-95 are: ICI Fibres (relegated from the Gloucestershire Northern Senior League), Charfield Junior Old Boys, Hillesley Utd Res., Sharpness 'A' and Ramblers 'A'.
Leaving the league are: Eastcombe (to the Gloucestershire Northern Senior League) and Old Barnwoodians (disbanded)

STROUD & DISTRICT CHARITY CUP FINALS

FOUNDED: 4th July, 1922

Harry Greening Trophy *(at Frampton Utd, 5th May)*:
Shortwood United 3, Wotton Rovers 1

Section 'A' Cup *(at Brimscombe & Thrupp, 4th May)*:
Shortwood United Res. 2, King's Stanley 0

Section 'B' Cup *(at GALA Wilton, 7th May)*:
Tuffley Rovers Res. 3, Upton St Leonards 2

Sec. 'C' Cup *(at Stonehouse Freeway, 3rd/10th May)*:
Charfield Res. 2, Nuclear Electric Res. 0 *(after 1-1)*

Section 'D' Cup *(at Shortwood Utd, 14th April)*:
NSSC 1, Horsley United Res. 0 *(aet)*

Bill Bick Trophy *(at Tuffley Rovers, 19th April)*:
Pressboard 3, Chalford Reserves 0

BERKELEY CHARITY CUP FINALS

FOUNDED: 23rd March, 1932

Premier Section Cup *(at Slimbridge, 9th May)*:
Stonehouse Freeway 2, Berkeley Town 1

Junior Section Cup *(at Stonehouse Freeway, 11th May)*:
Dursley Town 'A' 2, Kingswood Reserves 0

BRISTOL & DISTRICT LEAGUE

FOUNDED: 1892

SENIOR DIV.	P	W	D	L	F	A	PTS
Haynes Roofing	30	24	4	2	103	39	52
DRG Res.	30	21	3	6	89	35	45
BAWA Aces	30	17	8	5	67	40	42
Sth Brist. Cent.	30	15	7	8	72	55	37
Tormarton	30	16	3	11	69	46	35
Soundwell Vic. Utd	30	12	7	11	75	56	31
Wick Kingsway	30	12	7	11	53	38	29
Highridge U. Res.	30	12	5	11	56	55	29
Frampton A. Res.	30	11	6	13	62	49	28
Greyfriars Ath.	30	12	4	14	59	58	28
Winterbourne U. Res.	30	11	5	14	58	56	27
Made For Ever	30	10	7	13	49	67	27
Hartcliffe Com. C.	30	10	6	16	63	73	26
St Pancras	30	12	1	17	54	71	25
Iron Acton Res.	30	3	8	19	44	102	14
Hambrook Res.	30	1	1	28	32	165	3

DIV. ONE	P	W	D	L	F	A	PTS
Stapleton Res.	30	19	8	3	87	36	46
AEK Rangers	30	19	6	5	114	47	44
Roman Glass	30	18	6	6	67	35	#42
Crosscourt United	30	16	10	4	56	29	42
Seymour United	30	19	3	8	82	43	41
Totterdown Utd	30	16	7	7	59	41	39
Oldland Res.	30	13	10	7	73	61	36
Hanham Ath. Res.	30	16	2	12	66	58	34
Fishponds Ath.	29	12	5	13	70	71	29
St Stephens	30	10	5	15	55	60	25
IML Sports	30	6	9	15	50	70	21
Imperial Courage	30	7	5	18	48	101	19
Hillfields Park	29	9	4	17	48	77	*20
Parnalls	30	7	3	20	54	99	17
Eden Grove	30	4	7	19	36	76	15
Kingsgrove United	30	2	6	22	32	93	10

DIV. TWO	P	W	D	L	F	A	PTS
Nicholas Wdrs Res.	26	16	8	2	76	27	40
Hillfields OB Res.	26	15	5	6	63	28	35
Rangeworthy	26	13	6	7	59	40	32
Henbury OB 'A'	26	13	6	7	49	40	32
Bitton Res.	26	12	7	7	60	36	31
Knowle United	26	12	7	7	36	30	31
Lawrence R. Res.	26	13	4	9	45	37	30
Breakaways Rgrs	26	9	4	14	48	74	22
Westerleigh Spts	26	7	7	12	36	39	21
Olveston Utd Res.	26	8	5	13	50	58	21
Ace Kitchens LT	26	8	4	14	45	76	20
Quest Cleaning Serv.	26	5	6	15	42	65	16
Staple Hill Res.	26	6	7	13	38	63	*15
Dundridge Rovers	26	3	6	17	33	66	*8

DIV. THREE	P	W	D	L	F	A	PTS
Sea Mills Pk Res.	28	18	6	4	74	40	42
Barton Hill Rgrs	28	17	5	6	73	39	39
Longwell Gn Res.	28	14	8	6	63	57	36
Rotunda	28	15	4	9	78	49	34
Brist. Univ. Res.	28	13	3	12	67	56	29
S Brist. Cen. Res.	28	12	5	11	50	63	29
Clevedon T. 'A'	28	14	3	11	75	52	*27
Wick K'way Res.	28	10	5	13	45	51	25
Sun Life Res.	28	10	5	13	45	61	25
Brist. Union Res.	28	9	6	13	50	60	24
Cleevewood	28	11	2	15	51	67	24
Shaftesbury C. 'A'	28	9	7	12	47	47	*21
Made For Ever Res.	28	7	7	14	35	46	21
Chipping S'bury Res	28	7	10	11	52	67	*20
Nicholas Wdrs 'A'	28	3	4	21	34	83	10

DIV. FOUR	P	W	D	L	F	A	PTS
Hartcliffe Res.	30	21	4	5	122	38	46
Pucklechurch 'A'	30	20	6	4	93	43	46
Hilton Rangers	30	19	5	6	85	40	43
Sandringham Spts	30	19	5	6	100	60	43
Archway SP Res.	30	17	1	12	58	60	35
Long Ashton Res.	30	16	4	10	79	61	*34
Fry Club 'A'	30	14	3	13	75	61	31
Highridge U. 'A'	30	14	3	13	73	68	31
LA Sports	30	12	2	16	71	77	26
Soundwell VU Res.	30	11	4	15	55	79	26
Frampton Ath. 'A'	30	10	5	15	72	82	25
Oldland 'A'	30	9	6	15	74	80	24
DRG 'A'	30	10	2	18	52	68	22
Rangeworthy Res.	30	10	2	18	65	84	22
Old Sodbury	30	9	4	17	60	83	22
Bristol Albion	30	1	0	29	16	166	2

DIV. FIVE	P	W	D	L	F	A	PTS
Westerleigh S. Res.	30	19	6	5	77	47	44
Greyfriars A. Res.	30	18	7	5	91	37	43
Bendix Sports	30	18	6	6	82	33	42
Bitton 'A'	30	16	5	9	72	39	37
Bristol 5 OB Res.	30	17	3	10	72	51	37
Rail Bristol	30	14	7	9	70	47	35
AEK Rangers Res.	30	14	4	12	62	63	32
St Nicholas	30	14	3	13	65	58	31
Alveston Rangers	30	13	4	13	53	72	30
BAWA Aces Res.	30	11	5	14	66	87	27
Winterbourne U. 'A'	30	11	3	16	61	93	25
St Pancras Res.	30	8	7	15	46	81	23
Totterdown Utd Res.	30	10	4	16	56	75	22
Hanham Ath. 'A'	30	7	8	15	44	75	22
Avon St George	30	6	4	20	56	78	16
Dundridge R. Res.	30	5	2	23	52	89	12

DIV. SIX	P	W	D	L	F	A	PTS
Fry Club 'B'	30	26	1	3	96	42	53
Breakaways Res.	30	20	3	7	108	49	#45
Roman Glass Res.	30	20	5	5	124	52	*41
Hillfields OB 'A'	30	16	5	9	89	61	37
Sea Mills Pk 'A'	30	15	7	8	82	55	37
Haynes Roof. Res.	30	16	6	8	96	52	*36
Parnall Res.	30	16	2	12	84	62	34
Sun Life 'A'	30	11	6	13	50	59	28
Shireway Sports	30	9	9	12	53	65	27
Fishponds A. Res.	30	9	8	13	66	74	26
St Stephens Res.	30	9	6	15	50	61	24
Bristol Univ. 'A'	30	11	2	17	74	100	24
Bendix Spts Res.	30	8	4	18	54	89	20
Westbury Sports	30	7	6	17	50	88	20
Eden Grove Res.	30	5	4	21	44	104	14
Seymour Utd Res.	30	3	3	24	33	139	9

\# - points awarded
* - points deducted

BRISTOL & DISTRICT SUNDAY LEAGUE

FOUNDED: 1966

PREM. DIV.	P	W	D	L	F	A	PTS
Lebeq Tav. Courage	20	17	3	0	86	16	54
Friendship Spts	20	14	4	2	49	27	46
Broad Plain House	20	13	4	3	59	28	43
BRSC Aidan	20	9	5	6	41	33	32
Cabot Towers	20	8	3	9	41	45	27
Backwell Sunday	20	7	5	8	37	49	26
St Josephs	20	7	3	10	36	37	24
Hanham Sunday	20	6	1	13	32	52	19
Staple Hill	20	4	3	13	28	62	15
City Alarms	20	5	0	15	34	74	15
Sartan United	20	3	3	14	27	48	12

Lower Division Champions:
Senior Div. (10): George Inn
Div. 1 (10): Hallen United
Div. 2 (11): Shireway Sports
Div. 3 (11): AFC Hillfields
Div. 4 (10): Blackhorse
Div. 5 (13): Lawrence Weston

Cup Finals:
League Cup: Lebeq Tavern Courage 4, St Josephs 0
Evening Post Cup: AFC Hillfields 3, Lucas Sports 2
Charles Finch Memorial Cup: Shireway Sports 6, Chew Stoke Old Boys 0

GLOUCESTER & DISTRICT SUNDAY LEAGUE

FOUNDED: 1965

PREM. DIV.	P	W	D	L	F	A	PTS
Brockworth Parish	18	12	5	1	53	19	41
Jennings O.H.	18	11	2	5	49	40	35
Top Cue Hardwicke	18	9	4	5	42	18	31
Pikemen	18	8	3	7	42	39	27
Pint Pot Bowmen	18	7	5	6	43	40	26
DCSC Tartans	18	7	4	7	47	35	25
Longford	18	7	1	10	43	45	*21
Brockworth Nomads	18	6	2	10	39	45	20
Ermin Plant	18	4	4	10	28	55	16
Churchdown Parish	18	2	4	12	32	82	10

* - 1 point deducted

Lower Division Champions:
Div. 1 (12): Leyhill
Div. 2 (11): Windsor Drive
Div. 3 (12): AC Severn
Div. 4 (11): Forest Police
Div. 5 (12): Lydney Town Social
Div. 6 (10): John Carr
Div. 7 (10): Gloucester City Supporters

BRISTOL REGIONAL SUNDAY LEAGUE

FOUNDED: 1963

PREM. DIV.	P	W	D	L	F	A	PTS
TM Ceramics	18	13	2	3	49	22	28
Rangeworthy	18	12	4	2	54	31	28
Three Horseshoes	17	9	4	4	46	26	22
Ashton Vale Utd	17	5	7	5	28	23	17
The Fox	18	6	5	7	29	38	17
Dynamics	18	6	2	10	37	44	14
Bell Rhabits	18	5	4	9	32	44	14
New Inn Keynsham	17	5	3	9	37	36	13
Keyn. Venturers	18	5	3	10	27	43	13
Broomhill Wdrs	17	2	5	10	19	59	9

Lower Division Champions:
Div. 1 (12): Henbury Corinthians
Div. 2 (11): Bristol Irish
Div. 3 (12): Churngold Rangers
Div. 4 (12): Swan Inn
Div. 5 (14): Nat West Court
Div. 6 (14): New Inn Keynsham Reserves

G Pullin Cup: Three Horseshoes
G Pullin Cup R-up: Dynamics
KO Trophy: Churngold Rangers
KO Trophy R-up: New Inn Keynsham Reserves

C & G CHELTENHAM SUNDAY LEAGUE

FOUNDED: 1968

PREM. DIV.	P	W	D	L	F	A	PTS
Cat & Fiddle	14	11	0	3	54	27	33
Lokomotiv Bass	14	10	2	2	75	17	32
Charlton Sun. Bass	14	9	0	5	65	33	27
Endsleigh	14	9	1	4	46	30	**24
Whaddon Sunday	14	7	0	7	35	42	21
Typemasters	14	6	1	7	28	39	19
Grosvenor Batman	14	2	0	12	23	75	*4
Cheltenham Saras	14	0	0	14	12	75	*-2

* - 2 points deducted

Lower Division Champions:
Div. 1 (10): Tewkesbury YMCA
Div. 2 (10): Swindon Village
Div. 3 (10): Pump & Optic
Div. 4 (10): Whaddon Sunday Reserves
Div. 5 (11): Carpet Studio FC

Cup Finals:
Allan Duft Memorial Cup: Lokomotiv Bass 2, Charlton Sunday Bass 0
Intermediate KO Shield: Whaddon Sunday Reserves 3, Mitre United 1 *(aet)*
Junior KO Shield: Endsleigh 2, Cat & Fiddle 1

BRISTOL & WESSEX SUNDAY LEAGUE

FOUNDED: 1980

PREM. DIV.	P	W	D	L	F	A	PTS
Golden Bottle	18	15	1	2	72	17	46
Headley Park Utd	18	14	1	3	73	19	43
Cutters	18	14	0	4	70	14	42
Antelope Spartak	18	9	2	7	32	22	29
Shire Cricketers	18	9	2	7	36	31	29
London Pioneers	18	8	2	8	44	50	26
Portway Bristol	18	6	3	9	55	54	21
Southside Scaffolding	18	5	1	12	28	36	16
Azzurri	18	4	2	12	32	70	14
Morgan Westley	18	0	0	18	12	141	0

Lower Division Champions:
Div. 1 (11): Northavon Taverners
Div. 2 (12): Jessops Tavern
Div. 3 (14): Cutters Reserves
Div. 4 (11): Forest Police
Div. 5 (12): Lydney Town Social
Div. 6 (10): John Carr
Div. 7 (10): Gloucester City Supporters

League Cup: Golden Bottle
League Cup R-up: Cutters

COMMERCIAL SUNDAY LEAGUE

FOUNDED: 1978

PREM. DIV.	P	W	D	L	F	A	PTS
Clevedon Pier	18	15	2	1	84	26	32
Fortfield	18	14	4	0	59	25	32
Nailsea Glasshouse	18	9	6	3	46	28	24
Bridge Academicals	18	10	2	6	49	46	22
White Tree	18	7	5	6	45	40	17
Inter West	17	6	3	8	38	45	15
Severnside Surfacing	17	4	3	10	33	30	11
The Waltons	18	3	5	10	32	63	11
Crown Inn (Clapton)	18	3	0	15	15	47	6
Plough & Windmill	18	1	2	15	15	60	4

Lower Division Champions:
Div. 1 (11): Masons Arms
Div. 2 (11): Spiro Agnew
Div. 3 (11): Power Systems
Div. 4 (11): Baileys Caravans

GET ALL THE LATEST NEWS ON THE

F.A. COMPETITIONS NEWSLINE

Updated daily with Draws, Replay Dates, Results, Interviews from F.A. Cup, Trophy, Vase, Women's Challenge Cup, Sunday and Youth Cups

PHONE NOW

089166 44 33

Presented by Tony Incenzo

Marketed by Sportslines on 0386 47302 or 0831 464517

Calls cost 39p per minute cheap rate and 49p per minute at all other times.
Call costing correct at time of going to press.

HAMPSHIRE F.A.

Secretary: R G Barnes,
8 Ashwood Gardens, off Winchester Road, Southampton SO16 7PW (0703 791110).

SENIOR CUP 1993-94

First Round

AC Delco v Alresford Town	1-2
New Milton Town v Eastleigh	0-3
AFC Lymington v Portsmouth Royal Navy	3-0
AFC Totton v Jersey Wanderers	5-4
Andover v Hartley Wintney	5-1
Romsey Town v Winchester City	5-0
Christchurch *(w/o)* Sholing Sports *(scr)*	
Cove v Netley Central Sports	8-1
Horndean v Basingstoke Town	1-0
Locksheath v Bass Alton Town	0-3
Aerostructures Spts & Social v Bashley	2-4
New Street v Blackfield & Langley	0-0,3-2
Newport Isle of Wight v East Cowes Vics	4-2*(aet)*
Paulsgrove v Overton United	2-2,1-0
Brockenhurst v DCA Basingstoke	0-0*(B'hurst w'drew)*
Ryde Sports v Colden Common	4-1
Vale Recreation v Bournemouth	1-2
Waterlooville v Pirelli General	4-2

Second Round

AFC Totton v Bishops Waltham Town	4-3
Aldershot Town v DCA Basingstoke	4-1
Christchurch v Andover	4-2
Cove v BAT Sports	4-2
Cowes Sports v Bashley	0-1
Fareham Town v AFC Lymington	0-1
Farnborough Town v Bournemouth	7-0
Gosport Borough v Fleet Town	2-6
Havant Town v Bass Alton Town	3-0
Horndean v Malshanger	1-0
Eastleigh v Fleetlands	2-0
Newport Isle of Wight v Alresford Town	2-0
New Street v Portsmouth Civil Service	2-3
Ryde Sports v Romsey Town	3-1
Waterlooville v Petersfield Town	1-0
Whitchurch United v Paulsgrove	0-2

Third Round

AFC Totton v Bashley	1-5
Christchurch v AFC Lymington	1-4
Ryde Sports v Cove	2-1
Farnborough Town v Horndean	4-0
Waterlooville v Paulsgrove	9-1
Newport Isle of Wight v Eastleigh	6-0
Havant Town v Fleet Town	2-2,3-2
Aldershot Town v Portsmouth Civil Service	2-1

Quarter-Finals

Bashley v Eastleigh	1-3
Waterlooville v AFC Lymington	4-1
Havant Town v Ryde Sports	2-0
Farnborough Town v Aldershot Town	1-1,1-0

Semi-Finals

Eastleigh v Havant *(at Gosport 8/3/94)*	1-3
Waterlooville v Farnborough *(at Andover 16/3/94)*	2-4

Final *(at Southampton FC, Monday 25th April)*: Havant Town 1, Farnborough Town 0 *(att: 932)*

Cowes Sports - CBH Hampshire League champions 1993-94. *Photo - D W Hampton.*

C.H.B.
HAMPSHIRE LEAGUE

Chairman: Mr Norman White.

Vice-Chairman: Mr Geoff Cox.

Hon. Secretary: Mr John Moody,
13 Tadfield Cres., Romsey SO51 8AN
(0794 514073)

THREE EXCITING TITLE RACES

This season has probably been the most dramatic in the League's 98 year old history. The Management Committee found themselves without full-time office staff and equipment at a stroke after the Council of the Hampshire Football Association decided, by just two votes, to withdraw this facility from the League. As a consequence, the League also lost the services of a professional secretary in Ray Barnes and Treasurer in Julie Phippard.

The League's Management Committee had to take immediate steps to ensure the smooth running of the League and Cup competitions and were lucky to draw volunteers from their own ranks to take on the arduous positions of Officers. All the Secretaries were new to the posts and, because most also had full-time jobs and some of them also ran their own clubs, the posts and work previously undertaken by the HFA office staff were sub-divided to spread the load.

Having found their Officers, the League were then left in a situation of not having an office or even a paper clip or sheet of paper! A computer was bought as were desks and chairs, filing cabinets and other office equipment and in effect three small offices were set up; one in Romsey, one in Alton and one in Overton - all in the homes of the respective secretaries - not an ideal situation but one which subsequently worked well.

A new badge was designed and thousands of sheets of new stationery were printed and then the weather struck! We experienced one of the worst winters for many seasons and come January we still had a third of the season to complete. Our last league match was played on Tuesday 24th May, a day after the League Cup Final. Some Clubs had to play four games in a week and we even created history by playing the first ever Hampshire League game on a Sunday. My thanks go to all clubs for their co-operation in getting the games played during this difficlt period.

All three League titles were fought out right to the end of the season as were some of the relegation issues which kept interest alive. Congratulations go to Cowes Sports for taking the Division 1 championship and reaching the Trophyman League Cup final and the Isle of Wight Senior Cup final and for gaining promotion to the Jewson Wessex League. Cowes were pushed all the way by Blackfield & Langley and at one stage of the season Portsmouth Civil Service made it a three cornered fight.

There was a similar scrap for the Division 2 championship. Going into the last few games Ecchinswell, Hedge End and Hayling United could all have won it. Ecchinswell took the title to Berkshire for the first time.

The Division 3 championship followed last season's North Hants Senior League title to Ludgershall, but they were pressed all the way to the post by Bishopstoke Social who lost out when they had a win cancelled for playing an ineligible player and then lost the re-played match.

Congratulations also go to our clubs who have triumphed in Local Association and other cup competitions. Pride of place goes to Hedge End who won the Hampshire Intermediate Cup, the only County cup to be won by one of the League's clubs this season.

During the season the Grounds Committee visited a number of clubs and were impressed at the standards being achieved and maintained. Where faults were found, clubs responded well to rectify them.

We welcome back to the fold Whitchurch United who were unfortunately relegated from the Jewson Wessex League, but say goodbye to Romsey Town Reserves who were relegated to the Southampton Premier League. We also extend a welcome to four new clubs; Tadley (ex North Hants Senior League), Hythe & Dibden (Southampton Premier League), Four Marks (Aldershot Senior League) and Mayflower (Portsmouth League).

John Moody, Secretary

DIV. ONE	P	W	D	L	F	A	PTS
Cowes Sports	38	26	7	5	88	34	85
Blackfield & Langley	38	23	8	7	91	48	77
Portsmouth CS	38	21	9	8	80	44	72
Pirelli General	38	21	5	12	76	48	68
Bass Alton Town	38	19	10	9	84	60	67
Bishops Waltham T.	38	18	6	14	75	65	*59
Winchester City	38	17	7	14	75	59	58
Verwood Town	38	16	10	12	74	48	*57
Colden Common	38	14	11	13	63	59	53
New Street	38	14	8	16	64	63	50
Fleetlands	38	14	9	15	51	47	51
Paulsgrove	38	15	6	17	73	82	51
Overton United	38	14	6	18	61	63	48
Malshanger	38	12	9	17	53	68	45
New Milton Town	38	12	9	17	54	75	45
Alresford Town	38	12	8	18	53	88	44
AC Delco	38	9	9	20	35	72	36
Netley Cent. Spts	38	7	13	18	53	87	34
Romsey Town	38	7	12	19	48	83	33
Locksheath	38	3	10	25	48	106	19

* - 1 point deducted

DIV. TWO	P	W	D	L	F	A	PTS
Ecchinswell	32	23	6	3	97	33	75
Hayling United	32	21	7	4	71	26	70
Hedge End	32	18	8	6	85	41	62
Liss Athletic	32	17	9	6	77	46	*59
Stockbridge	32	18	3	11	71	52	57
St Mary's	32	17	6	9	94	55	*56
Basing Rovers	32	15	7	10	64	58	52
Nursling	32	13	8	11	55	34	47
Otterbourne	32	12	9	11	57	56	45
Fleets Spurs	32	13	5	14	70	68	44
Vosper Thornycroft	32	13	2	17	56	57	41
Broughton	32	11	8	13	68	69	41
Brading Town	32	11	8	13	43	49	41
West Wight	32	6	7	19	39	60	25
Awbridge	32	6	5	21	32	77	23
Ringwood Town	32	5	3	24	41	87	18
Braishfield	32	1	1	30	15	177	4

DIV. THREE	P	W	D	L	F	A	PTS
Ludgershall Sports	30	21	4	5	94	60	67
Bishopstoke Social	30	20	5	5	112	44	65
Hilsea Club	30	19	4	7	70	47	61
Esso Fawley	30	14	5	11	45	44	47
Portsmouth CS Res.	30	15	1	14	66	48	46
Winch. City Res.	30	13	6	11	51	70	45
Hamble Club	30	12	8	10	64	61	44
Swanmore	30	12	6	12	60	51	42
AFC Aldermaston	30	12	3	15	57	54	39
Compton	30	11	5	14	51	48	38
Bass Alton Res..	30	9	11	10	49	48	38
Fleetlands Res.	30	11	5	14	68	72	38
Covies	30	9	5	16	45	67	32
Netley Central Res.	30	8	5	17	34	55	29
Winchester Castle	30	8	5	17	57	101	29
Romsey Town Res.	30	3	6	21	37	90	15

* - 1 point deducted

DIVISION ONE RESULT CHART 1993-94

HOME TEAM	1	2	3	4	5	6	7	8	9	10	11	12	13	14	15	16	17	18	19	20
1. AC Delco	*	3-1	0-3	0-0	2-3	2-1	1-5	1-4	2-1	0-1	1-0	1-4	0-0	1-3	0-3	1-2	0-6	1-1	2-0	0-3
2. Alresford	3-1	*	1-1	1-2	0-3	3-4	3-4	2-1	2-2	2-1	1-0	1-4	1-3	1-0	3-2	2-1	0-4	1-1	0-0	3-3
3. Bass Alton	5-1	4-0	*	4-0	4-3	4-1	0-2	4-2	1-0	6-0	4-2	5-1	1-4	3-1	3-3	0-0	4-1	2-2	2-1	1-2
4. Bishops Waltham	1-0	6-1	1-2	*	2-3	0-0	3-6	3-1	3-1	2-4	3-2	4-2	0-1	2-4	5-2	1-3	4-1	2-1	1-0	2-0
5. Blackfield/Langley	2-2	4-2	2-2	5-1	*	2-1	1-1	2-1	8-0	2-2	4-1	5-0	0-1	2-3	1-0	6-0	4-2	4-1	3-1	3-0
6. Colden Common	1-1	3-0	1-1	0-2	3-1	*	2-0	1-1	0-0	2-1	0-2	2-2	4-2	2-2	5-3	3-0	1-1	4-0	2-1	0-1
7. Cowes Sports	0-0	2-0	3-1	0-0	1-1	2-1	*	2-0	2-0	1-0	3-0	3-0	3-2	1-2	5-0	2-0	1-0	9-1	3-0	2-0
8. Fleetlands	1-0	2-0	1-3	1-1	3-0	1-1	1-2	*	2-1	2-0	2-0	0-1	0-0	1-0	1-1	0-1	1-3	1-1	1-0	2-1
9. Locks Heath	0-2	2-2	6-2	0-4	1-3	1-3	2-4	2-3	*	2-1	1-2	2-1	1-2	1-4	2-6	3-3	2-2	2-2	0-1	1-7
10. Malshanger	4-0	2-3	2-0	2-0	0-2	3-2	0-5	0-2	1-0	*	0-2	1-2	2-1	2-2	2-2	4-0	1-2	1-1	0-2	2-1
11. Overton United	0-1	5-2	2-2	4-1	1-2	2-1	1-3	3-2	3-0	2-2	*	1-3	0-2	2-2	6-1	0-2	3-2	1-0	1-1	0-0
12. Paulsgrove	2-1	1-2	5-0	3-2	2-1	2-0	1-1	1-1	4-1	1-1	1-3	*	4-1	0-3	3-3	7-3	1-2	1-2	1-5	0-5
13. Pirelli General	5-0	0-1	1-0	1-3	0-2	2-2	2-0	2-0	8-1	4-0	3-0	1-2	*	0-4	4-0	3-4	5-0	2-0	1-1	3-1
14. Portsmouth CS	2-1	4-0	3-0	2-2	0-0	1-2	0-2	1-0	2-1	1-3	2-1	1-1	0-1	*	4-0	1-1	3-1	3-2	2-0	4-0
15. Netley Central	0-0	2-2	0-2	0-0	0-1	0-2	1-2	3-2	2-2	2-1	1-4	2-1	1-2	0-0	*	3-1	1-1	4-1	2-2	0-3
16. New Milton T.	2-1	1-1	0-0	0-3	1-1	2-2	1-0	2-0	3-1	1-2	2-2	2-4	1-2	0-6	6-0	*	0-1	1-1	0-4	0-1
17. New Street	0-1	2-3	1-1	2-0	0-1	0-1	3-1	0-0	3-3	2-2	3-2	3-0	3-0	1-1	4-1	3-2	*	1-0	1-5	0-1
18. Romsey Town	1-1	1-2	1-2	1-6	0-2	2-1	1-1	0-0	2-2	1-1	1-0	4-1	0-0	5-2	2-0	2-3	1-0	*	1-4	2-4
19. Verwood Town	1-1	4-0	1-1	1-2	6-1	7-2	1-1	0-3	1-1	3-1	0-1	2-1	3-1	0-2	1-1	2-1	3-1	7-2	*	1-0
20. Winchester City	1-1	3-1	1-4	4-1	1-1	2-0	2-3	2-3	5-0	1-1	2-0	5-3	3-4	2-3	1-1	0-2	3-2	2-1	2-2	*

DIV. TWO RESULTS 1993-94	1	2	3	4	5	6	7	8	9	10	11	12	13	14	15	16	17
1. Awbridge	*	1-3	1-0	0-0	1-1	1-1	1-6	0-2	0-3	1-2	0-5	1-2	4-2	0-1	0-4	0-1	4-1
2. Basing Rovers	5-0	*	0-0	3-0	5-1	0-2	1-1	1-1	2-6	0-0	0-2	2-2	3-1	2-7	1-2	0-2	2-2
3. Brading Town	1-1	0-2	*	3-0	2-2	0-0	5-2	1-1	2-0	0-2	1-0	1-1	2-1	3-0	4-0	2-1	2-1
4. Braishfield	1-2	0-4	2-1	*	1-9	0-9	0-3	0-5	1-3	0-7	0-7	0-6	0-5	0-7	0-5	0-3	1-2
5. Broughton	2-2	4-1	1-1	7-2	*	3-5	4-1	1-2	2-2	1-2	2-0	3-0	4-0	3-6	3-0	1-3	1-1
6. Ecchinswell	4-0	1-2	5-1	13-0	8-0	*	2-1	2-0	3-0	2-2	2-1	6-1	3-0	3-1	3-2	1-0	3-1
7. Fleet Spurs	4-3	2-3	4-2	6-1	4-2	3-4	*	2-2	3-1	1-4	1-1	3-1	6-1	1-4	1-2	0-4	2-1
8. Hayling United	4-0	2-1	2-0	6-2	5-0	1-2	2-0	*	1-2	3-1	1-0	2-0	5-1	5-0	2-0	3-1	0-0
9. Hedge End	3-0	1-1	6-1	14-0	6-1	0-1	4-0	2-2	*	4-0	2-2	3-0	4-1	1-1	2-1	0-1	2-0
10. Liss Athletic	3-1	5-0	1-1	8-0	2-1	3-2	1-2	1-2	2-2	*	1-0	1-1	3-0	2-2	5-2	3-3	4-2
11. Nursling	2-0	1-3	2-0	6-0	4-1	1-1	2-2	0-0	4-4	1-1	*	3-2	0-1	0-1	0-2	1-0	1-0
12. Otterbourne	3-1	1-5	3-0	6-1	0-5	1-1	0-0	2-2	2-1	2-2	1-1	*	4-1	1-1	1-2	3-0	4-0
13. Ringwood Town	2-1	1-2	0-2	4-0	0-0	0-1	1-2	0-2	3-4	2-3	0-4	0-1	*	2-4	1-4	5-0	2-2
14. St Marys	4-0	5-0	2-1	10-1	2-2	1-2	2-4	1-2	0-4	4-1	1-0	2-3	3-0	*	2-2	7-2	2-1
15. Stockbridge	0-2	2-4	1-2	5-2	2-0	5-1	3-0	2-1	2-2	2-0	1-2	3-1	8-2	0-6	*	3-1	2-0
16. Vosper Thornycroft	5-2	2-4	3-2	5-0	0-1	0-2	2-1	1-2	2-5	1-3	0-1	0-2	4-0	3-1	1-1	*	3-0
17. West Wight	0-2	1-2	1-0	3-0	1-2	2-2	4-3	0-1	0-2	1-2	3-1	1-0	2-2	4-4	0-1	0-1	*

DIV. 3. RESULTS 93-94.	1	2	3	4	5	6	7	8	9	10	11	12	13	14	15	16
1. AFC Aldermaston	*	3-3	1-5	1-0	2-0	0-1	3-1	3-3	2-3	1-5	2-0	4-2	4-0	0-0	3-1	0-3
2. Bass Alton Town Reserves	1-0	*	1-3	1-1	1-1	1-1	0-1	0-3	1-1	3-3	4-0	2-0	5-3	4-1	2-0	1-1
3. Bishopstoke Social	3-1	2-0	*	1-1	4-2	3-1	3-3	6-0	2-1	4-1	2-0	0-1	8-0	3-0	8-3	9-0
4. Compton	0-5	2-0	2-5	*	1-2	1-2	0-2	0-2	1-2	3-3	0-1	2-1	6-0	3-0	2-2	3-4
5. Covies	2-0	2-1	2-6	2-3	*	0-2	3-1	1-0	2-4	1-2	2-0	2-4	3-3	1-3	2-2	1-2
6. Esso Fawley	1-0	0-0	3-2	0-1	2-1	*	3-0	1-5	0-4	1-2	3-1	2-1	2-1	1-1	8-2	0-1
7. Fleetlands Reserves	3-1	2-0	3-2	1-4	3-0	3-1	*	4-5	1-3	3-5	1-3	0-3	4-1	2-2	10-5	1-3
8. Hamble Club	4-3	2-0	3-3	0-2	3-2	0-0	2-2	*	2-2	4-4	2-1	0-1	3-0	1-6	3-3	6-0
9. Hilsea Club	2-1	1-0	0-3	1-4	2-1	1-5	5-0	4-0	*	1-2	2-1	2-1	0-0	4-2	6-2	0-6
10. Ludgershall Sports	3-2	3-6	3-2	2-1	8-0	3-2	2-2	2-1	2-1	*	3-1	4-2	6-1	6-3	5-0	4-2
11. Netley Central Sports	1-4	1-3	5-3	1-0	0-0	0-0	3-2	1-1	1-1	0-1	*	0-4	1-1	1-4	1-2	2-3
12. Portsmouth Civil Service Reserves	2-0	2-2	0-3	3-2	1-3	1-0	4-5	2-0	0-2	5-0	0-2	*	4-2	4-0	6-3	4-0
13. Romsey Town Reserves	1-3	2-2	2-2	0-2	1-2	3-0	1-4	2-1	1-5	1-2	0-3	1-3	*	1-3	4-2	2-2
14. Swanmore	1-3	5-1	2-2	1-2	3-0	2-0	0-0	1-4	1-2	2-1	0-2	2-1	3-0	*	1-2	7-0
15. Winchester Castle	0-3	2-2	2-5	2-1	2-4	0-2	3-2	2-3	3-4	2-5	2-0	2-1	2-1	0-4	*	1-1
16. Winchester City Reserves	3-0	0-2	1-8	1-1	1-1	0-1	3-1	2-1	0-4	3-2	3-1	1-2	3-2	0-0	2-3	*

TROPHYMAN HAMPSHIRE LEAGUE CUP 1993-94

First Round

AFC Aldermaston v Broughton	3-1
Ecchinswell v Bradling Town	1-2*(aet)*
Liss Athletic v Esso Fawley	5-1
Malshanger v Bass Alton Town	0-2
Paulsgrove v West Wight	3-0
St Marys v Alresford Town	2-1
Wonchester City v New Street	2-1
Romsey Town v Pirelli General	0-2
Colden Common v Fleetlands	1-0
Fleet Spurs v Verwood Town	1-3
Ludgershall Sports v Netley Central Sports	1-0
Otterbourne v Swanmore	1-3
Portsmouth Civil Service v Hayling United	0-1
Winchester Castle v Overton United	2-3
Cowes Sports v Hedge End	4-2*(aet)*

(continued overleaf)

Trophyman Hampshire League Cup *(continuation)*

Second Round

Locks Heath v Cowes Sports	0-4	Hayling United v Covies	4-2
Brading Town v Winchester City	0-2	Ringwood Town v Bishops Waltham Town	0-2
Blackfield & Langley v New Milton Town	2-1	AFC Aldermaston v Verwood Town	1-2
Liss Athletic v Overton United	1-5	Nursling v Awbridge	2-1*(aet)*
Colden Common v Swanmore	2-1	Stockbridge v Bass Alton Town	2-3
Ludgershall Sports v AC Delco	1-0	Braishfield v Pirelli General	0-4
Bishopstoke Social v Compton	7-0	Paulsgrove v Basing Rovers	0-2
St Marys v Hilsea Club	3-0	Vosper Thornycroft v Hamble Club	2-1

Third Round

Colden Common v Winchester City	1-3	Nursling v Hayling United	3-2
Vosper Thornycroft v Bishopstoke Social	2-1	Verwood Town v Bass Alton Town	0-2
St Marys v Cowes Spts *(at Cowes Spts)*	2-4	Overton United v Blackfield & Langley	2-2,2-1
Ludgershall Sports v Pirelli General	1-2	Bishops Waltham Town v Basing Rovers	3-2

Quarter-Finals

Winchester City v Pirelli General	2-1	Bishops Waltham Town v Bass Alton Town	1-3
Vosper Thornycroft v Nursling	4-0	Cowes Sports v Overton United	2-1

Semi-Finals

Winchester City v Vosper Thornycroft	4-0	Bass Alton Town v Cowes Sports	2-2*(5-6 on pens)*

Final *(at Fareham Town FC)*: Winchester City 2, Cowes Sports 0

Winchester City celebrate after their Trophyman Cup win. *Photo - Innes Marlow*

DIVISION ONE CLUBS 1994-95

A.C. DELCO

Secretary: Adrian Gray, 51 Archery Grove, Woolston, Southampton SO19 9EW (0703 493955).
Ground: AC Delco Spts Ground, Stoneham Lane, Eastleigh (0703 613334).
Colours: Sky & white stripes/black/sky **Change:** Purple/white/purple
Programme: No **Midweek home matchday:** Wednesday.

ALRESFORD TOWN

Secretary: Mr M Chamberlain, 12 Bakers Drove, Rownhams, Southampton, Hants SO16 8AD (0703 730600).
Ground: Arlebury Park, Alresford, Hants (0962 735100).
Colours: White/black/black **Change:** Yellow/red/red
Programme: Yes **Midweek home matchday:** Tuesday/Thursday.

BASS ALTON TOWN

Secretary: A J M Hillman, 19a Beechwood Rd, Alton, Hants GU34 1RL (0420 87103).
Ground: Bass Spts Ground, Anstey Rd, Alton (0420 82465).
Colours: Black & white/black/black **Change:** Green & white & red & blue
Programme: No **Midweek home matchday:** Any.

BISHOPS WALTHAM TOWN

Secretary: Andy Spreadbury, 13 Tanners Rd, North Baddesley, Southampton, Hants SO52 9SD (0703 739034).
Ground: Hoe Road Spts Ground, Bishops Waltham (0489 891841).
Colours: Blue/blue/white **Change:** Gold/black/black
Programme: No **Midweek home matchday:** Wednesday.

BLACKFIELD & LANGLEY

Secretary: K O Bevis, 76 The Warren, Holbury, Southampton, Hants SO45 2QD (0703 891854).
Ground: Gang Warily Rec., Newlands Rd, Blackfield, Southampton, Hants (0703 893603).
Colours: Green/white/green **Change:** Yellow/blue/yellow
Programme: Yes **Midweek home matchday:** Wednesday.

COLDEN COMMON

Secretary: Mr C P Banford, 16 Hollies Way, North Baddesley, Southampton, Hants SO52 9NS (0703 730206).
Ground: Colden Common Recreation Ground, Main Road, Colden Common (0962 712365).
Colours: Red & white stripes/black/red **Change:** All yellow
Programme: Yes **Midweek home matchday:** Wednesday.

ECCHINSWELL

Secretary: Mr R Francis, 12 Willowmead Close, Wash Common, Newbury, Berks RG14 6RW (0635 48139).
Ground: Ecchinswell Rec, Ecchinswell, nr Newbury.
Colours: All red **Change:** White/navy/white.
Programme: Yes **Midweek home matchday:** Tuesday or Wednesday.

FLEETLANDS

Secretary: Mr Paul Coulter, 19 The Yews, Horndean, Waterlooville PO8 0BH (0705 599409).
Ground: Lederle Lane, Gosport, Hants (0329 239723).
Colours: Red & black/white/white **Change:** All blue
Programme: Yes **Midweek home matchday:** Any.

HAYLING UNITED

Secretary: Mrs S Westfield, 12 Wheatlands Ave., Hayling Island, Hants PO11 9SG (0705 463305).
Ground: Hayling Park, Hayling Island, Hants.
Colours: Red & navy/navy/navy **Change:** Blue & white/blue/blue
Programme: No **Midweek home matchday:** Tuesday.

MALSHANGER

Secretary: Fred Norris, 9 Goddards Firs, Oakley, Basingstoke, Hants RG23 7JL (0256 781697).
Ground: The Litchfield, Malshanger, Basingstoke (0256 780285).
Colours: Purple/purple/white **Change:** Orange/black/orange
Programme: **Midweek home matchday:** Tuesday.

NETLEY CENTRAL SPORTS

Secretary: Mr R W Crompton, 47 Station Rd, Netley Abbey, Southampton SO31 5AE (0703 452049).
Ground: Netley Rec, Station Rd, Netley Abbey, Southampton (0703 452267).
Colours: Royal & white/royal/royal **Change:** Red & white/red/red
Programme: Yes **Midweek home matchday:** Wednesday.

NEW MILTON TOWN

Secretary: Mr J A Wyatt, 12 Pinewood Rd, Hordle, Lymington, Hants SO41 0GP (0425 611670).
Ground: Fawcetts Spts Ground, Christchurch Rd, New Milton, Hants BH25 6QF (0425 628191).
Colours: Yellow & blue stripes/blue/blue **Change:** All maroon
Previous Name: New Milton FC (pre-1993) **Previous Ground:** Adjacent pitch (pre-1992)
Programme: Yes **Midweek home matchday:** Wednesday.

NEW STREET

Secretary: Mrs F J Waterman, 'Jorin Bay' 2 Pine Walk, Andover, Hants SP10 3PW (0264 362751)
Ground: Foxcotte Park, Charlton Down, Andover.
Colours: Green & black/black/green **Change colours:** Red & black/green/red.
Programme: Yes **Midweek home matchday:** Tuesday or Wednesday.

OVERTON UNITED

Secretary: Mr R Taylor, 18 Waltham Rd, Overton, Hants RG25 3NJ (0256 770835).
Ground: Recreation Centre, Bridge Street, Overton (0256 770561).
Colours: Blue & white stripes/white/blue **Change:** All yellow
Programme: No **Midweek home matchday:** Tuesday or Thursday

PAULSGROVE

Secretary: V Collins, 33 Portobello Grove, Portchester, Fareham PO16 8HX (0705 385538).
Ground: The Grove Club, Marsden Rd (off Allaway Avenue), Paulsgrove, Portsmouth (0705 324102).
Colours: Red & black/black/red **Change:** Sky & maroon/sky/maroon
Programme: **Midweek home matchday:** Wednesday.

PIRELLI GENERAL

Secretary: R W Hawkins, Pirelli General Spts & Social Club, The Pavilion, Dew Lane, Eastleigh, Hants SO5 5YE (0703 612721).
Ground: Jubilee Spts Ground, Chestnut Ave., Eastleigh (0703 612721).
Colours: Blue & white hoops/white/white **Change:** Yellow/black/yellow
Programme: Yes **Midweek home matchday:** Tuesday.

PORTSMOUTH CIVIL SERVICE

Secretary: P Shires, 242 Grafton Street, Mile End, Portsmouth PO2 7LH (0705 645813).
Ground: Portsmouth Civil Service Spts Ground, Copnor Rd, Hilsea, Portsmouth (0705 662538).
Colours: Yellow/navy/navy **Change:** Red/white/white
Programme: Yes **Midweek home matchday:** Wednesday.

VERWOOD TOWN

Secretary: Mrs J A Fry, 19a Noon Hill Rd, Verwood, Dorset BH31 7DB (0202 822826).
Ground: Pottern Park, Pottern Way, Verwood, Dorset.
Colours: Red & white/red/red **Change:** White & blue/blue/blue
Programme: Yes **Midweek home matchday:** Tuesday.

WHITCHURCH UNITED

Secretary: Mr N Spencer, 54 Winchester Rd, Whitchurch, Hants RG28 7HP (0256 896895).
Ground: Longmeadow, Winchester Road, Whitchurch, Hants (0256 892493).
Colours: White & red/black/red **Change:** All blue
Programme: Yes **Midweek home matchday:** Wednesday.

WINCHESTER CITY

Secretary: Geoffrey Cox, 9 Burnetts Gdns, Horton Heath, Eastleigh, Hants SO5 7BY (0703 693021).
Ground: Hillier Way, Abbotts Barton, Winchester (0962 863553).
Colours: Red & white/black/red **Change:** All blue
Programme: Yes **Midweek home matchday:** Tuesday or Wednesday.

DIVISION TWO CLUBS 1994-95

AWBRIDGE
Secretary: Miss Z C Wilson, 29 Borley Rd, Romsey, Hants SO51 8AG (0794 518969).
Ground: The Village Hall Field, Cross Roads, Awbridge, nr Romsey, Hants.
Colours: Red & black/black/black **Change:** Blue & white/white/white **Programme:** Yes

BASING ROVERS
Secretary: Mr C J Dale, 13 Howard View, Basingstoke, Hants RG22 6LF (0256 26604).
Ground: Old Basing Rec, The Street, Old Basing (0256 844254).
Colours: All red **Change:** Yellow/black/black
Programme: Yes **Midweek home matchday:** Wednesday.

BISHOPSTOKE SOCIAL
Secretary: Tony Boland, 34 Fryern Close, Chandlers Ford, Hants SO50 2LF (0703 262763).
Ground: Chicken Hall Lane, Bishopstoke, Eastleigh, Hants (0860 612038).
Colours: All blue **Change:** Red/black/black
Programme: Yes **Midweek home matchday:** Wednesday.

BRADING TOWN
Secretary: A F Harris, 56 New Street, Newport, Isle of Wight PO30 1BX (0983 522592).
Ground: Vicarage Lane, Brading, Isle of Wight (0983 405217).
Cols: Maroon & white stripes/white/white **Change:** All blue **Programme:** Yes

BROUGHTON
Secretary: A R Hammerton, 19 Plough Gdns, Broughton, Stockbridge, Hants SO20 8AF (0794 301495).
Ground: The Sports Field, Buckholt Rd, Broughton, Stockbridge, Hants.
Colours: Blue & white stripes/white/white **Change:** Green & white/green/green
Programme: Yes **Midweek home matchday:** Tuesday.

FLEET SPURS
Secretary: C R Filkins, 5 Byron Close, Fleet, Hants GU13 9QD (0252 627385).
Ground: Peter Driver Spts Ground, Bourley Rd, Church Crookham, Fleet, Hants.
Colours: Red & black stripes/black/red **Change:** Blue/white/white.
Programme: No **Midweek home matchday:** Wednesday.

HEDGE END
Secretary: M J Oliver, 25 Blossom Close, Botley, Southampton, Hants SO3 2FR (0489 786308).
Ground: Norman Rodaway Playing Fields, Heathouse Lane, Hedge End, Southampton.
Colours: Black & white stripes/black/black **Change:** Blue & white stripes/blue/blue
Programme: **Midweek home matchday:** Wednesday.

HILSEA CLUB
Secretary: Mr Terry Harwood, 147 Manners Rd, Southsea, Hants PO4 0BD (0705 785140).
Ground: Portsmouth Sailing Centre, Eastern Rd, Portsmouth PO3 5LY (0705 670119).
Colours: Yellow/sky/white **Change:** Blue/navy/navy.
Programme: Yes **Midweek home matchday:** Tuesday.

LISS ATHLETIC
Secretary: Alan Ridding, Imberdown, Woodlands Lane, Liss, Hants GU33 7EZ (0730 894007).
Ground: Newman Collard PF, Hill Brow Rd, Liss, Hants (0730 894022).
Colours: All blue **Change:** All yellow
Programme: No **Midweek home matchday:** Thursday.

LOCKS HEATH
Secretary: R H Setchfield, 58 Pimpernel Close, Priory Park, Locksheath SO3 6TN (0489 583229).
Ground: Locksheath Rec, Warsash Rd, Titchfield Common, Eastleigh (0489 581021).
Colours: Red/black/red **Change:** All white
Programme: Yes **Midweek home matchday:** Wednesday.

LUDGERSHALL SPORTS CLUB
Secretary: Mr B Roberts, 9 Martin Way, Harewood Park, Andover, Hants SP10 5PF (0264 338311).
Colours: Blue & black/black/black **Ground:** Astor Cres., Ludgershall (0264 790338).
Midweek home matchday: Wednesday. **Previous Lge:** Nth Hants (champs + Lge Cup winners 92-93)

NURSLING
Secretary: P E Hurst, 2 Horns Drove, Rownhams, Southampton, Hants SO1 8AH (0703 734061).
Ground: Nursling Recreation Ground, Nursling Str., Nursling, Southampton, Hants.
Colours: Orange/black/orange **Change:** Yellow/red/red.
Programme: No **Previous Name:** Nutfield FC (pre-1993).

OTTERBOURNE
Secretary: R J Broom, 249 Passfield Rd, Eastleigh, Hants SO5 5DE (0703 323992).
Ground: Oakwood Park, off Oakwood Ave., Otterbourne (0962 714681).
Colours: Blue & white stripes/blue/blue **Change:** Yellow/black/black.
Programme: Yes **Midweek home matchday:** Tuesday.

ROMSEY TOWN
Secretary: Mr Bill Clouder, 15 Malmesbury Rd, Romsey, Hants SO51 8FS (0794 518556).
Ground: The By-Pass Ground, South Front, Romsey, Hants (0794 512003).
Colours: White/black/black & white **Change:** All green
Programme: Yes **Midweek home matchday:** Tuesday.

St MARY'S
Secretary: Mr R W Chandler, 46 Stratford House, Sackville Street, Southsea, Portsmouth PO5 4BX (0705 812569).
Ground: Drayton Park, Lower Drayton Lane, East Cosham, Portsmouth, Hants (0705 827347).
Colours: Red & black stripes/black/red **Change:** Tangerine/white/tangerine
Programme: Yes **Previous Name:** Drayton Park (pre-1994).

STOCKBRIDGE
Secretary: Miss Noreen Durrant, 122 Buriton Rd, Harestock, Winchester, Hants SO22 6JG (0962 883772).
Ground: The Recreation Ground, High Street, Stockbridge, Hants.
Colours: All red **Change:** All blue **Programme:** Yes **Midweek home matchday:** Wednesday.

VOSPER THORNYCROFT

Secretary: Sean Jordan, 7 St Lawrence Close, Hedge End, Southampton SO3 4TJ (0489 780163).
Ground: Vosper Thornycroft Spts Ground, Portsmouth Rd, Sholing, Southampton (0489 403829).
Colours: Blue & black halves/black/blue **Change:** Yellow/red/red
Programme: Yes **Midweek home matchday:** Tuesday.

WEST WIGHT

Secretary: Gerry Beale, 75 Sandcroft Ave., Ryde, Isle of Wight PO33 2TU (0983 565956).
Ground: Camp Rd, Freshwater, Isle of Wight PO40 9HL (0983 754780).
Colours: White (navy trim)/navy/navy **Change:** All yellow
Programme: **Midweek home matchday:** Wednesday.

DIVISION THREE CLUBS 1994-95

A.F.C. ALDERMASTON

Secretary: Mr Gareth Dew, 58 Portway, Baughurst, Hants RG26 5PE (0734 811271).
Ground: Aldermaston, Recreation Society, Awe, Aldermaston (0734 814111 ex4544).
Colours: All blue **Change colours:** Red & white/white/white.
Programme: Yes **Midweek home matchday:** Monday or Wednesday.

BRAISHFIELD

Secretary: Mr W A Reid, 15 Addison Close, Romsey, Hants SO51 (0794 517991).
Ground: Braishfield Recreation Ground, Braishfield, Hants.
Colours: Yellow & emerald stripes/emerald/yellow & emerald. **Change:** Royal & black/stripes/royal/royal.
Programme: Yes **Midweek home matchday:** Wednesday.

COMPTON

Secretary: M Allerton, 28 Keats Close, Olivers Battery, Winchester SO22 4HR (0962 869574).
Ground: Shepherds Lane, Compton Down, nr Winchester (0962 712083).
Colours: All red **Change:** White/blue/blue
Programme: Yes **Midweek home matchday:** Wednesday.

COVIES

Secretary: Mr John Marchment, 4 Linstead Rd, Cove, Farnborough, Hants GU14 9HH (0276 34254).
Ground: Queens Road Recreation Ground, North Camp, Farnborough, Hants.
Colours: Yellow/green/green **Change:** All red
Programme: Yes **Midweek home matchday:** Tuesday or Wednesday.

ESSO (FAWLEY)

Secretary: Mr A Haws, 40 Hollybank Rd, Hythe, Southampton, Hants SO45 5FQ (0703 843402).
Ground: Esso Recreation Club, Long Lane, Holbury, Southampton, Hant (0705 893750).
Colours: White/blue/red **Change:** Red/white/red
Programme: No **Midweek home matchday:** Monday or Wednesday.

FOUR MARKS

Secretary: Mr Simon C Annetts, 5 Thorn Court, Four Marks, nr Alton, Hants (0420 562570).
Ground: The Recreation Ground, Uplands Lane, Brislands Lane, Four Marks, nr Alton, Hants.
Colours: Tangerine/black/tangerine **Change colours:** Navy/white/red
Programme: Yes **Midweek home matchday:** Tuesday or Thursday.

HAMBLE CLUB

Secretary: Paul John Smith, 100 Hamble Lane, Hamble, Southampton SO31 5HU (0703 452988).
Ground: Mount Pleasant Rec, Hamble Lane, Hanble, Southampton, Hants (0703 452327).
Colours: All red **Change:** Blue & white stripes/blue/blue.
Programme: No **Midweek home matchday:** Wednesday.

HYTHE & DIBDEN

Secretary: Mr A Moyst, 105 Hobart Drive, Hythe, Southampton, Hants SO40 6FD (0703 847335).
Ground: Ewart Rec Ground, Jones Lane, Hythe, Southampton (0703 845264 - matchdays only).
Colours: Green/green/yellow **Change:** Blue & white stripes/black/black.
Programme: Yes **Midweek home matchday:** Wednesday.

MAYFLOWER

Secretary: Mr C J Papadatos, 175 Chichester Rd, North End, Portsmouth PO2 0AJ (0705 793815).
Ground: Clarence Gardens, Southsea (0705 824696 - Mayflower Inn).
Colours: Blue & black stripes/black/blue **Change:** White/blue/red
Programme: Yes **Midweek home matchday:** Tuesday.

RINGWOOD TOWN

Secretary: N Crewe, 278 Windham Rd, Bournemouth, Dorset BH1 4QU (0202 398975).
Ground: Long Lane, Ringwood, Hants (0425 473448).
Colours: Red & white stripes/black/red **Change:** All blue
Programme: Yes **Midweek home matchday:** TBA.

SWANMORE

Secretary: Mrs Margaret Weavil, 69 Oak Rd, Bishops Waltham, Hants SO32 1ER (0489 894952).
Ground: The Recreation Ground, New Road, Swanmore, Hants.
Colours: White/navy/white **Change:** All yellow.
Programme: No **Midweek home matchday:** Wednesday.

TADLEY

Secretary: Mike Miller, Meadow View, West Heath, Baughurst, Hants RG26 5LE (0256 850700).
Ground: The Green, Tadley, Hants.
Cols: Blue & maroon stripes/maroon/maroon **Change:** Yellow/blue/blue
Programme: No **Midweek home matchday:** Wednesday.

WINCHESTER CASTLE

Secretary: A J Rutter, 31 Whistler Close, Basingstoke, Hants RG21 3HN (0256 50922).
Ground: Hants County Council Spts Ground, Petersfield Rd (A31) (Chilcomb), Winchester (0962 866989).
Colours: Red & white halves/black/red **Change:** Blue & white hoops/white/blue.
Programme: No **Midweek home matchday:** Wednesday.

This Division also contains the Reserve sides of: Bass Alton Town, Fleetlands, Netley Central Sports, Portsmouth Civil Service and Winchester City.

H.F.C. BANK SOUTHAMPTON LEAGUE (Est. 1894)

PREM. DIV.	P	W	D	L	F	A	PTS
Fair Oak	24	20	2	2	82	21	62
West End	24	15	3	6	64	36	48
Hythe & Dibden	24	13	6	5	54	34	45
Cadnam United	24	13	4	7	41	33	43
Old Tauntonians	24	10	5	9	46	47	35
Ordnance Survey	24	9	7	8	36	37	34
Queens Keep	24	9	6	9	48	44	33
Colden Com. Res.	24	8	5	11	40	43	29
AC Delco Res.	24	7	5	12	28	43	26
Pirelli Gen. Res.	24	8	2	14	33	51	26
Aztecs	24	6	5	13	41	68	23
Otterbourne Res.	24	4	7	13	20	48	19
Durley	24	5	1	18	35	63	16

SENIOR 1	P	W	D	L	F	A	PTS
BTC Southampton	24	17	4	3	58	23	55
Netley Vict. Ath.	24	15	4	5	52	31	49
North Baddesley	24	14	4	6	59	31	46
Brendon	24	12	5	7	58	39	41
East Boldre	24	12	5	7	59	62	41
Sarisbury Green	24	10	8	6	51	47	38
Bishopstoke S. Res.	24	7	7	10	64	48	28
Esso Fawley Res.	24	7	6	11	39	49	27
Netley RBL	24	7	6	11	38	48	27
Hamble Club Res.	24	7	5	12	37	62	26
Vosper Thorn. Res.	24	6	7	11	30	35	25
Ampfield	24	6	1	17	36	77	19
Bish. Waltham Res.	24	3	4	17	29	58	13

SENIOR 2	P	W	D	L	F	A	PTS
Lordswood Utd	26	21	2	3	103	38	65
Lyndhurst	26	20	0	6	99	32	60
Locomotive Testside	26	18	2	6	90	36	56
Hythe All Stars	26	15	6	5	93	36	51
Blackfield/L. Res.	26	16	3	7	59	37	51
O Taunton. Res.	25	12	2	11	59	70	+39
Swift Sporting	26	12	1	13	56	54	37
Horntree Sports	25	9	5	11	47	95	+33
West End Res.	26	9	3	14	58	93	30
Locks Heath Res.	26	8	5	13	57	70	29
Braishfield Res.	26	6	4	16	37	61	22
Michelmersh/Timsbury	26	5	4	17	39	76	19
MMI Sports	26	4	4	18	28	79	16
Warsash	26	4	3	19	29	77	15

JUNIOR 1	P	W	D	L	F	A	PTS
Hythe & Dib. Res.	24	21	2	1	96	31	65
Ford Sports	24	19	3	2	80	18	60
AFC Solent	24	18	4	2	67	23	58
Sholing Select	24	12	5	7	76	50	41
Queens Keep Res.	24	11	3	10	59	57	36
Hedge End Res.	24	8	6	10	49	54	30
Nursling Res.	24	9	5	10	60	51	#29
Ordnance S. Res.	24	8	4	12	47	71	28
Totton United	24	7	5	12	61	70	26
AFC Parkway	24	8	0	16	55	80	24
Swanmore Res.	24	6	3	15	24	54	21
Awbridge Res.	24	3	5	16	36	80	***11
Botley Park	24	1	5	18	24	103	*7

JUNIOR 2	P	W	D	L	F	A	PTS
Woodhouses Serv.	24	20	3	1	76	22	63
Four Star Sports	23	13	2	8	59	41	x44
Bishopstoke S. 'A'	24	13	4	7	62	43	43
Arrow	24	13	4	7	58	45	43
Albion Sports	24	13	3	8	48	40	42
AFC Dynamo	24	12	2	10	58	54	38
AFC Midanbury	23	10	1	12	65	55	x34
Easleigh Comrades	24	11	0	13	45	54	33
SDES	24	8	5	11	44	40	29
Compton Res.	24	7	4	13	43	59	25
Chartwell Gn Res.	24	6	3	15	27	60	21
Otterbourne 'A'	24	6	3	15	34	68	21
Old Issonians	22	3	4	15	37	80	#10

JUNIOR 3	P	W	D	L	F	A	PTS
BTM Sports	22	17	3	2	84	34	#51
BTC So'ton Res.	22	13	6	3	82	43	45
Mottisfont	22	11	8	3	50	24	41
Brendon Res.	22	11	7	4	52	32	40
Winsor Utd Spts	22	10	7	5	52	35	37
Vosper Thorn. 'A'	22	9	5	8	42	42	32
Bitterne Sports	22	8	5	9	53	56	29
Lordswood U. Res.	22	6	6	10	34	57	24
Brookwood .	22	7	3	12	32	60	24
Durley Res.	22	4	5	13	36	49	17
Aztecs Res.	22	5	1	16	37	76	16
Pirelli Gen. 'A'	22	1	4	17	39	88	7

JUNIOR 4	P	W	D	L	F	A	PTS
Wellow	22	14	7	1	65	25	49
AFC Marchwood	22	14	3	5	64	37	45
Nth Baddesley Res.	22	12	4	6	75	46	40
Inmar Electrical	22	11	6	5	62	36	39
Testwood United	22	11	5	6	48	41	38
Swift Sptng Res.	22	9	4	9	48	49	31
SUSA	22	6	7	9	39	51	25
Wildern	22	6	5	11	42	63	23
AFC Aldermoor	22	5	7	10	39	50	22
Botley Park Res.	22	6	2	14	34	63	20
Millbrook Furnishing	22	5	4	13	53	75	19
Langley Manor	22	4	4	14	40	73	16

JUNIOR 5	P	W	D	L	F	A	PTS
Fair Oak Res.	20	16	2	2	66	15	50
Loco Testside Res.	20	12	3	5	60	41	39
TBI Sports	20	11	3	6	53	39	36
Willis	20	10	3	7	55	28	33
Spartans	20	8	5	7	35	39	29
Woodmill Athletic	20	8	4	8	55	45	28
Burridge AFC	20	7	6	7	47	45	27
Michelmersh/T Res.	20	7	3	10	37	56	24
West End Sports	20	6	2	12	34	57	20
Eastleigh Ensigns	20	4	2	14	35	51	14
Cory Sports	20	4	1	15	34	95	13

JUNIOR 6	P	W	D	L	F	A	PTS
Aerostructures 'A'	22	18	2	2	71	23	56
Solent Youth	22	16	4	2	88	29	52
Mill Hill	22	16	1	5	73	40	49
Brendon 'A'	22	12	1	9	49	46	37
Regents Park Spts	22	9	6	7	58	49	33
Townhill Park	22	9	5	8	58	54	32
East Boldre Res.	22	10	3	9	53	62	#30
Queens Keep 'A'	22	9	2	11	46	55	29
Ordnance S. 'A'	22	8	0	14	40	60	24
RS Shirley	22	6	3	13	39	66	21
Mottisfont Res.	22	3	0	19	24	73	9
Compton 'A'	22	2	1	19	27	74	7

JUNIOR 7	P	W	D	L	F	A	PTS
Hythe & Dibden 'A'	20	16	2	2	86	20	50
Ford Sports Res.	20	15	4	1	66	23	49
AFC Hobury	20	11	3	6	69	52	36
Custom Covers	20	10	5	5	43	28	35
SDES Res.	20	11	1	8	55	50	34
Owslebury	20	7	3	10	33	54	24
Itchen	20	7	1	12	32	46	22
Four Star S. Res.	20	6	1	13	32	55	19
Willis Res.	20	6	1	13	23	70	19
Sporting B & Q	20	5	1	14	38	65	16
Gleneagles	20	5	0	15	45	59	15

JUNIOR 8	P	W	D	L	F	A	PTS
Lordshill S & S	20	18	1	1	116	19	55
Rownhams	20	18	0	2	100	25	54
Welcome Athletic	20	11	3	6	61	58	36
Progressive Club	20	10	4	6	65	38	34
P & P Sports	20	9	2	9	51	53	29
AFC Southside	20	8	2	10	46	43	26
Swift Sporting 'A'	20	7	5	8	53	61	26
Couch Green	20	6	4	10	35	84	22
Itchen Res.	20	6	2	12	46	63	20
Totton Utd Res.	20	2	2	16	26	91	8
Inmar Elect. Res.	20	1	3	16	32	96	6

JUNIOR 9	P	W	D	L	F	A	PTS
Bishopstoke S. 'B'	22	18	2	2	106	30	56
Warren United	22	14	2	6	71	39	44
Ordnance S. 'B'	22	13	3	6	72	38	42
Foresters	22	13	3	6	60	42	42
Millbrook Bedding	22	13	0	9	70	66	#36
Alma	22	10	2	10	49	50	32
Inter Notham	22	10	1	11	77	75	31
City Plumbing Supp	22	9	1	12	47	48	28
Eastleigh Town	22	11	4	7	69	51	=22
CAW	22	5	2	15	43	81	17
Brookwood Res.	22	2	3	17	27	99	9
Michelmersh & T. 'A'	22	2	1	19	18	95	7

x - 3pts awarded
+ - 1pt awarded
* - 1pt deducted
# - Goals & 3pts deducted
= - 15pts deducted

H.F.C. BANK SOUTHAMPTON LGE PREM. DIVISION CLUBS 1994-95

B.T.C. SOUTHAMPTON

Secretary: S Erskine, 12 Falkland Rd, Regents Park, Southampton SO15 4GZ (0703 490704).
Ground: BTC, Stonham Lane, Eastleigh **Colours:** Blue/black.

CADNAM UNITED

Secretary: L Diaper, 19 High View Way, Bitterne Park, Southampton SO18 4FE (0703 326992).
Ground: Bartley Avenue, Winsor Rd, Bartley **Colours:** Black & white stripes/black.

FAIR OAK (AMPLEVINE)

Secretary: H May, 21 Victoria Rd, Fair Oak, Eastleigh SO50 7FY (0703 693442).
Ground: BTC, Stonham Lane, Eastleigh **Colours:** All blue.

HYTHE AZTECS

Secretary: M Hawkins, 'Gray Helm', Chapel Lane, Langley, Southampton, Hants SO45 1YX (0703 897232).
Ground: Clay Fields, Dibden Purlieu **Colours:** All red.

NETLEY VICTORIA ATHLETIC

Secretary: L Bowers, 253 Kathleen Rd, Sholing, Southampton SO19 8LX (0703 394160).
Ground: Castle Rec., Netley Abbey **Colours:** White & black stripes/black.

NORTH BADDESLEY

Secretary: N Williams, 58 Middle Rd, North Baddesley, Southampton SO52 9JE (0703 733619).
Ground: Baddesley Rec., North Baddesley **Colours:** Royal/white.

OLD TAUNTONIANS

Secretary: K Wood, Flat 5, 50-52 Woodside Rd, Portswood, Southampton SO17 2GQ (0703 490095).
Ground: BTC, Stonham Lane, Eastleigh **Colours:** All blue.

ORDNANCE SURVEY

Secretary: G E Smith, 7a Greville Rd, Shirley, Southampton SO15 5AW (0703 339852).
Ground: Civil Service Ground, Shirley, Southampton **Colours:** Green/black.

QUEENS KEEP

Secretary: D Campbell, 81 Lumsden Ave., Shirley, Southampton SO15 5EJ (0703 781362).
Ground: Civil Service Ground, Shirley, Southampton **Colours:** Green & yellow stripes/green.

WEST END

Secretary: K Swain, 42 Exford Drive, Harefield, Southampton SO2 5DN (0703 464694).
Ground: Moor Green Road, West End **Colours:** Blue & white stripes/black

Plus the reserve sides of: AC Delco, Colden Common, Pirelli General and Romsey Town - refer to Hampshire League section for full club details.

Senior Division One 1994-95: Bishopstoke Social Res., Brendon, Durley, East Boldre, Esso Fawley Res., Hamble Club Res., Hythe All Stars, Locomotive Testside, Lordswood Utd, Lyndhurst, Netley RBL, Otterbourne Res., Sarisbury Green, Vosper Thornycroft Res.

Senior Division Two 1994-95: AFC Solent, Ampfield, Bishops Waltham Town Res., Blackfield & Langley Res., Braishfield Res., Ford Sports, Horntree Spts, Hythe & Dibden Res., Locks Heath Res., Michelmersh & Timsbury, Old Tauntonians Res., Sholing Select, Swift Sporting, West End Res.

NORTH HAMPSHIRE LEAGUE

FOUNDED: 1923

	P	W	D	L	F	A	PTS
Basing Rovers Res.	26	21	1	4	97	36	64
Tadley	26	19	4	3	101	27	61
Sherborne St John	26	19	3	4	100	29	60
AFC Aldermaston Res.	26	13	4	9	52	48	43
Overton Utd Res.	26	13	4	9	54	53	43
St Mary Bourne	26	10	3	13	68	55	#36
Alresford T. Res.	26	11	5	10	61	70	*35
Worthy Down	26	9	7	10	56	59	34
AFC Charlton	26	10	7	9	54	65	*34
Stockbridge Res.	26	7	6	13	46	79	27
Broughton Res.	26	7	5	14	45	77	26
Malshanger Res.	26	7	1	18	36	69	22
Winchester Cas. Res.	26	4	4	18	37	67	16
Kings Somborne	26	4	2	20	41	114	14

- 3 pts awarded * - 3 pts deducted

Leading Scorers:
35 - Lee Pomery (Sherborne), 24 Jason Schuster (Basing), Andy Gee (Tadley), 23 - Peter Courtnage (Tadley), 22 - Eddie Clegg (Basing), 19 - Mark Parry & Darren Clapson (Sherborne), 18 - Glen Damen (St Mary Bourne), 15 - Carlton Smith (Aldermaston), Jon Barnes (Kings Somborne), Lee Belbin (St MB), 14 - Dave Saunders & Mark Farry (Basing), 12 - Dave Pyle (Overton), Andy Kitson (St MB).

League Cup Final: Sherborne St John 2, Tadley 1

Tadley have been promoted to the Hampshire League, with their Reserves, from the Basingstoke League, replacing them. Wincastle Castle Reserves and Kings Somborne return to the Andover League with Andover Baptist Church making the reverse journey, and the other new arrival is Whitchurch United Reserves from the Jewson Wessex Combination.

GOSPORT & FAREHAM LEAGUE

FOUNDED: 1904

DIV. ONE	P	W	D	L	F	A	PTS
Ferndale	14	10	3	1	49	17	23
Royal FC	14	9	1	4	36	25	19
Phoenix	14	7	4	3	43	26	18
Rowner Rec	14	5	3	6	32	34	13
Castle AFC	14	6	1	7	28	46	13
Bridgemary	14	4	3	7	34	38	11
Stoke Select	14	3	3	8	25	35	9
Fareport	14	2	2	10	23	49	6

DIV. TWO	P	W	D	L	F	A	PTS
Foresters	15	13	2	0	65	16	28
Turnpike	15	11	1	3	71	20	23
GEC	15	6	1	8	44	49	13
Gosport Boro. 'A'	15	6	0	9	34	49	12
Three Tuns	15	4	3	8	36	39	11
Elliotts	15	1	1	13	15	92	3

GOSPORT & FAREHAM SUNDAY LEAGUE

FOUNDED: 1966

DIV. ONE	P	W	D	L	F	A	PTS
Wheatsheaf	16	14	2	0	75	15	30
Wallington	16	12	2	2	53	13	26
Salterns WMC	15	8	3	4	38	36	19
Junction	15	8	2	5	31	17	18
CS Crossways	16	8	0	8	45	31	16
Locksheath	16	5	4	7	45	32	14
Down End	16	4	3	9	24	37	11
Lee RBL	14	2	1	11	23	71	5
Wicor Mills	16	0	1	15	10	92	1

Lower Division Champions:
Div. 2: Iona Sports **Div. 3:** Locks Heath WMC

ISLE of WIGHT WIGHT F.A. (Est. 1898)

President:
P Hayward

Chairman:
A D King

Secretary:
B D Charman

The IWFA Senior (Gold) Cup is probably the most valuable trophy in the country, being valued at £20,000. It is kept in bank vaults and comes out only for presentation to the winners. Beazer Homes and Jewson Wessex League clubs are exempt until the Third Round (Quarter-Finals).

The Challenge Cup is for Moreys Saturday League Division One clubs and reserve teams who compete in the Jewson Wessex Combination or the CBH Hampshire League.

I.O.W. Senior (Gold) Cup 1993-94

First Round
Shanklin 6, Brighstone 1
Seaview 1, W & B Sports 4

Second Round
Shanklin 0, Cowes Sports 4
Sandown 3, Ventnor 1
Northwood 1, Brading Town 2
West Wight 0, Oakfield 1

Third Round
Oakfield 0, Ryde Sports 2
Newport IOW 2, East Cowes VA 1
Brading Town 0, Cowes Sports 6
W & B Sports 3, Sandown 0

Semi-Finals
Cowes Sports 5, W & B Sports 0
Ryde Sports 1, Newport IOW 2

Final:
Newport 3 *(Bale, Soares, Fearon)*, Cowes 0

I.O.W. Challenge Cup 1993-94

First Round
Ventnor 1, Sandown 4
Brading Town Res. 2, Cowes Spts Res. 4
Brighstone 1, Ryde Sports Res. 4
East Cowes VA Res. 1, Shanklin 5
Oakfield 0, Newport Res. 1 *(after 2-2 draw)*

Third Round
Seaview 0, Newport IOW Res. 6
Northwood SJ 0, Cowes Sports Res. 3
W & B Sports 1, Sandown 2
Shanklin 0, Ryde Sports Res. 4

Semi-Finals
Cowes Spts Res. 0, Ryde Sports Res. 3
Sandown 0, Newport IOW Res. 5

Final:
Ryde Sports Reserves 2, Newport IOW Reserves 1

MOREYS ISLE of WIGHT SATURDAY LEAGUE

FOUNDED: 1898

DIV. ONE	P	W	D	L	F	A	PTS
Oakfield	22	15	2	5	54	19	47
Shanklin	22	12	7	3	43	21	43
Cowes Spts Res.	22	11	7	4	40	26	40
Sandown	22	11	7	4	38	27	40
Wootton Bdge Spts	22	8	10	4	41	27	34
Ryde Sports Res.	22	8	8	6	38	24	32
Northwood	22	8	7	7	39	32	31
Ventnor	22	9	3	10	43	34	30
E Cowes VA Res.	22	7	3	12	32	42	24
Seaview	22	6	4	12	18	39	22
Brading T. Res.	22	3	5	14	21	54	14
Brighstone	22	2	1	19	12	75	7

Newport IOW Res. elected to Div. One

DIV. TWO	P	W	D	L	F	A	PTS
Binstead COB	22	20	0	2	115	24	60
St Helens	22	17	4	1	104	28	55
Brading Youth	22	11	3	8	50	40	36
Osborne Coburg	22	9	5	8	44	51	32
Carisbrooke Utd	22	9	4	9	62	61	31
West Wight Res.	22	8	6	8	48	37	30
Medina	22	9	3	10	37	42	30
Bembridge	22	8	4	10	58	77	28
Haylands	22	8	2	12	50	58	26
Westland	22	7	5	10	34	44	26
Newport IOW 'A'	22	5	4	13	40	54	***16
Wootton	22	1	0	21	13	144	3

Newport IOW 'A' have resigned from Lge

DIV. THREE	P	W	D	L	F	A	PTS
Newchurch	20	15	2	3	81	27	47
Niton	20	13	4	3	62	24	43
Plessey	20	12	3	5	59	33	39
Calbourne	20	12	0	8	57	36	36
Yarmouth Town	20	11	3	6	52	37	36
Red Star	20	10	4	6	45	41	34
Central Park	20	10	3	7	73	53	33
Wroxall	20	7	5	8	56	37	26
Rookley	20	5	2	13	46	63	17
Smallbrook	20	1	0	19	18	102	3
Shanklin Youth	20	1	0	19	22	122	3

Camp Hill and Cowes Old Boys are new clubs in Div.3 for 94-95. Shanklin Youth resign.

COMB. ONE	P	W	D	L	F	A	PTS
Binstead COB Res.	28	24	3	1	91	30	75
Northwood Res.	28	15	6	7	65	40	51
Ventnor Res.	28	15	5	8	43	47	50
Shanklin Res.	28	12	11	5	44	28	47
Oakfield Res.	28	13	7	8	48	36	46
Cowes Spts 'A'	28	12	7	9	59	50	43
Seaview Res.	28	12	7	9	42	40	43
Ryde Sports 'A'	28	11	5	12	57	44	38
Wootton Bdge Res.	28	10	7	11	67	65	37
Sandown Res.	28	10	4	14	57	59	34
Newport IOW 'B'	28	8	9	11	49	53	*32
Bembridge Res.	28	5	9	14	46	69	*23
Carisbrooke Res.	28	6	5	17	50	81	23
Medina Res.	28	6	3	19	39	66	21
St Helens Res.	28	5	4	19	49	87	19

COMB. TWO	P	W	D	L	F	A	PTS
Plessey Res.	28	21	2	5	99	20	*64
Westland Res.	28	20	2	6	80	33	62
West Wight 'A'	28	19	2	7	76	32	59
Brading Yth Res.	28	17	5	6	97	36	56
Osborne Co. Res.	28	17	4	7	83	36	**52
Wootton Res.	28	12	2	14	78	109	37
Calbourne Res.	28	10	3	13	65	67	35
Niton Res.	28	10	5	13	54	50	*34
Brading T. 'A'	28	9	4	15	42	53	31
Wroxall Res.	28	10	1	17	52	85	31
Yarmouth T. Res.	28	10	1	17	55	103	31
Newchurch Res.	28	8	5	15	56	65	29
Haylands Res.	28	9	2	17	47	123	29
Red Star Res.	28	8	3	17	37	73	27
Brighstone Res.	28	7	3	18	43	80	24

* - 1 point deducted

ISLE of WIGHT SUNDAY LEAGUE

FOUNDED: 1969

DIV. ONE	P	W	D	L	F	A	PTS
WASS	18	15	2	1	94	24	47
Northwood United	18	10	2	6	40	26	32
Plessey Sports	18	9	3	6	47	37	30
Havenstreet	18	8	3	7	51	36	27
Coppins Bridge	18	8	3	7	54	61	27
Castle	17	6	4	7	45	43	*#25
Osborne Athletic	18	6	3	9	51	53	21
Nomads XI	18	6	3	9	50	65	21
Fleming Estates	18	4	1	13	33	75	13
Columbia	17	4	2	11	25	69	*13

* - points deducted # - points awarded

Lower Division Champions:
Div. 2 (10): Shanklin **Div. 3** (12): Old Woottonians

Cup Finals: Albany: Plessey 2, WASS 0 *(after 1-1)*
Presidents': Manor House Spts 2, Cowes Soc. '92 0

PORTSMOUTH F.A. (Est. 1898)

SPORTIQUE PORTSMOUTH & DISTRICT LEAGUE

FOUNDED: 1895 (Re-formed 1974)

Mayflower (joining the CBH Hampshire League) and the reserve sides of George & Dragon and Havant Rangers all withdrew at the end of the season, and are replaced by Portsmouth Royal Navy Reserves (Premier Division), and Ventora Reserves and Corinthians (Junior Division Two). Because of the witdrawals and varying standards of the new entrants, no relegation was necessary.

PREM. DIV.	P	W	D	L	F	A	PTS
Ventora	18	13	3	2	53	25	29
Clanfield	18	13	1	4	56	27	27
Mayflower	18	11	3	4	58	29	25
Jubilee United	18	11	3	4	68	44	25
Paulsgrove Res.	18	8	4	6	42	41	20
Portchester Utd	18	3	8	7	28	35	14
Portchester	18	5	4	9	31	52	14
Wicor Mill	18	6	1	11	35	44	13
George & Dragon	18	3	1	14	27	55	7
Havant Rangers	18	2	2	14	21	66	6

JUNIOR ONE	P	W	D	L	F	A	PTS
Mayflower Res.	21	15	2	4	68	33	32
G & Dragon Res.	21	15	2	4	65	36	32
St Mary's Res.	21	9	4	8	36	39	22
Hayling Utd Res.	21	7	6	8	50	44	20
Carberry	21	8	4	9	50	55	20
RTC	21	8	2	11	51	50	18
Hilsea Club Res.	21	5	2	14	37	65	12
Clanfield Res.	21	2	6	13	32	65	10

JUNIOR TWO	P	W	D	L	F	A	PTS
Wicor Mill Res.	16	12	1	3	56	19	25
Sportsmans	16	11	1	4	51	31	23
Harbour Lights	16	11	0	5	54	41	22
IBM South Hants	16	10	1	5	48	34	21
Fawcett	16	8	3	5	41	33	19
Fleur de Lys	16	4	2	10	32	45	10
Bedhampton	16	4	1	11	35	53	9
Havant Rgrs Res.	16	4	1	11	29	54	9
Portchester Res.	16	1	4	11	14	50	6

Billy Head Cup Final: Mayflower 2, Clanfield 1
Len Day Cup winners: Wicor Mill Res.
Len Day Cup r-up: IBM South Hants

PORTSMOUTH NORTH END LGE

FOUNDED: 1905

DIV. ONE	P	W	D	L	F	A	PTS
Grant Thornton	16	14	1	1	96	19	29
Perseverance	16	8	4	4	63	40	20
Dunham Bush	16	9	2	5	54	48	20
Belle Vue	16	9	0	7	48	40	18
Sparta '81	16	7	1	8	72	65	15
Kingston Arrows	16	6	3	7	49	62	15
AES (Co-op EWA)	16	6	2	8	37	50	14
Phoenix	16	4	3	9	36	58	11
Invincible	16	1	0	16	19	92	2

DIV. TWO	P	W	D	L	F	A	PTS
Falcon	18	15	2	1	92	27	32
Somerstown '90	18	12	4	2	61	19	28
Portsmouth Nalgo	18	12	3	3	54	28	27
Curlew	18	12	2	4	53	30	26
S Co-op Dairies	18	6	2	10	34	59	14
St Helena Utd	18	4	5	9	36	50	13
Wightlink	18	5	3	10	35	61	13
Old Portmuthians	18	5	2	11	33	55	12
Sparta '81 Res.	18	3	2	13	35	57	8
Cosmos '87	18	2	3	13	33	81	7

DIV. THREE	P	W	D	L	F	A	PTS
Beehive	14	11	0	3	66	33	22
Oakville	14	8	3	3	60	37	19
Fountain	14	9	1	4	34	27	19
Uncle Toms Cabin	14	6	4	4	38	35	16
H & S Aviation	14	6	2	6	57	46	14
Advance Scaffold	14	4	3	7	42	52	11
Hilsea Club	14	4	1	9	42	64	9
South Coast	14	1	1	12	24	68	3

DIV. FOUR	P	W	D	L	F	A	PTS
British Star	18	17	0	1	113	19	34
Southside	18	14	1	3	89	26	29
Southsea Commoners	18	10	2	6	61	35	22
Old Portmuth. Res.	18	10	2	6	60	41	22
HPS	18	10	1	7	44	37	21
Spithead	18	7	1	10	58	45	15
Sparta '81 'A'	18	7	0	11	62	84	14
Oakville Res.	18	5	1	12	34	78	11
City Old Boys	18	2	2	14	27	81	6
Nautech	18	3	0	15	29	131	6

Cup Finals:
Father Purcell Chal. Cup: Grant Thornton 4, Falcon 2
Oscar Owers Mem. Inv. Tphy: Belle V. 7, Hilsea C. 1

CITY of PORTSMOUTH SUNDAY LEAGUE (Est. 1949)

PREM. DIV.	P	W	D	L	F	A	PTS
Portsmouth Civil S.	18	18	0	0	82	15	54
Wicor Mill	18	11	2	5	51	37	35
Havest Home	18	8	6	4	52	29	30
Manor Court	18	8	5	5	48	33	29
Havant Rovers	18	6	3	9	45	42	21
Marmion Tavern	18	6	3	9	23	31	21
Transfreight Express	18	5	4	9	31	47	19
Shaftesbury	18	5	2	11	24	42	17
Drayton	18	5	2	11	21	56	17
Cowplain Social	18	3	3	12	20	65	12

Lower Division Champions:
Senior Div.: Devonshire Arms
Div. 1: Admiral **Div. 2:** Queen Anne

PORTSMOUTH ROYAL DOCKYARD SUNDAY LEAGUE (Est. 1923)

PREM. DIV.	P	W	D	L	F	A	PTS
Grason	16	14	2	0	63	18	44
Riga	16	12	2	2	70	21	38
George & Dragon	16	10	3	3	50	30	33
Crown Sports	16	10	1	5	42	24	31
YO Oyster House	16	6	1	9	32	44	19
Mayflower	16	6	0	10	30	35	18
Victory Coatings	16	3	4	9	21	43	13
Strings	16	2	2	12	17	67	8
Horndean	16	1	1	14	19	62	4

Lower Division Champions:
Senior Div. (8): George & Dragon Res.
Junior Div. 1 (10): Oyster House Res.
Junior Div. 2 (9): Milton
Junior Div. 3 (9): Florist
Junior Div. 4 (10): Vectle Sports

HAVANT SUNDAY LGE (Est. 1967)

DIV. ONE	P	W	D	L	F	A	PTS
Pop Inn	20	16	3	1	105	29	51
Dresden	20	16	3	1	95	22	51
Stockheath Rovers	20	13	3	4	96	30	42
Ensinger	20	12	3	5	86	39	39
Prince of Wales	20	9	6	5	63	50	33
Stags Head	20	10	2	8	60	47	32
Rowlands Castle	20	8	2	10	69	60	25
Hide FC	20	8	1	11	60	88	*23
Barchrone-Smith	20	3	2	15	36	70	11
Kenwoods	20	2	1	17	36	87	7
Old House at Home	20	0	0	20	8	192	0

* - 2 points deducted

Division Two Champions: Warren

Cup Finals:
Havant Chall. Cup: Stockheath Rvrs 2, Dresden 1
Victory Cup: Stockheath Rvrs 2, Salterns WMC 1

BASINGSTOKE & DIST. LGE

FOUNDED: 1903

PREM. DIV.	P	W	D	L	F	A	PTS
Hook	20	18	1	1	64	14	55
Basing Rvrs Res.	20	15	0	5	81	53	45
Tadley	20	13	4	3	88	31	43
Sherborne SJ Res.	20	13	1	6	69	33	40
Burghclere	20	10	0	10	53	47	30
Wootton	20	9	2	9	50	44	29
Oakley Ath.	20	7	4	9	42	54	25
Kingsclere	20	6	3	11	44	63	21
B & T Winkle	20	6	3	11	43	67	21
Sherfield	20	2	0	18	30	99	6
Bramley United	20	1	2	17	28	87	5

DIV. ONE	P	W	D	L	F	A	PTS
Long Sutton	22	17	4	1	93	24	55
Impression	22	17	3	2	111	25	54
Tadley Res.	22	15	3	4	67	40	48
Hook Res.	22	15	1	6	81	38	46
Wootton Res.	22	11	4	7	49	44	37
Popinjay	22	9	4	9	51	62	31
Lightning Print	22	7	6	9	46	59	27
AFC A'maston 'A'	22	7	4	11	50	50	25
FC Winklebury	22	5	5	12	52	81	20
Sun Life Canada	22	5	3	14	42	75	18
Bas. Labour Club	22	2	2	18	48	97	8
Headley	22	1	3	18	28	123	6

DIV. TWO	P	W	D	L	F	A	PTS
Alpha Windows	22	17	3	2	83	26	54
Gordons Serv.	22	14	3	5	80	29	45
Priestley	22	12	5	5	68	36	41
Burghclere Res.	22	11	4	7	58	43	37
Overton Utd 'A'	22	12	0	10	72	52	36
Hart Rovers	22	10	6	6	62	47	36
Impression Res.	22	11	2	9	74	44	35
Sherborne SJ 'A'	22	11	2	9	62	59	35
Ropley	22	6	3	13	51	83	21
Hatch Warren	22	4	5	13	44	112	17
Mercantile Group	22	3	2	17	27	88	11
Unipath	22	1	5	16	36	98	8

DIV. THREE	P	W	D	L	F	A	PTS
Tadley 'A'	22	15	3	4	77	29	48
Hillborne	22	13	8	1	75	32	47
Kingsclere Res.	22	13	5	4	75	35	44
J Davy	22	11	5	6	75	35	38
Silchester	22	10	7	5	60	45	37
Southern Gas	22	10	5	7	67	48	35
Burghfield CS	22	11	2	9	66	55	35
Fox Newfound	22	9	1	11	47	56	28
Herriard Sports	22	7	5	10	46	61	26
Cromwell Inn	22	6	1	15	50	70	19
Bramley Utd Res.	22	4	3	15	31	63	*14
Uptown	22	0	1	21	15	155	1

* - 1 point deducted

Basingstoke 'A' Cup: Tadley
Basingstoke 'A' Cup R-up: Hook
Basingstoke 'B' Cup: Overton Utd 'A'
Bas. 'A' Cup R-up: Gordons Contract Services.
Supplementary 'A' Cup: Sherborne St John Res.
Supplementary 'A' Cup R-up: Oakley Athletic
Supplementary 'B' Cup: Tadley 'A'
Sup. 'B' Cup R-up: Gordons Contract Services

BASINGSTOKE SENIOR CUP: Overton United
B'STOKE SENIOR CUP R-up: DCA Basingstoke

BASINGSTOKE & D. SUNDAY LGE

FOUNDED: 1965

DIV. ONE	P	W	D	L	F	A	PTS
Buckskin	20	19	1	0	93	19	58
Rotherwick OB	20	15	2	3	60	19	47
Kingsclere	20	10	1	9	61	43	31
Kempshott	20	9	4	7	34	43	31
Network Sys.	20	8	1	11	39	42	25
Sherfield	20	8	1	11	40	54	25
Motorola	20	7	2	11	37	41	23
P Candover	20	7	1	12	39	43	22
Wellington	20	6	4	10	33	50	22
Chineham Arms	20	7	1	12	40	63	22
Danesmede	20	5	0	15	24	83	15

Lower Division Champions:
Div. 2 (9): North Warnborough
Div. 3 (11): Old Brewery
Div. 4 (12): Allison Suite Services
Div. 5 (13): White Hart Hotel
Div. 6 (11): Nth Warnborough Res.
Div. 7 (13): ESME

Kelvin Senior Cup: Rotherwick OB
Kelvin Senior Cup R-up: Ducal (Andover)
Bernard Cornish Cup: B'stoke Cricket Club
Bernard Cornish Cup R-up: Moat
Junior Cup: Allison Suite Services
Junior Cup R-up: Kingsclere Fieldgate.

A Two-up two-down promotion/relegation system applies throughout the divisions, except where a club already has a team at the higher level, i.e. Yateley Reserves are not promoted from Division One.

SENIOR DIV.	P	W	D	L	F	A	PTS
Tongham	20	17	1	2	63	23	52
Yateley Green	20	15	1	4	58	25	46
Hale	20	12	2	6	56	36	*40
Four Marks	20	10	4	6	57	34	34
Yateley	20	11	2	7	48	48	x34
Frimley Town	20	10	3	7	60	44	33
Liphook	20	9	4	7	59	40	31
Airborne United	20	6	0	14	61	64	18
Monteagle Arms	20	4	3	13	37	48	15
Border Sports	20	4	2	14	35	79	14
Bass Alton T. 'A'	20	0	2	18	23	116	2

* - 2pts awarded
x - 1pt deducted

DIV. ONE	P	W	D	L	F	A	PTS
Yateley Res.	22	15	1	6	75	38	46
Aldershot PO	22	14	2	6	71	29	44
Fleet Spurs Res.	22	12	6	4	51	33	42
Frimley Town Res.	22	10	9	3	41	35	39
Hartley Wintney 'A'	22	9	4	9	47	39	31
Covies Res.	22	9	4	9	34	36	31
Liphook Res.	22	9	4	9	44	52	31
Keogh	22	7	4	11	52	52	25
Yateley Green Res.	22	8	1	13	53	67	25
Pyestock	22	6	5	11	53	46	23
Binsted	22	7	2	13	44	64	23
Admel	22	4	2	16	32	86	14

DIV. TWO	P	W	D	L	F	A	PTS
Alton United	18	14	2	2	50	16	44
Fleet Spurs 'A'	18	11	4	3	43	13	37
Sandhurst T. 'A'	18	9	3	6	47	37	30
Froyle	18	9	2	7	33	34	29
Anchor Normandy	18	8	1	9	36	42	25
Puttenham	18	7	3	8	43	35	24
Tongham Res.	18	7	3	8	32	32	24
Lindford Ryl Exch.	18	6	3	9	34	66	21
Yateley 'A'	18	3	3	12	24	45	12
Headley	18	3	2	13	37	59	11

DIV. THREE	P	W	D	L	F	A	PTS
FTC United	20	17	1	2	60	23	52
Blackwater	20	15	2	3	60	30	47
Hale Res.	20	15	0	5	67	43	45
Old Dean	20	13	1	6	60	36	40
Airborne Utd Res.	20	9	1	10	66	60	28
Kings	20	9	1	10	66	60	26
Hartley Wintney 'B'	20	8	1	11	51	47	25
Four Marks Res.	20	6	1	13	47	62	19
Yateley Green 'A'	20	5	3	12	33	60	18
Farnham Athletic	20	3	3	14	37	69	12
Yateley 'B'	20	3	1	16	29	79	10

DIV. FOUR	P	W	D	L	F	A	PTS
Aldershot CC	20	15	2	3	82	29	47
Camberley Spartans	20	14	0	6	83	36	42
Eversley	20	13	3	4	67	32	42
Liphook 'A'	20	12	5	3	57	25	41
Lindford RE Res.	20	11	5	4	66	44	38
Fleet Spurs 'B'	20	9	2	9	61	45	29
Courtmoor	20	6	6	8	48	44	24
Anchor Norm. Res.	20	5	6	9	36	52	21
Queens Head	20	4	3	13	59	71	15
Crondall	20	3	4	14	44	62	13
Kings Res.	20	0	0	20	15	179	0

Divisional Cup Finals:
Senior: Tongham 3, Yateley Green 1 *(aet)*
Div. 1: Frimley T. Res. 2, Fleets Spurs Res. 1 *(aet)*
Div. 2: Sandhurst 'A' 2, Tongham Res. 1 *(aet)*
Div. 3: Airborne Utd Res. 6, Kings 2
Div. 4: Eversley 2, Liphook Res. 1

Other Awards:
Sportsmanship: Kings
Club Linesman: Anchor Normandy

WINCHESTER & DIST. LEAGUE

FOUNDED: 1891

DIV. ONE	P	W	D	L	F	A	PTS
Chandlers Ford	16	14	1	1	90	15	29
Twyford	16	13	1	2	64	18	27
Rising Sun	16	10	0	6	60	39	20
Littleton	16	7	2	7	52	37	16
Micheldever	16	8	0	8	42	39	16
Winch. City Res.	16	6	1	9	44	41	13
Upham	16	5	1	10	43	79	11
Sparsholt	16	4	0	12	29	90	8
Crusaders	16	2	0	14	27	93	4

DIV. TWO	P	W	D	L	F	A	PTS
Hyde United	16	12	1	3	63	24	25
Highcliffe	16	11	2	3	76	29	24
Twyford Res.	16	9	2	5	51	28	20
Chandlers Fd Res.	16	7	4	5	41	37	18
Sutton Scotney	16	6	5	5	34	27	17
Worthies Sports	16	8	1	7	35	38	17
Alresford	16	6	3	7	23	26	15
Winch. Castle Res.	16	2	2	12	16	45	6
Cheriton Sports	16	0	2	14	9	94	2

WINCHESTER & DISTRICT SUNDAY LEAGUE

FOUNDED: 1968

PREM. DIV.	P	W	D	L	F	A	PTS
Bakers Arms	22	16	4	2	92	30	36
Halfway Inn	22	14	5	3	75	40	33
Warrens	22	14	4	4	45	29	32
Fryern Sports	22	10	6	6	63	44	26
Ocean International	22	11	4	7	61	42	26
Compton	22	9	7	6	48	44	25
Rising Sun	22	9	5	8	53	31	23
Bitterne	22	6	4	12	42	61	16
St James Tavern	22	7	4	11	41	73	*16
Winter	22	5	4	13	43	64	14
Worthies	22	4	3	15	34	73	11
March Hare	22	1	2	19	33	109	4

* - 2 points deducted

Lower Division Champions:
Div. 2: Chestnut Sports
Div. 3: WCSC
Div. 4: Anglers

SPORTIQUE MEON VALLEY

SUNDAY LEAGUE

FOUNDED: 1906

DIV. ONE	P	W	D	L	F	A	PTS
Wickham Dynamos	22	17	3	2	83	30	37
Portsdown Inn	22	15	4	3	71	25	34
Seagull	22	14	5	3	62	35	33
Kennett Brothers	22	12	3	7	81	45	27
Black Horse	22	12	0	10	49	57	24
Sir J Paxton	22	11	1	10	52	38	23
Sportique	22	9	4	9	53	45	22
Timberland	22	7	4	11	34	45	18
Hunters Inn	22	6	5	11	35	38	17
New Casuals	22	5	2	15	31	83	12
Burridge FC	22	4	2	16	26	91	10
CPK	22	3	1	18	32	77	7

Lower Division Champions:
Div. 2 (11): Royal Oak
Div. 3 (12): Solent Club Sharks
Div. 4 (11): AFC Clanfield

Cup Winners (/runners-up)
Pink Cup: Wickham Dynamos (Kennett Bros)
Nicholson Cup: Royal Oak (Soberton)
Parker Cup: Solent Club Sharks (Wickham Utd)
Betteridge Cup: AFC Clanfield (Ship & Bell)
Blunt Cup: Hunters Inn (Portsdown Inn)

ANDOVER & DISTRICT

SUNDAY LEAGUE

FOUNDED: 1967

SENIOR DIV.	P	W	D	L	F	A	PTS
Broughton Sunday	16	14	1	1	57	16	43
Charlton Royal '89	16	13	3	0	96	13	42
Wherwell	16	9	0	7	65	21	27
Ducal	16	8	2	6	60	39	26
Southampton Arms	15	7	2	6	37	30	23
Fred Druce	16	7	0	9	34	58	21
Ludgershall Spts	15	5	1	9	52	45	19
Whitchurch RH	16	1	2	13	19	145	5
Andover Press	16	1	1	14	27	80	4

* - 3pts awarded - unplayed match

Lower Division Champions:
Junior Prem. Div. 2 (10): Kings Somborne
Junior Div. 1 (12): Central Club
Junior Div. 2 (11): Queens Head
Junior Div. 3 (14): Fred Druce '93

Cup Winners (/runners-up)
Presidents': Ludgershall Spts (Wherwell)
Jimmy Monro Memorial Open Challenge: Wherwell (Southampton Arms)
Divisions 2&3 Chal.: Queens Head (Fred Druce '93)
Junior Challenge: Blacksmiths Arms (Queens Head)

Sporting Award: Macaws
Secretary of the Year: Jimmy Pike (Fred Druce '93)

Covies FC - CBH Hampshire League. *Photo - Geoff Goddard.*

Portsmouth Civil Service - third-placed in the CBH Hampshire League 1993-94. *Photo - Eric Marsh.*

Bass Alton Town - CBH Hampshire League Division One. *Photo - Eric Marsh.*

CENTENARY YEAR
1893 – 1993

HEREFORDSHIRE F.A.

Secretary: E R Prescott,
7 Kirkland Close, Hampton Park, Hereford HR1 1XP.

COUNTY CHALLENGE CUP 1993-94

First Round

Weston v Bromyard Town 1-5

Second Round

Wellington v Ross Town 0-3
Colwall Rangers v Fownhope 2-1
Ewyas Harold v Ledbury Town 1-4
Hinton v Golden Valley 1-1,8-0
Redhill Lions v Bromyard Town 0-5
Hereford Lads Club v Woofferton 0-5
Kington Town v Leominster 0-2*(aet)*
Pegasus Juniors v Westfields 5-0

Quarter-Finals

Pegasus Juniors v Ross Town 8-1
Woofferton v Ledbury Town 3-1
Bromyard Town v Leominster 4-1
Hinton v Colwall Rangers 4-2

Semi-Finals

Bromyard Town v Pegasus Juniors 0-5
Hinton v Woofferton 2-1*(aet)*

Final *(at Hereford United FC, Tues 3rd May)*: Hinton 1, Pegasus Juniors 1
Replay *(at County Ground, Wed 25th May)*: Hinton 3, Pegasus Juniors 2 *(aet)*

COUNTY CHARITY BOWL 1993-94

First Round

Redhill Lions *(scr)* Bromyard Town *(w/o)*
Kington Town v Wellington 3-2
Leominster v Pegasus Juniors 2-1
Colwall Rangers v Ledbury Town 1-0
Fownhope v Golden Valley 2-1
Hinton v Ewyas Harold 4-0
Weston v Ross Town 3-2
Westfields *(bye)*

Quarter-Finals

Kington Town v Fownhope 4-3
Bromyard Town v Weston 3-1
Colwall Rangers v Leominster 5-2
Hinton v Westfields 5-0

Semi-Finals

Bromyard Town v Hinton 1-2
Kington Town v Colwall Rangers 4-2*(aet)*

Final *(at County Ground, Sat 23rd April)*: Hinton 2, Kington Town 1

Other County Finals:
Junior Cup *(at County Ground, Sat 30th April)*: Bulmers 2, Great Western 1
Burghill Cup *(at County Ground, Sat 7th May)*: Bromyard Town Reserves 1, Sutton United 0
Sunday Cup *(at County Ground, Sun 17th April)*: Black Lion Reserves 1, Green Dragon 0
Youth Cup *(at County Ground, Sun 1st January)*: Hereford Lads Club 1, Tupsley/Pegasus 0

HEREFORD TIMES HEREFORDSHIRE LEAGUE

President: Colin Shepherd, MP

Chairman: H J Handley

Vice-Chairman: M Magor

Secretary: J S Lambert,
16 Farr Close, Tupsley, Hereford HR1 1QF (0432 270308)

PREM. DIV.	P	W	D	L	F	A	PTS
Hinton	24	20	3	1	70	18	43
Bromyard Town	24	16	4	4	59	32	36
Ewyas Harold	24	14	4	6	59	36	32
Ross Town	24	14	4	6	64	43	32
Golden Valley	24	10	7	7	43	39	27
Pegasus Jnrs Res.	24	11	5	8	46	44	27
Colwall	24	9	3	12	44	58	21
Fownhope	24	7	6	11	41	45	20
Leominster	24	6	6	12	33	55	18
Conquest	24	4	7	13	24	37	15
Weston	24	5	5	14	32	49	15
Westfield Res.	24	4	7	13	31	54	15
Wellington	24	3	5	16	20	56	11

DIV. ONE	P	W	D	L	F	A	PTS
Bromyard T. Res.	20	14	4	2	52	24	32
Sutton United	20	9	6	5	45	31	24
Burghill	20	9	5	6	48	43	23
Leintwardine	20	10	3	7	38	38	23
Fownhope Res.	20	9	3	8	39	27	21
Stoke Prior	20	9	2	9	32	44	20
Holme Lacy	20	6	7	7	36	44	19
Civil Service	20	5	6	9	32	34	16
Hereford Tiles	20	7	2	11	34	44	16
Hereford Sports	20	4	6	10	39	52	14
Pegasus Colts	20	3	6	11	35	49	12

(tables continued overleaf)

DIV. TWO	P	W	D	L	F	A	PTS
Leominster Res.	18	12	3	3	54	28	27
Richards Castle	18	11	1	6	42	35	23
Wellington Res.	18	9	4	5	61	35	22
Ewyas Harold	18	9	2	7	45	40	20
Kingstone Rovers	18	9	2	7	49	49	20
Hinton Colts	18	7	5	6	62	37	19
Tupsley	18	8	0	10	46	47	16
Walford	18	6	1	11	42	55	13
Ross Town Res.	18	5	2	11	36	63	12
Ledbury T. Res.	18	3	2	13	27	75	8

DIV. THREE	P	W	D	L	F	A	PTS
Bulmers	22	15	5	2	66	33	35
Great Western	22	14	2	6	65	33	30
PO Sports	22	10	7	5	83	55	27
Dorstone United	22	12	2	8	52	38	26
Colwall Res.	22	12	2	8	44	44	26
Brinsty	22	9	6	6	50	26	24
Weston Res.	22	9	5	8	44	33	23
Woofferton	22	10	2	10	45	45	22
Pencombe	22	9	2	11	49	49	20
Civil Service Res.	22	3	7	12	33	67	13
Putson	22	5	1	15	29	83	11
Tram Rovers	22	1	3	18	21	75	5

DIV. FOUR	P	W	D	L	F	A	PTS
Shobdon	22	18	1	3	91	20	37
Three Elms	22	17	0	5	68	25	34
Kingstone Utd	22	14	3	5	78	35	31
Newtown	22	14	1	7	76	49	29
Orleton	22	12	2	8	53	36	26
Bromyard Colts	22	9	3	10	48	51	21
Bosbury	22	9	1	12	35	66	19
Eardisley	22	7	4	11	32	59	18
Wellington Colts	22	5	5	12	43	62	15
West St Regulars	22	5	5	12	40	73	15
Leominster Colts	22	5	1	16	32	63	11
Lads Club	22	3	2	17	24	81	8

DIV. FIVE	P	W	D	L	F	A	PTS
Golden Valley Res.	20	14	3	3	64	21	31
Hinton Juniors	20	14	2	4	67	40	30
Painters	20	13	2	5	47	31	28
Burghill Res.	20	8	6	6	48	40	22
Kington Colts	20	9	2	9	51	43	20
Shobdon Res.	20	8	3	9	58	48	19
Tupsley Colts	20	6	5	9	47	56	17
Sellack	20	8	1	11	44	63	17
Pegasus Youth	20	6	5	9	30	55	17
Bulmers Res.	20	4	3	13	41	66	11
Holme Lacy Res.	20	3	2	15	33	67	8

PREMIER DIVISION CLUBS 1994-95

BROMYARD TOWN

Secretary: D Harding, 20 Hardwick Close, Bromyard, Herefordshire (0885 482774).
Ground: Delahay Meadow, Bromyard **Colours:** Black & blue stripes/black.

COLWALL RANGERS

Secretary: P Butler, Ashfield, Colwall Green, Colwall, Worcs WR13 6DY (0684 40747).
Ground: Walwyn Rd, Colwall Elms Sch., Colwall, Worcs **Colours:** Black & white stripes/black

CONQUEST

Secretary: D Clayton, 15 Putson Ave., Putson, Hereford (0432 357173).
Ground: Stirling Lines, Ross Road, Hereford **Colours:** Sky & navy stripes/black

EWYAS HAROLD

Secretary: D Manning, 38 Elmdale, Ewyas Harold, Hereford HR2 0HZ (0981 240372).
Ground: Sports Field, Ewyas Harold, Hereford **Colours:** Amber/black.

FOWNHOPE

Secretary: N Walters, 68 Gorsty Lane, Hampton Dene, Hereford HR1 1UN (0432 275582).
Ground: Malt House Field, Fownhope, Hereford **Colours:** Green/white.

GOLDEN VALLEY

Secretary: J Price, Lansdown Villa, Clehonger, Hereford HR2 9TG (0981 250712).
Ground: Kingstone High School **Colours:** Red & blue stripes/blue.

HINTON

Secretary: Mrs M Hebbes, 3 Grafton Walk, Redhill, Hereford (0432 275949).
Ground: Broomy Hill, Hereford **Colours:** Red & black stripes/black.

LEOMINSTER

Secretary: R Weaver, 19 Castlefields, Leominster, Herefordshire HR6 8BG (0568 614450).
Ground: Bridge Street Park, Leominster **Colours:** Red/white.

PEGASUS JUNIORS RESERVES *(see page 621)*

ROSS TOWN '93

Secretary: Mrs M Jones, Bryntirion, Brookfield Rd, Ross-on-Wye, Herefordshire (0989 567417).
Ground: Ross Sports Centre, Ross-on-Wye **Colous:** All red.

WELLINGTON

Secretary: C Williams, Mandolin, Wellington, Hereford (0432 830620).
Ground: Wellington PF, Wellington, Hereford **Colours:** Orange/blue.

WESTFIELDS RESERVES *(see page 588)*

WESTON

Secretary: S Salmon, The Furze, Aston Crews, Lea, Ross-on-Wye, Herefordshire (0989 750672).
Ground: Weston Recreation Ground **Colours:** White & black stripes/black.

DIVISION ONE CLUBS 1994-95

BURGHILL

Secretary: I J Watkins, 1 Haven Cottages, Tillington, Hereford HR4 8LQ (0432 760887).
Ground: Burghill & Tillington CC, Lower House Farm **Colours:** White & black stripes/black.

CIVIL SERVICE

Secretary: D Blake, 37 Penn Grove Rd, Hereford (0432 343267).
Ground: Inco Spts Grnd, Grandstand Rd, Hereford **Colours:** Sky & navy stripes/navy.

HEREFORD TILES

Secretary: T Kelly, 4 Trenchard Ave., Credenhill, Hereford (0432 761708).
Ground: Holmer Sports Ground **Colours:** Yellow/green.

HOLME LACY

Secretary: K Ratcliffe, 28 Burdon Drive, Bartestree, Hereford HR1 4DL (0432 850995).
Ground: Holme Lacy Recreation Ground **Colours:** Yellow/black.

LEINTWARDINE COLTS

Secretary: G Vickress, 28 Rosemary, Leintwardine, Craven Arms, Shropshire SY7 0LR (0547 3345).
Ground: Paytoe Lane, Leintwardine, Craven Arms **Colours:** All red.

RICHARDS CASTLE

Secretary: B Giles, 36 Tollgate Rd, Ludlow, Shropshire SY8 1TQ (0584 875163).
Ground: Park Lane, Richards Castle **Colours:** Red & black stripes/black.

STOKE PRIOR

Secretary: R Painter, Causeway, Stoke Prior, Leominster, Herefordshire (0568 760329).
Ground: Wickton Lane, Stoke Prior Village Hall **Colours:** Green & white stripes/green.

SUTTON UNITED

Secretary: Miss J Williams, Janlyn, Sutton St Nicholas, Hereford HR1 3AU (0432 880568).
Ground: Amberley Park, Sutton St Nicholas, Hereford **Colours:** All blue.

This Division also includes the Reserve sides of: Bromyard Town, Fownhope, Leominster.

DIVISION TWO CLUBS 1994-95

BULMERS

Secretary: N Rivers, 24 Cheltenham Ave., Bobblestock, Hereford (0432 277811).
Ground: Bulmers Spts Grnd, Kings Acre Rd, Hereford **Colours:** White & blue/blue.

GREAT WESTERN

Secretary: N James, 34 Derwent Drive, Parkside, Hereford HR4 9PS (0432 351747).
Ground: City Spts Club, Grandstand Rd, Hereford **Colours:** Blue & black stripes/black.

HEARTS

Secretary: M Edwards, 56 Chatsworth Rd, Hereford HR4 9HZ (0432 341460).
Ground: Hereford Leisure Centre, Hereford **Colours:** Blue & white/black.

HEREFORD SPORTS

Secretary: A Burgess, 35 Stonebrow Rd, Hereford (0432 278154).
Ground: King George Playing Field, Hereford **Colours:** Yellow/black.

TUPSLEY

Secretary: S Paton, 2 Golden Lion Close, Hereford HR4 9NB (0432 351968).
Ground: Gorsty Lane, Tupsley **Colours:** Blue/navy.

WALFORD

Secretary: Mrs S Brooke, 9 Walford Rd, Ross-on-Wye, Herefordshire HR9 5PX (0989 566100).
Ground: Walford Village Hall **Colours:** All blue.

This Division also includes the Reserve sides of: Ewyas Harold, Hinton *(Hinton Colts)*, Pegasus Juniors *(Pegasus Colts)*, Ross Town '93, Wellington.
Leominster.

DIVISION THREE CLUBS 1994-95

BRINGSTY

Secretary: R Allsopp, 2 Awbrey Way, Bromyard, Herefordshire HR7 4UD (0885 488125).
Ground: Bringsty Common **Colours:** Black & blue stripes/black.

DORSTONE UNITED

Secretary: Mrs P Parry, Well Cottage, Preston-on-Wye, Hereford (0981 500617)
Ground: Dorstone Playing Field **Colours:** Green & yellow stripes/green.

PENCOMBE

Secretary: S Nicolson, 4 Wakefield, Pencombe, Herefordshire (0885 400686).
Ground: Pencombe Sports Ground **Colours:** Green & white stripes/white.

SHOBDON

Secretary: Mrs M Witts, 67 Withes Close, Withington, Hereford (0432 851059).
Ground: Shobdon Airfield **Colours:** Blue & black/black.

THREE ELMS

Secretary: C Haston, 12 Haston Close, Three Elms, Hereford (0432 352642).
Ground: Hereford City Sports Club **Colours:** Green/black.

TRAM ROVERS

Secretary: J Thomas, Caswell Terrace, Leominster (0568 614905).
Ground: Home Farm, Allensmore, Pateshall Allensmore **Colours:** Green/white.

WOOFFERTON

Secretary: H Wall, Grove Farm, Aynall Lane, Brimfield, Ludlow, Shropshire (0584 711271).
Ground: Aynall, Brimfield, Ludlow **Colours:** White/black.

This Division also includes the Reserve sides of: Civil Service, Colwall Rgrs, Ledbury Town *(see page 604)*, Weston.

DIVISION FOUR CLUBS 1994-95

BOSBURY

Secretary: K Panter, 59 Albert Rd, Ledbury, Herefordshire HR8 2DN (0531 631154).
Ground: Bosbury Village Hall **Colours:** All red.

EARDISLEY

Secretary: I L Clarke, 3 Cannonford Ave., Eardisley, Hereford HR3 6PL (0544 327285).
Ground: Sheepcroft, Eardisley, Hereford **Colours:** Green/black.

KINGSTONE UNITED

Secretary: Mrs J Morgan, Barmor, Yew Tree Close, Kingstone, Hereford HR2 9EX (0981 251001).
Ground: Seven Site, Kingstone, Hereford **Colours:** Black & white stripes/black.

NEWTOWN

Secretary: R H Styles, 1 Fillings Bridge, Stretton Grandison, Ledbury (0531 670635).
Ground: Moorend Farm, Woodsend **Colours:** Green & yellow stripes/green

ORLETON

Secretary: D J Saunders, 11 St Georges Cres., Orleton, Ludlow, Shropshire (0568 85609).
Ground: Recreation Ground, Orleton, Ludlow **Colours:** Yellow/black.

PAINTERS

Secretary: G Lloyd, 6 Plumpton Ave., Hillcrest, Hereford HR4 9TZ (0432 275640).
Ground: Painters Sports, Holmer Rd, Hereford **Colours:** Blue & white/blue.

This Division also includes the Reserve sides of: Bromyard Town *(Bromyard Colts)*, Burghill, Golden Valley, Hinton *(Hinton Juniors, playing at King Georges PF)*, Leominster *(Leominster Juniors)*, Wellington.

DIVISION FIVE CLUBS 1994-95

HEREFORD LADS CLUB

Secretary: S Millward, 65 Belmont Ave., Hereford HR2 7JQ (0432 268230).
Ground: Widemarsh Common, Hereford **Colours:** All blue.

KINGTON TOWN COLTS

Secretary: Mrs K Maygothling, Well's Cottage, Stanner Rd, Kington, Herefordshire (0544 231151).
Ground: Lady Hawkins School, Kington **Colours:** Yellow & black stripes/black.

ROSS UNITED SERVICES

Secretary: M Davies, Upton Park, 10 Oaklands Court, Brampton Rd, Ross-on-Wye (0989 565426).
Ground: John Kyrle School **Colours:** Red/white.

SKENFRITH UNITED

Secretary: D Woods, The Stores, Skenfrith, Abergavenny, Gwent NP7 8UH (0600 84201).
Ground: Skenfrith Village Hall, Skenfrith **Colours:** Red/black.

St MARTINS

Secretary: M Rone, 83-85 St Martins Street, Hereford HR2 7RG (0432 266022).
Ground: Kings Georges Playing Field, Hereford **Colours:** All navy

This Division also includes the Reserve sides of: Bulmers, Hereford Tiles, Holme Lacy, Leominster *(Leominster Colts)*, Pegasus Juniors *(Youth Team)*, Shobdon, Tupsley *(Tupsley Colts)*.

MALVERN GAZETTE & LEDBURY REPORTER SUNDAY LEAGUE

DIV. ONE	P	W	D	L	F	A	PTS
Castlemorton	18	17	1	0	104	23	35
Gas Tavern	18	15	1	2	81	31	31
Newtown Sports	18	13	0	5	45	32	26
New Inn Storridge	18	10	0	8	48	38	20
Much Marcle	18	9	1	8	46	43	19
Express 1988	18	6	2	10	44	51	14
Eastnor Stags	18	4	3	11	36	62	11
County Sports	18	5	0	13	31	56	10
Three Horseshoes	18	3	2	13	22	75	8
Albion Rovers	18	2	2	14	35	81	6

Lower Division Champions:
Div. 2 (12): Old Bush

HERTFORDSHIRE F.A.

Secretary: R G Kibble,
4 The Wayside, Leverstock Green,
Hemel Hempstead HP3 8NR.

SENIOR CUP 1993-94

First Round

Berkhamsted Town v Stevenage Boro. 0-0,1-2
Baldock Town v Tring Town 2-0
Bishop's Stortford v Hitchin Town 3-0
Hertford Town v St Albans City 3-5*(aet)*
Ware v Boreham Wood 1-2*(aet)*
Cheshunt v Watford 1-2
Royston Town v Hemel Hempstead 2-1

Quarter-Finals

Barnet v Watford 0-3
St Albans City v Baldock Town 1-3
Bishop's Stortford v Royston Town 2-0
Stevenage Borough v Boreham Wood 0-0,2-1

Semi-Finals

Baldock Town v Watford 2-2,0-1
Bishop's Stortford v Stevenage Borough 0-4

Final - Held over to start of 1994-95 season

CENTENARY TROPHY

First Round

Bushey Rangers v Letchworth Garden City 3-2
London Colney v Chipperfield Corinthians 1-2
Knebworth v Welwyn Garden City 1-1,1-3
Tring Athletic v Hoddesdon Town 0-3*(aet)*
Elliott Star v Potters Bar Town 1-5
Wormley Rovers v Cuffley 2-1
Oxhey Jets v Leverstock Green 1-0
Metropolitan Police (Bushey) v Bovingdon 0-3
BAC Stevenage v Roussel Sports 1-3
Kings Langley v Colney Heath 0-3
Sandridge Rangers v Croxley Guild 0-3
Harpenden Town v Bedmond Sports & Social 4-2

Second Round

St Margaretsbury v GDS Valmar 2-0
Bushey Rangers v Colney Heath 5-1
Hoddesdon Town v Oxhey Jets 1-0
Potters Bar Town v Croxley Guild 2-3
Harpenden Town v Sawbridgeworth Town 1-3
Chipperfield Corinthians v Sun Sports 2-1
Wormley Rovers v Welwyn Garden City 4-0
Roussel Sports v Bovingdon 0-2*(aet)*

Quarter-Finals

Croxley Guild v Hoddesdon Town 0-1
Sawbridgeworth T. v St Margaretsbury 5-1*(aet)*
Bovingdon v Bushey Rangers 2-3
Wormley Rovers v Chipperfield Corinthians 1-2

Semi-Finals

Bushey Rangers v Hoddesdon Town 2-1
Sawbridgeworth Town v Chipperfield Corinthians 2-1

Final *(at Ware FC, Sat 9th April)*: Sawbridgeworth Town 2, Bushey Rangers 1 *(aet)*

CHARITY CUP

First Round

Royston Town v Bishop's Stortford 0-6
Ware v Berkhamsted Town 2-0
Boreham Wood v Hemel Hempstead 2-2*(4-2 pens)*
St Albans City v Hitchin Town 4-3*(aet)*

Quarter-Finals

Hertford Town v Stevenage Borough 2-6
Bishop's Stortford v St Albans City 2-0
Tring Town v Baldock Town 0-3
Boreham Wood v Ware 4-0

Semi-Finals

Baldock T. v Boreham Wood 1-1*(4-2 pens)*
Stevenage Borough v Bishop's Stortford 2-0

Final *(at Baldock Town FC, Tues 26th April)*: Baldock Town 2, Stevenage Borough 1

CHARITY SHIELD

First Round

Sawbridgeworth Town v Sun Sports 2-0
Welwyn Garden City v London Colney 0-1
Cheshunt v Harpenden Town 5-0
Potters Bar Town v Letchworth Garden City 2-4

Quarter-Finals

Leverstock Green v Hoddesdon Town 0-1*(aet)*
Sawbridgeworth T. v Letchworth Gdn City 7-0
Bovingdon v St Margaretsbury 2-4
Cheshunt v London Colney 0-3

Semi-Finals

London Colney v Sawbridgeworth Town 2-1*(aet)*
St Margatesbury v Hoddesdon *(at Hoddesdon)* 0-3

Final *(at Welwyn Garden City FC, Tues 26th April)*: London Colney 2, Hoddesdon Town 0

OTHER COUNTY FINALS

Intermediate Cup: Bishop's Stortford Reserves 2, Sawbridgeworth Town Reserves 0
Junior Cup: Much Hadham 3, Argonauts 0
Saturday Inter-League Cup: North Herts FA 1, Herts Senior County League 0 *(aet)*
Sunday Cup: Gatecrashers 1, Elliott Bull & Tiger 0 *(aet)*
Sunday Intermediate Cup: John Gilpin beat Eleanor Cross 7-6 on penalties after 3-3 and 2-2 draws
Sunday Junior Cup: St Margaretsbury Reserves 2, Watford Golf Range 1
Sunday Inter-League Cup: Watford Sunday League XI 4, Welwyn Hatfield Sunday League XI 1 *(aet)*

HERTS SENIOR COUNTY LEAGUE

President: Mr W J R Veneear

Chairman: Mr C T Hudson

Secretary: Mr E H Dear,
48 Wilshere Road, Welwyn, Herts

DOMINANT SUN SPORTS DOUBLE UP AGAIN

The eleventh hour withdrawl of Little Gaddasden left the league with a balanced senior constitution of 36 teams divided into Premier and First Divisions of 18 apiece.

Early front-runners in the Premier were newly promoted Metropolitan Police (Bushey) but, as their early surge faded, Wormley Rovers took over at the top and soon they established a sizable lead. At the end of January, they stood 8 points clear of their nearest challengers with games in hand. However, five defeats in their last 14 games let in last season's champions Sun Sports who had started slowly but finished very strongly. Sun clinched their second successive title with a 3-0 home win over Rovers on the penultimate Saturday of the season. At the bottom, BAC Stevenage, Bushey Rangers and Elliott Star occupied the bottom three places for almost the entire season. A late burst of form from Bushey hoisted them out of a relegation spot at the expense of GDS Valmar who return to Division One after just a single season in the top flight.

On the way up from Division One are Somerset Ambury V & E who dominated their section losing just twice in 34 games with their first reverse not until 5th March. Their conquerors that day were runners-up Walkern. Their promotion was dependent on them meeting Premier ground standards which will entailed the installation of permanent post and rail around their pitch.

At the foot of the league, perenial strugglers Harpenden Rovers fought a season long battle with ICL Letchworth to see who would end with the wooden spoon. In the end, Rovers lost the fight, but neither club will grace County League soccer in 1994-95. Rovers are switching to the Mid Herts League whilst ICL sadly shut due to the loss of their ground.

In the Reserve section, Sun Sports dominated in Division One and emulated their seniors by winning a second successive championship. Runners-up, as in the seniors, were Wormley Rovers. At the foot of the table Dynamics pulled off a Houdini act to avoid relegation. After winning just once in their opening 17 games, three successive victories at the end of the season saw them condemn Met. Police, Elliott Star and Kodak to the drop.

From Reserve Division Two, a five team battle for the top saw Bushey Rangers clinch the championship on goal difference from Hertford Youth with Cuffley third.

The Aubrey Cup Final pitted Sun Sports against Roussel Sports on May Day Monday, 48 hours after the clubs had met in league action. Sun won the league encounter but, proving that "it's a funny old game", Roussel won the Cup 3-0 at Met. Police Bushey FC - their first triumph in the competition. The Reserve Cup provided a third time lucky for Wormley Rovers as they finally triumphed over Sun Sports, with a 2-1 scoreline at Colney Heath FC.

In Herts Cup competition, Bushey Rangers did well to reach the Senior Trophy Final and were unlucky to lose 2-1 after extra-time against Sawbridgeworth Town. Leading 1-0, Bushey conceded a rather harsh penalty in the final minute from which Sawbridgeworth levelled with the last kick of normal time. In the Inter-League Cup, the County League Rep. team reached the final but lost 1-0 to a late strike against the North Herts FA.

The 1994-95 season sees former South Midlands League club Ickleford join the league. Out of soccer completely in 1993-94, Ickleford are confident they can make an impression in County League football.

On the negative side, Harpenden Rovers cannot meet the standards of ground and facilities required by the league and have opted to switch to the Mid Herts League. ICL Letchworth have been forced to withdraw as their parent company have disposed of the sports facilities in Letchworth. Finally, Hertford Youth have been expelled after failing to fulfil financial commitments.

Kevin Folds, Management Committee

PREM. DIVISION	P	W	D	L	F	A	PTS
Sun Sports	34	23	7	4	68	25	76
Wormley Rovers	34	21	7	6	79	42	70
Chipperfield Cor.	34	19	8	7	76	47	65
Roussel Sports	34	19	4	11	72	52	61
Met Police Bushey	34	16	10	8	79	49	58
Bovingdon	34	16	9	9	60	45	57
Knebworth	34	16	8	10	62	55	56
Sandridge Rovers	34	15	8	11	73	62	53
Bedmond Social	34	13	9	12	52	57	48
Cuffley	34	12	9	13	58	59	45
Colney Heath	34	12	8	14	55	67	44
Oxhey Jets	34	11	7	16	47	56	40
Kings Langley	34	8	10	16	44	56	34
Bushey Rangers	34	9	6	19	52	72	33
Croxley Guild	34	8	8	18	41	52	32
GDS Valmar	34	8	6	20	33	72	30
Elliott Star	34	6	10	18	43	69	28
BAC Stevenage	34	5	4	25	43	100	19

Top Scorers: M Vidgen (Sandridge) 27, A Walker (Roussel) 26, P Rastrick (Chipperfield) 23, A Webb (Wormley) 22, K Lowe (Knebworth) 20, R Grant (Met Police) 19, L Edmunds (Bedmond) 19, S Kent (Sun) 18, M Graham (Oxhey) 18, S Read (Kings Langley) 17, A Foley (Bovingdon) 17, H Baldwin (Met Police) 15, B Mellor (Croxley) 14, A Wheeler (Cuffley) 14, S Fraser (Met Police) 13, P Clifford (Roussel) 12, C Smith (Chipperfield) 12.

DIVISION ONE	P	W	D	L	F	A	PTS
Somersett Ambury	34	25	7	2	94	33	82
Walkern	34	21	6	7	104	53	69
Welwyn	34	20	7	7	81	51	67
Allensbury Sports	34	20	4	10	93	54	64
Sarratt	34	19	4	11	61	44	61
Evergreen	34	18	5	11	82	57	59
Whitwell Ath.	34	17	5	12	78	53	56
Kodak Hemel Hem.	34	15	6	13	76	72	51
Kimpton Rovers	34	13	11	10	65	54	50
Standon & P'ridge	34	11	13	10	64	64	46
Codicote	34	13	5	16	51	60	44
Dynamics	34	11	9	14	45	59	42
St Peters	34	10	11	13	76	73	41
St Ippolytts	34	8	11	15	44	67	35
Hertford Youth	34	8	7	19	54	73	31
North Mymms	34	7	4	23	43	96	25
ICL Letchworth	34	5	5	24	25	90	20
Harpenden Rovers	34	2	6	26	35	118	12

Top Scorers: P Phillips (Somersett) 28, M Swaysland (Evergreen) 28, A McKellar (Allensbury) 25, A Kemp (Sarratt) 24, A Rowe (Walkern) 23, S Legate (Whitwell) 20, S Morley (Walkern) 20, D Boston (Whitwell) 19, J Valentine (Codicote) 18, P McCormack (Welwyn) 16, K Rehman (Allensburys) 15, G McGregor (St Peters) 15, J Fettus (Welwyn) 14, I Cooper (Somersett) 14, K Minnis (Whitwell) 13, D Brasewell (Evergreen) 12, M White (ICL) 12, S Manning (Kimpton) 12, W Morris (Somersett) 12, K Smith (Kimpton) 10, D Ridley (Welwyn) 10.

RESERVE DIV. 1	P	W	D	L	F	A	PTS
Sun Spts Res.	34	28	2	4	103	40	86
Wormley Rvrs Res.	34	26	4	4	106	30	82
Sandridge R. Res.	34	23	8	3	93	30	77
Bovingdon Res.	34	20	9	5	74	41	69
Bedmond Soc. Res.	34	19	3	12	96	62	60
Colney Heath Res.	34	15	6	13	82	71	51
Oxhey Jets Res.	34	16	3	15	67	63	51
Rossel Spts Res.	34	14	4	16	57	54	46
Kings Lang. Res.	34	13	5	16	54	62	44
Chipperfield Res.	34	11	9	14	52	61	42
Walkern Res.	34	11	6	17	51	73	39
BAC Stev. Res.	34	11	6	17	55	88	39
Knebworth Res.	34	11	6	17	48	81	39
Welwyn Res.	34	8	10	16	48	76	34
Dynamics Res.	34	7	9	18	44	84	30
Met Police Res.	34	8	5	21	52	83	29
Elliott Star Res.	34	7	6	21	47	74	27
Kodak HH Res.	34	6	3	25	42	98	21

Top Scorers: R Glavin (Sun) 46, N Layton (Wormley) 36, A Gallin (Sandridge) 35, D Morriott (Bedmond) 25, K Nguyen (Sandridge) 19, S Hancock (Kodak) 16, I Pepper (Sun) 15, G Donnison (Met Police) 15, P Kinchin (Bovingdon) 13, P Downing (Chipperfield) 12, J Duguid (Welwyn) 11, S Byford (Bedmond) 11, G Nicholson (Roussel) 10, K Wicks (Oxhey) 10

RESERVE DIV. 2	P	W	D	L	F	A	PTS
Bushey Rgrs Res.	30	24	2	4	97	32	74
Hertford Yth Res.	30	24	2	4	83	22	74
Cuffley Res.	30	21	6	3	92	25	69
Croxley G. Res.	30	20	5	5	74	26	65
Somersett A. Res.	30	20	4	6	74	23	64
St Peters Res.	30	12	6	12	70	63	42
Allensburys Res.	30	10	7	13	55	66	37
Whitwell A. Res.	30	11	4	15	60	76	37
Standon & P. Res.	30	11	2	17	53	70	35
Evergreen Res.	30	9	5	16	26	50	32
GDS Valmar Res.	30	9	4	17	51	71	31
Sarratt Res.	30	9	4	17	37	66	31
Kimpton Rvrs Res.	30	7	9	14	49	65	30
St Ippolyts Res.	30	8	4	18	38	77	28
Harpenden R. Res.	30	8	3	19	49	77	27
North Mymms Res.	30	2	3	25	29	128	9

Top Scorers: G Hall (Cuffley) 42, P Jackson (Somersett) 22, M Baker (Valmar) 22, D Campbell (Whitwell) 21, G Bartlett (Somersett) 16, A Trinder (Croxley) 15, D Quarman (Bushey) 14, L Fitzgerald (Croxley) 13, P Elliott (Bushey) 10, K Fletcher & P Mann (Hertford Yth) 10.

AUBREY (LEAGUE) CUP 1993-94

First Round

Kimpton Rovers v North Mymms 3-1
Sarratt v Codicote 2-4*(aet)*
St Ippolyts v Harpenden R. 2-2,3-3*(H on pens)*
Standon & Puckeridge v ICL Letchworth 2-1

Second Round

BAC Stevenage v Welwyn 4-2*(aet)*
Colney Heath v Elliott Star 5-0
Cuffley v Roussel Sports 1-2
Evergreen v Bedmond S. 2-2,2-2*(E on pens)*
Kings Langley v Walkern 2-0
Codicote v Kimpton Rovers 4-2
Standon & Puckeridge v Sandridge Rovers 0-5
GDS Valmar v St Peters 1-3*(aet)*
Chipperfield Corinthians v Wormley Rovers 3-1
Croxley Guild v Kodak Hemel Hempstead 4-0
Dynamics v Bovingdon 0-3
Hertford Youth v Bushey Rangers 0-3
Knebworth v Sun Sports 1-3
Harpenden Rovers v Oxhey Jets 0-6
Somersett Ambury V & E v Met Police (Bushey) 0-3
Whitwell Athletic v Allensbury Sports 1-2

Third Round

Sandridge Rovers v BAC Stevenage 0-3
Allensburys Sports v Met Police (Bushey) 3-1
Chipperfield Corinthians v Kings Langley 1-2
Oxhey Jets v St Peters 2-1
Sun Sports v Croxley Guild 2-1
Roussel Sports v Codicote 5-0
Bovingdon v Bushey Rangers 2-1
Evergreen v Colney Heath 1-0

Quarter-Finals

Sun Sports v Kings Langley 2-1
Bovingdon v Oxhey Jets 3-1
BAC Stevenage v Allensburys Sports 4-2
Roussel Sports v Evergreen 4-1

Semi-Finals

Roussel Sports v BAC Stevenage 7-0
Sun Sports v Bovingdon 4-2

Final *(at Met Police (Bushey) FC)*: Roussel Sports 3, Sun Sports 0

PREMIER DIV. RESULTS	1	2	3	4	5	6	7	8	9	10	11	12	13	14	15	16	17	18
1. BAC Stevenage Reserves	*	1-6	2-0	2-5	0-3	1-4	1-2	1-4	2-2	4-2	1-3	1-5	1-2	4-2	2-4	0-2	1-2	1-3
2. Bedmond Sports	0-0	*	2-1	3-3	0-2	1-1	1-0	2-1	0-0	2-4	1-2	2-0	1-1	1-0	0-3	1-2	4-0	1-2
3. Bovingdon	3-1	1-1	*	3-0	1-1	3-2	1-0	2-2	3-2	1-0	5-1	3-0	4-4	1-2	4-2	2-0	3-0	1-3
4. Bushey Rangers	9-3	1-2	0-1	*	1-2	0-3	2-1	0-2	2-0	2-1	2-2	0-0	2-0	3-1	1-4	0-1	2-1	0-3
5. Chipperfield Corinthians	4-1	6-1	1-0	3-0	*	4-2	2-0	4-3	2-2	0-2	3-3	1-1	1-0	4-1	0-2	0-3	5-3	3-2
6. Colney Heath	0-1	1-1	2-2	3-2	1-1	*	2-0	4-1	0-2	2-1	2-5	2-1	2-2	1-0	3-1	0-3	1-2	2-2
7. Croxley Guild of Sport	2-2	0-3	0-2	1-1	1-1	0-1	*	3-0	0-0	1-1	0-0	0-1	0-2	0-6	2-5	1-1	4-2	6-2
8. Cuffley	3-0	3-1	3-1	4-3	1-2	2-1	0-4	*	0-0	3-2	1-2	2-2	4-1	1-2	2-2	0-0	3-0	0-4
9. Elliott Star	1-3	1-2	3-2	2-2	1-2	1-1	0-4	4-1	*	3-5	1-1	1-0	2-4	0-5	2-3	1-2	2-1	0-1
10. Kings Langley	W-L	1-1	1-1	0-0	0-2	2-4	0-0	1-1	4-3	*	1-2	3-2	1-2	1-1	0-0	1-2	0-1	0-3
11. Knebworth	2-1	2-3	1-2	3-0	3-1	2-4	2-1	1-4	3-1	1-1	*	0-0	4-4	1-2	2-1	1-0	2-0	1-4
12. Metropolitan Police (Bushey)	8-1	4-1	0-0	2-1	1-1	3-1	2-0	3-3	7-1	2-1	1-4	*	1-0	4-1	4-2	2-3	6-2	1-3
13. Oxhey Jets	3-0	1-2	0-2	3-2	2-6	3-0	1-0	1-1	2-0	0-1	0-1	0-3	*	2-2	2-3	0-0	0-1	0-3
14. Roussel Sports	4-1	3-0	1-1	3-1	3-2	4-0	1-4	1-0	2-1	4-3	2-0	0-2	0-2	*	3-1	0-2	7-1	2-1
15. Sandridge Rovers	1-1	6-2	2-2	2-1	1-4	4-3	0-1	2-1	0-2	1-1	1-0	3-3	2-0	2-2	*	0-1	7-0	1-1
16. Sun Sports	6-2	1-0	2-0	4-1	5-2	4-1	2-1	2-0	1-0	3-0	0-1	3-3	1-0	2-3	6-1	*	1-1	3-0
17. (GDS) Valmar	1-0	0-1	0-1	1-2	0-0	0-0	2-1	1-2	1-1	0-2	3-2	2-2	1-2	3-1	0-3	0-0	*	0-2
18. Wormley Rovers	2-1	3-3	4-1	6-1	2-1	6-1	3-1	0-0	1-1	2-1	2-2	1-3	2-1	0-1	4-1	0-0	2-1	*

DIVISION ONE RESULTS	1	2	3	4	5	6	7	8	9	10	11	12	13	14	15	16	17	18
1. Allensbury Sports	*	3-1	3-0	1-2	6-2	1-2	6-2	1-2	2-0	0-1	1-1	3-3	1-3	1-5	4-0	0-3	1-0	6-2
2. Codicote	1-4	*	1-2	1-5	1-1	0-3	4-0	1-4	2-2	1-1	1-3	4-2	0-2	0-3	3-1	2-1	1-0	2-1
3. Dynamics	1-4	0-1	*	2-0	1-0	1-1	1-1	1-1	3-2	1-2	1-2	0-6	0-0	1-2	1-1	1-2	0-0	1-2
4. Evergreen	0-3	1-3	4-1	*	1-0	2-0	4-1	0-1	7-2	2-1	6-1	3-1	2-1	0-2	2-2	2-4	1-1	2-2
5. Harpenden Rovers	2-4	0-3	0-1	2-2	*	2-5	2-0	1-1	1-2	1-2	1-2	2-2	0-2	1-5	0-2	1-7	1-10	1-6
6. Hertford Youth	0-5	1-6	2-2	1-3	6-1	*	1-1	1-1	1-2	0-1	1-0	3-0	0-3	0-3	2-1	2-4	1-2	0-1
7. ICL Letchworth	0-3	1-0	1-2	0-6	1-0	W-L	*	0-5	2-3	4-1	1-2	0-1	0-0	0-5	0-3	0-5	1-2	0-3
8. Kimpton Rovers	0-0	1-1	1-3	3-2	3-2	2-5	3-0	*	2-2	3-1	3-0	3-1	0-3	0-5	2-2	2-2	2-2	1-1
9. Kodak Hemel Hempstead	1-2	1-0	2-3	5-3	3-3	2-1	3-0	3-2	*	6-2	3-1	4-2	1-2	2-5	1-1	2-3	2-1	2-0
10. North Mymms	0-7	2-4	3-1	1-2	1-2	3-2	2-0	0-1	2-5	*	0-2	0-5	2-3	0-2	2-4	2-5	3-5	0-8
11. St Ippolyts	0-3	0-1	0-3	1-4	2-2	3-3	2-2	1-1	2-2	3-1	*	2-2	1-0	1-3	1-1	3-1	0-1	0-4
12. St Peters	4-5	0-2	2-3	5-1	9-1	2-2	2-2	1-8	2-1	1-1	3-3	*	2-3	0-1	2-2	0-0	0-2	5-2
13. Sarratt	1-3	2-1	1-4	0-3	4-0	3-1	2-0	2-1	0-0	3-0	1-1	0-2	*	0-3	4-0	4-1	3-2	3-0
14. Somersett Ambury V & E	3-2	3-3	1-0	3-0	6-1	3-3	2-0	W-L	2-3	2-0	3-0	2-2	3-0	*	2-0	1-2	2-2	1-0
15. Standon & Puckeridge	3-2	4-0	2-2	4-3	2-0	4-1	1-2	1-4	4-2	1-1	1-1	1-1	4-2	2-2	*	1-1	1-5	2-2
16. Walkern	2-3	3-0	1-1	1-3	9-1	2-1	8-2	4-1	3-1	4-0	2-0	3-4	2-0	3-3	3-2	*	7-2	0-1
17. Welwyn	2-2	1-0	6-0	1-3	2-1	2-1	1-0	3-0	4-3	4-3	3-2	0-1	3-1	3-3	3-0	3-3	*	W-L
18. Whitwell Athletic	4-1	2-1	2-1	1-1	5-0	5-1	5-1	2-1	2-1	2-2	2-1	4-1	1-2	1-3	1-4	2-3	2-3	*

RES. DIV. ONE RESULTS	1	2	3	4	5	6	7	8	9	10	11	12	13	14	15	16	17	18
1. BAC Stevenage Reserves	*	3-2	2-6	3-1	0-5	1-1	5-3	1-1	4-1	2-1	2-1	1-0	7-1	0-3	2-6	3-2	0-0	0-9
2. Bedmond Social Reserves	9-0	*	4-5	5-0	6-1	3-2	3-3	3-1	4-0	4-3	3-1	3-1	W-L	3-1	1-2	6-3	4-0	1-3
3. Bovingdon Reserves	1-0	2-1	*	2-2	0-0	1-2	2-1	1-0	2-1	3-0	3-3	4-0	1-1	0-2	1-3	1-0	4-0	3-3
4. Chipperfield Cor. Reserves	3-0	1-2	2-2	*	2-2	1-1	1-3	5-4	2-1	3-0	3-1	4-0	0-0	1-1	2-4	1-1	1-1	0-3
5. Colney Heath Reserves	3-0	3-2	0-1	4-1	*	2-1	2-0	3-1	1-1	4-0	2-5	2-5	2-1	2-8	0-2	7-2	0-0	1-3
6. Dynamics Reserves	4-0	2-3	0-5	0-3	3-3	*	3-1	0-7	0-2	0-5	0-1	2-0	1-4	0-0	2-6	1-1	1-2	0-1
7. Elliott Star Reserves	0-0	4-0	2-2	0-1	3-2	1-1	*	0-1	1-4	0-0	4-1	3-2	0-1	1-4	0-2	2-2	1-3	0-5
8. Kings Langley Reserves	W-L	1-2	0-1	5-2	2-1	2-3	1-3	*	1-1	2-0	3-2	1-5	2-2	3-4	0-1	W-L	0-0	0-1
9. Knebworth Reserves	2-2	3-2	1-3	2-0	0-3	1-1	3-0	3-0	*	2-2	W-L	2-1	1-1	0-9	1-9	4-2	1-6	0-4
10. Kodak Hemel H. Reserves	4-3	0-10	1-1	1-3	1-4	0-1	2-1	0-2	3-2	*	5-1	2-3	0-2	0-1	0-4	0-1	0-3	1-6
11. Met Police (Bushey) Res.	3-1	0-2	0-4	1-2	3-5	3-1	3-1	2-3	0-3	3-1	*	5-5	0-2	1-1	1-6	1-5	0-2	1-1
12. Oxhey Jets Reserves	2-2	6-2	4-1	2-1	3-2	1-3	4-2	2-1	W-L	1-0	1-1	*	4-1	0-5	1-2	W-L	9-0	0-4
13. Roussel Sports Reserves	1-0	2-4	0-1	2-3	3-0	3-0	2-1	2-3	5-1	7-1	1-0	2-0	*	1-3	3-0	0-1	2-0	2-3
14. Sandridge Rovers Reserves	4-1	1-0	1-1	2-0	2-1	3-0	1-0	0-1	5-1	11-1	3-0	2-1	2-1	*	1-1	3-0	3-3	1-0
15. Sun Sports Reserves	4-2	2-0	1-0	3-0	4-1	3-0	5-1	1-3	4-3	3-2	1-0	1-2	2-1	1-1	*	4-0	4-0	2-5
16. Walkern	0-2	1-1	1-2	0-0	1-8	2-2	1-0	3-2	4-0	3-2	2-3	2-1	2-1	3-2	2-3	*	1-0	1-6
17. Welwyn	5-6	1-1	1-5	2-1	2-2	4-4	2-4	0-0	0-1	0-3	1-4	0-1	5-0	2-3	2-6	W-L	*	1-1
18. Wormley Rovers	W-L	4-0	2-3	1-0	3-4	9-2	3-1	7-1	W-L	2-1	4-1	W-L	5-0	0-0	0-1	5-2	3-0	*

RES. DIV. TWO RESULTS	1	2	3	4	5	6	7	8	9	10	11	12	13	14	15	16	17
1. Allensbury Sports Reserves	*	3-4	2-1	3-3	1-3	3-0	0-2		1-1	3-0	2-2	2-4	0-2	0-3	4-0	2-1	1-4
2. Bushey Rangers Reserves	4-1	*	0-2	0-3	4-1	7-2	2-1	4-1	3-2	6-0	2-0	2-1	6-1	2-1	4-0	5-1	7-0
3. Croxley Guild Reserves	5-0	0-5	*	0-1	1-0	4-1	0-0		5-1	4-0	5-0	6-0	1-0	2-2	3-1	W-L	W-L
4. Cuffley Reserves	3-0	0-0	1-1	*	6-0	3-2	0-1		5-3	5-1	5-1	2-1	4-0	1-1	5-0	1-1	5-0
5. Evergreen Reserves	2-0	2-1	0-3	0-1	*	2-1	0-1		0-0	2-1	1-1	1-6	2-2	0-2	1-3	2-1	2-1
6. Harpenden Rovers Reserves	4-4	1-4	1-1	0-4	9-0	*	1-3		W-L	5-0	2-0	2-2	0-1	0-3	2-4	3-7	3-5
7. Hertford Youth Reserves	3-0	2-0	0-2	3-2	W-L	3-2	*		5-1	3-0	4-0	2-1	5-1	2-0	4-0	2-3	1-1
8. ICL Letchworth Res. *(withdrew - recorded expunged & shown for interest only)*															3-0		2-1
9. Kimpton Rovers Reserves	0-3	2-3	2-1	1-1	1-1	0-1	0-4	0-1	*	8-0	2-0	3-3	1-1	0-1	2-6	1-1	1-0
10. North Mymms Reserves	2-2	0-3	1-0	0-4	1-2	0-3	0-9		3-3	*	2-4	0-3	3-3	2-6	1-4	1-5	0-4
11. St Ippolyts Reserves	1-3	0-3	1-6	0-3	1-1	0-1	1-6	4-2	1-3	10-1	*	1-4	0-4	1-0	1-3	1-4	2-2
12. St Peters Reserves	1-4	1-1	2-5	2-2	W-L	3-0	1-2		3-3	4-0	1-2	*	0-0	1-3	5-1	1-5	5-2
13. Sarratt Reserves	2-4	0-2	1-4	0-1	1-0	1-2	1-4		3-2	2-4	1-3	1-4	*	0-1	1-0	2-0	0-4
14. Somersett Ambury VE Res.	7-1	0-1	0-0	2-1	1-0	2-0	0-2	5-1	5-0	7-1	4-0	4-0	2-0	*	3-1	W-L	2-0
15. Standon & Puckeridge Res.	1-1	1-4	1-2	0-2	W-L	3-0	2-0		0-2	4-1	0-1	4-6	2-3	0-6	*	5-1	2-0
16. (GDS) Valmar Reserves	0-0	0-4	0-5	1-3	0-1	4-0	0-6		2-3	5-2	2-3	1-0	1-2	0-4	1-1	*	3-2
17. Whitwell Athletic Reserves	1-5	1-8	3-5	1-7	W-L	4-1	1-3		3-1	5-2	L-W	2-5	4-1	3-2	4-1	1-1	*

RESERVE CUP 1993-94

First Round

ICL Letch. Res. v Standon & Puckeridge Res. 1-3
Kimpton Rvrs Res. v Harpenden Rvrs Res. 3-1
St Ippolyts Res. v Whitwell Ath. Res. 1-2*(aet)*

Second Round

Allensburys Sports Res. v Cuffley Res. 0-7
Dynamics Res. v Sandridge Rovers Res. 1-5
Kings Langley Res. v Walkern Res. 0-1
Chipperfield Corinthians Res. v Colney Hth Res. 3-1
Hertford Yth Res. *(disq)* v Somersett *(reinstated)* 4-0
Kodak Hemel Hempstead Res. v Evergreen Res. 14-0

(continued opposite)

St Peters Res. v Sun Sports Res. 2-4*(aet)*
GDS Valmar Res. v BAC Stevenage Res. 1-3
Wormley Rovers Res. v Knebworth Res. 1-0
Bedmond Res. v Roussel Sports Res. 0-3
Bushey Rgrs Res. v North Mymms Res. 7-0
Sarratt Res. v Standon & Puckeridge Res. 3-2
Welwyn Res. v Elliott Star Res. 4-1
Kimpton Rovers Res. v Met Police Res. 1-2*(aet)*
Croxley Guild Res. v Bovingdon Res. 0-0,1-0
Oxhey Jets Res. *(w/o)* v Whitwell Ath. Res. *(scr)*

Third Round
Chipperfield Res. v Cuffley Rvrs Res. 2-4*(aet)*
Kodak HH Res. v BAC Stevenage Res. 0-1
Met Police (Bushey) Res. v Oxhey Jets Res. 0-1
Bushey Rgrs Res. v Wormley Rvrs Res. 2-2,1-4
Sarratt Res. v Walkern Res. 2-2*(Walkern then w'dew)*
Somersett Ambury VE Res. v Sandridge R. Res. 0-2
Roussel Spts Res. v Welwyn Res. 4-4,2-3
Sun Sports Res. v Croxley Guild Res. 8-0

Quarter-Finals
Sarratt Res. v Wormley Rovers Res. 0-5
Oxhey Jets Res. v BAC Stevenage Res. 2-3
Sun Sports Res. v Sandridge Rovers Res. 4-3
Cuffley Res. v Welwyn Res. 3-0

Semi-Finals
Sun Sports Res. v Cuffley Res. 2-0
BAC Stevenage Res. v Wormley Rovers Res. 1-2

Final *(at Colney Heath) FC)*: Wormley Rovers Reserves 2, Sun Sports Reserves 1

BAC Stevenage - who have changed their name to Bragbury Athletic for 1994-95. *Photo - Martin Wray.*

Paul Mann fires in an excellent shot to open the scoring for Premier Division leaders Wormley Rovers in their 2-1 win at home to Kings Langley on 8th January.
Photo - Martin Wray.

PREMIER DIVISION CLUBS 1994-95

BEDMOND SPORTS & SOCIAL

Secretary: Tom Payne, 339 Toms Lane, Bedmond, Abbots Langley, Herts WD5 0RA (0923 266358).
Ground: The Pavillion, Toms Lane, Bedmond (0923 267991).
Directions: M1 jct 8, then A4147 to 2nd r'bout, left on St Albans route (A414), bear right to Bedmond at church (Bedmond Rd), right in village into Toms Lane at mini r'bout, ground 300yds on left.
Seats: None **Cover:** Yes **Programme:** Yes **Nickname:** Mons **Founded:** pre-1913
Colours: Green & red/green/green **Change colours:** White (red pin stripes)/red/red
Previous Leagues: West Herts/ Watford & District **Hons:** Herts Lg 84-85 85-86 (Aubrey Cup 80-81)

BOVINGDON

Secretary: David Dawson, 9 Granville Dene, Bovingdon, Hemel Hempstead HP3 0JE (0442 834271).
Ground & Directions: Green Lane, Bovingdon (0442 832628). From Hemel Hempstead to Bovingdon, left by Halfway House then right into Green Lane. Ground on left at top of hill.
Seats: Yes **Cover:** Yes **Programme:** No **Nickname:** None
Colours: Green & white stripes/green/green **Change colours:** Tangerine/black/tangerine.
Previous League: West Herts **Hons:** Herts Lg Div 1 55-56 80-81 83-84 (Div 2 69-70).

BUSHEY RANGERS

Secretary: John Burrows, 56 Bournehall Ave., Bushey, Herts WD2 3BA (081 386 0295).
Ground: Moatfield, Bournehall Lane, Bushey (081 950 1875).
Directions: A41 to Hartspring Lane, into Aldenham Rd, left at r'bout into the Avenue, right at top into Herkomer Rd, take 4th left.
Seats: None **Cover:** Yes **Programme:** No **Nickname:** Rangers
Colours: Blue (white sleeves)/blue/white **Change colours:** Grey/black/black.

CHIPPERFIELD CORINTHIANS

Secretary: Stephen J Hall, 3 Rowley Close, Oxhey, Watford, Herts WD1 4DT (0923 253803).
Ground: Queen Street, Chipperfield.
Directions: To Chipperfield via Kings Langley. Take 1st left, over crossroads, ground 400yds on right.
Seats: None **Cover:** Yes **Programme:** Yes **Nickname:** None **Founded:** 1987
Colours: Red & black stripes/red/red **Change colours:** All sky.
Previous Leagues: None **Prev. Names:** Chipperfield FC, Tudor Corinthians (merged 1987)
Hons: Herts Lg Div 1 87-88 (Aubrey Cup 92-93), Herts Interm. Cup 87-88.

COLNEY HEATH

Secretary: Eddie Greywace, 28 Bullens Green Lane, Colney Heath, St Albans AL4 0QS (0727 822733).
Ground: The Pavillion Recreation Ground, High Street, Colney Heath (0727 826188).
Directions: Turn off A414 in Colney Heath village, ground behind school on left.
Seats: None **Cover:** Yes **Programme:** Yes **Nickname:** Magpies **Founded:** 1907
Colours: White & black stripes/black/black **Change cols:** Red & white stripes/red/red.
Previous Leagues: Nth Mymms & District/Mid Herts.
Hons: Herts Lg 58-59 (Div 1 55-56 88-89, Div 2 53-54, Aubrey Cup 53-54 59-60), Herts I'mediate Cup 59-60).

CROXLEY GUILD of SPORT

Secretary: Dave Rickman, 18 Tudor Walk, Watford, Herts WD2 4PA (0923 231543).
Ground: Croxley Guild of Sport, The Green, Croxley Green (0923 770534).
Directions: M25 to Chorleywood (jct 18), left off slip road (A404) to r'bout (2 miles), 1st exit to next r'bout, follow Watford sign (A412) to next r'bout, 1st exit, ground 300 yds on right opposite Artichoke pub.
Seats: None **Cover:** No **Programme:** No **Nickname:** Dicko's **Founded:** 1920
Previous Leagues: West Herts/Middx County. **Reformed:** 1983
Cols: Blue & black stripes/blue/blue **Change colours:** Sky/black/black.

CUFFLEY

Secretary: David C Chapman, 51 Woodlands Rd, Hertford, Herts SG13 7JF (0992 582358).
Ground: King Georges Playing Fields, Northaw Rd East, Cuffley (0707 875395).
Directions: A121 from Potters Bar or Cheshunt, 5 miles from either Jct 25 or 26 on M25.
Seats: None **Cover:** None **Programme:** No **Nickname:** Zeplins **Founded:** 1958
Colours: Maroon/sky/maroon **Change colours:** White & blue stripes/white/blue.
Previous Leagues: Barnet/ Nth London Combination. **Hons:** Herts Lg Div 2 77-78.

KINGS LANGLEY

Secretary: Brian Aldersley, 12 Elm Grove, Watford, Herts WD2 6QE (0923 251130).
Ground: Leavesden Hospital Ground, Woodside Rd, Abbots Langley.
Directions: A405 to Garston traffic lights. From Watford turn left (from St Albans, right) into Horseshoe Lane. Woodside Rd is one mile on right, ground quarter mile on left.
Seats: Yes **Cover:** Yes **Programme:** No **Nickname:** None **Founded:** 1886
Cols: Blue & white stripes/blue/white **Change colours:** Blue/black/black.
Previous League: West Herts.
Hons: Herts Lg 47-48 49-50 51-52 65-66 66-67 (Div 1 75-76, Aubrey Cup 67-68).

KNEBWORTH

Secretary: Steve Clarke, 34 Kerr Close, Knebworth, Herts SG3 6AB (0438 815406).
Ground: Old Knebworth Lane, Stevenage (0438 313320).
Directions: A1(M) to Stevenage South, A602 towards Hertford, 3rd exit at 2nd r'bout (B197). Follow to Roebuck Inn and turn right opposite pub into Old Knebworth Lane. Ground 200yds on left.
Seats: Yes **Cover:** Yes **Programme:** Yes **Nickname:** None **Founded:** 1901
Colours: Tangerine/black/black **Change colours:** Sky/blue/white
Previous Leagues: Nth Herts/Sth Mids. **Hons:** Herts Lg 73-74 (Div 1 76-77, Aubrey Cup 76-77).

METROPOLITAN POLICE (BUSHEY)

Secretary: Brian Southern, c/o Met Police Spts Club, Aldenham Rd, Bushey, Herts WD2 3TR (0923 243947).
Ground: Aldenham Road, Bushey (0923 243947).
Directions: M1 jct 5, A41 for Harrow/South Watford, at 1st r'bout right into Hartspring Lane which runs into Aldenham (A4008). Ground quarter mile on left opposite Caledonian School.
Seats: None **Cover:** No **Programme:** No **Nickname:** None
Colours: Sky/sky/navy **Change colours:** Green/black/green.
Hons: Herts County Lg Div 1 92-93.

OXHEY JETS

Secretary: John Elliott, 7 Brampton Rd, South Oxhey, Watford, Herts WD1 6PF (081 428 6382).
Ground: Chilwell Gardens, South Oxhey (081 421 4965).
Directions: Follow Bushey signs from Watford centre, at Bushey Arches turn right into Eastbury Rd, left into Brookdene Avenue, continue along Prestwick Rd past station, right into Northwick Rd and left into Chilwell Gdns.
Seats: None **Cover:** **Programme:** No **Nickname:** Jets **Founded:** 1972
Colours: All blue **Change colours:** All yellow.
Previous Leagues: Watford & District/West Herts.

ROUSSEL SPORTS

Secretary: Stephen Sells, 1 Robin Hill, Berkhamsted, Herts HP4 2HX (0442 864649).
Ground: Kitcheners Field, Castle Hill, Berkhamsted (0442 74937).
Directions: A41 into Berkhamsted. At main lights turn into Lower Kings Rd, at railway station turn left under bridge, then 2nd right. Entrance on next corner.
Seats: None **Cover:** None **Programme:** No **Nickname:** None **Founded:** 1967
Colours: All blue **Change colours:** All red.
Previous Name: Wellcome (pre-1993) **Previous League:** West Herts Sunday
Hons: Herts Lg Div 1 82-83 91-92 (Aubrey Cup 93-94, Div 2 81-82).

SANDRIDGE ROVERS

Secretary: Graham C Hardwick, 21 Woodcock Hill, Sandridge, St Albans AL4 9EF (0727 855334).
Ground: Spencer Recreation Ground, Sandridge (0727 55159).
Directions: B651 from St Albans or Wheathampstead to High Street. Ground at rear of public car park.
Seats: None **Cover:** Yes **Programme:** Yes **Nickname:** Rovers **Founded:** 1896
Colours: Black & white stripes/black/red **Change colours:** Green & white stripes/white/green.
Prev. Lge: Mid Herts **Hons:** Herts Lg 81-82 82-83 87-88 (Div 1 68-69), Herts Intermediate Cup 81-82.

SOMERSETT AMBURY V & E

Secretary: Ian Whittle, 21 Kilwardby Street, Ashby-de-la-Zouch, Leics LE65 2FR (0530 413471).
Ground: V & E Youth Club, Goffs Lane, Cheshunt (0992 624281).
Directions: M25 jct 25, A10 north, left at 1st r'bout onto Flamstead End relief road to r'bout with Goffs Lane. Right into Goffs Lane, clubhouse immediately on right.
Seats: None **Cover:** No **Programme:** Yes **Nickname:** **Founded:** 1960
Colours: White/blue/blue **Change colours:** Red/black/black.
Hons: Herts Lg Div 1 R-up 93-94 **Previous Leagues:** Enfield Alliance, Hertford & District.

SUN SPORTS

Secretary: Graham Stockinger, 30 Briar Rd, Watford, Herts (0923 465062).
Ground: Bellmont Wood Avenue, Watford (0703 254364).
Directions: From Kings Langley to Watford on Hempstead road, turn right at Langley lights, right at r'bout then 1st left. Entrance 50yds on right.
Seats: None **Cover:** Yes **Programme:** Yes **Nickname:** **Founded:**
Colours: Yellow/royal/yellow **Change colours:** White/navy/navy.
Previous Leagues: Watford & District/West Herts.
Hons: Herts Co. Snr Lg 92-93 93-94 (Aubrey Cup 88-89, Herts Intermediate Cup 75-76).

WELWYN

Secretary: Michael Pestle, 4 Marsden Close, Welwyn Garden City, Herts AL8 6YE (0707 335503).
Ground: Welwyn Playing Field, Ottway Walk, London Rd, Welwyn (0438 714183).
Directions: From A1(M) take A1000 turning 1st left off r'bout, then 1st right at Nodeway filling station into London Rd. Ground quarter mile on left opposite Steamer pub.
Seats: None **Cover:** No **Programme:** Yes **Nickname:** None **Founded:** 1893
Colours: All blue **Change colours:** All red.
Previous Leagues: North Herts/Mid Herts **Hons:** Herts Lg Div 1 79-80.

WORMLEY ROVERS

Secretary: David M Smith, 19 Nursery Gardens, Enfield, Middx EN3 5NG (081 804 3608).
Ground: Sports Club, Church Lane, Wormley (0992 460650).
Directions: From A10 take A1170 turning for Broxbourne and Turnford. Left at New River Arms, left again into Church Lane. Ground quarter mile on right.
Seats: None **Cover:** No **Programme:** No **Nickname:** Robins **Founded:** Unknown
Colours: Red/black/black **Change colours:** All blue.
Previous Leagues: Ware & District/Hertford & District/Northern Suburban.
Hons: Herts Lg Div 1 86-87 (Div 3 76-77).

DIVISION ONE CLUBS 1994-95

ALLENSBURYS SPORTS

Secretary: Simon Carr, 36 Starholme Court, Ware, Herts SG12 7EA (0920 484858).
Ground: Harris Lane, Ware (0920 462742).
Directions: From A10, take B1001 to Ware. 3rd right into Fanshawe Crescent, over crossroads into Harris Lane, ground on right.
Seats: None **Cover:** No **Programme:** No **Nickname:** None
Colours: Blue/blue/yellow **Change colours:** Yellow/blue/blue
Previous League: Hertford & District **Hons:** Herts Lg Div 2 90-91

BRAGBURY ATHLETIC

Secretary: Raymond C Poulter, 292 Jessop Rd, Stevenage, Herts SG1 5NA (0438 358078).
Ground & Directions: Bragbury End, Stevenage (0438 812985). A1(M) to Stevenage Sth (jct 7), A602 Hertford/Ware signs to Bragbury End, ground on left at just past golf course.
Seats: None **Cover:** Yes **Programme:** Yes **Nickname:** **Founded:** 1953
Colours: Red/white/white **Change colours:** Amber/black/amber.
Previous League: Nth Herts/Sth Mids **Previous Name:** BAC Stevenage (pre-1994)
Hons: Aubrey Cup 87-88.

CODICOTE

Secretary: Richard Hunt, 68a Vaughan Rd, Stotfold, Hitchin, Herts SG5 4EN (0462 835623).
Ground: Bury Lane, Codicote.
Directions: A1(M) jct 6, head for Welwyn and Codicote via B656, in village turn right into Bury Lane (after Bell pub), ground entrance opposite church.
Seats: None **Cover:** No **Programme:** Yes **Nickname:** None **Founded:** 1945
Cols: White & blue/white/blue & white **Change colours:** Green & white hoops/white/green.
Previous Leagues: North Herts.

DYNAMICS (SPACE SYSTEMS)

Secretary: Kevin Folds, 6 Lanthony Ct, High Street, Arlesey, Beds SG15 6TU (0462 834084).
Ground: Fairview Road, Stevenage, Herts (0438 736284).
Directions: A1(M) to Stevenage South (A602). Exit towards industrial area then turn left at next r'bout into Gunnelswood Rd. Take underpass and at following r'bout turn right into Fairlands Way. 1st left into Fairview Rd, ground 150yds on right.
Seats: None **Cover:** Yes **Programme:** No **Nickname:** None **Founded:** 1955
Colours: White/black/white **Change colours:** Claret/sky/claret.
Previous League: North Herts **Previous Name:** Dynamics (Stevenage) (pre-1994).

ELLIOTT STAR

Secretary: Raymond Capper, 28 Alban Cres., Boreham Wood, Herts WD6 5JF (081 207 3940).
Ground: GEC Sports Centre, Rowley Lane, Boreham Wood (081 953 5087).
Directions: A1 to Elstree Moat House, turn left (flyover) into town and turn into Elstree Way. Ground on right behind Clarenden Garage. One mile from Elstree & Boreham Wood (BR).
Seats: None **Cover:** None **Programme:** No **Nickname:** None **Founded:** 1957
Cols: Black & red hoops/black/black **Change colours:** Blue & navy/black/black.
Previous Lge: London Commercial **Hons:** FA Vase 2nd Rd 91-92.

EVERGREEN

Secretary: Dennis McCrystal, 76 Woodmere Ave., Watford, Herts WD2 4LW (0923 465750).
Ground: Southway, Abbots Langley (0927 767812).
Directions: A41 or A405 to r'bout junction and head for Leavesden. Right at next r'bout towards Abbots Langley, pass Rolls Royce works, then first left into Southway. Clubhouse entrance in Essex Lane at end of Southway.
Seats: None **Cover:** No **Programme:** No **Nickname:** None **Founded:** 1957
Cols: Green & white hoops/white/red **Change colours:** Black & blue stripes/black/black.
Previous Leagues: West Herts Youth. **Hons:** Herts Lg 64-65 67-88 68-69 69-70 70-71 71-72 79-80 (Aubrey Cup 64-65 66-67 69-70 70-71), Herts Intermediate Cup 79-80.

ICKLEFORD

Secretary: Peter Colderwood, 26 Sanfoine Close, Hitchin, Herts SG4 0NP (0462 434478).
Ground: Ickleford Sport Club, Chambers Lane, Ickleford (0462 420624).
Directions: A600 from Hitchin. First right into village then second left.
Seats: None **Cover:** None **Programme:** Yes **Nickname:** None **Reformed:** 1994
Colours: Red/white/red **Change colours:** Green/white/green.
Previous League: South Midlands (pre-1993)

KIMPTON ROVERS

Secretary: Neil Matthews, 30 Commons Lane, Kimpton, Herts SG4 8QG (0438 832625).
Ground: Recreation Ground, High Street, Kimpton.
Directions: Kimpton is between Stevenage, Luton & Welwyn on insection of B651 and B652. Ground is set back on hill off the High Street.
Seats: None **Cover:** No **Programme:** No **Nickname:** Rovers **Founded:** 1910
Colours: White/blue/white **Change colours:** All maroon.
Previous Leagues: Nth Herts/Mid Herts

KODAK HEMEL HEMPSTEAD

Secretary: Brian Pollard, The Laurels, Wood Rising Lodge, High Street Green, Hemel Hempstead HP2 7AA (0442 256720).
Ground: Kodak Sports Ground, Wood End Lane, off Maylands Avenue, Hemel Hempstead (0442 242597).
Directions: M1 jct 8, right at 2nd r'bout (A4147) to lights, then right into Wood End Lane. Ground quarter mile on right.
Seats: None **Cover:** No **Programme:** No **Nickname:** **Founded:** 1960
Colours: Blue/black/claret
Change colours: Green & black stripes/black/black.
Previous League: West Herts/Sth Mids **Hons:** Herts Lg Div 2 87-88.

NORTH MYMMS

Secretary: Mick Fitt, 61 Holloways Lane, North Mymms, Hatfield, Herts AL9 7NU (0707 269790).
Ground: Recreation Ground, Dellsome Lane, Welham Green (07072 66972/60338).
Directions: Welham Green is 2 miles south of Hatfield. At village crossroads turn north into Dellsome Lane. Ground on left.
Seats: None **Cover:** None **Programme:** No **Nickname:** None **Founded:** 1968
Colours: Sky/navy/sky **Change colours:** Red/red/red.

St IPPOLYTS

Secretary: Elizabeth Maxwell, 12 Orchard Close, St Ippolyts, Herts SG4 7RH (0462 453482).
Ground: Recreation Ground, Orchard Close, off Mill Road, St Ippolyts (0462 456748).
Directions: B656 from Welwyn. Left at St Ippolyts crossroads, right into The Crescent, left into Mill Rd. Orchard Close is a turning off this road.
Seats: None **Cover:** No **Programme:** No **Nickname:** Saints **Founded:** 1908
Colours: Black & red stripes/black/black **Change colours:** Blue/black/blue.
Previous League: North Herts.

St PETERS (St ALBANS)

Secretary: Peter Garden, 63 Ladies Grove, St Albans, Herts AL3 5TZ (0727 855286).
Ground: Toulmin Drive, St Albans, Herts (0727 852401).
Directions: St Albans ring-road towards Betchwood Golf Club. 20 yds from north entrance turn into Green Lane. At top of hill turn left into Toulmin Drive.
Seats: Yes **Cover:** Yes **Programme:** No **Nickname:** Saints **Founded:** pre-1904
Colours: Maroon & blue/white/maroon **Change colours:** Red/black/red.
Previous League: Mid Herts

SARRATT

Secretary: Mick Warner, 'Colinwood', 45 Church Lane, Sarratt, Herts WD3 6HN (0923 264618).
Ground: King George V Playing Fields, King George Avenue, Sarratt.
Directions: To Kings Langley, and then via Chipperfield.
Seats: None **Cover:** Yes **Programme:** No **Nickname:** **Founded:** Unknown
Colours: Black & amber/black/black **Change colours:** Red & black stripes/black/red.
Previous League: West Herts **Hons:** Herts Lg Div 2 79-80.

STANDON & PUCKERIDGE

Secretary: Jim Starks, 60 Batchelors, Puckeridge, Nr Ware, Herts SG11 1TJ (0920 821958).
Ground: Recreation Ground, Station Rd, Standon, Nr Ware (0920 822489.
Directions: A10 6 miles north of Ware or 4 miles south from Buntingford. Take A120 from A10 Bishop's Stortford r'bout. Over Standon Hill and into Station Rd (3rd left after r'bout), ground quarter mile on left.
Seats: None **Cover:** No **Programme:** No **Nickname:** None **Founded:** 1931
Colours: Blue & white/white/blue **Change colours:** White/green/green.
Previous League: Hertford & District/Norhern Suburban Intermediate.

(G.D.S.) VALMAR

Secretary: John Welsh, 44 Western Avenue, St Albans, Herts AL3 5HP (0727 833511).
Ground: Lemsford Village Hall, Brocket Road, Lemsford (0707 335548).
Directions: Welwyn Garden City exit from A1(M), left to Stanborough 'Ball' r'bout, 2nd exit towards Wheathipstead, Lemsford three quarters of a mile on the right.
Seats: None **Cover:** No **Programme:** No **Nickname:** None
Colours: Red & black hoops/black/black **Change colours:** Sky/navy/navy
Previous League: Mid Herts **Previous Name:** Valmar L.R. (pre-1993).
Hons: Herts County Lg Div 1 R-up 92-93.

WALKERN

Secretary: Ann Huggins, The Coach House, Todds Green, Stevenage, Herts SG1 2JE (0438 759171).
Ground: High Street, Walkern (0432 861615).
Directions: Leave A1(M) for Stevenage South, over 1st r'bout (A602), left at 2nd r'bout (Burger King), over next and right at swimming pool. Follow signs to Walkern (B1037) and in village turn right at junction. Ground 200yds on left.
Seats: None **Cover:** No **Programme:** No **Nickname:** None **Founded:** 1899
Colours: Yellow/sky/white **Change colours:** Sky/navy/navy.
Previous League: North Herts. **Honours:** Herts Lg Div 1 93-94.

RESERVE SECTION CONSTITUTIONS 1994-95

Division One
1. Bedmond Sports & Social Reserves
2. Bovingdon Reserves
3. Bragbury Athletic Reserves
4. Bushey Rangers Res.
5. Chipperfield Corinthians Reserves
6. Colney Heath Reserves
7. Cuffley Reserves
8. Kings Langley Reserves
9. Knebworth Reserves
10. Oxhey Jets Reserves
11. Roussel Sports Reserves
12. Sandridge Rovers Reserves
13. Sun Sports Reserves
14. Walkern Reserves
15. Welwyn Reserves
16. Wormley Rovers Reserves

Division Two
1. Allensbury Sports Reserves
2. Croxley Guild of Sports Reserves
3. Dynamics (Space Systems) Reserves
4. Elliott Star Rangers
5. Evergreen Reserves
6. Ickleford Reserves
7. Kimpton Rovers Reserves
8. Kodak Hemel Hempstead Reserves
9. Metropolitan Police (Bushey) Reserves
10. North Mymms Reserves
11. St Ippolyts Reserves
12. St Peters (St Albans) Reserves
13. Sarratt Reserves
14. Somersett Ambury V & E Reserves
15. Standon & Puckeridge Reserves
16. (G.D.S.) Valmar Reserves

NORTH HERTS LEAGUE (Est. 1910)

Chairman: J Burlison. **Vice-Chairman:** D E Hartley.

Hon. Secretary: R S Hyde,
35 Westmill Rd, Hitchin SG5 2SB (0462 435132)

Premier Division	P	W	D	L	F	A	PTS
Benington	21	18	3	0	65	13	57
Woolmer Green Rgrs	21	13	3	5	71	36	42
Shephall Ath.	21	12	3	6	57	35	39
Argonauts	21	11	3	7	51	33	36
Bridger Packaging	21	9	3	9	35	30	30
Squirrel	21	5	2	14	36	63	17
Sandon	21	4	0	17	17	73	12
Coopers Apprentice	21	2	3	16	29	78	9

Division One	P	W	D	L	F	A	PTS
Bridger Pack. Res.	21	14	3	4	73	31	45
Royston Town 'A'	21	14	2	5	69	46	44
Confederation Life	21	13	4	4	61	29	43
Pin Green	21	7	3	11	50	54	24
Steeple Morden	21	8	2	11	43	52	23
Dynamics 'A'	21	6	5	10	31	50	23
City Hearts	21	5	1	15	30	72	16
Wilbury Wanderers	21	5	4	12	30	53	15

Division Two	P	W	D	L	F	A	PTS
Neosid '92	21	17	0	4	76	26	51
Argonauts Res.	21	13	1	7	63	37	40
Woolmer GR Res.	21	12	2	7	67	41	38
Therfield & Kelshall	21	10	2	9	56	66	32
Johnson Matthey S.	21	10	1	10	58	62	31
Guilden Morden	21	9	3	9	61	48	30
Krypton Athletic	21	6	3	12	53	63	21
Ridlins Rovers	21	1	0	20	15	106	3

Division Three	P	W	D	L	F	A	PTS
Peartree Old Boys	21	20	0	1	105	26	60
WDT	21	16	1	4	80	39	49
Entreprize XI	21	16	0	5	87	15	48
Riverside	21	11	0	10	54	65	33
Pin Green Res.	21	6	1	14	37	78	19
Castle	21	4	2	15	34	69	14
White Lion	21	4	1	16	30	77	13
Wilbury Wdrs Res.	21	4	1	16	35	93	13

Division Four	P	W	D	L	F	A	PTS
Benington Res.	15	10	2	3	43	14	32
Squirrel Res.	15	10	1	4	36	16	31
Centurian	15	9	1	5	49	29	28
Symonds	15	7	1	7	47	35	22
Hitchin Reds	15	4	3	8	27	52	15
Steeple Morden Res.	15	0	2	13	17	73	2

Cygnet Rvrs, FC Ickleford - records expunged

Div 4 Supplem.	P	W	D	L	F	A	PTS
Hitchin Reds	4	3	0	1	15	8	9
Squirrel Res.	4	2	0	2	7	10	6
Symonds	4	1	2	1	11	11	5
Benington Res.	4	1	1	2	7	8	4
Centurian	4	1	1	2	8	11	4

CLUB DIRECTORY

ARGONAUTS

Secretary: Mr R W Hemmings, 13 Aubries, Walkern SG2 7NJ (0438 861792).
Ground: Knebworth Rec., Watton Rd, Knebworth **Colours:** White & black stripes.

BENINGTON

Secretary: R F White, 39 Blacksmiths Hill, Benington, SG2 7LQ (0438 869662).
Ground: Benington Rec. **Colours:** All red.

BRIDGER PACKAGING

Secretary: Paul Sale, 45 Mullway, Letchworth, SG6 4BQ (0462 674166).
Ground: 'Buffs' Ground, Clothall Rd, Baldock **Colours:** Yellow/sky.

CASTLE

Secretary: J P Wright, 33 Shackleton Spring, Stevenage SG2 9DF (0438 725322).
Ground: Shephalbury Park, Broadhall Way, Stevenage **Colours:** Yellow/green

CENTURIAN

Secretary: E Sinclair, 11 Constantine Close, Stevenage SG1 5LB (0438 749327).
Ground: TBA **Colours:** Sky (vertical black stripe)

CITY HEARTS

Secretary: G R Pettengell, 212 Chaucer Way, Hitchin SG4 0NY (0462 456963).
Ground: Hitchin Road Rec, Stotfold **Colours:** Sky/navy.

CONFEDERATION LIFE

Secretary: Warwick Sainter, 4 Colgrove, Welwyn Garden City AL8 6HU (0707 329534).
Ground: King George V PF, Sish Lane, Stev. (0430 354615) **Colours:** Blue (white trim).

COOPERS APPRENTICE

Secretary: Martin Shaw, 1 Robert Humbert House, Rushby Mead, Letchworth (0462 670729).
Ground: Ridlins End, Woodcock Rd, Stevenage **Colours:** Blue & white/blue.

DYNAMICS (SPACE SYSTEMS) 'A'

Secretary: Kevin Folds, 6 Lanthony Court, High Street, Arlesey, Beds SG15 6TU (0462 834084).
Ground: Shephalbury Park, Broadhall Way, Stevenage **Colours:** Claret/sky/claret.

ENTREPRIZE XI

Secretary: John Hooper, 57 Aylward Drive, Stevenage SG2 8US (0438 725201).
Ground: Wymondley Rec, Tower Close, Wymondley **Colours:** Yellow/navy/yellow

GUILDEN MORDEN

Secretary: Melvin Dellar, 40 Fox Hill Rd, Guilden Morden SG8 0JG (0763 852132).
Ground: Guilden Morden Rec. **Colours:** Red & white.

HARPENDEN ROVERS

Secretary: Fred Day, 69 Tassell Hall, Redbourn, St Albans, Herts AL3 7JD (0582 792408).
Ground: Aces Common, Cravells Road, Harpenden **Colours:** Red/white/red.

HITCHIN REDS

Secretary: P Calderwood, 26 Sanfoine Close, Hitchin, Herts SG4 0NP (0462 434478).
Ground: RAF Chicksands, near Shefford **Colours:** Red/black.

JOHNSON MATTHEY SPORTS

Secretary: Ian King, 11 Cockhall Close, Litlington, Royston SG8 0RB (0763 853337).
Ground: Johnson Matthey Spts Club, Orchard Rd, Royston **Colours:** Yellow & blue stripes.

KRYPTON ATHLETIC
Secretary: David Steven Page, 30 Uplands, Chells Manor, Stevenage SG2 7DN (0438 312380).
Ground: St Johns Road, Hitchin **Colours:** Blue/black.

NEOSID '92
Secretary: Andy Howell, 2 Monklands, Letchworth, SG6 4XF (0462 674398).
Ground: Baldock Rd Rec, Letchworth **Colours:** Amber & emerald/green.

PEARTREE OLD BOYS
Secretary: Grant Hazzard, 17 Greenways, Hertford SG14 2BS (0992 550007).
Ground: Shephalbury Park, Broadhall Way, Stevenage **Colours:** Red, white & Blue/blue.

PIN GREEN
Secretary: Chris Humphrey, 62 Brick Kiln Rd, Stevenage SG1 2NH (0438 724492).
Ground: Hampson Park, Webb Rise, Stev. (0438 351277) **Colours:** White/green.

RIDLINS ROVERS
Secretary: Roy Bowden, 68 Colestrete, Stevenage SG1 1RD (0438 315956).
Ground: Ridlins Ath. Grnd, Woodcock Rd, Stevenage **Colours:** White/blue.

RIVERSIDE
Secretary: Nicholas Hoffman, 77 Webb Rise, Stevenage SG1 5QE (0438 360429).
Ground: North Herts College, Cambridge Rd, Hitchin **Colours:** All white.

ROYSTON TOWN 'A'
Ground: Barkway Rec *(check main club entry for other details)*

SANDON
Secretary: Richard King, 23 Hay Green, Therfield, Royston SG8 9QL (0763 287558).
Ground: Roe Green, Sandon **Colours:** Red/black.

SHEPHALL ATHLETIC
Secretary: John Gardner, 33 Hillcrest, Stevenage SG1 1PU (0438 357535).
Ground: North Herts College, Shephalbury Park site, Stev. **Colours:** Red/black.

SQUIRREL
Secretary: R Wheeler, 22 Wigram Way, Stevenage SG2 9TS (0438 317998).
Ground: Chells Park, Gresley Way, Ferrier Rd, Stevenage **Colours:** Blue & black stripes/black

STEEPLE MORDEN
Secretary: Michael Dix, 27 Hillside, Orwell, Royston SG8 5QZ (0223 207938).
Ground: Steeple Morden Recreation Ground. **Colours:** Red/black.

THERFIELD & KELSHALL
Secretary: Trevor G Sharp, 17 Stamford Close, Royston SG8 7EJ (0763 244735).
Ground: The Rec, Police Row, Therfield **Colours:** White & green/green.

W.D.T.
Secretary: Nicholas Mitchell, 14 Constantine Place, Baldock SG7 6ST (0462 892519).
Ground: Weston Recreation Ground **Colours:** White & blue.

WHITE LION *(formerly MKK Colts)*
Secretary: Mrs Paulette Kane, 7 Hadrians Walk, Pacation Way, Stevenage SG2 5TU (0438 743686).
Ground: Hampson Park, Webb Rise, Stev. (0438 351277) **Colours:** Red & blue stripes/blue.

WILBURY WANDERERS
Secretary: Brian Bailey, 6 Broadwater Avenue, Letchworth SG6 3HE (0462 676620).
Ground: Stotfold Rd, Letchworth (by Two Chimneys pub) **Colours:** Black & white stripes/black

WOOLMER GREEN RANGERS
Sec: Peter Gillard, 29 Wadnall Way, Knebworth SG3 6DU (0438 814138).
Ground: Woolmer Green Rec, Bridge Road **Colours:** All green.

McMULLEN
HERTFORD & DISTRICT LEAGUE (Est. 1910)

President: R P Partridge
Chairman: J Burlison **Vice-Chairman:** R W Berry
Hon. Secretary: C R Smith,
26 Parker Ave., Bengeo, Hertford SG14 3LA (0992 583537)

Premier Division	P	W	D	L	F	A	PTS
Hertford Heath	20	13	6	1	72	14	32
Westmill	20	11	5	4	50	22	27
Broxbourne Badgers	20	10	5	5	58	38	25
Bengeo Trinity	20	9	6	3	58	42	24
St Margaretsbury 'A'	20	9	6	5	34	21	24
Greenbury	20	10	2	8	42	38	22
Herts Reg. College	20	8	3	9	45	42	19
Ware Lions St Marys	20	6	5	9	32	39	17
Albury	20	6	3	11	30	53	15
Thundridge United	20	5	2	13	22	69	12
Braughing Rovers	20	1	1	18	19	83	3

Division One	P	W	D	L	F	A	PTS
Much Hadham	26	18	3	5	97	24	39
Bury Rangers	26	17	2	7	71	47	36
Bengeo Trin. Res.	26	13	8	5	56	37	34
Ware Yth Club OB	25	13	5	7	47	34	31
Watton-at-Stone	26	10	9	7	61	53	29
Tesco	26	11	7	8	40	35	29
Sawbridgeworth Gate	26	12	5	9	52	55	29
Mangrove	26	10	3	13	36	43	23
Barclay	26	9	5	12	52	75	23
Westmills Res.	26	7	8	11	60	70	22
Greenbury Res.	25	7	5	13	41	54	19
Cottered	26	6	6	14	30	62	18
Barnsbury	26	7	3	16	43	55	17
Little Munden	26	4	5	17	26	71	13

Division Two	P	W	D	L	F	A	PTS
Hertford Hth Res.	25	22	1	2	97	27	45
Broxbourne B. Res.	26	21	3	2	100	30	45
Heron	26	17	5	4	110	31	39
Thundridge U. Res.	26	16	3	7	87	52	35
Roydon	26	11	8	7	78	43	30
Inter Unique	26	12	3	11	65	63	27
Merck Sharpe & Do.	26	11	4	11	61	67	26
Mangrove Res.	26	10	3	13	65	69	23
Hare St & Horemead	26	9	3	14	69	68	21
Barclay Res.	26	9	1	16	47	86	19
Buntingford	26	8	2	16	50	82	18
Albury Res.	26	7	3	16	56	78	17
County Hall Rgrs	25	8	0	17	53	86	16
Cottered Res.	26	0	1	25	25	181	1

Division Three	P	W	D	L	F	A	PTS
John Warner	26	21	4	1	124	19	46
Sainsbury Griffin	26	21	4	1	98	29	46
Ware Lions Res.	26	17	2	7	69	43	36
Herts R. Col. Res.	26	14	4	8	88	40	32
Bury Rangers Res.	26	13	4	9	66	46	30
Deaconsfield	26	11	6	9	68	58	28
Watton-at-Stone Res.	26	11	4	11	73	76	26
Buntingford Res.	26	10	3	13	50	70	23
Ware YCOB Res.	26	10	2	14	68	67	22
Much Hadham Res.	26	9	4	14	51	67	21
Braughing Res.	26	8	3	13	47	107	19
Little Munden Res.	26	5	3	18	34	60	13
Roydon Res.	26	5	1	20	55	126	11
Sawb. Gate Res.	26	5	1	20	30	110	11

CLUB DIRECTORY

ALBURY

Secretary: D J Wild, 9 Chestnut Close, Bishop's Stortford CM23 3SY (0279 503891).
Ground: Churchend, Albury, near Ware **Colours:** Lemon & blue stripes/blue.

BARCLAY

Secretary: Rose Winter, 210 Lampits, Hoddesdon EN11 8DU (0992 440585).
Ground: Wodson Park, Ware **Colours:** Royal & white/blue.

BARNSBURY

Secretary: Mrs P Dawson, 7 Hornbeam Way, Cheshunt EN7 6EZ (0992 634501).
Ground: Wormley Playing Fields **Colours:** Yellow/blue.

BENGEO TRINITY

Secretary: Mrs J I Carter, 119 Bentley Rd, Hertford SG14 2HJ (0992 584115).
Ground: Sports Ground, New Road, Bengeo **Colours:** White/black.

BRAUGHING ROVERS

Secretary: K Mardell, 30 Green Lane, Braughing, nr Ware SG11 2QW (0920 822133).
Ground: Green Lane PF, Braughing, nr Ware **Colours:** White/blue.

BROXBOURNE BADGERS

Secretary: Mrs Linda Wenborn, 15 Ashbourne Rd, Broxbourne EN10 7DF (0992 461409).
Ground: Station Road, Broxbourne **Colours:** Yellow/blue.

BUNTINGFORD TOWN

Secretary: F W Aylott, 2 High Street, Buntingford SG9 9AG (0763 271401).
Ground: Bowling Green Lane, off Baldock Rd, Buntingford. **Colours:** Gold (black trim).

BURY RANGERS

Secretary: Alan Fairbrother, 2 Foxholes Avenue, Hertford SG13 7JG (0992 583047).
Ground: Hartham Common, Hertford **Colours:** Maroon & sky

COTTERED

Secretary: David Gray, 13 Peasecroft, Cottered, near Buntingford, Herts SG9 9QS (0763 281347).
Ground: Cottered Recreation Ground. **Colours:** Green & black stripes.

COUNTY HALL RANGERS

Secretary: Andrew Cox, 13 Star Holme Court, Ware SG12 7EA (0920 469178).
Ground: Goldings, North Road, Hertford **Colours:** Yellow/blue.

DEACONSFIELD UNITED

Secretary: G Jenkin, 20 Berners Way, Wormley, Broxbourne EN10 6NP (0992 445159).
Ground: Wodson Park, Ware **Colours:** White/black.

GREENBURY UNITED

Secretary: Roy Gill, Sans Souci, Barrow Lane, Cheshunt, Herts EN7 5LN (0992 631734).
Ground: Cheshunt School, College Road, Cheshunt **Colours:** Green/black.

HARE STREET & HORMEAD

Secretary: D J Howard, 4 Barleycroft, Buntingford SG9 9SD (0763 289486).
Ground: The Meads, Hare Street **Colours:** Yellow/blue.

HERON SPORTS

Secretary: D E Gosling, 9 Plashes Close, Sandon, near Ware, Herts SG11 1QE (0920 821196).
Ground: Crouchfields, near Bengeo **Colours:** Maroon & navy/navy.

HERTFORD HEATH

Secretary: M D Newton, 38 Rushden Drive, Hertford Heath, Herts SG13 7BG (0992 558496).
Ground: Trinity Road, Hertford Heath. **Colours:** White/blue.

HERTFORD REGIONAL COLLEGE

Secretary: Mark Robinson, 16 Leaforis Road, Cheshunt, Herts EN7 6NB (0992 633665).
Ground: East Herts College, Turnford **Colours:** Yellow & blue/blue.

INTER-UNIQUE

Secretary: Angelo Tinnirello, 41 Lee Close, Mariners Walk, Stanstead Abbotts, Herts SG12 8JN.
Ground: Pound Close, Hoddesdon. **Colours:** Sky & navy stripes/black.

JOHN WARNER

Secretary: Gerry Brislin, John Warner Sports Centre, Stanstead Rd, Hoddesdon EN11 0RH (0992 445375).
Ground: John Sports Centre, Stanstead Rd, Hoddesdon **Colours:** Yellow/white.

LITTLE MUNDEN SPORTS

Secretary: A J Veryard, 52 Woodlands Road, Hertford SG13 7JF (0992 561049).
Ground: Prestdales, Hoe Lane, Ware **Colours:** Sky shadow stripes/blue.

MANGROVE

Secretary: Paul Rayment, 20 Rib Vale, Bengeo, Hertford SG14 3LF (0992 554643).
Ground: Hartham Common, Hertford **Colours:** Yellow (green trim).

MERCK SHARP & DOHME

Secretary: Neil Rissen, 73 Woodlands Rd, Hertford SG13 7JF (0992 553849).
Ground: Wormley Playing Fields **Colours:** Grey/blue.

MUCH HADHAM

Secretary: P Jarrett, 99 Honeybourne, Thorley, Bishop's Stortford, Herts CM23 4EF (0279 508283).
Ground: Much Hadham Sports Ground **Colours:** All white.

NAZEING

Secretary: D J Watts, 50 Trafalgar Avenue, Broxbourne, Herts EN10 7DL (0992 468973).
Ground: Bumbles Green, Nazeing, Essex **Colours:** White/navy.

ROYDON

Secretary: Raymond Saggers, 66 Parkfields, Roydon, Essex CM19 5JB (0279 793427).
Ground: Playing Fields, Roydon, Essex **Colours:** All blue.

SAINSBURY GRIFFIN

Secretary: S D Lewis, c/o SSA Office, J Sainsbury, Buntingford Depot, London Rd, Buntingford SG9 9JR.
Ground: Sainsburys Buntingford Depot, London Rd **Colours:** Yellow & black/black.

St MARGARETSBURY 'A'

Ground: St Margaretsbury Rec *(other details as per club's Spartan League entry)*

SAWBRIDGEWORTH GATE

Secretary: Gary Barnett, The Gate PH, 81 London Rd, Sawbridgeworth CM21 9JJ (0279 722313).
Ground: Grange Paddocks, Rye Street, Bishop's Stortford **Colours:** Sky & white stripes/black.

TESCO ATHLETIC

Secretary: D Lodge, 8 Burleigh Rd, Waltham Cross, Herts EN8 8TE (0992 631241).
G: Tesco Country Club, Flamstead End Refield Rd, Cheshunt **Colours:** Sky, white & navy/navy.

THUNDRIDGE UNITED

Secretary: P M Smith, 44 Cundalls Rd, Ware, Herts SG12 7DJ (0920 461169).
Ground: Thundridge Spts Field (off A10 opp. Village Hall) **Colours:** Yellow & black stripes/black.

TONWELL

Secretary: A J Andrews, 25 Ware Rd, Tonwell, Ware, Herts SG12 0HN (0920 463648).
Ground: Crouchfield, Chapmore End, Hertford **Colours:** Orange/blue.

WARE LIONS St MARY'S

Secretary: Brian Williams, 4 Rockfield Avenue, Ware, Herts SG12 0RG (0920 463836).
Ground: Prestdales, Hoe Lane, Ware **Colours:** Black & white (mottled)/black.

WARE YOUTH OLD BOYS

Secretary: R P Reed, 77 Kingsway, Ware, Herts SG12 0QJ (0920 465477).
Ground: Prestdales, Hoe Lane, Ware **Colours:** Blue & white hoops/blue.

WATTON-AT-STONE

Secretary: M Powell, 150 Hazeldell, Watton-at-Stone, Hertford SG14 3SP.
Ground: School Lane Rec, Watton-at-Stone, Hertford **Colours:** All blue.

WESTMILL

Secretary: J L Pegram, 3 The Rookery, Westmill, Buntingford, Herts SG9 9JL (0763 71166).
Ground: Westmill Recreation Ground **Colours:** White/navy.

EAST HERTS CORINTHIAN

SUNDAY LEAGUE

FOUNDED: 1993

PREM. DIV.	P	W	D	L	F	A	PTS
JLT	18	14	2	2	80	18	44
Greyhound	18	13	3	2	66	24	42
Warren House	18	13	2	3	73	33	41
Simson Pimm	18	9	4	5	70	46	31
Golden Griffin	18	9	2	7	104	43	29
Waitrose '175	18	9	2	7	52	35	29
White Hart	18	5	3	10	46	52	18
Hertford Post Office	18	5	1	12	53	131	16
Crown & Falcon	18	3	0	15	37	109	9
Old Bulls Head	18	0	1	17	23	107	1

HITCHIN GAZETTE HITCHIN SUNDAY LEAGUE

FOUNDED: 1977

PREM. DIV.	P	W	D	L	F	A	PTS
Westbury CA	18	14	3	1	67	17	31
Walsworth	18	11	2	5	54	32	24
Cricketers Hitchin	18	11	0	7	51	37	22
Angels	18	8	5	5	50	43	21
Offley Social	18	8	2	8	33	60	18
Chequers	18	7	2	9	27	50	16
Four Emblems	18	6	2	10	41	43	14
Westbury United	18	5	2	11	24	32	12
Wanderers	18	4	3	11	33	49	11
Bell	18	5	1	12	33	50	11

Lower Division Champions:
Div. 1 (11): Engineering Arms
Div. 2 (11): Letchworth Garden City
Div. 3 (11): Grange
Div. 4 (12): Two Chimneys Reserves

Cup Finals:
Gazette Challenge Cup: Angels 4, Westbury CA 3
George John Memorial Trophy: Westhill Athletic 5, Westbury United 4
Prem. Div. Cup: Westbury CA 6, Angels 3
Div. 1 Cup: Engineers Arms 3, Stevenage Police 0
Div. 2 Cup: Letchworth GC 1, Bell Res. 0
Div. 3 Cup: Hitchin Soc. 3, Ickwell Admirals 0 *(aet)*
Div. 4 Cup: White Horse Arlesey 3, Danesbury Utd 1
Reserve Team Cup: Offley Soc. 4, Two Chimneys 2

STEVENAGE & DISTRICT SUNDAY LEAGUE

FOUNDED: 1959

PREM. DIV.	P	W	D	L	F	A	PTS
Wagon	14	11	1	2	43	15	23
Benington	14	9	2	3	37	23	20
White Horse	14	6	3	5	33	24	15
Saints	14	6	3	5	29	27	15
Dynamics	14	3	4	7	32	30	10
Transpack	14	4	2	8	21	29	10
Manulife	14	4	2	8	21	56	10
Singh Sabbha	14	2	5	7	13	25	9

Lower Division Champions:
Div. 1 (9): Nemesis
Div. 2 (8): Stevenage Fencing
Div. 3 (11): Wagon & Horse
Div. 4 (11): Anglo Italians
Div. 3 (9): Broadhall

Cup Finals:
KLM Cup: Wagon 4, Stevenage Fencing 0
Prem. Div. Cup: Benington 1, Dynamics 0
Div. 1 Cup: Shephall Ath. OB 2, Athletico '85 0
Div. 2 Cup: Stevenage Fencing 5, CK Royals 1
Div. 3 Cup: AVC 3, Dixons 0
Div. 4 Cup: Anglo Italians 4, Stevenage Alarms 2
Div. 5 Cup: Broadhall 1, Stev. Gazza Lazio 0
ICL Invitation Cup: Hollybush 4, Benington 3

BARNET PRESS BARNET & DISTRICT SUNDAY LEAGUE

PREM. DIV.	P	W	D	L	F	A	PTS
Elliott Bull & Tiger	12	11	1	0	61	20	23
Prince of Wales	12	7	3	2	36	20	17
Conyers Park	12	6	2	4	25	29	14
Wood	12	6	0	6	35	35	12
East Barnet OG	12	2	3	7	9	23	7
Leevale	12	3	0	9	21	40	6
Hendon St Marys	12	2	1	9	30	50	5

Lower Division Champions:
Div. 1 (10): Old Elizabethans
Div. 2 (9): Locomotive Enfield
Div. 3 (10): Old Red Lion
Div. 4 (10): Finchley Town

HUNTINGDONSHIRE F.A.

ESTABLISHED: 1894

President: E P Brand

Secretary: M M Armstrong,
1 Chapel End, Gt Gidding, Huntingdon, Cambs.

SENIOR CUP 1993-94

First Round
Warboys Town v Earith United 11-1
Alconbury v Ramsey Town 0-2*(aet)*
St Ives Town v Godmanchester Rovers 4-2*(aet)*
Stilton United v Eynesbury Rovers 5-8
Hotpoint v Bluntisham Rangers 4-2

Quarter-Finals
ICA/Juventus v Somersham Town 0-3
Ramsey Town v Ortonians 2-4
Hotpoint v St Ives Town 4-5
Warboys Town v Eynesbury Rovers 0-2

Semi-Finals
Eynesbury Rovers v Somersham Town 0-1
St Ives Town v Ortonians 1-1,2-3*(aet)*

Final *(at Warboys Town FC, Mon 2nd May)*: Somersham Town 1, Ortonians 0

OTHER COUNTY FINALS:

Junior Cup: St Neots Town 3, Hotpoint Res. 2 *(aet)*
Lower Junior Cup: St Neots Town Reserves 2, Sun 0
Scott Gatty Cup *(at Somersham Town, Wed 4th May)*: Eynesbury Rovers Reserves 3, Ortonians Reserves 0
Benevolent Cup: BRJ 2, Huntingdon United 0
Sunday Cup: LT Pesler 2, Stilton United 0
Youth under-18 Cup *(at Eynesbury Rovers, Fri 6th May)*: St Neots Town Boys 5, ICA/Juventus 0
Youth under-16 Cup: ICA/Juventus 2, St Neots Town Boys 1
Youth under-15 Cup: Warboys Town Colts 1, Bushfield Park 0
Youth under-14 Cup: Rowden 2, Woodslen Dynamo 1
Youth under-12 Cup: Rowden 3, Brampton Sports 1

KENT F.A.

Secretary: K T Masters, 69 Maidstone Road, Chatham, Kent ME4 6DT (0634 843824)

SENIOR CUP 1993-94

First Round

Tonbridge AFC v Gillingham	2-1	Fisher '93 v Margate	0-1
Cray Wdrs v Welling Utd *(at Welling)*	1-3	Bromley v Dover Athletic	1-3
Canterbury City v Charlton Athletic	0-5	Sittingbourne v Erith & Belvedere	2-0

Quarter-Finals

Ashford Town v Dover Athletic	0-3	Welling v Gravesend	1-1,1-1,0-0*(at G'send, 7-6 pens)*
Charlton Athletic v Sittingbourne	3-1	Tonbridge AFC v Margate	2-4

Semi-Finals

Margate v Charlton Athletic	1-0	Welling United v Dover Athletic	0-1

Final *(at Gillingham FC, Mon 2nd May)*: Margate 3, Dover Athletic 2

SENIOR TROPHY

First Round

Headcorn v Folkestone Invicta	3-5	Greenwich Borough v Darenth Heathside	5-0
Thames Polytechnic v Herne Bay	0-5	Dartford v Chatham Town	2-0
West Wickham v Deal Town	4-2	Thamesmead Town v Crockenhill	1-3
Ramsgate v Alma Swanley	2-2,2-3	Sheppey United v Tunbridge Wells	2-0

Second Round

West Wickham v Alma Swanley	1-3	Slade Green v Corinthian	2-1
Whitstable Town v Herne Bay	0-1	Greenwich Borough v Furness	0-3
Beckenham Town v Crockenhill	1-0	Dartford v Folkestone Invicta	1-5
Midland Bank *(w/o)* Kent Police *(scr)*		Sheppey United v Faversham Town	1-3

Quarter-Finals

Folkestone Invicta v Furness	2-1	Slade Green v Beckenham Town	1-2
Faversham Town v Herne Bay	1-2	Alma Swanley v Midland Bank *(at Midland Bank)*	2-1

Semi-Finals

Herne Bay v Alma Swanley	4-6	Beckenham Town v Folkestone Invicta	2-3

Final *(at Gravesend & Northfeet FC, Sat 16th April)*: Alma Swanley 3, Folkestone Invicta 1

OTHER COUNTY FINALS 1993-94

Intermediate Cup *(at Chatham Town FC, Sat 26th March)*: Sevenoaks 3, Milton Athletic 1
Intermediate Shield *(at Tunbridge Wells FC, Sat 2nd April)*: Bromley Reserves 4, Whitstable Town Reserves 1
Junior Cup (A) *(at Herne Bay FC, Sat 7th May)*: Segas Bromley 1, Bishopsbourne 0
Junior Cup (B) *(at Thamesmead Town FC, Sat 30th April)*: Drummond Athletic 2, Ramsgate Albion 1
Junior Cup (C) *(at Sittingbourne FC, Sat 7th May)*: Findlay Athletic 4, Cricketers Arms 0
Sunday Premier Cup *(at Corinthian FC, Sun 8th May)*: Sun 3, Sheerness East 0
Sunday Junior Cup *(at Kent Police FC, Sun 1st May)*: Allington Athletic 4, Northfleet Rangers 1
Sunday Trophy *(at Corinthian FC, Sun 8th May)*: Creekside United 2, Broadway 0
Womens Cup *(at Welling Utd FC, Sun 24th April)*: Bromley Borough 2, Millwall Lionesses 1
Youth under-18 Cup *(at Thamesemead Town FC)*: Welling United 4, Maidstone Invicta 2
Youth under-16 Cup *(at Darenth Heathside FC, Sun 27th March)*: Chatham Town 10, Kingsdown Rac. 1

Sun FC, of the North Kent Sunday League, KFA Sunday Premier Cup winners 1993-94. They are now the second most successful club in the competition's history. *Photo - Richard Ralph.*

KENT COUNTY LEAGUE

President: A E Farmer.

Chairman: C T C Windiate

Press Officer: J C Mugridge, 14 Cherry Tree Rd, Tunbridge Wells, Kent TN2 5QA (0892 521578)

TEYNHAM & LYNSTED TAKE TITLE

The 1993/94 season started without a main sponsor despite excessive letter writing and visits to various companies by Chairman Cyril Windiate. However, the League was able to continue with its popular Manager of the Month Award when it announced that Aford Awards of Bearsted would be sponsoring this particular trophy. Fortunately, from the start of the new season, Nuclear Electric Dungeness has undertaken a three year sponsorship programme, and in future the League will be the Nuclear Electric Kent County League.

The League suffered an unusual number of withdrawals prior to a ball being kicked in earnest. The first to leave being Eastern Region Houchin Rovers, followed by Western Region Edenstone (two teams) and then Western Region Sherwood Park. None of these teams were in a position, in their opinion, to field teams of sufficient strength to make competing worthwhile. Another casualty was Western Region Strood County who departed during the season and, as they had not completed 75% of their fixtures, their playing record was expunged - much to the disgust of Ex Blues who felt that as they had beaten Strood, with whom Ten Em Bee had only drawn, they should have won the First Division and been promoted.

At least three clubs lost stalwarts during the season. Rusthall's Derek Seal passed away having suffered a heart attack whilst mowing the pitch at Jockey Farm, where his foresight and energy had seen many drastic changes in the last five years. Gordon Williams, secretary of Dunton Green FC and a member of the Western Region Management Committee, died suddenly on 29th October. Jimmy Gilham, who had a long association, with Tenterden Football Club having played for them in the 50's, was at Rye on 5th March supporting Tenterden when, towards the end of the second-half, he collapsed on the touch-line. Taken to hospital in an ambulance, he suffered a massive heart attack on the Sunday from which he did not recover.

Despite losing their first two games of the season, manager Kevin James had no doubts about Teynham & Lynsted's ability to win the Premier Division, but they were hard pushed at times by both runners-up, Greenways, and Lordswood. This means that Teynham & Lynsted, along with Sevenoaks Town, will be competing in the Kent Senior trophy next season.

VCD Athletic was no doubt the side to improve most during the season; on the 16th April they were third from bottom but, in the weeks to the end of the season, they won eight of their remaining ten games to put them in third place. Probably the most successful club in the competition was Eastern Region Lydd Town, closely followed by Western Region Maidstone Invicta. Lydd Town made a clean sweep of the Eastern Region trophies, winning the First Division without losing a game, the Les Leckie Cup, the Floodlit Cup, the Second Division and the Junior Cup. Maidstone Invicta went to

Teynham & Lynsted, League Champions, celebrate after receiving their trophies at the Presentation Evening. Photo - John Mugridge.

13th May before losing a League game, and by this time they had the Division Four championship in the bag. They were also successful in the West Kent Challenge Shield, beating Wellcome (Saturday) 3-1 after extra-time, and the Tunbridge Wells Intermediate Charity Cup. For the record, Matthew Toms netted ten hat-tricks during the season.

Sevenoaks Town made up for last year's disappointment in the Kent Intermediate Challenge Shield by beating Milton Athletic 3-1 in a final played in continuous rain at Chatham Town's ground. Bishopsbourne, runners-up in the Eastern First Division, were also beaten finalists in Group A of the Kent Junior Cup and the Eastern Region Junior Cup. Bearsted won the Inter Regional Challenge Cup for the second time in four years beating Rye United with a 64th minute goal from Gary Page and a second in the 88th minute from Keith Mottram.

Inter-League Team Manager Russ May, ably assisted by Brian Holman, took the League side through to win the Tom Stabler Trophy in the South Eastern Intermediate Inter-League Competition. Only dropping one point from four games, the Kent County League's results were; Middlesex (H) 2-4 *(Simon Brown (3), Phil Smith)*; Unijet Sussex County League (A) 2-0 *(Steve Warne & Sean Gentle)*, Johnson Wax Surrey County Premier League (A) 2-0 *(Steve Warne (2))*; Essex Intermediate League (H) 0-0.

Bruce Marchant of Lydd Town won the Aford Manager of the Year Award and NPI Football Club, who had an excellent disciplinary record, received the Fair Play Award. Both these awards were presented at the Annual General Meeting held on 20th June, 1994. Interest in the newsline (0891 800664) for which call charges are 39p per minute cheap rate and 49p at all other times, has increased during the season, and clubs and supporters have been glad of this facility that supplies results and news items.

J C Mugridge, Press Officer

Lydd Town - Eastern Region Division One champions. Back Row (L/R): Terry Mahoney, Chris Tosh, Dave Smith, Paul Chambers, Steve Ormerod, Bill Beaney, Kevin Tosh, Keith Taylor. Front: Shane Ashdown, Tim Barham, Phil Gore, Bruce Marchant, Kirt Byrne, Wayne Poetschke, Michael Barham.

Maidstone Invicta - Western Region Division Four champions. Back Row (L/R): A Gray, L Carey, M Toms, B Bennett, C Wilkins, N Byers, T Lungley. Front: J Brackpool, G Martin (Captain), P Churchill, M Holmes.

Photos - John Mugridge.

Premier Div.	P	W	D	L	F	A	PTS
Teynham & Lynsted	28	17	6	5	55	31	57
Greenways	28	16	5	7	42	27	53
VCD Athletic	28	15	4	9	70	39	49
Lordswood	27	15	4	8	61	39	49
New Romney	28	13	7	8	43	39	46
Stansfeld O & B.	27	14	4	9	49	48	46
Thames Poly.	28	13	4	11	46	36	43
Sevenoaks Town	28	12	5	11	45	36	41
Knockholt	28	11	6	11	43	45	39
Hythe United	28	11	5	12	37	37	38
Aylesford PM	28	9	4	15	34	41	31
Oakwood	28	8	6	14	30	45	30
Scott Spts & Soc.	28	6	11	11	41	44	29
Otford United	28	7	4	17	31	56	25
Woodnesborough	28	4	1	23	26	90	13

Eastern Div 1	P	W	D	L	F	A	PTS
Lydd Town	26	22	4	0	116	16	70
Bromley Green	26	20	4	2	92	22	64
Milton Athletic	26	17	1	6	82	41	52
Headcorn	26	15	6	5	63	36	51
Broomfield United	26	14	3	9	52	53	45
Rye United	25	11	7	7	71	39	40
Knatchbull	26	12	2	12	54	66	38
Cheriton	26	12	2	12	58	73	38
Tenterden	26	9	7	10	59	57	34
Kennington	26	7	4	15	42	59	25
Snowdown CW	25	7	3	15	30	54	24
Univ. of Kent	26	5	3	18	31	74	18
Walmer Rovers	26	3	1	22	28	102	10
New Romney Res.	26	2	3	21	23	109	9

Western Div 1	P	W	D	L	F	A	PTS
Ten Em Bee	18	12	3	3	54	33	39
Ex Blues	18	11	1	5	48	20	37
Phoenix Sports	18	10	5	3	39	25	35
Bearsted	18	8	6	4	43	28	30
AFC Egerton	18	8	3	7	55	35	27
Platt United	17	8	2	7	35	33	26
Westerham	18	6	3	9	46	41	21
Rusthall	18	5	6	7	31	37	21
Colts '85	17	3	2	12	23	69	11
Borough United	18	0	3	15	18	71	3

Eastern Div 2	P	W	D	L	F	A	PTS
Lydd Town Res.	30	24	2	4	91	35	74
Bishopsbourne	30	23	3	4	105	48	72
St Margarets	30	19	4	7	95	49	61
Sturry	29	16	3	10	72	44	51
Hythe Utd Res.	30	16	2	12	68	56	50
F'stone Inv. Res.	30	11	6	13	95	88	39
Teynham & L. Res.	29	11	6	12	56	57	39
Bond Sports	30	10	7	13	54	58	37
Kennington Res.	30	11	3	16	65	76	36
Headcorn Res.	26	9	8	9	68	65	35
Univ. Kent Res.	30	9	7	14	67	66	34
Tenterden Res.	30	9	7	14	56	74	34
Knatchbull Res.	30	8	9	13	56	73	33
Royal George	29	7	5	17	61	94	26
New Romney 'A'	29	7	4	18	52	92	25
Bromley Green Res.	28	5	4	19	44	130	19

Western Div 2	P	W	D	L	F	A	PTS
Sutton Athletic	20	14	4	2	78	31	46
Eynsford	20	13	3	4	63	34	42
Wellcome (Sat.)	20	11	7	2	57	37	40
Empire	20	11	3	6	54	38	36
Fleetdown United	20	9	4	7	31	23	31
Eltham Palace	19	7	5	7	41	44	26
Chislehurst	20	6	6	8	29	46	24
Edenbridge Utd	20	4	7	9	27	36	19
Paddock Wd Town	19	4	7	8	36	47	19
Moonshot Ath.	20	2	6	12	33	58	12
Halstead	20	0	4	16	21	76	4

Western Div 3	P	W	D	L	F	A	PTS
Tonbridge Rgrs	22	16	4	2	68	30	52
Swanscombe Utd	22	15	4	3	77	26	49
Dunton Green	22	12	1	9	59	64	37
Chipstead	22	10	5	7	47	40	35
Snodland	22	9	4	9	52	42	31
Joyce Green	22	7	9	6	41	39	30
Halls	22	8	3	11	41	55	27
NPI	22	8	3	11	38	57	27
Tonbridge Invicta	22	6	7	9	34	48	25
Wickham Park	22	6	6	10	39	49	24
St Georges	22	6	3	13	43	50	21
Nomads	22	1	7	14	18	57	10

Western Div 3	P	W	D	L	F	A	PTS
Maidstone Invicta	24	19	3	2	118	21	60
Greenways Res.	24	16	4	4	76	38	52
Lordswood Res.	24	14	6	4	58	37	48
Hawkenbury	24	14	0	10	62	48	42
Scott S & S Res.	24	12	4	8	45	42	40
Stansfeld Res.	23	11	6	6	52	33	39
VCD Ath. Res.	24	10	6	8	57	59	36
Sevenoaks T. Res.	23	6	7	10	48	66	25
Aylesford	24	7	4	13	56	76	25
Belvedere	24	6	5	13	39	73	23
Old Bexleians	24	5	2	17	47	76	17
Otford Utd Res.	24	5	2	17	25	56	17
Westerham Res.	24	4	3	17	25	93	15

Western Div 3	P	W	D	L	F	A	PTS
Rusthall Res.	22	15	5	2	73	22	50
Aylesford PM Res.	22	14	3	5	57	29	45
Thames Poly Res.	22	13	4	5	66	25	43
Phoenix Spts Res.	22	13	2	7	58	47	41
Platt Utd Res.	21	10	5	6	48	29	35
Bearsted Res.	22	10	5	7	41	42	35
Oakwood Res.	22	10	2	10	53	47	32
Borough Utd Res.	22	8	4	10	39	47	28
Fleetdown Res.	22	5	3	14	32	53	18
Joyce Green Res.	21	4	4	13	22	64	16
Colts '85 Res.	22	5	1	16	31	83	16
Nomads Res.	22	3	4	15	33	64	13

Below: *Greenways, Premier Division runners-up 1993-94. Back Row (L/R): R Hillier (Chairman), K Llewellyn, C Hearn, M Warner, D Harris, M Feakins, D Bourne, G Hollywood, W Miller (Secretary). Front: J Georgiou, T Hinds, W Heather, J Jenkins, C Freed, R Frost.*
Photo - John Mugridge.

PREM. DIV. RESULTS	1	2	3	4	5	6	7	8	9	10	11	12	13	14	15
1. Aylesford Paper Mills	*	1-3	0-1	2-0	0-2	0-0	1-3	3-1	1-3	3-1	6-0	0-1	2-3	1-3	2-1
2. Greenways	1-0	*	0-1	2-4	0-3	1-1	1-0	2-2	1-0	0-0	0-1	2-1	0-1	3-1	1-0
3. Hythe United	0-1	1-2	*	1-0	1-1	0-1	3-0	2-1	2-2	1-1	1-2	0-1	4-2	2-1	2-0
4. Knockholt	3-0	2-3	1-0	*	2-0	1-1	1-1	1-2	2-1	1-5	1-4	0-2	0-2	2-2	4-0
5. Lordwood	1-4	1-1	1-0	6-1	*	4-1	0-1	2-1	1-1	1-5		5-6	2-1	3-2	6-0
6. New Romney	1-1	0-1	1-1	1-0	4-3	*	2-1	1-2	1-0	1-0	1-1	1-1	3-1	1-3	6-1
7. Oakwood	0-0	1-1	3-4	1-1	0-3	0-2	*	2-0	2-0	1-3	1-0	1-3	0-3	1-1	0-3
8. Otford United	0-1	0-3	1-2	1-1	0-3	4-3	1-1	*	1-0	1-5	2-4	1-2	0-3	2-1	3-0
9. Scott Sports & Social	1-1	0-1	1-1	1-4	1-1	5-1	3-4	1-1	*	4-0	1-1	1-1	2-1	1-6	5-1
10. Sevenoaks Town	2-0	1-3	2-1	1-3	0-1	3-0	0-2	3-0	1-1	*	0-0	2-0	1-1	0-2	1-0
11. Stansfeld O. & B.	2-1	2-1	1-0	2-3	3-1	1-3	0-1	2-0	2-1	0-3	*	4-1	3-1	1-5	4-3
12. Teynham & Lynsted	1-0	2-0	5-1	1-1	0-4	2-0	1-0	2-0	1-1	2-0	2-1	*	4-2	2-2	5-0
13. Thames Polytechnic	2-0	0-1	3-1	0-1	0-1	0-2	5-2	2-1	0-0	1-0	3-1	0-0	*	1-3	4-0
14. VC Dartford Athletic	3-0	1-3	3-1	2-0	4-0	2-3	1-0	3-0	4-1	3-4	3-4	2-1	0-0	*	7-0
15. Woodnesborough	2-3	0-5	0-3	1-3	0-5	0-1	2-1	1-3	1-3	3-1	3-3	0-5	2-4	2-0	*

EAST DIV. 1 RESULTS	1	2	3	4	5	6	7	8	9	10	11	12	13	14
1. Bromley Green	*	4-0	7-0	1-0	1-0	5-0	1-4	2-1	10-0	2-1	4-2	1-1	4-0	5-1
2. Broomfield United	0-4	*	2-0	3-0	2-4	5-3	1-1	1-3	1-0	L-W	2-0	3-1	2-0	3-0
3. Cheriton	1-6	4-2	*	L-W	2-4	3-1	2-5	3-0	6-1	7-3	1-2	1-1	1-1	4-2
4. Headcorn	5-2	L-W	4-1	*	3-1	2-1	3-3	3-1	7-2	1-1	0-0	2-1	4-1	1-1
5. Kennington	0-5	1-3	0-1	0-5	*	1-2	0-4	1-3	7-2	2-3	2-1	2-2	2-1	3-1
6. Knatchbull	1-6	2-4	3-2	2-5	2-0	*	0-5	1-4	1-1	0-0	2-0	2-3	4-0	6-2
7. Lydd Town	0-0	9-0	6-0	0-0	3-0	9-2	*	3-1	7-1	2-0	5-0	2-1	3-1	6-0
8. Milton Athletic	1-1	5-1	10-1	4-0	2-1	1-3	0-2	*	7-1	4-1	5-0	5-0	4-3	4-1
9. New Romney Res.	1-5	1-4	0-2	2-6	0-0	0-1	0-10	2-5	*	1-4	3-2	0-3	1-4	2-0
10. Rye United	1-1	3-3	2-3	7-1	1-1	4-1	1-4	5-1	5-0	*		1-1	9-0	6-1
11. Snowdown Colliery W.	0-3	0-1	4-2	1-1	1-0	0-3	1-5	2-1	3-0	0-3	*	1-2	3-0	1-2
12. Tenterden & St M. U.	0-6	3-3	1-8	0-1	3-3	2-3	0-5	1-4	7-1	2-2	4-0	*	4-0	9-1
13. University of Kent	0-3	2-1	4-0	1-5	3-6	2-4	0-3	0-2	1-1	0-3	2-2	0-3	*	3-0
14. Walmer Rovers	2-3	3-5	2-3	0-4	3-1	0-4	1-10	2-4	1-0	1-5	1-4	0-4	0-2	*

EAST. DIV. 2 RESULTS	1	2	3	4	5	6	7	8	9	10	11	12	13	14	15	16
1. Bishopsbourne	*	0-2	8-0	3-1	4-1	3-2	4-1	1-0	1-4	9-1	4-2	4-1	2-2	3-0	2-1	2-1
2. Bond Sports	2-2	*	2-0	1-1	2-2	0-4	0-1	5-2	0-4	5-1	3-5	2-2	0-1	1-1	1-0	0-3
3. Bromley Green Res.	2-10	0-5	*	3-3	1-5	1-3	2-2	0-5	1-5	1-8	2-10	1-7	3-2	3-2	1-4	3-6
4. Folkestone Invicta 'A'	2-4	2-3	8-0	*	1-1	1-3	5-1	8-3	0-3	6-2	5-3	5-3	5-0	3-5	2-2	3-0
5. Headcorn Reserves	3-4	1-2		6-3	*	4-5	5-1	4-0	0-4			3-3		3-0	2-2	3-0
6. Hythe United Reserves	1-1	2-7	2-1	3-4	1-1	*	1-4	7-0	3-0	4-0	2-3	4-1	1-0	1-2	0-1	1-3
7. Kennington Reserves	5-2	2-0	2-2	7-2	6-0	1-3	*	0-1	0-2	7-3	2-1	1-3	1-2	2-3	2-0	2-5
8. Knatchbull Reserves	2-6	2-2	4-3	3-2	2-0	2-3	6-2	*	0-2	3-3	1-1	1-1	2-2	3-1	0-2	1-1
9. Lydd Town Reserves	1-2	3-2	1-3	6-1	3-3	2-1	7-3	2-0	*	6-2	3-1	4-2	3-1	3-2	3-1	2-0
10. New Romney 'A'	0-4	0-2	7-4	3-0	0-3	3-2	1-2	0-0	1-2	*	2-1	0-2	0-4	2-2	0-5	1-1
11. Royal George	1-6	3-0	2-2	4-4	4-7	2-0	1-5	1-1	0-5	2-3	*	2-9	1-1	1-2	2-1	1-7
12. St Margarets	1-3	5-2	4-0	2-4	6-0	1-2	3-0	5-0	2-1	2-0	4-2	*	1-0	2-2	4-1	1-0
13. Sturry	3-0	3-0	11-0	5-0	3-1	0-1	5-0	3-0	0-3	5-3	3-0	1-5	*	3-2	2-5	4-1
14. Tenterden & SM Res.	1-2	2-0	0-2	4-4	2-2	2-4	2-1	1-8	1-2	2-0	4-0	0-6	0-2	*	3-3	3-3
15. Teynsham & Lyn. Res.	2-3	2-2		4-3	3-5	1-2	1-1	1-0	0-3	4-3	6-4	1-3	0-3	2-1	*	0-0
16. University of Kent Res.	3-4	2-1	2-3	1-7	3-3	5-0	4-1	4-4	2-2	2-3	0-1	3-4	2-1	3-4	0-1	*

WEST DIV. 1 RESULTS	1	2	3	4	5	6	7	8	9	10	11
1. AFC Egerton	*	1-3	10-2	5-0	2-4	0-1	4-3	4-2		5-1	5-1
2. Bearsted	2-1	*	5-1	5-1	3-1	0-0	3-1	2-0		2-2	1-4
3. Borough United	1-4	2-2	*	0-1	0-3	0-2	0-2	1-1		0-9	0-3
4. Colts '85	1-4	2-7	5-1	*	0-2	2-2		1-2		1-7	1-12
5. Ex Blues	3-1	3-1	4-0	8-1	*	2-1	2-3	4-1		3-0	3-0
6. Phoenix Sports	2-2	1-1	2-1	7-2	2-1	*	3-1	3-2		1-2	4-2
7. Platt United	3-2	1-0	5-1	1-2	2-1	2-1	*	1-2		2-2	3-1
8. Rusthall	2-2	2-2	4-4	1-0	2-2	0-1	2-2	*		4-1	2-1
9. Strood County - *withdrew during season - record expunged*									*		
10. Ten Em Bee	3-2	4-3	3-1	4-2	1-0	2-2	4-1	3-0		*	4-3
11. Westerham	1-1	1-1	6-3	1-1	0-2	3-4	3-2	3-2		1-2	*

WEST DIV. 2 RESULTS	1	2	3	4	5	6	7	8	9	10	11
1. Chislehurst	*	0-0	2-1	1-7	2-2	1-0	4-4	2-1	0-3	1-5	1-2
2. Edenbridge United	1-3	*	3-0	3-3	1-2	0-2	1-1	1-1	1-0	0-0	1-3
3. Eltham Palace	2-0	3-4	*	2-0	0-3	1-0	5-0	5-1	2-2	3-3	1-1
4. Empire	2-2	4-2	2-0	*	4-0	2-0	4-0	5-1	3-2	6-3	2-2
5. Eynsford	4-1	1-1	11-3	5-2	*	3-1	5-0	2-1	3-1	4-2	2-4
6. Fleetdown United	2-0	3-2	0-1	2-1	1-0	*	5-0	4-2	0-0	2-2	0-1
7. Halstead	3-3	0-2	2-5	1-2	0-2	2-4	*	1-1	1-5	1-3	3-4
8. Moonshot Athletic	1-2	2-1	3-3	1-2	1-4	0-0	4-1	*	1-1	3-6	2-5
9. Paddock Wood United	2-3	1-1		2-0	3-6	1-3	4-1	3-3	*	0-2	3-3
10. Sutton Athletic	3-0	4-1	5-2	5-1	2-2	2-0	7-0	5-1	12-1	*	4-2
11. Wellcome (Saturday)	1-1	3-1	2-2	4-2	4-2	2-2	6-0	5-3	2-2	1-3	*

WEST DIV. 3 RESULTS	1	2	3	4	5	6	7	8	9	10	11	12
1. Chipstead	*	6-3	1-3	7-2	1-2	0-0	3-2	0-4	3-1	1-1	1-1	5-3
2. Dunton Green	1-3	*	2-3	3-2	6-1	2-1	1-1	6-3	2-1	1-4	1-8	1-4
3. Halls	1-2	4-5	*	0-3	0-2	6-2	2-5	4-1	0-4	1-4	0-0	2-1
4. Joyce Green	2-2	2-1	2-2	*	2-2	3-1	2-1	1-0	1-1	1-1	1-3	0-1
5. NPI	2-0	2-3	3-0	0-2	*	3-1	1-2	3-2	1-4	3-2	1-4	2-1
6. Nomads	1-4	1-4	0-2	1-1	1-1	*	1-2	0-4	1-5	0-0	0-3	0-0
7. Snodland	3-1	1-4	2-1	2-2	10-2	0-1	*	5-3	0-0	6-1	2-3	0-1
8. St Georges	2-3	1-2	2-3	2-2	4-2	3-2	0-3	*	3-3	1-2	1-2	3-1
9. Swanscombe United	1-0	11-2	8-1	3-1	1-0	4-0	5-1	1-1	*	6-0	3-2	6-0
10. Tonbridge Invicta	0-1	0-6	2-2	0-4	1-1	2-2	3-0	2-1	0-2	*	2-3	4-2
11. Tonbridge Rangers	4-2	4-1	3-2	2-2	5-0	6-0	3-2	1-2	4-2	3-2	*	2-1
12. Wickham Park	1-1	1-2	1-2	4-3	5-4	2-2	2-2	2-0	3-5	1-1	2-2	*

WEST DIV. 4 RESULTS	1	2	3	4	5	6	7	8	9	10	11	12	13
1. Aylesford	*	3-1	4-1	2-5	2-3	1-10	2-5	2-4	1-4	1-1	4-4	0-2	6-0
2. Belvedere	4-8	*	0-3	2-0	2-6	1-1	3-2	2-0	0-4	5-1	1-4	2-2	1-1
3. Greenways Reserves	1-0	5-1	*	2-4	4-1	3-1	2-1	3-0	3-1	6-0	2-0	3-3	7-0
4. Hawkenbury	2-4	1-4	1-3	*	2-1	0-3	3-2	2-0	2-0	6-4	2-0	2-5	7-0
5. Lordswood Reserves	1-0	6-0	3-2	3-2	*	2-2	2-1	2-1	6-1	1-3	2-0	4-1	2-2
6. Maidstone Invicta	12-1	8-0	10-2	2-1	1-1	*	9-0	1-0	7-0	5-1	2-1	5-0	4-1
7. Old Bexleians	5-2	1-0	2-3	0-4	0-4	0-5	*	3-5	2-4	3-3	1-1	3-4	1-2
8. Otford United Reserves	0-3	4-0	0-7	0-2	1-3	0-5	2-5	*	1-3	0-2	0-1	0-0	0-2
9. Scott Spts & Soc. Res.	2-2	1-1	1-4	3-1	0-0	4-3	3-1	0-3	*	4-0	1-2	1-0	3-1
10. Sevenoaks Town Res.	3-3	3-3	2-2	1-4	1-9	0-3	6-1	0-2	1-1	*		4-0	3-0
11. Stansfeld O & B Res.	1-0	1-2	1-1	2-0	5-2	1-6	4-1	1-1	1-0	3-3	*	1-1	6-0
12. VCD Athletic Res.	2-1	6-4	2-2	3-6	1-1	1-6	2-1	5-0	0-1	3-1	1-9	*	10-0
13. Westerham Res.	3-4	2-0	0-5	2-3	3-3	0-7	1-6	2-1	0-3	1-5	0-3	2-3	*

WEST RESERVE DIV.	1	2	3	4	5	6	7	8	9	10	11	12
1. Aylesford PM Res.	*	0-1	5-2	5-0	1-0	0-1	3-2	4-1	2-5	1-0	2-5	4-1
2. Bearsted Reserves	1-3	*	0-0	1-2	2-1	1-1	2-1	3-0	3-5	0-2	1-1	2-1
3. Borough United Reserves	0-0	2-1	*	5-1	1-0	3-0	3-2	5-3	0-2	0-4	0-6	0-2
4. Colts '85 Reserves	1-3	3-4	4-2	*	3-5	2-1	2-2	2-5	3-2	0-7	0-2	1-4
5. Fleetdown United	2-5	3-4	3-3	4-3	*	1-1	2-1	1-2	1-3	0-2	1-3	0-7
6. Joyce Green Reserves	1-3	0-3	0-4	1-0	1-3	*	2-0	1-3	1-4	4-4	1-4	2-1
7. Nomads Reserves	0-3	9-2	2-2	2-0	3-1	2-2	*	0-5	2-2	0-4	0-5	1-6
8. Oakwood Reserves	1-1	2-3	1-4	4-0	0-1	6-0	3-1	*	2-3	2-1	1-2	2-1
9. Phoenix Sports Reserves	0-5	0-2	3-1	12-1	3-1	2-1	3-0	1-5	*	3-2	1-1	2-0
10. Platt United Reserves	1-6	2-2	2-1	1-2	1-0		3-2	1-1	4-1	*	5-1	0-1
11. Rusthall Reserves	1-1	2-0	4-1	6-1	3-1	9-0	5-0	3-2	8-0	1-1	*	0-2
12. Thames Polytechnic Res.	3-1	2-2	2-0	6-0	1-1	9-1	4-1	9-2	2-1	1-1	1-1	*

INTER-REGIONAL CHALLENGE CUP 1993-94

First Round

Milton United v Woodnesborough 4-1
Aylesford Paper Mill v Sevenoaks Town 0-3
Greenways v Thames Polytechnic 6-0
Lordswood v VCD Athletic 1-2
Strood County v Colts '85 4-3
Tenterden & St Michaels v Kennington 4-0
Edenstone *(scr)* Rusthall *(w/o)*
Knockholt v Otford United 2-0
Scott Sports & Social v Ex Blues 1-1,1-0

Second Round

Bromley Green v University of Kent 0-1
Cheriton *(w/o)* Houchin Rovers *(scr)*
Lydd Town v Snowdown Colliery Welfare 3-1
Rye United v Teynham & Lynsted 2-1
Bearsted v Scott Sports & Social 3-1
Knockholt v AFC Egerton 2-1
Stansfeld O & B Club v Platt United 2-1
Ten Em Bee v Rusthall 4-0
Broomfield United v New Romney 1-2
Headcorn v Knatchbull 3-2
Milton Athletic v Walmer Rovers 9-1
Tenterden & St Michaels v Hythe United 3-1
Borough United v Oakwood 0-4
Pheonix Sports v Westerham 3-4
Strood County v Greenways 2-4
VCD Athletic v Sevenoaks Town 1-0

Third Round

Cheriton v Headcorn 1-6
Tenterden & St Michaels v Rye Utd 1-4*(aet)*
Bearsted v Knockholt 4-1
Stansfeld O & B Club v Ten Em Bee 0-2
Lydd Town v Milton Athletic 3-2
University of Kent v New Romney 0-1
Oakwood v Westerham 1-2
VCD Athletic v Greenways 1-1,1-1*(4-5 pens)*

Quarter-Finals

Bearsted v VCD Athletic 3-1
New Romney v Rye United 0-2
Headcorn v Westerham 4-0
Ten Em Bee v Lydd Town 1-4

Semi-Finals

Bearsted v Lydd Town 2-1
Headcorn v Rye United 0-1

Final *(at Gillingham FC, Fri 13th May)*: Bearsted 2 *(Spray, Mottram)*, Rye United 0

Bearsted - Inter-Regional Challenge Cup winners and Western Region Division One champions. Back Row (L/R): Charlie Ellmer (Physio), John Brook, Martin Cordrey, Marcel Payne, Phil Long, Michael Connelly, Gary Pace, Brian Palmer, Ray Hutchins (Manager). Front: Alan Swift, John Rigby, Richard Saysell, Ian Hamer, Graham Stonestreet, Keith Mottram. *Photo - John Mugridge.*

PREMIER DIVISION CLUBS 1994-95

AYLESFORD PAPER MILLS
Secretary: Mrs L Casey, 10 Ragstone Court, Ditton, Aylesford, Kent ME20 6AJ (0732 849476)
Ground: Cobdown, Station Road, Ditton, Nr. Maidstone (0622 717771) **Founded:** 1979
Colours: Red & white stripes/red/red **Change Colours:** Black & white stripes/black/black

GREENWAYS
Secretary: Mr W Miller, 14 Cygnet Gardens, Northfleet, Kent DA11 7DN (0474 560913)
Ground: Blue Circle Spts Ground, via Springhead Road, Northfleet (0474 534625) **Founded:** 1965
Colours: All red **Change Colours:** All blue

HYTHE UNITED (1992)
Secretary: Mrs L Hunter, 26 Adie Rd, Greatstone, Romney Marsh, Kent TN28 8SR (0797 363941)
Ground: Reachfields, Fort Rd, Hythe (0303 264932) **Founded:** 1992
Colours: White/red/red **Change Colours:** Blue & white/blue/blue.

KNOCKHOLT
Secretary: Mrs I Bryant, 4 Blair Court, The Knoll, Beckenham, Kent BR3 2JJ (081 650 7389)
Ground: Knockholt Village Club, Main Road, Knockholt (0959 532346) **Founded:** 1967
Colours: Red/black/black **Change Colours:** Grey & black/black/black

LORDSWOOD
Secretary: Mr S Lewis, Sunnybrook, Gorsewood Road, Hartley, Longfield (0474 708233)
Ground: Lordswood Spts & Social Club, North Dane Way, Walderslade (0634 669138)
Colours: Amber/black/black **Change Colours:** White/black/black **Founded:** 1968

LYDD TOWN
Secretary: Mr R W Hambley, 62 Roberts Road, Greatstone, Romney Marsh, Kent TN28 8RG (0797 366684)
Ground: The Rype, Manor Road, Lydd **Founded:** 1885
Colours: Red & green quarters/green/green **Change Colours:** All green

NEW ROMNEY
Secretary: Mr H Payne, 'Stonecrop', Grand Parade, Littlestone, New Romney, Kent TN28 8NQ (0679 366425)
Ground: Station Road, New Romney (0679 364858) **Founded:** 1895
Colours: All blue **Change Colours:** White/blue/blue

OAKWOOD
Secretary: Mr P Mannering, 24 Ellenswood Close, Otham, Maidstone, Kent ME15 9QA (0622 862482)
Ground: Honey Lane, Otham, Maidstone **Founded:** 1924
Colours: All red **Change Colours:** White/white/red

SCOTT SPORTS & SOCIAL
Secretary: Mr R Taylor, 24 Sun Lane, Gravesend, Kent DA12 5HG (0474 332208)
Ground: Scott Sports & Social Club, Nelson Road, Northfleet (0474 336456) **Founded:** 1927
Colours: Black & white stripes/black/black **Change Colours:** Blue & white hoops/white/blue

SEVENOAKS TOWN
Secretary: Mr E Diplock, 23 Holly Bush Lane, Sevenoaks, Kent TN13 3TH (0732 454280)
Ground: Greatness Park, Seal Road, Sevenoaks (0732 741987) **Founded:** 1883
Colours: Red & black/black/black **Change Colours:** Tangerine/black/tangerine.

STANSFELD OXFORD & BERMONDSEY CLUB
Sec: Mr E A Ellis, 40 Tillbrook Rd, Kidbrooke SE3 9QE (081 319 0903 - after 8pm). **Founded:** 1897
Ground: St James Squash & Leisure Club, Marvels Lane, Grove Park SE12 (081 851 3522)
Colours: Blue & yellow stripes/blue/blue **Change Colours:** All red.

TEN EM BEE
Secretary: Mr David Barnard, 120a Old Bromley Rd, Bromley, Kent BR1 4JY (081 313 9510).
Ground: Old Bromley Road Playing Fields, Old Bromley Road (081 460 0652) **Founded:** 1975
Colours: Blue/white/blue **Change Colours:** Green/black/black.

TEYNHAM & LYNSTED
Secretary: Mr M Ashworth, 74 Harold Road, Sittingbourne, Kent ME10 3AJ (0795 423986)
Ground: Frognal Lane, Teynham, Off A2 **Founded:** 1961
Colours: Sky & white stripes/maroon/sky **Change Colours:** Red & black/black/black

THAMES POLYTECHNIC
Secretary: Derek A Ingram, 8 St Josephs Close, Orpington, Kent BR6 9TY (0689 977162)
Ground: University of Greenwich, Avery Hill Rd **Founded:** 1888.
Colours: Yellow/green/green **Change Colours:** White & green/white/white.
Previous Lge: Kent (pre-1992) **Previous Ground:** Kidbrooke Lane, Eltham (pre-1993)

VICKERS CRAYFORD/DARTFORD ATHLETIC
Secretary: Mr R Bond, 97 Birkbeck Road, Sidcup, Kent DA14 4DJ (081 300 9943)
Ground: Oakwood, Old Road, Crayford (0322 524262) **Founded:** 1916
Colours: Green & white hoops/white/white **Change:** Yellow/black/black.

EASTERN FIRST DIVISION CLUBS 1994-95

BISHOPSBOURNE
Secretary: Mr Ray Fletcher, 120 The Street, Kingston, nr Canterbury, Kent CT4 6JD (0227 830044)
Ground: Canteen Meadow, The Street, Bishopsbourne, nr Canterbury, Kent **Founded:** 1963
Colours: Royal/royal/royal (white hoop) **Change Colours:** All green

BROMLEY GREEN
Secretary: Mr C McQuillian, 42 Fallon Way, Ashford, Kent TN23 2UR (0233 642941)
Ground: The Swan Centre, South Willesborough, Ashford. **Founded:** 1930
Colours: All green **Change Colours:** Orange/black/orange.

BROOMFIELD UNITED

Secretary: Mr J Edgington, 4 Damerham Close, Canterbury, Kent CT2 7SB (0227 452323)
Ground: Bridge Recreation Ground, Patrixbourne Road, Bridge, Nr Canterbury **Founded:** 1925
Colours: Red & white stripes/black/red & black **Change Colours:** Sky blue/black/navy

KENNINGTON

Secretary: Mr R Lancaster, 'Totternhoe', Goat Lees, Faversham Road, Kennington, Ashford (0233 624858)
Ground: Spearpoint Rec. Grnd, opposite Spearpoint Hotel, The Ridge, Kennington **Founded:** 1880
Colours: Amber **Change Colours:** All red

KNATCHBULL

Secretary: Mr D Howie, 13 Charminster, Washford Farm, Ashford, Kent TN23 2UH (0233 611207)
Ground: Hatch Park, Off A20, Mersham, Nr. Ashford **Founded:** 1981
Colours: White/white/maroon **Change Colours:** Maroon/white/maroon

LYDD TOWN RESERVES *(see Premier Division section)*

MILTON ATHLETIC

Secretary: Mr P Duffin, 18 Hales Rd, Tunstall, Sittingbourne, Kent ME10 1SR (0795 471260)
Ground: U.K.P. Sports Ground, Gore Court Rd, Sittingbourne (0795 477047) **Founded:** 1926.
Colours: Sky/navy/navy **Change Colours:** Red/white/white.

NEW ROMNEY RESERVES *(see Premier Division section)*

RYE UNITED

Secretary: Mr S Williams, 'Grovewood', Grove Lane, Iden, East Sussex TN31 7PX (0797 280509)
Ground: Rye Football and Cricket Salts **Founded:** 1938
Colours: Red & black/black/red & black **Change Colours:** All white

St MARGARETS

Secretary: Mr Bill Hay, The Free Down, St Margarets at Cliffe, nr Dover, Kent CT15 6BJ (0304 852386).
Ground: The Alexander Field, Kingsdown Rd, St Margarets at Cliffe, nr Dover. **Founded:** 1993
Colours: Blue & white/navy/sky **Change Colours:** Grey/black/black.

SNOWDOWN COLLIERY WELFARE

Secretary: Mr A Jones, 16 Ave Road, Dover, Kent CT16 2PX (0304 211856)
Ground: Spinney Lane, Aylesham, Canterbury (0304 840278) **Founded:** 1907
Colours: Black & white stripes/black/black **Change Colours:** Green & yellow/green/green.

TENTERDEN & ST MICHAELS

Secretary: Mr S Stevens, Kent House, Ashford Rd, St Michaels, Tenterden (0580 762703).
Ground: The Recreation Ground, Tenterden. **Founded:** 1890
Colours: Blue & white/navy/black **Change Colours:** Maroon/sky/maroon

UNIVERSITY OF KENT

Secretary: Mrs I Simmonds, Sports Federation, Sports Centre, University of Kent, Canterbury, Kent CT2 7NL (0227 768027)
Ground: The Playing Fields, University of Kent, Canterbury **Founded:** 1967.
Colours: Black & white stripes/black/black **Change Colours:** Red/black/black

WALMER ROVERS

Secretary: Mr B Skinner, 131 Downs Rd, Deal, Kent CT14 7TF (0304 361832)
Ground: Marke Wood, Dover Rd, Walmer (0304 374160) **Founded:** 1959.
Colours: All blue **Change Colours:** All red.

WOODNESBOROUGH

Secretary: Mr G Hunt, Hillcross Farm, Eastry, Sandwich, Kent CT13 0NY (0304 611311)
Ground: "Hillborough", Woodnesborough Road, Eastry (0304 614721) **Founded:** 1961
Colours: Yellow/blue/blue **Change Colours:** All blue

WESTERN FIRST DIVISION CLUBS 1994-95

A.F.C. EGERTON

Secretary: Mr S Parkes, 48 Oakdene Rd, St Mary Cray, Orpington, Kent BR5 2AN (0689 821737).
Ground: St Mary Cray Rec, Park Rd, St Mary Cray, Orpington **Founded:** 1971
Colours: Blue/blue/white **Change Colours:** White/blue/blue.

BEARSTED

Secretary: Mr J Scannel, 24 Fauchons Lane, Bearsted, Maidstone, Kent (0622 39072)
Ground: Bearsted Green, The Street, Bearsted **Founded:** 1895
Colours: White/white/blue **Change Colours:** Blue & yellow/blue/blue

EMPIRE

Secretary: Mrs Peter Danzey, 50 Challenge Close, Gravesend, Kent DA12 4RT (0474 567697)
Ground: Empire Fine Papers Sports Ground, Knockhall Road, A226, Greenhithe **Founded:** 1910
Colours: Blue/white/red **Change Colours:** Red/white/red

EX BLUES

Secretary: Mr M Harvey, 29 Crown Lane Bromley, Kent BR2 9PG (081 464 4815)
Ground: Hayes Country Club, West Common Road, Hayes, West Wickham, Kent.
Colours: White/blue/blue **Change Colours:** All blue **Founded:** 1945

EYNSFORD

Secretary: Mr D Wood, 76 Picardy Rd, Upper Belvedere, Kent (0322 442868). **Founded:** 1894
Ground: Harrow Meadow, Bower Lane, off Eynsford High Street
Colours: Black & white/black/black **Change Colours:** Blue & yellow/blue/blue

METROGAS

Secretary: Mr D Crouch, 100 Harland Ave., Sidcup, Kent (081 300 3814)
Ground: British Gas Conference Leisure Centre, 40 Footway, Avery Hill Rd, New Eltham SE9
Colours: Blue & white/blue/blue **Change Colours:** White & blue/blue/blue

OTFORD UNITED

Secretary: Mr R Gulliver, 22 Berwick Way, Sevenoaks, Kent TN14 5EY (0732 459064)
Ground: Recreation Ground, High Street, Otford (0959 524966) **Founded:** 1900
Colours: Amber/black/black **Change Colours:** Red/black/black

PHOENIX SPORTS

Secretary: Mr A Pearson, 4 Gainsborough Avenue, Dartford, Kent (0322 228625)
Ground: Phoenix Sports Ground, May Road East, Barnehurst. **Founded:** 1895
Colours: Red & white/black/red **Change Colours:** Green/red/red.

PLATT UNITED

Secretary: Mr G Broad, The Lilacs, Rowhill Rd, Hextable, Kent BR8 7RL (0322 662452).
Ground: Stonehouse Field, Longmill Lane, Platt **Founded:** 1930
Colours: White/blue/white **Change Colours:** Red/blue/red.

RUSTHALL

Secretary: Mr R Forbes, 27 Ashenden Walk, Tunbridge Wells, Kent TN2 3HR (0892 545075)
Ground: Jockey Farm, Newington Road, Rusthall **Founded:** 1899
Colours: All green **Change Colours:** Claret & blue/sky/sky.

SUTTON ATHLETIC

Secretary: Mr John F Willis, 6 Somerset Road, Dartford, Kent DA1 3DP (0322 222540)
Ground: The Roaches, Parsonage Lane, Sutton-at-Hone, nr Dartford (0322 280507) **Founded:** 1928
Colours: Green & yellow/green/green **Change Colours:** All blue

WELLCOME (SATURDAY)

Sec: Mr Roger Giles, 4 Wilkinson Close, Dartford DA1 5LH (0322 273974). **Founded:** 1985
Ground: Wellcome Club, Acacia Hall, opp. Dartford Church, Bottom East Hill, Dartford (0322 223488).
Colours: All yellow **Change Colours:** Blue & red/blue/blue

WESTERHAM

Secretary: Mr A Noad, 25 Croydon Road, Westerham, Kent (0959 62658)
Ground: King George Playing Fields, Costells Meadow, off Quebec Avenue, Westerham (0959 61106)
Colours: Red/black/black **Change Colours:** Green/black/black **Founded:** 1888

LOWER DIVISION CONSTITUTIONS 1994-95

Eastern 2nd	Western 2nd	Western 3rd	West Res. 1st:	West Res. 2nd.
Bond Sports	Borough United	Aylesford	Aylesford PM Res.	Bearsted Res.
Bromley Gn Res.	Chipstead	Belvedere	Greenways Res.	Borough Utd Res.
Broomfield Res.	Chislehurst	Halls	Lordswood Res.	Eynsford Res.
Hythe Utd Res.	Colts '85	Halstead	Oakwood Res.	Ex Blues Res.
Invicta	Dunton Green	Hawkenbury	Phoenox S. Res.	Fleetdown Utd Res.
Kennington Res.	Edenbridge Utd	Joyce Green	Rusthall Res.	Joyce Green Res.
Knatchbull Res.	Eltham Palace	NPI	Scott S. & S. Res.	Nomads Res.
Lydd Town 'A'	Fleetdown Utd	Nomads	Sevenoaks T. Res.	Otford Utd Res.
New Romney 'A'	Maidstone Inv.	Old Bexleians	Stansfeld O&B Res	Platt Utd Res.
Ocean Inn	Moonshot Ath.	Snodland	Thames Poly Res.	Tonbridge R. Res.
Ryl George (F'stone)	Paddock Wd Utd	St Geo. (Wrotham)	VCD Athletic Res.	Westerham Res.
Sturry	Swanscombe Utd	Tonbridge Inv.		
Tenterden SM Res.	Tonbridge Rgrs	Wickham Park		
Teynham & L. Res.				
Uni. of Kent Res.				

Bill Tucker of Maidstone Invicta (right) receives the first of his Afford Manager of the Month awards from League General Secretary Tony Scott.

Photo - Cyril Windiate.

D. & J. TYRES KENT YOUTH LEAGUE (FOUNDED: 1981)

NORTHERN	P	W	D	L	F	A	PTS
Millwall	30	25	3	2	127	36	53
Furness	30	24	4	2	116	30	52
Gillingham (N)	30	21	5	4	86	39	47
Charlton Ath.	30	15	8	7	88	46	38
Maidstone Invicta	30	16	5	9	80	58	37
Sittingbourne (N)	30	16	3	11	73	62	35
Beckenham Town	30	13	7	10	57	53	33
Fisher '93	30	12	5	13	66	77	29
Tonbridge Angels	30	10	7	13	52	55	27
Chatham Town (N)	30	11	5	14	49	67	27
Dartford	30	11	3	16	60	67	25
Thamesmead Town	30	8	4	18	51	80	20
Phoenix Sports	30	7	4	19	45	89	18
VCD Athletic	30	6	5	19	56	113	17
Knockholt	30	4	3	23	37	102	11
Corinthian	30	4	3	23	53	122	11

SOUTHERN	P	W	D	L	F	A	PTS
Whitstable Town	26	22	3	1	102	25	47
Dover Athletic	26	18	4	4	72	27	40
Gillingham (S)	26	16	6	4	52	24	38
Chatham Town (S)	26	11	7	8	52	45	29
Folkestone Invicta	26	11	7	8	65	62	29
Deal Town	26	13	2	11	63	43	28
Sittingbourne (S)	26	10	8	8	52	55	28
Margate	26	8	9	9	44	56	25
Ramsgate	26	4	11	11	34	54	19
Ashford Town	26	7	4	15	45	61	18
Lordswood	26	6	5	15	42	70	17
Herne Bay	26	5	6	15	31	57	16
Snowdown CW	26	5	5	16	44	72	15
Faversham Town	26	6	3	17	37	81	15

RESULT CHARTS 1993-94

NORTHERN SECTION	1	2	3	4	5	6	7	8	9	10	11	12	13	14	15	16
1. Beckenham Town	*	2-2	1-1	5-2	0-0	4-4	2-2	1-6	3-0	0-3	1-3	1-2	3-0	3-1	1-0	6-1
2. Charlton Athletic	1-0	*	4-1	9-2	3-0	4-1	1-3	2-2	1-1	3-2	0-1	4-2	1-2	5-1	5-1	7-1
3. Chatham Town (N)	0-1	0-3	*	1-0	1-3	4-1	0-3	1-3	5-1	1-1	1-4	1-1	2-0	1-0	1-0	4-0
4. Corinthian	3-4	1-1	1-4	*	2-5	3-4	0-6	0-7	4-2	1-4	0-9	2-2	2-4	2-1	1-0	4-4
5. Dartford	1-2	3-3	4-3	5-4	*	4-0	1-1	1-2	6-0	6-3	1-3	2-1	0-4	2-1	3-1	3-4
6. Fisher '93	2-1	2-3	3-0	6-1	2-0	*	1-5	2-5	4-1	2-2	1-4	1-2	2-2	0-5	1-1	5-1
7. Furness	5-1	0-0	8-1	6-2	4-0	4-1	*	2-2	7-0	5-2	1-3	7-0	5-1	3-2	3-0	2-1
8. Gillingham (N)	2-0	3-1	1-0	1-0	1-0	5-0	3-2	*	0-2	1-2	1-3	3-2	2-2	5-2	6-1	3-1
9. Knockholt	2-3	0-6	1-3	4-1	0-3	0-4	0-3	0-4	*	2-3	0-6	2-0	3-0	2-2	2-5	1-5
10. Maidstone Invicta	1-3	2-1	4-0	5-3	4-1	5-1	1-3	1-2	1-1	*	0-5	3-1	1-4	9-0	2-0	4-0
11. Millwall	3-0	2-3	3-3	5-3	4-1	3-0	2-4	6-2	5-2	3-2	*	4-0	9-1	3-2	1-1	7-0
12. Phoenix Sports	1-1	1-6	5-0	3-1	1-0	2-3	0-8	0-6	3-2	3-4	2-6	*	1-3	1-3	0-2	4-1
13. Sittingbourne (N)	0-4	3-1	6-1	3-2	3-2	1-4	1-2	0-2	6-1	3-4	1-3	5-1	*	3-0	3-1	5-0
14. Thamesmead Town	1-2	3-3	1-4	1-3	3-0	2-2	0-1	2-3	4-3	2-1	1-6	3-2	0-2	*	3-2	3-2
15. Tonbridge Angels	2-0	3-1	0-1	2-1	4-1	3-4	2-3	1-1	3-1	1-1	2-2	1-1	1-1	3-0	*	3-2
16. Vickers Crayford/Dartford Athletic	2-2	0-4	4-4	9-2	3-2	0-3	0-8	2-2	2-1	0-2	0-9	4-1	2-4	2-2	3-6	*

SOUTHERN SECTION	1	2	3	4	5	6	7	8	9	10	11	12	13	14
1. Ashford Town	*	2-1	1-0	2-4	2-3	2-1	0-2	2-0	4-3	2-3	0-0	1-2	2-3	1-6
2. Chatham Town	4-2	*	1-3	0-0	4-4	1-1	0-2	3-2	6-1	2-1	4-3	3-3	5-2	2-3
3. Deal Town	3-1	1-1	*	1-2	5-1	2-3	1-0	2-2	4-0	1-3	2-1	7-0	6-4	0-4
4. Dover Athletic	2-0	5-1	0-2	*	3-0	3-0	2-0	4-3	4-0	4-0	4-4	1-1	3-1	1-3
5. Faversham Town	0-4	1-2	0-6	0-6	*	4-3	0-6	1-3	4-2	1-2	3-3	1-9	3-2	1-2
6. Folkestone Inv.	5-4	2-0	4-3	2-1	3-0	*	2-2	4-1	5-2	0-0	3-0	1-3	2-2	2-6
7. Gillingham (S)	4-0	1-0	3-0	1-3	2-1	4-1	*	0-0	4-1	2-2	2-1	3-1	2-1	1-3
8. Herne Bay	3-2	0-2	1-2	0-1	1-0	0-5	0-2	*	1-1	1-0	2-1	2-3	1-3	1-4
9. Lordswood	2-1	3-1	2-1	0-3	0-2	5-2	1-1	1-1	*	1-2	2-2	2-3	4-1	2-5
10. Margate	2-7	1-1	1-4	3-4	1-1	3-5	0-0	1-1	3-1	*	2-2	1-2	5-4	2-9
11. Ramsgate	1-1	1-2	0-3	0-8	3-1	2-2	1-1	1-0	2-2	0-1	*	0-0	1-0	0-4
12. Sittingbourne (S)	1-1	0-4	2-1	0-0	2-0	4-4	0-1	7-4	4-1	0-1	1-3	*	2-2	0-5
13. Snowdown CW	2-1	0-1	3-2	0-2	1-3	3-3	2-3	4-0	0-3	2-2	0-0	2-3	*	0-5
14. Whitstable Town	5-0	0-0	3-1	3-2	4-2	5-0	1-3	1-1	4-0	1-1	4-2	4-0	8-0	*

HURST ELECTRICAL KENT MIDWEEK LEAGUE

FINAL TABLE	P	W	D	L	F	A	PTS
Hastings Town	18	14	1	3	46	20	29
Sittingbourne	18	11	3	4	49	18	25
Gravesend & N.	18	11	2	5	53	21	24
Margate	18	10	1	7	26	35	21
Deal Town	18	8	0	10	42	41	16
Corinthian	18	5	4	9	33	52	14
Faversham Town	18	5	3	10	40	41	13
Fisher '93	18	6	1	11	33	44	13
Thamesmead Town	18	5	3	10	26	44	13
Herne Bay	18	5	2	11	25	55	12

RESULTS	1	2	3	4	5	6	7	8	9	10
1. Corinthian	*	3-0	3-3	5-2	0-6	1-3	0-0	5-1	2-2	0-2
2. Deal Town	9-3	*	4-0	1-0	1-2	4-2	0-6	1-4	1-2	2-3
3. Faversham Town	5-0	0-1	*	3-4	0-4	0-1	1-3	3-5	0-2	3-2
4. Fisher '93	2-4	3-0	1-6	*	1-4	2-2	5-1	L-W	0-3	2-0
5. Gravesend & Northfleet	3-1	2-4	4-0	5-0	*	2-3	3-0	0-1	1-1	3-1
6. Hastings Town	6-0	4-0	2-0	W-L	4-3	*	W-L	2-0	3-2	6-1
7. Herne Bay	2-1	1-7	2-2	1-7	1-6	1-4	*	2-1	1-2	3-2
8. Margate	0-1	1-5	1-1	W-L	2-1	1-0	2-0	*	0-3	0-0
9. Sittingbourne	4-0	3-1	1-3	8-1	1-1	0-2	9-0	0-1	*	2-1
10. Thamesmead Town	2-2	2-1	1-1	1-3	0-3	3-2	4-0	1-7	0-4	*

PHOTOS OPPOSITE

Top: *Rye United FC - Kent County League*

Centre: *Tonbridge Rangers FC - Kent County League*

Foot: *Ex Blues FC - Kent County League.*

All Photos - John Mugridge.

POOLCARE

CANTERBURY & DIST. LEAGUE

Three games were left unplayed (Upper Red Lion v Canterbury PO in Division Two and Adisham v Staple and Albion Wanderers v Staple in Division Three). Promotion and relegation lines are marked on the tables, but some adjustments may be necessary as, although there has been no notice of any withdrawals, five new teams (including the reserve sides of Market Inn and Spartan Old Boys) have applied to join.

J F French, Secretary

PREM. DIV.	P	W	D	L	F	A	PTS
White Heathens	18	15	1	2	75	22	31
Sturry Road ASC	18	14	0	4	62	32	28
Sentinels	18	9	2	7	42	39	20
Beltinge	18	8	2	8	41	48	18
Chilham	18	7	3	8	35	43	17
Broomfield U. 'A'	18	7	3	8	30	40	17
Bellgrove	18	5	4	9	29	29	14
Pfizer Athletic	18	4	5	9	28	43	13
Herne United	18	5	1	12	35	50	11
Norton United	18	4	3	11	23	54	11

Faversham Town Res. withdrew - record expunged.

DIV. ONE	P	W	D	L	F	A	PTS
Spartan Old Boys	18	14	3	1	80	22	31
St Augustines	18	14	1	3	73	32	29
Selling Sports	18	9	4	5	48	34	22
Chartham Sports	18	10	1	7	52	31	21
Bekesbourne Sports	18	9	1	8	62	50	19
Univ. of Kent 'A'	18	9	1	8	39	41	19
Ash	18	7	3	8	33	45	17
Ickham	18	6	2	10	36	64	14
Sharsted Sports	18	1	2	15	28	67	4
Whitstable Eagles	18	2	0	16	31	96	4

DIV. TWO	P	W	D	L	F	A	PTS
Market Inn (Fav.)	16	15	0	1	53	19	30
Swingfield	16	10	4	2	59	31	24
Littlebourne	16	8	2	6	57	39	18
The Beckett	16	7	4	5	51	39	18
Univ. Staff Assoc.	16	7	3	6	32	28	17
Upper Red Lion	15	5	5	5	33	27	15
Chilham Res.	16	6	2	8	30	34	14
Sturry Res.	16	1	2	13	20	55	4
Canterbury PO	15	0	2	13	14	77	2

Graveney Sports withdrew - record expunged.

DIV. THREE	P	W	D	L	F	A	PTS
Staple	14	13	1	0	75	15	27
Adisham	15	12	0	3	63	21	24
Bishopsbourne Res.	16	8	4	4	41	28	20
Boughton Sports	16	8	2	6	48	58	18
Wingham	16	6	2	8	30	48	14
Albion Wanderers	15	6	1	8	34	46	13
Sentinels Res.	16	4	4	8	32	44	12
Blean United	16	3	1	12	34	63	7
St Nicholas	16	2	1	13	25	59	5

Herne United Res. withdrew - record expunged.

DIV. FIVE	P	W	D	L	F	A	PTS
Kennington 'A'	18	15	0	3	63	30	30
Pfizer Ath. Res.	18	12	2	4	61	28	26
Bekesbourne Res.	18	10	4	4	65	34	24
Academicals	18	9	4	5	57	32	22
Chartham Spts Res.	18	11	0	7	58	46	22
Charing	18	5	5	8	66	49	15
Whitstable E. Res.	18	6	2	10	34	53	14
Ospringe	18	6	1	11	42	64	13
Sharsted Res.	18	5	1	12	39	81	11
Metric Sports	18	1	1	16	24	92	3

League Challenge Trophy Final:
White Heathens 3, Spartan Old Boys 2

Reserve Trophy Final:
Chilham Reserves 1, Pfizer Ath. Res. 0 *(aet)*

Bert Dowell Cup Final:
Market Inn (Faversham) 2, Upper Red Lion 1

Anniversary Cup Final:
Pfizer Athletic Reserves 4, Bekesbourne Reserves 0

Faversham Charity Cup:
Senior sect.: White Heathens 3, UK Paper 0
Junior sect.: Market Inn (Faversham) 3, Swingfield 2

Whitstable Charity Cup Final:
Group A: Spartan Old Boys 4, Bellgrove 0
Group B: Market Inn (Faversham) 3, Littlebourne 0

SEVENOAKS & DIST. LEAGUE

FOUNDED: 1905

PREM. DIV.	P	W	D	L	F	A	PTS
Leaves Green	16	13	3	0	47	17	42
Eynsford 'A'	18	10	6	2	60	27	36
Tonbdge Bapt. Ch.	18	11	3	4	50	27	36
Ide Hill	17	10	2	5	52	35	32
Tatsfield Rovers	18	7	6	5	42	26	27
Kemsing United	18	6	6	6	52	38	23
Hever	17	5	3	9	28	50	18
Shoreham United	18	4	2	12	31	43	14
Seal	18	2	5	11	26	57	11
Ightham	18	1	2	15	22	90	5

DIV. ONE	P	W	D	L	F	A	PTS
Borough Green	18	14	3	1	69	12	45
Sevenoaks T. 'A'	18	12	2	4	53	30	38
Sevenoaks Weald	18	11	3	4	56	34	36
Halstead Utd Res.	18	9	3	6	48	49	30
St Lawrence	18	6	6	6	36	36	24
Westerham 'A'	18	7	2	9	40	55	23
St G. (Wrotham) Res.	18	5	4	9	38	43	19
Riverhead United	18	4	3	11	35	53	15
Chipstead Res.	18	3	3	12	28	49	12
Otford Utd 'A'	18	3	3	12	29	71	12

DIV. TWO	P	W	D	L	F	A	PTS
Tatsfield R. Res.	22	20	0	2	110	24	60
S'oaks Weald Res.	22	19	1	2	101	23	58
Wilderpark	22	12	2	8	95	62	38
Dunton Gn Res.	22	10	6	6	69	56	36
Borough Gn Res.	22	10	5	7	68	71	35
Kemsing Utd 'A'	22	7	6	9	56	60	27
Crockham Hill	22	6	6	10	57	55	24
Ide Hill Res.	22	6	5	11	53	74	23
Dowgate Priory	22	6	4	12	55	106	22
Sevenoaks T. 'B'	22	8	3	11	63	73	*21
Westerham 'B'	22	6	3	13	55	83	*18
Shoreham Utd Res.	22	1	1	20	27	122	4

DIV. THREE	P	W	D	L	F	A	PTS
Brasted/Sundridge	24	18	4	2	92	32	58
Leaves Green 'A'	23	18	2	3	92	28	*53
St Lawrence Res.	24	16	4	4	91	36	52
Am. & Tiger (Culv)	23	15	1	7	97	53	46
Platt Utd 'A'	21	13	2	6	75	38	*38
Borough Green 'A'	24	9	6	9	69	58	33
Tonb. Bapt. Res.	24	10	2	12	58	50	*29
Tatsfield R. 'A'	22	8	4	10	40	51	28
Ightham Res.	24	6	4	14	46	86	22
Chipstead 'A'	24	5	4	15	51	104	19
Riverhead Utd Res.	22	6	2	14	35	99	*11
Wilderpark Res.	24	4	1	9	38	95	*10
Nomads 'A'	21	2	4	15	25	79	*7

SMITHS CHARITY CUP (Founded: 1922)
Senior Final: Eynsford 3, Tatsfield Rovers 3 *(Eynsford won 4-2 on penalties)*
Premier Final: Sevenoaks Weald 2, Borough Green 1
Intermediate Final: Sevenoaks Weald Res. 1, Tatsfield Rovers Reserves 0
Junior Final: Amazon & Tiger (Culverstone) 3, Leaves Green 'A' 1

SEVENOAKS CHARITY CUP (Founded: 1894)
Centenary Final: Platt United 3, Sevenoaks Town 2
Junior Charity Cup (founded: 1923) **Final:** Sevenoaks Town Reserves 1, Bearsted Reserves 0

CRASKE & WELLS MEM. CUP (Founded: 1986)
Final: Platt United 6, Leaves Green 3

FISHER SHIELD (Founded: 1970)
Final: Tatsfield Rovers Reserves 5, Crockham Hill 2

HIRE-IT CHALLENGE CUP (Founded: 1988)
Final: Tatsfield Rovers 2, Leaves Green 1

SOUTHERN BUILDERS (CROYDON) INTER-LEAGUE COMPETITION

GROUP A.	P	W	D	L	F	A	PTS
Maidstone	4	2	1	1	7	2	5
Croydon	4	2	1	1	8	9	5
West Kent	4	1	2	1	8	5	4
Hythe	4	1	1	2	13	11	3
Medway	4	1	1	2	5	13	3

RESULTS	1	2	3	4	5
1. Croydon	*	3-3		3-3	
2. Hythe		*	1-3		3-3
3. Maidstone			*		1-1
4. Medway		1-6	1-1	*	
5. West Kent	0-1			4-0	*

GROUP B.	P	W	D	L	F	A	PTS
Croydon	4	3	0	1	11	7	6
Medway	4	2	1	1	11	8	5
Maidstone	4	1	1	2	7	8	4

RESULTS	1	2	3
1. Croydon	*	4-1	1-2
2. Maidstone	1-2	*	2-2
3. Medway	3-4	4-1	*

MAIDSTONE & DIST. LEAGUE

FOUNDED: 1892-93

PREM. DIV.	P	W	D	L	F	A	PTS
APS	16	14	1	1	55	18	43
Snodland Res.	16	11	3	2	70	30	36
Loose Rangers	16	10	2	4	33	19	32
West Farleigh	16	7	2	7	33	47	23
Staplehurst	16	6	3	7	29	27	21
MPE	16	5	3	8	30	37	18
Maidstone Rgrs	16	4	2	10	26	49	14
Blue Eagles	16	3	2	11	32	61	11
Barming	16	1	4	11	27	48	7

DIV. ONE	P	W	D	L	F	A	PTS
S'hurst Monarchs	18	12	3	1	65	24	39
Ulcombe	18	11	4	3	41	26	37
Shep. Eagles	18	9	3	4	57	34	30
E. Malling	18	8	3	7	42	54	27
Eccles	18	8	0	10	37	32	24
Lenham	18	6	6	6	57	56	24
Nu-Venture	18	6	4	8	41	47	22
Crosskeys	18	5	4	9	38	47	19
Malgo	18	5	3	10	19	50	18
Woodfield	18	4	2	12	24	52	14

DIV. TWO	P	W	D	L	F	A	PTS
Larkfield	18	15	0	3	81	19	45
YMCA	18	14	1	3	60	24	43
Ditton Village	18	12	3	3	47	20	39
Rose	18	10	1	7	56	60	31
Ditton Major	18	8	4	6	62	28	28
Headcorn 'A'	18	7	2	9	42	46	23
C/Sutton	18	6	3	9	37	48	21
Addington	18	6	2	10	40	55	20
Glydian	18	2	1	15	30	90	7
APM 'A'	18	1	1	16	19	84	4

DIV. THREE	P	W	D	L	F	A	PTS
APS Res.	20	16	2	2	77	25	50
Smarden	20	16	1	3	76	29	49
Staplehurst Res.	20	15	2	3	72	30	47
GSE	20	13	3	4	88	41	42
Hunton	20	9	4	7	48	33	31
Lashings	20	8	2	10	67	48	26
Coombe	20	7	3	10	55	44	24
YMCA Res.	20	5	1	14	38	80	16
Hospitals	20	4	1	15	22	77	13
Lenham Res.	20	4	0	16	25	92	12
Malgo Res.	20	3	1	16	17	82	10

DIV. FOUR	P	W	D	L	F	A	PTS
Marden	20	18	1	1	79	25	55
Barming Res.	20	14	2	4	76	36	44
S/Valence	20	14	2	4	70	43	44
Staplehurst M. Res.	20	8	6	6	52	61	30
W. Farleigh Res.	20	9	2	9	48	42	29
Union Flag	20	8	2	10	45	55	26
Thurnham	20	7	1	12	54	57	22
Leeds	20	5	5	10	34	48	20
Hollingbourne	20	5	2	13	38	77	17
Aylesford Res.	20	4	3	13	43	72	15
Take-off-Spts	20	4	2	14	48	72	14

DIV. FOUR	P	W	D	L	F	A	PTS
South Celtic	18	13	2	5	75	35	41
Ditton Mjrs Res.	18	13	2	5	63	25	41
Larkfield Res.	18	12	1	7	56	30	37
Safeway C/S	18	11	2	7	58	35	35
Snodland Nomads	18	8	4	12	71	44	28
Hunton Res.	18	7	4	9	52	44	25
Addington Res.	18	6	2	12	41	65	20
E. Malling Res.	18	5	0	15	37	53	15
Rose Res.	18	4	0	16	36	83	12
Paddock Wd U. 'A'	18	2	1	17	22	98	7

Challenge Cup Group 'A': APS
Challenge Cup Group 'B': Larkfield
Challenge Cup Group 'C': Marden
Benevolent Cup Group 'A': Staplehurst Monarchs

ASHFORD & DISTRICT LGE

PREM. DIV.	P	W	D	L	F	A	PTS
Quest International	20	18	0	2	119	33	36
Houchins Res.	20	16	2	2	103	28	34
Tech Pro.	20	15	2	3	102	31	32
Pullman	20	11	3	6	63	48	25
Orchard Rangers	20	8	3	9	65	59	19
Woodchurch	20	9	1	10	67	67	19
Bethersden	20	6	4	10	57	80	16
Portex Blue Liners	20	5	3	12	41	66	13
County Members	20	5	2	13	35	85	12
Cherry Pickers	20	3	2	15	38	132	8
Wye	20	2	2	16	45	108	6

DIV. ONE	P	W	D	L	F	A	PTS
Allied Foods	18	18	0	0	81	22	36
Addington	18	14	0	4	72	30	28
Tech Pro. Res.	18	11	0	7	75	47	22
Hamstreet	18	9	1	8	44	42	19
Ashford Dynamo	18	9	0	9	49	54	18
Ocean Inn	18	7	3	8	42	45	17
Churchills	18	6	2	10	42	55	14
Lydd Town 'A'	18	5	1	12	34	46	11
Ruckinge	18	5	0	13	25	67	10
Euro Tunnel	18	2	1	15	25	80	5

Cup Finals:
Prem. Div.: Tech Pro 3, Quest International 0
Div. 1: Allied Food 4, Tech Pro Reserves 1

NORTH KENT SUNDAY LEAGUE

PREM. DIV.	P	W	D	L	F	A	PTS
Sun	20	15	1	4	58	23	46
Scott	20	13	2	5	44	22	41
Welsh Tavern	20	11	3	6	42	30	36
Old Comrades	20	10	3	7	49	41	33
Northfleet Scotts	20	9	2	9	43	29	29
New Ash Green	20	9	2	9	38	36	29
Hollisters	20	7	4	9	31	34	25
Milton & Denton	20	7	2	11	29	50	20
Springvale	20	6	2	12	34	56	20
Wellcome Ath.	20	5	3	12	17	48	18
Guru Nanak	20	4	4	12	21	37	16

Lower Division Champions:
Div. 1: Crayford Athletic
Div. 2: Milton Ale Rangers
Div. 3: South Darenth
Div. 4: Northfleet Scotts Reserves
Combinastion Div.: Wellcome Ath. Reserves
Youth Div.: Swanscombe Tigers

Reporter Cup/Senior Cup: Sun
League Cup 'A': Milton Ale Rangers
League Cup 'B': Northfleet Rangers Reserves
Presidents Cup: Swanscombe Sun
Seeboard Cup: Gravesend United

LONDON & KENT BORDER SUNDAY LEAGUE

FOUNDED: 1964

SNR PREM. DIV.	P	W	D	L	F	A	PTS
Whitehouse Spts	21	15	3	3	95	41	33
Moves	22	15	3	4	76	27	33
Kenningwell Utd	20	11	4	5	43	29	26
Valley Valiants	20	12	2	7	49	39	26
Centaurs	21	11	3	7	57	40	25
Morley	22	10	3	9	49	61	23
Dolphin	22	8	3	11	32	42	19
Lesann United	21	9	1	11	45	53	19
Inter Royalle	22	6	4	12	34	55	16
Milldean	21	8	1	12	40	64	*13
Kingham	21	8	0	13	52	65	*12
Crown Rovers	22	1	1	20	16	72	***-3

* - 2 points deducted

Lower Division Champions:
Senior Div. 1 (11): Eltham United
Senior Div. 2 (12): Lordos
Senior Div. 3 (11): Mitre Athletic
Inter Div. 1 (12): Delta Sports
Inter Div. 2 (12): Gainsborough
Inter Div. 3 (11): South London Sports
Junior Div. 1 (11): Lynton
Junior Div. 2 (13): Seymour Villa
Junior Div. 3 (13): Norbury Royals

MEDWAY AREA SUNDAY LEAGUE

FOUNDED: 1960

Senior Sect.: Quested (R-up: St Mary's)
Prem. D.: Rainham Spts (R-up: Multi Trade Supplies)
Div. 1: Rainham '84 (R-up: Playa)
Div. 2: Palm Cottages (R-up: Eagles)
Div. 3: Strood Rangers (R-up: M2 Tune)
Div. 4: Spartac (R-up: Caulkers)
Div. 5: Real '60 (R-up: Burnt Oak)
Div. 6: Lansdowne Rgrs (R-up: River Valley Rgrs)
Comb.: M2 Tune Res. (R-up: Cuxton Social)

Cup Finals

Chall. Shield: Quested 2, ABC Sports 1
Hoo Peninsula Cup: Red Dog 4, Plough 0
Kent Today Cup: Woodcombe 4, Bly Spartans 2
Gillingham Cup: Cecil Arms 4, M2 Tune 1
Senior Charity Cup: Parkwood '79 beat Portland Arms 7-6 on penalties after a 1-1 draw.
Int. Charity Cup: Burnt Oak 7, Lansdowne Rgrs 1
Jnr Charity Cup: Red Dog 1, Lloyds 0 *(aet)*

Below: *Crockenhill FC - Winstonlead Kent League. Back Row (L/R): Kelvin Arnold, Colin Moriaty, Gary Wilders, Glen Cooper, Craig Townsend, Alan 'No Loyalty' Clarke, Kieran Murray. Front: Lee Hill, Mark Twiner, John Hibbert, John Reid, Steve Emery.*
Photo - Mike Floate.

Creekside Town FC, of the Metropolitan Sunday League - Kent Sunday Junior Trophy winners 1993-94.
Photo - Richard Ralph.

LANCASHIRE F.A.

FOUNDED: 28th September, 1878

Secretary: J Kenyon ACIS,
Northbank, 31a Wellington Street (St Johns),
Blackburn BB1 8AU (0254 264333)

ATS CHALLENGE TROPHY 1993-94

First Round

Atherton Laburnum Rovers v Nelson	0-1	Bacup Borough Atherton Collieries	1-0
Bamber Bridge v Blackpool Mechanics	6-2	Blackpool Wren Rovers v Barrow	1-2
Burscough v Darwen	1-0	Horwich RMI v Fleetwood Town	3-0
Lancaster City v Holker Old Boys	3-1	Rossendale United v Westhoughton Town	2-1

Second Round

Accrington Stanley v Nelson	4-1	Bamber Bridge v Burscough	5-4
Barrow v Horwich RMI	1-2	Clitheroe v Chorley	1-2
Morecambe v Bacup Borough	4-0	Gt Harwood Town v Lancaster City	2-2,3-3*(3-4 pens)*
Rossendale United v Radcliffe Borough	0-4	Southport v Marine	2-1

Quarter-Finals

Accrington Stanley v Southport	0-1	Bamber Bridge v Horwich RMI	1-3
Lancaster City v Chorley	3-0	Morecambe v Radcliffe Borough	2-0

Semi-Finals

Southport v Horwich RMI	2-0	Lancaster City v Morecambe	0-0,0-3

Final *(at Bolton Wanderers FC, Tues 26th April)*: Morecambe 4, Southport 3 *(aet)*

OTHER COUNTY FINALS:

Adidas Amateur Shield: Lancashire Constabulary 1, Wigan College 0
Whitbread Amateur Cup: St Dominics 5, Wythenshawe Amateurs 4
Royal Mail Sunday Trophy: Mammas 2, Masons Arms 1
Professional Youth Cup: Manchester United 4, Burnley 2
Inter-Lge under-18: Bolton Boys Federation 3, St Helens Combination 2
Inter-Lge under-16: Bury & Radcliffe Junior League 2, Blackpool & Dist. Junior League 1
Inter-Lge under-14: Presspart Hyndburn Junior Lge 2, Central Lancs Junior League 1
Under-18 Youth Cup: Southport 4, Chorley 2
Screen under-16 Youth Cup: Juniors Clarets 1, Crosby Stuart 0
Under-14 Youth Cup: Blackpool Rangers 2, Merrie England 0
Lancashire Floodlit League: Southport 2, Chorley 0
Lancashire under-14 One Day champions: Blackpool Rangers 2, Breightmet United 0

Little Hulton United - Centenary year winners of the Westhoughton Charity Cup.

Photo - John L Newton.

JOHN SMITH'S BITTER WEST LANCASHIRE LEAGUE (Est. 1905)

President: H Johnstone, Esq.
Chairman: D Procter, Esq.
Hon. Secretary: W Carr, Esq., 60 Selby Avenue, Blackpool.

Burnley United members of the First Division since 1972, won their first League championship. On the final day of the season, they needed at least a 4-0 win against Thornton International, who were sadly relegated despite accruing 37 points. However, despite their brave opposition Burnley, made sure of the title with a 6-0 result and pushing Turton into second place on goal difference only.

The Reserve teams of both clubs were also in the honours with Turton winning the Reserve Division One Championship and Burnley United winning the Reserve Division's Houston Cup by beating Poulton Town 2-1.

The loss of Haslinden to the CNWCL, and the resignations of Blackpool Rangers and BAE Warton, was more than compensated for by the return of Lancashire Constabulary and the addition of Charnock Richard and Fulwood Amateurs. The Police won Division Two ahead of Fulwood, whilst Charnock Richard finished in a very creditable 4th place so narrowly missing promotion at their first attempt. Blackrod Town, who had been among the leaders all season, finally won promotion, after many previous seasons of disappointments, by finishing in third place.

Leyland Motors Athletic won the First Division's Richardson Cup by beating Colne British Legion 1-0 in a good sporting encounter, whilst Blackrod Town were taken to extra-time by Padiham before winning the President's Cup 2-1. Leyland had the honour of representing the County in the Northern Counties competition, and were also selected to represent the League in the Sportslines Inter-League Challenge Cup. The club were a credit to the County and the League on both occasions.

The move to change the format of the reserve division from two geographical zones to Divisions One and Two with promotion and relegation, proved to be a success despite the extra travel for some clubs. Although the Reserve Division is restricted to member clubs, an increase in the number of teams is anticipated. Blackpool (Wren) Rovers won both the Fair Play Trophy and the award for Hospitality and goodwill, to establish an impressive record for this popular founder member club

The League provided both finalists for the third consecutive year for the prestigious Lancashire Challenge Shield when the Lancashire Constabulary completed a successful return to the league by beating Wigan College 1-0. No less than 12 clubs have represented the League in this competition in the past 9 seasons.

Derrick Procter, Chairman.

DIV. ONE	P	W	D	L	F	A	PTS
Burnley Utd	34	21	6	7	81	37	69
Turton	34	20	9	5	73	32	69
Eagley	34	20	8	6	79	45	*65
Wigan College	34	18	4	12	78	53	*55
Dalton United	34	14	10	10	58	46	52
Vickers SC	34	15	6	13	65	58	51
BAC Preston	34	14	7	13	68	63	49
Feniscowles	34	15	4	15	57	61	49
Poulton Town	34	13	9	12	62	49	48
Freckleton	34	14	6	14	59	56	48
Leyland Mtrs Ath.	34	12	11	11	65	45	47
Springfields	34	13	7	14	55	53	46
Kirkham & Wesham	34	13	7	14	46	60	46
Vernon Carus	34	12	8	14	52	55	44
Colne Brit. Legion	34	12	8	14	52	57	44
Thornton I'national	34	10	7	17	53	69	37
Lytham St Annes	34	8	2	24	48	96	*23
Glaxo Ulverston	34	1	3	30	18	134	*0

Richardson Cup Winners: Leyland Motors Ath.
Richardson Cup R-up: Colne British Legion
Top Scorers: A D Lean (Freckleton) 30, P Derbyshire (Eagley) 26, I McDonough (Turton) 25.

DIV. TWO	P	W	D	L	F	A	PTS
Lancs Constab.	32	24	6	2	107	27	78
Fulwood Amateur	32	21	9	2	84	31	72
Blackrod Town	32	22	6	4	66	24	72
Charnock Richard	32	17	9	6	65	57	*57
Tempest United	32	16	2	14	67	66	50
Multipart	32	14	4	14	77	80	46
Barrow Wanderers	32	13	6	13	70	76	45
BAe Canberra	32	12	7	13	62	56	43
Wyre Villa	32	12	7	13	54	63	43
Lansil	32	12	6	14	53	51	42
Blackpool Rvrs Res.	32	10	10	12	57	65	40
Hesketh Bank	32	12	4	16	62	72	40
Fleetwood Hesketh	32	10	6	16	42	67	36
Padiham	32	9	5	18	45	80	32
Norcross & Warbreck	32	8	6	18	54	77	30
Wigan Rovers	32	1	14	17	32	73	17
Carnforth Rgrs	32	3	5	24	30	74	14

Presidents Cup Winners: Blackrod Town
Presidents Cup Runners-up: Padiham
Top Scorers: P Goodall (Lancs Constab.) 33, M Mahoney (Blackrod) 32, L Allan (Fulwood) & C Shorrock (Multipart) 30.

RES. DIV. ONE	P	W	D	L	F	A	PTS
Turton Res.	24	17	5	2	63	26	56
BAC Preston Res.	24	16	4	4	75	30	52
Burnley Utd Res.	24	15	2	7	71	36	47
Eagley Res	24	13	6	5	76	43	45
Kirkham & W. Res.	24	13	4	7	58	36	43
Fleetwood Hesk. 'A'	24	11	5	8	50	43	38
Feniscowles Res.	24	11	5	8	67	68	38
Wyre Villa Res.	24	10	1	13	52	67	31
Poulton T. Res.	24	9	3	12	41	65	30
Freckleton Res.	24	8	2	14	35	50	26
Norcross & W. Res.	24	6	4	14	46	75	*19
Lytham SA Res.	24	4	0	20	25	76	12
Vickers SC Res.	24	1	3	20	29	73	*3

Houston Cup Winners: Burnley Utd Reserves
Top Scorers: M O'Hara (Burnley U. Res.) 31, P Hutton (Wyre V. Res.) 25, K Briggs (F'cowles Res.) 20.

RES. DIV. TWO	P	W	D	L	F	A	PTS
Blackrod T. Res.	22	16	1	5	66	39	49
Lansil Res.	22	14	4	4	60	28	46
Thornton I. Res.	16	14	2	6	65	34	44
Springfields Res.	22	14	1	7	61	51	43
Fulwood A. 'A'	22	11	2	9	51	42	35
Vernon Carus Res.	22	11	1	10	49	42	34
Hesketh Bk Res.	22	9	4	9	41	45	31
Tempest Utd Res.	22	8	6	8	47	38	30
Padiham Res.	22	7	3	12	38	52	24
Multipart Res.	22	7	2	13	45	59	23
Fleetwood Hes. 'B'	22	4	3	15	24	68	15
Fulwood A. 'B'	22	1	3	18	22	71	6

* - 3 points deducted

Houston Cup Runners-up: Poulton Town Res.
Top Scorers: S Donagey (Lansil Res.) 21, A Connolly (Springfields Res.) 20.

JOHN SMITHS WEST LANCASHIRE LEAGUE DIVISION ONE RESULT CHART 1993-94

HOME TEAM	1	2	3	4	5	6	7	8	9	10	11	12	13	14	15	16	17	18
1. BAC Preston	*	1-5	2-0	1-1	1-1	3-1	2-3	7-0	5-1	1-0	6-1	1-0	3-0	2-1	1-3	1-5	3-3	2-1
2. Burnley United	4-2	*	2-0	4-0	3-0	4-0	3-0	4-0	1-1	2-0	4-0	1-0	0-0	6-0	1-1	1-1	3-1	0-3
3. Colne British Legion	1-0	1-0	*	0-4	1-4	5-0	3-1	7-0	2-2	0-0	2-0	2-0	3-1	1-1	1-3	2-1	0-0	2-2
4. Dalton United	0-0	1-0	5-2	*	3-1	1-2	1-1	3-2	0-2	2-1	2-1	3-3	3-3	3-3	1-0	3-0	3-1	0-1
5. Eagley	4-3	2-1	2-1	4-1	*	4-0	1-0	11-0	3-1	2-0	3-2	2-3	1-1	2-0	2-2	2-2	3-0	2-1
6. Feniscowles	3-2	4-2	2-0	2-1	1-1	*	1-0	2-0	3-4	1-3	5-0	2-2	3-0	4-0	1-1	1-0	0-4	1-3
7. Freckleton	2-5	4-0	1-0	2-1	2-2	4-1	*	6-2	0-0	2-2	3-1	1-0	3-1	0-1	1-4	1-2	3-2	1-0
8. Glaxo Ulverston	0-0	3-4	0-2	0-5	0-2	1-5	0-2	*	0-4	1-1	0-7	0-3	1-6	0-3	0-2	0-5	0-1	0-2
9. Kirkham & Wesham	2-1	2-3	1-1	2-1	0-1	2-2	1-0	2-0	*	0-3	4-2	2-1	0-2	2-0	1-2	2-3	1-1	2-1
10. Leyland Motors Athletic	5-1	1-2	6-1	0-0	1-1	2-1	3-3	3-2	3-0	*	4-1	2-2	0-1	4-2	1-2	1-1	2-2	7-2
11. Lytham St Annes	1-4	0-4	2-1	2-3	1-5	1-3	0-4	3-1	1-3	0-4	*	4-1	0-3	0-4	0-2	2-1	0-2	5-3
12. Poulton Town	5-0	4-1	2-1	3-2	0-0	1-2	2-0	4-1	2-0	1-1	0-4	*	1-1	1-1	0-0	2-2	2-0	1-3
13. Springfields	2-2	1-1	3-2	0-1	1-2	0-1	4-2	2-3	3-0	1-0	2-1	1-3	*	4-1	0-1	0-1	2-3	0-4
14. Thornton International	3-0	1-1	1-1	1-1	1-5	3-2	2-3	3-0	3-0	0-1	2-3	4-3	1-3	*	0-1	3-0	0-1	2-0
15. Turton	2-2	0-1	2-2	0-0	0-3	2-0	3-1	1-1	5-0	3-1	4-0	1-2	4-0	4-3	*	2-1	3-0	3-0
16. Vernon Carus	0-2	1-3	2-3	1-0	2-1	1-0	2-2	5-0	0-2	2-2	1-1	1-0	0-1	2-2	0-6	*	2-1	1-2
17. Vickers SC	1-2	2-6	1-2	0-2	1-0	2-1	3-1	7-0	5-0	2-1	2-2	2-0	1-5	4-1	3-3	2-0	*	2-3
18. Wigan College	2-0	0-4	4-0	1-1	9-0	2-0	1-0	10-0	0-0	1-0	4-0	1-8	1-1	5-0	2-1	2-4	2-3	*

DIV. TWO RESULTS	1	2	3	4	5	6	7	8	9	10	11	12	13	14	15	16	17
1. BAe Canberra	*	2-2	0-4	4-2	3-1	1-0	0-1	2-3	4-0	1-1	2-0	2-4	3-0	3-0	1-2	1-1	4-1
2. Barrow Wanderers	2-0	*	3-3	0-2	2-1	1-3	4-2	1-6	2-1	3-7	2-1	5-3	5-1	3-1	5-3	0-0	3-2
3. Blackpool Rovers Reserves	2-1	3-3	*	1-1	0-1	0-1	4-0	3-3	4-3	2-7	2-1	1-5	2-2	5-0	1-1	1-1	1-0
4. Blackrod Town	4-1	3-1	3-1	*	3-1	0-0	3-3	2-1	1-0	0-0	5-1	2-0	4-0	2-0	2-1	1-0	1-0
5. Carnforth Rangers	0-1	2-3	1-3	0-1	*	0-1	2-1	0-2	0-1	0-8	1-1	0-2	0-1	1-1	3-0	2-2	0-1
6. Charnock Richard	1-3	4-1	5-1	1-1	5-3	*	1-1	1-2	3-2	2-5	1-0	2-2	4-0	4-1	3-4	1-1	4-3
7. Fleetwood Hesketh	2-1	0-1	2-3	0-1	1-0	1-2	*	0-3	3-6	1-1	1-0	2-0	1-3	2-1	0-1	2-0	1-1
8. Fulwood Amateurs	1-1	3-1	3-2	3-1	3-1	2-2	5-0	*	5-2	1-0	0-1	4-1	1-1	3-0	3-2	2-2	1-0
9. Hesketh Bank	2-2	3-1	3-0	0-4	1-1	0-4	2-5	0-0	*	1-5	2-2	1-2	3-0	3-1	0-1	3-0	5-3
10. Lancashire Constabulary	3-1	5-3	0-0	0-0	3-0	4-0	6-0	1-1	4-1	*	4-0	3-0	3-1	6-0	2-0	1-0	6-0
11. Lansil	6-2	2-2	3-0	0-3	3-1	0-1	1-2	1-1	6-0	1-1	*	1-3	2-1	2-3	3-1	2-1	2-0
12. Multipart	2-2	6-4	4-2	0-5	5-1	0-1	5-2	0-8	1-4	3-2	1-3	*	6-3	4-0	3-0	2-2	3-5
13. Norcross & Warbreck	0-3	3-1	2-3	0-2	3-0	1-1	0-0	1-3	3-4	2-3	1-2	5-1	*	4-0	1-5	4-1	4-3
14. Padiham	3-2	3-3	2-2	0-4	3-1	0-0	4-0	0-2	0-3	0-7	3-2	3-2	2-1	*	4-1	6-0	0-2
15. Tempest United	3-2	1-4	2-0	2-0	6-2	2-3	2-4	1-3	2-0	0-1	3-2	3-2	5-3	2-1	*	3-1	2-3
16. Wigan Rovers	0-4	1-0	1-1	0-1	0-3	2-3	2-2	1-6	1-5	0-3	0-1	1-1	3-3	2-2	3-3	*	1-2
17. Wyre Villa	3-3	3-2	1-0	3-1	3-0	1-1	2-0	0-1	2-1	3-5	1-1	1-4	0-0	2-1	1-3	2-2	*

DIVISION ONE CLUBS 1994-95

BLACKROD TOWN

G: Blackrod Community Centre, Vicarage Rd, Blackrod (0204 692614) **Sec:** Mr D Almond (0942 818663).

BRITISH AIRCRAFT CORPORATION PRESTON

Ground: Riverside Spts Grnd, Sth Meadow Lane, Preston (0772 51009) **Sec:** Mr F Heaton (0772 724751).

BURNLEY UNITED

Ground Barden Lane Spts Grnd, Burnley. **Sec:** Mr R Greenwood (0282 34739).

COLNE BRITISH LEGION

Ground Holt House (top of Harrison Drive), Colne (0282 862335) **Sec:** Mr W Alexander (0282 866638).

DALTON UNITED

Ground Railway Meadow, Beckside Rd, Dalton-in-Furness (0229 62799) **Sec:** Mr D Lacey (0229 64202).

EAGLEY

Ground Eagley Sports Complex, Dunscar Bridge, Bolton (0204 54191) **Sec:** Mr M Hackin (0204 595863).

FENISCOWLES

Ground Livsey Branch Road, Feniscowles, Blackburn (0254 208210) **Sec:** Mr A Akeroyd (0254 706931).

Feniscowles FC. *Photo - John L Newton.*

FRECKLETON

G: Hodgson Mem. Grnd, Bush Lane, Freckleton, Nr Preston (0772 67139) Mrs L O'Reilly (0772 634773).

FULWOOD AMATEURS

Ground Close to M6 jct 32 on M6 and A6-M55 junction **Sec:** Mr A Wilson (0772 798256).

KIRKHAM & WESHAM

Ground Coronation Rd Recreation Ground, Kirkham **Sec:** Mr E Pickton (0772 686264).

LANCASHIRE CONSTABULARY

G: Police HQ, Saunders Lane, off A59 at Hutton, nr Preston **Sec:** Mr B Woodburn (0772 652867).

LEYLAND MOTORS ATHLETIC

Ground Thurston Road, Leyland, Lancs (0772 422400) **Sec:** Mr J Hickson (0772 431066)

POULTON TOWN

Ground Cottam Hall PF, Blackpool Old Rd, Poulton-le-Fylde **Sec:** Mr M Sponder (0253 890284).

SPRINGFIELDS

G: S.S.R.A. Spts Grnd, Dodney Drive, Lea, Preston (0772 726131) **Sec:** Mr T Threlfall (0772 718959).

TURTON

Ground Moorfield, Edgworth. **Sec:** Mr L Donlan (0204 593387).

VERNON CARUS

Ground Factory Lane, Penwortham (0772 744006) **Sec:** Mr T Beswick (0772 745007).

VICKERS SPORTS CLUB

Ground Hawcoat Lane, Barrow-in-Furness (0229 825296) **Sec:** Mrs M Else (0229 834766).

WIGAN COLLEGE

Ground Christopher Park, Standish (0942 41140) **Sec:** Mr G T Reid (0942 208147).

DIVISION TWO CLUBS 1994-95

BRITISH AEROSPACE CANBERRA

Ground British Aerospace Samlesbury **Sec:** Mr S P Halse (0254 777050).

BARROW WANDERERS

Ground Lesh Lane, off Abbey Rd, Barrow-in-F. (0229 825224) **Sec:** Mr M Poole (0229 839148).

BLACKPOOL (WREN) ROVERS RESERVES *(see page 648)*

CARNFORTH RANGERS

Ground Close to town centre **Sec:** Mr K Webster (0524 735322).

CHARNOCK RICHARD

G: Charter Lane, off Chorley Lane, Charnock Richard (0257 79948) **Sec:** Mr G S Randle (0772 747129).

FLEETWOOD HESKETH

Ground Fylde Road, Southport (0704 27968) **Sec:** Mr B Charnock (0704 895588).

GARSTANG

Ground: Wyre Spts Ground, Main Street, Garstang **Sec:** Mr M Gornall (0995 605678).

GLAXCO SPORTS CLUB

Ground: Glaxco SC, Nth Lonsdale Rd, Ulverston (0229 582300) **Sec:** Mr M F Simpson (0229 870142).

HESKETH BANK

Ground Hesketh Spts Field, Station Rd, Hesketh Bank **Sec:** Mr D Hand (0772 813247).

LANSIL

Ground Lansil Sports Ground, Caton Rd, Lancaster **Sec:** Mr M E Miller (0524 33962).

LYTHAM St ANNES

G: Lytham Cricket & Spts Club, Church Rd, Lytham St A. (0253 734137) Mr S Broomfield (0772 632392).

MULTIPART

Ground St Georges Park, Duke Street, Chorley (0257 270103) **Sec:** Mr D Jolly (0257 270518).

NORCROSS & WARBRECK

Grnd: Anchorsholme Lane, Thornton Cleveleys, nr Blackpool **Sec:** Mr B Roberts (0253 825179).

PADIHAM

Ground: The Arbouries, Holland Street, Padiham (0282 773742) **Secretary:** Mr C D Barker (0282 452395).

TEMPEST UNITED

Ground: Tempest Rd, Chow Moor Village, Lostock (0942 811938) **Sec:** Mrs L Laird (0942 812772).

THORNTON INTERNATIONAL

Prev. Name: ICI Thornton **G:** Gamble Road, Thornton Cleveleys **Sec:** Mr J F Wright (0253 868430).

WEST END

Ground: Fishwick Bottoms, off London Rd, Preston (0772 715907) **Sec:** Mr S Robinson (0772 715907).

WYRE HILL

Ground: Stalmine Village, nr Knott End (0253 701468) **Secretary:** Mr G Bradley (0253 810637).

LANCASHIRE AMATEUR LEAGUE (Est. 1899)

PREM. DIV.	P	W	D	L	F	A	PTS
Leigh Athletic	26	19	2	5	93	35	40
Rochdale St Clem.	26	17	4	5	67	29	38
Burnley Belvedere	26	16	5	5	65	40	37
Royton Town	26	15	4	7	76	46	34
Bolton Wyresdale	26	16	2	8	70	44	34
Hesketh Casuals	26	12	5	9	68	48	29
Burnley GSOB	26	10	6	10	51	48	26
Walshaw SC	26	11	4	11	52	52	26
Rivington	26	9	6	11	44	61	24
Tarleton Corinthians	26	8	4	14	44	54	20
Old Gregorians	26	6	7	13	43	62	19
Broughton Amateurs	26	4	7	15	33	81	15
Old Blackburnians	26	4	5	17	30	85	13
Old Mostonians	26	3	3	20	42	93	9

DIV. ONE	P	W	D	L	F	A	PTS
Chaddertonians	26	17	5	4	90	41	39
Thornleigh	26	19	1	6	74	35	39
Rossendale Amtrs	26	17	5	4	68	30	39
Old Boltonians	26	15	5	6	79	38	35
Lymm HSA	26	12	4	10	54	51	28
Old Chorltonians	26	11	5	10	70	74	27
Old Smithillians	26	12	2	12	54	52	26
Old Sladians	26	9	6	11	56	55	24
Newman College	26	7	8	11	46	60	22
Southport Amateurs	26	8	6	12	48	62	22
Ashtonians	26	8	5	13	60	71	21
Preston GSA	26	5	6	15	34	60	16
Ainsdale United	26	4	7	15	49	95	15
Bury Amateurs	26	4	3	19	44	102	11

DIV. TWO	P	W	D	L	F	A	PTS
Hathershaw	26	21	4	1	93	34	46
Accrington Amtrs	26	18	3	5	74	31	39
Burnage GSOB	26	13	8	5	61	46	34
Nth Manchester	26	12	7	7	69	57	31
Bolton County	26	10	8	8	51	42	28
Old Mancunians	26	9	9	8	63	51	27
Oldham Hulmeians	26	10	6	10	68	61	26
Bury GSOB	26	11	4	11	61	55	26
Radcliffe Amtrs	26	10	5	11	50	52	25
Hayward	26	9	4	13	43	56	22
Little Lever SC	26	6	6	14	59	86	18
Roch Valley	26	7	2	17	55	74	16
Spotland Methodists	26	4	6	16	47	91	14
Old Salfordians	26	3	6	17	26	84	12

PREM. RESERVES	P	W	D	L	F	A	PTS
Rochdale St Clem.	26	20	3	3	85	23	43
Leigh Athletic	26	18	6	2	61	26	42
Old Gregorians	25	13	6	6	83	45	32
Old Boltonians	26	14	4	8	61	50	32
Hesketh Casuals	26	14	3	9	62	49	31
Rivington	26	11	7	8	63	52	29
Ashtonians	26	10	8	8	68	54	28
Ainsdale United	26	9	6	11	51	72	24
Rossendale Amtrs	26	8	6	12	53	51	22
Burnley Belvedere	26	7	7	12	53	60	21
Old Blackburnians	26	6	7	13	47	68	19
Burnley GSOB	26	5	6	15	47	72	16
Old Mostonians	26	5	4	17	35	84	14
Bury Amateurs	26	3	4	19	25	88	10

RES. DIV. ONE	P	W	D	L	F	A	PTS
Old Smithillians	26	18	3	5	74	41	39
Walshaw SC	26	17	4	5	75	41	38
Royton Town	26	16	4	6	69	31	36
Tarleton Corinthians	26	12	7	7	46	34	31
Bolton Wyresdale	26	11	5	10	56	52	27
Lymm HSA	26	10	6	10	68	66	26
Southport Amateurs	26	11	4	11	51	49	26
Bolton County	26	9	7	10	66	68	25
Newman College	26	10	3	13	55	54	23
Roch Valley	26	11	1	14	60	80	23
Broughton Amtrs	26	9	3	14	56	72	21
Preston GSA	26	5	10	11	52	73	20
Little Lever SC	26	8	2	16	46	69	18
Oldham Hulmeians	26	5	1	20	36	80	11

RES. DIV. TWO	P	W	D	L	F	A	PTS
Thornleigh	26	18	3	5	71	32	39
Old Sladians	26	16	6	4	71	34	38
Bury GSOB	26	16	2	8	72	46	34
Accrington Amtrs	26	14	6	6	66	41	34
Old Mancunians	26	12	8	6	67	41	32
Hayward	26	13	6	7	59	55	32
Hathershaw	26	13	5	8	72	50	31
Chaddertonians	26	12	3	11	74	60	27
Old Chorltonians	26	10	4	12	65	63	24
Radcliffe Amateurs	26	9	3	14	61	80	21
Burnage HSOB	26	7	7	12	50	71	21
North Manchester	26	5	4	17	48	79	14
Old Salfordians	26	5	1	20	41	106	11
Spotland Methodists	26	2	2	22	36	95	6

(continued)

DIV. 3A	P	W	D	L	F	A	PTS
Rochdale St C. 'A'	26	21	2	3	97	31	44
Old Blackburn. 'A'	26	16	6	4	58	35	38
O Gregorians 'A'	26	14	5	7	63	38	33
Burnley Bel. 'A'	26	12	5	9	65	52	29
O Gregorians 'B'	26	11	6	9	58	54	28
Old Sladians 'A'	26	10	6	10	53	65	26
Hesketh Cas. 'A'	26	9	7	10	40	40	25
O Smithill. 'A'	26	12	1	13	50	52	25
Ashtonians 'A'	26	10	2	14	70	68	22
Burnage HSOB 'A'	26	9	4	13	36	67	22
Walshaw SC 'A'	26	8	5	13	45	61	21
Bolton Wyres. 'A'	26	8	4	14	43	59	20
Rossendale A. 'A'	26	6	7	13	51	80	19
Rivington 'A'	26	3	6	17	43	70	12

DIV. 3B	P	W	D	L	F	A	PTS
Chaddertonians 'A'	26	19	5	2	88	45	43
O Boltonians 'B'	26	16	4	6	69	47	36
L. Lever SC 'A'	26	17	1	8	86	50	35
Burnley GSOB 'A'	26	16	2	8	89	55	34
Lymm HSA 'A'	26	13	5	8	76	51	31
Leigh Ath. 'A'	26	13	5	8	70	46	31
Rochdale SC 'B'	26	12	7	7	64	59	31
O Boltonians 'A'	26	9	7	10	59	60	25
Southport A. 'A'	26	9	6	11	60	70	24
Newman Coll. 'A'	26	8	5	13	73	80	21
Oldham Hulm. 'A'	26	7	3	16	48	95	17
O Chorlton. 'A'	26	6	1	19	58	94	13
Burnage HSOB 'B'	26	4	4	18	34	84	12
Broughton A. 'A'	26	4	3	19	68	106	11

STH DIV. 4A	P	W	D	L	F	A	PTS
Radcliffe Am. 'A'	24	20	2	2	104	28	42
O Gregorians 'C'	24	16	3	5	71	38	35
Roch Valley 'A'	24	15	2	7	92	48	32
Walshaw SC 'B'	24	12	5	7	65	51	29
O Mancunians 'A'	24	11	4	9	53	56	26
O Mostonians 'A'	24	9	6	9	58	63	24
Lymm HSA 'B'	24	9	4	11	68	80	22
Bury GSOB 'A'	24	9	3	12	46	63	21
Hayward 'A'	24	7	6	11	51	65	20
O Gregorians 'D'	24	7	5	12	38	58	19
Ashtonians 'B'	24	5	6	13	48	74	16
Leigh Ath. 'B'	24	5	4	15	42	77	14
Bolton County 'A'	24	4	4	16	38	73	12

STH DIV. 4B	P	W	D	L	F	A	PTS
Radcliffe Am. 'B'	22	16	3	3	74	41	35
Oldham Hulm. 'B'	22	15	1	6	75	55	31
O Chorlton. 'B'	22	11	4	7	67	40	26
Chaddertonians 'B'	22	11	4	7	63	42	26
Burnage HSOB 'C'	22	11	3	8	44	45	25
Roch Valley 'B'	22	10	4	8	58	65	24
Lymm HSA 'C'	22	7	6	9	47	55	20
Bury GSOB 'B'	22	6	6	10	46	53	18
Roch Valley 'C'	22	7	3	12	56	67	17
O Salfordians 'A'	22	8	1	13	61	66	17
O Chorltonians 'C'	22	7	1	14	37	59	15
Oldham Hulm. 'C'	22	4	2	16	42	72	10

NTH DIV. 4A	P	W	D	L	F	A	PTS
Preston GSA 'A'	22	16	3	3	78	39	35
Old Sladians 'B'	22	14	3	5	69	33	31
Burnley Bel. 'B'	22	12	6	4	69	34	30
Newman Coll. 'B'	22	11	6	5	70	44	28
Rossendale A. 'B'	22	10	6	6	63	53	26
O Blackburn. 'B'	22	7	6	9	48	48	20
Hesketh Cas. 'B'	22	7	5	10	45	58	19
Burnley GSOB 'B'	22	6	6	10	51	60	18
Broughton Am. 'B'	22	5	7	10	47	65	17
Preston GSA 'B'	22	7	3	12	50	71	17
Rivington 'B'	22	6	5	11	40	62	17
Burnley Bel. 'C'	22	2	2	18	34	97	6

NTH DIV. 4B	P	W	D	L	F	A	PTS
Accrington Am. 'B'	18	13	2	3	59	25	28
Thornleigh 'A'	18	12	4	2	64	31	28
Accrington Am. 'A'	18	10	4	4	59	27	24
L. Lever SC 'B'	18	10	3	5	70	55	23
Burnley GSOB 'C'	18	10	2	6	64	48	22
Tarleton C. 'A'	18	7	3	8	53	66	17
Thornleigh 'B'	18	7	2	9	44	46	10
Southport Am. 'B'	18	4	2	12	42	84	10
Newman Coll. 'C'	18	2	3	13	49	77	7
Burnley GSOB 'D'	18	2	1	15	29	74	5

EAST LANCASHIRE LEAGUE

President: Mr H Waddington.
Chairman: Mr R A Little.
Vice-Chairman: Mr K Dean.
Secretary: Mr J Constable,
66 Dukes Meadow, Ingol, Preston PR2 7AT (0772 727135).

DIV. ONE	P	W	D	L	F	A	PTS
Mill Hill St P.	28	22	4	2	85	22	48
Worsthorne	28	17	3	8	69	36	37
Sabden	28	15	5	8	66	48	35
Barnoldswick Utd	28	16	3	9	62	46	35
Foxhill	28	16	3	9	65	51	**33
Gt Harwood Utd	28	11	10	7	50	43	32
Clitheroe Res.	28	13	5	10	67	46	31
Colne United	28	14	2	12	58	47	30
Johnsons SC	28	9	9	10	55	58	27
Whalley	28	11	4	13	52	71	*26
Helmshore United	28	7	8	13	47	60	22
Ribchester	28	6	5	17	52	72	17
Rimington	28	7	3	18	51	78	17
Trawden Celtic	28	7	3	18	45	91	17
Rock Rovers	28	2	7	19	39	92	*10

* - 1 point deducted

Top Scorers:
Div 1: S Smith (Whalley)
Div 2: R Renshaw (Oswaldtwistle Town)

DIV. TWO	P	W	D	L	F	A	PTS
Crosshills	18	14	3	1	75	19	31
Settle United	18	13	3	2	54	17	29
Oswaldtwistle T.	18	13	1	4	58	24	27
Stacksteads St J.	18	11	3	4	51	35	25
Read United	18	11	1	6	44	35	23
Whinney Hill	18	6	0	12	44	48	12
Colne Legion Res.	18	4	3	11	29	64	11
Nelson Res.	18	4	1	12	24	60	9
Nelson GSOB	18	3	2	13	32	68	8
Pendle Forest	18	1	3	14	18	50	5

RESERVE DIV.	P	W	D	L	F	A	PTS
Barnoldswick Res.	16	14	0	2	62	18	28
Mill Hill SP Res.	16	11	2	3	66	20	24
Sabden Res.	16	7	3	6	49	35	17
Rock Rovers Res.	16	7	3	6	39	44	17
Helmshore U. Res.	16	7	2	7	43	36	16
Whalley Res.	16	6	3	7	43	37	15
Colne Utd Res.	16	4	6	6	27	34	14
Worsthorne Res.	16	5	3	8	31	40	13
Trawden C. Res.	16	0	0	16	13	110	0

DIVISION ONE RESULT CHART 1993-94

HOME TEAM	1	2	3	4	5	6	7	8	9	10	11	12	13	14	15
1. Barnoldswick United	*	0-4	2-2	3-2	0-0	3-0	2-3	0-1	4-2	3-4	5-4	5-3	3-0	0-1	0-3
2. Clitheroe Reserves	1-3	*	1-0	4-2	3-0	0-0	4-1	1-1	1-1	4-1	5-0	1-2	8-1	3-0	1-4
3. Colne United	1-4	3-2	*	0-1	1-5	2-4	3-1	0-1	1-1	3-0	6-2	0-2	4-1	3-0	1-2
4. Foxhill	1-4	3-2	2-0	*	2-0	3-2	4-3	2-2	7-5	3-1	6-0	0-2	3-0	2-1	2-1
5. Great Harwood United	1-2	1-0	2-1	2-2	*	2-2	2-2	1-4	3-0	1-1	1-1	1-1	8-2	1-1	1-2
6. Helmshore United	0-2	1-1	0-2	4-3	1-2	*	0-2	0-3	2-0	2-1	3-3	3-3	1-2	2-3	1-3
7. Johnsons SC	0-2	4-4	2-3	1-3	4-4	2-2	*	0-3	1-1	2-1	3-1	0-0	5-0	5-2	1-3
8. Mill Hill St Peters	4-2	3-0	1-0	4-1	0-1	4-0	3-0	*	5-1	4-1	2-2	1-0	8-1	4-1	0-4
9. Ribchester	0-3	6-3	1-3	2-1	0-1	2-2	2-3	0-3	*	2-1	4-1	2-2	5-3	2-3	2-3
10. Rimington	0-2	3-2	1-3	0-3	5-1	1-4	2-3	0-3	4-3	*	2-2	4-2	4-4	2-3	0-6
11. Rock Rovers	2-3	0-2	1-8	1-1	1-4	1-1	1-3	0-4	3-1	1-2	*	1-1	0-4	2-1	0-1
12. Sabden	0-2	1-3	3-0	4-1	1-2	3-0	2-0	1-7	1-0	5-4	10-6	*	3-0	6-3	0-1
13. Trawden Celtic	0-0	4-3	1-2	0-2	0-2	1-3	0-0	1-4	4-3	4-1	3-0	0-4	*	6-0	1-2
14. Whalley	4-1	1-3	1-2	2-3	1-1	4-3	2-2	2-6	1-0	2-1	4-3	1-2	3-2	*	2-1
15. Worsthorne United	3-2	0-1	3-4	1-0	3-0	2-4	2-2	0-0	3-4	1-4	2-0	0-2	10-0	3-3	*

DIV. TWO RESULTS	1	2	3	4	5	6	7	8	9	10
1. Colne RBL Reserves	*	2-2	1-3	2-2	0-4	2-2	3-2	1-7	1-5	1-4
2. Crosshills	7-1	*	2-1	6-1	1-2	7-1	4-0	2-2	3-1	5-3
3. Nelson Reserves	0-1	1-4	*	2-6	0-4	0-0	0-5	2-6	2-4	2-1
4. Nelson Grammar Sch. OB	2-4	0-7	1-3	*	2-7	1-4	0-3	1-4	1-1	1-2
5. Oswaldtwistle Town	7-0	1-5	4-1	3-1	*	6-0	2-3	0-1	4-0	3-2
6. Pendle Forest	1-5	1-4	0-1	1-4	1-2	*	0-6	0-4	1-3	0-5
7. Read United	4-2	0-4	3-1	4-2	1-4	2-0	*	0-2	5-3	2-1
8. Settle United	4-0	1-1	7-1	4-1	2-0	2-1	0-0	*	0-2	3-1
9. Stacksteads St Josephs	2-0	1-4	7-3	9-3	3-3	1-1	3-1	2-1	*	2-1
10. Whinney Hill	7-3	0-7	4-1	2-3	1-2	5-4	2-3	2-4	1-2	*

RESERVE DIV. RESULTS	1	2	3	4	5	6	7	8	9	
1. Barnoldswick Utd Reserves	*	9-2	2-3	2-1	4-0	5-1	6-0	2-1	4-0	
2. Colne United Reserves	0-2	*	1-1	1-1	0-4	1-1	4-0	1-2	0-2	
3. Helmshore United Reserves	1-2	5-3	*	1-2	2-0	0-6	11-1	1-2	4-1	
4. Mill Hill St Peters Res.	1-4	2-4	0-0	*	3-1	4-1	19-0	4-0	5-1	
5. Rock Rovers Reserves	1-9	2-2	5-3	2-4	*	3-1	5-3	1-1	6-3	
6. Sabden Reserves	0-5	0-0	5-0	0-7	5-2	*	12-0	2-2	1-3	
7. Trawden Celtic Reserves	0-4	1-3	2-4	2-8	0-1	0-6	*	1-7	0-4	
8. Whalley Reserves	6-0	1-4	3-2	1-4	2-5	1-3	10-2	*	2-2	
9. Worsthorne United Reserves	1-2	1-1	1-5	0-1	1-1	2-5	6-1	3-2	*	3-1

B.E.P. CUP 1993-94

First Round
Nelson Reserves v Whinney Hill 2-1
Settle United v Read United 2-2,4-0

Quarter-Finals
Settle United v Crosshills 0-1
Nelson GSOB v Oswaldtwistle Town 2-6
Nelson Reserves v Colne Legion Reserves 2-1
Stacksteads St Josephs v Pendle Forest 5-0

Semi-Finals
Crosshills v Nelson Reserves 3-1
Stacksteads St Josephs v Oswaldtwistle Town 6-1

Final: Stacksteads St Josephs 1, Crosshills 0

PRESIDENTS CUP 1993-94

First Round

Oswaldtwistle Town v Whinney Hill 1-0*(aet)*
Read United v Great Harwood United 0-3
Rimington v Crosshills 2-3*(aet)*
Clitheroe Reserves v Nelson Reserves 14-0
Settle Utd v Colne Utd 3-3*(Settle withdrew)*
Rock Rovers v Pendle Forest 6-0
Stacksteads St Josephs v Sabden 3-2
Johnsons SC v Nelson GS Old Boys 1-0
Ribchester v Cole RBL Reserves 9-1

Second Round

Barnoldswick United v Whalley 1-4
Helmshore United v Foxhill 1-3
Clitheroe Reserves v Stacksteads St J. 4-1
Worsthorne United v Great Harwood United 6-0
Ribchester v Rock Rovers 1-0
Colne Utd v Trawden C. 1-1*(Colne withdrew)*
Johnsons SC v Mill Hill St Peters 0-2
Crosshills v Oswaldtwistle Town 2-1

Quarter Finals

Foxhill v Worsthorne United 2-4
Ribchester v Mill Hill St Peters 1-2
Whalley v Clitheroe Reserves 2-3
Crosshills v Trawden Celtic 2-1

Semi-Finals

Crosshills v Mill Hill St Peters 2-1
Worsthorne Utd v Clitheroe Reserves 3-3,0-3

Final: Clitheroe Reserves 1, Crosshills 0

NORMAN SUPPLEMENTARY CUP 1993-94

GROUP 1.	P	W	D	L	F	A	PTS
Settle United	12	5	0	1			10
Worsthorne U. Res.	6	5	0	1			10
Pendle Forest	6	2	0	4			4
Trawden Celtic	6	0	0	6			0

GROUP 2.	P	W	D	L	F	A	PTS
Barnoldswick Res.	6	5	1	0			11
Nelson GSOB	8	4	1	3			9
Sabden Reserves	7	3	2	3			8
Whinney Hill	8	2	1	5			5
Read United	7	0	3	4			3

GROUP 3.	P	W	D	L	F	A	PTS
Oswaldtwistle T.	7	7	0	0			14
MH3P Reserves	8	4	2	2			10
Helmshore Utd Res.	8	3	3	2			9
Colne Legion Res.	8	2	1	5			5
Rock Rovers Res.	7	0	0	7			0

GROUP 4.	P	W	D	L	F	A	PTS
Crosshills	8	6	0	2			12
Stacksteads St J.	8	6	0	2			12
Whalley Reserves	6	2	0	4			4
Nelson Reserves	5	2	0	3			4
Colne Utd Reserves	7	1	0	6			2

Semi-Finals

Oswaldtwistle Town v Settle United 3-1
Barnoldswick Utd Reserves v Crosshills 2-1*(aet)*

Final: Oswaldtwistle Town 4, Barnoldswick United Reserves 1

RESERVES CUP 1993-94

First Round

Barnoldswick Utd Res. v Colne Utd Res. 6-1

Quarter-Finals

Helmshore United Res. v Sabden Reserves 2-1
Rock Rovers Reserves v Whalley Reserves 1-4
Barnoldswick Utd Res. v Mill Hill SP Res. 1-1,0-1
Worsthorne Utd Reserves v Trawden Celtic Res. 1-0

Semi-Finals

Whalley Reserves v Helmshore Utd Reserves 2-4
Mill Hill St Peters Res. v Worsthorne Utd Res.1-3*(aet)*

Final: Helmshore United Reserves 4, Worsthorne United Reserves 2

CLUB DIRECTORY

BARNOLDSWICK UNITED

Secretary: Mr D Bowditch, 10 Roundell Rd, Barnoldswick, Lancs BB8 6EB (0282 817278).
Ground: West Close, Victory Park, Barnoldswick.
Colours: All blue **Reserves colours:** Red & white.

CLITHEROE RESERVES *(see page 651)*

COLNE BRITISH LEGION RESERVES

Secretary: Mr W Alexander, 101 Keighley Rd, Colne, Lancs BB8 0QG (0282 866638).
Ground: Holt House, Colne *(former Colne Dynamoes ground)* (0282 862335. British Legion club: 863313).
Colours: All yellow. **Change Colours:** Blue & white/blue/blue.

COLNE UNITED

Secretary: Mr S Bannister, 13 Duke Str., Winewall, Colne, Lancs BB8 8AD (0282 871617).
Ground: Sough Park, Kelbrook, Earby, Colne.
Colours: All blue **Change colours:** Red & white/blue/blue

CROSSHILLS

Secretary: Mr A Knox, 33 Ash Grove, Sutton-in-Craven, Keighley, West Yorks (0535 632088).
Ground: Sutton Fields, Sutton-in-Craven, Keighley, West Yorkshire.
Colours: All red **Change colours:** Blue/black/red.

FOXHILL

Secretary: Mr A Dempsey, Heron Way, Oswaldtwistle, Accrington BB5 3AP (0254 394675).
Ground: Heys Playing Field, Heron Way, Oswaldtwistle, Accrington.
Colours: Green & yellow **Change colours:** All blue.

GREAT HARWOOD UNITED

Secretary: Mr W Holden, 21 Delph Mount, Great Harwood, Lancs BB6 7QF (0254 884758).
Ground: Lyndon House, Great Harwood.
Colours: Red & black/black/black **Change colours:** Blue/black.

HELMSHORE UNITED

Secretary: Mr I Walkden, 13 Piccadilly Str., Haslingden, Rossendale BB4 5LU (0706 226753).
Ground: Marl Pitts, Newchurch Rd, Rawtenstall.
Colours: Red & blue/red/red. **Change colours:** Blue & white/blue.

JOHNSONS S.C.

Secretary: Mr C Hayhurst, 182 New Line, Bacup, Lancs OL13 9RU (0706 878323).
Ground: Bacup Borough F.C. (see Bass North West Counties League section).
Colours: All blue **Change colours:** Grey/black/blue.

MILL HILL St PETERS

Secretary: Mr P Walsh, 187 St Aidans Avenue, Blackburn BB2 4EA (0254 260424).
Ground: Mill Hill, Blackburn.
Colours: All green **Change colours:** Claret & blue/maroon/blue.

NELSON RESERVES *(see page 660)*

NELSON GRAMMAR SCHOOL OLD BOYS

Secretary: Mr J Crabtree, 46 Borrowdale Rd, Reedley, Burnley BB10 2SG (0282 692211).
Ground: Surrey Rd, Nelson **Colours:** Red/black **Change:** Silver/black.

OSWALDTWISTLE TOWN

Ground: Mount Carmel School, Willows Lane, Accrington.
Secretary: T.B.A. **Colours:** All blue **Change colours:** All yellow.

PENDLE FOREST

Secretary: Mr L Townsend, 5 Rake Top Ave., Higham, Burnley BB12 9BB (0282 73904).
Ground: Old Laund Booth, Fence (off Padiham-Nelson by-pass).
Colours: All blue **Change colours:** All green.

READ UNITED

Secretary: Mr D Hacking, 39 Whalley Rd, Read. **Ground:** Rear of Read Cricket Club, Whalley Rd, Read.
Colours: Yellow/green/black **Change colours:** Green/black.

RIBCHESTER

Secretary: Mr A Walmsley, 47 Mardale Rd, Longridge, Preston, Lancs PR3 3EU (0772 784362).
Ground: Ribchester Playing Field (opposite car park).
Colours: Yellow/black **Change colours:** All blue.

RIMINGTON

Secretary: Mr L Whittaker, 2 Dorset Drive, Clitheroe, Lancs BB7 2BQ (0200 29112).
Ground: Coulthurst Memorial Field, Back Lane, Rimington (behind Black Bull).
Colours: Tangerine/black **Change colours:** Yellow/black.

ROCK ROVERS

Secretary: Mr R Davies, 2 Lancaster Str., Colne, Lancs BB8 9AZ (0282 864203).
Ground: As Colne R.B.L. (above). **Colours:** Blue/blue/yellow **Change:** All red.

SABDEN

Secretary: Mr T Bromley, 89 Whalley Rd, Sabden, Blackburn BB6 9EA (0282 76554).
Ground: Nutter Barn Field, Sabden, Blackburn.
Colours: Red & blue/blue/blue **Change colours:** Red & black/black/red.

TRAWDEN CELTIC

Secretary: Mr M Timberlake, 191 Cotton Tree Lane, Colne, Lancs BB8 7BN (0282 868143).
Ground: Trawden Recreation Ground, Rock Lane, Trawden.
Colours: Black & white/black/red **Change colours:** Red & blue/blue/blue.

WHALLEY

Secretary: Mrs A Bury, 59 Lord Str., Oswaldtwistle, Accrington, Lancs BB5 3EF (0254 235443).
Ground: Queen Elizabeth Playing Field, Mitton Rd, Whalley.
Change colours: Red & white/white/red. **Colours:** Blue & white/white/red

WORSTHORNE UNITED

Secretary: Mr K Stopforth, 43 Heckenhurst Ave., Worsthorne, Burnley BB10 1JN (0282 29092).
Ground: Worsthorne, Lennox Rd.
Colours: Yellow & green/green/yellow **Change colours:** Blue/black/black.

BLACKBURN SUNDAY LEAGUE

FOUNDED: 1970

DIV. ONE	P	W	D	L	F	A	PTS
Old Toll Bar	14	9	2	3	38	22	20
Darwen Sun Leisure	14	8	4	2	33	23	20
Gepal	14	8	2	4	32	20	18
Station	14	6	5	3	34	21	17
Foresters	14	6	3	5	22	19	*13
Arcade Bar	14	5	2	7	23	26	12
Jubilee	14	3	1	10	12	27	7
Cowies	14	1	1	12	14	50	3

* - 2 points deducted

N.b. Old Toll Bar won title after play-off

Lower Division Champions:
Div. 2 (11): Young Construction
Div. 3 (11): Tommy Balls

Blue & White Rosebowl Final:
Darwen Sun Leisure 3, Arcade Bar 1

HORWICH SUNDAY LEAGUE

PREM. DIV.	P	W	D	L	F	A	PTS
Pit Stop DIY	16	13	2	1	64	16	28
Albion	16	11	3	2	54	21	25
Schooner	16	10	1	5	45	35	21
Grey Mare	16	8	4	4	46	27	20
GAC Beaumont	16	7	2	7	41	38	16
White Horse Tavern	16	5	3	8	23	42	13
Arkwrights	16	4	4	8	33	51	12
Rose & Crown	16	2	1	13	26	57	5
Astley & Tyldesley	16	2	0	14	8	72	4

Bowling Green withdrew - record expunged

Lower Division Champions:
Div. 1 (9): Bay Mare **Div. 2** (11): Long Pull

BOLTON SPORTS FEDERATION OVER-35s VETERANS' LGE

	P	W	D	L	F	A	PTS
Breightmet United	14	12	1	1	71	14	25
Hayward AFC	14	9	2	3	40	18	20
Walkden Inter	14	8	2	4	37	21	18
Wyresdale	14	7	4	3	27	19	18
Walkden AFC	14	7	2	5	46	34	16
Horwich Town	14	4	1	9	19	47	9
Ainsworth Fossils	14	3	0	11	19	39	6
Wingate Wobblers	14	0	0	14	7	75	0

BOLTON & DISTRICT COMBINATION

FOUNDED: 1890

President: A Porter

Chairman: J R Stott JP

Treasurer: J Grundy

Hon. Secretary: Trevor Speak,
33 Brandwood Street, Bolton (0204 656932)

After many years in the Premier Division, Elton Fold, one of our oldest and most respected clubs, finally clinched their first championship. They were pushed all the way by former Accrington Combination champions, Whinney Hill who after three seasons in Bolton Combination are still looking for their first major trophy. Elton Fold's triumph follows on the heels of last season's Premier Division Challenge Cup victory and, with their current squad of players, they will again be the team to beat in 1994-95.

The first division campaign went all the way down to the wire, with the championship eventually being decided on the final evening of the league season. Tonge Ward clinched their second Division One championship after a 3-1 victory at Ainsworth. All credit to Bolton Wyresdale who kept plugging away in case of a slip up by Tonge Ward; they were hoping to better last season's second division championship, but in the end they failed by just two points.

The team of the season were Ambassadors FC who, after just four seasons in the league, have finally adjusted to the transition from Sunday to Saturday football. After chasing their rivals Antelope FC for much of the season they finally overhauled them in the final month, after accumulating a backlog of fixtures. This was mainly due to their success in lifting the national Church of England Challenge Cup where they beat Kings FC at the ground of St Albans City. They lifted their third trophy after they completed the league and cup double, and were further rewarded when they were presented with the league's Dobson Trophy which is awarded to the club who achieve an exemplary disciplinary and administration record.

The Bolton Combination set out into new and untried territory last season, when they formed a new division specifically for the reserve teams of clubs who compete in the GM Vauxhall Conference, the Northern Premier League and the Carling North West Counties League. The division commenced with a membership of 13 clubs all, with the exception of Lancaster City, within a 25 mile radius of Bolton. I am happy to report that the new venture was a complete success with all the clubs involved, who have given their support for the division. Flixton lifted the inaugural championship, after they chased and finally overtook long-time leaders Bamber Bridge, and the reports from the competing clubs have been glowing, both in their praise of the administration of the Division by Bolton Combination, but also to the match officials, who found the games a joy to officiate. The Division has enabled the clubs to view and try out new players, and to help bring existing first team players back to match fitness after injury. Due to the inevitable changes of policy that occur within clubs from time to time, there are a couple of clubs who will not be running reserve teams next season. However, we have gained three new members for this division next season, these being Accrington Stanley, Glossop North End and Netherfield FC, and I am sure the venture will continue to go from strength to strength.

Trevor Speak, Secretary

PREM. DIV.	P	W	D	L	F	A	PTS
Elton Fold	22	18	2	2	83	26	56
Whinney Hill	22	16	5	1	72	27	53
Stoneclough	22	15	2	5	62	39	47
VCS Walkers Leis.	22	12	3	7	65	41	39
Hindley Green	22	9	6	7	38	33	33
Walkden AFC	22	9	1	12	46	55	28
Bolton Lads COB	22	7	5	10	54	55	26
Little Lever	22	5	6	11	32	48	21
Farnworth CC	22	5	5	12	36	54	20
Sharples CC	22	6	1	15	33	65	19
Hindsford	22	5	3	14	33	76	18
Pallatech Villa	22	5	1	16	43	78	16

DIV. ONE	P	W	D	L	F	A	PTS
Tonge Ward	24	21	2	1	78	28	65
Bolton Wyresdale	24	21	0	3	99	39	63
British Aerospace	24	17	2	5	80	32	53
Ainsworth	24	16	2	6	77	35	50
Turton Res.	24	11	2	11	57	69	35
Hindley Gn Res.	24	10	3	11	52	54	33
Atherton C & N.	24	9	1	14	50	60	28
Bolton YMCA	24	7	6	11	45	66	27
Blackrod T. Res.	24	8	1	15	71	87	25
VCS Walkers Res.	24	6	5	13	49	76	23
Howe Bdge Mills	24	7	1	16	61	91	22
Silcoms Farnworth	24	5	2	17	44	92	17
Elton Fold Res.	24	3	3	18	44	77	12

DIV. TWO	P	W	D	L	F	A	PTS
Ambassadors	28	23	3	2	116	30	72
Antelope	28	21	1	6	141	44	64
Horwich Town	28	17	3	8	84	54	54
DF Aerospace	28	16	6	6	78	52	54
Tottington U. Res.	28	16	3	9	79	67	51
Stoneclough Res.	28	16	3	9	87	77	51
Walkden Res.	28	13	4	11	76	63	46
Adlington Athletic	28	13	3	12	74	69	42
Farnworth CC Res.	28	10	7	11	50	50	37
Church House	28	11	1	16	59	70	34
Hindsford Res.	28	10	4	14	51	68	34
Belmont	28	10	4	14	72	101	34
Ainsworth Res.	28	6	6	16	49	94	24
Watergate Toll	28	3	1	24	58	112	10
Howe Bdge M. Res.	28	0	3	25	20	134	3

N.W. ALLIANCE	P	W	D	L	F	A	PTS
Flixton Res.	22	17	3	2	53	20	54
Bamber Bridge Res.	22	14	5	3	54	19	47
Atherton LR Res.	22	12	2	8	46	30	38
Lancaster C. Res.	22	11	4	7	42	32	37
Cheadle Town Res.	22	8	9	5	41	36	33
Altrincham Res.	22	8	9	5	33	30	33
Southport Res.	22	7	7	8	36	31	28
Chorley Res.	22	7	7	8	35	33	28
Macclesfield Res.	22	7	5	10	35	40	26
Horwich RMI Res.	22	6	3	13	32	47	21
Northwich V. Res.	22	5	3	14	34	58	18
Westhoughton Res.	22	0	3	19	17	80	3

BOLTON COMBINATION RESULT GRIDS 1993-94

PREMIER DIV. RESULTS	1	2	3	4	5	6	7	8	9	10	11	12
1. Bolton Lads Club OB	*	2-3	3-1	2-1	5-0	2-2	3-1	2-4	5-6	1-1	3-2	3-5
2. Elton Fold	5-3	*	6-1	3-1	8-0	3-0	4-0	5-1	4-2	2-2	7-0	2-3
3. Farnworth CC	2-2	0-1	*	2-6	0-0	2-2	3-1	3-1	2-4	1-3	3-1	1-4
4. Hindley Green	2-0	1-3	0-0	*	2-3	1-1	3-2	4-2	1-3	1-0	0-1	0-0
5. Hindsford	5-2	0-2	5-3	2-2	*	2-7	4-2	3-4	0-3	3-5	0-3	2-4
6. Little Lever	2-2	1-6	3-1	0-2	2-2	*	2-3	1-2	0-4	0-1	3-1	2-2
7. Pallatech Villa	2-6	1-5	2-4	1-2	2-1	2-1	*	2-3	1-3	6-5	3-2	0-4
8. Sharples CC	2-1	1-2	1-5	1-2	0-1	0-1	4-4	*	1-4	0-8	0-3	2-4
9. Stoneclough	3-2	0-0	4-1	2-1	2-0	3-1	3-2	1-0	*	2-3	7-4	2-3
10. VCS Walkers Leisure	4-2	2-1	2-0	2-2	9-0	0-1	5-2	2-3	3-1	*	3-1	2-3
11. Walkden	1-2	3-8	1-1	2-3	5-0	2-0	3-1	2-1	4-2	4-2	*	1-3
12. Whinney Hill	1-1	2-3	2-0	1-1	4-0	5-0	8-3	5-0	1-1	5-1	3-0	*

DIV. ONE RESULTS	1	2	3	4	5	6	7	8	9	10	11	12	13
1. Ainsworth	*	6-0	2-0	1-2	6-1	2-0	2-1	0-0	4-1	0-3	1-3	4-2	2-4
2. Atherton C & N.	0-1	*	5-4	1-4	0-2	1-2	4-0	4-3	5-1	4-1	2-5	2-3	4-1
3. Blackrod Town Res.	2-7	2-1	*	1-3	3-3	2-4	4-7	4-2	3-8	6-2	3-5	6-3	6-3
4. Bolton Wyresdale	5-1	1-0	6-0	*	5-2	4-5	7-2	4-2	2-1	7-1	5-2	6-2	3-2
5. Bolton YMCA	0-2	2-2	6-3	0-5	*		2-1	1-3	3-2	3-4	0-3	0-3	2-2
6. British Aerospace	1-2	4-2	3-0	5-1	2-0	*	3-2	4-1	8-0	3-0	1-2	0-1	6-1
7. Elton Fold Reserves	1-2	1-3	3-2	1-5	4-4	0-5	*	2-3	4-6	3-0	0-4	3-4	3-5
8. Hindley Green Res.	2-1	3-1	3-1	0-3	2-2	1-6	0-0	*	6-1	4-2	0-2	2-3	3-0
9. Howe Bridge Mills	3-10	0-2	4-1	1-6	3-3	0-3	2-1	2-3	*	2-4	2-3	2-4	2-3
10. Silcoms Farnworth	1-11	1-3	1-10	1-4	4-5	3-3	3-2	4-1	3-4	*	0-2	1-2	0-1
11. Tonge Ward	2-2	3-0	3-2	4-2	2-0	1-0	2-0	3-1	9-1	6-2	*	3-1	3-0
12. Turton Reserves	0-3	3-1	1-3	2-4	2-3	3-3	3-1	0-4	0-11	4-0	2-5	*	8-1
13. VCS Walker Leis. Res.	1-5	7-3	2-3	2-5	0-1	3-6	2-2	4-3	1-2	2-2	1-1	1-1	*

DIV. TWO RESULTS	1	2	3	4	5	6	7	8	9	10	11	12	13	14	15
1. Adlington Athletic	*	4-2	0-4	0-1	4-1	2-0	1-1	3-1	2-0	0-1	5-1	2-6	0-2	4-4	4-1
2. Ainsworth	3-2	*	1-3	0-8	3-2	4-6	1-4	0-0	3-0	2-5	1-1	2-3	1-4	2-2	2-4
3. Ambassadors	5-3	7-1	*	7-0	4-1	5-2	2-1	4-1	6-1	4-3	5-0	12-2	1-0	1-5	5-0
4. Antelope	10-1	14-1	0-2	*	8-1	7-0	3-3	5-1	3-0	2-4	11-0	3-4	8-1	2-1	8-3
5. Belmont	3-1	0-0	1-1	0-4	*	7-4	1-1	6-3	6-2	1-1	11-1	0-4	5-3	5-3	4-2
6. Church House	1-3	2-1	2-1	0-3	6-1	*	1-3	2-4	0-2	3-4	4-0	5-3	3-1	0-0	4-0
7. DF Aerospace	3-0	3-1	1-4	0-3	7-5	2-1	*	3-1	7-1	2-4	4-2	5-1	2-1	3-1	3-1
8. Farnworth CC Reserves	5-4	1-1	0-0	3-2	3-0	2-1	1-1	*	1-1	4-1	6-1	0-0	1-2	0-2	2-0
9. Hindsford Reserves	3-3	0-3	0-3	0-2	4-1	4-1	4-2	1-0	*	4-0	4-0	0-2	2-2	2-2	2-1
10. Horwich Town	6-1	3-2	2-3	3-2	12-1	1-5	2-6	1-1	7-1	*	4-1	2-3	1-1	1-0	7-4
11. Howe Bdge Mills Res.	2-5	0-0	0-7	3-5	1-3	1-3	0-2	0-1	0-7	0-1	*	1-3	3-5	0-9	2-2
12. Stoneclough Reserves	1-7	3-6	0-0	2-5	4-1	3-2	1-1	2-5	2-0	0-2	12-0	*	4-1	7-5	4-2
13. Tottington Utd Res.	5-1	6-3	1-7	2-5	4-0	5-0	4-4	4-2	5-3	1-0	1-0	2-1	*	6-2	3-1
14. Walkden Reserves	3-2	5-1	1-4	1-4	5-0	1-0	3-1	2-0	3-1	1-2	2-0	1-4	5-4	*	4-1
15. Watergate Toll	0-7	1-2	1-9	1-9	2-4	1-3	2-3	0-2	1-2	0-5	11-0	5-6	2-3	6-3	*

N.W. ALLIANCE RESULTS	1	2	3	4	5	6	7	8	9	10	11	12
1. Altrincham Reserves	*	1-0	0-0	1-1	2-1	0-1	0-2	2-2	0-0	2-3	0-0	3-1
2. Atherton LR Reserves	0-1	*	1-1	7-1	1-0	3-1	3-2	2-1	1-2	7-2	2-1	7-0
3. Bamber Bdge Reserves	5-2	2-0	*	1-1	2-1	1-2	3-0	0-1	4-2	9-1	3-0	1-0
4. Cheadle Town Reserves	1-2	4-1	0-0	*	3-0	1-3	0-0	5-1	1-1	4-2	4-4	3-1
5. Chorley Reserves	1-1	3-1	0-2	2-2	*	0-1	1-2	1-1	5-0	2-1	1-1	3-1
6. Flixton Reserves	1-1	1-0	4-0	3-1	2-2	*	2-1	5-0	4-1	2-1	0-0	2-1
7. Horwich RMI Reserves	1-1	0-3	1-2	1-2	0-0	2-4	*	1-2	3-2	2-1	1-4	7-1
8. Lancaster City Reserves	1-3	3-0	1-2	0-0	5-1	2-1	6-2	*	1-2	1-0	5-1	1-0
9. Macclesfield Town Res.	1-3	1-2	1-1	2-3	1-2	1-2	3-1	2-1	*	3-1	1-2	2-2
10. Northwich Victoria Res.	7-2	2-3	0-1	1-1	1-4	0-3	3-1	0-0	0-3	*	1-5	4-3
11. Southport Reserves	1-1	0-1	1-2	3-0	1-3	0-1	4-0	0-3	1-1	1-1	*	3-1
12. Westhoughton Town Res.	1-5	1-1	0-11	0-3	2-2	2-8	0-2	0-4	0-3	0-2	0-3	*

MORECAMBE & LANCASTER SUNDAY LEAGUE

DIV. ONE	P	W	D	L	F	A	PTS
Moorlands Hotel	14	10	1	3	31	16	31
Royal Oak Hotel	14	9	3	2	68	22	30
The Traveller	14	8	3	3	42	23	*24
AFC Hydeaway	14	6	3	5	46	31	21
Mayfield United	14	5	4	5	27	24	*16
Slip Inn	14	6	1	7	38	43	*16
Uni-Sports Centre	14	3	2	9	32	36	11
PPC	14	0	1	13	7	96	*-2

* - 3 points deducted

Lower Division Champions:
Div. 2: Mitchells Brewery
Div. 3: Lancaster Farms
Div. 4: Upstairs/Downstairs

Cup Winners (/Runners-up):
Lge Chall. Cup: The Traveller (Slip Inn)
R Harrison Mem. Trophy: Mayfield Utd (Slip Inn)
J Bates Mem. Trophy: Mitchells Brewery (Freeholders Arms)
W. Walker Mem. Trophy: Lancaster Farms (Smiths Leisure)
K D Ormrod Mem. Trophy: Upstairs/Downstairs (AFC Britannia)

BOLTON & DISTRICT SUNDAY LEAGUE

Lyons & Mountford Jewellers Prem.	P	W	D	L	F	A	PTS
Antelope	15	12	2	1	70	18	38
Little Lever	15	8	5	2	35	24	29
Grange	15	6	3	6	31	32	21
Oxford Grove	15	4	2	9	27	35	14
Kearsley Town	15	3	4	6	33	46	13
Levers FC	15	3	2	10	20	61	11

Lower Division Champions:

Willie Containers of Bootle Div. 1 (11):
No Name FC

Morris Butchers of Farnworth Div. 2 (11):
Park FC

B & H Dairies Div. 3 (10):
Derby Ward Labour Club

Rileys Printers of Radcliffe Div. 4 (13):
Farnworth FC

THE FOOTBALL LEAGUE of WALES

KONICA LEAGUE of WALES

Registered Office: Plymouth Chambers, 3 Westgate Street, Cardiff CF1 1DD (0222 372325)

For the second consecutive season, Inter Cardiff were edged into the runners-up spot having looked title favourites for most of the season, and on this occasion they were particularly aggrieved as they felt that Haverfordwest County had fielded a weakened team in the 0-9 defeat at Bangor City that handed the title to the Farrar Road club. However, at least this time Inter Cardiff have the consolation of a European place after UEFA's decision to double the Konica League's allocation. In fact, three League of Wales clubs will be in Europe next season as promoted Barry Town qualify for the Cup-Winners Cup following their magnificent triumph in the Allbright Bitter Welsh Cup.

Maesteg Park and Briton Ferry finished in the relegation positions after a dogged battle at the bottom, but only the latter go down, Maesteg Park having been handed a reprieve by Haverfordwest's failure to arrange a groundshare deal whilst their new ground is under construction. Making the reverse journey are Barry Town, omnipotent champions of the Abacus League, and North Wales Joinery Cymru Alliance winners Rhyl - ironically both clubs who originally declined to join the Konica League at its inception in 1992.

Afan Lido retained the League Cup following a surprise win over 'double' chasing Bangor City in the final at Aberystwyth on 21st May.

FINAL TABLE	P	W	D	L	F	A	PTS
Bangor City	38	26	5	7	82	26	83
Inter Cardiff	38	26	3	9	97	44	81
Ton Pentre	38	21	8	9	62	37	71
Flint Town Utd	38	20	6	12	70	47	66
Holywell Town	38	18	10	10	74	57	64
Newtown	38	18	9	11	52	48	63
Connahs Quay N.	38	16	11	11	59	47	59
Cwmbran Town	38	16	9	13	51	46	57
Ebbw Vale	38	16	9	13	68	66	57
Aberystwyth Town	38	15	10	13	57	56	55
Porthmadog	38	14	7	17	90	71	49
Llanelli	38	14	4	20	76	100	46
Conwy United	38	13	6	19	55	70	45
Mold Alexandra	38	12	7	19	59	75	43
Haverfordwest Co.	38	10	10	18	40	81	40
Afan Lido	38	8	15	15	52	66	39
Caersws	38	9	12	18	39	56	39
Llansantffraid	38	9	7	22	46	77	34
Maesteg Park Ath.	38	8	9	21	43	71	33
Briton Ferry Ath.	38	8	9	21	53	84	33

League Cup Final *(at Aberystwyth, Sat 21st May)*
Afan Lido 1 *(Webber 26m.)*, Bangor City 0

RESULT CHART 1993-94

HOME TEAM	1	2	3	4	5	6	7	8	9	10	11	12	13	14	15	16	17	18	19	20
1. Aberystwyth Town	*	2-2	0-2	0-0	1-0	0-0	0-1	0-3	1-1	2-0	0-3	5-1	1-4	1-0	1-0	1-1	3-1	3-0	4-3	0-0
2. Afan Lido	2-4	*	2-3	1-3	0-0	0-1	2-2	1-1	1-1	1-1	3-3	0-2	1-3	2-2	3-0	1-0	1-2	3-1	2-2	3-1
3. Bangor City	1-1	2-1	*	2-0	1-1	2-0	2-1	2-1	1-0	1-0	9-0	2-1	1-1	5-1	8-0	6-1	3-0	0-0	2-1	1-0
4. Briton Ferry Athletic	2-2	0-3	0-4	*	1-0	2-2	2-4	1-1	2-1	3-3	3-1	2-4	2-9	2-3	2-3	3-0	1-2	1-3	3-6	0-1
5. Caersws	4-1	2-0	0-4	1-1	*	0-0	3-2	1-1	3-0	0-1	0-1	2-1	1-2	3-3	2-3	1-0	0-2	0-1	0-2	0-3
6. Connah's Quay N.	2-0	3-1	2-0	2-2	1-1	*	5-1	2-0	2-3	2-1	2-3	1-1	0-3	5-1	3-2	3-1	1-1	0-2	1-0	0-1
7. Conwy United	2-3	2-3	1-0	5-3	0-1	1-0	*	1-1	4-2	0-1	4-1	0-1	2-1	0-1	2-1	1-1	2-3	1-1	1-4	0-1
8. Cwmbran Town	1-1	1-0	1-0	3-1	4-1	1-0	0-2	*	2-2	3-2	0-3	1-1	1-1	3-1	2-1	1-1	4-0	1-0	0-1	2-1
9. Ebbw Vale	1-1	3-1	0-2	3-0	3-2	1-2	2-1	1-0	*	2-1	1-2	1-0	3-5	1-3	2-2	3-3	5-3	0-2	4-2	1-1
10. Flint Town United	0-3	5-0	1-0	0-1	0-0	2-1	3-3	2-1	2-1	*	4-0	3-1	4-0	3-1	1-1	0-3	2-0	4-1	3-1	3-1
11. Haverfordwest Co.	2-3	0-0	2-3	0-0	0-1	0-0	0-2	1-5	1-1	1-2	*	3-3	1-0	1-3	3-1	1-3	2-1	1-4	0-9	0-2
12. Holywell Town	3-1	4-0	3-0	1-3	1-1	1-1	3-1	3-1	4-2	2-2	4-0	*	1-0	6-1	0-0	2-1	1-0	2-2	3-2	4-1
13. Inter Cardiff	3-0	0-2	1-0	2-0	4-1	3-1	2-1	3-0	1-2	2-1	1-1	4-1	*	5-1	2-1	3-0	3-0	1-0	5-4	1-3
14. Llanelli	2-1	2-3	0-3	1-3	2-2	2-3	6-1	5-0	5-3	1-2	0-2	1-3	1-10	*	4-2	2-1	4-1	1-2	2-4	3-0
15. Llansantffraid	1-2	1-1	1-2	3-1	1-1	2-2	3-0	1-0	0-2	1-0	1-2	2-0	0-1	4-0	*	2-1	0-5	1-3	1-5	1-4
16. Maesteg Park Ath.	1-2	1-1	0-3	1-0	2-2	0-2	1-2	0-1	1-2	0-3	0-0	2-4	0-4	1-2	1-0	*	2-4	3-2	1-1	0-1
17. Mold Alexandra	1-3	2-2	0-1	3-1	1-2	2-4	1-1	1-2	0-2	1-4	1-0	1-1	3-2	1-1	2-1	4-5	*	0-0	4-0	1-4
18. Newtown	2-1	0-0	1-1	2-1	1-0	1-2	2-0	1-0	0-3	3-2	0-0	1-0	0-3	3-1	3-2	0-0	2-3	*	5-2	0-0
19. Porthmadog	2-1	2-2	0-2	1-1	2-0	1-1	0-1	1-0	1-2	0-2	5-1	7-1	1-2	5-6	4-0	0-2	1-1	0-1	*	5-2
20. Ton Pentre	2-1	2-1	2-1	1-0	3-0	2-0	4-0	0-2	1-1	3-0	0-0	0-0	1-0	3-1	0-0	1-2	2-1	5-0	2-2	*

KONICA LEAGUE of WALES CLUBS 1994-95

ABERYSTWYTH TOWN

President: Mrs D Richards **Chairman:** Mr D Dawson **Vice-Chairman:** Emyr James
Secretary: Arthur Griffiths, The Boars Head, Queens Rd, Aberystwyth, Dyfed SY23 2ET (0970 626106).
Manager: Tommy Morgan **Asst Manager:** Nipper Sutton **Physio:** Terry Edwards
Press Officer: Rhun Owens **Commercial Manager:** Clive Davies.
Ground: Park Avenue, Aberystwyth, Dyfed (0970 612122).
Directions: From south: A487, 1st right at Trefachan Bridge to r'bout, 1st right with Park Avenue being 3rd right. From north: A487 and follow one-way system to railway station, at r'bout 1st left with Park Avenue being 3rd right. 5 mins walk from Aberystwyth (BR) - follow as above.
Seats: 260 **Cover:** 1,500 **Capacity:** 6,000 **Floodlights:** Yes **Founded:** 1884.
Colours: Green & black stripes **Change colours:** Yellow & green **Nickname:** Seasiders
Previous League: Welsh 1896-97/ Nth Wales Comb. 99-1900/ Montgomeryshire & Dist. 04-20/ Central Wales 21-25 81-87/ Mid-Wales 26-32 51-81/ Cambrian Coast 32-51/ Welsh Lg South 51-63/ Abacus 87-92.
Programme: 26 pages, £1 **Programme Editor:** Steve Moore (0970 617705).
Club Sponsors: Meiron Motors **Club Shop:** Yes, selling replica kit, programmes, badges etc.
Prev. Ground: Vicarage Field 06-07 **Record Gate:** 4,500 v Hereford, Welsh Cup 1971.
Midweek matches: Wednesday **Local Press:** Cambrian News
Reserves' Lge: Mid-Wales **Clubhouse:** Open daily noon-3 & 7-12pm. Snacks available.
Record win: 21-1 v Machynlleth, Cambrian Coast League 13/3/37.
Record defeat: 1-20 v Caerws, Mid-Wales League 8/9/62.
Top Scorer 93-94: Kevin Morrison **Captain & P.o.Y. 93-94:** Neil O'Brien.
Record scorer: Eddie Ellis, 67 in 42 games, 1948-49. Career: David Williams, 476 in 433 games 1966-83.
Record appearances: David P Whitney 572, 1962-81.
Hons: Welsh Cup 1899-1900, Welsh I'mediate Cup 85-86 87-88, Mid Wales Lg(11) 22-24 25-28 32-33 48-50 58-59 83-85 (Lg Cup(7) 26-28 31-32 38-39 47-48 84-86), Welsh Amtr Cup 30-31 32-33 69-70, Welsh Lg Div 2 Sth 51-52, Cambrian Coast Lg(8) 32-37 49-50 56-57 58-59 (Lg Cup 35-36 49-50 56-57), Central Wales Chal. Cup(6) 75-76 81-83 84-85 86-88.

Aberystwyth Town FC. Back Row (L/R): Steve Williams, Neil O'Brien, David Morgan, Aneurin Thomas, Kevin Morrison, Jonathan Williams. Front: Martin Griffiths, Gari Lewis, Nigel Nicholas, Tommy Morgan (Player-Manager), Mark Devereux, Anthony Thomas, David Blair.

AFAN LIDO

Chairman: Andrew Edwards **President:** Jim Mahoney **Manager:** Paul Evans.
Secretary: Mr P Robinson, 56 Abbeyville Avenue, Sandfields Est., Port Talbot SA12 6PY (0639 885638).
Physio: Glyn Thomas **Press Officer:** Robert Clement.
Ground: Afan Lido Sports Centre, Princess Margaret Way, Aberavon Beach, Port Talbot (0639 892960).
Directions: M4 to Port Talbot centre, follow signs to Aberavon Beach - ground at Afan Lido Leisure complex.
Seats: 150 **Cover:** 150 **Capacity:** 1,500 **Floodlights:** Yes **Founded:** 1967.
Colours: Red/white/red **Change colours:** All blue. **Nickname:** The Lido
Previous Grounds: None **Previous Leagues:** Port Talbot/ Sth Wales Amtr/ Abacus
Sponsors: TBA **Record Gate:** 1,250 v Wrexham, official ground opener 1990.
Programme: 24 pages with entry **Programme Editor:** Alun Evans. **Club Shop:** No
Midweek matches: Tuesday. **Clubhouse:** No - use Grove Park Club.
Local Newspapers: Sth Wales Evening Post, Port Talbot Guardian, Port Talbot Tribune, Sth Wales Echo.
Reserves' Lge: Abacus Res. **Club Record Appearances:** David Rees.
Hons: Lg of Wales Cup 92-93 93-94, Abacus Lg Div 1(2) 87-89 (Yth Cup 91-92), Welsh I'mediate Cup 86-87.

BANGOR CITY

President: Lady Pennant **Chairman:** Gwyn Pierce Owen **Vice Chairman:** Keith Collier
Secretary: Alun Griffiths, 12 Lon-Y-Bryn, Menai Bridge, Anglesey, Gwynedd LL57 5NM (0248 712096).
Manager: Nigel Adkins **Asst Manager:** Steve Myers **Physio:** Arwel Jones
Comm. Manager: G Thomas. **Press Officer:** Alun Griffiths
Ground: The Stadium, Farrar Road, Bangor, Gwynedd (0248 355852).
Directions: Old A5 into Bangor, 1st left before railway station, ground on left by garage.
Seats: 900 **Cover:** 2,000 **Capacity:** 10,000 **Floodlights:** Yes **Founded:** 1876
Colours: All blue **Change colours:** All yellow **Nickname:** Citizens
Prev. Lges: N. Wales Coast 1893-98 1911-12/ The Comb. 1898-1910/ N. Wales Comb. 30-33/ W. Mids (B'gham) 32-38/ Lancs. Comb. 38-39 46-50/ Ches. Co. 50-68/ NPL 68-79 81-82 84-92/ Alliance Prem. 79-81 82-84.
Midweek matches: Tuesday **Record Gate:** 10,000 v Wrexham, Welsh Cup final 78-79.
Programme: 32 pages, 50p **Editor:** Alan Monument (0248 351528).
Clubhouse: Not on ground. **Club Shop:** Yes, selling programmes, badges and scarves.
Local Press: Bangor Mail, Holyhead & Anglesey Mail, Nth Wales Weekly News, Nth Wales Chronicle, Liverpool Daily Post.
Sponsors: Pentraeth Motors **Reserve team's League:** Welsh Alliance.
Captain 93-94: Dave Barnett **P.o.Y. 93-94:** Harry Wiggins **Top Scorer 93-94:** Frank Mottram 19.
Hons: FA Tphy R-up 83-84, Northern Prem. Lg 81-82 (R-up 86-87, Lg Cup 68-69, Presidents Cup 88-89, Chal. Shield 87-88), Cheshire Co. Lg R-up 53-54 58-59, Lancs Comb. R-up 30-31, League Cup Wales 93-94 (Lg Cup R-up 93-94), Welsh National Lg 27-28 (R-up 26-27), Nth Wales Coast Lg 1895-96, Welsh Cup 1888-89 95-96 1961-62 (R-up 27-28 60-61 63-64 72-73 77-78 84-85), Nth Wales Chal. Cup 26-27 35-36 36-37 37-38 46-47 51-52 57-58 64-65 67-68, Welsh Amtr Cup 1894-95 96-96 97-98 98-99 1900-01 02-03 04-05 05-06 11-12, Welsh Jnr Cup 1995-96 97-98 1919-20, Welsh All. Alves Cup 49-50 59-60 (Cookson Cup 61-62 68-69 84-85 86-87).

BARRY TOWN

Chairman: Neil O'Halloran. **President:**
Secretary: Alan Whelan, Jenner Park, Barry, South Glam. CF62 7HR (0446 737188).
Ground: Jenner Park, Barry (0446 721171).
Directions: M4 jct 33 via Wenvoe (A4050) to Barry. Left at 1st 2 r'bouts to Jenner Park. Nearest rail station is Cadoxton.
Capacity: 3,000 **Floodlights:** Yes **Cover:** Yes **Seats:** 800 **Founded:** 1923.
Colours: Red & white/white/white. **Change:** Yellow & blue/blue/blue. **Nickname:** Linnets
Sponsors: Pixie Tavern **Previous Name:** Barri FC, 1992-93 only. **Programme:** Yes
Previous Leagues: Western 08-13/ Southern 13-82 89-93/ Welsh 82-89 93-94.
Previous Ground: Worcester City, 92-93 **Record Gate:** 7,400 v Queens Park Rangers, FA Cup 1st Rd 1961.
Best FA Cup season: 2nd Rd 29-30. **Best FA Trophy season:** 3rd Qualifying Rd replay 90-91.
Midweek matches: Wednesday. **Clubhouse:** Open normal licensing hours.
Record transfer fee received: £1,000 for Derek Tapscott (Arsenal).
Players progressing to Football League: Chris Simmonds (Millwall) 1947, Jack Brown (Ipswich) 1948, Des Tennant (Brighton) 1948, Terry Elwell (Swansea) 1948, Rob McLaren (Cardiff) 1950, Ron Howells (Cardiff) 1950, Charles Cairney (Bristol Rovers) 1953, Derek Tapscott (Arsenal) 1953, Dai Ward (Bristol Rovers) 1954, Jim McGhee (Newport) 1954, Tom Quigley (Portsmouth) 1955, Brian Keating (Crewe) 1956, James Hartnett (Hartlepool) 1957, Richard Twigg (Notts County) 1957, Keith Webber (Everton) 1960, Peter Issac (Northampton) 1962, Laurie Sheffield (Newport) 1962, Gordon Fraser (Newport) 1966, Robert Ferguson (Newport) 1969, Robert Delgado (Luton) 1970, Gerry Jones (Luton) 1972, Roger Green (Newport) 1972, Mike Coslett (Newport) 1978, Phil Green (Newport) 1984, Chris Pike (Fulham) 1985, Ian Love (Swansea) 1986.
Club record scorer: Clive Ayres **Club record appearances:** Basil Bright.
Captain 93-94: Andy Beattie **Top Scorer 93-94:** David D'Auria.
Hons: Welsh Cup 54-55 93-94, Welsh Tphy 93-94, Southern Lg R-up 20-21, Western Lg R-up 11-12, Welsh Lg 82-83 83-84 84-85 85-86 86-87 88-89 93-94 (R-up 87-88, Lg Cup 34-35 46-47 82-83 93-94), South Wales Senior Cup 26-27 35-36 37-38 52-53 53-54 58-59 59-60 65-66 75-76 77-78 86-87 87-88 93-94, SA Brain Cup 78-79 82-83 86-87.

Jubilant Barry Town players salute their fans at the National Stadium, Cardiff, after their historic 2-1 win over Cardiff City in the Allbright Bitter Welsh Cup final.

Photo - Gavin Ellis-Neville.

CAERSWS

Chairman: Gareth Williams **Vice Chairman:** Hadyn Jones **President:** Dilwyn Jones
Secretary: T M B Jones, 3 Hafren Terrace, Caersws, Powys SY17 5ES (0686 688103).
Manager: Mickey Evans **Asst Manager:** Barry Harding **Coach:** W Jones.
Physio: John Wilden **Press Officer:** Ivor Williams (0686 420267).
Ground: The Recreation Ground, Caersws, Powys.
Directions: Entering Caersws (between Newtown & Llanidloes on A470) ground entrance on left by river bridge.
Seats: 150 **Cover:** 300 **Capacity:** 3,250 **Floodlights:** Yes **Founded:** 1887.
Colours: Blue/white/blue **Change colours:** All white. **Nickname:** Bluebirds
Previous Grounds: None **Previous Lges:** Mid-Wales (pre-1989)/Cymru Alliance 90-92.
Programme: 36 pages, 50p **Programme Editor:** Gareth Davies (0686 413219).
Record Gate: 2,795 v Swansea City, Welsh Cup 1990.
Midweek home matchday: Tuesday **Reserve team's League:** Mid-Wales.
Club Shop: No. **Record win:** 20-1 v Aberystwyth, Mid-Wales Lge 8/9/62.
Players progressing to Football League: P Woosnam (Leyton Orient, West Ham United, Aston Villa, Atalanta), M Evans (Wolverhampton Wanderers, Wrexham).
Clubhouse: Not on ground, but in village centre. Normal licensing hours. Food served.
Club Record Scorer: Gareth Davies. **Top Scorer 93-94:** Dave Griffiths
Captain 93-94: Ian Jones **P.o.Y. 93-94:** Kevin Lloyd.
Hons: Welsh Amtr Cup 60-61 (I'mediate Cup 88-89 (R-up 91-92)), Mid-Wales Lg(8) 59-61 62-63 77-78 82-83 85-86 88-90 (Lg Cup 79-80 82-83 87-88 89-90), Cent. Wales Challenge Cup 77-78 82-83 87-88 89-90 (Yth Cup 69-70 72-73), Montgomeryshire Challenge Cup(17) 52-53 59-60 62-63 69-72 74-75 76-78 83-89 90-91 93-94, Montgomeryshire Lg 77-78.

CONNAH'S QUAY NOMADS

Chairman: Mr R Morris **President:** Mr R Jones.
Secretary/Press Officer: Mr Robert Hunter, 40 Brookdale Avenue, Connah's Quay, Deeside, Clywd CH5 4LU (0244 831212(h)/ 520299(b)).
Manager: Neville Powell/Phil Evans **Physio:** Mr M Latter.
Ground: Halfway Ground, Connah's Quay, Deeside, Clwyd.
Directions: On main coast road (A548) from Chester to Rhyl west end of Connah's Quay behind Halfway Hotal.
Seats: 105 **Cover:** 500 **Capacity:** 1,500 **Floodlights:** Yes **Founded:** 1946
Colours: White/navy/white **Change colours:** Maroon & blue stripes/blue/maroon.
Previous Grounds: None **Prev. Lges:** Clywd/ Welsh Alliance/ Cymru Alliance 90-92.
Midweek home matchday: Tuesday **Record Gate:** 1,500 v Rhyl, Welsh Cup SF 29/3/93.
Sponsors: SLP Pumps Ltd **Reserve Team's League:** Sealink Welsh Alliance.
Programme: 26 pages, 50p **Programme Editor:** Don Fowler. **Club Shop:** No
Reserves' League: Clywd **Record win:** 16-0 v Rhydymwyn, 1949.
Nickname: Westenders **Clubhouse:** No, but Halfway Hotel is adjacent
Top Scorer 93-94: Scott Taylor **Captain & P.o.Y. 93-94:** Barry Thomas
Local Newspapers: Evening Leader, Deeside Chronicle, Liverpool Daily Post.
Hons: Welsh Amtr Cup 52-53 54-55, Nth Wales FA Amtr Cup 52-53 54-55, North Wales Coast Challenge Cup, Welsh Intermediate Cup 80-81, Welsh Alliance Cookson Cup 87-88, Welsh Youth Cup 47-48.

CONWY UNITED

Chairman: C R Jones **Vice Chairman:** G Evans **President:** K Davies
Secretary: Mr Cecil Jones, 'Iolyn', Iolyn Park, Conwy, Gwynedd LL32 8UX (0492 593496).
Manager: Paul Rowlands **Asst Manager:** John Hulse **Coach:** Chris Hayes
Press Officer: G Rees (0492 573080).
Ground: Morfa Ground, Conwy, Gwynedd (0492 593860).
Directions: Leave A55 on 1st slip road after river tunnel and turn left towards Conwy. Sharp left immediately after overhead railway bridge - ground 400yds on left of Penmaen Rd.
Seats: 120 **Cover:** 400 **Capacity:** 1,500 **Floodlights:** Yes **Founded:** 1977.
Colours: Tangerine/black/black **Change colours:** Claret & blue. **N'kname:** Musselmen
Previous Leagues: Vale of Conwy/ Gwynedd/ Welsh Alliance/ Cymru Alliance.
Previous Grounds: None **Record Gate:** 600 v Bangor City, Tyn Lyn Barritt Cup 1988.
Programme: 28 pages, 50p **Editor:** Martin Jones (0492 860166)
Club Shop: Yes, selling metal badges, programmes etc. Contact D Fare (0492 596109).
Reserves' Lge: Gwynedd League **Midweek matches:** Tuesday. **Clubhouse:** No
Sponsors: Crosville Wales Ltd **Record win:** 11-1 v British Steel Shotton, Welsh Cup 1979-80.
Players progressing to Football League: Neville Southall (via Winsford to Bury, Everton), Carl Dale (via Rhyl and Bangor to Chester City, Cardiff City).
Club record scorer: Carl Dale **Club record appearances:** Gwyn Williams.
Captain 93-94: Andy Harper **Top Scorer 93-94:** Peter Hughes **P.o.Y. 93-94:** Greg Moffatt.
Local Press: Liverpool Daily Post, Nth Wales Weekly News, Nth Wales Pioneer
Hons: Welsh Alliance 84-85 85-86, Barritt Cup 84-85, Welsh Intermediate Cup 81-82.

PHOTOS OPPOSITE:

Top: *Simon King makes a small piece of football history as he scores the first goal by a League of Wales club in Europe - a penalty during Cwmbran Town's 3-2 first-leg win at home to Cork City.*
Photo - Colin Stevens.

Foot: *David Evans of Connah's Quay Nomads gets in a shot during the 0-2 defeat at Ton Pentre.*
Photo - David Collins.

CWMBRAN TOWN

Chairman: George Thorneycroft **Vice Chairman:** Clive Edwards **President:** John Colley
Secretary: Mr Roy Langley, 2 Trafalgar Court, Penylan Rd, Penylan, Cardiff CF2 5RL (0222 483341).
Manager: Tony Wilcox **Coach:** John Relish **Physio:** John Prosser
Press Officer: Maurice Salway (0633 430065).
Ground: Cwmbran Stadium, Henllys Way, Cwmbran, Gwent (0633 866192/3).
Directions: M4 jct 26, follow signns to Cwmbran on A4042 & A4051, bear right after 3rd r'bout on A4051 to stadium. One and a half miles from Cwmbran (BR).
Seats: 3,200 **Cover:** 4,700 **Capacity:** 13,200 **Floodlights:** Yes **Founded:** 1951.
Colours: White/red/white **Change colours:** Blue/white/white **Nickname:** The Town
Previous Leagues: Monmouthshire Snr 51-59/ Welsh 60-92.
Record Gate: 3,582 v Cork City, European Cup Preliminary Round 1st leg 18/8/94.
Prev. Ground: Cwmbran Park 55-75 **Record win:** 11-0 v Gwynfi, Welsh Lg 21/9/68.
Programme: 28 pages, 50p **Programme Editor:** Maurice Salway (0633 430065).
Club Shop: Yes, selling programmes, badges, scarves etc. Contact Maurice Salway (above).
Midweek matches: Wednesday. **Clubhouse:** Pub hours, on ground. Catering facilities.
Sponsors: B.I.G. Batteries **Local Press:** South Wales Argus, Cwmbran Free Press.
Reserves' League: None **Record transfer paid:** £1,500 for Francis Ford (Briton Ferry 1992)
Players progressing to Football League: Simon King (Newport 1984), Mark Waite (Bristol Rovers 1984), Nathan Wigg (Cardiff 1993), Chris Watkins (Swansea 1993).
Record Scorer: Graham Reynolds **Record appearances:** Mostyn Lewis.
Captain 93-94: James Blackie **P.o.Y. 93-94:** Michael Copeman.
Top Scorer 93-94: Andrew Clissold **Hons:** Lg of W. 92-93, Welsh Lg Div 1 66-67 (Lg Cup 85-86 90-91).

EBBW VALE

President: J S Harrison **Vice Chairman:** M Carini
Secretary: D Coughlin, 107 Mount Pleasant Rd, Ebbw Vale, Gwent NP3 6JL (0495 305993).
Manager: Steve Williams **Assistant Manager:** Mick Martin.
Ground: Eugene Cross Park, Ebbw Vale, Gwent (0495 302995).
Directions: From A465 follow signs to Ebbw Vale, 1st left at next two r'bouts - ground on left.
Seats: 1,200 **Cover:** 1,200 **Capacity:** 10,000 **Floodlights:** Yes **Founded:** 1950
Cols: Amber & black/black/black **Change colours:** Sky/navy/grey. **Nickname:** Cowboys
Previous League: Abacus **Record Gate:** 1,762 v Wrexham, Welsh Cup 1989.
Programme: 25 pages, 50p **Midweek matches:** Wednesday **Club Shop:** No
Clubhouse: Pub hrs - shared with Rugby **Record win:** 10-0 v Briton Ferry Ath., Lge of Wales 6/1/93.
Captain 93-94: **Top Scorer & P.o.Y. 93-94:**
Hons: Abacus Lg 87-88 (Div 1 64-65, Southern Div 52-53, Div 2 East 60-61), Sth Wales Lg 03-04, Welsh Cup 25-26, South Wales Snr Cup 04-05, Gwent Snr Cup 24-25 26-27 28-29 32-33 45-46 50-51.

FLINT TOWN UNITED

Chairman: Mike Tierney **Vice Chairman:** Mike McClafferty **President:** David Hough.
Secretary: Howard Greenhough, 9 Broadacre Close, Bagillt, Clwyd CH6 6EA (0352 735889).
Mgr/Coach: Dixie McNeil **Asst Manager:** Graham A Jones **Physio:** Ray Marshall
Press Officer: Mike Cooper (0244 821083).
Commercial Manager: Ray Dodd (0352 730982).
Ground: Cae-Y-Castell, Marsh Lane, Flint, Clywd CH6 5JP (0352 730982).
Directions: Approaching Flint on A548 from Chester, turn right at signpost for Flint Castle. Ground to right of car park. Flint BR station and bus stops are adjacent to ground.
Seats: 300 **Cover:** 500 **Capacity:** 6,000 **Floodlights:** Yes **Founded:** 1886
Colours: Black & white stripes **Change colours:** All sky blue. **Nickname:** Silkmen
Reserves' League: Clywd **Previous Ground:** Holywell Road (until November 1993).
Record win: 15-0 v Rhos U., 1952 **Previous Leagues:** Clwyd/ Welsh Alliance/ Cymru Alliance 90-92.
Programme: 28 pages, 50p **Editor:** Graham George (0352 735148) **Sponsors:** None
Club Shop: Yes, selling replica kit, souvenirs & programmes. Contact Commercial Manager.
Midweek home matchday: Tuesday
Clubhouse: Flint Town United Social Club open every evening and matchdays. Two bars open to visiting supporters before & after game. Hot & cold food available. Stewart - Bryan Carroll (0352 762804).
Captain 93-94: Damian McKeown **Top Scorer 93-94:** Chris Davies 22
P.o.Y. 93-94: Dewi Parry.
Hons: Cymru Alliance 90-91, Welsh Cup 53-54, Welsh Amtr Cup 47-48, Welsh All.(4) 54-57 89-90 (Alves Cup 53-54 89-90, Cookson Cup 52-53 88-89), Welsh Championship Cup 90-91, N. Wales Coast Chal. Cup 90-91, Nth Wales Coast Amtr Cup(8) 09-10 30-36 68-69.

HOLYWELL TOWN

Chairman: Emile Moore **Vice Chairman:** Ian Ross **President:** Charles Meredith
Secretary: G M Davies, 45 Bron-Y-Wern, Bagillt, Clwyd CH6 6BS (0352 763571).
Manager: Glyn Griffiths **Asst Manager:** Mark Williams **Coach:** Colin Jones
Physio: Glyn Owen **Press Officer:** Sean Elliott (0352 712833)
Commercial Manager: Jackie Hough.
Ground: Halkyn Road, Holywell (0352 711411).
Directions: A55 Expressway to A5026 Holywell turn, turn right for ground just after Stanford Gate Hotel. Coming from town centre, turn left off ringroad at Victoria Hotel, pass Police Station and turn left for ground at the surgery.
Capacity: 3,000 **Seats:** 300 **Cover:** 500 **Floodlights:** Yes **Founded:** 1946
Colours: Red & white **Change colours:** All blue **Prev. Grounds:** None
Previous Lges: Welsh League North 50-60/ Clwyd 84-88/ Cymru Alliance 89-92.
Programme: 32 pages, 50p **Programme Editor:** Carl Lovell (0352 714581)
Club Shop: Yes, selling replica shirts, scarves, hats, T-shirts, sweaters, badges, old programmes. Contact Mr Malcolm Bell at club (matchdays only).
Sponsors: Business Systems (NW) **Clubhouse:** No - use Beaufort Hotel, West St. Snack bar on ground
Midweek home matchday: Tuesday **Reserve team's League:** Clwyd. **Nickname:** Wellmen
Captain 93-94: Pat Moran **Club record scorer:** Neil Davies
Top Scorer 93-94: Neil Davies **Player-of-the-Year 93-94:** Jimmy Griffith.
Hons: North Wales Coast Amtr Cup 13-14 21-22 57-58, North Wales Coast Jnr Cup 76-77, North Wales Coast Chal. Cup 86-87, Clywd Lg Presidents Cup 86-87 (Lg Cup 87-88, Yth Cup 92-93, Yth Auxiliary Cup 92-93), North Wales Coast Yth Cup 75-76.

INTER-CARDIFF

Chairman: Max James **President:** Len Carroll.
Secretary: Paul Woollacott, 7 Lloyd Ave., Barry, South Glamorgan (0446 734389).
Manager: Lyn Jones **Asst Manager:** Phil Hulme **Physio:** Ron Swain
Press Officer: Max James **Commercial Manager:** Terry Martin/ Dave Williams.
Ground & Directions: As Merthyr Tydfil FC *(see page 178)*. **Founded:** 1990.
Colours: White/black/red **Change colours:** Yellow/black/black.
Prev. Names: Lake Utd and Rumney Rgrs merged 1984 to form AFC Cardiff. This club merged with Sully in 1990.
Previous Grounds: Cwrt-yr-Ala, Fairwater (pre-1992)/ Cardiff Athletic Stadium, Leckwith Rd 92-93/ Cardiff City FC 93-94. *Sully: Burnham Ave.*
Previous Leagues: Barry & District/ South Wales Amateur/ Abacus **Nickname:** Seagulls
Sponsors: Brians Brewery **Record Gate:** 1,500 v Cardiff City, Sth Wales Snr Cup 1974.
Programme: 24 pages, 50p **Programme Editor:** Terry Martin. **Club Shop:** No.
Midweek matches: Wednesday. **Clubhouse:** Tues/Thurs/Sat 7-11pm at old ground (Cwrt-yr-Ala).
Rec. win: 11-1 v Abercynon 1990 **Top Scorer 93-94:**
Local Press: Sth Wales Echo, Cardiff Post, Western Mail.
Hons: League of Wales R-up 92-93 93-94, Abacus Lg Div 1 86-87, Sth Wales Amtr Lg 84-85 85-86. *As Sully: Sth Wales Amtr Lg Coronation Cup 69-70, Corinthian Cup 78-79, Abacus Lg Div 1 83-84 85-86 89-90 (Div 2 80-81), Sth Wales Snr Cup 80-81 81-82.*

LLANELLI

President: John James **Chairman:** Denley Mears.
Secretary: Roger Davies, 29 Pemberton Park, Llanelli, Dyfed SA14 8NH (0554 756176).
Manager: Gilbert Lloyd **Assistant Manager:** John Taylor
Physio: Robert Grant. **Coach:** Phil Davidson
Press Officer: Alan Evans.
Ground: Strebonheath Park, Llanelli, Dyfed (0554 772973).
Directions: M4 jct 48, link road to Llanelli for 4 miles, right at 1st lights, left after Esso garage (signed Strebonheath), ground 400yds on right. 2 miles from Llanelli (BR) station.
Seats: 700 **Cover:** 700 **Capacity:** 3,750 **Floodlights:** Yes **Founded:** 1896.
Colours: All red **Change:** All blue **Nickname:** Reds
Previous League: Southern/ Abacus **Record Gate:** 20,000 (before redevelopment).
Previous Name: Llanelly FC. **Previous Ground:** Halfway Park (1900-23).
Programme: 24 pages, 50p **Programme Editor:** Neil Richards. **Club Shop:** No
Midweek matches: Wednesday. **Local Newspapers:** Llanelli Star, Llanelli Weekly.
Record win: 17-0 v Treharris, Welsh League 1914
Club Sponsors: Classic Home Improvements Ltd
Clubhouse: Midweek evenings 6-11pm, weekends 1-11pm.
Captain 93-94: Gary Lloyd **Top Scorer 93-94:** Steven Morgan.
Hons: Welsh Lg 29-30 32-33 70-71 76-77 77-78 (Lg Cup 29-30 74-75), West Wales Snr Cup 30-31 47-48 50-51 52-53 63-64 67-68 70-71 76-77.

LLANSANTFFRAID

President: Mike Hughes. **Chairman:** Edgar Jones **Vice-Chairman:** Roger Morcton
Sec./Press Officer: Graham Ellis, Sarnall House, Sarnall, Llanymynech, Shropshire SY22 6QJ (0938 828583).
Manager: Ian Clarke **Asst Manager:** Bob Macaeley **Physio:** Noel Lloyd
Ground: Recreation Park, Treflan, Llansantffraid (0691 828112).
Directions: A470 between Welshpool and Oswestry, left for Llansantffraid at Llnmyrdach, over bridge into village, left thru village opposite silos, ground on right signed Community Centre.
Seats: 120 **Cover:** 250 **Capacity:** 1,500 **Floodlights:** Yes
Club Shop: Metal badges, scarves, hats available - contact secretary.
Colours: Green/black/black **Change:** White/black/black. **Nickname:** None
Rec. Gate: 475 v Rhyl, Welsh Cup '93 **Previous League:** Mid-Wales/ Cymru Alliance (pre-1993)
Programme: 24 pages, 50p **Sponsors:** Mike Hughes Construction.
Midweek matches: Tuesday. **Clubhouse:** Normal licensing hours.
Reserves' Lge: Mid-Wales
Club record scorer: Andy Oakley **Club record appearances:** Derek Arthur.
Captain 93-94: Graham Ellis **P.o.Y. 93-94:** Gary Jones **Top Scorer 93-94:** Billy Morris.
Honours: Cymru Alliance 92-93, Welsh Intermediate Cup 92-93, Central Wales Cup 92-93 (R-up 93-94), Central Wales Lg R-up 90-91, Montgomeryshire Amtr Lg 68-69 69-70 70-71 82-83 86-87 91-92 92-93 (R-up 72-73 73-74 74-75, Div 2 80-81, Lg Cup 62-63 65-66 69-70 70-71 73-74 75-76 91-92 92-93 (R-up 59-60 65-66 77-78 80-81 85-86 87-88 88-89)), J Emrys Morgan Cup 72-73 81-82 82-83 92-93, Montgomeryshire Cup R-up 82-83, Presteigne-Otway Cup 92-93, Tommy Jarman Cup 91-92 92-93.

Llansantffraid FC.

MAESTEG PARK ATHLETIC

Chairman: Brian Carpenter **Vice Chairman:** Michael O'Brien **President:** Anthony Richards.
Secretary: David Griffiths, 3 Padleys Close, Maesteg, Bridgend, Mid-Glamorgan CF34 0TX (0656 733000).
Manager: Mike Ellery **Press Officer:** David Griffiths.
Ground: Tudor Park, St Davids Place, Maesteg, Mid-Glamorgan (0656 732092-ground, 732029-club).
Directions: M6 jct 36, A4063 to Maesteg, top road into town past Gills garage, turn left at Royal Oak. At Gran pub turn left up hill to Red Cow pub, then right - ground on left.
Seats: 100 **Cover:** 200 **Capacity:** 2,000 **Floodlights:** Yes **Founded:** 1945.
Colours: Blue & white/blue/blue **Change:** Yellow & green stripes/green/yellow.
Previous Ground: South Parade 65-70 **Record Gate:** 1,100 v Cardiff, f'light opener 1981
Previous Leagues: Bridgend & Dist./ Port Talbot & Dist./ Abacus. **Nickname:** Park.
Programme: 24 pages, with entry **Programme Editor:** David Griffiths. **Club Shop:** No.
Local Press: South Wales Echo, Glamorgan Gazette, South Wales Eveing Post.
Midweek matches: Wed/tues **Reserves' League:** Welsh Lg Reserve Division.
Clubhouse: 1-4pm, 6-11pm daily (matchdays all day). Meals and snacks available always.
Top Scorer 93-94: **Record win:** 10-2 v Glyn Corrwg, 1967-68.
Hons: Welsh Cup SF 91-92, Sth Wales Snr Cup 78-79 90-91, Abacus Lg R-up 79-80 (Div 1 78-79), Sth Wales Cup 78-79 90-91 (R-up 92-93).

MOLD ALEXANDRA

Secretary: T Wynne, 1 Grays Rd, Mynydd Isa, nr Mold, Clwyd (0352 754531).
Manager: Mickey O'Brien/ Dave Allen **Ground:** Alyn Park, Maesydre, Mold (0352 4007).
Directions: Wrexham-Mold A541, follow signs to Flint, then Denbigh at Tescos r'bout, ground 200yds on right opposite Bryn Awel Hotel.
Seats: 100 **Cover:** 300 **Capacity:** 2,250 **Floodlights:** Yes **Founded:** 1929.
Colours: Royal/white/royal **Change colours:** All white **Nickname:** The Alex
Previous Grounds: None. **Previous Lges:** Welsh Nat. (Wrexham Area)/ Cymru Alliance
Midweek home matchday: Tuesday **Club Sponsors:** Synthrite Ltd.
Programme: 24 pages, 50p **Top Scorer 93-94:** **Clubhouse:** No.
Hons: Welsh National Lg (Wrexham Area) 89-90, Nth Wales Coast Chal. Cup 85-86 89-90, Barritt Cup 89-90, N.E. Wales Chal. Cup 89-90, Nth Wales Coast Jnr Cup 30-31.

NEWTOWN

President: Trevor Jones **Chairman:** Keith Harding **Manager:** Brian Coyne
Secretary: Shirley Reynolds, Brynwood Drive, Mitford Rd, Newtown, Powys (0686 628089).
Asst Manager: Jake King. **Physio:** Elwyn Morgan **Commercial Manager:** Phil Ledger
Press Officer/Team Secretary: John Annerean.
Ground: Latham Park, Newtown, Powys (0686 626159).
Directions: A43 to Newtown, right at 1st lights into Back Lane & town centre - 400yds left into Park St., 500yds right (at Library) into Park Lane - ground at end.
Seats: 200 **Cover:** 700 **Capacity:** 5,000 **Floodlights:** Yes **Founded:** 1875.
Colours: Red/white/white **Change colours:** White/red/white **Nickname:** Robins
Previous Leagues: The Combination/ Central Wales/ Northern Premier.
Previous Grounds: 24 Acres/ The Cummings/ Plantation Lane (pre-1950).
Previous Name: Newtown White Star. **Record Gate:** 5,002 v Swansea City, Welsh Cup 1954.
Best FA Trophy year: 3rd Qual. 89-90 **Best FA Cup year:** 2nd Rd 1884-85. Also 1st Rd 1885-86.
Players progressing to Football League: Clive Lloyd (Orient), John Lovent (C Palace & Exeter), Mike Bloor (Stoke & Lincoln), Ian Woan (Nottm Forest), Jonathan Hill (Rochdale), Ray Newlands (Plymouth), Mike Williams (Shrewsbury).
Programme: 36 pages, 50p **Programme Editor:** Keith Harding/ Nigel Bevan.
Club Shop: Yes. Open matchdays selling programmes etc. Contact Nigel Bevan.
Sponsors: Shell Gas **Clubhouse:** Open every evening. Hot/cold snacks, pool, darts.
Midweek matches: Tuesday. **Local Press:** Shropshire Times, County Times & Express.
Reserves' Lge: Central Wales
Captain 93-94: K Sherry **P.o.Y. 93-94:** Peter Wilding **Top Scorer 93-94:** Andy Cook.
Hons: Welsh Cup 1878-79 94-95 (R-up 85-65 87-88 96-97), Welsh Amtr Cup 1954-55, Central Wales Lg 75-76 78-79 81-82 86-87 87-88 (R-up 51-52 52-53 55-56 56-57 74-75 82-83, Lg Cup 54-55 56-57 74-75 75-76 81-82 83-84), Arthur Barritt Cup 86-87, Central Wales Cup 74-75 80-81 92-93, Emrys Morgan Cup 80-81.

PORTHMADOG

Chairman: Iwan Jones **President:** William Pike **Manager:** Ian Edwards
Secretary: Mr R I Griffiths, Llyn-yr-Eryr, Ynys, Cricieth, Gwynedd LL52 0PH (0766 810349).
Physio: Ifor Roberts **Press Officer:** Dylan Ellis (0978 853008).
Ground & Directions: Y Traeth, Porthmadog (0766 514687). At town centre crossroads (by Woolworths) into Snowdon Str., pass RBL/Craft Centre onto unmade track, over railway line - ground on right.
Seats: 140 **Cover:** 400 **Capacity:** 4,000 **Floodlights:** Yes **Founded:** 1884.
Colours: Red & black/black/black **Change:** Yellow & green/sky/white. **Nickname:** Porth.
Previous Grounds: None **Reserve team's league:** Gwynedd.
Prev. Lges: N. Wales/ Gwynedd/ Bangor & Dist./ Lleyn & Dist./ Cambrian Coast/ Welsh Alliance/ Cymru Alliance
Midweek home matchday: Tuesday **Record Gate:** 3,500 v Swansea, Welsh Cup 64-65.
Programme: 28 pages, 50p **Programme Editor:** Dylan Ellis. **Club Shop:** No.
Clubhouse: Not on ground (use Midland Hotel), but matchday refreshments available.
Local Newspapers: Caernarfon & Denbigh Herald/ Cambrian News/ Nth Wales Chronicle/ Y Wylan.
Captain 93-94: **Top Scorer 93-94:** David Taylor.
Hons: Welsh Amtr Cup(3) 55-58, N. Wales Amtr Cup 37-38 56-57 58-59 62-63, Lge of Wales Cup R-up 92-93, N. Wales Coast Chal. Cup(5) 55-56 73-75 76-78, Welsh All.(8) 02-03 37-38 66-69 74-76 89-90 (Cookson Cup 75-76 89-90, Barritt Cup 77-78, Alves Cup 65-66 73-74 76-77).

Porthmadog FC

RHYL

Chairman: Stuart McCallum. **President:**
Secretary: A R Hayes, 83 Grange Rd, Rhyl, Clwyd LL18 4BT (0745 330264).
Ground: Belle Vue, Grange Road, Rhyl, Clwyd (0745 338327).
Directions: A55 Expressway to Rhyl turn-off and follow signs thru Rhuddlan. Follow signs for Sun Centre along Pendyffryn Rd and turn left at junction - ground 200 yards on left.
Capacity: 4,000 **Floodlights:** Yes **Cover:** 1,200 **Seats:** 200 **Founded:** 1883.
Colours: All white. **Change:** Red & black stripes/black/red **Nickname:** Lilywhites
Sponsors: **Previous Name:** Rhyl Athletic. **Programme:** 50p
Previous Leagues: Cheshire County/ North West Counties/ Northern Premier/ Cymru Alliance 92-94.
Record Gate: 10,000 v Cardiff City, Welsh Cup 1953.
Best FA Cup season: 4th Rd Proper 56-57 (lost 0-3 at Bristol City).
Midweek matches: Wednesday. **Record transfer fee received:** £25,000.
Players progressing to Football League: Ian Edwards, Grenville Millington, Brian Lloyd, Andy Holden, Barry Horne, Andy Jones.
Club record scorer: Don Spendlove. **Club record appearances:** Not known.
Honours: Welsh Cup 51-52 52-53 (R-up 29-30 36-37 92-93), Welsh Amateur Cup 72-73, Northern Premier Lg Presidents Cup 84-85, North West Counties Lg R-up 82-83, North Wales Coast Challenge Cup, Cheshire County Lg 47-48 50-51 71-72 (R-up 48-49 49-50 51-52 55-56, Div 2 R-up 81-82, Lg Cup 48-49 51-52 70-71, Div 2 Shield 81-82), Cyrmu Alliance 93-94 (R-up 92-93, Lg Cup 92-93).

TON PENTRE

Chairman: Jeff Orrells **Vice Chairman:** Trevor Lowe **President:** Allan Rogers MP
Secretary/Press Officer: Paul Willoughby, 37 Bailey Street, Ton Pentre, Rhondda CF41 7EN (0443 438281).
Manager: John Emmanuel
Ground: Ynys Park, Ton Row, Ton Pentre, Rhondda (0443 432413).
Directions: A4058 Pontypridd to Treorchy Plain road, left at Thames Rico Garage then first left again. Ton Pentre (BR) station 400yds from ground.
Seats: 400 **Cover:** 800 **Capacity:** 2,750 **Floodlights:** Yes **Founded:** 1935
Colours: All red **Change colours:** All blue **Nickname:** Ton.
Previous Grounds: None.
Previous Leagues: Welsh (Abacus) pre-1993.
Programme: 28 pages, 50p **Club Shop:** No.
Club Sponsors: **Record Gate:** 2,900 v Cardiff City, F.A. Cup 1st Rd 1986.
Midweek home matchday: Wednesday **Reserve team:** None.
Clubhouse: Open normal licensing hours seven days a week. Food always available.
Captain 93-94: Brian Gullett. **Top Scorer 93-94:**
Hons: Welsh League 57-58 60-61 73-74 81-82 92-93, Welsh Amateur Cup 51-52, South Wales Senior Cup 47-48 60-61 61-62 63-64 83-84 92-93.

Ton Pentre's Jason Roberts waits for a cross with Leon Draper of Ebbw Vale.

Photo - Roger Turner.

KONICA LEAGUE of WALES TEN-YEAR RECORD (INCLUDES WELSH LEAGUE NATIONAL DIV. PRIOR TO 1992/93)

	84/5	85/6	86/7	87/8	88/9	89/0	90/1	91/2	92/3	93/4
Abergavenny Thursdays	-	-	-	-	7	3	1	1	20	-
Aberystwyth Town	-	-	-	4	2	2	2	3	3	10
Afan Lido	-	-	-	-	-	-	12	8	12	16
AFC Cardiff	-	-	-	7	13	7	-	-	-	-
Ammanford Town	-	-	-	-	-	14	16	-	-	-
Bangor City	-	-	-	-	-	-	-	-	5	1
Barry Town	1	1	1	2	1	-	-	-	-	-
Blaenrhondda	12	12	12	18	-	-	-	-	-	-
Brecon Corinthians	8	4	10	12	5	12	8	14	-	-
Bridgend Town	2	2	7	15	6	10	11	15	-	-
Briton Ferry Athletic	10	6	8	8	11	6	7	2	17	20
Caerau Athletic	11	16	17	-	-	-	-	-	-	-
Caerleon	5	15	14	16	16	-	-	-	-	-
Caersws	-	-	-	-	-	-	-	-	11	17
Caldicot Town	-	-	-	-	-	-	2	13	-	-
Connah's Quay Nomads	-	-	-	-	-	-	-	-	8	7
Conwy United	-	-	-	-	-	-	-	-	7	13
Cwmbran Town	15	5	3	5	14	4	9	7	1	8
Ebbw Vale	16	3	6	1	4	16	-	11	4	9
Ferndale Athletic	-	-	-	-	-	-	13	16	-	-
Flint Town United	-	-	-	-	-	-	16	4	-	-
Haverfordwest County	4	9	5	6	3	1	3	4	10	15
Holywell Town	-	-	-	-	-	-	-	-	6	5
Inter Cardiff	-	-	-	-	-	-	6	12	2	2
Llanelli	9	13	13	14	-	5	14	10	14	12
Llanidloes Town	-	-	-	-	-	-	-	-	19	-
Llansantffraid	-	-	-	-	-	-	-	-	-	18
Maesteg Park Athletic	6	11	4	10	10	13	5	6	15	19
Milford United	17	7	11	17	-	-	-	-	-	-
Mold Alexandra	-	-	-	-	-	-	-	-	13	14
Newtown	-	-	-	-	-	-	-	-	18	6
Pembroke Borough	14	10	16	9	9	8	10	9	-	-
Pontllanfraith	13	14	9	13	15	15	-	-	-	-
Porthmadog	-	-	-	-	-	-	-	-	9	11
Port Talbot Athletic	3	17	15	11	12	11	15	-	-	-
Ton Pentre	7	8	2	3	8	9	4	5	-	3
No. of clubs competing	**17**	**17**	**17**	**18**	**17**	**16**	**16**	**16**	**20**	**20**

LEICESTERSHIRE & RUTLAND F.A.

Secretary: Ron E Barston,
Holmes Park, Dog & Gun Lane, Whetstone LE8 3LJ (0533 867828).

SENIOR CUP 1993-94

First Round

Anstey Nomads v Earl Shilton	5-3	Cottesmore Amateurs v United Collieries	3-0
Birstall Utd v Friar Lane Old Boys	1-5	Hillcroft v Downes Sports	2-3
Burbage Old Boys v Asfordby Amateurs	2-4	Newfoundpool WMC v Aylestone Park	0-1
Castle Donnington Town v Sileby Town	2-7	Quorn v Huncote	3-1

Second Round

Barrow Town v Friar Lane Old Boys	1-2	Blaby & Whetstone v Syston St Peters	0-1
Harborough Town v Leics Constabulary	3-2	Highfield Rangers v Holwell Sports	3-2
Anstey Nomads v Downes Sports	2-5	Thringstone v Fosse Imps	1-0
Loughborough Dynamo v Quorn	0-3	Lutterworth Town v St Andrews SC	2-3
Barlestone St Giles v Asfordby Amateurs	1-4	Oadby Town v Sileby Town	7-1
Aylestone Park v Barwell	0-2	Houghton Rangers v North Kilworth	0-4
Anstey Town v Kirby Muxloe SC	1-2	Leicester YMCA v Ravenstone	1-13
Cottesmore A. v Narborough & Littlethorpe	1-2	Slack & Parr v Ibstock Welfare	0-5

Third Round

Ravenstone v Houghton Rangers	6-3*(aet)*	Syston St Peters v Thringstone	1-3
Barwell v North Kilworth	9-3	Ibstock Welfare v Harborough Town Imperial	7-0
Downes Sports v Asfordby Amateurs	3-4	Quorn v Narborough & Littlethorpe	3-0
St Andrews SC v Friars Lane Old Boys	4-2	Oadby Town v Kirby Muxloe SC	3-0

Quarter-Finals

Barwell v Thringstone	1-0	Quorn v Ravenstone	6-3
Ibstock Welfare v Asfordby Amateurs	4-1	St Andrews SC v Oadby Town	3-2

Semi-Finals

Ibstock Welfare v Quorn	4-0	St Andrews v Barwell	2-0

Final *(at Leics FA Ground, Holmes Park, Whetstone, 28th March)*: Ibstock Welfare 2, St Andrews SC 1

WESTERBY CUP 1993-94

First Round

Oadby Town v Hinckley Athletic	4-1	Hinckley Town v Friar Lane Old Boys	1-0
St Andrews SC v Birstall United	0-0,2-1	Barwell v Lutterworth Town	3-2

Quarter-Finals

Barwell v Oadby Town	3-2	Leicester City v Holwell Sports	3-2
Shepshed Albion v Leicester United	3-0	Birstall United v Hinckley Town	1-2

Semi-Finals

Shepshed Albion v Leicester City	1-2	Barwell v Hinckley Town	1-2

Final *(at Leicester City FC, Mon 25th April)*: Leicester City 0, Hinckley Town 0 *(att. 3,270)*

EVERARDS BREWERY LEICESTERSHIRE SENIOR LEAGUE

FOUNDED: 1896

President: J M Elsom Esq **Chairman:** P Henwood Esq

Secretary: Mr David Jamieson,
48 King George Road, Loughborough,
Leics LE11 2PA (0509 267912)

For the second time in five years St Andrews won the championship of the Premier Division. Although topping the Division by five points, it wasn't until they won their penultimate game, that they were certain. From the beginning of the season, they were never out of the top six and by the end of February they had moved into the top slot and, apart from the first week in April when Friar Lane moved one point ahead, they retained their position. St Andrews were a model of consistency throughout the season never losing at home in the league and only losing two League matches all season. Also, they were unfortunate not to do the double as they were beaten by an own-goal in the final of the Leicestershire Senior Cup in the last minute.

Friar Lane finished in second place with a superior goal difference over Oadby Town, who had the same number of points. The Friars headed the Premier Division until the middle of February, but losing key players through injuries did not help their cause.

Oadby Town had a very successful season, but reaching the last 16 of the FA Vase meant that they had only played nine league games by the middle of January, leaving 23 fixtures to fulfil by the end of April. Having no floodlights made the task very difficult but, with the co-operation of the clubs and the Management Committee and particularly Birstall United, who have floodlights and loaned their ground for some fixtures, Oadby accomplished their task. In addition to coming third they also won the Sportsworld League Cup beating Barrow in the final.

Holwell, champions for the past two seasons, started off very well being unbeaten in their first ten games and gaining 24 points, but they obtained only 33 points from their remaining 22 games. Inconsistency was their problem and, although top goal scorers in the division with 104 goals, their defence proved vulnerable and they conceeded 65. However, they finished in fourth spot.

Ibstock Welfare had a good season finishing fifth but drew nearly a third of their games. They drew great consolation by defeating St Andrews in the Senior Cup final. Newly promoted Barrow Town had a good season finishing 7th and reaching the final of the Sportsworld Cup. The other promoted club, Cottesmore Amateurs, finished in the lower half of the table, but could look upon the season with satisfaction.

Leicestershire Constabulary finished bottom of the table and struggled right from the start having lost a number of first team players. They went 11 games before securing their first point and just pipped Newfoundpool for the bottom spot.

In Division One, Asfordby Amateurs deservedly topped the table. They lost their first two games, the second on August 28th, but did not lose another League game until they visited Harborough Town Imperials on April 28th. They were very hard pressed until the last couple of weeks by Thringstone, who finished second, Sileby Town (third) and Loughborough Dynamo (fourth). It was a real dog fight for most of the season and particularly in the closing weeks with all of the teams changing positions each week. Ravenstone and Kirby Muxloe performed creditably to finish fifth and sixth respectively. Blaby & Whetstone, after having to seek re-election, did quite well and finished mid table.

Leicester YMCA, who finished at the bottom, and along with Earl Shilton Ablion had to apply for re-election, had a shocking start to the season, going to the 13th game before collecting any points. They never recovered from this dreadful start and, although they improved as the season went on, it proved too big a gap to close.

Earl Shilton gained 16 points from their first 14 games but only managed 10 from their remaining 22 games. Houghton Rangers, who had only 5 points from their first 20 games, improved to the extent of obtaining 25 from their last 16 games thus escaping re-election. United Collieries, newcomers to the League, battled along and finished on a comfortable 36 points and fifth from the bottom.

Many thanks to the sponsors of our League, Everards Brewery, who also sponsored our new floodlight competition, The Beacon Bitter Cup. Our thanks also go to Sportsworld, who sponsored our League Cup.

The upgrading of facilities of the Clubs is going ahead very well and by the beginning of June, the number of Clubs with floodlights should reach double figures.

David Jamieson, Secretary.

PREM. DIV.	P	W	D	L	F	A	PTS
St Andrews SC	32	27	3	2	95	28	*81
Friar Lane OB	32	25	1	6	100	26	76
Oadby Town	32	24	4	4	100	37	76
Holwell Sports	32	17	6	9	104	65	57
Ibstock Welfare	32	15	9	8	60	46	54
Anstey Nomads	32	17	3	12	67	62	54
Burbage Old Boys	32	15	6	11	61	68	51
Barrow Town	32	15	5	12	60	51	50
Highfield Rangers	32	12	7	13	48	57	43
Lutterworth Town	32	11	8	13	53	61	41
Cottesmore Amtrs	32	10	7	15	56	69	37
Birstall United	32	10	6	16	49	55	36
Downes Sports	32	7	9	16	45	78	30
Syston St Peters	32	8	4	20	34	62	28
North Kilworth	32	5	6	21	44	101	21
Newfounpool WMC	32	3	7	22	38	96	16
Leics Constabulary	32	3	5	24	32	84	14

* - points deducted

DIV. ONE	P	W	D	L	F	A	PTS
Asfordby Amateurs	36	27	6	3	113	37	87
Thringstone	36	27	3	6	92	42	84
Sileby Town	36	26	4	6	89	33	82
Loughborough Dyn.	36	26	3	7	109	40	81
Ravenstone	36	23	4	9	106	58	73
Kirby Muxloe SC	36	23	2	11	83	43	71
Narboro'/L'thorpe	36	19	4	13	77	60	61
Fosse Imps	36	17	5	14	65	53	56
Quorn	36	15	3	18	81	74	48
Blaby & Whetstone	36	13	5	18	53	68	44
Harborough Town I.	36	12	6	18	50	76	42
Hillcroft	36	11	6	19	58	84	39
Huncote S & S	36	11	5	20	40	77	38
Anstey Town	36	11	3	22	55	71	36
United Collieries	36	11	3	22	54	81	36
Aylestone Pk OB	36	10	4	22	57	88	34
Houghton Rangers	36	9	3	24	46	105	30
Earl Shilton Alb.	36	7	3	26	48	107	24
Leicester YMCA	36	7	2	26	48	127	23

PREMIER DIVISION CLUBS 1994-95

ANSTEY NOMADS

Secretary: Andy Coleman, 14 Church Lane, Anstey, Leicester LE7 7AF (0533 363191).
Ground: Cropston Road, Anstey, Leicester (0533 364868).
Directions: Anstey Lane from Leicester to Anstey, right at r'bout into Cropston Rd. 1 mile from London Road (BR).
Seats: None **Cover:** 100 **Capacity:** 2,500 **Floodlights:** No **Founded:** 1945.
Cols: Red & white stripes/black/black **Record Gate:** 4,500 v Hayes, FA Amtr Cup 53-54.
Programme: 12-14 pages, 25p **Hons:** Leics Snr Lg 51-52 53-54 81-82 82-83 (Div 2 73-74).

ASFORDBY AMATEURS

Secretary: Miss Alison Smith, 17 Cheviot Drive, Shepshed, Leics LE12 9ED (0509 502857).
Ground: Hoby Road Sports Ground, Asfordby, Melton Mowbray (0664 434545).
Colours: Green/black/black **Hons:** Leics Snr Lg Div 1 93-94

BARROW TOWN

Secretary: Nick J Freeman, 1 Beacon Drive, Loughborough, Leics LE11 2BD (0509 212853).
Ground: Riverside Park, Barrow Road, Quorn, Leics (0509 620650).
Colours: Red & white/black/red
Hons: Leics Snr Lg Div 1 92-93 (Lg Cup R-up 93-94), Loughborough Charity Cup R-up 92-93.

BIRSTALL UNITED

Secretary: Bob Garrard, 58 Halstead Rd, Mountsorrel, Leicester LE12 7HF (0533 376886).
Ground: Meadow Lane, Birstall (671230) **Directions:** Off Wanlip Lane, Birstall. **Floodlights:** Yes.
Colours: White/navy/white **Hons:** Leics Snr Lg Div 2 76-77.

BURBAGE OLD BOYS

Secretary: Mrs S Taylor, 8 Brockhurst Avenue, Burbage, Leics LE10 2HG (0455 633916).
Colours: Blue/white/royal **Ground:** Britannia Rd, Burbage, Leics (0455 890413).
Hons: Leics Snr Lg Div 1 91-92.

COTTESMORE AMATEURS

Secretary: K Nimmons, 17 Redwing Close, Oakham, Rutland LE15 6DA (0572 724582).
Ground: Rogues Park, Main Street, Cottesmore, Rutland (0572 813486).
Floodlights: Yes **Colours:** Green/black/green.

DOWNES SPORTS

Secretary: Stuart Millidge, 25 Elizabeth Rd, Hinckley, Leics LE10 0QY (0455 635808).
Colours: Tangerine/black/tangerine **Ground:** Leicester Rd, Hinckley *(adjacent Hinckley Town FC)*

FRIAR LANE OLD BOYS

Secretary: J Knibbs, 75 Brighton Avenue, Wigston Fields, Leicester LE18 1JB (0533 888928).
Ground: Knighton Lane East, Leicester (0533 833629).
Directions: Between A50 Welford Rd and Saffron Lane near Sports Centre.
Seats: None **Cover:** 250 **Capacity:** 3,500 **Floodlights:** No **Founded:** 1961.
Colours: Black & white stripes/black/black
Record Gate: 1,325 v Stamford, FA Vase Semi Final April 1975.
Hons: FA Vase SF(2) 74-76, Leics Snr Lg(7) 70-72 73-78 (R-up 92-93 93-94, Div 2 69-70), Leics Snr Cup(3) 73-75 91-92

HIGHFIELD RANGERS

Secretary: Maurice Christian, 18 Blanklyn Avenue, Leicester LE5 5FA (0533 734002).
Ground: 443 Gleneagles Ave., Rushey Mead, Leicester (0533 660009)
Directions: A6 to Leicester, 2nd left at Birstall r'bout into Watermead/Troon Way, right at 2nd lights, 1st left.
Colours: Yellow/black/yellow **Previous League:** Central Mids (until 1992).

HOLWELL SPORTS

Secretary: Mrs Margaret Hutton, 25 Welby Rd, Asfordby Hill, Melton Mowbray LE14 3RB (0664 812151).
Ground: Welby Road, Asfordby Hill, Melton Mowbray, Leics (0664 812663)
Directions: One and a half miles out of Melton Mowbray on A607 to Loughborough.
Previous Name: Holwell Works **Cols:** Green & gold/green/green & gold **Floodlights:** Yes.
Hons: Leics Snr Lg 11-12 86-87 91-92 92-93 (Div 1 84-85, Tebbutt Brown Cup R-up 92-93), Leics Snr Cup 54-55 56-57 57-58.

IBSTOCK WELFARE

Secretary: R A Wilkinson, 6 Valley Rd, Ibstock, Leicester LE67 6NY (0530 260744).
Ground: The Welfare, Leicester Road, Ibstock (0530 260656). **Colours:** All red.
Hons: Leics Snr Cup 93-94

LEICESTERSHIRE CONSTABULARY

Secretary: Mrs Judith Leacy, 6 Lena Drive, Groby, Leicester LE6 0FJ (0530 243110).
Colours: Yellow/green/green **Ground:** Police HQ, St Johns, Enderby (0533 482198).

LUTTERWORTH TOWN

Secretary: Kevin Zupp, 14 Swiftway, Lutterworth, Leics LE17 4PB (0455 550358).
Ground: Hall Lane, Bitteswell, Lutterworth, Leics (0455 554046)
Directions: M6 jct 1 or M1 jct 20, follow A426 through Lutterworth; Bitteswell signposted one and a half miles on beyond town.
Seats: None **Cover:** None **Capacity:** 3,000 **Floodlights:** Yes **Founded:** 1890.
Previous Ground: Dunley Way (pre-1991) **Programme:** 24 pages with admission.
Colours: White/navy/navy
Clubhouse: Normal licensing hours **Hons:** Leics Snr Lg 90-91 (Div 2 80-81).

NEWFOUNDPOOL W.M.C.

Secretary: Reg Molloy, 110 Wand Street, Leicester LE4 5BU (0533 665051).
Ground: Meadow Lane, Birstall (0533 673965).
Directions: Off Wanlip Lane, Birstall. First of two ground in Meadow Lane.
Colours: Green & yellow stripes/green/green & yellow.
Hons: Leics Snr Lg 65-66 69-70 (Div 2 82-83), Leics Snr Cup 68-69.

NORTH KILWORTH

Secretary: R Bell, 3 High Street, North Kilworth, Lutterworth, Leics LE17 6ET (0858 464048)(Steve Bell).
Ground: Rugby Road, North Kilworth, Lutterworth, Leics (0858 880890).
Cols: Blue & white halves/white/blue **Hons:** Leics Snr Lg Div 2 R-up 91-92.

OADBY TOWN

Secretary: D P Collins, 26 Hill Way, Oadby, Leics LE2 5YG (0533 713557).
Ground: Invicta Park, Wigston Road, Oadby, Leics (0533 715728)
Directions: Oadby is four miles south of Leicester on A6. From Oadby church in town centre follow signs for Wigston; ground three quarters of a mile on left.
Seats: None **Cover:** 200 **Capacity:** 2,000 **Prog:** 20 pages **Founded:** 1939.
Colours: Red/white/black **Clubhouse:** Matchdays only
Hons: Leics Snr Lg 63-64 67-68 68-69 72-73 (Div 2 51-52, Lg Cup 93-94), Leics Snr Cup 62-63 63-64 75-76 76-77 80-81, FA Vase 5th Rd 93-94.

St ANDREWS SOCIAL CLUB

Secretary: Martin Wilson, 3 Ainsdale Rd, Western Park, Leicester LE3 0UD (0533 858227).
Ground: Canal Street, Old Aylestone, Leicester (0533 839298).
Directions: Aylestone Rd at rear of Granby Street School.
Colours: Black & white/black/red **Floodlights:** Yes.
Hons: Leics Snr Lg 89-90 93-94 (Tebbutt Brown Cup 92-93), Leics Snr Cup R-up 93-94.

THRINGSTONE MINERS WELFARE

Secretary: Paul A Nelson, 30 Bardon Rd, Coalville, Leics (0530 838694).
Ground: Homestead Road, Thringstone (0530 223367).
Colours: Gold/black/gold. **Hons:** Leics Snr Lg 84-85 (Div 1 R-up 93-94, Div 2 71-72).

DIVISION ONE CLUBS 1994-95

ANSTEY TOWN

Secretary: G Ford, 99 Hollow Rd, Anstey, Leics LE7 7FR (0533 364170).
Ground: Leicester Road, Thurcaston (0533 368231) **Colours:** All blue

AYLESTONE PARK OLD BOYS

Secretary: Brendon Tyrrell, 8 Melbourne Close, Kibworth, Beauchamp, Leicester LE8 0JP (0533 793136).
Ground: Dorset Avenue, Fairfield Estate, Wigston, Leics (0533 775307)
Colours: Red & white/white/red **Floodlights:** Yes.

BARDON HILL

Secretary: Adrian Bishop, 138 Bradgate Drive, Coalville, Leics LE67 4HG (0530 815560).
Ground: Bardon Close, Coalville, Leicester (0530 815560).
Colours: Yellow & green/green/yellow **Previous League:** North Leics (pre-1994).

BLABY & WHETSTONE ATHLETIC

Secretary: Mrs S C Morris, 10 Winchester Road, Blaby, Leics LE8 3HJ (0533 773208).
Ground: Blaby & Whetstone Boys Club, Warwick Road, Whetstone (0533 864852). **Colours:** All blue

EARL SHILTON ALBION

Secretary: Adrian Knight, 19 Waverly Rd, Blaby, Leics LE8 3HH (0533 785042).
Ground: Stoneycroft Park, New Street, Earl Shilton, Leics (0455 844277).
Colours: All green **Hons:** Leics Snr Lg Div 2 68-69 79-80 88-89, Leics Snr Cup 72-73.

FOSSE IMPS

Secretary: Ivan V Colbourne, 55 Harrowgate Drive, Birstall, Leics LE4 3GQ (0533 671424).
Ground: Co-op Ground, Birstall Rd, Leicester (0533 674059) **Cols:** Red/white/black

HARBOROUGH TOWN IMPERIAL

Secretary: Gary Waterfield, 4 Lindsey Gdns, Market Harborough, Leics LE16 9JF (0858 431620).
Ground: Imperial Park, Northampton Road Sports Ground, Market Harborough, Leics.
Colours: Red & black stripes/black/black **Hons:** Leics Snr Lg Div 1 83-84.
Previous Ground: St Mary's Road (until 1992).

HILLCROFT

Secretary: Bruce Parry, 43 Blenheim Rd, Birstall, Leicester LE4 4FP (0533 677293).
Ground: Lawrence Park, Gipsy Lane, Leicester (0533 461209) **Colours:** Yellow & blue/blue/blue.

HOUGHTON RANGERS

Secretary: J P Silver, 'Red Roofs', 41 Main St., Houghton-on-the-Hill, Leics LE7 9GE (0533 433951).
Ground: Weir Lane, Houghton-on-the-Hill, Leics (0533 419551).
Colours: Blue/white/white **Hons:** Leics Snr Lg Div 2 90-91.

HUNCOTE SPORTS & SOCIAL

Secretary: D Russell, 72 Sycamore Way, Littlethorpe, Leics LE9 5HU (0533 841952).
Ground: Enderby Lane, Thurlaston, Leics (0455 888430). **Colours:** All blue.

KIRBY MUXLOE S.C.

Secretary: R Pallett, 184 Blackbird Road, Leicester LE4 0AF (0533 626020).
Ground: Ratby Lane, Kirby Muxloe (0533 393201) **Colours:** All blue.

LEICESTER Y.M.C.A.

Secretary: C W Chappell, 132 South Knighton Road, Leicester LE2 3LQ (0533 702721).
Ground: Belvoir Drive, Aylestone, Leicester (0533 440740) **Colours:** Red/white/red

LOUGHBOROUGH DYNAMO

Secretary: Max Hutchinson, 3 Wythburn Close, Loughborough, Leics LE11 3SZ (0509 266092).
Ground: Nanpanton Sport Ground, Loughborough (0509 612144).
Colours: Gold/black/gold. **Clubhouse:** Yes **Cover:** Yes **Programme:** Yes.

NARBOROUGH & LITTLETHORPE

Secretary: Ronald Bexley, 53 Trinity Rd, St Johns, Narborough, Leics LE9 5BW (0533 862818).
Ground: Leicester Road, Narborough (Near M1 bridge) (0533 751855).
Directions: M1 jct 21, follow signs to Narborough (2 miles).
Colours: All blue **Hons:** Leics Snr Lg Div 2 81-82.

QUORN

Secretary: W L Caunt, 64 Wood Lane, Quorn, Leics LE12 8DB (0509 414213).
Ground: Farley Way, Quorn, Leics (0533 620490).
Colours: Red/white/red **Previous Ground:** Warwick Av. (pre-1993) **Floodlights:** Yes
Hons: Leics Snr Cup 53-54.

RAVENSTONE

Secretary: Robert Brooks, 17 Ashland Drive, Coalville, Leics LE67 3NH (0530 833269).
Ground: Ravenslea Estate, Ravenstone, Leics.
Directions: A607 Leicester-Melton Mowbray road, on entering Syston take 1st fork left into Broad Street after railway bridge. Necton Street is third left.
Programme: 20 pages, 50p with entry **Prev. Lge:** Nth Leics (pre-1992) **Cover:** No.
Colours: Yellow & blue/blue/yellow.

SAFFRON DYNAMO

Secretary: Bob King, 14 Bramley Close, Broughton Astley, Leicester LE9 6QU (0455 284270).
Ground: Cambridge Road, Whetstone
Cols: Red & black stripes/black/black **Previous League:** Leicester & District (pre-1994).

SILEBY TOWN

Secretary: G Clarke, 123 Highgate Road, Sileby, Leics LE12 7PW (0509 813503).
Ground: Memorial Park, Seagrave Road, Sileby, Leics (0509 816104)
Colours: All blue. **Hons:** Leics Snr Lg Div 1 R-up 92-93.

SYSTON St PETERS

Secretary: Allan Walton, 73 Broad Str., Syston, Leicester (0533 696773).
Ground: Memorial Ground, Necton Street, Syston, Leics (0533 696773).
Directions: A607 Leicester-Melton Mowbray road, on entering Syston take 1st fork left into Broad Street after railway bridge. Necton Street is third left.
Colours: Red & black stripes/black/black **Hons:** Leics Snr Lg 61-62 (Div 2 60-61).

UNITED COLLIERIES

Secretary: John Meason, 29 Standard Hill, Coalville, Leics LE67 3HN (0530 810941).
Ground: 1 Terrace Rd, Ellistown, Coalville.
Previous Names: Bagworth Colliery/ Ellistown Colliery - clubs merged in 1993.
Colours: Yellow/royal/royal.
Previous Ground: Station Road, Bagworth (pre-1994).

Holwell Sports forward Spencer delivers a cross during his side's 4-1 win at Cottesmore Amateurs.
Photo - Martin Wray.

Dean Culpin's powerful shot is turned home by Simon Cook (No.9) for Oadby Town's third goal in their 5-1 win over Cogenhoe United at the Leicestershire FA ground. Oadby's win put them through to the last sixteen of the FA Vase - the best showing by a Senior League club in the competition for several seasons.
Photo - Chris Monument.

LEICESTER CITY

(Founded 1898)

LEAGUE

Cital Motor Insurance Prem. Div.

	P	W	D	L	F	A	PTS
New Parks	20	20	0	0	114	14	60
Wreake Valley	20	13	1	6	59	38	40
Rothley Imps	20	11	2	7	54	43	35
Wellington Vics '86	20	11	1	8	54	48	34
Premier Athletic	20	9	2	9	42	41	29
Anstey United	20	8	3	9	39	53	27
Ratby SC	20	7	3	10	33	51	24
GNG	20	7	1	12	39	51	22
St Patricks	20	6	2	12	40	54	20
Bharat	20	6	0	14	35	76	18
Goodwins	20	4	1	15	29	69	13

Top Scorers: S Glover (New Parks) 39, M Gotch (New Parks) 27, A Lucas (Rothley Imps) 18.

DIV. ONE	P	W	D	L	F	A	PTS
Oadby BC Old Boys	20	18	2	0	76	33	56
New Parks Res.	20	17	1	2	58	21	52
British United	20	9	6	5	57	46	33
FC Khalsa	20	10	1	9	52	44	31
Last Straw	20	9	1	10	62	61	28
Wigston '82	20	8	2	10	35	41	26
Glen Villa	20	7	3	10	39	42	24
FC Flamingo	20	7	2	11	44	45	23
FC Blaby	20	6	1	13	57	61	19
Kirkland	20	5	2	13	43	71	17
Victoria Pk Rgrs	20	3	1	16	34	92	10

Top Scorers: A Blanchard (Last Straw) 26, N Clarke (Oadby BCOB) 25, A Gokanile (FC Flamingo) 20.

Coalville Trophies D2	W	D	L	F	A	PTS	
Park End '74	26	14	5	7	126	76	47
Union Inn	26	13	6	7	70	56	45
Kirby Muxloe '87	26	14	5	7	80	67	*44
Leicester Fijian	26	13	4	9	90	73	43
Aylestone WMC	26	10	10	6	66	55	40
Buckminster Rgrs	26	11	5	10	83	71	38
Premier Ath. Res.	26	13	2	11	67	74	*38
Westhill United	26	11	3	12	61	63	36
Premier Percussion	26	11	2	13	85	79	35
Wreake Valley Res.	26	11	2	13	56	81	35
Ratby Sports Res.	26	9	4	13	61	69	31
FC Francis	26	8	4	14	61	89	28
Glen Hills	26	8	2	16	72	102	26
Rothly Imps Res.	26	7	4	15	60	83	25

* - 3 points deducted

Top Scorers: S Hope (Park End '74) 55, A Aldwinckle (Park End '74) 40, W Franklin (Buckminster Rgrs) 32.

DIV. THREE	P	W	D	L	F	A	PTS
FC Glen Parva	26	25	0	1	143	22	75
Hydroset	26	19	4	3	100	43	61
PSV Dominion	26	15	3	8	77	54	48
Metro '76	26	14	4	8	79	33	46
Vulcan	26	11	4	11	62	73	37
Primethorpe	26	10	6	10	71	54	36
Bowers	26	12	3	11	67	73	*36
Fresha Bakeries	26	11	3	12	57	69	36
Kirkland Res.	26	10	5	11	51	52	35
Wellington V. Res.	26	8	4	14	66	64	28
Wigston '82 Res.	26	7	5	14	37	66	26
Glen Villa Res.	26	8	2	16	42	80	26
Aylestone WMC Res.	26	7	3	16	43	87	*21
Leicester YMCA '90	26	1	2	23	36	161	5

* - 3 points deducted

Top Scorers: N Owen (FC Glen Parva) 46, G Higgins (Hydroset) 32, J McCabe (FC Glen Parva) 26.

DIV. FOUR	P	W	D	L	F	A	PTS
New Park 'A'	26	21	3	2	95	36	66
Ratby SC 'A'	26	18	3	5	75	29	57
FC Khalsa Res.	26	16	5	5	83	47	53
FC Francis Res.	26	16	4	6	76	49	*49
Corinthians	26	15	3	8	80	64	48
Willowbrook	26	14	4	8	94	65	46
Last Straw Res.	26	11	3	12	63	80	36
Southfields '92	26	11	1	14	79	99	34
Kirkland 'A'	26	9	4	13	51	68	31
Wreake Valley 'A'	26	6	7	13	73	84	25
Kirby Muxloe Res.	26	7	2	17	42	80	23
Glen Hills Res.	26	7	0	19	42	84	21
GNG Res.	26	5	4	17	63	78	19
Metro '76 Res.	26	3	3	20	42	95	12

* - 3 points deducted

Top Scorers: J Lyons (Ratby SC 'A') 32, H Smith (Willowbrook) 32, M Holder (FC Francis Res.) 28.

DIV. FIVE	P	W	D	L	F	A	PTS
Charnwood Rgrs	18	15	3	0	50	15	48
Elliott	18	13	2	3	81	25	41
Birstall Albion	18	12	1	5	58	29	37
FC Flamingo Res.	18	9	3	6	47	40	30
British Utd Res.	18	9	4	5	63	48	*28
Oadby BC '93	18	5	4	9	38	50	19
Belgrave Vics	18	5	3	10	46	45	18
Rushey Rangers	18	4	0	14	42	99	12
Ratby SC 'B'	18	3	2	13	35	70	11
Primethorpe Res.	18	3	2	13	19	58	11

* - 3 points deducted

Top Scorers: S Heggs (Elliott) 23, I Atkinson (Birstall Albion) 23, N Carson (Birstall Utd) 23, G Brindley (British Utd Res.) 17.

Steve Jones Mem. Cup winners: New Parks
Pinkerton League Cup: New Parks Res.

LEICESTER & DISTRICT MUTUAL LEAGUE (Est. 1900)

G H Electrical PD	W	D	L	F	A	PTS	
Scraptoft United	24	19	4	1	81	16	61
KRR WMC	24	19	3	2	123	30	60
Indiana	24	16	4	4	84	39	52
Spring Grove	24	16	3	5	82	39	*49
Highfield Rgrs Res.	24	14	1	9	57	38	43
Kibworth Town	24	13	3	8	88	36	42
Eastwood	24	10	4	10	55	74	34
Earl of Stamford	24	10	3	11	75	58	33
Wigston Couriers	24	7	1	16	44	83	22
Greensleeves	24	6	1	17	51	102	19
Spencers United	24	5	3	16	53	81	18
Enderby '93	24	4	1	19	45	145	13
Needham Rangers	24	1	1	22	36	133	4

* - 2 points deducted

DIV. ONE	P	W	D	L	F	A	PTS
Brookside	26	20	3	3	135	44	63
Sping Grove Res.	26	20	3	3	121	41	63
P D Imps	26	19	3	4	113	51	60
Parva Wayfarers	26	15	3	8	90	59	48
Saffron '85	26	13	4	9	70	69	43
Leicester Saints	26	11	7	8	77	60	40
Meridian	26	11	6	9	81	73	39
Pick Everard	26	11	4	11	63	76	37
Birstall OB	26	11	2	13	73	79	35
Cosby Utd 'A'	26	7	5	14	55	92	26
Hands Athletic	26	5	6	15	65	100	21
Huncote S & S 'A'	26	5	4	17	60	86	19
Barsby & District	26	4	6	16	52	103	18
Georges	26	1	2	23	33	155	5

DIV. TWO	P	W	D	L	F	A	PTS
AA Sports	24	20	1	3	129	40	61
Cosby United 'B'	24	17	3	4	84	35	54
Wyvern Rail	24	15	4	5	75	49	49
Kibworth T. Res.	24	14	4	6	70	28	46
Hinckley Central	24	13	5	6	73	56	44
Earl of Stam. Res.	24	11	2	11	86	65	35
Humberstone St M.	24	10	3	11	45	52	33
Pick Everard Res.	24	10	1	13	54	84	31
Spencers Utd Res.	24	8	6	10	40	65	30
Needham Rgrs Res.	24	9	1	14	45	75	28
Meridian Res.	24	8	3	13	69	58	27
Fisher Rosemount	24	2	2	20	30	108	8
Birstall OB Res.	24	1	1	22	41	126	4

T.M.S. MOTOR GROUP LEICESTER & DISTRICT LEAGUE

Volvo Prem.	P	W	D	L	F	A	PTS
Dunton Bassett	28	22	2	4	100	28	68
Croxton Kerrial	28	20	5	3	101	41	65
Cosby United	28	19	6	3	84	42	63
Saffron Dynamo	28	17	3	8	83	48	54
Greetham United	28	15	4	9	71	48	49
GEC Spts & Soc.	28	12	7	9	50	41	43
British Shoe	28	10	4	14	54	61	34
G & D United	28	9	6	13	48	54	33
Glenfield Town	28	10	3	15	55	62	33
City Gas	28	8	6	14	43	59	30
Blaby United	28	9	3	16	47	92	30
Uppingham Town	28	8	4	16	54	84	28
Syston Town	28	7	7	14	49	80	28
Birstall RBL	28	5	4	19	28	73	19
Sapcote United	28	5	4	19	50	104	19

Landrover D1	P	W	D	L	F	A	PTS
Magna '73	18	13	2	3	51	15	41
Stoney Stanton	18	11	3	4	51	20	36
Newbold Jubilee	18	10	1	7	37	30	31
Stoke Golding	18	10	0	8	46	43	30
County Hall	18	8	2	8	39	39	26
Epworth	18	8	0	10	29	34	24
Heather St Johns	18	7	2	9	42	47	23
Thurmaston SC	18	7	1	10	39	46	22
Queniborough	18	7	1	10	23	32	22
Fleckney	18	3	0	15	28	73	9

Nissan D2	P	W	D	L	F	A	PTS
DCE Thurmaston	20	15	4	1	68	27	49
Pedigree Petfoods	20	12	5	3	69	30	41
Desford Bucks	20	13	2	5	51	23	41
Frisby United	20	10	3	7	47	51	33
Welby Lane Utd	20	9	3	8	37	42	30
Hinckley Town Res.	20	10	2	8	57	44	*29
Lutterworth Ath.	20	6	3	11	32	39	21
Apollo	20	6	2	12	40	56	20
Tungstone '85	20	6	4	10	33	51	*19
Thurnby United	20	4	1	15	27	62	13
Dainite Sports	20	3	3	14	16	51	12

* - 3 points deducted

Reserve Prem.	P	W	D	L	F	A	PTS
Cosby United	24	17	5	2	74	22	56
Saffron Dynamo	24	12	9	3	61	29	45
GEC Spts & Soc.	24	12	7	5	45	28	43
Syston Town	24	10	7	7	42	35	37
G & D United	24	10	7	7	47	42	37
County Hall	24	8	10	6	41	37	34
City Gas	24	8	8	8	55	54	32
Epworth	24	6	8	10	32	44	26
Blaby United	24	6	7	11	51	55	25
British Shoe	24	5	9	10	45	62	24
Heather St Johns	24	5	8	11	51	63	23
Uppingham Town	24	7	1	16	46	88	22
Glenfield Town	24	4	6	14	38	68	18

Reserve Div 1.	P	W	D	L	F	A	PTS
Stoney Stanton	24	21	2	1	108	23	65
Desford Bucks	24	20	2	2	89	34	62
Dunton Bassett	24	15	4	5	72	44	49
Birstall RBL	24	13	3	8	70	61	42
Stoke Golding	24	11	6	7	74	39	39
Lutterworth Ath.	24	11	2	11	42	43	35
Magna '73	24	10	2	12	67	58	32
Thurmaston SSC	24	8	8	8	69	72	32
Queniborough	24	6	6	12	53	62	24
Newbold Jubilee	24	6	5	13	31	65	23
Fleckney	24	6	2	16	41	84	20
Dainite Sports	24	2	5	17	25	80	11
Sapcote United	24	1	5	18	34	110	8

Cup Finals:
League Cup: G & D Utd 7, Sapcote Utd 4
Threesons Trophy: Magna '73 3, County Hall 2
Chairman's Shield: Dunton Bassett Reserves 1, Stoney Stanton Reserves 0

MARCONI LEICESTERSHIRE YOUTH LEAGUE

U-18 PREM. DIV.	P	W	D	L	F	A	PTS
Seaton Youth	14	13	1	0	70	17	27
Woodgate '80	14	8	2	4	53	36	18
Queniborough Jnrs	14	8	1	5	36	31	17
Whitwick Juniors	14	7	2	5	42	36	16
Cosby United	14	6	3	5	33	34	15*
Glenfield Town	14	4	3	7	38	36	11
Fosse Rangers	14	1	2	11	16	55	4
Pedigree Petfoods	14	1	2	11	19	62	4

U-17 DIV. ONE	P	W	D	L	F	A	PTS
Magna '73 Youth	18	16	0	2	80	13	32
Hinckley Town	18	15	1	2	79	18	31
Queniborough Jnrs	18	11	2	5	58	27	24
Aylestone Imperials	18	10	4	4	60	36	24
Ratby Groby	18	10	1	7	58	51	21
Beaumont Royals	18	6	3	9	39	51	15
Asfordby Amtrs	18	3	6	9	46	64	12
Marlborough Rovers	18	4	2	12	29	53	10
Barrow Town	18	2	2	14	21	80	6
Humberstone Rgrs	18	2	1	15	32	111	5

U-16 DIV. ONE	P	W	D	L	F	A	PTS
Aylestone Imperials	16	13	3	0	80	16	29
Loughborough Dyn.	16	12	2	2	54	14	26
Sileby Town	16	9	2	5	38	29	20
Syston Town	16	7	4	5	47	42	18
Burbage & Wolvey	16	5	4	7	37	36	14
Oadby Town	16	5	3	8	28	37	13
Ratby Groby	16	5	2	9	36	52	12
Melton Foxes	16	4	3	9	32	52	11
Oadby Owls	16	0	1	15	14	88	1

Lower Division Champions:
U-17 Div. 2 (10): Ashby Road Spts Club
U-16 Div. 2 (9): Narborough & Littlethorpe
U-16 Div. 3 (8): Barwell Athletic.

COALVILLE SUNDAY YOUTH LEAGUE

'Central of Coalville'

Under-16s Div.	P	W	D	L	F	A	PTS
Hugglescote Manor	16	11	3	2	88	27	25
Merlin Boys	16	12	1	3	62	13	23
Anglesey Rovers	16	11	3	2	67	21	23
Moira United	16	10	1	5	67	23	21
Shelthorpe Hearts	16	8	0	8	50	52	16
Whitwick Juniors	16	7	0	9	69	35	14
Marlborough Rovers	16	4	0	12	41	81	8
ASC Dayncourt	16	4	0	12	26	79	8
Blackbird Youth	16	1	0	15	18	151	2

Merlin Boys beat Anglesey Rovers 1-0 in play-off for runners-up position.

Lower Division Champions:
Charnwood Home Centre u-15 (red) Div. (10): Burleigh Imps
Team Photographic 3 u-15 (blue) Div. (6): Merlin Boys
George Hind u-14 (red) Div. (10): Ashby Woulds
George Hind u-15 (blue) Div. (10): Ibstock Welfare
J F Lloyd & Sons u-13 (red) Div. (9): Marlborough Rovers
J F Lloyd & Sons u-13 (blue) Div. (11): Loughborough United
T R Farmer u-12 (red) Div. (10): Moira United
T R Farmer u-12 (blue) Div. (10): Rothley Imps
Mason & Son u-11 (red) Div. (9): Marlborough Rovers
A J Wagstaff u-11 (blue) Div. (9): Aston Juniors
Upton & Pegg u-10 Div. (12): Newhall Boys

LEICESTER SUNDAY LEAGUE

FOUNDED: 1989

Sportsworld Prem.	P	W	D	L	F	A	PTS
Westcotes United	18	16	0	2	105	26	48
Leicester Market	18	13	2	3	75	28	41
Mayflower Sunday	18	10	5	3	60	30	35
Saffron Dynamo	18	10	2	6	49	39	32
East Goscote	18	9	2	7	46	41	29
Leicester City Bus	18	8	3	7	46	43	27
Demes Athletic	18	5	3	10	41	55	18
Aylestone Pk Celtic	18	4	1	13	40	78	13
Knighton Athletic	18	3	2	13	32	67	*5
Leicester YMCA Sun.	18	2	0	16	20	107	*0

* - 6 points deducted

Lower Division Champions:
Div. 1 (11): Magna Windows
Sonney James D2 (11): Coach & Horses Anstey
Div. 3 (11): Syston RBL
Bells D4 (12): Dog & Gun Kilby
Div. 5 (12): Glenfield Rangers
Div. 6 (12): Park View
Div. 5 (12): GT Reserves

Cup Finals:
Everards Brewery Lge Cup: Leic City Bus 3, Demes 2
Griffin Senior Cup: Westcotes Utd 5, Demes Ath. 4
Andy Richardson Memorial Cup: Leicester Market 3, Westcotes United 2
Bostik Chairmans Cup: Dog & Gun Kilby 4, Glenfield Rangers 3
Presidents Cup: Charnwood Athletic '88 5, Leicester Market Reserves 1
Invitation Trophy: Aylestone United 2, Tower Hospital SSC Reserves 0

HINCKLEY SUNDAY LEAGUE

PREM. DIV.	P	W	D	L	F	A	PTS
Whetstone United	18	15	2	1	75	17	47
Scraptoft W.	18	13	3	2	81	26	42
Swan	18	10	1	7	57	30	31
Magna '73	18	9	2	7	53	35	29
Rutland Rovers	18	7	6	5	48	50	27
Tudor	18	8	1	9	55	75	25
Ambion BH	18	4	4	10	29	69	16
Cross Keys	18	4	2	12	29	57	14
Red Lion Earl Shilton	18	3	4	11	32	54	13
St Peters	18	3	3	12	27	72	12

Lower Division Champions:
Div. 1 (9): Sir Robert Peel
Div. 2 (12): Seaton United
Div. 3 (11): Parvia '87
Div. 4 (11): Oak Athletic
Div. 5 (13): Needham Rangers
Div. 6 (10): John Carr
Div. 7 (10): Gloucester City Supporters

Cup Winners:
Quality Roofing Senior Cup: Whetstone United (runners-up: Rutland Rovers).
Les Moore Memorial Cup: Polisox
Junior Cup: Countryman

Leicestershire Senior League side Oadby Town's exciting FA Vase run eventually came to end back at their own home ground, Invicta Park, against Arlesey Town in the Fifth Round. Here Oadby's tricky winger Chris Whitmore (right) battles for possession with an Arlesey opponent.

Photo - Chris Monument.

LINCOLNSHIRE F.A.

Secretary: Mr F S Richardson,
PO Box 26, 12 Dean Road, Lincoln LN2 4DP (0522 524917).

SENIOR CUP 1993-94

First Round

Scunthorpe Utd v Gainsborough Trinity	3-1	Lincoln City v Grantham Town	2-3

Semi-Finals

Boston United v Grantham Town	2-0	Grimsby Town v Scunthorpe United	2-0

Final *(at Grimsby Town FC, Tues 23rd November 1993)*: Grimsby Town 1, Boston United 0

SENIOR 'A' CUP 1993-94

Preliminary Round

Bourne Town v Mirrlees Blackstone	1-0	Stamford v Boston	1-2
Lincoln United v Spalding United	2-1	Nettleham v Louth United	1-2

Quarter-Finals

Brigg Town v Immingham Town	0-0,3-0	Winterton Rangers v Boston	0-4
Holbeach United v Louth United	2-1	Lincoln United v Bourne Town	5-2

Semi-Finals

Lincoln United v Boston	2-0	Holbeach United v Brigg Town	1-2

Final *(at Brigg Town FC, Tues 10th May)*: Brigg Town 5, Lincoln United 2

SENIOR 'B' CUP 1993-94

Preliminary Round

Bottesford Town v Grimsby Amateurs	7-2

First Round

Long Sutton Ath. v Hykeham United	3-0	Skegness Town v Deeping Rangers	4-1
Harrowby United v Wyberton	1-7	Limestone Rangers v Bottesford Town	0-3
Ruston Sports v Lincoln Moorlands	2-0	Spilsby Town v Immingham Blossom Way	0-2
Sleasford Town v Appleby Frodingham	3-0	Hykeham Town v Louth Old Boys	2-1

Quarter-Finals

Skegness Town v Ruston Sports	1-0	Long Sutton Ath. v Bottesford Town	3-1*(aet)*
Sleaford Town v Wyberton	3-4	Immingham Blossom Way Spts v Hykeham Town	0-2

Semi-Finals

Wyberton v Skegness Town	3-1	Hykeham Town v Long Sutton Ath.	1-1,2-0

Final *(at Boston Utd FC, Wed 30th March)*: Wyberton beat Hykeham Town 4-1 on pens after a 2-2 draw.

Wyberton FC - Lincolnshire Senior 'B' Cup winners 1993-94.

Photo - Martin Wray.

T.S.W. PRINTERS (SCUNTHORPE) LINCOLNSHIRE LEAGUE

President: Mr M Jackson

Hon. Secretary: Mr R Hewson, 'Raylaine', 219 Scotter Rd, Scunthorpe DN15 7EJ (0724 846166)

The season began on Saturday 14th August and closed on Saturday 7th May. Twenty teams took part including three new sides; Limestone Rangers, Lincoln Moorlands and Boston Reserves. Two of the newcomers (Limestone Rangers and Lincoln Moorlands) topped the table for a number of weeks giving the established clubs a run for their money. In all 374 matches were played, four results being awarded by the Committee when clubs were unable to raise teams.

Paul Birkitt, Hon. Assistant Secretary.

FINAL TABLE	P	W	D	L	F	A	PTS
Appleby Frodingham	38	28	3	7	107	39	87
Bottesford Town	38	26	6	6	100	45	#81
Wyberton	38	25	6	7	80	40	**81
Immingham BW Spts	38	24	8	6	107	47	80
Hykeham Town	38	24	5	9	118	37	77
Limestone Rangers	38	23	2	13	87	61	*71
Lincoln Moorlands	38	21	6	11	89	49	69
Boston United Res.	38	19	8	11	95	70	65
Sleaford Town	38	19	8	11	86	68	65
Lincoln Utd Colts	38	20	4	14	84	73	*64
Grimsby Amateurs	38	17	5	16	74	68	56
Louth Old Boys	38	11	6	21	54	86	+#41
Skegness Town	38	13	5	20	67	80	x#40
Louth Utd Amtrs	38	11	6	21	62	84	39
BRSA Retford	38	10	5	23	48	94	35
Ruston Sports	38	9	7	22	57	77	34
Nettleham Res.	38	10	4	24	62	118	34
Spilsby Town	38	8	7	23	62	90	31
Hykeham United	38	5	4	29	42	104	*22
Boston Res.	38	2	5	31	29	188	*14

* - 3 points awarded
\# - 3 points deducted
\+ - 2 points awarded
x - 1 point deducted

LEAGUE CHALLENGE CUP

First Round (11/9/93)
Lincoln Utd Colts 5, Spilsby Town 0 *(4/9/93)*
Appleby Frodingham Ath. 3, Boston Utd Res. 2
BRSA Retford 0, Bottesford Town 2
Sleaford Town 4, Wyberton 6

Second Round (16/10/93)
Grimsby Amateurs 2, Boston Res. 0
Louth Old Boys 3, Louth Utd Amateurs 1
Ruston Sports 6, Skegness Town 2
Wyberton 1, Bottesford Town 3
Hykeham Town 1, Appleby Frodingham Ath. 2
Lincoln Utd Colts 4, Limestone R. 0 *(19/10/93)*
Hykeham United 2, Immingham BW Spts *(30/10/93)*

Quarter-Finals (20/11/93)
Grimsby Amateurs 2, Ruston Sports 2
R: Ruston 8, Grimsby Amateurs 0 *(27/11/93)*
Bottesford Town 3, Louth Old Boys 1
Lincoln Moorlands 6, Lincoln Utd Colts 1
Appleby Frodlingham 0, Immingham BW Spts 1

Semi-Finals (3/3/94)
Bottesford Town 1, Immingham Blossom Way 3
Ruston Sports 0, Lincoln Moorlands 2 ***(Lincoln were removed for fielding 2 ineligible players)***

Final (at Scunthorpe Utd, Mon 11th April):
Immingham Blossom Way Spts 2, Ruston Spts 0

RESULT CHART 1993-94

HOME TEAM	1	2	3	4	5	6	7	8	9	10	11	12	13	14	15	16	17	18	19	20
1. Appleby Frodingham	*	10-1	3-3	2-0	8-1	3-1	2-0	3-1	1-0	3-2	2-1	4-1	2-0	5-1	10-0	2-0	3-0	2-1	5-2	1-2
2. Boston Reserves	0-5	*	0-5	1-5	0-0	1-6	1-11	1-0	0-2	0-4	3-5	1-4	1-3	2-1	0-5	1-2	0-4	2-2	2-2	1-1
3. Boston Utd Reserves	2-1	13-1	*	1-4	1-1	2-0	1-4	3-1	1-1	5-3	2-6	4-4	1-2	3-0	2-2	2-1	4-1	5-4	0-4	0-1
4. Bottesford Town	2-1	5-0	0-1	*	3-2	4-1	2-0	5-2	3-2	1-2	0-0	2-2	6-1	2-2	2-0	6-1	3-2	4-1	3-0	2-2
5. BRSA Retford	1-2	5-0	3-2	1-2	*	1-0	0-3	3-1	1-3	2-3	0-4	0-5	1-0	0-1	2-0	2-0	3-2	1-3	2-1	0-3
6. Grimsby Amateurs	1-4	2-1	1-1	1-1	0-2	*	2-3	3-2	2-3	3-2	2-4	1-1	1-3	3-2	4-1	4-1	2-3	3-2	1-1	1-2
7. Hykeham Town	3-0	11-0	0-2	1-1	6-0	2-3	*	5-0	3-0	2-0	2-3	0-1	8-0	3-0	5-1	1-0	5-1	1-2	3-1	1-1
8. Hykeham United	2-5	2-1	1-4	1-2	7-2	1-4	1-7	*	0-1	0-2	1-3	0-2	3-1	6-1	3-3	1-1	2-3	0-0	1-0	1-3
9. Immingham BW Spts	0-0	10-1	3-1	1-0	4-1	0-3	0-0	3-0	*	1-1	4-2	6-0	3-0	0-2	4-0	4-1	4-0	9-3	6-3	1-1
10. Limestone Rangers	3-0	9-3	1-2	2-4	2-1	2-0	0-1	3-0	0-0	*	2-0	4-2	4-0	2-4	5-2	0-1	6-1	4-1	0-3	1-0
11. Lincoln Moorlands	2-1	1-1	2-1	1-3	3-0	2-2	1-1	7-0	0-1	2-0	*	3-1	3-0	1-2	2-1	2-0	3-0	3-1	4-0	1-2
12. Lincoln United Colts	0-1	W-L	0-1	4-5	3-0	0-1	0-5	4-0	1-3	5-2	2-1	*	3-5	4-1	5-1	3-2	4-1	2-2	2-1	3-1
13. Louth Old Boys	1-2	2-1	3-2	1-5	1-1	3-0	1-4	1-0	2-0	1-2	4-3	2-4	*	2-3	3-0	0-2	0-2	1-3	1-1	0-2
14. Louth United Amtrs	0-2	8-0	3-4	0-2	1-0	0-1	2-4	5-1	1-6	L-W	0-4	0-1	2-2	*	1-2	4-1	0-2	1-1	1-1	2-3
15. Nettleham Reserves	1-4	4-0	2-4	2-5	2-2	1-3	0-5	3-1	1-5	0-2	1-7	2-4	4-3	4-1	*	2-0	3-0	0-3	4-0	1-2
16. Ruston Sports	4-2	7-0	2-2	0-2	4-1	0-2	1-1	2-0	2-2	2-3	0-1	2-3	1-1	2-2	0-2	*	3-5	0-1	0-4	1-3
17. Skegness Town	0-0	10-0	0-1	0-1	4-0	3-1	0-2	3-0	2-7	1-2	1-1	3-1	1-1	1-3	2-2	0-4	*	2-0	2-2	1-3
18. Sleaford Town	0-3	6-1	3-0	1-0	3-3	1-0	4-2	0-0	2-2	3-4	4-0	2-0	4-2	0-0	7-2	3-1	2-0	*	4-1	1-0
19. Spilsby Town	0-2	7-1	0-5	1-3	2-1	3-5	0-2	1-0	2-3	1-2	1-1	3-1	1-1	3-5	6-1	1-4	0-1	3-4	*	0-5
20. Wyberton	0-1	9-0	2-2	2-0	5-2	0-4	3-1	W-L	2-3	4-1	1-0	1-2	W-L	4-0	2-0	2-2	2-1	4-2	2-0	*

LINCOLNSHIRE LEAGUE CLUBS 1994-95

APPLEBY FRODINGHAM ATHLETIC

Chairman: G Keena **Manager:** Mr Walker
Secretary: Mr M D Mumby, 21 Messingham Rd, Scunthorpe, South Humbs DN17 2LL (0724 840117).
Ground: Brumby Hall, Ashby Rd, Scunthorpe (0724 843024).
Directions: A18 turn right at second circle, then 2nd left, left at next lights, straight on at next circle, 2nd left after circle.
Colours: Purple (thin white stripe)/purple **Change colours:** Red & blue stripes/blue

BOTTESFORD TOWN

Chairman: A Reeve **Manager:** P Ashworth
Secretary: Mr P Herrick, 22a Rooklands, Scotter, Gainsborough, Lincs DN21 3TT (0724 764183).
Ground: Ontario Road, Bottesford, Scunthorpe (0724 871883).
Directions: Berkeley Circle, Scotter Road South, Asda Circle, straight across 2nd left past Darby Glass Factory, turn right into Goodwood, turn right to Club.
Colours: Yellow & blue trim/blue **Change colours:** White/white

BOSTON UNITED RESERVES

Chairman: P Malkinson **Manager:** C Cook/D Creasey
Secretary: Mr J Blackwell, 14-16 Span Place, Boston PE21 6HN (0205 365652).
Ground: York Street, Boston (0205 365524/5)
Directions: A52 Sleaford-Boston Rd., 2nd left Brothertoft Rd., Argyle St. to Argyle Sluice Bridge. Immediately over bridge turn left Tattershall Rd., ground three quarters of a mile.
Colours: Amber/black **Change colours:** White/green

B.R.S.A. RETFORD

Chairman: S Pringle **Manager:** D Whalley
Secretary: Mr M Keeling, 18 Rutland Road, Retford, Notts DN22 7HF (0777 703929).
Ground: British Rail, Badworth Road, Retford.
Directions: Into centre of Retford, follow signs for Worksop A620. After crossing railway bridge, turn 1st left. Ground entrance on left under bridge.
Colours: Blue & black stripes/white **Change colours:** White/white

EPWORTH TOWN

Chairman: T Pyle **Manager:** P Deno
Secretary: Mr G Yeardley, 9 Hayfield Close, Haxey, Doncaster DN9 2NT (0427 753257).
Ground: Leisure Centre, Burnham Road, Epworth (0427 873945).
Directions: Main Road through village A161 Goole/Gainsborough Road becomes Burnham Road, ground behind South Axholme School access via Leisure Centre adj.
Colours: White/blue **Change colours:** Red/blue

GRANTHAM TOWN RESERVES

Chairman: A Prince **Manager:** T Eldred
Secretary: Mr P S Nixon, 72 Huntingtower Road, Grantham, Lincs NG31 7AU (0476 64408).
Ground: Trent Road, Grantham (0476 62011).
Directions: From A1 leave at A52 Nottingham. Turn, take 1st right after Nissan Garage in Barrowby Gate. At T junction turn right then left into Trent Road. From A607 Lincoln-Sleaford. Right at 3rd lights. Sign post A52 Nottingham. Over next lights on outskirts of town, turn right into Springfield Road, over next lights into Trent Road, half a mile on the right.
Colours: Black & white stripes/black **Change colours:** Yellow & blue or Red & white

GRIMSBY AMATEURS

Chairman: M Duckworth **Manager:** N Shackleton
Secretary: Mrs P Shackleton, 42 Campden Cres., Cleethorpes, S. Humbs DN35 2UL (0472 698351).
Ground: The Club, Wilton Road, Humberston (0472 872936).
Directions: From A16 Toll Bar circle, right for Cleethorpes, left when road forks. Next circle right Wilton Road, 1st right from A46 Nuns Corner College right at lights. Next circle 2nd exit. Next circle 2nd exit 1st right Wilton Road, Ground on left
Colours: White/navy **Change colours:** Yellow/navy

HYKEHAM TOWN

Chairman: M Clayton **Manager:** M Poucher
Secretary: Mr C Edwards, 5 Landsdowne Road, Lincoln (0522 520857).
Ground: Memorial Playing Fields, North Hykeham (0522 680193)
Directions: Off A46 opposite Kesteven Sports Centre - Memorial Playing Fields.
Colours: Blue/blue **Change colours:** Red/white

IMMINGHAM BLOSSOM WAY SPORTS

Chairman: N Day **Manager:** H Jacklin
Secretary: Mrs C Jacklin, 272 St. Nicholas Drive, Grimsby DN37 9RP (0472 882690).
Ground: Blossom Way, Immingham (0472 572612).
Directions: Enter Immingham from A180 -Blossom Way on right hand side.
Colours: White (black trim)/black **Change colours:** Red & white halves/red

LIMESTONE RANGERS

Chairman: P Wray **Manager:** D Andrews
Secretary: M Harty, 3 Brook Street, Hemswell, Gainsborough, Lincs DN21 5UT (0427 668382).
Ground: Willoughton.
Directions: Half way down Willoughton Hill, down Hollowgate Hill.
Colours: Red/black **Change colours:** Blue/black

LINCOLN MOORLANDS

Chairman: S Gordon **Manager:** S Gordon
Secretary: T Walshaw, 19 Spilsby Close, Hartsholme Field, Lincoln LN6 3YX (0522 501229).
Ground: Moorland Sports Ground, Newark Road, Lincoln (0522 520184)
Directions: The Moorland Club, Newark Road. Lincoln from Lincoln City Centre along A1434 towards Newark, Ground quarter mile passed Rooker Lane.
Colours: Red & white stripes/red **Change colours:** Blue/royal blue

LINCOLN UNITED COLTS

Chairman: K Roe **Manager:** P Tittcombe
Secretary: K Weaver, 22 Grainsby Close, Lincoln LN6 7QF (0522 531832).
Ground: Ashby Av., Hartsholme, Lincoln (0522 843024).
Directions: A46 Lincoln by-pass-circle exit marked Birchwood - 1 mile 30 mph sign turn right into Ashby Av., ground 200 yards on right.
Colours: White/white stripe **Change colours:** Yellow/yellow

LOUTH OLD BOYS

Chairman: A Roberson **Manager:** M Shackleton
Secretary: M Shackleton, 12 Tudor Drive, Louth, Lincs (0507 602929).
Ground: London Rd., Louth (0507 603928).
Directions: A16 road, ground one mile south of main church, sports ground.
Colours: Red & black stripe/black **Change colours:** Blue/blue

LOUTH UNITED AMATEURS

Chairman: C Horton **Manager:** T Porter
Secretary: P Smith, 84 Scartho Road, Grimsby DN33 2BG (0472 879356).
Ground: Park Avenue, Louth (0507 607351).
Directions: A16 from North or South to main Church traffic lights. Turn right or left into Eastgate - follow road through seeking ambulance/fire station on right, next turning on right Park Av. Ground at end of avenue turn right then left into ground entrance.
Colours: Royal blue/royal blue **Change colours:** Black & red stripes/black

NETTLEHAM RESERVES

Chairman: C Mason **Manager:** R Mason
Secretary: S W Timms, 5 Ash Tree Ave., Nettleham, Lincoln LN2 2TQ (0522 751140).
Ground: Mulsanne Park, Nettleham (0522 750007).
Directions: From A46 turn onto Washdyke Lane, name change to High Street, Mill Hill and Sudbrook Road, 2nd left into Greenfields, turn right into Field Close to Mulsanne Park.
Colours: Royal & white stripes/blue **Change colours:** Red/red

RUSTON SPORTS

Chairman: G Curtis **Manager:** B Linnicor
Secretary: P Dickson, 42 Fontwell Crescent, Lincoln LN6 7LE (0522 684738).
Ground: RMSC Club, Newark Road, Lincoln (0522 680057).
Directions: A46 road to Newark, left hand side of road approx 250 meters before City boundary.
Colours: Blue/white **Change colours:** White/white

SKEGNESS TOWN

Chairman: K Brearley **Manager:** B Ferguson
Secretary: M Brown, Nostro Demora, 10 Thames Meadow Drive, Hogsthorpe, Skegness, Lincs PE24 5PU (0754 73678).
Ground: Burgh Road, Skegness. (0754 4385).
Directions: A158 Road into Skegness, ground on the right hand side.
Colours: White/red **Change colours:** Green/white

SLEAFORD TOWN

Chairman: M Cameron **Manager:** B Rowland
Secretary: Miss J Muxlow, 7 Milton Way, Boston Road, Sleaford, Lincs NG34 7HX (0529 304502).
Ground: Boston Road, Sleaford.
Directions: A15 Lincoln to Sleaford centre, left at Hanley monument to Boston Road, Ground 800 yards on right.
Colours: Green & white stripes/white **Change colours:** Red/white

SPILSBY TOWN

Chairman: J Skinner **Manager:** D Wilkinson
Secretary: C Tempest, 59 Boston Road, Spilsby, Lincs PE25 5HQ (0790 53185).
Ground: Ancaster Ave., Spilsby.
Directions: Town centre for A16, Church Turn right, 2nd right Ancaster Ave., 100 meters to recreation ground.
Colours: Black & white stripes/black **Change colours:** Red (black trim).

WYBERTON

Chairman: I Smith **Manager:** M Scrupps
Secretary: Mrs C Scrupps, 52 Deldale Road, Wyberton, Boston, Lincs PE21 7BT (0205 367756).
Ground: Causeway, Wyberton (0522 353525).
Directions: From Boston take Spalding road, A16 to 1st circle, turn right onto B1397 Kirton end and proceed 1 mile to cross roads just before Pin Cushion Inn. Turn left into Saunder Gate Lane and turn immediately left again into the Causeway.
Colours: Black & white/black (white trim) **Change colours:** Red & blue stripes/blue

PHOTOS OPPOSITE:

Top: *Wyberton forward Reid (No.10) attacks a corner, but his side go down 0-4 at home to Grimsby Amateurs in this TSW Printers Lincolnshire League fixture on 21st August.*

Foot: *Grimsby Amateurs FC.*

Photos - Martin Wray.

CARR & CARR SUNDAY LEAGUE

FOUNDED: 1968

FINAL TABLE	P	W	D	L	F	A	PTS
Nunsthorpe Tavern	14	13	0	1	107	19	26
Rock Youth Club	14	10	3	1	53	27	23
Lloyds Arms	14	5	5	4	34	44	15
Humberston Roofing	14	7	0	7	46	59	14
Top Town Market	14	4	2	8	36	47	10
Wilton Cobley	14	2	5	7	27	43	9
Bradley Park	14	3	3	8	33	54	9
AC Dental	14	2	2	10	23	56	6

Cup Finals:

J Quickfall Senior Challenge Cup: Nunsthorpe Tavern 3, Lloyds Arms 1

T G Blow Junior Cup: Top Town Market 1, Bradley Park 0

Tom Fox Cup: Rock Youth Club 5, AC Dental 2

Chairmans Shield: Humberston Roofing 8, Wilton Cobley 5

GRIMSBY, CLEETHORPES & DIST.

SUNDAY LEAGUE

FOUNDED: 1961

DIV. ONE	P	W	D	L	F	A	PTS
Grimsby College	20	15	3	2	52	18	33
Youngs Ross	20	16	0	4	61	24	32
Blosson Way Spts	20	14	1	5	61	18	29
Swigs	20	11	3	6	47	39	25
Freetime Sports	20	9	5	6	35	35	23
Bradley Amateurs	20	8	2	10	41	53	18
Humberton	20	6	4	10	26	46	16
Axe & Cleaver	20	6	3	11	41	43	15
Healing	20	5	3	12	37	62	13
The Club	20	6	1	13	32	59	13
Athletico Trawl	20	1	1	18	17	53	3

Lower Division Champions:
Div. 2 (12): Jubilee Inn
Div. 3 (12): Diable Roofing
Div. 4 (10): Club '93 United
Div. 5 (12): Clee Motor Spares
Div. 6 (13): Newtons
Div. 7 (12): New Clee
Div. 8 (13): Valiant
Div. 9 (13): New Waltham
Div. 10 (13): White Hart Wanderers

Cup Finals:
Sports Supply Challenge Cup: Grimsby College 2, Blossom Way Sports 1 *(after 1-1 draw)*
Junior Cup: Longship 7, West Marsh Utd 1 *(after 1-1 draw)*
Challenge Trophy: Cross Keys 5, Westlands 1
Junior Shield: Conoco 4, White Hart Wanderers 1
Memorial Cup: Jubilee 4, Cross Keys 1
Inter-League Cup: Grimsby 4, Hull 0
Inter-League Cup (under-21): Grimsby 1, Hull 0

DEE JAYS SCUNTHORPE SUNDAY LEAGUE

DIV. ONE	P	W	D	L	F	A	PTS
Lions Head	12	10	0	2	46	16	20
Ashby Star	12	8	0	4	30	23	16
Queen Bess	12	5	3	4	28	19	13
Poachers	12	6	1	5	32	29	13
Keadby Club	12	4	2	6	18	23	10
Kypros	12	2	4	6	28	35	8
Comet Wanderers	12	1	2	9	23	60	4

Lower Division Champions:
Div. 2 (12): Broughton Clamart
Div. 3 (11): Messingham Trinity Old Boys
Div. 4 (11): Vandols
Div. 5 (12): Beacon
Div. 6 (8): Blue Bell
Div. 7 (9): Brigg Snooker Club
Div. 8 (12): Lion Head Reserves

Cup Finals:
Challenge Cup: Poachers 5, Trinity 1
Bob Bedford Cup: Broughton Clamart 4, Parkwood 0
Dave Ward Cup: Lions Head 3, Poachers 0
Geg McGowan Cup: Vandols 5, Parkwood 0
H (Nobby) Clark Cup: Blue Bell 3, Beacon 2
Ireson Cup: Mess. Trin. OB 3, Bloom & Billet Mill 2
Junior Cup: Brigg Snooker Club 2, Bridge OB 1
Ted Harrison Cup: Poachers Reserves 1, Winterton Rovers 0 *(after 2-2 draw)*

Below: *Trinity FC, who finished third in Division Two of the Scunthorpe Sunday League earning promotion to the First Division, pictured at Scunthorpe United's Glandford Park before the Challenge Cup final against Poachers. Keith Dixon, the League Secretary, who founded Trinity FC 21 years ago, is second from the left, back row.*

LIVERPOOL COUNTY F.A.

Secretary: Fred L J Hunter,
23 Greenfield Road, Liverpool L13 3BN (0051 220 6089).

SENIOR CUP 1993-94

First Round

Bootle v Formby	6-1	Knowsley United v St Helens Town	1-3
Marine v Burscough	4-0	Prescot AFC v Skelmersdale United	3-2

Quarter-Finals

Tranmere Rovers Reserves v Prescot AFC	2-0	Marine v Bootle	3-0
St Helens Town v Liverpool Reserves	1-2	Southport v Everton Reserves	2-1

Semi-Finals

Southport v Tranmere Rovers Reserves	4-1	Liverpool Reserves v Marine	0-2

Final *(at Everton FC, Mon 9th May)*: Marine 2, Southport 1

OTHER COUNTY FINALS:

Challenge Cup *(at Merseyside Police FC, Mon 25th April)*: Maghull 3, Remica United 1
Junior Cup *(at Merseyside Police FC, Mon 18th April)*: Layfield 1, East Lancs Crown 0
Intermediate Cup *(at Electric Supply FC, Sat 23rd April)*: Yorkshire Copper Tubes Reserves 3, Puma 2
Youth Cup *(at Maghull FC, Thurs 28th April)*: Aidans 2, Wynstay 2 *(Aidans won 4-3 on penalties)*
Sunday Premier Cup *(at Marine FC, Sun 24th April)*: Salerno 3, Walford Maritime 0
Sunday Junior Cup *(at B.R.N.E.S.C. FC, Sun 1st May)*: Breeze 1, Brook House 0
Sunday Intermediate Cup *(at Plessey GPT FC, Sun 17th April)*: Arc Joinery 2, Heath 1
Inter-Lge under-18 *(at Bellefield (Everton FC Training Ground), Fri 15th April)*: St Helens Combination 3, Bootle & Netherton Junior League 2
Inter-Lge under-16 *(at Cheshire Lines FC, Wed 4th May)*: St Helens Junior League 2, Craven Minor League 0
Inter-Lge under-14 *(at Melwood (Liverpool FC Training Ground), Wed 13th April)*: South Merseyside Junior League 3, West Derby Junior League 0
Inter-Lge under-12 *(at Melwood (Liverpool FC Training Ground), Wed 13th April)*: Craven Minor League 1, South Merseyside Junior League 0

Maghull FC - Liverpool Challenge Cup winners 1993-94.

Photo - John L Newton.

FRANK ARMITT LIVERPOOL COUNTY COMBINATION

DIV. ONE	P	W	D	L	F	A	PTS
St Dominics	30	21	2	7	95	42	65
Lucas Sports	30	22	2	6	82	37	*65
Ayone	30	17	6	7	71	46	57
Crawfords	30	17	5	8	67	41	56
Waterloo Dock	30	16	5	9	85	47	53
Chesh. Lines Sth Liv.	30	13	5	12	57	60	44
Yorks Cop. Tubes	30	13	4	13	67	77	43
Earle	30	13	3	14	62	56	42
Beesix	30	12	5	13	53	64	41
BRNESC	30	11	4	15	55	70	37
Ford Motors	30	10	4	16	63	67	34
Electric Supply	30	8	6	16	53	68	30
Mossley Hill	30	9	2	19	61	92	29
Crystal Villa	30	8	4	18	52	101	28
Littlewoods	30	8	6	16	67	91	*27
Speke	30	8	5	17	51	82	*26

DIV. TWO	P	W	D	L	F	A	PTS
Royal Seaforth	28	20	5	3	107	38	65
Stockbridge	28	19	6	3	98	44	63
Rainhill Town	28	18	5	5	76	37	59
Knowsley Utd Res.	28	15	5	8	86	56	50
Halewood Town	28	14	5	9	62	51	47
Camadale	28	13	5	10	65	53	*41
Plessey (GPT)	28	11	7	10	78	56	40
Elec. Supply Res.	28	10	9	9	53	56	39
Bootle Res.	28	10	5	13	63	66	35
BRNESC Res.	28	10	4	14	55	78	34
Yorkshire CT Res.	28	8	6	14	58	88	30
Eldonians	28	8	5	15	62	91	29
Mossley Hill Res.	28	8	4	16	42	57	*25
Avon Athletic	28	5	3	20	62	100	18
Speke Res.	28	3	2	23	36	132	*5

* - 3 points deducted

PETER COYNE (GEO MAHON) CUP

First Round:
Beesix 0, Speke 2
BRNESC 0, Crawfords 4
Cheshire Lines South Liverpool 2, Fords 0
Littlewoods 4, Earle 2
Lucas Sports 2, Crystal Villa 1
St Dominics 0, Ayone 2
Waterloo Dock 2, Mossley Hill 1
Electric Supply 0, Yorks Copper Tubes 2

Quarter Finals
Littlewoods 1, Ayone 2
Crawfords 3, Yorkshire Copper Tubes 2
Speke 3, Lucas Sports 10
Waterloo Dock 2, Cheshire Lines SL 1

Semi Finals
Crawfords 4, Waterloo Dock 2
Ayone 1, Lucas Sports 3

Final *(2/5/94)*: Crawfords 3, Lucas 1

FRED MICKLESFIELD CUP

First Round:
Yorks CT Res. 2, St Dominics 5
Avon Athletic 1, Beesix 3
Ford Motors 2, Electric Supply 1
Camadale 5, Eldonians 2
Bootles Res. 1, BRNESC 3 *(after 3-3 draw)*
Electric Supply 2, Mossley Hill 3
Earle 4, Speke Res. 2
Crystal Villa - bye

Quarter Finals
Ford Motors 1, Beesix 0
BRNESC 4, Mossley Hill 6
Crystal Villa 0, St Dominics 1
Earle 6, Camadale 1 *(after 3-3 draw)*

Semi Finals
Mossley Hill 3, Earle 2
Ford Motors 3, St Dominics 0

Final *(10/5/94)*: Mossley Hill 2, Ford Motors 1

MERSEYSIDE CERAMICS CUP

First Round
Avon Athletic 4, BRNESC Res. 5
Bootle Res. 1, Stockbridge 4
Camadale 0, Knowsley United Res. 2
Plessey (GPT) 4, Eldonians 1
El. Supp. Res. 3, Rainhill 4 *(after 2-2 draw)*
Yorkshire CT Res. 0, Royal Seaforth 6
Mossley Hill Res. 8, Speke Res. 0
Halewood Town - bye.

Quarter Finals
Royal Seaforth 3, Plesey (GPT) 1
Stockbridge 0, Halewood Town 3
Rainhill Town 2, BRNESC Res. 1
Mossley Hill Res. 3, Knowsley Utd Res. 2

Semi Finals
Mossley Hill Res. 3, Rainhill Town 2
Royal Seaforth 3, Halewood Town 1

Final *(26/4/94)*: Ryl Seaforth 1, Mossley Hill 0

DIVISION ONE CLUBS 1994-95

(Tel. codes 051 unless stated)

AYONE
Ground: Edinburgh Park (263 5267)
Secretary: J Doyle (207 1437)

BEESIX
Ground: Edinburgh Park (263 5267)
Secretary: D Brodie (256 8883)

B.R.N.E.S.C.
Ground: Melling Rd, Aintree (521 3330)
Secretary: G Riley (521 3526)

CHESHIRE LINES
Ground: Southmead Rd, Allerton (427 7126)
Secretary: H Humphries (722 6002)

CRAWFORDS U.B.
Ground: As Cheshire Lines (above)
Secretary: V Goodman (475 1563)

CRYSTAL VILLA
Ground: Orrell Lane, Bootle (525 5561)
Secretary: S Roberts (263 1545)

EARLE
Ground: Arncliffe Leisure Centre, Arncliffe Rd, Halewood (428 1929).
Secretary: W Hollerhead (489 9103)

ELECTRIC SUPPLY (MANWEB)
Ground: Thingwall Road
Secretary: J Shimmin (523 5593)

FORD MOTORS
Ground: Ford Sports & Social Club, Cronton Lane, Widnes (424 7078)
Secretary: T Doyle (0928 568329)

LUCAS SPORTS
Ground: Edenhurst Avenue (near Coronation Hotel), Liverpool 16 (480 6365)
Secretary: A Brodrick (423 4615)

MOSSLEY HILL
Ground: Mossley Hill Athletic Club, Mossley Hill Rd (724 4377)
Secretary: R Fitzpatrick (475 1934)

ROYAL SEAFORTH
Ground: Edinburgh Park (263 5185)
Secretary: A Stanton (489 9980)

St DOMINICS
Ground: St Dominics School, Lordens Rd, Huyton (489 2798)
Secretary: M Donohue (220 8180)

STOCKBRIDGE
Ground: Stockbridge Comprehensive School
Secretary: P Shaw (226 5857)

WATERLOO DOCK
Ground: Edinburgh Park (263 5267)
Secretary: J Davies (264 8179)

YORKSHIRE COPPER TUBE
Ground: Factory Site, East Lancashire Rd, Kirkby (545 5133)
Secretary: J Murray (228 6112)

DIVISION TWO CLUBS 1994-95

(Tel. codes 051 unless stated)

AVON ATHLETIC

Ground: St Maries RL Club, Brenfield, off Heath Rd, Widnes (424 3818)
Secretary: D Roylance (0925 264153)

CAMADALE

Ground: All Saints School, Kirkby
Secretary: R Murt (548 2236)

ELDONIANS

Ground: Edinburgh Park (263 5185)
Secretary: J Shea (207 1907)

HALEWOOD TOWN

Ground: Hollies Rd (487 5300)
Secretary: S Jones (486 4557)

PLESSEY (GPT)

Ground: 'Whitfield', Roby Rd, Huyton (489 1031)
Secretary: I Scholes (728 9848)

RAINHILL TOWN

Ground: Rainhill Recreation Club, Victoria Terrace (426 2805)
Secretary: S Lea (424 0400)

SELWYN

Ground: Bootle Stadium (523 4213).
Secretary: S Spencer (256 8255)

SOUTH LIVERPOOL

Ground: Blessed John Almond School, Horrocks Avenue, Liverpool L19
Secretary: J Stanway (733 1286)

SPEKE

Ground: Speke Hall Avenue (486 1588)
Secretary: W Locke (486 1954)

This Division also contains the Reserve sides of: Bootle *(see page 649)*, BRNESC, Electric Supply, Knowsley Utd *(page 272)*, Mossley Hill and Yorkshire Copper Tube.

Tony Pownall of Cheshire Lines South Liverpool (the club have now 're-separated') blasts an effort goalwards during the opening minutes of a 3-6 reverse at Waterloo Dock.

Andy Woods finishes a mazy dribble to score Cheshire Lines South Liverpool's final goal in their 6-3 win away to Electric Supply back in September.

Photos - Rob Ruddock.

ALEX STEWART ASSAYERS I ZINGARI LEAGUE

PREM. DIV.	P	W	D	L	F	A	PTS
REMYCA United	26	20	3	3	78	24	43
Liver Vaults	26	17	5	4	70	28	#39
Selwyn	26	15	7	4	65	23	37
Aigburth PH	26	14	5	7	56	29	33
East Villa	26	11	5	10	44	40	27
Liverpool Nalgo	26	9	9	8	55	61	27
Roma	26	10	6	10	51	79	#26
Leyfield	26	9	7	10	36	46	25
Quarry Bank OB	26	8	8	10	47	51	24
Unity BCOB	26	8	5	13	48	68	21
Warbreck	26	7	5	14	44	64	19
Stoneycroft	26	6	7	13	64	85	19
Collegiate OB	26	4	7	15	25	57	#15
Old Xaverians	26	3	3	20	33	61	9

DIV. ONE	P	W	D	L	F	A	PTS
Jabisco	26	21	3	2	89	37	45
Aintree Villa	26	20	4	2	99	40	44
Sefton & District	26	16	4	6	85	50	36
Blacklow Row	26	16	2	8	80	61	34
Edge Hill BCOB	26	11	7	8	60	59	29
St Marys COB	26	12	1	13	65	63	25
St Aloysius	26	10	5	11	59	64	25
Dove & Olive	26	10	5	11	57	72	25
De la Salle OB	26	10	4	12	55	56	24
Shrewsbury Hse OB	26	8	4	14	69	80	20
Old Bootleians	26	6	7	13	60	70	19
Essemmay OB	26	8	3	15	49	68	19
Walton Village	26	7	2	17	45	72	16
Alsop Old Boys	26	1	1	24	30	110	3

DIV. TWO	P	W	D	L	F	A	PTS
NELTC	26	19	2	5	83	40	40
Maghull Town	26	17	4	5	70	53	38
Liobians	26	16	5	5	75	48	37
Lee Jones OB	26	15	5	6	70	36	#35
Southport Trinity	26	15	5	6	87	53	35
Scare Coeur FP	26	12	4	10	92	58	28
Bluecoat OB	26	11	2	13	54	61	24
Old Holts	26	9	5	12	48	68	23
Riversdale College	26	9	6	11	45	67	*22
Hillfoot Hey OB	26	7	3	16	56	78	17
Oaks Institute	26	7	4	15	66	74	*16
Rockville (Wallasey)	26	6	4	16	42	75	16
Waterloo GSOB	26	6	4	16	47	85	16
Dista	26	4	5	17	34	73	13

- 2 points awarded   * - 2 points deducted

Challenge Cup Final: (at Lucas Sports):
REMYCA United 4, St Marys College Old Boys 0

Roy Wade Mem. Trophy Final: (at Lucas Sports):
Lee Jones OB 2, Stoneycroft 2 (after extra-time, Stoneycroft won 5-4 on penalties)

Senior Cup Final: (at Lucas Sports):
Aigburth PH 2, Lee Jones Old Boys 1

Hugh Latimer Sportsmanship Trophy: Alsop OB

Referee of the Year: G W Foulkes

Secretary of the Year: J Yates (Southport Trinity)

LIVERPOOL BUSINESS HOUSES SUNDAY LEAGUE

PREM. DIV.	P	W	D	L	F	A	PTS
A3	24	19	2	3	58	22	40
Nicosia	24	16	4	4	65	29	36
Manfast Kirkby	24	17	1	6	79	39	35
Littlewoods Ath.	24	15	3	6	64	43	33
Gt Eastern Hotel	24	15	1	8	59	40	31
BRNESC	24	13	4	7	77	35	30
Permatex	24	11	5	8	46	32	27
Walford Maritime	24	8	7	9	50	45	23
Clubmoor Nalgo	24	8	3	13	51	63	19
Seddons	24	7	2	15	39	65	16
Cadwa	24	2	5	17	48	98	9
Iron Bridge	24	2	3	19	25	97	7
Ford Motors	24	1	4	19	36	89	6

Lower Division Champions:
Div. 1 (13): Salerno
Div. 2 (13): CC Speke
Div. 3 (13): Halewood Labour
Div. 4 (13): Norcoast
Div. 5 (14): Stevenson R.

Cup Finals:
Senior: A3 beat Salerno 4-2 on pens after 1-1.
Junior: Venables Decorators 3, Halewood Labour 2
Minor: Arc Joinery 2, Heath 1
Cec Harrop Mem. Cup: BRNEC 5, Cadwa 1
Mid-Week Cup: Delta Taxis 1, Black Kabs Knowsley 0

CROSBY & DISTRICT SUNDAY LEAGUE

FOUNDED: 1967

DIV. ONE	P	W	D	L	F	A	PTS
Eden Vale	22	20	0	2	97	19	40
Lion Hotel	22	14	4	4	63	24	32
Carisbrooke Hotel	22	11	4	7	59	55	26
Tomlin	22	10	5	7	53	44	25
St Williams of York	22	8	7	7	59	55	23
Albion	22	9	4	9	63	57	22
Dominion	22	9	4	9	58	55	22
Strand Tavern	22	10	3	9	43	47	*21
Hawthorne	22	9	2	11	47	55	20
Chesterfield Park	22	5	5	12	35	53	15
Leamington	22	4	0	18	38	98	8
Lathom	22	3	2	17	19	72	8

* - 2 points deducted

Lower Division Champions:
Div. 2 (12): Thornton Rangers
Div. 3 (13): Jawbone

Cup Finals:
Lal Evans Mem. Cup: Lion Hotel 2, Strand Tavern 0
Canon Francis Cup: Lion Hotel 2, Eden Vale 0
League Challenge Cup: Alex beat Thornton Rangers on penalties after 1-1 draw
Lol Hunt Mem. Cup: Raven Hotel 1, Jawbone 0

LONDON F.A.

Secretary: Ron S Ashford,
Aldworth Grove, Lewisham, London SE13 6HY (081 690 9626)

CHALLENGE CUP 1993-94

First Round

Erith & Belvedere v Fisher '93	2-0
Hampton v Barking	2-4
Barnet v Dagenham & Redbridge	0-1
Southall v Uxbridge	1-6
Leyton v Bromley	1-2
Dulwich Hamlet v Leyton Orient	0-2
Welling United v Boreham Wood	2-1
Wealdstone v Tooting & Mitcham United	2-5

Quarter-Finals

Leyton Orient v Uxbridge	2-3
Tooting & Mitcham United v Barking	2-1
Welling United v Bromley	4-1
Erith & Belvedere v Dagenham & Redbridge	1-7

Semi-Finals

Tooting & Mitcham United v Welling United	0-3
Dagenham & Redbridge v Uxbridge	1-3

Final *(at Uxbridge FC, Tues 24th May)*: Uxbridge 3, Welling United 0

SENIOR CUP

First Round

Cockfosters v St Andrews	3-2
Cray Wanderers v Clapton	1-3
Haringey Borough v Croydon Athletic	0-1
Civil Service v Collier Row	1-2
Walthamstow Pennant v Furness	0-5
Ford United v Beckton United	3-1
Bedfont v Southgate Athletic	4-3

Second Round

Bedfont v Clapton	1-2
Brimsdown Rovers v Hanwell Town	1-2
Kingsbury Town v Collier Row	4-1
Tower Hamlets v Furness	1-3
Hoddesdon Town v Barkingside	4-2
East Ham United v Ford United	1-2
Wingate & Finchley v Corinthian-Casuals	0-4
Croydon Athletic v Cockfosters	2-1

Quarter-Finals

Ford United v Croydon Athletic	2-1
Clapton v Corinthian-Casuals	0-3
Hoddesdon Town v Hanwell Town	3-7
Furness v Kingsbury Town	4-1

Semi-Finals

Furness v Ford United	2-3
Hanwell Town v Corinthian-Casuals	2-0

Final *(at Leyton FC, Sat 21st May)*: Ford United 2, Hanwell Town 1

OTHER COUNTY FINALS:

Intermediate Cup *(at Fisher '93 FC, Sat 7th May)*: Clapton Villa 2, Walthamstow Trojans 1 *(after 1-1 draw at Brimsdown Rovers FC, Sat 23rd April).*
Midweek Cup *(at Thamesmead Town FC, Thurs 21st April)*: West Central Sports 3, Tottenham L.T. 1
Junior Cup *(at Cockfosters FC, Sat 30th April)*: Walthamstow St Marys 5, STC Ivor Grove 1
Sunday Challenge Cup *(at Wingate & Finchley FC, Sun 24th April)*: Ranelagh Sports 4, AEL 1
Sunday Intermediate Cup *(at Wingate & Finchley FC, Sun 3rd April)*: Samuel Lithgow 2, Thames Water (Essex) 1
Sunday Junior Cup *(at Dulwich Hamlet FC, Sun 17th April)*: Scotland Green 4, London Irish Accountants 1

Right: *Paul Evans of Ford United carries off the London Senior Cup after the Essex side had destroyed Hanwell Town's ambitions of completing an unprecedented hat-trick of wins in the competition.*
Photo - Richard Brock.

SOUTH LONDON

FOOTBALL FEDERATION

FOUNDED: 1991

PREM. DIV.	P	W	D	L	F	A	PTS
Cambdge Univ. Miss.	18	16	0	2	50	22	32
Keyworth	18	15	0	3	77	25	30
Albrighton	18	9	4	5	49	29	22
Bromley Baptist	18	11	0	7	55	38	22
Eltham Town	18	8	2	8	39	32	18
Cambridge	18	8	2	8	51	47	18
Staveley	18	7	2	9	42	54	16
Seven Seals Utd	18	5	1	12	35	59	11
Graham Athletic	18	2	1	12	30	70	5
Hitech Rangers	18	3	0	15	26	75	*4

DIV. ONE	P	W	D	L	F	A	PTS
Erith Albion	16	10	4	2	49	28	24
Green Eagles	16	8	7	1	44	27	23
Churchdown	16	6	7	3	39	37	19
Odua United	16	7	4	5	34	30	18
Selworthy Park	16	7	4	5	37	35	18
Umojah	16	4	6	6	33	38	14
Huntsman	16	2	7	7	32	46	11
PABYA	16	2	5	9	36	47	9
Red Star '87	16	1	6	9	27	43	8

DIV. TWO	P	W	D	L	F	A	PTS
Wagoners	20	16	2	2	109	29	34
Locksley	20	16	3	1	74	29	*33
AFC Sydenham	20	13	4	3	55	26	30
Eltham Palace Res.	20	12	4	4	55	34	28
Regal	20	9	5	6	55	39	#25
Eltham Invicta	20	8	1	11	38	56	17
Hilly Fields	20	7	2	11	55	50	16
Marseans	20	5	4	11	28	45	14
Marshall Res.	20	4	2	14	40	72	10
African Braves	20	3	2	15	22	94	8
Middle Pk Res.	20	2	1	17	21	78	5

DIV. THREE	P	W	D	L	F	A	PTS
Final Furlong	18	16	2	0	122	38	34
Catford Wdrs 'A'	18	11	4	3	68	40	26
Bostall Park	18	11	2	5	57	33	24
Havelock	18	10	3	5	53	28	23
Eltham Villa	18	10	3	5	57	38	23
Eltham Royals	18	5	4	9	45	56	14
Siemens Sports	18	5	4	9	42	59	14
Croydon Strikers	18	5	1	12	48	76	11
Swanley Town	18	4	2	12	30	58	10
Lower Sydenham	18	0	1	17	13	107	1

DIV. FOUR	P	W	D	L	F	A	PTS
Tressillian	18	13	5	0	68	34	31
North Kent	18	11	2	5	46	34	24
Santos United	18	10	2	6	54	32	22
Vista Colts	18	10	2	6	49	46	22
Brockley 'A'	18	8	4	6	53	46	20
Wagoners Res.	18	9	2	7	58	53	20
Eltham Palace 'A'	18	5	4	9	34	45	14
Marseans 'A'	18	4	2	12	20	60	10
Siemens Spts Res.	18	3	3	12	29	38	*7
Belvedere Res.	18	3	2	13	37	60	*6

* - 2 points deducted
# - 2 points awarded

Cup Finals

Federation Cup: Keyworth beat Eltham Town 5-4 on penalties after extra-time and a 1-1 draw.
Snr Cup: Cambridge 2, Cambridge Univ. Mission 0
Jnr Cup: Bostall Park 1, AFC Sydenham 0

MERCURY WALTHAM

FOOTBALL LEAGUE

PREM. DIV.	P	W	D	L	F	A	PTS
Enfield Royals	22	18	1	3	67	21	55
Somersett AVE Res.	22	17	2	3	68	31	53
Enfield Park	22	12	5	5	49	40	41
Bensons	22	10	5	7	47	34	35
Ninefields	22	10	5	7	36	35	35
Northmet	22	10	4	8	26	24	34
Pengelly	22	9	6	7	33	33	33
Abbey Youth	22	8	3	11	56	51	27
Clover	22	5	5	12	27	45	20
Newgate Street	22	6	0	16	35	69	18
JB's	22	4	2	16	20	48	14
Enfield Lock	22	3	2	17	37	70	11

DIV. ONE	P	W	D	L	F	A	PTS
Cheshunt Park	16	14	1	1	51	18	43
Arras	16	12	3	1	46	22	39
St Margaretsbury Res.	16	9	1	6	49	28	28
White Star	16	7	3	6	35	32	24
Royal Blues	16	7	1	8	34	31	22
Rosemill	16	5	1	10	28	62	16
JMC	16	4	2	10	38	53	14
Hadley Wood	16	3	2	11	34	51	11
Valencia	16	3	2	11	30	48	11

DIV. TWO	P	W	D	L	F	A	PTS
St Josephs	16	12	3	1	59	21	39
John Gilpin	16	10	2	4	43	19	32
Everest	16	10	1	5	28	26	31
Walton Athletic	16	7	3	6	31	21	24
Eleanor Cross	16	6	5	5	32	26	23
Dynamo Raiders	16	5	1	10	25	45	16
Salisbury	16	4	2	10	29	47	14
Gladiators	16	4	2	10	23	42	14
Nothaw	16	3	3	10	15	38	12

DIV. THREE	P	W	D	L	F	A	PTS
Winchmore Hill	18	14	1	3	57	20	43
Hoddesdon T. 'A'	18	14	1	3	48	18	43
St Margaretsbury 'A'	18	11	2	5	40	15	35
Northmet Res.	18	9	2	7	35	31	29
ESAB	18	8	3	7	45	37	27
Lea Valley Ryls	18	8	2	8	38	46	26
The Circus	18	8	1	9	49	46	25
Ninefield Res.	18	5	4	9	35	46	19
Botany Bay	18	3	1	14	22	56	10
Buryford	18	1	1	16	8	62	4

DIV. FOUR	P	W	D	L	F	A	PTS
Herts Reg. College	18	15	1	2	69	34	46
Percival	18	11	2	5	54	40	*34
Monarch	18	9	5	4	51	25	32
Botany Bay Res.	18	9	4	5	39	33	31
New Riverside	18	9	3	6	42	31	30
Addison	18	7	4	7	31	33	25
Leighton	18	5	4	9	28	41	19
Newgate St. Res.	18	5	4	9	29	28	*18
Astral United	18	4	4	10	40	49	16
Field End OB	18	0	1	17	27	96	1

* - Newgate Street Res. v Percival - match abandoned - no points awarded.

DIV. FIVE	P	W	D	L	F	A	PTS
Castle United	18	16	1	1	84	20	49
St Mary's	18	14	1	3	67	26	43
Oakwood	18	10	2	6	45	35	32
Edmonton Rovers	18	9	1	8	51	46	28
Goffs Oak Comrades	18	8	4	6	34	31	28
Old Bulls Head	18	7	2	9	39	44	23
AFC Astra	18	4	4	10	47	72	16
Cuffley 'A'	18	4	3	11	35	57	15
Enfield Park Res.	18	3	4	11	32	64	13
Hinton	18	2	4	12	40	79	10

DIV. SIX	P	W	D	L	F	A	PTS
Rangers	22	17	2	3	75	27	53
Somersett AVE 'A'	22	15	2	5	74	19	47
Tunfield	22	14	2	6	63	37	44
Wormley Rvrs 'A'	22	12	2	8	56	45	38
Turnford Rgrs	22	9	6	7	38	27	33
Northmet 'A'	22	10	3	9	42	52	33
Cheshunt Pk Res.	22	10	1	11	54	43	31
White Hart	22	8	5	9	52	56	29
Enfield Lock Res.	22	8	4	10	50	43	28
Woolpack Rgrs	22	7	1	14	40	60	22
Old Highway	22	5	0	17	36	106	15
Northaw Res.	22	1	4	17	18	82	7

DIV. SEVEN	P	W	D	L	F	A	PTS
Old Star Rgrs	18	14	1	3	91	37	43
DATA	18	12	3	3	72	26	39
Churchbury	18	11	3	4	65	39	36
Broxbourne Rgrs	18	11	1	6	83	46	34
Everest Res.	18	11	0	7	52	32	33
Beehive	18	10	3	5	54	35	33
Larsens	18	3	4	11	44	53	13
Rosemill Res.	18	4	1	13	30	85	13
John Gilpin Res.	18	3	3	12	33	74	12
Mead United	18	1	1	16	27	124	4

DIV. EIGHT	P	W	D	L	F	A	PTS
Myddleton	22	18	2	2	89	25	56
Enfield Ryls BL	22	17	3	2	85	30	54
Red Star Bell Lane	22	13	5	4	89	34	44
Hoddesdon United	22	13	4	5	62	36	43
Herts Reg C. Res.	22	13	3	6	87	43	42
Astral Res.	22	8	5	9	32	31	29
Oakwood Res.	22	8	5	9	43	51	29
Upshire	22	7	5	10	51	61	26
Haggs Lads	22	5	4	13	38	25	19
Lea Valley R. Res.	22	4	3	15	34	96	15
Larsens Res.	22	3	2	17	16	89	11
Abbey Res.	22	1	3	18	19	124	6

LONDON YOUTH

FOOTBALL ASSOCIATION

CUP FINALS 1993-94

U-18 Cup: Accra 2, Fisher 1
U-17 Cup: Kent Lions 1, Tudor Keys 0
U-16 Cup: Thamesmead Town 3, Puma 1
U-15 Cup: Parkmere 5, Wasps 2
U-14 Cup: Apex Arvensdale 4, Samuel Montague 1
U-13 Cup: Leaford 3, Valley Valiants 2
U-12 Cup: Teviot Rangers 1, Long Lane 0
U-11 Cup: S London Select 4, Valley Valiants 4
Replay: Sth London Select 2, Valley Valiants 0
U-10 Cup: YMCA Stars 2, Puma 0

BECKENHAM HOSPITAL CHARITY CUP

FOUNDED: 1903
(London's Oldest Charity Cup)

FINALS 1993-94

A: Eltham Palace 2, Bickley & Widmore 0 *(aet)*
B: Locksley 6, Wagoners 5
Veterans: Priory Vets 2, Keston Vets 0

CROYDON WEDNESDAY LEAGUE

FOUNDED: 1909

PREM. DIV.	P	W	D	L	F	A	PTS
Roys Rovers	14	10	3	1	40	21	23
Roma	14	8	4	2	42	22	20
WCDO	14	7	3	4	39	19	17
New Century	14	8	0	6	34	29	16
Croydon Postal	14	5	4	5	22	19	14
Beckenham Postal	14	4	4	6	33	29	12
Heathfield	14	3	1	10	15	53	7
Croydon Police	14	1	1	12	18	51	3

DIV. ONE	P	W	D	L	F	A	PTS
London FB Old Town	10	10	0	0	51	11	20
Croydon Postal Res.	10	5	2	3	29	18	12
Victoria Train Crew	10	4	2	4	22	18	10
Defiance	10	3	2	5	24	29	8
Carshalton College	10	2	3	5	18	34	7
SW Sports	10	1	1	8	12	36	3

Cup Finals:

Senior Cup: New Century beat Roys Rovers 9-8 on penalties after a 1-1 draw.
Junior Cup: London Fire Brigade Old Town 4, Victoria Train Crew 1
Charity Cup: Roys Rovers beat New Century 6-5 on penalties after a 1-1 draw.

Sportsmanship Trophy: New Century
Sportsmanship Runners-up: Carshalton Coll.
Secretary Award: Mr I Duncan (Vic. Train Crew)
Secretary R-up: Mr G Trayling (Croydon Police)
Referee Award: Mr B Woods
Referee Runner-up: Mr A Halfacre

SOUTHERN AREA SUNDAY LGE

FOUNDED: 1950

PREM. DIV.	P	W	D	L	F	A	PTS
Lewisham Way 'A'	16	12	2	2	59	21	26
Caribb	16	9	3	4	42	29	21
Man on the Moon	16	8	2	6	39	32	18
Portmanor	16	6	4	6	32	39	16
AMC Starline	16	5	5	6	26	37	15
Barracuda	16	6	3	7	35	48	15
AFC Flamingoes	16	4	3	9	43	47	11
Salters Hill	16	4	3	9	46	53	11
Mason Sports	16	4	3	9	38	54	11

Lower Division Champions:
Div. 1 (8): Horse & Groom
Div. 2 (11): Rising Sun
Div. 3 (12): Refuge AFC
Div. 4 (11): Southern Royals
Div. 5 (11): Manor Athletic
Div. 6 (11): Rapid Strikers

Cup Finals:

League Cup (Divs Prem-3): Lewisham Way IFC 'A' 1, Caribb 0 *(aet)*
Intermediate Cup (Divs 4-6): Southern Royals 4, William IV 2
Senior Cup (Prem & Div 1): Horse & Groom beat Caribb 4-3 on penalties after 1-1 draw
Chairmans Cup (Divs 2-3): Rising Sun 2, Mastercare 0
Presidents Cup (Divs 4-5): Herne Hill United 2, Lloyd Park Panthers 0 *(Match awarded to Lloyd Park Panthers - Herne Hill fielded an ineligible player).*
Junior Cup (Div 6): Selhurst Stewards 'B' beat Gipsy Wanderers 3-2 on penalties after 1-1 draw.

WEST FULHAM SUNDAY LGE

FOUNDED: 1932

PREM. DIV.	P	W	D	L	F	A	PTS
Horseferry	15	15	0	0	57	16	30
Mortlake	16	12	1	3	56	17	25
Westbourne Pk Villa	16	10	2	4	51	42	22
Riverside	15	8	1	6	52	44	17
O'Riordans	16	6	1	9	28	23	13
Hammersmith	15	5	2	8	32	17	12
Light Source	16	4	3	9	37	49	11
Elliott United	15	1	3	11	17	66	5
Heidleberg Griffin	16	2	1	13	20	76	5

Unplayed fixtures: Hammersmith v Elliott United, Horseferry v Riverside.

Lower Division Champions:
Div. 1 (9): White Ferry
Div. 2 (9): Masbro Mandela
Div. 3 (10): Bushville
Div. 4 (11): Elliott United Res.

Cup Finals:
Alf Dear Chal. Cup: Horseferry 4, White Ferry 0
Senior Cup: Horseferry 3, Mortlake 1
Intermediate Cup: White Ferry 3, Teddington Tgrs 2
Margaret Gray Cup: Barnes 2, Belgravia Brasserie 1

LONDON COMMERCIAL

LEAGUE

FOUNDED: 1912

DIV. ONE	P	W	D	L	F	A	PTS
Evershed Social	20	16	0	4	63	22	48
Meadhurst Sports	20	13	2	5	57	29	41
British Airways	20	12	2	6	66	31	38
Sudbury Court	20	11	2	7	46	32	35
57 Club	20	10	3	7	57	31	33
Charing Cross	20	9	0	11	51	56	27
District Line	20	7	3	10	40	34	24
Harrow Gas	20	7	3	10	40	59	*21
Barnet MO	20	6	3	11	32	64	21
Royal Mail (W12)	20	6	1	13	29	53	19
Hillingdon Irish	20	3	1	16	24	83	10

Lower Division Champions:
Div. 2 (11): Watneys Sports
Div. 3 (9): Hillingdon Irish Reserves
Div. 4 (11): Sandgate Old Boys
Div. 5 (10): Evershed Social 'A'
Div. 6 (12): District Line 'A'
Div. 7 (12): British Airways 'B'
Div. 8 (11): Osterley Town
Div. 9 (10): Racal Acoustics
Div. 10 (11): British Airways 'C'

Cup Finals:
Senior: Royal Mail (W12) 2, 57 Club 1
Intermediate: Sandgate OB 2, Meadhurst Spts Res. 0
Junior: Ealing OB 1, British Airways 'B' 0
Supplementary: Sudbury Court 2, Indian Gymkhana 1
Consolation: Hayes Villa 4, Blackstock Spts 0
Invitation: Glaxo Spts Res. 4, Taywood Spts Res. 0

DALSTON CROSS SHOPPING CENTRE EAST LONDON SUNDAY LEAGUE

FOUNDED: 1930

The League was founded in 1930 as the Stepney & District Sunday League, and is the oldest purely Sunday league in the country. The statute making Sunday football permissable was passed that year thanks to the efforts of later Prime Minister Clement Atlee.

Jim McCarroll, Secretary

DIV. ONE	P	W	D	L	F	A	PTS
Marquis of Salisbury	16	14	1	1	73	23	29
Bancroft United	18	12	1	5	68	33	25
JH Taverns	18	12	0	6	62	48	24
Gascoyne A.	17	9	2	6	65	44	20
Newington	17	9	2	6	50	43	20
Mile End Rangers	18	7	2	9	56	49	16
Meath	17	5	2	10	38	53	12
Barley Mow	18	4	2	12	24	56	10
Young Prince A.	16	3	3	10	33	67	9
The George	17	2	3	12	30	83	7

Lower Division Champions:
Div. 2 (9): Black Horse
Div. 3 (9): Crown & Dolphin
Div. 4 (10): Young Prince B.

Cup Finals:
Jubilee (all Divs): Bancroft United beat Marquis of Salisbury 4-2 on penalties after a 0-0 draw.
Senior (Divs 1 & 2): Bancroft 4, Marq. of Sal. 2
East London (Div 3): Duke of York (Bow) 2, Crown & Dolphin 1
Dick Coppick (Div 2): Younng Prince B. 2, Kingsbridge Arms 1

HENDON & DISTRICT SUNDAY LEAGUE

PREM. DIV.	P	W	D	L	F	A	PTS
West Hendon ESC	16	11	2	3	50	33	24
Samuel Lithgow	16	11	1	4	37	28	23
Rossmore	16	7	6	3	41	24	20
Linton	16	9	2	5	34	17	20
Pinner Town	16	8	3	5	27	21	19
Nissan	16	5	3	8	24	25	13
Maccabi	16	6	1	9	35	48	13
Kingfisher Yth	16	2	3	11	24	40	7
Kenboro'	16	0	5	11	14	50	5

Lower Division Champions:
Intermediate Div. (11): Wealdstone ESC
Div. 1 (10): West Hendon ESC Reserves
Div. 2 (9): St Andrews
Div. 3 (11): Starlight
Div. 4 (12): Plough (Ken)
Div. 5 (11): Crouch End Red Star

Cup Finals:
Mulston: Lynnpoint 2, White Bear (Hendon) 1
Presidents: St Andrews 4, W Hendon ESC Res. 0
Challenge: Nissan 3, Linton 2 *(aet)*
'Wishing Well' (7-a-side) **Cup:** LT (DVR) 1, Highgate Albion 0

MANCHESTER F.A.

Secretary: Fred Brocklehurst,
Sports Complex, Branthingham Rd,
Chorlton, Manchester M21 1TG (061 881 0299).

PREMIER CUP 1993-94

First Round

Curzon Aston v North Trafford	6-2	Radcliffe Borough v Flixton	2-0
Droylsden v Oldham Town	1-1,4-1	Mossley v Chadderton	2-1
Maine Road v Ashton United	0-2	Irlam Town v Salford City	4-5*(aet)*
Glossop NE *(w/o)* Atherton LR *(scr)*		Caernarfon v Hyde Utd	0-5*(see page 271)*

Quarter-Finals

Mossley v Hyde United	0-4	Glossop North End v Ashton United	1-4
Droylsden v Radcliffe Borough	1-0	Curzon Ashton v Salford City	3-0

Semi-Finals

Hyde United v Ashton United	3-0	Droylsden v Curzon Ashton	3-3,2-1*(aet)*

Final *(Wed 4th May, at Ashton United FC)*: Hyde United 4, Droylsden 1 *(aet)*

CHALLENGE TROPHY: **Winners:** Avro **Runners-up:** East Manchester

MANCHESTER LEAGUE (Est. 1893)

President: A Booth.
Vice-Presidents: G S Sinclair, W P D Haig.
Secretary: Mr F Fitzpatrick,
102 Victoria Rd, Stretford,
Manchester M32 0AD (061 865 2726).

PREM. DIV.	P	W	D	L	F	A	PTS
Abbey Hey	34	26	1	7	93	38	79
Wythenshaw Amtrs	34	24	6	4	96	36	78
Monton Amateurs	34	18	11	5	73	36	65
East Manchester	34	18	8	8	76	60	62
Wythenshawe Town	34	19	4	11	71	48	61
Springhead	34	17	7	10	56	42	58
Atherton Town	34	16	5	13	68	52	53
Woodley Sports	34	13	8	13	70	68	47
Little Hulton	34	14	5	15	74	82	47
Prestwich Heys	34	13	6	15	60	68	45
Dukinfield Town	34	13	5	16	52	66	44
BTCL	34	11	6	17	50	81	39
Stockport Georgians	34	9	11	14	46	54	38
Mitchell Shackleton	34	9	7	18	55	79	34
Ramsbottom United	34	9	4	21	49	78	31
Highfield United	34	8	6	20	43	60	30
Whitworth Valley	34	8	5	21	67	108	29
Gtr Man. Police	34	6	5	23	45	88	23

Gilgryst Cup: Little Hulton
Gilgryst Cup R-up: Dukinfield Town

DIV. ONE	P	W	D	L	F	A	PTS
Winton United	32	24	3	5	105	36	75
Sacred Heart	32	21	4	7	103	54	67
Whalley Range	32	19	4	9	72	46	61
Silcoms Woodside	32	17	6	9	72	48	57
Breightmet United	32	18	2	12	75	56	56
Zeneca	32	16	4	12	89	69	52
Pennington	32	14	6	12	90	65	48
Hollinwood	32	14	6	12	68	54	48
Avro	32	14	5	13	77	63	47
O Altrinchamians	32	14	3	15	71	59	45
Manchester Royal	32	13	6	13	77	76	45
New Mills	32	12	5	15	73	78	41
Stand Athletic	32	10	9	13	46	50	39
Ashton Athletic	32	11	5	16	66	78	38
Crompton	32	10	2	20	54	101	32
Milton	32	9	2	21	65	88	29
British Vita	32	0	0	32	29	211	0

Murray Trophy: Sacred Heart
Murray Trophy R-up: Avro

DIV. TWO	P	W	D	L	F	A	PTS
Abbey Hey Res.	30	25	3	2	95	36	78
W'shaw T. Res.	30	16	11	3	75	38	59
Monton Amtrs Res.	30	17	4	9	94	61	55
East Manch. Res.	30	15	8	7	66	45	53
W'shawe A. Res.	30	11	10	9	65	52	43
Dukinfield T. Res.	30	11	9	10	51	55	42
Skpt Georg. Res.	30	11	7	12	70	77	40
Ramsbottom Res.	30	9	9	12	53	66	36
Prestwich H. Res.	30	9	8	13	55	55	35
Whalley Rge Res.	30	9	8	13	54	76	35
Springhead Res.	30	9	7	14	50	57	34
Mit. Shack. Res.	30	9	7	14	47	71	34
Zeneca Res.	30	10	2	18	61	79	32
Highfield U. Res.	30	9	4	17	54	75	31
Manch. Royal Res.	30	8	6	16	55	78	30
Hollinwood Res.	30	8	5	17	50	74	29

Open Trophy: Atherton Town Reserves
Open Trophy R-up: Avro Reserves

DIV. THREE	P	W	D	L	F	A	PTS
Avro Res.	26	20	1	5	86	35	61
Atherton T. Res.	26	19	4	3	75	27	61
Woodley Spts Res.	26	16	6	4	77	31	54
Winton Utd Res.	26	15	3	8	83	53	48
Old Altrinch. Res.	26	12	6	8	61	36	42
Milton Res.	26	12	5	9	40	55	41
New Mills Res.	26	11	3	12	62	70	36
Stand Ath. Res.	26	9	6	11	45	53	33
Whitworth V. Res.	26	9	5	12	53	65	32
Sacred Heart Res.	26	8	6	12	45	55	30
Breightmet Res.	26	7	7	12	51	63	28
Pennington Res.	26	6	4	16	31	75	22
Crompton Res.	26	3	5	18	39	88	14
Ashton Ath. Res.	26	1	7	18	28	70	11

MANCHESTER LEAGUE PREMIER DIVISION CLUBS 1994-95

ABBEY HEY

Secretary: Mr G Lester, 6 Newhaven Ave., Higher Openshaw, Manchester M11 1HU.
Colours: Green & white/white/green **Ground:** Goredale Avenue, Gorton (061 231 7147).
Directions: A57 towards Hyde, right into Woodland Avenue approx one & a half miles past Belle Vue junction, right again into Ryder Brow Rd, 1st left after bridge into Goredale Ave.

ATHERTON TOWN

Secretary: G Butler, 43 Hope Fold Ave., Atherton, Lancs M29 0BW (0942 870326).
Colours: All royal **Ground:** Howe Bridge Spts Centre, Howe Bridge, Atherton (0942 870403).
Directions: A579 Atherton to Leigh road - Sports Centre on left approx one & a half miles from Atherton.

B.T.C.L.

Secretary: P Sinclair, 4 Printon Ave., Blackley, Manchester M9 3JH (061 740 3342).
Colours: Blue/white/blue **Ground:** G.M.T., White House, Middleton Rd, Crumpsall.
Directions: From Manchester via Cheetham Hill Rd to Half Way House hotel, right into Middleton Rd, ground entrance three quarters of a mile on left just before railway bridge.

DUKINFIELD TOWN

Secretary: L Walton, 280 Yew Tree Lane, Dukinfield, Cheshire SK16 5DN (061 338 6108).
Colours: Yellow/blue/yellow **Ground:** Blocksages Birch Lane, Dukinfield.
Directions: To Ashton along by-pass, right at 2nd island into Dewsnap Lane, left into Birch Lane, ground 100yds on lefy behind public baths and Colliers garage.

EAST MANCHESTER

Secretary: D Wilkinson, 76 Sandy Lane, Dukinfield, Cheshire SK16 5NL (061 330 4450).
Colours: Sky/navy/blue **Ground:** G.M.T. Tranport Ground, Mount Rd, Gorton (061 224 1176).
Directions: A57 from Manchester or Hyde to Belle Vue junction, turn into Mount Rd, ground 1 mile on left after Mellands Field.

LITTLE HULTON UNITED

Secretary: Mrs E Blood, 4 Cloudstock Grove, Little Hulton, Worsley M28 6DR (061 790 8925).
Colours: All royal **Change colours:** Sky & white stripes/white/white.
Ground: Avon Close, off Worsley Avenue, Little Hulton.
Directions: A6 from Manchester, two miles after Walkden turn left towards Tyldesley into Armitage Lane, left at Welcome pub after half mile into Madamswood Lane, 2nd right into Worsley Ave., 2nd right is Avon Close. Or, M61 jct 4, A6 towards Manchester, right into Armitage Lane and follow as above.

MITCHELL SHACKLETON

Secretary: C L Flynn, 3 Adelaide Str., Swinton, Manchester M27 3JW (061 794 7953).
Colours: Green & white hoops/white/green **Change colours:** All maroon.
Ground: Salteye Park, Peel Green, Eccles (061 788 8373).
Directions: Leave M63 at Peel Green r'bout (jct 2), take A57 Liverpool Road towards Irlam, ground entrance half mile on left behind Kara Cafew opposite Barton airport. Or, follow A57 from Manchester via Salford & Eccles, then follow Irlam signs.

MONTON AMATEURS

Secretary: T Lee, 28 Wheatley Rd, Swinton, Manchester M27 3RW (061 793 8033).
Colours: All royal **Ground:** As Mitchell Shackleton (above).

PRESTWICH HEYS

Secretary: M Johnston, 23 Fairways, Horwich, Bolton BL6 5QA (0204 692086).
Colours: Red & white stripes/black/red **Ground:** Sandgate Rd, Prestwich (061 773 8888).
Directions: Follow Old Bury Rd (A665) from Manchester to Prestwich, right into Heywood Rd, 3rd left into Mount Rd/Sandgate Rd - ground on right.

RAMSBOTTOM UNITED

Secretary: H Williams, 35 Nuttall Lane, Ramsbottom BL10 9JX (0706 823029).
Colours: Blue & white/blue & white/blue **Ground:** Ramsbottom Cricket Club (0706 822799).
Directions: M66 jct 1, A56 towards Ramsbottom, left down Bury New Rd after 1 mile, left again immediately after River Bridge.

SACRED HEART

Secretary: K D Devlin, 61 Buersil Ave., Balderstone, Rochdale, Lancs OL16 4TR (0706 313309).
Colours: Red/red/red & black **Ground:** Fox Park, Belfield Mill Lane, Rochdale.
Directions: M62 jct 21, follow Rochdale signs, right at 2nd lights into Albert Royds Street, ground half mile on right.

SPRINGHEAD

Secretary: K Gibson, 1 Little Oak Close, Lees, Oldham OL4 3LW (061 627 3760).
Colours: Red/white/red **Ground:** St John Str., Lees, Oldham (061 627 0260).
Directions: From Oldham (Mumps r'bout) follow A669 towards Lees for approx one & a half miles, left at St John Str., grounds 500yds on right.

STOCKPORT GEORGIANS

Secretary: M Kennedy, 45 Shakespeare Rd, Bredbury, Stockport SK6 2HS (061 494 5210).
Colours: Blue & white/blue/white **Ground:** Cromley Rd, Woodsmoor (061 483 6581).
Directions: Follow Stockport-Hazel Grove Rd (A6), right into Woodsmoor Lane at Davenport Theatre, 1st left into Moorland Rd, left at Flowery Field for Cromley Rd.

WOODLEY SPORTS

Secretary: D Dawson, 19 Woodstock Rd, Woodley, Stockport SK6 1QP (061 236 9177).
Colours: Orange/white/orange **Ground:** Lambeth Grove, off Mill Lane, Woodley (061 494 6429).
Directions: A560 from Stockport towards Woodley, left into Mill Str./Mill Lane at St Marks Church, Woodley, then 2nd right into Lambeth Grove.

WYTHENSHAWE AMATEURS

Secretary: S R Hall, 14 Southpark Rd, Gatley, Cheadle, Cheshire SK8 4AN (061 428 6074).
Colours: Blue & white stripes/blue/blue **Ground:** Longley Lane, Northenden (061 998 7268).
Directions: Princess Parkway from Manchester to Post House hotel, via Palatine Rd & Moor End Rd to Longley Lane - ground entrance opposite Overwood Rd.

WYTHENSHAWE TOWN

Secretary: P Whiles, 29 Lorna Rd, Cheadle Hulme SK8 5BJ (061 485 7380).
Colours: All royal **Ground:** Ericstan Park, Timpson Rd, Baguley, Manchester (061 998 5076).
Directions: Princess Parkway from Manchester, right into Altrincham Rd (A560), left into Southmoor Rd and 1st right into Timpson Rd - ground at end.

MANCHESTER LEAGUE DIVISION ONE CLUBS 1994-95

ASHTON ATHLETIC

Secretary: S Halliwell, 20 Kings Rd, Golborne, Warrington WA3 3PJ (0942 270778).
Colours: All green **Ground:** Brocstedes Park, Brocstedes Rd, North Ashton, Wigan (0942 716360).
Directions: A580 or M6 to Haydock Island, A49 to Ashton (Bryn Cross), left at lights onto Downall Green Rd, over M6, 2nd right, 2nd right is Brocstedes Rd.

AVRO

Secretary: D Kindon, 77 Hampton Rd, Failsworth, Manchester M35 9JA (061 688 8278).
Colours: All blue **Ground:** British Aerospace Sports Club, Broadway, Failsworth (061 681 3083).
Directions: A62 Manchester to Oldham road, left at Broadway (A663), ground entrance 200yds on left.

BREIGHTMET UNITED

Secretary: P G Lee, 37 Meadow Close, Little Lever, Bolton BL3 1LJ (0204 792280).
Colours: White/black/red **Ground:** Moss Park, Back Bury Rd, Breightmet, Bolton (0204 33930).
Directions: From Manchester follow A56 Bury road, at Whitefield take A665 towards Radcliffe, at Radcliffe proceed to Bolton Rd/Countess Lane and Radcliffe Moor Rd to A58 junction, left towards Bolton - ground half mile situated behind Coopers Egg Packing station.

COLDHURST UNITED

Secretary: Mr B Jackson, 526 Higginshaw Lane, Royton, Oldham OL2 6HW.
Colours: Blue & white/blue/blue **Ground:** Crompton Cricket Club, Glebe Str., Shaw (0706 847421).
Directions: From Manchester via Oldham road (A62) and Broadway/Shaw Rd (A663) to 'Big Lamp' r'bout near Shaw, by-pass Shaw centre, left into Salt Str., right into Glebe Street.
Previous Name: Crompton (pre-1994).

GREATER MANCHESTER POLICE

Secretary: P Davidson, 2 Oakwood, Sale M33 5RH (061 962 2327).
Colours: Green & white/white/green **Ground:** Hough End Police Club (061 856 1798).
Directions: Princess Parkway from central Manchester, right at Mauldeth Rd West, ground entrance half mile on left.

HIGHFIELD UNITED

Secretary: J Flynn, 58 Springside Rd, Bury BL9 5JQ (061 764 9986).
Colours: Red/white/red **Ground:** Bridge Hall Lane, Bury (061 797 2282).
Directions: A58 from Bury centre towards Heywood, at M66 junction pass under motorway and Bridge Hall Lane is first left - ground 200yds on left.

HOLLINWOOD

Secretary: K Evans, 20 Meadow Rise, High Crompton, Shaw, Oldham OL2 7QG (0706 840987).
Colours: All blue **Ground:** Lime Lane, Hollinwood (061 681 3385).
Directions: Oldham Road (A62) from Manchester to Roxy Cinema, right into Hollins Rd, 1st right into Albert Street, left at junction with Roman Road, 1st right into Lime Lane for quarter mile.

MANCHESTER ROYAL

Secretary: Mr A Royle, 34 Tennison Rd, Chedle SK8 2AR.
Colours: Red (black trim)/black/red (black trim) **Ground:** Barnes Hospital, Cheadle.
Directions: From Manchester, hospital entrance is on the left of Kingsway just after M63 jct 10. Keep left within hospital grounds, pitch is adjacent to motorway.

MILTON

Secretary: Mr R Curzon, 56 Abbey Crescent, Heywood OL10 4UG.
Cols: Green & yel. stripes/black/yel. **Grnd:** Athletic Stadium, Springfield Pk, off Bolton Rd, Rochdale.
Directions: From Manchester via Middleton (A664) to Hollins, A6046 towards Heywood then A58 towards Rochdale - Park on left after one and a half miles. Or, M62 jct 20 then follow Heywood signs (A58) - Park on right after one and a half miles.

NEW MILLS

Secretary: A Bowers, 5 Digland Villas, New Mills SK12 4HS (0663 744932).
Colours: Amber/black/black **Ground:** Church Lanw, New Mills (0663 747435).
Directions: A6 to Swan Hotel, left into Albion Rd, continue to Church Rd, left into Church Lane.

OLD ALTRINCHAMIANS

Secretary: K Ingham, 27 Oakleigh Ave., Timperley, Altrincham, Cheshire WA15 6QT (061 962 6496).
Colours: Black & white stripes/black/black **Ground:** Crossford Bridge P.F., Meadows Rd, Sale.
Directions: From Manchester via Stretford (A56), under M63, left at lights into Dane Rd, 1st left into Meadows Rd, ground entrance at end.

PENNINGTON

Secretary: K J Mullineaux, 271 Devonshire Rd, Atherton, Manchester M29 9QB (0942 879769).
Colours: Royal & white stripes/white/blue **Ground:** Jubilee Park, Leigh Rd, Atherton (0942 894703).
Directions: From Manchester follow East Lancs Rd towards Liverpool, right at Greyhound hotel towards Leigh, in Leigh take Atherton Rd (A579), ground on left after about one & a half miles before G.M.T. offices.

STAND ATHLETIC

Secretary: T H Edwards, 3 Burndale Drive, Unsworth, Bury BL9 8EN (061 766 3432).
Colours: All maroon **Ground:** Elms Playing Fields, George Street, Whitefield.
Directions: From Manc. city centre proceed via Bury New Rd (A56) to Whitefield. George St. is on right just before Fire Station. Car park & changing facilities are at Whitefield Community Centre in Green Lane, off George Str.

WHALLEY RANGE

Secretary: R Lapsley, 8 Withnell Rd, Burnage, Manchester M191GHN (061 432 6158).
Colours: Black & red stripes/black/black (red tops) **Ground:** King's Rd, Chorlton (061 881 2618).
Directions: Princess Parkway from Manchester, right at Wilbraham Rd, left at Withington Rd South, King's Rd is 1st right, ground entrance opposite Daventry Rd.

WHITWORTH VALLEY

Secretary: A Riley, 31 John Street, Whitworth, Rochdale OL12 8BT (0706 852619).
Colours: All royal **Ground:** Rawstron Str., Whitworth (0706 853030).
Directions: Bacup road (A671) from Rochdale, after just over 2 miles turn left at Whitworth centre into Tonge Lane then 3rd right left into Crown Park Way.

ZENECA (BLACKLEY)

Secretary: D McKay, 10 Lorraine Close, Hopwood, Heywood OL10 2JR (0706 368931).
Colours: White & blue hoops/white/white **Ground:** Hazelbottom Rd, Lower Crumpsall (061 205 5412).
Directions: A665 Cheetham Hill Rd froom Manchester, right into Queens Rd (A6010), left into Smedley Rd after half mile, fork right into Hazelbottom Rd, ground entrance 400yds on left.
Previous Name: ICI Blackley (pre-1993).

Division Two 1994-95 *(all Reserve teams)*: Abbey Hey, Atherton Town, Avro, Dukinfield Town, East Manchester, Highfield Utd, Mitchell Shackleton, Monton Amateurs, Prestwich Heys, Ramsbottom Utd, Springhead, Stockport Georgians, Whalley Range, Wythenshawe Amateurs, Wythenshawe Town, Zeneca (Blackley).

Division Three 1994-95 *(all Reserve teams)*: Ashton Ath., Breightmet Utd, Coldhurst Utd, Hollinwood, Little Hulton Utd, Manchester Royal, Milton, New Mills, Old Altrinchamians, Pennington, Sacred Heart, Stand Ath., Whitworth Valley, Woodley Sports.

Greater Manchester Police, who experienced relegation from the Premier Division after a disappointing season. Back Row (L/R): P Davidson (Manager), M Mangan, N Small, D Ewing, B Jefferson, M Bowring, M Bottrell, A Clarke, R Moulden (Asst Manager). Front: J Currie, T Timmons, I Arthur, S Currie, P Moore.
Photo - John L Newton.

Woodley Sports FC of the Manchester League Premier Division.
Photo - Colin Stevens.

LANCASHIRE & CHESHIRE

AMATEUR LEAGUE

FOUNDED: 1909

DIV. ONE	P	W	D	L	F	A	PTS
Cheadle Hth Nomads	24	17	5	2	57	24	39
Bedians	24	14	2	8	52	36	30
Oldham College	24	13	3	8	66	50	29
Old Standians	24	11	4	9	52	43	26
Disley	24	10	5	9	43	43	25
Old Ashtonians	24	9	6	9	40	34	24
Heaton Mersey	24	11	2	11	55	51	24
Pendle	24	10	2	12	53	48	22
West Didsbury	24	7	7	10	37	43	21
Cheadle Hulme	24	8	4	12	44	51	20
Heywood Town	24	9	2	13	41	68	20
Vymura Hyde	24	6	6	12	37	57	18
Mellor	24	6	2	16	28	57	14

DIV. TWO	P	W	D	L	F	A	PTS
Urmston	22	21	0	1	74	21	42
Gatley	22	13	4	5	46	29	30
Old Stoconians	22	11	3	8	45	43	25
South Manchester	22	11	2	9	38	37	24
Romiley	22	9	6	7	37	45	24
Bradford Parish	22	8	5	9	36	36	21
Old Stopfordians	22	7	5	10	52	49	19
Hazel Grove	22	7	3	12	39	52	17
Fletcher Bolton	22	6	5	11	40	59	17
Hooley Bdge Celtic	22	7	2	13	42	44	16
Old Stretfordians	22	4	7	11	30	54	15
Aldermere	22	5	4	13	30	40	14

DIV. THREE	P	W	D	L	F	A	PTS
Oldham Victoria	22	17	3	2	72	26	37
Metro	22	15	1	6	63	34	31
Parrswood Celtic	22	12	1	9	48	47	25
Moston Brook HSOB	22	11	2	9	49	36	24
Oldham Teachers	22	9	6	7	59	52	24
East Chorlton	22	9	2	11	56	59	20
Oldham Albion	22	9	2	11	36	43	20
Irlam/Cadishead Alb.	22	7	5	10	40	57	19
West Flixton	22	8	2	12	49	51	18
Clarksfield St Edw.	22	6	6	10	52	62	18
Manchester YMCA	22	6	2	14	46	70	14
Excise	22	4	6	12	23	56	14

DIV. A	P	W	D	L	F	A	PTS
O Ashtonians Res.	24	19	1	4	89	33	39
Bedians Res.	24	19	1	4	86	34	39
Cheadle HN Res.	24	15	4	5	78	34	34
Old Standians Res.	24	13	4	7	64	52	30
W Didsbury Res.	24	9	5	10	37	47	23
Pendle Res.	24	10	2	12	59	80	22
Cheadle Hulme Res.	24	9	3	12	50	59	21
Sth Manch. Res.	24	7	5	12	38	38	19
O Stoconians Res.	24	8	3	13	40	52	19
Hooley BC Res.	24	6	6	12	48	69	18
Vymura Hyde Res.	24	7	3	14	53	82	17
Disley Res.	24	6	5	13	51	82	17
Mellor Res.	24	5	4	15	49	80	14

DIV. B	P	W	D	L	F	A	PTS
Romiley Res.	22	14	4	4	58	27	32
Oldham Vict. Res.	22	14	3	5	58	29	31
Hazel Grove Res.	22	14	3	5	51	31	31
Heywood T. Res.	22	13	3	6	58	36	29
Oldham Coll. Res.	22	12	3	7	69	45	27
Fletcher B. Res.	22	9	4	9	65	61	22
Parrswood C. Res.	22	7	4	11	58	65	18
Oldham Albion Res.	22	7	4	11	52	60	18
Clarksfield SE Res.	22	6	5	11	54	59	17
Bdfd Parish Res.	22	6	4	12	57	71	16
Aldermere Res.	22	6	4	12	42	63	16
Mamch. YMCA Res.	22	3	1	18	35	110	7

DIV. C	P	W	D	L	F	A	PTS
Urmston Res.	22	16	4	2	95	22	36
Metro Res.	22	18	0	4	65	18	36
Oldham Teach. Res.	22	11	5	6	75	42	27
O Stretford. Res.	22	9	8	5	50	38	26
Gatley Res.	22	9	6	7	46	54	24
West Flixton Res.	22	9	4	9	52	44	22
Moston BHSOB Res.	22	8	5	9	45	47	21
O Stopford. Res.	22	8	5	9	42	55	21
Irlam/Cadishead Res.	22	6	4	12	35	59	16
Heaton Mersey Res.	22	6	4	12	39	64	16
Excise Res.	22	3	5	14	27	76	11
E Chorlton Res.	22	3	2	17	36	88	8

DIV. D	P	W	D	L	F	A	PTS
Old Ashtonians 'A'	22	16	3	3	80	38	35
Cheadle Hth N. 'A'	22	14	3	5	74	51	31
Mellor 'A'	22	12	5	5	67	40	29
Old Standians 'A'	22	13	1	8	74	49	27
Bedians 'A'	22	11	4	7	74	59	26
Cheadle Hulme 'A'	22	9	4	9	64	53	22
Oldham Teach. 'A'	22	8	4	10	70	67	20
O Stoconians 'A'	22	9	2	11	37	40	20
Parrswood C. 'A'	22	7	2	13	61	101	16
Hooley Bdge C. 'A'	22	6	3	13	40	72	15
Clarksfield SE 'A'	22	5	3	14	50	84	13
Vymura Hyde 'A'	22	4	2	16	46	83	10

DIV. E	P	W	D	L	F	A	PTS
Oldham Albion 'A'	22	17	2	3	85	32	36
Sth Manchester 'A'	22	16	1	5	105	43	33
Heywood T. 'A'	22	14	3	5	78	34	31
Hazel Grove 'A'	22	15	1	6	64	37	31
W Didsbury 'A'	22	12	5	5	77	55	29
Romiley 'A'	22	10	2	10	56	64	22
O Stretford. 'A'	22	8	3	11	55	56	19
Moston BHSOB 'A'	22	8	2	12	44	66	18
Aldermere 'A'	22	7	3	12	52	65	17
Disley 'A'	22	5	3	14	42	91	13
Oldham Teach. 'B'	22	2	4	16	39	90	8
Manch. YMCA 'A'	22	2	3	17	38	102	7

DIV. F	P	W	D	L	F	A	PTS
Old Ashtonians 'B'	20	18	2	0	90	26	38
Bedians 'B'	20	14	3	3	83	37	31
Vymura Hyde 'B'	20	11	5	4	60	36	27
Heywood Town 'B'	20	10	3	7	61	51	23
Mellor 'B'	20	8	3	9	80	60	19
Old Stoconians 'B'	20	7	5	8	49	40	19
Old Standians 'B'	20	9	1	10	54	47	19
Aldermere 'B'	20	8	1	11	50	51	17
Oldham Albion 'B'	20	6	0	14	40	104	12
Oldham Teach. 'C'	20	4	3	13	37	78	11
Moston BHSOB 'B'	20	1	2	17	25	99	4

STOCKPORT & DISTRICT SUNDAY LEAGUE

FOUNDED: 1957

PREM. DIV.	P	W	D	L	F	A	PTS
Offerton Utd	22	19	3	0	74	16	41
Norris Albion	22	19	2	1	89	18	40
Carnforth	22	14	2	6	61	27	30
Rifle Volunteer	22	10	5	7	54	25	25
Higher Poynton	22	8	6	8	42	50	22
Adswood United	22	8	5	9	40	40	21
Millbrow	22	9	2	11	40	65	20
Mount Villa	22	6	5	11	36	53	17
Medoak	22	6	3	13	39	76	15
Hindley Street	22	4	4	14	27	60	12
Ludworth	22	4	4	14	29	73	12
Dilke Celtic	22	3	3	16	35	63	9

Lower Division Champions:
Div. 1 (12): Handforth
Div. 2 (12): Devonshire
Div. 3 (12): Bramhall Queensgate
Div. 4 (12): Higher Poynton Reserves

HYDE & DISTRICT

SUNDAY LEAGUE

PREM. DIV.	P	W	D	L	F	A	PTS
Haughton Villa	18	14	2	2	59	22	30
Carters Bridge	18	12	2	4	69	31	26
Crown/Cush. Failsw.	18	11	3	4	61	28	25
Royal Oak Gorton	18	10	2	6	39	32	22
Lamb Hotel	18	6	7	5	33	34	19
Woodley	18	6	4	8	36	39	*14
Penny Farthing	18	3	8	7	35	33	*12
Grapes	18	4	4	10	32	44	12
Four in Hand	18	4	3	11	23	62	11
Sycamore	18	2	1	15	27	89	5

* - 2 points deducted

Lower Division Champions:
Div. 1 (12): Railway Hyde
Div. 2 (11): Old Ball
Div. 3 (13): White Horse
Div. 4 (14): New Inn Dukinfield
Div. 5 (13): Denton Masons
Div. 6 (12): Red Star United

Cup Finals:
Challenge Cup: Haughton Villa 2, Lamb Hotel 1
Rose Bowl: Charlesworth & Chisworth 4, Pear Tree Shadow 0
Reporter Cup: Haughton Villa 3, Woodley 2
Presidents Cup: Railway 3, Butchers Arms 1
John Wood Cup: Deltic 3, Haddon Hall 2
John Godley Cup: Pear Tree Shad. 2, White Gates 0
Dennis Woodley Mem. Tphy: Acres Inn 3, New Inn 2

CITY of MANCHESTER SUNDAY LEAGUE

Div. 1 Morning	P	W	D	L	F	A	PTS
Lord Lyon	26	23	1	2			47
Concert	26	22	1	3			45
Taymark	26	21	1	4			43
Manchester Appollo	26	15	2	9			32
Superstar	26	11	7	8			29
Rusholme OSB	26	11	6	9			28
Red Star C.	26	11	3	12			25
Victoria B.	26	10	4	12			24
Trafford H.	26	11	2	13			24
Birch Rovers	26	10	2	14			22
Mauldeth	26	8	5	13			21
St Crispens	26	6	3	17			15
Friday's	26	4	1	21			9
Jackson Old Boys	26	0	0	26			0

Div. 1 Afternoon	P	W	D	L	F	A	PTS
MSS Sports	22	18	2	2			38
Alpha Sports	22	14	5	3			33
Proctor's YC	22	14	5	3			33
Supreme United	22	13	2	7			28
AC Nova	22	9	6	7			24
Akal Zalam A.	22	10	4	8			24
Sporting YM	22	11	2	9			24
Saoirse	22	9	3	10			21
Manchester Raiders	22	9	3	10			21
Salutation	22	6	2	14			14
Withington S.	22	2	0	20			4
Errwood Celtic	22	0	0	22			0

Lower Division Champions:
Div. 2 Morning (13): Sporting BK
Div. 2 Afternoon (12): Chorlton
Div. 3 Afternoon (12): MSS Sports Res.

Cup Finals:
Manchester Utd: Grove Utd 3, Nelson Didsbury 0
Geoff Light: Seedley Rgrs 5, Taymark 4 *(aet)*
Roy Clarke: Sporting YM 3, Sporting BK 0
Dave Sterling: Lord Lyon 2, Rusholme OSB 1 *(aet)*
Jack Barlow: Akal Zalam A. 1, MSS Sports 0
Sportsman's Challenge: MSS Sports Reserves 3, Woodsend Villa 1

MANCHESTER AMATEUR

SUNDAY LEAGUE

DIV. ONE	P	W	D	L	F	A	PTS
Moss Side	20	15	4	1	65	19	34
East Levenshulme	20	15	0	5	58	28	30
Trafford Barons	20	10	5	5	57	35	25
Kearsley	20	11	3	6	55	43	25
Manchester Maccabi	20	10	4	6	51	39	24
Parrswood Mauldeth	20	6	6	8	34	28	18
Irish Association	20	5	5	10	31	37	15
Orion Villa	20	7	1	12	34	61	15
Burnage	20	5	4	11	28	47	14
Ellesmere	20	5	2	13	37	55	12
Stretford TL	20	1	6	13	26	83	8

Lower Division Champions:
D2 (7): Procter Gamble — **D3** (11): Portland
D4 (12): Albion Town — **D5** (9): Hurlford

Cup Finals:
J A Kennedy: East Levenshulme 5, Moss Side 4
John Old: Davyhulme Rangers 4, Nello James 3

Below: *East Levenshulme - J A Kennedy Cup winners 1993-94.* *Photo - Colin Stevens.*

MIDDLESEX F.A.

Secretary: Peter Clayton, 39 Roxborough Road, Harrow, Middlesex HA1 1NS (081 424 8524)

SENIOR CHALLENGE CUP 1993-94

First Preliminary Round

Hampton v Hillingdon Borough	2-1*(aet)*	North Greenford Utd v Feltham & Hounslow B.	1-3
Rayners Lane v Potters Bar Town	1-0	Southall v Cockfosters	3-0
Southgate v Harefield United	1-4	Willesden Hawkeye v Kingsbury Town	3-0
Wingate & Finchley v Viking Sports	3-4		

Second Preliminary Round

Ashford Town (Middx) v Rayners Lane	3-1	Brimsdown Rovers v Harefield United	3-2
Edgware Town v Ruislip Manor	2-1	Hampton v Viking Sports	1-0*(aet)*
Southall v Bedfont	0-1	Uxbridge v Brook House	0-0,4-2
Wealdstone v Hanwell Town	2-2,5-1	Willesden Hawkeye v Feltham	2-2,0-2

First Round

Bedfont v Feltham & Hounslow Borough	1-3	Edgware Town v Wembley	4-2
Enfield v Brimsdown Rovers	1-0	Hampton v Staines Town	0-1
Uxbridge v Northwood	5-2	Harrow Boro. v Hendon	0-1*(replay ordered)*,1-0
Wealdstone v Hayes	2-1	Yeading v Ashford Town (Middx)	6-0

Quarters-Finals

Edgware Town v Enfield	5-4*(aet)*	Harrow Borough v Staines Town	2-3
Uxbridge v Yeading	4-0	Wealdstone v Feltham & Hounslow Borough	2-1

Semi-Finals

Edgware Town v Uxbridge	3-2	Staines Town v Wealdstone	4-2*(aet)*

Final *(at Hayes FC, Mon 4th April)*: Staines Town 2, Edgware Town 1

SENIOR CHARITY CUP

First Round

Feltham & Hounslow Borough v Southgate	6-1	Hampton v Potters Bar Town	1-2
Harefield United v Ashford Town (Middx)	2-0	Kingsbury Town v Hillingdon Borough	2-4
Wingate & Finchley v Rayners Lane	0-1		

Second Round

Bedfont v North Greenford United	3-0	Harefield Utd v Feltham & Hounslow Borough	2-0
Hillingdon Borough v Hanwell Town	2-0	Northwood v Cockfosters	3-2
Potters Bar Town v Brook House	2-1	Staines Town v Brimsdown Rovers	1-0
Wembley v Rayners Lane	4-1	Willesden Hawkeye v Viking Sports	4-0

Third Round

Harefield United v Wembley	0-2	Harrow Borough v Bedfont	1-1*(7-6 on pens)*
Hayes v Potters Bar Town	3-0	Northwood v Yeading	6-2
Ruislip Manor v Hillingdon Borough	3-0	Staines Town v Edgware Town	1-0
Uxbridge v Chelsea	1-5	Willesden Hawkeye v Bedfont	4-1*(aet)*

Quarter-Finals

Ruislip Manor v Northwood	1-4	Staines Town v Hayes	2-0
Wembley v Harrow Borough	2-0	Willesden Hawkeye *(w/o)* Chelsea *(withdrew)*	

Semi-Finals

Staines Town v Willesden Hawkeye	4-0	Northwood v Wembley	2-2*(5-4 on penalties)*

Final *(at Harrow Borough FC, Fri 13th May)*: Staines Town 4, Northwood 0

OTHER COUNTY FINALS 1993-94

Premier Cup *(at Yeading FC)*: Evershed Soc. 3, Ruislip Mnr Res. 1 *(after game aban. 106 mins at 1-1)*
Intermediate Cup *(at Edgware Town FC)*: 57 Club Reserves 4, Slough Gas 2
Junior Cup *(at Northwood FC)*: Old Manorians 3, C B United 1
Junior Trophy *(at Harefield Utd FC)*: Acton Ealing Whistlers 5, Old Manorians Reserves 1
Midweek Cup *(at Northwood FC)*: Datacab 4, Willesden Hawkeye 1
Junior Inter-Lge Cup *(at Hillingdon Borough FC)*: West Middx Combination 3, Hounslow & Dist. Lge 1 *(aet)*
Veterans' Cup *(at Staines Town FC)*: Drayton Nomads 1, Northwood 0
Sunday Premier Cup *(at Uxbridge FC)*: Hampton Social 1, Plough Wanderers 0
Sunday Intermediate Cup *(at Northwood FC)*: West Hendon ESC Reserves 5, Stanmore Cosmos 2
Sunday Junior Cup *(at Kingsbury Town FC)*: Belstone Reserves 7, Mirrabeau 0
Sunday Junior Trophy *(at Edgware Town FC)*: Coningham Arms 2, Hope & Anchor 1
Sunday Inter-Lge Cup *(at Ashford Town)*: Hayes & District Lge 2, Hendon & District Lge 1
Ladies' Senior Cup *(at Wembley FC)*: Wembley Ladies 3, Millwall Lionesses 0

MIDDLESEX COUNTY LEAGUE

Patron: Russell Grant,
President: Peter Rogers,
Chairman: Fred Griggs,
Hon. Secretary: Keith Chamberlin,
4 Shelley Ave., Greenford, Middx UB6 8RU.

Founded 1984

New Hanford claimed their first-ever Middlesex County League championship last season. An impressive eight-match unbeaten start kept them in touch with Shamrock, the pace-setters and defending champions.

However, a mid-winter slump in form brought both clubs back to the other title contenders. During this spell, the leadership changed hands no fewer than eight times, between five teams. A gruelling run-in saw New Hanford pull clear again, fending off a strong three-way challenge from Scolar, Shamrock and Northolt Saints. They secured the title in the their final match, with a 2-2 draw against fellow contenders Northolt Saints, who themselves capped a glorious debut season in the top flight with runners-up spot.

The Division One championship race looked to be all but settled by Christmas, as Flackwell Heath Reserves raced to a nine-point lead, only for their campaign to falter in the second half of the season. The race was then on for the reserve teams of Rayners Lane and Northfield CAV. In the run-in, the former finally edged in front but, having finished their campaign a week early, had to sit out the last Saturday of the season before they could claim their crown.

In Division Two, a string of high-scoring victories saw Neasden's second team become the first side to secure any of the season's silverware. With two weeks of the title race still to go, yet another Neasden victory allowed them to claim their crown.

In the Alec Smith Cup, a three-year wait for a Premier Division side to win the League's senior challenge cup competition finally came to an end. Scolar, making their debut in the tournament, deservedly clinched the trophy with the only goal of the final against Osterley.

The President's Cup - the League's Junior knockout trophy - ended in a penalty shoot-out. Osterley's reserve side avenged their first XI's Alec Smith Cup final defeat the week before, after their duel with New Hanford's second team had ended deadlocked at two-each. It was the third season running that Osterley's second XI have overcome their rivals from New Hanford in this competition, including the 1991-92 final.

Elsewhere, the League's senior representative side claimed runners-up spot in the South Eastern Counties Intermediate Inter-League Competition - their best-yet performance. With next season's Premier Division being made up of the clubs who have attained intermediate status, plus Southgate and senior status club North Greenford United, the Middlesex County League can look forward to great things this coming season.

Nigel Hickes, League Registrar.

Premier Division	P	W	D	L	F	A	PTS
New Hanford	24	14	7	3	48	24	49
Northolt Saints	24	14	5	5	42	29	47
Scolar	24	14	3	7	53	28	45
Shamrock	24	12	6	6	42	33	42
Neasden	24	11	4	9	63	54	37
Nortfield CAV	24	11	3	10	40	33	36
Technicolor Spts	24	10	4	10	51	59	34
Hanworth Villa	23	8	6	9	51	56	31
Osterley	24	8	4	12	44	59	28
Broadwater United	23	7	4	12	35	46	24
Spelthorne Spts	24	6	6	12	29	43	24
Pitshanger	24	5	4	15	38	45	19
St Clarets (Hayes)	24	5	4	15	32	59	19

Broadwater Utd v Hanworth Villa unfulfilled - Hanworth awarded 1pt, Broadwater deducted 2pts. Simba All Stars were withdrawn and their record expunged.

Division One	P	W	D	L	F	A	PTS
Rayners Lane Res.	26	7	3	3	56	32	54
Nortfield CAV Res.	26	16	4	6	48	38	52
Willesden Constantine	26	15	4	7	78	44	49
Flackwell Hth Res.	26	15	3	8	56	36	48
Hounslow Town '91	26	13	8	5	57	35	47
Osterley Res.	26	12	5	9	65	44	41
N Greenford U. Res.	26	10	6	10	28	35	36
Harrow St Marys	26	10	3	13	38	62	33
Cockfosters Res.	26	9	5	12	40	42	32
Southgate Ath. Res.	26	9	4	13	52	57	31
Brook House Res.	26	8	6	12	38	49	30
Brimsdown Rvrs Res.	26	7	4	15	33	52	25
Amersham Town Res.	26	6	3	17	33	67	21
Scolar Res.	26	3	6	17	30	59	15

Division Two	P	W	D	L	F	A	PTS
Neasden Res.	26	20	1	5	85	39	61
New Hanford Res.	26	17	5	4	68	45	#58
Technicolor Res.	26	17	4	5	75	35	55
Southall Res.	26	13	7	6	85	50	46
Broadwater U. Res.	26	12	5	9	73	29	*40
Northolt Saints Res.	26	12	1	13	46	62	*36
St Clarets Res.	26	10	3	13	47	62	33
Spelthorne Spts Res.	26	10	3	13	38	43	33
Beaconsfield U. Res.	26	10	2	14	55	70	32
Pitshanger Res.	26	8	4	14	50	89	28
Brimsdown Rvrs 'A'	26	9	1	16	43	67	*27
Hanwell Town 'A'	26	6	5	15	45	66	*23
Circle	26	8	3	15	55	82	***23
Northolt Dynamo	26	7	2	17	44	69	*22

* - 1pt deducted # - 2pts awarded

PREMIER DIVISION RESULTS 1993-94

HOME TEAM	1	2	3	4	5	6	7	8	9	10	11	12	13
1. Broadwater United	*	#	4-1	0-2	1-0	0-0	2-1	4-2	1-2	2-3	0-2	1-2	4-3
2. Hanworth Villa	2-1	*	2-8	0-0	4-3	1-0	0-0	1-2	0-3	1-3	2-1	2-2	2-4
3. Neasden	3-1	3-2	*	1-4	1-2	0-2	7-0	1-5	0-3	0-0	2-2	5-3	3-2
4. New Hanford	1-1	2-0	2-1	*	1-0	2-2	1-0	1-0	2-0	1-2	4-1	1-1	6-0
5. Northfield CAV	4-1	4-3	1-1	2-3	*	0-1	5-2	2-0	0-1	1-4	2-0	3-1	4-1
6. Northolt Saints	1-1	5-5	2-1	0-3	1-0	*	0-3	4-1	1-0	1-1	3-1	2-3	2-0
7. Osterley	3-1	2-6	2-3	2-0	2-2	2-4	*	3-1	2-5	1-2	1-1	3-1	4-6
8. Pitshanger	8-0	1-3	1-1	2-3	1-2	0-2	2-3	*	1-3	0-0	1-3	0-3	3-0
9. Scolar	0-2	1-1	2-3	2-1	2-0	3-1	2-1	3-2	*	0-1	1-1	1-0	11-1
10. Shamrock	3-1	2-2	3-6	0-0	0-1	0-1	2-2	0-3	3-2	*	2-0	5-0	1-4
11. Spelthorne Spts	1-1	6-3	1-4	1-2	1-0	0-3	1-3	0-0	2-0	0-2	*	0-3	0-2
12. St Clarets (Hayes)	0-5	0-5	4-3	3-3	0-1	1-2	1-2	1-1	0-4	1-3	2-4	*	0-2
13. Technicolor Sports	2-1	3-4	4-5	3-3	1-1	1-2	4-0	2-1	2-2	3-0	0-0	1-0	*

- see explanation under league table on previous page.

DIVISION ONE RESULTS 1993-94

HOME TEAM	1	2	3	4	5	6	7	8	9	10	11	12	13	14
1. Amersham Town Res.	*	0-3	1-2	0-1	1-3	1-0	3-2	1-5	0-2	2-2	1-3	2-1	6-4	0-5
2. Brimsdown Rvrs Res.	4-0	*	0-0	1-7	0-1	2-0	0-2	2-0	1-1	3-1	1-3	0-0	1-2	0-4
3. Brook House Res.	1-0	2-1	*	0-2	1-0	4-3	1-1	1-2	1-2	1-1	4-2	2-2	1-2	3-2
4. Cockfosters Res.	2-1	2-3	1-2	*	0-2	2-2	0-2	0-0	3-5	0-2	0-1	1-4	2-0	0-0
5. Flackwell Hth Res.	3-1	5-0	1-0	0-2	*	9-1	2-2	0-1	2-1	2-1	0-4	3-1	3-0	0-6
6. Harrow St Mary's	2-1	2-1	5-4	1-5	1-0	*	2-0	1-2	2-2	0-5	0-2	2-2	3-2	2-1
7. Hounslow Town '91	0-0	4-1	5-1	0-0	3-0	2-1	*	4-0	3-0	2-2	1-2	2-1	2-1	2-2
8. N. Greenford Utd Res.	3-1	1-1	1-0	1-0	0-2	0-1	0-1	*	0-3	2-2	3-1	1-0	1-1	2-0
9. Northfield CAV Res.	6-0	3-2	3-2	4-1	2-1	2-0	2-1	0-0	*	0-5	1-5	0-1	1-0	0-5
10. Osterley Res.	3-4	3-0	3-1	4-2	3-4	6-2	3-2	3-0	0-2	*	0-2	2-1	2-4	2-2
11. Rayners Lane Res.	1-4	2-1	3-0	0-0	1-1	2-0	2-3	4-0	1-1	3-2	*	3-1	1-0	2-4
12. Scolar Res.	1-1	1-0	0-0	1-2	0-3	0-1	4-6	1-1	1-2	0-4	1-3	*	1-4	2-3
13. Southgate Ath. Res.	2-1	4-1	3-3	1-3	3-3	0-1	3-3	1-0	1-2	1-3	2-1	7-2	*	1-6
14. Willesden (Constantine)	6-1	1-4	3-1	5-2	1-6	5-3	2-2	4-2	0-1	2-1	1-2	4-1	4-2	*

DIVISION TWO RESULTS 1993-94

HOME TEAM	1	2	3	4	5	6	7	8	9	10	11	12	13	14
1. Beaconsfield Utd Res.	*	4-2	1-5	5-1	4-0	1-2	1-1	0-4	4-0	3-2	1-8	0-0	2-5	0-2
2. Brimsdown Rovers 'A'	5-2	*	0-10	0-2	1-3	0-3	1-2	2-0	4-1	1-4	2-1	3-1	2-1	1-4
3. Broadwater Utd Res.	L-W	5-0	*	L-W	1-1	L-W	1-1	1-2	L-W	L-W	4-1	2-2	2-4	2-3
4. Circle	2-6	2-3	0-6	*	5-2	4-5	2-5	4-3	3-1	2-4	2-2	4-2	9-0	0-3
5. Hanwell Town 'A'	1-3	1-6	1-5	0-0	*	1-4	1-4	5-1	0-1	7-1	3-3	1-3	0-4	1-2
6. Neasden Res.	6-2	7-0	4-1	2-1	0-2	*	6-3	4-2	3-4	5-1	1-1	3-1	5-0	3-1
7. New Hanford Res.	4-2	1-1	3-3	1-1	3-1	1-0	*	4-2	5-2	2-1	3-2	2-0	4-1	3-2
8. Northolt Dynamo	1-4	W-L	0-3	3-1	4-4	0-3	0-1	*	0-3	5-2	3-2	1-0	1-3	2-5
9. Northolt Saints Res.	3-2	5-4	0-6	3-2	0-3	3-0	2-7	4-1	*	4-1	L-W	0-3	4-2	0-1
10. Pitshanger Res.	5-3	3-1	2-6	3-2	1-1	0-7	5-0	3-3	2-1	*	2-9	0-4	2-2	1-6
11. Southall Res.	4-0	W-L	2-3	10-0	2-1	5-6	5-1	4-3	4-2	4-4	*	1-1	2-1	6-3
12. Spelthorne Spts Res.	2-0	1-0	0-1	1-4	2-0	1-3	1-4	2-1	4-1	3-1	0-3	*	1-2	2-1
13. St Clarets (Hayes) Res.	1-2	1-2	0-4	6-2	0-5	2-3	1-0	2-1	0-1	2-0	3-3	3-1	*	1-5
14. Technicolor Spts Res.	4-3	3-2	2-2	6-0	6-0	2-0	1-3	3-1	1-1	6-0	1-1	2-0	0-0	*

ALEC SMITH LEAGUE CUP 1993-94

First Round

St Clarets (Hayes) v Spelthorne Sports 1-0
Harrow St Mary's v Willesden (Constantine) 3-5
New Hanford v Simba All Stars 0-1
Brimsdown Rovers Reserves v Hanworth Villa 1-5
Broadwater United v Rayners Lane Res. 2-2,2-1
Flackwell Heath Reserves v Northolt Saints 1-2
Hounslow Town '91 v Pitshanger 2-0
North Greenford Utd Res. v Southgate Ath. Res. 1-0
Cockfosters Reserves v Technicolor Sports 5-5,1-2
All other clubs received byes

Second Round

St Clarets (Hayes) v Scolar 3-4
Neaden v Hounslow Town '91 2-1
North Greenford Utd Res. v Hanworth Villa 1-4
Broadwater United v Northfield CAV 1-2
Northolt Saints v Willesden (Constantine) 1-3
Simba All Stars *(scr)* Shamrock *(w/o)*
Amersham Town Reserves v Technicolor Sports 0-1
Brook House Reserves v Osterley 0-4

Quarter-Finals

Scolar v Willesden (Constantine) 4-2
Hanworth Villa v Technicolor Sports 3-1
Neasden v Shamrock 1-2
Northfield CAV v Osterley 0-1

Semi-Finals

Scolar v Shamrock 2-0
Hanworth Villa v Osterley 1-3

Final *(at Southall FC, Sat 30th April)*: Scolar 1, Osterley 0.

PRESIDENT'S CUP

Preliminary Round

Pitshanger Reserves v Northolts Saints Res. 4-2

First Round

Broadwater Utd Res. v Technicolor Spts Res. 1-2
Scolar Res. *(w/o)* Beacomnsfield Res. *(scr)*
Circle v Northolt Dynamo 2-5
Osterley Reserves v Spelthorne Spts Res. 10-0
Southall Reserves v Neasden Reserves 5-5,2-7
New Hanford Reserves v Brimsdown Rvrs Res. 4-2
St Clarets (Hayes) Reserves v Hanwell Town 'A' 0-5
Northfield CAV Reserves v Pitshanger Reserves 1-2

Quarter-Finals

Technicolor Sports Res. v Neasden Reserves 4-1
Northolt Dynamo v Hanwell Town 'A' 0-3
Beaconsfield Utd Res. v New Hanford Reserves 1-2
Osterley Reserves v Pitshanger Reserves 4-1

Semi-Finals

Hanwell Town 'A' v Osterley Reserves 1-3
Technicolor Sports Reserves v New Hanford Res. 0-1

Final *(at Nth Greenford Utd FC, Sat 7th May)*: Osterley Res. 2, New Hanford Res. 2 *(Osterley won 3-0 on pens).*

PREMIER DIVISION CLUBS 1994-95

BROADWATER UNITED

Secretary: Godfrey Lowe, 53 Rochford Griffin Road, Tottenham N17 6HX (081 801 7616).
Ground: Lordship Lane Recreation Ground, Lordship Lane, Tottenham, London N17 (081 880 3944).
Colours: Black & white/black/black **Change colours:** All blue.
Hons: Middx Lg R-up 92-93 (Div 1 91-92).

CIPPENHAM

Secretary: Tom Barclay, 127 Laughtons Meadow, Farnham Common, nr Slough SL2 3NS (0753 643949).
Ground: Cippenham Village Green, Cippenham, Slough, Berkshire (0628 660885).
Colours: Blue & white stripes/navy/navy **Change colours:** Blue & gold stripes/navy/navy.

HOUNSLOW TOWN '91

Secretary: Irene Ambrose, 171 Heath Rd, Hounslow, Middx TW3 2NR (081 568 9635).
Ground: Ingwood Park, Ingwood Road, Hounslow, Middx.
Colours: White/orange/orange & black **Change colours:** Red & black hoops/red/red.

NEW HANFORD

Secretary: Jerry Scanlon, 70 Bridge Avenue, Hanwell W7 3DJ (081 575 0113).
Ground: Drayton Manor Playing Fields, Greenford Ave., Hanwell, London W7 (081 578 5831).
Colours: Sky/navy/navy **Change Colours:** Red & black/black/black.
Previous Ground: Birkbeck College PF, Birkbeck Ave., Greenford (pre-1993).
Hons: Middx Co. Lg 93-94.

NORTH GREENFORD UNITED

Secretary: Reginald Johnson, 63 Berkeley Ave., Greenford, Middx UB6 0NY (081 864 2654).
Ground: Berkeley Fields, Berkeley Ave., Greenford, Middx (081 422 8923).
Colours: Royal & white stripes/royal/royal **Change colours:** Orange/black/orange
Previous League: Spartan (pre-1994).

NORTHFIELD C.A.V.

Secretary: Pauline Jones, 6 Siverst Close, Northolt, Middx UB5 4NJ (081 422 8012).
Ground: The Annexe, Yeading FC *(see page 458)*.
Colours: Yellow/black/yellow **Change Colours:** Blue/navy/navy.
Previous Names: CAV Northolt/ Northfield Rangers (clubs merged in 1993).
Previous Ground: (CAV Northolt): Armenian Community Centre, West End Rd, Northolt (pre-1993).
Hons: Middx Lg 91-92 (as Northfield Rgrs).

NORTHOLT SAINTS

Secretary: Robert Bevis, c/o Northolt Saints FC (address as below) (081 841 1249).
Ground: Lord Halsbury Playing Fields, Eastcote Lane, Northolt, Middx UB5 5DU (081 841 1249).
Colours: Yellow/blue/blue **Change colours:** All blue.
Hons: Middx Lg R-up 93-94 (Div 1 92-93, Alec Smith Cup 92-93).

OSTERLEY

Secretary: David Bull, 508 Great West Rd, Hounslow, Middx TW5 0TE (081 569 6889).
Ground: The White Lodge Club, Syon Lane, Osterley, Middx (081 758 1191).
Colours: Blue & white stripes/blue/blue **Change Colours:** Claret & sky stripes/sky/sky.
Hons: Middx Co. Lg Alec Smith Cup R-up 93-94.

PITSHANGER

Secretary: Chris Green, 14 Silver Birch Close, Ickenham, Middx UB10 8AP (0895 231796).
Ground: Pitshanger Park, Scotch Common, Ealing, London W13 (081 991 9826).
Colours: Tangerine/black/black **Club Colours:** White/white/orange.
Hons: Middx Lg Div 1 R-up 91-92 (Alec Smith Cup 91-92).

St CLARETS (HAYES)

Secretary: Paul Treanor, 310 Balmoral Drive, Hayes, Middx UB4 8DH (081 848 3500).
Ground: As Pitshanger FC (above)
Colours: Yellow/green/yellow **Change colours:** Sky/navy/sky.
Previous Ground: Cranford Comm. Sch., High Str., Cranford, Hounslow (pre-1993).
Hons: Middx County Lg Div 1 R-up 92-93.

SHAMROCK

Secretary: Nigel O'Connell, 24 Hawarden Hill, Brook Rd, London NW2 7BR (081 450 7886).
Ground: Shamrock Club House, Horn Lane, Acton, London W3 (081 993 1270).
Colours: Green/white/green. **Change colours:** White/green/white.
Hons: Middx County Lg 92-93 (R-up 91-92).

SOUTHGATE

Secretary: Kevin Cullen, 39 Hill Rise, Potters Bar, Herts EN6 2RX (0707 656136).
Ground: Tottenhall Rd Spts Ground, Tottenhall Rd, Palmers Green, London N13 (081 888 1542).
Colours: Amber/black/amber **Change Colours:** All blue.

SPELTHORNE SPORTS

Secretary: Ron Ford, 35 Walton Gardens, Feltham, Middx TW13 4QY (081 890 8346).
Ground: Spelthorne Spts Ground, 296 Staines Rd West, Ashford Common, Middx (0932 783625).
Colours: Sky/navy/navy **Club Colours:** Jade/jade/black.

TECHNICOLOR SPORTS

Secretary: Roy Shields, 26 Shorediche Road, Ickenham, Uxbridge UB10 8EB (0895 679031).
Ground: Technicolor Sports Ground, Springfield Road, Hayes, Middx (081 573 1203).
Cols: Claret & blue/white/claret & blue **Change Cols:** Black & white stripes/black/black.

Photo Opposite: *Jez Welsh of Hanworth Villa shows great poise during his side's 3-1 win at Pitshanger.*
Photo - Gavin Ellis-Neville.

DIVISION ONE CLUBS 1994-95

HANWORTH VILLA

Secretary: David Brown, 93 Tudor Drive, Kingston KT2 5NP (081 546 5979).
Ground: Rectory Meadows, Sunbury Road, Hanworth, Middlesex.
Colours: White (sky sleeves)/sky/sky **Change colours:** Red/black/black.
Prev. Ground: Twickenham Park Golf Club, Staines Road, Twickenham (pre-1994).

HARROW St MARY'S

Secretary: David Campbell, 11 Walford Road, Uxbridge UB8 2NF (0895 272473).
Ground: Harrow Recreation Ground, Roxborough Road, Harrow (081 427 0661).
Colours: Black & white stripes/black/black **Change colours:** Yellow/black/black.

NEASDEN

Secretary: Maurice Archer, 50 Woodcote Ave., Mill Hill, London NW7 (081 959 5217).
Ground: Chalkhill Youth Community Centre, Poplar Grove, Wembley, Middx (081 904 1974).
Colours: Green/black/red **Change colours:** Yellow/black/red.
Hons: Middx Co. Lg Alec Smith Cup R-up 92-93.

STONEBRIDGE (SCOLAR)

Secretary: Nick Christie, 45 Lee Road, Perivale, Greenford, Middx UB6 7BS(081 566 5176).
Ground: CRS Cardinals Club, 565 Great West Rd, Hounslow, Middx (081 572 8236). *Reserves: Bridge Park, Brentfield, Harrow Road, London NW10 0RG (081 961 5353).*
Colours: Red & grey/black/black **Change colours:** Sky & white/sky/sky
Previous Names: Bridge Park/ Scolar (clubs merged in 1993).
Hons: Middx County Lg Alec Smith Cup 93-94 (Div 2 91-92(Bridge Pk) 92-93(Scolar)).

WILLESDEN (CONSTANTINE)

Secretary: Dwight John, 29 Tangmere Gardens, Northolt UB5 6LS (081 845 9887).
Ground: Alperton Spts Ground, Alperton Lane, Alperton, Middx.
Directions: A4005 Hanger Lane turn off Hanger Lane Gyratory System, left by petrol station on left into Alperton Lane (B456), ground entrance 350m on right. Tube to Alperton (Piccadilly Line) or Hanger Lane (Central Line).
Colours: Gold/black/gold **Club Colours:** All white.
Previous Ground: Roe Green Park, Bacon Lane, Kingsbury (pre-1993).

This Division also incudes the Reserve sides of: Brimsdown Rovers *(see page 631)*, Brook House *(page 632)*, Cockfosters *(page 632)*, Flackwell Heath *(page 503)*, New Hanford, North Greenford Utd, Northfield CAV, Osterley, Rayners Lane *(page 626)*, Southgate, Technicolor Sports.

DIVISION TWO CLUBS 1994-95

NORTHOLT DYNAMO

Secretary: Martin Copeland, 19 Ribblesdale Avenue, Northolt, Middx UB5 4NF (081 423 1019).
Ground: As Osterley FC (opposite).
Colours: Red/white/red **Change colours:** Yellow/white/red.

WEST LONDON INSTITUTE

Secretary: Karl Ranalli, 7 College Rd, Isleworth, Middx (081 560 2731).
Ground: West London Institute Ground, Jersey Rd, Osterley, Middlesex.
Colours: All white **Change colours:** Yellow/black/black & white hoops.

This Division also incudes the Reserve sides of: Amersham Town *(see page 631)*, Cippenham, Hanwell Town *(page 634)*, Hounslow Town '91, Neasden, Northolt Saints, Pitshanger, Stonebridge (Scolar), Southall *(playing at Western Rd, Southall (081 574 1084))*, Spelthorne Sports, St Clarets (Hayes), Willesden (Constantine).

HOUNSLOW & DISTRICT LEAGUE

FOUNDED: 1897

PREM. DIV.	P	W	D	L	F	A	PTS
Park Celtic	20	13	2	5	41	24	28
Teddington Rgrs	20	11	5	4	43	27	27
Exxon Associaties	20	11	3	6	44	26	25
Northfield Shamrocks	20	9	4	7	39	29	22
Inwood Rangers	20	11	0	9	48	40	22
Phoenix	20	11	0	9	41	41	22
Abbey	20	8	4	8	34	38	20
Ashford United	20	7	4	9	27	28	18
CB United	20	7	2	11	27	38	16
East Fulham	20	5	3	12	30	54	13
Arya	20	3	1	16	19	48	7

DIV. ONE	P	W	D	L	F	A	PTS
The Bells	20	14	3	3	46	26	31
Young Sports	20	14	2	4	69	30	30
Marble Hill Rgrs	20	12	1	7	41	30	27
East Fulham Res.	20	11	4	5	58	38	26
Bedfont 'A'	20	9	3	8	41	38	21
J & S	20	9	3	8	42	36	19
Hanworth Villa Res.	20	8	2	10	39	48	18
Viaduct	20	7	2	11	46	40	16
Abbey Res.	20	6	4	10	36	40	16
Spelthorne S. 'A'	20	4	2	14	29	69	10
Islanders	20	2	2	16	25	77	6

DIV. TWO	P	W	D	L	F	A	PTS
Inwood Rgrs Res.	20	18	1	1	99	27	37
Orchard	20	18	0	2	86	28	36
Bison	20	13	3	4	76	29	29
Blondin	20	11	3	6	62	37	25
Ashur United	20	9	4	7	70	43	22
Heston Fire Station	20	10	2	8	63	56	22
Ashford Warriors	20	6	4	10	28	43	16
Abbey Veterans	20	5	3	12	35	41	13
Bedham Old Boys	20	5	2	13	48	52	12
Harrow Gaels	20	2	2	16	18	96	6
Bluepoint	20	1	0	19	15	148	2

DIV. THREE	P	W	D	L	F	A	PTS
Feltham Aces	18	15	2	1	77	20	32
Cedars United	18	10	4	4	68	35	24
CB United Res.	18	9	5	4	52	37	23
Hounslow Postal	18	7	5	6	40	38	19
Hoechst	18	6	5	7	48	44	17
Hounslow United	18	7	3	8	41	45	17
Laleham United	18	8	1	9	37	46	17
Eutectic	18	6	2	10	35	54	14
Good Old Boys	18	4	2	12	32	70	10
Feltham Flyers	18	1	5	12	32	73	7

Cup Finals:

Fred Barnard Cup: J & S 2, Exxon Associates 1
Jubilee Cup: Orchard 4, Ashur United 0
Ben Little Cup: Ashford Utd 6, Orchard 5
H & D Plate: J & S 1, Ashur United 0

HAYES & DISTRICT SUNDAY LEAGUE

FOUNDED: 1966

PREM. DIV.	P	W	D	L	F	A	PTS
Pinner	16	13	1	2	58	20	40
Beavers	16	12	2	2	48	21	38
Hillingdon Pk Rgrs	16	10	0	6	43	24	30
Eastcote United	16	9	2	5	38	34	29
Northolt United	16	6	1	9	42	54	19
White Lodge Sunday	16	5	2	9	21	36	17
Dawley Wanderers	16	4	3	9	42	51	15
Heathrow	16	4	0	12	39	56	12
Eastville (CDS)	16	3	1	12	27	62	10

Lower Division Champions:
Div. 1 (10): Drayton Nomads
Div. 2 (10): Beavers Res.
Div. 3 (10): The Vine
Div. 4 (10): White Horse Stallions
Div. 5 (8): Spartak Southall

Cup Finals:

Charles Nixon Insurance Presidents Cup: Drayton Nomads 2, Hillingdon Park Rangers 0
A J Newman Vice-Presidents Cup: The Vine 4, Floaters 2
Allied Dunbar Champions Cup: Drayton Nomads 3, St Marys Old Boys 2 *(aet)*
Jubilee Shield: Eastcote United 5, Infra 2
Prem. Div. Cup: Beavers 3, Drayton Wanderers 2
Div. 1 Cup: Drayton Nomads 2, Development '88 0
Div. 2 Cup: Beavers Res. 5, Heston Sportax 1
Div. 3 Cup: The Vine 5, Griffin Brewery SC 0
Div. 4 Cup: Tops 5, The Star 4
Div. 5 Cup: Spartak Southall 4, St Marys OB 1

MARATHON SUNDAY LEAGUE

FOUNDED: 1967

PREM. DIV.	P	W	D	L	F	A	PTS
Plough Wanderers	16	13	1	2	40	17	27
Belstone	16	10	4	2	42	26	24
Northfield Rgrs	16	10	2	4	29	21	22
Hatch End	16	6	4	6	28	23	16
Eastcote Manor	16	7	1	8	22	25	15
Bedfont Sunday	16	7	1	8	25	32	15
QPR LSA	16	4	4	8	27	34	12
Rayners L. Sunday	16	3	1	12	26	42	7
Hanworth Rgrs	16	2	2	12	16	35	6

Lower Division Champions:
Div. 1 (10): Shamrock Sunday
Div. 2 (9): Prestonians '57
Div. 3 (10): Belstone Reserves
Div. 4 (9): Thames Electric
Div. 5 (11): Zydeco
Div. 6 (11): Eastcote Manor Reserves

Cup Winners (Runners-up):
Chall. Cup: Belstone (Bedfont Sunday)
Charity Cup: Shamrock Sun. (Rayners L. Sun.)
Senior Cup: Belstone (Rayners L. Sun. Res.)
Intermediate Cup: St Nicholas (Prestonians '57)
Junior Cup: Thames Electric (108 Sports Club)

WEST MIDDX SUNDAY LEAGUE

FOUNDED: 1947

PREM. DIV.	P	W	D	L	F	A	PTS
Sunbury Park	22	18	2	2	85	24	38
Wayfarers	22	14	4	4	47	24	32
Chiswick Albion	22	14	4	4	65	34	32
Stanwell	22	12	3	7	58	40	27
Hayes & Harlington	22	12	1	9	58	49	25
Acton Saints	22	10	4	8	56	50	24
Sparrow Farm RA	22	11	0	11	56	60	22
Acton Wanderers	22	8	2	12	38	47	18
Northumberland	22	7	2	13	35	63	16
The Rising Sun	22	6	2	14	33	66	14
Ham	22	3	3	16	35	57	9
Osterley Sunday	22	2	3	17	26	78	7

Lower Division Champions:
Intermediate Div. 1 (11): Richings Park
Div. 1 (12): Bedfont Jays
Div. 2 (12): Red Lion Isleworth
Div. 3 (11): Pitshanger
Div. 4 (12): Cromwell Road

Cup Finals:

Ace Awards Open: Old Isleworthians 2, The Rising Sun 0 *(after extra-time and 2-2 draw and extra-time)*
President's: Three Horseshoes 1, Domine Ath. 0
Premier: Sunbury Park 6, West Middx Social 1
Keal: Red Lion Isleworth 4, Rectory Park 1
Kitson: Richings Pk Res. 2, Hampton Village Res. 0

MISCELLANEOUS

MIDLAND FLOODLIT CUP

Previous Winners: 1959-60: Peterborough U., 60-61: Worcester C., 61-62 & 62-63: Peterborough U. Res., 63-64: Cambridge U., 64-65: Worcester C., 65-66: Worcester C., 66-67: Wellington T., 67-68: Banbury U., 68-69: Nuneaton B., 69-70: Stafford R., 70-71 & 71-72: Telford U., 72-73: Atherstone T., 73-74: Nuneaton B., 74-75: Corby T., 75-76: Burton A., 76-77 & 77-78 & 78-79: Atherstone T., 79-80: Nuneaton B. 80-81 & 81-82: Kettering T., 82-83: Bedworth U., 83-84: Bedworth U./ Nuneaton B., 84-85: V.S. Rugby; 85-86 & 86-87 & 87-88: Cheltenham T., 88-89: Hinckley T., 89-90: V.S. Rugby, 90-91 & 91-92: Moor Green, 92-93: Bedworth U.

First Round (4 groups of 3)

Gp A: Leicester United v Tamworth 3-0
Gp A: Redditch United v Leicester United 2-0
Gp B: Moor Green v Dudley Town 1-0
Gp C: Willenhall Town v Hinckley Town 2-1
Gp C: Atherstone United v Willenhall Town 2-2
Gp D: Bedworth United v Hinckley Athletic 1-2
Gp A: Tamworth v Redditch United 3-2
Gp B: Brierley Hill Town v Moor Green 0-1
Gp B: Dudley Town v Brierley Hill Town 3-1
Gp C: Hinckley Town v Atherstone United 1-0
Gp D: Corby Town v Bedworth United 2-2
Gp D: Hinckley Athletic c Corby Town 1-1

Quarter-Finals

Redditch United v Dudley Town 2-0
Moor Green v Leicester United 1-2
Willenhall Town v Corby Town 1-2*(aet)*
Hinckley Athletic v Hinckley Town 2-2*(5-6 on pens)*

Semi-Finals

Redditch United v Hinckley Town 0-2
Leicester United v Corby Town 2-2*(5-4 on pens)*

Final *(at Leicester United FC, Fri 13th May)*: Leicester United 2, Hinckley Town 1

EVANS HALSHAW FLOODLIT CUP

By David Robinson

Eastwood Town were the winners but in a somewhat bizarre manner, one of their players being sent off during the penalty shoot-out for allegedly celebrating his goal in an obscene manner. The final itself was played on the New Manor Ground, home of losing finalists Ilkeston Town, after the two teams had tossed a coin to decide the venue. It proved a dour affair with few, if any, shots on target in the 120 minutes leading up to the penalty deciders. However most of the 1,000 plus crowd stayed on to see Eastwood take the cup by seven penalties to six, both teams experiencing crucial misses in reaching that point.

At the semi-final stage, Eastwood defeated Alfreton Town by two goals to nil with Browne and Clarke as their scorers, this being Alfreton's third cup semi-final loss of the season. Just to confirm that it was not their night, the ball burst as Johnson set off on a promising run at goal on their behalf.

The other semi saw Ilkeston beat Holbeach United 5-2, so the latter maintained their reputation for being involved in high scoring matches which startd back in the group games when they won 9-3 at Bourne Town.

Earlier in the competition, the weather was the problem as the rains produced a whole string of postponements, these usually affecting teams who were going well in other competitions.

Cup Competition Secretary David Harwood (left) takes control of the Evans Halshaw Cup from sponsor's representative Chris Blackshaw.

Granada Group	P	W	D	L	F	A	PTS
Eastwood Town	6	3	2	1	9	6	11
Matlock Town	6	3	0	3	13	8	9
Hucknall Town	6	2	2	2	4	6	8
Ashfield United	6	2	0	2	6	12	6

RESULTS	1	2	3	4
1. Ashfield United	*	0-2	1-0	2-4
2. Eastwood Town	3-1	*	1-1	1-0
3. Hucknall Town	2-0	0-0	*	1-0
4. Matlock Town	1-2	4-2	4-0	*

Escort Group	P	W	D	L	F	A	PTS
Holbeach United	6	4	1	1	14	5	13
Boston FC	6	3	0	3	9	12	9
Mirrlees Blackstone	6	2	1	3	10	7	7
Bourne Town	6	2	0	4	13	22	6

RESULTS	1	2	3	4
1. Boston FC	*	5-1	1-0	0-3
2. Bourne Town	2-3	*	3-9	3-1
3. Holbeach United	2-0	2-1	*	0-0
4. Mirrlees Blackstone	2-3	2-3	0-1	*

Mondeo Group	P	W	D	L	F	A	PTS
Alfreton Town	4	4	0	0	14	1	12
Belper Town	4	2	0	2	7	7	6
Rocester	4	0	0	4	1	14	0

RESULTS	1	2	3
1. Alfreton Town	*	4-0	4-0
2. Belper Town	1-2	*	4-1
3. Rocester	0-4	0-2	*

Semi-Final: Eastwood Town 2, Alfreton Town 0

Fiesta Group	P	W	D	L	F	A	PTS
Ilkeston Town	4	3	1	0	9	2	10
Stamford AFC	4	2	1	1	7	9	4
Arnold Town	4	0	0	4	5	10	0

RESULTS	1	2	3
1. Arnold Town	*	0-1	2-3
2. Ilkeston Town	3-1	*	5-1
3. Stamford AFC	3-2	0-0	*

Semi-Final: Ilkeston Town 5, Holbeach Utd 2

Final: Ilkeston Town 0, Eastwood Town 0
(Eastwood won 7-6 on penalties)

MIDLAND SUNDAY CUP

An Inter-League challenge cup, founded in 1964. Its geographical range stretches from Kidderminster and Stourport in the south to Barnsley and Sheffield in the north.

Midland Sunday Cup 1993-94

First Round

Greyhound '83 v Burlish Olympic	5-0	Warsop Town v Bedine Altone	3-4
Whetstone United v Brereton Town	2-1	Cheadle United v Darfield Station	3-0
AD Bulwell v Leefal	1-0	Rugeley Bell v Apollo Tavern	2-5*(aet)*
Nesbitt Rovers v Lodge Cottrell	2-4	Bournville Warriors v Dulwich	3-3,1-4
Birmingham Celtic v Demes Athletic	3-0	Hoyland T. Jaguars v Park & Arbourthorne	1-4*(aet)*
Cradley Olympic *(w/o)* Albion *(scr)*		Penn Old Boys v Trentham Romans	1-3*(aet)*
Half Moon v Westcotes	0-4	Ecclesfield Ball Inn *(scr)* Wedgewood *(w/o)*	
Rose United v Beechdale Social	1-2*(aet)*	Slade Celtic v Poplar Athletic	5-3*(aet)*

Second Round

Whetstone United v Dulwich	2-1	Beechdale Social v Apollo Tavern	4-5
Cradley Olympic v Westcotes United	2-4	Slade Celtic v Bedini Altone	5-3
Park & Arbourthorpe v Lodge Cottrell	1-3	AD Bulwell v Greyhound '83	1-2
Wedgewood v Trentham Romans	1-2	Birmingham Celtic v Cheade United	2-0

Quarter-Finals

Whetstone United v Greyhound '83	2-1	Trentham Romans v Lodge Cottrell	2-1*(aet)*
Brimingham Celtic v Apollo Tavern	4-1	Westcotes United v Slade Celtic	5-3

Semi-Finals

Trentham Romans v Birmingham Celtic	2-3	Westcotes United v Whetstone United	2-4

Final *(at Eastwood Town FC, Sun 10th April)*: Birmingham Celtic 4, Whetstone United 1

VARSITY MATCH 1994 By Rod Harrington

OXFORD UNIVERSITY 5, CAMBRIDGE UNIVERSITY 0 - March 26th 1994.

Answers please. At which annual match does the time of the kick-off depend on the tide, where women (the prettiest at that) nearly outnumber the men, where the crowd (all 2-3,000 of them) are fiercely partisan yet hugely good humoured and where the programme carries a half-page advertisement for the Concise Oxford Dictionary? There, I've given the game away. The Varsity match between Oxford and Cambridge has been played on the last four occasions at Craven Cottage to coincide with that major sporting non-event - The Boat Race.

After playing the game at Wembley Stadium from 1953-87 it would appear that attendances had dwindled so much that a more homely stadium was required. Even in the late seventies the match was pulling in 10,000 souls. However after a year at Highbury and at the Abbey Stadium, Cambridge, it has now settled at Fulham - at least for the foreseeable future. Since the first match at Fulham in there has even been a gradual increase in numbers attending. The crowd, if it can be called that, comprises essentially students, families and a smattering of old blues from previous years, some so old they must have pre-dated the glory days of Pegasus. Oh, yes, and I'm sure I spotted one groundhopper. Although the match does not seem to attract the punters (sorry!) picknicking in Bishops Park with their hampers and wine, it hauls in a few off the embankment, but even they are probably not regulars on the football terraces. Indeed one loud 'hooray henry' voice professed never to have seen a 'soccer' match in his life. Still he has broken his duck now. Also there are no tabloids here. A number of armpits were laden with the heavyweight Saturday editions of *The Independent* and *The Guardian*.

The most interesting sighting, however, was John Hollins of Chelsea, QPR and Arsenal fame whose son Chris, having attended that rugby stronghold of Tonbridge School, was turning out for Oxford. John could have sent him to Eton or Charterhouse where he could have practised his soccer skills. Perhaps to avoid the notoriety of his father's name and put us off the scent, he was labelled Chris Mellins in the programme. This was, incidentally, not the only spelling mistake. The Oxford University Press knows where to place its ads for its product.

The match was excellent entertainment if a little one-sided. History was made too. The first fixture was played in the 1873-74 season, and the 0-5 defeat suffered by Cambridge this year was their heaviest ever. The Oxford side played some attractive approach work and had a skilful striker in Andy Dechet (Princeton University and Jesus) whose deft touches showed a class or two above the average player on the field. The surprise was that it took Oxford forty minutes to score their first. Dechet took the ball into the box, sent a defender the wrong way and chipped a lovely little centre for Chris Hollins (Tonbridge and Keble) to head crisply home. Within four minutes, Dechet himself had increased the lead, so surely there was no route back for the light blues.

So it proved. Shortly after the interval Dave Ellidge (Handsworth Grammar, Birmingham and Jesus) had increased the lead but them the second surprise occurred. The game Cambridge side, led by their industrious midfield captain Sven Oestmann (Gymnasium Blankenesse and Gonville and Caius) startled the spectators by trying to make a real match of it. This led to an onslaught of some 15 minutes on the Oxford goal, but the lightweight and rather pedestrian attack could make no inroads into Oxford's well-marshalled defence. Oxford, of course, were sharp on the break and went further ahead with goals from Dechet again, a glancing header, and Andy Smith (St Marys VI Form College, Middlesborough and Jesus) added the fifth in the last few minutes.

So if you fancy honest endeavour, no little skill, no aggro, no gamesmanship (although I'm sure I glimpsed a Cambridge defender give Andy Dechet half a glare for about one second) and spectators who react with old-fashioned enthusiasm of the 'hats in the air' type, then get along to next year's Varsity match.

Oxford: *Phil Hazlewood, John Dunning, Hugh Campbell, Graham Box, Andrew Smith, Steve Smith, Dave Ellidge (Craig Mills 80), Doug Wills, Andy Dechet, Chris Hollins (Henrik Kraft 70), Matthew Sherrell. Scorers: Hollins 40, Dechet 44 66, Ellidge 51, A Smith 85.*

Cambridge: *John Park, Ian Ball, Phil Collins, Robert Luke, Mark Hargreaves, Sven Oestmann, Jeremy McCullough, Andy Miller (Graham Potts 80), Richard Taylor (David Walker 59), Mathias Deckers, Ian Riggs.*

NORFOLK F.A.

Secretary: Ray W Kiddell JP, ACII,
153 Middletons Lane, Hellesdon, Norwich NR6 5SF (0603 488222).

SENIOR CUP 1993-94

First Round

Wortwell v Reepham Town	0-2
Wymondham Town v Mattishall	5-3*(aet)*
Thorpe Village v Hellesdon	3-0
Wymondham Old Boys v Loddon United	2-1
Norwich Union v Bradenham Wanderers	0-2

Wymondham Old Boy J Parry rifles in a shot during the first round 2-1 home win over Loddon United.
Photo - Martin Wray.

Second Round

Lakenham Leisure v Dereham Town	0-1
Wymondham Old Boys v Coltishall HV '85	5-1
Overstrand v Thorpe Village	2-4
Newton Flotman v Lakeford Rangers	2-0
Mulbarton United v Downham Town	3-2
Swaffham Town v Horsford United	0-0,2-4
Thetford Town v Reepham Town	2-2,0-3
Blofield United v St Andrews	1-1,1-0
Bradenham Wanderers v Wymondham Town	0-4

Third Round

Watton United v Wymondham Old Boys	3-0
Reepham Town v Mulbarton United	1-3
Great Yarmouth Town v Gorleston	3-1
Norwich United v Fakenham Town	0-2
Thorpe Village v Wymondham Town	1-1,0-1
Blofield United v Diss Town	0-2
Newton Flotman v Dereham Town	0-2
King's Lynn v Horsford United	3-1

Quarter-Finals

King's Lynn v Wymondham Town	4-0
Dereham Town v Great Yarmouth Town	1-2
Mulbarton United v Fakenham Town	1-3
Watton United v Diss Town	1-3

Semi-Finals

King's Lynn v Great Yarmouth Town	2-1
Fakenham Town v Diss Town	1-0*(aet)*

Final *(at Norwich City FC, Tues 5th April)*: Fakenham Town 4, King's Lynn 0

OTHER COUNTY FINALS:

Invitation Cup *(at King's Lynn FC, Tues 22nd March)*: King's Lynn 2, Norwich City 1
Junior Cup *(at Norwich City FC, Mon 18th April)*: Stalham Town 2, Anglia Windows 0
Primary Cup *(at King's Lynn FC, Sat 23rd April)*: Stalham Town Reserves 2, Terrington St Clement 0
Thursday Cup *(at HM Prison Blundeston, Thurs 14th April)*: Lakeside 5, Great Yarmouth Postels 3
Sunday Senior Cup *(at Norwich City FC, Sun 17th April)*: Norwich Busmen 4, Wimsbotham 2
Sunday Intermediate Cup *(at Cromer Town FC, Sun 27th March)*: Black Swan 4, Aylsham Sunday 0
Sunday Junior Cup *(at Wymondham Town FC, Sun 10th April)*: Saham Sunday 3, Unicorns 1
Sunday Youth u-18 Cup *(at North Walsham Town FC, Sun 10th April)*: Gt Yarmouth Town 1, Sprowston Lads 0
John Savage u-16 Cup *(at East Harling FC, Sun 20th March)*: Old Catton Juniors 4, Scole Lads 0
Minor (u-14) Cup *(at Attleborough Town FC, Sun 27th March)*: Downham Youth Club 1, Fleggburgh Falcons 0
SRB Cowles (Schools' u-19) Cup *(at East Harling FC, 15th December)*: NORCAT 6, Hewett High 2

LOVEWELL BLAKE ANGLIAN COMBINATION

(AMALGAMATED EAST ANGLIA, NORFOLK AND SUFFOLK LEAGUES)

President: B A R Hansell.

Chairman: A J Dickerson.

Deputy Chairman: A J Fox.

Hon. Secretary: J C Harpley,
4 Harlington Avenue, Hellesdon, Norwich, NR6 5LJ (0603 408803).

LOYALTY PAYS DIVIDENDS FOR BLOFIELD UNITED

The season saw the fortunes slump of two of our most recent outstanding clubs, namely Overstrand and Mulbarton United. In season 1991/92 Overstrand did the double, winning the Premier Division and the Senior Knock-Out Cup. This season, because of difficulties over efforts to improve their sea-shore attractive ground, they decided to move to a sports ground at Knapton, some 7 or 8 miles from Overstrand, where there is more potential to implement their ambitions to get into the Jewson Eastern League. Sadly, they lost players to other clubs and struggled all season to avoid relegation. The last day of the season saw their opponents gain sufficient points and so relegate Overstrand to Division One.

Mulbarton United who won the Premier Division last year, also saw an exodus of players, mainly to Diss Town and Wroxham, and thus spent the season re-building and just gained points in their last two games to save them from relegation. They are, however, an ambitious club and next season will be installing floodlights as the next step to getting their ground in line with JELeague standards.

Lakenham Leisure (formally Carrow AFC) topped the Premier Division most of the season, but faltered during February and March to let in the consistent Blofield United who, with their policy of playing local talent which has created loyalty within the club and produces excellent team spirit spurred on by Manager Paddy Murphy, clinched the title by early April, finishing on 65 points from surprise runners-up Ashlea on 54 points. Blofield also won the 1st Division of the Reserve section. Dereham Town were hoping to make a serious challenge for the Sterry Trophy. They started the season well with a run of odd goal successes but, although being defensively sound, their goals for dried up and they finished in 4th place having drawn 11 of their 30 games. They did, however, win the Senior Knock-Out Cup, defeating Wymondham Town 3-0.

Divisioin One saw the Jewson League Reserve teams of Great Yarmouth, Fakenham and Lowestoft make all the running, with Mattishall vainly trying to keep in touch. Yarmouth Reserves lost their first 3 games, but then went 8 games without defeat and topped the Division most of the season, but Lowestoft Reserves came with a late run of 9 successive wins and pipped Yarmouth Reserves by 2 points. Fakenhanm Reserves came 3rd.

In the Junior sections, Stalham Town had an outstanding season in Cup competitions. They not only won the Norfolk Junior Cup defeating Anglian Windows, winners of our Division Three, by 2-0, but defeated Poringland Wanderers, winners of Division Two, by 2-0 in the League KO Cup final. To complete a unique double, their Reserves won the Norfolk Primary Cup, a feat never before achieved in 70 years since the inauguration of the Primary Cup.

The season completed 30 years of the Combination and Jim Harpley (Hononary Secretary) and his Assistant Don Frost are the only officers who remain since the amalgamation in 1964.

J C Harpley, Hon. Secretary.

Dereham Town FC - Senior Knock-Out Cup winners 1993-94. *Photo - Martin Wray.*

PREMIER DIV.	P	W	D	L	F	A	PTS
Blofield Utd	30	20	5	5	70	31	65
Ashlea	30	15	9	6	69	54	51
Lakenham Leisure	30	15	6	9	60	50	51
Dereham Town	30	13	11	6	52	26	50
St Andrews	30	14	7	9	46	39	49
Wroxham Res.	30	12	8	10	46	46	44
Newton Flotman	30	13	4	13	38	35	43
Kirkley	30	12	7	11	50	50	43
Diss Town Res.	30	11	7	12	52	45	40
Beccles Town	30	11	7	12	57	64	40
Mulbarton United	30	11	5	14	50	68	38
Wymondham Town	30	10	7	13	41	53	37
Lakeford Rangers	30	10	4	16	45	47	34
Horsford United	30	9	7	14	44	49	34
Overstrand	30	9	7	14	42	59	34
Coltishall HV '85	30	1	7	22	20	87	10

DIV. ONE	P	W	D	L	F	A	PTS
Lowestoft T. Res.	30	20	6	4	83	33	66
Gt Yarmouth Res.	30	20	4	6	65	28	64
Fakenham T. Res.	30	19	5	6	75	41	62
Mattishall	30	17	4	9	73	49	55
Thorpe Village	30	14	10	6	61	33	52
Loddon United	30	14	6	10	67	48	48
Hellesdon	30	13	5	12	54	67	44
Bradenham Wdrs	30	12	7	11	66	59	43
Wortwell	30	10	8	12	48	68	38
Watton Utd Res.	30	9	9	12	41	44	36
Brandon Town	30	10	6	14	58	65	36
Oulton Broad	30	10	6	14	38	53	36
Wymondham OB	30	9	4	17	44	70	31
Gorleston Res.	30	6	6	18	51	84	24
Reepham Town	30	5	6	19	49	85	21
Norwich Union	30	4	4	22	34	80	16

(JUNIOR SECTION TABLES ON PAGE 1044)

PREMIER DIVISION RESULT CHART 1993-94

HOME TEAM	1	2	3	4	5	6	7	8	9	10	11	12	13	14	15	16
1. Ashlea	*	2-2	4-0	8-0	1-1	1-1	0-0	1-1	0-1	3-2	2-0	2-0	3-0	2-3	1-3	5-0
2. Beccles Town	2-2	*	0-4	2-2	1-3	1-3	3-1	3-3	1-3	1-3	2-3	2-1	2-2	1-1	3-1	3-2
3. Blofield Utd	1-1	3-1	*	2-0	3-1	3-1	0-2	3-1	1-0	2-1	2-0	3-0	3-0	0-0	8-1	2-1
4. Coltishall	0-7	0-1	0-3	*	0-3	2-2	1-1	1-3	1-2	0-1	1-3	1-3	1-1	0-4	0-3	3-3
5. Dereham Town	2-1	2-2	3-0	7-0	*	2-1	4-0	1-1	0-1	3-3	0-1	1-1	1-1	1-1	0-0	1-0
6. Diss Town Res.	1-3	2-4	0-5	3-0	1-1	*	1-1	2-0	1-2	1-1	0-2	2-2	1-1	1-3	4-1	1-0
7. Horsford	2-4	1-2	3-1	0-2	0-2	0-5	*	3-5	1-0	2-1	8-0	0-2	1-2	1-0	1-1	3-0
8. Kirkley	1-2	3-2	2-1	2-0	1-1	0-2	3-1	*	2-5	1-2	2-1	0-3	1-0	1-3	1-1	0-2
9. Lakeford Rangers	2-3	0-2	3-4	3-0	1-2	3-2	1-1	0-1	*	1-2	3-1	0-3	0-1	2-0	1-1	2-2
10. Lakenham Leisure	2-3	3-4	1-1	1-1	1-0	3-1	2-1	1-1	3-2	*	3-3	1-1	1-2	1-3	3-1	4-1
11. Mulbarton Utd	1-4	5-2	1-1	3-1	1-0	1-4	1-3	0-6	0-4	3-1	*	1-5	4-0	1-4	1-2	4-1
12. Newton Flotman	0-0	2-1	0-2	4-1	0-1	0-2	0-2	1-0	2-1	2-4	0-0	*	2-0	0-1	0-4	0-1
13. Overstand	2-2	2-3	1-2	3-2	0-5	0-2	3-1	1-3	3-1	0-2	2-5	2-0	*	0-2	5-1	2-3
14. St Andrews	0-1	0-2	0-5	0-0	0-2	2-1	3-1	2-2	2-1	7-3	1-0	0-1	1-1	*	3-1	0-4
15. Wroxham Res.	2-1	3-1	1-3	6-0	1-1	1-0	1-0	1-3	2-1	3-0	0-1	1-0	1-1	1-1	*	1-1
16. Wymondham T.	1-0	2-1	2-2	3-0	1-0	0-4	1-1	1-1	0-1	1-4	1-1	0-3	3-4	2-0	2-0	*

DIVISION ONE RESULT CHART 1993-94

HOME TEAM	1	2	3	4	5	6	7	8	9	10	11	12	13	14	15	16
1. Bradenham	*	3-5	0-2	5-2	1-0	0-3	1-0	3-3	1-5	4-2	1-1	4-0	3-3	1-2	3-0	4-0
2. Brandon Town	7-5	*	1-1	5-1	0-4	1-2	4-2	1-1	0-1	4-2	6-1	5-0	0-2	1-2	0-0	1-4
3. Fakenham Town Res.	3-0	7-0	*	4-3	0-2	8-1	0-2	3-2	2-0	4-2	2-0	5-1	2-1	1-1	2-1	4-1
4. Gorleston Res.	0-5	1-2	2-3	*	0-2	7-3	2-2	1-3	1-6	3-2	4-1	4-2	2-4	1-0	2-2	2-2
5. Gt Yarmouth Res.	1-1	4-0	3-1	4-0	*	0-1	4-1	1-0	1-2	3-0	0-4	3-0	4-0	4-0	5-0	2-0
6. Hellesdon	2-1	1-1	0-0	3-1	2-4	*	1-3	4-1	3-3	1-4	2-0	2-1	1-1	1-5	1-3	1-0
7. Loddon United	5-1	3-1	3-4	3-0	6-0	2-3	*	2-2	3-0	3-1	0-1	4-1	1-3	3-2	0-1	5-2
8. Lowestoft T. Res.	2-0	2-1	4-1	2-1	1-1	5-2	5-2	*	4-0	6-0	5-0	1-0	1-0	1-0	9-1	3-0
9. Mattishall	0-5	3-1	2-3	4-3	1-1	2-2	1-2	2-1	*	4-0	1-1	2-0	3-2	3-0	4-1	1-3
10. Norwich Union	2-2	0-3	2-1	2-1	0-2	0-3	1-2	0-2	3-6	*	1-1	2-2	1-5	0-1	1-2	1-2
11. Oulton Broad	1-2	5-3	0-0	3-0	1-2	2-1	0-0	0-3	1-3	2-1	*	2-1	0-3	0-2	4-0	1-3
12. Reepham Town	4-3	1-1	1-4	5-1	1-2	4-1	1-1	2-2	1-5	2-3	2-2	*	0-4	3-3	2-4	1-4
13. Thorpe Village	1-1	0-1	2-2	2-2	0-2	3-1	0-0	2-2	2-0	4-0	3-0	4-2	*	0-0	3-0	3-0
14. Watton United Res.	0-0	2-1	1-3	1-1	2-2	0-1	3-1	0-1	2-0	0-0	0-1	1-2	1-3	*	1-2	4-2
15. Wortwell	0-2	2-2	2-3	1-1	3-0	4-0	3-3	2-6	0-2	2-0	2-1	4-3	0-0	4-4	*	2-2
16. Wymondham Old Boys	3-4	3-0	1-0	1-2	0-2	1-5	0-3	1-3	0-7	3-1	0-2	2-4	1-1	1-1	2-0	*

SENIOR KNOCK-OUT CUP 1993-94

First Round

Beccles Town v Watton United Res. 2-1
Thorpe Village v Kirkley 0-0*(aet)*,2-1
Hellesdon v Wymondham Old Boys 1-0
St Andrews v Coltishall HV '85 1-0
Mattishall v Great Yarmouth Town Reserves 4-1
Dereham Town v Gorleston Reserves 5-0
Blofield United v Norwich Union 5-4
Newton Flotman v Fakenham Town Res. 0-2*(aet)*
Lakeford Rangers v Diss Town Reserves 0-1
Ashlea v Mulbarton United 5-0
Brandon Town v Wroxham Reserves 4-3
Oulton Broad v Loddon United 0-2
Wortwell v Lakenham Leisure 2-3
Wymondham Town v Overstrand 2-1
Bradenham v Lowestoft Town Reserves 0-3
Horsford United v Reepham Town 5-3

Second Round

Blofield United v Hellesdon 1-0
Brandon Town v Ashlea 0-3
Mattishall v Lakenham Leisure 1-0
St Andrews v Dereham Town 1-4
Beccles T. v Lowestoft Town Reserves 4-4*(aet)*,0-4
Loddon United v Fakenham Town Reserves 0-4
Thorpe Village v Diss Town Reserves 2-3
Wymondham Town v Horsford United 2-1

Quarter-Finals

Mattishall v Lowestoft Town Reserves 4-1
Ashlea v Fakenham Town Reserves 4-2
Diss Town Reserves v Wymondham Town 1-1*(aet)*,0-1
Blofield United v Dereham Town 1-4

Semi-Finals

Ashlea v Dereham Town 1-2
Wymondham Town v Mattishall 3-2*(aet)*

Final *(at Wroxham FC)*: Dereham Town 3, Wymondham Town 0

DIV. TWO	P	W	D	L	F	A	PTS
Poringland Wdrs	30	23	4	3	94	36	73
Thetford Rovers	30	20	8	2	72	25	68
North Walsham T.	30	22	1	7	85	39	67
South Walsham	30	18	5	7	61	32	59
Hempnall	30	15	6	9	59	45	51
Stalham Town	30	14	6	10	80	52	48
Wells Town	30	14	5	11	50	50	47
Sprowston Wdrs	30	14	4	12	74	63	46
Corton	30	15	1	14	47	49	46
Caister United	30	11	2	17	64	69	35
Town Hall Scripts	30	9	8	13	52	61	35
Mundford	30	11	2	17	47	63	35
Bungay Town	30	7	4	19	44	77	25
Lakenheath	30	7	4	19	42	88	25
Scole United	30	5	6	19	49	99	21
Harleston Town	30	1	2	27	38	110	5

DIV. THREE	P	W	D	L	F	A	PTS
Anglia Windows	30	23	3	4	113	41	72
Holt United	30	22	3	5	74	38	69
Attleborough T.	30	21	1	8	91	49	64
City Norw. Sch. OBU	30	20	2	8	93	52	62
Swaffham T. Res.	30	19	5	6	74	33	62
Beccles Caxton	30	18	1	11	93	50	55
Acle United	30	14	3	13	59	48	45
Aylsham Wdrs	30	13	5	12	67	62	44
St Johns	30	12	2	16	51	75	38
CEYMS	30	9	4	17	58	60	31
Cromer Town	30	9	2	19	52	76	29
Norwich Utd Res.	30	10	3	17	52	105	**29
Thorpe SOB	30	8	3	19	49	90	27
Sheringham	30	7	3	20	34	87	24
East Harling	30	6	4	20	34	83	21
Buxton	30	6	2	22	43	88	20

DIV. FOUR	P	W	D	L	F	A	PTS
Halvergate	30	27	3	0	143	23	84
Southwold	30	20	5	5	81	22	65
Sprowston Ath.	30	20	5	5	79	22	65
Old Buckenham	30	17	8	5	81	32	59
Dereham United	30	18	5	7	66	27	59
Thetford T. Res.	30	16	4	10	75	47	52
Costessy	30	13	4	13	59	60	43
Rockland United	30	12	4	14	61	61	40
Shipdham	30	10	5	15	60	69	35
Norman Old Boys	30	10	5	15	54	89	35
Thurton & Ashby	30	9	5	16	55	99	32
Long Stratton	30	8	4	18	41	72	28
Hingham Athletic	30	8	4	18	60	102	28
Ashill	30	6	8	16	52	94	26
Dilham	30	4	6	20	36	92	18
Dickleburgh	30	2	5	23	34	126	11

RES. DIV. ONE	P	W	D	L	F	A	PTS
Blofield U. Res.	30	21	7	2	107	39	70
Wymondham T. Res.	30	18	5	7	64	45	59
St Andrews Res.	30	17	6	7	73	39	57
Mulbarton Res.	30	16	8	6	86	47	56
Norwich Union Res.	30	15	10	5	69	34	55
Oulton Bd Res.	30	17	2	11	74	49	*51
Loddon Utd Res.	30	15	4	11	63	57	49
Dereham T. Res.	30	13	5	12	60	53	44
Newton F'man Res.	30	12	7	11	60	46	43
Overstrand Res.	30	12	3	15	65	64	39
Lakenham L. Res.	30	10	5	15	61	78	35
Wymondham OB Res.	30	9	5	16	46	77	*30
Nth Walsham Res.	30	9	2	19	57	79	29
Beccles T. Res.	30	8	3	19	69	73	27
Bradenham W. Res.	30	4	7	19	28	94	*17
Coltishall Res.	30	3	3	24	27	135	12

RES. DIV. TWO	P	W	D	L	F	A	PTS
Thorpe Vill. Res.	30	22	6	2	74	25	72
Stalham T. Res.	30	21	3	6	98	51	66
Attleborough Res.	30	19	4	7	79	38	61
Kirkley Res.	30	17	5	8	69	41	56
Caister Utd Res.	30	14	6	10	56	49	48
Acle Utd Res.	30	13	5	12	53	58	44
Ashlea Res.	30	13	5	12	64	72	44
Horsford Utd Res.	30	12	5	13	63	47	41
Lakeford Res.	30	11	7	12	56	56	40
Holt Utd Res.	30	11	4	15	53	66	37
Sprowston A. Res.	30	11	3	16	63	78	36
Mattishall Res.	30	9	8	13	54	63	35
Poringland Res.	30	9	7	14	53	70	34
Thetford Rvrs Res.	30	10	2	18	64	82	32
Hempnall Res.	30	4	7	19	52	104	19
Long Stratt. Res.	30	2	7	21	37	88	13

RES. DIV. THREE	P	W	D	L	F	A	PTS
CEYMS Res.	28	18	6	4	72	45	60
Aylsham Utd Res.	28	18	5	5	89	40	59
Sth Walsham Res.	28	19	2	7	89	46	59
St Johns Res.	28	17	3	8	76	47	54
Mundford Res.	28	15	6	7	64	43	51
Sprowston W. Res.	28	12	6	10	59	49	42
East Harling Res.	28	13	3	12	74	67	42
CNSOBU Res.	28	11	5	12	74	61	38
Costessy Res.	28	11	2	15	61	61	35
Bungay T. Res.	28	9	5	14	55	62	32
Wortwell Res.	28	9	5	14	54	68	32
Reepham T. Res.	28	9	3	16	48	77	30
Rockland U. Res.	28	9	0	19	48	109	27
Harleston Res.	28	8	2	18	53	77	26
Thorpe SOB Res.	28	4	3	21	39	103	15

* - 2 points deducted

Overton (right) of Wroxham Reserves shrugs off a challenge during his side's 1-1 draw at Lakeford Rangers. Photo - Martin Wray.

PREMIER DIVISION CLUBS 1994-95

ASHLEA

Secretary: Mr S Gilder, 5 Back Lane, Lowestoft, Suffolk NR32 5NE (0502 731052).
Ground: Pitch I Normanston Park, Lowestoft. **Colours:** Yellow/blue/yellow.

BECCLES TOWN

Secretary: Mr J Humby, 11 Station Road, Beccles, Suffolk NR34 9QH (0502 713776).
Ground: College Meadow (0502 712016) **Colours:** White & black hoops/black

BLOFIELD UNITED

Secretary: Mrs K Hambling, 23 Rosemary Road, Blofield Heath, Norwich NR13 4QQ (0603 716893).
Ground: Gt Yarmouth Rd, Blofield (0603 712576) **Colours:** Red/black/black

DEREHAM TOWN

Secretary: Mr M Henman, 17 Hillcrest Avenue, Toftwood, Dereham, Norfolk NR19 1NF (0362 692242).
Ground: Recreation Ground, Commercial Road, Dereham. **Colours:** White/black.

DISS TOWN RESERVES *(see page 731)*

GREAT YARMOUTH TOWN *(see page 732)*

HORSFORD UNITED

Secretary: Mr G Soanes, 5 Bulwer Road, Buxton, Norwich NR10 5HG (0603 278156).
Ground: St Faiths Spts Centre, St Faiths (0603 898069) **Colours:** Jade/black/white

KIRKLEY

Secretary: Mr J W Dale, 8 Gorleston Rd, Oulton Broad, Lowestoft NR32 3AG (0502 572693).
Ground: Kirkley Rec., Walmer Rd, Lowestoft (0502 513549) **Colours:** All royal blue.

LAKEFORD RANGERS

Secretary: Mr R J Watling, 6 Cressener Close, Hellesdon, Norwich NR6 5RF (0603 405032).
Ground: Cringleford Rec, Oakfields Rd, Cringleford. **Colours:** Red (white trim)/white

LAKENHAM LEISURE

Secretary: Mr R Marcus, Apple Tree House, 1 Lawns Loke, Reepham, Norwich NR10 4QY (0603 872431).
Ground: Cricket Ground Road, Lakenham, Norwich. **Colours:** White/navy/navy
Previous Name: Carrow FC (pre-1993).

LOWESTOFT TOWN RESERVES *(see page 733)*

MULBARTON UNITED

Secretary: Mr J T Eastell, 'Erengon', 1 Cuckoofield Lane, Mulbarton, Norwich NR14 8AZ (0508 70832).
Grnd: Mulberry Pk (Village Hall facilities)(0508 570626) **Colours:** Sky & navy/blue/blue

NEWTON FLOTMAN

Secretary: Mr J Pomfret, 15 Joy Avenue, Newton Flotman, Norwich NR15 1RD (0508 470222).
Ground: Newton Flotman Village Centre, Grove Way. **Colours:** Yellow/royal.

St ANDREWS

Secretary: Mr I Bishop, Rose Acre, Broad Lane, Little Plumstead, Norwich NR13 5EJ (0603 720737).
Ground: Thorpe Rec., Laundry Lane, Thorpe (0603 300316) **Colours:** Sky & Navy/black/black.

WROXHAM RESERVES *(see page 736)*

WYMONDHAM TOWN

Secretary: Mr M B Utting, 52 Mill Lane, Attleborough, Norfolk NR17 2NW (0953 453146).
Ground: Kings Head Meadow, Wymondham (0953 607326). **Colours:** Red & black/black/red.

DIVISION ONE CLUBS 1994-95

BRADENHAM WANDERERS

Secretary: Mrs P Rowley, 8 Roger Ride, Toftwood, Dereham, Norfolk NR19 1SJ (0362 697757).
Ground: Hale Road, Bradenham. **Colours:** Amber & black.

BRANDON TOWN

Secretary: Mr P V Wright, Unit 6 Threxton Road Industrial Estate, Brandon Road, Watton, Norfolk IP25 6NG (0953 885463(day) 850149(evenings)).
Ground: Remembrance Playing Field, Church Road, Brandon (0842 813177) **Colours:** All blue.

COLTISHALL H.V. '85

Secretary: Mrs J Batch, 9 Burges Rd, Norwich NR3 2LL (0603 400065).
Ground: Rectory Road, Coltishall. **Colours:** Red & blue stripes/navy/navy

FAKENHAM TOWN RESERVES *(see page 731)*

GORLESTON RESERVES *(see page 737)*

HELLESDON

Secretary: Mr J Watson, 58 Northcote Road, Norwich NR3 4QE (0603 413486).
Ground: Coronation PF, Hellesdon (0603 413486) **Colours:** Royal blue/white.

LODDON UNITED

Secretary: Mr A Cook, 4 Crossway Terrace, Loddon, Norwich NR14 6JY (0508 28115).
Ground: Playing Field, George Lane, Loddon (0508 528115) **Colours:** All red.

MADRA UNITED

Secretary: Mr R Rounce, Turning Point, Norwich Road, Cromer NR27 0HF (0263 513715).
Ground: Madra Spts Field, Knapton, near North Walsham (0263 721870) **Cols:** Red/white.
Previous Name: Overstrand (pre-1994) **Previous Ground:** High Street, Overstrand (pre-1993).

MATTISHALL

Secretary: Mr R J Buxton, 17 Tilney Rd, East Tuddenham, Dereham, Norfolk NR20 3LZ (0603 880682).
Ground: Mattishall PF, South Green (0362 850246). **Colours:** All blue.

OULTON BROAD
Secretary: Mr D V Rackham, 339 Raglan Street, Lowestoft, Suffolk NR32 2LD (0502 563353).
Ground: Normanston Park, Lowestoft. **Colours:** Amber (black trim)/black.

PORINGLAND WANDERERS
Secretary: Mr Ben Casey, 8 Malten Close, Poringland, Norwich NR14 7RW (0508 493791).
Ground: Poringland Memorial Field (0508 495198). **Colours:** All royal

THETFORD ROVERS
Secretary: Mr E R Zipfel, 24 Williamson Crescent, Thetford, Norfolk IP24 3BE (0842 755781).
Ground: Euston Park, Near Thetford. **Colours:** Red/black/red.

THORPE VILLAGE
Secretary: Mr A Meek, 8 Birchwood, Thorpe, Norwich NR7 0RL (0603 35985).
Ground: Thorpe Recreation Ground. **Colours:** Claret & sky/sky.

WATTON UNITED RESERVES *(see page 735)*

WORTWELL
Secretary: Mr I Fisher, 18 Chestnut Road, Pulham St Mary, Diss, Norfolk IP21 4RA (0379 608401).
Ground: Wortwell Playing Field, opp. Bell PH. **Colours:** Green & white/green/green.

WYMONDHAM OLD BOYS
Secretary: Mr A Atkinson, 5 Perrings, Wymondham, Norwich NR18 4JR (0953 605171).
Ground: Browick Road, Recreation Ground, Wymondham. **Colours:** Sky & white stripes/navy.

JUNIOR CLUBS 1994-95

ACLE UNITED
Secretary: Mr J H Goward, 18 Reve Crescent, Blofield Corner, Norwich NR13 4RX (0603 712947).
Ground: Bridewell Lane, Acle. **Colours:** Black & white stripes/black

ANGLIAN WINDOWS
Secretary: Mr T M Cann, 83 Beverley Road, Norwich NR5 8AP (0603 58745).
Ground: Horsford Manor, Cromer Road, Norwich. **Cols:** Blue & black stripes/black

ASHILL
Secretary: Mr A Warby, 38 Swaffham Rd, Watton, Thetford, Norfolk IP25 (0953 882341).
Ground: Community Centre, Hale Road, Ashill. **Colours:** Yellow (blue trim)

ATTLEBOROUGH
Secretary: Mr K A Parsons, 45 Briton Way, Wymondham, Norfolk NR18 0TT (0953 603901).
Ground: Recreation Ground, Station Rd, Attleborough. **Colours:** White/blue/white.

AYLSHAM WANDERERS
Secretary: Mr P Hamilton, 6 Lancaster Gardens, Aylsham, Norwich NR11 6LD (0263 734904).
Ground: Recreation Ground, Sir Williams Lane, Aylsham. **Colours:** All red.

BECCLES CAXTON
Secretary: Mr A W Pasque, "Lauren", Bulls Green Lane, Toft Monks, Beccles, Suffolk NR34 0ER (0502 778116).
Grnd: Caxton Meadow, adj. Beccles Station (0502 712829) **Cols:** Green & white hooped/green/green.

BRADWELL T H SCRIPTS
Secretary: Mr A Algar, 7 Lincoln Ave., Gorleston, Gt Yarmouth NR31 7NL (0493 657278).
Ground: Bradwell Playing Field, Green Lane, Bradwell **Colours:** Sky/navy/navy.

BUNGAY TOWN
Secretary: Mr B Gower, 59 Garden Close, Bungay, Suffolk NR35 1JE (0986 892916).
Ground: Maltings Meadow, Ditchingham (0986 894028) **Colours:** All sky

BUXTON
Secretary: Miss G D Platford, Fat 2, 17 Beach Road, Mundesley, Norfolk NR11 8BG (0283 722206).
Ground: Buxton Playing Field, opposite church. **Colours:** Tangerine/black.

CAISTER UNITED
Secretary: Mr B Cork, 38 Upper Grange Crescent, Caister-on-Sea, Gt Yarmouth NR30 5AU (0493 728988).
Ground: Caister Playing Field, Off Allendale Road. **Cols:** Red & royal stripes/royal.

CITY of NORWICH SCHOOL OLD BOYS UNION
Secretary: Mr N Podolski, 27 Eaton Street, Norwich NR4 7LD (0603 502559).
Ground: Brittania Barracks. **Colours:** Red/black.

CORTON
Secretary: Mr D R Crisp, 10 Spencer Drive, Lowestoft, Suffolk NR32 4LS (0502 562599 Weekdays - 0502 517764 Saturdays).
Ground: Village Playing Field, Long Lane, Corton. **Cols:** White & red stripes/black/black

COSTESSEY SPORTS
Secretary: Mr A Page, 57 Sunny Grove, New Costessey, Norwich NR5 0EJ (0603 742749).
Ground: Breckland Rd Pk, Breckland Rd, New Costessey. **Colours:** Red/black.

CROMER TOWN
Secretary: Mr J R Baker, 32 Salisbury Road, Cromer, Norfolk NR27 0BW (0263 514405).
Ground: Cabbell Park, Mill Rd, Cromer (0263 512185) **Cols:** Yellow & black quarters/black/black

DICKLEBURGH
Secretary: Mr T J Leeder, 'Trev-Icia', Norwich Road, Dickleburgh, Diss, Norfolk IP21 4NR (0379 741444).
Ground: Playing Field, Harvey Lane, Dickleburgh. **Colours:** Yellow & green/yellow

DILHAM
Secretary: Mr K Sidell, No. 1 Ivy Farm, Dilham, North Walsham, Norfolk NR28 9PN (0692 536263).
Ground: The Rec., near Cross Keys PH (0692 536144) **Colours:** Red/green.

EAST HARLING
Secretary: Mrs D Jubb, 7 Drakes Close, East Harling, Norwich NR16 2JB (0953 717128).
Ground: Mem. Fields, Church Rd, E Harling (0953 718251) **Colours:** Green/white.

HALVERGATE UNITED
Secretary: Mr A Broom, 40 Churchill Road, Gt Yarmouth NR30 4NH (0493 850451).
Ground: Playing Field, Wickhampton Road, Halvergate. **Colours:** All blue.

HARLESTON TOWN
Secretary: Mr G N Page, 4a Station Road, Harleston, Norfolk IP20 9ES (0379 853929).
Ground: Rec. Ground & Memorial Leisure Centre, Off Wilderness Lane, Harleston (0379 854519).
Colours: Amber/black/black.

HEMPNALL
Secretary: Mr R C Youngman 'Dorchester', Sunnyside, Woodton, Bungay, Suffolk NR35 2LY (0508 482237).
Ground: Bungay Road, Hempnall. **Colours:** Maroon & sky/sky/maroon

HINGHAM ATHLETIC
Secretary: Mr M J Higgs, 6 Bond Street, Hingham, Norwich NR9 4HA (0953 850019).
Ground: Watton Road, Hingham. **Colours:** Red & black/black/black

HOLT UNITED
Secretary: Mr B Owen, 10 Mill Street, Holt, Norfolk NR25 6LB (0263 713914).
Ground: Sports Centre, Kelling Road, Holt (0263 711217) **Colours:** Green/black/black.

LAKENHEATH
Secretary: Mrs Peta Gyte, 5 Covey Way, Lakenheath, Suffolk IP27 9HJ (0842 860979).
Ground: Wings Road, Lakenheath. **Colours:** Blue & black/black.

LONG STRATTON
Secretary: Mr A South, 85 Manor Road, Long Stratton, Norwich NR15 2XS (0508 31744).
Ground: Playing Fields, Manor Road, Long Stratton. **Colours:** White/red.

MUNDFORD
Secretary: Mr J E Marston, 16 Impson way, Mundford, Thetford, Norfolk IP26 4JU (0842 878339).
Ground: The Glebe, Mundford. **Colours:** Red/black.

NORTH WALSHAM TOWN
Secretary: Mr J Hick, 9 Millard Close, North Walsham, Norfolk NR28 0HH (0692 404557).
Ground: Greens Road Spts Centre, N. Walsham (0692 406888) **Colours:** White/black.

NORWICH C.E.Y.M.S.
Secretary: Mr N D Laws, 14 Eastern Rd, Thorpe St Andrew, Norwich NR7 0UJ (0603 37229).
Ground: Hilltops Sports Centre, Swardeston **Colours:** Red & white stripes/black.

NORWICH St JOHNS
Secretary: Mr T Franklin, 35 Falcon Rd (East), Salhouse Road, Norwich NR7 8XZ (0603 429026).
Ground: Hewett Comp. School, Hall Road, Norwich. **Colours:** Amber/black/black.

NORWICH UNION
Secretary: Mr C McCullough, 10 Glenburn Court, Sprowston, Norwich NR7 8DR (0603 402242).
Ground: Pinebanks, School Lane, off Harvey Lane, Thorpe. **Colours:** Green & white/white/white.

NORWICH UNITED *(see page 738)*

OLD BUCKENHAM
Secretary: Mr A J Hales, 12 Steward Close, Wymondham, Norwich NR18 0EZ (0953 602377).
Ground: The Green, Dressing Acc. Church Hall. **Colours:** Amber & royal/royal/amber.

REEPHAM TOWN
Secretary: Mr D W Norris, 12 Silver End, Reepham, Norwich NR10 4LH (0603 870634).
Ground: Stimpsons Piece Recreation Ground. **Colours:** Red/white.

ROCKLAND UNITED
Secretary: Mr S J Fisher, 17 Rectory Road, Rocklands, Attleborough, Norfolk NR17 1XA (0953 483501).
Ground: Rocklands Playing Field. **Colours:** Blue (yellow trim).

SAHAM TONEY
Secretary: Mrs J Pitcher, 32 The Oval, Saham Toney, Thetford, Norfolk IP25 7HW (0953 885158).
Ground: Pavilion, Pages Lane PF, Saham Toney **Colours:** Yellow/blue/blue.

SCOLE UNITED
Secretary: Mr D Hill, 30 Ransome Ave., Scole, Diss, Norfolk IP21 4EA (0379 740696).
Ground: Playing Field, Ransome Ave., Scole (0379 741204) **Colours:** Royal/yellow.

SHERINGHAM
Secretary: Mr P R Bacon, 33 Nelson Road, Sheringham NR26 8BX (0263 823625).
Ground: High School, Holt Road, Sheringham. **Colours:** All red.

SHIPDHAM
Secretary: Mr R F Knights, Park Cottage, High Str., Shipdham, Thetford, Norfolk IP25 7PA (0362 820420).
Ground: Bullock Park, Mill Road, Shipdham. **Colours:** Green/white.

SOUTH WALSHAM
Secretary: Mrs J Bruce, 24 Borton Rd, Blofield Heath, Norwich NR13 4RU (0603 714220).
Ground: The Playing Field, South Walsham. **Colours:** Yellow/black.

SOUTHWOLD TOWN
Secretary: Miss Jo Crick, 2 Pier Avenue, Southwold, Suffolk IP18 6BX (0502 722872).
Ground: Southwold Common. **Colours:** Gold/black.

SPROWSTON ATHLETIC
Secretary: Mr C Thomson, 11 Fairfields, Cawston, Norwich NR10 4AS (0603 871404).
Ground: Blue Boar Lane, Sprowston. **Colours:** Tangerine/black.

SPROWSTON WANDERERS
Secretary: Mr R A Critten, 52 Cozens Hardy Road, Sprowston, Norwich NR7 8QG (0603 402928).
Ground: Barkers Lane, Sprowston (0603 404042) **Colours:** Red/black.

STALHAM TOWN
Secretary: Mr H Nicholson, 'Three Windows', Brumstead Rd, Stalham, Norwich NR12 9DE (0692 581529).
Ground: Rec. Ground, Recreation Rd, off St Johns Road, Stalham. **Colours:** All red.

SWAFFHAM TOWN RESERVES *(see page 739)*

THETFORD TOWN RESERVES *(see page 739)*

THORPE SCHOOL OLD BOYS

Secretary: Mr M Howe, 28 Julian Rd, Spixworth, Norwich NR10 3QA (0603 898549).
Ground: Thorpe School, Laundry Lane, Thorpe. **Colours:** Red/navy.

THURTON & ASHBY

Secretary: Mr A D Mobbs, Hill Cottage, Mill Rd, Ashby St Mary, Norwich NR14 7BN (0508 480338).
Ground: Thurton & Ashby PF, Ashby Rd, Thurton. **Colours:** Red/black/black

WELLS TOWN

Secretary: Mr P Barker, 3 Park Road, Wells-next-the-Sea, Norfolk NR23 1DQ (0328 711375).
Ground: Beach Road, Wells-next-the-Sea. **Colours:** Blue/white.

Horsford United FC, who narrowly avoided relegation from the Premier Division. *Photo - Martin Wray.*

CROMER LIFEBOAT CUP 1994-95

Details kindy supplied by Jon Weaver

The Cromer Lifeboat Cup is the Premier KO Cup in North Norfolk, and the final has been played on Cromer Town's ground since the competition's inception in 1947. For the past four years, it has produced an annual profit of £1,000 for the RNLI.

First Round

Blakeney v Holt United	3-4		
Sheringham v Briston	2-2*(5-6 on penalties)*	Runton v Aylsham Wanderers	0-6
Bodham v Buxton	0-5	Cromer Town v Bacton	6-0
Mundesley v Southrepps	0-1	Overstrand Reserves v Trunch	2-1

Quarter-Finals

Cromer Town v North Walsham Town	2-4	Southrepps v Holt United	0-1
Aylsham Wanderers v Overstrand Reserves	2-3	Buxton v Briston	3-1

Semi-Finals *(None played, as both Holt United and Buxton were removed from the competition)*

Final *(at Cromer Town FC, Mon 2nd May)*: North Walsham Town 2, Overstrand Reserves 0 *(att: 300)*

Former Norwich manager Ken Brown is presented to the North Walsham team before the Cromer Lifeboat Cup final.

Lakeford Rangers, of the Lovewell Blake Anglian Combination Premier Division. Back Row (L/R): S Moore, P Sylvester (Manager), R Dade, J Sinclair, I Sell, R Collins, R Sylvester, S Davison, J Clover (Physio). Front: L Walsh, P Hunt, L Miller, C Fynn, N Trett, M Nicholson.

Photo - Martin Wray.

NORWICH & SOUTH NORFOLK DISTRICT JUNIOR LEAGUE

FOUNDED: 1977

This has been a transitional season for the League pending the formation of a third division proper for 1994-95. Scole United Reserves are relegated from Division One with Dereham Town 'A' and Attleborough Town 'A' promoted (Overland Reserves cannot be promoted because their first team are already in the top division).

Division Two for next season will consist of Scole Reserves, the teams who finished in positions 2-6 in Division 2A, Overland Reserves, and the teams in positions 3-7 in Division 2B. Division Three will consist of the remaining clubs and any new acceptances (there have been seven applications).

The League as presently named was formed in 1977. However its predecessor, the Norwich & District League whose trophies are still used, was established in 1919.

J W Turner, Hon. Secretary

PREM. DIV.	P	W	D	L	F	A	PTS
Watton United 'A'	24	17	4	3	98	30	38
Yaxham	24	17	2	5	73	32	36
Toftwood United	24	14	5	6	70	36	33
Attleborough Ath.	24	14	4	6	60	39	32
Ditchingham	24	11	7	6	63	40	29
Diss Town 'A'	24	11	6	7	65	31	28
Mulbarton Utd 'A'	24	10	5	9	51	51	25
Overland	24	9	4	11	81	54	22
Saham Toney	24	9	3	12	62	65	21
Wymondham T. 'A'	24	9	3	12	50	57	21
Morley Village	24	5	3	16	37	79	13
Tacolneston	24	4	2	18	40	118	4
Scole United Res.	24	1	2	21	23	141	4

DIV. 2A	P	W	D	L	F	A	PTS
Dereham Town 'A'	16	12	2	2	70	16	26
Mayflair Blinds	16	11	2	3	63	22	24
Dereham Snooker C.	16	11	0	5	59	24	22
Attleborough A. Res.	16	9	3	4	56	19	21
Old Buckenham Res.	16	5	6	5	32	40	16
Saham Toney Res.	16	6	4	6	30	38	16
Yaxham Res.	16	4	3	9	29	47	11
Dereham Utd Res.	16	3	2	11	35	59	8
West End ST	16	0	0	16	9	118	0

Ashill Res. and Hingham Res. both withdrew during season - records expunged.

DIV. 2B	P	W	D	L	F	A	PTS
Overlands Res.	22	15	4	3	112	48	34
Attleborough T. 'A'	22	16	2	4	67	37	34
RL Rangers	22	15	3	4	84	40	33
Great Cressingham	22	10	5	7	51	49	25
Bridgham	22	11	2	9	84	52	24
Thetford Town 'A'	22	8	6	8	71	53	22
East Harling 'A'	22	8	6	8	49	59	22
Kenninghall	22	7	5	10	52	56	19
Shipdham Res.	22	8	3	11	50	56	19
Shotesham Rovers	22	8	2	12	61	65	18
Morley Vill. Res.	22	5	1	16	42	82	11
Bradenham Wdrs 'A'	22	1	1	20	21	147	3

Cup Finals:

Junior League Cup: Yaxham 3, Overland 0 *(after 0-0 draw)*
Primary League Cup: Overland Res. 4, Bridgham 2
Ben Smith Mem. Cup: Yaxham 4, Overland 0
Fen Regis Invitation Shield: Dereham Snooker Club 2, Morley Village 0

ANGLIA AUTO TRADER NORWICH & DISTRICT SUNDAY LEAGUE

FOUNDED: 1958

DIV. ONE	P	W	D	L	F	A	PTS
Norwich Busmen	24	18	5	1	98	18	41
Anglians	24	16	4	4	95	50	36
Bishopsgate Lions	24	14	4	6	73	35	32
Poringland Wdrs	24	12	6	6	96	45	30
Carrow RS	24	12	4	8	75	63	28
Hellesdon Sunday	24	10	7	7	69	59	27
Dereham Hobbies	24	10	5	9	44	51	25
Hellesdon HSOB	24	8	3	13	44	86	19
New Inn	24	7	4	13	48	59	18
Bastille	24	5	7	12	63	88	17
Saxlingham	24	5	6	13	50	78	16
Unity Emeralds	24	7	1	16	54	78	15
Costessey Sunday	24	2	4	18	31	130	8

Lower Division Champions:
Div. 2 (12): Spooner Row
Div. 3 (13): Edith Cavell
Div. 4 (14): Five Star
Div. 5 (14): CSSA
Div. 6 (13): Cranworth

NORTH EAST NORFOLK LEAGUE

FOUNDED: 1922

DIV. ONE	P	W	D	L	F	A	PTS
AFC Colts	24	21	1	2	117	26	64
Hindringham	24	21	0	3	100	25	63
East Ruston	24	12	5	7	75	48	41
Runton	24	12	4	8	46	48	40
Mundesley	24	12	3	9	74	56	39
Bacton	24	12	2	10	79	77	38
Erpingham	24	12	1	11	66	56	37
Southrepps	24	8	5	11	57	79	29
Swanton Abbott	24	5	6	13	37	65	21
Aldborough	24	6	3	15	36	74	21
Sheringham Res.	24	6	2	16	30	75	20
Happisburgh	24	5	4	15	40	67	19
Cromer Res.	24	3	6	15	31	92	15

DIV. TWO	P	W	D	L	F	A	PTS
Trunch	24	20	3	1	112	21	63
Hoveton	24	16	4	4	57	17	52
Gimingham	24	14	4	6	89	45	46
Wells Town Res.	24	15	1	8	74	46	46
Buxton Res.	24	12	3	9	77	47	42
Aylsham 'A'	24	12	4	8	83	55	40
Lyng	24	11	4	9	59	48	37
Mundesley Res.	24	10	4	10	61	63	34
Dilham Res.	24	9	3	12	48	64	30
Cromer 'A'	24	6	3	15	37	108	21
Stalham Town 'A'	24	6	2	16	48	91	20
Corpusty	24	3	2	19	41	110	11
Felmingham	24	3	1	20	36	105	10

DIV. THREE	P	W	D	L	F	A	PTS
Holt United 'A'	26	20	4	2	113	50	64
Horning	26	17	4	5	95	39	55
Bacton Res.	26	16	4	6	96	53	52
Hoveton Res.	26	15	3	8	66	48	48
Runton Res.	26	14	4	8	72	50	46
East Runton Res.	26	13	5	8	67	43	44
Marsham	26	12	6	8	88	75	42
Southrepps Res.	26	13	2	11	77	71	41
Nth Nflk Dist. Coun.	26	9	5	12	51	72	32
Dodham	26	8	2	16	40	82	26
Mundesley 'A'	26	4	6	16	54	94	18
Gimingham Res.	26	4	5	16	40	87	17
Happisburgh Res.	26	4	4	18	26	78	16
Trunch Res.	26	3	4	19	36	79	13

GREAT YARMOUTH & DISTRICT SUNDAY LEAGUE

FOUNDED: 1944

DIV. ONE	P	W	D	L	F	A	PTS
Schooners	18	14	3	1	65	20	45
Alleycats	18	10	4	4	40	36	34
Wheelwrights	18	9	4	5	44	25	31
Tudor Tavern	18	8	4	6	49	38	28
Acle Rangers	18	7	2	9	28	33	23
Halvagate	18	6	4	8	28	32	22
Tramway Rovers	18	6	2	10	36	53	20
Gorleston United	18	5	3	10	38	44	18
Bure Construction	18	5	2	11	35	52	17
Arches Academicals	18	4	4	10	26	56	16

Lower Division Champions:
Div. 2 (12): Camden Tavern
Div. 3 (11): Bohemians
Div. 4 (12): Ludham Reserves

Cup Winners:
KO Cup: Schooners
Div. 1 Cup: Tudor Tavern
Div. 2 Cup: Upton Sunday
Div. 3 Cup: Venture
Div. 4 Cup: Ludham Reserves

Below: *Loddon United - Lovewell Blake Anglian Combination Division One. Back Row (L/R): M Cracknell, M Fuller, D Mortimer, K Knights, W Clenell, N Banham, A Battison, P Cunningham. Front: M Butcher, T Fisher, J Makin, N Crocker, G Read, R McGregor. Photo - Martin Wray.*

NORTH RIDING F.A.

Secretary: P Kirby,
284 Linthorpe Rd, Middlesbrough TS1 3QU (0642 224585).

SENIOR CUP 1993-94

First Round

Nunthorpe Athletic v Tees Components	1-6	Acklam Steelworks v New Marske SC	3-4
Marske United v Fishburn Park	2-1	Dormans Athletic v North Ormesby Sports	2-7

Second Round

Northallerton Town v Guisborough Town	0-5	Pickering Town v Marske United	4-3
Tees Components v New Marske SC	3-0	North Ormesby Sports v Whitby Town	0-0,0-1
Stockton v Rowntrees	1-0		

Quarter-Finals

Guisborough Town v Stockton	1-1,2-0	Tees Components v Whitby Town	1-1,1-4
Scarborough v Pickering Town	1-3*(aet)*	York City v Middlesbrough	0-0,1-0

Semi-Finals

Whitby Town v Guisborough Town	0-1	York C. v Pickering T. *(at Pickering T.)*	1-3*(aet)*

Final *(Wed 20th April, at Whitby Town FC)*: Guisborough Town 2, Pickering Town 0

Guisborough Town FC - North Riding Senior Cup winners 1993-94. *Photo - Dave West.*

BSC Redcar Works - who achieved a commendable third place in the Teesside League in 1993-94.

CAMERONS BREWING COMPANY TEESSIDE LEAGUE (Est. 1891)

Hon. Secretary: R D Marsay, 12 Aislaby Court, Wilton Lane, Guisborough TS14 6TG.

	P	W	D	L	F	A	PTS
Rowntrees	32	24	4	4	100	30	*73
Grangetown BC	32	21	5	6	72	43	68
BSC Redcar Works	32	20	7	5	94	46	67
ICI Wilton	32	20	3	9	107	67	63
Fishburn Park	32	20	3	9	79	45	63
Tees Components	32	17	6	9	69	46	57
BEADS	32	16	4	12	60	53	52
Dormans Athletic	32	14	4	14	79	71	46
Stockton Supporters	32	13	6	13	46	67	45
Acklam Steelworks	32	12	8	12	66	46	44
Thornaby YC	32	13	5	14	57	58	44
Stokesley	32	12	3	17	45	54	39
Nunthorpe Athletic	32	9	7	16	47	62	34
Richmond Town	32	6	5	21	32	89	23
New Marske SC	32	5	7	20	42	89	22
North Ormesby	32	5	5	22	44	90	20
Moorcock Athletic	32	3	2	27	23	105	11

* - 3 points deducted

McMILLAN BOWL **Preliminary Round**
New Marske SC 1, Stokesley 5

First Round
Stokesley 0, Rowntrees 3
Dormans Athletic 3, Moorcock Athletic 0
Thornaby YC 5, BEADS 3
Tees Components 3, Richmond Town 2
ICI Wilton 4, Fishburn Park 1
North Ormesby 0, Acklam Steelworks 4
Stockton Supporters 3, Grangetown Boys Club 1
Nunthorpe Athletic 1, BSC Redcar 3

Quarter Finals
Acklam Steelworks 0, BSC Redcar 1
Tees Components 0, Thornaby YC 1
Dormans Athletic 0, ICI Wilton 6
Rowntrees 2, Stockton Supporters 1

Semi Finals
Rowntrees 1, Thornaby Youth Club 2
ICI Wilton 1, BSC Redcar 5 *(after 1-1 draw)*

Final: BSC Redcar 2, Thornaby YC 2 *(aet)*
Replay: Thornaby YC 1, BSC Redcar 1 *(aet, Thornaby Youth Club won 7-6 on penalties)*

R.T. RAINE CUP **Preliminary Round**
Moorcock Athletic 3, Richmond Town 1

Quarter Finals
Grangetown Boys Club 4, BEADS 0
New Marske SC 1, Nunthorpe Athletic 6
Stokesley 1, Moorcock Athletic 2
Fishburn Park 4, North Ormesby 0

Semi Finals
Moorcock Athletic 0, Fishburn Park 2
Nunthorpe Athletic 1, Grangetown 2 *(aet)*

Final: Fishburn Park 5, Grangetown BC 3

Top Scorers (league + cups): 38 - S Breckton (BSC Redcar), 26 - S Donoghue (Dormans), 23 - J Simpson (Fishburn Park), 20 - P Brough - Rowntrees.

RESULT CHART 1993-94	1	2	3	4	5	6	7	8	9	10	11	12	13	14	15	16	17
1. Acklam Steel Works	*	1-1	1-1	3-3	1-2	1-2	1-3	3-0	8-0	6-2	0-1	5-0	1-1	1-0	0-1	1-4	1-2
2. BEADS	1-1	*	1-3	0-3	0-5	0-2	3-3	0-0	6-3	3-0	3-1	5-0	1-0	4-0	1-0	1-3	3-0
3. BSC Redcar	2-1	2-1	*	6-0	4-1	4-2	7-2	3-1	1-1	6-3	1-1	5-1	1-1	0-2	2-0	1-0	1-3
4. Dormans Athletic	2-3	2-3	3-3	*	1-3	2-3	3-1	12-1	6-1	1-1	1-0	0-1	0-2	0-3	5-1	1-4	3-1
5. Fishburn Park	2-1	1-0	0-1	1-2	*	2-2	3-6	1-0	4-0	3-1	6-0	5-0	1-3	3-0	3-0	2-0	4-0
6. Grangetown Boys Club	2-1	5-2	1-2	6-0	3-5	*	2-4	4-1	1-0	3-1	3-0	1-0	2-1	3-1	2-1	3-0	3-0
7. ICI Wilton	1-3	2-0	4-4	9-3	6-1	0-1	*	4-0	6-1	6-2	8-0	2-0	2-4	4-1	3-0	0-2	4-3
8. Moorcock Athletic	0-4	1-2	1-8	0-2	0-5	0-3	2-3	*	1-1	1-2	1-5	1-3	0-6	1-2	2-1	0-4	0-1
9. New Marske SC	1-1	1-3	0-3	0-2	0-2	2-2	1-4	5-1	*	2-2	1-5	1-1	4-2	1-5	1-3	1-2	1-3
10. North Ormesby	1-4	2-3	1-5	2-5	2-3	0-3	2-3	4-1	1-2	*	1-3	3-1	2-0	1-2	2-3	0-5	1-3
11. Nunthorpe Athletic	2-2	2-1	3-2	1-1	1-1	2-2	1-3	2-3	4-1	0-0	*	6-2	0-1	0-1	1-3	0-3	1-2
12. Richmond Town	1-4	1-4	1-5	0-1	0-3	0-1	1-5	4-0	1-3	1-1	2-1	*	1-5	0-0	3-2	3-4	1-1
13. Rowntrees	3-0	5-1	0-0	2-0	3-3	4-0	4-2	3-0	2-1	4-0	1-0	7-0	*	9-0	1-0	7-2	2-0
14. Stockton Supporters	1-1	3-2	1-3	2-8	0-3	2-2	4-1	1-0	3-3	3-1	0-3	3-0	2-5	*	0-0	1-0	0-4
15. Stokesley	1-3	0-2	2-1	1-0	2-0	1-2	1-1	5-2	2-0	1-2	5-1	0-1	0-5	2-0	*	2-4	3-0
16. Tees Components	1-1	0-1	5-4	2-4	2-1	3-0	5-1	1-0	2-1	1-1	0-0	4-1	3-4	0-0	1-1	*	1-3
17. Thornaby Youth Club	1-2	1-1	2-3	3-5	4-1	1-1	2-4	1-2	2-3	3-0	1-0	1-1	1-3	2-3	3-1	1-1	*

Tees Components FC. *Photo - Richard Brock.*

TEESSIDE LEAGUE CLUBS 1994-95

ACKLAM STEELWORKS

Secretary: Dave Kane, 27 Edgeworth Court, Hemlington, Middlesbrough TS6 9EP (0642 596559).
Ground: Acklam Steelworks Club, Park Rd South, Middlesbrough (0642 818717).
Directions: When on Marton Rd (A172) follow route to M'bro centre, follow signs to County Sports Stadium, Steelworks club entrance along Park Rd South opposite main gate of stadium.
Colours: Red/blue/red **Change colours:** Black & blue/black/blue.

B.E.A.D.S.

Secretary: Dave Warwick, 13 Darnell Green, Easterside, Middlesbrough TS4 3NN (0642 321583).
Ground: Beechwood & Easterside SC, Marton Rd, Middlesbrough (0642 318789).
Directions: A172 into M'bro centre, pitch behind Beechwood & Easterside Social Club.
Colours: Red & black/black/red & black **Change colours:** Blue & white/blue/blue.

BILLINGHAM TOWN RESERVES *(see page 698)*

B.S.C. REDCAR WORKS

Secretary: Cliff Lampard, 60 Staintondale Ave., Dormanstown, Redcar TS10 5HU (0642 471537).
Ground: BSC Sports & Social Club, Dormanstown, Redcar (0642 486691).
Directions: Approaching Redcar from M'bro enter Dormanstown at BSC Steel House Works r'bout, 1st right then 1st left - pitch behind British Steel Club on right.
Colours: Blue/white/blue **Change colours:** All red.

DORMANS ATHLETIC

Secretary: Dennis Milburn, 20 Eton Rd, Linthorpe, Middlesbrough TS5 5EP (0642 822142).
Ground: Dormans Athletic Club, Oxford Rd, Middlesbrough (0642 817099).
Directions: Following A1032 down Acklam Rd towards M'bro centre, turn right on to Oxford Rd - Dormans Athletic Club on right before garage.
Colours: Red/white/red **Change colours:** Black & white/black/black.

FISHBURN PARK

Secretary: Ian Landers, 9 Pinewood Close, Whitby, North Yorkshire YO21 1LR (0947 600066).
Ground: Showfield Ground, White Leys, Whitby.
Directions: Following coast road into Whitby, Turnbull Ground (Whitby Town FC) quarter mile on left - Showfield Ground then 1st left on right.
Colours: Green/white/green **Change colours:** White/blue/blue.

GRANGETOWN BOYS CLUB

Secretary: Brian Honeywell, 11 Ambleside Rd, Normanby, Middlesbrough TS6 0DY (0642 458208).
Ground: Grangetown YCC, Trunk Road, Grangetown, Middlesbrough (0642 455435).
Directions: Follow the Trunk Rd to Redcar from M'bro, Grangetown YCC Club is on right after r'bout leading over bridge. Coming from Redcar, club on left before bridge.
Colours: Red/blue/red **Change colours:** Black & amber/black/black.

I.C.I. WILTON

Secretary: John Knott, 11 Howden Court, Hemlington, Middlesbrough TS8 9LR (0642 595598).
Ground: Wilton Recreation Club, Broadway, Grangetown, Middlesbrough (0642 453701).
Directions: Follow Trunk Rd from M'bro centre towards Redcar, past Grangetown YCC continue over r'bout to ICI Works r'bout, turn back towards M'bro on Trunk Rd, ICI Wilton Recreation Club is 1st left.
Colours: White/blue/blue **Change colours:** Yellow/black/yellow.

MOORCOCK ATHLETIC

Secretary: Linda Thomas, 23 Alloway Grove, Hemlington, Middlesbrough TS8 9HT (0642 596559).
Ground: King George V Playing Fields, Howlbeck Rd, Guisborough.
Directions: A171 into Guisborough from M'bro, left at 2nd lighs (opp. Moorcock Hotel), 3rd left (following signs to Swimming Baths) - pitch behind Guisborough Town FC.
Colours: Green/black/green **Change colours:** Yellow/green/yellow & green.

NEW MARSKE SPORTS CLUB

Secretary: Peter Whitaker, 28 High Str., Marske, Redcar TS11 7BE (0642 486770).
Ground: New Marske Sports Club, New Marske, Redcar (0642 479808).
Directions: From Whitby or M'bro follow the A174 to the r'bout junction with Longbeck Lane, turn right - ground on left. From Guisborough follow A173 and B1267 into New Marske - ground on right leaving New Marske.
Colours: Blue & white/blue/blue **Change colours:** Grey/red/red.

NUNTHORPE ATHLETIC

Secretary: Kevin Levitt, 131 Burlam Rd, Middlesbrough TS5 5AX (0642 824332).
Ground: Recreation Club, Guisborough Rd, Nunthorpe (0642 313251).
Directions: A172 (Dixons Bank) out of M'bro, left into Nunthorpe, ground on right 300yds after 2nd left. Approaching by A171 (Ormesby Bank) or from Guisborough, left into Nunthorpe and follow road over rail crossing - ground 200yds on left.
Colours: Yellow/black/black **Change colours:** All blue.

RICHMOND TOWN

Secretary: Geoff Hunter, 49 Willance Grove, Richmond, North Yorkshire DL10 4HA (0748 822657).
Ground: Earls Orchard Playing Fields, Sleegill, Richmond, North Yorkshire.
Directions: Entering town by A6108 follow road over 2 r'bouts, right at 3rd r'bout, 2nd left, follow downhill and cross Green Bridge to Hudswell Village - ground on left immediately after bridge.
Colours: Blue/white/blue **Change colours:** Black & red/black/black.

ROWNTREES

Secretary: Doug Jefferson, 18 North Eastern Terrace, Tadcaster Rd, York YO2 2HN (0904 703650).
Ground: Mille Crux Sports Ground, Haxby Road, York.
Directions: Approaching York by A19, take outer ring-road towards Scarborough, turn right to New Earswick, follow thru village - ground on left opposite large warehouse.
Colours: White/blue/blue **Change colours:** Blue/white/white.

STOCKTON SUPPORTERS

Secretary: Glen Youngman, 55 Aiskew Grove, Fairfield, Stockton, Cleveland TS19 7RB (0642 587871).
Ground & Colours: As Stockton FC *(see page 704)*

STOKESLEY

Secretary: Peter Grainge, 77 Darnton Drive, Easterside, Middlesbrough TS4 3RF (0642 316691).
Ground: Stokesley Sports Club, Broughton Rd, Stokesley (0642 710051).
Directions: Follow signs to Stokesley, take B1257 to Great Broughton at r'bout where A172 & A173 meet, ground on left next to cricket field.
Colours: All red **Change colours:** All blue.

TEES COMPONENTS

Secretary: Bryan Kitchen, 151 Guisborough Rd, Nunthorpe, Middlesbrough TS7 0JQ (0642 311358).
Ground: Recreation Ground, Machine Lane, North Skelton.
Directions: A173 into Skelton then North Skelton, ground off North Skelton High Street - follow lane between Boocock's Garage and church.
Colours: Navy/navy/sky **Change colours:** All white.

THORNABY YOUTH CLUB

Secretary: Mac Allan, 9 Bracknell Rd, Thornaby, Stockton TS17 9AW (0642 676653).
Ground: Dene School, Baysdale Rd, Thornaby.
Directions: Leaving A19 at Thornaby interchange, turn left at Roundel pub on to Mitchell Ave., proceed towards Thornaby town centre turning right at Baysdale Rd, follow road round to entrance of Youth Club.
Colours: Claret/claret/blue **Change colours:** All blue.

STOCKTON SUNDAY LEAGUE

FOUNDED: 1968

DIV. ONE	P	W	D	L	F	A	PTS
Oxbridge WMC	20	16	2	2	88	14	50
Buck Inn	20	15	4	1	96	21	49
Blue Nile	20	14	3	3	66	20	45
Principal Investments	20	9	2	9	49	36	29
Lord Nelson	20	9	2	9	53	61	29
Fairfield S & S	20	9	0	11	60	48	27
Gge & Dragon (Yarm)	20	8	1	11	42	53	25
Elm Tree	20	7	2	11	41	58	23
Churchills Ath.	20	7	2	11	37	57	23
Turks Head	20	6	1	13	36	58	19
Malleable Social	20	0	1	19	14	156	1

Lower Division Champions:
Div. 2 (10): Old Thornaby SC
Div. 3 (12): Norton Tavern
Div. 4 (14): CAB Glass

Cup Finals:
Ian Gorman Mem. Trophy (Lge Cup): Thrush Rovers beat Oxbridge WMC 5-4 on penalties after 4-4 draw
Norton Trophy: Elm Tree 4, Principal Investments 3

TEESSIDE & DISTRICT SUNDAY LEAGUE

FOUNDED: 1986

DIV. ONE	P	W	D	L	F	A	PTS
Clarendon	18	16	2	0	91	19	50
Flannagans Bar	18	13	3	2	110	18	42
Billingham Arms	18	12	2	4	65	26	38
Maple Hotel	18	11	1	6	58	33	34
Felching Rovers	18	7	4	7	46	45	25
Stoney Oak	18	7	3	8	36	42	24
Owington Farm	18	4	4	10	22	85	16
Billingham AC	18	3	4	11	17	49	13
Royal Snooker	18	2	3	13	27	73	9
Smiths Arms	18	2	0	16	19	101	6

Lower Division Champions:
Div. 2 (12): Photoworld

Near-post corner action from the Cleveland Sunday League Challenge Cup final between Grove Hill and Grangetown Social played at BSC Redcar Works.

Photo - Gavin Ellis-Neville.

NORTHAMPTONSHIRE F.A.

Secretary: Brian Walden, 2 Duncan Close,
Red House Rd, Moulton Park, Northampton NN3 6WL (0604 670741)

HILLIER SENIOR CUP 1993-94

First Round

Wellingborough Town v Long Buckby	1-2
Desborough Town v Raunds Town	2-4
Northampton Spencer v Stewarts & Lloyds	3-0
Brackley Town v Rothwell Town	0-7
Rushden & Diamonds v Cogenhoe United	4-2
Daventry Town v Corby Town	0-3

Quarters-Finals

Corby Town v Long Buckby	2-0
Northampton Spencer v Raunds Town	4-3*(aet)*
Rothwell Town v Rushden & Diamonds	0-1
Kettering Town *(bye)*	

Semi-Finals

Corby Town v Northampton Spencer	1-1,1-3*(aet)*
Rushden & Diamonds v Kettering Town	3-2

Final *(at Rushden & Diamonds FC, Tues 20th April)*: Rushden & Diamonds 5, Northampton Spencer 0

OTHER COUNTY FINALS 1993-94

Junior Cup *(at Northampton Town FC, Thurs 21st April)*: Northampton Vanaid 1, Northampton ON Chenecks 0
Lower Junior Cup *(at Rushden & Diamonds FC, Mon 14th March)*: Brotherhoods 4, Pitsford Eagles Reserves 1
Area Cup *(at Bugbrooke St Michael FC, Wed 20th April)*: Potterspury 2, Earls Barton 0
Sunday Cup *(at Cogenhoe Utd FC, Sun 16th March)*: Clicker Rangers 2, Wellingborough Valleybrook 1
Sunday Trophy *(at Long Buckby FC, Thurs 7th April)*: Daventry Dun Cow 2, Burton Band 0
Sunday Vase *(at Raunds Town FC, Wed 27th April)*: Hartwell 1, Pet. Railway 0
Sunday Shield *(at Wellingborough Town FC, Wed 4th & Tues 10th May)*: Kettering Rising Sun 2, Higham Ferrers 1 *(after 0-0 draw)*
Youth Invitation u-16 Cup *(at Desborough Town FC, Sun 24th April)*: Corby Town 2, Cogenhoe United 0
Youth Invitation u-14 Cup *(at Cogenhoe United FC, Sun 17th April)*: Corby Castle Rise 2, Northampton ON Chenecks 0

Weldon FC - champions of the East Midlands Alliance (see further on in this section for league tables). Weldon went into their last game of the season, away to Corby Danesholme, level on points with their opponents but with a superior goal difference. In front of 350 spectators, they held out for a draw to take the title.
Photo - Martin Wray.

DAVENTRY CHARITY CUP

The Daventry Charity Cup was made in London in 1901 and was originally presented as a shooting trophy to the Yeomanry by the citizens of the town. The cup was won outright by a Sergeant Goodman who then gave it to the borough to be used for charitable purposes.

Since the competition's inauguration in 1921, only three Daventry sides - The Vics (22-23), Dun Cow (78-79) and Timken Athletic (81-82) - have won the magnificent trophy which is ensured for over £10,000.

Former Northampton Town League giants Spencer School Old Boys have won the Cup a record eight times since the War, and Long Buckby have been victorious seven times in the last seventeen years. Yet, as recently as 1981, it was touch and go whether the competition would survive beyond its Diamond Jubilee. Out of the blue, the curator of the Northants Yeomanry Museum decided the silver cup should be allowed to gather dust in the Abingdon Park Museum alongside the defunct Northampton, Peterborough and Wellingborough Charity Cups. Fortunately, some common sense prevailed and, unable to provide written proof of ownership, the military brass hats beat a strategic retreat.

Due to the upsurge in Sunday football, it was decided to switch the competition to midweek in the early Eighties and invite Senior Clubs to compete. The organisers are grateful to clubs of the calibre of VS Rugby, Kettering, Banbury, Leamington and Wolverton who came to the assistance of the competition. Kettering emerged winners of the new style competition three times in the late 1980s, and in recent years several local charities have benefitted considerably.

Programme collectors can purchase copies of this season's Final issue (all proceeds to charity) from competition secretary Brian Sewell at 38 Foxons Barn Road, Rugby, Warks CV21 1JZ (0788 571738). Programmes are priced at 50p, or 3 for £1.

Daventry Charity Cup 1993-94

First Round

Folly Lane v Bilton Social	1-0	Milton v Olney Town	2-1
Dun Cow v Kislingbury	3-1	Rugby Town v Woodford United	1-0

Second Round

Bugbrooke St Michael v Rugby Town	0-2	Banbury United v Ford Sports	6-1
Brackley Town v Milton	1-0	Higham Town v Heyford Athletic	7-3
Newport Pagnell Town v Dun Cow	3-2*(aet)*	Lutterworth Town v Folly Lane	2-1
Wellingborough Town v Clifton	4-2	Cranfield United v British Timken	3-0

Third Round

Newport Pagnell Town v Higham Town	2-1	Daventry Town v Rothwell Town	1-5
Cogenhoe United v Banbury United	4-0	Lutterworth Town *(w/o)* Buckingham Town *(scr)*	
Wellingborough Town v Brackley Town	5-2	Northampton Spencer *(scr)* Rushden & Diamonds *(w/o)*	
Long Buckby v Rugby Town	4-0	Corby Town v Cranfield United	7-0

Quarter-Finals

Cogenhoe United v Newport Pagnell Town	0-1	Long Buckby v Wellingborough Town	6-1
Rothwell Town v Corby Town	1-2	Rushden & D. v Lutterworth *(at Lutterworth)*	3-2

Semi-Finals

Long Buckby v Corby Town	1-3	Rushden & Diamonds v Newport Pagnell Town	0-1

Final *(at Daventry Town FC, Wed 11th May)*: Corby Town 2, Newport Pagnell Town 0 *(aet)*

NORTHAMPTON TOWN LEAGUE

PREM. DIV.	P	W	D	L	F	A	PTS
Pitsford Eagles	26	21	4	1	91	21	46
Bective Wanderers	26	18	5	3	88	31	41
Queen Eleanor	26	19	3	4	91	40	41
Rosebery Rangers	26	18	4	6	90	44	38
Northampton Park	26	11	8	7	56	57	30
Foundry Generals	26	11	5	10	59	50	27
Crusaders	26	8	7	11	48	49	23
Queens Park WMC	26	7	8	11	60	62	22
Wootton	26	7	6	13	50	58	20
Hardingstone	26	8	3	15	45	83	19
Duston United	26	7	4	15	38	61	18
St Georges OB	26	6	5	15	43	58	17
St Mary's	26	5	4	17	41	72	14
Delapre Old Boys	26	3	2	21	39	136	8

DIV. ONE	P	W	D	L	F	A	PTS
Timken Duston	20	17	2	1	70	22	36
Rosebery Rgrs Res.	20	13	3	4	67	31	29
Pitsford E. Res.	20	11	5	4	68	32	27
ON Chenecks 'A'	20	12	1	7	43	34	25
Kingsthorpe Nomads	20	9	3	8	48	38	21
Foundry Gen. Res.	20	5	7	8	34	36	17
Ashley Rovers	20	6	4	10	28	40	16
Queen Eleanor Res.	20	6	4	10	39	54	16
N'pton Spencer 'A'	20	6	4	11	38	47	15
Crusaders Res.	20	5	2	13	14	46	12
N'pton Park Res.	20	2	2	16	22	36	6

DIV. TWO	P	W	D	L	F	A	PTS
Bective Wdrs Res.	20	15	3	2	96	25	33
Kingsthorpe Wdrs	20	10	8	2	61	23	28
New Duston Ath.	20	12	2	6	70	38	26
Duston United Res.	20	11	4	5	42	41	26
Cue Sports	20	8	4	8	47	42	20
Queens Pk WMC Res.	20	8	4	8	47	50	20
St Mary's Res.	20	5	7	8	32	58	17
St Georges OB Res.	20	6	4	10	23	65	16
SPA	20	6	3	11	38	52	15
United Castle	20	6	2	12	35	47	14
Northampton Amateurs	20	2	1	17	23	71	5

DIV. THREE	P	W	D	L	F	A	PTS
Strollers	20	17	3	0	84	13	37
Upper Mounts	20	16	2	2	76	26	34
Ango-Celtic	20	10	2	8	45	46	22
Wootton Res.	20	9	4	7	33	39	22
Victoria Rangers	20	9	3	8	44	35	21
Kings Wdrs Res.	20	10	1	9	37	42	21
United Co's Omni.	20	8	2	10	38	52	18
Ashley Rvrs Res.	20	7	1	12	33	47	15
Parkland Tigers	20	6	2	12	40	53	14
Kingsthorpe N. Res.	20	5	2	13	22	53	12
Hardingstone Res.	20	2	0	18	27	72	4

League KO Cup winners: Rosebery Rangers
Reserve Team's Cup: Rosebery Rgrs Reserves

EAST MIDLANDS ALLIANCE

FOUNDED: 1923

Promotion/relegation lines are marked on the tables. New entrants are Corby Grampian in the Intermediate Division, Corby Square Peg in Division One, and Corby Evapco in Division Two.

County Division	P	W	D	L	F	A	PTS
Weldon	24	17	4	3	77	23	38
Corby Danesholme	24	17	4	3	70	31	38
Rothwell Corries	24	15	4	5	50	27	34
Corby Strip Mills	24	16	1	7	68	37	33
Gretton	24	14	4	6	65	42	32
Corby Locomotives	24	13	0	11	47	41	26
Brixworth	24	12	1	11	66	54	25
Kettering Generals	24	11	1	12	53	50	23
Corby Pegasus	24	10	2	12	50	59	22
Kettering Nomads	24	6	2	16	36	52	14
Corby FC Fisher	24	5	2	17	43	84	12
Wellingboro. Gram.	24	3	4	17	46	84	10
Medbourne	24	2	1	21	21	106	5

I'mediate Div.	P	W	D	L	F	A	PTS
Kettering Reflections	24	17	5	2	91	33	39
Corby St Brendans	24	17	2	5	72	40	36
Corby Danes. Res.	24	14	3	6	75	36	33
Brixworth Res.	24	13	5	6	56	39	31
Gretton Res.	24	12	5	7	60	44	29
Barton Seagrave	24	13	2	9	70	54	28
Corby S. Mills Res.	24	12	2	10	69	49	26
Wilbarton Res.	24	7	5	12	40	53	19
Geddington WMC	24	8	1	15	41	51	17
Rothwell Cor. Res.	24	7	3	14	37	61	17
Kett. Orchard Park	24	6	2	16	37	90	14
Stanwick Rovers	24	6	1	17	27	67	13
Irthlingboro. Rgrs	24	4	2	18	36	83	10

Division One	P	W	D	L	F	A	PTS
Corby Darleydale	24	19	2	3	74	33	40
Weldon Res.	24	16	4	4	77	44	36
Corby Trades & Lbr	24	13	8	3	95	49	34
Kettering Briars	24	13	7	4	61	46	33
Ringstead Rangers	24	11	3	10	43	36	25
Kett. Nomads Res.	24	11	2	11	52	54	24
Corby Academicals	24	9	5	10	41	55	23
Corby Loco Res.	24	7	7	10	64	62	21
Corby Ex-Service	24	7	4	13	46	50	18
Kett. Emmaneff Utd	24	6	5	13	52	62	17
Kettering Park Rvrs	24	5	6	13	39	80	16
Corby Pegasus Res.	24	5	4	15	45	74	14
Corby Fisher Res.	24	1	9	14	32	74	11

Division Two	P	W	D	L	F	A	PTS
Corby Gainsboro. Rv.	26	22	4	0	102	26	48
Burton United	26	16	4	6	66	53	36
Corby Park Vale	26	13	8	5	58	51	34
Kett. Generals Res.	26	12	6	8	61	57	30
Corby T & L Res.	26	13	3	10	90	74	29
Wilbarston Res.	26	13	2	11	61	45	28
Stanion United	26	12	4	10	68	60	28
Corby Euramax	26	11	3	12	69	61	25
Kett. A/Harlequin	26	9	5	12	64	63	23
Corby Darley. Res.	26	9	3	14	63	81	21
Barton Seagrave Res.	26	8	4	14	39	46	20
Corby Linnco	26	8	4	14	64	76	20
Kett. Orchard Pk Res.	26	5	3	18	44	97	13
Islip United	26	3	3	20	36	93	9

Dr Martens Munton Cup (1st teams): Weldon
DM Munton Cup r-up: Wellingboro. Grammarians
Dr Martens Airwair Cup (Divisions One & Two): Kettering Avondale/Harlequin
DM Airwair Cup r-up: Kettering Briars
Dr Martens Doug Fairey Cup (Reserve teams): Corby Danesholme Reserves
DM Doug Fairey Cup r-up: Corby Strip Mills Res.

Opposite: *Andy Mann, captain of Weldon, receives the County Division championship trophy from Bill Quincey, League Registration Secretary, shortly after the title-clinching 1-1 draw at Danesholme.*
Photo - Martin Wray.

A.N.C. EXPRESS

EAST NORTHANTS LEAGUE

FOUNDED: 1920

PREM. DIV.	P	W	D	L	F	A	PTS
Wellingboro. Nucabs	18	16	1	1	70	16	33
Fox Sports	18	14	3	1	102	23	31
Wollaston Vics	18	12	1	5	48	28	25
AFC 2000	18	8	2	8	60	45	18
Wellingboro. Nalgo	18	8	2	8	35	33	18
Finedon Volta	18	8	1	9	41	41	17
Wellingboro. Castle	18	5	4	9	28	52	14
Rushden Park	18	3	3	11	31	59	9
Emberton Res.	18	4	1	13	21	93	9
Grammarians	18	1	4	13	17	60	6

DIV. ONE	P	W	D	L	F	A	PTS
Wellingboro. Wdrs	18	14	1	3	51	28	29
Finedon Volta Res.	18	11	4	3	50	29	26
Weavers Old Boys	18	11	0	7	41	29	22
Wollaston Res.	18	9	4	5	38	38	22
ANC International	18	9	1	8	61	44	19
Raunds Rangers	18	6	3	9	43	41	15
Green Dragon	18	6	3	9	44	54	15
Twywell	18	6	2	10	33	37	14
Woodford Stars	18	5	1	12	28	49	11
Podington	18	3	1	14	21	61	7

DIV. TWO	P	W	D	L	F	A	PTS
Rushden Band Club	12	11	1	0	81	23	23
Bozeat Phoenix	12	8	2	2	47	21	18
Great Doddington	12	5	3	4	29	29	13
Rushden Wanderers	12	3	3	6	31	46	9
Green Dragon Res.	12	3	3	6	29	48	9
Well. Castle Res.	12	2	4	6	40	41	8
Well. Nalgo Res.	12	1	2	9	15	64	4
Rushden Park	12	3	3	11	31	59	9

Cup Finals:
Senior Cup: Fox Spts 2, Huntingdon 0
Braybrook Cup: Wellingborough Wdrs 4, ANC Int. 0
Div. 2 Cup: Rushden Band 2, Great Doddington 0
Hamblin KO Cup: Well. Nucabs 2, Rushden Band 0

NON-LEAGUE TRAVELLER

The Weekly Magazine for the Non-League follower

Non-League Traveller will again be published weekly throughout the 1994-95 season and will include ...Up-to-date fixtures from around 90 different leagues in England, Scotland and Wales....The latest news from around the clubs....Programme Reviews......Club focuses and maps...... Cup Draws..... etc....etc.......

All for around £1 per week (incl. P & P). The cost of a half year subscription (until Christmas 1994 is just £18, or for the whole season (approx. 35 issues) £35-00.

Cheques or postal orders should be made payable to 'Non-League Traveller' and sent to the address below. For a free copy please write or give a call to the telephone number below. (Special Offer - next 6 issues for £5).

Top O' The Bank, Evesham Road, Broadway, Worcs. WR12 7DG :

0386 853289 Fax: 0386 858036

NORTHUMBERLAND F.A.

Secretary: Roland Maughan, Seymour House, 10 Brenkley Way, Blezard Business Park, Seaton Burn, Newcastle NE13 6DT (091 236 8020).

NORTH EAST FORD DEALERS SENIOR CUP 1993-94

First Round

Ashington v Bedlington Terriers	0-9	Seaton Delaval Amateurs v Prudhoe East End	1-4
Ponteland United v Morpeth Town	1-0	Alnwick Town v West Allotment Celtic	1-2

Quarter-Finals

Bedlington Terriers v Blyth Spartans	0-2	West Allotment Celtic v Newcastle Utd Reserves	1-4
Prudoe East End v Ponteland United	0-2	Newcastle Blue Star v Whitley Bay	6-2

Semi-Finals

Ponteland United v Newcastle Blue Star	1-3	Blyth Spartans v Newcastle United Reserves	4-1

Final *(at Blyth Spartans FC, Tues 26th April)*: Blyth Spartans 1, Newcastle Blue Star 0

WAUGH TRANSPORT BENEVOLENT BOWL

First Round

Longbenton v Forest Hall	5-2	Spittal Rovers v Newbiggin Central Welfare	3-1
Shankhouse v North Shields	4-3	Westerhope v Walker	4-2
Nth Shields St Columbas v Heaton Stann.	1-2	Seaton Terrace v Ashington Hirst Progressive	1-0
Newcastle Benfield Park v Wark	4-0	Haltwhistle Crown Paints v Blyth Kitty Brewster	0-1

Quarter Finals

Seaton Del. Seaton Terrace v Shankhouse	2-0	Spittal Rovers v Newcastle Benfield Park	2-1
Westerhope v Blyth Kitty Brewster	1-2	Longbenton v Heaton Stannington	5-0

Semi-Finals

Spittal Rovers v Shankhouse	6-1	Longbenton v Blyth Kitty Brewster	3-0

Final *(at Alnwick Town FC, Mon 9th May)*: Spittal Rovers 2, Longbenton 1 *(after 1-1 draw at same venue, Wed 27th April)*

OTHER COUNTY FINALS:

Sunday Cup *(at Whitley Bay FC)*: Newcastle Balloon 2, Wallsend Labour Club 1
Minor Cup *(at Morpeth Town FC)*: Orwin New Winning 1, Amble Town 0
Junior Cup *(at Seaton Delaval Amateurs FC)*: New Hartley 2, Wideopen & District 1
Rangers Cup *(at Ponteland Utd FC)*: Cramlington Blue Star 5, Wideopen & District 1
Colts Cup *(at Gosforth Bohemian FC)*: Bedlington 2, Killingworth BC 1
Clubs Cup *(at Heaton Stannington FC)*: Montagu & North Fenham 2, Cramlington 0

HALIFAX PROPERTY SERVICES NORTH NORTHUMBERLAND LEAGUE

President: H S Lancaster.

Chairman/Secretary: N Laidler, 29 Greyfield Estate, Embleton, Alnwick (0665 576343).

Press Officer/Fixture Secretary: C Sanderson, 10 Rydal Mount, Newbiggin-by-the-Sea (Ashington 855271).

The 1993/94 NNFL campaign was one of the most exciting seasons for many years with both the first and second division titles being decided in the final weeks of the season.

Alnwick Town Reserves were the early pace-setters in division one and by Christmas the main challengers were North Sunderland who, despite having three points deducted for a rule infringement, had put together a tremendous long run. With three games to go, North Sunderland led the table on goal difference and were now the favourites, but the Seahouses side slipped up drawing all three games while the Alnwick team won their remaining three games to clinch the title.

At the other end, newly promoted Belford were relegated after one season back in the top flight, but put a strong finish to the season although it was to be too late. Previous champions Alnmouth looked to be joining the Meadow Park side in division two but the 'Seasiders' won their last five matches to finish in mid-table.

The second division championship was won by Acklington HM Prison who romped home to the title with the free-scoring Derek Pouton netting an amazing tally of 40 goals. Craster Rovers claimed the runners-up spot after a late collapse cost them the title, and the free-scoring Stobhill Rangers claimed third place in their first season in the league.

In the Northumberland Minor Cup, both Rothbury and Springhill reached the third round, both defeating Northern Alliance League opposition on the way.

The honours in the five league cups were all shared evenly. Springhill retained the Bilclough Cup defeating Rothbury 2-1 after a replay, while Spittal Rovers 'A' edged out Berwick Harrow 3-2 in the Sanderson Cup Final and Amble Vikings lifted the Anderson Cup defeating North Sunderland 3-1. Embleton Whinstone Rovers shocked Craster Rovers 2-1 after a replay to lift the Runciman Cup - both games attracting record gates for the NNFL - while the Robson Cup final saw a battle of two of the new entrants in which Stobhill Rangers defeated Chevington Red Row 3-1.

The NNFL were hit hard with resignations in the past season. Percy Rovers Reserves resigned at the League AGM in May while Hedgeley folded a week before the season started and, four games into the season Ashington Town (formerly Ashington Reserves), folded due to administration problems. For season 1994/95 champions Alnwick Town Reserves (now known as Alnwick Aydon Forest) have tendered their resignation to join Northern Alliance, while for the league welcome new entrants in Morpeth Town Reserves and Craster Rovers Reserves.

For season 1994-95, the NNFL have negotiated a lucrative sponsorship deal with Halifax Property Services in a three-year agreement. The league will now be known as the Halifax Property Services North Northumberland Football League.

Chris Sanderson, Press Officer.

DIV. ONE	P	W	D	L	F	A	PTS
Alnwick Town Res.	20	16	2	2	55	22	50
North Sunderland	20	14	5	1	48	19	*44
Springhill	20	11	2	7	45	32	35
Berwick Harrow	20	10	4	6	35	19	34
Alnmouth	20	7	6	7	40	41	27
Amble Vikings	20	7	5	7	47	38	26
Rothbury	20	7	2	11	44	49	23
Spittal Rvrs 'A'	20	7	2	11	38	54	23
Wallington	20	5	5	10	38	49	20
Lowick	20	5	5	10	32	47	20
Belford	20	1	2	17	16	63	5

Top Scorers:

Jimmy Moffat (Wallington) 13
Ray Smith (Alnwick Town Res.) 13
Steven Tindale (Amble Vikings) 13
Nick Gay (Rothbury) 13

Good Conduct Winners:
Springhill

DIV. TWO	P	W	D	L	F	A	PTS
Acklington HMP	22	18	1	3	119	35	55
Craster Rovers	22	16	3	3	76	27	51
Stobhill Rangers	22	16	2	4	106	36	50
Berwick Allan Bros	22	14	3	5	89	42	46
Chevington Red Row	22	9	5	8	65	55	32
Wooler	22	8	5	9	51	42	29
Embleton Whinstone	22	9	4	9	50	59	*28
Longhoughton	22	8	4	10	40	60	28
Lowick Res.	22	6	4	12	34	83	*19
Rothbury Res.	22	5	1	16	55	100	16
Hedgeley Rovers	22	4	3	15	49	74	15
Alnmouth Res.	22	1	1	20	24	128	#2

* - 3 points deducted
# - 2 points deducted

Top Scorer:
Derek Poulton (Acklington HMP) 40

Good Conduct Winners:
Rothbury Reserves

DIVISION ONE RESULTS	1	2	3	4	5	6	7	8	9	10	11
1. Alnmouth	*	1-4	3-1	4-0	0-0	1-1	3-3	5-1	6-0	1-2	4-3
2. Alnwick Town Reserves	1-0	*	3-0	1-0	1-2	2-1	1-1	4-1	5-2	2-1	5-1
3. Amble Vikings	1-1	2-6	*	4-1	0-0	6-1	1-1	5-1	3-1	0-2	1-3
4. Belford	2-4	1-3	1-7	*	0-5	1-2	1-2	2-0	0-1	1-3	1-1
5. Berwick Harrow	4-0	1-2	1-2	2-0	*	2-2	0-5	1-0	6-0	1-0	0-2
6. Lowick	5-1	0-1	2-2	2-2	1-0	*	1-3	2-2	2-1	1-2	4-2
7. North Sunderland	1-1	2-0	1-0	1-0	2-0	5-0	*	5-2	5-2	2-0	2-0
8. Rothbury	1-2	2-3	5-1	5-1	1-2	6-3	3-0	*	4-2	1-2	3-3
9. Spittal Rovers 'A'	5-1	1-5	1-1	3-1	0-1	5-1	1-3	1-2	*	3-2	5-3
10. Springhill	4-0	3-3	5-3	7-0	0-6	1-0	1-1	4-2	1-2	*	4-1
11. Wallington	2-2	0-3	2-4	6-1	1-1	2-1	1-3	1-2	2-2	2-1	*

DIVISION TWO RESULTS	1	2	3	4	5	6	7	8	9	10	11	12
1. Acklington HM Prison	*	11-0	8-2	3-1	1-2	4-2	9-2	6-0	6-0	10-1	1-0	2-1
2. Alnmouth Reserves	2-5	*	0-10	1-8	1-11	2-3	1-13	1-2	0-1	2-6	0-5	3-1
3. Berwick Allan Brothers	2-4	12-1	*	3-0	4-1	4-0	2-0	2-3	7-1	4-2	3-3	3-2
4. Chevington Red Row	5-2	4-1	1-6	*	0-4	2-2	4-0	2-2	4-1	1-3	1-5	4-4
5. Craster Rovers	2-1	2-2	4-2	3-1	*	6-3	3-0	6-0	2-0	4-2	0-1	0-1
6. Embleton Whinstone Rovers	1-8	7-0	2-2	1-3	1-4	*	2-0	1-1	1-1	4-2	4-6	1-0
7. Hedgeley Rovers	4-6	7-2	2-3	3-5	2-8	0-1	*	2-1	3-3	1-4	2-6	3-3
8. Longhoughton	2-7	3-1	2-2	3-0	1-2	1-2	1-0	*	3-2	4-1	2-4	1-0
9. Lowick Reserves	0-11	2-1	1-6	1-1	1-4	3-5	0-0	2-1	*	4-2	1-12	4-3
10. Rothbury Reserves	1-6	2-1	1-6	2-11	0-4	4-3	0-2	5-5	2-5	*	2-5	2-3
11. Stobhill Rangers	2-3	10-1	5-1	2-4	1-2	5-1	7-1	8-1	6-2	8-1	*	4-2
12. Wooler	3-3	3-0	0-3	3-3	2-2	1-3	3-2	4-1	3-0	8-0	1-0	*

BILCLOUGH CUP 1993-94

First Round

Lowick Reserves v Wallington	1-7	Alnmouth Reserves v Chevington Red Row	4-2
Wooler v Belford	2-0	Berwick Allan Brothers v Ashington Town	0-4
Craster Rovers v Alnmouth	0-1	Amble Vikings v Rothbury Reserves	6-2
North Sunderland v Rothbury	0-1	Springhill v Lowick	5-2

Second Round

Alnmouth Reserves v Wallington	0-10	Amble Vikings v Alnwick Town Reserves	0-1
Rothbury v Stobhill Rangers	2-0	Wooler v Spittal Rovers 'A'	1-2
Longhoughton v Alnmouth	3-4	Springhill v Berwick Harrow	3-2

Quarter-Finals

Wallington v Alnmouth	1-2	Alnwick T. Res. v Embleton Whinstone Rovers	3-0
Rothbury v Spittal Rovers 'A'	2-0	Hedgeley Rovers v Springhill	1-2

Semi-Finals

Alnmouth v Rothbury	1-2	Springhill v Alnwick Town Reserves	3-1

Final: Springhill 2, Rothbury 1 *(after 2-2 draw)*

SANDERSON CUP 1993-94

First Round

Alnwick Town Reserves v Belford	4-0	Spittal Rovers 'A' v Alnmouth	5-4
Amble Vikings v Springhill	3-1	Lowick v Wallington	3-1

Quarter-Finals

Amble Vikings v Lowick	1-3	Spittal Rovers 'A' v Alnwick T. Reserves	3-2
Berwick Harrow v Rothbury	2-1	North Sunderland *(bye)*	

Semi-Finals

N Sunderland v Berwick H.	1-1,1-1*(BH on pens)*	Lowick v Spittal Rovers 'A'	1-2

Final: Spittal Rovers 'A' 3, Berwick Harrow 2

ANDERSON CUP 1993-94

First Round (Two-legged ties)

Wallington v Springhill	0-1,1-3	Nth Sunderland v Alnwick Res.	2-1,0-1*(NS on pens)*
Spittal Rovers 'A' v Rothbury	1-4,3-5	Belford *(w/o)* Ashington Town *(scr)*	

Quarter-Finals (Two-legged)

Rothbury v North Sunderland	2-2,1-3	Lowick v Springhill	1-1,2-1
Berwick Harrow v Amble Vikings	1-5,1-5	Alnmouth v Belford	1-1,0-1

Semi-Finals

Lowick v North Sunderland	1-3	Amble Vikings v Belford	2-1

Final: Amble Vikins 3, North Sunderland 1

RUNCIMAN CUP 1993-94

First Round

Berwick Allan Brothers v Hedgeley Rovers	6-1	Chevington Red Row v Wooler	6-2
Longhoughton v Lowick Reserves	7-1		

Quarter-Finals

Berwick Allan Brothers v Craster Rovers	0-3	Embleton Whinstone Rovers v Rothbury Reserves	2-1
Chevington Red Row v Alnmouth Reserves	14-3	Stobhill Rangers v Longhoughton	5-2

Semi-Finals

Craster Rovers v Stobhill Rangers	3-2	Embleton Whinstone Rovers v Chevington Red Row	3-2

Final: Embleton Whinstone Rovers 2, Craster Rovers 1 *(after 2-2 draw)*

ROBSON CUP 1993-94

First Round (Two-legged ties)

Alnmouth Reserves v Longhoughton	1-4,3-6	Hedgley Rovers v Berwick Allan Brothers	2-2,1-8
Stobhill Rangers v Lowick Reserves	4-2,1-0		

Quarter-Finals (Two-legged)

Craster Rovers v Embleton Whinstone R.	3-1,3-2	Stobhill Rangers v Wooler	5-1,0-3
Berwick Allan Brothers v Longhoughton	5-0,3-0	Chevington Red Row v Rothbury Reserves	5-1,5-2

Semi-Finals

Craster Rovers v Chevington Red Row	2-5	Berwick Allan Brothers v Stobhill Rangers	0-2

Final: Stobhill Rangers 3, Chevington Red Row 1

Ashington FC of the Federation Brewery Northern League, one of Northumberland most famous teams.
Photo - Gavin Ellis-Neville.

TSB BANK HEXHAM & NORTH TYNE LEAGUE

BY DAVID WALTON

TSB Hexham & North Tyne League reigning champions Hexham Town signed a sponsorship deal with local insurance company Border Counties and promptly changed their name to Hexham Border Counties. After a slow start, the team's class showed and they completed a League and Cup double and just missed out on the treble, losing to Haltwhistle Crown Paints 'A' in the Clayton Charity Cup final.

Three points were awarded for a win for the first time in this League. Hexham Border Counties were pushed all the way by Haltwhistle Red Star, but the latter lost their chance of the title with defeats at Hexhamshire and Corbridge although they were the only team to beat Border Counties in the league for eighteen months.

In the League Cup there were some good First Round matches with both Corbridge United and Hexhamshire, trailing from the first legs, coming good in the second legs to overcome Whitfield and Haltwhistle Red Star respectively. Hexham Border Counties brought Corbridge's gallant fight to an end in the semi-final. Wwith the score 2-2, Border Counties scored three times in the second period of extra-time to win 5-2, and went on to beat Haltwhistle CP 'A' in the final.

The same teams contested the Clayton Cup final, but Haltwhistle Crown Paints 'A' gained some revenge winning 3-1 although things may have been different if Rutherford had converted an 80th minute penalty for Border Counties.

Crown Berger were again the sponsors of the League Knockout Cup which saw Corbridge United 3-2 winners over Hexhamshire after extra-time thanks to a last minute penalty equaliser by Gardner; United grabbed the winner with only two minutes of extra-time left, Robert Noble scoring.

There was a new format for the Subsidiary Cup when the League joined the North Eastern Amateur League for an Inter-League Cup called the Hexham Challenge. North Eastern Amateur League clubs had the better of things and there seemed to be a great gulf in standards between the two Leagues. Haydon Bridge and Haltwhistle Crown Paints 'A' made the semi-finals, but were both well beaten.

The League were dealt a severe blow in November when Rochester resigned due to lack of players, leaving the league with only seven member clubs. Rochester rejoined the League in 1989 after an absence of nine years - they were the last club left from the North Tyne League. Between 1976 and 1978 they won three League Championships, losing only six times in those three seasons.

Hexham Border Counties have been elected to the Courage Northern Alliance League for next season. Alston Moor's application will be considered at the League AGM, and it is hoped that another two teams may join the League for the 1994/95 season.

FINAL TABLE

	P	W	D	L	F	A	PTS
Hexham Border Co's	12	10	0	2	47	27	30
Haltwhistle Red Star	12	7	2	3	36	22	23
Haltwhistle CP 'A'	12	6	0	6	26	27	18
Corbridge Utd	12	5	1	6	29	30	16
Hexhamshire	12	5	0	7	25	34	15
Haydon Bridge	12	4	2	6	11	16	14
Whitfield	12	1	1	10	15	39	4

RESULT GRID

Corbridge Utd	*	1-3	4-2	1-0	1-8	6-3	2-3
Haltwhistle CP 'A'	4-0	*	0-2	1-0	5-7	1-2	3-1
Haltwhistle Red Star	3-1	5-2	*	1-1	7-2	3-2	7-3
Haydon Bridge	0-0	0-1	1-0	*	1-4	4-2	2-1
Hexham Border Co's	3-2	3-2	2-3	2-1	*	2-1	5-2
Hexhamshire	1-5	2-3	3-2	3-0	1-4	*	2-0
Whitfield	0-6	3-4	1-1	0-1	1-5	1-2	*

CLAYTON CHARITY CUP

1st Round

Hexham Border Co's v Corbridge Utd	4-1
Haydon Bridge v Hexhamshire	0-1
Whitfield v Haltwhistle Red Star	2-4
Haltwhisite Crown Paints 'A' *(bye)*	

Semi-Finals

Hexhamshire v Haltwhistle CP 'A'	0-1
Haltwhistle RS v Hexham Border Counties	6-8

Final

Haltwhistle CP 'A' v Hexham Border Counties 3-1
Haltwhistle scorers: Armstrong 54m 89m, J Thompson 3m.
Hexham Border C. scorer: White 87m.

LEAGUE CHALLENGE CUP

1st Round	1st Leg	2nd Leg
Whitfield v Corbridge Utd	3-1	2-5
Haltwhistle RS v Hexhamshire	2-0	2-6
Haltwhistle CP 'A' v Haydon Bdge	0-0	2-0
Rochester *(scr)* Hexham Border Co's *(w/o)*		

Semi-Finals

Haltwhistle CP 'A' v Hexhamshire	4-1
Hexham Border C. v Corbridge Utd	5-2

Final

Hexham Border Co's v Haltwhistle CP 'A' 2-1
Hexham Border C. scorers: Marsden 36m, Smith 82m(p)
Haltwhistle scorer: Armstrong 89m.

CROWN BERGER KNOCKOUT CUP

Semi-Finals

Hexhamshire v Whitfield	3-2
Haydon Bridge v Corbridge United	2-5

Final

Corbridge Utd v Hexhamshire 3-2*(aet)*
Corbridge scorers: Kiery 20m, Gardner 89m, R Noble 118m.
Hexhamshire scorers: Scandle 65m 85m(p)

NOTTINGHAMSHIRE F.A.

Secretary: W T Annable,
7 Clarendon Street, Nottingham NG1 5HS (0602 418954).

SENIOR CUP 1993-94

First Round

John Player v Radford	3-5
Nuthall v Arnold Town	0-7
Sneinton v Gedling Town	3-2
Cotgrave Colliery v Ashfield United	0-3
Dunkirk v Radcliffe Olympic	7-1
Pelican v Ruddington	5-0
Kimberley Town v Clipstone Welfare	2-4
Wollaton v Basford United	0-1
Notts Police v Bulwell Forest Villa	2-1
Attenborough v City & Sherwood Hospital	3-1
GPT v Eastwood Town	0-2
Rainworth Miners Welfare v Hucknall Rolls Royce	3-1
Oakham United v Hucknall Town	3-4
Thoresby Colliery Welf. v Greenwood Meadows	0-1
Blidworth Welfare v Boots Athletic	1-5
Worthington Simpson v Priory (Eastwood)	4-0

Second Round

Sneinton v Ashfield Utd	0-0*(7-6 on penalties)*
Worthington Simpsons v Radford	1-4
Attenborough v Boots Athletic	2-4
Pelican v Dunkirk	3-2
Greenwood Meadows v Eastwood Town	2-4
Rainworth Miners Welfare v Hucknall Town	4-3
Clipstone Welfare v Notts Police	4-3
Arnold Town v Basford United	0-1

Quarter-Finals

Eastwood Town v Boots Athletic	0-1
Pelican v Rainworth Miners Welfare	2-0
Basford United v Sneinton	0-4
Clipstone Welfare v Radford	2-1

Semi-Finals

Clipstone Welfare v Sneinton	5-1*(aet)*
Pelican v Boots Athletic	1-1*(5-6 on penalties)*

Final *(Wed 27th April, at Eastwood Town FC)*: Clipstone Welfare 3, Boots Athletic 2

INTERMEDIATE CUP: Winners: Linby Colliery Welfare

MANULIFE
NOTTS FOOTBALL ALLIANCE

Established: 1894

President: R J Leafe

Chairman: A Wright **Vice-Chairman:** Bryn Richards

Secretary: E R Rudd, 18 Whitegate Vale,
Clifton Estate, Nottingham (0602 216382).

This season has been one of the best in my time as Secretary and Registrar dating back to the 1971 campaign. The outstanding performance was by Clipstone Miners Welfare in winning the treble of Nottinghamshire Senior Cup and the Notts Alliance championship and Senior Cup (beating Pelican in the final). Credit goes to manager John Slater and his team.

Neighbours Rainworth Miners Welfare did the treble in 1981 with John Slater in the side - Slater played in their team at Wembley that season when Rainworth were beaten 3-0 by Forest Green Rovers in the FA Vase final.

Another outstanding team was Dunkirk who reached the last sixteen of the FA Vase where they went down 0-2 to Tiverton Town. Dunkirk had enjoyed some cracking games throughout their run.

Linby Colliery Welfare won the Nottinghamshire Intermediate Cup by Sherwood Amateurs 2-1, whilst Welbeck Colliery, a new club to the League, gained a double in winning the Division Two title and beating holders Worthington Simpsons 3-2 in the final of the Alliance Intermediate Cup.

John Player, after beating relegated last season, fought back to take the Division One title, though only goal difference lifted them above Basford United.

E R Rudd, Hon. Secretary.

SENIOR DIV.	P	W	D	L	F	A	PTS
Clipstone MW	30	20	4	6	88	36	64
Rainworth MW	30	20	2	8	70	28	62
Ruddington	30	15	7	8	66	53	52
Dunkirk	30	14	8	8	68	46	50
Notts Police	30	13	9	8	47	32	48
Boots Athletic	30	13	6	11	63	44	45
GPT	30	11	8	11	53	41	41
Sneinton	30	13	6	11	59	55	**39
Pelican	30	10	9	11	42	50	39
Wollaton	30	10	8	12	57	55	38
Worthington Sim.	30	10	7	13	50	68	37
Cotgrave CW	30	9	9	12	36	49	36
Greenwood Meadows	30	9	5	16	27	57	32
Hucknall RR Welf.	30	9	3	18	42	69	30
Thorseby CW	30	8	5	17	39	72	29
Bulwell Forest V.	30	4	8	18	31	83	20

DIVISION ONE	P	W	D	L	F	A	PTS
John Player	30	21	3	6	93	40	66
Basford Utd	30	20	6	4	65	22	66
Awsworth Villa	30	20	1	9	89	48	61
Southwell City	30	19	2	9	76	47	59
Ollerton & Bever.	30	17	5	8	56	38	56
Keyworth United	30	15	9	6	56	38	51
Worthington S. Res.	30	14	4	12	80	87	46
Linby Colliery W.	30	13	5	12	51	47	44
Clipstone MW Res.	30	9	10	11	42	45	37
Radcliffe Olympic	30	10	7	13	48	63	37
Gedling CW	30	10	5	15	55	61	*32
Bilsthorpe CW	30	6	10	14	50	61	28
Stapleford Villa	30	5	8	17	39	75	23
City Sherwood Hos.	30	5	8	17	40	79	23
Carlton Athletic	30	4	7	19	46	93	19
Hucknall RRW Res.	30	5	6	19	28	70	*18

* - 3 points deducted

DIVISION TWO	P	W	D	L	F	A	PTS
Welbeck Colliery W.	32	23	6	3	111	35	75
Boots Athletic	32	21	6	5	79	29	69
Bestwood MW	32	19	4	9	69	38	61
Clifton All Whites	32	17	6	9	70	42	57
Fairham	32	16	6	10	74	48	54
Dunkirk Res.	32	13	12	7	81	64	51
Rainworth MW Res.	32	14	8	10	76	57	50
Attenborough	32	15	4	13	62	53	49
Abacus	32	13	7	12	77	71	46
Retford United	32	11	8	13	64	55	41
Teversal Grange	32	11	6	15	69	72	39
Pelican Res.	32	10	9	13	43	75	39
Ruddington Res.	32	11	2	19	55	74	35
Calverton CW	32	8	5	19	52	86	29
GPT Res.	32	8	4	20	52	98	28
John Player Res.	32	5	8	19	46	95	23
Greenwood M. Res.	32	5	3	24	37	126	*15

SENIOR DIVISION RESULTS	1	2	3	4	5	6	7	8	9	10	11	12	13	14	15	16
1. Boots Athletic	*	2-1	0-1	3-1	1-4	0-0	2-3	6-1	0-1	1-2	1-1	4-2	8-1	3-4	4-1	1-2
2. Bulwell Forest Villa	1-2	*	1-1	0-1	0-2	0-0	0-0	2-1	1-0	1-1	0-5	1-3	0-3	2-3	2-2	1-1
3. Clipstone Miners Welfare	3-1	9-0	*	3-0	2-1	1-0	3-0	6-1	2-1	1-2	1-3	7-0	5-2	5-1	4-2	1-1
4. Cotgrave Colliery Welfare	1-1	4-2	1-5	*	3-3	3-2	0-0	4-2	1-0	3-1	1-0	1-1	2-2	0-2	0-0	3-2
5. Dunkirk	0-0	4-1	1-3	1-1	*	2-1	2-3	4-0	3-2	2-2	2-1	1-2	2-3	5-0	1-2	6-1
6. Greenwood Meadows	2-4	1-2	0-2	1-0	3-3	*	1-0	1-3	1-6	2-2	0-5	1-2	1-2	0-3	1-0	1-0
7. GPT	1-2	10-2	1-1	2-1	1-1	1-2	*	1-0	0-2	3-1	0-2	1-1	1-0	6-0	5-0	1-2
8. Hucknall Rolls Royce Welfare	0-5	4-2	2-5	0-0	0-1	1-0	3-0	*	0-1	0-0	2-3	2-5	1-0	3-1	3-2	1-2
9. Notts Police	1-1	3-3	2-1	2-1	1-0	1-0	1-1	2-1	*	2-0	1-1	1-1	3-1	1-1	1-1	1-2
10. Pelican	1-0	6-1	4-2	4-0	2-2	0-1	0-0	2-1	1-1	*	2-1	0-5	0-3	1-0	3-6	0-2
11. Rainworth Miners Welfare	1-2	2-0	1-3	1-2	4-1	0-1	3-0	3-0	1-0	2-1	*	1-0	1-2	3-0	2-1	5-0
12. Ruddington	0-3	4-0	2-1	2-0	3-5	4-0	3-4	0-1	3-1	1-1	0-4	*	1-1	2-0	1-1	4-1
13. Sneinton	2-1	2-0	3-1	1-1	3-3	5-0	1-0	2-1	2-3	0-0	2-4	4-5	*	3-2	1-1	4-0
14. Thoresby Colliery Welfare	4-2	1-1	0-5	2-1	0-1	0-3	0-0	3-3	0-3	0-1	1-5	0-2	3-0	*	1-4	5-3
15. Wollaton	0-0	4-1	2-3	2-0	0-2	5-0	0-5	1-3	1-1	3-1	2-3	2-3	4-2	2-0	*	2-2
16. Worthington Simpson	2-3	2-3	1-1	2-0	1-3	0-0	5-3	5-2	0-3	4-1	0-2	4-4	1-0	2-2	0-4	*

DIV. ONE RESULTS 1993-94	1	2	3	4	5	6	7	8	9	10	11	12	13	14	15	16
1. Awsworth Villa	*	1-2	4-2	4-1	2-0	3-2	5-2	3-0	0-1	4-0	4-2	1-1	1-2	5-1	3-1	5-3
2. Basford United	1-0	*	3-1	3-0	2-2	1-1	3-1	0-1	1-2	0-1	3-2	3-0	2-0	4-0	4-1	6-0
3. Bilsthorpe Colliery Welfare	2-1	1-2	*	6-1	3-3	1-1	1-1	1-1	0-2	1-0	2-2	0-2	0-1	0-1	3-1	4-6
4. Carlton Athletic	1-6	0-5	3-2	*	7-4	1-1	1-3	3-2	1-1	0-1	0-2	2-1	1-2	1-4	1-5	4-4
5. City & Sherwood Hospital	1-7	0-2	1-1	4-3	*	0-2	1-4	0-1	1-5	1-1	2-0	0-2	1-1	1-3	3-3	4-0
6. Clipstone MW Reserves	3-1	1-1	0-2	2-0	3-0	*	2-1	0-2	3-1	2-2	0-1	0-0	2-1	2-3	0-0	2-2
7. Gedling Colliery Welfare	2-4	1-2	3-3	4-0	4-1	1-1	*	0-0	2-5	0-3	2-0	0-1	0-0	1-4	4-1	5-1
8. Hucknall Rolls Royce Reserves	3-4	1-4	0-1	2-2	1-3	0-0	3-2	*	0-4	1-2	2-3	1-5	1-3	0-2	1-1	0-2
9. John Player	2-3	2-3	2-2	4-0	5-1	2-0	6-1	10-0	*	3-4	3-0	4-2	3-1	1-0	2-1	2-5
10. Keyworth United	2-0	0-0	2-2	1-1	4-0	7-1	0-1	1-1	1-2	*	2-1	1-1	1-1	3-2	5-2	3-2
11. Linby Colliery Welfare	3-6	0-1	2-1	2-0	0-3	2-0	3-1	1-0	1-0	2-2	*	1-2	2-0	5-0	1-1	7-2
12. Ollerton & Bevercotes Miners Welfare	2-1	0-0	5-3	4-2	1-0	3-0	2-1	0-1	1-3	2-1	2-1	*	2-2	0-1	4-2	0-1
13. Radcliffe Olympic	3-2	0-1	2-2	4-4	1-1	0-3	2-1	3-1	0-7	1-2	3-2	0-3	*	3-1	1-1	3-0
14. Southwell City	2-3	2-1	2-1	4-4	5-1	2-1	3-0	5-0	1-2	1-0	0-1	2-4	3-1	*	7-1	4-0
15. Stapleford Villa	1-3	0-0	2-1	1-0	1-1	0-4	1-2	2-0	2-2	0-2	2-2	2-4	3-2	0-2	*	1-5
16. Worthington Simpson Reserves	0-3	1-5	5-1	6-2	5-0	5-3	2-5	3-2	3-5	3-2	1-1	2-0	2-1	3-3	3-1	*

DIV. TWO RESULTS 1993-94	1	2	3	4	5	6	7	8	9	10	11	12	13	14	15	16	17
1. Abacus	*	5-2	0-6	2-3	4-3	3-3	9-0	1-4	7-2	5-1	5-1	3-1	3-3	4-1	0-2	2-2	1-6
2. Attenborough	1-1	*	2-1	1-4	1-0	1-3	0-2	3-0	4-0	3-2	4-0	1-1	2-1	2-1	3-1	3-0	6-2
3. Bestwood Miners Welfare	4-1	2-1	*	4-0	2-1	1-2	1-2	0-1	5-2	4-1	3-0	0-0	3-2	3-1	3-1	4-2	1-0
4. Boots Athletic Reserves	5-0	4-0	1-0	*	2-0	0-4	1-2	1-1	5-0	4-1	4-2	7-1	2-2	2-0	2-1	2-0	1-1
5. Calverton Colliery Welfare	2-0	1-0	0-2	0-0	*	0-5	4-3	1-2	1-1	4-2	4-1	1-2	1-5	1-4	0-2	4-0	0-3
6. Clifton All Whites	0-1	1-0	2-2	3-2	4-1	*	4-1	0-2	3-3	4-1	3-0	4-0	5-1	1-2	3-0	2-0	2-2
7. Dunkirk Reserves	1-1	2-0	1-1	0-0	6-2	1-1	*	2-2	6-2	2-3	3-3	0-0	1-1	2-2	4-3	4-2	3-3
8. Fairham	1-1	3-1	3-1	0-2	5-4	1-1	0-1	*	8-2	1-2	9-0	1-2	0-1	4-1	2-4	3-1	0-4
9. Greenwood Meadows Reserves	2-7	0-3	0-2	0-5	2-5	4-1	0-4	0-4	*	4-3	3-2	1-0	0-2	0-2	2-0	0-7	0-7
10. GPT Reserves	1-1	2-0	1-4	0-2	2-2	0-3	1-6	1-5	4-3	*	3-2	5-3	1-5	3-4	4-2	3-2	0-0
11. John Player Reserves	0-3	1-3	1-4	0-2	3-3	0-2	5-4	0-0	4-0	1-1	*	0-2	3-1	2-1	4-3	1-1	2-2
12. Pelican Reserves	1-2	2-3	1-0	1-1	2-2	2-1	0-8	2-1	3-3	2-1	1-1	*	3-2	1-0	1-3	2-4	1-7
13. Rainworth Miners Welf. Reserves	4-0	5-5	1-0	0-3	3-0	3-1	1-1	0-3	4-0	6-1	4-2	1-2	*	2-0	4-1	2-2	3-2
14. Retford United	1-0	1-1	1-1	0-3	10-0	2-0	2-2	1-3	9-0	2-0	2-2	2-2	3-3	*	1-1	4-1	0-1
15. Ruddington Reserves	1-3	0-3	1-2	1-5	1-3	3-1	0-2	1-3	2-0	5-1	3-0	1-1	3-2	4-1	*	3-2	1-2
16. Teversal Grange	4-2	3-2	2-3	0-3	2-1	0-1	5-2	1-1	4-1	5-1	6-2	4-1	1-1	1-2	2-0	*	2-2
17. Welbeck Colliery Welfare	3-0	2-1	4-0	2-1	5-1	2-1	5-3	6-1	3-0	2-0	6-1	5-0	3-1	3-1	8-1	8-1	*

N.b. British Rail Newark resigned.

SENIOR DIVISION CLUBS 1994-95

BASFORD UNITED

Secretary: Paul Dobson, 26 Chevin Gardens, Top Valley, Nottm NG5 9ES (0602 274790).
Ground & Directions: Greenwich Ave., Sports Ground, Bagnall Road, Basford, Nottm (0602 423918). M1 (J26) follow signs 'A610 Nottingham' then 'B6004 Arnold' into Mill Street.
Colours: Yellow/black **Hons:** Notts Snr Cup 46-47 87-88, Notts Alliance Div 1 R-up 71-72 84-85 93-94.

BOOTS ATHLETIC

Secretary: Ian Whitehead, 21 Rosthwaite Close, West Bridgford, Nottingham NG2 6RA (0602 812380).
Ground: Lady Bay, West Bridgford, Nottingham (0602 822392). **Colours:** Blue & white/black
Hons: Notts Alliance Div 1 91-92 (Lg Cup 91-92, Div 2 R-up(res) 93-94), Notts Snr Cup R-up 93-94, Notts Intermediate Cup R-up 91-92.

COTGRAVE COLLIERY WELFARE

Secretary: Kevin Cooper, 18 Hawthorn Avenue, Cotgrave, Nottm NG12 3PY (0602 893396).
Ground: Cotgrave Miners Welfare. **Colours:** Yellow/blue

DUNKIRK

Secretary: Mr John G Peck, 5 Thistledown Rd, Clifton, Nottm NG11 9DP (0602 842147).
Ground & Directions: The Ron Steel Sports Ground, Trentside Farm, Clifton Bridge, Nottingham (0602 850803). Ring Road - Clifton Bridge (North End), Industrial Estate, Lenton Lane.
Colours: Red/Black
Hons: Notts Alliance Div 1 84-85 (Div 2 82-83, Lg Cup R-up 84-85), Notts I'mediate Cup 83-84.

Dunkirk FC - who brought much credit to the Notts Alliance with their thrilling FA Vase run.
Photo - Gavin Ellis-Neville.

G.P.T.

Secretary: Roger Marshall, Sports Office, GPT, Beeston, Nottm (0602 433669).
Colours: All sky **Ground:** Trent Vale Rd, Beeston, Nottm (0602 258320)
Hons: Notts Alliance 66-67 91-92 (R-up 92-93, Lg Cup 92-93).

GREENWOOD MEADOWS

Secretary: Eric Rust, 27 Turney Street, The Meadows, Nottm NG2 2LG (0602 528363).
Ground: Lenton Lane, Clifton Bridge, Nottm (0602 865913) **Colours:** Black & white.

HUCKNALL ROLLS ROYCE WELFARE

Secretary: Adrian Ward, 7 Redwood Court, Hucknall, Nottm (0602 637538).
Ground: Sports and Social Club, Entrance Watnall Road (0602 630134).
Colours: Yellow/burgundy/burgundy **Hons:** Notts I'mediate Cup 92-93

JOHN PLAYER

Secretary: Ron Walton, 27 St Margarets Ave., Aspley Lane, Nottm NG8 5GD (0602 292027).
Ground & Directions: Aspley Lane, Nottm (0602 294244). Corner of Nottingham ring road B690 turn towards City Centre.
Colours: Green & gold/green/green.
Hons: Notts Alliance 21-22 22-23 23-24 24-25 25-26 26-27 67-68 68-69 69-70 85-86 89-90 (Div 1 93-94).

NOTTINGHAMSHIRE POLICE

Secretary: Mr Bob Fawcett, 21 Bird Close, Kingshaven, Mansfield, Notts NG18 4AZ (0632 636911).
Ground & Directions: Force Training School, Epperstone Manor, Notts. On A60 Mansfield Road, on right from City Centre (2 miles).
Colours: White/black/black.
Hons: Notts Snr R-up 91-92, Notts All. Div 1 & Lge Snr Cup R-up 85-86, PAAN Nat. K-O Comp 63-64.

PELICAN

Secretary: Paul Asher, 14 Thaxted Close, Bilborough, Nottm NG8 4NG (0602 288625).
Ground: John Pearson Spts Ground, Lenton Lane, Nottm (0602 868255) **Colours:** All Blue.
Hons: Notts Alliance Lg Cup 90-91 (R-up 91-92 93-94).

RAINWORTH MINERS WELFARE

Secretary: Alan Wright, 10 Faraday Road, Mansfield NG18 4ES (0632 24379).
Ground & Directions: Kirklington Road, Rainworth. On A617 Mansfield - Newark Road.
Colours: All White
Hons: Notts Alliance 77-78 78-79 79-80 80-81 81-82 82-83 (R-up 93-94, Lg Cup 81-82), Notts Snr Cup 80-81 81-82 (R-up 82-83 92-93), FA Vase R-up 82-82, Thorn EMI F'lit Cup R-up 82-83 83-84 84-85.

RUDDINGTON UNITED

Secretary: John Fisk, 3 Savages Road, Ruddington, Nottm NG11 6EW (0602 842552).
Ground & Directions: The Elms Park Ground, Loughborough Road, Ruddington (0602 844976. On A60 Nottm to Loughborough, 5 miles out of Nottingham.
Previous Name: Ruddington FC (pre-1994).
Colours: Red & black/blue **Honours:** Notts Comb. Lg 79-80 (Lg Cup 70-71 76-77 80-81).

SNEINTON

Secretary: Paul Shelton, 28 Freda Close, Gedling, Nottm NG4 4GP (0602 877527).
Ground: Stoke Lane, Gedling, Nottingham. **Colours:** Blue & black stripes/black/black.
Hons: Notts Alliance Div 1 92-93, Notts Intermediate Cup 91-92.

THORESBY COLLIERY WELFARE

Secretary: Brian Wathall, 29 First Ave., Edwinstowe, Nr Mansfield NG21 9NZ (0632 823885).
Ground: Thoresby Colliery, Fourth Avenue, Edwinstowe, Nr Mansfield. **Colours:** Blue/navy

WOLLATON

Secretary: Andrew Moon, 150 Wollaton Vale, Wollaton, Nottm NG8 2PL (0602 287215).
Ground: Wollaton Sports Club, Wollaton Village, Nottm (0602 289748).
Colours: Sky/maroon **Hons:** Notts All. Div 1 R-up 92-93 (Div 2 91-92 (I'mediate Cup R-up 91-92)).

WORTHINGTON SIMPSONS

Secretary: Alan Toule, 54 Elterwater Drive, Gamston, Nottingham NG2 6PX (0602 810258).
Ground & Directions: Lowfields, off Hawton Lane, New Baldeton, Newark, Notts (0636 702672). From Newark, A6065 to Newark Hospital, right into Bowbridge Road, cont. 1 mile, left by timber yard, over bridge then right. From A1 (By-pass) A6065 Newark to lights. Ahead then left into Hawton Lane.
Colours: Maroon/sky **Hons:** Notts Alliance Lg Cup (Intermediate Cup(res) 92-93 (R-up 93-94)).

NOTTS ALLIANCE DIVISION ONE CLUBS 1994-95

AWSWORTH VILLA

Secretary: Keith Slaney, 24 Attewell Road, Awsworth, Nottm NG16 2SY (0602 302514).
Ground: Attewell Road, Awsworth. **Colours:** Yellow & black/black/yellow.

BESTWOOD MINERS WELFARE

Secretary: Mrs Alana Jackson, 9 Derwent Drive, Hucknall, Nottm NG15 6DS (0602 630189).
Ground: Bestwood Workshops, Park Rd, Bestwood (0602 273711) **Colours:** White/blue.

BILSTHORPE COLLIERY WELFARE

Secretary: Mr Les Lee, 42 Chapel Lane, Ravenshead, Mansfield NG15 9DA (0623 794442).
Ground: Bilsthorpe CW Ground, Eakring Road, Bilsthorpe. **Colours:** White/navy/navy.

CARLTON ATHLETIC

Secretary: Mr Roy Loach, 47 Fraser Rd, Carlton, Nottingham NG4 1NP (0602 872072).
Ground: Carlton Hill, Recreation Ground, Carlton (0602 615689). **Colours:** White/black

CITY & SHERWOOD HOSPITALS

Secretary: Mr Alan Bird, 72 Bilborough Rd, Nottm NG8 4DW (0602 285507).
Ground: COD Military Ground, Chilwell (0602 254811). **Colours:** All Royal blue

CLIFTON

Secretary: Keith Elliott, 61 Greencroft, Clifton Est., Nottm NG11 8GT (0602 215401).
Ground & Directions: Green Lane, Clifton Est., Nottm (0602 844903). Off A6005 Nottingham - Long Eaton Road.
Previous Name: Clifton All Whites (pre-1994).
Colours: All white **Hons:** Notts Alliance Div 1

GEDLING COLLIERY WELFARE

Secretary: Mrs Maureen Chambers, 8 Fraser Road, Carlton, Nottm NG4 1NJ (0602 612994).
Ground: Gedling Colliery Welfare, Plains Road, Mapperley (0602 266300) **Colours:** Yellow/blue

KEYWORTH UNITED

Secretary: Maurice G Simpson, 25 Waddington Drive, Wilford Hill, West Bridgford, Nottm NG2 7GT (0602 232921).
Ground: Platt Lane, Keyworth (0607 375998). **Colours:** Green/black

LINBY COLLIERY MINERS WELFARE

Secretary: D G Dickens, 4 Old Mill Close, Bestwood, Nottingham, NG6 8TA (0602 276598).
Ground: Church Lane, Linby **Colours:** Red/White
Hons: Notts Alliance Div 2 R-up 92-93, Notts Intermediate Cup 93-94.

OLLERTON & BEVERCOTES MINERS WELFARE

Secretary: Mr Jack Graham, 77 Petersmith Drive, New Ollerton, Newark NG22 9SD (0623 863127).
Ground: Walesby Lane, New Ollerton. **Colours:** Amber/black
Honours: Notts Alliance Div 2 92-93.

RADCLIFFE OLYMPIC

Secretary: C Johnson, 2 The Firs, Holme Pierrepont, Radcliffe-on-Trent NG12 2LT (0602 333791).
Ground: Wharf Lane, Radcliffe-on-Trent. **Colours:** Blue/red.

SOUTHWELL CITY

Secretary: P K Johnson, 63 The Ropewalk, Southwell, Notts NG25 0AL (0636 814386).
Ground: War Memorial Ground, Southwell (0636 4386) **Colours:** Black & white stripes/black

STAPLEFORD VILLA

Secretary: Mr Clyde Davis, 25 Grace Drive, Aspley, Nottm NG8 5AG (0602 290529).
Ground: Bramcote Park, Ilkeston Rd Entrance. **Colours:** White & blue/blue

WELBECK COLLIERY

Secretary: Mr Ron Turner, 1 Newcastle Str., Warsop, Mansfield, Notts NG20 0NQ (0623 846244).
Ground: Welbeck Colliery Pit (0623 842611). **Colours:** White/black.
Hons: Notts Alliance Div 2 93-94 (Intermediate Cup 93-94), Chesterfield & District Lg 92-93.

This Division also includes the Reserve sides of: Boots Athletic and Worthington Simpsons.

NOTTS ALLIANCE DIVISION TWO CLUBS 1994-95

ABACUS

Secretary: Mr Stephen Bingley, 6 Brisbane Close, Mansfield Woodhouse NG19 8QZ (0623 23072).
Ground: Sherwood Colliery Sports Ground, Debdale Lane, Mansfield Woodhouse, Notts.
Colours: Black & white stripes.

ATTENBOROUGH

Secretary: Terry Allen, 3 Firth Close, Arnold, Nottingham NG5 8RU (0602 200698).
Ground & Directions: The Village Green, The Strand, Attenborough, Beeston, Nottingham. Midway between Beeston & Long Eaton on A6005 - adjacent to Nature Reserve (via Attenborough Lane).
Colours: All blue **Change cols:** White/black/black. **Previous Lge:** Central Mids (pre-1992)

CALVERTON COLLIERY WELFARE

Secretary: Mr Mick Rippon, Cherry Tree, Collyer Rd, Calverton, Nottm (0602 655026).
Ground: Calverton MW Rec. Centre (0602 654390) **Colours:** White/blue/white.

RETFORD UNITED

Secretary: Jeff Lamb, 18 Northumbria Drive, Retford, Notts, DN22 7PR (0602 705833).
Ground: Oaklands Lane (Off London Road), Retford, (enter via Caledonian Road).
Colours: Black & white stripes/black

TEVERSAL GRANGE

Secretary: Kevin Newton, 8 Vere Ave., Sutton in Ashfield, Notts NG17 2ES (0623 511402).
Ground: Carnarvon Street, Sutton in Ashfield. **Colours:** Red & black hoops/red/red.

This Division also includes the Reserve sides of: Dunkirk, GPT, Hucknall Rolls Royce Welfare, John Player, Pelican, Rainworth Miner Welfare, Ruddington United.

Right: *Edge of the area action from Boots Athletic Reserves' 5-0 win away to Greenwood Meadows Reserves on 5th February.*
Photo - Gavin Ellis-Neville.

LONG EATON SUNDAY LEAGUE

FOUNDED: 1970

PREM. DIV.	P	W	D	L	F	A	PTS
Grandstand '83	24	18	2	4	73	23	56
Stapleford Con Rgrs	24	17	5	2	78	32	56
Stapleford Boro.	24	17	2	5	76	34	53
Sandiacre Town	24	16	3	5	84	33	51
Castle Donnington	24	12	6	6	55	45	42
Sportsman	24	13	2	9	56	34	41
Bracken Park	24	7	6	11	35	37	27
Railway	24	6	7	11	28	47	***22
Squires United	24	5	6	13	38	59	21
Ladywood	24	5	6	13	26	55	21
Barge	24	7	3	14	38	68	*21
Athletica	24	4	3	17	27	78	15
Greenwich Albion	24	3	1	20	19	86	10

* - 3 points deducted

Lower Division Champions:
Div. 1 (13): Carson Athletic
Div. 2 (14): Longmoor Plough
Div. 3 (14): Olympic
Div. 4 (13): Melfin Sports

Cup Finals:
Snowball: Grandstand '83 3, Stapleford Con. Rangers 2 *(aet)*
Premier: Sandiacre Town 3, Grandstand '83 0
Senior: Attenborough Cavs 2, Longmoor Plough 0
Junior: Ladywood Res. 2, Sutton Acads 1

NOTTINGHAMSHIRE SUNDAY LGE

FOUNDED: 1956

PREM. DIV.	P	W	D	L	F	A	PTS
Rolls Royce Celtic	22	17	4	1	64	20	55
Jolly Farmers	22	17	2	3	68	25	53
Spot On	22	13	4	5	45	24	48
Phoenix	22	11	6	5	54	40	39
Clifton Albion	22	12	3	7	52	49	39
Cotgrave Welf. Sun.	22	8	2	12	34	45	26
AD Bulwell	22	7	3	12	39	50	24
Grange	22	6	6	10	44	59	24
Radford Park Rgrs	22	6	4	12	38	58	22
Gedling United	22	4	6	12	27	47	18
Bingham Town	22	2	7	13	28	54	13
Clumber	22	2	7	13	24	46	*10

* - 3 points deducted

Lower Division Champions:
Premier Div. 1 (12): Poets Corner
Premier Div. 2 (11): Earl Decorators
Premier Div. 3 (11): Robin Hood & LJ
Premier Div. 4 (11): Windsor
Senior Div. 1 (12): Clifton Albion Res.
Senior Div. 2 (11): Redhill
Senior Div. 3 (12): Keyworth Tavern
Senior Div. 4 (11): Sunday Post
Intermediate Div. 1 (12): John Barleycorn
Intermediate Div. 2 (12): Highbury Vale
Intermediate Div. 3 (12): Crusaders
Intermediate Div. 4 (11): Dale
Intermediate Div. 5 (12): Carlton Valley Rovers
Junior Div. 1 (12): Olympic Shaver Centre
Junior Div. 2 (11): Beeston White Lion
Junior Div. 3 (12): The Beechos
Junior Div. 4 (12): Marks & Spencer
Junior Div. 5 (12): Waggon & Horses
Afternoon Prem. Div. (5): Friary Rovers
Afternoon Div. (6): Fox & Hounds Blidworth

Majestic Cup: Rolls Royce Celtic (r-up: Clifton Alb.)
Secretary of the Year: G Mascia (Al Italia)
Top Scorer: N Blanchard (Windsor)

NON-LEAGUE FOOTBALL RESULTS MAGAZINE

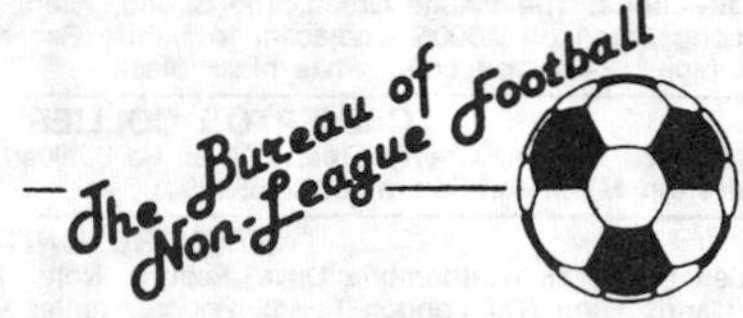

The Country's Longest Running National Non-League Football Monthly Magazine

Nearing its Fifteenth Year, BNLF is by far the most established and up to-date for Tables and Results each month covering the whole of the non-league Pyramid, including Scotland & Wales. Continually published since 1981 it has proven track record second to none Regularly features over 50/60 Tables, All the COUNTY FA SENIOR CUP draws & results, plus regular up-dates & news snippets.

INCLUDING ALL THE F A CUP, TROPHY & VASE, SCOTTISH JUNIOR CUP, WELSH CUP & TROPHY, DRAWS & RESULTS THROUGHOUT THE SEASON

MIDLANDS / SOUTH WEST / NORTH EAST
SOUTH EAST / NORTH WEST

Are You Missing Out ?
Stay on the Ball with The BNLF. 1994-95 Subscription £16-00

August to June Inc. Start your subscription when you like, The seasons back issues available if required.

Previous Seasons issues also available - Send your Name & address Now To;-

THE BUREAU OF NON-LEAGUE FOOTBALL
173,LEYTONSTONE ROAD,LONDON, E15 1LH.

OXFORDSHIRE F.A.

Secretary: Mr P J Ladbrook,
3 Wilkins Rd, Cowley, Oxford OX4 2HY.

SENIOR CUP 1993-94

First Round

Launton Sports v Yarnton 4-1
Ardley United v Clanfield '85 2-1
Blackbird Leys *(scr)* Henley Town *(w/o)*
Oxford University Press v Pressed Steel 5-4
Worcester College Old Boys v Peppard 0-3
Bicester Town *(w/o)* Chipping Norton Town *(scr)*
Quarry Nomads v Easington Sports 5-4
Eynsham v Kidlington 2-1

Second Round

Ardley United v Banbury United 0-2
Oxford University Press v Peppard 0-1
Eynshan v Garsington 1-2
Oxford City v Bicester Town 2-0
Bletchington v Headington Amateurs 1-2
Watlington v Old Woodstock 1-4
North Leigh v Henley Town 3-1
Quarry Nomads v Chinnor 3-1
Carterton Town v Launton Sports 2-0*(aet)*
AP Sports v Woodstock Town 0-5

Third Round

Banbury United v Woodstock Town 9-1
North Leigh v Carterton Town 0-2
Garsington v Peppard 0-5
Oxford City v Old Woodstock 6-2
Headington Amtrs v Quarry N. 2-0*(H'ton expelled)*

Quarter-Finals

Quarry Nomads v Witney Town 1-3*(aet)*
Banbury United v Oxford City 0-1
Carterton Town v Oxford United 1-0*(aet)*
Peppard v Thame United 2-0

Semi-Finals

Carterton Town v Witney Town 1-2
Oxford City v Peppard 1-1,1-3

Final *(at Oxford United FC, Wed 27th April)*: Witney Town 1, Peppard 0

CHARITY CUP First Round

Ruscote Sports v Woodstock Town 5-0
Quarry Nomads v Launton Sports 0-2
Hook Norton v AP Sports & Social 5-1
Chadlington v Old Woodstock 4-1
Oxford University Press v Wheatley United 3-2
Worcester College Old Boys v Adderbury 8-1
Pressed Steel Fisher v Barton Youth 5-1
West Witney v Wardington 11-0
Hanborough v Charlton United 3-0
KEA United v Blackbird Leys ASC 4-5

First Round

Ruscote United v West Witney 2-6
Watlington v Brize Norton 2-1
Pressed Steel Fisher v Chadlington 3-0
Garsington v Launton Sports 4-2
Worcester College Old Boys v Milcombe 3-1
Bletchington v Hanborough 0-2
Oxford University Press v Blackbird Leys ASC 3-1
Hook Norton v Eynsham 2-1

Quarter-Finals

Hanborough v Oxford University Press 2-4
West Witney v Pressed Steel Fisher 5-2
Watlington v Worcester College Old Boys 0-3
Hook Norton v Garsington 1-0

Semi-Finals

West Witney v Oxford University Press 6-2
Hook Norton v Worcester College Old Boys 1-0

Final *(at Oxford University Press FC, Mon 2nd May)*: West Witney 2, Hook Norton 0

INTERMEDIATE CUP Preliminary Round

Clanfield '85 Res. v Ardley United Res. 1-2
Launton Sports Res. v Thame United Res. 2-4
Newtown Henley v Sonning Common 2-3
Quarry Nomads Res. v Nettlebed United 5-4
Charlton United Res. v Bicester Civil Service 1-2
Benson Amateurs v Watlington Res. 0-1
Woodstock Town Res. v Chinnor Res. 0-2
Headington Amtrs Res. v Salesians 4-2
Eynsham Res. v Checkendon Sports 0-7

First Round

Worcester College Old Boys Res. *(bye)*
Bletchington Res. v Headington Amtrs Res. 0-6
Oxford Univ. P. Res. v Thame United Res. 1-7
Woodcote v Marlborough 1-0
Easington Spts Res. v Marston Saints 0-5
AP Spts & Soc. Res. v Old Woodstock Res. 3-2
Garsington Res. v Oxford City Res. 1-6
North Leigh Res. v Kidlington Res. 4-1
Berinsfield v Checkendon Sports 4-3
Bicester Civil Service v Bicester Town Res. 2-4
Ardley United Res. v Wheatley United 4-1
Yarnton Res. v Sonning Common 3-5
John Radcliffe v Carterton Town Res. 2-3
Henley Town Res. v Chinnor Res. 2-1
Peppard Res. v Quarry Nomads Res. 6-1
Watlington v Witney Town Res. 0-2

Second Round

North Leigh Res. v Ardley United Res. 3-0
AP Sports & Soc. Res. v Carterton T. Res. 1-7
Henley Town Res. v Thame United Res. 3-1
Sonning Common v Bicester Town Res. 3-2
Witney Town Res. v Berinsfield 2-8
Woodcote v Marston Saints 3-1
Headington Amtrs Res. v Oxford City Res. 0-3
Peppard Res. v Worcester College Old Boys Res. 5-0

Quarter-Finals

Carterton Town Res. v Woodcote Res. 2-1
Peppard Res. v Henley Town Res. 8-0
Berinsfield v Sonning Common 2-1
Oxford City Res. v North Leigh Res. 6-1

Semi-Finals

Carterton Town Res. v Berinsfield 4-2
Oxford City Res. v Peppard Res. 2-1

Final *(at Witney Town FC, Thurs 5th May)*: Oxford City Reserves 8, Carterton Town Reserves 0

OTHER COUNTY FINALS

Junior Shield *(at Oxford City FC, Sat 23rd April)*: Hook Norton 2, Brize Norton 1
Sam Waters Sunday Cup *(at Oxford City FC, Sun 10th April)*: Deddington Town 4, Chinnor Exiles 0

OXFORDSHIRE SENIOR LEAGUE

President: Mr R A Brock.
Chairman: Mr G Hayes.
Hon. Secretary: Mr K Rogers,
65 Bagley Close, Kennington, Oxford OX1 5LT (0865 739173)

PREM. DIVISION	P	W	D	L	F	A	PTS
Quarry Nomads	26	16	7	3	76	25	55
Old Woodstock	26	16	5	5	72	28	53
Garsington	26	15	6	5	65	24	51
Oakley United	26	14	9	3	57	22	51
AP Spts & Social	26	15	6	5	74	43	51
Launton Sports	26	14	6	6	58	32	48
Pressed Steel	26	11	8	7	39	29	41
Worcester COB	26	10	5	11	49	42	35
Oxford UP	26	9	6	11	45	46	33
Woodstock Town	26	8	4	14	54	54	28
Eynsham	26	7	4	15	46	66	25
Watlington	26	5	7	14	40	57	22
Bletchington	26	3	3	20	21	70	12
Blackbird Leys	26	1	0	25	22	179	3

Division One	P	W	D	L	F	A	PTS
Kennington Utd	26	20	2	4	86	19	62
Wheatley United	26	19	3	4	81	32	60
Long Crendon	26	19	0	7	66	29	57
Marlborough	26	15	6	5	66	33	51
Bicester CS	26	14	4	8	76	70	46
Marston Saints	26	11	4	11	72	54	37
Garsington	26	10	5	11	55	60	35
John Radcliffe	26	11	1	14	57	71	34
W'cester COB Res	26	9	4	13	37	62	31
Quarry Nomads Res	26	8	5	13	50	53	29
Charlton United	26	6	6	14	46	67	24
Woodstock T. Res	26	7	1	18	44	92	22
Salesians Res	26	4	6	16	28	66	18
Eynsham Res.	26	4	3	19	34	90	15

Division Two	P	W	D	L	F	A	PTS
Kennington Res	28	22	4	2	94	33	70
Old Woodstock Res	28	21	6	1	102	22	69
Marston Sts Res	28	18	5	5	82	36	59
AP Spts & Soc. Res	28	17	3	8	86	39	54
Launton Spts Res	28	12	9	7	72	49	45
Bletchington Res	28	14	3	11	71	58	45
Oxford UP Res	28	13	5	10	73	47	44
Lg Crendon Res	28	11	3	14	46	55	36
John R'cliffe Res	28	9	3	16	47	82	30
Marlborough Res	28	7	7	14	52	75	28
Watlington Res	28	8	3	17	43	61	27
Salesians Res	28	8	3	17	33	70	27
Bicester CS Res	28	8	2	18	55	100	26
Oakley Utd Res	28	7	2	19	51	100	23
Charlton Utd Res	28	4	4	20	38	118	16

PREMIER DIVISION RESULTS 1993-94

HOME TEAM	1	2	3	4	5	6	7	8	9	10	11	12	13	14
1. A P Sports	*	5-3	2-1	2-1	2-1	1-4	2-2	2-2	1-1	6-2	1-2	5-1	0-2	2-1
2. Blackird Leys ASC	0-11	*	2-1	1-5	0-5	1-6	1-2	1-14	0-3	0-5	2-11	1-8	0-9	1-8
3. Bletchington	1-3	6-1	*	1-5	0-1	0-2	1-3	0-3	0-4	2-1	0-3	1-1	0-4	0-3
4. Eynsham	3-3	6-2	0-2	*	1-6	3-6	0-5	1-1	1-4	4-1	1-0	1-1	2-1	1-1
5. Garsington	2-2	16-2	6-0	2-1	*	3-0	1-1	2-1	0-0	0-0	0-2	4-0	0-1	1-2
6. Launton Sports	1-1	9-0	2-0	4-1	0-1	*	0-4	1-0	5-1	0-1	1-1	0-0	2-1	3-1
7. Oakley United	4-0	9-1	1-0	4-0	0-0	1-1	*	0-0	2-1	1-1	3-0	1-0	1-1	3-2
8. Old Woodstock	1-2	4-0	4-1	3-2	1-3	3-1	3-1	*	2-0	3-2	1-1	3-0	5-1	4-1
9. Oxford University Press	0-4	2-1	1-1	2-1	1-2	1-2	2-2	1-2	*	1-3	1-3	2-2	3-3	1-3
10. Pressed Steel Fisher	2-3	4-1	1-0	2-0	1-2	0-0	1-0	2-1	0-1	*	0-0	3-0	3-2	0-0
11. Quarry Nomads	2-1	15-0	5-0	4-2	1-1	0-2	2-0	3-3	2-1	1-1	*	3-1	6-0	4-1
12. Watlington	3-4	7-0	1-1	4-1	1-2	4-2	0-3	0-3	2-4	0-0	0-0	*	0-4	2-1
13. Woodstock Town	0-6	5-0	7-2	1-3	2-3	2-3	1-3	0-2	1-2	1-1	1-3	3-1	*	1-3
14. Worcester College OB	1-3	3-0	4-0	3-0	2-1	1-1	1-1	0-3	1-5	0-2	1-2	5-1	0-0	*

DIVISION ONE RESULTS 1993-94

HOME TEAM	1	2	3	4	5	6	7	8	9	10	11	12	13	14
1. Bicester Civil Service	*	4-1	4-1	4-2	4-2	0-3	3-0	2-0	3-4	5-2	2-2	0-3	8-3	3-3
2. Charlton United	2-2	*	0-0	1-3	5-0	1-6	0-6	2-2	2-5	3-1	3-3	0-3	5-2	6-2
3. Eynsham Reserves	0-8	1-4	*	4-2	0-2	0-5	0-2	0-4	2-3	1-5	3-1	1-4	7-0	1-2
4. Garsington Reserves	1-2	3-1	3-2	*	4-3	1-2	1-3	1-4	2-2	1-1	2-1	2-2	3-1	6-1
5. John Radcliffe	4-5	1-0	2-5	1-3	*	0-2	2-1	2-5	5-1	1-3	2-1	1-3	3-0	1-2
6. Kennington United	6-1	6-1	9-0	3-0	5-1	*	4-2	4-2	1-3	2-0	2-0	1-1	3-0	6-0
7. Long Crendon	1-2	2-0	8-0	1-2	0-1	1-0	*	2-1	4-3	2-1	2-0	1-0	2-1	6-0
8. Marlborough	4-3	4-1	3-0	5-1	6-2	1-1	3-0	*	2-1	4-2	1-0	2-3	0-0	4-1
9. Marston Saints	0-3	2-1	5-0	3-5	3-3	0-3	0-1	0-0	*	6-0	6-1	2-5	13-1	0-1
10. Quarry Nomads Res.	9-1	2-0	1-1	2-2	2-3	1-0	2-3	2-2	1-3	*	1-2	2-4	0-3	0-0
11. Salesians	0-4	1-1	0-0	2-2	2-4	0-4	1-6	1-4	2-2	0-4	*	1-4	3-1	2-0
12. Wheatley United	9-0	2-2	3-2	3-0	1-3	1-0	0-5	1-0	2-4	3-1	3-0	*	7-0	5-2
13. Woodstock Town Res.	5-1	3-1	7-3	4-2	4-5	0-5	1-3	0-2	2-1	1-4	1-2	0-6	*	1-2
14. Worcester COB Res.	2-2	1-3	3-0	2-1	4-3	2-3	1-2	1-1	2-0	0-1	2-0	0-3	1-2	*

DIVISION TWO RESULTS 1993-94

	HOME TEAM	1	2	3	4	5	6	7	8	9	10	11	12	13	14	15
1.	AP Sports & Soc. Res	*	3-2	3-0	7-1	0-1	1-2	4-1	5-1	2-0	2-5	10-0	1-1	4-2	1-1	2-0
2.	Bicester Civil S. Res	2-3	*	9-2	2-3	3-1	1-7	4-4	0-3	1-1	1-5	1-0	0-8	2-7	2-0	0-9
3.	Bletchingdon Res	3-0	6-0	*	6-1	6-5	4-2	3-1	1-2	0-1	0-2	5-0	1-8	1-1	1-0	5-1
4.	Charlton United Res	4-2	2-4	4-6	*	3-5	0-5	0-10	1-6	5-0	1-5	1-5	0-3	0-10	1-1	0-1
5.	John Radcliffe Res.	0-8	2-1	2-1	0-0	*	2-4	0-1	2-2	6-2	0-3	1-5	0-5	0-2	3-2	3-0
6.	Kennington Utd Res	2-2	3-2	3-2	4-1	10-1	*	2-1	2-0	2-0	2-2	4-1	2-2	2-2	4-0	2-1
7.	Launton Sports Res	3-2	4-1	1-1	1-1	5-0	1-5	*	3-1	2-4	2-2	5-1	1-3	2-2	3-0	2-1
8.	Long Crendon Res	0-4	3-0	1-0	7-0	0-2	0-1	0-4	*	2-1	1-3	6-3	0-1	2-1	0-1	2-1
9.	Marlborough Res	0-3	2-3	0-2	10-2	3-2	1-5	3-3	2-2	*	2-2	1-4	2-2	0-2	4-1	1-0
10.	Marston Saints Res	1-2	6-2	1-1	4-0	2-0	0-2	2-5	5-1	3-0	*	4-1	1-2	1-0	3-1	3-0
11.	Oakley United Res	1-3	2-5	2-6	2-2	7-1	0-2	1-3	4-0	2-2	0-9	*	0-2	1-3	3-2	1-2
12.	Old Woodstock Res.	1-0	9-1	2-3	3-1	3-3	1-0	0-0	4-0	4-1	4-2	11-1	*	0-0	5-0	7-1
13.	Oxford UP Res	5-2	2-4	1-2	4-1	1-0	1-4	2-0	1-1	9-1	2-3	5-1	0-5	*	3-0	2-0
14.	Salesians Res.	0-8	1-0	3-2	1-3	2-1	2-6	2-2	3-1	1-5	1-2	4-1	0-3	3-1	*	0-2
15.	Watlington Res	0-2	3-2	2-1	4-0	1-4	2-5	2-2	0-2	3-3	1-1	0-2	1-3	5-2	0-2	*

PRESIDENTS CUP 1993-94

First Round

John Radcliffe v Watlington 1-2
Worcester College Old Boys v Oakley Utd 4-2
Kennington United v Bletchington 1-0
Marlborough v Blackbird Leys ASC 5-2
Wheatley United v Garsington 1-4*(aet)*
Quarry Nomads v AP Sports & Social 1-3
Eynsham v Woodstock Town 2-4
Long Crendon v Bicester Civil Service 2-4
Salesians v Marston Saints 4-2
Launton Sports v Old Woodstock 0-2
Oxford University Press v Charlton United 5-2
Pressed Steel Fisher *(bye)*

Second Round

Old Woodstock v Watlington 4-1
Worcester College Old Boys *(bye)*
Woodstock Town *(bye)*
Pressed Steel Fisher v Long Crendon 4-3
Garsington *(bye)*
AP Sports & Social *(bye)*
Salesians v Oxford University Press 1-5
Marlborough v Kennington United 1-1,4-2*(aet)*

Quarter Finals

Oxford University Press v Garsington 1-2
Woodstock Town v Worcester College OB 2-0
Marlborough v AP Sports & Social 0-1
Old Woodstock v Pressed Steel Fisher 2-2,3-1*(aet)*

Semi-Finals

Old Woodstock v Garsington 1-1,2-0
Woodstock Town v AP Sports & Social 3-3,1-3

Final: Garsington 6, AP Sports & Social 2

BEN TURNER CUP (for Presidents Cup First Round losers)

First Round

Oakley United v Marston Saints 2-1
John Radcliffe v Launton Sports 1-5
Eynsham v Blackbird Leys ASC 6-2
All others *(byes)*

Quarter Finals

Wheatley United v Charlton United 0-2
Launton Sports v Quarry Nomads 0-4
Bletchington v Bicester Civil Service 1-5
Eynsham v Oakley United 0-3

Semi-Finals

Charlton United v Oakley United 0-1
Bicester Civil Service v Quarry Nomads 2-3

Final: Quarry Nomads 2, Oakley 1

CLARENDON CUP 1993-94

First Round

AP Sports Res v Oxford Univ. P. Res 5-2
Bicester CS Res v Salesians Res 3-2
Marlborough Res v Eynsham Res 1-2
Long Crendon Res v Kennington Utd Res 3-1
Watlington Res v Marston Saints Res 2-3
Garsington Res v John Radcliffe Res 4-0
Old Woodstock Res v Quarry Nomads Res 0-1
Launton Spts Res v Bletchingdon Res 2-0
Woodstock T. Res v Oakley Utd Res 2-1
Charlton Utd Reserves, Worcester COB Res *(byes)*

Second Round

Worcester COB Res v Bicester CS Res 6-1
All other clubs - byes
Woodstock Town Res v Garsington Res 3-2*(aet)*
Launton Spts Res v Old Woodstock Res 9-2

Quarter Finals

Woodstock T. Res v Charlton Utd Reserves 4-2
Long Crendon Res v Marston S. Res 1-2*(aet)*
Worcester COB Res v Eynsham Reserves 2-4
Launton S. Reserves v AP Sports Res 6-0

Semi-Finals

Woodstock T. Reserves v Launton Spts Res 4-3
Marston Saints Res v Eynsham Reserves 1-0

Final: Marston Saints Reserves 3, Woodstock Town Reserves 2 *(aet)*

IVOR GUBBINS CUP (for Clarendon Cup First Round losers)

First Round

John Radcliffe Res v Oxford UP Reserves 2-1
All others - byes
Marlborough Reserves v Watlington Reserves 2-0

Quarter Finals

Bletchingdon Res. v John Radcliffe Reserves 4-3
Kennington Utd Res v Salesians Reserves 3-0
Quarry Nomads Reserves v Marlborough Reserves 4-0
Oakley United Reserves *(bye)*

Semi-Finals

Kennington United Res v Bletchingdon Res 6-0
Oakley Utd Reserves v Quarry Nomads Res 2-3*(aet)*

Final: Quarry Nomads Reserves 3, Kennington United Reserves 0

PREMIER DIVISION CLUBS 1994-95

A.P. SPORTS & SOCIAL

Secretary: S Maycock, 3 The Camellias, Banbury, Oxon OX16 7YT (0295 275124).
Ground: Croughton, Nr Banbury.
Colours: Blue/black/blue **Reserve's colours:** All yellow.

BLETCHINGDON

Secretary: J Clack, 111 Woodstock Rd, Yarnton, Oxford (08675 71228).
Ground: Oxford Road, Bletchingdon.
Colours: Sky & claret/claret/blue (Res: yellow & green/green/yellow) **Change colours:** All red.

EYNSHAM

Secretary: G Bailey, 8 Stratford Drive, Eynsham, Oxford OX8 1QJ (0865 882829).
Ground: Eynsham P.F., Oxford Road, Eynsham, Oxford.
Colours: White/black/black. **Reserves' colours:** Yellow/black/yellow.

GARSINGTON

Secretary: C Moss, 8 Birch Rd, Garsington, Oxford (086736 704).
Ground: Off Denton Lane, Garsington (086736 720).
Colours: All green. **Change colours:** White/black/black

KENNINGTON UNITED

Secretary: Mr A Lawson, 1 Hound Close, Abingdon, Oxon OX14 2LU (0235 559864).
Ground: Playfield Rd, Kennington, Oxford.
Colours: Green & yellow/green/yellow **Change colours:** All sky.

LAUNTON SPORTS

Secretary: C R Thompson, 24 Tweed Crescent, Bicester, Oxon.
Ground: Launton Playing Field, Launton, Bicester, Oxon.
Colours: Red/black/black **Change colours:** Grey/black/black.

OAKLEY UNITED

Secretary: A J Walker, 6 Brookside, Oakley, Aylesbury, Bucks HP18 9PN (0844 238355).
Ground: Recreation Ground, Oxford Road, Oakley, Aylesbury, Bucks.
Colours: All white (Res: Orange/black/red) **Change colours:** blue.

OLD WOODSTOCK

Secretary: T Halls, 20 Oxford Rd, Farmoor, Oxford OX2 9NN (0865 863871).
Ground: Marlborough School, Shipton Rd, Woodstock, Oxon.
Colours: Blue & white/red/red (Res: Blue & white/green/green) **Change colours:** Red/black/red.

OXFORD UNIVERSITY PRESS

Secretary: I Weston, 63 Jordan Hill, Banbury Rd, Oxford OX2 8EU (0865 510500).
Ground: Oxford University Press Sports Ground, Jordan Hill, Banbury Rd, Oxford (0865 562421).
Colours: All royal (Res: Yellow/red/red) **Change colours:** Reverse.

PRESSED STEEL FISHER

Secretary: Mrs J A Measor, 1 Vicarage Close, Chalgrove, Oxon OX9 7RD (0865 890793).
Ground: Roman Way, Cowley.
Colours: Sky/blue/blue **Change colours:** Red/black/black.

WATLINGTON

Secretary: S Muir, 9 Shirburn Str., Watlington, Oxon (0491 612644).
Ground: Shirburn Road, Watlington, Oxon (B4009).
Colours: Red & black/black/black (Res: blue & white/blue/blue) **Change:** All yellow.

WHEATLEY UNITED

Secretary: K Creed, 2 Fernhill Close, Tiddington, Oxon OX9 2NA (0844 338832).
Colours: All blue **Ground:** Holton Sports Field, Wheatley.

WOODSTOCK TOWN

Secretary: M J Turner, 22 Cockpit Close, Woodstock, Oxon. **Ground:** New Road, Woodstock.
Colours: All red (Res: Red & black/red/red) **Change colours:** All white.

WORCESTER COLLEGE OLD BOYS

Secretary: G Heppell, 1 Bampton Close, Littlemore, Oxford OX4 5NN (0865 779433).
Ground: Roman Way, Cowley.
Colours: Sky/navy/navy **Change colours:** Yellow/black/black.

DIVISION ONE CLUBS 1994-95

BICESTER CIVIL SERVICE

Secretary: I Moore, 50 Wear Rd, Bicester, Oxon (0869 248765).
Ground: Rodney House, London Road, Bicester, Oxon.
Colours: Red & white/blue/blue (Res: all blue) **Change colours:** White/blue/red.

BLACKBIRD LEYS A.S.C.

Secretary: P Courtnage, 126 Pegasus Rd, Oxford.
Ground: Pegasus Road, Blackbird Leys, Oxford.
Colours: Mauve/black/black **Change colours:** Black & red/black/black.

CHARLTON UNITED

Secretary: Ms J Cooper, Gorsewood, High Street, Charlton-on-Otmoor, Oxon OX5 2UQ.
Ground: Charlton-on-Otmoor Playing Fields.
Colours: Blue & white/white/blue **Change colours:** All red.

CHINNOR

Secretary: F C Saulsbury, 86 Station Rd, Chinnor, Oxon OX9 4HA (0844 351073).
Ground: Chinnor Playing Fields (0844 352579).
Colours: All blue **Change colours:** Yellow/blue/blue.

CHIPPING NORTON TOWN

Secretary: R J Tanner, 3 Cotswold Terrace, Chipping Norton, Oxon OX7 5DU (0608 641490).
Ground: Hailey Rd (0608 642562).
Colours: Black & white stripes/white/white **Change colours:** Red/blue/white.

FRITWELL

Secretary: E S Gordon, 5 Fewcott Rd, Fritwell, Bicester, Oxon OX6 9QA.
Ground: Fritwell Playing Field, Fewcott Road.
Colours: White/blue/blue **Previous League:** Lord Jersey FA (pre-1994).

JOHN RADCLIFFE

Secretary: A Glass, Unit 6, Fitzharris Trading Est., Wootton Rd, Abingdon, Oxon (0865 247573).
Ground: John Radcliffe Hospital Grounds.
Colours: All blue **Change colours:** Black & white/black/black.

LONG CRENDON

Secretary: R Gower, 26 Friars Furlong Rd, Long Crendon, Aylesbury (0844 208642).
Ground: Chearsley Rd, Long Crendon, Aylesbury, Bucks.
Colours: Green & white/black/black (Res: Red & white/black/black) **Change:** Blue & white/blue/white.

MARLBOROUGH

Secretary: C Disley, 21 Herschel Cres., Littlemore, Oxford (0865 770223)
Ground: Orchard Way, Littlemore, Oxford
Colours: Blue/white/blue (Res: Red/black/Grey) **Change cols:** Yellow & blue/blue/blue.

MARSTON SAINTS

Secretary: Miss E Davonport, 32 Elms Drive, Old Marston, Oxford OX3 0NJ (0865 249575).
Grnd: Boults Lane, Old Marston, Oxford **Colours:** All red **Reserves' cols:** Yellow/blue/blue

SALESIANS

Secretary: Mr C Nelson, 21 Trinity Street, Oxford (0865 250169).
Ground: Westminster College, Westminster Way, Oxford.
Colours: Red & blue/blue/blue **Change colours:** All yellow.

This Division also includes the Reserve sides of: Garsington, Kennington Utd, Old Woodstock, Woodstock Town, Worcester College Old Boys.

Division Two 1994-95: A P Sports Res., Bletchingdon Res., Charlton Utd Res., Chinnor Res., Eynsham Res., Fritwell Res., John Radcliffe Res., Launton Sports Res., Long Crendon Res., Marlborough Res., Marston Saints Res., Oakley Utd Res., Oxford University Press Res., Salesians Res., Watlington Res.

WITNEY & DISTRICT F.A.

PREM. DIV.	P	W	D	L	F	A	PTS
West Witney	20	16	2	2	72	17	34
Hanborough	20	16	1	3	58	25	33
Chadlington	20	11	4	5	58	32	26
Brize Norton	20	12	2	6	49	27	26
Enstone Sports	20	9	3	8	36	29	21
Hailey	20	6	7	7	30	34	19
Ducklington	20	7	3	10	36	43	17
Spartan Rangers	20	6	1	13	34	52	13
Charlbury Town	20	5	3	12	29	73	13
Bampton Town	20	4	2	14	28	61	10
Carterton Eagles	20	3	2	15	22	57	8

DIV. ONE	P	W	D	L	F	A	PTS
Aston	20	13	4	3	58	25	30
Witney Royals	20	11	8	1	57	33	30
Tackley	20	12	5	3	57	28	29
FC Mills	20	8	7	5	27	34	23
Minster Lovell	20	9	4	7	46	52	22
Kingham All Blacks	20	7	5	8	50	38	19
West Witney Res.	20	7	5	8	38	39	19
Hanborough Res.	20	6	3	11	39	54	15
Alvescot	20	4	4	12	36	45	12
Stonesfield	20	4	4	12	43	59	12
Milton	20	3	3	14	24	68	9

DIV. TWO	P	W	D	L	F	A	PTS
Chip. Norton Utd	24	19	1	4	124	28	39
North Leigh 'A'	24	17	5	2	80	29	39
Allandale	24	18	3	3	73	32	39
Carterton T. 'A'	24	14	1	9	75	44	29
Spartan Rgrs Res.	24	13	3	8	73	69	29
FC Mills Res.	24	10	4	10	57	76	24
Charlbury T. Res.	24	10	3	11	51	53	23
Swinbrook	24	8	4	12	53	73	20
Bladon	24	9	1	14	53	50	19
Ducklington Res.	24	4	8	12	42	65	16
Chadlington Res.	24	6	2	16	43	67	14
Cassington	24	5	3	16	31	77	13
Crusaders	24	4	0	20	29	121	8

DIV. THREE	P	W	D	L	F	A	PTS
Ascott	24	18	3	3	74	30	39
West Witney 'A'	24	12	5	7	70	55	29
Hailey Res.	24	11	4	9	58	42	26
Stonesfield Res.	24	10	5	9	48	46	25
Enstone Spts Res.	24	11	2	11	56	70	24
Adlestrop	24	10	3	11	46	60	23
Fieldtown	24	8	2	14	64	71	18
Brize Norton Res.	24	7	3	14	56	85	17
Alvescot Res.	24	6	3	15	38	51	15

DIV. FOUR	P	W	D	L	F	A	PTS
Freeland	18	10	7	1	56	28	27
FC Mills 'A'	18	11	4	3	50	27	26
C. Norton U. Res.	18	10	3	5	52	38	23
Kingham AB Res.	18	9	3	6	54	40	21
Newland	18	8	5	5	54	40	21
Carterton T. 'B'	18	7	5	6	52	50	19
Witney Royals Res.	18	7	3	8	51	42	17
Stanton Harcourt	18	5	4	9	40	43	14
Swinbrook Res.	18	2	2	14	27	72	6
Charlbury T. 'A'	18	1	4	13	20	77	6

DIV. FIVE	P	W	D	L	F	A	PTS
Napier Royals	20	19	3	3	69	29	31
Aston Res.	20	14	3	3	69	29	31
AFC Eynsham	20	14	0	6	77	20	28
Fieldtown Res.	20	10	2	8	47	39	22
Tackley Res.	20	9	3	8	40	41	21
Hanborough 'A'	20	9	1	10	47	60	19
Bampton T. Res.	20	7	4	9	38	49	18
Minster L. Res.	20	7	1	12	32	71	15
Bladon Res.	20	5	2	13	25	52	12
Allandale Res.	20	4	3	13	48	65	11
Alvescot 'A'	20	2	1	17	35	105	5

LORD JERSEY F.A.

(Est. 1887)

The Lord Jersey Association has been in existence for over 100 years, the first Jersey Cup being in 1887-88 when Middleton Stoney beat Deddington 4-2. The Association is named after Lord Jersey whose seat and estate is in the area covered by the Association.

League football did not appear to start until around the time of the Second World War. At first, there was only one division, but in 52-53 there were three. The Association peaked in 1983 when a 4th Division was added. To be correct, the divisions are called Jersey Shields and the whole set-up is never referred to as a league.

The area covered is from the Chilterns in the east to the Cotswolds in the West and Oxford in the south. Rules state that clubs should refrain spectators from entering the field of play, i.e. most pitches are roped. Most clubs have social facilities.

In the past, Brill United have progressed to the Chiltonian League plus at least six of the current Oxon Senior League clubs have played in the Lord Jersey. At the end of the season numerous Cup are played, all with evening kick-offs except the Jersey Cup which is played on Easter Monday or May Bank Holiday Monday. A programme is issued for each final.

Details supplied by Andy Molden.

Division One	P	W	D	L	F	A	PTS
Middle Barton	14	10	3	1	36	18	33
Fritwell	14	9	3	2	35	14	30
Bardwell	14	7	5	2	35	14	26
Heyford Athletic	14	5	5	4	29	27	20
Hethe	14	4	2	8	26	41	14
KEA United	14	4	2	8	39	34	14
Arncott	14	3	3	8	17	46	12
Kirklington	14	1	3	10	22	45	6

Division Two	P	W	D	L	F	A	PTS
Forest Hill	22	15	5	2	70	23	50
Wise Alderman	22	15	3	4	92	38	48
Bardwell Res.	22	13	4	5	66	40	43
Fairview	22	12	4	6	70	48	40
Souldern	22	10	4	8	50	47	34
Red Lion M'ders	22	10	3	9	57	51	33
Fritwell Res.	22	10	0	12	41	48	30
Wootton Sports	22	7	5	10	36	42	26
Hethe Res.	22	7	3	12	37	57	24
Viking Spts Utd	22	7	2	13	34	67	23
AFC Weston	22	5	4	13	41	68	19
Highfield OB	22	1	3	18	23	88	6

Division Three	P	W	D	L	F	A	PTS
Kirklington Res.	20	14	5	1	74	24	47
Steeple Aston	20	15	2	3	65	26	47
Merton	20	11	2	7	52	33	35
Middle Barton Res.	20	10	3	7	66	19	33
Finmere	20	10	2	8	57	37	32
Heyford A. Res.	20	8	5	7	53	47	29
Morton Foods	20	7	3	10	39	57	24
Team Unipart	20	7	3	10	30	49	24
Crusaders	20	6	5	9	39	58	23
Arncott Res.	20	4	5	11	42	56	17
Heyford United	20	0	1	19	15	126	1

CLUB DIRECTORY

(Tel. codes 0869 unless stated)

ARNCOTT
Ground: Arncott Rec. **Sec:** D Cox (249095)
BARDWELL
G: Pingle Field, Bicester **S:** A Simpson (246785)
CRUSADERS
Skimmingdish Lane, Bicester B Monk (243174)
FAIRVIEW (formerly Lynx)
Sandy Lane, Blackbird Leys S Hands(0865 244365)
FINMERE
Water Stratford Rd B Cranfield (0280 847056)
FOREST HILL
G: Stanton Rd **S:** P Hines (0865 778564)
HETHE
G: Hardwick Rd PF **S:** W Mansfield (277219)
HEYFORD ATHLETIC
G: Lower Heyford PF **S:** A Jupp (320151)
HEYFORD UNITED
Somerton Rd, Upper Heyf. I Lough-Scott (232788)
HIGHFIELD OLD BOYS
Sunderland Drive, Bicester R Gilbert (245205)
K.E.A. UNITED
G: Ashdene Rd, Bicester Mrs H Horner (244186)
KIRKLINGTON
G: Kirklington Spts Field **S:** M Mowat (50525)
MERTON
G: Merton PF **S:** W Jenser (47388)
MIDDLE BARTON
G: Worton Rd **S:** Ms J Reed (47388)
MORTON FOODS
G: Merton PF **S:** N Allen (320056)
RED LION MARAUDERS
G: Church Lane, Islip **S:** D Cowan (0867 571695)
SOULDERN
G: Souldern PF **S:** M Lillis (346715)
STEEPLE ASTON
G: Robinsons Close **S:** A Peckham (47756)
TEAM UNIPART
G: Court Place Farm, Marston, Oxford **S:** TBA
VIKING SPORTS UNITED
G: As Team Unipart **S:** A Kingston (0867 77643)
(A.F.C.) WESTON
Weston-on-the-Green Rec. Mrs O'Brien (50884)
WISE ALDERMAN
Cuttleslowe Pk, Oxfd S Middleditch (0993 706316)
WOOTTON SPORTS
G: Castle Rd PF **S:** M Tilsley (0867 578052)

R T HARRIS OXFORD CITY JUNIOR F.A.

White Eagles did the double of League title and Premier Division Cup, whilst North Oxford won the Chairmans Cup. Horspath, in their first season in the league, won Division One after the closest finish in years. A single goal from Wayne Shorter did the trick against Shelley Arms who needed just a draw.

PREM. DIV.	P	W	D	L	F	A	PTS
White Eagles	16	12	1	3	66	25	25
Princes of Wales	16	11	3	2	53	25	25
Port Mahon United	16	10	2	4	73	32	22
Chequers (Quarry)	16	9	3	4	57	22	21
Barton Youth	16	8	1	7	42	44	17
East Oxford	16	6	1	9	36	52	13
North Oxford	16	5	1	10	37	49	11
Marston	16	4	2	10	39	69	10
Oxford Gas Spts	16	0	0	16	15	106	0

DIV. ONE	P	W	D	L	F	A	PTS
Horspath	16	12	3	1	50	19	27
Shelley Arms	16	13	0	3	63	16	26
Tetsworth	16	11	3	2	51	17	25
Great Milton	16	8	3	5	62	42	19
Risinghurst	16	6	4	6	49	43	16
Beckley Sports	16	4	2	10	32	66	10
North Oxford Res.	16	4	1	11	21	58	9
Black Boy Celtic	16	3	1	12	35	61	7
Plough (Ltle Milton)	16	3	1	12	35	61	7

MORRELLS OXFORD SUNDAY LEAGUE

PREM. DIV.	P	W	D	L	F	A	PTS
Horspath Road	20	12	7	1	87	25	31
Six Bells Kidlington	20	13	4	3	72	29	30
Saxon Warriors	20	12	2	6	49	30	26
Rose Hill	20	11	3	6	64	29	25
Star Wanderers	20	10	3	7	53	47	23
Leafield Athletic	20	7	5	8	48	32	19
Star Royal	20	6	5	9	46	43	17
Oxford Nondes	20	7	3	10	44	73	17
Highfield SC	20	4	3	13	36	86	11
Cold Arbour	20	3	5	12	33	87	11
Wheatley '84	20	4	2	14	40	71	10

Lower Division Champions:
Div. 1 (11): Town Furze
Div. 2 (11): Shelley Arms
Div. 3 (11): Masons Arms
Div. 4 (13): Red Lion (Eynsford)
Div. 5 (12): Bull (Great Milton)
Div. 6 (12): Stadhampton

RESERVE AND YOUTH TEAM COMPETITIONS

F.A. YOUTH CHALLENGE CUP 1993-94

(Attendances in brackets throughout)

Extra-Preliminary Round

Petersfield Utd *(scr)* Woking *(w/o)*	
Sutton Coldfield Town v Bedworth United (59)	4-0

Preliminary Round

Darlington v Blackpool Mechanics (30)	7-1
Prudhoe East End v Atherton LR (36)	3-2
Bolton Wanderers v Marine (129)	3-1
Chadderton v Rochdale *(at Rochdale)*(124)	1-4
Wrexham v Southport (45)	7-1
Stockport County v Warrington Town (91)	2-3
Mansfield Town v Hinckley Athletic (82)	9-1
Burton Albion v Lutterworth Town (51)	6-1
Stratford Town v Corby Town (57)	4-0
Chasetown v Rothwell Town (55)	0-1
Nuneaton Borough v Wednesfield (35)	4-1
Pershore Town v Willenhall Town (35)	3-1
Stewarts & Lloyds v Leighton Town (22)	0-1
Baldock Town v Kempston Rovers	1-2
Braintree Town v Peterborough United (103)	2-8
King's Lynn v Saffron Walden Town (87)	1-2
Wivenhoe Town v Stevenage Borough (29)	1-2
Grays Athletic v Waltham Abbey (60)	1-3
Brook Hse v Wingate & F.	1-1,3-4*(aet, att: 60)*
Royston Town v Northwood	5-0
Hanwell Town v Ruislip Manor	3-4
Kingsbury Town v Staines Town (62/51)	1-1,4-3
Dover Athletic v Herne Bay (55)	5-0
Corinthian v Gillingham (27)	0-7
Bracknell T. *(w/o)* Peacehaven & Tels. *(scr)*	
Croydon Athletic v Thamesmead Town (38)	7-1
Kingstonian v Whitehawk (40)	10-0
Oakwood v Whitstable Town (28)	1-6
Shoreham *(scr)* Welling United *(w/o)*	
Whyteleafe *(w/o)* Walton & Hersham *(scr)*	
Wick v Thatcham Town (37)	2-1
Basingstoke Town v Wokingham Town (39)	1-4
Havant Town v Frome Town (62)	3-0
Romsey Town v Yate Town (29)	3-5*(aet)*
Cheltenham T. v Worcester C. (94/63)	1-1,2-4*(aet)*
Torquay United v Yeovil Town (234)	2-1
Guisborough Town v Huddersfield Town (67)	1-5
Hartlepool United v Carlisle United (117)	1-3
Burscough v Grimsby Town (21)	0-5
Bury v Altrincham (105)	7-1
Wigan Athletic v Prescot AFC	5-2
Stalybridge Celtic v Lincoln City (204)	1-6
Port Vale v Hednesford Town (200)	2-0*(aet)*
Bridgnorth Town v Worksop Town (60)	0-3
Boldmere St Michaels v Hinckley Town (37)	3-5
Bromsgrove Rovers v Sutton Coldfield (105)	2-1
Brierley Hill Town v Redditch United (46)	2-4
Pelsall Villa v Lye Town (52)	2-5
Banury United v Dunstable (40)	3-0
Eynesbury Rovers v Rushden & Diamonds (29)	1-6
Canvey Island v March Town United (80)	2-8
Gt Yarmouth Town v Bishop's Stortford (59)	2-1
Barkingside v Leyton (43)	5-1
East Thurrock United v Wisbech Town (37)	3-0
Edgware Town v Uxbridge (33)	4-0
Enfield v Beaconsfield United (45)	10-0
Hanwell Town v Marlow (35)	5-0
Hillingdon Borough v Hampton	1-3
Newhaven v Faversham Town (40)	3-0
Ringmer v Ashford Town (35)	2-3
Chatham Town v Egham Town (28)	2-0
Chipstead v Bedfont (22)	3-2
Malden Vale v Three Bridges (46)	2-4
Molesey *(scr)* Farnborough Town *(w/o)*	
Slough Town v Worthing (56)	0-1
Steyning Town v Redhill (20)	5-1
Fleet Town v Maidenhead United (25)	3-5
Aldershot Town v Woking (117)	6-1
Newbury Town v Chippenham Town (31)	2-4
Oxford City v Dorchester Town (55/33)	1-1,3-1
Gloucester City v Weston-super-Mare (58)	3-0
Hereford Utd v Bristol Rovers (62/44)	1-1,3-5

First Qualifying Round

Huddersfield Town v Carlisle United (100)	2-1
Grimsby Town v Bury	4-1
Wigan Athletic v Lincoln City (31)	3-4
Port Vale v Worksop Town (153)	5-0
Hinckley Town v Bromsgrove R. (30/57)	1-1,2-0
Redditch United v Lye Town (44)	0-1
Banbury United v Rushden & Diamonds (45)	2-1
March TU v Gt Yarmouth Town (55/30)	0-0,1-5
Barkingside v East Thurrock United (51)	0-5
Edgware Town v Enfield (35)	1-2
Harefield United v Hampton	4-1
Newhaven v Ashford (56)	3-2*(ab. 45m)*,3-1
Chatham Town v Chipstead (35)	0-3*(ab. 45m)*,1-3
Three Bridges v Farnborough Town (26)	3-1
Worthing v Steyning Town (45)	3-1
Maidenhead U. v Aldershot Town (39/58)	4-4,0-4
Chippenham Town v Oxford City (57)	4-3
Gliucester City v Bristol Rovers (125)	1-6
Darlington v Prudhoe East End (60)	9-0
Bolton Wanderers v Port Vale (141)	1-2
Wrexham v Warrington Town (43)	1-2
Burton Albion v Mansfield Town (110)	2-1
Stratford Town v Rothwell Town (39)	3-1
Nuneaton Borough v Pershore Town (37)	6-3
Leighton Town v Kempston Rovers (111)	5-0
Peterborough Utd v Saffron Walden T. (491)	6-1
Stevenage Borough v Waltham Abbey (54)	3-1
Wingate & Finchley v Royston Town (45)	0-4
Ruislip Manor v Kingsbury Town (39)	1-2
Dover Athletic v Gillingham (35)	0-5
Bracknell Town v Croydon Athletic (22)	1-3
Kingstonian v Whitstable Town (42)	4-1
Welling United v Whyteleafe (50)	3-0
Wick v Wokingham Town (28)	2-5
Havant Town v Yate Town (65)	1-0*(aet)*
Worcester City v Torquay United (172)	1-2

Second Qualifying Round

Huddersfield Town v Darlington (99)	5-1
Lincoln C. v Warrington T. (77/218)	2-2,3-1
Hinckley Town v Stratford Town (48)	0-2
Banbury United v Leighton Town (47)	1-3
East Thurrock v Stevenage Boro. (94/65)	1-1,2-1
Harefield United v Kingsbury Town (43)	5-0
Chipstead v Croydon Athletic (21)	1-4
Worthing v Welling United (72)	1-2
Chippenham Town v Havant Town (50)	0-1
Grimsby Town v Rochdale (174)	1-0
Port Vale v Burton Albion (134/168)	1-1,2-0
Lye Town v Nuneaton Borough (72)	0-1
Gt Yarmouth v Peterborough Utd (53/549)	2-2,0-8
Enfield v Royston Town (53)	4-3
Newhaven v Gillingham (30)	0-4
Three Bridges v Kingstonian (18)	1-5
Aldershot Town v Wokingham Town (69)	0-2
Bristol Rovers v Torquay United (38/256)	0-0,1-3

First Round

Tranmere R. v Huddersfield T. (491/160)	1-1,1-3
Rotherham United v Preston North End (127)	2-1
Blackburn Rovers v Sheffield Wed. (201)	1-0
Doncaster Rovers v Lincoln City (190)	2-0
Bradford City v Barnsley (95)	2-1
Newcastle Utd v Burnley (628)	1-1,0-3

Oldham Athletic v Hull City (361) 3-2
Scunthorpe United v Sunderland (183) 0-3
Kidderminster Harriers v Peterborough (30) 0-2
Cambridge United v Aston Villa (268) 1-4
Luton Town v Derby (149/256/168) 1-1,1-1,0-1
Cambridge City v Leighton Town (75/100) 3-3,0-1
Ipswich Town v Carshalton Athletic (227) 8-0
Dulwich H. v East Thurrock (141/141) 2-2,4-2*(aet)*
Herefield Utd v St Albans C. (51/135) 1-1,1-0
Croydon Athletic v Epsom & Ewell (85) 3-1
Reading v Charlton Ath. (50/512) 2-2,3-2*(aet)*
Portsmouth v Bashley (155) 4-0
Torquay United v Oxford United (305) 3-2
Havant T. v Wokingham T. (107/83) 0-0,1-2
Blackpool v Grimsby Town (124) 0-1
Stratford Town v Nuneaton B. (54/115) 2-2,1-2
Stoke City v Shrewsbury Town (229) 3-1
Birmingham City v Wolves (70) 4-1
Northampton Town v Leicester City (142) 1-3
Walsall v Port Vale (151) 0-1
Gillingham v Lewes (49) 3-0
Brighton & Hove Albion v Fulham (115) 3-1
Boreham Wood v Enfield 1-2
Sutton United v Wycombe Wanderers (47) 0-2
Kingstonian v Welling United 2-5
Southampton v AFC Bournemouth (251) 1-0
Cardiff City v Witney Town (105) 5-0
Exeter City v Swansea City (275) 4-2

Second Round
Middlesbrough v Oldham Athletic 2-0
Bradford City v Manchester United 2-0
York v Blackburn (149/165/144) 0-0,1-1,1-2
Everton v Grimsby Town 0-2
Sheffield United v Liverpool 1-2
Ipswich Town v Queens Park Rangers 1-0
West Bromwich Albion v Leighton Town 2-1
Watford v Aston Villa (232) 1-3
Port Vale v Southend United (112) 1-3
Nottm Forest v Nuneaton Borough (154) 3-1
Colchester United v Arsenal 2-3
Torquay United v Enfield 3-1
Reading v Bristol City 0-1
Dulwich Hamlet v Crystal Palace 0-5
Welling United v Portsmouth (227) 4-6
Brentford v Exeter City 5-1
Burnley v Leeds United (1,084) 3-0
Crewe Alexandra v Huddersfield Town 4-2
Doncaster Rovers v Manchester City (181) 1-4
Rotherham United v Sunderland 2-4
Coventry City v Leicester City (208) 2-1
Tottenham Hotspur v Stoke City (229) 1-2
West Ham United v Leyton Orient 6-0
Birmingham C. v Peterborough 1-1,1-1,1-2
Chelsea v Norwich City 1-1,0-1
Notts County v Derby County 0-3
Southampton v Wimbledon (89) 2-6
Croydon Athletic v Wycombe Wanderers (89) 2-3
Gillingham v Swindon Town (54) 1-2
Cardiff City v Harefield United 2-0
Brighton & Hove Albion v Wokingham Town (124) 1-8
Plymouth Argyle v Millwall 3-3,1-2

Third Round
Manchester City v Norwich City (227) 0-2
Middlesbrough v Nottm F. 2-2,3-3,2-1
Wimbledon v Burnley (247) 3-4
Grimsby Town v Torquay United 3-1
Liverpool v West Ham United 2-2,2-3
Swindon Town v Brighton & HA (172) 0-1
Cardiff City v Coventry City 1-2
Southend United v Stoke City 0-4
Bristol City v Aston Villa 1-4
Blackburn Rovers v Bradford City (896) 1-1,0-4
Ipswich v Peterboro. 1-1*(att: 472)*,0-0*(att: 1,489)*,1-0
West Bromwich Albion v Crewe Alexandra 2-1
Brentford v Arsenal 1-1,1-3
Sunderland v Derby County (333) 0-1
Millwall v Wycombe Wanderers 2-2,5-0
Portsmouth v Crystal Palace 2-0

Fourth Round
Coventry City v Norwich City 0-2
Middlesbrough v West Bromwich (984) 2-0
Grimsby Town v Bradford City 1-1,0-2
Stoke City v Derby County (1,198) 3-1
Brighton & Hove Albion v Millwall (540) 3-4
Ipswich Town v Portsmouth 2-4
Aston Villa v West Ham United 1-2
Burnley v Arsenal (4,943) 0-1

Quarter-Finals
Arsenal v Stoke City 3-1
Middlesbrough v Portsmouth (1,522) 5-0
West Ham United v Bradford City (780) 0-1
Millwall v Norwich City 2-0

Semi-Finals
Middlesbrough v Millwall (6,111/2,342) 1-1,1-3
Bradford City v Arsenal 0-1*(att: 2,746)*,0-1

Final. 1st leg: Millwall 3, Arsenal 2 *(att: 6,098)*
Final. 2nd leg: Arsenal 3, Millwall 0 *(att: 4,705)*

F.A. COUNTY YOUTH CUP

First Round
Nottinghamshire v Manchester 2-3*(aet)*
Birmingham v Cheshire 1-2
Shropshire v Northamptonshire 3-6
Berks & Bucks v Cambridgeshire 1-0
Surrey v Hampshire 7-2
Gloucestershire v Devon 0-3
Derbyshire v West Riding 0-5
Staffordshire v Westmorland 9-1
Oxfordshire v Hertfordshire 4-1
Bedfordshire v Kent 0-2
Dorset v Royal Navy 1-0
Sussex v Wiltshire 4-0

Second Round
Cumberland v Manchester 0-2
East Riding v Liverpool 3-4
North Riding v Cheshire 3-2
Sheffield & Hallamshire v Northampshire 3-2
Worcestershire v Berks & Bucks 1-1,2-0
Hertfordshire v Suffolk 1-1,3-5
London v Dorset 1-0
Middlesex v Devon 3-3,1-3*(aet)*
Lincolnshire v Durham 0-4
Northumberland v West Riding 3-5
Lancashire v Staffordshire 2-3
Leicestershire & Rutland v Oxfordshire 2-0
Norfolk v Kent 0-3
Essex v Surrey 2-4
Huntingdonshire v Somerset & Avon 1-3
Cornwall v Sussex 0-2

Third Round
Liverpool v North Riding 4-2
Leicestershire & Rutland v Staffordshire 0-3
Kent v Worcestershire 1-0*(aet)*
Sussex v Somerset & Avon (South) 1-0
Durham v Manchester 0-1
Suffolk v London 1-2
Middlesex v Surrey 0-3
Sheffield & Hallamshire v West Riding 1-3*(aet)*

Quarter-Finals
Surrey v West Riding 0-1
Kent v London 2-2*(aet)*,2-1
Staffordshire v Manchester (150) 2-1
Sussex v Liverpool (85) 3-2

Semi-Finals
Sussex v Kent *(at Lancing, att: 150)* 2-1
West Riding v Staffs *(at Stafford Rgrs, att: 150)* 4-0

Final *(at Bradford City FC, Sat 30th April)*: West Riding 3, Sussex 1

AVON INSURANCE

FOOTBALL COMBINATION

DIV. ONE	P	W	D	L	F	A	PTS
Chelsea Res.	38	24	8	6	79	41	80
Ipswich Town Res.	38	19	8	11	71	52	65
Tottenham H. Res.	38	19	6	13	69	47	63
Crystal Pal. Res.	38	17	11	10	63	40	62
Norwich City Res.	38	18	7	13	68	54	61
Wimbledon Res.	38	16	13	9	53	48	61
QPR Res.	38	17	8	13	58	49	59
West Ham Utd Res.	38	16	10	12	59	45	58
Swindon Town Res.	38	18	4	16	54	53	58
Bristol Rvrs Res.	38	15	12	11	50	52	57
Southampton Res.	38	15	10	13	62	66	55
Millwall Res.	38	12	11	15	57	67	47
Charlton A. Res.	38	13	7	18	61	62	46
Luton Town Res.	38	12	9	17	64	70	45
Arsenal Res.	38	13	6	19	67	76	45
Oxford Utd Res.	38	11	10	17	53	66	43
Portsmouth Res.	38	10	11	17	43	60	41
Brighton & HA Res.	38	9	10	19	38	58	37
Watford Res.	38	9	8	21	49	75	35
Bristol City Res.	38	8	9	21	47	84	33

DIV. TWO	P	W	D	L	F	A	PTS
Birmingham C. Res.	18	13	1	4	53	17	40
Plymouth A. Res.	18	12	2	4	63	18	38
Swansea City Res.	18	11	4	3	47	26	37
Torquay Utd Res.	18	11	2	5	33	18	35
AFC B'mouth Res.	18	8	3	7	33	38	27
Exeter City Res.	18	7	2	9	40	41	26
Cardiff C. Res.	18	5	4	9	29	44	19
Hereford Utd Res.	18	6	1	11	36	52	19
Yeovil Town Res.	18	4	2	12	21	47	14
Cheltenham T. Res.	18	2	1	15	14	69	7

LGE CUP Gp A	P	W	D	L	F	A	PTS
Torquay Utd Res.	8	5	2	1	17	9	17
AFC B'mouth Res.	8	4	1	3	10	11	13
Exeter City Res.	8	3	2	3	15	17	11
Plymouth A. Res.	8	3	1	4	15	14	10
Yeovil Town Res.	8	2	1	6	11	18	6

LGE CUP Gp B	P	W	D	L	F	A	PTS
Birmingham C. Res.	8	6	2	0	22	10	20
Cardiff City Res.	8	4	1	3	8	10	13
Swansea City Res.	8	3	3	2	20	9	12
Cheltenham T. Res.	8	1	2	5	9	18	5
Hereford Utd Res.	8	1	2	5	15	27	5

League Cup Final *(at Torquay Utd FC)*:
Birmingham City beat Torquay on aggregate

SPRINGHEATH PRINT

CAPITAL LEAGUE

FOUNDED: 1984

FINAL TABLE	P	W	D	L	F	A	PTS
Gillingham	24	17	2	5	55	27	53
Southend United	24	14	7	3	77	22	49
Brentford	24	15	2	7	63	28	47
Woking	24	13	2	9	40	33	41
Leyton Orient	24	12	4	8	48	38	40
Cambridge United	24	13	1	10	62	54	40
Wycombe Wdrs	24	11	2	11	49	41	35
Sutton United	24	10	5	9	48	45	35
Barnet	24	10	4	10	40	44	34
Colchester Utd	24	9	3	12	42	37	30
Enfield	24	3	6	15	39	56	15
St Albans City	24	5	0	19	28	105	15
Wokingham Town	24	4	2	18	26	72	14

COLBOURNE TROPHIES PRESIDENTS CUP

First Round
Wycombe Wanderers 3, Cambridge Utd 7 *(aet)*
Southend United 4, Gillingham 0
Brentford 1, Leyton Orient 2
Barnet 1, Colchester United 2
Woking 9, St Albans City 1

Quarter-Finals
Cambridge U. 3, Southend 3 *(aet, 3-2 on pens)*
Enfield 0, Leyton Orient 1
Colchester United 2, Woking 4 *(aet)*
Wokingham Town 4, Sutton United 1

Semi-Finals
Woking 3, Wokingham Town 2
Leyton Orient 1, Cambridge United 2

Final *(at Woking FC, Sun 24th April)*:
Woking 0, Cambridge 1 *(Michael Kyd, 61m)* Att: 310.

Below: *Woking Reserves - Capital League Cup finalists.*
Photo - Eric Marsh.

SOUTH EAST COUNTIES LEAGUE

SECL SJFC

Founded: 1954

Secretary: Alan Leather, 66 Green Acres, Chichester Road, Croydon, Surrey CR0 5UX.

The South Counties League is geographically the largest youth league in the country. In general, matches are played at 11am on Saturdays. A club directory is included on the next page, but it is imperative to check fixtures with the clubs as kick-offs and venues are liable to be changed at very short notice.

DIVISION ONE	P	W	D	L	F	A	PTS
Queens Park Rgrs	30	24	2	4	121	49	50
Tottenham Hotspur	30	20	4	6	85	40	44
West Ham United	30	19	5	6	78	44	43
Chelsea	30	19	3	8	67	39	41
Millwall	30	18	4	8	86	59	40
Fulham	30	19	2	9	59	46	40
Arsenal	30	15	7	8	66	42	37
Ipswich Town	30	11	8	11	50	49	30
Watford	30	11	5	14	52	63	27
Norwich City	30	11	2	17	42	60	24
Cambridge United	30	6	9	15	40	69	21
Portsmouth	30	7	5	18	44	76	19
Southend United	30	8	3	19	40	78	19
Leyton Orient	30	6	6	18	32	65	18
Charlton Athletic	30	6	3	21	46	87	15
Gillingham	30	4	4	22	30	72	12

DIVISION TWO	P	W	D	L	F	A	PTS
Crystal Palace	26	15	5	6	56	32	35
Swindon Town	26	14	6	6	49	26	34
Wimbledon	26	15	1	10	61	44	31
Reading	26	10	9	7	39	36	29
Oxford United	26	11	6	9	46	38	28
Brentford	26	10	8	8	40	34	28
Luton Town	26	11	4	11	40	47	26
Brighton & Hove A.	26	10	6	10	37	44	26
Southampton	26	8	7	11	29	30	23
Bristol Rovers	26	9	5	12	40	48	23
Bristol City	26	8	6	12	35	44	22
AFC Bournemouth	26	9	2	15	40	53	20
Tottenham Hotspur	26	8	4	14	35	49	20
Colchester Utd	26	6	7	13	33	55	19

DIV. ONE RESULTS 93-94	1	2	3	4	5	6	7	8	9	10	11	12	13	14	15	16
1. Arsenal	*	1-2	3-1	0-2	2-2	3-1	1-2	1-1	2-2	2-0	1-1	1-2	7-1	0-2	0-2	3-3
2. Cambridge United	1-1	*	4-2	3-0	1-4	3-3	0-0	0-0	2-2	0-1	4-2	1-3	0-0	1-3	1-2	1-4
3. Charlton Athletic	2-5	5-0	*	0-5	0-1	2-1	2-3	0-2	3-6	1-5	3-2	1-9	0-1	1-3	2-0	0-5
4. Chelsea	1-3	4-0	3-1	*	1-0	1-0	2-3	3-0	0-2	3-0	4-1	4-1	2-0	4-2	4-1	2-2
5. Fulham	3-0	4-0	3-2	4-0	*	1-0	2-1	2-1	2-1	1-0	4-1	1-2	1-0	2-5	2-0	1-5
6. Gillingham	0-2	2-2	0-2	2-4	1-3	*	2-1	4-2	0-3	1-2	2-1	0-4	1-3	1-2	0-1	0-2
7. Ipswich Town	2-3	0-0	3-1	1-1	1-1	1-1	*	1-1	4-1	2-1	0-1	4-0	1-1	1-2	5-2	2-1
8. Leyton Orient	0-0	0-3	1-3	0-1	1-3	1-0	2-1	*	1-3	4-1	4-1	1-4	2-0	2-2	1-3	2-4
9. Millwall	0-3	4-2	4-1	0-5	6-1	5-1	1-0	3-0	*	3-2	2-0	1-6	4-1	1-1	4-3	3-4
10. Norwich City	1-2	0-1	2-1	3-1	3-2	2-0	1-0	0-0	1-3	*	3-2	1-4	4-2	2-5	2-3	0-3
11. Portsmouth	0-3	3-0	3-2	3-2	1-2	2-2	5-2	3-1	1-7	0-0	*	2-6	1-3	2-1	2-2	1-2
12. Queens Park Rangers	1-3	4-2	4-3	5-2	2-0	6-1	8-3	3-0	3-3	5-0	2-2	*	9-0	1-6	3-1	4-0
13. Southend United	1-5	2-1	3-3	1-2	2-5	1-0	0-3	2-0	2-4	2-4	3-0	3-4	*	2-1	0-2	1-4
14. Tottenham Hotspur	2-0	7-1	4-0	1-3	0-2	4-1	5-0	6-0	4-2	2-1	4-0	2-5	2-0	*	1-0	1-1
15. Watford	3-6	2-2	1-1	0-1	2-0	2-3	1-1	4-0	1-4	3-0	1-0	0-5	4-2	4-4	*	2-3
16. West Ham United	1-3	4-2	1-1	0-0	5-0	4-0	0-2	4-2	3-2	2-0	4-1	1-6	2-1	0-1	4-0	*

DIV. TWO RESULTS 93-94	1	2	3	4	5	6	7	8	9	10	11	12	13	14
1. AFC Bournemouth	*	0-3	2-1	2-4	1-3	2-3	1-5	1-2	1-2	3-2	1-2	4-1	1-0	0-3
2. Brentford	1-0	*	1-0	2-2	3-0	3-0	1-0	4-1	1-3	2-2	1-1	2-2	2-0	1-2
3. Brighton & Hove Albion	1-6	2-0	*	3-0	1-1	1-1	1-1	3-2	2-0	3-3	1-0	3-2	2-1	1-0
4. Bristol City	0-1	1-0	4-0	*	1-0	1-1	1-0	5-1	0-0	0-0	1-1	1-2	0-2	1-3
5. Bristol Rovers	2-3	1-1	2-1	1-2	*	2-1	2-3	5-0	4-0	0-4	1-0	0-0	2-1	6-3
6. Colchester United	2-2	1-1	4-1	2-1	2-2	*	0-2	0-3	1-3	0-2	1-0	0-3	2-3	1-3
7. Crystal Palace	2-0	3-1	1-3	1-0	6-2	2-2	*	1-2	2-0	1-1	0-1	2-2	3-1	3-1
8. Luton Town	3-2	1-1	1-4	4-0	1-0	5-3	1-1	*	1-1	2-1	2-1	2-0	0-1	1-0
9. Oxford United	3-1	2-4	4-1	2-3	3-0	5-1	1-2	4-1	*	1-1	1-1	0-1	3-0	1-3
10. Reading	0-0	3-0	0-0	4-1	0-2	1-2	2-0	2-1	1-1	*	2-0	0-0	4-2	0-2
11. Southampton	0-1	4-1	2-1	3-1	0-0	0-0	2-3	2-1	0-2	0-1	*	0-2	1-1	3-2
12. Swindon Town	3-0	1-0	4-0	3-1	3-0	1-2	1-4	1-1	1-1	6-0	1-0	*	1-0	5-0
13. Tottenham Hotspur	1-3	1-1	1-1	2-2	2-0	2-1	1-4	2-0	2-3	2-3	0-3	3-2	*	1-4
14. Wimbledon	4-2	1-3	1-0	4-2	6-2	4-0	2-4	2-1	3-0	5-0	2-2	0-1	1-3	*

SOUTH EAST COUNTIES LEAGUE CUP

First Round

Southampton v Portsmouth	0-1	Oxford United v Fulham	1-0
Reading v Gillingham	0-1	Tottenham Hotspur *(bye)*	
West Ham United v AFC Bournemouth	3-0	Arsenal v Bristol City	1-1,2-3
Cambridge United v Brighton & Hove Albion	3-1	Norwich City v Brentford	1-2
Bristol Rovers v Leyton Orient	4-1	Queens Park Rangers *(bye)*	
Swindon Town v Southend United	2-1	Watford *(bye)*	
Colchester United v Millwall	3-6	Wimbledon v Ipswich Town	3-2
Luton Town v Charlton Athletic	3-1	Crystal Palace v Chelsea	2-6

Second Round

Portsmouth v Oxford United	1-1,2-3	Gillingham v Tottenham Hotspur	0-3
West Ham United v Bristol City	6-2	Cambridge United v Brentford	2-1
Bristol Rovers v Queens Park Rangers	1-4	Swindon Town v Watford	1-0
Millwall v Wimbledon	3-0	Luton Town v Chelsea	2-5

Quarter-Finals

Oxford United v Tottenham Hotspur	2-1	West Ham United v Cambridge United	3-0
Queens Park Rangers v Swindon Town	2-0	Millwall v Chelsea	4-0

Semi-Finals

Oxford United v West Ham United	3-4	Queens Park Rangers v Millwall	4-0

Final: West Ham United 2, QPR 3. QPR 3, West Ham Utd 2 *(Queens Park Rangers win 6-4 on aggregate).*

AFC Bournemouth: Bournemouth Spts Club, Chapel Gate, West Parley, Wimborne, Dorset.

Arsenal: University College Sports Ground, London Colney, Herts (0727 823352).

Brentford: London Transport Spts Grnd (CRS Cardinals Club), 565 Great North Rd, Hounslow, Middx.

Brighton & Hove Albion: University of Sussex, Falmer (0273 606755) *or the Goldstone Ground (0273 739535).*

Bristol City: Failand, Bristol.

Bristol Rovers: Cadbury Schweppes, Somerdale, Keynsham, Bristol (0272 352508/352303).

Cambridge United: Queens College, Barton Rd, Cambridge.

Charlton Athletic: Charlton Training Ground, Sparrows Lane, New Eltham SE9 2JR (081 859 8888).

Chelsea: Imperial College, Simpson Lane, Harlington, Middlesex (081 897 9844).

Colchester United: Essex University, Wivenhoe Park, Colchester, Essex CO4 3SQ (0206 872165) *or Layer Road if the 1st team are away (0206 574042).*

Crystal Palace: Imperial Sports Ground, Bishopsford Rd, Mitcham, Surrey (081 648 5893).

Fulham: London Fire Brigade Spts Grnd, Banstead Rd, Ewell, Surrey (081 394 1946).

Gillingham: Garrison Stadium, Brompton, Gillingham, Kent (0634 717307).

Ipswich Town: Training ground adjacent to Portman Road, Ipswich IP1 2DA (0473 219211).

Leyton Orient: Douglas Eyre Spts Centre, Coppermill Lane, Walthamstow E17 (081 520 4918).

Luton Town: Electrolux Training Ground, Ely Way, off Oakley Rd, Luton (0582 561141).

Millwall: Royal Imperial Spts Ground, Footscray Rd, London SE9 (081 850 6744).

Norwich City: Trowse Training Ground, The Street, Trowse, Norwich (0603 623612).

Oxford United: Brasenose College Spts Grnd, Abingdon Rd, Oxford (0865 243478).

Portsmouth: Royal Marine Barracks, Eastney, Portsmouth (0705 822351x24286).

Queens Park Rangers: Guinness Spts & Social Club, Twyford Abbey Rd, London NW10 (081 965 7700).

Reading: Coombe Park, Whitchurch, Pangbourne, nr Reading (0734 843940).

Southampton: Wellington Spts Grnd, Stoneham Lane, Eastleigh, Southampton (0703 612309).

Southend United: Access Spts Club, Eastern Ave., Southend-on-Sea (0702 613434).

Swindon Town: Allied Dunbar Training Centre, Wanborough, nr Swindon (0793 791282).

Tottenham Hotspur (both teams): Chase Lodge, Page Street NW7 (081 959 6741).

Watford: Woodside Stadium, Horseshoe Lane, Garston, Herts

West Ham United: Saville Rd Ground, Chadwell Heath, Essex (081 590 4441).

Wimbledon: Richard Evans Sports Ground, Roehampton Vale SW15 (081 788 7547).

SOUTHERN JUNIOR FLOODLIT CUP 1993-94

Preliminary Round

Cardiff City v Colchester United	1-0
Norwich City v Portsmouth	2-2,3-2
Brighton & Hove Albion v Leyton Orient	2-0

First Round

AFC Bournemouth v Brentford	3-1
Cardiff City v Gillingham	1-3
Coventry City v Brighton & Hove Albion	0-2
West Ham United v Luton Town	1-1,1-3
Wimbledon v Oxford United	1-1,1-2
Cambridge United v Reading	0-1
Southend United v Millwall	4-3
Chelsea v Watford	1-1,5-1
Aston Villa v Fulham	2-1
Charlton Athletic v Bristol C. *(at Bristol City)*	0-3
Wycombe Wanderers v Birmingham City	0-0,2-3
Arsenal v Ipswich Town	2-1
Tottenham Hotspur v Crystal Palace	6-1
Swindon Town v West Bromwich Albion	1-2
Queens Park Rangers v Northampton Town	3-0
Norwich City v Southampton	2-1

Second Round

AFC Bournemouth v Aston Villa	1-2
Brighton & Hove Albion v Birmingham City	5-3
Oxford United v Tottenham Hotspur	2-4
Southend United v Queens Park Rangers	2-4
Gillingham v Bristol City	1-1,0-2
Luton Town v Arsenal	1-2
Reading v West Bromwich Albion	0-2
Chelsea v Norwich City	2-2,3-4*(replay ordered)*,1-2

Quarter-Finals

Aston Villa v Bristol City	2-0
Tottenham Hotspur v West Bromwich Albion	2-0
Brighton & Hove Albion v Arsenal	1-0
Queens Park Rangers v Norwich City	3-1

Semi-Finals

Aston Villa v Brighton & Hove Albion	2-2,2-1
Tottenham Hotspur v Queens Park Rangers	2-1

Final: Aston Villa 1, Tottenham 0 Tottenham 2, Aston Villa 2 - *Aston Villa win on aggregate*

LANCASHIRE LEAGUE

DIV. ONE	P	W	D	L	F	A	PTS
Burnley 'A'	28	19	6	3	79	24	63
Crewe Alex. Res.	28	19	3	6	71	27	60
Everton 'A'	28	16	8	4	61	30	56
Manchester Utd 'A'	28	15	7	6	58	34	52
Blackburn Rvrs 'A'	28	14	3	11	44	52	45
Liverpool 'A'	28	14	2	12	66	42	44
Oldham Athletic 'A'	28	13	3	11	61	49	43
Tranmere Rvrs 'A'	28	12	6	10	44	41	42
Manchester C. 'A'	28	9	8	11	42	45	35
Bury Res.	28	10	5	13	55	61	35
Rochdale Res.	28	9	2	17	60	90	29
Chester City 'A'	28	8	3	17	39	72	27
Marine Res.	28	7	4	17	29	53	25
Blackpool 'A'	28	4	10	14	34	58	22
Morecambe Res.	28	5	1	22	20	85	16

DIV. TWO	P	W	D	L	F	A	PTS
Preston N.E. 'A'	34	22	7	5	89	42	73
Manchester Utd 'B'	34	20	8	6	111	44	68
Liverpool 'B'	34	20	7	7	92	48	67
Everton 'B'	34	19	6	9	70	49	63
Carlisle Utd 'A'	34	19	5	10	83	54	62
Wigan Athletic 'A'	34	17	6	11	67	62	57
Burnley 'B'	34	15	11	8	67	41	56
Tranmere Rvrs 'B'	34	17	5	12	65	56	56
Oldham Athletic 'B'	34	14	8	12	65	73	50
Bolton Wdrs 'A'	34	12	9	13	51	55	45
Crewe Alex. Res.	34	12	5	17	64	67	41
Manchester C. 'B'	34	11	7	16	59	66	40
Blackpool 'B'	34	10	9	15	59	77	39
Blackburn Rvrs 'B'	34	9	11	14	50	48	38
Stockport Co. 'A'	34	9	7	18	59	87	34
Rochdale 'A'	34	7	8	19	58	111	29
Bury 'A'	34	6	6	22	39	75	24
Marine 'Youth'	34	2	5	27	28	121	11

SOUTHERN COUNTIES FLOODLIT YOUTH LEAGUE

FOUNDED: 1985

	P	W	D	L	F	A	PTS
Stevenage Borough	18	14	4	0	67	17	46
Boreham Wood	18	12	4	2	54	16	40
Hoddesdon Town	18	11	2	5	46	19	35
Wingate & Finchley	18	11	1	6	49	33	34
Kingsbury Town	18	8	7	3	46	19	31
Enfield	18	6	3	9	32	31	21
Welwyn Gdn City	18	5	4	9	22	25	19
Hemel Hempstead	18	5	1	12	30	67	16
Dunstable	18	4	1	13	15	56	13
Beaconsfield Utd	18	0	1	17	10	89	1

Brian Hitchings Challenge Cup:
First Round:
Beaconsfield United 0, Enfield 3
Dunstable 0, Hemel Hempstead 3

Second Round:
Enfield 2, Stevenage Borough 3
Wingate & Finchley 1, Hoddesdon Town 5
Hemel Hempstead 3, Kingsbury Town 0
Boreham Wood 2, Welwyn Garden City 0

Semi-Finals:
Stevenage Borough 2, Hoddesdon Town 3 *(aet)*
Hemel Hempstead 2, Boreham Wood 4

Final: Boreham Wood 1, Hoddesdon Town 0

SUBURBAN LEAGUE

SOUTH DIV.	P	W	D	L	F	A	PTS
Sutton Utd Res.	32	25	7	0	113	31	82
Carshalton A Res.	32	24	2	6	99	30	74
Bromley Res.	32	20	6	6	91	42	66
Tooting & MU Res.	32	20	4	8	80	44	64
Dulwich H. Res.	32	17	7	8	62	34	*55
Crawley T. Res.	32	15	10	7	66	42	55
Whyteleafe Res.	32	14	6	12	67	58	*45
Cor.-Casuals Res.	32	11	11	10	55	57	44
Dorking Res.	32	11	4	17	61	76	37
Chipstead Res.	32	11	4	17	52	80	37
Banstead Ath. Res.	32	10	6	16	53	88	36
Malden Vale Res.	32	10	3	19	51	81	33
Epsom & Ewell Res.	32	7	10	15	56	74	31
Croydon Ath. Res.	32	8	5	19	49	73	29
Leatherhead Res.	32	8	2	22	36	93	26
Redhill Res.	32	6	6	20	36	71	24
Three Bdges Res.	32	6	5	21	44	97	23

NORTH DIV.	P	W	D	L	F	A	PTS
Ruislip Mnr Res.	30	21	5	4	90	40	68
Molesey Res.	30	18	7	5	72	26	61
Edgware T. Res.	30	18	5	7	88	51	59
Wembley Res.	30	18	8	4	64	29	*59
Met Police Res.	30	17	7	6	78	30	58
Northwood Res.	30	17	6	7	66	40	57
Hayes Res.	30	16	6	8	71	44	54
Kingsbury T. Res.	30	15	5	10	62	52	50
Uxbridge Res.	30	14	5	11	46	41	47
Staines Res.	30	8	9	13	58	63	33
Hampton Res.	30	8	7	15	44	65	31
Hanwell Town Res.	30	8	6	16	48	91	30
Hillingdon B. Res.	30	6	2	22	40	76	20
Feltham & H. Res.	30	4	6	20	59	115	18
Chalfont St P. Res.	30	4	4	22	34	94	16
Walton & H. Res.	30	2	4	14	29	92	10

WEST DIV.	P	W	D	L	F	A	PTS
Newbury T. Res.	34	28	2	4	134	51	86
Aldershot T. Res.	34	23	2	9	95	45	71
Fleet Town Res.	34	21	4	9	91	56	67
Woking Res.	34	20	5	9	90	48	65
Thame Utd Res.	34	19	6	9	66	50	63
Marlow Res.	34	19	5	10	95	62	62
Wokingham T. Res.	34	19	5	10	74	43	62
Slough T. Res.	34	17	4	13	70	73	55
Abingdon T. Res.	34	13	8	13	64	62	47
Windsor & E. Res.	34	12	6	16	67	75	42
Thatcham T. Res.	34	9	10	15	57	78	37
Maidenhead U. Res.	34	11	4	19	68	92	37
Burnham Res.	34	11	6	17	52	72	*36
Egham Town Res.	34	7	10	17	41	74	31
Camberley T. Res.	34	9	3	22	45	96	30
Bracknell T. Res.	34	7	7	20	51	77	28
Cove Res.	34	6	7	21	49	109	25
Hungerford T. Res.	34	6	4	24	42	88	22

League Cup: Tooting & Mitcham Utd Res.
League Cup R-up: Metropolitan Police
Champions Cup: Hayes
Champions Cup R-up: Sutton United

ESSEX & HERTS BORDER COMBINATION

FOUNDED: 1971

EASTERN DIV.	P	W	D	L	F	A	PTS
Ford Utd Res.	32	24	6	2	68	25	78
Heybridge S. Res.	32	24	2	6	94	30	74
Dag. & Redbdg Res.	32	22	1	9	107	37	67
Braintree T. Res.	32	19	3	10	71	48	60
Hornchurch Res.	32	15	9	8	49	49	54
Grays Ath. Res.	32	15	6	11	86	55	51
E. Thurrock U. Res.	32	13	7	12	59	61	46
Chelmsford C. Res.	32	13	5	14	58	53	44
Tilbury Res.	32	12	7	13	56	70	43
Collier Row Res.	32	11	8	13	52	67	41
Aveley Res.	32	10	7	15	51	54	37
Witham Town Res.	32	9	8	15	35	63	35
Clapton Res.	32	9	5	18	43	69	32
Tiptree United Res.	32	7	9	16	44	69	30
Billericay T. Res.	32	6	10	16	57	67	28
Barkingside Res.	32	6	7	19	35	78	25
Wivenhoe T. Res.	32	6	2	24	43	113	20

WESTERN DIV.	P	W	D	L	F	A	PTS
Berkhamsted Res.	28	19	7	2	73	33	#*65
B. Stortford Res.	28	19	7	2	77	33	64
Leyton Res.	28	17	7	4	91	30	58
Stevenage B. Res.	28	18	3	7	84	40	57
Baldock Town Res.	28	18	2	8	60	41	56
Boreham Wd Res.	28	17	3	8	71	35	54
Harlow Town Res.	28	13	7	8	48	42	46
Ware Res.	28	12	3	13	60	59	39
Walt. Pennant Res.	28	8	4	16	53	91	28
Royston Town Res.	28	8	2	18	57	76	26
Wingate & Fin. Res.	28	7	4	17	35	63	25
Hertford Town Res.	28	6	5	17	41	84	23
Hemel Hemp. Res.	28	5	6	17	42	77	*20
Saffron Walden Res.	28	5	3	20	37	85	18
Hoddesdon T. Res.	28	3	7	18	30	70	16

- 2 points awarded   * - 1 point deducted

Ford United Reserves beat **Berkhamsted Town Reserves** in play-off to become overrall champions.

Fred Budden Trophy: Berkhamsted Town Res.
Fred Budden Trophy r-up: Heybridge Swifts Res.
Combination Cup: Ford United Res.
Combination Cup r-up: Braintree Town Res.

YOUTH DIV.	P	W	D	L	F	A	PTS
East Thurrock	14	9	4	1	38	10	31
Saffron Walden	14	7	4	3	25	29	25
Royston	14	5	4	5	17	18	19
Clapton	14	3	8	3	17	14	17
Cambridge	14	4	5	5	22	32	17
Grays	14	4	4	6	19	26	16
Norwich	14	4	3	7	26	23	15
Bishop's Stortford	14	0	8	6	5	26	8

Tooting & Mitcham United Reserves - Suburban League Cup winners 1993-94.

SHEFFIELD & HALLAMSHIRE F.A.

Secretary: G Thompson JP,
Clegg House, 5 Onslow Rd, Sheffield S11 7AF (0742 670068)

SENIOR CUP 1993-94

First Qualifying Round

Avesta Sheffield v Frecheville CA	2-5
Kiveton Park v Grapes Northern Central	0-1
Treeton Welfare v Wombwell Town	5-1
Rossington Main v Staveley Miners Welfare	3-9
Rawmarsh & Ryecroft W. v Oughtibridge MWSC	0-5
Mexborough Main St. *(w/o)* Mexborough Town *(scr)*	

Second Qualifying Round

High Green Villa v Phoenix	1-2*(aet)*
Parramore Sports v British Gas Sheffield	2-4*(aet)*
Swinton Athletic v Abbeydale	1-0*(aet)*
Wath St James v Frechevilla CA	1-4
Yorkshire Main v Sheffield Centralians	1-0
Staveley MW v Harworth Colliery Institute	5-2
Old Edwardians v Grapes Northern Central	2-3
Davy v Pinegrove	3-1
Treeton Welfare *(w/o)* Thurcroft Ivanhoe *(scr)*	
Mexborough Main St. v Ecclesfield Red Rose	4-0
Goldthorpe Colliery v Sheffield Oakhouse	2-3
Caribbean Sports v Ash House	0-4
Norton Woodseats v Woodsetts Welfare	3-4
Sheffield Bankers v Clifton Rovers	6-0
Sheffield PO v Grimethorpe Miners Welfare	3-2
Throstles Ridgeway v Sheffield Aurora	1-3
Penistone Church v Wath Saracens	2-4
Denaby & Cadeby Miners Welfare v Rossington	3-1
Brunsmeer Athletic v Oughtibridge WMSC	3-0

First Round Proper

Swinton Athletic v Frecheville CA	0-8
Brodsworth Miners Welfare v Hallam	2-4
Sheffield Aurora v Grapes Northern Central	10-1
Wath Saracens v Treeton Welfare	1-2
Maltby Miners Welfare v Rossington Main	5-2
Denaby & Cadeby MW v Mexborough MS	3-1
Davy v Yorkshire Main	4-1
Brunsmeer Ath. v Stocksbridge Park Steels	0-2
Sheffield Bankers *(w/o)* Bridlington Town *(scr)*	
Worsborough Bdge MW v Worksop Town	2-3
Frickley Athletic v Emley	2-1
Staveley MW v Sheffield Oakhouse	0-0,3-0
RES Parkgate v Sheffield	0-6
Wooddsetts Welfare v Phoenix	1-3
Sheffield PO v British Gas Sheffield	2-6
Denaby United v Ash House	4-0

Second Round Proper

British Gas v Sheffield Bankers	5-2*(aet)*
Worksop Town v Denaby United	3-2
Stocksbridge Park Steels v Davy	6-1
Hallam v Frickley Athletic	2-6
Frecheville CA v Treeton Welfare	3-3,5-1
Staveley Miners Welfare v Maltby Miners Welf.	2-1
Phoenix v Denaby & Cadeby Miners Welfare	1-2
Sheffield v Sheffield Aurora	6-2

Quarter-Finals

Sheffield v Denaby & Cadeby Miners Welf.	3-2
Frecheville CA v Frickley Athletic	1-3
Stocksbridge PS v Staveley MW	1-1,3-2
Worksop Town v British Gas Sheffield	12-0

Semi-Finals (two legs)

Worksop Town v Stocksbridge PS	1-1,3-2
Sheffield v Frickley Athletic	2-1,0-0

Final *(at Sheffield Wednesday FC, Tues 5th May)*: Sheffield beat Worksop Town 6-5 on penalties after 1-1 draw, after extra-time.

WHITBREAD COUNTY SENIOR LEAGUE

Secretary: Mr R A Bowler,
1 Holbein Close, Dronfield Woodhouse, Sheffield S18 6QH.

Press Officer: Mr J Hamer,
3 Ians Way, Ashgate, Chesterfield S40 4PY.

Mexborough Main Street, consistently a top six side in recent campaigns, won their first Premier Division title since 1986-87, and proved their dominance by adding the Whitbread Trophy to complete only the third double in the League's history. Ironically on the first occasion, when Reserves Parkgate took both prizes in 1985-86, they had as their manager Steve Sigsworth - the same man who led Main Street to the dual triumph in 1994.

The early months of the campaign saw four-times winners Ash House setting the pace, but top flight debutants High Green Villa took over pole position in January and stayed there for seven weeks until a defeat at Main Street saw them toppled. High Green had the consolation of taking runners-up spot, with Ash House maintaining their high level of consistency by finishing third after last time's runners up placing.

Villa had surged into the Premier only three seasons after joining the League lifting a title in each of their highly successful terms, and still looked a good bet to make it four when they regained the leadership in mid-April. But at this stage Main Street had the games in hand to overtake them and were in the driving seat.

Mexborough knew they would be champions with a victory at Denaby & Cadeby MW on the final Saturday in April. But deadly local rivals Denaby had won nine out eleven home games and were certain to be in no mood to give their neighbours anything, and so it proved with Welfare grabbing a 1-0 victory to take the title chase to the wire. The following Wednesday, Main Street had their final game - a home clash with the League's most successful side, Ash House. Mexborough, who have a good record against Ash over the years, overcame their rivals with a 1-0 victory to lift the title and complete the double.

At the other end of the table, Rotherham based clubs Treeton Welfare and Reserves Parkgate, had been rooted to the foot of the table for over three months, but Welfare had a host of games in hand and clung to the hope that they could pull clear. Thirteen defeats in seventeen games meant that there would be no escape, but they did climb over Parkgate when the pair clashed on the last Saturday in April and Treeton came away with a 3-2 win to leave Reserves with the wooden spoon.

Goldthorpe Colliery (to be renamed Dearne CMW for 1994-95), who were rock bottom for the first two months of the campaign, got going in mid term when they took 13 points from 18 to climb to seventh. But they hit a late season slump when they managed just one point from seven games which proved disastrous leaving them in the bottom three at the final reckoning.

The First Division title went to Penistone Church, who set a tremendous pace through to February when they took 37 points from a possible 39 to look odds-on title favourites. But then Church faltered alarmingly and their overwhelming advantage was whittled away when they took just one point in five outings. But they held on to take first prize, two points ahead of runners-up Stocksbridge Park Steels. Relegated were Swinton Athletic and Rawmarch & Ryecroft WMC who were never able to meet the demands of their Division, both only managing a first win at the end of the campaign.

The top three in the Second Division had taken their berths six months prior to the final reckoning and always looked like the promotion candidates. Newcomers from Barnsley, the former NCEL side Grimethorpe MW, won their first thirteen games to top the table all season, while Pinegrove, the only side to beat them, never gave up the chase to finish runners-up. Debutants Grapes Northern General were never able to match the pace of the top pair but were always a good bet for the third spot, where they finished, ten points clear.

J Hamer, Publicity Officer.

PREM. DIVISION	P	W	D	L	F	A	PTS
Mexboro. Main St.	26	18	5	3	56	27	59
High Green Villa	26	16	7	3	51	28	55
Ash House	26	15	4	7	65	33	49
Frecheville CA	26	14	3	9	69	42	45
Parramore Sports	26	12	6	8	51	44	42
Denaby & Cadeby	26	12	4	10	48	54	40
Brunsmeer Ath.	26	11	6	9	54	41	39
Phoenix	26	8	8	10	53	42	32
Hallam Res.	26	10	2	14	46	63	32
Wath Saracens Ath.	26	8	7	11	36	40	31
Worboro. BMW Res.	26	8	3	15	35	53	27
Goldthorpe Colliery	26	7	4	15	40	77	25
Treeton Welfare	26	4	6	16	49	68	18
RES Parkgate Res.	26	4	5	17	35	76	17

DIV. ONE	P	W	D	L	F	A	PTS
Penistone Church	24	15	3	6	74	35	48
Stocksbdge PS Res.	24	14	4	6	65	36	46
Throstles Ridgeway	24	13	6	5	56	28	45
Oughtibdge WMSC	24	12	3	9	45	42	39
Wath St James	24	12	3	9	43	41	39
Ecclesfield Red Rose	24	11	5	8	45	26	38
Yorkshire Main	24	11	3	10	47	50	36
British Gas	24	9	6	9	45	52	33
Caribbean Sports	23	8	8	7	45	32	32
Wombwell Town	24	10	2	12	42	45	32
Woodsetts Sports	24	8	6	10	38	47	30
Swinton Athletic	24	1	6	17	26	74	9
Rawmarsh/Ryecroft	23	1	5	17	19	82	8

DIV. TWO	P	W	D	L	F	A	PTS
Grimethorpe MW	26	23	2	1	93	20	71
Pinegrove	26	23	1	2	97	25	70
Grapes Northern	26	16	5	5	80	37	53
Davy	26	12	8	6	46	32	*43
Sheff. Centralians	26	11	5	10	42	39	38
Sheffield Bankers	26	10	7	9	54	44	37
Sheffield Oakhouse	26	9	7	10	51	55	34
Avesta Sheffield	26	9	7	10	49	59	34
Kiveton Park Res.	26	10	2	14	42	57	32
Clifton Rovers	26	7	5	14	45	87	26
Rossington M. Res.	26	6	5	15	33	57	23
P'stone Church Res.	26	5	6	15	36	61	21
Abbeydale	26	5	6	15	36	67	21
Old Edwardians	26	2	2	22	20	84	8

PREMIER DIVISION RESULT CHART 1993-94

HOME TEAM	1	2	3	4	5	6	7	8	9	10	11	12	13	14
1. Ash House	*	3-1	6-2	1-0	9-0	2-3	1-1	3-4	1-1	3-0	2-0	2-0	2-1	2-0
2. Brunsmeer Athletic	0-1	*	2-2	3-0	4-2	1-4	2-2	3-4	0-4	2-2	6-0	0-0	5-2	4-1
3. Denaby & Cadeby MW	0-3	2-1	*	1-0	3-2	3-0	0-0	1-0	5-2	1-0	7-5	6-4	1-3	2-1
4. Frecheville CA	2-3	2-1	4-4	*	7-2	10-4	1-2	1-4	2-2	3-0	4-1	3-2	0-1	8-1
5. Goldthorpe Colliery	2-0	0-0	2-0	0-3	*	5-0	1-4	1-2	0-1	2-10	4-2	2-2	0-4	0-3
6. Hallam Reserves	1-5	2-3	0-1	1-4	0-1	*	2-2	0-4	6-3	3-1	4-1	2-1	2-1	2-0
7. High Green Villa	2-1	2-1	3-1	3-1	2-2	1-0	*	3-2	2-0	0-4	0-1	1-1	3-0	2-0
8. Mexborough Main St.	1-0	1-1	2-0	1-0	2-0	1-0	1-0	*	2-2	5-1	2-2	5-2	1-1	2-0
9. Parramore Sports	4-3	0-2	3-0	1-3	2-0	2-1	1-4	1-2	*	3-0	2-2	3-2	2-1	2-2
10. Phoenix	1-0	0-4	3-1	1-2	9-2	2-2	1-1	0-2	0-0	*	6-1	0-2	0-0	2-0
11. RES Parkgate Res.	3-3	0-1	1-0	0-4	1-3	3-1	2-3	1-2	1-4	1-8	*	2-3	2-2	0-2
12. Treeton Welfare	2-2	3-4	2-4	1-2	3-4	2-3	1-2	1-2	3-2	1-1	2-2	*	1-4	3-2
13. Wath Sarecens Ath.	0-2	0-2	1-1	2-2	2-1	1-2	0-1	1-1	0-1	1-1	1-0	5-3	*	0-3
14. Worsboro. Bdge MW	2-5	2-1	4-0	0-1	2-2	3-1	1-5	2-1	0-3	0-0	0-1	3-2	1-2	*

DIV. ONE RESULTS	1	2	3	4	5	6	7	8	9	10	11	12	13
1. British Gas	*	1-5	1-1	2-0	1-1	6-1	1-4	1-1	2-2	3-3	2-0	1-3	5-1
2. Caribbean Sports	2-2	*	0-2	0-0	3-0	4-1	1-1	4-2	1-1	3-2	4-1	1-1	3-1
3. Ecclesfield Rose Rose	0-1	1-0	*	2-0	2-1	4-0	1-3	2-1	4-0	1-3	1-2	1-1	2-3
4. Oughtibridge WMSC	2-1	3-1	0-8	*	6-1	5-2	2-1	3-0	0-3	2-0	2-4	6-4	1-2
5. Penistone Church	4-1	3-0	2-2	1-4	*	9-1	5-0	7-0	0-2	4-0	4-0	4-2	2-1
6. Rawmarsh & Ryecroft	1-4	2-2	0-3	1-1	0-4	*	0-4	3-3	1-1	0-2	3-3	0-1	0-9
7. Stocksbridge PS Res.	4-2	1-0	1-4	1-1	4-3	4-0	*	4-0	3-2	3-1	5-0	4-1	6-1
8. Swinton Athletic	1-3	2-2	0-0	1-2	1-3	1-1	1-6	*	0-5	5-2	0-5	1-2	1-3
9. Throstles Ridgeway	4-0	1-1	2-2	2-0	2-3	5-1	2-1	6-1	*	3-0	4-0	2-2	2-1
10. Wath St James	5-0	0-6	2-0	4-1	2-2	3-1	1-0	2-0	1-0	*	4-1	2-2	1-3
11. Wombwell Town	6-0	3-2	0-1	0-2	0-2	0-1	2-0	3-0	0-1	0-2	*	2-2	2-1
12. Woodsetts Sports	1-3	2-1	1-0	1-0	1-6	4-1	2-2	3-2	0-1	0-1	0-2	*	1-2
13. Yorkshire Main	0-2	1-1	2-1	0-2	0-3	2-0	3-3	2-2	4-3	1-0	2-6	2-1	*

DIV. TWO RESULTS	1	2	3	4	5	6	7	8	9	10	11	12	13	14
1. Abbeydale	*	2-2	4-4	1-2	2-3	0-3	4-5	3-2	2-1	0-3	2-2	0-4	0-1	1-3
2. Avesta Sheffield	1-0	*	4-2	5-3	0-5	1-5	2-3	2-0	1-1	3-2	3-3	3-3	0-0	2-3
3. Clifton Rovers	2-2	2-6	*	0-5	0-2	0-9	2-2	3-0	3-0	1-11	3-1	3-3	1-3	1-5
4. Davy	3-0	1-0	3-0	*	2-1	0-2	3-1	3-0	0-0	0-3	1-3	1-1	1-1	1-1
5. Grapes Northern Cen.	5-1	5-1	5-1	4-4	*	0-0	5-1	4-1	6-1	1-2	5-0	4-1	6-3	4-0
6. Grimethorpe Miners W.	5-1	4-2	5-0	1-0	3-0	*	4-1	4-0	1-0	3-1	8-1	3-2	4-2	3-2
7. Kiveton Park Res.	1-2	3-1	1-2	0-2	2-2	0-7	*	2-0	2-0	1-2	4-1	2-0	0-4	0-1
8. Old Edwardians	0-2	1-3	1-3	1-1	1-4	2-5	0-3	*	0-4	2-5	2-1	0-4	2-0	0-2
9. Penistone Church Res.	0-3	2-2	3-2	0-3	2-2	0-6	3-4	3-1	*	2-4	1-1	1-2	2-1	4-4
10. Pinegrove	6-2	4-0	5-0	4-1	4-2	3-0	3-0	7-0	3-0	*	2-1	5-1	3-0	1-1
11. Rossington Main Res.	0-0	1-2	2-3	0-2	2-0	0-2	0-2	3-0	2-1	1-5	*	1-0	0-1	2-3
12. Sheffield Bankers	5-0	2-0	2-1	1-1	1-1	0-3	2-1	6-1	3-1	1-3	2-2	*	1-2	4-1
13. Sheffield Centralians	2-0	0-1	0-0	1-1	1-2	1-2	3-0	4-0	2-1	1-4	2-1	2-2	*	2-1
14. Sheffield Oakhouse	2-2	2-2	3-6	1-2	1-2	1-1	2-1	3-3	1-3	1-2	1-2	2-1	4-3	*

WHITBREAD TROPHY 1993-94

Third Round

Ash House v Hallam Reserves 2-0
Frecheville CA v Penistone Church 4-4,3-0
Parramore Sports v Sheffield Bankers 3-0
Pinegrove v British Gas 4-3
Avesta Sheffield v Caribbean Sports 1-4
Mexborough Main Street v Sheffield Oakhouse 3-0
Penistone Church Res. v Grapes Northern Central 0-2
Woodsetts Sports v Abbeydale 4-1

Quarter-Finals

Ash House v Pinegrove 4-3
Woodsetts Sports v Parramore Sports 0-4
Caribbean Sports v Frechevilla Community Assoc. 1-2
Mexborough Main Street v Grapes Northern Centra 3-1

Semi-Finals

Ash House v Frecheville Community Assoc. 1-3
Mexborough Main Street v Parramores Sports 4-1

Final *(at Worsbrough Bridge Miners Welfare)*: Mexborough Main Street 3, Frecheville CA 2

Mexborough Main Street sealed the Whitbread Trophy final at Worsbrough Bridge against old adversaries Frecheville CA on 18th when they came from two goals down to run out 3-2 winners in extra-time. Frecheville raced into a 2-0 lead after 21 minutes courtesy of a well-struck shot from the edge of the area from Darren Kennedy, and a Mark Thompson snap volley that caught Dave Neal off his line. Not to be deterred, Main Street were level before the break. Ian Cotton headed home after 27 minutes, with David Kelly converting a 25-yard free-kick on 43 minutes. The tie was sealed two minutes into extra-time, another header from Cotton doing the trick.

PREMIER DIVISION CLUBS 1994-95

ASH HOUSE
Secretary: T Cottam, 41 Pleasant Rd, Sheffield S12 2BD (0742 390897).
Ground: Sheffield Transport, Meadowhead, Sheffield.
Directions: Sheffield A61 Chesterfield road, 4 miles to r'bout, right off Greenhill Main Road on left.

BRUNSMEER ATHLETIC
Secretary: Mr M Newton, 1 Skelton Way, Sheffield S13 7QW (0742 697900).
Ground: As Ash House (above)

DENABY & CADEBY MINERS WELFARE
Secretary: Mr D Steer, 27 Tickhill Square, Denaby Main, Doncaster DN12 4AW (0709 867824).
Ground & Directions: Denaby United FC *(see page 758).*

FRECHEVILLE C.A.
Secretary: Mr R Davenport, 45 Aspen Close, Killamarsh, Sheffield S31 8TA (0742 470937).
Ground: Silkstone Road, Frecheville, Sheffield.
Directions: From city A616 for 4 miles on Newark Road, left opposite shopping precinct into Silkstone Road.

HIGH GREEN VILLA
Secretary: T Staples, 41 Woodburn Drive, Chapeltown S30 4YT (0742 468560).
Ground: High Green Playing Fields, Mortomley Close.
Directions: A61 north for 5 miles, right at Howbrook crossroads into Greengate Lane.

MEXBOROUGH MAIN STREET
Secretary: Mr T Staples, 41 Woodburn Drive, Chapeltown, Sheffield S30 4YT (0742 468560).
Ground & Directions: As Mexborough Athletic (Oakhouse) *(see page 780)*

PARRAMORES SPORTS
Secretary: R Blagden, 15 Moor Farm Ave., Musborough Moor, Sheffield S19 5JP (0742 476757).
Ground: Prince of Wales Road, Sheffield.

PENISTONE CHURCH
Secretary: Mr D Hampshire, 36 Park Ave., Penistone, Sheffield S30 6DN (0226 764689).
Ground: Church View Road, Penistone.

PHOENIX
Secretary: D M Taylor, 22 Wilding Way, Kimberworth, Rotherham S61 1PQ (0709 555451).
Ground: Phoenix Sports Ground, Pavilion Lane, Bawtry Road, Brinsworth, Rotherham.
Directions: M1 jct 34, A631 to Rotherham - turn left after British Oxygen.

THROSTLES RIDGEWAY
Secretary: Mr P Crookes, Oak House, The Ford, Ridgeway, Sheffield S12 3YD (0246 434646).
Ground: Ridgeway Sports Ground, Main Road, Ridgeway, Sheffield.

WATH SARACENS
Secretary: Mr J L Mower, 163 Oak Rd, Wath-upon-Dearne, Rotherham S63 7JX (0709 876464).
Ground: Wath Sports Centre, Moor Road, Wath-upon-Dearne.
Directions: Rotherham, A633 through Rawmarsh, left at r'bout, left at next r'bout, Moor Road 400 yds on right.

THE DIVISION ALSO CONTAINS THE RESERVE SIDES OF: HALLAM *(see page 759)*, STOCKSBRIDGE PARK STEELS *(see page 763)*, WORSBOROUGH BRIDGE MINERS WELFARE ATHLETIC *(see page 768)*.

MEXBOROUGH & DISTRICT SUNDAY LEAGUE

FOUNDED: 1968

PREM. DIV.	P	W	D	L	F	A	PTS
Dearne CMW	20	16	3	1	72	18	35
Groves Social	20	15	2	3	76	29	32
Conisbrough Ivanhoe	20	14	1	5	54	23	29
The Gate	20	9	5	6	44	38	23
Robin Hood	20	10	2	8	40	47	22
LNER Athletic	20	6	7	7	37	36	19
Edlington WMC	20	7	4	9	47	52	18
Wath Saracens	20	8	2	11	39	38	17
Darfield Station	20	4	2	14	43	73	10
Station Athletic	20	3	3	14	28	72	9
New Masons	20	1	5	14	20	68	7

Lower Division Champions:
Div. 1 (12): Queens United
Div. 2 (11): Rock '86
Div. 3 (10): Denaby M. Hotel

ROTHERHAM & D. SUNDAY LGE

FOUNDED: 1966

Barlow Handling PD		W	D	L	F	A	PTS
Horse & Tiger	22	19	1	2	82	16	39
Three Magpies '89	22	17	4	1	77	22	38
Thurcroft Hotel	22	15	3	4	84	21	33
Maltby Miners Welf.	22	12	4	6	73	39	28
Aston Rangers	22	11	4	7	86	44	26
Treeton Welfare	22	11	2	9	60	53	24
Joker	22	8	3	11	57	59	19
Red Lion	22	6	3	11	33	56	15
Rawmarsh Earl Grey	22	6	3	13	33	56	15
Brinsworth Albion	22	5	3	14	64	59	13
Domino Rangers	22	3	1	18	40	106	7
Drawbridge	22	1	0	21	20	207	2

Lower Division Champions:
Allen Eng. D1 (12): Wickersley 3 Horse Shoes 'A'
Banks Brewery D2 (11): Hares '92
S T Sports D3 (11): Wickersley THS 'B'
Hastings D4 (11): Reresby Arms Athletic
Motorway Service Station D5 (12): Brewer '89
R C Snow D6 (12): Brecks Beefeaters
Div. 7 (12): Homestead Athletic
Burton & Jackson D8 (11): Swindon House S & S
Advertiser KO Cup winners: Thurcroft Hotel
Advertiser KO Cup runners-up: Aston Rangers
Sporting Award: Drawbridge

DONCASTER SENIOR LEAGUE

PREM. DIV.	P	W	D	L	F	A	PTS
Kinsley Boys	26	20	3	3	82	30	63
Hemsworth MW	26	18	5	3	75	31	59
Fishlake	26	15	6	5	50	36	51
Sth Kirkby Coll.	26	13	5	8	56	42	44
Hemsworth Town	26	13	5	8	60	48	44
Carcroft Village	26	11	6	9	61	41	39
Northgate WMC	26	11	5	10	51	48	38
Hemsworth St Pats	26	10	7	9	61	51	37
Worksop T. Res.	26	10	4	12	67	50	34
Goole Town Res.	26	9	5	12	54	69	32
Askern Welf. Res.	26	8	4	14	43	60	28
Peglers	26	4	8	14	31	58	20
Frickley Ath. Res.	26	3	3	20	28	66	12
Ings Lane	26	4	0	22	22	111	12

PREMIER DIVISION CUP First Round
Hemsworth Town 1, Northgate WMC 2
Worksop T. Res. 0, Goole Town Res. 1
Askern Welfare Res. 3, Ings Lane 0
Carcroft Village 2, Fishlake 3
Hemsworth St Pats 4, Hemsworth MW 1
Kinsley Boys 4, Peglers 1

Quarter Finals
Northgate WMC 1, Goole Town Res. 4
Askern Welfare Res. 0, Fishlake 1
Frickley A. Res. 3, Hemsworth St Pats 2
Kinsley Boys 3, South Kirkby Colliery 1

Semi Finals
Frickley Ath. Res. 0, Kinsley Boys 4
Goole Town Res. 1, Fishlake 2

Final (13/5/93 at Hesworth Town)
Kinsley Boys 3, Fishlake 1

DIV. ONE	P	W	D	L	F	A	PTS
Brookside WMC	24	20	4	0	63	21	64
Sutton Rovers	24	14	7	3	67	39	49
Plant Works	24	12	4	8	43	40	40
Scawthorpe Social	24	11	6	7	68	44	39
Highfields MW	24	10	7	7	48	38	37
Skellow Grange	24	8	11	5	50	32	35
Edlington WMC	24	10	2	12	52	59	32
Edlington B. Legion	23	8	6	9	44	42	30
Lodge	24	8	5	11	48	56	29
Tickhill Town	24	8	3	13	44	55	27
Scawsby United	24	6	5	13	44	73	23
White Hart United	24	5	6	13	40	63	21
Hatfield Main Res.	23	1	2	20	28	81	5

DIVISION ONE CUP First Round
Tickhill Town 6, White Hart Utd 3
Sutton Rovers 4, Scawsby Utd 2
Edlington WMC 6, Highfields MW 1
Skellow Grange 3, Edlington BL 0
Plant Works 0, Lodge 1

Quarter Finals
Scawthorpe Social 2, Tickhill Town 1
Brookside WMC 1, Sutton Rovers 2
Edlington WMC 1, Skellow Grange 2
Lodge 2, Hatfield Main Res. 1

Semi Finals
Scawthorpe Social 2, Sutton Rovers 3
Skellow Grange 5, Lodge 1 *(after 2-2 draw)*

Final (29/4/93 at Yorkshire Main FC)
Sutton Rovers 2, Skellow Grange 1 *(aet)*

DIV. TWO	P	W	D	L	F	A	PTS
Upton & Harewood	24	19	3	2	76	31	60
Ackworth United	24	17	3	4	74	29	54
Kinsley Boys Res.	24	15	5	4	58	38	50
Bentley Colliery	24	14	2	8	65	44	44
Hemsworth MW Res.	24	12	4	8	37	30	40
Tally Ho	24	9	6	9	58	54	33
White Hart Res.	24	9	3	12	60	68	30
S. Kirkby C. Res.	24	8	5	11	62	50	29
Kingshead	24	8	5	11	67	68	29
Cantley Hawthorn	24	7	8	9	58	65	29
RFS	24	4	6	14	31	60	18
Hemsworth T. Res.	24	4	1	19	39	81	13
Hemsworth SP Res.	24	3	3	18	52	119	12

DIVISION TWO CUP First Round
Ackworth Utd 1, Upton & Harewood 0
RFS 2, Cantley Hawthorn 3
Sth Kirkby Coll. Res. 3, Tally Ho 2
Hemsworth St Pats Res. 0, Bentley C. 2
Hemsworth MW Res. 4, Hemsworth T. Res. 2

Quarter Finals
Hemsworth Kingshead 4, Ackworth Utd 5
Kinsley Boys Res. 2, Cantley Hawthorn 1
White Hart Res. 2, S Kirkby C. Res. 0
Bentley Colliery 3, Hemsworth MW Res. 0

Semi Finals
Ackworth Utd Res. 3, Kinsley Boys Res. 2
White Hart Utd Res. 3, Bentley Colliery 1

Final (6/5/93 at Brodsworth MW)
Ackworth beat White Hart Utd Res. 4-2 on penalties after a 3-3 draw.

CHALLENGE CUP First Round
Kinsley Boys Res. 1, Fishlake 4
Northgate WMC 3, Kinsley Boys 1
White Hart Utd Res. 0, Carcroft Village 2
Hemsworth MW 8, White Hart United 1
Peglers 4, Askern Welfare Res. 0
Sutton Rovers 2, Hemsworth MW Res. 0
Yorkshire Main 4, South Kirkby Coll. 1
Hemsworth St Pats 1, Plant Works 2
Ackworth United 6, RFS 0

Second Round
Fishlake 2, Edlington BL 1 *(after 2-2 draw)*
Northgate WMC 3, Skellow G. 0 *(after 1-1 draw)*
Carcroft Village 2, Worksop T. Res. 1
Hemsworth MW 4, Hatfield Main Res. 0
Peglers 2, South Kirkby Colliery Res. 1
Tally Ho 2, Sutton Rovers 1
Brookside WMC 2, Highfields MW 0
Frickley Ath. Res. 5, Hemsworth SP Res. 1
Hemsworth Town Res. 1, Yorkshire Main 3
Hemsworth Town 4, Bentley Colliery 1
Scawthorpe Social 2, Tickhill Town 3
Plant Works 7, Cantley Hawthorn 2
Lodge 4, Edlington WMC 6
Upton & Harewood 5, Ings Lane 2
Scawsby United 4, Goole Town Res. 3
replay ordered: Scawsby 0, Goole 3
Hemsworth Kingshead 0, Ackworth United 1

Third Round
Fishlake 2, Northgate WMC 1
Carcroft Village 2, Hemsworth MW 1
Tally beat Peglers on pens after two 2-2s
Brookside WMC 2, Frickley Athletic Res. 1
Yorkshire Main 0, Hemsworth Town 1
Tickhill Town 1, Plant Works 3
Edlington WMC 0, Upton & Harewood 5
Ackworth 2, Goole Res. 1 *(after 1-1 draw)*

Quarter Finals
Fishlake 2, Carcroft Village 6
Tally Ho 1, Brookside WMC 3
Hemsworth Town 0, Plant Works 1
Upton & Harewood 2, Ackworth United 0

Semi Finals
Carcroft Village 2, Brookside WMC 1
Plant Works 1, Upton & Harewood 2

Final (11/5/93 at Yorkshire Main)
Carcroft Village WMC 5, Upton & Harewood Soc. 1

(result grids overleaf)

DONCASTER SENIOR LEAGUE PREMIER DIVISION RESULTS 1993-94

	HOME TEAM	1	2	3	4	5	6	7	8	9	10	11	12	13	14
1.	Askern Welfare Res.	*	1-4	0-2	2-1	2-2	0-4	3-2	5-1	8-1	L-W	L-W	1-1	2-2	1-14
2.	Carcroft Village WMC	4-0	*	1-4	5-2	9-0	0-0	1-0	1-1	3-4	1-3	1-0	4-0	2-4	1-1
3.	Fishlake	3-0	2-2	*	0-0	0-4	1-3	0-0	4-2	W-L	0-1	1-0	1-0	2-2	2-1
4.	Frickley Athletic Res.	1-3	0-2	2-3	*	0-1	1-5	0-3	0-5	7-0	0-2	1-1	2-0	0-0	0-5
5.	Goole Town Res.	2-5	4-3	2-2	2-1	*	0-2	4-5	1-2	9-1	1-0	0-5	2-3	1-3	1-4
6.	Hemsworth Miners W.	1-1	1-0	3-1	7-1	1-1	*	3-3	2-0	6-0	2-1	5-6	6-2	5-1	2-1
7.	Hemsworth St Pats	1-0	3-2	3-6	5-2	2-2	1-3	*	4-0	7-1	0-1	2-2	2-2	2-4	2-1
8.	Hemsworth Town	2-0	1-1	5-1	2-1	6-1	2-0	1-0	*	3-2	3-5	1-1	3-1	1-0	3-2
9.	Ings Lane	0-2	0-3	0-4	1-4	0-3	3-2	0-6	0-8	*	1-3	1-3	4-1	0-4	2-1
10.	Kinsley Boys	5-3	1-0	0-2	6-0	5-2	1-1	6-1	1-1	9-1	*	7-2	3-1	3-1	6-1
11.	Northgate WMC	2-3	0-3	3-4	W-L	2-3	0-2	2-1	7-2	4-0	2-7	*	1-1	3-0	3-1
12.	Peglers	2-1	1-1	0-2	2-1	2-2	1-3	1-2	1-1	6-0	1-1	1-2	*	1-1	0-5
13.	South Kirkby Colliery	W-L	2-4	1-2	2-0	3-1	1-2	3-3	4-2	3-0	1-2	1-0	4-0	*	5-2
14.	Worksop Town Res.	3-0	6-3	1-1	2-1	1-3	2-4	1-1	3-2	2-0	2-3	0-0	3-0	2-4	*

DONCASTER SENIOR LEAGUE DIVISION ONE RESULTS 1993-94

	HOME TEAM	1	2	3	4	5	6	7	8	9	10	11	12	13
1.	Brookside WMC	*	W-L	7-1	2-0	2-1	3-0	3-1	4-2	0-0	2-1	3-0	1-0	3-1
2.	Edlington British Leg.	0-5	*	3-1	4-1	1-2	2-2	2-0	2-1	3-2	0-0	1-1	4-1	4-4
3.	Edlington WMC	2-3	3-2	*	4-2	1-2	3-1	1-2	4-0	4-3	2-4	1-2	3-2	1-3
4.	Hatfield Main Res.	3-4		2-2	*	0-3	1-2	4-3	1-6	2-4	0-4	1-3	2-3	0-1
5.	Highfields Miners Welf.	0-1	2-1	5-1	2-0	*	2-3	1-1	2-2	2-2	2-2	3-4	4-1	3-1
6.	Lodge	3-5	1-1	3-2	4-2	4-0	*	0-1	1-3	1-6	2-2	1-5	5-1	6-3
7.	Plant Works	1-1	3-2	0-2	3-1	1-4	2-1	*	2-1	3-2	0-1	1-3	3-0	4-3
8.	Scawsby United	0-3	1-0	3-3	3-3	4-3	2-4	1-1	*	1-2	0-3	3-7	L-W	1-9
9.	Scawthorpe Social	2-3	1-2	1-0	6-0	0-1	1-1	4-4	6-3	*	4-4	2-4	5-0	4-0
10.	Skellow Grange	0-3	2-2	5-0	4-0	0-0	4-0	1-2	1-1	1-2	*	1-1	1-1	3-1
11.	Sutton Rovers	1-1	4-2	1-2	8-1	3-1	2-1	2-1	2-3	2-2	3-3	*	3-0	2-2
12.	Tickhill Town	1-1	0-3	2-4	5-2	2-2	1-0	0-2	9-1	2-3	4-3	1-2	*	6-2
13.	White Hart United	1-3	5-3	1-5	1-0	1-1	2-2	0-2	1-2	1-4	0-0	2-2	1-2	*

DONCASTER SENIOR LEAGUE DIVISION TWO RESULTS 1993-94

	HOME TEAM	1	2	3	4	5	6	7	8	9	10	11	12	13
1.	Ackworth United	*	3-0	5-3	0-1	10-0	3-0	2-1	1-2	3-0	4-2	4-2	0-2	4-3
2.	Bentley Colliery	0-5	*	6-1	3-0	2-2	6-2	2-0	0-1	3-1	3-1	5-1	0-1	1-5
3.	Cantley Hawthorn	0-0	4-3	*	0-0	2-2	1-4	1-1	0-4	2-2	3-2	2-2	1-1	4-2
4.	Hemsworth MW Res.	0-2	1-0	2-1	*	3-0	6-1	1-2	2-2	1-0	1-0	1-2	0-1	1-1
5.	Hemsworth St P. Res.	2-7	3-6	3-5	3-5	*	2-1	2-7	3-5	1-3	1-5	1-5	2-4	2-5
6.	Hemsworth Town Res.	0-3	2-3	1-5	0-2	5-0	*	0-8	1-2	0-2	3-4	2-1	0-1	5-6
7.	Hemsworth Kingshead	3-3	2-6	2-1	3-3	4-4	2-4	*	0-1	4-0	2-5	6-0	3-6	3-5
8.	Kinsley Boys Res.	2-5	3-4	2-1	0-1	5-3	7-1	3-1	*	3-3	2-1	W-L	2-2	2-4
9.	RFS	1-3	1-2	3-3	3-1	0-1	2-2	0-3	1-2	*	1-0	1-4	0-6	1-3
10.	South Kirkby Col. Res.	0-0	3-3	11-1	1-2	2-2	4-2	6-2	1-3	4-0	*	1-3	0-3	2-1
11.	Tally Ho	2-4	1-3	2-2	3-1	6-1	7-1	2-2	2-2	2-2	2-2	*	1-6	2-1
12.	Upton & Harewood S.	3-1	2-1	1-3	0-1	8-6	2-1	7-1	1-1	4-1	3-2	3-2	*	6-0
13.	White Hart Utd Res.	0-2	1-3	4-2	2-1	4-6	2-1	4-5	0-2	3-3	3-3	1-3	2-3	*

WORKSOP GUARDIAN SERIES
WORKSOP & DISTRICT SUNDAY LEAGUE

DIV. ONE	P	W	D	L	F	A	PTS
Worksop Borough	20	16	2	2	69	33	34
Lord Conyers Arms	20	16	2	2	79	26	34
GR Stein	18	9	5	4	36	18	23
Smokeys	17	7	4	6	41	32	18
Movietime Video	20	8	2	10	35	43	18
Rockware Glass	19	7	4	8	29	41	18
Sherwood Rgrs	17	7	3	7	39	29	17
Glassworks SC	15	6	2	7	44	29	14
Foresters	20	5	3	12	27	65	13
Greendale Oak	20	2	6	12	12	49	10
West End	20	2	3	15	17	63	7

Hodthorpe Miners Welfare - resigned

Title Play-off: Worksop Borough 3, Lord Conyers 0

Lower Division Champions:
Div. 2 (12): Ken Ward Sports
Div. 3 (14): Royal Oaks
Div. 4 (13): King Edward

Cup Finals:
Challenge Cup: Lord Conyers 3, Ken Ward Spts 2
Benevolent Cup: Worksop Boro. 1, Glassworks SC 0

SHROPSHIRE F.A.

Secretary: A W Brett,
10-11 High Str., Shrewsbury SY1 1SG (0743 362769).

SENIOR CUP 1993-94

Semi-Final

Bridgnorth Town v Shrewsbury Town 0-4

Final *(at Telford United FC, Sat 7th August 1993)*: Telford United 2, Shrewsbury Town 1

COUNTY CUP

First Round

Ludlow Town v Ludlow Colts	2-1
Wem Town v Little Drayton Rangers	2-3
Morda United v Oswestry Town	3-2*(aet)*
Shifnal Town v Clun Valley	12-0
Snailbeach White Star v Belle Vue OB	2-1
Donnington Town v Weston Rhyn United	1-4
Newport v Church Stretton Town	1-2
Meole Brace v Whitchurch Alport	4-2
Tibberton v Wellington Amateurs	2-3

Second Round

Little Drayton R. v Snailbeach WS	1-3
Clun Valley v Madeley Town	0-4
Clun Valley v Madeley Town	0-4
Ellesmere Rangers v Weston Rhyn United	5-1
Wellington Amateurs v Morda United	0-2
Star Aluminium v Oakengates Town	3-4
Albrighton S & S v Bridgnorth T. Res.	4-1
Ludlow Town v Donnington Wood	2-1
Ludlow Town v Donnington Wood	2-1
Church Stretton Town v Meole Brace	0-5

Quarter-Finals

Albrighton S & S v Morda United	0-3
Madeley Town v Meole Brace	4-2
Snailbeach White Star v Ludlow Town	1-1,0-5
Oakengates Town v Ellesmere Rangers	6-1

Semi-Finals

Ludlow T. v Madeley T. *(at Star Aluminium)*	4-1
Morda Utd v Oakengates T. *(at Ellesmere Rgrs)*	1-0

Final *(at Shrewsbury Town FC, Thurs 24th March)*: Ludlow Town 1, Morda United 0

SHROPSHIRE COUNTY LEAGUE

By Pat Brunning

With 1992/93 champions Shifnal Town moving on to the Midland Combination, the championship battle was to be far more open with no clear favourites. The first to show were Albrighton, and in the first few weeks of the season they and Meole Brace took turns to hold sway at the top of the table, with Belle Vue and Little Drayton snapping at their heels.

As the winter months approached, Albrighton took command and, due to Meole's Cup commitments and postponements, they pulled clear at the top. However, as Meole began to catch up with their fixtures, Albrighton went through a poor spell. This enabled Little Drayton and Meole to catch up, with the latter regaining top spot in December when they travelled to Albrighton and came away with a 3-2 victory. This put the Shrewsbury-based side a couple of points clear with four games in hand. From this point on, Meole never looked back finally taking the championship by some 12 points. Surprisingly, this was the first time for 23 seasons that a side from the County Town has won the County League. Second and third spots were, however, much tighter with Little Drayton needing to win at Meole Brace in order to pip Albrighton on goal difference on the last day of the season. Meole had other ideas and, much to the delight of the watching Albrighton players, they beat the Market Drayton side 2-1.

In the Premier Division League Cup there were no shocks in the first round but in the second, two of the favourites - Meole and Little Drayton - went out to less fancied sides. In the semis, Albrighton saw off Wellington 2-0 whilst Belle Vue beat Oakengates 2-1 in a replay after drawing 1-1. The final, played at the Gay Meadow, turned out to be a tight affair with Albrighton coming out on top 2-1.

FINAL TABLES

DIV. ONE	P	W	D	L	F	A	PTS
Meole Brace	26	20	2	4	67	33	62
Albrighton S & S	26	15	5	6	57	36	50
Little Drayton Utd	26	15	2	9	77	48	47
Ellesmere Rgrs	26	13	4	9	60	45	43
Wellington Amtrs	26	13	4	9	43	38	43
Belle Vue Old Boys	26	10	7	9	44	33	37
Star Aluminium	26	10	6	10	51	59	36
Oakengates Town	26	8	8	10	39	42	32
Madeley Town	26	9	4	12	48	52	32
Tibberton	26	10	2	14	49	56	*29
Snailbeach White S.	26	7	7	12	44	61	28
Donnington Town	26	7	5	14	48	66	26
Church Stretton T.	26	7	4	15	44	70	25
Newport	26	5	5	16	38	68	20

DIV. TWO	P	W	D	L	F	A	PTS
Hadley Keys	24	14	6	4	74	31	48
Hanwood United	24	15	2	7	54	30	47
St Martins	24	10	5	9	46	54	35
Morda United Res.	24	9	3	12	40	39	30
Weston Rhyn Utd	24	8	3	13	38	54	27
Donnington Park	24	8	2	14	35	55	26
Telford Juniors	24	7	5	12	33	57	*23

* - Three points deducted

SHROPSHIRE COUNTY LEAGUE CLUB DIRECTORY

ALBRIGHTON SPORTS & SOCIAL

Secretary: J Rhoden, 17 Bushfield Rd, Albrighton, Wolverhampton (0902 372730).
Ground: Loak Road, Albrighton, Wolverhampton.
Colours: All red | **Change colours:** All blue. | **Programme:** No.
Cover: No | **Clubhouse:** No. | **Tea Bar:** Yes.

BELLE VUE OLD BOYS

Secretary: P W Davies, 9 Millmead Drive, Sutton Rd, Shrewsbury, Shropshire (0743 362103).
Ground: Springfield, Mereside, Shrewsbury, Shropshire.
Colours: Red/blue | **Change colours:** All blue. | **Programme:** No.
Cover: No | **Clubhouse:** No. | **Tea Bar:** No.

CHURCH STRETTON TOWN

Secretary: K Hartley, Wheelridge, Watling Street South, Church Stretton (0694 724281).
Ground: Russells Meadow, Church Stretton.
Colours: White/navy | **Change colours:** Orange/black | **Programme:** No.
Cover: Yes - overhang | **Clubhouse:** Yes | **Tea Bar:** Yes.

DONNINGTON PARK

Secretary: D Johns, 30 Wrekin Drive, Donnington, Telford, Shropshire (0952 603929).
Ground: Idsall Sports Centre, Shifnal.
Colours: Black & white/red & black | **Change colours:** All blue. | **Programme:** No.
Cover: No | **Clubhouse:** No. | **Tea Bar:** No.

DONNINGTON TOWN

Secretary: B Rose, 68 Stafford Rd, Oakengates, Telford, Shropshire (0952 618204).
Ground: Donnington Recreation Ground, Donnington, Telford.
Colours: Red/black | **Change colours:** Blue/white. | **Programme:** No.
Cover: No | **Clubhouse:** No. | **Tea Bar:** No.

ELLESMERE RANGERS

Secretary: J Edge, 21 Hillcrest, Ellesmere (0691 623587).
Ground: Beech Grove Sports Field, Ellesmere.
Colours: Yellow/blue | **Change colours:** Sky/navy. | **Programme:**
Cover: No | **Clubhouse:** No. | **Tea Bar:** Yes.

HADLEY KEYS

Secretary: J Newbrook, 107 Hadley Park, Hadley, Telford, Shropshire (0952 244711).
Ground: Leegomery Playing Fields, Telford.
Colours: Blue & black/black | **Change colours:** Yellow/blue. | **Programme:** No.
Cover: No | **Clubhouse:** No. | **Tea Bar:** No.

HANWOOD UNITED

Secretary: G L Evans, 7 Hordley Avenue, Shrewsbury (0743 343124).
Ground: Recreation Ground, Hanwood.
Colours: White/red | **Change colours:** All blue. | **Programme:** No.
Cover: No | **Clubhouse:** No. | **Tea Bar:** No.

LITTLE DRAYTON RANGERS

Secretary: B Garratt, Garlow, Quarry Bank Rd, Market Drayton (0630 654618).
Ground: Greenfield Sports Ground, Market Drayton.
Colours: Red/white | **Change colours:** Yellow/black. | **Programme:** No.
Cover: Yes | **Clubhouse:** No. | **Tea Bar:** Yes.

MADELEY TOWN

Secretary: N Broome, 1 Severn Way, Little Dawley, Telford, Shropshire (0952 587620).
Ground: Sutton Park, Sutton Park, Telford.
Colours: All green | **Change colours:** All blue. | **Programme:** No.
Cover: No | **Clubhouse:** No. | **Tea Bar:** No.

MEOLE BRACE

Secretary: L W Rowlinson, 50 Alberbury Drive, Sundorne, Shrewsbury, Shropshire (0743 248962).
Ground: Church Road, Meole Brace, Shrewsbury.
Colours: Coral, purple & white/purple | **Change colours:** Grey/red. | **Programme:** Yes.
Cover: No | **Clubhouse:** No. | **Tea Bar:** Yes.

MORDA UNITED RESERVES *(see page 590)*

NEWPORT

Secretary: Mrs J Henry, 2 Meadow Rd, Newport (0952 825006).
Ground: Shukers Field, Newport.
Colours: Blue & white/black or white | **Change colours:** All red. | **Programme:** Yes.
Cover: No | **Clubhouse:** No. | **Tea Bar:**

OAKENGATES TOWN

Secretary: Mrs P Hickman, 6 Hatton Common, Hinstock, Market Drayton (0952 78282).
Ground: off School Grove, Oakengates.
Colours: Sky & navy/navy | **Change colours:** | **Programme:** Yes.
Cover: Yes. | **Clubhouse:** Yes. | **Tea Bar:** Yes.

St MARTINS

Secretary: D Stokes, 49 Garden Village, St Martins, Oswestry (0691 772699).
Ground: Gatacre Playing Fields, Oswestry.
Colours: Yellow/green **Change colours:** Blue/black.

SNAILBEACH WHITE STARS

Secretary: V Jones, 125 Lythwood Rd, Bayston Hill, Shrewsbury, Shropshire (0743 872672).
Ground: The Coates, Snailbeach.
Colours: Green/black **Change colours:** Blue & grey/blue. **Programme:** No.
Cover: No **Clubhouse:** Yes. **Tea Bar:** Yes.

STAR ALUMINIUM

Secretary: D J Rymer, 6 Callaughton, Much Wenlock, Shropshire (0952 727542).
Ground: Stourbridge Road, Bridgnorth, Shropshire.
Colours: Blue & white/black **Change colours:** Yellow/navy. **Programme:** No.
Cover: No **Clubhouse:** Yes. **Tea Bar:**

TELFORD JUNIORS

Secretary: G Griffiths, 7 Concorde, Dawley Bank, Telford (0952 503672).
Ground: Doseley Road, Dawley, Telford.
Colours: Tangerine/green **Change colours:** White/green **Programme:** No.
Cover: No **Clubhouse:** No. **Tea Bar:** No.

TIBBERTON

Secretary: D Waites, 9 Tudor Close, Newport (0952 813776).
Ground: Maslan Crescent, Tibberton, near Newport.
Colours: Black & blue/black **Change colours:** White/blue. **Programme:** Yes.
Cover: No **Clubhouse:** No. **Tea Bar:** Yes.

WELLINGTON AMATEURS

Secretary: G Richards, 7 Kings Court, Wellington, Shropshire (0952 245464).
Ground: Leegomery Playing Fields, Telford.
Colours: Navy & white/navy & red **Change colours:** Green & navy. **Programme:** Yes.
Cover: No **Clubhouse:** No. **Tea Bar:** No.

WESTON RHYN UNITED

Secretary: C W Mottram, Delamere, Old Chirk Rd, Gobowen, Oswestry (0691 661648).
Ground: Recreation Ground, Weston Rhyn, Oswestry.
Colours: All blue **Change colours:** Red/black.

SHREWSBURY HOTEL SHREWSBURY & DISTRICT SUNDAY LEAGUE

PREM. DIV.	P	W	D	L	F	A	PTS
Monkmeer	20	18	2	0	63	19	36
Plough	20	13	4	3	52	26	29
Instones United	20	11	7	2	62	40	24
Belle Vue Sunday	20	10	7	3	65	42	23
Ford	20	9	8	3	40	38	21
Brick Sports	20	10	10	0	50	64	20
Nalgo Sunday	20	8	10	2	46	48	18
The Apprentice	20	8	10	2	36	43	18
Pontesbury	20	7	10		40	58	17
Bayston Hill Clt	20	3	14	3	25	52	9
Cruckton Rovers	20	2	17	1	22	73	5

Lower Division Champions:
Div. 1 (11): Grove
Div. 2 (10): Meole '86
Div. 3 (11): Harry Hotspur
Div. 4 (11): Brick Rangers
Div. 5 (11): Compasses Bridgnorth

KEEP IN TOUCH with the latest developments on the non-League football scene

Make sure you get your copy of

TEAM TALK MAGAZINE

Incorporating
Non-League Football
Magazine

84 pages per month for £2.20. Available from your local newsagent, your local Non-League club, or the address on Page 3 of this book.

Team Talk features Conference to County League football

STAFFORDSHIRE F.A.

Secretary: C S Brookes,
County Showground, Weston Rd, Stafford ST18 0DB (0785 56994).

SENIOR CUP 1993-94

First Round

Match	Score	Match	Score
Armitage '90 v Blakenall	1-2	Dudley Town v Boldmere St Michaels	3-1
Chasetown v Bilston Town	1-1,2-0	Sutton Coldfield Town v Macclesfield Town	2-5
Kidsgrove Athletic v Walsall Wood	0-0,2-1	Halesowen Town v Halesowen Harriers	3-1
Newcastle Town v Hednesford Town	1-3	Tamworth v Pelsall Villa	0-1
Rushall Olympic v Stourport Swifts	2-3	Brierley Hill v Knypersley	2-2*(7-6 on pens)*
Stoke City v Paget Rangers	0-1	Congleton Town v Rocester	3-3,3-3,1-2
Redditch United v Stourbridge	1-3	Wednesfield v Port Vale	1-0
Oldbury United v Stafford Rangers	0-2	Eastwood Hanley v Leek Town	1-2

Second Round

Match	Score	Match	Score
Dudley Town v Chasetown	2-2,2-1	Blakenall v Brierley Hill Town	2-2,1-3
Paget Rangers v Stourport Swifts	1-1,2-1	Hednesford Town v Leek Town	3-4
Pelsall Villa v Macclesfield Town	1-1,1-3	Kidsgrove Athletic v Wednesfield	0-3
Halesowen Town v Rocester	4-0	Stourbridge v Stafford Rangers	1-2

Quarter-Finals

Match	Score	Match	Score
Paget Rangers v Leek Town	3-0	Brierley Hill Town v Wednesfield	1-3
Macclesfield Town v Halesowen Town	4-1	Stafford Rangers v Dudley Town	1-1,1-3

Semi-Finals

Match	Score	Match	Score
Macclesfield v Dudley Town	2-0	Wednesfield v Paget Rangers	1-0

Final - Held over to 1994-95 season.

STAFFORDSHIRE F.A. VASE: Meir KA (runners-up: Ball Haye Green).

REFUGE ASSURANCE MIDLAND LEAGUE

(Formerley Staffs Senior League)

President: P Keller
Chairman: F Askey
Vice-Chairman: A Key
Secretary: J K Johnson,
149 St Nicholas Ave., Norton, Stoke-on-Trent ST6 8JW (534866)

The league kicked off without Stafford Town and Walsall Wood who had left for the West Midland League, Stafford living up to the Refuge tradition set by first Rocester then Knypersley Victoria, by taking the Division One title of the West Midland League in their first season.

There were two newcomers. Cannock Town, who had to bring their Avon Road ground and facilities up to standard before getting the nod, were turned off mid-way through the season when their landlords, British Coal, closed down Littleton Mine. Cannock Stadium came to their rescue, but even that was short-lived, just enabling them to complete the season. Parkway Clayton, who share the impressive Lyme Valley Stadium with North West Counties side Newcastle Town, were the other newcomers. Having a strong local pedigree, the Parkway club were expected to do well.

Champions in both 1992 and 1993, Redgate Clayton were firm pre-season favourites to make it three in a row. Without the likes of Stafford Town and Walsall Wood, it was difficult to see from where others with the necessary championship aspirations could come. Norton United and Brocton were possible contenders, but in the end the main challenge came from a totally unexpected quarter.

Having ended the previous season on a high note, Goldenhill Wanderers received some support as potential challengers, but this did not last long as they received a 6-1 thrashing in the opening game at Redgate. It was a defeat that set the pattern for the Wanderers, struggling to make their mark throughout the season.

Audley, another side who usually start well and finish badly, did just the opposite this time. With just three wins from twelve outings, they were having a torrid time, but to their credit they pulled themselves together, stringing a run of seventeen games without defeat. Fighting their way into four cup semi finals, the Audley club ended the season dissapointed, losing three of the semis and the final that they did reach. A long run of drawn and lost games after a bright start, caused in the main by the conceding of goals at the death, saw Norton United's chances melt away before the half way-stage of the season. Like many other sides in the league they were constantly having to fight off approachs for their players by contributory teams in which money did the talking.

Although a good cup side, Brocton do not impress as championship contenders and so it again proved. With a third of the programme completed, Brocton had won just three games, yet still contrived to reach the semi-final of the Staffs FA Vase. An interesting aspect to the season was the number of away games won in comparison to home games, a situation that brought its fair share of shock resultes. *(continued overleaf)*

FINAL TABLE	P	W	D	L	F	A	PTS
Redgate Clayton	32	21	6	5	101	30	69
Ball Haye Green	32	19	7	6	68	30	64
Leek CSOB	32	16	7	9	62	39	55
Norton United	32	14	10	8	61	46	52
Parkway Clayton	32	15	7	10	52	41	52
Brocton	32	14	7	10	52	47	49
Audley	32	14	7	11	50	46	49
Rists United	32	16	1	15	45	56	49
Staffs Police	32	12	8	12	61	59	44
Eccleshall	32	12	8	12	59	61	44
Milton United	32	11	10	11	44	55	43
Goldenhill Wdrs	32	11	9	12	42	43	42
Congleton Hornets	32	11	8	13	44	50	41
Cannock Town	32	9	3	20	50	78	30
Hanford	32	7	7	18	37	59	28
Heath Hayes	32	6	9	17	34	81	27
Brereton Social	32	3	8	21	34	75	17

In consecutive seasons Hanford and Ball Haye Green had pleaded for re-election. Both clubs of long standing and successful history of honours in the past, they repaid the faith shown in them by the league with vastly improved performances. In Hanford's case it was not so much their results that set the league alight, but the fact that they moved grounds - to Northwood Stadium, complete with an 800 seater stand and floodlights to boot, a positive way to ensure that the only way Hanford will be going from now on is up.

In one season Balle Haye Green went from second bottom to second top. They thrust themselves into a potential championship position with a influx of new players that brought new life into a club with a 113 year history. For much of the season 'Green' led that table, but there was always the threat of Redgate Clayton breathing down their necks and, despite gaining full points from their visit to Northwood Lane they ended up one place short of the top. Consolation came in reaching the final of the Staffs Vase, a success made sweeter as thei win came against arch opponents and neighbours Leek CSOB.

Despite going down to Ball Haye Green in the Leek Cup, Leek CSOB finished in their highest-ever position. Led by ex-Leek Town captain Chris McMullin, Old Boys delighted with their neat football, but lacked the experience necessary to capitalise on their ability.

Another surprise team were Rists United. After tightening up an early season leaky defence with the inclusion of ex-Port Vale defender Ripley, a string of wins spiralled them up the table. Newcomers Parkway Clayton had a good first season, giving tidy performances including reaching the semi-finals of the League Cup, but fellow freshmen Cannock Town found the going very difficult, not helped by the loss of Avon Road. Town consistently threw away first-half leads by failing to stay the course.

There was never any chance of Brereton Social lifting themselves away from the bottom of the table, making the position theirs from day one. Heath Hayes, their companions in distress, started reasonably brightly, but a disastrous run of nineteen games without a win left them too much to do to escape joining Brereton.

Staffordshire Police turned out to be a real Jekyl and Hyde side. Good performances one week would be followed by quite the opposite the next, and their results merited their mid-table position. Of the others, Congleton Hornets had the consolation of winning their Cheshire County Cup although they were never a force in the League.

The season belonged to Redgate Clayton. They claimed their third consecutive title with a side blessed by a strong defence allied to speedy forwards. It was not a season without its set-backs for the 'Gate', however. Lowly Hanford comprehensively dispatched them dispatched them from the Staffs FA Vase, while progress in the Leek Cup came to an end in a replay at Ball Haye Green.

The League next season will be without Cannock Town and Brereton Town, both having gone defunct due to ground problems with the former and financial restraints for the latter. Nine new clubs have been accepted for 1994-95; Adderley Green, Baddeley Green Rangers, Biddulph Victoria, Cheadle Old Boys, Cheadle Rovers, GEC Alsthom, Florence, Nantwich and Stallington.

J K Johnson, Secretary.

RESULTS 1993-94	1	2	3	4	5	6	7	8	9	10	11	12	13	14	15	16	17
1. Audley	*	1-0	2-2	0-1	4-2	1-2	5-1	2-2	2-1	4-1	1-1	0-0	4-3	2-0	1-1	2-1	4-0
2. Ball Haye Green	2-0	*	2-0	0-0	3-0	1-1	3-1	4-1	5-1	2-0	3-0	1-0	2-2	4-1	1-2	0-1	0-0
3. Brereton Social	0-2	0-3	*	1-2	1-2	3-1	1-1	1-2	0-1	3-1	0-3	0-1	2-2	2-2	0-3	6-2	1-4
4. Brocton	3-0	3-4	3-0	*	0-1	1-1	1-2	0-1	1-3	1-1	0-1	2-1	1-0	1-3	3-3	0-2	2-1
5. Cannock Town	4-1	2-5	1-1	1-2	*	2-3	1-3	3-2	1-1	1-2	2-3	4-1	0-0	2-3	0-2	2-0	0-3
6. Congleton Hornets	2-2	4-2	2-2	1-3	3-0	*	2-4	0-1	2-1	2-1	0-2	0-1	0-2	1-0	3-3	1-2	2-1
7. Eccleshall	4-2	2-2	3-2	1-2	2-4	2-2	*	0-4	1-1	1-2	0-1	1-1	0-2	3-1	1-2	2-0	6-0
8. Goldenhill Wanderers	1-3	1-1	2-0	1-3	0-1	2-0	1-1	*	2-1	8-0	1-2	0-2	1-2	0-0	0-1	1-0	1-0
9. Hanford	1-0	0-1	2-1	1-3	3-0	0-3	0-1	0-1	*	1-2	2-2	1-1	3-4	0-2	2-4	0-1	1-1
10. Heath Hayes	0-1	0-2	2-2	2-2	1-2	1-0	3-3	0-0	1-1	*	0-4	0-1	3-4	0-2	0-7	2-0	1-1
11. Leek CS Old Boys	4-0	1-0	3-0	1-3	7-2	0-1	0-1	2-2	3-0	1-1	*	0-0	1-2	3-0	1-5	5-0	3-2
12. Milton United	2-0	0-2	1-1	3-2	5-4	1-1	2-4	0-0	0-3	6-2	0-0	*	1-1	3-0	0-5	1-3	3-3
13. Norton United	1-2	1-3	1-0	1-1	3-2	2-0	3-1	1-1	4-0	1-2	1-1	5-0	*	1-1	3-3	3-0	1-1
14. Parkway Clayton	1-0	0-0	4-0	0-0	2-0	3-2	2-2	2-0	5-1	1-1	4-2	1-2	1-2	*	0-3	2-3	3-0
15. Redgate Clayton	3-0	2-3	6-0	6-0	5-0	3-0	3-0	6-0	0-0	9-0	3-1	2-0	5-2	1-2	*	1-2	1-1
16. Rists United	0-2	0-5	7-1	1-4	2-1	0-0	2-0	4-2	2-1	2-0	2-1	2-4	1-0	0-3	2-0	*	1-2
17. Staffordshire Police	0-0	3-2	2-1	3-2	5-3	1-2	4-5	1-1	3-4	6-2	1-3	5-1	3-1	0-1	2-1	2-0	*

LEAGUE CUP 1994-95 Preliminary Round

Staffordshire Police v Ball Haye Green 3-6

First Round

Audley v Ball Haye Green 1-1,3-2*(aet)*
Congleton Hornets v Milton United 4-1
Hanford v Heath Hayes 4-2
Parkway Clayton v Rists United 1-1,2-1
Brocton v Eccleshall 2-1
Goldenhill Wanderers v Cannock Town 2-1
Norton United v Leek CS Old Boys 0-1
Redgate Clayton v Brereton Social 4-0

Quarter-Finals

Brocton v Audley 1-1,1-2
Hanford v Goldenhill Wanderers 1-1,0-4
Redgate Clayton v Leek CS Old Boys 3-3,1-0
Parkway C. v Congleton 1-1,2-2*(aet, Parkway on away goals)*

Semi-Finals

Redgate Clayton v Parkway Clayton 2-0
Audley v Goldenhill Wanderers 1-0

Final *(at Eastwood Hanley FC)*: Redgate Clayton 4, Audley 0

DIVISION ONE CLUBS 1994-95

AUDLEY

Chairman: M Cork **Manager:** Wayne Smith **Founded:** 1985
Secretary: Alan Smith, Frensham, Newfold Cres., Brown Edge, Stoke-on-Trent ST6 8QZ (0782 782108).
Ground: Old Road, Bignall End, Stoke-on-Trent (0782 723482).
Directions: M6 jct 16, A500 (Stoke), take 1st exit for Alsager/Audley, after 1 and a half miles (next junction) turn left, left into ground after brow of hill.
Colours: Red/navy/red **Midweek home matchday:** Wednesday **Floodlights:** No.
Previous Leagues: Fenton & Dist., Newcastle & Dist., North Staffs Alliance, Staffs Co.
Hons: Staffs Snr Lg Cup 89-90 (R-up 93-94, Chall. Shield 90-91), Staffs Co. Lg R-up 89-90, Bourne Sports Trophy 89-90 (R-up 90-91), Fenton & Dist. Lg R-up 85-86.

BALL HAYE GREEN

Chairman: John K Murfin **Manager:** Peter Booth **Founded:** 1880
Secretary: Michael Naylor, 27 Wallbridge Close, Leek ST13 8HZ (0538 383711).
Ground: Rear Balle Haye Green WMC, Leek (0538 371926).
Directions: M6 jct 15 or 16, A500, A53, 7 miles over flyover into Leek. 2nd exit at town centre r'bout, straight thru lights to Balle Haye Green WMC - ground at rear.
Colours: Green & white/green/green **Midweek home matchday:** Wednesday **Floodlights:** Yes
Previous Leagues: Leek & Moorland, Staffs Co., Manchester.
Hons: Staffs Snr Lg R-up 93-94 (Lg Cup R-up 89-90), Staffs Co. Lg 83-84 (Lg Cup 83-84), Leek Cup 83-84 93-94, Staffs Vase R-up 93-94.

BROCTON

Chairman: Nigel Pepper **Manager:** Trevor Cook **Founded:** 1937
Secretary: T J Homer, 124 John Street, Chadsmoor, Cannock WS11 2HR (0543 571964).
Ground: Rowley Park Stadium, Stafford (0785 51060).
Directions: M6 jct 13, 2 miles on A449 to Stafford, left after Royal Oak into West Way, right into Averill Rd after half mile - leads direct to Rowley Park Stadium.
Cols: Green & white/white/green & white **Midweek home matchday:** Monday **Floodlights:** No.
Previous League: Staffs Co. (South) **Hons:** Staffs Snr Lg Cup 92-93.

CONGLETON TOWN HORNETS

Chairman: Peter Farrow **Manager:** Alan Hughes **Founded:** 1896
Secretary: David Wilcock, 4 Maxwell Road, Congleton, Cheshire CW12 3HY (0260 276347).
Ground: Booth Street, Congleton (0260 274460)*(see page 296 for directions)*
Colours: Black & white/black/black. **Midweek home matchday:** Tuesday **Floodlights:** Yes
Previous Leagues: Macclesfield & District, Mid-Cheshire.
Honours: Macclesfield FA Cup 93-94.

ECCLESHALL

Chairman: R M Lloyd **Manager:** Barry Lowe **Founded:** 1971
Secretary: Jed C Atkins, 30 School Road, Eccleshall ST21 6AS (0785 851016).
Ground: Pershall Park, Near Eccleshall.
Directions: M6 jct 14, A5013 to Eccleshall, right at T-junction, left at cross-roads into High Street (B5026) for 1 mile - ground on right.
Colours: Blue & black/blue/blue **Midweek home matchday:** Wednesday **Floodlights:** No.
Previous Leagues: Stafford & District, Staffs Alliance, Staffs County (North).
Hons: Staffs Snr Lg 89-90, Staffs Vase R-up 84-85 85-86.

GOLDENHILL WANDERERS

Chairman: Joseph Birchall **Manager:** Bryan Finney **Founded:** 1885
Secretary: Michael J Goodwin, 4 Russell Place, Sandyford ST6 5LS (0782 824838).
Ground: Shelford Road, Sandyford (0782 811977).
Directions: M6 jct 16, A500, 2nd exit (signed Kidsgrove), 2nd left at r'bout, right at next r'bout, left at next 2 r'bouts, right after 50yds (by Hop Inn) into Sheldon Rd - ground at end.
Colours: Blue/white/blue **Midweek home matchday:** Wednesday **Floodlights:** No.
Previous Leagues: Staffs Co. (North) **Hons:** Staffs Snr Lg Cup R-up 85-86, Staffs Vase 83-84.

HANFORD

Chairman: D Finney **Manager:** Alan Ryder **Founded:** 1959
Secretary: Ian Bradbury, 9 Frenchmore Grove, Lightwood, Longton ST3 7SF (0782 341877).
Ground: Northwood Stadium (0782 269773).
Directions: M6 jct 15, A500 to Stoke, over flyover then right at r'bout, 200yds on left at r'bout, after 400yds bear right at lights on to Leek Rd, left at next lights into Bucknall Rd then 1st right into Keelings Rd - ground on right.
Colours: All blue **Midweek home matchday:** Wednesday **Floodlights:** Yes.
Previous Leagues: Fenton & Dist., Staffs County (North).
Honours: Staffs Co. North Lg 83-84 85-86.

HEATH HAYES

Chairman: John Weddon **Manager:** Garry Jones **Founded:** 1965
Secretary: Peter J Francis, 191 Hednesford Road, Heath Hayes (0543 274212).
Ground: Newlands Lane, Heath Hayes.
Directions: M6 jct 11 for Cannock, follow signs for Lichfield for two & a half miles, 1st right after Texaco garage into Newlands Lane, ground 50yds ahead on left past public pitch.
Colours: Blue & white/blue/blue **Midweek home matchday:** Wednesday **Floodlights:** No.
Previous League: Staffs Co. (South)

LEEK C.S.O.B.

Chairman: Kenneth J Hill **Manager:** Chris McMullin **Founded:** 1945
Secretary: Stanley H Lockett, 5 Fitzherbert Close, Swynnerton, Stone ST15 0PQ (0782 796551).
Ground & Directions: As Leek Town FC (see page 346).
Colours: Red/white/white **Midweek home matchday:** Wednesday **Floodlights:** Yes
Honours: Leek Cup R-up 93-94. **Prev. Lgs:** Leek & Moorland, Staffs All., Staffs Co. (N).

MILTON UNITED

Chairman: Maurice Sherratt **Manager:** Craig Vernon **Founded:** 1985
Secretary: Maurice Sherratt, 3 Clifford Avenue, Norton Green (0782 533775).
Ground: Leek Road, Milton End.
Directions: M6 on to A500 past Stoke City FC, right at r'bout for 200yds then left at next r'bout to lights, follow signs for Leek straight ahead at next r'bout & thru lights getting into lane marked Milton, ahead for 2 miles, ground 100yds on right after crematorium.
Colours: Blue & white/white/white **Midweek home matchday:** Wednesday **Floodlights:** No.
Previous Leagues: Staffs County, Mid-Cheshire.
Hons: Staffs Snr Lg R-up 84-85 (Lg Cup 87-87 88-89, Chall. Shield 87-88 89-90), Staffs Vase 88-89 89-90.

NORTON UNITED

Chairman: Alan Tittensor **Manager:** Neil Dundas **Founded:** 1989
Secretary: Dennis Vickers, 86 Ford Green Road, Smallthorne, S.-on-T. ST6 1NX (0782 822727)
Ground: Norton CC & MW Institute, Community Drive, Smallthorne (0782 838290).
Directions: M6 jct 15, A500 for 4 miles to Tunstall turn-off, right at r'bout, half mile to Burslem, thru light in town centre towards Smallthorne, 3rd exit at mini-r'bout at top of hill proceeding 500yds to pedestrian crossing before turning right into Community Drive - ground 200yds on left.
Colours: Red & black/black/black **Midweek home matchday:** Wednesday **Floodlights:** No.
Hons: Staffs Snr Lg R-up 92-93 (Lg Cup 91-92 (R-up 92-93), Chall. Shield 92-93(shared)).

PARKWAY CLAYTON

Chairman: Eric Whitmore **Manager:** Glyn Chamberlain **Founded:** 1964
Secretary: Arthur Carr, 7 Hackney Close, Longton, S.-on-T. ST3 1LT (0782 594688)
Ground: As Newcastle Town FC (see page 653)
Colours: Blue/white/blue. **Midweek home matchday:** Wednesday **Floodlights:** Yes
Previous League: Mid-Cheshire
Honours: None.

REDGATE CLAYTON

Chairman: Arthur Jackson **Manager:** Bernard Bramwell **Founded:** 1969
Secretary: Roger Farr, 9 Winnipeg Close, Trentham, Stoke-on-Trent ST4 8UE (0782 641334).
Ground: Northwood Lane, Clayton, Newcastle-under-Lyme (0782 717409).
Directions: M6 jct 15, left for Newcastle, past Post House Hotel, ground on right at 1st r'bout.
Colours: Red/blue/red **Midweek home matchday:** Wednesday **Nickname:** Gate
Previous Name: Manor Park **Prev. Grnds:** St Josephs College 84-87/ Oldfields Spts Grnd
Previous Leagues: Fenton & District, Longton & District, Staffs County.
Hons: Staffs Snr 87-88 91-92 92-93 93-94 (R-up 86-87 90-91, Lg Cup 90-91 93-94 (R-up 87-88 91-92 92-93), Challenge Shield 88-89), Walsall Snr Cup 89-90, Staffs Vase 91-92.

RISTS UNITED

Chairman: Gordon Attwood **Manager:** Peter Hall **Founded:** 1956
Secretary: Graham Michael Rutter, 46 James Street, Wolstanton ST5 0BX (0782 619567).
Ground: Lower Milehouse Lane, Newcastle-under-Lyme (0782 563366x4405).
Directions: M6 jct 15 then follow signs for Newcastle town centre then Congleton (A34), approx 2 miles from Newcastle centre turn left by Berni Tavern then 2nd right - ground in Rists factory. From M6 jct 16 take A500 then 2nd exit (Newcastle & Congleton), turn right for Newcastle, over r'bout, lights, r'bout turning right at third r'bout then follow above from 'Berni Tavern'.
Colours: All green **Midweek home matchday:** Wednesday **Floodlights:** No.
Previous Leagues: Newcastle & District, Staffs Co. (North).
Honours: Staffs Co. (North) Lg 88-89 (Lg Cup 85-86).

STAFFORDSHIRE POLICE

Chairman: R A Woolwich **Manager:** Peter Dent **Founded:** 1953
Secretary: Chris Haines, Police House, Blythe Bridge Rd, Caverswall, Stoke-on-Trent ST11 9ET (0782 397678).
Ground: Silkmore Lane, Stafford (0785 58386).
Directions: M6 jct 14, A5013 Eccleshall Rd towards Stafford, A34 signs along Kingsway then Lichfield Rd towards Cannock, right at Queensvilla r'bout into Silkmore Lane turning left into ground immediately after Lancaster Rd.
Colours: Blue & black/black/black **Midweek home matchday:** Wednesday **Floodlights:** No.
Previous Leagues: Staffs County, West Midlands (Regional)
Hons: Staffs Snr Lg R-up 90-91 (Lg Cup 87-88 (R-up 86-87), Challenge Shield 88-89).

DIVISION TWO CLUBS 1994-95

ADDERLEY GREEN

Chairman: John Sherratt **Manager:** D Minshall/Gary Woolrich
Secretary: Ross Crawford, 42 Cranford Way, Bucknall, Stoke-on-Trent ST2 9PY (0782 303218).
Ground & Directions: As Norton United (above)
Colours: Red & yellow/red/red **Midweek home matchday:** Monday **Floodlights:** No.
Previous League: Staffs Co. (North)
Hons: Staffs Co. (North) Lg R-up 88-89 90-91 (Lg Cup 93-94).

BADDELEY GREEN RANGERS

Chairman: David Perkins **Manager:** Darren Stair
Secretary: Anthony Munday, 6 Edge View Rd, Baddeley Green, Stoke-on-Trent ST2 7JX (0782 570603).
Ground: Abbey Lane, Abbey Hulton, Hanley, Stoke-on-Trent (0782 267234).
Directions: M6 jct 15, A500, over flyover taking outside lane for a right turn at r'bout, keep in inside lane for a left turn at next r'bout, take outside lane for right turn at lights (Leek Rd), proceed for two and a half miles going across major r'bout before taking outside lane at lights one mile further on, right at lights taking inside lane for left fork at next lights, 2nd left after lights into Fellbrook Rd, ground 3rd left.
Colours: All blue **Midweek home matchday:** Wednesday **Floodlights:** No
Previous League: Staffs Alliance.
Hons: None.

BIDDULPH VICTORIA

Chairman: Alan Farr **Manager:** Michael Carr
Secretary: Richard Baskeyfield, 9 Norfolk Drive, Biddulph, Stoke-on-Trent ST8 6DQ (0782 515368).
Ground & Directions: As Knypersley Victoria FC (see page 574).
Colours: Blue/maroone/blue **Midweek home matchday:** Wednesday **Floodlights:** Yes
Previous League: None **Hons:** None.

CHEADLE OLD BOYS

Chairman: D Lawrence **Manager:** Kevin Rogers
Secretary: J Brown, 11 Hawfinch Road, Cheadle, Stoke-on-Trent ST10 1RV (0538 755304).
Ground: Cheadle Leisure Centre (0538 753331)
Directions: M6 jct 15, A500, over flyover past Stoke City FC, right for 100yds the left at r'bout, proceed to lights bearing right past University, continue to lights and turn right on to A52, left fork at next lights, after 4 miles straight over crossroads (Leek-Cheadle-Weston Coyney), into Cheadle, after 5 miles at junction turn into Tape Street, left into Plant Street which leads to ground.
Colours: All blue. **Midweek home matchday:** Wednesday **Floodlights:** No.
Previous Leagues: Leek & Moorland, Staffs Alliance, Staffs County (North).
Honours: Staffs Alliance R-up 88-89 (Lg Cup R-up 89-90), Staffs FA Presidents Cup R-up 88-89, Leek Cup R-up 88-89 90-91.

CHEADLE ROVERS

Chairman: P Frith **Manager:** Melvyn Barks
Secretary: Stephen T Hilton, 34 Aldersleigh Drive, Wildwood, Stafford ST17 4RY (0785 664979).
Ground: (0782 388465).
Directions: M6 jct 15, A500, right at Hanford r'bout on to A34, left at Trentham r'bout, A5035 to Meir, right on to A520 towards Stone at town centre lights, A5060 towards Hilderstone at double mini-r'bout, ground 1 mile on right.
Colours: Blue & black/black/black **Midweek home matchday:** Wednesday **Floodlights:** No.
Previous Leagues: Leek & Moorland, Staffs Alliance, Staffs County (North).
Hons: Staffs Co. (North) Lg 92-93, Staffs Vase 92-93, Staffs Alliance 86-87, Leek & Moorland Lg 84-85 85-86, Leek Cup R-up 86-87 87-88.

FLORENCE

Chairman: A R Wakeham **Manager:** Michael Bailey
Secretary: Edward Preece, 36 Middlefield Rd, Bucknall, Stoke-on-Trent ST2 0BZ (0782 261561).
Ground: Florence Welfare Club.
Directions: M6 jct 15, A500, 1st exit turning right at r'bout on to A34, left at next r'bout (A5035), right at 2nd lights after 3 miles, right at r'bout into Lightwood Rd - ground 50yds on right.
Colours: All red **Midweek home matchday:** Wednesday **Floodlights:** No.
Previous Leagues: Longton & District, Staffs Alliance, Staffs Co. (North), Staffs Senior.
Hons: Staffs Co. (North) Lg 93-94, Staffs FA Challenge Cup 93-94.

G.E.C. ALSTHOM

Chairman: Mrs Fiona Matthew-Wilkes **Manager:** C G Simmons
Secretary: Mrs Fiona Matthew-Wilkes, 96d Wolverhampton Rd, Stafford ST17 4AH (0785 226512).
Ground: Salt Avenue, Stafford (0785 57111).
Directions: M6 jct 14, follow signs to Stafford centre then Wolverhampton (A449), left at Victoria Wine into Meyrick Rd, follow road to right before immediate left into Salt Avenue - ground at end.
Colours: Blue & white/black/black **Midweek home matchday:** Wednesday **Floodlights:** Yes.
Previous Leagues: Staffs County (South).
Honours: None.

NANTWICH TOWN RESERVES

Chairman: Albert Pye **Manager:** Alan Thompson
Secretary & Ground: As first team (see page 653).
Cols: Green/green & white/green & white **Midweek home matchday:** Tuesday **Floodlights:** Yes
Previous League: Crewe & District
Honours: Crewe & District Lg 93-94, Inter-League Cup 93-94.

STALLINGTON

Chairman: Terrence Balderstone **Manager:** Michael Poxon
Secretary: Kevin S Barnett, 43 Oak Place, Meir, Stoke-on-Trent ST3 5PN (0782 319670).
Ground: (0782 394573).
Directions: M6 jct 15, A500, right at 1st r'bout on to A34 for Stone, left at Tittensor Village for Barlaston, thru village to Meir Heath Rought Close, right into Hilderstone Rd at mini-r'bouts then left by Wheatsheaf Inn for Stallington Hospital, 1st right after hospital, ground 400yds on right.
Colours: Blue & white/blue/blue **Midweek home matchday:** Wednesday **Floodlights:** No.
Previous League: Staffs Co. (North).
Honours: Staffs Co. (North) Lg 89-90 90-91 (Lg Cup 92-93), Staffs Challenge Cup 89-90 90-91 92-92.

WALSALL & DISTRICT LEAGUE

DIV. ONE	P	W	D	L	F	A	PTS
Beechdale Soc. 'A'	14	11	3	0	51	15	36
Riley Sports	14	8	2	4	28	25	26
Colter Engineering	14	7	3	4	39	30	24
Bentley	14	8	3	3	40	11	*23
Bridge '92	14	6	1	7	20	31	19
Bentley Moor	14	5	1	8	32	30	16
Direct Alarms	14	4	1	9	29	41	13
High Heath	14	0	0	14	11	67	0

* - 4 points deducted

Lower Division Champions:
Div. 2 (8): New Fullbrook
Div. 3 (10): West Midlands Travel
Div. 4 (11): Crabtree
Div. 5 (12): Butts Tavern
Div. 6 (13): Beechdale Social 'B'

Cup Winners:
Wernick Cup: Beechdale Social 'A'
Div. 1 Cup: Beechdale Social 'A'
Div. 2 Cup: Homestead Rangers
Div. 3 Cup: Highgate (Duke of Wellington)
Div. 4 Cup: Chuckery WMC Old Boys
Div. 6 Cup: Beechdale Social 'B'

STAFFORDSHIRE COUNTY LEAGUE (SOUTH)

President: Mr W Davis **Vice-Chairman:** Mr R Smart
Secretary: Mr A Payne, 7 Norton Grange,
7 Norton Canes, Cannock WS11 3QZ (0543 279080)

The championship was a closely contested competition as seen in this league for some considerable time, with three teams being prominent from start to finish. Tipton Sports & Social were the early leaders followed by Brownhills Town after two games then Tipton after three, and so on.

Coming into September, Beechdale Social were lying in seventh place, but a good string of results saw them leading the table by October 23rd. Beechdale remained there throughout the month before Tipton Sports regained top spot on 6th November, but their stay was again short-lived, Brownhills ousting them by the 20th. The lead changed hands twice more before Beechdale became the settled leaders on 18th December and stayed there for the remainder of the season.

But with two other sides breathing down their necks, the championship went to the last games of the season, on 27th April. Beechdale won 4-3 at Sikh Hunters while Brownhills lost 0-2 at Mahal on the same evening. As Tipton Sports had lost 2-3 at Toll End Wesley the previous Saturday, Beechdale Social were the new champions.

Tipton Sports, having contested an epic semi-final against Brownhills Town, went on to record a 3-1 extra-time win over Beechdale in the final of the League Shield, this coming ten days after their success in the final of the Penkridge Charity Cup. Beechdale Social then met in-form Mahal in the final of the Premier Trophy and were convincingly beaten 4-2.

Brownhills Town defeated Sikh Hunters in a penalty shoot-out after the final of the Bloxwich Charity Cup on Easter Tuesday, but the Hunters did gain some silverware when they beat Newtown United in the West Bromwich Charity Cup final.

Only one team, Brownhills Town, was invited to apply for promotion to the West Midlands (Regional) League, but unfortunately their ground could not be brought up to standard by the specified deadline. They do, however, move to the Skol Midland Combination, and other departures are GEC Stafford (now GEC Alsthom) to the Refuge Assurance Midland League, Rugeley Athletic (folded) and Sikh Hunters. Joining the League for 1994-95 are newly formed sides Bustleholme and Willenhall Town Reserves, and two former Wolverhampton Works League clubs; Chubb Sports and Union Locks.

Alan Payne, League Secretary

Final Table	P	W	D	L	F	A	PTS
Beechdale Social	22	14	5	3	59	37	33
Tipton Spts & Soc.	22	14	3	5	72	35	31
Brownhills Town	22	13	3	6	49	27	29
Mahal	22	11	6	5	57	40	28
Toll End Wesley	22	9	9	4	56	40	27
GEC Stafford	22	7	10	5	40	39	24
Tipton Rovers	22	6	8	8	42	44	20
Sikh Hunters	22	7	4	11	57	55	18
West Bromwich BH	22	7	4	11	44	62	18
Rugeley Athletic	22	6	5	11	45	63	17
Tipton Town Res.	22	5	4	13	26	44	14
Rocket Pool	22	1	3	18	32	93	5

PREMIER TROPHY First Round

Rocket Pool v Beechdale Social	2-7
Sikh Hunters v GEC Stafford	1-3
Brownhills Town v Tipton Town Reserves	2-3
Tipton Sports & Social v Toll End Wesley	2-1

Quarter-Finals

GEC Stafford v West Bromwich BH	1-4
Beechdale Social v Rugeley Athletic	5-0
Tipton Town Reserves v Mahal	0-2
Tipton Rovers v Tipton Sports & Social	1-2*(aet)*

Semi-Finals

West Bromwich BH v Mahal	1-4
Tipton Sports & Social v Beechdale Social	1-2

Final *(at Willenhall Town FC, Tues 10th May)*:
Mahal 4, Beechdale Social 2

RESULT CHART 1993-95		1	2	3	4	5	6	7	8	9	10	11	12
1.	Beechdale Social	*	2-0	1-1	0-2	5-2	5-2	4-0	3-3	1-1	2-1	1-1	2-2
2.	Brownhills Town	3-1	*	0-0	5-1	6-2	2-1	1-0	1-1	3-1	1-0	1-1	4-2
3.	GEC Stafford	0-2	1-5	*	3-3	5-2	2-1	2-1	2-0	4-1	2-1	1-1	7-0
4.	Mahal	1-3	2-0	5-0	*	4-1	1-5	4-4	2-2	0-1	4-1	1-1	3-0
5.	Rocket Pool	0-3	2-6	3-3	0-3	*	2-2	2-4	1-2	0-9	2-4	3-5	2-1
6.	Rugeley Athletic	2-4	1-5	2-2	1-2	3-2	*	5-2	1-3	5-2	0-0	1-9	1-5
7.	Sikh Hunters	3-4	0-3	3-1	1-2	5-0	3-3	*	4-1	3-1	7-3	3-3	1-4
8.	Tipton Rovers	1-2	3-0	1-1	4-4	2-2	1-2	3-3	*	1-3	2-0	2-3	2-1
9.	Tipton Sports & Social	5-2	1-0	4-0	1-1	9-2	4-0	4-2	3-3	*	4-1	3-2	5-1
10.	Tipton Town Reserves	1-2	1-2	0-0	1-4	2-0	1-2	1-0	2-1	0-3	*	2-2	2-2
11.	Toll End Wesley	3-4	3-1	2-2	1-4	5-0	3-3	3-2	2-1	3-2	0-1	*	2-2
12.	West Bromwich BH	3-6	1-0	1-1	5-4	5-2	3-2	1-6	2-3	1-5	2-1	0-1	*

LEAGUE SHIELD 1993-94

First Round

GEC Stafford v Mahal	2-1
Sikh Hunters v Toll End Wesley	3-1
Rocket Pool v Tipton Rovers	1-2
Rugeley Athletic *(scr)* v Brownhill Town *(w/o)*	

Quarter-Finals

Beechdale Social v West Bromwich BH	3-2
Tipton Rovers v Tipton Sports & Social	1-2
GEC Stafford v Sikh Hunters	4-2
Tipton Town Reserves v Brownhills Town	0-2

Semi-Finals

Beechdale Social v GEC Stafford	2-0
Tipton S. v Brownhills	0-0*(ab. after 10m ET)*,2-0

Final *(at Chasetown FC, Sat 23rd April)*: Tipton S & S 3, Beechdale Social 1 *(aet, 1-1 after 90 mins)*.

CLUB DIRECTORY

BEECHDALE SOCIAL

Chairman: Mark Neville **Manager:** Gary Blland **Founded:** 1984
Secretary: Mr P R Jenkins, 150 Bloxwich Lane, Beechdale, Walsall (0922 21066)
Ground: Bloxwich Town FC (see page 597)
Colours: All white **Change colours:** Blue/white/blue **Programme:** No.
Previous Name: Walsall MA (pre-1993) **Previous Ground:** Pleck Park, Walsall (pre-1994).
Hons: Staffs Co. (Sth) Lg 93-94 (Div 1 R-up 90-91, Lge Shield 91-92 (R-up 93-94), Premier Cup R-up 93-94, Edge Cup 90-91, Ike Cooper Tphy R-up 90-91).

BUSTLEHOLME

Manager: S Glover **Asst Manager:** M Stanyer **Founded:** 1994
Secretary: Mr G Benbow, 123 Coles Lane, Hill Top, West Bromwich (021 556 9625)
Ground: Spear & Jackson, St Pauls Rd, Wood Green, Wednesbury.
Colours: Yellow/green/yellow **Change colours:** White/green/yellow

CHUBB SPORTS

Treasurer: S Martin **Manager:** P Lees.
Secretary: Mr P Clarke, 7 Nightingale Place, Bilston, West Mids WV14 6LZ (0902 343544)
Ground: Chubb Sports, Wooden Road, Wednesfield, Wolverhampton.
Colours: Red & white stripes/white/white **Change colours:** Blue & white/blue/white.
Previous League: Wolverhampton Works (pre-1994).

MAHAL

Secretary: Mr Sukhdev Pal, 1 St George Drive (off Perry Str.), Smethwick, West Mids B66 1DN (021 565 4556)
Ground: Wood Lane Playing Fields, Romilley Ave., Handsworth Wood, Birmingham.
Directions: M5 jct 1, A41 to Handsworth, A4040 to Handsworth Wood, left at island into Handsworth Wood Rd, follow road to right then 2nd left into Romilly Ave., ground on left.
Cover: No **Capacity:** 300 **Floodlights:** No **Clubhouse:** No **Programme:** No.
Colours: Red & blue stripes/red/red **Change:** Blue & white stripes/blue/blue **Founded:** 1979.
Hons: Staffs Co. (Sth) Lg Div 1 92-93 (Premier Cup 93-94, Edge Cup R-up 91-92, Ike Cooper Tphy R-up 92-93).

ROCKET POOL

Chairman/Manager: Mr W Holyhèad **Founded:** 1989
Secretary: Mr S Simkins, 72 Meldon Drive, Bradley, Bilston (0902 495946)
Ground: MEB Sports Ground, Bayles Lane, Tipton.
Cols: Green & white stripes/white/white **Change colours:** Red/black **Programme:** No.
Previous Ground: Bilston College, Westfield Rd, Bilston (pre-1994).

TIPTON ROVERS

Chairman: P Harris **Manager:** R Harris
Secretary: Mr T G Harris, 10 Lime Close, Tipton, West Midlands DY4 8NY (021 557 9503)
Ground: Newbury Lane Stadium, Newbury Lane, Oldbury.
Cover: **Capacity:** **Floodlights:** Yes **Clubhouse:** **Programme:**
Colours: Blue & claret/claret/claret **Change colours:** Red/white/white.

TIPTON SPORTS & SOCIAL

Chairman: Mr H Lucas **Manager:** Wally Twist **Founded:** 1964
Secretary: Mr W Andrews, 42 Ambleside Close, Bradley, Bilston, West Mids WV14 0SN (0902 497404)
Ground: Coneygre Rd, Tipton.
Directions: M5 jct 2, A4123 Birmingham New Rd to Burnt Tree island, A461 Coneygre Rd, ground entrance 200yds on left between terraced house and new Estate on left.
Cover: No **Capacity:** 500 **Floodlights:** No **Clubhouse:** Yes **Programme:** No.
Colours: Sky/navy/navy **Change colours:** Green & white stripes/navy/navy.
Hons: Staffs Co. Lg (Sth) R-up 93-94 (Div 1 88-89, Lge Shield 93-94), Penkridge Charity Cup 93-94.

TIPTON TOWN RESERVES

Manager: G Harris *(other details as first team - see page 591)*

TOLL END WESLEY

Chairman: Mr S Page **Manager:** A Cartwright/ M Smith **Founded:** 1905
Secretary: Mr B Walker, 23 Gospel Oak Rd, Ocker Hill, Tipton, West Mids DY4 0DR (021 556 7711).
Ground: Union Locks (Josiah Parks), Willenhall.
Directions: M6 jct 10, A454 to Willenhall, thru town centre, straight on towards Wolverhampton, entrance on right just before island on main A454 dual c'way.
Cover: No **Capacity:** 500 **Floodlights:** No **Programme:** No.
Clubhouse: Hospitality lounge & bar.
Colours: White/navy/navy **Change colours:** All blue.
Hons: Staffs Co. Lg (Sth) R-up 88-89 91-92 (Div 1 R-up 87-88, Edge Cup 91-92, Ike Cooper Tphy R-up 91-92).

UNION LOCKS

Secretary: Mr D Swatman, 71 Lincoln Ave., County Bridge, Willenhall, West Mids WV13 1JQ (0902 60395).
Ground: Union Locks (Josiah Parks), Willenhall.
Directions: M6 jct 10, A454 to Willenhall, thru town centre, straight on towards Wolverhampton, entrance on right just before island on main A454 dual c'way.
Cover: No **Capacity:** 500 **Floodlights:** No **Programme:** No.
Clubhouse: Hospitality lounge & bar. **Previous League:** Wolverhampton Works (pre-1994).
Colours: Navy/white/white **Change colours:** Royal/navy/navy.

WILLENHALL TOWN RESERVES *(see page 578)*

YEW TREE ALBION

Chairman: Clive Peel **Programme:** No **Founded:** 1985
Secretary: Mr C Peel, 12 Beechwood Rd, West Bromwich B70 8QJ (021 553 3701)
Ground: As Park Rangers FC (see page 606).
Colours: White/black/white **Change colours:** Yellow/blue/yellow.
Previous Name: West Bromwich BH (pre-1994).
Hons: Staffs Co. (Sth) Lg Div 1 R-up 92-93, West Bromwich Charity Cup 92-93.

STAFFORD & DISTRICT

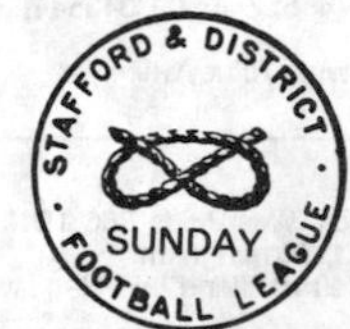

SUNDAY LEAGUE

FOUNDED: 1969

DIV. ONE	P	W	D	L	F	A	PTS
Nesbitt Rovers	18	14	2	2	64	20	30
Greyhound Yarlet	18	11	2	5	39	19	27
Waggon	18	13	5	0	65	27	26
Cross Keys	18	11	5	2	60	25	24
Seighford	18	6	9	3	25	57	15
Littleton Arms	18	6	10	2	42	58	14
Stafford Celtic	18	6	11	1	37	55	13
GEC Woolpack	18	4	10	4	38	54	12
Vine Stone	18	4	11	3	27	56	11
Lamb Stone	18	3	13	2	27	53	8

Lower Division Champions:
Div. 2 (10): Radford Rangers
Div. 3 (11): Wetwood
Div. 4 (11): Strollers
Div. 5 (11): Pheasant Stone
Div. 6 (11): AFC Eccleshall
Div. 7 (10): Gloucester City Supporters

Divisional Cup winners (runners-up):
Div. 1: Nesbitt Rovers (Waggon)
Div. 2: Oxleathers (Radford Rangers)
Div. 3: Wetwood (Horns Gnosall)
Div. 4: Staffordshire Bull (Woodseaves)
Div. 5: Pheasant Stone (Holmcroft Northend)
Div. 6: AFC Eccleshall (Clifford Arms)

Divisional Top-Scorers:
Div. 1: Michael Stark (Greyhound Yarlet) 21
Div. 2: Glen Doran (Rifleman Bushes) 20
Div. 3: Mick McHale (Rugeley Athletic) 28
Div. 4: Anthony Powell (Dorman Diesels) 36
Div. 5: Lee Hodson (Mossley Tavern) 25
Div. 6: Tracey Fife (Gilligans) 26

Secretary of the Year:
Michael Smith (Yarnfield)

HANLEY & DISTRICT SUNDAY LEAGUE

FOUNDED: 1967

PREM. DIV.	P	W	D	L	F	A	PTS
Thurston '92	22	19	2	1	90	26	59
Rose & Crown	22	16	2	4	65	28	50
Birches Hd Gdnrs	22	13	3	6	66	50	*39
Bench & Bar	22	10	5	7	61	49	35
Hillberry	22	9	5	8	55	49	32
Leigh Red Lion	22	9	3	10	44	47	30
Auctioneers Arms	22	8	4	10	48	42	28
YMCA (Hanley)	22	8	4	10	44	58	28
Fegg Hayes S & S	22	7	3	12	45	58	24
MESC	22	6	2	14	38	67	20
Birches Head YAC	22	4	4	14	47	90	16
West End Burslem	22	4	1	17	38	79	13

* - 3 points deducted

Lower Division Champions:
Div. 1 (13): Coalville Wanderers

Cup Finals:
Lge Cup: Leigh Red Lion 3, Birches Head Gdnrs 2
Subsidiary Cup: Auctioneers Arms 3, Duke of Wellington 2

SUFFOLK F.A.

Secretary: William M Steward,
2 Millfields, Haughley, Stowmarket IP14 3PU (0449 673481)

PREMIER CUP 1993-94

Preliminary Round

Bury Town v Lowestoft Town	1-1,0-2

First Round

Cornard United v Newmarket Town	1-3
Sudbury Town v Stowmarket Town	2-0
Lowestoft Town v Haverhill Rovers	0-0,1-3
Sudbury Wanderers v Felixstowe Town	0-2

Semi-Finals

Sudbury Town v Felixstowe Town	2-1
Haverhill Rovers v Newmarket Town	1-2

Final *(at Sudbury Town FC, Tues 2nd May)*: Sudbury Town 1, Newmarket Town 2

SENIOR CUP

First Round

Beccles Town v Sudbury Town Res.	1-5
Framlingham Town v Stutton	0-2
Felixstowe Town Res. v Sudbury Lucas Ath.	2-1

First Round

Ipswich Wanderers v Walsham-le-Willows	3-1
Kirkley v Achilles	1-0
Halesworth Town v Long Melford	4-0
Lowestoft T. Res. v Ashlea	3-3,0-4
Grundisburgh v Needham Market	0-1
Felixstowe T. Res. v Woodbridge T. Res.	0-2
Haverhill R. Res. v Brantham Athletic	1-2
Melton St Audrys v BS Fonnereau Ath.	1-4
Whitton United v Stowmarket Town Reserves	1-0
Haughley United v Mildenhall Town	1-1,1-2
Old Newton Utd v BT Research	0-3
Westerfield United v Brandon Town	4-2
Hadleigh United v Oulton Broad	5-0
Bury Town Reserves v Sudbury T. Reserves	2-4
Sudbury Wdrs Reserves v Saxmundham Spts Res.	1-3
Stutton v Stonham Aspal	3-0

Second Round

Hadleigh United v Ashlea	3-0
Needham Market v Haleworth Town	0-2
Whitton United v Kirkley	2-1
BS Fonnereau Ath. v Brantham Athletic	0-0,0-2
Stutton v Woodbridge Town	0-1
Westerfield United v Sudbury T. Reserves	2-3
Mildenhall Town v Saxmundham Sports	0-0,1-3
Ipswich Wanderers v BT Research	6-1

Quarter-Finals

Ipswich Wanderers v Hadleigh United	1-3
Brantham Athletic v Woodbridge Town	1-1,2-4
Whitton United v Sudbury Town Reserves	1-4
Saxmundham Sports v Halesworth Town	2-1

Semi-Finals

Hadleigh Utd v Woodbridge *(at Felixstowe T.)*	2-4
Sax'ham v Sudbury *(at Whitton)*	1-4*(Sud. expelled)*

Final *(at Ipswich Town FC, Tues 19th April)*: Woodbridge Town 4, Saxmundham Sports 0

Woodbridge Town celebrate their convincing victory over Saxmundham Sports at Portman Road in the final of the Suffolk Senior Cup. It was a fabulous season for the club as they also won the Jewson Eastern Counties League Cup and promotion to the JECL Premier Division.

Photo - Martin Wray.

BRITISH SUGAR
SUFFOLK & IPSWICH LEAGUE

Patron: W C A Snook
President: G Harper.
Chairman: P M Cocker.
Vice Chairman: G Whight.
Hon. Secretary: Alan Gorham,
179 Cauldwell Hall Road, Ipswich, Suffolk IP4 5DA (0473 723685).

The outstanding feature of the season's Senior Division was not the title race, which was won by Grundisburgh at a reasonably early date, but that even late into March, eight clubs were still fighting to avoid the drop to Division One. Finally two last day results settled the fate of Walsham-le-Willows and Saxmundham Sports. For Saxmundham it was a sad end to their first season in Senior Football, in which they had created a very good impression both on and off the field of play. The playing staff, at least, had Suffolk Senior Cup Runners-up medals as a reminder of their first Senior experience.

The title race involved Grundisburgh, Stutton (who for the second year running filled second spot), Achilles, Whitton United and Needham Market. The latter two met in the League's major KO cup, the Mick McNeil, and, in front of a record crowd, Whitton won with an extra-time strike by three goals to two.

With the McNeil Cup won, Whitton United also lifted the Intermediate 'A' title retaining the trophy they won in 1992/1993, while the clubs 'A' string were runners-up in Divison Three - enough success to edge them ahead of Grundisburgh to win the Senior Club of the Year award.

The Junior Award went to Ufford, winners of Division Three and Division Seven. The Mann Broadbent Cup was won by Achilles, 2-0 winners over Woodbridge Town. The Town were also runners-up in the Orwell League cup being defeated by East Bergholt by 3-0.

The League were successful in both Inter League matches this season, the Senior defeating the Essex & Suffolk Border League while the Juniors had quite an easy passage against the Bury & District League.

With just over 12 months to go before the League's Centenary Year, much work is going into the planning with confirmation that two books will be published - 'The History of the League' and a Year Book cum programme of the Year. In the latter book, many of the Leagues famous sons will be featured and research has shown that four of the players who featured in the Ipswich Town Wembley success of 1978 against Arsenal have played in our League. Two - Brian Talbot and Roger Osborne - in fact began their football in this League. Centenary details can be obtained from Alan Gorham, 179 Cauldwell Hall Road, Ipswich, IP4 5DA.

Alan Gorham, Secretary

SENIOR DIV.	P	W	D	L	F	A	PTS
Grundisburgh	30	23	5	2	67	18	51
Stutton	30	16	8	6	62	35	40
Achilles	30	18	3	9	69	43	39
Whitton United	30	14	10	6	58	30	38
Needam Market	30	15	7	8	42	36	37
Haughley	30	13	7	10	64	50	33
Westerfield	30	11	6	13	43	41	28
Melton St Audrys	30	10	6	14	43	49	26
Old Newton Utd	30	11	4	15	37	56	26
BS Fonnereau A.	30	10	6	14	51	72	26
Halesoworth Town	30	9	6	15	49	56	24
Framlingham	30	7	10	13	50	62	24
Stonham Aspal	30	8	8	14	43	57	24
BT Research	30	9	4	17	45	60	22
Saxmundham Spts	30	8	6	16	37	62	22
Walsham-le-Willows	30	8	4	18	43	76	20

DIV. ONE	P	W	D	L	F	A	PTS
Nicholians	26	21	3	2	76	34	45
Walton United	26	18	4	4	72	26	40
Stanton	26	18	1	7	76	33	37
Ipswich Athletic	26	15	7	4	59	40	37
Bramford United	26	10	7	9	44	43	27
Elmsett	26	12	2	12	55	58	26
Wenhaston	26	8	7	11	38	43	23
Suffolk Police	26	8	7	11	45	60	23
Willis Corroon	26	9	4	13	47	56	22
Ransomes	26	8	6	12	45	54	22
Coplestonians	26	6	9	11	47	64	21
Leiston	26	7	6	13	27	48	20
Crane Sports	26	3	6	17	29	57	12
Rushmere Athletic	26	1	7	18	29	73	9

SENIOR DIV. RESULTS 93-94	1	2	3	4	5	6	7	8	9	10	11	12	13	14	15	16
1. Achilles	*	5-1	3-2	3-2	2-4	2-1	4-2	1-2	1-2	5-0	4-0	2-3	2-0	3-0	3-0	4-2
2. British Sugar Fonnereau Ath.	1-3	*	2-2	1-2	0-3	4-1	4-3	2-0	2-2	1-2	1-0	2-2	2-3	2-0	0-4	2-6
3. British Telecom Research	2-4	2-3	*	1-1	1-2	0-2	0-4	2-0	0-1	3-1	2-2	3-1	1-5	0-1	1-2	2-3
4. Framlingham Town	2-0	3-3	3-0	*	2-1	3-1	2-4	2-3	1-1	2-0	1-2	1-3	1-1	0-2	0-2	1-4
5. Grundisburgh	3-1	3-1	2-0	5-0	*	3-2	0-0	2-2	1-0	1-0	5-1	1-0	1-1	1-0	1-0	0-0
6. Halesworth Town	3-4	2-0	3-0	1-1	0-1	*	3-2	1-3	0-1	1-1	2-0	0-0	0-3	5-1	2-3	1-1
7. Haughley United	2-1	6-1	4-0	5-2	0-5	1-1	*	0-1	1-2	2-1	2-0	2-3	0-0	2-0	1-1	4-1
8. Melton St Audrys	2-1	1-2	0-3	1-1	1-3	2-2	2-3	*	0-1	1-1	0-0	3-2	1-3	2-2	3-0	0-2
9. Needham Market	1-2	1-1	2-6	4-0	1-0	0-3	1-1	2-1	*	4-2	2-1	2-1	0-2	3-1	1-1	1-0
10. Old Newton United	2-4	2-0	1-4	1-1	0-3	3-2	3-1	1-0	1-2	*	3-2	0-2	2-1	1-2	0-4	0-3
11. Saxmundham Sports	1-1	2-1	3-1	0-5	1-4	2-3	2-3	0-3	3-2	1-2	*	1-1	1-0	0-1	3-2	2-1
12. Stonham Aspal	0-0	2-4	2-0	4-3	0-3	2-4	1-3	3-1	2-2	0-2	1-1	*	0-2	1-1	4-3	0-0
13. Stutton	2-0	5-1	1-1	2-2	0-3	2-0	3-1	2-1	0-0	1-2	4-2	4-0	*	8-3	0-0	2-2
14. Walsham-le-Willows	1-2	3-4	2-3	2-2	1-2	3-1	4-3	1-4	0-1	2-2	2-3	3-2	1-3	*	0-2	0-5
15. Westerfield United	0-2	1-2	0-1	1-0	0-3	5-1	0-3	0-3	1-0	0-1	1-1	3-1	1-1	2-3	*	0-0
16. Whitton United	0-0	1-1	0-1	4-4	1-1	2-1	0-0	4-0	1-0	1-0	2-0	1-0	4-0	7-1	0-2	*

ONE HUNDRED YEARS

To celebrate this important milestone, the **Suffolk & Ipswich Football League** will be publishing a prestigious, glossy hard back comprising 360 pages packed with stories, both strange and true, related to the League and it's players. Player profiles, acknowledgements, all the League tables, a year by year report, words and pictures of famous personalities, all the winners and every Club that ever played in the League, make this a truly important history of Suffolk Football.

All players, ex players, their relatives and the entire football community in Suffolk are invited to become **Subscribers** and be guaranteed a copy of this limited edition of such a notable chronicle.

All **Subscribers** will have their names included in the acknowledgement page.

Become a subscriber now, and pay by easy direct debit.

Please contact:
The Centenary Organiser
Mr Alan Gorham,
Cambridge Villas,
179 Cauldwell Hall Road,
Ipswich IP4 5DA

Below: *Stutton FC - League runners-up 1993-94. Back Row (L/R): N King, C Smith, M Webb, A Powell, R Mann, A Norman, S Farthing. Front: K Oxbrow, K Faiers, K Layne, A Harris, J Coupe, A Curtis.*
Photo - Martin Wray.

SUFFOLK & IPSWICH LEAGUE SENIOR DIVISION 1994-95

ACHILLES

Secretary: Carl Snowling, 149 Freehold Rd, Ipswich, Suffolk IP4 5JP (0473 727114).
Ground: Pauls SC, Stonelodge Lane, Ipswich, Suffolk.
Colours: Red/black **Change Colours:** Yellow/red/black.

BRITISH SUGAR FONNEREAU ATHLETIC

Secretary: David Knights, 16 Speedwell Rd, Ipswich, Suffolk IP2 0LP (0473 601543).
Ground: British Sugar Plc, Sproughton Road, Ipswich, Suffolk.
Colours: All royal blue **Change Colours:** All white.
Previous Names: Silent Youth/ Fonnereau Ath./ YMCA Fonnereau Ath.

B.T. RESEARCH

Secretary: Richard Field, 26 Harvesters Way, Martlesham Heath, Ipswich, Suffolk IP5 7UP (0473 610663).
Ground: The Hollies, Straight Road, Bucklesham.
Colours: Yellow/blue/blue **Change Colours:** All red.
Previous Names: British Telecom **Programme Editor:** Julian Catt (0473 252239).

FRAMLINGHAM TOWN

Secretary: Mrs Fiona Whatling, 46 College Rd, Framlingham, Woodbridge IP13 9ES (0728 723524).
Ground: Sports Field, Badlingham Road, Framlingham, Woodbridge, Suffolk.
Colours: Green & white/white/white **Change Colours:** Maroon & blue/blue/blue.

GRUNDISBURGH

Secretary: Malcolm Harris, 70 Post Mill Gardens, Grundisburgh, Woodbridge IP13 6UP (0473 35422).
Ground: The Playing Field, Grundisburgh, Woodbridge.
Colours: All rblue **Change Colours:** Red/red/black.

HALESWORTH TOWN

Secretary: Paul Collier, 98 Dukes Drive, Halesworth IP19 8DR (0986 872015).
Ground: Playing Fields, Dairy Hill, Bungay Road, Halesworth.
Colours: White/navy/red **Change Colours:** Maroon & royal/royal/royal.

HAUGHLEY UNITED

Secretary: David Tricker, 49 Union Str., Stowmarket, Suffolk IP14 1HE (0449 675741).
Ground: British Sugar Plc, Sproughton Road, Ipswich, Suffolk.
Colours: All white **Change Colours:** Red/white/red.

MELTON St AUDRY

Secretary: Leon Chmiel, 36 Mildmay Rd, Ipswich, Suffolk IP3 9PG (0473 718776).
Ground: St Audrys Hospital Sports Field, Melton, Nr Woodbridge, Suffolk.
Colours: Red/black/black **Change Colours:** Grey & white stripes/black/black.
Programme Editor: Michael Milbourne (Woodbridge 380146).

NEEDHAM MARKET

Secretary: Ian Croft, 30 Masefield Rd, Stowmarket, Suffolk IP14 1TH (0449 676517).
Ground: Barretts Lane, Needham Market, Suffolk. **Programme Editor:** Alan Parson (0449 720468).
Colours: Red/red/black **Change Colours:** Green/green/grey.

NICHOLIANS LOCOMOTIVE

Secretary: Mrs Jean McNally, 42 Rectory Rd, Ipswich, Suffolk IP2 8EQ (0473 601725).
Ground: YMCA Club, Rushmere Street, Rushmere St Andrew.
Colours: White/blue/blue **Change Colours:** Sky/red.

OLD NEWTON UNITED

Secretary: John Thorndyke, 13 Winchester Close, Stowmarket, Suffolk IP14 1SH (0449 675653).
Ground: Playing Field, Church Road, Old Newton.
Colours: Amber/amber/blue **Change Colours:** All blue.
Programme Editor: Rob Atherton (0449 673105).

STONHAM ASPAL

Secretary: Eric Cousins, 2 Holly Green, Mickfield, Stowmarket, Suffolk IP14 5LH (0449 711884).
Ground: Delsons Meadow, Three Crossways, Stonham Aspal.
Colours: Blue/blue/white **Change Colours:** All yellow.

STUTTON

Secretary: Michael Coombs, 4 Crowcroft Glebe, Nedging Tye, Ipswich, Suffolk IP7 7LH (0449 741200).
Ground: Hall Park, Stutton. **Programme Editor:** Ivan Ransby (0473 47645).
Colours: White/black/black **Change Colours:** Gold/black/black.

WALTON UNITED

Secretary: Tony Barnes, 63 Hintlesham Drive, Felixstowe IP11 8YW (0394 276407).
Ground: Recreation Ground, Walton, Felixstowe.
Colours: Red & white/white/white **Change Colours:** Sky/navy/blue.

WESTERFIELD UNITED

Secretary: Andrew Howes, 44 Foden Ave., Town End Fields, Ipswich, Suffolk IP1 5DL (0473 740275).
Ground: SEH Sports Centre, Humber Doucy Lane, Rushmere.
Colours: All blue **Change Colours:** Red & black stripes/black/red.

WHITTON UNITED

Secretary: David Gould, 7 Karen Close, Ipswich, Suffolk IP1 4LP (0473 253838).
Ground: King Geore V Playing Field, Norwich Road, Ipswich, Suffolk.
Colours: Green & white hoops/white/green **Change Colours:** Blue/white/green.
Previous Name: Whitton FC **Programme Editor:** Ian Vernau (0473 680592).

Saxmundham Town FC, who have sadly been relegated after just one season in the top flight. Back Row (L/R): I Fryer, R Hall, M Scopes, R Nettlingham, A Brown, K Goddard, J Behling, J Gibbons. Front: R Baker, D Blades, D Horner, C Page, D Fisher.

Photo - Martin Wray.

Achilles FC - who, by contrast, achieved an excellent third place after promotion to the Senior Division. Back Row (L/R): G Westley, M Laws, G Thrower, P Carter, R Barber, T Childs, R Steel, I Crick (Coach). Front: A Sayer, D Barber, K Tilley, A Hill, I Abbott, P Flegg.

Photo - Martin Wray.

Melton St Audrys FC. *Photo - Martin Wray.*

WIMPEY HOMES
ESSEX & SUFFOLK BORDER LEAGUE

President: B R Tatum Esq.
Hon. Secretary: K G Bulow Esq.,
13 Kingswood Road, Mile End, Colchester CO4 5JX Tel: 0206 851733

Premier Division - Last season's champions Little Oakley were again at the forefront this term thanks largely to some favourable performances by their fellow high-flyers on the few occasions when they were found lacking. In the end, only a fine 4-1 away win at runners-up West Bergholt maintained their dominance of the league. Clacton Town Reserves' usual late escape act was insufficient to prevent them making the drop to Division One along with Boxted Lodgers.

Division One - Leaders Halstead Town Reserves went much of the season unbeaten and in the end were only three goals short of a century as they took the title by four clear points ahead of runners-up Stanway Rovers Reserves. Following Anchor Press's withdrawal from the league early in the season, only one club was relegated to Division Two, Long Melford Reserves trailing second from bottom West End United by just one point.

Division Two - Lawford Lads made a swift return to the First Division, sustaining a healthy lead throughout the season. In the dog fight for second place, Gas Recreation Reserves made their games in hand tell to overhaul fellow hopefuls Cavendish although, earlier in the season, no less than half a dozen clubs were within sight of the promotion placings. Kelvedon and St Johns's second strings were relegated after finishing nearly ten points short of their nearest fellow strugglers.

Division Three - Finchingfield dominated from the start with only one defeat all season and were promoted along with fellow new-boys Hadleigh United Reserves and Bradfield Rovers. Dedham Old Boys Reserves also went up after finishing third with fourth placed Bradfield's promotion coming only after a decision to enlarge the league. At a special meeting held at the end of May, bottom club Rowhedge Reserves were re-elected to the league along with new clubs Foxash Reserves, Ipswich Wanderers Reserves, Kirby United and Weeley Reserves.

Steve Adlem, Press Officer.

PREM. DIV.	P	W	D	L	F	A	PTS
Little Oakley	30	19	5	6	72	36	62
West Bergholt	30	17	9	4	66	40	60
Haverhill Rvrs Res.	30	17	4	9	56	38	55
Dedham Old Boys	30	14	5	11	69	54	47
Long Melford	30	13	8	9	52	39	47
Stowmarket T. Res.	30	12	10	8	49	41	46
Sudbury Wdrs Res.	30	12	7	11	63	52	43
Gas Recreation	30	11	10	9	52	43	43
Alresford Colne R.	30	12	5	13	45	52	41
St Johns (Clacton)	30	11	8	11	58	68	41
Harwich P'ton Res.	30	12	4	14	54	64	40
Felixstowe T. Res.	30	10	9	11	56	50	39
Sudbury Athletic	30	9	5	16	41	56	32
Kelvedon Social	30	7	8	15	32	55	29
Clacton Town Res.	30	7	5	18	42	72	26
Boxted Lodgers	30	4	4	22	40	87	16

DIV. TWO	P	W	D	L	F	A	PTS
Lawford Lads	28	20	4	4	74	29	64
Gas Recreation Res.	28	18	5	5	82	42	59
Cavendish	28	17	4	7	62	30	55
Mersea Island Res.	28	15	7	6	54	33	52
Bures United	28	13	2	13	56	50	41
Hedinghames Utd	28	11	8	9	63	59	41
Alresford CR Res.	28	12	5	11	51	52	41
Earls Colne	28	12	5	11	51	53	41
Silver End	28	11	4	13	39	47	37
Little Oakley Res.	28	11	3	14	52	60	36
Great Bentley	28	10	6	12	46	66	36
Tiptree Heath Res.	28	9	2	17	46	66	29
Boxted Lodgers Res.	28	8	4	16	41	58	28
Kelvedon S. Res.	28	6	1	21	33	59	19
St Johns (C.) Res.	28	5	4	19	37	83	19

DIV. ONE	P	W	D	L	F	A	PTS
Halstead T. Res.	28	21	5	2	97	32	68
Stanway Rvrs Res.	28	20	4	4	73	28	64
Tiptree Heath	28	17	5	6	51	22	56
Mistley United	28	14	6	8	64	45	48
Bramston CML	28	13	9	6	51	42	48
Brantham Ath. Res.	28	11	9	8	37	31	42
Rowhedge	28	11	6	11	64	58	39
Mersea Island	28	10	7	11	46	44	37
West Bergholt Res.	28	10	6	12	52	52	36
Royal London	28	10	4	14	56	62	34
Foxash Social	28	8	6	14	40	56	30
Weeley Athletic	28	9	3	16	48	72	30
Cornard Utd Res.	28	7	6	15	35	66	27
West End United	28	4	3	21	35	86	15
Long Melford Res.	28	3	5	20	25	78	14

DIV. THREE	P	W	D	L	F	A	PTS
Finchingfield Rvrs	26	20	5	1	94	24	65
Hadleigh Utd Res.	26	17	4	5	78	29	55
Dedham OB Res.	26	13	8	5	59	44	47
Bradfield Rovers	26	14	4	8	54	37	46
Bramston CML Res.	26	14	3	9	57	45	45
Severalls	26	10	8	8	56	49	38
Walton Town	26	11	3	12	43	46	36
Sudbury Ath. Res.	26	10	3	13	62	57	33
Mistley United Res.	26	10	3	13	44	53	33
St Osyth	26	8	8	10	53	71	32
Lawford Lads Res.	26	9	1	16	24	47	28
Wormingford	26	7	3	16	36	87	24
Coggeshall Town	26	6	2	18	44	75	20
Rowhedge Res.	26	4	3	19	32	69	15

Rowhedge Reserves re-elected along with Foxash Reserves, Ipswich Wanderers Reserves, Kirby United and Weeley Athletic Reserves.

KNOCK-OUT CUP 1993-94

Preliminary First Round

Alresford Colne Rgrs v Bures United	5-0
Great Bentley v Mistley United	0-2
Severalls v Gas Recreation	1-7
Clacton Town Res. v Bradfield	2-0
Tiptree Heath v Silver End	4-0
Felixstowe Town Res. v Long Melford	0-3
Cavendish v Rowhedge	2-3
Finchingfield v Foxash Social	5-3
Stowmarket Town Res. v Harwich & P. Res.	4-3
Bramston CML v Mersea Island	1-2
Wormingford v Stanway Rovers Reserves	1-5
Weeley Athletic v St Johns	1-2

First Round

Alresford Colne Rgrs v Rowhedge	3-2
Gas Recreation v Brantham Ath. Reserves	1-2
Earls Colne v Clacton Town Reserves	0-1
Mistley United v Finchingfield	3-4
Lawford Lads v Stowmarket Town Reserves	0-1
Mersea Island v Hadleigh United Reserves	3-5

(continued opposite)

St Osyth v Little Oakley 1-10
West Bergholt v West End United 4-2
Stanway Rovers Reserves v Kelvedon Soc. 2-0
Haverhill R. Res. v Royal London 5-1
Cornard United Res. v St Johns 1-2

Sudbury Athletic v Coggeshall 3-1
Boxted Lodgers v Sudbury Wdrs Reserves 1-2
Walton Town v Long Melford 0-2
Hedinghams v Halstead Town Reserves 0-1
Tiptree Heath v Dedham Old Boys 0-1

Second Round

Alresford Colne Rgrs v Finchingfield 1-2
Clacton Town Res. v Hadleigh Utd Reserves 2-4
West Bergholt v Sudbury Wdrs Reserves 2-4
Long Melford v Haverhill Rovers Reserves 1-3

Brantham Athletic Res. v Stowmarket T. Res. 0-3
Little Oakley v Sudbury Athletic 4-2
Dedham Old Boys v Stanway Rovers Reserves 3-1
Halstead Town Reserves v St Johns 2-1

Quarter Finals

Finchingfield v Stowmarket Town Res 1-0
Sudbury Wdrs Reserves v Dedham Old Boys 1-2

Hadleigh United Res. v Little Oakley 2-2,3-4
Haverhill Rovers Res. v Halstead Town Reserves 0-5

Semi-Finals

Finchingfield v Little Oakley 1-3

Dedham Old Boys v Halstead Town Reserves 2-3*(aet)*

Final *(at Sudbury Wanderers FC, Wed 4th May)*: Halstead Town Reserves 2, Little Oakley 0

RESERVE KNOCK-OUT CUP 1993-94

First Round

Mersea Island Res. v Sudbury Ath. Res. 3-0
Rowhedge Res. v Little Oakley Res. 0-3
Dedham OB Reserves v Boxted Lodgers Res. 7-0
Alresford CR Reserves v Bramston CML Res. 0-2

Tiptree H. Res. v St Johns Res. 5-1*(Tiptree expelled)*
Lawford Lads Res. v Kelvedon Social Res. 0-1
Gas Recreation Res. v Mistley Utd Reserves 2-3
West Bergholt Res. v Long Melford Reserves 3-5

Quarter Finals

Mersea Island Res. v St Johns Reserves 6-0
Dedham OB Res. v Mistley Utd Reserves 1-5

Little Oakley Reserves v Kelvedon Social Res. 1-2
Bramston CML Res. v Long Melford Reserves 2-0

Semi-Finals

Mersea Island Res.v Kelvedon Social Res. 3-1

Mistley Utd Reserves v Bramston CML Reserves 0-1

Final *(at Stanway Rovers FC, Thurs 21st April)*:
Mersea Island Reserves beat Bramston CML Reserves 4-2 on penalties after 1-1 draw and extra-time.

TOMMY THOMPSION CUP 1993-94

First Round

Bures United v Hedinghams 1-3
Earls Colne v Kelvedon Social Reserves 5-6
Dedham Old Boys Res. v Alresford CR Res. 1-3
Cavendish v Rowhedge Reserves 3-1
Mistley United Reserves v Boxted Ldgrs Res. 2-1
Hadleigh Utd Reserves v Coggeshall 2-1

Tiptree Heath v Mersea Island Reserves 1-2
St Johns Reserves v Severalls 0-1
Wormingford v Silver End 2-5
Gas Reacreation Res. v Finchingfield 1-0
Little Oakley Res. v St Osyth 2-2,0-2
Walton Town v Bradfield 10-0

Second Round

Hedinghams v Mersea Island Reserves 1-3
Severalls Res. v Alresford CR Reserves 3-1
Gas Recreation Res. v Bramston CML Res. 6-2
Hadleigh Utd Reserves v Walton Town 7-0

Great Bentley v Kelvedon Social Res. 1-0
Silver End v Cavendish 0-3
Mistley Utd Res. v St Osyth 4-0
Lawford Lads v Sudbury Athletic Res. 7-2

Quarter Finals

Mersea Island Res. v Great Bentley 2-3*(aet)*
Gas Recreation Reserves v Mistley Utd Res. 4-1

Severalls v Cavendish 1-0
Hadleigh United Res. v Lawford Lads 0-1

Semi-Finals

Gas Recreation Res. v Lawford Lads 3-3,3-0

Great Bentley v Severalls 0-1*(aet)*

Final *(at Little Oakley FC, Mon 2nd May)*: Gas Recreation Reserves 4, Severalls 1

ALBERT LEE MEMORIAL TROPHY:

(at Sudbury Wanderers FC, 15th Sept. 1993): Alresford Colne Rangers 1, Little Oakley 0

ESSEX & SUFFOLK BORDER PREMIER DIVISON RESULTS 1993-94

HOME TEAM	1	2	3	4	5	6	7	8	9	10	11	12	13	14	15	16
1. Alresford Colne Rangers	*	1-3	3-2	2-1	1-5	1-0	3-1	0-3	0-0	1-2	0-1	2-1	1-1	2-2	1-3	1-2
2. Boxted Lodgers	3-1	*	7-1	0-3	2-1	2-3	0-5	0-4	0-0	1-3	1-1	0-1	1-2	1-4	0-5	1-3
3. Clacton Town Reserves	1-4	2-2	*	2-2	2-0	2-1	0-4	0-1	2-0	1-4	2-3	2-2	0-0	3-1	2-1	2-3
4. Dedham Old Boys	2-2	3-0	6-2	*	2-2	1-0	2-3	2-3	5-1	0-2	3-1	2-5	2-3	2-4	5-2	0-2
5. Felixstowe Town Reserves	3-1	7-2	4-1	4-1	*	2-2	3-0	0-2	0-0	1-1	1-4	2-2	1-1	2-0	1-4	2-2
6. Gas Recreation	2-1	6-0	2-0	0-3	2-0	*	2-3	1-1	4-1	2-2	1-1	3-1	2-3	6-4	1-1	0-0
7. Harwich & Parkeston Res.	0-1	2-1	5-2	2-4	1-1	3-0	*	2-0	3-3	4-1	0-2	1-3	1-3	1-0	0-1	1-4
8. Haverhill Rovers Reserves	2-4	2-1	W-L	1-0	2-2	4-2	3-1	*	3-0	0-1	1-3	4-1	2-3	4-1	4-0	0-3
9. Kelvedon Social	2-1	0-1	2-1	3-1	1-4	1-1	0-0	0-2	*	1-4	0-2	4-0	1-1	1-0	2-0	0-0
10. Little Oakley	3-1	6-0	4-1	2-3	3-0	0-3	3-4	1-0	2-0	*	4-1	1-2	W-L	1-0	3-3	2-2
11. Long Melford	0-1	3-1	0-2	0-0	1-2	1-1	4-0	0-1	2-1	0-4	*	5-0	1-1	3-1	4-1	1-1
12. St Johns (Clacton)	1-1	5-3	2-3	1-5	2-0	1-1	3-5	4-0	2-0	2-2	2-2	*	1-5	3-1	1-6	1-3
13. Stowmarket Town Reserves	0-1	3-2	1-1	1-2	2-1	0-0	6-1	1-1	0-1	0-5	1-1	1-3	*	0-1	2-1	3-2
14. Sudbury Athletic	0-2	2-2	3-2	1-2	0-1	0-1	0-0	0-3	4-2	1-0	1-2	1-3	3-2	*	1-3	2-1
15. Sudbury Wanderers Res.	3-1	3-2	2-1	1-3	0-1	1-3	8-1	1-1	5-2	1-2	2-1	1-1	1-1	1-1	*	1-1
16. West Bergholt	3-1	2-1	3-0	2-2	5-4	3-0	1-0	4-2	5-3	1-4	2-1	2-2	1-2	1-1	2-0	*

DIVISION ONE RESULTS

	1	2	3	4	5	6	7	8	9	10	11	12	13	14	15	16
1. Anchor Press - *withdrew*	*															
2. Bramston CML		*	3-2	1-1	3-0	1-3	4-2	2-2	1-0	0-1	3-3	1-1	1-1	5-0	0-0	4-0
3. Brantham Athletic Reserves		0-1	*	4-0	4-1	0-0	3-1	0-0	1-1	2-0	0-0	0-2	1-1	2-2	4-0	2-1
4. Cornard United Reserves		0-3	1-2	*	2-0	1-2	4-2	2-0	1-5	1-1	2-2	0-3	0-2	2-0	3-2	3-3
5. Foxash Social		4-0	1-1	2-4	*	1-2	4-1	3-3	0-1	2-0	1-2	2-3	3-2	1-0	2-0	4-1
6. Halstead Town Reserves		3-1	1-1	7-1	4-0	*	8-0	2-2	5-2	2-2	4-2	2-3	3-1	6-1	3-2	5-1
7. Long Melford Reserves		0-4	0-0	0-0	1-1	0-3	*	1-2	1-1	1-4	3-1	1-2	0-1	0-2	4-0	1-2
8. Mersea Island		1-3	0-1	0-1	2-2	1-3	2-0	*	3-0	3-1	2-1	2-3	4-2	5-0	2-3	2-1
9. Mistley United		0-1	1-1	2-1	3-0	2-2	4-0	1-0	*	4-1	7-0	2-4	0-3	2-1	1-1	3-1
10. Rowhedge		1-1	2-1	2-1	3-1	0-6	5-1	2-1	2-3	*	6-1	0-2	1-1	3-8	1-1	11-1
11. Royal London		1-1	2-0	3-0	2-0	2-4	11-1	1-1	2-5	4-1	*	1-3	0-1	3-1	2-1	2-3
12. Stanway Rovers Reserves		8-1	1-0	4-0	2-2	0-3	0-1	4-0	3-2	1-1	3-2	*	0-0	3-0	3-1	5-0
13. Tiptree Heath		0-0	4-0	2-0	3-0	1-3	3-0	4-1	3-0	2-1	2-0	2-0	*	3-2	3-1	1-0
14. Weeley Athletic		1-2	4-0	3-1	0-1	0-5	3-1	1-4	3-3	3-6	4-2	0-5	2-1	*	3-3	5-2
15. West Bergholt Reserves		5-1	1-2	6-0	7-2	2-1	2-2	0-0	2-6	1-0	0-2	2-1	1-0	1-0	*	6-1
16. West End United		2-3	0-1	3-3	0-0	2-5	2-0	0-1	2-3	3-6	1-2	0-4	0-2	0-1	3-1	*

DIVISION TWO RESULTS

	1	2	3	4	5	6	7	8	9	10	11	12	13	14	15
1. Alresford Colne Rgrs Reserves	*	1-1	0-1	1-0	0-2	1-3	5-0	0-1	1-2	3-2	0-1	5-1	1-0	2-0	5-2
2. Boxted Lodgers Reserves	3-3	*	0-1	0-6	4-1	0-4	6-2	0-4	3-3	0-1	7-4	1-1	2-2	2-1	0-4
3. Bures United	3-1	1-0	*	1-3	0-3	3-5	0-1	7-1	4-2	2-3	4-2	1-3	5-0	3-0	2-0
4. Cavendish	0-2	0-0	3-0	*	4-2	1-2	1-0	2-1	6-1	0-0	4-1	1-0	2-1	3-1	2-0
5. Earls Colne	4-1	2-0	1-0	2-2	*	1-3	2-1	2-2	0-3	2-1	2-3	0-4	4-1	0-0	4-0
6. Gas Recreation Reserves	0-0	1-0	3-1	3-5	7-2	*	3-1	2-2	3-1	1-1	5-2	4-0	5-2	2-1	1-4
7. Great Bentley	1-1	2-1	2-2	3-1	0-3	4-3	*	1-1	W-L	2-4	2-2	1-1	3-2	2-4	1-3
8. Hedinghams United	0-5	2-1	4-3	0-4	1-2	0-5	3-3	*	4-1	1-1	4-2	2-4	8-1	5-2	5-1
9. Kelvedon Social Reserves	2-4	1-3	L-W	0-2	2-1	1-4	1-2	1-1	*	0-1	0-3	0-2	2-3	L-W	2-1
10. Lawford Lads	13-1	2-1	4-1	2-0	5-2	3-1	4-1	1-1	7-2	*	3-2	2-0	3-1	1-2	2-0
11. Little Oakley Reserves	1-1	2-1	2-0	0-3	2-1	3-3	0-3	0-2	4-1	0-3	*	0-1	0-2	3-0	5-1
12. Mersea Island Reserves	3-3	4-1	2-2	2-1	1-1	1-1	5-1	3-1	1-0	2-0	1-3	*	5-0	1-0	3-1
13. St Johns (Clacton) Reserves	2-3	4-0	2-5	1-3	1-2	0-7	2-3	2-2	1-5	0-2	2-0	0-0	*	1-1	4-3
14. Silver End	2-0	1-0	3-1	2-1	2-2	2-1	2-3	3-1	0-1	3-1	0-2	0-3	2-0	*	3-4
15. Tiptree Heath Reserves	2-0	1-6	0-3	2-2	3-1	L-W	4-1	0-4	1-4	0-2	1-2	1-0	5-0	2-2	*

DIVISION THREE RESULTS

	1	2	3	4	5	6	7	8	9	10	11	12	13	14	15
1. Anchor Press Res. - *withdrawn*	*														
2. Bradfield Rovers		*	3-1	4-1	1-1	0-3	0-3	0-1	4-3	5-1	3-0	2-1	5-2	2-0	7-0
3. Bramston CML Reserves		0-4	*	4-3	6-1	1-0	1-4	3-0	0-1	3-3	2-0	2-5	3-3	1-2	0-1
4. Coggeshall Town		0-2	3-5	*	2-3	0-5	0-4	1-0	4-2	2-1	1-3	1-6	3-1	1-0	8-2
5. Dedham Old Boys Reserves		0-0	1-1	6-2	*	2-2	1-3	4-3	0-3	4-0	2-2	2-1	2-1	5-0	4-0
6. Finchingfield Rovers		2-0	4-0	W-L	1-1	*	1-0	3-0	4-3	6-1	4-0	4-1	3-1	5-0	9-2
7. Hadleigh United Reserves		1-1	3-6	3-1	5-0	2-2	*	6-1	3-0	5-0	1-1	3-3	3-0	0-2	3-0
8. Lawford Lads Reserves		1-0	1-0	2-0	0-2	0-2	0-4	*	0-1	1-0	1-3	3-1	2-0	0-3	2-1
9. Mistley United Reserves		0-1	0-1	5-4	0-4	2-3	1-6	1-1	*	0-0	2-1	4-0	2-1	1-0	3-3
10. Rowhedge Reserves		1-4	1-3	3-1	1-2	1-3	0-2	1-2	0-4	*	7-0	1-1	0-3	2-4	1-0
11. St Osyth		5-0	1-2	2-2	3-3	0-10	2-3	4-3	5-2	1-4	*	1-1	3-3	2-1	5-3
12. Severalls		5-2	0-2	2-0	0-0	4-4	2-0	3-0	4-2	3-0	2-2	*	1-4	2-2	3-1
13. Sudbury Athletic Reserves		6-1	0-1	6-1	2-6	0-2	4-2	2-0	1-2	2-1	7-4	3-0	*	7-2	1-2
14. Walton Town		0-1	0-3	3-2	1-2	2-2	0-1	1-0	2-0	3-0	1-1	3-4	4-1	*	3-1
15. Wormingford		3-1	1-6	1-1	4-1	1-7	0-8	1-0	1-0	5-2	1-2	1-1	1-5	0-4	*

Little Oakley forward N Aldridge tries to find a way through as the Premier Division champions-elect are held to a 3-3 draw at home to Sudbury Wanderers Reserves.

Photo - Martin Wray.

MOTORSPARES
BURY & DISTRICT LEAGUE

FOUNDED: 1907

DIV. ONE	P	W	D	L	F	A	PTS
Cockfield United	22	19	0	3	78	37	38
Thomas Ridley	22	17	3	2	85	36	37
St Edmunds (1965)	22	15	3	4	88	31	33
Wanderers SC	22	13	3	6	71	37	29
Thurston	22	10	5	7	67	38	25
Northbury	22	9	4	9	49	43	22
Sporting '87	22	9	4	9	39	39	22
Hepworth	22	8	1	13	50	58	17
Old Burians	22	6	5	11	48	65	17
Lakenheath Res.	22	7	0	15	47	74	14
Hundon	22	3	1	18	29	88	7
Pot Black Utd	22	1	1	20	26	128	3

Div 1 Cup Final: Thomas Ridley 2, St Edmunds 1

DIV. TWO	P	W	D	L	F	A	PTS
Wickhambrook	26	25	0	1	170	32	50
Ixworth	26	20	1	5	95	44	41
Eastgate Athletic	26	15	3	8	76	51	33
KJM Landscapes	26	13	3	8	76	52	31
Bury United	26	12	3	11	68	57	26
Next Installations	26	10	7	9	55	56	26
Advanced Air	26	12	1	13	51	65	25
Barons	26	9	5	12	47	73	23
Brandon Town 'A'	26	9	4	13	43	66	22
Eastbury	26	7	5	14	49	55	19
Silver Spoon	26	7	5	14	60	83	19
Lakenheath 'A'	26	6	4	16	29	70	16
Priors Inn	26	7	2	17	53	112	16
Beck Row	26	4	7	15	34	91	15

Div 2 Cup Final: Wickhambrook 3, Ixworth 0

DIV. THREE	P	W	D	L	F	A	PTS
Barrow	26	24	2	0	124	29	50
Cockfield Utd Res.	26	17	4	5	82	37	38
Royal Mail	26	15	7	4	115	38	37
Fornham St Martin	26	16	5	5	64	33	37
Helmsman	26	12	6	8	63	61	30
Great Barton	26	13	3	10	60	57	29
Cadogan Arms	26	12	5	9	53	52	29
Black Eagles	26	12	3	11	88	80	27
Sporting '87 Res.	26	9	3	14	60	61	21
Lucky Break	26	8	2	16	29	57	18
Padleys S & S	26	8	2	16	38	83	18
Hundon Res.	26	5	3	18	32	90	13
Ickworth	26	3	4	19	24	72	10
Next Instal. Res.	26	2	2	22	22	98	6

Div 3 Cup Final: Barrow 6, Lucky Break 1

Other Cup Finals:

Mick McNeil KO Cup: Wickhambrook 3, Cockfield United 0

Bill Utting Trophy: Thomas Ridley 2, Northbury 1

St Edmunds KO Cup: St Edmunds (1965) 4, Wickhambrook 2

Gratix Charity Cup: Ixworth 3, Thurston 2

Below: *Wickhambrook, Division Two champions, celebrate their Mick McNeil Cup final victory over Premier Division champions Cockfield United.*

Photo - Martin Wray.

S.E.H WINDOWS AND DOORS IPSWICH SUNDAY MORNING LGE

DIV. ONE	P	W	D	L	F	A	PTS
Heathfield	22	15	4	3	70	33	49
Melton YCOB	22	15	3	4	64	33	48
Capel Plough	22	13	4	5	61	34	43
Port of Felixstowe	22	12	2	8	55	42	38
Stowmarket Vandals	22	9	6	7	60	42	33
Eastern Eagles	22	9	6	7	43	38	33
Norbridge	22	8	6	8	56	57	30
Needham Market	22	8	4	10	51	50	28
Haughley Utd	22	7	5	10	40	49	26
Blandford	22	4	6	12	32	50	18
Belstead Arms	22	4	5	13	31	54	17
John Player	22	2	1	19	22	103	7

Lower Division Champions:
Div. 2 (12): Taverners
Div. 3 (11): Dickerson
Div. 4 (12): Leiston Athletic
Div. 5 (12): Stoke Athletic
Div. 6 (11): Wracc FC
Div. 7 (10): Schlumberger
Div. 8 (12): Walton Feathers
Div. 9 (11): Orford Sports
Div. 10 (11): Charsfield Reserves
Div. 11 (12): Warwick

Cockfield United - Motorspares Bury St Edmunds & District League champions 1993-94. Back Row (L/R): R Goldy (Manager), G Brinkley, S Langston, M Steggles, K Orriss, D Bush, T Nice, A Golding, T Bannon (Vice-Chairman), B Buckle (Physio). Front: J Whight, S Taylor, I Gooderham, S Arbon, R Dook, I Ramsbottom.

Sudbury Wanderers Reserves - Wimpey Homes Essex & Suffolk Border League. Back Row (L/R): N Theobald, R Dane, B McAnally, A Bowes, S Hughes, T Nippress, S Plowman, T Parsons, N Salt (Coach). Front: S Taylor, S Kilbourn, P Swain, C Wilde, J Howe.

Photos - Martin Wray.

SURREY F.A. (Est. 1877)

Secretary: Peter Adams,
321 Kingston Road, Leatherhead,
Surrey KT22 7TU (0372 373543)

SENIOR CUP 1993-94

First Qualifying Round

Chipstead v Banstead Athletic	0-5	Ash United v Kew Association	5-1
Westfield v Cranleigh	2-0	Godalming & Guildford v Shene Old Grammarians	2-1
Redhill v Old Suttonians	2-1		

Second Qualifying Round

Ditton v Westfield	0-2	St Andrews v Banstead Athletic	0-6
Cobham v Molesey *(at Molesey)*	0-4	Virginia Water v Merton	2-0
Farnham Town v Redhill	1-2	Merstham v Ash United	4-7*(aet)*
Farleigh Rovers v Frimley Green	3-0	Horley Town v Corinthian Casuals	0-5
Ashford Town (Middx) v Carshalton	3-1	Camberley Town v Godalming & Guildford	2-2,3-2

Third Qualifying Round

Virginia Water v Ash United	3-8	Redhill v Westfield	2-1*(aet)*
Farleigh Rovers v Ashford Town (Middx)	0-1	Corinthian Casuals v Banstead Athletic	2-2,0-1
Molesey v Camberley Town	4-1		

Fourth Qualifying Round

Chertsey Town v Ashford Town (Middx)	1-0	Banstead Athletic v Epsom & Ewell	2-2,0-1
Ash United v Redhill	4-0	Tooting & Mitcham United v Walton & Hersham	1-4
Leatherhead v Molesey	0-3		

First Round

Walton & Hersham v Kingstonian	2-0	Metropolitan Police v Croydon	4-0
Chertsey Town v Crystal Palace	1-1,3-4	Egham Town v Epsom & Ewell	2-1*(aet)*
Molesey v Carshalton Athletic	2-2,2-0	Whyteleafe v Sutton United	0-3
Ash United v Malden Vale	2-3	Woking v Dorking	3-1

Quarter-Finals

Egham Town v Sutton United	0-3	Metropolitan Police v Crystal Palace	2-2,1-3
Malden Vale v Molesey	1-2	Woking v Walton & Hersham	3-0

Semi-Finals

Crystal Palace v Sutton United	0-4	Molesey v Woking	0-3

Final *(at Kingstonian FC, Tues 10th May)*: Woking 3, Sutton United 1

OTHER COUNTY FINALS:

Premier Cup *(at Molesey FC, Wed 20th April)*: Sutton United Reserves 4, Woking Reserves 1
Intermediate Cup *(at Egham Town FC, Wed 4th May)*: Racal Dacca 1, Shottermill 0
Junior Cup *(at Merstham FC, Sat 7th May)*: Warbank Sports 3, St Ebbas 1
Lower Junior Cup *(at Horley Town FC, Sat 30th April)*: Sheen Athletic 2, FCA Highbury 0
Sunday Senior Cup *(at Molesey FC, Sunday 1st May)*: Ranelagh Sports 3, British Rail SA 0
Sunday Intermediate Cup *(at Tooting & Mitcham Utd FC, Sunday 8th May)*: AFC Mitcham 2, Melwood Ath. 1
Sunday Junior Cup *(at Chipstead FC, Sunday 24th April)*: Everest 2, Ashtead Park 1
Sunday Lower Junior Cup *(at Cobham FC, Sunday 15th May)*: Chessington White Hart 3, All Seasons Ath. 2 *(aet)*
Midweek Cup *(at Chipstead FC, Wed 11th May)*: Roehampton 2, Croydon Postal 0
Veterans Cup *(at Banstead Athletic FC, Fri 29th April)*: Manor Athletic 5, Merstham 2 *(aet)*
Saturday Inter-Lge Cup *(at Malden Vale FC, Mon 23rd May)*: Surrey SE Comb. 6, Surrey Int. (West) Lge 1
Sunday Inter-Lge Cup *(at Malden Vale FC, Tues 24th May)*: Leatherhead & Dist. 3, Mitcham & Dist. Lge 2

Ranelagh Sports - Surrey Senior Sunday Cup winners 1993-94. *Photo - Eric Marsh.*

S.C. JOHNSON SURREY COUNTY PREMIER LEAGUE

Founded: 1982

President: L F J Smith.

Chairman: R Clune.

Hon. Secretary: D Havenhand, 2 Balmoral Cres., Farnham GU9 0DN (0252 722798)

NETHERNE THE BEST OF UNLUCKY THIRTEEN

Last season, our 12th, was probably the most difficult and disappointing in our brief history. After congratulating ourselves the previous year on having our full complement of 16 clubs in the League, this season, because of the refusal of the Parasol Combined Counties League to relegate a club as a replacement for our champions, we were down to 15 clubs after the AGM. Within a few weeks, BT FC had their ground sold from beneath them and went out of existence and, only six weeks into the season, Frinton Rovers FC folded leaving us with only 13 clubs.

Perhaps it was a blessing in disguise, as the now customary monsoon season took a large number of Saturdays out of the fixture list and it was a struggle for our Fixtures Secretary, Alan Constable, and the clubs to get all the games played, the last one being on Tuesday 31st May!

The Premier Division was eventually won by Netherne, but only after much chopping and changing at the top, with Chobham, Burpham and, briefly, Holmesdale in the frame. Netherne were always favourites to win the title, especially when they snapped up several of the "stars" from the defunct Frinton Rovers, but they must have been concerned about Chobham, who went unbeaten in the League until April. Sadly for Chobham, although they lost only the once, they drew eight times, against Netherne's three, thus handing the title to Netherne by four points. The champions now leave us for the Combined Counties League, where we are confident that they will give a good account of themselves.

The Reserve Division was always a two horse race between the eventual winners, Vandyke, and Hinchley Wood, Vandyke going to the top in mid April when Hinchley Wood had unexpected home reverses against Chobham and Burpham. The fact that Hinchley Wood took four of the six points from Vandyke, before the two met in the Challenge Cup final, indicates how closely matched they were.

The cup competitions resulted in two of last season's winners retaining their trophies and new names appearing on the other two. The Premier final was a very competitive affair in which Walton Casuals led Holmesdale by 2-0 in the first game before being clawed back. They did not make the same mistake in the replay, running out worthy 2-0 winners. In the Reserve final, Hinchley Wood had the opportunity to gain revenge on Vandyke for pipping them in the League. Sadly for Hinchley Wood, they met an inspired Vandyke who won comfortably 4-1 to retain the Trophy. The two supplementary cup finals were very close, Holmesdale beating Raynes Park on penalties after a 2-2 draw to win the Richard Partington Memorial Cup, and Ottershaw retaining the Reserves' Charity Cup by beating Hinchley Wood 1-0. Thus Hinchley Wood Reserves ended as runners-up in all three competitions!

On the Sportsmanship side, unfortunately on-the-field discipline was the worst that this League has ever experienced, hence the Sportsmanship marks were very low. Nevertheless, the winners - Walton Casuals - were comfortable winners and receive the customary £150 award.

It would have been expecting a great deal for the Leagues' Representative side to continue where they left off the previous season and win everything in sight. The bubble has to burst sometime and it did, with a vengeance. After five seasons undefeated in the South Eastern Counties Intermediate Inter-League Compeition, we lost twice and finished only third. In the Surrey Inter-League Competiion, we were beaten in the second round. Nevertheless, congratulations and thanks are due to Managers Mick Taylor and Robin Denman and the players.

In the county cups, Chobham and Netherne both reached the semi-finals of the Surrey Premier Cup, losing to Woking Reserves and Sutton United Reserves respectively, but only after replays. In the Surrey Intermediate Cup, Chobham Reserves progressed the furthest - to the 4th Round.

Finally, we must thank our sponsors, SC Johnson (Johnson Wax) for their invaluable support and encouragement.

Shortly after the season finished, we were shocked and saddened by the sudden death of our popular Chairman - Reg Mendham. Reg was completing only his third season as chairman, but his influence on the League was significant. He will be sorely missed.

D Havenhand, Hon. Secretary.

PREM. DIV.	P	W	D	L	F	A	PTS
Netherne	24	18	3	3	56	23	57
Chobham	24	15	8	1	77	28	53
Holmesdale	24	15	5	4	60	32	50
Burpham	24	11	5	8	51	41	38
Walton Casuals	24	11	3	10	42	46	36
Vandyke	24	10	6	9	48	55	36
Ottershaw	24	9	5	10	39	36	32
Raynes Park	24	9	3	12	42	43	30
Croydon MO	24	8	5	11	47	55	29
Bisley Sports	24	8	3	13	50	53	27
Hersham RBL	24	5	4	15	40	69	19
Hinchley Wood	24	5	4	15	39	69	19
Battersea Ironsides	24	4	2	18	30	71	14

RESERVE DIV.	P	W	D	L	F	A	PTS
Vandyke Res.	24	16	3	5	69	40	51
Hinchley Wd Res.	24	15	5	4	63	35	50
Walton Cas. Res.	24	14	6	4	55	30	48
Holmesdale Res.	24	14	2	8	49	29	44
Chobham Res.	24	14	1	9	45	38	43
Burpham Res.	24	12	5	7	44	36	41
Raynes Pk Res.	24	12	3	9	46	38	39
Ottershaw Res.	24	10	7	7	38	35	37
Croydon MO Res.	24	11	3	10	47	41	36
Battersea I. Res.	24	6	5	13	27	45	23
Netherne Res.	24	5	4	15	26	49	19
Bisley Spts Res.	24	3	2	19	28	74	11
Hersham RBL Res.	24	0	2	22	20	67	2

PREMIER DIVISION RESULT CHART 1993-94

HOME TEAM		1	2	3	4	5	6	7	8	9	10	11	12	13
1.	Battersea Ironsides	*	3-2	1-3	1-4	3-4	1-7	5-2	3-2	0-5	1-3	1-3	2-4	0-3
2.	Bisley Sports	3-0	*	3-3	2-3	4-0	5-2	1-3	1-2	0-1	2-1	2-2	5-0	6-2
3.	Burpham	2-0	4-0	*	1-4	4-1	3-2	2-0	1-2	2-2	3-1	2-1	5-0	2-2
4.	Chobham	7-0	9-0	0-0	*	3-3	6-2	6-2	1-1	1-1	1-1	2-1	2-0	1-1
5.	Croydon Mun. Officers	3-1	2-5	3-2	0-1	*	3-0	1-2	1-1	1-2	2-1	1-3	1-3	3-1
6.	Hersham Ryl British L.	2-2	1-0	0-2	1-10	3-3	*	2-0	1-4	1-2	1-2	0-3	1-2	0-2
7.	Hinchley Wood	1-0	2-0	3-3	2-5	1-6	3-3	*	1-1	2-4	3-4	1-6	4-1	2-4
8.	Holmesdale	3-1	2-2	5-2	3-1	2-1	1-1	3-1	*	2-0	2-1	3-0	6-1	0-2
9.	Netherne	2-1	2-1	3-1	2-2	5-0	2-3	3-1	1-0	*	2-1	2-0	3-1	0-2
10.	Ottershaw	0-1	1-0	3-1	2-3	1-1	5-1	1-0	1-3	0-3	*	4-1	0-0	0-0
11.	Raynes Park	1-1	0-2	1-2	0-2	2-5	5-0	2-1	1-2	0-3	2-1	*	2-2	4-0
12.	Vandyke	4-2	4-3	3-1	2-2	2-2	2-1	2-2	4-1	0-3	2-2	4-1	*	2-3
13.	Walton Casuals	1-0	4-1	1-0	0-1	3-0	1-5	4-0	3-9	1-3	1-3	0-1	1-3	*

RESERVE DIVISION RESULT CHART 1993-94

HOME TEAM		1	2	3	4	5	6	7	8	9	10	11	12	13
1.	Battersea Ironsides Res.	*	3-0	1-1	2-4	0-3	3-2	3-4	0-0	0-1	1-0	0-4	1-2	1-4
2.	Bisley Sports Res.	1-2	*	5-3	0-1	1-2	2-0	0-1	1-5	0-2	1-1	0-4	1-4	1-2
3.	Burpham Res.	1-1	3-0	*	0-2	3-1	2-1	2-2	0-1	4-0	3-2	0-0	0-4	4-3
4.	Chobham Res.	2-0	3-1	1-0	*	2-1	3-2	0-4	1-0	3-1	1-2	1-2	2-5	1-1
5.	Croydon MO Res.	2-2	5-1	0-2	2-5	*	3-1	2-5	2-0	2-0	1-1	1-0	4-0	2-3
6.	Hersham RBL Res.	0-3	1-5	1-4	0-1	1-4	*	0-4	0-1	0-5	2-3	1-2	2-6	1-2
7.	Hinchley Wood Res.	1-1	4-2	3-4	1-4	1-0	1-0	*	3-0	4-1	2-2	2-5	2-2	2-2
8.	Holmesdale Res.	2-0	6-0	2-0	2-1	3-0	5-0	0-4	*	0-1	3-1	2-2	5-0	2-4
9.	Netherne Res.	1-2	2-2	1-2	2-3	0-3	1-1	0-4	1-3	*	1-1	2-1	1-3	0-1
10.	Ottershaw Res.	2-1	1-0	0-1	2-0	2-1	3-2	0-4	2-3	4-1	*	1-2	1-1	1-1
11.	Raynes Park Res.	1-0	6-1	1-2	3-2	3-4	1-0	1-2	0-1	3-1	1-1	*	2-3	1-0
12.	Vandyke Res.	1-0	7-3	2-1	4-2	3-0	1-1	1-2	4-3	3-1	2-3	6-0	*	1-2
13.	Walton Casuals Res.	6-0	6-0	2-2	1-0	2-2	2-1	3-1	2-0	0-0	0-2	5-1	1-4	*

PREMIER CHALLENGE CUP 1993-94

First Round

Vandyke *(w/o)* Frinton Rovers *(scr)*		Holmesdale v Battersea Ironsides	1-1*(aet)*,3-0
Walton Casuals v Chobham	1-0	Netherne v Burpham	3-0
Raynes Park v Bisley Sports	2-1	Hersham Royal British Legion v Croydon MO	1-0

Quarter-Finals

Holmesdale v Vandyke	2-1	Ottershaw v Netherne	1-2
Walton Casuals v Hinchley Wood	9-1	Raynes Park v Hersham Royal British Legion	1-0

Semi-Finals

Walton Casuals v Netherne	3-1	Hersham Royal British Legion v Holmesdale	0-1

Final *(at Dorking FC)*: Walton Casuals 2, Holmesdale 2 *(aet)*
Replay *(at Ashford Town (Middx) FC)*: Walton Casuals 2, Holmesdale 0

RESERVE CHALLENGE CUP 1993-94

First Round

Vandyke Res. *(w/o)* Frinton R. Res. *(scr)*		Holmesdale Res. v Chobham Res.	2-3
Ottershaw Res. v Hinchley Wood Res.	2-3	Hersham RBL Res. v Croydon MO Res.	0-1
Netherne Res. v Walton Casuals Res.	4-5	Raynes Park Res. v Burpham Res.	5-1

Quarter-Finals

Vandyke Res. v Raynes Park Res.	4-0	Bisley Spts Res. v Croydon MO Res.	1-2
Walton Casuals Res. v Chobham Res.	3-1	Battersea Ironsides Res. v Hinchley Wood Res.	0-1

Semi-Finals

Croydon MO Res *(scr)* Vandyke Res. *(w/o)*		Hinchley Wood Res. v Walton Casuals Res.	4-2

Final *(at Dorking FC)*: Vandyke Reserves 3, Hinchley Wood Reserves 0

RICHARD PARTINGTON CUP 1993-94

First Round

Vandyke v Holmesdale	3-5	Walton Casuals v Hinchley Wood	5-2

Quarter-Finals

Bisley Sports v Holmesdale	2-5	Hersham RBL v Walton Casuals	0-3
Ottershaw v Croydon MO	2-0	Battersea Ironsides v Raynes Park	1-5

Semi-Finals

Ottershaw v Raynes Park	0-4	Holmesdale v Walton Casuals	3-1

Final *(at Malden Vale FC)*: Holmesdale beat Raynes Park 4-3 on penalties after 2-2 draw and extra-time

RESERVE CHARITY CUP 1993-94

First Round
Burpham Res. v Walton C. Res. 0-0*(4-3 pens)*
Netherne Res. v Raynes Pk Res. 0-0*(aet)*,0-2
Hinchley Wood Res. v Bisley Spts Res. 3-2

Quarter-Finals
Vandyke Res. v Hinchley Wood Res. 1-3
Battersea Ironsides Res. v Croydon MO Res. 2-1
Ottershaw Res. v Raynes Park Res. 1-0
Holmesdale Res. v Burpham Res. 2-4

Semi-Finals
Ottershaw Res. v Burpham Res. 3-1
Hinchley Wood Res. v Battersea Ironside Res. 6-1

Final *(at Ashford Town (Middx) FC)*: Ottershaw Reserves 1, Hinchley Wood Reserves 0

SURREY COUNTY PREMIER LEAGUE CLUBS 1994-95

BISLEY SPORTS

Chairman: Michael Lawry
Secretary: Mrs Julie Robertson, 17 Cobbetts Walk, Bisley, Woking GU24 9DT (0483 481345).
Ground: Recreation Ground, Guildford Rd, Bisley.
Colours: Blue & black stripes/black/black.
Previous League: Surrey Intermediate (West)(pre-1993).

BURPHAM

Chairman: Jim Curtis.
Secretary: Kevin Brookham, 104 Manor Rd, Guildford GU2 6NR (0483 36713).
Ground: Sutherland Playing Fields, Clay Lane, Burpham, Guildford.
Colours: Yellow/green/yellow **Change colours:** Blue/black/black.

CHESSINGTON & HOOK UNITED

Secretary: Alan Warwick, 38 Hartfield Rd, Chessington, Surrey KT9 2PW (081 397 1843).
Ground: Chalky Lane, Chessington, Surrey (0372 729892).
Directions: Chalky Lane is off A243 opposite Chessington World of Adventure Theme Park. BR to Chessington South station.
Colours: All blue **Previous League:** Surrey South Eastern Combination (pre-1994)

CHOBHAM

Secretary: Mrs Daisey Walley, 8 Brook Green, Chertsey Rd, Chobham GU24 8PN (0276 858039).
Ground: Recreation Ground, Station Road, Chobham (0276 857876)
Cols: White (blue pin stripe)/navy/navy **Change colours:** Blue/white/blue.
Previous League: Combined Counties (pre-1990).

CONEY HALL

Secretary: Bill Lennox, 1 Southway, Hayes, Kent BR2 7LR (081 462 7514).
Ground: Tiepigs Lane, Coney Hall, West Wickham, Kent (081 462 9103).
Directions: Gravel Hill continue along Kent Gate Way, across r'bout along Addington Village Rd and Addington Rd until next r'bout, continue ahead, 2nd left down Tiepigs Lane, ground on left before railway bridge.
Colours: Red & black stripes/black/black.
Honours: Surrey South Eastern Combination 93-94.

CROYDON MUNICIPAL OFFICERS

Chairman: Terry Osborn.
Secretary: Tony Osborn, 15 Long Lane, Croydon CR0 7AR (081 6566120).
Ground: Russell Hill Reservoir, Pampisford Road, Purley.
Colours: Blue & white/blue/blue.

DITTON

Secretary: L Edwards, 83 Ravenswood Ave., Long Ditton, Surrey (081 391 1265).
Ground: Ditton Recreation Ground, Windmill Lane, Long Ditton, Surbiton, Surrey (081 398 7428).
Directions: At A307/A309 'Scilly Isles' r'bout east of Esher, take A307 towards Surbiton. Windmill Lane is one and a half miles on right. One and a half miles from Surbiton (BR); turn left into Victoria Rd, right at crossroads, left into Balaclava, right into Effingham Rd and right into Windmill Lane.
Seats: None **Cover:** No **Capacity:** 1,000 **Floodlights:** No **Founded:** 1912
Colours: Yellow/green/yellow **Change cols:** Black & white/black/white **Programme:** TBA
Previous Leagues: Kingston & Dist./ Middx Snr/ Surrey I'mediate/ Surrey Comb. 72-85/ Surrey Premier/ Combined Counties.
Club record appearances: Andy Boxall. **Record Gate:** 200 v Malden T., Comb. Co's Lg 1/1/92.
Hons: Surrey Premier Lg 85-86 88-89 89-90 (Lg Cup 87-88 88-89 90-91), Surrey Co. Premier Cup R-up 85-86, Surrey I'mediate Cup R-up 53-54 81-82 83-84, Surrey Comb. 84-85, Surrey Jnr Charity Cup 22-23 (R-up 21-22 44-45), Surrey Lower Jnr Cup 81-82, War Emergency Cup 46-47.

FARLEIGH ROVERS

Secretary: Barry Gibson, 3 Iris Close, Shirley Oaks Village, Shirley, Croydon, CR0 8XW (081 655 2031).
Ground: Parsonage Field, Harrow Road, Warlingham, Surrey (0883 626483).
Directions: Limpsfield Road (B269) south eastwards, left into Farleigh Rd, left at T-junction, right into Harrow Rd, right into Green Lane. Three miles from Upper Warlingham (BR); left into Chelsham Rd 1 mile left into Harrow Rd. Bus 403 to Harrow Rd.
Seats: None **Cover:** 50 **Capacity:** 2,000 **Floodlights:** No **Founded:** 1922
Colours: Red & navy/navy/navy **Change colours:** White & black/black/black.
Previous Name: Farleigh & Chelsham Utd (pre-1929) **Previous Ground:** Farleigh Common (pre-1925).
Prev. Lges: Surrey Prem./ Comb. Co's **Record Gate:** 130 v Chipstead, League 28/12/87.
Midweek matchday: Tuesday **Hons:** Combined Co's Lg Cup R-up 91-92.

HERSHAM ROYAL BRITISH LEGION

Secretary: Rod Stevens, 13 Leybourne Ave., Byfleet, Surrey KT14 7HB (0932 351725).
Ground: Coronation PF, Molesey Rd, Hersham (0932 227014-club, 223037-ground).
Directions: On left hand of Molesey Rd coming from Hersham BR midway between station & Barley Row r'bout.
Colours: Sky/navy/navy *(Reserves: Sky/maroon/sky).*

HINCHLEY WOOD

Secretary: Tony Arnold, 30 Cheshire Gdns, Chessington, Surrey KT9 2PR (081 397 9965)
Ground: Strenue Association, Lynwood Rd, Hinchley Wood, Esher (off Claygate Lane)(081 398 5374)
Directions: A3 southbound, bear left on Esher Rd (A309) directly after Aces of Spades underpass, right at 1st r'bout into Claygate Lane - Lynwood Rd turning off Claygate Lane (signposted Strenue Association).
Colours: Blue & black/black/black **Change colours:** White/blue/blue.
Previous Name: Surbiton Town (pre-1993).

HOLMESDALE

Chairman: Tony Roberts
Secretary: Mark Hayes, 45 Acacia Rd, Mitcham, Surrey CR4 1LS (081 715 7679)
Ground: John Ruskin PF, Combe Lodge, Oaks Rd, Shirley, Croydon (081 654 3804).
Colours: Yellow & green stripes/yellow/yellow. **Change colours:** White/navy/navy.
Previous League: Surrey South Eastern Combination (pre-1993).
Previous Ground: Croydon College, Coopers Rd, Waddon (pre-1992).

OTTERSHAW

Secretary: Steve Caswell, 16 The Maples, Ottershaw KT16 0NU (0932 872133).
Ground: Woodham Court Sports Club, Martyrs Lane, Woodham, Woking.
Colours: Yellow/blue/yellow.
Previous Ground: Abbeylands, School Lane, Addlestone.

RAYNES PARK

Secretary: Paul Armour, 6 Woodstock Rise, Sutton, Surrey SM3 3JE (081 644 2444).
Ground: Raynes Park Sports Ground, Taunton Avenue, Raynes Park SW20 (081 946 8385).
Colours: Red & black stripes/black/black. **Change colours:** White/black.black.

SHEERWATER

Chairman: T Bristow.
Secretary: Trevor Wendon, 24 North Rd, Guildford GU2 6PU (0483 38686).
Ground: Sheerwater Rec., Blackmore Crescent, Sheerwater Estate, Woking.
Colours: Royal & white/white/white *(Reserves: Maroon/white/blue)*
Previous League: Surrey Intermediate (West)(pre-1994).

SHOTTERMILL

Secretary: Dave Williams, 2 Church Green Cottages, Tanners Lane, Haslemere GU27 1BN (0428 651664).
Ground: Wooler Hill Sports Ground, Haslemere.
Colours: White/navy/navy **Change colours:** All green
Previous League: Surrey Intermediate (West).

VANDYKE

Manager: S Lundy.
Secretary: Paul Smith, 76 Court Ave., Old Coulsdon CR3 1HE (0737 552617).
Ground: London Fire Brigade Ground, Banstead Road, Ewell.
Colours: Blue/white/blue *(Reserves: Blue & yellow/blue/yellow)*
Previous Grounds: West Park Hosp., Horton Lane, Epsom (pre-1993), Bodnant Gardens, Raynes Park 93-94.

VIRGINIA WATER

Secretary: Ron Fisher, Butlers Cottage, Thorpe Green, Egham, Surrey TW20 8QN (0344 842518).
Ground: 'The Timbers', Crown Rd, Virginia Water, Surrey (0344 843811).
Directions: M25 jct 11, follow signs to Chertsey, Thorpe, then Virginia Water. From A30 - B389 to island, into Wellington Ave., 3rd left is Crown Rd. BR to Virginia Water.
Seats: None **Cover:** No **Capacity:** 2,000 **Floodlights:** No **Founded:** 1921
Colours: Red & green/red/red **Change colours:** White/grey/grey
Previous Leagues: Surrey Snr 68-75/ Combined Co's 79-87 93-94/ Surrey Comb. 87-91/ Surrey South Eastern Comb. 91-92/ Surrey Premier 92-93.
Rec. Gate: 250 v Raynes Park, 27/4/93. **Nickname:** Waters
Record win: 9-1 (reserves: 11-0) **Record defeat:** 1-4 (reserves: 0-6).
Club record scorer: Nigel Kaye **Club record appearances:** Sammy Eason.
Hons: Surrey Premier Lg 92-93, Surrey County Cup 90-91, Surrey S.E. Comb. R-up 91-92 (Lg Cup R-up 91-92).

WALTON CASUALS

Secretary: Stuart Roberts, 47 Foxholes, Weybridge KT13 0BN (0932 845923).
Ground: Franklyn Road Sports Ground, off Waterside Drive, Walton-on-Thames (0932 247318).
Colours: Orange & white/white/white **Change colours:** White/blue/white

SURREY SOUTH EASTERN COMBINATION LEAGUE

Presidents: L P Leech, B F Scott

Chairman: G E Ellis

Hon. Secretary: G W Worsfold, 41 Ballards Way, South Croydon, CR2 7JP (081 6510856)

The season provided more than its fair share of 'downs', with the withdrawal of clubs and the frequent inclement weather, and then finally the tragic collapse of Paul Ford of Woodmansterne Sports during a league game, and his subsequent death some weeks later in hospital.

However, the clubs put all the problems behind them and provided some exciting, and in some cases nail-biting, finishes. Intermediate Division One and Junior Divisions One, Three and Four all rested on the final games of the season, as did runners-up spot in Intermediate Division Three and Junior Division Two. In Intermediate Division One, Coney Hall and Chessington & Hook United provided a finish that could not have been bettered, playing each other in the final divisional game and eventually being separated by just one goal. Both clubs have now been promoted to the Surrey Premier League, and our best wishes go with them for a successful first season at the higher level.

All the five main finals were close games with four being decided, for the second year running, by a single goal. Additionally, all ten finalists actually scored. This year, both of the senior finals provided well-balanced and even games with some excellent and exciting football. In the Senior League Cup, Colliers Wood United just edged out Chessington & Hook United in the only final to go to extra-time. In the Ellis Printers Senior Shield final, Reigate Town came back well in the second-half to snatch victory against AFC Wandgas. In the junior finals, Coney Hall Reserves did a double winning the Junior League Cup and Ellis Printers Intermediate Shield, while Raynes Park 'A' did the 'double' nobody wants in becoming runners-up in both Junior League Cup and Ellis Printers Shield.

A number of clubs had multiple successes; Coney Hall won Intermediate Division One, the Junior League Cup, Ellis Printers Intermediate Shield and the Junior Division One Sportsmanship Trophy; Chessington & Hook United were runners-up in Intermediate Division One, the Senior League Cup and Junior Division One, whilst winning Junior Division Two; AFC Wandgas won Intermediate Division Two, were runners-up in the Ellis Printers Senior Shield and the 'Golden Goals' competition and won Junior Division Four; Reigate Town were runners-up in Intermediate Division Two, and won the Ellis Printers Senior Shield and the Junior Division Four Sportsmanship Trophy; Chessington White Hart won Intermediate Division Three and also took the Linesman's Award in their first season in the League; Racal Decca, another club in their first season, were runners-up Intermediate Division Three (also taking the Sportsmanship Trophy) and Junior Division Two; Raynes Park 'A', in addition to the two cup finals mentioned earlier, won Junior Division Three; Holmesdale 'A' were runners-up in Junior Division Four, but won the Ellis Printers Junior Shield and the 'Golden Goals' competition; Bookham Reserves were runners-up in the Ellis Printers Intermediate Shield and won the Junior Charity Cup, their appearance in the Intermediate final being the first in living memory of older club members.

One multiple winner more than worthy of a mention is South Godstone who, despite a very bad season on the pitch (bottom of Intermediate Division One and second-bottom of Junior Division Three), showed that the game can still be played within the rules, winning both their divisional sportsmanship awards and the overall Les Chapman Sportsmanship Trophy. Despite the number of multiple winners, a total of nineteen clubs received a trophy at the end of the season. As this is nearly half of those in membership, it is an encourageing sign.

The League had a betther season in the Surrey FA cups, with Racal Decca winning the Intermediate Cup in their first season. On the night, they put on an excellent show. The League Representative team won the County Inter-League Cup, and after last season's dismal performance in the competition, this was a real bonus.

In common with most competitions, misconduct showed an increase. The fact that ours was lower than most across the county is no reason for complacency and should be used as a base for improvement.

After only three seasons, this league has earned itself a good name, as is proved by the number of applicants to join once again this year. We will all be aiming to improve even further next season and beyond.

Gordon Worsfold, Hon. General Secretary.

PHOTOS OPPOSITE:

Top: *Coney Hall Reserves - Ellis Printers Intermediate Shield winners.*

Centre: *Holmesdale 'A' - Ellis Printers Junior Shield winners.*

Foot: *Raynes Park 'A' - Ellis Printers Junior Shield runners-up.*
All Photos - Dave West.

FINAL TABLES

* points adjusted

INT. DIV. ONE	P	W	D	L	F	A	PTS
Coney Hall	24	17	2	5	53	21	36
Chess. & Hook U.	24	16	4	4	60	29	36
Crescent Rovers	24	13	7	4	46	23	33
Colliers Wd Utd	24	11	8	5	56	38	30
Perrywood Spts	24	13	3	8	56	37	29
Worcester Park	24	9	6	9	54	52	24
Bookham	24	9	3	12	49	44	21
Ashstead	24	9	2	13	43	54	20
Greenside	24	7	5	12	33	45	19
Battersea Pk Corona	24	6	7	11	31	53	19
Beaufoy United	24	6	6	12	35	41	18
Sutton Athletic	24	6	5	13	43	67	17
South Godstone	24	4	2	18	34	89	10

INT. DIV. TWO	P	W	D	L	F	A	PTS
AFC Wandgas	24	19	3	2	100	31	41
Reigate Town	24	15	5	4	74	32	35
RAS Accra Utd	24	13	5	6	70	40	31
Oxted & District	24	14	3	7	62	37	31
Eversley Rangers	24	12	5	7	51	45	29
Halliford	24	9	9	6	56	45	27
Caius	24	11	5	8	46	54	27
Sutton High	24	11	1	12	52	46	23
Bletchingley	24	5	7	12	52	74	17
Hinchley Wood Utd	24	7	3	14	41	71	17
Hook Venturers	24	6	4	14	40	59	16
Fetcham	24	4	2	18	43	90	10
Verdayne	24	2	4	18	39	102	8

INT. DIV. THREE	P	W	D	L	F	A	PTS
Chess. White Hart	22	18	2	2	71	13	38
Racal Decca	22	16	3	3	76	28	35
Chipstead 'A'	22	16	1	5	79	36	33
Warlingham	22	12	2	8	42	25	26
Woodmansterne Spts	22	10	6	6	51	40	26
Charlwood	22	9	2	11	41	40	20
Tadworth	22	6	8	8	42	49	20
Thornton Hth Rvrs	22	7	4	11	43	59	18
St Andrews Res.	22	6	4	12	37	64	16
Three Bridges 'A'	22	5	3	14	31	82	13
Cobham 'A'	22	5	2	15	32	67	12
Cheam Vill. Warr.	22	2	3	17	28	70	7

JNR. DIV. ONE	P	W	D	L	F	A	PTS
Worcester Pk 'A'	20	15	3	2	66	22	33
Chess. & Hook Res.	20	14	3	3	54	14	31
Coney Hall Res.	20	11	3	6	48	21	25
Crescent Rvrs Res.	20	10	4	6	45	27	24
Greenside Res.	20	10	3	7	61	32	23
Battersea Pk C. Res.	20	11	1	8	46	43	23
Beaufoy Utd Res.	20	8	4	8	46	35	20
RAS Accra U. Res.	20	7	3	10	35	64	17
Ashtead Res.	20	5	0	15	24	57	10
Sutton High Res.	20	4	1	15	19	69	9
Hinchley Wd U. Res.	20	1	3	16	18	78	5

JNR. DIV. TWO	P	W	D	L	F	A	PTS
Chess. & Hook 'A'	16	11	4	1	65	15	26
Racal Decca Res.	16	10	2	4	62	29	22
Warlingham Res.	16	10	2	4	47	30	22
Cheam Vill. W. Res.	16	10	1	5	36	33	21
Netherne 'A'	16	7	5	4	41	31	19
Sutton Athletic 'A'	16	5	3	8	43	42	13
Bookham Res.	16	4	2	10	35	45	10
Hersham RBL 'A'	16	3	1	12	14	56	7
Bletchingley Res.	16	2	0	14	23	81	4

JNR. DIV. THREE	P	W	D	L	F	A	PTS
Raynes Park 'A'	20	14	3	3	67	23	*30
Perrywood Spts Res.	20	14	0	6	55	29	28
Colliers Wood Res.	20	11	2	7	36	30	*26
Worcester Pk 'A'	19	15	1	3	70	31	*25
Vandyke 'A'	20	9	1	10	54	47	*21
Coney Hall 'A'	20	8	4	8	40	52	*21
Battersea Pk C. 'A'	20	6	4	10	35	52	*18
Chess. & Hook 'B'	20	8	1	11	38	37	17
Woodmansterne Res.	20	7	0	13	46	56	*16
Sth Godstone Res.	20	6	2	12	36	61	14
Verdayne Res.	19	2	0	17	21	80	2

JNR. DIV. FOUR	P	W	D	L	F	A	PTS
AFC Wandgas	20	14	3	3	58	28	31
Holmesdale 'A'	20	14	2	4	78	31	30
Chess. White H. Res.	20	14	2	4	62	26	30
Thornton HR Res.	20	12	3	5	59	36	27
Tadworth Res.	20	10	1	9	61	46	21
Chipstead 'B'	20	8	5	7	40	37	21
Eversley Rgrs Res.	20	8	2	10	47	61	18
Charlwood Res.	20	7	3	10	42	38	17
Reigate T. Res.	20	5	2	13	28	89	12
Oxted & Dist. Res.	20	3	2	15	31	73	8
Crescent Rovers 'A'	20	1	3	16	23	64	5

INTERMEDIATE DIV. ONE RESULT CHART 1993-94

HOME TEAM		1	2	3	4	5	6	7	8	9	10	11	12	13
1.	Ashtead	*	4-0	0-2	1-2	2-5	2-4	2-5	1-0	5-1	2-3	2-0	2-1	0-3
2.	Battersea Park Corona	1-0	*	0-0	1-5	1-5	2-5	1-3	3-3	0-0	1-2	1-1	3-3	1-1
3.	Beaufoy United	0-1	2-1	*	4-3	2-2	0-0	0-3	1-1	1-3	0-2	1-2	0-1	3-3
4.	Bookham	5-0	2-0	0-3	*	2-2	2-0	1-3	2-0	0-1	0-2	10-1	4-1	3-2
5.	Chessington & Hook	6-0	1-3	2-1	1-0	*	1-0	1-0	4-3	2-0	1-0	3-4	4-4	6-1
6.	Colliers Wood United	2-2	1-1	1-0	2-0	1-1	*	2-3	2-2	2-1	4-1	3-0	5-3	1-1
7.	Coney Hall	2-0	3-1	1-1	2-1	2-0	1-1	*	0-1	1-0	1-2	5-0	3-0	1-0
8.	Crescent Rovers	3-1	0-1	3-1	2-0	1-0	3-1	1-0	*	2-0	1-1	2-0	3-0	2-2
9.	Greenside	2-2	1-3	2-0	2-2	0-1	2-6	2-1	2-3	*	1-1	4-0	3-3	1-4
10.	Perrywood Sports	1-2	2-3	5-3	7-2	0-4	1-0	1-2	1-1	3-1	*	10-0	2-0	0-2
11.	South Godstone	1-6	0-1	1-5	1-1	1-4	3-6	1-2	0-5	3-0	1-2	*	8-0	1-7
12.	Sutton Athletic	3-2	3-1	4-1	3-0	0-2	4-4	1-3	0-4	0-1	2-5	4-2	*	1-3
13.	Worcester Park	2-4	6-1	0-4	3-2	1-2	2-3	1-6	0-0	0-3	3-2	5-3	2-2	*

Bradbank Sports withdrew - record expunged

INTERMEDIATE DIV. TWO RESULT CHART 1993-94

HOME TEAM		1	2	3	4	5	6	7	8	9	10	11	12	13
1.	AFC Wandgas	*	4-0	4-1	4-1	5-2	1-1	5-2	3-1	3-5	3-3	4-0	3-2	3-0
2.	Bletchingley	2-6	*	2-3	2-3	11-2	0-8	2-2	3-1	2-4	2-6	4-4	1-0	5-5
3.	Caius	2-8	6-2	*	1-5	2-2	4-1	3-2	3-3	2-0	2-0	1-1	2-4	W-L
4.	Eversley Rangers	W-L	3-3	0-1	*	1-0	3-3	3-0	1-0	2-2	0-4	1-1	0-2	7-3
5.	Fetcham	1-6	5-1	1-1	2-3	*	4-5	2-5	5-1	1-3	0-5	2-3	0-5	4-1
6.	Halliford	0-3	2-2	2-0	1-1	3-1	*	2-0	3-3	0-2	3-3	0-5	2-3	5-0
7.	Hinchley Wood Utd	1-7	2-0	3-0	2-0	1-4	2-2	*	3-0	2-0	0-4	0-1	1-5	4-4
8.	Hook Venturers	2-2	0-1	3-4	0-1	3-2	0-0	5-1	*	0-3	2-3	1-8	1-0	6-3
9.	Oxted & District	1-4	2-1	1-1	1-2	16-0	2-1	2-1	0-2	*	4-3	2-2	1-0	4-1
10.	RAS Accra United	1-5	2-2	5-1	1-4	W-L	1-2	8-1	4-0	3-0	*	1-1	2-2	2-1
11.	Reigate Town	2-4	0-1	2-0	7-1	W-L	4-6	4-0	1-0	2-1	2-1	*	3-2	10-0
12.	Sutton High	0-6	2-1	1-3	5-0	6-1	0-3	5-1	3-0	1-3	0-2	0-7	*	4-2
13.	Verdayne	1-7	2-2	2-3	0-9	3-2	1-1	3-5	2-6	1-3	3-6	0-4	1-0	*

Merton Town withdrew without playing a game

INT. DIV. 3 RESULTS	1	2	3	4	5	6	7	8	9	10	11	12
1. Charlwood	*	0-0	1-3	1-3	4-1	0-1	2-1	0-1	3-4	6-0	1-0	4-0
2. Cheam Village Warriors	1-1	*	0-7	0-4	1-2	0-3	5-1	1-1	1-2	2-3	1-8	2-5
3. Chessington White Hart	6-0	3-0	*	3-2	2-0	2-0	5-1	6-0	4-0	4-0	2-1	4-0
4. Chipstead 'A'	1-3	2-1	3-0	*	11-1	1-5	5-2	4-2	4-0	7-0	2-1	5-1
5. Cobham 'A'	1-3	4-1	0-6	2-5	*	1-2	1-2	1-4	2-0	1-2	2-3	0-0
6. Racal Decca	4-3	4-1	3-0	4-1	3-0	*	3-2	3-0	3-2	11-0	0-1	3-3
7. St Andrews Reserves	2-5	3-2	1-1	1-5	5-2	3-2	*	0-3	3-1	2-3	0-5	1-7
8. Tadworth	1-0	7-2	0-0	4-4	2-3	2-6	0-0	*	3-3	3-1	1-4	1-3
9. Thornton Heath Rovers	1-2	4-3	0-4	1-2	6-3	1-8	2-1	2-2	*	2-2	0-1	1-4
10. Three Bridges 'A'	3-2	0-4	1-5	1-5	1-3	2-5	1-1	2-2	3-6	*	4-1	1-2
11. Warlingham	1-0	5-0	0-3	1-0	2-0	2-2	1-2	1-0	1-1	2-1	*	1-2
12. Woodmansterne Sports	5-0	1-0	0-1	2-3	2-2	1-1	3-3	3-3	0-4	6-0	1-0	*

Southside withdrew - record expunged

JNR DIV. 1 RESULTS	1	2	3	4	5	6	7	8	9	10	11
1. Ashtead Reserves	*	3-0	1-5	0-2	2-1	1-7	2-3	3-1	L-W	7-1	0-4
2. Battersea Park C. Res.	3-1	*	3-2	2-1	2-0	1-3	2-11	5-0	7-4	4-0	0-1
3. Beaufoy Utd Reserves	3-0	2-1	*	0-3	1-1	0-0	0-1	3-1	7-1	5-0	4-4
4. Chess. & Hook Res.	3-1	4-0	W-L	*	1-0	2-1	3-1	9-0	W-L	3-0	2-2
5. Coney Hall Reserves	1-2	2-0	2-1	2-0	*	0-0	5-0	5-0	1-4	6-0	1-5
6. Crescent R. Reserves	7-0	0-2	4-1	2-1	1-2	*	0-2	2-1	2-2	2-0	0-3
7. Greenside Reserves	W-L	2-2	2-3	0-0	1-1	2-3	*	6-0	11-0	8-1	2-3
8. Hinchley Wd U. Res.	2-0	1-4	2-2	1-7	0-7	0-2	1-4	*	2-2	2-2	2-9
9. RAS Accra Utd Res.	3-1	0-3	5-2	1-8	0-7	2-2	2-1	3-1	*	3-0	0-2
10. Sutton High Reserves	2-0	4-1	0-4	0-6	1-3	2-5	0-4	3-0	3-2	*	0-2
11. Worcester Park Res.	9-0	2-4	4-1	1-1	0-1	3-2	4-0	2-1	4-1	2-0	*

Caius Reserves withdrew - record expunged

JNR DIV. 2 RESULTS	1	2	3	4	5	6	7	8	9
1. Bletchingley Reserves	*	2-7	0-5	0-17	6-0	2-6	2-7	0-5	1-2
2. Bookham Reserves	2-0	*	0-1	0-6	4-0	2-2	2-3	3-3	0-4
3. Cheam VW Reserves	5-1	2-0	*	2-2	3-2	3-1	3-2	6-0	0-3
4. Chess. & Hook 'A'	4-0	3-2	3-0	*	7-0	0-0	4-3	2-1	1-1
5. Hersham RBL 'A'	1-3	1-5	0-1	0-3	*	2-1ab	1-1	3-2	0-6
6. Netherne 'A'	5-3	3-2	3-0	3-3	4-2	*	2-2	3-4	0-2
7. Racal Decca Res.	6-0	5-1	7-0	2-1	7-0	1-4	*	6-2	3-4
8. Sutton Athletic Res.	4-0	5-3	7-1	0-2	1-2	2-2	1-2	*	2-3
9. Warlingham Res.	5-3	5-2	2-4	1-3	2-0	1-2	2-5	4-4	*

Battersea Ironsides 'A' and Merton Town Reserves withdrew without playing a game. Bradbank Sports Reserves withdrew - record expunged.

JNR DIV. 3 RESULTS	1	2	3	4	5	6	7	8	9	10	11
1. Battersea Pk Corona 'A'	*	1-0	0-3	1-1	3-2	0-6	1-1	1-1	6-2	W-L	3-8
2. Chess. & Hook 'B'	3-2	*	1-2	1-3	2-3	1-2	L-W	3-1	3-1	5-3	0-0
3. Colliers Wood U. Res.	5-2	1-2	*	2-1	1-0	2-1	1-0	1-4	3-1	0-4	0-1
4. Chess. & Hook Res.	1-0	1-7	1-1	*	0-5	1-4	2-2	5-4	W-L	1-3	1-5
5. Perrywood S. Res.	4-3	W-L	3-1	2-0	*	5-2	2-1	5-0	3-1	6-3	1-2
6. Raynes Park 'A'	3-3	2-1	1-1	2-2	2-0	*	7-2	4-0	12-0	4-1	1-4
7. Sth Godstone Reserves	2-1	10-0	2-6	0-6	3-1	0-4	*	0-2	4-2	2-5	0-3
8. Vandyke 'A'	3-0	1-4	2-1	3-4	3-0	0-2	8-2	*	9-0	3-1	2-7
9. Verdayne Reserves	1-2	2-1	1-4	0-5	1-5	0-4	2-3	0-5	*	1-2	
10. Woodmansterne S. Res.	1-4	0-3	3-2	2-3	1-4	0-2	8-2	4-1	0-3	*	1-4
11. Worcester Park 'A'	5-2	2-1	0-1	8-2	0-5	0-2	2-0	3-2	9-3	7-4	*

Fetcham Reserves withdrew - record expunged

JNR DIV. 4 RESULTS	1	2	3	4	5	6	7	8	9	10	11
1. AFC Wandgas Res.	*	3-2	2-0	0-2	W-L	4-0	1-2	5-2	5-1	4-3	3-3
2. Charlwood Reserves	1-1	*	2-2	3-0	4-0	2-3	1-2	1-0	9-1	5-2	0-3
3. Chess. White Hart Res.	0-2	2-1	*	1-0	7-0	2-0	1-6	4-0	9-0	2-1	2-1
4. Chipstead 'B'	1-6	4-0	2-2	*	3-2	W-L	1-3	5-1	6-1	2-2	4-2
5. Crescent Rvrs Res.	0-2	1-2	0-6	1-1	*	2-2	0-3	5-1	2-3	3-5	1-9
6. Eversley Rgrs Res.	4-3	5-2	3-7	3-2	1-1	*	1-3	3-2	8-2	0-2	6-4
7. Holmesdale Reserves	1-3	1-3	1-2	1-1	6-2	4-2	*	4-4	13-0	6-3	4-1
8. Oxted & District Res.	1-6	2-2	0-4	0-3	3-0	1-2	0-5	*	4-1	1-0	4-9
9. Reigate T. Reserves	0-1	2-1	1-2	1-1	3-2	4-2	1-6	5-4	*	2-6	0-0
10. Tadworth Reserves	3-5	2-0	4-3	3-1	2-1	9-1	1-5	7-1	5-0	*	0-2
11. Thornton Hth R. Res.	2-2	2-1	0-4	5-1	1-0	5-1	3-2	2-0	3-0	2-1	*

Hook Venturers Reserves withdrew - record expunged

JNR CHARITY CUP 1993-94

GROUP A.	P	W	D	L	F	A	PTS
Netherne 'A'	3	3	0	0	19	4	6
Sutton Ath. Res.	3	1	1	1	12	10	3
Hersham RBL 'A'	3	1	0	2	4	11	2
Bletchingley Res.	3	0	1	2	5	15	1

RESULTS	1	2	3	4
1. Bletchingley Reserves	*			
2. Hersham RBL 'A'	1-0	*	1-5ab.	
3. Netherne 'A'	10-1		*	
4. Sutton Athletic Reserves	4-4	6-2	2-4	*

GROUP B.	P	W	D	L	F	A	PTS
Bookham Reserves	3	2	1	0	8	5	5
Cheam VW Reserves	3	0	2	1	4	5	2
Chess. & Hook 'A'	2	1	0	1	2	3	2
Warlingham Res.	2	0	1	1	4	5	1

RESULTS	1	2	3	4
1. Bookham Reserves	*	2-2		3-2
2. Cheam Village W. Res.		*	0-1	
3. Chessington & Hook 'A'	1-3		*	
4. Warlingham Reserves		2-2		*

Final: Bookham Res. 2, Netherne 'A' 0

SENIOR LEAGUE CUP

First Round

Worcester Park v Bletchingley	5-2	Hook Venturers v Caius	1-0
Chessington White Hart v Sutton Athletic	6-0	Warlingham v Oxted & District	4-1
Southside *(scr)* Reigate Town *(w/o)*		South Godstone v Coney Hall	2-1
Tadworth v Tadworth	0-3	Hinchley Wood Utd v Battersea Park Corona	1-3
Ashtead v Eversley Rangers	4-3		

Second Round

Chipstead 'A' v Hook Venturers	4-2	Woodmansterne Spts v St Andrews Res.	2-1*(aet)*
RAS Accra United v Crescent Rovers	0-2	Chessington White Hart v Cheam Vill. Warriors	6-1
Battersea Park Corona v Reigate Town	1-2	Tadworth v Warlingham	0-3
AFC Wandgas *(w/o)* Merton Town *(scr)*		Chessington & Hook Utd v Fetcham	7-1
Ashtead v Racal Decca	1-5	Greenside v Halliford	4-1
Beaufoy United v Colliers Wood United	1-2	Bradbank Sports v Bookham	1-8
Three Bdges 'A' v Cobham 'A' 10-4*(TB expelled)*		Thornton Heath Rovers v South Godstone	2-1
Perrywood Sports v Worcester Park	1-3	Sutton High v Verdayne	6-4

Third Round

AFC Wandgas v Warlingham	2-0	Cobham 'A' v Chessington White Hart	0-2
Chipstead 'A' v Woodmansterne Sports	4-2	Greenside v Thornton Heath Rovers	3-3,4-0
Crescent Rovers v Racal Decca	2-3	Bookham v Worcester Park	2-2,2-5
Colliers Wood United v Sutton High	2-1	Reigate T. v Chessington & Hook United	1-3*(aet)*

Quarter-Finals

Chessington White Hart v Chipstead 'A'	1-2	Chessington & Hook United v Greenside	4-1
AFC Wandgas v Worcester Park	3-4*(aet)*	Racal Decca v Colliers Wood United	1-3

Semi-Finals

Colliers Wood United v Worcester Park	3-2	Chessington & Hook Utd v Chipstead 'A'	0-0,6-0

Final: Colliers Wood United 3, Chessington & Hook United 2 *(aet)*

JUNIOR LEAGUE CUP

First Round

Eversley Rgrs Res. v Greenside Res.	0-7	Sutton Ath. Res. v Holmesdale 'A'	2-1
Beaufoy United Res. v Netherne 'A'	2-1	Chessington & Hook Utd v Hook Venturers Res.	5-0
Oxted & Dist. Res. v Tadworth Reserves	1-3	Chessington & Hook 'A' v Chess. & Hook 'B'	1-3
Fetcham Reserves v Sutton High Res.	3-3,4-5	Worcester Park Res. v Coney Hall Reserves	5-2
Crescent Rvrs 'A' v Cheam Vill. W. Res.	1-1,2-5	Hersham RBL 'A' v Woodmansterne S. Res.	1-2*(aet)*
Bookham Res. v RAS Accra United Res.	3-2	Hinchley Wood Utd Res. v Sth Godstone Res.	4-3
Chessington WH Res. v Battersea PC 'A'	13-2	Racal Decca Res. v Crescent Rovers Res.	0-3
Reigate Town Res. v Ashtead Res.	1-9	AFC Wandgas Res. *(w/o)* Battersea Iron. 'A' *(scr)*	

Second Round

Worcester Park 'A' v Bookham Reserves	3-1	Caius Reserves v Bradbank Sports Res.	4-2
Cheam VW Res. *(w/o)* Merton T. Res. *(scr)*		Woodmansterne Spts Res. v Sutton Ath. Res.	1-7
Battersea Pk C. Res. v Colliers Wood Res.	3-0	Greenside Res. v Worcester Park Reserves	3-2
Charlwood Reserves v Tadworth Reserves	1-3	Perrywood Spts Res. v Bletchingley	5-2
Warlingham Reserves v Ashtead Reserves	5-2	Raynes Park 'A' v Sutton High Res.	3-0
Vandyke 'A' v Crescent Rovers Res.	4-0	Hinchley Wood Utd Res. v Chess. & Hook Res.	0-3
Verdayne Res. v AFC Wandgas Res.	1-7	Thornton Heath R. Res. v Chess. & Hook 'B'	5-1
Beaufoy Utd Res. v Chipstead 'B'	3-3,7-2	Chessington White Hart Res. v Coney Hall Res.	1-4

Third Round

Warlingham Res. v Worcester Park 'A'	0-1	Vandyke 'A' v Greenside Reserves	3-3,2-3
Chess. & Hook Utd Res. v Sutton Ath. Res.	5-0	Thornton Heath Rovers Res. v AFC Wandgas Res.	4-9
Raynes Park 'A' v Cheam Vill. Warriors Res.	1-0	Caius Reserves v Beaufoy United Reserves	3-7
Perrywood Spts Res. v Coney Hall Reserves	2-4	Battersea Pk Corona Res. v Tadworth Reserves	0-3

Quarter-Finals

Greenside Res. v Chess. & Hook Res.	3-2*(aet)*	Worcester Park 'A' v Coney Hall Reserves	1-3
Raynes Park 'A' v Beaufoy United Reserves	4-3	Tadworth Reserves v AFC Wandgas Reserves	1-5

Semi-Finals

Raynes Park 'A' v Greenside Reserves	3-2	AFC Wandgas Reserves v Coney Hall Reserves	0-2

Final: Coney Hall Reserves 2, Raynes Park 'A' 1

ELLIS PRINTERS SENIOR SHIELD

First Round

Fetcham *(w/o)* Southside *(scr)*		Warlingham v Hook Venturers	4-2*(aet)*
Reigate Town v St Andrews Reserves	9-2	Cheam Village Warriors v Racal Decca	2-6
Verdayne v Thornton Heath Rovers	3-2	Tadworth v Chessington White Hart	4-4,0-6
RAS Accra United v Bletchingley	2-0	Sutton High v Charlwood	2-1
Cobham 'A' v Chipstead 'A'	0-1	Hinchley Wood United v Three Bridges 'A'	3-1
Woodmansterne Spts v Oxted & District	3-2*(aet)*		

Second Round

Caius v AFC Wandgas	0-2	RAS Accra United v Sutton High	1-2
Fetcham v Reigate Town	1-5	Woodmansterne Sports v Eversley Rangers	3-2
Merton T. *(scr)* Chessington White Hart *(w/o)*		Racal Decca v Halliford	9-2
Hinchley Wood Utd v Warlingham	1-4	Chipstead 'A' v Verdayne	6-1

Quarter-Finals

Chipstead 'A' v Chessington White Hart	0-2	Warlingham v Racal Decca	0-0,2-1
Woodmansterne Spts v AFC Wandgas	0-5	Reigate Town v Sutton High	2-1

Semi-Finals

AFC Wandgas v Chessington White Hart	2-0	Reigate Town v Warlingham	5-2

Final: Reigate Town 2, AFC Wandgas 1

ELLIS PRINTERS INTERMEDIATE SHIELD

First Round

Cheam VW Res. v Chessington & Hook 'A' 2-1
Crescent R. Res. *(w/o)* Bradbank S. Res *(scr)*
Ashtead Reserves v Caius Reserves 1-6
RAS Accra Utd Res. v Hersham RBL 'A' 10-2
Netherne 'A' v Worcester P. Res. 5-2*(Neth. expelled)*
Battersea Iron. Res. *(scr)* Coney Hall Res. *(scr)*
Bletchingley Res. v Sutton High Reserves 1-0
Racal Decca Res. v Battersea PC Res. 2-2,4-3

Second Round

Greenside Res. v RAS Accra Utd Reserves 7-0
Cheam Village Warr. v Bletchingley Res. 5-3
Crescent R. Res. v Chessington & Hook Res. 1-3
Merton Town Res. *(scr)* Coney Hall Res. *(w/o)*
Bookham Res. v Sutton Athletic Reserves 2-1
Caius Reserves v Hinchley Wood Utd Res. 5-1
Racal Decca Res. v Beaufoy United Reserves 3-1
Worcester Park Res. v Warlingham Reserves 4-3

Quarter-Finals

Bookham Reserves v Caius Reserves 4-1
Worcester Park Res. v Coney Hall Res. 0-2
Cheam VW Reserves v Greenside Reserves 0-5
Racal Decca Res. v Chessington & Hook Res. 2-0

Semi-Finals

Coney Hall Res. v Greenside Reserves 5-0
Bookham Res. v Racal Decca Res. 3-1*(aet)*

Final: Coney Hall Reserves 3, Bookham Reserves 1

ELLIS PRINTERS JUNIOR SHIELD

First Round

AFC Wandgas Res. v Verdayne Reserves 3-2
Coney Hall 'A' v Worcester Park 'A' 1-2
Crescent R. 'A' *(w/o)* v Fetcham Reserves *(scr)*
Charlwood Res. v Colliers Wood Utd Res. 3-0
Chipstead 'B' v Perrywood Spts Res. 2-1*(ab)*,2-3
Hook Venturers Res. *(scr)* Raynes Park 'A' *(w/o)*
Holmesdale 'A' v Eversley Rgrs Reserves 5-2
Vandyke 'A' v Chessington & Hook Utd 'B' 2-5

Second Round

Chessington WH Res. v Thornton Hth R. Res. 1-6
Chess. & Hook 'B' v Crescent Rovers 'A' 5-1
Tadworth Reserves v Worcester Park 'A' 3-4
Reigate Town Res. v AFC Wandgas Reserves 1-4
Battersea PC 'A' v Charlwood Reserves 2-1
Raynes Park 'A' v South Godstone Reserves 4-2*(aet)*
Woodmansterne Spts Res. v Perrywood Res. 0-0,1-7
Holmesdale 'A' v Oxted & District Reserves 5-2

Quarter-Finals

AFC Wandgas Res. v Perrywood Res. 4-1*(aet)*
Holmesdale 'A' v Worcester Park 'A' 7-2
Chessington & Hook 'B' v Raynes Park 'A' 1-2
Battersea Park C. *(w/o)* Thornton Hth R. Res. *(scr)*

Semi-Finals

Holmesdale 'A' v AFC Wandgas Reserves 1-0
Battersea PC 'A' v Raynes Park 'A' 0-4

Final: Holmesdale 'A' 3, Raynes Park 'A' 2

INTERMEDIATE DIVISION ONE CLUBS 1994-95

A.F.C. WANDGAS

Secretary: B F Fry, Flat 2, 15 Effingham Rd, Long Ditton, Surrey KT6 5JZ (081 398 9673).
Ground: Wandgas Spts Ground, Grafton Rd, Worcester Park **Colours:** Claret & blue/blue/claret.
Directions: A2043 Central Rd, Worcester Park going towards A3, under railway bridge and left up The Avenue, at top of hill go down other side - Grafton Rd - ground at crossroads with Cromwell Rd.

ASHTEAD

Secretary: Ralph Grange, Homeside, 58 Leatherhead Rd, Ashtead, Surrey KT21 2SY (0372 276901).
Ground: Ashtead Rec., Barnett Wood Lane, Ashtead. **Colours:** Gold/black/black.
Directions: Epsom to Leatherhead road (A24), in Ashtead village turn right into Woodfield Lane, Barnett Wood Lane half mile on left, ground just along on left. Ashtead station 3 mins from ground. Bus 418 to The Woodman pub.

BATTERSEA IRONSIDES

Secretary: Les Barker, 165 Washington Rd, Worcester Park KT4 8JQ (081 337 8665).
Ground: Battersea Ironsides Sports Club, Open View, Burntwood Lane SW18 (081 874 9913).
Directions: The ground is on corner of Openview and Burntwood Lane (B229), opp. Springfield Hospital.
Colours: Green & white/green/green **Change colours:** All white, or blue & white stripes.
Previous Names: Springfield Hospital FC and Battersea Ironsides FC merged in 1992 to form Springfield Battersea Ironsides. Name now reverted to Battersea Ironsides.
Previous League: Surrey South Eastern Combination (pre-1992)/ Surrey County Prem. 92-94.

BATTERSEA PARK CORONA

Secretary: A Brown, 96 Ethelburga Tower, Rosenau Rd, Battersea SW11 4AB (071 252 8080).
Ground: Dundonald Rec, Avebury Rd SW19 (081 542 3282). **Colours:** White/blue/white.
Directions: A298 to Merton, turn into Merton Hall Rd (opposite Nelson Hosp.), Avebury Avenue is 2nd right. Nearest Station is Wimbledon Chase.

BEAUFOY UNITED

Secretary: Derek Dalrymple, 13a Bryne Rd, Balham, London SW12 (071 407 2264).
Ground: Raynes Park PF, Grand Drive SW19. **Colours:** Red & white/red/red.
Directions: A3 to Shannon Corner then A298, right into Grand Drive at 1st lights - ground just under 1 mile on left.
Previous Ground Ground: Morden Park School Spts Centre, Hillcross Avenue (pre-1994).

BOOKHAM

Secretary: Ian Waller, 8 Northumberland Rd, Bordon, Hants GU35 9TR (0420 487618).
Grnd: Chrystie Rd, Recreation Grnd, Dorking Rd, Bookham (0372 459482). **Cols:** Amber/black/black.
Directions: M25 jct 9, A246 Guildford road, left into Leatherhead Rd 400yds after 'Jet' garage in Bookham, 1st left into Dorking Rd - ground 100yds on left. Bookham Station. Buses 408, 478, 479.

COLLIERS WOOD UNITED

Secretary: Tony Hurrell, 1 Inglewood, Pixton Way, Forestdale, Croydon CR0 9LN (081 651 3259).
Ground: Wibbundune Spts Ground, Robin Hood Way (A3) SW20 (081 942 8062)
Colours: Sky & navy/black/black.
Directions: On A3 (Robin Hood Way) between Robin Hood Gate and Raynes Park junctions; turn left immediately at 2nd footbridge from the Robin Gate junction.

CRESCENT ROVERS

Secretary: M D Bishop, 64 Wolsey Crescent, New Addington, Surrey CR0 0PF (0689 842996).
Ground: Southern Rail Sports Club, Mollison Drive, Wallington. **Colours:** Green/black/black.
Directions: A232 from central Croydon, take B271 Stafford Rd opposite Wilson School, cross A23 to 1st lights, left into Mollison Drive, ground 300yds on right. Bus 154 from central Croydon passes ground.

GREENSIDE

Secretary: E G Moon, 10 Curran Ave., Wallington SM6 7JW (081 669 7985).
Ground: Mayfield Road, off Silverleigh Rd, Thornton Heath. **Colours:** All green.
Directions: Silverleigh Rd is off Thornton Rd (A23) near Thornton Pond, fork left into Mayfield Rd & follow to end, left into narrow track, past playground, ground on right.
Previous Ground: Orchard Spts Centre, William Booth Rd, Anerley (pre-1994).

MONOTYPE

Secretary: Michael Overmass, Caretakers Bungalow, 51 Holland Close, Redhill, Surrey RH1 1HT (0737 761555).
Ground: Perrywood Spts & Social Club, Honeycrock Lane, Salfords (0737 763250).
Colours: Amber & black/black/black. **Previous Name:** Perrywood Sports (pre-1994).
Directions: South on A23, Salfords is 5 miles beyond Redhill, left into Honeycrock Lane, ground entrance 1st right after railway bridge.

R.A.S. ACCRA UNITED

Secretary: R Morrison, 57 Trevelyan Rd, London SW17 9LR (081 767 3454).
Ground: Pynners PF, Dulwich Common **Cols:** Yellow/blue/blue *(Res: all red)*
Directions: A205 Sth Circular to West Dulwich, ground on right 500yds past Dulwich College. BR to West Dulwich or Forest Hill.
Previous Name: RAS Knights (pre'92).

REIGATE TOWN

Secretary: Mrs Anita Head, 82 The Crescent, Horley, Surrey RH6 7NU (0293 782084).
Ground: Reigate Heath, Flanchford Rd, Reigate **Cols:** Green, white & black/black/black.
Directions: A25 from Reigate towards Dorking, left at Black Horse into Flanchard Rd, grnd on right.

SUTTON ATHLETIC

Secretary: Mrs Diane Goff, 265 Malden Rd, Cheam SM3 8ET (081 715 5069).
Ground: Overton Rd Sports Ground, Sutton **Colours:** Red/blue/blue.
Directions: From Sutton BR take turning opposite station, Mulgrave Rd, Overton Rd 4th turning left, proceed to end of Overton Rd for ground.

WORCESTER PARK

Secretary: Frank Thompson, 6 Courtney Rd, Worcester Park, Surrey KT4 8RY (081 335 3379).
Ground: Skinners Field, Green Lane, Worcester Park KT4 8AJ (081 337 4995).
Directions: Off A3 at New Malden r'bout onto A2043, 1st left under 2nd railway bridge into Green Lane. Entrance opposite Brookside Crescent. Adjacent to Worcester Park (BR) station.
Colours: Blue & white/white/blue *(Reserves: Grey & black).*

INTERMEDIATE DIVISION TWO CLUBS 1994-95

BLETCHINGLEY

Secretary: Andy Skinner, 91 Kingsley Rd, Horley, Surrey RH6 8HP (0293 773317).
Ground: Grange Meadow, Bletchingley (0883 742844). **Colours:** Green & yellow stripes/green/yellow.
Directions: A23 to Redhill, turn onto A25 Westerham Road, approx. 5 miles Bletchingley, 'Plough' PH on left, ground opposite.

CAIUS

Secretary: John Holden, 18 East Hill, Wandsworth, London SW18 2HN (081 871 9654).
Ground: Richardson Evans PF (081 228 6642). **Colours:** Sky/navy/navy.
Directions: Roehampton Vale on A3 at the Robin Hood Gate.

CHESSINGTON WHITE HART

Secretary: Mrs Donna Joslyn, 80 Somerset Ave., Chessington, Surrey KT9 1PP (081 391 1517).
Ground: As Ditton FC (see page 1112) **Cols:** Green/white/green *(Res: Yellow/green/yellow)*
Previous Ground: Claygate Rec., Dalmore Ave., Claygate (pre-1994).

CHIPSTEAD 'A'

Ground & Directions: Corrigan Ave., Coulsdon - A23 to Coulsdon, into Chipstead Valley Rd at Red Lion, right at lights, up hill over railway bridge, left into Woodmansterne Rd, left into St Andrews Rd, 3rd left Alexander Rd leads into Whitehorn Ave. - Corrigan Ave. on left *(other details as per page 746).*

EVERSLEY RANGERS

Secretary: Malcolm Berks, Hillview, 101 The Glade, Shirley, Croydon, Sutton (081 654 8821).
Ground: Harvington Rec., South Eden Park Rd, Beckenham. **Cols:** Red & white & purple).
Directions: Upper Elmers End Rd (A214), under rail bridge at Eden Park, left onto A230 South End Park Rd, ground on left (Harvington Est.). BR to Eden Park station.

HALLIFORD

Secretary: Danny F Waite, 46 Halliford Rd, Sunbury, Middx TW16 6DR (0932 789286).
Ground: Cedars Recreation Ground. **Cols:** White (blue trim)/blue (white trim).
Directions: M3 jct 1 (Sunbury Cross r'bout), into Green Street over rail bridge, Cedars Rec is half mile on right, behind War Memorial.
Previous Ground: Kenyngton Rec. (pre-1994).

HOOK VENTURERS

Secretary: Malcolm A Benham, 11 Ellingham Rd, Chessington, Surrey KT9 2JA (081 397 3638).
Ground: St Francis Barker Rec., Leeatherhead Rd, Chessington **Colours:** Sky/navy/navy.
Directions: BR from Waterloo to Chessington South, right out of station, left at main road, ground on right. Bus 71 from Kingston, 468 from Epsom (both to Chessington World of Adventure, 465 or 466 Horsham-Kingston.
Previous Ground: King Edward Rec., Hook Way, Chessington (pre-1994).

OXTED & DISTRICT

Secretary: Pete King, 2 The Greenway, Oxted, Surrey RH8 0JY (0883 716001).
Ground: Master Park, Oxted, Surrey (0883 712792). **Colours:** All red.
Directions: Rail to Oxted, bus 410 to Master Park. Or, A25 from Westerham or Redhill to Church Lane, Oxted. Ground quarter mile on left.

RACAL DECCA

Sec: T J Hanlon, 86 Queens Drive, Surbiton, Surrey KT5 8PP (081 399 5319) *No calls after 9pm.*
Ground: Racal Decca Spts & Social Club, Old Kingston Rd, Tolworth (081 337 0519).
Colours: All blue *(Reserves: Red & black/black/black)*
Directions: A3 to Tolworth, Old Kingston Rd towards Epsom, left after 300yds (just after bridge), entrance to ground on left.

SOUTH GODSTONE

Secretary: Steve Scott-Douglas, 'Rowans', Eden Vale, East Grinstead, W. Sussex RH19 2JH (0342 314484).
Ground: Lagham Rd PF, Sth Godstone, Surrey (0342 892490). **Cols:** Red/blue/red *(res: all red)*
Directions: South from Godstone on A22 for about two and a half miles, as you enter South Godstone, 1st left into Harcourt Way, follow to end, pavillion immediately in front. 719 Green Line and 409 buses.

SUTTON HIGH

Secretary: Ian Daggett, 178 Stanley Park Rd, Carshalton Beeches, Surrey SM5 3JR (081 661 6323).
Ground: University of London Spts Grnd, Motspur Park *(Reserves: Tattenham Way Rec., The Drive, Banstead).*
Directions: From Grand Drive left into Westway, left at end into West Barnes Lane. Over level crossing, ground on right. Motspur Park (BR). *To Tattenham Way: From Tattenway turn into Piquets Way, left at end into The Drive, ground at end on left.*
Colours: Claret & blue/sky/sky.

WARLINGHAM

Secretary: Stan Smith, 14a Abbey Rd, Selsdon, Surrey CR2 8NG (081 651 2439).
Grnd: Church Lane, Warlingham (0883 622943) **Cols:** White & black stripes/black.
Directions: Bus 403.

INTERMEDIATE DIVISION THREE CLUBS 1994-95

A.F.C. EWELL

Secretary: Trevor Andrews, 38 Portland Rd, New Malden, Surrey KT3 6AX (081 715 8986).
Ground: London Fire Brigade (Ewell Spts & Social), Banstead Rd, East Ewell (081 394 1946).
Directions: Cheam Rd (A232) from Ewell bypass, pass Ewell East station, 1st right Banstead Rd, ground entrance immediate right. Direct access from Ewell East station.
Colours: Amber/black/black.

CHARLWOOD

Secretary: Neil Maguire, 26 Birkdale Drive, Ifield, Crawley, West Sussex RH11 0TS (0293 512765).
Ground: The Recreation Ground, The Street, Charlwood **Previous Lge:** Redhill & Dist. (champs 92-93).
Colours: Amber/black/black *(Reserves: Red & white/white/red).*
Directions: Gatwick Airport exit off M23, over 1st island, right at next for Redhill, join dual-c'way for 400yds, left at island to Charlwood (3 miles), pitch on left corner opposite Rising Sun. Via A23 to island at start of Gatwick. Straight over (signed Charlwood), then as above.

COBHAM 'A'

Secretary: Gerry Petit, 149 Bridge Rd, Chessington, Surrey KT9 2RT (081 397 0433).
Ground & Directions: Cobham Rec, Portsmouth Rd & Anvil Lane - opposite Police Station which is at junction of Portsmouth Rd & Northfield Rd *(other details as per page 746)*.

FETCHAM

Secretary: Howard Taylor, 53 Cock Lane, Fetcham, Surrey (0372 377557).
Ground: Cock Lane Rec., Fetcham, Surrey. **Colours:** All red *(Reserves: Blue/white/blue)*
Directions: Turn into The Street at Tudor Motors Garage in village centre, Cock Lane 1st right - ground 400yds on right. From Leatherhead bus 462 to Fetcham, or 416 (limited time) to Cock Lane.

MERTON TOWN

Secretary: Fred G Brockwell, 28 Wordsworth Drive, Cheam, Surrey SM3 8HF (081 715 5052).
Ground: Merton Town Rec., Middleton Rd, Merton. **Previous Name:** Merton Risley (pre'93)
Directions: Adjacent to St Helier BR station. Bus 93 to Central Rd from Morden tube; 5 mins from ground - turn right into Green Lane, Middleton Rd is 200yds on left, ground behind row of shops.
Colours: Yellow/navy/yellow & navy hoops *(Reserves: Red & black/black/black).*

St ANDREWS

Secretary: Martin Feeley, 98a Endymion Rd, Brixton, London SW2 2BP (081 671 8690).
Ground: Herne Hill Stadium, Burbage SE24.
Directions: From Herne Hill take A2214, Half Moon Lane, Burbage Rd quarter mile on right, ground on right.
Colours: Navy/white/red.

TADWORTH

Secretary: M Lippett, 28 Rushmere Ct, The Avenue, Worcester Park, Surrey KT4 7EP (081 337 4987).
Ground: Kingswood Rec., Buckland Rd, Lower Kingswood
Directions: From Burgh Heath lights take A217, down to Lower Kingswood, right by Fox pub, into Buckland Rd, recreation ground 400yds on left.
Colours: Green & white stripes/green/green *(Res: Green & black stripes/white/green).*
Previous Grounds: Tadworth Village Green (pre-1994).

THORNTON HEATH ROVERS

Secretary: Ron Jones, 38a Brighton Rd, Coulsdon, Surrey CR5 2BA (081 668 4895).
Ground: Highbury Ave., Thornton Heath (081 764 5445) **Colours:** Black & white/black/red.
Directions: Thornton Hth BR station, left to clock tower, left into Parchmore Rd, left into County Rd after 1 mile (opposite Bricklayers Arms), 1st right Highbury Ave., ground on right.

THREE BRIDGES 'A'

Ground & Directions: Three Bridges Rec, Three Bridges Rd. Right out of Three Bridges BR station into Three Bridges Rd, Rec 1st left past 'Downs TV Shop'. *(other details as page 672).*

VERDAYNE

Secretary: Andrew West, 11 Harrington Close, Beddington, Croydon CR0 4UN (081 680 5507).
Ground: Valley Spts, off White Knobs Way, Caterham **Cols:** Grey (red trim)*(Res: Blue & yellow).*
Directions: Thru Caterham on Godstone road, White Knobs Way on right just before A22 junction. Nb. Do not use Caterham bypass; no right turns on bypass.

WARBANK SPORTS

Secretary: P Webb, 3 Netley Close, New Addington, Croydon, Surrey CR0 0QR (0689 842309).
Ground: Warbank Sports & Social Club, Layhams Rd **Colours:** White/blue *(Reserves: Red/yellow).*
Directions: To New Addington up Lodge Lane to r'bout, left into King Henry's Drive, follow past factories, after houses 1st left Layhams Rd, club then signposted.

WOODMANSTERNE SPORTS

Secretary: David Pryor, 16 Tonbridge Close, Woodmansterne, Surrey SM7 3JD (0737 363330).
Ground: The Park, Woodmansterne Str., Woodmansterne (0737 350109). **Colours:** Gold/black/gold.
Directions: A2022 Purley-Epsom road, B278 Carshalton Rd to end, turn right past pub, clubhouse/car park on right.

JUNIOR DIVISION ONE CLUBS 1994-95

ANCORA

Secretary: A Brown, 96 Ethelburga Tower, Rosenau Rd, Battersea SW11 4AB (071 252 8080).
Ground: As Caius FC (above) **Colours:** Red & black stripes/blue & white.

Plus the Reserve teams of: Ashtead, Battersea Ironsides, Battersea Park Corona, Beaufoy United, Chessington & Hook Utd *('A' team)*, Crescent Rvrs, Greenside, RAS Accra Utd, Racal Decca, Warlingham, Worcester Park.

JUNIOR DIVISION TWO CLUBS 1994-95

ACCRA '94

Secretary: Horace Hiles, 40 Ederline Ave., Norbury, London SW16 4SA (081 679 7663).
Ground: Bellingham Community Rec. Project, Randlestown Rd, Bellingham SE6 (081 695 1603).
Directions: Randlestown Rd is off A21 - ground opposite Bellingham BR station.
Colours: Emerald/gold.

Plus the Reserve teams of: AFC Wandgas, Bookham, Chessington White Hart, Colliers Wood Utd, Hersham RBL *('A' team)*, Holmesdale *('A' team)*, Monotype, Netherne *('A' team)*, Raynes Park *('A' team)*, Sutton Ath., Sutton High.

Junior Division Three (Reserve teams unless stated): Battersea Park Corona 'A', Bletchingley Res., Chessington & Hook Utd 'B', Chipstead 'B', Coney Hall 'A', Merton Town, South Godstone, Tadworth, Thornton Heath Rovers, Vandyke 'A', Worcester Park 'A'.

Junior Division Four (Reserve teams unless stated): AFC Ewell, Ancora, Charlwood, Crescent Rovers 'A', Eversley Rgrs, Holmesdale 'B', Oxted & Dist., Racal Decca 'A', Reigate Town, Verdayne, Warbank Sports.

REDHILL & DISTRICT LEAGUE

PREM. DIV.	P	W	D	L	F	A	PTS
Godstone	22	17	4	1	76	20	38
Nutfield	22	14	3	5	89	45	31
Mickleham	22	14	1	7	57	36	29
Horley United	22	13	3	6	56	39	29
Walton Heath	22	10	4	8	48	33	24
Westcott '35	22	10	4	8	48	43	24
Nork Social	22	7	6	9	41	41	20
Holland Sports	22	6	5	11	44	64	17
Croydon United	22	7	1	14	27	61	15
South Park	22	4	6	12	40	71	14
Smallfield	22	6	1	15	24	57	13
Oddfellows	22	4	2	16	48	88	10

DIV. ONE	P	W	D	L	F	A	PTS
Whyteleafe 'A'	22	13	6	3	45	23	32
Caterham Old Boys	22	13	4	5	67	39	30
Limpsfield Blues	22	12	4	5	54	33	28
Watsons	22	12	0	10	72	49	24
Oakside	22	10	4	8	56	35	24
Coulsdon Mitre	22	9	6	7	59	45	24
Rail Club	22	10	4	8	56	55	24
Beechams	22	8	6	8	59	51	22
Brockham	22	7	3	12	39	61	17
South Park Res.	22	7	3	12	26	49	17
Godstone Res.	22	3	6	13	27	61	12
Horley Utd Res.	22	3	4	15	34	93	10

DIV. TWO	P	W	D	L	F	A	PTS
Merstham Newton	20	17	2	1	103	31	36
Cheam Vill. W. 'A'	20	12	3	5	48	26	27
Horley Town 'A'	20	12	3	5	57	41	27
Caterham OB Res.	20	11	2	7	68	37	24
Bookham 'A'	20	11	2	7	47	46	24
Westcott '35 Res.	20	9	4	7	45	42	22
Griffin Albion	20	8	3	9	40	36	19
Woodland Albion	20	5	1	14	33	57	11
Nork Social Res.	20	4	3	13	25	57	11
Warlingham 'A'	20	4	2	14	23	63	10
Sth Godstone 'A'	20	4	1	15	23	76	9

DIV. THREE	P	W	D	L	F	A	PTS
Woodmansterne 'A'	22	16	2	4	87	42	34
Walton Heath Res.	22	15	3	4	62	26	33
Waddon United	22	15	2	5	95	37	32
Redhill RBL	22	11	4	7	60	40	26
Godstone 'A'	22	11	3	8	64	51	25
Horley Utd 'A'	22	8	4	10	41	50	20
Rail Club Res.	22	8	4	10	48	67	20
Perrywood Spts	22	8	4	10	43	65	20
Oddfellows Res.	22	7	2	13	44	74	16
Brockham Res.	22	7	1	14	46	62	15
Tadworth 'A'	22	6	1	15	26	55	13
Warlingham 'B'	22	4	2	16	36	83	10

DIV. FOUR	P	W	D	L	F	A	PTS
South Park 'A'	22	18	2	2	78	36	38
Caterham OB 'A'	22	16	1	5	59	30	33
Bookham 'B'	22	13	4	5	78	61	30
Godstone 'B'	22	13	3	6	73	48	29
Nutfield Res.	22	11	3	8	80	64	25
Holland Spts Res.	22	7	6	9	56	49	20
Cheam Vill. W. 'B'	22	6	6	10	48	61	18
Coulsdon Mitre Res.	22	7	3	12	53	64	17
Limpsfield B. Res.	22	7	3	12	39	55	17
Redhill RBL Res.	22	7	0	15	41	65	14
Bletchingley 'A'	22	4	4	13	42	72	12
Oxted 'A'	22	4	3	15	48	90	11

DIV. FIVE	P	W	D	L	F	A	PTS
Paris Garden	20	17	1	2	83	26	35
Quadrant Sports	20	14	2	4	78	32	30
Merstham New. Res.	20	14	2	4	78	24	28
Woodmansterne 'B'	20	12	3	5	69	29	27
Mickleham Res.	20	11	3	6	51	34	25
Horley District	20	9	2	9	50	51	20
Westcott '35 'A'	20	7	2	11	25	56	16
Beechams Res.	20	6	3	11	35	48	15
Caterham OB 'B'	20	4	1	15	24	74	9
Smallfield Res.	20	2	4	14	28	73	8
Sth Godstone 'B'	20	3	1	16	26	82	7

THORNTON HEATH & DISTRICT LEAGUE

FOUNDED: 1909

PREM. DIV.	P	W	D	L	F	A	PTS
Warbank Sports	15	11	2	2	43	19	35
Cricketers Addiscombe	15	8	3	4	34	22	27
Sentrey	15	7	3	5	36	31	24
Phoenix Sun	15	6	3	6	43	34	21
BKT Wanderers	15	6	2	7	36	33	20
Heath Old Boys	15	0	1	14	12	65	1

DIV. ONE	P	W	D	L	F	A	PTS
Park Tavern	21	14	3	4	67	31	45
Sentrey Res.	21	12	3	6	53	42	39
Sanderstead Rgrs	21	11	2	8	58	40	35
Croydon MO 'A'	21	10	3	8	62	53	33
Ashburton OB	21	9	2	10	51	54	29
Phoenix Sun Res.	21	7	3	11	50	55	24
Cricketers Ad. Res.	21	4	6	11	37	69	18
AFC Klamper	21	4	4	13	45	79	16

DIV. TWO	P	W	D	L	F	A	PTS
Norwood Rangers	18	14	2	2	52	21	43
BKT Wanderers Res.	18	12	3	3	48	20	39
Croydon MO 'B'	18	8	2	8	56	46	26
KJR Rovers	18	7	1	10	38	42	22
Holmesdale OB	18	6	1	11	34	45	21
Seeboard Croydon	18	6	1	11	32	59	19
Woodpecker	18	4	0	14	29	56	12

CLUB DIRECTORY

A.F.C. KLAMPER
Secretary: Mr Steven Brown, 100 Dunsfold Way, New Addington, Croydon, Surrey CR0 0XN (0689 842218).
Ground: Warbank Spts Grnd, Warbank Cres., New Addington **Colours:** All white.

ASHBURTON OLD BOYS
Secretary: Alan Tilley, 6 Colchester Villas, Stanley Rd, Croydon, Surrey CR0 3QE (081 689 8316).
Ground: Ashburton Playing Fields, Addiscombe **Colours:** Yellow/black/black.

B.K.T. WANDERERS
Secretary: Kenneth Brown, 67 Eversley Rd, Upper Norwood, London SE19 3QS (081 653 3904).
Ground: Foster Park, Lewisham **Colours:** Red & black/black.

CASTLE HILL
Secretary: Alan Tolfrey, 20 Burford Way, New Addington, Croydon, Surrey CR0 0RR (0689 842293).
Ground: As AFC Klamper (above) **Colours:** Yellow/black/black.

CRICKETERS ADDISCOMBE
Secretary: Andy Hodgkinson, 8 Warren Rd, Croydon, Surrey CR0 6PE (081 656 4460).
Ground: As Ashburton Old Boys (above) **Colours:** Yellow/black/yellow

CROYDON MUNICIPAL OFFICERS 'A' & 'B' *(see Surrey County Premier League section)*

HEATH OLD BOYS
Secretary: Peter Price, 81a Northwood Rd, Thornton Heath, Croydon, Surrey CR7 8HW (081 653 0578).
Ground: Wandle Park, Westfield Rd, West Croydon **Colours:** Black & white stripes.

HOLMESDALE OLD BOYS
Secretary: Ray Tapping, 74 Sunnybank, South Norwood, London SE25 (081 654 9614).
Ground: Ashburton Playing Fields, Addiscombe **Colours:** Yellow & green/white.

K.J.R. ROVERS
Secretary: Barry Hughes, 75 Oaks Road, Kenley, Surrey (081 668 4868).
Ground: As Ashburton Old Boys (above) **Colours:** Green/black/black.

NORWOOD RANGERS
Secretary: Marion McLeish, 43b Clyde Rd, Addiscombe, Croydon, Surrey CR0 6SY (081 656 8939).
Ground: BR Sports Ground, Mollison Drive, Wallington **Colours:** Red/white/red.

PARK TAVERN
Secretary: Andrew McDougall, 113 Norbury Hill, London SW16 3SM (081 764 8452).
Ground: As Ashburton Old Boys (above) **Colours:** Green & yellow/green/green

PHOENIX SUN
Secretary: Alan Latter, 146 Northwood Rd, Thornton Heath, Croydon, Surrey CR7 8HS (081 653 4371).
Ground: Highbury Avenue, Thornton Heath **Colours:** White & navy/navy/navy.

SANDERSTEAD RANGERS
Secretary: Mark Hammond, 19 Northbrook Rd, West Croydon, Surrey CR0 2QL (081 683 2251).
Ground: Sanderstead Recreation Ground, Sanderstead **Colours:** Yellow/blue/white.

SEEBOARD CROYDON
Secretary: Vince Lydon, 10 Aschurch Rd, Addiscombe, Croydon, Surrey CR0 6JS (081 654 1639).
Ground: Ashburton Playing Fields, Addiscombe **Colours:** Sky/blue/blue.

SENTREY
Secretary: Steve Bristow, 13b Kendall Avenue South, Sanderstead, South Croydon CR2 0QR (081 668 7532).
Ground: Wandle Park, Westfield Rd, West Croydon **Colours:** Sky & white.

REDHILL & DISTRICT SUNDAY LEAGUE

Lower Division Champions:
Div. 2 (11): Grange Park
Div. 3 (11): Mogador
Div. 4 (11): The Ship

DIV. ONE	P	W	D	L	F	A	PTS
Iron Horse	20	16	2	2	74	29	34
Caterham Town	20	13	4	3	65	32	30
Mid Day Sun	20	13	1	6	65	37	27
Woodhatch	20	11	3	6	53	39	25
Tudor Athletic	20	10	4	6	51	36	24
Merstham Orion	20	9	3	8	46	42	21
Clarkson Hyde	20	7	6	7	60	51	20
Directors	20	5	3	12	36	50	13
Meadvale Eagles	20	5	3	12	34	66	13
Horley Park Rgrs	20	3	3	14	24	60	9
Nutfield	20	1	2	17	33	99	4

WIMBLEDON & DIST. LEAGUE

FOUNDED: 1898

PREM. DIV.	P	W	D	L	F	A	PTS
Parkside	20	16	4	0	75	28	36
Eleven Wise	20	15	2	3	61	29	32
Merton Town	20	12	5	3	55	24	29
Stapleton	18	8	4	6	59	36	22
Ancora	20	10	2	8	66	52	22
Putney Celtic	19	8	5	6	60	52	21
Baron Grove	18	7	1	10	45	57	15
Nascimento	19	4	3	12	33	62	11
Ellerton	16	6	0	10	34	54	10
Rusmill	18	2	3	13	35	58	7
Trollope/Colls Joinery	18	0	1	17	19	90	1

DIV. TWO	P	W	D	L	F	A	PTS
Cosmos United	12	9	2	1	45	14	20
Merton Town Res.	12	8	3	1	29	12	19
Wilf Kroucher Utd	12	6	4	2	59	22	16
Parkside Res.	12	6	1	5	33	18	13
BRF	12	5	1	6	26	35	11
The Jokers	12	1	1	10	18	50	3
BRF Reserves	12	1	0	11	10	69	2

Chiswick Celtic - withdrawn
Triangle Goaldiggers - withdrawn

CLUB DIRECTORY

BARON GROVE
Secretary: Mr Richard Marney, 59 Poplar Court, Wimbledon, London SW19 (081 879 7162).
Ground: Wimbledon Common Extension, Baron Hill Lane **Colours:** Red/black.

B.R.F.
Secretary: John Kennedy, 12 Palmerston Rd, Wimbledon, London SW19 1PQ (081 395 3371).
Ground: Morden Park, Hillcross Avenue **Cols:** Green & white hoops/white.

COSMOS UNITED
Secretary: Noel Valapinee, 5 Grange Garden, South Norwood SE25 6DL (081 771 9030).
Ground: Wandsworth Common **Colours:** Blue/white.

ELEVEN WISE
Secretary: Joe Attoh, 102 Chute House, Stockwell Park Estate, London SW9 8DW (071 733 5406).
Ground: Tooting Bec Common, Doctor Avenue **Colours:** Green & white stripes/green

ELLERTON
Secretary: Peter Crichlow, 22 Corrance Rd, Clapham, London SW2 5RH (081 733 9265).
Ground: King George's Park, Kimber Rd, Wandsworth **Colours:** Maroon/white.

NASCIMENTO
Secretary: Chris Mitchell, 66 Fullerton Rd, Wandsworth, London SW18 1BX (071 978 1425).
Ground: As Ellerton (above) **Colours:** Yellow/blue.

PARKSIDE
Secretary: Arthur Cresswell, 71 Grandison Rd, Battersea, London SW11 6LT (071 228 3202).
Ground: As Battersea Park Corona (page 1119) **Colours:** Blue (red & white trim).

RUSMILL
Secretary: Stephen Chinnappa, 14 Inglewood, Forestdale, Croydon CR0 9LP (081 651 4512).
Ground: Rylands Playing Fields, Woodside, Albert Rd, Croydon SE25 **Colours:** White/blue.

STAPLETON
Secretary: Martin Stevens, 6 Wheatlands Road, Tooting Bec SW17 8BB (081 649 8180).
Ground: As Eleven Wise (above) **Colours:** Blue & black/black.

THE JOKERS
Secretary: Chris Salmon, c/o 128c Belgrave Rd, London SW1 (071 601 4334).
Ground: Battersea Park **Colours:** Claret & blue/black.

TROLLOPE & COLLS JOINERY
Secretary: Steve Middleton, 7 Tarver Rd, Walworth, London SE17 (071 627 2703).
Ground: Honor Oak **Colours:** Blue & black/black

WILF KROUCHER UNITED
Secretary: Tony Ryland, 201a Selhurst Rd, South Norwood SE25 6LB (081 771 0964).
Ground: Ellerton (above) **Colours:** Red/black.

Virginia Water - who return to the Surrey Premier League after a season in the Parasol. Photo - Eric Marsh.

Farleigh Rovers FC, who also drop down from the Parasol League to the Surrey County Premier League. Back Row (L/R): Steve Murray (Player-Manager), Barry Gibson (Asst Manager), Tony Humberstone, Kel Couzens, Darren Benham, Philip Gilmore, Sean O'Reilly, Terry Humphries (Asst Coach). Front: Andy French, Robbie Horrocks, Ian Clements, Scott Hayworth, David Horrocks, Rob Wadey, Mark Benetar. *Photo - Dave West.*

Bookham FC - Surrey South Eastern Combination Intermediate Division One.

Photo - Dave West.

Battersea Ironsides FC, who return to the Surrey South Eastern Combination. *Photo - Dave West.*

SOUTHERN YOUTH LEAGUE

FOUNDED: 1975
REFORMED: 1982

EAST DIV.	P	W	D	L	F	A	PTS
Welling United	14	11	2	1	53	12	35
Crystal Palace	14	9	3	2	35	12	30
Dulwich Hamlet	14	9	2	3	36	19	29
Croydon Athletic	14	4	4	6	25	25	16
Carshalton Ath.	14	4	4	6	20	30	16
Whyteleafe	14	4	3	7	19	30	15
Bromley	14	4	1	9	16	46	13
Sutton United	14	1	1	12	12	44	4

RESULTS	1	2	3	4	5	6	7	8
1. Carshalton	*	6-0	2-2	1-2	1-6	0-6	0-2	3-2
2. Bromley	1-1	*	0-4	2-3	2-5	0-2	4-1	3-1
3. Croydon A.	0-2	5-0	*	1-4	0-5	3-0	2-2	3-1
4. Crystal P.	2-0	5-0	1-1	*	1-2	0-0	3-1	4-0
5. Dulwich H.	1-1	7-0	0-0	0-3	*	1-2	1-0	3-0
6. Welling U.	4-0	5-0	4-2	2-2	6-0	*	7-1	7-1
7. Whyteleafe	0-0	0-3	2-1	2-1	2-3	2-4	*	1-1
8. Sutton Utd	2-3	1-3	2-1	0-4	1-2	0-4	0-3	*

WEST DIV.	P	W	D	L	F	A	PTS
Epsom & Ewell	14	9	4	1	38	17	31
Kingstonian	14	10	1	3	37	16	31
Hampton	14	9	1	4	33	20	28
Dorking	14	8	3	3	33	17	27
Malden Vale	14	5	2	7	27	29	17
Corinthian-Cas.	14	4	3	7	25	39	15
Bedfont	14	3	0	11	16	44	9
Walton & Hersham	14	1	0	13	15	44	3

RESULTS	1	2	3	4	5	6	7	8
1. Bedfont	*	2-4	0-2	0-4	2-1	0-1	0-2	4-3
2. C-Casuals	2-0	*	0-3	3-5	2-4	2-2	1-2	3-1
3. Epsom & E.	7-2	2-2	*	2-1	3-1	4-1	1-3	5-1
4. Hampton	3-2	2-0	3-3	*	2-0	1-3	2-0	4-2
5. Malden V.	6-0	3-3	1-2	0-3	*	0-4	4-0	1-0
6. Dorking	6-2	3-1	0-0	2-1	3-3	*	0-1	6-1
7. Kingstonian	3-2	9-0	2-2	2-0	4-0	1-0	*	6-1
8. Walton & H.	0-2	1-2	0-2	1-2	1-3	0-2	3-2	*

SOUTH DIV.	P	W	D	L	F	A	PTS
Chipstead	12	10	0	2	43	16	30
Redhill	12	8	1	3	32	18	25
Three Bridges	12	7	1	4	36	29	22
Brighton & HA	12	6	1	5	42	22	19
East Grinstead	12	5	1	6	29	28	16
Merstham	12	2	2	8	20	42	8
Oakwood	12	0	2	10	14	61	2

RESULTS	1	2	3	4	5	6	7
1. Brighton	*	2-4	1-5	8-1	7-1	1-1	1-2
2. Chipstead	4-3	*	1-2	2-0	7-1	0-1	7-1
3. E Grinstead	0-2	1-3	*	1-2	8-1	1-2	2-2
4. Merstham	0-10	0-1	6-2	*	1-1	0-4	3-4
5. Oakwood	1-4	0-5	2-3	4-4	*	0-5	0-5
6. Redhill	2-1	2-3	5-2	2-1	5-2	*	2-4
7. Three Bdges	1-2	3-6	1-2	3-2	7-1	3-1	*

After play-offs, Welling United became the overrall champions with Epsom & Ewell as runners-up. Welling completed the double by beating Dorking in the League Cup final. It is hoped that the youth sides of Chertsey Town, Tooting & Mitcham United, Crawley Tow and Banstead Athletic will join the League for 1994-95.

Beddington FC of the Morden & District Sunday League pictured after being AFC Mitcham 3-1 at Carshalton Athletic FC to win the the final of the Lawson Premier Cup.

Photo - Dave West.

SUSSEX F.A.

Secretary: Mr D M Worsfold,
Culver Road, Lancing,
West Sussex BN15 9AX (0903 753547)

SENIOR CUP 1993-94

First Round

Mile Oak v Selsey	3-3*(aet)*,3-0	Lancing v Stamco	1-2
East Grinstead v Sidley United	2-0	Little Common Albion v Saltdean United	2-4
Steyning Town v Horsham YMCA	2-3	Storrington v Midhurst & Easebourne Utd	1-2
Horsham v Shoreham	2-1	Chichester City v Eastbourne Town	1-0
Withdean v Southwick	2-0	Broadbridge Heath v Crowborough Athletic	2-3
Hassocks v Eastbourne United	3-2	Ringmer v Worthing United	2-1

Second Round

Hailsham Town v Arundel	3-1	Mile Oak v Lewes	1-3
Wick v Oakwood	0-1	Crowbrough Athletic v Ringmer	3-1
Burgess Hill Town v Portfield	2-1	Pagham v Worthing	3-2
Whitehawk v Littlehampton Town	1-0	Langney Sports v Horsham	5-0
Hastings Town v Horsham YMCA	1-1,3-1	Hassocks v Peacehaven & Telscombe	1-2
Chichester City v Crawley Town	0-3	Withdean v Midhurst & Easebourne United	4-0
Bexhill Town v East Grinstead	2-1	Three Bridge v Stamco	4-6
Bognor Regis Town v Newhaven	5-2	Brighton & Hove Albion Res. v Saltdean Utd	2-0

First Round

Hastings Town v Whitehawk	0-1	Bexhill Town v Lewes	3-0
Hailsham Town v Pagham	2-1	Peacehaven & Telscombe v Langney Sports	4-2
Stamco v Oakwood	2-0	Crawley Town v Burgess Hill Town	3-0
Withdean v Crowborough Athletic	0-4	Brighton & Hove Albion Res. v Bognor Regis	6-0

Quarter-Finals

Bexhill Town v Hailsham Town	1-4	Crawley Town v Peacehaven & Telscombe	1-2
Crowborough Athletic v Stamco	0-3	Brighton & Hove Albion v Whitehawk	2-2,1-0

Semi-Finals

Brighton v Stamco *(at Lewes FC)*	4-0	Peacehaven v Hailsham T. *(at Lewes FC)*	2-0

Final *(at Brighton & Hove Albion FC, Mon 2nd May)*:
Brighton & Hove Albion Reserves 1, Peacehaven & Telscombe 0 *(att: 752)*

ROYAL ULSTER RIFLES CHARITY CUP 1993-94

Preliminary Round

Selsey v Littlehampton Town	2-1	Saltdean Utd v Little Common Albion	6-2
Bexhill Town v Crowborough Athletic	4-2	Arundel v Broadbridge Heath	4-1
Hassocks v Wick	3-2		

Second Round

Pagham v Midhurst & Easebourne Utd	3-0	Peacehaven & Telscombe v Newhaven	1-2
Three Bridges v Oakwood	0-1	Steyning Town v Mile Oak	0-0,1-1,1-0
Hassocks v Southwick	3-1	Eastbourne United v Stamco	1-4
Saltdean United v East Grinstead	2-1	Selsey v Burgess Hill Town	2-3
Bexhill Town v Whitehawk	0-3	Arundel v Storrington	0-1
Eastbourne Town v Hailsham Town	4-4,0-1	Chichester City v Horsham YMCA	0-2
Ringmer v Langney Sports	1-0	Portfield v Lancing	0-3
Withdean v Sidley United	3-2	Worthing United v Shoreham	1-4

Second Round

Newhaven v Saltdean United	5-2	Pagham v Burgess Hill Town	5-4*(aet)*
Hailsham Town v Whitehawk	1-2*(aet)*	Horsham YMCA v Storrington	3-1
Stamco v Ringmer	2-1	Hassocks v Lancing	2-0
Withdean v Oakwood	3-2	Shoreham v Steyning Town	0-1

Quarter-Finals

Newhaven v Horsham YMCA	4-1	Pagham v Stamco	6-2
Steyning Town v Withdean	7-1	Hassocks v Whitehawk *(at Whitehaw)*	3-1

Semi-Finals

Hassocks v Pagham	0-2*(aet)*	Newhaven v Steyning Town	4-2

Final *(at Lancing FC, Tues 1st March)*: Newhaven 4, Pagham 0

UNIJET MID-SUSSEX LEAGUE

FOUNDED: 1900

President: Ken Somerville. **Treasurer:** B B Bradford.
Chairman: Allen D Washer. **Vice-Chairman:** Brian Hall.
Secretary: P H Strange.

Plumpton Athletic secured the title after enduring two frustrating years as runners-up, but perhaps owe some of their success to the fact that Wealden, Pease Pottage Village and Nutley in particular were unable to capitalise on their own chances of league glory. Since three points for a win was introduced in 1984, never before has a team taken the championship with only 45 points.

Handcross Village did the double by winning Division One and the Mowatt Cup, while fellow Division One side Lindfield Rangers Reserves brought some pride to the League by becoming the first Mid-Sussex team to lift the Sussex Junior Cup since St Francis Hospital in 1987.

Simon Langston, Press Officer.

PREM. DIVISION	P	W	D	L	F	A	PTS
Plumpton Ath.	22	14	3	5	53	33	45
Wealden	22	12	4	6	50	29	40
Crawley Down Vill.	22	12	3	7	51	35	39
Pease Pottage Vill.	22	12	3	7	44	29	39
Nutley	22	11	5	6	48	38	38
Leftovers SC	22	10	6	6	41	38	36
Cuckfield	22	8	6	8	36	31	30
Southwater	22	7	5	10	38	38	26
Maresfield Village	22	7	5	10	39	41	26
Lewes Rovers	22	4	7	11	30	51	19
Chailey	22	4	3	15	22	49	15
Newick	22	3	6	13	30	70	15

DIVISION ONE	P	W	D	L	F	A	PTS
Handcross Village	24	19	3	2	72	28	60
Wisdom Sports	24	17	4	3	68	28	55
Ashurstwood	24	13	3	8	57	43	42
Ansty	24	12	4	8	58	43	40
Village of Ditchling	24	11	4	9	56	31	37
Leftovers SC Res.	24	10	6	8	43	41	36
Clayton	24	10	3	11	48	43	33
Lindfield	24	9	3	12	50	67	30
Uckfield Town	24	8	5	11	36	55	29
Lindfield Rgrs Res.	24	7	6	11	39	47	27
Felbridge	24	8	2	14	46	54	26
Wivelsfield Green	24	6	6	12	34	53	24
Heath Pilgrims	24	0	3	21	25	99	3

DIVISION TWO	P	W	D	L	F	A	PTS
St Francis H. Res.	22	16	3	3	90	25	51
Southwater Res.	22	16	2	4	75	26	50
Hurstpierpoint Res.	22	16	1	5	66	32	49
Hassocks 'A'	22	11	4	7	61	38	37
Plumpton Ath. Res.	22	10	4	8	56	46	34
Horley Athletico	22	10	2	10	50	47	32
West Hoatly	22	8	3	11	36	40	27
Wisdom Spts Res.	22	8	3	11	50	64	27
Buxted Res.	22	7	4	11	41	58	25
Bolney Rovers	22	7	2	13	31	46	23
Ardingly	22	6	3	13	41	75	21
Forest Row	22	1	1	20	26	128	4

DIVISION THREE	P	W	D	L	F	A	PTS
Balcombe	20	14	4	2	60	18	46
DMS Cuckfield	20	12	6	2	57	29	42
Ringmer 'A'	20	10	6	4	52	41	36
Sovereign Finance	20	9	4	7	36	34	31
Horsted Keynes	20	9	4	7	40	43	31
Danehill	20	8	2	10	38	38	26
Maresfield Vill.Res.	20	7	3	10	40	38	24
Leftovers SC 'A'	20	7	2	11	32	48	23
Lingfield Res.	20	6	3	11	37	42	21
Fairwarp	20	4	5	11	33	55	17
Turners Hill	20	3	3	14	29	68	12

DIVISION FOUR	P	W	D	L	F	A	PTS
Crowborough A. 'A'	22	14	4	4	78	41	46
Woodcock Athletic	22	14	4	4	62	30	46
AFC Peacehaven	22	13	4	5	67	36	43
Crawley DV Res.	22	10	3	9	58	51	33
St Francis H. 'A'	22	9	5	8	51	47	32
E. Grin. Mariners	22	9	4	9	53	60	31
Ashurstwood Res.	22	9	3	10	35	50	30
Rotherfield	22	7	6	9	57	51	27
Lewes Rovers Res.	22	9	0	13	53	74	27
Franklands V. Res.	22	8	1	13	44	77	25
Cuckfield Res.	22	6	5	11	49	62	23
Jarvis Brook	22	3	3	16	45	73	12

DIVISION FIVE	P	W	D	L	F	A	PTS
Barcombe	22	17	4	1	71	24	55
Bridgeview	22	16	3	3	60	27	51
Pease PV Res.	22	13	2	7	56	37	41
Hartfield	22	10	5	7	52	30	35
Vill. of Ditch. Res.	22	10	2	10	48	55	32
Newick Res.	22	8	5	9	45	49	29
Hurstpierpoint 'A'	22	9	2	11	46	66	29
Felbridge Res.	22	8	3	11	46	46	27
Uckfield Town Res.	22	7	1	14	44	64	22
Lindfield Res.	22	6	3	13	39	63	21
Groombridge	22	5	5	12	28	46	20
Southwater 'A'	22	5	1	16	36	64	16

DIVISION SIX	P	W	D	L	F	A	PTS
Clayton Res.	18	11	3	4	46	25	36
DMS Cuckfield Res.	18	11	2	5	55	39	35
Wisdom Spts 'A'	18	9	3	6	41	30	30
Sov. Finance Res.	18	9	2	7	41	30	29
Wealden Res.	18	9	0	9	31	38	27
Wivelsfield G. Res.	18	7	5	6	30	35	26
Leftovers SC 'B'	18	7	1	10	44	37	22
Hth Pilgrims Res.	18	7	1	10	46	58	22
Scaynes Hill Utd	18	6	3	9	24	34	21
Staxil Burgess Hill	18	3	2	13	26	58	11

DIVISION SEVEN	P	W	D	L	F	A	PTS
Hassocks 'B'	20	18	1	1	96	27	55
Handcross Vil. Res.	20	16	0	4	63	23	48
Dormansland Rockets	20	15	1	4	74	23	46
Cuckfield 'A'	20	11	3	6	40	39	36
Ansty Res.	20	9	3	8	61	42	30
Chailey Res.	20	9	1	10	42	47	28
Crawley Dn V. 'A'	20	6	3	11	37	57	21
Buxted 'A'	20	5	3	12	40	61	18
West Hoathly Res.	20	6	0	14	18	61	18
Turners Hill Res.	20	4	1	15	25	60	13
Lindfield 'A'	20	2	2	16	21	77	8

DIVISION EIGHT	P	W	D	L	F	A	PTS
Nutley Res.	20	18	0	2	71	14	54
Bridgeview Res.	20	15	3	2	66	24	48
Ashurstwood 'A'	20	14	2	4	59	31	44
Horsted Keynes Res.	20	12	2	6	70	37	38
Vill. of Ditch. 'A'	20	8	4	8	58	53	28
Ardingly Res.	20	8	2	10	51	47	26
Hartfield Res.	20	8	2	10	42	44	26
Maresfield V. 'A'	20	8	1	11	48	46	25
Fairwarp Res.	20	5	2	13	37	55	17
Lingfield 'A'	20	3	1	16	25	74	10
Uckfield T. 'A'	20	0	3	17	16	118	3

DIVISION NINE	P	W	D	L	F	A	PTS
Danehill Res.	20	15	3	2	64	23	48
Plumpton Ath. 'A'	20	15	3	2	65	26	48
Barcombe Res.	20	15	1	4	62	27	46
Jarvis Brook Res.	20	12	3	5	49	31	39
Wealden 'A'	20	8	4	8	40	37	28
Rotherfield Res.	20	9	0	11	64	58	27
Lewes Rovers 'A'	20	7	4	9	44	42	25
Maresfield V. 'B'	20	6	5	9	34	33	23
Hayward Rgrs Res.	20	7	1	12	42	53	22
Balcombe Res.	20	1	2	17	17	66	5
Scaynes Hill U. Res.	20	1	2	17	13	98	5

PREMIER DIVISION RESULT CHART 1993-94

HOME TEAM	1	2	3	4	5	6	7	8	9	10	11	12
1. Chailey	*	1-1	1-2	1-2	1-1	4-1	2-2	1-3	0-2	0-3	1-3	0-1
2. Crawley Down Village	4-1	*	2-2	0-1	3-1	2-2	6-1	2-3	3-0	1-3	1-0	1-0
3. Cuckfield	1-0	0-1	*	1-1	1-1	3-3	2-3	1-2	1-0	0-0	2-3	2-1
4. Leftovers Sports Club	2-0	1-3	2-1	*	1-0	1-1	2-2	4-0	2-2	2-2	1-3	0-2
5. Lewes Rovers	1-0	1-5	0-6	1-4	*	1-0	2-4	1-1	2-3	0-1	3-1	2-2
6. Maresfield Village	5-1	0-2	1-2	3-1	3-1	*	3-3	1-0	0-2	4-0	3-1	1-3
7. Newick	2-4	1-4	0-3	1-5	0-5	0-3	*	1-4	3-6	1-4	1-1	1-1
8. Nutley	0-2	5-2	1-0	1-3	2-2	5-1	2-2	*	1-2	3-0	3-1	5-4
9. Pease Pottage Village	0-1	4-2	0-2	1-2	8-1	1-0	0-1	1-1	*	1-0	0-0	4-1
10. Plumpton Athletic	7-0	3-1	3-1	1-1	3-2	3-2	4-0	5-3	4-1	*	1-3	2-1
11. Southwater	2-0	2-3	1-1	5-2	2-2	1-1	4-1	1-2	2-4	2-3	*	0-3
12. Wealden	4-1	3-2	5-2	7-1	0-0	4-1	3-0	1-1	0-2	4-1		*

DIVISION ONE RESULT CHART 1993-94

HOME TEAM	1	2	3	4	5	6	7	8	9	10	11	12	13
1. Ansty	*	3-1	2-2	5-3	2-3	3-1	2-0	5-1	5-0	2-0	3-2	2-4	1-1
2. Ashurst Wood	1-3	*	4-1	3-0	3-0	1-1	1-3	4-1	1-4	2-0	1-0	0-2	6-1
3. Clayton	2-1	1-2	*	3-0	0-5	7-1	1-2	2-3	0-3	1-2	2-1	0-1	3-0
4. Felbridge	2-0	1-4	1-2	*	0-1	3-2	1-2	5-1	1-1	1-2	1-5	2-4	4-2
5. Handcross Cross	1-0	1-0	5-0	4-3	*	9-2	5-2	3-1	3-1	4-2	2-0	4-1	2-2
6. Heath Pilgrims	1-7	1-3	2-3	2-5	1-3	*	0-5	1-4	1-6	0-4	1-3	0-4	4-4
7. Leftovers SC Reserves	2-2	0-4	1-1	1-0	0-3	3-1	*	2-2	3-0	2-5	1-1	2-2	4-1
8. Lindfield	6-3	2-3	1-6	1-4	0-2	2-1	0-4	*	3-0	1-1	1-0	2-1	4-2
9. Lindfield Rangers Res.	4-1	6-6	1-3	0-1	4-7	4-0	0-0	3-1	*	2-2	3-0	1-1	1-0
10. Uckfield Town	1-1	1-3	2-7	1-2	0-1	3-1	2-1	1-1	2-1	*	0-4	0-3	3-1
11. Village of Ditchling	5-1	5-2	0-0	1-1	1-0	8-0	0-2	5-3	7-0	2-2	*	1-3	0-1
12. Wisdom Sports	3-1	5-1	1-0	5-4	1-1	4-0	3-1	2-1	2-2	10-0	0-3	*	3-0
13. Wivelsfield Green	0-3	1-1	2-1	2-1	2-2	1-1	4-0	2-4	2-0	2-0	1-2	0-3	*

DIVISION TWO RESULT CHART 1993-94

HOME TEAM	1	2	3	4	5	6	7	8	9	10	11	12
1. Ardingly	*	0-0	1-2	3-0	1-8	3-5	2-1	2-2	0-1	3-7	1-1	1-5
2. Bolney Rovers	1-2	*	4-1	2-3	1-0	1-1	2-2	2-5	1-4	1-2	0-5	4-1
3. Buxted Reserves	5-1	1-4	*	1-1	0-2	0-5	4-2	2-2	2-4	1-3	1-0	2-3
4. Forest Row	2-8	1-2	3-6	*	0-6	2-5	3-6	2-6	0-8	1-4	1-5	3-4
5. Hassocks 'A'	7-0	3-1	4-1	5-0	*	2-3	2-2	3-2	2-1	0-3	2-1	2-2
6. Hurstpierpoint Reserves	2-1	2-0	0-3	8-1	2-2	*	2-0	2-1	1-2	4-0	2-0	7-1
7. Horley Athletico	3-2	0-1	5-2	6-0	3-2	5-2	*	0-1	0-7	2-3	5-3	3-1
8. Plumpton Athletic Reserves	7-2	2-3	2-2	4-0	2-1	2-5	5-1	*	1-1	2-0	2-3	4-1
9. St Francis Hospital Res.	10-3	1-1	5-1	15-0	3-4	2-0	1-0	3-1	*	1-1	4-0	7-0
10. Southwater Reserves	4-0	5-2	6-1	13-0	3-0	3-2	0-1	4-0	3-5	*	0-0	4-0
11. West Hoathly	0-1	2-0	1-1	5-1	4-1	0-2	1-0	4-1	1-4	0-4	*	0-1
12. Wisdom Spts Reserves	2-4	3-1	0-2	6-2	3-3	2-4	3-3	3-4	3-1	0-3	6-0	*

DIVISION THREE RESULT CHART 1993-94

HOME TEAM	1	2	3	4	5	6	7	8	9	10	11
1. Balcombe	*	3-3	8-0	1-1	2-2	9-1	2-1	2-0	W-L	1-3	1-1
2. DMS Cuckfield	3-0	*	3-3	5-0	3-0	2-1	0-0	0-1	4-2	1-1	5-0
3. Fairwarp	0-2	2-3	*	3-1	3-2	1-3	2-2	1-2	2-2	2-4	1-0
4. Horsted Keynes	0-4	4-4	5-3	*	1-5	2-1	2-3	2-1	0-0	3-1	3-1
5. Leftovers SC 'A'	1-2	0-4	2-2	1-3	*	1-3	0-5	1-3	1-4	0-4	1-2
6. Lingfield Reserves	0-4	0-1	5-6	5-0	1-3	*	2-1	5-3	2-2	0-0	9-0
7. Maresfield Village 'A'	0-1	3-4	3-3	0-4	1-3	2-0	*	1-0	1-4	2-3	7-1
8. Danehill	0-3	1-3	2-0	1-2	1-2	3-0	3-1	*	2-2	2-2	5-2
9. Ringmer 'A'	2-9	3-3	6-4	1-1	2-3	4-2	2-1	5-3	*	4-0	3-2
10. Sovereign Finance	0-3	4-1	2-0	2-1	0-1	2-3	1-4	3-1	0-2	*	3-3
11. Turners Hill	0-3	1-5	4-2	1-5	3-4	2-2	1-2	1-4	1-2	3-1	*

DIVISION FOUR RESULT CHART 1993-94

HOME TEAM	1	2	3	4	5	6	7	8	9	10	11	12
1. AFC Peacehaven	*	5-1	1-3	1-1	5-1	3-3	6-1	3-2	7-0	1-0	3-1	1-1
2. Ashurstwood Reserves	2-1	*	3-1	3-2	3-1	1-0	1-3	W-L	2-5	2-3	0-2	1-1
3. Crawley Down Village Res.	2-5	3-1	*	6-1	1-1	0-2	2-3	3-2	9-1	1-1	1-2	2-1
4. Crowborough Athletic 'A'	4-3	4-0	4-1	*	3-0	1-2	7-2	2-2	7-3	4-2	5-2	3-2
5. Cuckfield Reserves	3-2	1-2	3-4	1-1	*	4-4	2-3	1-10	3-1	6-1	1-1	1-2
6. East Grinstead Mariners	2-1	1-4	6-3	0-2	0-8	*	5-1	5-3	2-3	2-2	3-2	0-3
7. Franklands Village 'A'	2-4	3-3	0-4		2-3	4-2	*	3-0	2-1	5-1	2-3	0-7
8. Jarvis Brook	1-6	5-0	1-5	0-6	2-3	2-6	1-2	*	2-4	3-2	2-4	1-2
9. Lewes Rovers Reserves	1-2	2-4	1-4	0-6	4-2	7-1	4-3	3-2	*	4-3	2-0	2-3
10. Rotherfield	2-3	4-0	2-2	3-3	4-1	2-2	12-1	2-2	2-1	*	5-0	1-3
11. St Francis Hospital 'A'	1-1	2-1	1-1	5-6	1-1	1-3	2-1	10-1	4-3	1-1	*	1-3
12. Woodcock Athletic	2-3	1-1	7-0	3-1	6-2	3-2	2-1	1-1	4-1	4-0	1-5	*

DIVISION FIVE RESULT CHART 1993-94

HOME TEAM	1	2	3	4	5	6	7	8	9	10	11	12
1. Barcombe	*	2-2	6-1	2-1	5-0	3-1	7-1	5-0	1-1	1-0	4-2	2-0
2. Bridgeview	0-3	*	4-0	3-3	2-0	2-1	6-4	1-3	5-0	1-2	W-L	0-0
3. Uckfield Town Reserves	2-2	3-4	*	1-4	2-2	0-2	3-2	0-2	1-6	3-6	7-2	3-5
4. Felbridge Reserves	0-3	1-3	3-0	*	5-1	0-1	1-4	3-2	0-1	2-5	6-2	2-1
5. Groombridge	0-1	1-4	1-3	2-2	*	2-2	3-4	3-0	4-1	1-1	W-L	2-0
6. Hartfield	3-3	1-2	0-3	1-2	1-0	*	5-0	8-1	6-0	3-0	2-4	3-3
7. Hurstpierpoint 'A'	3-8	0-3	1-5	1-4	1-0	0-0	*	2-1	2-1	1-3	3-2	3-1
8. Lindfield Reserves	2-3	0-5	8-4	1-4	1-0	0-4	3-3	*	2-2	2-3	2-1	2-3
9. Newick Reserves	0-2	1-2	5-2	2-2	1-2	1-1	2-4	2-2	*	3-1	1-0	2-6
10. Pease Pottage V. Res.	4-1	1-4	2-1	4-2	1-1	0-2	3-1	4-0	1-2	*	4-0	4-1
11. Southwater 'A'	2-2	1-2	0-2	3-2	5-1	1-4	4-3	0-4	0-7	0-4	*	3-4
12. Village of Ditchling Res.	1-5	0-5	1-0	3-1	4-2	3-1	1-3	3-1	3-4	5-3	0-4	*

DIVISION SIX RESULT CHART 1993-94

HOME TEAM	1	2	3	4	5	6	7	8	9	10
1. Clayton Reserves	*	0-3	1-4	1-0	2-0	W-L	8-1	1-0	4-1	1-3
2. DMS Cuckfield Reserves	2-2	*	6-1	5-1	4-0	4-2	4-3	0-4	1-1	6-2
3. Heath Pilgrims Reserves	1-8	4-5	*	0-4	1-0	1-5	6-0	3-1	1-6	L-W
4. Leftovers Sports 'B'	1-4	3-4	6-1	*	2-4	3-2	7-3	0-1	3-0	6-1
5. Scaynes Hill United	0-2	2-1	2-2	1-0	*	1-4	2-1	0-3	2-1	1-1
6. Sovereign Finance Res.	4-1	3-5	4-2	4-2	2-0	*	1-1	0-3	1-3	L-W
7. Staxil Burgess Hill	2-5	3-4	0-4	0-1	1-5	1-3	*	0-1	1-2	2-0
8. Wealden Reserves	1-4	4-0	0-9	W-L	3-2	2-3	1-2	*	0-4	4-3
9. Wisdom Sports Reserves	1-1	3-1	2-3	4-3	3-1	1-1	3-4	3-1	*	0-1
10. Wivelsfield Green Res.	1-1	1-0	8-3	2-2	1-1	2-0	1-1	4-2	1-3	*

DIVISION SEVEN RESULT CHART 1993-94

HOME TEAM	1	2	3	4	5	6	7	8	9	10	11
1. Ansty Reserves	*	3-3	6-2	1-1	3-4	1-3	3-4	2-3	2-2	4-0	10-1
2. Buxted 'A'	3-6	*	0-2	2-9	1-3	2-4	0-3	0-5	3-0	4-4	3-0
3. Chailey Reserves	2-1	3-2	*	2-7	2-0	2-1	1-4	1-2	5-1	8-0	2-3
4. Crawley Down Vill. 'A'	1-3	1-3	0-0	*	0-2	0-6	1-6	2-8	4-0	4-3	0-1
5. Cuckfield 'A'	1-0	2-2	4-1	1-1	*	2-1	1-0	1-6	4-2	1-0	4-0
6. Dormansland Rockets	2-4	5-0	5-1	9-2	5-0	*	1-2	9-3	4-1	4-1	4-0
7. Handcross Village Reserves	4-1	1-0	2-1	2-1	4-0	1-2	*	2-5	8-1	2-0	1-0
8. Hassocks 'B'	4-2	4-1	6-0	5-1	6-1	1-1	2-1	*	10-1	2-1	3-0
9. Lindfield 'A'	1-3	2-4	0-3	2-0	2-2	0-2	1-5	0-9	*	2-1	2-3
10. Turners Hill Reserves	1-3	3-1	3-1	L-W	1-6	0-3	1-5	1-5	3-0	*	2-1
11. West Hoatly Reserves	0-3	1-6	0-3	1-2	1-0	0-3	1-6	0-7	1-0	4-0	*

DIVISION EIGHT RESULT CHART 1993-94

HOME TEAM	1	2	3	4	5	6	7	8	9	10	11
1. Ardingly Reserves	*	1-6	1-3	0-1	3-1	2-2	12-1	4-0	0-1	6-0	2-6
2. Ashurstwood 'A'	3-0	*	3-3	1-2	6-2	6-2	2-1	2-1	0-3	3-1	5-2
3. Bridgeview Reserves	2-0	5-0	*	3-1	4-1	3-1	3-2	4-1	3-1	12-1	4-2
4. Fairwarp Reserves	5-3	2-2	5-1	*	0-3	3-8	5-1	1-5	0-3	3-3	1-5
5. Hartfield Reserves	1-1	1-4	1-3	3-1	*	1-3	6-0	3-4	0-4	3-0	1-1
6. Horsted Keynes Reserves	5-0	1-2	2-1	3-1	1-4	*	3-1	6-1	1-3	1-1	6-3
7. Lingfield 'A'	1-3	0-2	L-W	4-2	2-4	1-4	*	1-2	0-2	W-L	3-3
8. Maresfield Village 'A'	1-2	0-1	1-1	2-1	0-2	0-3	6-0	*	3-5	14-0	2-4
9. Nutley Reserves	6-2	2-1	0-2	2-0	3-1	2-0	9-0	3-0	*	5-0	4-0
10. Uckfield Town 'A'	1-8	1-5	0-8	0-3	2-4	0-15	0-3	1-2	0-11	*	4-4
11. Village of Ditchling 'A'	2-1	1-5	1-1	3-1	2-0	2-3	6-4	2-3	1-2	8-1	*

DIVISION NINE RESULT CHART 1993-94

HOME TEAM	1	2	3	4	5	6	7	8	9	10	11
1. Balcombe Reserves	*	1-3	1-5	2-0	0-5	2-4	1-1	1-9	1-3	1-1	0-4
2. Barcombe Reserves	2-0	*	3-4	3-1	2-0	5-1	1-0	2-5	5-3	4-0	4-1
3. Danehill Reserves	2-1	3-3	*	3-0	3-1	3-1	2-0	2-2	5-1	9-0	1-0
4. Hayward Rangers	5-2	1-3	2-8	*	3-5	4-1	0-5	1-2	2-5.	5-1	3-2
5. Jarvis Brook Reserves	4-1	3-2	1-1	1-0	*	2-2	2-0	1-2	5-1	1-1	4-1
6. Lewes Rovers 'A'	2-0	0-3	2-3	2-1	2-1	*	1-3	2-2	6-2	12-0	0-1
7. Maresfield Village 'B'	1-0	0-3	0-2	2-2	2-3	2-2	*	0-5	8-1	6-1	1-1
8. Plumpton Athletic 'A'	3-0	1-0	1-0	2-5	6-0	1-0	2-1	*	4-2	6-0	1-5
9. Rotherfield Reserves	5-1	2-4	0-2	2-5	1-3	4-0	3-0	3-6	*	10-1	7-0
10. Scaynes Hill Utd Res.	3-1	0-7	0-6	0-1	0-4	2-3	1-2	0-4	0-5	*	0-4
11. Wealden 'A'	4-1	1-3	4-0	2-1	1-3	1-1	0-0	1-1	0-4	7-2	*

MONTGOMERY CHALLENGE CUP

First Round

Lindfield Rgrs Res. v Leftovers SC 2-3
Felbridge v Village of Ditchling 4-3
Nutley v Maresfield Village 2-0
Pease Pottage Village v Wivelsfield Gn 2-1
Ansty v Lindfield 4-2
Ashurstwood v Newick 4-0
Southwater v Hurstpierpoint Reserves 2-2,3-0
Plumpton Athletic v Cuckfield 3-0

Second Round

Forest Row v Chailey 0-9
Ansty v Lewes Rovers 2-0
Wealden v Ashurstwood 2-0
Nutley v Southwater 1-1,4-3
Leftovers SC v Crawley Down Village 3-1
Felbridge v Wisdom Sports 1-1,1-3
Handcross Village v Uckfield Town 0-2
Pease Pottage Village v Plumpton Athletic 0-1

Quarter-Finals

Chailey v Leftovers SC 1-2
Wealden v Uckfield Town 5-0
Ansty v Wisdom Sports 1-3
Nutley v Plumpton Athletic 4-0

Semi-Finals

Wealden v Nutley 6-1
Leftovers SC v Wisdom Sports 3-2

Final *(23/4/94)*: Wealden 3, Leftovers SC 1

MOWATT CHALLENGE CUP

First Round

West Hoatly v East Grinstead 'A' 8-0
Village of Ditchling v Felbridge 3-1
Southwater v Ashurstwood 3-4
Leftovers SC Reserves v Plumpton Res. 2-4
Balcombe v St Francis Hospital Res. 2-1
Lindfield v Hurstpierpoint Res. 2-1
Danehill v Ansty 1-2
Handcross Village v Uckfield Town 2-1
Bolney Rovers v Hassocks 'A' 3-1
Fairwarp v DMS Cuckfield 2-0
Forest Row v Wisdom Sports 0-8
Heath Pilgrims v Lindfield Rgrs Res. 3-5
Wivelsfield Green v Buxted Reserves 4-1
Clayton v Lingfield Reserves 6-0

Second Round

West Hoathly v Handcross Village 0-3
Village of Ditchling v Horley Athletico 3-5

Bolney Rovers v Ashurstwood	0-3	Fairwarp v PLumpton Athletic Reserves	2-3
Wisdom Sports v Balcombe	0-2	Lindfield Rgrs Res. v Lindfield	2-3
Wivelsfield Green v Ansty	1-3	Clayton v Ardingly	6-1

Quarter-Finals

Handcross Village v Horley Athletico	5-0	Ashurstwood v Plumpton Athletic Reserves	5-2
Balcombe v Lindfield	1-0	Ansty v Clayton	1-3

Semi-Finals

Balcombe v Clayton	2-4	Handcross Village v Ashurstwood	4-0

Final *(26/3/94)*: Handcross Village 3, Clayton 1

EDGAR GERMAN CHALLENGE CUP

First Round

Lewes Rovers Res. v Leftovers SC 'A'	4-1	East Grinstead 'A' *(scr)* Rotherfield *(w/o)*	
Forest Row v Turners Hill	0-6	Danehill v West Hoathly	1-2
Wisdom Sports Res. v Fairwarp	4-2	Southwater Reserves v Ringmer 'A'	4-0
Crowborough 'A' v East Grin. Mariners	1-4	Horley Athletico v St Francis Hosp. Res.	0-2
Crawley Down V. Res. v Lingfield Res.	3-3,1-0	Ashurstwood Reserves v Hassocks 'A'	3-1
Horsted Keynes v Hurstpierpoint Res.	2-0	Jarvis Brook v Bolney Rovers	5-3
Ardingly v Buxted Reserves	4-0	Balcombe v Plumpton Ath. Reserves	2-2,0-2
Maresfield Vill. Res. v AFC Peacehaven	2-4		

Second Round

Lewes Rovers Res. v Rotherfield	4-4,0-4	Turners Hill v West Hoathly	1-5
Wisdom Sports Res.v Southwater Res.	0-2	East Grinst. Mariners v St Francis H. Res.	1-2
Crawley Down Vill. Res. v DMS Cuckfield	2-4	Ashurstwood Reserves v Horsted Keynes	0-3
Jarvis Brook v Ardingly	4-2	Plumpton Ath. Res. v AFC Peacehaven	1-5

Quarter-Finals

Rotherfield *(w/o)* West Hoatly *(scr)*		Southwater Res. v St Francis Hosp. Reserves	0-1
DMS Cuckfield v Horsted Keynes	7-3	Jarvis Brook v AFC Peacehaven	1-1,0-2

Semi-Finals

Rotherfield v St Francis Hosp. Reserves	2-1	DMS Cuckfield v AFC Peacehaven	3-1

Final *(16/4/94)*: Rotherfield 3, DMS Cuckfield 1

SOMERVILLE CHALLENGE CUP

Preliminary Round

Staxil Burgess Hill v Lindfield Res.	1-0		

First Round

AFC Peacehaven v DMS Cuckfield	6-0	Hartfield v Crowborough Athletic 'A'	1-8
Felbridge Res. v St Francis Hospital 'A'	3-2	Newick Reserves v Wisdom Sports 'A'	4-3
Woodcock Athletic v Lewes Rovers Reserves	2-4	Clayton Reserves v Hurspierpoint Res.	1-2
Wivelsfield Green Res. v Uckfield T. Res.	6-0	Barcombe v Southwater 'A'	2-1
Scaynes Hill Utd *(w/o)* Forest Row Res. *(scr)*		Staxil Burgess Hill v Village of Ditchling Res.	2-5
Heath Pilgrims Res. v Leftovers SC 'B'	4-0	Cuckfield Res. v East Grinstead Mariners	1-2
Ashurstwood Res. v Sovereign Finance	4-3	Crawley Down V. Res. v Pease Pottage V. Res.	4-3
Groombridge v Wealden Reserves	4-0	Bridgeview *(bye)*	

Second Round

Felbridge Res. v Newick Reserves	3-1	AFC Peacehaven v Crowborough Ath. 'A'	0-5
Lewes Rovers Res.v Hurstpierpoint 'A'	6-1	Wivelsfield Green Res. v Barcombe	2-3
Scaynes Hill. Res. v Village of Dit. Res.	1-4	Heath Pilgrims Reserves v E Grin. Mariners	3-3,1-3
Ashurstwood Res. v Bridgeview	4-1	Crawley Down V. Res. v Groombridge	3-2

Quarter-Finals

Crowborough 'A' v Felbridge Reserves	2-4	Hurstpierpoint 'A' v Barcombe	2-1
Vil. of Dit. Res. *(w/o)* E Grin. Mariners *(scr)*		Ashurstwood Res. v Crawley Down V. Reserves	4-2

Semi-Finals

Felbridge Res. v Hurtpierpoint 'A'	4-4,1-2	Ashurstwood Res. v East Grinstead Mariners	2-1

Final *(27/4/94)*: Ashurstwood Reserves 2, Hurstpierpoint 'A' 1

STUBBINS CHALLENGE CUP

First Round

Danehill v Barcombe	1-0	St Francis H. 'A' v E Grin Mariners	2-2,3-3*(1-3 pens)*
Hurstpierpoint 'A' v Leftovers SC 'A'	2-4	Lewes Rovers Reserves v AFC Peacehaven	3-3,4-5
Balcombe v Lindfield Reserves	3-0	Southwater 'A' v Ringmer 'A'	2-0
Woodcock Athletic v Horsted Keynes	4-5	Sovereign Finance v Turners Hill	5-1
Crawley Down V. Res. v Franklands Vill. 'A'	3-2	Crowbrough Ath. 'A' v Ashurstwood Res.	3-2
Jarvis Brook v Village of Ditchling Res.	2-1	Groombridge v Cuckfield Reserves	2-1
Pease Pottage Res. v DMS Cuckfield	1-3	Rotherfield v Newick Reserves	1-0

Second Round

Danehill v East Grinstead Mariners	0-2	Leftovers SC 'A' v AFC Peacehaven	2-4
Balcombe v Southwater 'A'	8-0	Horsted Keynes v Sovereign Finance	1-3
Crawley Down V. Res. v Ashurstwood Res.	4-0	Maresfield Village Res. v Jarvis Brook	3-2
Groombridge v Hartfield	1-4	DMS Cuckfield v Rotherfield	2-3

Quarter-Finals

East Grinstead Mariners v AFC Peacehaven	4-2	Balcombe v Sovereign Finance	2-2,0-3
Crawley DV Res. v Maresfield V. Res.	3-3,2-0	Hartfield v Rotherfield	0-1

Semi-Finals

E Grin Mariners v Sovereign Finance	2-2,2-1	Crawley Down V. Res. v Rotherfield	2-1

Final *(30/4/94)*: East Grinstead Mariners 2, Crawley Down Village Reserves 1

STRATFORD CHALLENGE CUP

First Round

Chailey Reserves v Staxil Burgess Hill	2-2,1-0	Lindfield 'A' v Hartfield	0-3
Forest Row Res. *(scr)* Wisdom Spts 'A' *(w/o)*		Barcombe v Newick Reserves	6-2
Wivelsfield G. Res. v Pease Pott. V. Res.	2-5	Village of Dit. Res. v Crawley Down V. Res.	1-1,1-2
Sovereign F. Res. v Heath Pilgrims Reserves	3-1	Uckfield T. Reserves v Cuckfield 'A'	3-1
DMS Cuckfield 'A' v Clayton Reserves	1-3	Felbridge Res. v Dormansland Rockets	2-1
Groombridge v Southwater 'A'	2-3	Buxted 'A' v Wealden Reserves	0-5
Ansty Res. v Hassocks 'B'	0-6	Handcross Vill. Res. v West Hoathly Res.	3-3,8-1

Second Round

Staxil Burgess Hill v Hartfield	0-3	Wisdom Sports 'A' v Barcombe	1-3
Pease Pot. V. Res. v Crawley Down V. Res.	3-1	Sovereign Finance Res. v Uckfield Town Res.	5-3
Clayton Res. v Felbridge Res.	7-4	Southwater 'A' v Wealden Reserves	3-1
Hassocks 'B' v Handcross Village Res.	5-2	Turners Hill Res. v Leftovers SC Reserves	1-4

Quarter-Finals

Hartfield v Barcombe	0-3	Pease Pott. Vill. Res. v Uckfield Reserves	4-0
Clayton Reserves v Southwater 'A'	4-2	Hassocks v Leftovers 'B'	1-2

Semi-Finals

Barcombe Res. v Pease Pottage V. Res.	4-0	Clayton Res. v Leftovers SC Reserves	6-2

Final *(6/4/94)*: Barcombe 3, Clayton Reserves 1

MALINS CHALLENGE CUP

First Round

Clayton Reserves v Lindfield 'A'	4-1	DMS Cuckfield Res. *(w/o)* Forest Row Res. *(scr)*	
Crawley Down V. 'A' v Wealden Reserves	0-1	Village of Dit. 'A' v Handcross Village Res.	0-6
Wisdom Sports 'A' v Hassocks 'B'	2-5	Nutley Reserves v Hartfield Reserves	0-1
Chailey Reserves v Wivelsfield G. Res.	2-1	Ardlingly Reserves v Fairwarp	5-1
Ashurst Wood 'A' v Horsted K. Res.	3-3,2-1	Heath Pilgrims Res. v Bridgeview Res.	5-1
Lingfield 'A' v West Hoathly Res.	1-0	Turners Hill Res. v Sovereign Finance Res.	0-5
Buxted 'A' v Maresfield Village 'A'	2-1	Staxil Burgess Hill v Dormansland Rockets	2-3
Uckfield Town 'A' v Ansty Reserves	1-4		

Second Round

Clayton Res. v DMS Cuckfield Res.	7-1	Wealden Res. v Handcross Village Reserves	2-4
Hassocks 'A' v Hartfield Reserves	5-0	Chailey Reserves v Cuckfield 'A'	2-4
Ardlingly Res. v Ashurstwood 'A'	2-4	Heath Pilgrims Reserves v Lingfield 'A'	9-1
Sovereign F. Res. v Buxted 'A'	2-2,3-2	Dormansland Rockets v Ansty Reserves	5-0

Quarter-Finals

Clayton Reserves v Handcross V. Res.	4-0	Hassocks 'B' v Cuckfield 'A'	2-3
Ashurstwood 'A' v Heath Pilgrims Reserves	0-2	Sovereign F. Res. v Dormansland Rockets	4-2

Semi-Finals

Clayton Res. v Cuckfield 'A'	3-2	Heath Pilgrims Res. v Dormansland Rockets	2-1

Final *(26/3/94)*: Clayton Reserves 3, Heath Pilgrims Reserves 2

PARSONS CHALLENGE CUP

First Round

Maresfield Village 'A' v Buxted 'A'	4-1	Barcombe Reserves v Dormansland Rockets	1-3
Hartfield Reserves v Plumpton Ath. 'A'	3-1	West Hoathly v Village of Ditchling 'A'	2-0
Chailey Res. v Horsted Keynes Reserves	2-3	Hayward Rangers v Rotherfield Reserves	4-7
Danehill Reserves v Handcross Vill. Res.	1-2	Wealden 'A' v Lingfield 'A'	3-0
Ashurstwood 'A' v Lewes Rovers 'A'	6-4	Ardingly Reserves v Jarvis Brook Res.	0-3

Second Round

Scaynes Hill Res. v Maresfield V. 'B'	0-3	Dormansland Rockets v Hartfield Reserves	4-0
West Hoathly Res. v Horsted Keynes Res.	1-4	Rotherfield Res. v Handcross Village Reserves	1-3
Balcombe Res. v Uckfield Town 'A'	4-0	Wealden 'A' v Fairwarp Reserves	4-3
Ashurstwood 'A' v Jarvis Brook Res.	4-3	Nutley Res. v Cuckfield 'A'	5-3

Quarter-Finals

Maresfield V. 'B' v Dormansland Rockets	1-3	Horsted Keynes Res. v Handcross Village Res.	0-2
Balcombe Res. *(scr)* Wealden Res. *(w/o)*		Ashurstwood 'A' v Nutley Reserves	0-0,0-2

Semi-Finals

Dormansland R. v Handcross V. Res.	3-1	Wealden 'A' v Nutley Reserves	0-7

Final *(13/4/94)*: Dormansland Rocket 7, Nutley Reserves 0

VETERANS' CUP

Second Round

Ardingly v Maresfield Village	4-6	Wisdom Sports v Hurstpierpoint	0-2
Lewes Rovers v Handcross Village	2-1	Hassocks v Southwater	2-0
Village of Ditchling *(bye)*.		Pease Pottage Village *(bye)*	
Bridgeview v Newick	2-2,2-7	Plumpton Athletic *(w/o)* Barcombe *(scr)*	

Quarter-Finals

Maresfield Village v Hurstpierpoint	3-1	Lewes Rovers v Hassocks	2-1
Vil. of Dit. v Pease Pottage Village	2-4	Newick v Plumpton Athletic	5-3

Semi-Finals

Maresfield Village v Hassocks	2-1	Pease Pottage Village v Newick	2-1

Final *(20/4/94)*: Maresfield Village 1, Pease Pottage Village 0

PREMIER DIVISION CLUBS 1994-95

CHAILEY

Secretary: Mr D Foord, Broomfields Farm Cottage, South Chailey, Lewes BN8 4QJ (0273 890085).
Ground: Chailey Rec. **Colours:** Amber/black/amber

CRAWLEY DOWN VILLAGE

Secretary: Mr A Watkins, 7 Brooklands Rd, Crawley RH11 9QQ (0293 514409).
Ground: Haven Spts Field, Hophurst Lane, Crawley Down **Colours:** White/red/red.

CUCKFIELD

Secretary: Mr P Brooks, 8 Views Path, Haywards Heath RH16 3SF (0444 456479).
Ground: Cuckfield Recreation Ground **Colours:** White/blue/blue.

EAST GRINSTEAD UNITED

Secretary: Mr K Brown, 26 Cromwell Place, East Grinstead RH19 4SD (0342 328623).
Ground: Kings Centre, Moat Rd, East Grinstead **Colours:** Blue & black/black/black.
Previous Name: Leftovers SC (pre-1994) **Previous League:** Sussex County

HANDCROSS VILLAGE

Secretary: Mr D Sinclair, 1 Percy Cottages, London Rd, Cuckfield, West Sussex (0444 417164).
Ground: Handcross Rec. **Colours:** Amber & black/black/black.

LEWES ROVERS

Secretary: Miss A Kerr, 19 Greenbank Ave., Saltdean BN2 8QS.
Ground: Cooksbridge Rec. **Colours:** All yellow.

MARESFIELD VILLAGE

Secretary: Mr T Gee, 1 Park View Rd, Uckfield TN22 1JP (0825 764496).
Ground: Maresfield Rec. **Colours:** White/blue/blue.

NUTLEY

Secretary: Mr K Funnell, 21 Selhurst Rd, Woolingdean, Brighton BN2 6WE (0273 308127).
Ground: Fords Green, Nutley. **Colours:** Red/black/red.

PEASE POTTAGE VILLAGE

Secretary: Mr R Cornock, 41 Selsey Rd, Broadfield, Crawley RH11 9HP (0293 515112).
Ground: Finches Field, Pease Pottage **Colours:** Green & white/black/green.

PLUMPTON ATHLETIC

Secretary: Mrs Chris Brimicombe, 13 Riddens Lane, Plumpton Green BN7 3BH.
Ground: King George VI PF, Plumpton **Colours:** Blue & white stripes/blue/red.

WEALDEN

Secretary: David Jenner, 10 Cleve Close, Framfield, Uckfield TN22 5PQ (0825 890632).
Ground: Framfield Rec., Uckfield **Colours:** White & blue/blue/white.

WISDOM SPORTS

Secretary: Mr B Menzies, 15 Augustines Way, Haywards Heath RH16 3JQ (0444 456016).
Ground: Victoria Park, Haywards Heath **Colours:** All red.

DIVISION ONE CLUBS 1994-95

ANSTY

Secretary: Mrs J Bealey, 34a Old Shoreham Rd, Brighton BN1 5DD (0273 883210).
Ground: Deaks Lane, Ansty (0444 454010) **Colours:** Yellow/blue/blue.

ASHURSTWOOD

Secretary: A Goold, 5 Chestnut Close, East Grinstead RH19 3UW (0342 317533).
Ground: Isle of Thorns, Chelwood Gate **Colours:** Red/black/red.

CLAYTON

Secretary: Mr John Bushell, Sunrise, 36 Victoria Close, Burgess Hill RH15 9QS (0444 245940).
Ground: Belmont Ground, Belmont Rd, Hassocks **Colours:** Red & blue/blue/blue.

FELBRIDGE

Secretary: Mr N McKnight, 47 Orchard Way, East Grinstead RH19 1Ay (0342 311831).
Ground: Crawley Down Rd, Felbridge **Colours:** Blue & white/blue/blue.

LINDFIELD

Secretary: Darren Parris, 36 Larch Way, Haywards Heath RH16 3TY (0444 415036).
Ground: Lindfield Common **Colours:** Green/white/green.

NEWICK

Secretary: Mrs J Brown, 1 Arkendale, Felbridge RH19 2QU (0342 313531).
Ground: King George V Rec., Newick **Colours:** White/blue/white.

UCKFIELD TOWN

Secretary: Mr I Bohemen, 32 Farriers Way, Uckfield TN22 5BY (0825 767781).
Ground: Victoria Pleasure Ground, Uckfield **Colours:** Black/blue/red.

VILLAGE OF DITCHLING

Secretary: Mrs J Jenner, 21 Blackthorns, Hurstpierpoint, West Sussex BN6 9TF (0273 833930).
Ground: Ditchling Rec., Lewes Rd, Ditchling (0273 843423) **Cols:** White (black/blue piping)/royal/white.

Plus the Reserve sides of: East Grinstead Utd, Hurstpierpoint (see page 679), Lindfield Rangers (see page 679), St Francis Hospital (page 680).

DIVISION TWO CLUBS 1994-95

ARDINGLY

Secretary: Mark Evans, 18 North Rd, Haywards Heath RH16 3NH (0403 273733).
Ground: Ardingly Rec. **Colours:** Blue & white/blue/blue.

BALCOMBE

Secretary: Mr C Tester, 145 St Marys Drive, Pound Hill, Crawley RH10 3BG (0293 537103).
Ground: Balcombe Rec. **Colours:** Gold/black/black.

BURGESS HILL ATHLETIC

Secretary: Mrs J Stringer, 169 Maple Drive, Burgess Hill, West Sussex RH15 8DE (0444 239079).
Ground: Janes Lane, Burgess Hill. **Colours:** All sky.

D.M.S. CUCKFIELD

Secretary: Mr M Robson, 14 Wheatsheaf Lane, Cuckfield RH17 5TZ (0444 441064).
Ground: Hickmans Lane *(or Whitemans Green)*, Cuckfield **Colours:** Green/white/green.

HEATH PILGRIMS

Secretary: Mr A Parsons, 16 Rumbolds Lane, Hayworth Heath RH16 4NY (0444 453729).
Ground: Victoria Park, Haywards Heath. **Colours:** Claret & grey/claret/grey.

HORLEY ATHLETICO

Secretary: Mr P Woodburn, 16 Michael Cres., Horley, Surrey RH6 7LH (0293 784668).
Ground: Horley Youth Centre, Court Lodge, Horley **Colours:** Red/black/black.

WEST HOATHLY

Secretary: Mr D Dibble, 37 Forest View Rd, East Grinstead RH19 4AW (0342 312797).
Ground: West Hoathly Rec. **Colours:** White & black stripes/black/black.

WIVELSFIELD GREEN

Secretary: Mr Justin Morris, 28 Brookway, Burgess Hill RH15 0LN (0444 245342).
Ground: Wivelsfield Green Rec. **Colours:** Green & black/black/green.

Plus the Reserve sides of: Buxted (see page 678), Hassocks *('A' team)*(page 675), Plumpton Ath., Wisdom Sports *(playing at Hickmans Lane, Lindfield).*

DIVISION THREE CLUBS 1994-95

COPTHORNE ROVERS

Secretary: Mr D McCarthy, 49 West Way, Copthorne RH10 3QS (0342 714700).
Ground: King George V PF, Copthorne. **Colours:** Yellow/black/black.

DANEHILL

Secretary: Mr R Smith, 64 Queens Rd, Haywards Heath, West Sussex (0444 455647).
Ground: Isle of Thorns, Chelwood Gate. **Colours:** Blue & yellow/blue/yellow.

FAIRWARP

Secretary: Mr J Lazenby, 'Androse', 19 Old Forge Lane, Fairwarp TN22 3EW (0825 712188).
Ground: Fairwarp Sports Field **Colours:** Green/white/green.

FOREST ROW

Secretary: Mrs E Lawrence, 67 Maypole Rd, Ashurstwood RH19 3RD (0342 824123).
Ground: Memorial Ground, Chapel Lane, Forest Row **Colours:** Yellow & green/yellow/yellow.

HORSTED KEYNES

Secretary: Mr A V Barker, 36 Challoners, Horsted Keynes RH17 7DT (0825 790036).
Ground: Horsted Keynes Rec. **Colours:** Blue & white/blue/blue.

PEACEHAVEN UNITED

Secretary: Mr A Mills, 90a Hoddern Ave., Peacehaven BN10 7QU (0273 585577).
Prev. Name: AFC Peacehaven (pre-1994) **Ground:** Sports Park, Piddington Avenue, Peacehaven.
Colours: Black & white stripes/black.

SOVEREIGN FINANCE

Secretary: Mr S Scoble, 14 Maple Drive, East Grinstead RH19 3UR (0342 323637).
Ground: East Court, East Grinstead **Colours:** Yellow (red sleeves)/yellow/red.

WOODCOCK ATHLETIC

Secretary: Mr S Duly, 'The Shieling', Woodcock Hill, Felbridge RH19 2RD (0342 410474).
Ground: St Piers School, St Piers Lane, Lingfield. **Cols:** Green (white trim)/green/green.

Plus the Reserve side of: Maresfield Village, **and the 'A' sides of:** Crowborough Ath. (page 668), East Grinstead Utd, Ringmer (page 671, *playing at Ringmer Community College).*

DIVISION FOUR CLUBS 1994-95

BARCOMBE

Secretary: Mr R Hepple, 20 Grantham Bank, Barcombe BN8 5DJ (0293 400576).
Ground: Barcombe Rec. **Colours:** Yellow & black stripes/black/yellow.

EAST GRINSTEAD MARINERS

Secretary: Mr R Connor, 'The Ship Inn', Ship Str., East Grinstead RH19 4EG (0342 312089).
Ground: Imberhorne Sch., Imberhorne Lane, East Grinstead **Colours:** White/black/black.

JARVIS BROOK

Secretary: Mr C Frampton, 11 Windsor Place, Jarvis Brook, Crowborough TN6 2HU (0892 661413).
Ground: Limekiln PF, Palesgate, Crowborough **Colours:** All green.

LEWES BRIDGEVIEW

Secretary: William Richards, 15 Beckett Way, Malling, Lewes BN7 2EB (0273 478215).
Ground: Malling Comm. Centre, Spences Lane, Lewes **Colours:** Orange & black/black/black.
Previous Name: Bridgeview (pre-1994).

ROTHERFIELD

Secretary: Mr R Paige, 8 Brook Cottages, New Rd, Rotherfield TN6 3JT (0892 852931).
Ground: Rotherfield Recreation Ground, Rotherfield **Colours:** Green/white/green.

TURNERS HILL

Secretary: Mr M Purcell, 24 Bourg de Peage Ave., East Grinstead RH19 3YE (0342 301323).
Ground: Turners Hill Rec. **Colours:** Claret/white/claret.

Plus the Reserve sides of: Ashurstwood *(playing at Hammerwood Rd Rec, Ashurst wood)*, Crawley Down Village, Cuckfield, Lewes Rovers, **and the 'A' sides of:** Franklands Village (page 678), St Francis Hospital (page 680).

DIVISION FIVE CLUBS 1994-95

GROOMBRIDGE

Secretary: Mr A Tamkin, 40 Erskine Park Rd, Rusthall, Tunbridge Wells, Kent TN4 8UR (0892 541041).
Ground: The Tanyard, Corsley Rd, Groombridge. **Colours:** Sky/navy/navy.

HARTFIELD

Secretary: Mr B Moore, 19 Post Horn Lane, Forest Row RH18 5DD (0342 823571).
Ground: Town Croft, Hartfield **Colours:** White/black/white.

Plus the Reserve sides of: Burgess Hill Ath., Clayton, DMS Cuckfield, Felbridge, Lindfield, Newick, Pease Pottage Village, Uckfield Town, Village of Ditchling, **and the 'A' side of:** Hurstpierpoint (page 679).

DIVISION SIX CLUBS 1994-95

DORMANSLAND ROCKETS

Secretary: Mr S Hendry, 43 St Leonards Park, East Grinstead, West Sussex (0342 321185).
Cols: Red & white stripes/black/black **Ground:** Colin Anderson PF, Wilderwick Rd, Lingfield

SCAYNES HILL

Secretary: Mr J Jeremiah, 7 Hillcrest Rd, Scaynes Hill RH17 7PJ (0444 831437).
Ground: Scaynes Hill Rec. **Colours:** Red/black/red.

Plus the Reserve sides of: Copthorne Rovers, Heath Pilgrims *(playing at Barn Cottage, Haywards Heath)*, Handcross Village, Sovereign Finance, Wealden, Wivelsfield Green, **and the 'A' side of:** Haywards Heath Town (page 679), Wisdom Sports *(playing at Hickmans Lane, Lindfield)*, **and the 'B' sides of:** East Grinstead Utd, Hassocks (page 675).

DIVISION SEVEN CLUBS 1994-95

STAXIL (BURGESS HILL)

Secretary: Mr C Rogers, 143 Maples Drive, Burgess Hill RH15 8DE (0444 243487).
Ground: Fairfield Rd Rec, Burgess Hill **Colours:** Green/black/green.

WOODGATE RANGERS

Secretary: Mr A White, 52 Stonefield Way, Burgess Hill RH15 8SG (0444 246237).
Ground: Mayhew, 5 Ash Down, Uckfield **Colours:** All blue.

Plus the Reserve sides of: Ansty, Chailey, Lewes Bridgeview, Nutley, Turners Hill, West Hoathly, **and the 'A' sides of:** Ashurstwood *(same ground as Reserves)*, Buxted (page 678, *playing at Highhurst Rec)*, Crawley Down Village, Cuckfield *(playing at Whitemans Green)*.

DIVISION EIGHT CLUBS 1994-95

The Reserve sides of: Ardingly, Barcombe, Danehill, Fairwarp, Hartfield, Horsted Keynes, **and the 'A' sides of:** Lindfield, Lindfield Rgrs (page 679), Maresfield Village *(playing at Blanchette Snooker Club, Eastbourne Rd, Uckfield)*, Plumpton Ath. *(playing at Plumpton College)*, Village of Ditchling, **and the 'B' sides of:** St Francis Hospital (page 680).

DIVISION NINE CLUBS 1994-95

HAYWARD RANGERS

Secretary: Mr M Sutherland, 19 Samphire Close, Broadfields, Crawley RH11 9EN (0293 618152).
Colours: Amber/blue/blue. **Ground:** Barn Cottage, Haywards Heath.

Plus the Reserve sides of: Balcombe, Forest Row, Jarvis Brook, Rotherfield, Scaynes Hill, **and the 'A' sides of:** Lewes Rovers *(playing at Convent Field)*, Lingfield (page 675), Uckfield Town, Wealden, **and the 'B' side of:** Crawley Down Village, Maresfield Village *(same ground as 'A' team)*.

MID-SUSSEX F.A. SENIOR CUP First Round

Lewes Rovers *(scr)* Roffey *(w/o)*
Heath Pilgrims v Buxted 0-2
East Grinstead Res. v Lindfield Rangers 2-0
Broadbridge Heath Reserves v Town Mead 3-0
Phoenix v Franklands Village 0-1
Crawley Down Village v Lingfield 1-3
Furnace Green v Horsham YMCA Reserves 1-3
Ringmer Reserves v Hurstpierpoint 1-2
Crowborough Athletic Reserves v Wealden 1-2
Copthorne Rovers v Maresfield Village 1-3

Second Round
Forest v Roffey 6-2
Nutley v Lingfield 4-2
Horsham YMCA Res. v Hassocks Reserves 2-3
Ansty v East Grinstead Reserves 1-4
Broadbridge Heath Reserves v Wealden 2-2
Maresfield Village v Burgess Hill T. Reserves 3-4
Clayton v Cuckfield 3-1
Cowfold v Haywards Heath Town 0-1
Longley v Southwater 2-4
Buxted v Newick 7-1
Thomas Bennett v Edwards Sports 2-7
Plumpton Athletic v Hurstpierpoint 1-3
Leftovers SC v Franklands Village 3-2
Ifield Reserves v Burgess Hill Athletic 6-0
Pease Pottage Village v Chailey 0-1
St Francis Hospital v Felbridge 2-1

Third Round
Forest v Southwater 1-0
Hassocks Reserves v Edwards Sports 2-2,1-0
Wealden v Leftovers SC 1-2
Clayton v Chailey 2-0
Nutley v Buxted 3-2
East Grinstead Reserves v Hurstpierpoint 2-3
Burgess Hill Town Reserves v Ifield Reserves 8-0
Haywards Heath Town v St Francis Hospital 1-2

Quarter-Finals
Forest v Nutley 2-1
Leftovers SC v Burgess Hill Town Res. 1-2
Hassocks Reserves v Hurtspierpoint 1-0
Clayton v St Francis Hospital 1-3

Semi-Finals
Forest v Hassocks Reserves 1-2
Burgess Hill T. Res. v St Francis Hospital 4-5

Final *(at Haywards Heath Town FC, Fri 13th May)*: St Francis Hospital 2, Hassocks Reserves 1

MID-SUSSEX F.A. JUNIOR CUP

First Round

Pease Pott. V. Res. v Maresfield V. Res. 2-2,4-1
Sovereign Finance v Longley Reserves 3-2
Hughes Rediffusion Res. v Town Mead 'A' 9-1
Horley Athletico *(w/o)* Hassocks 'A' *(scr)*
Barcombe v Nutley Reserves 3-1
Bolney Rovers v Ringmer 'A' 2-2,3-4
Phoenix 'A' v Copthorne Rovers Res. 1-0
Burgess Hill Ath. Res. v Uckfield Res. 1-2
Franklands Vill. 'A' v Leftovers SC 'A' 1-3
Ashurstwood Reserves v Lindfield Reserves 3-1
Newick Reserves v West Hoathly 2-7
Forest Row v Roffey 'A' 0-4
Cuckfield Reserves v DMS Cuckfield 0-9
Fairwarp v East Grinstead Mariners 3-5
East Grinstead 'A' v Turners Hill 9-0
Horsted Keynes v Wisdom Sports Res. 6-1
Crowborough Ath. 'A' v Horsham Olympic 'A' 4-0
Ardingly v Plumpton Athletic Reserves 0-2

Second Round

Hurstpierpoint Res. v Pease Pot. V. Res. 4-1
Sovereign Finance v Paymaster 6-0
West Hoathly v Hughes Rediffusion Res. 2-0
Horley Athletico v DMS Cuckfield 0-3
Southwater Reserves v Ringmer 'A' 1-4
Phoenix 'A' v Horsted Keynes 0-2
Cowfold Reserves v Youngmans 0-4
Leftovers SC 'A' v Crawley Dn V. Res. 5-2
Buxted Reserves v Ashurstwood Reserves 1-2
Woodcock Athletic v Wealden Reserves 4-0
Roffey Reserves v Lewes Rovers Reserves 5-3
Barcombe v East Grinstead Mariners 1-5
Danehill *(w/o)* East Grinstead 'A' *(scr)*
Rotherfield Reserves v Hartfield 1-7
Uckfield Town Res. v Crowborough Athletic 'A' 0-8
Balcombe v Plumpton Athletic Reserves 4-2

Second Round

Hurstpierpoint Res. v Ashurstwood Res. 1-2
West Hoathly v Roffey Reserves 1-2
Ringmer 'A' v Danehill 3-0
Youngmans v Crowborough Ath. 'A' 3-5
Sovereign Athletic v Woodcock Athletic 0-1
DMS Cuckfield v East Grinstead Mariners 5-2
Horsted Keynes v Hartfield 1-0
Leftovers SC 'A' v Balcombe 1-5

Quarter-Finals

Ashurstwood Res. v Woodcock Athletic 1-5
Ringmer 'A' v Horsted Keynes 4-0
Roffey Reserves v DMS Cuckfield 2-1
Crowborough Athletic 'A' v Balcombe 2-3

Semi-Finals

Woodcock Athletic v Roffey Res. 1-4
Ringmer 'A' *(scr)* Balcombe *(w/o)*

Final *(29/4/94)*: Balcombe beat Roffey Reserves 4-3 on penalties after 0-0 draw *(aet)*

UNIJET BRIGHTON, HOVE & DISTRICT LEAGUE

(Est. 1903)

PREM. DIV.	P	W	D	L	F	A	PTS
University of Sussex	18	16	1	1	46	13	49
AFC Falcons	18	12	4	2	53	21	40
Patcham (1903) FC	18	9	4	5	44	32	31
Rottingdean '89	18	8	2	8	39	41	26
Endsleigh	18	7	4	7	34	31	25
Midway	18	5	8	5	37	36	23
Brighton BBOB	18	4	6	8	32	33	18
Old Varndeanians	18	4	3	11	27	57	15
American Express	18	3	4	11	31	51	13
Legal & General	18	2	4	12	27	55	10

DIV. ONE	P	W	D	L	F	A	PTS
Rutland	18	12	3	3	43	32	39
Portslade Athletic	18	11	3	4	57	38	36
AFC Bensleys	18	11	3	4	47	38	36
Shakespears Hd Ath.	18	9	5	4	41	28	32
The Hollingbury	18	9	2	7	51	33	29
Preston Village	18	8	3	7	45	29	27
Brighton Insurance	18	5	4	9	32	41	19
Sussex County Rgrs	18	5	2	11	28	47	17
Ericsson	18	3	2	13	32	52	11
Hanover	18	1	5	12	26	55	8

DIV. TWO	P	W	D	L	F	A	PTS
International Factors	18	13	4	1	61	31	43
Barclays	18	12	2	4	68	34	38
Uni. of Sussex Res.	18	11	4	3	67	32	37
Alliance & Leicester	18	8	3	7	53	42	27
American Exp. Res.	18	8	2	8	37	48	26
Ultracolour	18	8	1	9	44	40	25
Hove County	18	7	3	8	35	36	24
Grenadier	18	5	5	8	40	67	20
Burgess Hill Ath.	18	4	4	10	26	38	16
Brighton Electricity	18	0	0	18	10	75	0

DIV. THREE	P	W	D	L	F	A	PTS
Madison Tigers	14	10	2	2	51	18	32
Adur Athletic	14	8	4	2	36	26	28
Saltdean Utd 'A'	14	7	3	4	34	27	24
Lower Bevendean	14	6	4	4	42	35	22
Rottingdean '89 Res.	14	6	1	7	28	27	19
Shoreham United	14	5	1	8	22	41	16
Brighton Rangers	14	4	2	8	20	32	14
Portslade Ath. Res.	14	0	3	11	25	52	3

DIV. FOUR	P	W	D	L	F	A	PTS
Montpelier Villa	14	12	1	1	50	10	37
Downs Athletic	14	9	1	4	49	28	28
Brighton Telephones	14	8	2	4	39	29	26
Brighton Sports	14	8	0	6	48	20	24
Clarendon Church	14	5	1	8	23	39	16
Midway Res.	14	5	1	8	25	52	16
Old Varndean. Res.	14	3	1	10	16	38	10
Sx County Rgrs Res.	14	2	1	11	13	53	7

DIV. FIVE	P	W	D	L	F	A	PTS
Hove Streamline Utd	18	13	2	3	75	27	41
The Mile	18	11	2	5	51	35	35
Prima	18	9	6	3	53	40	33
Lower Beven. Res.	18	9	2	7	49	42	29
Legal & Gen. Res.	18	8	4	8	42	32	28
Burgess Hill A. Res.	18	7	3	8	36	32	24
Brighton Rgrs Res.	18	6	2	10	35	55	20
Brighton BBOB Res.	18	4	5	9	31	46	17
Portslade Ath. 'A'	18	4	4	10	23	46	16
Erib ETL	18	2	4	12	30	57	10

DIV. SIX	P	W	D	L	F	A	PTS
Jaycee Sports	16	12	4	0	65	16	40
Woodingdean (Sat)	16	13	1	2	45	23	40
Southern Rgrs OB	16	10	3	3	47	22	33
Rottingdean '89 'A'	16	10	2	4	39	23	32
Marrion	16	6	3	7	47	37	21
Bupa	16	4	2	10	30	64	14
Brighton Tele. Res.	16	3	2	11	31	64	11
Shoreham Utd Res.	16	2	4	10	23	41	10
Brighton Elec. Res.	16	0	3	13	13	50	3

DIV. SEVEN	P	W	D	L	F	A	PTS
Seaford Town 'A'	14	13	0	1	82	12	39
Lion & Unicorn	14	10	1	3	53	17	31
Norton Wanderers	14	7	3	4	52	43	24
American Express 'A'	14	6	3	5	42	41	21
Sussex Panthers	14	5	1	8	34	51	16
Sx County Rgrs 'A'	14	5	0	9	28	53	15
B'ton Insurance Res.	14	3	0	11	25	70	9
Legal & General 'A'	14	2	2	10	15	44	8

UNIJET WEST SUSSEX LEAGUE

PREM. DIVISION	P	W	D	L	F	A	PTS
South Bersted	22	17	3	2	55	20	37
Roffey	22	14	5	3	55	20	33
London & E Sports	22	12	6	4	49	25	30
Lancing United	22	12	6	4	46	28	30
North Holmwood	22	10	7	5	52	41	27
Claymore Swan	22	8	6	8	45	35	22
Steyning Old Gr.	22	6	5	11	49	59	17
SB Sports	22	6	5	11	38	62	17
Rustington	22	4	7	11	34	44	15
Cowfold	22	4	7	11	32	49	15
Barns Green	22	4	4	14	23	63	12
Ferring	22	1	7	14	15	47	9

DIVISION ONE	P	W	D	L	F	A	PTS
Chichester Hosp.	24	22	1	1	93	21	45
Oving SC	24	17	2	5	104	32	36
Wittering	24	15	2	7	67	35	32
Ifield Reserves	24	14	4	6	44	38	32
Milland	24	10	6	8	43	42	26
Warnham	24	10	5	9	47	46	25
Horsham Olympic	24	10	5	9	31	33	25
Stedham	24	9	6	9	68	53	24
Billingshurst	24	6	5	13	35	48	17
Henfield	24	7	3	14	31	56	17
Emsworth	24	6	4	14	40	55	16
Old Collyerians	24	5	3	16	30	75	13
Lurgashall	24	1	2	21	18	117	4

DIV. 2 SOUTH	P	W	D	L	F	A	PTS
Rogate	26	24	1	1	85	24	49
The Ship	26	17	3	6	74	38	37
Bracklesham	26	15	5	6	78	45	35
Maple Leaf Rgrs	26	16	2	8	70	40	34
Sth Bersted Res.	26	14	5	7	66	39	33
Clymping	26	15	2	9	63	43	32
Angmering	26	12	4	10	62	48	28
Worthing BCOB	26	10	3	13	47	55	23
Liss Athletic	26	9	4	13	49	66	22
Lancing Utd Res.	26	7	6	13	58	68	20
Rustington Res.	26	7	4	15	44	80	18
Eastergate	26	7	2	17	48	79	16
Sidlesham Res.	26	4	5	17	39	74	13
Lavant	26	2	0	21	26	110	4

DIV. 2 NORTH	P	W	D	L	F	A	PTS
Alford	22	17	2	3	74	20	36
Shipley	22	13	8	1	52	23	34
Sunallon Res.	22	14	3	5	63	29	31
Ashington Rovers	22	12	4	6	56	37	28
Ciba-Geigy	22	8	8	6	35	34	24
Capel	22	9	3	10	44	41	21
Petworth	22	7	6	9	45	53	20
Partridge Green	22	6	5	11	46	56	17
Horsham Baptists	22	5	6	11	25	45	16
Nth Holmwood Res.	22	5	6	11	31	59	16
Northchapel S.	22	6	2	14	55	82	14
Wisborough Gn	22	3	1	18	29	76	7

DIV. 3 CENTRAL	P	W	D	L	F	A	PTS
Fittleworth	20	16	1	3	62	28	33
Fernhurst	20	14	4	2	59	28	32
Alfold Res.	20	13	2	5	51	34	28
Harting	20	10	5	5	67	28	25
Pulborough	20	10	4	6	78	32	24
Lodsworth	20	10	2	8	50	33	22
Barns Green Res.	20	8	2	10	37	62	18
Milland Res.	20	3	6	11	34	50	12
East Dean	20	4	3	13	40	75	11
Shipley Res.	20	3	4	13	33	66	10
Stedham Res.	20	1	3	16	24	99	5

DIV. 3 SOUTH	P	W	D	L	F	A	PTS
Southbourne Spts	20	18	0	2	101	26	36
Oving SC Res.	20	11	9	2	51	30	31
Hunston United	20	12	3	5	75	38	27
Ford United	20	9	6	5	70	38	24
Slindon	20	9	3	8	51	55	21
East Preston 'A'	20	6	8	6	34	42	20
Bilsham United	20	6	4	10	48	64	16
Ferring Res.	20	5	4	11	28	57	14
Yapton	20	5	3	12	37	71	13
Amberley	20	4	5	11	26	61	13
Emsworth Res.	20	4	0	16	36	81	8

DIV. 3 NORTH	P	W	D	L	F	A	PTS
Roffey Res.	22	14	6	2	57	23	34
Cranleigh 'A'	22	15	4	3	62	30	34
Rudgwick	22	12	5	5	57	25	29
Forest Res.	22	10	7	5	54	32	27
Slinfold	22	10	3	9	66	36	23
Horsham Trinity	22	10	2	10	47	45	22
Ockley	22	9	4	9	42	54	22
Sunallon 'A'	22	6	5	11	36	52	17
East End United	22	3	9	10	31	61	15
Seelec Delta	22	6	3	13	29	66	15
Broadbrigh H. 'A'	22	6	2	14	34	53	14
Warnham Res.	22	4	4	14	30	68	12

DIV. 4 NORTH	P	W	D	L	F	A	PTS
Faygate	24	21	3	0	97	16	45
Seelec Delta Res.	24	19	1	4	109	24	39
Rusper Village	24	13	4	7	70	55	30
Newdigate	24	13	3	8	61	59	29
Partridge G. Res.	24	9	7	8	46	51	25
Friends Provident	24	11	2	11	54	49	24
Henfield Res.	24	12	0	12	56	60	24
Cowfold Res.	24	9	4	11	50	58	22
Capel Res.	24	8	4	12	40	64	20
Horsham Ol. Res.	24	7	5	12	46	74	19
Roffey Athletic	24	6	3	15	44	68	15
Bell Spartans	24	5	3	16	41	87	13
East End	24	2	3	19	29	78	7

DIV. 4 CENTRAL	P	W	D	L	F	A	PTS
W. Chiltington	22	18	2	2	86	19	38
Upper Beeding	22	17	2	3	85	27	36
Graffham	22	14	4	4	55	22	32
Loxwood	22	12	3	7	65	33	*25
Fittleworth Res.	22	9	5	8	55	44	23
Billinghurst Res.	22	8	5	9	51	61	21
Watersfield	22	10	1	11	52	67	21
Pulborough Res.	22	7	5	10	48	61	19
Lodsworth	22	6	6	10	39	54	18
Rudgwick Res.	22	5	2	15	18	43	12
Plaistow & K.	22	4	3	15	27	76	11
Fernhurst Res.	22	1	4	17	35	109	6

DIV. 4 SOUTH	P	W	D	L	F	A	PTS
Sth Bersted 'A'	20	14	6	2	60	25	34
Angmering Res.	20	14	4	4	58	34	32
Thatched Vill.	20	10	6	6	56	49	26
Rustington 'A'	20	10	6	6	52	36	*25
Wittering Res.	20	10	3	9	39	40	23
Broadwater S.	20	9	2	11	55	47	20
Corinthians	20	8	4	10	58	85	20
Chich. Hos. Res.	20	8	3	11	44	45	19
Clymping Res.	20	9	1	12	56	59	19
Boxgrove	20	7	4	11	49	58	18
Watersfield Res.	20	6	4	12	45	52	16

DIV. 5 SOUTH	P	W	D	L	F	A	PTS
Angmering 'A'	22	18	3	1	93	17	39
GCRI	22	18	2	2	81	29	38
Ambassadors	22	15	3	4	81	35	33
Southbourne Res.	22	14	3	5	102	40	31
Bilsham Utd Res.	22	13	1	8	71	41	27
Liss Ath. Res.	22	10	2	10	56	40	22
Boxgrove Res.	22	8	2	12	53	64	18
Yapton Res.	22	8	2	12	54	82	18
AW Mundham	22	5	2	15	59	86	12
Petworth Res.	22	3	6	13	40	81	12
Amberley Res.	22	5	1	16	50	88	11
Lavant Res.	22	1	1	20	23	160	3

(tables continued overleaf)

DIV. 5 CENTRAL	P	W	D	L	F	A	PTS
Cocking	24	17	6	1	107	34	40
Rogate Res.	24	17	3	4	73	33	37
Alford 'A'	24	15	5	4	109	36	35
Ashington R. Res.	24	11	6	7	61	44	28
Wisborough G. Res.	24	11	5	8	64	52	27
Barns Green 'A'	24	10	7	7	55	54	*25
Billingshurst 'A'	24	8	5	11	54	48	21
Northchapel Res.	24	8	5	11	65	78	21
Kirdford	24	9	1	14	58	79	19
Horsham Bapt. Res.	24	7	4	13	50	85	18
Ambassadors Res.	24	6	5	13	55	73	17
Graffham Res.	24	6	5	13	58	81	17
Petworth 'A'	24	2	1	21	32	144	5

DIV. 5 NORTH	P	W	D	L	F	A	PTS
Nth Holmwood Res.	26	23	1	2	93	23	47
Roffey 'A'	26	18	3	5	80	26	39
Horsham Bapt. 'A'	26	15	5	6	77	53	35
Horsham OS	26	12	7	7	60	49	31
Horsham Olympic 'A'	26	14	3	9	45	43	31
Slinfold Res.	26	12	6	8	51	39	30
Forest 'A'	26	11	5	10	41	50	27
Ockley Res.	26	10	5	11	67	76	25
O Colleyerians Res.	26	9	2	15	58	60	20
Ciba-Geigy Res.	26	7	4	15	52	82	18
Sunallon 'A'	26	7	3	16	37	55	17
Partridge G. 'A'	26	7	2	17	53	73	16
Broadbridge Hth 'B'	26	7	1	18	41	77	15
Horsham Trinity Res.	26	3	7	16	35	84	13

* - points adjusted

Malcolm Simmonds Cup: Roffey
Chichester City Cup: Maple Rgrs
Bareham Trophy: Southbourne Spts
Tony Kopp: Upper Beeding
Div. 3 Cup: Forest Res.
Div. 4 Cup: Faygate
Div. 5 Cup: Angmering.

CLUB DIRECTORY

A.W. MUNDHAM
Secretary: A Clarke, 54 Windsor Rd, Chichester PO19 2XL (0243 774609).
Ground: Oaklands Park, Chichester. **Colours:** White.

ALFORD
Secretary: A Erricker, Pond Cottage, Loxwood Rd, Alford, Cranleigh, Surrey GU6 8HP (0483 752317).
Ground: Alford Spts Ground (0483 753132). **Colours:** White *(Res: red)*

AMBASSADORS
Secretary: Mrs M J Pink, 34 Kendal Close, Littlehampton, West Sussex BN17 6SZ (0903 731820).
Ground: Avisford Park, Rose Green, Bognor Regis. **Colours:** Royal blue.

AMBERLEY
Secretary: Mrs S M Joad, 63 White Horses Way, Littlehampton BN17 6NJ (0903 722232).
Ground: Storrington Rd, Amberley. **Colours:** Yellow.

ANGMERING
Secretary: G Anscombe, 5 Mill Close, Rustington, Littlehampton BN16 3HR (0903 776886).
Ground: Palmer Rd Rec., Angmering Village **Colours:** Red

ASHINGTON ROVERS
Secretary: R M Vine, 91 Stone Lane, Worthing, West Sussex BN13 2BD (0903 267047).
Ground: Church Lane Rec., Ashington. **Colours:** Blue.

BARNS GREEN
Secretary: D J Strudwick, 25 Hornbeam Close, Horsham RH13 5NP RG4 0RD (0403 66718).
Ground: Barns Green PF, Horsham (Southwater 730473) **Colours:** Yellow *(Res: red)*.

BELL SPARTANS
Secretary: M Foreman, 61 Pilgrims Walk, West Worthing BN13 1RJ (0903 692900).
Ground: Horsham Park (0403 68561). **Colours:** Red & black stripes

BILLINGSHURST
Secretary: D S Glaysher, 10 Groomsland Drive, Billingshurst RH14 9HA (Billingshurst 782300).
Ground: Station Rd (Res & 'A' Lower Station Rd), Billingshurst. **Cols:** Blue & white stripes.

BILSHAM UNITED
Secretary: A K Misselbrook, Walene, Bilsham Rd, Yapton, Arundel BN18 0JN (0903 552715).
Grnd: King George V PF, Yapton (res: Southfields Rec., Littlehampton). **Cols:** Blue & white stripes.

BOXGROVE
Secretary: D R Westbrook, 1 The Glebe, Tangmere, Chichester PO20 6HD (0243 775546).
Ground: Boxgrove Spts Field, The Street, Boxgrove (0243 786611). **Colours:** Yellow *(Res: navy)*

BRACKLESHAM
Secretary: T I Sadler, 19 Saxon Meadow, Tangmere, Chichester PO20 6GA (0243 784052)
Ground: Stocks Lane, East Wittering **Colours:** Green.

BROADWATER SAINTS
Secretary: B Harris, 37 Twyford Rd, Worthing BN13 2NP (0903 260274).
Ground: Broadwater Green, Ardsheal Rd, Worthing **Colours:** Green.

CAPEL
Secretary: Mrs S Burlinson, 24 Littlehaven Lane, Roffey, Horsham RH12 4JA (0403 68930).
Ground: Recreation Grnd, The Street, Capel, Dorking, Surrey **Colours:** Yellow.

CHICHESTER HOSPITALS
Secretary: J Edwards, 78 Chatsworth Rd, Chichester PO19 2YJ (0243 533269).
Ground: Sports Field, Graylingwell Hospital **Colours:** Black & white stripes *(Res: red)*.

CIBA-GEIGY
Secretary: A Crisp, Computer Services, Ciba-Geigy, Wimblehurst Rd, Horsham RH12 3LD (0403 52273).
Grnd: Ciba-Geigy Spts & Social Club, Parsonage Rd, Horsham (0403 60943) **Colours:** Blue.

CLYMPING
Secretary: Mrs J Bethell, 17 Potters Mead, Wick, Littlehampton BN17 7HZ (0903 715423).
Ground: Church Lane, Clymping (0903 724877). **Colours:** Blue *(Res: red)*.

COCKING
Secretary: D P Waller, 25 The Croft, Cocking, Midhurst GU29 0HQ (Midhurst 814440).
Ground: Bell Lane, Covking. **Colours:** Red

CORINTHIANS

Secretary: J Shacklady, 23 Wainscott Rd, Southsea, Portsmouth, Hants PO4 9NN (0705 730198).
Grnd: Bourne Comm. School, Park Rd, Southbourne **Cols:** Amber.

COWFOLD

Secretary: Mrs D E Brockbank, 2 Oakfield Cottages, Bolney Rd, Cowfold, Horsham RH13 8AA (0403 864498).
Ground: Cowfold Rec, Bolney Rd, Cowfold. **Colours:** Navy blue

EAST DEAN

Secretary: P A Cooper, 1 Park Farm Cottages, Racton, Chichester PO18 9DP (0903 374278).
Ground: Gasson Meadow, East Dean (Singleton 750) **Colours:** Blue.

EAST END UNITED

Secretary: N D Painting, 113 Heath Way, Horsham RH12 5XQ (0403 55723).
Grnd: Bennetts Field PF, Horsham **Colours:** Black & white stripes *(Res: Sky & white stripes).*

EASTERGATE UNITED

Secretary: A Ebling, 12 Park Rd, Yapton, Arundel BN18 0JE (0903 863161).
Ground: Eastergate Rec., Eastergate, Chichester **Colours:** Red *(Res: blue).*

EMSWORTH

Secretary: L Wade, 2 Cumberland Ave., Emsworth, Hants PO10 7UH (Emsworth 375526).
Grnd: Horndean Rd Rec, Emsworth (Emsworth 372330). **Cols:** Black & white stripes *(Res: red)*

FERNHURST SPORTS

Secretary: G Puttick, Raemar, Hill House Hill, Headley Rd, Liphook, Hants GU30 7PX (Liphook 723347).
Grnd: Church Rd Rec, Fernhurst (Haslemere 642302). **Colours:** Green *(Res: red).*

FERRING

Secretary: Malcolm Gamien, 46 Sunningdale Rd, Durrington, Worthing BN12 2NE (0903 263655).
Ground: Glebelands, Greystoke Rd, Ferring (0903 53618). **Colours:** Blue.

FITTLEWORTH

Secretary: G B Rapson, 6 Greatpin Croft, Fittleworth, Pulborough RH20 1HX (Fittleworth 470).
Ground: Fittleworth Rec (Fittleworth 781) **Colours:** Green.

FORD UNITED

Secretary: K M Fletcher, PE Dept, HM Prison Ford, Arundel BN18 0BX.
Ground: H.M. Prison, Ford. **Colours:** Red.

FRIENDS' PROVIDENT

Secretary: D Spence, Flat 4, Simons Ct, Station Approach, Leatherhead, Surrey KT22 7TE (0372 386165).
Ground: Pixham End, Pixham Lane Dorking (0306 889020) **Colours:** Sky blue.

GLASSHOUSE CROPS RESEARCH INSTITUTE

Sec: T J Elliott, Horticulture Res. International, Worthing Rd, Littlehampton BN17 6LP (0903 715804)
Ground: Southfields Rec, Littlehampton. **Colours:** Red & black stripes

GRAFFHAM

Secretary: C Cobbold, 1 Hurlands Cottages, Selham, Petworth (Lodsworth 605).
Ground: Graffham Rec. **Colours:** Black & white stripes *(Res: white).*

HARTING

Secretary: D G Matthews, 51 Madeline Rd, Petersfield, Hants GU31 4AL (0730 60715).
Ground: War Memorial PF, South Harting **Colours:** White (green pinstripes)

HENFIELD ATHLETIC

Secretary: R Knight, 9 Lower Faircox, Henfield BN5 9UT (Henfield 492293).
Ground: Henfield Common (Henfield 492990) **Colours:** Red.

HORSHAM BAPTISTS

Secretary: Miss J R Nichols, 71 Clarence Rd, Horsham RH13 5SL (0403 53498).
Ground: Horsham Park (0403 68561) **Colours:** White.

HORSHAM OLYMPIC

Secretary: W H Lipyeat, 6 Swindon Rd, Horsham RH12 2HD (0403 51274).
Ground: Dutchell's Copse, Rusper Rd, Horsham **Colours:** Green *(Res: red).*

HORSHAM TRINITY

Secretary: B Knight, 9 Sycamore Ave., Roffey, Horsham RH12 4TP (0403 56046).
Ground: Victory Rd Rec, Horsham. **Colours:** Green *(Res: sky).*

HUNSTON UNITED

Secretary: R Netley, 51 Leodgars Way, Hunston, Chichester PO20 2PE (0243 786073).
Ground: Main Road, Hunston, Chichester. **Colours:** Black & white hoops

LANCING UNITED

Secretary: R D George, 12a Freshbrook Rd, Lancing BN15 8BL (0903 761879).
Ground: Croshaw Ground, Bounstone Lane, Lancing **Colours:** Gold.

LAVANT

Secretary: S J Massey, 57 Garland Square, Tangmere, Chichester PO20 6JF (0243 532730).
Ground: Lavant Village Green *(Res: Raughmere Park, Lavant).* **Colours:** Yellow.

LISS ATHLETIC

Secretary: A Ridding, Imberdown, Woodlands, Liss, Hants GU33 7EZ (Liss 894007).
Ground: Newman Collard PF, Hill Brow Rd, Liss (Liss 894022). **Colours:** Yellow.

LODSWORTH

Secretary: G Boardman, 6 Yew Tree Place, Liss, Hants GU33 7ET (Liss 893773).
Ground: Lodsworth Rec (Lodsworth 583) **Colours:** Blue (amber trim)*(Res: Yellow (blue trim)*

LONDON & EDINBURGH SPORTS

Secretary: P Stone, Windsor Cottage, Mouse Lane, Steyning BN44 3DG (0903 879800).
Grnd: The Warren, Warren Rd, Worthing - entrance Hill Barn Lane (0903 201323) **Cols:** Blue

LOXWOOD

Secretary: R Blackwell, 7 Forge Way, Billingshurst, RH14 9LJ (Billingshurst 783439).
Ground: Flitchfold, Plaistow Rd, Loxwood (Loxwood 753185) **Colours:** White.

LURGASHALL

Secretary: Mrs A E Wilson, 10 Greengate Cottages, Lurgashall, Petworth GU28 9ES (Northchapel 683).
Ground: Glebe Rd, Lurgashall **Colours:** Red.

MAPLE LEAF RANGERS

Secretary: P Cotten, 22 Cypress Ave., Worthing BN13 3PS (0903 268476).
Grnd: Worthing Leisure Centre, Shaftesbury Ave., Worthing (0903 502237) **Colours:** White.

MILLAND

Secretary: G Bray, 12 Carterlands Corner, Milland, Liphook, Hants (Milland 203).
Grnd: Spts Grnd, North End Cross Rds, Milland, Liphook, Hants **Cols:** Red *(Res: blue & white)*

NEWDIGATE

Secretary: A Roberts, 10 Nursery Close, Markham Park, Capel, Dorking, Surrey RH5 5JU (0306 711585).
Ground: Brows Field, Trigg Str., Newdigate, Dorking (Newdigate 566) **Colours:** White & blue.

NORTHCHAPEL SPORTS

Secretary: D G Dabbs, 13 Valentines Lea, Northchapel, Petworth GU28 9HY (Northchapel 721).
Grnd: Northchapel Village Green **Cols:** Wine *(Res: Sky & navy stripes)*.

NORTH HOLMWOOD

Secretary: E E Adams, 24 Carterdale Cottages, Capel, Dorking, Surrey RH5 5ES (0306 712395).
Grnd: Meadowbank Rec, Mill Lane Dorking *(Res: Big Fld, Kiln Lane Brockam)* **Cols:** Yellow *(Res: sky)*.

OCKLEY

Secretary: L P Figg, Village Hall Cottage, Stane Str., Ockley, Dorking, Surrey RH5 5SY (0306 712408).
Ground: The Village Green, Stane Lane, Ockley **Colours:** White.

OLD COLLYERIANS

Secretary: D P Bussey, 35 Goose Green Chase, Horsham RH12 5ZX (0403 69575).
Ground: Collyers VI Form Coll., Hurst Rd, Horsham **Cols:** Blue & black stripes *(Res: red)*.

OVING SOCIAL CLUB

Secretary: R G C Dorey, 19 High View Rd, Eastergate, Chichester PO20 6XB (0243 542086).
Ground: Village PF, Highfield Lane, Oving, Chichester **Colours:** Silver *(Res: tangerine)*

PARTRIDGE GREEN

Secretary: J G Gamble, 8 Little Oak, Partridge Green, Horsham RH13 8JY (0403 710598).
Grnd: King George V PF, Partridge Gn *('A': Ashurst Rec, School Lane, Ashurst)* **Cols:** Green & white

PETWORTH

Secretary: K A Lintill, 22 Littlecote, Petworth GU28 0EF (Petworth 42948).
Grnd: Petworth Pk, Midhurst Rd (Petworth 43743) **Cols:** Red & black stripes *('A': White (black trim)*

PLAISTOW

Secretary: A Simmonds, Boughs, Rickmans Lane, Plaistow, Billinghurst RH14 0NT (Plaistow 344).
Ground: Floxfield, Plaistow **Colours:** Blue *(Res: yellow)*.

PULBOROUGH

Secretary: C Cox, 8 Cousins Way, Pulborough RH20 2TB (Pulborough 875127).
Ground: Rectory Lane Rec, Pulborough (Pulborough 873020) **Colours:** Red.

ROFFEY

Secretary: V A Searle, 46 Bostock Ave., Roffey, Horsham (0403 62387).
Grnd: Roffey Rec, Leith View Rd, Horsham (0403 60775)*('A': Bennetts Rd PF, Horsham)* **Cols:** Blue

ROFFEY ATHLETIC

Secretary: S P Reeves, 2 Rangers Lodge, Oakhill Rd, Horsham RH13 5LF (0403 53178).
Ground: Horsham Park (0403 68561) **Colours:** White.

ROGATE

Secretary: P H Collins, 6 Terwick Rise, Rogate, Petersfield, Hants GU31 5DE (0730 821456).
Ground: North Street Rec, Rogate, Petersfield (0730 821347) **Colours:** Maroon

RUDGWICK

Secretary: J Houston, 15 The Copse, Southwater, Horsham RH13 7UG (Southwater 732620).
Ground: King George V Playing Field, Bucks Green **Colours:** White *(Res: claret & blue)*

RUSPER VILLAGE

Secretary: R Harlow, Elsinore, Horsham Rd, Rusper, Horsham RH12 4PR (0293 871495).
Ground: Rusper PF, High Str., Rusper **Colours:** Blue & white stripes.

RUSTINGTON

Secretary: G F Hixon, 2 Jubilee Ave., Littlehampton BN16 3NB (0903 787436).
Grnd: Jubilee Avenue Rec, Rustington (0903 770495) **Colours:** Blue

S.B. SPORTS

Secretary: K T Yeates, 101 Upton Rd, Worthing BN13 1BY (0903 262818).
Ground: S.B. Ground, Dominion Way, Worthing **Colours:** Blue & white.

SEELEC DELTA

Secretary: B F Burdfield, 13 Fairfield Drive, Dorking, Surrey RH4 1JQ (0306 884260).
Ground: Seeboard Spts Grnd, London Rd, Dorking **Colours:** Blue *(Res: yellow)*.

SHIPLEY

Secretary: R Jones, 20 Beechings, Henfield, BN5 9XB (Henfield 493027).
Ground: Dragons Green, Shipley (on A272) **Colours:** Red *(Res: Yellow)*

SLINDON

Secretary: Mrs K Collier, 10 Woodgate Park, Woodgate, Chichester PO20 6QP (0243 545154).
Ground: Mill Rd Rec, Slindon. **Colours:** Blue

SLINFOLD

Secretary: A Haines, 11 Charrington Way, Broadbridge Heath, Horsham RH12 3TJ (0403 56250).
Ground: Cherry Tree Farm, Hayes Lane, Slinfold **Colours:** Red & black.

SOUTH BERSTED

Secretary: P Curran, 4 Shearwater Drive, North Bersted, Bognor Regis PO22 9QP (0243 830008).
G: Jubilee PF, Chalcraft Lane, Nth Bersted *('A': Hampshire Ave, Bognor)* **C:** Red *(Res: white, 'A': blue)*

SOUTHBOURNE SPORTS

Secretary: D Wiesner, 41 Elm Park Rd, Havant, Hants PO9 2AD (0705 475948).
Ground: Bourne Park, Park Rd, Southbourne **Colours:** Sky *(Res: green).*

SOUTHWATER

Secretary: Mrs Lynda McPherson, Hopedene, Green Close, Southwater RH13 7HA (0403 730265).
Ground: Village Centre, Pevensey Rd *(or Church Lane)* **Colours:** Red & black/black/red.

STEDHAM UNITED

Secretary: G Baigent, c/o Stedham Collins & Spts Club, The Street, Stedham, Midhurst (0730 813458).
Ground: Sports Field, Stedham (0730 813458) **Colours:** Claret (Blue trim)*(Res: blue)*

STEYNING OLD GRAMMARIANS

Secretary: Mrs M J Bryant, 5 Thornscroft, Steyning BN44 3RP (0903 815824).
Ground: Steyning Grammar School, Shooting Field, Steyning **Colours:** Blue.

SWAN

Secretary: R Warner, 55 Woodlea Rd, Worthing (0903 203910).
Ground: Northbrook Park, Carisbrook Rd, Worthing **Colours:** Green, white & black.

TAVERN VILLA

Secretary: M Davies, 15 Sycamore Rd, North Bersted, Bognor Regis PO22 9LD (0243 862322).
Ground: West Meads PF, West Meads, Bognor Regis **Colours:** Blue & white stripes.

UPPER BEEDING

Secretary: R Patmore, 36 Saltings Way, Upper Beeding, Steyning BN44 3JH (0903 814560).
Ground: Memorial PF, High Str., Upper Beeding **Colours:** Yellow.

WARNHAM

Secretary: N P Taylor, 8 Vale Drive, Horsham RH12 2JX (0403 58765).
Ground: Warnham Court Sch., Church Str., Warnham **Colours:** Sky *(Res: claret & blue).*

WATERSFIELD

Secretary: N Lamb, 123 Clun Rd, Littlehampton BN17 7EP (0903 714304).
Ground: Alban Head PF, Watersfield **Colours:** Blue

WEST CHILTINGTON

Secretary: J T Jones, Quincys, Mill Rd, West Chiltington, Pulborough RH20 2PZ (0903 812371).
Ground: Mill Rd Rec, West Chiltington **Colours:** White *(Res: blue).*

WISBOROUGH GREEN

Secretary: T Fallows, Stane House, Kirdford Rd, Wisborough Green RH14 0DD (Wisborough Green 700283).
Grnd: Wisborough Green Village Green (Wisborough Green 700474) **Colours:** Green & white hoops

WITTERING UNITED

Secretary: D W Vine, 23 Mill Gardens, West Wittering, Chichester PO20 8PR (0243 672600).
Ground: Sports Field, Rookwood Rd, West Wittering **Colours:** Red.

WORTHING BOYS CLUB OLD BOYS

Secretary: Mrs S Woolgar, 21 Acacia Ave., Worthing BN13 2JB (0903 266519).
Ground: The Bowl, Pond Lane, Worthing **Colours:** Red.

YAPTON

Secretary: Mrs B Goss, 81 Hazel Rd, Bognor Regis (0243 866741).
Ground: King George V PF, Yapton, Arundel **Colours:** Red *(Res: red & blue stripes)*

Brighton & Hove Albion Reserves - Sussex Senior Cup winners 1993-94. *Photo - Gavin Ellis-Neville.*

EAST SUSSEX LEAGUE

(Est: 1896)

PREM. DIV.	P	W	D	L	F	A	PTS
Hollington United	18	15	2	1	66	22	47
Rock-a-Nore	18	13	1	4	68	31	40
Wadhurst United	18	11	5	2	59	33	38
Bodiam	18	9	2	7	37	35	29
Polegate	18	9	4	5	44	33	*28
Wadhurst TOC H	18	7	3	8	52	49	24
Punnetts Town	18	4	6	8	20	35	x21
Burwash	18	4	2	12	20	42	14
E'bourne Fishermen	18	2	3	13	22	59	9
Herstmonceux	18	1	2	15	26	75	5

* - 3 points deducted x - 3 points awarded

DIV. ONE	P	W	D	L	F	A	PTS
Rye United Res.	18	11	7	0	51	26	40
Icklesham Casuals	18	11	3	4	41	22	36
Willingdon	18	11	2	5	34	19	35
Shinewater A. Res.	18	8	2	8	34	26	26
Westfield	18	8	1	9	42	33	25
Langney Spts 'A'	18	6	7	5	33	34	25
Ninfield United	18	7	3	8	32	41	24
Hawkhurst United	18	5	3	10	28	39	18
Sandhurst	18	3	3	12	18	44	12
The JC Tackleway	18	3	3	12	33	62	12

DIV. TWO	P	W	D	L	F	A	PTS
Ticehurst	20	17	1	2	70	17	52
E'b. Rose & Crown	20	14	4	2	57	16	46
Peche Hill Select	20	11	5	4	52	28	38
Cranbrook Town	20	7	8	5	31	30	29
Mountfield United	20	7	2	11	39	52	23
Claverham	20	7	2	11	28	51	23
Mayfield	20	6	3	11	38	43	21
Northiam '75	20	6	3	11	33	63	21
Old Hastonians	20	5	5	10	36	62	20
Hastings Rangers	20	6	1	13	26	34	19
Magham Down	20	3	8	9	27	41	17

DIV. THREE	P	W	D	L	F	A	PTS
Pebsham-Sibex	20	17	3	0	81	25	54
Robertsbridge Utd	20	14	4	2	66	35	46
Old Centmodians	20	12	1	7	50	37	37
Hollington Utd Res.	20	11	3	6	73	43	36
Hillcrest	20	8	2	10	67	63	26
Battle Rangers	20	7	5	8	46	43	26
Beach	20	7	5	8	40	48	26
Hooe Sports	20	6	3	11	31	63	21
Iden	20	5	3	12	43	69	18
Wadhurst Utd Res.	20	5	2	13	32	66	17
Hawkhurst Utd Res.	20	2	1	17	27	64	7

DIV. FOUR	P	W	D	L	F	A	PTS
Old Town E'bourne	22	16	3	3	89	33	51
Travaux	22	14	3	5	80	35	45
East Hoathly	22	12	6	4	76	35	42
Westfield Res.	22	13	3	6	69	44	42
Wittersham	22	10	9	3	71	35	39
Polegate Res.	22	12	0	10	63	60	36
Rye United 'A'	22	9	4	9	57	53	31
Ninfield Utd Res.	22	8	4	10	39	49	28
Hellingly Hospital	22	6	4	12	52	69	22
Blacklands	22	3	4	15	14	83	13
Hurst G. Village '89	22	3	3	16	31	106	12
Bexhill AAC	22	2	5	15	24	63	11

DIV. FIVE	P	W	D	L	F	A	PTS
Willingdon Res.	20	15	4	1	64	23	49
Sedlescombe	20	14	1	5	71	31	43
Heathfield Hotspurs	20	13	3	4	67	33	42
Old Hastonians Res.	20	12	4	4	66	44	40
Nelson Tigers	20	11	3	6	48	24	36
Pevensey & Westham	20	7	3	10	41	66	24
Shinewater Assn 'A'	20	7	1	12	42	50	22
Catsfield	20	6	4	10	31	41	22
Heathfield United	20	4	3	13	30	49	15
Hastings Rgrs Res.	20	4	1	15	31	79	13
Herstmonceux Res.	20	2	3	15	24	75	9

DIV. SIX	P	W	D	L	F	A	PTS
Wadhurst TOC Res.	22	15	1	6	64	48	46
Castle	22	13	5	4	95	35	44
Beckley '92	22	12	6	4	64	37	42
Battle Rgrs Res.	22	14	0	8	88	66	42
Silverhill Rgrs	22	11	3	8	71	42	36
Frant	22	11	3	8	61	46	36
Dynamo CEF	22	10	4	8	60	37	34
Pebsham-Sibex Res.	22	8	6	8	53	44	30
Little Cmn Alb. 'A'	22	9	2	11	41	82	29
Seeboard (Hastings)	22	5	4	13	29	52	19
Staplecross	22	4	1	17	31	82	13
JC Tackleway Res.	22	1	3	18	28	114	6

DIV. SEVEN	P	W	D	L	F	A	PTS
Rolvenden	22	18	3	1	94	22	57
Tack United	22	16	3	3	88	30	51
Durgates	22	14	3	5	64	31	45
Old Centmod. Res.	22	11	2	9	40	38	35
Claverham Res.	22	10	2	10	33	41	32
Westfield 'A'	22	9	4	9	54	56	31
Cranbrook T. Res.	22	9	4	9	43	45	31
Burwash Res.	22	9	2	11	38	51	29
Travaux Res.	22	9	1	12	39	41	28
East Hoathly Res.	22	6	2	14	42	67	20
Hawkhurst Utd 'A'	22	5	2	15	37	65	17
Tenterden St M. 'A'	22	2	0	20	28	113	6

DIV. EIGHT	P	W	D	L	F	A	PTS
Robertsbridge Res.	22	16	3	3	109	36	51
Broad Oak United	22	16	2	4	122	40	50
Firehills	22	14	1	7	111	53	43
Sedlescombe Res.	22	13	2	7	97	50	41
Pebsham-Sibex 'A'	22	12	5	5	60	37	41
Hellingly Hosp. Res.	22	9	2	11	48	48	29
Northiam '75	22	9	2	11	45	61	29
Icklesham Cas. Res.	22	7	5	10	43	56	26
Magham Down Res.	22	8	1	13	57	88	25
Mayfield Res.	22	6	2	14	44	101	20
Pevensey & W. Res.	22	5	4	13	37	93	*16
Herstmonceux 'A'	22	2	1	19	23	133	x10

* - 3 points deducted x - 3 points awarded

DIV. NINE	P	W	D	L	F	A	PTS
Old Town E. Res.	24	19	3	2	122	33	60
Punnetts Town Res.	24	18	4	2	90	36	58
Castle Res.	24	15	4	5	86	56	x52
Bexhill AAC Res.	24	16	3	5	81	42	51
Bohemia United	24	13	1	10	88	68	40
Hillcrest Res.	24	13	1	10	93	74	40
Mountfield Utd Res.	24	12	2	10	78	60	38
Heathfield U. Res.	24	9	4	11	67	80	31
Old Hastonians 'A'	24	8	2	14	53	63	*23
Heathfield H. Res.	24	5	4	15	39	88	19
Wadhurst Utd Res.	24	6	1	17	40	98	19
Ticehurst Res.	24	3	4	17	36	81	13
JC Tackleway 'A'	24	1	3	20	32	126	6

* - 3 points deducted x - 3 points awarded

EAST SUSSEX LEAGUE CUPS

League Challenge Cup

First Round

Bodiam v Icklesham Casuals	0-2
Hawkhurst United v Polegate	0-9
Herstmonceux v Burwash	1-2
Rye United Reserves v Willingdon	1-3
Eastbourne Fishermen v Westfield	2-3
Eastbourne Rose & Crown v Bexhill AA Club	4-1
Ninfield United v Wadhurst TOC H	1-1,4-3
Sandhurst v Old Town Eastbourne	6-2

Second Round

Ninfield United v Icklesham Casuals	2-4
Peche Hill Select v Langney Spts 'A'	1-1,2-0
Rock-a-Nore v Burwash	8-1
Wadhurst United v Westfield	1-4
Hollington United v Eastbourne Rose & Crown	3-1
Punnetts Town v Polegate	1-3
Shinewater Association Reserves *(w/o)* Sandhurst *(scr)*	
Willingdon v The JC Tackleway	5-1

(continued opposite)

Quarter-Finals

Polegate v Icklesham Casuals 2-3
Willingdon v Westfield 2-2,1-4
SF: Icklesham Casuals v Westfield 0-4

Rock-a-Nore v Hollington United 0-8
Shinewater Association Res. v Peche Hill Select 4-0
Shinewater Association Reserves v Hollington Utd 2-6

Final: Hollington United 3, Westfield 0

The Talbot Cup (Divisions Two & Three) First Round

Hastings Rangers v Hollington Utd Res. 3-2
Magham Down v Wadhurst United Reserves 7-2
Peche Hill Select v Cranbrook Town 6-1
Hoe Sports v Old Centmodians 3-3,3-1
Mayfield *(w/o)* Iden *(scr)*
Ticehurst v Eastbourne Rose & Crown 1-4

Second Round

Beach v Hawkhurst United Reserves 9-2
Hastings Rangers v Claverham 3-4
Northiam v Hooe Sports 1-1,1-0
Peche Hill Select v Mayfield 3-3,0-1
Eastbourne Rose & Crown v Magham Down 2-1
Mountfield United v Hillcrest 5-3
Old Hastonians v Battle Rangers 3-2
Robertsbridge United v Pebsham-Sibex 1-2

Quarter-Finals

Eastbourne Rose & Crown v Old Hastonians 8-3
Mountfield United v Beach 4-0
SF: Northiam v Eastbourne Rose & Crown 0-3
Mayfield v Northiam 3-5
Pebsham-Sibex v Claverham 4-0
Pebsham-Sibex v Mountfield United 4-3

Final: Eastbourne Rose & Crown 3, Pebsham-Sibex 2

The Percy Chambers Cup (Divisions Four & Five) First Round

Blacklands v Hurst Green Village 1-3
Herstmonceux Res. v Old Town Eastbourne 2-10
Polegate *(w/o)* Bexhill AAC *(scr)*
Wittersham v Sedlescombe 1-9
Heathfield Hotspurs v Shinewater Association 'A' 3-1
Ninfield United Reserves v Pevensey & Westham 9-1
Willingdon v East Hoathly 2-3

Second Round

East Hoathly v Catsfield 6-1
Heathfield United v Old Town Eastbourne 1-2
Nelson Tigers v Sedlescombe 3-2
Old Hastonians Res. v Heathfield Hotspurs 2-6
Hastings Rangers Reserves v Rye United 'A' 0-7
Hurst Green Village v Westfield Reserves 1-6
Ninfield United Reserves v Hellingly Hospital 1-4
Travaux v Bexhill Amateur Athletic Club 4-2

Quarter-Finals

Heathfield Hotspurs v Rye United 'A' 5-1
Travaux v Hellingly Hospital 2-0
SF: Old Town Eastbne v Heathfield Hotspurs 4-2
Old Town Eastbourne v Nelson Tigers 3-1
Westfield Reserves v East Hoathly 1-4
Travaux v East Hoathly 2-1

Final: Travaux 3, Old Town Eastbourne 1

The Fred Eade Cup (Divisions Six & Seven) First Round

Beckley '92 v Claverham Reserves 3-2
Old Centmodians Reserves v Travaux Res. 1-2
Seeboard (Hastings) v Cranbrook Town Res. 5-2
Tack United v Rolvenden 1-1,0-5
Castle v Burwash Reserves 4-3
Pebsham-Sibex Reserves v East Hoathly Reserves 3-2
Staplecross v Frant 0-1
Tenterden & St Michaels 'A' v Silverhill Rangers 0-3

Second Round

Battle Rangers Reserves v Castle 2-3
Frant v Silverhill Rangers 1-3
Pebsham-Sibex Res. v Seeboard (Hastings) 5-0
Travaux Reserves v Beckley '92 3-3,3-3*(3-0 pens)*
Dynamo CEF v Little Common Albion 'A' 6-0
Hawkhurst United 'A' v Westfield 'A' 1-8
Rolvenden v The Junior Club Tackleway 10-0
Wadhurst TOC H Reserves v Durgates 1-6

Quarter-Finals

Castle v Rolvenden 3-2
Silverhill Rangers v Durgates 0-0*(5-6 pens)*
SF: Durgates v Westfield 'A' 3-2
Pebsham-Sibex Reserves v Westfield 'A' 0-2
Travaux Reserves v Dynamo CEF 1-4
Dynamo CEF v Castle 3-2

Final: Dynamo CEF 3, Durgates 1

The President's Cup (Divisions Eight & Nine) First Round

Bohemia United v Old Hastonians 'A' 0-2
Hillcrest Reserves v Magham Down Reserves 6-1
Mayfield v Heathfield Hotspurs Reserves 3-2
Pebsham-Sibex 'A' v Herstmonceux 'A' 9-0
Sedlescombe Reserves v Broad Oak United 3-2
Firehills v Castle Reserves 4-4,5-4
Icklesham Cas. Reserves v Robertsbridge Utd Res. 1-6
Northiam '75 Reserves v Ticehurst Reserves 11-1
Punnetts Town Reserves v The JC Tackleway 'A' 3-1

Second Round

Firehills v Punnetts Town Reserves 8-4
Hellingly Hospital Res. v Pebsham-Sibex 'A' 1-5
Old Town Ebne Res. v Sedlescombe Res. 2-3
Robertsbridge Utd Res. v Northiam '75 Res. 8-1
Heathfield United Reserves v Mountfield Utd Res. 0-12
Old Hastonians 'A' v Bexhill AAC Reserves 0-3
Pevensey & Westham Res. v Hillcrest Reserves 1-4
Wadhurst United 'A' v Mayfield Reserves 2-4

Quarter-Finals

Firehills *(w/o)* Mayfield Reserves *(scr)*
Mountfield Utd Res. v Sedlescombe Reserves 2-1
SF: Bexhill AAC Res. v Mountfield Utd Res. 2-0
Hillcrest Reserves v Bexhill AAC Reserves 5-7
Robertsbridge Utd Reserves v Pebsham-Sibex Res. 4-0
Firehills v Robertsbridge United Reserves 2-3

Final: Robertsbridge United Reserves 11, Bexhill Amateur Athletic Club Reserves 0

EAST SUSSEX LEAGUE CLUB DIRECTORY

BATTLE RANGERS

Secretary: Mr A Bashford, 6 Hoath Hill, Mountfield TN32 5LN (0580 880053).
Ground: Battle Rec. **Colours:** Green/black/green.

BEACH

Secretary: Mr T H Walker, 74 Beach Rd, Eastbourne BN22 7AB (0323 723542).
Ground: Hampden Park, Eastbourne. **Colours:** Red/white/blue & red.

BECKLEY '92

Secretary: Mr M J Wreford, c/o Manroy Engineering, Hobbs Lane, Beckley, Rye TN31 6TS (0892 529109).
Ground: Jubilee Field, Beckley, Rye **Colours:** White/black/white.

BEXHILL AMATEUR ATHLETIC CLUB

Secretary: Mr M Hyland, 18 Heather Close, Langney, Eastbourne BN23 8DF (0323 765479).
Ground: The Downs, Little Common Rd, Bexhill-on-Sea **Colours:** All red.

BLACKLANDS
Secretary: Mr H Rich, 64 Hughenden Rd, Hastings, TN34 3TE (0424 439622).
Ground: Tilekiln PF, Ingleside, St Leonards-on-Sea **Colours:** Red & white/white/white.

BODIAM
Secretary: Mrs M Ennis, The Maltings, Woodbury Rd, Hawkhurst, Kent TN18 4DD (0580 752803).
Ground: Bodiam Sports Field **Colours:** Claret/sky/sky.

BOHEMIA UNITED
Secretary: Mr H D Chapman, 25 Magdalen Rd, St Leonards-on-Sea TN37 6EP (0424 439403).
Ground: Sandhurst PF, The Ridge, Hastings. **Colours:** Blue/white/blue.

BROAD OAK UNITED OLD BOYS
Secretary: Mr B Hart, 'Wheatsheaves', Street End Lane, Broad Oak, Heathfield TN21 8RY (0435 862676).
Ground: Tower Rec, Tower Str., Heathfield **Colours:** Yellow/black/black.

BURWASH
Secretary: Mr K Bray, 7 Mayview Close, Broad Oak, Heathfield TN21 8SL (0435 864628).
Ground: Swan Meadow Ham Lane, Burwash. **Colours:** Blue & black stripes/black/blue

CASTLE
Secretary: Mr R B Woollven, 10 Grand Ave., Bexhill-on-Sea TN40 2PH (0424 733104).
Ground: Little Common Rec. **Colours:** Yellow & green/green/yellow.

CATSFIELD
Secretary: Mr M J Davey, Lower Hill Farm, Watermill Lane, Bexhill-on-Sea TN39 5JB (0424 830477).
Ground: Catsfield PF **Colours:** Amber/black/amber.

CLAVERHAM
Secretary: Mr G Wenham, 10 Martindale Close, St Leonards-on-Sea TN37 7SW (0424 753604).
Ground: Claverham Comm. College, Nth Trades Rd, Battle **Colours:** Maroon & sky stripes/sky/maroon.

CRANBROOK TOWN
Secretary: Mr G J Holmes, 'Elim', New Rd, Cranbrook, Kent TN17 3LE (0580 712653).
Ground: Big Ball Field, Waterloo Rd, Cranbrook **Colours:** Blue & black stripes/black/black.

DURGATES
Secretary: Mr C E Baker, 3 Orchard Cres., Horsmonden, Kent BN12 8LB (0424 722649).
Ground: Bayham Rd, Tunbridge Wells **Colours:** White/blue/white.

DYNAMO C.E.F.
Secretary: Mr S Millard, 2 Harlequin Gdns, St Leonards-on-Sea TN37 7PF (0424 752537).
Ground: Sandhurst PF, The Ridge, Hastings **Colours:** Coral & purple/purple/purple

EASTBOURNE ROSE & CROWN
Secretary: Mr F Woods, 10 North Ave., Old Town, Eastbourne BN20 8RD (0323 649986).
Ground: Eastbourne VI Form College, Kings Drive, Eastbourne **Colours:** Amber/black/black.

EAST HOATHLY
Secretary: Mr T Ginno, 106 Sorrel Drive, Eastbourne BN23 8BJ (0323 768920).
Ground: East Hoathly War Mem. PF **Colours:** All white.

EASTBOURNE FISHERMEN
Secretary: Mrs I Bennett, 106a Foxglove Rd, Eastbourne BN23 8BX (0323 762672).
Ground: Eastbourne VI Form College, Kings Drive, Eastbourne **Colours:** Yellow/blue/yellow.

FIREHILLS
Secretary: Mrs S Medhurst, 5 Playden Gdns, Hastings TN34 2SH (0424 434084).
Grnd: Bulverhythe PF, Bexhill Rd, St Leonards-on-Sea **Cols:** Green & white stripes/white/green.

FRANT
Secretary: Mr B Akehurst, 'Winster Cottage', Stonecross, Crowborough TN6 3SJ (0892 662741).
Ground: Church Field, Main Rd, Frant **Colours:** Black & white stripes/black/black.

HASTINGS RANGERS
Secretary: Mrs L J Major, 404 Bexhill Rd, St Leonards-on-Sea TN38 8AS (0424 446796).
Ground: Bulverhythe PF, Bexhill Rd, St Leonards. **Colours:** Red/black/black.

HAWKHURST UNITED
Secretary: Mr D D Saunders, 55 Cranford Rd, Tonbridge, Kent TN10 4HQ (0732 361398).
Ground: King George V PF, The Moor, Hawkhurst **Colours:** Red & white/white/red.

HEATHFIELD HOTSPURS
Secretary: Mr B V Hemsley, 6 Uplands Ct, Burwash Rd, Heathfield TN21 8SP (0435 864623).
Ground: Tower Rec, Tower Str., Heathfield **Colours:** Apple green/dark green/apple green.

HEATHFIELD UNITED
Secretary: Mr D C Wright, 3 Geerswood Cottages, Ghyll Rd TN21 0AH (0435 866696).
Ground: Comm. Centre, Sheepsetting Lane, Heathfield **Colours:** Yellow/blue/yellow.

HELLINGLY HOSPITAL
Secretary: Mr L Mansbridge, 63 LOndon Rd, Hailsham BN27 3DD (0323 846498).
Ground: Hellingly Hospital. **Colours:** Black & white stripes/black/black.

HERSTMONCEUX
Secretary: Mr D A Page, 2/3 Corner Cottage, West End, Herstmonceux BN27 4NG (0323 833152).
Ground: Lime Cross. **Colours:** Blue & white/blue/blue.

HILLCREST
Secretary: Mr C Banfield, 7 Emmanuel Rd, Hastings TN34 3LB (0424 424228).
Ground: Hillcrest Sch., Rye Rd, Hastings **Colours:** Amber/black/black.

HOLLINGTON UNITED
Secretary: Mr K S Dullaway, 10 Swynford Drive, St Leonards-on-Sea, East Sussex TN38 9NE (0424 852894).
Ground: Gibbons Mem. Field, Wishing Tree Rd, St Leonards-on-Sea. **Colours:** All royal blue.

HOOE SPORTS
Secretary: Mrs P Baker, 1 Sawpits, Hooe, Battle TN33 9HR (0424 892880).
Ground: Hooe Rec. **Colours:** Green & black stripes/black/black.

HURST GREEN VILLAGE '89

Secretary: Mrs M Goldfinch, 'Woodmans Cottage', Little Iridge Farm, Hurst Green TN19 7PX (0580 860418).
Ground: Drewetts Field, Hurst Green. **Colours:** Blue & white hoops/blue/blue.

ICKLESHAM CASUALS

Secretary: Mr D Mayne, 12 Mill Lane, Hastings TN35 4LJ (0424 812214).
Ground: Icklesham Rec. **Colours:** Green & white quarters/black/green.

IDEN

Secretary: Mr G B Say, 18 Parkwood, Iden, Rye TN31 7XE (0797 280495).
Ground: Iden Playing Field. **Colours:** Tangerine/black/black.

MAGHAM DOWN

Secretary: Mr B W Brady, 79 Shakespeare Walk, Langney, Eastbourne BN23 7PN (0323 765802).
Ground: Red Lion Field, Magham Down. **Colours:** Black & white stripes/black/black.

MAYFIELD

Secretary: Mr D G Baldock, 15 Southmead Close, Mayfield TN20 6UJ (0424 873460).
Ground: King George V PF, Mayfield. **Colours:** Gold/black/black.

MOUNTFIELD UNITED

Secretary: Mr G R Brooman, 27 Fair Lane, Robertsbridge TN32 5AT (0580 880759).
Ground: Riverhall, Mountfield. **Colours:** White (red trim)/white/red.

NELSON TIGERS

Sec.: Mr D J Weller, Flat 1, 33 High Str., Hastings TN34 3ER (0424 423280 'The Lord Nelson').
Ground: Bulverhythe PF, Bexhill Rd, St Leonards-on-Sea **Colours:** Black & yellow/black/yellow

NORTHIAM '75

Secretary: Mr Mr F Francis, 23 Goddens Gill, Northiam, Rye TN31 6QE (0797 252365).
Ground: The Playing Field, Main Str., Northiam, Rye **Colours:** All yellow.

OLD CENTMODIANS

Secretary: Mr K Edwards, 5 St Marys Terrace, Battle TN33 0BU (0424 774059).
Ground: Bulverhythe PF, Bexhill Rd, St Leonards-on-Sea. **Colours:** All blue

OLD HASTONIANS

Secretary: Mr P A King, 5 Gilbert Rd, St Leonards-on-Sea TN38 0RH (0424 428057).
Ground: Sandhurst PF, The Ridge, Hastings **Colours:** Red/black/black.

OLD TOWN EASTBOURNE

Secretary: Mr R Lade, 78 Brodrick Rd, Hampden Park, Eastbourne BN22 9NS (0323 505641).
Ground: Hindland PF, Polegate. **Colours:** Blue & black stripes/black/black.

PEBSHAM-SIBEX

Secretary: Mr K Fuller, 28 Alma Villas, St Leonards-on-Sea TN37 6QU (0424 442229).
Ground: Buxton Drive, Sidley. **Colours:** Sky/navy/navy

PECHE HILL SELECT

Secretary: Mr M Delpeache, 17 Burry Rd, St Leonards-on-Sea TN37 6QW (0424 431317).
Grnd: Tilekiln PF, Ingleside, St Leonards-on-Sea **Cols:** Red & black stripes/white/white.

PEVENSEY & WESTHAM

Secretary: Mr N Coombes, 2 Trossachs Close, Eastbourne BN23 8HA (0323 460997).
Ground: Pevensey Rec. **Colours:** Blue & claret/claret/claret & blue.

POLEGATE

Secretary: Mrs G C Smith, 193 Priory Rd, Langney, Eastbourne BN23 7TB (0323 760684).
Ground: Polegate Rec. **Colours:** Red & white/red & black/red & black.

PUNNETTS TOWN

Secretary: Mr M E Kent, 11 North Str., Punnetts Town, Heathfield TN21 9DT (0435 830374).
Ground: Punnetts Town Rec. **Colours:** Sky & black/black/black

ROBERTSBRIDGE UNITED

Secretary: Mrs A Hardy, 43 Coronation Gdns, Hurst Green, Etchingham TN19 7PH (0580 860543).
Ground: Robertsbridge Rec. **Colours:** Black & white stripes/black/black.

ROCK-A-NORE

Secretary: Mr H J Veness, 39 Royal Terrace, St Leonards-on-Sea TN37 6QH (0424 427500).
Ground: Tilekiln PF, Ingleside, St Leonards **Colours:** All sky.

ROLVENDEN

Secretary: Mr K Sims, 26 Sparkeswood Ave., Rolvenden, Cranbrook TN17 4LX (0580 241351).
Ground: Gatefield. **Colours:** Blue/blue/yellow.

SANDHURST

Secretary: Mrs S Kerry, 'Mount Pleasant', Cranbrook, Kent TN18 5LN (0580 850313).
Ground: Sandhurst PF, Sandhurst, Kent. **Colours:** Blue & white/blue/blue.

SEDLESCOMBE

Secretary: Mr G Buss, 39 East View Terrace, Sedlescombe, Battle TN33 0PY (0424 870432).
Ground: Oaklands Park, Sedlescombe, Battle **Colours:** Red & black stripes/black/black.

SEEBOARD (HASTINGS)

Secretary: Mr J G Vidler, 1 Ravine Close, Hastings TN34 2BH (0424 426570).
Ground: Bulverhythe PF, Bexhill Rd, St Leonards-on-Sea **Colours:** White/blue/blue & white.

SILVERHILL RANGERS

Secretary: Mrs C A Clark, 150 Athelstan Rd, Hastings TN35 5JE (0424 422265).
Ground: Bulverhythe PF, Bexhill Rd, St Leonards-on-Sea **Colours:** Sky & white/black/black.

STAPLECROSS

Secretary: Mr M A Chandler, 3 Cricketers Field, Staplecross, Robertsbridge TN32 5QQ (0580 830871).
Ground: Gate House Farm, Lordine Lane, Staplecross **Colours:** All blue.

TACK UNITED

Secretary: Mr R Acland, Flat 4, Stamford Court, Harold Rd, Hastings TN35 5PE (0424 426400).
Ground: Benenden, Kent **Colours:** Red & black stripes/black/black.

THE JUNIOR CLUB TACKLEWAY

Secretary: Mr A M Brown, 42 St Thomas's Rd, Hastings TN34 3LQ (0424 444391).
Ground: Sandhurst PF, The Ridge, Hastings. **Colours:** Yellow/black/black.

TICEHURST

Secretary: Mr A A Stanbridge, 'Tilsmore', Tilsmore Rd, Heathfield TN21 0XU (0435 866750).
Ground: Bell Field, Pickeforde Lane, Ticehurst **Colours:** Amber/black/amber.

TRAVAUX

Secretary: Mr D Andrews, Flat 3, 23 East Ascent, St Leonards-on-Sea TN38 0DS (0424 460773).
Ground: Tilekiln PF, Ingleside, St Leonards-on-Sea **Colours:** Sky & white stripes/black/sky.

WADHURST TOC H.

Secretary: Mr D Mallion, 27 Queens Cottages, Wadhurst TN5 6RN (0892 783363).
Ground: Sparrows Green PF, Wadhurst **Colours:** White/black/black.

WADHURST UNITED

Secretary: Mr J Barnes, 2 Crossways, High Street, Flimwell, Wadhurst TN5 7PB (0580 87620).
Ground: Washwell Lane, Wadhurst. **Colours:** White/black/black.

WESTFIELD

Secretary: Mr J M Drinkwater, 28 Churchfield, Hastings TN35 4SN (0424 754032).
Ground: Westfield Parish Field **Colours:** Green & yellow/black/black

WILLINGDON

Secretary: Mr D Roderick, 30 Freeman Ave., Eastbourne BN22 9NT (0323 506685).
Ground: Willingdon Rec. **Colours:** All green.

WITTERSHAM

Secretary: Mr C K Packham, 3 Forge Meads, Wittersham, Nr Tenterden, Kent TN30 6PE (0797 270239).
Ground: Wittersham Spts Ground **Colours:** Green & white/white/black.

CRAWLEY OBSERVER CRAWLEY & DIST. LEAGUE

FOUNDED: 1956

JOURNAL PREM.	P	W	D	L	F	A	PTS
Longley	22	17	1	4	64	21	52
Hughes Rediffusion	22	16	3	3	85	34	51
Phoenix	22	15	2	5	70	30	47
Thorn EMI	22	10	5	7	39	37	35
Thomas Bennett	22	10	4	8	51	40	34
Crawley Post Off.	22	10	2	10	63	55	32
Ifield 'A'	22	9	2	11	49	60	29
Edwards Spts Res.	22	7	6	9	43	49	27
Cherry Lane Ath.	22	5	5	12	36	58	20
BOC	22	6	2	14	28	68	20
Crawley Down	22	5	3	14	30	69	18
Town Mead	22	3	3	16	32	69	12

DIV. ONE	P	W	D	L	F	A	PTS
Longley Res.	18	13	4	1	49	23	43
Southgate Ath.	18	12	3	3	64	30	39
FC Moonrakers	18	11	0	7	48	30	33
Lower Beeding NUT	18	8	0	10	50	49	24
Ifield 'B'	18	7	3	8	42	45	24
Copthorne Rovers	18	7	2	9	35	33	23
Charleston	18	7	1	10	41	59	22
Thomas Benn. Res.	18	6	3	9	37	38	21
Furnace Green	18	6	2	10	33	42	20
Bluebird Rangers	18	2	4	14	29	79	10

DIV. TWO	P	W	D	L	F	A	PTS
Phoenix Res.	24	21	0	3	105	21	63
Paymaster	24	20	2	2	114	36	62
Hughes Red. Res.	24	18	3	3	82	20	57
Brentford Electric	24	15	5	4	72	38	50
Longley 'A'	24	12	3	9	72	51	39
Youngmans	24	11	2	11	60	71	35
Border Wanderers	24	9	2	13	60	67	29
Southgate A. Res.	24	8	4	12	45	63	28
Town Mead Res.	24	6	4	14	46	57	22
Copthorne R. Res.	24	5	5	14	46	84	20
Forte Airport Serv.	24	6	1	17	41	127	19
North Park Rgrs	24	3	6	15	51	87	15
Beehive Sports	24	2	3	19	38	110	9

DIV. THREE	P	W	D	L	F	A	PTS
Paymaster Res.	20	14	3	3	69	28	45
Faygate United	20	14	2	4	93	38	44
Cherry Lane Res.	20	14	2	4	86	42	44
Barton Albion	20	13	3	4	83	56	42
Virgin Atlantic A.	20	11	2	7	71	46	35
Phoenix 'A'	20	9	6	5	68	39	33
Crawley Sun	20	8	2	10	50	52	26
Stones	20	6	3	11	36	47	21
Philip Medical Soc.	20	4	1	15	31	76	13
Horley Town Post	20	4	0	16	35	99	12
Corinthians	20	0	2	18	27	126	2

Crawley Lge Cup Winners:
Senior Challenge Cup: Longley
Charity Shield: Longley
Jubilee Cup: Phoenix
Junior Cup: Southgate Athletic
Junior Shield: Phoenix Reserves
Charity Trophy: Paymaster
Invitation Cup: Southgate Athletic.

P.P.P. EASTBOURNE & DISTRICT LGE (Est. 1970)

	P	W	D	L	F	A	PTS
Hampden Park	22	18	4	0	86	20	58
CRB Contractors	22	14	5	3	82	47	47
Sussex Building	22	13	5	4	68	32	44
Hailsham	22	12	5	5	95	39	41
Ebne Fishermen Res.	22	13	3	6	58	34	*39
Old Town Ebne 'A'	22	7	6	9	49	48	27
Eastbourne Spartan	22	7	5	10	63	75	26
Parkfield Utd	22	7	3	12	61	77	24
Parkfield 'A'	22	7	2	13	32	61	23
Buccaneer	22	6	3	13	47	74	21
Seeboard SE Sus.	22	3	5	14	41	74	14
Parkfield 'B'	22	1	2	19	18	119	5

* - 3 points deducted

KO Cup winners: CRB Contractors
KO Cup r-up: Hampden Park

HASTINGS & EAST SUSSEX SUNDAY LGE (Est. 1964)

DIV. ONE	P	W	D	L	F	A	PTS
Oddfellows Arms	18	15	3	0	70	12	48
Kings Head (Ore)	18	11	4	3	50	34	37
Ellerhoop	18	12	0	6	41	34	36
Harrow	18	10	2	6	52	35	32
Hastings Postal	18	7	4	7	36	28	25
Hast. Fishermen	18	8	1	9	40	46	25
Bexhill AAC	18	7	2	9	37	39	23
Southern Boys Club	18	6	3	9	42	56	21
Viking	18	4	1	13	30	42	13
Kings Head (Battle)	18	0	0	18	11	83	0

Lower Division Champions:
Div. 2 (11): Oddfellows Arms
Div. 3 (11): Crown Rye
Div. 4 (12): Stamco Staff
Div. 5 (12): Fountain Inn

WEST RIDING F.A.

Secretary: G R Carpenter JP,
Unit 3, Low Mills Rd, Wortley, Leeds LS12 4UY (0532 310101).

COUNTY CUP 1993-94

First Round

Liversedge v Ossett Town	4-3	Armthorpe Welfare v Eccleshill United	3-1
Guiseley v Garforth Town	0-0,7-1		

First Round

Bradford Park Avenue v Thackley	1-0	Ossett Albion v Liversedge	3-1
Glasshoughton Welfare v Armthorpe Welfare	2-3	Hatfield Main v Harrogate Railway Athletic	2-0
Harrogate Town v Selby Town	1-2	Guiseley v Farsley Celtic *(at Farsley Celtic)*	1-0
Yorkshire Amateur v Goole Town	0-2	Pontefract Collieries v Tadcaster Albion	1-2

Quarter-Finals

Armthorpe Welfare v Selby Town	2-0	Hatfield Main v Goole Town	2-6
Guiseley v Tadcaster Albion	3-1	Ossett Albion v Bradford Park Avenue	3-2

Semi-Finals

Goole Town v Armthorpe Welfare	1-1*(aet)*,3-1	Guiseley v Ossett Albion *(at Ossett Albion)*	4-3

Final *(at Halifax Town FC, Mon 9th May)*: Guiseley 1, Goole Town 0

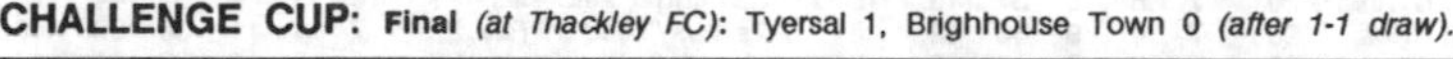

CHALLENGE CUP: Final *(at Thackley FC)*: Tyersal 1, Brighouse Town 0 *(after 1-1 draw)*.

WEST RIDING COUNTY AMATEUR LEAGUE (Est. 1922)

President: J Jones, Esq.

Hon. Secretary: Mr D H Humpleby,
1 The Leys, Baildon, Shipley, Bradford BD17 5PR.

PREM. DIVISION	P	W	D	L	F	A	PTS
Marsden	26	16	7	3	55	29	39
Field	26	16	5	5	78	34	37
Wibsey	26	14	6	6	47	32	34
Crag Road Utd	26	11	7	8	46	42	29
Campion	26	11	6	9	48	38	28
Tyersal	26	13	1	12	57	46	27
Brighouse Town	26	11	4	11	45	43	26
Ovenden W Riding	26	11	3	12	39	48	25
Salts	26	9	6	11	44	42	24
Halifax Irish	26	10	4	12	51	65	24
Ferrybridge Amtrs	26	9	5	12	47	46	23
Rawdon Old Boys	26	5	9	12	29	58	19
Farnley WMC	26	6	6	14	37	60	18
Aberford Albion	26	3	7	16	29	64	13

Div. Cup: Brighouse Town (R-up: Field)

Top Scorers:
C Aram (Field) 23, D Norman (Field) 16.

DIVISION ONE	P	W	D	L	F	A	PTS
Otley Town	26	21	5	0	79	30	47
Altofts	26	18	5	3	58	23	41
TS Harrison	26	18	2	6	83	34	38
Lower Hopton	26	12	6	8	52	42	30
Bowling Celtic	26	11	6	9	49	55	28
Ventus/Yeadon C.	26	11	5	10	55	59	27
Steeton	26	8	7	11	59	61	23
Morley Town	26	8	6	12	42	51	22
Westbrook Wdrs	26	7	7	12	43	47	21
Hall Green Utd	26	8	5	13	40	55	21
Brighouse T. Res.	26	6	7	13	48	59	19
Springfield YC	26	7	4	15	44	66	18
Allerton Bywater	26	4	8	14	42	72	16
Brook Motors	26	6	1	19	44	84	13

Div. Cup: Altofts (R-up: Steeton)

Top Scorers:
S Grey (Steeton) 23, C Farnell (Otley) 20.

Brighouse Town - Premier Division Cup winners. Back Row (L/R): Tony Lyons (Manager), Gary Lee, Nigel Parker, Andy Stewart, Nick Delaney, George Mulhall, Wayne Gibson, Leighton Armstrong, Chris Lister (Asst Manager). Front: Jimmy Hefferman, Mark Wood (Captain), Mick Phillips, Glen Lee, Andy Warnes, Sean O'Neill.

DIV. TWO	P	W	D	L	F	A	PTS
Phoenix	26	21	3	2	85	19	45
Ardsley Celtic	26	21	3	2	93	32	45
Golcar United	26	16	4	6	69	48	36
Eastmoor Albion	26	16	3	7	85	53	35
Dudley Hill Ath.	26	15	4	7	72	43	34
Allerton	26	10	7	9	54	50	27
Greetland	26	12	3	11	76	73	27
Littletown	26	11	2	13	65	69	24
Green Lane	26	10	2	14	55	81	22
Ovenden WR Res.	26	8	4	14	66	98	20
Selby RSSC	26	7	5	14	54	61	19
Bradford Rovers	26	6	2	18	47	90	14
Bowling	26	5	1	20	48	87	11
Aberford Alb. Res.	26	1	3	22	27	92	5

Div. Cup: Golcar Utd (R-up: Phoenix)

Top Scorers:
G McAllister (Golcar) 44, E Cassar (Ardsley) 27

DIV. THREE	P	W	D	L	F	A	PTS
Heckmondwike T.	24	19	2	3	93	48	40
Pontefract AFC	24	18	1	5	95	35	37
Salts GSOB	24	16	4	4	78	35	36
Wibsey 'A'	24	13	6	5	74	48	32
Trinity Ath. SC	24	11	5	8	50	39	27
Tyersal Res.	24	10	6	8	60	52	26
Pudsey Liberal	24	9	8	7	54	49	26
Field Res.	24	8	6	10	69	66	22
Salthorn	24	8	4	12	57	79	20
Hunsworth	24	6	4	14	60	76	16
Dynamoes	24	6	3	15	59	88	15
Altofts Res.	24	4	4	16	36	68	12
Bankfoot	24	1	1	22	16	118	8

Div. Cup: Pontefract (R-up: Wibsey 'A')

Top Scorers:
P Murphy (Wibsey) 33, P Safianyk (Salthorn) 26

DIV. FOUR (A)	P	W	D	L	F	A	PTS
Campion Res.	20	14	1	5	61	43	29
Ardsley C. Res.	20	11	6	3	48	31	28
Hall Green U. Res.	20	12	3	5	43	32	27
Westbrook W. 'A'	20	10	2	8	45	47	22
Salts Res.	20	8	5	7	41	37	21
Wibsey Res.	20	9	3	8	51	50	21
Crag Rd Utd Res.	20	7	5	8	51	43	19
Rawdon OB Res.	20	7	4	9	33	42	18
Otley Town Res.	20	5	6	9	52	50	16
Farnley Res.	20	7	2	11	40	47	16
Littletown Res.	20	0	3	17	24	67	3

Div. Cup: Salts (R-up: Pontefract AFC)
Supp. Cup: Hall Green (R-up: Farnley)

Top Scorers:
D Dalton (Campion) 28, C Prasher (Hall Green) 22

DIV. FOUR (B)	P	W	D	L	F	A	PTS
Phoenix Res.	22	16	4	2	89	26	36
TS Harrisons Res.	22	17	1	4	72	36	35
Lower Hopton Res.	22	15	4	3	64	30	34
Pontefract Res.	22	11	3	8	52	36	25
Salts GSOB Res.	22	10	5	7	51	38	25
Steeton Res.	22	9	5	8	55	44	23
Bowling Celtic Res.	22	10	3	9	52	44	23
Ventus/Yeadon Res.	22	7	4	11	36	53	18
Marsden Res.	22	5	4	13	32	54	14
Westbrook Wdrs 'B'	22	5	3	14	33	63	13
Bowling Res.	22	4	4	14	35	79	12
Trinity Ath. SC Res.	22	3	0	19	22	90	6

Top Scorers:
M Moss (Phoenix) 27, K Auty (Lower Hopton) 26

PREMIER DIVISION RESULT CHART 1993-94

HOME TEAM	1	2	3	4	5	6	7	8	9	10	11	12	13	14
1. Aberford Albion	*	3-2	2-2	2-3	3-3	0-2	1-6	1-2	1-4	0-2	1-2	2-1	2-2	2-4
2. Brighouse Town	1-0	*	2-1	1-1	3-3	4-0	1-3	1-1	0-2	1-2	1-0	1-0	1-2	2-1
3. Campion	3-0	3-1	*	1-0	2-2	1-0	0-0	5-2	0-1	3-0	2-1	3-0	1-0	1-2
4. Crag Road Utd	2-2	3-4	4-1	*	5-2	1-0	1-6	5-2	0-1	3-0	1-1	1-2	0-2	2-1
5. Farnley	0-2	3-2	1-0	3-2	*	0-2	1-4	5-4	0-2	1-2	1-2	1-0	0-4	0-1
6. Ferrybridge Amateurs	4-1	1-0	3-3	1-1	1-2	*	6-1	3-5	0-3	0-1	3-3	1-1	4-0	2-0
7. Field	6-0	1-1	3-3	1-1	3-1	2-1	*	1-2	1-1	6-1	7-2	1-1	5-1	2-1
8. Halifax Irish	4-0	0-2	2-1	1-1	3-3	4-1	1-6	*	1-3	3-1	4-2	4-2	1-3	1-4
9. Marsden	2-1	2-1	2-2	1-2	2-2	3-1	0-2	1-1	*	1-0	2-0	3-3	3-1	4-2
10. Ovenden West Riding	2-2	3-4	3-2	1-2	2-2	2-1	1-2	3-0	2-5	*	0-2	4-0	2-1	0-2
11. Rawdon Old Boys	0-0	0-3	4-2	2-3	1-0	2-2	2-1	0-2	1-1	1-1	*	0-7	0-3	1-1
12. Salts	0-0	2-1	2-1	3-0	2-0	2-3	0-2	2-1	1-3	4-2	1-1	*	5-1	1-1
13. Tyersal	3-1	3-1	1-2	1-2	4-1	2-4	5-3	6-1	1-0	0-1	6-0	3-1	*	0-1
14. Wibsey	2-0	3-4	2-1	0-0	2-0	2-1	2-1	3-0	3-3	0-0	1-1	2-1	4-2	*

DIVISION ONE RESULT CHART 1993-94

HOME TEAM	1	2	3	4	5	6	7	8	9	10	11	12	13	14
1. Allerton Bywater	*	2-3	3-3	1-1	2-1	0-1	2-4	2-2	1-3	3-1	2-6	1-6	2-4	1-1
2. Altofts	0-0	*	4-1	2-1	2-0	3-0	3-1	1-0	0-0	6-1	2-1	1-2	3-0	3-0
3. Bowling Celtic	3-2	1-0	*	5-1	3-6	2-1	0-2	3-3	0-2	2-1	3-1	0-2	0-0	1-0
4. Brighouse Town Res.	2-2	1-4	4-1	*	7-1	2-2	5-1	2-3	1-1	1-1	0-2	0-2	2-2	0-3
5. Brook Motors	3-1	2-5	1-2	4-5	*	1-3	0-3	4-2	0-3	0-3	4-0	1-5	3-4	1-5
6. Hall Green United	1-1	0-0	2-2	1-0	1-3	*	3-2	2-3	2-7	1-4	3-3	1-3	2-4	0-2
7. Lower Hopton	1-3	2-3	2-0	4-1	2-1	1-2	*	2-1	3-3	2-1	2-3	1-1	1-1	0-0
8. Morley Town	2-2	0-1	1-1	2-1	1-0	1-0	2-5	*	0-4	4-1	1-1	0-3	1-2	2-1
9. Otley Town	3-1	2-1	3-1	5-2	6-1	3-2	1-1	2-1	*	5-2	5-2	2-1	3-1	2-1
10. Springfield YC	3-0	1-1	2-4	2-3	5-1	1-2	0-0	2-0	0-2	*	2-2	1-6	4-2	1-5
11. Steeton	3-2	2-3	3-3	2-3	5-0	1-4	2-0	0-3	3-3	6-0	*	2-6	1-2	4-1
12. TS Harrisons	7-1	0-2	1-2	1-1	2-3	3-1	3-4	5-4	2-3	4-0	4-1	*	4-1	4-0
13. Ventus/Yeadon Celtic	7-3	1-3	1-5	3-2	5-1	0-1	0-4	4-3	1-2	3-2	1-1	1-3	*	1-1
14. Westbrook Wanderers	1-2	2-2	7-1	2-0	2-2	3-2	1-2	0-0	0-4	1-3	2-2	0-3	2-4	*

DIVISION TWO RESULT CHART 1993-94

HOME TEAM	1	2	3	4	5	6	7	8	9	10	11	12	13	14
1. Aberford Albion Res.	*	1-2	0-5	0-3	1-3	1-6	2-3	0-2	2-3	1-3	2-4	1-3	0-3	1-1
2. Allerton	3-2	*	2-2	3-2	4-0	2-2	3-4	0-2	0-2	3-1	5-1	4-5	1-1	3-1
3. Ardsley Celtic	4-0	3-1	*	5-4	5-0	2-0	2-1	1-2	7-0	5-3	4-1	8-2	1-0	2-1
4. Bowling	2-2	1-4	0-2	*	2-3	1-3	4-2	3-2	7-2	1-5	1-4	3-5	0-3	1-2
5. Bradford Rovers	5-1	1-2	1-3	3-0	*	1-9	1-2	3-4	7-2	1-2	1-3	3-2	1-3	2-3
6. Dudley Hill Athletic	9-1	1-1	3-6	7-0	3-3	*	2-0	2-2	2-0	3-1	2-0	1-2	1-0	1-0
7. Eastmoor Albion	9-1	2-2	2-4	3-1	6-0	5-4	*	3-4	5-0	2-5	3-2	3-1	3-3	3-1
8. Golcar United	3-0	2-0	1-2	4-1	2-0	4-1	3-3	*	6-1	1-1	0-7	1-2	2-2	3-0
9. Green Lane	2-1	0-1	1-1	3-0	3-2	0-1	1-2	2-7	*	8-3	3-3	4-2	0-2	5-1
10. Greetland	2-3	4-1	1-4	3-4	4-1	3-1	2-6	2-3	4-1	*	3-3	5-0	1-11	3-3
11. Littletown	6-2	4-2	0-3	4-3	3-4	2-4	1-4	2-4	4-0	0-5	*	5-2	0-3	3-1
12. Ovenden W Riding Res.	1-1	3-3	3-10	4-3	2-2	0-3	0-7	6-2	3-5	3-6	5-1	*	2-3	5-7
13. Phoenix	1-0	1-0	2-1	3-0	5-0	6-0	4-0	3-1	9-1	2-0	3-1	5-1	*	4-0
14. Selby RSSC	4-1	2-2	1-1	6-1	9-4	0-1	0-2	1-2	4-1	2-4	0-1	2-2	2-3	*

DIVISION THREE RESULT CHART 1993-94

HOME TEAM	1	2	3	4	5	6	7	8	9	10	11	12	13
1. Altofts Reserves	*	2-1	3-2	3-5	1-6	2-2	0-3	1-2	0-2	1-3	0-2	2-2	2-2
2. Bankfoot	1-2	*	3-1	0-6	1-3	0-10	0-4	2-2	0-4	0-4	1-3	2-8	0-7
3. Dynamoes	2-5	7-1	*	1-7	1-2	5-1	1-7	2-4	3-8	4-3	2-4	5-2	3-8
4. Field Reserves	3-0	5-0	2-2	*	1-1	5-3	0-9	1-3	4-2	0-1	1-2	2-3	0-0
5. Heckmondwicke Town	4-1	5-0	7-3	6-4	*	6-1	3-0	3-3	7-5	1-3	6-2	3-2	6-5
6. Hunsworth	3-1	2-0	3-1	7-7	1-4	*	0-3	4-4	1-1	1-3	5-1	5-2	0-4
7. Pontefract	5-0	5-2	3-1	8-2	2-1	6-2	*	1-2	5-0	5-3	2-1	3-3	2-4
8. Pudsey Libs Res.	3-1	5-0	0-2	2-5	3-5	3-2	1-2	*	3-2	3-1	2-2	0-0	2-3
9. Salthorn	3-2	4-2	2-5	4-4	2-5	2-1	1-8	2-1	*	1-9	1-2	3-2	2-2
10. Salts GSOB	3-0	11-0	3-3	2-1	2-3	3-2	2-1	1-1	6-2	*	2-1	2-1	2-1
11. Trinity Athletic SC	5-4	8-0	0-0	0-0	0-2	6-1	0-2	2-1	3-2	0-0	*	0-0	1-2
12. Tyersal Reserves	3-2	4-0	5-2	4-3	1-2	5-2	1-6	2-2	2-0	2-2	2-1	*	4-1
13. Wibsey 'A'	1-1	6-0	5-1	3-1	4-2	3-1	5-3	3-3	2-2	1-7	1-3	2-0	*

DIV. 4 'A' RESULTS	1	2	3	4	5	6	7	8	9	10	11
1. Ardsley Celtic Reserves	*	4-2	3-2	5-0	1-1	2-1	5-1	3-1	2-1	2-0	6-2
2. Campion Reserves	5-2	*	4-3	2-0	4-2	3-2	3-2	2-1	2-2	3-2	1-3
3. Crag Road Utd Reserves	3-4	2-3	*	2-2	2-0	2-2	1-1	6-1	3-1	5-0	2-2
4. Farnley Reserves	2-3	1-4	1-2	*	3-0	5-1	2-1	2-1	1-4	2-2	2-4
5. Hall Green Utd Reserves	2-1	5-3	3-2	2-3	*	4-2	2-2	2-2	3-1	1-0	1-0
6. Littletown Reserves	2-2	2-5	3-6	0-4	0-2	*	0-4	1-2	0-0	1-2	0-2
7. Otley Town Reserves	2-2	1-5	2-2	6-2	1-1	5-3	*	6-3	8-2	1-2	1-2
8. Rawdon Old Boys Res.	0-0	1-6	3-0	3-1	0-3	2-0	2-1	*	2-1	0-2	2-2
9. Salts Reserves	2-2	1-0	2-0	1-0	0-2	5-2	4-4	2-2	*	3 1	0 1
10. Westbrook Wdrs 'A'	0-0	1-3	5-2	2-1	5-1	4-2	4-1	0-4	1-6	*	6-4
11. Wibsey Reserves	3-0	6-1	2-3	2-6	1-6	4-0	3-2	2-2	1-3	5-6	*

DIV. 4 'B' RESULTS	1	2	3	4	5	6	7	8	9	10	11	12
1. Bowling Celtic Reserves	*	5-1	3-0	4-2	1-4	5-2	1-0	5-2	2-3	0-1	1-2	2-2
2. Bowling Reserves	3-3	*	1-2	1-1	1-5	1-5	1-7	1-4	2-4	4-1	2-2	3-1
3. Lower Hopton Reserves	3-1	5-1	*	2-0	0-0	2-1	3-3	1-2	3-2	4-1	3-0	1-0
4. Marsden Reserves	2-1	5-0	0-4	*	1-1	0-3	0-4	0-2	0-4	5-2	1-0	0-3
5. Phoenix Reserves	3-0	5-1	4-4	3-1	*	3-1	4-0	3-0	5-1	11-0	5-1	8-3
6. Pontefract Reserves	2-3	4-1	1-2	2-1	0-0	*	4-2	4-2	1-3	4-0	4-1	4-0
7. Salts GSOB Reserves	4-2	2-1	2-2	1-2	4-2	2-2	*	4-1	0-2	1-0	3-3	5-1
8. Steeton Reserves	2-2	6-1	1-6	2-2	4-1	1-1	1-2	*	5-2	11-0	2-2	2-1
9. TS Harrison Reserves	2-1	6-0	4-2	5-1	0-2	4-2	2-2	4-2	*	6-0	2-1	3-0
10. Trinity Athletic SC Res.	2-6	2-4	2-4	4-3	0-8	0-2	1-3	0-2	3-5	*	1-3	2-1
11. Ventus/Yeadon C. Res.	1-2	2-3	0-3	2-2	1-6	1-3	2-0	2-1	0-4	2-0	*	3-2

PREMIER DIVISION CLUBS 1994-95

ALTOFTS

Secretary: M Bell, 67 Churchfield Croft, Altofts, Normanton WF6 2QB (0924 893507).
Ground & Directions: Altofts Sports Club, Lock Lane, Altofts (0924 892708). M62, exit 31 (Normanton), A655 towards Castleford for half mile, left at Rising Sun and follow road 1 1/2 miles into Altofts. Lock Lane 2nd right after 'The Popular', ground 300yds on right.
Colours: Red & white/black/black **Change colours:** Blue/white.

BRIGHOUSE TOWN

Secretary: N Wilson, Lundy House, Limes Ave., Halifax HX3 0NT (0422 345057).
Ground & Directions: St Giles Road, Hove Edge, Brighouse. M62 jct 26, A58 to Hipperholme lights, left until Dusty Miller, 1st left and immediate left down Spout House Lane, past Old Pond Inn, ground quarter mile on right.
Colours: Tangerine/black/black **Change colours:** White/navy/navy.

CAMPION

Secretary: A Shepherd, 1 Avocet Close, Bradford BD8 0RB (0274 884152).
Ground & Directions: Manningham Mills CC, Scotchman Rd, Heaton, Bradford (0274 546726). Manningham Lane out of Bradford, at corner of Manningham Park turn left up Oak Lane, right at 1st lights into Heaton Rd, left up Scotchman Rd.
Change: Red/black/red. **Cols:** Blue & blue stripes/blue/blue

CRAG ROAD UNITED

Secretary: R Knight, 23 Easthorpe Court, Eccleshill, Bradford BD2 2PB (0274 635889).
Ground & Directions: Apperley Bridge, Greengates, Bradford. To Greengates traffic lights, 500 yards down Harrogate Road, ground on right after canal bridge.
Colours: Red/white/red **Change colours:** All white.

FIELD A.F.C.

Secretary: C Clough, 8 Hospital Rd, Riddlesden, Keighley BD20 5EP (0274 603782).
Ground & Directions: Hollingwood Lane, Lidget Green, Bradford (0274 571750). Clayton bus from city centre, alight at Works Ground behind new warehouse opposite works. By car leave Bradford on Thornton Rd, 1st left into Listerhills Rd, and continue forward to left turn into Hollingwood Lane, in front of Fields Printers.
Colours: Blue/blue/white **Change:** Green & white/green/green

HALIFAX IRISH CLUB

Secretary: R Stephenson, 10 Marldon Rd, Nothowram, Halifax HX3 7BP (0422 201594).
Ground & Directions: Natty Lane, Illingworth, Halifax (0422 360134). Keighley Rd (A629) out of Halifax for 3 miles. Fire station on left, 200yds turn right down Natty Lane. From Keighley/Thornton, Natty Lane 2nd left after 'Sportsman'.
Colours: Green/white/gold **Change colours:** Black & white.

MARSDEN

Secretary: D Warwick, 44 Western Rd, Cowlersley, Huddersfield HD7 5TH (0484 647807).
Ground & Directions: Fall Lane, Marsden, Huddersfield (0484 844191). A62 Huddersfield Ring Road (signed Oldham/Manchester) for 7 miles out of Huddersfd to Marsden, 1st turn left after Fire Station into Fall Lane, left at r'about into car park
Colours: Black & white stripes/black **Change colours:** All blue.

OTLEY TOWN

Secretary: G W Jones, 5 Cambridge Drive, Otley, Leeds LS21 1DD (0943 462380).
Ground & Directions: Old Show Field, Pool Rd, Otley (0943 461025). Harrogate road out of Otley, ground on right just after Garden centre.
Colours: Tangerine/black/tangerine **Change:** Blue & white/white/blue

OVENDEN WEST RIDING

Secretary: S Smith, 192 Illingworth Road, Bradshaw, Halifax HX2 9XH (0422 248753).
Ground & Directions: As Halifax Irish Club (above).
Colours: Red/black/black **Change colours:** Red & blue stripes.

RAWDON OLD BOYS

Secretary: D Saynor, 10 West Lea Grove, Yeadon, Leeds LS19 7EF (0532 506037).
Ground & Directions: Hanson Field, Rawdon. A658 from Bradford to Rawdon lights, right towards Leeds, then 100yds left (Over Lane) to Emmott Arms, left to ground. A65 from Leeds, right before Rawdon lights opposite Airedale Air Conditioning onto Layton Lane, left at top onto Town Str., right imm. before Emmott Arms.
Colours: Maroon & sky/sky/sky **Change colours:**

SALTS

Secretary: Brian Parker, 14 Northedge Meadow, Doctor Hill, Idle, Bradford BD10 8SF (0274 621167).
Ground & Directions: Salts Playing Fields, Hirst Lane, Shipley (0274 587427). From Bradford A650, from Leeds A657 to Saltaire, right at r'bout via Clarence Rd and Hirst Lane, cross canal bridge.
Colours: Yellow/blue/yellow **Change colours:** All blue.

T. S. HARRISON

Secretary: R Fisher, 32 Berwick Ave, Heckmondwike WF16 9AE (0924 402206).
Ground & Directions: T S Harrison Sports & Social Club, Healey Lane, Batley (0924 475859). From Heckmondwike Market Place travel up High Street signed to Batley, to Junction PH, left past Craven Heifer PH, left hand fork and ground left opposite Healey Junior School.
Colours: White/black **Change colours:** All red.

TYERSAL

Secretary: H Foster, 5 Norwood House, Sticker Lane, Bradford BD4 8DR (0274 666060).
Ground & Directions: Arkwright Street, off Dick Lane, Bradford 4. Leave Bradford on Leeds Road to large Phoenix Park r'bout, right onto Dick Lane. Please do not use pub car park.
Colours: White/blue/blue **Change:** Red & white/white/red & black.

WIBSEY

Secretary: D Nolan, 21 Glendale Drive, Bradford BD6 2LT (0274 602934).
Ground & Directions: Harold Park, Low Moor. From Odsal Top, Huddersfield road to Low Moor, right into Common Rd after 1 mile (Heaton Building Soc. on corner), Park Rd 100 yds on left - do not park on main road.
Colours: Blue & white halves/white **Change:** Red & black checks/black/red & black

FIRST DIVISION CLUBS 1994-95

ABERFORD ALBION

Secretary: P A Walton, 18 Highfield Rd, Aberford, Leeds LS25 (0532 813206).
Ground & Directions: The Willows, off A1 bypass, Aberford (0532 813248) Adjacent to Sewage Works; From Leeds on A64 and join A1 southbound, left into Yorkshire Water premises 1/4 mile past Aberford turn off. All others proceed North through Aberford village and join A1 south. (NB. All vehicles must turn left on leaving ground)
Colours: Yellow/yellow/red **Change colours:** All green.

ALLERTON BYWATER

Secretary: K Bowers, 4 Westfield Avenue, Allerton Bywater, Castleford WF10 2HA (0977 514493).
Ground & Directions: Ninevah Lane, Leeds Rd, Allerton Bywater. M62 exit 30, A642 to Rothwell for 2 miles, left at r'bout, right at next on A642 towards Garforth for 2 miles, at Pelican Crossing right towards Allerton Bywater. Right after 2 miles at 'T' junction and Ninevah Lane is 1/10th mile on right.
Colours: Sky/navy/navy **Change colours:** Yellow & blue/white/white

ARDSLEY CELTIC

Secretary: Stuart Scott, 31 Clifton Avenue, Stanley, Wakefield, WF3 4HB (0924 870993).
Ground & Directions: White Horse, Main Str., East Ardsley. From Tingley r'bout (M62 jct 28) A650 towards Wakefield for approx. 1 1/2 miles, turn right into East Ardsley Cricket Club opposite White Horse.
Colours: Green & white/white/green **Change:** Blue & white/white/blue.

BOWLING CELTIC

Secretary: Stewart Delaney, 557 Huddersfield Rd, Wyke, Braford BD12 (0274 605423).
Ground & Directions: Avenue Rd P.F., Bowling Park, West Bowling, Bradford. From Bradford via Manchester Road, after 1 mile left on Parkside Road, (opposite Admiral Nelson Pub) continue forward to Junction of Avenue Road. From top of M606 take 4th exit off Rooley r'bout then 1st left immediately after 'Rooley' pub, right onto Parkside Rd at t-junction, ground 500yds on left.
Colours: All green **Change:** Blue & white halves/black/black

DUDLEY HILL ATHLETIC

Secretary: C Cook, 12 Richardson Street, Oakenshaw, Bradford BD12 7EH (0274 394524).
Ground & Directions: Hunsworth Lane, East Bierley. From Bradford up Wakefield Rd thru Dudley Hill r'bout up Tong Street to Tong Cemetery, right to South View Road, then down Hunsworth Lane, ground 100yds left.
Cols: Black & white stripes/black/white **Change colours:** Green/black/green.

FARNLEY

Secretary: George Young, 22 Whincover, Farnley, Leeds LS12 5JR (0532 635333).
Ground & Directions: Lawns Lane, Farnley (0532 638826). Leeds-Bradford Ring Road, A6110 to Butt Lane r'bout (by Reservoir), up Butt Lane, cross Tong Rd to Club on right, left at top of hill, and Chapel Lane is 1st right, which becomes Lawns Lane after the Church.
Cols: Blue & white hoops/blue/blue **Change colours:** Yellow/black/black.

GOLCAR UNITED

Secretary: Margaret Whitaker, 8 Burcott Drive, Outlane, Huddersfield HD3 3FY (0422 378901).
Ground & Directions: Longfield Rec, Golcar. Manchester Road out of Huddersfield, right to Milnsbridge, left up Scar Lane, right at British Legion to Longfield Rec.
Colours: Green/black/black **Change colours:** Yellow/black/black

HALL GREEN UNITED

Secretary: S Marsden, 28 Church View, Crigglestone, Wakefield WF4 3PF (0924 253095).
Ground & Directions: Haslegrove Sports Ground, Criggleston (0924 254544). M1 jct 39, left to Wakefield, 1st right to Crigglestone, 1st right again to Crigglestone, past Empire Stores, 1st right after last house on right, to Haverold Lane, onto end to Painthorpe Country Club, left onto Painthorpe Lane, ground 300 yards on left
Colours: Yellow/blue/yellow **Change colours:** Red/black/black.

LOWER HOPTON

Secretary: Graham Preston, 14 Leonards Place, Bingley, Bradford BD16 1AD (0274 567239).
Ground & Directions: Woodend Rd, Lower Hopton, Mirfield (0924 492048). To Mirfield Town Centre, A644, turn down Newgate, under railway, over river, turn right & right again on Woodend Rd.
Colours: Red/blue/blue **Change colours:** All gold.

MORLEY TOWN

Secretary: Melvyn Hudson, 20 Brayshaw Rd, East Ardsley, nr Wakefield WF3 2JJ (0924 825833).
Ground & Directions: Brookes PF, Nepshaw Lane, Morley. A650 Bradford-Wakefield Road to Angel Pub, Bruntcliffe, turn left down Bruntcliffe Lane, and the Snooker Club is half mile on left. Ground across car park.
Colours: All maroon (sky trim) **Change colours:** All blue.

PHOENIX

Secretary: M Breeze, 17 Green Ave., Silsden, Keighley BD20 9LD (0535 669940).
Ground & D.: Utley, Keighley. Old Skipton road from Keighley, 2nd right after Roebuck Inn, ground on left.
Colours: Black & white stripes/black/black & white hoops **Change cols:** Silver grey & green.
Previous Ground: Beckfoot Grammar Sch., Wagon Lane, Bingley (pre-1993).

STEETON

Secretary: A Bates, 56 Eelholme View, Beechcliffe, Keighley BD20 6AY (0535 663397).
Ground & Directions: Summer Hill Lane, Steeton. A650 from Keighley towards Skipton, turn right at Steeton traffic lights, after 200 yards turn right opposite Steeton Hall Hotel.
Colours: Green & yellow/green/green **Change:** Black & blue/black/black.

VENTUS & YEADON CELTIC

Secretary: Frank Vento, 120 Pullan Ave., Eccleshill, Bradford BD2 3RN (0274 638346).
Ground & Directions: Dam Lane, Yeadon, Leeds. Right onto Rooley Lane (A6177), across 2 r'bouts, at 3rd lights right down Harrogate Rd (A658), 4 miles to Rawdon, thru 1st lights, left at next lights on High Street, right after The Swan (500m) onto Dam Lane, ground on right.
Colours: Black & white stripes/black/black (white band) **Change colours:** White/black.

This division also contains the reserve side of: Brighouse Town.

SECOND DIVISION CLUBS 1994-95

ALLERTON

Secretary: Barry Sutcliffe, 2 Tannerbrook Close, Calayton, Bradford BD14 6NJ (0274 884179).
Ground & Directions: Rhodesway School. From top of M606 left on Mayo Ave, over roundabout, thru 4 sets of lights, follow dual c'way (Allerton Rd) round to left, 1st turning after sharp bend is Rhodesway, school on right.
Colours: Grey/blue/blue **Change colours:** T.B.A.

BRADFORD ROVERS

Secretary: Lubo Simic, 47 Oaks Lane, Allerton, Bradford BD15 7RT (0274 499537).
Ground: As Campion (page 1149) **Previous Name:** Dubrovnic (pre-1992)
Colours: Blue & white stripes/blue **Change:** Red & black stripes/white.

BROOK MOTORS

Secretary: W Kaye, 31 Northwood Park, Kirkburton, Huddersfield HD8 0PY (0484 604122).
Ground & Directions: New Mill Rd, Brockholes, near Honley, Huddersfield. Leave Huddersfield centre/ring-road on A616 Sheffield Road, at Lockwood Bar lights bear left (still on A616), 4 miles from ring-road is Brockholes, ground on right of entrance to Brook Crompton Ltd.
Change: All white or all red. **Colours:** Blue & white stripes/white/blue

EASTMOOR ALBION

Secretary: D Liversedge, 16 Willow Grove Grove, Ossett, Wakefield WF5 0AB (0924 278881).
Ground: Eastmoor High School, Warmfield View, Wakefield (0924 364576). M62 jct 30 towards Wakefield, pass Pinderfields and Stanley Royd hospitals, left at lights and follow Queen Elizabeth Rd to Eastmoor School.
Colours: All sky **Change:** Red & black or Black & white

GREETLAND

Secretary: Peter Walker, 15 Sunnybank Drive, Greetland, Halifax HX4 8NB (0422 378203).
Ground & Directions: Greetland Community Centre, Rochdale Road, Greetland, Halifax (0422 370140). M62 jct 24, A629 towards Halifax, left signed Greetland after half mile, right at r'bout, after 400yds bear left following Greetland signs along Saddleworth Rd for 1 mile, right at lights by Shears Inn, right at next lights, left after 1 mile, Community Centre on right after St Thomas' Church.
Colours: White/green **Change colours:** Green/white

HECKMONDWIKE TOWN

Secretary: W Wright, 21 School St., Moorbottom, Cleckheaton BD19 6AF (0274 879702).
Ground & Directions: Heckmondwike Secondary School, Leeds Old Road, Heckmondwyke (0924 442907). A62 Leeds/Huddersfield Rd., at Half Way PH turn into White Lee Rd., 2nd right into Leeds Old Rd, school car park 200 yards on left
Cols: Sky & navy/navy/sky **Change:** Orange & white/black/black **Prev. Name:** Black Horse (pre-1993)

LITTLETOWN

Secretary: D Knight, 2 Norwood Drive, Moor Lane, Birkenshaw, Bfd BD11 2NS (0274 874915).
Ground & Directions: Beck Lane, Heckmondwike. From Bradford, thru Cleckheaton on A638 past Spenborough Baths, forward through 'Swan' traffic lights. Approx 1/4 mile past NEGAS Service Centre turn right down Wormald Street, to end, then Cross Union Road, through tunnel turn left, ground at end of road
Colours: Maroon/sky/sky **Change:** Red, white & blue stripes/blue/blue

PONTEFRACT

Secretary: Mark Scott, 6 Avenue Terrace, Halfpenny Lane, Pontefract WF8 4BE (0977 703141).
Ground & Directions: Pontefract Park (0977 702228). Next to racecourse. M62 jct 32 towards Pontefract, right at 1st lights, immediate right into park - follow road over racecourse to car park.
Colours: Royal & red stripes/royal **Change colours:** Grey/black/black.

SALTS GRAMMAR SCHOOL OLD BOYS

Secretary: P Hellewell, "Stonelands", 28 Belmont Rise, Baildon BD17 5AW (0274 583742).
Ground & Directions: Salts Grammar School, Higher Coach Road, Baildon, Shipley. From Shipley take A6038 Otley Road, and after 1/2 mile turn left into Green Lane. Continue straight ahead for 1 mile, and after Cup & Ring PH, Salts Grammar School on right.
Colours: White (navy stripe)/navy/white **Change:** Blue & black stripes/black.

SELBY R.S.S.C.

Secretary: Mark Pearce, 4 Meadow Drive, Thorpe, Willoughby, Selby, Nth Yorks YO8 9PN (0757 706406).
Ground & Directions: Denison Rd, Selby (00757 703880). M62 jct 34, A19 for 6 miles, right at 1st lights, over canal & level crossing, left at t-jct, 1st right into Abbotts Rd, right at t-jct, ground quarter mile on right..
Colours: Yellow/black/yellow **Change colours:** White/black/red.

TRINITY ATHLETIC

Secretary: Michael Armitage, 49 Valley View, Baildon BD17 5QT (0274 596148).
Ground & Directions: The Dell, Cliffe Lane West, Baildon. From Shipley lights along Otley Rd, left towards Baildon at 2nd lights (Junction pub), left into Cliffe Avenue at pelican crossing after 1 mile, Cliffe West 200yds on left, ground on left.
Colours: White/blue **Change colours:** All yellow.

WESTBROOK WANDERERS

Secretary: Paul Lewty, 20 Gladstone Str., Farsley, Pudsey, Leeds LS28 5HZ (0532 553451).
Ground: Horsforth School, Lea Lane East. Turn up Fink Hill from Leeds ring-road (adj. Eleventh Earl pub) signed Horsforth Centre, left after 600yds on St Margarets Ave., 1st left is Lea Lane East, school entrance 1st left.
Colours: Blue & white stripes/black/black **Change colours:** White/black/black.

This division also contains the reserve sides of: Ovenden West Riding *(playing at Shroggs Park, Lee Mount)*, Wibsey *('A' team).*

THIRD DIVISION CLUBS 1994-95

BIRSTALL CELTIC

Secretary: W R Cawtheray, 258 Upper Batley, Low Lane, Birstall, Batley WF15 0JF (0924 476822).
Ground & Directions: St Patricks Sports Ground, Mill Street, Birstall, nr Batley, West Yorkshire.
Colours: Black & white stripes/black **Change colours:** Blue & red stripes/blue.

BOWLING

Secretary: Neil Smith, 39 Lister Ave., East Bowling, Bradford BD4 7QP (0274 737895).
Ground & Directions: Fairfax Upper School, Lister Ave., Bradford. A650 Wakefield-Bradford road towards Bradford, left into Lister Ave. quarter mile on Bradford side of Dudley Hill (ring-road) flyover, school on left.
Colours: Navy & sky stripes/navy/navy **Change:** Black & white stripes/black/black

DYNAMOES

Secretary: Alan Brotherhead, 4 St Margarets Ave., Holmewood, Bradford BD4 9AJ (0274 823576).
Ground & Directions: Broomwood School. A650 Wakefield-Bradford road, Tong Street turn, down Dawson Lane near C D Bramalls or approach down Burnham Ave. from Bierley r'bout on ring-road.
Colours: Red & black stripes/black/red **Change colours:** All green

HOLMEWOOD ATHLETIC

Secretary: Steven Walker, 70 Holmewood Rd, Holmewood, Bradford BD4 9ED (0274 684701).
Ground & Directions: St Blaise Middle School, Bierley Lane, Bradford. Off Bradford ringroad Rooley Lane.
Colours: Black & white stripes/black **Change colours:** Blue & red stripes/blue.

HUNSWORTH

Secretary: Alan Hepworth, 217 Moor Lane, Birkenshaw, Bradford BD11 2NX (0274 682693).
Ground & Directions: Birkenshaw Middle School, Bradford Road, Birkenshaw (0274 852179). On A651 Bradford-Heckmondwike road at r'bout with A58.
Cols: Blue (white & red trim) **Change:** Red & white stripes/black/black **Prev. Name:** Savile (pre-1992)

KEIGHLEY SHAMROCKS

Secretary: Paul Milligan, 32 Grange Rd, Riddlesden, Keighley BD20 5AE (0535 670867).
Ground & Directions: Marley Stadium, Keighley. Bradford towards Keighley, at Magnet showrooms, Crossflatts, left onto new dual c'way, ground visible approaching 2nd r'bout - right at r'bout.
Colours: Green & white/white/white **Change colours:** Blue & red stripes/blue.

PUDSEY LIBERAL

Secretary: R Brook, 44 Brunswick Road, Pudsey LS28 7NA (0532 569059).
Ground & Directions: Pudsey Grangefield School (0532 577193). Travel from Thornbury Barracks along Galloway Lane towards Pudsey, fork left into Owlcotes Rd, over hill (becomes Cemetary Rd) go straigt over Richard Shaw Lane junction, 1st left, school 200yds on left.
Colours: Maroon & blue/blue/blue **Change:** Amber & black/black/black or white

SALTHORN

Secretary: Lawrence Barraclough, 7 Richardson Ave., Wibsey, Bradford BD6 1HF (0274 603286).
Ground & Directions: Victoria Park, Cleckheaton Rd, Oakenshaw, Bradford. From Odsal Top, Bradford, left down Cleckheaton Rd signed Dewsbury, ground 1 mile on right.
Colours: Red & white diamonds/red/red **Change colours:** Blue & white checks/blue/blue

This division also includes the reserve sides of: Aberford A., Campion, Field, Tyersal.

DIVISION FOUR (A) 1994-95

1. Ardsley Celtic Res.
2. Altofts Res.
3. Crag Rd United Res.
4. Farnley Res.
5. Hall Green Res.
6. Littletown Res.
7. Phoenix Res.
8. Rawdon OB Res.
9. Salts Res.
10. TS Harrison Res.
11. Westbrook 'A'
12. Wibsey Res.

DIVISION FOUR (B) 1994-95

1. Bowling Res.
2. Bowling Celtic Res.
3. Heckmondwike Res.
4. Lower Hopton Res.
5. Marsden Res.
6. Pontefract Res.
7. Salts GSOB Res.
8. Steeton Res.
9. Trinity Ath. Res.
10. Ventus & Yeadon C. Res.
11. Westbrook Wdrs 'B'

WEST YORKSHIRE LEAGUE

President: W Keyworth

Chairman: J Hill

Secretary: Kevin Parkinson,
9 Lake Lock Drive, Stanley, Wakefield WF3 4HN

PREMIER DIVISION

The division saw the inclusion of two new clubs, Knaresborough Town from North Yorkshire and Gascoigne United based in East Leeds. Both were to have mixed fortunes.

Current champions Beeston started the season well with a 5-0 win over new look Swillington Miners Welfare. Other fancied sides Horsforth St Margarets and Wakefield had a low key start, but by October the Division was beginning to take shape. Wakefield headed the table, but there was concern in their camp that too many draws would be their downfall. Remaining unbeaten for eight months they saw championship hopes disappear in a tense game at Beeston. Horsforth also suffered from too many draws and again they were another club to see their hopes disappear at Beeston. Carlton, on the other hand recovered from a bad start, investing in former professional and NCE players. They reached the top of the table in January after drawing with the champions. Eventually the Saints killed off their hopes winning 3-0 at Town Street in early March to put yet another pretender to their crown out of contention.

Sherburn White Rose showed considerable early season promise being tight at the back, and new manager Kevin Hayton guided the club to two cup finals. Newcomers Knarsborough Town had a very bad start, otherwise they may well have been title contenders. They remained unbeaten with two draws (1-1) against the champions. Whitkirk Wanderers and East End Park, two sleeping giants in East Leeds, managed to lower the colours of the Saints but could not consistently hit form. Swillington offered much early promise but faltered with a small squad, but did have the satisfaction of lifting the Barkston Ash Cup for the first time in twenty years. Newcomers Gascoigne started brightly but lost a number of players through injury and ended up having to apply for re-election. They too had cup success in the Barkston Ash Temple Newsam Cup. Featherstone Colliery ended up with the wooden spoon after winning their opening two games, being successful only once more in the division in 7 months.

Knaresborough rounded off a fine first season by beating Sherburn in the Premier Division Cup final, and have set their stall out for a title 'tilt' in 94-95. Robin Hood had a bad start and parted company with Manager Mally Jones. Steve Spooner took over the hot seat and the club's position improved, as they moved away from the bottom of the table.

DIVISION ONE

The division one title race was one of the closest for several years and was finally decided on goal difference on Cup final day.

The division saw the inclusion of five new teams, with Bramley expected to be one of the threats to current champions GN Prince Phillip who had been refused entry to the premier division because of their ground and changing facilities. Bramley however, with their armoury of ex-Farsley Celtic players, lost two out of their first three games against Horbury Town to severely dent their championship hopes. They did recover well to be in at the death, waiting on the GN score to see if they could add the title to their League cup success. Horbury Town, for their part were also in contention, but defeats to mid-table opposition were their downfall.

Rothwell Athletic, the fourth fancied club, also made a hash of it against mid-table opposition to end up in third position. But with ground improvements they were hoping this would help their Premier application. The surprise team was Beeston Reserves who inflicted defeats on all of the top four clubs, but lacked consistency dropping points to the relegated duo Whitkirk and Rothwell Town. Great Preston were everybodys favourite for the 'drop' but after a shaky start held on to a mid-table position following their fine run in February and March. Upper Armley were the League and cup double heroes only two seasons ago, but Manager Steve Thompson saw many of his squad unable to live up to those heights and they too ended in a disappointing lower reaches of the table. Barwick also had a new management team in Wayne Greenwood and Paul Todd. After much early season promise they too fell away to end up in the bottom half of the table.

Division Two champions from the previous year, Belle Isle WMC, found the loss of several players a problem and, although they only lost two more games than the eventual champions, they drew twelve to end in the bottom half of the table also. Armley Athletic found themselves rooted to the bottom of the table for most of the season, but League Cup finalists following a fine semi-final win over GN. In the final they went down 2-1 to Bramley, but managed to just scrape out of the relegation places. The two demoted clubs were Rothwell Town, who had an horrendous injury list, and Whitkirk Reserves.

So, to the championship. GN Prince Philip overcame the loss of several players to clubs higher up the pyramid to claim the title on goal difference on the last day of the season. Bramley, the team beaten for the second season running on goal difference, did, however have the distinction of beating the County Challenge Cup holders Thorne Colliery (Central Midlands League) to go with their League Cup success. Several clubs in this Division have the ability to do well in the Premier Division but the lack of facilities is going to hinder the progress of many.

Tony Rowe

PREM. DIV.	P	W	D	L	F	A	PTS
Beeston St Ant.	22	17	3	2	57	17	37
Carlton Athletic	22	14	3	5	55	34	31
Knaresborough T.	22	13	3	8	40	33	29
Wakefield	22	11	7	4	44	40	29
Whitkirk Wdrs	22	9	6	7	38	32	24
Horsforth St M.	22	7	9	6	33	27	23
Sherburn White R.	22	8	7	7	36	40	23
East End Pk WMC	22	7	2	13	33	42	18
Robin Hood Ath.	22	8	1	15	40	42	17
Swillington MW	22	6	4	12	29	43	16
Gascoigne United	22	3	3	16	32	61	9
Featherstone Coll.	22	3	2	17	13	50	8

DIV. ONE	P	W	D	L	F	A	PTS
GN Prince Philip	22	17	3	4	77	36	33
Bramley	22	15	3	4	70	28	33
Rothwell Ath.	22	13	4	5	59	33	30
Horbury Town	22	12	4	6	51	38	28
Beeston SA Res.	22	9	5	8	43	43	23
Great Preston	22	9	4	9	41	47	22
Upper Armley OB	22	8	4	10	37	44	20
Belle Isle WMC	22	4	12	6	42	59	20
Barwick	22	6	6	10	49	68	18
Armley Athletic	22	6	2	14	30	52	14
Rothwell Town	22	3	6	13	38	71	12
Whitkirk W. Res.	22	4	3	15	36	71	11

DIV. TWO	P	W	D	L	F	A	PTS
Wakefield Res.	24	19	1	4	88	34	39
Calverley Utd	24	17	4	4	90	33	38
Nostell MW	23	16	2	6	49	28	*36
Pontefract Town	24	16	2	6	70	34	34
Seacroft WMC	22	12	5	7	68	35	*33
Dewsbury Moor	24	15	2	7	71	41	32
BBA	22	8	4	12	46	66	*20
Monk Fryston Utd	24	6	5	13	37	51	17
Willowfield Celtic	24	6	4	14	40	68	16
Woodhouse Mr Meth	24	8	0	16	50	97	16
Upper Armley Res.	24	5	2	17	31	69	13
Oddyssey	23	4	2	16	41	94	*10
Carlton Ath. Res.	24	2	4	16	32	63	8

DIV. THREE	P	W	D	L	F	A	PTS
Leeds City	24	20	1	3	99	42	41
Woodhouse Hill	24	18	4	4	103	47	40
Mount St Mary	24	16	4	4	72	30	36
Garforth WMC	24	17	1	6	91	34	35
Rothwell A. Res.	24	15	2	7	52	42	32
Robin Hood Res.	24	10	5	9	63	59	25
Frank Ford	24	11	3	10	57	59	25
Horbury T. Res.	24	4	8	12	39	64	16
Sherburn WR Res.	24	7	2	15	44	76	16
Whitkirk W. 'A'	24	6	3	15	37	73	15
Belle Isle Res.	24	4	7	13	31	55	15
Barwick Res.	24	3	3	18	41	83	9
Yorks Copper Wks	24	1	5	18	26	80	7

DIV. FOUR	P	W	D	L	F	A	PTS
Nth Leeds WMC	22	18	2	2	106	24	38
Yorkshire Saints	22	16	6	0	78	23	38
AFC Whitecote	22	15	3	4	76	21	33
Garforth WMC Res.	22	11	4	7	93	59	26
Gt Preston Res.	22	11	2	9	48	39	24
Horsforth SM Res.	22	10	2	10	80	59	22
Swillington Res.	22	9	3	10	55	61	21
Pontefract T. Res.	21	6	6	10	48	43	*20
Dewsbury Moor Res	22	6	4	12	53	79	16
Seacroft WMC Res.	22	5	5	12	42	67	15
Holbeck WMC	21	3	2	16	31	84	*8
Frank Ford Res.	22	1	1	20	18	169	3

* - points deducted/added (unplayed games)

PREMIER DIV. RESULTS	1	2	3	4	5	6	7	8	9	10	11	12
1. Whitkirk Wanderers	*	1-1	4-0	4-0	2-1	2-0	2-0	3-1	5-2	2-1	1-1	2-3
2. Horsforth St M.	0-3	*	0-4	1-4	1-0	2-2	1-0	0-1	5-0	0-1	0-0	2-0
3. Carlton Athletic	1-1	1-1	*	3-1	4-3	3-1	3-0	0-3	4-1	3-1	4-2	2-3
4. Robin Hood Athletic	1-0	1-1	0-4	*	0-1	2-0	1-0	0-2	1-0	2-3	2-4	2-3
5. East End Park WMC	6-0	3-3	2-1	2-1	*	1-1	0-1	1-0	4-1	0-2	3-1	2-3
6. Sherburn White Rose	3-3	0-0	2-3	1-3	3-1	*	4-2	0-5	0-0	3-1	1-0	1-1
7. Featherstone Coll.	0-0	1-3	0-5	1-0	0-2	0-1	*	1-2	2-1	0-3	1-4	2-4
8. Beeston St Anthony	3-0	2-1	2-2	3-0	3-0	2-0	6-1	*	2-1	1-1	5-0	2-1
9. Gascoigne United	3-2	0-6	2-4	3-5	4-0	3-5	3-0	2-3	*	0-3	1-3	1-1
10. Knaresborough Town	2-0	2-4	1-2	4-1	3-0	0-1	2-0	1-1	2-1	*	2-1	2-0
11. Swillington Miners Welf.	1-0	0-0	1-2	0-2	3-1	3-4	0-0	1-6	3-2	0-2	*	1-3
12. Wakefield	1-1	1-1	3-0	2-1	5-0	3-3	3-1	1-2	1-1	1-1	1-0	*

DIV. ONE RESULTS	1	2	3	4	5	6	7	8	9	10	11	12
1. Beeston St A. Reserves	*	2-0	3-1	3-3	5-2	0-2	6-2	4-1	1-0	2-1	3-3	1-1
2. GN Prince Philip	3-2	*	4-1	3-0	6-4	2-4	9-1	7-1	0-2	5-3	5-2	2-0
3. Armley Athletic	2-3	1-2	*	0-1	3-4	0-2	1-1	3-0	3-2	1-2	3-1	1-0
4. Upper Armley Old Boys	4-1	0-0	1-0	*	1-0	0-4	5-1	1-2	1-2	2-1	0-3	0-2
5. Belle Isle WMC	1-1	1-8	2-2	2-2	*	2-2	2-2	3-2	2-2	1-1	4-1	4-2
6. Bramley	0-1	1-1	2-0	2-1	4-0	*	3-2	6-1	1-2	1-3	9-2	8-2
7. Rothwell Town	1-1	1-5	0-4	2-3	4-4	2-2	*	1-2	1-4	0-2	5-3	2-3
8. Whitkirk Wdrs Reserves	3-0	2-2	5-1	4-6	2-2	1-2	1-2	*	0-2	1-4	2-2	0-1
9. Rothwell Athletic	5-1	1-5	2-0	2-1	1-1	1-4	2-2	7-2	*	2-2	5-1	1-2
10. Horbury Town	2-0	1-2	2-1	4-1	5-2	2-1	5-2	4-2	0-6	*	1-1	2-3
11. Barwick	3-2	5-4	0-2	4-4	1-1	1-5	3-2	6-0	2-5	0-2	*	3-2
12. Great Preston	3-1	1-4	3-0	2-0	2-2	2-5	1-2	5-2	0-3	2-2	2-2	*

DIV. TWO RESULTS	1	2	3	4	5	6	7	8	9	10	11	12	13
1. Seacroft WMC	*	4-1	6-2	0-0	1-3	2-2	2-2	2-0		1-0	3-0	1-1	4-0
2. Oddyssey	1-4	*	1-1		3-5	2-6	1-11	0-8	2-5	4-1	3-0	2-3	1-2
3. Monk Fryston United	1-1	1-4	*	0-1	1-3	1-0	0-3	0-2	4-0	2-0	3-3	3-0	6-1
4. Nostell Miners Welfare	3-1	2-1	1-3	*	0-1	1-0	2-3	3-2	3-1	2-2	1-0	1-0	8-2
5. Wakefield Reserves	6-2	3-2	1-0	2-3	*	1-1	2-1	4-1	3-2	4-0	6-2	9-3	10-2
6. Pontefract Town	3-6	10-0	4-0	3-0	2-1	*	5-2	1-2	2-1	3-1	3-1	2-1	8-2
7. Calverley United	0-6	4-3	6-2	4-3	2-1	4-2	*	6-0	4-4	0-0	9-1	9-2	2-1
8. Dewsbury Moor	2-1	4-1	2-2	0-2	0-3	0-2	3-3	*	2-0	7-2	4-2	4-1	6-1
9. BBA		1-1	2-0	0-4	2-7	3-2	2-4	0-3	*	5-4	4-3	2-2	1-3
10. Carlton Athletic Reserves	1-3	6-1	0-0	1-2	0-5	0-1	0-4	2-3	0-3	*	2-3	5-0	2-4
11. Upper Armley OB Reserves	4-3	2-4	2-1	0-3	0-2	1-4	0-1	0-2	0-2	1-1	*	1-0	1-5
12. Willowfield	1-7	6-2	5-2	1-2	3-2	1-2	0-1	1-2	1-1	2-1	2-2	*	0-2
13. Woodhouse Moor Method.	2-6	5-1	3-2	1-2	1-4	1-2	1-5	2-12	2-5	3-1	1-2	3-4	*

DIV. THREE RESULTS	1	2	3	4	5	6	7	8	9	10	11	12	13
1. Mount St Mary	*	3-0	7-0	0-0	1-3	2-2	2-3	3-0	0-1	3-1	4-2	3-0	4-1
2. Rothwell Athletic Res.	2-1	*	3-2	2-1	2-1	3-1	2-3	3-2	3-1	3-2	2-1	1-0	2-4
3. Horbury Town Reserves	0-2	3-3	*	1-3	1-6	2-3	1-4	3-3	1-3	4-1	2-2	0-2	3-1
4. Barwick Reserves	2-3	1-6	0-2	*	2-3	1-5	0-9	2-5	2-3	2-2	3-8	1-1	4-2
5. Garforth WMC	5-2	6-0	2-2	8-1	*	6-1	1-3	1-2	2-0	5-0	4-2	5-1	8-0
6. Woodhouse Hill WMC	2-2	2-1	6-2	7-2	3-1	*	4-3	6-2	8-1	6-0	5-2	4-4	7-1
7. Leeds City	1-3	3-1	6-3	5-3	4-1	2-2	*	2-1	6-3	3-1	5-3	3-1	3-1
8. Whitkirk Wanderers 'A'	1-7	0-2	1-3	3-2	1-6	0-6	0-4	*	1-3	2-2	0-7	2-0	5-3
9. Frank Ford	1-3	1-0	1-1	6-2	1-2	2-6	3-5	2-0	*	1-0	1-6	5-2	6-4
10. Yorkshire Copper Works	0-3	0-1	2-2	4-2	1-4	2-7	0-9	2-2	0-4	*	2-3	1-3	0-4
11. Robin Hood Athletic Res.	2-6	2-2	1-1	2-1	1-5	2-4	4-3	1-0	2-1	4-2	*	1-1	1-4
12. Belle Isle WMC Res.	1-5	1-4	2-0	5-2	0-5	0-1	2-4	1-3	1-1	0-0	1-1	*	0-0
13. Sherburn White Rose Res.	0-2	2-4	0-0	1-2	3-1	4-5	0-6	2-1	1-6	3-1	0-3	3-2	*

DIV. FOUR RESULTS	1	2	3	4	5	6	7	8	9	10	11	12
1. Dewsbury Moor Reserves	*	5-1	1-1	0-2	0-3	2-1	2-2	2-3	0-7	2-4	7-6	1-4
2. Frank Ford Reserves	4-4	*	1-5	0-9	0-9	3-2	3-6	2-8	1-16	0-10	0-10	0-7
3. Swillington MW Res.	6-1	8-1	*	1-3	2-1	3-0	2-0	1-3	0-1	2-4	1-4	1-1
4. Great Preston Reserves	2-0	4-0	1-2	*	1-3	2-1	0-3	4-0	3-2	1-1	6-3	2-0
5. AFC Whitecote	6-2	7-0	3-0	2-0	*	8-0	7-1	3-3	1-2	2-4	1-1	2-0
6. Holbeck WMC	1-8	7-0	3-3	2-0	1-3	*	3-1	0-4	0-4	1-5	2-2	1-10
7. Seacroft WMC Reserves	2-3	3-0	0-5	1-2	0-4	5-2	*	4-4	1-5	0-5	2-3	1-2
8. Horsforth SM Reserves	1-4	17-1	14-2	4-1	1-2	7-0	1-3	*	1-2	0-5	0-10	3-2
9. North Leeds	9-2	16-1	5-1	6-2	1-0	4-1	8-1	3-0	*	1-4	6-4	2-0
10. Yorkshiro Saints	3-2	4-0	6-2	3-2	0-0	6-1	2-2	2-0	0-0	*	3-2	1-1
11. Garforth WMC Reserves	9-3	6-0	8-3	4-0	0-4	4-2	3-2	5-4	1-1	1-5	*	2-3
12. Pontefract Town Reserves	2-2	6-1	0-4	1-1	2-5		1-1	1-2	1-5	1-1	3-5	*

INGHAM'S SPORTS (OSSETT) PREMIER DIVISION CUP 1993-94 First Round

Carlton Athletic v Whitkirk Wanderers 1-4
Featherstone Colliery v Wakefield 1-4
East End Park WMC v Robin Hood Athletic 2-2,0-1
Swillington Miners W. v Beeston St Anthonys 0-3

Quarter-Finals
Gascoigne United v Knaresborough Town 1-3
Robin Hood Athletic v Whitkirk Wdrs 3-2
Beeston St Anthonys v Sherburn White Rose 0-1
Wakefield v Horsforth St Margarets 1-3

Semi-Finals
Knaresborough Town v Robin Hood Athletic 1-0
Sherburn White Rose v Hosforth St Margarets 1-0

Final: Knaresborough Town 3, Sherburn White Rose 1

DIVISION ONE CUP 1993-94 First Round

Barwick v Upper Armley Old Boys 6-2
GN Prince Philip v Rothwell Town 5-0
Belle Isle WMC v Rothwell Athletic 3-0
Great Preston v Whitkirk Wanderers Res. 1-0

Quarter-Finals
Belle Isle WMC v Barwick 1-2
Great Preston v GN Prince Philip 1-2
Armley Ath. v Beeston St Anthonys Reserves 4-2
Horbury Town v Bramley 0-3

Semi-Finals
Armley Athletic v GN Prince Philip 3-0
Bramley v Barwick 3-2

Final: Bramley 2, Armley Athletic 1

DIVISION TWO CUP 1993-94 First Round

Calverley United v Willowfield Celtic 3-0
Seacroft WMC v Upper Armley OB Reserves 5-2
Carlton Athletic Reserves v Pontefract Town 0-3
Nostell Miners Welfare v Wakefield Reserves 2-6
Woodhouse Moor Meths v Dewsbury Moor Ath. 2-1
0-3

Quarter-Finals
Calverley United v Wakefield Reserves 0-1
Seacroft WMC v Pontefract Town 6-0
Odyssey v BBA 1-2
Woodhouse Moor Meths v Monk Fryston United 0-5

Semi-Finals
Seacroft WMC *(scr)* BBA *(w/o)*
Monk Fryston United v Wakefield Reserves 1-3

Final: Wakefield Reserves 2, BBA 1

DIVISION THREE CUP 1993-94 First Round

Mount St Mary v Leeds City 2-1
Whitkirk Wanderers 'A' v Barwick Reserves 5-2
Belle Isle WMC v Garforth WMC 1-1,0-1
Rothwell Athletic Res. v Horbury Town Reserves 3-2
Woodhouse Hill WMC v Robin Hood Athletic Res. 5-0

Quarter-Finals
Frank Ford v Mount St Marys 1-3
Whitkirk Wanderers 'A' v Yorkshire Copper Works [illegible]
Sherburn WR Res. v Woodhouse Hill WMC 3-4
Garforth WMC v Rothwell Athletic Reserves 3-1

Semi-Finals
Woodhouse Hill WMC v Garforth WMC 2-3
Mount St Marys v Yorkshire Copper Works 0-1

Final: Garforth WMC 2, Yorkshire Copper Works 1 *(after 2-2 draw)*

DIVISION FOUR CUP 1993-94 First Round

AFC Whitecote v North Leeds WMC 1-2
Pontefract Town Res. v Frank Ford Reserves 4-1
Horsforth St Margarets v Swillington MW Res. 6-1
Yorks Copper Wks Res *(scr)* Garforth WMC Res. *(w/o)*

Quarter-Finals
Dewsbury Moor Res. v Horsforth SM Res. 2-3
Yorkshire Saints v Great Preston Reserves 6-3
Holbeck WMC v North Leeds WMC 3-3,0-2
Garforth WMC Res. v Pontefract Town Reserves 2-1

Semi-Finals
Horsforth SM Res. v Yorkshire Saints 2-5
North Leeds WMC v Garforth WMC Reserves 4-0

Final: North Leeds WMC 2, Yorkshire Saints 1

PREMIER DIVISION CLUBS 1994-95

BEESTON St ANTHONY'S

Secretary: N Hutton, 22 Sefton Terrace, Beeston, Leeds LS11 7EL (0532 703151).
Ground & Directions: Beggars Hill. Beggars Hill is situated behind Pullans Builders. from Leeds - A653 Dewsbury Road, right at Tommy Wass Pub (2.5 miles from Leeds) onto Old Lane, right at 'T' junction, left into Sunnyview Gdns at Beeston Manor Elderly Persons' Home, car park and dressing rooms 50yds on right.
Colours: Green/black/green **Change colours:** Red/black/red.

CARLTON ATHLETIC

Secretary: R Hargreaves, 11 Newton Drive, Outwood, Wakefield WF1 3HZ (0924 826141).
Ground & Directions: Carlton Cricket Club, Town Street, Carlton WF3 3QU (0113 282 1114). Via A61, Leeds/Wakefield Road, travel to Half Way House (Public House) at Robin Hood. Proceed to Rothwell down the A654, taking first right after approx. half a mile. This leads to Carlton, turn right to ground quarter mile on left. Via M62 or A642, Exit Motorway at junction 30. Travel towards Wakefield on A642 quarter mile only and then proceed towards Lofthouse along B6135. Continue for 1 mile passing under motorway to the top of the hill. Don't turn left to Lofthouse, but travel straight on with the ground in view on the right.
Colours: Red/navy/navy **Change colours:** Black & white stripes/white/white.

EAST END PARK W.M.C.

Secretary: D Dickinson, 20 Ecclesburn Avenue, Leeds LS9 9BZ (0532 485553).
Ground & Directions: Skelton Road. Buses from Leeds City Centre to White Horse Hotel, York Rd. Take bridge over main road into Skelton Terrace, then 2nd left & 1st right into Skelton Rd. Ground on left.
Colours: Sky & navy squares. **Change colours:** Maroon & navy blue.

FEATHERSTONE COLLIERY

Secretary: Mr M Smith, 11a Jardine Ave., Featherstone, West Yorks WF7 6LA (01977 796395).
Ground & Directions: Cressey's Corner. In Featherstone at the junction of Featherstone Lane and Green Lane, turn into Halfpenny Lane, 1st right down to rail crossing, ground over the crossing.
Colours: Maroon & sky/sky/maroon. **Change colours:** Blue & white stripes/white/blue.

HORSFORTH St MARGARETS

Secretary: R Cowling, 26 Victoria Walk, Horsforth, Leeds LS18 4PL (0113 2585356).
Ground & Directions: Cragg Hill Recreation Ground. Ground is situated on the Horsforth Ring Road A6120 (Broadway) halfway between the Ringway and the Eleventh Earl Public Houses.
Colours: Red/navy/navy **Change colours:** Blue & white stripes/blue/blue.

KNARESBOROUGH TOWN

Secretary: T Barrett, 26 Park House Green, Harrogate, North Yorkshire HG1 3HW (0423 509031).
Ground & Directions: Manse Lane. Via A1 or A59 from Leeds to Wetherby, follow signs for Knaresborough. Manse Lane is just before the Wetherby Road/York Road on the outskirts of town, one and a half a mile from the A1 (right by petrol station).
Cols: Red (white sleeves)/black/red. **Change colours:** White/black/white.

ROBIN HOOD ATHLETIC

Secretary: G Hart, 16 Belfry Court, Outwood, Wakefield WF1 3TY (01924 820635).
Ground & Directions: Coach & Horses Hotel. A61 Leeds/Wakefield Road to the Coach & Horses Public House at Robin Hood. Kettlethorpe Bus No.110 alighting at the Coach & Horses Public House.
Colours: Green/black/green **Change colours:** Red/black/black.

ROTHWELL ATHLETIC

Secretary: D Amann, 28 Haigh Rd, Rothwell, Leeds LS26 0NH (0113 2827322).
Ground & Directions: Rothwell Athletic Club. Rothwell is mid-way between Leeds and Wakefield. In Town centre turn of main road (Marsh Street) opp. Rothwell WMC into Royds Lane - ground 300yds on left at Rothwell Athletic Club.
Colours: Royal & red/royal/royal **Change colours:** Sky & white/navy/navy.

SHERBURN WHITE ROSE

Secretary: W Poskitt, 14 Deighton Avenue, Sherburn-in-Elmet, LS25 6BR (0977 684781).
Ground & Directions: Recreation Ground, Sherburn-in-Elmet. Take the Tadcaster Road from Sherburn traffic lights at main crossroads. Ground is on right just before de-restriction road sign *(HQ: Finkle Hill).*
Colours: White/blue/red. **Change colours:** Red/blue/red.

SWILLINGTON MINERS WELFARE

Secretary: F Boon, 39 Neville Grove, Swillington, Leeds LS26 8QN (0532 867833).
Ground & Directions: Welfare Sports Ground. From M62 exit junction 30 (A642) and follow signs fo Garforth. On entering village the Club is on the right. Ground to the rear of the club.
Colours: Red/white. **Change colours:** All blue.

WAKEFIELD

Secretary: A Wolfe, 28 Cliff Street, off Batley Road, Wakefield WF2 0DW (0924 364035).
Ground & Directions: Stanley Royd Hospital. M62 jct 30, A642 towards Wakefield for 2 miles. Pass Pinderfields and turn right at entrance to Stanley Royd Hospital and ground on left.
Colours: Red/navy/navy. **Change colours:** All blue.

WHITKIRK WANDERERS

Secretary: N S Beaumont, 7 Kingsway, Whitkirk, Leeds LS5 7BU (0532 644499).
Ground & Directions: Whitkirk Social & Sports Club.
Colours: All sky **Change colours:** All blue.

DIVISION ONE CLUBS 1994-95

ARMLEY ATHLETIC

Secretary: S Walker, 19 Otley Old Road, Leeds LS16 6HB (0532 672684).
Ground & Directions: Western Flatts Park. By road turn off Armley Gyratory r'bout left to Wortley via Wellington Rd, Oldfield Lane, Greenhill Lane to Western Flatts Park.
Colours: Navy/black/black **Change:** Green & yellow/green/yellow.

BARWICK
Secretary: B Kollesoff, 3 Leeds Rd, Barwick-in-Elmet, Leeds LS15 4JE (0532) 812638).
Ground & Directions: Back of Village Hall. From Leeds take A64 (York Rd) to Seacroft r'bout (6 miles) and follow signs for Barwick, right on entering Barwick at New Inn, 1st left into Chapel Lane.
Colours: Maroon/sky **Change colours:** Black & blue striped/black/black.

BELLE ISLE W.M.C.
Secretary: D Siddle, 53 Manor Farm Drive, Leeds LS10 3RE (0532 712214).
Ground & Directions: Belle Isle Road. A61 from Leeds (Hunslet Rd), right at Bowett Motors passing Hunslet shopping centre and bear left at lights into Belle Isle Rd, after Belle Isle Circus (r'bout) pitch 200yds on right. From Wakefield: to Half Way Garage, 1st left onto Sharp Lane past Omnibus Pub., travel down Belle Isle Rd - pitch on left.
Cols: Green & white hoops/green/green. **Change colours:** Black & white stripes/black/black.
Previous Ground: Belle Isle Primary School (pre-1994).

BRAMLEY
Secretary: B Davies, 43 Raynville Grange, Bramley, Leeds LS13 2QD (0532 744156).
Ground & Directions: Bramley Park, Town Street, Bramley. Entrance is from Moorfields, Town Street, Bramley (adjacent to Conservative Club and near to the Globe Hotel).
Colours: Orange/black/black **Change colours:** All red.

CALVERLEY UNITED
Secretary: D Young, 15 Warehouse Row, Calverley Bridge, Rodley, Leeds LS13 1NF (0532 561452).
Ground & Directions: Victoria Park. A647 Leeds/Greengates Rd past Calverley Church - ground on left.
Colours: Red/black/white. **Change colours:** Sky & white/white/white.

G.N. PRINCE PHILLIPS
Secretary: J Bravo, 7b Grange Crescent, Leeds LS7 4ET.
Ground & Directions: Prince Philip Centre. From Leeds City Centre take the main road to Harrogate (A61) onto Scott Hall Rd. Scott Hall Avenue is 2nd left turn which is signposted Prince Philip Centre.
Cols: Blue & white stripes/black/blue **Change colours:** All orange.

Previous Name: GN Khalsa (pre-1993)

GREAT PRESTON
Secretary: V Donnelly, 51 Hollinhurst, Allerton Bywater, Castleford WF10 2HY (0532 871713).
Ground & Directions: At side of New Inn. Berry Lane is off the main Leeds/Castleford Rd thru Gt Preston.
Cols: Green & yellow/green/green. **Change colours:** White/navy/navy.

HORBURY TOWN
Secretary: J Mosalski, Blake Hall Drive, Mirfield, West Yorks WF14 9NL(01924 495346).
Ground & Directions: Slazenger Sports & Social Club, Southfields, Addingford, Horbury (01924 274228). M1 jct 40, A638 towards Wakefield, 1st right at lights into Broadway, right on to Horbury Rd at end, under motorway and continue along Northfield/Southfield Lane (Horbury bypass) for 1 mile, left into Daw Lane (signed Horbury) taking immediate right on to Southfield Lane slip road, follow round for 200yds, over rail bridge and into Slazenger Sports Complex.
Cols: Blue & black/black/black **Change colours:** Red & black/black/black.
Previous Ground: Parker Road PF (pre-1994).

NOSTELL MINERS WELFARE
Secretary: R Winfield, 13 Edward Drive, Outwood, Wakefield WF1 2LL (01924 826408).
Ground & Directions: Nostell M.W. Leave Wakefield on A638 Doncaster Road. After approx. three and a half miles turn right opposite Crofton Arms into Crofton Village, one and a quarter miles to The Slipper pub, left and Welfare 400m away.
Colours: Red/white/red. **Change colours:** Orange/white/orange.

PONTEFRACT TOWN
Secretary: P Thorpe, 26 Windsor Rise, Pontefract, W.Yorkshire WF8 4PZ (0977 780359).
Ground & Directions: Pontefract Barracks PF. M62 jct 32, past racecourse to Pontefract for approx. 1 mile, right into Wakefield Rd, ground half mile on left.
Colours: Green & yellow stripes/green/green **Change:** Sky/navy/navy.

UPPER ARMLEY OLD BOYS
Secretary: J Plowright, 29 Armley Grange View, Leeds LS12 3QP. (0532 797134).
Ground & Directions: Moorfield Road, Leeds 12. From Leeds take Leeds/Bradford Rd thru Armley. Turn left at Kentucky Fried Chicken onto Armley Ridge Rd, club on left. *(HQ: Golden Lion Inn, Armley Rd, Leeds 12 (0113 263 0776).*
Colours: White/black/black. **Change colours:** Red & blue stripes/blue/blue.

This Division also includes the reserves sides of: Beeston St Anthonys and Wakefield Wdrs.

DIVISION TWO CLUBS 1994-95

B.B.A.
Secretary: J M Stead, 166 Whitechapel Rd, Cleckheaton, BD19 6HR (0274 879147).
Ground & Directions: B.B.A. Spts Centre. M62 jct 26 (Chain Bar), ground adjacent to r'bout.
Cols: Yellow & navy/navy/navy **Change colours:** Red & black stripes/black/black.

DEWSBURY MOOR ATHLETIC
Secretary: K Martin, 15 Park Avenue, Thornhill, Dewsbury WF13 0DA (01924 469923).
Ground & Directions: Pilgrim Park. M62 jct 28, A653 to Dewsbury, A644 for one and a half miles, right after Fire Station on to Ravenshouse Rd, at T-junction turn left, dressing rooms on right.
Colours: Blue & yellow/blue **Change colours:** Red & white/maroon.

GARFORTH W.M.C.
Secretary: A Fisher, 3 Summerhill Rd, Garforth, Leeds LS25 1AX (0532 869099)
Ground & Directions: Micklefield Welfare Ground. A63 (Selby Road) from Leeds passing Garforth, left to Micklefield just before A1, 1st left after rail bridge.
Cols: Green & gold stripes/green/green **Change colours:** White/black/black.
Previous Ground: Garforth Community College (pre-1994).

LEEDS CITY

Secretary: R Dixon, The Old Lodge, 151 Otley Road, Leeds LS6 3QG (0113 243 2100).
Ground & Directions: Bedquilts PF. Main Leeds to Otley Road, 1st right past Cemetery (St Helen's Lane), entrance to ground is on left hand side at first junction (Adel Lane).
Colours: Sky/navy/white or blue **Change colours:** White/navy/white or blue.

MONK FRYSTON UNITED

Secretary: P Collins, 7 York Rd, Monk Fryston, Leeds LS25 5JF (0977 685524).
Ground & Directions: Lowfield Lane, at the Selby Fork Motel. On A1 take A63 Selby Road, thru Monk Fryston village and after half-mile past Texaco Garage turn right into Lowfield Lane which is narrow and unmarked except for club sign.
Colours: Amber/black. **Change colours:** Black & white stripes/black.

MOUNT St MARY'S

Secretary: E J McDermott, 9 St Alban Grove, Leeds LS9 6LD (0113 243 3817).
Ground & Directions: Snake Lane. From York Road A64 follow signs for Pontefract down Pontefract Lane to the Bridgefield Pub, ground opposite. Bus No.63 from outside Bus Station or bus No.27 from Eastgate, alight at the Bridgefield Pub.
Colours: Green & white hoops/white. **Change colours:** Blue & black/black.

ROTHWELL TOWN

Secretary: P Richardson, 55 Meadowgate Drive, Lofthouse, Wakefield WF3 3SR (0924 870720).
Ground & Directions: Rothwell Labour Club, Fifth Avenue (off Leeds-Pontefract A639), Rothwell (0113 2822295).
Colours: Maroon & blue/blue/blue **Change colours:** Blue & black stripes/black/black.

WILLOWFIELD CELTIC

Secretary: K.Bush, 84 Roils Head Road, Norton Tower, Halifax HX2 0LH ((0422 380181).
Ground & Directions: Holmes Park. M62 jct 26, A58 to Halifax, A646 Todmorden/Burnley road for approx. three and a half miles to Luddendenfoot, left at British Furtex, over canal bridge to car park.
Colours: All white. **Change colours:** Green & white hoops.

WOODHOUSE HILL W.M.C.

Secretary: R Cunniff, 58 Garforth Drive, Altofts, Normanton WF6 2NQ.
Ground & Directions: Woodland Sch. PF. M62 jct 31, A655 towards Normanton for one and a half miles to Woodhouse Hill WMC. Dressing rooms are at rear of ground. Park cars in club car park.
Colours: Red/black/red. **Change colours:** Green & white hoops.

WOODHOUSE MOOR METHODISTS

Secretary: D Drake, 52 Moseley Wood Gdns, Leeds LS16 7HR (0113 230 1365).
Ground & Directions: Soldiers Field. Roundhay Rd out of Leeds, left at Oakwood Clock lights, ground on left.
Colours: White/blue. **Change colours:** Sky/navy.

This Division also includes the reserves sides of: Robin Hood Ath., Rothwell Ath., Upper Armley OB, Whitkirk Wanderers.

DIVISION THREE CLUBS 1994-95

(A.F.C.) WHITECOTE

Secretary: K J Hullock, 19 Brookfield Gdns, Leeds LS13 1NN (0113 256 7122).
Ground & Directions: Stanningley Park - Pitch No.4. From Leeds: Follow signs for Airport along Wellington Street, past Yorkshire Post and along Kirkstall Rd, past Yorkshire TV to left at Kirkstall lights, left past after Clover to next lights on bridge, follow right fork Leeds and Bradford road, past Acorn pub to second lights at Halfway House, turn right (Intake Lane) past pitches, 1st left, round bends, dressing rooms on right. From North: A6120 ringroad, follow A647 Bradford signs until Dawson's Corner/Nat. Breakdown r'bout, left signed Stanningley Village (B6157), past Tradex (on left) and carry on thru Stanningley village, left immediately after Sunwin Rover (on left), down Half Mile Lane, dressing-rooms on right. From South: A6110 ringroad follow A647 Bradford signs, pass ringways and Wickes to Dawson/Nat. Breakdown r'bout then as above. From Bradford: Follow Leeds A647 signs to Dawson/Nat. Breakdown r'bout, then as above.
Cols: Black & white half panels/black/black **Change cols:** Tangerine/black/tangerine.

BURMANTOFTS AMATEURS

Secretary: A Hawkhead, 1 Florence Street, Leeds LS9 7AW (0113 2485571).
Ground & Directions: Fearnville Sports Centre - Pitch No.5. From Leeds centre follow A58 Wetherby Rd, right at r'bout with Oakwood Lane, ground half mile on left.
Colours: Black & white stripes/black **Change colours:** Yellow/blue.

FRANK FORD

Secretary: T McIntyre, 13 Warley Rd, King Cross, Halifax HX1 3SU (0274 499821 W).
Ground & Directions: Saville Park, Halifax (changing rooms at Crossley Heath School). M62 jct 24, main Elland/Halifax road up Salterhebble Hill past Halifax Gen. Hosp., left up Dryclough Lane and Skircoat Moor Rd to Crossley Heath School at top of moor on right. *(HQ: Three Pigeons, South Parade, Halifax (01422 347001)).*
Colours: Maroon & sky/maroon/maroon **Change colours:** White & black stripes/black/black.
Previous Ground: Broomfield Avenue (pre-1994).

HARTSHEAD UNITED

Secretary: Mrs J Newman, 141 Church Rd, Hartshead, Liversedge WF15 8BB (01274 869162).
Ground & Directions: Hartshead WMC, Prospect Rd, Hartshead. M62 jct 27, A62 towards Huddersfield for 2 miles to lights at Swan pub, continue past Golden Fish Shop and turn right at sign to Robertstown, thru village turning right into Church Rd at Bluebell Florists, 3rd left, club on right down hill.
Colours: Blue/black **Change colours:** White/blue.

METHLEY RANGERS

Secretary: Mrs I Westmoreland, 29 Main Str., Methley, Leeds LS26 9JE (01977 515754).
Ground & Directions: Methley WMC, Pinfold Lane, Methley, Leeds (01977 553553). From Leeds via A639 Castleford-Pontefract road to Methley, left before cricket ground ground into Church Lane and continue down Saville Rd - ground entrance opp. Library on right.
Colours: All royal **Change colours:** White/black.

NORTH LEEDS W.M.C.

Secretary: K Pears, 2 Foundry Place, Leeds LS9 6DA (0532 403787).
Ground & Directions: Amaranth Cricket Club. Travel from Leeds A64 or via Ring Road to Crossgates. Turn down Austhorpe Rd which is adjacent to the Arndale Centre passing Vickers Tank Factory. Continue further along unmade road (Don't give up) to Farm gates. Go through gates and the ground is behind the Farm at Amaranth Cricket club.
Cols: Green & yellow/green/green **Change colours:** Black & blue stripes/black/black.

PONTEFRACT LABOUR CLUB

Secretary: M Downes, 36 Rookhill Rd, Pontefract WF8 2BY (01977 790187).
Ground & Directions: Pontefract Labour Club, Chequers Close, Pontefract. M62 jct 32 via A639 Leeds-Pontefracr road, Queens Hotel on right to 1st r'bout, left on A645 towards Knottingley, right at Fox pub for 2 miles passing Willow Park Hotel on left, right at Willow Park Club into Chequerfield Lane, at r'bout left and left again to Pontefract Labour Club.
Colours: Red & white/red/red **Change colours:** Amber/black/amber.

YORKSHIRE SAINTS

Secretary: J Dunne, 12 Longfellow Grove, Stanley, Wakefield WF3 4PL (01924 826795).
Ground & Directions: Fearnville Recreation Ground. From Leeds City Centre, follow A58 Wetherby Road. Turn right at roundabout with Oakwood Lane. Fearnville Rec half a mile on left.
Colours: Green/white/green. **Change colours:** White/black/red.

This Division also includes the reserve sides of: Belle Isle WMC, Carlton Ath., Garforth WMC, Horbury Town, Sherburn White Rose and Whitkirk Wanderers ('A' team).

DIVISION FOUR CLUBS 1994-95

HOLBECK W.M.C.

Secretary: G Dolphin, 8 Runswick Street, Holbeck, Leeds LS11 9LL (0113 245 0084)
Ground & Directions: Hunslet Boys Club. *(HQ: Holbeck WMC, Jenkinson Lawn, Holbeck, Leeds (0113 245 5136)).*
Colours: Blue & white/blue & white/blue & white
Change colours: Jade & white stripes/blue/white.
Previous Ground: Holbeck WMC (pre-1994).

YORKSHIRE COPPER WORKS

Secretary: R Lawrence, 56 Langdale Rd, Woodlesford, Leeds LS26 8XF (01924 826795).
Ground & Directions: Haigh Park Rd. A61 Leeds/Wakefield Road passing thru Hunslet to Stourton, at lights before John Waddington bear left on A639 Pontefract Rd, ground on left after half mile. Bus from Central Bus Station C Stand to Yorkshire Copper Works.
Colours: Green/white/green. **Change colours:** White/black/red.

This Division also includes the reserve sides of: Armley Ath., Barwick, Bramley, Dewsbury Moor Ath., Frank Ford, GN Prince Phillips, Great Preston, Horsforth St Margarets, Knaresborough T., Pontefract Town, Rothwell Ath., Swillington MW.

LEEDS RED TRIANGLE INVITATION LEAGUE

Founded: 1922

President: A West.

Chairman: R H Green.

Treasurer: D Nutter.

Secretary: B Ratcliffe, 97 Wakefield Rd, Drighlington BD11 1DH (853800).

The Leeds Red Triangle League, which was established in 1920, had Premier Division AFC Trotters at the top of the table with 52 points followed by Burmantofts Amateurs with 51.

In the Senior Division, Cavalier were at the with 88 points and unbeaten, Victoria finishing with 74 points. Other honours were the Ronnie Walker Trophy, won by Cavaliers with Victoria runners-up, the Senior Cup in which Middleton Social beat Wykebeck Arms, and the League Cup in Wykebeck Arms went one better pushing Middleton Social into the runners-up slot.

New League officials for the 1994-95 season will be Brian Ratcliffe as Secretary, Danny Law as Fixture Secretary and George Anslow as Registration Secretary.

Teams that have changed name are Vespar Gate to Headingley Rangers, Halfway House to Bramley Band, Travellers Crossgates to Brown Cow, Rocky's to Central United and Jimmy's to Malgate.

Burmantofts Amateurs (to the West Yorkshire League), Cross Green Dodgers, Moor Allerton, Tong Road Crown and GB3000 have all left the League, but a number of new teams have joined so an extra division will operate for 1994-95. The new teams are: Mandela Centre, Seacroft WMC (two teams), Beeston Old White Hart, Corpus Christi, Old Hembrigg, Calverley United Colts, Mason Arms, Wortley Star (two teams) and Oddfellows.

Peter Job.

(league tables overleaf on page 1160)

Leeds Red Triangle tables
(from page 1159)

PREM. DIV.	P	W	D	L	F	A	PTS
AFC Trotters	22	16	4	2	77	30	52
Burmantofts Amtrs	22	17	0	5	77	37	51
Wykebeck Arms	22	14	2	6	69	47	44
Middleton Social	22	12	4	6	48	33	40
Vesper Gate	22	9	7	6	62	43	34
Meanwood WMC	22	9	2	11	53	51	29
Halfway House	22	7	5	10	59	61	26
Merlins	22	6	5	11	47	66	23
Cross Green Ddgrs	22	6	5	11	35	44	23
Crossgate Travellers	22	5	4	13	44	83	19
Wortley Star	22	4	6	12	44	71	18
Moor Allerton	22	4	2	16	31	71	14

94-95 Constitution: Cavalier, FC Trotters, Headingley Rgrs (ex-Vesper Gate), Mandela Centre, Meanwood WMC, Merlins, Middleton Social, Seacroft WMC, Victoria, Wykebeck Arms.

SENIOR DIV.	P	W	D	L	F	A	PTS
Cavalier	30	29	1	0	134	37	88
Victoria	30	24	2	4	112	44	74
Tong Road Crown	30	22	4	4	156	52	70
Western United	30	19	5	6	112	60	62
Crossgates WMC	30	13	6	11	106	87	45
Wanderers	30	13	3	14	80	86	42
Morley CBA	30	12	4	14	97	95	40
Harehills Libs	30	12	4	14	86	73	40
Leeds Deaf	30	11	7	12	77	81	40
Woodhouse MM Res.	30	11	5	14	67	84	38
GB300	30	10	7	13	64	75	37
Jimmys DHQ	30	10	4	16	71	96	34
Leeds Coll. of Tech.	30	9	4	17	90	124	31
Moorside	30	7	2	21	51	90	23

94-95 Constitution: Beeston Old White Hart, Bramley Band (ex-Halfway House), Brown Cow (ex-Travellers Crossgates), Corpus Christi, Crossgates WMC, Harehills Liberals, Old Hemrigg, Seacroft WMC Res., Wanderers.

Div. One (new Div.) **94-95 Constitution:** Calverley Utd Colts, Central Utd (ex-Rockys), City of Mabgate (ex-Jimmys DHQ), Mason Arms, Leeds College of Technology), Leeds Deaf, Moorside, Morley CBA, Oddfellows, Sportinds LDS, Woodhouse Moor Methodists Reserves, Wortley Star Reserves.

LEEDS SUNDAY COMBINATION

JUBILEE PREMIER	P	W	D	L	F	A	PTS
Garforth Town	20	16	4	0	57	12	36
Monkbridge	20	9	7	4	50	28	25
Main Line	20	10	3	7	40	38	23
Roundhay	20	9	4	7	48	37	22
Lion Lamb	20	9	4	7	50	42	22
Prince Philip	20	9	3	8	36	47	21
Myrtle FC	20	8	3	9	51	57	19
Bird in Hand	20	5	7	8	38	47	17
Holbeck BC	20	6	0	14	32	47	12
Gildersome Taverners	20	3	6	11	27	49	12
Horsforth Bridge	20	4	3	13	22	47	11

Lower Division Champions:
Prem. Div. (12): Churwell
Div. 1 (10): Woodman
Div. 2 (12): HT Sports
Div. 3 (12): Burmantofts Sports
Div. 4 (12): Swinnow H.
Div. 5 (14): Merlins
Div. 6 (14): Garforth Liberals

HUDDERSFIELD & DISTRICT SUNDAY LEAGUE

DIV. ONE	P	W	D	L	F	A	PTS
Junction	16	9	5	2	33	23	32
Clayton West	16	9	1	6	39	25	28
Plumbers Arms	16	8	2	6	30	29	26
Wappy Springs	16	7	3	6	39	36	24
Rowley Hill	16	7	2	7	40	36	23
Railway Inn	16	5	4	7	33	39	19
Sikh Temple	16	5	3	8	25	36	18
Moldgreen Con.	16	4	5	7	26	30	17
Beaumont Arms	16	3	5	8	25	36	14

Lower Division Champions:
Div. 2 (11): Jacobs Well
Div. 3 (12): Ivy House
Div. 4 (11): Town Hall
Div. 5 (9): Deighton WMC

BRIGHOUSE SUNDAY LEAGUE

DIV. ONE	P	W	D	L	F	A	PTS
Star	18	15	3	0	83	11	33
Elland AFC	18	14	1	3	85	18	29
Rastrick CC	18	12	2	4	77	24	26
Thornhill Briggs	18	12	1	5	63	31	25
Triangle	18	6	5	7	42	33	17
Windmill	18	6	5	7	42	42	17
Sun Inn (L)	18	6	1	11	54	35	13
Pond	18	5	2	11	40	69	12
Holywell Green	18	4	0	14	26	116	8
Church Tavern	18	0	0	18	7	139	0

Lower Division Champions:
Div. 2 (12): Eastfield

WESTMORLAND F.A.

Founded: 1897.

Secretary: Mr J B Fleming,
Beezon Chambers, off Sandes Avenue,
Kendal, Cumbria (0539 730946).

SENIOR CUP 1993-94

First Round

Sedbergh v Netherfield Reserves	1-7	Kirkby Lonsdale v Shap	2-8
Heathwaite *(scr)* Penrith United *(w/o)*		Ambleside v Greystoke	4-0
Keswick v Ibis	11-2	Kendal County v Burton Thistle	2-4
Endmoor KGR v Staveley United	2-3	Kendal United v Lunesdale United	6-0
Corinthians v Windermere SC	1-3*(aet)*		

The Burton Thistle goalkeeper coolly claims a cross during his side's 4-2 First Round win at Kendal County. Photo - Gavin Ellis-Neville.

Second Round

Kendal United v Victoria Spts Club	9-3	Keswick v Kirkoswald	10-0
Ambleside v Wetheriggs	1-3	Burton Thistle v Coniston	2-4
Kirkby Stephen v Burneside	4-0	Windermere SC v Appleby	1-4
Shap v Penrith United	1-5	Netherfield Res. v Staveley United	2-0

Quarter-Finals

Netherfield Reserves v Wetheriggs	5-2	Keswick v Coniston	6-1
Appleby v Penrith United	6-4	Kirkby Stephen v Kendal United	3-4*(aet)*

Semi-Finals

Keswick v Appleby	2-1	Kendal United v Netherfield Reserves	1-0

Final *(at Netherfield FC, Sat 16th April)*: Kendal United 2, Keswick 0

OTHER COUNTY FINALS

Benevolent Trophy *(at Netherfield FC, Thurs 21st April)*: Kendal United 5, Sedbergh 0
Junior Cup *(at Appleby FC, Sat 30th April)*: Kendal United Reserves 2, Kirkby Stephen Reserves 1
Vaux Sunday Cup *(at Shap FC, Sun 20th March)*: Brough 6, Kendal Post Office 1
Minor Cup *(at Milnthorpe Corinthians FC, Thurs 24th March)*: Dallam Youth 1, Wattsfield Youth 0
Dallam Tower Youth Cup *(at Netherfield FC, Sun 17th April)*: Coniston Youth 4, Burton & Holme Youth 1
S M Jones Youth Cup *(at Netherfield FC, Sun 17th April)*: Wattsfield Youth 3, Ibis Youth 1

TALBOT INSURANCE WESTMORLAND LEAGUE

Hon. Secretary: Mr R Wilkinson,
High Sampool Farmhouse, Levens, Kendal, Cumbria LA8 8EQ.

Keswick were bottom of the League in September after losing their opening three fixtures, but just one defeat during the remainder of the season (to runners-up Kirkby Stephen), enabled them to complete the League and Cup double.

DIV. ONE	P	W	D	L	F	A	PTS
Keswick	26	22	0	4	85	28	44
Kirkby Stephen	26	19	2	5	86	41	40
Kendal County	26	15	5	6	52	39	35
Netherfield Res.	26	14	6	6	63	37	34
Kendal United	26	13	4	9	67	42	30
Ambleside	26	14	1	11	66	57	29
Coniston	26	11	3	12	49	47	25
Penrith United	26	12	1	13	63	74	25
Wetheriggs	26	8	6	12	42	54	22
Staveley	26	9	4	13	34	46	22
Kirkoswald	26	6	5	15	41	62	17
Appleby	26	7	3	16	39	87	17
Burneside	26	3	8	15	25	57	14
Sedbergh	26	4	2	20	46	87	10

DIV. TWO	P	W	D	L	F	A	PTS
Kendal Utd Res.	34	26	3	5	104	44	55
Windermere	34	23	3	8	95	49	49
Lunesdale Utd	34	22	4	8	106	53	48
Keswick Res.	34	22	2	10	108	63	46
Kirkby Stephen Res.	34	18	5	11	96	61	41
Penrith Utd Res.	34	18	4	12	95	76	40
Wetheriggs Res.	34	17	4	13	83	70	38
Greystoke	34	15	8	11	78	67	38
Endmoor	34	15	5	14	89	90	35
Braithwaite	34	14	5	15	72	77	33
Shap	34	15	2	17	80	74	32
Kendal Co. Res.	34	14	2	18	66	84	30
Victoria SC	34	14	2	18	73	102	30
Burneside Res.	34	10	5	19	46	73	25
Ambleside Res.	34	10	3	21	69	125	23
Coniston Res.	34	9	4	21	72	96	22
Eden Athletic	34	9	1	24	55	117	19
Ibis	34	3	2	29	34	100	8

DIV. THREE	P	W	D	L	F	A	PTS
Dent	32	23	4	5	86	30	50
Grasmere	32	20	8	4	68	29	48
Appleby Res	32	19	7	6	126	47	45
Kirkby Lonsdale	32	18	9	5	97	48	45
Windermere Res.	32	18	5	9	72	54	41
Ullswater United	32	18	5	9	60	46	41
Heathwaite	32	16	8	8	104	67	40
Staveley Res.	32	15	6	11	67	60	36
Greystoke Res.	32	13	6	13	111	76	32
Lunesdale U. Res.	32	11	7	14	65	62	29
Esthwaite Vale	32	10	8	14	84	89	28
Provincial	32	11	3	18	66	81	25
Shap Res.	32	9	5	18	59	114	23
Victoria CS Res.	32	9	3	20	56	124	*20
TFP	32	5	6	21	57	96	16
Langwathby	32	5	3	24	57	126	13
Lakes United	32	4	3	25	52	138	11

* - 1 point deducted

DIVISION ONE RESULTS 1993-94

HOME TEAM	1	2	3	4	5	6	7	8	9	10	11	12	13	14
1. Ambleside	*	7-3	6-2	0-3	3-0	4-2	2-3	5-3	1-2	5-1	2-6	3-1	3-3	3-1
2. Applely	1-4	*	2-1	3-1	0-2	0-0	0-7	1-4	0-4	0-5	1-5	2-1	3-0	1-1
3. Burneside	0-4	2-2	*	1-1	1-1	0-0	0-4	0-4	1-1	1-3	1-0	0-0	0-0	2-0
4. Coniston	5-0	2-0	2-0	*	1-3	0-5	2-4	1-2	2-0	3-2	2-3	4-0	1-0	3-3
5. Kendal County	2-0	1-1	3-2	3-1	*	1-1	1-2	0-1	3-1	1-1	2-1	1-0	4-1	6-4
6. Kendal United	3-1	7-3	2-0	4-3	1-2	*	3-1	4-0	1-4	1-1	1-2	1-3	4-1	1-0
7. Keswick	3-1	2-0	4-0	3-2	2-1	3-1	*	1-3	2-0	2-0	7-1	4-0	2-0	2-1
8. Kirkby Stephen	3-1	6-0	3-1	2-0	4-0	5-2	1-3	*	6-1	1-2	6-4	4-1	2-0	6-1
9. Kirkoswald	0-4	3-6	2-2	1-3	1-1	0-1	1-2	1-4	*	2-2	1-0	2-2	2-0	6-2
10. Netherfield Reserves	0-3	4-0	3-1	3-0	4-1	1-3	4-1	1-1	2-1	*	3-1	6-1	0-1	2-2
11. Penrith United	3-0	3-2	6-2	2-2	2-3	2-7	0-6	3-7	3-1	1-5	*	1-3	3-2	3-1
12. Sedbergh	1-2	3-5	0-3	2-3	3-4	1-3	2-10	4-6	6-3	2-5	3-5	*	1-3	2-3
13. Staveley United	0-1	3-1	2-1	0-2	1-5	1-1	2-1	2-0	3-1	1-2	3-1	4-2	*	1-1
14. Wetheriggs	6-1	0-2	2-1	1-0	0-1	2-1	0-4	2-2	3-0	1-1	1-2	2-1	2-0	*

DIVISION TWO RESULTS

	1	2	3	4	5	6	7	8	9	10	11	12	13	14	15	16	17	18
1. Ambleside Reserves	*	4-4	2-1	1-0	2-0	3-5	6-2	5-2	2-3	1-5	0-5	1-12	3-3	5-3	5-0	1-2	0-3	1-5
2. Braithwaite	2-6	*	2-0	5-1	5-1	3-4	1-5	3-2	0-1	2-2	0-3	1-3	0-2	1-5	3-2	4-3	2-0	2-1
3. Burneside Reserves	1-0	0-4	*	1-3	0-1	4-2	2-1	3-1	4-2	0-2	0-1	3-1	1-1	2-4	3-3	1-2	1-4	3-4
4. Coniston Reserves	7-1	1-1	0-1	*	7-0	3-3	5-2	2-3	0-2	1-2	2-4	4-2	0-4	3-7	5-3	2-3	2-3	2-6
5. Eden Athletic	4-1	1-5	5-2	1-3	*	2-8	0-4	3-0	8-0	4-2	1-0	0-3	3-5	0-1	0-4	0-4	1-4	3-5
6. Endmoor KGR	5-1	1-5	3-1	8-2	3-0	*	2-4	2-1	0-1	0-3	4-1	2-3	0-6	5-2	4-3	1-2	2-2	2-2
7. Greystoke	3-2	0-0	3-1	2-4	2-0	2-2	*	9-0	0-0	3-3	4-1	2-2	1-1	2-0	1-0	6-3	2-0	4-4
8. Ibis	0-1	2-4	0-2	1-1	3-1	0-1	0-1	*	2-3	1-2	2-3	2-3	1-5	2-4	0-2	1-3	0-4	0-4
9. Kendal County Reserves	2-3	3-1	3-1	3-3	2-3	0-3	2-1	2-0	*	0-1	2-0	1-2	4-1	1-3	3-5	2-4	2-4	3-2
10. Kendal Utd Reserves	10-0	3-0	1-1	4-1	9-0	3-0	5-2	2-0	4-1	*	1-0	1-0	1-4	5-6	3-2	5-1	3-1	1-0
11. Keswick Reserves	5-0	3-5	6-0	4-0	5-2	4-1	5-0	5-2	6-3	2-0	*	2-2	4-5	3-3	3-1	2-3	5-1	2-4
12. Kirkby Stephen Reserves	2-1	2-0	1-1	4-1	5-0	3-2	1-1	4-1	6-2	2-4	3-4	*	1-0	6-2	3-1	9-1	2-2	0-2
13. Lunesdale United	5-4	2-0	2-0	2-1	8-1	3-5	4-5	5-0	0-2	6-1	1-2	2-0	*	4-1	3-2	1-1	3-2	1-2
14. Penrith Utd Reserves	10-1	3-1	4-0	4-1	4-2	2-2	4-0	1-1	2-0	0-3	1-3	4-2	0-2	*	1-3	2-4	2-2	3-1
15. Shap	8-2	2-2	0-2	2-1	3-1	6-1	2-0	6-0	3-1	1-3	3-5	2-0	0-3	3-1	*	4-3	1-0	0-1
16. Victoria Sports Club	1-0	5-1	1-4	0-3	2-2	3-4	0-2	0-3	2-5	1-7	1-4	3-1	1-7	4-1	5-1	*	2-4	1-4
17. Wetheriggs Reserves	6-4	2-3	0-0	4-1	2-4	4-1	3-2	2-0	3-2	1-2	1-6	4-3	2-5	1-3	3-1	4-0	*	3-0
18. Windermere Sports Club	0-0	2-0	4-0	3-0	4-1	6-1	2-0	2-1	5-3	0-1	5-1	2-3	2-0	1-2	3-1	4-2	3-2	*

DIVISION THREE RESULTS

	1	2	3	4	5	6	7	8	9	10	11	12	13	14	15	16	17
1. Appleby Reserves	*	3-0	4-1	4-0	9-0	4-1	1-1	13-0	6-4	3-1	6-0	5-1	4-2	5-0	4-0	8-1	3-3
2. Dent	4-1	*	6-1	0-0	2-3	4-0	2-2	4-2	1-0	1-0	1-1	3-0	0-2	2-0	0-1	4-1	6-0
3. Esthwaite Vale	3-3	0-6	*	3-3	0-3	1-1	0-4	5-2	8-3	5-3	6-3	7-2	2-2	2-1	4-1	2-3	5-2
4. Grasmere	0-0	2-0	2-0	*	1-0	2-0	1-0	3-0	4-0	0-0	0-2	3-1	0-0	2-1	1-1	3-0	1-0
5. Greystoke Reserves	3-3	1-2	5-1	2-2	*	1-1	1-5	6-4	7-3	4-0	3-3	11-1	3-2	7-2	0-2	12-0	2-3
6. Heathwaite	1-3	3-5	5-1	1-4	1-1	*	5-3	9-1	12-1	4-2	3-2	4-1	3-3	5-0	3-1	5-4	2-2
7. Kirkby Lonsdale	1-0	1-3	3-1	2-2	3-2	2-2	*	2-2	5-1	4-0	5-3	3-0	7-1	2-0	1-1	10-2	3-2
8. Lakes United	2-9	2-4	4-4	0-3	1-8	2-3	1-7	*	0-5	2-4	4-3	3-1	0-1	5-0	1-4	2-5	2-2
9. Langwathby	2-3	1-2	4-4	0-5	1-9	2-2	1-7	5-0	*	2-0	1-5	7-0	0-0	1-3	1-3	0-3	2-5
10. Lunesdale United Reserves	0-5	1-1	1-1	2-0	3-2	0-5	1-1	10-1	3-1	*	3-1	8-2	4-0	2-2	0-2	1-1	3-1
11. Providential	3-1	0-3	4-3	3-4	2-1	2-1	3-2	0-1	1-2	3-2	*	2-3	0-3	4-4	2-3	2-1	0-3
12. Shap Reserves	2-2	1-8	3-3	0-5	6-2	1-3	2-2	2-1	1-0	2-4	1-0	*	1-1	4-2	0-1	7-2	3-0
13. Staveley United Reserves	3-2	0-4	2-1	5-2	3-1	2-3	1-2	5-1	5-0	1-5	4-1	5-1	*	3-2	1-0	2-3	1-3
14. TFP	2-1	1-4	1-5	1-5	4-2	2-2	1-1	4-2	9-1	0-0	1-4	3-3	1-3	*	1-3	2-4	1-3
15. Ullswater United	3-3	0-1	2-1	0-3	4-4	3-2	0-2	1-0	4-1	1-0	3-2	4-0	0-0	4-2	*	5-2	0-2
16. Victoria Sports Club Reserves	1-7	0-2	0-4	0-2	0-5	1-7	2-4	4-3	6-3	3-2	0-4	2-5	0-4	3-2	0-3	*	1-1
17. Windermere SC Reserves	2-1	0-1	1-0	1-3	2-0	4-5	4-0	2-1	3-2	1-0	3-1	8-2	4-0	3-2	2-0	1-1	*

HIGH SHERIFF'S CUP 1993-94

First Round

Ambleside v Sedbergh 2-1
Kendal County v Burneside 1-0
Netherfield Reserves v Keswick 1-3
Appleby v Ponteland United 2-4
Kirkoswald v Staveley United 4-0
Wetheriggs v Coniston 1-2

Quarter-Finals

Coniston v Kendal County 2-1
Kirkoswald v Ambleside 2-3
Kendal United v Kirkby Stephen 5-2
Penrith United v Keswick 2-4

Semi-Finals

Ambleside v Keswick 0-3
Kendal United v Coniston 5-3

Final: Keswick 2, Kendal United 0

MASON & FREEMAN CUP 1993-94

First Round

Ibis v Kendal United Reserves 4-5
Kendal County Reserves v Penrith Utd Reserves 3-5

Second Round

Braithwaite v Wetheriggs Reserves 0-2
Greystoke v Eden Athletic 2-0
Lunesdale United v Kirkby Stephen Res. 2-1
Shap v Endmoor KGR 8-4
Coniston Reserves v Victoria Sports Club 2-1
Keswick Reserves v Ambleside Reserves 5-0
Penrith Utd Reserves v Burneside Reserves 1-1,3-1
Windermere SC v Kendal United Reserves 0-3

Quarter-Finals

Coniston Reserves v Greystoke 2-2,1-8
Lunesdale United v Kendal United Reserves 3-1
Keswick Reserves v Penrith Utd Reserves 1-8
Wetheriggs Reserves v Shap 4-3

Semi Finals

Greystoke v Lunesdale United 0-5
Penrith United Reserves v Wetheriggs Res. 2-3

Final: Wetheriggs Reserves 3, Lunesdale United 1

PETER DAWS MEMORIAL SHIELD 1993-94

First Round

Victoria SC Res. v Greystoke Reserves 2-4

Second Round

Esthwaite Vale v Grasmere 3-2
Heathwaite v Provincial 5-1
Lakes United v Langwathby 6-5
Staveley Utd v Ullswater Utd 5-1
Greystoke Reserves v Dent 1-5*(aet)*
Kirkby Lonsdale Rangers v Appleby Reserves 0-1
Lunesdale Utd Reserves v Shap Reserves 4-0
TFP v Windermere SC Reserves 2-0

Quarter-Finals

Dent v TFP 3-2
Lunesdale Utd Res. v Lakes Utd 1-1,4-3
Esthwaite Vale v Appleby Reserves 4-3
Heathwaite v Staveley Utd Reserves 2-1*(aet)*

Semi-Finals

Esthwaite Vale v Lunesdale United 1-3
Dent v Heathwaite 1-2*(aet)*

Final: Heathwaite 2, Lunesdale United 0

DIVISIONAL CONSTITUTIONS 1994-95

Division One	Division Two	Division Three	Division Four
1. Ambleside	1. Appleby Res.	1. Ambleside Res.	1. Carleton Rangers
2. Appleby	2. Braithwaite	2. Burneside Res.	2. Dent Res.
3. Coniston	3. Burneside	3. Coniston Res.	3. Esthwaite Vale
4. Kendal County	4. Dent	4. Eden Athletic	4. Greystoke Res.
5. Kendal United	5. Endmoor	5. Heathwaite	5. Lakes United
6. Keswick	6. Grasmere	6. Ibis	6. Langwathby
7. Kirkoswald	7. Greystoke	7. Kendal County Res.	7. Lunesdale Utd
8. Kirkby Stephen	8. Kendal Utd Res.	8. Kirkby Lonsdale	8. Provincial
9. Lunesdale Utd	9. Keswick Res.	9. Staveley Utd	9. Sedbergh Res.
10. Netherfield Res.	10. Kirkby Stephen Res.	10. Ullswater Utd	10. Shap Res.
11. Penrith United	11. Penrith United Res.	11. Victoria SC	11. Victoria SC Res.
12. Staveley United	12. Sedbergh	12. Windermere Res.	12. TFP
13. Wetheriggs	13. Shap		
14. Windermere	14. Wetheriggs Res.		

A Kendal United forward outjumps his Lunesdale United marker during United's 6-0 home win in the First Round of the Westmorland Senior Cup. Kendal United went on to win the competition. They also won the County FA Benevolent Cup, and were denied a fine cup 'treble' only by league champions Keswick who defeated them in the final of the High Sherriff's Cup, the Westmorland League's major knock-out competition.

Photo - Gavin Ellis-Neville.

WILTSHIRE F.A.

Secretary: Mr E M Parry,
44 Kennet Ave., Swindon, Wilts SN2 3LG.

PREMIER SHIELD 1993-94

Preliminary Round

Warminster Town v Swindon Town 0-3

First Round

Swindon Town v Trowbridge Town	1-2	Salisbury City v Melksham Town	5-0
Westbury United v Chippenham Town	2-4	Devizes Town v Calne Town	0-3

Semi-Finals

Calne Town v Chippenham Town	1-2	Trowbridge Town v Salisbury City	2-0

Final: *(at Swindon Town FC, Thurs 14th April)*: Trowbridge Town 3, Chippenham Town 0

SENIOR CUP

First Round

Bradford Town v Tisbury United	2-0	Plessey Semics v Swindon Supermarine	1-3
Shrewton United v Dunbar Athletic	3-0	Walcot Athletic v Ferndale Athletic	1-2
Biddestone v Burmah Castrol	1-4	Pinehurst v Wootton Bassett Town	1-3
Highworth Town v Aldbourne Park	8-0	Wroughton v Bromham	0-2
Marlborough Town v Pewsey Vale	0-6	Wollen Sports v Downton	2-3
Dorcan *(w/o)* Chiseldon *(scr)*		Bemerton Heath Harlequins v Amesbury Town	0-1

Second Round

Malmesbury Victoria v Sanford	0-2	Wootton Bassett Town v Bromham	5-2
Highworth Town v Bradford Town	2-1	Amesbury Town v Pewsey Vale	2-1
Corsham Town v Burmah Castrol	0-1	Dorcan v Ferndale Athletic	1-2
Purton v Swindon Supermarine	1-4	Shrewton United v Downton	0-2

Quarter-Finals

Downton v Amesbury Town	0-2	Sanford v Ferndale Athletic	2-3
Burmah Castrol v Wootton Bassett Town	2-1	Highworth v Swindon Supermarine	1-1*(aet, 4-5 pens)*

Semi-Finals

Ferndale v Amesbury T. *(at Pewsey Vale)*	2-3*(aet)*	Swindon Sup. v Burmah C. *(at Wootton Bassett)*	2-1

Final *(at Calne Town FC, Wed 20th April)*: Amesbury Town 2, Swindon Supermarine 1

OTHER COUNTY FINALS:

Junior Cup *(at Trowbridge Town, Wed 6th April)*: South Newton & Wishford 1, Broughton Gifford 0
Sunday Cup *(at Wootton Bassett Town, Sun 10th April)*: Shaw & Whitley Hibs 3, Rodbourne Rangers 1
Youth Cup *(at Swindon Town FC, Sun 17th April)*: Rodbourne Mannington 4, Corsham Town 0
Minor Cup (under-15) *(at Swindon Supermarine, Sun 24th April)*: Highworth Jnrs 4, Stratton Red Eagles 0
Minor Cup (under-13) *(at Swindon Town FC, Sun 17th April)*: Corsham Boys 3, Devizes Town Minors 0

WILTSHIRE FOOTBALL LEAGUE

Founded: 1976

President: D S Paget

Chairman: D C Kilford

Vice-Chairman: C W Cousins

Hon. General Secretary: P J Ackrill,
3 Dallas Avenue, Swindon SN3 3NP (520334).

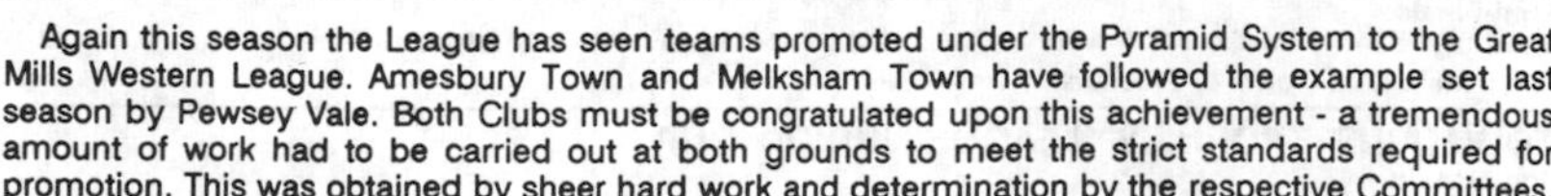

Again this season the League has seen teams promoted under the Pyramid System to the Great Mills Western League. Amesbury Town and Melksham Town have followed the example set last season by Pewsey Vale. Both Clubs must be congratulated upon this achievement - a tremendous amount of work had to be carried out at both grounds to meet the strict standards required for promotion. This was obtained by sheer hard work and determination by the respective Committees.

Fixture making has again provided many problems with clubs cancelling fixtures, and the inclement weather which hit the County mid-way through the season did nothing to help the situation.

The past season has seen all four divisional championships very closely contested, and many issues remained unresolved until final League games had been completed. The principal honours have been won by Melksham Town who became League Champions. Amesbury Town became runners-up after leading the table for most of the season. *(continued overleaf)*

Division Two was the first section to be decided with Bradford Town taking the honours in a dominate manner. Malmesbury Victoria have achieved their ambition since rejoining the League as a senior club by gaining promotion as runners-up. The other Divisions proved equally exciting. Division Three champions were National Semiconductor, who took the honours from Aldbourne Park Reserves. In Division Four, the newly-elected clubs all had a successful season with Ashton Keynes taking the title, closely followed by Raychem Sports & Social Club.

The Addkey Senior Knock-Out Competition proved interesting, with the final at Corsham Town's ground being won by Melksham Town who defeated Pinehurst FC by 4 goals to 1. The Fountain Trophies Junior Cup was staged in the evening following the Senior Cup final at Corsham, and this game resulted in a win for Melksham Town Reserves by 4 goals to 2 over National Semiconductor. The Floodlit Cup was won by Trowbridge Town who defeated Amesbury Town 2-0 at Calne.

Congratulations must be extended to Amesbury Town for winning the Wiltshire Senior Cup by defeating the Hellenic Premier Division Swindon Supermarine - this was an outsanding achievement.

P J Ackrill, Secretary.

DIV. ONE	P	W	D	L	F	A	PTS
Melksham Town	28	21	3	4	91	29	66
Amesbury Town	28	19	2	7	70	35	59
Pinehurst	28	17	3	8	50	41	54
Devizes Town Res.	28	15	2	11	37	32	47
Sanford	28	14	3	11	42	40	45
Tisbury United	28	12	8	8	57	45	44
Shrewton United	28	13	4	11	49	42	43
Ferndale Athletic	28	10	9	9	54	35	39
Calne Town Res.	28	10	8	10	40	48	38
Marlborough Town	28	10	6	12	41	51	36
Corsham Town	28	10	3	15	38	39	33
Aldbourne Park	28	7	3	18	26	75	24
Biddestone	28	6	5	17	35	54	23
Walcot Athletic	28	6	5	17	34	76	23
Burmah Castrol	28	5	6	17	37	59	21

DIV. TWO	P	W	D	L	F	A	PTS
Bradford Town	22	17	2	3	58	23	53
Malmesbury Victoria	22	12	6	4	40	22	42
Pewsey Vale Res.	22	12	5	5	34	20	41
Dorcan	22	12	4	6	34	27	40
Plessey Semics	22	11	5	6	43	25	38
Dunbar Athletic	22	8	7	7	35	31	31
Chippenham T. Res.	22	8	6	8	39	30	30
Wootton Bassett Res.	22	6	4	12	22	43	22
Purton Res.	22	6	3	13	22	39	21
Warminster T. Res.	22	5	6	11	32	50	21
Wroughton	22	5	3	14	26	46	18
Bromham	22	3	3	16	29	58	12

DIV. THREE	P	W	D	L	F	A	PTS
Nat. Semiconductor	24	18	3	3	66	18	57
Aldbourne P. Res.	24	14	5	5	55	26	47
West Swindon	24	13	4	7	46	32	43
Melksham T. Res.	24	13	3	8	57	37	42
Corsham Town Res.	24	13	2	9	49	39	41
Pinehurst Res.	24	11	4	9	42	36	37
Blunsdon United	24	9	4	11	40	51	31
Dorcan Res.	24	9	3	12	34	73	30
Wootton Bassett Spts	24	8	4	12	48	54	28
Burmah Castrol Res.	24	8	2	14	39	71	26
Sanford Res.	24	7	3	14	40	46	24
Marlborough Res.	24	5	6	13	45	61	21
Plessey Semics Res.	24	4	5	15	36	53	17
Ferndale Ath. Res. record expunged							

DIV. FOUR	P	W	D	L	F	A	PTS
Ashton Keynes	32	22	5	5	89	39	71
Raychem S & S	32	19	9	4	91	42	66
Cricklade Town	32	18	7	7	76	46	61
Minety	32	17	6	9	77	63	57
Down Ampney	32	17	4	11	91	54	55
Tidworth United	32	16	6	7	79	52	55
Highworth Athletic	32	16	5	11	81	56	53
Chippenham Boro.	32	15	7	10	78	51	52
Ramsbury	32	15	6	11	75	55	51
Sherston Town	32	13	12	7	66	56	51
Grove	32	14	3	15	75	88	45
Biddestone Res.	32	10	5	17	47	60	35
Walcot Ath. Res.	32	8	4	20	58	89	28
Dunbar Ath. Res.	32	7	5	20	51	79	26
Bromham Res.	32	6	7	19	39	98	25
Wroughton Res.	32	5	6	21	36	69	21
Chiseldon	32	3	4	25	35	147	13

'ADDKEY' LEAGUE SENIOR CUP 1993-94

First Round

Pinehurst v Aldbourne Park 5-0
Shrewton United v Plessey Semics 2-2,4-8
Warminster Town Reserves v Walcot Athletic 3-6
Amesbury Town v Biddestone 4-1
Sanford v Marlborough Town 2-4
Stratton Athletic *(scr)* v Ferndale Athletic *(w/o)*
Chiselden *(scr)* v Melksham Town *(w/)*
Bradford Town v Tisbury United 0-3
Pewsey Vale Reserves v Broughton 4-1
Wootton Bass. T. Res. v Chippenham T. Res. 2-2,1-0
Bromham v Calne Town Reserves 0-5
Purton Reserves v Malmesbury Victoria 1-2
Corsham Town v Devizes Town Reserves 3-1

Second Round

Amesbury Town v Dorcan 9-1
Corsham Town v Melksham Town 0-2
Pinehurst v Burmah Castrol 2-1
Tisbury United v Plessey Semics 2-0
Dunbar Athletic v Walcot Athletic 2-3
Calne Town Reserves v Marlborough Town 1-3
Pewsey Vale Res. v Wootton Bassett Town Res. 3-1
Malmesbury v Ferndale Ath. 2-5*(Ferndale disqualified)*

Quarter-Finals

Amesbury Town v Marlborough Town 2-0
Pinehurst v Tisbury United 3-0
Pewsey Vale Reserves v Walcot Athletic 1-2
Malmesbury Victoria v Melksham Town 0-6

Semi-Finals

Amesbury Town v Melksham Town 2-3
Pinehurst v Walcot Athletiv 3-1

Final: Melksham Town 4, Pinehurst 1

'FOUNTAINS TROPHIES' LEAGUE JUNIOR CUP

First Round

Melksham Town Reserves v Dorcan Res. 10-1
Walcot A. Res *(w/o)* v Biddestone Res. *(scr)*
Sherston Town v Minety 6-0
Grove v Sanford Reserves 3-1
Marlborough Town Res. v Ashton Keynes 2-1
Tidworth United v Chiseldon 5-0
West Swindon v Chippenham Borough 0-1
Wroughton Reserves v Wootton Bassett Spts 0-5
Bromham Reserves v Blundson United 2-4
Raychem S & S *(w/o)* v Ferndale Ath. Res. *(scr)*
Cricklade Town *(w/o)* v Pinehurst Res. *(scr)*
Burmah Castrol Res. v Plessey Semics Res. 1-3
Corsham Town Reserves v Dunbar Athletic 3-1
Ramsbury *(w/o)* v Box Rovers *(scr)*
Highworth Athletic v Down Ampney 5-1
Albourne Park Reserves v National Semiconductor 1-3

(continued opposite)

Second Round

Melksham Town Reserves v Blunsdon United	2-0	Walcot Athletic Res. v Raychem Sports & Soc.	1-2
Sherston Town v Cricklade Town	1-0	Grove v Plessey Semics Reserves	0-3
Marlborough T. Res. v Corsham Town Res.	1-0	Tidworth United v Ramsbury	1-3
Chippenham Borough v Highworth Athletic	2-1	Wootton Bassett Spts v Nat. Semiconductor	1-1,1-4

Quarter-Finals

Melksham Town Res. v Raychem Spts & S.	3-2	Sherston Town v Plessey Semics Reserves	1-2
Marlborough Town Reserves v Ramsbury	3-1	Chippenham Borough v National Semiconductor	1-2

Semi-Finals

Melksham Town Res. v Plessey Semics Res.	3-0	Marlborough Town Res. v National Semiconductor	1-5

Final: Melksham Town Reserves 4, National Semiconductor 2

SENIOR DIVISION ONE CLUBS 1994-95

ALDBOURNE FERNDALE
Secretary: Ms S Archer, 27 Claridge Close, Aldbourne, Swindon SN8 2DU.
Ground: Farm Lane, Aldbourne. **Colours:** Gold/black *(Res: red/black)*
Previous Names: Aldbourne Park/ Ferndale Athletic - clubs merged 1994.
Previous Ground: Ferndale Athletic - County Ground Extension (Swindon Town FC)(pre-1994).

BIDDESTONE
Secretary: Mr A Short, 1 Hartham Lane, Biddestone, Chippenham SN14 7EA (0249 714724).
Grnd: Yatton Rd, Cuttle Lane, Biddestone **Colours:** All white *(Res: yellow/blue/blue)*

BRADFORD TOWN
Secretary: Miss K Stevens, 12 Magnon Rd, Bradford-on-Avon BA15 1PT (0225 865526).
Ground: St Laurence School, Ashley Rd entrance, Bradford-on-Avon (0225 867691).
Colours: Blue & white/blue & white/blue & white *(Res: yellow/yellow/blue)*

CORSHAM TOWN
Secretary: Mrs P Kilmurray, 21 Telcroft Close, Corsham SN13 9JH (0249 714918).
Ground: Southbank, Lacock Rd (0249 715609) **Cols:** Red & white *(Res: White & black)*

MALMESBURY VICTORIA
Secretary: Mrs M Picter, 14 White Lion Park, Malmesbury SN16 0QW (0666 822623).
Grnd: Flying Monk Ground, Gloucester Rd, Malmesbury (0666 822141) **Cols:** White & black stripes/black.

MARLBOROUGH TOWN
Secretary: Mr D W G Cripps, 62 Five Stiles Rd, Marlborough SN8 4BE (0672 512741).
Ground: Elcot Lane (0672 513340) **Colours:** Blue & red stripes *(Res: all maroon).*

PINEHURST
Secretary: Mr N J Merrett, 21 Windflower Rd, Haydon Wick, Swindon SN1 2JU (0793 705304).
Ground: Pinehurst School Field, Beech Ave., Swindon.
Colours: White/blue/blue *(Res: Black & grey stripes/black/black).*

SANFORD
Secretary: Mr A L Pike, 41 Gays Place, Upper Stratton, Swindon SN2 6LN (0793 826082).
Ground: GWR Sports Club, Swindon (0793 523019) **Colours:** Red & black/black/red

SHREWTON UNITED
Secretary: Mrs M Withers, Fleming Farm, Shrewton, nr Salisbury SP3 4ER (0980 620065).
Ground: Shrewton Rec. **Colours:** Maroon & blue.

TISBURY UNITED
Secretary: Mr F L Hopgood, Hill-Tops, 1 Cuffs Lane, Tisbury SP3 6LG (0747 870246).
Ground: Station Rd Rec, Tisbury (0747 871314) **Colours:** All blue.

WALCOT ATHLETIC
Secretary: Mr P J Radley, 9 Colchester Close, Toothill, Swindon SN5 8AG (0793 488485).
Ground: Southbrook Rec, Pinehurst Rd, Swindon (0793 611171).
Colours: Red/blue/blue *(Res: Green/grey/green).*

Plus the Reserve sides of: *Calne Town (page 561), Devizes Town (page 567), Pewsey Vale (page 569).*

SENIOR DIVISION TWO CLUBS 1994-95

BROMHAM
Secretary: Mr R Witts, 2a Falcon Rd, Calne SN11 8PL (0249 813023).
Ground: Jubilee PF, New Rd, Bromham (0380 850671) **Cols:** Blue/white/maroon *(Res: white/black/red)*

BURMAH CASTROL
Secretary: Mr I G Watters, 15 Lucerne Close, Middleleaze, Swindon SN5 9GQ (0793 887628).
Ground: Burmah House, Pipers Way, Swindon (via Broome Manor Golf Club)(0793 523142).
Colours: Navy/black/black *(Res: Red & black hoops/red/red).*

DORCAN
Secretary: Mr T Smith, 69 Boadleas Park, Devizes SN1 3JR (0831 717336).
Grnd: Oakfield Sch., Marlowe Ave., Swindon (0793 535043) **Colours:** Sky/navy.

DUNBAR ATHLETIC
Secretary: Mr A M Pickett, 78 Southbrook Street Extension, Swindon SN2 1HG (0793 523980).
Grnd: King Edwards Place, Foxhill, nr Swindon (0793 791282) **Cols:** Tangerine/black/black.
Previous Name: Dunbar Wills (pre-1994).

PLESSEY SEMICS
Secretary: Mr C Bennett, 15 Mellow Ground, Haydon Wick, Swindon SN2 3QJ (0793 726715).
Ground: Plessey Spts Ground, Ermin Street, Stratton, Swindon **Colours:** All blue.

WROUGHTON

Secretary: Mr C G Swatton, 23 Lydiard Park, Hook Str.,, Wootton Bassett SN4 8EF (0793 855194).
Grnd: Weir Field, Wroughton **Colours:** White & blue.

Plus the Reserve sides of: *Amesbury Town (page 566), Chippenham Town (page 561), Melksham Town (page 569), Purton (page 626), Swindon Supermarine (page 622), Warminster Town (page 569), Wootton Bassett Town (page 628).*

JUNIOR DIVISION THREE CLUBS 1994-95

ASHTON KEYNES

Secretary: Mr D Young, Mayflower House, 3 Quater Row, Coates, Cirencester GL7 6JX (0285 770971).
Grnd: Bradstone Spts Field, Rixon Gate, Ashton Keynes **Colours:** Blue/white.

BLUNSDON UNITED

Secretary: Mr K Hobbs, 31 Burnet Close, Woodhall Park, Haydon Wick, Swindon SN2 2RT (0793 728059).
Ground: Recreation Park, Sams Lane, Blunsdon **Colours:** White/blue/white.

CRICKLADE TOWN

Secretary: Mr W J Locke, 11 Drew Str., Rodbourne, Swindon SN2 2HP (0793 520634).
Grnd: Cricklade Leisure Centre, Stones Lane, Cricklade (0793 750011) **Cols:** Green & white/green/green.

DOWN AMPNEY

Secretary: Mr D F Lawrence, 5 Limes Place, Latton, nr Cricklade, Swindon SN6 6DR (0793 751525).
Ground: Broadleaze, Down Ampney (0793 750414) **Colours:** All blue.

HIGHWORTH ATHLETIC

Secretary: Mr P D Hayward, 12 Brookfield, Highworth, Swindon SN6 7HY (0793 763012).
Ground: Barra Close Rec, Highworth **Colours:** White/blue/blue.

MINETY

Secretary: Mr C Henderson, 'Beechwood', Hornbury Hill, Minety, Malmesbury SN16 9QH (0666 860280).
Ground: Silver Street PF, Minety (0666 860802). **Colours:** Orange/black.

RAYCHEM SPORTS & SOCIAL

Secretary: Mr R J Wheatley, 18 Shapwick Close, Nythe, Swindon SN3 3RQ (0793 527500).
Ground: Crosslink Centre, Ermin Str., Swindon (0793 831511) **Colours:** Black & white stripes/black.

WEST SWINDON

Secretary: Mr M J Smyth, 130 Rosebery Street, Swindon SN1 2ET (0793 694253).
Ground: Greendown School, West Swindon (0793 874224) **Colours:** Claret/sky/claret.

WOOTTON BASSETT SPORTS

Secretary: Mr M Smedley, 31 Tennyson Rd, Wootton Bassett SN4 8HL (0793 852584).
Ground: Ballards Ash Spts Ground, W. Bassett (0793 849720) **Colours:** White & blue/blue/blue

Plus the Reserve sides of: *Aldbourne Ferndale, Burmah Castrol, Corsham Town, Dorcan, Marlborough Town, Pinehurst, Plessey Semics, Sanford.*

JUNIOR DIVISION FOUR CLUBS 1994-95

BOX ROVERS

Secretary: Mr P Goulding, 20 Sunderland Close, Melksham SN12 6TZ (0225 704988).
Ground: Box Recreation Ground **Colours:** All blue.

CHIPPENHAM BOROUGH

Secretary: Mr P Jefferies, 60 Park Avenue, Chippenham SN14 0HA (0249 655047).
Ground: West Mead Lane PF, Chippenham **Cols:** Blue & black stripes/black/black

CHISELDON

Secretary: Mr T J Townsend, 15 Tulip Tree Close, Swindon SN2 1RR (0793 520444).
Ground: Chiseldon Rec. **Colours:** Gold & black

LEISURE LINES SPORTS

Secretary: Mr T J Hunt, Flat 6, 12 Field Park Rd, Newport, Gwent NP9 0AY (0225 763994).
Ground: Holt Recreation Ground **Colours:** All green.

OLD TOWN RANGERS

Secretary: Miss C Axford, 26 Churchill, Wroughton, Swindon SN4 9JS (0793 814516).
Ground: Penhill Rec, Swindon (0793 722926)
Previous Name: Grove (pre-1994) **Colours:** Blue & black stripes/black/black.

RAMSBURY

Secretary: Mr R G Mills, 14 Swans Close, Ramsbury, Marlborough, Wilts SN8 2PH (0672 20468).
Ground: Hilldrop Lane Rec, Ramsbury, Marlborough **Colours:** Blue (white trim)

ROYAL MAIL

Secretary: Mr C Ballard, 11 Knolton Walk, Park South, Swindon SN3 2JN (0793 641873).
Ground: Nalgo Sports Ground, Cricklade Rd, Swindon **Cols:** Red & black/black/black.

SHERSTON TOWN

Secretary: Ms K Brock, 15 Portway, Chippenham SN14 0BQ (0249 660301).
Ground: Knockdown Rd, Sherston, Malmesbury (0666 840934) **Colous:** Red/black.

SUNSTRANDS

Secretary: Mr D Stradling, 17 Desborough, Freshbrook, Swindon SN3 8QR (0793 612391).
Ground: As Old Town Rgrs (above) **Colours:** Red & blue stripes/blue.

Plus the Reserve sides of: *Biddestone, Bradford Town, Bromham, Dunbar Ath., Malmesbury Victoria, Shrewton Utd, Walcot Ath., Wroughton.*

SWINDON & DISTRICT LEAGUE (Est. 1891)

President: J A Stephens, JP. **Chairman:** T D J Boffin. **Secretary:** J T Thorn.

PREM. DIVISION	P	W	D	L	F	A	PTS
Old Nick	20	16	2	2	75	20	*34
Ivy Leaf	20	16	2	2	84	19	34
Greatfield United	20	14	3	3	78	29	31
Copy Cats	19	12	2	5	46	23	26
Pinehurst Res.	20	11	2	7	37	38	24
Lower Stratton	20	5	6	9	35	43	16
Raychem SSC Res.	20	4	6	10	49	65	14
Walcot	20	3	7	10	40	60	13
Nat Semi-Con. Res.	20	4	5	11	38	59	13
AFC Rangers	20	3	3	14	23	77	9
Coleview United	19	2	0	17	19	91	4

* - Champions after play-off

DIVISION ONE	P	W	D	L	F	A	PTS
W H Smith	18	14	3	1	77	23	31
Boundary House	18	14	2	2	74	23	30
Salamandre	18	10	3	5	64	45	23
Bakers R.	18	7	5	6	40	37	19
AC Wanderers	18	8	2	8	51	52	18
Ridgeway	18	7	3	8	51	54	17
Sundstrand	18	7	2	9	49	48	16
SKS Blyskawica	18	4	4	10	25	41	12
Lower Stratton Res.	18	3	4	11	29	61	10
Copy Cats Res.	18	2	0	16	29	105	4

DIVISION TWO	P	W	D	L	F	A	PTS
Pinehurst Community	20	17	1	2	97	25	*35
NALGO Sports	20	17	1	2	84	23	35
Suffolk Arms	20	11	4	5	46	42	26
Spectrum XI	20	12	1	7	55	35	25
Royal Mail 419ers	20	11	2	7	66	46	24
Cricklade T. Res.	20	9	2	9	59	48	20
Farepak	20	9	2	9	49	62	20
Wroughton 'A'	20	5	4	11	50	81	14
Dunbar Ath. Res.	20	4	3	13	35	61	11
Bakers R. Res.	20	4	2	14	29	58	10
Trailers Res.	20	0	1	19	23	112	1

DIVISION THREE	P	W	D	L	F	A	PTS
John O'Flynn	24	21	1	2	78	18	43
Walcot Ath. Res.	23	18	2	3	100	25	38
Rodbourne Man'ton	24	17	3	4	97	38	37
Westbourne Park	24	16	3	5	102	38	35
Top Cue Wanderers	24	15	2	7	87	49	32
W. Bass. Spts Res.	24	9	7	8	86	69	25
P & O Excavations	24	12	1	11	68	64	25
Smith's Roofing	23	10	4	9	78	64	24
Prince of Wales	24	6	2	16	46	85	14
Coleview Utd Res.	24	4	4	16	32	82	12
Top Cue	24	4	3	17	46	93	11
Lydiard Sports	24	2	3	19	51	101	7
Toothill	24	3	1	20	35	180	7

PREMIER DIV. RESULTS	1	2	3	4	5	6	7	8	9	10	11
1. AFC Rangers	*	3-0	1-5	0-10	1-4	1-1	2-2	0-8	0-4	2-4	0-5
2. Coleview United	1-6	*	0-4	1-5	1-4	1-3	1-2	2-8	2-3	0-6	2-1
3. Copy Cats	4-0		*	0-2	1-1	2-1	1-0	0-1	0-1	8-1	2-2
4. Greatfield United	4-1	8-1	1-2	*	2-5	3-0	3-1	2-2	6-3	6-0	2-1
5. Ivy Leaf	7-1	14-0	3-1	1-3	*	3-0	6-0	4-0	0-1	5-2	5-0
6. Lower Stratton	4-0	2-2	1-2	3-3	1-5	*	2-1	0-5	1-2	2-2	3-3
7. Nat SemiConductor Res.	5-1	7-3	2-5	1-3	0-8	2-1	*	0-3	3-4	3-3	3-3
8. Old Nick	2-0	4-0	2-1	1-0	1-2	4-1	5-2	*	3-0	4-1	7-0
9. Pinehurst	5-0	3-0	0-1	2-6	0-3	1-1	3-2	0-4	*	3-3	W-L
10. Raychem S & SC Res.	1-1	1-0	1-2	2-7	2-2	1-2	1-1	1-7	3-1	*	10-2
11. Walcot	1-3	4-0	3-5	2-2	L-W	2-2	1-1	4-4	0-1	5-4	*

Old Nick defeated Ivy Leaf 4-2 in a play-off for the championship.

DIVISION ONE RESULTS	1	2	3	4	5	6	7	8	9	10
1. AC Wanderers	*	W-L	L-W	5-0	0-0	6-3	1-4	0-2	3-3	2-3
2. Bakers R.	5-1	*	1-1	2-0	2-1	3-1	6-4	1-1	0-1	2-3
3. Boundary House	5-3	7-0	*	10-2	2-1	3-2	8-1	6-2	3-2	2-1
4. Copy Cats Reserves	1-7	1-4	0-5	*	5-2	3-10	0-8	5-0	1-10	0-10
5. Lower Stratton Reserves	4-8	2-2	0-2	4-2	*	2-1	L-W	2-1	1-4	2-2
6. Ridgeway	2-3	6-5	0-7	4-2	3-1	*	4-2	2-2	5-0	0-6
7. Salamandre	4-5	3-2	3-2	15-2	5-2	3-3	*	0-0	3-2	1-3
8. SKS Blyskawica	2-3	1-2	3-3	W-L	6-2	1-2	2-4	*	1-0	0-3
9. Sundstrand	8-2	1-2	0-7	4-3	2-2	4-3	2-3	2-1	*	3-5
10. W H Smith	6-2	3-3	2-1	5-2	14-1	3-0	1-1	4-0	3-1	*

DIVISION TWO RESULTS	1	2	3	4	5	6	7	8	9	10	11
1. Baker R. Reserves	*	2-1	4-2	1-3	0-8	0-1	2-4	1-2	3-5	4-1	0-3
2. Cricklade Town Reserves	4-2	*	7-0	7-1	2-5	0-1	2-6	2-0	0-1	7-2	2-2
3. Dunbar Athletic Reserves	4-0	1-1	*	1-3	0-3	2-5	2-5	0-8	0-0	3-1	2-2
4. Farepak	3-1	2-7	3-2	*	1-4	3-5	0-3	4-3	1-2	4-4	4-4
5. NALGO Sports	3-0	3-1	4-1	1-2	*	3-1	4-3	3-0	2-1	13-1	7-0
6. Pinehurst Community	6-0	6-1	2-0	6-3	1-1	*	2-1	4-2	8-0	4-0	11-1
7. Royal Mail 419ers	1-1	1-4	3-7	4-3	2-0	2-7	*	1-2	5-2	5-1	9-0
8. Spectrum XI	4-2	5-1	2-0	2-3	1-7	2-1	2-1	*	0-2	9-1	5-0
9. Suffolk Arms	1-1	6-1	W-L	4-0	1-3	3-8	2-2	0-0	*	3-1	4-1
10. Trailers	0-5	1-4	2-5	1-2	2-6	0-12	1-2	0-4	2-4	*	0-7
11. Wroughton	2-0	1-5	6-3	0-4	3-4	1-6	2-6	L-W	4-5	9-2	*

Pinehurst Community defeated NALGO Sports 4-2 in a play-off for the championship.

DIV. THREE RESULTS	1	2	3	4	5	6	7	8	9	10	11	12	13
1. Coleview Utd Reserves	*	0-6	2-1	1-4	1-2	0-5	1-7	1-2	6-0	0-5	1-6	2-5	3-3
2. John O'Flynn	W-L	*	5-0	1-0	5-2	3-1	4-0	3-1	5-1	2-0	1-0	1-0	5-1
3. Lydiard Sports	1-1	0-2	*	1-5	3-6	1-4	5-4	1-4	2-3	3-4	3-5	5-5	2-11
4. P & O Excavations	5-1	2-4	3-1	*	W-L	1-3	1-2	13-0	5-3	1-6	0-2	4-2	4-1
5. Prince of Wales	1-2	0-6	3-2	2-2	*	2-4	3-1	2-1	4-5	1-8	0-14	0-9	1-4
6. Rodbourne Mannington	7-1	2-2	3-1	7-0	3-1	*	3-2	7-1	2-0	5-0	3-4	3-3	4-0
7. Smith's Roofing	2-2	1-0	5-4	3-1	3-2	3-6	*	16-4	6-7	0-2	2-10	0-0	4-1
8. Toothill	1-2	1-9	0-10	1-7	0-8	2-12	1-10	*	4-3	1-14	0-1	3-5	1-15
9. Top Cue	3-3	2-3	3-3	3-6	1-1	0-3	2-4	2-1	*	1-2	2-3	1-5	2-4
10. Top Cue Wanderers	W-L	3-1	7-2	0-1	3-1	1-4	2-2	9-1	5-1	*	0-3	0-6	6-6
11. Walcot Athletic Res.	4-0	0-4	8-0	8-0	2-0	2-0		14-2	4-0	2-0	*	1-3	3-3
12. Westbourne Park	8-0	0-1	4-0	4-1	3-2	6-4	3-1	13-0	6-0	1-3	0-3	*	9-2
13. Wootton B. Spts Res.	4-2	1-5	4-0	6-2	3-0	2-2	0-0	3-3	6-1	4-7	1-1	1-2	*

ADVERTISER CUP COMPETITION 1993-94

First Round

Walcot v Coleview United	8-0	SKS Blyskawica v Copy Cats	3-7
Ivy Leaf v Salamandre	9-1		

Second Round

Lower Stratton v Greatfield United	2-4	Walcot *(w/o)* Sanford Reserves *(scr)*	
Pinehurst v Copy Cats	4-5	National SemiConductor Reserves v W H Smith	3-5
Old Nick v AFC Rangers	3-1	Sundstrand v AC Wanderers	4-1
Ridgeway v Bakers R.	7-4	Boundary House v Ivy Leaf	1-2

Quarter-Finals

Greatfield United v Walcot	0-5	Copy Cats v W H Smith	2-3
Old Nick v Sundstrand	5-1	Rodbourne Mannington v Ivy Leaf	1-4

Semi-Finals

Walcot v W H Smith	6-3	Old Nick v Ivy Leaf	2-3

Final: Ivy Leaf 3, Walcot 2

SWINDON JUNIOR CUP COMPETITION 1993-94

First Round

Royal Mail 419ers v Lydiard Sports	5-3	Trailers *(w/o)* Asap Hotspurs *(scr)*	
Westbourne Park v Smith's Roofing	9-1	Farepak v Cricklade Town Reserves	1-2
Pinehurst Community v Pinehurst	12-0	Baker R. Reserves v Wootton Bassett Sports	4-2
Nalgo Spts v P & O Excavations	3-1	Wroughon v Dunbar Athletic	4-3
John Flynn v Crown	4-3	Top Cue Wdrs v Rodbourne Mannington	3-4
Spectrum XI v Toothill	6-3		

Second Round

Royal Mail 419ers v Trailers	3-0	Westbourne Park v Cricklade Town Reserves	7-1
Pinehurst Community v Bakers R. Res.	3-1	Coleview United Reserves v Nalgo Sports	0-6
Wroughton v Top Cue	7-3	Walcot Athletic Res. v John O'Flynn	2-0
Rodbourne Mannington *(w/o)* Prince of Wales *(scr)*		Suffolk Arms v Spectrum XI	0-1

Quarter-Finals

Royal Mail 419ers v Westbourne Park	2-3	Pinehurst Community v Nalgo Sports	4-1
Wroughton v Walcot Athletic Res.	1-3	Rodbourne Mannington v Spectrum XI	3-3,1-3

Semi-Finals

Westbourne Park v Pinehurst Community	0-4	Walcot Athletic Reserves v Spectrum XI	3-1

Final: Pinehurst Community 1, Walcot Athletic Reserves 0

SWINDON & DISTRICT LEAGUE MINOR SECTION TABLES

Under-13s	P	W	D	L	F	A	PTS
Westside Utd JFC	26	22	1	3	155	32	45
Hathaway Wdrs	26	22	0	4	121	32	44
Dorcan	26	22	0	4	141	54	44
Pinehurst	26	21	0	5	200	34	42
St Josephs YC	26	20	1	5	145	35	41
Wootton Bassett T.	26	12	2	12	80	60	26
Rodbourne Man'ton	26	10	4	12	107	63	24
Wroughton	26	10	3	13	96	117	23
Robins	26	10	1	15	87	132	21
Shrivenham	26	7	4	15	54	86	18
Ferndale YC	26	6	1	19	66	91	13
Nythe	26	4	1	21	58	190	9
West Swindon Jnrs	26	3	2	21	45	190	8
KC Rangers	26	1	0	25	11	264	2

Under-14s	P	W	D	L	F	A	PTS
Robins	12	12	0	0	84	10	24
Stratton Red Eagles	14	10	0	4	51	26	20
Dorcan	13	9	1	3	49	24	19
Ferndale YC	14	7	2	5	39	26	16
Pinehurst	14	6	2	6	37	48	14
Westside Utd JFC	14	3	2	9	26	37	8
Rodbourne Man'ton	13	2	0	11	26	89	4
Chiseldon Boys	14	1	1	12	7	58	3

Under-12s	P	W	D	L	F	A	PTS
Westside Utd JFC	14	14	0	0	80	4	28
Liden YC	14	10	1	3	62	22	21
St Josephs YC	14	8	1	5	58	46	17
Wootton Bassett T.	14	7	0	7	40	37	14
Wroughton	14	7	0	7	39	39	14
Ferndale YC	14	3	3	8	27	38	9
Eldene	14	2	1	11	17	72	5
Nythe	14	2	0	12	18	83	4

SWINDON SUNDAY LEAGUE

FOUNDED: 1962

DIV. ONE	P	W	D	L	F	A	PTS
Greyhound	16	13	3	0	59	12	29
New Century WMC	16	10	4	2	51	25	24
Athletico	16	8	1	7	41	41	17
Deers Leap	16	6	5	5	46	32	17
Juventus	16	6	2	8	29	39	14
Raychem Sunday	16	5	3	8	31	39	13
The Globe	16	3	6	7	28	41	12
AFC Cricklade	16	3	4	9	31	65	10
Bunsdonians	16	2	4	10	26	48	8

Lower Division Champions:
Div. 2 (12): The Windmill
Div. 3 (12): Steam Train
Div. 4 (13): Rodbourne Rangers
Div. 5 (12): Lechlade
Div. 6 (12): Aldbourne
Div. 7 (12): BT Union Nalgo
Div. 8 (13): Autoprime

Cup Finals:
KO Cup: Greyhound 3, Deer Leap 0
Chairman's Trophy: Jesters 2, Wanborough 1

WORCESTERSHIRE F.A.

Secretary: M R Leggett,
'Fermain', 12 Worcester Road,
Evesham, Worcs WR11 4JU.

SENIOR CUP 1993-94

First Round
Solihull Borough v Sutton Coldfield Town 4-0
Redditch United v Evesham United 2-2,3-2*(aet)*

Quarter-Finals
Kidderminster Harriers v Worcester City 4-2
Bromsgrove Rovers v Moor Green 3-0
Dudley Town v Solihull Borough 0-1
Reddditch United v Stourbridge 2-1

Semi-Finals
Redditch United v Kidderminster Harriers 2-3
Bromsgrove Rovers v Solihull Borough 3-0

Final First Leg *(Wed 11th May)*: Kidderminster Harriers 1, Bromsgrove Rovers 1
Final Second Leg *(Fri 13th May)*: Bromsgrove Rovers 4, Kidderminster Harriers 0

SENIOR URN 1993-94

First Round
Kiddersminster Res. v West Mids Police 1-1,4-3

Quarter-Finals
Stourport Swifts v Pershore. Town 3-0
Bromsgrove Rovers Reserves v Brierley Hill Town 5-3
Pegasus Juniors v Studley BKL 3-3,0-1

Semi-Finals
Bromsgrove Rovers Reserves v Studley BKL 4-1
Stourport Swifts v Kidderminster Harriers Res. 3-1

Final First Leg *(Thurs 21st April)*: Bromsgrove Rovers Reserves 1, Stourport Swifts 2
Final Second Leg *(Thurs 28th April)*: Stourport Swifts 1, Bromsgrove Rovers Reserves 1

Stourport Swifts, Worcestershire Senior Urn winners 1993-94.

OTHER COUNTY FINALS 1993-94

Junior Cup *(at Worcester City FC, Tues 3rd May)*: Colletts Green 3, Wyre Forest 2 *(aet)*
Minor Cup *(at Stourport Swifts FC, Sat 16th April)*: Worths 1, Perrywood 0
Youth Cup *(at Stourport Swifts FC, Fri 29th April)*: Kidderminster H. Yth 1, Redditch U. Yth 01
Sunday Prem. Cup *(at Kidderminster H. FC, Sun 1st May)*: Garringtons Sunday 3, Stourbridge Rolling Mills 1
Sunday Jnr Cup *(at Bromsgrove R. FC, Sun 10th April)*: Kingswinford Snooker Centre 3, Evesham WMC 1
Sunday Minor Cup *(at Pershore Town FC, Sun 24th April)*: Bredon 2, Studley Sporting 1
Sunday under-16s Cup *(at Archdales FC, Sun 17th April)*: Kidderminsters Harr. Boys 3, Kempsey Colts 0

WORCESTER & DISTRICT

LEAGUE

FOUNDED: 1893

PREM. DIV.	P	W	D	L	F	A	PTS
Tewkesbury YMCA	26	24	2	0	96	21	50
Bromsgrove Olympic	26	19	3	4	80	26	41
Feckenham	26	16	5	5	72	35	37
Bishampton Utd	26	16	4	6	82	39	36
Droitwich Spa	26	15	5	6	64	35	35
Chequers Fladbury	26	13	4	9	64	45	30
Inkberrow	26	12	1	13	52	64	25
Cooksons	26	8	3	15	47	69	19
Malvern Rangers	26	7	5	14	35	60	19
Hallow WMC	26	6	4	16	39	69	16
Ross Town '93	26	8	2	16	29	61	*#16
Hereford Lads Club	26	4	6	16	39	66	14
Malvern Radar	26	5	3	18	48	98	13
St Richards OB	26	4	3	19	33	97	#11

DIV. ONE	P	W	D	L	F	A	PTS
Littletons	22	18	2	2	74	28	38
BSK Castings	22	16	5	1	78	23	37
Pershore Town 'A'	22	13	4	5	51	31	30
Martley Spurs	22	10	5	7	57	60	25
Upton Sports	22	10	3	9	52	49	23
Perrywood	22	8	6	8	54	46	22
Tewk. YMCA Res.	22	10	2	10	48	50	22
Kempsey United	22	8	3	11	44	45	19
AFC Barbourne	22	7	5	10	49	56	*#17
County Sports	22	5	5	12	38	63	15
Ashchurch	22	2	4	16	30	70	8
Pershore New Inn	22	2	2	18	26	82	6

DIV. TWO	P	W	D	L	F	A	PTS
Comer Gardens	22	15	6	1	76	20	36
Avondale	22	16	5	1	85	20	*#35
Tewkesbury Town	22	15	2	5	87	38	32
Nelson	22	13	3	6	88	44	29
All Blacks	22	12	1	9	70	50	25
Vine Athletic	22	10	4	8	68	52	24
Hallow WMC Res.	22	9	4	9	46	45	22
Malvern Radar Res.	22	8	3	11	39	56	19
Malvern Victoria	22	8	2	12	52	63	18
Powick	22	7	0	15	44	76	14
West Malvern	22	3	0	19	24	91	6
FC Porto	22	1	0	21	15	144	2

* - Points deducted
\# - Goals deducted

Cup Finals:

Baylis Cup: Bromsgrove O. 4, Tewkesbury YMCA 1
Phipps Cup: Avondale 2, Comer Gardens 1

KIDDERMINSTER & DISTRICT LEAGUE

FOUNDED: 1894

(two promoted, two relegated throughout)

PREM. DIV.	P	W	D	L	F	A	PTS
Cradley Heath	24	16	5	3	74	24	53
Wyre Forest	24	17	3	4	76	30	*51
Bandon	24	14	3	7	48	26	45
Woofferton	24	14	3	7	68	49	45
Ludlow Colts	24	12	6	6	54	36	42
Bewdley Town	24	12	3	9	53	43	39
Brintons Chainwire	24	11	5	8	56	33	38
Black Cross '90	24	9	5	10	56	64	32
Highley Welfare	24	9	3	12	49	56	30
Parkdale Rovers	24	7	2	15	32	65	23
Dunns Bank Rovers	24	4	4	16	33	64	16
Netherton Libs	24	4	2	18	39	86	14
Two Gates	24	4	2	18	29	93	14

* - 3 points deducted

DIV. ONE	P	W	D	L	F	A	PTS
Edgecliff Eagles	22	15	4	3	82	40	49
Chaddesley Corbett	22	14	6	2	80	22	48
Wordsley Star	22	14	3	5	70	43	*42
Worths	22	13	5	4	58	33	*41
Kinver	22	12	1	9	53	50	37
Brin. Chainwire Res.	22	9	3	10	43	55	30
Ludlow Town Res.	22	8	4	10	55	58	28
Quarry Bank Labour	22	8	3	11	52	78	27
Springvale Rovers	22	7	4	11	48	51	25
Clee Hill United	22	6	4	12	53	57	22
Bewdley Town Res.	22	7	1	14	47	71	22
Bache Arms	22	0	0	22	25	119	0

* - 3 points deducted

DIV. TWO	P	W	D	L	F	A	PTS
Blackheath El. Res.	24	20	1	3	86	35	61
Cleobury. Town	24	16	1	7	102	35	49
Quarry Bank Celtic	24	16	1	7	83	31	49
Claines	24	14	3	7	67	49	45
Steelstock	24	14	2	8	51	42	44
Shakespeare Inn	24	11	5	8	65	57	38
Parkdale Rvrs Res.	24	10	4	10	53	51	34
Highley Welf. Res.	24	9	3	12	55	58	*27
Cradley Hth Res.	24	8	5	11	40	82	*26
Interlink	24	6	5	13	41	79	23
Landman	24	4	5	15	41	89	17
Clent	24	5	2	17	47	99	17
Horn & Trumpet	24	3	3	18	52	87	12

* - 3 points deducted

DIV. THREE	P	W	D	L	F	A	PTS
Ounsdale	16	14	2	0	81	20	**38
Wolverley Social	16	11	1	4	56	24	34
Tenbury United	16	9	3	4	47	37	30
Cleobury Town Res.	16	8	1	7	46	37	25
Furnace Sports	16	7	0	9	39	52	21
Broughton Shoes	16	5	2	9	29	66	17
Burlish Olympic	16	5	2	9	39	63	*14
Kinver Res.	16	4	0	12	32	60	12
Stourport Rangers	16	3	1	12	26	58	10

* - 3 points deducted

League Centenary Cup Finals:

Senior: Bewdley Town 2, Cradley Heath 0
Junior: Edgecliff Eagles 1, Bewdley Town Res. 0
Minor: Cleobury Town 3, Steelstock 2 *(aet)*
Subsidiary: Wordsley Star 2, Blackheath Elect. Res. 0

BROMSGROVE & DISTRICT LEAGUE

W A Harris Div.	P	W	D	L	F	A	PTS
Spar Barnt Green	18	16	1	1	102	19	33
Droitwich Hop Pole	18	14	0	4	73	25	28
Altered Images	18	13	1	4	64	26	27
Riflemans Arms	18	8	3	7	64	39	19
Droitwich Red Lion	18	8	2	8	37	32	18
Contract Foods	18	8	2	8	51	49	18
Crabbs Cross Rgrs	18	7	2	9	46	47	16
Ivy Cottage	18	6	1	11	40	65	13
Greyhound Hunters	18	4	0	14	27	75	8
Weary Traveller	18	0	0	18	20	147	0

Nth Worcs Div.	P	W	D	L	F	A	PTS
Catshill WMC	20	19	1	0	132	16	39
Greyhound	20	16	1	3	88	23	33
Blackwell	20	12	3	5	91	51	27
Star & Garter	20	13	1	6	68	49	27
AFC Winyates	20	10	2	8	78	42	22
Unity '93	20	10	2	8	77	47	22
Christian Salvesen	20	7	4	9	45	62	18
Hoobrook Sports	20	5	4	11	37	78	14
R L Millfields	20	2	4	14	41	93	8
Bromsgrove Rgrs	20	4	0	16	28	100	8
Ring O'Bells	20	1	0	19	18	142	2

Spar Barnt Green beat Catshill WMC in Frederick Smith Cup (championship play-off) to become overall champions.

Supplementary Div. (Rose Bowl)	P	W	D	L	F	A	PTS
Ivy Cottage	8	8	0	0	38	9	16
Crabbs Cross Rgrs	8	7	0	1	43	7	14
Christian Salvesen	8	5	1	2	24	11	11
Bromsgrove Rgrs	8	5	0	3	27	15	10
Greyhound Hunters	8	3	1	4	17	26	7
Hoobrook Sports	8	2	2	4	21	26	6
R L Millfields	7	1	2	4	23	38	4
Weary Traveller	8	1	0	6	10	38	2
Ring O'Bells	8	0	0	8	11	44	0

Bridgwater Cup Final: Catshill WMC 7, Droitwich Hop Pole 1 *(at Bromsgrove Rovers FC)*
LMS Shield Final: Spar Barnt Green 2, Contract Foods 0 *(at Redditch United FC)*
Sports Merit Cup: Star & Garter
Player of the Year: Denis Bird (Catshill)

KIDDERMINSTER & DISTRICT SUNDAY LEAGUE

PREM. DIV.	P	W	D	L	F	A	PTS
Cradley Olympic	26	20	3	3	84	20	63
SRM	26	20	3	3	76	21	63
Brintons A.	26	16	1	9	81	53	49
Cookley	26	14	6	6	42	29	48
Kingswinford	26	11	7	8	47	48	40
Burlish Olympic	26	10	8	8	55	55	38
Quarry Bank	26	10	6	10	48	50	36
Stourbridge United	26	10	4	12	53	53	34
Brickhouse	26	9	6	11	63	56	33
Norton	26	10	3	13	38	48	33
Wolverley Athletic	26	9	4	13	45	48	31
William Stevens	26	7	8	11	34	38	29
Gilt Edge '31	26	4	4	18	35	81	16
Swindon Greyhound	26	0	1	25	12	115	*0

* - 1 point deducted

Lower Division Champions:
Div. 1 (14): Round Oak
Div. 2 (14): Dibdale Rovers
Div. 3 (14): Pedmore
Div. 4 (14): Wilden Village
Div. 5 (13): Blue Ball Sports
Div. 6 (16): Victoria

Cup Finals:
Senior: Wolverley Ath. 1, Quarry Bank 0 *(aet)*
Junior: Pedmore 4, Dibdale Rovers 2
Minor: Belbroughton 2, Wilden Village 1
Fire Shield: Quarry Bank 3, Norton 1

WORCESTER & DISTRICT SUNDAY LEAGUE

PREM. DIV.	P	W	D	L	F	A	PTS
Southside Swifts	20	17	2	1	80	13	36
Bromyard Town	20	14	3	3	71	24	31
Warndon Youth	20	13	2	5	64	36	28
Droitwich Spa	20	9	5	6	50	43	23
Archdale '73	20	6	7	7	48	60	19
Droitwich '86	20	6	5	9	40	49	17
YMCA Comer Park	20	6	3	11	33	52	15
Upton Snodsbury	20	5	4	11	42	63	14
Hallow WMC	20	6	2	12	32	56	14
Kempsey United	20	5	3	12	28	52	13
AFC Barbourne	20	5	0	15	40	80	10

Lower Division Champions:
Div. 1 (13): Tolladine Sports
Div. 2 (14): Drifters
Div. 3 (13): Mayflower
Div. 4 (14): Cromwells
Div. 5 (14): Cutnall Green Res.

Cup Finals:
Katherine Rayer Cup: Tolladine Sports 2, Green Dragon 1
Bernard Finnegan Cup: Mostyn Ath. 2, Cromwells 0

JEWSON EVESHAM SUNDAY LEAGUE

FOUNDED: 1970

DIV. ONE	P	W	D	L	F	A	PTS
Evesham WMC	16	14	0	2	47	28	28
Bretforton Vic.	16	10	3	3	51	22	23
Moreton Youth	16	10	2	4	52	28	22
Ashchurch	16	7	4	5	26	28	18
Tewkesbury Town	16	7	3	6	36	24	17
Pershore Dynamo	16	4	4	8	22	39	12
Littleton	16	3	4	9	26	38	10
Pershore Harriers	16	2	5	9	11	43	9
Red Horse	16	1	3	12	20	56	5

Lower Division Champions:
Div. 2 (11): Bredon
Div. 3 (11): Stow Town
Div. 4 (12): Blockley Sports
Div. 5 (12): Moreton Town Colts

Cup Finals:
Birdseye Spts KO Cup: Moreton Yth 4, Evesham WMC 2 *(aet)*
Jewson Subsidiary Cup: Bretforton Sports Victoria 3, Pinvin United 2 *(aet)*
Bluck Cup: Lower Moor Utd 2, Blockley Spts 0

STOP PRESS LEAGUE TABLES

(Tables received too late for their appropriate sections)

SILHOUETTE SPORTS DUCHY LEAGUE

COUNTY: CORNWALL

PREM. DIV.	P	W	D	L	F	A	PTS
Biscovey	30	24	4	2	130	26	76
Probus	30	21	7	2	133	37	70
Fowey Town	30	22	1	7	129	56	67
Newmoor	30	19	2	9	82	46	59
Nanpean Rvrs Res.	30	17	7	6	74	51	58
Boscastle	30	14	6	10	64	56	48
Mevagissey	30	12	5	13	62	59	41
Roche Res.	30	13	3	14	75	74	*39
Godolphin	30	10	6	14	70	81	36
St Minver	30	9	5	16	62	83	32
Altarnum	30	9	5	16	53	107	32
Fowey RBL	30	9	4	17	64	110	31
Delabole	30	8	4	18	65	94	28
Grampound	30	7	3	20	38	92	24
St Mawes	30	7	2	21	55	121	23
Queens Rangers	30	6	2	22	47	100	20

DIV. ONE	P	W	D	L	F	A	PTS
St Dominic	28	22	5	1	120	32	71
Lanreath	28	21	3	4	85	33	66
Bude Res.	28	18	2	8	87	53	56
Looe	28	16	3	9	83	45	51
Lostwithiel	28	14	5	9	66	57	47
St Mawgan	28	11	9	8	71	54	42
St Stephen	28	11	7	10	63	62	40
Pensilva	28	12	4	12	41	57	40
Pelynt	28	11	5	12	52	50	38
Godolphin Res.	28	12	2	14	53	73	38
Barley	28	11	4	13	69	67	37
Tregony	28	7	3	18	55	101	24
Newmoor Res.	28	5	8	15	47	78	23
Bodmin Park	28	3	5	20	44	102	14
St Minver Res.	28	3	1	24	26	96	10

DIV. TWO 'A'	P	W	D	L	F	A	PTS
Stratton	22	19	2	1	100	21	59
Caradon	22	15	3	4	68	33	48
St Teath	22	13	3	6	54	36	42
Camelford Res.	22	13	2	7	67	32	41
Menheniot	22	12	3	7	74	45	39
Boscastle Res.	22	10	1	11	48	58	31
St Breward Res.	22	9	3	10	36	38	30
St Anns Chapel	22	9	3	10	45	55	30
St Lawrences	22	7	4	11	44	62	25
St Dominic Res.	22	4	6	12	33	52	18
Tintagel Res.	22	2	2	18	16	58	8
Altarnum Res.	22	1	4	17	25	120	7

DIV. TWO 'B'	P	W	D	L	F	A	PTS
Duke of Cornwall	24	19	4	1	66	23	61
Sticker Res.	24	18	4	2	78	25	*55
St Dennis Res.	24	16	3	5	85	44	51
Padstow Res.	24	14	6	4	88	37	48
Foxhole Stars Res.	24	14	4	6	71	34	46
St Austell Ath.	24	13	6	5	61	31	45
St Columb Minor	24	10	2	12	49	59	32
RAF St Mawgan Res.	24	10	0	14	35	44	30
Mevagissey Res.	24	6	5	13	37	44	23
Tregony Res.	24	5	4	15	34	88	19
Ladock	24	4	2	18	33	76	14
St Stephen Res.	24	3	3	18	27	84	12
St Teath Res.	24	1	3	20	22	96	6

* - Points adjusted

Dave Monks Cup Final *(at St Dominic FC)*: Menheniot 4, St Anns Chapel 1

MIDDLESEX ALLIANCE

PREM. DIV.	P	W	D	L	F	A	PTS
New Inn '90	20	16	1	3	60	22	49
Talbot All Stars	20	15	1	4	72	21	46
Chelsea Boys	20	14	2	4	46	27	44
Pars	20	13	3	4	64	24	42
Feltham Town	20	13	1	6	45	30	40
Internationals Utd	20	9	4	7	59	30	31
Assyrian	20	6	1	13	42	53	19
Parkside (Ealing)	20	6	1	13	23	45	19
Oghab	20	4	1	15	20	84	13
Northolt Saints	20	3	1	16	24	58	10
Vale	20	2	2	16	20	81	8

DIV. ONE	P	W	D	L	F	A	PTS
Acton/Ealing Whist.	18	16	0	2	100	13	48
Hanworth RBL	18	15	0	3	69	34	45
Simba All Stars	18	12	1	5	66	31	37
Talbot AS Res.	18	9	2	7	48	42	29
Chiswick Homefields	18	8	0	10	44	59	24
Hanworth	18	6	2	10	31	56	20
Feltham Town Res.	18	6	2	10	26	62	20
NCR Wanderers	18	6	0	12	29	54	18
GWR	18	3	6	9	26	37	15
Assoc. Academicals	18	1	3	14	20	71	6

Cup Finals

Snr Victory Cup: Talbot All Stars 2, Feltham T. 0
Jnr Victory Cup: Acton & Ealing Whistlers beat Simba All Stars on penalties after 3-3 draw.

WEST PENWITH LEAGUE

COUNTY: CORNWALL

	P	W	D	L	F	A	PTS
Pendeen Rvrs Res.	18	15	1	2	92	24	31
Mousehole Res.	18	13	4	1	66	13	30
Madron	18	13	2	3	65	16	28
St Buryan	16	8	4	4	57	29	*22
Cape Cornwall	18	8	2	8	49	45	18
Ludgvan Res.	17	4	5	8	34	43	13
Long Rock	17	6	1	10	35	59	13
Halsetown Res.	18	6	0	12	32	88	12
St Just Res.	18	3	4	11	47	56	10
Marazion Blues Res.	18	0	1	17	8	112	1

AMOR SHIELD	P	W	D	L	F	A	PTS
Ludgvan 'A'	16	13	0	3	66	21	26
Madron Res.	16	11	3	2	58	23	25
Hayle Res.	16	8	4	4	44	34	20
Sennen	16	9	1	6	46	22	19
Castle Utd Res.	16	7	3	5	34	28	17
Mousehole 'A'	16	7	1	6	49	47	15
St Buryan Res.	16	4	1	11	38	54	9
Long Rock Res.	16	4	1	11	33	63	9
Rosudgeon-Ken. Res.	16	1	0	15	22	97	2

Cup Finals

Charity Cup: Pendeen R. Res. 3, Mousehole Res. 2
Hanneford Cup: Mousehole Reserves 2, Pendeen Rovers Reserves 1
Marazion Cup: Madron Res. 4, Hayles Res. 0
Nicholas Cup: Madron 4, Pendeen Rovers Res. 0
Reynolds Cup: Ludgvan 'A' 3, Mousehole 'A' 2
West Cornwall Hosp. Cup: Mousehole Res. 1, Pendeen R. Res. 0

Appendix One
Welsh Football

(SEE ALSO PAGE 995 FOR KONICA LEAGUE of WALES)

Major Honours 1993-94

COMPETITION	WINNERS	RUNNERS-UP
Allbright Bitter Welsh Cup	Barry Town	Cardiff City
FAW Trophy	Barry Town	Aberaman Athletic
Konica League of Wales	Bangor City	Inter Cardiff
Konica League of Wales Cup	Afan Lido	Bangor City
NW Joinery Cymru Alliance	Rhyl	Welshpool Town
Abacus League Division One	Barry Town	Aberaman Athletic
Abacus League Division Two	Taff's Well	Treowen Stars
Abacus League Division Three	Penrhiwceiber Rgrs	Grange Harlequins
Sealink Welsh Alliance	Llangefni Town	Llanfairpwll
R.Con. Welsh Nat.Lge (Wrexham)	Penycae	Oswestry Town
R.Con. Welsh National Lge Cup	Penycae	Cefn Druids Reserves
Richards The Builders M.Wales Lge	Machynlleth	Llandrindod Wells
Mid-Wales League Cup	Morda United	Machynlleth

ALLBRIGHT BITTER WELSH CUP FINAL 1994

BARRY TOWN 2 **CARDIFF CITY 1**
D'Auria 40, Hough 61 — Stant 51

Referee: J W Lloyd (Wrexham) Att: 14,000
(at the National Stadium, Cardiff, Sunday 15th May)
Barry: Steve Morris, David Hough, Phil Williams, Ashley Griffiths, Terry Boyle, Paul Wimbleton, Alan Curtis (Smith 80), Chris Lillygreen, David D'Auria, Andy Beattie, Keith Bertschin (Sanderson 70).
Cardiff: Steve Williams, Wayne Fereday, Damon Searle, Mark Aizlewood, Jason Perry, Paul Millar, Gary Thompson (Anthony Bird 75), Nicky Richardson (Darren Adams 61), Phil Stant, Kevin Brock, Cohen Griffith.

As one of the Welsh 'irate eight' English Pyramid clubs who initially refused to join the League of Wales, Barry Town have had to swallow a lot of pride over the past two years. May 1994, however, must go down as the proudest month in the club's history.

Last season the Linnets were attracting miniscule gates to watch their Midlands-based team in Beazer Homes League action at their borrowed home of Worcester City. With the FAW showing no sign of clemency towards the exiled clubs, Barry decided to return home to Abacus League football. It was not, however, to the Abacus League they had last left in 1989. Now, instead of trips to comparatively salubrious venues such as Cwmbran, Aberystwyth and Ton Pentre, the diet was that of Llanwern, Cardiff Civil Service and Morriston, the league having been stripped of its 'big' clubs by the new Konica set-up.

Unperturbed, Barry invested strongly and wisely to ensure that their wait for Konica League football was a short one. The title was won at a canter, ensuring promotion and, on Saturday 7th May, victory over Aberaman in the FAW Trophy final brought the Linnets their first triumph in a national knock-out competition since 1955. The Cyril Rogers League Cup was also won, on Thursday 19th May, but by then Barry Town were already celebrating the most momentous achievement of the whole lot - victory in the Allbright Bitter Welsh Cup.

When inaugural Konica champions Cwmbran were dispatched 3-1 in Round Three, the omens were already looking good for Barry, but few would have predicted that the Linnets would see off a further three sides from the national league to reach only the second final in their history. North Walians Holywell Town and Flint Town United were both defeated at Jenner Park before Barry shook off the handicap of having a player sent off in both the home and away legs of the semi-final, and beat Konica champions-elect Bangor 2-1 on aggregate. The decisive goal in the second-leg came from former First Division star Keith Bertschin with just five minutes remaining, and triggered off scenes of celebration not witnessed at Jenner Park for many years.

Barry's run drew some interesting parallels with that of Rhyl last year but, unlike Rhyl, they were not content to play a gallant supporting role in an end-of-season Cardiff City party. One scan of the names on the team-sheet told you that here was a side full of talent and experience - professionals hungry for success.

It was one of Barry's best-known stars who set up the first goal, after forty minutes. Keith Bertschin dragged the ball in from the right and hit a low shot that was sneaking just inside the far post. Steve Williams managed to push it out, but only as far as **David D'Auria** and the former Swansea and Merthyr forward finished gleefully from a narrowing angle.

When Cardiff equalised early in the second-half with an almost identical goal - Steve Morris parried a long shot from Gary Thompson but **Phil Stant** pounced on the rebound - one felt that the non-Leaguers must buckle, but they regained the lead within ten minutes when **David Hough**, who had an outstanding match at left-back, moved up for a corner and lashed home a loose ball.

As the game wore on, Barry replaced two of their oldest heads, Bertschin and Alan Curtis, with Paul Sanderson and club stalwart Bobby Smith. It was a magnificent team display, from the impeccable keeping of Steve Morris through to the tireless foraging of Paul Wimbleton and Chris Lillygreen via the tenacious tackling of defenders David Hough, Ashley Griffiths and Phil Williams. The Man-of-the-Match award, however, went to captain and player-coach Andy Beattie for a typically illuminating midfield display.

The joy of Barry Town, players and fans alike, was unbounded at the final whistle. And why not? After all they had become only the second non-League club since 1963 (Merthyr in 1987 being the other) to lift the Welsh Cup. The Cardiff fans did their tarnished reputation no harm at all giving their victors a rousing standing ovation.

James Wright.

PHOTOS OPPOSITE

Top: *Keith Bertschin gets in a header at the Cardiff City goal.*

Centre: *Alan Curtis, Craig Gill and goalkeeper Steve Morris with the Welsh Cup.*

Foot: *Rhyl Ladies FC, who retained the Welsh Women's Cup in a curtain-raiser to the Allbright Bitter Cup final beating Inter-Cardiff Ladies in a penalty shoot-out after a thrilling 2-2 draw.*

All Photos - Gavin Ellis-Neville.

SERVICE TO BUSINESS

WELSH LEAGUE (Formerly Abacus League)

DIVISION ONE	P	W	D	L	F	A	PTS
Barry Town	34	27	4	3	94	27	85
Aberaman Ath.	34	20	4	10	71	49	64
AFC Porth	34	19	6	9	68	38	63
Caldicot Town	34	16	11	7	83	59	59
Pontypridd Town	34	15	8	11	53	43	*52
Pembroke Borough	34	15	6	13	59	49	51
Cardiff Civil S.	34	15	6	13	59	50	51
Llanwern	34	13	7	14	50	57	46
Ammanford	34	13	6	15	52	55	45
Caerleon	34	12	9	13	50	59	45
Morriston Town	34	11	10	13	45	49	43
Brecon Corinthians	34	11	8	15	57	68	41
Caerau	34	10	10	14	50	50	40
Abergavenny Thurs.	34	10	9	15	40	68	39
Ferndale Athletic	34	7	13	14	36	62	34
Port Talbot Ath.	34	9	7	18	43	71	34
Blaenrhondda	34	8	8	18	47	64	32
Bridgend Town	34	6	6	22	43	81	24

DIVISION ONE	P	W	D	L	F	A	PTS
Taff's Well	26	17	5	4	66	25	56
Treowen Stars	26	17	5	4	52	25	56
Carmarthen Town	26	15	3	8	58	47	48
Risca United	26	14	3	9	50	34	45
BP Llandarcy	26	12	6	8	50	37	42
Fields P/P'fraith	26	10	9	7	42	36	39
Garw	26	11	6	9	41	35	39
Skewen Athletic	26	10	8	8	44	43	38
Cardiff Corries	26	10	4	12	34	51	34
Pontyclun	26	7	7	12	33	37	28
Newport YMCA	26	7	6	13	36	50	27
Seven Sisters	26	7	1	18	30	54	22
Tonyrefail Welfare	26	6	3	17	36	54	21
Milford United	26	3	6	17	28	72	15

DIVISION TWO	P	W	D	L	F	A	PTS
Penrhiwceiber Rgrs	26	19	4	3	75	23	61
Grange Harlequins	26	17	3	4	92	29	57
Goytre United	26	18	3	5	81	31	57
Porth Tywyn Sub.	26	15	3	8	60	34	48
Tondu Robins	26	14	4	8	57	38	46
Pontlottyn BF	26	12	8	6	49	36	44
Pontardawe Ath.	26	11	5	10	45	50	38
Treharris Ath.	26	11	3	12	60	62	36
Albion Rovers	26	8	4	14	46	57	28
Abercynon	26	4	10	12	33	61	22
SW Constabulary	26	5	5	16	43	81	20
Cardiff Inst HE	26	4	6	16	28	72	18
Panteg	26	3	8	15	34	67	17
Trelewis Welfare	26	5	2	19	25	87	17

* - 1 point deducted

WELSH LEAGUE DIVISION ONE CLUBS 1994-95

ABERAMAN ATHLETIC

Secretary: Brian Fear, 28 Mostyn Street, Abercwmboi, Mid-Glamorgan (0443 472858).
Manager: John Herniman
Ground: Aberaman Park.
Colours: All royal blue. **Change colours:** Yellow/blue/yellow.
Programme: Yes **Floodlights:** No **Cover:** Yes **Seats:** No

ABERGAVENNY THURSDAYS

Secretary: David Morris, 48 Richmond Road, Abergavenny, Gwent, NP7 5RE (0873 854730).
Ground: Penypound Stadium, Penypond, Abergavenny, Gwent (0873 853906)
Colours: All white. **Change colours:** Navy/sky stripe/sky/navy.
Programme: Yes **Floodlights:** Yes **Cover:** Yes **Seats:** Yes

A.F.C. PORTH

Secretary: Robert Lewis, 11 Wyndham Street, Porth, Rhondda, Mid Glam. (0443) 687854).
Ground: Dinas Park, Dinas, Rhondda, Mid Glam.
Colours: Maroon & blue/blue/blue. **Change colours:** Red/blue/blue.
Programme: Yes **Floodlights:** 1994 scheduled. **Cover:** Yes **Seats:** No
Founded: 1987 (prev. Beatus Utd)

AMMANFORD

Secretary: John Thomas, 154 Hendre Rd, Capel Hendre, Ammanford, Dyfed SA18 3TE (0269 843712).
Player: Alan Walters
Ground: Betws Sports Club, Rice Road, Bettws, Ammanford, Dyfed (0269 592407).
Directions: From Quay Street Post Office head towards Bettws, cross railway line, left on sharp bend into Colonel Road, ground down narrow lane opposite Gwalia Stores.
Seats: Yes **Cover:** Yes **Floodlights:** No **Clubhouse:** Yes **Programme:** Yes
Club colours: Blue & white stripes/blue/blue **Change colours:** Black & white/white/black.
Founded: 1991 (Ammanford Town founded 1948 merged with Ammanford Athletic)

BRECON CORINTHIANS

Secretary: Terry Harley, 20 Charles Street, The Watton, Brecon, Powys LD3 7HF. (0874 624568)
Ground: The Rich Field, The Watton, Brecon. (0656 55097)
Directions: Head from town centre, turn at Rich Way Road. Hourly bus from Merthyr takes 40 minutes
Colours: All red. **Change colours:** All yellow. **Founded:** 1940
Programme: Yes **Floodlights:** Yes **Cover:** Yes **Seats:** Yes **Clubhouse:** In Town

BRITON FERRY ATHLETIC

Secretary: Graham Jenkins, 262 Neath Rd, Briton Ferry, West Glam. SA11 2SL (0639 814762).
Ground: Old Road, Briton Ferry, West Glamorgan (0639 812458)
Directions: M4 from Cardiff, on to A48 at r'bout (3rd exit) signed Briton Ferry, right at 1st traffic lights - ground half mile on right.
Programme: Yes **Floodlights:** Yes **Cover:** 350 **Seats:** 100 **Founded:** 1925.
Cols: Red & green quarters/white/white. **Change colours:** All blue.

CAERAU

Secretary: David Lewis, 19a Hermon Rd, Caerau, Mid-Glamorgan (0656 734388).
Ground: Humphreys Terrace, Caerau, Mid. Glam. (0656 732471)
Colours: All red **Change colours:** All blue **Founded:** 1901
Programme: Yes **Floodlights:** Yes **Cover:** Yes **Seats:** No

CAERLEON

Secretary: Ken Alden, 2 Conifer Close, Caerleon, Newport, gwent NP6 1RH (0633 **Ground:** Cold Bath Road, Caerleon, Gwent (0633 420074).
Colours: All green **Change colours:** Blue/white/blue
Programme: Yes **Floodlights:** Yes **Cover:** Yes **Seats:** Yes **Founded:** 1889.

CALDICOT TOWN

Secretary: Gordon Lewis, "Talfan", 83 Newport Road, Caldicot, Newport NP6 4BS (0291) 422035).
Ground: Jubilee Way, Caldicot, Gwent (0291 423519)
Directions: M4 - take Jnt 22 signs to town centre. Ground behind town centre car park.
Seats: No **Cover:** Yes **Programme:** Yes **Floodlights:** No **Founded:** 1953
Colours: Yellow/black/black **Club colours:** White/navy/navy

CARDIFF CIVIL SERVICE

Secretary: Bob Fry, 30 Flaxland Avenue, Heath, Cardiff CF4 3NT (0222 619192).
Ground: Civil Service Sports Ground, Santatorium Rd, Leckwith, Cardiff.
Directions: West side of Cardiff, near Cardiff City FC.
Seats: No **Cover:** No **Clubhouse:** Yes **Floodlights:** No **Programme:** Yes
Founded: 1963 **Colours:** Green & white hoops/white/white **Change colours:** red/white/red

CARMARTHEN TOWN

Secretary: Alan Latham, 3 Maes Dolau, Idole, Carmarthen SA32 8DQ (0267 232432).
Ground: Richmond Park, Priory Street, Carmarthen, Dyfed (0267 232101).
Colours: Gold/black/black **Change colours:** Blue/white/blue
Programme: Yes **Floodlights:** No **Cover:** Yes (1,000) **Seats:** Yes **Founded:** 1953

FERNDALE ATHLETIC

Secretary: Glyn Lewis, Dan-yr-allt, Brown Street, Ferndale, Rhondda CF43 4SF. (0443 730201)
Ground: TBA
Seats: **Cover:** **Programme:** Yes **Floodlights:** **Founded:** 1945.
Colours: Yellow/black/black **Club colours:** Blue/black/black

HAVERFORDWEST COUNTY

Secretary: Cliff Sales, 46 Wesley Place, Trecwn, Haverfordwest, Dyfed (0348 840083).
Ground: Haverfordwest West Rugby Club *(until move to new ground for 1995-96)*
Programme: Yes **Floodlights:** No **Cover:** Yes **Seats:** **Founded:** Pre-1936
Colours: All royal blue. **Change colours:** All white

LLANWERN

Secretary: John Fitzgerald, 3 Lansdowne Road, Gaer, Newport, Gwent (0633 257319).
Ground: British Steel Sports Club, Llanwern, Newport, Gwent (0633 273790).
Founded: 1962 (prev. Spencer Works)
Colours: Navy/white/navy **Change colours:** White/white/navy
Programme: Yes **Floodlights:** No **Cover:** Yes **Seats:** No

MORRISTON TOWN

Secretary: Lynford Owen, 33 Maes y gelynen, Morriston, Swansea SA6 6SD (0792 796640).
Ground: The Dingle, Morriston, Nr Swansea (0792 702033).
Directions: Through Morriston centre and bear right at foot of hill - ground quarter mile on left.
Seats: No **Cover:** No **Programme:** Yes **Floodlights:** No **Founded:** 1951.
Club colours: Red & black stripes/black/red. **Change colours:** Yellow/black/white

PEMBROKE BOROUGH

Secretary: Phil Tallet, 6 Shropshire Rd, Pembroke Dock, Dyfed (0646 682234).
Ground: London Road, Pembroke Dock, Pembroke. (0636 682239)
Directions: Take A477 from St Clears to Pembroke Dock (not Pembroke). Straight on at roundabout, pass rugby ground on right and football ground is also on right.
Cover: Yes **Programme:** Yes **Clubhouse:** Yes **Founded:** 1935. **Floodlights:** No
Colours: Black, white & blue stripes/black/white **Change colours:** Amber/black/black

PONTYPRIDD TOWN

Secretary: Peter Chalmers, 9 Silver Hill Close, Cilfynydd, Pontypridd, Mid. Glam. (0443 492354).
Ground: Ynysangharad Park, Pontypridd (0443 790204).
Colours: Black & white stripes/black/black **Change colours:** All sky blue
Previous Ground: Ynysbwl Rec. (pre-1992) **Previous Names:** Ynysbwl 1995-1991/ Pontypridd-Ynysbwl 91-92
Programme: Yes **Floodlights:** No **Cover:** Yes **Seats:** Yes

TAFF'S WELL

Secretary: Ray Toghill, 38 Heol Berry, Gwaelod-y-Garth CF4 8HB (0222 811356).
Ground: Rhiwddar, Parish Road, Taffs Well, Mid. Glam. (0222 811080)
Colours: Amber/black/black **Change colours:** All blue
Programme: Yes **Floodlights:** No **Cover:** No **Seats:** No **Founded:** 1947

TREOWEN STARS

Secretary: A.J.Davies, 19 Meredith Terrace, Newbridge, Gwent NP1 4FN (0495 245494).
Ground: Bush Park, Newbridge, Gwent (0495 248249).
Colours: Blue & white stripes/black/black **Change colours:** Grey & red/red/red
Programme: Yes **Floodlights:** No **Cover:** No **Seats:** No **Founded:** 1926

DIVISION TWO CLUBS 1994-95

BLAENRHONDDA

Secretary: Gwynne Davies, 60 Elizabeth Street, Pentre, Rhondda, Mid Glamorgan (0443 433901).
Ground: Blaenrhondda Park (0443 774772).
Colours: All royal blue. **Change colours:** All red.
Founded: 1934 **Programme:** Yes **Floodlights:** No **Cover:** Yes **Seats:** No

B.P. LLANDARCY

Secretary: David Maddock, 20 Brookfield, Neath Abbey, Neath SA10 7EG (0639 636327).
Ground: B.P. Sports Ground, Llandarcy (0792 812036)
Colours: White/white/yellow. **Change colours:** All light blue.
Programme: Yes **Floodlights:** No **Cover:** No **Seats:** No **Founded:** 1922

BRIDGEND TOWN

Secretary: Ray Warner, 1 Heol Treharne, Coytrahen, Bridgend, Mid Glam. CF32 0DS (0656 720618).
Ground: Coychurch Rd, Bridgend. (0656 655097)
Directions: M4 to Pencoed, left at Waterton Cross. 2nd right under railway brige.
Cover: Yes **Floodlights:** Yes **Clubhouse:** Yes **Programme:** Yes **Founded:** 1954.
Colours: Sky/navy/sky **Change colours:** All white

CARDIFF CORINTHIANS

Secretary: G Thomas, 9 Palace Rd, Llandaff, Cardiff (0222 562624).
Ground: Riverside Ground, Radyr, Cardiff (0222 843407). **Directions:** Left out of Radyr station, under railway - ground
through gate marked cricket club. **Colours:** Cardinal & Amber Quarters/Cardinal/Cardinal **Change:** All blue
Programme: Yes **Floodlights:** Yes **Cover:** Yes(150) **Seats:** No **Founded:** 1897

FIELDS PARK/PONTLLANFRAITH

Secretary: Paul Chiplin, 1 William Street, Cwmfrlinfach, Ynysddu, Newport NP1 7GY (0495 200349).
Ground: Islwyn Park, Pontllanfraith, Blackwood, Gwent (0495 224512)
Colours: All royal blue **Change colours:** Black & white stripes/black/black
Programme: Yes **Floodlights:** No **Cover:** No **Seats:** Yes (200) **Founded:** 1964

GARW

Secretary: Tecwyn Thomas, Drosglo, 5 Victoria Street, Pontycymmer, Nr. Bridgend (0656 870411).
Ground: Blandy Park, Pontycymmer (0656 720777)
Colours: Red/black/red **Change colours:** Yellow/blue/blue
Programme: Yes **Floodlights:** No **Cover:** Yes (100) **Seats:** No **Founded:** 1945

GOYTRE UNITED

Secretary: Boris Suhanski, 20 Goytre Cres., Port Talbot (0639 886826).
Ground: Glenhafod Park, Goytre, Port Talbot, West Glam. (0639 898983).
Colours: Blue & white stripes/blue/blue
Programme: Yes **Floodlights:** No **Cover:** No **Seats:** Yes (213) **Founded:** 1963

GRANGE HARLEQUINS

Secretary: Mike Smith-Phillips, 48 Penlan Road, Llandough, Nr. Penarth, South Glam. (0222 700200).
Ground: Cardiff Athletic Stadium, Leckwith Road, Cardiff (0222 225345).
Colours: All red **Change colours:** All blue
Programme: Yes **Floodlights:** Yes **Cover:** Yes **Seats:** Yes (2,500) **Founded:** 1948

MILFORD UNITED

Secretary: Ken Lowe, 17 Milton Crescent, Pill, Milford Haven SA73 2QS (0646 692194).
Ground: Marble Hall Road, Milford Haven, Dyfed (0646 693691)
Colours: Red/black/red **Change colours:** All blue
Programme: Yes **Floodlights:** No **Cover:** Yes (400) **Seats:** Yes (300) **Founded:** 1885

PENRHIWCEIBER RANGERS

Secretary: Chris Kerr, 8 Church Street, Penrhiwoeiber, Mountain Ash, Mid. Glam. (0443 476134).
Ground: Glasbrook Field, Glasbrook Terrace, Penrhiwoeiber (0443 473368).
Previous League: Sth Wales Amtr (champs 91-92). **Colours:** All red.
Programme: Yes **Floodlights:** No **Cover:** Yes (200) **Seats:** No **Founded:** 1945

PONTYCLUN

Secretary: Peter Shilton, 3 Lilac Drive, Chandlers Reach, Llantwit Fardre, Mid.Glam. (0443 831606).
Ground: Ivor Park, Cowbridge Road, Pontyclun, Mid.Glam (0443 222182)
Colours: Yellow/blue/blue **Change colours:** Blue/yellow/yellow
Programme: Yes **Floodlights:** No **Cover:** No **Seats:** No **Founded:** 1896

PORT TALBOT ATHLETIC

Secretary: Alf Germaine, 1 Bordsfield Cottage, Graig, Pontypridd CF37 1LE (0443 407868).
Ground: Victoria Park, Aberavon, Port Talbot (0639 8832465).
Directions: On left of main road from Port Talbot to Aberavon. 20 mins walk from Port Talbot (BR).
Cover: Yes **Programme:** Yes **Floodlights:** No **Clubhouse:** Yes **Founded:** 1901
Colours: All blue **Change colours:** Yellow/black/black

RISCA UNITED

Secretary: Mrs Ann Luckwell, 137 Ty Isaf Park Ave., Pontyminster, Risca, Gwent (0633 613434).
Ground: Ty Asaf Park, Risca, Gwent (0633 615081).
Colours: Black & white stripes/black/black **Change colours:** Yellow/black/black
Programme: Yes **Floodlights:** No **Cover:** Yes (250) **Seats:** No **Founded:** 1946

SKEWEN ATHLETIC

Secretary: Bob Smith, 50 Southall Avenue, Skewen, Neath, West Glam. SA10 6YW (0792 814518).
Ground: Tennant Park, Skewen, Neath, West Glam.
Colours: Blue/white/blue **Change colours:** Wine/white
Programme: Yes **Floodlights:** No **Cover:** Yes (100) **Seats:** No **Founded:** 1949

DIVISION THREE CLUBS 1994-95

ABERCYNON ATHLETIC

Secretary: Jeffrey Dudley, 131 Abercynon Rd, Abercynon. Mid. Glam CF45 4NE (0443 741433).
Ground: Parc Abercynon, Abercynon, Mid. Glam. (0443 740238).
Colours: Black & white/black/black **Change colours:** Yellow & black/black/red
Programme: Yes **Floodlights:** No **Cover:** No **Seats:** No **Founded:** 1933

ALBION ROVERS

Secretary: Mr N.A.Cueto, 37 Gilbert Close, Newport, Gwent (0633 275 785).
Ground: Spetty Stadium, Spetty. **Colours:** All red **Change colours:** All blue
Programme: Yes **Floodlights:** Yes **Cover:** Yes (3,000) **Seats:** Yes (1,500)

CARDIFF INSTITUTE OF HIGHER EDUCATION

Secretary: Lee Morgan, 96 Cowbridge Road West, Ely, Cardiff (0222 757223).
Ground: Cyncoed College, Cyncoed Rd, Cardiff (0222 757223).
Colours: Blue & white/blue/white **Change colours:** Maroon & gold stripes/maroon/Maroon
Programme: Yes **Floodlights:** No **Cover:** No **Seats:** No **Founded:** 1957

MONKTON SWIFTS

(promoted from Pembrokeshire League)

NEWPORT Y.M.C.A.

Secretary: Roy Leonard, 14 St.David's Crescent, Park Avenue, Newport, Gwent, NP9 3AW (0633 810783)
Ground: Y.M.C.A. Ground, Mendalgief Road, Newport, Gwent (0633 263387)
Colours: White & navy/navy/navy **Change colours:** All blue
Programme: Yes **Floodlights:** No **Cover:** No **Seats:** No **Founded:** 1971

PANTEG

Secretary: Bob Small, 26 Laburnum Drive, New Inn, Pontypool (0495 756280).
Ground: Panteg House, Greenhill Rd, Griffithstown, Pontypool. (0495 763605).
Colours: White & black/black/black. **Change colours:** Yellow/black/red.
Programme: Yes **Floodlights:** No **Cover:** No **Seats:** No **Founded:** 1940

PONTARDAWE ATHLETIC

Secretary: John Slater, 133 Lowe Road, Clydach, Swansea (0792 842530).
Ground: The Recreation Ground, Pontardawe Trading Estate, Pontardawe (0792 862228).
Colours: Black & white/black/black.
Programme: Yes **Floodlights:** No **Cover:** Yes (100) **Seats:** No **Founded:** 1947

PONTLOTTYN BLAST FURNACE

Secretary: Barry Horsman, Wordesley, Gwerthonor Road, Gilfach, Bargoed CF8 8JS (0443 831606).
Ground: Welfare Ground, Hill Road, Pontlottyn, Mid. Glam. (0685 841305).
Colours: Yellow/green/yellow. **Change colours:** White & red stripes/red/red.
Programme: Yes **Floodlights:** No **Cover:** Yes (100) **Seats:** No **Founded:** 1968

PORTH TYWYN SUBURBS

Secretary: Colin Jenkins, 25 St.Mary's Rise, Burry Port, Dyfed SA16 0SH (0554 832109).
Ground: Parc Tywyn, Woodbrook Terrace, Burry Port, Dyfed (0554 833991).
Colours: All green **Change colours:** All red
Programme: Yes **Floodlights:** No **Cover:** No **Seats:** No

PORTCAWL TOWN

(promoted from South Wales Amateur League)

SEVEN SISTERS

Secretary: Peter Warnes, 1 Mary Street, Seven Sisters, Neath, West Glam. (0639 700121).
Ground: Welfare Ground, Church Road, Seven Sisters, Neath (0639 700354).
Colours: Yellow/blue/yellow **Change colours:** Green/black/black
Programme: Yes **Floodlights:** No **Cover:** No **Seats:** No **Founded:** 1919

SOUTH WALES CONSTABULARY

Secretary: Alan Davies, 147 Bwlch Road, Fairwater, Cardiff CF5 3EE (0222 569105).
Ground: Police Sports Ground, Waterton Cross, Bridgend (0656 65555x218).
Colours: Red/blue/blue. **Change colours:** Yellow/blue/yellow/blue
Programme: Yes **Floodlights:** No **Cover:** No **Seats:** No **Founded:** 1969

TONDU ROBINS

Secretary: Dennis Jones, 66 Sunnyside, Bridgend, Mid. Glam. CF31 4AF (0656 658108).
Ground: Pandy Park, Aberkenfig, Bridgend, Mid. Glam (0656 720045).
Colours: All red **Change colours:** Yellow/black/black
Programme: Yes **Floodlights:** No **Cover:** No **Seats:** No **Founded:** 1897

TONYREFAIL WELFARE

Secretary: Peter Jones, 13 Rees Street, Treorchy, Rhondda, Mid Glam. (0443 773460).
Ground: Temporary ground in Pontypridd for 1994-95.
Colours: Red & black stripes/black/red **Change colours:** Yellow/black/black
Programme: Yes **Floodlights:** No **Cover:** No **Seats:** Yes (100) **Founded:** 1926

TREHARRIS ATHLETIC

Secretary: Mike Casey, 10 Windsor Rd, Edwardsville, Treharris (0443 411153).
Ground: Athletic Ground, Commercial Terrace, Treharris, Mid. Glam.
Colours: Blue & white stripes/blue/blue **Change colours:** Yellow/black/red
Programme: Yes **Floodlights:** No **Cover:** Yes (200) **Seats:** No **Founded:** 1889

TRELEWIS WELFARE

Secretary: Kyrien Thomas, 10 West Avenue, Maesycwmmer, Hengoed, Mid. Glam. CF8 7QN (0443 862876).
Ground: The Welfare Ground, Trelewis, Mid. Glam.
Directions: Through Trelewis village heading north and take sharp right after bridge - continue past houses to end of road, across wasteland to ground.
Colours: Red & white/red/red **Change colours:** Blue/black/blue.
Programme: Yes **Floodlights:** No **Cover:** No **Seats:** No **Founded:** 1966

Konica League of Wales action - Sean Wharton of Connah's Quay Nomads heads clear under pressure from Cwmbran Town forward Barry Thomas. *Photo - Paul Dennis.*

NORTH WALES JOINERY CYMRU ALLIANCE

	P	W	D	L	F	A	PTS
Rhyl	34	28	3	3	93	29	81
Welshpool Town	34	26	3	5	93	29	81
Wrexham Res.	34	20	6	8	83	38	66
Llandudno Town	34	20	5	9	91	48	65
Mostyn	34	20	3	11	85	67	63
Brymbo	34	15	10	9	53	34	55
Cemaes Bay	34	15	9	10	61	43	51
Cefn Druids	34	14	5	15	74	72	47
Lex XI	34	13	7	14	47	53	46
Penrhyncoch	34	12	8	14	51	60	44
Carno	34	12	6	16	57	76	42
Buckley Town	34	10	11	13	47	55	41
Rhayader Town	34	10	5	19	50	86	35
Llanidloes Town	34	8	10	16	42	71	34
Ruthin Town	34	8	8	18	49	79	32
Knighton Town	34	6	8	20	39	78	26
Rhos Aelwyd	34	6	6	22	30	81	21
Gresford Athletic	34	4	5	25	36	100	17

* - 3 points deducted

CYMRU ALLIANCE CLUBS 1994-95

BRYMBO

Secretary: N Jones, 29 Bryn Coed, Gwersyllt, Wrexham, Clwyd LL11 4UE (0978 753250).
Ground: Brymbo Sports Club, Tanyfron, Wrexham, (0978 755886).
Colours: Yellow/black/black **Change colours:** Black & blue/black/black
Programme: Yes **Floodlights:** No **Cover:** Yes (100) **Seats:** No **Founded:** 1943

BUCKLEY

Secretary: M Williams, 4 Hillany Grove, Western Park, Buckley, Clwyd (0244 546893).
Ground: Hawkesbury, Liverpool Road, Buckley.
Colours: Red & blue/blue/blue. **Change colours:** Amber/black/black.
Programme: Yes **Floodlights:** **Cover:** Yes **Seats:**

CARNO

Secretary: John Griffiths, Llwyneuron, Carno, Powys SY17 5LT (0686 420202).
Ground: Recreation Ground, Carno, Powys.
Colours: Green/black/black. **Change colours:** Red/black/black.
Programme: Yes **Floodlights:** No **Cover:** No **Seats:** Yes (105) **Founded:** 1960

CEFN DRUIDS

Secretary: Steve Williams, 9 Beacon Road, Pendine Park, Summerhill, Wrexham LL11 4UW (0978 752489).
Ground: Plaskynaston, Cefn Mawr (0978 820004).
Colours: White/black/black **Change colours:** Yellow & green/green/green
Programme: Yes **Floodlights:** No **Cover:** Yes (300) **Seats:** No
Founded: 1992 (Merger of Cefn Albion & Druids United).

CEMAES BAY

Secretary: Mrs N Hughes, 12 Maes Garnedd, Tregele, Anglesey, Gwynedd LL67 0DR (0407 710297).
Ground: School Lane, Cemaes Bay, Anglesey.
Colours: All red **Change colours:** All blue
Programme: Yes **Floodlights:** No **Cover:** Yes (300) **Seats:** Yes (100)

KNIGHTON TOWN

Secretary: Mrs C A Sutton, "Ashdown", 1 Underhill Cres., Knighton, Powys (0547 528953).
Ground: Bryn Y Castell, Knighton, Powys (0547 528339).
Colours: All red **Change colours:** Yellow/black/black
Programme: Yes **Floodlights:** Yes **Cover:** No **Seats:** Yes (100) **Founded:** 1881

LEX XI

Secretary: Phil Jones, 18 Mayflower Drive, Marford, Wrexham, Clwyd LL12 8LD (0978 854028).
Ground: Stansty Park, Mold Road, Wrexham (0978 261351).
Colours: Amber/black/black & amber **Change colours:** White/white/red
Programme: Yes **Floodlights:** No **Cover:** Yes (75) **Seats:** No **Founded:** 1965

LLANDRINDOD WELLS

Secretary: P Watkins, Camelot, Hillcrest Drive, Llandrindod Wells, Powys LD1 5DG (0597 823517)
Ground: Broadway, Lant Avenue, Llandrindod Wells (0597 823030).
Colours: Blue/white/blue & white **Change colours:** Red/white/red & white
Programme: Yes **Floodlights:** No **Cover:** Yes **Seats:** 250 **Founded:** 1888

LLANDUDNO TOWN

Secretary: E B Jarvis, 10 Howard Road, Llandudno, Gwynedd, LL30 1EA (0492 877113).
Ground: Maesdu Park, Maesdu Road, Llandudno.
Colours: White/navy blue/white **Change colours:** Red/navy/white
Programme: Yes **Floodlights:** No **Cover:** Yes (150) **Seats:** No

LLANIDLOES TOWN

Secretary: G E Parry, 22 Llysnant, Llanidloes, Powys, SY18 6BD (0551 225500).
Ground: Victoria Park, Victoria Avenue, Llanidloes (0551 222196).
Colours: Yellow/green/yellow **Change colours:** Green/white/white
Programme: Yes **Floodlights:** Yes **Cover:** Yes (100) **Seats:** Yes (240) **Founded:** 1875

MOSTYN

Secretary: Bryn Hughes, 11 Penrho Estate, Mostyn, Clwyd CH8 9QS (0745 560822).
Ground: Maes Pennant, Mostyn.
Colours: Red & black/black/black **Change colours:** Yellow & blue/blue/blue
Programme: Yes **Floodlights:** No **Cover:** Yes (100) **Seats:** No **Founded:** 1912

PENRHYNCOCH

Secretary: Rolant Ellis, 4 Maes Laura, Aberystwyth, Dyfed SY23 2AU (0970 617171).
Ground: Cae Baker, Penrhyncoch (0970 828992).
Colours: Yellow/blue/yellow **Change colours:** Red/black/red
Programme: Yes **Floodlights:** No **Cover:** Yes (100) **Seats:** No **Founded:** 1965

PENYCAE

Secretary: Mr S M Griffiths, 35 Chapel Street, Penycae, nr Wrexham, Clywd LL14 2RF (0978 842967).
Ground: Afoneitha Rd, Penycae, nr Wrexham, Clwyd (0970 828992).
Colours: All royal **Previous League:** Welsh (Wrexham Area)(Champions 93-94).
Programme: **Floodlights:** **Cover:** **Seats:** No **Founded:** 1982

RHAYADER TOWN

Secretary: Phil Woosman, 'Highlands', St.Harmon Road, Rhayader, Powys LD6 5PN (0597 811286).
Ground: The Weirglodd, Rhayader.
Colours: Red & white/white/red **Change colours:** Claret & blue/blue/blue
Programme: Yes **Floodlights:** Yes **Cover:** Yes (250) **Seats:** Yes (120)

RHOS AELWYD

Secretary: D Parry, "Penrallt", Queen Street, Rhos, Wrexham LL14 1PY (0978 845148).
Ground: Ponciau Park, Clarke Street, Ponciau.
Colours: Blue & black stripes/black/black **Change colours:** All green
Programme: Yes **Floodlights:** No **Cover:** No **Seats:** No **Founded:** 1948

RUTHIN TOWN

Secretary: B Lewis, 40 Maeshafod, Ruthin, Clwyd LL15 1LS (0824 702828).
Ground: Memorial Playing Fields, Parc-y-Dre, Ruthin (0824 702766).
Colours: Blue & white stripes/blue/blue **Change colours:** All red
Programme: Yes **Floodlights:** No **Cover:** No **Seats:** No **Founded:** 1951

WELSHPOOL TOWN

Secretary: J A Bartley, 24 Bryn Glas, Welshpool, Powys SY21 7TL (0938 552131).
Ground: Maesydre, Welshpool, Powys.
Colours: White/black/white **Change colours:** Red/navy/navy
Programme: Yes **Floodlights:** No **Cover:** Yes (100) **Seats:** No **Founded:** 1878

WREXHAM RESERVES

Secretary: David Rhodes, The Racecourse Ground, Mold Road, Wrexham Clwyd LL11 2AN (0978 262129).
Ground: The Racecourse Ground, Mold Road, Wrexham (0978 262129).
Colours: Red/white/red **Change colours:** Yellow & green/green/green
Programme: Yes **Floodlights:** Yes **Cover:** Yes (11,000) **Seats:** Yes (6,000) **Founded:** 1873

Brymbo FC, who had a greatly improved season finishing in the top half of the Cymru Alliance having only just been wooden-spoonists in 1992-93. *Photo - Colin Stevens.*

RICHARDS THE BUILDERS
MID WALES LEAGUE

FINAL TABLE	P	W	D	L	F	A	PTS
Machynlleth	30	22	5	3	123	32	71
Llandrindod Wells	30	22	4	4	95	26	70
Newtown Res.	30	21	3	6	85	36	66
Morda United	30	20	3	7	83	33	63
Caersws Res.	30	18	5	7	59	31	59
Llansantffraid Res.	30	15	6	9	72	41	51
Vale of Arrow	30	14	4	12	70	42	46
Waterloo Rovers	30	12	8	10	65	60	44
Berriew	30	11	6	13	67	55	39
Penparcau	30	11	5	14	54	58	38
Kington	30	11	3	17	37	82	35
Aberystwyth Res.	30	9	6	15	45	85	33
Builth Wells	30	10	2	18	64	87	32
Knighton Town Res.	30	6	5	19	27	90	23
Presteigne St A	30	3	4	23	26	107	13
Clun Valley	30	1	0	29	32	179	3

League Cup Final *(at Newtown)*:
Morda Utd 3 *(Evans, Clark, Houghton)*, Machynlleth 0

Youth League: Aberytwyth Town
Youth League R-up: Leintwardine

Summer Cup: Morda United
Summer Cup R-up: Machynlleth

Dias Williams Top Scorer Trophy:
Chris Evans (Machynlleth) 30

Manager of the Year:
Dai Eifion Davies (Machynlleth)

Player of the Year: Colin Jones (Berriew).

MID WALES LEAGUE CLUBS 1994-95

BERRIEW

Secretary: Miss A Jarman, Tyncoed, Llanwchaiarn, Newtown, Powys (0686 626881).
Ground: Berriew Recreation Ground.
Colours: White/navy/navy. **Change colours:** All blue.

BUILTH WELLS

Secretary: M L Jones, Bryncoed, 8 Irfon Bridge Rd, Builth Wells, Powys (0982 553673).
Ground: Thomas Lant Fields, Pendre, Builth Wells, Powys.
Colours: Amber/black/black. **Change colours:** Sky/black/black.

CLUN VALLEY

Secretary: V Burchell, 36 Henley Orchards, Ludlow, Shropshire (0584 877826).
Ground: Memorial Ground, Clun.
Colours: Maroon/claret/blue **Change colours:** All red

KINGTON TOWN

Secretary: Mrs P Shaw, 65 Greenfield, Kington, Herefordshire (0544 230191).
Ground: Mill Street, Kington, Herefordshire (0544 231007).
Colours: Amber & black/black/black **Change colours:** White & black/white/black

MACHYNLLETH

Secretary: G Evans, 4 Treowain, Machynlleth, Powys (0654 702734).
Ground: Cae Glas, Plas Ground, Machynlleth, Powys.
Colours: White & blue/blue/blue **Change colours:** All red

MONTGOMERY

Secretary:
Ground:

PENPARCAU

Secretary: N Gilbert, 19 Penrheidol, Penparcau, Aberystwyth (0970 617324).
Ground: Riverside Park, Manyddol, Aberystwyth.
Colours: White & black/black/red **Change colours:** Black & red/black/red.

PRESTEIGNE St ANDREWS

Secretary: Mrs D F Field, 14 Orchard Close, Presteigne, Powys (0544 360085).
Ground: Llanadras Park, Clatterbrune, Presteigne, Powys.
Colours: Red & black/black/black **Change colours:** Blue/white/white

U.C.W. ABERYSTWYTH

Ground: Vicarage Field, Llanbadarn, Aberystwyth (0970 623036).
Colours: All red **Change colours:** All green.

VALE of ARROW

Secretary: P Worts, Millside, Hundred House, Llandrindod Wells, Powys (0982 570409).
Ground: Cae Dressy, Gladestry, Kington (0544 22629).
Colours: White/navy/navy **Change colours:** White & navy/navy/navy.

WATERLOO ROVERS

Secretary: Cllr R Dart, 47 Erw Wen, Welshpool, Powys (0938 553688).
Ground: Maesydre Rec, off Severn Road, Welshpool, Powys.
Colours: All red **Change colours:** White/blue/blue

Plus the Reserve sides of: Aberystwyth Town *(see page 996)*, Caersws *(page 998)*, Knighton Town *(page 1183)*, Llansantffraid *(page 1001)*, Newtown *(page 1002)*.

SEALINK STENA WELSH ALLIANCE

	P	W	D	L	F	A	PTS
Llangefni Town	34	25	3	6			78
Llanfairpwll	34	24	6	4			78
Rhydymwyn	34	24	6	4			78
Loco Llanberis	34	23	8	3			77
Nefyn United	34	17	6	11			57
Llanfairfechan Town	34	17	5	12			56
Bangor City Res.	34	16	5	13			53
Nantlle Vale	34	15	7	12			51
Prestatyn Town	34	14	7	13			49
Connah's QN Res.	34	14	6	14			48
Holyhead Town	34	14	3	17			45
Llandyrnog United	34	12	5	17			41
Rhyl Res.	34	12	4	16			40
St Asaph City	34	9	9	16			39
Y Felinheli	34	9	5	20			32
Llanrwst United	34	8	3	23			27
Conwy Utd Res.	34	3	3	28			12
Penmaenmawr Phoe.	34	2	3	29			9

COPYRITE PANASONIC GWYNEDD LEAGUE

	P	W	D	L	F	A	PTS
Glaentraeth	34	27	2	7	153	44	83
Caernarfon Ath.	34	25	7	2	101	31	82
Porthmadog	34	25	4	5	138	40	79
Mountain Rangers	34	23	2	9	127	57	71
Penrhos United	34	22	5	7	128	62	71
Llandegfan	34	18	7	9	85	56	61
Llangefni Ath.	34	17	7	10	104	79	58
Hotpoint	34	17	5	12	92	71	56
Llanerchymedd	34	17	2	15	105	97	53
Pwllheli & Dist.	34	14	4	16	81	72	46
Crosville	34	14	4	16	92	99	46
Blaenau Amateurs	34	9	4	21	70	116	31
Bangor Coleg Normal	34	9	3	22	72	141	30
Pwllheli Borough	34	8	5	21	62	112	29
Llanrug United	34	7	4	23	86	120	25
P'rhyndeudraeth	34	5	7	22	47	112	22
Bangor University	34	3	9	22	49	109	18
Barmouth & D.	34	4	3	27	45	220	15

SAIN CAERNARFON & DISTRICT LEAGUE

	P	W	D	L	F	A	PTS
Caernarfon Borough	28	25	2	1	117	20	77
Deiniolen	28	24	3	1	106	18	75
Loco. Llanberis Res.	28	16	4	8	68	60	52
Bethesda Athletic	28	14	7	7	87	58	49
Llanrug Utd Res.	28	15	2	11	76	63	47
Harlech Town	28	14	4	10	88	53	46
Porthmadog Jnrs	28	15	1	12	72	87	46
Talysarn	28	12	5	11	65	57	41
Caernarfon Ath.	28	12	4	12	54	53	*37
Llanystumdwy	28	8	7	13	57	56	31
Nantlle Vale Res.	28	6	7	15	53	90	25
Y Felinheli Res.	28	5	5	18	56	72	20
Mountain R. Res.	28	4	5	19	48	120	*14
Nefyn United	28	3	7	18	56	93	*13
Bangor Univ. Res.	28	5	1	22	45	149	#1

* - 3pts deducted # - 15pts deducted

NURAS ANGLESEY LEAGUE

	P	W	D	L	F	A	PTS
Gwalchmai	32	29	2	1	147	31	89
Llanfairpwll Res.	32	25	4	3	113	36	79
Beaumaris Town	32	22	5	5	121	49	71
Gaerwen	32	20	4	8	119	43	64
Ll'erchymedd Res.	32	21	1	10	99	59	64
Holyhead M'tain Rgrs	32	19	6	7	87	54	63
Amlwch	32	16	8	8	86	55	56
Holyhead Hotspur	32	16	2	14	103	71	50
Moelfre	32	12	6	14	72	75	42
Holyhead T. Res.	32	12	7	13	68	84	**37
Trearddur Bay	32	10	5	17	75	92	35
Bodedern	32	9	7	16	51	94	34
Cemaes Bay Res.	32	9	6	17	74	114	33
Rhosneigr	32	9	1	22	62	88	28
Glantraeth Res.	32	3	2	27	52	140	11
Llangoed	32	3	2	27	40	154	*8
Bryngwran Bulls	32	2	2	28	44	185	8

* - 3pts deducted

O.C.S. CLWYD LEAGUE

PREM. DIV.	P	W	D	L	F	A	PTS
Flint Town U. Res.	22	18	2	2	76	18	56
Denbigh Town	22	15	5	2	69	28	50
Saltney CC	22	14	4	4	64	32	46
Halkyn United	22	11	3	8	46	36	36
Mochdre	22	10	3	9	67	45	33
Rhyl Delta	22	9	5	8	41	45	32
Point of Ayr	22	10	2	10	61	51	*29
Holywell T. Res.	22	7	3	12	39	63	24
Rhuddlan Town	22	6	5	11	40	61	23
Abergele Celts	22	7	1	14	41	62	22
Colwyn Bay YMCA	22	5	1	16	22	64	16
St Asaph C. Res.	22	2	2	18	26	87	*5

* - 1 point deducted

DIV. ONE	P	W	D	L	F	A	PTS
Meliden	18	15	1	2	65	33	46
Denbigh Town Res.	18	12	2	4	44	18	38
Northop Village	18	11	4	3	65	28	37
Rhyl Delta Res.	18	9	4	5	44	29	31
Golden Lions	18	6	5	7	38	39	23
Llandyrnog U. Res.	18	6	3	9	50	56	21
Halkyn Utd Res.	18	6	3	9	36	49	21
Bagillt Hotspurs	18	6	2	10	32	52	20
Caerwys	18	5	1	12	30	54	16
Tefnant Village	18	1	1	16	25	71	4

DIV. TWO	P	W	D	L	F	A	PTS
British Steel	16	12	3	1	83	21	39
Prestatyn T. Res.	16	12	2	2	75	12	38
Mostyn Lodge	16	9	4	3	47	26	31
Brynsford	16	9	1	6	34	33	28
Marsh Athletic	16	8	3	5	69	28	27
Mostyn Albion	16	4	2	10	26	45	14
Denbigh Albion	16	4	2	10	24	59	14
Golden Lions Res.	16	3	3	10	20	67	12
Tefnant Vil. Res.	16	1	0	15	16	103	3

THREEWAYS VALE of CONWY SUBARU LEAGUE

	P	W	D	L	F	A	PTS
Bro Cernyw	32	28	0	4			84
Machno United	32	24	4	4			76
Lansannan	32	23	1	8			70
Llandudno T. Res.	32	21	3	8			66
West Shore	32	19	5	7			62
Cerrigydrudion	32	18	7	7			61
Dolgarrog	32	18	3	11			57
Llan/Conwy	32	17	4	11			55
Rhos United	32	12	4	16			40
Betws-y-Coed	32	11	4	17			34
Dolwyddelan	32	10	3	19			33
Llanrwst Utd Res.	32	9	4	19			31
Llanfairfechan Res.	32	7	7	18			*25
Blaenau Am. Res.	32	8	1	23			*22
Hotpoint Res.	32	6	4	22			*19
Penmaenmawr Res.	32	4	6	22			18
Junction Labour	32	5	4	23			*16

* - Points adjusted

NORTH WALES CUP FINALS

Gwynedd Trophies North Wales Coast FA Challenge Cup: Connah's Quay Nomads 2, Conwy United 1

Gwynedd Trophies North Wales Coast FA Junior Cup: Deiniolen 2, Llansanan 0

North Wales Coast FA Youth under-18 Cup: Rhyl 2, Bangor City 1

Fitlock Cookson Cup: Llangefni Town 2, Bangor City 1

Fitlock Alves Cup: Prestatyn Town 1, St Asaph City 0

John Smith Gwynedd Cup: Glantraeth 3, Mountain Rangers 2

Tyn Lion Volvo Barritt Cup: Llanfairpwll 2, Rhydymwyn 1

Appendix Two Scottish Football

Major Honours 1993-94

COMPETITION	WINNERS	RUNNERS-UP
Tennents Qualifying Cup (South)	Whitehill Welfare	St Cuthberts Wanderers
Tennents Qualifying Cup (North)	Ross County	Huntly
OVD Scottish Junior Cup	Largs Thistle	Glenafton Athletic
Tennents Scottish Amateur Cup	Bannockburn Amateurs	Galston United
Press & Journal Highland League	Huntly	Caledonian
Highland League Cup	Huntly	Fraserburgh
South of Scotland League	Threave Rovers	Maxwelltown HSFP
East of Scotland League	Whitehill Welfare	Vale of Leithen
East of Scotland League Cup	Gala Fairydean	Whitehill Welfare
North of Scotland Cup	Caledonian	Forres Mechanics
West of Scotland Cup	Kilwinning Rangers	Shettleston
Ayrshire Region Junior League	Irvine Meadow	Auchinleck Talbot
Central Region Junior League	Arthurlie	Lesmahagow

TENNENTS SCOTTISH CUP 1993-94

Each year eight non-League clubs take part in the Scottish Cup. To get there they must reach at least the semi-final stage of one of two 'Qualifying Cups' - either the northern version or the southern.

The qualifying cups start in early September with the finals in November. Ross County beat holders Huntly to win the northern section, whilst Whitehill Welfare crushed St Cuthbert Wanderers 5-0 to triumph in the south.

SCOTTISH QUALIFYING CUP (SOUTH) 1993-94

First Round	Second Round	Third Round	Semi-Final	Final
	Wigtown & Blad. 1			
	Vale of Leithen 3			
Spartans 1		Vale of Leith. 0,1		
Whitehill Welf. 2	Whitehill Welf. 3	Whitehill 0,3		
	Hawick Ryl A. 0			
			Whitehill Welf. 2	
	Gala Fairydean 3		Gala Fairydean 0	
	Threave Rovers 0			
		Gala Fairydean 4		
	Newton Stewart 4	Newton Stewart 2		
	Girvan Amtrs 0			
				St Cuthbert Wdrs 0
Coldstream 3	Annan Ath. 0,4			Whitehill Welfare 5
Glasgow Univ. 1	Coldstream 0,3			
		Annan Athletic 0		
Selkirk 4	Selkirk 3	Selkirk 3		
Dalbeattie Star 1	Burntisland 2			
			Selkirk 0	
	Tarff Rovers 3		St Cuthbert W. 1	
	St Cuth. Wdrs 5			
		St Cuthbert 4		
	Edinb. Univ. 1	Civil Serv. S. 1		
	C.S. Strollers 2			

WINNERS: WHITEHILL WELFARE

SCOTTISH QUALIFYING CUP (NORTH) 1993-94

First Round	Second Round	Third Round	Semi-Final	Final
	Keith 2,1			
Deverondale 4	Ross County 2,2			
Elgin City 2		Ross County 1,4		
	Deverondale 2,1	Inverness This. 1,1		
Invern. Thistle 2	Invern. This. 2,6			
Caledonian 0			Ross County 5	
	Forres Mechan. 1		Rothes 0	
	Clachnacuddin 2			
		Clachnacuddin 0,1		
	Rothes 3	Rothes 0,3		
Fort William 4	Fort William 1			
Wick Academy 0				Huntly 1
	Lossiemouth 1,1			Ross County 2
	Fraserburgh 1,3			
		Fraserburgh 1		
	Huntly 3	Huntly 5		
Peterhead 1,2	Peterhead 1			
Golspie S. 1,1			Huntly 2	
	Buckie Thistle 1		Cove Rangers 1	
	Cove Rangers 3			
		Cove Rangers 4		
	Brora Rgrs 2,3	Brora Rangers 0		
	Nairn Co. 2,0			

WINNERS: ROSS COUNTY

In reaching the southern semi-finals, Selkirk qualified for their first appearance in the Scottish Cup since the infamous afternoon in December 1984 when they suffered the humiliation of being beaten 0-20 at Stirling Albion. Selkirk received a bye to the Second Round where, on Saturday 15th January, they entertained Arbroath in front of a 454 crowd. The match was in doubt in the preceding week as the pitch at the picturesque Ettrick Park was coated in ice, but Selkirk's jovial manager, Jackson Cockburn, cleared it almost single-handedly. The home side played well but in the end their opponents' superior fitness and experience told, and Arbroath ran out 3-0 winners. However, the Borders side had laid behind them the ghost of 1984.

Southern Qualifying Cup winners Whitehill Welfare were only twelve minutes away from a major surprise when they led 3-1 at high-flying Stranraer in the First Round. However, normality was restored a week later, on Saturday 18th December, when the Second Division leaders ran out 4-0 winners, Tommy Sloan getting all the goals, three of them with his head.

Huntly did extremely well to force a goalless draw with Albion Rovers in the First Round, and the replay received national exposure because of the inordinate number of postponements to which it was subjected. It eventually went ahead on Saturday 15th January and was well worth waiting for - the Highlanders thrilled a huge partisan crowd by scoring three times in the last ten minutes to come from behind to win. In the Second Round against Stranraer a week later, however, they received a dose of their own medicine. They were leading through an early Marco De Barros header until just sixteen minutes from time. Then, their experienced central defender Doug Rougvie pulled down Darren Henderson, and Graham Duncan equalised from the spot, and the hearts of the 2,400 fans packed into Christie Park were finally broken when, four minutes later, Tommy Sloan continued where he had left off against Whitehill, and headed the winner from an Alex Grant cross.

Ross County were the last surviving non-League club, and in Brian Grant had a striker even more prolific than Stranraer's Tommy Sloan. They disposed of St Cuthbert Wanderers at home to the tune of 11-0, with Grant striking five and all but two of the goals arriving before half-time, then beat Second Division Forfar Athletic 4-0 on their own patch. The home side did their cause no good when then had Eric Archibald sent off in the opening minutes, and Brian Grant weighed in with another hat-trick. The Press & Journal Highland League side then faced another away tie, on Tuesday 8th February, at Alloa Athletic who were lying second in the Second Division. With a trip to Ibrox for a money-spinning tie with Rangers at stake, County put the home side under some intense early pressure, but fell behind in the 17th minute when Mike McAnenay headed home a cross from Andy Willock. Neil McAvoy made it 2-0 seven minutes later, and although the Dingwall side dominated the second period, they could make no impact on Alloa's lead.

HOW THE NON-LEAGUERS FARED - FIRST ROUND

ALBION ROVERS	**0 v 0**	**HUNTLY**
-	Att:759	-
EAST FIFE	**5 v 0**	**ROTHES**
Scott 11 38 56, Hope 28, Hilersley 72		-
ROSS COUNTY	**11 v 0**	**St CUTHBERT W.**
Grant 1(p) 5 14 26 77, Williamson 4, Duff 25 27 47, Ferries 31 32,	Att:1800	-
STRANRAER	**3 v 3**	**WHITEHILL W.**
Sloan 7 78, Henderson 88	Att:760	Thorburn 29 55(ps), Sneddon 32

FIRST ROUND REPLAYS

WHITEHILL WELF.	**0 v 4**	**STRANRAER**
-	Att:750	Sloan 13 25 33 83
HUNTLY	**5 v 3**	**ALBION ROVERS**
De Barros 46, Stewart 47, Lennox 80, Murphy 83, Thomson 86	Att:2000	Fraser 26, Scott 58(p) McCaffrey 66

SECOND ROUND

ALLOA ATHLETIC	**4 v 0**	**GALA F'DEAN**
McCulloch 24 McCormick 30 49, Lamont 85	Att:805	-
SELKIRK	**0 v 3**	**ARBROATH**
-	Att:454	McKinnon 10, Adam 30, Buckley 80
HUNTLY	**1 v 2**	**STRANRAER**
De Barros 13	Att:2400	Duncan 74(p), Sloan 78
EAST STIRLING	**4 v 1**	**COVE RANGERS**
McAuley 48, Gerraghty 70, McCallum 78, Robertson 84	Att:867	Whyte 80
FORFAR ATHLETIC	**0 v 4**	**ROSS COUNTY**
-	Att:2439	Grant 16 50 71, Wilson 17,

THIRD ROUND

ALLOA ATHLETIC	**2 v 0**	**ROSS COUNTY**
McAvenay 17, McAvoy 25	Att:4169	-

LEWIS & HARRIS LEAGUE

The League runs with a summer season, and the table shown below is for 1993. The 1994 season will finish in September. All the clubs are named after towns, villages or areas of the islands of Lewis and Harris. The first competition on the islands was held in 1903-04, and the current league dates from 1908-09.

Malcolm McDonald

1993 TABLE	P	W	D	L	F	A	PTS
Point	18	15	2	1	60	17	32
Ness	18	13	1	4	74	21	27
Harris	18	12	2	4	51	23	26
Stornoway Ath.	18	10	3	5	44	27	23
Lochs	18	10	2	6	53	28	22
Stornoway Utd	18	5	3	10	29	39	13
Shawbost	18	6	1	11	27	59	13
Carloway	18	6	1	11	29	65	13
Back	18	4	1	13	24	59	9
West Side	18	0	2	18	16	19	72

1993 Cup Finals:

Acres Boys Club: Lochs beat Point 5-4 on penalties after a 1-1 draw.
Jock Stein Cup: Point 2, Ness 1
Lewis Cup: Ness beat Stornoway Athletic 6-5 on penalties after a 1-1 draw.
Eilean An Fhraoich Cup (rural teams only): Harris 6, Back 2 *(aet)*

O.V.D. SCOTTISH JUNIOR CUP 1993-94

First Round

Aberdeen LC v Neilston	1-3	Arniston R. v Newtongrange Star	2-3
Auchinleck Talbot v Formantine United	6-0	Banchory St T. v Crombie Sp.	4-2
Beith v FC Stonywood	2-2,2-0	Benburb v Annbank United	3-1
Bishopmill United v Edinburgh United	0-1	Blairgowrie v Bathgate Thistle	0-3
Buckie Rovers v Lesmahagow	0-3	Cambuslang Rangers v Petershill	0-2
Craigmark B. v Broxburn	2-2,1-4	Cumnock Juniors v RAF Kinloss	4-1
Darvel v Maybole	0-2	Downfield v Fauldhouse United	4-0
East Kilbride v Longside	4-1	Ellon United v Dalkeith Thistle	1-4
Elmwood v Tranent	1-3	Forfar Albion v Buchanhaven	1-2
Forfar West End v Pollok	0-3	Fraserburgh United v Maud	3-4
Glenrothes v Rosyth Recreation	1-0	Inch v Wishaw	1-1,0-1
Inverurie Juniors v Renfrew	1-7	Irvine Victoria v Kello Rovers	2-3
Islavale v Culter	0-2	Johnstone B. v Thornton H.	2-0
Kilbirnie Ladeside v Cuminestown	11-0	Kilsyth Rangers v Haddington	1-4
Kirrie Thistle v Lochee United	2-0	Lanark United v Port of Glasgow)	4-3
Livingston United v Hill of Beath Hawthorn	0-1	Lochee Harp v Aberdeen East End	1-0
Lochgelly Albion v Rob Roy	3-7	Lugar Boswell Thistle v St Rochs	2-1
Musselburgh A. v Parkvale	4-3	Ormiston Primrose v N. Elgin	1-1,8-1
Saltcoats Victoria v Dundee EC	5-1	Shettleston v Dundee Victoria	5-0
Shotts Bon Accord v Forth W.	0-0,1-0*(aet)*	Strathspey Thistle v Ardeer Thistle	1-1,0-4
Sunnybank v Stoneyburn	2-0	Yoker Athletic v Arthurlie	2-2,0-4

Second Round

Arbroath Victoria v Royal Albert	3-2	Ardrosson Winton R. v Port Gordon	13-0
Arthurlie v East Kilbride	6-0	Bankfoot Athletic v Kilwinning Rangers	2-6
Bellshill Athletic v Irvine Meadow	2-2	Benburb v Phumperston	2-0
Bonnybridge v Greenock	0-4	Bonnyrigg Rose v Dyce	9-0
Broxburn Athletic v Bathgate Thistle	1-2	Camelon v Tayport	3-3,0-0*(aet, 2-4 on penalties)*
Carluke Rovers v Dundonald B.	1-3	Clackmannan v Lossie United	2-2,5-1
Crossgates Primrose v Brechin Victoria	3-0	Cumbernauld United v Bo'ness United	3-1
Dairy Athletic v Dalskeith Thistle	0-2	Dundee Downfield v Bon Accord	2-1
Dunbar United v Whitburn	1-1,3-2	Dundee North End v Beith	0-0,1-4
Dundee St J. v Auchinleck Talbot	1-0	Forres Thistle v Larkhall Thistle	3-3,0-4
Glenafton Athletic v Dunipace	2-0	Hall Russell United v Deveronside	4-0
Hermes v Largs Thistle	1-2	Hill of Beath Hawthorn v Baillieston	4-1
Hurlford United v Buchanhaven	3-1	Inverurie Loco Works v Coltness United	2-1
Kelty Hearts v Rutherglen Glencairn	1-4	Kilbirnie Ladeside v Balbeggie	2-0
Kinnoull v Broughty Athletic	0-1	Kirkcaldy YMCA v Haddington	1-3
Kirrie Thistle v Luncarty	5-1	Lanark Utd v Blantyre Victoria	1-5
Lesmahagow v Arbroath SC	3-0	Linlithgow Rose v Lugar Boswell Thistle	5-0
Lochore Welfare v Vale of Leven	2-2,3-2	Maud v Maryhill	0-2
Montrose R. v Banchory	2-2,1-0	Muirkirk v Ashfield	3-1
Musselburgh A. v Cumnock Juniors	1-4	Neilston v Glenrothes	5-0
Newburgh v Maybole	3-2	Newtongrange Star v Culter	0-1
Oakley United v Jeanfield Swifts	3-1	Ormiston Primrose v Burghead Thistle	12-0
Petershill v Lochee Harp	1-2	Pollok v Carnoustie Primrose	2-1
RAF Lossie *(scr)* Kello Rovers *(w/o)*		Preston A. v Saltcoats	2-2*(at Arniston)*,1-2
Renfrew v Troon	3-1	Sauchie v Coupar Angus	7-2
Scone Thistle v Glasgow Perthshire	0-2	Shettleston v Nairn St Ninians	7-0
St Andrews United v Lewis United	2-1	Shotts Bon Accord v Ardeer Thistle	0-0,2-1
Stonehaven v Armadale Thistle	0-3	St Anthonys v Edinburgh Utd	2-2,1-1*(3-1 pens)*
Stonehouse Victoria v Blackburn United	0-2	Sunnybank v Harthill Rovers	0-1
Tranent v Thorniewood United	2-0	Tulliallan v Rob Roy *(at Rob Roy)*	0-3
Vale of Clyde v Johnstone B.	3-1	West Calder United v Banks O'Dee	1-2
Whitletts Victoria v Turriff United	1-1,0-2	Wishaw v Fochabers	3-1

Third Round

Bathgate Thistle v Clackmannan	4-2	Arthurlie v Ardrossan Winton Rovers	1-1,6-3*(aet)*
Beith v Newburgh	3-1	Blantyre Victoria v Kello Rovers	4-3
Bonnyrigg Rose v Larkhall Thistle	4-2	Crossgates Primrose v Inverurie Loco Works	8-1
Cumbernauld United v Blackburn United	1-1	Dundee Downfield v Arbroath Victoria	10-1
Dunbar United v Muirkirk	4-0	Glasgow Perthshire v Hurlford United	2-2,4-1
Greenock v Turriff United	0-2	Hall Russell United v Broughty Athletic	3-1
Harthill Rovers v Glenafton Athletic	2-3	Kilbirnie Ladeside v Renfrew	2-2,2-1
Kilwinning Rangers v St Andrews United	3-1	Rob Roy v Hill of Beath Hawthorn	0-1
Largs Thistle v St Anthonys	1-1,6-1	Lesmahagow v Tranent	2-0
Lochore Welfare v Lochee Harp	1-1,4-2	Linlithgow Rose v Irvine Meadow	0-0,1-0
Maryhill v Dundonald	3-3,4-2*(aet)*	Montrose R. v Benburb	2-2,0-4
Neilston v Shettleston	0-1	Oakley United v Kirrie Thistle	1-3
Ormiston Primrose v Haddington A.	2-1	Pollok v Sauchie	2-0
Rutherglen Glencairn v Culter	2-0	Saltcoats Victoria v Dalkeith	1-1,4-0
Shotts Bon Accord v Cumnock Juniors	2-0	Tayport v Armadale Thistle	1-2
Wishaw v Banks O'Dee	0-1	Vale of Clyde v Dundee St J.	2-1

Fourth Round

Arthurlie v Kilbirnie Ladeside	4-2	Bathgate Thistle v Bonnyrigg Rose	1-1,1-0
Beith v Shettleston	1-1,1-2	Blackburn United v Rutherglen Glencairn	0-5
Blantyre Victoria v Kilwinning Rangers	1-1,0-3	Dundee Downfield v Crossgates Primrose	2-1
Glenafton Athletic v Benburb	3-0	Lesmahagow v Hill of Beath Hawthorn	1-0
Linlithgow Rose v Kirrie Thistle	6-0	Lochore Welfare v Largs Thistle	0-6
Maryhill v Hall Russell United	1-2	Ormiston Primrose v Glasgow Perthshire	1-2
Pollok v Armadale Thistle	2-2,1-0	Saltcoats Victoria v Banks O'Dee	0-3
Shotts Bon Accord v Dunbar United	2-2,3-1	Turriff United v Vale of Clyde	3-1

Fifth Round

Bathgate Thistle v Pollok	0-1	Dundee Downfield v Lesmahagow	2-1
Kilwinning Rangers v Banks O'Dee	3-0	Largs Thistle v Hall Russell United	3-3,3-0
Linlithgow Rose v Glasgow Perthshire	2-1	Rutherglen Glencairn v Shettleston	0-3
Shotts Bon Accord v Arthurlie	1-1,0-1	Turriff United v Glenafton Athletic	3-4

Quarter-Finals

Glenafton Athletic v Shettleston	1-0	Kilwinning Rangers v Dundee Downfield	2-1
Linlithgow Rose v Arthurlie	1-2	Pollok v Largs Thistle	1-2

Semi-Finals.

Largs v Kilwinning *(at Ayr U., att: 6,151)*	2-1	Glenafton v Arthurlie *(at St Mirren, att: 7,192)*	4-0

Final *(at Ibrox Park, Sun 15th May, att: 8,668)*:
Largs Thistle 1 *(McCurdy 31)*,
Glenafton Athletic 0
Largs: *Barnstaple, A Elliott, Morrison, D Elliott, Feeney, Murray, McCurdy, Rodgers, Quigg (Phairs 88), Russell (Wall 61), Halley.*
Glenafton: *Kelly, Adams (Lowe 45), Gray, Renney, Kennedy, McFarlane, Walker, Archer, Moore (Montgomery 60), McVie, Miller.*
Referee: John Underhill.

Largs Thistle FC - OVD Scottish Junior Cup winners 1993-94.

THE SCOTTISH NON-LEAGUE REVIEW 93-94

The review contains dozens of final league tables and cup results from all over Scotland. It is obtainable for £2 from Stewart Davidson at: 12 Windsor Road, Renfrew PA4 0SS. Tel. 041 886 4856 (evenings only).

PRESS & JOURNAL HIGHLAND LEAGUE

FINAL TABLE	P	W	D	L	F	A	PTS
Huntly	34	27	4	3	95	21	85
Caledonian	34	20	7	7	80	44	67
Ross County	34	21	4	9	80	51	67
Cove Rangers	34	20	4	10	89	46	64
Lossiemouth	34	19	6	9	74	45	63
Elgin City	34	19	6	9	60	33	63
Keith	34	16	6	12	57	40	54
Buckie Thistle	34	16	6	12	54	48	54
Fraserburgh	34	15	8	11	52	36	53
Brora Rangers	34	13	9	12	60	61	48
Peterhead	34	12	8	14	55	56	44
Clachnacuddin	34	11	7	16	49	60	40
Forres Mechanics	34	11	6	17	56	67	39
Deverondale	34	7	8	19	46	84	29
Inverness Thistle	34	6	9	19	38	62	27
Fort William	34	8	3	23	26	78	27
Nairn County	34	6	3	25	30	114	21
Rothes	34	4	6	24	42	97	18

TENNENTS LEAGUE CUP Prelim. Round
Fraserburgh 6, Peterhead 1
Inverness Thistle 1, Ross County 4

First Round:
Elgin 2, Clachnacuddin 1 *(aet & 1-1 draw)*
Huntly 3, Cove Rangers 0
Deverondale 1, Fraserburgh 3
Lossiemouth 0, Buckie Thistle 1
Forres Mechanics 0, Nairn County 2
Caledonian 4, Ross County 3 *(after 1-1 draw)*
Brora Rgrs 8, Fort William 1 *(after 0-0 draw)*
Keith 1, Rothes 1 *(aet & 3-3 draw, 4-3 pens)*

Quarter-Finals: Caledonian 2, Brora Rangers 1
Keith 1, Huntly 2 *(after 1-1 draw)*
Fraserburgh 3, Buckie Thistle 0
Nairn County 1, Elgin City 8

Semi-Finals: Fraserburgh 3, Elgin City 2
Huntly 3, Caledonian 1

Final *(at Elgin City FC, Sept 18th)*:
Huntly 4, Fraserburgh 1

Gary Whyte heads clear for Huntly during their League Cup win over Cove Rangers.

Keith goalkeeper Ian Thain guesses correctly to save a penalty from Caledonian's Billy Skinner.
Photos - Alan Watson

SOUTH OF SCOTLAND LEAGUE

The South of Scotland League operated with eleven clubs in 1993-94 following the close season withdrawal of Queen of the South Reserves.

Early season attention was focussed on the League Cup competition. The final featured Threave Rovers and Wigtown & Bladnoch, both of whom had won their respective qualifying sections with difficulty. Threave were victorious over two legs in a scrappy final.

The Castle Douglas club were also favourites to retain the championship, but it was St Cuthberts Wanderers who set the pace in the league with seven straight wins only to falter after their Scottish Cup exploits had ended. Threave Rovers took over at the top and held off a strong challenge from Maxwelltown to finish worthy winners. Creetown and Tarff Rovers once again struggled at the foot of the table, but the 'Ferrymen' vacated bottom spot having been wooden-spooniss in each of the previous three seasons.

The cups were shared around three clubs. Stranraer's Scottish League side took the premier trophy, the Challenge Cup, and Annan Athletic's East of Scotland eleven won two trophies.

St Cuthbert Wanderers' Qualifying Cup run brought them national attention, and they became the first South League finalists since Girvan in 1976-77. The 11-0 thrashing they received at Ross County effectively ended their season, and the scoreline was later repeated against Threave in the league.

Malcolm Pagan.

FINAL TABLE	P	W	D	L	F	A	PTS
Threave Rovers	20	15	3	2	90	22	33
Maxwelltown HSFP	20	13	5	2	65	41	31
Wigtown & Bladnoch	20	13	3	4	57	27	29
St Cuthbert Wdrs	20	23	2	5	57	33	28
Dalbeattie Star	20	9	3	8	52	39	21
Newton Stewart	20	8	5	7	51	44	21
Annan Athletic	20	6	6	8	38	41	18
Girvan	20	8	0	12	45	71	16
Blackwood Dynamos	20	6	2	12	52	58	14
Creetown	20	2	1	17	25	99	5
Tarff Rovers	20	1	0	19	32	89	2

Top Scorer: Willie Best (Threave) 47

Lge Cup Sect. 1	P	W	D	L	F	A	PTS
Threave Rovers	8	7	1	0	35	8	15
Dalbeattie Star	8	6	1	1	22	11	13
Blackwood Dynamos	8	2	1	5	13	23	5
Maxwelltown HSFP	8	2	0	6	15	22	4
Annan Athletic	8	1	1	6	10	31	3

Lge Cup Sect. 2	P	W	D	L	F	A	PTS
Wigtown & Blad.	10	8	2	0	18	7	18
St Cuthberts Wdrs	10	5	1	4	29	16	11
Newton Stewart	10	5	0	5	35	22	10
Girvan	10	3	2	5	23	23	8
Tarff Rovers	10	3	2	5	14	27	8
Creetown	10	2	1	7	10	34	5

Final. 1st Leg: Threave Rovers 3, Wigtown & B. 1
Final. 2nd Leg: Wigtown & B. 0, Threave Rovers 1

EAST OF SCOTLAND LEAGUE

PREM. DIV.	P	W	D	L	F	A	PTS
Whitehill Welfare	18	13	4	1	58	17	30
Vale of Leithen	18	9	3	6	36	29	21
Gala Fairydea	18	7	5	6	28	18	19
Craigroyston	18	7	5	6	23	22	19
Annan Athletic	18	7	5	6	31	34	19
Spartans	18	6	6	6	30	30	18
CS Strollers	18	7	3	8	29	35	17
Easthouse Lily	17	5	5	7	19	29	15
Manor Thistle	17	4	4	9	21	39	12
Edinburgh City	18	4	0	14	22	44	8

DIV. ONE	P	W	D	L	F	A	PTS
Tollcross United	18	14	3	1	80	17	31
Edinburgh Univ.	18	11	5	2	54	21	27
Kelso United	18	9	4	5	37	23	22
Selkirk	18	9	4	5	35	25	22
Herriott Watt Univ.	18	7	5	6	28	34	19
Pencaitland	18	6	6	6	20	16	18
Coldstream	18	6	4	8	30	36	16
Peebles Rovers	18	3	4	11	17	35	10
Hawick Ryl Albert	18	4	1	13	34	63	9
Eyemouth United	18	1	4	13	16	51	6

Lge Cup Sect. 1	P	W	D	L	F	A	PTS
Gala Fairydean	6	4	2	0	26	6	10
Easthouses	6	3	1	2	13	13	7
Hawick Ryl Albert	6	1	2	3	7	15	4
Selkirk	6	1	1	4	6	18	3

Lge Cup Sect. 2	P	W	D	L	F	A	PTS
Tollcross United	6	4	2	0	14	4	10
Craigroyston	6	4	1	1	8	3	9
Peebles Rovers	6	1	1	4	8	13	3
Annan Athletic	6	1	0	5	6	16	2

Lge Cup Sect. 3	P	W	D	L	F	A	PTS
Whitehill Welfare	6	5	1	0	32	7	11
Vale of Leithen	6	4	1	1	26	9	9
Eyemouth United	6	2	0	4	6	30	4
Herriott Watt	6	0	0	6	5	23	0

Lge Cup Sect. 4	P	W	D	L	F	A	PTS
Edinburgh City	6	4	2	0	16	7	10
Spartans	6	2	2	2	10	9	6
Kelso United	6	2	2	2	5	7	6
Edinburgh Univ.	6	0	2	4	7	15	2

Lge Cup Sect. 5	P	W	D	L	F	A	PTS
CS Strollers	6	5	1	0	12	5	11
Pencaitland	6	2	3	1	9	5	7
Manor Thistle	6	2	1	3	8	7	5
Coldstream	6	0	1	5	4	16	1

Play-off:
CS Strollers 1, Edinburgh City 0 *(after 1-1 draw)*

Semi-Finals: CS Strollers 1, Whitehill Welf. 2
Tolcross U. 0, Gala Fairydean 4 *(after 1-1 draw)*

Final *(at Peebles Rovers FC, Sun 27th March)*:
Gala Fairydean beat Whitehill Welfare 4-2 on penalties after 0-0 draw.

KING CUP **First Round**

Easthouses Lily v Selkirk	1-0
Gala Fairydean v Vale of Leithen	3-0
Spartans v Civil Service Strollers	1-0

Second Round

Coldstream v Manor Thistle	3-0
Craigroyston v Easthouse Lily	1-0
Edinburgh City v Pencaitland	2-1
Edinburgh University v Spartans	0-2
Hawick Royal Albert v Gala Fairydean	2-3
Herriott Watt University v Whitehill Welfare	1-7
Kelso United v Eyemouth United	4-2
Tollcross United v Peebles Rovers	9-0

Quarter-Finals

Craigroyston v Kelso United	7-2
Gala Fairydean v Tolcross United	0-1
Spartans v Coldstream	3-1
Whitehill Welfare v Edinburgh City	4-2

Semi-Finals: Craigroyston v Tollcross Utd 2-0; Whitehill Welfare v Spartans 7-0

Final *(at Civil Service Strollers FC, Sat 7th May)*: Whitehill Welfare 3, Craigroyston 1

SCOTTISH JUNIOR LEAGUE TABLES

CENTRAL REGION
REEBOK LEAGUE

PREM. DIV.	P	W	D	L	F	A	PTS
Arthurlie	22	15	4	3	60	30	34
Lesmahagow	22	14	5	3	50	24	33
Shotts Bon Accord	22	12	6	4	40	20	30
Pollok	22	11	8	3	39	21	30
Rutherglen Glencairn	22	9	5	8	37	39	23
Shettleston	22	7	8	7	35	33	22
Petershill	22	9	4	9	36	38	22
Dunipace	22	8	5	9	27	30	21
Cambuslang Rgrs	22	6	5	11	29	38	17
Renfrew	22	2	12	8	23	42	16
Larkhall Thistle	22	3	3	16	28	53	9
E Kilbride This.	22	2	3	17	19	55	7

DIV. ONE	P	W	D	L	F	A	PTS
Maryhill	26	18	2	6	47	17	38
Baillieston	26	15	4	7	33	22	34
Vale of Clyde	26	14	4	8	42	37	32
Kilsyth Rangers	26	12	7	7	35	23	31
Benburb	26	12	4	10	47	36	28
Vale of Leven	26	13	2	11	40	34	28
Glasgow Perthshire	26	8	8	10	39	36	24
Ashfield	26	10	4	12	39	44	24
Neilston	26	10	4	12	40	53	24
Forth Wanderers	26	8	7	11	32	46	23
Lanark United	26	8	6	12	48	48	22
Thorniewood Utd	26	8	6	12	36	41	22
Kirkintilloch RR	26	7	4	15	39	57	18
Johnstone Burgh	26	6	4	16	30	52	16

DIV. TWO	P	W	D	L	F	A	PTS
Cumbernauld Utd	24	17	4	3	54	26	38
Port Glasgow	24	16	4	4	48	23	36
Blantyre Victoria	24	18	3	5	52	25	35
Yoker Athletic	24	14	3	7	49	33	31
Bellshill Ath.	24	12	7	5	36	21	31
Greenock	24	11	8	5	48	26	30
St Anthonys	24	7	5	12	25	37	19
Carluke Rovers	24	5	8	11	36	43	18
St Rochs	24	6	6	12	24	39	18
Royal Albert	24	4	10	10	24	39	18
Coltness United	24	6	5	13	27	43	17
Stonehouse Violet	24	4	6	14	34	51	14
Wishaw	24	2	4	19	16	57	7

Cup Finals:

Sectional Lge Cup *(at Clydebank FC, Oct 6th)*:
Lesmahagow 2, Petershill 1

MBM Hire Lge Cup *(at Pollok FC, May 20th)*:
Shotts BA bt Shettleston 4-2 on pens after 0-0 draw

Erskine Hosp. Cup *(at Vale of Clyde, June 17th)*:
Neilston 2, Johnstone Burgh 0

Maryhill Charity Cup *(at Petershill, May 28th)*:
Perthshire bt Ashfield 4-1 on pens after 0-0 draw

Evening Times Cup *(at Cambuslang, June 11th)*:
Arthurlie 3, Shotts Bon Accord 1

AYRSHIRE REGION
WESTERN SCOTTISH
OMNIBUSES LEAGUE

DIV. ONE	P	W	D	L	F	A	PTS
Irvine Meadow	20	14	3	3	63	28	31
Auchinleck Talbot	20	14	2	4	59	24	30
Beith	20	12	2	6	61	28	26
Kilwinning Rgrs	20	10	6	4	51	29	26
Ardrossan Winton R.	20	10	4	6	39	33	24
Glenafton Athletic	20	10	3	7	52	31	23
Maybole	20	8	3	9	37	48	19
Kilbirnie Ladeside	20	5	8	7	27	26	18
Cumnock Juniors	20	5	2	13	29	47	12
Saltcoats Vics	20	3	1	16	23	88	7
Kello Rovers	20	1	2	19	26	85	4

DIV. TWO	P	W	D	L	F	A	PTS
Largs Thistle	22	15	4	3	50	19	34
Darvel	22	15	4	3	47	22	34
Irvine Victoria	22	13	4	5	46	34	30
Ardeer Thistle	22	13	3	6	50	36	29
Craigmark Burnt.	22	10	6	6	62	40	26
Hurlford United	22	11	1	10	42	48	23
Dalry Athletic	22	8	4	10	37	42	20
Lugar Boswell Th.	22	8	2	12	32	51	18
Muirkirk	22	7	3	12	41	52	17
Annbank United	22	5	1	16	37	45	13
Troon	22	2	6	14	25	61	10
Whitletts Vics	22	3	4	15	24	53	10

Cup Finals:

Jackie Scarlett Lge Cup *(at Ayr Utd, Nov 16th)*:
Beith bt Auchinleck 4-3 on pens after 0-0 draw

Ayrshire Jnr Cup *(at Kilwinning Rgrs, June 12th)*:
Auchinleck Talbot 2, Irvine Meadow 0

Ayrshire Dist. Cup *(at Irvine Meadow, May 30th)*:
Glenafton bt Kilwinning 5-3 on pens after 2-2 draw

Cunninghame District Cup *(at Dalry, May 22nd)*:
Beith 2, Irvine Meadow 0

Cumnock & Doon Val. Cup *(at Auch'leck, May 13th)*:
Auchinleck Talbot 5, Muirkirk 0

Kyle & Carrick Cup *(at Dam Park, Ayr, April 25th)*:
Maybole 4, Troon 1

Kilmarnock & Louden & District Cup:
First Leg: Hurlford United 0, Darvel 3
Second Leg: Darvel 1, Hurlford United 0

Ayrshire Super Cup *(at Auchinleck, June 15th)*:
Auchinleck Talbot 1, Maybole 0

EAST REGION
JOHN WALKER LEAGUE

DIV. ONE	P	W	D	L	F	A	PTS
Camelon	22	15	4	3	49	17	34
Newtongrange S.	22	15	4	3	44	22	34
Whitburn	22	15	3	4	54	33	33
Linlithgow Rose	22	13	3	6	43	22	29
Fauldhouse United	22	8	7	7	39	35	23
Ormiston Primrose	22	7	5	10	32	37	19
Livingston United	22	8	3	11	30	51	19
Bonnyrigg Rose	22	6	6	10	37	43	18
Bo'ness United	22	5	6	11	34	40	16
Armadale Thistle	22	5	5	12	35	48	15
Harthill Royal	22	4	4	14	33	49	12
Edinburgh United	22	4	4	14	24	57	12

DIV. TWO	P	W	D	L	F	A	PTS
Dunbar United	28	18	6	4	68	34	42
Stoneyburn	28	19	4	5	61	31	42
Tranent	28	17	6	5	51	25	40
Arniston Rangers	28	17	3	8	57	30	37
Bathgate Thistle	28	16	5	7	45	34	37
Pumpherston	28	11	11	6	48	39	33
Haddington Ath.	28	10	8	10	52	43	28
Dalkeith Thistle	28	11	4	13	46	57	26
Broxburn Athletic	28	10	5	13	41	48	25
Musselburgh Ath.	28	9	4	15	53	57	22
West Calder Utd	28	9	3	16	39	54	21
Blackburn Utd	28	9	3	16	33	52	21
Bonnybridge	28	7	4	17	27	56	18
Sauchie	28	4	7	17	27	56	15
Preston Athletic	28	4	5	19	26	58	13

Cup Finals:

Skol Lge Cup *(at Falkirk FC, Feb 19th)*:
Camelon 2, Linlithgow Rose 0

National Steeplejacks Cup *(at Arniston, June 11th)*:
Newtongrange Star 3, Bo'ness United 2

Alloa Brewery Cup *(at Linlithgow, June 10th)*:
Camelon 2, Livingston United 1

Peter Craigie Cup *(at Bathgate, June 8th)*:
Livingston United 3, Dalkeith Thistle 1

FIFE REGION

	P	W	D	L	F	A	PTS
Hill of Bth H'thorn	28	23	1	4	72	22	*48
Oakley United	28	18	4	6	73	40	40
Dundonald Bluebell	28	15	7	6	51	36	37
St Andrews Utd	28	16	4	8	55	29	36
Kelty Hearts	28	14	7	7	68	35	35
Crossgates Primrose	28	13	5	10	57	44	31
Newburgh	28	15	4	9	57	43	*29
Glenrothes	28	10	8	10	51	42	28
Rosyth Recreation	28	11	4	13	50	45	*28
Lochgelly Albert	28	11	4	13	68	68	26
Thornton Hibs	28	8	9	11	60	59	25
Lochore Welfare	28	9	7	12	54	59	25
Clackmannan	28	6	6	16	42	78	18
Tulliallan Thistle	28	2	3	23	32	108	9
Kirkcaldy YM	28	0	5	23	24	106	5

Cup Finals:

Peddie Smith Maloco Fife Cup *(at Rosyth, May 26th)*:
Rosyth Recreation 2, Hill of Beath Hawthorn 3

John Fyfe Cowdenbeath Cup *(at Hill of B., June 4th)*:
Hill of Beath Hawthorn 3, St Andrews United 2

Clark Beckett Cup *(at Crossgates, May 27th)*:
Kelty Hearts 1, Oakley United 0

W T Menswear Cup *(at Hill of Beath, June 6th)*:
Hill of Beath Hawthorn 3, Rosyth Recreation 1

NORTH REGION
BON ACCORD GLASS LEAGUE

PREM. DIV.	P	W	D	L	F	A	PTS
Stonehaven	22	16	3	3	59	23	51
Sunnybank	22	15	5	2	50	17	50
FC Stoneywood	22	11	4	7	34	25	37
Culter	22	10	6	6	46	35	36
Aberdeen East End	22	8	6	8	36	40	30
Bon Accord	22	7	7	8	44	39	28
Lewis United	22	8	4	10	37	34	28
Turriff United	22	7	7	8	35	40	28
Inverurie Loco Wks	22	7	6	9	45	44	27
Buchanhaven Hearts	22	7	6	9	35	47	27
Banks O'Dee	22	6	4	12	22	31	22
Parkvale	22	0	2	20	18	86	2

DIV. ONE	P	W	D	L	F	A	PTS
Longside	26	20	3	3	73	26	63
Hall Russell Utd	26	17	7	2	47	24	58
Crombie Sports	20	10	5	5	60	22	53
Hermes	26	15	6	5	83	33	51
Banchory St Ternan	26	12	9	5	63	32	45
Ellon United	26	13	2	11	50	38	41
Aberdeen Lads Club	26	12	5	9	49	37	41
Fraserburgh Utd	26	12	4	10	51	38	40
Formantine United	26	8	6	12	44	46	30
Insch	26	8	6	12	47	57	30
Dyce	26	5	4	17	30	64	19
Maud	26	5	3	18	33	60	18
Inverurie Juniors	26	2	5	19	31	77	11
Cuminestown	26	2	5	19	22	128	11

Scotscoup North Section

	P	W	D	L	F	A	PTS
Deveronside	26	22	2	2	112	21	68
Lossiemouth Utd	26	18	3	5	62	36	57
Nairn St Ninian	26	17	3	6	82	43	54
Buckie Rovers	26	16	2	8	69	51	50
RAF Kinloss	26	16	2	8	66	49	50
Forres Thistle	26	14	4	8	62	38	46
Fochabers	26	13	2	11	63	45	41
New Elgin	26	11	2	13	46	43	35
Strathspey Thistle	26	9	5	12	43	54	32
Islavale	26	8	6	12	51	56	30
Bishopmill United	26	8	2	16	40	79	26
RAF Lossiemouth	26	5	2	19	33	82	17
Portgordon United	26	2	5	19	32	102	11
Burghead Thistle	26	1	4	21	41	103	7

Cup Finals:

North Regional Cup *(at Banks O'Dee FC, April 30th)*:
Sunnybank bt FC Stoneywood 2-0 on pens after 0-0

Grill Lge Cup *(at Bon Accord FC, Oct 3rd)*:
Sunnybank 1, FC Stoneywood 0

Aberdeen Cable Lge Cup *(at Hermes FC, June 16th)*:
FC Stoneywood 4, Hall Russell United 1

Acorn Heating Cup *(at Sunnybank FC, June 14th)*:
Stonehaven 3, Lewis United 1

Archibald Cup *(at Banks O'Dee FC, June 12th)*:
Aberdeen East End 4, Culter 2

Gordon Campbell Tphy *(at Banks O'Dee, June 8th)*:
FC Stoneywood bt Culter 3-2 on pens after 3-3 draw

Morrison Trophy *(at Sunnybank FC, June 17th)*:
Longside 3, Stonehaven 1

Robertson Cup *(at Merson Pk, Buckie, Sep 5th)*:
Deveronside 4, Nairn St Ninian 1

Championship Shield *(at Merson Park, June 11th)*:
Stonehaven bt Deveronside 5-3 on pens after 0-0 draw

Connon Cup *(at Foress Mechs FC, Oct 21st)*:
Focabers 4, New Elgin 0

Tom Gordon Cup *(at Burghead, June 17th)*:
Deveronside 7, RAF Kinloss 1

Matthew Cup *(at Forres Mechs FC, Dec 1st)*:
Buckie Rovers 3, Strathspey Thistle 2

Nicholson Cup *(at Merson Park, Buckie, May 25th)*:
Deveronside 3, Islavale 2

Stewart Mem. Trophy *(at Burghead, June 8th)*:
Deveronside 3, Fochabers 1

Gordon Williamson Cup *(at Forres Th., June 15th)*:
Kinloss 3, Lossiemouth United 2

Zamoyski Challenge Trophy (Tayside/North Region) *(at North End Park, Dundee, June 4th)*:
Dundee St Josephs 3, Dundee Downfield 1

TAYSIDE REGION

DIV. ONE	P	W	D	L	F	A	PTS
Tayport	26	20	5	1	79	15	45
Dundee Downfield	26	17	5	4	59	30	39
Dundee North End	26	12	5	9	45	42	29
Dundee St Josephs	26	12	4	10	59	35	28
Kinnoull	26	12	4	10	54	44	28
Arbroath SC	26	12	4	8	48	53	28
Forfar West End	26	9	9	8	45	40	27
Carnoustie Panmure	26	9	7	10	64	63	25
Dundee Violet	26	10	5	11	48	56	25
Jeanfield Swifts	26	9	7	10	39	55	25
Lochee Harp	26	8	6	12	34	57	22
Forfar Albion	20	7	5	14	42	55	19
Broughty Athletic	26	4	8	14	43	61	16
Arbroath Vics	26	2	4	20	31	82	8

DIV. TWO	P	W	D	L	F	A	PTS
Lochee United	22	15	6	1	60	26	36
Montrose Roselea	22	12	7	3	67	26	31
Kirrie Thistle	22	13	5	4	44	23	31
Bankfoot Athletic	22	11	5	6	41	23	27
Scone Thistle	22	11	4	7	46	29	26
East Craigie	22	8	7	7	36	36	23
Blairgowrie	22	9	5	8	40	44	23
Balbeggie	22	7	6	9	38	50	20
Brechin Victoria	22	6	3	13	27	47	15
Coupar Angus	22	3	7	12	32	50	13
Elmwood	22	5	3	14	37	61	13
Luncarty	22	2	2	18	20	73	6

Cup Finals:

Whyte & MacKay Cup *(at Lochee Utd, June 11th)*:
Tayport 3, Forfar West End 0

P'shire Advertiser Cup *(at St Johnstone, April 26th)*:
Downfield 2, St Josephs 0

Cream of the Barley *(at North End, June 7th)*:
Dundee Downfield 2, Carnoustie Panmure 1

Intersport Trophy *(at Carnoustie, June 15th)*:
Tayport 2, Dundee St Josephs 1

Winter Cup *(at Coupar Angus, June 9th)*:
Bankfoot Athletic 1, East Craigie 0 *(aet)*

Downfield SC Lge Cup *(at Downfield Park, May 8th)*:
Montrose Roselea 4, Blairgowrie 3

OTHER SCOTTISH LEAGUES

METRIK OFFICE SUPPLIES DUMFRIES AMATEUR LEAGUE

DIV. ONE	P	W	D	L	F	A	PTS
Kirkconnel	22	15	7	0	64	17	37
Lincluden Colts	22	16	2	4	79	31	34
Dumfries YMCA	22	12	8	2	47	25	*31
Abbey Vale	22	12	6	4	51	32	30
Dumfries High Sc. FP	22	7	8	7	58	39	22
Lochmaben	22	10	1	11	45	44	21
Galloway Rovers	22	7	6	9	43	38	20
Upper Annandale	22	7	4	11	22	33	18
Nithsdale	22	8	3	11	48	71	*18
Dumfries Acad. FP	22	4	7	11	45	67	15
Glenmarlin Thistle	22	6	2	14	36	70	**12
Glaxochem	22	0	2	20	26	98	2

* - 1 point deducted

DIV. TWO	P	W	D	L	F	A	PTS
Morton Thistle	22	15	5	2	70	38	35
Kirkton	22	14	5	3	57	32	33
Hoddom Rangers	22	12	6	4	40	30	30
Lochar Thistle	22	12	4	6	55	30	28
Maxwelltown HS Res.	22	9	6	7	44	38	24
St Josephs Col. FP	22	8	7	7	43	37	23
Mid Annandale	22	6	9	7	50	44	21
Noblehill	22	8	4	10	40	35	20
Kirkpatrick Fleming	22	8	3	11	46	47	19
Eastriggs	22	5	6	11	51	63	16
Terregles Athletic	22	3	4	15	40	86	10
Bellevue Rovers	22	0	5	17	21	74	5

Chapelcross - resigned

Cup Finals:

Queen of the South Cup: Kirkconnel 1, Abbey Vale 0
Lge Cup: K'connel 5, DHSFP 2 *(after match ab. at 0-1)*
Tayleurian Cup: Kirkconnel 1, Dumfries YMCA 0 *(aet)*
British Legion Cup: Dumfries YMCA beat Lochmaben
Nivison Cup: Abbey Vale 2, Mid Annandale 1 *(aet)*
McCall Cup: Maxwelltown HS Res. 3, Kirkpatrick F. 2
Presidents Cup: Hoddom Rgrs 2, Lochar Thistle 1

WEST OF SCOT. AMATEUR LGE

DIV. ONE	P	W	D	L	F	A	PTS
Denny Amtrs	22	14	5	3			33
Stedfast	22	12	5	5			29
Govanhill Victoria	22	12	4	6			28
St Patricks HSFP	22	10	6	6			26
Kilbowie Union	22	11	4	7			26
Bellaire	22	10	5	7			25
NM Rovers	22	11	4	7			**24
Possilpark YM	22	6	6	10			18
Whinnil	22	5	6	11			16
Barr & Stroud	22	6	1	15			13
Morriston YM	22	4	4	14			12
Rhu	22	3	6	13			12

* - 1 point deducted

AYRSHIRE AMATEUR LEAGUE

NORTH DIV. ONE	P	W	D	L	F	A	PTS
Shortlees Amtrs	22	16	4	2			36
Knockentiber	22	14	2	6			30
Girdle Toll Utd	22	12	5	5			29
Clark Drive	22	11	6	5			28
The Jets	22	12	0	10			24
Irvine Thistle	22	8	4	10			20
Johnnie Walker	22	8	4	10			20
Ardrossan CR	22	7	5	10			*17
Winlinton Wolves	22	7	3	12			17
Calderglen	22	5	6	11			16
Beith Amateurs	22	5	4	13			14
West Kilbride	22	3	5	13			11

* - 1 point deducted

SOUTH DIV. ONE	P	W	D	L	F	A	PTS
Heathside	22	20	1	1			41
Galston United	22	13	2	7			28
Dailly	22	11	5	6			27
Mossblown	22	7	10	5			24
Drongan United	22	9	5	8			23
Glenafton AFC	22	6	9	7			21
Auchinleck Curries	22	9	3	10			21
Minishant	22	8	5	9			21
Glenburn MW	22	4	8	10			16
Newmilns Vesuvias	22	6	4	12			16
Hurlford Thistle	22	5	5	12			15
Darvel Victoria	22	3	5	14			11

Div. 1 Play-off: Shortlees 1, Heathside 0
Div. 2 Play-off: Boutreehill 2, Mauchlins 1
Div. 3 Play-off: Kilwinning Town 6, Redbrae 1

Ayrshire Amateur Cup Final *(at Ayr Utd, 6th May)*: Knockentiber 1, The Jets 0

ABERDEENSHIRE AMATEUR LGE

	P	W	D	L	F	A	PTS
Kincorth	30	24	5	1			53
Glentanar	30	23	5	2			51
Skene/Bieldside	30	15	11	4			41
West End	30	16	7	7			39
Hatton	30	14	8	8			36
Gt Western Utd	30	12	9	9			33
Wilsons XI	30	12	7	11			31
Chatten Rovers	30	12	6	12			30
Inverurie FP	30	9	10	11			28
Walker Road	30	11	6	13			28
Grampian Police	30	9	7	14			25
Mugiemoss Amtrs	30	9	6	15			24
Portlethen Thistle	30	8	5	17			21
Raeden Thistle	30	6	7	17			19
Cults	30	4	10	16			18
Banchory Amateurs	30	0	3	27			3

Lower Division champions:

Div 2: Dyce Amateurs
Div 3: Hilton
Div 4: Echt
Div 5: RGu
Div 6: AC Mill Inn

MAKITA POWER DUMFRIES SUNDAY AMATEUR LEAGUE

	P	W	D	L	F	A	PTS
Maxwelltown Eagles	22	17	2	3	108	27	36
Castle Rovers	22	16	2	4	103	20	34
Kelloholm	22	15	4	3	100	26	34
Elopak	22	11	7	4	70	34	29
Moffat Thistle	22	10	6	6	63	36	26
Kirkholm	22	10	2	10	79	56	22
Moreig	22	8	6	8	54	49	22
Labour Club	22	8	3	11	54	71	19
Riverside Colts	22	6	6	10	57	46	18
Dynamo Oscars	22	5	5	12	66	75	15
Calside	22	3	1	18	17	158	7
Steamboat	22	1	0	21	26	199	2

Cup Finals:

League Cup: Kelloholm 1, Castle Rovers 0
Houliston Cup: Castle R. 3, Maxwelltown E. 3-2
Kirkcaldie Mem. Cup: Moreig 4, Kelloholm 0
Star Hotel Chal. Trophy: Moreig 4, Kirkholm 3
Peter Handley Mem. Trophy: Maxwelltown Eagles beat Kelloholm 3-2 on pens after 1-1 draw & extra-time.
Consolation Cup: Riverside C. 1, Dynamo Oscars 0

Appendix Two Women's Football

Doncaster Belles - Womens National League champions 1993-94.

DONCASTER MAKE IT NATIONAL PREMIER CHAMPIONSHIP NUMBER TWO, WHILST WOLVERHAMPTON AND BROMLEY EARN THEIR PLACES IN THE TOP FLIGHT.

CATHY GIBB TAKES A LOOK AT THE HIGHLIGHTS FROM THE 1993/94 SEASON IN THE WOMEN'S NATIONAL LEAGUE

The 1993/94 women's football season came to its eventual close when the last league match of the season was finished on the 12th of June 1994. And there was plenty that happened throughout, but to record the events in their entirety would take up the entire *Non-League Club Directory*. So here is just a brief resume of a compelling season.

First we had the Football Association taking over the running of the international side looking after the affairs of England. A new manager, Ted Copeland, was chosen for their entry into their 6th consecutive UEFA championship where they were placed in a relatively easy Group 7 - Spain the only tricky side holding them twice to a goalless draw en route through to the quarter finals where England's opponents could be Iceland or Holland, come September and October time this year.

The Women's FA Cup competition which is the equivalent of the men's FA Cup, and has been competed for since 1971, had also fallen into the hands of the FA who were quick to change it's name to 'The FA Women's Challenge Cup competition'.

Liverpool's Knowsley United who last year lost 3-0 in the League Cup final to Arsenal, more than made up for it this year. In a more prestigous event, they knocked out holders Arsenal at the semi-final stage, courtesy of a Cathy Gore goal.

But United's last hurdle was to overcome the five times winners Doncaster Belles who had reached their 11th final.

Just like last year against Arsenal, Doncaster's influential England midfielder Gillian Coultard was struck down with an injury, and so played no further part in the final. This should have favoured underdogs Knowsley. Yet the more United missed their chances, the more likely it was that Doncaster would score that killer goal and they did, through that deadly striker Karen Walker in the 38th minute.

Turning to the domestic scene, the Premier Division welcomed the two newcomers - the Division One North champions and the 1989 WFA cup winners Leasowe Pacific and the Division One South champions Wembley, formerly known as District Line.

And it seemed that Wembley fared the better of the two when they became the first side to defeat the defending league champions Arsenal this year and engaged the Gunners in one of the best cup matches of the season, witnessed on a cold winter's evening. They too won some silverware by winning the Middlesex cup defeating Millwall Lionesess 1-0 in the final.

Yet Wembley could well pay the penalty after fielding two unsigned reserves players for the senior side, and the consequences if they lose their hearing at Lancaster Gate would be a £100 fine and a six point deduction, which leave them in fifth spot behind Millwall.

The main intrigue of the season was whether Arsenal could repeat their phenomenal treble achievement of last season. There seemed every indication that they were intent on doing so after manager Vic Akers made two impressive pre-season signings by snapping up the England pair Marieanne Spacey from Wimbledon and Sam Britton from Bronte.

But Doncaster Belles, winners of the league in the first year of its inception, were surprisingly left empty handed last year and lost a remarkable unbeaten 15 year league record, when they were beaten by Wimbledon which paved the way for Arsenal to steal their league crown.

Doncaster were determined to claw themselves back to success this season by entering the league cup competition for the first time in three years and they too had collected two pre-season signings - Bronte's Chantel Woodhead (who became an England standby for one of their UEFA matches this year) and Stanton Rangers' Julie Goodman.

England training sessions intermittently devastated the Premier League programme with the majority of top sides like Arsenal, Doncaster and Knowsley United making up the England squad, and atrocious wintry conditions hit Doncaster the most, the Belles not playing competitively for four weeks.

It was the Gunners who did get off to a dream start winning 7-0 over Ipswich Town before an interruption of postponements for FA run England training sessions saw them drop a point against Stanton Rangers on October 24th.

They were then held 2-2 by Knowsley United who went on to knock out the league cup holders Arsenal from the competition winning 1-0 in the 6th round and were beaten for the first time this season by Wembley 3-2 on March 6th.

Despite these premature hiccups, Arsenal enjoyed a good run of results in the second half of the season.

A 4-1 triumph over Leasowe Pacific in the league cup semi-final and a 2-2 draw and a 3-1 victory over rivals Doncaster. By then Arsenal were without their England stars Debbie Bampton and goalkeeper Lesley Shipp who had left the club.

So by the 26th May the Gunners were sitting pretty at the top of the Premier Division having completed all their 18 league matches and having collected 45 points.

Realistically boss Vic Akers knew that his side had dropped too many points and was resigned to finishing as runners-up as they had to wait for their nearest challengers Doncaster Belles and Knowsley United to complete their league fixtures which was to decide their fate.

This year though the Belles were determined to put the record straight and continue where Arsenal left off last season.

When Doncaster did play their first league match of the season on Ocotober 17th they enjoyed a 7-1 victory over Millwall Lionesses.

On February 20th the league had a certain ring to it with Doncaster Belles at the top of the table with 24 points from eight matches.

A 6-1 league cup quarter final triumph over Millwall and a 2-2 draw with Arsenal still had Doncaster leading the Premier table with 25 points from nine matches.

By April 18th Arsenal had leapfrogged over Doncaster on the strength of playing three games more, while Doncaster had gone on to win the FA Women's Challenge Cup for a sixth time and had earned their first ever place in the League Cup final beating Knowsley United 4-0 on May 28th.

Doncaster Belles knew that they could afford to lose at least one of their five remaining league matches in their pursuit for the league championship title.

Doncaster Belles went on to reel off four consecutive victories - the 2nd last match on June 1st against Knowsley United, in which they won 7-0, clinched them the title.

But their last match in which they won 2-0 against a spirited Wembley side ensured that the Belles finished four points ahead of runners-up Arsenal.

Because of the nagging headache of having to re-schedule those postponed fixtures which meant the season spilling over into June, the league fixture secretary Alan Gardiner had to contact the FA who agreed to carry over the League Cup final at the start of next season.

This decision denied Doncaster Belles the opportunity of winning the treble, were they to beat Arsenal in the final, but this posed a couple of problems.

Both Arsenal and Doncaster Belles are bound to lose or gain new players during the pre-season so those players who played in the 1993/94 season will be denied a League Cup medal.

Also if Doncaster do win the League Cup and happen to go on to retain the FA Women's Challenge Cup, the league title and the League Cup during the 1994/95 season, does this mean that Doncaster Belles will pick up four trophies next year?

The team that brought most pleasure throughout the season was Millwall Lionesses whose talented youngsters possess great skill and could well be a threat to Doncaster and Arsenal in years to come.

And at Highbury after the FA Youth Cup Final on May 12th, Millwall played their part in producing one of the best matches of the season. They were very unlucky not to have at least snatched a point off Arsenal who, with five minutes remaining, clawed back a 1-0 deficit to win it 3-1 well into injury time.

How cruel a season can be for a team like Millwall who showed so much promise but they ended up losing two finals - The Kent County Cup final and the Middlesex Cup to Bromley Borough and

Wembley respectively.

Spare a thought for the two relegated sides from the Premier Division, Ipswich Town and Wimbledon, who collected six and three points respectively.

Both teams were going through periods of change in the big time of Premiership football. Ipswich, a young and inexperienced side just couldn't make any impact winning only one of their 18 league matches compared to bottom placed Wimbledon who did win two matches but had three points deducted for not fulfilling a fixture.

To make matters worse the Dons had lost, during the pre-season, the expertise of Manager Fred Brockwell who had resigned and players like England's talented Marieanne Spacey and Hannah Rushforth who had both moved on, plus their trusty defender and former international Terri Springett retired.

Premier Division	P	W	D	L	F	A	Pts
Doncaster Belles	18	16	1	1	110	16	49
Arsenal	18	14	3	1	85	15	45
Knowsley United	18	13	3	3	63	30	41
Wembley	18	9	2	7	35	34	29
Millwall Lionesses	18	9	1	8	42	48	28
Leasowe Pacific	18	7	2	9	42	48	23
Stanton Rangers	18	6	5	7	32	38	23
RS Southampton	18	2	3	13	25	70	6*
Ipswich Town	18	1	3	14	13	86	6
Wimbledon	18	2	0	16	16	81	3*

* - 3pts deducted.

Division One North ended in a two horse race, between Wolverhampton Wanderers and Sheffield Wednesday.

The early half of the season saw Wolves going great guns, leading the table up to December time with 16 points from six games, though their eventual nearest rivals Sheffield were placed in fifth place with nine points from five games.

A few key players departing midway through the season, which included goalkeeper Karen Ellis and manager Paul Broomhall resigning, left Wolves managerless throughout the rest of the season.

A 15 year old, Loraine Oliver deputised in goal and captain Nicola Gibson with the assistance of other team members chose the side from Sunday to Sunday.

A 2-0 defeat to second bottom placed Nottingham Argyle plus a shock 6-1 defeat to St. Helens temporarily saw Wolves displaced from the top by Sheffield Wednesday during the Easter break. Wolves did show great character to gradually hold off the challenge of a young and promising Wednesday side.

Both teams finished up on 40 points from 18 games but Wolves had the better goal difference which won them the Division One North league crown, and promotion to the Premier League.

Division One North	P	W	D	L	F	A	Pts
Wolverhampton	18	12	4	2	61	28	40
Sheffield Wed.	18	13	1	4	46	20	40
Abbeydale	18	9	2	7	38	31	29
Bronte	18	8	4	6	46	26	28
Cowgate Kestrels	18	9	1	8	38	41	28
Villa Aztecs	18	8	3	7	37	34	27
St. Helens	18	7	1	10	36	57	22
Langford	18	5	2	11	25	41	17
Nottingham Argyle	18	5	1	12	25	49	16
Kidderminster	18	3	3	12	24	49	12

Bottom placed Kidderminster Harriers remained in Division One North after surviving a play off encounter with the North West Division One league champions, Manchester Belle Vue, winning 2-1. Manchester had previously seen off the East Midlands Division One league champions, Notts County, after winning a thrilling 5-4 encounter.

The Division One South League emerged as a one horse race, despite the deserved winners Bromley Borough, tripping up on the odd game or two in their end of season run in, an inconsistent run that could be excused seeing as they had become champions with four games remaining.

It had taken Bromley Borough, who were made up mainly from Millwall's 1991 WFA Cup winning side, three seasons to gain Premiership status and admittedly they do possess talented players, like Brenda Sempare, England's Hope Powell and an impressive striker in Lynne McCormick who could make quite an impact next season.

As a harsh reminder to Bromley, they did lose heavily, 10-1, to Doncaster Belles in the 5th round of the FAW Cup competition.

Bromley would be the first to admit though, that they do need a couple of top players to strengthen their side somewhat and already they have picked up Arsenal's England star Debbie Bampton, a signing that could encourage other top players to join the Premiership newcomers.

And Bromley picked up another piece of silverware - The Kent County Cup after seeing off London rivals Millwall 2-1.

Hassocks were relegated from Division One South having only picked up one point and deciding not to enter the play-offs.

Division One South	P	W	D	L	F	A	Pts
Bromley Borough	18	14	3	1	68	16	45
Town & County	18	11	2	5	51	29	35
Bristol Backwell	18	11	1	6	50	34	34
Epsom & Ewell	18	10	2	6	37	26	32
Brighton & H.	18	9	4	5	36	23	31
Maidstone Tigresses	18	8	5	5	37	28	29
Hemel Hempstead	18	4	6	8	33	44	18
Horsham	18	4	4	10	14	33	16
Oxford United	18	3	4	11	17	37	13
Hassocks	18	0	1	17	7	90	1

Another London club will be playing in Division One South next year, Brentford, who had done the hard bit by beating the Eastern region Division One champions Dunstable, 3-0, then had to prove their worth against the supposedly impressive South East Counties Division One League champions and league cup winners, Whitehawk (previously known as Saltdean) who had not lost a game all season.

Brentford, influenced by captain Lisa King, were reduced to ten players in the latter stages of the game, but deservedly beat the favourites Whitehawk, 2-0.

Finally we end the women's football season how we began it with news that the Football Association are now taking over the running of the National League next season, which will begin on August 21st.

The league now becomes known as the Women's Premier League and it's the National Division One North and Division One South leagues.

Relegated Southern clubs, Wimbledon and Ipswich Town, will go into Division One South which means that runners-up Town & County who finished 10 points behind Bromley in that division, will have to compete in the National Division One North league next year.

GREATER LONDON REGIONAL WOMEN'S LEAGUE

Premier Div.	P	W	D	L	F	A	Pts
Arsenal Reserves	18	16	0	2	107	16	32
Brentford	18	15	1	2	103	23	31
Leyton Orient	18	14	1	3	112	20	29
Tottenham Hot.	18	14	0	4	81	38	28
Lambeth	18	8	2	8	47	47	18
Watford	18	6	1	11	42	74	13
Hackney	18	4	3	11	30	52	11
Wimbledon Reserves	18	4	1	13	29	52	9
Drayton Wanderers	18	4	1	13	22	68	9
Queens Pk Rgrs	18	0	0	18	4	187	0

Div. One	P	W	D	L	F	A	Pts
Wembley Reserves	18	18	0	0	98	11	36
Romford	18	14	1	3	71	24	29
Collier Row	18	14	0	4	77	28	28
Enfield	18	10	1	7	62	41	21
Newham	18	9	3	6	43	29	21
Southend Manor	18	7	1	10	32	37	15
Millwall Reserves	18	5	1	12	43	64	11
Basildon	18	3	2	13	24	68	8
Ealing	18	3	0	15	35	105	6
Pinewood	18	2	1	15	31	109	5

Div. Two	P	W	D	L	F	A	Pts
Mill Hill Utd	18	15	3	0	82	18	33
Leyton O. Res.	18	12	2	4	61	25	26
Chelmsford	18	10	4	4	57	29	24
Barnet	18	9	2	7	40	37	20
Walton & Hersham	18	9	2	7	40	45	20
Winchester All Stars	18	4	6	8	29	39	14
SE Rangers	18	3	7	8	26	48	13
Palace Eagles	18	5	3	10	30	60	13
Chislehurst Utd	18	3	5	10	20	37	11
Wimbledon 'A'	18	2	2	14	18	59	6

Div. Three	P	W	D	L	F	A	Pts
Chelsea	18	16	2	0	81	16	34
Greenwich	18	15	1	2	90	21	31
West Ham Utd	18	12	3	3	67	21	27
Hackney Reserves	18	9	1	8	50	46	19
Leyton Orient 'A'	18	8	1	9	42	40	17
Brentford Reserves	18	7	1	10	61	59	15
London	18	5	3	10	36	50	13
Palace Eagles Res.	18	5	3	10	22	59	13
Collier Row Res.	18	2	2	14	27	105	6
Newham Res.	18	2	1	15	13	72	5

Mill Hill United - Division Two champions 1993-94. *Photo - Dave West.*

LEAGUE INDEX

313 leagues are featured in this Directory, and all are listed alphabetically below with their relevant page numbers. Where a league entry runs to more than one page, the number indicated is that of the first page of the section.

105 leagues are Sunday competitions, and these are marked as 'SL'.

As in previous years, sponsors names have been omitted to ease reference. League sponsors, however, get their deserved recognition in the appropriate sections.

CLUB INDEX

A.

B.

C.

D.

E.

M.

N.

O.

P.

T.

U.

V.

W.

Y.

Z.